Christopher Peri Ph.D.

Sams Teach Yourself the Twitter API in 24 Hours

SAMS 800 East 96th Street, Indianapolis, Indiana 46240 USA

Sams Teach Yourself the Twitter API in 24 Hours

ISBN-13: 978-0-672-33110-7
ISBN-10: 0-672-33110-1

Library of Congress Cataloging-in-Publication Data

Peri, Christopher A., 1964-
Sams teach yourself the Twitter API in 24 hours / Christopher A. Peri, Bess P. Ho.
p. cm.
Includes index.
ISBN-13: 978-0-672-33110-7 (pbk. : alk. paper)
ISBN-10: 0-672-33110-1 (pbk. : alk. paper)
1. Application program interfaces (Computer software) 2. Twitter. I. Ho, Bess P., 1967- II. Title. III. Title: Teach yourself the Twitter API in 24 hours.
QA76.76.A63P47 2011
006.7'54—dc23
2011022576

Printed in the United States of America

First Printing June 2011

Trademarks

All terms mentioned in this book that are known to be trademarks or service marks have been appropriately capitalized. Sams Publishing cannot attest to the accuracy of this information. Use of a term in this book should not be regarded as affecting the validity of any trademark or service mark.

Warning and Disclaimer

Every effort has been made to make this book as complete and as accurate as possible, but no warranty or fitness is implied. The information provided is on an “as is” basis. The authors and the publisher shall have neither liability nor responsibility to any person or entity with respect to any loss or damages arising from the information contained in this book.

Bulk Sales

Sams Publishing offers excellent discounts on this book when ordered in quantity for bulk purchases or special sales. For more information, please contact

U.S. Corporate and Government Sales
1-800-382-3419
corpsales@pearsontechgroup.com

For sales outside of the U.S., please contact

International Sales
international@pearson.com

Associate Publisher
Mark Taub

Signing Editor
Trina MacDonald

Development Editor
Songlin Qiu

Managing Editor
Kristy Hart

Project Editor
Andy Beaster

Copy Editor
Barbara Hacha

Indexer
Erika Millen

Proofreader
Sarah Kearns

Technical Editors
Doug Jones
Ronan Schwartz
Ben Schupak

Publishing Coordinator
Olivia Basegio

Cover Designer
Gary Adair

Composition
Gloria Schurick

Contents at a Glance

Table of Contents

About the Author

Dr. Christopher Peri received his Doctorate from the University of California, Berkeley, in Architecture. His focus was on Collaboration in Virtual Environments delving into methods that facilitate designers and engineers to improve communication over remote networks.

He started playing with the Twitter API very early in the API release, creating his own Twitter client called TwittFilter, which is geared more to the occasional user then someone who uses Twitter all the time. As time went on, he added more and more features and functions for his own personal use, until one day he realized he had a fairly sophisticated application and opened it up to the general public to use. He learned quite a bit about the Twitter API the hard way—by simply coding things up and seeing what happens. Although TwittFilter is still a personal project, he has already created a number of private Twitter applications, robots, and smaller projects like NewsSnacker.com, which is open to the public.

About the Contributing Author

Bess Ho is a UI Engineer in mobile, tablet, TV, and web with a strong background in data analytic and consumer behavior. She received her Master Degree from the University of California, Davis in Food Science and Technology. Her focus was on Consumer Sensory Science and Engineering. She is the winner of Nokia Open Screen Project Fund and was elected as Samsung Star in the Samsung Mobile Innovator worldwide program. She served as technical editor for the book titled **Building OpenSocial Apps: A Field Guide to Working with MySpace Platform** (Addison Wesley, 2009). She has presented mobile technology at Stanford University, O'Reilly Web20 Expo SF, Where20 Conference, Silicon Valley China Wireless Conference, and many developer events. Currently, she is Mobile Architect (EIR) for Archimedes Ventures. She also advises many early-stage startups in UI/UXP design and mobile development in multiple platforms. She is actively teaching many mobile classes such as iOS SDK in Silicon Valley and online courses at Udemy.com. You can follow her at Twitter @Bess or Slideshare at www.slideshare.net/bess.ho. Her developer blog is at http://www.bess.co.

Acknowledgments

Christopher Peri—We would like to thank all the unknown coders on the interwebs who have contributed to not only Twitter's success, but creating mountains of technical information and code examples that allows a lowly hobby programmer, like myself, to learn how to work with Twitter API and one day...write a book on it. A number of people have helped with this book, but I want to call out three people specifically: @chiah for creating the foundation of Hour 1, @jon_wu for Hour 8 as well as helping with debugging and general feedback on technical issues, and @LanceNanek for debugging and researching Android in Hour 22.

We Want to Hear from You!

As the reader of this book, you are our most important critic and commentator. We value your opinion and want to know what we're doing right, what we could do better, what areas you'd like to see us publish in, and any other words of wisdom you're willing to pass our way.

You can email or write me directly to let me know what you did or didn't like about this book—as well as what we can do to make our books stronger.

Please note that I cannot help you with technical problems related to the topic of this book, and that due to the high volume of mail I receive, I might not be able to reply to every message.

When you write, please be sure to include this book's title and author as well as your name and phone or email address. I will carefully review your comments and share them with the author and editors who worked on the book.

Email: opensource@samspublishing.com

Mail: Mark Taub
Associate Publisher
Sams Publishing
800 East 96th Street
Indanapolis, IN 46240 USA

Reader Services

Visit our website and register this book at www.informit.com/title/9780672331107 for convenient access to any updates, downloads, or errata that might be available for this book.

Preface

This book on the Twitter API is geared to the programmer who is just a bit past beginner—who knows the basics of LAMP, including how to set up a basic server, PHP, JavaScript, HTML, and CSS. You do not have to be an expert programmer to use this book, but you should know how to look things up. In writing this book, we have tried to provide you with everything you need to get a simple Twitter client up and running. We include an hour on setting up your environment, as well as providing you with HTML and CSS codes to have something up and running. However, it's beyond the scope of this book to explain what is happening with these codes. Instead, we focus on the code surrounding the API calls, OAuth, and the returns. That does not mean that you could not use this book if you are a beginner programmer. Because we provide you with all the code and build an application up step by step, you can stop at any time and look up parts of the code you do not understand. However, if you have never coded anything before, you may find that this book moves far too fast. It may be better to get an introductory book on basic programming in PHP before reading this book.

In writing this book, we also kept in mind experienced programmers who have been asked to create a Twitter application or include Twitter support in a current application, even if they do not know much about Twitter. We believe it's important to understand what Twitter is, how it's being used, and what makes it different from other social media services. It's with this understanding that you will be able to approach your Twitter project with a more engaged understanding of what your application is trying to accomplish, which is the best way to not only satisfy product requirements, but also design future growth.

Sams Teach Yourself Twitter API in 24 Hours is a little different from most technical books in that the book is geared around creating a functional Twitter client, including all HTML, CSS, JavaScript, and PHP needed to create your own application. We also dedicated the last four hours of this book to getting you started with making API calls on the iPhone and Android OSes in case you want to make your own mobile Twitter application.

Unlike most books, this book was written as Twitter and the API set was going through major changes. As such, the book and the code used in the book have been edited many, many times. So much so that we expect there will be a technical oversight here and there. So be sure to check the book's website for changes and updates (http://www.twitterapi24.com/). Also, as much as we tried to keep up with all the changes happening with Twitter, we fully expect some details about the various API's to evolve from the time of the last edit to the time you have this book in your hands.

We hope you enjoy this book.

HOUR 1

What Is Twitter?

What You'll Learn in This Hour:

- What is Twitter?
- List of terms
- A brief history of Twitter
- How Twitter is different from other social media tools
- Example of how Twitter has been used

What Twitter Offers You

Twitter is a vast electronic conversation that is changing personal communications through the use of new social and mobile technologies. The idea is simple: The service enables users to post messages using 140 characters or fewer, resulting in short bursts of communication that can be transmitted through text, mobile apps, or the Web. Tweets can include links to video, photos, or other media hosted elsewhere on the Internet in addition to plain text. The text link URLs are included in the 140-character limit, so short URLs are obviously preferred.

Twitter is not designed to be any one thing; it's different things to different people. For some, it's a way to talk with their friends; for others, it's a way to broadcast out to the world, a way to consume information, or a way to share links. As such, the API has been designed and continues to be designed to be as agnostic as possible to how it's used.

For people who are not familiar with Twitter, it is a platform that allows one-to-many communication. It is a mashup of text, email, instant messages (IM), news, forum posts, social networks, public conversation, links, information sharing, and the world's biggest dinner party. The technology allows for almost instantaneous communication between an individual and a self-selected group. You can receive tweets through a variety of channels: the Twitter website, IM, SMS/text message, RSS, email, or third-party applications on computers and mobile devices.

A useful way to think about Twitter is to imagine that you are IMing or texting everyone you know, at the same time, in public.

The following is a list of common Twitter terms:

- **Twitter**—The service that allows you to communicate with anyone else who also signs up.
- **Tweets**—Messages of 140 characters or fewer that are sent through the Twitter service.
- **Follower**—Someone who opts in to receive your tweets.
- **Following**—The people whose tweets you opt in to receive.
- **@reply**—A public message sent as a tweet directed at one person, designated with @username typically as a response to a previous Tweet.
- **Direct messages (DMs)**—A message of fewer than 140 characters sent privately to one of your followers. You can send DMs only to people who are following you.
- **Private account**—An account whose tweets are not public. Only people who have accounts on Twitter *and* have been approved as a follower by the owner of the account can see what has been written.
- **Trending topics**—The most popular terms on Twitter at a moment in time.
- **Retweets (RTs)**—When users find an interesting tweet and share it with their followers.
- **Hashtag**—The convention of flagging a word with the hash character #topic. This was created on Twitter to aid with keyword search and the tagging of discussions. It came from users who used IRC regularly, where #topic indicates a channel where the topic is being discussed.

A Brief History of Twitter—or Why 140 Characters?

According to Dom Sagolla (www.140characters.com/2009/01/30/how-twitter-was-born/), Jack Dorsey came up with the idea of having a mobile text message-based communication tool for groups, because their podcasting startup Odeo was struggling to find a new direction. Text messages, also known as the Short Message System (SMS) protocol, are limited to 160 characters for historical reasons. In 1985, Friedhelm Hillebrand, chairman of the nonvoices services committee in the Global

System for Mobile Communications (GSM), tested his hypothesis that 160 characters were enough to communicate a complete thought. His group of researchers pushed forward their recommendation in 1986, and the modern text message length standard was born (http://latimesblogs.latimes.com/technology/2009/05/invented-text-messaging.html). Twitter's character limits resulted from that 160-character limitation: 20 characters are reserved for the username, leaving 140 characters for the message.

Even though Twttr, the original name for the project, was created in 2006, the service really took off a year later at SXSW Interactive in March of 2007. Attendees used it to keep track of other conference goers, and Twitter became the hit of the show, winning the SXSW Web Award in the Blog category.

One of the big reasons for Twitter's success is that it was first built as an SMS communication platform; only later did it turn into a web-based product with simple APIs. Because a very large user base of phones already existed that can only text, Twitter was often the only way to engage in social media without a computer. Keep in mind that this was before the iPhone and Android began their run to take over the phone market.

The service continued to gain popularity and obtained massive coverage from traditional media in the November 26 Mumbai attacks, when citizens on the ground used Twitter to relay eyewitness accounts well in advance of any reporters (see www.informationweek.com/blog/main/archives/2008/11/twitter_in_cont.html;jsessionid=4JPX5T2TTQKMHQE1GHPCKHWATMY32JVN). The resulting articles and TV news reports propelled the service into the mainstream. And the leap from technologists and bloggers continued, with celebrities like Ashton Kutcher and Oprah helping to highlight the service.

During the Iran elections, the use of Twitter by the opposition was deemed so critical that the U.S. government asked Twitter to delay an update to its services out of fear of compromising one of the few channels the opposition had to communicate and organize.

During the 2010 World Cup, traffic was so high that Twitter actually shelved one of its new features in order to focus time and resources on the spike in traffic.

How Is Twitter Different from Other Social Tools?

The newest social technologies take information that was once passed from one person to another and alter the format so the sharing is faster and more public. Now the news can spread through Twitter, Facebook, reddit, and Digg, taking personal, limited-distribution conversations and disseminating them to the entire world. Although word-of-mouth news has existed since the beginning of spoken language itself, it now accumulates in a written record, available to a much wider audience. In addition, social technologies not only make it easy for you to share with the people you know, it also allows the people you know to share with the people they know. What used to be a phone conversation, text, or IM can now propagate to a larger audience.

Social is also different from traditional media. Older media was a one-way communication channel in which a central authority sent out information for consumption by readers. Social media technologies allow unstructured conversations to happen, so information can flow both ways or be forwarded outward to others.

Twitter is a social networking site that is simple in format but allows each person to use the service differently. Other social sites have narrower applications: bookmarking sites, such as del.icio.us, or social news sites, such as Digg or reddit, are for sharing links. Media-sharing sites like YouTube or Flickr are for distributing videos or photos. Using Twitter, you can share any combination of links, news, photos, or videos with your network.

One of the biggest differences between Twitter and other networks is that the social relationship does not have to be symmetrical. You can opt in to see updates from other people by following them, and other users can see your updates by becoming followers. In other words, when you follow people, you receive their tweets or messages, and when they follow you, they receive your tweets or messages. As noted previously, you can choose to get these messages as text messages on your phone, tweets on the Web, or as output in a third-party application.

The two biggest social network platforms are Twitter and Facebook. They are different in two ways:

- Twitter has an inherent openness, unlike Facebook, and Twitter also offers nonreciprocal relationships that are very different from Facebook.
- Facebook began as a "walled garden," or a system that people from only certain universities or colleges could join, and it still hasn't lost that sense of protected information.

Most of the photos, status updates, or other content that you post on Facebook is accessible only to people who are connected to you. In contrast, you can always see users' tweets on their Twitter page or at the URL www.twitter.com/username, provided they have not made their account private. This is further reflected in the limits of what interactions from an API perspective are supported.

In the beginning, the power of Twitter was in the conversations and the networks of people who choose to participate. Twitter is closer to the old IRC channels than to any other form of communication. This means that for a user, the service is not useful without a meaningful social network, and so it's hard for a new user to understand what to do with it. However, as the acceptance of Twitter by mainstream media has grown, more and more users are finding Twitter as a great information resource for news, Hollywood rumors, stock tips, and general yelling—mostly during sporting events. Twitter has become so useful for gaining information that often a story will break on Twitter before making it onto traditional media.

Like most things on the Web, after a tweet is sent out, there is no way to edit its content; the only thing that can be changed is that the tweet can be deleted. And even in that case, if the tweet went out to mobile devices or third-party tools, those copies are not deleted. So, as with anything information you put out to the Internet, if you would not say it in public, don't say it on Twitter.

Twitter Use Case Study: #blamedrewscancer

On May 20, 2009, Drew Olanoff was diagnosed with Hodgkin's Lymphoma (www.drewolanoff.com/post/117383549/thats-not-what-i-ordered), and he decided to use his online presence to create awareness of his cancer. He chose to write a blog post and use Twitter to share his experience. To make it interesting, he created a hashtag, #blamedrewscancer, and encouraged his friends to blame whatever went wrong in their lives on his cancer.

Soon, hundreds of people were tweeting about lost keys, getting stuck in traffic, Mondays, and anything else going wrong, all using this tag. A website was created that showed the tweets in a fun way, and news outlets started picking up the story. In just 100 days, more than 11,000 people blamed more than 25,000 things on Drew's cancer (www.twitip.com/blamedrewscancer-for-this-case-study/). What started out as a personal story of a cancer diagnosis became a phenomenon on Twitter. People connected over their own stories of unfortunate experiences.

Twitter Use Case Study: Global Politics

On February 11th, 2011, Mubarak stepped down from his post of President that he held since 1981. With the military taking over power, it seemed almost all of Egypt erupted in celebration. Almost as soon as his plane reached cruising altitude, the news broke and Twitter went nuts. Here is a Tweet I sent out the day before where he gave a speech where everyone expected him to step down and then a Tweet after he did the following day (see Figure 1.1).

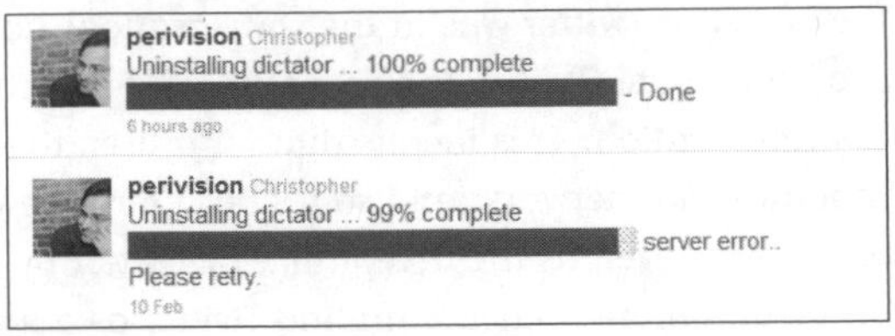

FIGURE 1.1 Tweets sent during the Egyptian revolution.

This is not the first time that Twitter, Facebook, and other social media services have had an influence on world events. If you remember, back to April 10th, 2008, a UC Berkeley student sent out a single tweet that saved him from an uncertain outcome. He tweeted the word "Arrested"...just as he was taken into custody. That single Tweet was enough to let people know in Egypt, and back in the U.S., what had happened; to hire a lawyer and to demand his release. Although even back then, Twitter had already proven itself as a medium for rapid dissemination of information unlike anything we have seen in the past; no one could have foreseen the impacts yet to come.

Fast forward to the beginning of 2011. The number of people on Twitter, Facebook, and other social media climbed to the hundred of millions. Twitter and Facebook alone, combined, claim just under one billion users. Combine those numbers along with the explosion of online mobile devices now capable of accessing these services and you have a flattening of communications never before seen since the advent of the printing press, the consumer grade photocopying machine, and email. Each of these revolutions in communication has had its impact on society; the Twitter revolution is no different.

The reach of social media, especially Twitter (since it supports communication with increasingly popular text messaging), has become so prevalent that the normal tools used by regimes to manage their population have become compromised. Usage of information is a tool; information control is paramount to controlling a population. The more control over information you can impress, the greater the likelihood the population will believe and act on whatever information you provide; or conversely, ensure it never gets disseminated in the first place. Just in the past year alone (2010-11), we have seen exceptional examples of states that had some form of control over information (typically by controlling the press), but lost that control over information because of networked communications like Twitter and Facebook. Even with efforts to shut down Twitter and other social media platforms, information still seems to find a way out. For example; in Egypt, access to Twitter was blocked. In 24 hours, it was announced on the Google Blog, that the search giant has teamed up with the SayNow team and Twitter to create a simple speak-to-tweet service for people currently engulfed in the turmoil in Egypt. From the Google post...

"It's already live and anyone can tweet by simply leaving a voicemail on one of these international phone numbers (+16504194196 or +390662207294 or +97316199855) and the service will instantly tweet the message using the hashtag #egypt. No Internet connection is required. People can listen to the messages by dialing the same phone numbers or going to twitter.com/speak2tweet."

We hope that this will go some way to helping people in Egypt stay connected at this very difficult time. Our thoughts are with everyone there.

At the time of this writing (early 2011), demonstrators have clashed with police in the Yemeni capital Sanaa, riot police in Algiers dispersed thousands of people who had defied a government ban to demand that President Abdelaziz Bouteflika step down, and President Mahmoud Abbas will immediately ask Prime Minister Salam Fayyad to appoint a new cabinet. And in Iran, reports say several opposition activists have been arrested and international broadcasters are being jammed. In Libya, the control of the country is currently in doubt and sections of the country are no longer in government control.

As much as it seems that the "tools" of social media was the foundation of the revolutions we have been talking about, and those that seem to be coming, it's not the service of Twitter, Facebook, YouTube, and Google but instead the change of thinking that these tools have helped evolve. By allowing people to exchange ideas and information quickly and easily and with greater reach, social media tools have given people a sense of community and strength. And it's this ability to create and inform communities through social media that is the real power of Twitter, not just sending 140 characters.

Summary

This hour introduced you to Twitter, gave a brief history of the service, covered the basics of social media, and described how Twitter is different from other social platforms. The common terms used on Twitter were defined, and you should now have an understanding of the functionality of the platform and some of the ways people use the medium for communication. We also discussed an example of how someone used Twitter to create a community and illustrated some of the social norms at play and reflected on how such a simple idea like Twitter and all the programmers the help made it grow can have an effect on world.

Q&A

Q. *What is an @ reply?*

A. It's a way to specify a username on Twitter. Typically, this is used to respond to a tweet created by the user referenced.

Q. *What is the character limit for a tweet?*

A. 140 characters.

Q. *What is a hashtag and why are they important?*

A. Hashtags are a way to indicate a keyword by putting # in front of it. They are important because it allows people to tag tweets, search for them, and also organize all tweets from an event or chat. Think of it as a way to indicate the subject or subjects of a tweet.

Q. *Do I have to already have a network of friends on Twitter before I begin to find the service useful?*

A. No, many Twitter users send no more than a handful of messages a month. More people read messages on Twitter than create them. There are services that are focused on presenting Twitter messages (and the content of their links) as stand-alone application for reading only.

Workshop

Quiz

1. Why is there a character limit in a tweet?

A. Twitter decided that's long enough for a thought.

B. Twitter wanted to save on server space.

C. There is a hard-character limit on SMS.

2. True or False: There are two types of accounts on Twitter: one that is open and another that is closed.

3. What is a direct message, or DM?

A. A tweet that doesn't go through Twitter's servers.

B. A private tweet that goes only to the person you are sending it to.

C. A message that comes from Twitter corporate.

Quiz Answers

1. C. Twitter started off as a text or SMS system, and mobile phones can accept only 160 characters; 20 are reserved by Twitter for the username.

2. True. There are private accounts that are not open to anyone who doesn't have permission to follow.

3. B. A direct message is not shown in the public timeline and goes only to the person you are sending it to. You can send it only to someone who is following you.

Exercises

1. Visit www.twitter.com and create an account. Then follow a few of the suggested users.

2. Use search.twitter.com to find keywords that are interesting.

HOUR 2

Twitter Out of the Box

What You'll Learn in This Hour:

- What Twitter offers you
- Creating a new account
- Skinning your account
- Registering your application

What Twitter Offers You

Unlike almost any other API, Twitter exposes almost everything. Basically, if it's on Twitter, there is an API for it. That includes account setup and customization information. This is one of the great approaches of Twitter—focusing on the network and allowing others to create applications on top, and you have that right out of the box. After you set up your account, you are ready to go with almost every function that Twitter offers. There are limits, of course. Here are the current limits from (http://dev.twitter.com/pages/rate-limiting):

> 1,000 total updates per day, on any and all devices (web, mobile web, phone, API, and so on)
>
> 250 total direct messages per day, on any and all devices
>
> 150 API requests per hour
>
> OAuth calls are permitted 350 requests per hour

Whitelisting

Here is the current policy from Twitter.com on whitelisting.
(http://groups.google.com/group/twitter-development-talk/browse_thread/thread/1acd954f8a04fa84?pli=1)

Watch Out!

> There is no general idea of a whitelist for the Search API as with the REST API. However, under extraordinary circumstances, Twitter will work with developers to raise rate limiting for Search requests.

"Beginning in February 2011, Twitter no longer grants whitelisting requests. We will continue to allow whitelisting privileges for previously approved applications; however, any unanswered requests recently submitted to Twitter will not be granted whitelist access.

Twitter whitelisting was originally created as a way to allow developers to request large amounts of data through the REST API. It provided developers with an increase from 150 to 20,000 requests per hour, at a time when the API had few bulk request options and the Streaming API was not yet available.

With authentication, an application can make 350 GET requests on a user's behalf every hour. This means that for every user of your service, you can request their timelines, followers, friends, lists, and saved searches up to 350 times per hour. Actions such as Tweeting, Favoriting, Retweeting, and Following do not count toward this 350 limit. Using authentication on every request is recommended, so that you are not affected by other developers who share an IP address with you."

Setting Up Your Account

Odds are that you have already done this. However, in an effort to be complete, we are going to briefly walk through setting up and configuring a new account.

Open up a web browser and go to www.twitter.com; then click on 'Sign Up'.

Account Information (shown in Figure 2.1) is pretty clear; thus, I will not go over every field. Keep in mind that these fields, with exception to email, are most likely not checked for proper format. For example, you can see that I used "the bay" for my location. Although there are plenty of other sites with the name of the city I live in, back when I first set up my account, I was being a little more cautious. Yes, there was a time when Twitter was yet just another startup. What is great about Twitter (and now other services are seeing the value of this) is the fact that your username is unique and part of your Twitter URL. In this case, my unique Twitter username is Perivision. Thus, my unique Twitter address is http://twitter.com/perivision.

Did You Know?

> Many system admins will set up an account using a user's name and adding a 1 or a 123 after it. For example, consider the username: myusername123. This is common practice, and hackers look for it. Do not set up an account for a new user using this technique. Many systems now create a completely random string of letters and numbers and then email the password. This is a more secure procedure.

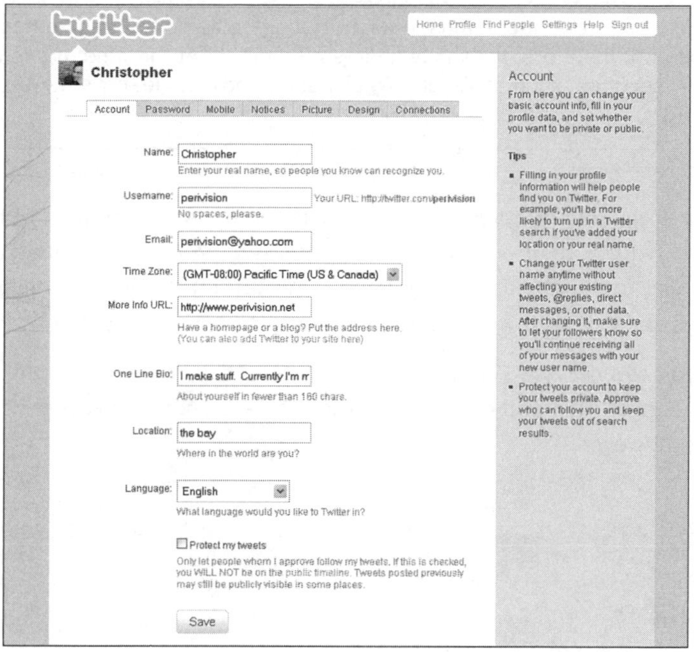

FIGURE 2.1 Example of the Twitter setup page.

We want to reinforce that you use a somewhat cryptic password when you get to this screen (see Figure 2.2). However, if you are setting up accounts for other users and use something simple for them with the expectation they will change it, double-check that they did change the password.

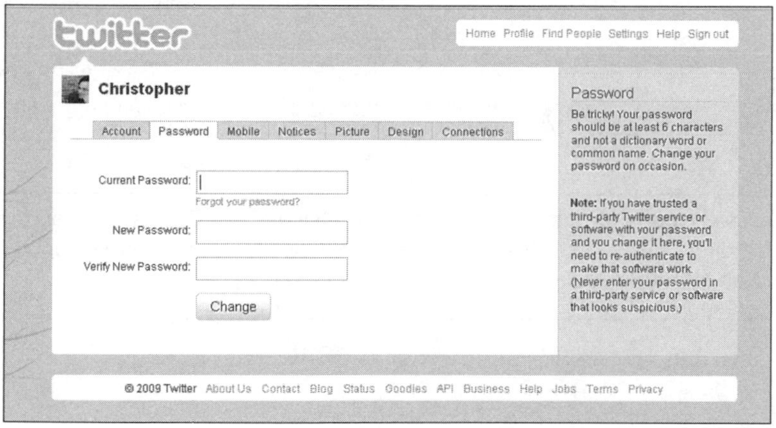

FIGURE 2.2 Screenshot of the password page.

Did you Know?

> Many people believe that one reason for Twitter's popularity is that usernames are unique and, therefore, the vanity address is unique. At the time of this writing, many other services, such as Facebook, LinkedIn, and Google, have moved to "vanity" URLs.

Twitter first started out as a text-messaging system only. Although most of the interactions with Twitter are through the Web, text messaging is still an option (see Figure 2.3). Be careful, though, if you do not have unlimited SMS messaging with your plan; it can get out of control, and thus very expensive, very quickly.

Although you can get New Follower email alerts and Direct Message email alerts, you can no longer get email alerts for mentions. There are third-party services that can do this, however.

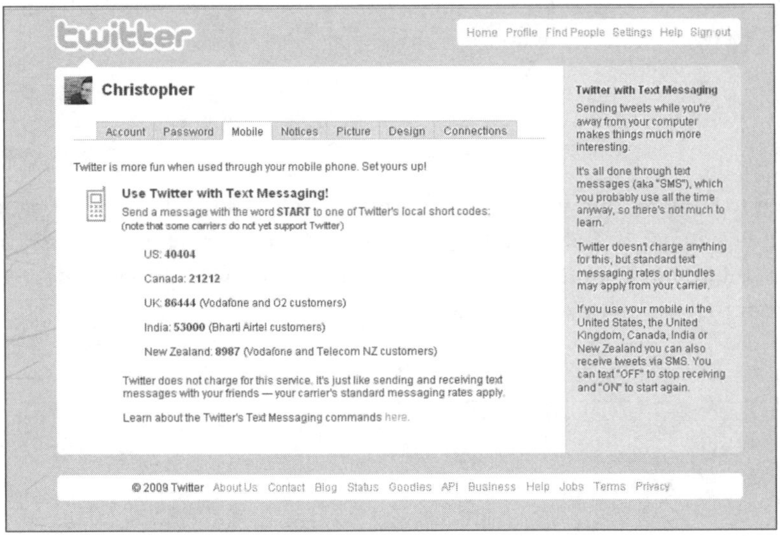

FIGURE 2.3
Screenshot of the mobile options on Twitter.

Did You Know?

> In the screenshot shown in Figure 2.4, the text "Direct Text Emails" is used to refer to "direct message." This terminology is a holdover from when Twitter started as an SMS service.

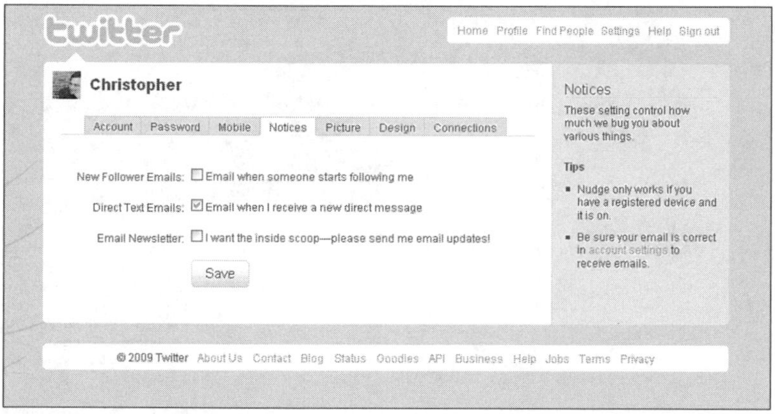

FIGURE 2.4
Notices screen in Twitter.com.

Registering Your Application

With Twitter, you can register your application at (http://twitter.com/apps/net) so a user can share OAuth credentials with you (we will cover this in later hours of this book) and that when someone gets a tweet, the person can see what application it came from. If you are going to create any type of Twitter client that can send messages, it's worth your time to set this up. Wait until you have a beta version of your site alive and running. You cannot register a nonfunctioning site. In addition, it is possible that Twitter may review your site for promotion on Twitter.com. So, make sure your beta is working well.

Twitter originally allowed a username-password combination for registering a new application, but no longer. The following is from the Twitter site:

> "We originally allowed applications to create a source parameter for non-OAuth use but that has been discontinued. Applications pre-OAuth source parameters will remain active, but new registrations are no longer accepted."

The registration process is simple enough: Provide the name of your application, OAuth information (http://oauth.net/about/), a short description, and a logo, and you are ready to go. As you can see in the screenshot (see Figure 2.5), I registered TwittFilter. I can, however, register more than one application if I choose.

You can also authorize other applications to have access to your account. Under the Settings and then Connections tab, you can see all applications you have authorized. It's a good idea to keep an eye on this for your own account as well as accounts you manage. Figure 2.6 is an example of applications registered to have access to the Perivision account.

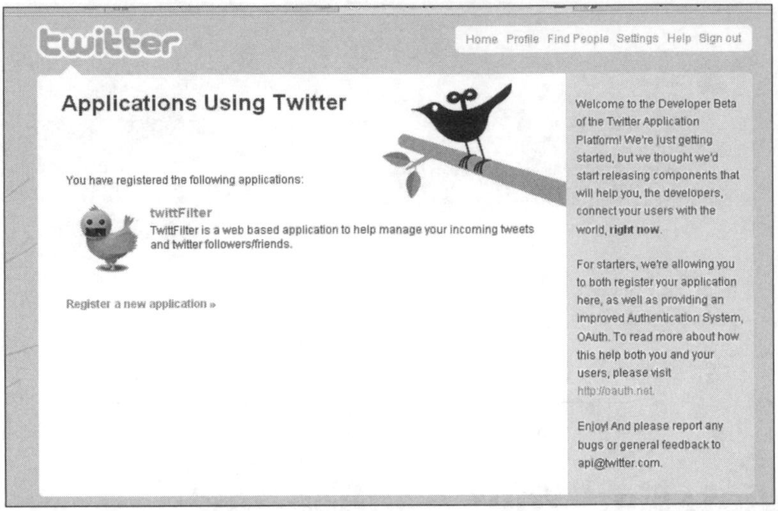

FIGURE 2.5
Example of a registered application.

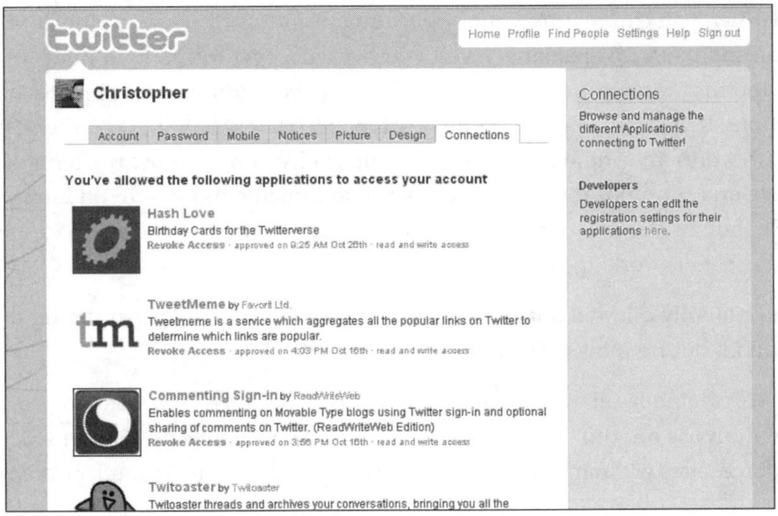

FIGURE 2.6
List of applications that have access to the Perivision Twitter account.

The Twitter Client

The default page of Twitter.com has changed a few times over the years, so what this page will look like by the time of this printing is unknown. However, as you can see from the screenshot shown in Figure 2.7, the folks at Twitter seem to be committed to making search and topic trending a major part of Twitter's offering. As such, when you are developing your application, understanding this direction is important so that you do not develop something that later becomes a native functionality within Twitter.

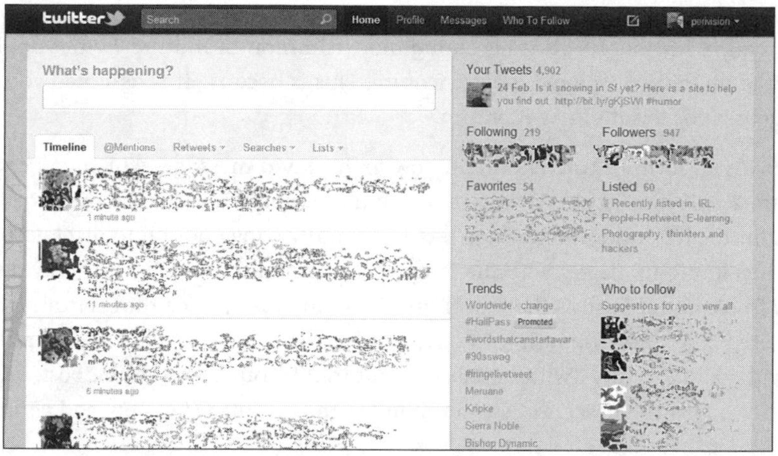

FIGURE 2.7 Example of the Twitter home page as of early 2011.

The web client that Twitter provides is bare bones and purposely so. However, most of the features and functions you need to fully engage with Twitter are here: reading your timeline, mentions, direct messages; managing your following and followers; as well as managing the recently added lists. Although the Twitter.com website is "bare bones," it serves as a great example of the minimum functionality a Twitter user would expect from a client, which is the following:

- Create a new tweet
- Create a new direct message
- Read your latest messages from your timeline
- Read your latest mentions
- Read your latest direct messages
- Read your lists
- Respond, reply, and retweet messages
- Reply to a direct message (which is different from replying to a public or mention)
- Search Twitter
- Edit your lists
- Follow/unfollow a tweeter
- Block a tweeter
- Create or remove Favorites

Notice that I did not include in the list anything about setting up and managing your account. Although this is becoming more common in mature Twitter applications, it is still not considered a basic feature. This is because it is assumed you can manage your account via Twitter.com.

There is also a form of convention on how to display a message, which you can see in Figure 2.7. Typically, the Twitter image of the person who sent the message is displayed on the left, and the message box is normally wide enough to display three lines, thus lining up nicely with the image. The date and source is normally displayed in a smaller font as the fourth line. You may also notice that certain words are colored blue, indicating they are hyperlinked. The current Twitter convention is to provide a link to any Twitter user's account that is found within the post, any term with a # as the first character, and any term with http:// as the lead characters.

Summary

Good job. You should have your account set up. You should also have a good idea of what basic features and functions your client or customers may expect if you decide to create a Twitter client. Although it's not necessary, skinning your Twitter page is a worthwhile exercise.

Q&A

Q. ***What is a vanity URL?***

A. A vanity URL is a URL unique to a user that employs the username in the URL structure.

Q. ***We know that there is a 150 API call limit. What are the other two limits at this time?***

A. 1,000 total updates per day, on any and all devices (web, mobile web, phone, API, and so on) and 250 total direct messages per day, on any and all devices.

Q. ***Can I use my login and password when I register my application?***

A. No, you need to have information from setting up OAuth within your application, including the URL that twitter will use to verify your application.

Workshop

Quiz

1. True or False: Twitter's main objective is to build a full-featured super client application.

2. True or False: It is never a good idea to create passwords that are easy to guess, even if you expect it to be changed later.

Quiz Answers

1. False. Twitter wants people to build interesting products on their service. The goal with twtter.com is to focus on an enjoyable experience.

2. True. Bots exist that try to guess common passwords.

Exercises

1. If you have not done so already, set up a Twitter account.

2. Take a look at various Twitter page designs. Can you figure out how they were done?

3. If you have an idea of what type of Twitter application or widget you want to build, what percentage of its features and functions are already supported on the Twitter.com site?

HOUR 3

Key Issues to Consider When Developing Twitter Applications

What You'll Learn in This Hour:

- Different types of Twitter users and how they impact code design
- Different types of Twitter applications and program architecture
- Things to consider if you are not building a web-based application

Types of Twitter Users

As one would expect with an API system as open as Twitter, and the explosion of interesting applications people have developed, we have also seen the development of different types of Twitter users. Understanding these types of users and knowing which of them we are trying to reach will inform how we may want to build our Twitter application framework. As with any large user base, there are a number of ways to set up categories. In this hour, we will break down and discuss the users in the following categories or types.

The News Reader

Twitter is a great source of breaking news, whether it's politics, business, sports, or following celebrities. Most users use searches to find what they are interested in, or they follow Twitter feeds that act like RSS readers. For example, BreakingNews is what you would guess it would be—a Twitter account publishing breaking news. Most news outlets have such accounts: CBSNews, ABC, BBC, and so on. The screen-shot of NewsSnacker, an application created by the author (shown in Figure 3.1) is a good example of a Twitter application that focuses on the news.

FIGURE 3.1
Screenshot of NewsSnacker.

Although making search and Twitter account API reads from Twitter does not require authentication, you can still get dinged going over the API limit because Twitter will limit calls from an IP address. So, you still need to keep in mind how often you make calls. In the case of NewsSnacker, we use a white-listed account because the user could exceed the API calls-per-hour limit since each news service is a separate call. Suppose that the user has 10 sources and refreshes every 30 minutes. That is 200 calls in an hour, which is over the current limit of 150 for non logged in users. This does not include normal calls to check for new mentions or direct messages from the user's chosen Twitter client application. An alternative approach is to create a list of twitter news accounts and then call that list. However since newsSnacker removes duplicate posts, a large number of returns on the list call would be required. Both approaches have their merits however; one feature of newsSnacker is to allow a custom list of sources. This can be done by having the user log into the application and then select which of their lists they would like to call thus the second approach is being pursued in the next version of the application.

Chatters

Twitter does allow for people to have conversations; it's called a *direct message*. However, many people like to hold their conversations in public and a big attraction for these people is conversation threading. This is a very complicated proposition, so much so that new APIs are being created to deal with this situation. We will cover retweeting in later hours, but this could cause quite an impact on your code's structure because of older reply techniques that use the letters RT for conversations instead of recent API methods that support replies formally. So, supporting Twitter conversation is a decision you will want to make early in your product's design.

Power Users and PR Managers

Although you will have a drag-out fight between the two because one is personal messaging and the other is more professional, the impact on product design is not that much different. PR (public relations) managers, power users, and anyone who consumes or monitors a lot of Twitter information will put special requirements on you as a product developer. Like the limits to the number of API calls mentioned in the section discussing the user group news readers, the issues with the power users and PR managers group will be the same, with the added requirements of being able to sort and search the stream of messages that come in. They may also need to send messages on a schedule or from people using the same account. There is usually no simple way around this issue other than to start thinking of a well laid-out database up front. You may want to also explore having your server make the API calls and relay the information to your Twitter application in the form of automatic processes or bots. Furthermore, set up your architecture to deal with a wide variety of API calls. We will cover this later in the hour. PR managers will want more than just searching the Twitter stream; they will want to make sense of it and make sense of who is on that stream and their influence. The API has just expanded to handle retweets, but not all Twitter clients will be updated to work with this API. As such, you still need to pay attention to RT (the current convention for a retweet) and hashtags. Plan for this up front. Also, plan to keep some of the user information in your database; you will want to use it for user profile and relationship analysis. Although the number of power users, compared to typical Twitter users, is quite low, having a power user using (and advocating) your application is highly desirable, and although every power user you talk to will have a different list of features and functions, there are some things you must be able to support—for example, dynamic search. Just providing a call and return to the search API is not good enough anymore. The current and future power users of Twitter are going to demand just as much power and feedback as they get using Google search. For example, power users would want links with the tweets that are returned to be followed and analyzed in some manner. Perhaps you should show a thumbnail of the site, or display the title and the first 50 words of the link. Be sensitive to nonstandard protocols, such as searching stock quotes using the $ sign in front of the stock market ID. For example, $aapl for Apple. Power users are going to demand speed and customization and will fully expect that your application understand the nonstandard features (social conventions) of Twitter.

Microbloggers

Microbloggers will want to take the time to craft each tweet carefully. Pay attention to the ease of creating a message—that is, allowing them to save as drafts, sending to multiple Twitter accounts, spell checking (yes, spell checking), and although this is not easy, a quick look up of the other tweeters or access to a list of tweeters. Especially for PR users, you may want to have a look at simple web-based CRM products to give you ideas. A new API to Twitter is the capability to store lists of tweeters. This is useful to all power users as well as microbloggers.

High-Frequency Users (TwitterHolics)

The current rules of the API system allow only 350 calls per hour if you are logged in, 150 if not. This may seem like a lot, but based on what features you are providing to your users, this can go very quickly. It's not unlikely that you could have five API calls per user action if you need to make follow-up calls. If they are high-frequency users, they may find themselves approaching the 350-call limit pretty quickly. Although there are calls that do not require credentials, you could still run up against this limit because Twitter does count the number of calls from an IP. As such, be sure you monitor the number of calls the user has left and deal with it accordingly. The good news is that an API call exists for checking how many API calls the user has left which does not count against your API limit. However, calling it over and over again too often (every 5 seconds, for example) could trigger other traffic limit controls.

New Users

This is less an API architecture question than a GUI issue. Although GUI design is not addressed directly in this book, consider using clear terms and common metaphors (like an email system, for example) for the layout and functionality of your application. Do not assume that your users will understand various social conventions in Twitter, so explain it up front and design your functions' intent clearly using tool tips for icons for example. If you are making an application that reflects some aspects of the Twitter.com site, be sure to follow the conventions Twitter uses.

Bots

Bots (programs that perform automated tasks), including creating spam or setting up phishing attacks, will always be an issue. A sophisticated Twitter application will be aware of some of these bots and try to protect users. You may, however, need to create your own bots (for good, not evil). For example, you might take a RSS feed and republish it to Twitter after passing it through a business rules filter which is something the main Author of this book does. Because a bot is nothing more than "rules" you have for dealing with reading or creating Twitter messages or lists, you will find creating automated processes very easy with the Twitter API.

Types of Twitter Applications

Normally, when I'm about to start writing a Twitter application, I already know what I want it to do. Thus, based on the features and functions I have in mind, I already know what platform and category of users I'm targeting. Because we cannot know what you, the reader, have in mind, we will try to set up a basic framework for thinking about the various things you can do with Twitter as we go through this book. Part of Twitter's success is its simplicity and wide-open API. As such, people have developed powerful, sophisticated applications, mashups, and simple widgets that run in other apps or on web pages. However, the approach you will take building a full-on application is different from building a simple mashup or widget.

By the Way

> A mashup is a web page or application that takes two or more data sources and combines them into a new service. Typically, mashups create a functionality not envisioned by the creators of the original sources. Twitter is a very popular mashup source.

Building a feature-rich Twitter application takes some planning. Although we will walk you through various examples of how to build apps around specific APIs, we want to bring focus, too. There is an overall approach you should determine before you write line one.

Widget

Let's talk about architecture around a simple widget. Suppose our simple widget is going to display the results of a search or the latest tweets from a user. This is the easiest to build. All we have to think about is four steps: make an API call to Twitter, parse the return, format it, and display it. That's it. We diagrammed this simple architecture in Figure 3.2.

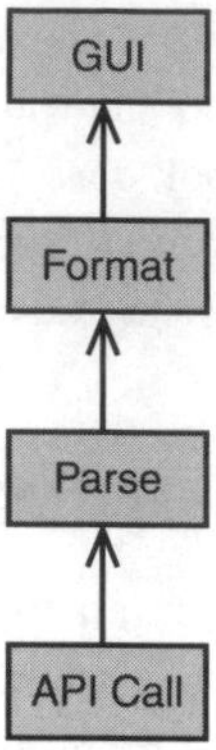

FIGURE 3.2
Example of a simple Twitter API diagram.

All API systems work this way, but what's great about Twitter is that the results are already of value. Quite often, blogging sites (mostly personal) have this type of widget. I have a widget like this on my blog (see Figure 3.3).

FIGURE 3.3
Screenshot of a Twitter widget on www.perivision.net/wordpress.

Mashup

Because a mashup can be the combination of anything, and that's kind of the point of mashups, we are going to think about our architecture a bit differently. Although technically, a mashup can be just two sources of information or very complex number and relationship of sources, we are going to stick with the spirit of what is considered a mashup by just thinking about mixing two data sources. For example, we can take our Twitter search feed and weather data and display tweets from places that are raining versus tweets from where it's sunny. In this case, we need to store our returns from Twitter somewhere while we get weather data. Then we need to perform some business logic on those returns.

By the Way

Business logic is a nontechnical term generally used to describe the functional algorithms that handle information exchange between a database and a user interface. It is distinguished from input/output data validation and product logic. *From Wikipedia, the free encyclopedia*

In this case, we need to hold our returns in an array so that when we get the weather data, we can reorganize our data. Because tweets are small, discrete messages, it makes sense to create a multidimensional array object that we can easily explore. So now, we will add one more layer to our diagram. As you can see in Figure 3.4, we are using arrays to store our parsed return so that we can apply some rules (business logic) to create a more valuable dataset.

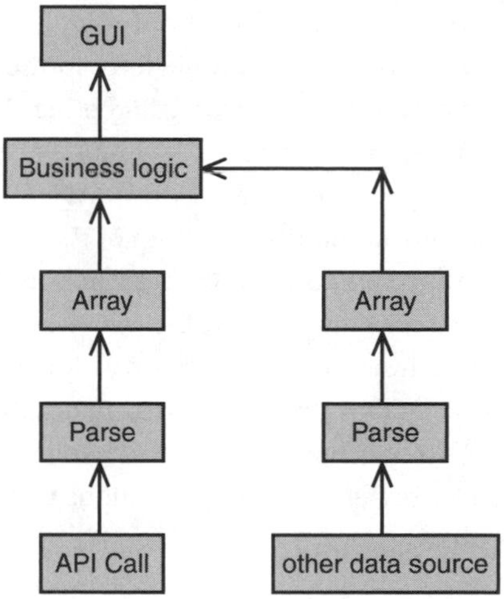

FIGURE 3.4
Example of combining two data streams.

Twitter Application

I would expect that only a small percentage of readers of this book are intending to build a full-featured Twitter client, but if you are, you want to approach building your application like any other application. Think about your calls to Twitter almost like calls to a database where you provide a set of parameters with your call and get a filtered response that can then be analyzed or applied to a set of rules. It is also well worth your time to set up your Twitter calls in a separate class to deal with errors and changes to the API. You should also set up another class to deal with converting your Twitter calls into multidimensional arrays and/or storing them in a database. The reason for this is that Twitter is still changing. Even during the writing of this book, we had to make adjustments to the book's index as new methods were introduced and other calls were deprecated. By keeping these two processes in standalone classes, you're going to save yourself some headaches down the road. If you are planning on building a full-scale Twitter app, we recommend bookmarking the website for this book and the Twitter API site. Really! It changes and grows that much.

Also, somewhat like a database, you can store information in Twitter. For example, a much-overlooked feature is favorites. This API call allows you to save tweets. This can be quite useful as a means of understanding which tweeters and types of tweets a user tends to favor. New to the API list is lists. This is a list of tweeters a user creates. Again, it's a powerful bit of information that can be quite useful in understanding users' preferences. What is more interesting, though, is using these two API calls as storage devices if your user is under your control—a corporate account, for example. Because the user of that account does not interact with the account personally, you can use these API calls to store tweets and lists that can have greater meaning than originally intended. For example, suppose you have a corporate account for company X. We can store in the favorite list all tweets that match a certain rule, like any tweet that has an unfavorable term in the tweet. Now you have a list of tweets that public relations can examine using other than the application you developed. Also, remember you have access to user bio, location, and other elements. Again, because of how open Twitter is with its API, you can use these fields for anything—for example, including the updating of the Twitter background based on the latest message from the company, or perhaps updating the location field if you're a mobile food van, or changing the profile image based on the time of day or your mood. Instant database functionality ... of sorts! Now this does not mean you should not have a database if you intended on storing anything beyond the simple examples provided here. Also, it is not recommended to abuse this open access by placing unrelated data in these fields. Most applications will follow a simple structure, as illustrated in Figure 3.5.

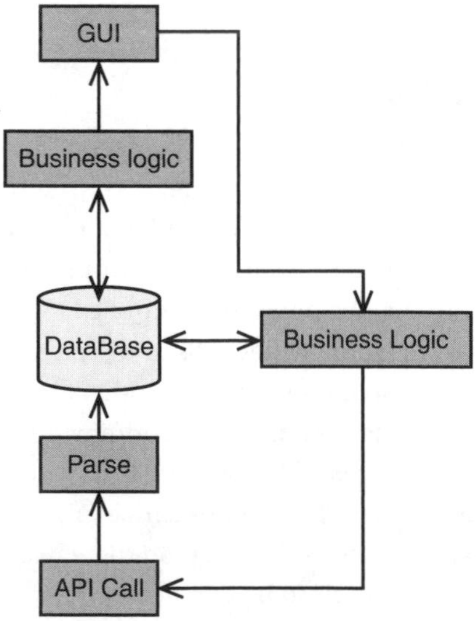

FIGURE 3.5 Example of an architecture placing a database between API calls and an application's business logic.

Pure Chat

This class of Twitter application is concerned with creating tweets, reading incoming tweets, searching Twitter, retweeting, setting/getting favorites, and displaying simple user account information. Everything can be done as a standalone command, meaning you do not need to store information outside of Twitter. Each command has only one or two API calls. The current Twitter.com main web page is this type of application. Since we do not need to keep track of a state or store data, we can create this application using nothing more than a simple collection of PHP calls. For this class of application, we want to think about our application as a series of standalone pages. It would be a good idea to use cookies on the user's computer in case you need to store last-seen dates or other simple pieces of information.

Structured Display

Very common with Twitter applications are the capabilities to save groups, perform more advanced searches, display only new information and some threaded conversations, and so on. Although some of these structured displays can be somewhat complex, the approach you would take as a programmer is not that much different. Many of these structured displays can be achieved without storing information on the server but by using API calls and cookies instead. Consider the following example: Suppose we want to display a column of unread tweets, tweets from our "top 10" friends, three or four saved searches, and your current favorites lists. All of these can be achieved by passing variables within the existing API calls. You will actually work far harder at the UI than the backend coding. For this class of application, we want to set up our code as a series of calls that are more or less self-contained. This will make dealing with the GUI less troublesome as redesign is requested or required.

Twitter Statistics

Collecting statistics from Twitter data provides great promise for research, improved discover and communications. However, this class of Twitter application is a bit harder. TwittFilter, another application created by this author is in this class as shown in Figure 3.6.

This class of Twitter application depends on creating new information through analyzing the return or returns from past Twitter calls, and storing or modifying this information on the server, typically in a database. This, however, is where we find Twitter to be the most interesting; because Twitter has such a large user base, you can gather enough data to infer information that does not have a direct user correlation. Did someone say mashup? For example, a very popular and now API-supported feature called "Trends" in Twitter is nothing more than a constant search across all messages being sent to Twitter, displaying the terms with the highest rate of occurrence. However, because of the large user base and ease of creating tweets, Trends tends to be one of the first places that news breaks.

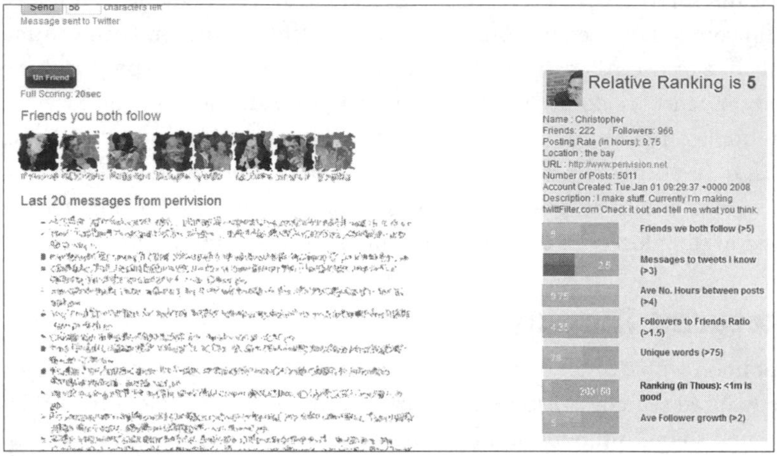

FIGURE 3.6
User Scoring screen of TwittFilter.

Because we need to store information as well as grab details for analysis, we need to think about how we structure our program differently. For this class of application, we want to think of Twitter as more of a database source. Setting up our arrays that allow for ease of use within formulas, as well as pulling and pushing into databases, will be a great benefit as our analytics become more and more complex. However, if you are not white listed, you will run into the API call limit quite quickly. It's recommended that if you plan to do statics that require large sample sets or recursive calls, that you explore the streaming API.

Platform

Now that we know the class of application we want to develop, we need to think about the delivery platform. If you are going to develop for UI-hosted apps, such as native mobile apps or Adobe Air, you may again want to modify how to approach your coding. Typically, when creating an app for the iPhone or other mobile platform, many of our UI elements are going to be handled on the device. You also will want to minimize the amount of traffic going back and forth as much as possible. Therefore, you should design your application around the output, which could be XML, JSON, or some custom bitcode. In this case, the organizational structure you choose will dictate how you structure your backend code. Because we have the luxury of storing information on our target platform, we can focus on speed and ease of architecture. Even though our backend code is not responsible for the presentation layer (display), you still need to follow the basic tenants of good programming design by keeping the business logic separate from the API calls; don't fall into the trap of making each call from your application as a separate instance, as you may with the Pure Chat approach. You never know when your application starts to take on more features than you planned.

Summary

In this hour, you were introduced to various types of Twitter users. Depending on your product's target market, you may need to think about how you will approach the design architecture of your product.

This was not intended to be an exhaustive list, nor an absolute one. One could easily break this list into smaller pieces or roll it up into more general categories; instead, it's to provide a framework to think about the application you intend to build. We broke this up into two sections because we want to make a distinction between the type of use and type of application, However, do not think you can explore one without the other. When designing any application, you should always start with the user. What is the value proposition you are offering users in order for them to use your application? Once you understand that, you can then move to the type of application you want to create. So, we started out with an exploration of types of Twitter users, and then types of Twitter applications. We ended this hour with a short conversation about platforms. If you are developing for anything other than the desktop, you are most likely already aware of these points, but we included them for less-experienced developers as good to know.

Now, hold on to your hats because in the following hours, we are going to start building code!

Q&A

Q. ***Should I apply for a white-list account before I start coding?***

A. No. White listed accounts are currents not available. However, you will find that having 350 calls per hour is plenty as you learn how to develop your program.

Q. ***I plan to make a simple Twitter application now, but I may expand it later. Should I bother setting up a separate twitterAPI class?***

A. Yes. If you have any plans, even just thoughts of doing something beyond a few different types of API calls, set up a separate class for your API calls. In addition to new APIs, current API calls can change.

Workshop

Quiz

1. What is meant by thinking about Twitter as a type of database?
2. I check my Twitter account only a few days a week on my iPhone. What kind of Twitter user am I?
3. Is it illegal to create bots?
4. What is the easiest type of Twitter application to create?

Quiz Answers

1. This is a two-part answer: 1) Although Twitter exposes everything, you still can only get detail data on users one at a time although this is changing. Thus, thinking about accessing user statistics as if you were accessing a database is a useful way to think about what you can do with Twitter. 2) If you have control over the Twitter account(s), you can use the fields in Twitter to store information instead of on your database.
2. You are a news reader. Even if you are reading only your timeline (people you follow), you are more of a consumer of information than a creator.
3. No—and not all bots are bad. However, the good folks at Twitter do actively look for automated processess that abuse the system.
4. A pure chat widget.

Exercises

1. Describe your typical target user and then determine the class of application you feel is appropriate for your user.
2. If you plan to create an automated process, write down each step and then count the number of times you will need to call Twitter to get information. What happens if the user hits refresh 10 times in 10 minutes? Will you go over the 150-API call limit if they are not logged in?

HOUR 4

Creating a Development Environment

What You'll Learn in This Hour:

- What is a LAMP stack?
- Setting up a local web server
- How to secure your web server
- How to choose the right development tools

Background of LAMP Stacks

If you've ever built a dynamic web application, it's no news to you that you need a web server to run your code; you can't just open files straight from Firefox like static HTML files. Most of the code we write in this book is in PHP, so you'll need an Apache web server with PHP installed to run the examples. If you already have a development environment in place, you can skip this hour.

So, before we get started, what is LAMP? From Wikipedia:

> LAMP is an acronym for a solution stack of free, open source software, originally coined from the first letters of Linux (operating system), Apache HTTP Server, MySQL (database software), and PHP, Python, or Perl (scripting language), principal components to build a viable general purpose web server.

Although the "P" in LAMP stands for PHP, Python, or Perl, it most commonly refers to PHP.

> **Did You Know?** PHP originally stood for Personal Home Page.

LAMP stack packages have become popular because configuring Apache, PHP, MySQL, and all the necessary components is no easy task. They offer developers a quick and easy way to get a web server running with everything they need on their local machines. Even if you have an existing web host with everything you need, it is often faster and more convenient to develop code locally.

Although there are entire books about LAMP, this hour will serve as a quick intro or refresher so you can follow along for the rest of the book, even if you're new to PHP. Before we set up our own server, here's an overview of each component:

- **Apache**—The most popular HTTP server on the Web since 1996; it currently serves the majority of sites on the Web.
- **MySQL**—A relational database management system (RDBMS) used for persistent storage in many applications.
- **PHP: Hypertext Processor**—A popular general-purpose scripting language generally used to create dynamic web applications often running on top of Apache and using a MySQL database for persistent storage.

Did You Know?

> *AMP is a term most commonly denoting the use of Apache, MySQL, and PHP regardless of the operating system. There are variants such as LAMP, WAMP, and MAMP for Linux, Windows, and Mac, respectively. All components are available on all major operating systems, although the majority of web servers running Apache use Linux.

Setting Up a Local Web Server

LAMP is a common term describing a web server using Apache, MySQL, and PHP, but there are a number of ways to set up a LAMP server. Although you could install Apache with PHP and a MySQL server independently, getting all the right components set up and working together can be a tricky process. The easiest way to get a web server up and running is to use one of many LAMP packages available, which will help you install everything you need to start testing your PHP code.

Running a local web server makes development easier and faster because files can be edited directly from your computer and do not have to be uploaded to another server. This is sometimes referred to as the *sandbox*. In many cases, you can also test your applications without Internet access, although you will need connectivity if you are making any calls to the Twitter API. After you have a live site, developing locally will also give you a chance to test out your code in a sandboxed environment before making changes on your actual site. However, you should also set up a testing area in the same environment as your live server because your local web server's configuration will differ from your webhost's.

By the Way

> Although LAMP packages are convenient and easy to install, they are typically used by developers looking to get a development environment up and running and may not be optimized for the best performance or security. Most production environments are set up carefully by an IT professional.

Introducing XAMPP

Our LAMP package of choice is called XAMPP, where the X is cross-platform and the extra "P" stands for Perl support (which we won't be utilizing in this book). It is one of the most popular LAMP distributions because it installs everything you'll need for most development with minimal effort, including phpMyAdmin, a popular web-based MySQL administration tool. Because it runs on Windows, Mac, Linux, and Solaris, you can be sure you'll have a consistent experience no matter what platform you're using.

Installing XAMPP

The XAMPP installation is so simple that it tricks you into thinking anybody could set up a web server. At the time of this writing, the current version is 1.7.2. Because XAMPP is frequently updated, your experience may differ slightly from what we describe here. To download the package, follow these steps:

1. Visit www.apachefriends.org.
2. Go to the XAMPP project page.
3. Click on the XAMPP icon at the top of the page to get to the links for the download page for your platform.
4. Depending on your platform, different options may be available. For your convenience, we've outlined quick installation tips for Windows, Mac, and Linux in the sections that follow.

Watch Out!

> Regardless of your operating system, installing XAMPP will overwrite any existing XAMPP installations. If you already have XAMPP, you can skip this section.

Windows

Windows users will see download options—XAMPP, XAMPP Lite, and XAMPP Add-Ons. For the purposes of this book, XAMPP Lite is fine. One of the biggest differences is that it doesn't include the FileZilla FTP Server or the Mercury Mail Transport System. The easiest option is to download the XAMPP Lite EXE, which includes an installer. Compared to the ZIP download, it is about half the download size because of better compression.

If you don't want XAMPP making changes to the Registry (required for all installed Windows applications), you can follow the instructions on the download page to install the ZIP version. You don't need the Mercury Mail Transport System to allow your applications to send emails. This is normally done using an existing SMTP server, such as one provided by Gmail or your web host.

Installing XAMPP Lite from the EXE installer is straightforward:

1. Fire up the downloaded XAMPP Lite EXE and click Install. The default option will extract all the files to `C:\xampplite`.
2. After the files are extracted, choose the default options in the command prompt windows that follow, until you reach the final menu, which has no default.
3. From the final menu, choose 1 to start the XAMPP control panel (shown in Figure 4.1).

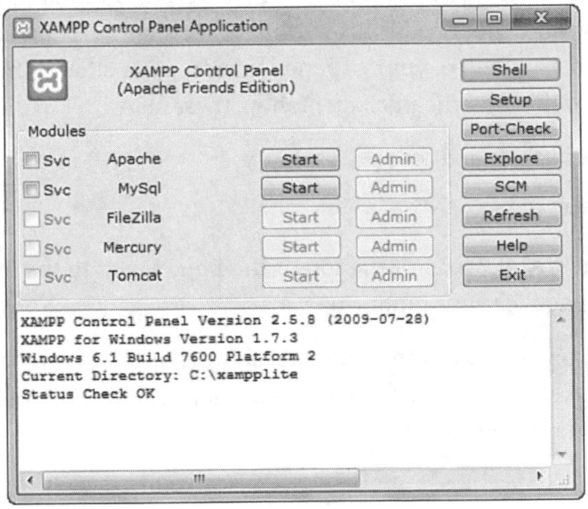

FIGURE 4.1
XAMPP Control Panel (Windows).

4. Check the Svc boxes for both Apache and MySQL and confirm the prompts that follow.
5. Click Start next to both Apache and MySQL to fire up both servers.
6. You may now exit the command prompt menu and the XAMPP control panel.

Did You Know?

A service is a program that starts with Windows and is often automatically run by the system even before a user logs in. If Apache and MySQL are not installed as system services, they must be started manually.

Mac

On the Mac download page, grab the Universal Binary—the file containing Apache, MySQL, and PHP. You do not need the developer package.

After you've downloaded the file, installing XAMPP on a Mac is just like installing any other application from a DMG file:

1. Open the downloaded DMG file.
2. Drag and drop the orange XAMPP folder into your Applications folder.
3. Open XAMPP Control in `/Applications/XAMPP` and start Apache and MySQL.

Linux

Download XAMPP Linux—the file containing Apache, MySQL, and PHP. If you're using Linux, we'll assume you pretty much know what you're doing, but we've outlined the installation steps to make sure we're all on the same page:

1. Open a terminal and switch users to root or run all the subsequent commands with `sudo`.
2. Extract the downloaded file to `/opt`:

   ```
   tar xvfz xampp-linux-1.7.4.tar.gz -C /opt
   ```

3. Start XAMPP using the following command:

   ```
   /opt/lampp/lampp start
   ```

   If everything went okay, you should see something like the following output:

   ```
   Starting XAMPP 1.7.4...

   LAMPP: Starting Apache...
   LAMPP: Starting MySQL...
   LAMPP started.
   Ready. Apache and MySQL are running.
   ```

If you encountered any errors during the preceding steps, make sure you were running all commands as root or prepending each command with `sudo`. Otherwise, take a look at the Linux FAQ at www.apachefriends.org/en/faq-xampp-linux.html#start.

Does It All Work?

Presumably, you now have a local PHP-enabled web server and a MySQL database. To see if it all works, open up a web browser and go to http://localhost.

If everything is working correctly, you'll be redirected to http://localhost/xampp/splash.php. If you see nothing, something is wrong. To troubleshoot, visit the download page for your platform on the XAMPP website for some tips, or try reinstalling XAMPP again from scratch using the directions on the XAMPP website. If you had an existing web server running on your machine, try uninstalling it and reinstalling XAMPP because they will conflict with each other if they are both using the default settings. You may also encounter a conflict if Skype is running because it uses ports 80 and 443 as alternative ports for incoming connections. If you are having trouble running XAMPP and have Skype installed, search the Skype documentation for "conflicts."

Take note of where XAMPP is installed. Inside the XAMPP root folder is a folder called `htdocs`. This is your web root, and files inside it are accessible via http://localhost. We'll be referring to the `htdocs` folder for the rest of the book; it's where all the code goes.

Securing Your Web Server

XAMPP is designed to be a convenient package to help web developers get a server running as easily as possible, but in many cases, convenience means risk. XAMPP's defaults leave your local web server open to risks on many fronts. Most people are behind a router that typically uses Network Address Translation (NAT) to share a single Internet connection. By default, NAT acts as a firewall by discarding all incoming requests to your network, including those bound for your web server.

Did You Know?

> If you are using a home router and want others to be able to access your web server, forward TCP requests on port 80 (HTTP) to the local IP of your computer on your router's port forwarding configuration page. In some cases, your ISP may block incoming requests to port 80, so you may want to try another port, such as 8080, to port 80 of your local IP. When setting up port forwarding, you should also assign your server a static IP to prevent it from changing and breaking your forwarding rules.

The following are security issues with the default installation of XAMPP:

- The MySQL root account has no password.
- MySQL is accessible via network.
- phpMyAdmin is accessible via network.
- The XAMPP demo page is accessible via network.

In general, you'll want to ensure that all your passwords are secure—containing some combination of uppercase and lowercase letters, numbers, symbols, and no words or names that could be found in a dictionary.

For the rest of this book, we will use the following credentials for everything, but feel free to use your own secure usernames and passwords:

- **Username**—`twitter` or `root` (MySQL)
- **Password**—`s0m3Th1ng`

Note that we are using the same credentials everywhere so that this book is easy to follow. On your own sites, it's a good idea to use different secure credentials for everything. If you're wondering why there are no symbols in our password, at the time of this writing, there is a bug in the XAMPP security console for Windows that prevents you from setting passwords with symbols in them.

XAMPP Security Console

Although we need to fix a number of things, XAMPP makes it easy for us to take care of everything at once. The XAMPP security console will guide you through securing your XAMPP installation on all OSes, although each package may differ because each uses slightly different components.

Next, we outline some steps you can take to secure your web server. If you'd like more detail about the security issues the XAMPP security console addresses, we explain the main issues in detail in the next few sections. Otherwise, you can skip ahead to the "Development Tools" section.

Windows

The Windows version of XAMPP has a web-based security console to help you secure your local development server. Go to http://localhost/security/ in your browser, and you will see a page with a title like "XAMPP SECURITY [Security Check 1.1]," which will give you a quick overview of security issues with your current configuration.

From here, you can click the link to http://localhost/security/xamppsecurity.php, which you'll be able to use in the following sections to secure MySQL and the XAMPP pages.

In the MYSQL SECTION, set the MySQL password to `s0m3Th1ng` using defaults for the rest of the options. If you'd like, you can store the password you set here in a text file by checking the last box before submitting the form. The saved password file cannot be accessed directly from your web server because it does not reside in `htdocs`.

Next, we need to secure the XAMPP directory in the second section. For simplicity's sake, we'll use the same login information we used for MySQL—`twitter` for the username and `s0m3Th1ng` for the password. Again, you can check the box if you want this login info saved to a text file.

After you've changed both passwords, you can go back to http://localhost/security/, and you'll notice that XAMPP has been secured. You may notice an UNKNOWN status by Tomcat because we have not installed that add-on.

Mac and Linux

Run `/Applications/XAMPP/xamppfiles/xampp security` (Mac) or `/opt/lampp/lampp security` (Linux) to secure your server. We assume that you use `twitter` for all usernames except for MySQL, which uses `root`, and `s0m3Th1ng` for all passwords.

XAMPP Pages

By default, all the pages under http://localhost/, including the demo pages at http://localhost/xampp/, are exposed and available to anybody who can see your computer on the network. Although the security page is available only from your local machine, other potentially sensitive information such as the `phpinfo()` page is still accessible without a password.

Did You Know?

> The `phpinfo()` function outputs all details of your current PHP configuration and is useful when reconfiguring PHP, checking to see if a certain extension is enabled, or checking the values of certain server-side variables. Although XAMPP includes a page already, all it takes is a PHP file containing `<?php phpinfo()`.

MySQL

There are two MySQL issues that we'll point out. The most urgent issue is that there is no root password, so anybody can log in to your MySQL server and make any changes if the person knows your IP address or hostname. Our other potential issue is that the MySQL server is accessible from other IP addresses. For the purposes of this book, no other computer will need access to your MySQL server, so we could restrict access to only localhost. However, because we have configured MySQL with a secure password, the default settings should be good enough for development purposes.

Did You Know?

> The `root` user is the default superuser for many systems, including MySQL and, most commonly, Linux.

phpMyAdmin

Leaving phpMyAdmin open is just as bad as leaving MySQL open to attack, because it is a web-based interface to your MySQL database. The good news is that with the default options, securing MySQL means that your phpMyAdmin installation is secured because you'll need to use your new MySQL login for phpMyAdmin. We'll discuss phpMyAdmin some more in the next section, "Development Tools."

Development Tools

Having a web server set up is a good first step, but it's about as useful as having a foundation to a house without any tools to build the house with. Seasoned developers have their favorite tools, but if you're just getting started or want to try something new, we've listed some of our favorites in this section.

Firefox

One of the most important tools in any web developer's kit is Firefox. Sure, it might be obvious that you need a web browser to test your code, but Firefox is really valuable to developers because it has a plethora of powerful extensions available to help out with debugging. In the end, you'll want to make sure your pages work in Firefox because it's the second most popular browser used today, with about one-fourth market share.

Firebug

Firebug is a must in every web developer's toolbox. It gives you tools for HTML, CSS, and JavaScript and allows you to edit your pages in the browser and preview changes live, debug code, and optimize performance. You can easily find the HTML for any element on the page and edit it live or modify CSS styles on the page so you can quickly see what the changes do before you hardcode them. In JavaScript, you can see scripts in one place, whether they're inline or in external files. The JavaScript debugger can watch variables, inspect objects, and set breakpoints so that you can step through your code when you run into complex issues. For performance optimization and AJAX development, the Net panel in Firebug allows you to monitor all network requests and see how long they look. This includes a visual graph of load and render time for all the initial elements on the page as well as all subsequent AJAX requests that occur in the background. Although Firebug adds important features to Firefox, it also slows it down significantly so it should only be enabled when needed.

Chrome

Google Chrome is quickly growing in popularity and like Safari, it is based on the Webkit rendering engine which is also used on many mobile devices. The two browsers account for more than 1 in 5 desktop users. Although it is important to test on all supported browsers, Chrome will often render sites similarly to Safari as well as the Android and iPhone browsers. Many web developers like Chrome too because it offers many developer tools that offer functionality similar to Firebug without the need for any add-ons or extensions.

Internet Explorer

Even if you think nobody uses Internet Explorer anymore, it still accounts for over one-third of all browser traffic on the Internet. If you're using Firefox to test most of the time, you'll often have to verify that everything works and looks the way it's supposed to from Internet Explorer. If you want to maximize your site's exposure, you should ensure that your site works in at least Internet Explorer (IE) 6 and later, since many machines running Windows XP still have IE 6.

phpMyAdmin

One of the most popular graphical MySQL administration tools is phpMyAdmin because it is open source, free, and web-based. It enables you to create and administer MySQL databases with minimal knowledge of MySQL, but it still has features useful to novices and professionals alike. As a result of phpMyAdmin's popularity, you will find it preinstalled on many web hosts. If not, installing it is as simple as extracting the files into a folder on a web server and entering the hostname and login credentials for your MySQL server.

For the rest of this book, phpMyAdmin will be our MySQL administration tool of choice, but if you already prefer using the command-line interface or some other tool, that will work equally well.

Text Editors

Although technically you can use any text editor (not a word processor) to write your code, using an editor with programming-specific features can help you code faster and more efficiently with features like syntax highlighting specific to each language. Hundreds of great text editors exist, and we've listed a few of our favorites for each platform:

- Notepad++ (Windows) is a lightweight text editor for Windows with many useful features for programmers, such as syntax highlighting in every major language and format, auto-completion, tabbed editors, and more. It comes with a variety of plug-ins, such as a simple FTP plug-in to let you edit remote files.
- TextMate (OS X) is a GUI editor much like Notepad++. Because of its rich feature set and extensive support for almost every language, many people who prefer a GUI-based editor and use a Mac stand by TextMate, even though it costs about $60 at the time of this writing.
- Vim (all platforms) is a powerful modal text editor that is most popular among Linux users who often prefer its command-line interface over GUI-based text editors. Although it is most popular on Linux, it has been ported to every major operating system, including Windows and Mac. Users accustomed to GUI editors might find it difficult to use because it makes use of many customizable keyboard shortcuts for much of its functionality. However, most people who want an editor like vim probably already use it or something similar; therefore, we do not recommend it for beginners.

Integrated Development Environments (IDEs)

Although a simple text editor is lightweight, fast, and gets the job done, many developers prefer IDEs for their additional features, such as syntax checking and intelligent code completion. These features often function like a spell checker for your code—identifying and underlining syntax errors before you even execute your code. Some other common features include integration with revision control, bug tracking, and the capability to upload files directly to a web server from your IDE.

There are a handful of popular IDEs supporting PHP, but Eclipse and Netbeans are our favorites, and they're both free and cross-platform. Both also support a variety of programming languages, including Java and C/C++, but they are also great for web programming:

- Eclipse is a popular IDE that supports development for many platforms, languages, and devices. If you're looking to try out an IDE for the first time, we'd recommend giving Eclipse for PHP Developers a shot; it is a copy of Eclipse that comes with all the necessary plug-ins needed for PHP and general web development. Speaking of plug-ins, there are hundreds of thousands available to extend Eclipse's abilities from support for new languages, to support for revision control systems, to task and bug management. Because Eclipse is popular outside of web development, getting comfortable with it while programming in PHP may help you in other unrelated endeavors, such as Android mobile development.
- Netbeans has been around for a long time but recently added support for PHP. It offers many of the same features that you'll find in Eclipse but would be well suited for anybody who has already used it with other programming languages. However, it's a close match with Eclipse, so we suggest giving it a shot and deciding what works best for yourself.

Revision Control Systems

Revision control systems, also known as source code management (SCM) systems, are used to store and manage changes to files or documents. They are most commonly used in software development to manage source code. Because every revision of each file is stored, developers can always revert changes back to an earlier version of the code if things don't go as planned. If multiple developers make edits to the same file, the revision control system will automatically merge the changes and, if needed, facilitate resolving any conflicts.

There are many more uses for revision control, and we encourage you to research using one of the revision control systems listed next—especially if you're working with other people. Even if you're working alone, you can save yourself the frustration of making a change that breaks everything and not knowing what code caused the problem:

- Subversion (SVN) is one of the most popular revision control systems today and is designed to improve on the older Concurrent Versions System (CVS).
- Git is much like SVN for basic revision control, but one of its strengths is that there is a local repository, so changes can be committed locally even if there is no network access to the main server. Another advantage of Git is access to GitHub, which is a social coding website that allows you to host, share, and collaborate on your code. At the time of this writing, if your code is open source, it's a free service; otherwise, there is a monthly fee.

Many other differences exist between Git and SVN; however, it is difficult to discuss them without going into more depth on version control. If you're interested, search online for the differences and do some research on your own. In general, you'll find that Git is more powerful than SVN and is rapidly becoming more popular, but it may be more confusing to new users. If you have no experience using version control, we recommend you start with SVN because it is widely used and there are clients for more platforms and programs than Git.

Our Recommended Toolbox

If you're new to web development, we don't want to scare you off with all these possibilities. If you're just starting off, we recommend that you install the following tools (described in the previous sections):

- **Firefox**—The second most popular browser in use today; it works on all platforms and supports a variety of extensions to aid you in web development and testing.
- **Firebug**—A popular Firefox extension for web developers; it helps you debug issues with HTML, CSS, and JavaScript.
- **Chrome**—The most popular Webkit based desktop browser has many integrated development tools to help you debug and tune your site and has similar behavior to Safari and many mobile devices.
- **Eclipse for PHP Developers**—This powerful IDE will help you program with code completion and help you quickly find mistakes with syntax checking.

We've recommended these tools because they'll work on all platforms and should get you through the entire book. However, you should always test all web pages in Internet Explorer because it is the most popular browser.

After you're comfortable with these tools, try using revision control to avoid irreversible changes and prepare yourself for working on a team of developers. Revision control systems are used by almost all professional software developers.

Summary

In this hour, we set you up with everything you need to start writing and testing PHP code. You learned about LAMP stacks and how to set up your own local web server for development purposes. You also learned about a few security vulnerabilities you'll encounter with a fresh XAMPP install and how to fix them. After configuring and testing your local web server, you learned about some of our favorite web development tools, which we will use for the rest of the book.

Q&A

Q. *Why are LAMP stacks so popular?*

A. It's no coincidence that LAMP stacks are popular in the web world. Because all of the technologies in LAMP are open source, free, and widely supported, they are cheap and easy to deploy.

Q. *If I already have an *AMP server set up, is there any reason to install XAMPP?*

A. In theory, almost any *AMP configuration with a current version of PHP should work with the examples in this book. However, because there are so many options to configure within Apache, MySQL, and PHP, we cannot guarantee that things will work unless you're using XAMPP.

Q. *Why do you recommend an IDE for beginners over a simple text editor?*

A. People generally take two sides when deciding what editor to recommend to beginners. There's no doubt that an IDE can offer useful tips and can help you find errors in your code faster, but some people argue that an IDE can become a crutch and others feel strongly against installing a large program with many features they will not use. For us, our recommendation is simple. We're here to teach you about the Twitter API, not to teach you PHP, HTML, CSS, or JavaScript. We want your full attention on the Twitter API, not the nuances of programming and markup languages we're using in this book; using an IDE can help you worry less about the code, and more about the API itself.

Workshop

Quiz

1. What does LAMP stand for?

  A. Linux Apache MySQL Python

  B. Linux Apache MySQL PHP

  C. Linux Apache MySQL Perl

  D. All of the above

2. In XAMPP, what is the name of the folder containing the files or scripts that you can access from http://localhost?

3. True or False: When testing a web page, you can safely assume that it will look the same in all web browsers as long as you are using valid HTML.

Quiz Answers

1. D. Although LAMP most commonly refers to the use of Linux, Apache, MySQL, and PHP, the "P" can also stand for Perl or Python—other popular scripting languages.

2. `htdocs` is the folder sometimes referred to as the web root, which is where you put all the files that are to be accessible from the web server. If you aren't using XAMPP, it's sometimes named www.

3. False. All web pages should be tested in at least Internet Explorer, Firefox, and Chrome as pages may render differently in every browser and on every operating system. If you want to be thorough, you should try your web pages in Safari as well as on Windows, Mac, and Linux. As a final check, you should test your site on a variety of popular mobile devices.

Exercises

1. Create your own phpinfo() page and access it from your browser. Read over the page as it contains interesting information about your server's configuration and environment variables. When you begin to develop more complex applications, this information will come in handy, especially if your application requires special PHP extensions.

2. Set up your development and testing environment, including an editor, Internet Explorer, Firefox, Chrome, Safari, and the Firebug browser extension we mentioned in this hour. When we get around to building, you don't want to be distracted by having to get your toolbox in order.

3. Try setting up a version control system. We recommend Git for more experienced users, but if you're just getting started and Git looks too complicated for you, try SVN first until you're comfortable with it. However, it is important to familiarize yourself with Git because it and other distributed version control systems are quickly gaining popularity for new projects due to their power, speed, and flexibility.

HOUR 5

Making Your First API Call

What You'll Learn in This Hour:

- ▶ How to make a simple URL call
- ▶ How to make a call in php

Making a Simple Twitter API Call

OK, it's time make a call to Twitter and get a response. Let's dive right in and make a simple call to the Twitter service to get the latest public timeline. Depending on your browser and its configuration you may need to view source to see the proper formatting.

Open a web browser, type in the following, and press Enter:

```
http://twitter.com/statuses/public_timeline.xml
```

You should get something like the following:


```
<statuses type="array">
<status>
  <created_at>Thu Dec 31 03:31:08 +0000 2009</created_at>
  <id>7220013867</id>
  <text>Lorem ipsum dolor sit amet, consectetur adipisicing elit, sed do
➥eiusmod tempor
incididunt ut labore et dolore magna aliqua.</text>
  <source>&lt;a href=&quot;http://apiwiki.twitter.com/&quot;
rel=&quot;nofollow&quot;&gt;API&lt;/a&gt;</source>
  <truncated>false</truncated>
  <in_reply_to_status_id></in_reply_to_status_id>
  <in_reply_to_user_id></in_reply_to_user_id>
  <favorited>false</favorited>
  <in_reply_to_screen_name></in_reply_to_screen_name>
  <user>
    <id>11710512</id>
    <name>Christopher</name>
```

```
    <screen_name>perivision</screen_name>
    <location>the bay</location>
    <description>I make stuff.  Currently I'm making twittFilter.com  Check
➥it out and
tell me what you think.</description>
    <pro
file_image_url>http://a1.twimg.com/profile_images/61029076/
chrisperi2_normal.jpg</profile_image_url>
    <url>http://www.perivision.net</url>
    <protected>false</protected>
    <followers_count>830</followers_count>
    <profile_background_color>C6E2EE</profile_background_color>
    <profile_text_color>663B12</profile_text_color>
    <profile_link_color>1F98C7</profile_link_color>
    <profile_sidebar_fill_color>DAECF4</profile_sidebar_fill_color>
    <profile_sidebar_border_color>C6E2EE</profile_sidebar_border_color>
    <friends_count>172</friends_count>
    <created_at>Tue Jan 01 09:29:37 +0000 2008</created_at>
    <favourites_count>26</favourites_count>
    <utc_offset>-28800</utc_offset>
    <time_zone>Pacific Time (US &amp; Canada)</time_zone>
    <pro
file_background_image_url>http://s.twimg.com/a/1262113883/images/themes/the
me2/bg.gif</profile_background_image_url>
    <profile_background_tile>false</profile_background_tile>
    <notifications>false</notifications>
    <geo_enabled>false</geo_enabled>
    <verified>false</verified>
    <following>false</following>
    <statuses_count>3416</statuses_count>
  </user>
  <geo/>
</status>
<status>
  <created_at>Thu Dec 31 03:30:37 +0000 2009</created_at> ...
```


Quite the mess, isn't it? Well, no worries. We are going to clean this up a bit so that you can see what's going on. First, we made a call request in XML format. We could have made that call in JSON, RSS, or ATOM, but we are sticking with XML for now.

The first thing you should notice is the nesting of information. To make this a bit easier to explore, let's remove the content and simplify this output:

Statuses

    created_at

    id

    text

    truncated

in_reply_to_status_id

in_reply_to_user_id

favourited

in_reply_to_screen_name

user

- id
- name
- screen_name
- location
- description
- url
- protected
- followers_count
- profile_background_color
- profile_text_color
- profile_link_color
- profile_sidebar_fill_color
- friends_count
- created_at
- favourites_count
- utc_offset
- time_zone
- profile_background_tile
- statuses_count
- notifications
- following
- verified

geo

..

Although this is a bit easier to read, we can pare this down even further by focusing on the key fields we would use to display a typical message:

Statuses

- created_at
- id
- text
- user
    - id
    - name
    - screen_name
    - utc_offset

..

Now we have something a bit easier to deal with. These will be the values we will want to read for each message, or statuses, that we get back from Twitter. So, let's go over each node of the XML schema quickly:

Created_at—This is the time the message was created in UTC Coordinated Universal Time.

Id—This is the numerical ID number of the message.

Text—This is the contents of the message.

User—This is the Twitter user who created the message. This node also has children. The nodes inside "user" contain information about the user.

User->id—This is the numerical id of the writer.

User->name—This is the name of the writer.

User->screen_name—This is the writer's screen name. The writer's name and screen_name are sometimes the same thing.

User->utc_offset—This is the time zone offset that is relative to the creator of the message. Because the created_at value is always at UTC, we need this value in order to display the created time relative to our own time zone.

Watch Out!

A Twitter screen name is restrictive. You cannot use the word "twitter," cannot have spaces, and certain characters are not allowed.

Making a Call in PHP

Now that we have connected to Twitter, it's time to do it using PHP code. You should have your development environment ready go, as outlined in Hour 4, "Creating a Development Environment." Let's create a new php file called `get_public_timeline.php`. The first line will read as follows:

```
<?php
```

This lets the server know that all the following lines are to be treated as PHP code. Next, type in the following line:

```
$api_url = 'http://twitter.com/statuses/public_timeline.xml';
```

Here we are setting the variable `$api_url` to the string http://twitter.com/statuses/public_timeline.xml. The next few lines might be a bit confusing for those who are not used to PHP. It's not in the scope of this book to go into great detail on the cURL library, but we will touch on it. Type these lines into your file:

```
$curl_handle = curl_init();
curl_setopt($curl_handle, CURLOPT_URL, $api_url);
curl_setopt($curl_handle, CURLOPT_RETURNTRANSFER, TRUE);
$twitter_data = curl_exec($curl_handle);
curl_close($curl_handle);
```

What Is cURL?

cURL, sometimes written as curl, is a set of C-based libraries in PHP that support http "get" and "post" protocol communication with a server. The name "curl" is the contraction of "client" and "URL." The outcome of this project is a set of routines referred to as the *libcurl*, which is shorthand for curl libraries. These libraries support FTP, FTPS, HTTP, HTTP POST, and many more. The library is also very well supported on various platforms: Windows, Mac OS X, Linux, Solaris, OpenBSD, and more. Even better, libcurl is free, thread-safe, and supports IPv6.

What's important to us is the PHP libcurl, which is typically included in any well-rounded PHP installation. This library and the functions within are how we are going to manage our communications with Twitter. So, let's go through the lines we just added to our `get_publictimeline.php` file.

This line creates a reference to the curl library and assigns that reference to the variable $curl_handle:

```
$curl_handle = curl_init();
```

These next two lines set options within our curl object. It's important to notice here that the CURLOPT URL is using a variable called $api_url:

```
curl_setopt($curl_handle, CURLOPT_URL, $api_url);
curl_setopt($curl_handle, CURLOPT_RETURNTRANSFER, TRUE);
```

These last two lines should be clear. The first makes the actual curl call to Twitter.com and assigns $twitter_data to results. The last line closes our reference object:

```
$twitter_data = curl_exec($curl_handle);
curl_close($curl_handle);
```

Okay, only two more lines to go. Type these in:

```
echo 'Public Stream <br>';
echo '<pre> '.htmlentities($twitter_data);
?>
```

The first line uses the command echo to print 'Public Stream' in your browser and the '<br>' is HTML to end that line and start a new one. The following line also uses echo to print information in the browser. The <pre> HTML tag and the `htmlentities()` function are there to make the display more readable for us.

Save your file. Make sure your local PHP server is up and running, and open a web browser. Open your file get_public_timeline.php in the browser.

Did you get an output of text similar to the text below? Great! This is pretty much the same thing we saw when we made this API call from the browser in the beginning of this hour:

```
<statuses type="array">
<status>
  <created_at>Thu Dec 31 03:31:08 +0000 2009</created_at>
  <id>7220013867</id>
  <text> Lorem ipsum dolor sit amet, consectetur adipisicing elit, sed do
➥eiusmod tempor
incididunt ut labore et dolore magna aliqua.</text>
  <source>&lt;a href=&quot;http://apiwiki.twitter.com/&quot;
rel=&quot;nofollow&quot;&gt;API&lt;/a&gt;</source>
  <truncated>false</truncated>
  <in_reply_to_status_id></in_reply_to_status_id>
  <in_reply_to_user_id></in_reply_to_user_id>
  <favorited>false</favorited>
  <in_reply_to_screen_name></in_reply_to_screen_name>
  <user>
    <id>11710512</id>
    <name>Christopher</name>
    <screen_name>perivision</screen_name>
    <location>the bay</location>
...
```

Congratulations! You just made your first Twitter API call from PHP using cURL. Now, let's make another API call to a specific Twitter account.

User_timeline API

The API call to get the public timeline is http://twitter.com/statuses/public_timeline.xml. The API call to get a specific twitter user's timeline is http://twitter.com/statuses/user_timeline/<users screen name>.xml. For example, if I wanted to see the timeline for perivision, I would type the following into a web browser:

http://twitter.com/statuses/user_timeline/perivision.xml.

However, we want to do this in our code. All we have to do is make one change in our code. So, let's create a new php file and call it get_user_timeline.php. Copy the lines from get_public_timeline.php into our new file.

Next, change this line:

```
$api_url = 'http://twitter.com/statuses/public_timeline.xml';
```

To this:

```
$api_url = 'http://twitter.com/statuses/user_timeline/perivision.xml';
```

Make the change in your code and give it a try. You should see basically the same XML schema we have been looking at throughout this hour, but with different content.

However, suppose you want to read *your* timeline. There is an API call for that too, called "../home_timeline." However, this XML structure is a little different from the other two. Also, readers who have used the Twitter API may be wondering why we are not using "../friends_timeline." The friends_timeline API call is still functional, but it's being deprecated in favor of "../home_timeline" because this new API call will include replies. Let's see what's different about "../home_timeline."

As you might recall, the simplified public_timeline XML schema from the beginning of this hour looks something like this:

Statuses

- created_at
- id
- text
- user
    - id

name

screen_name

utc_offset

...

Now, if a message was in reply to a previous message, a new child node will be presented. Here is the reply node in full:


```
<retweeted_status>
    <created_at>Wed Nov 18 18:36:34 +0000 2009</created_at>
    <id>5833513351</id>
    <text>
Lorem ipsum dolor sit amet, consectetur adipisicing elit, sed do eiusmod
➥tempor
incididunt ut labore et dolore magna aliqua.</text>
    <source><a href="http://www.hootsuite.com"
➥rel="nofollow">HootSuite</a></source>
    <truncated>false</truncated>
    <in_reply_to_status_id></in_reply_to_status_id>
    <in_reply_to_user_id></in_reply_to_user_id>
    <favorited>false</favorited>
    <in_reply_to_screen_name></in_reply_to_screen_name>
    <user>
      <id>2558...</id>
      <name> jfieuu uremd</name>
      <screen_name>jfieuu uremd</screen_name>
      <location></location>
      <description>jfisoje jilsifijis jifle<description>
      <pro
file_image_url>http://a3.twimg.com/profile_images/11621.../
➥hjkuyi_73x73_normal.jpg</pro
file_image_url>
      <url>http://www.trdytf.com</url>
      <protected>false</protected>
      <followers_count>1653473</followers_count>
      <profile_background_color>08a9e7</profile_background_color>
      <profile_text_color>000000</profile_text_color>
      <profile_link_color>ee0077</profile_link_color>
      <profile_sidebar_fill_color>ffee9a</profile_sidebar_fill_color>
      <profile_sidebar_border_color>ffcc66</profile_sidebar_border_color>
      <friends_count>406</friends_count>
      <created_at>Fri Mar 20 22:30:24 +0000 2009</created_at>
      <favourites_count>2</favourites_count>
      <utc_offset>-18000</utc_offset>
      <time_zone>Eastern Time (US & Canada)</time_zone>
      <pro
file_background_image_url>http://a1.twimg.com/profile_background_images/
➥6859.../bgpage.g
if</profile_background_image_url>
```

```
      <profile_background_tile>true</profile_background_tile>
      <statuses_count>1740</statuses_count>
      <notifications>false</notifications>
      <geo_enabled>false</geo_enabled>
      <verified>false</verified>
      <following>false</following>
    </user>
    <geo/>
  </retweeted_status>
```

Let's simplify this a bit more:

```
<retweeted_status>
    <created_at>Wed Nov 18 18:36:34 +0000 2009</created_at>
    <id>5833513351</id>
    <text>
Lorem ipsum dolor sit amet, consectetur adipisicing elit, sed do eiusmod
tempor
incididunt ut labore et dolore magna aliqua </text>
    <user>
      <id>255897...</id>
      <name>hkhukg</name>
      <screen_name>hjkhjiiu</screen_name>
    </user>
    <geo/>
  </retweeted_status>
```

We can see here that the reply node has some things in common with the message node structure we have seen before. However, for now, we are going ignore this node, but we will revisit it in later hours.

In addition to an additional node within the user_timeline API call, there is a new requirement we have not seen before: You must provide user credentials. When we first started writing this book, you could simply add your username and password along with the cURL request. This is no longer supported because Twitter has moved to an OAuth authentication protocol only. But don't worry—we will be covering that in Hour 8, "Twitter OAuth."

Summary

Great! We have just made two API calls in this hour, both from the browser and from PHP using cURL. Now it's time to take our return from Twitter and parse it so that we can display our returns in a format a little more user friendly than what we have seen so far.

Q&A

Q. ***Can we make only API calls in XML?***

A. No. You can use JSON, RSS, or ATOM. However, we have decided to stick with XML here because of how well known it is.

Q. ***What is the difference between a message and a status within Twitter?***

A. There is no difference. Although it can be confusing, a status is actually a message, not the actual status of the user.

Q. ***Do I have to pay for the cURL libraries in PHP?***

A. No, cURL is free.

Workshop

Quiz

1. What is the difference between a user ID, username, and user screen_name?
2. Why is the friends_timeline API call being deprecated for the new home_timeline API call?

Quiz Answers

1. The user ID is a numeric identifier for the user. The username is the name the user used when he or she registered. The user screen name is the actual Twitter handle used within the Twitter system.
2. The home_timeline API call now includes information about the original status if the status being viewed is a reply.

Exercise

Create an HTML text field that enables you to enter in a Twitter name and then make a Twitter API call to get the timeline of the Twitter name entered.

HOUR 6

Building a Simple Twitter Reader

What You'll Learn in This Hour:

- **How to set up a basic file structure for our Twitter client application**
- **How to parse returned data from Twitter**
- **What is an HTTP response code?**

Building Our First Twitter Client

We are in Hour 6 and, believe it or not, we already have the basics required to create our first simple Twitter Client. In this hour, we will create the basic file structure that you would see with any typical website: the HTML, CSS, and PHP code to create the content.

In the previous hour, we created a single standalone PHP file to make calls to and get data back from Twitter. However, this is not the proper way to structure a program. It is the goal of this book to have you create a Twitter client by the end of the 24 hours. As such, we are going to take a more structured approach to how we create our application framework. If it's been a while since you read Hour 3, "Key Issues to Consider When Developing Twitter Applications," I recommend that you go back and give it a quick review.

As we go through this Hour and the rest of the Hours in the book, more advanced programmers may be wondering why we took certain approached to our coding or choose to use what would seem overly simple techniques. After much debate by the writers and advisors, we decided that at the price of elegant coding, we would try to make things more clear to the beginning programmers.

Let's put our simple framework in place. It's a basic framework compared to more sophisticated applications. Our basic setup will have an HTML file that is called when the user first comes to the site, which will load main.php, as well as call three other files, each designed to perform a certain task, as you can see in Figure 6.1.

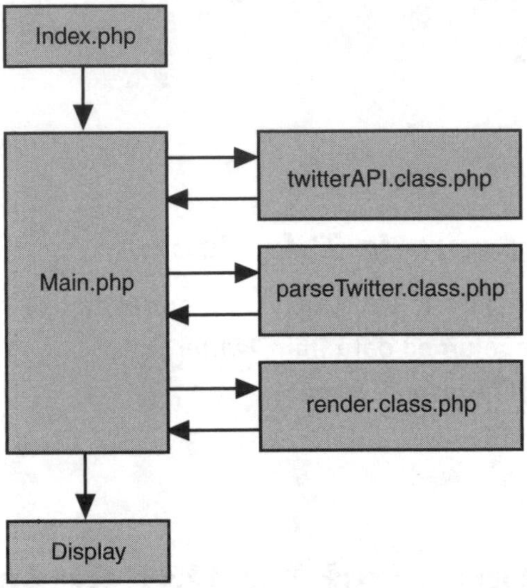

FIGURE 6.1
A simple client application framework.

We are going to create six files in this hour: the HTML page, the CSS file, and four PHP files. Three of the PHP files will live in a subdirectory called includes.

Creating index.php and main.css

First, lets create the HTML code. We are not going to go into detail about the HTML nor the CSS files, which is not in the scope of this book. You may have noticed that we are using index.php instead of index.html. Depending on your server's configuration, you can use either one, however convention is to use index.php if you have a php code in your file, and we very much do in our example. Create a new file called index.php in your editor and type in the following code:

Watch Out!

Recall That HTML Processors Ignore Extraneous Whitespace

Although most environments will allow you to mix HTML and PHP code by simply calling out the PHP code using <?php ... ?>, this is not true with all environments. If you find that your PHP codes are being displayed on your web page, change the name of index.html to index.php.

```
<meta charset="utf-8">
<html>
  <head>
```

```
        <title>twitterAPI 24 hours</title>
    <link href="css/main.css" rel="stylesheet" />
  </head>
```

Here we will make a PHP call to load the various files we need to run our application. As a means of clarity, we are going to place some of our new files into a folder called includes. We use this convention to refer to files and the functions that are not called on their own:

```
  <?php
        include 'includes/twitterAPI.php';
        include 'includes/parseTwitter.php';
        include 'includes/render.php';
        ?>
  <body>
    <div class="header">
        <div class="tweet">TwitterAPI24</div>
    </div>
    <div class="container">
```

Next, we make a call to main.php, which we will use to load our content:

```
    <? include 'main.php'; ?>
    </div>

  </body>
</html>
```

Creating main.css

It's not in the scope of this book to explain how CSS works, so we will simply provide the CSS code here. Create a folder called css and then create a file in that folder called main.css. Type in the following code:

```
/* Global Layout */
body {
        margin:0;
        padding:0;
        font:12px Arial, Helvetica, sans-serif;
        color:#999;
        width:100%;
}
/* End of Global Layout */

/* Global Styles */
/* Disable CSS Text Decoration Property */
a {
        text-decoration:none;
        color:#667;
}
```

```
/* Enable CSS Text Decoration Property and select underline */
a:hover {
          text-decoration:underline;
}

/* End of Global Styles */

/* Section: Header */
.header {
          margin:0 auto;
          padding:10px 10px;
          background:#333;
          overflow:hidden;
}
.tweet {
          padding:0 10px;
}

/* Section: Table */
/* Format the Detail Table with border */
#detail_table td{
          width:330px;
          padding-top:2px;
          padding-left:5px;
          padding-bottom:2px;
          vertical-align: top;
          color:#333;
          border-bottom:1px solid #DBDBDB;
          font-family: Trebuchet MS, Arial, Helvetica, sans-serif;
          valign: top;
}

/* Section: Messages */
/* Format the Message container */
.container{
          float:left;
          width:320px;
}
/* Format the Message image */
.mess-pic {
  background-color:#eee;
  padding-right: 5px;
  font-size: 10px;
  float:left;
}
/* Format the Message container */
.mess-container{
  float:left; width: 250px; padding-left:10px;
}
/* Format the Message content */
.mess-row-text{
float:right; padding-left:10px; width:250px;
}
```

Great. Now that we have the presentation layer out of the way, we can get to the actual code. We are going to create four more files: main.php, parseTwitter.php, render.php, and twitterAPI.php.

Creating main.php

First, let's start with main.php. This file will make calls to all other functions we need to support our simple Twitter client application. The main.php script should not do any tasks in and of itself, but instead serve as the traffic cop for calling other functions. In this example, main.php is going to make three calls: first to callTwitter() from twitterAPI.php to get the latest messages from the Twitter servers; then it will call parseTwitterReply () from parseTwitter.php to convert the returned data into something more usable within PHP; finally, it sends the formatted HTML code of renderTweets() of render.php to the user's browser.

To get started, let's create main.php and type in our first line of code:

```
<?php
```

In the next line, we manually defined $twitterName. BREAKINGNEWS is the name of a Twitter account. You could replace this with any valid Twitter account with public tweets. We appended .xml to let Twitter know we want the response to our request to be in XML format:

```
        $twitterName =
'http://api.twitter.com/1/statuses/user_timeline/BREAKINGNEWS.xml';
```

Next, we make a call to a function called callTwitter() in our twitterAPI.php file. It is here that we make the actual call to the Twitter servers. We will create this file later in this hour:

```
        $twitterRequest = callTwitter($twitterName);
```

After we get our return from the callTwitter() function, we call parseTwitterReply in our parseTwitter.php file to convert the XML text reply we got from Twitter into a structured PHP object that is easier to work with. Again, do not worry; we will create this file later in this hour:

```
        $twitterRequest = parseTwitterReply($twitterRequest);
```

After we have our reply from Twitter in a format we can use, we make a call to renderTweets in render.php to create the HTML code we will send to the user's browser:

```
        echo renderTweets($twitterRequest);

?>
```

Creating twitterAPI.php

Now that we have our main file, let's create the file twitterAPI.php that will be placed in the includes folder. We are going to use this file only twice. After this hour and the following hour, we will replace it with a collection of files that support OAuth authentication with Twitter. The twitterAPI.php file basically takes our request and makes a cURL call to Twitter for us, just as we did in Hour 5:

```
<?php

function callTwitter($api_url){
```

First, we create a curl object to allow us to communicate with the Twitter servers. That object is assigned to $curl_handle:

```
        $curl_handle = curl_init();
```

Next, set options for our new curl object. These are metadata elements we will send along with our request to the Twitter servers:

```
        curl_setopt($curl_handle, CURLOPT_URL, $api_url);
        curl_setopt($curl_handle, CURLOPT_RETURNTRANSFER, TRUE);
```

Here we set the variable $twitterResponseData to contain the data that Twitter has sent back to us:

```
        $twitterResponseData = curl_exec($curl_handle);
```

After a message is sent back to our cURL object, we can find out what the HTTP response code is. We can then use that code to determine if there was a problem with our request, what the problem was, and what we want to do about it. Don't worry about what an HTTP response code is at the moment; we will cover this later in this hour:

```
        $errCode=curl_getinfo($curl_handle, CURLINFO_HTTP_CODE);
```

Although we could set an action for each error code, we are only interested in whether the call was successful. So, if the response code is anything but 200, we will display an error message with whatever other information Twitter has sent us:

```
        if(!stristr($errCode,'200'))  {echo 'err '.$errCode;  return; }
```

Now that we are done with our API call, we do not need the connection any longer. So, here we close it:

```
        curl_close($curl_handle);
```

Assuming a successful API call, we return our data from Twitter to the function that called it:

```
        return $twitterResponseData;
}

?>
```

By the Way

> You may have noticed that we have not entered any authentication information. That is because the public and user API calls are public API calls, not requiring us to send login information.

Twitter HTTP Response Codes

Every time you make a restful call to the Twitter API service, you will get an 'HTTP response code' in addition to whatever data you requested. These response codes are important for letting the application, and the user, know when something did go as expected. Here is a list of the currently supplied codes from Twitter. These codes are based on the current standard for HTTP response codes; they are not specific to Twitter with exception to one:

200 OK—Success!

304 Not Modified—There was no new data to return.

400 Bad Request—The request was invalid. An accompanying error message will explain why. This is the status code will be returned during rate limiting.

401 Unauthorized—Authentication credentials were missing or incorrect.

403 Forbidden—The request is understood, but it has been refused. An accompanying error message will explain why. This code is used when requests are being denied due to update limits.

404 Not Found—The URI requested is invalid or the resource requested, such as a user, does not exist.

406 Not Acceptable—Returned by the Search API when an invalid format is specified in the request.

420 Enhance Your Calm—Returned by the Search and Trends API when you are being rate limited.

500 Internal Server Error—Something is broken. Please post to the group so the Twitter team can investigate.

502 Bad Gateway—Twitter is down or being upgraded.

503 Service Unavailable—The Twitter servers are up, but overloaded with requests. Try again later.

Depending on the amount of time you want to invest, you could write an exception for each code and present the user with a custom message, as well as perform follow-up actions. For example, codes 500, 502, and 503 have to do with Twitter being unable to fulfill a request. If you get one of these codes back, you can provide a message to your users that Twitter is unavailable. You could create a custom page to show the famous FailWhale as shown on the creators website (http://www.whatisfailwhale.info/). In our case, we will simply display whatever message Twitter gave back to us if the response code is not 200.

Did You Know?

> The HTTP response code 420 is not a standard response code. Instead, Twitter created it for their own use. We will cover this more in Hour 20.

Creating parseTwitter.php

Now let's create parseTwitter.php. This file should be in the includes folder. This file is focused on making calls to and parsing the returns from Twitter:

```
<?php
function parseTwitterReply($messages){
```

The variable $messages has the reply we got from Twitter. Because our reply is in XML, we are going to use a standard PHP 5 function called SimpleXMLElement() that will take our XML reply and convert it into an object we can work with more easily within PHP. Explaining the SimpleXMLElement object is not in the scope of this book. However, you can learn more at http://php.net/manual/en/book.simplexml.php.

```
        $twitterReturn = new SimpleXMLElement($messages);
        $i=0;
```

Now that we have our response in an object, we can get the values we are interested in. We will create a simple 'foreach' loop and grab the values for <created_at>, <text>, <profile_image_url>, and <screen_name>. These are the only four values we need to create our simple display.

In the following loop, we are going to create a set of array objects to hold each tweet as we loop through, the following are the values we are looking for:

$updateTime: the time a tweet was created.

$update: the content of the tweet.

$profile_image_url: the user's profile image.

$screen_name: the screen name of the user.

```
        foreach($twitterReturn->status as $status){
                $updateTime[$i] = $status->created_at;
                $update[$i] = $status->text;
                $profile_image_url[$i] = $status->user->profile_image_url;
                $screen_name[$i] = $status->user->screen_name;
                $i++;
        }
```

We now have all the tweets that Twitter gave us back into arrays. You may have noticed that we defined our array using $i. Not every element returned by Twitter will have a value, so we use $i to ensure that the arrays for the first tweet have information for the first tweet returned, and the second set of arrays contains information from the second tweet, and so on.

Now we will create a new array object called $parseReturn to hold the arrays we just created:

```
        $parsedReturn = array();
        $parsedReturn['updateTime']=$updateTime;
        $parsedReturn['update']=$update;
        $parsedReturn['profile_image_url']=$profile_image_url;
        $parsedReturn['screen_name']=$screen_name;

        return $parsedReturn;

}
?>
```

Creating render.php

Next, let's create render.php. This file will take the returns from parseTwitter.php and format them in HTML to be displayed on our page. This will also be in the includes folder:

```
<?php

function renderTweets($parsedReturn){
```

In this function, we are going to loop through each set of array objects that we created in parseTwitter. We will then create an object that will contain the HTML codes we need to display our tweets:

```
        $num = count ($parsedReturn['update']);
        $output="";
```

Notice that we are using $i again to control our loop. This is to make sure we get the correct values for each tweet. The first part of the loop will get the values from our $parseReturn object:

```
        for($i=0; $i<$num; $i++){
                $updateTime = $parsedReturn['updateTime'][$i];
                $update = $parsedReturn['update'][$i];
                $profile_image_url =
➥$parsedReturn['profile_image_url'][$i];
                $screen_name = $parsedReturn['screen_name'][$i];
                $textBody = $update.' '.$updateTime;
```

Because a screen name can be pretty long, we are going to cut it off at nine characters:

```
                $screen_name_abv="<a
➥href='http://www.twitter.com/$screen_name'
➥target='_blank'>".strtolower(substr($screen_name,0,8))."</a>";
```

Now that we have our values, we can populate $output with HTML code:

```
                $output.= "<tr><td><div id='$screen_name' class='mess-
➥pic' >
                  <img src='$profile_image_url'/ width='48px'
➥height='48px'>
                  <br>$screen_name_abv</div>
                <div class='mess-container'>
                <div class='mess-row-text'>$textBody</div></div>
                <div style='clear: both; padding-top:
➥10px'></div></td></tr>";
        }

        return $output;
}

?>
```

So, let's test out our code. Go to your browser and open index.html. You should see a stream of tweets from BREAKINGNEWS similar to Figure 6.2. Congratulations! You have made your first step in creating a basic Twitter client by creating a Twitter reader!

Did You Know?

Did you notice the +0000 after the date and time? This indicates the time zone that the displayed date is based on. +0000 means the time based on GMT—Greenwich Mean Time, also known as Coordinated Universal Time (UTC).

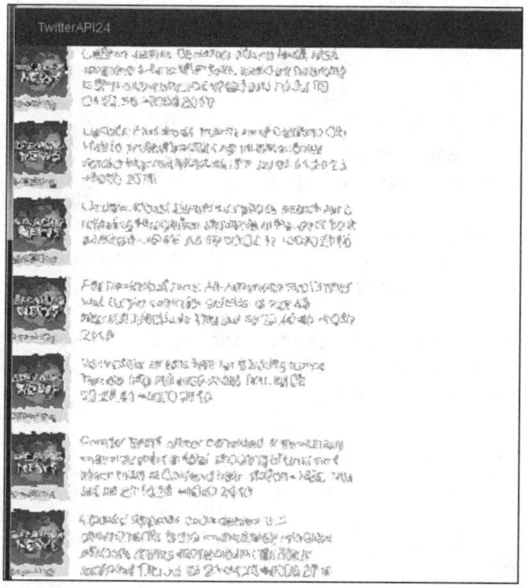

FIGURE 6.2
Example of tweets from BREAKINGNEWS.

Summary

In this hour, we created a basic Twitter reader. This will serve as the foundation for the rest of the examples we will use in the book. You were also introduced to file structure, making calls to Twitter, parsing the reply, and displaying the data in a web-friendly format.

PHP Code Created in This Hour

We created quite a number of files and lots of code in this hour. As such, we are showing all the code for this hour again for your convenience.

index.php:

```
<meta charset="utf-8">
<html>
  <head>
          <title>twitterAPI 24 hours</title>
    <link href="css/main.css" rel="stylesheet" />
  </head>
```

main.php:

```
<?php
          $twitterName =
'http://api.twitter.com/1/statuses/user_timeline/BREAKINGNEWS.xml';
          $twitterRequest = callTwitter($twitterName);
          $twitterRequest = parseTwitterReply($twitterRequest);
          echo renderTweets($twitterRequest);
```

```
?>
```

twitterAPI.php:

```
<?php
function callTwitter($api_url){
          $curl_handle = curl_init();

          curl_setopt($curl_handle, CURLOPT_URL, $api_url);
          curl_setopt($curl_handle, CURLOPT_RETURNTRANSFER, TRUE);
          $twitterResponseData = curl_exec($curl_handle);

          $errCode=curl_getinfo($curl_handle, CURLINFO_HTTP_CODE);
          if(!stristr($errCode,'200'))  {echo 'err '.$errCode;  return; }
          curl_close($curl_handle);

          return $twitterResponseData;
}
?>
```

parseTwitterReply.php:

```
<?php

function parseTwitter($messages){

          $twitterReturn = new SimpleXMLElement($messages);
          $i=0;
          foreach($twitterReturn->status as $status){
                    $updateTime[$i] = $status->created_at;
          $update[$i] = $status->text;
         $profile_image_url[$i] = $status->user->profile_image_url;
          $screen_name[$i] = $status->user->screen_name;
                    $i++;
          }

          $parsedReturn = array();
          $parsedReturn['updateTime']=$updateTime;
          $parsedReturn['update']=$update;
          $parsedReturn['profile_image_url']=$profile_image_url;
          $parsedReturn['screen_name']=$screen_name;

          return $parsedReturn;

}
?>
```

render.php:

```
<?php

function renderTweets($parsedReturn){
```

```
        $num = count ($parsedReturn['update']);
        $output="";

        for($i=0; $i<$num; $i++){
                $updateTime = $parsedReturn['updateTime'][$i];
                $update = $parsedReturn['update'][$i];
                $profile_image_url =
➥$parsedReturn['profile_image_url'][$i];
                $screen_name = $parsedReturn['screen_name'][$i];
                $textBody = $update.' '.$updateTime;

                $screen_name_abv="<a
➥href='http://www.twitter.com/$screen_name'
➥target='_blank'>".strtolower(substr($screen_name,0,8))."</a>";

                $output.= "<tr><td><div id='$screen_name' class='mess-
➥pic' >
                  <img src='$profile_image_url'/ width='48px'
➥height='48px'>
                  <br>$screen_name_abv</div>
                <div class='mess-container'>
                <div class='mess-row-text'>$textBody</div></div>
                <div style='clear: both; padding-top:
➥10px'></div></td></tr>";

        }

        return $output;
}
?>
```

Q&A

Q. ***Can I request my data from Twitter to be in any other format than XML?***

A. Yes. The API presently supports the following data formats: XML, JSON, and the RSS and Atom syndication formats, with some methods accepting only a subset of these formats.

Q. ***In theory, I could use a class object for almost everything in PHP. When should I use a class and when not?***

A. There is no hard and fast rule for when to use a class versus defining functions in separate PHP files and calling them using the include statement. In general, you should use class if what you are creating is going to be shared by other programmers or, as in our case, the functions and procedures are self-contained, numerous and may be replaced in the future

Q. ***Do I have to keep my class file in the same directory as my main files?***

A. No. In fact, it's better to keep as many files out of your first level (sometimes referred to as root) directory as possible. Standard practice is to create a folder called /Classes and place your file there.

Workshop

Quiz

1. True or False: With PHP, you have to break up your application into as many separate files as you can.
2. Can you make API calls to Twitter without authentication?
3. What does HTTP response code 502 mean?

Quiz Answers

1. False. If you wanted to, you could write a complete application in one file. Files are broken up to make it easier on the programmer to manage the code and to make it easier for other programmers to read and work on the code. As such, breaking key functions, like making calls to Twitter, is easier to modify if it's a single file.
2. Yes and no. There are only a few calls that you can make without providing Twitter with authentication; these include public_timeline, user_timeline, and search API calls.
3. Code 502 means Bad Gateway. This indicates that the Twitter service is down or cannot respond. It's normally a bad sign.

Exercise

Twitter returns an HTTP response code when a call is made. Create your equivalent of a FailWhale page for the correct HTTP response codes that indicate Twitter is unable to fulfill a request.

HOUR 7

Creating a Twitter API Framework

What You'll Learn in This Hour:

- ▶ What are Twitter API parameters?
- ▶ How to create an API function for Twitter method calls

Twitter API Parameters

In Hour 6, "Building a Simple Twitter Reader," we created a simple Twitter reader application. There are some shortcomings, however. Remember that we had to manually create the API call to the Twitter servers.

Here is the line just to remind you:

```
$name = 'http://api.twitter.com/1/statuses/user_timeline/BREAKINGNEWS.xml';
```

We created the API call, the value BREAKINGNEWS, and the return type .xml manually in one line. However, to make our system more useful, we need a better way to create this API call. In addition, we need a more dynamic framework for the various API calls we will want to support. However, it's not just API calls we want to support. There is something called *parameters* that can be sent along with an API call.

Not only can we make calls to the Twitter API to get messages, but we can also pass along parameters to refine that call. For example, here are the parameters that Twitter currently accepts for our *statuses/user_timeline* API call (the following are all optional parameters. Not all of these links will work directly in the browser anymore since basic authentication has been disabled):

- **ID:** Specifies the ID or screen name of the user's timeline. Example: http://api.twitter.com/1/statuses/user_timeline/11710512.xml or http://api.twitter.com/1/statuses/user_timeline/perivision.json.
- **User_ID:** Specifies the ID of the user's timeline. This is useful when a valid user ID is also a valid screen name. Example: http://api.twitter.com/1/statuses/user_timeline.xml?user_id=11710512.
- **Screen_name:** Specifies the screen name of the user's timeline. This is useful when a valid screen name is also a user ID. Example: http://api.twitter.com/1/statuses/user_timeline.xml?screen_name=perivision.
- **Since_ID:** Returns statuses with an ID greater than the specified ID. Example: http://api.twitter.com/1/statuses/user_timeline.xml?since_id=2000000 (this example does not work via webpage).
- **Max_ID:** Returns statuses with an ID less than or equal to the specified ID. Example: http://api.twitter.com/1/statuses/user_timeline.xml?max_id=123456 (this example does not work via webpage).
- **Count:** Specifies the number of statuses to return. This cannot be greater than 200. Note: The number of statuses returned might be fewer than requested because retweets are stripped out. Example: http://api.twitter.com/1/statuses/user_timeline.xml?count=200.
- **Page:** Specifies the page of results to retrieve. Keep in mind that there are pagination limits. Example: http://api.twitter.com/1/statuses/user_timeline.rss?page=3.

As you can see, there are a number of parameters at our disposal for tuning the reply we get from the Twitter servers.

Watch Out!

> Twitter has been growing so fast that the example numbers you see here for message ID are far larger than simply a five-digit number. At the time of this writing, a typical message ID is as high as 20000000000. That's 20 billion!

Because this is your first time creating a Twitter application, you might be wondering why we need so many parameters. Not every API call has these parameters—some have less, and some have more, but by having these parameters, we can set up some fairly complex and refined interaction with Twitter.

For example, if we keep track of the last message ID a user has seen, we can then request only the newest messages for that user by passing the last-known message ID plus one. This is very useful for keeping the number of replies from Twitter to a minimum, as well as letting us know if there are any new messages to act on or if Twitter provides an empty set of new messages.

Another example is pagination. If we ask for the last 20 messages, and then the user wants to look back 20 more messages, we can simply pass the value of '2' to the page parameter.

Watch Out!

> Although the current default reply is 20 messages on most API calls, this is not the case with all calls. If a tweet within the set is a retweet or deleted, it will not appear but will still count toward the returned set. In addition, Twitter could change this value in the future.

Creating an API Function for Twitter Function Calls

To manage all these parameters, we are going to expand our twitterAPI.php file, but before we show you the code for this API call, let's revisit some code from Hour 6. Remember that we had a function called callTwitter() in our php file main.php:

```
$twitterName = 'http://api.twitter.com/1/statuses/user_timeline/
BREAKINGNEWS.xml';
$twitterRequest = callTwitter($twitterName);
```

The callTwitter() function call would pass our $twitterName API request to a cURL function in twitterAPI.php. Now we need to update our twitterAPI.php file to support the various parameters we might want to pass to it.

Open the file twitterAPI.php and add the following code at the end of the file but before the '?>':

```
function getUserTimeline($format, $id = NULL, $count = NULL) {
```

Here we begin constucting our API statement. The following 'if' statement checks to see if a user ID was passed. If so, we append the user ID (in this case, 'BREAKINGNEWS') to the end of the API statement. We also append the end of the statement with a '`.`' and '`xml`':

```
        if ($id != NULL) {
            $api_call =
sprintf("http://api.twitter.com/1/statuses/user_timeline/%s.%s", $id,
$format);
        }
        else {
            $api_call =
```

```
sprintf("http://api.twitter.com/1/statuses/user_timeline.%s", $format);
        }
        if ($count != 20) {
            $api_call .= sprintf("?count=%d", $count);
        }
```

The next lines append the parameter options. You should already be familiar with '?' and '&' for sending requests over URL, but just to be complete, a ? after a URL statement indicates to the receiving server that parameters are being passed. The '&' allows us to pass more than one set of parameters.

Here we are using an echo statement so that you can see the API statement we have created. You can remove this later:

```
        echo "<h4>$api_call</h4>";
```

Finally, we return our results back to main.php:

```
        return callTwitter($api_call);
    }
```

Save this file and close it.

Because we have a function to create our API call for us, we no longer need to manually construct our API statement. So, open main.php and make a modification.

Delete these two lines:

```
    $name =
'http://api.twitter.com/1/statuses/user_timeline/BREAKINGNEWS.xml';
    $twitterRequest = callTwitter('xml', $name);
```

And replace them with these two:

```
    $name = 'BREAKINGNEWS';
    $twitterRequest = getUserTimeline('xml', $name);
```

Save the file and close it.

Now let's give our new code a test. Open your web browser and load index.php in your development environment. You should see a set of returns, shown in Figure 7.1, that look a lot like what we saw in Hour 6.

We now are making a call to getUserTimeline() and passing two values, as follows:

- **'xml'**—We want our reply to be in XML format. We could have used JSON if we wanted.
- **$name**—We redefined $name to be just BREAKINGNEWS. We could have used any value Twitter name.

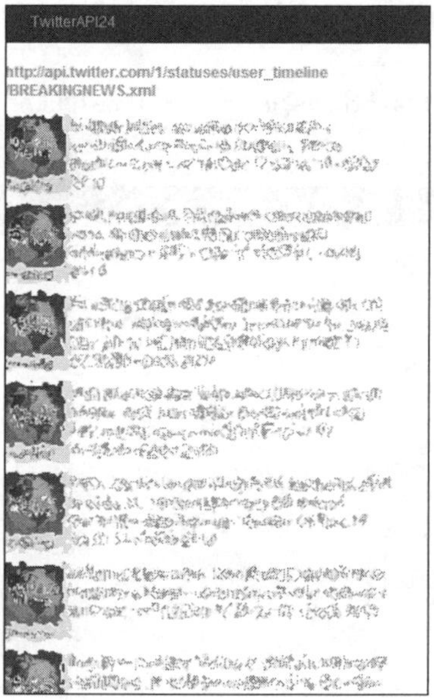

FIGURE 7.1 Example of tweets from BREAKINGNEWS.

Now let's open up main.php again and make a slight change to our code.

Modify this line:

```
$twitterRequest = getUserTimeline('xml', $name);
```

To read:

```
$twitterRequest = getUserTimeline('xml', $name, '3');
```

With this change, we now are making a call to getUserTimeline() and passing three values, as follows:

- **'xml'**—We want our reply to be in XML format. We could have used JSON if we wanted.
- **$name**—We redefined $name to be just BREAKINGNEWS. We could have used any value Twitter name.
- **'3'**—Here we are passing our first parameter: the number of tweets we want to get back. If we had left this empty, we would get the default 20 messages back.

We are done with our changes to main.php, so save and close the file.

Next, let's open our Twitter application and see what we get.

You should see something like Figure 7.2. Notice the following line at the top of the page:

```
http://api.twitter.com/1/statuses/user_timeline/BREAKINGNEWS.xml?count=3
```

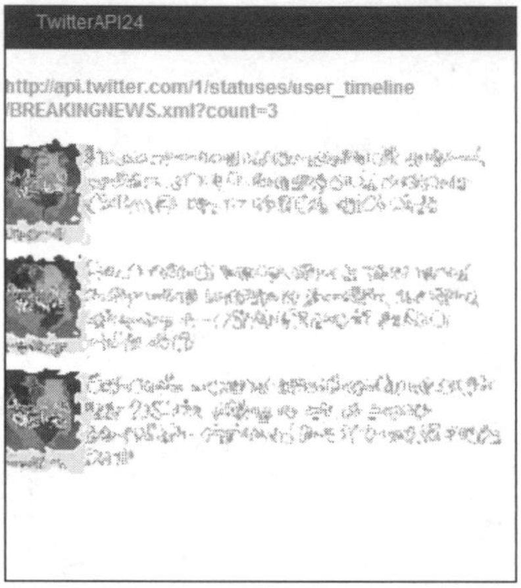

FIGURE 7.2 Example of three latest tweets from BREAKINGNEWS.

This is the actual request we are sending Twitter. Using 'echo' to see what commands are being sent to Twitter is a great debugging tool. We will leave this in for now, but do remember to remove it once you feel comfortable with what these calls look like.

Let's add one more API function.

Creating getPublicTime API Function

First, let's see what parameters Twitter supports for this API call. In this case, there is just one: 'since_id.'

This makes our function call pretty simple. Open up twitterAPI.php and add the following lines at the end of the file but before '?>':

```
function getPublicTimeline($format, $since_id = 0) {
    $api_call =
sprintf("http://api.twitter.com/1/statuses/public_timeline.%s",
$format);
    if ($since_id > 0) {
        $api_call .= sprintf("?since_id=%d", $since_id);
    }
    echo "<h4>$api_call</h4>";
    return callTwitter($api_call);
}
```

This should seem quite simple compared to all the parameters we had to worry about with 'user_timeline.'

Save the file and close it.

Now to test this new function call, all we have to do is change one line in main.php. Open main.php and delete (or comment out) the following line:

```
$twitterRequest = getUserTimeline('xml', $name, '3');
```

Then add this line:

```
$twitterRequest = getPublicTimeline('xml');
```

Save your file and close it. Now let's try our application again.

You should see the latest public tweets from Twitter, as shown in Figure 7.3. And all you had to do was change one line!

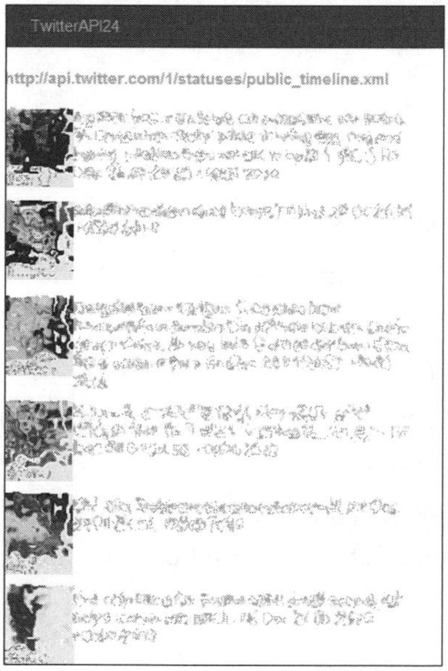

FIGURE 7.3
Example of latest public tweets.

This is going to be the basis of our framework going forward. We will create a UI that will enable users to click tabs to choose which API calls they want to make. We will get to that in later hours.

Summary

In this hour, we took the first steps in creating the twitterAPI portion of our framework. We also introduced the concept of parameters and a structured way of dealing with them. In addition, we discovered in this hour that we can make different API calls to Twitter by changing one line within our framework.

Q&A

Q. ***Can I use multiple parameters in a call? For example, can I use both since_id and max_id together?***

A. Technically, you can, but it's a bad idea. Twitter sometimes has issues with since_id and max_id, especially with search, so it's normally a good idea to use only one or the other. There are no known issues with mixing other parameters however, always test first.

Workshop

Quiz

1. True or False: You have to use at least one parameter when making an API call.
2. True or False: The XML return for all Twitter API calls is the same.

Quiz Answers

1. False. If you do not pass any parameters outside the normal API call, Twitter will assume default values for you.
2. False. Although the XML returns are similar and reflect the same basic constructs, there are subtle differences resulting from the ever-evolving API requirements and modifications.

Exercises

1. Try various calls with different parameters to see what you can do. There is a way to confuse and get nothing back from Twitter by asking for conflicting parameters. Try to do this.
2. Toward the end of this hour, we added support for the parameter since_id but did not actually use it. Try to find the most recent message ID and then make the call again. Try a number in the future and see what you get as a return.

HOUR 8

Twitter OAuth

What You'll Learn in This Hour:

- ▶ What is a class and why do we use it?
- ▶ What is OAuth? (Briefly)
- ▶ How to create a simple Twitter class object
- ▶ How to add new functions to your Twitter class object
- ▶ How our class deals with Twitter connection errors

What Is a Class and Why Do We Want to Use It?

The rewrite of PHP5 from PHP4 includes updating and upgrading the underlying Object model, which includes the class object. First, what is an object? Object-oriented programming, or OOP, has been around since the 1960s but did not really enter the mainstream until the early 1990s. OOP programming is pretty common in today's languages, and although we are using PHP in this book, most languages you may use to build your Twitter application will likely support the OOP constructs. So, what is an object? Let's look to Wikipedia.

> An object is actually a discrete bundle of functions and procedures, all relating to a particular real-world concept such as a bank account holder or hockey player in a computer game. Other pieces of software can access the object only by calling its functions and procedures that have been allowed to be called by outsiders. Isolating objects in this way makes their software easy to manage and keep track of. (http://en.wikipedia.org/wiki/Object-oriented_programming_language)

In our case, the object is a collection of Twitter API calls. The functions and procedures we will isolate will be the individual API calls, as well as a few procedures to deal with Twitter instability. A class is a type of object. Because it's not in the scope of this book to define OOP in depth, we will continue on from here.

The advantage of using a class is that it gives us a clean and clear way to think about our code, as well as ensuring that if you are working with others and thus sharing this code, that no confusion or duplication errors are introduced into the code set.

Now that we know what a class is, and the advantages it gives us, let's have a look at a class for handling the Twitter API.

What Is OAuth?

From the Oauth.net site:

> OAuth provides a method for clients to access server resources on behalf of a resource owner (such as a different client or an end-user). It also provides a process for end-users to authorize third-party access to their server resources without sharing their credentials (typically, a username and password pair), using user-agent redirections...
>
> In the traditional client-server authentication model, the client uses its credentials to access its resources hosted by the server. With the increasing use of distributed web services and cloud computing, third-party applications require access to these server-hosted resources.
>
> OAuth introduces a third role to the traditional client-server authentication model: the resource owner. In the OAuth model, the client (which is not the resource owner, but is acting on its behalf) requests access to resources controlled by the resource owner, but hosted by the server. In addition, OAuth allows the server to verify not only the resource owner authorization, but also the identity of the client making the request.
>
> (http://tools.ietf.org/html/rfc5849)

How to Register Your Application

To get the OAuth information for your application, you need to register it with Twitter.

Registering an application is fairly simple. Open your browser and go to this address: http://dev.twitter.com/apps/new.

Fill out your application as appropriate. If you are not sure, use the following:

Application Type: 'Browser'

Default Access Type: Read & Write

Don't worry; you can change these settings at any time.

After you have filled out the application, you should get something like the screenshot in Figure 8.1.

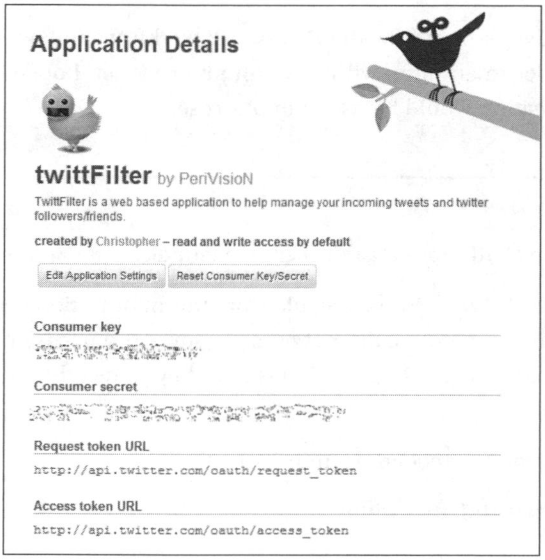

FIGURE 8.1 Twitter Application Registration screen.

Creating the OAuth Twitter Class

So, now that we know what a class is and we know what OAuth is, we need to create an OAuth class. However, creating our own OAuth class is outside the bounds of this book, so instead we will get one that is recommended from the Twitter.com site.

The example we are using here came from a class written by Abraham Williams | abraham@poseurte.ch | http://abrah.am twitter name: @abraham.

PHP Library for Working with Twitter's OAuth API

Documentation: http://wiki.github.com/abraham/twitteroauth/documentation

Source: http://github.com/abraham/twitteroauth

Twitter: http://apiwiki.twitter.com

It is not in the scope of this book to explain what OAuth is in detail, much less deconstruct Abraham's code. There are whole books dedicated to the subject. Instead, we are going to walk through the steps needed to get this working for us and then learn how to write API calls within this class.

First, the general overview of how the OAuth API works: the following steps come directly from the documentation within Abraham's code set. I added a few notes where I felt clarification would be useful in our case.

Flow Overview

1. Build TwitterOAuth object using client credentials.

This is where we start. Typically, you would store this information either in the cookie or in a database. In our case, we are not going to support a persistent login, so after the browser is closed, or the OAuth session is closed by some other means, the user will have to reauthenticate.

2. Request temporary credentials from Twitter.
3. Build authorize URL for Twitter.
4. Redirect user to authorize URL.

This URL is found in the config.php file.

5. User authorizes access and returns from Twitter.
6. Rebuild TwitterOAuth object with client credentials and temporary credentials.
7. Get token credentials from Twitter.
8. Rebuild TwitterOAuth object with client credentials and token credentials.
9. Query Twitter API.

A more detailed explanation of the preceding flow overview can be found in Abraham's documentation.

Setting Up the twitterOAuth Class

Now that we have an introductory understanding of what OAuth is and how it works, let's take Abraham's code, place it in our development environment, and test it out.

First, if you have not done so already, download his code from github. You should have the following:

images/

darker.png

lighter.png

twitteroauth/

OAuth.php

twitteroauth.php

DOCUMENTATION

LICENSE

README

callback.php

clearsessions.php

config.php

connect.php

html.inc

index.php

redirect.php

test.php

Copy these files into the root directly of your development environment. Now we need to modify a few things:

Open config.php.

In this file, you are going to put your CONSUMER_KEY and CONSUMER_SECRET that we got when registering our application.

The OAUTH_CALLBACK is the location of our root directory. For example, on my local build, it's the following:

```
define('OAUTH_CALLBACK', 'http://localhost/callback.php');
```

Note: Using localhost as a callback does not always work. If that happens, try using the following workaround: http://127.0.0.1:8000/twitter_callback.

If this does not work, try this. You can use bit.ly, a URL-shortening service. Just shorten the url "http://localhost:3000/twitter_callback" and register the shortened URL as the callback in your Twitter app. For this method, you have to create another Twitter OAuth app for development so that the callback URLs can differ. (Thanks to Toni for this workaround: http://www.tonyamoyal.com/2009/08/17/how-to-quickly-set-up-a-test-for-twitter-oauth-authentication-from-your-local-machine/.)

Save and close.

Now open a web browser and click index.php. You should see something like the screenshot in Figure 8.2. If you do not, there is one more thing you may want to check. Sometimes you need to set your system to GMT time. Another possibility is that you need to create a new Twitter application if you were trying to use an existing twitter application.

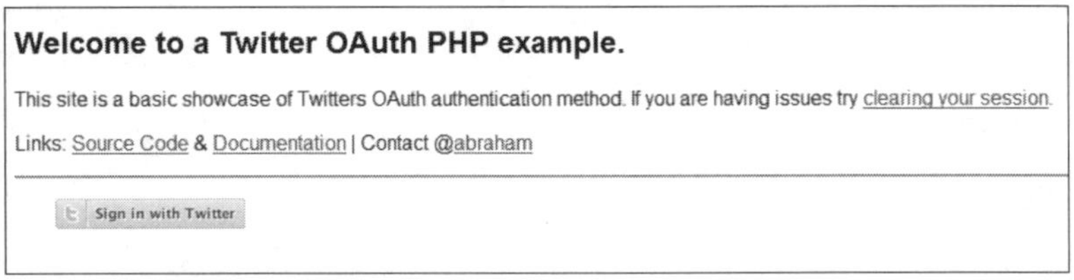
Welcome to a Twitter OAuth PHP example.
This site is a basic showcase of Twitters OAuth authentication method. If you are having issues try clearing your session.
Links: Source Code & Documentation | Contact @abraham
Sign in with Twitter

FIGURE 8.2
Abraham OAuth login screen.

Click the Sign In with Twitter button, and you will see a message from Twitter asking: An application would like to connect to your account. Select Allow. Next, you should see something like Figure 8.3.

If you got an error saying the curl could not be initiated, be sure you have the php_curl extension uncommented. For example:

Fatal error: Call to undefined function curl_init() in **C:\xampplite\htdocs\api\twitteroauth\twitteroauth.php** on line **199**

```
extension=php_curl.dll
```

By the Way

PHP supports libcurl, a library created by Daniel Stenberg that allows you to connect and communicate to many types of servers with many types of protocols.

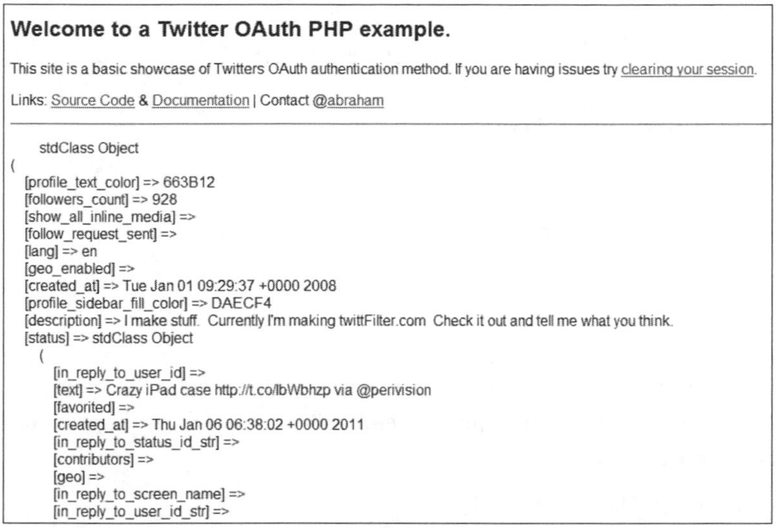
Welcome to a Twitter OAuth PHP example.
This site is a basic showcase of Twitters OAuth authentication method. If you are having issues try clearing your session.
Links: Source Code & Documentation | Contact @abraham
stdClass Object
(
[profile_text_color] => 663B12
[followers_count] => 928
[show_all_inline_media] =>
[follow_request_sent] =>
[lang] => en
[geo_enabled] =>
[created_at] => Tue Jan 01 09:29:37 +0000 2008
[profile_sidebar_fill_color] => DAECF4
[description] => I make stuff. Currently I'm making twittFilter.com Check it out and tell me what you think.
[status] => stdClass Object
(
[in_reply_to_user_id] =>
[text] => Crazy iPad case http://t.co/lbWbhzp via @perivision
[favorited] =>
[created_at] => Thu Jan 06 06:38:02 +0000 2011
[in_reply_to_status_id_str] =>
[contributors] =>
[geo] =>
[in_reply_to_screen_name] =>
[in_reply_to_user_id_str] =>

FIGURE 8.3 Your account information.

Great. Now that we have our OAuth class in place, we are going to add to it to support our API calls. But first, a little tweak.

Open index.php and save it under a new name. Call it oauth_index.php. We will be changing index.php. This will allow us to create our own index.php file. By the way, I used an underscore as a personal habit when I rename a core file from another framework.

Edit oauth_index.php

If you do not have it open already, open the file oauth_index.php. Change the variable $connection to $twitter in this line:

(old)

```
$connection = new TwitterOAuth(CONSUMER_KEY, CONSUMER_SECRET,
$access_token['oauth_token'], $access_token['oauth_token_secret']);
```

(new)

```
$twitter = new TwitterOAuth(CONSUMER_KEY, CONSUMER_SECRET,
$access_token['oauth_token'], $access_token['oauth_token_secret']);
```

Do the same for the following line:

(old)

```
$content = $connection->get('account/verify_credentials');
```

(new)

```
$content = $twitter->get('account/verify_credentials');
```

Finally, comment out the last line:

(old)

```
include('html.inc');
```

(new)

```
//include('html.inc');
```

We do not have to make this change. However, it's easier to read that you are opening a connection to Twitter. Thus, just for readability, we are changing the variable name. Save and close this file.

We have one more file to edit.

Edit twitteroauth.php

Open the file twitteroauth/twitteroauth.php.

Change the following line:

(old)

```
  public $format = 'json';
```

(new)

```
  public $format = 'xml';
```

We are making this change because it's easier to read raw XML than raw JSON.

Next, find the function `oAuthRequest()`.

We are going to change this line:

```
$url = "{$this->host}{$url}.{$this->format}";
```

To this line:

```
$url = "{$this->host}{$url}";
```

We are doing this because in later hours, we are going to make JSON calls, so we will define when to use XML and when to use JSON in another part of our code.

Now we are going to add some new lines.

At the end of the file, but *before* the last "}", add the following:

```
##########################################################################
###########################     New Code    ##############################
##########################################################################


         function getHomeTimeline($format, $id = NULL, $count = 60, $since
➥= NULL) {
                  if ($id != NULL) {
                           $api_call =
sprintf("statuses/home_timeline/%s.%s", $id, $format);
                  }
                  else {
                           $api_call =
sprintf("statuses/home_timeline.%s", $format);
return $this->get($api_call);                       }

}
```

We have added a function that will make the API call home_timeline for us. The reason we want to have a separate function here in the class is to give us maximum flexibility for default actions on an API call, as well as having all our calls in one place in case we need to make any changes or worry about scope. Do not worry about what this function is doing; we will cover it later in the hour.

Save and close.

Great! We have a basic working Twitter class object that we can call. So now, let's write some code to call it. Create a new file and call it firstcall.php. In this file, put the following code:

```
<?php
  ini_set('display_errors', '1');
  include 'oauth_index.php';
          global $twitter;
          $messages=$twitter->getHomeTimeline('xml');
          echo 'Home Timeline <br> ';
          print_r($messages);
?>
```

This first line is for reporting errors; this is useful for testing:

```
  ini_set('display_errors', '1');
```

This line is where we initiate our OAuth sessions:

```
  include 'oauth_index.php';
```

Now we set our $twitter object within scope of our function:

```
global $twitter;
```

And finally, we make our first API call using the OAuth class we put in place.

```
$messages=$twitter->getHomeTimeline('xml');
```

Save and close.

Open the file firstcall.php in your web browser, and you should see a stream of content from Twitter. Congratulations! You have a working Twitter class.

How to Add New Functions to Your Twitter Class Object

Now that we have a basic class, we can easily add more functions to it. So, let's add a function to allow us to get a user's timeline using the API call 'users_timeline'.

Edit twitteroauth.php

Let's open twitteroauth.php again and add a new function. At the end of the file, but *before* the last "}", add the following code:

```
function getUsersTimeline ($format, $id = NULL, $since = NULL) {
          if ($id != NULL) {
                    $api_call = sprintf("statuses/user_timeline/%s.%s", $id,
➥$format);
          }
          else {
                    $api_call = sprintf("statuses/user_timeline.%s",
➥$format);
          }
          if ($since != NULL) {
                    $api_call .= sprintf("?since=%s", urlencode($since));
          }
          return $this->get($api_call);
}
```

Next, open firstcall.php and find this line:

```
$messages=$twitter->getHomeTimeline('xml');
```

Comment out this line:

```
//$messages=$twitter->getHomeTimeline('xml');
```

Below the line that you commented out, add the following:

```
$messages=$twitter->getUsersTimeline('xml', 'perivision');
```

This new function we created in our Twitter class does look a little like the 'getHomeTimeline' function. Next, we need to look at a few new lines. Let's look at the second and third lines:

```
        if ($id != NULL) {
                $api_call = sprintf("statuses/user_timeline/%s.%s", $id,
➥$format);
        }
```

If we do not pass a value for $id in our function call, we will skip the following line because the curl object via OAuth already knows who we are when we first created the object. However, we will provide a value for $id, so let's look at the next line:

```
$api_call = sprintf("statuses/user_timeline/%s.%s", $id, $format);
```

Remember the new line we added in firstcall.php?

```
$messages=$twitter->getUsersTimeline('xml', 'perivision');
```

This line is going to call our new getUsersTimeline function in the Twitter class and pass two values: 'perivision', which is assigned to $id, and 'xml', which is assigned to $format. So, the variable $api_call will have the value of this string: statuses/user_timeline/perivision.xml.

Now if we did not provide a value for $id, the following lines in our new function will handle that contingency by assigning the viable $api_call with the string value of statuses/user_timeline.xml:

```
        else {
                $api_call = sprintf("statuses/user_timeline.%s",
➥$format);
        }
```

The Twitter API call user_timeline will provide the timeline of whichever credentials were passed if an ID is not provided.

The next lines in our new function deals with an attribute of the Twitter API that allows us to decide how far back in time to look for messages:

```
        if ($since != NULL) {
                $api_call .= sprintf("?since=%s", urlencode($since));
        }
```

In this case, we did not pass a value for $since, so this attribute will be ignored and the default value of 20 will be used.

The final line in our new function is something you have already seen before. This line calls the private function that makes the actual API call to twitter.com:

```
return $this->APICall($api_call, true);
```

Save both files and open or refresh the web page firstcall.php. You should get a stream of information, but this time from the Perivision Twitter account.

How Our Class Deals with Twitter Connection Errors

Twitter is a great service, but it's not perfect and sometimes is unavailable. When this first started to happen, Twitter.com provided an error page, sometimes with the picture of a whale trying to be supported by a collection of small birds, a.k.a the FailWhale.

So, what do we do when we try to make a call and Twitter does not give us a reply we expected? We place some code in our Twitter class to deal with this exception.

By the Way

> An exception is a generally accepted reserved word that deals with errors encountered by the program. In this case, we are taking exception a bit out of context because a return from Twitter is not an error as much as a message saying the system is not available.

Twitter.com's API provides a variety of replies, as do most HTTP-based services. However, in this hour, we will focus on whether we got a good reply.

Because Twitter provides a status code for each reply, we can check that status value to see if we got a good return. The status code for a good return from Twitter is '200'. So, all we need to do is check to see if we got '200' as a status code.

Insert the following code into twitteroauth/twitteroauth.php below these lines:

```
curl_setopt($ci, CURLOPT_URL, $url);
$response = curl_exec($ci);
$this->http_code = curl_getinfo($ci, CURLINFO_HTTP_CODE);
$this->last_api_call = $url;
```

Code to insert:

```
$http_status = curl_getinfo($ci, CURLINFO_HTTP_CODE);
echo 'status '.$http_status.'<br>';
if ($http_status!=200) return $http_status;
```

These three lines are fairly straightforward. The first line gets the status code from the curl object. The next line "prints" the value of $http_status on the screen. The third line is our 'if' statement. If the value of $http_status is *not* 200, then we return whatever the value is.

In a proper application, we will want to deal with this exception in a more proper manner; however, in our case, we simply want to know if the call worked.

There is no reason to keep this code because we will deal with this more properly toward the end of the book, but you can keep it for now it you like.

Summary

In this hour, we implemented our OAuth class object that we will reply on and expand upon throughout the rest of this book. Understanding the class object is not only useful to our goals here in building Twitter applications, but good programming in general. We also only touched on the basics of OAuth; however, there are many great sources of detailed information on how OAuth works. You will find many such links on docs.twitter.com.

Q&A

Q. ***When I first started programming with the Twitter API, I was using a simple username and password, and only recently it stopped working. Will they ever bring it back?***

A. Very unlikely. If you have any past code that used 'Basic Auth', you would be advised to go back and update that code. With exception to public streams and the various forms of search, access to Twitter requires the use of OAuth only.

Workshop

Quiz

1. What is a class object?
2. What is a callback URL?
3. What does the status code 200 mean?

Quiz Answers

1. An object is actually a discrete bundle of functions and procedures, all relating to a particular real-world concept, such as a bank account holder or player info in a computer game.
2. This is the URL Twitter will call when trying to verify your OAuth process.
3. It means the API cURL call you made resulted in a successful

return.

Exercises

1. Try changing the search from "perivision" to some other Twitter name.
2. Knowing the HTTP response code is very important when building a Twitter client, try to find where the HTTP response code is returned within the twitter.class and display it to the viewer using echo.

HOUR 9

Building a Simple Twitter Client, Part I

What You'll Learn in This Hour:

- How to create a simple framework for our Twitter client
- How to put tabs in HTML
- How to support parameters in your framework

Expanding the Index File to Support Tabs

First, we need to add a few tabs to our index.php file so that we can select between reading home_timeline, mentions, and our direct messages. So, let's create a new file called header.inc, and we will put it in the includes folder. By the way, it is not necessary to label header.inc with a .inc extension. This is a convention used by this Author.

To know what page the user wants, we passed that page identifier in the URL link and picked it up using the $_GET command:

```
<? $page = $_GET['page']; ?>

<div id="header">
          <div class="header-bg">
                    <div class="header">
                              twitterAPI in 24 hours. <br>
```

You can add the following line optionally to help keep track of what hour you are currently working on. Remember to update this as you move from hour to hour:

```
Hour 9 <br>
                    </div>
          </div>
```

```
<!— main navigation —>
     <div id="nav-box">
                    <ul id="main-nav">
```

Here you can see where we set the $page value:

```
                                  <li><a href="/" >Home</a></li>
                                  <li><a href="/?page=mentions"
>Mentions</a></li>
                                  <li><a href="/?page=direct" >Messages</a></li>
                    </ul>
          </div>
</div>
```

Save and close this file. Now let's open the file index.php and add this file we just created.

After this line:

```
include 'includes/render.php';
```

Add the following line:

```
include 'includes/header.inc';
```

Great. Save the file and close. Load index.php, and we should see our new tabs; they should look something like Figure 9.1.

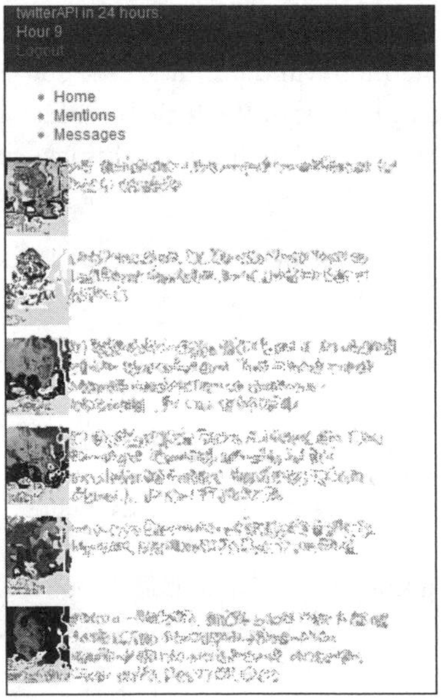

FIGURE 9.1
Tabs now added to the top of the web page.

Adding Support for Home Timeline

First, we need to set a switch to call the correct set of functions.

Open includes/parseTwitter.php in your editor and add the following code at the end of the file but before the ?>:

```
function getTwitterData($command) {

        global $twitter;
        switch ($command) {
    case 'timeline':
        { $messages=$twitter->getHomeTimeline('xml'); return
➥call_timeline($messages); }
        break;
    case 'mentions':
        { $messages=$twitter->getMentions('xml'); return
➥call_timeline($messages); }
        break;
    case 'direct':
        { $messages=$twitter->getMessages('xml'); return
➥call_direct($messages); }
        break;
}
}
```

This is a simple case routine that will not only make the correct API call for us, but also pass the returned data to the correct parsing function. Now we need to define the functions this case will call:

```
function call_timeline($messages){
```

We are going to use a PHP5 call called SimpleXMLElement(). Again, it's not in the scope of this book to explain PHP, but if you would like to know more, go to this site: http://us3.php.net/simplexml:

```
        $twitterReturn = new SimpleXMLElement($messages);
```

We are again using a counter ($i) to make sure our arrays are aligned:

```
          $i=0;
          foreach($twitterReturn->status as $status){
                   $updateTime[$i] = parseDate($status->created_at);
          $update[$i] = $status->text;
          $profile_image_url[$i] = $status->user->profile_image_url;
          $screen_name[$i] = $status->user->screen_name;
                   $i++;
          }
```

Now that we have Twitter attribute values in arrays, we are going to create another associative array to hold the ones we just defined:

```
        $parsedReturn = array();
        $parsedReturn['updateTime']=$updateTime;
        $parsedReturn['update']=$update;
        $parsedReturn['profile_image_url']=$profile_image_url;
        $parsedReturn['screen_name']=$screen_name;

        return $parsedReturn;

}
```

Save your file and now open main.php.

Delete everything between the <?php and the ?> and replace them with these two lines:

```
        $twitterReturn = getTwitterData($page);
        echo renderTweets ($twitterReturn);
```

This is the last file to edit. Open the file 'twitteroauth/twitteroauth.php' in your editor and add the following function at the bottom of the file but *before* the last "}": This will look alot like what we used in Hour 7 with the following exceptions:

```
        function getHomeTimeline($format, $id = NULL, $count = 60, $since
➥= NULL) {
                if ($id != NULL) {
```

Notice here that we have changed the first annotation to the $api_call variable. This is because this part of the API call http://api.twitter.com/1/ is handled in the OAuth class:

```
                        $api_call =
sprintf("statuses/home_timeline/%s.%s", $id, $format);
                }
                else {
                        $api_call =
sprintf("statuses/home_timeline.%s", $format);
                }
                if ($since != NULL){
                        $api_call .= sprintf("?since_id=%s",
urlencode($since));
                        $count=0;
                }
```

Notice that both if statements offer to add a question mark. A more proper programming technique would be to use switch or some control to change the question mark to an ampersand if more than one variable is passed to this function.

However, we want to keep this simple to get the idea across. In addition, it's not a great idea to stack parameters—the results are not always guaranteed:

```
if ($count != 60 AND $count!='') {
        $api_call .= sprintf("?count=%d", $count);
}
// Now we return this API call.
```

Here is the second change. We are now calling 'get' instead of 'call_twitter':

```
        return $this->get($api_call);
    }
```

Let's save and close our files and give this a go. Load index.php, and you should have something like we saw in Figure 9.1 but with different content. We have not added new functionality to our application, but instead we have made our framework a little more flexible.

Adding Support for Mentions

The next API call we are going to make is to get our mentions (*statuses/mentions*). Remember that a mention in Twitter is any tweet that has your Twitter name in it preceded by an ampersand. For example: "Chatted with @perivision at the twitter hackup today." This tweet will then show up in the *statuses/mentions* feed. If we have a look at the parameters that the mention API call accepts, we will see that they are the same as the home API call. These are the current parameters as listed in the Twitter docs (http://dev.twitter.com/doc/get/statuses/mentions).

Parameters:

- **since_id:** Returns only statuses with an ID greater than (that is, more recent than) the specified ID.

  Example: http://api.twitter.com/1/statuses/mentions.xml?since_id=12345

- **max_id:** Returns only statuses with an ID less than (that is, older than) or equal to the specified ID.

  Example: http://api.twitter.com/1/statuses/mentions.xml?max_id=54321

- **count:** Specifies the number of statuses to retrieve. May not be greater than 200.

  Example: http://api.twitter.com/1/statuses/mentions.xml?count=200

- **page:** Specifies the page or results to retrieve. Note: there are pagination limits. (More information on pagination limits can be found here: http:/ /apiwiki.twitter.com/Things-Every-Developer-Should-Know#6Therearepaginationlimits.)

  Example: http://api.twitter.com/1/statuses/mentions.xml?page=3

- **trim_user:** When set to either true, t or 1, each tweet returned in a timeline will include a user object including only the status authors numerical ID.

  Example: http://api.twitter.com/1/statuses/mentions.json?trim_user=true

- **include_rts:** When set to either true, t or 1,the timeline will contain native retweets (if they exist) in addition to the standard stream of tweets.

  Example: http://api.twitter.com/1/statuses/mentions.json?include_rts=true

- **include_entities:** When set to either true, t or 1, each tweet will include a node called "entities,". This node offers a variety of metadata about the tweet in a discreet structure, including: user_mentions, urls, and hashtags.

  Example: http://api.twitter.com/1/statuses/mentions.json?include_entities=true

We can use this to our advantage as we expand our classes, but for now, it's enough to make note of this, but the main point is to understand the variety of options we have available to us. Many of these parameters only became available just recently.

Here is the code for our new call. Open the file 'twitteroauth/twitteroauth.php' in your editor and add the following function at the bottom of the file but before the last "}":

```
function getMentions($format, $page = 0, $since_id=0) {
          $api_call = sprintf("statuses/mentions.%s", $format);
          if ($page) {
                  $api_call .= sprintf("?page=%d", $page);
          }
          if ($since_id) {
                  $api_call .= sprintf("?since_id=%d", $since_id);
          }
          return $this->get($api_call);
}
```

Notice that we did not write code to support all the parameters listed. However, the code should be clear enough to add new parameters if desired.

Because the XML return for mentions is very much like the return for home_timeline, we can use the same XML parser function as well as the same display. So revisiting our includes/parseTwitter.php file, we can use the same parsing XML for both home_timeline and mentions.

return call_ timeline($messages);

Let's save our code and close. Load your index.php file, select the Mentions tab, and you should see the 20 most recent messages with your Twitter name that you have received. If you have yet to receive a mention before, you may want to ask a friend to send you one or two.

Adding Support for Direct Messages

We have added two API calls, and now it's time to add a third. By now, you should see a pattern to how our framework is going to work. So, let's add the API call for getting direct messages that were sent to us.

Open the file 'twitteroauth/twitteroauth.php' in your editor and add the following function at the bottom of the file but before the last "}":

```
function getMessages($format, $page = 1, $since = NULL, $since_id = 0) {
          $api_call = sprintf("direct_messages.%s", $format);
          if ($since != NULL) {
                   $api_call .= sprintf("?since=%s", urlencode($since));
          }
          if ($since_id > 0) {
                   $api_call .= sprintf("%ssince_id=%d", (strpos($api_call,
"?since") === false) ? "?" : "&", $since_id);
          }
          if ($page > 1) {
                   $api_call .= sprintf("%spage=%d", (strpos($api_call,
"?since") === false) ? "?" : "&", $page);
          }
          return $this->get($api_call);
}
```

It looks pretty much like the rest of the API calls, doesn't it? However, again, the XML that is returned is slightly different, and again, we need to account for this.

What is different with the mention API call is the return. We cannot use the same parser call as we used for the home API call because the XML is structured a little differently.

Open 'includes/parseTwitter.class.php' in your editor and add the following code:

```
function call_direct($messages){

          $twitterReturn = new SimpleXMLElement($messages);
          $i=0;
```

Most of this code will look much like the function call_timeline() we defined in the beginning of this hour. However, you can see that because the returned XML is structured differently, we need to get our data differently:

```
            foreach($twitterReturn->direct_message as $status){
                    $updateTime[$i] = parseDate($status->created_at);
            $update[$i] = $status->text;
            $profile_image_url[$i] = $status->sender->profile_image_url;
            $screen_name[$i] = $status->sender->screen_name;
                    $i++;
            }

            $parsedReturn = array();
            $parsedReturn['updateTime']=$updateTime;
            $parsedReturn['update']=$update;
            $parsedReturn['profile_image_url']=$profile_image_url;
            $parsedReturn['screen_name']=$screen_name;

            return $parsedReturn;
}
```

Let's save our code and close. Load your index.php file, select the Messages tab, and you should see the 20 most direct messages to you. If you have yet to receive a direct message, you may want to ask a friend to send you one or two.

Summary

In this hour, we completed Part 1 of building a simple Twitter client. We added three new API calls: home, getMentions, and getMessages. You should now have a pretty good understanding of our Twitter framework and how to add new API calls to the framework.

Q&A

Q. ***Is there a way to ask for only the fields I want from Twitter?***

A. Unfortunately, no. Even if all you need is just a few fields, Twitter will provide a feed with everything included. This may change in the future, however.

Q. ***Is there a way to use just one XML parser call instead of having different ones for each API call?***

A. Yes. Because the XML returns for the API calls are mostly the same, you could write exception rules for various sets of API calls. However, this will make your code messy and difficult for others to understand. In the interest of simplicity and clarity, we have created separate function calls for various sets of API calls.

Workshop

Quiz

1. True or False: A mention is any time your name shows up in the Twitter stream.

2. True or False: The SimpleXMLElement is the only PHP library call I can use to parse replies from Twitter.

Quiz Answers

1. False. Remember that a mention in Twitter is any tweet that has your Twitter name in it with an 'at' symbol (@).

2. False. There are other XML parsing functions you can use. Also, Twitter can return JSON as well.

Exercise

As you read in this hour, there are a number of parameters you can pass to Twitter to refine what Twitter returns, including since_id, max_id, count, and page. Try each parameter one at a time so you can experience how the returns are affected.

HOUR 10

Building a Simple Twitter Client, Part II

What You'll Learn in This Hour:

- How to send a message to Twitter
- How to send a direct versus a normal tweet
- How to sanitize messages

Updating and Adding New Files to Support Input Text Field

Now that we have a simple Twitter client to read messages, we need to work on making our client application send messages. The good news is that we can still use our current framework with a few additional files. In addition, we will introduce a few JavaScript calls to support user interaction.

First, we need to add to our index.php file to allow a user to type in a message.

Edit index.php

Open the file index.php, and after this line:

```
<title>twitterAPI 24</title>
```

Add the following line:

```
<script type='text/javascript' src='js/base.js'></script>
```

Now we need to add a few more files to include; we will create them in a moment.

After the following line:

```
include 'includes/header.inc';
```

Add the following two lines:

```
include 'includes/createMessage.php';
include 'sendMessage.php';
```

Notice that we did not place sendMessage.php in the include folder. That is because this file will be called by JavaScript and, thus, for simplicity, needs to live in the same folder as our OAuth code.

Create createMessage.php

Let's add a new file. Create a new file called 'createMessage.php' within the includes folder and type in the following code:

```
<div class="sendMessage">
  <div class="messageTextBox">
    <form name="sendMessForm" method="get" action="" class="asholder">
➥<label id="prefex"></label>
      <textarea id="testinput" name="sendMessField" class="inputbox"
➥rows="2" cols="80" ></textarea>
      <br>
      <input class="inputbox" type="button" value="Send"
➥onmouseup="sendMessage()" />
      </font>
    </form>
              <div id="serverMessages">
              </div>
  </div>
 </div>
```

Then save this file and close it.

Edit main.css

Now let's open css/main.css and add two entries.

After the following lines:

```
.tweet {
          padding:0 10px;
}
```

Add the following lines:

```
.sendMessage {
 padding: 15px 10px 0px;
}
```

```
.messageTextBox {
 width: 600px;
}
```

Then save this file and close it.

Create base.js

Now that we have a text field and a Send button, we need some JavaScript code to catch the button click and pass the message to a new PHP file we will create soon. If you are not familiar with JavaScript, this might look a bit scary, but all we are really doing here is making a call to our server, getting the response, and putting that response on our page. This is known as an AJAX call:

```
<!--

function sendMessage(){
  message = document.getElementById("prefex").innerHTML;
  message += document.sendMessForm.sendMessField.value;
  url='sendMessage.php?message='+message;
  document.sendMessForm.sendMessField.value='';
  document.getElementById("prefex").innerHTML='';
  callPage(url, 'serverMessages');
}


//########################################################################
############


var k=0; req = Array();

function callPage(pageUrl, divElementId, loadingMessage, pageErrorMessage) {
  if(!loadingMessage || loadingMessage=='') loadingMessage = "ContentSet is
loading, Please Wait...";
  if(!pageErrorMessage || pageErrorMessage=='') pageErrorMessage="Error in
Loading page />";
  document.getElementById(divElementId).innerHTML = loadingMessage+'Calling
➥twitter...';
  try {
  req[k] = new XMLHttpRequest(); /* e.g. Firefox */
  } catch(e) {
   try {
   req[k] = new ActiveXObject('Msxml2.XMLHTTP');  /* some versions IE */
   } catch (e) {
     try {
     req[k] = new ActiveXObject('Microsoft.XMLHTTP');  /* some versions IE */
     } catch (E) {
      req[k] = false;
     }
   }
```

```
  }
  req[k].onreadystatechange = function() {responsefromServer(divElementId,
➥pageErrorMessage);};
  req[k].open('GET',pageUrl,true);
  req[k].send(null);
}

function responsefromServer(divElementId, pageErrorMessage) {
  var output = req[k].responseText;
   if(req[k].readyState == 4) {
      if(req[k].status == 200) {
         output = req[k].responseText;
         document.getElementById(divElementId).innerHTML = output;
         } else {
         document.getElementById(divElementId).innerHTML =
➥pageErrorMessage+'\n'+output;
      }
    }
}

-->
```

Now let's save and close the file.

Create sendMessage.php

This next file are going to create will be placed in the home or root directory of our development environment. Create a new file called sendMessage.php and add the following code:

```
<?php

include 'oauth_index.php';

$message=$_GET['message'];

$output=$twitter->updateStatus($message);
$twitterReturn = new SimpleXMLElement($output);
echo 'Twitter said ';
print_r ($twitterReturn);

?>
```

Save and close this file.

Sending a Message to Twitter

Finally, we need to have a file to catch the newly created message and make the API call. Open twitteroauth/twitteroauth.php.

At the end of the file, but before the "} ?>", add the following lines:

```
        function updateStatus($status) {
                $status = urlencode(stripslashes(urldecode($status)));
                $api_call = sprintf("statuses/update.xml?status=%s",
➥$status);
```

We are going to add an echo statement here so that you can see the structure of your API call, as we have done on other functions:

```
                  echo "<h4>$api_call</h4><br>";
                return $this->post($api_call);
        }
```

Save and close this file.

Open index.php, and let's try sending our first message. Type something into the text box and hit Send.

If you see something like Figure 10.1, you have successfully sent your first tweet from an API call!

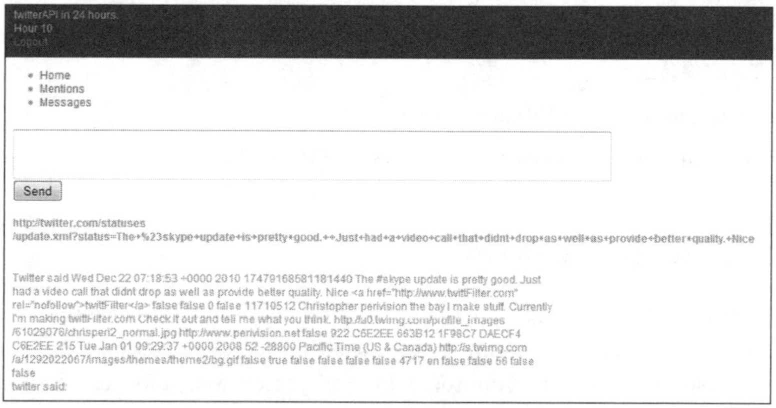

FIGURE 10.1
Raw return from sending a message.

API Call for Direct Messages

Sending a direct message is different from sending a regular message and thus requires a different API call. As such, we need to know when the user wants to send a direct message and when the user wants to send a regular message. There are a number of ways to approach this: One way is to simply look for a message that starts with the letter "d" followed by a space as an indicator that the user wants to send a direct message. Why is this? Because in the early days of Twitter, when it was SMS only, the only way to send a direct message was to use the letter "d" and a space followed by the Twitter name the message is to be delivered to, a space, and then your message. Even now, we can type d <twittername> and a message, and

Twitter will automatically treat this as a direct message. There is a downside to this, however. There are only 140 characters within a tweet, so we lose those characters to the “d,” the space, the Twitter username, and another space. This may not seem like much, but it adds up, especially if the Twitter user’s name is long.

To get around this, the Twitter API provides us with a separate API call for direct messages. Because this is a separate process, we will explore this API in Hour 12, “Direct Messages.” However, depending on what your Twitter client is going to do, you may want to look for the “d” shortcut pattern and extend the number of characters users can send in their message if you plan to implement a character counter in your application.

Sanitizing Messages

Although our current implementation works, we need to account for a few things. Because we are sending information over the Web back to our application, we need to make sure that the characters we use are web safe. So, let’s add the following code to our JavaScript to sanitize the message before we send it to our sendMessage.php file.

Edit base.js

Open base.js, and after the following line:

```
message += document.sendMessForm.sendMessField.value;
```

Add this line:

```
message=encodeURIComponent(message);
```

Just to be clear, the encodeURIComponent function will replace certain non-web safe symbols with a URI code. This is much like the string replace function here, $message = str_replace(“%23”, “#”, $message), but for all non web-safe characters.

Save and close this file.

Great! We now have a working Twitter client that can read messages as well as send messages. We also implemented AJAX within our application. And it’s only Hour 10.

Summary

In this hour, we have finished up the basics for our simple Twitter application and set the foundation for further expansion through the rest of book.

We also created our first AJAX call for sending messages, and we created a PHP file for responding to the requests that come from our JavaScript AJAX call.

Q&A

Q. ***How do you send a direct message from the message box in Twitter?***

A. Type d, then a space, and then your message. This is one of many shortcuts that you can use with Twitter.

Q. ***Why does Twitter have shortcuts?***

A. Twitter started out as a SMS-only communication system. Using a single letter was a simple way to send Twitter a command or indicate the type of message being sent.

Workshop

Quiz

1. True or False: If, for some reason, a non-web safe character is sent to Twitter, it will return an error.

2. True or False: If you wanted to, you could send a message through the normal API and place the letter d, a space, and then a valid username, and it would work just as well as using the direct message API call.

Quiz Answers

1. False. Most likely it will simply truncate the message and execute the requested API request. **However**, ALWAYS be sure that any message you send to Twitter is web-safe.

2. True for now. Although this can be done (there is no guarantee this will continue to work), it's not a good idea. However, many users still use short cuts, so it's in your best interest to look for a message that starts with a d, a space, and a valid username, and then send it as a direct message through the correct API call.

Exercise

In this hour, we simply displayed what Twitter returns after sending a direct message. Try displaying only the message you sent to Twitter. Hint: You would parse return in a similar manner as you have parsed other returns from Twitter.

HOUR 11

Expanding Our Client for More API Calls

What You'll Learn in This Hour:

- ▶ How to add multiple tabs to our UI
- ▶ More statuses API calls
- ▶ How to send a retweet through the API
- ▶ The various ways to handle retweets

Types of API Method Calls

Congratulations. This is Hour 11, and we have already created a Twitter client application. But we have only scratched the surface of what can be done with Twitter through the API set. We will not go through every API call in detail, because that would make this book so large we would have to break into multiple volumes. But we will list and discuss them all so that you can get an idea of what options you have for the Twitter application you would like to build. At the time of this writing, the Twitter development documents break up the API sets into the following groups: (http://dev.twitter.com/doc)

- ▶ Timeline
- ▶ Status
- ▶ User
- ▶ List Members
- ▶ List Subscribers
- ▶ Direct Message

- Friendship
- Social Graph
- Account
- Favorite
- Notification
- Block
- Spam
- Saved Searches
- OAuth
- Local Trends
- Geo
- Help
- Search

Quite a lot, isn't there? A vast majority of our time will be spent around the Timeline, Status, and Search methods. As such, we are going to spend this hour updating our User Interface (UI) so that we can support more API calls. By the end of this hour, we will have all the Timeline methods covered.

Adding Tabs to Our UI

To make it a bit easier for us to add new API calls, we need more buttons in our UI. We will also have these tabs organized such to reflect how Twitter currently has their API reference documents organized as well as the order of what we will be building in this book. So, let's open includes/header.inc and expand the code.

Edit header.inc

Erase everything after the line <!-- main navigation --> and add the following lines:

```
<div id="nav-box">
                <div class="nav-box">
    <ul id="globalnav">

      <li><a href="#" class="here">Timeline</a>
        <ul>
          <li><a href="#">Public</a></li>
          <li><a href="?page=timeline" >Home</a></li>
```

```
                              <li><a href="?page=mentions" >User</a></li>
                              <li><a href="?page=direct" >Mentions</a></li>
            <li><a href="?page=rt_by_me">Retweeted By Me</a></li>
            <li><a href="?page=rt_to_me">Retweeted To Me</a></li>
            <li><a href="?page=rt_of_me">Retweeted Of Me</a></li>
          </ul>
        </li>
        <li><a href="#">List</a>
        </li>
        <li><a href="#">User</a>
        </li>
        <li><a href="#">Direct Message</a>
        </li>
        <li><a href="#">Favorites</a>
        </li>
        <li><a href="#">Search</a>
        </li>
        <li><a href="#">Saved Search</a>
        </li>
      </ul>
                  </div>
         </div>
</div>
```

Save and close. Now let's create a new CSS file to support these tabs:

Create nav.css

Create a new file in your css folder called nav.css and add the following code:

```
#globalnav {
          position:relative;
          float:left;
          width:100%;
          padding:0 0 1.75em 1em;
          margin:0;
          list-style:none;
          line-height:1em;
}

#globalnav LI {
          float:left;
          margin:0;
          padding:0;
}

#globalnav A {
          display:block;
          color:#444;
          text-decoration:none;
          font-weight:bold;
          background:#c0deed;
```

```
            margin:0;
            padding:0.25em 1em;
            border-left:1px solid #fff;
            border-top:1px solid #fff;
            border-right:1px solid #aaa;
}

#globalnav A:hover,
#globalnav A:active,
#globalnav A.here:link,
#globalnav A.here:visited {
            background:#a8d0e3;
}

#globalnav A.here:link,
#globalnav A.here:visited {
            position:relative;
            z-index:102;
}

/*subnav*/

#globalnav UL {
            position:absolute;
            left:0;
            top:1.5em;
            float:left;
            background:#a8d0e3;
            width:100%;
            margin:0;
            padding:0.25em 0.25em 0.25em 1em;
            list-style:none;
            border-top:1px solid #fff;
}

#globalnav UL LI {
            float:left;
            display:block;
            margin-top:1px;
}

#globalnav UL A {
            background:#a8d0e3;
            color:#fff;
            display:inline;
            margin:0;
            padding:0 1em;
            border:0
}

#globalnav UL A:hover,
#globalnav UL A:active,
#globalnav UL A.here:link,
```

```
#globalnav UL A.here:visited {
        color:#444;
}
```

Save and close. We have one more file to go. We need to update index.php to see the new css file.

Edit index.php

After this line:

```
<link href="css/main.css" rel="stylesheet" type="text/css" media="screen" />
```

Add the following line:

```
    <link href="css/nav.css" rel="stylesheet" type="text/css"
media="screen" />
```

Save and close. Now open index.html in your browser, and you should see something like Figure 11.1.

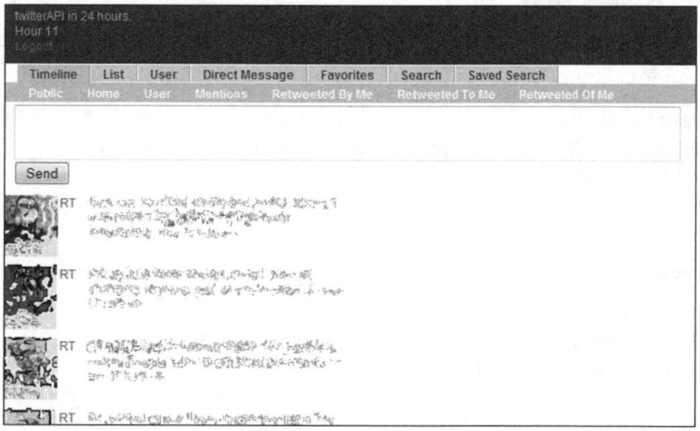

FIGURE 11.1
New tabs are now added to the top of the web page.

New Timeline API Calls: Retweeted

We are going to create three new API calls (retweeted by me, to me, and of me), and because of how we created our code structure, you will find that it will be very easy because we are cutting and pasting code from functions we have already created. However, let's explore these three calls first.

Retweeted by Me

Depending on the Twitter account you are using and the type of client application you have used, you may or may not get returns from this API call. That is because the retweeted_by_me API call relies on the application to send a retweet using a certain format. We will cover this later. If the application you have been using to retweet does not use the retweet API call, you may not see any returns, or they may be older returns. If this is the case, the best thing to do is log in to Twitter.com and retweet a message; then return to your code. You should see your retweeted message.

Retweeted to Me and of Me

The retweeted_to_me and retweeted_of_me API calls are very similar. So much so, you may find the same display when you click between the two buttons. That is because a message that is retweeted_to_me are retweets from people in your friends list. Message that are retweeted_of_me are from anyone—a slight but important difference.

Now let's add a few new API calls.

Edit parseTwitter.php

We have added new tabs to our UI. Now we need to account for the new tabs in our parsing statement. Open parseTwitter.php, and after the following lines:

```
    case 'direct':
        { $messages=$twitter->getMessages('xml'); return
➥call_direct($messages); }
        break;
```

Add these lines:

```
    case 'rt_by_me':
        { $messages=$twitter->getRTByMe('xml'); return
➥call_timeline($messages); }
        break;
    case 'rt_to_me':
        { $messages=$twitter-> getRTtoMe ('xml'); return
➥call_timeline($messages); }
        break;
    case 'rt_of_me':
        { $messages=$twitter-> getRTofMe ('xml'); return
➥call_timeline($messages); }
        break;
          }
```

As you can see, we have extended our case statement. Also, because the XML returns of the new API calls are similar to our home_timeline call, we will simply reuse the same function call to display our returns.

Save and close.

Edit twitteroauth.php

Now that we have the new API calls in parseTwitter, we need to add functions to twitteroauth.php to catch those calls.

Open twitteroauth.php and add the following lines at the end of the file, but before '} ?>':

```
function getRTByMe() {
                $api_call = ' statuses/retweeted_by_me.xml';
                return $this->get($api_call);
        }

        function getRTToMe() {
                $api_call = 'statuses/retweeted_to_me.xml';
                return $this->get($api_call);
        }

        function getRTOfMe() {
                $api_call = 'statuses/retweets_of_me.xml';
                return $this->get($api_call);
        }
```

If these functions seem a lot like our getHomeTimeline function call, it's because they are. Many API calls to Twitter are similar in fashion, and we get to take advantage of this. However, what is different is that we are not using the sprint() function anymore. Although we could have continued to use the sprint() functions, the extra code will only make reading more confusing as well as cause extra typing for you.

Save and close this file.

Now let's give it a try. Load index.php and click the three new function calls we just created. You have three new functional API calls!

New Status API Calls: Retweeted

The retweet API call is not required because it's still a convention to prepend a message with the letters 'rt' and the tweeter's name. However, this introduces extra characters, and if the original message is close to 140 characters, the addition of 'rt' and the tweeter's name could put it over. In addition, if you wanted to trace back a message that generated the retweet in the first place, you would have to search all tweets with this message or keep a log yourself. To deal with this issue, as well as make it more feasible to display related tweets inline, the Twitter API has a method called retweet that has one required input: the ID of the tweet to be retweeted.

Retweet

Now this is tricky; in order for our user to retweet a message, we need to offer a Retweet button, which needs to pass the ID of that message back to the server. There are two ways to do this. We can create a dumb button that makes a unique call back to the server with the message ID and thus load a new page, or we can make an AJAX call. The AJAX call is a bit more involved but provides a far superior user experience.

We need to add a few lines of code to our framework, so we are going to add a case switch here.

Edit sendMessages.php

After this line:

```
$message = $_GET['message'];
```

Add the following:

```
$id = $_GET['id'];
$command = $_GET['command'];
        switch ($command) {
        case '':
                  { echo 'Err: No command found'; }
                   break;
        case 'update':
                  { $output=$twitter->updateStatus($message); }
                  break;
        case 'retweet':
                  { $output=$twitter->retweet('xml', $id); }
                break;
        }
```

Save and close.

Edit twitteroauth.php

Next we need to pass the retweet request on to Twitter, so let's edit twitteroauth.php. Open twitteroauth.php and add the following lines at the end of the file, but before '} ?>':

```
          function retweet($format, $id = NULL) {
            if(!$id) { return 'Err; cannot retweet.  no id found'; }
                   $api_call = sprintf('statuses/retweet/%s.%s', $id,
➥$format);
                   return $this->post($api_call);
          }
```

Edit parseTwitter.php

Once we get our return from Twitter, we need to parse. Open parseTwitter.php:

After this:

```
        foreach($twitterReturn->status as $status){
                $updateTime[$i] = parseDate($status->created_at);
        $update[$i] = $status->text;
```

Add this:

```
        $id[$i] = $status->id;
```

After this:

```
        $parsedReturn = array();
        $parsedReturn['updateTime']=$updateTime;
        $parsedReturn['update']=$update;
```

Add this:

```
        $parsedReturn['id']=$id;
```

Edit render.php

And of course, we need to modify how we render so that we can provide the user with a retweet button. We are just using letters, here, but you could replace this with an icon. Open render.php:

After this:

```
        for($i=0; $i<$num; $i++){
                $updateTime = $parsedReturn['updateTime'][$i];
                $update = $parsedReturn['update'][$i];
```

Add the following line:

```
                $id = $parsedReturn['id'][$i];
```

After this:

```
                $output.= "<tr><td><div id='$screen_name' class='mess-
pic' >
                  <img src='$profile_image_url'/ width='48px'
height='48px'>
                  <br>$screen_name_abv</div>
```

Add the following lines:

```
                <div class='mess-actions'>
                <a href='#' onmouseup=\"retweet('$id')\">RT</a></div>
```

Edit main.css

We need to make some space for our retweet button, so lets make some via our CSS file. Open main.css:

Add this at the end of the file:

```
.mess-actions{
float:left; padding-left:3px; width:10px;
}
```

Edit base.js

We will add a function in our javascript file to catch the users click. Add this at the end of the file of base.js:

```
function retweet(mess_id){
          alert('retweet '+mess_id);
  url='sendMessage.php?command=retweet&id='+mess_id;
            callPage(url, mess_id);
}
```

If you did not already know, the JavaScript function 'alert()', which is built in to JavaScript, will pop up a window and stop any further execution of JavaScript code. This serves as a very useful debugging tool. If everything went well with this call, you can comment out or remove this line.

retweets/id, id/retweeted_by, id/retweeted by/ids

We are not going to write code for the next three API calls, but I do want to cover them briefly. You can find this and more information in the Twitter docs. (http://dev.twitter.com/doc/get/statuses/retweets/:id)

> **retweets/id**—http://api.twitter.com/1/statuses/retweets/id.format
>
> Retweets give up to 100 retweet status (messages) based on a given status ID. In other words, if we pass a status id, as we did to create a retweet to the status/retweets API call, we would get back up to 100 statuses that are retweets of the original status. The value of this is not the actual status, because they would all be the same, RT @<screen_name> <original message>, but instead the list of people who retweeted the original tweet.
>
> **id/retweeted_by**—http://api.twitter.com/1/statuses/id/retweeted_by.format
>
> Show user objects of up to 100 members who retweeted the status represented by ID.

id/retweeted_by/ids—http://api.twitter.com/1/statuses/id/retweeted_by/ids.format

Note ids here refers to the support of multiple ids that can be passed

Show user IDs of up to 100 users who retweeted the status represented by ID. Keep in mind this will only return users' IDs.

Summary

In this hour, we expanded the UI of our application to support tabs, which we will need as we include more and more API calls. We also introduced the concept of retweeting. The various ways to read a retweet include messages retweeted by the user, messages retweeted to the user, and retweets about the user.

We also dealt with passing a message ID back to our script from the client using JavaScript, which we will see again in coming hours.

Q&A

Q. ***Is 'RT' a shortcut like 'd'?***

A. No. RT was never officially supported by Twitter. It was a convention that many people and later Twitter programmers, like you, implemented.

Q. ***Because the difference between retweeted_to_me and retweeted_of_me is so slight, do I really need to support both in my application?***

A. It depends on what you are trying to accomplish, but for most basic applications, you could get away with just retweeted_of_me.

Workshop

Quiz

1. What are the three different types of retweeted messages?
2. Because 'RT' is only a convention, can I ignore it in my application?

Quiz Answers

1. The three types are retweeted_by_me, retweeted_to_me, and retweeted_of_me.
2. No, it's only a convention; however, many people and older programs still follow this convention, so you may want to look for a message starting with or containing a 'RT' and then decide what you should do based on what your application is trying to accomplish. Caution, many users will us RT but change the message somewhat.

Exercise

Although we did not code an example for any of the Retweet API methods, pick one and implement it into our sample application.

HOUR 12

Direct Messages

What You'll Learn in This Hour:

- Send direct messages through the API
- Test for the existence of friendships between users
- How to delete direct messages using destroy method

Sending a Direct Message

Although we have briefly discussed direct messages in Hour 10, in this hour we add support for sending direct messages, as well as a few other methods. We will also look at another set of API calls, called friends, in order to know if we can send a direct message in the first place.

Adding UI Elements for Direct Messages

However, the first thing we will do is revisit reading our direct messages. Because we already have this in our API set, we just need to populate the button on our UI.

Edit index.php

After this line:

```
<meta charset="utf-8">
```

Add this line:

```
$nav = $_GET['nav'];
```

Edit header.inc

After these lines:

```
      <li><a href="/?page=rt_of_me">Retweeted Of Me</a></li>
    </ul>
  <? } ?>
  </li>
```

Add the following lines:

```
  <li><a href="/?nav=direct" <? if($nav=='direct') echo
➥'class="here"'; ?> >Direct Message</a>
  <? if($nav=='direct') { ?>
    <ul>
      <li><a href="/?page=direct" >Direct Message</a></li>
    </ul>
  <? } ?>
  </li>
```

Testing if a Direct Message Can Be Sent

Now that we have that in place, let's create an API call that deals with sending direct messages.

In Twitter, you can send a direct message only to someone who follows you. If the Twitter user does not follow you, you will get back an error. So, before we send our direct message, we should check to see whether the Twitter user is following us. That means a new API call: friendships/exists.

This will be a new type of API call that we have not seen before. This call returns a simple true or false. We pass two parameters: the Twitter name of user A and the Twitter name of user B. If Twitter user A follows user B (A->B), Twitter will return a value of true. If not, it returns a value of false.

There are a few ways to determine if a direct message can be sent or not:

- Get a list of IDs of every follower a user has. Then check to see if the Twitter ID displayed in the message stream is contained within this list. The only problem with this option is what do you do if the user has a very large number of followers? The current paging limit is 5,000 IDs per page. This could become cumbersome if the user has a lot of followers: 20,000 followers is not that rare.
- Get a list and store it in a database. This would be the more typical solution for a high-level functioning Twitter application. You would go through the list of pages of follower IDs, store them in a database, and then make calls as each new Twitter ID is found in the incoming stream.
- Check one at a time at the moment the user tries to create a message. That is the approach we are going to use here. This keeps the API calls to a

minimum and is the easiest to code as a book example. However, this is not practical if we need to determine a large number of friendship relationships at once. It also has the drawback that you cannot indicate to the user ahead of time if someone can receive a direct message or not.

- Send the message and alert the user if an error has occurred. This is similar to the previous point but instead of testing is a friendship exists, you look for an error from Twitter. This is not recommended since it reflects poor coding techniques as well as depends on the Twitter error code not changing.

Because we are going to check the friendship status only after the direct message button or the letters DM in our case were clicked, we will have two events to manage. First, we are going to populate the message box with the "d" shorthand and the Twitter name we want to send the direct message to. Second, within the sendMessage.php file, we will detect for that shorthand and use the proper API method. The reason we want to do this is to support the older shorthand of using the letter d and the username that some Twitter users still employ. We are using this approach to help illustrate how to deal with short hand. In a typical application, you would use other means to indicate that a message is a direct message.

Here is what an example call would look like:

```
http://api.twitter.com/1/friendships/exists.xml?user_a=tweetapi24&user_b=
➥perivision
```

We need two Twitter names to make this work: the name of the user and the name of the person who we want to send the direct message to. We will pass those names to the API, and if we get a true value back, we will allow the user to send a message. If we get back a false value, we will pop up a warning that the direct message will not go through. Of course, we could accomplish the same thing by simply trying to send the message and look for the error response back from Twitter, but this is a book on Twitter API programming, so we are going to do it the more formal way.

Adding Direct Message API Support

In this section, we add direct message API support.

Edit Render.php

We are going to add another mouse rollover action to our UI. We will add the letters "DM" under the "RT" we created in Hour 11:

```
global $twitterName;
```

After this line:

```
function renderTweets ($parsedReturn){
```

Add this line:

```
global $twitterName;
```

Edit this line:

```
<a href='#' onmouseup=\"retweet('$id')\">RT</a></div>
```

To read:

```
<a href='#' onmouseup=\"retweet('$id')\">RT</a>
```

This will remove “</div>”.

Now add the following under the line we just edited:

```
<a href='#' onmouseup=\"direct('$screen_name' , '$twitterName')\">DM</a>
</div>
```

Open index.php, and we should now see a ‘DM’ under our ‘RT’ in the Twitter stream.

Edit base.js

The next step is to populate the message box with the letter “d” and the screen name of the person we want to send the direct message to. We also want to check to see whether the user is following us. We will initiate both actions in this JavaScript function call.

Add the following function after the ‘retweet()’ function:

```
function direct(nameA, nameB){

          document.getElementById("serverMessages").innerHTML =
➥'Checking... ';
          document.sendMessForm.sendMessField.value='d '+nameA+' ';
```

Here we are defining our URL to call sendMessage.php and pass the two names we want to compare:

```
          url = 'sendMessage.php?command=testFriendship&parameterA=
➥'+nameA+'&parameterB='+nameB;
          callPage(url, 'serverMessages');
}
```

Edit sendMessage.php

Now we need to catch our new DM request in the sendMessage.php file. So, let's add a few more lines of code.

After this line:

```
$id = $_GET['id'];
```

Add the following lines:

```
$parameterA = $_GET['parameterA'];
$parameterB = $_GET['parameterB'];
```

Notice that we have made our variables more generic; that will allow us to use these over again for other calls. We have chosen to make these variables generic for illustrative reason for this book.

Next, we need to add a new case to our switch.

After these lines:

```
    case 'retweet':
        { $output=$twitter->retweet('xml', $id); }
        break;
```

Add the following lines:

```
          case 'direct':
                   { $output=$twitter->sendDirectMessage('xml', $id,
➥$message); }
                   break;
          case 'testFriendship':
                   { $output=$twitter->friendshipExists($parameterA,
➥$parameterB);
                             if(stristr($output, 'false')) echo '<h3>This
➥person does not follow you. They may not receive the message</h3>';
                             return; }
                   break;
```

Edit twitteroauth.php

The friendships/exists API method we are going to call will be a bit different from the other API calls we have been making, mostly because all we need is a true or false based on two parameters.

At the end of the file, but before the last brace }, add the following lines:

```
        function friendshipExists($a, $b){
          $api_call = " friendships/exists.xml?user_a=$a&user_b=$b";
                 return $this->get($api_call);
        }
```

The friendships/exists is not the only API call we could have made here. We could have called friendships/show. Here is an example:

```
http://api.twitter.com/1/friendships/show.xml?source_id=3191321&target_scre
en_name=noradio
```

The reply would be the following:

```
<relationship>
-
<target>
<screen_name>ev</screen_name>
<id_str>20</id_str>
<followed_by type="boolean">true</followed_by>
<following type="boolean">true</following>
<id type="integer">20</id>
</target>
-
<source>
<want_retweets nil="true"/>
<marked_spam nil="true"/>
<all_replies nil="true"/>
<screen_name>noradio</screen_name>
<id_str>3191321</id_str>
<blocking nil="true"/>
<followed_by type="boolean">true</followed_by>
<notifications_enabled nil="true"/>
<can_dm type="boolean">true</can_dm>
<following type="boolean">true</following>
<id type="integer">3191321</id>
</source>
</relationship>
```

So, although we get more information this way, we do not get anything that we would act upon for our requirement. By using friendships/exits, we can use an 'if(stristr)' statement and look for true or false.

Okay, let's give it a try. Open index.php, and click DM from any Twitter name that you know does not follow you. You should get something like the screenshot in Figure 12.1.

Now let's try sending a direct message. Click the DM of a Twitter user who you know is following you and send them a message.

You should get something like the screenshot in Figure 12.2.

There are few other direct message API calls available to us, so let's add them to our application.

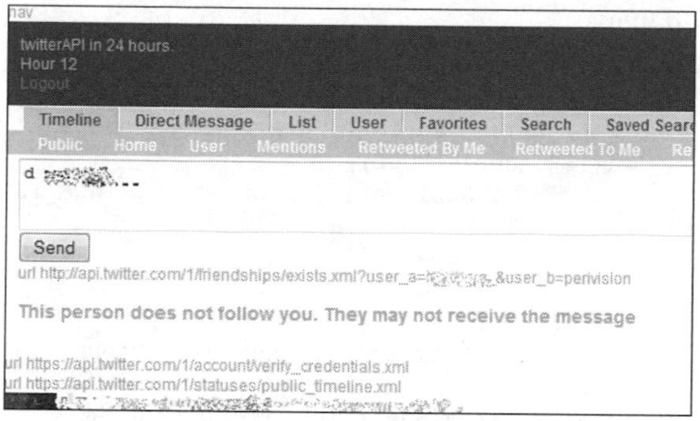

FIGURE 12.1 Screenshot showing the Not Following warning.

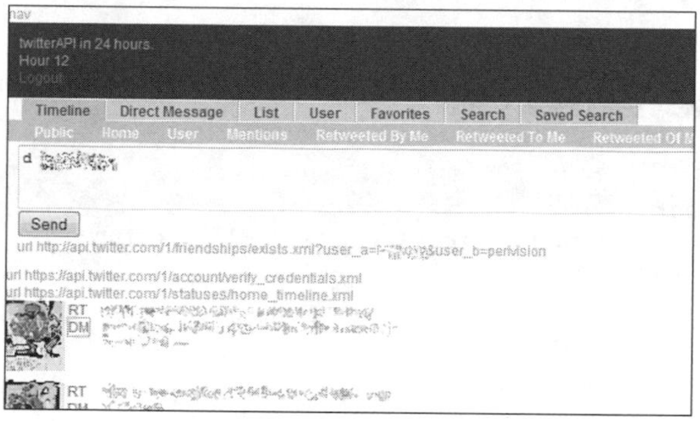

FIGURE 12.2 Screenshot showing the Following confirmed message.

Adding More Direct Message API Support

Now let's add more direct message API support.

Edit twitteroauth.php

After this code:

```
        function getMessages($format, $id = NULL, $count = 60, $since =
➥NULL) {
                $api_call = sprintf("direct_messages.%s", $format);
                if($since != NULL){
                        $api_call .= sprintf("?since_id=%s",
➥urlencode($since));
                        $count=0;
                }
                if ($count != 60 AND $count!='') {
                        $api_call .= sprintf("?count=%d", $count);
                }
                return $this->get($api_call);
        }
```

Add the following lines:

```
        function getMessagesSent($format, $id = NULL, $count = 20, $since
➥= NULL) {
                $api_call = sprintf("direct_messages/sent.%s", $format);
                if($since != NULL){
                        $api_call .= sprintf("?since_id=%s",
➥urlencode($since));
                        $count=0;
                }
                if ($count != 20 AND $count!='') {
                        $api_call .= sprintf("?count=%d", $count);
                }
                return $this->get($api_call);
        }
```

Edit parseTwitter.php

After this code:

```
    case 'direct':
        { $messages=$twitter->getMessages('xml'); return
➥call_direct($messages); }
        break;
```

Add the following lines:

```
    case 'directSent':
        { $messages=$twitter->getMessagesSent('xml'); return
➥call_direct($messages); }
        break;
```

Edit header.inc

After this code:

```
<li><a href="/?page=direct" >Direct Message</a></li>
```

Add the following line:

```
<li><a href="/?page=directSent" >Direct Messages Sent</a></li>
```

The Destroy API Method

There is one more direct message API method we did not cover: direct_messages/destroy. This is for direct messages that have been sent to you. Yes, it would be great if you could delete a direct message that you sent, but alas, that is not the case. So, never tweet in anger. In addition, your message is not removed off the server, it's simply marked as deleted. It's up to the client application to respect this tag. This may change in the future.

Here is the format of the destroy call:

```
http://api.twitter.com/version/direct_messages/destroy/:id.format
```

Summary

In this hour, we explored the direct message methods. To ensure that we can send a direct message, we also learned how to test whether two users are friends with each other—a requirement for a direct message to be successfully sent. We also learned that we cannot take back a direct message once it's sent. So, think before you tweet.

Q&A

Q. ***Can I send a direct message without using the API?***

A. Yes. You can send a normal message by placing a d and the name of a valid user who is following you. This is not recommended, however.

Q. ***Can I use Destroy to delete a direct message I sent?***

A. No. Destroy will delete messages sent to you.

Workshop

Quiz

1. True or False: For a friendship to exist, both you and you friend must follow each other.
2. True or False: Using the destroy method on a message you have sent will not remove the message.
3. True or False: If you send a direct message to someone who does not follow you, they will get a request to follow you so that your message can go through.

Quiz Answers

1. False. All that is required for someone to receive a direct message is that they follow the sender. The sender does not need to follow the recipient of the direct message.

2. True. You can only destroy messages that have been sent to you. Hopefully this is changed in the future.

3. False. The target of the direct message will not receive any alerts. As such, it's up to the sender to let the recipient know they cannot receive a direct message.

Exercises

1. We did not implement the Destroy method in this hour. As an exercise, let's implement it now.

   Because you can only destroy a direct message that was sent to you, you will need to create a second twitter account or get a friend to send you a few direct messages. Remember, you need the message ID to destroy this message. Look back to Hour 11 to remind yourself how to do this.

2. Because we can simply look for an error from Twitter when we try to send a direct message instead of checking for a friendship, try changing your code to skip the friendship checking procedures and instead simply display the error message Twitter provides you.

HOUR 13
Lists

What You'll Learn in This Hour:

- What is a Twitter list?
- The List Timeline resources
- The List Members resources
- The List Subscribers resources
- A new approach to restful calls not seen so far
- How to use the DELETE cURL method and what to do if your host environment does not support it

What Is a List?

Lists in Twitter are interesting—as you would guess, they are lists of Twitter accounts. For something so simple, there are lots of API methods to support it. Most of them around the identification of who is on a list or who is following a list. But first, let's get to know what a list is. On the @perivision account is a list called news-feeds. The members of this list are a few major news outlets. When you view a feed based on a list, it's the same as viewing any other feed.

Based on such a simple concept, you might be surprised at the number of API methods Twitters offers at http://dev.twitter.com/doc. Click on lists on the right. Here is the current list:

- http://dev.twitter.com/doc/post/:user/lists
- http://dev.twitter.com/doc/post/:user/lists/:id
- http://dev.twitter.com/doc/get/:user/lists
- http://dev.twitter.com/doc/get/:user/lists/:id

- http://dev.twitter.com/doc/delete/:user/lists/:id
- http://dev.twitter.com/doc/get/:user/lists/:id/statuses
- http://dev.twitter.com/doc/get/:user/lists/memberships
- http://dev.twitter.com/doc/get/:user/lists/subscriptions
- http://dev.twitter.com/doc/get/:user/:list_id/members
- http://dev.twitter.com/doc/post/:user/:list_id/members
- http://dev.twitter.com/doc/post/:user/:list_id/create_all
- http://dev.twitter.com/doc/delete/:user/:list_id/members
- http://dev.twitter.com/doc/get/:user/:list_id/members/:id
- http://dev.twitter.com/doc/get/:user/:list_id/subscribers
- http://dev.twitter.com/doc/post/:user/:list_id/subscribers
- http://dev.twitter.com/doc/delete/:user/:list_id/subscribers
- http://dev.twitter.com/doc/get/:user/:list_id/subscribers/:id

It would not be practical to try to add each method to our sample application, so we are going to add only the ones needed to create and display a list. But we will go through these in more detail at the end of the hour. However, we need to point out a few odd things about these methods and deal with them within our code.

Formal Use of GET, POST, and DELETE

You may notice that many of the methods defined here are duplicates. So, how do we tell them apart and what do they do differently? Let's take user/lists, for example.

The API method user/lists can do two things. It can create a list, or it can list a user's list—a list of a list if you like. Private lists are not included unless it's your own list you are accessing.

If this seems confusing, that's because it is. The difference between these two API calls is in the way you make the call. If you make a GET call, Twitter interprets this as a request to get a list of the user's lists. If you make a POST call, Twitter interprets this as a request to create a list.

If you look again at the list, you may notice that user/:id/subscribers is listed three times! We already know that there is a GET and a POST option. What would be the third? DELETE. DELETE unsubscribes the authenticated user from the specified list. But what if your cURL implementation does not support DELETE?

There is a workaround for clients that cannot issue `DELETE` requests; instead, use `POST` with the added parameter `_method=DELETE`.

Fortunately for us, taking the extra step of separating the function call from the actual API method request means we can deal with these new approaches fairly easily. So, let's add a few List methods to our application. We'll take a slightly different approach from the methods we have placed so far. This time, we are going to make a call to Twitter to get a list of our list. Yes, a list of a list. We will display the list and create a hyperlink on each list to make a call to that list and display the list's Twitter stream. That may sound a bit confusing, but it will make perfect sense after we put the code in place and try it out.

If you have not created a list before, it's easy to do so from the Twitter website, as you can see in Figure 13.1.

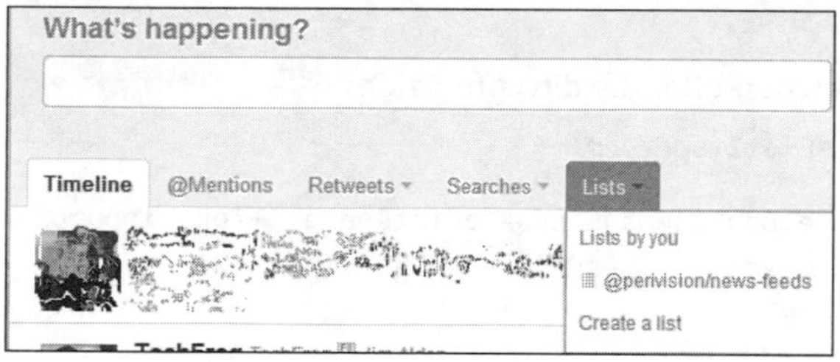

FIGURE 13.1 Creating a list on the Twitter website.

Implementing the List API into Our Application

Because we are here to learn about the Twitter API, let's create a list using an API call. We are going to take a slightly different approach. This time, we are going to create a new page when we click the List button. So, let's create that first. Open the index.php page and save that code as list.php. Basically we are making a copy of index.php and calling it list.php. Keep the file open; we need to edit a few things.

Edit list.php

Remove this line:

```
include 'includes/create_message.php';
```

Then remove this line:

```
<? include 'main.php'; ?>
```

After this line:

```
<div class="container">
```

Add the following lines:

```
      <p />
      <form name='createlist'>
      <input type="text" name="inputbox" value="">
      <input type=button OnClick="createListItem(this.form);" value="Create
➥a new list">
      </form>
      <?php getTwitterData(showList); ?>
```

Edit base.js

Now we need to add a few lines in our JavaScript file to support the button we just put in.

Let's add this function after the direct function:

```
function createListItem(form) {

url='commandLine.php?command=createList&name='+form.inputbox.value;
          callPage(url, 'serverMessages');
}
```

Because we are going to make an AJAX call, we need a file to call on the remote server just like we did with sendMessage.php. We will call this file commandLine.php because we will use this to respond to single requests that does not refresh the page.

Create commandLine.php

Let's create a new file at the root directory and call it 'commandLine.php'.

Add the following lines:

```
<?php

$command=$_GET['command'];
$name = $_GET['name'];
include 'oauth_index.php';

switch ($command) {
          case '';
          case 'createList':
              { $messages=$twitter->createList($name); echo ($messages); }
                   break;
          case 'deleteList':
```

```
    { $messages=$twitter->deleteList($name, $twitterName); echo
➥($messages); }
          break;
}
?>
```

Edit twitteroauth.php

To support our new call, let's add a new function at the end of the file twitteroauth.php but before the last }:

```
          function createList($name , $twitterName ){
            $api_call = $twitterName.'/lists/'.$name.'.xml';
            return $this->post($api_call);
          }
```

Now that we have created a few lists, let's edit our application to display that list and the feeds for each list item.

Edit header.inc

First, we need to add the correct UI elements. We are going to add only one button to our list tab, and that button will call our Twitter account and display the lists we can create.

After these lines:

```
        <li><a href="/?nav=direct" <? if($nav=='direct') echo
➥'class="here"'; ?> >Direct Message</a>
        <? if($nav=='direct') { ?>
          <ul>
            <li><a href="/?nav=direct&page=direct" >Direct Messages
➥received</a></li>
            <li><a href="/?nav=direct&page=directSent" >Direct Messages
➥Sent</a></li>
          </ul>
        <? } ?>
        </li>
```

Add the following lines:

```
        <li><a href="/?nav=list" <? if($nav=='list') echo 'class="here"';
➥?> >List</a>
        <? if($nav=='list') { ?>
          <ul>
            <li><a href="/?nav=list&page=showList" >Show a list of
➥lists</a></li>
          </ul>
        <? } ?>
```

Edit parseTwitter.php

Now that we have our UI in place, let's account for our new commands in our case switch. Open the file parseTwitter.php.

After the following lines:

```
    case 'rt_of_me':
        { $messages=$twitter->getMentions('xml'); return
➥call_timeline($messages); }
        break;
```

Add these lines:

```
    case 'showList':
        { $messages=$twitter->showLists(); return call_showList($messages); }
        break;
    case 'renderList':
        { $messages=$twitter->renderLists($name, $twitterName); return
➥call_timeline($messages); }
        break;
```

After this function:

```
function call_direct($messages){ ...
```

Add this function:

```
function call_showList($messages){
```

Notice that we have done something different here. Normally, we use the SimpleXMLElement() PHP call to parse our return from Twitter, but in this case we cannot. Here is the return the 'list.xml' <get> method returns us:

```
<lists_list>
<lists type="array">
<list>
  <id>20003603</id>
  <name>testlistno6</name>
  <full_name>@perivision/testlistno6</full_name>
  <slug>testlistno6</slug>
  <description></description>
  <subscriber_count>0</subscriber_count>
  <member_count>1</member_count>
  <uri>/perivision/testlistno6</uri>
  <following>false</following>
  <mode>public</mode>
  <user>
    <id>11710512</id>
    <name>Christopher</name>
    <screen_name>perivision</screen_name>
    <location>the bay</location>
```

The word 'list' is a reserved word with SimpleXMLElement(), so we are going to go with another XML parsing technique:

```
...
          $parser = xml_parser_create();
          xml_parser_set_option($parser,XML_OPTION_SKIP_WHITE,1);
          xml_parser_set_option($parser,XML_OPTION_CASE_FOLDING,0);
          xml_parse_into_struct($parser,$messages,$d_ar,$i_ar) or
➥print_error();
          xml_parser_free($parser);
```

Here we make another departure from how we have been doing things up to this point. Because all we are going to do is display a simple list of our Twitter list, we do not need to return back to main and render:

```
  $i=0;
          while($i_ar['name'][$i]){
          $user_name = $i_ar['slug'][$i];
           $user_name = $d_ar[$user_name][value];
            echo '<li><a href="/hour13/?nav=list&page=renderList&name='.
$user_name.'" >'.$user_name.'</a></li>';
                 $i++;
 }
}
```

Edit twitteroauth.php

Now let's add a new function to twitteroauth.php to support our request.

After this function:

```
          function friendshipExists($a, $b){
            $api_call = " friendships/exists.xml?user_a=$a&user_b=$b";
                   return $this->get($api_call);
          }
```

Add these functions:

```
          function showLists(){
            $api_call = 'lists.xml';
            return $this->get($api_call);
          }
          function renderLists($name, $twitterName){

            $api_call = $twitterName.'/lists/'.$name.'/statuses.xml';
            return $this->get($api_call);
          }
```

Three Types of List Methods

Twitter groups the List methods into three categories:

- List resources
- List Members resources
- List Subscribers resources

We have already gone through some of the methods as we added new functions to our application; however, we need to cover many more.

List Resources

List resources are methods that focus on managing the list; that is, creating, editing, and deleting the list.

Following is a summary of the methods from the Twitter docs:

- **GET user/:lists**—Lists the lists of the specified user. Private lists will be included if the authenticated user is the same as the user whose lists are being returned.
- **POST user/:lists**—Creates a new list for the authenticated user. Accounts are limited to 20 lists.
- **GET user/lists/:id**—Shows the specified list. Private lists will be shown only if the authenticated user owns the specified list.
- **POST user/lists/:id**—Updates the specified list.
- **DELETE user/lists/:id**—Deletes the specified list. Must be owned by the authenticated user.
- **GET user/lists/:id/statuses**—Shows tweet timeline for members of the specified list.
- **GET :user/lists/memberships**—Lists the lists the specified user has been added to.
- **GET :user/lists/subscriptions**—Lists the lists the specified user follows.

By the Way

> Clients who cannot issue DELETE requests can POST with the added parameter _method=DELETE.

List Members Resources

Members resources are the List methods that provide access to who is following a list as well as manipulating the members of a list. Although the use case is limited, the most common use would be for automatically updating a list based on other criteria. Perhaps you want to automatically create a list of the people you interact with most often. In this case, you could add a name to this list anytime you do a reply or send a direct message, and you can remove people from the list if they do not show up in any of your sent messages for a set of time or the last 100 messages.

Here is a brief summary of the list from the Twitter docs:

- **GET :user/:list_id/members**—Returns the members of the specified list.
- **POST :user/:list_id/members**—Adds a member to a list. The authenticated user must own the list to be able to add members to it. Lists are limited to having 500 members.
- **DELETE :user/:list_id/members**—Removes the specified member from the list. The authenticated user must be the list's owner to remove members from the list.
- **POST :user/:list_id/create_all**—Adds multiple members to a list by specifying a comma-separated list of member IDs or screen names. The authenticated user must own the list to be able to add members to it. Lists are limited to having 500 members, and you are limited to adding up to 100 members to a list at a time with this method.

List Subscribers Resources

The Subscribers method deals with the subscribers of a list. This is different from the List Members methods in that we are dealing with those who are following 'subscribed' to a list versus managing lists that a member is subscribed to. Again, this is a confusing but important distinction. Read through these carefully. You may need to read over this section more than once:

- **Member**—Adds a userID to a list.
- **Subscriber**—Adds a list to a userID's list of lists.

For example, the GET :user/:list_id/members method returns the members of a list, whereas the GET :user/:list_id/members/:id method checks to see if the user is a member of a list. Some methods seem to perform the same actions; however, they are different. POST :user/:list_id/members adds a member to a list. POST :user/:list_id/subscribers : makes the authenticated user follow the specified list. For example, if we have a list called football, we could pass the following to the Twitter servers:

```
http://api.twitter.com/1/twitterapi24/football/members.xml?id=12345
```

This would add the Twitter user 12345 to the list football. However, if we pass this request to Twitter:

```
http://api.twitter.com/1/twitterapi24/football/subscribers.xml?id=12345
```

It would add the list 'football' to the user '12345' list of lists.

Here is a brief summary of the list:

- **GET :user/:list_id/ subscribers /:id:** Checks if a user is a member of the specified list.
- **POST :user/:list_id/subscribers:** Makes the authenticated user follow the specified list.
- **DELETE :user/:list_id/subscribers:** Unsubscribes the authenticated user form the specified list.
- **GET :user/:list_id/subscribers/:id:** Checks if a user is a subscriber of the specified list.

Summary

In this hour, we learned about the three types of List methods: timeline, members, and subscribers. We also learned the numerous ways we can manage a list. This hour also saw us again using more advanced techniques of the REST protocol.

We also created a new file called commandLine.php, which we do not call directly, but instead make a call from a JavaScript action. We will use this file a few more times in the book.

Q&A

Q. ***Why did the good folks at Twitter start a new API method where API calls are the same name?***

A. The API is always evolving, and the list API calls are some of the most recent. Thus, it could be an indication of how future API calls will be designed.

Workshop

Quiz

1. Name the three list types.
2. List the three types of cURL request.
3. If your service does not support DELETE, what can you do?

Quiz Answers

1. List resources, List Members resources, and List Subscribers resources.
2. GET, POST, and DELETE.
3. A workaround for clients that cannot issue DELETE requests can use POST with the added parameter _method=DELETE instead.

Exercise

As suggested in an earlier part of this hour, add users to a list if you send them a message or retweet one of their messages. Remember to check to see if they are a member of the list first before adding.

Did you notice the function we called in the following lines?

```
.$parser = xml_parser_create();
xml_parser_set_option($parser,XML_OPTION_SKIP_WHITE,1);
xml_parser_set_option($parser,XML_OPTION_CASE_FOLDING,0);
xml_parse_into_struct($parser,$messages,$d_ar,
$i_ar) or print_error();
xml_parser_free($parser);
```

We did not define `'prtint_error()'`. Let's do that now.

HOUR 14

Favorites and User Methods

What You'll Learn in This Hour:

- What is a favorite?
- How to create, read, and destroy favorites
- Learn about user functions
- How to create an image-based address book of Twitter friends and followers

Favorites API Methods

One of the most underrated features of Twitter but yet has the most promise is favorites. Favorites are only just now beginning to surface as a powerful feature for both the user and those performing analytics on Twitter data. A favorite is a tweet that a user saves. It's somewhat like creating a bookmark of a web page, except the user saves a message ID instead of a URL. The only thing missing is the ability to see other peoples' favorites, but who knows? Perhaps that will change in the future.

The API method calls for favorites are pretty simple; there are only three:

- GET http://api.twitter.com/1/favorites.format
- POST http://api.twitter.com/1/favorites/create/*id.format*
- POST/DELETE http://api.twitter.com/1/favorites/destroy/*id.format*

These methods work much like the rest of the methods we have been working with, so let's get to coding and add these methods to our application.

Adding Favorites Methods to Our Application

Now that we understand what a favorite is, let's update our application to support these API calls. First, place the code to read your list of favorites.

Edit header.inc

Keeping with how we have been adding other methods, we are going to add a few lines to our header so that we can make the call to favorites. After the HTML tags <li> lists </li>, add the following lines:

```
        <li><a href="/?nav=showFavorites&page=showFavorites" <?
if($nav=='showFavorites') echo 'class="here"'; ?> >Favorites</a>
        <? if($nav=='showFavorites') { ?>
          <ul>
            <li><a href="/?nav=favorites&page=showFavorites" >Show
➥Favorites</a></li>
          </ul>
        <? } ?>
</li>
```

Edit parseTwitter.php

Now that we have our text button, let's edit parseTwitter.php to catch the user action. Because the return from Twitter will be a standard feed of tweets, we can use the 'call_timeline()' function to display our return.

After the case statement:

```
    case 'renderList':
        { $messages=$twitter->renderLists($name, $twitterName); return
call_timeline($messages); }
        break;
```

Add the following lines:

```
case 'showFavorites':
{ $messages=$twitter->showFavorites(); return call_timeline($messages); }
break;
```

Edit twitteroauth.php

Next, we need to support the showFavorites() we just created. Open twitteroath.php and add the following function at the end of the file but before the last '}':

```
function showFavorites(){
$api_call = 'favorites.xml';
          return $this->get($api_call);
}
```

Edit base.js

Next, let's add a function in our JavaScript file to accept the clicks we are setting up. Open base.js and add these two functions after the createListItem() function:

```
function favorite(mess_id){
  url='commandLine.php?command=createFavorite&id='+mess_id;
            callPage(url, mess_id);
}
```

Save and close your files and give it a test. This will work only if you have selected a few messages as favorites. If you have not, you will get nothing back. If you do not know how to create a favorite, go to Twitter and click the star of any tweet. The star will show up when you mouse over the tweet, as shown in Figure 14.1. Go ahead and favor a few tweets; then go back to our application and make sure they show up when you click on the tab titled "favorites."

FIGURE 14.1 Create a favorite on Twitter.

Create a Favorite Tweet Using the Twitter API Method

Now that you can get your favorites, we need to be able to create favorites via Twitter API method calls. To create a favorite, we need the message's ID. The easiest way to do that is similar to how we supported creating a retweet message and populating our message box to send a direct message. We are going to place a link within the message itself.

Edit render.php

Open the render.php file and remove the trailing </div> by editing the following line from:

```
<a href='#' onmouseup=\"direct('$screen_name', '$twitterName')\">DM</a></
div>
```

To:

```
<a href='#' onmouseup=\"direct('$screen_name', '$twitterName')\">DM</a>
```

Now add the following code:

```
<a href='#' onmouseup=\"favorite('$id')\">F</a></div>
```

Save your file and refresh or open index.php and then select Favorites. You should see your list of favorite Twitter messages with an "F" below the "RT" and the "DM." Clicking this F will not do anything yet because we need to capture this click in JavaScript, so let's add some code to both commandLine.php and twitteroath.php to execute the request.

Edit commandLine.php

After the case switch:

```
case 'deleteList':
    { $messages=$twitter->deleteList($name); echo ($messages); }
      break;
```

Add the following case switch:

```
case 'createFavorite':
    { $messages=$twitter->createFavorite($id); echo ($messages); }
      break;
```

Save and close this file.

Edit twitteroauth.php

Now let's add the method call to our twitteroauth class. Open twitteroauth.php and add the following code after the last function but before the last '}':

```
function createFavorite($id){
  $api_call = ' favorites/create/'.$id.'.xml';
  return $this->post($api_call);
}
```

Save and close this file.

We should now be able to create a favorite tweet from our application. Open your application and click the F from any tweet. You should get back an unstructured XML reply from Twitter, similar to Figure 14.2.

Pretty simple, right? To delete a favorite, we are going to destroy it. I'm guessing the good folks at Twitter decided that it was not good enough to delete a favorite—you have to go all out and destroy it. For this method, we can use either POST or DELETE; however, there is one tricky bit around the UI. To destroy a favorite, we need to have that message's ID, and the best way to capture that is when we are rendering the tweet stream. So, we are going to be a bit creative here and put an if statement in the render.php call so that we can offer to delete (destroy) a tweet.

24k
RT
DM
F
url http://api.twitter.com/1/favorites/create/47514069883817984.xml
Tue Mar 15 04:26:51 +0000 2011 47514069883817984 Create a chatroom in 12 lines of code with NowJS http://tnw.to/17ZIQ on @TheNextWeb #socialnetworking <a href="http://www.echofon.com/" rel="nofollow">Echofon</a> false true 0 false 17145442 Chris Rauschnot 24k Las Vegas, NV Web 2.0 & Social Media Guy. Speaker. Internet Entrepreneur for over 15 years. Certified Apple Tech. @24kMedia http://bit.ly/24kMediaFB #vegas #tech #celebrity http://a3.twimg.com/profile_images/1193040615/24k_normal.jpg http://TheMacWizard.com/ false 50595 9AE4E8 333333 0000ff DDFFCC BDDCAD 42760 Tue Nov 04 01:09:10 +0000 2008 3200 -28800 Pacific Time (US & Canada) http://a0.twimg.com /profile_background_images/183661076/CRK002_TwitterBGround2.jpg false true false true false true 38447 en false false 1206 false false SimpleXMLElement Object ([created_at] => Tue Mar 15 04:26:51 +0000 2011 [id] => 47514069883817984 [text] => Create a chatroom in 12 lines of code with NowJS http://tnw.to/17ZIQ on @TheNextWeb #socialnetworking [source] => Echofon [truncated] => false [favorited] => true [in_reply_to_status_id] => SimpleXMLElement Object ( ) [in_reply_to_user_id] => SimpleXMLElement Object ( ) [in_reply_to_screen_name] => SimpleXMLElement Object ( ) [retweet_count] => 0 [retweeted] => false [user] => SimpleXMLElement Object ([id] => 17145442 [name] => Chris Rauschnot [screen_name] => 24k [location] => Las Vegas, NV [description] => Web 2.0 & Social Media Guy. Speaker. Internet Entrepreneur for over 15 years. Certified Apple Tech. @24kMedia http://bit.ly/24kMediaFB #vegas #tech #celebrity [profile_image_url] => http://a3.twimg.com /profile_images/1193040615/24k_normal.jpg [url] => http://TheMacWizard.com/ [protected] => false [followers_count] => 50595 [profile_background_color] => 9AE4E8 [profile_text_color] => 333333 [profile_link_color] => 0000ff [profile_sidebar_fill_color] => DDFFCC [profile_sidebar_border_color] => BDDCAD [friends_count] => 42760 [created_at] => Tue Nov 04 01:09:10 +0000 2008 [favourites_count] => 3200 [utc_offset] => -28800 [time_zone] => Pacific Time (US & Canada) [profile_background_image_url] => http://a0.twimg.com /profile_background_images/183661076/CRK002_TwitterBGround2.jpg [profile_background_tile] => false [profile_use_background_image] => true [notifications] => false [geo_enabled] => true [verified] => false [following] => true [statuses_count] => 38447 [lang] => en [contributors_enabled] => false [follow_request_sent] => false [listed_count] => 1206 [show_all_inline_media] => false [is_translator] => false) [geo] => SimpleXMLElement Object ( ) [coordinates] => SimpleXMLElement Object ( ) [place] => SimpleXMLElement Object ( ) [contributors] => SimpleXMLElement Object ( ) [annotations] => SimpleXMLElement Object ( ))

FIGURE 14.2 XML return from creating a favorite on Twitter.

Edit render.php

We need to add one extra line of code to support this if statement. To know whether we are showing the favorite list, we are going to look at the URL and see if nav=showFavorites. If it does, instead of rendering the 'F' link, we will display a 'Del' (delete) link.

Open render.php and at the top of the file, find the following line:

```
global $twitterName;
```

Add the following code:

```
$nav = $_GET['nav'];
```

Now that we know what navigation page we are on, we can create our if statement.

Find the following line of code:

```
<a href='#' onmouseup=\"favorite('$id')\">F</a></div>
```

And add a trailing quote and semi colon as shown:

```
<a href='#' onmouseup=\"favorite('$id')\">F</a></div> ";
```

And add the following:

```
    if($nav=='showFavorites') { $output.="<a href='#'
➥onmouseup=\"destroyFavorite('$id')\">Del</a></div> ";
    } else { $output.="<a href='#'
➥onmouseup=\"favorite('$id')\">F</a></div> "; }
$output.="
```

Save and close the file.

Edit base.js

Now that we have created a new link, let's catch it in JavaScript. Open base.js and add the following function after the 'favorite' function:

```
function destroyFavorite(mess_id){
  url='commandLine.php?command=destroyFavorite&id='+mess_id;
  callPage(url, mess_id);
}
```

Save and close.

Edit twitteroauth.php

Just as we did before, we will add a function call in twitteroauth to catch and process the destroy request.

Open twitteroauth.php and add the following function at the end of the file but before the '}':

```
function destroyFavorite($id){
  $api_call = 'favorites/destroy/'.$id.'.xml';
  return $this->post($api_call);
}
```

If you remember our reference to the destroy method in the beginning of this hour, we could use either POST or DELETE for this method call. We are going to use DELETE because it's more informative when we read the code. Either way will work; however, using DELETE could prove to be more future proofed as Twitter continues to evolve the API set.

Save and close the file.

Now let's give it a shot. Open index.php and click Favorites. Now click 'Del' on one of the messages. You should get an XML return similar to Figure 14.3 that indicates you have destroyed that favorite message.

FIGURE 14.3 XML return from destroying a favorite on Twitter.

User API Methods

The user methods in Twitter are straightforward in that they are methods for getting information about a Twitter user. The user methods are as follows, all using the GET method:

- users/show
- users/lookup
- users/search
- users/suggestions
- users/suggestions/category
- statuses/friends
- statuses/followers

Add users/show to Our Application

The users/show method is much like the other API methods we have seen so far. Placing support for it in our application will take a familiar path. We will create a tab on the UI and then support the link with new code within parseTwitter.php and twitteroauth.php.

Edit header.inc

First, we'll add a new <li></li> tab. After the following code:

```
        <li><a href="/?nav=showFavorites&page=showFavorites" <?
if($nav=='showFavorites') echo 'class="here"'; ?> >Favorites</a>
        <? if($nav=='showFavorites') { ?>
          <ul>
            <li><a href="/?nav=favorites&page=showFavorites" >Show
➥Favorites</a></li>
          </ul>
        <? } ?>
          </li>
```

Add the following code:

```
        <li><a href="/?nav=user&page=showUser" <? if($nav=='user') echo
➥'class="here"'; ?> >User</a>
        <? if($nav=='user') { ?>
          <ul>
            <li><a href="/?nav=user&page=showUser" >Show Users</a></li>
          </ul>
        <? } ?>
          </li>
```

Save and close the file.

Edit parseTwitter.php

Open parseTwitter.php and add a new case switch using the following code:

```
    case 'showUser':
        { $messages=$twitter->showUser($twitterName); echo($messages); }
        break;
```

Save and close the file.

Edit twitteroauth.php

Finally, we will add support for the method call. Open twitteroauth.php and add the following function at the end of the file but before the last '}':

```
          function showUser($name){
            $api_call = 'users/show.xml?screen_name='.$name;
            return $this->get($api_call);
          }
```

Save and close the file.

Now open index.php and click the User tab. You should get an unstructured XML stream from Twitter with details on your Twitter account, similar to Figure 14.4.

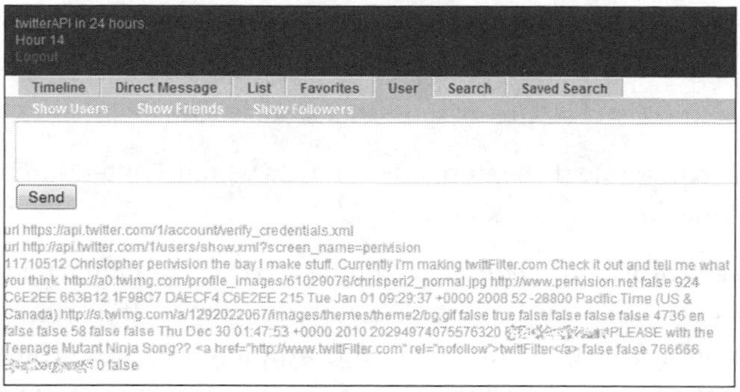

FIGURE 14.4
XML details on your Twitter account.

Accessing Other User Information

What if you wanted to get information on someone else? Easy enough—simply replace your Twitter name with another Twitter name or ID. You can also get more than one detailed report on a Twitter account at a time. With the API method call GET users/lookup, you can pass more than one screen_name or ID at a time. It's the same structure that we used for 'users/show', except we use 'users/lookup' and provide a list of names or IDs separated by commas. For example, we just used 'http://api.twitter.com/1/users/show.xml?screen_name=perivision', where 'perivision' is my account name. To construct a 'lookup' API call, it would look something like the following:

```
http://api.twitter.com/1/users/lookup.xml?screen_name=perivision,cbsnews,
➥abc,breakingnews, ...
```

You would then get a list of <users> in your XML return, each with details about the user. Notice that I did not include a space after the comma. This is an HTTP request, and there should never be a space—but you know that, didn't you?

Understanding More of the Users APIs

GET users/search is an interesting API method in that it will return the first 100 users that best match a search. This functions much like the Find People button on Twitter.com.

The next three methods are interesting, but useful only for targeted applications:

- **GET users/suggestions**—Access to Twitter's suggested user list. This returns the list of suggested user categories. The category can be used in the users/suggestions/category endpoint to get the users in that category. And where would we use this category? In the following method call:
- **GET users/suggestions/:slug**—Access the users in a given category of the Twitter suggested user list.

For example, we can get a list of Twitter recommended users based on the category 'books'. The API call would look like the following:

http://api.twitter.com/1/users/suggestions/books.xml

This API call would then return a list of users whom Twitter thinks is a best fit for the category 'books'.

- **GET users/profile_image/:screen_name**—Access the profile image in various sizes for the user with the indicated screen_name. If no size is provided, the normal image is returned. Note this warning from the Twitter docs: **This resource does not return JSON or XML, but instead returns a 302 redirect to the actual image resource.**

This method should be used only by application developers to look up or check the profile image URL for a user. This method must not be used as the image source URL presented to users of your application.

Basically, what the Twitter folks are saying here is DO NOT USE THIS! Really, there is very little reason to use this call.

Create a Simple Thumbnail Viewer in Our Application

We have two more calls to look at:

- **GET statuses/friends**—Returns a user's friends, each with current status inline. They are ordered by the order in which the user followed them; the most recently followed are first, 100 at a time.
- **GET statuses/followers**—Returns the authenticating user's followers, each with current status inline. They are ordered by the order in which they followed the user, 100 at a time.

These last two calls can be quite useful for creating an image thumbnail viewer which could be the foundation of an address book of sorts for our application. So, let's add these to our application. We'll create a page of Twitter images and screen names so that we can skim through the list to find the person we are interested in.

Edit header.inc

First, we need a button, so open the file header.inc, and after this line:

```
<li><a href="/?nav=user&page=showUser" >Show Users</a></li>
```

Add the following line:

```
<li><a href="/?nav=user&page=showFriends" >Show Friends</a></li>
<li><a href="/?nav=user&page=showFollowers" >Show Followers</a></li>
```

Save and close this file.

Edit parseTwitter.php

We will now add two new case switches for our new requests. Open parseTwitter.php, and after this case switch:

```
    case 'showUser':
        { $messages=$twitter->showUser($twitterName); echo $messages;
➥return; }
        break;
```

Add the following code:

```
    case 'showFriends':
        { $messages=$twitter->showFriends($twitterName); return
➥call_users($messages); }
        break;
    case 'showFollowers':
        { $messages=$twitter->showFollowers($twitterName); return
➥call_users($messages); }
        break;
```

Don't close just yet. We need to create a function to render our list of images and screen names. Within this same file, add the following function after the function 'call_showList($messages)':

```
function call_users($messages){
          $twitterReturn = new SimpleXMLElement($messages);
          foreach($twitterReturn->user as $status){
                    $profile_image_url = $status->profile_image_url;
                    $screen_name = $status->screen_name;
                    echo "
                              <div id='$screen_name' class='mess-pic' \" >
                              <a href='http://twitter.com/$screen_name'>
                      <img src='$profile_image_url'/ width='48px'
➥height='48px'>
                      <br>$screen_name</a>
                              </div>";
          }
}
```

Because each return is a 'user', we stepped through the XML return $twitterReturn setting $status to each 'user' node instead of 'status' node, as we have done in the past.

Save and close this file.

Edit twitteraouth.php

Finally, we need to implement the actual API method calls. Open twitteroauth.php and add the following functions at the end of the file but before the last '}':

```
function showFriends($name){
  $api_call = ' statuses/friends.xml?screen_name='.$name;
  return $this->get($api_call);
}
function showFollowers($name){
  $api_call = 'statuses/followers.xml?screen_name='.$name;
  return $this->get($api_call);
}
```

Save and close this file.

Now open index.php and click users, friends, or followers. Assuming you have at least one or more friends or followers, you should see something like the screenshot in Figure 14.5.

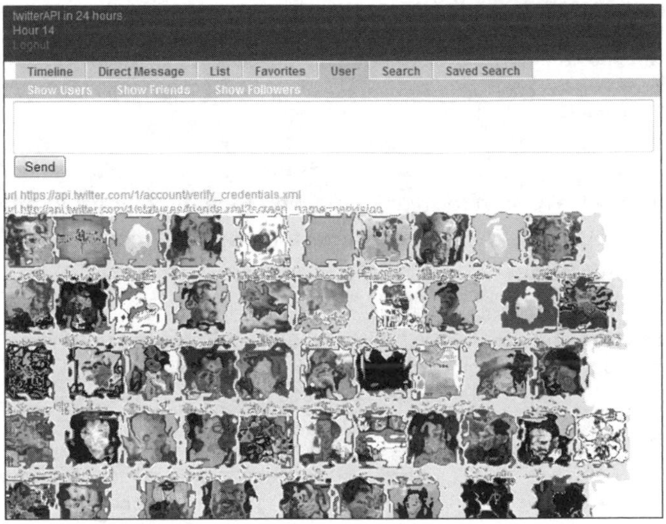

FIGURE 14.5
List of friends using images and screen names.

Summary

In this hour, we learned about favorites and how to create, edit, and destroy through the API. We also used the JavaScript to commandLine.php technique again because of the need to track message IDs. You should be fairly comfortable with this technique by now. If not, you should reread the past two hours because future Twitter API methods will rely more and more on IDs to perform actions as the API evolves.

We also explored users' methods in this hour. Unlike the methods we have been working with in the past two hours, the users' methods are based on GET only.

Q&A

Q. ***Can I send an update using 'F' like I can with 'D'?***

A. Yes. Any currently supported shortcut can be used via the update method.

Q. ***Because there is a way to use 'POST' to delete a favorite, why should I bother with DESTROY?***

A. Although either cURL call will work, we do not know what the future of the API will be, but indications are that more formal uses of the cURL protocol will be used, and that includes DESTROY.

Workshop

Quiz

1. Does 'GET users/profile_image/:screen_name' return JSON or XML?
2. How many returns do I get with the call 'GET statuses/friends'?
3. What does GET statuses/search do?

Quiz Answers

1. Neither. It returns the URL of an image only.
2. 100 at a time.
3. Returns the first 100 Twitter users that best match the search term provided.

Exercise

Now that know how to show friends and we can show followers, write a script that will check to see what user we both friend and follower. Create a new tab for this.

HOUR 15
Search

What You'll Learn in This Hour:

- The history of the Search API and why it's different from the other Twitter API methods
- About the single Search API call
- How to construct a search query using attributes
- How to convert characters not supported though REST requests
- How to make and parse a JSON request

History of Twitter Search API

Users who remember using Twitter from the very beginning know that Search was not a feature of Twitter. Many things were not a feature of Twitter in fact, and thus many other companies started writing software to fill this void. Summize was one of these companies. Like Twitter, Summize offered an API so other programmers could access the Summize Search service. Search is, as you would imagine, a means to search through the Twitter history of tweets. However, there are billions of tweets, and searching through all of them is simply not practical. But in the beginning, when the number was only in the six-figures range, not only was it practical, it was downright useful—so useful that Twitter made Summize its first major acquisition. Here is a bit more on Twitter Search from the site documents:

Twitter's Stance on Search

"The Twitter API consists of three parts: two REST APIs and a Streaming API. The two distinct REST APIs are entirely due to history. Summize, Inc. was originally an independent company that provided search capability for Twitter data. Summize was later acquired and rebranded as Twitter Search. Rebranding the site was easy; fully integrating Twitter Search and its API into the Twitter codebase is more difficult. It is in our pipeline to unify the APIs, but until resources allow, the REST API and Search API will remain as separate entities. The Streaming API is distinct from the two REST APIs as Streaming supports long-lived connections on a different architecture.

The Twitter REST API methods allow developers to access core Twitter data. This includes update timelines, status data, and user information. The Search API methods give developers methods to interact with Twitter Search and trends data. The concern for developers given this separation is the effects on rate limiting and output format."

The Lone Search API

The Search API has only one API method: search. That's it. However, the power of Search is within the options you pass to Twitter. First, let's have a look at the API definition and then the option list:

> **GET search**—Returns tweets that match a specified query.

Note that as of April 1, 2010, the Search API provides an option to retrieve "popular tweets" in addition to real-time search results. In an upcoming release, this will become the default, and clients that don't want to receive popular tweets in their search results will have to explicitly opt out. See the result_type parameter for more information.

Be aware that the user IDs in the Search API are different from those we have seen so far. This means that the to_user_id and from_user_id field vary from the actual user ID on Twitter.com. Applications will have to perform a screen name-based lookup with the users/show method to get the correct user ID if necessary.

The most typical search attribute you will use is `?q=`. q stands for query. However, there are other options. Let's have a look at the current list from the Twitter docs (http://dev.twitter.com/doc/get/search):

- **callback**—Available only for JSON format. If supplied, the response will use the JSON format with a callback of the given name.
- **lang**—Restricts tweets to the given language, given by an ISO 639-1 code.
- **locale**—Specifies the language of the query you are sending (only ja is currently effective). This is intended for language-specific clients, and the default should work in the majority of cases:

```
http://search.twitter.com/search.json?locale=ja
```

- **rpp**—The number of tweets to return per page, up to a max of 100:

```
http://search.twitter.com/search.json?rpp=100
```

- **page**—The page number (starting at 1) to return, up to a max of roughly 1,500 results (based on rpp * page):

```
http://search.twitter.com/search.json?page=10
```

- **since_id**—Returns results with an ID greater than (that is, more recent than) the specified ID. There are limits to the number of tweets that can be accessed through the API. If the limit of tweets has occurred since the since_id, the since_id will be forced to the oldest ID available. If the since_id used is too old, a HTTP 404 error will be returned:

```
http://search.twitter.com/search.json?since_id=12345
```

- **until**—Optional. Returns tweets generated before the given date. Date should be formatted as YYYY-MM-DD:

```
http://search.twitter.com/search.json?until=2010-03-28
```

- **geocode**—Returns tweets by users located within a given radius of the given latitude/longitude. The location is preferentially taking from the Geotagging API, but will fall back to the Twitter profile. The parameter value is specified by latitude,longitude,radius, where radius units must be specified as either mi (miles) or km (kilometers). Note that you cannot use the near operator via the API to geocode arbitrary locations; however, you can use this geocode parameter to search near geocodes directly:

```
http://search.twitter.com/search.json?geocode=37.781157,-122.398720,1mi
```

- **show_user**—When true, prepends ":" to the beginning of the tweet. This is useful for readers that do not display Atom's author field. The default is false.
- **result_type**—Optional. Specifies what type of search results you would prefer to receive. The current default is "mixed." Valid values include the following:
  - **mixed**—Includes both popular and real-time results in the response.
  - **recent**—Returns only the most recent results in the response.
  - **popular**—Returns only the most popular results in the response.

```
http://search.twitter.com/search.json?result_type=mixed
http://search.twitter.com/search.json?result_type=recent
http://search.twitter.com/search.json?result_type=popular
```

Quite a bit, right? We will go through this step by step and cover the major options you would most commonly use.

Search Request Parameters

First, let's have a look at a simple search request. Open up your web browser and type this into the URL address text field:

```
http://search.twitter.com/search?q=football
```

You should have a reply from the Twitter website that looks similar to Figure 15.1.

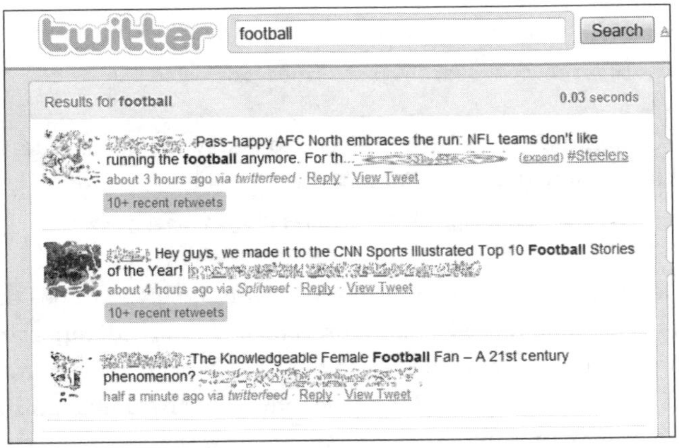

FIGURE 15.1
Search on Twitter.com.

Here we set the value of `q` to `football` and got a return of the latest searches with the keyword football in the latest tweet. This is not the only option for Search that is available to us. Consider the following search request:

```
http://search.twitter.com/search?q=football+bears
```

By using the '+' sign, we now get tweets that have both words. However, if we want to have two words in a specific order, we would use quotes, as in the following example:

```
http://search.twitter.com/search?q="cal+bears"
```

Watch Out!

Remember, you can only use web-safe symbols when making http calls.

You can see how this works. We control our Twitter search completely through the options we pass to Twitter. Let's have a look at the various options as described in the Twitter docs (http://search.twitter.com/api/):

- Find tweets **containing a word**:
  http://search.twitter.com/search.atom?q=twitter
- Find tweets **from a user**:
  http://search.twitter.com/search.atom?q=from%3Aalexiskold
- Find tweets **to a user**:
  http://search.twitter.com/search.atom?q=to%3Atechcrunch
- Find tweets **referencing a user**:
  http://search.twitter.com/search.atom?q=%40mashable
- Find tweets **containing a hashtag**:
  http://search.twitter.com/search.atom?q=%23haiku
- Combine any of the operators together:
  http://search.twitter.com/search.atom?q=movie+%3A%29

The API also supports the following optional URL parameters:

- **lang**—Restricts tweets to the given language, given by an ISO 639-1 code. For example: http://search.twitter.com/search.atom?lang=en&q=devo
- **rpp**—The number of tweets to return per page, up to a max of 100. For example: http://search.twitter.com/search.atom?lang=en&q=devo&rpp=15
- **page**—The page number to return, up to a max of roughly 1,500 results (based on rpp * page).
- **since_id**—Returns tweets with status IDs greater than the given ID.
- **geocode**—Returns tweets by users located within a given radius of the given latitude/longitude, where the user's location is taken from the Twitter profile. The parameter value is specified by "latitide,longitude,radius", where radius units must be specified as either "mi" (miles) or "km" (kilometers). For example: http://search.twitter.com/search.atom?geocode=40.757929%2C-73.985506%2C25km. Note that you cannot use the near operator via the API to geocode arbitrary locations; however, you can use this geocode parameter to search near geocodes directly.
- **show_user**—When "true", adds "<user>:" to the beginning of the tweet. This is useful for readers that do not display Atom's author field. The default is "false".

Integrating Search into Our Application

Now that we have a good idea about how Search works, we can start to get Search integrated into our application. We are going to take a slightly different approach from what we have been doing in this book so far, but we are still going to work within our normal framework.

Edit header.inc

Let's add a new button. After the last tag we created in Hour 14, `<li><a href="/?nav=user&page=showUser...`, we'll add the following code:

```
        <li><a href="/?nav=search&page=search" <? if($nav=='search') echo
'class="here"'; ?> >Search</a>
        <? if($nav=='search') { ?>
          <ul>
            <li><a href="/?nav=search&page=search" >Search</a></li>
          </ul>
        <? } ?>
         </li>
```

Save and close.

Edit parseTwitter.php

Now let's add a switch to our case statement to catch the new link we just created. Open parseTwitter.php and add the following case switch at the end of the switch statement:

```
    case 'search':
        { $messages=$twitter->search($options); return
➥call_search($messages); }
        break;
```

Don't save and close just yet. Remember that we are not dealing with the normal method calls we have seen throughout the book. Search does not have an option to return XML; instead, we can get only JSON, ATOM, or RSS. In our case, we are going to request a JSON feed.

Did You Know?

> JSON is one of the more popular formats for sending and receiving data over the web. It is based on a subset of the JavaScript Programming Language, Standard ECMA-262 3rd Edition - December 1999. You can learn more about JSON by going to this website:
>
> www.json.org/

To handle parsing JSON instead of XML as we have so far in the book, we need to make a few changes to our parse function. We are going to start with our `call_timeline()` function and then make some changes.

We'll create a new function below the function `call_users()` in this file. Add the following code:

```
function call_search($messages){
   $twitterReturn = json_decode($messages);
```

Here we have introduced a new PHP library call called `json_decode()`. This function will convert the json return into a PHP variable:

```
      $i=0;
   foreach($twitterReturn->results as $status){
```

Now that we have the return converted to a PHP object, we can step through each of the results and get our values, just as we did with our other parse functions:

```
    $updateTime[$i] = parseDate($status->created_at);
          $update[$i] = $status->text;
          $id[$i] = $status->id;
          $profile_image_url[$i] = $status->profile_image_url;
          $screen_name[$i] = $status->from_user;

          $i++;
   }

          $parsedReturn = array();
          $parsedReturn['updateTime']=$updateTime;
          $parsedReturn['update']=$update;
          $parsedReturn['id']=$id;
          $parsedReturn['profile_image_url']=$profile_image_url;
          $parsedReturn['screen_name']=$screen_name;

          return $parsedReturn;
}
```

Save and close.

Edit twitteroauth.php

Now we can put our Search API request function code in. Open twitteroauth.php and add the following function at the end of the file but before the last '}':

```
function search($options){
  $api_call = 'http://search.twitter.com/search.json?'.$options;
  return $this->get($api_call);
}
```

Did you notice that we are passing the variable `$options` to our API statement? We are going populate that using JavaScript. To do so, we need to edit a few more files. Also did you notice how we defined the $api_call varible? We used a full path instead of the short hand we have been using. Remember that the OAuth library we are using will supply the default https://api.twitter.com/1/ for us if we do not have http in our call. In this case we need to call search.twitter.com instead of api.twitter.com, thus the override.

Save and close.

Edit create_message.php

Open create_message.php. It's been a while since we have opened this file. We are going to make only a small change. We want to know when we are sending a normal message or requesting a search so that we can call the appropriate JavaScript function. We also want to keep the request in the text field after the page has reloaded. So, let's take care of that now.

Replace this line:

```
<textarea id="testinput" name='sendMessField' class='inputbox'
➥rows="2" cols="80" ></textarea>
```

With the following line:

```
<textarea id="testinput" name='sendMessField' class='inputbox'
➥rows="2" cols="80" ><? echo $_GET['options']; ?></textarea>
```

Remember that we are reloading this page, so this small bit of PHP will populate the text field box with whatever we typed in before. Now on to the next edit.

Find this line:

```
<input class='inputbox' type='button' value='Send'
➥onmouseup='sendMessage()' />
```

And replace it with the following code:

```
<? if($nav==search){ ?>
<input class='inputbox' type='button' value='Send'
➥onmouseup='sendSearch()' />
<? } else { ?>
<input class='inputbox' type='button' value='Send'
➥onmouseup='sendMessage()' />
<? } ?>
```

Here we are checking to see if we navigated to the Search tab, thus setting `$nav='search'`. If we want to submit the contents to search, we will call the JavaScript function `sendSearch` instead of `sendMessage` as we do for sending a tweet. Speaking of which, we should put some JavaScript code in place to catch this new `onmouseup()` request we just created.

Save and close this file.

Edit base.js

Open base.js and create a new function call after the `destroyFavorite()` call we created in the previous hour.

Put in the following code:

```
function sendSearch(){
  message = document.getElementById("prefex").innerHTML;
  message += document.sendMessForm.sendMessField.value;

  message=encodeURIComponent(message);

  trace(message);
  url = location.href.split("?");
  url = url[0]+'?nav=search&page=search&options='+message
  window.open(url, '_self');
}
```

This looks quite a bit like the JavaScript function `sendMessage()`, except we are not going to make an AJAX call here. Instead we are going to make a PHP request from our server passing the contents of our text box as an argument. We defined `url` as our current location, `location.href`; added `nav` and `page` identifiers, `?nav=search&page=search`; and finally, the contents of the text box, `&options='+message;`. This will allow us to experiment with Search options. Let's give it a try. Save and close this file.

Open index.php and click the Search tab. Do not worry if you do not see anything. We haven't populated a search request yet, but we'll do that now. In the text field, type in the following:

```
q='football'
```

Then click the Send button. Do note that the quotes (either single or double) are optional here. You could have typed q=football and would get the same result.

You should get something like Figure 15.2.

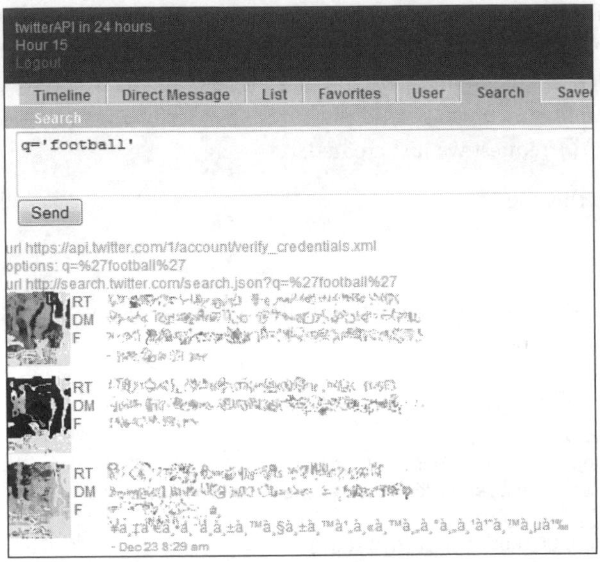

FIGURE 15.2 Search result from our application.

Now let's try some of the options we used earlier in this hour. Try typing the following content into the Search text box and see what kind of results you get:

- q=so+cool
- q="cal+bears"
- q=+junk+#food
- q=devo&rpp=3
- q=+good+#cal+since:<today's date>

Note that when using the since operator, there is little reason to set the date more than two days older than today's date. A typical search will go back only a few days, depending on how the Twitter Search servers are feeling that day. As of this writing, you cannot use time with the since operator.

A Quick Guide to More Information on Search from the Twitter Docs

Now that we have a basic understanding of how Search works, let's look at some of the more detailed notes from the Twitter documents. The following section is a pretty good reference, but keep in mind that docs change and update all the time, so be sure to check the following link for the most updated information. Here we have included only the core elements you should be aware of when thinking about your Search options. Let's again refer to the Twitter online docs (http://dev.twitter.com/doc/get/search)

GET Search

Required:

- **q**—Search query. Should be URL encoded. Queries will be limited by complexity:

```
http://search.twitter.com/search.json?q=@noradio
```

Optional:

- **callback**—Available only for JSON format. If supplied, the response will use the JSON format with a callback of the given name.
- **lang**—Restricts tweets to the given language, given by an ISO 639-1 code.
- **locale**—Specifies the language of the query you are sending (only ja is currently effective). This is intended for language-specific clients, and the default should work in the majority of cases:

```
http://search.twitter.com/search.json?locale=ja
```

- **rpp**—The number of tweets to return per page, up to a max of 100.

```
http://search.twitter.com/search.json?rpp=100
```

- **page**—The page number (starting at 1) to return, up to a max of roughly 1,500 results (based on rpp * page):

```
http://search.twitter.com/search.json?page=10
```

- **since_id**—Returns results with an ID greater than (that is, more recent than) the specified ID. There are limits to the number of tweets that can be accessed through the API. If the limit of tweets has occurred since the since_id, the since_id will be forced to the oldest ID available:

```
http://search.twitter.com/search.json?since_id=12345
```

- **until**—Optional. Returns tweets generated before the given date. Date should be formatted as YYYY-MM-DD:

```
http://search.twitter.com/search.json?until=2010-03-28
```

- **geocode**—Returns tweets by users located within a given radius of the given latitude/longitude. The location is preferentially taking from the Geotagging API, but will fall back to the Twitter profile. The parameter value is specified by "latitude,longitude,radius", where radius units must be specified as either "mi" (miles) or "km" (kilometers). Note that you cannot use the near operator via the API to geocode arbitrary locations; however, you can use this geocode parameter to search near geocodes directly:

```
http://search.twitter.com/search.json?geocode=37.781157,-122.398720,1mi
```

- **show_user**—When true, prepends ":" to the beginning of the tweet. This is useful for readers that do not display Atom's author field. The default is false.
- **result_type**—Optional. Specifies what type of search results you would prefer to receive. The current default is "mixed." Valid values include the following:
    - **mixed**—Includes both popular and real-time results in the response.
    - **recent**—Returns only the most recent results in the response.
    - **popular**—Returns only the most popular results in the response.

```
http://search.twitter.com/search.json?result_type=mixed
http://search.twitter.com/search.json?result_type=recent
http://search.twitter.com/search.json?result_type=popular
```

Usage Notes

Search does have a few issues and rules you need to be aware of. Most are common sense, such as knowing that your query string must be URL encoded. Some are trial and error, like the second item saying queries are limited by complexity. Sometimes you do not know what "complex" means until you try it. So, do not assume you can string some long query combination. Always test every possible combination you want to support first. Returning back to the Twitter docs:

- Query strings should be URL encoded.
- Queries may be limited by complexity.
- Some users may be absent from search results.
- The since_id parameter will be removed from the next_page element because it is not supported for pagination. If since_id is removed, a warning will be added to alert you.

- This method will return an HTTP 404 error if since_id is used and is too old to be in the Search index.
- If you are having trouble constructing your query, use the advanced search form to construct your search, which is located here: http://dev.twitter.com/console. Then add the format. For example, http://search.twitter.com/search?q=twitter would become http://search.twitter.com/search.json?q=twitter.
- Applications must have a meaningful and unique User Agent when using this method. An HTTP Referrer is expected but not required. Search traffic that does not include a User Agent will be rate limited to fewer API calls per hour than applications including a User Agent string. More information on rate limiting can be found here: https://dev.twitter.com/pages/rate-limiting.

More information on Twitter Search best practices can be found here: http://support.twitter.com/forums/10713/entries/42646.

Notes on Metadata in Responses

The metadata node will sometimes contain a result_type field with a value of either "recent" or "popular"—although other values may be possible in the future. Popular results are derived by an algorithm that Twitter computes, and up to three will appear in "mixed mode" at the top of the resultset. Popular results will also include another node to metadata called "recent_retweets" and will indicate how many retweets the tweet was bestowed recently. The metadata node will contain more fields as time goes on.

Refreshing Search Results

For those using client-side search widgets, by default the first request might include popular results. If you want to display these, you can use the result_type attribute to visually differentiate them. If you don't want to display these, you can always pass the "result_type" parameter with a value of "recent" along with your request, and they'll never be included.

Summary

In this hour, we learned about the Search method and why it's different from other Twitter method calls. We discovered that all searches are performed using only one method! Instead, Search queries are constructed through attributes passed through the single Search method call.

We also learned that despite having only one method call, we can use a rich variety of attributes for our search. However, we also discovered that there are certain restrictions on how many and what attributes we can use together in one call.

We also were introduced to the JSON protocol because XML is not supported in Search. In fact, many programmers prefer JSON over XML. So, we learned how to parse a JSON reply to be compatible with our rendering code.

Q&A

Q. ***Search is the only API method. Will there be others in the future?***

A. No one knows for sure, but in the short term, no—it will be only Search.

Workshop

Quiz

1. Who is Summize?
2. Twitter Search uses only one API call. Why?
3. What is the operator to search back tweets by time?

Quiz Answers

1. It is the name of a company that created a Twitter Search technology that was purchased by Twitter. Hopefully, you got the Jeopardy reference.
2. The Summize product was originally created to search only Twitter; thus, it needs to perform only one function: Search.
3. Trick question. You cannot. You can only search by date, not time.

Exercises

Try these various operators listed below. Remember, these are examples. For example, using the exact date as listed from some of these examples may not work. Be aware of context.

Operator	Finds Tweets...
twitter search	containing both "twitter" and "search." This is the default operator.
"happy hour"	containing the exact phrase "happy hour."
love **OR** hate	containing either "love" or "hate" (or both).
beer **-**root	containing "beer" but not "root."
#haiku	containing the hashtag "haiku."
from:alexiskold	sent from person "alexiskold."
to:techcrunch	sent to person "techcrunch."
@mashable	referencing person "mashable."
"happy hour" **near:**"san francisco"	containing the exact phrase "happy hour" and sent near "san francisco."
near:NYC **within:**15mi	sent within 15 miles of "NYC."
superhero **since:**2010-09-01	containing "superhero" and sent since date "2010-09-01" (year-month-day).
ftw **until:**2010-09-01	containing "ftw" and sent up to date "2010-09-01."
movie -scary **:)**	containing "movie," but not "scary," and with a positive attitude.
flight **:(**	containing "flight" and with a negative attitude.
traffic **?**	containing "traffic" and asking a question.
hilarious **filter:links**	containing "hilarious" and linking to URLs.
news **source:twitterfeed**	containing "news" and entered via TwitterFeed.

HOUR 16

Trends and GEO

What You'll Learn in This Hour:

- What is a Twitter trend?
- Not all returns from the Trend method are in order based on time.
- What is the WOEID format?
- GEO methods.

What Is a Trending Topic?

Trends are an interesting aspect of Twitter that has been originated and copied by many other services. A trend is just a type of search; a term that is trending is simply a term that appears in higher frequency than other terms over a set amount of time. For example, during the World Cup final of 2010, when Holland played Spain, the terms "holland," "spain," and "worldcup" would have been trending highly because Twitter was almost brought to its knees by the amount of traffic during the final. As you would expect, a trending topic term, more commonly referred to as a *trending topic*, tends to reflect the major events of the day. What is really fascinating is that trending topics on Twitter tend to beat most news outlets for fast-breaking news.

Supporting Trends in Our Application

The API for Trends is a lot like Search given that it's based on Search. So, as you would expect, we are going to use JSON and various operators to fine tune what we get back for Twitter.

To start out, let's add a new menu item to our application to display finding topics.

Edit header.inc

This should be almost routine at this point. Let's add a new button to our UI. Open header.inc and add a new <li> .. </li> tag set with the following code:

```
        <li><a href="/?nav=trends&page=trends" <? if($nav=='trends') echo
'class="here"'; ?> >Trends</a>
        <? if($nav=='trends') { ?>
          <ul>
            <li><a href="/?nav=trends&page=trends" >Trends</a></li>
          </ul>
        <? } ?>
          </li>
```

Save and close.

Edit parseTwitter.php

Now that we have our tab, let's add a switch to support our new request. There are no options with this method, so we will make an empty function call. Open parseTwitter.php and add the following case statement at the end of our switch:

```
    case 'trends':
        { $messages=$twitter->showTrends(); return call_trends($messages); }
        break;
```

Notice that we are making a call to the function `call_trends()`. A new parsing function is required for the JSON return we get back from Twitter. So, let's create a new function called `call_trends()` and add it after the function `call_search()`. Here is the code for our new function:

```
function call_trends($messages){
   $twitterReturn = json_decode($messages);
   foreach($twitterReturn->trends as $status){
          $query = explode('?',$status->url);
           echo "<p /><a href='/?nav=search&page=search&options=$query[1]'>
Term: $status->name</a>";
   }
}
```

Let's go through this function because there are some tricky things going on behind the scenes that you should be aware of. First, let's have a look a typical raw JSON return from the trends request using `var_dump()`:

```
<urlrequest>url
https://api.twitter.com/1/account/verify_credentials.xml</urlrequest><br>
➥<urlrequest>url
http://api.twitter.com/1/trends.json?</urlrequest><br>object(stdClass)#5
➥(2) {
  ["as_of"]=>
```

```
    string(31) "Sat, 04 Sep 2010 04:45:05 +0000"
    ["trends"]=>
    array(10) {
      [0]=>
      object(stdClass)#7 (2) {
        ["url"]=>
        string(53) "http://search.twitter.com/search?q=Duke+Nukem+Forever"
        ["name"]=>
        string(18) "Duke Nukem Forever"
      }
      [1]=>
      object(stdClass)#8 (2) {
        ["url"]=>
        string(51) "http://search.twitter.com/search?q=%23lessonlearned"
        ["name"]=>
        string(14) "#lessonlearned"
      }
      [2]=>
      object(stdClass)#9 (2) {
        ["url"]=>
        string(42) "http://search.twitter.com/search?q=Mitchie"
        ["name"]=>
        string(7) "Mitchie"
      }
      [3]=>
      object(stdClass)#10 (2) {
        ["url"]=>
        string(44) "http://search.twitter.com/search?q=Birdhouse"
        ["name"]=>
        string(9) "Birdhouse"
      }
...
      [9]=>
      object(stdClass)#16 (2) {
        ["url"]=>
        string(45) "http://search.twitter.com/search?q=Earthquake"
        ["name"]=>
        string(10) "Earthquake"
      }
    }
}
```

Notice that the "url" string has a full URL to `http://search.twitter.com/search?q=<term>`. This is great if we want our users to go to Twitter. However, if we want to keep the users on our application, we are going to need to parse this string to get the query value the text after the ?q=. So, we are using the PHP library call `explode` function to split all text after the '?' so that we can use our Search function that we created in Hour 15.

Save and close this file.

Edit twitteroauth.php

Let's add our API call. Open twitteroauth.php and add the following function at the end of the file but before the last '}':

```
function showTrends(){
  $api_call = 'trends.json';
  return $this->get($api_call);
}
```

Save and close this file.

Now we'll give it a go. Open index.php in your browser and click Trends. You should see something like Figure 16.1.

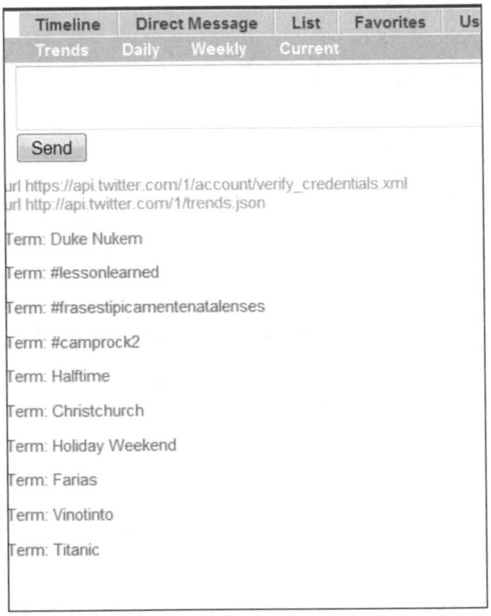

FIGURE 16.1
Screenshot of Trends.

Trends: Recent, Daily, Weekly

There are a few more Trend API calls we can make; however, its usefulness is most likely only within a select domain. The following three API calls return the same information in general: a collection of trending terms based on a segment of time—most recent, daily, and weekly. Let's have a look at the returns for trend/daily.json:

```
<urlrequest>url
https://api.twitter.com/1/account/verify_credentials.xml</urlrequest><br>
➥<urlrequest>url
http://api.twitter.com/1/trends/daily.json?</urlrequest><br>array(2) {
  ["trends"]=>
  array(24) {
```

```
  ["2010-09-04 03:40"]=>
  array(20) {
    [0]=>
    array(4) {
      ["events"]=>
      NULL
      ["query"]=>
      string(18) "Duke Nukem Forever"
      ["promoted_content"]=>
      NULL
      ["name"]=>
      string(18) "Duke Nukem Forever"
    }
    [1]=>
    array(4) {
      ["events"]=>
      NULL
      ["query"]=>
      string(14) "#lessonlearned"
      ["promoted_content"]=>
      NULL
      ["name"]=>
      string(14) "#lessonlearned"
    }
    [2]=>
    array(4) {
      ["events"]=>
      NULL
      ["query"]=>
      string(10) "#voltaxuxa"
      ["promoted_content"]=>
      NULL
      ["name"]=>
      string(10) "#voltaxuxa"
    }
    [3]=>
    array(4) {
      ["events"]=>
      NULL
      ["query"]=>
      string(10) "#camprock2"
      ["promoted_content"]=>
      NULL
      ["name"]=>
      string(10) "#camprock2"
    }
...
    [19]=>
    array(4) {
      ["events"]=>
      NULL
      ["query"]=>
```

```
        string(9) "Hurricane"
        ["promoted_content"]=>
        NULL
        ["name"]=>
        string(9) "Hurricane"
      }
    }
    ["2010-09-04 05:40"]=>
    array(20) {
      [0]=>
      array(4) {
        ["events"]=>
        NULL
        ["query"]=>
        string(10) "Duke Nukem"
        ["promoted_content"]=>
        NULL
        ["name"]=>
        string(10) "Duke Nukem"
      }
      [1]=>
      array(4) {
        ["events"]=>
        NULL
        ["query"]=>
        string(14) "#lessonlearned"
        ["promoted_content"]=>
        NULL
        ["name"]=>
        string(14) "#lessonlearned"
      }
...
```

The rest of the output is truncated.

There are 20 items per date. As you can imagine, this is quite a large dataset being returned. You may have also noticed that the key for the first array attribute is the date and time when those terms where trending. Let's have a look at the first five:

```
["2010-09-04 03:40"]=>
["2010-09-04 05:40"]=>
["2010-09-04 07:40"]=>
["2010-09-03 18:40"]=>
["2010-09-04 04:40"]=>
```

As you can see, the first three seem to respect a two-hour interval, but after that, it's fairly random which time slice is going to show up when. As such, you need to parse and convert these times into a date/time object so that you can sort them properly. In addition, the dates are not value pairs but the key of the nested array within the object. As such, we need to do a bit more work to parse these returns.

The value of looking at trending term data in time slices is to compare which terms are rising and which terms are declining and at what rate. Creating that capability in our application is a bit out of scope, but we still want to display the data, so let's instead display the returns separated by date but still linking to our search function.

Edit header.inc

Let's add a few more tabs to our Trends section. Under the following line:

```
<li><a href="/?nav=trends&page=trends" >Trends</a></li>
```

Add the following lines:

```
            <li><a href="/?nav=trends&page=trends_daily" >Daily</a></li>
            <li><a href="/?nav=trends&page=trends_weekly" >Weekly</a></li>
            <li><a href="/?nav=trends&page=trends_current" >Current</a></li>
```

Save and close.

Edit parseTwitter.php

Now let's add three new case statements to our switch. Open parseTwitter.php and add these case statements at the end of the switch function:

```
    case 'trends_daily':
        { $messages=$twitter->showTrends_daily($options); return
call_trends_time($messages); }
        break;
    case 'trends_weekly':
        { $messages=$twitter->showTrends_weekly($options); return
call_trends_time($messages); }
        break;
    case 'trends_current':
        { $messages=$twitter->showTrends_current($options); return
call_trends_time($messages); }
        break;
```

Notice that all three are sending the returns to the same function. Let's create that function now.

In this same file, create a new function under the previous function we created called 'call_trends()':

```
function call_trends_daily($messages){
   $twitterReturn = json_decode($messages, true);
```

Notice that I have used the option 'true' while using json_decode. I'm doing this because it's sometimes easier to work with an array than with an object. Because we want to display the date, we need the key as we loop through the nested arrays. The array_keys() function within PHP makes that very easy for us:

```
$keys=array_keys($twitterReturn['trends']);
```

Here we set $keys to the array of dates from our JSON return:

```
$i=0;
foreach($twitterReturn['trends'] as $foo){
                echo  '<br><b>'.$keys[$i].'<br></b> ';
                foreach($twitterReturn['trends'][$keys[$i]] as $trend){
```

Now that we know the time, we can access the nested array for each of the 20 returns per time segment:

```
          echo "<a
href='/?nav=search&page=search&options=q=".urlencode($trend['name'])."'>
Term: ".$trend['name']."</a>";
          echo '<p />';
          }
    $i++;
   }
}
```

Save and close the file.

Edit twitteroauth.php

Now that we have our parsing in place, let's insert the code to make the API requests to Twitter. Open twitteroauth.php and add the following three function calls at the end of the file but before the last '}':

```
function showTrends_daily($options){
  $api_call = 'trends/daily.json?'.$options;
  return $this->get($api_call);
}
function showTrends_weekly($options){
  $api_call = 'trends/weekly.json?'.$options;
  return $this->get($api_call);
}
function showTrends_current($options){
  $api_call = 'trends/current.json?'.$options;
  return $this->get($api_call);
}
```

Save and close this file.

Now let's see what we get when we run our application. Open index.php in your web browser, and you should see something similar to Figure 16.2. Remember to scroll down the page to see more returns and times.

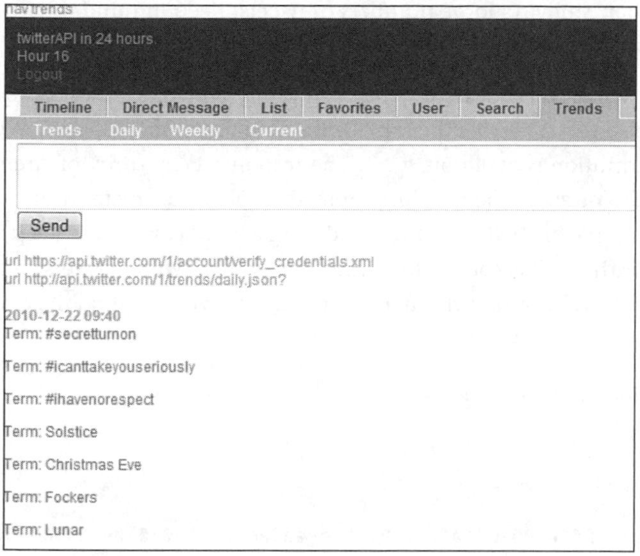

FIGURE 16.2 Screenshot of Trends/daily.

Click Trends/weekly, and you will see something very much like Trends/daily but again with some of the dates out of sequence.

Clicking Trends/current returns something very much like the generic 'trends' API call, but based on a time slice in the recent past. Note that you will only get the top ten with this API. I expect this to change in the future.

Trends/Available and WOEID

Let's have a look at the API call Trends/available from Twitter documents: http://dev.twitter.com/doc/get/trends/:woeid.

The API call trends/available returns the locations that Twitter has trending topic information for. The response is an array of "locations" that encode the location's `WOEID` and some other human-readable information, such as a canonical name and country the location belongs in. A `WOEID` is a Yahoo! Where On Earth ID.

Clearly there is something different here. The trends/available call relies on another API service from Yahoo! called "Yahoo! Where On Earth ID," or WOEID.

What is WOEID?—WOEID stands for Where On Earth ID by Yahoo!. It's a standalone integer that represents a place. A more detailed explanation relevant to Twitter was posted at http://engineering.twitter.com/2010/02/woeids-in-twitters-trends.html, by Raffi Krikorian @raffi.

Basically, Twitter will try to determine a location for a tweet based on its content, not just the location of the tweet's owner. This could be quite powerful and interesting when studying large numbers of tweets. Keep in mind that this applies only to trending topics, not ALL tweets.

The actual API method call, trends/:woeid is pretty typical, as most of the API calls we have seen so far. It returns the top 10 trending topics for a specific WOEID, if trending information is available for it. The response is an array of "trend" objects that encode the name of the trending topic, the query parameter that can be used to search for the topic on Twitter Search, and the Twitter Search URL. Keep in mind that return for this call is cached for 5 minutes on the Twitter servers so calling it more frequently will not return any more data, and will count against your rate limit usage.

Example: http://api.twitter.com/1/trends/23424975.xml

Output:


```
<matching_trends type="array">
-
<trends as_of="2010-09-04T01:12:21Z" created_at="2010-09-04T00:54:16Z">
-
<locations>
-
<location>
<woeid>23424975</woeid>
<name>United Kingdom</name>
</location>
</locations>
<trend url="http://search.twitter.com/search?q=Duke+Nukem+Forever"
query="Duke+Nukem+Forever">Duke Nukem Forever</trend>
<trend url="http://search.twitter.com/search?q=Dries+Roelvink"
query="Dries+Roelvink">Dries Roelvink</trend>
<trend url="http://search.twitter.com/search?q=Vanessa+Feltz"
query="Vanessa+Feltz">Vanessa Feltz</trend>
<trend url="http://search.twitter.com/search?q=Blues+Brothers"
query="Blues+Brothers">Blues Brothers</trend>
<trend url="http://search.twitter.com/search?q=Heart+Vacancy"
query="Heart+Vacancy">Heart Vacancy</trend>
<trend url="http://search.twitter.com/search?q=%23lessonlearned"
query="%23lessonlearned">#lessonlearned</trend>
<trend url="http://search.twitter.com/search?q=Cloverfield"
query="Cloverfield">Cloverfield</trend>
<trend url="http://search.twitter.com/search?q=Glyn"
query="Glyn">Glyn</trend>
<trend url="http://search.twitter.com/search?q=Cyril"
query="Cyril">Cyril</trend>
<trend url="http://search.twitter.com/search?q=ITV4"
query="ITV4">ITV4</trend>
</trends>
</matching_trends>
```


There are other API calls with trends that can be found here: http://dev.twitter.com/doc/get/trends.

Many of the Trends API functions are still in development, so I would expect that there will be some evolution of these methods as time goes on. Similar to WOEID, another API method we can look at is the GEO tag.

Understanding the GEO Tag

The GEO methods are very interesting in that you can filter tweets based on location. The most obvious example is to map tweets over a map. A typical example is Trendsmap.com. This site will take your location, if enabled, and provide all trending topics in this area.

So, let's have a look at GEO API call from the Twitter docs.

GET geo/search

The geo/search API call will search for places that can be attached to a status/update. Given a latitude and a longitude pair, an IP address, or a name, this request will return a list of all the valid places that can be used as the place_id when updating a status.

This is the recommended method to use to find places that can be attached to statuses/update. Unlike geo/reverse_geocode, which provides raw data access, this endpoint can potentially reorder places in regard to the user who is authenticated. This approach is also preferred for interactive place matching with the user.

As we have seen before with other switch operator, there are GEO-centric search operators we can look at. Here's the current list from the Twitter docs (http://dev.twitter.com/doc/get/geo/search):

- `lat`
- `long`
- `query`
- `ip`
- `granularity`
- `accuracy`
- `max_results`
- `contained_within`
- `attribute:street_address`
- `callback`

A rich list of operators, right? Let's take one and see what it looks like. Here is an example search using the attribute:street_address operator:

```
http://api.twitter.com/1/geo/search.json?attribute:street_address=795%
➥20Folsom%20St
```

If we look at the sample JSON return from the Twitter docs, we can see that we get a rich amount of information. First, here is the sample return:


```
{
  "result": {
    "places": [
      {
        "name": "Twitter HQ",
        "country": "The United States of America",
        "country_code": "US",
        "attributes": {
          "street_address": "795 Folsom St"
        },
        "url": "http://api.twitter.com/1/geo/id/247f43d441defc03.JSON",
        "id": "247f43d441defc03",
        "bounding_box": {
          "coordinates": [
            [
              [
                -122.400612831116,
                37.7821120598956
              ],
              [
                -122.400612831116,
                37.7821120598956
              ],
              [
                -122.400612831116,
                37.7821120598956
              ],
              [
                -122.400612831116,
                37.7821120598956
              ]
            ]
          ],
          "type": "Polygon"
        },
        "contained_within": [
          {
            "name": "San Francisco",
            "country": "The United States of America",
            "country_code": "US",
            "attributes": {
```

```
            },
            "url": "http://api.twitter.com/1/geo/id/5a110d312052166f.JSON",
            "id": "5a110d312052166f",
            "bounding_box": {
              "coordinates": [
                [
                  [
                    -122.51368188,
                    37.70813196
                  ],
                  [
                    -122.35845384,
                    37.70813196
                  ],
                  [
                    -122.35845384,
                    37.83245301
                  ],
                  [
                    -122.51368188,
                    37.83245301
                  ]
                ]
              ],
              "type": "Polygon"
            },
            "full_name": "San Francisco, CA",
            "place_type": "city"
          }
        ],
        "full_name": "Twitter HQ, San Francisco",
        "place_type": "poi"
      }
    ]
  },
  "query": {
    "url":
"http://api.twitter.com/1/geo/search.JSON?query=Twitter+HQ&accuracy=0&
➥autocomplete=false&granularity=neighborhood",
    "type":
"search",
    "params": {
      "granularity":
"neighborhood",
      "accuracy": 0,
      "autocomplete": false,
      "query":
"Twitter HQ"
    }
  }
}
```

What is interesting here is getting not only an area bounding box for the address, but also for the city in general where the address is located. The number of options for searching is quite useful. As we can see from the preceding options list, we can use lat, long, ip, and—what I would think would be the most useful—query.

Summary

In this hour, we learned about trending topic and some of the limitations of how returns are presented to us. We also discovered that trends do not provide a timeline themselves, but instead a set of terms that are trending that we can thus use with the search method to get a timeline of tweets using that term.

We also learned how to search Twitter using GEO codes, including using the WOEID protocol created by Yahoo!. You will have discovered that the returns from the GEO methods are rich with information that lends itself nicely to a mapping application.

Q&A

Q. ***Because a trending topic is much like a search, can I employ the same search parameters?***

A. No, although there are parameters you can use to refine the returns.

Q. ***Will we see other GEO tools that we can use with Twitter other than WOEID?***

A. Yes, in fact, as of the writing of this book, a new set of reference tools is being Alpha tested.

Workshop

Quiz

1. What does WOEID mean?
2. What is a trending topic?
3. Why do hash keywords seem to appear in trending topics so often?

Quiz Answers

1. Yahoo! Where On Earth ID.

2. A trending topic is a keyword that has appeared repeatedly in a given bracket of time.

3. Remember, a hash (#) is an unofficial convention to designate the subject of a Tweet. As such, a subject will appear more often than standalone words.

Exercises

1. When we get a return from a GEO method call, we get a return type 'Polygon'. Take the information from this return and draw a polygon using Google Maps API.

2. Create a simple script to display the top 10 trending topic keywords. For each topic, place code that will allow the user to perform a search of that keyword.

HOUR 17

Friendships, Notification, Block, and Account Methods

What You'll Learn in This Hour:

- How to follow and unfollow a user with the Friendships methods
- Notification methods
- Block methods
- Account methods

Friendships Methods

The Friendships methods are what you would expect: the ability to create or destroy a friendship, which is also known as following and unfollowing a user. This is a core functionality and something that is expected to be supported by most Twitter applications. There are two ways to approach supporting the friendships. First, we can try to find out if we are already following the user, and based on that condition, offer a follow or unfollow button. Or, we can provide one button that assumes to follow, and if we get an HTTP reply of 403, meaning we are already following the Twitter user, we can offer to unfollow. The second procedure is more useful for automated systems, so we are going to go with the first option—checking to see if we are following someone and then offering the appropriate button.

Implement Friendships Methods in Our Application

Although the notification API seems straightforward, not all API methods return the status of whether you are following someone. As such, we will have to write a nested `if()` statement within our function call of render.php.

Edit render.php

Because we are using letters for our action buttons, we are going to use 'FOL' for a follow request and 'LEV' for a leave request.

After the following line:

```
$textBody = formatUpdates($update, $updateTime);
```

Add this line:

```
$following = $parsedReturn['following'][$i];
```

Now we need to add the code to render the 'LEV' link. In the same file, find the following code:

```
    if($nav=='showFavorites') { $output.="<a href='#' on-
mouseup=\"destroyFavorite('$id')\">Del</a></div> ";
    } else { $output.="<a href='#'
onmouseup=\"favorite('$id')\">Fav</a></div> "; }
```

And replace it with the following, removing the trailing '</div>'s:

```
    if($nav=='showFavorites') { $output.="<a href='#'
onmouseup=\"destroyFavorite('$id')\">Del</a> ";
    } else { $output.="<a href='#' onmouseup=\"favorite('$id')\">Fav</a> "; }
```

Now we can add our new code. Add the following under the code you just changed:

```
    if($following==null) {$output.= '</div>'; } else {
                              if($following=='true') { $output.="<a
➥href='#' onmouseup=\"leave('$screen_name')\">LEV</a></div> ";
                } else { $output.="<a href='#'
➥onmouseup=\"follow('$screen_name')\">Fol</a></div> "; }
                    }
```

Save and close.

Edit base.js

Now we need to catch these links in JavaScript. Add the following function after the function sendGeoSearch() in base.js:

```
function follow(id){
  url='commandLine.php?command=follow&id='+id;

  callPage(url, 'serverMessages');
}
function leave(id){
  url='commandLine.php?command=leave&id='+id;

  callPage(url, 'serverMessages');
}
```

Save and close.

Edit commandLine.php

Now we need to catch the AJAX request we made in base.js. We will use the same approach as we have for the other AJAX calls.

At the end of the file, but before the last '}', add the following code:

```
case 'follow':
    { $messages=$twitter->follow($id); echo ($messages); }
      break;
case 'leave':
    { $messages=$twitter->leave($id); echo ($messages); }
      break;
```

Save and close.

Edit twitteroauth.php

Now let's put our notification methods into twitteroauth.php. Open twitteroauth.php and add these two functions at the end of the file but before the last '}':

```
      function follow($options){
              $api_call = "friendships/create.XML?screen_name=$options";
return $this->post($api_call);
      }
      function leave($options){
              $api_call = " friendships/destroy.XML?screen_name=$options";
return $this->post($api_call);
      }
```

Save and close.

Edit parseTwitter.php

Finally, we need to parse our return to find out whether the owner of the tweet in the returned stream is following us. Not all APIs return this value, so we are only going to put code into our function `call_timeline()`. Fortunately, this is a simple matter of adding two more lines.

After the following line:

```
$screen_name[$i] = $status->user->screen_name;
```

Add this line:

```
$following[$i] = $status->user->following;
```

And after this line:

```
$parsedReturn['screen_name']=$screen_name;
```

And this line:

```
$parsedReturn['following']=$following;
```

Save and close.

Now let's give it a try. You should see something like Figure 17.1.

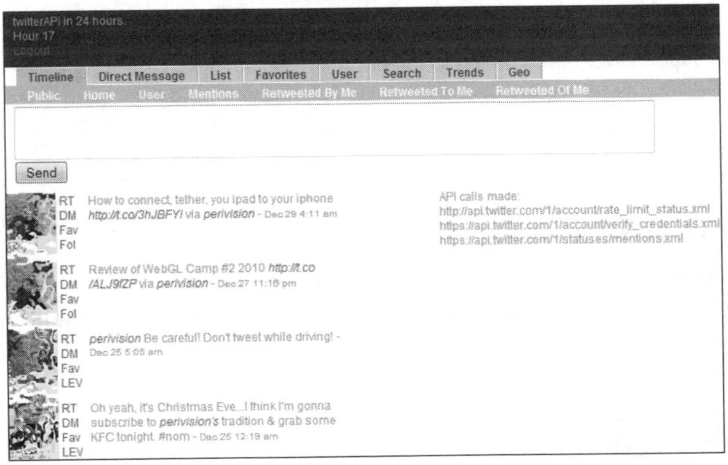

FIGURE 17.1
Screenshot of Following method buttons.

Try clicking on a FOL, and you should see a raw dump of the tweeter's information, as shown in Figure 17.2.

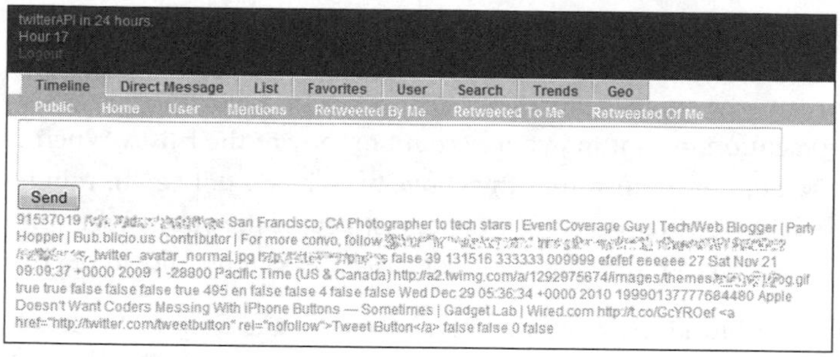

FIGURE 17.2
Screenshot showing user info from a notification call.

Notification Methods

The notification methods are somewhat like the account methods in that they are used to get information about or change the operation of a user's account. There are only two methods to review: notifications/follow and notifications/leave. They also work much the same as many of the API methods. Simply POST the proper http: request with either the user_id or screen_name, and you will get back a code 200 with profile information about the person you followed or left. Let's have a look at these methods and then we will add this feature to our application. First notifications/follow as defined in the Twitter docs:

- **POST notifications/follow:** Enables device notifications for updates from the specified user. Returns the specified user when successful.

Did You Know?

> We have a choice of operators for letting Twitter know who we want to follow. We can use either user_id or screen_name. In our example, let's use screen_name.

Example:

OK, now let's have a look at the API from the Twitter docs about notifications/leave:

- **POST notifications/leave:** Disables notifications for updates from the specified user to the authenticating user. Returns the specified user when successful.

Pretty simple, right? Sometimes, it's just that easy.

Block Methods

Blocking occurs when a user blocks another user from following you, sending you a @reply or @mention, or putting your account on any of their lists. When users are blocked, they are not notified that they have been blocked. Keep in mind, though, if you have a public Twitter account, which most people do, your tweets will still show up in the public stream and thus a blocked user will still be able to see them.

The methods for blocking are very similar to friends and follows. So, let's look at these methods from the Twitter docs:

- **POST blocks/create:** Blocks the user specified in the ID parameter as the authenticating user. Destroys a friendship to the blocked user if it exists. Returns the blocked user in the requested format when successful.

Now, the next one may seem confusing and, if so, don't feel bad. To remove a block, you do not unblock or delete the block—you destroy it! Let's look at blocks/destroy from Twitter docs:

- **POST (DELETE) blocks/destroy:** Unblocks the user specified in the ID parameter for the authenticating user. Returns the unblocked user in the requested format when successful.

We can also see if a block exists. Again, from the Twitter docs:

- **GET blocks/exists:** Returns if the authenticating user is blocking a target user. Returns the blocked user's object if a block exists, and returns an error with an HTTP 404 response code otherwise.

This next API is a bit different; blocks/blocking returns a list of blocked accounts:

- **GET blocks/blocking:** Returns an array of user objects that the authenticating user is blocking.

The blocks/blocking/ids is just like the blocks/blocking API call except the return is user IDs:

- **GET blocks/blocking/ids:** Returns an array of numeric user IDs the authenticating user is blocking.

There are quite a number of methods for blocking, right? And you may not even know right off what you may use blocking for, but once you start to build more complete Twitter applications, or integrations into a larger application, you will find these to be more useful than you think.

Account Methods

As we have mentioned before, Twitter exposed almost all the elements of its functionality through its API system. This includes managing a user's account. We have already used one of these methods: account/verify_credentials. There are a few other useful credentials we can access. For example, 'account/rate_limit_status' can be a useful warning to users that they are approaching the limit of how many API calls they can make for the hour or day.

Here is a list currently supported:

- account/verify_credentials
- account/rate_limit_status
- account/end_session
- account/update_delivery_device
- account/update_profile_colors
- account/update_profile_image
- account/update_profile_background_image
- account/update_profile

Just for fun, let's add a display in our application for displaying the rate limit of our user. We will make this call when we make the account/verify_credentials call.

Adding the Rate Status Method to Our Application

These next series of edits will be pretty simple because we are going to make a single API call and display the results, but no new menu items are needed. Also, it's good to note that making this API method call does not count against the user's API limit counts.

Edit header.inc

We'll do something a little different this time from a presentation point of view. We are going use the space on the right of our dark header bar to display this information. Let's open header.inc.

Near the top of the file, find this line:

```
TwitterAPI in 24 hours. <br>
```

Then add the following lines:

```
<div style='float: right'>
  <? echo getTwitterData('getUserRate'); ?>
</div>
```

Save and close.

Edit parseTwitter.php

Because we make a request of getTwitterData(), we need to create a switch to catch it. Open parseTwitter.php, and add this case to the switch function:

```
case 'getUserName':
    { $messages=$twitter->getVerifyCredentials('XML'); return
call_credentials($messages); }
    break;
```

Save and close.

Edit twitteroauth.php

Now we need to create the API method call to support our new request. Open twitteroauth.php and at the end of the file, but before the last '}', add the following function:

```
      function getUserRate() {
               $api_call = 'account/rate_limit_status.XML';
return $this->get($api_call);
      }
```

Save and close.

Now let's give it a try. Open index.php in your browser, and you should see something like Figure 17.3. Do not worry if you do not have as many calls as shown in the figure. This is from a whitelisted account.

FIGURE 17.3 Screenshot showing API calls remaining.

Additional Account Methods

For reference, let's have a look at some of the other methods we have access to via 'account' method calls from the Twitter docs. It is not likely you will use these methods in more typical Twitter client applications, but it's good to be aware of them. Again referencing the Twitter docs, let's have a quick look at some additional account methods that you have access to via the APIs:

- **POST account/end_session:** Ends the session of the authenticating user, returning a null cookie. Use this method to sign users out of client-facing applications like widgets.

  URL: http://api.twitter.com/version/account/end_session.format

Watch Out!

> This does not always work because of aggressive OAuth caching. Always provide an option to log out from Twitter.com.

- **POST account/update_profile_colors:** Sets one or more hex values that control the color scheme of the authenticating user's profile page on Twitter.com. Each parameter's value must be a valid hexadecimal value and may be either three or six characters (ex: #fff or #ffffff).

  URL: http://api.twitter.com/version/account/update_profile_colors.format

- **POST account/update_profile_image:** Updates the authenticating user's profile image. Note that this method expects raw multipart data, not a URL to an image. This method asynchronously processes the uploaded file before updating the user's profile image URL. You can either update your local cache the next time you request the user's information, or, at least 5 seconds after uploading the image, ask for the updated URL using users/profile_image/:screen_name.

  URL: http://api.twitter.com/version/account/update_profile_image.format

- **POST account/update_profile_background_image:** Updates the authenticating user's profile background image. Note that this method expects raw multipart data, not a URL to an image.

  URL: http://api.twitter.com/version/account/update_profile_background_image.format

- **POST account/update_profile:** Sets values that users are able to set under the Account tab of their settings page. Only the parameters specified will be updated.

  URL: http://api.twitter.com/version/account/update_profile.format

Summary

In this hour, we explored the Friendships and Notification methods, which are used to get information about or change the operation of a user's account. We looked at blocking and the methods associated with that account.

We also looked at the Account methods and how we can use some of those methods to track how many API calls a user has per hour. We also used a new portion of our UI to display API rate information in the upper right.

Q&A

Q. ***What API method would you use to change an account holder's email address?***

A. Trick question. You are not allowed to change a user's email address due to security reasons because a password reminder is sent to a user via email.

Q. ***What are the API method calls to follow and unfollow another twitter user?***

A. To follow a user: .. /friendships/create. To unfollow a user: .. /friendships/destroy.

Workshop

Quiz

1. What are the five profile colors methods we have access to?
2. When you block a user, will the user you block be notified?
3. Does the rate_limit_status API call count against your API limits?

Quiz Answers

1. They are as follows:

   Background_color

   Text_color

   Link_color

   Sidebar_fill_color

   Sidebar_border_color

2. No, the user is not notified.

3. No, but if you create a loop making this call too often, you can run into limits of any calls coming from the same IP too often, as well as other traffic monitoring tools that are not publicly expressed or have yet to be deployed.

Exercises

1. Check to see how many tweets a user has made in the past 24 hours and change the background color based on that number. For example, blue could mean 1 or less in 24; red could be 40 tweets or more. Use color gradation based on the number of tweets.

2. In the commandline.php file, we used echo to see the return after creating a friendship. Parse this return and provide the user with something more useful.

3. When we reviewed notification methods, we did not implement them into our application. Try to do that now.

HOUR 18

Twitter Documentation

What You'll Learn in This Hour:

- How to navigate the Twitter Development website
- How to use dev.twitter.com/console
- About the Tweet Button widget
- How to navigate Twitter documents
- Some recommended best practices from Twitter

The Twitter Dev Website

Twitter has been taking great pains to make working with the Twitter API as clear as possible. However, as the API evolves, so does the documentation; as of this writing, the documentation is evolving. Much of the information in this book is a combination of references from the old docs and the new docs. Both versions of the document will still be online by the time this book is published, so be sure to pay attention to the URL when you look things up. It should be dev.twitter.com.

Currently, Figure 18.1 is the front page when you go to dev.twitter.com.

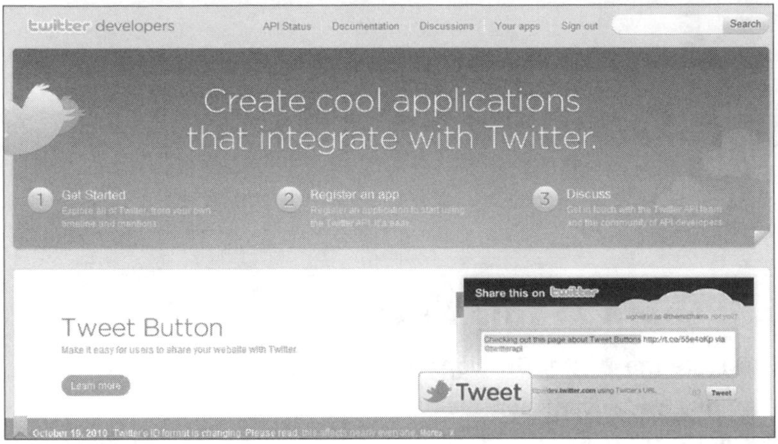

FIGURE 18.1
dev.twitter.com.

Getting Started

From dev.twitter.com, click Getting Started or navigate to dev.twitter.com/start. You might see something like Figure 18.2. Click Explore the API with the Twurl Web Console or navigate to dev.twitter.com/console. You should see something like Figure 18.3.

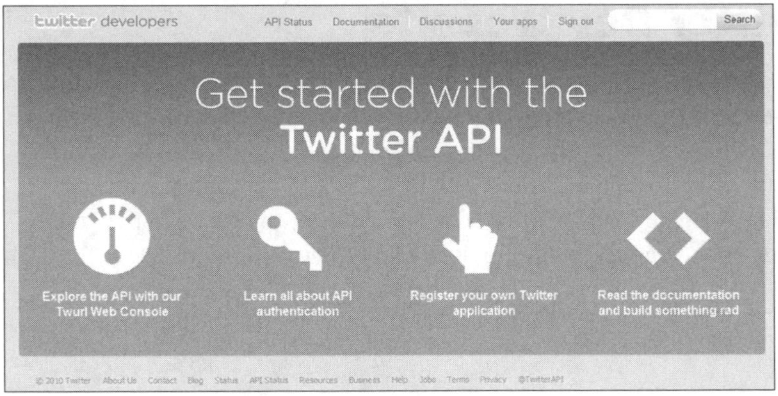

FIGURE 18.2
The dev.twitter.com/start page.

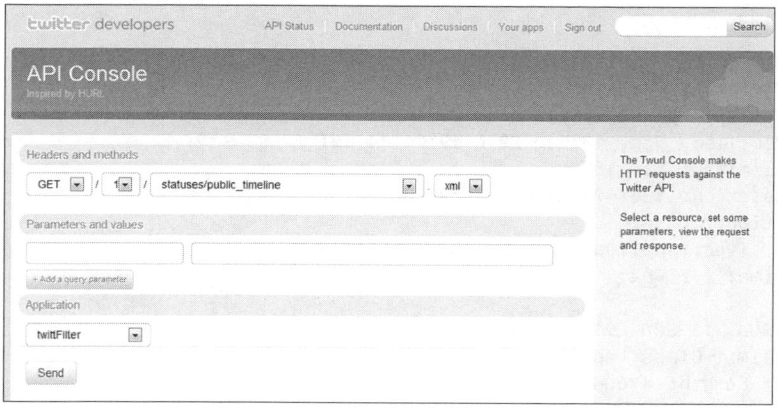

FIGURE 18.3 The dev.twitter.com/console page.

This is a useful tool for exploring exactly how the Twitter API is returning data at the moment. You need to have a registered application to use this tool. As you can see in this example, I'm using my own application twittFilter.com. If you have not done this already, you may want to refer back to Hour 2 on registering your application.

Something really useful with this tool is the display of the response headers. For example, here are the response headers I get when making the call '..statuses/user_timeline', as you can see in Figure 18.4.

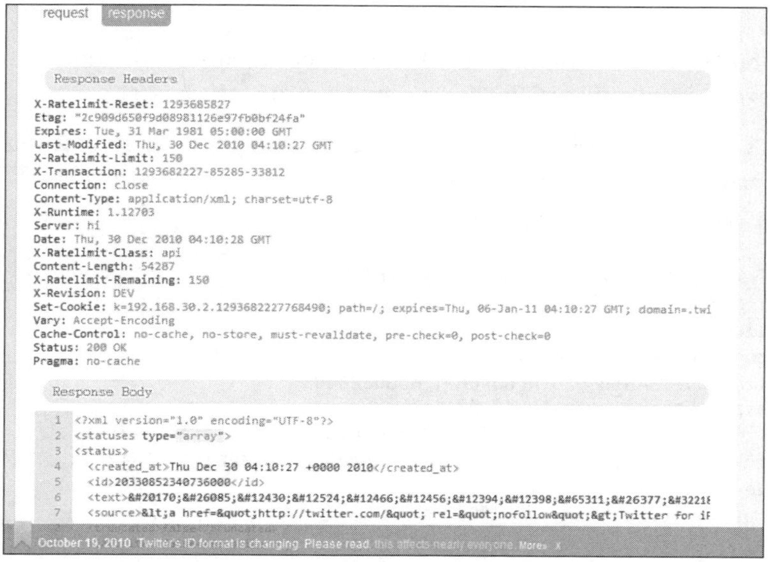

FIGURE 18.4 statuses/user_timeline console response.

Response headers:

```
X-Ratelimit-Reset: 1284408284
Etag: "f739af2f2888af9..."
Expires: Tue, 31 Mar 1981 05:00:00 GMT
Last-Modified: Mon, 13 Sep 2010 19:04:44 GMT
X-Ratelimit-Limit: 150
X-Transaction: 1284404684-62667-59215
Connection: close
Content-Type: application/xml; charset=utf-8
X-Runtime: 0.71764
Server: hi
Date: Mon, 13 Sep 2010 19:04:45 GMT
X-Ratelimit-Class: api
Content-Length: 47666
X-Ratelimit-Remaining: 150
X-Revision: DEV
Set-Cookie: k=192.168.30.2.1284404684672016; path=/; expires=Mon, 20-Sep-10
19:04:44
 GMT; domain=.twitter.com, guest_id=1284404684xxxxx; path=/; expires=Wed,
13 Oct 2010
19:04:44 GMT, lang=en; path=/,
_twitter_sess=BAh7CjoPY3JlYXRlZF9hdGwrCI8nfAwrAToTcGFzc3dxxxxxxxxxx...; do-
main=.twitter.com; path=/
Vary: Accept-Encoding
Cache-Control: no-cache, no-store, must-revalidate, pre-check=0, post-
check=0
Status: 200 OK
Pragma: no-cache
```

Notice that we use the 'status' element of the response header to determine whether we received a valid response. In this case, we got a 200, which is 'ok'.

Now let's click the Request tab. You should see something like Figure 18.5. You can see the actual HTTP GET request that we normally see in our application:

```
opening connection to api.local.twitter.com...
opened
<- "GET /1/statuses/user_timeline.xml HTTP/1.1
Accept: */*
Connection: close
User-Agent: OAuth gem v0.3.4.1
Authorization: OAuth oauth_nonce=\"moGd323sds...\",
oauth_signature_method=\"HMAC-SHA1\",
oauth_timestamp=\"1284404684\", oauth_consumer_key=\"wIRkjfiul...\",
oauth_token=\"1171057892...\", oauth_signature=\"sAnXnlTl6XY7s8s....\",
oauth_version=\"1.0\"
Host: api.local.twitter.com:9000
```

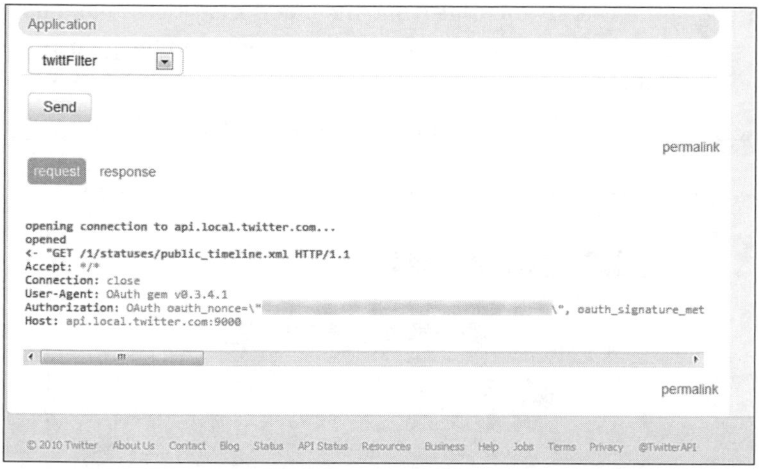

FIGURE 18.5 statuses/user_timeline console request.

The Tweet Button

Let's refer back to the main page dev.twitter.com. As you saw in Figure 18.1, there is more on this page than navigation options. Currently, Twitter's Tweet button is featured. Because it's here, let's have a look at it.

The Tweet button is a simple JavaScript call that you can place on your web page to allow a user to retweet web content. For example, on my personal blog, "As seen through PeriVisioN," I have a retweet button for each article, as shown in Figure 18.6.

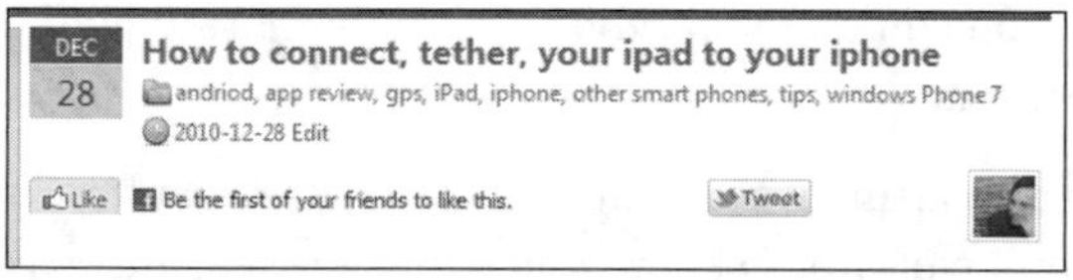

FIGURE 18.6 Retweet button on PeriVisioN.

The user experience for using the Tweet button is standard, as you can see from the following steps and Figure 18.7:

1. The user clicks the Tweet button.
2. The user is asked to log in to Twitter if the user isn't already logged in. The user who is new to Twitter can also create an account.
3. The Share box appears already completed with the information provided in the properties of the Tweet button. Users can change the content if they wish.

4. Posting of the Tweet is confirmed, and the user is suggested a maximum of two accounts the user may want to follow as provided in the properties of the Tweet button.
5. The Share box remains open until the user clicks Close.

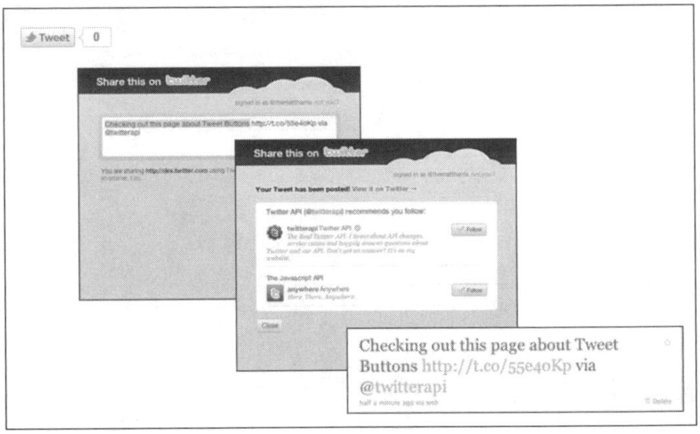

FIGURE 18.7
Retweet button experience.

Implementation is also easy. Here are three ways you can do it, as posted on http://dev.twitter.com/pages/tweet_button.

Using JavaScript

The easiest way to add the Tweet button to your website is to use JavaScript. This method requires adding a line of JavaScript and an HTML anchor to your web page. With this method, you can customize the Tweet button using data attributes and query string parameters.

Notice how the anchor element has a class of twitter-share-button. This is required for the Tweet button JavaScript to know which anchor elements to convert to buttons:

```
<script src="http://platform.twitter.com/widgets.js"
type="text/javascript"></script>
<a href="http://twitter.com/share" class="twitter-share-button">Tweet</a>
```

Using an iframe

If you prefer, you can add a Tweet button using an iframe. When using this method, you have to use query string parameters to customize the Tweet button's behavior:

```
<iframe allowtransparency="true" frameborder="0" scrolling="no"
        src="http://platform.twitter.com/widgets/tweet_button.html"
        style="width:130px; height:50px;"></iframe>
```

Building Your Own

If you want to be able to customize the way the Tweet button looks, you will want to use this basic format. When using this method, you have to use query string parameters to customize the Tweet button's behavior as well as handle the pop-up of the Share box.

The dimensions of the Share box are listed here in the FAQ: http://dev.twitter.com/pages/tweet_button_faq#dimensions.

Dev.twitter.com/doc

The current set of Twitter API docs that you would find on dev.twitter.com is not the same documents that Twitter started with. In fact, this collection is fairly recent; the original site was created using a wiki: http://apiwiki.twitter.com/. A screenshot of the original documentation resource can be seen in Figure 18.8, in contrast to the new system shown in Figure 18.9.

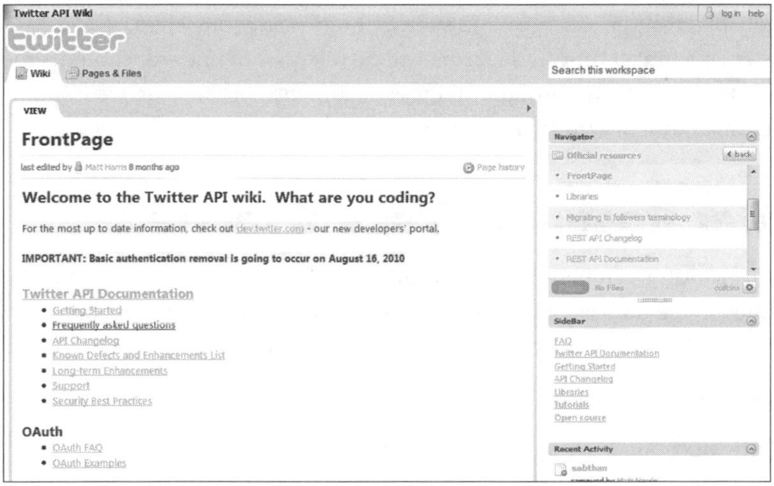

FIGURE 18.8
Twitter API wiki.

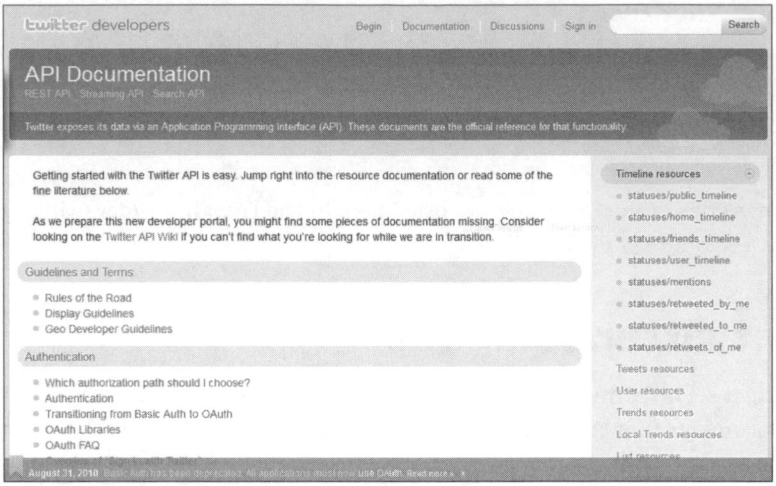

FIGURE 18.9
New twitter API page.

At the time of this writing, all the API methods have been moved, but not everything has been fully documented, and there are a few errors, omissions, and even grammatical errors, of which we are sure we have plenty ourselves, in the new document. It is anticipated that these errors will go away as the new documents mature. It's not in the scope to go through all these documents, but instead we'll highlight a few interesting and generally useful resources.

Twitter Resource Page Overview

Although the API Documentation (http://dev.twitter.com/doc) is still being created and refined, these documents are still a great resource for any programmer or product developer. The Twitter docs are broken up into seven sections:

- Guidelines and Terms
- Authentication
- REST API and General
- Streaming API and User Streams
- Search API
- @Anywhere and Tweet Button
- Ecosystem

Guidelines and Terms

There are three sections to Guidelines and Terms: Rules of the Road, Display Guidelines, and Geo Developer Guidelines.

Rules of the Road (http://dev.twitter.com/pages/api_terms) are "a set of ("Rules") that describe the policies and philosophy around what type of innovation is permitted with the content and information shared on Twitter." This section is the meatiest of the Guidelines. Here we can read about how and where you can use Twitter data. You will also discover what you CANNOT do with Twitter data, including trying to sell access to the Twitter API, and if you provide an API that returns Twitter data, you can only return IDs. Also from the docs, "Exporting Twitter Content to a datastore as a service or other cloud-based service, however, is not permitted." So, be sure you read ALL of the Twitter Content section before you even start to develop your application. You will also find information on commercial use as well as legal terms.

The Display Guidelines (http://dev.twitter.com/pages/display_guidelines) section is pretty straightforward and reflects the recommended way to display a tweet. You will notice that our application already follows most of these guidelines. At this point in the book, you should feel confident to make the modifications to satisfy this display requirement.

The Geo Developer Guidelines (http://dev.twitter.com/pages/geo_dev_guidelines) are more around privacy about a user's location as well as certain functions you should allow the user.

Authentication

We discussed OAuth in Hour 8. However, it is still a good idea to check the OAuth FAQ every now and again to see what has changed:

- Which authorization path should I choose?
- Authentication
- Transitioning from Basic Auth to OAuth
- OAuth Libraries
- OAuth FAQ
- Overview of "Sign in with Twitter"

It is strongly recommended that you look at the "OAuth Libraries" section to look for a more recent and feature-rich OAuth library than we used here now that you have a good idea of how OAuth works.

REST API and General

This area is where most programmers spend their time, and not just within the API section. Because these are new documents, a few corrections and annotations are expected:

- Recently Updated Documentation

  Whenever you find that something is not working the way you expect, it's a good idea to check the Recently Updated section in case something changed, updating your previous understanding on how the API functions.

- Introduction to @twitterapi

  A nice slideshow from @raffi on Twitter API development.

Watch Out!

> There are 99 slides in the deck at the time of this writing. Although they go fast, pace yourself.

- Things Every Developer Should Know
- Twitter API FAQ
- API Overview
- API Support
- Security Best Practices

  Whether you are a first-time coder or have been writing for years, it's a good idea to always have security in mind. Twitter provides a good checklist of things to keep in mind when building and testing your application. Even the outline from the site on its own serves as a good check-off list.

- Rate Limiting
- Rate Limiting FAQ
- HTTP Responses and Errors
- Counting Characters
- Tweet Entities

We did not spend much time on Tweet Entities in our previous hours because the feature is still in development and not fully live yet. Tweet Entities are additional structured data elements that automatically identify and reformat various known

Twitter conventions for you. For example, if a hyperlink is discovered within a tweet, that hyperlink will be provided via an attribute within JSON or XML. If the link is shorted, the full link will be provided as well. This is becoming necessary as well as useful to guard against malicious links being hidden in a URL-shortened link.

By the Way

From Wikipedia

URL shortening is a technique on the World Wide Web in which a URL may be made substantially shorter in length. This involves using an HTTP Redirect on a domain name that is short to link to a website that has a long URL. Domain names are linked to IP addresses; however, in order to be human friendly, the Latin alphabet can be used. Sometimes this can lead to extremely long URLs. For example, the URL http://en.wikipedia.org/w/index.php?title=TinyURL&diff=283621022&oldid=283308287 can be shortened to http://tinyurl.com/mmw6lb.

Streaming API Documentation and Search API

Streaming on Twitter is normally used only in very specific applications, and as such was not included in this book in detail. However, we will discuss it in Hour 19. As for search, we covered much of these sections in previous hours; however, the search API section is a very handy reference section for building a search query, so that is worth bookmarking.

@Anywhere and Tweet Button

@Anywhere and the Tweet Buttons are Twitter's early attempts at creating widgets for making the adding of Twitter functionality to a website easier. @Anywhere is an interesting effort by Twitter that will allow you to place Twitter widgets within other applications. For example, one of the @Anywhere widgets is a 'hovercard'. This widget pops up a simple Twitter card upon rollover, as shown in Figure 18.10.

The code to implement this is pretty easy:

```
<script type="text/javascript">

  twttr.anywhere(function (T) {
    T.hovercards();
  });

</script>
```

FIGURE 18.10
@Anywhere hovercard

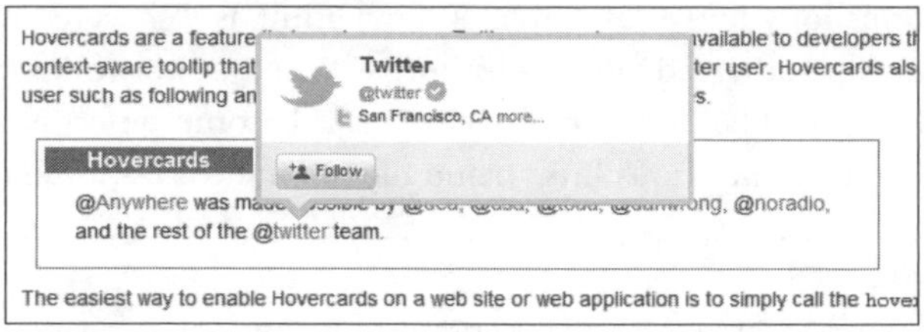

Watch Out!

> Twitter recommends that you set and register a separate application for use with @Anywhere

Ecosystem

This section contains information about non-programmatic issues, like libraries, where to find Developers, mention of @twitterapi - a twitter account about the Twitter API, and a mailing list.

As a developer, I'm on one of the mailing lists, but I caution you, there is a lot of traffic on these lists. I would strongly recommend that you select the option to receive only one email a day.

Summary

In this hour, we looked at many of the API resources that are made available on dev.twitter.com. Many of these documents we have referenced before. We explored the console page and looked at the Twitter widget Reweet button.

Also in this hour, we looked at the online Twitter docs and explored how they are structured. We also touched on recommended best practices and security recommendations.

Q&A

Q. ***Because the old API docs on apiwiki.twitter.com/ are being deprecated in favor of dev.twitter.com/docs, can we ignore the apiwiki completely?***

A. At some point, yes, but at the time of this writing, a few small details in the old docs have not made it to the new ones. So, if you do not find what you looking for, it may be worth the time to try the older docs.

Q. ***If the user does not have Tweeting With Location enabled, can I enable via API calls?***

A. At this time, you cannot, nor do I think you will able to in the future, but that could change.

Workshop

Quiz

1. If you wanted to look at response headers, what tool does Twitter offer to help with this?
2. What is a URL shortener?
3. What are the "Rules of the Road?"

Quiz Answers

1. Dev.twitter.com/console.
2. URL shortening is a technique on the Web in which a URL may be made substantially shorter in length. This involves using an HTTP Redirect on a domain name that is short to link to a website that has a long URL.
3. A set of ("Rules") that describes the policies and philosophy around what type of innovation is permitted with the content and information shared on Twitter. Make sure you read them.

Exercise

We did not do this in our sample program, so as an exercise, put the Retweet button in your application. Use either the JavaScript or iframe version.

HOUR 19

Streaming API

What You'll Learn in This Hour:

- The three types of streaming APIs
- The user streams and site streams
- The Firehose, Gardenhose, Birddog, and Shadow

The Three Types of Streaming APIs

Because search was never designed to support large-scale queries or the volume of tweets Twitter has seen recently, the streaming architecture was put in place.

There are three Twitter API sets: the RESTful APIs, Search, and the streaming APIs. Streaming is as it sounds, opening up a connection to the Twitter servers and getting a stream of information back.

There are three main streaming products: the Streaming API, user streams, and sites streams. How we would call and work with each type of stream is basically the same, but each one has its own particular focus. Let's have a look at these as defined in the Twitter docs. http://dev.twitter.com/pages/streaming_api:

- **Streaming API**—Public statuses from all users, filtered in various ways: by userid, by keyword, by random sampling, by geographic location, and so on.
- **User streams**—Nearly all data required to update a user's display. This requires the user's OAuth token. It provides public and protected statuses from followings, direct messages, mentions, and other events taken on and by the user. A large number of user streams may not be created from the same host or service. For example, an application that displays a few

accounts at once may open a connection per account. The primary use case is providing updates to a Twitter client.

- **Site streams**—Allows multiplexing of multiple user streams over a site stream connection. When more than a handful of user stream connections are opened from the same host or service, site streams must be used. The primary use case is website and other service integrations.

Although there are three types of streams listed, the streaming and user streams API's would be the ones you would most likely be interested in. You can think of the Streaming API and the incoming stream from Twitter and the user streams as outgoing or what you would provide to Twitter. We will get into the particulars of how to use these API calls later in this hour.

Who Would Normally Use Streaming?

Streaming is mostly targeted to people who make the same search over and over or who need a large dataset for research or data analysis. For example, suppose you want to track the performance of a keyword over time. You would open a stream and pass the results through a set of business rules and thus update a log file(s) or a database. Trends are done somewhat like this. A stream of tweets is tracked and all found keywords are logged, so you could create your own trending application using streaming.

As stated in the Twitter docs, each of the three products has its intended uses.

The Streaming API is very useful for data analysis. To discover interesting trends in the Twitter universe, you may need quite a bit of data. For example, a very interesting experiment was done to track the movement of the swine flu virus by tracking people who tweeted the words "swine" or "flu" and displaying that information on a map.

The user streams product has a different objective. It's intended to give you everything you need or want to know about a user. This includes nonpublic information like DMs, private tweets, and so on, so you will need the user's OAuth information. Remember, we already have access to this information through our Twitter application for anyone who logs in. The user streams enable us to get much of the information that takes many API calls using just one call.

Site streams is basically user streams en mass. A vast majority of developers would not need to use site streams, but large-scale integration operations or those clients with many users would use this product.

What Makes Streaming Different?

The Streaming API methods are similar to search methods, with one major exception. This is a streaming connection, not your normal REST connection where we pass a request and we get a response. Instead, we are opening a socket connection (or a stream) to Twitter, and the Twitter servers will happily continue to feed us data for as long as we (or Twitter) keep the connection open. Keep in mind that in comparison to REST where you parse the complete response when the connection is closed, you just create a single persistent connection that has responses separated by carriage returns \r (http://dev.twitter.com/pages/streaming_api_concepts#parsing-responses).

It's important to stress that you only get one connection per account. From the Twitter docs: "Each account may create only one standing connection to the Streaming API. Subsequent connections from the same account may cause previously established connections to be disconnected. Excessive connection attempts, regardless of success, will result in an automatic ban of the client's IP address. Continually failing connections will result in your IP address being blacklisted from all Twitter access."

Pre-Launch Checklist

Within the Twitter docs we visited in the previous section, there is a checklist of things to consider before you start your streaming request. At the time of this writing, there are 11 items on the checklist. Why 11 and not the traditional 10? Actually, it was 10 when we first started writing this book, and now they have added another one—yet another indication of how fast things with Twitter change and get updated. That or it's an homage to Spinal Tap. Look it up.

1. Using the correct product?
2. Not purposefully attempting to circumvent access limits and levels?
3. Creating the minimal number of connections?
4. Avoiding duplicate logins?
5. Avoiding needless reconnection?
6. Backing off from failures: none for first disconnect, seconds for repeated network (TCP/IP) level issues, minutes for repeated HTTP (4XX codes)?
7. Using long-lived connections?
8. Tolerant of other objects and newlines in markup stream (non <status> objects...)?

9. Tolerant of duplicate and out-of-order messages?
10. Carefully monitoring the Twitter-API-Announce mailing list and using the Twitter-Dev-Talk list for questions?
11. Following @twitterapi and the @sitestreams accounts?

Item 6 is of the most important in my opinion, although I'm sure you will not be making any friends by violating item 2. Before you make *any* calls, make sure you have a timeout switch to kill the connection before trying to make a new one. Although you can use cURL to make this call, using cURL tends to have operational gotchas, so it's best to use cURL for debugging. It would also be a good idea to limit how long you keep the stream open if you are storing the information to a file. Keep in mind that Twitter will hold a connection indefinitely short of server-side errors. However, what item 6 is referring to is failing gracefully. There are plenty of reasons a connection can fail: network errors, server overload, or perhaps your client cannot keep up with the traffic flow. The best solution is to look for any HTTP response code that is over 200 and have your script pause before trying to reconnect again. It is suggested to start at 250 milliseconds and continue to up the wait time to around 16 seconds. I would recommend that after 10 consecutive errors, send a message to a human to look at the issue. Keep a log of the errors.

Parsing JSON responses from the Streaming API is simple: Every object is returned on its own line and ends with a carriage return. Newline characters (`\n`) may occur in object elements (the `text` element of a status object, for example), but carriage returns (`\r`) should not.

Not listed on the checklist, but probably should be, is planning for growth. Every time we think Twitter has gotten as big as it's going to get, it doubles again. You should make sure that whatever system you put in place to read and process the stream has enough hardware power and storage space to handle three times whatever you are experiencing now.

Streaming Methods

There are a number of API methods available to us within the stream.twitter.com API call. Each type of stream is geared to a particular use. Unlike any of the other API calls we have seen in Twitter, these types of streams all have names. For example, the most common and simple method to use is called Spritzer. This API stream provides a sample of tweets from the Twitter stream.

Keep in mind that sometimes a status will come with a delete status or a delete location. Twitter requests that you honor this delete status and remove statuses from your client and storage. Some of these delete and scrub requests can come significantly out of order. Try to account for this. Here are examples of the delete status and delete geo attributes.

Delete Status:

```
JSON : { "delete": { "status": { "id": 1234, "user_id": 3 } } }
```

Delete Geo (scrub):

```
JSON: {"scrub_geo":{"user_id":14090452,"up_to_status_id":23260136625}}
```

Watch Out!

> Remember that the API is changing all the time, so make sure your code can handle unexpected attributes that will be coming in the future.

Watch Out!

> Because of volume, the Twitter stream may not provide each status update in exactly the correct chronological order. It is not unusual to have status updates delivered 3 seconds or more out of order. If the order of the status is critical to your application, you may want to delay updates for 5 seconds to be sure that statuses are presented based on creation date, not the order it was delivered.

Types of Stream Methods

Given the enormous volume of status updates flowing through the Twitter servers, it's not necessary or practical to provide everyone with a stream of every status update. As such, Twitter provides different levels of samples from the stream. All accounts may access the statuses/sample and statuses/filter methods at default access levels. To apply for greater level access, refer to the support page (http://dev.twitter.com/pages/support) or email Twitter directly at api@twitter.com.

The Streaming methods are similar to the search methods, including supporting only JSON. Let's have a look at these methods as currently documented in Twitter docs (http://dev.twitter.com/pages/streaming_api_methods).

POST statuses/filter: Returns public statuses that match one or more filter predicates. At least one predicate parameter, follow, locations, or track must be specified. Multiple parameters may be specified, which allows most clients to use a single connection to the Streaming API. Placing long parameters in the URL may cause the request to be rejected for excessive URL length. Use a POST request header parameter to avoid long URLs.

There are various levels of access (or roles) you can apply for with the API filter:

- The default access level allows up to 400 track keywords, 5,000 follow userids, and 25 0.1-360 degree location boxes.
- Shadow role allows 100,000 follow userids.
- Birddog role allows 400,000 follow userids.
- Restricted track role allow for 10,000 track keywords.
- Partner Track role allows for 200,000 track keywords.
- LocRestricted role supports 200 0.1-360 degree location boxes.

Any increased track access levels also pass a higher proportion of statuses before limiting the stream. You can apply for greater tracking and access by filling out the online form currently found here:
https://spreadsheets.google.com/viewform?hl=en&formkey=dFBTbHZIMVhseUtqS2NkT283RTluX3c6MQ&ndplr=1#gid=0.

Here is an abbreviated list of parameters statuses/filter supports. Details on these parameters can be found in the referenced Twitter docs:

- **count**—Indicates the number of previous statuses to consider for delivery before transitioning to live stream delivery.
- **delimited**—Indicates that statuses should be delimited in the stream. Statuses are represented by a length, in bytes, a newline, and the status text that is exactly length bytes.
- **follow**—Returns public statuses that reference the given set of users. Users are specified by a comma-separated list.
- **locations**—Specifies a set of bounding boxes to track. Only tweets that are both created using the Geotagging API and are placed from within a tracked bounding box will be included in the stream.
- **track**—Specifies keywords to track. Keywords are specified by a comma-separated list.

GET statuses/firehose: Returns all public statuses. The Firehose is not a generally available resource. Few applications require this level of access. Creative use of a combination of other resources and various access levels can satisfy nearly every application use case.

Here is an abbreviated list of parameters statuses/firehose supports. Details on these parameters can be found in the referenced Twitter docs:

- **count**—Indicates the number of previous statuses to consider for delivery before transitioning to live stream delivery.
- **delimited**—Indicates that statuses should be delimited in the stream. Statuses are represented by a length, in bytes, a newline, and the status text that is exactly length bytes.

GET statuses/links: Returns all statuses containing http: and https:. The links stream is not a generally available resource.

Here is an abbreviated list of parameters statuses/retweet supports. Details on these parameters can be found in the referenced Twitter docs:

- **count**—Indicates the number of previous statuses to consider for delivery before transitioning to live stream delivery.
- **delimited**—Indicates that statuses should be delimited in the stream. Statuses are represented by a length, in bytes, a newline, and the status text that is exactly length bytes.

GET statuses/retweet: Returns all retweets. The retweet stream is not a generally available resource. Few applications require this level of access. Creative use of a combination of other resources and various access levels can satisfy nearly every application use case.

Here is an abbreviated list of parameters statuses/retweet supports. Details on these parameters can be found in the referenced Twitter docs:

- **delimited**—Indicates that statuses should be delimited in the stream. Statuses are represented by a length, in bytes, a newline, and the status text that is exactly length bytes.

GET statuses/sample: Returns a random sample of all public statuses. The default access level provides a small proportion of the Firehose. The "Gardenhose" access level provides a proportion more suitable for data mining and research applications that desire a larger proportion to be statistically significant sample.

Here is an abbreviated list of parameters statuses/sample supports. Details on these parameters can be found in the referenced Twitter docs:

- **count**—Indicates the number of previous statuses to consider for delivery before transitioning to live stream delivery.

- **delimited**—Indicates that statuses should be delimited in the stream. Statuses are represented by a length, in bytes, a newline, and the status text that is exactly length bytes.

Summary

In this hour, we learned about the Streaming API and the three main products of the Streaming API: the Streaming API, user streams, and site streams. We also learned about a very useful pre-launch checklist provided by Twitter.

In addition, we learned about filtering the stream and the various parameters we can employ.

Q&A

Q. ***If I'm building a normal Twitter client, do I really need to employ streaming?***

A. No. Streaming is typically used for special purposes where you need lots of data for analysis.

Q. ***What is the advantage of using streaming?***

A. In addition to a far greater amount of data being available to you, it also is a persistent connection, meaning that you do not have to keep making cURL calls to maintain a flow of data. If your application requires real-time data or a large amount of data, streaming is worth the extra work required to support it.

Workshop

Quiz

1. Twitter gave you a list of 11 things you need to consider before you start streaming. Can you list five of them without looking back at the text?
2. What are the sampling rates for Spritzer and Gardenhose?
3. What type of connection gives you everything?

Quiz Answers

1. Things to consider before streaming include the following:
   - Using the correct product?
   - Not purposefully attempting to circumvent access limits and levels?
   - Creating the minimal number of connections?
   - Avoiding duplicate logins?
   - Avoiding needless reconnection?
   - Backing off from failures: none for first disconnect, seconds for repeated network (TCP/IP) level issues, minutes for repeated HTTP (4XX codes)?
   - Using long-lived connections?
   - Tolerant of other objects and newlines in markup stream (non <status> objects...)?
   - Tolerant of duplicate and out-of-order messages?
   - Using JSON if at all possible?
   - Planning for growth.
2. ~1% for Spritzer, ~5% for Gardenhose.
3. Firehose, but this is only by request.

Exercises

Create a test page that opens up a stream for 3 seconds and then displays the result. Do not worry about displaying formatting for this exercise; the key is to open a connection, process the data, and then close the connection. After you have done it for 3 seconds, try 15, and then try 5 minutes. You may find it easier to open and write the output to a file.

HOUR 20

FailWhale and the Future of the API

What You'll Learn in This Hour:

- The History of the FailWhale
- How to get your application to retry if Twitter is not working
- What 420 really means
- The future of the Twitter API

What Is Spotting the FailWhale?

We touched this briefly in Hour 6, but now it's time to formalize how we deal with getting replies back from Twitter that are other than what we expect, and twitter servers being over capacity; sometimes referred to as spotting the FailWhale. First, what is the FailWhale?

The designer behind the FailWhale, Yiying Lu (http://www.yiyinglu.com/sc/illustration) had posted the image to the stock photo website, iStockPhoto (that image is now removed). The original title of this artwork was "Lifting a Dreamer." Twitter adapted this image for its 502 and 503 HTTP response pages. In a discussion thread on FriendFeed about Twitter's downtime art, Robert Scoble deemed that it should be called FailWhale, and it stuck. "Fail" was already an existing Internet meme, at the time used for anything that was not successful in one way or another. For a brief time, Twitter tried to get rid of the FailWhale with a generic overcapacity message, and later other graphics, but user backlash caused it to be reinstated. The FailWhale has become so popular that it even has a fan club, failwhale.com (http://failwhale.com/). Because Twitter's growth and popularity exceeded anyone's expectations, the FailWhale was seen over and over again, and it became a reference for Twitter being down.

The FailWhale has become so well known that other variations have appeared, including Homer Simpson as the whale, a beer called Fail Whale Pale Ale, cakes, pumpkins, and of course printed on t-shirts, jackets, and coffee mugs.

Now that we know the history of the FailWhale, and why it appears, let's figure out a way to deal with it so we can have our own "Fail" art pages.

Just a reminder, the following are the currently supported HTTP response codes from Twitter:

- **200 OK**—Success!
- **304 Not Modified**—There was no new data to return.
- **400 Bad Request**—The request was invalid. An accompanying error message will explain why. This is the status code that will be returned during rate limiting.
- **401 Unauthorized**—Authentication credentials were missing or incorrect.
- **403 Forbidden**—The request is understood, but it has been refused. An accompanying error message will explain why. This code is used when requests are being denied because of update limits.
- **404 Not Found**—The URI requested is invalid or the resource requested, such as a user, does not exist.
- **406 Not Acceptable**—Returned by the Search API when an invalid format is specified in the request.
- **420 Enhance Your Calm**—Returned by the Search and Trends API when you are being rate limited.
- **500 Internal Server Error**—Something is broken. Please post to the group so the Twitter team can investigate.
- **502 Bad Gateway**—Twitter is down or being upgraded.
- **503 Service Unavailable**—The Twitter servers are up, but overloaded with requests. Try again later.

Did You Know?

There is a standard for what HTTP response codes are supposed to indicate, but it's up to the one who set up the server configuration to decide what they will mean. For example, 420 used by Twitter is not a standard response code. There is even a 418 code saying, I'm a teapot: The HTCPCP server is a teapot. The responding entity may be short and stout. Defined by the April Fools specification RFC 2324. See Hypertext Coffee Pot Control Protocol for more information: http://en.wikipedia.org/wiki/Hyper_Text_Coffee_Pot_Control_Protocol.

Review of the Application We Just Built

It's Hour 20, and we have covered a lot of ground in very little time. It's a good time to step back to review what we have built, how we are using the API currently, and how we may want to use it in the future.

Application Architecture

In Hour 3, we talked about the various types of Twitter applications. So, what did we just build over the past 20 hours? Well, believe it or not, we created a functioning Twitter application. Notice I did not say full featured because there are some elements we glossed over in the interest of time.

Did You Know?

The first Twitter.com website had fewer features than what we have created here. Only recently has Twitter.com updated its site's features and functions with a major upgrade in the fall of 2010.

So, let's take a look at a diagram of our application architecture, as shown in Figure 20.1.

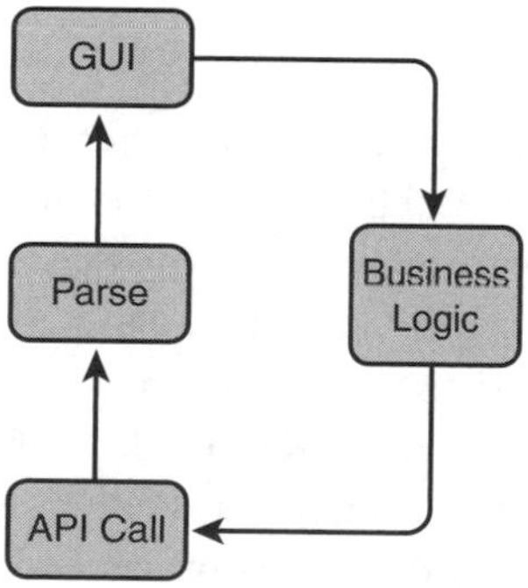

FIGURE 20.1 High-level architectural view of our Twitter application.

We have a straightforward application structure that can support almost any future API methods that Twitter will come up with. Let's take a closer look at the API Call box in our architecture diagram in Figure 20.2.

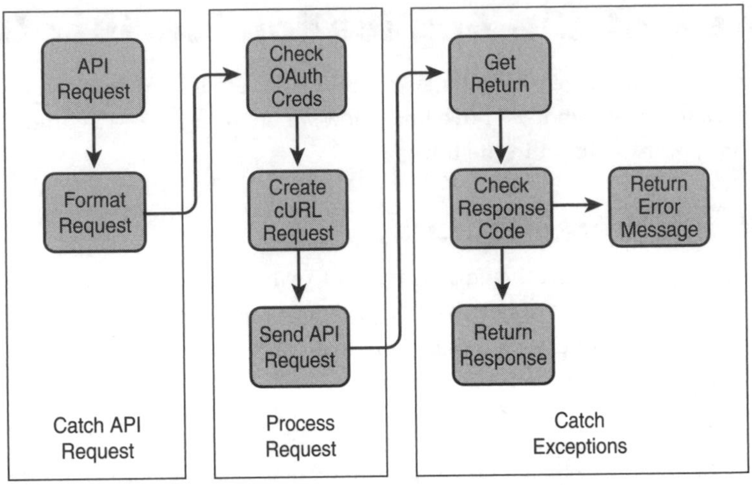

FIGURE 20.2 Architecture of our API class.

As we can see from the diagram, we have three main parts of the class: Catch API Request, Process Request, and Catch Exceptions. In Hour 8, we explored Abraham Williams' OAuth class and talked a little bit about how it worked, but now that we have learned about the API, it's a good idea revisit this class and understand it within the larger context of developing a Twitter application.

Catch API Request

Almost all our work on the file twitteroauth.php has been around defining function calls to catch requests from our application. A good question to ask is, "Why didn't we just build the request in the application?" The reason is that the Twitter API is ever evolving. Twitter makes a great effort to make sure its changes will not break things, but as Twitter continues its massive growth and evolution of product offerings, we have to be prepared. Another reason to keep the API class outside the application is the ease of replacing the current class with a more updated class library. Although the class library we used in this book serves our purpose in its clarity and simplicity, you may be well served to explore more recent and sophisticated classes to use with your application. So, let's take a look at one of the functions we use to format our API call for catching API calls:

```
function showgeo_search($options){
  $api_call = '/geo/search.json?query='.$options;
  return $this->get($api_call);
}
```

This should be old hat to you by now. We have our function call, the options we want to pass, construction of the $api_call variable, and the actual call to the function that begins the Process Request part of our class. This is pretty typical, but do you remember this function call?

```
function getMentions($format, $id = NULL, $count = 60, $since = NULL) {
        if ($id != NULL) {
                $api_call = sprintf("statuses/mentions/%s.%s", $id,
➥$format);
        }
        else {
                $api_call = sprintf("statuses/mentions.%s", $format);
        }

        if($since != NULL){
                $api_call .= sprintf("?since_id=%s", urlencode($since));
                $count=0;
        }

        if ($count != 60 AND $count!='') {
                $api_call .= sprintf("?count=%d", $count);
        }

        return $this->get($api_call);
}
```

Not every API request catch function is a few simple lines. As Twitter starts to get more and more RESTful, we will see more attributes that will be passed to Twitter after the initial REST call. Also, by keeping these calls separate, we can customize our default setting based on our needs. For example, we may write a function knowing the default response from Twitter is 20 statuses. Then, it changes to 60, but our application is not set up to handle that many status updates. By explicitly stating how many returns we expect to get back by default, we can better manage changes in how Twitter provides returns to us.

What to Do When the Twitter Service Is Down

From time to time, the Twitter servers will not be able to respond to your API request. There will also be times when your users have used more than the current limit of Twitter API calls. To deal with this, we need to examine the HTTP response codes we talked about at the top of this hour and respond accordingly.

First, we'll add a few simple lines of code to allow us to respond to the unexpected.

Edit twitteroauth.php

Open the twitteroauth.php file and add some code. Find the following lines:

```
curl_setopt($ci, CURLOPT_URL, $url);
$response = curl_exec($ci);
$this->http_code = curl_getinfo($ci, CURLINFO_HTTP_CODE);
$this->last_api_call = $url;
```

Add the following lines, including the comment text:

```
$errCode = $this->http_code;
/*
200 OK: Success!
304 Not Modified: There was no new data to return.
400 Bad Request: The request was invalid. An accompanying error message
will explain why. This is the status code will be returned during rate
limiting.
401 Not Authorized: Authentication credentials were missing or incorrect.
403 Forbidden: The request is understood, but it has been refused. An
accompanying error message will explain why. This code is used when
requests are being denied due to update limits.
404 Not Found: The URI requested is invalid or the resource requested, such
as a user, does not exist.
406 Not Acceptable: Returned by the Search API when an invalid format is
specified in the request.
420 Enhance Your Calm—Returned by the Search and Trends API when you are
being rate limited.
500 Internal Server Error: Something is broken. Please post to the group so
the Twitter team can investigate.
502 Bad Gateway: Twitter is down or being upgraded.
503 Service Unavailable: The Twitter servers are up, but overloaded with
requests. Try again later. The search and trend methods use this to
indicate when you are being rate limited.
*/
                    switch ($errCode) {
                                        case '400':
                                            { return $response; }
                            break;
                                        case '401':
                                            { return $response; }
                            break;
                                        case '403':
                                            { return '<err>403</err> '; }
                            break;
                    }
                    if(stristr($errCode,'200') ) {} else {
                      print '<h4>status '.$response.'</h4><br>';
                      print "Calling Twitter again ...<p>";
                      $i++; if ($i>2) { print 'Giving up'; return; }
         sleep(2);
         curl_setopt($ci, CURLOPT_CONNECTTIMEOUT , $timeout);
➥//CURLOPT_TIMEOUT
         $response = curl_exec($ci);
```

```
        if (empty($response)){
          print "<h4>Sorry, twitter just does not want to talk now. Try
➥again in a few min? <p></h4>";
          break;
        }
                    }
```

Save your file and close.

The commented code is clear enough. We are keeping a log of the existing possible HTTP response codes that Twitter will return. This is useful for when new error codes come into being, such as the 420 code: Enhance your calm.

Did You Know?

> 420 is a fairly well-known shorthand in the Internet community to represent smoking, planting, or just identifying the use of marijuana. The joke here is that you are trying to hit the Search and Trends servers too often and need to slow down. Who says the people at Twitter do not have a sense of humor?

The next lines are pretty straightforward. We are using a case switch for some of the 40x conditions. We also set up the switch to make one of the exercises at the end of the hour easier for some beginning programmers.

The next line, however, is more interesting:

```
if(stristr($errCode,'200') ) {} else {
```

Here we are checking to see if we have any response code other than '200'. Remember that we already have accounted for 400–403, so all other current and future codes will be handled here.

We want to catch the unknown exceptions here because often, and more often than Twitter would like, the service will be come unavailable. However, waiting one or two seconds can be enough that the service will come back on again. So, we want to put our script to sleep for two seconds and then try the API call again. You can see how we are doing by using $i as a counter to keep track of how many times we retry hitting the Twitter servers, as you can see in the following lines:

```
              $i++; if ($i>2) { print 'Giving up'; return; }
sleep(2);
curl_setopt($ci, CURLOPT_CONNECTTIMEOUT , $timeout); //CURLOPT_TIMEOUT
$twitter_data = curl_exec($ci);
```

Notice that if $i is greater than 2, we printed 'Giving up' and then return the function call. You could set this higher and keep hitting Twitter over and over, but this is frowned upon and considered bad practice. In addition, if Twitter finds that you are constantly hitting the servers and the same non-200 response code is given, you may find yourself flagged and have your privileges revoked.

We also have a check for when 'nothing' comes back:

```
if (empty($twitter_data)){
  print "<h4>Sorry, twitter just does not want to talk now.. Try again in a
few min? <p></h4>";
  break;
}
```

Although here we print a simple message saying that Twitter does not want to talk right now, we could also put our own version of a FailWhale at this point.

Where Is the Twitter API Going?

Those of us who have been using the Twitter API since the beginning have seen some interesting changes in the approach and style of how the API is designed and implemented. Although Twitter tries not to break past applications with API changes, it has happened and most likely will happen again. Greater and greater load requirements exist for Twitter to make changes to support the growing user base and expand Twitter's functionality.

First, if you were to ask 10 people at Twitter where the API is going, you will get 11 responses back, most likely because at least one person will change his or her mind. That is not unexpected because right now the major focus of Twitter is to keep the system stable. Changes in the API, however, can give us clues about where it will be in the future.

Have a look at the List API methods. Remember from Hour 13 that we had an approach to the API we had not seen before. With the List API, we use the same URL method call for :user/:lists/:id, but to accomplish three different tasks. This is because we would use different cURL protocols; for example, GET: Shows the specified list; POST: Updates the specified list; and DELETE: Deletes the specified list.

Although there is no official position on this, I would expect that we will see future API calls working this way.

Remember Search? The search and trend protocols do not work like the rest of the Twitter API family because of search having been developed by an outside company. There have been intentions to revise the search API to work more like the rest of the Twitter API, but because of the amount of work required to keep Twitter running and to update features and functions, it is simply not worth the time and effort to revise something that already works. Will we see major changes in the search or trends APIs in the future? Not likely. Instead, Twitter has invested significant time and effort in its streaming functionality, which has taken a good deal of pressure off the search API methods.

Attributes

Twitter has been working to expand the functionality of the API set to allow users to become even more creative. One idea was to allow users to define their own attributes that would be attached to each status. It was a great idea but had to be put on the shelf because of some technical difficulties and yet another massive traffic growth spike. Although on the sideline for now, I fully expect user-defined attributes at some point in the future. A user-defined attribute could be quite interesting and allow tweets to become more self-defining. Imagine a tweet having meta information about the tweet. Perhaps the tweet is a headline and the attribute contains more information like the source of the story, or type of tweet (that is, funny, business, stock, and so on). How would this work with the API? Most likely the same way we have seen all the other API calls: perhaps /userDefined?

Widgets and a New Web Interface

In 2010, two big changes happened with Twitter, but not around the API. Twitter introduced widgets. We discussed them briefly in Hour 18. We can expect a few more widgets to be released by Twitter, and perhaps an API that is dedicated to interacting with special functions on these widgets. We also saw a new web interface in mid-2010 that did not expose more API calls; however, as Twitter starts to put more effort into its web-based tools, as well as its recently released iPhone and iPad applications, perhaps we can look forward to new features and functionality that can be exposed via the API.

Speaking of iPhones, it's clear that mobile devices and thin tablets will become more and more prevalent. There are features and functions that lend themselves to mobile and tablet devices that are not needed or well supported with a web-based client. As Twitter matures its current offering in this sphere, new features and functions will come online and, hopefully, the API will expand to support information generated or unique to its display.

Summary

In this hour, we learned that Twitter shows a graphic when something is wrong on the server side, normally overcapacity. This image was coined the FailWhale and gained a significant level of popularity as a standalone meme.

We learned how to catch HTTP response codes that are not 200, meaning everything seems fine, and perform different actions based on the response code. We also learned how to pause and resend our request to Twitter as a workaround incase the Twitter servers are not able to fulfill our API requests.

Q&A

Q. ***If the Twitter servers are not responding, and given the massive growth Twitter has experienced, what would be the most likely HTTP response code you would see when Twitter is overloaded?***

A. 502 or 503.

Q. ***What is the advantage of keeping our API library separated from our application code?***

A. The advantage is making changes, upgrade, or complete library replacement easier. Given the rapid changes at Twitter, this is highly recommended.

Q. ***What is the future of Twitter?***

A. Trick question. No one knows the future of Twitter, not even the people at Twitter.

Workshop

Quiz

1. Of the HTTP response codes we have explored in this hour, which one is not standard HTTP response code?
2. Why is it not a good idea to build API calls directly in the application?
3. What is the HTTP response code 304, and what type of error page should be created for it?

Quiz Answers

1. 420 Enhance Your Calm. It is returned by the Search and Trends API when you are being rate limited.

2. It's not a good idea because the API is always evolving and expanding. Also, new libraries are created and old ones are updated often, so it's to your advantage to make updating and changing the API library as easy as possible.

3. Not Modified—There was no new data to return. Unlike other HTTP Response codes, 304 as well as 200 are not errors; thus, an error page would not be appropriate for this response.

Exercise

Build your own custom pages for each error message. Try to come up with an image for each.

HOUR 21

Getting Started in Twitter Android Application

What You'll Learn in This Hour:

- Creating an AVD
- Using the Android Development Tools (ADT) plug-in for Eclipse
- Building your first Hello Android application
- Using Eclipse and Android Emulator
- Getting Twitter Java library and OAuth Java library

Introducing Android

We have spent the last 20 hours learning about the Twitter API and how to employ it using the LAMP stack. Now we are going spend the last 4 hours learning how to set up a Twitter library for mobile devices, in our case, Android and iOS4. Unless you decided to skip ahead directly to this hour, you should already be comfortable with the various API calls and how to employ them, so we will instead focus on simply getting you up and running on your mobile platform with OAuth.

Before we get started, a few words of warning. As we have stated before, this book is not intended for beginners, but those that have some experienced with programming. However, we did try to accommodate beginning programmers who are willing to look up terms and concepts that they do not understand. In the following 4 hours, we took the same approach; however, these hours are very dense with information and move quite quickly. Although a beginning programmer could successfully navigate the mobile section with the step by step technique used throughout this book, you may find yourself getting lost in the flurry of terminology used. Do not despair, you will get through it, just have a little faith and do LOTS of web searches for terms you do not understand. Also, be sure to check this book's website (http://www.twitterapi24.com/) for any changes or update since this book has gone to print. Doing so may save you some headaches down the road.

First, we are going to start with the Android SDK and Eclipse IDE, by creating a Hello Android application. A simple Hello Android application contains the basic Android application functionality and prints out the text "Hello Android" on the device screen.

You can download the Android SDK at http://developer.android.com/sdk/. Follow the Official Android documentation to install Android SDK at http://developer.android.com/sdk/installing.html. You can download the Eclipse IDE at http://www.eclipse.org/downloads/. The preferred Eclipse version for mobile development is Eclipse Classic.

It's important that you set up your Android Development Environment properly before we start working on Twitter API: Android SDK (Software Development Kit), AVD (Android Virtual Devices) Manager, Eclipse IDE (Integrated Development Environment), and ADT (Android Development Tools) plug-in.

Android ADT Plug-In

The ADT (Android Development Tools) plug-in provides the tools to develop, compile, package, and deploy Android applications:

- The Android Project Wizard
- The Android SDK (Software Development Kit) and AVD (Android Virtual Devices) Manager
- The Eclipse DDMS (Dalvik Debug Monitor Service) for monitoring and debugging Android applications
- The Android LogCat logging
- Automated builds and application deployment to Android emulators and devices
- Packing and code-signing tools for application deployment

Creating an AVD

Before you can launch the Android Emulator, you have to create an Android Virtual Device (AVD). This AVD defines the system image and device settings used by the emulator.

To create an AVD, follow these steps:

1. In Eclipse, select Window, Android SDK and AVD Manager.
2. In the left panel, select Virtual devices.
3. Click New.

4. Enter the name of AVD.

5. Select the target of platform (version of Android SDK) for the Android emulator.

6. Click Create AVD.

Creating the Hello Android Project

The Android Project Wizard creates all the required files for an Android application. Before you can create an Android project from Eclipse, ADT plug-in for Eclipse must be installed properly. Follow these steps to create a new project:

1. In Eclipse, select File, New, Project.

2. Select the Android folder and choose Android Project, as shown in Figure 21.1. Click Next.

Did You Know?

In the Build Target, you can select Android X.X or Google APIs. If you decide to use Google Map in your Android Application, select Google APIs. If you would like to use Google Android Market License APIs, select Google APIs.

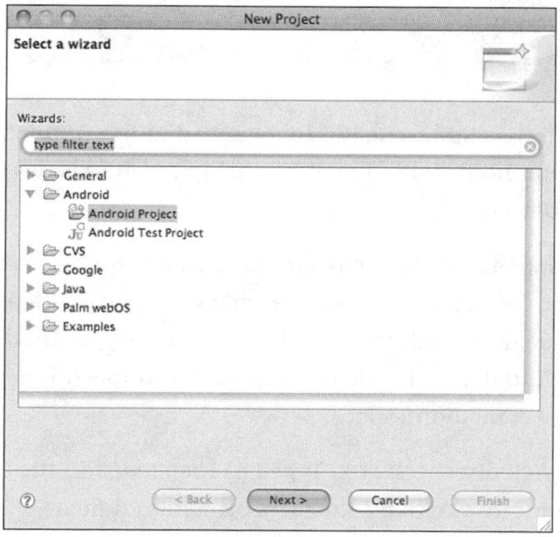

FIGURE 21.1
Selecting Android Project in the Android Project Wizard.

3. Enter `HelloAndroid` in the project name.

4. Select Create new project in workspace.

5. Select the Use default location check box.

6. In the Build Target section, select Android 2.2 on Platform 2.1 or Google APIs on Platform 2.1, as shown in Figure 21.2.

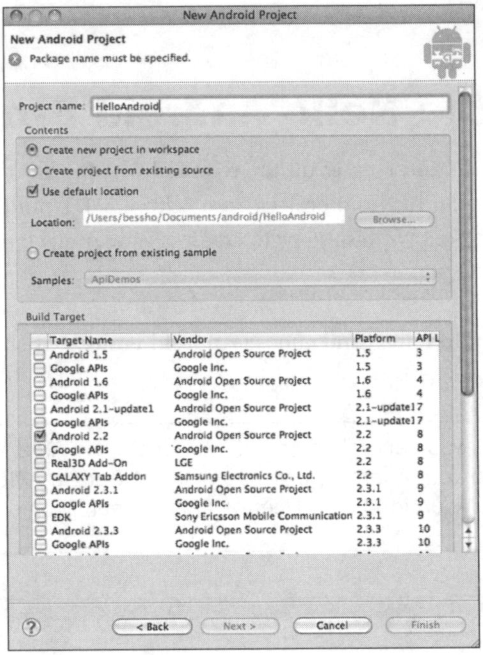

FIGURE 21.2
Creating a New Android Project in the Android Project Wizard.

7. In the Properties section, type `Hello Android` in the Application name. This application name will appear on the application screen of Android Emulator or Device.

8. Type `com.example.helloandroid` in the Package name. This is the package namespace where all your source code will reside. The package name must be unique across all packages installed on the Android. It is suggested to use a standard domain-style package for the application such as "com.example.com" namespace.

9. Select Create Activity check box. Type `helloandroid` in the Create Activity. This is for your main Activity class. It's an optional field.

10. Enter a Min SDK Version. Type `8`. This is an integer to indicate the minimum API Level required to run your application. This value will automatically set the minSdkVersion attribute in the <uses-sdk> of your Android Manifest file.

11. Click Finish.

> If you don't see the Android folder in the Android Project Wizard, you may not have a properly installed ADT plug-in.

Watch Out!

Exploring the helloandroid.java File

By now, your Android project should be created. It should be visible in the Package Explorer in the left panel. You can find the helloandroid.java file at helloandroid, src, com.example.helloandroid.

This helloandroid.java file contains the following source code:

```
package com.example.helloandroid;

import android.app.Activity;
import android.os.Bundle;

public class helloandroid extends Activity {
    /** Called when the activity is first created. */
    @Override
    public void onCreate(Bundle savedInstanceState) {
        super.onCreate(savedInstanceState);
        setContentView(R.layout.main);
    }
}
```

The class is based on the Activity class. The onCreate() method will be called by the Android system after the activity starts. This is where you initialize and set up the UI.

> To add import packages to your project, you can use Ctrl+Shift+O (PC) or Cmd-Shift-O (Mac). It's an Eclipse short key to identify missing packages based on your code and add them.

Did You Know?

Eclipse detects the missing packages and added android.R package to the code. Eclipse adds the import statement of android.R package to the helloandroid.java file:

```
package com.example.helloandroid;

import android.R;
import android.app.Activity;
import android.os.Bundle;

public class helloandroid extends Activity {
    /** Called when the activity is first created. */
    @Override
    public void onCreate(Bundle savedInstanceState) {
        super.onCreate(savedInstanceState);
        setContentView(R.layout.main);
    }
}
```

Watch Out!

> If you run the HelloAndroid application now, you will encounter an error: R.layout.main cannot be resolved in helloandroid.java line 12. You can view the error description in the Problem window.

Creating the Hello Android Application

After creating the HelloAndroid project, it's time to add your own codes.

The Android UI is composed of hierarchies of objects named Views. A view is a drawable object in the UI layout element, such as a button, image, or text label. The subclass that handles text is TextView.

You create a TextView with the class constructor that takes Android Context instance as its parameter. Define the text content with the setText() method. Display the content by passing TextView to the setContentView() method for the Activity UI.

In helloandroid.java, you will create a TextView, define the text in the setText() method, and display the content in the setContentView() method:

```
package com.example.helloandroid;

import android.app.Activity;
import android.os.Bundle;
import android.widget.TextView;

public class helloandroid extends Activity {
    /** Called when the activity is first created. */
    @Override
    public void onCreate(Bundle savedInstanceState) {
        super.onCreate(savedInstanceState);
        TextView viewHello = new TextView(this);
        viewHello.setText("Hello Android");
        setContentView(viewHello);
    }
}
```

Eclipse detects the missing packages and adds android.widget.TextView. We can now remove the unnecessary android.R package:

1. In Eclipse, select the HelloAndroid project on the left panel. Select Run, Run As, Android Application.
2. Select Android Application and click OK.
3. In your first time, the Android AVD Error window will appear and show "Do you wish to add a new Android Virtual Device?" Click Yes.

4. In the Android Device Choose window, select Launch a new Android Virtual Device.
5. Select New.
6. In the Create new Android Virtual Device (AVD), enter `Android`.
7. In the Target drop-down list, select Android 2.2 – API Level 8.
8. In the SD Card section, select Size and MiB and enter 20.
9. Leave Skin as Built-in Default (WVGA800).
10. Click Create AVD.
11. Select Android from the list of existing Android Virtual Devices.
12. Click Start.
13. Android emulator starts and launches the Android operating system, as shown in Figure 21.3.
14. Click the Menu button to unlock the home screen.

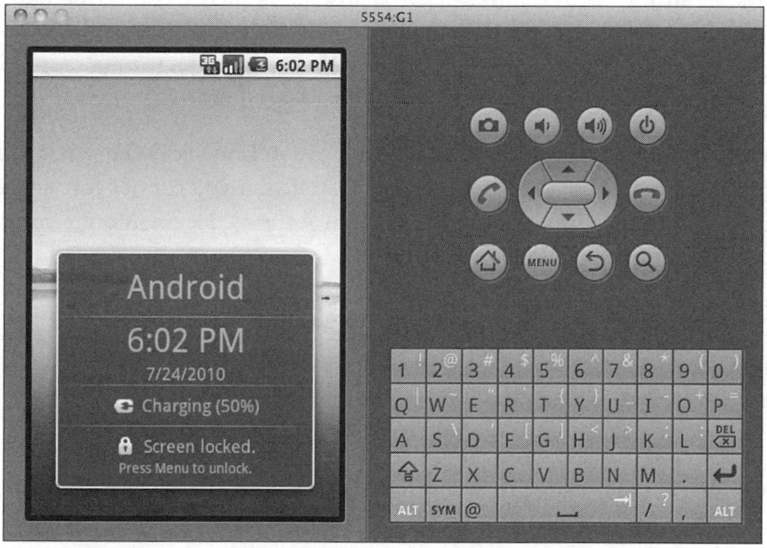

FIGURE 21.3
Unlocking the screen on the Android home screen.

15. After unlocking the home screen, the text string "Hello Android" inside the TextView appears on the screen, as shown in Figure 21.4.

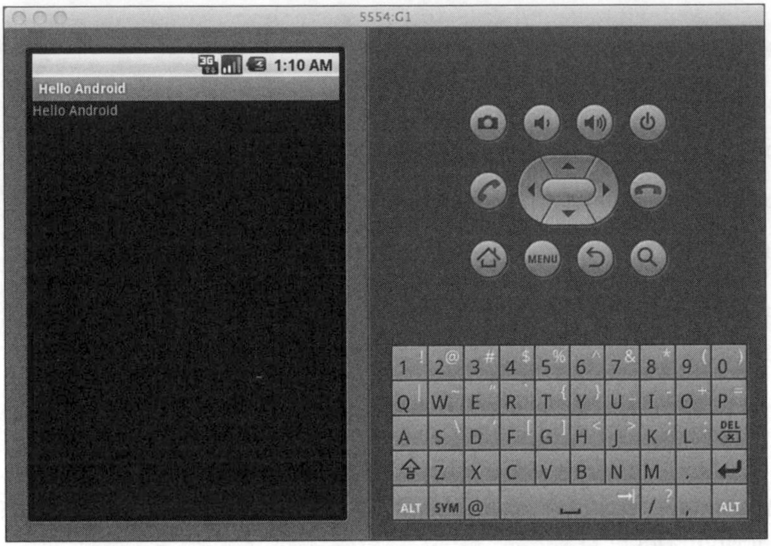

FIGURE 21.4 Launching HelloAndroid application.

The Eclipse plug-in generates the Title Bar in gray below the Status Bar. The Title Bar shows the string "Hello Android". The Eclipse plug-in creates the Title Bar automatically based on the string defined in the res/values/strings.xml file and AndroidManifest.xml file. The text below the Title Bar is the text string you have created in the TextView object.

The purpose of running the Hello Android application is to verify that your Eclipse, Android SDK, and Android ADT are properly installed. If you cannot run the Hello Android application, be sure you use the Official Android documentation as a guide and repeat the entire installation.

Watch Out!

> You must enter at least 9 MiB in size in your SD Card section.

If you have created an AVD, you can select an existing AVD in the Android Device Chooser window. Click OK. Be sure your selected AVD Target API Level matches your android:minSdkVersion in your AndroidManifest.xml file.

Android automatically generates this manifest.xml file for new Android project. To check your minimal SDK version of your Android project, open the AndroidManifest.xml file. Check the value in the <uses-sdk> tag.

1. In the Package Explorer, select and double-click to open the AndroidManifest.xml file in your HelloAndroid project folder.

2. Select the AndroidManifest.xml tab below the window to view the file in XML format.

In HelloAndroid Manifest:

```
<?xml version="1.0" encoding="utf-8"?>
<manifest xmlns:android="http://schemas.android.com/apk/res/android"
      package="com.example.helloandroid"
      android:versionCode="1"
      android:versionName="1.0">
    <uses-sdk android:minSdkVersion="8" />

    <application android:icon="@drawable/icon"
android:label="@string/app_name">
        <activity android:name=".HelloAndroid"
                  android:label="@string/app_name">
            <intent-filter>
                <action android:name="android.intent.action.MAIN" />
                <category android:name="android.intent.category.LAUNCHER" />
            </intent-filter>
        </activity>

    </application>
</manifest>
```

In the AndroidManifest.xml <uses-sdk> tag, always check if your android:minSdk Version matches your selected AVD Target API Level. If it doesn't, change the android:minSdkVersion.

This list specifies the API Level supported by each version of the Android platform:

- Android 3.0—API Level: 11
- Android 2.3.3—API Level: 10
- Android 2.3.1—API Level: 9
- Android 2.2—API Level: 8
- Android 2.1—API Level: 7
- Android 2.0.1—API Level: 6
- Android 2.0—API Level: 5
- Android 1.6—API Level: 4
- Android 1.5—API Level: 3
- Android 1.1—API Level: 2
- Android 1.0—API Level: 1

You can always find more updates and information about API Levels at the Android developer site: http://developer.android.com/guide/appendix/api-levels.html.

To understand the landscape of device distribution and prioritize the development of your Android application features, let's reveal the current distribution published by Android on May 2, 2011:

- Android 1.5 API Level 3—Distribution: 2.3%
- Android 1.6 API Level 4—Distribution: 3.0%
- Android 2.1 API Level 7—Distribution: 24.5%
- Android 2.2 API Level 8—Distribution: 65.9%
- Android 2.3 API Level 9—Distribution: 1.0%
- Android 2.3.3 API Level 10—Distribution: 3.0%
- Android 3.0 API Level 11—Distribution: 0.3%

You can always find up-to-date data at the Android developer site: http://developer.android.com/resources/dashboard/platform-versions.html.

Resolving Any AVD-Related Issues

Sometimes you may not set up everything properly to match API levels in your application. You need to start fresh. To do so, follow these steps:

1. Select the gen folder of your Android project in the Package Explorer, and right-click to select Delete.
2. Click OK.
3. Disable Project Build Automatically by selecting Project, Build Automatically.
4. Clean the project by selecting Project, Clean.
5. Select Project, Build All.
6. Debug by checking the Console window for any errors.

Resolving Any Android SDK Issues

Sometimes you will run into problems in Android ADT relating to upgrading your Android SDK or Android ADT or Eclipse. Sometimes the latest Android SDK will require a newer version of Eclipse. You would have to download and install the newer Eclipse version and then install Android ADT. To resolve any Android ADT issues, follow these steps:

1. Start a terminal window.
2. Locate your directory where you save the Android SDK. You can find the path of /android-sdk-mac_x86/platform-tools/android.
3. At the terminal prompt, type `ls -a` to view the file list.
4. Type `rm -rf .android` to remove the entire directory.

Downloading the Twitter4J Library

The Twitter developer website suggests a list of Twitter Libraries at http://dev.twitter.com/pages/libraries. Among the Java libraries, Twitter4J is widely accepted by Android developers.

Twitter4J is a Java library for the Twitter API. You can download the latest version of Twitter4J file twitter4j-core-<version>.jar at http://twitter4j.org/en/index.html#download.

A list of Twitter APIs supported by Twitter4J is documented at http://twitter4j.org/en/api-support.html.

> **Did You Know?**
> Twitter4J is thread-safe, and you can make method calls concurrently.

Downloading the OAuth Library for Java

Oauth-signpost is a simple OAuth message signing for Java. Signpost is widely accepted by Android developers. The latest version can be downloaded at http://code.google.com/p/oauth-signpost/downloads/list. Download both signpost-core-<version>.jar and signpost-commonshttp4-<version>.jar. Documentation of Signpost is available at http://kaeppler.github.com/signpost/index.html.

Summary

Congratulations! You are now an Android developer. You have downloaded tools, created a development environment and created your first Android project, however this is just the start. You still have to attach an OAuth library to allow messages to be sent back and forth to the Twitter API servers. We will cover this in the next hour.. Finally, you have run your newly created Android application on the Android Emulator. You also have downloaded Twitter libraries for Android.

Q&A

Q. ***What kind of a development environment do I need for creating an Android application?***

A. You need the JDK, Android SDK, Eclipse IDE, Android Developer Tools (ADT) plug-in, and SDK components.

Q. ***What operating systems are supported for Android application development?***

A. It is supported by Microsoft Windows XP, Vista and Windows 7, Mac OS X, and Linux.

Q. ***What features does the Android ADT plug-in provide?***

A. The Android ADT plug-in adds capacity to Eclipse to create new projects, create UIs, add components based on the Android Framework API, manage installed APIs, manage AVDs, debug using Android SDK tools, and export signed or unsigned APKs to distribute application.

Workshop

Quiz

1. Which programming languages do I use to code and develop an Android application?

A. Objective-C

B. Java

C. HTML / JavaScript / CSS

D. C++

2. Which file do you use to create the layout of the Android application?

A. helloandroid.java

B. main.xml

C. AndroidManifest.xml

3. Which element attribute in the XML<uses-sdk> tag of the AndroidManifest.xml file specifies the minimum API Level that the application is able to run?

   A. android:minSdkVersion

   B. android:targetSdkVersion

   C. android:maxSdkVersion

Quiz Answers

1. B. Use Java to write the code for the Android application.
2. B. Use main.xml to create the layout.
3. A. Use android:minSdkVersion in the <uses-sdk> tag.

Exercises

1. Install JDK, Android SDK, Eclipse, ADT plug-in, and SDK components. Create a HelloAndroid application.
2. Build Project and run the application in the Android Emulator.

HOUR 22

Building Android Applications with Twitter

What You'll Learn in This Hour:

- Creating the Android OAuth application
- Adding Java library
- Creating a layout in main.xml
- Adding Intent Filters and Permission
- Using the Java OAuth library
- Posting a tweet from an Android application
- Using xAuth in an Android application

Using Twitter OAuth in Android

At the launch of the Twitter API platform, Twitter introduced Basic Authentication. Twitter allows developers to capture and save the username and password in the native app and use them to make all API calls directly. In August 2010, Twitter banned the use of Basic Auth due to security concerns. Twitter now supports both OAuth and xAuth.

Twitter accepts the use of OAuth and xAuth to authenticate the application in a device. OAuth (Open Authorization) is an open standard for authorization that was initially designed for web authentication.

After the Android application initiates a request token, it sends the user to the Twitter website to authorize the request token in exchange for returning the access token to the user.

OAuth-Signpost is a simple HTTP message signing on the Java platform in conformance with the OAuth Core 1.0a standard. OAuth-Signpost has been widely used in Android.

Selecting Twitter Java Libraries

The most popular Twitter Java libraries, Twitter4J and JTwitter, support Android implementation. OAuth Java library OAuth-Signpost works well with these Twitter Java libraries.

Creating an Android OAuth Application

It's time to start a new Android project and add the external libraries. Be sure you follow these steps:

1. In the Package Explorer panel, right-click the project and select New, Folder.
2. Enter lib in the folder name field and click Finish.
3. Open the folder where you keep the downloaded libraries.
4. Select the signpost-commonshttp4-<version>.jar, signpost-core-<version>.jar, and twitter4j-core-<version>.jar files.
5. Drag these files from the folder to the lib folder inside the Package Explorer panel.
6. In the Package Explorer panel, right-click the project and select Properties.
7. Select Java Build Path and select the Libraries tab.
8. Click the Add JARs button.
9. Expand the Android project until you see the lib folder. Select all .jar files and click OK.
10. You should see the added .jar files, as shown in Figure 22.1.
11. Click OK.

After adding the external libraries, you will find that a new folder, Referenced Libraries, is created by Eclipse.

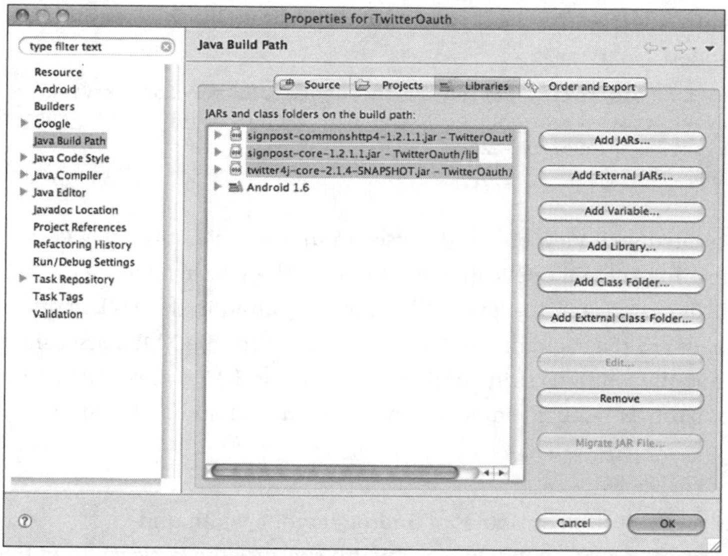

FIGURE 22.1 Adding external libraries to the Android project.

Creating the Layout

The layout is the architecture for the user interface in an Activity. The layout also defines the layout structure and holds all the visible UI elements. You can declare UI elements in XML or instantiate layout elements at runtime. You can create and manipulate the View and ViewGroup objects and its properties programmatically.

In this Android application, we declare the UI in XML. The advantage is that it separates the presentation layer from your behavior, similar to the MVC model. It allows you to create XML layouts for different screen orientations, different device screen sizes, and different languages. It is much easier to debug layout issues to visualize the UI structure in XML.

Each layout file must contain only one root element of a View or ViewGroup object. In this XML layout, we use a vertical LinearLayout to hold a TextView and a Button. The layout file is located in res/layout/main.xml:

```
<LinearLayout xmlns:android="http://schemas.android.com/apk/res/android"
    android:orientation="vertical"
    android:layout_width="fill_parent"
    android:layout_height="fill_parent"
> </LinearLayout>
```

In this app layout, we first create a text label "Twitter OAuth" by using a TextView tag with an id "TextView":

```
<TextView android:text="Twitter OAuth" android:id="@+id/TextView" an-
droid:layout_width="wrap_content" android:layout_height="wrap_content" an-
droid:layout_marginBottom="20dp">
</TextView>
```

ID is associated with View object. It is used to uniquely identify the View within the tree. When the Android application is compiled, the ID is referenced as an integer, but the ID is assigned in the layout XML file as a string in the XML id attribute. The at symbol (@) at the beginning of the string states that the XML parser should parse and expand the entire ID string and identify it as an ID resource. The plus-symbol (+) refers to a new resource name that must be created and added to the R.java file:

```
android:id="@+id/TextView"
```

TextView contains XML attributes of android:layout_width and android:layout_height. android:layout_width specifies the basic width of the TextView. It is a required attribute for any view inside of a containing layout manager. Available units are px (pixels), dp (density-independent pixels), sp (scaled pixels based on preferred font size), in (inches), and mm (millimeters). wrap_content defines to size itself to the dimension required by its content (with padding). Another option is fill_parent (renamed match_parent in API Level 8), which resizes the view as big as its parent view group (without padding). Similar rules apply to android:layout_height.

TextView contains XML attributes of android:layout_marginBottom. android:layout_marginBottom specifies the extra space on the bottom side of the view, and this space is outside the view's bounds. Other options are android:layout_marginLeft, android:layout_marginRight, and android:layout_marginTop.

Next, we create a button with the text label "Authenticate" by using a <Button> tag with an id "ButtonLogin":

```
<Button android:text="Authenticate" android:id="@+id/ButtonLogin" an-
droid:layout_width="wrap_content" android:layout_height="wrap_content" an-
droid:layout_marginBottom="50dp">
</Button>
```

Last, we create an empty text label by using a <TextView> tag with an id "tweet":

```
<TextView android:text="" android:id="@+id/tweet" an-
droid:layout_width="wrap_content" android:layout_height="wrap_content">
</TextView>
```

The order of the codes in the layout main.xml is shown here:

> **Did You Know?**
> Both Data Scheme and Data Authority matching are case sensitive. It is recommended to use all lowercase letters.

```
<?xml version="1.0" encoding="utf-8"?>
<LinearLayout xmlns:android="http://schemas.android.com/apk/res/android"
    android:orientation="vertical"
    android:layout_width="fill_parent"
    android:layout_height="fill_parent"
><TextView android:text="Twitter OAuth" android:id="@+id/TextView" an-
➥droid:layout_width="wrap_content" android:layout_height="wrap_content"
➥android:layout_marginBottom="20dp">
</TextView>
<Button android:text="Authenticate" android:id="@+id/ButtonLogin" an-
➥droid:layout_width="wrap_content" android:layout_height="wrap_content"
➥android:layout_marginBottom="50dp">
</Button>
<TextView android:text="" android:id="@+id/tweet" an-
➥droid:layout_width="wrap_content" android:layout_height="wrap_content">
</TextView>
</LinearLayout>
```

Adding Intent Filters and Permission

Intent is an abstract description of a performed operation. It is heavily used in launching activities and is sometimes described as the glue between activities.

IntentFilter objects are XML <intent-filter> tags in the AndroidManifest.xml file. You can filter Intent into three areas: action, data, and categories.

Action matches if any values match the Intent action or if no actions were specified in the filter. Categories match if all categories in the Intent match categories given in the filter. Data Type matches if any values match the Intent type. Data Type is classified into Data Scheme, Data Authority, and Data Path.

> **Did You Know?**
> It is not recommended to use absolute units such as pixels in specifying a layout width and height. It is highly recommended to use relative measurements, such as density-independent pixel units in dp, wrap_content, or fill_parent.

android.intent.action.VIEW is Activity Action that displays the data to the user. android.intent.category.DEFAULT is set if the activity should be an option for the default action to perform on data. android.intent.category.BROWSABLE is activities that invoke from a browser.

android:scheme is scheme part of a URI and used as a filter. android: host is the host part of a URI authority. This android: host attribute is meaningless unless android:scheme scheme attribute is also specified in the filter.

android.permission.INTERNET allows applications to open network sockets. This gives permission to access the Internet.

An Android application uses the android:minSdkVersion attribute to indicate the lowest system API Level it supported. System checks the value of android:minSdkVersion and allows the install only if the referenced integer is less than or equal to the API Level integer stored in the system. The Minimal SDK version level is set at 4 in the <uses-sdk> tag.

In this AndroidManifest.xml, it shows intent filter and permission required to integrate Twitter. The <uses-permission> tag is used to give the app permission on internet. In the <activity> tag, the single instance is added in the android:launchMode. This is to restrict the main activity to one stance:

```
<?xml version="1.0" encoding="utf-8"?>
<manifest xmlns:android="http://schemas.android.com/apk/res/android"
      package="com.example.twitteroauth"
      android:versionCode="1"
      android:versionName="1.0">
    <application android:icon="@drawable/icon"
➥android:label="@string/app_name">
        <activity android:name=".TwitterOauth"
                  android:label="@string/app_name"
                  android:launchMode="singleInstance">
            <intent-filter>
                <action android:name="android.intent.action.MAIN" />
               <category android:name="android.intent.category.LAUNCHER" />
            </intent-filter>
            <intent-filter>
              <action android:name="android.intent.action.VIEW" />
              <category android:name="android.intent.category.DEFAULT" />
              <category android:name="android.intent.category.BROWSABLE" />
              <data android:scheme="myapp" android:host="twitteroauth" />
            </intent-filter>
        </activity>

    </application>
<uses-sdk android:minSdkVersion="4" />
<uses-permission android:name="android.permission.INTERNET"></uses-
permission>
</manifest>
```

Loading the XML Resource

The Android application main Java file is located in src/com.example.twitteroauth/TwitterOauth.java. When the Android application is compiled, each XML layout file is compiled into a View resource. Calling setContentView() method will load the referenced layout resource in the form of R.layout.<layout_filename>, such as R.layout.main. onCreate() method in the Activity is called by the Android framework when your Activity is launched. Keep in mind that the activity will be destroyed and re-created in an orientation change or if a physical keyboard is opened (even if the orientation is locked).

This is the default TwitterOauth.java file that is created by Android project. This is your starting point where we would include packages and add codes to support Twitter authentication and posting tweet. Let's put this class in place:

```
package com.example.twitteroauth;

import android.app.Activity;
import android.os.Bundle;

public class TwitterOauth extends Activity {
    /** Called when the activity is first created. */
    @Override
    public void onCreate(Bundle savedInstanceState) {
        super.onCreate(savedInstanceState);
        setContentView(R.layout.main);

    }
}
```

Importing Packages

Java classes are groups in packages. A package is the same as the directory name that contains the .java file. You declare the packages when you define the Android application. Name the packages from other libraries in an import statement. Activity class is in the app package, which is located in the Android package. Android.app.Activity is a standard screen with no specialization.

It's time to add the additional packages from other libraries we need from Twitter4J, Signpost, and additional Android packages.

In TwitterOauth.java:

```
package com.example.twitteroauth;

import java.sql.Date;
```

```
import oauth.signpost.OAuthConsumer;
import oauth.signpost.OAuthProvider;
import oauth.signpost.commonshttp.CommonsHttpOAuthConsumer;
import oauth.signpost.commonshttp.CommonsHttpOAuthProvider;
import twitter4j.Twitter;
import twitter4j.TwitterFactory;
import twitter4j.auth.AccessToken;
import twitter4j.conf.ConfigurationBuilder;
import android.app.Activity;
import android.content.Intent;
import android.net.Uri;
import android.os.Bundle;
import android.util.Log;
import android.view.View;
import android.view.View.OnClickListener;
import android.widget.Button;
import android.widget.TextView;
import android.widget.Toast;

public class TwitterOauth extends Activity {
    /** Called when the activity is first created. */
    @Override
    public void onCreate(Bundle savedInstanceState) {
        super.onCreate(savedInstanceState);
        setContentView(R.layout.main);

    }
}
```

Adding OAuth

First, we declare APP as string in the private static final statement. Private indicates that it is visible only to the objects of the same class. Static gives only one instance of this member. Final allows it to be assigned once.

Next, we declare twitter as Twitter, provider as OAuthProvider, and consumer as CommonsHttpOAuthConsumer:

```
private Twitter twitter;
private OAuthProvider provider;
private OAuthConsumer consumer;
```

We also declare the CONSUMER_KEY in string, CONSUMER_SECRET in string, and CALLBACK_URL in string. This is where you insert your Twitter Application consumer key, consumer secret, and callback url from the application settings from your Twitter app:

```
private String CONSUMER_KEY = "<Consumer Key>";
private String CONSUMER_SECRET = "<Consumer Secret>";
private String CALLBACK_URL = "http://www.twitter.com";
```

Now we declare variables tweetTextView as TextView, and buttonLogin as Button used in the layout. In the app, we are adding a label and a button:

```
private TextView tweetTextView;
private Button buttonLogin;
```

onCreate(Bundle) is where you initialize the activity. Call setContentView(int) to define the UI from the layout resource. Call findViewById(int) to retrieve the UI widget.

This onClick(View v) method is called when a view has been clicked:

```
public void onClick(View v){}
```

In TwitterOauth.java:

```
package com.example.twitteroauth;

import java.sql.Date;

import oauth.signpost.OAuthConsumer;
import oauth.signpost.OAuthProvider;
import oauth.signpost.commonshttp.CommonsHttpOAuthConsumer;
import oauth.signpost.commonshttp.CommonsHttpOAuthProvider;
import twitter4j.Twitter;
import twitter4j.TwitterFactory;
import twitter4j.auth.AccessToken;
import twitter4j.conf.ConfigurationBuilder;
import android.app.Activity;
import android.content.Intent;
import android.net.Uri;
import android.os.Bundle;
import android.util.Log;
import android.view.View;
import android.view.View.OnClickListener;
import android.widget.Button;
import android.widget.TextView;
import android.widget.Toast;

/**
 * Using Twitter4J Java library and Signpost OAuth library to access
Twitter
 */
public class TwitterOauth extends Activity {

       private static final String APP =  "TWITTEROAUTH";

       private Twitter twitter;
       private OAuthProvider provider;
       private OAuthConsumer consumer;

       private String CONSUMER_KEY =             "v7xwr2xFzDEsgDvg962Paw";
```

```
        private String CONSUMER_SECRET =
➥"YlbknWgtA9t5u4q6q18IwHTQ2vtOlHesVBO9u5EtEy4";
        private String CALLBACK_URL =           "myapp://twitteroauth";

        private TextView tweetTextView;
        private Button buttonLogin;

        @Override
        public void onCreate(Bundle savedInstanceState) {
                super.onCreate(savedInstanceState);
                setContentView(R.layout.main);
                tweetTextView = (TextView)findViewById(R.id.tweet);
                buttonLogin = (Button)findViewById(R.id.ButtonLogin);
                buttonLogin.setOnClickListener(new OnClickListener() {
                        public void onClick(View v) {
                               askOAuth();
                        }
                });
        }
```

Authenticating the Application

To focus on illustrating the Twitter authentication process, we will not go into details in explaining Java programming line by line. Instead, we will highlight a few things that are unique or key to understand for implementing this framework. We also include the section code so you can see the logic and workflow in the codes.

To authenticate the Android application, we add a private method askOAuth() to verify against the Twitter application consumer key and secret:

```
askOAuth();
```

This is a key section where we declare the objects for the OAuth HTTP messaging for the consumer and provider. To make it more secure, we are using "https" version of Twitter urls for request token, access token, and authorize. We define a string object authURL after authentication is completed:

```
// Use Apache HttpClient for HTTP messaging
consumer = new CommonsHttpOAuthConsumer(CONSUMER_KEY, CONSUMER_SECRET);
provider = new CommonsHttpOAutProvider
("https://api.twitter.com/oauth/request_token",
"https://api.twitter.com/oauth/access_token",
"https://api.twitter.com/oauth/authorize");
String authUrl = provider.retrieveRequestToken(consumer, CALLBACK_URL);
```

Here we introduce the android.widget class Toast. A toast is a view containing a quick message to the user. This class creates and shows this message. It appears as a floating view, and it is unobtrusive to the user, as shown in Figure 22.2.

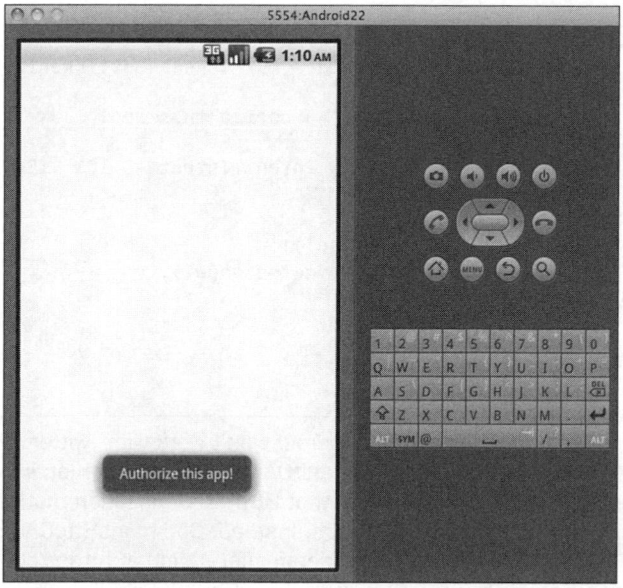

FIGURE 22.2 Showing the Toast class on the app.

Toast.makeText() is to make a standard toast that contains a text view. We want to show the message "Authorize this app!" as text:

```
Toast.makeText(this, "Authorize this app!", Toast.LENGTH_LONG).show();
```

Toast.LENGTH_LONG is a constant, showing the text notification for a long period of time. Another option is LENGTH_SHORT. Toast.show() is to show the view for the specified duration.

```
this.startActivity(new Intent(Intent.ACTION_VIEW, Uri.parse(authUrl)));
```

The startActivity (Intent intent) method is to launch a new activity. The intent is ACTION_VIEW displaying the data to the user. authUrl is a URI string. The Uri.parse() method is to create a Uri that parses the given encoded URI string of authUrl variable:

```
/**
 * Direct to Twitter to authenticate the user
 */
private void askOAuth() {
       try {
              // Use Apache HttpClient for HTTP messaging
              consumer = new CommonsHttpOAuthConsumer(CONSUMER_KEY,
➥CONSUMER_SECRET);
              provider = new
➥CommonsHttpOAuthProvider("https://api.twitter.com/oauth/request_token",

"https://api.twitter.com/oauth/access_token",
```

```
"https://api.twitter.com/oauth/authorize");
                String authUrl = provider.retrieveRequestToken(consumer,
➥CALLBACK_URL);
                Toast.makeText(this, "Authorize this app!",
➥Toast.LENGTH_LONG).show();
                this.startActivity(new Intent(Intent.ACTION_VIEW,
➥Uri.parse(authUrl)));
        } catch (Exception e) {
                Log.e(APP, e.getMessage());
                Toast.makeText(this, e.getMessage(),
➥Toast.LENGTH_LONG).show();
        }
}
```

Watch Out!

The default OAuth implementation in Android won't work with Twitter API. It is highly recommended not to use the DefaultOAuth* implementation in Android because there is a bug in Android's java.net.HttpURLConnection that keeps it from working with some service providers. Instead, CommonsHttpOAuth* classes are used in Android. You can find more detail information at http://code.google.com/p/oauth-signpost. You can find examples at http://github.com/kaeppler/signpost-examples.

Responding After Authentication

We add another onNewIntent() method to process after authenticating the Android application:

```
@Override
        protected void onNewIntent(Intent intent) {
}
```

We retrieve the URI by using intent.getData() method. If the returning URL is not null and it matches the CALLBACK_URL string, we define the string variable verifier from oauth.signpost.OAuth.OAUTH_VERIFIER parameter:

```
Uri uri = intent.getData();
if (uri != null && uri.toString().startsWith(CALLBACK_URL))
```

This getQueryParameter(String key) method is to search the query string for the first value with the given key. We create a string object "verifier" to keep the returning query string from the search:

```
String verifier = uri.getQueryParameter(oauth.signpost.OAuth.OAUTH_
VERIFIER);
```

We populate the token and token_secret from the consumer object:

```
// Populate token and token_secret in consumer
provider.retrieveAccessToken(consumer, verifier);

// TODO: you might want to store token and token_secret in you app settings!
AccessToken a = new AccessToken(consumer.getToken(),
consumer.getTokenSecret());
```

Then we initialize Twitter4J:

```
// Initialize Twitter4J
ConfigurationBuilder confbuilder  = new ConfigurationBuilder();
confbuilder.setOAuthAccessToken(a.getToken())
.setOAuthAccessTokenSecret(a.getTokenSecret())
.setOAuthConsumerKey(CONSUMER_KEY)
.setOAuthConsumerSecret(CONSUMER_SECRET);
twitter = new TwitterFactory(confbuilder.build()).getInstance();
```

The System.*currentTimeMillis*() method retrieves the date from the standard "wall" clock date/time in milliseconds since the epoch:

```
Date d = new Date(System.currentTimeMillis());
```

The toLocaleString() method (replaced by DateFormat) formats the date to the current Locale. Date/time is added to the end of the string as tweet.

We are creating a string object "tweet" for posting the message to a Twitter update. First, we include the Twitter message we like to post in a string `"Twitter API 24 HRS: TwitterOAuth works on Android "`. We add the d.toLocaleString() to the end. Twitter API has a detecting mechanism to prevent you from posting the same tweet message more than once in a given time period. By adding a date time string, each message we define will be different at a different date time. We will be able to pass the Twitter filtering system to show the message from our API call:

```
String tweet = "Twitter API 24 HRS: TwitterOAuth works on Android " +
d.toLocaleString();
```

The tweet is posted using updateStatus() method in twitter class:

```
twitter.updateStatus(tweet);
```

We display the tweet object inside the tweetTextView:

```
tweetTextView.setText(tweet);
```

We add the Toast to show the tweet object as an indicator of success:

```
Toast.makeText(this, tweet, Toast.LENGTH_LONG).show();
```

setVisibility(int visibility) method is to set the enabled state of the view. Options are VISIBLE, INVISIBLE, or GONE. GONE refers to invisible, but it doesn't take any space for layout. Basically, we make the button disappear from the layout in the last step:

```
buttonLogin.setVisibility(Button.GONE);
```

Now let's wrap this section. Here is the complete set of codes so you can follow and understand the order:

```
       /**
        * Get the verifier from the callback URL.
        * Retrieve token and token_secret.
        * Feed them to twitter4j along with consumer key and secret
        */
       @Override
       protected void onNewIntent(Intent intent) {

              super.onNewIntent(intent);

              Uri uri = intent.getData();
              if (uri != null && uri.toString().startsWith(CALLBACK_URL)) {

                     String verifier =
➥uri.getQueryParameter(oauth.signpost.OAuth.OAUTH_VERIFIER);

                     try {
                            // Populate token and token_secret in consumer
                            provider.retrieveAccessToken(consumer,
➥verifier);

                            // TODO: you might want to store token and
➥token_secret in you app settings!
                            AccessToken a = new
➥AccessToken(consumer.getToken(), consumer.getTokenSecret());

                            // Initialize Twitter4J
                            ConfigurationBuilder confbuilder  = new
➥ConfigurationBuilder();
                            confbuilder.setOAuthAccessToken(a.getToken())

➥.setOAuthAccessTokenSecret(a.getTokenSecret())
                                   .setOAuthConsumerKey(CONSUMER_KEY)
                                   .setOAuthConsumerSecret(CONSUMER_SECRET);
                            twitter = new
➥TwitterFactory(confbuilder.build()).getInstance();

                            // Create a tweet
                            Date d = new Date(System.currentTimeMillis());
                            String tweet = "Twitter API 24 HRS: TwitterOAuth
➥works on Android " + d.toLocaleString();

                            // Post the tweet
```

```
                        twitter.updateStatus(tweet);

                        // Show message
                        tweetTextView.setText(tweet);
                        Toast.makeText(this, tweet,
➥Toast.LENGTH_LONG).show();
                        buttonLogin.setVisibility(Button.GONE);

                    } catch (Exception e) {
                        Log.e(APP, e.getMessage());
                        Toast.makeText(this, e.getMessage(),
➥Toast.LENGTH_LONG).show();
                    }
               }
          }
}
```

Complete Code

This is the complete code in the TwitterOAuth.java file. It combines all the code we have discussed and explained in each section earlier:

```
package com.example.twitteroauth;

import java.sql.Date;

import oauth.signpost.OAuthConsumer;
import oauth.signpost.OAuthProvider;
import oauth.signpost.commonshttp.CommonsHttpOAuthConsumer;
import oauth.signpost.commonshttp.CommonsHttpOAuthProvider;
import twitter4j.Twitter;
import twitter4j.TwitterFactory;
import twitter4j.auth.AccessToken;
import twitter4j.conf.ConfigurationBuilder;
import android.app.Activity;
import android.content.Intent;
import android.net.Uri;
import android.os.Bundle;
import android.util.Log;
import android.view.View;
import android.view.View.OnClickListener;
import android.widget.Button;
import android.widget.TextView;
import android.widget.Toast;

/**
 * Using Twitter4J Java library and Signpost OAuth library to access
Twitter
 */
public class TwitterOauth extends Activity {

       private static final String APP =  "TWITTEROAUTH";
```

```
	private Twitter twitter;
	private OAuthProvider provider;
	private OAuthConsumer consumer;

	private String CONSUMER_KEY =			"v7xwr2xFzDEsgDvg962Paw";
	private String CONSUMER_SECRET =
➥"YlbknWgtA9t5u4q6q18IwHTQ2vt0lHesVBO9u5EtEy4";
	private String CALLBACK_URL =			"myapp://twitteroauth";

	private TextView tweetTextView;
	private Button buttonLogin;

	@Override
	public void onCreate(Bundle savedInstanceState) {
		super.onCreate(savedInstanceState);
		setContentView(R.layout.main);
		tweetTextView = (TextView)findViewById(R.id.tweet);
		buttonLogin = (Button)findViewById(R.id.ButtonLogin);
		buttonLogin.setOnClickListener(new OnClickListener() {
			public void onClick(View v) {
				askOAuth();
			}
		});
	}

	/**
	 * Direct to Twitter to authenticate the user
	 */
	private void askOAuth() {
		try {
			// Use Apache HttpClient for HTTP messaging
			consumer = new CommonsHttpOAuthConsumer(CONSUMER_KEY,
➥CONSUMER_SECRET);
			provider = new
➥CommonsHttpOAuthProvider("https://api.twitter.com/oauth/request_token",

➥"https://api.twitter.com/oauth/access_token",

➥"https://api.twitter.com/oauth/authorize");
			String authUrl =
➥provider.retrieveRequestToken(consumer, CALLBACK_URL);
			Toast.makeText(this, "Authorize this app!",
➥Toast.LENGTH_LONG).show();
			this.startActivity(new Intent(Intent.ACTION_VIEW,
➥Uri.parse(authUrl)));
		} catch (Exception e) {
			Log.e(APP, e.getMessage());
			Toast.makeText(this, e.getMessage(),
➥Toast.LENGTH_LONG).show();
		}
	}
```

```
        /**
         * Get the verifier from the callback URL.
         * Retrieve token and token_secret.
         * Feed them to twitter4j along with consumer key and secret
         */
        @Override
        protected void onNewIntent(Intent intent) {

               super.onNewIntent(intent);

               Uri uri = intent.getData();
               if (uri != null && uri.toString().startsWith(CALLBACK_URL)) {

                      String verifier =
➥uri.getQueryParameter(oauth.signpost.OAuth.OAUTH_VERIFIER);

                      try {
                            // Populate token and token_secret in consumer
                            provider.retrieveAccessToken(consumer,
➥verifier);

                            // TODO: you might want to store token and
➥token_secret in you app settings!
                            AccessToken a = new
➥AccessToken(consumer.getToken(), consumer.getTokenSecret());

                            // Initialize Twitter4J
                            ConfigurationBuilder confbuilder  = new
➥ConfigurationBuilder();
                            confbuilder.setOAuthAccessToken(a.getToken())

➥.setOAuthAccessTokenSecret(a.getTokenSecret())
                                    .setOAuthConsumerKey(CONSUMER_KEY)
                                    .setOAuthConsumerSecret(CONSUMER_SECRET);
                            twitter = new
➥TwitterFactory(confbuilder.build()).getInstance();

                            // Create a tweet
                            Date d = new Date(System.currentTimeMillis());
                            String tweet = "Twitter API 24 HRS: TwitterOAuth
➥works on Android " + d.toLocaleString();

                            // Post the tweet
                            twitter.updateStatus(tweet);

                            // Show message
                            tweetTextView.setText(tweet);
                            Toast.makeText(this, tweet,
➥Toast.LENGTH_LONG).show();
                            buttonLogin.setVisibility(Button.GONE);

                      } catch (Exception e) {
                            Log.e(APP, e.getMessage());
```

```
                                Toast.makeText(this, e.getMessage(),
➥Toast.LENGTH_LONG).show();
                        }
                }
        }
}
```

Did You Know?

Older versions of Twitter4J library use the setOAuthAccessToken(AccessToken accessToken) method. This method is deprecated. Use the TwitterFactory.getInstance(twitter4j.http.Authorization) method. Keep in mind that the Twitter4J library author is updating the library regularly, including changing methods without notice on each update. It's important that you understand how this works and be able to make any necessary changes in your own code.

Whew, quite a lot of code, eh? But now we are ready to build and run the Android app. By now, you should know the steps to run the Android app in Android Emulator inside Eclipse. In this Android example, we are creating a simple app with a text label and an Authenticate button, as shown in Figure 22.3. Once the button is pressed, it calls the method we explained previously.

FIGURE 22.3 Launching the Twitter OAuth in the Android emulator.

In this Android example, we are using OAuth to authenticate the user by redirecting to the Android browser that is pointing to the Twitter OAuth mobile page, as shown in Figure 22.4.

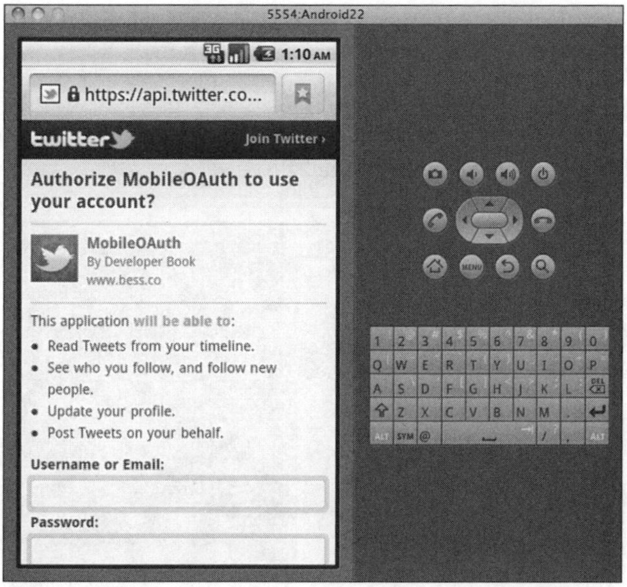

FIGURE 22.4 Showing Twitter authentication in the Android emulator.

As we can see in Figure 22.4, Twitter shows an OAuth page that is optimized for mobile devices. It shows the Twitter application name, developer name, and website. It also shows what the Twitter application is allowed to do if the user grants authentication. This is where you enter your Twitter account username and password, as shown in Figure 22.5.

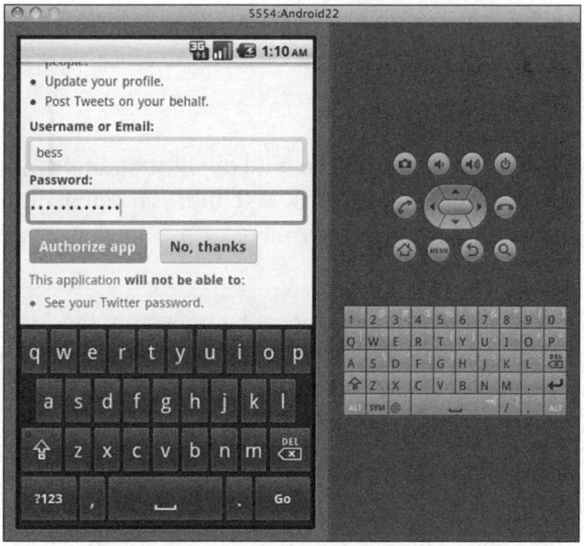

FIGURE 22.5 Entering your Twitter account and pressing the Authorize button in the Android emulator.

Scroll down to see the bottom of the Twitter OAuth page. After entering your username or email and password, press Authorize app button.

The Confirm dialog box will appear, asking if the user wants to keep the password on the browser or not. After closing this dialog box, you will be re-directed to another Twitter mobile page, as shown in Figure 22.6.

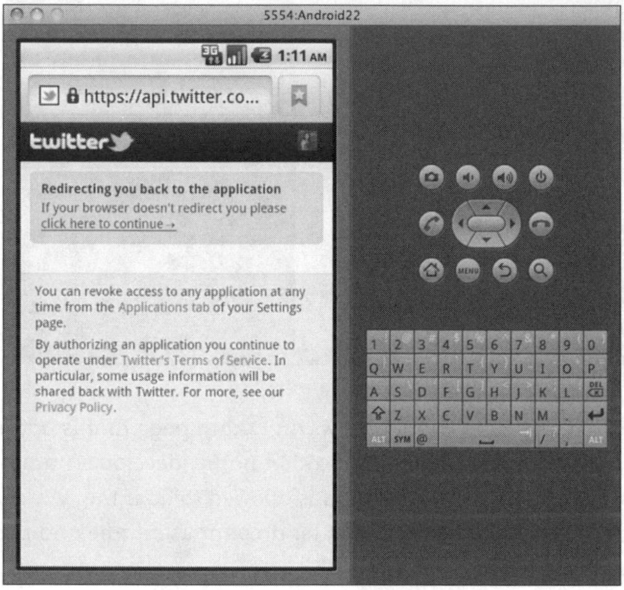

FIGURE 22.6 Showing the Twitter redirecting page to the app in the Android emulator.

After waiting a few seconds, you will be redirected from the device browser back to the Twitter Android app you defined in the code:

```
private String CALLBACK_URL = "myapp://twitteroauth";
```

After you launch and authenticate the Android application in the Android emulator, you will be redirected to the CALLBACK_URL that you define in the TwitterOauth.java file. This overrides the callback URL that you save in your Twitter Application setting.

Twitter4J library allows developers to re-direct the browser to the Android app without any additional modifications. In this chapter, we intend to show you the simplest method to authenticate OAuth. Ideally, you would create a WebView to show the Twitter OAuth screen within the same Android app.

After the user successfully grants authorization by verifying his or her Twitter account and then get redirected to the Twitter app, we hide the Authenticated button. Instead, we show him or her the posted tweet in the TextView in the place of the

Authenticated button and the Toast indicator at the bottom of the app, as shown in Figure 22.7. A successful posted tweet includes the date time stamp at the end of the tweet string you defined in the code.

Congratulations! You have a working Twitter OAuth app in Android.

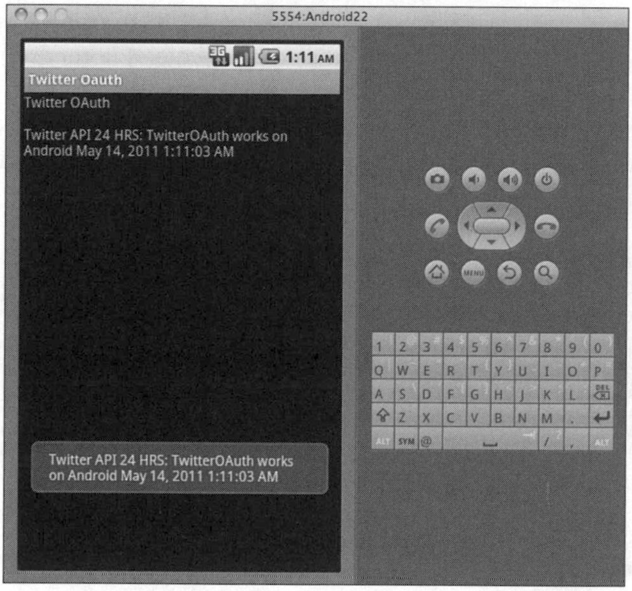

FIGURE 22.7 Showing the Twitter redirecting page to the app in the Android emulator.

xAuth

xAuth is alternative authenticate method. This method is available only to desktop or mobile apps. xAuth requires the developer to request permission to use it. Twitter will review your xAuth submission before granting its use. Your xAuth enabled or disabled status will not show in your Twitter application settings.

xAuth for Twitter is not the same as Xauth (http://xauth.org/). xAuth is still OAuth. The only difference is you skip the request_token and authorize steps of the OAuth flow. xAuth allows the mobile app to exchange the username and password for an OAuth access token.

According to Twitter's recommendation, once the access token is retrieved, Twitter suggests for developers to dispose of the username and password. Twitter also suggests for you to consider the standard web OAuth flow or PIN-code out-of-band flow before considering xAuth. xAuth requires you to use header-based OAuth authentication against an SSL access token endpoint, using the POST HTTP method. More details are at http://dev.twitter.com/pages/xauth.

The Twitter4J library does support xAuth as well as OAuth. In order to implement xAuth, you would have to create a new layout to provide a user interface to enter the Twitter account username and password. Due to the limitation of this hour's space, we decided not to cover xAuth. As such, we decided to use the OAuth method in our example.

The Twitter4J library enables you to use a CALLBACK_URL to redirect user from the Android browser to the Android app on the device. Twitter4J library supports the OAuth method without requiring the user to perform any steps to open the same Android app and without requiring developers to do any extra work to close the browser. Thus, because of this simplicity, we decided to go with the OAuth method.

Summary

Congratulations! You've added Twitter Java library and OAuth Java library to your Android OAuth project. You've created an Android application using the OAuth Consumer key and Consumer secret. And last, you have posted a tweet from your Android application using Android Emulator.

Q&A

Q. ***What are the supporting Java libraries for Twitter API integration?***

A. Twitter4J library and JTwitter library.

Q. ***What is the most accepting Java OAuth library for Android?***

A. Oauth-signpost library.

Workshop

Quiz

1. What authentication type does Twitter not support?

A. Basic Auth

B. OAuth

C. xAuth

2. What must be included in an Android application to request an OAuth token?

   A. Consumer key

   B. Consumer secret

   C. Both

3. Which tab should you use to add third-party Java libraries (JARs) in the project's properties of Java Build Path?

   A. Source

   B. Projects

   C. Libraries

   D. Order and Export

Quiz Answers

1. A. Twitter does not accept Basic Auth due to security concerns.
2. C. You are required to include Consumer key and Consumer secret from your Twitter application settings.
3. C. You use the Libraries tab of Java Build Path inside Project's properties to add all the third-party Java libraries (JARs) for OAuth and Twitter libraries.

Exercises

1. Add Twitter Java libraries into your Android application.
2. Create a new Twitter application in your Twitter developer account. Save the Consumer key and Consumer secret into your Android application.
3. Create an Android application to send a tweet using OAuth.

HOUR 23

Getting Started with Twitter Using iOS

What You'll Learn in This Hour:

- Building your first Hello World application
- Using the Xcode and Interface Builder
- Requesting Twitter xAuth
- Using Twitter Objective-C library
- Verifying your Twitter xAuth

Introducing iOS

In 2007, Apple released iOS as its mobile operating system. In early 2008, Apple released the beta iPhone SDK for native application development. Apple announced the iPad as a tablet in early 2010 and iPhone 4 in the summer of 2010. Apple also renamed iPhone SDK to iOS SDK. iOS SDK supports iPhone, iPod Touch, iPad, and iPhone 4. iOS SDK is written in C, C++, and Objective-C. iOS SDK includes Xcode, Interface Builder, Instruments, and iPhone and iPad Simulator.

To learn about the iOS SDK and Xcode, we will start by creating a Hello World application on the iPhone. A simple Hello World application contains the basic iPhone application functionality and prints out the text "Hello World" on the screen—typically the first program you would create when learning any language. Because setting up the iOS environment is a bit tricky, we will spend a bit more time trying to get you up and running.

Creating a Hello World Application

We are sure you already know this, but you need to have a computer that can run the Apple OS X operating system running Snow Leopard or better, and you must have a license to publish iOS applications. Currently, a license will run you $99.00 a year. You can download a copy of the iOS SDK without the license, but you will not be able to put anything in the store. So, if you have not done so already, download and install Xcode OS4 and let's get going.

Open Xcode to create a new project. Xcode will create all the required files for an iOS iPhone application. Follow these steps to create a new project:

1. In Xcode, select File, New, New Project....
2. In the New Project window, select iOS, Application on the OS panel, as shown in Figure 23.1.

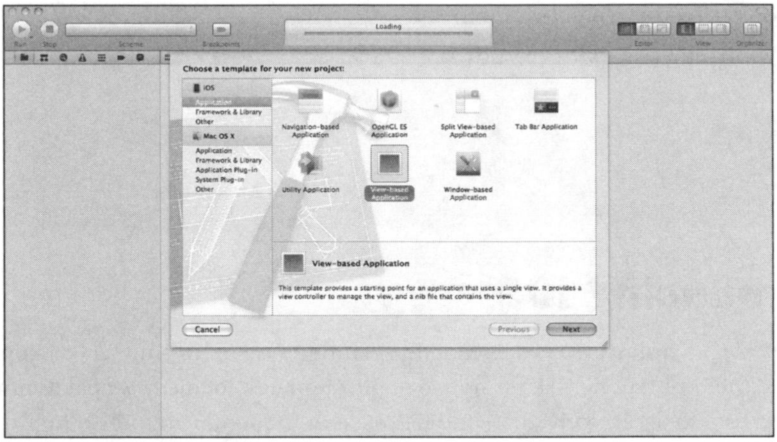

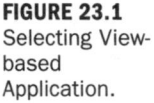

FIGURE 23.1
Selecting View-based Application.

3. In the template panel, select View-based Application. Click Next.
4. In the Project Options window, enter `helloworld` in the Product Name field. Leave the Company Identifier field as it is as shown in Figure 23.2.
5. Select iPhone in the Device Family drop-down menu. Click Next.
6. Select the directory to which you would like to save the Xcode project. Save the project by clicking Create.
7. In the Xcode's Project Navigator inside the Xcode project, the template files are created inside the Group folder named helloworld, as shown in Figure 23.3.

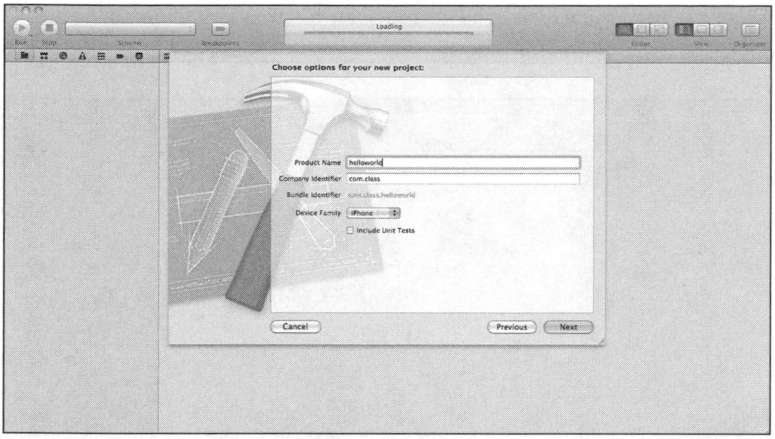

FIGURE 23.2
Naming the helloworld in the Product Name field.

FIGURE 23.3
Showing Xcode project summary panel after creating the project.

8. Click the file helloworldViewController.xib to launch Interface Builder in the editor area of the workspace window.
9. Click the View Right Panel icon in the Selector Bar to show the Utility area.
10. Select the Attributes icon in the Inspector Selector Bar to show the Attributes Inspector.
11. Click on the Interface Builder object View inside the Editor area. Attributes Inspector will display the UIView's details.
12. In the View section, select Default in the Background drop-down menu to switch away from the gray background. It gives a white background.
13. Select the Object icon in the Library selector bar to show the Object Library.

14. Select the Icon View icon or List View icon to show the Object Library objects, as shown in Figure 23.4.

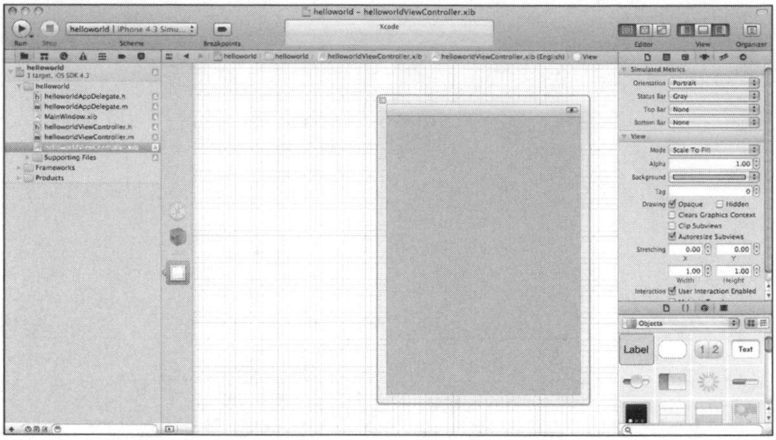

FIGURE 23.4
Showing Attributes Inspector and Object Library in Utility area.

15. Select the Label and drag it to the View inside the Editor area.

16. Double-click the Label object until the entire label is selected in the View object.

17. Enter the text "`Hello World`" inside the Label object (as shown in Figure 23.5) and press Enter on the keyboard.

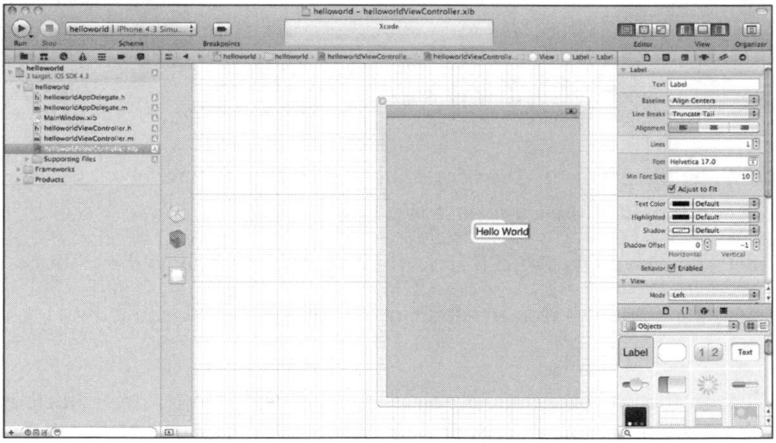

FIGURE 23.5
Showing the "Hello World" label on the view in the Editor area.

18. Select File, Save or hold both <Command>+S key buttons to save the file.

19. In the Xcode, select Product, Run, or click the Run button at the top left of the Xcode window.

If everything went well, you should have a working application displaying the text "Hello World," as shown in Figure 23.6.

FIGURE 23.6 Showing "Hello World" in the iPhone Simulator.

Did You Know?

Objects will not be displayed on the iPhone Simulator in the Run and Build process until the objects inside the Interface Builder are properly saved. When the file icon is highlighted in gray in the Project Navigator, it indicates that the file changes are not saved in Xcode. Build and Run won't render the updates.

Creating a Twitter Application for xAuth Request

Before you can request and activate xAuth, you need to create a Twitter application. You should have done this already in Hour 8, "Twitter OAuth," but if not, be sure to do this now.

To do so, go to http://twitter.com/apps.

1. Click the link "Register a new application" at the bottom of the page.
2. Complete the application form.
3. Click Save.

Requesting Twitter xAuth

In Hour 8, we discussed registering your application and getting an OAuth number. In most cases, this should be fine. However, you can also request something called xAuth, which is more tailored for mobile apps. However, this spec is ever-changing and evolving. Be sure to check Twitter for the latest updates with xAuth.

You can request for xAuth activation by opening a support ticket at http://support.twitter.com/forms. Select "Everything else" in the menu. Include your App ID of your app in your support ticket. Your App ID is the number at the end of the URL of your app:

http://twitter.com/oauth_clients/details/<your app id>

Twitter xAuth API

After it is approved, you will be able to make a call to the following API method:

```
http://api.twitter.com/oauth/access_token
```

and send three parameters:

```
x_auth_username - username
x_auth_password - password
x_auth_mode - set the value to "client_auth"
```

This API method returns the authorized access token similar to OAuth. xAuth authorized tokens can be saved and reused for any subsequent API calls because the tokens do not expire.

Retrieving Consumer Key and Consumer Secret

After Twitter API approves your xAuth request and activates xAuth on your Twitter application, you can retrieve your Consumer key and Consumer secret by visiting http://dev.twitter.com/apps/<your app id> or http://twitter.com/oauth_clients/details/<your app id>.

Now let's log into your Twitter account to retrieve your App ID, the Consumer key, and Consumer secret and copy them into a text file, as we did in Hour 8. We will use them in the code later:

1. Log in to your Twitter account.
2. Select your xAuth-activated application at http://twitter.com/apps.

   After selecting your application, you should see the Application Details. This is where you find the Consumer key and Consumer secret.

3. Retrieve your App ID by looking up the application URL. Your App ID is the number at the end of the URL of your app: http://twitter.com/oauth_clients/details/<your app id>.

4. Copy the Consumer key and Consumer secret and store them into a notepad.

5. Click Edit Application Settings.

   The Application Settings is where you define the Application Type and Default Access Type. You should choose Client as Application Type to support xAuth on iPhone app. You should choose Read & Write on Default Access Type in this application.

6. Select Client as the Application Type.

7. Select Read & Write on Default Access Type.

Downloading MGTwitterEngine Library

The Twitter developer website suggests a list of Twitter Libraries at http://dev.twitter.com/pages/libraries. MGTwitterEngine is the most accepted Objective-C Cocoa library by iOS developers. This Twitter library includes OAuth and xAuth support for Mac OS X and iOS.

MGTwitterEngine is an Objective-C Cocoa library for the Twitter API. You can download the latest version of MGTwitterEngine at https://github.com/mattgemmell/MGTwitterEngine.

xAuth implementation in iOS application requires additional resources in addition to the MGTwitterEngine library.

Downloading MGTwitterEngineDemo

MGTwitterEngineDemo is a complete Xcode project packaged with additional resources to support Twitter xAuth on an iPhone application. You can download the latest version of MGTwitterEngineDemo at https://github.com/aral/MGTwitterEngineDemo.

It also allows you to verify your Twitter application xAuth activation and test your Consumer key and Consumer secret.

By the Way

> Twitter application settings do not support xAuth status. The only method to verify your xAuth approval and activation is the email confirmation from Twitter API.

Targeting Active SDK

The latest build on MGTwitterEngineDemo may not support your latest or previous iOS SDK you installed for your Xcode. You would need to take additional steps to select the Base SDK:

1. Launch the MGTwitterEngineDemo project in Xcode by opening MGTwitterEngineDemo.xcodeproj in the folder.
2. TARGETS should be selected by Default, showing the Summary tab.
3. Select the Building Settings tab.
4. In Architectures, Base SDK, select the latest iOS Device SDK version from the drop-down list.
5. Click on the Scheme button at the top left of Xcode. Select iPhone Simulator from the drop-down list to set the active scheme.
6. Click the Run button at the top left of the Xcode to run the project.

Verifying xAuth

MGTwitterEngineDemo requires xAuth-activated Consumer key and Consumer secret to call Twitter API. Twitter is no longer allowing apps to store Twitter usernames and passwords on the device to log into the user's Twitter account for the Basic Auth method. In order to integrate xAuth, you are required to include the Twitter OAuth Consumer key and Consumer secret in the app to authenticate the app.

Inside the MGTwitterEngineDemoViewController.h file, #define statement is where you define the constant of Twitter OAuth Consumer key and Consumer secret.

In MGTwitterEngineDemoViewController.h:

```
#define kOAuthConsumerKey        @""
#define kOAuthConsumerSecret     @""
```

If you run the project without including your application Twitter OAuth Consumer key and Consumer secret, you will be receiving an alert box with a title "Missing oAuth details," as shown in Figure 23.7.

FIGURE 23.7 Showing the Missing oAuth details in iPhone Simulator alert.

Now you retrieve the Consumer key and Consumer secret you saved in the text file. Copy those values inside the Objective-C String. The value should be copied inside the double quotes after the @ symbol:

1. In MGTwitterEngineDemoViewController.h, enter your Consumer key in the Objective-C string @"" of kOAuthConsumerKey constant.
2. Enter your Consumer secret in the Objective-C string @"" of kOAuthConsumerSecret constant.
3. Click the Run button at the top left of the Xcode.

   After running the project, you will see two empty text field input boxes in the iPhone Simulator. Enter your valid Twitter username and password under the title "Twitter account details," as shown in Figure 23.8.

FIGURE 23.8
Showing the Twitter account form in the iPhone Simulator.

4. Enter your valid Twitter username and password in the iPhone Simulator.
5. Click the Get xAuth Access Token button.

   Selecting the Get xAuth Access Token button will send a Twitter API request to Twitter to authenticate your app based on your Twitter OAuth Consumer key and Consumer secret. Before selecting the Get xAuth Access Token button, the Send Test Tweet button is disabled and is grayed out. After the xAuth is successfully authenticated by Twitter, the Send Test Tweet button will be enabled.
6. Click the Send Test Tweet button when it is enabled.

   The Send Test Tweet button will send a hard-coded Twitter message to your Twitter account. You will receive an alert box title "Tweet sent!," as shown in Figure 23.9.

FIGURE 23.9 Showing the success alert message in the iPhone Simulator.

7. Log in to your Twitter account to verify the successful tweet message in your Twitter timeline feed, as shown in Figure 23.10.

   You can log into your Twitter account to see the test message on your Home Timeline status. A random number is generated at the end of the message to avoid Twitter from blocking any duplicated message.

FIGURE 23.10 Showing the successful tweet message on Twitter feed.

Summary

Congratulations! You are now an iOS developer. You've created your first iPhone project. You also have created a Twitter application and requested xAuth from Twitter. Finally, you learned how to verify your xAuth tokens by testing your application's Consumer key and Consumer secret.

Q&A

Q. ***What kind of a development environment do I need for creating an iPhone application?***

A. You need the latest iOS SDK, Xcode, Interface Builder, and iPhone Simulator.

Q. ***What operating systems are supported for iOS application development?***

A. Mac OS X Snow Leopard.

Q. ***What is xAuth?***

A. xAuth is Twitter's preferred authentication method for iOS native app after Twitter discontinued the support in Basic Authentication.

Workshop

Quiz

1. Which programming languages do I use to code and develop an iPhone application?

   A. Objective-C

   B. Java

   C. HTML / JavaScript / CSS

   D. C++

2. What are the types of authentications Twitter accepts?

   A. Basic Authentication

   B. OAuth

   C. xAuth

   D. B and C only

3. How do you request Twitter xAuth?

   A. Twitter generates xAuth when you create your Twitter developer account.

   B. Twitter generates xAuth when you create a new Twitter application.

   C. Email Twitter at api@twitter.com with your application ID to request xAuth.

Quiz Answers

1. A. Use Objective-C to write the code for the iOS application.
2. D. Twitter accepts OAuth and xAuth and bans the use of Basic Authentication.
3. C. Twitter manually approves xAuth on each request.

Exercises

1. Register the Apple developer account. Install your iOS SDK. Create a view-based template project in Xcode. Create a hello iPhone application.
2. Build and run the application in the iPhone Simulator.
3. Create a new Twitter application. Find your application's Consumer key and Consumer secret, and your App ID.
4. Request xAuth from Twitter.
5. Verify your xAuth after Twitter activates your xAuth.

HOUR 24

Building an iPhone and iPod Touch Application with Twitter

What You'll Learn in This Hour:

- ▶ Creating an iPhone xAuth application
- ▶ Adding Objective-C library
- ▶ Creating layout in Interface Builder
- ▶ Using Objective-C xAuth library
- ▶ Posting a Tweet from iPhone application

Introducing Twitter xAuth

Twitter introduces and extends xAuth to support mobile application and authenticates the mobile application without storing the username and password in the application.

In the iOS application, the Twitter OAuth authentication process forces the user to exit the app and to authorize the request on the Twitter website in an opened Safari browser. Initially, the Twitter OAuth web interface was not optimized for mobile. The option of using UIWebView to request and exchange OAuth tokens within the same iOS application is considered a hacked approach. Developers have reported that it takes a default preset 10 seconds for Twitter to redirect to the OAuth successful page within UIWebView. Twitter has not responded to any suggestion to shorten or optimize the 10-second redirect for mobile native apps.

Because Twitter bans the use of Basic Auth and disallows storing Twitter usernames and passwords on devices, the next option Twitter embraced for mobile native apps is xAuth.

xAuth is a preferred authentication method for iOS application. Developers can exchange both usernames and passwords for authorized tokens in one API call using xAuth.

Benefits of Using Twitter xAuth

Using xAuth enhances your organic marketing effort by displaying the source parameter at the bottom of every tweet (display as "via My App").

Did You Know?

> Twitter initially allowed applications to create a source parameter for non-OAuth use. Twitter no longer accepts new registrations for source request. However, applications using pre-OAuth source parameters will remain active.

xAuth improves security in case of a stolen device. You can revoke access to your application by visiting your Twitter account settings; select the Connections tab at http://twitter.com/settings/connections to see the list of Twitter applications. Use the "Revoke Access" button on the right side of the application to enable Revoke Access, as shown in Figure 24.1.

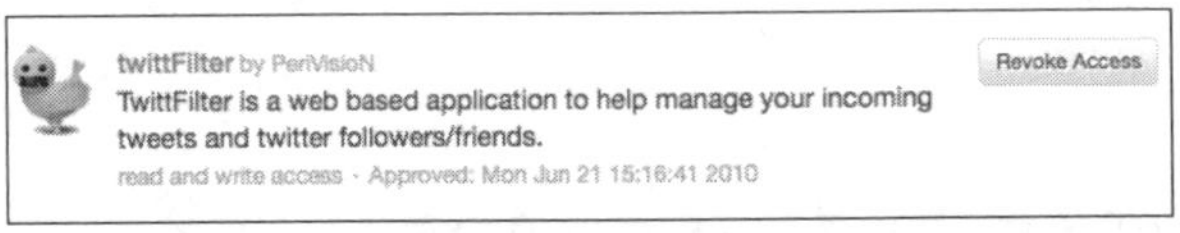

FIGURE 24.1 Showing the Revoke Access in Connections panel for Twitter account settings.

Selecting Twitter Objective-C Libraries

MGTwitterEngine is one of the few Objective-C libraries supporting Twitter APIs. MGTwitterEngine supports OAuth and xAuth, as well as iOS SDK for iPhone, iTouch, and iPad applications. MGTwitterEngineDemo contain the JSON library, OAuth library, and helper files to support MGTwitterEngine Twitter library.

Creating xAuth Application

MGTwitterEngineDemo is a nice way to verify your xAuth activation, validate your Consumer key and Consumer secret, and confirm your Twitter username and password. However, it is not for designing commercial application containing many alerts for debugging. Let's start with a new project:

1. In Xcode, select File, New, New Project....
2. Select the View-based Application template in the New Project window.
3. Click Next.
4. Enter `xauth` in the Product Name input box. Select iPhone in the drop-down menu of Device Family.
5. Click Next.
6. Select the directory to save the Xcode project.
7. Click Create.
8. Click Build Phases tab under Project TARGETS.
9. Expand the arrow icon next to Link Binary With Libraries item.
10. Click + icon to open the Frameworks & Libraries drop-down list.

    MGTwitterEngine requires additional frameworks to support the Twitter OAuth library. Security.framework and libxml2.dylib are added to the Project TARGETS in the Build Phases tab. You can add each framework one by one or you can hold down the Command key on the keyboard to select more than one framework, as shown in Figure 24.2.

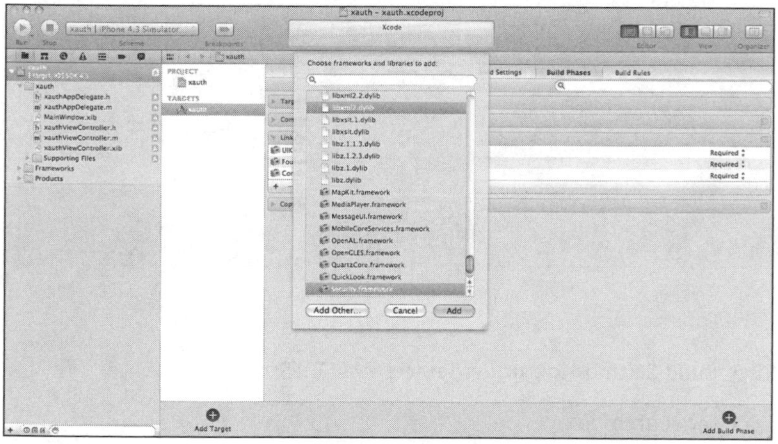

FIGURE 24.2 Adding Frameworks to Xcode project.

11. Select Security.framework and click Add.
12. Select libxml2.dylib and click Add.

13. Select both Security.framework and libxml2.dylib and drag them into the Frameworks Group.
14. Open the MGTwitterEngineDemo Xcode project. Select the Libraries Group from the Project Navigator panel. Drag the entire Libraries Group from the MGTwitterEngineDemo Xcode project into your xauth Group of your new Xcode project inside the Project Navigator panel. You should see a green + icon when you drag the folder into the Project Navigator panel.
15. Check the Destination box Copy items into destination group's folder (if needed).
16. The Folder radio button should be selected for Create groups for any added folders, as shown in Figure 24.3.

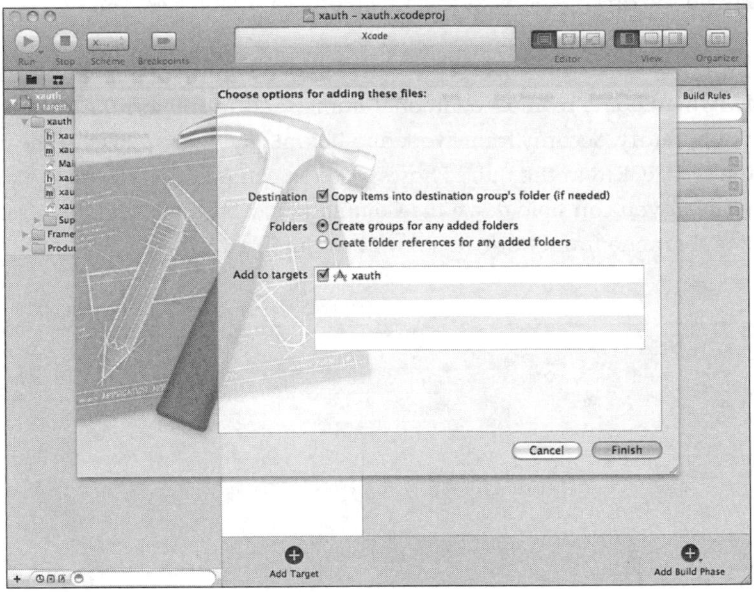

FIGURE 24.3 Copying the library.

17. Click Finish.
18. Click Build Settings tab under Project TARGETS.
19. Click the search box.
20. Enter `Header Search Paths` into the search box.
21. Enter return.
22. Select Header Search Paths in the Setting Column, as shown in Figure 24.4.
23. Add `$(SDKROOT)/usr/include/libxml2` in the column Value.

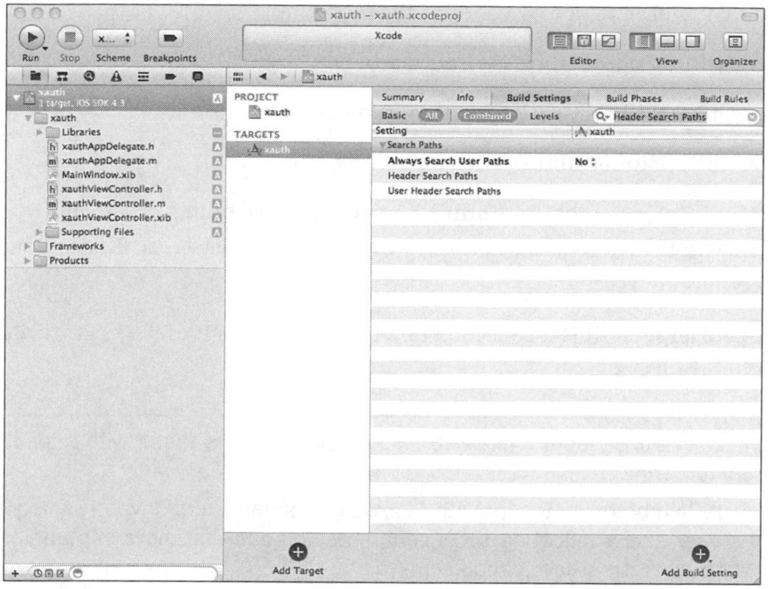

FIGURE 24.4 Targeting Header Search Paths in the Build tab.

Watch Out!

> If you build the project now without libXML framework libxml2.dylib, you will get hundreds of errors. The classes from MGTwitterEngineDemo require libXML to be a target of the project build. Make sure you add the framework libxml2.dylib.

The MGTwitterEngineDemo library uses third-party libraries OAuth Consumer library to support OAuth and scifihifi-iphone-security library to store account information in the keychain for security. Both OAuth Consumer library and scifihifi-iphone-security library require iOS SDK Security framework (Security.framework).

MGTwitterEngineDemo library is required to parse Twitter XML responses. Based on the MGTwitterEngineDemo recommendation, LibXML parser is preferred over the NSXMLParser. Libxml2 included by Apple in the iOS SDK is used to perform tree-based parsing. Because libxml2 is a .dylib and is not an iOS SDK framework, it is necessary to include libxml2 path in the Project Target's Build Settings tab in the "Header Search Paths".

Now we have added the missing Security Framework and LibXML parser .dylib to the project. We can explore the files inside the MGTwitterEngineDemo library.

MGTwitterEngineDemo library is consisting of several third-party libraries. These libraries are grouped together inside Twitter+OAuth and CocoaHelpers Groups.

MGTwitterEngineDemo library includes Twitter+OAuth and CocoaHelpers folders.

MGTwitterEngineDemo library contains the following:

- **MGTwitterEngine library**—It supports Twitter APIs.
- **TouchJSON library**—It supports JSON parsing.
- **OAuthConsumer library**—It supports Twitter OAuth.
- **scifihifi-iphone-security library**—It supports Keychain storage and retrieval. Source code is at https://github.com/ldandersen/scifihifi-iphone/tree/master/security/.
- **CocoaHelpers**—It is a collection of Objective-C class files to generate alerts to inform users.

Did You Know?

LibXML is a native parser. Unlike NSXMLParser, LibXML is faster with a smaller memory footprint.

YAJL is JSON library written in ANSI C. YAJL is a small event-driven (SAX-style) JSON parser and a validating JSON generator. You can find more info about YAJL library at http://lloyd.github.com/yajl/.

The MGTwitterEngine library does not include the source files from the TouchJSON library and YAJL library. The MGTwitterEngine library requires users to include the source files in your Xcode project. Because both TouchJSON and YAJL libraries are JSON parsers, there is no reason to keep two similar JSON libraries in the same Xcode project. In this xAuth implementation, the TouchJSON library is used as a JSON parser instead of YAJL library. It is necessary to remove all the YAJL dependency files from the compile sources in the project target in order to run the xAuth version of MGTwitterEngine in MGTwitterEngineDemo.

So, let's remove those dependency files in the following steps:

1. Click Build Phases tab of Project TARGETS.
2. Click the arrow next to Compile Sources item.
3. Delete the following YAJL dependency files by selecting the file and click the minus sign button to delete the file:
    - MGTwitterMessagesYAJLParser.m
    - MGTwitterStatusesYAJLParser.m
    - MGTwitterYAJLParser.m
    - MGTwitterSearchYAJLParser.m

- MGTwitterUsersYAJLParser.m
- MGTwitterMiscYAJLParser.m

4. Click Run icon to run the project.

> The latest release of YAJL is not compatible with the MGTwitterEngine library. It is best to remove all the YAJL dependency files at the target.

Watch Out!

Exploring ViewController.h

The view-based application template generates both header (.h) and implementation (.m) files for your <project name>ViewController in Xcode project. In the Header file, you declare variable instances, properties, and methods.

In xauthViewController.h:

```
#import <UIKit/UIKit.h>

@interface xauthViewController : UIViewController {

}

@end
```

Importing Libraries to Header Files

Add the libraries from MGTwitterEngine and OAuth in the ViewController.h file.

In xauthViewController.h, add the import statements of header files:

```
#import "MGTwitterEngineDelegate.h"
#import "OAToken.h"
```

Add the following constants:

```
#define kOAuthConsumerKey                    @"<Consumer key>"
#define kOAuthConsumerSecret                 @"<Consumer secret>"
#define kTokenKey                            @"tokenKey"
#define kHaveCachedToken                     @"haveCachedToken"
#define kMGTwitterEngineDemoServiceName      @"MGTwitterEngineDemoService"
```

Add class MGTwitterEngineDelegate:

```
@class MGTwitterEngine;
```

Add MGTwitterEngineDelegate protocol to the @interface:

```
@interface xauthViewController : UIViewController
<MGTwitterEngineDelegate> {

}
```

Declare Variable Instances

Before we can use any objects such as TextField, TextView, or Button in ViewController, we need to declare each object type and object variable instance in @interface directive.

In xauthViewController.h, add the following variable instances:

```
@interface xauthViewController : UIViewController
<MGTwitterEngineDelegate> {
     UITextField *usernameTextField;
     UITextField *passwordTextField;
     UITextView *messageTextView;
     UIButton *postButton;
     MGTwitterEngine *twitterEngine;}
```

Declare Properties and Methods

We declare the property types and add IBOutlet to each object. We also declare the method used in ViewController's implementation .m file.

In xauthViewController.h, add the following @property and methods:

```
@property (nonatomic, retain) IBOutlet UITextField *usernameTextField;
@property (nonatomic, retain) IBOutlet UITextField *passwordTextField;
@property (nonatomic, retain) IBOutlet UITextView *messageTextView;
@property (nonatomic, retain) IBOutlet UIButton *postButton;
@property (nonatomic, retain) MGTwitterEngine *twitterEngine;

- (IBAction)postMessage;
```

Exploring ViewController.m

The implementation .m file of ViewController is where you execute the Objective-C methods. The view-based template you selected in creating the new Xcode project would generate some templates files including xauthViewController.m file. The codes you see in xauthViewController.m are default codes from the view-based template.

In xauthViewController.m:

```
#import "xauthViewController.h"
@implementation xauthViewController
```

```
- (void)didReceiveMemoryWarning {
    [super didReceiveMemoryWarning];
}
- (void)viewDidUnload {
}
- (void)dealloc {
    [super dealloc];
}
@end
```

Importing Libraries to Implementation File

Include the supporting libraries once with the #import directive" above the @implementation directive in xauthViewController.m:

```
#import "MGTwitterEngine.h"
#import "SFHFKeychainUtils.h"
#import "UIAlertView+Helper.h"
#import "OAToken.h"
```

After the @implementation directive, add the following to xauthViewController.m:

```
@synthesize usernameTextField;
@synthesize passwordTextField;
@synthesize messageTextView;
@synthesize postButton;
@synthesize twitterEngine;
```

@synthesize directive will generate getter and setter methods for the property you defined in the header .h file.

Adding Pragma Mark Directive

#pragma mark is a simple directive that helps us to organize our implementation code. It functions similar to bookmarks. It helps developers to jump to user-defined sections by adding #pragma mark in the project navigation toolbar above the Xcode's Editor area. #pragma mark adds a line, and #pragma mark <title> adds a title to the project navigation toolbar drop-down menu.

Add the following Pragma Mark directives to xauthViewController.m:

```
#pragma mark -
#pragma mark Memory management
```

Managing Memory

The viewDidUnload method is called when controller's view is released from memory. This method resets the objects on the view.

The Dealloc method is called when controller deallocates the memory occupied by the receiver. This method releases the memory of the objects on the view.

After @synthesize, add the following in xauthViewController.m:

```
- (void)viewDidUnload {
     self.usernameTextField = nil;
     self.passwordTextField = nil;
     self.messageTextView = nil;
     self.postButton = nil;
}

- (void)dealloc {
     [usernameTextField release];
     [passwordTextField release];
     [messageTextView release];
     [postButton release];
     [twitterEngine release];
    [super dealloc];
}
```

Initializing MGTwitterEngine

The initWithCoder: method is used to create a variable instance of the MGTwitterEngine object called twitterEngine.

Add #pragma mark directives and the initWithCoder: method in xauthViewController.m:

```
-(id)initWithCoder:(NSCoder *)aDecoder{
     self = [super initWithCoder:aDecoder];
     if (self)
     {
            // Custom initialization
            self.twitterEngine = [[[MGTwitterEngine alloc]
initWithDelegate:self] autorelease];
     }
     return self;
}
```

Loading xAuth Token

The viewDidLoad method is called after the controller's view is loaded into memory. This method is where we handle the success and error if there is any missing Consumer key and Consumer secret in the application, and if xAuth token is cached and loaded from the Keychain.

Token key is saved in NSUserDefaults and token secret is stored in the Keychain using SFHFKeychainUtils. SFHFKeychainUtils offers better security than storing both token keys and secrets in NSUserDefaults.

The xAuth access token is stored as an NSString object. This cached token is used for future sessions.

Twitter apps that use multiple accounts, or apps allowing users to change the account in apps with a single account, update the xAuth access token manually within the session.

The view-based template generates commented viewDidLoad method by default. Delete the entire default viewDidLoad method and add our own viewDidLoad method instead.

Add the following viewDidLoad method in xauthViewController.m:

```
- (void)viewDidLoad {
    [super viewDidLoad];

     // Sanity check
     if ([kOAuthConsumerKey isEqualToString:@""] || [kOAuthConsumerSecret
➥isEqualToString:@""])
     {
            NSLog(@"Twitter Consumer key or Consumer secret is missing!");
     }
     else
     {
            [self.twitterEngine setConsumerKey:kOAuthConsumerKey
➥secret:kOAuthConsumerSecret];
     }

        NSUserDefaults *userDefaults = [NSUserDefaults
➥standardUserDefaults];
     if ([userDefaults boolForKey:kHaveCachedToken])
     {
            // Get the cached (saved) token.
                     NSString *tokenKey = [userDefaults
➥objectForKey:kTokenKey];

                     NSError *error = nil;
                     NSString *tokenSecret = [SFHFKeychainUtils
➥getPasswordForUsername:tokenKey
➥andServiceName:kMGTwitterEngineDemoServiceName
➥sharedKeychainAccessGroupName:nil error:&error];
            if (error)
            {
                   // Error loading oAuth token from keychain
                   NSLog( Can't load OAuth token from Keychain %d: %@",
➥[error code], [error localizedDescription]);
            }
            else
```

```
            {
                    // Success in loading OAuth token from keychain
                    OAToken *token = [[OAToken alloc] initWithKey:tokenKey
➥secret:tokenSecret];

                    self.twitterEngine.accessToken = token;

                    NSLog( xAuth token cached");
                    self.postButton.enabled = YES;
            }
    }

        // Set initial focus.
    [self.usernameTextField becomeFirstResponder];
}
```

Did You Know?

MGTwitterEngineDemo uses UIAlert to display messages for debugging. NSLog is replacing UIAlert displaying messages in Console for debugging.

Posting Tweet

A new method postMessage is created to connect the UIButton named postButton created in Interface Builder via (IBAction).

First, the username, password, and message are stored in NSString objects. Then, the `getXAuthAccessTokenForUsername:password:` method retrieves xAuth access token from Twitter API.

To avoid Twitter's 403 Status Is a Duplicate error, we add a random number to the end of the message using random generator `arc4random()%144`. Display the entire message in an NSString object named tweetText.

Finally, use sendUpdate: method to post the message to Twitter feed in Timeline. Immediately release all the NSString object memory.

Add #pragma mark directives and a postMessage method in xauthViewController.m:

```
#pragma mark -
#pragma mark Actionable methods

- (IBAction)postMessage {
    // Retrieve your username and password from Textfields
    NSString *username = self.usernameTextField.text;
    NSString *password = self.passwordTextField.text;
    NSString *message = self.messageTextView.text;

    // Retrieve xAuth access token from username and password
```

```
    NSLog( %@ Password: %@", username, password);
    NSLog( %@", message);
    [self.twitterEngine getXAuthAccessTokenForUsername:username
➥password:password];

    // Adding random number to the tweet to avoid Twitter's 403 "Status is
➥a duplicate" error.
    NSString *tweetText = [NSString stringWithFormat:@"%@ %d", message,
➥arc4random()%144];

    NSLog(@"About to post message to Twitter: \"%@\"", tweetText);

    [self.twitterEngine sendUpdate:tweetText];
    [username release];
    [password release];
    [message release];
    [tweetText release];
}
```

Adding MGTwitterEngine Delegate Methods

These are the MGTwitterEngine Delegate methods that would return the resulting responses from Twitter APIs. Each Delegate method will return a specific message in an alert window:

- statusesReceived:(NSArray *)statuses forRequest:(NSString *)connectionIdentifier
- accessTokenReceived:(OAToken *)token forRequest:(NSString *)connectionIdentifier
- requestSucceeded:(NSString *)connectionIdentifier
- requestFailed:(NSString *)connectionIdentifier withError:(NSError *)error

Add #pragma mark directives and MGTwitterEngine Delegate method in xauthViewController.m:

```
#pragma mark -
#pragma mark MGTwitterEngineDelegate methods

- (void)statusesReceived:(NSArray *)statuses forRequest:(NSString
*)connectionIdentifier{
        // Since we're just sending a tweet in this example, we can
➥assume that's the tweet that's returned
        // and use this as a success handler.
        UIAlertViewQuick(@"Tweet sent!", @"The tweet was successfully
➥sent. Everything works!", @"OK");
```

```
}

- (void)accessTokenReceived:(OAToken *)token forRequest:(NSString
*)connectionIdentifier{
        //
        // We've got an oAuth access token from Twitter. Let's save it.
        //
        NSString *tokenKey = token.key;
        NSString *tokenSecret = token.secret;

        // Save the token securely in the keychain.
        // (Note: this SFHFKeychainUtils method doesn't return a value.)
        NSError *error = nil;
        [SFHFKeychainUtils storeUsername:tokenKey andPassword:tokenSecret
➥forService-Name:kMGTwitterEngineDemoServiceName
➥sharedKeychainAccessGroupName:nil updateExist-ing:YES error:&error];
        if (error)
        {
                NSString *errorMessage = [NSString
➥stringWithFormat:@"Error saving to-ken", @"I couldn't save the oAuth
➥token to the keychain. %d: %@", [error code], [errorlocalized
➥Description]];
                UIAlertViewQuick(@"Error saving token", errorMessage,
➥@"OK");
        }
        else
        {
                // Save the token key and flag that we have a cached
➥token.
                NSLog(@"Got the oAuth token and about to save it.");
                NSUserDefaults *userDefaults = [NSUserDefaults
➥standardUserDefaults];
                [userDefaults setObject:tokenKey forKey:kTokenKey];
                [userDefaults setBool:YES forKey:kHaveCachedToken];
                [userDefaults synchronize];
        }

        // Set the access token on the twitter engine
        // (Why doesn't MGTwitterEngine do this automatically?)
        self.twitterEngine.accessToken = token;
}

- (void)requestSucceeded:(NSString *)connectionIdentifier{
        NSLog(@"Twitter request succeeded: %@", connectionIdentifier);
}

- (void)requestFailed:(NSString *)connectionIdentifier withError:(NSError
➥*)error{
        NSLog(@"Twitter request failed: %@ with error:%@",
➥connectionIdentifier, error);

        if ([[error domain] isEqualToString: @"HTTP"])
        {
```

```
            switch ([error code]) {

                    case 401:
                    {
                            // Unauthorized. The user's
➥credentials failed to verify.
                            UIAlertViewQuick(@"Oops!", @"Your
➥username and pass-word could not be verified. Double check that you
➥entered them correctly and tryagain.", @"OK");
                            break;
                    }

                    case 502:
                    {
                            // Bad gateway: twitter is down or
➥being upgraded.
                            UIAlertViewQuick(@"Fail whale!",
@"Looks like Twitteris down or being updated. Please wait a few seconds and
try again.", @"OK");
                            break;
                    }

                    case 503:
                    {
                            // Service unavailable
                            UIAlertViewQuick(@"Hold your taps!",
@"Looks likeTwitter is overloaded. Please wait a few seconds and try
➥again.", @"OK");
                            break;
                    }

                    default:
                    {
                            NSString *errorMessage = [[NSString
alloc] initWith-Format: @"%d %@", [error  code], [error
localizedDescription]];
                            UIAlertViewQuick(@"Twitter error!",
➥errorMessage, @"OK");

                            [errorMessage release];
                            break;
                    }
            }

        }
        else
        {
            switch ([error code]) {

                    case -1009:
                    {
                            UIAlertViewQuick(@"You're offline!",
@"Sorry, it lookslike you lost your Internet connection. Please reconnect
and try again.", @"OK");
```

```
                                break;
                        }

                        case -1200:
                        {
                                UIAlertViewQuick(@"Secure connection
failed", @"Icouldn't connect to Twitter. This is most likely a temporary
issue, please try again.",@"OK");
                                break;
                        }

                        default:
                        {
                                NSString *errorMessage = [[NSString
➥alloc] initWith-
Format:@"%@ xx %d: %@", [error domain], [error code], [error
➥localizedDescription]];
                                UIAlertViewQuick(@"Network Error!",
errorMessage ,@"OK");
                                [errorMessage release];
                        }
                }
        }

}
```

Now we finish all the codes in .h and .m files for the xauthViewController.

Creating Objects in Interface Builder

It's time to create all the objects required in the Interface Builder for the xauthViewController:

1. Click the interface builder file named xauthViewController.xib in Xcode's Project Navigator.

2. Select View, Utilities, Object Library or click on View Right Panel icon at the top right of Xcode to show the Utility panel and select the Object Library icon to open the Object Library, as shown in Figure 24.5.

3. Create a UILabel by dragging a Label from the Object Library to the View within the Interface Builder Editor.

4. Create a UIText field for username by dragging a TextField from the Objective Library to the View. Create another text field for password.

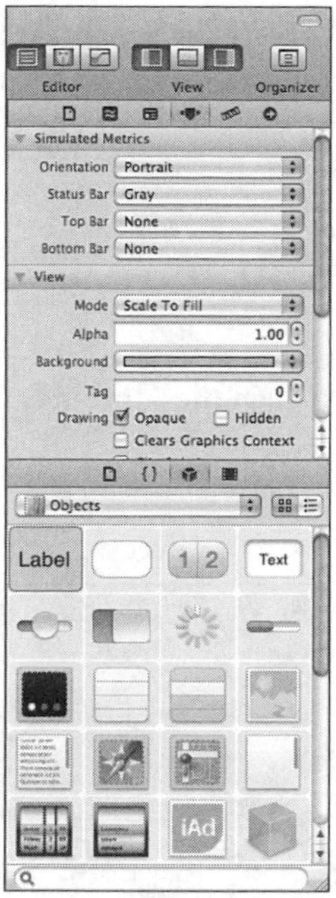

FIGURE 24.5
Selecting the UILabel in Library.

5. Create a UIText view for the message by dragging a TextView from the Object Library to the View.
6. Create a UIButton by dragging a Button from the Object Library to the View.
7. Select File, Save.
8. Click Run icon to run the project.

Did You Know?

The View in Interface Builder is laid out to give sufficient space for the Keyboard to display in the lower half of View. The Keyboard in iPhone OS is 216 pixels high. You can use Size Inspector to guide you on the layout dimension.

Did You Know?

UITextField object is designed for one line only. To display multiple lines, you would have to use UITextView object. UITextView object is filled with random text by default. The default text is longer than Twitter messages, which are restricted to 140 characters. The example is using only 140 characters from the default random text to guide the layout. 140 characters fit well in four lines in the UITextView object.

Defining Object Attributes in Interface Builder

After the objects are created on the View, it's time to define the object attributes:

1. Click xauthViewController.xib in the Xcode's Project Navigator to open the file.
2. Select the username UITextField object in the View inside Interface Builder Editor.
3. Select the Attributes icon to open the Attributes Inspector in the Utilities area.
4. In the Attributes Inspector, enter `Username` in Placeholder, as shown in Figure 24.6.

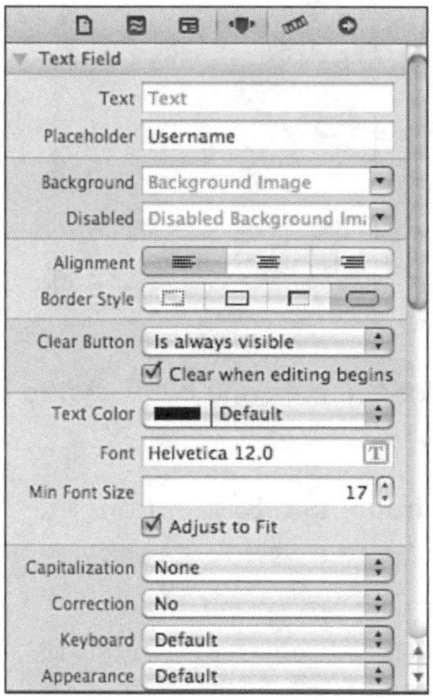

FIGURE 24.6
Setting the properties for username Text Field in Attributes Inspector.

5. In the Clear Button menu, select Is Always Visible.
6. Click the check box Clear When Editing Begins.
7. In the Correction menu, select No.
8. Select the password UITextField object in the View inside Interface Builder Editor.
9. In the Attributes Inspector, enter `Password` in Placeholder.
10. In the Clear Button menu, select Is Always Invisible.

11. Click the check box Clear When Editing Begins.
12. In the Correction menu, select No.
13. Click the check box Secure.
14. Select the message UITextView object in the View within Interface Builder Editor.
15. Click the check box Editable.
16. Delete all the characters longer than 140 characters in the Text box. Adjust the TextView object size by dragging the object handlers until it is 300 pixels wide and 98 pixels high. Now remove all the characters in the Text box.
17. In the Correction menu, select No.
18. In the Return Key menu, select Done.
19. In Scrollers of the Scroll View section, remove all the default settings from the Scroller check boxes.
20. Select Button object in the View within Interface Builder Editor.
21. In the Attributes Inspector, enter `Post` in Title.
22. Save all the changes by selecting File, Save in File menu.

Connecting Objects in Interface Builder

Everything is in place now. It's time to connect the objects in Interface Builder to the methods in Xcode:

1. Select the username UITextField object in the View within Interface Builder Editor, as shown in Figure 24.7.
2. Click the Connections icon to open the Connections Inspector in the Utilities area. In the Connections Inspector, mouse over the circle next to New Referencing Outlet until it appears as a plus (+) sign (see Figure 24.8).
3. Click and hold the mouse down. Drag it outside the circle until you see a blue line. Drag the blue line across the interface builder Editor area to the orange cube File's Owners icon. It is the first icon at the top of the vertical bar in the interface builder dock bar.

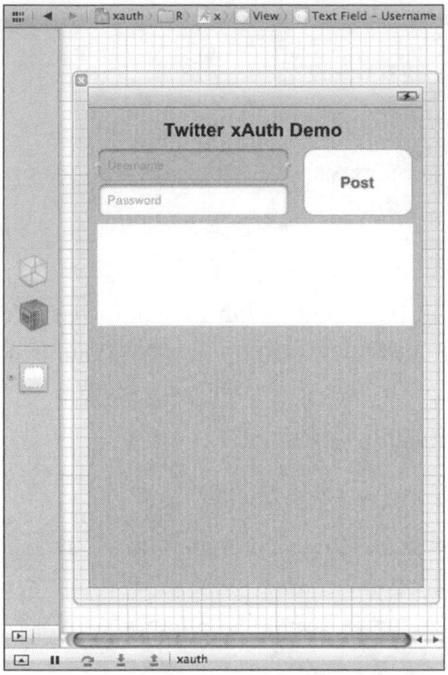

FIGURE 24.7 Selecting Username UITextField in the View in Interface Builder.

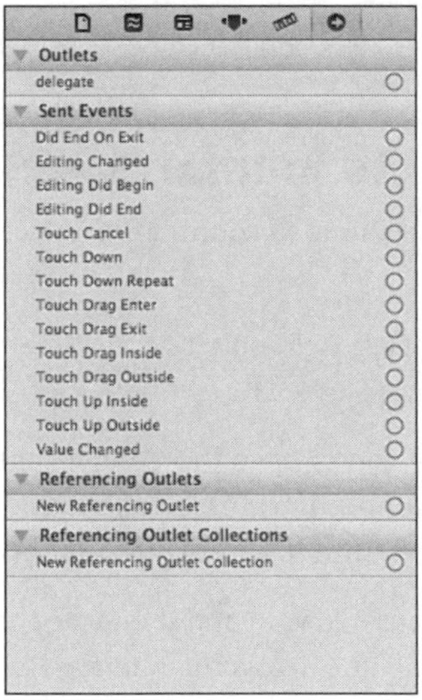

FIGURE 24.8 Selecting New Referencing Outlet for Text Field in Connections Inspector.

4. Release the mouse until you see a pop-up menu showing the Text Field objects, as shown in Figure 24.9.
5. Select usernameTextField to connect the username UITextField object. You should see usernameTextField is connected to File's Owner in the Connections Inspector.

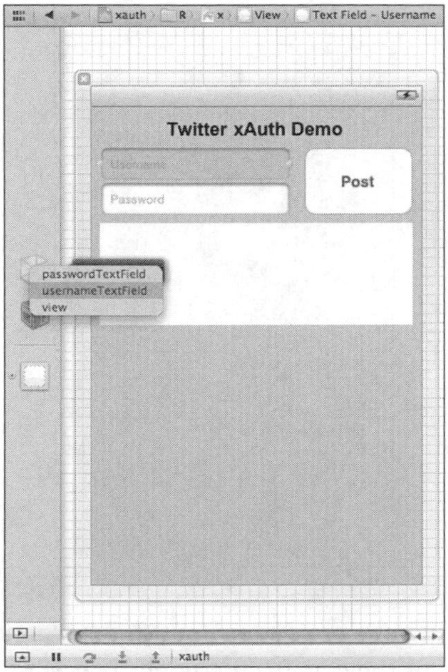

FIGURE 24.9 Selecting usernameTextField in File's Owner.

6. Repeat the same for the password UITextField object. Connect it to passwordTextField of the File's Owner icon.
7. Select the UITextView object in the View within Interface Builder Editor.
8. Connect it from Referencing Outlet in Connections Inspector to messageTextView at the File's Owner icon.
9. Select the UIButton object in the View within Interface Builder Editor.
10. Connect it from Referencing Outlet in Connections Inspector to postButton at the File's Owner icon.
11. Select the UIButton object in the View again within the Interface Builder Editor.
12. Connect it from Touch Up Inside under Events in the Connections Inspector to postMessage at the File's Owner icon.
13. Select File, Save in the File menu. If you open the Connections Inspector, you should see that the postButton method is connected to the File's Owner of UIButton object, and the postMessage method is connected to the Touch Up Inside on the Sent Events list, as shown in Figure 24.10.

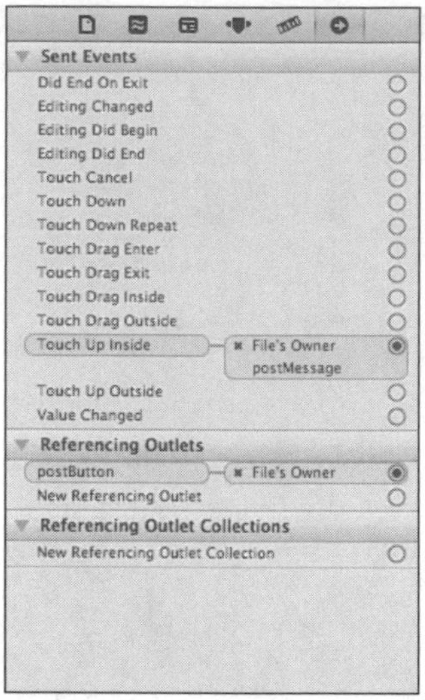

FIGURE 24.10 Showing the connections of UIButton in the Connections Inspector.

14. Click Run icon to run the project and launch the iPhone Simulator. You should see the app is showing the username, password, message, and post button objects inside the iPhone Simulator, as shown in Figure 24.11.

FIGURE 24.11 Showing the completed app in iPhone Simulator.

15. In the iPhone Simulator, enter a valid Twitter username and password.
16. Enter a text message under 140 characters.
17. Click the Post button. You should see the successful alert message in the app, as shown in Figure 24.12. It indicates that your xAuth is properly implemented and your Twitter account is valid.

FIGURE 24.12 Showing the Successful message in Alert view on the iPhone Simulator.

18. Log in to your Twitter account to view the Send Tweet submitted from the iPhone Simulator. Bask in the glow of your success.

Summary

Congratulations! You've added Twitter Objective-C library, JSON Objective-C library, and OAuth Objective-C library to your iPhone xAuth project. You've created an iPhone xAuth application using your activated xAuth Consumer key and Consumer secret. Last, you have posted a Tweet from your iPhone application in the iPhone Simulator.

Q&A

Q. ***Why is xAuth the preferred authentication method in the iOS application?***

A. xAuth library authenticates the iOS application without requiring users to visit the Twitter OAuth page. It is considered a better user experience.

Q. ***Why is the xAuth token stored in the Keychain?***

A. It is a better security practice to store the xAuth token in the Keychain than in user defaults.

Workshop

Quiz

1. Which parsing method(s) are integrated in processing Twitter resulting responses in MGTwitterEngine library?

A. XML

B. JSON

C. Both

2. What must be included in the iOS application to request an xAuth token?

A. Consumer key

B. Consumer secret

C. Both

3. What Inspector do you use to connect the interface builder object to the File's Owner?

A. Attributes Inspector

B. Size Inspector

C. Connection Inspector

D. Identity Inspector

Quiz Answers

1. C. libxml2.dylib framework is added to parse Twitter XML results, and TouchJSON is included to parse Twitter JSON results.
2. C. Twitter requires both the Consumer key and Consumer secret to generate xAuth access tokens.
3. C. The Connection Inspector provides the interface to connect the interface builder object in the view to the File's Owner.

Exercises

1. Create an xAuth Xcode project using the View-based template.
2. Add the entire MGTwitterDemo library into your iPhone Xcode project.
3. Add the application's Consumer key and Consumer secret into your iPhone application.
4. Complete an iPhone application to send a Tweet using xAuth.
5. Add another View Controller to show your Twitter timeline feed.

Index

Symbols

A

D

E

F

I

N

O

P

Q-R

V

W

X-Y-Z

Pocket Oxford American Thesaurus

SECOND EDITION

OXFORD
UNIVERSITY PRESS

OXFORD
UNIVERSITY PRESS

Oxford University Press, Inc., publishes works that further
Oxford University's objective of excellence
in research, scholarship, and education.

Oxford New York

Auckland Cape Town Dar es Salaam Hong Kong Karachi
Kuala Lumpur Madrid Melbourne Mexico City Nairobi
New Delhi Shanghai Taipei Toronto

With offices in

Argentina Austria Brazil Chile Czech Republic France Greece
Guatemala Hungary Italy Japan Poland Portugal Singapore
South Korea Switzerland Thailand Turkey Ukraine Vietnam

First edition 2002
Second edition 2008

Published by Oxford University Press, Inc.
198 Madison Avenue, New York, NY 10016
www.oup.com

The Library of Congress Cataloging-in-Publication Data

Data available

ISBN 978-0-19-530169-4

3 5 7 9 8 6 4 2

Printed in the United States of America
on acid-free paper

Contents

Contributors

Project Manager
Maurice Waite

Senior Editor
Christine A. Lindberg

Editor
Benjamin G. Zimmer

For the *Concise Oxford American Thesaurus*:

Editor in Chief
Erin McKean

Managing Editor
Constance Baboukis

Senior Editor
Christine A. Lindberg

Preface

This new edition of the *Pocket Oxford American Thesaurus*, with more than 15,000 main entries and over 350,000 synonyms, will help you enrich your writing and express yourself more effectively. Example sentences or phrases for virtually every sense guide you to the right synonym, the synonyms are arranged in order of usefulness and closeness to the target word, and antonyms are provided for many senses.

Two kinds of featured note help you still further: "The Right Word" describes the subtle differences between a group of similar synonyms (for example, ***replace***, ***displace***, ***supersede***, and ***supplant***), and each "Usage Note," specially written by Brian Garner, the author of *Garner's Modern American Usage*, gives guidance on a tricky or disputed point of English, such as the expression ***the reason is because...*** and the use of ***but*** at the start of a sentence.

The compilers have been able to make full use of the worldwide resources of Oxford University Press, including work carried out for the *Concise Oxford American Thesaurus* (2006). This has ensured that the *Pocket* is fully informed by analysis of both the Oxford English Corpus, a two-billion-word database of many different types of real English, and the database of the Oxford Reading Program.

The brand new *Wordfinder* section in the center of the thesaurus contains hundreds of lists of words that are not normally found as synonyms in a thesaurus. The lists of Dogs, Fruit, Boats, etc., are grouped in thematic categories such as Animals, Food, and Transportation to make them interesting to browse, while an index enables you to go straight to a particular list. This section forms an invaluable additional resource for finding the word you need, especially for word puzzles such as crosswords.

Trademarks

This thesaurus includes some words that have, or are asserted to have, proprietary status as trademarks or otherwise. Their inclusion does not imply that they have acquired for legal purposes a nonproprietary or general significance, nor any other judgment concerning their legal status. In cases where the editorial staff have some evidence that a word has proprietary status, this is indicated by the label trademark, but no judgment concerning the legal status of such words is made or implied thereby.

Guide to the Thesaurus

entry word

phrase for which synonyms are given

approve ▸ verb **1** *his boss doesn't approve of his lifestyle* **agree with,** endorse, support, back, uphold, subscribe to, recommend, advocate, be in favor of, favor, think well of, like, appreciate, go for, hold with, take kindly to; be pleased with, admire, applaud, praise.
ANTONYMS condemn, disapprove.
2 *the government approved the proposals* **accept,** agree to, consent to, assent to, give one's blessing to, bless, rubber-stamp; ratify, sanction, endorse, authorize, validate, pass; support, back; informal give the nod to, give the go-ahead to, give the green light to, give the OK to, give the thumbs-up to.
ANTONYMS refuse.

example of use, to help distinguish different senses

label indicating the style of English in which the following synonym(s) are used (see page ix for explanations)

note helping you choose between similar words

> CHOOSE THE RIGHT WORD
>
> **approve, certify, commend, endorse, ratify, sanction**
>
> There are a number of ways to show your support for something. The most general way is to **approve** it, a term that covers

adorable ▸ adjective *adorable little kittens* **lovable,** appealing, charming, cute, cuddly, sweet, enchanting, bewitching, captivating, engaging, endearing, dear, darling, delightful, lovely, beautiful, attractive, gorgeous, winsome, winning, fetching; Scottish bonny.
ANTONYMS repulsive, hateful.

word(s) meaning the opposite of the entry word; most have entries of their own, where a wider choice will be found

label indicating the region of the world in which the following synonym(s) are used

part of speech of the entry word

aggravate ▸ verb **1** *the new law could aggravate the situation* **worsen,** make worse, exacerbate, inflame, compound; add fuel to the fire/flames, add insult to injury, rub salt in the wound.
ANTONYMS alleviate, improve.
2 informal *you don't have to aggravate people to get what you want* **annoy,** irritate, exasperate, bother, put out, nettle, provoke, antagonize, get on someone's nerves, ruffle (someone's feathers), try someone's patience; informal peeve, needle, bug, miff, get under someone's skin; tick off.
ANTONYMS calm, conciliate.

numbered sense of the entry word

core synonym—the closest synonym to the entry word

note giving help with a particular point of usage

> USAGE
>
> **aggravate, aggravation**
>
> Though documented as existing since the 1600s, *aggravate* for *annoy* or *irritate* has never gained the approval of stylists and

authority ▶ **noun 1** *a rebellion against those in authority* **power,** jurisdiction, command, control, charge, dominance, rule, sovereignty, supremacy; influence; informal clout. See note at JURISDICTION.
2 *the authority to arrest drug traffickers* **authorization,** right, power, mandate, prerogative, license, permission.
3 (authorities) *they failed to report the theft to the authorities* **officials,** officialdom; government, administration, establishment; police; informal the powers that be.
4 *an authority on the stock market* **expert,** specialist, aficionado, pundit, guru, sage.
5 *on good authority* **evidence,** testimony, witness, attestation, word, avowal; Law deposition.

cross reference to a note at another entry

form of the entry word for which the following synonym(s) can be used

label indicating the specialist field in which the following synonym(s) are used

Most of the synonyms given are part of standard English, but some are suitable only in certain contexts. These are grouped at the end of their synonym set and given the following labels:

formal	e.g., *cognizance* as a synonym for *knowledge*: normally used only in writing, such as official documents or academic works.
informal	e.g., *cornball* as a synonym for *sentimental*: normally used only in speaking or in informal writing such as email.
vulgar slang	informal language that may cause offense, usually because it refers to bodily functions.
technical	e.g., *annular* as a synonym for *round*: normally used only in technical and specialist language, though not necessarily restricted to any specific field. Words used in specific fields are given appropriate labels, e.g., Medicine, Nautical.
literary	e.g., *strand* as a synonym for *beach*: found only or mainly in literature.
dated	e.g., *gay* as a synonym for *cheerful*: no longer used by most, but still sometimes by older people.
historical	e.g., *alms* as a synonym for *charity*: still used today, but only to refer to some activity or article that is no longer part of the modern world.
rare	e.g., *flexuous* as a synonym for *winding*: not in normal use, either today or in previous times.
humorous	e.g., *libation* as a synonym for *drink*: intended to sound funny or playful.
archaic	e.g., *bootless* as a synonym for *futile*: old-fashioned language found in literature of the past, but not in ordinary use today except for an old-fashioned effect.
derogatory	e.g., *brat* as a synonym for *child*: intended to insult or offend the person or thing referred to.
euphemistic	e.g., *neutralize* as a synonym for *kill*: used in place of a more direct or vulgar term.

Synonyms are also labeled Canadian, Brit. (British), Scottish, Irish, or Austral. (Australian) if they are used exclusively or mainly in those particular parts of the world.

Aa

abandon ▸ verb **1** *the party abandoned policies that made it unelectable* **renounce,** relinquish, dispense with, disclaim, forgo, disown, disavow, discard, wash one's hands of; give up, withdraw, drop, jettison, do away with; informal ax, ditch, dump, scrap, scrub, junk, deep-six; formal forswear, abjure. See note at RELINQUISH.
ANTONYMS keep, retain.
2 *by that time, she had abandoned painting* **give up,** stop, cease, drop, forgo, desist from, dispense with, have done with, abstain from, discontinue, break off, refrain from, set aside; informal cut out, kick, pack in, quit.
ANTONYMS take up, continue.
3 *he abandoned his wife and children* **desert,** leave, leave high and dry, turn one's back on, cast aside, break (up) with; jilt, strand, leave stranded, leave in the lurch, throw over; informal walk out on, run out on, dump, ditch; literary forsake.
4 *the skipper gave the order to abandon ship* **vacate,** leave, depart from, withdraw from, quit, evacuate.
5 *a vast expanse of territory was abandoned to the invaders* **relinquish,** surrender, give up, cede, yield, leave.
ANTONYMS keep, claim.
6 *she **abandoned herself to** the sensuousness of the music* **indulge in,** give way to, give oneself up to, yield to, lose oneself to/in.
ANTONYMS control oneself.
▸ noun *at age sixty he had no less abandon than when he was twenty* **uninhibitedness,** recklessness, lack of restraint, lack of inhibition, wildness, impulsiveness, impetuosity, immoderation, wantonness.
ANTONYMS self-control.

abandoned ▸ adjective **1** *an abandoned child* **deserted,** forsaken, cast aside/off; jilted, stranded, rejected; informal dumped, ditched.
2 *an abandoned tin mine* **unused,** disused, neglected, idle; deserted, unoccupied, uninhabited, empty.
3 *an abandoned dance* **uninhibited,** reckless, unrestrained, wild, unbridled, impulsive, impetuous; immoderate, wanton.

abase ▸ verb **1** *Dunlap had a reputation for openly abasing his employees* **humble,** humiliate, belittle, demean, lower, degrade, debase, cheapen, discredit, bring low. See note at HUMBLE.
2 *I'd rather lose my job than continue to **abase myself*** grovel, kowtow, bow and scrape, toady, fawn; informal crawl, suck up to someone, lick someone's boots.

abasement ▸ noun *only a fiend delights in the abasement of his children* **humiliation,** humbling, belittlement, lowering, degradation, debasement.
ANTONYMS pride.

abashed ▸ adjective *Iris was positively abashed when she rose only to realize another nominee had won the award* **embarrassed,** ashamed, shamefaced, remorseful, conscience-stricken, mortified, humiliated, humbled, chagrined, crestfallen, sheepish, red-faced, blushing, put out of countenance, with one's tail between one's legs; taken aback, disconcerted, discomfited, fazed, disturbed; informal floored.

abate ▸ verb **1** *the storm had abated* **subside,** die down/away/out, lessen, ease (off), let up, decrease, diminish, moderate, decline, fade, dwindle, recede, tail off, peter out, taper off, wane, ebb, weaken, come to an end; archaic remit. See note at ALLEVIATE.
ANTONYMS intensify.
2 *nothing abated his crusading zeal* **decrease,** lessen, diminish, reduce, moderate, ease, soothe, dampen, calm, tone down, allay, temper.
ANTONYMS increase.

abatement ▸ noun **1** *the storm rages with no sign of abatement* **subsiding,** dying down/away/out, lessening, easing (off), letup, decrease, moderation, decline, ebb.
2 *noise abatement* **decrease,** reduction, lowering.

abbey ▸ noun *the brothers had been hiding refugees in the abbey's catacombs* **monastery, convent,** priory, cloister, friary, nunnery; historical charterhouse; rare cenobium.

abbreviate ▸ verb *please abbreviate your essays to a length of no more than two pages* **shorten,** reduce, cut, contract, condense, compress, abridge, truncate, pare down, prune, shrink, telescope; summarize, abstract, précis, synopsize, digest, edit.
ANTONYMS lengthen, expand, elongate.

abbreviation ▸ noun **1** *the abbreviation for 'teaspoon' is 'tsp.' or just 't.'* **shortened form,** short form, contraction, acronym, initialism, symbol, diminutive; elision.
ANTONYMS full form.
2 *'Desi Arnaz' was an abbreviation of the bandleader's full name, 'Desiderio Alberto Arnaz y de Acha III'* **shortening,** reduction, cutting, contraction, condensation, abridgment, truncation, cropping, paring down.
ANTONYMS expansion.

abdicate ▸ verb **1** *the king abdicated in 1936* **resign,** retire, stand down, step down, bow out, renounce the throne; archaic demit.

ANTONYMS be crowned.
2 *Ferdinand abdicated the throne* **resign from,** relinquish, renounce, give up, surrender, vacate, cede; Law disclaim; formal abjure.
ANTONYMS accede to.
3 *the state abdicated all responsibility for their welfare* **disown,** reject, renounce, give up, refuse, relinquish, repudiate, abandon, turn one's back on, wash one's hands of; forgo, waive; formal abjure; literary forsake.
ANTONYMS accept, take on.

abdication ▶ **noun 1** *Edward VIII's abdication* **resignation,** retirement; relinquishment, renunciation, surrender; formal abjuration; archaic demission.
ANTONYMS coronation.
2 *an abdication of responsibility* **disowning,** renunciation, rejection, refusal, relinquishment, repudiation, abandonment.
ANTONYMS acceptance.

abdomen ▶ **noun** *a firm abdomen* **stomach,** belly, gut, middle, intestines; informal tummy, insides, guts, maw, breadbasket, pot, paunch.

abdominal ▶ **adjective** *abdominal pains* **gastric,** intestinal, stomach, stomachic, enteric, duodenal, visceral, celiac, ventral.

abduct ▶ **verb** *police were tipped off that Kiley was planning to abduct the congressman's wife* **kidnap,** carry off, seize, capture, run away/off with, make off with, spirit away; informal snatch, shanghai.

aberrant ▶ **adjective** *eating on the floor with the dogs is just one example of his aberrant behavior* **deviant,** deviating, divergent, abnormal, atypical, anomalous, irregular; nonconformist, rogue; strange, odd, peculiar, uncommon, freakish, quirky; twisted, warped, perverted.
ANTONYMS normal, typical.

aberration ▶ **noun** *a statistical aberration* **anomaly,** deviation, departure from the norm, divergence, abnormality, irregularity, variation, digression, freak, rogue, rarity, oddity, peculiarity, curiosity, quirk; mistake.

abet ▶ **verb** *I refused to abet the neighbors in their scheme to sabotage the construction site* **assist,** aid, help, lend a hand to, support, back, encourage; cooperate with, collaborate with, work with, connive with, collude with, go along with, be in collusion with, be hand in glove with, side with; second, endorse, sanction; promote, incite, champion, further, expedite.
ANTONYMS hinder.

abeyance ▶ **noun** *expansion plans for the middle school are **in abeyance*** **in suspension,** in a state of suspension, in a state of dormancy, in a state of uncertainty, in remission; pending, suspended, deferred, postponed, put off, put to one side, unresolved, up in the air; informal in cold storage, on ice, on the back burner. See note at LATENT.

abhor ▶ **verb** *I abhor the taste of liver* **detest,** hate, loathe, despise, execrate, regard with disgust, shrink from, recoil from, shudder at; formal abominate. See note at DESPISE.
ANTONYMS love, admire.

abhorrent ▶ **adjective** *he continued to find war morally abhorrent* **detestable,** hateful, loathsome, despicable, abominable, execrable, repellent, repugnant, repulsive, revolting, disgusting, distasteful, horrible, horrid, horrifying, awful, heinous, reprehensible, obnoxious, odious, nauseating, offensive, contemptible. See note at OFFENSIVE.
ANTONYMS admirable.

abide ▶ **verb 1** *he expected everybody to **abide by** the rules* **comply with,** obey, observe, follow, keep to, hold to, conform to, adhere to, stick to, stand by, act in accordance with, uphold, heed, accept, go along with, acknowledge, respect, defer to.
ANTONYMS flout, disobey.
2 informal *I can't abide the smell of cigarettes* **tolerate,** bear, stand, put up with, endure, take, countenance; informal stomach; formal brook; archaic suffer.
ANTONYMS enjoy, relish.
3 *the memory of our parting will abide* **continue,** remain, survive, last, persist, stay, live on.
ANTONYMS fade, disappear.

abiding ▶ **adjective** *theirs is an abiding friendship* **enduring,** lasting, persisting, long-lasting, lifelong, continuing, remaining, surviving, standing, durable, everlasting, perpetual, eternal, unending, constant, permanent, unchanging, steadfast, immutable.
ANTONYMS short-lived, ephemeral.

ability ▶ **noun 1** *the ability to read and write* **capacity,** capability, potential, potentiality, power, faculty, aptness, facility; wherewithal, means.
2 *the president's leadership ability* **talent,** skill, expertise, adeptness, aptitude, skillfulness, savoir faire, prowess, mastery, accomplishment; competence, proficiency; dexterity, adroitness, deftness, cleverness, flair, finesse, gift, knack, genius; qualification, resources; informal know-how.

abject ▶ **adjective 1** *abject poverty* **wretched,** miserable, hopeless, pathetic, pitiful, pitiable, piteous, sorry, woeful, lamentable, degrading, appalling, atrocious, awful.
2 *an abject sinner* **contemptible,** base, low, vile, worthless, debased, degraded, despicable, ignominious, mean, unworthy, ignoble.
3 *an abject apology* **obsequious,** groveling, fawning, toadyish, servile, cringing, sycophantic, submissive, craven.

abjure ▶ **verb** formal *she has abjured the doctrines of her parents' faith* **renounce,** relinquish, reject, forgo, disavow, abandon, deny, repudiate, give up, wash one's hands of; eschew, abstain from, refrain from; informal kick, pack in; Law disaffirm; literary forsake; formal forswear, abnegate.

ablaze ▶ **adjective 1** *several vehicles were ablaze* **on fire,** alight, aflame, in flames, flaming, burning, fiery, blazing; literary afire, igneous.
2 *every window was ablaze with light* **lit up,** alight, gleaming, glowing, aglow, illuminated, bright, shining, radiant, shimmering, sparkling, flashing, dazzling, luminous, incandescent.
3 *his eyes were ablaze with fury* **passionate,** impassioned, aroused, excited, adrenalized, stimulated, eager, animated, intense, ardent, fiery, fervent, frenzied.

able ▶ **adjective 1** *he will soon be able to resume his*

duties **capable of,** competent to, equal to, up to, fit to, prepared to, qualified to; allowed to, free to, in a position to.
ANTONYMS incapable.
2 *an able student* **intelligent,** clever, talented, skillful, skilled, accomplished, gifted; proficient, apt, good, adroit, adept; capable, competent, efficient, effective.
ANTONYMS incompetent.

able-bodied ▶ **adjective** *we'll need at least six able-bodied men and women for the expedition* **healthy, fit,** in good health, robust, strong, sound, sturdy, vigorous, hardy, hale and hearty, athletic, muscular, strapping, burly, brawny, lusty; in good shape, in good trim, in fine fettle, fighting fit, as fit as a fiddle; informal husky; dated stalwart.
ANTONYMS infirm, frail, disabled.

abnegation ▶ **noun** formal **1** *a serious abnegation of their responsibilities* **renunciation,** rejection, refusal, abandonment, abdication, surrender, relinquishment, repudiation, denial; formal abjuration.
ANTONYMS acceptance.
2 *people capable of abnegation and unselfishness* **self-denial,** self-sacrifice, abstinence, temperance, continence, asceticism, austerity, abstemiousness.
ANTONYMS self-indulgence.

abnormal ▶ **adjective** *an increased appetite during pregnancy is not abnormal | she speaks Spanish with a Swedish accent, which is pretty abnormal* **unusual,** uncommon, atypical, untypical, nontypical, unrepresentative, rare, isolated, irregular, anomalous, deviant, divergent, aberrant, freak, freakish; **strange,** odd, peculiar, curious, bizarre, weird, queer; eccentric, idiosyncratic, quirky; unexpected, unfamiliar, unconventional, surprising, unorthodox, singular, exceptional, extraordinary, out of the ordinary, out of the way; unnatural, perverse, perverted, twisted, warped, unhealthy, distorted; informal freaky.
ANTONYMS normal, typical, common.

abnormality ▶ **noun 1** *born with a heart abnormality* **malformation,** deformity, irregularity, flaw, defect, anomaly.
2 *the abnormality of such behavior* **unusualness,** uncommonness, atypicality, irregularity, anomalousness, deviation, divergence, aberrance, aberration, freakishness; strangeness, oddness, peculiarity, unexpectedness, singularity.

abode ▶ **noun** *welcome to my humble abode* **home,** house, place of residence, accommodations; quarters, lodgings, domicile, rooms; address; informal pad, digs; formal dwelling, dwelling place, residence, habitation.

abolish ▶ **verb** *the governor never fulfilled his promise to abolish the state income tax* **put an end to,** get rid of, scrap, end, stop, terminate, ax, eradicate, eliminate, exterminate, destroy, annihilate, stamp out, obliterate, wipe out, extinguish, quash, expunge, extirpate; annul, cancel, invalidate, negate, nullify, void, dissolve; rescind, repeal, revoke, overturn; discontinue, remove, excise, drop, jettison; informal do away with, ditch, junk, scrub, dump; formal abrogate.
ANTONYMS retain, create.

abolition ▶ **noun** *the abolition of slavery did not guarantee equality* **scrapping,** ending, termination, eradication, elimination, extermination, abolishment, destruction, annihilation, obliteration, extirpation; annulment, cancellation, invalidation, nullification, dissolution; revocation, repeal, discontinuation, removal; formal abrogation.

abominable ▶ **adjective** *Caligula was among the most abominable figures in history* **loathsome,** detestable, hateful, odious, obnoxious, despicable, contemptible, damnable, diabolical; disgusting, revolting, repellent, repulsive, offensive, repugnant, abhorrent, reprehensible, atrocious, horrifying, execrable, foul, vile, wretched, base, horrible, awful, dreadful, appalling, nauseating; horrid, nasty, disagreeable, unpleasant, distasteful; informal terrible, shocking, godawful; beastly; dated cursed, accursed. See note at **OFFENSIVE.**
ANTONYMS good, admirable.

abominate ▶ **verb** formal *I truly abominate her use of coarse language* **detest,** loathe, hate, abhor, despise, execrate, shudder at, recoil from, shrink from, be repelled by.
ANTONYMS like, love.

abomination ▶ **noun 1** *in both wars, internment was an abomination* **atrocity,** disgrace, horror, obscenity, outrage, evil, crime, monstrosity, anathema, bane.
2 *she looked upon his kitschy decor with abomination* **detestation,** loathing, hatred, aversion, antipathy, revulsion, repugnance, abhorrence, odium, execration, disgust, horror, hostility.
ANTONYMS liking, love.

aboriginal ▶ **adjective 1** *the area's aboriginal inhabitants* **indigenous,** native; original, earliest, first; ancient, primitive, primeval, primordial; rare autochthonous.
2 *Aboriginal soldiers serving in the Canadian forces* **native,** indigenous, First Nations, Indian, Inuit, Metis. See note at **NATIVE.**
▶ **noun** *the social structure of the aboriginals* **native,** aborigine, original inhabitant; rare autochthon, indigene.

abort ▶ **verb** *the crew aborted the takeoff* **halt,** stop, end, ax, call off, cut short, discontinue, terminate, arrest, cancel, scrub; informal pull the plug on.

abortion ▶ **noun** *her first pregnancy resulted in a spontaneous abortion* **termination,** miscarriage.

abortive ▶ **adjective** *the abortive coup was crushed after two days of fighting* **unsuccessful,** failed, vain, thwarted, futile, useless, worthless, ineffective, ineffectual, to no effect, inefficacious, fruitless, unproductive, unavailing, to no avail, sterile, nugatory; archaic bootless.
ANTONYMS successful, fruitful.

abound ▶ **verb 1** *cafés and bars abound in the narrow streets* **be plentiful,** be abundant, be numerous, proliferate, superabound, be thick on the ground; informal grow on trees.
2 *the stream* ***abounds with*** *trout and eels* **be full of,** overflow with, teem with, be packed

with, be crowded with, be thronged with; be alive with, be crawling with, be overrun by/with, swarm with, bristle with, be infested with, be thick with; informal be stuffed with, be jam-packed with, be chockablock with, be chock-full of.

about ▶ preposition **1** *a book about needlecraft* **regarding,** concerning, with reference to, referring to, with regard to, with respect to, respecting, relating to, on, touching on, dealing with, relevant to, connected with, in connection with, on the subject of, in the matter of, apropos, re.
2 *two hundred people were milling about the room* **around,** round, throughout, over, through, on every side of.
▶ adverb **1** *there were babies crawling about in the grass* **around,** here and there, to and fro, back and forth, from place to place, hither and thither, in all directions.
2 *I knew he was somewhere about* **near,** nearby, around, hereabouts, not far (off/away), close by, in the vicinity, in the neighborhood.
3 *the explosion caused about $15,000 worth of damage* **approximately,** roughly, around, round about, in the region of, circa, of/on the order of, something like; or so, or thereabouts, there or thereabouts, more or less, give or take a few, not far off; informal in the ballpark of.
4 *there's a lot of gossip about* **around,** in circulation, in existence, current, going on, prevailing, prevalent, happening, in the air, abroad.
– PHRASES **about to** *I'm about to leave* **(just) going to,** ready to, all set to, preparing to, getting ready to, intending to, soon to; on the point of, on the verge of, on the brink of; informal fixing to.

above ▶ preposition **1** *a tiny window above the door* **over,** higher (up) than; on top of, atop, on, upon.
ANTONYMS below, under, beneath.
2 *those above the rank of colonel* **superior to,** senior to, over, higher (up) than, more powerful than; in charge of, commanding.
ANTONYMS below, junior to.
3 *you must be above suspicion* **beyond,** not liable to, not open to, not vulnerable to, out of reach of; immune to, exempt from.
4 *the Chinese valued pearls above gold* **more than,** over, before, rather than, in preference to, instead of.
5 *an increase above the rate of inflation* **greater than,** more than, higher than, exceeding, in excess of, over, over and above, beyond, surpassing, upwards of.
ANTONYMS below, less than.
▶ adverb **1** *in the darkness above, something moved* **overhead,** on/at the top, high up, on high, up above, (up) in the sky, high above one's head, aloft.
2 *the two cases described above* **earlier,** previously, before, formerly.
▶ adjective *the above example* **preceding,** previous, earlier, former, foregoing, prior, above-stated, above-mentioned, aforementioned, aforesaid.
– PHRASES **above all** *above all, deactivate the alarm before attempting to open the door* **most importantly,** before everything, beyond everything, first of all, most of all, chiefly, primarily, in the first place, first and foremost, mainly, principally, predominantly, especially, essentially, basically, in essence, at bottom; informal at the end of the day, when all is said and done.

aboveboard ▶ adjective *the proceedings were completely aboveboard* **legitimate,** lawful, legal, licit, honest, fair, open, frank, straight, overt, candid, forthright, unconcealed, trustworthy, unequivocal; informal legit, kosher, by the book, street legal, fair and square, square, on the level, on the up and up, upfront.
ANTONYMS dishonest, shady.

abrasion ▶ noun **1** *his knees were marked up with abrasions* **graze,** cut, scrape, scratch, gash, laceration, injury, contusion; sore, ulcer.
2 *the metal is resistant to abrasion* **erosion,** wearing away/down, corrosion, scraping, scouring.

abrasive ▶ adjective **1** *abrasive cleanser* **corrosive,** corroding, erosive; caustic, harsh, scratching, coarse.
ANTONYMS gentle.
2 *her abrasive manner* **caustic,** cutting, biting, acerbic; rough, harsh, hard, tough, sharp, grating, curt, brusque, stern, severe; wounding, nasty, cruel, callous, insensitive, unfeeling, unsympathetic, inconsiderate.
ANTONYMS kind, gentle.

abreast ▶ adverb **1** *they walked three abreast* **in a row,** side by side, alongside, level, beside each other, shoulder to shoulder.
2 *try to keep **abreast of** current affairs* **up to date with,** up with, in touch with, informed about, acquainted with, knowledgeable about, conversant with, familiar with, au courant with, au fait with.

abridge ▶ verb *she was hired to abridge the works of Shakespeare for a children's book club* **shorten,** cut, cut short, cut down, curtail, truncate, trim, crop, clip, pare down, prune; abbreviate, condense, contract, compress, reduce, decrease, shrink; summarize, sum up, abstract, précis, synopsize, give a digest of, put in a nutshell, edit; rare epitomize.
ANTONYMS lengthen.

abridgment ▶ noun *an abridgment of the full report* **summary,** abstract, synopsis, précis, outline, résumé, sketch, compendium, digest.

abroad ▶ adverb **1** *he regularly travels abroad* **overseas,** out of the country, to/in foreign parts, to/in a foreign country, to/in a foreign land.
2 *rumors were abroad* **in circulation,** circulating, widely current, everywhere, in the air, 'here, there, and everywhere'; about, around; at large.

abrogation ▶ noun formal *such a defense system would require amendment or abrogation of the 1972 antiballistic missile treaty* **repeal,** revocation, repudiation, rescinding, overturning, annulment, overruling, cancellation, invalidation, nullification, negation, dissolution, discontinuation; reversal, retraction, removal, withdrawal, abolition; formal rescission; rare deracination.

abrupt ▶ adjective **1** *an abrupt halt* | *an abrupt change of subject* **sudden,** unexpected,

without warning, unanticipated, unforeseen, precipitate, precipitous, surprising, startling; quick, swift, rapid, hurried, hasty, immediate, instantaneous.
ANTONYMS gradual, unhurried.
2 *an abrupt manner* **curt,** brusque, blunt, short, sharp, terse, crisp, gruff, rude, discourteous, uncivil, snappish, unceremonious, offhand, rough, harsh; bluff, no-nonsense, to the point; informal snappy.
ANTONYMS friendly, expansive.
3 *abrupt, epigrammatic paragraphs* **disjointed,** jerky, uneven, disconnected, inelegant.
ANTONYMS smooth, flowing.
4 *an abrupt slope* **steep,** sheer, precipitous, bluff, sharp, sudden; perpendicular, vertical, dizzy, vertiginous.
ANTONYMS gradual, gentle.

abscess ▶ **noun** *the abscess is what's causing the pain* **ulcer,** ulceration, cyst, boil, blister, sore, pustule, carbuncle, pimple, wen, whitlow, canker; inflammation, infection, eruption.

abscond ▶ **verb** *it seems that the one they entrusted with their stolen goods has absconded* **run away,** escape, bolt, flee, make off, take flight, take off, decamp; make a break for it, take to one's heels, make a quick getaway, beat a hasty retreat, run for it, make a run for it; disappear, vanish, slip away, split, steal away, sneak away; clear out, duck out; informal cut and run, skedaddle, skip, skip town, head for the hills, do a disappearing act, fly the coop, take French leave, vamoose, take a powder.

absence ▶ **noun 1** *what excuse has he given for his absence this time? | an extended absence* **nonattendance,** nonappearance, absenteeism; **truancy,** playing truant; leave, holiday, vacation, sabbatical.
ANTONYMS presence, attendance.
2 *the absence of suitable candidates* **lack,** want, nonexistence, unavailability, deficiency, dearth; need.
ANTONYMS presence, availability.

absent ▶ **adjective 1** *she was absent from work | an absent parent* **away,** off, out, nonattending, truant; off duty, on holiday, on leave; gone, missing, unavailable, nonexistent; informal AWOL, playing hooky.
ANTONYMS present.
2 *an absent look* **distracted,** preoccupied, inattentive, vague, absorbed, abstracted, unheeding, oblivious, distrait, absentminded, dreamy, far away, in a world of one's own, lost in thought, in a brown study; blank, empty, vacant; informal miles away.
ANTONYMS attentive, alert.
▶ **verb** (**absent oneself**) *Rose absented herself from the occasion* **stay away,** be absent, withdraw, retire, take one's leave, remove oneself.

absentminded ▶ **adjective** *I tend to be most absentminded in school* **forgetful,** distracted, preoccupied, inattentive, vague, abstracted, daydreaming, unheeding, oblivious, distrait, in a brown study; lost in thought, moony, pensive, thoughtful, brooding; informal scatterbrained, out of it, out to lunch, miles away, having a mind/memory like a sieve, spacey.
ANTONYMS alert, observant.

absolute ▶ **adjective 1** *absolute silence | an absolute disgrace* **complete,** total, utter, out-and-out, outright, entire, perfect, pure, decided; thorough, thoroughgoing, undivided, unqualified, unadulterated, unalloyed, unmodified, unreserved, downright, undiluted, consummate, unmitigated, sheer, arrant, rank, dyed-in-the-wool.
ANTONYMS partial, qualified.
2 *the absolute truth* **definite,** certain, positive, unconditional, categorical, unquestionable, incontrovertible, undoubted, unequivocal, decisive, conclusive, confirmed, infallible.
ANTONYMS partial, qualified.
3 *absolute power* **unlimited,** unrestricted, unrestrained, unbounded, boundless, infinite, ultimate, total, supreme, unconditional.
ANTONYMS limited, conditional.
4 *an absolute monarch* **autocratic,** despotic, dictatorial, tyrannical, tyrannous, absolutist, authoritarian, arbitrary, autonomous, sovereign, autarchic, autarchical, omnipotent.
ANTONYMS constitutional.
5 *absolute moral standards* **universal,** fixed, independent, nonrelative, nonvariable, absolutist.
ANTONYMS relative, flexible.

absolutely ▶ **adverb** *you're absolutely right* **completely,** totally, utterly, perfectly, entirely, wholly, fully, quite, thoroughly, unreservedly; definitely, certainly, positively, unconditionally, categorically, unquestionably, undoubtedly, without (a) doubt, without question, surely, unequivocally; exactly, precisely, decisively, conclusively, manifestly, in every way, in every respect, one hundred percent, every inch, to the hilt; informal dead.
ANTONYMS partially, in no way.
▶ **exclamation** informal *"Have I made myself clear?" "Absolutely!"* **yes,** indeed, of course, definitely, certainly, quite, without (a) doubt, without question, unquestionably; affirmative, by all means.
ANTONYMS by no means.

absolution ▶ **noun** Christianity *Father, I am a sinful man in need of absolution* **forgiveness,** pardon, exoneration, remission, dispensation, indulgence, clemency, mercy; discharge, acquittal; freedom, deliverance, release; vindication; formal exculpation; archaic shrift.
ANTONYMS punishment, condemnation.

absolve ▶ **verb 1** *this fact does not absolve you from responsibility* **exonerate,** discharge, acquit, vindicate; release, relieve, liberate, free, deliver, clear, exempt, let off; formal exculpate.
ANTONYMS blame, condemn.
2 Christianity *I **absolve** you of your sins* **forgive,** pardon.
ANTONYMS punish, condemn.

CHOOSE THE RIGHT WORD

absolve, acquit, exempt, exonerate, forgive, pardon, vindicate

To varying degrees, all of these words mean to free from guilt or blame, and some are most frequently heard in a legal or political context. **Absolve** is the most general term, meaning to set free or release—not only from guilt or blame, but from a duty or obligation (*absolved from her promise to serve on the committee*) or from the penalties for their violation. **Pardon** is usually associated with the actions of a government or military official (*he was convicted of murder but later pardoned*) and specifically refers to a release from prosecution or punishment. It is usually a legal official who decides to **acquit** someone—that is, release someone from a specific and formal accusation of wrongdoing (*the court acquitted the accused due to lack of evidence*). **Exonerate** suggests relief (its origin suggests the lifting of a burden), often in a moral sense, from a definite charge so that not even the suspicion of wrongdoing remains (*completely exonerated from the accusation of cheating*). A person who is **vindicated** is also off the hook, usually due to the examination of evidence (*she vindicated herself by producing the missing documents*). **Exempt** has less to do with guilt and punishment and more to do with duty and obligation (*exempt from paying taxes*). To **forgive**, however, is the most magnanimous act of all: It implies not only giving up on the idea that an offense should be punished, but also relinquishing any feelings of resentment or vengefulness (*"To err is human; to forgive divine"*).

absorb ▸ **verb 1** *a spongelike material that absorbs water* **soak up,** suck up, draw up/in, take up/in, blot up, mop up, sop up.
ANTONYMS exude.
2 *she absorbed the information in silence* **assimilate,** digest, take in.
3 *the company was absorbed into the new concern* **incorporate,** assimilate, integrate, take, appropriate, subsume, include, co-opt, swallow up.
4 *these roles absorb most of his time and energy* **use (up),** consume, take (up), occupy.
5 *she was totally* ***absorbed in*** *her book* **engross in,** captivate by, occupy with, preoccupy with, engage in, rivet by, grip by, hold by, interest in, intrigue by/with, immerse in, involve in, enthrall by, spellbind by, fascinate by/with.

absorbent ▸ **adjective** *absorbent towels* **porous,** spongy, spongelike, permeable, pervious, absorptive; technical spongiform.
ANTONYMS waterproof.

absorbing ▸ **adjective** *an absorbing spy novel* **fascinating,** interesting, captivating, gripping, engrossing, compelling, compulsive, enthralling, riveting, spellbinding, consuming, intriguing, thrilling, exciting; informal unputdownable.
ANTONYMS boring, uninteresting.

absorption ▸ **noun 1** *the absorption of water* **soaking up,** sucking up; technical osmosis.
2 *by 1543, Scottish fears of absorption by England were allayed* **incorporation,** assimilation, integration, appropriation, inclusion.
3 *her total* ***absorption in*** *the music* **involvement in,** immersion in, raptness in, engrossment in, occupation with, preoccupation with, engagement in, captivation with, fascination with, enthrallment with.

abstain ▸ **verb 1** *Benjamin* ***abstained from*** *wine* **refrain from,** desist from, hold back from, forbear; give up, renounce, avoid, shun, eschew, forgo, go without, do without; refuse, decline; informal cut out; formal abjure.
ANTONYMS indulge in.
2 *pregnant women are encouraged to abstain* **not drink,** be teetotal, take the pledge; informal be on the wagon.
ANTONYMS drink.
3 *262 voted against, 38 abstained* **not vote,** decline to vote.
ANTONYMS vote.

abstemious ▸ **adjective** *the monks here have willingly chosen this abstemious life* **self-denying,** temperate, abstinent, moderate, self-disciplined, restrained, self-restrained, sober, austere, ascetic, puritanical, spartan, hair-shirt.
ANTONYMS self-indulgent.

abstinence ▸ **noun 1** *AA endorses a path of abstinence* **teetotalism,** temperance, sobriety, abstemiousness, abstention; rare nephalism.
2 *of course abstinence is the most effective form of birth control, but is it the most realistic?* **celibacy,** chastity, virginity, self-restraint, self-denial.
ANTONYMS promiscuity.
3 *three days of* ***abstinence from*** *solid food* **refraining from,** desisting from, holding back from, withholding; **renunciation of,** refusal of, declining, avoidance of, eschewal of, abjuration of; forgoing, shunning, going without, doing without.
ANTONYMS indulgence.

CHOOSE THE RIGHT WORD

abstinence, abnegation, abstemiousness, continence, forbearance, moderation, temperance

Abstinence implies voluntary self-denial and is usually associated with the non-indulgence of an appetite (*total abstinence from cigarettes and alcohol*). **Abstemiousness** is the quality or habit of being abstinent; an abstemious person would be one who is moderate when it comes to eating and drinking. **Continence**, **temperance**, and **moderation** all imply various forms of self-restraint or self-denial: *moderation* is the avoidance of extremes or excesses (*he drank in moderation*); *temperance* is habitual moderation, or even total abstinence, particularly with regard to alcohol (*the nineteenth-century temperance movement*); and *continence* (in this regard) refers to self-restraint with regard to sexual activity. **Forbearance** is self-control, the patient endurance that characterizes deliberately holding back from action or response. **Abnegation** is the rejection or renunciation of something that is generally held in high esteem (*abnegation of the Christian Church*), although it can also mean to refuse or deny oneself a particular right, claim, or convenience (*abnegation of worldly goods*).

abstract ▶ adjective **1** *abstract concepts* **theoretical,** conceptual, notional, intellectual, metaphysical, ideal, philosophical, academic; rare ideational.
ANTONYMS actual, concrete.
2 *abstract art* **nonrepresentational,** nonpictorial.
ANTONYMS representational.
▶ verb **1** *we'll be abstracting material for an online database* **summarize,** précis, abridge, condense, compress, shorten, cut down, abbreviate, synopsize; rare epitomize.
2 *he abstracted the art of tragedy from its context* **extract,** isolate, separate, detach.
▶ noun *an abstract of her speech* **summary,** synopsis, précis, résumé, outline, abridgment, digest, summation; wrap-up.

abstracted ▶ adjective *I apologize for being so abstracted when you were talking* **absentminded,** distracted, preoccupied, in a world of one's own, with one's head in the clouds, daydreaming, dreamy, inattentive, thoughtful, pensive, lost in thought, deep in thought, immersed in thought, in a brown study, musing, brooding, absent, oblivious, moony, distrait; informal miles away, out to lunch.
ANTONYMS attentive.

abstraction ▶ noun **1** *philosophical abstractions* **concept,** idea, notion, thought, theory, hypothesis.
2 *she sensed his momentary abstraction* **absentmindedness,** distraction, preoccupation, dreaminess, inattentiveness, inattention, woolgathering; thoughtfulness, pensiveness.
3 *the abstraction of metal from ore* **extraction,** removal, separation.

abstruse ▶ adjective *her abstruse arguments were hard to follow* **obscure,** arcane, esoteric, little known, recherché, rarefied, recondite, difficult, hard, puzzling, perplexing, cryptic, enigmatic, Delphic, complex, complicated, involved, over/above one's head, incomprehensible, unfathomable, impenetrable, mysterious. See note at OBSCURE.

absurd ▶ adjective *what an absurd idea!* **preposterous,** ridiculous, ludicrous, farcical, laughable, risible, idiotic, stupid, foolish, silly, inane, imbecilic, insane, harebrained, cockamamie; unreasonable, irrational, illogical, nonsensical, incongruous, pointless, senseless; informal crazy, daft.
ANTONYMS reasonable, sensible.

CHOOSE THE RIGHT WORD

absurd, foolish, ludicrous, preposterous, ridiculous, unreasonable

We call something **absurd** when it is utterly inconsistent with what common sense or experience tells us (*she found herself in the absurd position of having to defend the intelligence of a cockroach*). **Ludicrous** applies to whatever is so incongruous that it provokes laughter or scorn (*a ludicrous suggestion that he might escape unnoticed if he dressed up as a woman*), and **ridiculous** implies that ridicule or mockery is the only appropriate response (*she tried to look younger, but succeeded only in making herself look ridiculous*). **Foolish** behavior shows a lack of intelligence or good judgment (*it was foolish to keep that much money under a mattress*), while **unreasonable** behavior implies that the person has intentionally acted contrary to good sense (*his response was totally unreasonable in view of the fact that he'd asked for their honest opinion*). **Preposterous** should be reserved for those acts or situations that are glaringly absurd or ludicrous. For example, it might be *unreasonable* to judge an entire nation on the basis of one tourist's experience and *foolish* to turn down an opportunity to visit that country on those grounds alone, but it would be *preposterous* to suggest that everyone who comes to the United States will be robbed at gunpoint.

absurdity ▶ noun *these artworks convey a sense of the absurdity of contemporary life* **preposterousness,** ridiculousness, ludicrousness, incongruity, inappropriateness, risibility, idiocy, stupidity, foolishness, folly, silliness, inanity, insanity; unreasonableness, irrationality, illogicality, pointlessness, senselessness; informal craziness.

abundance ▶ noun *the abundance of donated funds was completely unexpected* **profusion,** plentifulness, profuseness, copiousness, amplitude, lavishness, bountifulness, bounty; host, cornucopia, riot; plenty, quantities, scores, multitude; informal millions, sea, ocean(s), wealth, lot(s), heap(s), mass(es), stack(s), pile(s), load(s), bags, mountain(s), ton(s), slew, scads, oodles, gobs; formal plenitude.
ANTONYMS lack, scarcity.

abundant ▶ adjective *an abundant supply of food* **plentiful,** copious, ample, profuse, rich, lavish, abounding, liberal, generous, bountiful, large, huge, great, bumper, overflowing, prolific, teeming; in plenty, in abundance; informal galore; literary plenteous, bounteous. See note at PREVALENT.
ANTONYMS scarce, sparse.

abuse ▶ verb **1** *the judge abused his power* **misuse,** misapply, misemploy; exploit, take advantage of.
2 *he was accused of abusing children* **mistreat,** maltreat, ill-treat, treat badly; molest, interfere with, indecently assault, sexually abuse, sexually assault; injure, hurt, harm, damage.
ANTONYMS look after, nurture.
3 *the referee was abused by players from both teams* **insult,** be rude to, swear at, curse, call someone names, taunt, badmouth, dis, shout at, revile, inveigh against, bawl out, vilify, slander, cast aspersions on.
ANTONYMS compliment, flatter.
▶ noun **1** *the abuse of power* **misuse,**

misapplication, misemployment; exploitation.
2 *the abuse of children* **mistreatment,** maltreatment, ill-treatment; molestation, interference, indecent assault, sexual abuse, sexual assault; injury, hurt, harm, damage.
ANTONYMS care, nurturing.
3 *the scheme is open to administrative abuse* **corruption,** injustice, wrongdoing, wrong, misconduct, misdeed(s), offense(s), crime(s), sin(s).
4 *torrents of abuse* **insults,** curses, jibes, expletives, swear words; swearing, cursing, name-calling; invective, vilification, vituperation, slander; informal trash talk; archaic contumely.
ANTONYMS compliments, flattery.
5 *alcohol abuse* **addiction,** dependency, overuse, misuse, problems.

abusive ▸ **adjective** *such abusive language will not be tolerated in this workplace* **insulting,** rude, vulgar, offensive, disparaging, belittling, derogatory, opprobrious, disrespectful, denigratory, uncomplimentary, censorious, pejorative, vituperative; defamatory, slanderous, libelous, scurrilous, blasphemous; informal bitchy; archaic contumelious.

abut ▸ **verb** *two rows of forsythia abut one another where the driveway meets the sidewalk* **adjoin,** be adjacent to, butt against, border, neighbor, join, touch, meet, reach, be contiguous with.

abysmal ▸ **adjective** informal *some of the teaching was abysmal* **very bad,** dreadful, awful, terrible, frightful, atrocious, disgraceful, deplorable, shameful, hopeless, lamentable; informal rotten, appalling, crummy, pathetic, pitiful, woeful, useless, lousy, dire, the pits.

abyss ▸ **noun** *a recurring nightmare in which he falls into an abyss* **chasm,** gorge, ravine, canyon, fissure, rift, crevasse, hole, gulf, pit, cavity, void, bottomless pit.

academic ▸ **adjective 1** *an academic institution* **educational,** scholastic, instructional, pedagogical.
2 *his academic turn of mind* **scholarly,** studious, literary, well-read, intellectual, clever, erudite, learned, educated, cultured, bookish, highbrow, pedantic, donnish, cerebral; informal brainy, inkhorn; dated lettered.
3 *the debate has been largely academic* **theoretical,** conceptual, notional, philosophical, hypothetical, speculative, conjectural, suppositional; impractical, unrealistic, ivory-tower.
▸ **noun** *a group of Russian academics* **scholar,** lecturer, teacher, tutor, professor, fellow, man/woman of letters, don, bluestocking; informal egghead, bookworm; formal pedagogue.

accede ▸ **verb** formal **1** *he **acceded to** the government's demands* **agree to,** consent to, accept, assent to, acquiesce in, comply with, go along with, concur with, surrender to, yield to, give in to, give way to, defer to.
2 *Elizabeth I **acceded to** the throne in 1558* **succeed to,** come to, assume, inherit, take.
3 *Albania **acceded to** the IMF in 1990* **join,** become a member of, sign on to, sign up for.

accelerate ▸ **verb 1** *the car accelerated down the hill* **speed up,** go faster, gain momentum, increase speed, pick up speed, gather speed, put on a spurt.
ANTONYMS decelerate, slow down.
2 *inflation started to accelerate* **increase,** rise, go up, leap up, surge, escalate, spiral.
ANTONYMS slow down, drop.
3 *the university accelerated the planning process* **hasten,** expedite, precipitate, speed up, quicken, make faster, step up, advance, further, forward, promote, give a boost to, stimulate, spur on; informal crank up, fast-track.
ANTONYMS slow down, delay.

acceleration ▸ **noun 1** *the acceleration of the industrial process* **hastening,** precipitation, speeding up, quickening, stepping up, advancement, furtherance, boost, stimulation, spur.
2 *an acceleration in the divorce rate* **increase,** rise, leap, surge, escalation.

accent ▸ **noun 1** *a Bronx accent* **pronunciation,** intonation, enunciation, articulation, inflection, tone, modulation, cadence, timbre, manner of speaking, delivery; brogue, burr, drawl, twang.
2 *the accent is on the first syllable* **stress,** emphasis, accentuation, force, prominence; beat; technical ictus.
3 *the accent is on comfort* **emphasis,** stress, priority; importance, prominence.
4 *an acute accent* **mark,** diacritic, diacritical mark.
▸ **verb** *fabrics that accent the background colors in the room* **focus attention on,** draw attention to, point up, underline, underscore, accentuate, highlight, spotlight, foreground, feature, play up, bring to the fore, heighten, stress, emphasize.

accentuate ▸ **verb** *a haircut that accentuates your cheekbones* **focus attention on,** draw attention to, point up, underline, underscore, accent, highlight, spotlight, foreground, feature, play up, bring to the fore, heighten, stress, emphasize.

accept ▸ **verb 1** *she accepted a pen as a present* **receive,** take, get, gain, obtain, acquire.
ANTONYMS refuse, reject.
2 *he accepted the job immediately* **take on,** undertake, assume, take responsibility for.
ANTONYMS turn down, refuse.
3 *she accepted an invitation to lunch* **say yes to,** agree to.
ANTONYMS turn down, refuse.
4 *she was accepted as one of the family* **welcome,** greet, receive, receive favorably, embrace, adopt.
ANTONYMS reject.
5 *he accepted Ellen's explanation* **believe,** regard as true, give credence to, credit, trust; informal buy, swallow.
ANTONYMS reject, doubt.
6 *we have agreed to accept his decision* **go along with,** agree to, consent to, acquiesce in, concur with, assent to, acknowledge, comply with, abide by, follow, adhere to, act in accordance with, defer to, yield to, surrender to, bow to, give in to, submit to, respect; formal accede to.
ANTONYMS defy, go against.
7 *she will just have to accept the consequences* **tolerate,** endure, put up with, bear, take,

submit to, stomach, swallow; reconcile oneself to, resign oneself to, get used to, adjust to, learn to live with, make the best of; face up to.

acceptable ▶ adjective **1** *an acceptable standard of living* **satisfactory,** adequate, reasonable, quite good, fair, decent, good enough, sufficient, sufficiently good, fine, not bad, all right, average, tolerable, passable, middling, moderate; informal OK, jake, so-so, 'comme ci, comme ça', fair-to-middling.
2 *the risk had seemed acceptable at the time* **bearable,** tolerable, allowable, admissible, sustainable, justifiable, defensible.

acceptance ▶ noun **1** *the acceptance of an award* **receipt,** receiving, taking, obtaining.
2 *the acceptance of responsibility* **undertaking,** assumption.
3 *acceptances to an invitation* **yes,** affirmative reply, confirmation.
4 *her acceptance into the group* **welcome,** favorable reception, adoption.
5 *his* ***acceptance of*** *Thom's promise* **belief in,** trust in, faith in, confidence in, credence in, giving of credence to.
6 *their* ***acceptance of*** *the ruling* **compliance with,** acquiescence in, agreement with, consent to, concurrence with, assent to, acknowledgment of, adherence to, deference to, surrender to, submission to, respect for, adoption of, buy-in to.
7 *the acceptance of pain* **toleration,** endurance, forbearance, sufferance.

accepted ▶ adjective *newspaper ads from the 1700s show that, even in New England, the brokering of slaves was an accepted practice* **recognized,** acknowledged, established, traditional, orthodox, sanctioned; usual, customary, habitual, common, current, normal, general, prevailing, accustomed, familiar, wonted, popular, expected, routine, standard, stock.

access ▶ noun **1** *the building has a side access* **entrance,** entry, way in, means of entry; approach, means of approach.
2 *they were denied access to the stadium* **admission,** admittance, entry, entrée, ingress, right of entry.
3 *students have* ***access to*** *a photocopier* **(the) use of,** permission to use/visit.
▶ verb **1** *the program is used to access data* **retrieve,** gain access to, obtain; read.
2 *you access the building from the south side* **enter,** approach, gain entry to.

> USAGE
>
> **access**
>
> Although the verb *access* is standard and common in computing and related terminology (*only subscribers may access the full text online*), the word is primarily a noun. Outside computing contexts, its use as a verb in the sense of 'approach or enter a place' is often regarded as nonstandard (*you must use a key card to access the lounge*). Even weaker is its use in an abstract sense (*access the American dream*). It is usually clear enough to say 'enter' or 'gain access to.'

accessible ▶ adjective **1** *the village is accessible only on foot* | *an easily accessible reference tool* **reachable,** attainable, approachable; obtainable, available; informal get-at-able.
2 *his accessible style of writing* **understandable,** comprehensible, easy to understand, intelligible; formal exoteric.
3 *Professor Cooper is very accessible* **approachable,** friendly, agreeable, obliging, congenial, affable, cordial, welcoming, easygoing, pleasant.

accession ▶ noun **1** *the Queen's* ***accession to*** *the throne* **succession to,** assumption of, inheritance of.
2 *accession to the Treaty of Rome was effected in 1971* **assent to,** consent to, agreement to; acceptance of, acquiescence in, compliance with, concurrence with.
3 *recent museum accessions* **addition,** acquisition, new item, gift, purchase.

accessory ▶ noun **1** *camera accessories such as tripods* **attachment,** extra, addition, add-on, adjunct, appendage, appurtenance, fitment, supplement.
2 *fashion accessories* **adornment,** embellishment, ornament, ornamentation, decoration; frills, trimmings.
3 *two days after the murder, she was charged as an accessory* **accomplice,** partner in crime, associate, collaborator, abettor, fellow conspirator, co-conspirator; henchman.
▶ adjective *an accessory gearbox* **additional,** extra, supplementary, supplemental, auxiliary, ancillary, secondary, subsidiary, reserve, add-on.

accident ▶ noun **1** *an accident at work* **mishap,** misadventure, unfortunate incident, mischance, misfortune, disaster, tragedy, catastrophe, calamity; technical casualty.
2 *she was injured in a highway accident* **crash,** collision, smash, bump, car crash; wreck; informal smash-up, pileup, fender bender.
3 *it is no accident that there is a similarity between them* **(mere) chance,** coincidence, twist of fate, freak; fluke, bit of luck, serendipity; fate, fortuity, fortune, providence, happenstance.

accidental ▶ adjective **1** *an accidental meeting* **fortuitous,** chance, adventitious, fluky, coincidental, casual, serendipitous, random; unexpected, unforeseen, unanticipated, unlooked-for, unintentional, unintended, inadvertent, unplanned, unpremeditated, unthinking, unwitting.
ANTONYMS intentional.
2 *the location is accidental and contributes nothing to the poem* **incidental,** unimportant, by the way, by the by, supplementary, subsidiary, subordinate, secondary, accessory, peripheral, tangential, extraneous, extrinsic, irrelevant, nonessential, inessential.
ANTONYMS deliberate.

> CHOOSE THE RIGHT WORD
>
> **accidental, adventitious, casual, contingent, fortuitous, incidental**
>
> Things don't always go as planned, but there are many ways to describe the role that

chance plays. **Accidental** applies to events that occur entirely by chance (*an accidental encounter with the candidate outside the men's room*); but it is so strongly influenced by the noun "accident" that it carries connotations of undesirable or possibly disastrous results (*an accidental miscalculation of the distance he had to jump*). A **casual** act or event is one that is random or unpremeditated (*a casual conversation with her son's teacher in the grocery store*), in which the role that chance plays is not always clear. Something that is **incidental** may or may not involve chance; it typically refers to what is secondary or nonessential (*incidental expenses in the budget*) or what occurs without design or regularity (*incidental lighting throughout the garden*). **Adventitious** also implies the lack of an essential relationship, referring to something that is a mere random occurrence (*adventitious circumstances that led to victory*). In contrast, **contingent** points to something that is entirely dependent on an uncertain event for its existence or occurrence (*travel plans that are contingent upon the weather*). **Fortuitous** refers to chance events of a fortunate nature; it is about as far as one can get from *accidental* (*a fortuitous meeting with the candidate outside the men's room just before the press conference*).

acclaim ▸ verb *the booklet has been widely acclaimed by teachers* **praise,** applaud, cheer, commend, approve, welcome, pay tribute to, speak highly of, eulogize, compliment, celebrate, sing the praises of, rave about, heap praise on/upon, wax lyrical about, lionize, exalt, admire, hail, extol, honor, hymn; informal ballyhoo; formal laud. See note at **PRAISE**.
ANTONYMS criticize.

▸ noun *she has won acclaim for her commitment to democracy* **praise,** applause, cheers, ovation, tribute, accolade, acclamation, salutes, plaudits, bouquets; approval, approbation, admiration, congratulations, commendation, kudos, welcome, homage; compliment, a pat on the back.
ANTONYMS criticism.

acclamation ▸ noun *the proposal was received with considerable acclamation* **praise,** applause, cheers, ovation, tribute, accolade, acclaim, salutes, plaudits, bouquets; approval, admiration, approbation, congratulations, commendation, homage; compliment, a pat on the back.
ANTONYMS criticism.

– PHRASES **by acclamation** *she won reelection by acclamation* **by oral vote,** by a verbal vote, without a ballot, by nonballot; Canadian without opposition, as the only candidate.

acclimatize ▸ verb *the panda Ling Ling will acclimatize to the environment in Mexico before choosing a mate* **adjust,** acclimate, adapt, accustom, accommodate, habituate, acculturate, assimilate, attune; get used, become inured, reconcile oneself, resign oneself; familiarize oneself; get one's bearings, become seasoned, become naturalized.

accommodate ▸ verb **1** *refugees were accommodated in army camps* **lodge,** house, put up, billet, quarter, board, take in, shelter, give someone a roof over their head; harbor.
2 *each cottage accommodates up to six people* **hold,** take, have room for.
3 *our staff will make every effort to accommodate you* **help,** assist, aid, oblige; meet the needs/wants of, satisfy.
4 *she tried to* ***accommodate herself to*** *her new situation* **adjust to,** adapt to, accustom oneself to, habituate oneself to, acclimatize (oneself) to, acclimate (oneself) to, acculturate to, get (oneself) accustomed to, get used to, come to terms with.
5 *the bank would be glad to accommodate you with a loan* **provide,** supply, furnish, grant.

accommodating ▸ adjective *her in-laws were far more accommodating than her own parents* **obliging,** cooperative, helpful, eager to help, adaptable, amenable, considerate, unselfish, inclusionary, generous, willing, compliant, kindly, hospitable, neighborly, kind, friendly, pleasant, agreeable.

accommodation ▸ noun **1** (**accommodations**) *temporary accommodations* **housing,** lodging(s), living quarters, quarters, rooms; place to stay, billet; shelter, roof over one's head; informal digs, pad; formal abode, residence, place of residence, dwelling, dwelling place, habitation.
2 *lifeboat accommodations for 1,178 people* **space,** room, seating; places.
3 *an accommodation between the two parties was reached* **arrangement,** understanding, settlement, accord, deal, bargain, compromise.
4 *their accommodations to changing economic circumstances* **adjustment,** adaptation, habituation, acclimatization, acclimation, acculturation; inurement.

accompaniment ▸ noun **1** *a musical accompaniment* **backing,** support, background, backup, soundtrack.
2 *the wine makes a superb accompaniment to cheese* **complement,** supplement, addition, adjunct, appendage, companion, accessory.

accompany ▸ verb **1** *I accompanied my brother to the audition* **go with,** travel with, keep someone company, tag along with, hang out with; partner, escort, chaperone, attend, show, see, usher, conduct.
2 *the illness* ***is often accompanied by*** *nausea* **occur with,** co-occur with, coexist with, go with, go together with, go hand in hand with, appear with, be attended by.
3 *he accompanied the choir on the piano* **back,** play with, play for, support.

accomplice ▸ noun *police have reason to believe that Johnson had two accomplices, possibly his wife and brother* **partner in crime,** associate, accessory, abettor, confederate, collaborator, fellow conspirator, co-conspirator; henchman; informal sidekick.

accomplish ▸ verb *the planes accomplished their mission* **fulfill,** achieve, succeed in, realize, attain, manage, bring about/off, carry out/through, execute, effect, perform, do, discharge, complete, finish, consummate, conclude; informal pull off, nail; formal effectuate.

accomplished ▸ adjective *an accomplished bassoonist* **expert,** skilled, skillful, masterly, successful, virtuoso, master, consummate, complete, proficient, talented, gifted, adept, adroit, deft, dexterous, able, good, competent, capable, efficient, experienced, seasoned, trained, practiced, professional, polished, ready, apt; informal great, mean, nifty, crack, ace, wizard; informal crackerjack.

accomplishment ▸ noun **1** *the reduction of inflation was a remarkable accomplishment* **achievement,** act, deed, exploit, performance, attainment, effort, feat, move, coup.
2 *a poet of considerable accomplishment* **expertise,** skill, skillfulness, talent, adeptness, adroitness, deftness, dexterity, ability, prowess, mastery, competence, capability, proficiency, aptitude, artistry, art; informal know-how.

accord ▸ verb **1** *the national assembly accorded him more power* **give,** grant, present, award, vouchsafe; confer on, bestow on, vest in, invest with.
ANTONYMS withhold.
2 *his views **accorded with** mine* **correspond to,** agree with, match up with, concur with, be consistent with, harmonize with, be in harmony with, be compatible with, chime in with, be in tune with, correlate with, dovetail with; conform to; suit, fit, parallel, match; informal square with, jibe with.
ANTONYMS disagree, contrast.
▸ noun **1** *a peace accord* **pact,** treaty, agreement, settlement, deal, entente, concordat, protocol, contract, convention.
2 *the two sides failed to reach accord* **agreement,** consensus, unanimity, harmony, unison, unity; formal concord.
– PHRASES **of one's own accord** *Nels offered to fix the gate of his own accord* **voluntarily,** of one's own free will, of one's own volition, by choice; willingly, freely, readily. **with one accord** *the committee decided with one accord to approve the drainage plans* **unanimously,** in complete agreement, with one mind, without exception, as one, of one voice, to a man.

accordance ▸ noun *a ballot held **in accordance with** union rules* **in agreement with,** in conformity with, in line with, true to, in the spirit of, observing, following, heeding.

according ▸ adjective **1** *she had a narrow escape, **according to** the doctors* **as stated by,** as claimed by, on the authority of, in the opinion of.
2 *cook the rice **according to** the instructions* **as specified by,** as per, in accordance with, in compliance with, in agreement with.
3 *salary will be fixed **according to** experience* **in proportion to,** proportional to, commensurate with, in relation to, relative to, in line with, corresponding to.

accordingly ▸ adverb **1** *they appreciated the danger and acted accordingly* **appropriately,** correspondingly, suitably.
2 *accordingly, he returned home to Kingston* **therefore,** for that reason, consequently, so, as a result, as a consequence, in consequence, hence, thus, that being the case, ergo.

accost ▸ verb *police accosted him in the street* **confront,** call to, shout to, hail, address, speak to; approach, detain, stop, waylay; informal buttonhole, collar, bend someone's ear.

account ▸ noun **1** *an account of the extraordinary events* **description,** report, version, story, narration, narrative, statement, explanation, exposition, delineation, portrayal, tale; chronicle, history, record, log; view, impression.
2 *the firm's quarterly accounts* **financial record,** ledger, balance sheet, financial statement; (**accounts**) books.
3 *I pay the account off in full each month* **bill,** invoice, tally; debt, charges; informal tab.
4 *his background is of no account* **importance,** import, significance, consequence, substance, note; formal moment.
5 *efforts to keep our most important accounts happy* **client,** customer.
▸ verb *her visit could not be accounted a success* **consider,** regard as, reckon, hold to be, think, look on as, view as, see as, judge, adjudge, count, deem, rate.
– PHRASES **account for 1** *they must account for the delay* **explain,** answer for, give reasons for, rationalize, justify. **2** *taxes account for much of the price of gasoline* **constitute,** make up, form, compose, represent. **on account of** *I was invited on account of my friendship with her parents* **because of,** owing to, due to, as a consequence of, thanks to, by/in virtue of, in view of. **on no account** *on no account sign a document without reading it* **never,** under no circumstances, not for any reason.

accountability ▸ noun *there must be accountability for the expenditure of every public cent* **responsibility,** liability, answerability.

accountable ▸ adjective **1** *the government was held accountable for the food shortage* **responsible,** liable, answerable; to blame. See note at RESPONSIBLE.
2 *the game's popularity is barely accountable* **explicable,** explainable; understandable, comprehensible.

accredited ▸ adjective *an accredited preschool* **official,** appointed, recognized, authorized, approved, certified, licensed.

accrue ▸ verb **1** *financial benefits will **accrue from** restructuring* **result from,** arise from, follow from, ensue from; be caused by, attend.
2 *interest is added to the account as it accrues* **accumulate,** collect, build up, mount up, grow, increase.

accumulate ▸ verb *he has accumulated thousands of frequent-flier miles | mother whales transfer chemicals accumulated in their tissue to their offspring during gestation* **gather,** collect, assemble; amass, stockpile, pile up, heap up, store (up), hoard, cumulate, lay in/up; increase, mass, multiply, accrue, snowball; run up; informal stash (away).
ANTONYMS dissipate.

accumulation ▸ noun *the accumulation of illegal funds | an accumulation of debris* **buildup,** mass, pile, heap, stack, collection, stock, store, stockpile, reserve, hoard; amassing, gathering, cumulation, accrual, accretion.

accuracy ▶ noun *the accuracy of their lead story is being questioned* **correctness,** precision, preciseness, exactness, exactitude; factuality, literalness, fidelity, faithfulness, truth, truthfulness, veracity, closeness, authenticity, realism, verisimilitude.

accurate ▶ adjective **1** *accurate information | an accurate representation of the situation* **correct,** precise, exact, right, error-free, perfect; **factual,** fact-based, literal, faithful, true, truthful, true to life, authentic, realistic; informal on the mark, bang on, on the money, on the button; formal veracious.
2 *an accurate shot* **well-aimed,** on target, unerring, deadly, lethal, sure, true, on the mark.

accursed ▶ adjective dated **1** *that accursed woman* **hateful,** detestable, loathsome, foul, abominable, damnable, odious, obnoxious, despicable, horrible, horrid, ghastly, awful, dreadful, terrible; annoying, irritating, vile, infuriating, exasperating; informal damned, damn, blasted, pesky, pestilential, infernal, beastly.
ANTONYMS pleasant.
2 literary *he and his line are accursed* **cursed,** damned, doomed, condemned, ill-fated, ill-omened, jinxed.
ANTONYMS blessed.

accusation ▶ noun *the bishop has denied accusations of genocide* **allegation,** charge, claim, assertion, imputation; indictment, arraignment, incrimination, recrimination, inculpation; suit, lawsuit, impeachment; informal rap.

accuse ▶ verb **1** *four people were* ***accused of*** *assault* **charge with,** indict for, arraign for; summons for, cite for, prefer charges against for; impeach for.
ANTONYMS absolve, exonerate.
2 *the companies were* ***accused of*** *causing job losses* **blame for,** lay/pin the blame on for, hold responsible for, inculpate for, hold accountable for; condemn for, criticize for, denounce for; informal point the finger at for.
ANTONYMS defend, hold blameless.

accustom ▶ verb *she couldn't* ***accustom herself to*** *city life* **adapt to,** adjust to, acclimatize to, acclimate to, habituate oneself to, accommodate oneself to, acculturate to; reconcile oneself to, become reconciled to, get used to, come to terms with, learn to live with, become inured to.

accustomed ▶ adjective **1** *his accustomed lifestyle* **customary,** usual, normal, habitual, regular, routine, ordinary, typical, traditional, established, common, general; literary wonted.
2 *she's* ***accustomed to*** *hard work* **used to,** habituated to, acclimatized to, no stranger to, familiar with, acquainted with, in the habit of, experienced in.
ANTONYMS unfamiliar.

ace ▶ noun informal *a snowboarding ace* **expert,** master, genius, virtuoso, maestro, adept, past master, doyen, champion, star; informal demon, hotshot, wizard, pro, whiz; informal maven, crackerjack.
ANTONYMS amateur, beginner.
▶ adjective *an ace tennis player* **excellent,** first-rate, first-class, marvelous, wonderful, magnificent, outstanding, superlative, formidable, virtuoso, masterly, expert, champion, consummate, skillful, adept; great, terrific, tremendous, superb, fantastic, sensational, fabulous; informal fab, crack, hotshot, A1, mean, demon, awesome, magic, tip-top, top-notch; killer, blue-ribbon, blue-chip, brilliant, wicked.
ANTONYMS mediocre.

acerbic ▶ adjective *soaring melodies built around acerbic lyrics* **sharp,** sarcastic, sardonic, mordant, trenchant, cutting, razor-edged, biting, piercing, stinging, searing, scathing, caustic, bitter, acrimonious, astringent, abrasive, harsh, wounding, hurtful, unkind, cruel, virulent, vitriolic, venomous, malicious, vicious; informal bitchy; rare acidulous, mordacious.
ANTONYMS mild, kind.

ache ▶ noun **1** *a stomachache* **pain,** cramp, twinge, pang; gnawing, stabbing, stinging, smarting; soreness, tenderness, irritation, discomfort.
2 *the ache in her heart* **sorrow,** sadness, misery, grief, anguish, suffering, pain, agony, torture, hurt.
▶ verb **1** *my legs were aching* **hurt,** be sore, be painful, be in pain, pain, throb, pound, twinge; smart, burn.
2 *her heart ached for poor Philippa* **grieve,** sorrow, be in distress, be miserable, be in anguish, bleed.
3 *I* ***ached for*** *her affection* **long for,** yearn for, hunger for, thirst for, hanker for, pine for, itch for; crave, desire, covet.

achieve ▶ verb *the legal resources are inadequate to achieve our public health objectives* **attain,** reach, arrive at; realize, bring off/about, pull off, accomplish, carry off/out/through, fulfill, execute, perform, engineer, conclude, complete, finish, consummate; earn, win, gain, acquire, obtain, score, come by, get, secure, clinch, net; informal wrap up, wangle, swing; formal effectuate.

achievement ▶ noun **1** *the achievement of a high rate of economic growth* **attainment,** realization, accomplishment, fulfillment, implementation, execution, performance; conclusion, completion, close, consummation.
2 *they felt justifiably proud of their achievement* **accomplishment,** attainment, feat, performance, undertaking, act, action, deed, effort, exploit, success, triumph; work, handiwork.

acid ▶ adjective **1** *a slightly acid flavor* **acidic, sour,** tart, bitter, sharp, acrid, pungent, acerbic, vinegary, acetic, acetous.
ANTONYMS sweet.
2 *acid remarks* **acerbic,** sarcastic, sharp, sardonic, scathing, cutting, razor-edged, biting, stinging, caustic, trenchant, mordant, bitter, acrimonious, astringent, harsh, abrasive, wounding, hurtful, unkind, vitriolic, venomous, waspish, spiteful, malicious; informal bitchy, catty; snarky.
ANTONYMS pleasant.

acknowledge ▶ verb **1** *the government acknowledged the need to begin talks* **admit,** accept, grant, allow, concede, accede to, confess,

own, recognize.
ANTONYMS reject, deny.
2 *he did not acknowledge Colin, but hurried past* **greet,** salute, address; nod to, wave to, raise one's hat to, say hello to.
ANTONYMS ignore.
3 *Douglas was glad to acknowledge her help* **express gratitude for,** show appreciation for, thank someone for.
4 *nobody acknowledged my letters* **answer,** reply to, respond to.
ANTONYMS overlook.

acknowledged ▸ **adjective** *the acknowledged leader of the Turkish community* **recognized,** accepted, approved, accredited, confirmed, declared, confessed, avowed.

acknowledgment ▸ **noun 1** *acknowledgment of the need to take new initiatives* **acceptance,** recognition, admission, concession, confession.
2 *a smile of acknowledgment* **greeting,** welcome, salutation.
3 *she left without a word of acknowledgment* **thanks,** gratitude, appreciation, recognition.
4 *I sent off the form, but there was no acknowledgment* **answer,** reply, response.

acme ▸ **noun** *the acme of her career* **peak,** pinnacle, zenith, height, high point, crown, crest, summit, top, apex, apogee; climax, culmination.
ANTONYMS nadir.

acolyte ▸ **noun** *surrounded by eager acolytes* **assistant,** helper, attendant, aide, minion, underling, lackey, henchman; follower, disciple, supporter, votary; informal sidekick, groupie, hanger-on.

acquaint ▸ **verb** *this exercise will* ***acquaint*** *you* ***with*** *the food groups* **familiarize with,** make familiar with, make aware of, inform of, advise of, apprise of, let know, get up to date on; brief on, prime on; informal fill in on, clue in on.

acquaintance ▸ **noun 1** *a business acquaintance | friends and acquaintances* **contact,** associate, ally, connection, colleague.
2 *my acquaintance with George* **association,** relationship, contact; fellowship, companionship.
3 *the students had little* ***acquaintance with*** *the language* **familiarity with,** knowledge of, experience with/of, awareness of, understanding of, comprehension of, grasp of.

acquiesce ▸ **verb** *he would eventually* ***acquiesce in*** *promoting their product* **accept,** consent to, agree to, allow, concede, assent to, concur with, give the nod to; comply with, cooperate with, give in to, bow to, yield to, submit to; informal go along with.

acquiescence ▸ **noun** *its commercial success depends on the acquiescence of the consumer* **consent,** agreement, acceptance, concurrence, assent, leave; compliance, concession, cooperation, buy-in; submission.

acquiescent ▸ **adjective** *the apolitical and acquiescent masses* **compliant,** complying, consenting, cooperative, willing, obliging, agreeable, amenable, tractable, persuadable, pliant, flexible, unprotesting; **submissive,** servile, subservient, obsequious, self-effacing, unassertive, yielding, biddable, docile, deferential; rare obeisant, longanimous.

acquire ▸ **verb** *the library's goal is to acquire eight new or upgraded computers in this fiscal year* **obtain,** come by, get, receive, gain, earn, win, come into, be given; buy, purchase, procure, possess oneself of, secure, pick up, adopt; informal get one's hands on, get hold of, land, bag, cop, score. See note at **GET**.
ANTONYMS lose, get rid of.

acquisition ▸ **noun 1** *the boat is a new acquisition* **purchase,** buy, gain, accession, addition, investment, possession.
2 *the acquisition of funds* **obtaining,** acquirement, gaining, earning, winning, procurement, collection.

acquisitive ▸ **adjective** *his acquisitive wife has left him for a Denver architect* **greedy,** covetous, avaricious, possessive, grasping, grabbing, predatory, avid, rapacious, mercenary, materialistic; informal money-grubbing. See note at **GREEDY**.

acquisitiveness ▸ **noun** *their three children seem to possess none of the acquisitiveness so typical of Hollywood brats* **greed,** greediness, covetousness, cupidity, possessiveness, avarice, avidity, rapaciousness, rapacity, materialism; informal affluenza.

acquit ▸ **verb 1** *the jury acquitted her* **clear,** exonerate, find innocent, absolve; discharge, release, free, set free; informal let off (the hook); formal exculpate. See note at **ABSOLVE**.
ANTONYMS convict.
2 *the boys* ***acquitted themselves*** *well* **behave (oneself),** conduct oneself, perform, act; formal comport oneself.

acquittal ▸ **noun** *the acquittal of the defendants* **clearing,** exoneration, absolution; discharge, release, freeing; formal exculpation.
ANTONYMS conviction.

acrid ▸ **adjective** *the fruit's acrid taste was a bad surprise* **pungent,** bitter, sharp, sour, tart, caustic, harsh, irritating, acid, acidic, vinegary, acetic, acetous; stinging, burning.

acrimonious ▸ **adjective** *a heated and acrimonious discussion* **bitter,** angry, rancorous, caustic, acerbic, scathing, sarcastic, acid, harsh, sharp, cutting; virulent, spiteful, vicious, vitriolic, hostile, venomous, nasty, bad-tempered, ill-natured, mean, malign, malicious, malignant, waspish; informal bitchy, catty.

acrimony ▸ **noun** *the meeting ended with acrimony on both sides* **bitterness,** anger, rancor, resentment, ill feeling, ill will, bad blood, animosity, hostility, enmity, antagonism, waspishness, spleen, malice, spite, spitefulness, peevishness, venom.
ANTONYMS goodwill.

acrobatics ▸ **plural noun 1** *staggering feats of acrobatics* **gymnastics,** tumbling; agility; rare funambulism.
2 *the acrobatics required to negotiate an international contract* **mental agility,** skill, quick thinking, fancy footwork, alertness, inventiveness.

act ▸ **verb 1** *the government must act to remedy the situation* **take action,** take steps, take measures, move, react.

2 *he was **acting on** the orders of the party leader* **follow,** act in accordance with, obey, heed, comply with; fulfill, meet, discharge.
3 *a real estate agent **acting for** a prospective buyer* **represent,** act on behalf of; stand in for, fill in for, deputize for, take the place of.
4 *Alison began to act oddly* **behave,** conduct oneself, react; formal comport oneself.
5 *the scents act as a powerful aphrodisiac* **operate,** work, function, serve.
6 *the drug **acted** directly **on** the blood vessels* **affect,** have an effect on, work on; have an impact on, impact on, influence.
7 *he acted in a highly successful film* **perform,** play a part, play-act, take part, appear; informal tread the boards, ham it up.
8 *we laughed, but most of us were just acting* **pretend,** play-act, put it on, fake it, feign it, dissemble, dissimulate.
▶ **noun 1** *acts of kindness | a criminal act* **deed,** action, feat, exploit, move, gesture, performance, undertaking, stunt, operation; achievement, accomplishment.
2 *the act raised the tax on tobacco* **law,** decree, statute, bill, act of Congress, enactment, resolution, edict, dictum, ruling, measure; ordinance.
3 *the first act of the play* **division,** section, subsection, part, segment.
4 *a music hall act* **performance,** routine, number, sketch, skit, shtick, turn.
5 *it was all just an act* **pretense,** show, front, facade, masquerade, charade, posture, pose, affectation, sham, fake; informal put-on.
– PHRASES **act up** informal **1** *all children act up from time to time* **misbehave,** behave badly, be up to mischief, become unruly. **2** *the engine was acting up* **malfunction,** go wrong, be defective, be faulty; informal be on the blink, be on the fritz.

acting ▶ **noun** *the theory and practice of acting* **drama,** the theater, the stage, the performing arts, thespianism, dramatics, dramaturgy, stagecraft, theatricals; informal treading the boards.
▶ **adjective** *the bank's acting governor* **temporary,** interim, caretaker, pro tem, pro tempore, provisional, stopgap; deputy, stand-in, fill-in; informal pinch-hitting.
ANTONYMS permanent.

action ▶ **noun 1** *there can be no excuse for their actions* **deed,** act, move, undertaking, exploit, maneuver, endeavor, effort, exertion; behavior, conduct, activity.
2 *the need for local community action* **measures,** steps, activity, movement, work, operation.
3 *a man of action* **energy,** vitality, vigor, forcefulness, drive, initiative, spirit, liveliness, vim, pep; activity; informal get-up-and-go.
4 *the action of hormones on the pancreas* **effect,** influence, working; power.
5 *he missed all the action while he was away* **excitement,** activity, happenings, events, incidents; informal goings-on.
6 *twenty-nine men died in the action* **fighting,** hostilities, battle, conflict, combat, warfare; engagement, clash, encounter, skirmish.
7 *a civil action for damages* **lawsuit,** legal action, suit, case, prosecution, litigation, proceedings.

activate ▶ **verb** *the alarm system can be activated remotely* **operate,** switch on, turn on, start (up), set going, trigger (off), set in motion, initiate, actuate, energize; trip.

active ▶ **adjective 1** *despite her illness she remained active* **energetic,** lively, sprightly, spry, mobile, vigorous, vital, dynamic, sporty; busy, occupied; informal on the go.
ANTONYMS listless.
2 *an active member of the union* **hard-working,** busy, industrious, diligent, tireless, contributing, effective, enterprising, involved, enthusiastic, keen, committed, devoted, zealous.
ANTONYMS passive, indifferent.
3 *the mill was active until 1960* **operative,** working, functioning, functional, operating, operational, in action, in operation, running; live; informal up and running.
ANTONYMS inoperative.

activity ▶ **noun 1** *there was a lot of activity in the area* **bustle,** hustle and bustle, busyness, action, liveliness, movement, life, stir, flurry; happenings, occurrences, proceedings, events, incidents; informal toing and froing, comings and goings.
2 *a wide range of activities* **pursuit,** occupation, interest, hobby, pastime, recreation, diversion; venture, undertaking, enterprise, project, scheme, business, entertainment; act, action, deed, exploit.

actual ▶ **adjective** *be honest—how much of this wild story is actual?* **real,** true, genuine, authentic, verified, attested, confirmed, definite, hard, plain, veritable; existing, existent, manifest, substantial, factual, de facto, bona fide; informal honest-to-goodness, real live. See note at **GENUINE**.
ANTONYMS notional.

actually ▶ **adverb** *believe it or not, George actually remembered our anniversary* **really,** in (actual) fact, in point of fact, as a matter of fact, in reality, in actuality, in truth, if truth be told, to tell the truth; literally; truly, indeed; archaic in sooth.

acumen ▶ **noun** *noted for her business acumen* **astuteness,** shrewdness, acuity, sharpness, sharp-wittedness, cleverness, smartness, brains; judgment, understanding, awareness, sense, common sense, canniness, discernment, wisdom, wit, sagacity, perspicacity, insight, perception, penetration; savvy, know-how, horse sense, smarts, street smarts.

acute ▶ **adjective 1** *acute food shortages* **severe,** critical, drastic, dire, dreadful, terrible, awful, grave, bad, serious, desperate, dangerous. See note at **CRUCIAL**.
ANTONYMS negligible.
2 *acute stomach pains* **sharp,** severe, stabbing, piercing, excruciating, agonizing, racking, keen, shooting, searing. See note at **KEEN**.
ANTONYMS mild, dull.
3 *an acute mind* **astute,** shrewd, sharp, sharp-witted, razor-sharp, rapierlike, quick, quick-witted, agile, nimble, clever, intelligent,

brilliant, keen, smart, canny, discerning, perceptive, perspicacious, penetrating, insightful, incisive, piercing, discriminating, sagacious, wise, judicious; informal on the ball, quick off the mark, quick on the uptake, streetwise, savvy.
ANTONYMS slow-witted.
4 *an acute sense of smell* **keen,** sharp, good, penetrating, discerning, sensitive.
ANTONYMS poor, weak.

acutely ▶ **adverb** *our trust in you has become acutely shaken* **extremely,** exceedingly, very, markedly, severely, intensely, deeply, profoundly, keenly, painfully, desperately, tremendously, enormously, thoroughly, heartily; informal awfully, terribly; slang majorly.
ANTONYMS slightly.

adage ▶ **noun** *I should have remembered the old adage 'look before you leap'* **saying,** maxim, axiom, proverb, aphorism, saw, dictum, byword, precept, motto, truism, platitude, cliché, apophthegm, commonplace.

adamant ▶ **adjective** *he begged his mother to let him try out for the football team, but she was adamant* **unshakable,** immovable, inflexible, unwavering, unswerving, uncompromising, insistent, resolute, resolved, determined, firm, steadfast; stubborn, unrelenting, diehard, unyielding, unbending, rigid, obdurate, inexorable, intransigent, (dead) set.

adapt ▶ **verb 1** *we've adapted the procedures to suit their needs* **modify,** alter, change, adjust, readjust, convert, redesign, restyle, refashion, remodel, reshape, revamp, rework, rejig, redo, reconstruct, reorganize; customize, tailor; improve, amend, refine, tweak.
2 *he has **adapted** well **to** his new home* **adjust to,** acclimatize oneself to, acclimate to, accommodate oneself to, attune to, conform to, habituate oneself to, become habituated to, get used to, orient oneself in, reconcile oneself to, come to terms with, get one's bearings in, find one's feet in, acculturate to, assimilate to, blend in to, fit in to.

adaptable ▶ **adjective 1** *competent and adaptable staff* **flexible,** versatile, cooperative, accommodating, amenable.
2 *an adaptable piece of furniture* **versatile,** modifiable, convertible, alterable, adjustable, changeable; multipurpose, all-purpose.

adaptation ▶ **noun 1** *an adaptation of a Scandinavian folk tale* **alteration,** modification, redesign, remodeling, revamping, reworking, reconstruction, conversion.
2 *the cubs' adaptation to the zoo environment* **adjustment,** acclimatization, acclimation, accommodations, habituation, acculturation, assimilation, integration.

add ▶ **verb 1** *the back room was added in 1971 | add more sugar to the mix* **attach,** build on, join, append, affix, connect, annex; include, incorporate, throw in, toss in; admix.
ANTONYMS remove.
2 *they added all the numbers* **total,** add up, count, count up, compute, calculate, reckon, tally; dated cast up.
ANTONYMS subtract.
3 *the subsidies **added up to** $1,700* **amount to,** come to, run to, make, total, equal, number.
4 *it all **adds up to** a deepening crisis* **amount to,** constitute; signify, signal, mean, indicate, denote, point to, be evidence of, be symptomatic of; informal spell.
5 *her decision just **added to** his woe* **increase,** magnify, amplify, augment, intensify, heighten, deepen; compound, reinforce; add fuel to the fire of, fan the flames of, rub salt on the wound of.
6 *she added that she had every confidence in Laura* **go on to say,** state further, continue, carry on.
– PHRASES **add up** informal *the situation just didn't add up* **make sense,** stand to reason, hold up, hold water, ring true, be convincing.

addendum ▶ **noun** *we can add the list of sponsors as an addendum to the program* **appendix,** codicil, postscript, afterword, tailpiece, rider, coda, supplement; Law adhesion; adjunct, appendage, addition, add-on, attachment.

addict ▶ **noun 1** *stealing money for your next high, just like the addicts out in the street | a barbiturate addict* **abuser,** user, drug addict; informal junkie, druggie, -head, -freak, pill-popper, dope fiend.
2 informal *skiing addicts* **enthusiast,** fan, lover, devotee, aficionado; informal freak, buff, nut, fiend, bum, junkie, fanatic, maniac.

addicted ▶ **adjective 1** *he was addicted to tranquilizers* **dependent on**; informal hooked on, strung out on.
2 *she became **addicted to** the theater* **devoted to,** obsessed with, fixated on, dedicated to, fanatical about, passionate about, enamored of, a slave to; informal hooked on, wild about, mad about, crazy about, nuts about.
ANTONYMS indifferent.

addiction ▶ **noun 1** *his heroin addiction* **dependency,** dependence, habit, problem.
2 *a slavish **addiction to** fashion* **devotion to,** dedication to, obsession with, infatuation with, passion for, love of, mania for, enslavement to.

addition ▶ **noun 1** *the soil is improved by the addition of compost* **adding,** incorporation, inclusion, introduction.
2 *an addition to the existing regulations* **supplement,** adjunct, addendum, adhesion, appendage, add-on, extra, attachment; rider, appurtenance.
– PHRASES **in addition 1** *the wind was frigid and, in addition, the sky threatened rain* **additionally,** as well, what's more, furthermore, moreover, also, into the bargain, to boot, likewise. **2** *three presidential hopefuls **in addition to** the vice president* **besides,** as well as, along with, other than, apart from, on top of, plus, over and above, not to mention, to say nothing of.

additional ▶ **adjective** *six additional tables will be necessary to accommodate the entire crew* **extra,** added, supplementary, supplemental, further, auxiliary, ancillary; more, other, another, new, fresh; informal bonus.

additionally ▶ **adverb** *additionally, there will be live entertainment every Thursday* **also,** in addition, as well, too, besides, on top (of that), moreover, further, furthermore, what's more, over and above that, into the bargain, to boot, likewise; archaic withal.

additive ▸ noun *our flours have no additives* **added ingredient,** addition; preservative, coloring.

address ▸ noun 1 *the address on the envelope* inscription, superscription; directions, number.
2 *our officers arrived at the address* **house,** apartment, home; formal residence, dwelling, dwelling place, habitation, abode, domicile.
3 *her address to the board members* **speech,** lecture, talk, monologue, dissertation, discourse, oration, peroration; slang spiel, chalk talk; sermon, homily, lesson; harangue.
▸ verb 1 *I addressed the envelope by hand* inscribe, superscribe.
2 *Rev. Lally addressed a crowded congregation* **talk to,** give a talk to, speak to, make a speech to, give a lecture to, lecture, hold forth to; **preach to,** give a sermon to; informal buttonhole, collar.
3 *the question of how to address one's parents-in-law* **call,** name, designate; speak to; formal denominate.
4 *correspondence should be addressed to the Personnel Department* **direct,** send, forward, communicate, convey, route, remit.
5 *the selectmen failed to address the issue of subsidies* **attend to,** apply oneself to, tackle, see to, deal with, confront, come to grips with, get down to, turn one's hand to, take in hand, undertake, concentrate on, focus on, devote oneself to.

adduce ▸ verb *evidence adduced to support their argument* **cite,** quote, name, mention, instance, point out, refer to; put forward, present, offer, advance, propose, proffer.

adept ▸ adjective *an adept negotiator* **expert,** proficient, accomplished, skillful, talented, masterly, masterful, consummate, virtuoso; adroit, dexterous, deft, artful; brilliant, splendid, marvelous, formidable, outstanding, first-rate, first-class, excellent, fine; informal great, top-notch, tip-top, A1, ace, mean, hotshot, crack, nifty, deadly; informal crackerjack.
ANTONYMS inept.
▸ noun *figure-skating adepts* **expert,** past master, master, genius, maestro, doyen, virtuoso; informal wizard, demon, ace, hotshot, whiz, maven, crackerjack.
ANTONYMS amateur.

adequacy ▸ noun 1 *the adequacy of the existing services* **satisfactoriness,** acceptability, acceptableness; sufficiency.
2 *he had deep misgivings about his own adequacy* **capability,** competence, ability, aptitude, suitability; effectiveness, fitness; formal efficacy.

adequate ▸ adjective 1 *he lacked adequate financial resources* **sufficient,** enough, requisite.
2 *the company provides an adequate service* **acceptable,** passable, reasonable, satisfactory, tolerable, fair, decent, quite good, pretty good, moderate, unexceptional, unremarkable, undistinguished, ordinary, average, not bad, all right, middling; informal OK, so-so, 'comme ci, comme ça', fair-to-middling, nothing to write home about.
3 *the workstations were small but seemed **adequate to** the task* **equal to,** up to, capable of, suitable for, able to do, fit for, sufficient for.

adhere ▸ verb 1 *a dollop of cream adhered to her nose* **stick (fast),** cohere, cling, bond, attach; be stuck, be fixed, be glued, be cemented.
2 *they **adhere to** Judaic law* **abide by,** stick to, hold to, comply with, act in accordance with, conform to, submit to, hew to; follow, obey, heed, observe, respect, uphold, fulfill.
ANTONYMS flout, ignore.

adherent ▸ noun *adherents of the Catholic faith* **follower,** supporter, upholder, defender, advocate, disciple, votary, devotee, partisan, member, friend, stalwart; believer, true believer, worshiper; rare sectary.
ANTONYMS opponent.

adhesive ▸ noun *a spray adhesive* **glue,** fixative, gum, paste, cement, mucilage; informal stickum.
▸ adjective *adhesive paper* **sticky,** tacky, gluey, gummed, stick-on, self-stick, gooey; viscous, viscid; technical adherent.

adieu ▸ noun & exclamation *with a cheery "adieu," they were gone* **goodbye,** farewell, until we meet again; bye-bye, bye, cheers, ciao, au revoir, adios, sayonara, so long, ta-ta, cheerio, toodle-oo.

adjacent ▸ adjective *adjacent angles | a patio **adjacent to** the greenhouse* **adjoining,** neighboring, next-door, abutting, contiguous, proximate; (**adjacent to**) close to, near, next to, by, by the side of, bordering on, beside, alongside, attached to, touching, cheek by jowl with.

adjoining ▸ adjective *adjoining hotel rooms* **connecting,** connected, interconnecting, adjacent, en suite, neighboring, bordering, next-door; contiguous, proximate; attached, touching.

adjourn ▸ verb 1 *the meeting was adjourned for lunch* **suspend,** break off, discontinue, interrupt, prorogue, stay, recess.
2 *sentencing was adjourned until June 9* **postpone,** put off, put back, defer, delay, hold over, shelve. See note at POSTPONE.
3 *they adjourned to the sitting room for liqueurs* **withdraw,** retire, retreat, take oneself; formal repair, remove; literary betake oneself.

adjournment ▸ noun *if not now signed into law, the legislation will die with the adjournment of this Congress* **suspension,** discontinuation, interruption, postponement, deferment, deferral, stay, prorogation; break, pause, recess.

adjudicate ▸ verb *this court cannot proceed to **adjudicate on** a matter when the accused does not have a counsel* **judge,** try, hear, examine, arbitrate, referee, umpire; pronounce on, give a ruling on, pass judgment on, decide, determine, settle, resolve.

adjudication ▸ noun *some newspapers do not publish the names of defendants in such cases until adjudication* **judgment,** decision, pronouncement, ruling, settlement, resolution, arbitration, finding, verdict, sentence; Law determination.

adjunct ▸ noun *the oral medication is used as an adjunct to the insulin* **supplement,** addition,

extra, add-on, accessory, accompaniment, complement, appurtenance; attachment, appendage, addendum.
▶ adjective *an adjunct professor of entomology* **subordinate,** auxiliary, assistant; temporary, provisional.

adjust ▶ verb 1 *Nanfeldt never quite* ***adjusted*** *to military life* **adapt to,** become accustomed to, get used to, accommodate oneself to, acclimatize to, acclimate to, orient oneself to, reconcile oneself to, habituate oneself to, assimilate to, familiarize oneself with; come to terms with, fit in with, find one's feet in.
2 *he adjusted the harness* **modify,** alter, regulate, tune, fine-tune, calibrate, balance; adapt, arrange, rearrange, change, rejig, rework, revamp, remodel, reshape, convert, tailor, improve, enhance, customize; repair, fix, correct, rectify, overhaul, put right; informal tweak.

adjustable ▶ adjective *adjustable seats* **alterable,** adaptable, modifiable, convertible, changeable, variable, multiway, versatile.

adjustment ▶ noun 1 *a period of adjustment* **adaptation,** accommodations, acclimatization, acclimation, habituation, acculturation, naturalization, assimilation.
2 *they had to make some adjustments to their strategy* **modification,** alteration, regulation, adaptation, rearrangement, change, reconstruction, customization, refinement; repair, correction, amendment, overhaul, improvement.

ad lib ▶ verb *halfway through the speech, she started ad libbing* **improvise,** extemporize, speak impromptu, play it by ear, make it up as one goes along, wing it.
▶ adverb *she spoke ad lib* **impromptu,** extempore, without preparation, without rehearsal, extemporaneously; informal off the cuff, off the top of one's head; ad libitum.
▶ adjective *a live, ad lib commentary* **impromptu,** extempore, extemporaneous, extemporary, improvised, unprepared, unrehearsed, unscripted; informal off-the-cuff, spur-of-the-moment.
ANTONYMS rehearsed.

administer ▶ verb 1 *the union is administered by a central executive | Leighton administers an entire department* **manage,** direct, control, operate, regulate, conduct, handle, run, organize, supervise, superintend, oversee, preside over, govern, rule, lead, head, steer; be in control of, be in charge of, be responsible for, be at the helm of; informal head up.
2 *the lifeboat crew administered first aid* **dispense,** issue, give, provide, apply, allot, distribute, hand out, dole out, disburse.
3 *a gym shoe was used to administer punishment* **inflict,** mete out, deal out, deliver.

administration ▶ noun 1 *the day-to-day administration of the company* **management,** direction, control, command, charge, conduct, operation, running, leadership, government, governing, superintendence, supervision, regulation, overseeing.
2 *the previous administration left a legacy of reckless spending* **government,** cabinet, ministry, regime, executive, authority, directorate, council, leadership, management; parliament, congress, senate; rule, term of office, incumbency.
3 *the administration of anti-inflammatory drugs* **provision,** issuing, issuance, application, dispensing, dispensation, distribution, disbursement.

administrative ▶ adjective *strong administrative skills* **managerial,** management, directorial, executive, organizational, bureaucratic, supervisory, regulatory.

administrator ▶ noun *he became the team's top administrator in 1973* **manager,** director, executive, controller, head, chief, leader, governor, superintendent, supervisor; informal boss.

admirable ▶ adjective *having done an admirable job of teaching preschoolers* **commendable,** praiseworthy, laudable, estimable, meritorious, creditable, exemplary, honorable, worthy, deserving, respectable, worthwhile, good, sterling, fine, masterly, great.
ANTONYMS deplorable.

admiration ▶ noun *it is with much admiration that we dedicate tonight's concert to Dr. Woods* **respect,** appreciation, (high) regard, esteem, veneration; commendation, acclaim, applause, praise, compliments, tributes, accolades, plaudits.
ANTONYMS scorn.

admire ▶ verb 1 *I admire your courage* **esteem,** approve of, respect, think highly of, rate highly, hold in high regard, applaud, praise, commend, acclaim. See notes at ESTEEM, REVERE.
ANTONYMS despise, disapprove of.
2 *we're just admiring your garden* **delight in,** appreciate, take pleasure in.

admirer ▶ noun *a great admirer of William Finn* **fan,** devotee, enthusiast, aficionado; supporter, adherent, follower, disciple.

admissible ▶ adjective *an admissible claim for damages* **valid,** allowable, allowed, permissible, permitted, acceptable, satisfactory, justifiable, defensible, supportable, appropriate, well-founded, tenable, sound; legitimate, lawful, legal, licit; informal OK, legit, kosher.

admission ▶ noun 1 *membership entitles you to free admission* **admittance,** entry, entrance, right of entry, access, right of access, ingress; entrée.
2 *the admission was $8* **entrance fee,** entry charge, cover (charge), ticket.
3 *a written admission of guilt* **confession,** acknowledgment, mea culpa, acceptance, concession, disclosure, divulgence.

admit ▶ verb 1 *he unlocked the door to admit her* **let in,** allow entry, permit entry, take in, usher in, show in, receive, welcome.
ANTONYMS exclude.
2 *she was admitted to law school* **accept to/into,** receive into, enroll in, enlist into, register into.
ANTONYMS expel.
3 *Paul admitted that he was angry* **confess,** acknowledge, own, concede, grant, accept, allow; reveal, disclose, divulge; plead guilty.
ANTONYMS deny.

admittance ▶ noun *no one is granted admittance*

without a pass **entry,** right of entry, admission, entrance, access, right of access, ingress; entrée.
ANTONYMS exclusion.

admonish ▸ verb **1** *he was severely admonished by his father* **reprimand,** rebuke, scold, reprove, reproach, upbraid, chastise, chide, berate, criticize, take to task, read the riot act to, rake/haul over the coals; dress down, bawl out, rap over the knuckles, give someone hell; chew out; formal castigate; rare reprehend. See note at REBUKE.
2 *she admonished him to drink less* **advise,** recommend, counsel, urge, exhort, bid, enjoin; caution, warn; formal adjure.

adolescence ▸ noun *the lack of adequate sleep in adolescence is a growing health problem largely ignored by the public school system* **teenage years,** teens, youth; pubescence, puberty; rare juvenescence, juvenility.

adolescent ▸ noun *an awkward adolescent* **teenager,** youngster, young person, youth, boy, girl; juvenile, minor; informal teen, teeny-bopper.
▸ adjective **1** *an adolescent boy* **teenage,** pubescent, young; juvenile; informal teen.
2 *adolescent silliness* **immature,** childish, juvenile, infantile, puerile, jejune. See note at YOUTHFUL.
ANTONYMS adult, mature.

adopt ▸ verb **1** *we adopted Sasha in 1996* **take as one's child,** be adoptive parents to, take in, take care of.
ANTONYMS abandon.
2 *they adopted local customs* **espouse,** take on/up, embrace, assume; appropriate, arrogate.
ANTONYMS abandon, reject.
3 *the people adopted him as their patron saint* **choose,** select, pick, vote for, elect, settle on, decide on, opt for; name, nominate, appoint.
ANTONYMS reject.

adorable ▸ adjective *adorable little kittens* **lovable,** appealing, charming, cute, cuddly, sweet, enchanting, bewitching, captivating, engaging, endearing, dear, darling, delightful, lovely, beautiful, attractive, gorgeous, winsome, winning, fetching; Scottish bonny.
ANTONYMS repulsive, hateful.

adoration ▸ noun **1** *the girl gazed at him with adoration* **love,** devotion, care, fondness; admiration, high regard, awe, idolization, worship, hero-worship, adulation.
2 *our day of prayer and adoration* **worship,** glory, glorification, praise, thanksgiving, homage, exaltation, veneration, reverence.

adore ▸ verb **1** *he adored his mother* **love dearly,** love, be devoted to, dote on, hold dear, cherish, treasure, prize, think the world of; admire, hold in high regard, look up to, idolize, worship; informal put on a pedestal.
ANTONYMS hate, detest.
2 *we adore thee, Lord God* **worship,** glorify, praise, revere, reverence, exalt, extol, venerate, pay homage to; formal laud; archaic magnify. See note at REVERE.
3 informal *I adore oysters* **like,** love, be very fond of, be very keen on, be partial to, have a weakness for; delight in, relish, savor; informal be crazy about, be wild about, have a thing about/for/with, be hooked on.
ANTONYMS hate, detest.

adorn ▸ verb *we'll adorn the hall with tiny lights and ropes of pine* **decorate,** embellish, ornament, enhance; beautify, prettify, grace, bedeck, deck (out), dress (up), trim, swathe, wreathe, festoon, garland, array, emblazon, titivate.
ANTONYMS disfigure.

adornment ▸ noun *why all the adornment just for a casual dinner party?* | *we purchased way more adornments than we could ever use* **decoration,** embellishment, ornamentation, ornament, enhancement; beautification, prettification; frill, accessory, doodad, fandangle, frippery; trimmings, finishing touches.

adrift ▸ adjective **1** *their empty boat was spotted adrift* **drifting,** unmoored, unanchored.
2 *adrift in a strange country* **lost,** off course; disoriented, confused, at sea; drifting, rootless, unsettled, directionless, aimless, purposeless, without purpose.

adroit ▸ adjective *an adroit politician* | *adroit social commentary* **skillful,** adept, dexterous, deft, nimble, able, capable, skilled, expert, masterly, masterful, master, practiced, handy, polished, slick, proficient, accomplished, gifted, talented; quick-witted, quick-thinking, clever, smart, sharp, cunning, wily, resourceful, astute, shrewd, canny; informal nifty, crack, mean, ace, A1, clueful, on the ball, savvy, crackerjack.
ANTONYMS inept, clumsy.

adroitness ▸ noun *there is an undeniable adroitness in his economic plan* **skill,** skillfulness, prowess, expertise, adeptness, dexterity, deftness, nimbleness, ability, capability, mastery, proficiency, accomplishment, artistry, art, facility, aptitude, flair, finesse, talent; quick-wittedness, cleverness, sharpness, cunning, astuteness, shrewdness, resourcefulness, savoir faire; informal know-how, savvy.

adulation ▸ noun *unspoiled by all the adulation he's received* **hero-worship,** worship, idolization, adoration, admiration, veneration, awe, devotion, glorification, praise, flattery, blandishments.

adult ▸ adjective **1** *an adult woman* **mature,** grown-up, fully grown, full-grown, fully developed, of age, of legal age.
2 *an adult movie* **sexually explicit,** pornographic, obscene, smutty, dirty, rude, erotic, sexy, suggestive, titillating; porn, porno, naughty, blue, X-rated.

adulterate ▸ verb *some of the drinks had been adulterated with tranquilizers* **make impure,** degrade, debase, spoil, taint, contaminate; doctor, tamper with, dilute, water down, weaken; bastardize, corrupt; informal cut, spike, lace, dope. See note at POLLUTE.
ANTONYMS purify.

advance ▸ verb **1** *the battalion advanced rapidly* **move forward,** proceed, press on, push on, push forward, make progress, make headway, gain ground, approach, come closer, draw nearer, near.
ANTONYMS retreat.

2 *the court may advance the date of the hearing* **bring forward**, put forward, move forward.
ANTONYMS postpone.
3 *the move advanced his career* **promote**, further, help, aid, assist, boost, strengthen, improve, benefit, foster.
ANTONYMS impede, hinder.
4 *our technology has advanced in the last few years* **progress**, make progress, make headway, develop, evolve, make strides, move forward (in leaps and bounds), move ahead; improve, thrive, flourish, prosper.
ANTONYMS stagnate.
5 *the hypothesis I wish to advance in this article* **put forward**, present, submit, suggest, propose, introduce, offer, adduce, moot.
ANTONYMS retract.
6 *a relative advanced him some money* **lend**, loan, put up, come up with.
ANTONYMS borrow.
▶ **noun 1** *the advance of the aggressors* **progress**, forward movement; approach.
2 *a significant medical advance* **breakthrough**, development, step forward, step in the right direction, (quantum) leap; find, finding, discovery, invention.
3 *share prices showed significant advances* **increase**, rise, upturn, upsurge, upswing, growth; informal hike.
4 *the writer is going to be given a huge advance* **down payment**, retainer, prepayment, deposit, front money, money up front.
5 *unwelcome sexual advances* **pass**, proposition.
▶ **adjective 1** *an advance party of settlers* **preliminary**, sent (on) ahead, first, exploratory; pilot, test, trial.
2 *advance warning* **early**, prior, beforehand.
– PHRASES **in advance** *rental skis and boots can be reserved in advance* **beforehand**, before, ahead of time, earlier, previously; in readiness.

advanced ▶ **adjective 1** *advanced manufacturing techniques* **state-of-the-art**, new, modern, developed, cutting-edge, leading-edge, up-to-date, up-to-the-minute, the newest, the latest; progressive, avant-garde, ahead of the times, pioneering, innovative, sophisticated.
2 *advanced further-education courses* **higher-level**, higher.
ANTONYMS primitive.

advancement ▶ **noun 1** *the advancement of computer technology* **development**, progress, evolution, growth, improvement, advance, furtherance; headway.
2 *employees must be offered opportunities for advancement* **promotion**, preferment, career development, upgrading, a step up the ladder, progress, improvement, betterment, growth.

advantage ▶ **noun 1** *the advantages of belonging to a union* **benefit**, value, good point, strong point, asset, plus, bonus, boon, blessing, virtue; attraction, beauty, usefulness, helpfulness, convenience, advantageousness, profit.
ANTONYMS disadvantage, drawback.
2 *they appeared to be gaining the advantage over their opponents* **upper hand**, edge, lead, whip hand, trump card; superiority, dominance, ascendancy, supremacy, power, mastery; informal inside track, catbird seat.
3 *there is no advantage to be gained from delaying the process* **benefit**, profit, gain, good; informal mileage.
ANTONYMS detriment.

advantageous ▶ **adjective 1** *an advantageous position* **superior**, dominant, powerful; good, fortunate, lucky, favorable.
ANTONYMS inferior.
2 *the arrangement is advantageous to both sides* **beneficial**, of benefit, helpful, of assistance, useful, of use, of value, of service, profitable, fruitful; convenient, expedient.
ANTONYMS detrimental.

advent ▶ **noun** *the advent of a new school year* **arrival**, appearance, emergence, materialization, occurrence, dawn, birth, rise, development; approach, coming.
ANTONYMS disappearance.

adventitious ▶ **adjective** *he felt that the conversation was not entirely adventitious* **unplanned**, unpremeditated, accidental, chance, fortuitous, serendipitous, coincidental, casual, random. See note at ACCIDENTAL.
ANTONYMS premeditated.

adventure ▶ **noun 1** *they set off in search of adventure* **excitement**, thrill, stimulation; risk, danger, hazard, peril, uncertainty, precariousness.
2 *her recent adventures in Italy* **exploit**, escapade, deed, feat, experience.

adventurous ▶ **adjective 1** *an adventurous traveler* **daring**, daredevil, intrepid, venturesome, bold, fearless, brave, unafraid, unshrinking, dauntless; informal gutsy, spunky.
ANTONYMS cautious.
2 *adventurous activities* **risky**, dangerous, perilous, hazardous, precarious, uncertain; exciting, thrilling.
ANTONYMS tame.

adversary ▶ **noun** *once his devoted comrade at West Point, Arthur was now his adversary at Bull Run* **opponent**, rival, enemy, antagonist, combatant, challenger, contender, competitor, opposer; opposition, competition, foe.
ANTONYMS ally, supporter.

adverse ▶ **adjective 1** *adverse weather conditions* **unfavorable**, disadvantageous, inauspicious, unpropitious, unfortunate, unlucky, untimely, untoward.
ANTONYMS favorable, auspicious.
2 *the drug's adverse side effects* **harmful**, dangerous, injurious, detrimental, hurtful, negative, deleterious.
ANTONYMS beneficial.
3 *an adverse response from the public* **hostile**, **unfavorable**, antagonistic, unfriendly, ill-disposed, negative. See note at HOSTILE.
ANTONYMS positive, friendly.

adversity ▶ **noun** *the studio made sure the public saw only the manufactured glamour and none of the real adversity of her private life* **misfortune**, ill luck, bad luck, trouble, difficulty, hardship, distress, disaster, suffering, affliction, sorrow, misery, tribulation, woe, pain, trauma; mishap, misadventure, accident, upset, reverse, setback, crisis, catastrophe, tragedy, calamity, trial, cross, burden, blow; hard times, trials and tribulations; informal ill wind.

advertise ▶ **verb** *you should advertise the contest*

on your local radio station **publicize,** make public, make known, announce, broadcast, proclaim, trumpet, call attention to, bill, promulgate; promote, market, beat/bang the drum for, huckster; informal push, plug, hype, boost; ballyhoo, flack.

advertisement ▸ noun *it looked like the phone bill, but it was just an advertisement* **ad,** announcement, notice; commercial, infomercial, promotion, endorsement, blurb, write-up; poster, leaflet, pamphlet, flyer, bill, handbill, handout, fact sheet, circular, bulletin, brochure, sign, placard, junk mail; informal plug.

advice ▸ noun *they give excellent advice on running a small business* **guidance,** counseling, counsel, help, direction; information, recommendations, guidelines, suggestions, hints, tips, pointers, ideas, opinions, views, input, words of wisdom.

advisable ▸ adjective *it is advisable to book a table in advance* **judicious,** desirable, preferable, well, best, sensible, prudent, proper, appropriate, apt, suitable, fitting, wise, recommended, suggested; expedient, politic, advantageous, beneficial, profitable, in one's (best) interest.

advise ▸ verb **1** *her grandmother advised her about marriage* **counsel,** give guidance, guide, offer suggestions, give hints, give tips, give pointers.
2 *he advised caution* **advocate,** recommend, suggest, urge, encourage, enjoin.
3 *you will be* ***advised of*** *the requirements* **inform of,** notify about/of, give notice of, apprise of, warn of, forewarn of; acquaint with, make familiar with, keep posted about, update about/on; informal fill in on.

advisory ▸ adjective *she agreed to serve in an advisory role* **consultative,** advising.
ANTONYMS executive.

advocacy ▸ noun *his* ***advocacy of*** *animal rights* **support for,** backing of, promotion of, championing of; argument for, push for; informal boosterism of.

advocate ▸ noun *an advocate of children's rights* **champion,** upholder, supporter, backer, promoter, proponent, exponent, spokesman, spokeswoman, spokesperson, campaigner, fighter, crusader; propagandist, apostle, apologist, booster, flag-bearer; informal libber.
ANTONYMS critic.
▸ verb *heart specialists advocate a diet low in cholesterol* **recommend,** prescribe, advise, urge; support, back, favor, espouse, endorse, uphold, subscribe to, champion, campaign on behalf of, speak for, argue for, lobby for, promote.

aegis ▸ noun *they had wrongly assumed that Lincoln Beach fell under the aegis of the Parks Department* **protection,** backing, support, patronage, sponsorship, charge, care, guidance, control, guardianship, trusteeship, agency, safeguarding, shelter, umbrella, aid, assistance; auspices.

affable ▸ adjective *he would have us believe that his sexual advances were merely the charming excesses of an affable rogue* **friendly,** amiable, genial, congenial, cordial, warm, pleasant, nice, likable, personable, charming, agreeable, sympathetic, simpatico, good-humored, good-natured, jolly, kindly, kind, courteous, civil, gracious, approachable, accessible, amenable, sociable, hail-fellow-well-met, outgoing, gregarious, neighborly.
ANTONYMS unfriendly.

affair ▸ noun **1** *what you do is your own affair* **business,** concern, matter, responsibility, province, preserve; problem, worry.
2 (**affairs**) *his financial affairs* **transactions,** concerns, matters, activities, dealings, undertakings, ventures, business.
3 *the board admitted responsibility for the affair* **event,** incident, happening, occurrence, eventuality, episode; case, matter, business.
4 *his affair with Monica was over* **relationship,** love affair, affaire de coeur, romance, fling, flirtation, dalliance, liaison, involvement, intrigue, amour; informal hanky-panky.

affect[1] ▸ verb **1** *this development may have affected the judge's decision* **have an effect on,** influence, act on, work on, have an impact on, impact; change, alter, modify, transform, form, shape, sway, bias.
2 *he was visibly affected by the experience* **move,** touch, make an impression on, hit (hard), tug at someone's heartstrings; **upset,** trouble, distress, disturb, agitate, shake (up).
3 *the disease affected his lungs* **attack,** infect; hit, strike. See note at **EMOTION**.

affect[2] ▸ verb **1** *he deliberately affected a Republican stance* **assume,** take on, adopt, embrace, espouse.
2 *Paul affected an air of injured innocence* **pretend,** feign, fake, simulate, make a show of, make a pretense of, sham; informal put on, make like.

affectation ▸ noun **1** *the affectations of a prima donna* **pretension,** pretentiousness, affectedness, artificiality, posturing, posing; airs (and graces).
2 *an affectation of calm* **facade,** front, show, appearance, pretense, simulation, posture, pose.

affected ▸ adjective *that affected voice of his really grates on me* **pretentious,** artificial, contrived, unnatural, stagy, studied, mannered, ostentatious; insincere, unconvincing, feigned, false, fake, sham, simulated; informal la-di-da, phony, pretend, put on.
ANTONYMS natural, unpretentious, genuine.

affecting ▸ adjective *an affecting piece of music* **touching,** moving, emotive, emotional; stirring, soul-stirring, heartwarming; poignant, pathetic, pitiful, piteous, tear-jerking, heart-rending, gut-wrenching, heartbreaking, disturbing, distressing, upsetting, sad, haunting. See note at **MOVING**.

affection ▸ noun *the affection they share is obvious* **fondness,** love, liking, tenderness, warmth, devotion, endearment, care, caring, attachment, friendship; warm feelings.

affectionate ▸ adjective *an affectionate handshake | golden retrievers are known for being affectionate* **loving,** fond, adoring, devoted, caring, doting, tender, warm, warmhearted, softhearted, friendly; demonstrative, cuddly; informal touchy-feely, lovey-dovey.

ANTONYMS cold.

affiliate ▸ verb *the college is **affiliated with** the University of Wisconsin* **associate with,** unite with, combine with, join (up) with, link up with, team up with, ally with, align with, band together with, federate with, amalgamate with, merge with; attach to, annex to, incorporate into, integrate into.

▸ noun *Conklin Textiles is their largest Midwest affiliate* **partner,** branch, offshoot, subsidiary.

affiliation ▸ noun *the project's **affiliation with** the town's welfare department | the newspaper's obvious **affiliation to** the Republican Party* **association with,** connection with/to, alliance with/to, alignment with, link with/to, attachment to, tie with/to, relationship with/to, fellowship with, partnership with, coalition with, union with; amalgamation with, incorporation into, integration into, federation with, confederation with.

affinity ▸ noun **1** *her **affinity with** animals and birds | an **affinity for** opera* **empathy for,** rapport with, sympathy for, accord with, harmony with, relationship with, bond with, fellow feeling for, closeness with/to, understanding of/for; liking of/for, fondness of/for; informal chemistry with.
ANTONYMS aversion, dislike.
2 *the semantic affinity between the two words* **similarity,** resemblance, likeness, kinship, relationship, association, link, analogy, similitude, correspondence. See note at **LIKENESS**.
ANTONYMS dissimilitude, dissimilarity.

affirm ▸ verb **1** *he affirmed that they would lend military assistance* **declare,** state, assert, proclaim, pronounce, attest, swear, avow, guarantee, pledge, give an undertaking; formal aver.
ANTONYMS deny.
2 *the referendum affirmed the republic's right to secede* **uphold,** support, confirm, ratify, endorse, sanction.

affirmation ▸ noun **1** *an affirmation of faith* **declaration,** statement, assertion, proclamation, pronouncement, attestation; oath, avowal, guarantee, pledge; deposition; formal averment, asseveration.
ANTONYMS denial.
2 *the poem ends with an affirmation of pastoral values* **confirmation,** ratification, endorsement.

affirmative ▸ adjective *an affirmative answer* **positive,** assenting, consenting, corroborative, favorable.
ANTONYMS negative.

▸ noun *she took his grunt as an affirmative* **agreement,** acceptance, assent, acquiescence, concurrence; OK, yes, thumbs-up.
ANTONYMS disagreement.

affix ▸ verb **1** *he affixed a stamp to the envelope* **stick,** glue, paste, gum; attach, fasten, fix; clip, tack, pin; tape.
ANTONYMS detach.
2 formal *affix your signature to the document* **append,** add, attach.

afflict ▸ verb *arthritis can afflict people of all ages* **trouble,** burden, distress, cause suffering to, beset, harass, worry, oppress; torment, pester, plague, blight, bedevil, rack, smite, curse; archaic ail.

affliction ▸ noun **1** *a common herb reputed to cure a variety of afflictions* **disorder,** disease, malady, complaint, ailment, illness, indisposition, handicap; scourge, plague, trouble.
2 *he bore his affliction with great dignity* **suffering,** distress, pain, trouble, misery, wretchedness, hardship, misfortune, adversity, sorrow, torment, tribulation, woe.

affluent ▸ adjective *the affluent families of Newport* **wealthy,** rich, prosperous, well off, moneyed, well-to-do; propertied, substantial, of means, of substance, plutocratic; informal well-heeled, rolling in it, made of money, filthy rich, stinking rich, loaded, on easy street; upper-class, upscale. See note at **WEALTHY**.
ANTONYMS poor, impoverished.

afford ▸ verb **1** *I can't afford a new car* **pay for,** bear the expense of, have the money for, spare the price of.
2 *it took more time than he could afford* **spare,** allow (oneself).
3 *the rooftop terrace affords beautiful views* **provide,** supply, furnish, offer, give, make available, yield. See note at **GIVE**.

affront ▸ noun *an affront to public morality* **insult,** offense, indignity, slight, snub, put-down, provocation, injury; outrage, atrocity, scandal; informal slap in the face, kick in the teeth.

▸ verb *she was affronted by his familiarity* **insult,** offend, mortify, provoke, pique, wound, hurt; put out, irk, displease, bother, rankle, vex, gall; outrage, scandalize, disgust; informal put someone's back up, needle.

afoot ▸ adjective & adverb *evil plans are afoot* **going on,** happening, around, about, abroad, stirring, circulating, in circulation, at large, in the air/wind; brewing, looming, in the offing, on the horizon.

aforesaid ▸ adjective *the policy insures the aforesaid items* **previously mentioned,** aforementioned, aforenamed; foregoing, preceding, earlier, previous; above.

afraid ▸ adjective **1** *they ran away because they were afraid* **frightened,** scared, terrified, fearful, petrified, scared witless, scared to death, terror-stricken, terror-struck, frightened out of one's wits, scared out of one's wits, shaking in one's shoes, shaking like a leaf; intimidated, alarmed, panicky; faint-hearted, cowardly; informal scared stiff, in a cold sweat, spooked; chicken; archaic afeared, affrighted.
ANTONYMS brave, confident.
2 *don't be afraid to ask questions* **reluctant,** hesitant, unwilling, disinclined, loath, slow, chary, shy.
ANTONYMS confident.
3 *I'm afraid that your daughter is ill* **sorry,** sad, distressed, regretful, apologetic.
ANTONYMS pleased.

afresh ▸ adverb *let's start afresh* **anew,** again, over again, once again, once more, another time.

after ▸ preposition **1** *she made a speech after the performance* **following,** subsequent to, at the close/end of, in the wake of; formal posterior to.
ANTONYMS before, preceding.

2 *Guy shut the door after them* **behind,** following.
ANTONYMS in front of.
3 *after the way he treated my sister, I never want to speak to him again* **because of,** as a result of, as a consequence of, in view of, owing to, on account of.
4 *is he still going to marry her, after all that's happened?* **despite,** in spite of, regardless of, notwithstanding.
5 *the policeman ran after him* **in pursuit of,** in someone's direction, following.
ANTONYMS away from, in front of.
6 *I'm after information, and I'm willing to pay for it* **in search of,** in quest of, in pursuit of, trying to find, looking for, hunting for; desirous of, wanting.
7 *they asked after Dad* **about,** concerning, regarding, with regard to, with respect to, with reference to.
8 *the village was named after a Roman officer* **in honor of,** as a tribute to.
▶ **adverb 1** *the week after, we went to Madrid* **later,** afterward, after this/that, subsequently.
ANTONYMS previously, before.
2 *porters were following on after with their bags* **behind,** in the rear, at the back, in someone's wake.
ANTONYMS ahead, in front.
– PHRASES **after all** *I couldn't stay mad—after all, we're best friends* **above all,** most important, most importantly, beyond everything, ultimately; informal when all is said and done, at the end of the day, when push comes to shove.

afterlife ▶ **noun** *they shared their personal beliefs about the afterlife* **life after death,** the next world, the hereafter, the afterworld, eternity, kingdom come; immortality.

aftermath ▶ **noun** *the Red Cross is a prominent presence in the aftermath of last week's earthquake* **repercussions,** aftereffects, consequences, effects, results, fruits; wake.

again ▶ **adverb 1** *her spirits lifted again* **once more,** another time, afresh, anew.
2 *this can add half as much again to the price* **extra,** in addition, additionally, on top.
3 *again, evidence was not always consistent* **also,** furthermore; moreover, besides.
– PHRASES **again and again** *I've warned you again and again about that loose step* **repeatedly,** over and over (again), time and (time) again, many times, many a time; often, frequently, continually, constantly.

against ▶ **preposition 1** *a number of delegates were against the motion* **opposed to,** in opposition to, hostile to, averse to, antagonistic toward, inimical to, unsympathetic to, resistant to, at odds with, in disagreement with, dead set against; informal anti.
ANTONYMS in favor of, pro.
2 *he was swimming against the tide* **in opposition to,** counter to, contrary to, in the opposite direction to.
ANTONYMS with.
3 *his age is against him* **disadvantageous to,** unfavorable to, damaging to, detrimental to, prejudicial to, deleterious to, harmful to, injurious to, a drawback for.
ANTONYMS advantageous to.
4 *she leaned against the wall* **touching,** in contact with, up against, on, adjacent to.

age ▶ **noun 1** *he is 35 years of age | his wife is the same age* **number of years,** length of life; stage of life, generation, age group.
2 *her hearing had deteriorated with age* **elderliness,** old age, oldness, senescence, dotage, seniority, maturity; one's advancing/advanced/declining years; literary eld; archaic caducity.
3 *the Elizabethan age* **era,** epoch, period, time, eon.
4 informal **(ages)** *you haven't been in touch with me for ages* **a long time,** days/months/years on end, an eternity, an eon; informal ages and ages, donkey's years, a coon's age, a month of Sundays, forever.
▶ **verb 1** *Cabernet Sauvignon ages well* **mature,** mellow, ripen, season.
2 *Leila has aged a lot since the last time I saw her* **grow/become/get old,** mature, (cause to) decline, weather, fade; grow up, come of age.
See note at **MATURE**.

aged ▶ **adjective** *an aged relative* **elderly,** old, mature, older, senior, hoary, ancient, senescent, advanced in years, in one's dotage, long in the tooth, as old as the hills, past one's prime, not as young as one used to be, getting on, over the hill, no spring chicken. See note at **OLD**.
ANTONYMS young.

agency ▶ **noun 1** *an advertising agency* **business,** organization, company, firm, office, bureau.
2 *the infection is caused by the agency of insects* **action,** activity, means, effect, influence, force, power, vehicle, medium.
3 *regional policy was introduced through the agency of the Board of Trade* **intervention,** intercession, involvement, good offices; auspices, aegis.

agenda ▶ **noun 1** *the next topic on the agenda* **list of items,** schedule, program, timetable, itinerary, lineup, list, plan.
2 *their hidden agenda* **plan,** scheme, motive.

agent ▶ **noun 1** *the sale was arranged through an agent* **representative,** emissary, envoy, go-between, proxy, negotiator, broker, liaison, spokesperson, spokesman, spokeswoman; informal rep.
2 *a travel agent* **agency,** business, organization, company, firm, bureau.
3 *a CIA agent* **spy,** secret agent, undercover agent, operative, fifth columnist, mole, Mata Hari; informal G-man.
4 *the agents of destruction* **performer,** author, executor, perpetrator, producer, instrument, catalyst.
5 *a cleansing agent* **medium,** means, instrument, vehicle.

aggravate ▶ **verb 1** *the new law could aggravate the situation* **worsen,** make worse, exacerbate, inflame, compound; add fuel to the fire/flames, add insult to injury, rub salt in the wound.
ANTONYMS alleviate, improve.
2 informal *you don't have to aggravate people to get what you want* **annoy,** irritate, exasperate, bother, put out, nettle, provoke, antagonize, get on someone's nerves, ruffle (someone's feathers), try someone's patience; informal peeve,

needle, bug, miff, get under someone's skin; tick off.
ANTONYMS calm, conciliate.

USAGE

aggravate, aggravation

Though documented as existing since the 1600s, *aggravate* for *annoy* or *irritate* has never gained the approval of stylists and should be avoided in formal writing. Strictly speaking, *aggravate* means "make worse; exacerbate": *writing a second apology might just aggravate the problem.* Even the eloquent American jurist Oliver Wendell Holmes, Jr., nodded once, using *aggravate* for *irritate* in a letter penned in 1895: "Our two countries aggravate each other from time to time."

In some contexts, it's genuinely difficult to tell whether the word *aggravating* is a present participle or an adjective—e.g.: "The City of Washington is notorious for aggravating allergies, and Mr. Clinton said he expected his to be more severe there than in Arkansas." (*New York Times;* Oct. 14, 1996.) The second half of that compound sentence suggests that the writer is using *aggravating* correctly. But taken alone, the phrase in the first half of the sentence ("Washington is notorious for aggravating allergies") could refer to either (1) making allergies worse (the preferred usage), or (2) allergies that are irritating or frustrating.

The confusion also occurs between the noun forms—e.g.: "Rush Limbaugh . . . has an extra tone of aggravation [read *irritation*] as he denounces the unyielding poll leads of 'the Schlickmeister' and 'noted hetero fun-seeker,' President Clinton." (*New York Times;* Sept. 25, 1996.)

Perhaps *exasperate* contributes to the misuse of *aggravate* (which sounds a bit like *exasperate*) in the sense of *irritate* (which is close in meaning to *exasperate*). Also, when *aggravate* is used in this sense it often implies something more intense than merely *irritate*. It is closer in meaning to *exasperate*.
— BG

aggravation ▶ **noun 1** *the recession led to the aggravation of unemployment problems* **worsening,** exacerbation, compounding.
2 informal *it's not worth the aggravation* **nuisance,** annoyance, irritation, hassle, headache, trouble, difficulty, inconvenience, bother, pain, distress.

aggregate ▶ **noun 1** *the specimen is an aggregate of rock and mineral fragments* **collection,** mass, agglomeration, conglomerate, assemblage; mixture, mix, combination, blend, accumulation; compound, alloy, amalgam.
2 *he won with an aggregate of 325* **total,** sum total, sum, grand total.
▶ **adjective** *an aggregate score* **total,** combined, gross, overall, composite.

aggression ▶ **noun 1** *an act of aggression* **hostility,** aggressiveness, belligerence, bellicosity, force, violence; pugnacity, pugnaciousness, militancy, warmongering; attack, assault.
2 *he played the game with unceasing aggression* **confidence,** self-confidence, boldness, determination, forcefulness, vigor, energy, zeal.

aggressive ▶ **adjective 1** *aggressive behavior* **hostile,** belligerent, bellicose, antagonistic, truculent; pugnacious, combative, two-fisted, violent; macho; confrontational; quarrelsome, argumentative.
ANTONYMS meek, friendly.
2 *aggressive foreign policy* **warmongering,** warlike, warring, belligerent, bellicose, hawkish, militaristic; offensive, expansionist.
ANTONYMS peaceable, peaceful.
3 *an aggressive promotional drive* **assertive,** pushy, forceful, vigorous, energetic, dynamic; bold, audacious; informal in-your-face, feisty. See note at BOLD.
ANTONYMS submissive, diffident.

aggressor ▶ **noun** *England was the aggressor in a succession of wars* **attacker,** assaulter, assailant; invader, instigator, warmonger.

aggrieved ▶ **adjective 1** *the manager looked aggrieved at the suggestion* **resentful,** affronted, indignant, disgruntled, discontented, upset, offended, piqued, riled, nettled, vexed, irked, irritated, annoyed, put out, chagrined; informal peeved, miffed, in a huff, sore, steamed.
ANTONYMS pleased.
2 *the aggrieved party* **wronged,** injured, mistreated, ill-treated, abused, harmed.

aghast ▶ **adjective** *eyewitnesses to the explosion were aghast* **horrified,** appalled, dismayed, thunderstruck, stunned, shocked, staggered; informal flabbergasted.

agile ▶ **adjective 1** *she was as agile as a monkey* **nimble,** lithe, supple, limber, acrobatic, fleet-footed, light-footed, light on one's feet; literary fleet, lightsome.
ANTONYMS clumsy, stiff.
2 *an agile mind* **alert,** sharp, acute, shrewd, astute, perceptive, quick-witted.
ANTONYMS slow, dull.

agitate ▶ **verb 1** *any mention of Clare agitates my grandmother* **upset,** perturb, fluster, ruffle, disconcert, unnerve, disquiet, disturb, distress, unsettle, unhinge; informal rattle, faze; discombobulate.
2 *she agitated for the appointment of more women* **campaign,** strive, battle, fight, struggle, push, press.
3 *agitate the water to disperse the oil* **stir,** whisk, churn, beat.

agitator ▶ **noun** *tell your band of agitators that my generals are heavily armed and most unsympathetic* **troublemaker,** rabble-rouser, agent provocateur, demagogue, incendiary; revolutionary, firebrand, rebel, insurgent, subversive; informal disturber.

agnostic ▶ **noun** *as far as I know, Stevens was an atheist, or at least an agnostic* **skeptic,** doubter, doubting Thomas, cynic; unbeliever, nonbeliever, rationalist; rare nullifidian.
ANTONYMS believer, theist.

ago ▶ **adverb** *years ago, on this very site, was a small stone cottage* **in the past,** before, earlier, back, since, previously; formal heretofore.

agog ▶ adverb *tell us what happened—we're all agog!* **eager,** excited, impatient, keen, anxious, avid, in suspense, on tenterhooks, on the edge of one's seat, on pins and needles, waiting with bated breath.

agonizing ▶ adjective *agonizing pain* **excruciating,** harrowing, racking, searing, extremely painful, acute, severe, torturous, tormenting, piercing; informal hellish.

agony ▶ noun *the agony was both mental and physical* **pain,** hurt, suffering, torture, torment, anguish, affliction, trauma; pangs, throes.

agree ▶ verb **1** *I agree with you* **concur,** be of the same mind/opinion, see eye to eye, be in sympathy, be united, be as one man.
ANTONYMS differ.
2 *they had **agreed to** a cease-fire* **consent to,** assent to, acquiesce to, accept, approve, say yes to, give one's approval to, give the nod to; informal OK; formal accede to.
ANTONYMS reject.
3 *the plan and the drawing do not agree with each other* **match (up),** jibe, accord, correspond, chime in, conform, coincide, fit, tally, be in harmony/agreement, harmonize, be consistent/equivalent; informal square.
ANTONYMS differ, contradict.
4 *they **agreed on** a price* **settle on,** decide on, arrive at, work out, negotiate, reach an agreement on, come to terms on, strike a bargain on, make a deal on, shake hands on.

agreeable ▶ adjective **1** *an agreeable atmosphere of rural tranquility* **pleasant,** pleasing, enjoyable, pleasurable, nice, to one's liking, appealing, charming, delightful. See note at PLEASANT.
ANTONYMS unpleasant.
2 *an agreeable fellow* **likable,** charming, amiable, affable, pleasant, nice, friendly, good-natured, sociable, genial, congenial, simpatico.
ANTONYMS unpleasant.
3 *we should get together for a talk, if you're agreeable* **willing,** amenable, in accord/agreement, compliant, consenting.
ANTONYMS unwilling.

agreement ▶ noun **1** *all heads nodded in agreement* **accord,** concurrence, consensus; assent, acceptance, consent, acquiescence, endorsement, like-mindedness.
2 *an agreement on military cooperation* **contract,** compact, treaty, covenant, pact, accord, concordat, protocol.
3 *there is some agreement between my view and that of the author* **correspondence,** consistency, compatibility, accord; similarity, resemblance, likeness, similitude.
ANTONYMS discord.

agriculture ▶ noun *the mechanization of agriculture* **farming,** cultivation, tillage, tilling, husbandry, land/farm management, horticulture; agribusiness, agronomy.

aground ▶ adverb & adjective *the ship was aground when we spotted it* **grounded,** ashore, beached, stuck, shipwrecked, high and dry, on the rocks, on the ground/bottom.

ahead ▶ adverb **1** *he peered ahead, but could see nothing* **forward,** toward the front, frontward, onward, along.
ANTONYMS behind.
2 *he had ridden on ahead* **in front,** at the head, in the lead, at the fore, in the vanguard, in advance.
ANTONYMS behind, at the back.
3 *she was preparing herself for what lay ahead* **in the future,** in time, in time to come, in the fullness of time, at a later date, after this, henceforth, later on, in due course, next.
ANTONYMS in the past.
4 *they are ahead by six points* **leading,** winning, in the lead, (out) in front, first, coming first.
ANTONYMS trailing, losing.
– PHRASES **ahead of 1** *Blanche went ahead of the others* **in front of,** before. **2** *we have a demanding trip ahead of us* **in store for,** waiting for. **3** *two months ahead of schedule* **in advance of,** before, earlier than.

aid ▶ noun **1** *with the aid of his colleagues he prepared a manifesto* **assistance,** support, help, backing, cooperation; a helping hand.
ANTONYMS hindrance.
2 *humanitarian aid* **relief,** charity, financial assistance, donations, contributions, subsidies, handouts, subvention, succor; historical alms.
▶ verb **1** *he provided an army to aid the King of England* **help,** assist, abet, come to someone's aid, give assistance, lend a hand, be of service; avail, succor, sustain.
ANTONYMS hinder.
2 *certain teas can aid restful sleep* **facilitate,** promote, encourage, help, further, boost; speed up, hasten, accelerate, expedite.
ANTONYMS discourage, hinder.

aide ▶ noun *an aide to the supervisor* **assistant,** helper, adviser, right-hand man, man/girl Friday, adjutant, deputy, second-in-command, second; subordinate, junior, underling, acolyte.

ailing ▶ adjective **1** *his ailing mother* **ill,** sick, unwell, sickly, poorly, weak, indisposed, in poor/bad health, infirm, debilitated, diseased, delicate, valetudinarian, below par, bedridden; informal laid up, under the weather.
ANTONYMS healthy.
2 *the country's ailing economy* **failing,** in poor condition, weak, poor, deficient.
ANTONYMS strong.

ailment ▶ noun *a common stomach ailment* **illness,** disease, sickness, disorder, condition, affliction, malady, complaint, infirmity; informal bug, virus.

aim ▶ verb **1** *he aimed the rifle* **point,** direct, train, sight, line up.
2 *she **aimed at** the target* **take aim at,** fix on, zero in on, draw a bead on.
3 *undergraduates **aiming for** a degree* **work toward,** be after, set one's sights on, try for, strive for, aspire to, endeavor to achieve; formal essay for.
4 *this system is **aimed at** the home entertainment market* **target at,** intend for, destine for, direct at, design for, tailor for, market to, pitch to/at.
5 *we aim to give you the best possible service* **intend,** mean, have in mind/view; plan, resolve, propose, design. See note at INTEND.

▶ noun *our aim is to develop gymnasts to the top level* **objective,** object, goal, end, target, design, desire, desired result, intention, intent, plan, purpose, object of the exercise; ambition, aspiration, wish, dream, hope, raison d'être.

aimless ▶ adjective **1** *Flavia set out on an aimless walk* **purposeless,** goalless, without purpose, haphazard, wandering, without goal, desultory.
ANTONYMS purposeful.
2 *aimless men standing outside the bars* **unoccupied,** idle, at a loose end; purposeless, undirected.
ANTONYMS determined.

air ▶ noun **1** *hundreds of birds hovered in the air* **sky,** atmosphere; heavens, ether.
2 *open the windows to get some air into the room* **breeze,** draft, wind; breath/blast of air, gust of wind.
3 *an air of defiance* **expression,** appearance, look, impression, aspect, aura, mien, countenance, manner, bearing, tone.
4 (**airs**) *putting on airs* **affectations,** pretension, pretentiousness, affectedness, posturing, airs and graces.
5 *a traditional Scottish air* **tune,** melody, song; literary lay.
▶ verb **1** *a chance to air your views* **express,** voice, make public, ventilate, articulate, state, declare, give expression/voice to; have one's say about.
2 *the windows were opened to air the room* **ventilate,** freshen, refresh, cool.
3 *the film was aired nationwide* **broadcast,** transmit, screen, show, televise, telecast, podcast.

airily ▶ adverb *the sparrow hopped airily along | the composer meant for the piece to be played airily* **lightly,** breezily, flippantly, casually, nonchalantly, heedlessly, without consideration.
ANTONYMS seriously.

airtight ▶ adjective **1** *an airtight container* **sealed,** hermetically sealed, closed tight, shut tight.
2 *an airtight alibi* **indisputable,** unquestionable, incontrovertible, undeniable, incontestable, irrefutable, watertight, beyond dispute, beyond question, beyond doubt.

airy ▶ adjective **1** *the conservatory is light and airy* **well ventilated,** fresh; spacious, uncluttered; light, bright.
ANTONYMS stuffy.
2 *an airy gesture* **nonchalant,** casual, breezy, flippant, insouciant, heedless.
ANTONYMS serious.
3 *airy clouds* **delicate,** soft, fine, feathery, insubstantial.
ANTONYMS heavy, dense.

aisle ▶ noun *there is no sitting allowed in the aisle* **passage,** passageway, gangway, walkway, corridor.

ajar ▶ adjective & adverb *with shutters ajar, we got only a glimpse of the morning sun | use the flatiron to keep the door ajar* **slightly open,** half open.
ANTONYMS closed, wide open.

akin ▶ adjective *much of the vegetation here is akin to that of southern California* **similar,** related, close, near, corresponding, comparable, equivalent; connected, alike, analogous.
ANTONYMS unlike.

alacrity ▶ noun *I am confident that Liberia is going to move forward now with alacrity at the peace table* **eagerness,** willingness, readiness; enthusiasm, ardor, avidity, fervor, keenness; promptness, haste, swiftness, dispatch, speed.

alarm ▶ noun **1** *we spun around in alarm* **fear,** anxiety, apprehension, trepidation, nervousness, unease, distress, agitation, consternation, disquiet, perturbation, fright, panic.
ANTONYMS calmness, composure.
2 *sound the alarm | a smoke alarm* **warning,** alert, distress signal; **siren,** bell, horn, whistle; archaic tocsin.
▶ verb *the news had alarmed her* **frighten,** scare, panic, unnerve, distress, agitate, upset, disconcert, shock, dismay, disturb; informal rattle, spook, scare the living daylights out of.
ANTONYMS calm, reassure.

alarming ▶ adjective *the latest statistics on deaths from AIDS are more than just a little alarming* **frightening,** unnerving, shocking; distressing, upsetting, disconcerting, perturbing, worrisome, worrying, dismaying, disquieting, startling, disturbing; informal scary.
ANTONYMS reassuring.

alarmist ▶ noun *until I saw the map and radar photos of the hurricane, I thought he was being an alarmist* **scaremonger,** doomster, doomsayer, Cassandra, Chicken Little.
ANTONYMS optimist.

alcohol ▶ noun *the doctor told him to avoid alcohol* **liquor,** intoxicating drink/beverage(s), strong drink, alcoholic drink/beverage(s), drink, spirits; informal booze, hooch, the hard stuff, firewater, rotgut, moonshine, white lightning, grog, the demon rum, the bottle, the sauce; technical ethyl alcohol, ethanol.

alcoholic ▶ adjective *alcoholic drinks* **intoxicating,** inebriating, containing alcohol, fermented; strong, hard, stiff; formal spirituous.
▶ noun *he is an alcoholic* **dipsomaniac,** drunk, drunkard, heavy/hard/serious drinker, problem drinker, alcohol abuser, person with a drinking problem; tippler, sot, inebriate; informal boozer, lush, alky, boozehound, dipso, juicer, wino, barfly.

alcove ▶ noun *nestled on a cushion in the alcove, reading a book* **recess,** niche, nook, bay; arbor, bower.

alert ▶ adjective **1** *police have asked neighbors to stay alert* **vigilant,** watchful, attentive, observant, wide awake, circumspect; on the lookout, on one's guard, on one's toes, on the qui vive; informal heads-up, keeping one's eyes open/peeled, bright-eyed and bushy-tailed. See note at VIGILANT.
ANTONYMS inattentive.
2 *mentally alert* **quick-witted,** sharp, bright, quick, keen, perceptive, wide awake, on one's toes; informal on the ball, quick on the uptake, all there, with it.
ANTONYMS inattentive, slow-witted.
▶ noun **1** *a state of alert* **vigilance,** watchfulness, attentiveness, alertness, circumspection.
2 *a flood alert* **warning,** notification, notice; siren, alarm, signal, danger signal, distress signal.
▶ verb *police were alerted by a phone call* **warn,**

notify, apprise, forewarn, put on one's guard, put on the qui vive; informal tip off, clue in.

alias ▶ noun *he is known under several aliases* **assumed name,** false name, pseudonym, sobriquet, incognito; pen name, stage name, nom de plume, nom de guerre; rare allonym, anonym.

▶ adverb *Lester Gillis, alias Baby Face Nelson* **also known as,** aka, also called, otherwise known as.

alibi ▶ noun *we've both got a good alibi for last night* **defense,** justification, explanation, reason; informal story, line.

alien ▶ adjective 1 *an alien landscape* **unfamiliar,** unknown, strange, peculiar; exotic, foreign.
ANTONYMS familiar.
2 *a vicious role* ***alien to*** *his nature* **incompatible with,** unusual for, opposed to, conflicting with, contrary to, in conflict with, at variance with, out of step with; rare oppugnant to.
ANTONYMS familiar.
3 *alien beings* **extraterrestrial,** unearthly, otherworldly; Martian, Jovian, Venutian.
ANTONYMS earthly.

▶ noun 1 *an illegal alien* **foreigner,** nonnative, immigrant, emigrant, émigré.
2 *the alien's spaceship* **extraterrestrial,** ET; Martian, Jovian, Venutian; informal little green man.

alienate ▶ verb *was it the dispute over the inheritance that has alienated these two brothers?* **estrange,** divide, distance, put at a distance, isolate, cut off; set against, turn away, turn off, drive apart, marginalize, disunite, set at variance/odds, drive a wedge between.

alienation ▶ verb *my deep sense of alienation* **isolation,** detachment, estrangement, distance, separation, division; cutting off, turning away. See note at SOLITUDE.

alight[1] ▶ verb 1 *he* ***alighted from*** *the train* **get off,** step off, disembark from, pile out of; detrain, deplane; dismount.
ANTONYMS get on, board.
2 *a swallow alighted on a branch* **land,** come to rest, settle, perch, light.
ANTONYMS fly off.

alight[2] ▶ adjective 1 *the bales of hay were alight* **burning,** ablaze, aflame, on fire, in flames, blazing; literary afire.
2 *her face was alight with laughter* **lit up,** gleaming, glowing, aglow, ablaze, bright, shining, resplendent, radiant.

align ▶ verb 1 *the desks are aligned in straight rows* **line up,** put in order, put in rows/columns, straighten, place, position, situate, set, range.
2 *he* ***aligned himself*** *with the workers* **ally oneself,** affiliate oneself, associate oneself, join, side, unite, combine oneself, join forces, form an alliance, team up, band together, throw in one's lot, make common cause.

alike ▶ adjective *all the doors looked alike* **similar,** (much) the same, indistinguishable, identical, uniform, interchangeable, cut from the same cloth; informal like (two) peas in a pod, like Tweedledum and Tweedledee, much of a muchness.
ANTONYMS different.

▶ adverb *great minds think alike* **similarly,** (just) the same, in the same way/manner/fashion, equally, likewise, identically.

alimony ▶ noun *he has failed to pay alimony for more than two years* **financial support,** maintenance, support; child support.

alive ▶ adjective 1 *he was last seen alive on Labor Day | when mastodons were alive* **living,** live; breathing, vital, functioning; animate, sentient; existing; informal alive and kicking, in the land of the living, among the living; archaic quick.
ANTONYMS dead, inanimate, extinct.
2 *the association has kept her dream alive* **in existence,** existing, active, existent, extant, ongoing, abiding, functioning, in operation; current, contemporary; informal on the map.
ANTONYMS inactive, obsolete.
3 *it was Judith's great love that made Marty so alive* **animated,** lively, full of life, alert, active, energetic, vigorous, spry, sprightly, vital, vivacious, buoyant, exuberant, ebullient, zestful, spirited; informal full of beans, bright-eyed and bushy-tailed, chirpy, chipper, peppy, full of vim and vigor.
ANTONYMS listless, lethargic.
4 *the place was alive with mice* **teeming,** swarming, overrun, bristling, infested; crowded, packed; informal crawling, lousy; rare pullulating.

> CHOOSE THE RIGHT WORD
>
> **alive, animate, animated, living, vital**
>
> Dead is dead, but one can be **alive** to varying degrees. The broadest of these terms describing what has life or shows signs of having it, *alive* can refer to what barely exists (*he was unconscious but still alive when they found him*) as well as to what is bursting with (literal or figurative) life (*her face was alive with excitement and anticipation*). **Living**, on the other hand, is more limited in scope and implies the condition of not being dead (*at 92, she was the oldest living member of the family*) or a state of continued existence or activity (*America's greatest living historian*). **Animate** has fewer connotations than *living* or *alive*; though rare, it is used to distinguish living organisms as opposed to dead ones (*one of the few animate creatures after the devastating explosion*). **Animated**, on the other hand, is used to describe inanimate things to which life or the appearance of life has been given (*an animated cartoon*), or things that are vigorous and lively (*an animated debate on the death penalty*). Anything that is essential to life is **vital** (*vital functions; vital organs*), but it can also be used to describe the energy, activity, and alertness of living things (*an aging but vital member of the historical society*).

all ▶ adjective 1 *all the children went home | all creatures need sleep* **each of,** each one of, every one of, every single one of; every (single), each and every.
ANTONYMS no, none of.
2 *the sun shone all week* **the whole of the,** every

bit of the, the complete, the entire.
ANTONYMS none of.
3 *in all honesty | with all speed* **complete,** entire, total, full; greatest (possible), maximum.
ANTONYMS no, little.
▶ **pronoun 1** *all are welcome* **everyone,** everybody, each person, every person.
ANTONYMS none, nobody.
2 *all of the cups were broken* **each one,** the sum, the total, the whole lot.
ANTONYMS none.
3 *they took all of it* **everything,** every part, the whole amount, the (whole) lot, the entirety.
ANTONYMS none, nothing.
▶ **adverb** *he was dressed all in black* **completely,** fully, entirely, totally, wholly, absolutely, utterly; in every respect, in all respects, without reservation, without exception.
ANTONYMS partly.

allay ▶ **verb** *nothing would allay his fears* **reduce,** diminish, decrease, lessen, assuage, alleviate, ease, relieve, soothe, soften, calm, take the edge off. See note at ALLEVIATE.
ANTONYMS increase, intensify.

allegation ▶ **noun** *not one of the allegations against my client has been substantiated* **claim,** assertion, charge, accusation, declaration, statement, contention, deposition, argument, affirmation, attestation, grievance; formal averment.

allege ▶ **verb** *both children allege that the babysitter had left them alone for hours at a time* **claim,** assert, charge, accuse, declare, state, contend, argue, affirm, maintain, attest, testify, swear; formal aver.

alleged ▶ **adjective** *did Mr. Ramirez tell you what time this alleged crime took place?* **supposed,** so-called, claimed, professed, purported, ostensible, putative, unproven.

allegiance ▶ **noun** *allegiance to the queen* **loyalty,** faithfulness, fidelity, obedience, homage, devotion; historical fealty; formal troth.
ANTONYMS disloyalty, treachery.

allegorical ▶ **adjective** *an allegorical painting* **symbolic,** metaphorical, figurative, representative, emblematic.

allegory ▶ **noun** *Saramago's latest novel is an allegory of social disintegration* **parable,** analogy, metaphor, symbol, emblem.

allergy ▶ **noun 1** *an allergy to feathers* **hypersensitivity,** sensitivity, allergic reaction; anaphylaxis.
2 informal *their allergy to free enterprise* **aversion,** antipathy, opposition, hostility, antagonism, dislike, distaste.

alleviate ▶ **verb** *use ice to alleviate the swelling* **reduce,** ease, relieve, take the edge off, deaden, dull, diminish, lessen, weaken, lighten, attenuate, mitigate, allay, assuage, palliate, damp, soothe, help, soften, temper.
ANTONYMS aggravate.

CHOOSE THE RIGHT WORD

alleviate, abate, allay, assuage, mitigate, relieve, temper

To **alleviate** is to make something easier to endure (*alleviate the pain following surgery*); **allay** is often used interchangeably, but it also means to put to rest, to quiet or calm (*to allay their suspicions*). **Assuage** and *allay* both suggest the calming or satisfying of a desire or appetite, but *assuage* implies a more complete or permanent satisfaction (*we allay our hunger by nibbling hors d'oeuvres, but a huge dinner assuages our appetite*). To **relieve** implies reducing the misery or discomfort to the point where something is bearable (*relieve the monotony of the cross-country bus trip*) and **mitigate,** which comes from a Latin word meaning to soften, usually means to lessen in force or intensity (*mitigate the storm's impact*). **Abate** suggests a progressive lessening in degree or intensity (*her fever was abating*). To **temper** is to soften or moderate (*to temper justice with mercy*), but it can also mean the exact opposite: to harden or toughen something (*tempering steel; a body tempered by lifting weights*).

alley ▶ **noun** *he disappeared down an alley on his motorbike* **passage,** passageway, alleyway, back alley, back lane, laneway, backstreet, lane, path, pathway, walk, allée.

alliance ▶ **noun 1** *a defense alliance* **association,** union, league, confederation, federation, confederacy, coalition, consortium, affiliation, partnership.
2 *an alliance between medicine and morality* **relationship,** affinity, association, connection.

allied ▶ **adjective 1** *a group of allied nations* **federated,** confederated, associated, in alliance, in league, in partnership; unified, united, integrated.
ANTONYMS hostile.
2 *agricultural and allied industries* **associated,** related, connected, interconnected, linked; similar, like, comparable, equivalent.
ANTONYMS dissimilar, unrelated.

allocate ▶ **verb** *how funds will be allocated is dependent on which budget gets approved* **allot,** assign, distribute, apportion, share out, portion out, dispense, deal out, dole out, give out, dish out, parcel out, ration out, divide up/out; informal divvy up.

allocation ▶ **noun 1** *the efficient allocation of resources* **allotment,** assignment, distribution, apportionment, sharing out, handing out, dealing out, doling out, giving out, dishing out, parceling out, rationing out, dividing up/out; informal divvying up.
2 *our annual allocation of funds* **allowance,** allotment, quota, share, ration, portion, grant, slice; informal cut.

allot ▶ **verb** *Councilwoman Crane has asked why so much tax revenue was* ***allotted to*** *park restoration* **allocate to,** assign to, apportion to, distribute to, issue to, grant to; earmark for, designate for, set aside for; hand out to/for, deal out to/for, dish out to/for, dole out to/for, give out to/for; informal divvy up for.

allotment ▶ **noun 1** *the allotment of shares by a company* **allocation,** assignment, distribution,

apportionment, issuing, sharing out, handing out, dealing out, doling out, giving out, dishing out, parceling out, rationing out, dividing up/out; informal divvying up.
2 *each member received an allotment of new shares* **quota,** share, ration, grant, allocation, allowance, slice; informal cut.

all out ▶ **adverb** *I'm working all out to finish my novel* **strenuously,** energetically, vigorously, hard, with all one's might (and main), at full speed, in high gear, eagerly, enthusiastically, industriously, diligently, assiduously, sedulously, indefatigably; informal like mad, like crazy.
ANTONYMS lackadaisically.
▶ **adjective** *an all-out attack* **strenuous,** energetic, vigorous, forceful, forcible; spirited, mettlesome, plucky, determined, resolute, wholehearted, unrestrained, aggressive, eager, keen, enthusiastic, zealous, ardent, fervent.
ANTONYMS halfhearted.

allow ▶ **verb 1** *we don't allow open fires at this campground* **permit,** let, authorize, give permission for, give authorization for, sanction, license, enable, entitle; consent to, assent to, give one's consent to/for, give one's assent to/for, give one's blessing to/for, give the nod to, acquiesce to, agree to, approve; tolerate, brook; informal give the go-ahead to/for, give the thumbs up to/for, OK, give the OK to/for, give the green light to/for; formal accede to.
ANTONYMS prevent, forbid.
2 *allow an hour or so for driving* **set aside,** allocate, allot, earmark, designate, assign, leave.
3 *she allowed that all people had their funny little ways* **admit,** acknowledge, recognize, agree, accept, concede, grant.
ANTONYMS deny.

allowable ▶ **adjective** *the maximum allowable number of users* **permissible,** permitted, allowed, admissible, acceptable, legal, lawful, legitimate, licit, authorized, sanctioned, approved, in order; informal OK, legit.
ANTONYMS forbidden.

allowance ▶ **noun 1** *your baggage allowance* **permitted amount/quantity,** allocation, allotment, quota, share, ration, grant, limit, portion, slice.
2 *she spent her allowance on paperbacks* **payment,** pocket money, sum of money, contribution, grant, subsidy, stipend, maintenance, remittance, financial support, per diem.
3 *a tax allowance* **concession,** reduction, decrease, discount.
– PHRASES **make allowance(s) for 1** *you must make allowances for delays* **take into consideration,** take into account, bear in mind, have regard to, provide for, plan for, make plans for, get ready for, allow for, make provision for, make preparations for, prepare for. **2** *she made allowances for his faults* **excuse,** make excuses for, forgive, pardon, overlook.

alloy ▶ **noun** *modern pewter is an alloy of tin, copper, and antimony* **mixture,** mix, amalgam, fusion, meld, blend, compound, combination, composite, union; technical admixture.

all right ▶ **adjective 1** *the tea was all right* **satisfactory,** acceptable, adequate, fairly good, passable, reasonable; informal so-so, 'comme ci, comme ça', OK, jake.
ANTONYMS unsatisfactory.
2 *are you all right?* **unhurt,** uninjured, unharmed, unscathed, in one piece, safe, safe and sound; well, fine, alive and well, OK.
ANTONYMS hurt, in danger.
3 *it's all right for you to go now* **permissible,** permitted, allowed, allowable, admissible, acceptable, legal, lawful, legitimate, licit, authorized, sanctioned, approved, in order, OK, legit.
ANTONYMS forbidden.
▶ **adverb 1** *the system works all right* **satisfactorily,** adequately, fairly well, passably, acceptably, reasonably; OK.
ANTONYMS unsatisfactorily.
2 *it's him all right* **definitely,** certainly, unquestionably, undoubtedly, indubitably, undeniably, assuredly, for sure, without (a) doubt, beyond (any) doubt, beyond the shadow of a doubt; archaic in sooth, verily.
ANTONYMS possibly.
▶ **exclamation** *all right, I'll go* **very well (then),** fine, good, yes, agreed, right (then); informal OK, okey-dokey, roger, wilco.
ANTONYMS no.

allude ▶ **verb** *the prosecutor* ***alluded to*** *Dixon's past* **refer to,** touch on, suggest, hint at, imply, mention (in passing), make an allusion to; formal advert to.

allure ▶ **noun** *the allure of Paris* **attraction,** lure, draw, pull, appeal, allurement, enticement, temptation, charm, seduction, fascination.
ANTONYMS repulsion.
▶ **verb** *will sponsors be allured by such opportunities?* **attract,** lure, entice, tempt, appeal to, captivate, draw, win over, charm, seduce, inveigle, beguile, fascinate, whet the appetite of, make someone's mouth water. See note at **TEMPT**.
ANTONYMS repel.

alluring ▶ **adjective** *an alluring hostess* **enticing,** tempting, attractive, appealing, inviting, captivating, fetching, seductive; enchanting, charming, fascinating; informal come-hither.

allusion ▶ **noun** *the town's name is an* ***allusion to*** *its founding family* **reference to,** mention of, suggestion of, hint to, intimation of, comment on, remark on.

ally ▶ **noun** *close political allies* **associate,** colleague, friend, confederate, partner, supporter.
ANTONYMS enemy, opponent.
▶ **verb 1** *he allied his racing experience with business acumen* **combine,** marry, couple, merge, amalgamate, join, fuse.
ANTONYMS split.
2 *the Catholic powers allied with Philip II* **unite,** combine, join (up), join forces, band together, team up, collaborate, side, align oneself, form an alliance, throw in one's lot, make common cause.
ANTONYMS split.

almanac ▶ **noun** *we consult the almanac for planting times* **yearbook,** calendar, register, annual; manual, handbook.

almighty ▸ adjective **1** *I swear by almighty God* **all-powerful,** omnipotent, supreme, preeminent.
ANTONYMS powerless.
2 informal *an almighty explosion* **very great,** huge, enormous, immense, colossal, massive, prodigious, stupendous, tremendous, monumental, mammoth, vast, gigantic, giant, mighty, Herculean, epic; very loud, deafening, ear-splitting, ear-piercing, booming, thundering, thunderous; informal whopping, thumping, astronomical, mega, monster, humongous, jumbo, ginormous.
ANTONYMS insignificant.

almost ▸ adverb *we're almost done with the attic* **nearly,** (just) about, more or less, practically, virtually, all but, as good as, close to, near, not quite, roughly, not far from, for all intents and purposes; approaching, bordering on, verging on; informal pretty near, pretty nearly, pretty much, pretty well; literary well-nigh, nigh on.

alone ▸ adjective & adverb **1** *she lived alone | he came to the party alone* **by oneself,** on one's own, all alone, solitary, single, singly, solo, solus; unescorted, unaccompanied, partnerless, companionless, by one's lonesome.
ANTONYMS with others, accompanied.
2 *he managed the store alone* **unaided,** unassisted, without help, without assistance, single-handedly, solo, on one's own.
ANTONYMS with help.
3 *Klein felt terribly alone* **lonely,** isolated, solitary, deserted, abandoned, forsaken, forlorn, friendless.
ANTONYMS loved, wanted, among friends.
4 *a house standing alone* **apart,** by itself/oneself, separate, detached, isolated.
ANTONYMS among others.
5 *you alone inspire me* **only,** solely, just; and no one else, and nothing else, and no one but, and nothing but.

along ▸ preposition **1** *she walked along the corridor* **down,** from one end of —— to the other.
2 *trees grew along the river bank* **beside,** by the side of, on the edge of, alongside.
3 *they'll stop along the way* **on,** at a point on, in the course of.
▸ adverb **1** *Maurice moved along past the other exhibits* **onward,** on, ahead, forward, forth.
2 *I invited a friend along* **as company,** with one, to accompany one, as a partner.
– PHRASES **along with** *he backpacked, along with Kate and Sean, across northern Vermont* **together with,** accompanying, accompanied by; at the same time as; as well as, in addition to, plus, besides.

aloof ▸ adjective *part of their strategy is to remain aloof during the first stages of negotiation* **distant,** detached, unfriendly, antisocial, unsociable, remote, unapproachable, formal, stiff, withdrawn, reserved, unforthcoming, uncommunicative, unsympathetic; informal standoffish.
ANTONYMS familiar, friendly.

aloud ▸ adverb *please don't read aloud* **audibly,** out loud, for all to hear.
ANTONYMS silently.

already ▸ adverb **1** *Anna had already suffered a great deal* **by this/that time,** by now/then, thus/so far, before now/then, until now/then, up to now/then.
2 *is it 3 o'clock already?* **as early as this/that,** as soon as this/that, so soon.

also ▸ adverb *she plays basketball also | gummy bears, candy corn, and also licorice whips* **too,** as well, besides, in addition, additionally, furthermore, further, moreover, into the bargain, on top (of that), what's more, to boot, equally; informal and all, likewise; archaic withal.

alter ▸ verb **1** *Eliot was persuaded to alter the opening passage to his sermon* **change,** make changes to, make different, make alterations to, adjust, make adjustments to, adapt, amend, modify, revise, revamp, rework, redo, refine, vary, transform; informal tweak; technical permute.
ANTONYMS preserve.
2 *the state of affairs has altered* **change,** become different, undergo a change, undergo a sea change, adjust, adapt, transform, evolve.
ANTONYMS stay the same.

alteration ▸ noun *the library was lovely, but they had not anticipated such extensive alterations* **change,** adjustment, adaptation, modification, variation, revision, amendment; rearrangement, reordering, restyling, rejigging, reworking, revamping; sea change, transformation; humorous transmogrification.

altercation ▸ noun *an unruly passenger got into an altercation with the flight crew* **argument,** quarrel, squabble, fight, shouting match, disagreement, contretemps, difference of opinion, falling-out, dispute, disputation, clash, fracas, wrangle, blowup, skirmish, run-in, war of words, donnybrook; informal tiff, scrap, spat, row, rhubarb. See note at QUARREL.

alternate ▸ verb **1** *rows of trees alternate with dense shrub* **be interspersed,** occur in turn, rotate, follow one another; take turns, take it in turns, work/act in sequence; oscillate, fluctuate.
2 *we could alternate the groups so that no one feels left out* **give turns to,** take in turn, rotate, take in rotation; swap, exchange, interchange.
▸ adjective **1** *she attended on alternate days* **every other,** every second.
2 *place the leeks and noodles in alternate layers* **alternating,** interchanging, following in sequence, sequential, occurring in turns.
3 *just in case, let's come up with a couple of alternate plans | an alternate crossing guard* **alternative,** other, another, second, different, substitute, replacement, deputy, relief, proxy, surrogate, cover, fill-in, stand-in, standby, emergency, reserve, backup, auxiliary, fallback; informal pinch-hitting.

alternative ▸ adjective **1** *an alternative route* **different,** other, another, second, possible, substitute, replacement, alternate; standby, emergency, reserve, backup, auxiliary, fallback.
2 *an alternative lifestyle* **unorthodox,** unconventional, nonstandard, unusual, uncommon, out of the ordinary, radical, revolutionary, nonconformist, avant-garde; informal off the wall, oddball, offbeat, way-out.
▸ noun *we have no alternative* **option,** choice, other possibility; substitute, replacement.

alternatively ▸ adverb *alternatively, you can*

build your own barbecue **on the other hand,** as an alternative, or; otherwise, instead, if not, then again, alternately.

although ▸ conjunction *although I'm not a fan of country music, I thoroughly enjoyed his lively performance* **in spite of the fact that,** despite the fact that, notwithstanding (the fact) that, even though/if, for all that, while; chiefly Brit. whilst.

altitude ▸ noun *clouds are classified according to form and altitude* **height,** elevation, distance above the sea/ground; loftiness.

altogether ▸ adverb 1 *he wasn't altogether happy* **completely,** totally, entirely, absolutely, wholly, fully, thoroughly, utterly, perfectly, one hundred percent, in all respects.
2 *we have five offices altogether* **in all,** all told, in toto.
3 *altogether it was a great evening* **on the whole,** overall, all in all, all things considered, on balance, on average, for the most part, in the main, in general, generally, by and large.

altruistic ▸ adjective *a team of altruistic doctors who left their lucrative practices to open a clinic in Zambia* **unselfish,** selfless, compassionate, kind, public-spirited; charitable, benevolent, beneficent, philanthropic, humanitarian; literary bounteous.

always ▸ adverb 1 *he's always late* **every time,** each time, at all times, all the time, without fail, consistently, invariably, regularly, habitually, unfailingly.
ANTONYMS never, seldom, sometimes.
2 *she's always complaining* **continually,** continuously, constantly, forever, perpetually, incessantly, ceaselessly, unceasingly, endlessly, the entire time; informal 24-7.
ANTONYMS never, on and off.
3 *the place will always be dear to me* **forever,** for always, for good (and all), forevermore, for ever and ever, until the end of time, eternally, for eternity, until hell freezes over; informal for keeps, until the cows come home; archaic for aye.
ANTONYMS never.
4 *you can always take it back to the shop* **as a last resort,** no matter what, in any event, in any case, come what may.

amalgamate ▸ verb *the two departments were amalgamated | various companies amalgamated* **combine,** merge, unite, fuse, blend, meld; join (together), join forces, band (together), link (up), team up, go into partnership; literary commingle.
ANTONYMS separate.

amass ▸ verb *the squirrels have amassed a huge quantity of acorns* **gather,** collect, assemble; accumulate, aggregate, stockpile, store (up), pile up, heap, cumulate, accrue, lay in/up, garner; informal stash (away).
ANTONYMS dissipate.

amateur ▸ noun 1 *the crew were all amateurs* **nonprofessional,** nonspecialist, layman, layperson; dilettante; informal greenhorn.
ANTONYMS professional.
2 *what a bunch of amateurs* **bungler,** incompetent, bumbler.
ANTONYMS expert.
▸ adjective 1 *an amateur sportsman* **nonprofessional,** nonspecialist, lay; dilettante.
2 *their amateur efforts* **incompetent,** inept, unskillful, inexpert, amateurish, clumsy, maladroit, bumbling.

amaze ▸ verb *this shy, gawky teenager gets on the stage and amazes everyone with the best Elvis impersonation of the evening* **astonish,** astound, surprise, stun, stagger, shock, stupefy, awe, stop someone in their tracks, leave open-mouthed, leave aghast, take someone's breath away, dumbfound; informal bowl over, flabbergast, blow away.

amazement ▸ noun *we watched in amazement as Yvonne took her first steps since the accident* **astonishment,** surprise, shock, stupefaction, incredulity, disbelief, speechlessness, awe, wonder, wonderment.

ambassador ▸ noun 1 *the American ambassador* **envoy,** plenipotentiary, emissary, (papal) nuncio, representative, high commissioner, consul, consul general, diplomat; archaic legate.
2 *a great ambassador for the sport* **campaigner,** representative, promoter, champion, supporter, backer, booster.

ambiguity ▸ noun *the ambiguity of the rule made it impossible to follow* **vagueness,** obscurity, abstruseness, doubtfulness, uncertainty; formal dubiety; ambivalence, equivocation, double meaning.

ambiguous ▸ adjective *an ambiguous explanation* **equivocal,** ambivalent, open to debate/argument, arguable, debatable; obscure, unclear, imprecise, vague, abstruse, doubtful, dubious, uncertain. See note at DOUBTFUL.
ANTONYMS clear.

ambition ▸ noun 1 *young people with ambition* **drive,** determination, enterprise, initiative, eagerness, motivation, resolve, enthusiasm, zeal, hunger, commitment, a sense of purpose; informal get-up-and-go.
2 *her ambition was to become a diplomat* **aspiration,** intention, goal, aim, objective, object, purpose, intent, plan, desire, wish, design, target, dream.

ambitious ▸ adjective 1 *an energetic and ambitious politician* **aspiring,** determined, forceful, pushy, enterprising, motivated, enthusiastic, energetic, zealous, committed, purposeful, power-hungry; informal go-getting, go-ahead.
ANTONYMS lazy, laid-back.
2 *he was ambitious to make it to the top* **eager,** determined, enthusiastic, anxious, hungry, impatient, striving.
3 *an ambitious task* **difficult,** exacting, demanding, formidable, challenging, hard, arduous, onerous, tough; archaic toilsome.
ANTONYMS easy.

ambivalent ▸ adjective *the need to relocate has made her ambivalent about the promotion* **equivocal,** uncertain, unsure, doubtful, indecisive, inconclusive, irresolute, of two minds, undecided, torn, in a quandary, on the fence, hesitating, wavering, vacillating, equivocating, blowing/running hot and cold; informal iffy.
ANTONYMS unequivocal, certain.

amble ▸ verb *ambling through the park* **stroll,**

saunter, wander, ramble, promenade, walk, go for a walk, take a walk; informal mosey, toddle, tootle; formal perambulate.

ambush ▶ noun *the soldiers were killed in an ambush* **surprise attack,** trap; archaic ambuscade. ▶ verb *twenty youths ambushed the patrol car* **attack by surprise,** surprise, pounce on, fall upon, lay a trap for, set an ambush for, lie in wait for, waylay, bushwhack; archaic ambuscade.

amenable ▶ adjective **1** *an amenable child* **cooperative,** acquiescent, compliant, accommodating, obliging, biddable, manageable, controllable, governable, persuadable, tractable, responsive, pliant, malleable, complaisant, easily handled; rare persuasible.
ANTONYMS uncooperative.
2 *many cancers are amenable to treatment* **susceptible,** receptive, responsive; archaic susceptive.
ANTONYMS unresponsive, resistant.

amend ▶ verb *the membership application was recently amended* **revise,** alter, change, modify, qualify, adapt, adjust; edit, copyedit, rewrite, redraft, rephrase, reword, rework, revamp.

amends ▶ plural noun
– PHRASES **make amends** *after all the pain I've caused, is it possible to make amends? | he's obviously trying to make amends for what he's done* **make good,** atone, make up, indemnify, expiate. **make amends to** *it's up to you to make amends to those you've hurt* **compensate,** recompense, redress, indemnify, make it up to.

amenity ▶ noun *basic amenities* **facility,** service, convenience, resource, appliance, aid, comfort, benefit, feature, advantage.

amiable ▶ adjective *you'll find that the folks in this department are genuinely amiable* **friendly,** affable, amicable, cordial; warm, warmhearted, good-natured, nice, pleasant, agreeable, likable, genial, good-humored, charming, easy to get along with, companionable, sociable, personable; informal chummy, simpatico.
ANTONYMS unfriendly, disagreeable.

amicable ▶ adjective *the relationship between the kids and their stepfather is an amicable one* **friendly,** good-natured, cordial, easy, easygoing, neighborly, harmonious, cooperative, civilized.
ANTONYMS unfriendly.

amid ▶ preposition **1** *the jeep was concealed amid pine trees* **in the middle of,** surrounded by, among, amongst; literary amidst, in the midst of.
2 *the truce collapsed amid fears of a revolt* **at a time of,** in an atmosphere of, against a background of; as a result of.

amiss ▶ adjective *an inspection revealed nothing amiss* **wrong,** awry, faulty, out of order, defective, flawed, unsatisfactory, incorrect, not right; inappropriate, improper.
ANTONYMS right, in order.
– PHRASES **take something amiss** *we were only kidding, but I think he took it amiss* **be offended,** take offense, be upset.

ammunition ▶ noun *police seized arms and ammunition* **bullets,** shells, projectiles, missiles, rounds, shot, slugs, cartridges, munitions; informal ammo.

amnesty ▶ noun *the governor has granted amnesty to seven of the prisoners* **pardon,** pardoning, reprieve; grace; release, discharge.

amok ▶ adverb
– PHRASES **run amok** *the robot is running amok in Sector B* **go berserk,** get out of control, rampage, riot, run riot, go on the rampage, behave like a maniac, behave wildly, behave uncontrollably, become violent, become destructive; informal raise hell, go postal.

amorous ▶ adjective *amorous advances* **romantic,** lustful, sexual, erotic, amatory, ardent, passionate, impassioned; in love, enamored, lovesick; informal lovey-dovey, kissy, smoochy, hot.

amorphous ▶ adjective *an amorphous lump of clay* **shapeless,** formless, structureless, indeterminate; vague, nebulous, indefinite.

amount ▶ noun *a fair amount of roast beef | we sold a comparable amount in the second quarter* **quantity,** number, total, aggregate, sum, quota, group, size, mass, weight, volume, bulk, lot, quantum.
– PHRASES **the full amount** *we can't make a payment schedule until we know the full amount* **the grand total,** the total, the aggregate; informal the whole kit and caboodle, the whole shebang, the whole nine yards. **amount to 1** *the bill amounted to $50* **add up to,** come to, run (to), be, total. **2** *a result that amounted to complete failure* **constitute,** be tantamount to, come down to, boil down to; signify, signal, mean, indicate, suggest, denote, point to, be evidence of, be symptomatic of; literary betoken. **3** *her relationships had never amounted to anything significant* **become,** develop into, develop into, prove to be, turn out to be.

ample ▶ adjective **1** *there is ample time for discussion* **enough,** sufficient, adequate, plenty of, more than enough, enough and to spare.
ANTONYMS insufficient.
2 *an ample supply of wine* **plentiful,** abundant, copious, profuse, rich, lavish, liberal, generous, bountiful, bounteous, large, huge, great, bumper; literary plenteous.
ANTONYMS meager.

amplify ▶ verb **1** *the sound from an electric guitar was meant to be amplified* **make louder,** louden, turn up, magnify, intensify, increase, boost, step up, raise.
ANTONYMS quieten.
2 *these notes amplify our statement* **expand,** enlarge upon, elaborate on, add to, supplement, develop, flesh out, add detail to, go into detail about.
ANTONYMS condense.

amputate ▶ verb *doctors had to amputate two fingers* **cut off,** sever, remove (surgically), dismember, saw/chop off.

amuse ▶ verb **1** *the ugliest dog contest amused him* **entertain,** make laugh, delight, divert, cheer (up), please, charm, tickle; informal tickle pink, crack up.
ANTONYMS bore, depress.
2 *he amused himself by writing poetry* **occupy,** engage, busy, employ, distract, absorb, engross; interest, entertain, divert.

amusement ▶ noun **1** *we looked with amusement at the cartoon* **mirth,** merriment, lightheartedness, hilarity, glee, delight, gaiety, joviality, fun; enjoyment, pleasure, high spirits, cheerfulness.
2 *I read the book for amusement* **entertainment,** pleasure, leisure, relaxation, fun, enjoyment, interest, diversion; informal R and R; archaic disport.
3 *a wide range of amusements* **activity,** entertainment, diversion; game, sport.

amusing ▶ adjective *an amusing story* **entertaining,** funny, comical, humorous, lighthearted, jocular, witty, mirthful, hilarious, droll, diverting; laughable; informal wacky, side-splitting, rib-tickling.
ANTONYMS boring, solemn.

analogous ▶ adjective *their lab results were analogous* **comparable,** parallel, similar, like, akin, corresponding, related, kindred, equivalent.
ANTONYMS unrelated.

analogy ▶ noun *there's a thinly veiled analogy between his fiction and his real life* **similarity,** parallel, correspondence, likeness, resemblance, correlation, relation, kinship, equivalence, similitude, metaphor, simile. See note at **LIKENESS**.
ANTONYMS dissimilarity.

analysis ▶ noun *an interesting analysis of England's tax laws* **examination,** investigation, inspection, survey, study, scrutiny; exploration, probe, research, review, evaluation, interpretation, dissection.

analyze ▶ verb *chemists are analyzing the substance* **examine,** inspect, survey, study, scrutinize, look over; investigate, explore, probe, research, go over (with a fine-tooth comb), review, evaluate, break down, dissect, anatomize.

anarchic ▶ adjective *an anarchic society has replaced the despotism* **lawless,** without law and order, in disorder, in turmoil, unruly, disordered, disorganized, chaotic, turbulent; mutinous, rebellious.

anarchist ▶ noun *police said they arrested ten self-styled anarchists* **nihilist,** insurgent, agitator, subversive, terrorist, revolutionary, revolutionist, insurrectionist.

anarchy ▶ noun *conditions are dangerously ripe for anarchy* **lawlessness,** nihilism, mobocracy, revolution, insurrection, disorder, chaos, mayhem, tumult, turmoil.
ANTONYMS government, order.

anathema ▶ noun *the rise of taxes was anathema to most small business owners* **an abomination,** an outrage, an abhorrence, a disgrace, an evil, a bane, a bugbear, a bête noire; adjectives **abhorrent,** hateful, repugnant, odious, repellent, offensive.

anatomy ▶ noun *the anatomy of a frog* **bodily structure,** makeup, composition, constitution, form, structure.

ancestor ▶ noun **1** *he could trace his ancestors back to colonial Boston* **forebear,** forefather, predecessor, antecedent, progenitor, primogenitor.
ANTONYMS descendant, successor.
2 *the instrument is an ancestor of the lute* **forerunner,** precursor, predecessor.

ancestral ▶ adjective *their ancestral hunting grounds* **inherited,** hereditary, familial; rare lineal.

ancestry ▶ noun *our Polish ancestry* **ancestors,** forebears, forefathers, progenitors, antecedents; family tree; lineage, parentage, genealogy, descent, roots, stock, line.

anchor ▶ noun **1** *the anchor of the new coalition* **mainstay,** cornerstone, linchpin, bulwark, foundation.
2 *a TV news anchor* **presenter,** announcer, anchorman, anchorwoman, broadcaster.
▶ verb **1** *the ship was anchored in the bay* **moor,** berth, be at anchor; dated harbor.
2 *the fish anchors itself to the coral* **secure,** fasten, attach, affix, fix.

ancient ▶ adjective **1** *in ancient times* **of long ago,** early, prehistoric, primeval, primordial, primitive; literary of yore; archaic foregone.
ANTONYMS recent, contemporary.
2 *an ancient custom* **old,** very old, age-old, archaic, timeworn, time-honored, venerable. See note at **OLD**.
ANTONYMS recent, new, modern.
3 informal *I feel positively ancient* **old,** aged, elderly, antiquated, decrepit, antediluvian, in one's dotage; old-fashioned, out of date, outmoded, obsolete, passé, démodé; informal horse-and-buggy.
ANTONYMS youthful, up to date.

ancillary ▶ adjective *the Administrative Procedures Act and ancillary documents* **additional,** auxiliary, supporting, helping, extra, supplementary, supplemental, accessory, attendant; subsidiary, secondary; Medicine adjuvant; rare adminicular.

and ▶ conjunction *coffee and a scone* **together with,** along with, with, as well as, in addition to, also; besides, furthermore; informal plus.

USAGE

and

It is rank superstition that this coordinating conjunction cannot properly begin a sentence:

- "Another stumbling-block to a certain type of academic mind is the conjunction *and*. It is often laid down as a rigid rule that a sentence should never begin with *and*. This was a point on which my own schoolmaster was inflexible. And quite recently a training college student whom I asked to comment on a passage from Malory condemned him for using 'the objectionable conjunction *and*.' And printers have an ugly trick of emasculating my meaning by turning my periods into commas because they happen to be followed by *and*. Taking down my Bible and opening it at random, I find that the eighth chapter of Exodus contains thirty-two sentences, twenty-five of which begin with *and*." (Philip Boswood Ballard, *Teaching and*

Testing English; 1939.)

- "Many years ago schoolteachers insisted that it was improper to begin a sentence with *and*, but this convention is now outmoded. Innumerable respected writers use *and* at the beginning of a sentence." (William Morris and Mary Morris, *Harper Dictionary of Contemporary Usage*, 2d ed.; 1985.)
- "And the idea that *and* must not begin a sentence, or even a paragraph, is an empty superstition. The same goes for *but*. Indeed either word can give unimprovably early warning of the sort of thing that is to follow." (Kingsley Amis, *The King's English*; 1997.)

Schoolteachers may have laid down a prohibition against the initial *and* to counteract elementary-school students' tendency to begin every sentence with *and*. The same superstition has plagued *but* (see BUT). But the very best writers find occasion to begin sentences with *and*—e.g.: "And one had better make use of whatever beauty, elegance, riches the translator's language possesses, and hope that something emotionally, intellectually, aesthetically equivalent will emerge." (John Simon, *The Sheep from the Goats*; 1989.)

Oddly, *and* is frequently misused for *or* where a singular noun, or one of two nouns, is called for—e.g.: "While third-party candidates have mounted serious challenges for senator and governor in almost two dozen states this year, building an effective third-party apparatus is rare." (*New York Times*; Oct. 5, 1994.) The phrase should be "senator *or* governor"; as written, the sentence says that in each of almost 24 states, third-party candidates were running for *both* senator *and* governor—an idea belied by the context of the article.

Some writers have a tendency, especially in long enumerations, to omit *and* before the final element. To do so is often infelicitous: the reader is jarred by the abrupt period ending the sentence and may even wonder whether something has been omitted. One may occasionally omit *and* before the final element in an enumeration with a particular nuance in mind. Without *and*, the implication is that the series is incomplete—rhetoricians call this construction "asyndeton." With *and*, the implication is that the series is complete. This shade in meaning is increasingly subtle in modern prose. — **BG**

anecdote ▸ noun *amusing anecdotes* **story,** tale, narrative, incident; urban myth/legend; informal yarn.

anemic ▸ adjective **1** *his anemic face* **colorless,** bloodless, pale, pallid, wan, ashen, gray, sallow, pasty-faced, whey-faced, peaked, sickly, etiolated.
2 *an anemic description of her feelings* **feeble,** weak, insipid, wishy-washy, vapid, bland; lame, tame, lackluster, spiritless, languid, lifeless, ineffective, ineffectual, etiolated; informal pathetic.

anew ▸ adverb *may we please begin anew?* **again,** afresh, another time, once more/again, over again.

angel ▸ noun **1** *an angel appeared in the heavens* **messenger of God,** divine/heavenly messenger, divine being.
ANTONYMS devil, demon.
2 *she's an absolute angel* **saint,** paragon of virtue; gem, treasure, darling, dear; informal star.
3 informal *a financial angel* **backer,** sponsor, benefactor, fairy godmother, promoter, patron; rare Maecenas.

angelic ▸ adjective **1** *angelic beings* **divine,** heavenly, celestial, holy, seraphic, cherubic; spiritual.
ANTONYMS demonic, infernal.
2 *Sophie's angelic appearance* **innocent,** pure, virtuous, good, saintly, wholesome; beautiful.

anger ▸ noun *his face was livid with anger* **rage,** vexation, exasperation, displeasure, crossness, irritation, irritability, indignation, pique; annoyance, fury, wrath, ire, outrage, irascibility, ill temper/humor; informal slow burn, aggravation; literary choler.
ANTONYMS pleasure, good humor.
▸ verb *she was angered by his terse reply* **infuriate,** irritate, exasperate, irk, vex, peeve, madden, put out; enrage, incense, annoy; rub the wrong way; informal make someone's blood boil, get someone's back up, make someone see red, get someone's dander up, rattle someone's cage, make someone's hackles rise; aggravate, get someone, rile, tick off, tee off, burn up.
ANTONYMS pacify, placate.

angle ▸ noun **1** *the wall is sloping at an angle of 33°* **gradient,** slant, inclination.
2 *the angle of the roof* **corner,** intersection, point, apex.
3 *consider the problem from a different angle* **perspective,** point of view, viewpoint, standpoint, position, aspect, slant, direction.
▸ verb **1** *Anna angled her camera toward the tree* **tilt,** slant, direct, turn.
2 *angle your answer so that it is relevant* **present,** slant, orient, twist, bias.
3 *he was angling for an invitation* **try to get,** seek to obtain, fish for, hope for, be after.

angry ▸ adjective **1** *Vivienne got angry* **irate,** mad, annoyed, cross, vexed, irritated, indignant, irked; furious, enraged, infuriated, in a temper, incensed, raging, fuming, seething, beside oneself, choleric, outraged; livid, apoplectic; informal hot under the collar, up in arms, in high dudgeon, foaming at the mouth, doing a slow burn, steamed up, in a lather, fit to be tied, seeing red; sore, bent out of shape, ticked off, teed off, PO'd; literary wrathful; archaic wroth.
ANTONYMS pleased.
2 *an angry debate* **heated,** passionate, stormy, "lively"; bad-tempered, ill-tempered, ill-natured, acrimonious, bitter.
ANTONYMS good-humored.
– PHRASES **get angry** *my father almost never gets angry* **lose one's temper,** become enraged, go into a rage, go berserk, flare up; informal go crazy, go bananas, hit the roof, go through the roof, go

up the wall, see red, go off the deep end, fly off the handle, blow one's top, blow a fuse/gasket, flip out, have a fit, foam at the mouth, explode, go ballistic, go postal, flip one's wig, blow one's stack, have a conniption.

angst ▸ noun *business leaders expressed their angst over war and recession* **anxiety,** fear, apprehension, worry, foreboding, trepidation, malaise, disquiet, disquietude, unease, uneasiness.

anguish ▸ noun *the anguish of the hostages' families* **agony,** pain, torment, torture, suffering, distress, angst, misery, sorrow, grief, heartache, desolation, despair; literary dolor.
ANTONYMS happiness.

angular ▸ adjective **1** *an angular shape* **sharp-cornered,** pointed, V-shaped, Y-shaped.
ANTONYMS rounded, curving.
2 *an angular face* **bony,** rawboned, lean, spare, thin, skinny, gaunt.
ANTONYMS plump, curvy.

animal ▸ noun **1** *endangered animals* **creature,** beast, living thing; informal critter, beastie; (**animals**) wildlife, fauna.
2 *the man was an animal* **brute,** beast, monster, devil, demon, fiend; informal swine, bastard, pig.
▸ adjective *a grunt of animal passion* **carnal,** fleshly, bodily, physical; brutish, beastly, bestial, unrefined, uncultured, coarse.

animate ▸ verb *a sense of excitement animated the whole school* **enliven,** vitalize, breathe (new) life into, energize, invigorate, revive, vivify, liven up; inspire, inspirit, exhilarate, thrill, excite, fire, arouse, rouse, quicken, stir; light a fire under. See note at QUICKEN.
ANTONYMS depress.
▸ adjective *an animate being* **living,** alive, live, breathing; archaic quick. See note at ALIVE.
ANTONYMS inanimate.

animated ▸ adjective *an animated discussion | his animated walk* **lively,** spirited, high-spirited, energetic, adrenalized, full of life, excited, enthusiastic, eager, alive, active, vigorous, vibrant, vital, vivacious, buoyant, exuberant, ebullient, effervescent, bouncy, bubbly, perky; informal bright-eyed and bushy-tailed, bright and breezy, chirpy, chipper, peppy; heated. See note at ALIVE.
ANTONYMS lethargic, lifeless.

annals ▸ plural noun *the annals of the town's history* **records,** archives, chronicles, accounts, registers; Law muniments.

annex ▸ verb **1** *Charlemagne annexed northern Italy* **take over,** take possession of, appropriate, seize, conquer, occupy.
2 *ten amendments were annexed to the constitution* **add,** append, attach, tack on, tag on.
▸ noun *the new annex will house four classrooms and a computer lab* **extension,** addition, bump-out; wing; ell.

annihilate ▸ verb *an ungodly tornado touched down, annihilating everything in its path* **destroy,** wipe out, obliterate, wipe off the face of the earth; eliminate, liquidate, defeat. See note at DESTROY.
ANTONYMS create.

annotate ▸ verb *annotate the text in Chapters 4 and 5* **comment on,** add notes/footnotes to, gloss, interpret, mark up.

annotation ▸ noun *the teacher's copy has annotations in the margins* **note,** notation, comment, gloss, footnote; commentary, explanation, interpretation.

announce ▸ verb **1** *their financial results were announced* **make public,** make known, report, declare, divulge, state, give out, notify, publicize, broadcast, publish, advertise, circulate, proclaim, blazon.
2 *Victor announced the guests* **introduce,** present, name.
3 *strains of music announced her arrival* **signal,** indicate, give notice of, herald, proclaim; literary betoken.

> CHOOSE THE RIGHT WORD
>
> **announce, blazon, declare, proclaim, promulgate, publish**
>
> When you **announce** something, you communicate it in a formal and public manner, often for the first time (*to announce the arrival of the guest of honor*). But just how you go about announcing something depends on what you're trying to convey. If you want to make sure no one misses your message, use **blazon** (*signs along the highway blazoned the local farmers' complaints*). If you plan to make your views known to the general public through the medium of writing, use **publish** (*to publish a story on drunk driving in the local newspaper*). Use **proclaim** if you have something of great importance that you want to announce very formally and officially (*proclaim a national day of mourning*). Although **declare** also implies a very formal announcement (*declare war*), it can refer to any clear and explicit statement (*declare one's love*). **Promulgate** is usually associated with the communication of a creed, doctrine, or law (*promulgate the views of the Democratic Party*).

announcement ▸ noun **1** *an announcement by the dean* **statement,** report, declaration, proclamation, pronouncement, rescript; bulletin, communiqué.
2 *the announcement of the decision* **declaration,** notification, reporting, publishing, broadcasting, proclamation; archaic annunciation.

announcer ▸ noun *the announcer's voice sounds familiar* **presenter,** anchorman, anchorwoman, anchor, anchorperson; news reader, newscaster, broadcaster; host, master of ceremonies; informal MC, emcee.

annoy ▸ verb *their barking dog annoys me | where the movie attempts to amuse, it only annoys* **irritate,** vex, make angry/cross, anger, exasperate, irk, gall, pique, put out, antagonize, get on someone's nerves, get to, ruffle someone's feathers, make someone's hackles rise, nettle; rub the wrong way; informal aggravate, peeve, hassle, miff, rile, needle, frost, bug, get someone's goat, get someone's back up,

get in someone's hair, give someone the gears, drive mad/crazy/bananas, drive around the bend, drive up the wall, tee off, tick off, burn up, rankle. See note at **AGGRAVATE**.
ANTONYMS please, gratify.

annoyance ▶ noun 1 *much to his annoyance, Louise didn't even notice* **irritation,** exasperation, vexation, indignation, anger, displeasure, chagrin; informal aggravation.
2 *they found him an annoyance* **nuisance,** pest, bother, irritant, inconvenience, palaver; informal pain, pain in the neck/butt/ass, hassle; nudnik, burr under someone's saddle.

annual ▶ adjective 1 *the annual company picnic* **yearly,** once-a-year, every twelve months; year-end.
2 *an annual subscription to the alumni newsletter* **year-long,** twelve-month.

annually ▶ adverb *we renew our membership annually* **yearly,** once a year, each year, per annum, per year; every year.

annul ▶ verb *their parents wanted to get the marriage annulled* **declare invalid,** declare null and void, nullify, invalidate, void, disallow; repeal, reverse, rescind, revoke; Law vacate; formal abrogate; recall. See note at **VOID**.
ANTONYMS restore, enact.

anoint ▶ verb *he was anointed and crowned* **consecrate,** bless, ordain; formal hallow.

anomalous ▶ adjective *it's an anomalous birthmark* **abnormal,** atypical, irregular, aberrant, heteroclite, exceptional, freak, freakish, odd, bizarre, peculiar, unusual, out of the ordinary; deviant, mutant.
ANTONYMS normal, typical.

anomaly ▶ noun *the growth on the duck's bill is a harmless anomaly* **oddity,** peculiarity, abnormality, irregularity, inconsistency, incongruity, aberration, quirk, rarity.

anonymous ▶ adjective 1 *an anonymous donor* **unnamed,** of unknown name, nameless, incognito, unidentified, unknown, secret.
ANTONYMS known, identified.
2 *an anonymous letter* **unsigned,** unattributed.
ANTONYMS signed.
3 *an anonymous housing development* **characterless,** nondescript, impersonal, faceless.

another ▶ adjective *have another drink* **one more,** a further, an additional.

answer ▶ noun 1 *her answer was unequivocal* **reply,** response, rejoinder, reaction; retort, riposte; informal comeback.
ANTONYMS question.
2 *a new filter is the answer* **solution,** remedy, key.
▶ verb 1 *Steve was about to answer* **reply,** respond, make a rejoinder, rejoin; retort, riposte, return.
2 *she has yet to answer the charges* **rebut,** defend oneself against.
3 *a man answering this description* **match,** fit, correspond to, be similar to.
4 *we're trying to answer the needs of our audience* **satisfy,** meet, fulfill, fill, measure up to.
5 *I **answer to** the commissioner* **report to,** work for/under, be subordinate to, be accountable to, be answerable to, be responsible to.
6 *he will answer for his crime* **pay,** be punished, suffer; make amends, make reparation, atone.
7 *the government has a lot to answer for* **be accountable,** be responsible, be liable, take the blame; informal take the rap.

answerable ▶ adjective *the ensign is answerable to the captain* **accountable,** responsible, liable; subject. See note at **RESPONSIBLE**.

antagonism ▶ noun *a long history of antagonism between the two nations* **hostility,** friction, enmity, antipathy, animus, opposition, dissension, rivalry; acrimony, bitterness, rancor, resentment, animosity, aversion, dislike, ill feeling, ill will, bad blood.
ANTONYMS rapport, friendship.

antagonist ▶ noun *only in our political life are we antagonists* **adversary,** opponent, enemy, foe, rival, competitor; (**antagonists**) opposition, competition.
ANTONYMS ally.

antagonistic ▶ adjective 1 *he was **antagonistic to** the reforms* **hostile to,** against, (dead) set against, opposed to, inimical to, antipathetic to, ill-disposed to, resistant to, in disagreement with; informal anti.
ANTONYMS sympathetic, pro.
2 *an antagonistic group of bystanders* **hostile,** aggressive, belligerent, bellicose, pugnacious; rare oppugnant.

antagonize ▶ verb *have I done something to antagonize you?* **arouse hostility in,** alienate; anger, annoy, provoke, vex, irritate; rub the wrong way; informal aggravate, rile, needle, rattle someone's cage, get someone's back up.
ANTONYMS pacify, placate.

antedate ▶ verb *a civilization that antedates the Roman Empire* **precede,** predate, come/go before, be earlier than.

antediluvian ▶ adjective *her antediluvian attitudes* **out of date,** outdated, outmoded, old-fashioned, antiquated, behind the times, passé. See note at **OLD**.

anteroom ▶ noun *guests will be met in the anteroom* **antechamber,** vestibule, lobby, foyer, outer room; Architecture narthex.

anthem ▶ noun *a patriotic anthem* **hymn,** song, chorale, psalm, paean.

anthology ▶ noun *an anthology of American poetry* **collection,** selection, compendium, treasury, miscellany; archaic garland.

anticipate ▶ verb 1 *we don't anticipate any trouble* **expect,** foresee, predict, be prepared for, bargain on, reckon on; informal figure on.
2 *the defender must anticipate the attacker's moves* **preempt,** forestall, second-guess; informal beat someone to the punch.
3 *we enthusiastically anticipate your arrival* **look forward to,** await, count the days until; informal lick one's lips over.

anticipation ▶ noun *her eyes sparkled with anticipation* **expectancy,** expectation, excitement, suspense.
– PHRASES **in anticipation of** *we bought plenty of food in anticipation of holiday visitors* **in the expectation of,** in preparation for, in case of, ready for.

anticlimax ▶ noun *for me, the anticlimax is*

when Reggie—for no apparent purpose to the plot—suddenly decides to quit school **letdown,** disappointment, comedown, nonevent; bathos.

antics ▸ plural noun *someday you'll be too old to get away with such antics* **capers,** pranks, larks, hijinks, frolicking, skylarking, foolery, tomfoolery.

antidote ▸ noun **1** *the antidote to this poison* **antitoxin,** antiserum, antivenin.
2 *laughter is a good antidote to stress* **remedy,** cure, nostrum.

antipathy ▸ noun *I never encountered racial antipathy until I went to college* **hostility,** antagonism, animosity, aversion, animus, enmity, dislike, distaste, hatred, hate, abhorrence, loathing.
ANTONYMS liking, affinity.

antiquated ▸ adjective *his views on single parenthood are antiquated* **outdated,** out of date, outmoded, outworn, old, stale, behind the times, old-fashioned, anachronistic, old-fangled, antique, antediluvian, passé, démodé, obsolete; informal out of the ark, moldy, horse-and-buggy. See note at OLD.
ANTONYMS modern, up to date.

antique ▸ noun *the zither is a lovely antique* **collector's item,** period piece, antiquity, heirloom.
▸ adjective **1** *antique furniture* **old,** antiquarian, collectable, old-fashioned.
ANTONYMS modern, new.
2 *statues of antique gods* **ancient,** of long ago; literary of yore.
3 *antique work practices* See ANTIQUATED.
ANTONYMS modern, current.

antiseptic ▸ adjective **1** *an antiseptic substance* **disinfectant,** germicidal, bactericidal, antibacterial, antibiotic.
2 *antiseptic bandages* **sterile,** aseptic, germ-free, uncontaminated, disinfected. See note at SANITARY.
ANTONYMS contaminated.
3 *their antiseptic surroundings* **characterless,** colorless, soulless; clinical, institutional; dispassionate, detached.
ANTONYMS colorful.
▸ noun **disinfectant,** germicide, bactericide.

antisocial ▸ adjective **1** *worrisome antisocial behavior* **sociopathic,** distasteful, disruptive, rebellious, misanthropic, asocial.
2 *I'm feeling a bit antisocial* **unsociable,** unfriendly, uncommunicative, reclusive, withdrawn; standoffish.

antithesis ▸ noun *friends of the actress say she is quite the antithesis of her giddy and frivolous character* (**complete**) **opposite,** converse, contrary, reverse, inverse, obverse, other side of the coin; informal flip side.

anxiety ▸ noun **1** *his anxiety grew* **worry,** concern, apprehension, apprehensiveness, uneasiness, unease, fearfulness, fear, disquiet, disquietude, inquietude, perturbation, agitation, angst, misgiving, nervousness, nerves, tension, tenseness; informal heebie-jeebies, butterflies (in one's stomach), jitteriness, the jitters, twitchiness.
ANTONYMS calmness, serenity.
2 *an anxiety to please* **eagerness,** keenness, desire.

anxious ▸ adjective **1** *her fever has us all a little anxious* **worried,** concerned, uneasy, apprehensive, fearful, perturbed, troubled, bothered, disturbed, distressed, disquieted, fretful, agitated, nervous, edgy, antsy, unquiet, on edge, tense, overwrought, worked up, keyed up, jumpy, worried sick, with one's stomach in knots, with one's heart in one's mouth; informal uptight, on tenterhooks, with butterflies in one's stomach, trepidatious, jittery, twitchy, in a dither, in a lather, in a tizzy, het up; strung out, having kittens; antsy, spooked, squirrelly.
ANTONYMS carefree, unconcerned.
2 *she was anxious for news* **eager,** keen, desirous, impatient.

USAGE

anxious

The word *anxious* has a range of meaning. As the adjective corresponding to *anxiety*, it has long meant "uneasy, disquieted." In the most unimpeachable uses, the word stays close to that association—e.g.: "The latest holdup is the EPA's final approval of the companies' plans to test for lead at the 150 homes . . . . Some residents are getting anxious." (*Atlanta Journal Constitution*; Sept. 13, 2002.)

Today the word typically encompasses both worry and anticipation—e.g.: "Creator and anchorman Brian Lamb, the prince of un-chic, tirelessly fields the remarks of obnoxious callers, preening journalists, and anxious authors." (*National Review*; Mar. 24, 1997.)

The word carries a sense of expectation, as when discussing a major life change. But when no sense of uneasiness is attached to the situation, *anxious* isn't the best word. In those instances, it displaces a word that might traditionally have been considered its opposite—namely, eager—e.g.: "Three years ago, the Latin music industry was caught up in crossover mania, anxious [read *eager*] to ride the popularity of singers such as Ricky Martin and Enrique Iglesias by selling their English-language albums to the American mainstream." (*Sun-Sentinel* [Fort Lauderdale]; Sept. 13, 2002.) — **BG**

any ▸ adjective **1** *is there any cake left?* **some,** a piece of, a part of, a bit of.
2 *it doesn't make any difference* **the slightest bit of,** a scrap of, a shred of, a whit of, a particle of, an iota of, a jot of.
3 *any job will do* **whichever,** no matter which, never mind which; informal any old.
▸ pronoun **1** *you don't know any of my friends* **a single one,** one, even one.
2 *we no longer give to any, unless they represent one of our top five charities* **anyone,** anybody, any individual/person; any group.
▸ adverb *is your father any better?* **at all,** in the least, to any extent, in/to any degree.

anyhow ▸ adverb **1** *anyhow, it doesn't really matter* **anyway,** in any case, in any event, at any rate; however, be that as it may, regardless; informal still and all, anyways.

2 *her clothes were strewn about anyhow* **haphazardly,** carelessly, heedlessly, negligently, in a muddle; informal all over the place, every which way.

apart ▸ adverb 1 *the villages are two miles apart* **away from each other,** distant from each other.
2 *Isabel stood apart* **to one side,** aside, separately, alone, by oneself/itself.
3 *his parents are living apart* **separately,** independently, on one's own.
4 *the car was blown apart* **to pieces,** to bits, up; literary asunder.
– PHRASES **apart from** *apart from the broken headlight, the car seems to be OK* **except for,** but for, aside from, with the exception of, excepting, excluding, bar, barring, besides, other than; informal outside of; formal save.

apartment ▸ noun 1 *a rented apartment* informal pad.
2 *the royal apartments* **suite (of rooms),** rooms, living quarters, accommodations.

apathetic ▸ adjective *an apathetic workforce* **uninterested, indifferent,** unconcerned, unmoved, uninvolved, disinterested, unemotional, emotionless, dispassionate, lukewarm, unmotivated, halfhearted; informal couldn't-care-less; rare Laodicean. See note at CARE.

apathy ▸ noun *widespread apathy among the voters* **indifference,** lack of interest, lack of enthusiasm, lack of concern, unconcern, uninterestedness, unresponsiveness, impassivity, dispassion, lethargy, languor, ennui; rare acedia.

ape ▸ noun **primate,** simian; monkey; technical anthropoid.
▸ verb *he aped Barbara's accent* **imitate,** mimic, copy, parrot, do an impression of, parody, mock; informal take off, send up. See note at IMITATE.

aperture ▸ noun *adjusting the aperture of the camera* **opening,** hole, gap, slit, slot, vent, crevice, chink, crack, interstice; technical orifice, foramen.

apex ▸ noun 1 *the apex of a pyramid* **tip,** peak, summit, pinnacle, top, vertex.
ANTONYMS bottom.
2 *the apex of his career* **climax,** culmination; peak, top, pinnacle, zenith, acme, apogee, high(est) point, capstone.
ANTONYMS nadir.

aphrodisiac ▸ noun **love potion,** philter; informal passion potion.

apiece ▸ adverb *the caps are $10 apiece* **each,** respectively, per item, individually; informal a pop, a throw, per; formal severally.

aplomb ▸ noun *the judges were especially impressed by her aplomb* **poise,** self-assurance, self-confidence, calmness, composure, collectedness, levelheadedness, sangfroid, equilibrium, equanimity; informal unflappability.

apocryphal ▸ adjective *an apocryphal account of Jesus' childhood* **fictitious,** made-up, untrue, fabricated, false, spurious; unverified, unauthenticated, unsubstantiated; bogus. See note at SPURIOUS.
ANTONYMS authentic.

apologetic ▸ adjective *the students who defaced the lockers seemed truly apologetic* **regretful,** sorry, contrite, remorseful, rueful, penitent, repentant; conscience-stricken, compunctious, shamefaced, ashamed.
ANTONYMS unrepentant.

apologize ▸ verb *please allow me to apologize for my wrongful accusations* **say (one is) sorry,** express regret, be apologetic, make an apology, ask forgiveness, ask for pardon; informal eat one's words, eat humble pie.

apology ▸ noun 1 *I owe you an apology* **expression of regret,** one's regrets.
2 *an apology for capitalism* **defense of,** explanation of, justification of, vindication of, apologia for.

apostle ▸ noun 1 *the twelve apostles* **disciple,** follower.
2 *the apostles of the Slavs* **missionary,** evangelist, proselytizer.
3 *an apostle of capitalism* **advocate,** apologist, proponent, exponent, promoter, supporter, upholder, champion, booster.

appall ▸ verb *it doesn't take much to appall her* **horrify,** shock, dismay, distress, outrage, scandalize; disgust, repel, revolt, sicken, nauseate, offend, make someone's blood run cold.

appalling ▸ adjective 1 *an appalling crime* **shocking,** horrific, horrifying, horrible, terrible, awful, dreadful, ghastly, hideous, horrendous, frightful, atrocious, abominable, abhorrent, outrageous, gruesome, grisly, monstrous, heinous, egregious.
2 informal *your schoolwork is appalling* **bad,** dreadful, awful, terrible, frightful, atrocious, disgraceful, deplorable, hopeless, lamentable; informal rotten, crummy, pathetic, pitiful, woeful, useless, lousy, abysmal, dire.

apparatus ▸ noun 1 *laboratory apparatus* **equipment,** gear, rig, tackle, gadgetry; appliance, instrument, machine, mechanism, device, contraption, gadget, gizmo, doohickey. See note at TOOL.
2 *the apparatus of government* **structure,** system, framework, organization, network.

apparel ▸ noun formal *the senator is noted for her snazzy apparel* **clothes,** clothing, garments, dress, attire, wear, garb, getup; informal gear, togs, duds, threads; archaic raiment, habit, habiliments.

apparent ▸ adjective 1 *their relief was all too apparent* **evident,** plain, obvious, clear, manifest, visible, discernible, perceptible; unmistakable, crystal clear, palpable, patent, blatant, writ large; informal as plain as the nose on one's face, written all over one's face. See note at OSTENSIBLE.
ANTONYMS unclear, obscure.
2 *his apparent lack of concern* **seeming,** ostensible, outward, superficial; supposed, alleged, professed.
ANTONYMS genuine.

apparently ▸ adverb *apparently, no one had ever told him that he had a half-sister in San Diego* **seemingly,** evidently, it seems (that), it appears (that), it would seem (that), it would appear (that), as far as one knows, by all accounts; ostensibly, outwardly, supposedly, on the face of it, so the story goes, so I'm told; allegedly, reputedly.

apparition ▶ **noun** *a monstrous apparition* **ghost,** phantom, specter, spirit, wraith; vision, hallucination; informal spook, chimera; literary phantasm, revenant, shade, visitant; rare eidolon.

appeal ▶ **verb 1** *police are appealing for information* **ask urgently/earnestly,** make an urgent/earnest request, call, make a plea, plead.
2 *Stuart **appealed to** me to help them* **implore,** beg, entreat, call on, plead with, exhort, ask, request, petition; formal adjure; literary beseech.
3 *the idea of traveling **appealed to me*** **attract,** be attractive to, interest, take someone's fancy, fascinate, tempt, entice, allure, lure, draw, whet someone's appetite.
▶ **noun 1** *an appeal for help* **plea,** urgent/earnest request, entreaty, cry, call, petition, supplication, cri de coeur.
2 *the cultural appeal of the island* **attraction,** attractiveness, allure, charm; fascination, magnetism, drawing power, pull.
3 *the court allowed the appeal* **retrial,** reexamination.

appear ▶ **verb 1** *a cloud of dust appeared on the horizon* **become visible,** come into view, come into sight, materialize, pop up.
ANTONYMS vanish.
2 *fundamental differences were beginning to appear* **be revealed,** emerge, surface, manifest itself, become apparent, become evident, come to light; arise, crop up.
3 informal *Bill still hadn't appeared* **arrive,** turn up, put in an appearance, come, get here/there; informal show (up), roll in, blow in.
4 *they **appear to be** completely devoted* **seem to be,** look to be, give the impression of being, come across as being, strike someone as being.
5 *the paperback edition didn't appear for two years* **become available,** come on the market, go on sale, come out, be published, be produced.
6 *she appeared on Broadway* **perform,** play, act.

appearance ▶ **noun 1** *her disheveled appearance* **look(s),** air, aspect, mien.
2 *they tried to maintain a respectable appearance* **impression,** air, image, show, outward show; semblance, facade, veneer, front, pretense.
3 *the sudden appearance of her daughter* **arrival,** advent, coming, emergence, materialization.
4 *the appearance of these symptoms* **occurrence,** manifestation, development.

appease ▶ **verb 1** *an attempt to appease his critics* **conciliate,** placate, pacify, mollify, propitiate, reconcile, win over. See note at PACIFY.
ANTONYMS provoke, inflame.
2 *I'd wasted a lot of money to appease my vanity* **satisfy,** fulfill, gratify, indulge; assuage, relieve.

appeasement ▶ **noun** *a policy of appeasement* **conciliation,** placation, concession, pacification, propitiation, reconciliation; fence-mending.
ANTONYMS provocation.

append ▶ **verb** *the teacher may append comments to the final report* **add,** attach, affix, tack on, tag on; formal subjoin.

appendage ▶ **noun 1** *I am not just an appendage to the family* **addition,** attachment, adjunct, addendum, appurtenance, accessory.
2 *a pair of feathery appendages* **protuberance,** projection; technical process.

appendix ▶ **noun** *there is a windchill table in the appendix* **supplement,** addendum, postscript, codicil; coda, epilogue, afterword, tailpiece, back matter; attachment.

appertain ▶ **verb**
– PHRASES **appertain to** *how do these articles appertain to the topic of our discussion?* **pertain to,** be pertinent to, apply to, relate to, concern, be concerned with, have to do with, be relevant to, have reference to, have a bearing on, bear on; regard.

appetite ▶ **noun 1** *a walk sharpens the appetite* **hunger,** ravenousness, hungriness; taste, palate.
2 *my appetite for learning* **craving,** longing, yearning, hankering, hunger, thirst, passion; enthusiasm, keenness, eagerness, desire; informal yen.

appetizer ▶ **noun** *tonight's featured appetizer is a dish of grilled oysters and roasted mushrooms* **starter,** first course, hors d'oeuvre, antipasto, amuse-gueule.

appetizing ▶ **adjective 1** *an appetizing lunch* **mouthwatering,** inviting, tempting; tasty, delicious, flavorful, toothsome, delectable, succulent; informal scrumptious, yummy, delish, lip-smacking.
ANTONYMS bland, off-putting.
2 *the least appetizing part of election campaigns* **appealing,** attractive, inviting, alluring.
ANTONYMS unappealing.

applaud ▶ **verb 1** *the audience applauded* **clap,** give a standing ovation, put one's hands together; show one's appreciation; informal give someone a big hand.
ANTONYMS boo.
2 *police have applauded the decision* **praise,** commend, acclaim, salute, welcome, hail, celebrate, express admiration for, express approval of, look on with favor at, approve of, sing the praises of, pay tribute to, speak highly of, take one's hat off to, express respect for.
ANTONYMS criticize.

applause ▶ **noun 1** *a massive round of applause* **clapping,** hand clapping, (standing) ovation; acclamation.
2 *the museum's design won general applause* **praise,** acclaim, acclamation, admiration, commendation, adulation, favor, approbation, approval, respect; compliments, accolades, tributes; informal props.

appliance ▶ **noun** *domestic appliances* **device,** machine, instrument, gadget, contraption, apparatus, utensil, implement, tool, mechanism, contrivance, labor-saving device; informal gizmo. See also note at TOOL.

applicable ▶ **adjective** *the laws applicable to the dispute* **relevant,** appropriate, pertinent, appurtenant, apposite, germane, material, significant, related, connected; fitting, suitable, apt, befitting, useful, helpful.
ANTONYMS inappropriate, irrelevant.

applicant ▶ **noun** *first-time applicants must have an appointment* **candidate,** interviewee, competitor, contestant, contender, entrant;

claimant, suppliant, supplicant, petitioner, postulant; prospective student, prospective employee, job-seeker, job-hunter, auditioner.

application ▶ noun **1** *an application for a loan* **request,** appeal, petition, entreaty, plea, solicitation, supplication, requisition, suit, approach, claim, demand.
2 *the application of official rules* **implementation,** use, exercise, employment, utilization, practice, applying, discharge, execution, prosecution, enactment; formal praxis.
3 *the argument is clearest in its application to the theater* **relevance,** relevancy, bearing, significance, pertinence, aptness, appositeness, germaneness, importance.
4 *the application of makeup* **putting on,** rubbing in, applying.
5 *a smelly application to relieve muscle pain* **ointment,** lotion, cream, rub, salve, emollient, preparation, liniment, embrocation, balm, unguent, poultice.
6 *a vector graphics application* **program,** software, routine.

apply ▶ verb **1** *more than 300 people* ***applied for*** *the job* **put in an application for,** put in for, try (out) for, bid for, appeal for, petition for, sue for, register for, audition for; request, seek, solicit (for), claim, ask for, try to obtain.
2 *the third paragraph applies only to returning students* **be relevant,** have relevance, have a bearing, appertain, pertain, relate, concern, affect, involve, cover, deal with, touch; be pertinent, be appropriate, be significant.
3 *she applied some ointment* **put on,** rub in, work in, spread, smear.
4 *a steady pressure should be applied* **exert,** administer, implement, use, exercise, employ, utilize, bring to bear.
– PHRASES **apply oneself** *if Palermo applies himself, he has an excellent shot at the scholarship* **be diligent,** be industrious, be assiduous, show commitment, show dedication; work hard, exert oneself, make an effort, try hard, do one's best, give one's all, put one's shoulder to the wheel, put one's nose to the grindstone; strive, endeavor, struggle, labor, toil; pay attention, commit oneself, devote oneself; persevere, persist; informal put one's back into it, knuckle down, buckle down, hunker down.

appoint ▶ verb **1** *he was appointed chairman* **nominate,** name, designate, install as, commission, engage, co-opt; select, choose, elect, vote in; Military detail.
ANTONYMS reject.
2 *the arbitrator shall appoint a date for the meeting* **specify,** determine, assign, designate, allot, set, fix, arrange, choose, decide on, establish, settle, ordain, prescribe, decree.

appointment ▶ noun **1** *a six o'clock appointment* **meeting,** engagement, interview, arrangement, consultation, session; date, rendezvous, assignation; commitment, fixture.
2 *the appointment of directors* **nomination,** naming, designation, installation, commissioning, engagement, co-option; selection, choosing, election, voting in; Military detailing.
3 *he held an appointment at the university* **job,** post, position, situation, employment, place, office; dated station.

apportion ▶ verb *the proceeds from the sale of the restaurant will be apportioned equally among the siblings* **share,** divide, allocate, distribute, allot, assign, give out, hand out, mete out, deal out, dish out, dole out, parcel out, prorate; ration, measure out; split; informal divvy up.

apposite ▶ adjective *an apposite caption accompanies each photo* **appropriate,** suitable, fitting, apt, befitting; relevant, pertinent, appurtenant, to the point, applicable, germane, material, congruous, felicitous; formal ad rem.
ANTONYMS inappropriate.

appraisal ▶ noun **1** *an objective appraisal of the book* **assessment,** evaluation, estimation, judgment, rating, gauging, sizing up, summing-up, consideration.
2 *a free insurance appraisal* **valuation,** estimate, estimation, quotation, pricing; survey.

appraise ▶ verb **1** *they appraised their handiwork* **assess,** evaluate, judge, rate, gauge, review, consider; informal size up.
2 *the goods were appraised at $1,800* **value,** price, estimate, quote; survey.

appreciable ▶ adjective *there is an appreciable amount of sugar in the lemonade* **considerable,** substantial, significant, sizable, goodly, fair, reasonable, marked; perceptible, noticeable, visible, discernible; informal tidy. See note at TANGIBLE.
ANTONYMS negligible.

appreciate ▶ verb **1** *I'd appreciate your advice* **be grateful for,** be thankful for, be obliged for, be indebted for, be in your debt for, be appreciative of.
ANTONYMS disparage.
2 *the college appreciated her greatly* **value,** treasure, admire, respect, hold in high regard, think highly of, think much of. See note at ESTEEM.
3 *we appreciate your difficulty* **recognize,** acknowledge, realize, know, be aware of, be conscious of, be sensitive to, understand, comprehend, grasp, fathom; informal be wise to.
4 *a home that will appreciate in value* **increase,** gain, grow, rise, go up, escalate, soar, rocket.
ANTONYMS depreciate, decrease.

appreciation ▶ noun **1** *he showed his appreciation* **gratitude,** thanks, gratefulness, thankfulness, recognition, sense of obligation.
ANTONYMS ingratitude.
2 *her appreciation of literature* **valuing,** treasuring, admiration, respect, regard, esteem, high opinion.
3 *an appreciation of the difficulties involved* **acknowledgment,** recognition, realization, knowledge, awareness, consciousness, understanding, comprehension.
ANTONYMS unawareness.
4 *a critical appreciation of the professor's work* **review,** critique, criticism, critical analysis, assessment, evaluation, judgment, rating.

appreciative ▶ adjective **1** *we are* ***appreciative of*** *all your efforts* **grateful for,** thankful for, obliged for, indebted for, in someone's debt for.

ANTONYMS ungrateful.
2 *an appreciative audience* **supportive,** encouraging, sympathetic, responsive; enthusiastic, admiring, approving, complimentary.

apprehend ▶ verb **1** *the thieves were quickly apprehended* **arrest,** catch, capture, seize; take prisoner, take into custody, detain, put in jail, put behind bars, imprison, incarcerate; informal bag, collar, nab, nail, run in, bust, pick up, pull in.
2 *they are slow to apprehend danger* **appreciate,** recognize, discern, perceive, make out, take in, realize, grasp, understand, comprehend; informal get the picture.

apprehension ▶ noun **1** *he was filled with apprehension* **anxiety,** worry, unease, nervousness, nerves, misgivings, disquiet, concern, tension, trepidation, perturbation, consternation, angst, dread, alarm, fear, foreboding; informal butterflies, jitters, the willies, the creeps, the shivers, the heebie-jeebies.
ANTONYMS confidence.
2 *the apprehension of a perpetrator* **arrest,** capture, seizure; detention, imprisonment, incarceration; informal collar, nabbing, bagging, busting.

apprehensive ▶ adjective *dentists know that many of their patients are apprehensive* **anxious,** worried, uneasy, nervous, concerned, agitated, tense, afraid, scared, frightened, fearful; informal on tenterhooks, trepidatious.
ANTONYMS confident.

apprentice ▶ noun *she worked with the great violin maker as his apprentice* **trainee,** learner, probationer, novice, beginner, starter, cadet, tenderfoot; pupil, student; informal rookie, newbie, greenhorn. See note at NOVICE.
ANTONYMS veteran.

apprise ▶ verb *we'll apprise you of any changes in your husband's condition* **inform,** tell, notify, advise, brief, make aware, enlighten, update, keep posted; informal clue in, fill in, bring up to speed.

approach ▶ verb **1** *she approached the altar* **move toward,** come/go toward, advance toward, inch toward, go/come/draw/move nearer, go/come/draw/move closer, near; close in, gain on; reach, arrive at.
ANTONYMS leave.
2 *the trade deficit is approaching $20 million* **border on,** verge on, approximate, touch, nudge, near, come near to, come close to.
3 *she approached him about leaving his job* **speak to,** talk to; make advances to, make overtures to, make a proposal to, sound out, proposition.
4 *he approached the problem in the best way* **tackle,** set about, address oneself to, undertake, get down to, launch into, embark on, go about, come to grips with.
▶ noun **1** *a typical male approach* **method,** procedure, technique, modus operandi, MO, style, way, manner; strategy, tactic, system, means.
2 *the dog barked at the approach of any intruder* **advance,** coming, nearing; arrival, appearance; advent.
3 *the approach to the castle* **driveway,** drive, access road, road, avenue; way.

appropriate ▶ adjective *this isn't the appropriate time* **suitable,** proper, fitting, apt, right; relevant, pertinent, apposite; convenient, opportune; seemly, befitting; formal ad rem; archaic meet.
ANTONYMS unsuitable.
▶ verb **1** *the barons appropriated church lands* **seize,** commandeer, expropriate, annex, arrogate, sequestrate, sequester, take over, hijack.
2 *he had allegedly appropriated company funds* steal, take; informal swipe, nab, bag, pinch.
3 *his images have been appropriated by advertisers* **plagiarize,** copy; poach, steal, borrow; informal rip off.
4 *we are appropriating funds for these expenses* **allocate,** assign, allot, earmark, set aside, devote, apportion.

approval ▶ noun **1** *their proposals went to the board for approval* **acceptance,** agreement, consent, assent, permission, leave; sanction, endorsement, ratification, authorization, validation; support, backing; informal the go-ahead, the green light, the nod, the rubber stamp, the OK, the say-so, the thumbs up.
ANTONYMS refusal.
2 *Lily looked at him with approval* **approbation,** appreciation, favor, liking, admiration, regard, esteem, respect, praise.
ANTONYMS dislike.

approve ▶ verb **1** *his boss doesn't **approve of** his lifestyle* **agree with,** endorse, support, back, uphold, subscribe to, recommend, advocate, be in favor of, favor, think well of, like, appreciate, go for, hold with, take kindly to; be pleased with, admire, applaud, praise.
ANTONYMS condemn, disapprove.
2 *the government approved the proposals* **accept,** agree to, consent to, assent to, give one's blessing to, bless, rubber-stamp; ratify, sanction, endorse, authorize, validate, pass; support, back; informal give the nod to, give the go-ahead to, give the green light to, give the OK to, give the thumbs-up to.
ANTONYMS refuse.

CHOOSE THE RIGHT WORD

approve, certify, commend, endorse, ratify, sanction

There are a number of ways to show your support for something. The most general way is to **approve** it, a term that covers everything from simple, technical agreement (*to approve the plan*) to enthusiastic support (*she was quick to approve her son's decision to marry*). **Endorse** implies a more public and official expression of support and is used primarily in reference to things that require promotion or publicity (*endorse a political candidate*), while **commend** is to make a formal and usually public statement of approval or congratulation (*he was commended for his heroism*). **Sanction**, **certify**, and **ratify** imply that approval is not only official but that it makes something legal. To *sanction* is not only to *approve* but to authorize (*school authorities would not sanction the wearing of hats in class*), while *certify* implies conformity with certain standards (*certified to teach in the State of New York*). *Ratify* is usually confined to only the most official and authoritative settings. For example, an employer might *sanction* the idea of hiring a woman to perform a job that only men have performed in the past, and the woman in question might have to *certify* that she possesses the necessary training and qualifications. But to *ratify* a constitutional amendment granting equal rights to women requires a lengthy set of legislative procedures.

approximate ▶ adjective *approximate dimensions* **estimated,** rough, imprecise, inexact, indefinite, broad, loose; informal ballpark.
ANTONYMS precise.
▶ verb *the sound approximates that of a cow* **resemble,** be similar to, be not unlike; be/come close to, be/come near to, approach, border on, verge on.

approximately ▶ adverb *there are approximately 24 children per classroom* **roughly,** about, around, circa, more or less, in the neighborhood of, in the region of, of/on the order of, something like, around/round about, give or take (a few); near to, close to, nearly, almost, approaching; informal pushing, in the ballpark of.
ANTONYMS precisely.

approximation ▶ noun 1 *the figure is only an approximation* **estimate,** estimation, guess, rough calculation; informal guesstimate, ballpark figure.
2 *an approximation to the truth* **semblance,** resemblance, likeness, similarity, correspondence.

appurtenances ▶ plural noun *artist's studio with appurtenances for rent* **accessories,** trappings, appendages, accouterments, equipment, paraphernalia, impedimenta, bits and pieces, things; informal stuff.

apropos ▶ preposition *he was asked a question apropos his resignation* **with reference to,** with regard to, with respect to, regarding, concerning, on the subject of, connected with, about, re.
▶ adjective *the word "conglomerate" was decidedly apropos* **appropriate,** pertinent, relevant, apposite, apt, applicable, suitable, germane, fitting, befitting, material; right on.
ANTONYMS inappropriate.
– PHRASES **apropos of nothing** *apropos of nothing, she started speaking only in rhyme* **irrelevantly,** arbitrarily, at random, for no reason, illogically.

apt ▶ adjective 1 *a very apt description of how I felt* **suitable,** fitting, appropriate, befitting, relevant, germane, applicable, apposite.
ANTONYMS inappropriate.
2 *they're apt to get a bit sloppy* **inclined,** given, likely, liable, disposed, predisposed, prone.
ANTONYMS unlikely.
3 *an apt pupil* **clever,** quick, bright, sharp, smart, intelligent, able, gifted, adept, astute.
ANTONYMS slow.

aptitude ▶ noun *an aptitude for higher mathematics* **talent,** gift, flair, bent, skill, knack, facility, ability, proficiency, capability, potential, capacity, faculty, genius.

aquatic ▶ adjective *seals and other aquatic mammals* **marine,** water, saltwater, freshwater, seawater, sea, oceanic, river; technical pelagic, thalassic.

aqueduct ▶ noun *our paper boats went through the aqueduct* **conduit,** race, channel, chute, watercourse, sluice, sluiceway, spillway.

arable ▶ adjective *arable soil* **farmable,** cultivable; fertile, productive.

arbiter ▶ noun 1 *an arbiter between Moscow and Washington* See ARBITRATOR.
2 *the great arbiter of fashion* **authority,** judge, controller, director; master, expert, pundit.

arbitrary ▶ adjective 1 *an arbitrary decision* **capricious,** whimsical, random, chance, unpredictable; casual, wanton, unmotivated, motiveless, unreasoned, unsupported, irrational, illogical, groundless, unjustified; personal, discretionary, subjective.
ANTONYMS reasoned, rational.
2 *the arbitrary power of the prince* **autocratic,** dictatorial, autarchic, undemocratic, despotic, tyrannical, authoritarian, high-handed; absolute, uncontrolled, unlimited, unrestrained.
ANTONYMS democratic.

arbitrate ▶ verb *a third and disinterested party was brought in to arbitrate* **adjudicate,** judge, referee, umpire; mediate, conciliate, intervene, intercede; settle, decide, resolve, pass judgment.

arbitration ▶ noun *the council called for arbitration to settle the dispute* **adjudication,** judgment, arbitrament; mediation, mediatorship, conciliation, settlement, intervention.

arbitrator ▶ noun *the litigants met with a court-appointed arbitrator* **adjudicator,** arbiter, judge, referee, umpire; mediator, conciliator, intervenor, intercessor, go-between.

arbor ▶ noun *the arbor was overgrown with wisteria and bittersweet* **bower,** pergola; alcove, grotto, recess; gazebo.

arc ▶ noun *the arc of a circle* **curve,** arch, crescent, semicircle, half-moon; curvature, convexity.
▶ verb *I sent the ball arcing out over the river* **curl,** curve; arch.

arcade ▶ noun 1 *a classical arcade* **colonnade,** gallery, cloister, loggia, portico, peristyle, stoa.
2 *playing hooky at the arcade* **video arcade,** midway.

arcane ▶ adjective *processes as old and arcane as the language of the law* **mysterious,** secret; enigmatic, esoteric, cryptic, obscure, abstruse, recondite, recherché, impenetrable, opaque.

arch[1] ▶ noun 1 *a stone arch* **archway,** vault, span, dome.
2 *the arch of his spine* **curve,** bow, bend, arc, curvature, convexity; hunch, crook.
▶ verb *she arched her eyebrows* **curve,** arc.

arch[2] ▶ adjective *an arch grin* **mischievous,** teasing, saucy, knowing, playful, roguish, impish, cheeky, tongue-in-cheek.

arch- ▶ combining form *his archenemy* **chief,** principal, foremost, leading, main, major, prime, premier, greatest; informal number-one, numero uno.
ANTONYMS minor.

archaic ▶ adjective *archaic conventions* **obsolete,** out of date, old-fashioned, outmoded, behind the times, bygone, anachronistic, antiquated, superannuated, antediluvian, old world, old-fangled; ancient, old, extinct, defunct; prehistoric; literary of yore. See note at **OLD**.
ANTONYMS modern.

archetype ▶ noun *the archetype of Southern hospitality* **quintessence,** essence, representative, model, embodiment, prototype, stereotype; original, pattern, standard, paradigm. See note at **MODEL**.

architect ▶ noun **1** *the architect of St. Mary's Cathedral* **designer,** planner, draftsman.
2 *Andrew was the architect of the plan* **originator,** author, creator, founder, father, founding father; engineer, inventor, mastermind; literary begetter.

architecture ▶ noun **1** *modern architecture* **building design,** building style, planning, building, construction; formal architectonics.
2 *the architecture of a computer system* **structure,** construction, organization, layout, design, build, anatomy, makeup; informal setup.

arctic ▶ adjective **1** (**Arctic**) *Arctic waters* **polar,** far northern, boreal; literary hyperborean.
2 *arctic weather conditions* (**bitterly**) **cold,** wintry, freezing, frozen, icy, glacial, hypothermic, gelid, subzero, polar, Siberian, bone-chilling.
ANTONYMS Antarctic, tropical.
▶ noun (**the Arctic**) *a research station in the Arctic* **far north,** High Arctic, North Pole, Arctic Circle, North of Sixty.
ANTONYMS Antarctic.

ardent ▶ adjective *an ardent soccer fan* **passionate,** fervent, zealous, fervid, wholehearted, vehement, intense, fierce, fiery; enthusiastic, keen, eager, avid, committed, dedicated; literary perfervid. See note at **EAGER**.
ANTONYMS apathetic.

ardor ▶ noun *approaching the project with ardor* **passion,** fervor, zeal, vehemence, intensity, verve, fire, emotion; enthusiasm, eagerness, avidity, gusto, keenness, dedication.

arduous ▶ adjective *an arduous journey* **onerous,** taxing, difficult, hard, heavy, laborious, burdensome, strenuous, vigorous, backbreaking; demanding, tough, challenging, formidable; exhausting, tiring, punishing, grueling; uphill, steep; informal killing; toilsome. See note at **HARD**.
ANTONYMS easy.

area ▶ noun **1** *an inner-city area* **district,** region, zone, sector, quarter, precinct; locality, locale, neighborhood, parish, patch; tract, belt; informal neck of the woods, turf.
2 *specific areas of scientific knowledge* **field,** sphere, discipline, realm, domain, sector, province, territory, line.
3 *the dining area* **section,** space; place, room.
4 *the area of a circle* **expanse,** extent, size, scope, compass; dimensions, proportions.

arena ▶ noun **1** *a hockey arena* **stadium;** amphitheater, coliseum; sportsplex; field, ring, court; bowl, park, ground; rink, ice rink; historical circus.
2 *the political arena* **scene,** sphere, realm, province, domain, sector, forum, territory, world.

argue ▶ verb **1** *they argued that the government was to blame* **contend,** assert, maintain, insist, hold, claim, reason, allege; formal aver, represent, opine.
2 *the children are always arguing* **quarrel,** disagree, squabble, bicker, fight, wrangle, dispute, feud, have words, cross swords, lock horns, be at each other's throats; informal spat.
3 *it is hard to argue the point* **dispute,** debate, discuss, controvert, deny, question.

argument ▶ noun **1** *he had an argument with Tony* **quarrel,** disagreement, squabble, fight, dispute, wrangle, clash, altercation, feud, contretemps, disputation, falling-out; informal tiff, row, blowup, rhubarb.
2 *arguments for the existence of God* **reasoning,** justification, explanation, rationalization; case, defense, vindication; evidence, reasons, grounds.
3 *the argument of the book* **theme,** topic, subject matter; summary, synopsis, précis, gist, outline.

argumentative ▶ adjective *the futility of dealing with argumentative people* **quarrelsome,** disputatious, captious, contrary, cantankerous, contentious; belligerent, bellicose, combative, antagonistic, truculent, pugnacious.

arid ▶ adjective **1** *an arid landscape* **dry,** dried up, bone-dry, waterless, moistureless, parched, scorched, baked, thirsty, droughty, desert; **barren,** infertile. See note at **DRY**.
ANTONYMS wet, fertile.
2 *this town has an arid, empty feel* **dreary,** dull, drab, dry, sterile, colorless, unstimulating, uninspiring, flat, boring, uninteresting, lifeless, emotionless, plain-vanilla.
ANTONYMS vibrant.

arise ▶ verb **1** *many problems arose* **come to light,** become apparent, appear, emerge, crop up, turn up, surface, spring up; occur; literary befall, come to pass.
2 *injuries arising from defective products* **result,** proceed, follow, ensue, derive, stem, originate; be caused by.
3 *the beast arose* **stand up,** rise, get to one's feet, get up.

aristocracy ▶ noun *she was quite at home with the aristocracy* **nobility,** peerage, gentry, gentility, upper class, ruling class, elite, high society, establishment, haut monde; aristocrats, lords, ladies, peers, peers of the realm, nobles, noblemen, noblewomen; informal upper crust, top drawer, aristos.
ANTONYMS working class.

aristocrat ▶ noun *the son of aristocrats* **nobleman,** noblewoman, lord, lady, peer, peeress, peer of the realm, patrician, grandee; blue blood; informal aristo.
ANTONYMS commoner.

aristocratic ▶ adjective **1** *an aristocratic family* **noble,** titled, upper-class, blue-blooded,

high-born, well-born, elite; informal upper-crust, top-drawer.
ANTONYMS working-class.
2 *an aristocratic manner* **refined,** polished, courtly, dignified, posh, decorous, gracious, fine; haughty, proud.
ANTONYMS vulgar.

arm ▶ **noun 1** *an arm of the sea* **inlet,** creek, cove, fjord, bay; estuary, strait(s), sound, channel.
2 *the political arm of the group* **branch,** section, department, division, wing, sector, detachment, offshoot, extension.
3 *the long arm of the law* **reach,** power, authority, influence.
▶ **verb** *he armed himself with a revolver* **equip,** provide, supply, furnish, issue, outfit, fit out.

armada ▶ **noun** *the world's largest armada of warships* **fleet,** flotilla, squadron, navy.

armaments ▶ **plural noun** *a shortage of armaments* **arms,** weapons, weaponry, firearms, guns, ordnance, artillery, munitions, matériel, hardware.

armistice ▶ **noun** *the armistice was declared on November 11* **truce,** cease-fire, peace, suspension of hostilities.

armor ▶ **noun** *a suit of armor | protected by his armor* **protective covering,** armor plate, shield; chain mail, coat of mail, panoply; carapace.

armory ▶ **noun** *a Civil War exhibition at the old armory* **arsenal,** arms depot, arms cache, ordnance depot, magazine, ammunition dump.

arms ▶ **plural noun 1** *the illegal export of arms* **weapons,** weaponry, firearms, guns, ordnance, artillery, armaments, munitions, matériel.
2 *the family arms* **crest,** emblem, coat of arms, heraldic device, insignia, escutcheon, shield.

army ▶ **noun 1** *the invading army* **armed force,** military force, land force, military, soldiery, infantry, militia; troops, soldiers; archaic host.
2 *an army of tourists* **crowd,** swarm, multitude, horde, mob, gang, throng, mass, flock, herd, pack.

aroma ▶ **noun** *the wonderful aroma of warm bread* **scent,** fragrance, perfume, smell, bouquet, balm, nose, odor, whiff; literary redolence. See note at **SMELL**.

aromatic ▶ **adjective** *aromatic wood chips* **fragrant,** scented, perfumed, fragranced, odorous; literary redolent.

around ▶ **adverb 1** *there were houses scattered around* **on every side,** on all sides, throughout, all over (the place), everywhere; about, here and there.
2 *he turned around* **in the opposite direction,** to face the other way, backward, to the rear.
3 *there was no one around* **nearby,** near, about, close by, close, close at hand, at hand, in the vicinity, at close range.
▶ **preposition 1** *the palazzo is built around a courtyard* **on all sides of,** about, encircling, surrounding, enclosing.
2 *they drove around town* **about,** all over, in/to all parts of.
3 *around three miles* **approximately,** about, around/round about, circa, roughly, something like, more or less, in the region of, in the neighborhood of, give or take (a few); nearly, close to, approaching; getting on for; informal in the ballpark of.
– PHRASES **around the clock 1** *we're working around the clock* **day and night,** night and day, round the clock, all the time, [morning, noon, and night], continuously, nonstop, steadily, unremittingly; informal 24-7. **2** *around-the-clock supervision* **continuous,** round-the-clock, constant, nonstop, continual, uninterrupted.

arouse ▶ **verb 1** *they had aroused his suspicion* **induce,** prompt, trigger, stir up, bring out, kindle, fire, spark off, provoke, engender, cause, foster; literary enkindle.
ANTONYMS allay.
2 *his ability to arouse the masses* **stir up,** rouse, galvanize, excite, electrify, stimulate, inspire, inspirit, move, fire up, whip up, get going, inflame, agitate, goad, incite; rare inspirit. See note at **INCITE**.
ANTONYMS pacify.
3 *his touch aroused her* **excite,** stimulate, titillate; informal turn on, get going, give a thrill to, light someone's fire.
ANTONYMS turn off.
4 *she was aroused from her sleep* **wake (up),** awaken, bring to, rouse; literary waken.

arraign ▶ **verb 1** *he was **arraigned for** murder* **indict for,** prosecute for, put on trial for, bring to trial for, take to court for, lay/file/prefer charges against for, summons for, cite for; accuse of, charge with, incriminate with; archaic inculpate for.
ANTONYMS acquit.
2 *they bitterly arraigned the government* **criticize,** censure, impugn, attack, condemn, chastise, lambaste, rebuke, admonish, remonstrate with, take to task, berate, reproach; informal knock, slam, blast, lay into; castigate, excoriate.
ANTONYMS praise.

arrange ▶ **verb 1** *she arranged the flowers* **order,** set out, lay out, array, position, dispose, present, display, exhibit; group, sort, organize, tidy.
2 *they hoped to arrange a meeting* **organize,** fix (up), plan, schedule, pencil in, contrive, settle on, decide, determine, agree.
3 *he arranged the piece for a full orchestra* **adapt,** set, score, orchestrate, transcribe, instrument.

arrangement ▶ **noun 1** *the arrangement of the furniture* **positioning,** disposition, order, presentation, display; grouping, organization, alignment.
2 (**arrangements**) *the arrangements for my trip* **preparations,** plan(s), provision(s); planning, groundwork.
3 *we had an arrangement* **agreement,** deal, understanding, bargain, settlement, pact, modus vivendi.
4 *an arrangement of Beethoven's symphonies* **adaptation,** orchestration, instrumentation.

arrant ▶ **adjective** *what arrant nonsense!* **utter,** complete, total, absolute, downright, outright, thorough, out-and-out, sheer, pure, unmitigated, unqualified; blatant, flagrant.

array ▶ **noun 1** *a huge array of cars* **range,** collection, selection, assortment, diversity, variety; arrangement, assemblage, lineup,

formation; display, exhibition, exposition.
2 *she arrived in silken array* **dress,** attire, clothing, garb, garments; finery, apparel.
▶ **verb 1** *a buffet was arrayed on the table* **arrange,** assemble, group, order, place, position, set out, exhibit, lay out, dispose; display.
2 *he was arrayed in gray flannel* **dress,** attire, clothe, garb, deck (out), outfit, get up, turn out; archaic apparel.

arrears ▶ **plural noun** *rent arrears* **money owing,** outstanding payment(s), debt(s), liabilities, dues.
ANTONYMS credit.
– PHRASES **in arrears** *the personal accounts are fine, but the business is in arrears* **behind,** behindhand, late, overdue, in the red, in debt.

arrest ▶ **verb 1** *police arrested him for murder* **apprehend,** take into custody, take prisoner, imprison, incarcerate, detain, jail, put in jail; informal pick up, pull in, run in, pinch, bust, nab, collar.
ANTONYMS release.
2 *the spread of the disease can be arrested* **stop,** halt, check, block, hinder, restrict, limit, inhibit, impede, curb; prevent, obstruct; literary stay.
3 *she tried to arrest his attention* **attract,** capture, catch, hold, engage; absorb, occupy, engross.
▶ **noun 1** *a warrant for your arrest* **detention,** apprehension, seizure, capture, takedown.
2 *a cardiac arrest* **stoppage,** halt, interruption.

arresting ▶ **adjective** *an arresting image* **striking,** eye-catching, impactful, conspicuous, engaging, engrossing, fascinating, impressive, imposing, spectacular, dramatic, breathtaking, dazzling, stunning, awe-inspiring; remarkable, outstanding, distinctive.
ANTONYMS inconspicuous.

arrival ▶ **noun 1** *they awaited Ruth's arrival* **coming,** appearance, entrance, entry, approach.
ANTONYMS departure.
2 *staff greeted the late arrivals* **comer,** entrant, incomer; visitor, caller, guest.

arrive ▶ **verb 1** *more police arrived* **come,** turn up, get here/there, make it, appear, enter, present oneself, come along, materialize; informal show (up), roll in/up, blow in, show one's face.
ANTONYMS depart.
2 *we* ***arrived at*** *his house* **reach,** get to, come to, make it to, end up at; informal wind up at.
ANTONYMS leave.
3 *they* ***arrived at*** *an agreement* **reach,** achieve, attain, gain, accomplish; work out, draw up, put together, strike, settle on; informal clinch.
4 *the wedding finally arrived* **happen,** occur, take place, come about; present itself, crop up; literary come to pass.
5 *CD-ROMs arrived in the late eighties* **emerge,** appear, surface, come on the scene, dawn, be born, come into being, arise.
6 informal *their Rolls Royce proved that they had arrived* **succeed,** be a success, do well, reach the top, make good, prosper, thrive; informal make it, make one's mark, do all right for oneself.

arrogant ▶ **adjective** *success has made him arrogant* **haughty,** conceited, self-important, egotistic, full of oneself, superior; overbearing, pompous, bumptious, presumptuous, imperious, overweening; proud, immodest; informal high and mighty, too big for one's britches, too big for one's boots, bigheaded, puffed-up; rare hubristic. See note at **PRIDE**.
ANTONYMS modest.

arrogate ▶ **verb** *the Church* ***arrogated to itself*** *the power to create kings* **assume,** take, claim, appropriate, seize, expropriate, wrest, usurp, commandeer.

arrow ▶ **noun 1** *a bow and arrow* **shaft,** bolt, dart; historical quarrel.
2 *the arrow pointed right* **pointer,** indicator, marker, needle.

arsenal ▶ **noun 1** *Britain's nuclear arsenal* **weapons,** weaponry, arms, armaments.
2 *mutineers broke into the arsenal* **armory,** arms depot, arms cache, ordnance depot, magazine, ammunition dump.

arson ▶ **noun** *the fire is being treated as arson* **pyromania,** incendiarism; informal torching.

art ▶ **noun 1** *he studied art* **fine art,** artwork.
2 *the art of writing* **skill,** craft, technique, knack, facility, ability, know-how.
3 *she uses art to achieve her aims* **cunning,** artfulness, slyness, craftiness, guile; deceit, duplicity, artifice, wiles.

artful ▶ **adjective 1** *artful politicians* **sly,** crafty, cunning, wily, scheming, devious, Machiavellian, sneaky, tricky, conniving, designing, calculating; canny, shrewd; deceitful, duplicitous, disingenuous, underhanded; informal foxy, shifty; archaic subtle.
ANTONYMS ingenuous.
2 *artful precision* **skillful,** clever, adept, adroit, skilled, expert.

article ▶ **noun 1** *small household articles* **item,** thing, object, artifact, commodity, product.
2 *an article in the paper* **report,** account, story, write-up, feature, item, piece, column, review, commentary.
3 *the crucial article of the treaty* **clause,** section, subsection, point, item, paragraph, division, subdivision, part, portion.

articulate ▶ **adjective** *an articulate speaker* **eloquent,** fluent, effective, persuasive, lucid, expressive, silver-tongued; intelligible, comprehensible, understandable.
ANTONYMS unintelligible.
▶ **verb** *they were unable to articulate their emotions* **express,** voice, vocalize, put in words, communicate, state; air, ventilate, vent, pour out; utter, say, speak, enunciate, pronounce; informal come out with.

artifice ▶ **noun** *in our trade, artifice is an asset* **trickery,** deceit, deception, duplicity, guile, cunning, artfulness, wiliness, craftiness, slyness, chicanery; fraud, fraudulence.

artificial ▶ **adjective 1** *artificial flowers* **synthetic,** fake, imitation, mock, ersatz, faux, substitute, replica, reproduction; man-made, manufactured, fabricated, inorganic; plastic; informal pretend, phony. See note at **SPURIOUS**.
ANTONYMS natural.
2 *an artificial smile* **insincere,** feigned, false, unnatural, contrived, put-on, exaggerated, forced, labored, strained, hollow; informal pretend, phony, bogus.
ANTONYMS genuine.

artisan ▶ **noun** *artisans from around North*

America will demonstrate their crafts **craftsman,** craftswoman, craftsperson; skilled worker, technician; smith, wright, journeyman; archaic artificer.

artist ▶ **noun 1** *a mural artist* **designer,** creator, originator, producer; old master.
2 *the surgeon is an artist with the knife* **expert,** master, maestro, past master, virtuoso, genius; informal pro, ace.
ANTONYMS novice.

artistic ▶ **adjective 1** *he's very artistic* **creative,** imaginative, inventive, expressive; sensitive, perceptive, discerning; informal artsy.
ANTONYMS unimaginative.
2 *artistic touches* **aesthetic,** aesthetically pleasing, beautiful, attractive, fine; decorative, ornamental; tasteful, stylish, elegant, exquisite.
ANTONYMS inelegant.

artistry ▶ **noun** *one immediately notices the sheer artistry in her music* **creative skill,** creativity, art, skill, talent, genius, brilliance, flair, proficiency, virtuosity, finesse, style; craftsmanship, workmanship.

artless ▶ **adjective** *there is a no-nonsense, artless flavor to his memoirs* **natural,** ingenuous, naive, simple, innocent, childlike, guileless; candid, open, sincere, unaffected.
ANTONYMS scheming.

as ▶ **conjunction 1** *she looked up as he entered the room* **while,** just as, even as, (just) when, at the time that, at the moment that.
2 *we all felt as Frank did* **in the (same) way that,** the (same) way; informal like.
3 *do as you're told* **what,** that which.
4 *they were free, as the case had not been proved* **because,** since, seeing that/as, in view of the fact that, owing to the fact that; informal on account of; literary for.
5 *try as she did, she couldn't smile* **though,** although, even though, in spite of the fact that, despite the fact that, notwithstanding that, for all that, albeit, however.
6 *relatively short distances, as Hartford to New Haven* **such as,** like, for instance, e.g., for example.
7 *I'm away a lot, as you know* **which,** a fact which.
▶ **preposition 1** *he was dressed as a policeman* **like,** in the guise of, so as to appear to be.
2 *I'm speaking to you as your friend* **in the role of,** being, acting as.
– PHRASES **as for/as to** *as for interior paint, I prefer a semigloss latex* **concerning,** with respect to, on the subject of, in the matter of, as regards, with regard to, regarding, with reference to, re, in re, apropos to, vis-à-vis. **as it were** *the guests were chosen, as it were, by an almost random process* **so to speak,** in a manner of speaking, to some extent, so to say; informal sort of. **as yet** *there is no sign of them as yet* **so far,** thus far, yet, still, up till now, up to now.

USAGE

as to

First, it must be said that *as to* is an all-purpose preposition to be avoided whenever a more specific preposition will do. But *as to* isn't always indefensible. The phrase is most justifiable when introducing something previously mentioned only cursorily: "As to concerns the fair might lose on-track business if it offered its signal to the OTBs, [Dun said]: 'I figured we were going to lose the handle either way.' (*Portland Press Herald* [ME]; Sept. 7, 1997.) In beginning sentences this way, *as to* is equivalent to the more colloquial *as for*. In effect, the phrase is a passable shorthand form of *regarding, with regard to*, or *on the question of*.

The phrase is also (minimally) defensible when used for *about*, but that word is stylistically preferable in most contexts. *As to* smells of jargon—e.g.: "The bill carries no presumptions as to [read *about*] the effect of incorporation." (*News & Observer* [Raleigh]; Mar. 17, 1997.)

The main problem with *as to* is that it doesn't clearly establish syntactic or conceptual relationships, so it can hamper comprehensibility. In each of the following examples, another preposition would more directly and forcefully express the thought:

- "There's no rule as to [read *about*] how long you have to wait before you can enjoy your creation." (*Florida Times-Union*; Aug. 14, 1997.)
- "It is always possible that your neighbor is not aware of how disturbing his or her behavior is and that he or she can be more sensitive to your concerns, or you can agree as to [read *on*] certain time parameters or (if music is the culprit) what is an acceptable volume level." (*San Diego Union-Tribune*; Aug. 24, 1997.)
- "The same is true as to [read *of*] other cases finding for leaders by applying the regulation." (*Bankruptcy Court Decisions*; Mar. 24, 1994.)
- "There is no change in the prior IRA rules with regard to an individual's participation in other qualifying retirement plans. As such, the rules remain the same as to [read *for*] the maximum amount of adjusted gross income a taxpayer can have before the IRA deduction begins to phase out." (*Gazette-Telegraph* [Colorado Springs]; Mar. 12, 1997.)
- "Some people are a little surprised as to [read *by* or *at*] how quickly Veniard has gotten to his present level." (*Florida Times-Union*; June 28, 1997.)
- "During a trip to the Mars Pathfinder Mission Control Center in Pasadena this summer, House Aeronautics and Space Subcommittee member Sheila Jackson-Lee, D-Texas, inquired as to [read *into*] whether the Pathfinder Mission had taken pictures of the American flag planted by Neil Armstrong in 1969." (*San Francisco Chronicle*; Sept. 15, 1997.) (In this case, the better rewording of "inquired as to whether" would have been "asked whether.") — **BG**

ascend ▶ verb *ascending the stairs | we watched the missiles ascend* **climb,** go up/upward, move up/upward, rise (up), clamber (up); mount, scale, conquer; take to the air, take off; rocket.
ANTONYMS descend.

ascertain ▶ verb *first let's ascertain when it was that you last saw Vince* **find out,** discover, get to know, work out, make out, fathom, learn, deduce, divine, discern, see, understand, comprehend; establish, determine, verify, confirm; figure out.

ascetic ▶ adjective *an ascetic life* **austere,** self-denying, abstinent, abstemious, self-disciplined, self-abnegating; simple, puritanical, monastic; reclusive, eremitic, hermitic; celibate, chaste. See note at SEVERE.
ANTONYMS sybaritic.
▶ noun *a desert ascetic* **abstainer,** puritan, recluse, hermit, anchorite, solitary; fakir, Sufi, dervish, sadhu; archaic eremite.
ANTONYMS sybarite.

ascribe ▶ verb *much of our success can be* ***ascribed to*** *the generosity of the Fords* **attribute to,** assign to, put down to, accredit to, credit to, chalk up to, impute to; blame on, lay at the door of; connect with, associate with.

ashamed ▶ adjective *I was too ashamed to return her call* **sorry,** shamefaced, abashed, sheepish, guilty, contrite, remorseful, repentant, penitent, regretful, rueful, apologetic; **embarrassed,** mortified, humiliated, chagrined, discomfited; rare compunctious.
ANTONYMS proud, unabashed.

ashen ▶ adjective *an ashen complexion* **pale,** wan, pasty, gray, ashy, colorless, sallow, pallid, anemic, white, waxen, ghostly, pale-faced, bloodless; rare etiolated, lymphatic. See note at PALE².

ashore ▶ adverb *passengers may now go ashore* **on to (the) land,** on to the shore, aground; shoreward, landward; on the shore, on (dry) land.

aside ▶ adverb **1** *they stood aside* **to one side,** to the side, on one side; apart, away, separately.
2 *that aside, he seemed a nice man* **apart,** notwithstanding.
▶ noun *"Her parents died," he said in an aside* **whispered remark,** confidential remark, stage whisper; digression, incidental remark, obiter dictum.
– PHRASES **aside from** *aside from the mess in the garage, this place is looking good* **apart from,** besides, in addition to, not counting, barring, other than, but (for), excluding, not including, except (for), excepting, leaving out, save (for).

asinine ▶ adjective *an asinine stunt* **stupid,** foolish, brainless, mindless, senseless, idiotic, imbecilic, ridiculous, ludicrous, absurd, nonsensical, fatuous, silly, inane, witless, empty-headed; informal halfwitted, dimwitted, dumb, moronic. See note at STUPID.
ANTONYMS intelligent, sensible.

ask ▶ verb **1** *he asked what time we opened* **inquire,** query, want to know; question, interrogate, quiz.
ANTONYMS answer.
2 *they want to ask a few questions* **put forward,** pose, raise, submit.
ANTONYMS answer.
3 *don't be afraid to* ***ask for*** *advice* **request,** demand; solicit, seek, crave, apply for, petition for, call for, appeal for, beg (for), sue for.
4 *let's ask them to dinner* **invite,** bid, summon, have someone over/around.

askance ▶ adverb *they look askance at anything foreign* **suspiciously,** skeptically, cynically, mistrustfully, distrustfully, doubtfully, dubiously; disapprovingly, contemptuously, scornfully, disdainfully.
ANTONYMS approvingly.

askew ▶ adjective *the pictures are askew* **crooked,** lopsided, tilted, angled, at an angle, skew, skewed, slanted, aslant, awry, oblique, out of true, to/on one side, uneven, off-center, asymmetrical; informal cockeyed, wonky.
ANTONYMS straight.

asleep ▶ adjective **1** *she was asleep in bed* **sleeping,** in a deep sleep, napping, catnapping, dozing, drowsing; informal snoozing, catching some Zs, zonked, hibernating, dead to the world, comatose, in the land of Nod, in the arms of Morpheus; literary slumbering.
ANTONYMS awake.
2 *my leg's asleep* **numb,** with no feeling, numbed, benumbed, dead, insensible; rare torpefied.

aspect ▶ noun **1** *the photos depict every aspect of life* **feature,** facet, side, characteristic, particular, detail; angle, slant.
2 *his face had a sinister aspect* **appearance,** look, air, cast, mien, demeanor, expression; atmosphere, mood, quality, ambience, feeling.

asperity ▶ noun *he replied with some asperity in his tone* **harshness,** sharpness, abrasiveness, roughness, severity, acerbity, astringency, tartness, sarcasm.

aspersions ▶ plural noun
– PHRASES **cast aspersions on** *in saying this, I do not mean to cast aspersions on the Senator* **vilify,** disparage, denigrate, defame, run down, impugn, belittle, criticize, condemn, decry, denounce, pillory; malign, slander, libel, discredit; informal pull apart, throw mud at, knock, badmouth, dis.

asphyxiate ▶ verb *they were nearly asphyxiated from the fumes* **choke (to death),** suffocate, smother, stifle; throttle, strangle.

aspiration ▶ noun *his greatest aspiration is to win an Olympic gold medal* **desire,** hope, dream, wish, longing, yearning; aim, ambition, expectation, goal, target.

aspire ▶ verb *Jen* ***aspires to*** *a career in veterinary medicine* **desire,** hope for, dream of, long for, yearn for, set one's heart on, wish for, want, be desirous of; aim for, seek, pursue, set one's sights on.

aspiring ▶ adjective *an aspiring journalist* **would-be,** aspirant, hopeful, budding; potential, prospective, future; ambitious, determined, upwardly mobile; informal wannabe.

ass ▶ noun **1** *he rode on an ass* **donkey,** jackass, jenny; burro.
2 informal *don't be a silly ass* **fool,** idiot, dolt, simpleton, imbecile; dimwit, halfwit, dummy, dum-dum, loon, jackass, cretin, jerk, fathead,

blockhead, jughead, boob, bozo, buffoon, numbskull, numbnuts, lummox, dunce, moron, meatball, doofus, ninny, nincompoop, dipstick, lamebrain, chump, peabrain, thickhead, dumbass, wooden-head, pinhead, airhead, birdbrain; nitwit, twit, turkey, goofball, putz; dated tomfool, muttonhead.
3 informal *I'm tired of sitting around on my big fat ass* See **BUTTOCKS**.

> USAGE
> **ass, arse**
> *Arse* is the spelling of the British slang term—in the anatomical sense, that is, not in the horse sense. In American English, *ass* is the spelling for both meanings. There's a story behind this. Today *ass* means both (1) "donkey" and (2) "a person's bottom." Sense 1 is the historical one; sense 2 originated in the mid-eighteenth century as the result of a phonological change, as *arse* and *ass* became homophones. By the early nineteenth century, it was possible to engage in wordplay between the words—as in an 1802 cartoon ("Neddy [a donkey] Paces at Tunbridge Wells [in Kent, England]"), in which one female rider says to another, "I'll show my Ass against any Lady's at Wells."
> **— BG**

assail ▶ **verb 1** *the army moved in to assail the enemy* **attack,** assault, pounce on, set upon/about, fall on, charge, rush, storm; informal lay into, tear into, pitch into. See note at **ATTACK**.
2 *she was assailed by doubts* **plague,** torment, rack, beset, dog, trouble, disturb, worry, bedevil, nag, vex.
3 *critics assailed the policy* **criticize,** censure, attack, condemn, pillory, revile; informal knock, slam.

assailant ▶ **noun** *he recognized his assailant* **attacker,** mugger, assaulter.

assassin ▶ **noun** *the presumed assassin, Oswald, was gunned down* **murderer,** killer, gunman; executioner; informal hit man, hired gun; dated homicide.

assassinate ▶ **verb** *a plot to assassinate the premier* **murder,** kill, slaughter; eliminate, execute; liquidate; informal hit, terminate, knock off; literary slay. See note at **KILL**.

assault ▶ **verb 1** *he assaulted a police officer* **attack,** hit, strike, punch, beat up, thump; pummel, pound, batter; informal clout, wallop, belt, clobber, hammer, bop, sock, deck, slug, plug, lay into, do over, rough up; literary smite.
2 *they regrouped to assault the hill* **attack,** assail, pounce on, set upon, strike, fall on, swoop on, rush, storm, besiege. See note at **ATTACK**.
3 *he has no memory of assaulting the victim* **rape,** sexually assault, molest.
▶ **noun 1** *he was charged with assault* **battery,** violence; sexual assault, rape.
2 *an assault on the city* **attack,** strike, onslaught, offensive, charge, push, thrust, invasion, bombardment, sortie, incursion, raid, blitz, campaign.

assay ▶ **noun** *this brand of herbal supplement will undergo independent assay* **evaluation,** assessment, appraisal, analysis, examination, test/tests, testing, inspection, scrutiny.
▶ **verb** *gold is assayed to determine its purity* **evaluate,** assess, appraise, analyze, examine, test, inspect, scrutinize, probe.

assemblage ▶ **noun** *an assemblage of protestors* **collection,** accumulation, conglomeration, gathering, group, grouping, cluster, aggregation, mass, number; assortment, selection, array, miscellany.

assemble ▶ **verb 1** *a crowd had assembled* **gather,** collect, get together, congregate, convene, meet, muster, rally. See note at **GATHER**.
ANTONYMS disperse.
2 *he assembled the suspects* **bring together,** call together, gather, collect, round up, marshal, muster, summon; formal convoke.
ANTONYMS disperse.
3 *how to assemble the kite* **construct,** build, fabricate, manufacture, erect, set up, put together, piece together, connect, join.
ANTONYMS dismantle.

assembly ▶ **noun 1** *an assembly of civil servants* **gathering,** meeting, congregation, convention, rally, convocation, assemblage, group, body, crowd, throng, company; informal get-together.
2 *the labor needed in car assembly* **construction,** manufacture, building, fabrication, erection.

assent ▶ **noun** *they are likely to give their assent* **agreement,** acceptance, approval, approbation, consent, acquiescence, compliance, concurrence; sanction, endorsement, confirmation; permission, leave, blessing; informal the go-ahead, the nod, the green light, the OK, the thumbs up.
ANTONYMS dissent, refusal.
▶ **verb** *he* ***assented to*** *the change* **agree to,** accept, approve, consent to, acquiesce in, concur in, give one's blessing to; sanction, endorse, confirm; informal give the go-ahead to, give the nod to, give the green light to, give the OK to, OK, give the thumbs up to; formal accede to.
ANTONYMS refuse.

assert ▶ **verb 1** *they asserted that all aboard were safe* **declare,** maintain, contend, argue, state, claim, propound, proclaim, announce, pronounce, swear, insist, avow; formal aver, opine; rare asseverate.
2 *we find it difficult to assert our rights* **insist on,** stand up for, uphold, defend, contend, establish, press for, push for, stress.
– PHRASES **assert oneself** *she was finally asserting herself, just like everyone told her to* **behave confidently, speak confidently,** be assertive, put oneself forward, take a stand, make one's presence felt; informal put one's foot down.

assertive ▶ **adjective** *an assertive sales team* **confident,** self-confident, bold, decisive, assured, self-assured, self-possessed, forthright, firm, emphatic; authoritative, strong-willed, forceful, insistent, determined, commanding; informal feisty, pushy.
ANTONYMS timid.

assess ▶ **verb 1** *we need more time to assess the situation* **evaluate,** judge, gauge, rate,

estimate, appraise, consider, get the measure of, determine, analyze; informal size up.
2 *the damage was assessed at $5 million* **value,** calculate, work out, determine, fix, cost, price, estimate.

assessment ▸ noun **1** *a teacher's assessment of the student's abilities* **evaluation,** judgment, rating, estimation, appraisal, analysis, opinion.
2 *some assessments valued the estate at $2 million* **valuation,** appraisal, calculation, costing, pricing, estimate.

asset ▸ noun **1** *he sees his age as an asset* **benefit,** advantage, blessing, good point, strong point, selling point, strength, forte, virtue, recommendation, attraction, resource, boon, merit, bonus, plus, pro.
ANTONYMS liability, handicap.
2 (**assets**) *the seizure of all their assets* **property,** resources, estate, holdings, possessions, effects, goods, valuables, belongings, chattels.
ANTONYMS liability.

assiduous ▸ adjective *she was assiduous in pointing out every feature* **diligent,** careful, meticulous, thorough, sedulous, attentive, conscientious, punctilious, painstaking, rigorous, particular; persevering. See note at BUSY.

assign ▸ verb **1** *a young doctor was assigned the task* **allocate,** allot, give, set to; charge with, entrust with.
2 *she was **assigned to** a new post* **appoint to,** promote to, delegate to, commission to, post to, co-opt to; select for, choose for, install in; Military detail to.
3 *we **assign** large sums of money **to** travel budgets* **earmark for,** designate for, set aside for, reserve for, appropriate for, allot to/for, allocate for, apportion for.
4 *he **assigned** the opinion **to** the prince* **ascribe to,** attribute to, put down to, accredit to, credit to, chalk up to, impute to; pin on, lay at the door of.
5 *he may assign the money to a third party* **transfer,** make over, give, pass, hand over, hand down, convey, consign.

assignation ▸ noun *their secret assignation* **rendezvous,** date, appointment, meeting; literary tryst.

assignment ▸ noun **1** *I'm going to finish this assignment tonight* **task,** piece of work, job, duty, chore, mission, errand, undertaking, exercise, business, endeavor, enterprise; project, homework.
2 *the assignment of tasks* **allocation,** allotment, issuance, designation; sharing out, apportionment, distribution, handing out, dispensation.
3 *the assignment of property* **transfer,** making over, giving, hand down, consignment; Law conveyance, devise, attornment.

assimilate ▸ verb **1** *the amount of information he can assimilate* **absorb,** take in, acquire, soak up, pick up, grasp, comprehend, understand, learn, master; digest, ingest.
2 *many tribes were assimilated by Turkic peoples* **subsume,** incorporate, integrate, absorb, engulf, acculturate; co-opt, adopt, embrace, admit.
3 *after arriving, it took us some time to assimilate* **integrate,** blend in.

assist ▸ verb **1** *I spend my time assisting the chef* **help,** aid, lend a (helping) hand to, oblige, accommodate, serve; collaborate with, work with; support, back (up), second; abet; informal pitch in with.
ANTONYMS hinder.
2 *the exchange rates assisted the firm's expansion* **facilitate,** aid, ease, expedite, spur, promote, boost, benefit, foster, encourage, stimulate, precipitate, accelerate, advance, further, forward.
ANTONYMS impede.

assistance ▸ noun *the governor has requested federal assistance* **help,** aid, support, backing, reinforcement, succor, relief, TLC, intervention, cooperation, collaboration; a (helping) hand, a good turn; social security, benefits; informal a break, a leg up; the dole.
ANTONYMS hindrance.

assistant ▸ noun *a photographer's assistant* **helper,** deputy, second-in-command, second, number two, right-hand man/woman, aide, attendant, mate, apprentice, junior, auxiliary, subordinate; hired hand, hired help, man/girl Friday; informal sidekick, gofer.

associate ▸ verb **1** *the colors that we associate with fire* **link,** connect, relate, identify, equate, bracket, set side by side.
2 *I was forced to associate with them* **mix,** keep company, mingle, socialize, go around, rub shoulders, rub elbows, fraternize, consort, have dealings; informal hobnob, hang out/around.
3 *the firm is associated with a local charity* **affiliate,** align, connect, join, attach, team up, be in league, ally; merge, integrate, confederate.
▸ noun *his business associate* **partner,** colleague, coworker, workmate, comrade, ally, affiliate, confederate; connection, contact, acquaintance; collaborator; informal crony.

assorted ▸ adjective *the ribbons are available in assorted colors* **various,** miscellaneous, mixed, varied, heterogeneous, varying, diverse, eclectic, multifarious, sundry; literary divers.

assortment ▸ noun *an assortment of antique buttons* **mixture,** variety, array, mixed bag, mix, miscellany, selection, medley, diversity, hodgepodge, mishmash, potpourri, salmagundi, farrago, gallimaufry, omnium gatherum.

assuage ▸ verb **1** *a pain that could never be assuaged* **relieve,** ease, alleviate, soothe, mitigate, allay, palliate, abate, suppress, subdue; moderate, lessen, diminish, reduce. See note at ALLEVIATE.
ANTONYMS aggravate.
2 *her hunger was quickly assuaged* **satisfy,** gratify, appease, fulfill, indulge, relieve, slake, sate, satiate, quench, check.
ANTONYMS intensify.

assume ▸ verb **1** *I assumed he wanted me to keep the book* **presume,** suppose, take it (as given), take for granted, take as read, conjecture, surmise, conclude, deduce, infer, reckon, reason, think, fancy, believe, understand, gather, figure.

2 *he assumed a Southern accent* **affect,** adopt, impersonate, put on, simulate, feign, fake.
3 *the disease may assume epidemic proportions* **acquire,** take on, come to have.
4 *they are to assume more responsibility* **accept,** shoulder, bear, undertake, take on/up, manage, handle, deal with.
5 *he assumed control of their finances* **seize,** take (over), appropriate, commandeer, expropriate, hijack, wrest, arrogate, usurp.

assumed ▶ **adjective** *an assumed name* **false,** fictitious, invented, made-up, fake, bogus, sham, spurious, make-believe, improvised, adopted; informal pretend, phony.
ANTONYMS genuine.

assumption ▶ **noun 1** *an informed assumption* **supposition,** presumption, belief, expectation, conjecture, speculation, surmise, guess, premise, hypothesis; conclusion, deduction, inference; rare illation, notion, impression.
2 *the assumption of power by revolutionaries* **seizure,** arrogation, appropriation, expropriation, commandeering, confiscation, hijacking, wresting.
3 *the early assumption of community obligation* **acceptance,** shouldering, tackling, undertaking.

assurance ▶ **noun 1** *her calm assurance* **self-confidence,** confidence, self-assurance, self-possession, nerve, poise, aplomb, levelheadedness; calmness, composure, sangfroid, equanimity; informal cool, unflappability.
ANTONYMS self-doubt.
2 *you have my assurance* **word of honor,** word, promise, pledge, vow, avowal, oath, bond, undertaking, guarantee, commitment.
3 *there is no assurance of getting one's money back* **guarantee,** certainty, certitude, surety, confidence, expectation.
ANTONYMS uncertainty.

assure ▶ **verb 1** *we must assure him of our loyal support* **reassure,** convince, satisfy, persuade, guarantee, promise, tell; affirm, pledge, swear, vow.
2 *he wants to assure a favorable vote* **ensure,** secure, guarantee, seal, clinch, confirm; informal sew up.

assured ▶ **adjective 1** *an assured demeanor* **confident,** self-confident, self-assured, self-possessed, poised, phlegmatic, levelheaded; calm, composed, equanimous, imperturbable, unruffled; informal unflappable, together.
ANTONYMS doubtful.
2 *an assured supply of weapons* **guaranteed,** certain, sure, secure, reliable, dependable, sound; infallible, unfailing; informal sure-fire.
ANTONYMS uncertain.

astonish ▶ **verb** *the NYPD astonished many with the success of its aggressive crime-fighting tactics* **amaze,** astound, stagger, surprise, startle, stun, confound, dumbfound, strike dumb, boggle, stupefy, daze, shock, take aback, leave open-mouthed, leave aghast; informal flabbergast, blow away, bowl over, floor.

astonishing ▶ **adjective** *she's read an astonishing number of books* **amazing,** astounding, staggering, surprising, breathtaking; remarkable, extraordinary, incredible, unbelievable, phenomenal; informal mind-boggling.

astonishment ▶ **noun** *we stared in astonishment* **amazement,** surprise, stupefaction, incredulity, disbelief, speechlessness, awe, wonder, wonderment.

astound ▶ **verb** *the dogs' tricks will astound you* **amaze,** astonish, stagger, surprise, startle, stun, confound, dumbfound, boggle, stupefy, shock, daze, take aback, leave open-mouthed, leave aghast; informal flabbergast, blow away, bowl over, floor.

astounding ▶ **adjective** *his speed and fitness were astounding* **amazing,** astonishing, staggering, surprising, breathtaking, remarkable, extraordinary, incredible, unbelievable, phenomenal; informal mind-boggling.

astray ▶ **adverb 1** *the shots went astray* **off target,** wide of the mark, awry, off course; amiss.
2 *the older boys led him astray* **into wrongdoing,** into error, into sin, into iniquity, away from the straight and narrow, off the right course.

astringent ▶ **adjective 1** *the lotion has an astringent effect on pores* **constricting,** constrictive, contracting; styptic.
2 *her astringent words* **severe,** sharp, stern, harsh, acerbic, acidulous, caustic, mordant, trenchant; scathing, spiteful, cutting, incisive, waspish.

astronaut ▶ **noun** **spaceman, spacewoman,** cosmonaut, space traveler, space cadet.

astute ▶ **adjective** *an astute investor* **shrewd,** sharp, acute, adroit, quick, clever, crafty, intelligent, bright, smart, canny, intuitive, perceptive, insightful, incisive, sagacious, wise; informal on the ball, quick on the uptake, savvy; heads-up. See note at **KEEN**.
ANTONYMS stupid.

asunder ▶ **adverb** literary *the fabric of society may be torn asunder* **apart,** up, in two; to pieces, to shreds, to bits.

asylum ▶ **noun 1** *he appealed for political asylum* **refuge,** sanctuary, shelter, safety, protection, security, immunity; a safe haven.
2 *he was confined to an asylum* **psychiatric hospital,** mental hospital, mental institution, mental asylum; informal madhouse, loony bin, funny farm, nuthouse, bughouse; dated lunatic asylum; archaic bedlam.

asymmetrical ▶ **adjective** *the quilt pattern is asymmetrical* **lopsided,** unsymmetrical, uneven, unbalanced, crooked, awry, askew, skew, misaligned; disproportionate, unequal, irregular; informal cockeyed, wonky.

atheism ▶ **noun** *atheism was not freely discussed in his community* **nonbelief,** disbelief, unbelief, irreligion, skepticism, doubt, agnosticism; nihilism.

atheist ▶ **noun** *why is it often assumed that a man of science is probably an atheist?* **nonbeliever,** disbeliever, unbeliever, skeptic, doubter, doubting Thomas, agnostic; nihilist.
ANTONYMS believer.

athlete ▶ **noun** *the school's top athletes*

sportsman, sportswoman, sportsperson; jock; Olympian; runner.

athletic ▸ adjective **1** *his athletic physique* **muscular,** muscly, sturdy, strapping, well-built, strong, powerful, robust, able-bodied, vigorous, hardy, lusty, hearty, brawny, burly, broad-shouldered, Herculean; **fit,** in good shape, in trim; informal sporty, husky, hunky, beefy; literary thewy.
ANTONYMS puny.
2 *athletic events* **sporting,** sports; Olympic.

athletics ▸ plural noun **sports,** sporting events, games, races; track and field events, track; contests; working out, exercising.

atmosphere ▸ noun **1** *the gases present in the atmosphere* **air,** aerospace; sky; literary heavens, firmament, blue, azure, ether.
2 *the hotel has a relaxed atmosphere* **ambience,** air, mood, feel, feeling, character, tone, tenor, aura, quality, undercurrent, flavor; informal vibe.

atom ▸ noun **1** *they build tiny circuits atom by atom* **particle,** molecule, bit, piece, fragment, fraction.
2 *there wasn't an atom of truth in the allegations* **grain,** iota, jot, whit, mite, scrap, shred, ounce, scintilla, trace, smidgen, modicum.

atone ▸ verb *how shall I* ***atone for*** *my mistakes?* **make amends for,** make reparation for, make restitution for, make up for, compensate for, pay for, recompense for, expiate, redress, make good, offset; do penance for.

atrocious ▸ adjective **1** *atrocious cruelties* **brutal,** barbaric, barbarous, savage, vicious, beastly; wicked, cruel, nasty, heinous, monstrous, vile, inhuman, black-hearted, fiendish, ghastly, horrible; abominable, outrageous, hateful, disgusting, despicable, contemptible, loathsome, odious, abhorrent, sickening, horrifying, unspeakable, execrable, egregious.
ANTONYMS admirable, kindly.
2 *the weather was atrocious* **appalling,** dreadful, terrible, very bad, unpleasant, miserable; informal abysmal, dire, rotten, lousy, godawful.
ANTONYMS superb.

atrocity ▸ noun *such atrocity happens again and again in war* **abomination,** cruelty, enormity, outrage, horror, monstrosity, obscenity, violation, crime, abuse; barbarity, barbarism, brutality, savagery, inhumanity, wickedness, evil, iniquity.

atrophy ▸ verb *muscles atrophy in microgravity* **waste away,** become emaciated, wither, shrivel (up), shrink; decay, decline, deteriorate, degenerate, weaken.
ANTONYMS strengthen, flourish.
▸ noun *muscular atrophy* **wasting,** emaciation, withering, shriveling, shrinking; decay, decline, deterioration, degeneration, weakening, debilitation, enfeeblement.
ANTONYMS strengthening.

attach ▸ verb **1** *a lead weight is attached to the cord* **fasten,** fix, affix, join, connect, link, couple, secure, make fast, tie, bind, chain; stick, adhere, glue, fuse; append.
ANTONYMS detach.
2 *they attached importance to research* **ascribe,** assign, attribute, accredit, impute.
3 *the medical officer attached to HQ* **assign,** appoint, allocate, second; Military detail.

attached ▸ adjective **1** *I'm not interested in you—I'm attached* **spoken for,** married, engaged, promised in marriage; going out, involved, seeing someone; informal hitched, spliced, shackled, going steady; dated betrothed; formal wed, wedded; literary affianced; archaic espoused.
ANTONYMS single.
2 *she was very* ***attached to*** *her brother* **fond of,** devoted to; informal mad about, crazy about.

attachment ▸ noun **1** *he has a strong* ***attachment to*** *his mother* **bond with,** closeness to/with, devotion to, loyalty to; fondness for, love for, affection for, feeling for; relationship with.
2 *the shower had a massage attachment* **accessory,** fitting, extension, add-on, appendage.
3 *the attachment of safety restraints* **fixing,** fastening, linking, coupling, connection.

attack ▸ verb **1** *Chris had been brutally attacked* **assault,** assail, set upon, beat up; batter, pummel, punch; informal do over, work over, rough up.
2 *they attacked along a 10-mile front* **strike,** charge, pounce; bombard, shell, blitz, strafe, fire, besiege.
ANTONYMS defend.
3 *the clergy attacked government policies* **criticize,** censure, condemn, pillory, savage, revile, vilify; informal knock, slam, blast, bash, lay into.
ANTONYMS praise.
4 *they have to attack the problem soon* **address,** attend to, deal with, confront, apply oneself to, get to work on, undertake, embark on; informal get cracking on.
▸ noun **1** *the attack began at dawn* **assault,** onslaught, offensive, strike, blitz, raid, charge, rush, invasion, incursion.
2 *she wrote a hostile attack against him* **criticism,** censure, rebuke, admonishment, reprimand; condemnation, denunciation, vilification; tirade, diatribe, polemic; informal roasting, caning, hatchet job.
ANTONYMS defense, commendation.
3 *an asthmatic attack* **fit,** seizure, spasm, convulsion, paroxysm, outburst, bout.

CHOOSE THE RIGHT WORD

attack, assail, assault, beset, besiege, bombard, charge, molest, storm

There is no shortage of "fighting words." **Attack** is the most general verb, meaning to set upon someone or something in a violent, forceful, or aggressive way (*the rebels attacked at dawn*); but it can also be used figuratively (*attack the government's policy*). **Assault** implies a greater degree of violence or viciousness and the infliction of more damage. As part of the legal term "assault and battery," it suggests an attempt or threat to injure someone physically. **Molest** is another word meaning to *attack* and is used today almost exclusively of sexual molestation (*she had been molested as a child*). **Charge** and **storm** are primarily military words, both suggesting a forceful assault on a fixed position. To *charge* is to make a violent onslaught (*the infantry charged the enemy camp*) and is often used as a command (*"Charge!" the general cried*). To *storm* means to take by force, with all the momentum and fury of a storm (*after days of planning, the soldiers stormed the castle*), but there is often the suggestion of a last-ditch, all-out effort to end a long siege or avoid defeat. To **assail** is to attack with repeated thrusts or blows, implying that victory depends not so much on force as on persistence. To **bombard** is to assail continuously with bombs or shells (*they bombarded the city without mercy for days*). **Besiege** means to surround with an armed force (*to besiege the capital city*). When used figuratively, its meaning comes close to that of *assail*, but with an emphasis on being hemmed in and enclosed rather than punished repeatedly (*besieged with fears*). **Beset** also means to attack on all sides (*beset by enemies*), but it is also used frequently in other contexts to mean set or placed upon (*a bracelet beset with diamonds*).

attacker ▸ noun *the attacker escaped with her purse* **assailant,** assaulter, aggressor; mugger, rapist, killer, murderer.

attain ▸ verb *attempts to attain a promotion* **achieve,** accomplish, reach, obtain, gain, procure, secure, get, hook, net, win, earn, acquire; realize, fulfill; informal clinch, bag, snag, wrap up. See note at GET.

attainable ▸ adjective *a challenging but attainable target* **achievable,** obtainable, accessible, within reach, securable, realizable; practicable, workable, realistic, reasonable, viable, feasible, possible; informal doable, get-at-able.

attempt ▸ verb *I attempted to answer the question* **try,** strive, aim, venture, endeavor, seek, undertake, make an effort; have a go at, try one's hand at; informal go all out, bend over backwards, bust a gut, hazard; formal essay; archaic assay.

▸ noun *an attempt to improve the economy* **effort,** endeavor, try, venture, trial; informal crack, go, bid, shot, stab; formal essay; archaic assay.

attend ▸ verb **1** *they attended a carol service* **be present at,** sit in on, take part in; appear at, present oneself at, turn up at, visit, go to; informal show up at, show one's face at.
ANTONYMS miss.
2 *he had not **attended to** the regulations* **pay attention to,** pay heed to, be attentive to, listen to; concentrate on, take note of, bear in mind, take into consideration, heed, observe, mark.
ANTONYMS disregard, ignore.
3 *the wounded were **attended to** nearby* **care for,** look after, minister to, see to; tend (to), treat, nurse, help, aid, assist, succor; informal doctor.
4 *he **attended to** the boy's education* **deal with,** see to, manage, organize, sort out, handle, take care of, take charge of, take in hand, tackle.
ANTONYMS neglect.
5 *the princess was attended by an usher* **escort,** accompany, chaperone, squire, guide, lead, conduct, usher, shepherd; assist, help, serve, wait on.
6 *her weakness **was attended with** a fever* **be accompanied by,** occur with, coexist with, be associated with, connected with, be linked with; be produced by, originate from/in, stem from, result from, arise from.

attendance ▸ noun **1** *please confirm your attendance* **presence,** appearance.
2 *the attendance was dismal* **turnout,** audience, house, gate, box office; crowd, congregation, gathering.
ANTONYMS absence.
– PHRASES **in attendance** *three doctors are in attendance* **present,** here, there, at hand, available; assisting.

attendant ▸ noun *your attendant will be Edward* **steward,** waiter, waitress, garçon, porter, servant, waitperson, stewardess; escort, companion, retainer, aide, lady-in-waiting, equerry, chaperone; manservant, valet, butler, maidservant, maid, footman; busboy, houseman; lackey.

▸ adjective *new discoveries and the attendant excitement* **accompanying,** associated, related, connected, concomitant, coincident; resultant, resulting, consequent.

attention ▸ noun **1** *the issue needs further attention* **consideration,** contemplation, deliberation, thought, study, observation, scrutiny, investigation, action.
2 *he tried to attract the attention of a policeman* **awareness,** notice, observation, heed, regard, scrutiny, surveillance.
3 *adequate medical attention* **care,** treatment, ministration, succor, relief, aid, help, assistance.
4 (**attentions**) *he was effusive in his attentions* **overtures,** approaches, suit, wooing, courting; compliments, flattery; courtesy, politeness.

attentive ▸ adjective **1** *a bright and attentive scholar* **perceptive,** observant, alert, acute, aware, heedful, vigilant; intent, focused, committed, studious, diligent, conscientious, earnest; wary, watchful; informal not missing a trick, on the ball.
2 *the most attentive of husbands* **conscientious,** considerate, thoughtful, kind, caring, solicitous, understanding, sympathetic, obliging, accommodating, courteous, gallant, chivalrous; dutiful, responsible.
ANTONYMS inconsiderate.

attenuated ▸ adjective **1** *attenuated fingers* **thin,** slender, narrow, slim, skinny, spindly, bony; rare attenuate.
ANTONYMS plump, broad.
2 *his muscle activity was much attenuated* **weakened,** reduced, lessened, decreased, diminished, impaired.
ANTONYMS strengthened.

attest ▸ verb *I can **attest to** her fitness as a mother* **certify,** corroborate, confirm, verify, substantiate, authenticate, evidence, demonstrate, show, prove; endorse, support, affirm, bear out, give credence to, vouch for;

formal evince.
ANTONYMS disprove.

attic ▶ **noun** *the Christmas lights are in the attic* **loft**, garret.

attire ▶ **noun** *Thomas preferred formal attire* **clothing**, clothes, garments, dress, wear, outfits, garb, costume; *informal* gear, duds, getup, threads; *formal* apparel; *archaic* raiment, habiliments.
▶ **verb** *she was attired in black crepe* **dress**, dress up, clothe, garb, robe, array, costume, swathe, deck, deck out, turn out, fit out, trick out; *archaic* apparel, invest, habit.

attitude ▶ **noun 1** *you seem ambivalent in your attitude* **view**, viewpoint, outlook, perspective, stance, standpoint, position, inclination, temper, orientation, approach, reaction; opinion, ideas, convictions, feelings, thinking.
2 *an attitude of prayer* **position**, posture, pose, stance, bearing.
3 *their music is hard rock with plenty of attitude* **hostility**, anger, venom, vitriol, rancor, spunk, spirit; *informal* 'tude.

attract ▶ **verb 1** *positive ions are attracted to the negatively charged terminal* **draw**, pull; magnetize.
ANTONYMS repel.
2 *he was attracted by her smile* **entice**, allure, lure, tempt, charm, win over, woo, engage, enthrall, enchant, entrance, captivate, beguile, bewitch, seduce.
ANTONYMS repel.

attraction ▶ **noun 1** *the stars are held together by gravitational attraction* **pull**, draw; magnetism.
ANTONYMS repulsion.
2 *she had lost whatever attraction she once had* **appeal**, attractiveness, desirability, seductiveness, seduction, allure, animal magnetism; charisma, charm, beauty, good looks, eye-appeal.
ANTONYMS repulsion.
3 *the fair offers sideshows and other attractions* **entertainment**, activity, diversion, interest.

attractive ▶ **adjective 1** *a more attractive career* **appealing**, inviting, tempting, irresistible; agreeable, pleasing, interesting. See note at PLEASANT.
ANTONYMS uninviting.
2 *she has no idea how attractive she is* **good-looking**, beautiful, pretty, handsome, lovely, stunning, striking, arresting, gorgeous, prepossessing, fetching, captivating, bewitching, beguiling, engaging, charming, enchanting, enticing, appealing, delightful, winning, photogenic, telegenic; sexy, seductive, alluring, tantalizing, irresistible, ravishing, desirable; *informal* drop-dead gorgeous, foxy; *literary* beauteous; *archaic* comely, fair.
ANTONYMS ugly.

attribute ▶ **verb** *they attributed their success to him* **ascribe to**, assign to, accredit to, credit to, impute to; put down to, chalk up to; hold responsible for, blame on, pin on; connect with, associate with.
▶ **noun 1** *he has all the attributes of a top player* **quality**, characteristic, trait, feature, element, aspect, property, sign, hallmark, mark, distinction.
2 *the hourglass is the attribute of Father Time* **symbol**, mark, sign, hallmark, trademark. See note at EMBLEM.

attrition ▶ **noun 1** *the battle would result in further attrition of their already lame naval force* **wearing down, wearing away,** weakening, debilitation, enfeebling, sapping, attenuation; gradual loss.
2 *the skull shows attrition of the teeth* **abrasion,** friction, erosion, corrosion, corroding, grinding; wearing away, deterioration; *rare* detrition.

attune ▶ **verb** *we are finally attuned to city life* **accustom**, adjust, adapt, acclimatize, condition, accommodate, assimilate; acclimate.

auburn ▶ **adjective** *auburn hair* **reddish-brown,** red-brown, Titian (red), tawny, russet, chestnut, copper, coppery, rufous, rust.

audacious ▶ **adjective 1** *an audacious remark* **impudent**, impertinent, insolent, presumptuous; cheeky, irreverent, discourteous, disrespectful, insubordinate, ill-mannered, unmannerly, rude, brazen, shameless, pert, defiant, cocky, bold (as brass); *informal* fresh, lippy, mouthy, saucy, sassy, nervy, ballsy; *archaic* contumelious.
ANTONYMS polite.
2 *his audacious exploits* **bold**, daring, fearless, intrepid, brave, courageous, valiant, heroic, plucky; daredevil, devil-may-care, reckless, madcap; venturesome, mettlesome; *informal* gutsy, spunky, ballsy; *literary* temerarious. See note at BOLD.
ANTONYMS timid.

audacity ▶ **noun 1** *he had the audacity to contradict me* **impudence**, impertinence, insolence, presumption, cheek, bad manners, effrontery, nerve, gall, defiance, temerity; *informal* chutzpah, sass. See note at TEMERITY.
2 *a traveler of extraordinary audacity* **boldness,** daring, fearlessness, intrepidity, bravery, courage, heroism, pluck, grit; recklessness; spirit, mettle; *informal* guts, gutsiness, spunk, moxie.

audible ▶ **adjective** *the radio is barely audible* **hearable,** perceptible, discernible, detectable, appreciable; clear, distinct, loud.
ANTONYMS faint.

audience ▶ **noun 1** *the audience applauded* **spectators, listeners,** viewers, onlookers, patrons; crowd, throng, congregation, turnout; house, gallery.
2 *the radio station has a teenage audience* **market, public,** following, fans; listenership, viewership.
3 *an audience with the Pope* **meeting,** consultation, conference, hearing, reception, interview; *informal* meet-and-greet.

audit ▶ **noun** *an audit of the party accounts* **inspection,** examination, verification, scrutiny, probe, investigation, assessment, appraisal, evaluation, review, analysis; *informal* going-over, once-over.
▶ **verb** *we audited their books* **inspect**, examine, survey, go through, scrutinize, check, probe, vet, investigate, inquire into, assess, verify, appraise, evaluate, review, analyze, study; *informal* give something a/the once-over, give something a going-over.

augment ▶ **verb** *moonlighting helps augment her*

income **increase,** add to, supplement, build up, enlarge, expand, extend, raise, multiply, swell, grow; magnify, amplify, escalate; improve, boost; informal up, jack up, hike up, bump up.
ANTONYMS decrease.

augur ▶ verb *the war heightened anxiety and augured higher taxes* **bode,** portend, herald, be a sign of, warn of, forewarn of, foreshadow, be an omen of, presage, indicate, signify, signal, promise, threaten, spell, denote; predict, prophesy; literary betoken, foretoken, forebode. See note at PREDICT.

august ▶ adjective *our august guests* **distinguished,** respected, eminent, venerable, hallowed, illustrious, prestigious, renowned, celebrated, honored, acclaimed, esteemed, exalted; great, important, lofty, noble; imposing, impressive, awe-inspiring, stately, grand, dignified.

aura ▶ noun *an aura of sophistication* **atmosphere,** ambience, air, quality, character, mood, feeling, feel, flavor, tone, tenor; emanation; informal vibe.

auspices ▶ plural noun *talks were to be held under the auspices of the UN* **patronage,** aegis, umbrella, protection, keeping, care; support, backing, guardianship, trusteeship, guidance, supervision.

auspicious ▶ adjective *thanks for joining us on this auspicious occasion* **favorable,** propitious, promising, rosy, good, encouraging; opportune, timely, lucky, fortunate, providential, felicitous, advantageous. See note at OPPORTUNE.

austere ▶ adjective **1** *an outwardly austere man* **severe,** stern, strict, harsh, steely, flinty, dour, grim, cold, frosty, unemotional, unfriendly; formal, stiff, reserved, aloof, forbidding; grave, solemn, serious, unsmiling, unsympathetic, unforgiving; hard, unyielding, unbending, inflexible; informal hard-boiled. See note at SEVERE.
ANTONYMS genial.
2 *an austere life* **ascetic,** self-denying, self-disciplined, nonindulgent, frugal, spartan, puritanical, abstemious, abstinent, self-sacrificing, strict, temperate, sober, simple, restrained; celibate, chaste.
ANTONYMS immoderate.
3 *the buildings were austere* **plain,** simple, basic, functional, modest, unadorned, unembellished, unfussy, restrained; stark, bleak, bare, clinical, spartan, ascetic; informal no-frills, bare-bones.
ANTONYMS ornate.

authentic ▶ adjective **1** *an authentic document* **genuine,** real, bona fide, true, veritable; legitimate, lawful, legal, valid; informal the real McCoy, the real thing, kosher. See note at GENUINE.
ANTONYMS fake.
2 *an authentic depiction of the situation* **reliable,** dependable, trustworthy, authoritative, honest, faithful; accurate, factual, true, truthful; formal veridical, veracious.
ANTONYMS unreliable.

authenticate ▶ verb **1** *the evidence will authenticate his claim* **verify,** validate, prove, substantiate, corroborate, confirm, support, back up, attest to, give credence to.
2 *a mandate authenticated by the popular vote* **validate,** ratify, confirm, seal, sanction, endorse.

authenticity ▶ noun **1** *the authenticity of the painting* **genuineness,** bona fides; legitimacy, legality, validity.
2 *the authenticity of this account* **reliability,** dependability, trustworthiness, credibility; accuracy, truth, veracity, fidelity.

author ▶ noun **1** *modern Latin American authors* **writer;** novelist, playwright, poet, essayist, biographer; columnist, reporter; wordsmith; bard; informal scribe, scribbler.
2 *the author of the peace plan* **originator,** creator, instigator, founder, father, architect, designer, deviser, producer; cause, agent.

authoritarian ▶ adjective *his authoritarian manner* **autocratic,** dictatorial, despotic, tyrannical, draconian, oppressive, repressive, illiberal, undemocratic; disciplinarian, domineering, overbearing, high-handed, peremptory, imperious, strict, rigid, inflexible; informal bossy, iron-fisted.
ANTONYMS democratic, liberal.
▶ noun *the army is dominated by authoritarians* **autocrat,** despot, dictator, tyrant; disciplinarian, martinet.

authoritative ▶ adjective **1** *authoritative information* **reliable,** dependable, trustworthy, sound, authentic, valid, attested, verifiable; accurate.
ANTONYMS unreliable.
2 *the authoritative edition* **definitive,** most reliable, best; authorized, accredited, recognized, accepted, approved, standard, canonical.
3 *his authoritative manner* **assured,** confident, assertive; commanding, masterful, lordly; domineering, imperious, overbearing, authoritarian; informal bossy.
ANTONYMS diffident, timid.

authority ▶ noun **1** *a rebellion against those in authority* **power,** jurisdiction, command, control, charge, dominance, rule, sovereignty, supremacy; influence; informal clout. See note at JURISDICTION.
2 *the authority to arrest drug traffickers* **authorization,** right, power, mandate, prerogative, license, permission.
3 (**authorities**) *they failed to report the theft to the authorities* **officials,** officialdom; government, administration, establishment; police; informal the powers that be.
4 *an authority on the stock market* **expert,** specialist, aficionado, pundit, guru, sage.
5 *on good authority* **evidence,** testimony, witness, attestation, word, avowal; Law deposition.

authorize ▶ verb **1** *they authorized further action* **sanction,** permit, allow, approve, consent to, assent to; ratify, endorse, validate; informal give the green light to, give the go-ahead to, OK, give the thumbs up to.
ANTONYMS forbid.
2 *the troops were authorized to fire* **empower,** mandate, commission; entitle.

autobiography ▶ noun *the actor's autobiography* **memoirs,** life story, personal history.

autocratic ▶ adjective *autocratic governments*

despotic, tyrannical, dictatorial, totalitarian, autarchic; undemocratic, one-party, monocratic; domineering, draconian, overbearing, high-handed, peremptory, imperious; harsh, rigid, inflexible, illiberal, oppressive, iron-fisted.

autograph ▸ noun *fans pestered him for his autograph* **signature**; informal John Hancock.
▸ verb *Jack autographed copies of his book* **sign**, sign one's name to.

automatic ▸ adjective 1 *automatic garage doors* **mechanized,** mechanical, automated, computerized, electronic, robotic; self-activating.
ANTONYMS manual.
2 *an automatic reaction* **instinctive,** involuntary, unconscious, reflex, knee-jerk, instinctual, subconscious; spontaneous, impulsive, unthinking; mechanical; informal gut.
ANTONYMS conscious, deliberate.
3 *he is the automatic choice for the team* **inevitable,** unavoidable, inescapable, mandatory, compulsory; certain, definite, undoubted, assured.

autonomy ▸ noun *the region's claims for political autonomy are rooted in a strong sense of ethnic identity* **self-government,** self-rule, home rule, self-determination, independence, sovereignty, freedom.

available ▸ adjective 1 *refreshments will be available | don't worry ladies, Bryan is still available* **obtainable,** accessible, at hand, at one's disposal, handy, convenient; on sale, procurable; untaken, unengaged, unused; informal up for grabs, on tap, gettable.
2 *I'll see if he's available* **free,** unoccupied; present, in attendance; contactable; unattached, single.
ANTONYMS busy, engaged.

avarice ▸ noun *the job had become less about integrity and more about avarice* **greed,** greediness, acquisitiveness, cupidity, covetousness, rapacity, materialism, mercenariness; rare pleonexia; informal money-grubbing, affluenza. See note at **GREEDY**.
ANTONYMS generosity.

average ▸ noun *the price is above the national average* **mean,** median, mode; norm, standard, rule, par.
▸ adjective 1 *the average temperature in May* **mean,** median, modal.
2 *a woman of average height* **ordinary,** standard, normal, typical, regular. See note at **NORMAL**.
3 *a very average director* **mediocre,** second-rate, undistinguished, ordinary, middle-of-the-road, unexceptional, unexciting, unremarkable, unmemorable, indifferent, pedestrian, lackluster, forgettable, amateurish; informal OK, so-so, 'comme ci, comme ça', fair-to-middling, no great shakes, underwhelming, plain-vanilla.
ANTONYMS outstanding, exceptional.
– PHRASES **on average** *on average, we get about two million visitors each year* **normally,** usually, ordinarily, generally, in general, for the most part, as a rule, typically; overall, by and large, on the whole.

aversion ▸ noun *an aversion to the use of force* **dislike of,** antipathy for, distaste for, abhorrence of, hatred of, odium of, loathing of, detestation of, hostility toward; reluctance toward, unwillingness for, disinclination toward.
ANTONYMS liking.

avid ▸ adjective *an avid reader of science fiction* **keen,** eager, enthusiastic, ardent, passionate, zealous, hard-core; devoted, dedicated, wholehearted, earnest. See note at **EAGER**.
ANTONYMS apathetic.

avoid ▸ verb 1 *I avoid situations that stress me out* **keep away from, stay away from,** steer clear of, give a wide berth to, fight shy of.
ANTONYMS confront.
2 *he is trying to avoid responsibility* **evade,** dodge, sidestep, escape, run away from; informal duck, wriggle out of, get out of, cop out of.
ANTONYMS face up to.
3 *he jerked back to avoid a wild pitch* **dodge,** duck, get out of the way of.
4 *you've been avoiding me all evening* **shun,** stay away from, evade, keep one's distance from, elude, hide from; ignore, give the cold shoulder.
ANTONYMS seek out.
5 *he should avoid drinking alcohol* **refrain from,** abstain from, desist from, eschew.
ANTONYMS indulge in.

aware ▸ adjective 1 *she is **aware of** the dangers* **conscious of,** mindful of, informed about, acquainted with, familiar with, alive to, alert to; informal clued in to, wise to, in the know about, hip to; formal cognizant of; archaic ware of.
ANTONYMS ignorant, oblivious.
2 *we need to be more environmentally aware* **knowledgeable,** enlightened, well-informed, au fait; informal clued in, tuned in, plugged in.
ANTONYMS ignorant.

awe ▸ noun *we watched in awe* **wonder,** wonderment; admiration, reverence, respect, esteem; dread, fear.

awful ▸ adjective 1 *the place smelled awful* **disgusting,** horrible, terrible, dreadful, ghastly, nasty, vile, foul, revolting, repulsive, repugnant, odious, sickening, nauseating; informal yucky, gross, beastly.
ANTONYMS wonderful, lovely.
2 *an awful book* **terrible,** atrocious, dreadful, frightful, execrable, abominable; inadequate, inferior, substandard, lamentable; informal crummy, pathetic, rotten, woeful, lousy, appalling, abysmal.
ANTONYMS good, excellent.
3 *an awful accident* **serious,** dreadful, grave, terrible, bad, critical.
ANTONYMS minor.
4 *you look awful—go lie down* **ill,** unwell, sick, queasy, nauseous; poorly; informal lousy, rotten, terrible, dreadful.
5 *I felt awful for getting so angry* **remorseful,** guilty, ashamed, contrite, sorry, regretful, repentant.
6 archaic *the awful sights of nature* **awe-inspiring,** awesome, impressive; dread, fearful.

awkward ▸ adjective 1 *the box was awkward to carry* **difficult,** tricky; cumbersome, unwieldy.
ANTONYMS easy.
2 *an awkward time* **inconvenient,** inappropriate, inopportune, unseasonable, difficult.

ANTONYMS convenient.
3 *he put her in a very awkward position* **embarrassing,** uncomfortable, unpleasant, delicate, tricky, problematic, troublesome, thorny; humiliating, compromising; informal sticky, dicey, hairy.
4 *she felt awkward alone with him* **uncomfortable,** uneasy, tense, nervous, edgy, unquiet; self-conscious, embarrassed.
ANTONYMS relaxed, at ease.
5 *his awkward movements* **clumsy,** ungainly, uncoordinated, graceless, inelegant, gauche, gawky, wooden, stiff; unskillful, maladroit, inept, blundering; informal clodhopping, ham-fisted, ham-handed, heavy-handed; informal all thumbs.
ANTONYMS adroit, graceful.

awry ▶ adjective **1** *something was awry* **amiss,** wrong; informal up.
2 *his wig looked awry* **askew,** crooked, lopsided, tilted, skewed, skew, to one side, off-center, uneven; informal cockeyed, wonky.
ANTONYMS straight, symmetrical.

Bb

babble ▶ verb **1** *Betty babbled about the stupidest things* **prattle,** rattle on, chatter, jabber, twitter, go on, run on, prate, ramble, burble, blather; informal gab, yap, yak, yabber, yatter, yammer, blabber, jaw, gas, shoot one's mouth off, run off at the mouth.
2 *a brook babbled gently* **burble,** murmur, gurgle, tinkle; literary plash.
▶ noun *his inarticulate babble* **prattle,** chatter, jabber, prating, rambling, blather; informal gab, yabbering, yatter.

babe ▶ noun **1** literary *a babe in arms* See BABY (sense 1 of the noun).
2 informal *what a babe!* **beauty**; informal hottie, looker, bombshell, heartthrob, knockout, fox, (piece of) arm candy, eye-catcher, dish, boy toy, hunk.

babel ▶ noun *I can't hear you above this babel* **clamor,** din, racket, confused noise, tumult, uproar, hubbub; babble, babbling, shouting, yelling, screaming; informal hullabaloo.

baby ▶ noun **1** *a newborn baby* **infant,** newborn, child, tot, little one; informal rug rat; Scottish bairn; literary babe, babe in arms, suckling; papoose; technical neonate.
2 *don't be such a baby* **sissy,** wimp, wuss, milquetoast; pantywaist.
▶ adjective *baby carrots* **miniature,** mini, little, small, small-scale, scaled-down, toy, pocket, vest-pocket, midget, dwarf; informal teeny, teeny-weeny, teensy, teensy-weensy, itsy-bitsy, itty-bitty, little-bitty, bite-sized.
ANTONYMS large.
▶ verb *her aunt babied her* **pamper,** mollycoddle, spoil, cosset, coddle, indulge, overindulge, nanny, pander to.

babyish ▶ adjective *she hated the babyish remarks he would make about her friends* **childish,** immature, infantile, juvenile, puerile, adolescent.
ANTONYMS mature.

back ▶ noun **1** *she's broken her back* **spine,** backbone, spinal column, vertebral column.
2 *the back of the house* **rear,** rear side, other side; Nautical stern.
ANTONYMS front.
3 *the back of the line* **end,** tail end, rear end, rear, tail, tag end.
ANTONYMS front, head.
4 *the back of a postcard* **reverse,** other side, underside; verso; informal flip side.
ANTONYMS front, face.
▶ adverb **1** *he pushed his chair back* **backward,** behind one, to one's rear, rearward; away, off.
ANTONYMS forward.
2 *a few months back* **ago,** earlier, previously, before, in the past.
▶ verb **1** *the government backed the initiative with $4 million* **sponsor,** finance, put up the money for, fund, subsidize, underwrite, be a patron of, act as guarantor of; informal foot the bill for, pick up the tab for; bankroll, stake.
2 *most people backed the idea* **support,** endorse, sanction, approve of, give one's blessing to, smile on, favor, advocate, promote, uphold, champion; vote for, ally oneself with, stand behind, stick by, side with, be on the side of, defend, take up the cudgels for; second; informal throw one's weight behind.
ANTONYMS oppose.
3 *he backed the horse at 33–1* **bet on,** gamble on, stake money on.
4 *he backed out of the garage* **reverse,** draw back, step back, move backward, back off, pull back, retreat, withdraw, give ground, backtrack, retrace one's steps, recede.
ANTONYMS move forward, advance.
▶ adjective **1** *the back seats* **rear,** rearmost, backmost, hind, hindmost, hinder, posterior.
ANTONYMS front.
2 *a back copy* **past,** old, previous, earlier, former, out of date.
ANTONYMS future.
– PHRASES **back away** *there's no need to back away—he's a very gentle dog* **draw back,** step back, move away, withdraw, retreat, pull back, give ground; shrink back, cower, quail, quake. **back down** *all your begging is useless because I am not going to back down* **give in,** concede defeat, surrender, yield, submit, climb down, concede, reconsider; backtrack, backpedal. **back out of** *Charlie's backed out of the original agreement* **renege on,** go back on, withdraw from, pull out of, retreat from, fail to honor, abandon, default on, repudiate, backpedal on. **back someone up** *I was surprised when it turned out to be Dina who backed me up* **support,** stand by, give one's support to, side with, be on someone's side, take someone's side, take someone's part; vouch for. **back something up** *can you back up that statement with any real evidence?* **substantiate,** corroborate, confirm, support, bear out, endorse, bolster, reinforce, lend weight to. **behind someone's back** *the takeover was planned behind the plant manager's back* **secretly,** without someone's knowledge, on the sly, slyly, sneakily, covertly, surreptitiously, furtively.

backbiting ▶ noun *the backbiting between candidates has become tiresome* **malicious**

talk, spiteful talk, slander, libel, defamation, abuse, character assassination, disparagement, denigration, vilification, vituperation, calumny; slurs, aspersions; informal bitching, bitchiness, cattiness, mudslinging, bad-mouthing, dissing.

backbone ▶ noun **1** *an injured backbone* **spine,** spinal column, vertebral column, vertebrae; back; Anatomy dorsum, rachis.
2 *the infantry is the backbone of our army* **mainstay,** cornerstone, foundation, chief support, buttress, pillar, tower of strength.
3 *he has enough backbone to see us through* **strength of character,** strength of will, firmness, resolution, resolve, determination, fortitude, pluck, pluckiness, nerve, courage, mettle, spirit, moral fiber; informal guts, spunk, grit, true grit.

backer ▶ noun **1** *the backers of the proposition* **supporter,** defender, advocate, promoter, proponent; seconder; booster.
2 *$3 million was provided by the project's backers* **sponsor,** investor, underwriter, financier, patron, benefactor, benefactress; informal angel.

backfire ▶ verb *Bernard's plan backfired* **rebound,** boomerang, come back; fail, miscarry, go wrong; informal blow up in someone's face.

background ▶ noun **1** *a background of palm trees* **backdrop,** backcloth, surrounding(s), setting, scene.
2 *students from many different backgrounds* **social circumstances,** family circumstances; environment, class, culture, tradition; upbringing.
3 *her nursing background* **experience,** record, history, past, training, education, grounding, knowledge; backstory.
4 *the political background* **circumstances,** context, conditions, situation, environment, milieu, scene, scenario.
– PHRASES **in the background** *maybe there was a sugar daddy in the background* **behind the scenes,** out of the public eye, out of the spotlight, out of the limelight, backstage; inconspicuous, unobtrusive, unnoticed.

backhanded ▶ adjective *a backhanded compliment* **indirect,** ambiguous, oblique, equivocal; double-edged, two-edged, left-handed; tongue-in-cheek.
ANTONYMS direct.

backing ▶ noun **1** *he has the backing of his colleagues* **support,** help, assistance, aid; approval, endorsement, sanction, blessing.
2 *financial backing* **sponsorship,** funding, patronage; money, investment, funds, finance; grant, contribution, subsidy.
3 *musical backing* **accompaniment**; harmony, obbligato.

backlash ▶ noun *the move provoked a backlash from union leaders* **adverse reaction,** adverse response, counterblast, comeback, repercussion; retaliation, reprisal.

backlog ▶ noun *Stella's been gone for one day and there's already a backlog of messages* **accumulation,** logjam, pileup, pile, mountain.

backpedal ▶ verb *they agreed to the peace initiative, but soon after they backpedaled* **change one's mind,** backtrack, back down, climb down, (do an) about-face, reverse course, do a U-turn, renege, go back (on), back out (of), fail to honor something, withdraw, default (on).

backslide ▶ verb *many things can cause dieters to backslide* **relapse,** lapse, regress, weaken, lose one's resolve, give in to temptation, go astray, leave the straight and narrow, fall off the wagon.
ANTONYMS persevere.

backslider ▶ noun *I'll have no backslider like you in my family* **recidivist,** regressor; defector, deserter, turncoat, apostate, fallen angel.

backward ▶ adjective **1** *a backward look* **rearward,** to/toward the rear, to/toward the back, behind one, reverse.
ANTONYMS forward.
2 *the decision was a backward step* **retrograde,** retrogressive, regressive, for the worse, in the wrong direction, downhill, negative.
ANTONYMS progressive.
3 *an economically backward country* **underdeveloped,** undeveloped; primitive, unsophisticated, benighted.
ANTONYMS advanced, sophisticated.
4 *he was not backward in displaying his talents* **hesitant,** reticent, reluctant; shy, diffident, bashful, timid; unwilling, afraid, loath, averse.
ANTONYMS bold, confident.
▶ adverb (also **backwards**) **1** *Penny glanced backward* **toward the rear,** rearward, behind one.
ANTONYMS forward.
2 *count backward from twenty to ten* **in reverse,** in reverse order; informal ass-backward, bassackward.
ANTONYMS forward.

> USAGE
>
> **backward, backwards**
>
> In British English, the spelling *backwards* is more common than *backward*. In American English, the adverb form is sometimes spelled *backwards* (*the ladder fell backwards*), but the adjective is almost always *backward* (*a backward glance*). Directional words using the suffix *-ward* tend to have no *s* ending in American English, although *backwards* is more common than *afterwards, towards,* or *forwards*. The *s* ending often (but not always) appears in the phrases *backwards and forwards* and *bending over backwards*.

backwash ▶ noun **1** *a ship's backwash* **wake,** wash, slipstream.
2 *the backwash of the Cuban missile crisis* **repercussions,** reverberations, aftereffects, aftermath, fallout.

backwoods ▶ plural noun *they're bringing cable TV to the backwoods* **back of beyond,** remote areas, wilds, bush, bush country, bushland, hinterlands, backwater; backcountry, backlands; middle of nowhere; informal sticks, boondocks, boonies, tall timbers.

bacteria ▶ plural noun *a different strain of bacteria* **microorganisms,** microbes, germs, bacilli, pathogens, prokaryotes; informal bugs.

bad ▸ adjective **1** *bad workmanship* **substandard,** poor, inferior, second-rate, second-class, unsatisfactory, inadequate, unacceptable, not up to scratch, not up to par, deficient, imperfect, defective, faulty, shoddy, amateurish, careless, negligent, miserable, sorry; incompetent, inept, inexpert, ineffectual; awful, atrocious, appalling, execrable, deplorable, terrible, abysmal, godawful; informal crummy, rotten, pathetic, useless, woeful, bum, lousy, not up to snuff.
ANTONYMS good, excellent, skilled.
2 *the alcohol had a really bad effect on me* **harmful,** damaging, detrimental, injurious, hurtful, inimical, destructive, ruinous, deleterious; unhealthy, unwholesome.
ANTONYMS good, beneficial.
3 *the bad guys* **wicked,** evil, sinful, immoral, morally wrong, corrupt, base, black-hearted, reprobate, amoral; criminal, villainous, nefarious, iniquitous, dishonest, dishonorable, unscrupulous, unprincipled; informal crooked, dirty; dated dastardly.
ANTONYMS virtuous.
4 *you bad girl!* **badly behaved,** naughty, ill-behaved, disobedient, wayward, willful, self-willed, defiant, unruly, insubordinate, undisciplined.
ANTONYMS well-behaved.
5 *bad news* **unpleasant,** disagreeable, unwelcome; unfortunate, unlucky, unfavorable; terrible, dreadful, awful, grim, distressing.
ANTONYMS good.
6 *a bad time to arrive* **inauspicious,** unfavorable, inopportune, unpropitious, unfortunate, disadvantageous, adverse, inappropriate, unsuitable, untoward.
ANTONYMS good, auspicious.
7 *a bad accident* **severe,** serious, grave, critical, acute; formal grievous.
ANTONYMS minor, slight.
8 *the meat's bad* **rotten,** decayed, decomposed, decomposing, putrid, putrefied, off, moldy; sour, spoiled, rancid, rank, unfit for human consumption; (of an egg) addled; (of beer) skunky.
ANTONYMS fresh.
9 *if you still feel bad, stay in bed* See ILL (sense 1 of the adjective).
10 *a bad knee* **injured,** wounded, diseased; dated game.
11 *I felt bad about leaving them* **guilty,** conscience-stricken, remorseful, guilt-ridden, ashamed, contrite, sorry, full of regret, regretful, shamefaced.
ANTONYMS unrepentant.
12 *a bad check* **invalid,** worthless; counterfeit, fake, false, bogus, fraudulent; informal phony, dud.
ANTONYMS valid.
13 *bad language* **offensive,** vulgar, crude, foul, obscene, rude, coarse, smutty, dirty, filthy, indecent, indecorous; blasphemous, profane.
– PHRASES **not bad** *hey, this curried octopus is not bad | the movie's not bad, but the book's much better* **all right,** adequate, good enough, pretty good, reasonable, fair, decent, average, tolerable, acceptable, passable, middling, moderate, fine; informal OK, so-so, 'comme ci, comme ça', fair-to-middling, satisfactory.

badge ▸ noun **1** *the badge on her jacket was earned in combat* pin, brooch, button, emblem, crest.
2 *a badge of success* **sign,** symbol, indication, signal, mark; hallmark, trademark.

badger ▸ verb *stop badgering us* **pester,** harass, bother, plague, torment, hound, nag, harry, tease, go on at; informal hassle, bug, get on someone's case.

badly ▸ adverb **1** *the job had been very badly done* **poorly,** incompetently, ineptly, inexpertly, inefficiently, imperfectly, deficiently, defectively, unsatisfactorily, inadequately, incorrectly, faultily, shoddily, amateurishly, carelessly, negligently; abominably; informal crummily, pitifully, woefully.
ANTONYMS well.
2 *try not to think badly of me* **unfavorably,** ill, critically, disapprovingly.
3 *stop behaving badly* **naughtily,** disobediently, willfully, reprehensibly, mischievously.
4 *he had been badly treated* **cruelly,** wickedly, unkindly, harshly, shamefully; unfairly, unjustly, wrongly, improperly.
5 *it turned out badly* **unsuccessfully,** unfavorably, adversely, unfortunately, unhappily, unluckily.
6 *some of the victims are badly hurt* **severely,** seriously, gravely, acutely, critically; formal grievously.
ANTONYMS slightly.
7 *she badly needs help* **desperately,** sorely, intensely, seriously, very much, greatly, exceedingly.

baffle ▸ verb *his explanations baffle the class* **perplex,** puzzle, bewilder, mystify, bemuse, confuse, confound, disconcert; informal flummox, faze, stump, make someone scratch their head, be all Greek to, floor, discombobulate. See note at THWART.
ANTONYMS enlighten.

bag ▸ noun **1** *I dug around in my bag for a lipstick* **handbag,** purse, shoulder bag, clutch bag/purse, minaudière; sack, pouch; historical reticule.
2 *she began to unpack her bags* **suitcase,** case, valise, portmanteau, grip, overnighter; backpack, rucksack, knapsack, haversack, carryall, kit bag, duffel bag; satchel; (**bags**) luggage, baggage.
3 informal *mystery novels just aren't my bag* **interest,** preoccupation, concern; informal thing.
▸ verb **1** *locals bagged the most fish* **catch,** land, capture, trap, snare, ensnare; kill, shoot.
2 *he bagged seven medals* **get,** secure, obtain, acquire, pick up; win, achieve, attain; commandeer, grab, appropriate, take; informal get one's hands on, land, net.

baggage ▸ noun *leave your baggage with the inspectors* **luggage,** suitcases, cases, bags.

baggy ▸ adjective *baggy pants* **loose-fitting,** loose, roomy, full, ample, voluminous, billowing; oversized, shapeless, ill-fitting, tentlike, sacklike.
ANTONYMS tight, form-fitting.

bail ▸ noun *he was released on bail* **surety,**

security, assurance, indemnity, indemnification; bond, guarantee, pledge; archaic gage.
– PHRASES **bail out** *the pilot bailed out* **eject,** parachute to safety; desert, get out, escape. **bail someone/something out** *the state was called in to bail out the foundering housing project* **rescue,** save, relieve; finance, help (out), assist, aid; informal save someone's bacon/neck/skin.

bait ▶ **noun 1** *the fish let go of the bait* **lure,** decoy, fly, troll, jig, plug.
2 *was she the bait to lure him into a trap?* **enticement,** lure, decoy, snare, trap, siren, carrot, attraction, draw, magnet, incentive, temptation, inducement; informal come-on.
▶ **verb** *he was baited at school* **taunt,** tease, goad, pick on, torment, persecute, plague, harry, bother, harass, hound; informal needle.

bake ▶ **verb 1** *bake the fish for 15–20 minutes* **cook,** oven-bake, roast, dry-roast.
2 *the earth was baked by the sun* **scorch,** burn, sear, parch, dry (up), desiccate; broil.

balance ▶ **noun 1** *I tripped and lost my balance* **stability,** equilibrium, steadiness, footing.
ANTONYMS instability.
2 *political balance in broadcasting* **fairness,** justice, impartiality, evenhandedness, egalitarianism, equal opportunity; parity, equity, equilibrium, equipoise, evenness, symmetry, correspondence, uniformity, equality, equivalence, comparability.
ANTONYMS imbalance.
3 *this stylistic development provides a balance to the rest of the work* **counterbalance,** counterweight, stabilizer, compensation.
4 *the food was weighed on a balance* **scale(s),** weighing machine.
5 *the balance of the rent* **remainder,** outstanding amount, rest, residue, difference, remaining part.
▶ **verb 1** *she balanced the book on her head* **steady,** stabilize, poise, level.
2 *he balanced his radical remarks with more familiar declarations* **counterbalance,** balance out, offset, even out/up, counteract, compensate for, make up for.
3 *their income and expenditure do not balance* **correspond,** agree, tally, match up, concur, coincide, be in agreement, be consistent, equate, be equal.
4 *you need to balance cost against benefit* **weigh,** weigh up, compare, evaluate, consider, assess, appraise, judge.
– PHRASES **in the balance** *thanks to these dismal sales figures, everyone's job is in the balance* **uncertain,** undetermined, unsettled, unresolved, unsure, pending, in limbo, up in the air, at a turning point, critical, at a critical stage, at a crisis. **on balance** *on balance, I'd say the scenery for Act II is coming along great* **overall,** all in all, all things considered, taking everything into consideration/account, by and large, on average.

balcony ▶ **noun 1** *the balcony of the hotel* veranda, terrace, balustrade, patio.
2 *the applause from the balcony* **gallery,** dress circle, loge, upper tier, upper deck; choir loft; informal gods.

bald ▶ **adjective 1** *a bald head* **hairless,** smooth, shaven, depilated; bald-headed; informal chrome-domed; technical glabrous; archaic bald-pated.
ANTONYMS hairy, hirsute.
2 *a few bald bushes* **leafless,** bare, uncovered.
ANTONYMS lush, leafy.
3 *the bald prairie* **treeless,** naked, barren. See note at **NAKED**.
ANTONYMS lush.
4 *a bald statement* **plain,** simple, unadorned, unvarnished, unembellished, undisguised, unveiled, stark, severe, austere, brutal, harsh; blunt, direct, forthright, plain-spoken, straight, straightforward, candid, honest, truthful, realistic, frank, outspoken; informal upfront.
ANTONYMS vague.

balderdash ▶ **noun** See **NONSENSE** (sense 1 of the noun).

bale ▶ **noun** *a bale of cotton* **bundle,** bunch, pack, package, parcel.

baleful ▶ **adjective** *she saw her rival's reddened, baleful face* **menacing,** threatening, unfriendly, hostile, antagonistic, evil, evil-intentioned, vindictive, wicked, nasty, bitter, acrimonious, malevolent, malicious, malignant, malign, sinister; harmful, injurious, dangerous, destructive, noxious, pernicious, deadly, venomous, poisonous, vitriolic; literary malefic, maleficent.
ANTONYMS benevolent, friendly.

balk ▶ **verb 1** *I balk at paying that much* **be unwilling to (be),** draw the line at, be reluctant to (be), hesitate over; eschew, resist, refuse to (be), take exception to; draw back from, flinch from, shrink from, recoil from, demur from, hate to (be).
ANTONYMS accept.
2 *they were balked by traffic* **impede,** obstruct, thwart, hinder, prevent, check, stop, curb, halt, bar, block, forestall, frustrate. See note at **THWART**.
ANTONYMS assist.

ball ▶ **noun 1** *a ball of dough* **sphere,** globe, orb, globule, spherule, spheroid, ovoid.
2 *a musket ball* **bullet,** pellet, slug, projectile.
3 *a costume ball* **dance,** dinner dance, masked ball, formal, prom, masquerade; informal hop, bop.
4 *everyone had a ball* **good time,** blast, riot.

ballad ▶ **noun** *a ballad sung by Burl Ives* **song,** folk song, chantey, ditty, canzone; poem, tale, saga.

ballast ▶ **noun** *the third balloonist appears to be in need of ballast* **stabilizer,** counterbalance, counterweight.

balloon ▶ **noun** *sailing by in a balloon* hot-air balloon, barrage balloon; airship, dirigible, Zeppelin, blimp; weather balloon.
▶ **verb 1** *her long skirt ballooned in the wind* **swell (out),** puff out/up, bulge (out), bag, belly (out), fill (out), billow (out), distend.
2 *the company's debt has ballooned* **increase rapidly,** soar, rocket, shoot up, escalate, mount, surge, spiral; informal go through the ceiling, go through the roof, skyrocket.
ANTONYMS plummet.

ballot ▶ **noun** *the ballot results will be announced soon* **vote,** poll, election, referendum, plebiscite; show of hands.

ballyhoo ▶ **noun** informal *after all the ballyhoo,*

the movie was a flop **publicity,** advertising, promotion, marketing, propaganda, push, puffery, buildup, boosting; fuss, excitement; informal hype, spiel, hullabaloo, splash.

balm ▶ **noun 1** *skin balm* **ointment,** lotion, cream, salve, liniment, embrocation, rub, gel, emollient, unguent, balsam, moisturizer; dated pomade; archaic unction.
ANTONYMS astringent, irritant.
2 *balm for troubled spirits* **relief,** comfort, ease, succor, consolation, cheer, solace.
ANTONYMS exacerbation, misery.

balmy ▶ **adjective** *the balmy breezes of the West Indies* **mild,** gentle, temperate, summery, calm, tranquil, clement, fine, pleasant, benign, soothing, soft.
ANTONYMS harsh, wintry.

bamboozle ▶ **verb** informal See **TRICK** (verb).

ban ▶ **verb 1** *smoking was banned* **prohibit,** forbid, veto, proscribe, disallow, outlaw, make illegal, embargo, bar, debar, block, stop, suppress, interdict; Law enjoin, restrain. See note at **PROHIBIT**.
ANTONYMS permit.
2 *Gary was banned from the playground* **exclude,** banish, expel, eject, evict, drive out, force out, oust, remove, get rid of; informal boot out, kick out.
ANTONYMS admit.
▶ **noun 1** *a ban on soliciting* **prohibition,** veto, proscription, embargo, bar, suppression, stoppage, interdict, interdiction, moratorium, injunction.
2 *a ban from international competition* **exclusion,** banishment, expulsion, ejection, eviction, removal.

banal ▶ **adjective** *banal lyrics* **trite,** hackneyed, clichéd, platitudinous, vapid, commonplace, ordinary, common, stock, conventional, stereotyped, overused, overdone, overworked, stale, worn out, timeworn, tired, threadbare, hoary, hack, unimaginative, humdrum, ho-hum, unoriginal, uninteresting, dull, trivial; informal old hat, corny, cornball, played out; dated dime-store; rare truistic, bromidic.
ANTONYMS original.

banality ▶ **noun 1** *the banality of most sitcoms* **triteness,** vapidity, staleness, unimaginativeness, lack of originality, prosaicness, dullness; informal corniness.
ANTONYMS originality.
2 *they exchanged banalities* **platitude,** cliché, truism, old chestnut, stock phrase, bromide, commonplace.
ANTONYMS epigram, witticism.

band[1] ▶ **noun 1** *a band around her waist* **belt,** sash, girdle, strap, tape, ring, hoop, loop, circlet, circle, cord, tie, string, thong, ribbon, fillet, strip; literary cincture.
2 *the sweater is white with a green band* **stripe,** strip, streak, line, bar, swathe; technical stria, striation.

band[2] ▶ **noun 1** *a band of robbers* **group,** gang, mob, pack, troop, company, party, crew, body, working party, posse; team, side, lineup; association, society, club, circle, fellowship, partnership, guild, lodge, order, fraternity, confraternity, sodality, brotherhood, sisterhood, sorority, union, alliance, affiliation, institution, league, federation, clique, set, coterie; informal bunch.
2 *the band played on* **(musical) group,** pop group, ensemble, orchestra; informal combo.
▶ **verb** *local people* ***banded together*** **join (up),** team up, join forces, pool resources, get together; amalgamate, unite, form an alliance, form an association, affiliate, federate.
ANTONYMS split up.

bandage ▶ **noun** *she had a bandage on her foot* **dressing,** covering, gauze, compress, plaster, tourniquet; trademark Band-Aid; trademark Ace bandage.
▶ **verb** *she bandaged my knee* **bind,** bind up, dress, cover, wrap, swaddle, strap (up).

bandit ▶ **noun** *masked bandits held up the train* **robber,** thief, outlaw, gunman, crook, mugger, gangster, raider, freebooter, hijacker, looter, marauder; dated desperado; literary brigand; historical rustler, highwayman, reaver.

bandy[1] ▶ **adjective** *bandy legs* **bowed,** curved, bent; bow-legged, bandy-legged.
ANTONYMS straight.

bandy[2] ▶ **verb 1** *a figure of $40,000 has been* ***bandied about*** | *what's the latest story being* ***bandied about***? **toss around/about,** put about, spread (around), discuss, rumor, mention, repeat; literary bruit about/abroad.
2 *I'm not going to bandy words with you* **exchange,** swap, trade.

bane ▶ **noun** *scurvy was the bane of these seafarers* **scourge,** plague, curse, blight, pest, nuisance, headache, nightmare, trial, hardship, cross to bear, burden, thorn in one's flesh/side, bitter pill, affliction, trouble, misery, woe, tribulation, misfortune, pain.

bang ▶ **noun 1** *the door slammed with a bang* **thud,** thump, bump, crack, crash, smack, boom, clang, clap, knock, tap, clunk; stamp, stomp, bam, kaboom, kapow, wham, whump, whomp; report, explosion, detonation.
2 *a nasty bang on the head* **blow,** knock, thump, bump, hit, smack, bonk, crack, bash, whack, thwack.
▶ **verb 1** *he banged the table with his fist* **hit,** strike, beat, thump, hammer, knock, rap, pound, thud, punch, bump, smack, slap, slam, cuff, pummel, buffet, bash, whack, thwack, clobber, clout, clip, wallop, belt, bop, sock, whomp, bust, slug, whale.
2 *fireworks banged in the air* **go bang,** thud, thump, boom, clap, pound, crack, crash, explode, detonate, burst, blow up.
▶ **adverb** informal *the library is bang in the center of town* | *the train arrived bang on time* **precisely,** exactly, right, directly, immediately, squarely, dead; promptly, prompt, dead on, sharp, on the dot; informal smack, slap, smack dab, plumb, on the button, on the nose.

bangle ▶ **noun** *the familiar jingle of Nana's silver bangles* **bracelet,** wristlet, anklet, armlet.

banish ▶ **verb 1** *he was banished for his crime* **exile,** expel, deport, eject, expatriate, ostracize, extradite, repatriate, transport; cast out, oust, evict, throw out, exclude, shut out, ban.

ANTONYMS admit, readmit.
2 *he tried to banish his fear* **dispel,** dismiss, disperse, scatter, dissipate, drive away, chase away, shut out, quell, allay.
ANTONYMS engender.

bank[1] ▶ **noun 1** *the bank of the great river* **edge,** side, shore, coast, embankment, bankside, levee, border, verge, boundary, margin, rim, fringe; literary marge, skirt.
2 *a grassy bank* **slope,** rise, incline, gradient, ramp; mound, ridge, hillock, hummock, knoll; bar, reef, shoal, shelf; accumulation, pile, heap, mass, drift.
3 *a bank of switches* **array,** row, line, tier, group, series.
▶ **verb 1** *they* ***banked up*** *the earth* **pile (up),** heap (up), stack (up); accumulate, amass, assemble, put together.
2 *the aircraft banked* **tilt, lean,** tip, slant, incline, angle, slope, list, camber, pitch, dip, cant.

bank[2] ▶ **noun 1** *money in the bank* **financial institution,** merchant bank, savings bank, finance company, trust company, credit union.
2 *a blood bank* **store,** reserve, accumulation, stock, stockpile, supply, pool, fund, cache, hoard, deposit; storehouse, reservoir, repository, depository.
▶ **verb** *I banked the money* **deposit,** pay in, invest, lay away.
– PHRASES **bank on** *can the senator bank on your support?* **rely on,** depend on, count on, place reliance on, bargain on, plan on; anticipate, expect; be confident of, be sure of, pin one's hopes/faith on, figure on.

bankrupt ▶ **adjective 1** *the company was declared bankrupt* **insolvent,** failed, ruined, in debt, owing money, in the red, in arrears, in receivership; informal bust, belly up, broke, cash-strapped, flat broke.
ANTONYMS solvent, in the black.
2 *this government is* ***bankrupt of*** *ideas* **bereft of,** devoid of, empty of, destitute of; completely lacking in, without, in need of, wanting.
ANTONYMS teeming with.
▶ **verb** *the strike nearly bankrupted the union* **ruin,** impoverish, reduce to penury/destitution, bring to ruin, bring someone to their knees, wipe out, break; rare beggar, pauperize.

bankruptcy ▶ **noun** *many companies were facing bankruptcy* **insolvency,** liquidation, failure, ruin, financial ruin, collapse, receivership.
ANTONYMS solvency.

banner ▶ **noun 1** *students waved banners* **sign,** placard, poster, notice.
2 *banners fluttered above the troops* **flag,** standard, ensign, color(s), pennant, banderole, guidon; Nautical burgee.

banquet ▶ **noun** *the awards banquet* **feast,** dinner; informal spread, blowout.
ANTONYMS snack.

banter ▶ **noun** *a brief exchange of banter* **repartee,** witty conversation, raillery, wordplay, cut and thrust, kidding, ribbing, badinage, joshing.
▶ **verb** *sightseers were bantering with the guards* **joke,** jest, quip; informal josh, wisecrack.

baptism ▶ **noun 1** *the baptism ceremony* **christening,** naming.
2 *his baptism as a politician* **initiation,** debut, introduction, inauguration, launch, rite of passage.

baptize ▶ **verb 1** *he was baptized as a baby* **christen.**
2 *they were baptized into the church* **admit,** initiate, enroll, recruit, convert.
3 *he was baptized Enoch* **name,** give the name, call, dub; formal denominate.

bar ▶ **noun 1** *an iron bar* **rod,** pole, stick, batten, shaft, rail, paling, spar, strut, crosspiece, beam.
2 *a bar of chocolate* **block,** slab, cake, tablet, brick, loaf, wedge, ingot.
3 *your drinks are on the bar* **counter,** table, buffet, stand.
4 *she had a drink in a bar* **tavern,** cocktail lounge, barroom, taproom, pub, after-hours club, lounge, nightclub, speakeasy, roadhouse, beer hall, boîte, club, inn, rathskeller, cantina, bodega; singles bar, sports bar; informal watering hole, gin mill, dive, nineteenth hole; Brit. public house; historical saloon, alehouse.
5 *a bar to promotion* **obstacle,** impediment, hindrance, obstruction, block, hurdle, barrier, stumbling block.
ANTONYMS aid.
6 *members of the Bar* **lawyers,** barristers, advocates, counsel, counselors; chiefly Brit. solicitors.
7 *the bar across the river mouth* **sandbar,** sandbank, shoal, shallow, reef.
▶ **verb 1** *they have barred the door* **bolt,** lock, fasten, secure, block, barricade, obstruct.
ANTONYMS open, unlock.
2 *I was barred from entering* **prohibit,** debar, preclude, forbid, ban, interdict, inhibit; exclude, keep out; obstruct, hinder, block; Law enjoin.
ANTONYMS accept, admit.
▶ **preposition** *everyone bar me* See EXCEPT (preposition).

barb ▶ **noun 1** *the hook has a nasty barb* **spike,** prong, spur, thorn, needle, prickle, spine, quill.
2 *the barbs from his critics* **insult,** sneer, jibe, cutting remark, shaft, slight, brickbat, slur, jeer, taunt; informal dig, put-down; **(barbs)** abuse, disparagement, scoffing, scorn, sarcasm, goading.

barbarian ▶ **noun** *the city was besieged by barbarians* **savage,** heathen, brute, beast, wild man/woman; ruffian, thug, lout, vandal, boor, hoodlum, hooligan, Neanderthal, troglodyte; philistine; informal roughneck, lowlife; knuckle-dragger.
▶ **adjective** *the barbarian hordes* **savage,** uncivilized, barbaric, primitive, heathen, vulgar, wild, brutish, Neanderthal.
ANTONYMS civilized.

barbaric ▶ **adjective** *barbaric crimes* **brutal,** barbarous, brutish, bestial, savage, vicious, wicked, cruel, ruthless, merciless, villainous, murderous, heinous, monstrous, vile, inhuman, infernal, dark, fiendish, diabolical.
ANTONYMS civilized.

barbarity ▶ **noun** *the barbarity of slavery* **brutality,** brutalism, cruelty, bestiality, barbarism, barbarousness, savagery, viciousness, wickedness, villainy, baseness,

inhumanity; atrocity.
ANTONYMS benevolence.

barbarous ▶ adjective See **BARBARIC**.

barbecue ▶ noun *a backyard barbecue* **cookout,** wiener/wienie/weenie roast; BBQ.
▶ verb *they barbecued some steaks* **grill,** spit-roast, broil, charbroil.

bare ▶ adjective 1 *a giggling bare infant in her arms* **naked,** unclothed, undressed, uncovered, stripped, having nothing on, nude, in the nude, stark naked; informal without a stitch on, buck-naked, butt-naked, mother-naked, in one's birthday suit, in the raw, in the altogether, in the buff. See note at **NAKED**.
ANTONYMS clothed.
2 *a bare room* **empty,** unfurnished, cleared; stark, austere, spartan, unadorned, unembellished, unornamented, plain.
ANTONYMS furnished, embellished.
3 *a cupboard* ***bare of food*** **empty of,** devoid of, bereft of; without, lacking, wanting, free from.
ANTONYMS containing.
4 *a bare landscape* **barren,** bleak, exposed, desolate, stark, arid, desert, lunar; treeless, deforested, bald.
ANTONYMS lush.
5 *the bare facts* **plain,** essential, fundamental, basic, straightforward, simple, pure, stark, bald, cold, hard, brutal, harsh.
6 *a bare lead in the race* **mere,** no more than, simple; slim, slight, slender, paltry, minimum.
ANTONYMS comfortable.
▶ verb *he bared his arm* **uncover,** strip, lay bare, undress, unclothe, denude, expose.
ANTONYMS cover.

barefaced ▶ adjective *a barefaced lie* **flagrant,** blatant, glaring, obvious, undisguised, unconcealed, naked; shameless, unabashed, unashamed, impudent, audacious, unblushing, brazen.

barely ▶ adverb *former hurricane Patricia was barely at tropical storm force* **hardly,** scarcely, just, only just, narrowly, by a very small margin, by the narrowest of margins, by the skin of one's teeth, by a hair's breadth, by a nose; almost not; informal by a whisker.
ANTONYMS easily.

bargain ▶ noun 1 *this binder is a bargain at $1.98* **good buy,** (good) value for the money, surprisingly cheap; informal steal, deal, giveaway, best buy.
ANTONYMS rip-off.
2 *I'll make a bargain with you* **agreement,** arrangement, understanding, deal; contract, pact, compact; pledge, promise.
▶ verb *they bargained over the contract* **haggle,** negotiate, discuss terms, hold talks, deal, barter, dicker; formal treat.
– PHRASES **bargain for/on** *a whole new roof is more than we bargained for* **expect,** anticipate, be prepared for, allow for, plan for, reckon with, take into account, take into consideration, contemplate, imagine, envisage, foresee, predict; count on, rely on, depend on, bank on, plan on, reckon on, figure on. **in(to) the bargain** *we went to pick out one puppy and came home with two more in the bargain* **also,** as well, in addition, additionally, besides, on top of that, over and above that, to boot, for good measure.

barge ▶ noun *a barge carrying lumber and dry goods* lighter, canal boat, wherry, scow.
▶ verb *he* ***barged into us*** **push,** shove, force, elbow, shoulder, jostle, bulldoze, muscle.
– PHRASES **barge in** *sorry for barging in* **burst in,** break in, butt in, cut in, interrupt, intrude, encroach; informal horn in.

bark[1] ▶ noun *the bark of a dog* **woof,** yap, yelp, bay.
▶ verb 1 *the collie barked* **woof,** yap, yelp, bay.
2 *"Get out!" he barked* **say brusquely,** say abruptly, say angrily, snap; shout, bawl, cry, yell, roar, bellow, thunder; informal holler.
ANTONYMS whisper.

bark[2] ▶ noun *the bark of a tree* **rind,** skin, peel, covering; integument; cork; technical cortex.

barn ▶ noun *the loft in the barn* **outbuilding,** shed, cowshed, shelter; stable, stall, outhouse; archaic grange, garner.

baron ▶ noun 1 *she married a baron* **lord,** noble, nobleman, aristocrat, peer.
2 *a steel baron* **magnate,** tycoon, mogul, captain of industry, nabob, mandarin.

barracks ▶ plural noun *confined to the barracks* **garrison,** camp, encampment, depot, billet, quarters, fort, cantonment.

barrage ▶ noun 1 *an artillery barrage* **bombardment,** cannonade; gunfire, shelling; salvo, volley, fusillade; historical broadside.
2 *a barrage of criticism* **deluge,** stream, storm, torrent, onslaught, flood, shower, spate, tide, avalanche, hail, blaze; abundance, mass, profusion.

barrel ▶ noun *oak barrels* **cask,** keg, butt, vat, tun, drum, hogshead, kilderkin, barrique, pipe; historical firkin.
▶ verb *barreling down the road* **charge,** plow, stampede, rush, go headlong; zoom.

barren ▶ adjective 1 *barren land* **unproductive,** infertile, unfruitful, sterile, arid, desert. See note at **NAKED**.
ANTONYMS fertile.
2 archaic *a barren woman* **infertile,** sterile, childless; technical infecund.
ANTONYMS fertile.
3 *a barren exchange of courtesies* **pointless,** futile, worthless, profitless, valueless, unrewarding, purposeless, useless, vain, aimless, hollow, empty, vacuous, vapid.
ANTONYMS fruitful.

barricade ▶ noun *a barricade across the street* **barrier,** roadblock, blockade; obstacle, obstruction.
▶ verb *they barricaded the building* **seal (up),** close up, block off, shut off/up; defend, protect, fortify.

barrier ▶ noun 1 *the barrier across the entrance* **fence,** railing, barricade, hurdle, bar, blockade, roadblock.
2 *a barrier to international trade* **obstacle,** obstruction, hurdle, stumbling block, bar, block, impediment, hindrance, curb.

barter ▶ verb 1 *they bartered grain for salt* **trade,** swap, exchange, sell.
2 *you can barter for souvenirs* **haggle,** bargain,

negotiate, discuss terms, deal, dicker; formal treat.

base[1] ▶ noun 1 *the base of the tower* **foundation,** bottom, foot, support, stand, pedestal, plinth.
ANTONYMS top.
2 *the system uses existing technology as its base* **basis,** foundation, bedrock, starting point, source, origin, root(s), core, key component, heart, backbone.
3 *the troops returned to their base* **headquarters,** camp, site, station, settlement, post, center, starting point.
▶ verb 1 *he based his idea on a movie* **found,** build, construct, form, ground, root; use as a basis; (**be based on**) derive from, spring from, stem from, originate in, have its origin in, issue from.
2 *the company was based in Quebec* **locate,** situate, position, install, station, site, establish; garrison.

base[2] ▶ adjective *base motives* **sordid,** ignoble, low, low-minded, mean, immoral, improper, unseemly, unscrupulous, unprincipled, dishonest, dishonorable, shameful, bad, wrong, evil, wicked, iniquitous, sinful.
ANTONYMS noble.

baseless ▶ adjective *baseless accusations* **groundless,** unfounded, ill-founded, without foundation; unsubstantiated, unproven, unsupported, uncorroborated, unconfirmed, unverified, unattested; unjustified, unwarranted; speculative, conjectural; unsound, unreliable, spurious, specious, trumped up, fabricated, untrue.
ANTONYMS valid.

bashful ▶ adjective *the superhero's alter ego is a sweetly bashful science dork* **shy,** reserved, diffident, inhibited, retiring, reticent, reluctant, shrinking; hesitant, timid, apprehensive, nervous, wary, demure, coy, blushing.
ANTONYMS bold, confident.

basic ▶ adjective 1 *basic human rights* **fundamental,** essential, primary, principal, cardinal, elementary, elemental, quintessential, intrinsic, central, pivotal, critical, key, focal; vital, necessary, indispensable.
ANTONYMS secondary, unimportant.
2 *basic cooking facilities* **plain,** simple, unsophisticated, straightforward, adequate; unadorned, undecorated, unornamented, without frills; spartan, stark, severe, austere, limited, meager, rudimentary, patchy, sketchy, minimal; unfussy, homely, homespun, meat-and-potatoes, bread-and-butter; rough, rough and ready, crude, makeshift.
ANTONYMS elaborate.

basically ▶ adverb *he's basically a well-behaved dog* **fundamentally,** essentially, in essence; firstly, first of all, first and foremost, primarily; at heart, at bottom, au fond; principally, chiefly, above all, most of all, mostly, mainly, on the whole, by and large, substantially; intrinsically, inherently; informal at the end of the day, when all is said and done.

basics ▶ plural noun *this woodworking class is recommended for those who already know the basics* **fundamentals,** essentials, rudiments, (first) principles, foundations, preliminaries, groundwork; essence, basis, core; informal nitty-gritty, brass tacks, nuts and bolts, meat and potatoes, bread and butter, ABCs.

basin ▶ noun 1 *she poured water into the basin* **bowl,** dish, pan; sink, washtub.
2 *a basin among low hills* **valley,** hollow, dip, depression.

basis ▶ noun 1 *the basis of his method* **foundation,** support, base; reasoning, rationale, defense; reason, grounds, justification, motivation.
2 *the basis of discussion* **starting point,** base, point of departure, beginning, premise, fundamental point/principle, principal constituent, main ingredient, cornerstone, core, heart, thrust, essence, kernel, nub.
3 *on a part-time basis* **footing,** condition, status, position; arrangement, system, method.

bask ▶ verb 1 *I basked in the sun* **laze,** lie, lounge, relax, sprawl, loll, wallow; sunbathe, sun oneself.
2 *she's **basking in** all the glory* **revel in,** delight in, luxuriate in, wallow in, take pleasure in, rejoice in, glory in, indulge oneself in; enjoy, relish, savor, lap up.

basket ▶ noun *baskets decorated with ribbons* hamper, creel, pannier, bushel; wicker basket.

bass ▶ adjective *his beautiful bass voice* **low,** deep, low-pitched, resonant, sonorous, rumbling, booming, resounding; baritone.
ANTONYMS high.

bastard ▶ noun 1 archaic *he had fathered a bastard* **illegitimate child,** child born out of wedlock; dated love child, by-blow; natural child/son/daughter.
2 informal *he's a real bastard* **scoundrel,** villain, rogue, rascal, weasel, snake, snake in the grass, miscreant, good-for-nothing, reprobate; informal lowlife, creep, nogoodnik, scamp, scalawag, jerk, beast, rat, ratfink, louse, swine, dog, skunk, heel; slimeball, son of a bitch, SOB, scumbag, scumbucket, scuzzball, scuzzbag, dirtbag, sleazeball, sleazebag; dated hound, cad; archaic blackguard, knave, varlet, whoreson.
▶ adjective 1 archaic *a bastard child* **illegitimate,** born out of wedlock; dated natural.
2 *a bastard socialism* **adulterated,** alloyed, impure, inferior; hybrid, mongrel, patchwork.

bastardize ▶ verb *it is unthinkable that I would bastardize my values* **adulterate,** corrupt, contaminate, weaken, dilute, taint, pollute, debase, distort.

bastion ▶ noun 1 *fortified with ditches and bastions* **projection,** outwork, breastwork, barbican; Architecture bartizan.
2 *a bastion of respectability* **stronghold,** bulwark, defender, support, supporter, guard, protection, protector, defense, prop, mainstay.

batch ▶ noun *when can we expect the next batch of invoices?* **group,** quantity, lot, bunch, mass, cluster, raft, set, collection, bundle, pack; consignment, shipment.

bath ▶ noun 1 *he lay soaking in the bath* **bathtub,** tub, hot tub, whirlpool, sauna, steam bath, Turkish bath; trademark Jacuzzi.
2 *give it a bath* **wash,** soak, cleansing, soaking, scrubbing, ablutions; dip; shower.

bathe ▶ verb 1 *she bathed and dressed* **have/take**

a **bath,** wash; shower.
2 *I bathed in the local swimming pool* **swim,** go swimming, take a dip.
3 *they bathed his wounds* **clean,** cleanse, wash, rinse, wet, soak, immerse.
4 *the room was bathed in light* **suffuse,** permeate, pervade, envelop, flood, cover, wash, fill; literary mantle.

bathing suit ▶ **noun** *bring a bathing suit and a towel* **swimsuit;** bikini, monokini, maillot, swimming trunks, swim trunks; swimwear.

bathos ▶ **noun** *the story ends with such a stroke of bathos, you're not sure whether to laugh or scream* **anticlimax,** letdown, disappointment, disillusionment; absurdity; informal comedown.

bathroom ▶ **noun** *excuse me, where's the bathroom?* **washroom,** toilet, ladies'/men's room, restroom, lavatory, powder room, comfort station; urinal; informal facilities; little girls'/boys' room, can, john; Brit. water closet; Brit. informal WC, loo, ladies'/gents'; Military latrine; Nautical head; dated commode, privy, outhouse.

baton ▶ **noun 1** *the conductor's baton* **stick,** rod, staff, wand.
2 *police batons* **truncheon,** club, billy club, cudgel, bludgeon, stick, nightstick, blackjack, mace; Irish shillelagh.

battalion ▶ **noun 1** *an infantry battalion* regiment, brigade, force, division, squadron, squad, company, section, detachment, contingent, legion, corps, cohort.
2 *a battalion of supporters* See CROWD (sense 1 of the noun).

batten ▶ **noun** *two boards joined with battens* **bar,** bolt, rail, shaft; board, strip.
▶ **verb** *Stephen was **battening down** the shutters* **fasten,** fix, secure, clamp (down), lash, make fast, nail (down), seal.

batter ▶ **verb** *they took turns battering the effigy* **pummel,** pound, hit repeatedly, buffet, thrash, beat up, clobber, trounce, rain blows on; informal knock around/about, beat the living daylights out of, give someone a good hiding, lay into, lace into, do over, rough up.

battered ▶ **adjective** *a battered boat drifted to shore* **damaged,** shabby, run-down, worn out, beat-up, falling to pieces, falling apart, dilapidated, rickety, ramshackle, crumbling, the worse for wear, on its last legs; **abused.**

battery ▶ **noun 1** *insert fresh batteries* **storage cell,** cell.
2 *a gun battery* **emplacement,** artillery unit; cannonry, ordnance.
3 *a battery of equipment* **array,** series, set, bank, group, row, line, lineup, collection.
4 *a battery of tests* **series,** sequence, cycle, string, succession.
5 *assault and battery* **violence,** assault, mugging.

battle ▶ **noun 1** *he was killed in the battle* **fight,** armed conflict, clash, struggle, skirmish, engagement, fray, duel; war, campaign, crusade; fighting, warfare, combat, action, hostilities; informal scrap, dogfight, shoot-out; brawl.
2 *a battle at the office* **conflict,** clash, contest, competition, struggle, turf war; disagreement, argument, altercation, dispute, controversy, tug-of-war.
▶ **verb 1** *he has been battling cancer* **fight,** combat, contend with; resist, withstand, stand up to, confront; war with, feud with; struggle with, strive against.
2 *Mark battled his way to the podium* **force,** push, elbow, shoulder, fight; struggle, labor.

battle-ax ▶ **noun 1** *a severe blow from a battle-ax* **poleax,** ax, pike, halberd, tomahawk.
2 informal *she's a real battle-ax* See HARRIDAN.

battle cry ▶ **noun 1** *the army's battle cry* **war cry,** war whoop, rallying call/cry; rebel yell.
2 *the battle cry of the feminist movement* **slogan,** motto, watchword, catchphrase, mantra.

battlefield ▶ **noun** *what were Vietnam battlefields then are now tourist sites* **battleground,** field of battle, field of operations, combat zone, theater of war, arena of war, front.

battlement ▶ **noun** *the battlements were abandoned* **castellation,** crenellation, parapet, rampart, balustrade, bulwark, wall, bastion, fortification.

batty ▶ **adjective** informal See MAD (sense 1).

bauble ▶ **noun** *gift-shop baubles* **trinket,** knickknack, ornament, frippery, gewgaw, gimcrack, bibelot, kickshaw, tchotchke.

bawdy ▶ **adjective** *bawdy jokes* **ribald,** indecent, risqué, racy, rude, spicy, sexy, suggestive, titillating, naughty, improper, indelicate, indecorous, off-color, earthy, barnyard, broad, locker-room, Rabelaisian; pornographic, obscene, vulgar, crude, coarse, lewd, dirty, filthy, smutty, unseemly, salacious, prurient, lascivious, licentious, X-rated, blue, raunchy; euphemistic adult.
ANTONYMS clean, innocent.

bawl ▶ **verb 1** *"Come on!" he bawled* **shout,** yell, roar, bellow, screech, scream, shriek, howl, whoop, bark, trumpet, thunder; informal yammer, holler.
ANTONYMS whisper.
2 *the children continued to bawl* **cry,** sob, weep, shed tears, wail, whine, howl, squall; rare ululate.
– PHRASES **bawl someone out** informal See REPRIMAND.

bay[1] ▶ **noun** *ships were anchored in the bay* **cove,** inlet, estuary, indentation, gulf, bight, basin, fjord, arm; natural harbor, anchorage.

bay[2] ▶ **noun** *there was a bay set into the wall* **alcove,** recess, niche, nook, oriel, opening, hollow, cavity, inglenook; compartment.

bay[3] ▶ **verb** *coyotes baying at the moon* **howl,** bark, yelp, yap, cry, bellow, roar.
– PHRASES **at bay** *the smoke did little to keep the mosquitoes at bay* **at a distance,** away, off, at arm's length.

bayonet ▶ **noun** *a man armed with a bayonet* sword, knife, blade, spear, lance, pike, javelin.

bazaar ▶ **noun 1** *a Turkish bazaar* **market,** marketplace, mart, exchange, souk.
2 *the church bazaar* **rummage sale,** garage sale, yard sale; fundraiser, charity event; flea market, swap meet; fair, carnival.

be ▶ verb **1** *there was once a king* **exist,** have being, have existence; live, be alive, have life, breathe, draw breath, be extant.
2 *the trial is tomorrow at half past one* **occur,** happen, take place, come about, arise, crop up, transpire, fall, materialize, ensue; literary come to pass, befall, betide.
3 *the bed is over there* **be situated,** be located, be found, be present, be set, be positioned, be placed, be installed.
4 *it has been like this for hours* **remain,** stay, last, continue, survive, endure, persist, prevail; wait, linger, hold on, hang on.

beach ▶ noun *a sandy beach* **seaside,** seashore, shore, coast, waterfront, lakeshore, coastline, coastal region, littoral, seaboard, foreshore, water's edge; sands; literary strand.
▶ verb *they beached the boat* **land,** ground, strand, run aground, run ashore.

beached ▶ adjective *rescuing the beached whale* **stranded,** grounded, aground, ashore, marooned, high and dry, stuck, washed up, washed ashore.

beacon ▶ noun *the beacon penetrated the fog* **lighthouse**; signal light, signal fire, danger signal, bonfire, warning light, warning fire; spotlight, searchlight.

bead ▶ noun **1** *a string of beads* **ball,** pellet, pill, globule, sphere, spheroid, oval, ovoid, orb, round; (**beads**) necklace, rosary, chaplet.
2 *beads of sweat* **droplet,** drop, blob, dot, dewdrop, teardrop.
– PHRASES **draw/get a bead on** *I drew a bead on the figure in the attic window* **aim at,** fix on, focus on, zero in on, sight.

beak ▶ noun *a bird's beak* **bill,** nib, mandible.

beam ▶ noun **1** *an oak beam* **joist,** lintel, rafter, purlin; spar, girder, balk, timber, two-by-four, plank; support, strut; scantling, transom, stringer, collar beam, I-beam.
2 *a beam of light coming from the window* **ray,** shaft, stream, streak, pencil, finger; flash, gleam, glow, glimmer, glint, flare.
3 *the beam on her face* **grin,** smile, happy expression, bright look.
ANTONYMS frown.
▶ verb **1** *the signal is* **beamed out** **broadcast,** transmit, relay, emit, send/put out, disseminate; direct, aim.
2 *the sun* **beamed down** **shine,** radiate, give off light, glare, gleam.
3 *he beamed broadly* **grin,** smile, smirk; informal be all smiles.
ANTONYMS frown.

bear ▶ verb **1** *I come bearing gifts* **carry,** bring, transport, move, convey, take, fetch, deliver, tote, lug.
2 *the bag bore my name* **display,** exhibit, be marked with, show, carry, have.
3 *will it bear his weight?* **support,** carry, hold up, prop up.
4 *they can't bear the cost alone* **sustain,** carry, support, shoulder, absorb, take on.
5 *she bore no grudge* **harbor,** foster, entertain, nurse, nurture, brood over.
6 *such a solution does not bear close scrutiny* **withstand,** stand up to, stand, put up with, take, cope with, handle, sustain, accept.
7 *I can't bear having him around* **endure,** tolerate, put up with, stand, abide, submit to, experience, undergo, go through, countenance, brave, weather, stomach; informal hack, swallow; formal brook; archaic suffer.
8 *she bore a son* **give birth to,** bring forth, deliver, be delivered of, have, produce, spawn, birth; informal drop; literary beget.
9 *a shrub that bears yellow berries* **produce,** yield, give forth, give, grow, provide, supply.
10 *bear left at the junction* **veer,** curve, swerve, fork, diverge, deviate, turn, bend.
– PHRASES **bear oneself** *if you bear yourself like a bum, expect to treated as a bum* **conduct oneself,** carry oneself, acquit oneself, act, behave, perform; formal comport oneself. **bear down on** *we knew that Sherman's men would be bearing down on us by dawn* **advance on,** close in on, move in on, converge on. **bear fruit** *we're always amazed when one of her crazy ideas actually bears fruit* **yield results,** get results, succeed, meet with success, be successful, be effective, be profitable, work, go as planned; informal pay off, come off, pan out, do the trick. **bear something in mind** *the meals are free, but please bear in mind that you are expected to tip the servers* **take into account,** take into consideration, remember, consider, be mindful, mind, mark, heed. **bear on** *I fail to see how Hugh's personal problem bears on our final decision* **be relevant to,** appertain to, pertain to, relate to, have a bearing on, have relevance to, apply to, be pertinent to. **bear something out** *we're hoping you can bear out his statement* **confirm,** corroborate, substantiate, endorse, vindicate, give credence to, support, ratify, warrant, uphold, justify, prove, authenticate, verify. **bear with** *if you'll just bear with us, I'm sure the lights will be back on soon* **be patient with,** show forbearance toward, make allowances for, tolerate, put up with, endure. **bear witness/testimony to** *the majestic windows bear witness to the architect's fascination with natural light* **testify to,** be evidence of, be proof of, attest to, evidence, prove, vouch for; demonstrate, show, establish, indicate, reveal, bespeak.

bearable ▶ adjective *volunteer staff can make a hospital stay bearable* **tolerable,** endurable, supportable, sustainable, sufferable, brookable; acceptable, admissible, manageable.
ANTONYMS intolerable.

beard ▶ noun *a black beard* **facial hair,** whiskers, stubble, five o'clock shadow, bristles; goatee, imperial, Vandyke.
▶ verb *it was up to me to beard the bully* **confront,** face, challenge, brave, come face to face with, meet head on; defy, oppose, stand up against, dare, throw down the gauntlet to.

bearded ▶ adjective *bearded men* **unshaven,** whiskered, whiskery, bewhiskered; stubbly, bristly.
ANTONYMS clean-shaven.

bearer ▶ noun **1** *a lantern-bearer* **carrier,** porter.
2 *the bearer of bad news* **messenger,** agent, conveyor, carrier, emissary.
3 *the bearer of the documents* **holder,** possessor, owner.

bearing ▶ noun **1** *a man of military bearing* **posture,** stance, carriage, gait, deportment; formal comportment.
2 *a regal bearing* **demeanor,** manner, air, aspect, attitude, behavior, mien, style.
3 *this has no bearing on the matter* **relevance,** pertinence, connection, appositeness, germaneness, importance, significance, application.
4 *a bearing of 15°* **direction,** orientation, course, trajectory, heading, tack, path, line, run.
5 *he tormented her beyond bearing* **endurance,** tolerance, toleration.
6 (**bearings**) *I lost my bearings* **orientation,** sense of direction; whereabouts, location, position.

beast ▶ noun **1** *the beasts of the forest* **animal,** creature; informal critter, varmint.
2 *he is a cruel beast* **monster,** brute, savage, barbarian, animal, swine, pig, ogre, fiend, demon, devil.

beastly ▶ adjective **1** *politics is a beastly profession* **awful,** horrible, rotten, nasty, foul, objectionable, unpleasant, disagreeable, offensive, vile, abominable, hateful, detestable, terrible, godawful.
ANTONYMS pleasant.
2 *he was beastly to her* **unkind,** malicious, mean, nasty, unpleasant, unfriendly, spiteful, cruel, vicious, base, foul, malevolent, despicable, contemptible, horrible, horrid, rotten.
ANTONYMS kind.

beat ▶ verb **1** *they were beaten with truncheons* **hit,** strike, batter, thump, bang, hammer, punch, knock, thrash, pound, pummel, slap, smack, rain blows on; assault, attack, abuse; cudgel, club, birch; informal wallop, belt, bash, whack, thwack, clout, clobber, slug, tan, bop, sock, deck, plug, beat the living daylights out of; dated chastise.
2 *the waves **beat upon** the shore* **break on/upon/against,** dash against; lash against, strike, lap (upon), wash against; splash on/upon/against, roll upon; literary plash upon/against, lave against.
3 *the metal is beaten into a die* **hammer,** forge, form, shape, mold, work, stamp, fashion, model.
4 *her heart was still beating* **pulsate,** pulse, palpitate, vibrate, throb; pump, pound, thump, thud, hammer, drum; pitter-patter.
5 *the eagle beat its wings* **flap,** flutter, thresh, thrash, wave, vibrate, oscillate.
6 *beat the cream into the mixture* **whisk,** mix, blend, whip.
7 *she beat a path through the grass* **tread,** tramp, trample, wear, flatten, press down.
8 *the team they need to beat* **defeat,** conquer, win against, get the better of, vanquish, trounce, rout, overpower, overcome, subdue; informal lick, thrash, whip, wipe the floor with, clobber, cream, shellac, skunk.
9 *he beat the record* **surpass,** exceed, better, improve on, go one better than, eclipse, transcend, top, trump, cap.
▶ noun **1** *the song has a good beat* **rhythm,** pulse, meter, time, measure, cadence; stress, accent.
2 *the beat of hooves* **pounding,** banging, thumping, thudding, booming, hammering, battering, crashing.
3 *the beat of her heart* **pulse,** pulsating, vibration, throb, palpitation, reverberation; pounding, thump, thud, hammering, drumming; pitter-patter.
4 *a cop on his beat* **circuit,** round, route, way, path.
▶ adjective informal *phew, I'm beat!* See EXHAUSTED (sense 1).
– PHRASES **beat a (hasty) retreat** See RETREAT (sense 1 of the verb). **beat it** informal See RUN (sense 2 of the verb). **beat someone up** *he just snapped and started beating up his abusive father* **assault,** attack, mug, thrash, do over, work over, rough up, lay into, lace into, sail into, beat the living daylights out of, let someone have it, beat up on, knock around/about.

beaten ▶ adjective **1** *the beaten team* **defeated,** losing, unsuccessful, conquered, bettered, vanquished, trounced, routed, overcome, overwhelmed, overpowered, overthrown, bested, subdued, quashed, crushed, broken, foiled, hapless, luckless; informal licked, thrashed, losingest, clobbered.
ANTONYMS victorious, winning.
2 *a beaten dog* **abused,** battered, maltreated, ill-treated, mistreated, misused, downtrodden; **assaulted,** thumped, whacked, hit, thrashed, pummeled, smacked, drubbed; informal walloped, belted, bashed, clobbered, knocked around/about, roughed up.
3 *gradually stir in the beaten eggs* **whisked,** whipped, stirred, mixed, blended; frothy, foamy.
4 *a beaten path* **trodden,** trampled; well-trodden, much trodden, well-used, much traveled, worn, well-worn.
ANTONYMS untouched.
– PHRASES **off the beaten track/path** *we tried to find a campsite off the beaten track* **out of the way,** isolated, quiet, private, remote, unfrequented, outlying, secluded, hidden, backwoods, in the back of beyond, in the middle of nowhere, in the hinterlands; informal in the sticks.
ANTONYMS busy, popular.

beatific ▶ adjective **1** *a beatific smile* **rapturous,** joyful, ecstatic, seraphic, blissful, serene, happy, beaming.
2 *a beatific vision* **blessed,** exalted, sublime, heavenly, holy, divine, celestial, paradisical, glorious.

beatitude ▶ noun *the everlasting beatitude* **blessedness,** benediction, grace; bliss, ecstasy, exaltation, supreme happiness, divine joy, divine rapture; saintliness, sainthood.

beau ▶ noun dated **1** *Sally and her beau* **boyfriend,** sweetheart, lover, darling, partner, significant other, escort, young man, admirer, suitor; informal main squeeze, boy toy.
2 *an eighteenth-century beau* **dandy,** fop; dated swell, coxcomb, popinjay.

beautiful ▶ adjective *beautiful fashion models | a beautiful crystal vase* **attractive,** pretty, handsome, good-looking, alluring, prepossessing; lovely, charming, delightful, appealing, engaging, winsome; ravishing, gorgeous, stunning, arresting, glamorous, bewitching, beguiling; graceful, elegant,

exquisite, aesthetic, artistic, decorative, magnificent; informal divine, drop-dead gorgeous, easy on the eye, killer, cute, foxy; formal beauteous; archaic comely, fair.
ANTONYMS ugly.

beautify ▶ **verb** *efforts to beautify the town center* **adorn,** embellish, enhance, decorate, ornament, garnish, gild, smarten up, prettify, enrich, glamorize, spruce up, spiff up, deck (out), trick out, grace; informal do up, tart up, pimp.
ANTONYMS spoil.

beauty ▶ **noun 1** *the beauty of the scenery* **attractiveness,** prettiness, good looks, comeliness, allure; loveliness, charm, appeal, eye-appeal, heavenliness; winsomeness, grace, elegance, exquisiteness; splendor, magnificence, grandeur, impressiveness, decorativeness; gorgeousness, glamour; literary beauteousness, pulchritude.
ANTONYMS ugliness.
2 *she is a beauty* **beautiful woman,** belle, vision, Venus, goddess, beauty queen, picture; informal babe, hottie, looker, good looker, beaut, siren, doll, arm candy, lovely, stunner, knockout, bombshell, dish, peach, eyeful, fox.
ANTONYMS hag.
3 *the beauty of this plan* **advantage,** attraction, strength, benefit, boon, blessing, good thing, strong point, virtue, merit, selling point.
ANTONYMS drawback.

becalmed ▶ **adjective** *the boats remained becalmed* **motionless,** still, at a standstill, at a halt, unmoving, stuck.

because ▶ **conjunction** *your photos won because they're the best* **since,** as, in view of the fact that, inasmuch as, owing to the fact that, seeing that/as; informal on account of, cuz; literary for.
ANTONYMS despite.
– PHRASES **because of** *because of her exceptionally high scores, she was able to start at Level 3* **on account of,** as a result of, as a consequence of, owing to, due to; thanks to, by/in virtue of; formal by reason of.

beckon ▶ **verb 1** *the guard beckoned to Benny* **gesture,** signal, wave, gesticulate, motion.
2 *the countryside beckons you* **entice,** invite, tempt, coax, lure, charm, attract, draw, call.

become ▶ **verb 1** *she became rich* **grow,** get, turn, come to be, get to be; literary wax.
2 *he became a tyrant* **turn into,** change into, be transformed into, be converted into.
3 *he became Louisiana's attorney general* **be appointed (as),** be assigned as, be nominated, be elected (as), be made.
4 *the dress becomes her* **suit,** flatter, look good on; set off, show to advantage; informal do something for.
5 *it ill becomes him to preach the gospel during a board meeting* **befit,** suit, behoove.
– PHRASES **become of** *whatever became of the guy who designed your terrace?* **happen to,** be the fate of, be the lot of, overtake; literary befall, betide. See note at HAPPEN.

becoming ▶ **adjective** *that suit's very becoming* **flattering,** attractive, lovely, pretty, handsome, fetching; stylish, elegant, chic, fashionable, tasteful; archaic comely.

bed ▶ **noun 1** *she got into her bed* cot, cradle, crib, berth; brass bed, bunk bed, camp bed, canopy bed, captain's bed, daybed, featherbed; trademark Hide-A-Bed, Murphy bed, sofa bed, spool bed, trundle bed, waterbed, divan, futon, four-poster; informal the sack, the hay.
2 *a flower bed* **patch,** plot, border, strip.
3 *built on a bed of stones* **base,** foundation, support, prop, substructure, substratum.
4 *a river bed* **bottom,** floor, ground.
– PHRASES **go to bed** *time to go to bed* **retire,** call it a day; go to sleep, have/take a nap, get some sleep; informal hit the sack, hit the hay, turn in, go (to) beddy-bye, crash, catch forty winks, get some shut-eye, catch some Zs, beat the sheets, meet the sandman, go to slumberland; literary slumber.

bedeck ▶ **verb** *a church bedecked with flowers* **decorate,** adorn, ornament, embellish, furnish, garnish, trim, deck, grace, enrich, dress up, trick out; swathe, wreathe, festoon; informal do up.

bedevil ▶ **verb** *past mistakes that continue to bedevil her | he accused Congress of allowing "single-interest-group" politics to bedevil U.S. foreign policy* **afflict,** torment, beset, assail, beleaguer, plague, blight, rack, oppress, harry, curse, dog; harass, distress, trouble, worry, torture; frustrate, vex, annoy, irritate, irk.

bedlam ▶ **noun** *there was bedlam in the stadium* **uproar,** pandemonium, commotion, mayhem, confusion, disorder, chaos, anarchy, lawlessness; furor, upheaval, hubbub, hoopla, turmoil, riot, ruckus, rumpus, tumult, hullabaloo.
ANTONYMS calm.

bedraggled ▶ **adjective** *the bedraggled search party* **disheveled,** disordered, untidy, unkempt, tousled, disarranged, in a mess, mussed.
ANTONYMS neat, clean.

bedridden ▶ **adjective** *Jake will be bedridden for weeks* **confined to bed,** sick in bed, laid up, immobilized, flat on one's back.

bedrock ▶ **noun 1** *we're digging till we hit bedrock* **substratum,** substructure, understructure, solid foundation, base, rock base.
2 *the bedrock of our society* **core,** basis, base, foundation, roots, heart, backbone, principle, essence, nitty-gritty; informal nuts and bolts.

beef ▶ **noun 1** *there's plenty of beef on him* **muscle,** brawn, bulk; strength, power.
2 *his beef was about the cost* **complaint,** criticism, objection, cavil, quibble, grievance, grumble, gripe, grouse.
▶ **verb 1** *security was being* ***beefed up*** **toughen up,** strengthen, build up, reinforce, consolidate, augment, improve.
2 *they're constantly beefing about the neighbor's dog* **complain,** grumble, whine, carp, bitch, gripe, bellyache.

beefy ▶ **adjective** informal *the beefy right fielder* **muscular,** brawny, hefty, burly, hulking, strapping, well-built, hard-bodied, solid, stalwart, strong, powerful, heavy, robust, sturdy; informal hunky, husky.
ANTONYMS puny.

beer ▶ **noun** *pizza and beer* **ale,** brew; informal brewski, suds, pint.

befall ▶ verb literary **1** *the same fate befell him* **happen to,** overtake, come upon, be visited on.
2 *tell us what befell* **happen,** occur, take place, come about, transpire, materialize; ensue, follow, result; informal go down; literary come to pass, betide.

befitting ▶ preposition *this is an automobile befitting your fine taste* **in keeping with,** as befits, appropriate to, fit for, suitable for, suited to, proper to, right for, compatible with, consistent with, in character with; archaic meet for.

before ▶ preposition **1** *he dressed up before going out* **prior to,** previous to, earlier than, preparatory to, in preparation for, preliminary to, in anticipation of, in expectation of; in advance of, ahead of, leading up to, on the eve of; rare anterior to.
ANTONYMS after.
2 *he appeared before the judge* **in front of,** in the presence of, in the sight of.
3 *death before dishonor* **in preference to,** rather than, sooner than.
▶ adverb *she has ridden before* **previously,** before now/then, until now/then, up to now/then; earlier, formerly, hitherto, in the past, in days gone by; formal heretofore.

beforehand ▶ adverb *bring any notes you compiled beforehand* **in advance,** ahead of time, in readiness; before, before now/then, earlier (on), previously, already, sooner.
ANTONYMS afterward.

befriend ▶ verb *a charming story in which the toys befriend one another* **make friends with,** make a friend of; look after, keep an eye on; be of service to, lend a helping hand to, help, protect; side with, stand by, encourage.

befuddled ▶ adjective *befuddled from the anesthesia* **confused,** muddled, addled, bewildered, disorientated, fazed, perplexed, dazed, dizzy, stupefied, groggy, muzzy, foggy, fuddled, fuzzy, dopey, woozy, befogged, mixed up, discombobulated.
ANTONYMS clear.

beg ▶ verb **1** *he begged on the streets* **panhandle,** ask for money, seek charity, seek alms; informal sponge, cadge, scrounge, bum, mooch.
2 *we begged for mercy* **ask for,** request, plead for, appeal for, call for, sue for, solicit, seek, press for.
3 *he begged her not to go* **implore,** entreat, plead with, appeal to, supplicate, pray to, importune; ask, request, call on, petition; literary beseech.

CHOOSE THE RIGHT WORD

beg, entreat, plead, beseech, implore, importune, petition, solicit

How badly do you want something? You can **beg** for it, which implies a humble and earnest approach. If you **entreat**, you're trying to get what you want by ingratiating yourself (*she entreated her mother to help her prepare for the exam*). To **plead** involves more urgency (*he pleaded with the judge to spare his life*) and is usually associated with the legal system (*she was advised to plead guilty*). **Beseech** also suggests urgency, as well as an emotional appeal (*he beseeched her to tell the truth*). **Implore** is still stronger, suggesting desperation or great distress (*the look in his mother's eyes implored him to have mercy*). If you really want to get your way, you can **importune**, which means to *beg* not only urgently but persistently and to risk making a pest of yourself (*he importuned her daily to accept his invitation*). **Petition** suggests an appeal to authority (*to petition the government to repeal an unjust law*), while **solicit** suggests petitioning in a courteous, formal way (*soliciting financial support for the school carnival*).

beget ▶ verb **1** literary *he begat a son* **father,** sire, have, bring into the world, give life to, bring into being, spawn.
2 *violence begets violence* **cause,** give rise to, lead to, result in, bring about, create, produce, generate, engender, spawn, occasion, bring on, precipitate, prompt, provoke, kindle, trigger, spark off, touch off, stir up, whip up, induce, inspire, promote; literary enkindle.

beggar ▶ noun *he never turned any beggar from his door* **panhandler,** mendicant, tramp, vagrant, vagabond, hobo; informal scrounger, sponger, cadger, freeloader, bum, moocher, mooch.

begin ▶ verb **1** *we began work* **start,** commence, set about, go about, embark on, launch into, get down to, take up; initiate, set in motion, institute, inaugurate, get ahead with; informal get cracking on, get going on.
ANTONYMS cease.
2 *he began by saying hello* **open,** lead off, get underway, get going, get off the ground, start, start off, go ahead, commence; informal start the ball rolling, kick off, get the show on the road, fire away, take the plunge.
ANTONYMS finish, conclude.
3 *when did the illness begin?* **appear,** arise, become apparent, make an appearance, spring up, crop up, turn up, come into existence, come into being, originate, start, commence, develop; literary come to pass.
ANTONYMS disappear.

beginner ▶ noun *a yoga video for beginners* **novice,** newcomer, fledgling, neophyte, starter, learner, student, apprentice, trainee; recruit, raw recruit, initiate, freshman; tenderfoot, tyro; postulant, novitiate; informal rookie, newbie, cub, greenhorn, new kid (on the block). See note at NOVICE.
ANTONYMS expert, veteran.

beginning ▶ noun **1** *the beginning of socialism* **dawn,** birth, inception, conception, origination, genesis, emergence, rise, start, commencement, starting point, launch, onset, outset; day one; informal kickoff
ANTONYMS end.
2 *the beginning of the article* **opening,** introduction, start, first part, preamble, opening statement.
ANTONYMS end, conclusion.

3 (**beginnings**) *the therapy has its beginnings in China* **origin,** source, roots, starting point, birthplace, cradle, spring, fountainhead; genesis, creation; literary fount, well spring.

begrudge ▶ **verb 1** *she begrudged Brian his affluence* **envy,** resent, grudge.
2 *don't begrudge the cost* **resent,** feel aggrieved about, feel bitter about, be annoyed about, be resentful of, grudge, mind, object to, take exception to, regret.

beguile ▶ **verb 1** *she was beguiled by his beauty* **charm,** attract, enchant, entrance, win over, woo, captivate, bewitch, spellbind, dazzle, hypnotize, mesmerize, seduce. See note at **TEMPT**.
ANTONYMS repel.
2 *the program has been beguiling children for years* **entertain,** amuse, delight, please, occupy, absorb, engage, distract, divert, fascinate, enthrall, engross.
ANTONYMS bore.

behalf ▶ **noun**
– PHRASES **on behalf of/on someone's behalf**
1 *I am writing on behalf of my client* **as a representative of,** as a spokesperson for, for, in the name of, in place of, on the authority of, at the behest of. **2** *a campaign on behalf of recycling* **in the interests of,** in support of, for, for the benefit of, for the good of, for the sake of.

behave ▶ **verb 1** *she behaved badly* **conduct oneself,** act, acquit oneself, bear oneself; formal comport oneself; archaic deport oneself.
2 *the children behaved themselves* **act correctly,** act properly, conduct oneself well, be well-behaved, be good; be polite, show good manners, mind one's manners.
ANTONYMS misbehave.

behavior ▶ **noun 1** *his behavior was inexcusable* **conduct,** deportment, bearing, actions, doings; manners, ways; formal comportment.
2 *the behavior of these organisms* **functioning,** action, performance, operation, working, reaction, response.

behead ▶ **verb** *dissidents were beheaded* **decapitate,** cut/chop/lop someone's head off, guillotine.

behest ▶ **noun** *the plan is being pushed through the legislature at the behest of a few members* **instruction,** requirement, demand, insistence, bidding, request, wish, desire, will; command, injunction, order, decree, ruling, directive, mandate; informal say-so; rare rescript.

behind ▶ **preposition 1** *he hid behind a tree* **at the back/rear of,** beyond, on the far/other side of, in back of.
ANTONYMS in front of.
2 *a guard ran behind him* **after,** following, at the back/rear of, (hard) on the heels of, in the wake of.
ANTONYMS ahead of.
3 *he was behind the bombings* **responsible for,** at the bottom of, the cause of, the source of, the organizer of; to blame for, culpable of, guilty of.
4 *we're behind you all the way* **supporting,** backing, for, on the side of, in agreement with; financing; informal rooting for.
▶ **adverb 1** *a man followed behind* **after,** afterward, at the back/end, in the rear.
ANTONYMS in front, ahead.
2 *I looked behind* **over one's shoulder,** to/toward the back, to/toward the rear, backward.
ANTONYMS ahead.
3 *we're behind, so don't stop* **late,** running late, behind schedule, behindhand, not on time, behind time.
4 *he was behind with his subscription* **in arrears,** overdue; late, unpunctual, behindhand.
▶ **noun** informal *he sat on his behind* See **BUTTOCKS**.
– PHRASES **put something behind one** *they put last night's loss to the Orioles behind them* **consign to the past,** put down to experience, regard as water under the bridge, forget about, ignore.

behold ▶ **verb** literary *no eyes beheld them* **see,** observe, view, look at, watch, survey, witness, gaze at/upon, regard, contemplate, inspect, eye; catch sight of, glimpse, spot, spy, notice; informal clap eyes on, have/take a gander at, get a load of, eyeball; literary espy, descry.
▶ **exclamation** archaic *behold, the prince returns!* **look,** see; archaic lo.

beholden ▶ **adjective** *he is beholden to no one in his determination to defend Malaysia's rights* **indebted,** in someone's debt, obligated, under an obligation; grateful, owing a debt of gratitude.

behoove ▶ **verb 1** *it behooves me to go* **be incumbent on,** be obligatory for, be required of, be expected of, be appropriate for.
2 *it ill behooves them to comment* **befit,** become, suit.

beige ▶ **adjective** *beige curtains* **fawn,** pale brown, buff, sand, sandy, oatmeal, khaki, biscuit, coffee, coffee-colored, café au lait, camel, ecru.

being ▶ **noun 1** *she is warmed by his very being* **existence,** living, life, reality, actuality.
2 *God is alive in the being of man* **soul,** spirit, nature, essence, inner being, inner self, psyche; heart, bosom, breast; Philosophy quiddity, pneuma.
3 *an enlightened being* **creature,** life form, living entity, living thing, soul, living soul, individual, person, human being, human.

belabor ▶ **verb** *don't belabor the point* **overelaborate,** labor, dwell on, harp on about, hammer away at; overdo, overplay, overdramatize, make too much of, place too much emphasis on; informal beat to death, drag out, make a big thing of, blow out of proportion.
ANTONYMS understate.

belated ▶ **adjective** *a belated anniversary dinner* **late,** overdue, behindhand, behind time, behind schedule, delayed, tardy, unpunctual.
ANTONYMS early.

belch ▶ **verb 1** *onions make me belch* **burp**.
2 *the furnace belched flames* **emit,** give off, give out, pour out, discharge, disgorge, spew out, spit out, vomit, gush, cough up.
▶ **noun** *he gave a loud belch* **burp**; formal eructation.

beleaguered ▶ **adjective 1** *the beleaguered garrison* **besieged,** under siege, blockaded, surrounded, encircled, beset, hemmed in, under attack.

2 *a beleaguered government* **hard-pressed,** troubled, in difficulties, under pressure, under stress, with one's back to the wall, in a tight corner, in a tight spot, up against it; beset, assailed.

belie ▶ verb *his eyes belied his words* **contradict,** be at odds with, call into question, show/prove to be false, disprove, debunk, discredit, controvert, negate; formal confute.
ANTONYMS testify to, reveal.

belief ▶ noun **1** *it's my belief that age is irrelevant* **opinion,** view, conviction, judgment, thinking, way of thinking, idea, impression, theory, conclusion, notion. See note at **OPINION**.
2 *belief in God* **faith,** trust, reliance, confidence, credence.
ANTONYMS disbelief, doubt.
3 *traditional beliefs* **ideology,** principle, ethic, tenet, canon; doctrine, teaching, dogma, article of faith, creed, credo.

believable ▶ adjective *contestant number 3 tells the most believable anecdotes | she was completely believable in her role as a federal marshal* **credible,** plausible, likely, tenable, able to hold water, conceivable, imaginable, convincing, creditable, probable, possible, feasible, reasonable, rational, sound, within the bounds of possibility, with a ring of truth.
ANTONYMS inconceivable.

> CHOOSE THE RIGHT WORD
>
> **believable, cogent, convincing, credible, creditable, plausible, valid**
>
> **Believable** is the most general of these terms, used to describe anything we accept as true, even in the absence of absolute proof (*a believable story about why she was late*). **Credible** also means worthy of belief or confidence and is often used interchangeably with *believable,* but it goes one step further: a *credible* excuse is one that is supported by known facts. **Creditable**, often confused with *credible,* at one time meant worthy of belief but nowadays is used to mean respectable or decent, deserving of honor, reputation, or esteem (*leading a creditable life*). Something that is **convincing** is *believable* because it overcomes doubts or opposition (*a convincing performance*), while something that is **plausible** may appear to be convincing or believable on the surface, but may not be so upon closer examination. **Valid** means legally sound, just, or authoritative; a *valid* criticism seldom provokes opposition. **Cogent**, on the other hand, means having the power to convince; a *cogent* argument is believable because of its clear, forceful, or incisive presentation.

believe ▶ verb **1** *I don't believe you* **be convinced by,** trust, have confidence in, consider honest, consider truthful.
2 *do you believe that story?* **regard as true,** accept, be convinced by, give credence to, credit, trust, put confidence in; informal swallow, buy, go for.
3 *I believe he worked for you* **think,** be of the opinion that, have an idea that, imagine, suspect, suppose, assume, presume, take it, conjecture, surmise, conclude, deduce, understand, be given to understand, gather, fancy, guess, dare say; informal reckon, figure; archaic ween.
ANTONYMS doubt.
– PHRASES **believe in 1** *she believed in God* **be convinced of the existence of,** be sure of the existence of. **2** *I believe in lots of exercise* **have faith in,** pin one's faith on, trust in, have every confidence in, cling to, set (great) store by, value, be convinced by, be persuaded by; subscribe to, approve of; informal swear by.

believer ▶ noun *a cause with few believers* **devotee,** adherent, disciple, follower, supporter.
ANTONYMS infidel, skeptic.

belittle ▶ verb *Mr. Reese had been warned on two previous occasions to stop belittling his students* **disparage,** denigrate, run down, deprecate, depreciate, downgrade, play down, trivialize, minimize, make light of, pooh-pooh, treat lightly, scoff at, sneer at; formal derogate; rare misprize.
ANTONYMS praise, magnify.

belligerent ▶ adjective **1** *a belligerent attitude* **hostile,** aggressive, threatening, antagonistic, warlike, warmongering, hawkish, pugnacious, bellicose, truculent, confrontational, contentious, militant, combative; informal spoiling for a fight, trigger-happy, scrappy. See note at **HOSTILE**.
ANTONYMS peaceable, friendly.
2 *belligerent nations* **warring,** at war, combatant, fighting, battling.
ANTONYMS peaceful, neutral.

bellow ▶ verb *she bellowed in his ear* **roar,** shout, bawl, thunder, trumpet, boom, bark, yell, shriek, howl, scream; raise one's voice; informal holler.
ANTONYMS whisper.
▶ noun *a bellow of pain* **roar,** shout, bawl, bark, yell, yelp, shriek, howl, scream.
ANTONYMS whisper.

belly ▶ noun *he scratched his belly* **stomach,** abdomen, paunch, middle, midriff, girth; informal tummy, tum, breadbasket, gut, guts, insides, pot, potbelly, beer belly, spare tire.
▶ verb *her skirt bellied out* **billow (out),** bulge (out), balloon (out), bag (out); distend.
ANTONYMS sag, flap.

belong ▶ verb **1** *the house belongs to his mother* **be owned by,** be the property of, be the possession of, be held by, be in the hands of.
2 *I belong to a book club* **be a member of,** be in, be affiliated to/with, be allied to, be associated with, be linked to, be an adherent of.
3 *the atlas belongs with the reference books* **be classed,** be classified, be categorized, be included, have a place, be located, be situated, be found, lie.
4 *she doesn't belong here* **fit in,** be suited to,

have a rightful place, have a home; informal go, click.

belongings ▶ plural noun *she could fit all her belongings in one bag* **possessions,** effects, worldly goods, assets, chattels, property; informal gear, tackle, kit, things, stuff.

beloved ▶ adjective *her beloved brother* **darling,** dear, dearest, precious, adored, much loved, cherished, treasured, prized, highly regarded, admired, esteemed, worshiped, revered, venerated, idolized.
ANTONYMS hated.
▶ noun *he watched his beloved* **sweetheart,** love, darling, dearest, lover, girlfriend, boyfriend, young lady, young man, beau, lady friend; informal steady, main squeeze, swain; archaic paramour, doxy.

below ▶ preposition **1** *the water rushed below them* **beneath,** under, underneath, further down than, lower than.
ANTONYMS above, over.
2 *the result is below average* **less than,** lower than, under, not as much as, smaller than.
ANTONYMS above, more than.
3 *a captain is below a major* **lower than,** under, inferior to, subordinate to, subservient to.
ANTONYMS above.
▶ adverb **1** *I could see what was happening below* **further down,** lower down, in a lower position, underneath, beneath.
2 *read the statements below* **underneath,** following, further on, at a later point.

belt ▶ noun **1** *the belt of her coat* **sash,** girdle, strap, cummerbund, band; literary cincture; historical baldric.
2 *farmers in the cotton belt* **region,** area, district, zone, sector, territory; tract, strip, stretch.
▶ verb **1** *she belted them in* **fasten,** tie, bind; literary gird.
2 informal *a guy belted him in the face* **hit,** strike, smack, slap, bang, beat, punch, thump; informal clout, bash, whack, thwack, wallop, sock, clobber, bop, larrup, slug; archaic smite.
– PHRASES **below the belt** *bringing up Dana's past to the boss was below the belt* **unfair,** unjust, unacceptable, inequitable; unethical, unprincipled, immoral, unscrupulous, unsporting, sneaky, dishonorable, dishonest, underhanded; informal lowdown, dirty.

bemoan ▶ verb *it does no good to bemoan the loss of that job* **lament,** bewail, mourn, grieve over, sorrow over, regret, cry over; deplore, complain about; archaic plain over. See note at MOURN.
ANTONYMS rejoice at, applaud.

bemused ▶ adjective *bemused expressions on their faces* **bewildered,** confused, puzzled, perplexed, baffled, mystified, nonplussed, muddled, befuddled, dumbfounded, at sea, at a loss, taken aback, disoriented, disconcerted; informal flummoxed, bamboozled, clueless, fazed, discombobulated.

bench ▶ noun **1** *he sat on a bench* **pew,** stall, settle, seat; bleacher.
2 *a laboratory bench* **workbench,** work table, worktop, work surface, counter.
3 *the bench heard the evidence* **judges,** magistrates, judiciary; court.
▶ verb *the coach benched him for two games* **sideline,** sit out, cut.

benchmark ▶ noun *the settlement became the benchmark for all future negotiations* **standard,** point of reference, gauge, guide, guideline, guiding principle, norm, touchstone, yardstick, barometer, indicator, measure, model, exemplar, pattern, criterion, specification, convention.

bend ▶ verb **1** *the frames can be bent to fit your face* **curve,** angle, hook, bow, arch, flex, crook, hump, warp, contort, distort, deform.
ANTONYMS straighten.
2 *the highway bends to the left* **turn,** curve, incline, swing, veer, deviate, diverge, fork, change course, curl, loop.
3 *he bent down to tie his shoe* **stoop,** bow, crouch, hunch, lean down/over.
ANTONYMS straighten up.
4 *they want to bend me to their will* **mold,** shape, manipulate, direct, force, press, influence, incline, sway.
▶ noun *he came to a bend in the road* **curve,** turn, corner, jog, kink, dogleg, oxbow, zigzag, angle, arc, crescent, twist, crook, deviation, deflection, loop, hairpin turn, hairpin.
– PHRASES **bend over backwards** informal *we've bent over backwards to give you a second chance* **try one's hardest,** do one's best, do one's utmost, do all one can, give one's all, make every effort; informal do one's damnedest, go all out, pull out all the stops, bust a gut, move heaven and earth.

beneath ▶ preposition **1** *we sat beneath the trees* **under,** underneath, below, at the foot of, at the bottom of; lower than.
ANTONYMS above.
2 *made to feel beneath them* **inferior to,** below, not so important as, lower in status than, subordinate to, subservient to.
ANTONYMS above.
3 *such an attitude was beneath her* **unworthy of,** unbecoming to, degrading to, below.
ANTONYMS above.
▶ adverb *sand with rock beneath* **underneath,** below, further down, lower down.
ANTONYMS above.

benediction ▶ noun **1** *the priest pronounced the benediction* **blessing,** prayer, invocation; grace, benedicite.
2 *filled with heavenly benediction* **blessedness,** beatitude, bliss, grace.

benefactor, benefactress ▶ noun *an anonymous benefactor* **patron,** supporter, backer, sponsor; donor, contributor, subscriber; informal angel.

beneficial ▶ adjective *ladybugs and other species beneficial to the garden | this information has been highly beneficial* **advantageous,** favorable, helpful, useful, of use, of benefit, of assistance, valuable, of value, profitable, rewarding, gainful.
ANTONYMS detrimental, disadvantageous.

beneficiary ▶ noun *her beneficiaries include several godchildren | about three in five Medicare beneficiaries do not have dependable drug coverage* **heir,** heiress, inheritor, legatee; recipient, receiver, payee, donee, assignee; Law devisee, grantee.

benefit ▶ noun **1** *for the benefit of others* **good,** sake, welfare, well-being, advantage, comfort, ease, convenience; help, aid, assistance, service; profit.
ANTONYMS detriment.
2 *the benefits of working for a large firm* **advantage,** reward, merit, boon, blessing, virtue; bonus; value; informal perk; formal perquisite.
ANTONYMS drawback, disadvantage.
3 *have you applied for this benefit?* **social security,** welfare, assistance, employment insurance, unemployment, food stamps; charity, donations, gifts, financial assistance.
4 *we have four tickets for tonight's benefit* **fundraiser,** fundraising event, charity affair, charity event.
▶ verb **1** *the deal benefited them both* **be advantageous to,** be beneficial to, be of advantage to, be to the advantage of, profit, do good to, be of service to, serve, be useful to, be of use to, be helpful to, be of help to, help, aid, assist, be of assistance to; better, improve, strengthen, boost, advance, further.
ANTONYMS damage.
2 *they may **benefit from** the scheme* **profit from,** gain from, reap benefits from, reap reward(s) from, make money from; make the most of, exploit, turn to one's advantage, put to good use, do well out of; informal cash in on, make a killing from.
ANTONYMS suffer.

benevolence ▶ noun *the benevolence of local businesses* **kindness,** kindheartedness, bigheartedness, goodness, goodwill, charity, altruism, humanitarianism, compassion, philanthropy; generosity, magnanimity, munificence, unselfishness, openhandedness, beneficence; literary bounty, bounteousness. See note at MERCY.
ANTONYMS spite, miserliness.

benevolent ▶ adjective **1** *a benevolent patriarch* **kind,** kindly, kindhearted, bighearted, good-natured, good, benign, compassionate, caring, altruistic, humanitarian, philanthropic; generous, magnanimous, munificent, unselfish, openhanded, beneficent; literary bounteous.
ANTONYMS unkind, tightfisted.
2 *a benevolent institution* **charitable,** nonprofit, not-for-profit; formal eleemosynary.

benign ▶ adjective **1** *a benign grandfatherly role* **kindly,** kind, warmhearted, good-natured, friendly, warm, affectionate, agreeable, genial, congenial, cordial, approachable, tenderhearted, gentle, sympathetic, compassionate, caring, well-disposed, benevolent.
ANTONYMS unfriendly, hostile.
2 *a benign climate* **temperate,** mild, gentle, balmy, soft, pleasant, favorable; healthy, wholesome, salubrious.
ANTONYMS harsh, unhealthy, unfavorable.
3 Medicine *a benign tumor* **harmless,** nonmalignant, noncancerous; Medicine benignant.
ANTONYMS malignant.

bent ▶ adjective *the bucket had a bent handle* **twisted,** crooked, warped, contorted, deformed, misshapen, out of shape, irregular; bowed, arched, curved, angled, hooked, kinked; informal pretzeled.
▶ noun *an artistic bent* **inclination,** leaning, tendency; talent, gift, flair, aptitude, facility, skill, capability, capacity; predisposition, disposition, instinct, orientation, predilection, proclivity, propensity.
– PHRASES **bent on** *he's bent on going to law school* **intent on,** determined on, set on, insistent on, resolved on, hell-bent on; committed to, single-minded about, obsessed with, fanatical about, fixated on.

bequeath ▶ verb *I **bequeath** the northern campgrounds **to** the Yellow Birch Fishing Club* **leave to,** leave in one's will to, hand on/down to, will to, make over to, pass on to, entrust to, grant to, transfer to; donate to, give to; endow on, bestow on, confer on; Law demise to, devise to, convey to.

bequest ▶ noun *they received a bequest of more than $300,000* **legacy,** inheritance, endowment, settlement; estate, heritage; bestowal; Law devise; Law dated hereditament.

berate ▶ verb *she berates him so often, he barely hears the words anymore* **scold,** rebuke, reprimand, reproach, reprove, admonish, chide, criticize, upbraid, take to task, read someone the riot act, haul over the coals; castigate; informal tell off, give someone a talking-to, give someone what for, dress down, give someone a dressing-down, give someone a tongue-lashing, rap over the knuckles, bawl out, come down on, tear into, blast; ream out, chew out, zing, take to the woodshed; dated call down, rate; rare reprehend. See note at SCOLD.
ANTONYMS praise.

bereavement ▶ noun *slowly getting over his bereavement* **loss,** deprivation, dispossession, privation; grief, sorrow, sadness, suffering.

bereft ▶ adjective *are you totally **bereft of** common sense?* **deprived of,** robbed of, stripped of, devoid of, bankrupt of; wanting, in need of, lacking, without; informal minus, sans, clean out of.

berserk ▶ adjective *one of the inmates is berserk* **frenzied,** raving, wild, out of control, amok, on the rampage, frantic, crazy, raging, insane, out of one's mind, hysterical, mad, crazed, maniacal, manic; informal bananas, bonkers, nuts, loco, hyper, postal.

berth ▶ noun **1** *a four-berth cabin* **bunk,** bed, cot, couch, hammock.
2 *the vessel left its berth* **mooring,** dock, slip, anchorage; wharf, pier, jetty, quay.
▶ verb *they berthed at a jetty in Ram's Head Bay* **dock,** moor, land, tie up, make fast.
– PHRASES **give someone/something a wide berth** *they learned to give those gang members a wide berth* **avoid,** shun, keep away from, stay away from, steer clear of, keep at arm's length, have nothing to do with; dodge, sidestep, circumvent, skirt around.

beseech ▶ verb literary *we beseech your help in permitting us the right to live in a country where human rights are respected* **implore,** beg, entreat, importune, plead with, appeal to, exhort, call on, supplicate, importune, pray to, ask, request, petition; rare obtest, impetrate, obsecrate. See note at BEG.

beset ▶ verb **1** *he is beset by fears* **plague,** bedevil, assail, beleaguer, afflict, torment, rack, oppress, trouble, worry, harass, dog, harry.
2 *they were beset by enemy forces* **surround,** besiege, hem in, shut in, fence in, box in, encircle. See note at ATTACK.

beside ▶ preposition **1** *Kate walked beside him* **alongside,** by/at the side of, next to, parallel to, abreast of, at someone's elbow; adjacent to, next door to, cheek by jowl with; bordering, abutting, neighboring.
2 *beside Paula, she felt clumsy* **compared with/to,** in comparison with/to, by comparison with, next to, against, contrasted with, in contrast to/with.
– PHRASES **beside oneself** *she was beside herself with worry* **distraught,** overcome, out of one's mind, frantic, desperate, distracted, at one's wits' end, frenzied, wound up, worked up; hysterical, unhinged, mad, crazed. **beside the point** See POINT[1].

besides ▶ preposition *who did you ask besides Mary?* **in addition to,** as well as, over and above, above and beyond, on top of; apart from, other than, aside from, but for, save for, not counting, excluding, not including, except, with the exception of, excepting, leaving aside; informal outside of.
▶ adverb **1** *there's a lot more besides* **in addition,** as well, too, also, in/into the bargain, on top of that, to boot; archaic therewithal.
2 *besides, he's always late* **furthermore,** moreover, further; anyway, anyhow, in any case, be that as it may; informal what's more, anyways.

besiege ▶ verb **1** *the Romans besieged Carthage* **lay siege to,** beleaguer, blockade, surround; archaic invest.
2 *fans besieged his hotel* **surround,** mob, crowd around, swarm around, throng around, encircle. See note at CIRCUMSCRIBE.
3 *guilt besieged him* **oppress,** torment, torture, rack, plague, afflict, haunt, harrow, hound, beset, beleaguer, trouble, bedevil, prey on.
4 *he was besieged with requests* **overwhelm,** inundate, deluge, flood, swamp, snow under; bombard.

besmirch ▶ verb literary *I'm not trying to besmirch the victim, but the woman had an extensive history of drug-related arrests* **sully,** tarnish, blacken, drag through the mud/mire, stain, taint, smear, disgrace, dishonor, bring discredit to, damage, debase, ruin; slander, malign, defame; literary besmear, smirch; archaic breathe on.
ANTONYMS honor, enhance.

besotted ▶ adjective *the poor boy is so obviously besotted with Miss O'Toole* **infatuated with,** smitten with, in love with, head over heels in love with, obsessed with; doting on, greatly enamored of; informal swept off one's feet by, crazy about, mad about, wild about, carrying a torch for, gaga about/for/over, stuck on, gone on.

bespeak ▶ verb *a tree-lined road which bespoke money* **indicate,** be evidence of, be a sign of, denote, point to, testify to, evidence, reflect, demonstrate, show, manifest, display, signify; reveal, betray; informal spell; literary betoken.
ANTONYMS belie.

best ▶ adjective **1** *the best hotel in Rhode Island* **finest,** greatest, top, foremost, leading, preeminent, premier, prime, first, chief, principal, supreme, of the highest quality, superlative, par excellence, unrivaled, second to none, without equal, nonpareil, unsurpassed, peerless, matchless, unparalleled, unbeaten, unbeatable, optimum, optimal, ultimate, incomparable, ideal, perfect; highest, record-breaking; informal star, number-one, a cut above the rest, top-drawer, the Cadillac of, the Rolls-Royce of.
ANTONYMS worst.
2 *do whatever you think best* **most advantageous,** most useful, most suitable, most fitting, most appropriate; most prudent, most sensible, most advisable.
▶ adverb **1** *the best-dressed man* **to the highest standard,** in the best way.
ANTONYMS worst.
2 *the food he liked best* **most,** to the highest/greatest degree.
ANTONYMS least.
3 *this is best done at home* **most advantageously,** most usefully, most suitably, most fittingly, most appropriately; most sensibly, most prudently, most wisely; better.
▶ noun **1** *only the best will do* **finest,** choicest, top, cream, choice, prime, elite, crème de la crème, flower, jewel in the crown, nonpareil; informal tops, pick of the bunch.
2 *she dressed in her best* **best clothes,** finery, Sunday best; informal glad rags.
3 *give her my best* **best wishes,** regards, kind/kindest regards, greetings, compliments, felicitations, respects; love.
▶ verb informal *she was not to be bested* **defeat,** beat, get the better of, outdo, outwit, outsmart, worst, be more than a match for, prevail over, vanquish, trounce, triumph over; surpass, outclass, outshine, put someone in the shade, overshadow, eclipse; informal lick.
– PHRASES **do one's best** *we'll do our best to make sure you get a good education* **do one's utmost,** try one's hardest, make every effort, do all one can, give one's all; informal bend over backwards, do one's damnedest, go all out, pull out all the stops, bust a gut, break one's neck, move heaven and earth. **had best** *you had best look elsewhere* **ought to,** should.

bestial ▶ adjective *Stanley's bestial behavior* **savage,** brutish, brutal, barbarous, barbaric, cruel, vicious, violent, inhuman, subhuman; depraved, degenerate, perverted, debauched, immoral, warped.
ANTONYMS civilized, humane.

bestow ▶ verb *the honor bestowed upon him* **confer on,** grant, accord, afford, endow someone with, vest in, present, award, give, donate to, entrust with, vouchsafe. See note at GIVE.

bet ▶ verb **1** *he bet $10 on the favorite* **wager,** gamble, stake, risk, venture, hazard, chance; put/lay money, speculate.

2 informal *I bet it was your idea* **be certain,** be sure, be convinced, be confident; expect, predict, forecast, guess.
▶ **noun 1** *a $20 bet* **wager,** gamble, stake, ante.
2 informal *my bet is that they'll lose* **prediction,** forecast, guess; opinion, belief, feeling, view, theory.
3 informal *your best bet is to go early* **option,** choice, alternative, course of action, plan.

betoken ▶ **verb** literary **1** *a small gift betokening regret* **indicate,** be a sign of, be evidence of, evidence, manifest, mean, signify, denote, represent, show, demonstrate, bespeak.
2 *the blue sky betokened a day of good weather* **foretell,** signal, give notice of, herald, proclaim, prophesy, foreshadow, presage, be a harbinger of, portend, augur, be an omen of, be a sign of, be a warning of, warn of, bode; literary foretoken, forebode.

betray ▶ **verb 1** *he betrayed his own brother* **be disloyal to,** be unfaithful to, double-cross, cross, break faith with, inform on/against, give away, denounce, sell out, stab in the back, break one's promise to; informal rat on, fink on, sell down the river, squeal on, rat on/out, finger.
ANTONYMS be loyal to.
2 *he betrayed a secret* **reveal,** disclose, divulge, tell, give away, leak; unmask, expose, bring out into the open; let slip, let out, let drop, blurt out; informal blab, spill, kiss and tell.
ANTONYMS conceal, hide.

betrayal ▶ **noun** *betrayal in the workplace | the CIA leak was a serious act of betrayal* **disloyalty,** treachery, bad faith, faithlessness, falseness, duplicity, deception, double-dealing; breach of faith, breach of trust, stab in the back; double-cross, sellout; literary perfidy.
ANTONYMS loyalty.

betrothal ▶ **noun** dated *the betrothal was announced on St. Swithin's Day* **engagement,** marriage contract; archaic espousal.

better ▶ **adjective 1** *better facilities* **superior,** finer, of higher quality; preferable; informal a cut above, head and shoulders above, ahead of the pack/field.
ANTONYMS worse, inferior.
2 *there couldn't be a better time* **more advantageous,** more suitable, more fitting, more appropriate, more useful, more valuable, more desirable.
ANTONYMS worse.
3 *are you better?* **healthier,** fitter, stronger; well, cured, healed, recovered; recovering, on the road to recovery, making progress, improving; informal on the mend.
ANTONYMS worse, sicker.
▶ **adverb 1** *I played better today* **to a higher standard,** in a superior/finer way.
2 *this may suit you better* **more,** to a greater degree/extent.
3 *the money could be better spent* **more wisely,** more sensibly, more suitably, more fittingly, more advantageously.
▶ **verb 1** *he bettered the record* **surpass,** improve on, beat, exceed, top, cap, trump, eclipse.
2 *refugees who want to better their lot* **improve,** ameliorate, raise, advance, further, lift, upgrade, enhance.
ANTONYMS worsen.

betterment ▶ **noun** *he spoke of his desire for the betterment of the country* **improvement,** amelioration, advancement, change for the better, furtherance, upgrading, enhancement; reform, rectification.

between ▶ **preposition 1** *Philip stood between his parents* **in the space separating,** in the middle of, with one on either side; amid, amidst; archaic betwixt.
2 *the bond between Amy and her mother* **connecting,** linking, joining; uniting, allying; among.

bevel ▶ **noun** *the bevel that borders the mirror* **slope,** slant, angle, cant, miter, chamfer, bezel.

beverage ▶ **noun** *soda and other beverages* **drink,** liquid refreshment; humorous libation; archaic potation.

bevy ▶ **noun** *a bevy of Vegas headliners* **group,** crowd, herd, flock, horde, army, galaxy, assemblage, throng, company, gathering, band, body, pack, covey; knot, cluster; informal bunch, gaggle, posse.

bewail ▶ **verb** *they bewailed the loss of their cherished freedoms* **lament,** bemoan, mourn, grieve over, sorrow over, cry over; deplore, complain about, wail about; archaic plain over.
ANTONYMS rejoice at, applaud.

beware ▶ **verb** *there are loose rocks underfoot, so beware!* **be on your guard,** watch out, look out, be alert, be on the lookout, keep your eyes open/peeled, keep an eye out, keep a sharp lookout, be on the qui vive; take care, be careful, be cautious, watch your step; Golf fore.

bewilder ▶ **verb** *Sally's words bewildered him* **baffle,** mystify, bemuse, perplex, puzzle, addle, confuse, confound; informal flummox, faze, stump, beat, fox, make someone scratch their head, be all Greek to, floor, discombobulate.
ANTONYMS enlighten.

bewildered ▶ **adjective** *she looked completely bewildered* **baffled,** mystified, bemused, perplexed, puzzled, confused, nonplussed, dumbfounded, at sea, at a loss, disorientated, taken aback; informal flummoxed, bamboozled; discombobulated.

bewitch ▶ **verb 1** *the villagers were certain that Ramara had bewitched him* **cast/put a spell on,** enchant; possess, curse, hex; archaic witch.
2 *we were bewitched by the surroundings* **captivate,** enchant, entrance, enrapture, charm, beguile, delight, fascinate, enthrall.
ANTONYMS repel.

beyond ▶ **preposition 1** *beyond the trees* **on the far side of,** on the other side of, further away than, behind, past, after, over.
2 *inflation beyond 10 percent* **greater than,** more than, exceeding, in excess of, above, over and above, above and beyond, upwards of.
3 *little beyond food was provided* **apart from,** except, other than, besides; informal outside of; formal save.
▶ **adverb** *a house with a garden beyond* **further away,** further off.

bias ▶ **noun 1** *he accused the media of bias* **prejudice,** partiality, partisanship, favoritism, unfairness, one-sidedness; bigotry, intolerance,

discrimination, leaning, tendency, inclination, predilection.
ANTONYMS impartiality.
2 *a dress cut on the bias* **diagonal,** cross, slant, angle.
▶ **verb** *this may have biased the result* **prejudice,** influence, color, sway, weight, predispose; distort, skew, slant.

> CHOOSE THE RIGHT WORD
>
> **bias, bigotry, intolerance, narrow-mindedness, parochialism, partiality, prejudice, provincialism**
>
> **Bias** is a predisposition either for or against something; one can have a *bias* against police officers or a *bias* for French food and wines. **Partiality**, on the other hand, is a favorable *bias* (*the partiality of parents for their own children; the partiality of Americans for fast food*), while **prejudice** implies a preconceived and usually negative judgment or opinion (*a decision motivated by racial prejudice*). **Bigotry** is an even stronger term, referring to an intense dislike and often violent hatred for the members of a particular race, religion, or ethnic group. **Narrow-mindedness** also points to rigidly preconceived ideas, but implies that they are the result of lack of education or understanding, rather than outright hostility (*her parents' narrow-mindedness prevented her from meeting any boys her age*). **Parochialism** is another term meaning excessive narrowness of mind (from "parochial," pertaining to a parish or parishes; that is, concerned mainly about local issues), while **provincialism** is narrow-mindedness that results from lack of exposure to cultural or intellectual activity, characteristic of a province or non-urban area. **Intolerance** is a broad term used to describe the inability to put up with almost anything (*parents' intolerance of their children's misbehavior*).

biased ▶ **adjective** *a biased view of the situation* **prejudiced,** partial, partisan, one-sided, blinkered; bigoted, intolerant, discriminatory; distorted, warped, twisted, skewed.
ANTONYMS impartial.

Bible ▶ **noun 1** *he read the Bible* **(Holy) Scriptures,** Holy Writ, Good Book, Book of Books.
2 informal (**bible**) *the taxi driver's bible* **handbook,** manual, ABCs, companion, guide, primer, vade mecum; rare enchiridion.

bicker ▶ **verb** *they never bickered before they were married* **quarrel,** argue, squabble, wrangle, fight, disagree, dispute, spar, have words, be at each other's throats, lock horns; informal scrap, spat.
ANTONYMS agree.

bicycle ▶ **noun** *her first bicycle was a Schwinn* **bike,** cycle, two-wheeler, mountain bike, ten-speed, racing bike, recumbent; historical penny-farthing, ordinary, velocipede.

bid[1] ▶ **verb 1** *we bid $650 for the antique table* **offer,** make an offer of, put in a bid of, put up, tender, proffer, propose.
2 *she is **bidding for** a place on the UConn team* **try to obtain,** try to get, make a pitch for, make a bid for.
▶ **noun 1** *a bid of $3,000* **offer,** tender, proposal.
2 *a bid to cut crime* **attempt,** effort, endeavor, try; informal crack, go, shot, stab; formal essay.

bid[2] ▶ **verb 1** *she bid him farewell* **wish**; utter.
2 literary *I did as he bade me* **order,** command, tell, instruct, direct, enjoin, charge.
3 literary *he bade his companions enter* **invite to,** ask to, request to.

bidding ▶ **noun** *let's make it clear that I am not here at your bidding* **command,** order, instruction, decree, injunction, demand, mandate, direction, summons, call; wish, desire; request; literary behest; archaic hest.

big ▶ **adjective 1** *a big building* **large,** sizable, substantial, great, huge, immense, enormous, extensive, colossal, massive, mammoth, vast, tremendous, gigantic, giant, monumental, mighty, gargantuan, elephantine, titanic, mountainous, Brobdingnagian; towering, tall, high, lofty; outsize, oversized; goodly; capacious, voluminous, spacious; king-size(d), man-size, family-size(d), economy-size(d); informal jumbo, whopping, mega, humongous, monster, astronomical, ginormous; formal commodious.
ANTONYMS small, little.
2 *clothing for big people* **well-built,** sturdy, brawny, burly, broad-shouldered, muscular, muscly, rugged, Herculean, bulky, hulking, strapping, thickset, stocky, solid, hefty, large; tall, huge, gigantic; fat, stout, portly, plump, fleshy, paunchy, corpulent, obese; full-figured, big-boned, buxom; roly-poly, rotund, well-fed; informal hunky, beefy, husky; literary thewy.
ANTONYMS small, slight, diminutive.
3 *my big sister* **elder,** older; grown-up, adult, mature, grown.
4 *a big decision* **important,** significant, major, momentous, weighty, consequential, far-reaching, impactful, key, vital, critical, crucial, life-and-death.
ANTONYMS unimportant, minor, trivial.
5 informal *a big man in the government* **powerful,** important, prominent, influential, high-powered, leading, preeminent; major-league.
ANTONYMS unimportant, obscure.
6 informal *she has big plans* **ambitious,** far-reaching, grandiose, on a grand scale.
ANTONYMS modest.
7 *he's got a big heart* **generous,** kind, kindly, caring, compassionate, loving.
8 informal *East Coast bands are big across the country* **popular,** successful, in demand, sought-after, all the rage; informal hot, in, cool, trendy, now, hip.
– PHRASES **too big for one's britches/boots** informal *sudden popularity has made Scully too big for his britches* **conceited,** full of oneself, cocky, arrogant, cocksure, above oneself, self-important, puffed-up; vain, self-satisfied, pleased with oneself, smug, complacent; informal

bigheaded; literary vainglorious.

bigot ▶ noun *he was denounced as an anti-Catholic bigot* **chauvinist,** partisan, sectarian; racist, sexist, homophobe, dogmatist, jingoist. See note at ZEALOT.

bigoted ▶ adjective *his bigoted father-in-law* **prejudiced,** biased, partial, one-sided, sectarian, discriminatory; opinionated, dogmatic, intolerant, narrow-minded, blinkered, illiberal; racist, sexist, chauvinistic, jingoistic; warped, twisted, distorted. See note at BIAS.
ANTONYMS open-minded.

bigwig ▶ noun informal *the company bigwigs are flying in for the annual meeting* **VIP,** (very) important person, notable, dignitary, grandee; celebrity; informal somebody, heavyweight, big shot, big gun, big cheese, big fish, big kahuna, big wheel, top gun.
ANTONYMS nonentity.

bilious ▶ adjective **1** *I felt bilious* **nauseous,** sick, queasy, nauseated, green around the gills; rare qualmish.
ANTONYMS well.
2 *his bilious disposition* See IRRITABLE.
3 *a bilious green and pink color scheme* **nauseating,** sickly, distasteful, dreadful; lurid, garish, loud.
ANTONYMS subtle, muted.

bilk ▶ verb informal See SWINDLE (verb).

bill[1] ▶ noun **1** *a bill for $60* **invoice,** account, statement, list of charges; check, tab; archaic reckoning, score.
2 *a congressional bill* **draft law,** proposed piece of legislation, proposal, measure.
3 *a $20 bill* **banknote,** note.
4 *he had been posting bills* **poster,** advertisement, ad, public notice, announcement; flyer, leaflet, handbill.
▶ verb **1** *please bill me for the work* **invoice,** charge, debit, send a statement to.
2 *the concert went ahead as billed* **advertise,** announce; schedule, program, timetable; slate.
3 *he was* **billed as** *the new Sean Connery* **describe as,** call, style, label, dub; promote as, publicize as, talk up as, hype as.

bill[2] ▶ noun *a bird's bill* **beak,** neb; technical mandibles.

billet ▶ noun *the troop's billet* **quarters,** rooms; accommodations, lodging, housing; barracks, cantonment.
▶ verb *two soldiers were billeted here* **accommodate,** quarter, put up, lodge, house; station, garrison.

billow ▶ noun **1** *billows of smoke* **cloud,** mass.
2 archaic *the billows that break upon the shore* **wave,** roller, breaker.
▶ verb **1** *her dress billowed around her* **puff up/out,** balloon (out), swell, fill (out), belly out.
2 *smoke billowed from the chimney* **swirl,** spiral, roll, undulate, eddy; pour, flow.

bin ▶ noun *the onions go in a bin* **container,** receptacle, holder; drum, canister, box, caddy, can, crate, chest, tin.

bind ▶ verb **1** *they bound our hands and feet* **tie (up),** fasten (together), hold together, secure, make fast, attach; rope, strap, lash, fetter, truss, hog-tie, tether.
ANTONYMS untie, release.
2 *the experience had* **bound them together** **unite,** join, bond, knit together, draw together, yoke together.
ANTONYMS separate.
3 *we were bound by a rigid timetable* **constrain,** restrict, restrain, trammel, tie hand and foot, tie down, fetter, shackle, hog-tie; hamper, hinder, inhibit.
4 *the edges are bound in a contrasting color* **trim,** hem, edge, border, fringe; finish; archaic purfle.
▶ noun *we're in a terrible bind* **predicament,** awkward situation, difficult situation, quandary, dilemma, plight, spot, tight spot; informal Catch-22, fix, hole.

binding ▶ adjective *the agreement is binding* **irrevocable,** unalterable, inescapable, unbreakable, contractual; compulsory, obligatory, mandatory, incumbent.

binge ▶ noun **1** *she was afraid that Howie was on another of his all-night binges* **drinking bout,** debauch; informal bender, jag, toot, session; dated souse; literary bacchanal, bacchanalia; archaic wassail.
2 *a two-day shopping binge* **spree**; informal splurge, spendfest, orgy.
▶ verb *we binged on all the free food* **overindulge,** overeat, gorge; informal pig out.

biography ▶ noun *an unauthorized biography always sounds more interesting* **life story,** life history, life, memoir; informal bio.

bird ▶ noun *feeding the birds* fowl; chick, fledgling, nestling; informal feathered friend, birdie; budgie; technical (**birds**) avifauna.

birth ▶ noun **1** *Nick arrived just in time for the birth* **childbirth,** delivery, nativity, birthing; blessed/happy event; formal parturition; dated confinement; archaic accouchement, childbed.
ANTONYMS death.
2 *the birth of science* **beginning(s),** emergence, genesis, dawn, dawning, rise, start, onset, commencement.
ANTONYMS demise, end.
3 *he is of noble birth* **ancestry,** lineage, blood, descent, parentage, family, extraction, origin, genealogy, heritage, stock, kinship.
– PHRASES **give birth to** *she gave birth to twins* **have,** bear, produce, be delivered of, bring into the world; birth; informal drop; dated mother; archaic bring forth.

birthmark ▶ noun *a birthmark shaped like an apple* **beauty spot/mark,** mole, blemish, nevus.

birthright ▶ noun *the presidency of this firm is my birthright* **patrimony,** inheritance, heritage; right, due, prerogative, privilege; primogeniture.

bisect ▶ verb *bisect the exterior angle* **cut in half,** halve, divide/cut/split in two, split down the middle; cross, intersect.

bit ▶ noun **1** *a bit of bread* **piece,** portion, segment, section, part; chunk, lump, hunk, slice; fragment, scrap, shred, crumb, grain, speck; spot, drop, pinch, dash, soupçon, modicum; morsel, mouthful, bite, sample; iota, jot, tittle, whit, atom, particle, trace, touch, suggestion, hint, tinge; snippet, snatch, smidgen, tad.

ANTONYMS lot.
2 *wait a bit* **moment,** minute, second, (little) while; informal sec, jiffy, jiff.
– PHRASES **a bit** *he's a bit forgetful* **somewhat,** fairly, slightly, rather, quite, a little, moderately; informal pretty, sort of, kind of, kinda. **bit by bit** *bit by bit, the truth came out* **gradually,** little by little, in stages, step by step, piecemeal, slowly. **in a bit** *I'll see you in a bit* **soon,** in a (little) while, in a second, in a minute, in a moment, shortly, in no time, before you know it, before long, directly; informal in a jiffy/jiff, in two shakes, in a snap; literary ere long, anon.

bitch ▶ noun informal **1** *she's such a bitch* **witch,** shrew, vixen, she-devil, hellcat, harridan, termagant, virago, harpy; archaic grimalkin.
2 *a bitch of a job* **nightmare**; informal bastard, bummer, —— from hell, stinker.
▶ verb *they bitched about the price of oil* **complain,** whine, grumble, grouse; informal whinge, moan, grouch, gripe.

bitchy ▶ adjective informal See SPITEFUL.

bite ▶ verb **1** *the dog bit his arm* **sink one's teeth into,** chew, munch, crunch, chomp, tear at, snap at.
2 *the acid* ***bites into*** *the copper* **corrode,** eat into, eat away at, burn (into), etch, dissolve.
3 *a hundred or so retailers should bite* **accept,** agree, respond; be lured, be enticed, be tempted; take the bait.
▶ noun **1** *he took a bite of his sandwich* **munch,** chew, nibble, nip, snap.
2 *he ate it in two bites* **mouthful,** piece, bit, morsel.
3 *let's go out for* ***a bite*** **a snack,** a light meal, a quick meal; refreshments; informal a little something.
4 *we came back from the picnic covered in insect bites* **sting.**
5 *the appetizer had a fiery bite* **piquancy,** pungency, spiciness, strong flavor, tang, zest, sharpness, tartness; informal kick, punch, edge, zing.

biting ▶ adjective **1** *biting comments* **vicious,** harsh, cruel, savage, cutting, sharp, bitter, scathing, caustic, acid, acrimonious, acerbic, stinging; vitriolic, hostile, spiteful, venomous, mean, nasty; informal bitchy, catty.
ANTONYMS mild, gentle.
2 *the biting wind* **freezing,** icy, arctic, glacial; bitter, piercing, penetrating, raw, wintry.
ANTONYMS mild, balmy.

bitter ▶ adjective **1** *a bitter aftertaste* **sharp,** acid, acidic, acrid, tart, sour, biting, unsweetened, vinegary; technical acerbic.
ANTONYMS sweet.
2 *a bitter woman* **resentful,** embittered, aggrieved, begrudging, rancorous, spiteful, jaundiced, ill-disposed, sullen, sour, churlish, morose, petulant, peevish, with a chip on one's shoulder.
ANTONYMS magnanimous, content.
3 *a bitter blow* **painful,** unpleasant, disagreeable, nasty, cruel, awful, distressing, upsetting, harrowing, heartbreaking, heart-rending, agonizing, traumatic, tragic, chilling; formal grievous.
ANTONYMS welcome.
4 *a bitter wind* **freezing,** icy, arctic, glacial; biting, piercing, penetrating, raw, wintry.
ANTONYMS warm, balmy.
5 *a bitter dispute* **acrimonious,** virulent, angry, rancorous, spiteful, vicious, vitriolic, savage, ferocious, hate-filled, venomous, poisonous, acrid, nasty, ill-natured.
ANTONYMS amicable.

bitterness ▶ noun **1** *the bitterness of the medicine* **sharpness,** acidity, acridity, tartness, sourness, harshness; technical acerbity.
ANTONYMS sweetness.
2 *there was no bitterness between them* **resentment,** rancor, indignation, grudge, spite, sullenness, sourness, churlishness, moroseness, petulance, pique, peevishness; **acrimony,** hostility, malice, virulence, antipathy, antagonism, enmity, animus, friction, vitriol, hatred, loathing, venom, poison, nastiness, ill feeling, ill will, bad blood.
ANTONYMS magnanimity, contentment, goodwill.
3 *the bitterness of war* **trauma,** pain, agony, grief; unpleasantness, disagreeableness, nastiness; heartache, heartbreak, distress, desolation, despair, tragedy.
ANTONYMS delight.

bizarre ▶ adjective *bizarre sculptures* **strange,** peculiar, odd, funny, curious, outlandish, outré, abnormal, eccentric, unconventional, unusual, unorthodox, queer, extraordinary; informal weird, wacky, bizarro, oddball, way out, kooky, freaky, off the wall, offbeat.
ANTONYMS normal, conventional.

black ▶ adjective **1** *a black horse* **dark,** pitch-black, jet-black, coal-black, ebony, sable, inky.
ANTONYMS white.
2 *a black night* **unlit,** dark, starless, moonless, wan; literary tenebrous, Stygian.
ANTONYMS clear, bright.
3 *thirty-seven percent of our advanced-study students are black* See note on BLACK below.
4 *the blackest day of the war* **tragic,** disastrous, calamitous, catastrophic, cataclysmic, fateful, wretched, woeful, awful, terrible; formal grievous.
ANTONYMS joyful.
5 *Mary was in a black mood* **miserable,** unhappy, sad, wretched, broken-hearted, heartbroken, grief-stricken, grieving, sorrowful, sorrowing, anguished, desolate, despairing, disconsolate, downcast, dejected, sullen, cheerless, melancholy, morose, gloomy, glum, mournful, doleful, funereal, dismal, forlorn, woeful, abject; informal blue; literary dolorous.
ANTONYMS cheerful.
6 *black humor* **cynical,** macabre, weird, unhealthy, ghoulish, morbid, perverted, gruesome; informal sick.
7 *a black look* **angry,** vexed, cross, irritated, incensed. See also ANGRY (sense 1).
ANTONYMS pleased.
8 archaic *a black deed* **wicked,** evil, heinous, villainous, bad. See also WICKED (sense 1).
ANTONYMS virtuous.
– PHRASES **black out** *he blacked out from the*

pain **faint,** lose consciousness, pass out, swoon; informal go out. **black something out** *we blacked out our homes during the war* **darken,** shade, turn off the lights in; keep the light out of. **in the black** *our business is finally in the black* **solvent,** debt-free, out of debt, in credit, financially sound, able to pay one's debts, creditworthy. **black and white 1** *a black-and-white picture* **monochrome,** gray-scale.
2 *I wish to see the proposals in black and white* **in print,** printed, written down, set down, on paper, recorded, on record, documented.
3 *in black-and-white terms* **categorical,** unequivocal, absolute, uncompromising, unconditional, unqualified, unambiguous, clear, clear-cut.

> USAGE
> **black**
> *Black*, designating Americans of African heritage, became the most widely used and accepted term in the 1960s and 1970s, replacing *Negro*. It is not usually capitalized: *black Americans*. Through the 1980s, the more formal *African American* replaced *black* in much usage, but both are now generally acceptable. *Afro-American*, an earlier alternative to *black*, is heard mostly in anthropological and cultural contexts. *Colored people*, common earlier in the twentieth century, is now usually regarded as derogatory, although the phrase survives in the full name of the NAACP, the National Association for the Advancement of Colored People. An inversion, *people of color*, has gained some favor, but is also used in reference to other nonwhite ethnic groups: *a gathering spot for African Americans and other people of color interested in reading about their cultures.*

blackball ▶ **verb** *Zabel could not support the group's intention to blackball Curtis* **reject,** debar, bar, ban, vote against, blacklist, exclude, shut out; ostracize, expel.
ANTONYMS admit.

blacken ▶ **verb 1** *they blackened their faces* **black,** darken; dirty, make sooty, make smoky, stain, grime, soil.
ANTONYMS whiten, clean.
2 *the sky blackened* **grow/become black,** darken, dim, grow dim, cloud over.
ANTONYMS lighten, brighten.
3 *someone has blackened my name* **sully,** tarnish, besmirch, drag through the mud/mire, stain, taint, smear, disgrace, dishonor, bring discredit to, damage, ruin; slander, defame.
ANTONYMS clear, honor.

blacklist ▶ **verb** *the club blacklisted Edwards soon after his arrest* **boycott,** ostracize, blackball, spurn, avoid, embargo, steer clear of, ignore; stigmatize; refuse to employ.

blackmail ▶ **noun** *he was accused of blackmail* **extortion;** informal hush money; formal exaction.
▶ **verb 1** *he was blackmailing the murderer* **extort money from,** threaten; informal demand hush money from.
2 *she blackmailed me to work for her* **coerce,** pressurize, pressure, force; informal lean on, put the screws on, twist someone's arm.

blackout ▶ **noun 1** *there must have been a blackout—all the clocks are blinking* **power failure,** power outage, brownout.
2 *a news blackout* **suppression,** silence, censorship, gag order, reporting restrictions.
3 *he had a blackout* **fainting spell,** faint, loss of consciousness, passing out, swoon, collapse; Medicine syncope.

blame ▶ **verb 1** *he always blames others* **hold responsible,** hold accountable, condemn, accuse, find/consider guilty, assign fault/liability/guilt to, indict, point the finger at, finger, incriminate; archaic inculpate.
ANTONYMS absolve.
2 *they* **blame** *youth crime* **on** *unemployment* **ascribe to,** attribute to, impute to, lay at the door of, put down to; informal pin.
▶ **noun** *he was cleared of all blame | Ullman took the blame* **responsibility,** guilt, accountability, liability, culpability, fault; informal rap.

blameless ▶ **adjective** *the company conceded that it was not entirely blameless* **innocent,** guiltless, above reproach, irreproachable, unimpeachable, in the clear, exemplary, perfect, virtuous, pure, impeccable, faultless; informal squeaky clean; trademark Teflon.
ANTONYMS blameworthy.

blameworthy ▶ **adjective** *there is no longer any no doubt that Otis is the blameworthy individual* **culpable,** reprehensible, indefensible, inexcusable, guilty, criminal, delinquent, wrong, evil, wicked; to blame, at fault, reproachable, responsible, answerable, erring, errant, in the wrong.
ANTONYMS blameless.

blanch ▶ **verb 1** *the moonlight blanches her hair* **turn pale,** whiten, lighten, wash out, fade.
ANTONYMS darken.
2 *his face blanched* **pale,** turn pale, turn white, whiten, lose its color, lighten, fade.
ANTONYMS color, darken.
3 *blanch the spinach leaves* **scald,** boil briefly.

bland ▶ **adjective 1** *bland food* **tasteless,** flavorless, insipid, weak, watery, spiceless; informal wishy-washy.
ANTONYMS tangy, tasty.
2 *a bland film* **uninteresting,** dull, boring, tedious, monotonous, monochrome, dry, drab, dreary, wearisome; unexciting, unimaginative, uninspiring, uninspired, lackluster, vapid, flat, stale, trite; informal blah, plain-vanilla, white-bread, banal, commonplace, humdrum, ho-hum, vacuous, wishy-washy.
ANTONYMS interesting, stimulating.
3 *a bland expression* **unemotional,** emotionless, dispassionate, passionless; inexpressive, cool, impassive; expressionless, blank, wooden, stony, deadpan, hollow, undemonstrative, imperturbable.
ANTONYMS emotional, expressive.

blandishments ▶ **plural noun** *the blandishments of advertisers* **flattery,** cajolery, coaxing, wheedling, persuasion, palaver, honeyed words, smooth talk, blarney; informal sweet talk, soft soap, buttering up, smarm.

blank ▶ adjective 1 *a blank sheet of paper* **empty,** unmarked, unused, clear, free, bare, clean, plain.
ANTONYMS full.
2 *a blank face* **expressionless,** deadpan, wooden, stony, impassive, unresponsive, poker-faced, vacuous, empty, glazed, fixed, lifeless, inscrutable.
ANTONYMS expressive.
3 *"What?" said Maxim, looking blank* **baffled,** mystified, puzzled, perplexed, stumped, at a loss, stuck, bewildered, dumbfounded, nonplussed, bemused, lost, uncomprehending, at sea, confused; informal flummoxed, bamboozled.
4 *a blank refusal* **outright,** absolute, categorical, unqualified, complete, flat, straight, positive, certain, explicit, unequivocal, clear, clear-cut.
▶ noun *leave a blank where the address will go* **space,** gap, blank space, empty space; lacuna.

blanket ▶ noun *a blanket of cloud* **covering,** layer, coating, carpet, overlay, cloak, mantle, veil, pall, shroud.
▶ adjective *blanket coverage* complete, total, comprehensive, overall, general, mass, umbrella, inclusive, all-inclusive, all-around, wholesale, outright, across-the-board, sweeping, indiscriminate, thorough; universal, international, worldwide, global, nationwide, countrywide, coast-to-coast.
ANTONYMS partial, piecemeal.
▶ verb *snow blanketed the mountains* **cover,** coat, carpet, overlay; cloak, shroud, swathe, envelop; literary mantle.

blare ▶ verb *sirens blared* **blast,** sound loudly, trumpet, bray, clamor, boom, blat, roar, thunder, bellow, resound.
ANTONYMS murmur.
▶ noun *the blare of the siren* **blast,** trumpeting, clamor, boom, roar, thunder, bellow, blat.
ANTONYMS murmur.

blaspheme ▶ verb *would you dare to blaspheme in the House of the Lord?* **swear,** curse, take the Lord's name in vain; informal cuss; archaic execrate.

blasphemous ▶ adjective *a blasphemous mock communion* **sacrilegious,** profane, irreligious, irreverent, impious, ungodly, godless.
ANTONYMS reverent.

blasphemy ▶ noun *the nuns would punish me at least three times a week for my blasphemy* **profanity,** sacrilege, irreligion, irreverence, taking the Lord's name in vain, swearing, curse, cursing, impiety, desecration; archaic execration.
ANTONYMS reverence.

blast ▶ noun 1 *the blast from the bomb* **shock wave,** pressure wave.
2 *Friday's blast killed two people* **explosion,** detonation, discharge, burst.
3 *a sudden blast of cold air* **gust,** rush, gale, squall, wind, draft, waft, puff.
4 *the shrill blast of the trumpets* **blare,** wail, roar, screech, shriek, hoot, honk, beep.
5 *we had a blast* **good time,** ball, riot.
▶ verb 1 *bombers were blasting enemy airfields* **blow up,** bomb, blow to pieces, dynamite, shell, explode.
2 *guns were **blasting away*** **fire,** shoot, blaze, let fly, discharge.
3 *he blasted his horn* **honk,** beep, toot, sound.
4 *radios blasting out pop music* **blare,** boom, roar, thunder, bellow, pump, shriek, screech.
5 informal *the opposition blasted the government over the deal* See **BERATE**.
– PHRASES **blast off** *the rocket blasted off at 8:02* **be launched,** take off, lift off, leave the ground, become airborne, take to the air.

blatant ▶ adjective *it was a blatant lie* **flagrant,** glaring, obvious, undisguised, unconcealed, open; shameless, barefaced, naked, unabashed, unashamed, unblushing, brazen.
ANTONYMS inconspicuous, shamefaced.

blaze ▶ noun 1 *firemen fought the blaze* **fire,** flames, conflagration, inferno, holocaust; forest fire, wildfire, bush fire.
2 *a blaze of light* **glare,** gleam, flash, burst, flare, streak, radiance, brilliance, beam.
▶ verb 1 *the fire blazed for hours* **burn,** be alight, be on fire, be in flames, flame.
2 *headlights blazed* **shine,** flash, flare, glare, gleam, glint, dazzle, glitter, glisten.

blazon ▶ verb *their name is blazoned across the sails* **display,** exhibit, present, spread, emblazon, plaster; announce, proclaim. See note at **ANNOUNCE**.

bleach ▶ verb *the blinds had been bleached by the sun* **turn white,** whiten, turn pale, blanch, lighten, fade, decolorize, peroxide.
ANTONYMS darken.
▶ noun *a bottle of bleach* chlorine bleach; trademark Clorox.

bleak ▶ adjective 1 *a bleak landscape* **bare,** exposed, desolate, stark, desert, lunar, open, empty, windswept; treeless, without vegetation, denuded.
ANTONYMS lush.
2 *the future is bleak* **unpromising,** unfavorable, unpropitious, inauspicious; discouraging, disheartening, depressing, dreary, dim, gloomy, black, dark, grim, hopeless, somber.
ANTONYMS promising.
3 *a bleak wind* **cold,** bitter, biting, raw, freezing, icy.

bleary ▶ adjective *his eyes were bleary from exhaustion* **blurred,** blurry, unfocused; fogged, clouded, dull, misty, watery, rheumy; archaic blear.
ANTONYMS clear.

bleed ▶ verb 1 *his arm was bleeding* **lose blood,** hemorrhage.
2 *the doctor bled him* **draw blood from;** Medicine exsanguinate; archaic phlebotomize.
3 *one color bled into another* **flow,** run, seep, filter, percolate, leach.
4 *sap was bleeding from the trunk* **flow,** run, ooze, seep, exude, weep.
5 *the country was **bled dry** by poachers* **drain,** sap, deplete, milk, exhaust.
6 *my heart **bleeds for** them* **grieve for,** ache for, sorrow for, mourn for, lament for, feel for, suffer for; sympathize with, pity.

blemish ▶ noun 1 *not a blemish marred her skin* **imperfection,** flaw, defect, fault, deformity, discoloration, disfigurement; bruise, scar, pit, pock, pimple, blackhead, wart, scratch, cut,

gash; mark, streak, spot, smear, speck, blotch, smudge, smut; birthmark, mole; Medicine stigma.
2 *the mayor's record is not without blemish* **defect,** fault, failing, flaw, imperfection, foible, vice; shortcoming, weakness, deficiency, limitation; taint, blot, stain, dishonor, disgrace.
ANTONYMS virtue.
▶ **verb 1** *nothing blemished the coast* **mar,** spoil, impair, disfigure, blight, deface, mark, scar; ruin.
ANTONYMS enhance.
2 *his reign has been blemished by controversy* **sully,** tarnish, besmirch, blacken, blot, taint; spoil, mar, ruin, disgrace, damage, degrade, dishonor; formal vitiate.

blend ▶ **verb 1** *blend the ingredients until smooth* **mix,** mingle, combine, merge, fuse, meld, coalesce, integrate, intermix; stir, whisk, fold in; technical admix; literary commingle.
2 *the new buildings blend with the older ones* **harmonize,** go (well), fit (in), be in tune, be compatible; coordinate, match, complement.
▶ **noun** *a blend of bananas, raisins, and ginger* **mixture,** mix, combination, amalgamation, amalgam, union, marriage, fusion, meld, synthesis, concoction; technical admixture.

bless ▶ **verb 1** *the chaplain blessed the couple* **ask/invoke God's favor for,** give a benediction for; **consecrate,** sanctify, dedicate (to God), make holy, make sacred; formal hallow.
ANTONYMS curse.
2 *bless the name of the Lord* **praise,** worship, glorify, honor, exalt, pay homage to, venerate, reverence, hallow; archaic magnify.
3 *the gods **blessed** us **with** magical voices* **endow with,** bestow with, furnish with, accord, give, favor with, grace with; confer on; literary endue with.
4 *I bless the day you came here* **give thanks for,** be grateful for, thank; appreciate.
ANTONYMS rue.

blessed ▶ **adjective 1** *a blessed place* **holy,** sacred, hallowed, consecrated, sanctified; ordained, canonized, beatified.
ANTONYMS cursed.
2 *blessed are the meek* **favored,** fortunate, lucky, privileged, enviable, happy.
ANTONYMS wretched.

blessing ▶ **noun 1** *may God give us his blessing* **protection,** favor.
ANTONYMS condemnation.
2 *a special blessing from the priest* **benediction,** invocation, prayer, intercession; grace.
ANTONYMS anathema.
3 *she gave the plan her blessing* **sanction,** endorsement, approval, approbation, favor, consent, assent, agreement; backing, support; informal thumbs up, OK, nod.
4 *it was a blessing they didn't have far to go* **godsend,** boon, advantage, benefit, help, bonus, plus; stroke of luck, unmixed blessing, (lucky) break, windfall; literary benison.
ANTONYMS affliction.

blight ▶ **noun 1** *potato blight* **disease,** canker, infestation, fungus, mildew, mold.
2 *the blight of aircraft noise* **affliction,** scourge, bane, curse, plague, menace, misfortune, woe, trouble, ordeal, trial, nuisance, pest.
ANTONYMS blessing.
▶ **verb 1** *a tree blighted by leaf curl* **infect,** mildew; kill, destroy.
2 *scandal blighted the careers of several politicians* **ruin,** wreck, spoil, mar, frustrate, disrupt, undo, end, scotch, destroy, shatter, devastate, demolish; informal mess up, foul up, stymie.

blind ▶ **adjective 1** *he has been blind since birth* **sightless,** unsighted, visually impaired, visionless, unseeing; partially sighted, purblind; informal as blind as a bat.
ANTONYMS sighted.
2 *the government must be blind* **imperceptive,** unperceptive, insensitive, slow, obtuse, uncomprehending; stupid, unintelligent; informal dense, dim, thick, dumb, dopey, dozy.
ANTONYMS perceptive.
3 *he was **blind to** her shortcomings* **unmindful of,** mindless of, careless of, heedless of, oblivious to, insensible to, unconcerned about, indifferent to.
ANTONYMS mindful.
4 *blind acceptance of conventional opinion* **uncritical,** unreasoned, unthinking, unconsidered, mindless, undiscerning, indiscriminate.
ANTONYMS discerning.
5 *a blind rage* **impetuous,** impulsive, uncontrolled, uncontrollable, wild, unrestrained, immoderate, intemperate, irrational, unbridled.
▶ **verb 1** *he was blinded in a car crash* **make blind,** deprive of sight, render sightless; put someone's eyes out.
2 *he was blinded by his faith* **deprive of judgment,** deprive of perception, deprive of reason, deprive of sense.
3 *they try to blind you with science* **overawe,** intimidate, daunt, deter, discourage, cow, subdue, dismay; disquiet, discomfit, unsettle, disconcert; disorient, stun, stupefy, confuse, bewilder, bedazzle, confound, perplex, overwhelm; informal faze, psych out.
▶ **noun 1** *a window blind* **shade,** screen, sunshade, shutter, curtain, awning, canopy; louver, jalousie; Venetian blind, miniblind, vertical blind.
2 *some crook had sent the basketball tickets as a blind* **deception,** smokescreen, front, facade, cover, pretext, masquerade, feint, camouflage; trick, ploy, ruse, machination.

blindly ▶ **adverb** *they blindly followed central policy* **uncritically,** unthinkingly, mindlessly, indiscriminately.

blink ▶ **verb 1** *his eyes did not blink* flutter, flicker, wink, bat.
2 *several red lights began to blink* **flash,** flicker, wink.
3 *no one even blinks at the estimated cost* **be surprised,** look twice; informal boggle.
4 *after a tense standoff, the union blinked* **back down,** give in, knuckle under, submit, relent.

bliss ▶ **noun 1** *she gave a sigh of bliss* **joy,** happiness, pleasure, delight, ecstasy, elation, rapture, euphoria. See note at **RAPTURE**.
ANTONYMS misery.
2 *religions promise perfect bliss after death*

blessedness, benediction, beatitude, glory, heavenly joy, divine happiness; heaven, paradise.
ANTONYMS hell.

blister ▶ noun **1** *a blister on each heel* vesicle, vesication; pustule, abscess.
2 *check for blisters in the wall covering* **bubble,** swelling, bulge, protuberance.

blistering ▶ adjective **1** *blistering heat* **intense,** extreme, ferocious, fierce; **scorching,** searing, blazing, burning, fiery; informal boiling, baking, roasting, sweltering.
ANTONYMS mild, icy.
2 *a blistering attack on the government* **savage,** vicious, fierce, bitter, harsh, scathing, devastating, caustic, searing, vitriolic.
ANTONYMS mild.
3 *a blistering pace* **very fast,** breakneck; informal blinding.
ANTONYMS leisurely.

blithe ▶ adjective **1** *a blithe disregard for the rules* **casual,** indifferent, unconcerned, unworried, untroubled, uncaring, careless, heedless, thoughtless; nonchalant, blasé.
ANTONYMS thoughtful.
2 literary *his blithe, smiling face* **happy,** cheerful, jolly, merry, joyful, joyous, blissful, ecstatic, euphoric, elated; dated gay.
ANTONYMS sad.

blitz ▶ noun **1** *the 1940 blitz on London* **bombardment,** bombing, onslaught, barrage; attack, assault, raid, strike, blitzkrieg.
2 *an expensive new marketing blitz* **campaign,** effort, operation, undertaking.

blizzard ▶ noun **snowstorm,** whiteout, snow squall, snowfall; nor'easter, northeaster.

blob ▶ noun **1** *a blob of cold gravy* **drop,** droplet, globule, bead, bubble; informal glob.
2 *a blob of ink* **spot,** dab, blotch, blot, dot, smudge; informal splotch.

bloc ▶ noun *a free-trade bloc* **alliance,** coalition, federation, confederation, league, union, partnership, axis, body, association, group.

block ▶ noun **1** *a block of cheese* **chunk,** hunk, lump, wedge, cube, brick, slab, bar, piece.
2 *an apartment block* **building,** complex, structure, development.
3 *a block of shares* **batch,** group, set, quantity.
4 *a block to Third World development* **obstacle,** bar, barrier, impediment, hindrance, check, hurdle, stumbling block, handicap, deterrent.
ANTONYMS aid.
5 *a block in the pipe* **blockage,** obstruction, stoppage, clog, congestion, occlusion, clot.
▶ verb **1** *weeds can block drainage ditches* **clog (up),** stop up, choke, plug, obstruct, gum up, dam up, congest, jam, close; informal gunge up; technical occlude.
ANTONYMS open.
2 *picket lines blocked access to the factory* **hinder,** hamper, obstruct, impede, inhibit, restrict, limit; halt, stop, bar, check, prevent.
ANTONYMS facilitate.
3 *he blocked a shot on the goal line* **stop,** deflect, fend off, hold off, repel, parry, repulse.
– PHRASES **block something off** *the bridge was blocked off* **close up,** shut off, seal off, barricade, bar, obstruct. **block something out** *trees blocked out the light* **conceal,** keep out, blot out, exclude, obliterate, blank out, stop.

blockade ▶ noun **1** *a naval blockade of the island* **siege;** rare besiegement.
2 *they erected blockades in the streets* **barricade,** barrier, roadblock; obstacle, obstruction.
▶ verb *rebels blockaded the capital* **barricade,** block off, shut off, seal; **besiege,** surround.

blockage ▶ noun *a blockage of leaves in the storm drain* **obstruction,** stoppage, block, occlusion, clog, congestion.

blockhead ▶ noun informal See IDIOT.

blood ▶ noun **1** *he had lost too much blood* **plasma,** vital fluid, gore; literary lifeblood, ichor.
2 *a woman of noble blood* **ancestry,** lineage, bloodline, descent, parentage, family, birth, extraction, origin, genealogy, heritage, stock, kinship.

blood-curdling ▶ adjective *a blood-curdling scream* **terrifying,** frightening, bone-chilling, spine-tingling, chilling, hair-raising, horrifying, alarming; eerie, sinister, horrible; informal spooky.

bloodless ▶ adjective **1** *a bloodless revolution* **nonviolent,** peaceful, peaceable, pacifist.
ANTONYMS bloody, violent.
2 *his face was bloodless* **anemic,** pale, wan, pallid, ashen, colorless, chalky, waxen, white, gray, pasty, drained, drawn, deathly.
ANTONYMS ruddy.
3 *a bloodless production* **feeble,** spiritless, lifeless, listless, halfhearted, unenthusiastic, lukewarm.
ANTONYMS powerful.

bloodshed ▶ noun *another day of bloodshed in Beirut* **slaughter,** massacre, killing, wounding; carnage, butchery, bloodletting, bloodbath; violence, fighting, warfare; literary slaying.

bloodthirsty ▶ adjective *bloodthirsty Vikings* **murderous,** homicidal, violent, vicious, barbarous, barbaric, savage, brutal, cutthroat; fierce, ferocious, inhuman.

bloody ▶ adjective **1** *his bloody nose* **bleeding.**
2 *bloody medical waste* **bloodstained,** blood-soaked, gory; archaic sanguinary.
3 *a bloody civil war* **vicious,** ferocious, savage, fierce, brutal, murderous, barbarous, gory; archaic sanguinary.
4 Brit. informal *a bloody nuisance!* See DAMNED (sense 2).

bloom ▶ noun **1** *orchid blooms* **flower,** blossom, floweret, floret.
2 *a girl in the bloom of youth* **prime,** perfection, acme, peak, height, heyday; salad days.
3 *the bloom of her skin* **radiance,** luster, sheen, glow, freshness; **blush,** rosiness, pinkness, color.
▶ verb **1** *the geraniums bloomed* **flower,** blossom, open; mature.
ANTONYMS wither.
2 *their health bloomed in the mountain air* **flourish,** thrive, prosper, progress, burgeon; informal be in the pink.
ANTONYMS decline.

blossom ▶ noun *pink blossoms* **flower,** bloom, floweret, floret.
▶ verb **1** *the trilliums have blossomed* **bloom,**

flower, open, unfold; mature.
ANTONYMS fade.
2 *the whole region had blossomed* **develop,** grow, mature, progress, evolve; flourish, thrive, prosper, bloom, burgeon.
ANTONYMS decline.
– PHRASES **in blossom** *the cactus is in blossom* **in flower,** flowering, blossoming, blooming, in (full) bloom, abloom, open, out; formal inflorescent.

blot ▶ noun **1** *an ink blot* **spot,** dot, mark, blotch, smudge, patch, dab; informal splotch.
2 *the only blot on a clean campaign* **blemish,** taint, stain, blight, flaw, fault; disgrace, dishonor.
▶ verb **1** *blot the excess water* **soak up,** absorb, sponge up, mop up; dry up/out; dab, pat.
2 *he had blotted our name forever* **tarnish,** taint, stain, blacken, sully, mar; dishonor, disgrace, besmirch.
ANTONYMS honor.
– PHRASES **blot something out 1** *Mary blotted out her picture* **erase,** obliterate, delete, efface, rub out, blank out, expunge, eradicate; cross out, strike out, wipe out.
2 *clouds were starting to blot out the stars* **conceal,** hide, obscure, exclude, obliterate; shadow, eclipse.

blotch ▶ noun **1** *pink flowers with dark blotches* **patch,** smudge, dot, spot, blot, dab, daub; informal splotch.
2 *his face was covered in blotches* **patch,** mark, freckle, birthmark, discoloration, eruption, nevus.
▶ verb *her face was blotched and swollen* **spot,** mark, smudge, streak, blemish.

blow ▶ verb **1** *the icy wind blew around us* **gust,** bluster, puff, blast, roar, rush, storm.
2 *his ship was blown on to the rocks* **sweep,** carry, toss, drive, push, force.
3 *leaves blew across the road* **drift,** flutter, waft, float, glide, whirl, move.
4 *he blew a smoke ring* **exhale,** puff, breathe out; emit, expel, discharge, issue.
5 *he blew a trumpet* **sound,** blast, toot, pipe, trumpet; play.
6 *a rear tire had blown* **burst,** explode, blow out, split, rupture, puncture.
7 informal *he blew his money on gambling* **squander,** waste, misspend, throw away, fritter away, go through, lose, lavish, dissipate, use up; spend recklessly; informal splurge.
8 informal *don't blow this opportunity* **spoil,** ruin, bungle, mess up, fudge, muff; **waste,** lose, squander; informal botch, screw up, foul up.
9 *his cover was blown* **expose,** reveal, uncover, disclose, divulge, unveil, betray, leak.
▶ noun **1** *a blow on the head* **knock, bang,** hit, punch, thump, smack, crack, rap, karate chop; informal whack, thwack, bonk, bash, clout, sock, wallop.
2 *losing his wife must have been a blow* **shock,** surprise, bombshell, thunderbolt, jolt; calamity, catastrophe, disaster, upset, setback.
3 *a blow on the guard's whistle* **toot,** blast, blare; whistle.
– PHRASES **blow out 1** *the matches will not blow out in a strong wind* **be extinguished,** go out, be put out, stop burning. **2** *the front tire blew out* See **BLOW** (sense 6 of the verb). **3** *the windows blew out* **shatter,** rupture, crack, smash, splinter, disintegrate; burst, explode, fly apart; informal bust. **blow something out** *blow the candles out* **extinguish,** put out, snuff, douse, quench, smother. **blow over** *the storm will blow over soon* **abate,** subside, drop off, lessen, ease (off), let up, diminish, fade, dwindle, slacken, recede, tail off, peter out, pass, die down, fizzle out; dated remit. **blow up 1** *a truckload of shells blew up* **explode,** detonate, go off, ignite, erupt. **2** *he blows up over every little thing* **lose one's temper,** get angry, rant and rave, go berserk, flare up, erupt; informal go mad, go crazy, go wild, hit the roof, fly off the handle. **3** *a crisis blew up* **break out,** erupt, flare up, boil over; emerge, arise. **blow something up 1** *they blew the plane up* **bomb,** blast, destroy; explode, detonate. **2** *blow up the balloons* **inflate,** pump up, fill up, puff up, swell, expand. **3** *I blew the picture up on a photocopier* **enlarge,** magnify, expand, increase. **blow out of proportion** *it was an innocent passing remark that he's blown out of proportion* **exaggerate,** overstate, overstress, overestimate, magnify, amplify; aggrandize, embellish, elaborate.

blowout ▶ noun **1** *the steering is automatic in the event of blowouts* **puncture,** flat tire, burst tire; informal flat.
2 informal *this meal is our last real blowout* **feast,** banquet, celebration, party; informal shindig, do, binge.
3 *the game turned into a 17–3 blowout* **rout,** whitewash, walkover, landslide.

bludgeon ▶ noun *hooligans wielding bludgeons* **cudgel,** club, stick, truncheon, baton; nightstick, billy club, blackjack.
▶ verb *he was bludgeoned to death* **batter,** cudgel, club, beat, thrash; clobber, pummel.

blue ▶ adjective **1** *bright blue eyes* sky blue, azure, cobalt, sapphire, navy, powder blue, midnight blue, Prussian blue, electric blue, indigo, royal blue, ice-blue, baby blue, air force blue, robin's egg blue, peacock blue, ultramarine, aquamarine, steel blue, slate blue, cyan; chiefly Brit. Oxford blue, Cambridge blue; literary cerulean.
2 informal *Mom was feeling a bit blue* **depressed,** down, sad, unhappy, melancholy, miserable, gloomy, dejected, dispirited, downhearted, downcast, despondent, low, glum; informal down in the dumps.
ANTONYMS happy.

blueprint ▶ noun **1** *blueprints of the aircraft* **plan,** design, diagram, drawing, sketch, map, layout, representation.
2 *a blueprint for similar measures in other countries* **model,** plan, template, framework, pattern, example, guide, prototype, pilot.

blues ▶ plural noun informal *a fit of blues* **depression,** sadness, unhappiness, melancholy, misery, sorrow, gloom, dejection, despondency, despair; the doldrums, the dumps, a blue funk.

bluff[1] ▶ noun *this threat was dismissed as a bluff* **deception,** front, subterfuge, pretense,

posturing, sham, fake, deceit, feint, hoax, facade, fraud, charade; trick, ruse, scheme, machination; informal put-on.
▶ **verb 1** *they are bluffing to hide their guilt* **pretend,** sham, fake, feign, lie, hoax, pose, posture, masquerade, dissemble.
2 *I managed to bluff the board into believing me* **deceive,** delude, mislead, trick, fool, hoodwink, dupe, hoax, beguile, gull; informal con, kid.

bluff² ▶ **adjective** *a bluff man* **plain-spoken,** straightforward, blunt, direct, no-nonsense, frank, open, candid, forthright, unequivocal; hearty, genial, good-natured; informal upfront. See note at BRUSQUE.

bluff³ ▶ **noun** *an impregnable high bluff* **cliff,** promontory, ridge, headland, crag, bank, height, peak, escarpment, scarp, overhang; rare eminence.

blunder ▶ **noun** *he shook his head at his blunder* **mistake,** error, gaffe, slip, oversight, faux pas, misstep, infelicity; informal botch, slip-up, boo-boo, blooper, boner, flub. See note at MISTAKE.
▶ **verb 1** *the government admitted it had blundered* **make a mistake,** err, miscalculate, bungle, trip up, be wrong; informal slip up, screw up, blow it, goof.
2 *she blundered down the steps* **stumble,** lurch, stagger, flounder, struggle, fumble, grope.

blunt ▶ **adjective 1** *a blunt knife* **unsharpened,** dull, worn, edgeless.
ANTONYMS sharp.
2 *the leaf is broad with a blunt tip* **rounded,** flat, obtuse, stubby.
ANTONYMS pointed.
3 *a blunt message* **straightforward,** frank, plain-spoken, candid, direct, bluff, forthright, unequivocal; **brusque,** abrupt, curt, terse, bald, brutal, harsh; stark, unadorned, undisguised, unvarnished; informal upfront. See note at BRUSQUE.
ANTONYMS subtle.
▶ **verb 1** *ebony blunts tools very rapidly* **dull,** make less sharp.
ANTONYMS sharpen.
2 *age hasn't blunted my passion for life* **dull,** deaden, dampen, numb, weaken, sap, cool, temper, allay, abate; diminish, reduce, decrease, lessen, deplete.
ANTONYMS intensify.

blur ▶ **verb 1** *tears blurred her vision* **cloud,** fog, obscure, dim, make hazy, unfocus, soften; literary bedim; archaic blear.
ANTONYMS sharpen, focus.
2 *movies blur the difference between villains and victims* **obscure,** make vague, confuse, muddle, muddy, obfuscate, cloud, weaken.
▶ **noun** *a blur on the horizon* **indistinct shape,** smudge; haze, cloud, mist.

blurred ▶ **adjective** *a blurred photograph* **indistinct,** blurry, fuzzy, hazy, misty, foggy, shadowy, faint; unclear, vague, indefinite, unfocused, obscure, nebulous.

blurt ▶ **verb**
– PHRASES **blurt something out** *he blurted out his story* **burst out with,** exclaim, call out; **divulge,** disclose, reveal, betray, let slip, give away; informal blab, gush, let on, spill the beans (about), let the cat out of the bag (about).

blush ▶ **verb** *Joan blushed at the compliment* **redden,** turn/go pink, turn/go red, flush, color, burn up; feel shy, feel embarrassed.
▶ **noun** *a blush spread across his face* **flush,** rosiness, pinkness, bloom, (high) color.

bluster ▶ **verb 1** *he started blustering about the general election* **rant,** rave, thunder, bellow, sound off; be overbearing; informal throw one's weight around/about.
2 *storms bluster in from the sea* **blast,** gust, storm, roar, rush.
▶ **noun** *his bluster turned to cooperation* **ranting,** thundering, hectoring, bullying; bombast, bravado, bumptiousness, braggadocio.

blustery ▶ **adjective** *a blustery autumn day* **stormy,** gusty, blowy, windy, squally, wild, tempestuous, turbulent; howling, roaring.
ANTONYMS calm.

board ▶ **noun 1** *a wooden board* **plank,** beam, panel, slat, batten, timber, lath.
2 *the board of directors* **committee,** council, panel, directorate, commission, executive, group.
3 *your room and board will be free* **food,** meals, provisions, diet, table, bread, rations; keep, maintenance; informal grub, nosh, eats, chow.
▶ **verb 1** *he boarded the aircraft* **get on,** go aboard, enter, mount, ascend; embark, emplane, entrain; catch; informal hop on.
2 *a number of students boarded with them* **lodge,** live, reside, be housed, room; informal be put up.
3 *they run a facility for boarding dogs* **accommodate,** lodge, take in, put up, house; keep, feed, cater for, billet.
– PHRASES **board something up/over** *shoreline residents are boarding up their windows* **cover up/over,** close up, shut up, seal.

boast ▶ **verb 1** *his mother had been boasting about him* **brag,** crow, swagger, swank, gloat, show off; exaggerate, overstate; informal talk big, blow one's own horn, lay it on thick.
2 *the hotel boasts a fine restaurant* **possess,** have, own, enjoy, pride oneself/itself on.
▶ **noun 1** *everyone has tired of listening to your boast* **brag,** self-praise; exaggeration, overstatement, grandiloquence, fanfaronade.
2 *the hall is the boast of the county* **pride,** joy, wonder, delight, treasure, gem.

boastful ▶ **adjective** *in the first debate he came across as aggressive and boastful* **bragging,** swaggering, bumptious, puffed up, full of oneself; cocky, conceited, arrogant, egotistical; informal swanky, bigheaded, blowhard; literary vainglorious.
ANTONYMS modest.

boat ▶ **noun** *a rowing boat* **vessel,** craft, watercraft, ship; literary keel.
▶ **verb** *they were out boating for hours* **sail,** yacht, paddle, row, cruise.

bob ▶ **verb** *the bottle bobbed in the water* **move up and down,** bounce, toss, skip, dance, jounce; wobble, jiggle, joggle, jolt, jerk; **nod,** incline, dip; wag, waggle.

bode ▶ **verb** *it's that unsettling kind of silence that bodes danger* **augur,** portend, herald, be a sign of, warn of, foreshadow, be an omen of, presage, indicate, signify, promise, threaten, spell, denote, foretell; prophesy, predict; literary betoken, forebode.

bodily ▶ adjective *bodily sensations* **physical,** corporeal, corporal, somatic, fleshly; concrete, real, actual, tangible.
ANTONYMS spiritual, mental.

body ▶ noun **1** *the human body* **figure,** frame, form, physique, anatomy, skeleton; soma; informal bod.
2 *he was hit by shrapnel in the head and body* **torso,** trunk.
3 *the body was exhumed* **corpse,** carcass, skeleton, remains; informal stiff; Medicine cadaver.
4 *the body of the essay* **main part,** central part, core, heart.
5 *a body of water* **expanse,** mass, area, stretch, tract, sweep, extent.
6 *a growing body of evidence* **quantity,** amount, volume, collection, mass, corpus.
7 *the representative body of the employers* **association,** organization, group, party, company, society, circle, syndicate, guild, corporation, contingent.
8 *add body to your hair* **fullness,** thickness, substance, bounce, lift, shape.
– PHRASES **body and soul** *these young men and women belong to the Corps, body and soul* **completely,** entirely, totally, utterly, fully, thoroughly, wholeheartedly, unconditionally, to the hilt.

CHOOSE THE RIGHT WORD

body, cadaver, carcass, corpse, cremains, remains

The problem of what to call the human **body** after it has departed this life is a delicate one. Although a *body* can be either dead or alive, human or animal, a **corpse** is most definitely a dead human body and a **carcass** is the body of a dead animal. The issue has been confused, of course, by the figurative use of *carcass* as a term of contempt (*"Get your carcass out of bed and come down here!"*). While *carcass* is often used humorously, there's nothing funny about *corpse*, a no-nonsense term for a lifeless physical body (*the battlefield was littered with corpses*). A funeral director is likely to prefer the term **remains**, which is a euphemism for the body of the deceased (*he had his wife's remains shipped home for burial*), or **cremains**, if the body has been cremated. A medical student, on the other hand, is much more likely to use the term **cadaver**, which is a corpse that is dissected in a laboratory for scientific study.

bog ▶ noun *the bogs were alive with chirring insects and croaking frogs* **marsh,** swamp, muskeg, mire, quagmire, morass, slough, fen, wetland, bogland.
– PHRASES **bogged down** *bogged down with endless paperwork* **mired,** stuck, entangled, ensnared, embroiled; hampered, hindered, impeded, delayed, stalled, detained; swamped, overwhelmed.

boggle ▶ verb **1** *this data makes the mind boggle* **marvel,** wonder.
2 *it boggles my mind* **baffle,** astonish, astound, amaze, stagger, overwhelm.

bogus ▶ adjective *a bogus insurance claim | a bogus lottery ticket* **fake,** spurious, false, fraudulent, sham, deceptive; **counterfeit,** forged, feigned; make-believe, dummy, pseudo, phony, pretend, fictitious.
ANTONYMS genuine.

bohemian ▶ noun *he is an artist and a Bohemian* **nonconformist,** free spirit, dropout; hippie, beatnik; informal boho.
ANTONYMS conservative.
▶ adjective *a Bohemian student life* **unconventional,** nonconformist, unorthodox, avant-garde, irregular, offbeat, alternative; artistic; informal boho, artsy, artsy-fartsy, way-out.
ANTONYMS conventional.

boil[1] ▶ verb **1** *boil the potatoes* **bring to a boil,** simmer, parboil, poach; cook.
2 *the soup is boiling* **simmer,** bubble, stew.
3 *a huge cliff with the sea boiling below* **churn,** seethe, froth, foam; literary roil.
▶ noun *bring the stock to a boil* **boiling point,** rolling boil.
– PHRASES **boil something down** *you have to boil down a lot of tomatoes to make just a few tablespoons of tomato paste* **condense,** reduce, concentrate, distill, thicken, compress.
boil down to *it all boils down to how much money you're willing to spend* **come down to,** amount to, add up to, be in essence.

boil[2] ▶ noun *a boil on her neck* **swelling,** spot, pimple, blister, pustule, eruption, carbuncle, wen, abscess, ulcer; technical furuncle.

boiling ▶ adjective **1** *boiling water* **at boiling point,** at 212 degrees Fahrenheit, at 100 degrees Celsius/centigrade; very hot, piping hot; bubbling.
ANTONYMS freezing, ice-cold.
2 informal *it was a boiling day* **very hot,** scorching, blistering, sweltering, sultry, torrid; informal broiling, roasting, baking, sizzling.
ANTONYMS cold, freezing.

boisterous ▶ adjective **1** *a boisterous game of handball* **lively,** animated, exuberant, spirited, rambunctious; rowdy, unruly, wild, uproarious, unrestrained, undisciplined, uninhibited, uncontrolled, rough, disorderly, riotous, knockabout; noisy, loud, clamorous. See note at VOCIFEROUS.
ANTONYMS restrained, quiet.
2 *a boisterous wind* **blustery,** gusty, windy, stormy, wild, squally, tempestuous; howling, roaring; informal blowy.
ANTONYMS calm.

bold ▶ adjective **1** *bold adventurers* **daring,** intrepid, brave, courageous, valiant, valorous, fearless, dauntless, audacious, daredevil; adventurous, heroic, plucky, spirited, confident, assured; informal gutsy, spunky, feisty; literary temerarious.
ANTONYMS timid, unadventurous.
2 *don't be so bold in public* **impudent,** insolent, impertinent, brazen, brash, disrespectful, presumptuous, forward; cheeky, fresh.

3 *a bold pattern* **striking,** vivid, bright, strong, eye-catching, prominent, impactful; gaudy, lurid, garish.
ANTONYMS pale.
4 *departure times are in bold type* **heavy,** thick, pronounced, conspicuous.
ANTONYMS light, roman.

> CHOOSE THE RIGHT WORD
> **bold, aggressive, audacious, bumptious, brazen, intrepid, presumptuous**
> Is walking up to an attractive stranger and asking him or her to have dinner with you tonight a **bold** move or merely an **aggressive** one? Both words suggest assertive, confident behavior that is a little on the shameless side, but *bold* has a wider range of application. It can suggest self-confidence that borders on impudence (*to be so bold as to call the president by his first name*), but it can also be used to describe a daring temperament that is either courageous or defiant (*a bold investigator who would not give up*). *Aggressive* behavior, on the other hand, usually falls within a narrower range, somewhere between menacing (*aggressive attacks on innocent villagers*) and just plain pushy (*an aggressive salesperson*). **Brazen** implies a defiant lack of modesty (*a brazen stare*), and **presumptuous** goes even further, suggesting overconfidence to the point of causing offense (*a presumptuous request for money*). **Bumptious** behavior can also be offensive, but it is usually associated with the kind of cockiness that can't be helped (*a bumptious young upstart*). An **audacious** individual is bold to the point of recklessness (*an audacious explorer*), which brings it very close in meaning to **intrepid**, suggesting fearlessness in the face of the unknown (*the intrepid settlers of the Great Plains*).

bolster ▶ verb *an occasional word of thanks would really bolster the staff's morale* **strengthen,** reinforce, boost, fortify, renew; support, sustain, buoy up, prop up, shore up, maintain, aid, help; augment, increase.
ANTONYMS undermine.

bolt ▶ noun 1 *the bolt on the shed door* **bar, lock,** catch, latch, fastener, deadbolt.
2 *nuts and bolts* **rivet,** pin, peg, screw.
3 *a bolt whirred over my head* **arrow,** quarrel, dart, shaft.
4 *a bolt of lightning* **flash,** thunderbolt, shaft, streak, burst, flare.
5 *Mark made a bolt for the door* **dash,** dart, run, sprint, leap, bound.
6 *a bolt of cloth* **roll,** reel, spool; quantity, amount.
▶ verb 1 *he bolted the door* **lock,** bar, latch, fasten, secure.
2 *the lid was bolted down* **rivet,** pin, peg, screw; fasten, fix.
3 *Anna bolted from the room* **dash,** dart, run, sprint, hurtle, careen, rush, fly, shoot, bound; flee; informal tear, scoot, leg it.
4 *he bolted down his breakfast* **gobble up,** gulp down, wolf down, guzzle (down), devour; informal demolish, polish off, shovel in/down, scarf up.
– PHRASES **a bolt (from) out of the blue** *the department shutdown came as a bolt out of the blue* **shock,** surprise, bombshell, thunderbolt, revelation. **bolt upright** *in Scene 2, the corpse is supposed to sit suddenly bolt upright* **straight,** rigidly, stiffly.
ANTONYMS slouching.

bomb ▶ noun 1 *they saw bombs bursting on the runway* **explosive,** incendiary (device); missile, projectile; dated blockbuster, bombshell.
2 *countries with the bomb* **nuclear weapons,** nuclear bombs, atom bombs, A-bombs.
3 informal *their next film was a bomb* **failure,** flop, megaflop, fiasco, bust, dud, washout, debacle, turkey, dog, clunker.
▶ verb 1 *their headquarters were bombed* **bombard,** blast, shell, blitz, strafe, pound; attack, assault; blow up, destroy, demolish, flatten, devastate.
2 informal *the show bombed at the box office* **fail,** flop, fall flat, founder.

bombard ▶ verb 1 *gun batteries bombarded the islands* **shell,** pound, blitz, strafe, bomb; assail, attack, assault, batter, blast, pelt. See note at ATTACK.
2 *we were bombarded with information* **inundate,** swamp, flood, deluge, snow under; besiege, overwhelm.

bona fide ▶ adjective *the table is definitely an imitation Chippendale, but the chairs are bona fide | a bona fide endorsement* **authentic,** genuine, real, true, actual; legal, legitimate, lawful, valid, proper; informal legit, the real McCoy. See note at GENUINE.
ANTONYMS bogus.

bonanza ▶ noun *those grisly murders of 1872 turned into quite a bonanza for the town, which has thrived as a center of tourism ever since* **windfall,** godsend, boon, blessing, bonus, stroke of luck, jackpot.

bond ▶ noun 1 *the bond between Moira and her son* **relationship,** tie, link, friendship, fellowship, partnership, association, affiliation, alliance, attachment.
2 *the prisoner struggled with his bonds* **chains,** fetters, shackles, manacles, irons, restraints.
3 *you've broken your bond* **promise,** pledge, vow, oath, word (of honor), guarantee, assurance; agreement, contract, pact, bargain, deal.
▶ verb *the extensions are bonded to your hair* **join,** fasten, fix, affix, attach, secure, bind, stick, fuse.

bondage ▶ noun *our own freedom is not so gratifying when we must look upon the bondage of others* **slavery,** enslavement, servitude, subjugation, subjection, oppression, domination, exploitation, persecution; enthrallment, thraldom; historical serfdom, vassalage.
ANTONYMS liberty.

bonus ▶ noun 1 *the extra space is a real bonus* **benefit,** advantage, boon, blessing, godsend, stroke of luck, asset, attraction; informal plus, pro, perk, gravy; formal perquisite.
ANTONYMS disadvantage.

2 *she's on a good salary and she gets a bonus* **gratuity,** gift, present, reward, prize, lagniappe; incentive, inducement, handout; informal sweetener. See note at PRESENT[3].
ANTONYMS penalty.

bony ▶ **adjective** *his pale, bony face* **gaunt, angular,** skinny, thin, lean, spare, spindly, skin-and-bones, skeletal, emaciated, underweight; informal like a bag of bones; rare starveling, macilent, gracile.
ANTONYMS plump.

book ▶ **noun 1** *Nadine and Ian have recommended some good books* **volume,** tome, publication, title; novel, storybook, anthology, treatise, manual; paperback, hardback, pocket book, e-book.
2 *he scribbled in his book* **notebook,** notepad, pad, memo pad, exercise book, workbook; logbook, ledger, journal, diary.
3 *enter a $400 deposit in the book | the council had to balance its books* **ledger,** account book, record book, balance sheet; (**books**) **accounts,** records.
▶ **verb 1** *Dan and Veronica booked a table at the restaurant* **reserve,** make a reservation for, prearrange, order; formal bespeak.
2 *we booked a number of events for the festival* **arrange,** program, schedule, timetable, line up, pencil in, slate.
– PHRASES **by the book** *he's a cop who does everything by the book* **according to the rules,** within the law, lawfully, legally, legitimately; honestly, fairly; informal on the level, fair and square.

bookish ▶ **adjective** *Swann was always the bookish one in our group* **studious,** scholarly, academic, intellectual, highbrow, erudite, learned, lettered, educated, well-read, knowledgeable; cerebral, serious, earnest; pedantic.

boom ▶ **noun 1** *the boom of the thunder* **reverberation,** resonance, thunder, echoing, crashing, drumming, pounding, roar, rumble, explosion.
2 *an unprecedented boom in sales* **upturn,** upsurge, upswing, increase, advance, growth, boost, escalation, improvement, spurt.
ANTONYMS slump.
▶ **verb 1** *thunder boomed overhead* **reverberate,** resound, resonate; rumble, thunder, blare, echo; crash, roll, clap, explode, bang.
2 *a voice boomed at her* **bellow,** roar, thunder, shout, bawl; informal holler.
ANTONYMS whisper.
3 *the market continued to boom* **flourish,** burgeon, thrive, prosper, progress, improve, pick up, expand, mushroom, snowball.
ANTONYMS slump.

boomerang ▶ **verb** *their tax-evading scheme boomeranged, and now they're facing serious legal trouble* **backfire,** recoil, reverse, rebound, ricochet; be self-defeating; informal blow up in one's face.

boon ▶ **noun** *their help was such a boon* **blessing,** godsend, bonus, plus, benefit, advantage, help, aid, asset; stroke of luck, windfall.
ANTONYMS curse.

boor ▶ **noun** *a civilized affair guaranteed to separate the boors from the gentlemen* **lout,** oaf, ruffian, thug, yahoo, barbarian, Neanderthal, brute, beast, lubber; informal clod, roughneck, troglodyte, knuckle-dragger, pig, peasant.

boorish ▶ **adjective** *we will not tolerate such boorish behavior from our officers* **coarse,** uncouth, rude, ill-bred, ill-mannered, uncivilized, unrefined, rough, thuggish, loutish, oafish, lubberly, lumpen; vulgar, unsavory, gross, brutish, Neanderthal; informal cloddish.
ANTONYMS refined.

boost ▶ **noun 1** *a boost to one's morale | just the boost I needed* **uplift,** lift, spur, encouragement, help, inspiration, stimulus, pick-me-up; informal shot in the arm.
2 *a boost in sales* **increase,** expansion, upturn, upsurge, upswing, rise, escalation, improvement, advance, growth, boom; hike, jump.
ANTONYMS decrease.
▶ **verb 1** *he phoned to boost her spirits* **improve,** raise, uplift, increase, enhance, encourage, heighten, help, promote, foster, stimulate, invigorate, revitalize; informal buck up.
2 *they used advertising to boost sales* **increase,** raise, escalate, improve, strengthen, inflate, push up, promote, advance, foster, stimulate, maximize; facilitate, help, assist, aid; jump-start; informal hike, bump up.
ANTONYMS decrease.

boot ▶ **noun** *muddy boots*
▶ **verb 1** *his shot was booted away by the goalkeeper* **kick,** punt; propel, drive.
2 ***boot up*** *your computer* **start up,** fire up, reboot.
– PHRASES **give someone the boot** informal See DISMISS (sense 1).

booth ▶ **noun 1** *booths for different vendors* **stall,** stand, kiosk.
2 *a phone booth* **cubicle,** kiosk, box, enclosure.

booty ▶ **noun** *divvying up the booty* **loot,** plunder, pillage, haul, spoils, stolen goods, ill-gotten gains, pickings; informal swag.

bordello ▶ **noun** *she's currently on Broadway, playing the feisty madam of a bordello* **brothel,** whorehouse; informal cathouse; euphemistic massage parlor; dated bawdy house, house of ill repute; Law dated disorderly house.

border ▶ **noun 1** *the border of a medieval manuscript* **edge, margin,** perimeter, circumference, periphery; rim, fringe, verge; sides.
2 *the Canadian border* **frontier,** boundary; borderline, perimeter; marches, bounds.
▶ **verb 1** *the fields were bordered by hedges* **surround,** enclose, encircle, circle, edge, fringe, bound, flank.
2 *the straps are bordered with gold braid* **edge,** fringe, hem; trim, pipe, finish.
3 *the property* ***bordered on*** *the state park* **adjoin,** abut, be next to, be adjacent to, be contiguous with, touch, join, meet, reach.
– PHRASES **border on** *his tone bordered on contempt* **verge on,** approach, come close to, be comparable to, approximate to, be tantamount to, be similar to, resemble.

> CHOOSE THE RIGHT WORD
>
> **border, brim, brink, edge, margin, rim, verge**
>
> A **border** is the part of a surface that is nearest to its boundary (*a rug with a flowered border*)—although it may also refer to the boundary line itself (*the border between Vermont and New Hampshire*). A **margin** is a *border* of a definite width that is usually distinct in appearance from what it encloses; but unlike *border*, it usually refers to the blankness or emptiness that surrounds something (*the margin on a printed page*). While *border* and *margin* usually refer to something that is circumscribed, **edge** may refer to only a part of the perimeter (*the edge of the lawn*) or the line where two planes or surfaces converge (*the edge of the table*). *Edge* can also connote sharpness (*the edge of a knife*) and can be used metaphorically to suggest tension, harshness, or keenness (*there was an edge in her voice; take the edge off their nervousness*). **Verge** may also be used metaphorically to describe the extreme limit of something (*on the verge of a nervous breakdown*), but in a more literal sense, it sometimes is used of the line or narrow space that marks the limit or termination of something (*the verge of a desert or forest*). **Brink** denotes the edge of something very steep or an abrupt division between land and water (*the brink of the river*), or metaphorically the very final limit before an abrupt change (*on the brink of disaster*). **Rim** and **brim** apply only to things that are circular or curving. But while *rim* describes the edge or lip of a rounded or cylindrical shape (*the rim of a glass*), *brim* refers to the inner side of the rim when the container is completely full (*a cup filled to the brim with steaming coffee*). However, when one speaks of the *brim* of a hat, it comes closer to the meaning of *margin* or *border*.

bore ▶ verb **1** *the movie bored us* **stultify,** pall on, stupefy, weary, tire, fatigue, send to sleep, leave cold; bore to death, bore to tears; informal turn off.
2 *bore a hole in the ceiling* **drill,** pierce, perforate, puncture, punch, cut; tunnel, burrow, mine, dig, gouge, sink.
▶ noun *you can be such a bore* **tedious person/thing,** tiresome person/thing, dull person/thing, yawn, bother, nuisance, wet blanket.

boredom ▶ noun *his eyes were glassy with boredom* **weariness,** ennui, apathy, unconcern; frustration, dissatisfaction, restlessness, restiveness, lethargy, lassitude; tedium, dullness, monotony, repetitiveness, flatness, dreariness; informal deadliness.

boring ▶ adjective *a boring one-man play* **tedious,** dull, monotonous, repetitive, unrelieved, unvaried, unimaginative, uneventful; characterless, featureless, colorless, lifeless, insipid, uninteresting, unexciting, uninspiring, unstimulating; unreadable, unwatchable; jejune, flat, bland, dry, stale, tired, banal, lackluster, stodgy, vapid, monochrome, dreary, humdrum, mundane; mind-numbing, wearisome, tiring, tiresome, irksome, trying, frustrating; informal deadly, ho-hum, dullsville, dull as dishwater, plain-vanilla.

borrow ▶ verb **1** *we borrowed a lot of money* take as a loan; lease, hire; informal scrounge, bum, cadge, mooch.
ANTONYMS lend.
2 informal *they "borrowed" all of his tools* **take,** help oneself to, appropriate, commandeer, abscond with, carry off; steal, purloin; informal filch, rob, swipe, nab, rip off, lift, "liberate", pinch, heist.
3 *adventurous chefs borrow foreign techniques* **adopt,** take on, acquire, embrace.
ANTONYMS impart.

bosom ▶ noun **1** *the gown was set low over her bosom* **bust,** chest; breasts, mammary glands; informal boobs, knockers, mammaries, bazooms.
2 literary *the family took Gill into its bosom* **protection,** shelter, safety, refuge; heart.
3 *love was kindled within his bosom* **heart,** breast, soul, core, spirit.
▶ adjective *bosom friends* **close,** intimate, inseparable, faithful, constant, devoted; good, best, favorite.

boss ▶ noun *the boss of a large company* **head,** chief, director, president, principal, chief executive, chair, manager; supervisor, foreman, overseer, controller; employer, owner, proprietor; informal number one, kingpin, boss man, boss lady, top dog, bigwig, big cheese, head honcho, big kahuna.
▶ verb *you have no right to* ***boss*** *me* ***around*** **order around,** dictate to, lord it over, bully, push around, domineer, dominate, pressurize, browbeat; call the shots for, lay down the law on, bulldoze, walk all over, railroad.

bossy ▶ adjective *we're hiding from his bossy sister* **domineering,** pushy, overbearing, imperious, officious, high-handed, authoritarian, dictatorial, controlling; informal high and mighty.
ANTONYMS submissive.

botch ▶ verb *examiners botched the test scores* **bungle,** mismanage, mishandle, make a mess of, mess up, make a hash of, muff, fluff, foul up, screw up, flub.

bother ▶ verb **1** *no one bothered her* **disturb,** trouble, inconvenience, pester, badger, harass, molest, plague, nag, hound, harry, annoy, upset, irritate, hassle, bug, get in someone's hair, get on someone's case, get under a someone's skin, ruffle someone's feathers, rag on, ride.
2 *the incident was too small to bother about* **mind,** care, concern oneself, trouble oneself, worry oneself; informal give a damn, give a hoot.
3 *there was something bothering him* **worry,** trouble, concern, perturb, disturb, disquiet, disconcert, unnerve; fret, upset, distress, agitate, gnaw at, weigh down; informal rattle.
▶ noun **1** *I don't want to put you to any bother* **trouble,** effort, exertion, inconvenience, fuss, pains.
2 *the food was such a bother to cook* **nuisance,** hassle, pain in the neck, headache, pest, palaver,

rigmarole, job, trial, drag, chore, inconvenience, trouble, problem.

bottle ▶ noun **1** *a bottle of whiskey* carafe, flask, decanter, canteen, vessel, pitcher, flagon, magnum, carboy, demijohn.
2 informal *a world blurred by the bottle* See ALCOHOL.
– PHRASES **bottle something up** *don't bottle up your emotions* **suppress,** repress, restrain, withhold, hold in, rein in, inhibit, smother, stifle, contain, conceal, hide, cork, keep a lid on.

bottleneck ▶ noun *there's a bottleneck at the intersection of I-91 and I-84* **traffic jam,** jam, congestion, tie-up, holdup, snarl-up, gridlock, logjam, constriction, narrowing, restriction, obstruction, blockage, choke point.

bottom ▶ noun **1** *the bottom of the stairs* **foot,** lowest part, lowest point, base; foundation, substructure, underpinning.
ANTONYMS top.
2 *the bottom of the car* **underside,** underneath, undersurface, undercarriage, underbelly.
3 *the bottom of Lake Ontario* **floor,** bed.
ANTONYMS surface.
4 *the bottom of the standings in the Eastern League* **lowest position,** lowest level.
ANTONYMS top.
5 *I enjoyed the horseback ride, except for my sore bottom* **rear,** rear end, backside, seat, buttocks, rump, derrière; informal cheeks, behind, butt, booty, fanny, keister, tush, tail, buns, caboose, duff, heinie, ass, fundament, posterior, gluteus maximus, sit-upon, stern; Brit. informal bum, arse; Anatomy nates.
6 *police got to the bottom of the mystery* **origin,** cause, root, source, basis, foundation; heart, kernel; essence.
▶ adjective *she sat on the bottom step* **lowest,** last, bottommost; technical basal.
ANTONYMS highest, top.

bottomless ▶ adjective **1** *the bottomless pits of hell* **fathomless,** unfathomable, endless, infinite, immeasurable.
2 *George's appetite was bottomless* **unlimited,** limitless, boundless, infinite, inexhaustible, endless, never-ending, everlasting; vast, huge, enormous.
ANTONYMS limited.

bough ▶ noun *snow-laden pine boughs* **branch,** limb, arm, offshoot.

boulder ▶ noun *a natural formation of boulders* **rock,** stone.

boulevard ▶ noun *the third right off of the boulevard* **avenue,** street, road, drive, thoroughfare, way.

bounce ▶ verb **1** *the ball bounced* **rebound,** spring back, ricochet, jounce, carom; reflect.
2 *William bounced down the stairs* **bound,** leap, jump, spring, bob, hop, skip, trip, prance.
▶ noun **1** *he reached the door in a single bounce* **bound,** leap, jump, spring, hop, skip.
2 *she had lost her bounce* **vitality,** vigor, energy, vivacity, liveliness, animation, sparkle, verve, spirit, enthusiasm, dynamism; cheerfulness, happiness, buoyancy, optimism; exuberance, ebullience; informal get-up-and-go, pep, zing.
– PHRASES **bounce back** *despite our optimistic predictions, sales never bounced back* **recover,** revive, rally, pick up, be on the mend; perk up, cheer up, brighten up, liven up; informal buck up.

bouncing ▶ adjective *can we expect a bouncing economy within the next five years?* **vigorous,** thriving, flourishing, blooming; **healthy,** strong, robust, fit, in fine fettle; informal in the pink.

bound[1] ▶ adjective **1** *his bound ankles* **tied,** chained, fettered, shackled, secured, tied up.
2 *she seemed bound to win* **certain,** sure, very likely, destined, fated, doomed.
3 *you're bound by the law to keep quiet* **obligated,** obliged, compelled, required, constrained, forced.
4 *the unrest was* **bound up** *with the region's economic stagnation* **connected,** linked, tied, united, allied.

bound[2] ▶ verb *hares bound in the fields* **leap,** jump, spring, bounce, hop; skip, bob, dance, prance, gambol, gallop.
▶ noun *he crossed the room with a single bound* **leap,** jump, spring, bounce, hop.

bound[3] ▶ verb **1** *corporate freedom is bounded by law* **limit,** restrict, confine, circumscribe, demarcate, delimit.
2 *the garden is bounded by a hedge* **enclose,** surround, encircle, circle, border; close in/off, hem in.
– PHRASES **out of bounds** *this building is out of bounds for all nonmilitary personnel | harassment of our waitresses is strictly out of bounds* **off limits,** restricted, closed off; forbidden, banned, proscribed, illegal, illicit, unlawful, unacceptable, taboo; informal no go; rare non licet.

boundary ▶ noun **1** *the boundary between Alaska and the Yukon Territory* **border,** frontier, borderline, partition; fenceline.
2 *the boundary between art and advertising* **dividing line,** divide, division, borderline, cutoff point.
3 *the boundary of his estate* **bounds,** confines, limits, margins, edges, fringes; border, periphery, perimeter.
4 (**boundaries**) *the boundaries of acceptable behavior* **limits,** parameters, bounds, confines; ambit, compass.

boundless ▶ adjective *the pups have boundless energy* **limitless,** unlimited, unbounded, untold, immeasurable, abundant; inexhaustible, endless, infinite, interminable, unfailing, ceaseless, everlasting.
ANTONYMS limited.

bountiful ▶ adjective **1** *their bountiful patron* **generous,** magnanimous, munificent, openhanded, unselfish, unstinting, lavish; benevolent, beneficent, charitable, philanthropic; rare eleemosynary, benignant.
ANTONYMS mean, stingy.
2 *a bountiful supply of fresh food* **abundant,** plentiful, ample, copious, bumper, superabundant, inexhaustible, prolific, profuse; lavish, generous, handsome, rich; informal whopping; literary plenteous.
ANTONYMS meager.

bouquet ▶ noun **1** *her bridal bouquet* **bunch**

of flowers, posy, nosegay, spray, corsage, boutonniere.
2 *bouquets go to Ann for a well-planned event* **compliment**, commendation, tribute, accolade; praise, congratulations, applause.
3 *the Chardonnay has a fine bouquet* **aroma**, nose, smell, fragrance, perfume, scent, odor. See note at SMELL.

bourgeois ▶ **adjective 1** *a bourgeois family* **middle-class**, propertied; **conventional**, conservative, conformist; provincial, suburban, small-town; informal white-bread.
ANTONYMS proletarian, unconventional.
2 *bourgeois decadence* **capitalistic**, materialistic, money-oriented, commercial.
ANTONYMS communist.
▶ **noun** *a proud bourgeois* **member of the middle class**, property owner.

bout ▶ **noun 1** *a bout of dysentery* **attack**, fit, spasm, paroxysm, convulsion, eruption, outburst; period, session, spell.
2 *he is fighting his fifth bout* **contest**, match, fight, prizefight, competition, event, meeting.

bovine ▶ **adjective 1** *large, bovine eyes* **cowlike**, calflike, taurine.
2 *an expression of bovine amazement* **stupid**, slow, ignorant, unintelligent, imperceptive, vacuous, mindless, witless, doltish, dumb, dense, dim, dimwitted, dopey, birdbrained, peabrained, dozy.
▶ **noun** *a beautiful bovine* **cow**, heifer, bull, bullock, calf, ox, bison.

bow[1] ▶ **verb 1** *the officers bowed* **incline the body**, incline the head, nod, salaam, kowtow, curtsy, bob, genuflect.
2 *the government* ***bowed to*** *foreign pressure* **yield to**, submit to, give in to, surrender to, succumb to, capitulate to, defer to, conform to; comply with, accept, heed, observe.
▶ **noun** *a perfunctory bow* **obeisance**, salaam, bob, curtsy, nod; archaic reverence.
– PHRASES **bow out** *he bowed out of the election before he got beaten* **withdraw**, resign, retire, step down, pull out, back out; give up, quit, leave, pack it in.

bow[2] ▶ **noun** *the bow of the tanker* **prow**, front, stem, nose, head, cutwater.

bow[3] ▶ **noun 1** *she tied a bow in her hair* **loop**, knot; ribbon.
2 *he bent the rod into a bow* **arc**, curve, bend; crescent, half-moon.
3 *an archer's bow* **longbow**, crossbow; Archery recurve.

bowdlerize ▶ **verb** *the English translation was bowdlerized beyond recognition* **expurgate**, censor, blue-pencil, cut, edit; purge, sanitize, water down; informal clean up.

bowel ▶ **noun 1** (also **bowels**) *a disorder of the bowels* **intestine**(s), entrails, innards, small intestine, large intestine, colon; informal guts, insides, viscera.
2 (**bowels**) *the bowels of the ship* **interior**, inside, core, belly; depths, recesses; informal innards.

bower ▶ **noun** *a rose-scented bower* **arbor**, pergola, grotto, alcove, sanctuary; gazebo.

bowl ▶ **noun 1** *she cracked two eggs into a bowl* **dish**, basin, pot, crock, mortar; container, vessel, receptacle; rare jorum, porringer.
2 *the Hollywood Bowl* **stadium**, arena, amphitheater, colosseum.
▶ **verb**
– PHRASES **bowl someone over 1** *the explosion bowled us over* **knock down/over**, fell, floor, prostrate. **2** informal *I have been bowled over by your generosity* **overwhelm**, astound, astonish, overawe, awe, dumbfound, stagger, stun, amaze, daze, shake, take aback, leave aghast; informal floor, flabbergast, blow away.

box[1] ▶ **noun** *a box of cigars* **carton**, pack, packet; case, crate, chest, coffer, casket; container, receptacle.
▶ **verb** *Muriel* ***boxed up*** *his clothes* **package**, pack, parcel, wrap, bundle, crate, bin.
– PHRASES **box something/someone in** *those two vans have boxed in my car* **hem in**, fence in, close in, shut in; trap, confine, imprison, intern; surround, enclose, encircle, circle.

box[2] ▶ **verb 1** *he began boxing professionally* **fight**, prizefight, spar; brawl; informal scrap.
2 *he boxed my ears* **strike**, smack, cuff, hit, thump, slap, swat, punch, jab, wallop; informal belt, bop, sock, clout, clobber, whack, slug; literary swinge, smite.

boxer ▶ **noun** *a professional boxer* **fighter**, pugilist, prizefighter, kick-boxer; informal bruiser, scrapper.

boy ▶ **noun** *the tallest boy in our class* **lad**, schoolboy, male child, youth, young man, laddie, stripling. See also CHILD.

boycott ▶ **verb** *they boycotted the elections* **spurn**, snub, shun, avoid, abstain from, wash one's hands of, turn one's back on, reject, veto.
ANTONYMS support.
▶ **noun** *a boycott of imported lumber* **ban**, veto, embargo, prohibition, sanction, restriction; avoidance, rejection, refusal.

boyfriend ▶ **noun** *her old boyfriend was at the reunion* **lover**, sweetheart, beloved, darling, dearest, young man, man friend, man, guy, escort, suitor; **partner**, significant other, companion; informal fella, (main) squeeze, flame, steady, toy boy, boy toy, sugar daddy; literary swain; dated beau; archaic paramour.

boyish ▶ **adjective** *his boyish good looks* **youthful**, young, childlike, adolescent, teenage; immature, juvenile, infantile, childish, babyish, puerile.

brace ▶ **noun** *the aquarium is supported by wooden braces* **prop**, beam, joist, batten, rod, post, strut, stay, support, stanchion, bracket.
▶ **verb 1** *the plane's wing is braced by a system of rods* **support**, shore up, prop up, hold up, buttress, underpin; strengthen, reinforce.
2 *he braced his hand on the railing* **steady**, secure, stabilize, fix, poise; tense, tighten.
3 *brace yourself for disappointment* **prepare**, get ready, gear up, nerve, steel, galvanize, gird, strengthen, fortify; informal psych oneself up.

bracelet ▶ **noun** *gold bracelets* **bangle**, band, circlet, armlet, wristlet, anklet.

bracing ▶ **adjective** *a bracing jog through the snowy field* **invigorating**, refreshing, stimulating, energizing, exhilarating, reviving, restorative, rejuvenating, revitalizing, rousing, fortifying, strengthening; **fresh,** brisk, keen.

bracket ▶ noun **1** *each speaker is fixed on a separate bracket* **support,** prop, stay, batten, joist; rest, mounting, rack, frame.
2 *put the words in brackets* **parenthesis,** square bracket; Printing brace.
3 *a higher tax bracket* **group,** category, grade, classification, set, division, order.

brackish ▶ adjective *several species of crab inhabit the brackish water* **slightly salty,** saline, salt, briny.

brag ▶ verb *he liked to brag about his business connections* **boast,** crow, swagger, swank, bluster, gloat, show off; blow one's own horn, sing one's own praises; informal talk big, lay it on thick.

braggart ▶ noun *Jeff is a prodigious braggart and a liar* **boaster,** bragger, swaggerer, egotist; informal big head, loudmouth, show-off, showboat, blowhard.

braid ▶ noun *her hair is in braids* **plait,** pigtail, twist; cornrows, dreadlocks.
▶ verb **1** *she began to braid her hair* **plait,** entwine, intertwine, interweave, weave, twist, twine.
2 *the sleeves are braided in scarlet* **trim,** edge, border, pipe, hem, fringe.

brain ▶ noun **1** *the disease attacks certain cells in the brain* **cerebrum,** cerebral matter, encephalon; informal gray matter.
2 (also **brains**) *success requires brains as well as brawn* **intelligence,** intellect, brainpower, IQ, cleverness, wit(s), reasoning, wisdom, acumen, discernment, judgment, understanding, sense; informal gray matter, savvy; smarts.
3 informal (**brains**) *Janice is the brains of the family* **clever person,** intellectual, intellect, thinker, mind, scholar; genius, Einstein; informal egghead, brainiac, rocket scientist.
ANTONYMS dunce.

brainy ▶ adjective informal *behind every successful machine is a brainy scientist* **clever,** intelligent, smart, bright, brilliant, gifted; intellectual, erudite, academic, scholarly, studious, bookish.
ANTONYMS stupid.

brake ▶ noun *a brake on research* **curb,** check, restraint, restriction, constraint, control, limitation.
▶ verb *she braked at the traffic lights* **slow down,** slow, decelerate, reduce speed, stop.
ANTONYMS accelerate.

branch ▶ noun **1** *the branches of a tree* **bough,** limb, arm, offshoot.
2 *a branch of the river* **tributary,** feeder, side stream, fork, side channel, influent.
3 *the judicial branch of government* **division,** subdivision, section, subsection, subset, department, sector, part, side, wing.
4 *the corporation's New York branch* **office,** bureau, agency; subsidiary, affiliate, offshoot, satellite.
▶ verb **1** *the place where the road branches* **fork,** bifurcate, divide, subdivide, split.
2 *narrow paths **branched off** the road* **diverge from,** deviate from, split off from; fan out from, radiate from.
– PHRASES **branch out** *the company is branching out into the European market* **expand,** open up, extend; diversify, broaden one's horizons.

brand ▶ noun **1** *a new brand of margarine* **make,** line, label, marque; type, kind, sort, variety; trade name, trademark, proprietary name.
2 *her particular brand of humor* **type,** kind, sort, variety, class, category, genre, style, ilk, stripe.
3 *the brand on a sheep* **identification,** marker, earmark.
▶ verb **1** *the letter M was branded on each animal* **mark,** stamp, burn, sear.
2 *the scene was branded on her brain* **engrave,** stamp, etch, imprint.
3 *the media branded us as communists* **stigmatize,** mark out; denounce, discredit, vilify; label.

brandish ▶ verb *brandishing a sword* **flourish,** wave, shake, wield; swing, swish; display, flaunt, show off.

brash ▶ adjective *a brash man* **self-assertive,** pushy, cocksure, cocky, self-confident, arrogant, bold, audacious, brazen, bumptious, overweening, puffed-up; forward, impudent, insolent, rude.
ANTONYMS meek.

brassy ▶ adjective *we're not at all pleased with your brassy new friends* **brazen,** forward, bold, self-assertive, pushy, cocksure, cocky, cheeky, saucy, brash; shameless, immodest; loud, vulgar, showy, ostentatious; informal flashy.
ANTONYMS demure, modest.

brat ▶ noun *now that I've met his two little brats, I'm not so sure about this relationship* **badly behaved child,** spoiled child; rascal, wretch, imp, scamp, scapegrace, whippersnapper; minx; informal monster, horror, hellion; archaic jackanapes.

bravado ▶ noun *his bravado seems so phony and overplayed* **boldness,** swaggering, bluster; machismo; boasting, bragging, bombast, braggadocio; informal showing off.

brave ▶ adjective **1** *they put up a brave fight* **courageous,** valiant, valorous, intrepid, heroic, lionhearted, bold, fearless, gallant, daring, plucky, audacious; unflinching, unshrinking, unafraid, dauntless, doughty, mettlesome, stouthearted, spirited; informal game, gutsy, spunky.
ANTONYMS cowardly.
2 literary *his medals made a brave show* **splendid,** magnificent, impressive, fine, handsome.
▶ noun dated *an Indian brave* **warrior,** soldier, fighter.
▶ verb *fans braved freezing temperatures to see them play* **endure,** put up with, bear, withstand, weather, suffer, go through; face, confront, defy.

bravery ▶ noun *the bravery witnessed here today will never be forgotten* **courage,** valor, intrepidity, nerve, daring, fearlessness, audacity, boldness, dauntlessness, stoutheartedness, heroism; backbone, grit, true grit, pluck, spine, spirit, mettle; informal guts, balls, cojones, spunk.

bravo ▶ exclamation *chants of "Bravo!" went*

on for several minutes **well done,** splendid, congratulations, brava; encore, take a bow; informal attaboy, attagirl.

brawl ▶ **noun** *a drunken brawl* **fight,** skirmish, scuffle, tussle, fray, melee, free-for-all, donnybrook; fisticuffs; informal scrap, set-to.
▶ **verb** *he ended up brawling with photographers* **fight,** skirmish, scuffle, tussle, exchange blows, grapple, wrestle; informal scrap.

brawn ▶ **noun** *he has certainly developed his brawn since high school* **physical strength,** muscle(s), burliness, huskiness, toughness, power, might; vigor, punch; informal beef, beefiness.

brawny ▶ **adjective** *the brawny young hunks at the gym* **strong,** muscular, muscly, well-built, hard-bodied, powerful, mighty, Herculean, strapping, burly, sturdy, husky, rugged; hefty, solid; informal beefy, hunky.
ANTONYMS puny, weak.

bray ▶ **verb 1** *a donkey brayed* **neigh,** whinny, hee-haw.
2 *Billy brayed with laughter* **roar,** bellow, trumpet.

brazen ▶ **adjective** *brazen defiance* **bold, shameless,** unashamed, unabashed, unembarrassed; defiant, impudent, impertinent, cheeky, saucy, insolent, in-your-face; barefaced, blatant, flagrant. See note at **BOLD**.
ANTONYMS timid.
– PHRASES **brazen it out** *we were shaking in our boots, but we brazened it out* **put on a bold front,** stand one's ground, be defiant, be unrepentant, be unabashed.

breach ▶ **noun 1** *a clear breach of the regulations* **contravention,** violation, infringement, infraction, transgression, neglect; Law delict.
2 *a breach between government and Church* **rift,** schism, division, gulf, chasm; disunion, estrangement, discord, dissension, disagreement; split, break, rupture, scission.
3 *a breach in the sea wall* **break,** rupture, split, crack, fracture; opening, gap, hole, fissure.
▶ **verb 1** *the river breached its bank* **break (through),** burst (through), rupture; informal bust (through).
2 *the changes breached union rules* **break,** contravene, violate, infringe; defy, disobey, flout, fly in the face of; Law infract.

bread ▶ **noun 1** *may I have some bread with my soup?* rye (bread), pumpernickel, French bread, Italian bread, focaccia, pita (bread), cornbread, soda bread.
2 *his job puts bread on the table* See **FOOD** (sense 1).
3 informal *I hate doing this, but I need the bread* See **MONEY** (sense 1).

breadth ▶ **noun 1** *a breadth of 100 meters* **width,** broadness, wideness, thickness; span; diameter.
2 *the breadth of his knowledge* **range,** extent, scope, depth, reach, compass, scale, degree.

break ▶ **verb 1** *the mirror broke* **shatter,** smash, crack, snap, fracture, fragment, splinter, fall to bits, fall to pieces; split, burst; informal bust.
2 *she had broken her leg* **fracture,** crack.
ANTONYMS mend.
3 *the bite had barely broken the skin* **pierce,** puncture, penetrate, perforate; cut.
4 *the coffee machine has broken* **stop working,** break down, give out, go wrong, malfunction, crash; informal go kaput, conk out, go/be on the blink, go/be on the fritz, give up the ghost.
5 *traders who break the law* **contravene,** violate, fail to observe, fail to comply with, infringe, breach; defy, flout, disobey, fly in the face of.
ANTONYMS abide by, keep.
6 *his concentration was broken* **interrupt,** disturb, interfere with.
7 *they broke for coffee* **stop,** pause, have a rest, recess; informal take a breather, take five.
ANTONYMS resume.
8 *a pile of carpets broke his fall* **cushion,** soften the impact of, take the edge off.
9 *the movie broke box-office records* **exceed,** surpass, beat, better, cap, top, outdo, outstrip, eclipse.
10 *habits are difficult to break* **give up,** relinquish, drop; informal kick, shake, quit.
11 *the strategies used to break the union* **destroy,** crush, quash, defeat, vanquish, overcome, overpower, overwhelm, suppress, cripple; weaken, subdue, cow, undermine.
12 *her self-control finally broke* **give way,** crack, cave in, yield, go to pieces.
13 *four thousand dollars wouldn't break him* **bankrupt,** ruin, pauperize.
14 *he tried to break the news gently* **reveal,** disclose, divulge, impart, tell; announce, release.
15 *he broke the encryption code* **decipher,** decode, decrypt, unravel, work out; informal figure out.
16 *the day broke fair and cloudless* **dawn,** begin, start, emerge, appear.
17 *a political scandal broke* **erupt,** break out.
18 *the weather broke* **change,** alter, shift.
19 *waves broke against the rocks* **crash,** dash, beat, pound, lash.
20 *her voice broke as she relived the experience* **falter,** quaver, quiver, tremble, shake.
▶ **noun 1** *the magazine has been published without a break since 1950* **interruption,** interval, gap, hiatus; discontinuation, suspension, disruption, cutoff; stop, stoppage, cessation.
2 *a break in the weather* **change,** alteration, variation.
3 *let's have a break* **rest,** respite, recess; stop, pause; interval, intermission; informal breather, time out, down time; coffee break.
4 *a weekend break* **time off,** vacation, holiday, leave, getaway.
5 *a break in diplomatic relations* **rift,** schism, split, breakup, severance, rupture.
6 *the actress got her first break in 1951* **opportunity,** chance, opening.
– PHRASES **break away 1** *she attempted to break away* **escape,** get away, run away, flee, make off; break free, break loose, get out of someone's clutches; informal cut and run. **2** *a group broke away from the main party* **leave,** secede from, split off from, separate from, part company with, defect from; Politics cross the floor from.
break down 1 *his van broke down* See **BREAK** (sense 4 of the verb).

2 *pay negotiations broke down* **fail,** collapse, founder, fall through, disintegrate; informal fizzle out. **3** *Vicky broke down, sobbing loudly* **burst into tears**; lose control, be overcome, go to pieces, crumble, disintegrate; informal crack up, lose it. **break something down 1** *the police broke the door down* **knock down,** kick down, smash in, pull down, tear down, demolish. **2** *break big tasks down into smaller parts* **divide,** separate. **3** *graphs show how the information can be broken down* **analyze,** categorize, classify, sort out, itemize, organize; dissect. **break in 1** *thieves broke in and took her checkbook* **commit burglary,** break and enter; force one's way in. **2** *"I don't want to interfere," Mrs. Hendry broke in* **interrupt,** butt in, cut in, interject, interpose, intervene, chime in. **break someone in** *it's Edgar's responsibility to break in the new cooks* **train,** initiate; informal show someone the ropes. **break into 1** *thieves broke into a house on Park Street* **burgle,** burglarize, rob; force one's way into. **2** *Phil broke into the discussion* **interrupt,** butt into, cut in on, intervene in. **3** *he broke into a song* **burst into,** launch into. **break off** *the cup handle just broke off* **snap off,** come off, become detached, become separated. **break something off 1** *I broke off a branch from the tree* **snap off,** pull off, sever, detach. **2** *they threatened to break off diplomatic relations* **end,** terminate, stop, cease, call a halt to, finish, dissolve; **suspend,** discontinue; informal pull the plug on. **break out 1** *he **broke out of** the detention center* **escape from,** abscond from, flee from; get free of. **2** *fighting broke out* **flare up,** start suddenly, erupt, burst out. **break up 1** *the meeting broke up* **end,** finish, stop, terminate; adjourn; recess. **2** *the crowd began to break up* **disperse,** scatter, disband, part company. **3** *Danny and I broke up last year* **split up,** separate, part, part company; divorce. **4** informal *the whole cast broke up* **burst out laughing,** crack up, dissolve into laughter. **break something up 1** *police tried to break up the crowd* **disperse,** scatter, disband. **2** *I'm not going to let you break up my marriage* **wreck,** ruin, destroy.

breakable ▶ adjective *pack the breakable items in bubble wrap* **fragile,** delicate, flimsy, destructible, brittle, easily broken, easily damaged; formal frangible.
ANTONYMS shatterproof.

breakdown ▶ noun **1** *the breakdown of the negotiations* **failure,** collapse, disintegration, foundering.
2 *on the death of her father she suffered a breakdown* **nervous breakdown,** collapse; informal crack-up.
3 *the breakdown of the computer system* **malfunction,** failure, crash.
4 *a breakdown of the figures* **analysis,** classification, examination, investigation, dissection.

breaker ▶ noun *breakers crashed against the cliff* **wave,** roller, comber, whitecap; informal (big) kahuna.

break-in ▶ noun *the break-in occurred just before midnight* **burglary,** robbery, theft, raid, breaking and entering, forced entry, break and enter.

breakneck ▶ adjective *the breakneck pace of change* **extremely fast,** rapid, speedy, high-speed, lightning, whirlwind.

breakthrough ▶ noun *the breakthroughs that will lead us to the cure for this disease cannot happen without adequate funding* **advance,** development, step forward, success, improvement; discovery, innovation, revolution; progress, headway.
ANTONYMS setback.

breakup ▶ noun **1** *the breakup of negotiations* **end,** dissolution; breakdown, failure, collapse, disintegration.
2 *their breakup was very amicable* **separation,** split, parting, divorce; estrangement, rift; informal splitsville.

breakwater ▶ noun *she found a submerged breakwater, constructed of parallel stone walls filled with rubble* **sea wall,** jetty, barrier, mole, bulwark, groin, pier.

breast ▶ noun **1** *a baby at her breast* mammary gland, mamma; (**breasts**) **bosom**(s), bust, chest; informal boobs, knockers, bazooms, hooters.
2 *feelings of frustration were rising up in his breast* **heart,** bosom, soul, core.

breath ▶ noun **1** *I took a deep breath* **inhalation,** inspiration, gulp of air; exhalation, expiration; Medicine respiration.
2 *a breath of wind* **puff,** waft, faint breeze.
3 *a breath of scandal* **hint,** suggestion, trace, touch, whisper, murmur, suspicion, whiff, undertone.
4 *there was no breath left in him* **life,** life force.
– PHRASES **take someone's breath away** *his solo on the sax took our breath away* **astonish,** astound, amaze, stun, startle, stagger, shock, take aback, dumbfound, jolt, shake up; awe, overawe, thrill, flabbergast, blow away, bowl over, stop someone in their tracks, leave someone speechless.

breathe ▶ verb **1** *she breathed deeply* inhale and exhale, respire, draw breath; puff, pant, blow, gasp, wheeze, huff; Medicine inspire, expire.
2 *at least I'm still breathing* **be alive,** be living, live.
3 *she would breathe new life into the firm* **instill,** infuse, inject, inspire, impart, imbue.
4 *"Together at last," she breathed* **whisper,** murmur, purr, sigh, say.

breather ▶ noun *we could all use a breather* **break, rest,** respite, breathing space, pause, interval, recess.

breathless ▶ adjective **1** *Will arrived flushed and breathless* **out of breath,** panting, puffing, gasping, wheezing, hyperventilating; winded, short of breath.
2 *the crowd was breathless with anticipation* **agog,** open-mouthed, waiting with bated breath, on the edge of one's seat, on tenterhooks, in suspense; excited, impatient.

breathtaking ▶ adjective *the breathtaking view from the tower* **spectacular,** magnificent, wonderful, awe-inspiring, awesome, astounding, astonishing, amazing, stunning, incredible; thrilling, exciting; informal sensational, out of this world, jaw-dropping; literary wondrous.

breed ▶ verb 1 *elephants breed readily in captivity* **reproduce,** produce/bear/generate offspring, procreate, multiply, propagate; mate.
2 *she was born and bred in the village* **bring up,** rear, raise, nurture.
3 *the political system bred discontent* **cause,** bring about, give rise to, lead to, produce, generate, foster, result in; stir up; literary beget.
▶ noun 1 *a breed of cow* **variety,** stock, strain; type, kind, sort.
2 *a new breed of journalist* **type,** kind, sort, variety, class, brand, genre, generation.

breeding ▶ noun 1 *the birds pair for breeding* **reproduction,** procreation; mating.
2 *the breeding of laboratory rats* **rearing,** raising, nurturing.
3 *her aristocratic breeding* **upbringing,** rearing; parentage, family, pedigree, blood, birth, ancestry.
4 *people of rank and breeding* **(good) manners,** gentility, refinement, cultivation, polish, urbanity; informal class.
ANTONYMS bad manners, vulgarity.

breeze ▶ noun 1 *a breeze ruffled the leaves* **gentle wind,** puff of air, gust, cat's paw; Meteorology light air; literary zephyr.
2 informal *getting your child in and out of the seat is a breeze* **easy task,** child's play, nothing; informal piece of cake, cinch, snap, kids' stuff, cakewalk, five-finger exercise, duck soup.
▶ verb informal *Roger breezed into her office* **saunter,** stroll, sail, cruise.

breezy ▶ adjective 1 *a bright, breezy day* **windy,** fresh, brisk, airy; blowy, blustery, gusty.
2 *his breezy manner* **jaunty, cheerful,** cheery, brisk, carefree, easy, casual, relaxed; informal lighthearted, lively, buoyant, blithe, spirited, sunny, jovial; informal upbeat, bright-eyed and bushy-tailed; dated gay.

brevity ▶ noun 1 *the report is notable for its brevity* **conciseness,** concision, succinctness, economy of language, pithiness, incisiveness, shortness, compactness.
ANTONYMS verbosity.
2 *the brevity of human life* **shortness,** briefness, transience, ephemerality, impermanence.
ANTONYMS lengthiness, permanence.

brew ▶ verb 1 *this beer is brewed in Oshkosh* **ferment,** make.
2 *I'll brew some tea* **prepare,** infuse, make, steep, stew.
3 *there's trouble brewing* **develop,** loom, threaten, impend, be imminent, be on the horizon, be in the offing.
▶ noun 1 *a home brew* **beer,** ale.
2 *a piping hot brew* **drink,** beverage; tea, coffee.
3 *a dangerous brew of political turmoil and violent conflict* **mixture,** mix, blend, combination, amalgam, mishmash, hodgepodge.

bribe ▶ verb *he used his wealth to bribe officials* **buy off,** pay off, suborn; informal grease someone's palm, fix, square.
▶ noun *she accepted bribes* **inducement,** incentive, payola; informal payoff, kickback, boodle, sweetener.

bridal ▶ adjective *the bridal party* **wedding,** nuptial, marriage, matrimonial, marital, conjugal.

bride ▶ noun *Ben's lovely bride* **wife,** marriage partner; newlywed.

bridge ▶ noun 1 *a bridge over the river* **viaduct,** overpass, fixed link, aqueduct.
2 *a bridge between rival groups* **link,** connection, bond, tie.
▶ verb 1 *a walkway bridged the highway* **span,** cross (over), extend across, traverse, arch over.
2 *an attempt to bridge the gap between cultures* **join,** link, connect, unite; straddle; overcome, reconcile.

bridle ▶ noun *a horse's bridle* **harness,** headgear; hackamore.
▶ verb 1 *William seemed to bridle at the brusque manner of questioning* **bristle,** take offense, take umbrage, be affronted, be offended, get angry.
2 *he bridled his indignation* **curb,** restrain, hold back, control, check, rein in/back; suppress, stifle; informal keep a/the lid on.

brief ▶ adjective 1 *a brief account* **concise,** succinct, short, pithy, incisive, abridged, condensed, compressed, abbreviated, compact, thumbnail, capsule, potted; formal compendious.
ANTONYMS lengthy, long-winded.
2 *a brief visit* **short,** flying, fleeting, hasty, hurried, quick, cursory, perfunctory; temporary, short-lived, momentary, transient; informal quickie.
ANTONYMS long, lengthy.
3 *a pair of brief shorts* **skimpy,** scanty, short; revealing.
4 *the boss was rather brief with him* **brusque,** abrupt, curt, short, blunt, sharp.
▶ noun 1 *a lawyer's brief* **summary,** case, argument, contention; dossier.
2 *a brief of our requirements* **outline,** summary, synopsis, précis, sketch, digest.
▶ verb *employees were briefed about the decision* **inform,** tell, update, notify, advise, apprise; prepare, prime, instruct; informal fill in, clue in, put in the picture.

briefing ▶ noun *a press briefing* **conference,** meeting, interview; orientation; informal backgrounder, Q & A session.

briefly ▶ adverb 1 *Henry paused briefly* **momentarily,** temporarily, for a moment, fleetingly.
2 *briefly, the plot is as follows* **in short,** in brief, to make/cut a long story short, in a word, in sum, in a nutshell, in essence.

brigade ▶ noun 1 *a brigade of soldiers* **unit,** contingent, battalion, regiment, division, squadron, company, platoon, section, corps, troop.
2 *the volunteer ambulance brigade* **squad,** team, group, band, party, crew, force, outfit.

brigand ▶ noun literary See BANDIT.

bright ▶ adjective 1 *the bright surface of the metal* **shining,** brilliant, dazzling, beaming, glaring; sparkling, flashing, glittering, scintillating, gleaming, glowing, luminous, radiant, undimmed; shiny, lustrous, glossy; literary coruscating.
ANTONYMS dull, dark.
2 *a bright morning* **sunny,** sunshiny, cloudless,

clear, fair, fine.
ANTONYMS cloudy, overcast.
3 *bright crayons* **vivid,** brilliant, intense, strong, bold, glowing, rich; gaudy, lurid, garish; **colorful,** vibrant; dated gay.
ANTONYMS drab.
4 *a bright guitar sound* **clear,** vibrant, pellucid; high-pitched.
5 *a bright young graduate* **clever,** intelligent, quick-witted, smart, canny, astute, intuitive, perceptive; ingenious, resourceful; gifted, brilliant; informal brainy.
ANTONYMS dimwitted, stupid.
6 *a bright smile* **happy,** cheerful, cheery, jolly, merry, sunny, beaming; lively, exuberant, buoyant, bubbly, bouncy, perky, chirpy; dated gay.
ANTONYMS cheerless.
7 *a bright future* **promising,** rosy, optimistic, hopeful, favorable, propitious, auspicious, encouraging, good, golden.
ANTONYMS dismal, pessimistic.
▶ **adverb** literary *the moon shone bright* **brightly,** brilliantly, intensely, undimmed.

CHOOSE THE RIGHT WORD

bright, brilliant, effulgent, luminous, lustrous, radiant, refulgent, resplendent, shining

Looking for just the right word to capture the quality of the light on a moonlit night or a summer day? All of these adjectives describe an intense, steady light emanating (or appearing to emanate) from a source. **Bright** is the most general term, applied to something that gives forth, reflects, or is filled with light (*a bright and sunny day*; *a bright star*). **Brilliant** light is even more intense or dazzling (*the brilliant diamond on her finger*), and **resplendent** is a slightly more formal, even poetic, way of describing a striking brilliance (*the sky was resplendent with stars*). Poets also prefer adjectives like **effulgent** and **refulgent**, both of which can be applied to an intense, pervading light, sometimes from an unseen source (*her effulgent loveliness*); but *refulgent* specifically refers to reflected light (*a chandelier of refulgent crystal pendants*). **Radiant** is used to describe the power of giving off light, either literally or metaphorically (*a radiant June day*; *the bride's radiant face*); it describes a steady, warm light that is emitted in all directions. Like *radiant*, **luminous** suggests sending forth light, but light of the glow-in-the-dark variety (*the luminous face of the alarm clock*). While diamonds are known for being *brilliant*, fabrics like satin and surfaces like polished wood, which reflect light and take on a gloss or sheen, are often called **lustrous**. If none of these words captures the exact quality of the light you're trying to describe, you can always join the masses and use **shining**, a word that has been overworked to the point of cliché (*my knight in shining armor*).

brighten ▶ **verb 1** *sunshine brightened the room* **illuminate,** light up, lighten, make bright, make brighter, cast/shed light on; formal illume.
2 *Sarah **brightened up** as she thought of her mother's words* **cheer up,** perk up, rally; be enlivened, feel heartened, be uplifted, be encouraged, take heart; informal buck up, pep up.

brilliance ▶ **noun 1** *a philosopher of great brilliance* **genius,** intelligence, wisdom, sagacity, intellect; talent, ability, prowess, skill, expertise, aptitude; flair, finesse, panache; greatness.
2 *the brilliance and beauty of Paris* **splendor,** magnificence, grandeur, resplendence.
3 *the brilliance of the sunshine* **brightness,** vividness, intensity; sparkle, glitter, glittering, glow, blaze, luminosity, radiance.

brilliant ▶ **adjective 1** *a brilliant student* **bright,** intelligent, clever, smart, astute, intellectual; gifted, talented, able, adept, skillful; elite, superior, first-class, first-rate, excellent; informal brainy.
ANTONYMS stupid.
2 *his brilliant career* **superb,** glorious, illustrious, impressive, remarkable, exceptional.
ANTONYMS unremarkable.
3 *a shaft of brilliant light* **bright,** shining, blazing, dazzling, vivid, intense, gleaming, glaring, luminous, radiant; literary irradiant, coruscating. See note at **BRIGHT**.
ANTONYMS obscure, dark.
4 *brilliant green* **vivid,** intense, bright, bold, dazzling.
ANTONYMS dull, dark.

brim ▶ **noun 1** *the brim of his hat* peak, visor, shield, shade; fringe.
2 *the cup was filled to its brim* **rim,** lip, brink, edge, margin. See note at **BORDER**.

bring ▶ **verb 1** *he brought a tray* **carry,** fetch, bear, take; convey, transport, tote; move, haul, shift, lug.
2 *Seth brought his bride to the club* **escort,** conduct, guide, lead, usher, show, shepherd.
3 *the wind changed and brought rain* **cause,** produce, create, generate, precipitate, lead to, give rise to, result in; stir up, whip up, promote; literary beget.
4 *the police contemplated bringing charges* **put forward,** prefer, lay, submit, present, initiate, institute.
5 *this job brings him a regular salary* **earn,** make, fetch, bring in, yield, net, gross, return, produce; command, attract.
– PHRASES **bring about** *the events that brought about her death* **cause,** produce, give rise to, result in, lead to, occasion, bring to pass; provoke, generate, engender, precipitate, bring on; formal effectuate. **bring around 1** *she administered CPR and brought him around* **wake up,** return to consciousness, rouse, bring to. **2** *we would have brought him around, given time* **persuade,** convince, win over, sway, influence. **bring back 1** *the smell brought back memories* **remind one of,** put one in mind of, bring/call to mind, conjure up, evoke, summon up. **2** *bring back capital punishment* **reintroduce,** reinstate, reestablish, revive, resurrect. **bring down 1** *he was brought*

down by his own teammate **trip,** knock over, knock down; foul. **2** *I couldn't bear to bring her down* **depress,** sadden, upset, get down, dispirit, dishearten, discourage. **3** *we will bring down the price* **decrease,** reduce, lower, cut, drop; informal slash. **4** *the unrest brought down the government* **unseat,** overturn, topple, overthrow, depose, oust. **bring forward** *why wasn't this brought forward at the last meeting?* **propose,** suggest, advance, raise, present, move, submit, lodge. **bring in** *the event brings in a million dollars each year* See **BRING** (sense 5). **bring on** *what could have brought on this fever?* See **BRING ABOUT**. **bring out 1** *they were bringing out a new magazine* **launch,** establish, begin, start, found, set up, instigate, inaugurate, market; publish, print, issue, produce. **2** *the shawl brings out the color of your eyes* **accentuate,** highlight, emphasize, accent, set off. **bring oneself to** *she could not bring herself to complain* **force oneself to,** make oneself, bear to. **bring up 1** *she and Lenny brought up her brother's four children* **rear,** raise, care for, look after, nurture, provide for. **2** *I wonder if he'll bring up the matter of the grocery bill* **mention,** allude to, touch on, raise, broach, introduce; voice, air, suggest, propose, submit, put forward, bring forward.

brink ▶ **noun 1** *the brink of the abyss* **edge,** verge, margin, rim, lip; border, boundary, perimeter, periphery, limit(s).
2 *two countries on the brink of war* **verge,** threshold, point, edge. See note at **BORDER**.

brisk ▶ **adjective 1** *a brisk pace* **quick,** rapid, fast, swift, speedy, hurried; energetic, lively, vigorous.
ANTONYMS slow, sluggish.
2 *business was brisk at the bar* **busy,** bustling, lively, hectic; good.
ANTONYMS slow.
3 *a brisk breeze* **bracing,** fresh, crisp, invigorating, refreshing, stimulating, energizing; biting, keen, chilly, cold; informal nippy.
ANTONYMS sultry.

bristle ▶ **noun 1** *the bristles on his chin* **hair,** whisker; (**bristles**) stubble, five o'clock shadow; Zoology seta/setae.
2 *a hedgehog's bristles* **spine,** prickle, quill, barb.
▶ **verb 1** *the hair on the back of his neck bristled* **rise,** stand up, stand on end; literary horripilate.
2 *she bristled at his tone* **take offense,** bridle, take umbrage, be affronted, be offended; get angry, be irritated.
3 *the roof bristled with antennas* **abound,** overflow, be full, be packed, be crowded, be jammed, be covered; informal be thick, be jam-packed, be chock-full.

bristly ▶ **adjective 1** *bristly little bushes* **prickly,** spiky, thorny, scratchy, brambly.
2 *the bristly skin of his cheek* **stubbly,** hairy, fuzzy, unshaven, whiskered, whiskery; scratchy, rough, coarse, prickly; Biology setaceous, hispid.
ANTONYMS smooth.

brittle ▶ **adjective 1** *glass is a brittle material* **breakable,** fragile, delicate; splintery; formal frangible.
ANTONYMS flexible, resilient.
2 *a brittle laugh* **harsh,** hard, sharp, grating.
ANTONYMS soft.
3 *a brittle young woman* **edgy,** anxious, unstable, high-strung, tense, excitable, jumpy, skittish, neurotic; informal uptight.
ANTONYMS relaxed.

broach ▶ **verb 1** *I broached the matter with my parents* **bring up,** raise, introduce, talk about, mention, touch on, air.
2 *he broached a barrel of beer* **pierce,** puncture, tap; **open,** uncork; informal crack open.

broad ▶ **adjective 1** *a broad flight of steps* **wide.**
ANTONYMS narrow.
2 *the leaves are two inches broad* **wide,** across, in breadth, in width.
3 *a broad expanse of prairie* **extensive,** vast, immense, great, spacious, expansive, sizable, sweeping, rolling.
4 *a broad range of opportunities* **comprehensive,** inclusive, extensive, wide, all-embracing, eclectic, unlimited.
ANTONYMS limited.
5 *this report gives a broad outline* **general,** nonspecific, unspecific, rough, approximate, basic; loose, vague.
ANTONYMS detailed.
6 *a broad hint* **obvious,** unsubtle, explicit, direct, plain, clear, straightforward, bald, patent, transparent, undisguised, overt.
ANTONYMS subtle.
7 *a broad Latvian accent* **pronounced,** noticeable, strong, thick.
ANTONYMS slight.
8 *he was attacked in broad daylight* **full,** complete, total; clear, bright.

broadcast ▶ **verb 1** *the show will be broadcast worldwide* **transmit,** relay, air, beam, show, televise, telecast, webcast, podcast, simulcast, cablecast, screen.
2 *the result was broadcast far and wide* **report,** announce, publicize, proclaim; spread, circulate, air, blazon, trumpet. See note at **SCATTER**.
▶ **noun** *radio and television broadcasts* **program,** show, production, transmission, telecast, webcast, podcast, simulcast, screening.

broaden ▶ **verb 1** *her smile broadened* **widen,** expand, stretch (out), draw out, spread; deepen.
2 *the government tried to broaden its political base* **expand,** enlarge, extend, widen, swell; increase, augment, add to, amplify; develop, enrich, improve, build on.

broad-minded ▶ **adjective** *our broad-minded English professor* **liberal,** tolerant, open-minded, freethinking, progressive, permissive, unprejudiced, unbiased, unbigoted.
ANTONYMS intolerant.

broadside ▶ **noun 1** historical *the gunners fired broadsides* **salvo,** volley, cannonade, barrage, blast, fusillade.
2 *a broadside against the economic reforms* **criticism,** censure, polemic, diatribe, tirade; attack, onslaught; literary philippic.

brochure ▶ **noun** *college recruitment brochures* **booklet,** pamphlet, leaflet, flyer, handbill, catalog, handout, prospectus, fact sheet, folder.

broil ▶ verb *broil the lamb chops* **grill,** toast, barbecue; cook.

broiling ▶ adjective *the sweaty nights and broiling days* **hot,** scorching, roasting, baking, boiling (hot), blistering, sweltering, parching, searing, blazing, sizzling, burning (hot), sultry, torrid, tropical, like an oven, like a furnace.
ANTONYMS cold, cool.

broke ▶ adjective *have you so easily forgotten what it's like to be broke?* **penniless,** moneyless, bankrupt, insolvent, ruined, down-and-out, without a penny to one's name, without a cent, without one red cent, without two pennies to rub together; poor, poverty-stricken, impoverished, impecunious, penurious, indigent, in penury, needy, destitute; informal cleaned out, flat broke, strapped (for cash), bust, busted, hard up, stone broke, as poor as a church mouse.

broken ▶ adjective **1** *a broken bottle* **smashed,** shattered, fragmented, splintered, crushed, snapped; in bits, in pieces; destroyed, disintegrated; cracked, split; informal in smithereens.
ANTONYMS whole.
2 *a broken arm* **fractured,** damaged, injured.
3 *this TV's broken* **inoperative,** not working, malfunctioning, faulty, defective, in disrepair, damaged, out of order, broken-down, down; informal on the blink, on the fritz, kaput, bust, busted, conked out, acting up, done for.
ANTONYMS working, fixed.
4 *broken skin* **cut,** ruptured, punctured, perforated.
5 *a broken marriage* **failed,** ended.
6 *broken promises* **flouted,** violated, infringed, contravened, disregarded, ignored, unkept.
ANTONYMS kept, honored.
7 *he was left a broken man* **defeated,** beaten, subdued; **demoralized,** dispirited, discouraged, crushed, humbled; dishonored, ruined.
8 *a night of broken sleep* **interrupted,** disturbed, fitful, disrupted, discontinuous, intermittent, unsettled, troubled.
ANTONYMS uninterrupted.
9 *he pressed on over the broken ground* **uneven,** rough, irregular, bumpy; rutted, pitted.
ANTONYMS smooth.
10 *she spoke in broken English* **halting,** hesitating, disjointed, faltering, imperfect.
ANTONYMS perfect.

broken-down ▶ adjective **1** *a broken-down hotel* **dilapidated,** run-down, ramshackle, tumbledown, in disrepair, beat-up, battered, crumbling, deteriorated, gone to rack and ruin; informal fleabag.
2 *a broken-down car* **defective,** broken, faulty; not working, malfunctioning, inoperative, nonfunctioning; informal kaput, conked out, done for.

broken-hearted ▶ adjective *his broken-hearted family* **heartbroken,** grief-stricken, desolate, devastated, despondent, inconsolable, disconsolate, miserable, depressed, melancholy, wretched, sorrowful, forlorn, heavy-hearted, woeful, doleful, downcast, woebegone, sad, down; informal down in/at the mouth; literary heartsick.
ANTONYMS overjoyed.

broker ▶ noun *a top Wall Street broker* **dealer,** agent; middleman, intermediary, mediator; liaison; stockbroker.
▶ verb *an agreement brokered by the secretariat* **arrange,** organize, orchestrate, work out, settle, clinch, bring about; negotiate, mediate.

brooch ▶ noun *her great aunt's ivory brooch* pin, clip, clasp, badge; historical fibula.

brood ▶ noun **1** *the bird flew to feed its brood* **offspring,** young, progeny; family, hatch, clutch.
2 informal *Gill was the youngest of the brood* **family**; children, offspring, youngsters, progeny; informal kids.
▶ verb **1** *once the eggs are laid, the male broods them* **incubate,** hatch.
2 *he slumped in his armchair, brooding* **worry,** fret, agonize, mope, sulk; think, ponder, contemplate, meditate, muse, ruminate.

brook[1] ▶ noun *a babbling brook* **stream,** creek, streamlet, rivulet, rill, brooklet, runnel; Brit. bourn, burn, beck.

brook[2] ▶ verb formal *we brook no violence* **tolerate,** allow, stand, bear, abide, put up with, endure; accept, permit, countenance; informal stomach, stand for, hack; archaic suffer.

brothel ▶ noun *young foreign girls are sold to the owners of these brothels* **whorehouse,** bordello, massage parlor, cathouse, bagnio; dated bawdy house, house of ill repute; Law dated disorderly house.

brother ▶ noun **1** *then Steve and his brother Dan showed up* **sibling**; informal bro, sib.
2 *they were brothers in crime* **comrade,** colleague, partner, associate, fellow, friend; informal pal, chum, mate.
3 *a brother of the order* **monk,** cleric, friar, religious, monastic.

brotherhood ▶ noun **1** *the ideals of justice and brotherhood* **comradeship,** fellowship, brotherliness, fraternalism, kinship; camaraderie, friendship.
2 *a masonic brotherhood* **society,** fraternity, association, alliance, union, league, guild, order, body, community, club, lodge, circle.

brotherly ▶ adjective **1** *brotherly rivalry* **fraternal,** sibling.
2 *brotherly love* **friendly,** comradely; affectionate, amicable, kind, devoted, loyal.

brow ▶ noun **1** *the doctor wiped his brow* **forehead,** temple; Zoology frons.
2 *heavy black brows* **eyebrow.**
3 *the brow of the hill* **summit,** peak, top, crest, crown, head, pinnacle, apex.

browbeat ▶ verb *they browbeat the witness into changing her testimony* **bully,** intimidate, force, coerce, compel, hector, dragoon, bludgeon, pressure, pressurize, tyrannize, terrorize, menace; harass, harry, hound; informal bulldoze, railroad.

brown ▶ adjective *she has brown eyes* hazel, chocolate-colored, coffee-colored, cocoa-colored, nut-brown; brunette; sepia, mahogany, umber, burnt sienna; beige, buff, tan, fawn, camel, café au lait, caramel, chestnut.

browse ▶ verb **1** *I visited all the little boutiques, just to browse* **look around,** window-shop, peruse.
2 *she* ***browsed through*** *the newspaper* **scan (through),** skim through, glance through, look through, peruse; thumb through, leaf through, flick through; dip into.
3 *three cows were browsing in the meadow* **graze,** feed, nibble, crop; ruminate.
4 *he spent hours browsing online* **surfing,** go from site to site.

bruise ▶ noun *a bruise across her forehead* **contusion,** lesion, mark, black-and-blue mark, discoloration, blackening; injury; swelling, lump, bump, welt; Medicine ecchymosis.
▶ verb **1** *her face was badly bruised* injure, mark, discolor.
2 *every one of the apples is bruised* **mark,** discolor, blemish; damage, spoil.
3 *Eric's ego was bruised* **upset,** offend, insult, affront, hurt, wound, injure, crush.

brunette ▶ adjective *a brunette woman* **brown-haired,** dark, dark-haired.

brunt ▶ noun *the brunt of the downsizing was felt most by the warehouse crew* **full force,** force, impact, shock, burden, pressure, weight; effect, repercussions, consequences.

brush ▶ noun **1** *a styling brush | camel-hair brushes | a brush and dustpan* hairbrush; toothbrush; paintbrush; scrub brush; whisk broom, sweeper, broom.
2 *he gave the seat a brush with his hand* **sweep,** wipe, dust.
3 *the brush of his lips against her cheek* **touch,** stroke, skim, graze, nudge, contact; kiss.
4 *a brush with the law* **encounter,** clash, confrontation, conflict, altercation, incident; informal run-in.
▶ verb **1** *she brushed her hair* **groom,** comb, neaten, tidy, smooth, arrange, fix, do; curry.
2 *she felt his lips brush her cheek* **touch,** stroke, caress, skim, sweep, graze, contact; kiss.
3 *she brushed a wisp of hair away* **push,** move, sweep, clear.
– PHRASES **brush something aside** *she brushed aside his repeated warnings* **disregard,** ignore, dismiss, shrug off, wave aside; overlook, pay no attention to, take no notice of, neglect, forget about, turn a blind eye to, turn a deaf ear to; reject, spurn; laugh off, make light of, trivialize; informal pooh-pooh. **brush someone off** *he tried to help, but she brushed him off* **rebuff,** dismiss, spurn, reject; slight, scorn, disdain; ignore, disregard, snub, turn one's back on, give someone the cold shoulder, freeze out; jilt, cast aside, discard. **brush up (on)** *I'm brushing up on my French before our trip to Paris* **relearn,** read up (on), go over, study; improve, sharpen (up), polish up; hone, refine, perfect; informal bone up (on).

brusque ▶ adjective *his brusque manners* **curt,** abrupt, blunt, short, sharp, terse, peremptory, gruff; offhand, discourteous, impolite, rude; informal snappy.
ANTONYMS polite.

> CHOOSE THE RIGHT WORD
>
> **brusque, blunt, bluff, curt, gruff, surly**
>
> **Brusque**, which comes from an Italian word meaning rude, describes an abruptness of speech or manner that is not necessarily meant to be rude (*a brusque handshake; a brusque reply*). **Curt** is more deliberately unfriendly, suggesting brevity and coldness of manner (*a curt dismissal*). There's nothing wrong with being **blunt**, although it implies an honesty and directness that can border on tactlessness (*a blunt reply to his question about where the money went*). Someone who is **bluff** is usually more likable, possessing a frank, hearty manner that may be a little too outspoken but is seldom offensive (*a bluff man who rarely minced words*). Exhibiting **gruff** or **surly** behavior will not win friends, since both words suggest bad temper if not rudeness. But *gruff* is used to describe a rough or grouchy disposition and, like *bluff*, is applied more often to a man. Anyone who has had to deal with an overworked store clerk while shopping during the holidays knows the meaning of *surly*, which is worse than *gruff*. It describes not only a sour disposition but an outright hostility toward people, and it can apply to someone of either sex (*that surly woman at the customer service desk*).

brutal ▶ adjective **1** *a brutal attack* **savage,** cruel, vicious, ferocious, brutish, barbaric, barbarous, wicked, murderous, bloodthirsty, cold-blooded, callous, heartless, ruthless, merciless, sadistic; heinous, monstrous, abominable, atrocious.
ANTONYMS gentle, humane.
2 *brutal honesty* **unsparing,** unstinting, unembellished, unvarnished, bald, naked, stark, blunt, direct, straightforward, frank, outspoken, forthright, plain-spoken; complete, total.

brute ▶ noun *a callous brute* **savage,** beast, monster, animal, barbarian, fiend, ogre; sadist; thug, lout, ruffian; informal swine, pig.
▶ adjective *brute strength* **physical,** bodily; crude, violent.

bubble ▶ noun *the bubbles rose in the glass* globule, bead, blister; air pocket; (**bubbles**) sparkle, fizz, effervescence, froth, head.
▶ verb **1** *the champagne bubbled nicely on the tongue* **sparkle,** fizz, effervesce, foam, froth.
2 *the milk was bubbling above the flame* **boil,** simmer, seethe, gurgle.
3 *she was* ***bubbling over*** *with enthusiasm* **overflow,** brim over, be filled, gush.

bubbly ▶ adjective **1** *a bubbly wine* **sparkling,** bubbling, fizzy, effervescent, gassy, aerated, carbonated; spumante, frothy, foamy.
ANTONYMS flat.
2 *she was bubbly and full of life* **vivacious,** animated, ebullient, exuberant, lively, high-spirited, zestful; sparkling, bouncy, buoyant, carefree; merry, happy, cheerful, perky, sunny,

bright; informal upbeat, chirpy.
ANTONYMS dull, listless.
▶ **noun** informal *a bottle of bubbly* **champagne,** sparkling wine, spumante, cava.

buck ▶ **verb** *it takes guts to buck the system* **resist,** oppose, defy, fight, kick against.
– PHRASES **buck up** informal *don't worry, I'll buck up soon* **cheer up,** perk up, take heart, pick up, bounce back. **buck someone up** informal *how can we buck you up, pal?* **cheer up,** buoy up, perk up, hearten, uplift, encourage, enliven, give someone a lift; informal pep up; rare inspirit.

bucket ▶ **noun 1** *a bucket of cold water* **pail,** scuttle, can, tin, tub; ice bucket, wine cooler.
2 informal *everyone wept buckets* **floods,** gallons, oceans.

buckle ▶ **noun** *a belt buckle* **clasp,** clip, catch, hasp, fastener.
▶ **verb 1** *he buckled the belt around his waist* **fasten,** do up, hook, strap, secure, clasp, clip.
2 *the front axle buckled* **warp,** bend, twist, curve, distort, contort, deform; bulge, arc, arch; crumple, collapse, give way.
– PHRASES **buckle down** *Isaac finally began to buckle down in his junior year* **get (down) to work,** set to work, get down to business; work hard, apply oneself, make an effort, be industrious, be diligent, focus.

bucolic ▶ **adjective** *their farm had been used as the bucolic setting for two major motion pictures* **rustic,** rural, pastoral, country, countryside; literary Arcadian, sylvan, georgic.

bud ▶ **noun** *fresh buds* **sprout,** shoot, blossom; Botany plumule.
▶ **verb** *trees began to bud* **sprout,** shoot, germinate.

budding ▶ **adjective** *a budding artist* **promising,** up-and-coming, rising, in the making, aspiring, emerging, fledgling, developing, blossoming; informal would-be, wannabe.

budge ▶ **verb 1** *the horses wouldn't budge* **move,** shift, stir, go.
2 *I couldn't budge the door* **dislodge,** shift, move, reposition.
3 *they refuse to budge on the issue* **give in,** give way, yield, change one's mind, acquiesce, compromise, do a U-turn.

budget ▶ **noun 1** *your budget for the week* **financial plan,** forecast; accounts, statement.
2 *a cut in the defense budget* **allowance,** allocation, quota; grant, award, funds, resources, capital.
▶ **verb 1** *we have to budget $7,000 for the work* **allocate,** allot, allow, earmark, designate, set aside.
2 *budget your finances* **schedule,** plan, cost, estimate; ration.
▶ **adjective** *a budget hotel* **cheap,** inexpensive, economy, affordable, low-cost, low-price, cut-rate, discount, bargain, downmarket.
ANTONYMS expensive.

buff ▶ **adjective** *a plain buff envelope* **beige,** yellowish, yellowish-brown, light brown, fawn, sandy, wheaten, biscuit, camel.
▶ **verb** *he buffed the glass* **polish,** burnish, shine, clean, rub.
▶ **noun** informal *a film buff* **enthusiast,** fan, devotee, lover, admirer; expert, aficionado, authority, pundit; informal freak, nut, fanatic, fiend, addict, junkie, bum.
– PHRASES **in the buff** informal See **NAKED** (sense 1).

buffer ▶ **noun** *a buffer against market fluctuations* **cushion,** bulwark, shield, barrier, guard, safeguard.
▶ **verb** *she tried to buffer the children from the troubles* **shield,** protect, defend, cushion, insulate, screen, guard.

buffet[1] ▶ **noun 1** *a sumptuous buffet* **smorgasbord,** self-serve meal, serve-yourself meal, spread.
2 *the plates are kept in the buffet* **sideboard,** cabinet, cupboard.

buffet[2] ▶ **verb 1** *rough seas buffeted the coast* **batter,** pound, lash, strike, hit.
2 *he has been buffeted by bad publicity* **afflict,** trouble, harm, burden, bother, beset, harass, assail, harry, plague, torment, blight, bedevil.

buffoon ▶ **noun 1** archaic *the king's buffoon* **clown,** jester, fool, comic, comedian, wag, wit, merry-andrew, harlequin, Punchinello, Pierrot.
2 *they regarded him as a buffoon* **fool,** idiot, dolt, dunce, dunderhead, dullard, ignoramus, dummy, simpleton, jackass; informal chump, blockhead, jughead, boob, bozo, doofus, nincompoop, numbskull, numbnuts, dope, twit, nitwit, halfwit, birdbrain. See also **ASS** (sense 2).

bug ▶ **noun 1** *bugs were crawling everywhere* **insect,** mite; informal creepy-crawly, beastie.
2 informal *a stomach bug* **illness,** ailment, disorder, infection, disease, sickness, complaint, upset, condition; bacterium, germ, virus.
3 informal *he caught the journalism bug* **obsession,** enthusiasm, craze, fad, mania, passion, fixation.
4 *the bug planted in his phone* **listening device,** hidden microphone, wire, wiretap, tap.
5 *a bug in the software* **fault,** error, defect, flaw; virus; informal glitch, gremlin.
▶ **verb 1** *her conversations were bugged* **record,** eavesdrop on, spy on, overhear; wiretap, tap, monitor.
2 informal *she really bugs me* See **ANNOY**.

bugbear ▶ **noun** *pseudoscience is a perennial bugbear for legitimate researchers* **pet peeve,** hate, bête noire, anathema, aversion, bugaboo; bane, bane of one's life/existence, irritant, irritation, vexation, thorn in one's flesh/side; nightmare, torment; informal pain, pain in the neck, hang-up.

build ▶ **verb 1** *they were building a tree house* **construct,** erect, put up, assemble; make, form, create, fashion, model, shape.
2 *they are building a business strategy* **establish,** found, set up, institute, inaugurate, initiate.
3 *the pressure was building* **increase,** mount, intensify, escalate, grow, rise.
▶ **noun** *a man of slim build* **physique,** frame, body, figure, form, shape, stature, proportions; informal vital statistics.
– PHRASES **build something in/into** *emergency procedures must be built into every plan* **incorporate in/into,** include in, absorb into, subsume into, assimilate into. **build on** *we are now in a position to build on all the wonderful*

legwork that our staff has accomplished **expand on,** enlarge on, develop, elaborate, flesh out, embellish, amplify; refine, improve, perfect. **build up** *the traffic continues to build up* **increase,** grow, mount (up), intensify, escalate; strengthen. **build something up 1** *he built up a huge business* **establish,** set up, found, institute, start, create; develop, expand, enlarge. **2** *she built up her stamina* **boost,** strengthen, increase, improve, augment, raise, enhance, swell; informal beef up. **3** *I have built up a collection of prints* **accumulate,** amass, collect, gather; stockpile, hoard.

building ▶ **noun 1** *a brick building* **structure,** construction, edifice, erection; property, premises, establishment.
2 *the building of power stations* **construction,** erection, fabrication, assembly.

buildup ▶ **noun 1** *the buildup of military strength* **increase,** growth, expansion, escalation, development, proliferation.
2 *the buildup of carbon dioxide* **accumulation,** accretion.
3 *the buildup for the World Cup* **publicity,** promotion, advertising, marketing; informal hype, ballyhoo, brouhaha, to-do.

built-in ▶ **adjective 1** *a built-in cupboard* integrated, integral, incorporated.
2 *built-in advantages* **inherent,** intrinsic, inbuilt, innate; essential, implicit, basic, fundamental, deep-rooted.

bulge ▶ **noun 1** *a bulge in the tire* **swelling,** bump, lump, protuberance, prominence, tumescence.
2 informal *a bulge in the population* **surge,** upsurge, rise, increase, escalation.
▶ **verb** *his eyes were bulging* **swell,** stick out, puff out, balloon (out), bug out, fill out, belly, distend, tumefy, intumesce; project, protrude, stand out.

CHOOSE THE RIGHT WORD

bulge, project, protrude, protuberate

While all of these verbs mean to extend outward, beyond the normal line or surface of something, it is almost impossible not to associate the word **bulge** with the human body (*a stomach that bulges over a waistband, muscles that bulge beneath a shirt*). *Bulge* suggests a swelling out that is quite noticeable or even abnormal, and that may be the result of internal pressure, although a brick wall can *bulge*, as can a bicep muscle. **Protuberate** is a less common word meaning to swell or stick out, but it does not necessarily imply that anything is abnormal or radically wrong (*he was so thin that his knees protuberated*). To **protrude** is to thrust forth in an unexpected way or to stick out in a way that is abnormal or disfiguring (*her eyes protruded from her skull*). **Project** is the least upsetting of all these words, probably because it is used less often with reference to the human body. Anything that juts out abruptly beyond the rest of a surface is said to *project* (*the balcony projected from the south side of the house*).

bulk ▶ **noun 1** *the sheer bulk of the bags* **size,** volume, dimensions, proportions, mass, scale, magnitude, immensity, vastness.
2 *the bulk of entrants were women* **majority,** main part, major part, lion's share, preponderance, generality; most, almost all.
ANTONYMS minority.

bulky ▶ **adjective** *bulky items* **large,** big, huge, sizable, substantial, massive; king-size, economy-size(d), outsize, oversized, considerable, voluminous; **cumbersome,** unmanageable, unwieldy, ponderous, heavy, weighty; informal jumbo, whopping, hulking, humongous, ginormous.
ANTONYMS small, slight.

bulldoze ▶ **verb 1** *they plan to bulldoze the park* **demolish,** knock down, tear down, pull down, flatten, level, raze, clear.
2 *he bulldozed his way through* **force,** push, shove, barge, elbow, shoulder, jostle, muscle; plunge, crash, sweep, bundle.
3 informal *she tends to bulldoze everyone* **bully,** browbeat, intimidate, dragoon, domineer, hector, pressurize, tyrannize, strong-arm, push around, walk all over; railroad, steamroller, lean on, boss.

bullet ▶ **noun** *the bullet was taken to the police lab* ball, shot, cartridge; informal slug; (**bullets**) lead, ammunition, ammo.

bulletin ▶ **noun 1** *a news bulletin* **report,** dispatch, story, press release, newscast, flash; statement, announcement, message, communication, communiqué.
2 *the society's monthly bulletin* **newsletter,** proceedings; newspaper, magazine, digest, gazette, review; tipsheet.

bullish ▶ **adjective** *another bullish candidate has thrown her hat into the ring* **confident,** positive, assertive, self-assertive, assured, self-assured, bold, determined; optimistic, buoyant, sanguine; informal feisty, upbeat.

bully ▶ **noun** *the school bully* **persecutor,** oppressor, tyrant, tormentor, intimidator; tough guy, thug, ruffian, strong-arm.
▶ **verb 1** *the others bully him* **persecute,** oppress, tyrannize, browbeat, harass, torment, intimidate, strong-arm, dominate; informal push around, bullyrag.
2 *she was bullied into helping* **coerce,** pressure, pressurize, press, push; force, compel; badger, goad, prod, browbeat, intimidate, dragoon, strong-arm; informal bulldoze, railroad, lean on.

bulwark ▶ **noun 1** *ancient bulwarks* **wall,** rampart, fortification, parapet, stockade, palisade, barricade, embankment, earthwork.
2 *a bulwark of liberty* **protector,** defender, protection, guard, defense, supporter, buttress; mainstay, bastion, stronghold.

bum¹ ▶ **noun** informal **1** *the bums sleeping on the sidewalk* See TRAMP (sense 1 of the noun).

2 *you lazy bum* **idler,** loafer, slacker, good-for-nothing, ne'er-do-well, layabout, lounger, shirker; loser.
3 *a ski bum* **enthusiast,** fan, aficionado, lover, freak, nut, buff, fanatic, addict.
▶ **verb 1** *that summer he bummed around Montreal* **loaf,** lounge, idle, wander, drift, meander, dawdle; informal mooch, lollygag.
2 *they bummed money off him* **beg,** borrow; informal scrounge, cadge, sponge, mooch.
▶ **adjective** *a bum deal* **crummy,** rotten, pathetic, lousy, pitiful; **bad,** poor, second-rate, tinpot, third-rate, second-class, unsatisfactory, inadequate, unacceptable; dreadful, awful, terrible, deplorable, lamentable.
ANTONYMS excellent.

bum² ▶ **noun** Brit. informal *next time I go skating, I'm tying a pillow to my bum!* See BUTTOCKS.

bumbling ▶ **adjective** *the bumbling Inspector Clouseau* **blundering,** bungling, inept, clumsy, maladroit, awkward, muddled, klutzy; oafish, clodhopping, lumbering; botched, ham-handed, ham-fisted.
ANTONYMS efficient, debonair.

bump ▶ **noun 1** *I landed with a bump* **bang,** crash, smash, smack, crack, jolt, thud, thump; informal whack, thwack, bash, bonk, wallop.
2 *a bump in the road | the bump on his head* **hump,** lump, ridge, bulge, knob, protuberance; swelling.
▶ **verb 1** *cars* ***bumped into*** *each other* **hit,** crash into, smash into, smack into, slam into, bang into, knock into, run into, plow into; ram into, collide with, strike.
2 *a cart bumping along the road* **bounce,** jolt, jerk, rattle, shake.
3 *she got bumped in favor of a rookie* **displace,** demote, dislodge, supplant.
– PHRASES **bump into** informal *you'll never guess who we bumped into at the theater* **meet,** meet by chance, encounter, run into/across, come across, chance on, happen on.

bumpkin ▶ **noun** *he was very bright, but a bit of a bumpkin* **yokel,** peasant, provincial, rustic, country cousin, hayseed, hillbilly, hick, rube.

bumptious ▶ **adjective** *our bumptious cousin thinks she's God's gift to men* **self-important,** conceited, arrogant, self-assertive, pushy, pompous, overbearing, cocky, swaggering; proud, haughty, overweening, egotistical; informal snooty, uppity. See note at BOLD.
ANTONYMS modest.

bumpy ▶ **adjective 1** *a bumpy road* **uneven,** rough, rutted, rutty, pitted, potholed, holey; lumpy, rocky.
ANTONYMS smooth, level.
2 *a bumpy ride* **bouncy,** rough, uncomfortable, jolting, lurching, jerky, jarring, bone-shaking.
ANTONYMS smooth, comfortable.

bunch ▶ **noun 1** *a bunch of flowers* **bouquet,** posy, nosegay, spray, corsage; wreath, garland.
2 *a bunch of grapes | a bunch of keys* **cluster,** clump; knot; group, assemblage.
3 informal *we invited the whole bunch* **group,** set, circle, company, collection, bevy, band, party; gang, crew, pack; crowd, throng, multitude.
4 informal *I bought* ***a bunch of*** *used books* **an assortment of,** a bundle of, a collection of; many, lots of, a lot of, loads of, a load of, tons of, a ton of, an abundance of; informal a bucketload of, a shedload of.
▶ **verb 1** *he bunched the reins in his hand* **bundle,** clump, cluster, group, gather; pack.
2 *her skirt bunched at the waist* **gather,** ruffle, pucker, fold, pleat.
3 *the runners* ***bunched up*** *behind him* **cluster,** huddle, gather, congregate, collect, amass, group, crowd.

bundle ▶ **noun** *a bundle of clothes* **bunch,** roll, clump, wad, parcel, sheaf, bale, bolt; package; pile, stack, heap, mass; informal load.
▶ **verb 1** *she bundled up her things* **tie,** pack, parcel, wrap, roll, fold, bind, bale, package.
2 *she was bundled in furs* **wrap,** envelop, clothe, cover, muffle, swathe, swaddle, shroud, drape, enfold.
3 informal *he was bundled into a van* shove, push, thrust, manhandle, hurry, rush.

bungle ▶ **verb** *they bungled the robbery* **mishandle,** mismanage, mess up, spoil, ruin, blunder; informal botch, muff, fluff, make a hash of, foul up, screw up, flub, goof up.

bungling ▶ **adjective** *the work of a bungling amateur* **incompetent,** blundering, amateurish, inept, unskillful, maladroit, clumsy, klutzy, awkward, bumbling; informal ham-handed, ham-fisted.

bunk ▶ **noun 1** *there were twelve bunks per dormitory* **berth,** cot, bed.
2 informal *the idea was sheer bunk* See NONSENSE (sense 1 of the noun). See also note at NONSENSE.

bunkum ▶ **noun** informal dated See NONSENSE (sense 1 of the noun).

buoy ▶ **noun** *a mooring buoy* **float,** marker; bellbuoy, nun buoy, sonobuoy.
▶ **verb** *the party was buoyed by an election victory* **cheer,** cheer up, hearten, rally, invigorate, uplift, lift, encourage, stimulate, inspirit; informal pep up, perk up, buck up.
ANTONYMS depress.

buoyant ▶ **adjective 1** *a buoyant substance* **able to float,** floating, floatable.
ANTONYMS leaden.
2 *a buoyant mood* **cheerful,** cheery, happy, lighthearted, carefree, bright, merry, joyful, bubbly, bouncy, sunny, jolly; lively, jaunty, high-spirited, perky; optimistic, confident, positive; informal peppy, upbeat.
ANTONYMS depressed, optimistic.

burden ▶ **noun 1** *a financial burden* **encumbrance,** strain, care, problem, worry, difficulty, trouble, millstone; **responsibility,** onus, charge, duty, obligation, liability.
2 *they shouldered their burdens* **load,** weight, cargo, freight.
▶ **verb** *she thought nothing of burdening us with yet another mouth to feed* **load,** charge, weigh down, encumber, hamper; overload, overburden; **oppress,** trouble, worry, harass, upset, distress; haunt, afflict, strain, stress, tax, overwhelm.

bureau ▶ **noun 1** *an oak bureau* **dresser,** chest of drawers, cabinet, tallboy, highboy.
2 *the tourism bureau* **agency,** service, office, business, company, firm; **department,** division, branch, section.

bureaucracy ▶ noun **1** *the ranks of the bureaucracy* **civil service,** government, administration; establishment, system, powers that be; ministries, authorities.
2 *unnecessary bureaucracy* **red tape,** rules and regulations, protocol, officialdom, paperwork.

bureaucrat ▶ noun *Washington bureaucrats* **official,** officeholder, administrator, public servant, civil servant, functionary; mandarin; derogatory apparatchik, bean counter, paper shuffler.

burgeon ▶ verb *the toy industry is burgeoning* **flourish,** thrive, prosper, improve, develop; expand, escalate, swell, grow, boom, mushroom, snowball, rocket.

burglar ▶ noun *the burglar escaped through the bedroom window* **robber,** housebreaker, cat burglar, thief, raider, looter, safecracker, intruder, prowler; informal second-story man, yegg.

burglary ▶ noun **1** *serving time for burglary* **housebreaking,** breaking and entering, theft, stealing, robbery, larceny, thievery, looting, pilferage.
2 *a series of burglaries* **break-in,** theft, robbery, raid; informal heist.

burial ▶ noun *a private burial at Vineyard Point Cemetery* **burying,** interment, committal, entombment; funeral, obsequies; formal inhumation; archaic sepulture. See note at INTERMENT.
ANTONYMS exhumation.

burlesque ▶ noun *a rather risqué burlesque* **parody,** caricature, satire, lampoon, skit, farce; sendup, takeoff, spoof; striptease, strip. See note at CARICATURE.

burly ▶ adjective *his burly bodyguards* **strapping,** well-built, sturdy, brawny, strong, muscular, muscly, thickset, blocky, big, hefty, bulky, stocky, stout, Herculean; informal hunky, beefy, husky, hulking; literary stalwart, thewy; technical mesomorphic.
ANTONYMS puny.

burn ▶ verb **1** *the shed was burning* **be on fire,** be alight, be ablaze, blaze, go up, go up in smoke, be in flames, be aflame; smolder, glow.
2 *he burned the letters* **set fire to,** set on fire, set alight, light, ignite, touch off; incinerate; informal torch.
3 *I burned my dress with the iron* **scorch,** singe, sear, char, blacken, brand, sizzle; scald.
4 *her face burned* **be hot,** be warm, be feverish, be on fire; blush, redden, go red, flush, color.
5 *she is* ***burning with*** *curiosity* **be consumed by/with,** be eaten up by/with, be obsessed by/with, be tormented by/with, be beside oneself with.
6 *the energy they* ***burn up*** **consume,** use up, expend, go/get through, eat up; dissipate.
ANTONYMS conserve.

> CHOOSE THE RIGHT WORD
>
> **burn, cauterize, char, scald, scorch, sear, singe**
>
> If you're not an experienced cook, you're likely to **burn** your vegetables, **char** your meat, and, if you put your face too close to the stove, you might even **singe** your eyebrows. All of these verbs mean to injure or bring about a change in something by exposing it to fire or intense heat. *Burn*, which is the most comprehensive term, can mean to change only slightly (*she burned her face by staying out in the sun*) or to destroy completely (*the factory was burned to the ground*). To *char* is to convert a substance to carbon or charcoal (*the beams in the ceiling were charred by the fire*). Like *char*, **singe** and **scorch** mean to burn only partially or superficially (*scorched the blouse while ironing it; singe the chicken before cooking it*). *Singeing* is often done deliberately to remove the hair, bristles, or feathers from the carcass of an animal or bird. **Scald** refers specifically to burning with, or as if with, a hot liquid or steam (*the cook scalded herself when she spilled the boiling water*); it can also mean to parboil or heat to a temperature just below boiling (*scald the milk to make the sauce*). **Sear** is also a term used in cooking, where it means to brown the outside of a piece of meat by subjecting it briefly to intense heat to seal in the juices. When it's human flesh that's being seared in surgery, the correct verb is **cauterize**, which means to burn for healing purposes (*the doctor cauterized the wound to ward off infection*).

burning ▶ adjective **1** *burning coals* **blazing,** flaming, fiery, ignited, glowing, red-hot, smoldering, igneous; raging, roaring.
2 *burning desert sands* **extremely hot,** red-hot, fiery, blistering, scorching, searing, sweltering, torrid; informal baking, boiling (hot), broiling, roasting, sizzling.
ANTONYMS freezing.
3 *a burning desire* **intense,** passionate, deep-seated, profound, wholehearted, strong, ardent, fervent, urgent, fierce, eager, frantic, consuming, uncontrollable.
4 *burning issues* **important,** crucial, significant, vital, essential, pivotal; urgent, pressing, compelling, critical.

burnish ▶ verb *marks can be removed by burnishing the metal* **polish,** shine, buff, rub, gloss.

burp ▶ verb informal *cucumbers make me burp* **belch**; formal eructate; rare eruct; archaic bolk, rout, ruck.
▶ noun *he let out a loud burp* **belch**; formal eructation; rare ventosity; archaic bolk.

burrow ▶ noun *a rabbits' burrow* **hole,** tunnel, warren, dugout; lair, set, den, earth.
▶ verb *the mouse burrows a hole* **tunnel,** dig (out), excavate, grub, mine, bore, channel; hollow out, gouge out.

burst ▶ verb **1** *one balloon burst* **split open,** rupture, break, tear.
2 *a shell burst in the distance* **explode,** blow up, detonate, go off.
3 *water burst through the hole* **break,** erupt, surge, gush, rush, stream, flow, pour, spill; spout, spurt, jet, spew.

4 *he burst into the room* **barge,** charge, plunge, plow, hurtle, career, careen, rush, dash, tear.
5 *they* ***burst into*** *tears* **break out in,** launch into, erupt in, have a fit of.

▶ **noun 1** *mortar bursts* **explosion,** detonation, blast, eruption, bang.
2 *a burst of gunfire* **volley,** salvo, fusillade, barrage, discharge; hail, rain.
3 *a burst of activity* **outbreak,** eruption, flare-up, blaze, attack, fit, rush, gale, storm, surge, upsurge, spurt.

– PHRASES **burst out** *"I don't care!" she burst out* **exclaim,** blurt, cry, shout, yell; dated ejaculate.

bury ▶ **verb 1** *the dead were buried* **inter,** lay to rest, entomb; informal put six feet under; literary inhume.
ANTONYMS exhume.
2 *she buried her face in her hands* **hide,** conceal, cover, enfold, engulf, tuck, cup, sink; literary enshroud.
ANTONYMS reveal.
3 *the bullet buried itself in the wood* **embed,** sink, implant, submerge; drive into.
ANTONYMS extract.
4 *he buried himself in his work* **absorb,** engross, immerse, occupy, engage, busy, involve.

bush ▶ **noun 1** *a rose bush* **shrub,** brier; (**bushes**) undergrowth, shrubbery.
2 *out in the bush* **wilds,** wilderness, forest, woodland, timberland, bush country, bushland; backwoods, hinterland(s), backcountry, backlands; informal the sticks, boondocks, boonies.

bushy ▶ **adjective** *Groucho's trademark greasepaint mustache and bushy eyebrows* **thick,** shaggy, unruly, fuzzy, bristly, fluffy, woolly; luxuriant.
ANTONYMS sleek, wispy.

business ▶ **noun 1** *Bill's business is electrical engineering* **work,** line of work, occupation, profession, career, employment, job, position; vocation, calling; field, sphere, trade, métier, craft; informal biz, racket, game.
2 *whom do you do business with?* **trade,** trading, commerce, dealing, traffic, merchandising; dealings, transactions, negotiations.
3 *her own business* **company,** firm, concern, enterprise, venture, organization, operation, corporation, undertaking; office, agency, franchise, practice; informal outfit.
4 *none of your business* **concern,** affair, responsibility, duty, function, obligation; problem, worry; informal beeswax, bailiwick.
5 *this thing about the disappearing furniture is a strange business* **affair,** matter, thing, case, circumstance, situation, event, incident, happening, occurrence; episode.

businesslike ▶ **adjective** *our meetings are usually conducted in a more businesslike fashion* **professional,** efficient, competent, methodical, disciplined, systematic, orderly, organized, structured, practical, pragmatic, routine, slick.

bust[1] ▶ **noun 1** *an empire waistline accentuates the bust* **chest,** bosom, breasts.
2 *a bust of Caesar* **sculpture,** carving, effigy, statue; head and shoulders.

bust[2] ▶ **verb** informal **1** *I didn't mean to bust your DVD player* **break,** smash, fracture, shatter, crack, disintegrate, snap; split, burst.
2 *he promised to bust the counterfeit ring* **overthrow,** destroy, topple, bring down, ruin, break, overturn, overcome, defeat, get rid of, oust, dislodge.
3 *they were busted for drugs* See ARREST (sense 1 of the verb).

▶ **noun** *a cache of guns was discovered in the bust* **raid,** search; informal takedown, shakedown.

– PHRASES **go bust** *their flower shop went bust* **fail,** collapse, fold, go under, founder; go bankrupt, go into receivership, go into liquidation, be wound up; informal crash, go broke, go belly up, flop, bomb.

bustle ▶ **verb** *people bustled about* **rush,** dash, hurry, scurry, scuttle, hustle, scamper, scramble; run, tear, charge; informal scoot, beetle, buzz, zoom.

▶ **noun** *the bustle of the market* **activity,** action, liveliness, hustle and bustle, excitement; tumult, hubbub, whirl, commotion; informal toing and froing, comings and goings.

bustling ▶ **adjective** *the mall is bustling with holiday shoppers* **busy,** crowded, swarming, teeming, thronged; buzzing, abuzz, buzzy, hectic, lively.
ANTONYMS deserted.

busy ▶ **adjective 1** *the campaign volunteers have been busy* **occupied,** engaged, involved, employed, working, hard at work; rushed off one's feet, hard-pressed, swamped, up to one's neck; on the job, absorbed, engrossed, immersed, preoccupied; informal (as) busy as a bee, on the go, hard at it.
ANTONYMS idle.
2 *sorry, she's busy at the moment* **unavailable,** engaged, occupied; working, in a meeting, on duty; informal tied up.
ANTONYMS free.
3 *the busy streets of Toronto* **hectic,** active, lively; crowded, bustling, abuzz, swarming, teeming, full, thronged.
4 *a busy design* **ornate,** overelaborate, overblown, overwrought, overdone, fussy, cluttered, overworked.
ANTONYMS restrained, quiet.

▶ **verb** *he busied himself with paperwork* **occupy,** involve, engage, concern, absorb, engross, immerse, preoccupy; distract, divert.

CHOOSE THE RIGHT WORD

busy, assiduous, diligent, engaged, industrious, sedulous

There are varying degrees of busyness. **Busy** implies actively and attentively involved in work or a pastime (*too busy to come to the phone*). It can also be used to describe intensive activity of any kind (*a busy intersection; a busy day*). Someone who is **engaged** is also *busy*, but in a more focused way (*engaged in compiling a dictionary*). **Diligent** is used to describe earnest and constant effort, and it often connotes enjoyment of or dedication to what one is doing (*diligent efforts to rescue injured animals*). To be **industrious** is to be more focused still, often with a definite goal in mind (*an industrious employee working for a promotion*). **Sedulous** also applies to goal-oriented activity, but it suggests more close care and perseverance than *industrious* does (*a sedulous investigation of the accident*). The award for concentrated effort goes to the person who is **assiduous**, which suggests painstaking preoccupation with a specific task (*an assiduous student is the one most likely to win his or her teacher's favor*).

busybody ▶ noun *I was labeled a snob because I didn't care to belong to her nest of busybodies* **meddler,** interferer, mischief-maker, troublemaker; gossip, scandalmonger; eavesdropper; informal kibitzer, buttinsky, snoop, snooper, Nosy Parker, yenta.

but ▶ conjunction **1** *he stumbled but didn't fall* **yet,** nevertheless, nonetheless, even so, however, still, notwithstanding, despite that, in spite of that, for all that, all the same, just the same; though, although.

2 *this one's expensive, but this one isn't* **whereas,** conversely, but then, then again, on the other hand, by/in contrast, on the contrary.

▶ preposition *everyone but him* **except (for),** apart from, other than, besides, aside from, with the exception of, bar, excepting, excluding, leaving out, save (for), saving.

▶ adverb *he is but a shadow of his former self* **only,** just, simply, merely, no more than, nothing but; a mere.

– PHRASES **but for** *I would not have survived but for your selfless courage* **except for,** if it were not for, were it not for, barring, notwithstanding.

USAGE

but

It is a gross canard that beginning a sentence with *but* is stylistically slipshod. In fact, doing so is highly desirable in any number of contexts, as many stylebooks have said (many correctly pointing out that *but* is more effective than *however* at the beginning of a sentence)—e.g.:

- "The group of Adversative conjunctions represented by BUT (called Arrestive) very often fulfil [sic] the office of relating consecutive sentences. . . . An entire paragraph is not infrequently devoted to arresting or preventing a seeming inference from one preceding, and is therefore appropriately opened by But, Still, Nevertheless, &c." (Alexander Bain, *English Composition and Rhetoric*, 4th ed.; 1877.)
- "*But* (not followed by a comma) always heads its turning sentence; *Nevertheless* usually does (followed by a comma). I am sure, however, that *however* is always better buried in the sentence between commas; *But* is for the quick turn; the inlaid *however* for the more elegant sweep." (Sheridan Baker, *The Practical Stylist*;1962.)
- "Of the many myths concerning 'correct' English, one of the most persistent is the belief that it is somehow improper to begin a sentence with *and, but, for, or*, or *nor*. The construction is, of course, widely used today and has been widely used for generations, for the very good reason that it is an effective means of achieving coherence between sentences and between larger units of discourse, such as paragraphs." (R. W. Pence and D. W. Emery, *A Grammar of Present-Day English*, 2d ed.; 1963.)
- "I can't overstate how much easier it is for readers to process a sentence if you start with *but* when you're shifting direction." (William Zinsser, *On Writing Well*, 6th ed.; 1998.)
- "If you want to begin a sentence by contradicting the last, use *but* instead of *however*." (Christopher Lasch, *Plain Style*; 2002.)

Good writers often begin sentences with *but* and have always done so. Samples from twentieth- and twenty-first-century writers follow:

- "But such simplicity of instinct is scarcely possible for human beings." (Bertrand Russell, *Education and the Good Life*; 1926.)
- "But it must not be assumed that intelligent thinking can play no part in the formation of the goal and of ethical judgments." (Albert Einstein, "Science and Religion" (1939), in *Ideas and Opinions*; 1954.)
- "But he had got used to that and it did not disquiet him." (Ursula K. Le Guin, *The Other Wind*; 2001.)

These are not good writers on bad days. No: they were having good days. In 1963, researcher Francis Christensen found that 8.75% of the sentences in the work of first-rate writers—including H. L. Mencken, Lionel Trilling, and Edmund Wilson—began with coordinating conjunctions (i.e., *and* and *but*). In *The New York Times* (front page during the 1990s) and *U.S. News & World Report* (in 1997), the figure is about the same. To the professional rhetorician, these figures aren't at all surprising.

All this enthusiasm for the construction, though, needs to be tempered to this extent: don't start consecutive sentences with *but*. Also, putting this subordinating conjunction twice in one sentence invariably makes the sentence unwieldy and less easy to read—e.g.: "But this opening misleads because the focus dissipates as the play progresses and the scattershot climax drips with sentiment but is ultimately unsatisfying." (*Pittsburgh Post-Gazette*; Oct. 10, 1997.) (A possible revision: "But this opening misleads because the focus dissipates as the play progresses. Although the scattershot climax drips with sentiment, it's ultimately unsatisfying.")

The surprisingly common misuse of *but* for *and* often betrays the writer's idiosyncratic prejudice. That is, if you write that someone is "attractive but smart," you're suggesting that this combination of characteristics is atypical—e.g.: "Billy's father . . . is a man of sterling rectitude, poor but honest [read *poor and honest*], determined to pass his upcoming naturalization exams." (*Chicago Tribune*; Oct. 24, 1997.) Is the writer really suggesting that poor people are typically dishonest?

The use of *but* in a negative sense after a pronoun has long caused confusion. Is it "No one but she" or "No one but her"? When *but* is a preposition (meaning "except"), the objective *her* (or *him*) follows. But when *but* is a conjunction, the nominative *she* (or *he*) is proper. The correct form depends on the structure of the sentence. If the verb precedes the *but* phrase, the objective case should be used: "None of the defendants were convicted but him." But if the *but* phrase precedes the verb, the nominative case is proper: "None of the defendants but he were convicted." That sentence is considered equivalent to "None of the defendants were convicted, but he was convicted." (Although that rewording doesn't seem to make literal sense—given that he was one of the defendants—it serves to show the grammar of the sentence excepting him from the absolute word *none*.) *But* thus acts as a conjunction when it precedes the verb in a sentence, as in this one from Thomas Jefferson: "Nobody but we of the craft can understand the diction, and find out what [the statute] means." Here the subject of *can understand* is *nobody*, and the *but* heads the understood clause: "nobody can understand, but we can understand."

The logic here is based on syntax: the native English speaker instinctively rejects as alien-sounding the constructions *me know* in "No one but you and I know what is on these notice boards" and *him knew* in "No one but he knew what this had cost him." **— BG**

butch ▶ adjective informal *a butch haircut* **masculine,** manly; mannish, manlike; informal macho.
ANTONYMS effeminate.

butcher ▶ noun **1** *a butcher's shop* **meat seller,** meat vendor, meat trader.
2 *the local occupying commander was a psychotic butcher* **murderer,** slaughterer, killer, assassin; literary slayer; dated cutthroat, homicide.
▶ verb **1** *the goat was butchered* **slaughter,** cut up, carve up.
2 *they butchered 150 people* **massacre,** murder, slaughter, kill, destroy, exterminate, assassinate; literary slay.
3 *the studio butchered the film* **spoil,** ruin, mutilate, mangle, mess up, wreck; informal make a hash of, screw up, botch.

butt ▶ noun **1** *the butt of a joke* **target,** victim, object, subject, dupe; laughingstock.
2 *the butt of a gun* **stock,** end, handle, hilt, haft, helve.
3 *a cigarette butt* **stub,** end, tail end, stump, remnant.
4 informal *sitting on his butt* See BUTTOCKS.
▶ verb **1** *the shop **butts up against** the house* **adjoin,** abut, be next to, be adjacent to, border (on), be connected to; join, touch.
2 *students butting everyone with their backpacks* **ram,** headbutt, bunt; bump, buffet, push, shove.
– PHRASES **butt in** *I've asked you not to butt in when your father and I are talking* **interrupt,** break in, cut in, chime in, interject, intervene, interfere, interpose; informal poke one's nose in, put one's oar in.

buttocks ▶ plural noun *stand with your heels and buttocks against the wall* **backside,** rear end, rear, seat, bottom, rump, cheeks, behind, derrière; informal butt, booty, fanny, keister, tush, tail, buns, heinie, ass, caboose; fundament, posterior, haunches, gluteus maximus, sit-upon, stern, wazoo; Brit. informal bum, arse; Anatomy nates. See note at ASS.

button ▶ noun **1** *shirt buttons* **fastener,** stud, toggle; hook, catch, clasp, snap fastener, pin.
2 *press the button* **switch,** knob, control; lever, handle; icon, box.

buttonhole ▶ verb informal See ACCOST.

buttress ▶ noun **1** *stone buttresses* **prop,** support, abutment, brace, shore, pier, reinforcement, stanchion.
2 *a buttress against social collapse* **safeguard,** defense, protection, guard; support, prop; bulwark.
▶ verb *authority was buttressed by religion* **strengthen,** reinforce, fortify, support, bolster, shore up, underpin, cement, uphold, prop up, defend, sustain, back up.

buxom ▶ adjective *a buxom lingerie model* **large-breasted,** big-breasted, bosomy, big-bosomed; shapely, ample, plump, rounded, full-figured, voluptuous, curvaceous, Rubenesque; informal busty, built, stacked, chesty, well-endowed, curvy.

buy ▶ verb *they bought a new house* **purchase,** acquire, obtain, get, pick up; take, procure, pay for; invest in; informal get hold of, snatch up, snap up, grab, score.
ANTONYMS sell.
▶ noun informal *a good buy* **purchase,** investment, acquisition, gain; deal, value, bargain.

buzz ▶ noun **1** *the buzz of the bees* **hum,** humming, buzzing, murmur, drone.
2 *the buzz of the doorbell* **ring,** purr, note, tone, beep, bleep, warble, alarm, warning sound.
3 informal *give me a buzz* **call,** ring, phone call, telephone call.
4 informal *the buzz is that he's gone* See RUMOR.
5 informal *get a buzz out of flying* **thrill,** stimulation, glow, tingle; informal kick, rush, high, charge.
▶ verb **1** *bees buzzed* **hum,** drone, bumble, murmur.
2 *the intercom was buzzing* **purr,** warble, sound, ring, beep, bleep.
3 informal *he buzzed around the mall* **bustle,** scurry, scuttle, hurry, rush, race, dash, tear, chase; informal scoot, beetle, whiz, zoom, zip.
4 *the town is buzzing with excitement* **hum,** throb, vibrate, pulse, bustle, be abuzz.
– PHRASES **buzz off** *I told that little pest to buzz off* **scram,** go away, be gone/begone, be off; informal get lost, take a hike, beat it, bug off, go

fly a kite, go suck an egg, vamoose.

by ▶ preposition **1** *I broke it by forcing the lid* **through,** as a result of, because of, by dint of, by way of, via, by means of; with the help of, with the aid of, by virtue of.
2 *be there by midday* **no later than,** in good time for, at, before.
3 *a house by the lake* **next to,** beside, alongside, by/at the side of, adjacent to, side by side with; near, close to, neighboring, adjoining, bordering, overlooking; connected to, contiguous with, attached to.
4 *go by the building* **past,** in front of, beyond.
5 *all right by me* **according to,** with, as far as —— is concerned.
▶ adverb *people hurried by* **past,** on, along.
– PHRASES **by and by** *by and by, you'll learn the routine* **eventually,** ultimately, finally, in the end, one day, some day, sooner or later, in time, in a while, in the long run, in the fullness of time, in time to come, at length, in the future, in due course, over the long haul. **by oneself** *I built the fireplace by myself* **alone,** on one's own, singly, separately, solitarily, unaccompanied, companionless, unattended, unescorted, solo; unaided, unassisted, without help, by one's own efforts, under one's own steam, independently, single-handed(ly), on one's own initiative; informal by one's lonesome.

bygone ▶ adjective *it recaptures a bygone era* **past,** former, olden, earlier, previous, one-time, long-ago, of old, ancient, antiquated; departed, dead, extinct, defunct, out of date, outmoded; literary of yore.
ANTONYMS present, recent.

bypass ▶ noun *follow the signs for the bypass* **detour,** alternate route, alternative route, diversion, shortcut.
▶ verb **1** *bypass the farm* **go around,** go past, make a detour around; avoid.
2 *an attempt to bypass the problem* **avoid,** evade, dodge, escape, elude, circumvent, get around, shortcut around, skirt, sidestep, steer clear of; informal duck.
3 *they bypassed the regulations* **ignore,** pass over, neglect, go over the head of; informal short-circuit.

bystander ▶ noun *bystanders witnessed the accident* **onlooker,** looker-on, passerby, nonparticipant, observer, spectator, eyewitness, witness, watcher, gawker; informal rubbernecker.

byword ▶ noun **1** *their office was a byword for delay* **perfect example,** classic case, model, exemplar, embodiment, incarnation, personification, epitome.
2 *'vigor' was the byword of the Kennedy years* **slogan,** motto, maxim, mantra, catchword, watchword, formula; middle name; proverb, adage, saying, dictum.

Cc

cab ▶ noun *she hailed a cab* **taxi,** taxicab, hack; rickshaw, trishaw, pedicab.

cabal ▶ noun *a cabal of dissidents* **clique,** faction, coterie, cell, sect, junta, camarilla; lobby (group), pressure group. See note at PLOT.

cabaret ▶ noun **1** *the evening's cabaret* **entertainment,** show, floor show, performance.
2 *the cabarets of New Orleans* **nightclub,** dinner theater, club, boîte, café; informal nightspot, clip joint, honky-tonk.

cabin ▶ noun *a cabin by the lake* **cottage,** log cabin, shack, chantey, hut; chalet; cabana; historical caboose.

cabinet ▶ noun **1** *a walnut cabinet* **cupboard,** bureau, bookcase, chest of drawers, sideboard, buffet, dresser, credenza, highboy, tallboy, wardrobe, chiffonier, armoire, wall unit; china cabinet, file cabinet, medicine cabinet.
2 *a meeting of the new cabinet* **council,** administration, ministry, executive, senate.

cable ▶ noun **1** *a thick cable moored the ship* **rope,** cord, line, guy, wire; hawser, stay, bridle; choker.
2 *electric cables* **wire,** lead; power line, hydro line, transmission line.

cache ▶ noun *a cache of arms* **hoard,** store, stockpile, stock, supply, reserve; arsenal; informal stash.

cachet ▶ noun *for more than fifty years, their winery enjoyed the cachet that others could only envy* **prestige,** status, standing, clout, kudos, snob value, stature, preeminence, eminence; street credibility.

cackle ▶ verb **1** *the geese cackled at him* **squawk,** cluck, gabble.
2 *Noel cackled with glee* **laugh loudly,** guffaw, chortle, chuckle.

cacophony ▶ noun *despite the cacophony, Rita slept on* **din,** racket, noise, clamor, discord, dissonance, discordance, uproar.

cad ▶ noun dated See BASTARD (sense 2 of the noun).

cadaver ▶ noun Medicine *each student is assigned a cadaver* **corpse,** body, dead body, remains, carcass; informal stiff; archaic corse. See note at BODY.

cadaverous ▶ adjective *his cadaverous face* **(deathly) pale,** pallid, ashen, gray, whey-faced, sallow, wan, anemic, bloodless, etiolated, corpselike, deathlike; bony, skeletal, emaciated, skin-and-bones, haggard, gaunt, drawn, pinched, hollow-cheeked, hollow-eyed; informal like a bag of bones, anorexic.
ANTONYMS rosy, plump.

cadence ▶ noun *there is a musical cadence in her speech* **intonation,** modulation, lilt, accent, inflection; rhythm, tempo, meter, beat, pulse; Music resolution.

cafeteria ▶ noun **lunchroom,** luncheonette, lunch counter; snack bar, canteen, café; informal caf.

cage ▶ noun *animals in cages* **enclosure,** pen, pound; coop, hutch; birdcage, aviary; corral.
▶ verb *many animals are caged* **confine,** shut in/up, pen, coop up, fence in, immure, impound, corral.

cajole ▶ verb *I hate it when he cajoles me to go out with his friends* **persuade,** wheedle, coax, talk into, prevail on, sweet-talk, butter up, soft-soap, seduce, inveigle.

cake ▶ noun **1** *cakes from the bakery* cupcake, sponge cake, angel food cake, layer cake, fruitcake, gingerbread, shortcake.
2 *a cake of soap* **bar,** block, brick, slab, tablet, lump.
▶ verb **1** *boots caked with mud* **coat,** encrust, plaster, cover.
2 *the blood was beginning to cake* **clot,** congeal, coagulate, solidify, set, inspissate.

calamitous ▶ adjective *their calamitous adventure became legendary* **disastrous,** catastrophic, cataclysmic, devastating, dire, tragic; literary direful.

calamity ▶ noun *she has survived more calamities in the past three months than most people experience in a lifetime* **disaster,** catastrophe, tragedy, cataclysm, adversity, tribulation, affliction, misfortune, misadventure.
ANTONYMS godsend.

calculate ▶ verb **1** *the interest is calculated on a daily basis* **compute,** work out, reckon, figure; add up/together, count up, tally, total, tote, tot up.
2 *his words were calculated to wound her* **intend,** mean, aim, design.
3 *we had **calculated on** a quiet Sunday* **expect,** count on, anticipate, reckon on, bargain on, figure on.

calculated ▶ adjective *a vicious and calculated assault* **deliberate,** premeditated, planned, preplanned, preconceived, intentional, intended, willful; Law prepense.
ANTONYMS unintentional.

calculating ▶ adjective *a crime that only a calculating mind could have planned* **cunning,** crafty, wily, shrewd, sly, scheming, devious, designing, conniving, Machiavellian; informal foxy; archaic subtle.
ANTONYMS ingenuous.

calculation ▶ noun **1** *the calculation of the*

overall cost **computation,** reckoning, adding up, counting up, working out, figuring, totaling up, totting up.
2 *political calculations* **assessment,** judgment; forecast, projection, prediction.

caliber ▶ noun **1** *a man of his caliber* **quality,** merit, distinction, stature, excellence, preeminence; ability, expertise, talent, capability, capacity, proficiency.
2 *questions about the caliber of the officiating* **standard,** level, quality.
3 *the caliber of a gun* **bore,** diameter, gauge.

call ▶ verb **1** *"Wait for me!" she called* **cry out,** cry, shout, yell, hail, bellow, roar, bawl, vociferate; informal holler.
2 *I'll call you tomorrow* **phone,** telephone, get someone on the phone, give someone a call, give someone a ring, give someone a buzz.
3 *dinner's ready—call the kids* **summon,** send for, assemble, muster, invite, order.
4 *the vice president called a meeting* **convene,** summon, assemble; formal convoke.
5 *they called their son Liam* **name,** christen, baptize; designate, style, term, dub; formal denominate.
6 *yes, I would call him a friend* **describe as,** regard as, look on as, consider to be.
▶ noun **1** *I heard calls from the auditorium* **cry,** shout, yell, roar, scream, exclamation, vociferation; informal holler.
2 *the call of the loon* **cry,** song, sound.
3 *I'll give you a call tomorrow* **phone call,** telephone call, ring; informal buzz.
4 *he paid a call on Harold* **visit,** social call.
5 *a call for party unity* **appeal,** request, plea, entreaty.
6 *the last call for passengers on flight 701* **summons,** request.
7 *there's no call for expensive wine here* **demand,** desire, market.
8 *the call of the sea* **attraction,** appeal, lure, allure, spell, pull, draw.
9 *it's your call* **decision,** ruling, judgment, verdict.
– PHRASES **call for** *desperate times call for desperate measures* **require,** need, necessitate; justify, warrant. **call off** *we had to call off the trip to Maryland* **cancel,** abandon, scrap, drop, ax, scrub, nix; end, terminate. **call on 1** *I might call on her later* **visit,** pay a visit to, go and see, drop in on, pop in on, visit with. **2** *he called on the government to hold a plebiscite* **appeal to,** ask, request, petition, urge, exhort. **3** *we are able to call on qualified staff* **have recourse to,** avail oneself of, draw on, make use of. **call the shots** *if she's gonna call the shots from now on, I'm not gonna stick around* **be in charge,** be in control, be the boss, be at the helm/wheel, be in the driver's seat, pull the strings, run the show, rule the roost. **call to mind** *this calls to mind the last constitutional debate* **evoke,** bring to mind, call up, conjure up. **call up 1** *Roland called me up to ask me out* See CALL (sense 2 of the verb). **2** *they called up the reservists* **enlist,** recruit, conscript; draft. **3** *he was called up from the minors* **select,** pick, choose. **on call** *Dr. Merton is on call this evening* **on duty,** on standby, available.

calling ▶ noun *when I was four, I knew my calling was photography* **profession,** occupation, vocation, call, summons, career, work, employment, job, business, trade, craft, line, line of work; informal bag; archaic employ.

callous ▶ adjective *his callous disregard for other people's feelings* **heartless,** unfeeling, uncaring, cold, cold-hearted, hard, as hard as nails, hard-hearted, insensitive, lacking compassion, hard-bitten, hard-nosed, hard-edged, unsympathetic.
ANTONYMS kind, compassionate.

callow ▶ adjective *she toyed with the emotions of Laughton when he was a callow and insecure young man* **immature,** inexperienced, juvenile, adolescent, naive, green, raw, untried, unworldly, unsophisticated; informal wet behind the ears. See notes at GULLIBLE, RUDE, YOUTHFUL.
ANTONYMS mature.

calm ▶ adjective **1** *she seemed very calm* **serene,** tranquil, relaxed, unruffled, unperturbed, unflustered, untroubled; equable, even-tempered; placid, unexcitable, unemotional, phlegmatic; composed, 'calm, cool, and collected', coolheaded, self-possessed; informal unflappable, unfazed, nonplussed.
ANTONYMS excited, nervous, upset.
2 *the night was calm* **windless,** still, tranquil, serene, quiet.
ANTONYMS windy, stormy.
3 *the calm waters of the lake* **tranquil,** still, smooth, glassy, like a millpond; literary stilly.
ANTONYMS rough, stormy.
▶ noun **1** *calm prevailed* **tranquility,** stillness, calmness, quiet, quietness, quietude, peace, peacefulness.
2 *his usual calm deserted him* **composure,** coolness, calmness, self-possession, sangfroid; serenity, tranquility, equanimity, equability, placidness, placidity; informal cool, unflappability.
▶ verb **1** *I tried to* ***calm*** *him* ***down*** **soothe,** pacify, placate, mollify, appease, conciliate, quiet (down), relax.
ANTONYMS excite, upset.
2 *she forced herself to* ***calm down*** **compose oneself,** recover/regain one's composure, control oneself, pull oneself together, simmer down, cool down/off, take it easy; informal get a grip, keep one's shirt on, chill (out), take a chill pill, cool one's jets, hang/stay loose, decompress.

CHOOSE THE RIGHT WORD

calm, halcyon, peaceful, placid, serene, tranquil

We usually speak of the weather or the sea as **calm**, meaning free from disturbance or storm. When applied to people and their feelings or moods, *calm* implies an unruffled state, often under disturbing conditions (*to remain calm in the face of disaster*). **Halcyon** is another adjective associated with the weather (*the halcyon days of summer*); it comes from the name of a mythical bird, usually identified with the kingfisher, that builds its nest on the sea and possesses a magical power to calm the winds and waves. **Peaceful** also suggests a lack of turbulence or disorder, although it is usually applied to situations, scenes, and activities rather than to people (*a peaceful gathering of protesters; a peaceful resolution to their problems*). **Serene, tranquil,** and **placid** are more often used to describe human states of being. *Serene* suggests a lofty and undisturbed calmness (*he died with a serene look on his face*), while *tranquil* implies an intrinsic calmness (*they led a tranquil life in the country*). **Placid** usually refers to a prevailing tendency and is sometimes used disparagingly to suggest a lack of responsiveness or a dull complacency (*with her placid disposition, she seldom got involved in family arguments*).

calumny ▶ noun *voters were tired of the candidates' endless barrage of calumny* **slander,** defamation (of character), character assassination, libel; vilification, traducement, obloquy, verbal abuse; informal mudslinging, trash-talk; rare contumely. See note at MALIGN.

camaraderie ▶ noun *he enjoyed the camaraderie of army life* **friendship,** comradeship, fellowship, companionship, fraternity, conviviality; mutual support, team spirit, esprit de corps.

camouflage ▶ noun 1 *pieces of mossy turf served for camouflage* **disguise,** concealment, cover, screen.
2 *her indifference was merely camouflage* **a facade,** a front, a false front, a smokescreen, a cover-up, a mask, a blind, a screen, a masquerade, a dissimulation, a pretense.
▶ verb *the van was camouflaged with branches* **disguise,** hide, conceal, keep hidden, mask, screen, cover (up).

camp[1] ▶ noun 1 *a kids' camp* **campsite,** campground, encampment, bivouac.
2 *the liberal and conservative camps* **faction,** wing, group, lobby, caucus, bloc, party, coterie, sect, cabal.
▶ verb *they camped in a field* **pitch tents,** set up camp, encamp, bivouac.

camp[2] ▶ adjective informal 1 *the camp humor became tiresome after the first twenty minutes* **exaggerated,** theatrical, affected; informal over the top, OTT, camped up, hammy.
2 *a highly camp actor* **effeminate,** effete, mincing; informal campy.
ANTONYMS macho.
– PHRASES **camp it up** *he camped it up for the cameras* **posture,** behave theatrically/affectedly, overact; informal ham it up.

campaign ▶ noun 1 *Napoleon's Russian campaign* **military operation**(s), maneuver(s); crusade, war, battle, offensive, attack.
2 *the campaign to reduce vehicle emissions* **crusade,** drive, push, struggle; operation, strategy, battle plan.
▶ verb 1 *they are campaigning for political reform* **crusade,** fight, battle, push, press, strive, struggle, lobby.
2 *she campaigned as a political outsider* **run for office,** stand for office, canvass, barnstorm, electioneer, stump, go on the hustings.

can ▶ noun *a bag of empty cans for recycling* tin can, aluminum can; canister; spray can; garbage can, trash can.
▶ verb informal *he was canned after being caught stealing office supplies* **fire,** dismiss, ax, let go, lay off, sack.

canal ▶ noun 1 *barges chugged up the canal* **inland waterway,** watercourse, channel.
2 *the ear canal* **duct,** tube, passage.

cancel ▶ verb 1 *the meeting was canceled* **call off,** abandon, scrap, drop, ax, scrub, nix.
2 *his visa has been canceled* **annul,** invalidate, nullify, declare null and void, void; revoke, rescind, retract, countermand, withdraw; Law vacate.
3 *rising unemployment* **cancelled out** *earlier economic gains* **neutralize,** counterbalance, counteract, balance (out), countervail, compensate for; negate, nullify, wipe out.

cancer ▶ noun 1 *most skin cancers are curable if detected early* **malignant growth,** cancerous growth, tumor, malignancy; technical carcinoma, sarcoma, melanoma, lymphoma, myeloma.
2 *the cancer of slavery spread across the continent* **evil,** blight, scourge, poison, canker, plague; archaic pestilence.

candid ▶ adjective 1 *his responses were remarkably candid* **frank,** outspoken, forthright, blunt, open, honest, truthful, sincere, direct, plain-spoken, straightforward, ingenuous, bluff; informal upfront, on the level, on the up and up.
ANTONYMS guarded.
2 *candid shots* **unposed,** informal, uncontrived, impromptu, natural.

candidate ▶ noun *candidates should be computer-literate* **applicant,** job applicants, job-seeker, interviewee; contender, contestant, nominee.

candle ▶ noun *hand-dipped white candles* taper, votive candle; archaic glim.

candor ▶ noun *I'm not sure he appreciated my candor* **frankness,** openness, honesty, candidness, truthfulness, sincerity, forthrightness, directness, plain-spokenness, bluntness, straightforwardness, outspokenness; informal telling it like it is.

candy ▶ noun *chocolate candy* bonbon, confectionery, sweet.

cane ▶ noun 1 *a silver-topped cane* **walking stick,** staff; alpenstock; crook, pikestaff.
2 *he was beaten with a cane* **stick,** rod, birch; historical ferule.
▶ verb *Matthew was caned for bullying* **beat,** strike, hit, flog, thrash, lash, birch, flagellate; informal belt, whale.

canker ▶ noun 1 *this plant is susceptible to canker* **fungal disease,** plant rot; blight.
2 *ear cankers* **ulcer,** ulceration, infection, sore, abscess, noma.
3 *racism remains a canker* See CANCER (sense 2).

cannibal ▶ noun *overblown tales of savage cannibals* **man-eater,** people-eater; rare anthropophagite, anthropophagist.

cannon ▶ noun *a Civil War cannon sits near the entrance to the armory* **mounted gun,** field gun, piece of artillery; mortar, howitzer; historical culverin, falconet.
▶ verb *the couple behind* **cannoned into** *us* **collide with,** hit, run into, crash into, plow into.

cannonade ▶ noun *the distant cannonade kept us alert all night* **bombardment,** shelling, gunfire, artillery fire, barrage, pounding.

canny ▶ adjective *canny investors* **shrewd,** astute, smart, sharp, sharp-witted, discerning, penetrating, discriminating, perceptive, perspicacious, wise, worldly-wise, sagacious; cunning, crafty, wily, as sharp as a tack, savvy; dated long-headed.
ANTONYMS foolish.

canon ▶ noun 1 *the canons of fair play and equal opportunity* **principle,** rule, law, tenet, precept; standard, convention, criterion, measure.
2 *a set of ecclesiastical canons* **law,** decree, edict, statute, dictate, decretal.
3 *the Shakespeare canon* **list of works,** works, writings, oeuvre.

canopy ▶ noun *the canopy gave us some relief from the sun* **awning,** shade, sunshade; marquee; chuppah.

cant[1] ▶ noun 1 *religious cant* **hypocrisy,** sanctimoniousness, sanctimony, pietism.
2 *thieves' cant* **slang,** jargon, idiom, argot, patois, speech, terminology, language; informal lingo, -speak, -ese. See note at DIALECT.

cant[2] ▶ verb *the deck canted some twenty degrees* **tilt,** lean, slant, slope, incline; tip, list, bank, heel.
▶ noun *the cant of the walls* **slope,** slant, tilt, angle, inclination.

cantankerous ▶ adjective See GRUMPY.

canvass ▶ verb 1 *he's canvassing for the Green Party* **campaign,** electioneer, stump, barnstorm.
2 *they promised to canvass all members* **poll,** question, ask, survey, interview.
3 *they're canvassing support* **seek,** try to obtain.

canyon ▶ noun *burros can be negotiated through the canyon* **ravine,** gorge, gully, defile, couloir; chasm, abyss, gulf, gulch, coulee.

cap ▶ noun 1 *his cap blew off in the wind*
2 *a white plastic cap* **lid,** top; stopper, cork, bung.
3 *the cap on spending* **limit,** upper limit, ceiling; curb, check.
▶ verb 1 *mountains capped with snow* **top,** crown, cover, coat.
2 *his breakaway goal capped a great game* **round off,** crown, top off, be a fitting climax to.
3 *they tried to cap each other's stories* **beat,** better, improve on, surpass, outdo, outshine, outstrip, top, upstage.
4 *budgets will be capped* **set a limit on,** limit, restrict; curb, control.

capability ▶ noun *her professional capabilities | their capability and willingness to tackle tough issues* **ability,** capacity, power, potential; competence, proficiency, adeptness, aptitude, faculty, wherewithal, experience, skill, skillfulness, talent, flair; informal know-how.

capable ▶ adjective *a capable young woman* **competent,** able, efficient, effective, proficient, accomplished, adept, handy, experienced, skillful, skilled, talented, gifted; informal useful.
ANTONYMS incompetent.
– PHRASES **be capable of** *I'm capable of looking after myself* **have the ability to,** be equal to (the task of), be up to, have what it takes to (be).

capacious ▶ adjective *a capacious hotel suite* **roomy,** spacious, ample, big, large, sizable, generous; formal commodious.
ANTONYMS cramped, small.

capacity ▶ noun 1 *the capacity of the freezer* **volume,** size, magnitude, dimensions, measurements, proportions.
2 *his capacity to inspire trust* See CAPABILITY.
3 *in his capacity as head librarian* **position,** post, job, office; role, function.

cape[1] ▶ noun *a woolen cape* **cloak,** mantle, cope, wrap, stole, poncho, shawl, tippet, capelet; historical pelisse, mantelet.

cape[2] ▶ noun *the ship rounded the cape* **headland,** promontory, point, spit, head, foreland, horn, hook.

caper ▶ verb *children were capering about* **skip,** dance, romp, frisk, gambol, cavort, prance, frolic, leap, hop, jump, rollick.
▶ noun 1 *she did a little caper* **dance,** skip, hop, leap, jump.
2 informal *I'm too old for this kind of caper* **stunt,** monkey business, escapade, prank, trick, mischief, foolery, tomfoolery, antics, hijinks, skylarking, lark, shenanigans.

capital ▶ noun 1 *Warsaw is the capital of Poland* **first city,** seat of government, metropolis.
2 *she had the capital to pull off the deal* **money,** finance(s), funds, wherewithal, means, assets, wealth, resources, investment capital; informal cash, dough, bread, loot, bucks.
3 *he wrote the name in capitals* **capital letters,** uppercase letters, block letters; informal caps.

capitalism ▶ noun *the capitalism of emerging nations* **free enterprise,** private enterprise, the free market.
ANTONYMS communism.

capitalist ▶ noun *a capitalist who made his fortune in textiles* **financier,** investor, industrialist; magnate, tycoon, entrepreneur, businessman, businesswoman.

capitalize ▶ verb *the capacity to capitalize new ventures* **finance,** fund, underwrite, provide capital for, back; informal bankroll, stake, grubstake.
– PHRASES **capitalize on** *she tried to capitalize on Sam's misfortune by offering him a high-interest loan* **take advantage of,** profit from, make the most of, exploit; informal cash in on.

capitulate ▶ verb *the rebels had been forced to capitulate* **surrender,** give in/up, yield, concede defeat, give up the struggle, submit, knuckle under; lay down one's arms, raise/show the white flag, throw in the towel.
ANTONYMS resist, hold out.

caprice ▶ noun 1 *his wife's caprices* **whim,** whimsy, vagary, fancy, fad, quirk, eccentricity, foible.
2 *the staff tired of his caprice* **fickleness,** changeableness, volatility, capriciousness, unpredictability.

capricious ▶ adjective *the capricious workings of fate* **fickle,** inconstant, changeable, variable, mercurial, volatile, unpredictable, temperamental; whimsical, fanciful, flighty, quirky, faddish.
ANTONYMS consistent.

capsize ▶ verb *gale-force winds capsized their small craft* **overturn,** turn over, turn upside down, upend, flip/tip/keel over, turn turtle; Nautical pitchpole; archaic overset.
ANTONYMS right.

capsule ▶ noun **1** *he swallowed a capsule* **pill,** tablet, lozenge, pastille, drop; informal tab.
2 *a space capsule* **module,** craft, probe.

captain ▶ noun **1** *the ship's captain* **commander,** master; informal skipper.
2 *the team captain* **leader,** head; informal boss, skipper.
3 *a captain of industry* **magnate,** tycoon, industrialist; chief, head, leader, principal; informal boss, number one, bigwig, big shot, big gun, big cheese, big kahuna, honcho, top dog, top banana.
▶ verb *a vessel captained by a cutthroat* **command,** run, be in charge of, control, manage, govern; informal skipper.

caption ▶ noun *the captions are written in German* **title,** heading, wording, head, legend, subtitle; rubric, slogan.

captivate ▶ verb *audiences are captivated by his energy* **enthrall,** charm, enchant, bewitch, fascinate, beguile, entrance, enrapture, delight, attract, allure; engross, mesmerize, spellbind, hypnotize.
ANTONYMS repel, bore.

captive ▶ noun *release the captives* **prisoner,** convict, detainee, inmate, abductee; prisoner of war, POW, internee; informal jailbird, con, yardbird, lifer.
▶ adjective *captive wild animals* **confined,** caged, incarcerated, locked up; jailed, imprisoned, in prison, interned, detained, in captivity, under lock and key, behind bars.

captivity ▶ noun *these creatures will languish in captivity* **imprisonment,** confinement, internment, incarceration, detention, custody.
ANTONYMS freedom.

capture ▶ verb **1** *the spy was captured in Moscow* **catch,** apprehend, seize, arrest; take prisoner, take captive, imprison, detain, put/throw in jail, put behind bars, put under lock and key, incarcerate; informal nab, collar, bag, pick up.
ANTONYMS free.
2 *guerrillas captured a strategic district* **occupy,** invade, conquer, seize, take, take over, take possession of.
3 *the music captured the atmosphere of a summer morning* **express,** reproduce, represent, encapsulate.
4 *the tales of pirates captured the children's imaginations* **engage,** attract, catch, seize, hold.
▶ noun *he tried to evade capture* **arrest,** apprehension, seizure, being taken prisoner, being taken captive, imprisonment.

car ▶ noun **1** *he drove up in his car* **automobile,** motor vehicle, vehicle; dated motorcar; informal auto, wheels, gas guzzler; jalopy, lemon, junker, clunker, Tin Lizzie, rustbucket.
2 *the dining car* **carriage,** coach.

carafe ▶ noun *a carafe of hot coffee* **flask,** jug, pitcher, decanter, flagon.

caravan ▶ noun *a refugee caravan* **convoy,** procession, column, train, cavalcade.

carcass ▶ noun *a mule carcass* **corpse,** dead body, body, remains; Medicine cadaver; informal stiff, roadkill; archaic corse. See note at **BODY**.

card ▶ noun **1** *a piece of stiff card* **cardboard,** pasteboard, board, Bristol board.
2 *I'll send her a card* **greeting card,** postcard, notecard.
3 *she produced her card* **identification (card),** ID, credentials, pass, key card; business card, calling card.
4 *she paid with her card* **credit card,** debit card, bank card, charge card, gold card, platinum card; phone card; informal plastic.
5 *the cards were dealt* **playing card**; tarot card; **(cards)** deck/pack of cards.
6 informal *she's such a card!* **eccentric,** character; **joker,** wit, wag, jester, clown, comedian; informal laugh, scream, hoot, riot, jokester.

cardinal ▶ adjective *you've broken one of the cardinal rules* **fundamental,** basic, main, chief, primary, crucial, pivotal, prime, principal, paramount, preeminent, highest, key, essential.
ANTONYMS unimportant.

care ▶ noun **1** *the care of the child* **safekeeping, supervision,** custody, charge, protection, control, responsibility; guardianship, wardship.
ANTONYMS neglect.
2 *handle with care* **caution,** carefulness, heedfulness, heed, attention, attentiveness.
ANTONYMS carelessness.
3 *she chose her words with care* **discretion,** judiciousness, forethought, thought, regard, heed, mindfulness; accuracy, precision, discrimination.
ANTONYMS carelessness.
4 *the cares of the day* **worry,** anxiety, trouble, concern, stress, pressure, strain; sorrow, woe, hardship.
5 *care for the elderly* **help,** aid, assistance, succor, support; concern, consideration, thought, regard, solicitude; informal TLC.
ANTONYMS disregard.
▶ verb *the teachers didn't care about our work* **be concerned,** worry (oneself), trouble oneself, concern oneself, bother, mind, be interested; informal give a damn, give a hoot.
– PHRASES **care for 1** *he cares for his children* **love,** be fond of, be devoted to, treasure, adore, dote on, think the world of, worship, idolize. **2** *would you care for a cup of coffee?* **like,** want, desire, fancy, feel like. **3** *hospices care for the terminally ill* **look after,** take care of, tend (to), attend to, minister to, nurse; be responsible for, keep safe, keep an eye on.

USAGE

couldn't care less

Couldn't care less is the correct and logical phrasing, not *could care less*—e.g.: "The American people could care less [read *couldn't care less*] who's White House Chief of Staff." (George Will, on "This Week with David Brinkley"; July 3, 1994.) If you *could care less*, you're saying that you do care some. Invariably, though, writers and speakers who use the phrase mean that they don't care at all. Although some apologists argue that *could care less* is meant to be sarcastic and not to be taken literally, a more plausible explanation is that the *-n't* of *couldn't* has been garbled in sloppy speech and sloppy writing. As American linguist Atcheson L. Hench explains: "A listener has not heard the whole phrase; he has heard a slurred form. *Couldn't care* has two dental stops practically together, *dnt*. This is heard only as *d* and slurring results. The outcome is *I c'd care less*." (*American Speech*, 159; 1973.) — **BG**

career ▶ noun **1** *a business career* **profession,** occupation, job, vocation, calling, employment, line, line of work, walk of life, métier.
2 *a checkered career* **history,** existence, life, course, passage, path.
▶ adjective *a career politician* **professional,** permanent, full-time.
ANTONYMS permanent.

cargo ▶ noun *they work on the docks loading cargo* **freight,** load, haul, consignment, delivery, shipment; goods, merchandise, payload, lading.

caricature ▶ noun *a caricature of the famous brothers* **cartoon,** parody, satire, lampoon, burlesque; informal sendup, takeoff.
▶ verb *she has turned to caricaturing her fellow actors* **parody,** satirize, lampoon, make fun of, burlesque, mimic; informal send up, take off.

CHOOSE THE RIGHT WORD

caricature, burlesque, lampoon, mimicry, parody, travesty

Skilled writers and artists who want to poke fun at someone or something have a number of weapons at their disposal. An artist might come up with a **caricature,** which is a drawing or written piece that exaggerates its subject's distinguishing features or peculiarities (*the cartoonist's caricature of the presidential candidate*). A **parody** is similar to a caricature in purpose, but is used of written work, or performances that ridicule an author or performer's work by imitating its language and style for comic effect (*a parody of the scene between Romeo and Juliet*). While a *parody* concentrates on distorting the content of the original work, a **travesty** retains the subject matter but imitates the style in a grotesque or absurd way (*their version of the Greek tragedy was a travesty*). A **lampoon** is a strongly satirical piece of writing that attacks or ridicules an individual or an institution; it is more commonly used as a verb (*to lampoon the government in a local newspaper*). While a *caricature*, a *parody*, and a *travesty* must have an original to imitate, a **burlesque** can be an independent creation or composition; it is a comic or satiric imitation, often a theatrical one, that treats a serious subject lightly or a trivial subject with mock seriousness (*the play was a burlesque of Homer's great epic*). **Mimicry** is something you don't have to be an artist, a writer, or an actor to be good at. Anyone who successfully imitates another person's speech or gestures is a good mimic or impressionist, whether the intent is playful or mocking (*he showed an early talent for mimicry; entertaining his parents with imitations of their friends*).

carefree ▶ adjective *she's nothing like her carefree mother* **unworried,** untroubled, blithe, airy, nonchalant, insouciant, happy-go-lucky, free and easy, easygoing, relaxed, mellow; informal laid-back, loosey-goosey.
ANTONYMS careworn.

careful ▶ adjective **1** *be careful when you go up the stairs* **cautious,** heedful, alert, attentive, watchful, vigilant, wary, on guard, circumspect. See note at VIGILANT.
ANTONYMS careless.
2 *she'd always been careful with money* **prudent,** thrifty, frugal, economical, economizing, scrimping, abstemious, sensible; mean, miserly, penny-pinching, parsimonious, niggardly; informal stingy.
ANTONYMS extravagant.
3 *careful consideration of the facts* **attentive,** conscientious, painstaking, meticulous, diligent, deliberate, assiduous, sedulous, scrupulous, punctilious, methodical; informal persnickety.
ANTONYMS inattentive.

careless ▶ adjective **1** *careless motorists* **inattentive,** incautious, negligent, absentminded, remiss; heedless, irresponsible, impetuous, reckless, foolhardy; cavalier, supercilious, devil-may-care.
ANTONYMS careful, attentive.
2 *careless work* **shoddy,** slapdash, slipshod, slovenly, negligent, lax, slack, disorganized, hasty, hurried; informal sloppy, slaphappy.
ANTONYMS meticulous.
3 *a careless remark* **thoughtless,** insensitive, indiscreet, unguarded, incautious, inadvertent.
ANTONYMS judicious.
4 *she carried on,* ***careless of*** *the time* **heedless of,** unconcerned with, indifferent to, oblivious to.

caress ▶ verb *his hands caressed her back* **stroke,** touch, fondle, brush, pet; hug, embrace; nuzzle.

caretaker ▶ noun **janitor,** custodian, superintendent, maintenance man/woman; curator; concierge, attendant, porter; informal super.
▶ adjective *a caretaker government* **temporary,** short-term, provisional, substitute, acting, interim, pro tem, stand-in, fill-in, stopgap.

carnage ▶ noun *an unforgettable scene of carnage* **slaughter,** massacre, mass murder, butchery, bloodbath, bloodletting, gore; holocaust, pogrom, ethnic cleansing.

carnal ▶ adjective *his carnal desires* **sexual,** sensual, erotic, lustful, lascivious, libidinous, lecherous, licentious; physical, bodily, corporeal, fleshly.
ANTONYMS spiritual.

carnival ▶ noun **1** *the town's carnival* **festival,** fiesta, fête, gala, jamboree, celebration, fest.
2 *he worked at a carnival* **fair,** amusement park,

fun fair, ex, amusement show, circus, big top, midway.

carol ▶ noun *children sang carols* **Christmas song,** hymn, canticle.

carouse ▶ verb *it was pretty stupid to carouse the night before an exam* **drink and make merry,** go on a drinking bout, go on a spree; revel, celebrate, roister; informal party, booze, go boozing, binge, go on a binge, go on a bender, paint the town red, rave, whoop it up; archaic wassail.

carp ▶ verb *they could always find something to carp about* **complain,** cavil, grumble, grouse, whine, bleat, nag; informal gripe, grouch, beef, bellyache, moan, bitch, whinge, kvetch.
ANTONYMS praise.

carpenter ▶ noun *you'll need a carpenter to repair those joists* **woodworker,** cabinetmaker.

carpet ▶ noun **1** *a Turkish carpet* **rug,** mat, floor covering.
2 *a carpet of wildflowers* **covering,** blanket, layer, cover, cloak, mantle.
▶ verb *the gravel was carpeted in moss* **cover,** coat, overlay, overspread, blanket.

carriage ▶ noun **1** *a horse and carriage* **coach,** coach-and-four, stagecoach; hansom, hackney, gig, surrey.
2 *a railroad carriage* **coach,** car, passenger car; flatcar, boxcar.

carry ▶ verb **1** *she carried the box into the kitchen* **convey,** transfer, move, take, bring, bear, lug, tote, fetch, cart.
2 *a cruise line carrying a million passengers a year* **transport,** convey, move, handle.
3 *satellites carry the signal across the country* **transmit,** conduct, relay, communicate, convey, dispatch, beam.
4 *the dinghy can carry the weight of the baggage* **support,** sustain, stand; prop up, shore up, bolster.
5 *managers carry most of the responsibility* **bear,** accept, assume, undertake, shoulder, take on (oneself).
6 *she was carrying twins* **be pregnant with,** bear, expect; technical be gravid with.
7 *she carried herself with assurance* **conduct,** bear, hold; act, behave, acquit; formal comport.
8 *a resolution was carried* **approve,** vote for, accept, endorse, ratify, pass; agree to, assent to, rubber-stamp; informal OK, give the thumbs up to.
9 *I carried the whole audience* **win over,** sway, convince, persuade, influence; motivate, stimulate.
10 *today's paper carried an article on housing policy* **publish,** print, communicate, distribute; broadcast, transmit.
11 *we carry a wide range of linens* **sell,** stock, keep, keep in stock, offer, have, have for sale, retail, supply.
12 *most toxins carry warnings* **display,** bear, exhibit, show, be marked with.
13 *it carries a penalty of two years' imprisonment* **entail,** involve, result in, occasion, have as a consequence.
14 *his voice carried across the field* **be audible,** travel, reach.
– PHRASES **be/get carried away** *I'm afraid I get a bit carried away* **lose self-control,** get overexcited, go too far; informal flip, lose it. **carry something off** *she carried off four awards* **win,** secure, gain, achieve, collect; informal land, net, bag, scoop. **carry on 1** *they carried on arguing* **continue,** keep (on), go on; persist in, persevere in, stick with/at. **2** informal *she was carrying on with other men* **have an affair,** commit adultery, have a fling, play around, mess around, fool around. **3** informal *I was always carrying on* **misbehave,** behave badly, get up to mischief, cause trouble, get up to no good, be naughty; clown around, fool around, mess around, act up. **4** *we carried on a conversation* **engage in,** conduct, undertake, be involved in, carry out, perform. **carry out 1** *operations were carried out in secret* **conduct,** perform, implement, execute. **2** *I carried out my promise to her* **fulfill,** carry through, honor, redeem, make good; keep, observe, abide by, comply with, adhere to, stick to, keep faith with.

cart ▶ noun **1** *a horse-drawn cart*
2 *carts lined up at the checkout* **shopping cart,** handcart, pushcart.
▶ verb informal *he had the wreckage carted away* **transport,** convey, haul, move, shift, take; carry, lug.

carton ▶ noun *a carton of empty whiskey bottles* **box,** package, cardboard box, container, pack, packet.

cartoon ▶ noun **1** *a cartoon of the defense secretary* **caricature,** parody, lampoon, satire; informal takeoff, sendup.
2 *he was reading cartoons* **comic strip,** comic, funnies, graphic novel.
3 *they watched cartoons on television* **animated film,** animation; informal toon.

cartridge ▶ noun **1** *a toner cartridge* **cassette,** canister, container, magazine.
2 *a rifle cartridge* **bullet,** round, shell, charge, shot.

carve ▶ verb **1** *she carved horn handles* **sculpt,** sculpture; cut, hew, whittle; form, shape, fashion.
2 *I carved my initials on the tree* **engrave,** etch, incise, score.
3 *he carved the roast chicken* **slice,** cut up; chop.
– PHRASES **carved in stone** *these are merely suggestions, they're not carved in stone* **unalterable,** immutable, unchangeable, irreversible, irrevocable.

cascade ▶ noun *a roaring cascade* **waterfall,** cataract, falls, rapids, white water.
▶ verb *rain cascaded from the roof* **pour,** gush, surge, spill, stream, flow, issue, spurt.

case[1] ▶ noun **1** *a classic case of overreaction* **instance,** occurrence, manifestation, demonstration, exposition, exhibition; example, illustration, specimen, sample, exemplification.
2 *if that is the case, I will have to find somebody else* **situation,** position, state of affairs, lay of the land; circumstances, conditions, facts; way things stand; informal score.
3 *the officers on the case* **investigation,** inquiry, examination, exploration, probe, search, inquest.
4 *only urgent cases were admitted for immediate*

examination **patient,** sick person, invalid, sufferer, victim.
5 *she lost her case* **lawsuit,** (legal) action, legal dispute, suit, trial, legal/judicial proceedings, litigation.
6 *a strong case* **argument,** contention, reasoning, logic, defense, justification, vindication, exposition, thesis.

case² ▶ **noun 1** *a cigarette case* **container,** box, canister, receptacle, holder.
2 *a seed case* **casing,** cover, covering, sheath, sheathing, envelope, sleeve, jacket, integument.
3 *a case of wine* **crate,** box, pack.
4 *a glass display case* **cabinet,** cupboard, buffet.
▶ **verb** informal *a thief casing the joint* **reconnoiter,** inspect, examine, survey, explore, check out.

cash ▶ **noun 1** *a wallet stuffed with cash* **money,** currency, hard cash; notes, bank notes, bills; coins, change; informal dough, bread, loot, moolah, bucks, dinero, lucre.
ANTONYMS check, credit.
2 *a lack of cash* **finance**(s), money, resources, funds, assets, the means, the wherewithal.
▶ **verb** *the bank cashed her check* **exchange,** change, convert into cash/money; honor, pay, accept.
– PHRASES **cash in on** *the band is cashing in on merchandising* **take advantage of,** exploit, milk; make money from, profit from, make a killing from.

cashier ▶ **noun** *the cashier took the check* **checkout girl/boy/person,** clerk; bank clerk, teller, banker, treasurer, bursar, purser.

casino ▶ **noun** *playing the slots in her favorite casino* **gambling establishment,** gambling club, gambling den, gaming house.

cask ▶ **noun** *casks of ale for the crew* **barrel,** keg, butt, tun, vat, drum, hogshead; historical firkin.

casket ▶ **noun 1** *the casket of a dead soldier* **coffin,** sarcophagus; informal box; humorous wooden overcoat.
2 *a small casket of jewels* **box,** chest, case, container, receptacle.

cast ▶ **verb 1** *he cast the stone into the stream* **throw,** toss, fling, pitch, hurl, lob; informal chuck.
2 *fishermen cast their nets* **spread,** throw, open out.
3 *she cast a fearful glance over her shoulder* **direct,** shoot, throw, send.
4 *each citizen cast a vote* **register,** record, enter, file, vote.
5 *the fire cast a soft light* **emit,** give off, send out, radiate.
6 *the figures cast shadows* **form,** create, produce; project, throw.
7 *the stags' antlers are cast each year* **shed,** lose, discard, slough off.
8 *a figure cast by hand* **mold,** fashion, form, shape, model; sculpt, sculpture, forge.
9 *they were cast as extras* **choose,** select, pick, name, nominate.
▶ **noun 1** *a cast of the writer's hand* **mold,** die, matrix, shape, casting, model.
2 *a cast of the dice* **throw,** toss, fling, pitch, hurl, lob; informal chuck.
3 *an inquiring cast of mind* **type,** sort, kind, character, variety, class, style, stamp, nature.
4 *the cast of our spring musical* **actors,** performers, players, company, troupe; dramatis personae, characters.
– PHRASES **cast aside** *cast aside the pages marked with an "X"* **discard,** reject, throw away/out, get rid of, dispose of, abandon.

caste ▶ **noun** *she could not marry outside her caste* **class,** social class, social order, rank, level, stratum, echelon, status; dated estate, station.

castigate ▶ **verb** *Leopold castigated his son for leaving the archbishop's service* **reprimand,** rebuke, admonish, chastise, chide, censure, upbraid, reprove, reproach, scold, berate, take to task, lambaste, give someone a piece of one's mind; informal rake/haul over the coals, tell off, give someone an earful, give someone a tongue-lashing, give someone a roasting, rap someone on the knuckles, slap someone's wrist, dress down, bawl out, give someone hell, blow up at, lay into, blast, zing, have a go at, give someone what for, chew out, ream out; rare reprehend.
ANTONYMS praise, commend.

castle ▶ **noun** *a drafty old Scottish castle* **fortress,** fort, stronghold, fortification, keep, citadel.

casual ▶ **adjective 1** *a casual attitude to life* **indifferent,** apathetic, uncaring, unconcerned; lackadaisical, blasé, nonchalant, insouciant, offhand, flippant; easygoing, free and easy, blithe, carefree, devil-may-care; informal laid-back, loosey-goosey, Type-B.
ANTONYMS careful, concerned.
2 *a casual remark* **offhand,** spontaneous, unpremeditated, unthinking, unconsidered, impromptu, throwaway, unguarded; informal off-the-cuff.
ANTONYMS premeditated.
3 *a casual glance* **cursory,** perfunctory, superficial, passing, fleeting; hasty, brief, quick.
ANTONYMS careful, thorough.
4 *a casual acquaintance* **slight,** superficial.
ANTONYMS intimate, close.
5 *casual work* **temporary,** part-time, freelance, impermanent, irregular, occasional.
ANTONYMS permanent, full-time.
6 *casual sex* **promiscuous,** extramarital, free.
7 *a casual meeting changed his life* **chance,** accidental, unplanned, unintended, unexpected, unforeseen, unanticipated, fortuitous, serendipitous, adventitious. See note at **ACCIDENTAL**.
ANTONYMS intentional, planned.
8 *a casual shirt* **informal,** comfortable, leisure, everyday; informal sporty.
ANTONYMS formal, dressy.
9 *the inn's casual atmosphere* **relaxed,** friendly, informal, unceremonious, easygoing, free and easy; informal laid-back.
ANTONYMS formal.

casualty ▶ **noun** *a casualty of war | a record of the casualties* **victim,** fatality, loss, MIA; (**casualties**) dead and injured, missing in action, missing.

cat ▶ **noun** *their pet cats* **feline,** tomcat, tom, kitten, mouser; informal pussy (cat), puss, kitty; alley cat; archaic grimalkin.

catacombs ▶ **plural noun** *they unearthed the catacombs of an apparently prominent family* **underground cemetery,** crypt, vault, tomb, ossuary.

catalog ▶ **noun 1** *a library catalog* **directory,**

register, index, list, listing, record, archive, inventory.
2 *a mail-order catalog* **brochure,** mailer, wish book.
▶ **verb** *the collection is fully cataloged* **classify,** categorize, systematize, index, list, archive, make an inventory of, inventory, record, itemize.

catapult ▶ **verb** *the boulder was catapulted into the sea* **propel,** launch, hurl, fling, send flying, fire, blast, shoot.

cataract ▶ **noun** *the glistening cataract made a spectacular backdrop for our photo shoot* **waterfall,** cascade, falls, rapids, white water.

catastrophe ▶ **noun** *the flood of '82 was the worst catastrophe in the town's history* **disaster,** calamity, cataclysm, holocaust, havoc, ruin, ruination, tragedy; adversity, blight, trouble, trial, tribulation.

catcall ▶ **noun** *the young comics have to learn how to withstand the inevitable catcalls* **whistle,** boo, hiss, jeer, raspberry, taunt; (**catcalls**) scoffing, abuse, taunting, derision.

catch ▶ **verb 1** *he caught the ball* **seize,** grab, snatch, take hold of, grasp, grip, trap, clutch, clench; receive, get, intercept.
ANTONYMS drop.
2 *we've caught the thief* **capture,** seize; apprehend, arrest, take prisoner/captive, take into custody; trap, snare, ensnare; net, hook, land; informal nab, collar, run in, bust.
ANTONYMS release.
3 *her heel caught in a hole* **become trapped,** become entangled, snag.
4 *she caught the last bus* **be in time for,** make, get; board, get on, step aboard.
ANTONYMS miss.
5 *they were caught siphoning gas* **discover,** find, come upon/across, stumble on, chance on; surprise, catch red-handed, catch in the act.
6 *it caught his imagination* **engage,** capture, attract, draw, grab, grip, seize; hold, absorb, engross.
7 *she caught a trace of aftershave* **perceive,** notice, observe, discern, detect, note, make out.
ANTONYMS miss.
8 *I couldn't catch what she was saying* **hear,** perceive, discern, make out; understand, comprehend, grasp, apprehend; informal get, get the drift of, figure out.
9 *it caught the flavor of the sixties* **evoke,** conjure up, call to mind, recall, encapsulate, capture.
10 *the blow caught her on the side of her face* **hit,** strike, slap, smack, bang.
ANTONYMS miss.
11 *he caught malaria* **become infected with,** contract, get, fall ill with, be taken ill with, develop, come down with, be struck down with.
ANTONYMS escape.
12 *the kindling wouldn't catch* **ignite,** start burning, catch fire, kindle.
▶ **noun 1** *he inspected the catch* **haul,** net, bag, yield.
2 *he secured the catch* **latch,** lock, fastener, clasp, hasp.
3 *it looks great, but there's a catch* **snag,** disadvantage, drawback, stumbling block, hitch, fly in the ointment, pitfall, complication, problem, hiccup, difficulty; trap, trick, snare; informal catch-22.
– PHRASES **catch on 1** *radio soon caught on* **become popular,** become fashionable, take off, boom, flourish, thrive. **2** *I caught on fast* **understand,** comprehend, learn, see the light; informal latch on, get the picture, get the message, get wise. **catch up to** *police didn't catch up to Swanson until he stopped for gas and food in Great Neck* **reach**; be even with; gain on, close in on.

catching ▶ **adjective** informal *my rash is not catching* **infectious,** contagious; communicable, transmittable, transmissible, infective.

catchy ▶ **adjective** *I'm not sure what their product is, but they've got a catchy little jingle* **memorable,** unforgettable, haunting; appealing, popular; singable, melodious, tuneful, foot-tapping.

categorical ▶ **adjective** *a categorical assurance that annual premiums would not increase* **unqualified,** unconditional, unequivocal, absolute, explicit, express, unambiguous, definite, direct, downright, outright, emphatic, positive, point-blank, conclusive, without reservations, out-and-out.
ANTONYMS qualified, equivocal.

categorize ▶ **verb** *we should first categorize them by years of experience* **classify,** class, group, grade, rate, designate; order, arrange, sort, rank; file, catalog, list, index; typecast, pigeonhole, stereotype.

category ▶ **noun** *his music doesn't fit into any conventional category* **class,** classification, group, grouping, bracket, heading, set; type, sort, kind, variety, species, breed, brand, make, model; grade, order, rank; informal pigeonhole.

cater ▶ **verb 1** *we cater for vegetarians* **provide food for,** feed, serve, cook for.
2 *a resort catering to older travelers* **serve,** provide for, meet the needs/wants of, accommodate; satisfy, indulge, pander to, gratify.
3 *he seemed to cater to all tastes* **take into account,** take into consideration, allow for, consider, bear in mind, make provision for, have regard for.

catharsis ▶ **noun** *the hope was that hypnosis would bring about a catharsis* **emotional release,** relief, release, venting; purging, purgation, purification, cleansing; Psychoanalysis abreaction.

catholic ▶ **adjective** *her musical tastes are quite catholic* **universal,** diverse, diversified, wide, broad, broad-based, eclectic, liberal, latitudinarian; comprehensive, all-encompassing, all-embracing, all-inclusive. See note at **UNIVERSAL**.
ANTONYMS narrow.

cattle ▶ **plural noun** **cows,** bovines, oxen, bulls; stock, livestock.

catty ▶ **adjective** informal See **SPITEFUL**.

caucus ▶ **noun 1** *the conservative caucus* **members,** party, faction, camp, bloc, group, set, band, ring, cabal, coterie, pressure group.
2 *caucuses will be held in eleven states* **meeting,**

assembly, gathering, congress, conference, convention, rally, convocation.

cause ▶ noun **1** *the cause of the fire* **source,** root, origin, beginning(s), starting point; mainspring, base, basis, foundation, fountainhead; originator, author, creator, producer, agent.
ANTONYMS effect, result.
2 *there is no cause for alarm* **reason,** grounds, justification, call, need, necessity, occasion; excuse, pretext.
3 *the cause of human rights | a good cause* **principle,** ideal, belief, conviction; object, end, aim, objective, purpose, mission; charity.
4 *he went to plead his cause* **case,** suit, lawsuit, action, dispute.
▶ verb *this disease can cause blindness* **bring about,** give rise to, lead to, result in, create, produce, generate, engender, spawn, bring on, precipitate, prompt, provoke, trigger, make happen, induce, inspire, promote, foster; literary beget, enkindle.
ANTONYMS result from.

caustic ▶ adjective **1** *a caustic cleaner* **corrosive,** corroding, abrasive, mordant, acid.
2 *a caustic comment* **sarcastic,** cutting, biting, mordant, sharp, bitter, scathing, derisive, sardonic, ironic, scornful, trenchant, acerbic, abrasive, vitriolic, acidulous.

caution ▶ noun *proceed with caution* **care,** carefulness, heedfulness, heed, attention, attentiveness, alertness, watchfulness, vigilance, circumspection, discretion, prudence.
▶ verb *you were cautioned against taking such rash action* **advise,** warn, counsel; admonish, exhort.

cautious ▶ adjective *a cautious driver* **careful,** heedful, attentive, alert, watchful, vigilant, circumspect, prudent; cagey, canny. See note at VIGILANT.
ANTONYMS reckless.

cavalcade ▶ noun *bystanders cheered as the cavalcade passed by* **procession,** parade, motorcade, cortège.

cavalier ▶ noun archaic *foot soldiers and cavaliers* **horseman,** equestrian; cavalryman, trooper, knight.
▶ adjective *a cavalier disregard for danger* **offhand,** indifferent, casual, dismissive, insouciant, unconcerned; supercilious, patronizing, condescending, disdainful, scornful, contemptuous; informal couldn't-care-less, devil-may-care.

cavalry ▶ plural noun *he rode with the cavalry during the Mexican War* **mounted troops,** cavalrymen, troopers, horse; historical dragoons, lancers, hussars.

cave ▶ noun *the caves at the bottom of the cliff* **cavern,** grotto, underground chamber; cellar, vault, crypt.
– PHRASES **cave in 1** *the roof caved in* **collapse,** fall in/down, give, give way, crumble, subside.
2 *the manager caved in to their demands* **yield,** surrender, capitulate, submit, give in, back down, make concessions, throw in the towel.

caveat ▶ noun *he added the caveat that the results still had to be corroborated* **warning,** caution, admonition; proviso, condition, stipulation, provision, clause, rider, qualification.

caveman, cavewoman ▶ noun *were these the drawings of a caveman?* **cave dweller,** troglodyte, primitive man/woman, prehistoric man/woman; Neanderthal.

cavern ▶ noun *the crude stone steps led down to a dank and cold cavern* **large cave,** grotto, underground chamber/gallery, vault.

cavernous ▶ adjective *dinner was served in a cavernous hall* **vast,** huge, large, immense, spacious, roomy, airy, capacious, voluminous, extensive, deep; hollow, gaping, yawning; formal commodious.
ANTONYMS small.

cavil ▶ verb *He caviled at the cost* See CARP.

cavity ▶ noun *microscopic photos show a surface full of nodes and cavities* **space,** chamber, hollow, hole, pocket, pouch; orifice, aperture; socket, gap, crater, pit.

cease ▶ verb **1** *hostilities had ceased* **come to an end,** come to a halt, end, halt, stop, conclude, terminate, finish, draw to a close, be over.
ANTONYMS start, continue.
2 *they ceased all military activity* **bring to an end,** bring to a halt, end, halt, stop, conclude, terminate, finish, wind up, discontinue, suspend, break off; informal leave off.
ANTONYMS start, continue.
– PHRASES **without cease** *they have worked without cease on these prototypes* **continuously,** incessantly, unendingly, unremittingly, without a pause, without a break, on and on.

ceaseless ▶ adjective *a ceaseless flow of questions* **continual,** constant, continuous; incessant, unceasing, unending, endless, never-ending, interminable, nonstop, uninterrupted, unremitting, relentless, unrelenting, unrelieved, sustained, persistent, eternal, perpetual.
ANTONYMS intermittent.

cede ▶ verb *the library has ceded ten parking spaces to the hearing clinic* **surrender,** concede, relinquish, yield, part with, give up; hand over, deliver up, give over, make over, transfer; abandon, forgo, sacrifice; literary forsake. See note at RELINQUISH.

ceiling ▶ noun *a ceiling was to be set on prices* **upper limit,** maximum, limitation.

celebrate ▶ verb **1** *they were celebrating their wedding anniversary* **commemorate,** observe, mark, keep, honor, remember, memorialize.
2 *let's all celebrate!* **enjoy oneself,** have fun, have a good time, have a party, revel, roister, carouse, make merry; informal party, go out on the town, paint the town red, whoop it up, make whoopee, live it up, have a ball.
3 *he was celebrated for his achievements* **praise,** extol, glorify, eulogize, reverence, honor, pay tribute to; formal laud.

celebrated ▶ adjective *a celebrated hero* **acclaimed,** admired, highly rated, lionized, revered, honored, esteemed, exalted, vaunted, well-thought-of, ballyhooed; eminent, great, distinguished, prestigious, illustrious, preeminent, estimable, notable, of note, of repute; formal lauded.
ANTONYMS unsung.

celebration ▶ noun **1** *the celebration of his*

50th birthday **commemoration,** observance, marking, keeping.
2 *a birthday celebration for the twins* **party,** gathering, festivities, festival, fête, carnival, gala, jamboree, function; informal do, bash, shindig, rave.
3 *the celebration of the Eucharist* **observance,** performance, officiation, solemnization.

celebrity ▶ **noun 1** *a sports celebrity* **famous person,** VIP, very important person, personality, name, big name, famous name, household name, star, superstar; informal celeb, somebody, someone, megastar.
ANTONYMS nonentity.
2 *his celebrity grew* **fame,** prominence, renown, eminence, preeminence, stardom, popularity, distinction, note, notability, prestige, stature, repute, reputation.
ANTONYMS obscurity.

celestial ▶ **adjective 1** *a celestial body* **(in) space,** heavenly, astronomical, extraterrestrial, stellar, astral, planetary.
ANTONYMS earthly, terrestrial.
2 *celestial beings* **heavenly,** holy, saintly, divine, godly, godlike, ethereal, otherworldly; immortal, angelic, seraphic, cherubic.
ANTONYMS mundane, hellish.

cell ▶ **noun 1** *a prison cell* **room,** cubicle, chamber; dungeon, oubliette, lockup.
2 *each cell of the honeycomb* **compartment,** cavity, hole, hollow, section.
3 *terrorist cells* **unit,** faction, arm, section, ring, coterie, group.

cement ▶ **noun** *don't step in the wet cement* **mortar,** grout, concrete; **adhesive,** glue, fixative, gum, paste; superglue; mucilage.
▶ **verb** *he cemented the sample to a microscope slide* **stick,** bond; fasten, fix, affix, attach, secure, bind, glue, gum, paste.

cemetery ▶ **noun** *we gather at the cemetery on Memorial Day* **graveyard,** churchyard, burial ground, burying ground, necropolis, memorial park/garden; informal boneyard; historical potter's field; archaic God's acre.

censor ▶ **noun** *the film censors* **expurgator,** bowdlerizer; examiner, inspector, editor.
▶ **verb** *letters home were censored* **cut,** delete parts of, make cuts in, blue-pencil; edit, expurgate, bowdlerize, sanitize; informal clean up.

censorious ▶ **adjective** *the appointment of censorious watchdogs over the broadcasters* **hypercritical,** overcritical, fault-finding, disapproving, condemnatory, denunciatory, deprecatory, disparaging, reproachful, reproving, censuring, captious, carping, sitting in judgment.
ANTONYMS complimentary.

censure ▶ **verb** *he was censured for his conduct* See REPRIMAND (verb). See also note at REBUKE.
▶ **noun** *a note of censure* **condemnation,** criticism, attack, abuse; reprimand, rebuke, admonishment, reproof, upbraiding, disapproval, reproach, scolding, obloquy; informal flak, dressing-down, tongue-lashing; formal excoriation, castigation.
ANTONYMS approval.

center ▶ **noun** *the center of the town* **middle,** nucleus, heart, core, hub; middle point, midpoint, halfway point, mean, median.
ANTONYMS edge.
▶ **verb** *the story centers on a doctor* **focus,** concentrate, pivot, hinge, revolve, be based.

> USAGE
>
> **center around**
>
> The construction *center around* (as opposed to *center on,* or *revolve around*) has been denounced as incorrect and illogical since it first appeared in the mid-nineteenth century. Although the phrase is common, it defies geometry by confusing the orbit with the fixed point: *the earth revolves around* (or *its revolution centers on*) *the sun.* A careful writer will use a precise expression, such as *centers on, revolves around, concerns,* or *involves.*

central ▶ **adjective 1** *occupying a central position* **middle,** center, halfway, midway, mid, median, medial, mean; Anatomy mesial.
ANTONYMS side, extreme.
2 *central Fargo* **inner,** innermost, middle, mid; downtown.
ANTONYMS outer.
3 *their central campaign issue* **main,** chief, principal, primary, leading, foremost, first, most important, predominant, dominant, key, crucial, vital, essential, basic, fundamental, core, prime, premier, paramount, major, overriding; informal number-one.
ANTONYMS minor, subordinate.

centralize ▶ **verb** *the state is to centralize its communications network* **concentrate,** consolidate, amalgamate, condense, unify, streamline, focus; Brit. rationalize.
ANTONYMS devolve.

ceramics ▶ **plural noun** *an exhibit of Armenian ceramics* **pottery,** pots, china, terra cotta.

ceremonial ▶ **adjective** *a ceremonial occasion* **formal,** official, state, public; ritual, ritualistic, prescribed, stately, courtly, solemn. See note at FORMAL.
ANTONYMS informal.

ceremonious ▶ **adjective** *a ceremonious affair at the White House* **dignified,** majestic, imposing, impressive, solemn, ritualistic, stately, formal; courtly, regal, imperial, elegant, grand, glorious, splendid, magnificent, resplendent, portentous; informal starchy. See note at FORMAL.

ceremony ▶ **noun 1** *a wedding ceremony* **ritual,** rite, ceremonial, observance; service, sacrament, liturgy, worship, celebration.
2 *the new queen was proclaimed with due ceremony* **pomp,** protocol, formalities, niceties, decorum, etiquette, punctilio, politesse.

certain ▶ **adjective 1** *I'm certain he's guilty* **sure,** confident, positive, convinced, in no doubt, satisfied, assured, persuaded.
ANTONYMS doubtful.
2 *it is certain that more changes are in the offing* **unquestionable,** sure, definite, beyond question, not in doubt, indubitable, undeniable, irrefutable, indisputable; obvious, evident, recognized, confirmed, accepted, acknowledged, undisputed, undoubted,

unquestioned.
ANTONYMS doubtful, possible, unthinkable.
3 *they are certain to win* **sure,** very likely, bound, destined.
ANTONYMS unlikely.
4 *certain defeat* **inevitable,** assured, destined, predestined; unavoidable, inescapable, inexorable, ineluctable; informal in the bag.
ANTONYMS possible, unlikely.
5 *there is no certain cure for this* **reliable,** dependable, trustworthy, foolproof, tried and tested, effective, guaranteed, sure, unfailing, infallible; informal sure-fire, idiot-proof, goof-proof.
ANTONYMS unreliable.
6 *a certain sum of money* **determined,** definite, fixed, established, precise.
ANTONYMS undefined, undetermined.
7 *a certain lady* **particular,** specific, individual, special.
8 *to a certain extent that is true* **moderate,** modest, medium, middling; limited, small.
ANTONYMS great.

certainly ▶ **adverb** *this is certainly a forgery* **unquestionably,** surely, assuredly, definitely, beyond/without question, without doubt, indubitably, undeniably, irrefutably, indisputably; obviously, patently, evidently, plainly, clearly, unmistakably, undisputedly, undoubtedly; informal sure as shootin', for sure.
ANTONYMS possibly.
▶ **exclamation** *"May I have one?" "Certainly."* **yes,** definitely, absolutely, sure, by all means, indeed, of course, naturally; affirmative; informal OK, okay.

certainty ▶ **noun 1** *she knew with certainty that he was telling the truth* **confidence,** sureness, positiveness, conviction, certitude, assurance.
ANTONYMS doubt.
2 *he accepted defeat as a certainty* **inevitability,** foregone conclusion; informal sure thing, sure bet, no-brainer.
ANTONYMS impossibility, possibility.

certificate ▶ **noun** *do you have any type of certificate that proves your ownership?* **guarantee,** certification, document, authorization, registration, authentication, credentials, accreditation, license, diploma.

certify ▶ **verb 1** *the aircraft was certified as airworthy* **verify,** guarantee, attest, validate, confirm, substantiate, endorse, vouch for, testify to; provide evidence, give proof, prove, demonstrate.
2 *a certified hospital* **accredit,** recognize, license, authorize, approve, warrant. See note at **APPROVE**.

cessation ▶ **noun** *the cessation of hostilities* **end,** ending, termination, stopping, halting, ceasing, finish, finishing, stoppage, conclusion, winding up, discontinuation, abandonment, suspension, breaking off, cutting short.
ANTONYMS start, resumption.

chafe ▶ **verb 1** *the collar chafed his neck* **abrade,** graze, rub against, gall, scrape, scratch; Medicine excoriate.
2 *material chafed by the rock* **wear away/down,** erode, abrade, scour, scrape away.
3 *the bank chafed at the restrictions* **be angry,** be annoyed, be irritated, fume, be exasperated, be frustrated.

chaff ▶ **noun 1** *separating the chaff from the grain* **husks,** hulls, pods, shells, bran, shucks.
2 *the proposals were so much chaff* **garbage,** dross, rubbish, trash; informal junk, crap, schlock.
3 *good-natured chaff* **banter,** repartee, teasing, ragging, joking, jesting, raillery, badinage, wisecracks, witticism(s); informal kidding, ribbing; formal persiflage.
▶ **verb** *the pleasure of chaffing your buddies* **tease,** make fun of, poke fun at, make sport of; informal rib, razz, kid, josh, have on, pull someone's leg, pull/jerk/yank someone's chain, goof on.

chagrin ▶ **noun** *Sean showed up at the party, to everyone's chagrin* **annoyance,** irritation, vexation, exasperation, displeasure, dissatisfaction, discontent; anger, rage, fury, wrath, indignation, resentment; embarrassment, mortification, humiliation, shame.
ANTONYMS delight.

chain ▶ **noun 1** *he was held in chains* **fetters,** shackles, irons, leg irons, manacles, handcuffs; informal cuffs, bracelets; historical bilboes.
2 *a chain of events* **series,** succession, string, sequence, train, course.
▶ **verb** *she chained her bicycle to the railing* **secure,** fasten, tie, tether, hitch; restrain, shackle, fetter, manacle, handcuff.

chair ▶ **noun** *he sat down on a chair* **seat**; armchair, easy chair, rocking chair; stool, bench.
▶ **verb** *she chairs the economic committee* **preside over,** take the chair of; lead, direct, run, manage, control, be in charge of.

chalk ▶ **verb**
– PHRASES **chalk something up 1** *he has chalked up another success* **achieve,** attain, accomplish, gain, earn, win, succeed in making, make, get, obtain, rack up. **2** *I forgot completely—chalk it up to age* **attribute,** assign, ascribe, put down; blame on, pin on, lay at the door of.

chalky ▶ **adjective 1** *chalky skin* **pale,** bloodless, pallid, colorless, wan, ashen, white, pasty.
2 *chalky bits at the bottom of the glass* **powdery,** gritty, granular.

challenge ▶ **noun 1** *he accepted the challenge* **dare,** provocation; summons.
2 *a challenge to his leadership* **test,** questioning, dispute, stand, opposition, confrontation.
3 *it was proving quite a challenge* **problem,** difficult task, test, trial.
▶ **verb 1** *we challenged their statistics* **question,** disagree with, dispute, take issue with, protest against, call into question, object to.
2 *he challenged one of my men to a duel* **dare,** summon, throw down the gauntlet to.
3 *changes that would challenge them* **test,** tax, strain, make demands on; stretch, stimulate, inspire, excite.

USAGE

challenged

The use of *challenged* with a preceding adverb, e.g., *physically challenged,* originally intended to give a more positive tone than such terms as *disabled* or *handicapped*, arose in the U.S. in the 1980s. Despite the originally serious intention, the term rapidly became stalled by uses whose intention was to make fun of the attempts at euphemism and whose tone was usually clearly ironic: examples include *cerebrally challenged, follicularly challenged,* etc.

chamber ▶ **noun 1** *a debating chamber* **room,** hall, assembly room, auditorium.
2 archaic *we slept safely in our chamber* **bedroom,** room; literary bower; historical boudoir; archaic bedchamber.
3 *the left chamber of the heart* **compartment,** cavity; Anatomy auricle, ventricle.

champion ▶ **noun 1** *the world champion* **winner,** titleholder, defending champion, gold medalist, titleist; prizewinner, victor; informal champ, number one, king.
2 *a champion of change* **advocate,** proponent, promoter, supporter, defender, upholder, backer, exponent; campaigner, lobbyist, crusader, apologist, booster, flag-bearer.
3 historical *the king's champion* **knight,** man-at-arms, warrior.
▶ **verb** *championing the rights of refugees* **advocate,** promote, defend, uphold, support, back, stand up for, take someone's part; campaign for, lobby for, fight for, crusade for, stick up for.
ANTONYMS oppose.

chance ▶ **noun 1** *there was a chance he might be released* **possibility,** prospect, probability, likelihood, likeliness, expectation, anticipation; risk, threat, danger.
2 *I gave her a chance to answer* **opportunity,** opening, occasion, turn, time, window (of opportunity); informal shot.
3 *Nichola took an awful chance* **risk,** gamble, venture, speculation, long shot, shot in the dark.
4 *pure chance* **accident,** coincidence, serendipity, fate, destiny, fortuity, providence, happenstance; good fortune, luck, good luck, fluke.
▶ **adjective** *a chance discovery* **accidental,** fortuitous, adventitious, fluky, coincidental, serendipitous; unintentional, unintended, inadvertent, unplanned.
ANTONYMS intentional.
▶ **verb 1** *I chanced to meet him* **happen.**
2 *she chanced another look* **risk,** hazard, venture, try; formal essay.
– PHRASES **by chance** *we found a signed first edition completely by chance* **fortuitously,** by accident, accidentally, coincidentally, serendipitously; unintentionally, inadvertently.
chance on/upon *if you should chance upon a copy of the book, please let me know* **come across/upon,** run across/into, happen on, light on, stumble on, find by chance, meet (by chance), bump into.

chancy ▶ **adjective** informal *these investments seem too chancy for me* **risky,** unpredictable, uncertain, precarious; unsafe, insecure, tricky, high-risk, hazardous, perilous, parlous; informal dicey, hairy.
ANTONYMS predictable.

change ▶ **verb 1** *this could change the face of television | things have changed* **alter,** make/become different, adjust, adapt, amend, modify, revise, refine; reshape, refashion, redesign, restyle, revamp, rework, remodel, reorganize, reorder; vary, transform, transfigure, transmute, metamorphose, evolve; informal tweak, doctor, rejig; technical permute.
ANTONYMS preserve, stay the same.
2 *they've changed places* **exchange,** substitute, swap, switch, replace, alternate, interchange.
ANTONYMS keep.
▶ **noun 1** *a change of plan* **alteration,** modification, variation, revision, amendment, adjustment, adaptation; remodeling, reshaping, rearrangement, reordering, restyling, reworking; metamorphosis, transformation, evolution, mutation; informal transmogrification.
2 *a change of government* **exchange,** substitution, swap, switch, changeover, replacement, alternation, interchange.
3 *I don't have any change* **coins,** loose/small change, silver; cash, petty cash; formal, specie.
– PHRASES **have a change of heart** See **HEART**.

changeable ▶ **adjective 1** *the weather will be changeable | changeable moods* **variable,** inconstant, varying, changing, fluctuating, irregular; erratic, inconsistent, unstable, unsettled, turbulent, protean; fickle, capricious, temperamental, volatile, mercurial, unpredictable, blowing hot and cold; informal up and down.
ANTONYMS constant.
2 *the colors are changeable* **alterable,** adjustable, modifiable, variable, mutable, exchangeable, interchangeable, replaceable.
ANTONYMS invariable.

channel ▶ **noun 1** *sailing the North Channel* **strait(s),** sound, narrows, passage, sea passage.
2 *the water ran down a channel* **duct,** gutter, conduit, trough, culvert, sluice, spillway, race, drain.
3 *a channel for their extraordinary energy* **use,** medium, vehicle, way of harnessing; release (mechanism), safety valve, vent.
4 *a channel of communication* **means,** medium, instrument, mechanism, agency, vehicle, route, avenue.
▶ **verb 1** *she* **channeled out** *a groove* **hollow out,** gouge (out), cut (out).
2 *many countries channel their aid through charities* **convey,** transmit, conduct, direct, guide, relay, pass on, transfer.

chant ▶ **noun 1** *the protesters' chants* **shout,** cry, call, rallying call, cheer, slogan.
2 *the melodious chant of the monks* **incantation,** intonation, singing, song, plainsong, recitative.
▶ **verb 1** *protesters were chanting slogans* **shout,** chorus, repeat.
2 *the choir chanted Psalm 118* **sing,** intone, incant.

chaos ▶ **noun** *police were called in to quell the chaos* **disorder,** disarray, disorganization, confusion, mayhem, bedlam, pandemonium, havoc, turmoil, tumult, commotion, disruption, upheaval, uproar, maelstrom; muddle, mess,

shambles, free-for-all; anarchy, lawlessness, entropy; informal hullabaloo, hoopla, all hell broken loose.
ANTONYMS order.

chaotic ▶ adjective *the whole town was chaotic* **disorderly,** disordered, in disorder, in chaos, in disarray, disorganized, topsy-turvy, in pandemonium, in turmoil, in an uproar; in a muddle, in a mess, messy, in a shambles; anarchic, lawless.

chap ▶ verb *my skin chapped in the wind* **become raw,** become sore, become inflamed, chafe, crack.

chapter ▶ noun 1 *the first chapter of the book* **section,** division, part, portion.
2 *a new chapter in our history* **period,** phase, page, stage, epoch, era.
3 *a local chapter of the American Cancer Society* **branch,** division, subdivision, section, department, lodge, wing, arm.
4 *the cathedral chapter* **governing body,** council, assembly, convocation, synod, consistory.

char ▶ verb *the steaks should be slightly charred* **scorch,** burn, singe, sear, blacken; informal toast. See note at BURN.

character ▶ noun 1 *a forceful character | the character of a town* **personality,** nature, disposition, temperament, temper, mentality, makeup; features, qualities, properties, traits; spirit, essence, identity, ethos, complexion, tone, feel, feeling.
2 *a woman of character* **integrity,** honor, moral strength, moral fiber, rectitude, uprightness; fortitude, strength, backbone, resolve, grit, willpower; informal guts, gutsiness.
3 *a stain on his character* **reputation,** name, good name, standing, stature, position, status.
4 informal *a bit of a character* **eccentric,** oddity, madcap, crank, individualist, nonconformist, rare bird, free spirit; informal oddball.
5 *a boorish character* **person,** man, woman, soul, creature, individual, customer.
6 *the characters develop throughout the play* **persona,** role, part; (**characters**) dramatis personae.
7 *thirty characters per line* **letter,** figure, symbol, sign, mark.

characteristic ▶ noun *interesting characteristics* **attribute,** feature, quality, essential quality, property, trait, aspect, element, facet; mannerism, habit, custom, idiosyncrasy, peculiarity, quirk, oddity, foible.
▶ adjective *his characteristic eloquence* **typical,** usual, normal, predictable, habitual; distinctive, particular, special, especial, peculiar, idiosyncratic, defining, singular, unique.

characterize ▶ verb 1 *the period was characterized by scientific advancement* **distinguish,** make distinctive, mark, typify, set apart.
2 *the women are characterized as prophets of doom* **portray,** depict, present, represent, describe; categorize, class, style, brand.

charade ▶ noun *our entire relationship is a charade* **farce,** pantomime, travesty, mockery, parody, pretense, act, masquerade.

charge ▶ verb 1 *he didn't charge much* **ask in payment,** ask, levy, demand, want, exact; bill, invoice.
2 *the subscription will be charged to your account* **bill,** debit from, take from.
3 *two men were charged with theft* **accuse,** indict, arraign; prosecute, try, put on trial, inculpate.
4 *they charged him with reforming the system* **entrust,** burden, encumber, saddle, tax.
5 *the cavalry charged the tanks* **attack,** storm, assault, assail, fall on, swoop on, descend on; informal lay into, tear into. See note at ATTACK.
6 *we charged into the crowd* **rush,** storm, stampede, push, plow, launch oneself, go headlong, steam, barrel, zoom.
7 *his work was charged with energy* **suffuse,** pervade, permeate, saturate, infuse, imbue, load, fill.
8 *I charge you to stop* **order,** command, direct, instruct, enjoin; formal adjure; literary bid.
▶ noun 1 *all customers pay a charge* **fee,** payment, price, tariff, amount, sum, fare, levy.
2 *he pleaded guilty to the charge* **accusation,** allegation, indictment, arraignment.
3 *an infantry charge* **attack,** assault, offensive, onslaught, drive, push, thrust.
4 *the child was in her charge* **care,** protection, safekeeping, control; custody, guardianship, wardship; hands.
5 *his charge was to save the business* **duty,** responsibility, task, job, assignment, mission, function; informal marching orders.
6 *the safety of my charge* **ward,** protégé, dependent.
7 *the judge gave a careful charge to the jury* **instruction,** direction, directive, order, command, dictate, exhortation.
8 informal *I get a real charge out of working hard* **thrill,** tingle, glow; excitement, stimulation, enjoyment, pleasure; informal kick, buzz, rush.
– PHRASES **in charge of** *I'm in charge of museum security* **responsible for,** in control of, in command of, at the helm/wheel of; **managing,** running, administering, directing, supervising, overseeing, controlling.

charitable ▶ adjective 1 *charitable activities* **philanthropic,** humanitarian, altruistic, benevolent, public-spirited; nonprofit; formal eleemosynary.
2 *charitable people* **bighearted,** generous, openhanded, free-handed, munificent, bountiful, beneficent; literary bounteous.
3 *he was charitable in his judgments* **magnanimous,** generous, liberal, tolerant, easygoing, broad-minded, considerate, sympathetic, lenient, indulgent, forgiving, kind.

charity ▶ noun 1 *a children's charity* **nonprofit organization,** voluntary organization, charitable institution; fund, trust, foundation.
2 *we don't need charity* **financial assistance,** aid, welfare, relief, financial relief; handouts, gifts, presents, largesse; historical alms.
3 *his actions are motivated by charity* **philanthropy,** humanitarianism, humanity, altruism, public-spiritedness, social conscience, benevolence, beneficence, munificence.
4 *show a bit of charity* **goodwill,** compassion, consideration, concern, kindness, kindheartedness, tenderness,

tenderheartedness, sympathy, indulgence, tolerance, leniency, caritas; literary bounteousness. See note at **MERCY**.

charlatan ▶ noun *the doc didn't go to no fancy halls of ivy, but he was no charlatan* **quack,** sham, fraud, fake, impostor, hoaxer, cheat, deceiver, double-dealer, swindler, fraudster, mountebank; informal phony, shark, con man, con artist, scam artist, flimflammer, bunco artist, snake oil salesman; dated confidence man/woman. See note at **QUACK**.

charm ▶ noun **1** *people were captivated by her charm* **attractiveness,** beauty, glamour, loveliness; appeal, allure, desirability, seductiveness, magnetism, charisma.
2 *these traditions retain a lot of charm* **appeal,** drawing power, attraction, allure, fascination.
3 *magical charms* **spell,** incantation, conjuration, magic formula, magic word, mojo, hex.
4 *a lucky charm* **talisman,** fetish, amulet, mascot, totem, juju.
▶ verb **1** *he charmed them with his singing* **delight,** please, win (over), attract, captivate, allure, lure, dazzle, fascinate, enchant, enthrall, enrapture, seduce, spellbind.
2 *he charmed his mother into agreeing* **coax,** cajole, wheedle; informal sweet-talk, soft-soap; archaic blandish.

charming ▶ adjective *a charming inn on the cape | their charming daughter* **delightful,** pleasing, pleasant, agreeable, likable, endearing, lovely, lovable, adorable, appealing, attractive, good-looking, prepossessing; alluring, delectable, ravishing, winning, winsome, fetching, captivating, enchanting, entrancing, fascinating, seductive; informal heavenly, divine, gorgeous; literary beauteous; archaic fair, comely.
ANTONYMS repulsive.

chart ▶ noun **1** *check your ideal weight on the chart* **graph,** table, diagram, histogram; bar chart, pie chart, flow chart; Computing graphic.
2 (**charts**) *the song hit the charts at number twelve* top twenty, top ten, list, listing; dated hit parade.
▶ verb **1** *the changes were charted accurately* **tabulate,** plot, graph, record, register, represent; make a chart/diagram of.
2 *the book charted his progress* **follow,** trace, outline, describe, detail, record, document, chronicle, log.

charter ▶ noun **1** *a royal charter* **authority,** authorization, sanction, dispensation, consent, permission; permit, license, warrant, franchise.
2 *the UN Charter* **constitution,** code, canon; fundamental principles, rules, laws.
3 *the charter of a yacht* **hire,** hiring, lease, leasing, rent, rental, renting; booking, reservation, reserving.
▶ verb *they chartered a bus* **hire,** lease, rent; book, reserve.

chary ▶ adjective *he was chary of broaching the subject* **wary,** cautious, circumspect, heedful, careful, on one's guard; distrustful, mistrustful, skeptical, suspicious, dubious, hesitant, reluctant, leery, canny, nervous, apprehensive, uneasy; informal cagey, iffy.

chase ▶ verb **1** *the cat chased the mouse* **pursue,** run after, give chase to, follow; hunt, track, trail; informal tail.
2 *chasing young girls* **pursue,** run after, make advances to, flirt with; informal come on to, hit on; dated woo, court, romance, set one's cap for/at, make love to.
3 *she **chased away** the donkeys* **drive away,** drive off, send away, scare off; informal shoo (away), send packing.
4 *she **chased away** all thoughts of him* **dispel,** banish, dismiss, drive away, shut out, put out of one's mind.
▶ noun *they gave up the chase* **pursuit,** hunt, trail.

chasm ▶ noun **1** *a deep chasm* **gorge,** abyss, canyon, ravine, gully, gulf, defile, couloir, crevasse, fissure, crevice, gulch, coulee.
2 *the chasm between their views* **breach,** gulf, rift; difference, separation, division, dissension, schism, scission.

chassis ▶ noun *the chassis of the car is in mint condition* **framework,** frame, structure, substructure, shell, casing.

chaste ▶ adjective **1** *her determination to remain chaste* **virginal,** virgin, intact, maidenly, unmarried, unwed; celibate, abstinent, self-restrained, self-denying, continent; innocent, virtuous, pure, pure as the driven snow, sinless, undefiled, unsullied, immaculate; literary vestal.
ANTONYMS promiscuous, immoral.
2 *a chaste kiss on the cheek* **nonsexual,** platonic, innocent.
ANTONYMS passionate.
3 *the dark, chaste interior* **plain,** simple, bare, unadorned, undecorated, unornamented, unembellished, functional, no-frills, austere.
ANTONYMS ostentatious.

USAGE

chaste, celibate

Chaste (= untainted by unlawful sexual intercourse; virtuous; sexually continent) is a word that applies to males and females alike—e.g.: "As a young and chaste boy, Yava said, he would often be called on to help construct the sand painting, lending the power of his purity." (*Phoenix Gazette*; June 4, 1993.) Unfortunately, however, a bias pervades the word's usual applications so that it typically refers to women and girls—e.g.: "One view is that a fallen woman who has fully reformed is chaste, while another is that chastity before marriage means physical virginity—a woman can be seduced only once. There is nothing unchaste about marital intercourse and hence, under either view, a widow or divorcee may be an unmarried female of previously chaste character." (Rollin M. Perkins and Ronald N. Boyce, *Criminal Law*, 3d ed.; 1982.)

There is also some confusion about the sense of *chaste*, as opposed to *celibate*. A person who is *chaste* is innocent of unlawful sex—that is, does not engage in sex with anyone other than the person's spouse. So, in both secular law and church law, a person who frequently has sex, but only with his or her spouse, is *chaste*. By contrast, a person who is *celibate* (in the word's original sense and still the only definition in the *Oxford English Dictionary*) abstains from marrying—and sex, too, but only as a consequence of the choice not to marry. The times have passed that meaning by, and today this traditional sense is obsolescent at best. It may remain current with the vow of celibacy that Catholic priests make (i.e., a promise not to marry). But it is almost universally understood, even in that context, to mean "abstaining from sex"—e.g.: "His case underscores the growing debate within the church over whether there is a place in the priesthood for gay men, even celibate ones." (*Boston Globe*; Nov. 25, 2002.) And while many word extensions result in the loss of a useful and unique term, here the shift in meaning of *celibate* has resulted in the creation of a term that has no good substitute—especially since *chaste* sounds archaic, carries outdated connotations about sex, and has drifted toward becoming gender-specific. — **BG**

chasten ▶ verb **1** *both men were chastened* **subdue,** humble, cow, squash, deflate, abase; informal flatten, take down a peg or two, put someone in their place, cut down to size, settle someone's hash.
2 archaic *the Heaven that chastens us* See CHASTISE.

chastise ▶ verb *the staff were chastised for arriving late* **scold,** upbraid, berate, reprimand, reprove, rebuke, admonish, chide, censure, lambaste, castigate, lecture, give someone a piece of one's mind, give someone a tongue-lashing, take to task, rake/haul over the coals; informal tell off, dress down, bawl out, blow up at, give someone an earful, give someone a roasting, come down on someone like a ton of bricks, slap someone's wrist, rap over the knuckles, give someone hell, give someone what for, chew out, ream out, zing; archaic chasten; rare reprehend.
ANTONYMS praise.

chastity ▶ noun *a vow of chastity* **celibacy,** chasteness, virginity, abstinence, self-restraint, self-denial, continence; innocence, purity, virtue, morality.

chat ▶ noun *I popped in for a chat* **talk,** conversation, chitchat, gossip, chatter, heart-to-heart, tête-à-tête; informal jaw, confab, chinwag, rap, bull session; formal confabulation, colloquy. See note at CONVERSATION.
▶ verb *they chatted with their guests* **talk,** gossip, chatter, speak, converse, engage in conversation, tittle-tattle, prattle (on), jabber, babble; informal gas, jaw, chew the fat, yap, yak, yatter, yammer, shoot the breeze; formal confabulate.

chatter ▶ noun *she tired him with her chatter* **chat,** talk, gossip, chitchat, jabbering, jabber, prattling, prattle, babbling, babble, tittle-tattle, blathering, blather; informal yammering, yattering, yapping, jawing, chewing the fat; formal confabulation, colloquy.
▶ verb *they chattered excitedly* See BLATHER (verb).

chatterbox ▶ noun informal *he was the office chatterbox* **talker,** chatterer, prattler; informal windbag, bigmouth, gasbag, blabbermouth, motormouth.

chatty ▶ adjective **1** *he was a chatty person* **talkative,** communicative, expansive, unreserved, gossipy, gossiping, garrulous, loquacious, voluble, verbose; informal mouthy, talky, gabby, motormouthed.
ANTONYMS taciturn.
2 *a chatty letter* **conversational,** gossipy, informal, casual, familiar, friendly; informal newsy.
ANTONYMS formal.

chauvinism ▶ noun *they have a tendency toward small-mindedness and chauvinism* **jingoism,** excessive patriotism, blind patriotism, excessive nationalism, sectarianism, isolationism, flag-waving; xenophobia, racism, ethnocentrism, ethnocentricity; **partisanship,** partiality, prejudice, bias, discrimination, bigotry; male chauvinism, antifeminism, misogyny, sexism.

USAGE

chauvinism, jingoism

Most traditionally, *chauvinism* (/**shoh**-vuh-niz-uhm/) refers to fanatical patriotism. The word is an eponym from Nicolas Chauvin, a French soldier who was ridiculed for being excessively devoted to Napoleon. By metaphorical extension, the word was broadened to denote excessive pride in people like oneself, especially in reference to males. Today *male chauvinism,* which (as a phrase, not a phenomenon) dates back to the late 1960s, is something of a cliché, being the word's most frequent application. Indeed, some writers have come to use *chauvinism* as if it were synonymous with *male chauvinism*—e.g.: "He betrayed his chauvinism by expressing surprise that I [Diane McFarlin] was an editor." (*Sarasota Herald-Tribune*; Nov. 8, 1998.) To the linguistic traditionalist, these uses (or misuses) are arrant nonsense.

The void left by the shift in the meaning of *chauvinism* from national pride to supposed sexual superiority has been filled by *jingoism*. Essentially synonymous with *chauvinism* in its traditional sense, *jingoism* has the added layer of xenophobic and aggressive attitudes toward foreign policy—e.g.: "Gilmour goes overboard in trying to rationalize and justify Kipling's racism and jingoism. He argues, for example, that 'white' in *The White Man's Burden* does not refer to skin color but rather to 'civilization and character' and that Kipling's imperialistic beliefs were essentially humane and benevolent rather than based on greed, paternalism and self-interest." (*Houston Chronicle*; June 23, 2002.) Sometimes the word takes on an even softer sense, suggesting a provincialism or regionalism that is broader than national sovereignty—e.g.: "The prime minister's evident glee that the BA order had gone to a 'European' company is mere jingoism at bottom." (*Wall Street Journal Europe*; Aug. 27, 1998.) — **BG**

cheap ▶ adjective **1** *cheap tickets* **inexpensive,** low-priced, low-cost, economical, competitive, affordable, reasonable, reasonably priced, budget, economy, bargain, downmarket, cut-rate, reduced, discounted, discount, rock-bottom, giveaway, bargain-basement, low-end, dirt cheap.
ANTONYMS expensive.
2 *cheap furniture* **poor-quality,** second-rate, third-rate, tinpot, substandard, low-grade, inferior, vulgar, shoddy, trashy, tawdry, meretricious, cheapjack, gimcrack, pinchbeck; informal rubbishy, chintzy, cheapo, junky, tacky, cheesy, ticky-tacky, kitsch, kitschy, two-bit, dime-store, schlocky.
ANTONYMS high-class.
3 *she was too cheap to contribute to the fund* **miserly,** stingy, parsimonious, tightfisted, niggardly, chintzy, frugal, penny-pinching, cheeseparing.
ANTONYMS generous.
4 *the cheap exploitation of suffering* **despicable,** contemptible, immoral, unscrupulous, unprincipled, unsavory, distasteful, vulgar, ignoble, shameful.
ANTONYMS admirable.
5 *he made me feel cheap* **ashamed,** humiliated, mortified, debased, degraded.

cheapen ▶ verb **1** *Hetty never cheapened herself* **demean,** debase, degrade, lower, humble, devalue, abase, discredit, disgrace, dishonor, shame, humiliate, mortify, prostitute.
2 *cheapening the cost of exports* **reduce,** lower (in price), cut, mark down, discount; informal slash.

cheat ▶ verb **1** *customers were cheated* **swindle,** defraud, deceive, trick, scam, dupe, hoodwink, double-cross, gull; informal rip off, con, fleece, shaft, hose, sting, bilk, diddle, rook, gyp, finagle, bamboozle, flimflam, put one over on, pull a fast one on, sucker, stiff, hornswoggle; formal mulct; literary cozen.
2 *the boy cheated death* **avoid,** escape, evade, elude; foil, frustrate, thwart.
3 *it's not the first time her husband has cheated* **commit adultery,** be unfaithful, stray; informal two-time, play around; archaic cuckold.
▶ noun *a liar and a cheat* **swindler,** cheater, fraudster, trickster, deceiver, hoaxer, double-dealer, double-crosser, sham, fraud, fake, charlatan, quack, crook, snake oil salesman, mountebank; informal con man, con artist, scam artist, shark, sharper, phony, flimflammer, bunco artist; dated confidence man/woman.

check ▶ verb **1** *troops checked all vehicles | I checked her background* **examine,** inspect, look at/over, scrutinize, survey; study, investigate, research, probe, look into, inquire into; informal check out, give something a once-over.
2 *he checked that the gun was cocked* **make sure,** confirm, verify.
3 *two defeats checked their progress* **halt,** stop, arrest, cut short; bar, obstruct, hamper, impede, inhibit, frustrate, foil, thwart, curb, block, stall, hold up, retard, delay, slow down; literary stay.
4 *her tears could not be checked* **suppress,** repress, restrain, control, curb, rein in, stifle, hold back, choke back; informal keep a lid on.
▶ noun **1** *a check of the records* **examination,** inspection, scrutiny, perusal, study, investigation, probe, analysis; test, trial, monitoring; checkup; informal once-over, look-see.
2 *a check on the abuse of authority* **control,** restraint, constraint, curb, limitation.
3 *write a check in the amount of $150* bank draft; traveler's check, certified check, bank check; paycheck.
4 *the waitress arrived with the check* **bill,** account, invoice, statement, tab.
– PHRASES **check in** *I checked in at two o'clock sharp* **report (one's arrival),** sign in, register. **check out 1** *we'll be checking out in the morning* **leave,** vacate, depart; pay the bill, settle up.
2 *the police checked out dozens of leads* **investigate,** look into, inquire into, probe, research, examine, go over; assess, analyze, evaluate; follow up; informal give something a once-over, scope out. **3** *she checked herself out in the mirror* **look at,** survey, regard, inspect, contemplate; informal eyeball. **keep in check** *I try to keep my temper in check* **curb,** restrain, hold back, keep a tight rein on, rein in/back; control, govern, master, suppress, stifle; informal keep a lid on.

checkered ▶ adjective **1** *a checkered tablecloth* **checked,** plaid, tartan, multicolored, many-colored.
2 *a checkered history* **varied,** mixed, up and down, full of ups and downs, vicissitudinous; unstable, irregular, erratic, inconstant.

checkup ▶ noun *I saw the doctor for my annual checkup* **examination,** inspection, evaluation, analysis, survey, probe, test, appraisal; check, health check; informal once-over, going-over.

cheek ▶ noun *that's enough of your cheek!* See IMPUDENCE.

cheeky ▶ adjective See IMPUDENT.

cheep ▶ verb *the summer sounds of bees buzzing and birds cheeping* **chirp,** chirrup, twitter, tweet, peep, chitter, chirr, trill, warble, sing.

cheer ▶ noun **1** *the cheers of the crowd* **hurray,** hurrah, whoop, bravo, shout, roar; hosanna, alleluia; (**cheers**) applause, acclamation, clamor, acclaim, ovation.
ANTONYMS boo.
2 *a time of cheer* **happiness,** joy, joyousness, cheerfulness, cheeriness, gladness, merriment, gaiety, jubilation, jollity, jolliness, high spirits, joviality, jocularity, conviviality, lightheartedness; merrymaking, pleasure, rejoicing, revelry.
ANTONYMS sadness.
3 *Christmas cheer* **fare,** food, foodstuffs, eatables, provender; drink, beverages; informal eats, nibbles, nosh, grub, chow; formal victuals, comestibles.
▶ verb **1** *they cheered their team* **applaud,** hail, salute, shout for, root for, hurrah, hurray, acclaim, clap for; encourage, support; bring the house down for, holler for, give someone a big hand, put one's hands together for.
ANTONYMS boo.
2 *the bad weather did little to cheer me* **raise someone's spirits,** make happier, brighten, buoy up, enliven, exhilarate, hearten, gladden, uplift, perk up, boost, encourage, inspirit; informal buck up.

ANTONYMS depress.

– PHRASES **cheer on** *my friends were there to cheer me on* **encourage,** urge on, spur on, drive on, motivate, inspire, fire (up), inspirit, light a fire under. **cheer up** *Leslie cheered up as soon as the grades were posted* **perk up,** brighten (up), become more cheerful, liven up, rally, revive, bounce back, take heart; informal buck up.

cheerful ▶ adjective **1** *he arrived looking cheerful* **happy,** jolly, merry, bright, glad, sunny, joyful, joyous, lighthearted, in good/high spirits, sparkling, bubbly, exuberant, buoyant, ebullient, elated, gleeful; breezy, cheery, jaunty, animated, radiant, smiling; jovial, genial, good-humored; carefree, unworried, untroubled, without a care in the world; informal upbeat, chipper, chirpy, peppy, bright-eyed and bushy-tailed, full of beans; dated gay; formal blithe, jocund.
ANTONYMS sad.
2 *a cheerful room* **pleasant,** attractive, agreeable, cheering, bright, sunny, happy, friendly, welcoming.
ANTONYMS drab, dreary.

cheerless ▶ adjective *visitors often remarked that the interior of the castle was more cheerless than they had expected* **gloomy,** dreary, dull, dismal, bleak, drab, somber, dark, dim, dingy, funereal; austere, stark, bare, comfortless, unwelcoming, uninviting; miserable, wretched, joyless, depressing, disheartening, dispiriting.

cheers ▶ exclamation informal *from Bertie's table we could hear the clinking of glasses and a rousing "Cheers!"* **here's to you,** good health, your health, skol, prosit, salut, l'chaim; informal bottoms up, down the hatch, here's mud in your eye.

cheery ▶ adjective See CHEERFUL (sense 1).

chef ▶ noun *he was the ambasssador's personal chef* **cook,** food preparer; chef de cuisine, pastry chef, sous-chef, short-order cook, cordon bleu cook; informal cookie.

cherish ▶ verb **1** *a woman he could cherish* **adore,** hold dear, love, dote on, be devoted to, revere, esteem, admire; think the world of, set great store by, hold in high esteem; care for, tend to, look after, protect, preserve, keep safe.
2 *I cherish her letters* **treasure,** prize, value highly, hold dear.
3 *they cherished dreams of glory* **harbor,** entertain, possess, hold (on to), cling to, keep in one's mind, foster, nurture.

cherub ▶ noun **1** *she was borne up to heaven by cherubs* **angel,** seraph.
2 *a cherub of 18 months* **baby,** infant, toddler, little angel, (tiny) tot; literary babe, babe in arms.

chest ▶ noun **1** *a bullet wound in the chest* **breast,** upper body, torso, trunk; technical thorax.
2 *her matronly chest* **bust,** bosom; breasts.
3 *an oak chest* **box,** case, casket, crate, trunk, coffer, strongbox.

– PHRASES **get off one's chest** informal *I've known what really happened for years, and I'd like to finally get it off my chest* **confess,** disclose, divulge, reveal, make known, make public, make a clean breast of, bring into the open, tell all about, get a load off one's mind.

chew ▶ verb *Carolyn chewed a mouthful of toast* munch, chomp, champ, crunch, nibble, gnaw, eat, consume; formal **masticate,** manducate.

– PHRASES **chew over** *go home and chew it over* **meditate on,** ruminate on, think about/over/through, mull over, consider, ponder on, deliberate on, reflect on, muse on, dwell on, give thought to, turn over in one's mind; brood over, puzzle over, rack one's brains about; informal kick around, bat around; formal cogitate about. **chew the fat** informal See CHAT (verb).

chic ▶ adjective *a chic yellow belt* **stylish,** elegant, sophisticated, dressy, smart; fashionable, high-fashion, in vogue, up-to-date, up-to-the-minute, contemporary, à la mode, chi-chi, au courant; dapper, dashing, trim; informal trendy, with it, happening, snappy, snazzy, modish, du jour, in, funky, natty, swish, fly, spiffy, kicky, tony.
ANTONYMS unfashionable.

chicanery ▶ noun *we didn't catch on to his chicanery until it was too late* **trickery,** deception, deceit, deceitfulness, duplicity, dishonesty, deviousness, unscrupulousness, underhandedness, subterfuge, fraud, fraudulence, swindling, cheating, duping, hoodwinking; informal crookedness, monkey business, hanky-panky, shenanigans, skulduggery, monkeyshines; archaic management, knavery.

chide ▶ verb *he wasn't expecting her to chide him right there in front of everyone* **scold,** chastise, upbraid, berate, reprimand, reprove, rebuke, admonish, censure, lambaste, lecture, give someone a piece of one's mind, take to task, rake/haul over the coals; informal tell off, dress down, bawl out, blow up at, give someone an earful, give someone a roasting, give someone a tongue-lashing, come down on someone like a ton of bricks, slap someone's wrist, rap over the knuckles, give someone hell, take to the woodshed, have a go at, give someone what for, chew out, ream out; formal castigate; archaic chasten; rare reprehend. See note at SCOLD.
ANTONYMS praise.

chief ▶ noun **1** *a Wampanoag chief* **leader,** chieftain, grand chief, sachem, sagamore, head, headman, ruler, overlord, master, commander, seigneur, liege lord, liege, potentate, cacique.
2 *the chief of the central bank* **head,** principal, chief executive, chief executive officer; CEO, president, chair, chairman, chairwoman, chairperson, governor, director, manager; employer, proprietor; informal big cheese, big shot, bigwig, skipper, numero uno, honcho, head honcho, boss, padrone.

▶ adjective **1** *the chief rabbi* **head,** leading, principal, premier, highest, foremost, supreme, arch.
ANTONYMS subordinate.
2 *their chief aim* **main,** principal, most important, primary, prime, first, cardinal, central, key, crucial, essential, predominant, preeminent, paramount, overriding, number-one.
ANTONYMS secondary, minor.

chiefly ▶ adverb *we are interested chiefly in waterfront properties* **mainly,** in the main, primarily, principally, predominantly, mostly, for the most part; usually, habitually, typically, commonly, generally, on the whole, largely, by and large, almost always.

child ▶ noun *a well-behaved child | his estate goes directly to his children* **youngster,** little one, boy, girl; baby, newborn, infant, toddler; cherub, angel; schoolboy, schoolgirl; minor, junior, preteen; son, daughter, descendant; informal kid, kiddie, tot, tyke, young 'un, lad, rug rat, ankle-biter; derogatory brat, guttersnipe, urchin, gamin, gamine; literary babe, babe in arms; (**children**) offspring, progeny, issue, brood, descendants.

childbirth ▶ noun *complications during childbirth have been drastically reduced* **labor,** delivery, giving birth, birthing, child-bearing; formal parturition; dated confinement; literary travail; archaic lying-in, accouchement, childbed.

childhood ▶ noun *born into a war-torn environment, they are subject to experiences inappropriate for anyone's childhood* **youth,** early years, early life, infancy, babyhood, boyhood, girlhood, prepubescence, minority; springtime of life, salad days; formal nonage, juvenescence.
ANTONYMS adulthood.

childish ▶ adjective **1** *childish behavior* **immature,** babyish, infantile, juvenile, puerile; silly, inane, jejune, foolish, irresponsible.
ANTONYMS mature.
2 *a round childish face* **childlike,** youthful, young, young-looking, girlish, boyish, baby.
ANTONYMS adult.

childlike ▶ adjective **1** *his grandmother looked almost childlike* **youthful,** young, young-looking, girlish, boyish.
2 *geniuses tend to be rather childlike* **innocent,** artless, guileless, unworldly, unsophisticated, naive, ingenuous, trusting, unsuspicious, unwary, credulous, gullible; unaffected, without airs, uninhibited, natural, spontaneous; informal wet behind the ears.

chill ▶ noun **1** *a chill in the air* **coldness,** chilliness, coolness, iciness, rawness, bitterness, nip.
ANTONYMS warmth.
2 *he had a chill* **a cold,** (the) sniffles, (the) shivers, (the) flu/influenza, a fever; archaic (the) grippe.
3 *the chill in their relations* **unfriendliness,** lack of warmth, lack of understanding, chilliness, coldness, coolness.
ANTONYMS friendliness.
▶ verb **1** *the dessert is best chilled* **make cold,** make colder, cool (down/off); refrigerate, ice.
ANTONYMS warm.
2 *his quiet tone chilled Ruth* **scare,** frighten, petrify, terrify, alarm; make someone's blood run cold, chill to the bone, make someone's flesh crawl; informal scare the pants off; archaic affright.
ANTONYMS comfort, reassure.
▶ adjective *a chill wind* **cold,** chilly, cool, fresh; wintry, frosty, icy, ice-cold, icy-cold, glacial, polar, arctic, raw, bitter, bitterly cold, biting, freezing, frigid, gelid, hypothermic; informal nippy.
– PHRASES **chill out** informal *a place to chill out* See RELAX (sense 1).

chilly ▶ adjective **1** *the weather had turned chilly* **cool,** cold, crisp, fresh, wintry, frosty, brisk, icy, ice-cold, icy-cold, chill, glacial, polar, arctic, raw, bitter, bitterly cold, freezing, frigid, gelid, hypothermic; informal nippy.
ANTONYMS warm.
2 *a chilly reception* **unfriendly,** unwelcoming, cold, cool, frosty, gelid; informal standoffish, offish.
ANTONYMS warm, friendly.

chime ▶ verb **1** *the bells began to chime* **ring,** peal, toll, sound; ding, dong, clang, boom, bong; literary knell.
2 *the clock chimed eight o'clock* **strike,** sound.
▶ noun *the chimes of the bells* **peal,** pealing, ringing, carillon, toll, tolling; ding-dong, clanging, tintinnabulation; literary knell.
– PHRASES **chime in** *"Yes, you do that," Doreen chimed in* **interject,** interpose, interrupt, butt in, cut in, join in.

china ▶ noun **1** *a cup made of fine china* **porcelain.**
2 *a table laid with the best china* **dishes,** plates, cups and saucers, tableware, chinaware, dinner service; chiefly Brit. crockery.

chink ▶ noun *a chink in the curtains* **opening,** gap, space, hole, aperture, crack, fissure, crevice, cranny, cleft, split, slit, slot.
▶ verb *the glasses chinked* **jingle,** jangle, clink, tinkle.

chip ▶ noun **1** *wood chips* **fragment,** sliver, splinter, shaving, paring, flake.
2 *a chip in the glass* **nick,** crack, scratch, notch; flaw, fault.
3 chiefly Brit. *fish and chips* French fries, fries, home fries, frites, pommes frites.
4 *gambling chips* **counter,** token, check.
▶ verb **1** *a stone chipped my windshield* **nick,** crack, scratch; damage.
2 *the plaster had chipped* **break (off),** crack, crumble.
3 *chip the flint to the required shape* **whittle,** hew, chisel, carve.
– PHRASES **chip away at** *chipping away at their defenses* erode, wear down, wear away, whittle down, corrode, gnaw away at. **chip in** *we can afford the new dishwasher if everybody chips in* **contribute,** make a contribution, make a donation, pay; informal fork out, shell out, cough up, kick in.

chirp ▶ verb *winter is officially over when I hear the robins chirping* **tweet,** twitter, cheep, peep, chitter, chirrup, chirr; sing, warble, trill.

chit-chat ▶ noun informal *we ran into each other at the pharmacy and had a little chit-chat* **small talk,** chatter, gossip, chat, chatting, prattle.

chivalrous ▶ adjective **1** *his chivalrous treatment of women* **gallant,** gentlemanly, honorable, respectful, considerate; courteous, polite, gracious, well-mannered, mannerly; archaic gentle.
ANTONYMS rude.
2 *chivalrous pursuits* **knightly,** noble, chivalric; brave, courageous, bold, valiant, valorous, heroic, daring, intrepid.
ANTONYMS cowardly.

chivalry ▶ noun **1** *acts of chivalry* **gallantry,** gentlemanliness, courtesy, courteousness,

politeness, graciousness, mannerliness, good manners.
ANTONYMS rudeness.
2 *the values of chivalry* **knight errantry,** courtly manners, knightliness, courtliness, nobility; bravery, courage, boldness, valour, heroism, daring, intrepidity; bushido.

choice ▶ **noun 1** *it's your choice | freedom of choice* **selection,** election, choosing, picking; decision, say, vote.
2 *you have no other choice* **option,** alternative, possible course of action.
3 *an extensive choice of wines* **range,** variety, selection, assortment.
4 *the critics' choice* **preference,** selection, pick, favorite.
▶ **adjective** *choice plums* **superior,** first-class, first-rate, prime, premier, grade A, best, finest, excellent, select, quality, high-quality, top, top-quality, high-grade, prize, fine, special; hand-picked, carefully chosen; informal tip-top, A1, top-notch, blue-ribbon, blue-chip.
ANTONYMS inferior.

choke ▶ **verb 1** *Christopher started to choke* **gag,** retch, cough, fight for breath.
2 *thick dust choked her* **suffocate,** asphyxiate, smother, stifle.
3 *she had been choked to death* **strangle,** throttle; asphyxiate, suffocate; informal strangulate.
4 *the gutters were choked with leaves* **clog (up),** stop up, block, obstruct, plug, bung up; technical occlude.
5 *the Rangers choked in the playoffs* **underachieve,** underperform, disappoint, lose, collapse, fall apart.
– PHRASES **choke back** *we could see that he was choking back tears* **suppress,** hold back, fight back, bite back, swallow, check, restrain, control, repress, smother, stifle; informal keep a lid on.

choose ▶ **verb 1** *we chose a quiet country inn* **select,** pick (out), opt for, settle on, decide on, fix on, take; appoint, name, nominate, vote for, elect.
2 *I'll stay as long as I choose* **wish,** want, desire, feel/be inclined, please, like, see fit.

choosy ▶ **adjective** *my cat Kiki was never too choosy when it came to leftovers* **fussy,** finicky, fastidious, overparticular, difficult/hard to please, demanding; informal picky, persnickety.

chop ▶ **verb 1** *chop the potatoes into small pieces* **cut up,** cut into pieces, chop up, cube, dice, hash.
2 *they were out back chopping wood* **chop up,** cut up, cut into pieces, hew, split.
3 *four fingers were* ***chopped off*** **sever,** cut off, hack off, slice off, lop off, saw off, shear off.
4 *they chopped down large areas of rain forest* **cut down,** fell, hack down, clear-cut, harvest.
5 *their training courses were chopped* **cut,** ax, abolish, scrap, slash, cancel, terminate, ditch, dump, pull the plug on.

choppy ▶ **adjective** *sailing on choppy waters* **rough,** turbulent, heavy, heaving, stormy, tempestuous, squally; uneven.
ANTONYMS calm.

chore ▶ **noun 1** *he was not accustomed to doing the chores that were now expected of him* **task,** job, duty, errand; (**chores**) work, domestic work, drudgery.
2 informal *spending the afternoon with Millie was a chore* drag, bore, pain.

chortle ▶ **verb** *they were chortling behind their hands, as if we didn't notice* **chuckle,** laugh, giggle, titter, tee-hee, snigger.

chorus ▶ **noun 1** *the chorus sang powerfully* **choir,** ensemble, choral group, choristers, (group of) singers, voices, glee club.
2 *Nancy sang the chorus* **refrain.**
– PHRASES **in chorus** *at least on the library parking issue, we were in chorus* **in unison,** together, simultaneously, as one, united; in concert, in harmony.

christen ▶ **verb 1** *she was christened Sara* **baptize,** name, give the name of, call.
2 *a group who were christened "The Magic Circle"* **call,** name, dub, style, term, designate, label, nickname, give the name of; formal denominate.

chronic ▶ **adjective 1** *a chronic illness* **persistent,** long-standing, long-term; incurable; Medicine immedicable.
ANTONYMS acute.
2 *chronic economic problems* **constant,** continuing, ceaseless, unabating, unending, persistent, long-lasting; severe, serious, acute, grave, dire.
ANTONYMS temporary.
3 *a chronic liar* **inveterate,** hardened, dyed-in-the-wool, incorrigible; compulsive; informal pathological.
ANTONYMS occasional.

> USAGE
> **chronic**
> *Chronic* is often used to mean 'habitual, inveterate,' e.g., *a chronic liar.* Some consider this use incorrect. The precise meaning of *chronic* is 'persisting for a long time,' and it is used chiefly of illnesses or other problems: *more than one million people in the United States have chronic bronchitis.*

chronicle ▶ **noun** *a chronicle of the region's past* **record,** written account, history, annals, archive(s); log, diary, journal.
▶ **verb** *the events that followed have been chronicled* **record,** put on record, write down, set down, document, register, report.

chronological ▶ **adjective** *put these eight historical events in chronological order, beginning with the earliest* **sequential,** consecutive, in sequence, in order (of time).

chubby ▶ **adjective** *look how chubby Dad was as a baby!* **plump,** fat, rotund, portly, dumpy, chunky, well-upholstered, well-rounded; informal roly-poly, tubby, pudgy, blubbery, big-boned, full-figured; zaftig, corn-fed.
ANTONYMS skinny.

chuck ▶ **verb** informal **1** *he chucked the letter onto the table* **throw,** toss, fling, hurl, pitch, cast, lob.
2 *I chucked the old comics* **throw away/out,** discard, dispose of, get rid of, dump, scrap, jettison; informal ditch, junk, deep-six, trash.

3 *Mary chucked him for another guy* **leave,** throw over, finish with, break off with, jilt; informal dump, ditch.

chuckle ▶ verb *Adam chuckled to himself as he drove away* **giggle,** chortle, titter, tee-hee, snicker, snigger.

chum ▶ noun informal *he's having lunch with a few of his old army chums* **friend,** buddy, bud, pal; companion, sidekick, intimate; playmate, classmate, schoolmate, workmate; mate; crony; amigo, compadre.
ANTONYMS enemy, stranger.

chunk ▶ noun *a chunk of cheese* **lump,** hunk, wedge, block, slab, square, nugget, brick, cube, bar, cake.

church ▶ noun 1 *a village church* **place of worship,** house of God, house of worship; cathedral, abbey, chapel, basilica; synagogue, mosque.
2 *the Methodist Church* **denomination,** ecclesial community; creed, faith.

churlish ▶ adjective *it seemed churlish to refuse her invitation* **rude,** ill-mannered, ill-bred, discourteous, impolite, unmannerly, uncivil, unchivalrous; inconsiderate, uncharitable, surly, sullen.
ANTONYMS polite.

churn ▶ verb 1 *Mae churned the milk* **stir,** agitate, beat, whip, whisk.
2 *the sea churned* **heave,** boil, swirl, toss, seethe; literary roil.
3 *propellers churned up the water* **disturb,** stir up, agitate; literary roil.
– PHRASES **churn out** *they churn out at least twenty romance novels a year* **produce,** make, turn out; informal crank out.

cigarette ▶ noun *he's outside, having a cigarette* informal smoke, butt, ciggie/ciggy, cancer stick, coffin nail; Brit. informal fag.

cinema ▶ noun 1 chiefly Brit. *the local cinema* **movie theater,** theater, multiplex, movie house; historical nickelodeon.
2 *Italian cinema* **films,** movies, pictures, motion pictures.

cipher ▶ noun 1 *information in cipher* **code,** secret writing, cryptograph, cryptogram.
2 dated *a row of ciphers* **zero,** o, nil, naught/nought.

circle ▶ noun 1 *a circle of gold stars* **ring,** band, hoop, circlet; halo, disc; technical annulus.
2 *her circle of friends* **group,** set, company, coterie, clique; crowd, band; informal gang, bunch, crew.
3 *I don't move in such illustrious circles* **sphere,** world, milieu; society.
▶ verb 1 *seagulls circled above* **wheel,** move around, revolve, rotate, whirl, spiral.
2 *satellites circling the earth* **go around,** travel around, circumnavigate; orbit, revolve around.
3 *the abbey was circled by a wall* **surround,** encircle, ring, enclose, encompass; literary gird.

circuit ▶ noun 1 *two circuits of the course* **lap,** turn, round, circle.
2 *a racing circuit* **track,** racetrack, raceway, running track, course.
3 *the judge's circuit* **tour,** tour of duty, rounds, regular journey; informal beat.

circuitous ▶ adjective 1 *a circuitous route* **roundabout,** indirect, winding, meandering, serpentine, tortuous.
ANTONYMS direct, straight.
2 *a circuitous discussion* **indirect,** oblique, roundabout, circumlocutory, periphrastic.
ANTONYMS to the point.

circular ▶ adjective *a circular window* **round,** disk-shaped, ring-shaped, annular. See note at ROUND.
▶ noun *handing out circulars at the mall* **leaflet,** pamphlet, handbill, flyer, mailer, folder.

circulate ▶ verb 1 *the news was widely circulated* **spread (around/about),** communicate, disseminate, make known, make public, broadcast, publicize, advertise, propagate, promulgate; distribute, give out, pass around.
2 *fresh air circulates freely* **flow,** course, move around.
3 *they circulated among their guests* **socialize,** mingle.

circumference ▶ noun 1 *the circumference of the pit* **perimeter,** border, boundary; edge, rim, verge, margin, fringe; literary marge.
2 *the circumference of his arm* **girth,** width.

circumlocution ▶ noun *when you've finished your circumlocution, maybe you could just get to the point* **periphrasis,** discursiveness, long-windedness, verbosity, verbiage, wordiness, prolixity, redundancy, pleonasm, tautology, repetitiveness, repetitiousness.

circumscribe ▶ verb *the power of the local agency has been circumscribed by the national organization* **restrict,** limit, keep within bounds, curb, confine, restrain; regulate, control.

CHOOSE THE RIGHT WORD

circumscribe, encircle, enclose, encompass, envelop, surround

Strictly speaking, to **circumscribe** is to draw a line around something to mark its limits or boundary (*a square circumscribed by a circle*). Beyond the realm of geometry, however, it suggests something that is hemmed in on all sides (*a lake circumscribed by mountains*). **Encompass** is used when something is set within a circle or within limits (*a road that encompassed the grounds of the estate; a view that encompassed the harbor*). **Surround** is a less formal word for *circumscribe*, but it can also refer to an undesirable, threatening, or dangerous situation (*surrounded by angry demonstrators; surrounded by skyscrapers*). **Encircle** is similar to *surround* in meaning, but it suggests a tight or quite circular clustering around a central object (*a bowl of fruit encircled by flowers*) or a deliberate attempt to surround someone or something for a definite reason (*to encircle the enemy camp*). **Envelop** is the right word if something is surrounded to the point where it can barely be seen (*a lonely figure enveloped in fog*) or if it is surrounded by layers or folds of an amorphous material (*enveloped in soft cotton to prevent breakage*). **Enclose** is very similar to *envelop*, but it suggests that something has been especially designed to fit around something else for protection or containment (*a ship model enclosed in a glass case*).

circumspect ▶ adjective *she would have to be circumspect in her dealings with Catherine* **cautious,** wary, careful, chary, guarded, on one's guard; watchful, alert, attentive, heedful, vigilant, leery; informal cagey, playing one's cards close to one's chest. See note at **VIGILANT**.
ANTONYMS unguarded.

circumstances ▶ plural noun **1** *favorable economic circumstances* **situation,** conditions, state of affairs, position; events, turn of events, incidents, occurrences, happenings; factors, context, background, environment.
2 *Jane explained* ***the circumstances*** *to him* **the facts,** the details, the particulars, how things stand, the lay of the land; informal what's what, the score.
3 *reduced circumstances* **financial position,** lot, lifestyle; resources, means, finances, income.

circumstantial ▶ adjective **1** *they have only circumstantial evidence* **indirect,** inferred, deduced, conjectural; inconclusive, unprovable.
2 *a circumstantial account* **detailed,** particularized, comprehensive, thorough, exhaustive; explicit, specific.

citadel ▶ noun *they were prisoners within their own citadel* **fortress,** fort, stronghold, fortification, castle; archaic hold.

citation ▶ noun **1** *a citation from an eighteenth-century text* **quotation,** quote, extract, excerpt, passage, line; reference, allusion.
2 *a citation for gallantry* **commendation,** mention, honorable mention.
3 Law *a traffic citation* **summons, ticket,** subpoena, writ, court order.

cite ▶ verb **1** *cite the passage in full* **quote,** reproduce.
2 *he cited the case of Roe v. Wade* **refer to,** make reference to, mention, allude to, adduce, instance; specify, name.
3 *he has been cited many times* **commend,** pay tribute to, praise.
4 Law *the writ cited four of the signatories* **summon,** summons, serve with a summons, serve with a writ, subpoena.

citizen ▶ noun **1** *a Japanese citizen* **national,** subject, passport holder, native.
2 *the citizens of Amsterdam* **inhabitant,** resident, native, townsman, townswoman, townsperson, denizen; taxpayer; burgher.

city ▶ noun *Phoenix is my favorite city in the Southwest* **town,** municipality, metropolis, megalopolis, megacity; conurbation, urban area, metropolitan area, urban municipality; borough, township; informal burg.

civic ▶ adjective *they encourage their children to participate in civic affairs* **municipal,** city, town, urban, metropolitan; public, civil, community, local.

civil ▶ adjective **1** *a civil marriage* **secular,** nonreligious, lay; formal laic.
ANTONYMS religious.
2 *civil aviation* **nonmilitary,** civilian.
ANTONYMS military.
3 *a civil war* **internal,** domestic, interior, national.
ANTONYMS international, foreign.
4 *he behaved in a civil manner* **polite,** courteous, well-mannered, well-bred, chivalrous, gallant; cordial, genial, pleasant, affable; gentlemanly, ladylike.
ANTONYMS discourteous, rude.

civilian ▶ noun *family members and other civilians were quickly evacuated from the post* **noncombatant,** nonmilitary person, ordinary citizen, private citizen; informal civvy.

civility ▶ noun **1** *he treated me with civility* **courtesy,** courteousness, politeness, good manners, graciousness, consideration, respect, politesse, comity.
ANTONYMS disrespect, rudeness.
2 *she didn't waste time on civilities* **polite remark,** politeness, courtesy; formality.

civilization ▶ noun **1** *a higher stage of civilization* **human development,** advancement, progress, enlightenment, culture, refinement, sophistication.
2 *ancient civilizations* **culture,** society, nation, people.

civilize ▶ verb *they were trying to civilize people who strongly resented the intrusion* **enlighten,** edify, improve, educate, instruct, refine, cultivate, polish, socialize, humanize.

civilized ▶ adjective *his civilized behavior | a civilized society* **polite,** courteous, well-mannered, civil, gentlemanly, ladylike, mannerly; cultured, cultivated, refined, polished, sophisticated; enlightened, educated, advanced, developed.
ANTONYMS rude, unsophisticated.

clad ▶ adjective *he's clad in a hunting outfit* **dressed,** clothed, attired, got up, garbed, rigged out, togged out, costumed; archaic appareled; (**clad in**) wearing, sporting.

claim ▶ verb **1** *Davies claimed that she was lying* **assert,** declare, profess, maintain, state, hold, affirm, avow; argue, contend, allege; formal aver.
2 *no one claimed the items* **lay claim to,** assert ownership of, formally request.
3 *you can claim compensation* **request,** ask for, apply for; demand, exact.
4 *the fire claimed four lives* **take,** result in the loss of, cause the loss of.
▶ noun **1** *her claim that she was unaware of the problem* **assertion,** declaration, profession, affirmation, avowal, protestation; contention, allegation.
2 *a claim for damages* **request,** application; demand, petition.
3 *we have first* ***claim on*** *their assets* **entitlement to,** title to, right to.

claimant ▶ noun *the claimant was a passenger on the derailed train* **applicant,** candidate, supplicant; petitioner, plaintiff, litigant, appellant.

clairvoyance ▶ noun *I'm not sure how much confidence I have in Miss ZuZu's clairvoyance* **ESP,** extrasensory perception, sixth sense, psychic powers, second sight; telepathy.

clamber ▶ verb *Frankie clambered up to the top bunk* **scramble,** climb, scrabble, claw one's way.

clammy ▶ adjective **1** *his clammy hands* **moist,** damp, sweaty, sticky; slimy, slippery.
ANTONYMS dry.
2 *the clammy atmosphere* **damp,** dank, wet; humid, close, muggy, heavy.

clamor ▶ noun **1** *her voice rose above the clamor* **din,** racket, rumpus, loud noise, uproar, tumult, shouting, yelling, screaming, roaring; commotion, brouhaha, hue and cry, hubbub, hullabaloo, hoopla.
2 *the clamor for her resignation* **demand(s),** call(s), urging.
3 *the clamor of the workers* **protests,** complaints, outcry.
▶ verb **1** *clamoring crowds* **yell,** shout loudly, bay, scream, roar.
2 *scientists are clamoring for a ban* **demand,** call for, press for, push for, lobby for.

clamp ▶ noun *if the clamp is too loose, its function becomes useless* **brace,** vice, press, clasp; Music capo (tasto); Climbing jumar.
▶ verb **1** *the sander is clamped on to the workbench* **fasten,** secure, fix, attach; screw, bolt.
2 *a pipe was clamped between his teeth* **clench,** grip, hold, press, clasp.
– PHRASES **clamp down on** *they promised to clamp down on the drug trafficking in this neighborhood* **suppress,** prevent, stop, put a stop/end to, stamp out; crack down on, limit, restrict, control, keep in check.

clampdown ▶ noun informal *Barone's clampdown on graft rooted out a lot of unexpected dirt in the department* **suppression,** prevention, stamping out; crackdown, restriction, restraint, curb, check.

clan ▶ noun **1** *the Macleod clan* **group of families,** sept; family, house, dynasty, tribe; Anthropology kinship group.
2 *a clan of art collectors* **group,** set, circle, clique, coterie; crowd, band; informal gang, bunch.

clandestine ▶ adjective *their clandestine meetings* **secret,** covert, furtive, surreptitious, stealthy, cloak-and-dagger, hole-and-corner, closet, backstairs, backroom; hush-hush. See note at SECRET.

clang ▶ noun *the clang of the church bells* **reverberation,** ringing, ring, ding-dong, bong, peal, chime, toll.
▶ verb *the huge bells clanged* **reverberate,** resound, ring, bong, peal, chime, toll.

clank ▶ noun *the clank of rusty chains* **jangling,** clanging, rattling, clinking, jingling; clang, jangle, rattle, clangor, clink, jingle.
▶ verb *I could hear the chain clanking* **jangle,** rattle, clink, clang, jingle.

clannish ▶ adjective *your daughter is part of a very clannish group of girls* **cliquey,** cliquish, insular, exclusive; unfriendly, unwelcoming.

clap ▶ verb **1** *the audience clapped* **applaud,** clap one's hands, give someone a round of applause, put one's hands together; informal give someone a big hand.
2 *he clapped Owen on the back* **slap,** strike, hit, smack, thump; pat; informal whack, thwack.
3 *the dove clapped its wings* **flap,** beat, flutter.
▶ noun **1** *everybody gave him a clap* **round of applause,** handclap; informal hand.
2 *a clap on the shoulder* **slap,** blow, smack, thump; pat; informal whack, thwack.
3 *a clap of thunder* **crack,** crash, bang, boom; thunderclap.

claptrap ▶ noun *sentimental claptrap* See NONSENSE (sense 1 of the noun).

clarify ▶ verb **1** *their report clarified the situation* **make clear,** shed/throw light on, elucidate, illuminate; **explain,** explicate, define, spell out, clear up.
ANTONYMS confuse.
2 *clarify the butter* **purify,** refine; filter, fine.

CHOOSE THE RIGHT WORD

clarify, construe, elucidate, explain, explicate, interpret

When a biology teacher gets up in front of a class and tries to **explain** how two brown-eyed parents can produce a blue-eyed child, the purpose is to make an entire process or sequence of events understandable. In a less formal sense, to *explain* is to make a verbal attempt to justify certain actions or to make them understood (*she tried to explain why she was so late*). That same teacher might **clarify** a particular exam question that almost everyone in the class got wrong—a word that means to make an earlier event, situation, or statement clear. **Elucidate** is a more formal word meaning to *clarify*, but where the root of the latter refers to clearness, the root of the former refers to light; to *elucidate* is to shed light on something through explanation, illustration, etc. (*the principal's comments were an attempt to elucidate the school's policy on cheating*). A teacher who **explicates** something discusses a complex subject in a point-by-point manner (*to explicate a poem*). If a personal judgment is inserted in making such an explication, the correct word is **interpret** (*to interpret a poem's symbolic meanings*). To **construe** is to make a careful interpretation of something, especially where the meaning is ambiguous. For example, when a class misbehaves in front of a visitor, the teacher is likely to *construe* that behavior as an attempt to cause embarrassment or ridicule.

clarity ▶ noun **1** *the clarity of his account* **lucidity,** lucidness, clearness, coherence; formal perspicuity.
ANTONYMS vagueness, obscurity.
2 *the clarity of the image* **sharpness,** clearness, crispness, definition.
ANTONYMS blurriness.
3 *the crystal clarity of the water* **limpidity,** limpidness, clearness, transparency, translucence, pellucidity.
ANTONYMS murkiness, opacity.

clash ▶ noun **1** *clashes between armed gangs* **confrontation,** skirmish, fight, battle, engagement, encounter, conflict.
2 *an angry clash* **argument,** altercation,

confrontation, shouting match; contretemps, quarrel, disagreement, dispute, run-in.
3 *a clash of tweeds and a striped shirt* **mismatch,** discordance, discord, lack of harmony.
4 *the clash of cymbals* **striking,** bang, clang, crash.
▶ **verb 1** *protesters clashed with police* **fight,** skirmish, contend, come to blows, come into conflict; do battle.
2 *the mayor clashed with union leaders* **disagree,** differ, wrangle, dispute, cross swords, lock horns, be at loggerheads.
3 *her red scarf clashed with her coat* **be incompatible,** not match, not go, be discordant.
4 *she clashed the cymbals together* **bang,** strike, clang, crash.

clasp ▶ **verb 1** *Ruth clasped his hand* **grasp,** grip, clutch, hold tightly; take hold of, seize, grab.
2 *he clasped Joanne in his arms* **embrace,** hug, enfold, fold, envelop; hold, squeeze.
▶ **noun 1** *a gold clasp* **fastener,** fastening, catch, clip, pin; buckle, hasp.
2 *his tight clasp* **embrace,** hug, cuddle; grip, grasp.

class ▶ **noun 1** *a hotel of the first class* **category,** grade, rating, classification, group, grouping.
2 *a new class of heart drug* **kind,** sort, type, variety, genre, brand; species, genus, breed, strain, stripe.
3 *the middle class* **social division,** social stratum, rank, level, echelon, group, grouping, income group; social status; dated estate; archaic condition.
4 *a math class* **lesson,** period; seminar, tutorial, workshop, study group.
5 informal *a woman of class* **style,** stylishness, elegance, chic, sophistication, taste, refinement, quality, excellence.
▶ **verb** *the 12-seater is classed as a commercial vehicle* **classify,** categorize, group, grade; order, sort, codify; bracket, designate, label, pigeonhole.
▶ **adjective** informal *a class player* **classy,** decent, gracious, respectable, noble.

classic ▶ **adjective 1** *the classic work on the subject* **definitive,** authoritative; outstanding, first-rate, first-class, best, finest, excellent, superior, masterly.
2 *a classic example of Norman design* **typical,** archetypal, quintessential, vintage; model, representative, perfect, prime, textbook.
ANTONYMS atypical.
3 *a classic style* **simple,** elegant, understated; traditional, timeless, ageless.
▶ **noun** *a classic of the genre* **definitive example,** model, epitome, paradigm, exemplar; great work, masterpiece.

classical ▶ **adjective 1** *classical mythology* ancient Greek, Hellenic, Attic; Latin, ancient Roman.
2 *classical music* **traditional,** long-established; serious, highbrow.
ANTONYMS modern.
3 *a classical style* **simple,** pure, restrained, plain, austere; well-proportioned, harmonious, balanced, symmetrical, elegant.

classification ▶ **noun 1** *the classification of diseases* **categorization,** categorizing, classifying, grouping, grading, ranking, organization, sorting, codification, systematization.
2 *a series of classifications* **category,** class, group, grouping, grade, grading, ranking.

classify ▶ **verb** *we can classify the students into two groups* **categorize,** group, grade, rank, rate, order, organize, range, sort, type, codify, bracket, systematize, systemize; catalog, list, file, index, lump.

clatter ▶ **verb** *the cups clattered on the tray* **rattle,** clank, clink, clunk, clang.

clause ▶ **noun** *a new clause in the treaty* **section,** paragraph, article, subsection; stipulation, condition, proviso, rider.

claw ▶ **noun 1** *a bird's claw* **talon,** nail; technical unguis.
2 *a crab's claw* **pincer,** nipper; technical chela.
▶ **verb** *her fingers clawed his shoulders* **scratch,** lacerate, tear, rip, scrape, graze, dig into.

clay ▶ **noun 1** *the soil is mainly clay* **earth,** soil, loam.
2 *potter's clay* china clay, kaolin, adobe, ball clay, argil, pug; fireclay.

clean ▶ **adjective 1** *keep the wound clean* **washed,** scrubbed, cleansed, cleaned; spotless, unsoiled, unstained, unsullied, unblemished, immaculate, pristine, dirt-free; hygienic, sanitary, disinfected, sterilized, sterile, aseptic, decontaminated; laundered; informal squeaky clean, as clean as a whistle.
ANTONYMS dirty.
2 *a clean sheet of paper* **blank,** empty, clear, plain; unused, new, pristine, fresh, unmarked.
ANTONYMS used.
3 *clean air* **pure,** clear, fresh, crisp, refreshing; unpolluted, uncontaminated.
ANTONYMS polluted.
4 *a clean life* **virtuous,** good, upright, upstanding; honorable, respectable, reputable, decent, righteous, moral, exemplary; innocent, pure, chaste; informal squeaky clean.
ANTONYMS guilty.
5 *the firm is clean* **innocent,** guiltless, blameless, guilt-free, crime-free, above suspicion; informal squeaky clean.
ANTONYMS dirty, polluted.
6 *a good clean fight* **fair,** honest, sporting, sportsmanlike, honorable, according to the rules; informal on the level.
ANTONYMS dirty, unfair.
7 informal *they are trying to stay clean* **sober,** teetotal, dry, nondrinking; **drug-free,** off drugs; informal on the wagon.
8 *a clean cut* **neat,** smooth, crisp, straight, precise.
ANTONYMS ragged.
9 *a clean break* **complete,** thorough, total, absolute, conclusive, decisive, final, irrevocable.
ANTONYMS partial.
10 *clean lines* **simple,** elegant, graceful, streamlined, smooth.
ANTONYMS complex, elaborate.
▶ **adverb** informal *I clean forgot* **completely,** entirely, totally, fully, quite, utterly, absolutely.
▶ **verb 1** *Dad cleaned the windows* **wash,** cleanse, wipe, sponge, scrub, mop, rinse, scour, swab, hose down, sluice (down), disinfect; shampoo;

literary lave.
ANTONYMS dirty, soil.
2 *I got my clothes cleaned* **launder,** dry-clean.
3 *she cleaned the fish* **gut,** draw, dress; formal eviscerate.
– PHRASES **clean out** informal *those grifters cleaned him out* **bankrupt,** ruin, make insolvent, make penniless, wipe out. **come clean** informal *if you don't come clean, they're going to pin all of this on Kerry* **tell the truth,** tell all, make a clean breast of it; confess, own up, admit guilt, admit to one's crimes/sins; informal fess up.

cleanse ▶ verb **1** *the wound was cleansed* **clean (up),** wash, bathe, rinse, disinfect.
2 *cleansing the environment of traces of lead* **rid,** clear, free, purify, purge.

clear ▶ adjective **1** *clear instructions* **understandable,** comprehensible, intelligible, plain, uncomplicated, explicit, lucid, coherent, simple, straightforward, unambiguous, clear-cut, crystal clear; formal perspicuous.
ANTONYMS vague.
2 *a clear case of harassment* **obvious,** evident, plain, crystal clear; sure, definite, unmistakable, manifest, indisputable, patent, incontrovertible, irrefutable, beyond doubt, beyond question; palpable, visible, discernible, conspicuous, overt, blatant, glaring; as plain as day, as plain as the nose on one's face.
ANTONYMS vague, possible.
3 *clear water* **transparent,** limpid, pellucid, translucent, crystal clear; unclouded.
ANTONYMS murky, opaque.
4 *a clear blue sky* **bright,** cloudless, unclouded, without a cloud in the sky.
ANTONYMS cloudy.
5 *her clear complexion* **unblemished,** spot-free.
ANTONYMS spotty, pimply.
6 *Rosa's clear voice* **distinct,** bell-like, as clear as a bell.
ANTONYMS muffled.
7 *the road was clear | a clear view* **unobstructed,** unblocked, passable, unrestricted, open, unhindered.
ANTONYMS limited, obstructed.
8 *a clear conscience* **untroubled,** undisturbed, unperturbed, unconcerned, having no qualms; peaceful, at peace, tranquil, serene, calm, easy.
ANTONYMS guilty.
▶ adverb **1** *stand clear of the doors* **away from,** apart from, at a (safe) distance from, out of contact with.
2 *Tommy's voice came loud and clear* **distinctly,** clearly, as clear as a bell, plainly, audibly.
3 *he has time to get clear away* **completely,** entirely, fully, wholly, totally, utterly; informal clean.
▶ verb **1** *the sky cleared briefly* **brighten (up),** lighten, clear up, become bright/brighter, become light/lighter, become sunny.
2 *the drizzle had cleared* **disappear,** go away, end; peter out, fade, wear off, decrease, lessen, diminish.
3 *together they cleared the table* **empty,** unload, unburden, strip.
4 *clearing drains* **unblock,** unstop.
5 *staff cleared the building* **evacuate,** empty; leave.
6 *Karen cleared the dirty dishes* **remove,** take away, carry away, tidy up.
7 *I cleared the bar on my first attempt* **go over,** pass over, sail over; jump (over), vault (over), leap (over), hurdle.
8 *he was cleared by an appeals court* **acquit,** declare innocent, find not guilty; absolve, exonerate; informal let off (the hook); formal exculpate.
9 *I was cleared to work on the atomic project* **authorize,** give permission, permit, allow, pass, accept, endorse, license, sanction, give approval, give consent; informal OK, give the OK, give the thumbs up, give the green light, give the go-ahead.
10 *I cleared $50,000 profit* **net,** make/realize a profit of, take home, pocket; gain, earn, make, get, bring in, pull in.
– PHRASES **clear out 1** informal *we were told to clear out immediately* See LEAVE[1] (sense 1).
2 *we cleared out the junk room* **empty (out);** tidy (up), clean up, clear up, declutter.
3 *clear out the old equipment* **get rid of,** throw out/away, discard, dispose of, dump, scrap, jettison; informal chuck (out), deep-six, ditch, trash. **clear up 1** *I hope it clears up before the party* See CLEAR (sense 1 of the verb).
2 *we've cleared up the problem* **solve,** resolve, straighten out, find an/the answer to; get to the bottom of, explain; informal crack, figure out.

clearance ▶ noun **1** *slum clearance* **removal,** clearing, demolition.
2 *you must have clearance to enter* **authorization,** permission, consent, approval, blessing, leave, sanction, license, dispensation, assent, agreement, endorsement; informal the green light, the go-ahead, the thumbs up, the OK, the say-so.
3 *the clearance of a debt* **repayment,** payment, paying (off), settling, discharge.
4 *there is plenty of clearance* **space,** room, room to spare, margin, leeway.

clear-cut ▶ adjective *a clear-cut objective* **definite,** distinct, clear, well-defined, precise, specific, explicit, unambiguous, unequivocal, black and white, cut and dried.
ANTONYMS vague.

clearly ▶ adverb **1** *write clearly* **intelligibly,** plainly, distinctly, comprehensibly, with clarity; legibly, audibly; formal perspicuously.
2 *clearly, substantial changes are needed* **obviously,** evidently, patently, unquestionably, undoubtedly, without doubt, indubitably, plainly, undeniably, incontrovertibly, irrefutably, doubtless, it goes without saying, needless to say.

USAGE

clearly

Exaggerators like this word, along with its cousins (*obviously, undeniably, undoubtedly,* and the like). Often a statement prefaced with one of these words is conclusory, and sometimes even exceedingly dubious. As a result—though some readers don't consciously realize it—*clearly* and its ilk are 'weasel words'—that is, unnecessary words that supposedly intensify the meaning of a statement, but actually weaken it. Just how much *clearly* can weaken a statement is evident in the following example, in which the author uses the word to buttress a claim about his own state of mind: "Clearly, I am not to be convinced that this is a small matter." (Stephen White, *The Written Word*; 1984.) — **BG**

cleave[1] ▶ verb **1** *cleaving wood for the fire* **split (open)**, cut (up), hew, hack, chop up; literary rive.
2 *cleaving a path through the traffic* **plow,** drive, bulldoze, carve.

cleave[2] ▶ verb
– PHRASES **cleave to** literary **1** *her tongue clove to the roof of her mouth* **stick (fast)**, adhere, be attached. **2** *cleaving too closely to Moscow's line* **adhere to,** hold to, abide by, be loyal to, be faithful to.

cleaver ▶ noun *the butcher's cleaver* **chopper,** hatchet, ax, knife; butcher's knife, kitchen knife.

cleft ▶ noun **1** *a deep cleft in the rocks* **split,** slit, crack, fissure, crevice, rift, break, fracture, rent, breach.
2 *the cleft in his chin* **dimple**.
▶ adjective *a cleft tail* **split,** divided, cloven, bifid.

clemency ▶ noun *a fallen dictator who now seeks the clemency he withheld from others* **mercy,** mercifulness, leniency, mildness, indulgence, quarter; compassion, humanity, pity, sympathy. See note at MERCY.
ANTONYMS ruthlessness.

clench ▶ verb **1** *he stood there clenching his hands* **squeeze together,** clamp together, close/shut tightly; make into a fist.
2 *he clenched the iron bar* **grip,** grasp, grab, clutch, clasp, hold tightly, seize, press, squeeze.

clergy ▶ noun *a group of clergy who want to promote religious tolerance* **clerics,** clergymen, clergywomen, churchmen, churchwomen, priests, ecclesiastics, men/women of God; ministry, priesthood, holy orders, the church, the cloth.
ANTONYMS laity.

clerical ▶ adjective **1** *typing, filing, and other clerical jobs* **office,** desk, back-room; administrative, secretarial; white-collar.
2 *her clerical duties as the associate pastor* **ecclesiastical,** church, priestly, religious, spiritual, sacerdotal; holy, divine.
ANTONYMS secular.

clever ▶ adjective **1** *a clever young woman* **intelligent,** bright, smart, astute, sharp, quick-witted, shrewd; talented, gifted, brilliant, capable, able, competent, apt; educated, learned, knowledgeable, wise; informal brainy, clueful, savvy.
ANTONYMS stupid.
2 *a clever scheme* **ingenious,** canny, cunning, crafty, artful, slick, neat.
ANTONYMS ill-advised, foolish.
3 *she was clever with her hands* **skillful,** dexterous, adroit, adept, deft, nimble, handy; skilled, talented, gifted.
4 *a clever remark* **witty,** amusing, droll, humorous, funny.
ANTONYMS witless.

click ▶ noun *the click of the timer* **clack,** snap, pop, tick; clink.
▶ verb **1** *cameras clicked* **snap,** clack, tick, pop; clink.
2 informal *that night it clicked* **become clear,** fall into place, come home, make sense, dawn, register, get through, sink in.
3 informal *we just clicked* **take to each other**, get along, be compatible, be like-minded, feel a rapport, see eye to eye; informal hit it off, be on the same wavelength.
4 informal *this issue hasn't clicked with the voters* **go down well,** prove popular, be a hit, succeed.

client ▶ noun *the waiting room was designed to put the clients at ease* **customer,** buyer, purchaser, shopper, consumer, user; patient; patron, regular; **(clients)** clientele, patronage, public, market; Law vendee.

cliff ▶ noun *the cliffs of the Southwest are breathtaking* **precipice,** rock face, crag, bluff, ridge, escarpment, scar, scarp, ledge, overhang.

climate ▶ noun **1** *the mild climate* **weather conditions,** weather; atmospheric conditions.
2 *they come from a colder climate* **region,** area, zone, country, place; literary clime.
3 *the political climate* **atmosphere,** mood, feeling, ambience, tenor; tendency, ethos, attitude; milieu; informal vibe(s).

climax ▶ noun *the climax of his career* **peak,** pinnacle, height, high(est) point, top; acme, zenith; culmination, crowning point, crown, crest; highlight, high spot, high-water mark.
ANTONYMS nadir.
▶ verb *the event will climax with a concert* **culminate,** peak, reach a pinnacle, come to a crescendo, come to a head.

climb ▶ verb **1** *we climbed the hill* **ascend,** mount, scale, scramble up, clamber up, shinny up; go up, walk up; conquer, gain.
ANTONYMS descend.
2 *the plane climbed* **rise,** ascend, go up, gain altitude.
ANTONYMS descend, dive.
3 *the road climbs steeply* **slope upward,** rise, go uphill, incline upward.
ANTONYMS drop.
4 *the shares climbed to $10.77* **increase,** rise, go up; shoot up, soar, rocket.
ANTONYMS decrease, fall.
5 *he climbed through the ranks* **advance,** rise, move up, progress, work one's way (up).
6 *he climbed out of his car* **clamber,** scramble; step.
▶ noun *a steep climb* **ascent,** clamber.
ANTONYMS descent.
– PHRASES **climb down** *Sandy climbed down the ladder* **descend,** go/come down, move down, shinny down.

clinch ▶ verb **1** *he clinched the deal* **secure,** settle, conclude, close, pull off, bring off, complete, confirm, seal, finalize; informal sew up, wrap up.
2 *these findings clinched the matter* **settle,** decide, determine; resolve; informal sort out.
3 *Wisconsin State clinched the title* **win,** secure; be victorious, come first, triumph, prevail.
ANTONYMS lose.
4 *the boxers clinched* **grapple,** wrestle, struggle, scuffle.

cling ▶ verb *rice grains tend to cling together* **stick,** adhere, hold, cohere, bond, bind.
– PHRASES **cling (on) to 1** *she clung to him* **hold on to,** clutch, grip, grasp, clasp, attach oneself to, hang on to; embrace, hug. **2** *they clung to their beliefs* **adhere to,** hold to, stick to, stand by, abide by, cherish, remain true to, have faith in; informal swear by, stick with.

clinic ▶ noun *we took Ralph to the clinic for stitches* **medical center,** health center, doctor's office.

clinical ▶ adjective **1** *he seemed so clinical* **detached,** impersonal, dispassionate, objective, uninvolved, distant, remote, aloof, removed, cold, indifferent, neutral, unsympathetic, unfeeling, unemotional.
ANTONYMS emotional.
2 *the room was clinical* **plain,** simple, unadorned, unembellished, stark, austere, spartan, bleak, bare; clean; functional, utilitarian, basic, institutional, impersonal, characterless.
ANTONYMS luxurious.

clip[1] ▶ noun **1** *a briefcase clip* **fastener,** clasp, hasp, catch, hook, buckle, lock.
2 *a mother-of-pearl clip* **brooch,** pin, badge.
3 *his clip was empty* **magazine,** cartridge, cylinder.
▶ verb *he clipped the pages together* **fasten,** attach, fix, join; pin, staple, tack.

clip[2] ▶ verb **1** *I clipped the hedge* **trim,** prune, cut, snip, shorten, crop, shear, pare; lop; neaten, shape.
2 *clip the coupon below* **remove,** cut out, snip out, tear out, detach.
3 *his trailer clipped a parked van* **hit,** strike, touch, graze, glance off, run into.
4 *Mom clipped his ear* **hit,** cuff, strike, smack, slap, box; informal clout, whack, wallop, clobber, sock.
▶ noun **1** *I gave the dog a clip* **trim,** cut, crop, haircut; shear.
2 *a film clip* **extract,** excerpt, snippet, cutting, fragment; trailer.
3 informal *a clip to the ear* **smack,** cuff, slap; informal clout, whack, wallop, sock.
4 informal *the truck went at a good clip* **speed,** rate, pace, velocity; informal lick.
– PHRASES **clip someone's wings** *if you try to clip her wings, neither one of you will ever be happy* **restrict someone's freedom,** impose limits on, keep under control, stand in the way of; obstruct, impede, frustrate, thwart, fetter, hamstring, handcuff.

clique ▶ noun *almost no one from her clique showed up at the reunion* **coterie,** set, circle, ring, in-crowd, group; club, society, fraternity, sorority; cabal, caucus; informal gang.

cloak ▶ noun **1** *the cloak over his shoulders* **cape,** poncho, serape, shawl, mantle, wrap, pelisse, burnoose, cope, robe, cowl, djellaba, tippet; cassock, chasuble, pallium; historical cardinal.
2 *a cloak of secrecy* **cover,** veil, mantle, shroud, screen, mask, shield, blanket.
▶ verb *a peak cloaked in mist* **conceal,** hide, cover, veil, shroud, mask, obscure, cloud; envelop, swathe, surround.

clock ▶ noun *a grandfather clock* **timepiece,** timekeeper, timer; chronometer, chronograph.
▶ verb informal *his fastball was clocked at 92 mph* **time,** measure.

clog ▶ noun *dancing in clogs takes a lot of practice* **sabot,** wooden shoe.
▶ verb *the pipes were clogged* **block,** obstruct, congest, jam, choke, bung up, plug, stop up, fill up, gunge up.

cloister ▶ noun **1** *the convent's shadowed cloisters* **walkway,** covered walk, arcade, loggia, gallery.
2 *I was educated in the cloister* **abbey,** monastery, friary, convent, priory, nunnery.

cloistered ▶ adjective *the cloistered life of a writer* **secluded,** sequestered, sheltered, protected, insulated; shut off, isolated, confined, incommunicado; solitary, monastic, reclusive.

close[1] ▶ adjective **1** *the town is **close to** Paris* **near,** adjacent to; in the vicinity of, in the neighborhood of, within reach of; neighboring, adjoining, abutting, alongside, on the doorstep, a stone's throw (away) from/to, 'a hop, skip, and a jump from'; nearby, at close quarters to; informal within spitting distance from/to; archaic nigh to.
ANTONYMS far, distant.
2 *flying in close formation* **dense,** compact, tight, close-packed, packed, solid; crowded, cramped, congested.
ANTONYMS sparse.
3 *I was **close to** tears* **near,** on the verge of, on the brink of, on the point of.
4 *a very close match* **evenly matched,** even, with nothing to choose between them, neck and neck; informal even-steven.
ANTONYMS one-sided.
5 *close relatives* **immediate,** direct, near.
ANTONYMS distant.
6 *close friends* **intimate,** dear, bosom; close-knit, tight-knit, inseparable, attached, devoted, faithful; special, good, best, fast, firm; informal (as) thick as thieves.
ANTONYMS casual.
7 *a close resemblance* **strong,** marked, distinct, pronounced.
ANTONYMS slight.
8 *a close examination* **careful,** detailed, thorough, minute, searching, painstaking, meticulous, rigorous, scrupulous, conscientious; attentive, focused.
ANTONYMS casual.
9 *keep a close eye on them* **vigilant,** watchful, keen, alert.
10 *a close translation* **strict,** faithful, exact, precise, literal; word for word, verbatim.
ANTONYMS loose.
11 *the weather was hot and close* **humid,** muggy, stuffy, airless, heavy, sticky, sultry, oppressive, stifling.
ANTONYMS fresh.

close[2] ▶ verb **1** *she closed the door* **shut,** pull (shut), push (shut), slam; fasten, secure.
ANTONYMS open.
2 *close the hole* **block (up/off),** stop up, plug, seal (up/off), shut up/off, cork, stopper, bung (up); clog (up), choke, obstruct.
ANTONYMS open, unblock.
3 *the enemy was closing fast* **catch up,** close in, creep up, near, approach, gain on someone.
4 *the gap is closing* **narrow,** reduce, shrink,

lessen, get smaller, diminish, contract.
ANTONYMS widen.
5 *his arms closed around her* **meet,** join, connect; form a circle.
6 *he closed the meeting* **end,** conclude, finish, terminate, wind up, break off, halt, discontinue, dissolve; adjourn, suspend.
ANTONYMS open, begin.
7 *the factory is to close* **shut down,** close down, cease production, cease trading, go out of business, go bankrupt, go into receivership, go into liquidation; informal fold, go bust.
ANTONYMS open.
8 *he closed a deal* **clinch,** settle, secure, seal, confirm, establish; transact, pull off; complete, conclude, fix, agree, finalize; informal wrap up.
▶ **noun** *the close of the talks* **end,** finish, conclusion, termination, cessation, completion, resolution, climax, denouement; informal outro.
ANTONYMS beginning.

closet ▶ **noun** *a clothes closet* **cabinet,** cupboard, wardrobe, armoire, locker.
▶ **adjective** *a closet Sherlock Holmes fan* **secret,** covert, private; surreptitious, clandestine, underground, furtive.
▶ **verb** *David was closeted in his den* **shut away,** sequester, seclude, cloister, confine, isolate.

closure ▶ **noun** *the closure of rural schools* **closing down,** shutdown; termination, discontinuation, cessation, finish, conclusion; failure; informal folding.

clot ▶ **noun** *blood clots* **lump,** clump, mass; thrombus, thrombosis, embolus; informal glob, gob.
▶ **verb** *the blood is likely to clot* **coagulate,** set, congeal, curdle, thicken, solidify.

cloth ▶ **noun 1** *a maker of cloth* **fabric,** material; textile(s), soft goods.
2 *a cloth to wipe the table* **rag,** wipe, duster, sponge; towel; chamois.

clothe ▶ **verb 1** *they were clothed in silk* **dress,** attire, robe, garb, array, costume, swathe, deck (out), turn out, fit out, rig (out); informal get up; archaic apparel, habit, invest.
2 *a valley clothed in conifers* **cover,** blanket, carpet; envelop, swathe.

clothes ▶ **plural noun** *his clothes are too big for him* **clothing,** garments, attire, garb, dress, wear, costume; informal gear, togs, duds, threads, getup; formal apparel; archaic raiment, habiliments, vestments.

clothing ▶ **noun** See CLOTHES.

cloud ▶ **noun 1** *dark clouds* storm cloud, cloudbank, cloud cover; mackerel sky.
2 *a cloud of exhaust smoke* **mass,** billow; pall, mantle, blanket.
▶ **verb 1** *the sky clouded* **become cloudy,** cloud over, become overcast, lower, blacken, darken.
2 *the sand is churned up, clouding the water* **make cloudy,** make murky, dirty, darken, blacken.
3 *anger clouded my judgment* **confuse,** muddle, obscure, fog, muddy, mar.
– PHRASES **on cloud nine** *Amy was on cloud nine when she passed the bar exam* **ecstatic,** rapturous, joyful, elated, blissful, euphoric, in seventh heaven, walking on air, transported, in raptures, delighted, thrilled, overjoyed, over the moon, on top of the world, tickled pink.

cloudy ▶ **adjective 1** *a cloudy sky* **overcast,** clouded; dark, gray, black, leaden, murky; somber, dismal, heavy, gloomy; sunless, starless; hazy, misty, foggy.
ANTONYMS clear, bright.
2 *cloudy water* **murky,** muddy, milky, dirty, opaque, turbid.
ANTONYMS clear.
3 *his eyes grew cloudy* **tearful,** teary, weepy, lachrymose; moist, watery; misty, blurred.
ANTONYMS clear, dry.

clout informal ▶ **noun 1** *a clout on the ear* **smack,** slap, thump, punch, blow, hit, cuff, box, clip; informal whack, wallop.
2 *her clout in the business world* **influence,** power, weight, sway, leverage, control, say; dominance, authority; informal teeth, muscle.
▶ **verb** *he clouted me* **hit,** strike, punch, smack, slap, cuff, thump, buffet; informal wallop, belt, whack, clobber, sock, bop.

clown ▶ **noun 1** *a circus clown* **comedian**; jester, fool, zany.
2 *the class clown* **joker,** comedian, comic, humorist, wag, wit, prankster, jester, buffoon; informal laugh, kidder, wisecracker.
3 *bureaucratic clowns* **fool,** idiot, dolt, ass, simpleton, ignoramus; bungler, blunderer; informal moron, meatball, bozo, jackass, chump, numbskull, numbnuts, nincompoop, halfwit, bonehead, knucklehead, fathead, birdbrain, twit, nitwit, twerp.
▶ **verb** *Harvey* ***clowned around*** **fool around,** play the fool, play around, monkey around; joke (around), jest; informal mess around, horse around.

cloying ▶ **adjective** *her romance novels are too cloying for my taste* **sickly,** syrupy, saccharine, oversweet; sickening, nauseating; mawkish, sentimental, twee; informal over the top, mushy, slushy, sloppy, gooey, cheesy, corny, cornball, sappy.

club[1] ▶ **noun 1** *a canoeing club* **society,** association, organization, institution, group, circle, band, body, ring, crew; alliance, league, union.
2 *the city has great clubs* **nightclub,** disco, discotheque, bar.
3 *the top club in the league* **team,** squad, side, lineup, franchise.

club[2] ▶ **noun** *a wooden club* **cudgel,** truncheon, bludgeon, baton, stick, mace, bat, blackjack, nightstick.
▶ **verb** *he was clubbed with an iron bar* **cudgel,** bludgeon, bash, beat, hit, strike, batter, belabor; informal clout, clobber.

clue ▶ **noun 1** *give me just one clue | police are searching for clues* **hint,** indication, sign, signal, pointer, trace, indicator; lead, tip, tipoff; (**clues**) **evidence,** information.
2 *a crossword clue* **question,** problem, puzzle, riddle, poser, conundrum.
– PHRASES **clue in** informal *if you're missing any of the facts, we can clue you in* **inform,** notify, make aware, prime; keep up to date, keep posted; informal tip off, give the lowdown, fill in on, put in the picture, put wise, get/keep up to speed. **not have a clue** informal *you expect me*

to explain her motives, but I do not have a clue **have no idea,** be ignorant, not have an inkling; be baffled, be mystified, be at a loss; informal be clueless, not have the faintest/foggiest/slightest idea.

clump ▶ noun **1** *a clump of trees* **cluster,** thicket, group, bunch, assemblage.
2 *a clump of earth* **lump,** clod, mass, wad, glob, gob.
▶ verb **1** *galaxies clump together* **cluster,** group, collect, gather, assemble, congregate, mass.
2 *they were clumping around upstairs* **stamp,** stomp, clomp, tramp, lumber; thump, thud, bang; informal galumph.

clumsy ▶ adjective **1** *she was terribly clumsy* **awkward,** uncoordinated, ungainly, graceless, inelegant; inept, maladroit, unskillful, unhandy, accident-prone, like a bull in a china shop, all thumbs; informal ham-fisted, butterfingered, having two left feet, klutzy.
ANTONYMS graceful.
2 *a clumsy contraption* **unwieldy,** cumbersome, bulky, awkward.
ANTONYMS elegant.
3 *a clumsy remark* **gauche,** awkward, graceless; unsubtle, uncouth, boorish, crass; tactless, insensitive, thoughtless, undiplomatic, indelicate, ill-judged.
ANTONYMS tactful.

cluster ▶ noun **1** *clusters of berries* **bunch,** clump, mass, knot, group, clutch, bundle, truss.
2 *a cluster of spectators* **crowd,** group, knot, huddle, bunch, throng, flock, pack, band; informal gang, gaggle.
▶ verb *they clustered around the television* **congregate,** gather, collect, group, assemble; huddle, crowd, flock.

clutch[1] ▶ verb *she clutched his arm* **grip,** grasp, clasp, cling to, hang on to, clench, hold.
– PHRASES **clutch at** *she saved herself by clutching at a branch* **reach for,** snatch at, make a grab for, catch at, claw at.

clutch[2] ▶ noun **1** *a clutch of eggs* **group,** batch.
2 *a clutch of awards* **group,** collection; raft, armful; informal load, bunch, ton.

clutches ▶ plural noun *she's married to a hateful man who has her in his clutches* **power,** control, domination, command, rule, tyranny; hands, hold, grip, grasp, claws, jaws, tentacles; custody.

clutter ▶ noun **1** *a clutter of toys* **mess,** jumble, litter, heap, tangle, muddle, hodgepodge.
2 *a desk full of clutter* **disorder,** chaos, disarray, untidiness, mess, confusion; litter, rubbish, junk.
▶ verb *the garden was cluttered with tools* **litter,** mess up, disarrange; be strewn, be scattered; literary bestrew.

coach[1] ▶ noun **1** *an air-conditioned coach shuttled us to the casino* **bus,** minibus; dated omnibus.
2 chiefly Brit. *a railroad coach* **car,** carriage, wagon, compartment, van, Pullman.
3 *a coach and horses* **horse-drawn carriage,** hackney, hansom, gig, landau, brougham.

coach[2] ▶ noun *a football coach* **instructor,** trainer, manager; teacher, tutor, mentor, guru.
▶ verb *she coached Richard in math* **instruct,** teach; tutor, school, educate; drill; train.

coagulate ▶ verb *a drug that helps the blood to coagulate* **congeal,** clot, thicken, jell; solidify, harden, set, dry.

coalesce ▶ verb *the puddles had coalesced into shallow streams* **merge,** unite, join together, combine, fuse, mingle, blend; amalgamate, consolidate, integrate, homogenize, converge.

coalition ▶ noun *the ruling four-party coalition* **alliance,** union, partnership, bloc, caucus; federation, league, association, confederation, consortium, syndicate, combine; amalgamation, merger.

coarse ▶ adjective **1** *coarse blankets* **rough,** scratchy, prickly, wiry.
ANTONYMS soft.
2 *his coarse features* **large,** rough, rough-hewn, heavy; ugly.
ANTONYMS delicate.
3 *a coarse boy* **oafish,** loutish, boorish, uncouth, rude, impolite, ill-mannered, uncivil; vulgar, common, rough, uncultured, crass.
ANTONYMS sophisticated, refined.
4 *a coarse innuendo* **vulgar,** crude, rude, off-color, dirty, filthy, smutty, indelicate, improper, unseemly, crass, tasteless, lewd, prurient, blue, farmyard.

coarsen ▶ verb **1** *hands coarsened by work* **roughen,** toughen, harden.
ANTONYMS soften.
2 *I had been coarsened by the army* **desensitize,** dehumanize; dull, deaden.
ANTONYMS refine.

coast ▶ noun *the houses along the coast* **seaboard,** coastal region, coastline, seashore, shore, foreshore, shoreline, seaside, waterfront, littoral; literary strand.
▶ verb *the car coasted down a hill* **freewheel,** cruise, taxi, drift, glide, sail.

coat ▶ noun **1** *a winter coat* **overcoat,** jacket.
2 *a dog's coat* **fur,** hair, wool, fleece; hide, pelt, skin.
3 *a coat of paint* **layer,** covering, coating, skin, film, wash; plating, glaze, varnish, veneer, patina; deposit.
▶ verb *the tube was coated with wax* **cover,** paint, glaze, varnish, wash; surface, veneer, laminate, plate, face; daub, smear, cake, plaster.

coating ▶ noun See COAT (sense 3 of the noun).

coax ▶ verb *you have to coax some of the children to speak* **persuade;** wheedle, cajole, get around; beguile, seduce, inveigle, maneuver; informal sweet-talk, soft-soap, butter up, twist someone's arm.

cock ▶ noun *strutting around like a barnyard cock* **rooster,** cockerel, capon.
▶ verb **1** *he cocked his head* **tilt,** tip, angle, incline, dip.
2 *she cocked her little finger* **bend,** flex, crook, curve.
3 *the dog cocked its leg* **lift,** raise, hold up.

cocky ▶ adjective *military school has certainly made him less cocky* **arrogant,** conceited, overweening, overconfident, cocksure, self-important, egotistical, presumptuous, boastful, self-assertive; bold, forward, insolent, cheeky, puffed-up.
ANTONYMS modest.

coddle ▶ verb *your sons are too old for you to be coddling them* **pamper,** cosset, mollycoddle; spoil, indulge, overindulge, pander to; baby, mother, wait on hand and foot.
ANTONYMS neglect.

code ▶ noun **1** *a secret code* **cipher,** key; hieroglyphics; cryptogram.
2 *a strict social code* **morality,** convention, etiquette, protocol, value system.
3 *the penal code* **law(s),** rules, regulations; constitution, system.

coerce ▶ verb *he was coerced into giving evidence* **pressure,** pressurize, press, push, constrain; force, compel, oblige, browbeat, bludgeon, bully, threaten, intimidate, dragoon, twist someone's arm; informal railroad, squeeze, lean on. See note at COMPEL.

coffer ▶ noun **1** *every church had a coffer* **strongbox,** money box, cashbox, money chest, treasure chest, safe; casket, box.
2 (**coffers**) *the government coffers* **fund(s),** reserves, resources, money, finances, wealth, cash, capital, purse; treasury, exchequer; informal pork barrel.

coffin ▶ noun *a simple pine coffin* casket; sarcophagus; informal box; humorous wooden overcoat.

cogent ▶ adjective *a cogent argument* **convincing,** compelling, strong, forceful, powerful, potent, weighty, effective; valid, sound, plausible, telling; impressive, persuasive, eloquent, credible, influential; conclusive, authoritative; logical, reasoned, rational, reasonable, lucid, coherent, clear. See note at BELIEVABLE.

cogitate ▶ verb formal *I may have to cogitate on that one for a bit* **think about/on/over,** contemplate, consider, mull over, meditate on, muse on/over, ponder, reflect on, deliberate on/over, ruminate on/over; dwell on, brood on, chew over; informal put on one's thinking cap for.

cognate ▶ adjective formal *the cognate words in English and German* **associated,** related, connected, allied, linked; similar, like, alike, akin, kindred, comparable, parallel, corresponding, analogous.

cognition ▶ noun *the head injury has impaired his speech and cognition* **perception,** discernment, apprehension, learning, understanding, comprehension, insight; reasoning, thinking, thought.

cognizant ▶ adjective formal See AWARE (sense 1).

cohabit ▶ verb *her brother James and this Marilyn Monroe lookalike are cohabiting in Soho* **live together,** live as a couple; informal shack up; dated live in sin.

coherent ▶ adjective *the patient's speech is more coherent today* **logical,** reasoned, reasonable, rational, sound, cogent, consistent, consilient; clear, lucid, articulate; intelligible, comprehensible.
ANTONYMS muddled.

cohort ▶ noun **1** *a Roman army cohort* **unit,** force, corps, division, brigade, battalion, regiment, squadron, company, troop, contingent, legion, phalanx.
2 *the 1940–44 birth cohort of women* **group,** grouping, category, class, set, division, batch, list; age group, generation.
3 *a party thrown by her departmental cohorts* **colleague,** companion, associate, friend.

coil ▶ noun *coils of rope* **loop,** twist, turn, curl, convolution; spiral, helix, corkscrew.
▶ verb *he coiled her hair around his finger* **wind,** loop, twist, curl, curve, bend, twine, entwine; spiral, corkscrew.

coin ▶ noun **1** *coins in my pocket* penny, nickel, dime, quarter; piece.
2 *large amounts of coin* **coinage,** coins, specie; change, loose change, small change; silver, gold.
▶ verb **1** *dimes were coined* **mint,** stamp, strike, cast, punch, die, mold, forge, make.
2 *he coined the term* **invent,** create, make up, conceive, originate, think up, dream up.

coincide ▶ verb **1** *the events coincided* **occur simultaneously,** happen together, be concurrent, concur, coexist.
2 *their interests do not always coincide* **correspond,** tally, agree, accord, concur, match, fit, be consistent, equate, harmonize, be compatible, dovetail, correlate; informal square.
ANTONYMS differ.

coincidence ▶ noun **1** *too close to be mere coincidence* **accident,** chance, serendipity, fortuity, providence, happenstance, fate; a fluke.
2 *the coincidence of inflation and unemployment* **co-occurrence,** coexistence, conjunction, simultaneity, contemporaneity, concomitance.
3 *a coincidence of interests* **correspondence,** agreement, accord, concurrence, consistency, conformity, harmony, compatibility.

coincidental ▶ adjective **1** *a coincidental resemblance* **accidental,** chance, fluky, random; fortuitous, adventitious, serendipitous; unexpected, unforeseen, unintentional, inadvertent, unplanned.
2 *the coincidental disappearance of the two men* **simultaneous,** concurrent, coincident, contemporaneous, concomitant.

cold ▶ adjective **1** *a cold day* **chilly,** chill, cool, freezing, icy, snowy, wintry, frosty, frigid, gelid; bitter, biting, raw, bone-chilling, nippy, arctic.
ANTONYMS hot.
2 *I'm very cold* **chilly,** chilled, cool, freezing, frozen, shivery, numb, benumbed; hypothermic.
ANTONYMS hot.
3 *a cold reception* **unfriendly,** inhospitable, unwelcoming, forbidding, cool, frigid, frosty, glacial, lukewarm, indifferent, unfeeling, unemotional, formal, stiff.
ANTONYMS friendly, warm.

cold-blooded ▶ adjective *a cold-blooded killer* **cruel,** callous, sadistic, inhuman, inhumane, pitiless, merciless, ruthless, unforgiving, unfeeling, uncaring, heartless; savage, brutal, barbaric, barbarous; cold, cold-hearted, unemotional.

collaborate ▶ verb **1** *they collaborated on the project* **co-operate,** join forces, team up, band together, work together, participate, combine, ally; pool resources, put —— heads together.
2 *they collaborated with the enemy* **collude,** conspire, fraternize, co-operate, consort, sympathize; informal be in cahoots.

collaborator ▶ noun **1** *his collaborator on the*

book **coworker,** partner, associate, colleague, confederate; assistant.
2 *a wartime collaborator* **quisling,** fraternizer, collaborationist, colluder, (enemy) sympathizer; traitor, fifth columnist.

collapse ▶ **verb 1** *the roof collapsed* **cave in,** fall in, subside, fall down, give (way), crumple, buckle, sag, slump.
2 *he collapsed last night* **faint,** pass out, black out, lose consciousness, keel over, swoon; informal conk out.
3 *he collapsed in tears* **break down,** go to pieces, lose control, be overcome, crumble; informal crack up.
4 *peace talks collapsed* **break down,** fail, fall through, fold, founder, miscarry, come to grief, be unsuccessful; end; informal flop, fizzle out.
▶ **noun 1** *the collapse of the roof* **cave-in,** subsidence.
2 *her collapse on stage* **fainting fit,** faint, blackout, loss of consciousness, swoon; Medicine syncope.
3 *the collapse of the talks* **breakdown,** failure, disintegration; end.
4 *he suffered a collapse* **breakdown,** nervous breakdown, personal crisis, psychological trauma; informal crack-up.

collar ▶ **noun 1** *a shirt collar* **neckband,** choker; historical ruff, gorget, bertha.
2 *a collar around the pipe* **ring,** band, collet, sleeve, flange.
▶ **verb** informal **1** *he collared a thief* **apprehend,** arrest, catch, capture, seize; take prisoner, take into custody, detain; informal nab, pinch, bust, pick up, pull in.
2 *she collared me in the street* **accost,** waylay, hail, approach, detain, stop, halt, catch, confront, importune; informal buttonhole.

collate ▶ **verb 1** *the system is used to collate information* **collect,** gather, accumulate, assemble; combine, aggregate, put together; arrange, organize.
2 *we must collate these two sources* **compare,** contrast, set side by side, juxtapose, weigh against.

collateral ▶ **noun** *she put up her house as collateral for the loan* **security,** surety, guarantee, guaranty, insurance, indemnity, indemnification; backing.

colleague ▶ **noun** *the Professor's colleagues started a scholarship fund in his name* **coworker,** fellow worker, workmate, teammate, associate, partner, collaborator, ally, confederate.

collect ▶ **verb 1** *he collected the rubbish | she collects Hummel figurines* **gather,** accumulate, assemble; amass, stockpile, pile up, heap up, store (up), hoard, save; mass, accrue. See note at GATHER.
ANTONYMS squander, distribute.
2 *a crowd collected in the square* **gather,** assemble, meet, muster, congregate, convene, converge, flock together.
ANTONYMS disperse.
3 *I must collect the children* **fetch,** go/come to get, call for, meet.
ANTONYMS take, drop off.
4 *they collect money for charity* **raise,** appeal for, ask for, solicit; obtain, acquire, gather.
ANTONYMS give away, distribute.
5 *he paused to* ***collect himself*** **recover,** regain one's composure, pull oneself together, steady oneself; informal get a grip (on oneself).
ANTONYMS disperse, distribute.
6 *she collected her thoughts* **gather,** summon (up), muster, get together, marshal.
ANTONYMS disperse, distribute.

collected ▶ **adjective** *she is the most collected gymnast on the team* **calm,** cool, self-possessed, self-controlled, composed, poised; serene, tranquil, relaxed, unruffled, unperturbed, untroubled; placid, quiet, sedate, phlegmatic; informal unfazed, nonplussed, together, laid-back.
ANTONYMS excited, hysterical.

collection ▶ **noun 1** *a collection of stolen items* **hoard,** pile, heap, stack, stock, store, stockpile; accumulation, reserve, supply, bank, pool, fund, mine, reservoir.
2 *a collection of shoppers* **group,** crowd, body, assemblage, gathering, throng; knot, cluster; multitude, bevy, party, band, horde, pack, flock, swarm, mob; informal gang, load, gaggle.
3 *a collection of Victorian dolls* **set,** series; array, assortment.
4 *a collection of short stories* **anthology,** selection, compendium, treasury, compilation, miscellany, potpourri.
5 *a collection for the poor* **donations,** contributions, gifts, subscription(s); historical alms.
6 *a church collection* **offering,** offertory, tithe.

collective ▶ **adjective** *our collective interests* **common,** shared, joint, combined, mutual, communal, pooled; united, allied, cooperative, collaborative.
ANTONYMS individual.

college ▶ **noun 1** *a college of technology* **school,** academy, university, polytechnic, institute, seminary, conservatoire, conservatory.
2 *the college of physicians* **association,** society, club, institute, body, fellowship, guild, lodge, order, fraternity, league, union, alliance.

collide ▶ **verb 1** *the trains* ***collided with*** *each other* **crash into,** hit, strike, impact, run into, bump into, meet head-on, cannon into, plow into, barrel into.
2 *in her work, politics and metaphysics collide* **conflict,** clash; differ, diverge, disagree, be at odds, be incompatible.

collision ▶ **noun 1** *a collision in the passing lane* **crash,** accident, impact, smash, bump, hit, fender bender, wreck, pileup.
2 *a collision between two ideas* **conflict,** clash; disagreement, incompatibility, contradiction.

colloquial ▶ **adjective** *she just loved the colloquial expressions of her Southern in-laws* **informal,** conversational, everyday, nonliterary; unofficial, idiomatic, slangy, vernacular, popular, demotic.
ANTONYMS formal.

collusion ▶ **noun** *there has been collusion between the security forces and paramilitary groups* **conspiracy,** connivance, complicity, intrigue, plotting, secret understanding, collaboration, scheming.

colonize ▶ **verb** *the Germans colonized Tanganyika in 1885* **settle (in),** people, populate; occupy, take over, seize, capture, subjugate.

colonnade ▶ noun *we took a stroll through the colonnade* **row of columns**; portico, gallery, stoa, peristyle; arcade.

colony ▶ noun 1 *a French colony* **settlement,** dependency, protectorate, satellite, territory, outpost, province.
2 *an artists' colony* **community,** commune; quarter, district, ghetto.

color ▶ noun 1 *the lights changed color* **hue,** shade, tint, tone, coloration.
2 *oil color* **paint,** pigment, colorant, dye, stain, tint, wash.
3 *the color in her cheeks* **redness,** pinkness, rosiness, ruddiness, blush, flush, bloom.
4 *people of every color* **skin coloring,** skin tone, coloring; race, ethnic group.
5 *anecdotes add color to the text* **vividness,** life, liveliness, vitality, excitement, interest, richness, zest, spice, piquancy, impact, force; informal oomph, pizzazz, punch, kick; literary salt.
▶ verb 1 *the wood was colored blue* **tint,** dye, stain, paint, pigment, wash.
2 *she colored* **blush,** redden, go pink, go red, flush.
3 *the experience colored her outlook* **influence,** affect, taint, warp, skew, distort, bias, prejudice.
4 *they color evidence to make a story sell* **exaggerate,** overstate, embroider, embellish, dramatize, enhance, varnish; falsify, misreport, manipulate.

colorful ▶ adjective 1 *a colorful picture* **brightly colored,** vivid, vibrant, brilliant, radiant, rich; gaudy, glaring, garish; multicolored, multicolor, rainbow, varicolored, harlequin, polychromatic, psychedelic, neon, jazzy.
2 *a colorful account* **vivid,** graphic, lively, animated, dramatic, fascinating, interesting, stimulating, scintillating, evocative.

colorless ▶ adjective 1 *a colorless liquid* **uncolored,** white, bleached; literary achromatic.
ANTONYMS colored.
2 *her colorless face* **pale,** pallid, wan, anemic, bloodless, ashen, white, waxen, pasty, peaked, sickly, drained, drawn, ghostly, deathly.
ANTONYMS rosy.
3 *a colorless personality* **uninteresting,** dull, boring, tedious, dry, dreary; unexciting, bland, weak, insipid, vapid, vacuous, feeble, wishy-washy, lame, lifeless, spiritless, anemic, bloodless; nondescript, characterless, plain-vanilla.
ANTONYMS colorful.

colossal ▶ adjective *a colossal building | we made some colossal mistakes* **huge,** massive, enormous, gigantic, giant, mammoth, vast, immense, monumental, prodigious, mountainous, titanic, towering, king-size(d), economy-size(d); informal monster, whopping, humongous, jumbo, ginormous.
ANTONYMS tiny.

column ▶ noun 1 *arches supported by massive columns* **pillar,** post, support, upright, baluster, pier, pile, pilaster, stanchion; obelisk, monolith; Doric column, Ionic column, Corinthian column, Tuscan column.
2 *a column in the paper* **article,** piece, item, story, report, account, write-up, feature, review, notice, editorial.
3 *we walked in a column* **line,** file, queue, procession, train, cavalcade, convoy.

coma ▶ noun *doctors do not expect him to come out of the coma* state of unconsciousness; Medicine persistent vegetative state.

comatose ▶ adjective 1 *he was comatose after the accident* **unconscious,** in a coma, insensible, insensate.
2 informal *she lay comatose in the sun* **inert,** inactive, lethargic, sluggish, torpid, languid; somnolent, sleeping, dormant.

comb ▶ verb 1 *she combed her hair* **groom,** brush, untangle, smooth, straighten, neaten, tidy, arrange; curry.
2 *police combed the area* **search,** scour, explore, sweep, probe, hunt through, forage through, poke around in, go over, go over with a fine-tooth comb; leave no stone unturned.

combat ▶ noun *he was killed in combat* **battle,** fighting, action, hostilities, conflict, war, warfare.
▶ verb *they tried to combat the disease* **fight,** battle, tackle, attack, counter, resist, withstand; impede, block, thwart, inhibit; stop, halt, prevent, check, curb.

combatant ▶ noun 1 *a combatant in the war* **fighter,** soldier, serviceman, servicewoman, warrior, trooper.
2 *combatants in the computer market* **contender,** adversary, opponent, competitor, challenger, rival.
▶ adjective *combatant armies* **warring,** at war, opposing, belligerent, fighting, battling.

combative ▶ adjective *the dictator's combative language* **pugnacious,** aggressive, antagonistic, quarrelsome, argumentative, contentious, hostile, truculent, belligerent, bellicose, militant; informal spoiling for a fight.
ANTONYMS conciliatory.

combination ▶ noun 1 *a combination of ancient and modern* **amalgamation,** amalgam, merger, merging, blend, mixture, mix, fusion, marriage, coalition, integration, incorporation, synthesis, composite; informal combo.
2 *he acted in combination with his brother* **cooperation,** collaboration, association, union, partnership, league.

combine ▶ verb 1 *he combines comedy with tragedy* **amalgamate,** integrate, incorporate, merge, mix, fuse, blend; bind, join, marry, unify. See note at JOIN.
2 *teachers combined to tackle the problem* **co-operate,** collaborate, join forces, get together, unite, team up, throw in one's lot; informal gang up.

combustible ▶ adjective *piles of combustible material* **inflammable,** flammable, incendiary, ignitable.

combustion ▶ noun *the combustion of fossil fuels* **burning**; kindling, ignition.

come ▶ verb 1 *come and listen* **move nearer,** move closer, approach, advance, draw close/closer, draw near/nearer; proceed; archaic draw nigh.
ANTONYMS go away.

2 *they came last night* **arrive,** get here/there, make it, appear, come on the scene; approach, enter, turn up, come along, materialize; informal show (up), roll in/up, blow in, show one's face. ANTONYMS leave.
3 *they **came to** a stream* **reach,** arrive at, get to, make it to; come across, run across, happen on/upon, chance on/upon, come upon, stumble on/upon; end up at, wind up at.
4 *the dress **comes to** her ankles* **extend to,** stretch to, reach, come as far as.
5 *she **comes from** Italy* **be from,** be a native of, hail from, originate in; live in, reside in.
6 *attacks came without warning* **happen,** occur, take place, come about, transpire, fall, present itself, crop up, materialize, arise, arrive, appear; ensue, follow; literary come to pass, befall.
7 *the shoes come in black and brown* **be available,** be for sale; be made, be produced.
– PHRASES **come about** *the change came about in 1989* **happen,** occur, take place, transpire, fall; crop up, materialize, arise, arrive, appear, surface; ensue, follow; literary come to pass, befall. **come across 1** *they came across his friends* **meet/find by chance,** meet, run into, run across, come upon, chance on/upon, stumble on/upon, happen on/upon; discover, encounter, find, locate; informal bump into. **2** *the emotion comes across* **be communicated,** be perceived, get across, be clear, be understood, register, sink in, strike home. **3** *she came across as cool* **seem,** appear, look, sound, look to be. **come along 1** *the puppies are coming along nicely* **progress,** develop, shape up; come on, turn out; improve, get better, pick up, rally, recover. **2** *come along!* **hurry (up),** be quick, get a move on, come on, look lively, speed up, move faster; informal get moving, get cracking, step on it, move it, shake a leg, make it snappy; dated make haste. **come apart** *if the straw is too short, the bales will come apart* **break apart,** break up, fall to bits/pieces, fall apart, disintegrate, come unstuck, separate, split, tear. **come around 1** *the smelling salts helped him come around* **regain consciousness,** recover consciousness, come to, come to one's senses, recover, revive, awake, wake up. **2** *I **came around to** her view* **be converted to,** be won over by, agree with, change one's mind to, be persuaded by; give way to, yield to, relent to. **3** *Friday the 13th comes around every few months* **occur,** take place, happen, come up, crop up, arise; recur, reoccur, return, reappear. **4** *come around for a drink* **visit,** stop by, drop by/in/over, come over, pop in/over. **come back** *are you coming back before dinner?* **return,** get back, arrive home, come home; come again. **come between** *I let my drinking come between me and my family* **alienate,** estrange, separate, divide, split up, break up, disunite, set at odds. **come by** *where did you ever come by such a magnificent horse?* **obtain,** acquire, gain, get, find, pick up, procure, secure; buy, purchase; informal get one's hands on, get hold of, bag, score, swing. **come down** *the report comes down against a zoning variance in the wetlands* **decide,** conclude, settle; choose, opt, plump. **come down on** *she came down on him like a ton of bricks* See REPRIMAND (verb). **come down to** *it comes down to two choices: stay in school or find another place to live* **amount to,** add up to, constitute, boil down to, be equivalent to. **come down with** *the whole family has come down with chicken pox* **fall ill with,** fall sick with, be taken ill with, show symptoms of, become infected with, get, catch, develop, contract, fall victim to. **come forward** *Vera is always the first to come forward* **volunteer,** offer one's services, make oneself available. **come in** *you can't come in without a pass* **enter,** gain admission, cross the threshold. **come into** *Jerry came into a small fortune when his grandfather died* **inherit,** be left, be willed, be bequeathed. **come off** *if you make this meeting come off, you're probably looking at a promotion* **succeed,** work, turn out well, work out, go as planned, produce the desired result, get results. **come on** *the new bookcases are coming on nicely* **progress,** develop, shape up, take shape, come along, turn out; improve. **come out 1** *it came out that he'd been to Rome* **become known,** become apparent, come to light, emerge, transpire; get out, be discovered, be uncovered, be revealed, leak out, be disclosed. **2** *my book is coming out* **be published,** be issued, be released, be brought out, be printed, go on sale. **3** *the flowers have come out* **bloom,** flower, open. **4** *it will come out all right* **end,** finish, conclude, work out, turn out; informal pan out. **5** *the councilman came out voluntarily* disclose one's homosexuality; informal come out of the closet. **come out with** *I didn't really mean to come out with those stupid remarks* **utter,** say, let out, blurt out, burst out with; issue, present. **come through 1** *we came through it OK* **survive,** get through, ride out, weather, live through, pull through; withstand, stand up to, endure, surmount, overcome; informal stick out. **2** *you **came through for** us* **help,** be there for. **come to 1** *the bill came to $17.50* **amount to,** add up to, total, run to, equal. **2** *I came to in the ambulance* **regain consciousness,** recover consciousness, come around, come to one's senses, recover, revive, awake, wake up. **come up** *whatever comes up, we'll be ready* **arise,** occur, happen, come about, transpire, emerge, surface, crop up, turn up, pop up. **come up to 1** *she came up to his shoulder* **reach,** come to, be as tall as, extend to. **2** *he never came up to her expectations* **measure up to,** match up to, live up to, fulfill, satisfy, meet, equal, compare with; be good enough for; informal hold a candle to. **come up with** *Miranda has come up with a terrific idea* **produce,** devise, think up; propose, put forward, submit, suggest, recommend, advocate, introduce, moot.

comeback ▶ **noun 1** *he made a determined comeback* **resurgence,** recovery, return, rally, upturn.
2 informal *one of my best comebacks* **retort,** riposte, return, rejoinder; answer, reply, response.

comedian, comedienne ▶ **noun 1** *a famous comedian* **comic,** comedienne, funny man,

funny woman, humorist, gagster, stand-up.
2 *Dad was such a comedian* **joker,** jester, wit, wag, comic, wisecracker, jokester; prankster, clown, fool, buffoon; informal laugh, hoot, riot; informal dated card.

comedown ▶ noun informal **1** *a bit of a comedown for a sergeant* **loss of status,** loss of face, humiliation, belittlement, demotion, degradation, disgrace.
2 *it's such a comedown after Christmas* **anticlimax,** letdown, disappointment, disillusionment, deflation, decline.

comedy ▶ noun **1** *he excels in comedy* **light entertainment,** comic theater, farce, situation comedy, satire, pantomime, comic opera; burlesque, slapstick; informal sitcom.
ANTONYMS tragedy, drama.
2 *the comedy in their work* **humor,** fun, funny side, comical aspect, absurdity, drollness, farce.
ANTONYMS gravity.

comely ▶ adjective archaic See ATTRACTIVE (sense 2).

come-on ▶ noun informal *the $200 rebate is a come-on for prospective car buyers* **inducement,** incentive, attraction, lure, pull, draw, enticement, bait, carrot, temptation; fascination, charm, appeal, allure.

comeuppance ▶ noun informal *the bad guys always get their comeuppance in the final scene* **just deserts,** just punishment, due, retribution, requital, what's coming to one.

comfort ▶ noun **1** *travel in comfort* **ease,** relaxation, repose, serenity, tranquility, contentment, coziness; luxury, opulence, prosperity; bed of roses.
2 *words of comfort* **consolation,** solace, condolence, sympathy, commiseration; support, reassurance, cheer.
▶ verb *a friend tried to comfort her* **console,** solace, condole with, commiserate with, sympathize with; support, succor, ease, reassure, soothe, calm; cheer, hearten, uplift.
ANTONYMS distress, depress.

comfortable ▶ adjective **1** *a comfortable lifestyle* **pleasant,** free from hardship; affluent, well-to-do, luxurious, opulent.
ANTONYMS harsh.
2 *a comfortable room* **cozy,** snug, warm, pleasant, agreeable; restful, homelike, homely; informal comfy.
ANTONYMS spartan.
3 *comfortable clothes* **loose,** loose-fitting, casual; informal comfy.
4 *a comfortable pace* **leisurely,** unhurried, relaxed, easy, gentle, sedate, undemanding, slow; informal laid-back.
5 *they feel comfortable with each other* **at ease,** relaxed, secure, safe, unworried, contented, happy.
ANTONYMS vulnerable, tense.

comforting ▶ adjective *Anne gave her a comforting hug* **consoling,** sympathetic, compassionate, solicitous, tender, warm, caring, loving; supportive, reassuring, soothing, calming; cheering, heartening, encouraging.

comic ▶ adjective *a comic play* **humorous,** funny, droll, amusing, hilarious, uproarious; comical, farcical, silly, slapstick, zany; witty, jocular; informal priceless, side-splitting, rib-tickling; informal dated killing.
ANTONYMS serious.
▶ noun **1** *a professional comic* **comedian,** comedienne, funny man/woman, humorist, wit; joker, clown; informal kidder, wisecracker.
2 *the paper no longer runs his favorite Sunday comic* comic strip, cartoon, comic book; informal funny.

comical ▶ adjective **1** *he could be quite comical* **funny,** comic, humorous, droll, witty, jocular, hilarious, amusing, diverting, entertaining; informal jokey, wacky, waggish, side-splitting, rib-tickling, priceless, a scream, a laugh; informal dated killing, a card, a caution.
ANTONYMS sensible.
2 *they look comical in those suits* **silly,** absurd, ridiculous, laughable, risible, ludicrous, preposterous, foolish; informal wacky, crazy.
ANTONYMS sensible.

coming ▶ adjective *the coming election* **forthcoming,** imminent, impending, approaching; future, expected, anticipated; close, at hand, in store, in the offing, in the pipeline, on the horizon, on the way; informal in the cards.
▶ noun *the coming of spring* **approach,** advance, advent, arrival, appearance, emergence, onset.

command ▶ verb **1** *he commanded his men to retreat* **order,** tell, direct, instruct, call on, require; literary bid.
2 *Jones commanded a tank squadron* **be in charge of,** be in command of, be the leader of; head, lead, control, direct, manage, supervise, oversee; informal head up.
3 *they command great respect* **receive,** get, gain, secure.
▶ noun **1** *officers shouted commands* **order,** instruction, directive, direction, commandment, injunction, decree, edict, demand, stipulation, requirement, exhortation, bidding, request.
2 *he had 160 men under his command* **authority,** control, charge, power, direction, dominion, guidance; leadership, rule, government, management, supervision, jurisdiction.
3 *a brilliant command of Italian* **knowledge,** mastery, grasp, comprehension, understanding.

commandeer ▶ verb *dozens of private homes were commandeered by the army* **seize,** take, requisition, appropriate, expropriate, sequestrate, sequester, confiscate, annex, take over, claim, preempt; hijack, arrogate, help oneself to; informal walk off with; Law distrain.

commander ▶ noun *he is commander of an intelligence unit in Bogotá* **leader,** head, chief, overseer, controller; commander-in-chief, C in C, commanding officer, CO, officer; informal boss, boss man, skipper, numero uno, number one, top dog, kingpin, head honcho, big kahuna.

commanding ▶ adjective **1** *a commanding position* **dominant,** dominating, controlling, superior, powerful, prominent, advantageous, favorable.
2 *a commanding voice* **authoritative,** masterful, assertive, firm, emphatic, insistent, imperative; peremptory, imperious, dictatorial; informal bossy.

commemorate ▶ verb *an annual festival to commemorate the liberation of our town* **celebrate,** pay tribute to, pay homage to, honor, salute, toast; remember, recognize, acknowledge, observe, mark.

commemorative ▶ adjective *a commemorative coin that depicts the raising of the flag on Iwo Jima* **memorial,** remembrance; celebratory.

commence ▶ verb *the meeting will commence at noon* **begin,** start; get the ball rolling, get going, get underway, get off the ground, set about, embark on, launch into, lead off; open, initiate, inaugurate; informal kick off, get the show on the road.
ANTONYMS conclude.

commend ▶ verb **1** *we should commend him* **praise,** compliment, congratulate, applaud, salute, honor; sing the praises of, pay tribute to, take one's hat off to, pat on the back; formal laud. See note at PRAISE.
ANTONYMS criticize.
2 *I commend her to you without reservation* **recommend,** suggest, propose; endorse, advocate, vouch for, speak for, support, back. See note at APPROVE.
3 formal *I commend them to your care* **entrust,** trust, deliver, commit, hand over, give, turn over, consign, assign.

commendable ▶ adjective *he tackled the tests with commendable zeal* **admirable,** praiseworthy, creditable, laudable, estimable, meritorious, exemplary, noteworthy, honorable, respectable, fine, excellent.
ANTONYMS reprehensible.

commendation ▶ noun **1** *letters of commendation* **praise,** congratulation, appreciation; acclaim, credit, recognition, respect, esteem, admiration, homage, tribute.
2 *a commendation for bravery* **award,** accolade, prize, honor, honorable mention, mention, citation.

commensurate ▶ adjective **1** *they had privileges but commensurate duties* **equivalent,** equal, corresponding, correspondent, comparable, proportionate, proportional.
2 *a salary* ***commensurate with*** *your qualifications* **appropriate to,** in keeping with, in line with, consistent with, corresponding to, according to, relative to; dependent on, based on.

comment ▶ noun **1** *their comments on her appearance* **remark,** observation, statement, utterance; pronouncement, judgment, reflection, opinion, view; criticism.
2 *a great deal of comment* **discussion,** debate; interest.
3 *a comment in the margin* **note,** annotation, footnote, gloss, commentary, explanation.
▶ verb **1** *they* ***commented on*** *the food* **remark on,** speak about, talk about, discuss, mention.
2 *"It will soon be night," he commented* **remark,** observe, reflect, say, state, declare, announce; interpose, interject.

commentary ▶ noun **1** *the soccer commentary* **narration,** description, account, report, review.
2 *textual commentary* **explanation,** elucidation, interpretation, exegesis, analysis; assessment, appraisal, criticism; notes, comments.

commentator ▶ noun **1** *a television commentator* **narrator,** announcer, presenter, anchor, anchorman, anchorwoman; reporter, journalist, newscaster, sportscaster; informal talking head.
2 *a political commentator* **analyst,** pundit, monitor, observer; writer, speaker.

commerce ▶ noun **1** *industry and commerce* **trade,** trading, buying and selling, business, dealing, traffic; (financial) transactions, dealings.
2 dated *human commerce* **relations,** dealings, socializing, communication, association, contact, intercourse.

commercial ▶ adjective **1** *a vessel built for commercial purposes* **trade,** trading, business, private enterprise, mercantile, sales.
2 *a commercial society* **profit-oriented,** money-oriented, materialistic, mercenary.
▶ noun *a TV commercial* **advertisement,** promotion, display; informal ad, plug, infomercial.

commission ▶ noun **1** *the dealer's commission* **percentage,** brokerage, share, portion, dividend, premium, fee, consideration, bonus; informal cut, take, rake-off, slice.
2 *the commission of building a palace* **task,** employment, job, project, mission, assignment, undertaking; duty, charge, responsibility; informal marching orders.
3 *items made under state commission* **warrant,** license, sanction, authority.
4 *an independent commission* **committee,** board, council, panel, directorate, delegation.
5 *the commission of an offense* **perpetration,** committing, committal, execution.
▶ verb **1** *he was commissioned to paint a portrait* **engage,** contract, charge, employ, hire, recruit, retain, appoint, enlist, book, sign up.
2 *they commissioned a sculpture* **order;** authorize; formal bespeak.
– PHRASES **in commission** *the new bathrooms are now in commission* **in service,** in use; working, functional, operative, up and running, in operation, in working order. **out of commission** *more than half of our original computers are out of commission* **not in service,** not in use, unserviceable; not working, inoperative, out of order, malfunctioning, broken, down.

commit ▶ verb **1** *he committed a murder* **carry out,** do, perpetrate, engage in, enact, execute, effect, accomplish; be responsible for; informal pull off.
2 *she was committed to their care* **entrust,** consign, assign, deliver, give, hand over, relinquish; formal commend.
3 *they committed themselves to the project* **pledge,** devote, apply, give, dedicate.
4 *the judge committed him to prison* **consign,** send, deliver, confine.
5 *her husband had her committed* **hospitalize,** confine, institutionalize, put away; certify.

commitment ▶ noun **1** *the pressure of his commitments* **responsibility,** obligation, duty, tie, liability; task; engagement, arrangement.
2 *her commitment to her students* **dedication,** devotion, allegiance, loyalty, faithfulness, fidelity.
3 *he made a commitment* **vow,** promise, pledge, oath; contract, pact, deal; decision, resolution.

commodious ▶ adjective formal *a commodious armchair* **roomy,** capacious, spacious, ample,

generous, sizable, large, big, extensive.
ANTONYMS cramped.

commodity ▶ noun *Australian wools are among our most popular foreign commodities* **item,** material, product, article, object; import, export.

common ▶ adjective 1 *the common folk* **ordinary,** normal, average, unexceptional; simple.
2 *a very common art form* **usual,** ordinary, familiar, regular, frequent, recurrent, everyday; standard, typical, conventional, stock, commonplace, run-of-the-mill; informal garden variety. See note at PREVALENT.
ANTONYMS unusual.
3 *a common belief* **widespread,** general, universal, popular, mainstream, prevalent, prevailing, rife, established, conventional, traditional, orthodox, accepted. See note at UNIVERSAL.
ANTONYMS rare.
4 *the common good* **collective,** communal, community, public, popular, general; shared, combined.
ANTONYMS individual, private.
5 *they are far too common* **uncouth,** vulgar, coarse, rough, boorish, unladylike, ungentlemanly, ill-bred, uncivilized, unrefined, unsophisticated; lowly, low-born, low-class, inferior, proletarian, plebeian.
ANTONYMS refined.

common sense ▶ noun *well, at least you had the common sense to call 911* **good sense,** sense, native wit, sensibleness, judgment, levelheadedness, prudence, discernment, canniness, astuteness, shrewdness, wisdom, insight, perception, perspicacity; practicality, capability, resourcefulness, enterprise; informal horse sense, gumption, savvy, smarts, street smarts.
ANTONYMS folly.

commotion ▶ noun *what's all that commotion in the parking lot?* **disturbance,** uproar, tumult, rumpus, ruckus, brouhaha, hoopla, furor, hue and cry, fuss, stir, storm; turmoil, disorder, confusion, chaos, mayhem, havoc, pandemonium; unrest, fracas, riot, breach of the peace, donnybrook; informal ruction, ballyhoo, hoo-ha, to-do, hullabaloo.

communal ▶ adjective 1 *the kitchen was communal* **shared,** joint, common.
ANTONYMS private.
2 *they farm on a communal basis* **collective,** cooperative, community, communalist, combined.
ANTONYMS individual.

commune ▶ noun *she lives in a commune* **collective,** cooperative, communal settlement, kibbutz.
▶ verb 1 *we pray to commune with God* **communicate,** speak, talk, converse, interface.
2 *she likes to* **commune with** *nature* **empathize with,** identify with, have a rapport with, feel at one with; relate to, feel close to.

communicable ▶ adjective *the spread of communicable diseases* **contagious, infectious,** transmittable, transmissible, transferable, spreadable; informal catching.

communicate ▶ verb 1 *he communicated the news to his boss* **convey,** tell, impart, relay, transmit, pass on, announce, report, recount, relate, present; divulge, disclose, mention; spread, disseminate, promulgate, broadcast.
2 *they communicate daily* **be in touch,** be in contact, have dealings, interface, interact, commune, meet, liaise; talk, speak, converse; informal have a confab, powwow.
3 *learn how to communicate better* **get one's message across,** explain oneself, be understood, get through to someone.
4 *the disease is communicated easily* **transmit,** transfer, spread, carry, pass on.
5 *each bedroom communicates with a bathroom* **connect with,** join up with, open on to, lead into.

communication ▶ noun 1 *the communication of news* **transmission,** conveyance, divulgence, disclosure; dissemination, promulgation, broadcasting.
2 *there was no communication between them* **contact,** dealings, relations, connection, association, socializing, intercourse; correspondence, dialogue, talk, conversation, discussion.
3 *an official communication* **message,** statement, announcement, report, dispatch, communiqué, letter, bulletin, correspondence.

communicative ▶ adjective *we find that teenage boys tend to be less communicative* **forthcoming,** expansive, expressive, unreserved, uninhibited, vocal, outgoing, frank, open, candid; talkative, chatty, loquacious; informal gabby.

communion ▶ noun 1 *a sense of communion with others* **affinity,** fellowship, kinship, friendship, fellow feeling, togetherness, closeness, harmony, understanding, rapport, connection, communication, empathy, accord, unity. See note at CONVERSATION.
2 *Christ's presence at Communion* **the Eucharist,** Holy Communion, the Lord's Supper, Mass.

community ▶ noun 1 *work done for the community* **public,** general public, populace, people, citizenry, population, collective; residents, inhabitants, citizens.
2 *a suburban community* **district,** region, zone, area, locality, locale, neighborhood; informal neck of the woods, hood.
3 *concerns in the immigrant community* **group,** body, set, circle, clique, faction; informal gang, bunch.
4 *a monastic community* **brotherhood,** sisterhood, fraternity, sorority, sodality; order, congregation, abbey, convent.

commute ▶ verb 1 *they commute by train* **travel to and from work,** travel to and fro, travel back and forth.
2 *his sentence was commuted* **reduce,** lessen, lighten, shorten, cut, attenuate, moderate.
ANTONYMS increase, uphold.
3 *his jail sentence was commuted to a fine* **exchange,** change, substitute, swap, trade, switch.

commuter ▶ noun *commuters may see an increase in train fares this spring* **daily traveler,** traveler, passenger; informal straphanger.

compact[1] ▶ adjective 1 *a compact rug* **dense,** close-packed, tightly packed; thick, tight, firm.
ANTONYMS loose.
2 *a compact camera* **small,** little, petite, miniature, mini, small-scale; informal teeny, teeny-weeny; little-bitty, itty-bitty; Scottish wee.
ANTONYMS large.
3 *her overview is compact* **concise,** succinct, condensed, brief, pithy; short and sweet; informal snappy; formal compendious.
ANTONYMS rambling.
▶ verb *the snow has been compacted* **compress,** condense, pack down, press down, tamp (down), flatten; informal smoosh.

compact[2] ▶ noun *the warring states signed a compact* **treaty,** pact, accord, agreement, contract, bargain, deal, settlement, covenant, concordat; pledge, promise, bond.

companion ▶ noun 1 *Harry and his companion* **associate,** partner, escort, compatriot, confederate; friend, intimate, confidant, confidante, comrade; informal pal, chum, crony, sidekick, mate, buddy, amigo, compadre.
2 *a lady's companion* **attendant,** aide, helper, assistant, valet, equerry, lady-in-waiting; chaperone; minder.
3 *the tape is a companion to the book* **complement,** counterpart, twin, match; accompaniment, supplement, addition, adjunct, accessory.
4 *The Gardener's Companion* **handbook,** manual, guide, reference book, ABC, primer, vade mecum; informal bible.

companionship ▶ noun *the volunteers do various errands for our elderly clients and provide some much-appreciated companionship* **friendship,** fellowship, closeness, togetherness, amity, intimacy, rapport, camaraderie, brotherhood, sisterhood; company, society, social contact.

company ▶ noun 1 *an oil company* **firm,** business, corporation, establishment, agency, office, bureau, institution, organization, concern, enterprise; conglomerate, consortium, syndicate, multinational; informal outfit.
2 *I enjoy his company* **companionship,** friendship, fellowship, amity, camaraderie; society, association.
3 *I'm expecting company* **guests,** house guests, visitors, callers, people; someone.
4 *a company of poets* **group,** crowd, party, band, assembly, cluster, flock, herd, troupe, throng, congregation; informal bunch, gang.
5 *a company of infantry* **unit,** section, detachment, troop, corps, squad, squadron, platoon, battalion, division.

comparable ▶ adjective 1 *comparable incomes* **similar,** close, near, approximate, akin, equivalent, commensurate, proportional, proportionate; like, matching, homologous.
2 *nobody is **comparable with** him* **equal to,** as good as, in the same league as, able to hold a candle to, on a par with, on a level with; a match for.

comparative ▶ adjective *they left the city for the comparative quiet of the country* **relative,** in/by comparison.

compare ▶ verb 1 *we compared the data sets* **contrast,** juxtapose, collate, differentiate.
2 *he was **compared to** Wagner* **liken to,** equate to, analogize to; class with, set side by side with.
3 *the porcelain **compares with** Dresden's fine china* **be as good as,** be comparable to, bear comparison with, be the equal of, match up to, be on a par with, be in the same league as, come close to, hold a candle to, be not unlike; match, resemble, emulate, rival, approach.
– PHRASES **beyond compare** *their peach cobbler is beyond compare* **without equal,** second to none, in a class of one's own; peerless, matchless, unmatched, incomparable, inimitable, supreme, outstanding, consummate, unique, singular, perfect.

comparison ▶ noun 1 *a comparison of the results* **juxtaposition,** collation, differentiation.
2 *there's no comparison between them* **resemblance,** likeness, similarity, correspondence, correlation, parallel, parity, comparability.

compartment ▶ noun 1 *a secret compartment* **section,** part, bay, recess, chamber, cavity; pocket.
2 *they put science and religion in separate compartments* **domain,** field, sphere, department; category, pigeonhole, bracket, group, set.

compass ▶ noun *faith cannot be defined within the compass of human thought* **scope,** range, extent, reach, span, breadth, ambit, limits, parameters, bounds. See note at RANGE.

compassion ▶ noun *have you no compassion for a fellow human being?* **pity,** sympathy, empathy, fellow feeling, care, concern, solicitude, sensitivity, warmth, love, tenderness, mercy, leniency, tolerance, kindness, humanity, charity. See note at MERCY.
ANTONYMS indifference, cruelty.

compassionate ▶ adjective *a compassionate concern for the victims* **sympathetic,** empathetic, understanding, caring, solicitous, sensitive, warm, loving; merciful, lenient, tolerant, considerate, kind, humane, charitable, bighearted.

compatible ▶ adjective 1 *they were never compatible* **well suited,** suited, well matched, like-minded, in tune, in harmony; reconcilable.
2 *her bruising is compatible with a fall* **consistent,** congruous, congruent; in keeping.

compatriot ▶ noun *Sampras defeated his compatriot Agassi in the final* **fellow countryman,** fellow countrywoman, countryman, countrywoman, fellow citizen.

compel ▶ verb 1 *he compelled them to leave their land* **force,** pressure, press, push, urge; dragoon, browbeat, bully, intimidate, strong-arm; oblige, require, make; informal lean on, put the screws on.
2 *they can compel compliance* **exact,** extort, demand, insist on, force, necessitate.

CHOOSE THE RIGHT WORD

compel, coerce, constrain, force, necessitate, oblige

A parent faced with a rebellious teenager may try to **compel** him to do his homework by threatening to take away his allowance. *Compel* commonly implies the exercise of authority, the exertion of great effort, or the impossibility of doing anything else (*compelled to graduate from high school by her eagerness to leave home*). It typically requires a personal object, although it is possible to *compel* a reaction or response (*she compels admiration*). **Force** is a little stronger, suggesting the exertion of power, energy, or physical strength to accomplish something or to subdue resistance (*his mother forced him to confess that he'd broken the basement window*). **Coerce** can imply the use of force, but often stops short of using it (*she was coerced into obedience by the threat of losing her telephone privileges*). **Constrain** means *compel*, but by means of restriction, confinement, or limitation (*constrained from dating by his parents' strictness*). **Necessitate** and **oblige** make an action necessary by imposing certain conditions that demand a response (*Her mother's illness obliged her to be more cooperative; it also necessitated giving up her social life*).

compelling ▶ **adjective 1** *a compelling performance* **enthralling,** captivating, gripping, riveting, spellbinding, mesmerizing, absorbing, irresistible.
ANTONYMS boring.
2 *a compelling argument* **convincing,** persuasive, cogent, irresistible, powerful, strong, weighty, plausible, credible, sound, valid, telling, conclusive, irrefutable, unanswerable.
ANTONYMS weak.

compensate ▶ **verb 1** *you must compensate for what you did* **make amends,** make up, make reparation, recompense, atone, requite, pay; expiate, make good, rectify.
2 *we agreed to compensate him for his loss* **recompense,** repay, pay back, reimburse, remunerate, recoup, requite, indemnify.
3 *his flair* ***compensated for*** *his faults* **balance (out),** counterbalance, counteract, offset, make up for, cancel out, neutralize, negative.

compensation ▶ **noun** *my client has not received compensation for the legal fees incurred in 1998* **recompense,** repayment, reimbursement, remuneration, requital, indemnification, indemnity, redress; damages; informal comp.

compete ▶ **verb 1** *they competed in a tennis tournament* **take part,** participate, play, be a competitor, be involved; enter.
2 *they had to* ***compete with*** *other firms* **contend with,** vie with, battle (with), wrangle with, jockey with, go head to head with; strive against, pit oneself against; challenge, take on.
3 *no one can* ***compete with*** *Elaine* **rival,** challenge, keep up with, keep pace with, compare with, match, be in the same league as, come near to, come close to, touch; informal hold a candle to.

competence ▶ **noun 1** *my technical competence* **capability,** ability, competency, proficiency, accomplishment, expertise, adeptness, skill, prowess, mastery, talent; informal savvy, know-how.
2 *the competence of the system* **adequacy,** appropriateness, suitability, fitness; effectiveness; formal efficacy.
3 *matters within the competence of the courts* **authority,** power, control, jurisdiction, ambit, scope.

competent ▶ **adjective 1** *a competent carpenter* **capable,** able, proficient, adept, adroit, accomplished, complete, skillful, skilled, credentialed, gifted, talented, expert; good, excellent; informal great, mean, wicked, nifty, ace.
2 *she spoke competent French* **adequate,** acceptable, satisfactory, reasonable, fair, decent, not bad, all right, average, tolerable, passable, moderate, middling; informal OK, okay, so-so, 'comme ci, comme ça'.
ANTONYMS inadequate.
3 *the court was not competent to hear the case* **fit,** suitable, suited, appropriate; qualified, empowered, authorized.
ANTONYMS unfit.

competition ▶ **noun 1** *Stephanie won the competition* **contest,** tournament, match, game, heat, fixture, event.
2 *I'm not interested in competition* **rivalry,** competitiveness, vying; conflict, feuding, fighting; informal keeping up with the Joneses.
3 *we must stay ahead of the competition* **opposition,** other side, field; enemy; challengers, opponents, rivals, adversaries; literary foe.

competitive ▶ **adjective 1** *a competitive player* **ambitious,** zealous, keen, pushy, combative, aggressive.
ANTONYMS apathetic.
2 *a highly competitive industry* **ruthless,** aggressive, fierce; Darwinian; informal dog-eat-dog, cutthroat.
3 *competitive prices* **reasonable,** moderate; low, inexpensive, cheap, budget, bargain, reduced, discount; rock-bottom, bargain-basement, downmarket.
ANTONYMS exorbitant.

competitor ▶ **noun 1** *the competitors in the race* **contestant,** contender, challenger, participant, entrant; runner, player.
ANTONYMS spectator.
2 *our European competitors* **rival,** challenger, opponent, adversary; competition, opposition.
ANTONYMS ally.

compilation ▶ **noun** *a compilation of their greatest hits* **collection,** selection, anthology, treasury, compendium, album, corpus; potpourri.

compile ▶ **verb** *he compiled a dossier of patients with tropical diseases* **assemble,** put together, make up, collate, compose, organize, arrange; gather, collect.

complacent ▶ **adjective** *in this competitive field we can't afford to be complacent* **smug,** self-satisfied, self-congratulatory, self-regarding; gloating, triumphant, proud; pleased, satisfied, content, contented.

complain ▶ **verb** *his dogs were always roaming until someone finally complained* **protest,** grumble, whine, bleat, carp, cavil, grouse, make a fuss; object, speak out, criticize, find fault; informal kick up a fuss, raise a stink, bellyache, moan, snivel, beef, bitch, sound off, gripe, kvetch.

complaint ▶ noun 1 *they lodged a complaint* **protest,** objection, grievance, grouse, cavil, quibble, grumble; charge, accusation, criticism; jeremiad; informal beef, gripe, whinge; Law plaint.
2 *little cause for complaint* **protestation,** objection, exception, grievance, grumbling; criticism, fault-finding, condemnation, disapproval, dissatisfaction; informal grousing, bellyaching, nitpicking.
3 *a kidney complaint* **disorder,** disease, infection, affliction, illness, ailment, sickness; condition, problem, upset, trouble.

complement ▶ noun 1 *the perfect complement to the food* **accompaniment,** companion, addition, supplement, accessory, trimming.
2 *a full complement of lifeboats* **amount,** total, contingent, capacity, allowance, quota.
▶ verb *this sauce complements the dessert* **accompany,** go with, round off, set off, suit, harmonize with; enhance, complete.

complementary ▶ adjective *decorating in complementary colors and patterns* **harmonious,** compatible, corresponding, matching, twin; supportive, reciprocal, interdependent.
ANTONYMS incompatible.

complete ▶ adjective 1 *the complete interview* **entire,** whole, full, total; uncut, unabridged.
2 *their research was complete* **finished,** ended, concluded, completed, finalized; accomplished, achieved, discharged, settled, done; informal wrapped up, sewn up, polished off.
ANTONYMS unfinished.
3 *a complete fool* **absolute,** out-and-out, utter, total, real, downright, thoroughgoing, veritable, prize, perfect, unqualified, unmitigated, sheer, arrant, full-out.
ANTONYMS partial.
▶ verb 1 *he had to complete his training* **finish,** end, conclude, finalize, wind up; informal wrap up, sew up, polish off.
2 *the outfit was completed with a veil* **finish off,** round off, top off, crown, cap, complement.
3 *complete the application form* **fill in/out,** answer.

completely ▶ adverb *he'd always been completely honest with her* **totally,** entirely, wholly, thoroughly, fully, utterly, absolutely, perfectly, unreservedly, unconditionally, quite, altogether, downright; in every way, in every respect, one hundred percent, every inch, to the hilt; informal dead, deadly, to the max.

completion ▶ noun *the money ran out before the project's completion* **realization,** accomplishment, achievement, fulfillment, consummation, finalization, resolution; finish, end, conclusion, close, cessation.

complex ▶ adjective 1 *a complex situation* **complicated,** involved, intricate, convoluted, elaborate, impenetrable, Gordian; difficult, knotty, tricky, thorny.
ANTONYMS simple.
2 *a complex structure* **compound,** composite, multiplex.
▶ noun 1 *a complex of roads* **network,** system, nexus, web, tissue; combination, aggregation.
2 informal *he had a complex about losing his hair* **obsession,** fixation, preoccupation; neurosis; informal hang-up, thing, bee in one's bonnet.

complexion ▶ noun 1 *a pale complexion* **skin,** skin color, skin tone; pigmentation.
2 *this puts an entirely new complexion on things* **perspective,** angle, slant, interpretation; appearance, light, look.
3 *governments of all complexions* **type,** kind, sort; nature, character, stamp, ilk, kidney.

complexity ▶ noun *an issue of great complexity* **complication,** problem, difficulty; twist, turn, intricacy.

compliance ▶ noun 1 *compliance with international law* **obedience to,** observance of, adherence to, conformity to, respect for.
ANTONYMS violation.
2 *he mistook her silence for compliance* **acquiescence,** agreement, assent, consent, acceptance; complaisance, pliability, docility, meekness, submission.
ANTONYMS defiance.

complicate ▶ verb *involvement with Adam could only complicate her life* **make (more) difficult,** make complicated, mix up, confuse, muddle; informal mess up, screw up, snarl up.
ANTONYMS simplify.

complicated ▶ adjective *the complicated election process* **complex,** intricate, involved, convoluted, tangled, impenetrable, knotty, tricky, thorny, labyrinthine, tortuous, Gordian; confusing, bewildering, perplexing.
ANTONYMS straightforward.

complication ▶ noun 1 *a complication concerning ownership* **difficulty,** problem, obstacle, hurdle, stumbling block; drawback, snag, catch, hitch; informal fly in the ointment, headache.
2 *the complication of life in our society* **complexity,** complicatedness, intricacy, convolutedness.

complicity ▶ noun *they've been accused of complicity in the destruction of damning evidence* **collusion,** involvement, collaboration, connivance; conspiracy; informal being in cahoots.

compliment ▶ noun 1 *an unexpected compliment | he enjoyed the compliments* **flattering remark,** tribute, accolade, commendation, bouquet, pat on the back; (**compliments**) praise, acclaim, admiration, flattery, blandishments, honeyed words.
ANTONYMS insult.
2 (**compliments**) *my compliments on your cooking* **congratulations,** commendations, praise; informal props, kudos.
3 (**compliments**) *Margaret sends her compliments* **greetings,** regards, respects, good wishes, best wishes, salutations, felicitations.
▶ verb *they complimented his performance* **praise,** pay tribute to, speak highly/well of, flatter, wax lyrical about, make much of, commend, acclaim, applaud, salute, honor; congratulate someone on.
ANTONYMS criticize.

complimentary ▶ adjective 1 *complimentary remarks* **flattering,** appreciative,

congratulatory, admiring, approving, commendatory, favorable, glowing, adulatory; informal rave.
ANTONYMS derogatory.
2 *complimentary tickets* **free,** free of charge, gratis, for nothing; courtesy; informal on the house.

comply ▶ verb *Myra complied with his wishes* **abide by,** observe, obey, adhere to, conform to, hew to, follow, respect; agree to, assent to, go along with, yield to, submit to, defer to; satisfy, fulfill.
ANTONYMS ignore, disobey.

component ▶ noun *the components of electronic devices* **part,** piece, bit, element, constituent, ingredient, building block; unit, module, section.
▶ adjective *the molecule's component elements* **constituent,** integral; basic, essential.

compose ▶ verb **1** *a poem composed by Shelley* **write,** formulate, devise, make up, think up, produce, invent, concoct; pen, author, draft; score, orchestrate, choreograph.
2 *compose a still life* **organize,** arrange, set out.
3 *the subcommittee is composed of ten senators* **make up,** constitute, form.
– PHRASES **compose oneself** *you have to compose yourself before you take the stand* **calm down,** control oneself, regain one's composure, pull oneself together, collect oneself, steady oneself, keep one's head, relax; informal get a grip, take a chill pill, keep one's cool, cool one's jets, decompress.

composed ▶ adjective *she remained composed throughout the ordeal* **calm,** collected, cool, cool as a cucumber, 'cool, calm, and collected', self-controlled, self-possessed; serene, tranquil, relaxed, at ease, unruffled, unperturbed, untroubled; equable, even-tempered, imperturbable; informal unflappable, together, laid-back.
ANTONYMS excited.

composite ▶ adjective *a composite structure* **compound,** complex; combined, blended, mixed.
▶ noun *a composite of plastic and metal* **amalgamation,** amalgam, combination, compound, fusion, synthesis, mixture, blend; alloy.

composition ▶ noun **1** *the composition of the council* **makeup,** constitution, configuration, structure, formation, form, framework, fabric, anatomy, organization; informal setup.
2 *a literary composition* **work,** work of art, creation, opus, oeuvre, piece, arrangement.
3 *we all participated in the composition of the school song* **writing,** creation, formulation, invention, concoction, orchestration.
4 *a school composition* **essay,** paper, study, piece of writing, theme.
5 *the composition of the painting* **arrangement,** disposition, layout; proportions, balance, symmetry.
6 *an adhesive composition* **mixture,** compound, amalgam, blend, mix.

compost ▶ noun *all of our organic garbage is converted to compost* **fertilizer,** mulch, manure, bone meal, fish meal, blood meal, guano; humus, peat; plant food, top-dressing.

composure ▶ noun *most people would have lost their composure after such a disappointing defeat* **self-control,** self-possession, calm, equanimity, equilibrium, serenity, tranquility; aplomb, poise, presence of mind, sangfroid; imperturbability, placidness, impassivity; informal cool.

compound ▶ noun **1** *a compound of two elements* **amalgam,** amalgamation, combination, composite, blend, mixture, mix, fusion, synthesis; alloy.
2 *they were contained in the compound* **enclosure,** pound, coop; estate, cloister.
▶ adjective *a compound substance* **composite,** complex; blended, fused, combined.
ANTONYMS simple.
▶ verb **1** *soap compounded with disinfectant* **mix,** combine, blend, amalgamate, fuse, synthesize.
2 *his illness compounds their problems* **aggravate,** exacerbate, worsen, add to, augment, intensify, heighten, increase, magnify; complicate.
ANTONYMS alleviate.
– PHRASES **compounded of** *a smell compounded of dust and mold* **composed of,** made up of, formed from.

comprehend ▶ verb **1** *Katie couldn't comprehend his message* **understand,** grasp, take in, see, apprehend, follow, make sense of, fathom, get to the bottom of; unravel, decipher, interpret; informal work out, figure out, make head(s) or tail(s) of, get one's head around, get the drift of, catch on to, get.
2 formal *a divine order comprehending all men* **comprise,** include, encompass, embrace, involve, contain.
ANTONYMS exclude.

comprehensible ▶ adjective *the information must be accurate and comprehensible* **intelligible,** understandable, accessible; lucid, coherent, clear, plain, explicit, unambiguous, straightforward, fathomable.
ANTONYMS opaque.

comprehension ▶ noun *matters that seemed beyond her comprehension* **understanding,** grasp, conception, apprehension, cognition, ken, knowledge, awareness, perception; interpretation.
ANTONYMS ignorance.

comprehensive ▶ adjective *a comprehensive review of our defense policy* **inclusive,** all-inclusive, complete; thorough, full, extensive, all-embracing, exhaustive, detailed, in-depth, encyclopedic, universal, catholic; far-reaching, radical, sweeping, across the board, wholesale; broad, wide-ranging; informal wall-to-wall.
ANTONYMS limited.

compress ▶ verb **1** *the skirt can be compressed into a small bag* **squeeze,** press, squash, crush, cram, jam, stuff; tamp, pack, compact; constrict; informal scrunch, smoosh.
2 *the text was compressed* **abridge,** condense, shorten, cut, abbreviate, truncate; summarize, précis.
ANTONYMS expand.

comprise ▶ verb **1** *the country comprises twenty states* **consist of,** be made up of, be composed of, contain, encompass, incorporate; include;

formal comprehend.
2 informal *this breed comprises half the herd* **make up,** constitute, form, compose; account for. See note at INCLUDE.

compromise ▶ noun **1** *they reached a compromise* **agreement,** understanding, settlement, terms, deal, trade-off, bargain; middle ground, happy medium, balance.
2 *a happy marriage needs compromise* **give and take,** concession, cooperation.
ANTONYMS intransigence.
▶ verb **1** *we compromised* **meet each other halfway,** come to an understanding, make a deal, make concessions, find a happy medium, strike a balance; give and take.
2 *his actions could compromise his reputation* **undermine,** weaken, damage, harm; jeopardize, prejudice; discredit, dishonor, shame, embarrass.

compulsion ▶ noun **1** *he is under no compulsion to go* **obligation,** constraint, coercion, duress, pressure, intimidation.
2 *a compulsion to tell the truth* **urge,** impulse, need, desire, drive; obsession, fixation, addiction; temptation.

compulsive ▶ adjective **1** *a compulsive desire* **irresistible,** uncontrollable, compelling, overwhelming, urgent; obsessive.
2 *compulsive eating* **obsessive,** obsessional, addictive, uncontrollable.
3 *a compulsive liar* **inveterate,** chronic, incorrigible, incurable, hardened, hopeless, persistent; obsessive, addicted, habitual; informal pathological.
4 *it's compulsive viewing* **fascinating,** compelling, gripping, riveting, engrossing, enthralling, captivating.

compulsory ▶ adjective *the wearing of seat belts is compulsory* **obligatory,** mandatory, required, requisite, necessary, essential; imperative, unavoidable, enforced, demanded, prescribed.
ANTONYMS optional.

compunction ▶ noun *she had no compunction about deceiving them* **scruples,** misgivings, qualms, worries, unease, uneasiness, doubts, reluctance, reservations; guilt, regret, contrition, self-reproach. See note at QUALMS.

compute ▶ verb *we compute our expenses at the close of each day* **calculate,** work out, reckon, determine, evaluate, quantify; add up, count up, tally, total, totalize, tot up.

comrade ▶ noun *we became comrades back in 1943, working in a field hospital in the Philippines* **companion,** friend; colleague, associate, partner, coworker, workmate; informal pal, crony, mate, chum, buddy.

con ▶ verb informal *we got conned* See SWINDLE.
▶ noun **1** *an ex-con* See CONVICT.
2 *a public relations con* See SWINDLE.

concave ▶ adjective *a small concave area now filled with rainwater* **incurvate,** curved inward, hollow, depressed, sunken; indented, recessed.
ANTONYMS convex.

conceal ▶ verb **1** *clouds concealed the sun* **hide,** screen, cover, obscure, block out, blot out, mask, shroud, secrete.
ANTONYMS reveal.
2 *he concealed his true feelings* **hide,** cover up, disguise, mask, veil; keep secret, draw a veil over; suppress, repress, bottle up; informal keep a lid on, keep under one's hat.
ANTONYMS reveal, confess.

concealed ▶ adjective *another piece of concealed evidence was disclosed to Sgt. Kahn* **hidden,** not visible, out of sight, invisible, covered, disguised, camouflaged, obscured; private, secret.

concealment ▶ noun **1** *the concealment of his weapon* **hiding,** secretion.
2 *the deliberate concealment of facts* **suppression,** hiding, cover-up, hushing up; whitewash.

concede ▶ verb **1** *I had to concede that I'd overreacted* **admit,** acknowledge, accept, allow, grant, recognize, own, confess; agree.
ANTONYMS deny.
2 *he conceded the Auvergne to the king* **surrender,** yield, give up, relinquish, cede, hand over.
ANTONYMS retain.
– PHRASES **concede defeat** *Colonel Morris vowed never to concede defeat* **capitulate,** give in, give, surrender, yield, give up, submit, raise the white flag; back down, climb down; informal throw in the towel.

conceited ▶ adjective *she's too conceited to think she might not get the lead role* **vain,** narcissistic, self-centered, egotistic, egotistical, egocentric; proud, arrogant, boastful, full of oneself, self-important, immodest, swaggering; self-satisfied, smug; supercilious, haughty, snobbish; informal bigheaded, too big for one's britches, stuck-up, high and mighty, uppity, snotty; literary vainglorious.

conceivable ▶ adjective *is there any conceivable justification for betraying your family?* **imaginable,** possible; plausible, tenable, credible, believable, thinkable, feasible; understandable, comprehensible.

conceive ▶ verb **1** *they were unable to conceive* **become pregnant,** become impregnated.
2 *the project was conceived in 1977* **think up,** think of, dream up, devise, formulate, design, originate, create, develop; informal cook up, hatch.
3 *I can hardly conceive what it must be like* **imagine,** envisage, visualize, picture, think, envision; grasp, appreciate, apprehend; formal ideate.

concentrate ▶ verb **1** *the government concentrated its efforts* **focus,** direct, center, centralize.
ANTONYMS dissipate.
2 *she* ***concentrated on*** *the movie* **focus on,** pay attention to, keep one's mind on, devote oneself to; be absorbed in, be engrossed in, be immersed in.
3 *troops concentrated on the horizon* **collect,** gather, congregate, converge, mass, cluster, rally.
ANTONYMS disperse.
4 *the liquid is filtered and concentrated* **condense,** boil down, reduce, thicken.
ANTONYMS dilute.
▶ noun *a fruit concentrate* **extract,** decoction, distillation.

concentrated ▶ adjective **1** *a concentrated effort* **strenuous,** concerted, intensive, intense; informal all-out.
ANTONYMS halfhearted.
2 *a concentrated solution* **condensed,** reduced, evaporated, thickened; undiluted, strong.
ANTONYMS diluted.

concentration ▶ noun **1** *a task requiring concentration* **close attention,** attentiveness, application, single-mindedness, tunnel vision, absorption.
ANTONYMS inattention.
2 *the concentration of effort* **focusing,** centralization.
3 *concentrations of seals* **gathering,** cluster, mass, congregation, assemblage.

concept ▶ noun *Freud's concept of the superego* **idea,** notion, conception, abstraction; theory, hypothesis; belief, conviction, opinion; image, impression, picture. See note at **IDEA**.

conception ▶ noun **1** *from conception until natural death* **inception of pregnancy,** conceiving, fertilization, impregnation, insemination.
2 *the product's conception* **inception,** genesis, origination, creation, invention; beginning, origin.
3 *his original conception* **plan,** scheme, project, proposal; intention, aim, idea. See note at **IDEA**.
4 *my conception of democracy* **idea,** concept, notion, understanding, abstraction; theory, hypothesis; perception, image, impression.
5 *they had no conception of our problems* **understanding,** comprehension, appreciation, grasp, knowledge; idea, inkling; informal clue.

concern ▶ verb **1** *the report concerns the war* **be about,** deal with, have to do with, cover; discuss, go into, examine, study, review, analyze; relate to, pertain to.
2 *that doesn't concern you* **affect,** involve, be relevant to, apply to, have a bearing on, impact on; be important to, interest.
3 *I won't* ***concern myself with*** *your affairs* **involve oneself in,** take an interest in, busy oneself with, devote one's time to, bother oneself with.
4 *one thing still concerns me* **worry,** disturb, trouble, bother, perturb, unsettle, make anxious.
▶ noun **1** *a voice full of concern* **anxiety,** worry, disquiet, apprehensiveness, unease, consternation.
ANTONYMS peace of mind.
2 *his concern for others* **solicitude,** consideration, care, sympathy, regard.
ANTONYMS indifference.
3 *housing is the concern of the council* **responsibility,** business, affair, charge, duty, job; province, preserve; problem, worry; informal bag, bailiwick.
4 *issues that are of concern to women* **interest,** importance, relevance, significance.
5 *Aboriginal concerns* **affair,** issue, matter, question, consideration.
6 *a publishing concern* **company,** business, firm, organization, operation, corporation, establishment, house, office, agency; informal outfit.

concerned ▶ adjective **1** *her mother looked concerned* **worried,** anxious, upset, perturbed, troubled, distressed, uneasy, apprehensive, agitated.
2 *he is concerned about your welfare* **solicitous,** caring; attentive to, considerate of.
3 *all concerned parties* **interested,** involved, affected; connected, related, implicated.

concerning ▶ preposition *we have new information concerning his disappearance* **about,** regarding, relating to, with reference to, referring to, with regard to, as regards, with respect to, respecting, dealing with, on the subject of, in connection with, re, apropos of.

concert ▶ noun *a concert at Woolsey Hall featuring a pianist from Estonia* **musical performance,** show, production, presentation; recital; informal gig.
– PHRASES **in concert** *we must take stronger action in concert with our European allies* **together,** jointly, in combination, in collaboration, in cooperation, in league, side by side; in unison.

concerted ▶ adjective **1** *make a concerted effort* **strenuous,** vigorous, intensive, intense, concentrated; informal all-out.
ANTONYMS halfhearted.
2 *concerted action* **joint,** united, collaborative, collective, combined, cooperative.
ANTONYMS individual.

concession ▶ noun **1** *the government made several concessions* **compromise,** allowance, exception.
2 *a concession of failure* **admission,** acknowledgment, acceptance, recognition, confession.
ANTONYMS denial.
3 *the concession of territory* **surrender,** relinquishment, sacrifice, handover.
ANTONYMS retention, acquisition.
4 *tax concessions* **reduction,** cut, discount, deduction, decrease; rebate; informal break.
5 *a fast-food concession* **stand,** kiosk, stall, counter, vendor.
6 *a logging concession* **right,** privilege; license, permit, franchise, warrant, authorization.

conciliate ▶ verb **1** *he tried to conciliate the peasantry* **appease,** placate, pacify, mollify, assuage, soothe, humor, reconcile, win over, make peace with. See note at **PACIFY**.
ANTONYMS provoke.
2 *he conciliated in the dispute* **mediate,** act as peacemaker, arbitrate; pour oil on troubled waters.

conciliatory ▶ adjective *a conciliatory gesture* **propitiatory,** placatory, appeasing, pacifying, mollifying, peacemaking.

concise ▶ adjective *a concise account* **succinct,** pithy, incisive, brief, short and to the point, short and sweet; abridged, condensed, compressed, abbreviated, compact; informal snappy. See note at **TERSE**.
ANTONYMS lengthy, wordy.

conclave ▶ noun *a conclave of American and Japanese business leaders* **(private) meeting,** gathering, assembly, conference, council, summit; informal parley, powwow, get-together.

conclude ▶ verb **1** *the meeting concluded at ten*

finish, end, draw to a close, be over, stop, cease.
ANTONYMS commence, start, begin.
2 *she concluded the press conference* **bring to an end,** close, wind up, terminate, dissolve; informal wrap up.
ANTONYMS open, start, begin.
3 *an attempt to conclude a cease-fire* **negotiate,** broker, agree, come to terms on, settle, clinch, finalize, tie up; bring about, arrange, effect, engineer; informal sew up.
4 *I concluded that he was rather unpleasant* **deduce,** infer, gather, judge, decide, conjecture, surmise, extrapolate, figure, reckon.

conclusion ▶ noun **1** *the conclusion of his speech* **end,** ending, finish, close, termination, windup, cessation; culmination, denouement, peroration, coda; informal outro.
ANTONYMS beginning.
2 *the conclusion of a trade agreement* **negotiation,** brokering, settlement, completion, arrangement, resolution.
3 *his conclusions have been verified* **deduction,** inference, interpretation, reasoning; opinion, judgment, verdict; assumption, presumption, supposition; rare illation.
– PHRASES **in conclusion** *in conclusion, I'd like to remind you that Mr. Clark will be signing books in the cafeteria* **finally,** in closing, to conclude, last but not least; to sum up, in short, to make a long story short.

conclusive ▶ adjective **1** *conclusive proof* **incontrovertible,** undeniable, indisputable, irrefutable, unquestionable, unassailable, convincing, certain, decisive, definitive, definite, positive, categorical, unequivocal; airtight, watertight.
ANTONYMS unconvincing.
2 *a conclusive win* **emphatic,** resounding, convincing.
ANTONYMS narrow.

concoct ▶ verb **1** *he planned to concoct a dessert* **prepare,** make, assemble; informal fix, rustle up.
2 *this story she has concocted* **make up,** dream up, fabricate, invent, trump up; formulate, hatch, brew, cook up.

concoction ▶ noun **1** *a concoction containing gin and vodka* **mixture,** brew, preparation, potion.
2 *a strange concoction of folk pop and Gregorian chant* **blend,** mixture, mix, combination, hybrid.
3 *her story is an improbable concoction* **fabrication,** invention, falsification; informal fairy tale.

concomitant ▶ adjective formal *the rise of urbanism brought a concomitant risk of crime* **attendant,** accompanying, associated, related, connected; resultant, consequent.
ANTONYMS unrelated.

concord ▶ noun *council meetings rarely ended in concord* **agreement,** harmony, accord, consensus, concurrence, unity.
ANTONYMS discord.

concrete ▶ adjective **1** *concrete objects* **solid,** material, real, physical, tangible, palpable, substantial, visible, existing.
ANTONYMS abstract, imaginary.
2 *concrete proof* **definite,** firm, positive, conclusive, definitive; real, genuine, bona fide.
ANTONYMS vague.

concubine ▶ noun archaic *she was the reluctant concubine of Prince Percival* **mistress,** courtesan, kept woman; lover; archaic paramour, doxy; historical hetaera.

concur ▶ verb **1** *we concur with this view* **agree,** be in agreement, go along, fall in, be in sympathy; see eye to eye, be of the same mind, be of the same opinion.
ANTONYMS disagree.
2 *the two events concurred* **coincide,** be simultaneous, be concurrent, coexist.

concurrent ▶ adjective **1** *nine concurrent life sentences* **simultaneous,** coincident, contemporaneous, parallel.
2 *concurrent lines* **convergent,** converging, meeting, intersecting.

concussion ▶ noun **1** *he suffered a concussion* temporary unconsciousness; brain injury.
2 *the concussion of the blast* **force,** impact, shock, jolt.

condemn ▶ verb **1** *he condemned the suspended players* **censure,** criticize, denounce, revile, blame, chastise, berate, reprimand, rebuke, reprove, take to task, find fault with; informal slam, blast, lay into; formal castigate.
ANTONYMS praise.
2 *he was condemned to death* **sentence**; convict, find guilty.
ANTONYMS acquit.
3 *the house has been condemned* **declare unfit,** declare unsafe.
4 *her mistake had condemned her* **incriminate,** implicate; archaic inculpate.
5 *his illness condemned him to a lonely life* **doom,** destine, damn; consign, assign.

condensation ▶ noun **1** *windows misty with condensation* **moisture,** water droplets, steam.
2 *the condensation of the vapor* **precipitation,** liquefaction, deliquescence.
3 *a condensation of recent literature* **abridgment,** summary, synopsis, précis, digest.
4 *the condensation of the report* **shortening,** abridgment, abbreviation, summarization.

condense ▶ verb **1** *the water vapor condenses* **precipitate,** liquefy, become liquid, deliquesce.
ANTONYMS vaporize.
2 *he condensed the play* **abridge,** shorten, cut, abbreviate, compact; summarize, synopsize, précis; truncate, curtail.
ANTONYMS lengthen, expand.

condescend ▶ verb **1** *don't condescend to your readers* **patronize,** talk down to, look down one's nose at, look down on, put down.
2 *he condescended to see us* **deign,** stoop, descend, lower oneself, demean oneself; vouchsafe, see fit, consent.

condescending ▶ adjective *she looked us up and down in a condescending manner* **patronizing,** supercilious, superior, snobbish, snobby, disdainful, lofty, haughty; informal snooty, stuck-up.

condition ▶ noun **1** *check the condition of your wiring* **state,** shape, order.
2 *they lived in appalling conditions* **circumstances,** surroundings, environment, situation, setup, setting, habitat.

3 *she was in top condition* **fitness,** health, form, shape, trim, fettle.
4 *a liver condition* **disorder,** problem, complaint, illness, disease, ailment, sickness, affliction, infection, upset.
5 *a condition of membership* **stipulation,** constraint, prerequisite, precondition, requirement, rule, term, specification, provision, proviso.
▶ verb 1 *their choices are conditioned by the economy* **constrain,** control, govern, determine, decide; affect, touch; form, shape, guide, sway, bias.
2 *our minds are conditioned by habit* **train,** teach, educate, guide; accustom, adapt, habituate, mold, inure.
3 *condition the boards with water* **treat,** prepare, prime, temper, process, acclimatize, acclimate, season.
4 *a product to condition your skin* **improve,** nourish, tone (up), moisturize.

conditional ▶ adjective 1 *their approval is* ***conditional on*** *success* **subject to,** dependent on, contingent on, based on, determined by, controlled by, tied to.
2 *a conditional offer* **contingent,** dependent, qualified, with reservations, limited, provisional, provisory.

condom ▶ noun *using a condom is only one part of safe sex* **contraceptive,** prophylactic, sheath; trademark Trojan; informal **rubber**; chiefly Brit. informal French letter.

condone ▶ verb *we cannot condone such dreadful behavior* **disregard,** accept, allow, let pass, turn a blind eye to, overlook, forget; forgive, pardon, excuse, let go.
ANTONYMS condemn.

conducive ▶ adjective *an environment that is* ***conducive to*** *learning* **favorable to,** beneficial to, advantageous to, opportune to, propitious to, encouraging to, promising to, convenient for, good for, helpful, instrumental in, productive of, useful for.
ANTONYMS unfavorable.

conduct ▶ noun 1 *they complained about her conduct* **behavior,** performance, demeanor; actions, activities, deeds, doings, exploits; habits, manners; formal comportment.
2 *the conduct of the elections* **management,** running, direction, control, supervision, regulation, administration, organization, coordination, orchestration, handling.
▶ verb 1 *the election was conducted lawfully* **manage,** direct, run, administer, organize, coordinate, orchestrate, handle, control, oversee, supervise, regulate, carry out/on.
2 *he was conducted through the corridors* **escort,** guide, lead, usher, show; shepherd, see, bring, take, help.
3 *aluminum conducts heat* **transmit,** convey, carry, transfer, impart, channel, relay; disseminate, diffuse, radiate.
– PHRASES **conduct oneself** *I am proud of the way they conducted themselves* **behave,** act, acquit oneself, bear oneself; formal comport oneself.

conduit ▶ noun *spring water enters the brewery through a conduit* **channel,** duct, pipe, tube, gutter, trench, culvert, cut, sluice, spillway, flume, chute.

confederacy ▶ noun *a confederacy of Indian tribes* **federation,** confederation, alliance, league, association, coalition, consortium, syndicate, group, circle; bloc, axis.

confederate ▶ adjective *confederate councils* **allied,** in alliance, in league, cooperating, associated, united, combined, amalgamated.
▶ noun *he was a confederate of the James brothers* **associate,** partner, accomplice, helper, assistant, ally, collaborator, colleague.

confer ▶ verb 1 *she went to confer with her colleagues* **consult,** talk, speak, converse, have a chat, have a tête-à-tête, parley; informal have a confab, powwow.
2 *she* ***conferred*** *a knighthood* ***on*** *him* **bestow on,** present to, grant to, award to, decorate with, honor with, give to, endow with, extend to. See note at GIVE.

conference ▶ noun 1 *an international conference* **congress,** meeting, convention, seminar, colloquium, symposium, forum, summit.
2 *he gathered them for a conference* **discussion,** consultation, debate, talk, conversation, dialogue, chat, tête-à-tête, parley; informal confab; formal confabulation.

confess ▶ verb 1 *he confessed that he had done it* **admit,** acknowledge, reveal, disclose, divulge, avow, declare, profess; own up, tell all.
ANTONYMS deny.
2 *they could not make him confess* **own up,** plead guilty, accept the blame; tell the truth, tell all, make a clean breast of it; informal come clean, spill the beans, let the cat out of the bag, get something off one's chest, let on, fess up.
3 *I confess I don't know* **acknowledge,** admit, concede, grant, allow, own, declare, affirm.

confession ▶ noun *they soon got a confession out of him* **admission,** acknowledgment, profession; revelation, disclosure, divulgence, avowal; guilty plea.

confide ▶ verb 1 *he confided his fears to his mother* **reveal,** disclose, divulge, lay bare, betray, impart, declare, intimate, uncover, expose, vouchsafe, tell; confess, admit, give away; informal blab, spill.
2 *I need him to* ***confide in*** **open one's heart to,** unburden oneself to, confess to, tell all to.

confidence ▶ noun 1 *I have little confidence in these figures* **trust,** belief, faith, credence, conviction.
ANTONYMS skepticism, distrust.
2 *she's brimming with confidence* **self-assurance,** self-confidence, self-possession, assertiveness; poise, aplomb, phlegm; courage, boldness, mettle, nerve.
ANTONYMS uncertainty, doubt.
3 *the girls exchanged confidences* **secret,** confidentiality, intimacy.

confidential ▶ adjective 1 *a confidential chat* **private,** personal, intimate, quiet; secret, sensitive, classified, restricted, unofficial, unrevealed, undisclosed, unpublished; informal hush-hush, mum; formal sub rosa; archaic privy.
2 *a confidential friend* **trusted,** trustworthy, trusty, faithful, reliable, dependable; close, bosom, intimate.

confidentially ▶ adverb *I thought we were speaking confidentially* **privately,** in private, in confidence, between ourselves/themselves, off the record, quietly, secretly, in secret, behind closed doors; between you and me and the lamppost; formal sub rosa.

confine ▶ verb **1** *they were confined in the house* **enclose,** incarcerate, imprison, intern, impound, hold captive, trap; shut in/up, keep, lock in/up, coop (up); fence in, hedge in, wall in/up.
2 *he confined his remarks to the weather* **restrict,** limit.

confinement ▶ noun **1** *solitary confinement* **imprisonment,** internment, incarceration, custody, captivity, detention, restraint; house arrest.
2 *the confinement of an animal* **caging,** enclosure; quarantine.
3 dated *she went to the hospital for her confinement* **labor,** delivery, birthing; birth, childbirth; formal parturition; archaic lying-in, childbed.

confirm ▶ verb **1** *records confirm the latest evidence* **corroborate,** verify, prove, validate, authenticate, substantiate, justify, vindicate; support, uphold, back up.
ANTONYMS contradict, repudiate.
2 *he confirmed that help was on the way* **affirm,** reaffirm, assert, assure someone, repeat; promise, guarantee.
ANTONYMS deny.
3 *his appointment was confirmed by the president* **ratify,** validate, sanction, endorse, formalize, authorize, warrant, accredit, approve, accept.
ANTONYMS revoke.

confirmation ▶ noun **1** *independent confirmation of the deaths* **corroboration,** verification, proof, testimony, endorsement, authentication, substantiation, evidence.
2 *confirmation of your appointment* **ratification,** approval, authorization, validation, sanction, endorsement, formalization, accreditation, acceptance.

confirmed ▶ adjective *he's a confirmed gambler* **established,** long-standing, committed, dyed-in-the-wool, through and through; staunch, loyal, faithful, devoted, dedicated, steadfast; habitual, compulsive, persistent; unapologetic, unashamed, inveterate, chronic, incurable; informal card-carrying.

confiscate ▶ verb *the guards confiscated his camera* **impound,** seize, commandeer, requisition, appropriate, expropriate, sequester, sequestrate, take (away); Law distrain.
ANTONYMS return.

conflagration ▶ noun *the conflagration spread rapidly through the wooden buildings* **fire,** blaze, flames, inferno, firestorm.

conflict ▶ noun **1** *industrial conflicts* **dispute,** quarrel, squabble, disagreement, dissension, clash; discord, friction, strife, antagonism, hostility, disputation, contention; feud, schism.
ANTONYMS agreement.
2 *the Vietnam conflict* **war,** campaign, battle, fighting, (armed) confrontation, engagement, encounter, struggle, hostilities; warfare, combat.
ANTONYMS peace.
3 *a conflict between his business and domestic life* **clash,** incompatibility, incongruity, friction; mismatch, variance, difference, divergence, contradiction, inconsistency.
ANTONYMS harmony.
▶ verb *their interests sometimes conflict* **clash,** be incompatible, vary, be at odds, be in conflict, differ, diverge, disagree, contrast, collide.

conflicting ▶ adjective *the two suspects gave conflicting stories* **contradictory,** incompatible, inconsistent, irreconcilable, incongruous, contrary, opposite, opposing, antithetical, clashing, discordant, divergent; at odds.

conform ▶ verb **1** *visitors have to* ***conform to*** *our rules* **comply with,** abide by, obey, observe, follow, keep to, stick to, adhere to, uphold, heed, accept, go along with, fall in with, respect, defer to; satisfy, meet, fulfill.
ANTONYMS flout.
2 *they refuse to conform* **follow convention,** be conventional, fit in, adapt, adjust, follow the crowd; comply, acquiesce, toe the line, follow the rules; submit, yield; informal play it by the book, play by the rules.
ANTONYMS rebel.
3 *goods must* ***conform to*** *their description* **match,** fit, suit, answer, agree with, be like, correspond to, be consistent with, measure up to, tally with, square with.
ANTONYMS differ.

conformist ▶ noun *he was too much of a conformist to wear anything but a suit* **traditionalist,** conservative, stickler, formalist, diehard, reactionary; informal stick-in-the-mud, stuffed shirt.
ANTONYMS eccentric, rebel.

confound ▶ verb **1** *the figures confounded analysts* **amaze,** astonish, dumbfound, stagger, surprise, startle, stun, throw, shake, discompose, bewilder, bedazzle, baffle, mystify, bemuse, perplex, puzzle, confuse; take aback, shake up, catch off balance; informal flabbergast, blow someone's mind, blow away, flummox, faze, stump, beat, fox, discombobulate.
2 *he has always confounded expectations* **contradict,** counter, invalidate, negate, go against, quash, explode, demolish, shoot down, destroy, disprove; informal poke holes in.

confront ▶ verb **1** *Jones confronted the intruder* **challenge,** face (up to), come face to face with, meet, accost; stand up to, brave; tackle; informal collar.
ANTONYMS avoid.
2 *the problems that confront us* **trouble,** bother, burden, distress, worry, oppress, annoy, strain, stress, tax, torment, plague, blight, curse; face, beset.
3 *they must confront their problems* **tackle,** address, face, come to grips with, grapple with, take on, attend to, see to, deal with, take care of, handle, manage.
ANTONYMS avoid.
4 *she confronted him with the evidence* **present,** face.

confrontation ▶ noun *I've been trying to avoid a confrontation with his new girlfriend* conflict, clash, fight, battle, encounter, faceoff, engagement, skirmish; hostilities, fighting; informal set-to, run-in, dust-up, showdown.

confuse ▶ verb 1 *don't confuse students with too much detail* **bewilder,** baffle, mystify, bemuse, perplex, puzzle, confound; informal flummox, faze, stump, fox, discombobulate, bedazzle.
ANTONYMS enlighten.
2 *the authors have confused the issue* **complicate,** muddle, jumble, garble, blur, obscure, cloud.
ANTONYMS simplify.
3 *some people* ***confuse*** *strokes* ***with*** *heart attacks* **mistake for,** take for, misinterpret as; mix up with, muddle up with, confound with.

confused ▶ adjective 1 *they are confused about what is going on* **bewildered,** bemused, puzzled, perplexed, baffled, mystified, nonplussed, muddled, dumbfounded, at sea, at a loss, taken aback, disoriented, disconcerted; informal flummoxed, clueless, fazed, discombobulated.
2 *her confused elderly mother* **demented,** bewildered, muddled, addled, befuddled, disoriented, disorientated; unbalanced, unhinged; senile.
ANTONYMS lucid.
3 *a confused recollection* **vague,** unclear, indistinct, imprecise, blurred, hazy, woolly, shadowy, dim; imperfect, sketchy.
ANTONYMS clear, precise.
4 *a confused mass of bones* **disorderly,** disordered, disorganized, disarranged, out of order, untidy, muddled, jumbled, mixed up, chaotic, topsy-turvy; informal shambolic.
ANTONYMS neat.

confusing ▶ adjective *the instructions are confusing* **bewildering,** baffling, unclear, perplexing, puzzling, mystifying, disconcerting; ambiguous, misleading, inconsistent, contradictory; unaccountable, inexplicable, impenetrable, unfathomable; complex, complicated.

confusion ▶ noun 1 *there is confusion about the new system* **uncertainty,** incertitude, unsureness, doubt, ignorance; formal dubiety.
ANTONYMS certainty.
2 *she stared in confusion* **bewilderment,** bafflement, perplexity, puzzlement, mystification, befuddlement; shock, daze, wonder, wonderment, astonishment; informal head-scratching, discombobulation.
3 *I could not live in this kind of confusion* **disorder,** disarray, disorganization, untidiness, chaos, mayhem; turmoil, tumult, disruption, upheaval, uproar, muddle, mess, shambles; informal three-ring circus.
ANTONYMS order.
4 *a confusion of boxes* **jumble,** muddle, mess, heap, tangle; informal shambles. See note at JUMBLE.

congeal ▶ verb *the gravy is starting to congeal* **coagulate,** clot, thicken, jell, cake, set, curdle.

congenial ▶ adjective 1 *very congenial people* **hospitable,** genial, personable, agreeable, friendly, pleasant, likable, amiable, nice; companionable, sociable, sympathetic, comradely, convivial, simpatico; **like-minded,** compatible, kindred, well-suited. See note at PLEASANT.
ANTONYMS disagreeable.
2 *a congenial environment* **pleasant,** pleasing, agreeable, enjoyable, pleasurable, nice, appealing, satisfying, gratifying, delightful, relaxing, welcoming, hospitable; suitable, well-suited, favorable.
ANTONYMS unpleasant.

congenital ▶ adjective 1 *congenital defects* **inborn,** inherited, hereditary, innate, inbred, constitutional, inbuilt, natural, inherent. See note at INHERENT.
ANTONYMS acquired.
2 *a congenital liar* **inveterate,** compulsive, persistent, chronic, regular, habitual, obsessive, confirmed; incurable, incorrigible, irredeemable, hopeless; unashamed, shameless, pathological.

congested ▶ adjective *the tunnels are congested with holiday traffic* **crowded,** overcrowded, full, overflowing, packed, jammed, thronged, teeming, swarming; obstructed, blocked, clogged, choked; informal snarled up, gridlocked, jam-packed.
ANTONYMS clear.

congestion ▶ noun *the congestion on I-95 is especially bad near exit 34* **crowding,** overcrowding; obstruction, blockage; traffic jam, bottleneck; informal snarl-up, gridlock.

conglomerate ▶ noun 1 *the conglomerate was broken up* **corporation,** company, business, multinational, combine, group, consortium, partnership; firm.
2 *a conglomerate of disparate peoples* **mixture,** mix, combination, amalgamation, union, marriage, fusion, composite, synthesis; miscellany, hodgepodge. See note at JUMBLE.
▶ adjective *a conglomerate mass* **aggregate,** agglomerate, amassed, combined.
▶ verb *the debris conglomerated into planets* **coalesce,** unite, join, combine, merge, fuse, consolidate, amalgamate, integrate, mingle, intermingle.

congratulate ▶ verb 1 *she congratulated him on his marriage* **send one's best wishes to,** wish someone good luck, wish someone joy; drink to someone's health, toast.
ANTONYMS curse.
2 *they are to be congratulated* **praise,** commend, applaud, salute, honor; pay tribute to, regard highly, pat on the back, take one's hat off to.
ANTONYMS criticize.
– PHRASES **congratulate oneself** *you should* ***congratulate yourself on*** *this wonderful accomplishment* **take pride in,** feel proud of, flatter oneself on, pat oneself on the back for; take/feel satisfaction in, take pleasure in, glory in, bask in, delight in.

congratulations ▶ plural noun 1 *her congratulations on their wedding* **good wishes,** best wishes, compliments, felicitations.
2 *you all deserve congratulations* **praise,** commendation, applause, salutes, honor, acclaim, cheers; approval, admiration, compliments, bouquets, kudos, adulation; a pat on the back.
▶ exclamation *Congratulations! You did it!* **bravo,** brava, mazel tov, kudos; informal congrats,

attaboy, attagirl, way to go.

congregate ▶ verb *war protesters congregated in front of the recruiting office* **assemble,** gather, collect, come together, convene, rally, rendezvous, muster, meet, cluster, group. See note at GATHER.
ANTONYMS disperse.

congregation ▶ noun 1 *the chapel congregation* **parishioners,** parish, churchgoers, flock, faithful, followers, believers, fellowship, communicants, laity, brethren, membership; throng, company, assemblage, audience.
2 *congregations of birds* **gathering,** assembly, flock, swarm, bevy, pack, group, body, crowd, mass, multitude, horde, host, mob, throng.

congress ▶ noun 1 *a congress of mathematicians* **conference,** convention, seminar, colloquium, symposium, forum, meeting, assembly, gathering, rally, summit.
2 *elections for the new Congress* **legislature,** legislative assembly, senate, house, house of representatives, parliament, convocation, diet, council, chamber.

conjecture ▶ noun *the information is merely conjecture* **speculation,** guesswork, surmise, fancy, presumption, assumption, theory, postulation, supposition; inference, (an) extrapolation; an estimate; informal a guesstimate, a shot in the dark, a ballpark figure.
ANTONYMS fact.
▶ verb *I conjectured that the game was over* **guess,** speculate, surmise, infer, fancy, imagine, believe, think, suspect, presume, assume, hypothesize, suppose.
ANTONYMS know.

conjugal ▶ adjective *the conjugal bond must be a two-way relationship* **marital,** matrimonial, nuptial, marriage, bridal; Law spousal; literary connubial.

conjunction ▶ noun 1 *a theory that the Americas were formed by a conjunction of floating islands* **coming together,** convergence, union, confluence.
2 *a conjunction of planets* **co-occurrence,** concurrence, coincidence, coexistence, simultaneity, contemporaneity, concomitance, synchronicity, synchrony.
– PHRASES **in conjunction with** *in conjunction with our Native American Day, there will be an exhibit of Pequot art in the gymnasium* **together with,** along with, accompanying, accompanied by; as well as, in addition to, plus.

conjure ▶ verb 1 *he conjured a cigarette out of the air* **produce,** make appear, materialize, summon.
2 *the picture that his words* ***conjured up*** **bring to mind,** call to mind, evoke, summon up, recall, recreate; echo, allude to, suggest, awaken.

connect ▶ verb 1 *electrodes were connected to the device* **attach,** join, fasten, fix, affix, couple, link, secure, hitch; stick, adhere, fuse, pin, screw, bolt, clamp, clip, hook (up); add, append. See note at JOIN.
2 *rituals* ***connected with*** *Easter* **associate with,** link to/with, couple with; identify with, equate with, relate to.

connection ▶ noun 1 *the connection between commerce and art* **link,** relationship, relation, interconnection, interdependence, association; bond, tie, tie-in, correspondence, parallel, analogy.
2 *a poor connection in the plug* **attachment,** joint, fastening, coupling.
3 *he has the right connections* **contact,** friend, acquaintance, ally, colleague, associate; relation, relative, kin.
– PHRASES **in connection with** *a man is being questioned in connection with the murder* **regarding,** concerning, with reference to, with regard to, with respect to, respecting, relating to, in relation to, on, connected with, on the subject of, in the matter of, apropos, re.

connive ▶ verb *it is now known that at least two of the directors connived with Officer Cutler in the cover-up* **conspire,** collude, collaborate, intrigue, be hand in glove, plot, scheme; informal be in cahoots.

conniving ▶ adjective *his conniving brother planned the whole dirty affair* **scheming,** cunning, crafty, calculating, devious, wily, sly, tricky, artful, guileful; manipulative, Machiavellian, disingenuous, deceitful, underhanded, treacherous; informal foxy.

connoisseur ▶ noun *a connoisseur of fine wines* **expert,** authority, specialist, pundit, savant; arbiter of taste, aesthete; gourmet, epicure, gastronome; informal buff, maven.

connotation ▶ noun *there was a connotation of distrust in his voice* **overtone,** undertone, undercurrent, implication, hidden meaning, nuance, hint, echo, vibrations, association, intimation, suggestion, suspicion, insinuation.

conquer ▶ verb 1 *the Franks conquered the Visigoths* **defeat,** beat, vanquish, trounce, triumph over, be victorious over, get the better of, worst; overcome, overwhelm, overpower, overthrow, subdue, subjugate, quell, quash, crush, rout; informal lick, best, hammer, clobber, thrash, paste, demolish, annihilate, wipe the floor with, walk all over, make mincemeat of, massacre, slaughter, cream, shellac, skunk.
2 *Peru was conquered by Spain* **seize,** take (over), appropriate, subjugate, capture, occupy, invade, annex, overrun.
3 *the first men to conquer Mount Everest* **climb,** ascend, mount, scale, top, crest.
4 *the way to conquer fear* **overcome,** get the better of, control, master, get a grip on, deal with, cope with, surmount, rise above, get over; quell, quash, beat, triumph over; informal lick.

conqueror ▶ noun *they may have uncovered the burial ground of legendary conqueror Genghis Khan* **vanquisher,** conquistador; victor, winner, champion, conquering hero.

conquest ▶ noun 1 *the conquest of the Aztecs* **defeat,** vanquishment, annihilation, overthrow, subjugation, rout, mastery, crushing; victory over, triumph over.
2 *their conquest of the valley* **seizure,** takeover, capture, occupation, invasion, acquisition, appropriation, subjugation, subjection.
3 *the conquest of K2* **ascent,** climbing, scaling.
4 *she's his latest conquest* **catch,** acquisition, prize, slave; admirer, fan, worshiper; lover, boyfriend, girlfriend.

conscience ▶ noun *her conscience would not*

allow her to remain silent **sense of right and wrong,** moral sense, inner voice; morals, standards, values, principles, ethics, beliefs; compunction, scruples, qualms.

conscience-stricken ▶ **adjective** *the conscience-stricken teens who set fire to the gazebo* **guilt-ridden,** remorseful, ashamed, shamefaced, apologetic, sorry; chastened, contrite, guilty, regretful, rueful, repentant, penitent, abashed, sheepish, compunctious.
ANTONYMS unrepentant.

conscientious ▶ **adjective** *even Douglas, the most conscientious worker in our department, was laid off* **diligent,** industrious, punctilious, painstaking, sedulous, assiduous, dedicated, careful, meticulous, thorough, attentive, hard-working, studious, rigorous, particular; religious, strict.
ANTONYMS casual.

conscious ▶ **adjective 1** *the patient was conscious* **aware,** awake, alert, responsive, sentient, compos mentis.
2 *he became conscious of people talking* **aware,** mindful, sensible; formal cognizant; rare regardful.
ANTONYMS unaware.
3 *a conscious effort* **deliberate,** intentional, intended, purposeful, purposive, knowing, considered, calculated, willful, premeditated, planned, volitional.

conscript ▶ **verb** *they were conscripted into the army* **call up,** enlist, recruit, draft; historical press, impress.
▶ **noun** *an army conscript* compulsorily enlisted soldier, recruit, draftee.
ANTONYMS volunteer.

consecrate ▶ **verb** *the bishop had consecrated two cathedrals in his time* **sanctify,** bless, make holy, make sacred; dedicate to God, devote, reserve, set apart; anoint, ordain; formal hallow. See note at **DIVINE.**

consecutive ▶ **adjective** *share prices fell for three consecutive days* **successive,** succeeding, following, in succession, running, in a row, one after the other, back-to-back, continuous, straight, uninterrupted.

consensus ▶ **noun 1** *there was consensus among delegates* **agreement,** harmony, concurrence, accord, unity, unanimity, solidarity; formal concord.
ANTONYMS disagreement.
2 *the consensus was that they should act* **general opinion,** majority opinion, common view.

consent ▶ **noun** *the consent of all members* **agreement,** assent, acceptance, approval, approbation; permission, authorization, sanction, leave; backing, endorsement, support; informal go-ahead, thumbs up, green light, OK.
ANTONYMS dissent.
▶ **verb** *she* ***consented to*** *surgery* **agree to,** assent to, yield to, give in to, submit to; allow, give permission for, sanction, accept, approve, go along with.
ANTONYMS forbid.

consequence ▶ **noun 1** *a consequence of inflation* **result,** upshot, outcome, effect, repercussion, ramification, corollary, concomitant, aftermath, aftereffect; fruit(s), product, by-product, end result; informal payoff; Medicine sequela.
ANTONYMS cause.
2 *the past is of no consequence* **importance,** import, significance, account, substance, note, mark, prominence, value, concern, interest; formal moment.

consequent ▶ **adjective** *heavy rains and consequent flash flooding are tonight's lead stories* **resulting,** resultant, ensuing, consequential; following, subsequent, successive; attendant, accompanying, concomitant; collateral, associated, related.

consequently ▶ **adverb** *the doctor has had two emergencies this morning and consequently is running behind schedule* **as a result,** as a consequence, so, thus, therefore, ergo, accordingly, hence, for this/that reason, because of this/that, on this/that account; inevitably, necessarily.

conservation ▶ **noun** *the conservation of tropical forests* **preservation,** protection, safeguarding, safekeeping; care, guardianship, husbandry, supervision; upkeep, maintenance, repair, restoration; ecology, environmentalism.

conservative ▶ **adjective 1** *the conservative wing of the party* **right-wing,** reactionary, traditionalist; Republican; Brit. Tory; informal redneck.
ANTONYMS socialist.
2 *our more conservative neighbors may object to the modern architecture being proposed* **traditionalist,** traditional, conventional, orthodox, old-fashioned, dyed-in-the-wool, hidebound, unadventurous, set in one's ways; moderate, middle-of-the-road, buttoned-down; informal stick-in-the-mud.
ANTONYMS radical.
3 *he wore a conservative blue suit* **conventional,** sober, modest, plain, unobtrusive, restrained, subtle, low-key, demure; informal square, straight.
ANTONYMS ostentatious.
4 *a conservative estimate* **low,** cautious, understated, moderate, reasonable.
▶ **noun** *liberals and conservatives have found common ground* **right-winger,** reactionary, rightist, diehard; Republican; Brit. Tory.

conservatory ▶ **noun 1** *a frost-free conservatory* **summer house,** belvedere; glasshouse, greenhouse, hothouse.
2 *a teaching job at the conservatory* **conservatoire,** music school, drama school.

conserve ▶ **verb** *fossil fuel should be conserved* **preserve,** protect, save, safeguard, keep, look after; sustain, prolong, perpetuate; store, reserve, husband.
ANTONYMS squander.
▶ **noun** *cherry conserve* **jam,** preserve, jelly, marmalade.

consider ▶ **verb 1** *Isabel considered her choices* **think about,** contemplate, reflect on, examine, review; mull over, ponder, deliberate on, chew over, meditate on, ruminate on; assess, evaluate, appraise; informal size up.
2 *I consider him irresponsible* **deem,** think, believe, judge, adjudge, rate, count, find; regard as, hold to be, reckon to be, view as, see as.
3 *he considered the ceiling* **look at,** contemplate, observe, regard, survey, view, scrutinize, scan, examine, inspect; informal check out, eyeball.

4 *the inquiry will consider those issues* **take into consideration,** take account of, make allowances for, bear in mind, be mindful of, remember, mind, mark, respect, heed, note, make provision for.
ANTONYMS ignore.

considerable ▶ adjective **1** *a considerable amount of money* **sizable,** substantial, appreciable, significant; goodly, fair, hefty, handsome, decent, worthwhile; ample, plentiful, abundant, great, large, generous; informal tidy, not to be sneezed at.
ANTONYMS paltry.
2 *considerable success* **much,** great, a lot of, lots of, a great deal of, plenty of, a fair amount of.
ANTONYMS minor.
3 *a considerable player in the game of politics* **distinguished,** noteworthy, important, significant, prominent, eminent, influential, illustrious; renowned, celebrated, acclaimed.
ANTONYMS insignificant.

considerably ▶ adverb *alcoholic drinks vary considerably in strength* **greatly,** much, very much, a great deal, a lot, lots; significantly, substantially, appreciably, markedly, noticeably; informal plenty, seriously.

considerate ▶ adjective *the doorman was considerate enough to call her when the mail was delivered* **attentive,** thoughtful, solicitous, mindful, heedful; obliging, accommodating, helpful, cooperative, patient; kind, unselfish, compassionate, sympathetic, caring, charitable, altruistic, generous; polite, sensitive, tactful.

consideration ▶ noun **1** *your case needs careful consideration* **thought,** deliberation, reflection, contemplation, rumination, meditation; examination, inspection, scrutiny, analysis, discussion; attention, regard; formal cogitation.
2 *his health is the prime consideration* **factor,** issue, matter, concern, detail, aspect, feature.
3 *firms should show more consideration* **attentiveness,** concern, care, thoughtfulness, solicitude; kindness, understanding, respect, sensitivity, tact, discretion; compassion, charity, benevolence.
– PHRASES **take into consideration** *the company was willing to take her extended illness into consideration* **consider,** give thought to, take into account, allow for, provide for, plan for, make provision for, accommodate, bargain for, reckon with; foresee, anticipate.

considering ▶ preposition *considering his size, he was speedy* **bearing in mind,** taking into consideration, taking into account, keeping in mind, in view of, in light of.
▶ adverb informal *he's been lucky, considering* **all things considered,** all in all, on the whole, at the end of the day, when all is said and done.

consign ▶ verb **1** *he was **consigned to** Sing Sing* **send to,** deliver to, hand over to, turn over to, sentence to; confine in, imprison in, incarcerate in, lock up in; (**consign to prison/jail**) informal put away, put behind bars, send up the river.
2 *the picture was consigned to the gallery* **assign,** allocate, place, put, remit, commit.
3 *the package was consigned by a local company* **send (off),** courier, dispatch, transmit, convey, mail, post, ship.
4 *I consigned her picture to the garbage can* **deposit,** commit, banish, relegate.

consignment ▶ adjective *a consignment clothing shop* **secondhand,** used, preowned, castoff, hand-me-down.
▶ noun *Dexter has to initial the paperwork for any consignment* **delivery,** shipment, load, boatload, truckload, cargo; batch; goods.

consist ▶ verb **1** *the exhibition **consists of** 180 drawings* **be composed of,** be made up of, be formed of; comprise, contain, include, incorporate.
2 *style **consists in** the choices that writers make* **be inherent in,** lie in, reside in, be present in, be contained in; be expressed by.

consistency ▶ noun **1** *the trend shows a degree of consistency* **uniformity,** constancy, regularity, evenness, steadiness, stability, equilibrium; dependability, reliability.
2 *mix until the batter is of pouring consistency* **thickness,** density, viscosity, heaviness, texture; firmness, solidity.

consistent ▶ adjective **1** *consistent opinion-poll evidence* **constant,** regular, uniform, steady, stable, even, unchanging, undeviating, unfluctuating; dependable, reliable, predictable.
ANTONYMS irregular.
2 *her injuries were **consistent with** a knife attack* **compatible with,** congruous with, consonant with, in tune with, in line with, reconcilable with; corresponding to, conforming to.
ANTONYMS incompatible.

consolation ▶ noun *I realize that mere words are of little consolation* **comfort,** solace, sympathy, compassion, pity, commiseration, empathy; relief, help, support, moral support, encouragement, reassurance.

console ▶ verb *she tried to console him* **comfort,** solace, sympathize with, commiserate with, show compassion for, condole with; help, support, cheer (up), hearten, encourage, reassure, soothe.
ANTONYMS upset.

consolidate ▶ verb **1** *we consolidated our position in the market* **strengthen,** secure, stabilize, reinforce, fortify; enhance, improve.
2 *consolidate the results into an action plan* **combine,** unite, merge, integrate, amalgamate, fuse, synthesize, bring together, unify. See note at JOIN.

consonant ▶ adjective
– PHRASES **consonant with** *these findings are consonant with recent research* **in agreement with,** consistent with, in accordance with, in harmony with, compatible with, congruous with, in tune with.

consort ▶ noun *the queen and her consort* **partner,** life partner, companion, mate; spouse, husband, wife, helpmate.
▶ verb *he consorted with other women* **associate,** keep company, mix, go around, spend time, socialize, fraternize, have dealings; informal run around, hang around/out, be thick.

conspicuous ▶ adjective *a tropical vine with conspicuous blossoms* **easily seen,** clear, visible, noticeable, discernible, perceptible, detectable; obvious, manifest, evident, apparent, marked, pronounced, prominent, patent, crystal clear; striking, eye-catching, impactful, overt, blatant; distinct, recognizable, unmistakable, inescapable; informal as plain as the nose on one's face, standing/sticking out like a sore thumb. See note at **NOTICEABLE**.

conspiracy ▶ noun 1 *a conspiracy to manipulate the results* **plot,** scheme, plan, machination, ploy, trick, ruse, subterfuge; informal racket. See note at **PLOT**.
2 *conspiracy to commit murder* **plotting,** collusion, intrigue, connivance, machination, collaboration; treason.

conspirator ▶ noun *is there any credible evidence of a conspirator working with Oswald?* **plotter,** schemer, intriguer, colluder, collaborator, conniver.

conspire ▶ verb 1 *they admitted conspiring to steal cars* **plot,** scheme, plan, intrigue, machinate, collude, connive, collaborate, work hand in glove; informal be in cahoots.
2 *circumstances conspired against them* **act together,** work together, combine, unite, join forces; informal gang up.

constancy ▶ noun 1 *constancy between lovers* **fidelity,** faithfulness, loyalty, commitment, dedication, devotion; dependability, reliability, trustworthiness.
2 *the constancy of Henry's views* **steadfastness,** resolution, resolve, firmness, fixedness; determination, perseverance, tenacity, doggedness, staunchness, staying power, obstinacy.
3 *the constancy of their doubt* **consistency,** permanence, persistence, durability, endurance; uniformity, immutability, regularity, stability, steadiness.

constant ▶ adjective 1 *the constant background noise* **continual,** continuous, persistent, sustained, around/round-the-clock; ceaseless, unceasing, perpetual, incessant, never-ending, eternal, endless, unabating, nonstop, unrelieved; interminable, unremitting, relentless. See note at **RESOLUTE**.
ANTONYMS fitful, inconstant.
2 *a constant speed* **consistent,** regular, steady, uniform, even, invariable, unvarying, unchanging, undeviating, unfluctuating.
ANTONYMS variable.
3 *a constant friend* **faithful,** loyal, devoted, true, fast, firm, unswerving; steadfast, staunch, dependable, trustworthy, trusty, reliable, dedicated, committed.
ANTONYMS fickle.
4 *constant vigilance* **steadfast,** steady, resolute, determined, tenacious, dogged, unwavering, unflagging.
▶ noun *dread of cancer has been a constant* **unchanging factor,** given.

constantly ▶ adverb *the language is constantly in flux* **always,** all the time, continually, continuously, persistently; around/round the clock, night and day, 'morning, noon, and night'; endlessly, nonstop, incessantly, unceasingly, perpetually, eternally, forever; interminably, unremittingly, relentlessly; informal 24-7.
ANTONYMS occasionally.

consternation ▶ noun *much to his colleagues' consternation, Victor was awarded the job in Paris* **dismay,** perturbation, distress, disquiet, discomposure; surprise, amazement, astonishment; alarm, panic, fear, fright, shock.
ANTONYMS satisfaction.

constituent ▶ adjective *constituent parts* **component,** integral; elemental, basic, essential, inherent.
▶ noun 1 *representatives must listen to their constituents* **voter,** elector, member of a constituency.
2 *the constituents of tobacco* **component,** ingredient, element; part, piece, bit, unit; section, portion.

constitute ▶ verb 1 *farmers constituted 10 percent of the population* **amount to,** add up to, account for, form, make up, compose.
2 *this constitutes a breach of copyright* **be equivalent to,** be, embody, be tantamount to, be regarded as.
3 *the courts were constituted in 1875* **inaugurate,** establish, initiate, found, create, set up, start, form, organize, develop; commission, charter, invest, appoint, install, empower.

constitution ▶ noun 1 *the constitution guarantees our rights* **charter,** social code, law; bill of rights; rules, regulations, fundamental principles.
2 *the chemical constitution of the dye* **composition,** makeup, structure, construction, arrangement, configuration, formation, anatomy.
3 *she has the constitution of an ox* **health,** physical condition, fettle; physique.

constitutional ▶ adjective 1 *constitutional powers* **legal,** lawful, legitimate, authorized, permitted; sanctioned, ratified, warranted, constituted, statutory, chartered, vested, official; by law.
2 *a constitutional weakness* **inherent,** intrinsic, innate, fundamental, essential, organic; congenital, inborn, inbred.
▶ noun dated *she went out for a constitutional* See **WALK** (sense 1 of the noun).

constrain ▶ verb 1 *he felt constrained to explain* **compel,** force, drive, impel, oblige, coerce, prevail on, require; press, push, pressure. See note at **COMPEL**.
2 *prices were constrained by government controls* **restrict,** limit, curb, check, restrain, contain, rein in, hold back, keep down.

constrained ▶ adjective *she was uncharacteristically constrained whenever her in-laws were visiting* **unnatural,** awkward, self-conscious, forced, stilted, strained; restrained, reserved, reticent, guarded.
ANTONYMS relaxed.

constraint ▶ noun 1 *financial constraints* **restriction,** limitation, curb, check, restraint, control, damper, rein; hindrance, impediment, obstruction, handicap.
2 *they were able to talk without constraint* **inhibition,** uneasiness, embarrassment; restraint, reticence, guardedness, formality; self-consciousness, awkwardness, stiltedness.

constrict ▶ verb **1** *fat constricts the blood vessels* **narrow,** make narrower, tighten, compress, contract, squeeze, strangle, strangulate; archaic straiten.
ANTONYMS expand, dilate.
2 *fear of crime constricts many people's lives* **restrict,** impede, limit, inhibit, obstruct, interfere with, hinder, hamper.

construct ▶ verb **1** *a new high-rise was being constructed* **build,** erect, put up, set up, raise, establish, assemble, manufacture, fabricate, create, make.
ANTONYMS demolish.
2 *he constructed a faultless argument* **formulate,** form, put together, create, devise, design, compose, work out; fashion, mold, shape, frame.

construction ▶ noun **1** *the construction of a new airport* **building,** erection, putting up, setting up, establishment; assembly, manufacture, fabrication, creation.
2 *the station was a spectacular construction* **structure,** building, edifice, pile.
3 *you could put an honest construction on their conduct* **interpretation,** reading, meaning, explanation, explication, construal; informal take, spin.

constructive ▶ adjective *constructive criticism* **useful,** helpful, productive, positive, encouraging; practical, valuable, profitable, worthwhile.

consul ▶ noun *he was posing as the French consul* **ambassador,** diplomat, chargé d'affaires, attaché, envoy, emissary, plenipotentiary.

consult ▶ verb **1** *you need to consult a lawyer* **seek advice from,** ask, take counsel from, call on/upon, speak to, turn to, have recourse to; informal pick someone's brains.
2 *the government must consult with interested parties* **confer,** have discussions, talk things over, exchange views, communicate, parley, deliberate; informal put their heads together.
3 *she consulted her diary* **refer to,** turn to, look at.

consultant ▶ noun *she freelanced as a communications consultant* **adviser,** expert, specialist, authority, pundit.

consultation ▶ noun **1** *the need for further consultation with industry* **discussion,** dialogue, discourse, debate, negotiation, deliberation.
2 *a 30-minute consultation* **meeting,** talk, discussion, interview, audience, hearing; appointment, session; formal confabulation, colloquy.

consume ▶ verb **1** *vast amounts of food and drink were consumed* **eat,** devour, ingest, swallow, gobble up, wolf down, guzzle, feast on, snack on; **drink,** gulp down, imbibe; informal tuck into, put away, polish off, dispose of, pig out on, down, swill, scarf (down/up).
2 *natural resources are being consumed at an alarming rate* **use (up),** utilize, expend; deplete, exhaust; waste, squander, drain, dissipate, fritter away.
3 *the fire consumed fifty houses* **destroy,** demolish, lay waste, wipe out, annihilate, devastate, gut, ruin, wreck.
4 *Carolyn was consumed with guilt* **eat up,** devour, obsess, grip, overwhelm; absorb, preoccupy.

consumer ▶ noun *if you're a satisfied consumer, we've done our job | they provide what consumers ask for* **purchaser,** buyer, customer, shopper; user, end user; client, patron; (**the consumer** or **consumers**) the public, the market.

consuming ▶ adjective *his consuming passion for opera* **absorbing,** compelling, compulsive, obsessive, overwhelming; intense, ardent, strong, powerful, burning, raging, fervid, profound, deep-seated.

consummate ▶ verb *the deal was finally consummated* **complete,** conclude, finish, accomplish, achieve; execute, carry out, perform; informal sew up, wrap up; formal effectuate.
▶ adjective *his consummate skill | a consummate politician* **supreme,** superb, superlative, superior, accomplished, expert, proficient, skillful, skilled, masterly, master, first-class, talented, gifted, polished, practiced, perfect, ultimate; complete, total, utter, absolute, pure.

consumption ▶ noun **1** *food unfit for human consumption* **eating,** drinking, ingestion.
2 *the consumption of fossil fuels* **use,** using up, utilization, expending, depletion; waste, squandering, dissipation.

contact ▶ noun **1** *a disease transmitted through casual contact* **touch,** touching; proximity, exposure.
2 *foreign diplomats were asked to avoid all contact with him* **communication,** correspondence, touch; association, connection, intercourse, relations, dealings; archaic traffic.
3 *he had many contacts in Germany* **connection,** acquaintance, associate, friend.
▶ verb *anyone with information should contact the police* **get in touch with,** communicate with, make contact with, approach, notify; telephone, phone, call, speak to, talk to, write to, get hold of.

contagious ▶ adjective *the disease is highly contagious* **infectious,** communicable, transmittable, transmissible, spreadable; informal catching; dated infective.

contain ▶ verb **1** *the archive contains much unpublished material* **include,** comprise, take in, incorporate, involve, encompass, embrace; consist of, be made up of, be composed of.
2 *the boat contained four people* **hold,** carry, accommodate, seat.
3 *he must contain his anger* **restrain,** curb, rein in, suppress, repress, stifle, subdue, quell, swallow, bottle up, hold in, keep in check; control, master.

container ▶ noun *a container of leftover beets* **receptacle,** vessel, canister, can, box, holder, repository.

contaminate ▶ verb *the river was contaminated with photographic chemicals* **pollute,** adulterate; defile, debase, corrupt, taint, infect, foul, spoil, soil, stain, sully; poison; literary befoul. See note at **POLLUTE**.
ANTONYMS purify.

contemplate ▶ verb 1 *she contemplated her image in the mirror* **look at,** view, regard, examine, inspect, observe, survey, study, scrutinize, scan, stare at, gaze at, eye.
2 *he contemplated his fate* **think about,** ponder, reflect on, consider, mull over, muse on, dwell on, deliberate over, meditate on, ruminate on, chew over, brood on/about, turn over in one's mind; formal cogitate.
3 *he was contemplating action for damages* **consider,** think about, have in mind, intend, propose; envisage, foresee.

contemplation ▶ noun 1 *the contemplation of beautiful objects* **viewing,** examination, inspection, observation, survey, study, scrutiny.
2 *the monks sat in quiet contemplation* **thought,** reflection, meditation, consideration, rumination, deliberation, reverie, introspection, brown study; formal cogitation, cerebration.

contemplative ▶ adjective *a peaceful, contemplative mood* **thoughtful,** pensive, reflective, meditative, musing, ruminative, introspective, brooding, deep/lost in thought, in a brown study.

contemporary ▶ adjective 1 *contemporary sources* **of the time,** of the day, contemporaneous, concurrent, coeval, coexisting, coexistent.
2 *contemporary society* **modern,** present-day, present, current, present-time.
3 *a very contemporary design* **modern,** up-to-date, up-to-the-minute, fashionable; modish, latest, recent; informal trendy, with it, du jour.
ANTONYMS old-fashioned, out of date.
▶ noun *Chaucer's contemporaries* **peer,** fellow; formal compeer.

contempt ▶ noun 1 *she regarded him with contempt* **scorn,** disdain, disrespect, scornfulness, contemptuousness, derision; disgust, loathing, hatred, abhorrence.
ANTONYMS respect.
2 *he is guilty of contempt of court* **disrespect,** disregard, slighting.
ANTONYMS respect.

contemptible ▶ adjective *what they said to poor old Mr. Ortiz was contemptible* **despicable,** detestable, hateful, reprehensible, deplorable, unspeakable, disgraceful, shameful, ignominious, abject, low, mean, cowardly, unworthy, discreditable, petty, worthless, shabby, cheap, beyond contempt, beyond the pale, sordid; archaic scurvy.
ANTONYMS admirable.

contemptuous ▶ adjective *the contemptuous look on your face says it all* **scornful,** disdainful, disrespectful, insulting, insolent, derisive, mocking, sneering, scoffing, withering, scathing, snide; condescending, supercilious, haughty, proud, superior, arrogant, dismissive, aloof; informal high and mighty, snotty, sniffy.
ANTONYMS respectful.

contend ▶ verb 1 *the pilot had to contend with torrential rain* **cope with,** face, grapple with, deal with, take on, pit oneself against.
2 *three main groups were contending for power* **compete,** vie, contest, fight, battle, tussle, go head to head; strive, struggle.
3 *he contends that the judge was wrong* **assert,** maintain, hold, claim, argue, insist, state, declare, profess, affirm; allege; formal aver.

content[1] ▶ adjective *she seemed content with life* **contented,** satisfied, pleased, gratified, fulfilled, happy, cheerful, glad; unworried, untroubled, at ease, at peace, tranquil, serene.
ANTONYMS discontented, dissatisfied.
▶ verb *her reply seemed to content him* **satisfy,** please; soothe, pacify, placate, appease, mollify.
▶ noun *a time of content* See CONTENTMENT.

content[2] ▶ noun 1 *foods with a high fiber content* **amount,** proportion, quantity.
2 (**contents**) *the contents of a vegetarian sausage* **constituents,** ingredients, components, elements.
3 (**contents**) *the book's table of contents* **chapters,** sections, divisions.
4 *the content of the essay* **subject matter,** subject, theme, argument, thesis, message, thrust, substance, matter, material, text, ideas.

contented ▶ adjective *a contented man* See CONTENT[1] (adjective).

contention ▶ noun 1 *a point of contention* **disagreement,** dispute, disputation, argument, discord, conflict, friction, strife, dissension, disharmony.
ANTONYMS agreement.
2 *we questioned the validity of his contention* **argument,** claim, plea, submission, allegation, assertion, declaration; opinion, stand, position, view, belief, thesis, case.
– PHRASES **in contention** *the sisters are in contention for the top ranking* **in competition,** competing, contesting, contending, vying; striving, struggling.

contentious ▶ adjective 1 *a contentious issue* **controversial,** disputable, debatable, disputed, open to debate, vexed.
2 *a contentious debate* **heated,** vehement, fierce, violent, intense, impassioned.
3 *contentious people* See QUARRELSOME.

contentment ▶ noun *finally being alone brought her a contentment she'd never known* **contentedness,** content, satisfaction, gratification, fulfillment, happiness, pleasure, cheerfulness; ease, comfort, well-being, peace, equanimity, serenity, tranquility.

contest ▶ noun 1 *a boxing contest* **competition,** match, tournament, game, meet, event, trial, bout, heat, race.
2 *the contest for the party leadership* **fight,** battle, tussle, struggle, competition, race.
▶ verb 1 *he intended to contest the seat* **compete for,** contend for, vie for, fight for, try to win, go for.
2 *we contested the decision* **oppose,** object to, challenge, take a stand against, take issue with, question, call into question.
3 *the issues have been hotly contested* **debate,** argue about, dispute, quarrel over.

contestant ▶ noun *the celebrity contestants play for their favorite charities* **competitor,** participant, player, contender, candidate, aspirant, hopeful, entrant.

context ▶ noun 1 *the wider historical context* **circumstances,** conditions, factors, state of affairs, situation, background, scene, setting.

2 *a quote taken out of context* **frame of reference,** contextual relationship; text, subject, theme, topic.

contiguous ▶ **adjective** *the contiguous Gulf states* **adjacent,** neighboring, adjoining, bordering, next-door; abutting, connecting, touching, in contact, proximate.

contingency ▶ **noun** *we've tried to imagine and provide for all possible contingencies* **eventuality,** (chance) event, incident, happening, occurrence, juncture, possibility, fortuity, accident, chance, emergency.

contingent ▶ **adjective 1** *the merger is contingent on government approval* **dependent on,** conditional on, subject to, determined by, hinging on, resting on.
2 *contingent events* **chance,** accidental, fortuitous, possible, unforeseeable, unpredictable, random, haphazard. See note at ACCIDENTAL.
▶ **noun 1** *a contingent of Japanese businessmen* **group,** party, body, band, company, cohort, deputation, delegation; informal bunch, gang.
2 *a contingent of soldiers* **detachment,** unit, group.

continual ▶ **adjective** *a service disrupted by continual breakdowns* **frequent,** repeated, recurrent, recurring, intermittent, regular.
ANTONYMS occasional, sporadic.

USAGE

continual, continuous

Continual = frequently recurring; intermittent—e.g.: "And [the police are] removing [the homeless]—by police rides to the edge of town, by continual issuing of citations for camping, by mass towing of vehicles and by routine discarding of people's belongings." (*USA Today*; Dec. 3, 1997.) *Continuous* = occurring without interruption; unceasing—e.g.: "Crow Canyon archaeologists want to study the twelfth- and thirteenth-century village to determine exactly when it was inhabited and whether it was occupied continuously or intermittently." (*Santa Fe New Mexican*; Sept. 8, 1996.) A good mnemonic device is to think of the *-ous* ending as being short for "one uninterrupted sequence."

The two words are frequently confused, usually with *continuous* horning in where *continual* belongs—e.g.:

- "Minutes after the arrest, Wayne Forrest, a Deputy Attorney General helping prosecute the case, told the presiding judge, Charles R. DiGisi, that the sheriff's office had been engaged in a 'continuous [read *continual*] course of misconduct' in the Spath case." (*New York Times*; Jan. 18, 1992.)
- "Continuous [read *Continual*] interruptions are frustrating because it often means [read *they often mean*] you have to warm up all over again or don't get a complete workout." (*Montgomery Advertiser*; Jan. 1, 1996.)

The two-word phrase *almost continuous* is correctly replaced by the single word *continual*—e.g.: "The antidepressant Prozac has been in the news almost continuously [read *continually*] since it was introduced in Belgium in 1986." (*Tampa Tribune*; Nov. 24, 1996.)

A related mistake is to use *continuous* for something that happens at regular (e.g., annual) intervals—e.g.: "The White House tree-lighting ceremony has been held continuously [read *annually*] since 1923." (*Herald-Sun* [Durham, NC]; Dec. 6, 1996.) — **BG**

continually ▶ **adverb 1** *security measures are continually updated and improved* **frequently,** regularly, repeatedly, recurrently, again and again, time and (time) again; constantly.
ANTONYMS occasionally, sporadically.
2 *patients were monitored continually* **constantly,** continuously, around/round the clock, day and night, night and day, 'morning, noon, and night', without a break, nonstop; all the time, the entire time, always, forever, at every turn, incessantly, ceaselessly, endlessly, perpetually, eternally, 24-7.
ANTONYMS occasionally, sporadically.

continuance ▶ **noun 1** *concerned with the continuance of life* See CONTINUATION.
2 *the prosecution sought a continuance* **adjournment,** postponement, deferment, stay.

continuation ▶ **noun** *the continuation of our relationship seems futile* **carrying on,** continuance, extension, prolongation, protraction, perpetuation.
ANTONYMS end.

continue ▶ **verb 1** *he was unable to continue with his job* **carry on,** proceed, go on, keep on, persist, press on, persevere; informal stick, soldier on.
ANTONYMS stop.
2 *discussions continued throughout the night* **go on,** carry on, last, extend, be prolonged, run on, drag on.
ANTONYMS stop, cease.
3 *we are keen to continue this relationship* **maintain,** keep up, sustain, keep going, keep alive, preserve.
ANTONYMS suspend, break off.
4 *his willingness to continue in office* **remain,** stay, carry on, keep going.
5 *we continued our conversation after supper* **resume,** pick up, take up, carry on with, return to, recommence.
ANTONYMS end.

continuity ▶ **noun** *a breakdown in the continuity of care* **continuousness,** uninterruptedness, flow, progression.

continuous ▶ **adjective** *the rain has been continuous since early this morning* **unceasing,** uninterrupted, unbroken, constant, ceaseless, incessant, steady, sustained, solid, continuing, ongoing, without a break, nonstop, around/round-the-clock, persistent, unremitting, relentless, unrelenting, unabating, unrelieved, without respite, endless, unending, never-ending, perpetual, everlasting, eternal, interminable; consecutive, rolling, running;

archaic without surcease. See note at CONTINUAL.
ANTONYMS momentary, temporary.

contort ▶ verb *her face was contorted with grief* **twist,** bend out of shape, distort, misshape, warp, buckle, deform.

contour ▶ noun *the contour of the moon's surface* **outline,** shape, form; lines, curves, figure; silhouette, profile.

contraband ▶ noun 1 *contraband was suspected* **smuggling,** illegal traffic, black marketeering, bootlegging; the black market.
2 *they confiscated the contraband* **stolen goods,** swag, bootleg.
▶ adjective *contraband goods* **smuggled,** black-market, bootleg, under the counter, illegal, illicit, unlawful; prohibited, banned, proscribed, forbidden; informal hot.

contraceptive ▶ noun *what type of contraceptive did you use?* **birth control**; prophylactic, condom, birth control pill, the pill, diaphragm, the sponge, female condom, IUD, cervical cap, morning-after pill, BC/BCP; trademark Plan B.

contract ▶ noun *a legally binding contract* **agreement,** commitment, arrangement, settlement, understanding, compact, covenant, bond; deal, bargain; Law indenture.
▶ verb 1 *the market for such goods began to contract* **shrink,** get smaller, decrease, diminish, reduce, dwindle, decline.
ANTONYMS expand, increase.
2 *her stomach muscles contracted* **tighten,** tense, flex, constrict, draw in, narrow.
ANTONYMS relax.
3 *she contracted her brow* **wrinkle,** knit, crease, purse, pucker.
4 *his name was soon contracted to "Rob"* **shorten,** abbreviate, cut, reduce; elide.
ANTONYMS expand, lengthen.
5 *the company contracted to rebuild the stadium* **undertake,** pledge, promise, covenant, commit oneself, engage, agree, enter an agreement, make a deal.
6 *she contracted rubella* **develop,** catch, get, pick up, come down with, be struck down by, be stricken with, succumb to.
7 *he contracted a debt of $3,300* **incur,** run up.
– PHRASES **contract out** *trash collection is contracted out by the town* **subcontract,** outsource, farm out.

contraction ▶ noun 1 *the contraction of the industry* **shrinking,** shrinkage, decline, decrease, diminution, dwindling.
2 *the contraction of muscles* **tightening,** tensing, flexing.
3 *my contractions started at midnight* **labor pains,** labor; cramps.
4 *"goodbye" is a contraction of "God be with you"* **abbreviation,** short form, shortened form, elision, diminutive.

contradict ▶ verb 1 *he contradicted the government's account of the affair* **deny,** rebut, dispute, challenge, counter, controvert; formal gainsay.
ANTONYMS confirm, agree with.
2 *nobody dared to contradict him* **argue against,** go against, challenge, oppose; formal gainsay.
3 *this research contradicts previous assertions* **conflict with,** be at odds with, be at variance with, be inconsistent with, run counter to, disagree with.
ANTONYMS corroborate, support.

contradiction ▶ noun 1 *the contradiction between his faith and his lifestyle* **conflict,** clash, disagreement, opposition, inconsistency, mismatch, variance.
ANTONYMS agreement.
2 *a contradiction of his statement* **denial,** refutation, rebuttal, countering.
ANTONYMS confirmation, reaffirmation.

contradictory ▶ adjective *their contradictory accounts angered the lieutenant* **opposed,** in opposition, opposite, antithetical, contrary, contrasting, conflicting, at variance, at odds, opposing, clashing, divergent, discrepant, different; inconsistent, incompatible, irreconcilable. See note at OPPOSITE.

contraption ▶ noun *he's driving around the yard in another one of his wild contraptions* **device,** gadget, apparatus, machine, appliance, mechanism, invention, contrivance; informal gizmo, widget, doohickey.

contrary ▶ adjective 1 *contrary views* **opposite,** opposing, opposed, contradictory, clashing, conflicting, antithetical, incompatible, irreconcilable. See note at OPPOSITE.
ANTONYMS compatible, same.
2 *she was sulky and contrary* **perverse,** awkward, difficult, uncooperative, unhelpful, obstructive, disobliging, recalcitrant, willful, self-willed, stubborn, obstinate, defiant, mulish, pigheaded, intractable; formal refractory; archaic froward.
ANTONYMS cooperative, accommodating.
▶ noun *in fact, the contrary is true* **opposite,** reverse, converse, antithesis.
– PHRASES **contrary to** *contrary to what we had predicted, the lemon potatoes were very popular* **in conflict with,** against, at variance with, at odds with, in opposition to, counter to, incompatible with.

contrast ▶ noun 1 *the contrast between rural and urban trends* **difference,** dissimilarity, disparity, distinction, contradistinction, divergence, variance, variation, differentiation; contradiction, incongruity, opposition, polarity.
ANTONYMS similarity.
2 *Jane was a complete contrast to Sarah* **opposite,** antithesis; foil, complement.
▶ verb 1 *a view that* **contrasts with** *his earlier opinion* **differ from,** be at variance with, be contrary to, conflict with, go against, be at odds with, be in opposition to, disagree with, clash with.
ANTONYMS resemble, echo.
2 *people* **contrasted** *her* **with** *her sister* **compare with/to,** set side by side with, juxtapose with/to; measure against; distinguish from, differentiate from.
ANTONYMS liken.

contravene ▶ verb 1 *he contravened several laws* **break,** breach, violate, infringe; defy, disobey, flout.
ANTONYMS comply with, uphold.
2 *the prosecution contravened the rights of the individual* **conflict with,** be in conflict with, be at odds with, be at variance with, run counter to.

contretemps ▶ noun *her little contretemps with Terry* **argument,** quarrel, squabble, disagreement, difference of opinion, dispute; informal tiff, set-to, run-in, spat, row.

contribute ▶ verb **1** *the government contributed a million dollars* **give,** donate, put up, subscribe, hand out, grant, bestow, present, provide, supply, furnish; informal chip in, pitch in, fork out, shell out, cough up, kick in, ante up, pony up.
2 *an article contributed by Dr. Clouson* **supply,** provide, submit.
3 *numerous factors contribute to job satisfaction* **play a part in,** be instrumental in, be a factor in, have a hand in, be conducive to, make for, lead to, cause.

contribution ▶ noun **1** *voluntary financial contributions* **donation,** gift, offering, present, handout, grant, subsidy, allowance, endowment, subscription; formal benefaction.
2 *contributions from local authors* **article,** piece, story, item, chapter, paper, essay.

contributor ▶ noun **1** *the magazine's regular contributors* **writer,** columnist, correspondent.
2 *campaign contributors* **donor,** benefactor, subscriber, supporter, backer, patron, sponsor.

contrite ▶ adjective *Joey was so contrite we had to conceal our amusement* **remorseful,** repentant, penitent, regretful, sorry, apologetic, rueful, sheepish, hangdog, ashamed, chastened, shamefaced, conscience-stricken, guilt-ridden.

contrivance ▶ noun **1** *a mechanical contrivance* **device,** gadget, machine, appliance, contraption, apparatus, mechanism, implement, tool, invention; informal gizmo, widget, doohickey.
2 *her matchmaking contrivances* **scheme,** stratagem, tactic, maneuver, move, plan, ploy, gambit, wile, trick, ruse, plot, machination.

contrive ▶ verb *his opponents contrived a cabinet crisis* **bring about,** engineer, manufacture, orchestrate, stage-manage, create, devise, concoct, construct, plan, fabricate, plot, hatch; informal wangle, set up.

contrived ▶ adjective *the story's contrived ending is a big letdown* **forced,** strained, studied, artificial, affected, put-on, phony, pretended, false, feigned, fake, manufactured, unnatural; labored, overdone, elaborate.
ANTONYMS natural.

control ▶ noun **1** *the Aztec Empire lost its control of Mexico in 1521* **jurisdiction,** sway, power, authority, command, dominance, government, mastery, leadership, rule, sovereignty, supremacy, ascendancy; charge, management, direction, supervision, superintendence.
2 *strict import controls* **restraint,** constraint, limitation, restriction, check, curb, brake, rein; regulation.
3 *her control deserted her* **self-control,** self-restraint, self-possession, composure, calmness; informal cool.
4 *easy-to-use controls* **switch,** knob, button, dial, handle, lever.
5 *mission control* **headquarters,** HQ, base, center of operations, command post, nerve center.
▶ verb **1** *one family had controlled the company since its formation* **be in charge of,** run, manage, direct, administer, head, preside over, supervise, superintend, steer; command, rule, govern, lead, dominate, hold sway over, be at the helm; informal head up, be in the driver's seat, run the show.
2 *she struggled to control her temper* **restrain,** keep in check, curb, check, contain, hold back, bridle, rein in, suppress, repress, master.
3 *public spending was controlled* **limit,** restrict, curb, cap, constrain; informal put the brakes on.

controversial ▶ adjective *controversial issues such as abortion* **contentious,** disputed, at issue, disputable, debatable, arguable, vexed, tendentious; informal hot.

controversy ▶ noun *being drawn into the political controversy* **disagreement,** dispute, argument, debate, dissension, contention, disputation, altercation, wrangle, wrangling, quarrel, quarreling, war of words, storm; cause célèbre; informal hot potato, minefield.

contusion ▶ noun *a minor contusion on his elbow* **bruise,** discoloration, injury.

conundrum ▶ noun **1** *the conundrums facing policy-makers* **problem,** difficult question, difficulty, quandary, dilemma; informal poser.
2 *Rod enjoyed conundrums and crosswords* **riddle,** puzzle, word game; informal brainteaser. See note at RIDDLE.

convalescence ▶ noun *a long period of convalescence* **recuperation,** recovery, return to health, rehabilitation, improvement.

convene ▶ verb **1** *he convened a secret meeting* **summon,** call, call together, order; formal convoke.
2 *the committee convened for its final session* **assemble,** gather, meet, come together, congregate. See note at GATHER.

convenience ▶ noun **1** *the convenience of the arrangement* **expedience,** advantage, propitiousness, timeliness; suitability, appropriateness.
2 *for convenience, the handset is wall-mounted* **ease of use,** usability, usefulness, utility, serviceability, practicality.
3 *the kitchen has all the modern conveniences* **appliance,** device, labor-saving device, gadget; amenity; informal gizmo.

convenient ▶ adjective **1** *a convenient time* **suitable,** appropriate, fitting, fit, suited, opportune, timely, well-timed, favorable, advantageous, seasonable, expedient.
2 *a hotel that's **convenient for** public transit* **near (to),** close to, within easy reach of, well situated for, handy for, not far from, just around the corner from; informal a stone's throw from, within spitting distance of.

convent ▶ noun *even the hardest work at the convent gave her a sense of peace and fulfillment* **nunnery, monastery,** priory, abbey, cloister, religious community.

convention ▶ noun **1** *social conventions* **custom,** usage, practice, tradition, way, habit, norm; rule, code, canon, punctilio; propriety, etiquette, protocol; formal praxis; (**conventions**) mores.
2 *a convention signed by 74 countries* **agreement,** accord, protocol, compact, pact, treaty, concordat, entente; contract, bargain, deal.

3 *the party's biennial convention* **conference,** meeting, congress, assembly, gathering, summit, convocation, synod, conclave.

conventional ▶ adjective **1** *the conventional wisdom of the day* **orthodox,** traditional, established, accepted, received, mainstream, prevailing, prevalent, accustomed, customary.
ANTONYMS unorthodox.
2 *a conventional railroad* **normal,** standard, regular, ordinary, usual, traditional, typical, common.
3 *a very conventional woman* **conservative,** traditional, traditionalist, conformist, bourgeois, old-fashioned, of the old school, small-town, suburban; informal straight, buttoned-down, square, stick-in-the-mud, fuddy-duddy.
ANTONYMS radical, Bohemian.
4 *a conventional piece of work* **unoriginal,** formulaic, predictable, stock, unadventurous, unremarkable; informal humdrum, run-of-the-mill.
ANTONYMS original.

converge ▶ verb **1** *the tracks converge at Union Station* **meet,** intersect, cross, connect, link up, coincide, join, unite, merge.
ANTONYMS diverge.
2 *5,000 protesters* ***converged on*** *Capitol Hill* **close in on,** bear down on, approach, move toward.
ANTONYMS diverge, leave.

conversant ▶ adjective *the students are* ***conversant with*** *a wide range of math skills* **familiar with,** acquainted with, au fait with, au courant with, at home with, well versed in, well-informed about, knowledgeable about, informed about, abreast of, up-to-date on; informal up to speed on, in the loop about; formal cognizant of.

conversation ▶ noun *he may have overheard our conversation* **discussion,** talk, chat, gossip, tête-à-tête, heart-to-heart, exchange, dialogue; informal confab, jaw, chitchat, chinwag, gabfest; formal confabulation, colloquy.

CHOOSE THE RIGHT WORD

conversation, chat, colloquy, communion, dialogue, parley, tête-á-tête

It is nearly impossible for most people to get through a day without having a **conversation** with someone, even if it's only a **chat** with the mailman. Although *conversation* can and does take place in all sorts of contexts, both formal and informal, the word usually implies a relaxed, casual exchange. A *chat* is the least formal of all conversations, whether it's a father talking to his son about girls or two women having a **tête-á-tête** (French for "head to head," meaning a confidential conversation) about their wayward husbands. Men, of course, often complain that women don't understand the meaning of **dialogue**, which is a two-way conversation that may involve opposing points of view. Argument is even more likely to play a role in a **parley**, which formally is a discussion between enemies regarding the terms of a truce. A **colloquy** is the most formal of all conversations (*a colloquy on nuclear disarmament*); it can also be used to jocularly describe a guarded exchange (*a brief colloquy with the arresting officer*). **Communion** is a form of conversation as well—one that may take place on such a profound level that no words are necessary (*communion with nature*).

conversational ▶ adjective **1** *conversational English* **informal,** chatty, relaxed, friendly; colloquial, idiomatic.
2 *a conversational man* **talkative,** chatty, communicative, forthcoming, expansive, loquacious, garrulous.

converse[1] ▶ verb *they conversed in low voices* **talk,** speak, chat, have a conversation, discourse, communicate; informal chew the fat, jaw, visit, shoot the breeze; formal confabulate.

converse[2] ▶ noun *the converse is also true* **opposite,** reverse, obverse, contrary, antithesis, other side of the coin, flip side.

conversion ▶ noun **1** *the conversion of waste into energy* **change,** changing, transformation, metamorphosis, transfiguration, transmutation, sea change; humorous transmogrification.
2 *the conversion of the building* **adaptation,** alteration, modification, reconstruction, rebuilding, redevelopment, redesign, renovation, rehabilitation.
3 *his religious conversion* **rebirth,** regeneration, reformation.

convert ▶ verb **1** *plants convert the sun's energy into chemical energy* **change,** turn, transform, metamorphose, transfigure, transmute; humorous transmogrify; technical permute.
2 *the factory was converted into lofts* **adapt,** turn, change, alter, modify, rebuild, reconstruct, redevelop, refashion, redesign, restyle, revamp, renovate, rehabilitate; informal do up, rehab.
3 *they sought to convert sinners* **proselytize,** evangelize, bring to God, redeem, save, reform, re-educate, cause to see the light.
▶ noun *Christian converts* **proselyte,** neophyte, new believer; Christianity catechumen.

convey ▶ verb **1** *taxis conveyed guests to the station* **transport,** carry, bring, take, fetch, bear, move, ferry, shuttle, shift, transfer.
2 *he conveyed the information to me* **communicate,** pass on, make known, impart, relay, transmit, send, hand on/off, relate, tell, reveal, disclose.
3 *it's impossible to convey how I felt* **express,** communicate, get across/over, put across/over, indicate, say.
4 *he conveys an air of competence* **project,** exude, emit, emanate.

conveyance ▶ noun **1** *the conveyance of agricultural produce* **transportation,** transport, carriage, carrying, transfer, movement, delivery; haulage, portage, cartage, shipment.
2 formal *three-wheeled conveyances* **vehicle,** means/method of transport.

convict ▶ verb *he was convicted of sexual assault* **find guilty,** sentence.
ANTONYMS acquit.

▶ **noun** *two escaped convicts* **prisoner,** inmate; criminal, offender, lawbreaker, felon; informal jailbird, con, crook, lifer, yardbird.

conviction ▶ **noun 1** *his conviction for murder* **declaration of guilt,** sentence, judgment.
ANTONYMS acquittal.
2 *his political convictions* **belief,** opinion, view, thought, persuasion, idea, position, stance, article of faith. See note at **OPINION**.
3 *she spoke with conviction* **certainty,** certitude, assurance, confidence, sureness, no shadow of a doubt.
ANTONYMS uncertainty.

convince ▶ **verb 1** *he convinced me that I was wrong* **make certain,** persuade, satisfy, prove to; assure, put/set someone's mind at rest.
2 *I convinced her to marry me* **persuade,** induce, prevail on/upon, get, talk into, win over, cajole, inveigle.

> CHOOSE THE RIGHT WORD
>
> **convince, persuade**
>
> Although it is common to see **convince** and **persuade** used interchangeably, there are distinctions in meaning that careful writers and speakers try to preserve. **Convince** derives from a Latin word meaning 'to conquer, overcome.' **Persuade** derives from a Latin word meaning 'to advise, make appealing, sweeten.' One can **convince** or **persuade** someone with facts or arguments, but, in general, *convincing* is limited to the mind, while *persuasion* results in action (just as *dissuasion* results in nonaction): *the prime minister convinced the council that delay was pointless; the senator persuaded her colleagues to pass the legislation.*

convincing ▶ **adjective 1** *a convincing argument* **cogent,** persuasive, plausible, powerful, potent, strong, forceful, compelling, irresistible, telling, conclusive. See note at **BELIEVABLE**.
2 *a convincing 5–0 win* **resounding,** emphatic, decisive, conclusive.

convivial ▶ **adjective** *our convivial host* **friendly,** genial, affable, amiable, congenial, agreeable, good-humored, cordial, warm, sociable, outgoing, gregarious, companionable, clubby, hail-fellow-well-met, cheerful, jolly, jovial, lively; enjoyable, festive.

convocation ▶ **noun 1** *the students gathered for their convocation* **graduation (ceremony),** commencement.
2 *a convocation of church leaders* **assembly,** gathering, meeting, conference, convention, congress, council, symposium, colloquium, conclave, synod.

convolution ▶ **noun 1** *crosses adorned with elaborate convolutions* **twist,** turn, coil, spiral, twirl, curl, helix, whorl, loop, curlicue; Architecture volute.
2 *the convolutions of the plot* **complexity,** intricacy, complication, twist, turn, entanglement.

convoy ▶ **noun** *a convoy of vehicles* **group,** fleet, cavalcade, motorcade, cortège, caravan, line, train.
▶ **verb** *the ship was convoyed by army gunboats* **escort,** accompany, attend, flank; protect, defend, guard.

convulse ▶ **verb** *his whole body convulsed* **shake uncontrollably,** go into spasms, shudder, jerk, thrash about.

convulsion ▶ **noun 1** *she had convulsions* **fit,** seizure, paroxysm, spasm, attack; Medicine ictus.
2 (**convulsions**) *the audience collapsed in convulsions* **fits of laughter,** paroxysms of laughter, uncontrollable laughter; informal hysterics.
3 *the political convulsions of the period* **upheaval,** eruption, cataclysm, turmoil, turbulence, tumult, disruption, agitation, disturbance, unrest, disorder.

cook ▶ **verb 1** *Scott cooked dinner* **prepare,** make, put together; informal fix, rustle up.
2 informal *he's been cooking the books* **falsify,** alter, doctor, tamper with, interfere with, massage, manipulate, fiddle.
3 informal (**cookin'**/**cooking**) *we just stopped by to see what's cookin'* **happening,** going on, taking place, occurring; informal going down.
▶ **noun chef,** food preparer, short-order cook, pastry chef; chef de cuisine, sous-chef, cordon bleu cook; informal cookie.
– PHRASES **cook up** informal *he cooked up an alibi so ludicrous that even his own attorney laughed* **concoct,** devise, contrive, fabricate, trump up, hatch, plot, plan, invent, make up, think up, dream up.

cool ▶ **adjective 1** *a cool breeze* **chilly,** chill, cold, bracing, brisk, crisp, fresh, refreshing, invigorating, nippy.
ANTONYMS warm, hot.
2 *a cool response* **unenthusiastic,** lukewarm, tepid, indifferent, uninterested, apathetic, halfhearted; unfriendly, distant, remote, aloof, cold, chilly, frosty, unwelcoming, unresponsive, uncommunicative, undemonstrative, standoffish.
ANTONYMS enthusiastic, friendly.
3 *his ability to keep cool in a crisis* **calm,** 'calm, cool, and collected', composed, as cool as a cucumber, collected, coolheaded, levelheaded, self-possessed, controlled, self-controlled, poised, serene, tranquil, unruffled, unperturbed, unmoved, untroubled, imperturbable, placid, phlegmatic; informal unflappable, together, laid-back.
ANTONYMS panic-stricken, agitated.
4 *a cool lack of morality* **bold,** audacious, nerveless; brazen, shameless, unabashed.
5 informal *she thinks she's so cool* **fashionable,** stylish, chic, up-to-the-minute, sophisticated; informal trendy, funky, with it, hip, big, happening, groovy, phat, kicky, fly.
6 informal *a cool song* See **EXCELLENT**.
▶ **noun 1** *the cool of the evening* **chill,** chilliness, coldness, coolness.
ANTONYMS warmth.
2 *Ken lost his cool* **self-control,** control, composure, self-possession, calmness, equilibrium, calm; aplomb, poise, sangfroid, presence of mind.
▶ **verb 1** *cool the sauce in the fridge* **chill,** refrigerate.

ANTONYMS heat.
2 *her reluctance did nothing to cool his interest* **lessen,** moderate, diminish, reduce, dampen.
ANTONYMS inflame, arouse.
3 *Simon's ardor had cooled* **subside,** lessen, diminish, decrease, abate, moderate, die down, fade, dwindle, wane.
ANTONYMS intensify.
4 *after a while, she* ***cooled off*** **calm down,** recover/regain one's composure, compose oneself, control oneself, pull oneself together, simmer down; informal take a chill pill.

coop ▶ noun *a chicken coop* **pen,** run, cage, hutch, enclosure.
▶ verb *he hates being* ***cooped up*** *at home* **confine,** shut in/up, cage (in), pen up/in, keep, detain, trap, incarcerate, immure.

cooperate ▶ verb **1** *police and social services cooperated in the operation* **collaborate,** work together, work side by side, pull together, band together, join forces, team up, unite, combine, pool resources, make common cause, liaise.
2 *he was happy to cooperate* **be of assistance,** assist, help, lend a hand, be of service, do one's bit; informal play ball.

cooperation ▶ noun **1** *cooperation between management and workers* **collaboration,** joint action, combined effort, teamwork, partnership, coordination, liaison, association, synergy, synergism, give and take, compromise.
2 *thank you for your cooperation* **assistance,** helpfulness, help, helping hand, aid.

cooperative ▶ adjective **1** *a cooperative effort* **collaborative,** collective, combined, common, joint, shared, mutual, united, concerted, coordinated.
2 *pleasant and cooperative staff* **helpful,** eager to help, glad to be of assistance, obliging, accommodating, willing, amenable, adaptable.
▶ noun *a housing cooperative | a farm cooperative* **complex,** commune, collective; joint venture, cooperative enterprise; credit union; pool; informal **co-op.**

coordinate ▶ verb **1** *exhibitions coordinated by a team of international scholars* **organize,** arrange, order, systematize, harmonize, correlate, synchronize, bring together, fit together, dovetail.
2 *care workers coordinate at a local level* **cooperate,** liaise, collaborate, work together, negotiate, communicate, be in contact.
3 *floral designs coordinate with the decor* **match,** complement, set off; harmonize, blend, fit in, go.

cope ▶ verb **1** *she couldn't cope on her own* **manage,** survive, subsist, look after oneself, fend for oneself, carry on, get by/through, bear up, hold one's own, keep one's end up, keep one's head above water; informal make it, hack it.
2 *his inability to cope with the situation* **deal with,** handle, manage, address, face (up to), confront, tackle, come to grips with, get through, weather, come to terms with.

copious ▶ adjective *she took copious notes* **abundant,** superabundant, plentiful, ample, profuse, full, extensive, generous, bumper, lavish, fulsome, liberal, overflowing, in abundance, many, numerous; informal galore; literary plenteous. See note at **PREVALENT.**
ANTONYMS sparse.

copse ▶ noun *tall firs form a copse at the back of the house* **thicket,** grove, wood, coppice, stand, bush, woodlot, brake, brush; archaic hurst, holt, boscage.

copy ▶ noun **1** *a copy of the report* **duplicate,** facsimile, photocopy, transcript, reprint; Computing download; trademark Xerox; dated carbon (copy), mimeograph, mimeo.
2 *a copy of a sketch by Leonardo da Vinci* **replica,** reproduction, replication, print, imitation, likeness; counterfeit, forgery, fake; informal knockoff.
▶ verb **1** *each form had to be copied* **duplicate,** photocopy, xerox, run off, reproduce, replicate; Computing download; dated mimeograph.
2 *portraits copied from original paintings by Reynolds* **reproduce,** replicate; forge, fake, counterfeit.
3 *their sound was copied by a lot of jazz players* **imitate,** reproduce, emulate, follow, echo, mirror, parrot, mimic, ape; plagiarize, steal; informal rip off. See note at **IMITATE.**

cord ▶ noun *a two-foot cotton cord* **string,** thread, thong, lace, ribbon, strap, tape, tie, line, rope, cable, wire, ligature; twine, yarn; braid, braiding; elastic, bungee (cord).

cordial ▶ adjective *a cordial welcome* **friendly,** warm, genial, affable, amiable, pleasant, fond, affectionate, warmhearted, good-natured, gracious, hospitable, welcoming, hearty.
▶ noun *fruit cordial* **liqueur,** drink.

cordon ▶ noun *a cordon of 500 police* **barrier,** line, row, chain, ring, circle; picket line.
▶ verb *troops* ***cordoned off*** *the area* **close off,** shut off, seal off, fence off, separate off, isolate, enclose, surround.

core ▶ noun **1** *the earth's core* **center,** interior, middle, nucleus; recesses, bowels, depths; informal innards; literary midst.
2 *the core of the argument* **heart,** heart of the matter, nucleus, nub, kernel, marrow, meat, essence, quintessence, crux, gist, pith, substance, basis, fundamentals; informal nitty-gritty, brass tacks, nuts and bolts.
▶ adjective *the core issue* **central,** key, basic, fundamental, principal, primary, main, chief, crucial, vital, essential; informal number-one.
ANTONYMS peripheral.

cork ▶ noun *the cork from the wine bottle went flying across the room* **stopper,** stop, plug, peg, spigot, spile.

corner ▶ noun **1** *the cart lurched around the corner* **bend,** curve, crook, dog-leg; turn, turning, jog, junction, fork, intersection; hairpin turn.
2 *a charming corner of Italy* **district,** region, area, section, quarter, part; informal neck of the woods.
3 *he found himself in a tight corner* **predicament,** plight, tight spot, mess, can of worms, muddle, difficulty, problem, dilemma, quandary; informal pickle, jam, stew, fix, hole, hot water, bind.
▶ verb **1** *he was eventually cornered by police dogs* **drive into a corner,** bring to bay, cut off, block off, trap, hem in, pen in, surround, enclose;

capture, catch.
2 *crime syndicates have cornered the stolen car market* **gain control of,** take over, control, dominate, monopolize; capture; informal sew up.

corny ▶ **adjective** informal *most of our outdoors play was inspired by those corny TV westerns* **banal,** trite, hackneyed, commonplace, clichéd, predictable, hoary, stereotyped, platitudinous, tired, stale, overworked, overused, well-worn; mawkish, sentimental, cloying, syrupy, sugary, saccharine; informal cheesy, schmaltzy, mushy, sloppy, cutesy, soppy, cornball, hokey.

corollary ▶ **noun** *job losses are the unfortunate corollary of budget cutting* **consequence,** result, end result, upshot, effect, repercussion, product, by-product, offshoot.

coronet ▶ **noun** See CROWN (sense 1 of the noun).

corporation ▶ **noun** *the chairman of the corporation* **company,** firm, business, concern, operation, house, organization, agency, trust, partnership; conglomerate, group, chain, multinational; informal outfit, setup.

corps ▶ **noun 1** *an army corps* **unit,** division, detachment, section, company, contingent, squad, squadron, regiment, battalion, brigade, platoon.
2 *a corps of trained engineers* **group,** body, band, cohort, party, gang, pack; team, crew.

corpse ▶ **noun** *the corpse was stolen from the morgue* **dead body,** body, carcass, skeleton, remains, mortal remains; informal stiff; Medicine cadaver. See note at BODY.

corpulent ▶ **adjective** *they provide ample seating for their corpulent clients* **fat,** obese, overweight, plump, portly, stout, chubby, paunchy, beer-bellied, heavy, bulky, chunky, well-upholstered, well padded, well covered, meaty, fleshy, rotund, broad in the beam; informal tubby, pudgy, beefy, porky, roly-poly, blubbery, corn-fed; rare abdominous.
ANTONYMS thin.

correct ▶ **adjective 1** *the correct answer* **right,** accurate, true, exact, precise, unerring, faithful, strict, faultless, flawless, error-free, perfect, letter-perfect, word-perfect; informal on the mark, on the nail, bang on, (right) on the money, on the button.
ANTONYMS wrong, inaccurate.
2 *correct behavior* **proper,** seemly, decorous, decent, respectable, right, suitable, fit, fitting, befitting, appropriate, apt; approved, accepted, conventional, customary, traditional, orthodox, comme il faut.
ANTONYMS improper.
▶ **verb 1** *proofread your work and correct any mistakes* **rectify,** put right, set right, right, amend, emend, remedy, repair.
2 *an attempt to correct the trade imbalance* **counteract,** offset, counterbalance, compensate for, make up for, neutralize.
3 *the thermostat needs correcting* **adjust,** regulate, fix, set, standardize, normalize, calibrate, fine-tune.

corrective ▶ **adjective** *corrective shoes* **remedial,** therapeutic, restorative, curative, reparative, rehabilitative.

correctly ▶ **adverb 1** *the questions were answered correctly* **accurately,** right, unerringly, precisely, faultlessly, flawlessly, perfectly, without error; dated aright.
2 *she behaved correctly at all times* **properly,** decorously, with decorum, decently, suitably, fittingly, appropriately, well.

correlate ▶ **verb 1** *postal codes correlate with geographic location* **correspond to/with,** match, parallel, agree with, tally with, tie in with, be consistent with, be compatible with, be consonant with, coordinate with, dovetail (with), relate to, conform to; informal square with, jibe with.
ANTONYMS contrast.
2 *we can correlate good health and physical fitness* **connect,** analogize, associate, relate, compare, set side by side.

correlation ▶ **noun** *the correlation between smoking and lung cancer* **connection,** association, link, tie-in, tie-up, relation, relationship, interrelationship, interdependence, interaction, interconnection; correspondence, parallel.

correspond ▶ **verb 1** *their policies do not correspond with their statements* **correlate with,** agree with, be in agreement with, be consistent with, be compatible with, be consonant with, accord with, be in tune with, concur with, coincide with, tally with, tie in with, dovetail (with), fit in with; match, parallel; informal square with, jibe with.
2 *a rank corresponding to the American rank of corporal* **be equivalent,** be analogous, be comparable, equate.
3 *Debbie and I corresponded for years* **exchange letters,** write, communicate, keep in touch, keep in contact.

correspondence ▶ **noun 1** *there is some correspondence between the two variables* **correlation,** agreement, consistency, compatibility, consonance, conformity, similarity, resemblance, parallel, comparability, accord, concurrence, coincidence.
2 *his private correspondence* **letters,** messages, missives, mail, post; communication.

correspondent ▶ **noun** *the paper's foreign correspondent* **reporter,** journalist, columnist, writer, contributor, newspaperman, newspaperwoman, commentator; informal stringer, newshound.

corridor ▶ **noun** *the conference room is at the end of the corridor* **passage,** passageway, aisle, gangway, hall, hallway, gallery, arcade.

corroborate ▶ **verb** *the witness can corroborate Brueller's story* **confirm,** verify, endorse, ratify, authenticate, validate, certify; support, back up, uphold, bear out, bear witness to, attest to, testify to, vouch for, give credence to, substantiate, sustain.
ANTONYMS contradict.

corrode ▶ **verb 1** *the iron had corroded* **rust,** become rusty, tarnish; wear away, disintegrate, crumble, perish, spoil; oxidize.
2 *acid rain corrodes buildings* **wear away,** eat away (at), gnaw away (at), erode, abrade, consume, destroy.

corrosive ▶ **adjective** *corrosive chemicals* **caustic,** corroding, erosive, abrasive, burning, stinging;

destructive, damaging, harmful, harsh.

corrugated ▶ adjective *panels of corrugated fiberglass* **ridged,** fluted, grooved, furrowed, crinkled, crinkly, puckered, creased, wrinkled, wrinkly, crumpled; technical striated.

corrupt ▶ adjective **1** *a corrupt official | corrupt practices* **dishonest,** unscrupulous, dishonorable, unprincipled, unethical, amoral, untrustworthy, venal, underhanded, double-dealing, fraudulent, bribable, criminal, illegal, unlawful, nefarious; informal crooked, shady, dirty, sleazy.
ANTONYMS honest, law-abiding.
2 *the earth was corrupt in God's sight* **immoral,** depraved, degenerate, reprobate, vice-ridden, perverted, debauched, dissolute, dissipated, bad, wicked, evil, base, sinful, ungodly, unholy, irreligious, profane, impious, impure; informal warped. See note at **DEPRAVED**.
ANTONYMS moral.
3 *a corrupt text* **impure,** bastardized, debased, adulterated.
ANTONYMS pure.
▶ verb **1** *a book that might corrupt its readers* **deprave,** pervert, debauch, degrade, warp, lead astray, defile, pollute, sully.
2 *the apostolic writings had been corrupted* **alter,** tamper with, interfere with, bastardize, debase, adulterate.

corruption ▶ noun **1** *political corruption* **dishonesty,** unscrupulousness, double-dealing, fraud, fraudulence, misconduct, crime, criminality, wrongdoing; bribery, venality, extortion, profiteering, payola; informal graft, grift, crookedness, sleaze.
ANTONYMS honesty.
2 *his fall into corruption* **immorality,** depravity, vice, degeneracy, perversion, debauchery, dissoluteness, decadence, wickedness, evil, sin, sinfulness, ungodliness; formal turpitude.
ANTONYMS morality, purity.
3 *these figures have been subject to corruption* **alteration,** bastardization, debasement, adulteration.

corset ▶ noun dated **girdle,** panty girdle, foundation garment, foundation, corselette; historical stays.

cosmetic ▶ adjective *most of the changes were merely cosmetic* **superficial,** surface, skin-deep, outward, exterior, external.
▶ noun (**cosmetics**) *a new range of cosmetics* **makeup,** beauty products, beauty aids; informal war paint; rare maquillage.

cosmic ▶ adjective **1** *cosmic bodies* **extraterrestrial,** in space, from space.
2 *an epic of cosmic dimensions* **vast,** huge, immense, enormous, massive, colossal, prodigious, immeasurable, incalculable, unfathomable, fathomless, measureless, infinite, limitless, boundless.

cosmonaut ▶ noun See **ASTRONAUT**.

cosmopolitan ▶ adjective **1** *the student body has a cosmopolitan character* **multicultural,** multiracial, international, worldwide, global.
2 *a cosmopolitan audience* **worldly,** worldly-wise, well traveled, experienced, unprovincial, cultivated, cultured, sophisticated, suave, urbane, glamorous, fashionable; informal jet-setting, cool, hip, stylish. See note at **URBANE**.

cost ▶ noun **1** *the cost of the equipment* **price,** asking price, market price, selling price, unit price, fee, tariff, fare, toll, levy, charge, rental; value, valuation, quotation, rate, worth; informal humorous damage.
2 *the human cost of the conflict* **sacrifice,** loss, expense, penalty, toll, price.
3 (**costs**) *we need to make $10,000 to cover our costs* **expenses,** disbursements, overheads, running costs, operating costs, fixed costs; expenditure, spending, outlay.
▶ verb **1** *the chair costs $186* **be priced at,** sell for, be valued at, fetch, come to, amount to; informal set someone back, go for.
2 *the proposal has not yet been costed* **put a price on,** price, value, put a value on, put a figure on.

costly ▶ adjective **1** *costly machinery* **expensive,** dear, high-priced, highly priced, overpriced; informal steep, pricey, costing an arm and a leg, costing the earth.
ANTONYMS cheap, inexpensive.
2 *a costly mistake* **catastrophic,** disastrous, calamitous, ruinous; damaging, harmful, injurious, deleterious, woeful, awful, terrible, dreadful; formal grievous.
ANTONYMS beneficial.

costume ▶ noun *each contestant wore a costume depicting her state* **outfit,** garments, (set of) clothes, ensemble; dress, clothing, attire, garb, uniform, livery; informal getup, gear, togs, threads; formal apparel; archaic habit, habiliments, raiment.

coterie ▶ noun *a coterie of kindred spirits* **clique,** set, circle, inner circle, crowd, in-crowd, band, community, gang.

cottage ▶ noun *summers up at Anna and Renzo's cottage* **cabin,** lodge; bungalow, country house; shack, chantey.

couch ▶ noun *she seated herself on the couch* **sofa,** divan, settee, love seat, chesterfield, daybed, davenport, studio couch.
▶ verb *his reply was couched in deferential terms* **express,** phrase, word, frame, put, formulate, style, convey, say, state, utter.

cough ▶ verb *he coughed loudly* **hack,** hawk, bark, clear one's throat, hem.
▶ noun *a loud cough* **hack,** bark.
– PHRASES **cough up** *we need to cough up the rent by next Thursday* **pay,** pay up, come up with, hand over, dish out, part with; fork out, shell out, lay out, ante up, pony up.

council ▶ noun **1** *the town council* **local authority,** municipal authority, local government, administration, executive, chamber, assembly, corporation.
2 *the Student Council* **advisory body,** board, committee, brain trust, commission, assembly, panel; synod, convocation.
3 *that evening, she held a family council* meeting, gathering, conference, conclave, assembly.

counsel ▶ noun **1** *his wise counsel* **advice,** guidance, counseling, direction, information; hints, recommendations, suggestions, guidelines, tips, pointers, warnings.
2 *the counsel for the defense* **lawyer,** advocate,

attorney, attorney-at-law, counselor; chiefly Brit. solicitor, barrister.
▶ **verb** *he counseled the team to withdraw from the deal* **advise,** recommend, direct, advocate, encourage, urge, warn, caution; guide, give guidance.

counselor ▶ **noun** *I discussed college choices with my counselor* **adviser,** consultant, guide, mentor; expert, specialist.

count ▶ **verb 1** *Vern counted the money again* **add up,** add together, reckon up, total, tally, calculate, compute, tot up; census; formal enumerate; dated cast up.
2 *a company with 250 employees, not counting overseas staff* **include,** take into account, take account of, take into consideration, allow for.
3 *I count it a privilege to be asked* **consider,** think, feel, regard, look on as, view as, hold to be, judge, deem, account.
4 *it's your mother's feelings that count* **matter,** be of consequence, be of account, be significant, signify, be important, carry weight.
▶ **noun 1** *at last count, the committee had 57 members* **calculation,** computation, reckoning, tally; formal enumeration.
2 *her white blood cell count* **amount,** number, total.
– PHRASES **count on/upon 1** *you can count on me* **rely on,** depend on, bank on, trust (in), be sure of, have (every) confidence in, believe in, put one's faith in, take for granted, take as read.
2 *they hadn't counted on his indomitable spirit* **expect,** reckon on, anticipate, envisage, allow for, be prepared for, bargain for/on, figure on.
down for the count informal See **UNCONSCIOUS** (sense 1 of the adjective).

countenance ▶ **noun** *his strikingly handsome countenance* **face,** features, physiognomy, profile; (facial) expression, look, appearance, aspect, mien; informal mug, puss; literary visage, lineaments.
▶ **verb** *he would not countenance the use of force* **tolerate,** permit, allow, agree to, consent to, give one's blessing to, go along with, hold with, put up with, endure, stomach, swallow, stand for; formal brook.

counter[1] ▶ **noun** *the sugar is in a canister on the counter* **work surface,** countertop, work table; bar; checkout (counter).

counter[2] ▶ **verb 1** *workers countered accusations of dishonesty* **respond to,** parry, hit back at, answer, retort to.
2 *the second argument is more difficult to counter* **oppose,** dispute, argue against/with, contradict, controvert, negate, counteract; challenge, contest; formal gainsay, confute.
ANTONYMS support.
▶ **adjective** *a counter bid* **opposing,** opposed, opposite.
– PHRASES **counter to** *nearly all of his proposals are counter to our original agreement* **against,** in opposition to, contrary to, at variance with, in defiance of, in contravention of, in conflict with, at odds with.

counteract ▶ **verb 1** *new measures to counteract drug trafficking* **prevent,** thwart, frustrate, foil, impede, curb, hinder, hamper, check, put a stop to, put/bring a end to, defeat.
ANTONYMS encourage.
2 *a drug to counteract the side effects* **offset,** counterbalance, balance (out), cancel out, even out, counterpoise, countervail, compensate for, make up for, remedy; neutralize, nullify, negate, invalidate.
ANTONYMS enhance, exacerbate.

counterbalance ▶ **verb** *the risk is counterbalanced by the potential high yields* **compensate for,** make up for, offset, balance (out), even out, counterpoise, counteract, equalize, neutralize; nullify, negate, undo.

counterfeit ▶ **adjective** *counterfeit $100 bills* **fake,** faked, bogus, forged, imitation, spurious, substitute, ersatz, phony. See note at **SPURIOUS**.
ANTONYMS genuine.
▶ **noun** *the notes were counterfeits* **fake,** forgery, copy, reproduction, imitation; fraud, sham; informal phony, knockoff.
ANTONYMS original.
▶ **verb 1** *his signature was hard to counterfeit* **fake,** forge, copy, reproduce, imitate.
2 *he grew tired of counterfeiting interest* **feign,** simulate, pretend, fake, sham.

countermand ▶ **verb** *orders were being issued and then countermanded* **revoke,** rescind, reverse, undo, repeal, retract, withdraw, quash, overturn, overrule, cancel, annul, invalidate, nullify, negate; Law disaffirm, discharge, vacate; formal abrogate.
ANTONYMS uphold.

counterpart ▶ **noun** *the minister held talks with his French counterpart* **equivalent,** opposite number, peer, equal, coequal, parallel, complement, analog, match, twin, mate, fellow, brother, sister; formal compeer.

countless ▶ **adjective** *bringing relief to countless patients* **innumerable,** numerous, untold, a legion of, without number, numberless, unnumbered, limitless, multitudinous, incalculable; informal umpteen, no end of, a slew of, loads of, stacks of, heaps of, masses of, oodles of, zillions of, gazillions of; literary myriad.
ANTONYMS few.

country ▶ **noun 1** *foreign countries* **nation,** (sovereign) state, kingdom, realm, territory, province, principality, palatinate, duchy.
2 *he risked his life for his country* **homeland,** native land, fatherland, motherland, the land of one's fathers.
3 *every election year, these guys claim to know what the country wants* **the people,** the public, the population, the populace, citizenry, the nation, the body politic; the electors, the voters, the taxpayers, the grass roots; informal John Q. Public, Joe Blow, Joe Schmo.
4 *thickly forested country* **terrain,** land, territory, parts; landscape, scenery, setting, surroundings, environment.
5 *she hated living in the country* **countryside,** greenbelt, great outdoors; rural areas, back woods, back of beyond, hinterland, bush, backcountry; informal sticks, middle of nowhere, boondocks, boonies; Austral. outback.
▶ **adjective** *country pursuits* **rural,** countryside, outdoor, rustic, pastoral, bucolic; literary sylvan, Arcadian, georgic.
ANTONYMS urban.

countryside ▶ noun 1 *beautiful unspoiled countryside* **landscape,** scenery, surroundings, setting, environment; country, terrain, land.
2 *I was brought up in the countryside* See COUNTRY (sense 5 of the noun).

county ▶ noun *families from neighboring counties* **region,** province, administrative unit, territory, district, area.

coup ▶ noun 1 *a violent military coup* **seizure of power,** coup d'état, putsch, overthrow, takeover, deposition; revolution, palace revolution, rebellion, revolt, insurrection, mutiny, insurgence, uprising.
2 *a major publishing coup* **success,** triumph, feat, accomplishment, achievement, scoop, master stroke, stroke of genius.

couple ▶ noun 1 *the next couple is a sister act from Trenton* **pair,** duo, twosome, two; archaic twain, brace.
2 *a honeymoon couple* **husband and wife,** twosome, partners, lovers; informal item.
3 *I have **a couple of** things to do* **some,** a few, a handful of, one or two.
▶ verb 1 *a sense of hope **coupled with** a sense of loss* **combine with,** accompany with, mix with, incorporate with, link with, associate with, connect with/to, ally with; add to, join to; formal conjoin with.
2 *a cable is coupled to one of the wheels* **connect,** attach, join, fasten, fix, link, secure, tie, bind, strap, rope, tether, truss, lash, hitch, yoke, chain, hook (up).
ANTONYMS detach.

coupon ▶ noun 1 *grocery coupons* **voucher,** token, ticket; informal comp, rain check.
2 *fill in the coupon below* **form,** tear-off card.

courage ▶ noun *the courage of firefighters is just awesome* **bravery,** courageousness, pluck, pluckiness, valor, fearlessness, intrepidity, nerve, daring, audacity, boldness, grit, true grit, hardihood, heroism, gallantry; informal guts, spunk, moxie, cojones, balls.
ANTONYMS cowardice.

CHOOSE THE RIGHT WORD

courage, fortitude, guts, nerve, pluck, resolution, tenacity

Courage is what makes someone capable of facing extreme danger and difficulty without retreating (*the courage to confront the enemy head-on*). It implies not only bravery and a dauntless spirit but the ability to endure in times of adversity (*a mother's courage in the face of her loss*). Someone who has **guts**, a slang word indicating an admirable display of courage when it really counts (*having the guts to stand up to one's boss*), might also be described as having "intestinal fortitude," a cliché that is more formal and means the same thing. **Fortitude** is the most formal of any of these words; it suggests firmness or strength of mind rather than physical bravery (*the fortitude to stand up for his beliefs*). **Resolution** also implies firmness of mind rather than fearlessness, but the emphasis is on the determination to achieve a goal in spite of opposition or interference (*a woman of strong resolution, not easily held back by her male superiors*). **Tenacity** goes one step beyond *resolution*, adding stubborn persistence and unwillingness to acknowledge defeat (*the tenacity of a bulldog*). **Nerve** and **pluck** are informal words. *Pluck* connotes high spirits, conviction, and eagerness (*the pluck to volunteer her time even after she'd been laid off*), while *nerve* is the cool, unflappable daring with which someone takes a calculated risk (*the nerve to take over the controls and land the plane safely*). *Nerve* can also refer to brashness or even rudeness in social situations (*She had the nerve to go to his house without calling first*).

courageous ▶ adjective *these Special Olympians are among the most courageous individuals on the planet* **brave,** plucky, fearless, valiant, valorous, intrepid, heroic, lionhearted, bold, daring, daredevil, audacious, undaunted, unflinching, unshrinking, unafraid, dauntless, indomitable, doughty, mettlesome, venturesome, stouthearted, gallant; informal game, gutsy, spunky, ballsy.
ANTONYMS cowardly.

courier ▶ noun *the documents were sent by courier* **messenger,** runner; letter carrier, mail carrier, delivery man/woman; delivery service.

course ▶ noun 1 *the island was not far off our course* **route,** way, track, direction, tack, path, line, trail, trajectory, bearing, heading, orbit.
2 *the course of history* **progression,** development, progress, advance, evolution, flow, movement, sequence, order, succession, rise, march, passage, passing.
3 *what is the best course to adopt?* **procedure,** plan, plan of action, course of action, line of action, MO, modus operandi, practice, approach, technique, way, means, policy, strategy, program; formal praxis.
4 *a waterlogged course* **racecourse,** raceway, racetrack, track, ground.
5 *I'm taking a French course* **class,** course of study, program of study, curriculum, syllabus; classes, lectures, studies.
6 *a course of antibiotics* **program,** series, sequence, system, schedule, regimen.
▶ verb *tears coursed down her cheeks* **flow,** pour, stream, run, rush, gush, cascade, flood, roll.
– PHRASES **in due course** *I look forward to hearing from you in due course* **at the appropriate time,** when the time is ripe, in time, in the fullness of time, in the course of time, at a later date, by and by, sooner or later, in the end, eventually. **of course** *there are, of course, exceptions to the rule* **naturally,** as might be expected, as you/one would expect, needless to say, certainly, to be sure, as a matter of course, obviously, it goes without saying; informal natch.

court ▶ noun 1 *the court found him guilty* **court of law,** bench, bar, judicature, tribunal; chiefly Brit. law court, chancery.
2 *the court of Louis IX* **royal household,** retinue, entourage, train, suite, courtiers, attendants.

3 *she made her way to the queen's court* **royal residence,** palace, castle, chateau.
▶ verb 1 *a newspaper editor who was courted by senior politicians* **curry favor with,** cultivate, try to win over, make up to, ingratiate oneself with; informal suck up to, butter up.
2 *he was busily courting public attention* **seek,** pursue, go after, strive for, solicit.
3 *he has often courted controversy* **risk,** invite, attract, bring on oneself.
4 dated *he's courting her sister* **go out with,** pursue, run after, chase; informal date, see, go steady with; dated woo, set one's cap for, romance, seek the hand of.

courteous ▶ adjective *our courteous staff is available 24 hours a day* **polite,** well-mannered, civil, respectful, well-behaved, well-bred, well-spoken, mannerly; gentlemanly, chivalrous, gallant; gracious, obliging, considerate, pleasant, cordial, urbane, polished, refined, courtly, civilized.
ANTONYMS rude.

courtesan ▶ noun archaic See PROSTITUTE (noun).

courtesy ▶ noun *our customers will be treated with courtesy* **politeness,** courteousness, good manners, civility, respect, respectfulness; chivalry, gallantry; graciousness, consideration, thought, thoughtfulness, cordiality, urbanity, courtliness.

courtier ▶ noun *the princess's courtiers* **attendant,** lord, lady, lady-in-waiting, steward, page, squire.

courtly ▶ adjective *he gave a courtly bow* **refined,** polished, suave, cultivated, civilized, elegant, urbane, debonair; polite, civil, courteous, gracious, well-mannered, well-bred, chivalrous, gallant, gentlemanly, ladylike, aristocratic, dignified, decorous, formal, stately, ceremonious.
ANTONYMS uncouth.

courtship ▶ noun 1 *a whirlwind courtship* **romance,** love affair, affair; engagement.
2 *his courtship of Emma* **wooing,** courting, suit, pursuit.

courtyard ▶ noun *India and I met in the courtyard for lunch* **quadrangle,** cloister, square, plaza, piazza, close, enclosure, yard; informal quad.

cove ▶ noun *a small sandy cove* **bay,** inlet, fjord, anchorage.

covenant ▶ noun *a breach of the covenant* **contract,** agreement, undertaking, commitment, guarantee, warrant, pledge, promise, bond, indenture; pact, deal, settlement, arrangement, understanding.
▶ verb *the landlord covenants to repair the property* **undertake,** contract, guarantee, pledge, promise, agree, engage, warrant, commit oneself, bind oneself.

cover ▶ verb 1 *she covered her face with a towel* **protect,** shield, shelter; hide, conceal, veil.
ANTONYMS expose, reveal.
2 *his car was covered in mud* **cake,** coat, encrust, plaster, smother, daub, bedaub.
3 *snow covered the fields* **blanket,** overlay, overspread, carpet, coat; literary mantle.
4 *a course covering all aspects of the business* **deal with,** consider, take in, include, involve, comprise, incorporate, embrace.
5 *the trial was covered by several newspapers* **report on,** write about, describe, commentate on, publish/broadcast details of.
6 *he turned on the radio to cover the noise of the air conditioner* **mask,** disguise, hide, camouflage, muffle, block out, stifle, smother.
7 *I'm covering for Jill* **stand in for,** fill in for, deputize for, take over from, relieve, take the place of, sit in for, understudy, hold the fort; informal sub for, pinch-hit for.
8 *can you make enough to cover your costs?* **pay (for),** be enough for, fund, finance; pay back, make up for, offset.
9 *your home is covered against damage and loss* **insure,** protect, secure, underwrite, assure, indemnify.
10 *we covered ten miles each day* **travel,** journey, go, do, traverse.
▶ noun 1 *a protective cover | a manhole cover* See COVERING (sense 1 of the noun).
2 *a book cover* **binding,** jacket, dust jacket, dust cover, wrapper.
3 (**covers**) *she pulled the covers over her head* **bedding,** bedclothes, sheets, blankets.
4 *a thick cover of snow* **coating,** coat, covering, layer, carpet, blanket, overlay, dusting, film, sheet, veneer, crust, skin, cloak, mantle, veil, pall, shroud.
5 *panicking onlookers ran for cover* **shelter,** protection, refuge, sanctuary, haven, hiding place.
6 *there is considerable game cover around the lake* **undergrowth,** vegetation, greenery, woodland, trees, bushes, brush, scrub, plants; covert, thicket, copse.
7 *the company was a cover for an international swindle* **front,** facade, smokescreen, screen, blind, camouflage, disguise, mask, cloak.
8 *on weekends there's a cover to get in the bar* **cover charge,** entry charge, entrance fee, admission charge, price of admission.
– PHRASES **cover up** *the government has tried to cover up the army's role* **conceal,** hide, keep secret, hush up, draw a veil over, suppress, sweep under the carpet, gloss over, keep dark; informal whitewash, keep a/the lid on.

coverage ▶ noun 1 *up-to-the-minute coverage of the situation* **reportage,** reporting, description, treatment, handling, presentation, investigation, commentary; reports, articles, pieces, stories, ink.
2 *your policy provides coverage against damage by fire* **insurance,** protection, security, assurance, indemnification, indemnity, compensation.

covering ▶ noun 1 *a plastic covering* **awning,** canopy, tarpaulin, cowling, cowl, casing, housing; wrapping, wrapper, cover, envelope, sheath, sleeve, jacket, lid, top, cap.
2 *a covering of snow* **layer,** coating, coat, carpet, blanket, overlay, topping, dusting, film, sheet, veneer, crust, skin, cloak, mantle, veil.
▶ adjective *a covering letter* **accompanying,** explanatory, introductory, prefatory.

coverlet ▶ noun *a queen-size flannel coverlet* **bedspread,** bedcover, cover, throw, duvet, quilt, eiderdown, comforter; dated counterpane.

covert ▶ adjective *covert plans to sell arms* **secret,** furtive, clandestine, surreptitious, stealthy, cloak-and-dagger, hole-and-corner, backstairs, backroom, hidden, under-the-table, concealed, private, undercover, underground; informal hush-hush. See note at SECRET.
ANTONYMS overt.

covet ▶ verb *even with all they have, they covet the wealth of others* **desire,** yearn for, crave, have one's heart set on, want, wish for, long for, hanker after/for, hunger after/for, thirst for.

covetous ▶ adjective *this covetous man will never be satisfied* **grasping,** greedy, acquisitive, desirous, possessive, envious, green with envy, green-eyed. See notes at GREEDY, JEALOUS.

cow ▶ verb *has he cowed you all with his threats?* **intimidate,** daunt, browbeat, bully, tyrannize, scare, terrorize, frighten, dishearten, unnerve, subdue; informal psych out, bulldoze.

coward ▶ noun *the cowards were the first to give up* **weakling,** milksop, namby-pamby, mouse; informal chicken, scaredy-cat, yellow-belly, sissy, baby, candy-ass, milquetoast.
ANTONYMS hero.

cowardly ▶ adjective *he made a cowardly dash for the exit, leaving everyone else behind* **faint-hearted,** lily-livered, spineless, chicken-hearted, craven, timid, timorous, fearful, pusillanimous; informal yellow, chicken, weak-kneed, gutless, yellow-bellied, wimpish, wimpy.
ANTONYMS brave.

cowboy ▶ noun *cowboys on horseback* **cattleman,** cowhand, cowman, cowherd, herder, herdsman, drover, stockman, rancher, gaucho, vaquero; informal cowpuncher, cowpoke, broncobuster; dated buckaroo.
▶ adjective informal *a cowboy pilot* **maverick,** original, nonconformist, unorthodox, rebel, rebellious.

cower ▶ verb *they cowered at the sound of gunfire* **cringe,** shrink, crouch, recoil, flinch, pull back, draw back, tremble, shake, quake, blench, quail, grovel. See note at WINCE.

coy ▶ adjective *her coy demeanor is just an act* **arch,** simpering, coquettish, flirtatious, kittenish; demure, shy, modest, bashful, reticent, diffident, self-effacing, shrinking, timid.
ANTONYMS brazen.

cozen ▶ verb literary See TRICK (verb).

cozy ▶ adjective **1** *a cozy country cottage* **snug,** comfortable, warm, homelike, homey, homely, welcoming; safe, sheltered, secure, down-home, homestyle; informal comfy, toasty, snug as a bug (in a rug).
2 *a cozy chat* **intimate,** relaxed, informal, friendly.

crabbed ▶ adjective **1** *her crabbed handwriting* **cramped,** ill-formed, bad, illegible, unreadable, indecipherable, hieroglyphic; shaky, spidery.
2 *a crabbed old man* See CRABBY.

crabby ▶ adjective *sorry, I didn't mean to be so crabby* **irritable,** cantankerous, irascible, bad-tempered, grumpy, grouchy, crotchety, tetchy, testy, crusty, curmudgeonly, ill-tempered, ill-humored, peevish, cross, fractious, pettish, crabbed, prickly, waspish; informal snappish, snappy, cranky, ornery.
ANTONYMS affable.

crack ▶ noun **1** *a crack in the glass* **split,** break, chip, fracture, rupture; crazing.
2 *a crack between two rocks* **space,** gap, crevice, fissure, cleft, breach, rift, cranny, chink, interstice.
3 *the crack of a rifle* **bang,** report, explosion, detonation, pop; clap, crash.
4 *a crack on the head* **blow,** bang, hit, knock, rap, punch, thump, bump, smack, slap; informal bash, whack, thwack, clout, wallop, clip, bop.
5 informal *we'll have a crack at it* **attempt,** try; informal go, shot, stab, whack; formal essay.
6 informal *cheap cracks about her clothes* **joke,** witticism, quip; jibe, barb, taunt, sneer, insult; informal gag, wisecrack, funny, dig.
▶ verb **1** *the glass cracked in the heat* **break,** split, fracture, rupture, snap.
2 *she cracked him across the forehead* **hit,** strike, smack, slap, beat, thump, knock, rap, punch; informal bash, whack, thwack, clobber, clout, clip, wallop, belt, bop, sock, boff, bust, slug.
3 *the witnesses cracked* **break down,** give way, cave in, go to pieces, crumble, lose control, yield, succumb.
4 informal *the naval code proved harder to crack* **decipher,** interpret, decode, break, solve, resolve, work out, find the key to; informal figure out.
▶ adjective *a crack shot* **expert,** skilled, skillful, formidable, virtuoso, masterly, consummate, excellent, first-rate, first-class, marvelous, wonderful, magnificent, outstanding, superlative; deadly; informal great, superb, fantastic, ace, hotshot, mean, demon, brilliant, crackerjack, bang-up.
ANTONYMS incompetent.
– PHRASES **crack down on** *a campaign to crack down on crime* **suppress,** prevent, stop, put a stop to, put an end to, stamp out, eliminate, eradicate; clamp down on, get tough on, come down hard on, limit, restrain, restrict, check, keep in check, control, keep under control.
crack up informal *I feel as if I'm about to crack up* **break down,** have a breakdown, lose control, go to pieces, go out of one's mind, go mad; informal lose it, fall/come apart at the seams, go crazy, freak out.

cracked ▶ adjective **1** *a cracked cup* **chipped,** broken, crazed, fractured, splintered, split; damaged, defective, flawed, imperfect.
2 informal *you're cracked!* See MAD (sense 1).

crackle ▶ verb *bits of dried mosses crackled in the fire* **sizzle,** fizz, hiss, crack, snap, sputter, crepitate.

cradle ▶ noun **1** *the baby's cradle* **crib,** bassinet, cot, rocker.
2 *the cradle of democracy* **birthplace,** fount, fountainhead, source, spring, fountain, origin, place of origin, seat; literary wellspring.
▶ verb *she cradled his head in her arms* **hold,** support, pillow, cushion, shelter, protect; rest, prop (up).

craft ▶ noun **1** *a player with plenty of craft* **skill,** skillfulness, ability, capability, competence, art, talent, flair, artistry, dexterity, craftsmanship,

expertise, proficiency, adroitness, adeptness, deftness, virtuosity.
2 *the historian's craft* **activity,** occupation, profession, work, line of work, pursuit.
3 *she used craft to get what she wanted* **cunning,** craftiness, guile, wiliness, artfulness, deviousness, slyness, trickery, duplicity, dishonesty, deceit, deceitfulness, deception, intrigue, subterfuge; wiles, ploys, ruses, schemes, stratagems, tricks.
4 *a sailing craft* **vessel,** ship, boat; literary bark/barque.

craftsmanship ▶ **noun** *a fine example of modern craftsmanship* **workmanship,** artistry, craft, art, handiwork, work; skill, skillfulness, expertise, technique.

crafty ▶ **adjective** *a couple of crafty rogues* **cunning,** wily, guileful, artful, devious, sly, tricky, scheming, calculating, designing, sharp, shrewd, astute, canny; duplicitous, dishonest, deceitful; informal foxy.
ANTONYMS honest.

crag ▶ **noun** *the crag is a popular nesting site for eagles* **cliff,** bluff, ridge, precipice, height, peak, tor, escarpment, scarp.

cram ▶ **verb 1** *closets crammed with clothes* **fill,** stuff, pack, jam, fill to overflowing, fill to the brim, overload; crowd, overcrowd.
2 *they all crammed into the car* **crowd,** pack, pile, squash, squish, squeeze, wedge oneself, force one's way.
3 *he crammed his clothes into a suitcase* **thrust,** push, shove, force, ram, jam, stuff, pack, pile, squash, compress, squeeze, wedge.
4 *most of the students are cramming for exams* **study,** review, bone up.

cramp ▶ **noun** *stomach cramps* **muscle/muscular spasm,** pain, shooting pain, pang, stitch; Medicine hyperkinesis.
▶ **verb** *tighter rules will cramp economic growth* **hinder,** impede, inhibit, hamper, constrain, hamstring, interfere with, restrict, limit, shackle; slow down, check, arrest, curb, retard.

cramped ▶ **adjective 1** *cramped accommodations* **confined,** uncomfortable, restricted, constricted, small, tiny, narrow; crowded, packed, congested; archaic strait.
ANTONYMS spacious.
2 *cramped handwriting* **small,** crabbed, illegible, unreadable, indecipherable, hieroglyphic.

crane ▶ **noun** *the cargo is lifted by a crane* **derrick,** winch, hoist, davit, windlass; block and tackle.

cranium ▶ **noun** *a blow to his cranium* **skull,** head, brain case; informal noggin, brainpan.

crank[1] ▶ **verb** *you crank the engine by hand* **start,** turn (over), get going.
– PHRASES **crank up** informal *crank up the volume, Steve* **increase,** intensify, amplify, heighten, escalate, add to, augment, build up, expand, extend, raise; speed up, accelerate; up, jack up, hike up, step up, bump up, pump up.

crank[2] ▶ **noun** *they're nothing but a bunch of cranks* **eccentric,** oddity, madman/madwoman, lunatic; informal oddball, freak, weirdo, crackpot, loony, nut, nutcase, fruit loop, head case, maniac, screwball, kook.

cranky ▶ **adjective** informal *the children were tired and cranky* See CRABBY.

cranny ▶ **noun** *every little cranny was filled with drifted snow* **chink,** crack, crevice, slit, split, fissure, rift, cleft, opening, gap, aperture, cavity, hole, hollow, niche, corner, nook, interstice.

crash ▶ **verb 1** *the car* ***crashed into*** *a tree* **smash into,** collide with, be in collision with, hit, strike, ram, cannon into, plow into, meet head-on, run into, impact.
2 *he crashed his car* **smash,** wreck; informal total.
3 *waves* ***crashed against*** *the shore* **dash against,** batter, pound, lash (against), slam (against), be hurled against.
4 *thunder crashed overhead* **boom,** crack, roll, clap, explode, bang, blast, blare, resound, reverberate, rumble, thunder, echo.
5 informal *his clothing company crashed* **collapse,** fold, fail, go under, go bankrupt, become insolvent, cease trading, go into receivership, go into liquidation; informal go broke, go bust, go belly up.
▶ **noun 1** *a crash on the highway* **accident,** collision, road traffic accident, derailment, wreck; informal pileup, smash-up, rear-ender.
2 *a loud crash* **bang,** smash, smack, crack, bump, thud, clatter, clunk, clang; report, detonation, explosion; noise, racket, clangor, din.
3 *the stock market crash* **collapse,** failure, bankruptcy.
▶ **adjective** *a crash course* **intensive,** concentrated, rapid, short; accelerated, immersion.

crass ▶ **adjective** *crass assumptions about women* **stupid,** insensitive, mindless, thoughtless, ignorant, witless, oafish, boorish, asinine, coarse, gross, graceless, tasteless, tactless, clumsy, heavy-handed, blundering.
ANTONYMS intelligent.

crate ▶ **noun** *a crate for their good china* **case,** packing case, chest, box; container, receptacle.

crater ▶ **noun** *the crater has become a lake* **hollow,** bowl, basin, hole, cavity, depression; Geology caldera.

crave ▶ **verb** *he craved professional recognition* **long for,** yearn for, desire, want, wish for, hunger for, thirst for, sigh for, pine for, hanker after, covet, lust after, ache for, set one's heart on, dream of, be bent on; informal have a yen for, have a jones for, itch for, be dying for.

craven ▶ **adjective** *a craven surrender* **cowardly,** lily-livered, faint-hearted, chicken-hearted, spineless, timid, timorous, fearful, pusillanimous, weak, feeble; informal yellow, chicken, weak-kneed, gutless, yellow-bellied, wimpish; contemptible, abject, ignominious.
ANTONYMS brave.

craving ▶ **noun** *a craving for chocolate* **longing,** yearning, desire, want, wish, hankering, hunger, thirst, appetite, greed, lust, ache, need, urge; informal yen, itch, jones.

crawl ▶ **verb 1** *they crawled under the table* **creep,** worm one's way, go on all fours, go on hands and knees, wriggle, slither, squirm, scrabble.
2 informal *I'm not going to go* ***crawling to him*** **grovel to,** ingratiate oneself with, be obsequious to, kowtow to, pander to, toady to, truckle to, bow and scrape to, dance attendance on, curry favor with, make up to, fawn on/over;

informal suck up to, lick someone's boots, butter up.
3 *the place was **crawling with** soldiers* **be full of,** overflow with, teem with, be packed with, be crowded with, be alive with, be overrun with, swarm with, be bristling with, be infested with, be thick with; informal be lousy with, be jam-packed with, be chock-full of.

craze ▶ noun *the latest fitness craze* **fad,** fashion, trend, vogue, enthusiasm, mania, passion, rage, obsession, compulsion, fixation, fetish, fancy, taste, fascination, preoccupation; informal thing.

crazed ▶ adjective *a crazed murderer* **mad,** insane, out of one's mind, deranged, demented, certifiable, psychopathic, lunatic; wild, raving, berserk, manic, maniac, frenzied; informal crazy, mental, out of one's head, raving mad, psycho. See also CRAZY (sense 1).
ANTONYMS sane.

crazy ▶ adjective informal **1** *he was acting like a crazy person* **mad,** insane, out of one's mind, deranged, demented, not in one's right mind, crazed, lunatic, non compos mentis, unhinged, mad as a hatter, mad as a March hare; informal mental, nutty, nutty as a fruitcake, off one's rocker, not right in the head, round/around the bend, raving mad, batty, bonkers, cuckoo, loopy, ditzy, loony, bananas, loco, with a screw loose, touched, gaga, not all there, out to lunch, crackers, nutso, out of one's tree, wacko, gonzo.
ANTONYMS sane.
2 *Andrea had a crazy idea* **stupid,** foolish, idiotic, silly, absurd, ridiculous, ludicrous, preposterous, farcical, laughable, risible, nonsensical, imbecilic, harebrained, cockamamie, half-baked, impracticable, unworkable, ill-conceived, senseless; informal cockeyed, daft, kooky.
ANTONYMS sensible.
3 *he's **crazy about** her* **passionate about,** (very) keen on, enamored of, infatuated with, smitten with, devoted to; (very) enthusiastic about, fanatical about; informal wild about, mad about, nuts about, hog-wild about, gone on.
ANTONYMS indifferent, apathetic.

creak ▶ verb *the rusty gate creaked in the wind* **squeak,** grate, rasp; groan, complain.

cream ▶ noun **1** *skin creams* **lotion,** ointment, moisturizer, emollient, unguent, cosmetic; salve, rub, embrocation, balm, liniment.
2 *the cream of the crop* **best,** finest, pick, flower, crème de la crème, elite.
ANTONYMS dregs.
▶ adjective *a cream dress* **off-white,** whitish, cream-colored, creamy, ivory, yellowish-white, ecru.

crease ▶ noun **1** *pants with knife-edge creases* **fold,** line, ridge; pleat, tuck; furrow, groove, corrugation.
2 *the creases at the corners of her eyes* **wrinkle,** line, crinkle, pucker; (**creases**) crow's feet.
▶ verb *her skirt was creased and stained* **crumple,** wrinkle, crinkle, line, scrunch up, rumple, ruck up.

create ▶ verb **1** *she has created a work of stunning originality* **produce,** generate, bring into being, make, fabricate, fashion, build, construct; design, devise, originate, frame, develop, shape, form, forge.
2 *regular socializing creates good team spirit* **bring about,** give rise to, lead to, result in, cause, breed, generate, engender, produce, make for, promote, foster, sow the seeds of, contribute to.
ANTONYMS destroy.
3 *the governments planned to create a free-trade zone* **establish,** found, initiate, institute, constitute, inaugurate, launch, set up, form, organize, develop.

creation ▶ noun **1** *the creation of a coalition government* **establishment,** formation, foundation, initiation, institution, inauguration, constitution; production, generation, fabrication, fashioning, building, construction, origination, development.
ANTONYMS destruction.
2 *the whole of creation* **the world,** the universe, the cosmos; the living world, the natural world, nature, life, living things.
3 *Margaret Atwood's literary creations* **work,** work of art, production, opus, oeuvre; achievement, intellectual property; informal brainchild.

creative ▶ adjective *our students are encouraged to be creative* **inventive,** imaginative, innovative, experimental, original; artistic, expressive, inspired, visionary; enterprising, resourceful.

CHOOSE THE RIGHT WORD

creative, inventive, original, resourceful, imaginative, ingenious

Everyone likes to think that he or she is **creative**, which is used to describe the active, exploratory minds possessed by artists, writers, and inventors (*a creative approach to problem-solving*). Today, however, *creative* has become an advertising buzzword (*creative cooking, creative hair-styling*) that simply means new or different. **Original** is more specific and limited in scope. Someone who is *original* comes up with things that no one else has thought of (*an original approach to constructing a doghouse*), or thinks in an independent and creative way (*a highly original filmmaker*). **Imaginative** implies having an active and creative imagination, which often means that the person visualizes things quite differently than the way they appear in the real world (*imaginative illustrations for a children's book*). The practical side of *imaginative* is **inventive**; the *inventive* person figures out how to make things work (*an inventive solution to the problem of getting a wheelchair into a van*). But where an *inventive* mind tends to come up with solutions to problems it has posed for itself, a **resourceful** mind deals successfully with externally imposed problems or limitations (*A resourceful child can amuse herself with simple wooden blocks*). Someone who is **ingenious** is both *inventive* and *resourceful*, with a dose of cleverness thrown in (*the ingenious idea of using recycled plastic to create a warm, fleecelike fabric*).

creator ▶ noun **1** *the creator of the series* **author,** writer, designer, deviser, maker, producer; originator, inventor, architect, mastermind, prime mover; literary begetter.
2 (**the Creator**) *the Sabbath is kept to honor the Creator* See **GOD** (sense 1).

creature ▶ noun **1** *the earth and its creatures* **animal,** beast, brute; living thing, living being; informal critter, varmint.
2 *you're such a lazy creature!* **person,** individual, human being, character, soul, wretch, customer; informal devil, beggar, sort, type.
3 *the boss's truckling creatures* **lackey,** minion, hireling, servant, puppet, tool, cat's paw, pawn; informal stooge, yes-man.

credence ▶ noun **1** *the government placed little credence in the scheme* **belief,** faith, trust, confidence, reliance.
2 *later reports lent credence to this view* **credibility,** plausibility, believability; archaic credit.

credentials ▶ plural noun *checking the driver's credentials* **documents,** documentation, papers, identity papers, bona fides, ID, ID card, identity card, passport, proof of identity; certificates, diplomas, certification, references.

credibility ▶ noun **1** *the whole tale lacks credibility* **plausibility,** believability, tenability, probability, feasibility, likelihood, credence; authority, cogency.
2 *does he possess the moral credibility the party is looking for?* **trustworthiness,** reliability, dependability, integrity; reputation, status.

credible ▶ adjective *only one of the so-called witnesses could provide a credible story* **believable,** plausible, tenable, able to hold water, conceivable, likely, probable, possible, feasible, reasonable, with a ring of truth, persuasive. See note at **BELIEVABLE**.

credit ▶ noun **1** *he never got the credit he deserved* **praise,** commendation, acclaim, acknowledgment, recognition, kudos, glory, esteem, respect, thanks, admiration, tributes, gratitude, appreciation; informal bouquets, brownie points, marks.
2 *the speech did his credit no good* **reputation,** repute, image, name, good name, character, prestige, standing, status, estimation, credibility.
3 archaic *his theory has been given very little credit* **credence,** belief, faith, trust, reliance, confidence.
4 *she bought her new car on credit* **loan,** advance, financing; installments; informal plastic.
▶ verb **1** *the wise will seldom credit all they hear* **believe,** accept, give credence to, trust, have faith in; informal buy, swallow, fall for, take something as gospel (truth).
2 *the scheme's success can be credited to the team's frugality* **ascribe,** attribute, assign, accredit, chalk up, put down.

creditable ▶ adjective *her forty years of creditable stage work* **commendable,** praiseworthy, laudable, admirable, honorable, estimable, meritorious, worthy, deserving, respectable. See note at **BELIEVABLE**.
ANTONYMS deplorable.

credulous ▶ adjective *he sold 'miracle' cures to desperate and credulous clients* **gullible,** naive, too trusting, easily taken in, impressionable, unsuspecting, unsuspicious, unwary, unquestioning; innocent, ingenuous, inexperienced, unsophisticated, unworldly, wide-eyed; informal born yesterday, wet behind the ears. See note at **GULLIBLE**.
ANTONYMS suspicious.

creed ▶ noun **1** *people of many creeds and cultures* **faith,** religion, religious belief, religious persuasion, church, denomination, sect.
2 *his political creed* **system of belief,** set of beliefs, beliefs, principles, articles of faith, ideology, credo, doctrine, teaching, dogma, tenets, canons.

creek ▶ noun *marsh marigolds grow along the creek* **stream,** river, brook, rivulet, freshet, runnel, rill, tributary, watercourse, bourn; informal crick.
– PHRASES **up a/the creek** *when I saw the condition of the spare tire, I knew we were up a creek* **in trouble,** in difficulty/difficulties, in a mess, in a predicament; informal in a pickle, in a jam, in a fix.

creep ▶ verb *Tim crept out of the house* **tiptoe,** steal, sneak, slip, slink, sidle, pad, edge, inch; skulk, prowl.
▶ noun informal *he's such a creep!* See **BASTARD** (sense 2 of the noun).

creeps ▶ plural noun
– PHRASES **give someone the creeps** informal *Pam says he's a nice guy, but he still gives me the creeps* **repel,** repulse, revolt, disgust, sicken, nauseate, make someone's flesh creep, make someone's skin crawl; scare, frighten, terrify, horrify; informal gross out, freak out, creep out.

creepy ▶ adjective informal *the old apple trees look creepy in the dim moonlight* **frightening,** eerie, disturbing, sinister, weird, hair-raising, menacing, threatening, eldritch; informal spooky, scary, freaky.

crescent ▶ noun *she carved a small crescent into the lid of the box* **half-moon,** sickle-shape, lunula, lunette; arc, curve, bow.

crest ▶ noun **1** *the bird's crest* **comb,** plume, tuft of feathers.
2 *the crest of the hill* **summit,** peak, top, tip, pinnacle, brow, crown, apex.
3 *our family crest* **insignia,** regalia, badge, emblem, heraldic device, coat of arms, arms.

crestfallen ▶ adjective *he was crestfallen after his mediocre performance at the tryouts* **downhearted,** downcast, despondent, disappointed, disconsolate, disheartened, discouraged, dispirited, dejected, depressed, desolate, in the doldrums, sad, glum, gloomy, dismayed, doleful, miserable, unhappy, woebegone, forlorn; informal blue, bummed, in a blue funk, down in/at the mouth, down in the dumps.
ANTONYMS cheerful.

crevice ▶ noun *the termites crawled into a crevice* **crack,** fissure, cleft, chink, interstice, cranny, nook, slit, split, rift, fracture, breach; opening, gap, hole.

crew ▶ noun **1** *the ship's crew* **sailors,** mariners,

hands, ship's company, ship's complement.
2 *a crew of cameramen and sound engineers* **team,** group, company, unit, corps, party, gang.
3 informal *they were a motley crew* **crowd,** group, band, gang, mob, pack, troop, swarm, herd, posse; informal bunch, tribe.

crib ▶ **noun 1** *the baby's crib* **cradle,** cot, bassinet.
2 *the oxen's crib* **manger,** stall, feeding trough.
▶ **verb** informal *she cribbed the plot from a Shakespeare play* **copy,** plagiarize, poach, appropriate, steal, "borrow"; informal rip off, lift, pinch.

crick ▶ **noun** *a crick in my neck* **kink,** pinch, knot, strain, stiffness.

crime ▶ **noun 1** *kidnapping is a very serious crime* **offense,** unlawful act, illegal act, felony, misdemeanor, misdeed, wrong; informal no-no.
2 *the increase in crime* **lawbreaking,** delinquency, wrongdoing, criminality, misconduct, illegality, villainy; informal crookedness; Law malfeasance.
3 *a crime against humanity* **sin,** evil, immoral act, wrong, atrocity, abomination, disgrace, outrage. See note at **SIN**.

criminal ▶ **noun** *a convicted criminal* **lawbreaker,** offender, villain, delinquent, felon, convict, malefactor, wrongdoer, culprit, miscreant; thief, burglar, robber, armed robber, gunman, gangster, terrorist; informal crook, con, jailbird, hood, yardbird, perp; Law malfeasant.
▶ **adjective 1** *criminal conduct* **unlawful,** illegal, illicit, lawless, felonious, delinquent, fraudulent, actionable, culpable; villainous, nefarious, corrupt, wrong, bad, evil, wicked, iniquitous; informal crooked; Law malfeasant.
ANTONYMS lawful.
2 informal *a criminal waste of taxpayers' money* **deplorable,** shameful, reprehensible, disgraceful, inexcusable, unforgivable, unconscionable, unpardonable, outrageous, monstrous, shocking, scandalous, wicked.
ANTONYMS commendable.

crimp ▶ **verb** *crimp the edges of the pie crust* **pleat,** flute, corrugate, ruffle, fold, crease, crinkle, pucker, gather; pinch, compress, press together, squeeze together.

cringe ▶ **verb 1** *she cringed as he bellowed in her ear* **cower,** shrink, recoil, shy away, flinch, blench, draw back; shake, tremble, quiver, quail, quake.
2 *it makes me cringe when I think of it* **wince,** shudder, squirm, feel embarrassed, feel mortified. See note at **WINCE**.

crinkly ▶ **adjective** *a stiff, crinkly fabric* **wrinkled,** wrinkly, crinkled, creased, crumpled, rumpled, crimped, corrugated, fluted, puckered, furrowed; wavy.

cripple ▶ **verb 1** *the accident crippled her* **disable,** paralyze, immobilize, make lame, incapacitate, handicap, leave someone a paraplegic/quadriplegic.
2 *the company had been crippled by the recession* **devastate,** ruin, destroy, wipe out; paralyze, hamstring, bring to a standstill, put out of action, sideline, put out of business, bankrupt, break, bring someone to their knees.

crippled ▶ **adjective** *crippled soldiers* **disabled,** paralyzed, incapacitated, physically handicapped, lame, immobilized, bedridden, in a wheelchair, paraplegic, quadriplegic; euphemistic physically challenged.

crisis ▶ **noun 1** *the situation had reached a crisis* **critical point,** turning point, crossroads, watershed, head, moment of truth, zero hour, point of no return, Rubicon, doomsday; informal crunch; Medicine climacteric. See note at **CRUCIAL**.
2 *the current economic crisis* **emergency,** disaster, catastrophe, calamity; predicament, plight, mess, trouble, dire straits, difficulty, extremity.

crisp ▶ **adjective 1** *Sarah ordered scrambled eggs and crisp bacon* **crunchy,** crispy, brittle, crumbly, friable, breakable; firm, dry.
ANTONYMS soft.
2 *Grace and Elijah enjoyed the crisp autumn day* **invigorating,** bracing, brisk, fresh, refreshing, exhilarating, tonic, energizing; cool, chill, chilly, cold, nippy.
ANTONYMS sultry.
3 *Ms. Stevens's answers were crisp and to the point* **brisk,** decisive, businesslike, no-nonsense, incisive, to the point, matter-of-fact, brusque; terse, succinct, concise, brief, short, short and sweet, laconic, snappy.
ANTONYMS soft, sultry, rambling.
4 *crisp white bed linen* **smooth,** uncreased, ironed; starched.
ANTONYMS wrinkled.

criterion ▶ **noun** *academic ability is not the sole criterion for allocating funds* **standard,** specification, measure, gauge, test, scale, benchmark, yardstick, touchstone, barometer; principle, rule, law, canon.

critic ▶ **noun 1** *a literary critic* **reviewer,** commentator, evaluator, analyst, judge, pundit.
2 *critics of the government* **detractor,** attacker, fault-finder, backseat driver, gadfly.

critical ▶ **adjective 1** *a highly critical report* **censorious,** condemnatory, condemning, denunciatory, disparaging, disapproving, scathing, fault-finding, judgmental, accusatory, negative, unfavorable; informal nitpicking, picky.
ANTONYMS complimentary.
2 *a critical essay* **evaluative,** analytical, interpretative, expository, explanatory.
3 *the situation is critical* **grave,** serious, dangerous, risky, perilous, hazardous, precarious, touch-and-go, in the balance, uncertain, parlous, desperate, dire, acute, life-and-death.
ANTONYMS safe.
4 *the choice of materials is critical for product safety* **crucial,** vital, essential, of the essence, all-important, paramount, fundamental, key, pivotal, decisive, deciding, climacteric.
ANTONYMS unimportant.

criticism ▶ **noun 1** *she was stung by his criticism* **censure,** condemnation, denunciation, disapproval, disparagement, opprobrium, fault-finding, attack, broadside, stricture, recrimination; informal flak, bad press, panning, put down, knock, slam, brickbats, potshot(s); formal excoriation.
2 *literary criticism* **evaluation,** assessment, appraisal, analysis, judgment; commentary, interpretation, explanation, explication,

elucidation.

criticize ▶ verb *must you criticize everything she does?* **find fault with,** censure, denounce, condemn, attack, lambaste, pillory, rail against, inveigh against, arraign, cast aspersions on, pour scorn on, disparage, denigrate, give bad press to, run down; informal knock, pan, maul, slam, roast, hammer, lay into, lace into, flay, crucify, take apart, pull to pieces, pick holes in, pummel, trash, nitpick; formal excoriate.
ANTONYMS praise.

critique ▶ noun *a critique of North American culture* **analysis,** evaluation, assessment, appraisal, appreciation, criticism, review, study, commentary, exposition, exegesis.

croak ▶ verb **1** *"Thank you," I croaked* **rasp,** squawk, caw, wheeze, gasp.
2 informal *I thought that old mule croaked years ago* See DIE (sense 1).

crock ▶ noun **1** *a crock of honey* **pot,** jar; jug, pitcher, ewer; container, receptacle, vessel.
2 chiefly Brit. (**crocks**) *a pile of dirty crocks* See CROCKERY.
3 informal *his story was a total crock* **lie,** falsehood, fib, made-up story, invention, fabrication, deception, (piece of) fiction; (little) white lie, half-truth; informal tall tale, whopper.

crockery ▶ noun chiefly Brit. *a sink filled with crockery* **dishes,** china, tableware; plates, bowls, cups, saucers; chiefly Brit. crocks.

crony ▶ noun informal *he's playing pool with his cronies* **friend,** companion, bosom friend, intimate, confidant, confidante, familiar, associate, accomplice, comrade; informal pal, chum, sidekick, partner in crime, buddy, amigo, compadre, mate; archaic compeer.

crook ▶ noun **1** informal *a small-time crook* **criminal,** lawbreaker, offender, villain, delinquent, felon, convict, malefactor, culprit, wrongdoer; rogue, scoundrel, shyster, cheat, scam artist, swindler, racketeer, confidence trickster, snake oil salesman; thief, robber, burglar; informal shark, con man, con, jailbird, hood, yardbird; Law malfeasant.
2 *the crook of a tree branch* **bend,** fork, curve, angle.
▶ verb *he crooked his finger and called the waiter* **cock,** flex, bend, curve, curl.

crooked ▶ adjective **1** *narrow, crooked streets* **winding,** twisting, zigzag, meandering, tortuous, serpentine.
ANTONYMS straight.
2 *a crooked spine* **bent,** twisted, misshapen, deformed, malformed, contorted, out of shape, wry, warped, bowed, distorted.
3 *the picture over the bed looked crooked* **lopsided,** askew, awry, off-center, uneven, out of line, asymmetrical, tilted, at an angle, aslant, slanting, cockeyed, wonky.
4 informal *a crooked cop | crooked deals* **dishonest,** unscrupulous, unprincipled, untrustworthy, corrupt, corruptible, venal; criminal, illegal, unlawful, nefarious, fraudulent; informal shady, dodgy, hinky.
ANTONYMS law-abiding, honest.

croon ▶ verb *she'd sit by the old phonograph for hours, listening to Rudy Vallee croon* **sing softly,** hum, warble, trill.

crop ▶ noun **1** *some farmers lost their entire crop* **harvest,** year's growth, yield; fruits, produce.
2 *a bumper crop of mail* **batch,** lot, assortment, selection, collection, supply, intake.
3 *a rider's crop* **whip,** switch, cane, stick.
▶ verb **1** *she's had her hair cropped* **cut short,** cut, clip, shear, shave, lop off, chop off, hack off; dock, bob.
2 *a flock of sheep were cropping the turf* **graze on,** browse on, feed on, nibble, eat.
3 *the hay was cropped several times this summer* **harvest,** reap, mow; gather (in), collect, pick, bring home.
– PHRASES **crop up** *things kept cropping up to delay their work* **happen,** occur, arise, turn up, spring up, pop up, emerge, materialize, surface, appear, come to light, present itself; literary come to pass, befall.

cross ▶ noun **1** *a bronze cross* **crucifix,** rood.
2 *we all have our crosses to bear* **burden,** trouble, worry, trial, tribulation, affliction, curse, bane, misfortune, adversity, hardship, vicissitude; millstone, albatross, thorn in one's flesh/side; misery, woe, pain, sorrow, suffering; informal hassle, headache.
3 *a cross between a yak and a cow* **hybrid,** hybridization, cross-breed, half-breed, mongrel; mixture, amalgam, blend, combination.
▶ verb **1** *they crossed the hills on foot* **travel across,** traverse, range over; negotiate, navigate, cover.
2 *a lake crossed by a fine stone bridge* **span,** bridge; extend across, stretch across, pass over.
3 *the point where the two roads cross* **intersect,** meet, join, connect, crisscross.
4 *no one dared cross him* **oppose,** resist, defy, obstruct, impede, hinder, hamper; contradict, argue with, quarrel with, stand up to, take a stand against, take issue with; formal gainsay.
5 *the breed was crossed with the similarly colored Holstein* **hybridize,** cross-breed, interbreed, cross-fertilize, cross-pollinate.
▶ adjective *Jane was getting cross* **angry,** annoyed, irate, irritated, in a bad mood, vexed, irked, piqued, out of humor, put out, displeased; irritable, short-tempered, bad-tempered, snappish, snappy, crotchety, grouchy, grumpy, fractious, testy, crabby, cranky, mad, hot under the collar, peeved, riled, on the warpath, up in arms, steamed up, sore, bent out of shape, teed off, ticked off, pissed off.
ANTONYMS pleased.
– PHRASES **cross out** *looking at the manager's starting lineup, it seems that Mitchell's name has been crossed out* **delete,** strike out, ink out, score out, edit out, cancel, obliterate.

cross-examine ▶ verb *when McCoy cross-examines a witness, it's not a pretty sight* **interrogate,** question, cross-question, quiz, catechize, give someone the third degree; informal grill, pump, put someone through the wringer.

crossing ▶ noun **1** *there should be a traffic light at this crossing* **intersection,** crossroads, junction, interchange.
2 *a short ferry crossing* **journey,** passage, voyage, trip.

crotchety ▶ adjective *it's the dreadful arthritis that has made him so crotchety* **bad-tempered,** irascible, irritable, grumpy, grouchy,

cantankerous, short-tempered, tetchy, testy, curmudgeonly, ill-tempered, ill-humored, ill-natured, cross-grained, peevish, cross, fractious, pettish, waspish, crabbed, crabby, crusty, prickly, touchy, snappish, snappy, cranky, ornery.
ANTONYMS good-humored.

crouch ▶ verb *the umpire crouches just enough to get a good view of the strike zone* **squat**, bend (down), hunker down, scrunch down, hunch over, stoop, kneel (down); duck, cower.

crow ▶ verb **1** *a cock crowed* **cry**, squawk, screech, caw, call.
2 *crowing about your success* **boast**, brag, trumpet, swagger, swank, gloat, show off, preen oneself, sing one's own praises; informal talk big, blow one's own horn.

crowd ▶ noun **1** *a crowd of people* **throng**, horde, mass, multitude, host, army, battalion, herd, flock, drove, swarm, sea, troupe, pack, press, crush, mob, rabble; collection, company, gathering, assembly, audience, assemblage, congregation; informal gaggle, bunch, gang, posse.
2 *she wanted to stand out from the crowd* **majority**, multitude, common people, populace, general public, masses, rank and file, hoi polloi; informal Joe Public, John Q. Public.
3 *he's been hanging round with a bad crowd* **set**, group, circle, clique, coterie; camp; informal gang, crew, lot.
4 *the spectacle attracted a capacity crowd* **audience**, spectators, listeners, viewers; house, turnout, attendance, gate; congregation.
▶ verb **1** *reporters crowded around her* **cluster**, flock, swarm, mill, throng, huddle, gather, assemble, congregate, converge.
2 *the guests all crowded into the dining room* **surge**, push one's way, jostle, elbow one's way; squeeze, pile, cram.
3 *stop crowding me* pressure; harass, hound, pester, harry, badger, nag; informal hassle, lean on.

crowded ▶ adjective *the pizza place is crowded after every home game | a crowded bus | our villa was crowded with uninvited guests* **packed**, full, mobbed, filled to capacity, full to bursting, congested, overcrowded, overflowing, teeming, swarming, thronged, populous, overpopulated; busy; informal jam-packed, stuffed, chockablock, chock-full, bursting at the seams, wall-to-wall, standing room only, SRO; (**crowded with**) full of; informal crawling with, lousy with.
ANTONYMS deserted.

crown ▶ noun **1** *a jeweled crown* **coronet**, diadem, circlet, tiara; literary coronal.
2 *the world heavyweight crown* **title**, award, accolade, distinction; trophy, cup, medal, plate, shield, belt, prize; laurels, bays, palm(s).
3 *he and his family were loyal servants of the Crown* **monarch**, sovereign, king, queen, emperor, empress; monarchy, royalty; informal royals.
4 *the crown of the hill* **top**, crest, summit, peak, pinnacle, tip, head, brow, apex.
▶ verb **1** *David II was crowned in 1331* **enthrone**, install; invest, induct.
2 *a teaching post at Harvard crowned his career* **round off**, cap, be the climax of, be the culmination of, top off, consummate, perfect, complete, put the finishing touch(es) on/to.
3 *a steeple crowned by a gilded cross* **top**, cap, tip, head, surmount.
4 informal *someone crowned him with a poker* See HIT (sense 1 of the verb).

crucial ▶ adjective **1** *negotiations were at a crucial stage* **pivotal**, critical, key, climacteric, decisive, deciding; life-and-death.
ANTONYMS minor, unimportant.
2 *confidentiality is crucial in this case* **all-important**, of the utmost importance, of the essence, critical, preeminent, paramount, essential, vital.
ANTONYMS unimportant.

CHOOSE THE RIGHT WORD

crucial, acute, critical, deciding, pressing, urgent

In any emergency or crisis situation, there is usually a turning point. Such an event is called **critical** if it determines the outcome of a situation (*a critical point in the nuclear disarmament negotiations; a critical election for the Democratic Party*). **Crucial** can also refer to a turning point, but it emphasizes the necessity of something happening before a result can be achieved (*the battle was crucial to their victory*), while *critical* suggests more of a balance between positive and negative outcomes (*a critical debate on foreign policy*). **Acute** describes the intensification of a situation that is rapidly approaching a climax (*an acute shortage of O-negative blood*), while **deciding** refers to something that forces a certain outcome (*a deciding factor in his recovery*). **Pressing** and **urgent** are milder words. A situation that is *pressing* may be chronic rather than *acute* (*a pressing need for changes in the political system*), while an *urgent* situation may be approaching a crisis without reference to a specific turning point (*an urgent meeting between the two presidents*). While *urgent* expresses more intensity than *pressing*, neither adjective conveys the same sense of intensity as *crucial, critical,* or *acute*.

crucify ▶ verb **1** *two thieves were crucified with Jesus* **nail to a cross**; execute, put to death, kill.
2 *she had been crucified by his boastful admission of adultery* **devastate**, crush, shatter, cut to the quick, wound, pain, harrow, torture, torment, agonize, persecute.
3 informal *the fans would crucify us if we lost* See CRITICIZE.

crude ▶ adjective **1** *crude oil* **unrefined**, unpurified, unprocessed, untreated; unmilled, unpolished; coarse, raw, natural.
ANTONYMS refined.
2 *a crude barricade* **primitive**, simple, basic, homespun, rudimentary, rough, rough and ready, rough-hewn, make-do, makeshift, improvised, unfinished, jury-rigged, jerry-built, slapdash; dated rude.
ANTONYMS sophisticated.
3 *crude jokes* **vulgar**, rude, naughty, suggestive, bawdy, off-color, indecent, obscene, offensive,

lewd, salacious, licentious, ribald, coarse, uncouth, indelicate, tasteless, crass, smutty, dirty, filthy, scatological; informal blue. See note at **RUDE**.
ANTONYMS decent, inoffensive.

cruel ▶ **adjective 1** *a cruel man* **brutal,** savage, inhuman, barbaric, barbarous, brutish, bloodthirsty, murderous, vicious, sadistic, wicked, evil, fiendish, diabolical, monstrous, abominable; callous, ruthless, merciless, pitiless, remorseless, uncaring, heartless, stony-hearted, hard-hearted, cold-blooded, cold-hearted, unfeeling, unkind, inhumane; dated dastardly; literary fell.
ANTONYMS compassionate.
2 *her death was a cruel blow* **harsh,** severe, bitter, harrowing, heartbreaking, heart-rending, painful, agonizing, traumatic; formal grievous.
ANTONYMS mild.

cruelty ▶ **noun** *he treated her with cruelty* **brutality,** savagery, inhumanity, barbarity, barbarousness, brutishness, sadism, bloodthirstiness, viciousness, wickedness; lack of compassion, callousness, ruthlessness.

cruise ▶ **noun** *a cruise to the islands* **boat trip,** sea trip; voyage, journey.
▶ **verb 1** *she cruised across the Atlantic* **sail,** voyage, journey.
2 *a taxi cruised past* **drive slowly,** drift; informal mosey, toodle.

crumb ▶ **noun** *we haven't got a crumb of evidence* **fragment,** bit, morsel, particle, speck, scrap, shred, sliver, atom, grain, trace, tinge, mite, iota, jot, whit, ounce, scintilla, soupçon; informal smidgen, tad, titch.

crumble ▶ **verb** *the old barn is slowly crumbling* **disintegrate,** fall apart, fall to pieces, fall down, break up, collapse, fragment; decay, fall into decay, deteriorate, degenerate, go to rack and ruin, decompose, rot, molder, perish.

crumple ▶ **verb 1** *she crumpled the note in her fist* **crush,** scrunch up, screw up, squash, squeeze.
2 *his pants were dirty and crumpled* **crease,** wrinkle, crinkle, rumple.
3 *her resistance crumpled* **collapse,** give way, cave in, go to pieces, break down, crumble, be overcome.

crunch ▶ **verb** *she hungrily crunched the apple* **munch,** chomp, bite into.
▶ **noun** informal *when the crunch comes, she'll be forced to choose* **moment of truth,** critical point, crux, crisis, decision time, zero hour, point of no return; showdown.

crusade ▶ **noun 1** *the medieval crusades* **holy war**; jihad.
2 *a crusade against crime* **campaign,** drive, push, movement, effort, struggle; battle, war, offensive.
▶ **verb** *she likes crusading for the cause of the underdog* **campaign,** fight, do battle, battle, take up arms, work, strive, struggle, agitate, lobby, champion, promote.

crusader ▶ **noun** *she was a crusader against domestic violence* **campaigner,** fighter, champion, advocate; reformer.

crush ▶ **verb 1** *essential oils are released when the herbs are crushed* **squash,** squeeze, press, compress; pulp, mash, macerate, mangle; flatten, trample on, tread on; informal smush, smoosh.
2 *your dress will get crushed* **crease,** crumple, rumple, wrinkle, crinkle, scrunch (up).
3 *crush the cookies with a rolling pin* **pulverize,** pound, grind, break up, smash, crumble; mill; technical comminute.
4 *he crushed her in his arms* **hug,** squeeze, hold tight, embrace, enfold.
5 *the new regime crushed all popular uprisings* **suppress,** put down, quell, quash, stamp out, put an end to, overcome, overpower, defeat, triumph over, break, repress, subdue, extinguish.
6 *Alan was crushed by her words* **mortify,** humiliate, abash, chagrin, deflate, flatten, demoralize, squash; devastate, shatter; informal shoot down in flames, knock the stuffing out of.
▶ **noun 1** *the crush of people* **crowd,** throng, horde, swarm, sea, mass, pack, press, mob.
2 informal *a teenage crush* **infatuation,** obsession, love, passion; informal puppy love.

crust ▶ **noun** *a thin crust will form where the twig was snapped off* **covering,** layer, coating, cover, coat, sheet, thickness, film, skin, topping; incrustation, scab.

crusty ▶ **adjective 1** *crusty French bread* **crisp,** crispy, well baked; crumbly, brittle, friable.
ANTONYMS soft, soggy.
2 *a crusty old man* **irritable,** cantankerous, irascible, bad-tempered, ill-tempered, grumpy, grouchy, crotchety, short-tempered, testy, crabby, curmudgeonly, peevish, cross, fractious, pettish, crabbed, prickly, waspish, peppery, cross-grained; informal snappish, cranky, ornery.
ANTONYMS affable, good-natured.

cry ▶ **verb 1** *Mandy started to cry* **weep,** shed tears, sob, wail, cry one's eyes out, bawl, howl, snivel, whimper, squall, mewl, bleat; lament, grieve, mourn, keen; informal boo-hoo, blubber, turn on the waterworks; literary pule.
ANTONYMS laugh.
2 *"Wait!" he cried* **call,** shout, exclaim, sing out, yell, shriek, scream, screech, bawl, bellow, roar, vociferate, squeal, yelp, holler; dated ejaculate.
ANTONYMS whisper.
▶ **noun 1** *Leonora had a good cry* **sob,** weep, crying fit, crying jag; Technical vagitus.
2 *a cry of despair* **call,** shout, exclamation, yell, shriek, scream, screech, bawl, bellow, roar, howl, yowl, squeal, yelp, interjection, holler; dated ejaculation.
3 *they've issued a cry for help* **appeal,** plea, entreaty, cry from the heart, cri de cœur.

crypt ▶ **noun** *the fraternity pledges had to spend the night in a crypt* **tomb,** vault, mausoleum, burial chamber, sepulcher, catacomb, ossuary, undercroft.

cub ▶ **noun 1** *a lioness and her cubs* (**cubs**) **young,** offspring, pups; archaic whelps.
2 *don't waste our top writer's time with a routine story—give it to one of the cubs | a cub reporter* **trainee,** apprentice, probationer, novice, tyro, learner, beginner, tenderfoot; informal rookie, newbie, greenhorn.
ANTONYMS veteran.

cubbyhole ▶ **noun** *the glass-partitioned*

cubbyhole he called an office **small room,** booth, cubicle; den; informal cubby.

cube ▶ noun **1** *I like my ice to be in conventional cubes* **hexahedron,** cuboid, parallelepiped.
2 *a cube of soap* **block,** lump, chunk, brick.

cuddle ▶ verb **1** *she picked up the baby and cuddled him* **hug,** embrace, clasp, hold tight, hold/fold in one's arms, snuggle.
2 *the pair were kissing and cuddling* **embrace,** hug, caress, pet, fondle; informal canoodle, smooch; informal dated spoon, bill and coo.
3 *I cuddled up to him* **snuggle,** nestle, curl, nuzzle.

cuddly ▶ adjective *a cute and cuddly teddy bear* **huggable,** soft, warm, cuddlesome, snuggly, cushy; attractive, endearing, lovable.

cudgel ▶ noun *a thick wooden cudgel* **club,** bludgeon, stick, truncheon, baton, mace, blackjack, billy club, nightstick, shillelagh.
▶ verb *the victim was cudgeled to death* **bludgeon,** club, beat, batter, bash.

cue ▶ noun *the blinking blue light is my cue to lower the volume* **signal,** sign, indication, prompt, reminder; nod, word, gesture.

USAGE

cue, queue

Though pronounced the same, these words have different meanings. *Cue* = (1) a signal to begin; a hint; or (2) a stick used in billiards, pool, or shuffleboard. *Queue* = (1) a line of people or things waiting their turn; or (2) a hanging braid of hair. Not surprisingly, the two are sometimes confused—e.g.:

- "Like most birds, teal don't start their migration based on air temperatures, but take their queue [read *cue*] to head south from the shortening hours of daylight." (*Times-Picayune* [New Orleans]; Sept. 25, 1994.)
- "People were forced to stand in long cues [read *queues*] at five emergency water stations in Amagasaki." (*Daily Yomiuri* [English language/Japan]; Jan. 19, 1995.)

To *cue up* a videotape, an audiotape, or a compact disc is to have it ready for playing at a particular point—e.g.: "His brother cued up the tape, the rousing theme song from 'Rocky.' (*Hartford Courant*; Sept. 17, 1996.)

To *queue up* is to line up—e.g.: "Florida State students queued up for probably the most prized ticket they would ever use." (*Sports Illustrated*; Dec. 2, 1996.)

The braid of hair is spelled *queue*, not *cue*—e.g.: "Instructed by French dancing masters in the stately steps and deep curtsies of the minuet, the young men had indeed to mind their pieds (feet) and queues (pigtails) to keep from losing their balance or their huge wigs." (*Press-Enterprise* [Riverside, CA]; Nov. 15, 1995.) — **BG**

cuff ▶ verb *Chris cuffed him on the head* **hit,** strike, slap, smack, thump, beat, punch; informal clout, wallop, belt, whack, thwack, bash, clobber, bop, sock, boff, slug; archaic smite.
– PHRASES **off the cuff** informal **1** *an off-the-cuff remark* **impromptu,** extempore, ad lib; unrehearsed, unscripted, unprepared, improvised, spontaneous, unplanned.
2 *I spoke off the cuff* **without preparation,** without rehearsal, impromptu, ad lib; informal off the top of one's head.

cuisine ▶ noun *authentic Vietnamese cuisine* **cooking,** cookery, food, dishes.

cul-de-sac ▶ noun *this is not a through street, it's a cul-de-sac* **dead end,** no exit; blind alley.

culminate ▶ verb *two hours and ten minutes of toe-tapping merriment culminating in the grandest musical finale on Broadway* **come to a climax,** come to a head, peak, climax, reach a pinnacle; build up to, lead up to; end with, finish with, conclude with.

culmination ▶ noun *the gold medal at Nagano was the culmination of her amateur career* **climax,** pinnacle, peak, high point, highest point, height, high-water mark, top, summit, crest, apex, zenith, crowning moment, apotheosis, apogee; consummation, completion, finish, conclusion.
ANTONYMS nadir.

culpable ▶ adjective *I hold you personally culpable* **to blame,** guilty, at fault, in the wrong, answerable, accountable, responsible, blameworthy, censurable.
ANTONYMS innocent.

culprit ▶ noun *police are doing all they can to catch the culprit* **guilty party,** offender, wrongdoer, perpetrator, miscreant; criminal, malefactor, felon, lawbreaker, delinquent; informal baddy, crook, perp.

cult ▶ noun **1** *a religious cult* **sect,** denomination, group, movement, church, persuasion, body, faction.
2 *the cult of eternal youth in Hollywood* **obsession with,** fixation on, mania for, passion for, idolization of, devotion to, worship of, veneration of.

cultivate ▶ verb **1** *the peasants cultivated the land* **till,** plow, dig, hoe, farm, work, fertilize, mulch, weed.
2 *they were encouraged to cultivate basic food crops* **grow,** raise, rear, plant, sow.
3 *Tessa tried to cultivate her as a friend* **win someone's friendship,** woo, court, curry favor with, ingratiate oneself with; informal get in good with someone, butter up, suck up to.
4 *he wants to cultivate his mind* **improve,** better, refine, elevate; educate, train, develop, enrich.

cultivated ▶ adjective *believe it or not, Mrs. Cleasby, there are some cultivated young ladies in the Ozarks* **cultured,** educated, well-read, civilized, enlightened, discerning, discriminating, refined, polished; sophisticated, urbane, cosmopolitan.

cultural ▶ adjective **1** *cultural differences* **ethnic,** racial, folk; societal, lifestyle.
2 *cultural achievements* **aesthetic,** artistic, intellectual; educational, edifying, civilizing.

culture ▶ noun **1** *exposing their children to culture* **the arts,** the humanities, intellectual achievement; literature, music, painting, philosophy, the performing arts.

2 *a man of culture* **intellectual/artistic awareness,** education, cultivation, enlightenment, discernment, discrimination, good taste, taste, refinement, polish, sophistication.
3 *Afro-Caribbean culture* **civilization,** society, way of life, lifestyle; customs, traditions, heritage, habits, ways, mores, values.
4 *the culture of crops* **cultivation,** farming; agriculture, husbandry, agronomy.

cultured ▶ adjective *she got her love of art and music from her mother, a vibrant and cultured woman* **cultivated,** intellectually/artistically aware, artistic, enlightened, civilized, educated, well-educated, well-read, well-informed, learned, knowledgeable, discerning, discriminating, refined, polished, sophisticated; informal artsy.
ANTONYMS ignorant.

culvert ▶ noun *they were concerned with the foul smell from the water in the culvert* **channel,** conduit, watercourse, trough; drain, gutter, ditch.

cumbersome ▶ adjective **1** *a cumbersome diving suit* **unwieldy,** unmanageable, awkward, clumsy, inconvenient, incommodious; bulky, large, heavy, hefty, weighty, burdensome; informal hulking, clunky. See note at HEAVY.
ANTONYMS manageable.
2 *cumbersome procedures* **complicated,** complex, involved, inefficient, unwieldy, slow.
ANTONYMS straightforward.

cumulative ▶ adjective *the effects of pollution are cumulative* **increasing,** accumulative, growing, mounting; collective, aggregate, amassed.

cunning ▶ adjective *a cunning scheme* **crafty,** wily, artful, guileful, devious, sly, scheming, designing, calculating, Machiavellian; shrewd, astute, clever, canny; deceitful, deceptive, duplicitous, foxy; archaic subtle.
ANTONYMS honest.
▶ noun *his political cunning* **guile,** craftiness, deviousness, slyness, trickery, duplicity; shrewdness, astuteness.

cup ▶ noun **1** *a cup and saucer* teacup, coffee cup, demitasse; mug; historical chalice.
2 *the winner was presented with a silver cup* **trophy,** loving cup, award, prize.

cupboard ▶ noun *there are clean potholders in the cupboard* **cabinet,** sideboard, buffet; dresser, armoire, credenza, chiffonier, closet, wardrobe, commode.

cupidity ▶ noun *he did not really see her cupidity until they'd been married for several years* **greed,** avarice, avariciousness, acquisitiveness, covetousness, rapacity, materialism, Mammonism; informal money-grubbing.
ANTONYMS generosity.

cur ▶ noun **1** *a mangy cur* **mongrel,** mutt.
2 informal *Neil was beginning to feel like a cur* See BASTARD (sense 2 of the noun).

curative ▶ adjective *the natives have used these curative herbs for centuries* **healing,** therapeutic, medicinal, remedial, corrective, restorative, tonic, health-giving.

curb ▶ noun *a curb on public spending* **restraint,** restriction, check, brake, rein, control, limitation, limit, constraint; informal crackdown; literary trammel.
▶ verb *he tried to curb his temper* **restrain,** hold back/in, keep back, repress, suppress, fight back, bite back, keep in check, check, control, rein in, contain, bridle, subdue; informal keep a/the lid on.

curdle ▶ verb *the milk was left out so long that it curdled* **clot,** coagulate, congeal, solidify, thicken; turn, sour, ferment.

cure ▶ verb **1** *after a long course of treatment, he was cured* **heal,** restore to health, make well/better; archaic cleanse.
2 *economic equality cannot cure all social ills* **rectify,** remedy, put/set right, right, fix, mend, repair, heal, make better; solve, sort out, be the answer/solution to; eliminate, end, put an end to.
3 *the farmers cured their own bacon* **preserve,** smoke, salt, dry, pickle.
▶ noun **1** *a cure for cancer* **remedy,** medicine, medication, medicament, antidote, antiserum; treatment, therapy; archaic physic.
2 *interest rate cuts are not the cure for the problem* **solution,** answer, antidote, nostrum, panacea, cure-all; informal quick fix, magic bullet, silver bullet.

curio ▶ noun *a dusty old room full of forgotten curios* **trinket,** knickknack, bibelot, ornament, bauble; objet d'art, collector's item, rarity, curiosity, oddity, kickshaw, tchotchke.

curiosity ▶ noun **1** *his evasiveness roused my curiosity* **interest,** spirit of inquiry, inquisitiveness.
2 *the shop is a treasure trove of curiosities* See CURIO.

curious ▶ adjective **1** *she was curious to know what had happened* **intrigued,** interested, eager to know, dying to know, agog; inquisitive.
ANTONYMS uninterested.
2 *her curious behavior* **strange,** odd, peculiar, funny, unusual, bizarre, weird, eccentric, queer, unexpected, unfamiliar, extraordinary, abnormal, out of the ordinary, anomalous, surprising, incongruous, unconventional, offbeat, unorthodox.
ANTONYMS ordinary.

curl ▶ verb **1** *smoke curled up from his cigarette* **spiral,** coil, wreathe, twirl, swirl; wind, curve, bend, twist, twist and turn, loop, meander, snake, corkscrew, zigzag.
2 *Ruth curled her arms around his neck* **wind,** twine, entwine, wrap.
3 *she washed and curled my hair* **crimp,** perm, wave.
4 *they curled up together on the sofa* **nestle,** snuggle, cuddle.
▶ noun **1** *the tangled curls of her hair* **ringlet,** corkscrew, kink, wave.
2 *a curl of smoke* **spiral,** coil, twirl, swirl, twist, corkscrew, curlicue, helix.

curly ▶ adjective *thick, curly hair* **wavy,** curling, curled, ringlety, crimped, permed, frizzy, kinky, corkscrew.
ANTONYMS straight.

currency ▶ noun **1** *foreign currency* **money,** legal tender, cash, banknotes, bills, notes, coins, coinage, specie.

2 *a term that has gained new currency* **prevalence,** circulation, exposure; acceptance, popularity.

current ▶ adjective 1 *current events* **contemporary,** present-day, modern, present, contemporaneous; topical, in the news, live, burning.
ANTONYMS past.
2 *the idea is still current* **prevalent,** prevailing, common, accepted, in circulation, circulating, on everyone's lips, popular, widespread.
ANTONYMS obsolete.
3 *a current driver's license* **valid,** usable, up-to-date.
ANTONYMS expired.
4 *the current prime minister* **incumbent,** present, in office, in power; reigning.
ANTONYMS past, former.
▶ noun 1 *a current of air* **flow,** stream, backdraft, slipstream; airstream, thermal, updraft, draft; undercurrent, undertow, tide.
2 *the current of human life* **course,** progress, progression, flow, tide, movement.
3 *the current of opinion* **trend,** drift, direction, tendency.

curse ▶ noun 1 *she put a curse on him* **malediction,** hex, jinx; formal imprecation; literary anathema; (**a curse**) the evil eye.
2 *the curse of racism* **evil,** blight, scourge, plague, cancer, canker, poison.
3 *the curse of unemployment* **affliction,** burden, cross to bear, bane.
4 *muffled curses* **obscenity,** swear word, expletive, oath, profanity, four-letter word, dirty word, blasphemy; informal cuss, cuss word; formal imprecation.
▶ verb 1 *it seemed as if the family had been cursed* **put a curse on,** put the evil eye on, anathematize, damn, hex, jinx; archaic imprecate.
2 *she was cursed with feelings of inadequacy* **afflict,** trouble, plague, bedevil.
3 *drivers cursed and honked their horns* **swear,** blaspheme, take the Lord's name in vain; informal cuss; archaic execrate.

cursed ▶ adjective *a cursed city* **under a curse,** damned, doomed, ill-fated, ill-starred, jinxed, blighted; literary accursed, star-crossed.

cursory ▶ adjective *a cursory inspection* **perfunctory,** desultory, casual, superficial, token; hasty, quick, hurried, rapid, brief, passing, fleeting. See note at SUPERFICIAL.
ANTONYMS thorough.

curt ▶ adjective *after a curt response to Mary's accusation, he grabbed his coat and headed for the door* **terse,** brusque, abrupt, clipped, blunt, short, monosyllabic, summary; snappish, snappy, sharp, tart; gruff, offhand, unceremonious, ungracious, rude, impolite, discourteous, uncivil. See note at BRUSQUE.
ANTONYMS expansive.

curtail ▶ verb 1 *economic policies designed to curtail spending* **reduce,** cut, cut down, decrease, lessen, pare down, trim, retrench; restrict, limit, curb, rein in; informal slash.
ANTONYMS increase.
2 *his visit was curtailed* **shorten,** cut short, truncate.
ANTONYMS lengthen.

curtain ▶ noun *he drew the curtains* **drape,** drapery; window treatment, window hanging, screen, blind(s), shade; valance, café curtain.
▶ verb *the bed was* **curtained off** *from the rest of the room* **conceal,** hide, screen, shield; separate, isolate.

curve ▶ noun *the serpentine curves of the river* **bend,** turn, loop, curl, twist, hook; arc, arch, bow, undulation, curvature, meander.
▶ verb *the road curved back on itself* **bend,** turn, loop, wind, meander, undulate, snake, spiral, twist, coil, curl; arc, arch.

curved ▶ adjective *use a large curved needle for the upholstery* **bent,** arched, bowed, crescent, curving, wavy, sinuous, serpentine, meandering, undulating, curvilinear, curvy.
ANTONYMS straight.

cushion ▶ noun *a cushion against inflation* **protection,** buffer, shield, defense, bulwark.
▶ verb 1 *she cushioned her head on her arms* **support,** cradle, prop (up), rest.
2 *to cushion the blow, wages and pensions were increased* **soften,** lessen, diminish, decrease, mitigate, temper, allay, alleviate, take the edge off, dull, deaden.
3 *residents are cushioned from the outside world* **protect,** shield, shelter, cocoon.

custody ▶ noun *the parent who has custody of the child* **care,** guardianship, charge, keeping, safekeeping, wardship, responsibility, protection, tutelage; custodianship, trusteeship.
– PHRASES **in custody** *the carjacker is in custody* **in prison,** in jail, imprisoned, incarcerated, locked up, under lock and key, interned, detained; on remand; informal behind bars, doing time, inside.

custom ▶ noun 1 *his unfamiliarity with the local customs* **tradition,** practice, usage, observance, way, convention, formality, ceremony, ritual; sacred cow, unwritten rule; mores; formal praxis.
2 *it is our custom to visit the Adirondacks in October* **habit,** practice, routine, way, wont; policy, rule.

customarily ▶ adverb *we customarily leave at least a fifteen-percent tip* **usually,** traditionally, normally, as a rule, generally, ordinarily, commonly; habitually, routinely.
ANTONYMS occasionally.

customary ▶ adjective 1 *customary social practices* **usual,** traditional, normal, conventional, familiar, accepted, routine, established, time-honored, regular, prevailing.
ANTONYMS unusual.
2 *her customary good sense* **usual,** accustomed, habitual, wonted.
ANTONYMS unusual.

customer ▶ noun *Mr. Kanter is one of our best customers* **consumer,** buyer, purchaser, patron, client, subscriber; shopper.

customs ▶ plural noun See TAX (sense 1 of the noun).

cut ▶ verb 1 *the knife slipped and cut his finger* **gash,** slash, lacerate, sever, slit, pierce, penetrate, wound, injure; scratch, graze, nick, incise, score; lance.
2 *cut the pepper into small pieces* **chop,** cut up, slice, dice, cube, mince; carve, hash.

3 *cut back the new growth to about half its length | he should get his hair cut* **trim,** snip, clip, crop, barber, shear, shave; pare; prune, lop, dock; mow.
4 *I went to cut some flowers* **pick,** pluck, gather; literary cull.
5 *lettering had been cut into the stonework* **carve,** engrave, incise, etch, score; chisel, whittle.
6 *the government cut public spending* **reduce,** cut back/down on, decrease, lessen, retrench, trim, slim down; rationalize, downsize, lower, slash, chop.
7 *the text has been substantially cut* **shorten,** abridge, condense, abbreviate, truncate; edit; bowdlerize, expurgate.
8 *you need to cut at least ten lines per page* **delete,** remove, take out, excise, blue-pencil, chop.
9 *oil supplies to the area had been cut* **discontinue,** break off, suspend, interrupt; stop, end, put an end to.
10 *the point where the line cuts the vertical axis* **cross,** intersect, bisect; meet, join.
11 *she was suspended for cutting classes* **skip,** miss, play truant from; informal ditch, play hooky from.

▶ **noun 1** *a cut on his jaw* **gash,** slash, laceration, incision, wound, injury; scratch, graze, nick.
2 *a cut of beef* piece, section.
3 informal *the directors are demanding their cut* **share,** portion, bit, quota, percentage; informal slice, piece of the pie, piece of the action.
4 *his hair was in need of a cut* **haircut,** trim, clip, crop.
5 *a smart cut of the whip* **blow,** slash, stroke.
6 *he followed this with the unkindest cut of all* **insult,** slight, affront, slap in the face, jibe, barb, cutting remark, put-down, dig.
7 *a cut in interest rates* **reduction,** cutback, decrease, lessening, rollback.
8 *the elegant cut of his jacket* **style,** design; tailoring, lines, fit.

– PHRASES **cut back** *if profits don't soon improve, we'll have to find ways to cut back | they cut back on medical benefits* **economize,** downsize, pull/draw in one's horns, tighten one's belt, slim down, scale down; (**cut back on**) cut, cut down, decrease, lessen, retrench, reduce, trim; informal slash. **cut down 1** *24 hectares of trees were cut down* **fell,** chop down, hack down, saw down, hew. **2** *he was cut down in his prime* **kill,** slaughter, shoot down, mow down, gun down; informal take out, blow away; literary slay. **cut and dried** *the answers to such questions are not always cut and dried* **definite,** decided, settled, explicit, specific, precise, unambiguous, clear-cut, unequivocal, black and white, hard and fast. **cut in** *excuse me for cutting in, but Glenda says that dinner's ready* **interrupt,** butt in, break in, interject, interpose, chime in. **cut off 1** *how did this doll's arm get cut off?* **sever,** chop off, hack off; amputate. **2** *oil and gas supplies were cut off* **discontinue,** break off, disconnect, suspend; stop, end, bring to an end. **3** *a community cut off from the mainland by the floodwaters* **isolate,** separate, keep apart; seclude, closet, cloister, sequester. **cut out 1** *the lifeboat's engines cut out* **stop working,** stop, fail, give out, break down; informal die, give up the ghost, conk out. **2** *cut out all the diseased wood* **remove,** take out, excise, extract; snip out, clip out. **3** *it's best to cut out alcohol altogether* **give up,** refrain from, abstain from, go without; informal quit, lay off, knock off. **cut out of** *his mother cut him out of her will* **exclude from,** leave out of, omit from, eliminate from. **cut short 1** *they cut short their vacation* **break off,** shorten, truncate, curtail, terminate, end, stop, abort, bring to an untimely end. **2** *several award recipients were cut short during their acceptance speeches* **interrupt,** cut off, butt in on, break in on.

cut-rate ▶ **adjective** *sorry, but I'm not interested in cut-rate tires* **cheap,** marked down, reduced, discount, bargain.

cutthroat ▶ **noun** dated *a band of robbers and cutthroats* **murderer,** killer, assassin; informal hit man.
▶ **adjective** *cutthroat competition between rival firms* **ruthless,** merciless, fierce, intense, aggressive, dog-eat-dog.

cutting ▶ **noun 1** *plant cuttings* **scion,** slip; graft.
2 *fabric cuttings* **piece,** bit, fragment; trimming.
▶ **adjective 1** *a cutting remark* **hurtful,** wounding, barbed, pointed, scathing, acerbic, mordant, caustic, acid, sarcastic, sardonic, snide, spiteful, malicious, mean, nasty, cruel, unkind; informal bitchy, catty.
ANTONYMS friendly, pleasant.
2 *cutting winter winds* **icy,** icy-cold, freezing, arctic, Siberian, glacial, hypothermic, bitter, chilling, chilly, chill; biting, piercing, penetrating, raw, keen, sharp.
ANTONYMS balmy, warm.

cycle ▶ **noun 1** *the cycle of birth, death, and rebirth* **round,** rotation; pattern, rhythm.
2 *the painting is one of a cycle of seven* **series,** sequence, succession, run; set.
▶ **verb** *Patrick cycled 10 miles each day* **ride (a bicycle),** bike, pedal.

cyclone ▶ **noun** See STORM (sense 1 of the noun).

cynic ▶ **noun** *he was a cynic who deflated all the hopeful aspirations of his children* **skeptic,** doubter, doubting Thomas; pessimist, prophet of doom, doomsayer, Cassandra, Chicken Little.
ANTONYMS idealist, Pollyanna.

cynical ▶ **adjective** *losing her job after fifteen years of loyal service had left her bitter and cynical* **skeptical,** doubtful, distrustful, suspicious, disbelieving; pessimistic, negative, world-weary, disillusioned, disenchanted, jaundiced, sardonic.
ANTONYMS idealistic.

cynicism ▶ **noun** *theirs was a childhood of absent parents and broken promises, so cynicism was hardly a surprise* **skepticism,** doubt, distrust, mistrust, suspicion, disbelief; pessimism, negativity, world-weariness, disenchantment.
ANTONYMS idealism.

Dd

dab ▶ verb *she dabbed disinfectant on the cut* **pat,** press, touch, blot, mop, swab; daub, apply, wipe, stroke.
▶ noun **1** *a dab of glue* **drop,** spot, smear, splash, speck, taste, trace, touch, hint, bit; informal smidgen, tad, lick.
2 *apply concealer with light dabs* **pat,** touch, blot, wipe.

dabble ▶ verb **1** *they dabbled their feet in rock pools* **splash,** dip, paddle, trail; immerse.
2 *he* ***dabbled in*** *politics* **toy with,** dip into, flirt with, tinker with, trifle with, play with, dally with.

dabbler ▶ noun *I'm no expert astronomer, just a dabbler* **amateur,** dilettante, layman, layperson; trifler, nonprofessional, nonspecialist.
ANTONYMS professional.

daft ▶ adjective **1** *a daft idea* **absurd,** preposterous, ridiculous, ludicrous, farcical, laughable; idiotic, stupid, foolish, silly, inane, fatuous, harebrained, cockamamie, half-baked, crazy, cockeyed.
ANTONYMS sensible.
2 *are you daft?* **simpleminded,** stupid, idiotic, slow, witless, feebleminded, empty-headed, vacuous, vapid; unhinged, insane, mad; informal thick, dim, dopey, dumb, dimwitted, halfwitted, birdbrained, pea-brained, slow on the uptake, soft in the head, brain-dead, not all there, touched, crazy, mental, nuts, batty, bonkers, crackers, dumb-ass.

daily ▶ adjective *a daily event* **everyday,** day-to-day, quotidian, diurnal, circadian.
▶ adverb *the museum is open daily* **every day,** once a day, day after day, diurnally.

dainty ▶ adjective **1** *a dainty china cup* **delicate,** fine, neat, elegant, exquisite.
ANTONYMS unwieldy.
2 *a dainty morsel* **tasty,** delicious, choice, palatable, luscious, mouthwatering, delectable, toothsome; appetizing, inviting, tempting; informal scrumptious, yummy, finger-licking, melt-in-your-mouth.
ANTONYMS tasteless, unpalatable.
3 *a dainty eater* **fastidious,** fussy, finicky, particular, discriminating; informal choosy, persnickety, picky.
ANTONYMS undiscriminating.
▶ noun *homemade dainties* **delicacy,** tidbit, fancy, luxury, treat; nibble, appetizer; confection, bonbon, goody; archaic sweetmeat.

dais ▶ noun *each speaker is allowed ten minutes on the dais* **platform,** stage, podium, rostrum, stand; soapbox.

dale ▶ noun *the green lushness of the dale in springtime* **valley,** vale; hollow, basin, gully, gorge, ravine, glen; literary dell.

dally ▶ verb **1** *don't dally on the way to work* **dawdle,** delay, loiter, linger, waste time; lag, trail, straggle, fall behind; amble, meander, drift; informal dilly-dally; archaic tarry. See note at LOITER.
ANTONYMS hurry.
2 *he likes dallying with film stars* **trifle,** toy, amuse oneself, flirt, play fast and loose, philander, carry on, play around.

dam ▶ noun *the dam burst* **barrage,** barrier, wall, embankment, barricade, obstruction.
▶ verb *the river was dammed* **block (up),** obstruct, bung up, close; technical occlude.

damage ▶ noun **1** *did the thieves do any damage?* **harm,** destruction, vandalism; injury, impairment, desecration, vitiation, detriment; ruin, havoc, devastation.
2 informal *what's the damage?* **cost,** price, expense, charge, total.
3 (**damages**) *she won $4,300 in damages* **compensation,** recompense, restitution, redress, reparation(s); indemnification, indemnity.
▶ verb *the parcel had been damaged* **harm,** deface, mutilate, mangle, impair, injure, disfigure, vandalize; tamper with, sabotage; ruin, destroy, wreck, trash; formal vitiate.
ANTONYMS repair.

damn ▶ verb **1** *they were all damning him* **curse,** put the evil eye on, anathematize, hex, jinx.
ANTONYMS bless.
2 *we are not going to damn the new product before we try it* **condemn,** censure, criticize, attack, denounce, revile; find fault with, deprecate, disparage; informal slam, lay into, blast.
ANTONYMS acclaim, praise.
▶ noun informal *it's not worth a damn* **jot,** whit, iota, rap, scrap, bit; informal hoot, two hoots; dated a tinker's damn.
▶ exclamation *Damn! I forgot the keys* **darn,** damn it, dammit, drat, shoot, blast, doggone (it), goddammit, hell, rats.
– PHRASES **give a damn** *the only thing she gives a damn about is herself* **care,** mind, concern oneself; informal give a hoot.

damnable ▶ adjective *a damnable nuisance* **unpleasant,** disagreeable, objectionable, horrible, horrid, awful, nasty, dreadful, terrible; annoying, irritating, maddening, exasperating; hateful, detestable, loathsome, abominable, beastly.

damned ▶ adjective **1** *damned souls* **cursed,** doomed, lost, condemned to hell;

anathematized; literary accursed.
2 informal *this damned car won't start* **blasted,** damn, damnable, confounded, rotten, wretched; informal blessed, bloody; dated accursed.

damning ▶ **adjective** *Erlich's family was stunned to hear the damning new evidence against her* **incriminating,** condemnatory, damnatory; damaging, derogatory; conclusive, strong.

damp ▶ **adjective** *her hair was damp* **moist,** moistened, wettish, dampened, dampish; humid, steamy, muggy, clammy, sweaty, sticky, dank, moisture-laden, wet, wetted; rainy, drizzly, showery, misty, foggy, vaporous, dewy.
ANTONYMS dry.
▶ **noun** *the damp in the air* **moisture,** dampness, humidity, wetness, wet, water, condensation, steam, vapor; clamminess, dankness; rain, dew, drizzle, precipitation, spray; perspiration, sweat.
ANTONYMS dryness.
▶ **verb 1** *sweat damped his hair* See DAMPEN (sense 1).
2 *nothing damped my enthusiasm* See DAMPEN (sense 2).

dampen ▶ **verb 1** *the rain dampened her face* **moisten,** damp, wet, dew, water; literary bedew.
ANTONYMS dry.
2 *nothing could dampen her enthusiasm* **lessen,** decrease, diminish, reduce, moderate, damp, put a damper on, throw cold water on, cool, discourage; suppress, extinguish, quench, stifle, curb, limit, check, restrain, inhibit, deter.
ANTONYMS heighten.

damper ▶ **noun** *the presence of the wretched Inez puts a damper on our fun* **curb,** check, restraint, restriction, limit, limitation, constraint, rein, brake, control, impediment; chill, pall, gloom.

dampness ▶ **noun** See DAMP (noun).

damsel ▶ **noun** literary See GIRL (sense 2).

dance ▶ **verb 1** *he danced with Katherine* sway, trip, twirl, whirl, pirouette, gyrate; informal bop, disco, rock, boogie, shake a leg, hoof it, cut a/the rug, trip the light fantastic, get down, mosh, groove.
2 *little girls danced around me* **caper,** cavort, frisk, frolic, skip, prance, gambol, jig; leap, jump, hop, bounce.
3 *flames danced in the fireplace* **flicker,** leap, dart, play, flit, quiver; twinkle, shimmer.
▶ **noun 1** *they met at a dance* **ball,** masquerade, prom, hoedown, disco; dated hop, sock hop.
2 *the last dance had been played* (**piece of**) **dance music.**

dandy ▶ **noun** *he became something of a dandy* **fop,** man about town, glamour boy, rake; informal sharp dresser, snappy dresser, trendy, dude, pretty boy; informal dated swell; dated beau; archaic buck, coxcomb, popinjay.
▶ **adjective** informal *our trip was dandy* See EXCELLENT.

danger ▶ **noun 1** *an element of danger* **peril,** hazard, risk, jeopardy; perilousness, riskiness, precariousness, uncertainty, instability, insecurity.
ANTONYMS safety.
2 *that car is a danger on the roads* **menace,** hazard, threat, risk; informal death trap, widow-maker.
3 *a serious danger of fire* **possibility,** chance, risk, probability, likelihood, fear, prospect.

dangerous ▶ **adjective 1** *a dangerous animal* **menacing,** threatening, treacherous; savage, wild, vicious, murderous, desperate.
ANTONYMS harmless.
2 *dangerous wiring* **hazardous,** perilous, risky, high-risk, unsafe, unpredictable, precarious, insecure, touch-and-go, chancy, treacherous; informal dicey, hairy.
ANTONYMS safe.

dangle ▶ **verb 1** *a chain dangled from his belt* **hang (down),** droop, swing, sway, wave, trail, stream.
2 *he dangled the keys* **wave,** swing, jiggle, brandish, flourish.
3 *he dangled money in front of the locals* **offer,** hold out; entice someone with, tempt someone with.

dangling ▶ **adjective** *her dangling earrings* **hanging,** drooping, droopy, suspended, pendulous, pendent, trailing, flowing, tumbling.

dank ▶ **adjective** *the dank basement* **damp,** musty, chilly, clammy, moist, wet, unaired, humid.
ANTONYMS dry.

dapper ▶ **adjective** *doesn't Norm look dapper in his new suit?* **smart,** spruce, trim, debonair, neat, well-dressed, well-groomed, well turned out, elegant, chic, dashing; informal snazzy, snappy, natty, sharp, spiffy, fly.
ANTONYMS scruffy.

dapple ▶ **verb** *we dappled the wall by gently flicking the paintbrushes* **dot,** spot, fleck, streak, speck, speckle, mottle, marble.

dappled ▶ **adjective** *a dappled horse* **speckled,** blotched, blotchy, spotted, spotty, dotted, mottled, marbled, flecked, freckled; piebald, pied, brindle, pinto, tabby, calico; patchy, variegated; informal splotchy.

dare ▶ **verb 1** *everyone wanted to say something, but nobody dared* **be brave enough,** have the courage; venture, have the nerve, have the temerity, be so bold as, have the audacity; risk, hazard, take the liberty, stick one's neck out, go out on a limb.
2 *she dared him to go* **challenge,** defy, invite, bid, provoke, goad; throw down the gauntlet.
▶ **noun** *she accepted the dare* **challenge,** provocation, goad; gauntlet, invitation.

USAGE

dare

It's been called "one of the subtlest and most variegated verbs in the language" (Robert W. Burchfield, *Points of View*; 1992) and also "one of the trickiest" (William Safire, "Love That Dare," *New York Times*; May 17, 1987). The subtleties arise because *dare* is both an ordinary verb (*he dares you to pick up the snake*) and a modal verb (*he dare not do it himself*). And the form it takes (*dares* vs. *dare* in those examples) changes with that grammatical function.

When *dare* is used as a full verb, it behaves just like most other verbs: it takes an *-s* with a third-person singular subject (*Robert always speaks his mind bluntly and dares anyone to disagree*). The form is identifiable by the presence of an explicit infinitive (with *to*) after *dare* (here, *to disagree*).

Dare was an Old English modal. When it is used as an auxiliary verb (like the modern modals *will, must,* and, more closely, *ought*), the infinitive either is missing its *to* (*dare he disagree with Robert?*) or is missing altogether but understood (*he dare not!*). This occurs chiefly, but not only, in interrogative or negative sentences. In those sentences, the form *dares*—although sometimes used mistakenly in striving for correctness—would be unidiomatic, because *dare* in this usage behaves like other uninflected modals (*will he disagree with Robert?* | *he must not*)

As a modal verb, *dare* raises an interesting question of tense: in reference to past time, should one write (1) "Although challenged to do it, he dare not," or (2) "Although challenged to do it, he dared not"? The *Oxford English Dictionary* endorses the first and calls the second "careless," but that advice was written when that part of the great dictionary was published in 1894 (and the dandy but now archaic *durst* was still available). More recent grammarians are more lenient—e.g.: "As a modal, *dare* exhibits abnormal time reference in that it can be used, without inflection, for past as well as present time: 'The king was so hot-tempered that no one dare tell him the bad news.' The main verb form *dared* (*to*) might also occur here." (Randolph Quirk et al., *A Comprehensive Grammar of the English Language*; 1985.)

These more modern grammarians' analyses are borne out by actual usage—e.g.: "Mayo said he dared not declare it a little blue heron without confirmation from others." (*Hartford Courant*; Dec. 23, 2001.)

It is odd, however, to see the past-tense form in the set phrase *how dare you*—e.g.: " 'How dared you!' Jon shouted, waving his arms for emphasis. 'That dish was ours, the property of the entire Order! How dared you even think to appropriate it for your own uses!' " (Patricia C. Wrede, *Mairelon the Magician*; 1991.)

The form *durst*, which is a past indicative and past subjunctive along with *dared*, is obsolete in American English. In British English, it still occurs rarely, always in a negative sentence or conditional clause in which there is an infinitive either understood or having no *to* (*none durst answer him*).

The exclamatory construction *How dare he do that!* is an idiomatic phrasing of the interrogative *How* (*does/did he*) *dare* (*to*) *do that?* The subject/actor (*he*) appears after the verb (*dare*) and is always in the nominative case—e.g.: "How dare she tell taxpayers to take on more responsibility to help neighborhood kids? How dare she be right?" (*Cincinnati Enquirer*; Aug. 18, 2002.) — **BG**

daredevil ▸ noun *a young daredevil crashed his car* **thrill-seeker,** adventurer, madcap, exhibitionist, swashbuckler; stuntman; informal show-off.

▸ adjective *a daredevil skydiver* **daring,** bold, audacious, intrepid, fearless, madcap, dauntless; heedless, reckless, rash, impulsive, impetuous, foolhardy, incautious, imprudent, harum-scarum.

ANTONYMS cowardly, cautious.

daring ▸ adjective *a daring attack* **bold,** audacious, intrepid, venturesome, fearless, brave, unafraid, undaunted, dauntless, valiant, valorous, heroic, dashing; madcap, rash, reckless, heedless; informal gutsy, spunky, ballsy.

▸ noun *his sheer daring* **boldness,** audacity, temerity, fearlessness, intrepidity, bravery, courage, valor, heroism, pluck, spirit, mettle; recklessness, rashness, foolhardiness; informal nerve, guts, spunk, grit, moxie, sand, balls.

dark ▸ adjective **1** *a dark night* **black,** pitch-black, jet-black, inky; unlit, unilluminated, underlit; starless, moonless; dingy, gloomy, dusky, shadowy, shady; literary Stygian.

ANTONYMS bright.

2 *a dark secret* **mysterious,** secret, hidden, concealed, veiled, covert, clandestine; enigmatic, arcane, esoteric, obscure, abstruse, impenetrable, incomprehensible, cryptic.

3 *dark hair* **brunette,** dark brown, chestnut, sable, jet-black, ebony.

ANTONYMS blond/blonde.

4 *dark skin* **swarthy,** dusky, olive, brown, black, ebony; tanned, bronzed.

ANTONYMS pale.

5 *dark days* **tragic,** disastrous, calamitous, catastrophic, cataclysmic; dire, awful, terrible, dreadful, horrible, horrendous, atrocious, nightmarish, harrowing; wretched, woeful.

ANTONYMS happy.

6 *dark thoughts* **gloomy,** dismal, pessimistic, negative, downbeat, bleak, grim, fatalistic, black, somber; despairing, despondent, hopeless, cheerless, melancholy, glum, grave, morose, mournful, doleful.

ANTONYMS optimistic.

7 *a dark look* **moody,** brooding, sullen, dour, scowling, glowering, angry, forbidding, threatening, ominous.

8 *dark deeds* **evil,** wicked, sinful, immoral, bad, iniquitous, ungodly, unholy, base; vile, unspeakable, sinister, foul, monstrous, shocking, atrocious, abominable, hateful, despicable, odious, horrible, heinous, execrable, diabolical, fiendish, murderous, barbarous, black; sordid, degenerate, depraved; dishonorable, dishonest, unscrupulous; informal lowdown, dirty, crooked, shady.

ANTONYMS virtuous, good.

▸ noun **1** *he's afraid of the dark* **darkness,** blackness, gloom, murkiness, shadow, shade; dusk, twilight, gloaming.

ANTONYMS light.

2 *she went out after dark* **night,** nighttime, darkness; nightfall, evening, twilight, sunset.

ANTONYMS dawn, day.

– PHRASES **in the dark** informal *all those months that Luis was running guns for the Contras, his family was completely in the dark* **unaware,** ignorant, incognizant, oblivious, uninformed, unenlightened, unacquainted, unconversant.

darken ▶ verb **1** *the sky darkened* **grow dark,** blacken, dim, cloud over, lower; shade, fog.
2 *his mood darkened* **blacken,** become angry, become annoyed; sadden, become gloomy, become unhappy, become depressed, become dejected, become dispirited, become troubled.

darkness ▶ noun **1** *lights shone in the darkness* **dark,** blackness, gloom, dimness, murkiness, shadow, shade; dusk, twilight, gloaming.
2 *darkness fell* **night,** nighttime, dark.
3 *the forces of darkness* **evil,** wickedness, sin, iniquity, immorality; devilry, the Devil.

darling ▶ noun **1** *good night, my darling* **dear,** dearest, love, lover, sweetheart, sweet, beloved; informal honey, hon, angel, pet, sweetie, sugar, babe, baby, treasure.
2 *the darling of the media* **favorite,** pet, idol, hero, heroine; informal blue-eyed boy/girl, fair-haired boy.
▶ adjective **1** *his darling wife* **dear,** dearest, precious, adored, loved, beloved, cherished, treasured, esteemed, worshiped.
2 *a darling little hat* **adorable,** appealing, charming, cute, sweet, enchanting, bewitching, endearing, dear, delightful, lovely, beautiful, attractive, gorgeous, fetching; Scottish bonny.

darn ▶ verb *he was darning his socks* **mend,** repair, reinforce; sew up, stitch, patch.
▶ exclamation *oh, darn!* See DAMN.

dart ▶ noun **1** *a poisoned dart* **small arrow,** missile, projectile, flechette.
2 *she made a dart for the door* **dash,** rush, run, bolt, break, start, charge, sprint, bound, leap, dive; scurry, scamper, scramble.
▶ verb **1** *Karl darted across the road* **dash,** rush, tear, run, bolt, fly, shoot, charge, race, sprint, bound, leap, dive, gallop, scurry, scamper, scramble; informal scoot.
2 *he darted a glance at her* **direct,** cast, throw, shoot, send, flash.

dash ▶ verb **1** *he dashed home* **rush,** race, run, sprint, bolt, dart, gallop, career, charge, shoot, hurtle, careen, fly, speed, zoom, scurry, scuttle, scamper; informal tear, belt, scoot, zip, whip, hotfoot it, leg it, bomb, barrel.
ANTONYMS dawdle.
2 *he dashed the glass to the ground* **hurl,** smash, crash, slam, throw, toss, fling, pitch, cast, project, propel, send; informal chuck, heave, sling, peg.
3 *rain dashed against the walls* **be hurled,** crash, smash; batter, strike, beat, pound, lash.
4 *her hopes were dashed* **shatter,** destroy, wreck, ruin, crush, devastate, demolish, blight, overturn, scotch, spoil, frustrate, thwart, check; informal blow a hole in, scuttle.
ANTONYMS raise.
▶ noun **1** *a dash for the door* **rush,** race, run, sprint, bolt, dart, leap, charge, bound, break; scramble.
2 *a dash of salt* **pinch,** touch, sprinkle, taste, spot, drop, dab, speck, smattering, sprinkling, splash, bit, modicum, little; informal smidgen, tad, lick.
3 *he led off with such dash* **verve,** style, flamboyance, gusto, zest, confidence, self-assurance, élan, flair, vigor, vivacity, sparkle, brio, panache, éclat, vitality, dynamism; informal pizzazz, pep, oomph.

dashing ▶ adjective **1** *a dashing pilot* **debonair,** devil-may-care, raffish, sporty, spirited, lively, dazzling, energetic, animated, exuberant, flamboyant, dynamic, bold, intrepid, daring, adventurous, plucky, swashbuckling; romantic, attractive, gallant.
2 *he looked exceptionally dashing* **stylish,** smart, elegant, chic, dapper, spruce, trim, debonair; fashionable, modish, voguish; informal trendy, with it, hip, sharp, snazzy, classy, natty, swish, fly, spiffy.

dastardly ▶ adjective dated *their dastardly plan to kidnap Hayes* **wicked,** evil, heinous, villainous, diabolical, fiendish, barbarous, cruel, black, dark, rotten, vile, monstrous, abominable, despicable, degenerate, sordid; bad, base, mean, low, dishonorable, dishonest, unscrupulous, unprincipled; informal lowdown, dirty, shady, rascally, crooked; beastly.
ANTONYMS noble.

> USAGE
>
> **dastard, dastardly**
>
> *Dastard* (= coward) is commonly muddled because of the sound association with its harsher rhyme, *bastard*. Although English usage authority H. W. Fowler insisted that *dastard* should be reserved for "one who avoids all personal risk," modern American writers tend to use it as a printable euphemism for the more widely objectionable epithet—e.g.: "Samuel Ramey is the dastard of the piece, the treacherous, lecherous, murderous Assur." (*Los Angeles Times*; May 22, 1994.) British writers, on the other hand, have remained truer to the word's original sense—e.g.: "Last week I moved house from London to Brighton but like a genuine spineless dastard I flatly denied its implications on personal relationships to the last." (*Times* [London]; Feb. 8, 1994.) Recent American dictionaries record one meaning of *dastard* as being "dishonorable, despicable" or "treacherously underhanded." So the new meaning should probably now be considered standard.
>
> Like the noun form, the adjective *dastardly* has been subjected to slipshod extension. Although most dictionaries define it merely as "cowardly," it is now often used as if it meant "sneaky and underhanded; treacherous"—e.g.: "He's b-a-a-a-c-k. Dastardly J. R. Ewing and his oft-manipulated clan rise from TV dustdom to air three times a day on TNN, Cable Channel 37, beginning Monday." (*Tulsa World*; Sept. 27, 1996.) — **BG**

data ▶ plural noun (often as singular) *a lack of data on the drug's side effects* **facts,** figures, statistics, details, particulars, specifics; information, intelligence, material, input; informal info.

USAGE

data

Whether you write "data are" or "data is," you're likely to make some readers raise their eyebrows. Technically a plural, *data* has, since the 1940s, been increasingly treated as a mass noun taking a singular verb. But in more or less formal contexts it is preferably treated as a plural—e.g.: "The data are derived from tests performed on expectant mothers." (*Economist*; Mar. 24, 2001.) Many writers use it as a singular, however, risking their credibility with some readers (admittedly a shrinking minority)—e.g.: "No data is offered to suggest that women are being adversely hit by the dearth of articles." (*Globe and Mail* [Canada]; Aug. 24, 1993.)

In the context of computing and related disciplines, the singular use of *data* is common and comfortable—e.g.: "Every time you synchronize your PDA, the data gets backed up to your PC." (PCWorld.com; Feb. 8, 2001.) In one particular use, *data* is rarely treated as a singular: when it begins a clause and is not preceded by the definite article—e.g.: "Data over the last two years suggest that the rate at which gay men get AIDS has finally begun to flatten out." (*New York Times*; Feb. 5, 1989.)

Datum, the "true" singular, is sometimes used when a single piece of information is referred to—e.g.: "We accept the law as a necessary datum, but that is not to say that we are required to accept it in abeyance of our critical faculties." (F. R. Leavis, *The Common Pursuit*; 1952.) Still, in nonscientific contexts, *datum* is likely to sound pretentious.

Because *data* can be either a plural count noun or a singular mass noun, both *many data* and *much data* are correct—e.g.:

- "Numerous expert and representative interests are consulted, and many data assembled, often over a long period." (Carleton K. Allen, *Law in the Making*, 7th ed.; 1964.)
- "But much of the data in present personnel files is highly subjective." (William O. Douglas, *Points of Rebellion*; 1970.) As Albert C. Baugh, a historian of the English language, put it in 1962, "A student with one year of Latin [knows] that *data* and *phenomena* are plural." Whatever you do, if you use *data* in a context in which its number becomes known, you'll bother some of your readers. Perhaps 50 years from now—maybe sooner, maybe later—everybody will accept it as a collective. But not yet. — **BG**

date ▶ **noun 1** *the only date he has to remember* **day,** day of the month, occasion, time; year; anniversary.
2 *a later date is suggested for this artifact* **age,** time, period, era, epoch, century, decade, year.
3 *a lunch date* **appointment,** meeting, engagement, rendezvous, assignation; commitment.
4 informal *he's my date for tonight* **partner,** escort, girlfriend, boyfriend, steady.
▶ **verb 1** *the sculpture can be dated accurately* **assign a date to,** ascertain the date of, put a date on.
2 *the building* ***dates from*** *the sixteenth century* **was made in,** was built in, originates in, comes from, belongs to, goes back to.
3 *the best films don't date* **become old-fashioned,** become outmoded, become dated, show its age.
4 informal *he's dating Jill* **go out with,** take out, go around with, be involved with, see, go steady with; dated woo, court.
– PHRASES **to date** *this is all the information we have to date* **so far,** thus far, yet, as yet, up to now, till now, until now, up to the present (time), hitherto.

dated ▶ **adjective** *the graphics look somewhat dated* **old-fashioned,** outdated, outmoded, passé, behind the times, archaic, obsolete, antiquated; unfashionable, unstylish, untrendy; crusty, old world, prehistoric, antediluvian; informal old hat, out, uncool.
ANTONYMS modern.

daub ▶ **verb** *he daubed a rock with paint* **smear,** bedaub, plaster, splash, spatter, splatter, cake, cover, smother, coat.
▶ **noun** *daubs of paint* **smear,** smudge, splash, blot, spot, patch, blotch, splotch.

daunt ▶ **verb** *wintry conditions did not daunt the runners* **discourage,** deter, demoralize, put off, dishearten, dispirit; intimidate, abash, take aback, throw, cow, overawe, awe, frighten, scare, unman, dismay, disconcert, discompose, perturb, unsettle, unnerve; throw off balance; informal rattle, faze, shake up.
ANTONYMS hearten.

dawdle ▶ **verb 1** *they dawdled over breakfast* **linger,** dally, take one's time, be slow, waste time, idle; delay, procrastinate, stall, dilly-dally, lollygag; archaic tarry. See note at LOITER.
ANTONYMS hurry.
2 *Ruth dawdled home* **amble,** stroll, trail, walk slowly, move at a snail's pace; informal mosey, toodle.
ANTONYMS hurry, speed.

dawn ▶ **noun 1** *we got up at dawn* **daybreak,** sunrise, first light, daylight; first thing in the morning, sun-up.
ANTONYMS dusk.
2 *the dawn of civilization* **beginning,** start, birth, inception, origination, genesis, emergence, advent, appearance, arrival, dawning, rise, origin, onset; unfolding, development, infancy; informal kickoff.
ANTONYMS end.
▶ **verb 1** *Thursday dawned crisp and sunny* **begin,** break, arrive, emerge.
ANTONYMS end.
2 *a bright new future has dawned* **begin,** start, commence, be born, appear, arrive, emerge; arise, rise, break, unfold, develop.
ANTONYMS end.
3 *the reality dawned on him* **occur to,** come to, strike, hit, enter someone's mind, register with,

enter someone's consciousness, cross someone's mind, suggest itself.

day ▶ **noun 1** *I stayed for a day* **a twenty-four-hour period,** twenty-four hours.
2 *enjoy the beach during the day* **daytime,** daylight; waking hours.
ANTONYMS night.
3 *the leading architect of the day* **period,** time, age, era, generation.
4 *in his day he had great influence* **heyday,** prime, time; peak, height, zenith, ascendancy; youth, springtime, salad days.
ANTONYMS decline.
– PHRASES **day after day** *day after day, we learn of new allegations* **repeatedly,** again and again, over and over (again), time and (time) again, frequently, often, time after time; 'day in, day out', night and day, all the time; persistently, recurrently, constantly, continuously, continually, relentlessly, regularly, habitually, unfailingly, always, oftentimes; informal 24-7; literary oft, ofttimes. **day by day 1** *day by day they were forced to retreat* **gradually,** slowly, progressively; bit by bit, inch by inch, little by little. **2** *they follow the news day by day* **daily,** every day, day after day; diurnally.

daybreak ▶ **noun** *we'll be packed and ready to go by daybreak* **dawn,** crack of dawn, sunrise, first light; daylight, sunup.
ANTONYMS nightfall.

daydream ▶ **noun 1** *she was lost in a daydream* (a) **reverie,** a trance, (a) fantasy, a vision, fancy, (a) brown study; inattentiveness, woolgathering, preoccupation, absorption, self-absorption, absentmindedness, abstraction.
2 *winning the lottery is just a daydream* **a dream,** a pipe dream, a fantasy, a castle in the air, a fond hope; wishful thinking; informal pie in the sky.
▶ **verb** *stop daydreaming!* **dream,** muse, stare into space; fantasize, build castles in the air.

daylight ▶ **noun 1** *do the test in daylight* **natural light,** sunlight.
ANTONYMS darkness.
2 *she went there only in daylight* **daytime,** day; broad daylight.
ANTONYMS nighttime.
3 *police moved in at daylight* **dawn,** daybreak, (the) break of day, (the) crack of dawn, sunrise, first light, early morning, sunup.
ANTONYMS nightfall.

daze ▶ **verb 1** *he was dazed by his fall* **stun,** stupefy; knock unconscious, knock out; informal knock the stuffing out of.
2 *she was dazed by the revelations* **astound,** amaze, astonish, startle, dumbfound, stupefy, overwhelm, stagger, shock, confound, bewilder, bedazzle, take aback, shake up; informal flabbergast, bowl over, blow away.
▶ **noun** *she is in a daze* **stupor,** trance, haze; spin, whirl, muddle, jumble.

dazzle ▶ **verb 1** *she was dazzled by the headlights* **blind temporarily,** deprive of sight.
2 *I was dazzled by the exhibition* **overwhelm,** overcome, impress, move, stir, affect, touch, awe, overawe, leave speechless, take someone's breath away; spellbind, hypnotize; informal bowl over, blow away, knock out.
▶ **noun 1** *dazzle can be a problem to sensitive eyes* **glare,** brightness, brilliance, shimmer, radiance, shine.
2 *the dazzle of the limelight* **sparkle,** glitter, brilliance, glory, splendor, magnificence, glamour; attraction, lure, allure, draw, appeal; informal razzle-dazzle, razzmatazz.

dead ▶ **adjective 1** *my parents are dead* **passed on/away,** expired, departed, gone, no more; late, lost, lamented; perished, fallen, slain, slaughtered, killed, murdered; lifeless, extinct; informal (as) dead as a doornail, six feet under, pushing up daisies; formal deceased; euphemistic with God, asleep.
ANTONYMS alive, living.
2 *patches of dead ground* **barren,** lifeless, bare, desolate, sterile.
ANTONYMS fertile, lush.
3 *a dead language* **obsolete,** extinct, defunct, disused, abandoned, discarded, superseded, vanished, forgotten; archaic, antiquated, ancient; literary of yore.
ANTONYMS modern, current.
4 *the phone was dead* **not working,** out of order, inoperative, inactive, in disrepair, broken, malfunctioning, defective; informal kaput, conked out, on the blink, on the fritz, bust, busted.
ANTONYMS in working order.
5 *a dead leg* **numb,** numbed, deadened, desensitized, unfeeling; paralyzed, crippled, incapacitated, immobilized, frozen.
6 *she has dead eyes* **emotionless,** unemotional, unfeeling, impassive, unresponsive, indifferent, dispassionate, inexpressive, wooden, stony, cold; deadpan, flat; blank, vacant.
ANTONYMS passionate.
7 *his affection for her was dead* **extinguished,** quashed, stifled; finished, over, gone, no more; a thing of the past, ancient history.
8 *a dead town* **uneventful,** uninteresting, unexciting, uninspiring, dull, boring, flat, quiet, sleepy, slow, lackluster, lifeless; informal one-horse, dullsville.
ANTONYMS lively.
9 *dead silence* **complete,** absolute, total, utter, out-and-out, thorough, unmitigated.
ANTONYMS partial.
10 *a dead shot* **unerring,** unfailing, impeccable, sure, true, accurate, precise; deadly, lethal, bang on.
ANTONYMS poor.
▶ **adverb 1** *he was dead serious* **completely,** absolutely, totally, utterly, deadly, perfectly, entirely, quite, thoroughly; definitely, certainly, positively, categorically, unquestionably, undoubtedly, surely; in every way, one hundred percent.
2 *flares were seen dead ahead* **directly,** exactly, precisely, immediately, right, straight, due, squarely; informal smack dab.
3 informal *it's dead easy* See VERY.

deaden ▶ **verb 1** *surgeons tried to deaden the pain* **numb,** dull, blunt, suppress; alleviate, mitigate, diminish, reduce, lessen, ease, soothe, relieve, assuage, kill.
ANTONYMS intensify.
2 *the wood paneling deadened any noise* **muffle,** mute, smother, stifle, dull, dampen; silence,

quieten, soften; cushion, buffer, absorb.
ANTONYMS amplify.
3 *laughing might deaden us to the moral issue* **desensitize,** numb, anesthetize; harden (one's heart), toughen, inure.
ANTONYMS sensitize.

deadlock ▶ **noun** *the negotiations reached a deadlock* **stalemate,** impasse, standoff, logjam; standstill, halt, stop, full stop, dead end.

deadly ▶ **adjective 1** *these drugs can be deadly* **fatal,** lethal, mortal, death-dealing, life-threatening; dangerous, injurious, harmful, detrimental, deleterious, unhealthy; noxious, toxic, poisonous; literary deathly.
ANTONYMS harmless, beneficial.
2 *deadly enemies* **mortal,** irreconcilable, implacable, unappeasable, unforgiving, remorseless, merciless, pitiless; bitter, hostile, antagonistic.
3 *I noticed their deadly seriousness* **intense,** great, marked, extreme.
ANTONYMS mild.
4 *he was deadly pale* **deathly,** ghostly, ashen, white, pallid, wan, pale; ghastly.
5 *his aim is deadly* **unerring,** unfailing, impeccable, perfect, flawless, faultless; sure, true, precise, accurate, exact, bang on.
ANTONYMS inaccurate, poor.
6 informal *life here can be deadly* See **BORING**.
▶ **adverb** *deadly calm* **completely,** absolutely, totally, utterly, perfectly, entirely, wholly, quite, dead, thoroughly; in every way, one hundred percent, to the hilt.

deaf ▶ **adjective 1** *she is deaf and blind* **hearing impaired,** hard of hearing; informal deaf as a post.
2 *she was* ***deaf to*** *their pleading* **unmoved by,** untouched by, unaffected by, indifferent to, unresponsive to, unconcerned by; unaware of, oblivious to, incognizant of, impervious to.

deafen ▶ **verb** *they were deafened by the explosion* **make deaf,** deprive of hearing, impair someone's hearing.

deafening ▶ **adjective** *the deafening noise from the construction site* **very loud,** very noisy, overloud, ear-splitting, overwhelming, almighty, mighty, tremendous; booming, thunderous, roaring, resounding, resonant, reverberating.
ANTONYMS quiet.

deal ▶ **noun** *completion of the deal* **agreement,** understanding, pact, bargain, covenant, contract, treaty; arrangement, compromise, settlement; terms; transaction, sale, account; Law indenture.
▶ **verb 1** *how to* ***deal with*** *difficult children* **cope with,** handle, manage, treat, take care of, take charge of, take in hand, sort out, tackle, take on; control; act toward, behave toward.
2 *the article* ***deals with*** *advances in chemistry* **concern,** be about, have to do with, discuss, consider, cover, pertain to; tackle, study, explore, investigate, examine, review, analyze.
3 *the company* ***deals in*** *high-tech goods* **trade in,** buy and sell; sell, purvey, supply, stock, market, merchandise; traffic, smuggle; informal push, flog.
4 *the cards were dealt* **distribute,** give out, share out, divide out, hand out, pass out, pass around, dole out, dispense, allocate; informal divvy up.
5 *the court dealt a blow to government reforms* **deliver,** administer, dispense, inflict, give, impose; aim.
– PHRASES **a great deal/a good deal** *under a great deal of pressure | there's a good deal of unfinished work here* **a lot,** a large amount, a fair amount, much, plenty; informal lots, loads, heaps, bags, masses, tons, stacks.

dealer ▶ **noun 1** *an antique dealer* **trader,** merchant, salesman, saleswoman, seller, vendor, purveyor, peddler, hawker; buyer, merchandiser, distributor, supplier, shopkeeper, retailer, wholesaler.
2 *a drug dealer* **trafficker,** supplier.

dealing ▶ **noun 1** *dishonest dealing* **business methods,** business practices, business, commerce, trading, transactions; behavior, conduct, actions.
2 (**dealings**) *Canada's dealings with China* **relations,** relationship, association, connections, contact, intercourse; negotiations, bargaining, transactions; trade, trading, business, commerce, traffic; informal truck, doings.

dean ▶ **noun 1** *students must have the consent of the dean* **faculty head,** department head, college head, provost, university official; chief, director, principal, president, chancellor, governor.
2 *the dean of Russian literature* **doyen/doyenne,** elder statesman, grande dame, grand old man, veteran.

dear ▶ **adjective 1** *a dear friend* **beloved,** loved, adored, cherished, precious; esteemed, respected, worshiped; close, intimate, bosom, best.
ANTONYMS hated.
2 *her pictures were too dear to part with* **precious,** treasured, valued, prized, cherished, special.
3 *such a dear man* **endearing,** adorable, lovable, appealing, engaging, charming, captivating, winsome, lovely, nice, pleasant, delightful, sweet, darling.
ANTONYMS disagreeable.
4 *the meals are rather dear* **expensive,** costly, high-priced, overpriced, exorbitant, extortionate; informal pricey, steep, stiff.
ANTONYMS inexpensive, cheap.
▶ **noun 1** *don't worry, my dear* **darling,** dearest, love, beloved, sweetheart, sweet, precious, treasure; informal sweetie, sugar, honey, hon, baby, pet.
2 *he's such a dear* **lovable person**; darling, sweetheart, pet, angel, gem, treasure, star.

dearly ▶ **adverb 1** *I love my son dearly* **very much,** a great deal, greatly, deeply, profoundly, extremely; fondly, devotedly, tenderly.
2 *our freedom has been bought dearly* **at great cost,** at a high price, with much suffering, with much sacrifice.

dearth ▶ **noun** *a dearth of trained specialists* **lack,** scarcity, shortage, shortfall, want, deficiency, insufficiency, inadequacy, paucity, sparseness, scantiness, rareness; absence. See note at **LACK**.
ANTONYMS surfeit.

death ▶ **noun 1** *her father's death* **demise,** dying,

end, passing, loss of life; eternal rest, quietus; murder, assassination, execution, slaughter, massacre; informal curtains; formal decease; archaic expiry.
ANTONYMS life.
2 *the death of their dream* **end,** finish, termination, extinction, extinguishing, collapse, destruction, eradication, obliteration.
ANTONYMS birth.
3 *Death gestured toward a grave* **the Grim Reaper,** the Dark Angel, the Angel of Death.
– PHRASES **put to death** *the czar and his family were put to death* **execute,** hang, behead, guillotine, decapitate, electrocute, shoot, gas, crucify, stone; kill, murder, assassinate, eliminate, terminate, exterminate, destroy; informal bump off, polish off, do away with, do in, knock off, string up, take out, croak, stiff, blow away, ice, rub out, waste, whack, smoke; literary slay.

deathless ▶ adjective *our deathless souls* **immortal,** undying, imperishable, indestructible; enduring, everlasting, eternal; timeless, ageless.
ANTONYMS mortal, ephemeral.

debacle ▶ noun *the Watergate break-in became a debacle of the highest order* **fiasco,** failure, catastrophe, disaster, mess, ruin; downfall, collapse, defeat; informal foul-up, screw-up, hash, botch, washout, snafu.

debar ▶ verb **1** *women were debarred from the club* **exclude,** ban, bar, disqualify, declare ineligible, preclude, shut out, lock out, keep out, reject, blackball.
ANTONYMS admit.
2 *the unions were debarred from striking* **prevent,** prohibit, proscribe, disallow, ban, interdict, block, stop; Law enjoin, estop.
ANTONYMS allow.

debase ▶ verb **1** *the moral code has been debased* **degrade,** devalue, demean, cheapen, prostitute, discredit, drag down, tarnish, blacken, blemish; disgrace, dishonor, shame; damage, harm, undermine. See notes at **DEPRAVED, HUMBLE.**
ANTONYMS enhance.
2 *the added copper debases the silver* **reduce in value,** reduce in quality, depreciate; contaminate, adulterate, pollute, taint, sully, corrupt; dilute, alloy.

debatable ▶ adjective *the historical accuracy of this account is debatable* **arguable,** disputable, questionable, open to question, controversial, contentious; doubtful, dubious, uncertain, unsure, unclear; borderline, inconclusive, moot, unsettled, unresolved, unconfirmed, undetermined, undecided, up in the air, iffy.

debate ▶ noun *a debate on the reforms* **discussion,** discourse, parley, dialogue; argument, dispute, wrangle, war of words; argumentation, disputation, dissension, disagreement, contention, conflict; negotiations, talks; informal confab, powwow.
▶ verb **1** *they will debate the future of rail transport* **discuss,** talk over/through, talk about, thrash out, hash out, argue, dispute; informal kick around, bat around.
2 *he debated whether to call her* **consider,** think over/about, chew over, mull over, ponder, revolve, deliberate, contemplate, muse, meditate; formal cogitate.

debauched ▶ adjective *a fleet commanded by debauched young men* **dissolute,** dissipated, degenerate, corrupt, depraved, sinful, unprincipled, immoral; lascivious, lecherous, lewd, lustful, libidinous, licentious, promiscuous, loose, wanton, abandoned; decadent, profligate, intemperate, sybaritic.
ANTONYMS wholesome.

debauchery ▶ noun *a life of self-absorption and debauchery* **dissipation,** degeneracy, corruption, vice, depravity; immodesty, indecency, perversion, iniquity, wickedness, sinfulness, impropriety, immorality; lasciviousness, salaciousness, lechery, lewdness, lust, promiscuity, wantonness, profligacy; decadence, intemperance, sybaritism; formal turpitude.

debilitate ▶ verb *can't you see how these drugs have debilitated you?* **weaken,** enfeeble, enervate, devitalize, sap, drain, exhaust, weary, fatigue, prostrate; undermine, impair, indispose, incapacitate, cripple, disable, paralyze, immobilize; informal knock out, do in. See note at **WEAK.**
ANTONYMS invigorate.

debility ▶ noun *Sam's obvious debility came as a shock to us* **frailty,** weakness, enfeeblement, enervation, devitalization, lassitude, exhaustion, weariness, fatigue, prostration; incapacity, indisposition, infirmity, illness, sickness, sickliness; Medicine asthenia.

debonair ▶ adjective *as debonair as Cary Grant* **suave,** urbane, sophisticated, cultured, self-possessed, self-assured, confident, charming, gracious, courteous, gallant, chivalrous, gentlemanly, refined, polished, well-bred, genteel, dignified, courtly; well-groomed, elegant, stylish, smart, dashing; informal smooth, sharp, cool, slick, fly.
ANTONYMS unsophisticated.

debris ▶ noun *the irrigation channels were blocked with debris* **detritus,** refuse, rubbish, waste, litter, scrap, dross, chaff, flotsam and jetsam; rubble, wreckage; remains, scraps, dregs, trash, garbage, dreck, junk.

debt ▶ noun **1** *he couldn't pay his debts* **bill,** account, dues, arrears, charges; financial obligation, outstanding payment; check, tab.
2 *his debt to the author* **indebtedness,** obligation; gratitude, appreciation, thanks.
– PHRASES **in debt** *the medical bills left them hopelessly in debt* **owing money,** in arrears, behind with payments, overdrawn; insolvent, bankrupt, ruined; informal in the red. **in someone's debt** *Chris would be forever in his debt* **indebted to,** beholden to, obliged to, duty-bound to, honor-bound to, obligated to; grateful (to), thankful (to), appreciative (of).

debunk ▶ verb *even the most successful hoax will eventually be debunked* **explode,** deflate, quash, discredit, disprove, contradict, controvert, invalidate, negate; challenge, call into question, poke holes in; formal confute.
ANTONYMS confirm.

debut ▶ noun *her acting debut was in a*

forgettable play in Pittsburgh **first appearance,** first performance, launch, coming out, entrance, premiere, introduction, inception, inauguration; informal kickoff.

decadence ▶ noun **1** *the decadence of modern society* **dissipation,** degeneracy, debauchery, corruption, depravity, vice, sin, moral decay, immorality; immoderateness, intemperance, licentiousness, self-indulgence, hedonism.
ANTONYMS morality.
2 *the decadence of nations* **deterioration,** fall, decay, degeneration, decline, degradation, retrogression.
ANTONYMS rise.

decadent ▶ adjective **1** *decadent city life* **dissolute,** dissipated, degenerate, corrupt, depraved, sinful, unprincipled, immoral; licentious, abandoned, profligate, intemperate; sybaritic, hedonistic, pleasure-seeking, self-indulgent.
2 *the decadent empire* **declining,** decaying, ebbing, degenerating, deteriorating.

decamp ▶ verb **1** *he decamped with the profits* **abscond,** make off, run off/away, flee, bolt, take flight, disappear, vanish, steal away, sneak away, escape, make a run for it, leave, depart; informal split, scram, vamoose, cut and run, do a disappearing act, head for the hills, go AWOL, take a powder, go on the lam.
2 archaic *the armies decamped* **strike one's tents,** break camp, move on.

decant ▶ verb *the wine was decanted into a flask* **pour off,** draw off, siphon off, drain, tap; transfer.

decapitate ▶ verb *traitors were publicly decapitated* **behead,** guillotine, put on the block.

decay ▶ verb **1** *the corpses had decayed* **decompose,** rot, putrefy, go bad, go off, spoil, fester, perish, deteriorate; degrade, break down, molder, shrivel, wither.
2 *the cities continue to decay* **deteriorate,** degenerate, decline, go downhill, slump, slide, go to rack and ruin, go to seed; disintegrate, fall to pieces, fall into disrepair; fail, collapse; informal go to pot, go to the dogs, go into/down the toilet.
▶ noun **1** *signs of decay* **decomposition,** putrefaction, festering; rot, mold, mildew, fungus.
2 *tooth decay* **rot,** corrosion, decomposition; caries, cavities, holes.
3 *the decay of American values* **deterioration,** degeneration, debasement, degradation, decline, weakening, atrophy; crumbling, disintegration, collapse.

decease ▶ noun formal *her decease was imminent* **death,** dying, demise, end, passing, loss of life, quietus; informal curtains, croaking, snuffing; archaic expiry.

deceased ▶ adjective formal *his deceased relatives* **dead,** expired, departed, gone, no more, passed on/away; late, lost, lamented; perished, fallen, slain, slaughtered, killed, murdered; lifeless, extinct; informal (as) dead as a doornail, six feet under, pushing up daisies; euphemistic with God, asleep.

deceit ▶ noun **1** *her endless deceit* **deception,** deceitfulness, duplicity, double-dealing, fraud, cheating, trickery, chicanery, deviousness, slyness, wiliness, guile, bluff, lying, pretense, treachery; informal crookedness, monkey business, monkeyshines.
ANTONYMS honesty.
2 *their life is a deceit* **sham,** fraud, pretense, hoax, fake, blind, artifice; trick, stratagem, device, ruse, scheme, dodge, machination, deception, subterfuge; cheat, swindle; informal con, setup, scam, flimflam, bunco. See note at **FICTION**.

deceitful ▶ adjective **1** *a deceitful woman* **dishonest,** untruthful, mendacious, insincere, false, disingenuous, untrustworthy, unscrupulous, unprincipled, two-faced, duplicitous, double-dealing, underhanded, crafty, cunning, sly, scheming, calculating, treacherous, Machiavellian, sneaky, tricky, foxy, crooked.
2 *a deceitful allegation* **fraudulent,** counterfeit, fabricated, invented, concocted, made up, trumped up, untrue, false, bogus, fake, spurious, fallacious, deceptive, misleading; euphemistic economical with the truth.

deceive ▶ verb **1** *she was deceived by a con man* **swindle,** defraud, cheat, trick, hoodwink, hoax, dupe, take in, mislead, delude, fool, outwit, lead on, inveigle, beguile, double-cross, gull; informal con, bamboozle, do, gyp, diddle, rip off, shaft, pull a fast one on, take for a ride, pull the wool over someone's eyes, sucker, snooker, stiff.
2 *he deceived her with another woman* **be unfaithful to,** cheat on, betray, play someone false; informal two-time.

decelerate ▶ verb *decelerate when approaching the curve* **slow down,** slow up, ease up, slack up, reduce speed, brake.

decency ▶ noun **1** *standards of taste and decency* **propriety,** decorum, good taste, respectability, dignity, correctness, good form, etiquette; morality, virtue, modesty, delicacy.
2 *he didn't have the decency to tell me* **courtesy,** politeness, good manners, civility, respect; consideration, thoughtfulness, tact, diplomacy.

decent ▶ adjective **1** *a decent burial* **proper,** correct, appropriate, apt, fitting, suitable; respectable, dignified, decorous, seemly; nice, tasteful; conventional, accepted, standard, traditional, orthodox; comme il faut.
2 *a very decent fellow* **honorable,** honest, trustworthy, dependable; respectable, upright, clean-living, virtuous, good; obliging, helpful, accommodating, unselfish, generous, kind, thoughtful, considerate; neighborly, hospitable, pleasant, agreeable, amiable.
ANTONYMS dishonest, disobliging.
3 *a job with decent pay* **satisfactory,** reasonable, fair, acceptable, adequate, sufficient, ample; not bad, all right, tolerable, passable, suitable; informal OK, okay, up to snuff.
ANTONYMS unsatisfactory.

deception ▶ noun **1** *they obtained money by deception* **deceit,** deceitfulness, duplicity, double-dealing, fraud, cheating, trickery, chicanery, deviousness, slyness, wiliness, guile, bluff, lying, pretense, treachery; informal

crookedness, monkey business, monkeyshines.
2 *it was all a deception* **trick,** deceit, sham, fraud, pretense, hoax, fake, blind, artifice; stratagem, device, ruse, scheme, dodge, machination, subterfuge; cheat, swindle; informal con, setup, scam, flimflam, bunco.

deceptive ▶ **adjective 1** *distances are very deceptive* **misleading,** illusory, illusionary, specious; ambiguous; distorted; literary illusive.
2 *deceptive practices* **deceitful,** duplicitous, fraudulent, counterfeit, underhanded, cunning, crafty, sly, guileful, scheming, treacherous, Machiavellian; disingenuous, untrustworthy, unscrupulous, unprincipled, dishonest, insincere, false; informal crooked, sharp, shady, sneaky, tricky, foxy.

> USAGE
> **deceptively**
> *Deceptively* belongs to a very small set of words whose meaning is genuinely ambiguous in that it can be used in similar contexts to mean both one thing and also its complete opposite. A *deceptively smooth surface* is one that appears smooth but in fact is not smooth at all, while a *deceptively spacious room* is one that does not look spacious but is in fact *more* spacious than it appears. But what is a *deceptively steep gradient*? Or a person who is described as *deceptively strong*? To avoid confusion, use with caution (or not at all) unless the context makes clear in what way the thing modified is not what it first appears to be.

decide ▶ **verb 1** *she decided to become a writer* **resolve,** determine, make up one's mind, make a decision; elect, choose, opt, plan, aim, have the intention, have in mind.
2 *research to decide a variety of questions* **settle,** resolve, determine, work out, answer; informal sort out, figure out.
3 *the court is to decide the case* **adjudicate,** arbitrate, adjudge, judge; hear, try, examine; sit in judgment on, pronounce on, give a verdict on, rule on.

decided ▶ **adjective 1** *they have a decided advantage* **distinct,** clear, marked, pronounced, obvious, striking, noticeable, unmistakable, patent, manifest; definite, certain, positive, emphatic, undeniable, indisputable, unquestionable; assured, guaranteed.
2 *he was very decided* **determined,** resolute, firm, strong-minded, strong-willed, emphatic, dead set, unwavering, unyielding, unbending, inflexible, unshakable, unrelenting, obstinate, stubborn, rock-ribbed.
3 *our future is decided* **settled,** established, resolved, determined, agreed, designated, chosen, ordained, prescribed; set, fixed; informal sewn up, wrapped up.

decidedly ▶ **adverb** *they were decidedly hostile to one another* **distinctly,** clearly, markedly, obviously, noticeably, unmistakably, patently, manifestly; definitely, certainly, positively, absolutely, downright, undeniably, unquestionably; extremely, exceedingly, exceptionally, particularly, especially, very; informal terrifically, devilishly, ultra, mega, majorly, ever so, dead, real, mighty, awful.

deciding ▶ **adjective** *the deciding factor may be the size of your budget* **determining,** decisive, conclusive, key, pivotal, crucial, critical, significant, major, chief, principal, prime. See note at CRUCIAL.

decipher ▶ **verb 1** *he deciphered the code* **decode,** decrypt, break, work out, solve, interpret, unscramble, translate; make sense of, get to the bottom of, unravel; informal crack, figure out.
ANTONYMS encode.
2 *the writing was hard to decipher* **make out,** discern, perceive, read, follow, fathom, make sense of, interpret, understand, comprehend, grasp.

decision ▶ **noun 1** *they came to a decision* **resolution,** conclusion, settlement, commitment, resolve, determination; choice, option, selection.
2 *the judge's decision* **verdict,** finding, ruling, recommendation, judgment, judgment call, pronouncement, adjudication, order, rule, resolve; findings, results; Law determination.
3 *his order had a ring of decision* **decisiveness,** determination, resolution, resolve, firmness; strong-mindedness, purpose, purposefulness.

decisive ▶ **adjective 1** *a decisive man* **resolute,** firm, strong-minded, strong-willed, determined; purposeful, forceful, dead set, unwavering, unyielding, unbending, inflexible, unshakable, obstinate, stubborn, rock-ribbed. See note at RESOLUTE.
2 *the decisive factor* **deciding,** conclusive, determining; key, pivotal, critical, crucial, significant, influential, major, chief, principal, prime.

deck ▶ **verb 1** *the street was decked with streamers* **decorate,** bedeck, adorn, ornament, trim, trick out, garnish, cover, hang, festoon, garland, swathe, wreathe; embellish, beautify, prettify, enhance, grace, set off; informal get up, do up, tart up; literary bejewel, bedizen, caparison.
2 *Ingrid was* ***decked out*** *in blue* **dress (up),** clothe, attire, garb, robe, drape, turn out, fit out, outfit, costume; informal doll up, get up, do up, gussy up, pimp.
3 *he got up from the table and decked me* See HIT (sense 1 of the verb).
▶ **noun** *they were lounging on the deck* **terrace,** balcony, veranda, porch, patio.

declaim ▶ **verb 1** *a preacher declaiming from the pulpit* **make a speech,** give an address, give a lecture, deliver a sermon; speak, hold forth, orate, preach, lecture, sermonize, moralize; informal sound off, spout, speechify, preachify.
2 *they loved to hear Garfield declaim his poetry* **recite,** read aloud, read out loud, read out; deliver; informal spout.
3 *he* ***declaimed against*** *the evils of society* **speak out against,** rail against, inveigh against, fulminate against, rage against, thunder against; rant about, expostulate against; condemn, criticize, attack, decry, disparage.

declamation ▶ **noun** *he delivered a passionate declamation* **speech,** address, lecture, sermon, homily, discourse, oration, recitation, disquisition, monologue.

declaration ▶ noun 1 *they issued a declaration* **announcement,** statement, communication, pronouncement, proclamation, communiqué, edict, advisory.
2 *the declaration of war* **proclamation,** notification, announcement, revelation, disclosure, broadcasting.
3 *a declaration of faith* **assertion,** profession, affirmation, acknowledgment, revelation, disclosure, manifestation, confirmation, testimony, validation, certification, attestation; pledge, avowal, vow, oath, protestation.

declare ▶ verb 1 *she declared her political principles* **proclaim,** announce, state, reveal, air, voice, articulate, express, vent, set forth, publicize, broadcast; informal come out with, shout from the rooftops. See note at ANNOUNCE.
2 *he declared that they were guilty* **assert,** maintain, state, affirm, contend, argue, insist, hold, profess, claim, avow, swear; formal aver.
3 *his speech* ***declared*** *him* ***to be*** *a gentleman* **show to be,** reveal as, confirm as, prove to be, attest to someone's being.

decline ▶ verb 1 *she declined all invitations* **turn down,** reject, brush aside, refuse, rebuff, spurn, repulse, dismiss; forgo, deny oneself, pass up; abstain from, say no to; informal give the thumbs down to, give something a miss.
ANTONYMS accept.
2 *the number of traders has declined* **decrease,** reduce, lessen, diminish, dwindle, contract, shrink, fall off, tail off; drop, fall, go down, slump, plummet; informal nosedive, take a header, crash.
ANTONYMS increase.
3 *standards steadily declined* **deteriorate,** degenerate, decay, crumble, collapse, slump, slip, slide, go downhill, worsen; weaken, wane, ebb; informal go to pot, go to the dogs, go into/down the toilet.
ANTONYMS rise.
▶ noun 1 *a decline in profits* **reduction,** decrease, downturn, downswing, downtrend, devaluation, depreciation, diminution, ebb, drop, slump, plunge; informal nosedive, crash.
2 *forest decline* **deterioration,** degeneration, degradation, shrinkage; death, decay.
– PHRASES **in decline** *sadly, our volunteer program is in decline* **declining,** decaying, crumbling, collapsing, failing; disappearing, dying, moribund; informal on its last legs, on the way out.

decompose ▶ verb 1 *the carcasses will not decompose in these subzero temperatures* **decay,** rot, putrefy, go bad, go off, spoil, fester, perish, deteriorate; degrade, break down, molder, shrivel, wither.
2 *some minerals decompose rapidly* **break up,** fragment, disintegrate, crumble, dissolve; break down, decay.

decomposition ▶ noun 1 *an advanced state of decomposition* **decay,** putrefaction, putrescence, putridity.
2 *the decomposition of granite* **disintegration,** dissolution; breaking down, decay.

decor ▶ noun *the decor in the family room is just awful* **decoration,** furnishing, ornamentation; color scheme.

decorate ▶ verb 1 *the door was decorated with a wreath* **ornament,** adorn, trim, embellish, garnish, furnish, enhance, grace, prettify; festoon, garland, bedeck.
2 *he started to decorate his home* **paint, wallpaper,** paper; refurbish, furbish, renovate, redecorate; informal do up, spruce up, do over, fix up, give something a facelift.
3 *he was decorated for courage* **give a medal to,** honor, cite, reward.

decoration ▶ noun 1 *a ceiling with rich decoration* **ornamentation,** adornment, trimming, embellishment, garnishing, gilding; beautification, prettification; enhancements, enrichments, frills, accessories, trimmings, finery, frippery.
2 *internal decoration* See DECOR.
3 *a Christmas tree decoration* **ornament,** bauble, trinket, knickknack, spangle; trimming, tinsel.
4 *a decoration won on the battlefield* **medal,** award, star, ribbon; laurel, trophy, prize.

decorative ▶ adjective *mirrors were used as decorative features* **ornamental,** embellishing, garnishing; fancy, ornate, attractive, pretty, showy.
ANTONYMS functional.

decorous ▶ adjective *he behaved toward her in a decorous manner* **proper,** seemly, decent, becoming, befitting, tasteful; correct, appropriate, suitable, fitting; tactful, polite, well-mannered, genteel, respectable; formal, restrained, modest, demure, gentlemanly, ladylike.
ANTONYMS unseemly.

decorum ▶ noun 1 *he had acted with decorum* **propriety,** seemliness, decency, good taste, correctness; politeness, courtesy, good manners; dignity, respectability, modesty, demureness.
ANTONYMS impropriety.
2 *a breach of decorum* **etiquette,** protocol, good form, custom, convention; formalities, niceties, punctilios, politeness.
ANTONYMS impropriety.

decoy ▶ noun *a decoy to distract their attention* **lure,** bait, red herring; enticement, inducement, temptation, attraction, carrot; snare, trap.
▶ verb *he was decoyed to the mainland* **lure,** entice, allure, tempt; entrap, snare, trap.

decrease ▶ verb 1 *pollution levels decreased* **lessen,** reduce, drop, diminish, decline, dwindle, fall off; die down, abate, subside, tail off, ebb, wane; plummet, plunge.
ANTONYMS increase.
2 *decrease the amount of fat in your body* **reduce,** lessen, lower, cut (back/down), curtail; slim down, tone down, deplete, minimize, slash.
ANTONYMS increase.
▶ noun *a decrease in crime* **reduction,** drop, decline, downtrend, downturn, cut, falloff, cutback, diminution, ebb, wane.
ANTONYMS increase.

decree ▶ noun 1 *a presidential decree* **order,** edict, command, commandment, mandate, proclamation, dictum, fiat; law, bylaw, statute, act; formal ordinance.

2 *a court decree* **judgment,** verdict, adjudication, ruling, resolution, decision.
▶ verb *he decreed that a stadium should be built* **order,** command, rule, dictate, pronounce, proclaim, ordain; direct, decide, determine.

decrepit ▶ adjective 1 *a decrepit old man* **feeble,** infirm, weak, weakly, frail; disabled, incapacitated, crippled, doddering, tottering; old, elderly, aged, ancient, senile; informal past it, over the hill, no spring chicken. See note at WEAK.
ANTONYMS strong, fit.
2 *a decrepit house* **dilapidated,** rickety, run-down, tumbledown, beat-up, ramshackle, derelict, ruined, in (a state of) disrepair, gone to rack and ruin; battered, decayed, crumbling, deteriorating.
ANTONYMS sound.

decry ▶ verb *she decried the double standards* **denounce,** condemn, criticize, censure, attack, rail against, run down, pillory, lambaste, vilify, revile; disparage, deprecate, cast aspersions on; informal slam, blast, knock.
ANTONYMS praise.

dedicate ▶ verb 1 *she dedicated her life to the sick* **devote,** commit, pledge, give, surrender, sacrifice; set aside, allocate, consign.
2 *a book dedicated to his muse* **inscribe,** address; assign.
3 *the chapel was dedicated to the Virgin Mary* **devote,** assign; bless, consecrate, sanctify; formal hallow.

dedicated ▶ adjective 1 *a dedicated socialist* **committed,** devoted, staunch, firm, steadfast, resolute, unwavering, loyal, faithful, true, dyed-in-the-wool; wholehearted, enthusiastic, single-minded, keen, earnest, zealous, ardent, passionate, fervent; informal card-carrying, hardcore.
ANTONYMS indifferent.
2 *data is accessed by a dedicated machine* **exclusive,** custom built, customized.

dedication ▶ noun 1 *athletic excellence requires dedication* **commitment,** application, diligence, industry, resolve, enthusiasm, zeal, conscientiousness, perseverance, persistence, tenacity, drive, staying power; hard work, effort.
ANTONYMS apathy, laziness.
2 *her dedication to the job* **devotion,** commitment, loyalty, adherence, allegiance.
ANTONYMS indifference.
3 *the book has a dedication to her husband* **inscription,** address, message.
4 *the dedication of the church* **blessing,** consecration, sanctification, benediction.

deduce ▶ verb *we can deduce from the evidence that Harding was indeed present at the time of the murder* **conclude,** reason, work out, infer; glean, divine, intuit, understand, assume, presume, conjecture, surmise, reckon; informal figure out.

deduct ▶ verb *we'll deduct ten percent from the total* **subtract,** take away, take off, debit, dock, discount; abstract, remove, knock off.
ANTONYMS add.

deduction ▶ noun 1 *the deduction of tax* **subtraction,** removal, debit, abstraction.
2 *gross pay, before deductions* **subtraction.**
3 *she was right in her deduction* **conclusion,** inference, supposition, hypothesis, assumption, presumption; suspicion, conviction, belief, reasoning; archaic illation.

deed ▶ noun 1 *kindly deeds* **act,** action; feat, exploit, achievement, accomplishment, endeavor, undertaking, enterprise.
2 *unity must be established in deed and word* **fact,** reality, actuality.
3 *a deed to the property* **legal document,** contract, indenture, instrument.

deem ▶ verb *many of these campaigns have been deemed successful* **consider,** regard as, judge, adjudge, hold to be, view as, see as, take for, class as, count, find, suppose, reckon; think, believe to be, feel to be; formal esteem.

deep ▶ adjective 1 *a deep ravine* **cavernous,** yawning, gaping, huge, extensive; bottomless, fathomless, unfathomable.
ANTONYMS shallow.
2 *two inches deep* **in depth,** downward, inward, in vertical extent.
3 *deep affection* **intense,** heartfelt, wholehearted, deep-seated, deep-rooted; sincere, genuine, earnest, enthusiastic, great.
ANTONYMS insincere, superficial.
4 *a deep sleep* **sound,** heavy, intense.
5 *a deep thinker* **profound,** serious, philosophical, complex, weighty; abstruse, esoteric, recondite, mysterious, obscure; intelligent, intellectual, learned, wise, scholarly; discerning, penetrating, perceptive, insightful.
6 *he was deep in concentration* **rapt,** absorbed, engrossed, preoccupied, immersed, lost, gripped, intent, engaged.
7 *a deep mystery* **obscure,** mysterious, secret, unfathomable, opaque, abstruse, recondite, esoteric, enigmatic, arcane; puzzling, baffling, mystifying, inexplicable.
8 *his deep voice* **low-pitched,** low, bass, rich, powerful, resonant, booming, sonorous.
ANTONYMS high.
9 *a deep red* **dark,** intense, rich, strong, bold, warm.
ANTONYMS light.
▶ noun 1 literary *creatures of the deep* **sea,** ocean; informal drink, briny; literary profound.
2 *the deep of night* **middle,** midst; depths, dead, thick.
▶ adverb 1 *I dug deep* **far down,** way down, to a great depth.
2 *he brought them deep into woodland* **far,** a long way, a great distance.

deepen ▶ verb 1 *his love for her had deepened* **grow,** increase, intensify, strengthen, heighten, amplify, augment; informal step up.
2 *they deepened the hole* **dig out,** dig deeper, excavate.

deeply ▶ adverb *I am deeply grateful* **profoundly,** greatly, enormously, extremely, very much; strongly, powerfully, intensely, keenly, acutely; thoroughly, completely, entirely; informal well, seriously, majorly.

deface ▶ verb *the kids were caught defacing a school building with spray paint* **vandalize,**

disfigure, mar, spoil, ruin, sully, damage, blight, impair, trash.

de facto ▶ **adverb** *the republic is de facto two states* **in practice,** in effect, in fact, in reality, really, actually.
ANTONYMS de jure.
▶ **adjective** *de facto control* **actual,** real, effective.
ANTONYMS de jure.

defamation ▶ **noun** *he sued the newspaper for defamation* **libel,** slander, calumny, character assassination, vilification; scandalmongering, malicious gossip, aspersions, muckraking, abuse; disparagement, denigration; smear, slur; informal mudslinging.

defamatory ▶ **adjective** *the candidates abused the debate forum by exchanging defamatory remarks* **libelous,** slanderous, calumnious, scandalmongering, malicious, vicious, backbiting, muckraking; abusive, disparaging, denigratory, insulting; informal mudslinging, bitchy, catty.

defame ▶ **verb** *she has defamed my character* **libel,** slander, malign, cast aspersions on, smear, traduce, give someone a bad name, run down, speak ill of, vilify, besmirch, stigmatize, disparage, denigrate, discredit, decry; informal do a hatchet job on, drag through the mud, slur; informal badmouth, dis; formal calumniate. See note at MALIGN.
ANTONYMS compliment.

default ▶ **noun 1** *the incidence of defaults on loans* **nonpayment,** failure to pay, bad debt.
2 *Browne lost the case by default* **inaction,** omission, lapse, neglect, negligence, disregard; failure to appear, absence, nonappearance.
▶ **verb 1** *the customer defaulted* **fail to pay,** not pay, renege, back out; go back on one's word; informal welsh, bilk.
2 *the program will default to its own style* **revert,** select automatically.

defeat ▶ **verb 1** *the army that defeated the rebels* **beat,** conquer, win against, triumph over, get the better of, vanquish; rout, trounce, overcome, overpower, crush, subdue; informal lick, thrash, whip, wipe the floor with, make mincemeat of, clobber, slaughter, demolish, cream, skunk, nose out.
2 *these complex plans defeat their purpose* **thwart,** frustrate, foil, ruin, scotch, debar, derail; obstruct, impede, hinder, hamper; informal put the kibosh on, stymie, scuttle.
3 *the motion was defeated* **reject,** overthrow, throw out, dismiss, outvote, turn down; informal give the thumbs down.
4 *how to make it work defeats me* **baffle,** perplex, bewilder, mystify, bemuse, confuse, confound, throw; informal beat, flummox, faze, stump.
▶ **noun 1** *a crippling defeat* **loss,** conquest, vanquishment; rout, trouncing; downfall; informal thrashing, hiding, drubbing, licking, pasting, massacre, slaughter.
ANTONYMS victory.
2 *the defeat of his plans* **failure,** downfall, collapse, ruin; rejection, frustration, abortion, miscarriage; undoing, reverse.
ANTONYMS success.

defeatist ▶ **adjective** *a defeatist attitude* **pessimistic,** fatalistic, negative, cynical, despondent, despairing, hopeless, bleak, gloomy.
ANTONYMS optimistic.
▶ **noun** **pessimist,** fatalist, cynic, prophet of doom, doomster; misery, killjoy, worrier; informal quitter, wet blanket, worrywart.
ANTONYMS optimist.

defecate ▶ **verb** *nobody wants to see dogs defecating on the beach* **excrete feces,** have a bowel movement, have a BM, evacuate one's bowels, relieve oneself, go to the bathroom; informal do/go number two, poop, take a crap, take a dump.

defect[1] ▶ **noun** *he spotted a defect in my work* **fault,** flaw, imperfection, deficiency, weakness, weak spot, inadequacy, shortcoming, limitation, failing; kink, deformity, blemish; mistake, error; informal glitch; Computing bug.

defect[2] ▶ **verb** *his chief intelligence officer defected* **desert,** change sides, turn traitor, rebel, renege; abscond, quit, jump ship, escape; break faith; secede from, revolt against; Military go AWOL; Politics cross the floor; literary forsake.

defection ▶ **noun** *his defection to the United States* **desertion,** absconding, decamping, flight; apostasy, secession; treason, betrayal, disloyalty; literary perfidy.

defective ▶ **adjective 1** *a defective seat belt* **faulty,** flawed, imperfect, shoddy, inoperative, malfunctioning, out of order, unsound; in disrepair, broken; informal on the blink, on the fritz.
ANTONYMS perfect.
2 *these methods are defective* **lacking,** wanting, deficient, inadequate, insufficient.

defector ▶ **noun** *the defector, identified only as G.K., fled his homeland in 1994* **deserter,** turncoat, traitor, renegade, Judas, quisling; informal rat.

defend ▶ **verb 1** *a fort built to defend the border* **protect,** guard, safeguard, secure, shield; fortify, garrison, barricade; uphold, support, watch over.
ANTONYMS attack.
2 *he defended his policy* **justify,** vindicate, argue for, support, make a case for, plead for; excuse, explain.
ANTONYMS attack, criticize.
3 *the manager defended his players* **support,** back, stand by, stick up for, stand up for, argue for, champion, endorse; informal throw one's weight behind.
ANTONYMS criticize.

defendant ▶ **noun** *does the defendant have counsel?* **accused,** prisoner (at the bar); appellant, litigant, respondent; suspect.
ANTONYMS plaintiff.

defender ▶ **noun 1** *defenders of the environment* **protector,** guard, guardian, preserver; custodian, watchdog, keeper, overseer.
2 *a defender of colonialism* **supporter,** upholder, backer, champion, advocate, apologist, proponent, exponent, promoter; adherent, believer.

defense ▶ **noun 1** *the defense of the fortress* **protection,** guarding, security, fortification;

resistance, deterrent.
2 *the enemy's defenses* **barricade,** fortification; fortress, keep, rampart, bulwark, bastion.
3 *he spoke in defense of his boss* **vindication,** justification, support, advocacy, endorsement; apology, explanation, exoneration.
4 *more spending on defense* **armaments,** weapons, weaponry, arms; the military, the armed forces.
5 *the prisoner's defense* **vindication,** explanation, mitigation, justification, rationalization, excuse, alibi, reason; plea, pleading; testimony, declaration, case.

defenseless ▶ adjective **1** *defenseless animals* **vulnerable,** helpless, powerless, impotent, weak, susceptible.
ANTONYMS resilient.
2 *the country is wholly defenseless* **undefended,** unprotected, unguarded, unshielded, unarmed; vulnerable, assailable, exposed, insecure.
ANTONYMS well-protected.

defensible ▶ adjective **1** *a defensible attitude* **justifiable,** arguable, tenable, defendable, supportable; plausible, sound, sensible, reasonable, rational, logical; acceptable, valid, legitimate; excusable, pardonable, understandable.
ANTONYMS untenable.
2 *a defensible territory* **secure,** safe, fortified; invulnerable, impregnable, impenetrable, unassailable.
ANTONYMS vulnerable.

defensive ▶ adjective **1** *troops in defensive positions* **defending,** protective; wary, watchful.
2 *a defensive response* **self-justifying,** oversensitive, prickly, paranoid, neurotic; informal uptight.

defer[1] ▶ verb *the committee will defer its decision* **postpone,** put off, delay, hold over, hold off (on), put back; shelve, suspend, stay, put over, table; informal put on ice, put on the back burner, back-burner, put in cold storage, mothball. See note at POSTPONE.

defer[2] ▶ verb *they deferred to Joseph's judgment* **yield to,** submit to, give way to, give in to, surrender to, capitulate to, acquiesce to; respect, honor.

deference ▶ noun *his writings show excessive deference to the wealthy* **respect,** respectfulness, dutifulness; submissiveness, submission, obedience, surrender, accession, capitulation, acquiescence, complaisance, obeisance. See note at HONOR.
ANTONYMS disrespect.

deferential ▶ adjective *the hotel's deferential treatment of its elite clientele* **respectful,** humble, obsequious; dutiful, obedient, submissive, subservient, yielding, acquiescent, complaisant, compliant, tractable, biddable, docile.

deferment ▶ noun *they sought a temporary deferment of the loan payments* **postponement,** deferral, suspension, delay, adjournment, interruption, pause; respite, stay, moratorium, reprieve, grace.

defiance ▶ noun *he wasn't used to such outspoken defiance* **resistance,** opposition, noncompliance, disobedience, insubordination, dissent, recalcitrance, subversion, rebellion; contempt, disregard, scorn, insolence, truculence.
ANTONYMS obedience.

defiant ▶ adjective *he is defiant in the face of critics* **intransigent,** resistant, obstinate, uncooperative, noncompliant, recalcitrant; obstreperous, truculent, dissenting, disobedient, insubordinate, subversive, rebellious, mutinous, feisty.
ANTONYMS cooperative.

deficiency ▶ noun **1** *a vitamin deficiency* **insufficiency,** lack, shortage, want, dearth, inadequacy, deficit, shortfall; scarcity, paucity, absence, deprivation, shortness.
ANTONYMS surplus.
2 *the team's big deficiency* **defect,** fault, flaw, imperfection, weakness, weak point, inadequacy, shortcoming, limitation, failing.
ANTONYMS strength.

deficient ▶ adjective **1** *a diet deficient in vitamin A* **lacking,** wanting, inadequate, insufficient, limited, poor, scant; low.
2 *deficient leadership* **defective,** faulty, flawed, inadequate, imperfect, shoddy, weak, inferior, unsound, substandard, second-rate, poor.

deficit ▶ noun *a large deficit in the federal budget* **shortfall,** deficiency, shortage, debt, arrears; negative amount, loss.
ANTONYMS surplus.

defile ▶ verb **1** *her capacity for love had been defiled* **spoil,** sully, mar, impair, debase, degrade; poison, taint, tarnish; destroy, ruin.
ANTONYMS purify.
2 *the sacred bones were defiled* **desecrate,** profane, violate; contaminate, pollute, debase, degrade, dishonor. See note at POLLUTE.
ANTONYMS sanctify.
3 archaic *she was defiled by a married man* **rape,** violate; literary ravish; dated deflower.

definable ▶ adjective *she had no definable illness* **determinable,** ascertainable, known, definite, clear-cut, precise, exact, specific.

define ▶ verb **1** *the dictionary defines it succinctly* **explain,** expound, interpret, elucidate, describe, clarify; give the meaning of, put into words.
2 *he defined the limits of the law* **determine,** establish, fix, specify, designate, decide, stipulate, set out; demarcate, delineate.
3 *the farm buildings defined against the fields* **outline,** delineate, silhouette.

definite ▶ adjective **1** *a definite answer* **explicit,** specific, express, precise, exact, clear-cut, direct, plain, outright; fixed, established, confirmed, concrete.
ANTONYMS vague.
2 *definite evidence* **certain,** sure, positive, conclusive, decisive, firm, concrete, unambiguous, unequivocal, clear, unmistakable, proven; guaranteed, assured, cut and dried.
ANTONYMS uncertain, ambiguous.
3 *she had a definite dislike for dogs* **unmistakable,** certain, unequivocal, unambiguous, undisputed, decided, marked, distinct.
ANTONYMS vague, slight.

4 *a definite geographical area* **fixed,** marked, demarcated, delimited, stipulated, particular.
ANTONYMS indeterminate.

definitely ▶ adverb *it was definitely a case of exploiting child labor* **certainly,** surely, for sure, unquestionably, without doubt, without question, undoubtedly, indubitably, positively, absolutely; undeniably, unmistakably, plainly, clearly, obviously, patently, palpably, transparently, unequivocally.

definition ▶ noun **1** *the definition of "intelligence"* **meaning,** denotation, sense; interpretation, explanation, elucidation, description, clarification, illustration.
2 *the definition of the picture* **clarity,** visibility, sharpness, crispness, acuteness; resolution, focus, contrast.

definitive ▶ adjective **1** *a definitive decision* **conclusive,** final, ultimate; unconditional, unqualified, absolute, categorical, positive, definite.
2 *the definitive guide* **authoritative,** exhaustive, best, finest, consummate; classic, standard, recognized, accepted, official.

deflate ▶ verb **1** *he deflated the tires* **let down,** flatten, void; puncture.
ANTONYMS inflate.
2 *the balloon deflated* **go down,** collapse, shrink, contract.
ANTONYMS inflate, expand.
3 *the news had deflated him* **subdue,** humble, cow, chasten; dispirit, dismay, discourage, dishearten; squash, crush, bring down, take the wind out of someone's sails, knock the stuffing out of.
ANTONYMS aggrandize.
4 *the budget deflated the economy* **reduce,** slow down, diminish; devalue, depreciate, depress.
ANTONYMS inflate.

deflect ▶ verb **1** *she wanted to deflect attention from herself* **turn aside/away,** divert, avert, sidetrack; distract, draw away; block, parry, fend off, stave off.
2 *the ball deflected off the wall* **bounce,** glance, ricochet, carom; diverge, deviate, veer, swerve, slew.

deform ▶ verb *shoes that will not cramp or deform the toes* **disfigure,** bend out of shape, contort, buckle, warp; damage, impair.

deformed ▶ adjective *a deformed skeleton* **misshapen,** distorted, dysmorphic, malformed, contorted, out of shape; twisted, crooked, warped, buckled, gnarled; crippled, humpbacked, hunchbacked, disfigured, grotesque; injured, damaged, mutilated, mangled.

deformity ▶ noun *a brace used to correct spinal deformities* **malformation,** misshapenness, distortion, crookedness; imperfection, abnormality, irregularity; disfigurement; defect, flaw, blemish.

defraud ▶ verb *they defrauded thousands of investors* **swindle,** cheat, rob, embezzle; deceive, dupe, hoodwink, double-cross, trick; informal con, do, sting, diddle, rip off, shaft, bilk, rook, gyp, pull a fast one on, put one over on, sucker, snooker, stiff.

deft ▶ adjective *a deft piece of footwork | his deft handling of the situation* **skillful,** adept, adroit, dexterous, agile, nimble, handy; able, capable, skilled, proficient, accomplished, expert, polished, slick, professional, masterly; clever, shrewd, astute, canny, sharp; informal nifty, neat.
ANTONYMS clumsy.

defunct ▶ adjective *the original contract is defunct* **disused,** unused, inoperative, nonfunctioning, unusable, obsolete; no longer existing, discontinued; extinct.
ANTONYMS working, extant.

defy ▶ verb **1** *he defied local law* **disobey,** go against, flout, fly in the face of, disregard, ignore; break, violate, contravene, breach, infringe.
ANTONYMS obey.
2 *his actions defy belief* **elude,** escape, defeat; frustrate, thwart, baffle.
3 *he glowered, defying her to mock him* **challenge,** dare.

degeneracy ▶ noun *the sexual degeneracy and intellectual deterioration of the time* **corruption,** decadence, moral decay, dissipation, dissolution, profligacy, vice, immorality, sin, sinfulness, ungodliness; debauchery; formal turpitude.

degenerate ▶ adjective **1** *a degenerate form of classicism* **debased,** degraded, corrupt, impure; formal vitiated.
ANTONYMS pure.
2 *her degenerate brother* **corrupt,** decadent, dissolute, dissipated, debauched, reprobate, profligate; sinful, ungodly, immoral, unprincipled, amoral, dishonorable, disreputable, unsavory, sordid, low, ignoble. See note at **DEPRAVED**.
ANTONYMS moral.
▶ noun *a group of degenerates* **reprobate,** debauchee, profligate, libertine, roué.
▶ verb **1** *their quality of life had degenerated* **deteriorate,** decline, slip, slide, worsen, lapse, slump, go downhill, regress, retrogress; go to rack and ruin; informal go to pot, go to the dogs, hit the skids, go into/down the toilet.
ANTONYMS improve.
2 *the muscles started to degenerate* **waste (away),** atrophy, weaken.

degradation ▶ noun **1** *poverty brings with it degradation* **humiliation,** shame, loss of self-respect, abasement, indignity, ignominy.
2 *the degradation of women* **demeaning,** debasement, discrediting.
3 *the degradation of the tissues* **deterioration,** degeneration, atrophy, decay; breakdown.

degrade ▶ verb **1** *prisons should not degrade prisoners* **demean,** debase, cheapen, devalue; shame, humiliate, humble, mortify, abase, dishonor; dehumanize, brutalize. See note at **HUMBLE**.
ANTONYMS dignify.
2 *the polymer will not degrade* **break down,** deteriorate, degenerate, decay.

degraded ▶ adjective **1** *I feel so degraded* **humiliated,** demeaned, cheapened, cheap, ashamed.
ANTONYMS proud.
2 *his degraded sensibilities* **degenerate,** corrupt,

depraved, dissolute, dissipated, debauched, immoral, base, sordid.
ANTONYMS pure, moral.

degrading ▶ adjective *accepting our assistance should not be a degrading experience* **humiliating,** demeaning, shameful, mortifying, ignominious, undignified, inglorious, wretched.

degree ▶ noun **1** *to a high degree* **level,** standard, grade, mark; amount, extent, measure; magnitude, intensity, strength; proportion, ratio.
2 *she completed her degree in three years* **diploma,** academic program; baccalaureate, bachelor's, master's, doctorate, Ph.D..
– PHRASES **by degrees** *rivalries and prejudice were by degrees fading out* **gradually,** little by little, bit by bit, inch by inch, step by step, slowly; piecemeal. **to a degree** *without proper instruction, you can operate the machinery only to a degree* **to some extent,** to a certain extent, up to a point, somewhat.

dehydrate ▶ verb **1** *alcohol dehydrates the skin* **dry (out),** desiccate, dehumidify, effloresce. See note at DRY.
ANTONYMS hydrate.
2 *frogs can dehydrate quickly* **dry up/out,** lose water.

deify ▶ verb **1** *she was deified by the early Romans* **worship,** revere, venerate, reverence, hold sacred; immortalize.
2 *he was deified by the press* **idolize,** lionize, extol, hero-worship; idealize, glorify, aggrandize, put on a pedestal.
ANTONYMS demonize.

deign ▶ verb *he'll never deign to return to his father's house* **condescend,** stoop, lower oneself, demean oneself, humble oneself; consent, vouchsafe; informal come down from one's high horse.

deity ▶ noun *everyone cracked up when Coolidge said she worshiped a deity named Grover* **god,** goddess, divine being, supreme being, divinity, immortal; creator, demiurge; godhead.

dejected ▶ adjective *the dejected look on Thomas's face* **downcast,** downhearted, despondent, disconsolate, dispirited, crestfallen, disheartened; depressed, crushed, desolate, heartbroken, in the doldrums, sad, unhappy, doleful, melancholy, miserable, woebegone, forlorn, wretched, glum, gloomy; informal blue, down in/at the mouth, down in the dumps, in a blue funk.
ANTONYMS cheerful.

delay ▶ verb **1** *we were delayed by the traffic* **detain,** hold up, make late, slow up/down, bog down; hinder, hamper, impede, obstruct.
2 *they delayed no longer* **linger,** dally, drag one's feet, be slow, hold back, dawdle, waste time; procrastinate, stall, hang fire, mark time, temporize, hesitate, dither, shilly-shally, dilly-dally; archaic tarry.
ANTONYMS hurry.
3 *he may delay the cut in interest rates* **postpone,** put off, defer, hold over, shelve, suspend, stay; reschedule, put over, push back, table; informal put on ice, back-burner, put on the back burner, put in cold storage. See note at POSTPONE.
ANTONYMS advance.
▶ noun **1** *drivers will face lengthy delays* **holdup,** wait, detainment; hindrance, impediment, obstruction, setback.
2 *the delay of his trial* **postponement,** deferral, deferment, stay, respite; adjournment.
3 *I set off without delay* **procrastination,** stalling, hesitation, dithering, dallying, lollygagging, dawdling.

delectable ▶ adjective **1** *a delectable meal* **delicious,** mouthwatering, appetizing, flavorful, toothsome, palatable; succulent, luscious, tasty; informal scrumptious, delish, yummy, finger-licking, lip-smacking, melt-in-your-mouth.
ANTONYMS unpalatable.
2 *the delectable Ms. Davis* **delightful,** pleasant, lovely, captivating, charming, enchanting, appealing, beguiling; beautiful, attractive, ravishing, gorgeous, stunning, alluring, sexy, seductive, desirable, luscious; informal divine, heavenly, dreamy.
ANTONYMS unattractive.

delectation ▶ noun chiefly humorous *they had all manner of goodies for our delectation* **enjoyment,** gratification, delight, pleasure, satisfaction, relish; entertainment, amusement, titillation.

delegate ▶ noun *union delegates* **representative,** envoy, emissary, commissioner, agent, deputy, commissary; spokesperson, spokesman, spokeswoman; ambassador, plenipotentiary.
▶ verb **1** *she must delegate routine tasks* **assign,** entrust, pass on, hand on/over, turn over, devolve, depute, transfer.
2 *they were delegated to negotiate with the Slavs* **authorize,** commission, depute, appoint, nominate, mandate, empower, charge, choose, designate, elect.

delegation ▶ noun **1** *the delegation from South Africa* **deputation,** legation, mission, diplomatic mission, commission; delegates, representatives, envoys, emissaries, deputies; contingent.
2 *the delegation of tasks to others* **assignment,** entrusting, giving, devolution, deputation, transference.

delete ▶ verb *the offending paragraph was deleted* **remove,** cut out, take out, edit out, expunge, excise, eradicate, cancel; cross out, strike out, blue-pencil, ink out, scratch out, obliterate, white out; rub out, erase, efface, wipe out, blot out; Printing dele.
ANTONYMS add.

deleterious ▶ adjective *the deleterious effects of smoking* **harmful,** damaging, detrimental, injurious; adverse, disadvantageous, unfavorable, unfortunate, undesirable, bad.
ANTONYMS beneficial.

deliberate ▶ adjective **1** *a deliberate attempt to provoke him* **intentional,** calculated, conscious, intended, planned, studied, knowing, willful, purposeful, purposive, premeditated, preplanned; voluntary, volitional.
ANTONYMS accidental, unintentional.
2 *small, deliberate steps* **careful,** cautious; measured, regular, even, steady.

ANTONYMS hasty.
3 *a deliberate worker* **methodical,** systematic, careful, painstaking, meticulous, thorough.
ANTONYMS careless.
▶ verb *she* ***deliberated on*** *his words* **think about/over,** ponder, consider, contemplate, reflect on, muse on, meditate on, ruminate on, mull over, give thought to, brood over, dwell on, think on.

deliberately ▶ adverb **1** *he deliberately hurt me* **intentionally,** on purpose, purposely, by design, knowingly, wittingly, consciously, purposefully; willfully; Law with malice aforethought.
2 *he walked deliberately down the aisle* **carefully,** cautiously, slowly, steadily, evenly.

deliberation ▶ noun **1** *after much deliberation, I accepted* **thought,** consideration, reflection, contemplation, meditation, rumination; formal cogitation.
2 *he replaced the glass with deliberation* **care,** carefulness, caution, steadiness.

delicacy ▶ noun **1** *the fabric's delicacy* **fineness,** exquisiteness, daintiness, airiness; flimsiness, gauziness, silkiness.
2 *the children's delicacy* **sickliness,** ill health, frailty, fragility, weakness, debility; infirmity, valetudinarianism.
3 *the delicacy of the situation* **difficulty,** trickiness; sensitivity, ticklishness, awkwardness.
4 *treat this matter with delicacy* **care,** sensitivity, tact, discretion, diplomacy, subtlety, sensibility.
5 *an Australian delicacy* **choice food,** gourmet food, treat, luxury, specialty.

delicate ▶ adjective **1** *delicate embroidery* **fine,** exquisite, intricate, dainty; flimsy, gauzy, filmy, floaty, diaphanous, wispy, insubstantial.
ANTONYMS coarse, crude.
2 *a delicate shade of blue* **subtle,** soft, muted; pastel, pale, light.
ANTONYMS bold, lurid, vibrant.
3 *delicate china cups* **fragile,** breakable, frail; formal frangible.
ANTONYMS strong, durable.
4 *his wife is delicate* **sickly,** unhealthy, frail, feeble, weak, debilitated; unwell, infirm; formal valetudinarian.
ANTONYMS strong, robust, healthy.
5 *a delicate issue* **difficult,** tricky, sensitive, ticklish, awkward, problematic, touchy, prickly, thorny; embarrassing; informal sticky, dicey.
6 *the matter required delicate handling* **careful,** sensitive, tactful, diplomatic, discreet, kid-glove.
ANTONYMS inept, clumsy.
7 *his delicate palate* **discriminating,** discerning; **fastidious,** fussy, finicky, dainty; informal picky, choosy, persnickety.
8 *a delicate mechanism* **sensitive,** precision, precise.

delicious ▶ adjective **1** *Ezio's delicious sausages* **delectable,** mouthwatering, appetizing, tasty, flavorful, toothsome, palatable; succulent, luscious; informal scrumptious, delish, yummy, finger-licking, nummy, lip-smacking, melt-in-your-mouth.
ANTONYMS unpalatable.
2 *a delicious languor stole over her* **delightful,** exquisite, lovely, pleasurable, pleasant; informal heavenly, divine.
ANTONYMS unpleasant.

delight ▶ verb **1** *her manners delighted him* **please greatly,** charm, enchant, captivate, entrance, thrill; gladden, gratify, appeal to; entertain, amuse, divert; informal send, tickle pink, bowl over.
ANTONYMS dismay, disgust, displease.
2 *Meg* ***delighted in*** *his touch* **take pleasure in,** revel in, luxuriate in, wallow in, glory in; adore, love, relish, savor, lap up; informal get a kick out of, get a thrill out of, get a charge out of, dig.
ANTONYMS loathe, dislike.
▶ noun *she squealed with delight* **pleasure,** happiness, joy, glee, gladness; excitement, amusement; bliss, rapture, elation, euphoria.
ANTONYMS displeasure.

delighted ▶ adjective *a delighted child | the Fitzgeralds were delighted with the kitchen remodeling* **pleased,** glad, happy, thrilled, overjoyed, ecstatic, elated; on cloud nine, walking on air, in seventh heaven, jumping for joy; enchanted, charmed; amused, diverted; gleeful; informal over the moon, tickled pink, as pleased as punch, on top of the world, blissed out, on a high.

delightful ▶ adjective **1** *a delightful evening* **pleasant,** lovely, pleasurable, enjoyable; amusing, entertaining, diverting; gratifying, satisfying; marvelous, wonderful, splendid, sublime, thrilling; informal great, super, fabulous, fab, terrific, heavenly, divine, grand, brilliant, peachy, ducky.
2 *the delightful Sally* **charming,** enchanting, captivating, bewitching, appealing; sweet, endearing, cute, lovely, adorable, delectable, delicious, gorgeous, ravishing, beautiful, pretty; informal dreamy, divine.

delineate ▶ verb **1** *the aims of the study as delineated by the boss* **describe,** set forth/out, present, outline, sketch, depict, represent; map out, define, specify, identify.
2 *a section delineated in red pen* **outline,** trace, block in, mark (out/off), delimit.

delinquency ▶ noun **1** *teenage delinquency* **crime,** wrongdoing, lawbreaking, lawlessness, misconduct, misbehavior; misdemeanors, offenses, misdeeds.
2 formal *grave delinquency on the host's part* **negligence,** dereliction of duty, irresponsibility.

delinquent ▶ adjective **1** *delinquent teenagers* **lawless,** lawbreaking, criminal; errant, badly behaved, troublesome, difficult, unruly, disobedient, uncontrollable.
ANTONYMS well-behaved.
2 formal *delinquent parents face tough penalties* **negligent,** neglectful, remiss, irresponsible, lax, slack, derelict.
ANTONYMS dutiful.
▶ noun *young delinquents* **offender,** wrongdoer, malefactor, lawbreaker, culprit, criminal; hooligan, vandal, mischief-maker, ruffian, hoodlum, lowlife, punk; young offender.

delirious ▶ adjective **1** *she was delirious but had lucid intervals* **incoherent,** raving, babbling, irrational; feverish, frenzied; deranged,

demented, unhinged, mad, insane, out of one's mind.
2 *the crowd was delirious during the concert* **ecstatic,** euphoric, elated, thrilled, overjoyed, beside oneself, walking on air, on cloud nine, in seventh heaven, carried away, transported, rapturous; hysterical, wild, frenzied; informal blissed out, over the moon, on a high.

delirium ▶ noun **1** *she had fits of delirium* **derangement,** dementia, madness, insanity; incoherence, irrationality, hysteria, feverishness, hallucination.
ANTONYMS lucidity.
2 *the delirium of desire* **ecstasy,** rapture, transports, wild emotion, passion, wildness, excitement, frenzy, feverishness, fever; euphoria, elation.

deliver ▶ verb **1** *the parcel was delivered to his house* **bring,** take, convey, carry, transport, courier; send, dispatch, remit.
2 *the money was* ***delivered up*** *to the official* **hand over,** turn over, make over, sign over; surrender, give up, yield, cede; consign, commit, entrust, trust.
3 *he was delivered from his enemies* **save,** rescue, free, liberate, release, extricate, emancipate, redeem.
4 *the court delivered its verdict* **utter,** give, make, read, broadcast; pronounce, announce, declare, proclaim, hand down, return, set forth.
5 *she delivered a deadly blow to his head* **administer,** deal, inflict, give; informal land.
6 *he delivered the ball* **throw,** pitch, hurl, launch, cast, lob, aim.
7 *the trip delivered everything she wanted* **provide,** supply, furnish.
8 *we must* ***deliver on*** *our commitments* **fulfill,** live up to, carry out, carry through, make good on.
9 *she returned home to deliver her child* **give birth to,** bear, have, bring into the world, birth; informal drop; dated be delivered of.

deliverance ▶ noun **1** *their deliverance from prison* **liberation,** release, delivery, discharge, rescue, emancipation; salvation; informal bailout.
2 *the tone he adopted for such deliverances* **utterance,** statement, announcement, pronouncement, declaration, proclamation; lecture, speech.

delivery ▶ noun **1** *the delivery of the goods* **conveyance,** carriage, transportation, transport, distribution; dispatch, remittance; haulage, shipment.
2 *we get several deliveries a day* **consignment,** load, shipment.
3 *the midwife had assisted at four deliveries* **birth,** childbirth; formal parturition.
4 *her delivery was stilted* **speech,** pronunciation, enunciation, articulation, elocution; utterance, recitation, recital, execution.

delude ▶ verb *Arthur's children were convinced that his young bride was deluding him* **mislead,** deceive, fool, take in, trick, dupe, hoodwink, gull, lead on; informal con, pull the wool over someone's eyes, lead up the garden path, take for a ride, sucker, snooker.

deluge ▶ noun **1** *homes were swept away by the deluge* **flood,** torrent, spate.
2 *the deluge turned the field into a swamp* **downpour,** torrential rain; thunderstorm, thundershower, rainstorm, cloudburst.
3 *a deluge of complaints* **barrage,** volley; flood, torrent, avalanche, stream, spate, rush, outpouring, niagara.
▶ verb **1** *homes were deluged by the rains* **flood,** inundate, submerge, swamp, drown.
2 *we have been deluged with calls* **inundate,** overwhelm, overrun, flood, swamp, snow under, engulf, bombard.

delusion ▶ noun *was her belief in his fidelity just a delusion?* **misapprehension,** misconception, misunderstanding, mistake, error, misinterpretation, misconstruction, misbelief; fallacy, illusion, fantasy.

deluxe ▶ adjective *deluxe accommodations* **luxurious,** luxury, sumptuous, palatial, opulent, lavish; grand, high-class, quality, exclusive, choice, fancy; expensive, costly, upscale, upmarket; high-end, top-line, top-notch, five-star; informal plush, posh, classy, ritzy, swanky, pricey, swank.
ANTONYMS basic, cheap.

delve ▶ verb **1** *she* ***delved into*** *her pocket* **rummage (around/about) in,** search, hunt in, scrabble around in, root around/about in, ferret (about/around) in, fish about/around in, dig into/in; go through, rifle through.
2 *we must* ***delve into*** *the matter more deeply* **investigate,** inquire into, probe, explore, research, look into, go into.

demagogue ▶ noun *he was drawn into a circle of campus demagogues* **rabble-rouser,** agitator, political agitator, soapbox orator, firebrand, fomenter, provocateur.

demand ▶ noun **1** *I gave in to her demands* **request,** call, command, order, dictate, ultimatum, stipulation.
2 *the demands of a young family* **requirement,** need, desire, wish, want; claim, imposition.
3 *there is a big demand for such toys* **market,** call, appetite, desire.
▶ verb **1** *workers demanded wage increases* **call for,** ask for, request, push for, hold out for; insist on, claim.
2 *Harvey demanded that I tell him the truth* **order,** command, enjoin, urge; literary bid.
3 *"Where is she?" he demanded* **ask,** inquire, question, interrogate; challenge.
4 *an activity demanding detailed knowledge* **require,** need, necessitate, call for, involve, entail.
5 *they demanded complete anonymity* **insist on,** stipulate, make a condition of; expect, look for.
– PHRASES **in demand** *the clerk at Buchanan's said that red kitchen accessories were suddenly in demand* **sought-after,** desired, coveted, wanted, requested; marketable, desirable, popular, all the rage, at a premium, big, trendy, hot.

demanding ▶ adjective **1** *a demanding task* **difficult,** challenging, taxing, exacting, tough, hard, onerous, burdensome, formidable; arduous, uphill, rigorous, grueling, back-breaking, punishing.
ANTONYMS easy, effortless.
2 *a demanding child* **nagging,** clamorous,

importunate, insistent; trying, tiresome, hard to please; informal high-maintenance.
ANTONYMS easygoing.

demarcation ▶ noun 1 *clear demarcation of function* **separation,** distinction, differentiation, division, delimitation, definition.
2 *territorial demarcations* **boundary,** border, borderline, frontier; dividing line, divide.

demean ▶ verb *such actions demean him in the eyes of the public* **debase,** lower, degrade, discredit, devalue; cheapen, abase, humble, humiliate, disgrace, dishonor. See note at HUMBLE.
ANTONYMS dignify.

demeanor ▶ noun *his normally calm demeanor* **manner,** air, attitude, appearance, look; bearing, carriage; behavior, conduct; formal comportment.

demented ▶ adjective *many of her patients were too demented to benefit from group therapy* **mad,** insane, deranged, out of one's mind, crazed, lunatic, unbalanced, unhinged, disturbed, non compos mentis; informal crazy, mental, psycho, off one's rocker, nutty, around the bend, raving mad, batty, cuckoo, loopy, loony, bananas, screwy, touched, gaga, not all there, out to lunch, bonkers, crackers, cracked, buggy, nutso, squirrelly, wacko.
ANTONYMS sane.

dementia ▶ noun *her failing memory is not necessarily a symptom of dementia* **mental illness,** madness, insanity, derangement, lunacy.

demise ▶ noun 1 *her tragic demise* **death,** dying, passing, loss of life, end, quietus; formal decease; archaic expiry.
ANTONYMS birth.
2 *the demise of the Ottoman Empire* **end,** breakup, disintegration, fall, downfall, collapse.
ANTONYMS start.

democracy ▶ noun *freedom of speech is essential to democracy* **representative government,** elective government; self-government, government by the people; republic, commonwealth.
ANTONYMS dictatorship.

democratic ▶ adjective *a young democratic government* **elected,** representative, popular, parliamentary; egalitarian, classless; self-governing, autonomous, republican.

demolish ▶ verb 1 *they demolished the building* **knock down,** pull down, tear down, bring down, destroy, flatten, raze (to the ground), level, bulldoze, topple; blow up; dismantle, disassemble. See note at DESTROY.
ANTONYMS construct.
2 *he demolished her credibility* **destroy,** ruin, wreck; refute, disprove, discredit, overturn, explode; informal poke holes in.
ANTONYMS confirm, strengthen.
3 informal *our team was demolished* See TROUNCE.
4 informal *she demolished a bagel* See DEVOUR (sense 1).

demon ▶ noun 1 *the demons from hell* **devil,** fiend, evil spirit; incubus, succubus.
ANTONYMS angel.
2 *the man was a demon* **monster,** ogre, fiend, devil, brute, savage, beast, barbarian, animal.
ANTONYMS saint.
3 *she's a demon on the tennis court* **pro,** ace, expert, genius, master, virtuoso, maestro, past master, marvel; star; informal hotshot, whiz, buff.

demonstrable ▶ adjective *the demonstrable links between French and American art* **verifiable,** provable, attestable; verified, proven, confirmed; obvious, clear, clear-cut, evident, apparent, manifest, patent, distinct, noticeable; unmistakable, undeniable.

demonstrate ▶ verb 1 *his findings demonstrate that boys commit more crimes than girls* **show,** indicate, determine, establish, prove, confirm, verify, corroborate, substantiate.
2 *she was asked to demonstrate quilting* **give a demonstration of,** show how something is done; display, show, illustrate, exemplify, demo.
3 *his work demonstrated an analytical ability* **reveal,** bespeak, indicate, signify, signal, denote, show, display, exhibit; bear witness to, testify to; imply, intimate, give away.
4 *they demonstrated against the government* **protest,** rally, march; stage a sit-in, picket, strike, walk out; mutiny, rebel.

demonstration ▶ noun 1 *a dubious demonstration of God's existence* **proof,** substantiation, confirmation, affirmation, corroboration, verification, validation; evidence, indication, witness, testament.
2 *a demonstration of woodcarving* **exhibition,** presentation, display, exposition, teach-in, demo, expo.
3 *his paintings are a demonstration of his talent* **manifestation,** indication, sign, mark, token, embodiment; expression.
4 *an anti-racism demonstration* **protest,** march, rally, lobby, sit-in; stoppage, strike, walkout, picket (line); informal demo.

demonstrative ▶ adjective 1 *a very demonstrative family* **expressive,** open, forthcoming, communicative, unreserved, emotional, effusive, gushing; affectionate, cuddly, loving, warm, friendly, approachable; informal touchy-feely, lovey-dovey, huggy.
ANTONYMS reserved.
2 *the successes are demonstrative of their skill* **indicative,** suggestive, illustrative.
3 *demonstrative evidence of his theorem* **convincing,** definite, positive, telling, conclusive, certain, decisive; incontrovertible, irrefutable, undeniable, indisputable, unassailable.
ANTONYMS inconclusive.

demoralize ▶ verb *the celebratory fuss made about young Browning's promotion has demoralized many of the older employees* **dishearten,** dispirit, deject, cast down, depress, dismay, daunt, discourage, unman, unnerve, crush, shake, throw, cow, subdue; break someone's spirit, knock the stuffing out of.
ANTONYMS hearten.

demote ▶ verb *Calvin was demoted to second lieutenant* **downgrade,** relegate, declass, reduce in rank; depose, unseat, displace, oust; Military cashier.
ANTONYMS promote.

demur ▶ verb *Steve demurred when the suggestion was made* **object,** take exception, take issue, protest, cavil, dissent; voice reservations, be unwilling, be reluctant, balk, think twice; drag one's heels, refuse; informal boggle, kick up a fuss.
▶ noun *they accepted without demur* **objection,** protest, protestation, complaint, dispute, dissent, opposition, resistance; reservation, hesitation, reluctance, disinclination; doubts, qualms, misgivings, second thoughts; a murmur, a word. See note at QUALMS.

demure ▶ adjective *a demure Victorian miss* **modest,** unassuming, meek, mild, reserved, retiring, quiet, shy, bashful, diffident, reticent, timid, shrinking, coy; decorous, decent, seemly, ladylike, respectable, proper, virtuous, pure, innocent, chaste; sober, sedate, staid, prim, goody-goody, straitlaced.
ANTONYMS brazen.

den ▶ noun 1 *the mink left its den* **lair,** set, earth, burrow, hole, dugout, covert, shelter, hiding place, hideout.
2 *a notorious drinking den* **haunt,** site, nest, pit, hole; hotbed; informal joint, dive.
3 *he scribbled a letter in his den* **study,** studio, library; family room, living room; sanctum, retreat, sanctuary, hideaway.

denial ▶ noun 1 *the reports met with a denial* **contradiction,** refutation, rebuttal, repudiation, disclaimer; negation, dissent.
2 *the denial of insurance to certain people* **refusal,** withholding; rejection, rebuff, repulse, veto, turndown; formal declination.
3 *the denial of worldly values* **renunciation,** eschewal, repudiation, disavowal, rejection, abandonment, surrender, relinquishment.

denigrate ▶ verb *it amused him to denigrate his guests* **disparage,** belittle, deprecate, decry, cast aspersions on, criticize, attack; speak ill of, give someone a bad name, defame, slander, libel; run down, abuse, insult, revile, malign, vilify, slur; informal badmouth, dis, pull to pieces.
ANTONYMS extol.

denizen ▶ noun formal *the denizens of Grant's Hollow were a quirky lot* **inhabitant,** resident, townsman, townswoman, native, local; occupier, occupant, dweller; archaic burgher.

denomination ▶ noun 1 *a Christian denomination* **religious group,** sect, cult, movement, body, branch, persuasion, order, school; church.
2 *they demanded bills in small denominations* **value,** unit, size.

denote ▶ verb 1 *the headdresses denoted warriors* **designate,** indicate, be a mark of, signify, signal, symbolize, represent, mean; typify, characterize, distinguish, mark, identify.
2 *his manner denoted an inner strength* **suggest,** point to, smack of, indicate, show, reveal, intimate, imply, convey, betray, bespeak, spell.

denouement ▶ noun 1 *the film's denouement* **finale,** final scene, epilogue, coda, end, ending, finish, close; culmination, climax, conclusion, resolution, solution.
ANTONYMS beginning.
2 *the debate had an unexpected denouement* **outcome,** upshot, consequence, result, end; informal payoff.
ANTONYMS origin.

denounce ▶ verb 1 *the Pope denounced abortion* **condemn,** criticize, attack, censure, decry, revile, vilify, discredit, damn, reject; proscribe; malign, rail against, run down, slur; informal knock, slam, hit out at, lay into; formal castigate.
ANTONYMS praise.
2 *he was denounced as a traitor* **expose,** betray, inform on; incriminate, implicate, cite, name, accuse.

dense ▶ adjective 1 *a dense forest* **thick,** close-packed, tightly packed, closely set, close-set, crowded, crammed, compact, solid, tight; overgrown, jungly, impenetrable, impassable.
ANTONYMS sparse.
2 *dense smoke* **thick,** heavy, opaque, soupy, murky, smoggy; concentrated, condensed.
ANTONYMS thin, light.
3 informal *they were dense enough to believe me* **stupid,** unintelligent, ignorant, brainless, mindless, foolish, slow, witless, simpleminded, empty-headed, vacuous, vapid, idiotic, imbecilic; informal thick, dim, moronic, dumb, dopey, dozy, wooden-headed, lamebrained, birdbrained, pea-brained; daft. See note at STUPID.
ANTONYMS clever.

deny ▶ verb 1 *the report was denied by witnesses* **contradict,** controvert, repudiate, challenge, counter, contest, oppose, rebut; informal poke holes in; formal gainsay.
ANTONYMS confirm.
2 *he denied the request* **refuse,** turn down, reject, rebuff, repulse, decline, veto, dismiss; informal give the thumbs down to, give the red light to, nix.
ANTONYMS accept.
3 *she had to deny her parents* **renounce,** eschew, repudiate, disavow, disown, wash one's hands of, reject, discard, cast aside, abandon, give up; formal forswear; literary forsake.

deodorant ▶ noun *an underarm deodorant* **antiperspirant,** body spray, perfume, scent; informal roll-on.

depart ▶ verb 1 *James departed after lunch* **leave,** go (away), withdraw, absent oneself, abstract oneself, quit, exit, decamp, retreat, retire; make off, run off/away; set off/out, get underway, be on one's way; informal make tracks, clear off/out, take off, split.
ANTONYMS arrive.
2 *the budget departed from the norm* **deviate,** diverge, digress, drift, stray, veer; differ, vary.

departed ▶ adjective *her dear departed father* **dead,** expired, gone, no more, passed on/away; perished, fallen; informal six feet under, pushing up daisies; formal deceased; with God, asleep.

department ▶ noun 1 *the public health department* **division,** section, sector, unit, branch, arm, wing; office, bureau, agency, ministry.
2 *the food is Kay's department* **domain,** territory, province, area, line; responsibility, duty, function, business, affair, charge, task, concern; informal baby, bag, bailiwick.

departure ▶ noun 1 *he tried to delay her*

departure **leaving,** going, leave-taking, withdrawal, exit, egress, retreat.
2 *a departure from the norm* **deviation,** divergence, digression, shift; variation, change.
3 *an exciting departure for filmmakers* **change,** innovation, novelty, rarity.

depend ▶ verb 1 *her career* ***depends on*** *a good reference* **be contingent on,** be conditional on, be dependent on, hinge on, hang on, rest on, rely on; be decided by.
2 *my family* ***depends on*** *me* **rely on,** lean on; count on, bank on, trust (in), have faith in, believe in; pin one's hopes on.

dependable ▶ adjective *a dependable worker* **reliable,** trustworthy, trusty, faithful, loyal, unfailing, sure, steadfast, stable; honorable, sensible, responsible.

dependence ▶ noun See DEPENDENCY.

dependency ▶ noun 1 *her* ***dependency on*** *her husband* **dependence on,** reliance on; need for.
2 *the association of retirement with dependency* **helplessness,** dependence, weakness, defenselessness, vulnerability.
ANTONYMS independence.
3 *drug dependency* **addiction,** dependence, reliance; craving, compulsion, fixation, obsession; abuse.

dependent ▶ adjective 1 *your placement is* ***dependent on*** *her decision* **conditional on,** contingent on, based on; subject to, determined by, influenced by.
2 *the army is* ***dependent on*** *volunteers* **reliant on,** relying on, counting on; sustained by.
3 *she is* ***dependent on*** *drugs* **addicted to,** reliant on; informal hooked on.
4 *he is ill and dependent* **reliant,** needy; helpless, weak, infirm, invalid, incapable; debilitated, disabled.
▶ noun *providing for his dependents* **child,** minor; ward, charge, protégé; relative; (**dependents**) offspring, progeny.

depict ▶ verb 1 *the painting depicts the Last Supper* **portray,** represent, picture, illustrate, delineate, reproduce, render; draw, paint; literary limn.
2 *the process depicted by Darwin's theory* **describe,** detail, relate; present, set forth, set out, outline, delineate; represent, portray, characterize.

deplete ▶ verb *the food supply has been depleted* **exhaust,** use up, consume, expend, drain, empty, milk; reduce, decrease, diminish; slim down, cut back.
ANTONYMS augment.

depletion ▶ noun *the depletion of our natural resources* **exhaustion,** use, consumption, expenditure; reduction, decrease, diminution; impoverishment.

deplorable ▶ adjective 1 *your conduct is deplorable* **disgraceful,** shameful, dishonorable, unworthy, inexcusable, unpardonable, unforgivable; reprehensible, despicable, abominable, contemptible, execrable, heinous, beyond the pale.
ANTONYMS admirable.
2 *the garden is in a deplorable state* **lamentable,** regrettable, unfortunate, wretched, atrocious, awful, terrible, dreadful, diabolical; sorry, poor, inadequate; informal appalling, dire, abysmal, woeful, lousy; formal grievous.
ANTONYMS excellent.

deplore ▶ verb 1 *we deplore violence* **abhor,** find unacceptable, frown on, disapprove of, take a dim view of, take exception to; detest, despise; condemn, denounce.
ANTONYMS applaud, admire.
2 *he deplored their lack of flair* **regret,** lament, mourn, rue, bemoan, bewail, complain about, grieve over, sigh over.
ANTONYMS applaud.

deploy ▶ verb 1 *forces were deployed at strategic points* **position,** station, post, place, install, locate, situate, site, establish; base; distribute, dispose.
2 *she deployed all her skills* **use,** utilize, employ, take advantage of, exploit; bring into service, call on, turn to, resort to.

deport ▶ verb 1 *they were fined and deported* **expel,** banish, exile, transport, expatriate, extradite, repatriate; evict, oust, throw out; informal kick out, boot out, send packing.
ANTONYMS admit.
2 archaic *he deported himself with dignity* See BEHAVE (sense 1).

deportment ▶ noun *unprofessional deportment* **behavior,** conduct, performance; manners, practices, actions.

depose ▶ verb 1 *the president was deposed* **overthrow,** unseat, dethrone, topple, remove, supplant, displace; dismiss, oust, drum out, throw out, expel, eject; informal chuck out, boot out, get rid of, show someone the door.
2 Law *a witness deposed that he had seen me* **swear,** testify, attest, assert, declare, claim.

deposit ▶ noun 1 *a thick deposit of ash* **accumulation,** sediment; layer, covering, coating, blanket.
2 *a copper deposit* **seam,** vein, lode, layer, stratum, bed, pipe.
3 *they paid a deposit* **down payment,** advance payment, prepayment, installment, retainer, stake.
▶ verb 1 *she deposited her books on the table* **put (down),** place, set (down), unload, rest; drop; informal dump, park, plonk, plunk.
2 *the silt deposited by floodwater* **leave (behind),** precipitate, dump; wash up, cast up.
3 *the gold was deposited at the bank* **house,** bank, store, stow, put away; informal stash, squirrel away.

deposition ▶ noun 1 Law *depositions from witnesses* **statement,** affidavit, attestation, affirmation, assertion; allegation, declaration; testimony, evidence; rare asseveration.
2 *the deposition of calcium* **depositing,** accumulation, buildup, precipitation.

depository ▶ noun *a book depository* **repository,** cache, store, storeroom, storehouse, warehouse; vault, strongroom, safe, treasury; container, receptacle.

depot ▶ noun 1 *the bus depot* **terminal,** terminus, station, garage; headquarters, base.
2 *an arms depot* **storehouse,** warehouse, store, repository, depository, cache; arsenal, magazine,

armory, ammunition dump, drop-off.

deprave ▶ verb *young minds depraved by pornography* **corrupt,** lead astray, warp, subvert, pervert, debauch, debase, degrade, defile, sully, pollute.

depraved ▶ adjective *the character does come across as a depraved alcoholic* **corrupt,** perverted, deviant, degenerate, debased, immoral, unprincipled; debauched, dissolute, licentious, lecherous, prurient, indecent, sordid; wicked, sinful, vile, iniquitous, nefarious; informal warped, twisted, sick.

CHOOSE THE RIGHT WORD

depraved, corrupt, debased, degenerate, perverted, vile

There are many terms to describe the dark side of human nature. Someone who preys on young children would be considered **depraved**, a term that means totally immoral and implies a warped character or a twisted mind (*a depraved man who stole money from his own mother and eventually murdered her*). While *depraved* suggests an absolute condition, **degenerate** is a relative term that implies deterioration from a mental, moral, or physical standard (*her degenerate habits eventually led to her arrest for possession of drugs*). **Corrupt** also suggests a deterioration or loss of soundness, particularly through a destructive or contaminating influence. But unlike *depraved*, which usually applies to the lower end of the human spectrum, people in high positions are often referred to as *corrupt* (*a corrupt politician from a prominent family*). To say that someone or something is **debased** suggests a lowering in quality, value, dignity, or character (*debased by having to spend time in prison*). **Perverted** and **vile** are the strongest of these words describing lack of moral character. *Perverted* suggests a distortion of someone or something from what is right, natural, or true; in a moral sense, it means to use one's appetites or natural desires for other ends than those which are considered normal or natural (*a perverted individual who never should have been left alone with young children*). Most people find criminals who prey on either very old or very young victims to be **vile**, a more general term for whatever is loathsome, repulsive, or utterly despicable (*a vile killer who deserved the maximum sentence*).

depravity ▶ noun *the depravity of white slavers* **corruption,** vice, perversion, deviance, degeneracy, immorality, debauchery, dissipation, profligacy, licentiousness, lechery, prurience, obscenity, indecency; wickedness, sin, iniquity; formal turpitude.

deprecate ▶ verb **1** *the school deprecates this behavior* **deplore,** abhor, disapprove of, frown on, take a dim view of, take exception to, detest, despise; criticize, censure.
ANTONYMS praise, overrate.
2 *he deprecates the value of television* See DEPRECIATE (sense 3).

USAGE

deprecate, depreciate

The first of these has increasingly encroached on the figurative senses of the second, while the second has retreated into financial contexts. *Deprecate* means "disapprove earnestly"—e.g.: " 'Well,' he admitted, deprecatingly, 'one can't suppress one's natural instincts altogether; even if one's reason and self-interest are all the other way.' " (Dorothy L. Sayers, *Gaudy Night*; 1936.)

Depreciate, transitively, means "belittle, disparage"; and intransitively, "fall in value" (used in reference to assets or investments).

The familiar phrase *self-deprecating* is, literally speaking, a virtual impossibility, except perhaps for those suffering from extreme neuroses. Thus *self-depreciating*, with *depreciate* in its transitive sense, has historically been viewed as the correct phrase—e.g.: "Sadly, Grizzard did not have the self-depreciating humor of a Jeff Foxworthy, the self-proclaimed redneck comedian." (*St. Louis Post-Dispatch*; July 25, 1996.)

Unfortunately, though, the form *self-deprecating*—despite its mistaken origins—is now 50 times as common in print as *self-depreciating*. Speakers of American English routinely use *self-deprecating*. However grudgingly, we must accord to it the status of standard English—e.g.: "He's smart, articulate, funny, alternately self-deprecating and proud of his success." (*Los Angeles Times*; Sept. 1, 1996.) — **BG**

deprecatory ▶ adjective **1** *deprecatory remarks* **disapproving,** censorious, critical, scathing, damning, condemnatory, denunciatory, disparaging, denigrating, derogatory, negative, unflattering; disdainful, derisive, snide.
2 *a deprecatory smile* **apologetic,** rueful, regretful, sorry, remorseful, contrite, penitent, repentant; shamefaced, sheepish.

depreciate ▶ verb **1** *these cars will depreciate quickly* **decrease in value,** lose value, fall in price.
2 *the decision to depreciate property* **devalue,** cheapen, reduce, lower in price, mark down, discount.
3 *they depreciate the importance of art* **belittle,** disparage, denigrate, decry, deprecate, underrate, undervalue, underestimate, diminish, trivialize; disdain, sneer at, scoff at, scorn; informal knock, badmouth, sell short, pooh-pooh. See note at DEPRECATE.
ANTONYMS overrate.

depreciation ▶ noun *we are concerned about the depreciation of residential properties* **devaluation,** devaluing, decrease in value, lowering in value, reduction in value, cheapening, markdown, reduction; decline, downturn, downswing, drop, slump, plunge, tumble, nosedive, crash.

depredation ▶ noun *the depredation of the barbarian invasion* **plundering,** plunder, looting, pillaging, robbery; devastation, destruction, damage, rape; ravages, raids.

depress ▶ verb **1** *the news depressed him* **sadden,** dispirit, cast down, get down, dishearten, demoralize, crush, shake, desolate, weigh down, oppress; upset, distress, grieve, haunt, harrow; informal give someone the blues.
ANTONYMS cheer (up).
2 *new economic policies depressed sales* **slow down,** reduce, lower, weaken, impair; limit, check, inhibit, restrict.
ANTONYMS encourage.
3 *foreign imports will depress domestic prices* **reduce,** lower, cut, cheapen, keep down, discount, deflate, depreciate, devalue, diminish, ax, slash.
ANTONYMS raise.
4 *depress each lever in turn* **press,** push, hold down; thumb, tap; operate, activate.
ANTONYMS lift.

depressant ▶ noun *they were found guilty of drugging Jefferson's horse with depressants* **sedative,** tranquilizer, calmative, sleeping pill, soporific, opiate, hypnotic; informal downer, trank/tranq; trademark Valium; Medicine neuroleptic.
ANTONYMS stimulant.

depressed ▶ adjective **1** *he felt lonely and depressed* **sad,** unhappy, miserable, gloomy, glum, melancholy, dejected, disconsolate, downhearted, downcast, down, despondent, dispirited, low, heavy-hearted, morose, dismal, desolate; tearful, upset; informal blue, down in the dumps, down in/at the mouth.
ANTONYMS cheerful.
2 *a depressed economy* **weak,** enervated, devitalized, impaired; inactive, flat, slow, slack, sluggish, stagnant.
ANTONYMS strong.
3 *depressed prices* **reduced,** low, cut, cheap, marked down, discounted, discount; informal slashed.
ANTONYMS inflated.
4 *a depressed part of town* **poverty-stricken,** poor, disadvantaged, underprivileged, deprived, needy, distressed; run-down, slummy.
ANTONYMS prosperous.
5 *the removal of the tree left a depressed patch of ground* **sunken,** hollow, concave, indented, recessed.
ANTONYMS raised.

depressing ▶ adjective **1** *depressing thoughts* **upsetting,** distressing, painful, heartbreaking; dismal, bleak, black, somber, gloomy, grave, unhappy, melancholy, sad; wretched, doleful; informal morbid, blue.
2 *a depressing room* **gloomy,** bleak, dreary, grim, drab, somber, dark, dingy, funereal, cheerless, joyless, comfortless, uninviting.

depression ▶ noun **1** *she seems to be suffering from depression* **unhappiness,** sadness, melancholy, melancholia, misery, sorrow, woe, gloom, despondency, low spirits, a heavy heart, despair, desolation, hopelessness; upset, tearfulness; informal the dumps, the doldrums, the blues, a funk, a blue funk; Psychiatry dysthymia, seasonal affective disorder, SAD.
2 *an economic depression* **recession,** slump, decline, downturn, standstill; stagnation; the Great Depression; Economics stagflation.
3 *a depression in the ground* **hollow,** indentation, dent, cavity, concavity, dip, pit, hole, sinkhole, trough, crater; basin, bowl.

deprivation ▶ noun **1** *unemployment and deprivation* **poverty,** impoverishment, penury, privation, hardship, destitution; need, want, distress, indigence, beggary, ruin; straitened circumstances.
ANTONYMS wealth.
2 *deprivation of political rights* **dispossession,** withholding, withdrawal, removal, divestment, expropriation, seizure, confiscation; denial, forfeiture, loss; absence, lack.
ANTONYMS possession.

deprive ▶ verb *Adams was **deprived of** her civil rights* **dispossess of,** strip of, divest of, relieve of, deny, rob of; cheat out of; informal do out of.

deprived ▶ adjective *society's deprived classes* **disadvantaged,** underprivileged, poverty-stricken, impoverished, poor, destitute, needy, unable to make ends meet.

depth ▶ noun **1** *the depth of the caves* **deepness,** distance downward, distance inward; drop, vertical extent; archaic profundity.
ANTONYMS shallowness.
2 *the depth of his knowledge* **extent,** range, scope, breadth, width; magnitude, scale, degree.
3 *her lack of depth* **profundity,** deepness, wisdom, understanding, intelligence, sagacity, discernment, penetration, insight, astuteness, acumen, shrewdness; formal perspicuity.
ANTONYMS shallowness.
4 *a work of great depth* **complexity,** intricacy; profundity, gravity, weight.
ANTONYMS triviality.
5 *depth of color* **intensity,** richness, deepness, vividness, strength, brilliance.
6 (**depths**) *the depths of the sea* **deepest part,** bottom, floor, bed; abyss.
ANTONYMS surface.
– PHRASES **in depth** *choose one aspect of the case and investigate it in depth* **thoroughly,** extensively, comprehensively, rigorously, exhaustively, completely, fully; meticulously, scrupulously, painstakingly.

deputation ▶ noun *a deputation on behalf of disabled veterans* **delegation,** legation, commission, committee, mission, diplomatic mission; contingent, group, party.

depute ▶ verb **1** *he was deputed to handle negotiations* See DESIGNATE (sense 1).
2 *the judge deputed smaller cases to others* See DELEGATE (sense 1 of the verb).

deputy ▶ noun *he handed over his duties to his deputy* **second,** second-in-command, number two; substitute, stand-in, fill-in, relief, understudy, locum tenens; representative, proxy, agent, spokesperson; informal sidekick, locum.
▶ adjective *her deputy editor* **assistant,** substitute, stand-in, acting, reserve, fill-in, caretaker, temporary, provisional, stopgap, surrogate, interim; informal second-string.

deranged ▸ adjective *her deranged cousin has finally been locked up* **insane,** mad, disturbed, unbalanced, unhinged, unstable, irrational; crazed, demented, berserk, frenzied, lunatic, certifiable; non compos mentis; informal touched, crazy, wacko, mental, psycho.
ANTONYMS rational.

derelict ▸ adjective **1** *a derelict building* **dilapidated,** ramshackle, run-down, tumbledown, in ruins, falling apart; rickety, creaky, deteriorating, crumbling; neglected, untended, gone to rack and ruin.
2 *a derelict airfield* **disused,** abandoned, deserted, discarded, rejected, neglected, untended.
3 *he was derelict in his duty* **negligent,** neglectful, remiss, lax, careless, sloppy, slipshod, slack, irresponsible, delinquent.
▸ noun *the derelicts who survive on the streets* **tramp,** vagrant, vagabond, down and out, homeless person, drifter; beggar, mendicant; outcast; informal bag lady, hobo, bum.

dereliction ▸ noun **1** *buildings were reclaimed from dereliction* **dilapidation,** disrepair, deterioration, ruin, rack and ruin; abandonment, neglect, disuse.
2 *dereliction of duty* **negligence,** neglect, delinquency, failure; carelessness, laxity, sloppiness, slackness, irresponsibility; oversight, omission.

deride ▸ verb *the kid I used to deride in junior high is now my boss* **ridicule,** mock, scoff at, jibe at, make fun of, poke fun at, laugh at, hold up to ridicule, pillory; disdain, disparage, denigrate, dismiss, slight; sneer at, scorn, insult; informal knock, pooh-pooh.
ANTONYMS praise.

derision ▸ noun *Quincy's memoirs incited the derision of his siblings* **mockery,** ridicule, jeers, sneers, taunts; disdain, disparagement, denigration, disrespect, insults; scorn, contempt; lampooning, satire.

derisive ▸ adjective *shouting derisive comments* **mocking,** jeering, scoffing, teasing, derisory, snide, sneering; disdainful, scornful, contemptuous, taunting, insulting; scathing, sarcastic.

derisory ▸ adjective **1** *a derisory sum* **inadequate,** insufficient, tiny, small; trifling, paltry, pitiful, miserly, miserable; negligible, token, nominal; ridiculous, laughable, ludicrous, preposterous, insulting; informal measly, stingy, lousy, pathetic, piddling, piffling, mingy.
2 *derisory calls from the crowd* See DERISIVE.

derivation ▸ noun **1** *the derivation of theories from empirical observation* **deriving,** induction, deduction, inference; extraction, eliciting.
2 *the derivation of a word* **origin,** etymology, root, etymon, provenance, source; origination, beginning, foundation, basis, cause; development, evolution.

derivative ▸ adjective *her poetry was derivative* **imitative,** unoriginal, uninventive, unimaginative, uninspired; copied, plagiarized, plagiaristic, secondhand; trite, hackneyed, clichéd, stale, stock, banal; informal copycat, me-too, cribbed, old hat.
ANTONYMS original.
▸ noun *a derivative of opium* **by-product,** subsidiary product; spin-off.

derive ▸ verb **1** *he derives consolation from his poetry* **obtain,** get, take, gain, acquire, procure, extract, attain, glean.
2 *"coffee"* ***derives from*** *the Turkish "kahveh"* **originate in,** stem from, descend from, spring from, be taken from.
3 *his fortune* ***derives from*** *real estate* **originate in,** be rooted in; stem from, come from, spring from, proceed from, issue from.

derogate ▸ verb formal **1** *his contribution was derogated by critics* **disparage,** denigrate, belittle, deprecate, deflate; decry, discredit, cast aspersions on, run down, criticize; defame, vilify, abuse, insult, attack, pour scorn on; informal drag through the mud, knock, slam, bash, badmouth, dis.
ANTONYMS praise.
2 *the act would* ***derogate from*** *the king's majesty* **detract from,** devalue, diminish, reduce, lessen, depreciate; demean, cheapen.
ANTONYMS improve, increase.
3 *behaviors that* ***derogate from*** *the norm* **deviate from,** diverge from, depart from, digress from, stray from; differ from, vary from; conflict with, be incompatible with.

derogatory ▸ adjective *a derogatory remark* **disparaging,** denigratory, deprecatory, disrespectful, demeaning; critical, pejorative, negative, unfavorable, uncomplimentary, unflattering, insulting; offensive, personal, abusive, rude, nasty, mean, hurtful; defamatory, slanderous, libelous; informal bitchy, catty.
ANTONYMS complimentary.

descend ▸ verb **1** *the plane started descending* **go down,** come down; drop, fall, sink, dive, plummet, plunge, nosedive.
ANTONYMS ascend, climb.
2 *she descended the stairs* **climb down,** go down, come down.
ANTONYMS ascend, climb.
3 *the road descends to a village* **slope,** dip, slant, go down, fall away.
4 *she saw Herb* ***descend from*** *the bus* **alight from,** disembark, get down from, get off, dismount.
ANTONYMS climb aboard, board.
5 *they would not descend to such mean tricks* **stoop,** lower oneself, demean oneself, debase oneself; resort, be reduced.
6 *the army descended into chaos* **degenerate,** deteriorate, decline, sink, slide, fall.
7 *they* ***descended on*** *the fortress* **come in force on/upon,** arrive in hordes on; attack, assail, assault, storm, invade, swoop (down) on, charge.
8 *he* ***is descended from*** *a Flemish family* **be a descendant of,** originate from, issue from, spring from, derive from.
9 *his estates descended to his son* **be handed down,** be passed down; be inherited by.

descent ▸ noun **1** *the plane began its descent* **dive,** drop; fall, pitch, nosedive.
2 *their descent of the mountain* **downward climb.**
3 *a steep descent* **slope,** incline, dip, drop,

gradient, declivity, slant; hill.
4 *his descent into alcoholism* **decline,** slide, fall, degeneration, deterioration, regression.
5 *she is of Italian descent* **ancestry,** parentage, ancestors, family, antecedents; extraction, origin, derivation, birth; lineage, line, genealogy, heredity, stock, pedigree, blood, bloodline; roots, origins.
6 *the descent of property* **inheritance,** succession.
7 *the sudden descent of the cavalry* **attack,** assault, raid, onslaught, charge, thrust, push, drive, incursion, foray.

describe ▶ **verb 1** *he described his experiences* **report,** recount, relate, tell of, set out, chronicle; detail, catalog, give a rundown of; explain, illustrate, discuss, comment on.
2 *she described him as a pathetic figure* **designate,** pronounce, call, label, style, dub; characterize, class; portray, depict, brand, paint; literary limn.
3 *the pen described a circle* **delineate,** mark out, outline, trace, draw.

description ▶ **noun 1** *a description of my travels* **account,** report, rendition, explanation, illustration; chronicle, narration, narrative, story, commentary; portrayal, portrait; details.
2 *the description of horse racing as "the sport of kings"* **designation,** labeling, naming, dubbing, pronouncement; characterization, classification, branding; portrayal, depiction.
3 *vehicles of every description* **sort,** variety, kind, type, category, order, breed, class, designation, specification, genre, genus, brand, make, character, ilk, stripe.

descriptive ▶ **adjective** *descriptive prose* **illustrative,** expressive, graphic, detailed, lively, vivid, striking; explanatory, explicative.

descry ▶ **verb** literary See NOTICE (verb). See also note at DISTINGUISH.

desecrate ▶ **verb** *invaders desecrated the temple* **violate,** profane, defile, debase, degrade, dishonor; vandalize, damage, destroy, deface.

desert[1] ▶ **verb 1** *his wife deserted him* **abandon,** leave, turn one's back on; throw over, jilt, break up with; leave high and dry, leave in the lurch, leave behind, strand; informal walk out on, run out on, drop, dump, ditch; literary forsake.
2 *his allies were deserting the cause* **renounce,** repudiate, relinquish, wash one's hands of, abandon, turn one's back on, betray, disavow; formal abjure; literary forsake.
3 *soldiers deserted in droves* **abscond,** defect, run away, make off, decamp, flee, turn tail, take French leave, depart, quit, jump ship; Military go AWOL.

desert[2] ▶ **noun** *an expanse of desert* **wasteland,** wastes, wilderness, wilds, barren land; dust bowl.
▶ **adjective 1** *desert conditions* **arid,** dry, moistureless, parched; scorched, hot; barren, bare, stark, infertile, unfruitful, dehydrated, sterile.
ANTONYMS fertile.
2 *an uncharted desert island* **uninhabited,** empty, lonely, desolate, bleak; wild, uncultivated.

deserted ▶ **adjective 1** *a deserted wife* **abandoned,** thrown over, jilted, cast aside; neglected, stranded, marooned, forlorn, bereft; informal dumped, ditched, dropped; literary forsaken.
2 *a deserted village* **empty,** uninhabited, unoccupied, unpeopled, abandoned, evacuated, vacant; untenanted, tenantless, neglected; desolate, lonely, godforsaken.
ANTONYMS populous.

deserter ▶ **noun** *deserters were shot in full view of their fellow soldiers* **absconder,** runaway, fugitive, truant, escapee; renegade, defector, turncoat, traitor.

desertion ▶ **noun 1** *McKinley's desertion of her family* **abandonment,** leaving, jilting.
2 *the desertion of the president's colleagues* **defection;** betrayal, renunciation, repudiation, apostasy; formal abjuration.
3 *soldiers were prosecuted for desertion* **absconding,** running away, truancy, going absent without leave, taking French leave, escape; defection, treason; Military going AWOL.

deserve ▶ **verb** *the book deserves our greatest praise* **merit,** earn, warrant, rate, justify, be worthy of, be entitled to, have a right to, be qualified for.

deserved ▶ **adjective** *they clinched a deserved victory* **well-earned,** merited, warranted, justified, justifiable; rightful, due, right, just, fair, fitting, appropriate, suitable, proper, apt; archaic meet.

deserving ▶ **adjective 1** *the deserving workers* **worthy,** meritorious, commendable, praiseworthy, admirable, estimable, creditable; respectable, decent, honorable, righteous.
2 *a lapse deserving punishment* **meriting,** warranting, justifying, suitable for, worthy of.

design ▶ **noun 1** *a design for the offices* **plan,** blueprint, drawing, sketch, outline, map, plot, diagram, draft, representation, scheme, model.
2 *tableware with a gold design* **pattern,** motif, device; style, composition, makeup, layout, construction, shape, form.
3 *his design of reaching the top* **intention,** aim, purpose, plan, intent, objective, object, goal, end, target; hope, desire, wish, dream, aspiration, ambition.
▶ **verb 1** *the church was designed by Hicks* **plan,** outline, map out, draft, draw.
2 *they designed a new engine* **invent,** originate, create, think up, come up with, devise, formulate, conceive; make, produce, develop, fashion; informal dream up.
3 *this paper is designed to provoke discussion* **intend,** aim; devise, contrive, purpose, plan; tailor, fashion, adapt, gear; mean, destine. See note at INTEND.
– PHRASES **by design** *things worked out more by accident than by design* **deliberately,** intentionally, on purpose, purposefully; knowingly, wittingly, consciously, calculatedly.

designate ▶ **verb 1** *she designated her successor* **appoint,** nominate, depute, delegate; select, choose, pick, elect, name, identify, assign.
2 *the building was designated a historical site* **classify,** class, label, tag; name, call, entitle, term, dub; formal denominate.

designation ▶ noun 1 *the designation of a leader* **appointment,** nomination, naming, selection, election.
2 *the designation of wildlife preserves* **classification,** specification, definition, earmarking, pinpointing.
3 *the designation "Generalissimo"* **title,** name, epithet, tag; nickname, byname, sobriquet; informal moniker, handle; formal denomination, appellation.

designer ▶ noun 1 *a designer of office furniture* **creator,** planner, deviser, inventor, originator; maker; architect, builder.
2 *young designers made the dress* **couturier,** tailor, dressmaker.

designing ▶ adjective *he couldn't compete with the designing young executives he encountered in Washington* **scheming,** calculating, conniving; cunning, crafty, artful, wily, devious, guileful, manipulative; treacherous, sly, underhanded, deceitful, double-dealing; informal crooked, foxy.

desirability ▶ noun 1 *the desirability of the property* **appeal,** attractiveness, allure; agreeableness, worth, excellence.
2 *they debated the desirability of gay marriage* **advisability,** advantage, expedience, benefit, merit, value, profit, profitability.
3 *her obvious desirability* **attractiveness,** sexual attraction, beauty, good looks; charm, seductiveness; informal sexiness.

desirable ▶ adjective 1 *a desirable location* **attractive,** sought-after, in demand, popular, desired, covetable, coveted, enviable; appealing, agreeable, pleasant; valuable, good, excellent; informal to die for.
2 *it is desirable that they should meet* **advantageous,** advisable, wise, sensible, recommendable; helpful, useful, beneficial, worthwhile, profitable, preferable.
ANTONYMS disadvantageous.
3 *a very desirable woman* **sexually attractive,** attractive, beautiful, pretty, appealing; seductive, alluring, enchanting, beguiling, captivating, bewitching, irresistible; informal sexy, beddable.
ANTONYMS unattractive, ugly.

desire ▶ noun 1 *a desire to see the world* **wish,** want, aspiration, fancy, inclination, impulse; yearning, longing, craving, hankering, hunger; eagerness, enthusiasm, determination; informal yen, itch, jones.
2 *his eyes glittered with desire* **lust,** sexual attraction, passion, sensuality, sexuality; lasciviousness, lechery, salaciousness, libidinousness; informal the hots, raunchiness, horniness.
▶ verb 1 *they desired peace* **want,** wish for, long for, yearn for, crave, hanker after, be desperate for, be bent on, covet, aspire to; fancy; informal have a yen for, have a jones for, yen for, hanker after/for.
2 *she desired him* **be attracted to,** lust after, burn for, be infatuated by; informal fancy, have the hots for, have a crush on, be mad about, be crazy about.

desired ▶ adjective 1 *cut the cloth to the desired length* **required,** necessary, proper, right, correct; appropriate, suitable; preferred, chosen, selected.
2 *the desired results* **wished for,** wanted, coveted; sought-after, longed for, yearned for; informal must-have.

desirous ▶ adjective *he was* ***desirous of*** *change* **eager for,** desiring, anxious for, keen for, craving, yearning for, longing for, hungry for; ambitious for, aspiring to; covetous of, envious of; informal dying for, itching for.

desist ▶ verb *manufacturers were ordered to* ***desist from*** *dumping chemicals in the river* **abstain from,** refrain from, forbear from, hold back from, keep from; stop, cease, discontinue, suspend, give up, break off, drop, dispense with, eschew; informal lay off, quit.
ANTONYMS continue.

desolate ▶ adjective 1 *the desolate prairie* **bleak,** stark, bare, dismal, grim; wild, inhospitable; deserted, uninhabited, godforsaken, abandoned, unpeopled, untenanted, empty, barren; unfrequented, unvisited, isolated, remote.
ANTONYMS populous.
2 *the news of Rudolph's disappearance left them desolate* **miserable,** despondent, depressed, disconsolate, devastated, despairing, inconsolable, broken-hearted, grief-stricken, crushed, bereft; sad, unhappy, downcast, down, dejected, forlorn, upset, distressed; informal blue, cut up.
ANTONYMS joyful.
▶ verb 1 *droughts desolated the plains* **devastate,** ravage, ruin, lay waste to; level, raze, demolish, wipe out, obliterate.
2 *she was desolated by the loss of her husband* **dishearten,** depress, sadden, cast down, make miserable, weigh down, crush, upset, distress, devastate; informal shatter.

desolation ▶ noun 1 *the desolation of the Gobi Desert* **bleakness,** starkness, barrenness, sterility; wildness; isolation, loneliness, remoteness. See note at SOLITUDE.
2 *a feeling of utter desolation* **misery,** sadness, unhappiness, despondency, sorrow, depression, grief, woe; broken-heartedness, wretchedness, dejection, devastation, despair, anguish, distress.

despair ▶ noun *let me help you during this time of your despair* **hopelessness,** disheartenment, discouragement, desperation, distress, anguish, unhappiness; despondency, depression, disconsolateness, melancholy, misery, wretchedness; defeatism, pessimism.
ANTONYMS hope, joy.
▶ verb *don't despair if you can't find a job right away* **lose hope,** abandon hope, give up, lose heart, lose faith, be discouraged, be despondent, be demoralized, resign oneself; be pessimistic.

despairing ▶ adjective *a despairing look came over his face* **hopeless,** in despair, dejected, depressed, despondent, disconsolate, gloomy, miserable, wretched, desolate, inconsolable; disheartened, discouraged, demoralized, devastated, suicidal; defeatist, pessimistic.

desperado ▶ noun dated *a band of armed desperados* **bandit,** criminal, outlaw, lawbreaker, villain, renegade; robber, cutthroat, gangster, pirate.

desperate ▸ adjective 1 *a desperate look* **despairing,** hopeless; anguished, distressed, wretched, desolate, forlorn, distraught, fraught; out of one's mind, at one's wits' end, beside oneself, at the end of one's rope/tether.
2 *a desperate attempt to escape* **last-ditch,** last-gasp, eleventh-hour, do-or-die, final; frantic, frenzied, wild; futile, hopeless, doomed.
3 *a desperate shortage of teachers* **grave,** serious, critical, acute, risky, precarious; dire, awful, terrible, dreadful; urgent, pressing, crucial, vital, drastic, extreme; informal chronic.
4 *they were* ***desperate for*** *food* **in great need of,** urgently requiring, in want of; eager for, longing for, yearning for, hungry for, crying out for; informal dying for.
5 *a desperate act* **violent,** dangerous, lawless; reckless, rash, hasty, impetuous, foolhardy, incautious, hazardous, risky; do-or-die.

desperately ▸ adverb 1 *he screamed desperately for help* **in desperation,** in despair, despairingly, in anguish, in distress; wretchedly, hopelessly, desolately, forlornly.
2 *they are desperately ill* **seriously,** critically, gravely, severely, acutely, dangerously, perilously; very, extremely, dreadfully; hopelessly, irretrievably; informal terribly.
3 *he desperately wanted to talk* **urgently,** pressingly; intensely, eagerly.

desperation ▸ noun *her family failed to see her state of desperation* **hopelessness,** despair, distress; anguish, agony, torment, misery, wretchedness; discouragement, disheartenment.

despicable ▸ adjective *despicable crimes* **contemptible,** loathsome, hateful, detestable, reprehensible, abhorrent, abominable, awful, heinous; odious, vile, low, mean, abject, shameful, ignominious, shabby, ignoble, disreputable, discreditable, unworthy; informal dirty, rotten, lowdown, lousy; beastly; archaic scurvy.
ANTONYMS admirable.

despise ▸ verb *he despised weakness* **detest,** hate, loathe, abhor, execrate, deplore, dislike; scorn, disdain, look down on, deride, sneer at, revile; spurn, shun; formal abominate; archaic, or literary contemn.
ANTONYMS adore.

CHOOSE THE RIGHT WORD

despise, abhor, contemn, detest, disdain, loathe, scorn

It's one thing to dislike someone; it's quite another to **despise** or **detest** the person. Both are strong words, used to describe extreme dislike or hatred. *Detest* is probably the purest expression of hatred (*she detested the woman who had raised her, and longed to find her own mother*), while *despise* suggests looking down with great contempt and regarding the person as mean, petty, weak, or worthless (*he despised men whose only concern was their own safety*). **Disdain** carries even stronger connotations of superiority, often combined with self-righteousness (*to disdain anyone lacking a college education*). **Scorn** is a stronger word for *disdain*, and it implies an attitude of not only contempt but of haughty rejection or refusal (*to scorn the woman he'd once loved*). To **loathe** something is to feel utter disgust toward it (*he grew to loathe peanut butter and jelly sandwiches*) and to **abhor** it is to feel a profound, shuddering, repugnance (*she abhorred the very idea of asking her husband for the money*). **Contemn** is a more literary word meaning to treat with disdain, scorn, or contempt.

despite ▸ preposition *despite his lack of enthusiasm, Zachary had a pretty good time* **in spite of,** notwithstanding, regardless of, in the face of, for all, even with.

despoil ▸ verb 1 *a village despoiled by invaders* **plunder,** pillage, rob, ravage, raid, ransack, rape, loot, sack; devastate, lay waste, ruin. See note at RAVAGE.
2 *the thief despoiled him of all he had* **rob,** strip, deprive, dispossess, denude, divest, relieve, clean out.

despondency ▸ noun *the despondency of the refugees was captured in this documentary* **hopelessness,** despair, discouragement, low spirits, wretchedness; melancholy, gloom, misery, desolation, disappointment, disheartenment, dejection, sadness, unhappiness; informal blues, heartache.

despondent ▸ adjective *they were tired and despondent* **disheartened,** discouraged, dispirited, downhearted, downcast, crestfallen, down, low, disconsolate, despairing, wretched; melancholy, gloomy, morose, dismal, woebegone, miserable, depressed, dejected, sad; informal blue, down in/at the mouth, down in the dumps.
ANTONYMS hopeful, cheerful.

despot ▸ noun *when one despot is deposed for another, the cycle of repression continues* **tyrant,** oppressor, dictator, absolute ruler, totalitarian, autocrat; informal slave driver.

despotic ▸ adjective *a despotic regime* **autocratic,** dictatorial, totalitarian, absolutist, undemocratic, unaccountable; one-party, autarchic, monocratic; tyrannical, tyrannous, oppressive, repressive, draconian, illiberal.
ANTONYMS democratic.

destination ▸ noun *our original destination was Richmond* **journey's end,** end of the line; terminus, stop, stopping place, port of call; goal, purpose, target, end.

destined ▸ adjective 1 *he is destined to lead a charmed life* **fated,** ordained, predestined, meant; certain, sure, bound, assured, likely; doomed.
2 *computers destined for Europe* **heading,** bound, en route, scheduled; intended, meant, designed, designated, allotted, reserved.

destiny ▸ noun 1 *master of his own destiny* **future,** fate, fortune, doom; lot; archaic portion.
2 *she believed their meeting was destiny* **fate,** providence; predestination; God's will,

kismet, the stars; luck, fortune, chance; karma, serendipity.

destitute ▶ adjective **1** *she was left destitute* **penniless,** poor, impoverished, poverty-stricken, impecunious, without a cent/penny (to one's name); needy, in straitened circumstances, distressed, badly off; informal hard up, broke, flat broke, strapped (for cash), without a red cent, dirt poor.
ANTONYMS rich.
2 *we were* ***destitute of*** *clothing* **devoid of,** bereft of, deprived of, in need of; lacking, without, deficient in, wanting.

destroy ▶ verb **1** *their offices were destroyed by bombing* **demolish,** knock down, level, raze (to the ground), fell; wreck, ruin, shatter; blast, blow up, dynamite, explode, bomb.
ANTONYMS build, reconstruct.
2 *the new highway would destroy the conservation area* **spoil,** ruin, wreck, disfigure, blight, mar, impair, deface, scar, injure, harm, devastate, damage, wreak havoc on; informal total.
ANTONYMS restore, preserve.
3 *illness destroyed his career* **wreck,** ruin, spoil, disrupt, undo, upset, put an end to, put a stop to, terminate, frustrate, blight, crush, quash, dash, scotch; devastate, demolish, scuttle, sabotage; informal mess up, foul up, put the kibosh on, fry, do for, blow a hole in; archaic bring to naught.
ANTONYMS bolster, help.
4 *the horse had to be destroyed* **kill,** put down, put to sleep, slaughter, terminate, exterminate, euthanize.
5 *we will destroy the enemy* **annihilate,** wipe out, obliterate, wipe off the face of the earth, eliminate, eradicate, liquidate, finish off, erase; kill, slaughter, massacre, exterminate; informal take out, rub out, snuff out, waste, fry, nuke, zap.
ANTONYMS spare.

CHOOSE THE RIGHT WORD

destroy, annihilate, demolish, eradicate, exterminate, extirpate, raze

If you're interested in getting rid of something, you've got a number of options at your disposal. **Destroy** is a general term covering any force that wrecks, ruins, kills, etc. (*to destroy an ant hill by pouring boiling water on it*). If it's a building, you'll want to **demolish** or **raze** it, two words that are generally applied only to very large things. *Raze* is used almost exclusively with structures; it means to bring something down to the level of the ground (*they razed the apartment building to make way for the new hospital*). *Demolish* implies pulling or smashing something to pieces; when used with regard to buildings, it conjures up a vision of complete wreckage and often a heap of rubble (*their new house was demolished by the first hurricane of the season*). But unlike *raze, demolish* can also be applied to nonmaterial things (*to demolish the theory with a few simple experiments*). If you **eradicate** something, you eliminate it completely, literally or figuratively, pull it out by the roots (*to eradicate smallpox with a vaccine*) and prevent its reappearance. **Extirpate**, like *eradicate*, implies the utter destruction of something (*the species was extirpated from the park by the flooding*). If you're dealing with cockroaches, you'll probably want to **exterminate** them, which means to wipe out or kill in great numbers. Or better yet, you'll want to **annihilate** them, which is the most extreme word in this group and literally means to reduce to nothingness.

destruction ▶ noun **1** *the destruction by allied bombers* **demolition,** wrecking, ruination, blasting, bombing; wreckage, ruins.
2 *the destruction of the countryside* **devastation,** ruination, blighting, disfigurement, impairment, scarring, harm, desolation.
3 *the destruction of cattle* **slaughter,** killing, putting down, extermination, termination.
4 *the destruction of the enemies' forces* **annihilation,** obliteration, elimination, eradication, liquidation; killing, slaughter, massacre, extermination.

destructive ▶ adjective **1** *the most destructive war* **devastating,** ruinous, disastrous, catastrophic, calamitous, cataclysmic; harmful, damaging, detrimental, deleterious, injurious, crippling; violent, savage, fierce, brutal, deadly, lethal.
2 *destructive criticism* **negative,** hostile, vicious, unfriendly; unhelpful, obstructive, discouraging.

desultory ▶ adjective *the desultory interest you have in your child's welfare is appalling* **casual,** cursory, superficial, token, perfunctory, half-hearted, lukewarm; random, aimless, erratic, unmethodical, unsystematic, chaotic, inconsistent, irregular, intermittent, sporadic, fitful.
ANTONYMS keen.

detach ▶ verb *he detached the lamp from its bracket* **unfasten,** disconnect, disengage, separate, uncouple, remove, loose, unhitch, unhook, free, pull off, cut off, break off.
ANTONYMS attach.
– PHRASES **detach oneself from 1** *she detached herself from the crowd* **free oneself from,** separate oneself from, segregate oneself from; move away from, split off from; leave, abandon.
2 *he has detached himself from his family* **dissociate oneself from,** divorce oneself from, alienate oneself from, separate (oneself) from, segregate oneself from, isolate oneself from, cut oneself off from; break away from, disaffiliate oneself from, defect from; leave, quit, withdraw from, break with.

detached ▶ adjective **1** *a detached collar* **unfastened,** disconnected, separated, separate, loosened; untied, unhitched, undone, unhooked, unbuttoned; free, severed, cut off.
2 *a detached observer* **dispassionate,** disinterested, objective, uninvolved, outside, neutral, unbiased, unprejudiced, impartial,

nonpartisan; indifferent, aloof, remote, distant, impersonal; informal cool.
3 *a detached house* **standing alone,** separate.

detachment ▸ noun **1** *she looked on everything with detachment* **objectivity,** dispassion, disinterest, open-mindedness, neutrality, impartiality; indifference, aloofness.
2 *a detachment of soldiers* **unit,** detail, squad, troop, contingent, outfit, task force, patrol, crew; platoon, company, corps, regiment, brigade, battalion.
3 *retinal detachment* **loosening,** disconnection, disengagement, separation; removal.

detail ▸ noun **1** *the picture is correct in every detail* **particular,** respect, feature, characteristic, attribute, specific, aspect, facet, part, unit, component, constituent; fact, piece of information, point, element, circumstance, consideration.
2 *that's just a detail* **unimportant point,** trivial fact, triviality, technicality, nicety, subtlety, trifle, fine point, incidental, inessential, nothing.
3 *records with a considerable degree of detail* **precision,** exactness, accuracy, thoroughness, carefulness, scrupulousness, particularity.
4 *a guard detail* **unit,** detachment, squad, troop, contingent, outfit, task force, patrol.
5 *I got kitchen detail* **duty,** task, job, chore, charge, responsibility, assignment, function, mission, engagement, occupation, undertaking, errand.
▸ verb **1** *the report details our objections* **describe,** explain, expound, relate, catalog, list, spell out, itemize, particularize, identify, specify; state, declare, present, set out, frame; cite, quote, instance, mention, name.
2 *troops were detailed to prevent their escape* **assign,** allocate, appoint, delegate, commission, charge; send, post; nominate, vote, elect, co-opt.
– PHRASES **in detail** *this will be examined in detail in the next chapter* **thoroughly,** in depth, exhaustively, minutely, closely, meticulously, rigorously, scrupulously, painstakingly, carefully; completely, comprehensively, fully, extensively.

detailed ▸ adjective *a detailed description of the assailants* **comprehensive,** full, complete, thorough, exhaustive, all-inclusive; elaborate, minute, intricate; explicit, specific, precise, exact, accurate, meticulous, painstaking; itemized, blow-by-blow.
ANTONYMS general.

detain ▸ verb **1** *they were detained for questioning* **hold,** take into custody, take (in), confine, imprison, lock up, put in jail, intern; arrest, apprehend, seize; informal pick up, run in, haul in, nab, collar.
ANTONYMS release.
2 *don't let me detain you* **delay,** hold up, make late, keep, slow up/down; hinder, hamper, impede, obstruct.

detect ▸ verb **1** *no one detected the smell of gas* **notice,** perceive, discern, be aware of, note, make out, spot, recognize, distinguish, remark, identify, diagnose; catch, sense, see, smell, scent, taste.
2 *they are responsible for detecting fraud* **discover,** uncover, find out, turn up, unearth, dig up, root out, expose, reveal.
3 *the hackers were detected* **catch,** hunt down, track down, find, expose, reveal, unmask, smoke out; apprehend, arrest; informal nail.

detection ▸ noun **1** *the detection of methane* **discernment,** perception, awareness, recognition, identification, diagnosis; sensing, sight, smelling, tasting.
2 *the detection of insider trading* **discovery,** uncovering, unearthing, exposure, revelation.
3 *he managed to escape detection* **capture,** identification, exposure; apprehension, arrest; notice.

detective ▸ noun *they hired a detective to track down Polk's former partner* **investigator,** private investigator, private detective, police detective, operative; informal private eye, PI, sleuth, snoop, shamus, gumshoe, Sherlock; informal dated dick, private dick.

detention ▸ noun *he was released after spending a year in detention* **custody,** imprisonment, confinement, incarceration, internment, detainment, captivity; arrest, house arrest; quarantine; punishment, discipline.

deter ▸ verb **1** *the high cost deterred many* **discourage,** dissuade, put off, scare off; dishearten, demoralize, daunt, intimidate.
ANTONYMS encourage.
2 *the presence of a guard deters crime* **prevent,** stop, avert, fend off, stave off, ward off, block, halt, check; hinder, impede, hamper, obstruct, foil, forestall, counteract, inhibit, curb.
ANTONYMS encourage.

detergent ▸ noun *laundry detergent* **cleaner,** cleanser, cleaning agent; soap, soap powder, dish soap, soap flakes.

deteriorate ▸ verb **1** *his health deteriorated* **worsen,** decline, degenerate; fail, slump, slip, go downhill, wane, ebb; informal go to pot.
ANTONYMS improve.
2 *these materials deteriorate if stored wrongly* **decay,** degrade, degenerate, break down, decompose, rot, go off, spoil, perish; break up, disintegrate, crumble, fall apart.

deterioration ▸ noun **1** *a deterioration in market conditions* **decline,** collapse, failure, drop, downturn, slump; informal slip, retrogression.
2 *deterioration of the main structure* **decay,** degradation, degeneration, breakdown, decomposition, rot; atrophy, weakening; breakup, disintegration, dilapidation; entropy.

determination ▸ noun **1** *it took great determination to win* **resolution,** resolve, willpower, strength of character, single-mindedness, purposefulness, intentness; staunchness, perseverance, persistence, tenacity, staying power; strong-mindedness, backbone; stubbornness, doggedness, obstinacy; spirit, courage, pluck, grit, stout-heartedness; informal guts, spunk, balls, moxie; formal pertinacity.
2 *the determination of the rent* **setting,** specification, settlement, designation, arrangement, establishment, prescription.
3 *the determination of the speed of light* **calculation,** discovery, ascertainment,

establishment, deduction, divination, diagnosis, discernment, verification, confirmation.

determine ▶ verb **1** *chromosomes determine the sex of the embryo* **control,** decide, regulate, direct, dictate, govern; affect, influence, mold.
2 *he determined to sell* **resolve,** decide, make up one's mind, choose, elect, opt; formal purpose.
3 *the sum will be determined by an accountant* **specify,** set, fix, decide on, settle, assign, designate, arrange, choose, establish, ordain, prescribe, decree.
4 *determine the composition of the fibers* **ascertain,** find out, discover, learn, establish, calculate, work out, make out, deduce, diagnose, discern; check, verify, confirm; informal figure out.

determined ▶ adjective **1** *he was determined to have his way* **intent on,** bent on, set on, insistent on, resolved to, firm about, committed to; single-minded about, obsessive about.
2 *a very determined man* **resolute,** purposeful, purposive, adamant, single-minded, unswerving, unwavering, undaunted, intent, insistent; steadfast, staunch, stalwart; persevering, persistent, indefatigable, tenacious; strong-minded, strong-willed, unshakable, steely, four-square, dedicated, committed; stubborn, dogged, obstinate, inflexible, intransigent, unyielding, immovable, rock-ribbed; formal pertinacious. See note at RESOLUTE.

determining ▶ adjective *money is the determining factor* **deciding,** decisive, conclusive, final, definitive, key, pivotal, crucial, critical, major, chief, prime.

deterrent ▶ noun *the high rate of interest is a deterrent to first-time home buyers* **disincentive,** discouragement, damper, curb, check, restraint; obstacle, hindrance, impediment, obstruction, block, barrier, inhibition.
ANTONYMS incentive.

detest ▶ verb *the only vegetable I truly detest is turnip* **abhor,** hate, loathe, despise, shrink from, be unable to bear, find intolerable, dislike, disdain, have an aversion to; formal abominate. See note at DESPISE.
ANTONYMS love.

detestable ▶ adjective *civilized people must not tolerate such detestable inhumanity* **abhorrent,** hateful, loathsome, despicable, abominable, execrable, repellent, repugnant, repulsive, revolting, disgusting, distasteful, horrible, horrid, awful; heinous, reprehensible, obnoxious, odious, offensive, contemptible. See note at OFFENSIVE.

detonate ▶ verb **1** *the charge detonated on impact* **explode,** go off, blow up, shatter, erupt; ignite; bang, blast, boom.
2 *they detonated the bomb* **set off,** explode, discharge, let off, touch off, trigger; ignite, kindle.

detour ▶ noun *the detour will add another twenty minutes to the trip* **diversion,** circuitous route, indirect route, scenic route; bypass; digression, deviation, shortcut.

detract ▶ verb *my reservations should not detract from the book's excellence* **belittle,** take away from, diminish, reduce, lessen, minimize, play down, trivialize, decry, depreciate, devalue, deprecate.

detractor ▶ noun *detractors never deterred me from pursuing my art* **critic,** disparager, denigrator, deprecator, belittler, attacker, fault-finder, backbiter; slanderer, libeler; informal knocker.

detriment ▶ noun *local merchants fear the detriment to business that one of these superstores could bring about* **harm,** damage, injury, hurt, impairment, loss, disadvantage, disservice, mischief.
ANTONYMS benefit.

detrimental ▶ adjective *erosion can have a detrimental effect on our water* **harmful,** damaging, injurious, hurtful, inimical, deleterious, destructive, ruinous, disastrous, bad, malign, adverse, undesirable, unfavorable, unfortunate; unhealthy, unwholesome.
ANTONYMS benign.

detritus ▶ noun *areas littered with military detritus* **debris,** waste, refuse, rubbish, litter, scrap, flotsam and jetsam, rubble; remains, remnants, fragments, scraps, dregs, leavings, sweepings, dross, scum, trash, garbage; informal dreck.

devastate ▶ verb **1** *the city was devastated by an earthquake* **destroy,** ruin, wreck, lay waste, ravage, demolish, raze (to the ground), level, flatten; informal trash, total. See note at RAVAGE.
2 *he was devastated by the news* **shatter,** shock, stun, daze, dumbfound, traumatize, crush, overwhelm, overcome, distress.

devastating ▶ adjective **1** *a devastating cyclone* **destructive,** ruinous, disastrous, catastrophic, calamitous, cataclysmic; harmful, damaging, injurious, detrimental; crippling, violent, savage, fierce, dangerous, fatal, deadly, lethal.
2 *devastating news* **shattering,** shocking, traumatic, overwhelming, crushing, distressing, terrible.
3 informal *he presented devastating arguments* **incisive,** highly effective, penetrating, cutting; withering, blistering, searing, scathing, fierce, savage, stinging, biting, caustic, harsh, unsparing.

devastation ▶ noun **1** *the hurricane left a trail of devastation* **destruction,** ruin, desolation, havoc, wreckage; ruins, ravages.
2 *the devastation of Prussia* **destruction,** wrecking, ruination; demolition, annihilation; despoliation, plunder, pillaging, plundering.
3 *the devastation you have caused the family* **shock,** trauma, distress, stress, strain, pain, anguish, suffering, upset, agony, misery, heartache.

develop ▶ verb **1** *the industry developed rapidly* **grow,** expand, spread; advance, progress, evolve, mature; prosper, thrive, flourish, blossom. See note at MATURE.
2 *a plan was developed* **initiate,** instigate, set in motion; originate, invent, form, establish, generate.
3 *children should develop their talents* **expand,** augment, broaden, supplement, reinforce; enhance, refine, improve, polish, perfect.

4 *a fight developed* **start,** begin, emerge, erupt, break out, burst out, arise, break, unfold, happen.
5 *he developed the symptoms last week* **fall ill with,** be stricken with, succumb to; contract, catch, get, pick up, come down with, become infected with.

development ▶ noun **1** *the development of the firm* **evolution,** growth, maturation, expansion, enlargement, spread, progress; success.
2 *the development of an idea* **forming,** establishment, initiation, instigation, origination, invention, generation.
3 *keep abreast of developments* **event,** occurrence, happening, circumstance, incident, situation, issue.
4 *a housing development* **complex,** site.

deviant ▶ adjective *deviant behavior* **aberrant,** abnormal, atypical, anomalous, irregular, nonstandard; nonconformist, perverse, uncommon, unusual; freakish, strange, odd, peculiar, bizarre, eccentric, idiosyncratic, unorthodox, exceptional; warped, perverted; informal kinky, quirky.
ANTONYMS normal.
▶ noun *we were seen as deviants* **nonconformist,** eccentric, maverick, individualist; outsider, misfit; informal oddball, weirdo, freak, screwball, kook, odd duck.

deviate ▶ verb *do not* ***deviate from*** *the original plan* **diverge from,** digress from, drift from, stray from, veer from, swerve from; get sidetracked from, branch off from; differ from, vary from, run counter to, go in opposition to, contrast with.

deviation ▶ noun *the slightest deviation could prove disastrous* **divergence,** digression, departure; difference, variation, variance; aberration, abnormality, irregularity, anomaly, inconsistency, discrepancy.

device ▶ noun **1** *a device for measuring pressure* **implement,** gadget, utensil, tool, appliance, apparatus, instrument, machine, mechanism, contrivance, contraption; informal gizmo, widget, doohickey.
2 *an ingenious legal device* **ploy,** tactic, move, stratagem, scheme, plot, plan, trick, ruse, maneuver, machination, contrivance, expedient, dodge, wile.
3 *their shields bear his device* **emblem,** symbol, logo, badge, crest, insignia, coat of arms, escutcheon, seal, mark, design, motif; monogram, hallmark, trademark.

devil ▶ noun **1** *God and the Devil* **Satan,** Beelzebub, Lucifer, the Prince of Darkness, the Evil One; informal Old Nick.
2 *he drove out the devils from their bodies* **evil spirit,** demon, fiend, bogie; informal spook.
3 *look what the cruel devil has done* **brute,** beast, monster, fiend; villain, sadist, barbarian, ogre.
4 *he's a naughty little devil* **rascal,** rogue, imp, fiend, monkey, wretch; informal monster, horror, scamp, tyke, varmint.
5 informal *the poor devils looked ill* **wretch,** unfortunate, creature, soul, person, fellow; informal thing, beggar.

devilish ▶ adjective **1** *a devilish grin* **diabolical,** fiendish, demonic, satanic, demoniac, demoniacal; hellish, infernal; **mischievous,** wicked, impish, roguish.
2 *a devilish job* **difficult,** tricky, ticklish, troublesome, thorny, awkward, problematic.

devil-may-care ▶ adjective *devil-may-care stunt pilots* **reckless,** rash, incautious, heedless, impetuous, impulsive, daredevil, hotheaded, wild, foolhardy, audacious, nonchalant, casual, breezy, flippant, insouciant, happy-go-lucky, easygoing, unworried, untroubled, unconcerned, harum-scarum.

devious ▶ adjective **1** *the devious ways in which they bent the rules* **underhanded,** deceitful, dishonest, dishonorable, unethical, unprincipled, immoral, unscrupulous, fraudulent, dubious, unfair, treacherous, duplicitous; crafty, cunning, calculating, artful, conniving, scheming, sly, wily; sneaky, furtive, secret, clandestine, surreptitious, covert, snide; informal crooked, shady, dirty, lowdown.
2 *a devious route around the coast* **circuitous,** roundabout, indirect, meandering, winding, tortuous.

devise ▶ verb *they have devised a way to recycle contaminated oil* **conceive,** think up, dream up, work out, formulate, concoct; design, invent, coin, originate; compose, construct, fabricate, create, produce, develop; discover, hit on; hatch, contrive; informal cook up.

devoid ▶ adjective *your argument is* ***devoid of*** *logic* **free of,** empty of, vacant of, bereft of, deprived of, destitute of, bankrupt of; lacking, without, wanting; informal minus.

devolve ▶ verb *the move would devolve responsibility to local units* **delegate,** depute, pass (down/on), download, hand down/over/on, transfer, transmit, assign, consign, convey, entrust, turn over, give, cede, surrender, relinquish, deliver; bestow, grant.

devote ▶ verb *they devoted considerable time to the matter* **allocate,** assign, allot, commit, give (over), apportion, consign, pledge; dedicate, consecrate; set aside, earmark, reserve, designate.

devoted ▶ adjective *a devoted follower of the writer* **loyal,** faithful, true, staunch, steadfast, constant, committed, dedicated, devout; fond, loving, affectionate, caring, admiring.

devotee ▶ noun **1** *a devotee of rock music* **enthusiast,** fan, lover, aficionado, admirer; informal buff, bum, freak, nut, fiend, fanatic, addict, maniac.
2 *devotees thronged the temple* **follower,** adherent, supporter, advocate, disciple, votary, member, stalwart, fanatic, zealot; believer, worshiper.

devotion ▶ noun **1** *her devotion to her husband* **loyalty,** faithfulness, fidelity, constancy, commitment, adherence, allegiance, dedication; fondness, love, admiration, affection, care.
2 *a life of devotion* **devoutness,** piety, religiousness, spirituality, godliness, holiness, sanctity.
3 *morning devotions* **religious worship,** worship, religious observance; prayers; prayer meeting, church service.

devour ▶ verb **1** *he devoured his meal* **eat**

hungrily, eat greedily, gobble (up/down), guzzle, gulp (down), bolt (down), gorge oneself on, wolf (down), feast on, consume, eat up; informal demolish, dispose of, make short work of, polish off, shovel down, stuff oneself with, pig out on, put away; informal scarf (down/up).
2 *flames devoured the house* **consume,** engulf, envelop; destroy, demolish, lay waste, devastate; gut, ravage, ruin, wreck.
3 *he was devoured by remorse* **afflict,** plague, bedevil, trouble, harrow, rack; consume, swallow up, overcome, overwhelm.

devout ▶ adjective **1** *a devout Christian* **pious,** religious, devoted, dedicated, reverent, God-fearing; holy, godly, saintly, faithful, dutiful, righteous, churchgoing, orthodox.
2 *a devout family man* **dedicated,** devoted, committed, loyal, faithful, staunch, genuine, firm, steadfast, unwavering, sincere, wholehearted, keen, enthusiastic, zealous, passionate, ardent, fervent, active, sworn, pledged; informal card-carrying, true blue.

dexterity ▶ noun **1** *painting china demanded dexterity* **deftness,** adeptness, adroitness, agility, nimbleness, handiness, ability, talent, skill, proficiency, expertise, experience, efficiency, mastery, delicacy, knack, artistry, finesse.
2 *his political dexterity* **shrewdness,** astuteness, acumen, acuity, intelligence; ingenuity, inventiveness, cleverness, smartness; canniness, sense, discernment, insight, understanding, penetration, perception, perspicacity, discrimination; cunning, artfulness, craftiness; informal horse sense, savvy, street smarts.

dexterous ▶ adjective **1** *a dexterous flick of the wrist* **deft,** adept, adroit, agile, nimble, neat, handy, able, capable, skillful, skilled, proficient, expert, practiced, polished; efficient, effortless, slick, professional, masterly; informal nifty, mean, ace.
ANTONYMS clumsy.
2 *his dexterous accounting abilities* **shrewd,** ingenious, inventive, clever, intelligent, brilliant, smart, sharp, acute, astute, canny, intuitive, discerning, perceptive, insightful, incisive, judicious; cunning, artful, crafty, wily; informal on the ball, quick off the mark, quick on the uptake, brainy, savvy.
ANTONYMS stupid.

diadem ▶ noun *the queen's jeweled diadem* **crown,** coronet, tiara, circlet, chaplet; literary coronal.

diagnose ▶ verb *perhaps he diagnosed the condition incorrectly* **identify,** determine, distinguish, recognize, detect, pinpoint.

diagnosis ▶ noun **1** *the diagnosis of celiac disease* **identification,** detection, recognition, determination, discovery, pinpointing.
2 *the results confirmed his diagnosis* **opinion,** judgment, verdict, conclusion.

diagonal ▶ adjective *the diagonal stripes on the wall make me dizzy* **crosswise,** crossways, slanting, slanted, aslant, oblique, angled, at an angle; cater-cornered, kitty-cornered.

diagram ▶ noun *Jackson's diagrams show the dramatic effects of erosion since 1948* **drawing,** line drawing, sketch, representation, draft, illustration, picture, plan, outline, delineation, figure; Computing graphic.

dialect ▶ noun *the island dialect was influenced by the Spanish in the sixteenth century* **regional language,** local language, local speech, vernacular, patois, idiom; regionalisms, localisms; informal lingo.

CHOOSE THE RIGHT WORD

dialect, argot, cant, jargon, lingo, slang, vernacular

When a New York City cab driver calls out the window, "Hey, wassa madda wichoo?" he is using the **vernacular**, which is the authentic, natural pattern of speech among those belonging to a certain community. In some areas of London, on the other hand, one might hear the Cockney **dialect**, which is a form or variety of a language that is confined to a specific group or locality; it has its own pronunciation, usage, and vocabulary, and may persist for generations or even centuries (*he spoke in the dialect of the Appalachian backwoodsman*). A teenager who tells his parents to "Chill out" is using **slang**, which is a very informal language that includes "substitute" vocabulary ("wheels" for *car*, "rug" for *toupee*), grammatical distortions, and other departures from formal or polite usage. **Argot** refers to the slang of a group that feels threatened by the hostility of society as a whole; it traditionally refers to the slang used by criminals and thieves, although it may refer to any peculiar language that a clique or other closely knit group uses to communicate with each other. At one time **cant** was a synonym for *argot*, but now it usually refers to pompous, inflated language or the hackneyed use of words and phrases by members of a particular class or profession (*the cant of the fashion industry*). In contrast to *cant*, which can at least be understood, **jargon** is nearly impossible for the average person to decipher. This term refers to the technical or highly specialized language used by members of an occupational or professional group (*medical jargon, the jargon of the theater*). If you are frustrated because you can't understand the language used by a particular class or group, you're apt to refer to their way of talking as **lingo**, which is a term for any language that is not readily understood (*she tried to reason with the cab driver, but she couldn't understand his lingo*).

dialectic ▶ noun *feminism has of course contributed to this dialectic* **discussion,** debate, dialogue, logical argument, reasoning, argumentation, polemics; formal ratiocination.

dialogue ▶ noun **1** *a book consisting of a series of dialogues* **conversation,** talk, discussion, interchange, discourse; chat, tête-à-tête, heart-to-heart; informal confab, chinwag; formal colloquy, confabulation. See note at CONVERSATION.

2 *they called for a serious political dialogue* **discussion,** exchange, debate, exchange of views, talk, consultation, conference, parley; talks, negotiations; informal powwow, skull session.

diameter ▶ **noun** *the diameter of the hole is less than two inches* **breadth,** width, thickness; caliber, bore, gauge.

diametrical, diametric ▶ **adjective** *politically, Taylor was in diametrical opposition to her parents* **direct,** absolute, complete, exact, extreme, polar, antipodal.

diaphanous ▶ **adjective** *a diaphanous dress* **sheer,** fine, delicate, light, thin, insubstantial, floaty, flimsy, filmy, silken, chiffony, gossamer, gossamer-thin, gauzy; translucent, transparent, see-through.
ANTONYMS thick, opaque.

diarrhea ▶ **noun** *an outbreak of diarrhea in the camp* loose stools; informal the runs, the trots, the squirts, Montezuma's revenge, turista; Medicine dysentery; archaic the flux.
ANTONYMS constipation.

diary ▶ **noun 1** *he put the date in his diary* **appointment book,** engagement book, organizer, personal organizer, daybook, PDA.
2 *her World War II diaries* **journal,** memoir, chronicle, log, logbook, history, annal, record.

diatribe ▶ **noun** *he launched into a diatribe against the Catholic Church* **tirade,** harangue, onslaught, attack, polemic, denunciation, broadside, fulmination, condemnation, censure, criticism; informal blast; literary philippic.

dicey ▶ **adjective** informal *refueling at sea is a bit dicey in bad weather* **risky,** uncertain, unpredictable, touch-and-go, precarious, unsafe, dangerous, fraught with danger, hazardous, perilous, high-risk, difficult; informal chancy, hairy, iffy, gnarly.
ANTONYMS safe.

dictate ▶ **verb 1** *the president's attempts to dictate policy* **prescribe,** lay down, impose, set down, order, command, decree, ordain, direct, determine, decide, control, govern.
2 *you are in no position to dictate to me* **give orders to,** order around/about, lord it over; lay down the law to; informal boss around/about, push around/about; (**dictate to someone**) throw one's weight around/about.
3 *choice is often dictated by availability* **determine,** control, govern, decide, influence, affect.
▶ **noun** *the dictates of his superior* **order,** command, commandment, decree, edict, ruling, dictum, diktat, directive, direction, instruction, pronouncement, mandate, requirement, stipulation, injunction, demand; formal ordinance; literary behest.

dictator ▶ **noun** *a regime that has survived under one dictator for more than forty years* **autocrat,** absolute ruler, despot, tyrant, oppressor, autarch.

dictatorial ▶ **adjective 1** *a dictatorial regime* **autocratic,** undemocratic, totalitarian, authoritarian, autarchic, despotic, tyrannical, tyrannous, absolute, unrestricted, unlimited, unaccountable, arbitrary; informal iron-fisted.
ANTONYMS democratic.
2 *his dictatorial manner* **domineering,** autocratic, authoritarian, oppressive, imperious, officious, overweening, overbearing, peremptory, dogmatic, high and mighty; severe, strict; informal bossy, high-handed.
ANTONYMS meek.

dictatorship ▶ **noun** *growing up in the shadow of dictatorship* **absolute rule,** undemocratic rule, despotism, tyranny, autocracy, autarchy, authoritarianism, totalitarianism, fascism; oppression, repression.
ANTONYMS democracy.

diction ▶ **noun 1** *his careful diction* **enunciation,** articulation, elocution, locution, pronunciation, speech, intonation, inflection; delivery.
2 *her diction was archaic* **phraseology,** phrasing, turn of phrase, wording, language, usage, vocabulary, terminology, expressions, idioms.

dictionary ▶ **noun** *dictionaries created by Oxford's American lexicographers* **lexicon,** wordbook, word list, glossary; thesaurus.

dictum ▶ **noun 1** *he received the dictum with evident reluctance* **pronouncement,** proclamation, direction, injunction, dictate, command, commandment, order, decree, edict, mandate, diktat.
2 *the old dictum "might is right"* **saying,** maxim, axiom, proverb, adage, aphorism, saw, precept, epigram, motto, truism, commonplace, platitude; expression, phrase, tag.

didactic ▶ **adjective** *the reforming, didactic function of art* **instructive,** instructional, educational, educative, informative, informational, edifying, improving, preceptive, pedagogic, moralistic.

die ▶ **verb 1** *her father died last year* **pass away,** pass on, lose one's life, expire, breathe one's last, meet one's end, meet one's death, lay down one's life, perish, go the way of all flesh, go to one's last resting place, go to meet one's maker, cross the great divide, slip away; informal give up the ghost, kick the bucket, croak, buy it, turn up one's toes, cash in one's chips, bite the big one, check out, buy the farm; archaic depart this life.
ANTONYMS live, survive.
2 *the wind had **died down*** **abate,** subside, drop, lessen, ease (off), let up, moderate, fade, dwindle, peter out, wane, ebb, relent, weaken; melt away, dissolve, vanish, disappear; archaic remit.
ANTONYMS intensify.
3 informal *the engine died* **fail,** cut out, give out, stop, break down, stop working; informal conk out, go kaput, give up the ghost.
4 informal *she's dying to meet you* **long,** yearn, burn, ache; informal itch.

diehard ▶ **adjective** *a diehard hockey fan* **hardline,** reactionary, ultraconservative, conservative, traditionalist, dyed-in-the-wool, intransigent, inflexible, uncompromising, rigid, entrenched, set in one's ways; staunch, steadfast.

diet[1] ▶ **noun** *health problems related to your diet* **selection of food,** food, foodstuffs; informal grub, nosh.
▶ **verb** *she dieted for most of her life* **be on a diet,**

eat sparingly; lose weight, watch one's weight, reduce, slenderize.

diet² ▶ **noun** *the diet's lower house* **legislative assembly,** legislature, congress, senate, parliament, council, assembly.

differ ▶ **verb 1** *the second set of data* ***differed from*** *the first* **contrast with,** be different from, be dissimilar to, be unlike, vary from, diverge from, deviate from, conflict with, run counter to, be incompatible with, be at odds with, go against, contradict.
ANTONYMS resemble.
2 *the two sides differed over this issue* **disagree,** conflict, be at variance, be at odds, be in dispute, not see eye to eye.
ANTONYMS agree.

difference ▶ **noun 1** *the difference between the two sets of data* **dissimilarity,** contrast, distinction, differentiation, variance, variation, divergence, disparity, deviation, polarity, gulf, gap, imbalance, contradiction, contradistinction.
ANTONYMS similarity.
2 *we've had our differences in the past* **disagreement,** difference of opinion, dispute, argument, quarrel, wrangle, contretemps, altercation; informal tiff, set-to, run-in, spat, row.
3 *I am willing to pay the difference* **balance,** remainder, rest, remaining amount, residue.

different ▶ **adjective 1** *people with different lifestyles* **dissimilar,** unalike, unlike, contrasting, contrastive, divergent, differing, varying, disparate; poles apart, incompatible, mismatched, conflicting, clashing.
ANTONYMS similar.
2 *suddenly everything in her life was different* **changed,** altered, transformed, new, unfamiliar, unknown, strange.
ANTONYMS the same.
3 *two different occasions* **distinct,** separate, individual, discrete, independent.
ANTONYMS similar, related.
4 informal *he wanted to try something different* **unusual,** out of the ordinary, unfamiliar, novel, new, fresh, original, unconventional, exotic, uncommon.
ANTONYMS ordinary.

differential ▶ **adjective** technical **1** *the differential achievements of boys and girls* **different,** dissimilar, contrasting, unalike, divergent, disparate, contrastive.
ANTONYMS similar.
2 *the differential features of benign and malignant tumors* **distinctive,** distinguishing.
ANTONYMS similar.

differentiate ▶ **verb 1** *he was unable to differentiate between fantasy and reality* **distinguish,** discriminate, make/draw a distinction, tell the difference, tell apart. See note at DISTINGUISH.
2 *this differentiates their business from all other booksellers* **make different,** distinguish, set apart, single out, separate, mark off.

difficult ▶ **adjective 1** *a very difficult job* **hard,** strenuous, arduous, laborious, tough, onerous, burdensome, demanding, punishing, grueling, back-breaking, exhausting, tiring, fatiguing, wearisome; informal hellish, killing; archaic toilsome.
ANTONYMS easy.
2 *she found math very difficult* **hard,** complicated, complex, involved, impenetrable, unfathomable, over/above one's head, beyond one, puzzling, baffling, perplexing, confusing, mystifying; problematic, intricate, knotty, thorny, ticklish. See note at HARD.
ANTONYMS simple, straightforward.
3 *a difficult child* **troublesome,** tiresome, trying, exasperating, awkward, demanding, perverse, contrary, recalcitrant, unmanageable, obstreperous, unaccommodating, unhelpful, uncooperative, disobliging; hard to please, fussy, finicky; formal refractory.
ANTONYMS accommodating.
4 *you've come at a difficult time* **inconvenient,** awkward, inopportune, unfavorable, unfortunate, inappropriate, unsuitable, untimely, ill-timed.
ANTONYMS convenient.
5 *the family has been through a difficult year* **bad,** tough, grim, dark, black, hard, adverse, distressing; straitened.
ANTONYMS happy.

difficulty ▶ **noun 1** *the difficulty of balancing motherhood with a career* **strain,** trouble, problems, toil, struggle, laboriousness, arduousness; informal hassle, stress.
ANTONYMS ease.
2 *the project has met with one difficulty after another* **problem,** complication, snag, hitch, pitfall, handicap, impediment, hindrance, obstacle, hurdle, stumbling block, obstruction, barrier; informal fly in the ointment, headache; growing pains.
3 (**difficulties**) *Charles got into difficulties* **trouble,** predicament, plight, hard times, dire straits; quandary, dilemma; informal deep water, a fix, a jam, a spot, a scrape, a stew, a hole, a pickle.

diffidence ▶ **noun** *her diffidence was out of place in this outgoing group* **shyness,** bashfulness, modesty, self-effacement, meekness, unassertiveness, timidity, humility, hesitancy, reticence, insecurity, self-doubt, uncertainty, self-consciousness.

diffident ▶ **adjective** *underneath his diffident exterior was a passionate temperament* **shy,** bashful, modest, self-effacing, unassuming, meek, unconfident, unassertive, timid, timorous, humble, shrinking, reticent, hesitant, insecure, self-doubting, doubtful, uncertain, unsure, self-conscious; informal mousy.
ANTONYMS confident.

diffuse ▶ **verb** *such ideas were diffused widely in the 1970s* **spread,** spread around, send out, disseminate, scatter, disperse, distribute, put about, circulate, communicate, purvey, propagate, transmit, broadcast, promulgate. See note at SCATTER.
▶ **adjective 1** *a diffuse community centered on the church* **spread out,** scattered, dispersed, diasporic.
2 *a diffuse narrative* **verbose,** wordy, prolix, long-winded, long-drawn-out, discursive, rambling, wandering, meandering, maundering,

digressive, circuitous, roundabout, circumlocutory, periphrastic.

diffusion ▶ noun *the diffusion of Marxist ideas* **spread,** dissemination, scattering, dispersal, diaspora, distribution, circulation, propagation, transmission, broadcasting, promulgation.

dig ▶ verb **1** *she began to dig the heavy clay soil* **turn over,** work, break up; till, harrow, plow, shovel.
2 *he took a spade and dug a hole* **excavate,** dig out, quarry, hollow out, scoop out, gouge out; cut, bore, tunnel, burrow, mine.
3 *the bodies were hastily* ***dug up*** **exhume,** disinter, unearth.
4 *Winnie dug her elbow into his ribs* **poke,** prod, jab, stab, shove, ram, push, thrust, drive.
5 *he'd been* ***digging into*** *my past* **delve into,** probe into, search into, inquire into, look into, investigate, research, examine, scrutinize, check up on; informal check out.
6 *I* ***dug up*** *some disturbing information* **uncover,** discover, find (out), unearth, dredge up, root out, ferret out, turn up, reveal, bring to light, expose.
7 informal dated *I dig talking with him* See **ENJOY** (sense 1).
▶ noun **1** *a dig in the ribs* **poke,** prod, jab, stab, shove, push.
2 informal *they're always making digs at each other* **snide remark,** cutting remark, jibe, jeer, taunt, sneer, insult, barb, insinuation; informal wisecrack, crack, put-down.

digest ▶ verb *Liz digested this information* **assimilate,** absorb, take in, understand, comprehend, grasp; consider, think about, reflect on, ponder, contemplate, mull over.
▶ noun *a digest of their findings* **summary,** synopsis, abstract, précis, résumé, summation; compilation; informal wrap-up.

dignified ▶ adjective *a dignified and courteous butler* **stately,** noble, courtly, majestic, distinguished, proud, august, lofty, exalted, regal, lordly, imposing, impressive, grand; solemn, serious, grave, formal, proper, ceremonious, decorous, reserved, composed, sedate.

dignify ▶ verb *shall we dignify their arrival with some music?* **ennoble,** enhance, distinguish, add distinction to, honor, grace, exalt, magnify, glorify, elevate.

dignitary ▶ noun *the studio is being visited by a bunch of foreign dignitaries* **worthy,** personage, VIP, grandee, notable, pillar of society, luminary, leading light, big name; informal heavyweight, bigwig, top brass, top dog, big gun, big shot, big cheese, big chief, supremo, big wheel, big kahuna, big enchilada, top banana.

dignity ▶ noun **1** *the dignity of the proceedings* **stateliness,** nobility, majesty, regality, courtliness, augustness, loftiness, lordliness, grandeur; solemnity, gravity, gravitas, formality, decorum, propriety, sedateness.
2 *he had lost his dignity* **self-respect,** pride, self-esteem, self-worth.

digress ▶ verb *I have digressed from the original plan* **deviate,** go off on a tangent, get off the subject, get sidetracked, lose the thread, turn aside/away, depart, drift, stray, wander.

digression ▶ noun *a book full of long digressions* **deviation,** detour, diversion, departure, divergence, excursus; aside, incidental remark.

dilapidated ▶ adjective *a row of dilapidated houses* **run-down,** tumbledown, ramshackle, broken-down; in disrepair, shabby, battered, beat-up, rickety, shaky, unsound, crumbling, in ruins, ruined, decayed, decaying, decrepit; neglected, uncared-for, untended, the worse for wear, falling to pieces, falling apart, gone to rack and ruin, gone to seed.

dilate ▶ verb **1** *her nostrils dilated* **enlarge,** widen, expand, distend.
ANTONYMS contract.
2 *Diane dilated on the joys of her married life* **expatiate,** expound, enlarge, elaborate, speak/write at length.
ANTONYMS contract.

dilatory ▶ adjective **1** *he had been dilatory in appointing an executor* **slow,** tardy, unhurried, sluggish, sluggardly, snaillike, lazy.
ANTONYMS fast, prompt.
2 *dilatory procedural tactics* **delaying,** stalling, temporizing, procrastinating, time-wasting, filibustering.

dilemma ▶ noun *a discussion with a colleague resolved her dilemma* **quandary,** predicament, Catch-22, vicious circle, plight, mess, muddle; difficulty, problem, trouble, perplexity, confusion, conflict; informal no-win situation, fix, tight spot, tight corner, can of worms.

> USAGE
> **dilemma**
> *Dilemma* should be reserved for reference to a predicament in which a difficult choice must be made between undesirable alternatives: *You see his dilemma? If he moves to London, he may never see his parents again. But if he stays in Seattle, he may be giving up the best job offer of his life.* The weakened use of *dilemma* to mean simply "a difficult situation or problem" (*the dilemma of a teacher shortage*) is recorded as early as the first part of the seventeenth century, but many regard this use as unacceptable and it should be avoided in written English.

dilettante ▶ noun *there is no room for the dilettante in this business* **dabbler,** amateur, nonprofessional, nonspecialist, layman, layperson.
ANTONYMS professional.

diligence ▶ noun *they set about their tasks with diligence* **conscientiousness,** assiduousness, assiduity, hard work, application, concentration, effort, care, industriousness, rigor, meticulousness, thoroughness; perseverance, persistence, tenacity, dedication, commitment, tirelessness, indefatigability, doggedness.

diligent ▶ adjective *diligent workers* **industrious,** hard-working, assiduous, conscientious,

particular, punctilious, meticulous, painstaking, rigorous, careful, thorough, sedulous, earnest; persevering, persistent, tenacious, zealous, dedicated, committed, unflagging, untiring, tireless, indefatigable, dogged; archaic laborious. See note at **BUSY**.
ANTONYMS lazy.

dilly-dally ▶ **verb** informal *we can't dilly-dally when there are critical decisions to be made* **waste time,** dally, dawdle, loiter, linger, take one's time, delay, temporize, stall, procrastinate, pussyfoot around, drag one's feet; dither, hesitate, falter, vacillate, waver, hem and haw; informal shilly-shally, lollygag, let the grass grow under one's feet; archaic tarry.
ANTONYMS hurry.

dilute ▶ **verb 1** *strong bleach can be diluted with water* **make weaker,** weaken, water down; thin out, thin; doctor, adulterate; informal cut.
2 *the original plans have been diluted* **weaken,** moderate, tone down, water down.

dim ▶ **adjective 1** *the dim light* **faint,** weak, feeble, soft, pale, dull, subdued, muted.
ANTONYMS bright.
2 *long dim corridors* **dark,** badly lit, ill-lit, underlit, dingy, dismal, gloomy, murky; literary tenebrous.
ANTONYMS bright.
3 *a dim figure* **indistinct,** ill-defined, unclear, vague, shadowy, nebulous, obscured, blurred, blurry, fuzzy.
ANTONYMS distinct.
4 *dim memories* **vague,** imprecise, imperfect, unclear, indistinct, sketchy, hazy, blurred, shadowy.
ANTONYMS clear, distinct.
5 informal *is she a bit dim?* See **STUPID** (sense 1).
6 *their prospects for the future looked dim* **gloomy,** unpromising, unfavorable, discouraging, disheartening, depressing, dispiriting, hopeless.
ANTONYMS encouraging.
▶ **verb 1** *the lights were dimmed* **turn down,** lower, soften, subdue, mute; literary bedim.
ANTONYMS turn up.
2 *my memories have not dimmed with time* **fade,** become vague, dwindle, blur.
ANTONYMS sharpen.
3 *the fighting dimmed hopes of peace* **diminish,** reduce, lessen, weaken, undermine.
ANTONYMS intensify.

dimension ▶ **noun 1** *the dimensions of the room* **size,** measurements, proportions, extent; length, width, breadth, depth, area, volume, capacity; footage, acreage.
2 *the dimension of the problem* **size,** scale, extent, scope, magnitude; importance, significance.
3 *the cultural dimensions of the problem* **aspect,** feature, element, facet, side.

diminish ▶ **verb 1** *the pain will gradually diminish* **decrease,** lessen, decline, reduce, subside, die down, abate, dwindle, fade, slacken off, moderate, let up, ebb, wane, recede, die away/out, peter out; archaic remit.
ANTONYMS increase.
2 *new legislation diminished the courts' authority* **reduce,** decrease, lessen, curtail, cut, cut down/back, constrict, restrict, limit, curb, check; weaken, blunt, erode, undermine, sap.
ANTONYMS increase.
3 *she lost no opportunity to diminish him* **belittle,** disparage, denigrate, defame, deprecate, run down; decry, demean, cheapen, devalue; formal derogate.
ANTONYMS boost.

diminution ▶ **noun** *a diminution of freedom reduces the quality of life* **reduction,** decrease, lessening, decline, dwindling, moderation, fading, fade-out, weakening, ebb.

diminutive ▶ **adjective** *a diminutive breed of parrot* **tiny,** small, little, petite, elfin, minute, miniature, mini, minuscule, compact, pocket, toy, midget, undersized, short; informal teeny, weeny, teeny-weeny, teensy-weensy, itty-bitty, itsy-bitsy, baby, pint-sized, knee-high to a grasshopper, little-bitty; Scottish wee. See note at **SMALL**.
ANTONYMS enormous.

din ▶ **noun** *he shouted above the din* **noise,** racket, rumpus, ruckus, cacophony, babel, hubbub, tumult, uproar, commotion, clatter; shouting, yelling, screaming, caterwauling, clamor, clangor, outcry; informal hullabaloo.
ANTONYMS silence.
▶ **verb 1** *she had had the evils of drink dinned into her* **instill,** inculcate, drive, drum, hammer, drill, ingrain; indoctrinate, brainwash.
2 *the sound dinning in my ears* **blare,** blast, clang, clatter, crash, clamor.

dine ▶ **verb 1** *we dined at a restaurant* **have dinner,** have supper, eat; dated sup, break bread.
2 *they dined on lobster* **eat,** feed on, feast on, banquet on, partake of; informal tuck into, chow down on.

dingy ▶ **adjective** *their secret hiding place was a dingy room in the basement* **gloomy,** dark, dull, badly/poorly lit, murky, dim, dismal, dreary, drab, somber, grim, cheerless; dirty, grimy, shabby, faded, worn, dowdy, seedy, run-down; informal grungy.
ANTONYMS bright.

dinky ▶ **adjective** informal *as usual, he made a dinky contribution* **trifling,** trivial, insignificant, unimportant, negligible, of no account.

dinner ▶ **noun** *dinner will be served on the terrace* **evening meal,** supper, main meal; lunch, midday meal; feast, banquet, dinner party; informal spread; humorous din-din; formal repast.

dip ▶ **verb 1** *he dipped a rag in the water* **immerse,** submerge, plunge, duck, dunk, lower, sink.
2 *the sun dipped below the horizon* **sink,** set, drop, go/drop down, fall, descend; disappear, vanish.
ANTONYMS rise.
3 *the president's popularity has dipped* **decrease,** fall, drop, fall off, decline, diminish, dwindle, slump, plummet, plunge.
ANTONYMS rise, increase.
4 *the road dipped* **slope down,** descend, go down; drop away, fall, sink.
ANTONYMS rise.
5 *you might have to* **dip into** *your savings* **draw on,** use, make use of, have recourse to, spend.
▶ **noun 1** *a relaxing dip in the pool* **swim,** bathe; splash, paddle.

2 *give the fish a ten-minute dip in a salt bath* **immersion,** plunge, ducking, dunking.
3 *chicken satay with peanut dip* **sauce,** dressing.
4 *the hedge at the bottom of the dip* **slope,** incline, decline, descent; hollow, concavity, depression, basin, indentation.
5 *a dip in sales* **decrease,** fall, drop, downturn, decline, falling-off, slump, reduction, diminution, ebb.

diplomacy ▶ noun **1** *diplomacy failed to win them independence* **statesmanship,** statecraft, negotiation(s), discussion(s), talks, dialogue; international relations, foreign affairs.
2 *Jack's quiet diplomacy* **tact,** tactfulness, sensitivity, discretion, subtlety, finesse, delicacy, savoir faire, politeness, thoughtfulness, care, judiciousness, prudence.

diplomat ▶ noun *a British diplomat working in Germany* **ambassador,** attaché, consul, chargé d'affaires, envoy, nuncio, emissary, plenipotentiary; archaic legate.

diplomatic ▶ adjective **1** *diplomatic activity* **ambassadorial,** consular.
2 *he tried to be diplomatic* **tactful,** sensitive, subtle, delicate, polite, discreet, thoughtful, careful, judicious, prudent, politic, clever, skillful.
ANTONYMS tactless.

dire ▶ adjective **1** *the dire economic situation* **terrible,** dreadful, appalling, frightful, awful, atrocious, grim, alarming; grave, serious, disastrous, calamitous, ruinous, hopeless, irretrievable, wretched, desperate, parlous; formal grievous.
2 *he was in dire need of help* **urgent,** desperate, pressing, crying, sore, grave, serious, extreme, acute, drastic.
3 *dire warnings of fuel shortages* **ominous,** gloomy, grim, dismal, unpropitious, inauspicious, unfavorable, pessimistic.

direct ▶ adjective **1** *the most direct route* **straight,** undeviating, unswerving; shortest, quickest.
2 *a direct flight* **nonstop,** unbroken, uninterrupted, through.
3 *he is very direct* **frank,** candid, straightforward, honest, open, blunt, plain-spoken, outspoken, forthright, downright, no-nonsense, matter-of-fact, not afraid to call a spade a spade; informal upfront.
4 *direct contact with the president* **face to face,** personal, immediate, firsthand.
5 *a direct quotation* **verbatim,** word for word, to the letter, faithful, exact, precise, accurate, correct.
6 *the direct opposite* **exact,** absolute, complete, diametrical.
▶ verb **1** *an economic elite directed the nation's affairs* **manage,** govern, run, administer, control, conduct, handle, be in charge/control of, preside over, lead, head, rule, be at the helm of; supervise, superintend, oversee, regulate, orchestrate, coordinate; informal run the show, call the shots, be in the driver's seat.
2 *was that remark directed at me?* **aim at,** target at, address to, intend for, mean for, design for.
3 *a man in uniform directed them to the hall* **give directions,** show the way, guide, lead, conduct, accompany, usher, escort.
4 *the judge directed the jury to return a 'not guilty' verdict* **instruct,** tell, command, order, charge, require; literary bid.

direction ▶ noun **1** *a northerly direction* **way,** route, course, line, run, bearing, orientation.
2 *the direction of my research* **orientation,** inclination, leaning, tendency, bent, bias, preference; drift, tack, attitude, tone, tenor, mood, current, trend.
3 *his direction of the project* **administration,** management, conduct, handling, running, supervision, superintendence, regulation, orchestration; control, command, rule, leadership, guidance.
4 *explicit directions about nursing care* **instruction,** order, command, prescription, rule, regulation, requirement.

directive ▶ noun *a directive from the front office* **instruction,** direction, command, order, charge, injunction, prescription, rule, ruling, regulation, law, dictate, decree, dictum, edict, mandate, fiat; formal ordinance.

directly ▶ adverb **1** *they flew directly to New York* **straight,** right, as the crow flies, by a direct route.
2 *I went directly after breakfast* **immediately,** at once, instantly, right away, straightaway, posthaste, without delay, without hesitation, forthwith; quickly, speedily, promptly; informal pronto.
3 *the houses directly opposite* **exactly,** right, immediately; diametrically; informal bang.
4 *she spoke simply and directly* **frankly,** candidly, openly, bluntly, forthrightly, without beating around the bush.

director ▶ noun *the director of the museum* **administrator,** manager, chairman, chairwoman, chairperson, chair, head, chief, principal, leader, governor, president; managing director, chief executive (officer), CEO; supervisor, controller, overseer; informal boss, kingpin, top dog, head honcho, numero uno.

dirge ▶ noun *a lone bagpiper played the woeful dirge* **elegy,** lament, burial hymn, threnody, requiem, funeral march; Irish keen.

dirt ▶ noun **1** *his face was streaked with dirt* **grime,** filth; dust, soot, smut; muck, mud, mire, sludge, slime, ooze, dross; smudges, stains; informal crud, yuck, grunge; Brit. gunge.
2 *the packed dirt of the road* **earth,** soil, loam, clay, silt; ground.
3 informal *dog dirt* See EXCREMENT.
4 informal *they tried to dig up dirt on the president* **a scandal,** gossip, revelations, a rumor, rumors; information.

dirty ▶ adjective **1** *a dirty sweatshirt | dirty water* **soiled,** grimy, grubby, filthy, mucky, stained, unwashed, greasy, smeared, smeary, spotted, smudged, cloudy, muddy, dusty, sooty; unclean, sullied, impure, tarnished, polluted, contaminated, defiled, foul, unhygienic, unsanitary; informal cruddy, yucky, icky, grotty, grungy; literary befouled, besmirched, begrimed.
ANTONYMS clean.
2 *a dirty joke* **indecent,** obscene, rude, naughty, vulgar, smutty, coarse, crude, filthy, bawdy, suggestive, ribald, racy, salacious, risqué,

offensive, off-color, lewd, pornographic, explicit, X-rated; informal blue, triple-X, XXX; euphemistic adult.
ANTONYMS clean.
3 *dirty tricks* **dishonest,** deceitful, unscrupulous, dishonorable, unsporting, ungentlemanly, below the belt, unfair, unethical, unprincipled; crooked, double-dealing, underhanded, sly, crafty, devious, sneaky.
ANTONYMS honest, decent.
4 informal *a dirty cheat* **despicable,** contemptible, hateful, vile, low, mean, unworthy, worthless, beyond contempt, sordid; informal rotten; archaic scurvy.
ANTONYMS trustworthy, decent.
5 *a dirty look* **malevolent,** resentful, hostile, black, dark; angry, cross, indignant, annoyed, disapproving; informal peeved.
▶ **verb** *he dirtied her nice clean towels* **soil,** stain, muddy, blacken, mess up, mark, spatter, bespatter, smudge, smear, splatter; sully, pollute, foul, defile; literary befoul, besmirch, begrime.
ANTONYMS clean.

disability ▶ **noun** *my disability makes getting into bed a slow process* **handicap,** disablement, incapacity, impairment, infirmity, defect, abnormality; condition, disorder, affliction.

disable ▶ **verb 1** *an injury that could disable somebody for life* **incapacitate,** put out of action, debilitate; handicap, cripple, lame, maim, immobilize, paralyze.
2 *the bomb squad disabled the device* **deactivate,** defuse, disarm.
3 *he was disabled from holding public office* **disqualify,** prevent, preclude.

disabled ▶ **adjective 1** *a disabled athlete* **handicapped,** incapacitated; debilitated, infirm, out of action; crippled, lame, paralyzed, immobilized, bedridden, paraplegic, quadriplegic, in a wheelchair; euphemistic physically challenged, differently abled.
ANTONYMS able-bodied.
2 *a disabled cargo ship* **broken down,** out of service, out of commission, wrecked.
ANTONYMS functioning.

disabuse ▶ **verb** *it isn't easy to disabuse people of something they've been taught to believe in* **disillusion about,** undeceive about, set straight on/about, open someone's eyes about, correct on, enlighten on/about, disenchant about, shatter someone's illusions about.

disadvantage ▶ **noun** *the long commute is a big disadvantage of this job* **drawback,** snag, downside, stumbling block, fly in the ointment, catch, hindrance, obstacle, impediment; flaw, defect, weakness, fault, handicap, con, trouble, difficulty, problem, complication, nuisance; informal minus.
ANTONYMS benefit.

disadvantaged ▶ **adjective** *disadvantaged families will not be helped by these measures* **deprived,** underprivileged, depressed, in need, needy, poor, impoverished, indigent, hard up.

disadvantageous ▶ **adjective** *this puts us in a disadvantageous position* **unfavorable,** adverse, unfortunate, unlucky, bad; detrimental, prejudicial, deleterious, harmful, damaging, injurious, hurtful; inconvenient, inopportune, ill-timed, untimely, inexpedient.

disaffected ▶ **adjective** *a plot by disaffected soldiers* **dissatisfied,** disgruntled, discontented, malcontent, frustrated, alienated; disloyal, rebellious, mutinous, seditious, dissident, up in arms; hostile, antagonistic, unfriendly. See note at **SOLITUDE**.
ANTONYMS contented.

disagree ▶ **verb 1** *no one was willing to disagree with him* **take issue with,** challenge, contradict, oppose; be at variance with, be at odds with, not see eye to eye with, differ with, dissent from, be in dispute with, debate with, argue with, quarrel with, wrangle with, clash with, be at loggerheads with, cross swords with, lock horns with; formal gainsay.
2 *their accounts disagree on details* **differ,** be dissimilar, be different, vary, diverge; contradict each other, conflict, clash, contrast.
3 *the spicy food disagreed with her* **make ill,** make unwell, nauseate, sicken, upset.

disagreeable ▶ **adjective 1** *a disagreeable smell* **unpleasant,** displeasing, nasty, offensive, off-putting, obnoxious, objectionable, horrible, horrid, dreadful, frightful, abominable, odious, repugnant, repulsive, repellent, revolting, disgusting, foul, vile, nauseating, sickening, unpalatable.
ANTONYMS pleasant.
2 *a disagreeable man* **bad-tempered,** ill-tempered, curmudgeonly, cross, crabbed, irritable, grumpy, peevish, sullen, prickly; unfriendly, unpleasant, nasty, mean, mean-spirited, ill-natured, rude, surly, discourteous, impolite, brusque, abrupt, churlish, disobliging.
ANTONYMS pleasant.

disagreement ▶ **noun 1** *there was some disagreement over possible solutions* **dissent,** dispute, difference of opinion, variance, controversy, discord, contention, division.
2 *a heated disagreement* **argument,** debate, quarrel, wrangle, squabble, falling-out, altercation, dispute, disputation, war of words, contretemps; informal tiff, set-to, blowup, spat, row.
3 *the disagreement between the results of the two assessments* **difference,** dissimilarity, variation, variance, discrepancy, disparity, divergence, deviation, nonconformity; incompatibility, contradiction, conflict, clash, contrast.

disallow ▶ **verb** *Nguyen's testimony will be disallowed* **reject,** refuse, dismiss, say no to; ban, bar, block, debar, forbid, prohibit; cancel, invalidate, overrule, quash, overturn, countermand, reverse, throw out, set aside; informal give the thumbs down to, veto, nix. See note at **PROHIBIT**.

disappear ▶ **verb 1** *by 4 o'clock the mist had disappeared* **vanish,** pass from sight, be lost to view/sight, recede from view; fade (away), melt away, clear, dissolve, disperse, evaporate, dematerialize; literary evanesce.
ANTONYMS materialize.
2 *this way of life has disappeared* **die out,** die, cease to exist, come to an end, end, pass away, pass into oblivion, perish, vanish.

ANTONYMS survive.

disappoint ▶ verb **1** *I'm sorry to have disappointed you* **let down,** fail, dissatisfy, dash someone's hopes; upset, dismay, sadden, disenchant, disillusion, shatter someone's illusions, disabuse.
ANTONYMS please, satisfy.
2 *his hopes were disappointed* **thwart,** frustrate, foil, dash, put a damper on; informal throw cold water on.
ANTONYMS fulfill.

disappointed ▶ adjective *it was hard to look into those disappointed faces* **upset,** saddened, let down, cast down, disheartened, downhearted, downcast, depressed, dispirited, discouraged, despondent, dismayed, crestfallen, distressed, chagrined; disenchanted, disillusioned; displeased, discontented, dissatisfied, frustrated, disgruntled; informal choked, bummed (out), miffed, cut up.
ANTONYMS pleased.

disappointing ▶ adjective *a pretty good movie up until the disappointing ending* **regrettable,** unfortunate, sorry, discouraging, disheartening, dispiriting, depressing, dismaying, upsetting, saddening; unsatisfactory; informal not all it's cracked up to be.

disappointment ▶ noun **1** *his disappointment in the outcome was obvious* **sadness,** regret, dismay, sorrow; dispiritedness, despondency, distress, chagrin; disenchantment, disillusionment; displeasure, dissatisfaction, disgruntlement.
ANTONYMS satisfaction.
2 *the trip was a bit of a disappointment* **letdown,** nonevent, anticlimax, washout; informal bummer.

disapproval ▶ noun *their strong disapproval of the law* **disapprobation,** objection, dislike; dissatisfaction, disfavor, displeasure, distaste; criticism, censure, condemnation, denunciation, deprecation; informal thumbs down.

disapprove ▶ verb **1** *he disapproved of gamblers* **object to,** have a poor opinion of, look down one's nose at, take exception to, dislike, take a dim view of, look askance at, frown on, be against, not believe in; deplore, criticize, censure, condemn, denounce, decry, deprecate.
2 *the board disapproved the plan* **reject,** veto, refuse, turn down, disallow, throw out, dismiss, rule against; informal nix.

disarm ▶ verb **1** *the UN must disarm the country* **demilitarize,** demobilize.
2 *the militia refused to disarm* **lay down one's arms,** demilitarize; literary beat one's swords into plowshares.
3 *police disarmed the bomb* **defuse,** disable, deactivate, put out of action, make harmless.
4 *the warmth in his voice disarmed her* **win over,** charm, persuade, thaw; mollify, appease, placate, pacify, conciliate, propitiate.

disarmament ▶ noun *the public wanted peace and disarmament* **demilitarization,** demobilization, decommissioning; arms reduction, arms limitation, arms control; the zero option.

disarming ▶ adjective *a disarming smile* **winning,** charming, irresistible, persuasive, beguiling; conciliatory, mollifying.

disarrange ▶ verb *every year the festival gets bigger, and every year the town gets more disarranged* **disorder,** throw into disarray/disorder, put out of place, disorganize, disturb, displace; mess up, make untidy, make a mess of, jumble, mix up, muddle, turn upside-down, scatter; dishevel, tousle, rumple; informal turn topsy-turvy, make a shambles of, muss up.

disarray ▶ noun *the room was in disarray* **disorder,** confusion, chaos, untidiness, disorganization, dishevelment, mess, muddle, clutter, jumble, tangle, shambles. See note at JUMBLE.
ANTONYMS tidiness.

disaster ▶ noun **1** *a subway disaster* **catastrophe,** calamity, cataclysm, tragedy, act of God, holocaust; accident.
2 *a string of personal disasters* **misfortune,** mishap, misadventure, mischance, setback, reversal, stroke of bad luck, blow.
ANTONYMS blessing.
3 informal *the film was a disaster* **failure,** fiasco, catastrophe, debacle; informal flop, megaflop, dud, bomb, washout, dog, turkey, dead loss.
ANTONYMS success.

disastrous ▶ adjective *a series of disastrous floods* **catastrophic,** calamitous, cataclysmic, tragic; devastating, ruinous, harmful, dire, terrible, awful, shocking, appalling, dreadful; black, dark, unfortunate, unlucky, ill-fated, ill-starred, inauspicious; formal grievous.

disavowal ▶ noun *it's a complete disavowal of responsibility* **denial,** rejection, repudiation, renunciation, disclaimer.

disband ▶ verb *the unit was scheduled to disband* **break up,** disperse, demobilize, dissolve, scatter, separate, go separate ways, part company.
ANTONYMS assemble.

disbelief ▶ noun **1** *she stared at him in disbelief* **incredulity,** astonishment, amazement, surprise, incredulousness; skepticism, doubt, doubtfulness, dubiousness; cynicism, suspicion, distrust, mistrust; formal dubiety.
2 *I guess I'll burn in hell for my disbelief* **atheism,** nonbelief, unbelief, godlessness, irreligion, agnosticism, nihilism.

disbelieve ▶ verb *we've learned to disbelieve most of Hubert's explanations* **not believe,** give no credence to, discredit, discount, doubt, distrust, mistrust, be incredulous, be unconvinced; reject, repudiate, question, challenge; informal take with a pinch of salt.

disbeliever ▶ noun *they promised to pray for us disbelievers* **unbeliever,** nonbeliever, atheist, nihilist; skeptic, doubter, agnostic, doubting Thomas, cynic.

disburse ▶ verb *the proceeds were disbursed weekly* **pay out,** spend, expend, dole out, dish out, hand out, part with, donate, give; informal fork out/over, shell out, lay out, ante up, pony up.

discard ▶ verb *his old suit has been discarded* **dispose of,** throw away/out, get rid of, toss out,

jettison, scrap, dispense with, cast aside/off, throw on the scrap heap; reject, repudiate, abandon, drop, have done with, shed; informal chuck, dump, ditch, junk, trash, deep-six.
ANTONYMS keep.

discern ▶ verb *they could discern a slender figure, probably a woman, slowly approaching* **perceive,** make out, pick out, detect, recognize, notice, observe, see, spot; identify, determine, distinguish; literary descry, espy. See note at DISTINGUISH.

discernible ▶ adjective *in the fog our flares may be barely discernible* **visible,** detectable, noticeable, perceptible, observable, distinguishable, recognizable, identifiable; apparent, evident, distinct, appreciable, clear, obvious, manifest, conspicuous.

discerning ▶ adjective *some real treasures for the discerning collector* **discriminating,** judicious, shrewd, clever, astute, intelligent, sharp, selective, sophisticated, tasteful, sensitive, perceptive, percipient, perspicacious, wise, aware, knowing; informal clueful.

discharge ▶ verb **1** *after his third violation, Vance was discharged* **dismiss,** eject, expel, throw out, give someone notice; release, let go, fire, terminate; Military cashier; informal sack, give someone the sack, boot out, give someone the boot, turf out, give someone their marching orders, show someone the door, send packing, pink-slip, give some the (old) heave-ho.
ANTONYMS recruit, engage.
2 *he was discharged from prison* **release,** free, set free, let go, liberate, let out.
ANTONYMS imprison.
3 *oil is routinely discharged from ships* **send out,** release, eject, let out, pour out, void, give off.
4 *the swelling will burst and discharge pus* **emit,** exude, ooze, leak.
ANTONYMS absorb.
5 *he accidentally discharged the gun* **fire,** shoot, let off; set off, trigger, explode, detonate.
6 *the ferry was discharging passengers* **unload,** offload, put off; remove.
ANTONYMS load.
7 *they discharged their duties efficiently* **carry out,** perform, execute, conduct, do; fulfill, accomplish, achieve, complete.
8 *the executor must discharge the funeral expenses* **pay,** pay off, settle, clear, honor, meet, liquidate, defray, make good; informal square.
▶ noun **1** *his discharge from the service* **dismissal,** release, removal, ejection, expulsion; Military cashiering; informal the sack, the boot, the ax, a/the pink slip.
2 *her discharge from prison* **release,** liberation.
3 *a discharge of diesel oil into the river* **leak,** leakage, emission, release, flow.
4 *a watery discharge from the eyes* **emission,** secretion, excretion, seepage, suppuration; pus, matter; Medicine exudate.
5 *a single discharge of his gun* **shot,** firing, blast; explosion, detonation.
6 *the discharge of their duties* **carrying out,** performance, performing, execution, conduct; fulfillment, accomplishment, completion.
7 *the discharge of all debts* **payment,** repayment, settlement, clearance, meeting, liquidation.

disciple ▶ noun **1** *the disciples of Jesus* **apostle,** follower.
2 *a disciple of Rousseau* **follower,** adherent, believer, admirer, devotee, acolyte, votary; pupil, student, learner; upholder, supporter, advocate, proponent, apologist.

disciplinarian ▶ noun *Mr. Chips was the antithesis of the stern disciplinarian that the boys had come to expect* **martinet,** hard taskmaster, authoritarian, stickler for discipline; tyrant, despot, ramrod; informal slave driver.

discipline ▶ noun **1** *a lack of proper parental discipline* **control,** training, teaching, instruction, regulation, direction, order, authority, rule, strictness, a firm hand; routine, regimen, drill, drilling.
2 *he was able to maintain discipline among his men* **good behavior,** orderliness, control, obedience; self-control, self-discipline, self-government, self-restraint.
3 *sociology is a fairly new discipline* **field (of study),** branch of knowledge, subject, area; specialty.
▶ verb **1** *she had disciplined herself to ignore the pain* **train,** drill, teach, school, coach; regiment.
2 *she learned to discipline her emotions* **control,** restrain, regulate, govern, keep in check, check, curb, keep a tight rein on, rein in, bridle, tame, bring into line.
3 *he was disciplined by management* **punish,** penalize, bring to book; reprimand, rebuke, reprove, chastise, upbraid; informal dress down, give someone a dressing-down, rap on/over the knuckles, give someone a roasting, call (up) on the carpet; formal castigate.

disclaimer ▶ noun **1** *a disclaimer of responsibility* **denial,** refusal, rejection.
ANTONYMS acceptance, acknowledgment.
2 Law *a deed of disclaimer* **renunciation,** relinquishment, resignation, abdication; repudiation, abjuration, disavowal.

disclose ▶ verb **1** *the information must not be disclosed to anyone* **reveal,** make known, divulge, tell, impart, communicate, pass on, vouchsafe; release, make public, broadcast, publish, report, unveil; leak, betray, let slip, let drop, give away; informal let on, blab, spill the beans, let the cat out of the bag; archaic discover, unbosom.
ANTONYMS conceal.
2 *exploratory surgery disclosed an aneurysm* **uncover,** reveal, show, expose, bring to light.

disclosure ▶ noun **1** *she was embarrassed by this unexpected disclosure* **revelation,** declaration, announcement, news, report; leak.
2 *the disclosure of official information* **publishing,** broadcasting; revelation, communication, release, uncovering, unveiling, exposure, exposé; leakage.

discolor ▶ verb *smoke will discolor the fabric* **stain,** mark, soil, dirty, streak, smear, spot, tarnish, sully, spoil, mar, blemish; blacken, char; fade, bleach.

discoloration ▶ noun *a brown discoloration on the skin* **stain,** mark, streak, spot, blotch, tarnishing; blemish, flaw, defect, bruise, contusion; birthmark, nevus; liver spot, age spot; informal splotch.

discomfit ▶ verb *her kiss on the cheek discomfited him even more* **embarrass,** abash, disconcert, discompose, discomfort, take aback, unsettle, unnerve, put someone off their game, ruffle, confuse, fluster, agitate, disorient, upset, disturb, perturb, distress; chagrin, mortify; informal faze, rattle, discombobulate.

discomfiture ▶ noun *I admit we were somewhat amused by his discomfiture* **embarrassment,** unease, uneasiness, awkwardness, discomfort, discomposure, abashment, confusion, agitation, nervousness, disorientation, perturbation, distress; chagrin, mortification, shame, humiliation; informal discombobulation.

discomfort ▶ noun 1 *abdominal discomfort* **pain,** aches and pains, soreness, tenderness, irritation, stiffness; ache, twinge, pang, throb, cramp.
2 *the discomforts of life at sea* **inconvenience,** difficulty, bother, nuisance, vexation, drawback, disadvantage, trouble, problem, trial, tribulation, hardship; informal hassle.
3 *she was unable to hide her discomfort* **embarrassment,** discomfiture, unease, uneasiness, awkwardness, discomposure, confusion, nervousness, perturbation, distress, anxiety; chagrin, mortification, shame, humiliation.
▶ verb *his purpose was to discomfort the president* See DISCOMFIT.

discomposure ▶ noun *she laughed to cover her discomposure* **agitation,** discomfiture, discomfort, uneasiness, unease, confusion, disorientation, perturbation, distress, nervousness; anxiety, worry, consternation, disquiet, disquietude; embarrassment, abashment, chagrin, loss of face; informal discombobulation.

disconcert ▶ verb *Sheila's unexpected appearance disconcerted him* **unsettle,** discomfit, throw/catch off balance, take aback, rattle, unnerve, disorient, perturb, disturb, perplex, confuse, bewilder, baffle, fluster, ruffle, shake, upset, agitate, worry, dismay, surprise, take by surprise, startle, put someone off (their game), distract; informal throw, faze, discombobulate.

disconcerting ▶ adjective *the intense scrutiny was disconcerting* **unsettling,** unnerving, discomfiting, disturbing, perturbing, troubling, upsetting, worrying, alarming, distracting, off-putting; confusing, bewildering, perplexing.

disconnect ▶ verb 1 *the trucks were disconnected from the train* **detach,** disengage, uncouple, decouple, unhook, unhitch, undo, unfasten, unyoke.
ANTONYMS attach.
2 *she felt as if she were disconnected from the real world* **separate,** cut off, divorce, sever, isolate, divide, part, disengage, dissociate, disassociate, remove.
3 *an engineer disconnected the power source* **deactivate,** shut off, turn off, switch off, unplug.

disconnected ▶ adjective 1 *a world that seemed disconnected from reality* **detached,** separate, separated, divorced, cut off, isolated, dissociated, disengaged; apart.
2 *a disconnected narrative* **disjointed,** incoherent, garbled, confused, jumbled, mixed up, rambling, wandering, disorganized, uncoordinated, ill-thought-out.

disconsolate ▶ adjective *his partner had to face the disconsolate investors on his own* **sad,** unhappy, doleful, woebegone, dejected, downcast, downhearted, despondent, dispirited, crestfallen, cast down, depressed, down, disappointed, disheartened, discouraged, demoralized, low-spirited, forlorn, in the doldrums, melancholy, miserable, long-faced, glum, gloomy; informal blue, choked, down in/at the mouth, down in the dumps, in a blue funk; literary dolorous.
ANTONYMS cheerful.

discontent ▶ noun *the workers' discontent could no longer be overlooked* **dissatisfaction,** disaffection, discontentment, discontentedness, disgruntlement, grievances, unhappiness, displeasure, bad feelings, resentment, envy; restlessness, unrest, uneasiness, unease, frustration, irritation, annoyance; informal a chip on one's shoulder.
ANTONYMS satisfaction.

discontented ▶ adjective *discontented parents attended the meeting in record numbers* **dissatisfied,** disgruntled, fed up, disaffected, discontent, malcontent, unhappy, aggrieved, displeased, resentful; restless, frustrated, irritated, annoyed; informal fed up (to the teeth), teed off, ticked off.
ANTONYMS satisfied.

discontinue ▶ verb *the ferry service was discontinued* **stop,** end, terminate, put an end to, put a stop to, finish, call a halt to, cancel, drop, abandon, dispense with, do away with, get rid of, ax, abolish; suspend, interrupt, break off, withdraw; informal cut, pull the plug on, scrap, nix.

discord ▶ noun 1 *stress resulting from family discord* **strife,** conflict, friction, hostility, antagonism, antipathy, enmity, bad feeling, ill feeling, bad blood, argument, quarreling, squabbling, bickering, wrangling, feuding, contention, disagreement, dissension, dispute, difference of opinion, disunity, division, opposition; infighting.
ANTONYMS accord, harmony.
2 *the music faded in discord* **dissonance,** discordance, disharmony, cacophony.
ANTONYMS harmony.

discordant ▶ adjective 1 *the messages from Washington and Ottawa were discordant* **different,** in disagreement, at variance, at odds, divergent, discrepant, contradictory, contrary, in conflict, conflicting, opposite, opposed, opposing, clashing; incompatible, inconsistent, irreconcilable.
ANTONYMS harmonious, compatible.
2 *discordant sounds* **inharmonious,** tuneless, off-key, dissonant, harsh, jarring, grating, jangling, jangly, strident, shrill, screeching, screechy, cacophonous; sharp, flat.
ANTONYMS harmonious, dulcet.

discount ▶ noun *students get a 10 percent discount* **reduction,** deduction, markdown, price cut, cut, rebate.

▶ verb 1 *I'd heard rumors, but I discounted them* **disregard,** pay no attention to, take no notice of, take no account of, dismiss, ignore, overlook, disbelieve, reject; informal take with a pinch of salt, pooh-pooh.
ANTONYMS believe.
2 *the actual price is discounted in many stores* **reduce,** mark down, cut, lower; informal knock down.
ANTONYMS increase.
3 *show your card and they'll discount 40 percent* **deduct,** take off, rebate; informal knock off, slash off.
ANTONYMS add.

discourage ▶ verb 1 *we want to discourage children **from** smoking* **deter from,** dissuade from, disincline from, put off, talk out of; advise against, urge against; archaic discountenance from.
ANTONYMS encourage.
2 *she was discouraged by his hostile tone* **dishearten,** dispirit, demoralize, cast down, depress, disappoint; put off, unnerve, daunt, intimidate, cow, crush.
ANTONYMS encourage, hearten.
3 *he sought to discourage further conversation* **prevent,** stop, put a stop to, avert, fend off, stave off, ward off; inhibit, hinder, check, curb, put a damper on, throw cold water on.
ANTONYMS encourage.

discouraged ▶ adjective *Doug must be feeling pretty discouraged* **disheartened,** dispirited, demoralized, deflated, disappointed, let down, disconsolate, despondent, dejected, cast down, downcast, depressed, crestfallen, dismayed, low-spirited, gloomy, glum, pessimistic, unenthusiastic; put off, daunted, intimidated, cowed, crushed; informal down in/at the mouth, down in the dumps, unenthused, bummed.

discouraging ▶ adjective *most reports from the area are discouraging* **depressing,** demoralizing, disheartening, dispiriting, disappointing, gloomy, off-putting; unfavorable, unpromising, inauspicious.
ANTONYMS encouraging.

discourse ▶ noun 1 *they prolonged their discourse outside the door* **discussion,** conversation, talk, dialogue, conference, debate, consultation; parley, powwow, chat, confab; formal confabulation, colloquy.
2 *a discourse on critical theory* **essay,** treatise, dissertation, paper, study, critique, monograph, disquisition, tract; lecture, address, speech, oration; sermon, homily.

▶ verb 1 *he discoursed at length on his favorite topic* **hold forth,** expatiate, pontificate; talk, give a talk, give a speech, lecture, sermonize, preach; informal spout, sound off; formal perorate.
2 *Edward was discoursing with his friends* **converse,** talk, speak, debate, confer, consult, parley, chat.

discourteous ▶ adjective *it would be discourteous to ignore her* **rude,** impolite, ill-mannered, bad-mannered, disrespectful, uncivil, unmannerly, unchivalrous, ungentlemanly, unladylike, ill-bred, churlish, boorish, crass, ungracious, graceless, uncouth; insolent, impudent, cheeky, audacious, presumptuous; curt, brusque, blunt, offhand, unceremonious, short, sharp; ignorant.
ANTONYMS polite.

discourtesy ▶ noun *these parents seemed unfazed by the discourtesy of their children* **rudeness,** impoliteness, bad manners, incivility, disrespect, ungraciousness, churlishness, boorishness, ill breeding, uncouthness, crassness; insolence, impudence, impertinence; curtness, brusqueness, abruptness.

discover ▶ verb 1 *firemen discovered a body in the debris* **find,** locate, come across/upon, stumble on, chance on, light on, bring to light, uncover, unearth, turn up; track down.
2 *eventually, I discovered the truth* **find out,** learn, realize, recognize, fathom, see, ascertain, work out, dig up/out, ferret out, root out; informal figure out, dope out.
3 *scientists discovered a new way of dating fossil crustaceans* **hit on,** come up with, invent, originate, devise, design, contrive, conceive of; pioneer, develop.

discoverer ▶ noun *the discoverer of penicillin* **originator,** inventor, creator, deviser, designer; pioneer, explorer.

discovery ▶ noun 1 *the discovery of the body* **finding,** location, uncovering, unearthing.
2 *the discovery that she was pregnant* **realization,** recognition; revelation, disclosure.
3 *the discovery of new drugs* **invention,** origination, devising; pioneering.
4 *he failed to take out a patent on his discoveries* **find,** finding; invention, breakthrough, innovation.

discredit ▶ verb 1 *an attempt to discredit him and his company* **bring into disrepute,** disgrace, dishonor, damage the reputation of, blacken the name of, put/show in a bad light, reflect badly on, compromise, stigmatize, smear, tarnish, taint, slur.
2 *that theory has been discredited* **disprove,** invalidate, explode, refute; informal debunk, poke holes in; formal confute.

▶ noun 1 *crimes that brought discredit on the administration* **dishonor,** disrepute, disgrace, shame, humiliation, ignominy, infamy, notoriety; censure, blame, reproach, opprobrium; stigma; dated disesteem.
ANTONYMS honor.
2 *the ships were a discredit to the country* **disgrace,** source of shame, reproach.
ANTONYMS glory.

discreet ▶ adjective 1 *discreet inquiries* **careful,** circumspect, cautious, wary, chary, guarded; tactful, diplomatic, prudent, judicious, strategic, politic, delicate, sensitive, kid-glove.
2 *discreet lighting* **unobtrusive,** inconspicuous, subtle, low-key, understated, subdued, muted, soft, restrained.

discrepancy ▶ noun *the discrepancy between the two sets of figures* **difference,** disparity, variance, variation, deviation, divergence, disagreement, inconsistency, dissimilarity, mismatch, discordance, incompatibility, conflict.
ANTONYMS correspondence.

discrete ▶ adjective *discrete units of sound*

separate, distinct, individual, detached, unattached, disconnected, discontinuous, disjunct, disjoined.
ANTONYMS connected.

discretion ▶ noun 1 *you can rely on his discretion* **circumspection,** carefulness, caution, wariness, chariness, guardedness; **tact,** tactfulness, diplomacy, delicacy, sensitivity, prudence, judiciousness.
2 *his sentence would be determined at the discretion of the court* **choice,** option, preference, disposition, volition; pleasure, liking, wish, will, inclination, desire.

discretionary ▶ adjective *a discretionary service charge* **optional,** voluntary, at one's discretion, elective.
ANTONYMS compulsory.

discriminate ▶ verb 1 *he cannot discriminate between fact and fiction* **differentiate,** distinguish, draw a distinction, tell the difference, tell apart; separate, separate the sheep from the goats, separate the wheat from the chaff. See note at DISTINGUISH.
2 *existing employment policies discriminate against women* **be biased against,** be prejudiced against; treat differently, treat unfairly, put at a disadvantage, single out; victimize.

discriminating ▶ adjective *she had discriminating tastes* **discerning,** perceptive, astute, shrewd, judicious, perspicacious, insightful, keen; selective, fastidious, tasteful, refined, sensitive, cultivated, cultured, artistic, aesthetic.
ANTONYMS indiscriminate.

discrimination ▶ noun 1 *racial discrimination* **prejudice,** bias, bigotry, intolerance, narrow-mindedness, unfairness, inequity, favoritism, one-sidedness, partisanship; sexism, chauvinism, misogyny, racism, racialism, anti-Semitism, heterosexism, ageism, classism; in South Africa historical apartheid.
ANTONYMS impartiality.
2 *a bland man with no discrimination* **discernment,** judgment, perception, perceptiveness, perspicacity, acumen, astuteness, shrewdness, judiciousness, insight; selectivity, (good) taste, fastidiousness, refinement, sensitivity, cultivation, culture.

discriminatory ▶ adjective *the decision against Ms. Rodriquez was discriminatory* **prejudicial,** biased, prejudiced, preferential, unfair, unjust, invidious, inequitable, weighted, one-sided, partisan; sexist, chauvinistic, chauvinist, racist, racialist, anti-Semitic, ageist, classist.
ANTONYMS impartial.

discursive ▶ adjective 1 *dull, discursive prose* **rambling,** digressive, meandering, wandering, maundering, diffuse, long, lengthy, wordy, verbose, long-winded, prolix; circuitous, roundabout, circumlocutory; informal waffly.
ANTONYMS concise.
2 *an elegant discursive style* **fluent,** flowing, fluid, eloquent, expansive.
ANTONYMS terse.

discuss ▶ verb 1 *I discussed the matter with my wife* **talk over,** talk about, talk through, converse about, debate, confer about, deliberate about, chew over, consider, consider the pros and cons of, thrash out; informal kick around, hash out, bat around.
2 *the third chapter discusses this topic in detail* **examine,** explore, study, analyze, go into, deal with, treat, consider, concern itself with, tackle.

discussion ▶ noun 1 *a long discussion with her husband* **conversation,** talk, dialogue, discourse, conference, debate, exchange of views, consultation, deliberation; powwow, chat, tête-à-tête, heart-to-heart, huddle; negotiations, parley; informal confab, chitchat, rap (session), skull session, bull session; formal confabulation, colloquy.
2 *the book's candid discussion of sexual matters* **examination,** exploration, analysis, study; treatment, consideration.

disdain ▶ noun *she looked at him with disdain* **contempt,** scorn, scornfulness, contemptuousness, derision, disrespect; disparagement, condescension, superciliousness, hauteur, haughtiness, arrogance, snobbishness, indifference, distaste, dislike, disgust.
ANTONYMS respect.
▶ verb 1 *she disdained vulgar exhibitionism* **scorn,** deride, pour scorn on, regard with contempt, sneer at, sniff at, curl one's lip at, look down one's nose at, look down on; despise; informal turn up one's nose at, pooh-pooh. See note at DESPISE.
2 *we disdained his invitation* **spurn,** reject, refuse, rebuff, disregard, ignore, snub; decline, turn down, brush aside.

disdainful ▶ adjective *Tyler was offended by his disdainful expression* **contemptuous,** scornful, derisive, sneering, withering, slighting, disparaging, disrespectful, condescending, patronizing, supercilious, haughty, superior, arrogant, proud, snobbish, lordly, aloof, indifferent, dismissive; informal high and mighty, hoity-toity, sniffy, snotty; archaic contumelious.
ANTONYMS respectful.

disease ▶ noun *herbal preparations to treat tropical diseases* **illness,** sickness, ill health; infection, ailment, malady, disorder, complaint, affliction, condition, indisposition, upset, problem, trouble, infirmity, disability, defect, abnormality; pestilence, plague, cancer, canker, blight; informal bug, virus; dated contagion.

diseased ▶ adjective *the diseased trees have been marked with red paint* **unhealthy,** ill, sick, unwell, ailing, sickly, unsound; infected, septic, contaminated, blighted, rotten, bad, abnormal.

disembark ▶ verb *passengers are asked to disembark in single file* **get off,** step off, leave, pile out; go ashore, debark, detrain, deplane; land, arrive, alight.

disembodied ▶ adjective *disembodied faces floated through the smoky mist* **bodiless,** incorporeal, discarnate, spiritual; intangible, insubstantial, impalpable; ghostly, spectral, phantom, wraithlike.

USAGE

disembodied, dismembered

Disembodied = separated from the physical body, esp. as a spirit. The word is stretched too far when used to describe a body part severed from the torso—e.g.: "Having said all that, did we really need to see the disembodied [read *severed*] heads? In a word: yuck. We got the idea with the hacksaw and the meat cleaver, thanks." (*Arizona Republic*; Nov. 21, 2002.)

Dismembered = (1) (of bodily limbs) cut from the torso; or (2) (of a torso) characterized by having had limbs cut off. This term does not work well with heads—e.g.: "In a flurry of recent TV appearances promoting his new book on families, the former vice president has been seen . . . floating as a dismembered [read *detached*] head in a jar on the Fox cartoon show 'Futurama,' where he's dubbed 'the inventor of the environment.' " (*Christian Science Monitor*; Nov. 19, 2002.) — **BG**

disembowel ▶ verb *we cleaned and disemboweled the game before returning to the campsite* **gut,** draw, remove the guts from; formal eviscerate.

disenchanted ▶ adjective *disenchanted with politics, he retired from the foreign service* **disillusioned,** disappointed, disabused, let down, fed up, dissatisfied, discontented; cynical, soured, jaundiced, sick, indifferent, blasé.

disenchantment ▶ noun *the disenchantment of a first love gone sour* **disillusionment,** disappointment, dissatisfaction, discontent, discontentedness, rude awakening; cynicism.

disengage ▶ verb **1** *I disengaged his hand from mine* **remove,** detach, disentangle, extricate, separate, release, free, loosen, loose, disconnect, unfasten, unclasp, uncouple, undo, unhook, unhitch, untie, unyoke.
ANTONYMS attach.
2 *UN forces* ***disengaged from*** *the country* **withdraw from,** leave, pull out of, quit, retreat from.
ANTONYMS enter.

disentangle ▶ verb **1** *Allen was disentangling a coil of rope* **untangle,** unravel, untwist, unwind, undo, untie, straighten out, smooth out; comb.
2 *he disentangled his fingers from her hair* **extricate,** extract, free, remove, disengage, untwine, release, loosen, detach, unfasten, unclasp, disconnect.

disfavor ▶ noun *the disfavor of his fellow students* **disapproval,** disapprobation; dislike, displeasure, distaste, dissatisfaction, low opinion; dated disesteem.

disfigure ▶ verb *junkyards disfigure the landscape* **mar,** spoil, deface, scar, blemish, uglify; damage, injure, impair, blight, mutilate, deform, maim, ruin; vandalize.
ANTONYMS adorn.

disfigurement ▶ noun **1** *the disfigurement of Victorian buildings* **defacement,** spoiling, scarring, uglification, mutilation, damage, vandalizing, ruin.
2 *a permanent facial disfigurement* **blemish,** flaw, defect, imperfection, discoloration, blotch; scar, pockmark; deformity, malformation, abnormality, injury, wound.

disgorge ▶ verb **1** *the combine disgorged a stream of grain* **pour out,** discharge, eject, throw out, emit, expel, spit out, spew out, belch forth, spout; vomit, regurgitate.
2 *they were made to disgorge all the profits* **surrender,** relinquish, hand over, give up, turn over, yield; informal cough up, fork over.

disgrace ▶ noun **1** *he brought disgrace on the family* **dishonor,** shame, discredit, ignominy, degradation, disrepute, ill repute, infamy, scandal, stigma, opprobrium, obloquy, condemnation, vilification, contempt, disrespect; humiliation, embarrassment, loss of face; dated disesteem.
ANTONYMS honor.
2 *the unemployment figures are a disgrace* **scandal,** outrage; discredit, reproach, affront, insult; stain, blemish, blot, black mark; informal crime, sin.
ANTONYMS credit.
▶ verb **1** *you have disgraced the family name* **bring shame on,** shame, dishonor, discredit, bring into disrepute, degrade, debase, defame, stigmatize, taint, sully, tarnish, besmirch, stain, blacken, drag through the mud/mire.
ANTONYMS honor.
2 *he was publicly disgraced* **discredit,** dishonor, stigmatize; humiliate, cause to lose face, chasten, humble, demean, put someone in their place, take down a peg or two, cut down to size.
ANTONYMS honor.
– PHRASES **in disgrace** *Benjamin couldn't bear to return home in disgrace* **out of favor,** unpopular, under a cloud, disgraced; informal in the doghouse.

disgraceful ▶ adjective *they caught Warren's disgraceful behavior on videotape* **shameful,** shocking, scandalous, deplorable, despicable, contemptible, beyond contempt, beyond the pale, dishonorable, discreditable, reprehensible, base, mean, low, blameworthy, unworthy, ignoble, shabby, inglorious, outrageous, abominable, atrocious, appalling, dreadful, terrible, disgusting, shameless, vile, odious, monstrous, heinous, iniquitous, unspeakable, loathsome, sordid, nefarious; archaic scurvy.
ANTONYMS admirable.

disgruntled ▶ adjective *poor service was the primary complaint of these disgruntled customers* **dissatisfied,** discontented, aggrieved, resentful, fed up, displeased, unhappy, disappointed, disaffected; angry, irate, annoyed, cross, exasperated, indignant, vexed, irritated, piqued, irked, put out, peeved, miffed, bummed, aggravated, hacked off, riled, peed off, PO'd, hot under the collar, in a huff, cheesed off, shirty, sore, teed off, ticked off.

disguise ▶ verb *his controlled voice disguised his true feelings* **camouflage,** conceal, hide, cover up, dissemble, mask, screen, shroud, veil, cloak; gloss over, put up a smokescreen to hide/mask.
ANTONYMS expose.
– PHRASES **disguise oneself as** *Eleanor disguised herself as a man* **dress up as,** pretend to be, pass oneself off as, impersonate, pose as; formal personate.

disgust ▶ noun *a look of disgust* **revulsion,**

repugnance, aversion, distaste, nausea, abhorrence, loathing, detestation, odium, horror; contempt, outrage.
ANTONYMS delight.
▶ verb 1 *the hospital food disgusted me* **revolt,** repel, repulse, sicken, nauseate, turn someone's stomach; informal turn off, gross out.
2 *Toby's foul language disgusted her* **outrage,** shock, horrify, appall, scandalize, offend.

disgusting ▶ adjective 1 *the food was disgusting* **revolting,** repellent, repulsive, sickening, nauseating, stomach-churning, stomach-turning, off-putting, unpalatable, distasteful, foul, nasty, vomitous; informal yucky, icky, gross.
ANTONYMS delicious, appealing.
2 *I find racism disgusting* **abhorrent,** loathsome, offensive, appalling, outrageous, objectionable, shocking, horrifying, scandalous, monstrous, unspeakable, shameful, vile, odious; obnoxious, detestable, hateful, sickening, contemptible, despicable, deplorable, abominable, beyond the pale; informal gross, ghastly, sick.
ANTONYMS commendable.

dish ▶ noun 1 *a china dish* **bowl,** plate, platter, salver, paten; container, receptacle, casserole, tureen; archaic trencher, charger; historical porringer.
2 *vegetarian dishes* **recipe,** meal, course; (**dishes**) food, fare.
3 informal *she's quite a dish* See BEAUTY (sense 2).
– PHRASES **dish out** *they dished out free coffee and bagels to the volunteers* **distribute,** dispense, issue, hand out/around, give out, pass out/around; deal out, dole out, share out, allocate, allot, apportion.

dishearten ▶ verb *poor reviews disheartened the young author* **discourage,** dispirit, demoralize, cast down, depress, disappoint, dismay, dash someone's hopes; put off, deter, unnerve, daunt, intimidate, cow, crush.
ANTONYMS encourage.

disheveled ▶ adjective *long and disheveled hair* **untidy,** unkempt, scruffy, messy, in a mess, disordered, disarranged, rumpled, bedraggled; uncombed, tousled, tangled, tangly, knotted, knotty, shaggy, straggly, windswept, wind-blown, wild; slovenly, slatternly, blowsy, frowzy, mussed (up), mussy.
ANTONYMS tidy.

dishonest ▶ adjective *accused of dishonest business practices* **fraudulent,** corrupt, swindling, cheating, double-dealing; underhanded, crafty, cunning, devious, treacherous, unfair, unjust, dirty, unethical, immoral, dishonorable, untrustworthy, unscrupulous, unprincipled, amoral; criminal, illegal, unlawful; false, untruthful, deceitful, deceiving, lying, mendacious; informal crooked, hinky, shady, tricky, sharp, shifty; literary perfidious.

dishonesty ▶ noun *Richard was a victim of his business manager's dishonesty* **fraud,** fraudulence, corruption, cheating, chicanery, double-dealing, deceit, deception, duplicity, lying, falseness, falsity, falsehood, untruthfulness; craft, cunning, trickery, artifice, underhandedness, subterfuge, skulduggery, treachery, untrustworthiness, unscrupulousness, criminality, misconduct; informal crookedness, dirty tricks, shenanigans; literary perfidy.
ANTONYMS probity.

dishonor ▶ noun *the incident brought dishonor upon the police department* **disgrace,** shame, discredit, humiliation, degradation, ignominy, scandal, infamy, disrepute, ill repute, loss of face, disfavor, ill favor, debasement, opprobrium, obloquy; stigma; dated disesteem.
▶ verb *his family name has been dishonored* **disgrace,** shame, discredit, bring into disrepute, humiliate, degrade, debase, lower, cheapen, drag down, drag through the mud, blacken the name of, give a bad name to; sully, stain, taint, besmirch, smear, mar, blot, stigmatize.

dishonorable ▶ adjective *dishonorable conduct cost Major Pierce her commission* **disgraceful,** shameful, disreputable, discreditable, degrading, ignominious, ignoble, blameworthy, contemptible, despicable, reprehensible, shabby, shoddy, sordid, sorry, base, low, improper, unseemly, unworthy; unprincipled, unscrupulous, corrupt, untrustworthy, treacherous, traitorous; informal shady, dirty; literary perfidious; archaic scurvy.

disillusion ▶ verb *we pretended to have a happy marriage because we didn't want to disillusion the children* **disabuse,** enlighten, set straight, open someone's eyes; disenchant, shatter someone's illusions, disappoint, make sadder and wiser.
ANTONYMS deceive.

disincentive ▶ noun *high interest rates are a disincentive to investment* **deterrent,** discouragement, damper, brake, curb, check, restraint, inhibitor; obstacle, impediment, hindrance, obstruction, block, barrier.

disinclination ▶ noun *they show a disinclination to face the truth* **reluctance,** unwillingness, lack of enthusiasm, indisposition, hesitancy; aversion, dislike, distaste; objection, demur, resistance, opposition.
ANTONYMS enthusiasm.

disinclined ▶ adjective *she was disinclined to abandon the old ways* **reluctant,** unwilling, unenthusiastic, unprepared, indisposed, ill-disposed, not in the mood, hesitant; loath, averse, antipathetic, resistant, opposed.
ANTONYMS willing.

disinfect ▶ verb *use bleach to disinfect your kitchen surfaces* **sterilize,** sanitize, clean, cleanse, purify, decontaminate; fumigate.
ANTONYMS contaminate.

disinfectant ▶ noun *vinegar is a natural disinfectant* **antiseptic,** germicide, sterilizer, cleanser, decontaminant; fumigant.

disingenuous ▶ adjective *that innocent, teary-eyed look is just part of a disingenuous act* **insincere,** dishonest, untruthful, false, deceitful, duplicitous, lying, mendacious; hypocritical.

disinherit ▶ verb *Harrison's parents disinherited him when he joined a neo-Nazi cult* **cut someone out of one's will,** cut off, dispossess; disown, repudiate, reject, cast off/aside, wash one's hands of, have nothing more to do with, turn one's back on; informal cut off without a penny.

disintegrate ▶ verb *steam causes the substance to disintegrate* **break up,** break apart, fall apart, fall to pieces, fragment, fracture, shatter, splinter; explode, blow up, blow apart, fly apart; crumble, deteriorate, decay, decompose, rot, molder, perish, dissolve, collapse, go to rack and ruin, degenerate; informal bust, be smashed to smithereens.

disinterested ▶ adjective **1** *disinterested advice* **unbiased,** unprejudiced, impartial, neutral, nonpartisan, detached, uninvolved, objective, dispassionate, impersonal, clinical; open-minded, fair, just, equitable, balanced, evenhanded, with no ax to grind.
2 *he looked at her with disinterested eyes* **uninterested,** indifferent, incurious, uncurious, unconcerned, unmoved, unresponsive, impassive, passive, detached, unenthusiastic, lukewarm, bored, apathetic; informal couldn't-care-less.

USAGE

disinterested, uninterested

Disinterest = (1) impartiality or freedom from bias or from chance of financial benefit; or (2) lack of concern or attention. Leading writers and editors almost unanimously reject sense 2, for which *uninterest* is the better term. Given the overlapping nouns, writers have found it difficult to keep the past-participial adjectives entirely separate, and many have given up the fight to preserve the distinction between them. But the distinction is still best recognized and followed because *disinterested* captures a nuance that no other word quite does. Many influential writers have urged the preservation of its traditional sense. The typically understated A. R. Orage rhapsodized over the word: "No word in the English language is more difficult [than *disinterestedness*] to define or better worth attempting to define. Somewhere or other in its capacious folds it contains all the ideas of ethics and even, I should say, of religion. . . . I venture to say that whoever has understood the meaning of 'disinterestedness' is not far off understanding the goal of human culture." (*Readers and Writers: 1917–1921*; 1922.)

A *disinterested* observer is not merely "impartial" but has nothing to gain from taking a stand on the issue in question. The illustrative quotation that follows deals with journalists' disinterest: "In the film, Wexler's directorial debut, a cameraman portrayed by Robert Forster must wrestle with being a disinterested observer or becoming emotionally involved with what he sees through his lens." (*Los Angeles Times*; Aug. 26, 1996.)

Yet *disinterested* is frequently used (or, in traditionalists' eyes, misused) for *uninterested*—e.g.: "On a day when seeded players fell by the wayside like overripe tomatoes, Agassi looked sickly and almost disinterested [read *uninterested*]." (*Toronto Sun*; June 25, 1996.) — **BG**

disjointed ▶ adjective *the discussion was too disjointed to follow* **unconnected,** disconnected, disunited, discontinuous, fragmented, disorganized, disordered, muddled, mixed up, jumbled, garbled, incoherent, confused; rambling, wandering.

dislike ▶ verb *a man she had always disliked* **find distasteful,** regard with distaste, be averse to, have an aversion to, have no liking/taste for, disapprove of, object to, take exception to; hate, detest, loathe, abhor, despise, be unable to bear/stand, shrink from, shudder at, find repellent; informal be unable to stomach; formal abominate.
▶ noun *she viewed the other woman with dislike* **distaste,** aversion, disfavor, disapproval, disapprobation, enmity, animosity, hostility, antipathy, antagonism; hate, hatred, detestation, loathing, disgust, repugnance, abhorrence, disdain, contempt.

dislocate ▶ verb **1** *she dislocated her hip* **put out of joint;** informal put out; Medicine luxate.
2 *trade was dislocated by a famine* **disrupt,** disturb, throw into disarray, throw into confusion, play havoc with, interfere with, disorganize, upset, disorder; informal mess up.

dislodge ▶ verb **1** *replace any stones you dislodge* **displace,** knock out of place/position, move, shift; knock over, upset.
2 *economic sanctions failed to dislodge the dictator* **remove,** force out, drive out, oust, eject, get rid of, evict, unseat, depose, topple, drum out; informal kick out, boot out.

disloyal ▶ adjective *once judged disloyal, you will never be welcome in this group* **unfaithful,** faithless, false, false-hearted, untrue, inconstant, untrustworthy, unreliable, undependable, fickle; treacherous, traitorous, subversive, seditious, unpatriotic, two-faced, double-dealing, double-crossing, deceitful; dissident, renegade; adulterous; informal backstabbing, two-timing; literary perfidious.

disloyalty ▶ noun *the investigation uncovered more cases of disloyalty than anyone had originally suspected* **unfaithfulness,** infidelity, inconstancy, faithlessness, fickleness, unreliability, untrustworthiness, betrayal, falseness; duplicity, double-dealing, treachery, treason, subversion, sedition, dissidence; adultery; informal backstabbing, two-timing; literary perfidy, perfidiousness.

dismal ▶ adjective **1** *a dismal look* **gloomy,** glum, melancholy, morose, doleful, woebegone, forlorn, dejected, depressed, dispirited, downcast, despondent, disconsolate, miserable, sad, unhappy, sorrowful, desolate, wretched; informal blue, down in the dumps, down in/at the mouth; literary dolorous.
ANTONYMS cheerful.
2 *a dismal hall* **dingy,** dim, dark, gloomy, dreary, drab, dull, bleak, cheerless, depressing, uninviting, unwelcoming.
ANTONYMS cheerful, bright.
3 informal *a dismal performance* See **POOR** (sense 2).

dismantle ▶ verb *the old opera house was dismantled* **take apart,** pull apart, pull to pieces, disassemble, break up, break down, strip

(down); knock down, pull down, demolish.
ANTONYMS assemble, build.

dismay ▶ verb *he was dismayed by the change in his friend* **appall,** horrify, shock, shake (up); disconcert, take aback, alarm, unnerve, unsettle, throw off balance, discompose; disturb, upset, distress; informal rattle, faze.
ANTONYMS encourage, please.
▶ noun *they greeted his decision with dismay* **alarm,** shock, surprise, consternation, concern, perturbation, disquiet, discomposure, distress.
ANTONYMS pleasure, relief.

dismiss ▶ verb 1 *the president dismissed five aides* **give someone their notice,** get rid of, discharge, terminate; lay off; informal sack, give someone the sack, fire, boot out, give someone the boot, give someone their marching orders, show someone the door, can, pink-slip; Military cashier.
ANTONYMS engage.
2 *the guards were dismissed* **send away,** let go; disband, dissolve, discharge. See note at EJECT.
ANTONYMS assemble.
3 *he dismissed all morbid thoughts* **banish,** set aside, disregard, shrug off, put out of one's mind; reject, deny, repudiate, spurn.
ANTONYMS entertain.

dismissal ▶ noun 1 *the threat of dismissal* **termination,** discharge, one's notice; redundancy, laying off; informal the sack, sacking, firing, the boot, the ax, one's marching orders, the pink slip; Military cashiering.
ANTONYMS recruitment.
2 *a condescending dismissal* **rejection,** repudiation, repulse, nonacceptance; informal kiss-off, brush-off.
ANTONYMS acceptance.

disobedient ▶ adjective *he had never been punished for being disobedient* **insubordinate,** unruly, wayward, badly behaved, naughty, delinquent, disruptive, troublesome, rebellious, defiant, mutinous, recalcitrant, uncooperative, truculent, willful, intractable, obstreperous; archaic contumacious.

disobey ▶ verb *she was put on report for willfully disobeying a superior officer* **defy,** go against, flout, contravene, infringe, transgress, violate; disregard, ignore, pay no heed to.

disobliging ▶ adjective *our disobliging neighbors* **unhelpful,** uncooperative, unaccommodating, unreasonable, awkward, difficult; discourteous, uncivil, unfriendly.
ANTONYMS helpful.

disorder ▶ noun 1 *he hates disorder* **untidiness,** disorderliness, mess, disarray, chaos, confusion; clutter, jumble; a muddle, a shambles.
ANTONYMS tidiness.
2 *incidents of public disorder* **unrest,** disturbance, disruption, upheaval, turmoil, mayhem, pandemonium; violence, fighting, rioting, lawlessness, anarchy; breach of the peace, fracas, rumpus, ruckus, melee.
ANTONYMS order, peace.
3 *a blood disorder* **disease,** infection, complaint, condition, affliction, malady, sickness, illness, ailment, infirmity, irregularity.

disorderly ▶ adjective 1 *a disorderly desk* **untidy,** disorganized, messy, cluttered; in disarray, in a mess, in a jumble, in a muddle, at sixes and sevens; informal shambolic, like a bomb went off.
ANTONYMS tidy.
2 *disorderly behavior* **unruly,** boisterous, rough, rowdy, wild, riotous; disruptive, troublesome, undisciplined, lawless, unmanageable, uncontrollable, out of hand, out of control.
ANTONYMS peaceful.

disorganized ▶ adjective 1 *a disorganized toolbox* **disorderly,** disordered, unorganized, jumbled, muddled, untidy, messy, chaotic, topsy-turvy, haphazard, ragtag; in disorder, in disarray, in a mess, in a muddle, in a shambles, shambolic.
ANTONYMS orderly.
2 *muddled and disorganized* **unmethodical,** unsystematic, undisciplined, badly organized, inefficient; haphazard, careless, slapdash; informal sloppy, hit-and-miss.
ANTONYMS organized.

disown ▶ verb *he has been disowned by his parents* **reject,** cast off/aside, abandon, renounce, deny; turn one's back on, wash one's hands of, have nothing more to do with; literary forsake.

disparage ▶ verb *they disparage Lawrence and his achievements* **belittle,** denigrate, deprecate, trivialize, make light of, undervalue, underrate, play down; ridicule, deride, mock, scorn, scoff at, sneer at; run down, defame, discredit, speak badly of, cast aspersions on, impugn, vilify, traduce, criticize, slur; informal pick holes in, knock, slam, pan, badmouth, dis, pooh-pooh; formal calumniate, derogate.
ANTONYMS praise, overrate.

disparity ▶ noun *a disparity between their stories* **discrepancy,** inconsistency, imbalance; variance, variation, divergence, gap, gulf; difference, dissimilarity, contrast.
ANTONYMS similarity.

dispassionate ▶ adjective 1 *a calm, dispassionate manner* **unemotional,** emotionless, impassive, cool, calm, 'calm, cool, and collected', unruffled, unperturbed, composed, self-possessed, self-controlled, unexcitable; informal laid-back.
ANTONYMS emotional.
2 *a dispassionate analysis* **objective,** detached, neutral, disinterested, impartial, nonpartisan, unbiased, unprejudiced; scientific, analytical.
ANTONYMS biased.

dispatch ▶ verb 1 *all the messages were dispatched* **send (off),** post, mail, forward, transmit, email.
2 *the business was dispatched in the morning* **deal with,** finish, conclude, settle, discharge, perform; expedite, push through; informal make short work of.
3 *the hero dispatched a host of villains* **kill,** put to death, take/end the life of; slaughter, butcher, massacre, wipe out, exterminate, eliminate; murder, assassinate, execute; informal bump off, do in, do away with, take out, blow away, ice, rub out, waste; literary slay. See note at KILL.
▶ noun 1 *files ready for dispatch* **sending,** posting, mailing, e-mailing.
2 *efficiency and dispatch* **promptness,** speed, speediness, swiftness, rapidity, briskness, haste,

hastiness; literary fleetness, celerity.
3 *the latest dispatch from the front* **communication,** communiqué, bulletin, report, statement, letter, message; news, intelligence; informal memo, info, story, lowdown, scoop; literary tidings.
4 *the capture and dispatch of the rogue bull* **killing,** slaughter, massacre, extermination, elimination; murder, assassination, execution; literary slaying.

dispel ▶ **verb** *allow me to dispel your fears* **banish,** eliminate, drive away/off, get rid of; relieve, allay, ease, quell. See note at SCATTER.

dispensable ▶ **adjective** *any goods deemed dispensable will not be allowed on board* **expendable,** disposable, replaceable, inessential, nonessential, noncore; unnecessary, redundant, superfluous, surplus to requirements.

dispensation ▶ **noun 1** *the dispensation of supplies* **distribution,** supply, supplying, issue, issuing, handing out, doling out, dishing out, sharing out, dividing out; division, allocation, allotment, apportionment.
2 *the dispensation of justice* **administration,** administering, delivery, discharge, dealing out, meting out.
3 *a dispensation from the Pope* **exemption,** immunity, exception, exoneration, reprieve, remission.
4 *the new constitutional dispensation* **system,** order, arrangement, organization.

dispense ▶ **verb 1** *servants dispensed the drinks* **distribute,** pass around, hand out, dole out, dish out, share out; allocate, supply, allot, apportion.
2 *the soldiers dispensed summary justice* **administer,** deliver, issue, discharge, deal out, mete out.
3 *dispensing medicines* **prepare,** make up; supply, provide, sell.
4 *the Pope dispensed him from his impediment* **exempt,** excuse, except, release, let off, reprieve, absolve.
– PHRASES **dispense with 1** *let's dispense with the formalities* **waive,** omit, drop, leave out, forgo; do away with, give something a miss.
2 *he dispensed with his crutches* **get rid of,** throw away/out, dispose of, discard; manage without, cope without; informal ditch, scrap, dump, deep-six, chuck.

disperse ▶ **verb 1** *the crowd began to disperse* | *police dispersed the demonstrators* **break up,** split up, disband, scatter, leave, go their separate ways; drive away/off, chase away.
ANTONYMS assemble.
2 *the fog finally dispersed* **dissipate,** dissolve, melt away, fade away, clear, lift.
3 *seeds dispersed by birds* **scatter,** disseminate, distribute, spread, broadcast. See note at SCATTER.
ANTONYMS gather.

displace ▶ **verb 1** *roof tiles displaced by gales* **dislodge,** dislocate, move, shift, reposition; move out of place, knock out of place/position.
ANTONYMS replace.
2 *the director was displaced* **depose,** dislodge, unseat, remove (from office), dismiss, eject, oust, expel, force out, drive out; overthrow, topple, bring down; informal boot out, give someone the boot, show someone the door, bump.
ANTONYMS reinstate.
3 *English displaced the local language* **replace,** take the place of, supplant, supersede. See note at REPLACE.

display ▶ **noun 1** *a display of lights* **exhibition,** exposition, array, arrangement, presentation, demonstration; spectacle, show, parade, pageant.
2 *they vied to outdo each other in display* **ostentation,** showiness, extravagance, flamboyance, lavishness, splendor; informal swank, flashiness, glitziness.
3 *his display of concern* **manifestation,** expression, show.
▶ **verb 1** *the paintings are displayed in the art gallery* **exhibit,** show, put on show/view; arrange, array, present, lay out, set out.
2 *the play displays his many theatrical talents* **show off,** parade, flaunt, reveal; publicize, make known, call/draw attention to.
ANTONYMS hide.
3 *she displayed a caustic sense of humor* **manifest,** show evidence of, reveal; demonstrate, show; formal evince.
ANTONYMS conceal.

displease ▶ **verb** *I'd never seen his mom when she wasn't displeased about something* **annoy,** irritate, anger, irk, vex, pique, gall, nettle; put out, upset, aggravate, peeve, needle, bug, rile, miff; informal tee off, tick off, piss off.

displeasure ▶ **noun** *the scowl on his face indicated displeasure* **annoyance,** irritation, crossness, anger, vexation, pique, rancor; dissatisfaction, discontent, discontentedness, disgruntlement, disapproval; informal aggravation.
ANTONYMS satisfaction.

disposable ▶ **adjective 1** *disposable plates* **throwaway,** expendable, single-use.
2 *disposable income* **available,** usable, spendable.

disposal ▶ **noun 1** *garbage ready for disposal* **throwing away,** discarding, jettisoning, scrapping, recycling; informal dumping, ditching, chucking, deep-sixing.
2 *the disposal of the troops in two lines* **arrangement,** arranging, positioning, placement, lining up, disposition, grouping.
– PHRASES **at someone's disposal** *the van will be at your disposal all weekend* **for use by,** in reserve for, in the hands of, in the possession of.

dispose ▶ **verb 1** *he disposed the pictures in sequence* **arrange,** place, put, position, array, set up, form; marshal, gather, group.
2 *the experience disposed him to be kind* **incline,** encourage, persuade, predispose, make willing, prompt, lead, motivate; sway, influence.
– PHRASES **dispose of 1** *the waste was disposed of* **throw away/out,** get rid of, discard, jettison, scrap, junk; informal dump, ditch, chuck, trash, deep-six. **2** *he had disposed of all his assets* **part with,** give away, hand over, deliver up, transfer;

sell, auction. **3** informal *she disposed of a fourth cupcake* See CONSUME (sense 1).

disposed ▶ adjective **1** *they are philanthropically disposed* **inclined,** predisposed, minded.
2 *we are not disposed to argue* **willing,** inclined, prepared, ready, minded, in the mood.
3 *he was disposed to be cruel* **liable,** apt, inclined, likely, predisposed, prone, tending; capable of.

disposition ▶ noun **1** *a nervous disposition* **temperament,** nature, character, constitution, makeup, mentality.
2 *his disposition to generosity* **inclination,** tendency, proneness, propensity, proclivity.
3 *the disposition of the armed forces* **arrangement,** positioning, placement, configuration; setup, lineup, layout, array; marshaling, mustering, grouping; Military dressing.
4 Law *the disposition of the company's property* **distribution,** disposal, allocation, transfer; sale, auction.

dispossess ▶ verb *the peasants have been dispossessed of their land* **divest,** strip, rob, cheat (out), deprive; informal do out.

disproportionate ▶ adjective *the sentence is disproportionate to the offense committed* **out of proportion to,** not appropriate to, inappropriate to, not commensurate with, incommensurate with, relatively too large/small for; inordinate for, unreasonable for, excessive for, undue for.

disprove ▶ verb *Wesley's version of the story should be easy to disprove* **refute,** prove false, falsify, debunk, negate, invalidate, contradict, confound, controvert, discredit; informal poke holes in, blow out of the water, shoot down; formal confute.

disputable ▶ adjective *some of these figures are disputable* **debatable,** open to debate, open to discussion, open to question, arguable, contestable, moot, questionable, doubtful; informal iffy.

disputation ▶ noun *we'll have no religious disputation in this house* **debate,** discussion, dispute, argument, arguing, altercation, dissension, disagreement, controversy; polemics.

dispute ▶ noun **1** *a subject of dispute* **debate,** discussion, disputation, argument, controversy, disagreement, quarreling, dissension, conflict, friction, strife, discord.
ANTONYMS agreement.
2 *they have settled their dispute* **quarrel,** argument, altercation, squabble, falling-out, disagreement, difference of opinion, clash, wrangle; informal tiff, spat, blowup, scrap, row, rhubarb. See note at QUARREL.
ANTONYMS agreement.
▶ verb **1** *George disputed with him* **debate,** discuss, exchange views; quarrel, argue, disagree, clash, fall out, wrangle, bicker, squabble; informal have words, have a tiff, have a spat.
2 *they disputed his proposals* **challenge,** contest, question, call into question, impugn, quibble over, contradict, controvert, argue about, disagree with, take issue with; formal gainsay.
ANTONYMS accept.

disquiet ▶ noun *grave public disquiet* **unease,** uneasiness, worry, anxiety, anxiousness, concern, disquietude; perturbation, consternation, upset, malaise, angst; agitation, restlessness, fretfulness; informal jitteriness.
ANTONYMS calm.
▶ verb *I was disquieted by the news* **perturb,** agitate, upset, disturb, unnerve, unsettle, discompose, disconcert; make uneasy, worry, make anxious; trouble, concern, make fretful, make restless.

disregard ▶ verb *Annie disregarded the remark* **ignore,** take no notice of, pay no attention/heed to; overlook, turn a blind eye to, turn a deaf ear to, shut one's eyes to, gloss over, brush aside, shrug off; informal sneeze at. See note at NEGLECT.
ANTONYMS heed.
▶ noun *blithe disregard for the rules* **indifference,** nonobservance, inattention, heedlessness, neglect.
ANTONYMS attention.

disrepair ▶ noun *the outbuildings are in disrepair* **dilapidation,** decrepitude, shabbiness, collapse, ruin; abandonment, neglect, disuse.

disreputable ▶ adjective **1** *he fell into disreputable company* **of bad reputation,** infamous, notorious, louche; dishonorable, dishonest, untrustworthy, unwholesome, villainous, corrupt, immoral; unsavory, slippery, seedy, sleazy; informal crooked, shady, shifty, dodgy.
ANTONYMS respectable, smart.
2 *filthy and disreputable* **scruffy,** shabby, down-at-heel, down-at-the-heel(s), seedy, untidy, unkempt, disheveled.
ANTONYMS respectable, smart.

disrepute ▶ noun *she had brought the family name into disrepute* **disgrace,** shame, dishonor, infamy, notoriety, ignominy, bad reputation; humiliation, discredit, ill repute, low esteem, opprobrium, obloquy.
ANTONYMS honor.

disrespect ▶ noun **1** *disrespect for authority* **contempt,** lack of respect, scorn, disregard, disdain.
ANTONYMS esteem.
2 *he meant no disrespect to anybody* **discourtesy,** rudeness, impoliteness, incivility, ill/bad manners; insolence, impudence, impertinence.
ANTONYMS esteem.

disrespectful ▶ adjective *no one had ever heard him utter a disrespectful word* **discourteous,** rude, impolite, uncivil, ill-mannered, bad-mannered; insolent, impudent, impertinent, cheeky, flippant, insubordinate.
ANTONYMS polite.

disrupt ▶ verb **1** *the strike disrupted public transit* **throw into confusion,** throw into disorder, throw into disarray, cause confusion/turmoil in, play havoc with; disturb, interfere with, upset, unsettle; obstruct, impede, hold up, delay, interrupt, suspend; informal throw a (monkey) wrench into the works of.
2 *the explosion disrupted the walls of the crater*

distort, damage, buckle, warp; shatter; literary sunder.

disruptive ▶ adjective *he's the most disruptive student in the school* **troublesome,** unruly, badly behaved, rowdy, disorderly, undisciplined, wild; unmanageable, uncontrollable, uncooperative, out of control/hand, obstreperous, truculent; formal refractory.
ANTONYMS well-behaved.

dissatisfaction ▶ noun *widespread dissatisfaction with the new law* **discontent,** discontentment, disaffection, disquiet, unhappiness, malaise, disgruntlement, vexation, annoyance, irritation, anger; disapproval, disapprobation, disfavor, displeasure.

dissatisfied ▶ adjective *no one could handle a dissatisfied customer better than Angie* **discontented,** malcontent, unsatisfied, disappointed, disaffected, unhappy, displeased; disgruntled, aggrieved, vexed, annoyed, irritated, angry, exasperated, fed up.
ANTONYMS contented.

dissect ▶ verb **1** *the body was dissected* **anatomize,** cut up/open, dismember; vivisect. **2** *the text of the gospels was dissected* **analyze,** examine, study, scrutinize, pore over, investigate, go over with a fine-tooth comb.

dissection ▶ noun **1** *the dissection of corpses* **cutting up/open,** dismemberment; autopsy, postmortem, necropsy, anatomy, vivisection. **2** *a thorough dissection of their policies* **analysis,** examination, study, scrutiny, investigation; evaluation, assessment.

disseminate ▶ verb *much of our funding is used to disseminate information where it is most needed* **spread,** circulate, distribute, disperse, promulgate, propagate, publicize, communicate, pass on, put about, make known. See note at SCATTER.

dissension ▶ noun *there was dissension within the cabinet* **disagreement,** difference of opinion, dispute, dissent, conflict, friction, strife, discord, antagonism, infighting; argument, debate, controversy, disputation, contention.

dissent ▶ verb *two members dissented* **differ,** disagree, demur, fail to agree, be at variance/odds, take issue; decline/refuse to support, protest, object, dispute, challenge, quibble.
ANTONYMS agree, accept.
▶ noun *murmurs of dissent* **disagreement,** difference of opinion, argument, dispute; disapproval, objection, protest, opposition, defiance; conflict, friction, strife, infighting.
ANTONYMS agreement.

dissenter ▶ noun *a chorus of criticism from dissenters* **dissident,** objector, protester, disputant; rebel, renegade, maverick, independent; apostate, heretic.

dissertation ▶ noun *a fascinating dissertation on the fall of Communism* **essay,** thesis, treatise, paper, study, discourse, disquisition, tract, monograph.

disservice ▶ noun *the posting of inaccurate information does a great disservice to the patrons* **unkindness,** bad turn, ill turn, disfavor; injury, harm, hurt, damage, wrong, injustice.
ANTONYMS favor.

dissident ▶ noun *a jailed dissident* **dissenter,** objector, protester; rebel, revolutionary, recusant, subversive, agitator, insurgent, insurrectionist, refusenik.
ANTONYMS conformist.
▶ adjective *dissident intellectuals* **dissenting,** disagreeing; opposing, objecting, protesting, rebellious, rebelling, revolutionary, recusant, nonconformist, dissentient.
ANTONYMS conforming.

dissimilar ▶ adjective *families of dissimilar backgrounds* **different,** differing, unalike, variant, diverse, divergent, heterogeneous, disparate, unrelated, distinct, contrasting; literary divers.

dissimilarity ▶ noun *the enzymes' structural dissimilarity* **difference(s),** variance, diversity, heterogeneity, disparateness, disparity, distinctness, contrast, nonuniformity, divergence.

dissipate ▶ verb **1** *his anger dissipated* **disappear,** vanish, evaporate, dissolve, melt away, melt into thin air, be dispelled; disperse, scatter; literary evanesce. See note at SCATTER. **2** *he dissipated his fortune* **squander,** fritter (away), misspend, waste, be prodigal with, spend recklessly/freely, spend like water; expend, use up, consume, run through, go through (like water); informal blow, splurge.

dissipated ▶ adjective *it was in college that he became a dissipated young man* **dissolute,** debauched, decadent, intemperate, profligate, self-indulgent, wild, depraved; licentious, promiscuous; drunken.
ANTONYMS ascetic.

dissociate ▶ verb *the word "spiritual" has become dissociated from religion* **separate,** detach, disconnect, sever, cut off, divorce; isolate, alienate, disassociate.
ANTONYMS relate.
– PHRASES **dissociate oneself from 1** *he dissociated himself from the Catholic Church* **break away from,** end relations with, sever connections with; withdraw from, quit, leave, disaffiliate from, resign from, pull out of, drop out of, defect from. **2** *he dissociated himself from the statement* **disown,** reject, disagree with, distance oneself from.

dissolute ▶ adjective *the problems of dissolute teens have become epidemic* **dissipated,** debauched, decadent, intemperate, profligate, self-indulgent, wild, depraved; licentious, promiscuous; drunken.
ANTONYMS ascetic.

dissolution ▶ noun **1** *the dissolution of the legislative session* **cessation,** conclusion, end, ending, termination, winding up/down, discontinuation, suspension, disbanding; prorogation, recess.
2 technical *the dissolution of a polymer in a solvent* **dissolving,** liquefaction, melting, deliquescence; breaking up, decomposition, disintegration.
3 *the dissolution of the empire* **disintegration,**

breaking up; decay, collapse, demise, extinction.

dissolve ▶ verb **1** *sugar dissolves in water* **go into solution,** break down; liquefy, deliquesce, disintegrate.
2 *his hopes dissolved* **disappear,** vanish, melt away, evaporate, disperse, dissipate, disintegrate; dwindle, fade (away), wither; literary evanesce.
3 *the crowd dissolved* **disperse,** disband, break up, scatter, go in different directions.
4 *the assembly was dissolved* **disband,** disestablish, bring to an end, end, terminate, discontinue, close down, wind up/down, suspend; prorogue, adjourn.
5 *their marriage was dissolved* **annul,** nullify, void, invalidate, overturn, revoke.
– PHRASES **dissolve into/in** *she dissolved into tears* **burst into,** break (down) into, be overcome with.

dissuade ▶ verb *his colleagues did nothing to dissuade him from quitting* **discourage from,** deter from, prevent from, divert from, stop from; talk out of, persuade against, advise against, argue out of.
ANTONYMS encourage.

distance ▶ noun **1** *they measured the distance* **interval,** space, span, gap, extent; length, width, breadth, depth; range, reach.
2 *our perception of distance* **remoteness;** closeness.
3 *there is a distance between them* **aloofness,** remoteness, detachment, unfriendliness; reserve, reticence, restraint, formality; informal standoffishness.
▶ verb *he distanced himself from her* **withdraw,** detach, separate, dissociate, disassociate, isolate, put at a distance.
– PHRASES **in the distance** *there was a cabin in the distance* **far away/off,** afar, just in view; on the horizon; dated yonder.

distant ▶ adjective **1** *distant parts of the world* **faraway,** far-off, far, far-flung, remote, out of the way, outlying, extrasolar.
ANTONYMS near.
2 *the distant past* **long ago,** bygone, olden; ancient, prehistoric; literary of yore, olden.
ANTONYMS recent.
3 *half a mile distant* **away,** off, apart.
4 *a distant memory* **vague,** faint, dim, indistinct, unclear, indefinite, sketchy, hazy.
ANTONYMS strong, clear.
5 *a distant family connection* **remote,** indirect, slight.
ANTONYMS close.
6 *father was always distant* **aloof,** reserved, remote, detached, unapproachable; withdrawn, reticent, taciturn, uncommunicative, undemonstrative, unforthcoming, unresponsive, unfriendly; informal standoffish.
ANTONYMS friendly, close.
7 *a distant look in his eyes* **distracted,** absentminded, faraway, detached, distrait, vague; informal spacey.
ANTONYMS attentive.

distaste ▶ noun *they make little secret of their distaste for returning exiles now looking for power* **dislike for,** aversion to/toward, disinclination to/toward, disapproval of, disapprobation of, disdain for, repugnance at/toward, hatred for/of, loathing of.
ANTONYMS liking.

distasteful ▶ adjective **1** *distasteful behavior* **unpleasant,** disagreeable, displeasing, undesirable; objectionable, offensive, unsavory, unpalatable, obnoxious; disgusting, repellent, repulsive, revolting, repugnant, abhorrent, loathsome, vile.
ANTONYMS agreeable, pleasant.
2 *their eggs are distasteful to predators* **unpalatable,** unsavory, unappetizing, inedible, disgusting.
ANTONYMS tasty.

distended ▶ adjective *a distended abdomen* **swollen,** bloated, dilated, engorged, enlarged, inflated, expanded, extended, bulging, protuberant.

distill ▶ verb **1** *the water was distilled* **purify,** refine, filter, treat, process; evaporate and condense.
2 *oil distilled from marjoram* **extract,** press out, squeeze out, express.
3 *whiskey is distilled from barley* **brew,** ferment.
4 *the solvent is distilled to leave the oil* **boil down,** reduce, concentrate, condense; purify, refine.

distinct ▶ adjective **1** *two distinct categories* **discrete,** separate, different, unconnected; precise, specific, distinctive, individual, contrasting.
ANTONYMS overlapping.
2 *the tail has distinct black tips* **clear,** well-defined, unmistakable, easily distinguishable; recognizable, visible, obvious, pronounced, prominent, striking.
ANTONYMS indistinct, indefinite.

distinction ▶ noun **1** *class distinctions* **difference,** contrast, dissimilarity, variance, variation; division, differentiation, dividing line, gulf, gap.
ANTONYMS similarity.
2 *a painter of distinction* **importance,** significance, note, consequence; renown, fame, celebrity, prominence, eminence, preeminence, repute, reputation; merit, worth, greatness, excellence, quality.
ANTONYMS mediocrity.
3 *he had served with distinction* **honor,** credit, excellence, merit.

distinctive ▶ adjective *the distinctive design in the lace* **distinguishing,** characteristic, typical, individual, particular, peculiar, unique, exclusive, special.
ANTONYMS common.

distinctly ▶ adverb **1** *there's something distinctly odd about him* **decidedly,** markedly, definitely; clearly, noticeably, obviously, plainly, evidently, unmistakably, manifestly, patently.
2 *Laura spoke quite distinctly* **clearly,** plainly, intelligibly, audibly, unambiguously.

distinguish ▶ verb **1** *distinguishing reality from fantasy* **differentiate,** tell apart, discriminate between, tell the difference between.
2 *he could distinguish shapes in the dark* **discern,** see, perceive, make out; detect, recognize, identify; literary descry, espy.

3 *this is what distinguishes history from other disciplines* **separate,** set apart, make distinctive, make different; single out, mark off, characterize.

– PHRASES **distinguish oneself** *she distinguished herself in the air corps* **attain distinction,** be successful, bring fame/honor to oneself, become famous.

> CHOOSE THE RIGHT WORD
>
> **distinguish, descry, differentiate, discern, discriminate**
>
> What we **discern** we see apart from all other objects (*to discern the lighthouse beaming on the far shore*). **Descry** puts even more emphasis on the distant or unclear nature of what we're seeing (*the lookout was barely able to descry a man approaching in the dusk*). To **discriminate** is to perceive the differences between or among things that are very similar; it may suggest that some aesthetic evaluation is involved (*to discriminate between two painters' styles*). **Distinguish** requires making even finer distinctions among things that resemble each other even more closely (*unable to distinguish the shadowy figures moving through the forest*). *Distinguish* can also mean recognizing by some special mark or outward sign (*the sheriff could be distinguished by his silver badge*). **Differentiate**, on the other hand, suggests the ability to perceive differences between things that are easily confused. In contrast to *distinguish, differentiate* suggests subtle differences that must be compared in some detail (*the color of her dress was difficult to differentiate from the color of the chair in which she was seated; it took a sharp eye to distinguish where her skirt ended and the upholstery began*). If you have trouble *differentiating* among these closely related verbs, you're not alone.

distinguishable ▶ adjective *the differences between the original and the copy were only slightly distinguishable* **discernible,** recognizable, identifiable, detectable.

distinguished ▶ adjective *our distinguished guests* **eminent,** famous, renowned, prominent, well-known; esteemed, respected, illustrious, acclaimed, celebrated, great; notable, important, influential.
ANTONYMS unknown, obscure.

distinguishing ▶ adjective *does he have any distinguishing features, such as a scar or a birthmark?* **distinctive,** differentiating, characteristic, typical, peculiar, singular, unique.

distract ▶ verb *let's not distract Dionne while she's painting* **divert,** sidetrack, draw away, disturb, put off.

distracted ▶ adjective **1** *she seemed distracted today* **preoccupied,** inattentive, vague, abstracted, distrait, absentminded, faraway, in a world of one's own; bemused, confused, bewildered; troubled, harassed, worried, anxious; informal miles away, not with it.
ANTONYMS attentive.
2 *she was distracted with worry* **crazed,** mad, insane, wild, out of one's head, crazy.

distraction ▶ noun **1** *a distraction from the real issues* **diversion,** interruption, disturbance, interference, hindrance.
2 *frivolous distractions* **amusement,** entertainment, diversion, recreation, leisure pursuit, divertissement.
3 *he was driven to distraction* **frenzy,** hysteria, mental distress, madness, insanity, mania; agitation, perturbation.

distress ▶ noun **1** *she concealed her distress* **anguish,** suffering, pain, agony, torment, heartache, heartbreak; misery, wretchedness, sorrow, grief, woe, sadness, unhappiness, desolation, despair.
ANTONYMS happiness.
2 *a ship in distress* **danger,** peril, difficulty, trouble, jeopardy, risk.
ANTONYMS safety.
3 *the distress of the refugees* **hardship,** adversity, poverty, deprivation, privation, destitution, indigence, impoverishment, penury, need, dire straits.
ANTONYMS prosperity.
▶ verb *he was distressed by the trial* **cause anguish to,** cause suffering to, pain, upset, make miserable; trouble, worry, bother, perturb, disturb, disquiet, agitate, harrow, torment.
ANTONYMS calm, please.

distressing ▶ adjective *the news was terribly distressing* **upsetting,** worrying, disturbing, disquieting, painful, traumatic, agonizing, harrowing; sad, saddening, heartbreaking, heart-rending; informal gut-wrenching.
ANTONYMS comforting.

distribute ▶ verb **1** *the proceeds were distributed among his creditors* **give out,** deal out, dole out, dish out, hand out/around; allocate, allot, apportion, share out, divide out/up, parcel out.
ANTONYMS collect.
2 *the newsletter is distributed free* **circulate,** issue, hand out, deliver.
3 *more than 130 different species are distributed worldwide* **disperse,** scatter, spread.

distribution ▶ noun **1** *the distribution of charity* **giving out,** dealing out, doling out, handing out/around, issue, issuing, dispensation; allocation, allotment, apportioning, sharing out, dividing up/out, parceling out.
2 *the geographical distribution of plants* **dispersal,** dissemination, spread; placement, position, location, disposition.
3 *centers of food distribution* **supply,** supplying, delivery, transport, transportation.
4 *the statistical distribution of the problem* **frequency,** prevalence, incidence, commonness.

district ▶ noun *the most respected contractor in our district* **neighborhood,** area, region, locality, locale, community, quarter, sector, zone, territory; ward; informal neck of the woods.

distrust ▶ noun *the general distrust of authority* **mistrust,** suspicion, wariness, chariness, leeriness, lack of trust, lack of confidence; skepticism, doubt, doubtfulness, cynicism;

misgivings, qualms, disbelief; formal **dubiety.**
▶ verb *Louise distrusted him* **mistrust,** be suspicious of, be wary/chary of, be leery of, regard with suspicion, suspect; be skeptical of, have doubts about, doubt, be unsure of/about, have misgivings about, wonder about, disbelieve (in).

disturb ▶ verb **1** *let's go somewhere where we won't be disturbed* **interrupt,** intrude on, butt in on, barge in on; distract, disrupt, bother, trouble, pester, harass; informal hassle.
2 *don't disturb his papers* **disarrange,** muddle, rearrange, disorganize, disorder, mix up, interfere with, throw into disorder/confusion, turn upside down.
3 *waters disturbed by winds* **agitate,** churn up, stir up; literary roil.
4 *he wasn't disturbed by the allegations* **perturb,** trouble, concern, worry, upset; agitate, fluster, discomfit, disconcert, dismay, distress, discompose, unsettle, ruffle.

disturbance ▶ noun **1** *we are concerned about the disturbance to local residents* **disruption,** distraction, interference; bother, trouble, inconvenience, upset, annoyance, irritation, intrusion, harassment, hassle.
2 *disturbances among the peasantry* **riot,** fracas, upheaval, brawl, street fight, melee, free-for-all, ruckus, rumpus, rumble, ruction.
3 *emotional disturbance* **trouble,** perturbation, distress, worry, upset, agitation, discomposure, discomfiture; neurosis, illness, sickness, disorder, complaint.

disturbed ▶ adjective **1** *disturbed sleep* **disrupted,** interrupted, fitful, intermittent, broken.
2 *the children seemed disturbed* **troubled,** distressed, upset, distraught; unbalanced, unstable, disordered, dysfunctional, maladjusted, neurotic, unhinged; informal screwed up, mixed up.

disturbing ▶ adjective *he gave us some disturbing information* **worrying,** perturbing, troubling, upsetting; distressing, discomfiting, disconcerting, disquieting, unsettling, dismaying, alarming, frightening.

disuse ▶ noun *many of the mills fell into disuse* **nonuse,** nonemployment, lack of use; neglect, abandonment, desertion, obsolescence; formal desuetude.

disused ▶ adjective *a disused building* **unused,** no longer in use, unemployed, idle; abandoned, deserted, vacated, unoccupied, uninhabited.

ditch ▶ noun *she rescued a cat from the ditch* **trench,** trough, channel, dike, drain, gutter, gully, watercourse, conduit; Archaeology fosse.
▶ verb **1** *they started ditching the coastal areas* **dig a ditch in,** trench, excavate, drain.
2 informal *she ditched her old curtains* **throw out,** throw away, discard, get rid of, dispose of, do away with, deep-six, shed; abandon, drop, shelve, scrap, jettison, throw on the scrap heap; informal dump, junk, chuck, pull the plug on, trash.
3 informal *she ditched her husband* See ABANDON (sense 3 of the verb).

diurnal ▶ adjective *the patient's moods are determined by diurnal events* **daily,** everyday, quotidian, occurring every/each day.

divan ▶ noun *have a rest on the divan* **settee,** sofa, couch, chesterfield; sofa bed, daybed, studio couch.

dive ▶ verb **1** *they dived into the clear water | the plane was diving toward the ground* **plunge,** nosedive, jump head first, bellyflop; plummet, fall, drop, pitch, dive-bomb.
2 *the islanders dive for oysters* **swim under water;** snorkel, scuba dive.
3 *they dove for cover* **leap,** jump, lunge, launch oneself, throw oneself, go headlong, duck.
▶ noun **1** *a dive into the pool* **plunge,** swan dive, nosedive, jump, bellyflop; plummet, fall, drop, swoop, pitch.
2 *a sideways dive* **lunge,** spring, jump, leap.
3 informal *John got into a fight in some dive* **sleazy bar/nightclub,** seedy bar/nightclub; informal (drinking) joint, hole.

diverge ▶ verb **1** *the two roads diverged* **separate,** part, fork, divide, split, bifurcate, go in different directions.
ANTONYMS converge.
2 *areas where our views diverge* **differ,** be different, be dissimilar; disagree, be at variance, be at odds, conflict, clash.
ANTONYMS agree.
3 *he diverged from his script* **deviate,** digress, depart, veer, stray; stray from the point, get off the subject.

divergence ▶ noun **1** *the divergence of the human and ape lineages* **separation,** dividing, parting, forking, bifurcation.
2 *a marked political divergence* **difference,** dissimilarity, variance, disparity; disagreement, incompatibility, mismatch.
3 *divergence from standard behavior* **deviation,** digression, departure, shift, straying; variation, change, alteration.

divergent ▶ adjective *divergent points of view* **differing,** varying, different, dissimilar, unalike, disparate, contrasting, contrastive; conflicting, incompatible, contradictory, at odds, at variance.
ANTONYMS similar.

divers ▶ adjective literary *Mr. Roosevelt's divers areas of expertise* **several,** many, numerous, multiple, manifold, multifarious, multitudinous; sundry, miscellaneous, assorted, various; literary myriad.

diverse ▶ adjective *managing data from diverse databases* **various,** sundry, manifold, multiple; varied, varying, miscellaneous, assorted, mixed, diversified, divergent, heterogeneous, a mixed bag of; different, differing, distinct, unlike, dissimilar; literary divers, myriad.

diversify ▶ verb **1** *farmers looking for ways to diversify* **branch out,** expand, extend operations.
2 *a plan aimed at diversifying the economy* **vary,** bring variety to; modify, alter, change, transform; expand, enlarge.

diversion ▶ noun **1** *the diversion of 19 rivers* **rerouting,** redirection, deflection, deviation, divergence.
2 *traffic diversions* **detour,** bypass, deviation, alternative route.

3 *the noise created a diversion* **distraction,** disturbance, smokescreen, feint.
4 *a city full of diversions* **entertainment,** amusement, pastime, delight, divertissement; fun, recreation, rest and relaxation, pleasure; informal R and R; dated sport.

diversity ▶ **noun** *a diversity of design styles* **variety,** miscellany, assortment, mixture, mix, mélange, range, array, multiplicity; variation, variance, diversification, heterogeneity, difference, contrast.
ANTONYMS uniformity.

divert ▶ **verb 1** *a plan to divert the Fraser River* **reroute,** redirect, change the course of, deflect, channel.
2 *he diverted her from her studies* **distract,** sidetrack, disturb, draw away, be a distraction, put off.
3 *the story diverted them* **amuse,** entertain, distract, delight, enchant, interest, fascinate, absorb, engross, rivet, grip, hold the attention of.

diverting ▶ **adjective** *a diverting musical* **entertaining,** amusing, enjoyable, pleasing, agreeable, delightful, appealing; interesting, fascinating, intriguing, absorbing, riveting, compelling; humorous, funny, witty, comical.
ANTONYMS boring.

divest ▶ **verb** *he intends to* ***divest*** *you* ***of*** *your power* **deprive of,** strip of, dispossess of, rob of, cheat out of, trick out of.

divide ▶ **verb 1** *he divided his estate into separate holdings* **split (up),** cut up, carve up; dissect, bisect, halve, quarter; literary sunder.
ANTONYMS unify, join, converge.
2 *a curtain divided her cabin from the galley* **separate,** segregate, partition, screen off, section off, split off.
ANTONYMS unify, join, converge.
3 *the stairs divide at the mezzanine* **diverge,** separate, part, branch (off), fork, split (in two), bifurcate.
ANTONYMS unify, join, converge.
4 *Jack* ***divided up*** *the cash* **share out,** allocate, allot, apportion, portion out, ration out, parcel out, deal out, dole out, dish out, distribute, dispense; informal divvy up.
5 *he aimed to divide his opponents* **disunite,** drive apart, break up, split up, set at variance, set at odds; separate, isolate, estrange, alienate; literary tear asunder.
ANTONYMS unify, unite.
6 *living things are divided into three categories* **classify,** sort (out), categorize, order, group, grade, rank.
ANTONYMS combine.
▶ **noun** *the sectarian divide* **breach,** gulf, gap, split; borderline, boundary, dividing line.

dividend ▶ **noun 1** *an annual dividend* **share,** portion, premium, return, gain, profit, commission; informal cut.
2 *the research will produce dividends in the future* **benefit,** advantage, gain; bonus, extra, plus.

divine ▶ **adjective 1** *a divine being* **godly,** angelic, seraphic, saintly, beatific; heavenly, celestial, supernal, holy.
ANTONYMS mortal.
2 *divine worship* **religious,** holy, sacred, sanctified, consecrated, blessed, devotional.
3 informal *this food is divine* See **EXCELLENT**.
▶ **noun** dated *puritan divines* **theologian,** clergyman, clergywoman, member of the clergy, churchman, churchwoman, cleric, minister, man/woman of the cloth, preacher, priest; informal reverend.
▶ **verb 1** *Fergus divined how afraid she was* **guess,** surmise, conjecture, deduce, infer; discern, intuit, perceive, recognize, see, realize, appreciate, understand, grasp, comprehend; informal figure (out), savvy.
2 *they divined that this was an auspicious day* **foretell,** predict, prophesy, forecast, foresee, prognosticate. See note at **PREDICT**.

> CHOOSE THE RIGHT WORD
>
> **divine, holy, sacred, hallowed, consecrated**
>
> **Holy** is the only one of these words associated with religion and worship that may be applied directly to the Supreme Being. Something that is *holy* is regarded with the highest reverence because of its connection with God or a god (*Christmas is a holy day in the Christian calendar*). Something that is **sacred**, on the other hand, is set apart as *holy* or is dedicated to some exalted purpose (*sacred music*) but may derive its holiness from a human source rather than from God (*a sacred oath between brothers*). In its strictest sense, **divine** means associated with or derived from God (*the divine right of kings*), but it has also been used to describe anything that is admirable or treasured (*her wedding dress was divine*). **Hallowed** and **consecrated** refer to what has been made sacred or holy, with *hallowed* connoting intrinsic holiness (*they walked on hallowed ground*) and *consecrated* meaning blessed by a formal rite or formally dedicated to some religious use (*the old building had been consecrated as a church*).

divinity ▶ **noun 1** *they denied Christ's divinity* **divine nature,** godliness, deity, godhead, holiness.
2 *the study of divinity* **theology,** religious studies, religion, scripture.
3 *a female divinity* **deity,** god, goddess, divine being, supreme being.

division ▶ **noun 1** *the division of the island | cell division* **dividing (up),** breaking up, breakup, carving up, splitting, dissection, bisection; partitioning, separation, segregation.
2 *the division of his assets* **sharing out,** dividing up, parceling out, dishing out, allocation, allotment, apportionment; splitting up, carving up; informal divvying up.
3 *the division between nomadic and urban cultures* **dividing line,** divide, boundary, borderline, border, demarcation line.
4 *each class is divided into nine divisions* **section,** subsection, subdivision, category, class, group, grouping, set, subset, family.

5 *an independent division of the company* **department,** branch, arm, wing, sector, section, subsection, subdivision, subsidiary.
6 *the causes of social division* **disunity,** disunion, conflict, discord, disagreement, dissension, disaffection, estrangement, alienation, isolation.

divisive ▶ adjective *a divisive scheme to set his rivals against each other* **alienating,** estranging, isolating, schismatic.
ANTONYMS unifying.

divorce ▶ noun 1 *she wants a divorce* **dissolution,** annulment, (official) separation.
ANTONYMS marriage.
2 *a growing divorce between the church and people* **separation,** division, split, disunity, estrangement, alienation; schism, gulf, chasm.
ANTONYMS unity.
▶ verb 1 *her parents have divorced* **dissolve one's marriage,** annul one's marriage, end one's marriage, get a divorce.
2 *religion cannot be divorced from morality* **separate,** disconnect, divide, dissociate, disassociate, detach, isolate, alienate, set apart, cut off.

divulge ▶ verb *he refused to divulge Father O'Neill's whereabouts* **disclose,** reveal, tell, communicate, pass on, publish, broadcast, proclaim; expose, uncover, make public, give away, let slip; informal spill the beans about, let on about, let the cat out of the bag about.
ANTONYMS conceal.

dizzy ▶ adjective 1 *she felt dizzy* **giddy,** lightheaded, faint, unsteady, shaky, muzzy, wobbly; informal woozy.
2 *dizzy heights* **causing dizziness,** causing giddiness, vertiginous.

do ▶ verb 1 *she does most of the manual work* **carry out,** undertake, discharge, execute, perform, accomplish, achieve; bring about/off, engineer; informal pull off; formal effectuate.
2 *they can do as they please* **act,** behave, conduct oneself, acquit oneself; formal comport oneself.
3 *regular coffee will do* **suffice,** be adequate, be satisfactory, fill/fit the bill, serve one's purpose, meet one's needs.
4 *the boys will do the dinner* **prepare,** make, get ready, see to, arrange, organize, be responsible for, be in charge of; informal fix.
5 *the company is doing a new range of footwear | a portrait I am doing* **make,** create, produce, turn out, design, manufacture; paint, draw, sketch; informal knock off.
6 *each room was done in a different color* **decorate,** furnish, ornament, deck out, trick out; informal do up.
7 *the maid did her hair* **style,** arrange, adjust; brush, comb, wash, dry, cut; informal fix.
8 *I am doing a show to raise money* **put on,** present, produce; perform in, act in, take part in, participate in.
9 *you've done me a favor* **grant,** pay, render, give.
10 *show me how to do these equations* **work out,** figure out, calculate; solve, resolve.
11 *she's doing archaeology* **study,** learn, take a course in.
12 *what does he do?* **have as a job,** have as a profession, be employed at, earn a living at.
13 *he is doing well at college* **get on/along,** progress, fare, manage, cope; succeed, prosper.
14 *he was doing 25 mph over the speed limit* **drive at,** travel at, move at.
15 *the cyclists do 30 kilometers per day* **travel (over),** journey, cover, traverse, achieve, notch up, log; informal chalk up.
16 informal *we're doing Scotland this summer* **visit,** tour, sightsee in.
▶ noun informal *he invited us to a grand do* **party,** reception, gathering, celebration, function, social event/occasion, social, soiree; informal bash, shindig.
– PHRASES **do away with 1** *they want to do away with the old customs* **abolish,** get rid of, discard, remove, eliminate, discontinue, stop, end, terminate, put an end to, put a stop to, dispense with, drop, abandon, give up; informal scrap, ditch, dump, deep-six. **2** informal *she tried to do away with her husband* See KILL (sense 1 of the verb). **do in** informal **1** *the poor devil's been done in* See KILL (sense 1 of the verb). **2** *the long walk home did me in* **wear out,** tire out, exhaust, fatigue, weary, overtire, drain; informal take it out of. **3** *I did my back in* **injure,** hurt, damage. **do out of** informal *she nearly succeeded in doing Martin out of his inheritance* **swindle out of,** cheat out of, trick out of, deprive of; informal con out of, diddle out of. **do up 1** *she did up her bootlace* **fasten,** tie (up), lace, knot; make fast, secure. **2** informal *he's had his house done up* **renovate,** refurbish, refit, redecorate, decorate, revamp, make over, modernize, improve, spruce up, smarten up; informal give something a facelift, rehab, tart up, pimp. **do without** *we learned to do without many of the luxuries we had become accustomed to* **forgo,** dispense with, abstain from, refrain from, eschew, give up, cut out, renounce, manage without; formal forswear.

docile ▶ adjective *his docile children do everything he asks of them* **compliant,** obedient, pliant, dutiful, submissive, deferential, unassertive, cooperative, amenable, accommodating, biddable, malleable. See note at OBEDIENT.
ANTONYMS disobedient, willful.

dock[1] ▶ noun *his boat was moored at the dock* **harbor,** marina, port, anchorage; wharf, quay, pier, jetty, landing stage.
▶ verb *the ship docked* **moor,** berth, put in, tie up, anchor.

dock[2] ▶ verb 1 *they docked the money from his salary* **deduct,** subtract, remove, debit, take off/away, garnishee; informal knock off.
2 *workers had their pay docked* **reduce,** cut, decrease.
3 *the dog's tail was docked* **cut off,** cut short, shorten, crop, lop; remove, amputate, detach, sever, chop off, take off.

docket ▶ noun 1 *he opened a new docket for the account* **file,** dossier, folder.
2 *I looked my name up on the docket* **list,** index; schedule, agenda, program, timetable.
▶ verb *docket the package* **document,** record, register; label, tag, tab, mark.

doctor ▶ noun *Claudio went to see a doctor*

physician, MD, medical practitioner, clinician; general practitioner, GP; medic, intern; informal doc, medico, quack, sawbones.
▶ **verb 1** informal *he doctored their wounds* **treat,** medicate, cure, heal; tend, attend to, minister to, care for, nurse.
2 *he doctored Stephen's drink* **adulterate,** contaminate, tamper with, lace; informal spike, dope.
3 *the reports have been doctored* **falsify,** tamper with, interfere with, alter, change; forge, fake; informal cook, fiddle with.

doctrinaire ▶ **adjective** *doctrinaire Marxists* **dogmatic,** rigid, inflexible, uncompromising; authoritarian, intolerant, fanatical, zealous, extreme.

doctrine ▶ **noun** *the doctrine of the Trinity* **creed,** credo, dogma, belief, teaching, ideology; tenet, maxim, canon, principle, precept.

document ▶ **noun** *their lawyer drew up a document* **official paper,** legal paper, certificate, deed, contract, legal agreement; Law instrument, indenture.
▶ **verb** *many aspects of school life have been documented* **record,** register, report, log, chronicle, archive, put on record, write down; detail, note, describe.

documentary ▶ **adjective 1** *documentary evidence* **recorded,** documented, registered, written, chronicled, archived, on record, on paper, in writing.
2 *a documentary film* **factual,** nonfictional.
▶ **noun** *a documentary about rural West Virginia* **factual program,** factual film; program, film, broadcast.

dodder ▶ **verb** *doddering along the sidewalk* **totter,** teeter, toddle, hobble, shuffle, shamble, falter.

doddering, doddery ▶ **adjective** *a doddering patient who needs constant supervision* **tottering,** tottery, staggering, shuffling, shambling, faltering, shaky, unsteady, wobbly; feeble, frail, weak.

dodge ▶ **verb 1** *she dodged into a crowded restaurant* **dart,** bolt, dive, lunge, leap, spring.
2 *he could easily dodge the two cops* **elude,** evade, avoid, escape, run away from, lose, shake (off), jink; informal give someone the slip, ditch.
3 *the mayor tried to dodge the debate* **avoid,** evade, get out of, back out of, sidestep, do an end run; informal duck, wriggle out of.
▶ **noun 1** *a dodge to the right* **dart,** bolt, dive, lunge, leap, spring.
2 *a clever dodge | a tax dodge* **ruse,** ploy, scheme, tactic, stratagem, subterfuge, trick, hoax, wile, cheat, deception, blind; swindle, fraud; informal scam, con, bunco, grift.

doer ▶ **noun 1** *the doer of unspeakable deeds* **performer,** perpetrator, executor, accomplisher, agent.
2 *Daniel is a thinker more than a doer* **worker,** organizer, man/woman of action; informal mover and shaker, busy bee.

doff ▶ **verb** literary *he doffed his cap as we walked past* **take off,** remove, strip off, pull off; raise, lift, tip; dated divest oneself of.
ANTONYMS don.

dog ▶ **noun 1** *she went for a walk with her dog* hound, canine; mongrel, cur; pup, puppy; informal doggy/doggie, pooch.
2 informal *you black-hearted dog!* See **BASTARD** (sense 2 of the noun).
3 informal *you're a lucky dog!* See **FELLOW** (sense 1).
▶ **verb 1** *they dogged him the length of the country* **pursue,** follow, track, trail, shadow, hound; informal tail.
2 *the scheme was dogged by bad weather* **plague,** beset, bedevil, beleaguer, blight, trouble.

dogged ▶ **adjective** *what he lacks in natural talent he makes up for in dogged spirit* **tenacious,** determined, resolute, resolved, purposeful, persistent, persevering, single-minded, tireless; strong-willed, steadfast, staunch; formal pertinacious. See note at **STUBBORN**.
ANTONYMS halfhearted.

dogma ▶ **noun** *a dogma of the Sikh religion* **teaching,** belief, tenet, principle, precept, maxim, article of faith, canon; creed, credo, set of beliefs, doctrine, ideology.

dogmatic ▶ **adjective** *your being so dogmatic does not attract me to your religious philosophy* **opinionated,** peremptory, assertive, insistent, emphatic, adamant, doctrinaire, authoritarian, imperious, dictatorial, uncompromising, unyielding, inflexible, rigid.

doing ▶ **noun 1** *the doing of the act constitutes the offense* **performance,** performing, carrying out, execution, implementation, implementing, achievement, accomplishment, realization, completion; formal effectuation.
2 *an account of his doings in Boston* **exploit,** activity, act, action, deed, feat, achievement, accomplishment; informal caper.
3 *that would take some doing* **effort,** exertion, work, hard work, application, labor, toil, struggle.

doldrums ▶ **plural noun** *winter doldrums* **depression,** melancholy, gloom, gloominess, downheartedness, dejection, despondency, low spirits, despair; inertia, apathy, listlessness, blahs, blue funk, blues.
– PHRASES **in the doldrums** *overseas stocks are in the doldrums* **inactive,** quiet, slow, slack, sluggish, stagnant.

dole ▶ **verb** *we dole out fresh soup and bread every afternoon* **deal out,** share out, divide up, allocate, allot, distribute, dispense, hand out, give out, dish out/up, divvy up.

doleful ▶ **adjective** *her doleful eyes* **mournful,** woeful, sorrowful, sad, unhappy, depressed, gloomy, morose, melancholy, miserable, forlorn, wretched, woebegone, despondent, dejected, disconsolate, downcast, crestfallen, downhearted; informal blue, down in/at the mouth, down in the dumps; literary dolorous, heartsick.
ANTONYMS cheerful.

doll ▶ **noun 1** *the child was hugging a doll* **figure,** figurine, action figure, model; toy, plaything; informal dolly.
2 informal *she was quite a doll* See **BEAUTY** (sense 2).
– PHRASES **doll oneself up** informal *you don't need to doll yourself up for me* **dress up**; informal do

oneself up, dress up to the nines, put on one's glad rags.

dolor ▶ noun literary See MISERY (sense 1).

dolt ▶ noun See IDIOT.

domain ▶ noun 1 *they extended their domain* **realm,** kingdom, empire, dominion, province, territory, land.
2 *the domain of art* **field,** area, sphere, discipline, province, world.

dome ▶ noun *the distinctive dome of the cathedral* **cupola,** vault, arched roof, rotunda.

domestic ▶ adjective 1 *domestic commitments* **family,** home, household.
2 *she was not at all domestic* stay-at-home, home-loving, homey, housewifely; humorous domesticated.
3 *small domestic animals* **domesticated,** tame, pet, household.
4 *the domestic car industry* **national,** home, internal.
5 *domestic plants* **native,** indigenous.
▶ noun *they worked as domestics* **servant,** domestic worker, domestic help, maid, housemaid, cleaner, cleaning lady, housekeeper.

domesticated ▶ adjective 1 *domesticated animals* **tame,** tamed, pet, domestic, trained.
ANTONYMS wild.
2 *domesticated crops* **cultivated,** naturalized.
ANTONYMS foreign, wild.
3 humorous *I'm happily domesticated* See DOMESTIC (sense 2 of the adjective).

domicile ▶ noun formal *changes of domicile* **residence,** home, house, address, residency, lodging, accommodations; informal digs; formal dwelling (place), abode, habitation.
▶ verb *he is domiciled in Australia* **is settled,** live, make one's home, take up residence.

dominant ▶ adjective 1 *the dominant classes* **presiding,** ruling, governing, controlling, commanding, ascendant, supreme, authoritative.
ANTONYMS subservient.
2 *he has a dominant personality* **assertive,** authoritative, forceful, domineering, commanding, controlling, pushy.
ANTONYMS submissive.
3 *the dominant issues in psychology* **main,** principal, prime, premier, chief, foremost, primary, predominant, paramount, prominent; central, key, crucial, core; informal number-one.
ANTONYMS secondary.

dominate ▶ verb 1 *the Russians dominated Iran in the nineteenth century* **control,** influence, exercise control over, command, be in command of, be in charge of, rule, govern, direct, have ascendancy over, have mastery over; informal head up, be in the driver's seat, be at the helm of, rule the roost (in), wear the pants (in), have someone in one's hip pocket; literary sway.
2 *it dominates the sports scene* **predominate,** prevail, reign, be prevalent, be paramount, be preeminent; informal kick butt.
3 *the village is dominated by the viaduct* **overlook,** command, tower above/over, loom over.

domination ▶ noun *she was put off by the male domination sanctioned by her boyfriend's family* **rule,** government, sovereignty, control, command, authority, power, dominion, dominance, mastery, supremacy, superiority, ascendancy, sway.

domineer ▶ verb *his mother had always sought out men she could domineer* **browbeat,** bully, intimidate, push around/about, order about/around, lord it over; dictate to, be overbearing, have under one's thumb, rule with a rod of iron; informal boss about/around, walk all over.

domineering ▶ adjective *a domineering father and a meek mother had turned her against the idea of marriage* **overbearing,** authoritarian, imperious, high-handed, autocratic; masterful, dictatorial, despotic, oppressive, iron-fisted, strict, harsh, bossy.

dominion ▶ noun 1 *France had dominion over Laos* **supremacy,** ascendancy, dominance, domination, superiority, predominance, preeminence, hegemony, authority, mastery, control, command, power, sway, rule, government, jurisdiction, sovereignty, suzerainty. See note at JURISDICTION.
2 *a British dominion* **dependency,** colony, protectorate, territory, province, possession; historical tributary.

don ▶ verb *he donned an overcoat* **put on,** get dressed in, dress (oneself) in, get into, slip into/on.

donate ▶ verb *the proceeds were donated to the American Red Cross* **give,** give/make a donation of, contribute, make a contribution of, gift, pledge, grant, bestow; informal chip in, pitch in, kick in. See note at GIVE.

donation ▶ noun *a tax-deductible donation* **gift,** contribution, present, pledge, handout, grant, offering; formal benefaction; historical alms. See note at PRESENT[3].

done ▶ adjective 1 *the job is done* **finished,** ended, concluded, complete, completed, accomplished, achieved, fulfilled, discharged, executed; informal wrapped up, sewn up, polished off.
ANTONYMS incomplete.
2 *is the meat done?* **cooked (through),** ready.
ANTONYMS raw, underdone.
3 *those days are done* **over,** over and done with, at an end, finished, ended, concluded, terminated, no more, dead, gone, in the past.
ANTONYMS to come, ongoing.
4 informal *that's just not done* **proper,** seemly, decent, respectable, right, correct, in order, fitting, appropriate, acceptable, the done thing.
– PHRASES **be/have done with** *she was done with him* **be/have finished with,** be through with, want no more to do with. **done for** informal *if you get caught, you'll be done for* **ruined,** finished, destroyed, undone, doomed, lost; informal washed up.

donkey ▶ noun 1 *the cart was drawn by a donkey* **ass,** jackass, jenny; mule, hinny, burro.
2 informal *you silly donkey!* See FOOL (sense 1 of the noun).

donor ▶ noun *an anonymous donor* **giver,** contributor, benefactor, benefactress; supporter, backer, patron, sponsor, friend, member; informal angel.

doom ▶ noun 1 *his impending doom* **destruction,**

downfall, ruin, ruination; extinction, annihilation, death.
2 archaic *the day of doom* **Judgment Day,** the Last Judgment, doomsday, Armageddon.
▶ **verb** *we were doomed to fail* **destine,** fate, predestine, preordain, foredoom, mean; condemn, sentence.

doomed ▶ **adjective** *a doomed voyage* **ill-fated,** ill-starred, cursed, jinxed, foredoomed, damned; literary star-crossed.

door ▶ **noun** *many a weary traveler has walked through that door* **doorway,** portal, opening, entrance, entry, exit.
– PHRASES **out of doors** *if the weather's nice, we'll have our dinner out of doors* **outside,** outdoors, in/into the open air, alfresco.

dope ▶ **noun** informal **1** *he was caught smuggling dope* **(illegal) drugs,** narcotics; cannabis, heroin, cocaine.
2 *what a dope!* See **FOOL** (sense 1 of the noun).
3 *give me the dope on Mr. Dixon* See **INTELLIGENCE** (sense 2).
▶ **verb 1** *the horse was doped* **drug,** administer drugs/narcotics to, tamper with, interfere with; sedate.
2 *they doped his drink* **add drugs to,** tamper with, adulterate, contaminate, lace; informal spike, doctor.

dormant ▶ **adjective** *the tubers lie dormant in the soil until spring* **asleep,** sleeping, resting; **inactive,** passive, inert, latent, quiescent. See note at **LATENT**.
ANTONYMS awake, active.

dose ▶ **noun** *do not exceed the prescribed dose* **measure,** measurement, portion, dosage, shot; informal hit, fix.

dot ▶ **noun** *a pattern of tiny dots* **spot,** speck, fleck, speckle; decimal point, period, pixel.
▶ **verb 1** *spots of rain dotted his shirt* **spot,** fleck, mark, stipple, freckle, sprinkle; literary bestrew, besprinkle.
2 *the streets are dotted with restaurants* **scatter,** pepper, sprinkle, strew.
– PHRASES **on the dot** informal *ring the bell at 1:15 on the dot* **precisely,** exactly, sharp, prompt, dead on, on the stroke of——; informal on the button, on the nose.

dotage ▶ **noun** *the memoirs she began in her dotage* **declining years,** winter of one's life, autumn of one's life; advanced years, old age; literary eld.

dote ▶ **verb**
– PHRASES **dote on** *she doted on the boy* **adore,** love dearly, be devoted to, idolize, treasure, cherish, worship, hold dear; indulge, spoil, pamper.

doting ▶ **adjective** *all her doting admirers* **adoring,** loving, besotted, infatuated; affectionate, fond, devoted, caring; uxorious.

double ▶ **adjective 1** *a double garage | double yellow lines* **dual,** duplex, twin, binary, duplicate, in pairs, coupled, twofold.
ANTONYMS single.
2 *a double helping* **doubled,** twofold.
3 *a double meaning* **ambiguous,** equivocal, dual, two-edged, double-edged, ambivalent, cryptic, enigmatic.
ANTONYMS unambiguous.
4 *a double life* **deceitful,** double-dealing, two-faced, dual; hypocritical, false, duplicitous, insincere, deceiving, dissembling, dishonest.
ANTONYMS simple, honest.
▶ **adverb** *we had to pay double* **twice (over),** twice the amount, doubly.
▶ **noun 1** *if it's not her, it's her double* **look-alike,** twin, clone, duplicate, exact likeness, replica, copy, facsimile, doppelgänger; informal spitting image, dead ringer.
2 *she used a double for the stunts* **stand-in,** substitute.
▶ **verb 1** *they doubled his salary* **multiply by two,** increase twofold.
2 *the bottom sheet had been doubled up* **fold (back/up/down/over/under),** turn back/up/down/over/under, tuck back/up/down/under.
3 *the kitchen can double as a dining room* **function,** do, (also) serve.
– PHRASES **on the double** *hold tight, we'll be there on the double* **very quickly,** as fast as one's legs can carry one, at a run, at a gallop, fast, swiftly, rapidly, speedily, at full speed, at full tilt, as fast as possible; informal like (greased) lightning, like the wind, like a bat out of hell, lickety-split, PDQ (pretty damn quick).

double-cross ▶ **verb** *he was double-crossing his family behind their backs* **betray,** cheat, defraud, trick, hoodwink, mislead, deceive, swindle, be disloyal to, be unfaithful to, play false; informal sell down the river.

double-dealing ▶ **noun** *your double-dealing will eventually be your undoing* **duplicity,** treachery, betrayal, double-crossing, unfaithfulness, untrustworthiness, infidelity, bad faith, disloyalty, breach of trust, fraud, underhandedness, cheating, dishonesty, deceit, deceitfulness, deception, falseness; informal crookedness.
ANTONYMS honesty.

double entendre ▶ **noun** *much of the comedy is derived from racy double entendres* **ambiguity,** double meaning, innuendo, play on words.

doubt ▶ **noun 1** *there was some doubt as to the caller's identity* **uncertainty,** unsureness, indecision, hesitation, dubiousness, suspicion, confusion; queries, questions; formal dubiety. See note at **UNCERTAINTY**.
ANTONYMS certainty.
2 *a weak leader racked by doubt* **indecision,** hesitation, uncertainty, insecurity, unease, uneasiness, apprehension; hesitancy, vacillation, irresolution.
ANTONYMS confidence, conviction.
3 *there is doubt about their motives* **skepticism,** distrust, mistrust, doubtfulness, suspicion, cynicism, uneasiness, apprehension, wariness, chariness, leeriness; reservations, misgivings, suspicions; formal dubiety.
ANTONYMS trust.
▶ **verb 1** *they doubted my story* **disbelieve,** distrust, mistrust, suspect, have doubts about, be suspicious of, have misgivings about, have qualms about, feel uneasy about, feel apprehensive about, query, question, challenge.
ANTONYMS trust.
2 *I doubt whether he will come* **think something**

unlikely, have (one's) doubts about, question, query, be dubious.
ANTONYMS be confident.
3 *stop doubting and believe!* **be undecided,** have doubts, be irresolute, be ambivalent, be doubtful, be unsure, be uncertain, be of two minds, hesitate, shilly-shally, waver, vacillate.
ANTONYMS believe.
– PHRASES **in doubt 1** *the issue was in doubt* **doubtful,** uncertain, open to question, unconfirmed, unknown, undecided, unresolved, in the balance, up in the air; informal iffy.
2 *if you are in doubt, ask for advice* **irresolute,** hesitant, vacillating, dithering, wavering, ambivalent; doubtful, unsure, uncertain, of two minds, shilly-shallying, undecided, in a quandary, in a dilemma; informal sitting on the fence. **no doubt** *he's no doubt read the note by now* **doubtless,** undoubtedly, indubitably, doubtlessly, without (a) doubt; unquestionably, undeniably, incontrovertibly, irrefutably; unequivocally, clearly, plainly, obviously, patently.

doubter ▶ noun *this is his chance to confound the doubters* **skeptic,** doubting Thomas, nonbeliever, unbeliever, disbeliever, cynic, scoffer, questioner, challenger, dissenter.
ANTONYMS believer.

doubtful ▶ adjective **1** *I was doubtful about going* **irresolute,** hesitant, vacillating, dithering, wavering, in doubt, unsure, uncertain, of two minds, shilly-shallying, undecided, in a quandary, in a dilemma, blowing hot and cold.
ANTONYMS confident, decisive.
2 *at this point, the verdict is still doubtful* **in doubt,** uncertain, open to question, unsure, unconfirmed, not definite, unknown, undecided, unresolved, debatable, in the balance, up in the air; informal iffy.
ANTONYMS certain.
3 *the whole trip is looking rather doubtful* **unlikely,** improbable, dubious, impossible.
ANTONYMS probable.
4 *they are doubtful of the methods used* **distrustful,** mistrustful, suspicious, wary, chary, leery, apprehensive; skeptical, unsure, ambivalent, dubious, cynical; informal trepidatious.
ANTONYMS trusting.
5 *this decision is of doubtful validity* **questionable,** arguable, debatable, controversial, contentious; informal iffy.
ANTONYMS sound.

CHOOSE THE RIGHT WORD

doubtful, ambiguous, dubious, enigmatic, equivocal, problematic, questionable

If you are **doubtful** about the outcome of a situation, you might be understandably **dubious** about getting involved in it. While all of these adjectives express suspicion, indecision, or a lack of clarity, *doubtful* carries such strong connotations of uncertainty that the thing being described is as good as worthless, unsound, invalid, unlikely, or doomed to fail (*it was doubtful that the plane could land safely*). *Dubious* is not quite as strong, suggesting suspicion, mistrust, or hesitation (*a dubious reputation*). It can also mean inclined to doubt or full of hesitation. If you're *doubtful* about the outcome of a particular situation, it means that you are fairly certain it will not turn out well. If you're *dubious*, on the other hand, it means that you're wavering or hesitating in your opinion. **Questionable** may merely imply the existence of doubt (*a questionable excuse*), but like *dubious*, it also has connotations of dishonesty and immorality (*a place where questionable activities were going on*). **Problematic**, in contrast to both *dubious* and *questionable*, is free from any suggestion of moral judgment or suspicion. It is applied to things that are genuinely uncertain, and to outcomes that are as likely to be positive as negative (*getting everyone in the family to agree could be problematic*). **Ambiguous** and **equivocal** refer to lack of clarity. But while *ambiguous* can refer to either an intentional or unintentional lack of clarity (*her ambiguous replies to our questions*), *equivocal* suggests an intentional wish to remain unclear (*his equivocal responses indicated that he wasn't keen to cooperate*). It can also mean capable of different interpretations (*an equivocal statement that could be taken to mean opposite things*). Something that is **enigmatic** is likely to be intentionally unclear as well (*an enigmatic statement designed to provoke controversy*), although *enigmatic* can also mean perplexing or mysterious.

doubtless ▶ adverb *Henry was doubtless glad of the opportunity* **undoubtedly,** indubitably, doubtlessly, no doubt; unquestionably, indisputably, undeniably, incontrovertibly, irrefutably; certainly, surely, of course, indeed.

dour ▶ adjective *they were barely acknowledged by the dour receptionist* **stern,** unsmiling, unfriendly, severe, forbidding, gruff, surly, grim, sullen, solemn, austere, stony. See note at GLUM.
ANTONYMS cheerful, friendly.

dovetail ▶ verb **1** *the ends of the logs were dovetailed* **joint,** join, fit together, splice, mortise, tenon.
2 *this will dovetail well with the company's existing activities* **fit in,** go together, be consistent, match, conform, harmonize, be in tune, correspond; informal square, jibe.

dowdy ▶ adjective *a makeover that took her from dowdy to wow-dy* **unfashionable,** frumpy, old-fashioned, outmoded, out-of-date, inelegant, shabby, frowzy.
ANTONYMS fashionable.

down[1] ▶ adverb **1** *they went down in the elevator* **toward a lower position,** downward, downstairs.
ANTONYMS up.
2 *she fell down* **to the ground,** to the floor, over.
ANTONYMS up.
▶ preposition **1** *the elevator plunged down the shaft* **to a lower position in,** to the bottom of.

2 *I walked down the street* **along,** to the other end of, from one end of—— to the other.
3 *down the years* **throughout,** through, during.
▶ adjective 1 *I'm feeling a bit down* **depressed,** sad, unhappy, melancholy, miserable, wretched, sorrowful, gloomy, dejected, downhearted, despondent, dispirited, low; informal blue, down in the dumps, down in/at the mouth.
ANTONYMS elated.
2 *the computer is down* **not working,** inoperative, malfunctioning, out of order, broken; not in service, out of action, out of commission; informal conked out, bust, busted, (gone) kaput, on the fritz, on the blink.
ANTONYMS working.
▶ verb informal 1 *antiaircraft missiles downed the fighter jet* **knock down/over,** knock to the ground, bring down, topple; informal deck, floor, flatten.
2 *he downed his beer* **drink (up/down),** gulp (down), guzzle, quaff, drain, chugalug, slug, finish off; informal knock back, put away, scarf (down/up).
▶ noun *the ups and downs of running a business* **setbacks,** upsets, reverses, reversals, mishaps, vicissitudes; informal glitches.
– PHRASES **be down on** informal *why do you have to be down on your parents all the time?* **disapprove of,** be against, feel antagonism to, be hostile to, feel ill will toward; informal have it in for.

down[2] ▶ noun *goose down* **soft feathers,** fine hair; fluff, fuzz, floss, lint.

downbeat ▶ adjective *the mood is decidedly downbeat* **pessimistic,** gloomy, negative, defeatist, cynical, bleak, fatalistic, dark, black; despairing, despondent, depressed, dejected, demoralized, hopeless, melancholy, glum.

downcast ▶ adjective *it's too nice a day to be looking so downcast* **despondent,** disheartened, discouraged, dispirited, downhearted, crestfallen, down, low, disconsolate, despairing; sad, melancholy, gloomy, glum, morose, doleful, dismal, woebegone, miserable, depressed, dejected; informal blue, down in/at the mouth, down in the dumps.
ANTONYMS elated.

downfall ▶ noun *the shah's downfall* **undoing,** ruin, ruination; defeat, conquest, deposition, overthrow; nemesis, destruction, annihilation, elimination; end, collapse, fall, crash, failure; debasement, degradation, disgrace; Waterloo.
ANTONYMS rise.

downgrade ▶ verb 1 *plans to downgrade three workers* **demote,** lower, reduce/lower in rank; relegate.
ANTONYMS promote.
2 *I won't downgrade their achievement* **disparage,** denigrate, detract from, run down, belittle; informal badmouth, dis.
ANTONYMS praise.

downhearted ▶ adjective *of the children, little Robbie was the most downhearted* **despondent,** disheartened, discouraged, dispirited, downcast, crestfallen, down, low, disconsolate, wretched; melancholy, gloomy, glum, morose, doleful, dismal, woebegone, miserable, depressed, dejected, sorrowful, sad; informal blue, down in/at the mouth, down in the dumps.
ANTONYMS elated.

downpour ▶ noun *they met when huddled under an awning during a sudden downpour* **rainstorm,** cloudburst, deluge, shower; thunderstorm, thundershower; torrential/pouring rain.

downright ▶ adjective 1 *downright lies* **complete,** total, absolute, utter, thorough, out-and-out, outright, sheer, arrant, pure, real, veritable, categorical, unmitigated, unadulterated, unalloyed, unequivocal.
2 *her downright attitude* See **FORTHRIGHT**.
▶ adverb *that's downright dangerous* **thoroughly,** utterly, positively, profoundly, really, completely, totally, entirely; unquestionably, undeniably, in every respect, through and through; informal plain.

down-to-earth ▶ adjective *I guess we weren't expecting the son of those weirdos to be so charming and down-to-earth* **practical,** sensible, realistic, matter-of-fact, responsible, reasonable, rational, logical, balanced, sober, pragmatic, levelheaded, commonsensical, sane.
ANTONYMS idealistic.

downtrodden ▶ adjective *thousands of downtrodden families arrived at the border, only to be turned away* **oppressed,** subjugated, persecuted, repressed, tyrannized, crushed, enslaved, exploited, victimized, bullied; disadvantaged, underprivileged, powerless, helpless; abused, maltreated.

downward ▶ adjective *profits are in a downward trend* **descending,** downhill, falling, sinking, dipping; earthbound, earthward.

dowry ▶ noun *Belinda's dowry included an acre of fertile pasture and two young mules* **marriage settlement,** (marriage) portion; archaic dot.

doze ▶ verb *she was dozing at her desk when the supervisor walked by* **catnap,** nap, drowse, sleep lightly, rest; informal snooze, catch forty winks, get some shut-eye, catch some Zs; literary slumber.
▶ noun *a little doze before dinner might be just what you need* **catnap,** nap, siesta, light sleep, drowse, rest; informal snooze, forty winks; literary slumber.
– PHRASES **doze off** *the guy in front of us would doze off between all the musical numbers* **fall asleep,** go to sleep, drop off; informal nod off, drift off, sack out, conk out.

drab ▶ adjective 1 *a drab interior* **colorless,** gray, dull, washed out, muted, lackluster; dingy, dreary, dismal, cheerless, gloomy, somber.
ANTONYMS bright, cheerful.
2 *a drab existence* **uninteresting,** dull, boring, tedious, monotonous, dry, dreary; unexciting, unimaginative, uninspiring, insipid, lackluster, flat, stale, wishy-washy, colorless; lame, tired, sterile, anemic, barren, tame; middle-of-the-road, run-of-the-mill, mediocre, nondescript, characterless, mundane, unremarkable, humdrum, plain-vanilla.
ANTONYMS interesting.

draft[1] ▶ noun 1 *the draft of his speech* **preliminary version,** rough outline, plan, skeleton, abstract; main points, bare bones.

2 *a draft of the building* **plan,** blueprint, design, diagram, drawing, sketch, map, layout, representation.
3 *a bank draft* **check,** order, money order, bill of exchange.

draft² ▶ noun 1 *the draft made Robyn shiver* **current of air,** rush of air; waft, wind, breeze, gust, puff, blast; informal blow.
2 *a deep draft of beer* **gulp,** drink, swallow, mouthful, slug; informal swig, swill.

drag ▶ verb 1 *she dragged the chair backward* **haul,** pull, tug, heave, lug, draw; trail, trawl, tow; informal yank.
2 *the day dragged* **become tedious,** pass slowly, creep along, hang heavy, wear on, go on too long, go on and on.
▶ noun 1 *the drag of the air brakes* **pull,** resistance, tug.
2 informal *work can be a drag* **bore,** nuisance, bother, trouble, pest, annoyance, trial, chore, vexation; informal pain, pain in the neck, headache, hassle.
– PHRASES **drag on** *their feud has dragged on for years* **persist,** continue, go on, carry on, extend, run on, be protracted, endure, prevail. **drag out** *let's not drag out the Q and A session with issues that can't be addressed at this point* **prolong,** protract, draw out, spin out, string out, extend, lengthen, carry on, keep going, continue.

dragoon ▶ noun historical *the dragoons charged* **cavalryman,** mounted soldier; historical knight, chevalier, hussar; archaic cavalier.
▶ verb *he dragooned his friends into participating* **coerce,** pressure, press, push; force, compel, impel; hound, harass, nag, harry, badger, goad, pester; browbeat, bludgeon, bully, twist someone's arm, strong-arm; informal railroad.

drain ▶ verb 1 *a valve for draining the tank* **empty (out),** void, clear (out), evacuate, unload.
ANTONYMS fill.
2 *drain off any surplus liquid* **draw off,** extract, withdraw, remove, siphon off, pour out, pour off; milk, bleed, tap, void, filter, discharge.
3 *the water drained away to the sea* **flow,** pour, trickle, stream, run, rush, gush, flood, surge; leak, ooze, seep, dribble, issue, filter, bleed, leach.
4 *more people would just drain our resources* **use up,** exhaust, deplete, consume, expend, get through, sap, strain, tax; milk, bleed.
ANTONYMS replenish.
▶ noun 1 *the drain filled with water* **sewer,** channel, conduit, ditch, culvert, duct, pipe, gutter, trough; sluice, spillway, race, flume, chute.
2 *a drain on the battery* **strain,** pressure, burden, load, tax, demand.

drama ▶ noun 1 *a television drama* **play,** show, piece, theatrical work, dramatization.
2 *he is studying drama* **acting,** the theater, the stage, the performing arts, dramatic art(s), stagecraft.
3 *she liked to create a drama* **incident,** scene, spectacle, crisis; excitement, thrill, sensation; disturbance, commotion, turmoil; dramatics, theatrics.

dramatic ▶ adjective 1 *dramatic art* **theatrical,** theatric, thespian, stage, dramaturgical; formal histriônic.
2 *a dramatic increase* **considerable,** substantial, sizable, goodly, marked, tectonic, obvious, appreciable; significant, notable, noteworthy, remarkable, extraordinary, exceptional, phenomenal; informal tidy.
ANTONYMS insignificant.
3 *dramatic scenes set in the city* **exciting,** stirring, action-packed, sensational, spectacular; startling, unexpected, tense, gripping, riveting, fascinating, thrilling, hair-raising; rousing, lively, electrifying, impassioned, moving.
ANTONYMS boring.
4 *dramatic headlands* **striking,** impressive, imposing, spectacular, breathtaking, dazzling, sensational, awesome, awe-inspiring, impactful, remarkable, outstanding, incredible, phenomenal.
ANTONYMS unimpressive.
5 *a dramatic gesture* **exaggerated,** theatrical, ostentatious, actressy, stagy, showy, splashy, melodramatic, overdone, histrionic, affected, mannered, artificial; informal hammy, ham, campy.
ANTONYMS natural, unaffected.

dramatist ▶ noun *a great German dramatist, poet, and novelist* **playwright,** writer, scriptwriter, screenwriter, scenarist, dramaturge.

dramatize ▶ verb 1 *the novel was dramatized* **turn into a play/movie/motion picture/film,** adapt for the stage/screen.
2 *the tabloids dramatized the event* **exaggerate,** overdo, overstate, hyperbolize, magnify, amplify, inflate; sensationalize, embroider, color, aggrandize, embellish, elaborate; informal blow up (out of all proportion).

drape ▶ verb 1 *she draped a shawl around her* **wrap,** wind, swathe, sling, hang.
2 *the chair was draped with dirty laundry* **cover,** envelop, swathe, shroud, deck, festoon, overlay, cloak, wind, enfold, sheathe.
3 *he draped one leg over the arm of his chair* **dangle,** hang, suspend, droop, drop.

drastic ▶ adjective *drastic measures were necessary* **extreme,** serious, desperate, radical, far-reaching, impactful, momentous, substantial; heavy, severe, harsh, rigorous; oppressive, draconian.
ANTONYMS moderate.

draw ▶ verb 1 *he drew the house* **sketch,** make a drawing (of), delineate, outline, draft, rough out, illustrate, render, represent, trace; portray, depict.
2 *she drew her chair closer to the fire* **pull,** haul, drag, tug, heave, lug, trail, tow; informal yank.
3 *the train drew into the station* **move,** go, come, proceed, progress, travel, advance, pass, drive; inch, roll, glide, cruise; forge, sweep; back.
4 *she drew the curtains* **close,** shut, lower; open, part, pull back, pull open, fling open, raise.
5 *the doctor drew some fluid off the knee* **drain,** extract, withdraw, remove, suck, pump, siphon, milk, bleed, tap.
6 *he drew his gun* **pull out,** take out, produce, fish out, extract, withdraw; unsheathe.
7 *I drew on my line of credit* **withdraw,** take out.
8 *while I draw breath* **breathe in,** inhale, inspire, respire.
9 *she was drawing huge audiences* **attract,**

interest, win, capture, catch, engage, lure, entice; absorb, occupy, rivet, engross, fascinate, mesmerize, spellbind, captivate, enthrall, grip.
10 *what conclusion can we draw?* **deduce,** infer, conclude, derive, gather, glean.
▶ **noun 1** *the match ended in a draw* **tie,** dead heat, stalemate.
2 *the draw of the city* **attraction,** lure, allure, pull, appeal, glamour, enticement, temptation, charm, seduction, fascination, magnetism.
– PHRASES **draw on** *you can always draw on your carpentry skills* **call on,** have recourse to, avail oneself of, turn to, look to, fall back on, rely on, exploit, use, employ, utilize, bring into play. **draw out 1** *he drew out a gun* See DRAW (sense 6 of the verb). **2** *they always drew out their goodbyes* **prolong,** protract, drag out, spin out, string out, extend, lengthen. **3** *you'll have to carefully draw him out with specific questions* **encourage to talk,** put at ease. **draw up 1** *a car drew up beside us* **stop,** pull up, halt, come to a standstill, brake, park; arrive. **2** *we drew up a list* **compose,** formulate, frame, write down, draft, prepare, think up, devise, work out; create, invent, design. **3** *he drew up his forces in battle array* **arrange,** marshal, muster, assemble, group, order, range, rank, line up, dispose, position, array.

drawback ▶ **noun** *one of the drawbacks of the bigger screen is a slight loss in resolution* **disadvantage,** snag, downside, stumbling block, catch, hitch, pitfall, fly in the ointment; weak spot/point, weakness, imperfection; handicap, limitation, trouble, difficulty, problem, complication; hindrance, obstacle, impediment, obstruction, inconvenience, discouragement, deterrent; informal minus, hiccup, (monkey) wrench in the works.
ANTONYMS benefit.

drawing ▶ **noun 1** *a drawing of our poodles, Skibby and Popo* **sketch,** picture, illustration, representation, portrayal, delineation, depiction, composition, study; diagram, outline, design, plan.
2 *she won the Christmas drawing* **raffle,** lottery, sweepstake, sweep, ballot, lotto.

drawl ▶ **verb** *by the time he drawls a complete sentence, I'll be old and gray* **say slowly,** speak slowly; drone.

drawn ▶ **adjective** *she looked pale and drawn* **pinched,** haggard, drained, wan, hollow-cheeked; fatigued, tired, exhausted; tense, stressed, strained, worried, anxious, harassed, fraught; informal hassled.

dread ▶ **verb** *I used to dread going to school* **fear,** be afraid of, worry about, be anxious about, have forebodings about; be terrified by, tremble/shudder at, shrink from, recoil from, quail from, flinch from; informal get cold feet about.
▶ **noun** *she was filled with dread* **fear,** apprehension, trepidation, anxiety, worry, concern, foreboding, disquiet, unease, angst; fright, panic, alarm; terror, horror; informal the jitters, the creeps, the shivers, the heebie-jeebies.
ANTONYMS confidence.
▶ **adjective** *the dread disease* **awful,** frightful, terrible, horrible, dreadful; feared, frightening, alarming, terrifying, dire, dreaded.

dreadful ▶ **adjective 1** *a dreadful accident* **terrible,** frightful, horrible, grim, awful, dire; horrifying, alarming, shocking, distressing, appalling, harrowing; ghastly, fearful, horrendous; tragic, calamitous; formal grievous.
ANTONYMS mild.
2 *a dreadful meal* **unpleasant,** disagreeable, nasty; frightful, shocking, awful, abysmal, atrocious, disgraceful, deplorable, very bad, repugnant; poor, inadequate, inferior, unsatisfactory, distasteful; informal pathetic, woeful, crummy, rotten, sorry, third-rate, lousy, godawful.
ANTONYMS pleasant, agreeable.
3 *you're a dreadful flirt* **outrageous,** shocking; inordinate, immoderate, unrestrained.

dream ▶ **noun 1** *I awoke from my dreams* REM sleep; nightmare; vision, fantasy, hallucination.
2 *she went around in a dream* **daydream,** reverie, trance, daze, stupor, haze.
3 *he realized his childhood dream* **ambition,** aspiration, hope; goal, aim, objective, grail, intention, intent, target; desire, wish, yearning; daydream, fantasy, pipe dream.
4 *he's an absolute dream* **delight,** joy, marvel, wonder, gem, treasure; beauty, vision.
▶ **verb 1** *she dreamed about her own funeral* **have a dream,** have a nightmare.
2 *I **dreamt of** making the Olympic team* **fantasize about,** daydream about; **wish for,** hope for, long for, yearn for, hanker after, set one's heart on; aspire to, aim for, set one's sights on.
3 *she's always dreaming* **daydream,** be in a trance, be lost in thought, be preoccupied, be abstracted, stare into space, muse, be in la-la land.
4 *I wouldn't dream of being late* **think,** consider, contemplate, conceive.
▶ **adjective** *his dream home* **ideal,** perfect, fantasy.
– PHRASES **dream up** *I dreamed up some new excuse* **think up,** invent, concoct, devise, hatch, contrive, create, work out, come up with; informal cook up.

dreamer ▶ **noun** *part of me will always be a dreamer* **fantasist,** daydreamer; romantic, sentimentalist, idealist, wishful thinker, Don Quixote; Utopian, visionary.
ANTONYMS realist.

dreamland ▶ **noun 1** *I drift off to dreamland* **sleep;** humorous the land of Nod.
2 *they must be living in dreamland* **the land of make-believe,** fairyland, cloudland, la-la land, never-never land, paradise, Utopia, heaven, Shangri-La.

dreamy ▶ **adjective 1** *a dreamy expression* **daydreaming,** dreaming; pensive, thoughtful, reflective, meditative, ruminative; lost in thought, preoccupied, distracted, rapt, inattentive, woolgathering, vague, absorbed, absentminded, with one's head in the clouds, in a world of one's own; informal miles away.
ANTONYMS alert, attentive.
2 *you and your ideas are a bit too dreamy for me* **idealistic,** romantic, starry-eyed, impractical,

unrealistic, Utopian, quixotic; chiefly Brit. informal airy-fairy.
ANTONYMS realistic, practical.
3 *a dreamy recollection* **dreamlike,** vague, dim, hazy, shadowy, faint, indistinct, unclear.
ANTONYMS clear, sharp.
4 informal *Tasha's friend Rick is really dreamy* **attractive,** handsome, good-looking; appealing, lovely, delightful; informal heavenly, divine, gorgeous, hot, cute.
ANTONYMS unattractive, ugly.

dreary ▶ **adjective 1** *the dreary hours spent in a jail cell* **dull,** drab, uninteresting, flat, tedious, wearisome, boring, unexciting, unstimulating, uninspiring, soul-destroying; humdrum, monotonous, uneventful, unremarkable, featureless, ho-hum.
ANTONYMS exciting.
2 *she thought of dreary things* **sad,** miserable, depressing, gloomy, somber, grave, mournful, melancholic, joyless, cheerless.
ANTONYMS cheerful.
3 *a dreary day* **gloomy,** dismal, dull, dark, dingy, murky, overcast; depressing, somber.
ANTONYMS bright.

dregs ▶ **plural noun 1** *the dregs from a bottle of wine* **sediment,** deposit, residue, accumulation, sludge, lees, grounds, remains; technical residuum.
2 *the dregs of humanity* **scum,** refuse, riffraff, outcasts, deadbeats; underclass, untouchables, lowest of the low, great unwashed, hoi polloi; informal trash.

drench ▶ **verb** *the rain has drenched us to the bone* **soak,** saturate, wet through, permeate, douse, souse; drown, swamp, inundate, flood; steep, bathe.

dress ▶ **verb 1** *he dressed quickly* **put on clothes,** clothe oneself, get dressed.
2 *she was dressed in a suit* **clothe,** attire, garb, deck out, trick out, costume, array, robe; informal get up, doll up.
3 *they dress for dinner every day* **wear formal clothes,** wear evening dress, dress up.
4 *dressing the house for the holidays* **decorate,** trim, deck, adorn, ornament, embellish, beautify, prettify; festoon, garland, garnish.
5 *they dressed his wounds* **bandage,** cover, bind, wrap, swathe; doctor, care for.
6 *dress the chicken* **prepare,** get ready; clean.
7 *the field was dressed with manure* **fertilize,** enrich, manure, mulch, compost, top-dress.
8 *he dressed Michelle's hair* **style,** groom, arrange, do; comb, brush; preen, primp; informal fix.
9 Military *the battalion dressed its ranks* **line up,** align, straighten, arrange, order, dispose; fall in.
▶ **noun 1** *a long blue dress* gown, robe, shift, frock.
2 *fancy dress* **clothes,** clothing, garments, attire; costume, outfit, ensemble, garb; informal gear, getup, togs, duds, glad rags, threads, Sunday best; formal apparel; archaic raiment.
– PHRASES **dress down 1** *even the execs dress down on Fridays* **dress informally,** dress casually. **2** *never dress down an employee in front of his colleagues* See REPRIMAND (verb).
dress up 1 *Angela loved dressing up* **dress smartly,** dress formally, wear evening dress; informal doll oneself up, put on one's glad rags, gussy oneself up. **2** *Hugh dressed up as Santa Claus* **disguise oneself,** dress; put on fancy dress, put on a costume.

dressing ▶ **noun 1** *salad dressing* **sauce,** condiment, dip.
2 *they put fresh dressings on her burns* **bandage,** covering, plaster, gauze, lint, compress; trademark Band-Aid.
3 *an organic dressing for the vegetable garden* **fertilizer,** manure, compost, dung, guano; bone meal, blood meal, fish meal; mulch; top-dressing.

dressmaker ▶ **noun** *her dressmaker was the young widow of Colonel Wilcox* **tailor,** seamstress, needlewoman; clothier; couturier, designer.

dribble ▶ **verb 1** *the baby started to dribble* **drool,** slaver, slobber, salivate, drivel.
2 *rainwater dribbled down her face* **trickle,** drip, fall, drizzle; ooze, seep.
3 *dribble the ball* **bounce.**
▶ **noun 1** *there was dribble on his chin* **saliva,** spittle, spit, slaver, slobber, drool.
2 *a dribble of sweat* **trickle,** drip, driblet, stream, drizzle; drop, splash.

drift ▶ **verb 1** *his raft drifted down the river* **be carried,** be borne; float, bob, waft, meander.
2 *the guests drifted away* **wander,** meander, stray, putter, dawdle.
3 *don't allow your attention to drift* **stray,** digress, deviate, diverge, veer, get sidetracked.
4 *snow drifted over the path* **pile up,** bank up, heap up, accumulate, gather, amass.
▶ **noun 1** *a drift from the country to urban areas* **movement,** shift, flow, transfer, relocation, gravitation.
2 *the pilot had not noticed any drift* **deviation,** digression.
3 *he caught her drift* **gist,** essence, meaning, sense, substance, significance; thrust, import, tenor; implication, intention; direction, course.
4 *a drift of deep snow* **pile,** heap, bank, mound, mass, accumulation.

drill ▶ **noun 1** *a hydraulic drill* **drilling tool,** boring tool, auger, (brace and) bit, gimlet, awl, bradawl.
2 *they learned military drills* **training,** instruction, coaching, teaching; (physical) exercises, workout.
3 *Estelle knew the drill* **procedure,** routine, practice, regimen, program, schedule; method, system.
▶ **verb 1** *drill the piece of wood* **bore a hole in,** make a hole in; bore, pierce, puncture, perforate.
2 *a sergeant drilling new recruits* **train,** instruct, coach, teach, discipline; exercise, put someone through their paces.
3 *his mother had drilled politeness into him* **instill,** hammer, drive, drum, din, implant, ingrain; teach, indoctrinate, brainwash.

drink ▶ **verb 1** *she drank her coffee* **swallow,** gulp down, quaff, guzzle, imbibe, sip, consume; informal swig, down, knock back, put away, swill, chug.
2 *he never drank* **drink alcohol,** tipple, indulge;

carouse; informal hit the bottle, booze, booze it up, knock a few back, get tanked up, go on a bender, bend one's elbow.
3 *let's* ***drink to*** *success* **toast,** salute.
▶ **noun 1** *he took a sip of his drink* **beverage,** liquid refreshment; bracer, nightcap, nip; humorous libation; archaic potation.
2 *she turned to drink* **alcohol,** liquor, alcoholic drink; informal booze, hooch, the hard stuff, firewater, rotgut, moonshine, the bottle, the sauce.
3 *she took a drink of her wine* **swallow,** gulp, sip, draft, slug; informal swig, swill.
4 informal *he fell into* ***the drink*** **the sea,** the ocean, the water; informal the briny, Davy Jones's locker; literary the deep.
– PHRASES **drink something in** *I'll just sit here and drink in the scenery* **absorb,** assimilate, digest, ingest, take in; be rapt in, be lost in, be fascinated by, pay close attention to.

drinkable ▶ **adjective** *running low on drinkable water* **potable,** fit to drink, palatable; pure, clean, safe, unpolluted, untainted, uncontaminated.

drinker ▶ **noun** *I had no idea he was such a drinker* See DRUNK (noun).

drip ▶ **verb 1** *there was a faucet dripping* **dribble,** leak.
2 *sweat dripped from his chin* **drop,** dribble, trickle, drizzle, run, splash, plop; leak, emanate, issue.
▶ **noun 1** *a bucket to catch the drips* **drop,** dribble, spot, trickle, splash.
2 informal *that drip who fancies you* bore; ninny, milksop, namby-pamby; informal creep; wimp, sissy, wuss, candy-ass, pantywaist.

drive ▶ **verb 1** *I can't drive a car* **operate,** handle, manage; pilot, steer.
2 *he drove to the police station* **travel by car,** motor.
3 *I'll drive you to the airport* **chauffeur,** run, give someone a lift/ride, take, ferry, transport, convey, carry.
4 *the engine drives the front wheels* **power,** propel, move, push.
5 *he drove a nail into the board* **hammer,** screw, ram, sink, plunge, thrust, propel, knock.
6 *she drove her cattle to market* **impel,** urge; herd, round up, shepherd.
7 *a desperate mother driven to crime* **force,** compel, prompt, precipitate; oblige, coerce, pressure, goad, spur, prod.
8 *he drove his staff extremely hard* **work,** push, tax, exert.
▶ **noun 1** *an afternoon drive* **excursion,** outing, trip, jaunt, tour; ride, run, journey; informal spin.
2 *the house has a long drive* **driveway,** approach, access road.
3 *sexual drive* **urge,** appetite, desire, need; impulse, instinct.
4 *she lacked the drive to succeed* **motivation,** ambition, single-mindedness, willpower, dedication, doggedness, tenacity; enthusiasm, zeal, commitment, aggression, spirit; energy, vigor, verve, vitality, pep; informal getup-and-go.
5 *an anticorruption drive* **campaign,** crusade, movement, effort, push, appeal.
– PHRASES **drive at** *I can see what you're driving at, but you're wrong* **suggest,** imply, hint at, allude to, intimate, insinuate, indicate; refer to, mean, intend; informal get at.

drivel ▶ **noun** *he was talking complete drivel* **nonsense,** twaddle, claptrap, balderdash, gibberish, rubbish, mumbo-jumbo, garbage; informal poppycock, piffle, tripe, bull, hogwash, baloney, codswallop, flapdoodle, jive, guff, bushwa; informal dated tommyrot, bunkum. See note at NONSENSE.
▶ **verb** *you always* ***drivel on*** **talk nonsense,** talk rubbish, babble, ramble, gibber, blather, prattle, gabble, waffle.

driver ▶ **verb** *the driver failed to signal* **motorist,** chauffeur; pilot, operator.

drizzle ▶ **noun 1** *they shivered in the drizzle* **fine rain,** light shower, spray, mist.
2 *a drizzle of syrup* **trickle,** dribble, drip, stream, rivulet; sprinkle, sprinkling.
▶ **verb 1** *it's beginning to drizzle* **rain lightly,** shower, spot, spit, sprinkle.
2 *drizzle the cream over the fruit* **trickle,** drip, dribble, pour, splash, sprinkle.

droll ▶ **adjective** *a droll remark that started everyone laughing* **funny,** humorous, amusing, comic, comical, mirthful, hilarious; clownish, farcical, zany, quirky; jocular, lighthearted, facetious, witty, whimsical, wry, tongue-in-cheek; informal waggish, wacky, side-splitting, rib-tickling.
ANTONYMS serious.

drone ▶ **verb 1** *a plane droned overhead* **hum,** buzz, whirr, vibrate, murmur, rumble, purr.
2 *he* ***droned on*** *about right and wrong* **speak boringly,** go on and on, talk at length; intone, pontificate; informal spout, sound off, jaw, spiel, speechify.
▶ **noun 1** *the drone of aircraft taking off* **hum,** buzz, whirr, vibration, murmur, purr.
2 *drones supported by taxpayers' money* **hanger-on,** parasite, leech, passenger, bottom feeder; idler, loafer, layabout, good-for-nothing, do-nothing; informal lazybones, scrounger, sponger, freeloader, slacker.

droop ▶ **verb 1** *the dog's tail is drooping* **hang (down),** dangle, sag, flop; wilt, sink, slump, drop.
2 *his eyelids were drooping* **close,** shut, fall.
3 *the news made her droop* **be despondent,** lose heart, give up hope, become dispirited, become dejected; flag, languish, wilt.

drop ▶ **verb 1** *Eric dropped the box* **let fall,** let go of, lose one's grip on; release, unhand, relinquish.
ANTONYMS lift, hold on to.
2 *water drops from the cave roof* **drip,** fall, dribble, trickle, run, plop, leak.
3 *a plane dropped out of the sky* **fall,** descend, plunge, plummet, dive, nosedive, tumble, pitch.
ANTONYMS rise.
4 *she dropped to her knees* **fall,** sink, collapse, slump, tumble.
ANTONYMS rise.
5 informal *I was so tired I thought I would drop* **collapse,** faint, pass out, black out, swoon, keel over; informal conk out.
6 *the track drops from the ridge* **slope downward,** slant downward, descend, go down,

fall away, sink, dip.
ANTONYMS lift.
7 *the exchange rate dropped* **decrease,** lessen, reduce, diminish, depreciate; fall, decline, dwindle, sink, slump, plunge, plummet, drop off.
ANTONYMS increase.
8 *you can drop algebra if you wish* **give up,** drop out of, finish with, withdraw from; discontinue, end, stop, cease, halt; abandon, forgo, relinquish, dispense with, have done with; informal pack in, quit.
ANTONYMS take up, continue.
9 *he was dropped from the team* **exclude,** discard, expel, oust, throw out, leave out; dismiss, discharge, let go; informal boot out, kick out.
ANTONYMS pick, keep.
10 *he dropped his unsuitable friends* **abandon,** desert, throw over; renounce, disown, turn one's back on, wash one's hands of; reject, give up, cast off; neglect, shun; literary forsake.
ANTONYMS keep.
11 *he dropped all reference to compensation* **omit,** leave out, eliminate, take out, delete, cut, erase.
ANTONYMS insert, include.
12 *the taxi* ***dropped*** *her* ***off*** **deliver,** bring, take, convey, carry, transport; leave, unload.
ANTONYMS pick up.
13 *drop the gun on the ground* **put,** place, deposit, set, lay, leave; informal pop, plonk.
ANTONYMS pick up.
14 *she dropped names* **mention,** refer to, hint at; bring up, raise, broach, introduce; show off.
15 *the team has yet to drop a point* **lose,** concede, give away.
ANTONYMS gain, win.
▶ **noun 1** *a drop of water* **droplet,** blob, globule, bead, bubble, tear, dot; informal glob; (**drops of water/rain**) rare stillicide.
2 *it needs a drop of oil* **small amount,** little, bit, dash, spot; dribble, driblet, sprinkle, trickle, splash; dab, speck, smattering, sprinkling, modicum; informal smidgen, tad.
ANTONYMS great deal.
3 *a lemon drop* **candy,** lozenge, pastille.
4 *a small drop in profits* **decrease,** reduction, decline, falloff, downturn, slump; cut, cutback, curtailment; depreciation.
ANTONYMS increase.
5 *I walked to the edge of the drop* **cliff,** abyss, chasm, gorge, gully, precipice; slope, descent, incline.
– PHRASES **drop back/behind** *he dropped back and was soon lost in the crowd* **fall back/behind,** get left behind, lag behind; straggle, linger, dawdle, dally, hang back, loiter, bring/take up the rear, dilly-dally. **drop off 1** *trade dropped off sharply* See DROP (sense 7 of the verb).
2 *she kept dropping off* **fall asleep,** doze (off), nap, catnap, drowse; informal nod off, drift off, snooze, take forty winks. **drop out of** *he dropped out of his studies* See DROP (sense 8 of the verb).

drought ▶ **noun** *this year's drought was devastating to cotton growers* **dry spell,** lack of rain, shortage of water.

drove ▶ **noun 1** *a drove of cattle* **herd,** flock, pack.
2 *they came in droves* **crowd,** swarm, horde, multitude, mob, throng, host, mass, army, herd.

drown ▶ **verb 1** *he nearly drowned* **suffocate in water,** inhale water; go to a watery grave.
2 *the valleys were drowned* **flood,** submerge, immerse, inundate, deluge, swamp, engulf.
3 *his voice was* ***drowned out*** *by the music* **make inaudible,** overpower, overwhelm, override; muffle, deaden, stifle, extinguish.

drowsy ▶ **adjective 1** *the pills made her drowsy* **sleepy,** dozy, groggy, somnolent; tired, weary, fatigued, exhausted, yawning, nodding; lethargic, sluggish, torpid, listless, languid; informal snoozy, dopey, yawny, dead beat, all in, dog-tired, bone-weary.
ANTONYMS alert.
2 *a drowsy afternoon* **soporific,** sleep-inducing, sleepy, somniferous; narcotic, sedative, tranquilizing; lulling, soothing.
ANTONYMS invigorating.

drubbing ▶ **noun 1** *I gave him a good drubbing* **beating,** thrashing, walloping, thumping, battering, pounding, pummeling, slapping, punching, pelting; informal hammering, licking, clobbering, belting, bashing, pasting, tanning, kicking.
2 informal *New York's 8–1 drubbing by Anaheim* See DEFEAT (sense 1 of the noun).

drudge ▶ **noun** *a household drudge* **menial worker,** slave, lackey, servant, laborer, worker, cog; informal gofer, runner, bottle-washer, serf.
▶ **verb** archaic *he drudged in the fields* See TOIL (sense 1 of the verb).

drudgery ▶ **noun** *she swore her daughters would never be condemned to a life of drudgery* **hard work,** menial work, donkey work, toil, labor; chores. See note at LABOR.

drug ▶ **noun 1** *drugs prescribed by doctors* **medicine,** medication, medicament, pharmaceutical; remedy, cure, antidote.
2 *she was under the influence of drugs* **narcotic,** stimulant, hallucinogen; informal dope.
▶ **verb 1** *he was drugged* **anesthetize,** narcotize; poison; knock out, stupefy; informal dope.
2 *she drugged his coffee* **add drugs to,** tamper with, adulterate, contaminate, lace, poison; informal dope, spike, doctor.

drugged ▶ **adjective** *they found Tom and his drugged friends camped out in the living room* **stupefied,** insensible, befuddled; delirious, hallucinating, narcotized; anesthetized, knocked out; informal stoned, coked, high (as a kite), doped, tripping, spaced out, wasted, wrecked.
ANTONYMS sober.

drum ▶ **noun 1** *the beat of a drum* percussion instrument; bongo, tom-tom, snare drum, kettledrum, bodhrán; historical tambour.
2 *the steady drum of raindrops* **beat,** rhythm, patter, tap, pounding, thump, thud, rattle, pitter-patter, pit-a-pat, rat-a-tat, thrum.
3 *a drum of radioactive waste* **canister,** barrel, cylinder, tank, bin, can; container.
▶ **verb 1** *she drummed her fingers on the desk* **tap,** beat, rap, thud, thump; tattoo, thrum.
2 *the rules were drummed into us at school* **instill,** drive, din, hammer, drill, implant, ingrain, inculcate.
– PHRASES **drum out of** *Kazwell was running the organization into the ground, until the other*

members drummed him out **expel,** dismiss, throw out, oust; drive out, get rid of; exclude, banish; informal give someone the boot, boot out, kick out, give someone their marching orders, show someone the door, send packing. **drum up** *leaflets were distributed in hopes of drumming up support for the campaign* **round up,** gather, collect; summon, attract; canvass, solicit, petition.

drunk ▶ **adjective** *he was so drunk he couldn't stand up* **intoxicated,** inebriated, inebriate, impaired, drunken, tipsy, under the influence; informal plastered, smashed, bombed, sloshed, sozzled, sauced, lubricated, well-oiled, wrecked, juiced, blasted, stinko, blitzed, half-cut, fried, wasted, hopped up, gassed, polluted, pissed, tanked (up), soaked, out of one's head/skull, loaded, trashed, hammered, soused, buzzed, befuddled, besotted, pickled, pixilated, canned, cockeyed, blotto, blind drunk, roaring drunk, dead drunk, punch-drunk, ripped, stewed, tight, merry, the worse for wear, far gone, pie-eyed, in one's cups, three sheets to the wind; Brit. informal bladdered, lashed; literary crapulous.
ANTONYMS sober.
▶ **noun** *a brilliant artist, he was also a tortured drunk* **drunkard,** inebriate, drinker, tippler, imbiber, sot; heavy drinker, problem drinker, alcoholic, dipsomaniac; informal boozer, soak, lush, wino, alky, rummy, barfly; archaic toper.
ANTONYMS teetotaler.

CHOOSE THE RIGHT WORD

drunk, blotto, drunken, inebriated, intoxicated, tight, tipsy

Anyone who is obviously or legally under the influence of alcohol is said to be **drunk**. **Drunken** means the same thing, but only *drunk* should be used predicatively, that is, after a linking verb (*she was drunk*) while *drunken* is more often used to modify a noun (*a drunken sailor*) and, in some cases, to imply habitual drinking to excess. *Drunken* is also used to modify nouns that do not refer to a person (*a drunken celebration*). To say **intoxicated** or **inebriated** is a more formal and less offensive way of calling someone *drunk*, with *intoxicated* implying that the individual is only slightly drunk, and *inebriated* implying drunkenness to the point of excitement or exhilaration (*the streets were filled with inebriated revelers*). **Tight** and **tipsy** are two of the more common slang expressions (there are literally hundreds more) meaning *drunk*. Like *intoxicated*, *tipsy* implies that someone is only slightly drunk, while *tight* implies obvious drunkenness but without any loss of muscular coordination. An elderly woman who has had one sherry too many might be described as *tipsy*, but someone who has been drinking all evening and is still able to stand up and give a speech might be described as *tight*. Either condition is preferable to being **blotto**, a word that means drunk to the point of incomprehensibility or unconsciousness.

drunken ▶ **adjective 1** *drunken revelers* See DRUNK (adjective). See also note at DRUNK.
2 *a drunken all-night party* **debauched,** dissipated, carousing, roistering, intemperate, unrestrained, uninhibited, abandoned; bacchanalian, Bacchic; informal boozy.

drunkenness ▶ **noun** *his bouts of drunkenness* **intoxication,** inebriation, insobriety, tipsiness, impairment; intemperance, overindulgence, debauchery; heavy drinking, alcoholism, dipsomania.

dry ▶ **adjective 1** *the dry desert* **arid,** parched, droughty, scorched, baked; waterless, moistureless, rainless; dehydrated, desiccated, thirsty, bone dry.
ANTONYMS wet.
2 *dry leaves* **parched,** dried, withered, shriveled, wilted, wizened; crisp, crispy, brittle; dehydrated, desiccated.
ANTONYMS fresh.
3 *the rolls were dry* **hard,** stale, old, past its best.
ANTONYMS moist, fresh.
4 *a dry well* **waterless,** empty.
5 *I'm really dry* **thirsty,** dehydrated; informal parched, gasping.
6 *it was dry work* **thirsty,** thirst-making; hot; strenuous, arduous.
7 *dry toast* **unbuttered,** butterless, plain.
8 *the dry facts* **bare,** simple, basic, fundamental, stark, bald, hard, straightforward.
ANTONYMS embellished.
9 *a dry debate* **dull,** uninteresting, boring, unexciting, tedious, tiresome, wearisome, dreary, monotonous; unimaginative, sterile, flat, bland, lackluster, stodgy, prosaic, humdrum, mundane; informal deadly.
ANTONYMS lively, interesting.
10 *a dry sense of humor* **wry,** subtle, laconic, sharp; ironic, sardonic, sarcastic, cynical; satirical, mocking, droll; informal waggish.
11 *a dry response to his cordial advance* **unemotional,** indifferent, impassive, cool, cold, emotionless; reserved, restrained, impersonal, formal, stiff, wooden.
ANTONYMS emotional, expressive.
12 *this is a dry state* **teetotal,** prohibitionist, alcohol-free, nondrinking, abstinent, sober; informal on the wagon.
13 *dry white wine* **crisp,** sharp, piquant, tart, bitter.
ANTONYMS sweet.
▶ **verb 1** *the sun dried the ground* **parch,** scorch, bake; dehydrate, desiccate, dehumidify.
ANTONYMS moisten.
2 *dry the leaves completely* **dehydrate,** desiccate; wither, shrivel.
ANTONYMS moisten.
3 *he dried the spills with a paper towel* **towel,** rub; mop up, blot up, soak up, absorb.
4 *she dried her eyes* **wipe,** rub, dab.
5 *methods of drying meat* **desiccate,** dehydrate; preserve, cure, smoke.
– PHRASES **dry out** *she dried out on her thirtieth birthday and has been sober ever since* **give up drinking,** give up alcohol, become a teetotaler, go on the wagon. **dry up** *foreign investment may dry up* **dwindle,** subside, peter out, wane, taper off, ebb, come to a halt/end, run out, give out, disappear, vanish.

CHOOSE THE RIGHT WORD

dry, arid, dehydrated, desiccated, parched, sere

Almost anything lacking in moisture (in relative terms)—whether it's a piece of bread, the basement of a house, or the state of Arizona—may be described as **dry**, a word that also connotes a lack of life or spirit (*a dry lecture on cell division*). **Arid**, on the other hand, applies to places or things that have been deprived of moisture and are therefore extremely or abnormally *dry* (*one side of the island was arid*); it is most commonly used to describe a desertlike region or climate that is lifeless or barren. **Desiccated** is used as a technical term for something from which moisture has been removed, and in general use it suggests lifelessness, although it is applied very often to people who have lost their vitality (*a desiccated old woman who never left her house*) or to animal and vegetable products that have been completely deprived of their vital juices (*desiccated oranges hanging limply from the tree*). **Dehydrated** is very close in meaning to *desiccated* and is often the preferred adjective when describing foods from which the moisture has been extracted (*they lived on dehydrated fruit*). *Dehydrated* may also refer to an unwanted loss of moisture (*the virus had left him seriously dehydrated*), as may the less formal term **parched**, which refers to an undesirable or uncomfortable lack of water in either a human being or a place (*parched with thirst; the parched landscape*). **Sere** is associated primarily with places and means *dry* or *arid* (*a harsh, sere land where few inhabitants could survive*).

dual ▶ adjective *a futuristic car with dual engines* **double,** twofold, binary; duplicate, twin, matching, paired, coupled.
ANTONYMS single.

dub ▶ verb **1** *he was dubbed "the world's sexiest man"* **nickname,** call, name, label, christen, term, tag, entitle, style; designate, characterize, nominate; formal denominate.
2 *she dubbed him a Knight of the Garter* **create,** invest.

dubiety ▶ noun formal *the dubiety of Henry's fate* **doubtfulness,** uncertainty, unsureness, incertitude; ambiguity, ambivalence, confusion; hesitancy, doubt. See note at UNCERTAINTY.

dubious ▶ adjective **1** *I was rather dubious about the idea* **doubtful,** uncertain, unsure, hesitant; undecided, indefinite, unresolved, up in the air; vacillating, irresolute; skeptical, suspicious; informal iffy. See note at DOUBTFUL.
ANTONYMS certain, definite.
2 *dubious business practices* **suspicious,** suspect, untrustworthy, unreliable, questionable; informal shady, fishy.
ANTONYMS trustworthy.

duck ▶ noun *a pair of ducks were nesting on the edge of our pond* male drake; female duck; young duckling.

duct ▶ noun *a ventilation duct* **tube,** channel, canal, vessel; conduit, culvert; pipe, pipeline, outlet, inlet, flue, shaft, vent; Anatomy ductus.

ductile ▶ adjective **1** *ductile metals* **pliable,** pliant, flexible, supple, plastic, tensile; soft, malleable, workable, bendable; informal bendy.
ANTONYMS brittle.
2 *efforts to keep the oppressed people ductile* **docile,** obedient, submissive, meek, mild, lamblike; willing, accommodating, amenable, cooperative, compliant, malleable, tractable, biddable, persuadable.
ANTONYMS intransigent.

dud ▶ noun *their new product is a dud* **failure,** flop, letdown, disappointment; informal washout, lemon, no-hoper, nonstarter, dead loss, clunker.
ANTONYMS success.
▶ adjective **1** *a dud typewriter* **defective,** faulty, unsound, inoperative, broken, malfunctioning; informal bust, busted, kaput, conked out.
ANTONYMS sound.
2 *a dud $50 bill* **counterfeit,** fraudulent, forged, fake, faked, false, bogus; invalid, worthless; informal phony.
ANTONYMS genuine.

dudgeon ▶ noun
– PHRASES **in high dudgeon** *the sponsors from Cleveland stormed out in high dudgeon* **indignantly,** resentfully, angrily, furiously; in a temper, in anger, with displeasure; informal in a huff, seeing red.

due ▶ adjective **1** *their fees were due* **owing,** owed, payable; outstanding, overdue, unpaid, unsettled, undischarged, delinquent.
2 *the chancellor's statement is due today* **expected,** anticipated, scheduled for, awaited; required.
3 *the respect due to a great artist* **deserved by,** merited by, warranted by; appropriate to, fit for, fitting for, right for, proper to.
4 *he drove without due care* **proper,** correct, rightful, suitable, appropriate, apt; adequate, sufficient, enough, satisfactory, requisite.
▶ noun **1** *he attracts more criticism than is his due* **rightful treatment,** fair treatment, just punishment; right, entitlement; just deserts; informal comeuppance.
2 *members have paid their dues* **fee,** subscription, charge; payment, contribution.
▶ adverb *he hiked due north* **directly,** straight, exactly, precisely, dead.
– PHRASES **due to 1** *her death was due to an infection* **attributable to,** caused by, ascribed to, because of, put down to. **2** *the train was canceled due to staff shortages* **because of,** owing to, on account of, as a consequence of, as a result of, thanks to, in view of; formal by reason of.

USAGE

due to

The use of *due to* as a prepositional phrase meaning 'because of,' as in *he had to retire due to an injury* first appeared in print in 1897, and traditional grammarians have opposed this prepositional usage for a century on the grounds that it is a misuse of the adjectival phrase *due to* in the sense of 'attributable to, likely or expected to' (*the train is due to arrive at 11:15*), or 'payable to' (*render unto Caesar what is due to Caesar*). Nevertheless, this prepositional usage is now widespread and common in all types of literature and must be regarded as standard English.

Avoid the wordy phrase *due to the fact that* and use *because* instead, especially in writing.

duel ▶ noun **1** *he was killed in a duel* **affair of honor**; single combat; (sword) fight, confrontation, face-off, shoot-out.
2 *a chess duel* **contest,** match, game, meet, encounter.
▶ verb *they dueled with swords* **fight a duel,** fight, battle, combat, contend.

dulcet ▶ adjective *the dulcet sounds of the zither* **sweet,** soothing, mellow, honeyed, mellifluous, euphonious, pleasant, agreeable; melodious, melodic, lilting, lyrical, silvery, golden.
ANTONYMS harsh.

dull ▶ adjective **1** *a dull novel* **uninteresting,** boring, tedious, monotonous, unrelieved, unvaried, unimaginative, uneventful; characterless, featureless, colorless, lifeless, insipid, unexciting, uninspiring, unstimulating, jejune, flat, bland, dry, stale, tired, banal, lackluster, ho-hum, stodgy, dreary, humdrum, mundane; mind-numbing, wearisome, tiring, tiresome, irksome; dullsville.
ANTONYMS interesting.
2 *a dull morning* **overcast,** cloudy, gloomy, dark, dismal, dreary, somber, gray, murky, sunless.
ANTONYMS sunny, bright.
3 *dull colors* **drab,** dreary, somber, dark, subdued, muted, lackluster, faded, washed out, muddy, dingy.
ANTONYMS bright.
4 *a dull sound* **muffled,** muted, quiet, soft, faint, indistinct; stifled, suppressed.
ANTONYMS loud, resonant.
5 *the chisel became dull* **blunt,** unsharpened, edgeless, worn down.
ANTONYMS sharp.
6 *a rather dull child* **unintelligent,** stupid, slow, witless, vacuous, empty-headed, stunned, brainless, mindless, foolish, idiotic; informal dense, dim, moronic, halfwitted, thick, dumb, dopey, dozy, bovine, slow on the uptake, wooden-headed, fat-headed. See note at STUPID.
ANTONYMS clever.
7 *her cold made her feel dull* **sluggish,** lethargic, enervated, listless, languid, torpid, slow, sleepy, drowsy, weary, tired, fatigued; apathetic; informal dozy, dopey, yawny, logy.
ANTONYMS lively.
▶ verb **1** *the pain was dulled by drugs* **lessen,** decrease, diminish, reduce, dampen, blunt, deaden, allay, ease, soothe, assuage, alleviate.
ANTONYMS intensify.
2 *sleep dulled her mind* **numb,** benumb, deaden, desensitize, stupefy, daze.
ANTONYMS enliven.
3 *rain dulled the sky* **darken,** blacken, dim, veil, obscure, shadow, fog.
ANTONYMS brighten.
4 *the somber atmosphere dulled her spirit* **dampen,** lower, depress, crush, sap, extinguish, smother, stifle.
ANTONYMS raise, brighten.

duly ▶ adverb **1** *the document was duly signed* **properly,** correctly, appropriately, suitably, fittingly.
2 *he duly arrived to collect Alice* **at the right time,** on time, punctually.

dumb ▶ adjective **1** *she stood dumb while he shouted* **mute,** speechless, tongue-tied, silent, at a loss for words; taciturn, uncommunicative, untalkative, tight-lipped, close-mouthed; informal mum.
2 informal *he is not as dumb as you'd think* **stupid,** unintelligent, ignorant, dense, brainless, mindless, foolish, slow, dull, simple, empty-headed, stunned, vacuous, vapid, idiotic, half-baked, imbecilic, bovine; informal thick, dim, moronic, dopey, dozy, thickheaded, fat-headed, birdbrained, pea-brained; daft. See note at STUPID.
ANTONYMS clever.

dumbfound ▶ verb *she was dumbfounded by Bruce's actions* **astonish,** astound, amaze, stagger, surprise, startle, stun, confound, stupefy, daze, take aback, stop someone in their tracks, strike dumb, leave open-mouthed, leave aghast; informal flabbergast, floor, bowl over.

dummy ▶ noun **1** *a store-window dummy* **mannequin,** model, figure.
2 *the book is just a dummy* **mock-up,** imitation, likeness, look-alike, representation, substitute, sample; replica, reproduction; counterfeit, sham, fake, forgery; informal dupe.
3 informal *you're a dummy* See IDIOT.
▶ adjective *a dummy attack on the airfield* **simulated,** feigned, pretended, practice, trial, mock, make-believe; informal pretend, phony, virtual.
ANTONYMS real.

dump ▶ noun **1** *take the garbage to the dump* **transfer station,** garbage dump, landfill (site), rubbish heap, dumping ground; dustheap, slag heap.
2 informal *the house is a dump* **hovel,** shack, slum; mess; hole, pigsty.
▶ verb **1** *he dumped his bag on the table* **put down,** set down, deposit, place, unload; drop, throw down; informal park, plonk (down), plunk (down).
2 *they will dump asbestos at the site* **dispose of,** get rid of, throw away/out, discard, jettison; informal ditch, junk, deep-six.
3 informal *he dumped her* **abandon,** desert, leave, jilt, break up with, finish with, throw over; informal walk out on, rat on, drop, ditch.

dumps ▶ plural noun
– PHRASES **down in the dumps** informal *why so down in dumps, Mrs. Herbert?* **unhappy,** sad, depressed, gloomy, glum, melancholy, miserable, dejected, despondent, dispirited, downhearted, downcast, down, low, heavy-hearted, dismal, desolate; tearful, upset, blue, down in/at the mouth.

dun ▶ adjective *a dun cow* **grayish-brown,** brownish, mousy, muddy, khaki, umber.

dunce ▶ noun *Uncle Abraham was a bit of a dunce, but most people got along with him* **fool,** idiot, stupid person, simpleton, ignoramus, dullard; informal dummy, dumbo, thickhead, nitwit, dimwit, halfwit, moron, cretin, imbecile, dope, boob, chump, numbskull, numbnuts, nincompoop, fathead, airhead, birdbrain, peabrain, ninny, ass, doofus, goof, meatball, schmuck, bozo, lummox.
ANTONYMS genius.

dungeon ▶ noun *the castle dungeon is now a tourist attraction* **underground prison,** oubliette; cell, jail, lockup.

duplicate ▶ noun *a duplicate of the invoice* **copy,** photocopy, facsimile, reprint; replica, reproduction, clone; Computing download; dated carbon copy; informal dupe; trademark Xerox.
▶ adjective *duplicate keys* **matching,** identical, twin, corresponding, equivalent.
▶ verb 1 *she will duplicate the newsletter* **copy,** photocopy, xerox, reproduce, replicate, reprint, run off; Computing download; dated mimeograph.
2 *a feat difficult to duplicate* **repeat,** do again, redo, replicate.

duplicity ▶ noun *he got caught up in the duplicity of his crooked partners* **deceitfulness,** deceit, deception, double-dealing, underhandedness, dishonesty, fraud, fraudulence, sharp practice, chicanery, trickery, subterfuge, skulduggery, treachery; informal crookedness, shadiness, dirty tricks, shenanigans, monkey business; literary perfidy.
ANTONYMS honesty.

durable ▶ adjective 1 *durable carpets* **hardwearing,** long-lasting, heavy-duty, industrial-strength, tough, resistant, imperishable, indestructible, strong, sturdy.
ANTONYMS delicate.
2 *a durable peace* **lasting,** long-lasting, long-term, enduring, persistent, abiding; stable, secure, firm, deep-rooted, permanent, undying, everlasting.
ANTONYMS short-lived.

duress ▶ noun *their confessions were extracted under duress* **coercion,** compulsion, force, pressure, intimidation, constraint; threats; informal arm-twisting.

during ▶ preposition *the museum is closed during December* **throughout,** through, in, in the course of, for the time of.

dusk ▶ noun *we launch the patrol boats at dusk* **twilight,** nightfall, sunset, sundown, evening, close of day; semidarkness, gloom, murkiness; literary gloaming, eventide.
ANTONYMS dawn.

dusky ▶ adjective 1 *the dusky countryside* **shadowy,** dark, dim, gloomy, murky, shady; unlit, unilluminated; sunless, moonless.
ANTONYMS bright.
2 dated *a dusky complexion* **dark-skinned,** dark, olive-skinned, swarthy, ebony, black; tanned, bronzed, coppery, brown.
ANTONYMS fair.

dust ▶ noun 1 *the desk was covered in dust* **dirt,** grime, filth, smut, soot; fine powder.
2 *they fought in the dust* **earth,** soil, dirt; ground.
▶ verb 1 *she dusted her mantelpiece* **wipe,** clean, brush, sweep, mop.
2 *dust the cake with powdered sugar* **sprinkle,** scatter, powder, dredge, sift, cover, strew.

dusty ▶ adjective 1 *the floor was dusty* **dirty,** grimy, grubby, unclean, soiled, mucky, sooty; undusted; informal grungy, cruddy.
ANTONYMS clean.
2 *dusty sandstone* **powdery,** crumbly, chalky, friable; granular, gritty, sandy.
3 *a dusty pink* **muted,** dull, faded, pale, pastel, subtle; grayish, darkish, dirty.
ANTONYMS bright.

dutiful ▶ adjective *Clarence's dutiful niece* **conscientious,** responsible, dedicated, devoted, attentive; obedient, compliant, submissive, biddable; deferential, reverent, reverential, respectful, good. See note at **OBEDIENT**.
ANTONYMS remiss.

duty ▶ noun 1 *she was free of any duty* **responsibility,** obligation, commitment; allegiance, loyalty, faithfulness, fidelity, homage.
2 *it was his duty to attend the king* **job,** task, assignment, mission, function, charge, place, role, responsibility, obligation; dated office.
3 *the duty was raised on alcohol* **tax,** levy, tariff, excise, toll, fee, payment, rate, countervail; dues.
– PHRASES **off duty** *I'll be off duty at midnight* **not working,** at leisure, on leave, off (work), free. **on duty** *there is always a supervisor on duty* **working,** at work, busy, occupied, engaged; informal on the job.

dwarf ▶ noun 1 *she married a dwarf who worked in her father's circus* **small person,** short person; midget, pygmy, manikin, homunculus.
2 *the wizard captured the dwarf* **gnome,** goblin, hobgoblin, troll, imp, elf, brownie, leprechaun.
▶ adjective *dwarf conifers* **miniature,** small, little, tiny, toy, pocket, diminutive, baby, pygmy, stunted, undersized, undersize; informal mini, teeny, teeny-weeny, itsy-bitsy, pint-sized, little-bitty, vertically challenged; Scottish wee.
ANTONYMS giant.
▶ verb 1 *the buildings dwarf the trees* **dominate,** tower over, loom over, overshadow, overtop.
2 *her progress was dwarfed by her sister's success* **overshadow,** outshine, surpass, exceed, outclass, outstrip, outdo, top, trump, transcend; diminish, minimize.

dwell ▶ verb formal *gypsies dwell in these caves* **reside,** live, be settled, be housed, lodge, stay; informal put up; formal abide, be domiciled.
– PHRASES **dwell on** *I'm not one to dwell on the past* **linger over,** mull over, muse on, brood about/over, think about; be preoccupied by, be obsessed by, eat one's heart out over; harp on about, discuss at length.

dwelling ▶ noun formal *their dwellings were simple but pristine, both inside and out* **residence,** home, house, accommodations; quarters, rooms, lodgings; informal place, pad, digs; formal abode, domicile, habitation.

dwindle ▶ verb 1 *the population dwindled* **diminish,** decrease, reduce, lessen, shrink; fall off, tail off, drop, fall, slump, plummet; disappear, vanish, die out; informal nosedive.

ANTONYMS increase.
2 *her career dwindled* **decline,** deteriorate, fail, slip, slide, fade, go downhill, go to rack and ruin; informal go to pot, go to the dogs, hit the skids, go down the tubes, go down the drain, go down the toilet.
ANTONYMS flourish.

dye ▶ **noun** *a blue dye* **colorant,** coloring, color, dyestuff, pigment, tint, stain, wash.
▶ **verb** *the gloves were dyed* **color,** tint, pigment, stain, wash.

dyed-in-the-wool ▶ **adjective** *a dyed-in-the-wool socialist* **inveterate,** confirmed, entrenched, established, long-standing, deep-rooted, diehard; complete, absolute, thorough, thoroughgoing, out-and-out, true blue; firm, unshakable, staunch, steadfast, committed, devoted, dedicated, loyal, unswerving, full bore; informal card-carrying.

dying ▶ **adjective 1** *his dying aunt* **terminally ill,** at death's door, on one's deathbed, near death, fading fast, expiring, moribund, not long for this world, in extremis; informal on one's last legs, having one foot in the grave.
2 *a dying art form* **declining,** vanishing, fading, ebbing, waning; informal on the way out.
ANTONYMS thriving.
3 *her dying words* **final,** last; deathbed.
ANTONYMS first.
▶ **noun** *he took her dying very hard* **death,** demise, passing, loss of life, quietus; formal decease.

dynamic ▶ **adjective** *he was eclipsed by his more dynamic colleagues* **energetic,** spirited, active, lively, zestful, vital, vigorous, forceful, powerful, positive; high-powered, aggressive, bold, enterprising; magnetic, passionate, fiery, high-octane; informal go-getting, peppy, full of get-up-and-go, full of vim and vigor, gutsy, spunky, feisty, go-ahead.
ANTONYMS halfhearted.

dynasty ▶ **noun** *the fourth king of the Shang dynasty* **bloodline,** line, ancestral line, lineage, house, family, ancestry, descent, succession, genealogy, family tree; regime, rule, reign, empire, sovereignty.

Ee

each ▶ pronoun *there are 47 books and each must be read* **every one,** each one, each and every one, all, the whole lot.

▶ adjective *he visited each month* **every,** each and every, every single.

▶ adverb *they gave $10 each* **apiece,** per person, per capita, from each, individually, respectively, severally.

eager ▶ adjective 1 *small eager faces* **keen,** enthusiastic, avid, fervent, ardent, motivated, wholehearted, dedicated, committed, earnest; informal gung-ho.
ANTONYMS apathetic.
2 *we were eager for news* **anxious,** impatient, longing, yearning, wishing, hoping, hopeful; on the edge of one's seat, on tenterhooks, on pins and needles; informal itching, gagging, dying.
ANTONYMS uninterested.

> CHOOSE THE RIGHT WORD
>
> **eager, ardent, avid, enthusiastic, fervent, keen, zealous**
>
> You've heard of the "eager beaver"? Anyone who has a strong interest or an impatient desire to pursue or become involved in something is called **eager** (*eager to get started; an eager learner*). Someone who is especially *eager* might be called **avid**, a word that implies greed or insatiable desire (*an avid golfer, he was never at home on weekends*). **Ardent** combines eagerness with intense feelings of passion or devotion (*an ardent lover; an ardent theatergoer*), while **fervent** suggests an eagerness that is ready, at least figuratively, to boil over (*their fervent pleas could not be ignored*). Anyone who is deeply interested in something or who shows a spirited readiness to act is called **keen** (*he was keen on bicycling*), while **zealous** implies the kind of eagerness that pushes all other considerations aside (*a zealous environmentalist*). **Enthusiastic** may connote participation rather than expectation: One can be *eager* to take a trip to Switzerland, an *ardent* student of Swiss history, and an *avid* outdoorsperson who is *keen* on hiking, but one is usually called *enthusiastic* about a trip to Switzerland when it is under way or is over; *enthusiastic* also very often applies to someone who outwardly and forcefully expresses eagerness.

eagerness ▶ noun *the eagerness of potential buyers* **keenness,** enthusiasm, avidity, fervor, zeal, wholeheartedness, earnestness, commitment, dedication; impatience, desire, longing, yearning, hunger, appetite, ambition, yen.

ear ▶ noun 1 *an infection of the ear* inner ear, middle ear, outer ear.
2 *he had the ear of the president* **attention,** notice, heed, regard, consideration.
3 *he has an ear for a good song* **appreciation,** discrimination, perception.
– PHRASES **play it by ear** *until we know all the facts, we'll have to play it by ear* **improvise,** extemporize, ad lib; make it up as one goes along, think on one's feet, wing it, fly by the seat of one's pants.

early ▶ adjective 1 *early copies of the book* **advance,** forward; initial, preliminary, first; pilot, trial.
ANTONYMS late.
2 *an early death* **untimely,** premature, unseasonable, before time.
3 *early man* **primitive,** ancient, prehistoric, primeval; literary of yore.
ANTONYMS modern.
4 *an early official statement* **prompt,** timely, quick, speedy, rapid, fast.
ANTONYMS overdue.

▶ adverb 1 *Rachel has to get up early* **in the early morning**; at dawn, at daybreak, at first light.
ANTONYMS late.
2 *they hoped to leave school early* **before the usual time**; prematurely, too soon, ahead of time, ahead of schedule; literary betimes.

earmark ▶ verb *the cash had been earmarked for the firm* **set aside,** keep (back), reserve; designate, assign, mark; allocate, allot, devote, pledge, give over.

▶ noun *he has all the earmarks of a leader* **characteristics,** attribute, feature, hallmark, quality.

earn ▶ verb 1 *they earned $20,000* **be paid,** take home, gross, net; receive, get, make, obtain, collect, bring in; informal pocket, bank, rake in.
2 *he has earned their trust* **deserve,** merit, warrant, justify, be worthy of; gain, win, secure, establish, obtain, procure, get, acquire; informal clinch.
ANTONYMS lose.

earnest ▶ adjective 1 *he is dreadfully earnest* **serious,** solemn, grave, sober, humorless, staid, intense; committed, dedicated, keen, diligent, zealous; thoughtful, cerebral, deep, profound.
ANTONYMS frivolous, apathetic.
2 *earnest prayer* **devout,** heartfelt, wholehearted, sincere, impassioned, fervent,

ardent, intense, urgent.
ANTONYMS halfhearted.
– PHRASES **in earnest 1** *we are in earnest about stopping crime* **serious,** sincere, wholehearted, genuine; committed, firm, resolute, determined. **2** *he started writing in earnest* **zealously,** purposefully, determinedly, resolutely; passionately, wholeheartedly.

earnings ▶ plural noun *their combined earnings paid for this house* **income,** wages, salary, stipend, pay, payment, fees; revenue, yield, profit, takings, proceeds, avails, dividends, return, remuneration.

earth ▶ noun **1** *the moon orbits the earth* **world,** globe, planet.
2 *a trembling of the earth* **land,** ground, terra firma; floor.
3 *he plowed the earth* **soil,** clay, loam; dirt, sod, turf; ground.
4 *the earth rejoiced* **humanity,** humankind, mankind, (all) people; humorous earthlings.
5 *the fox's earth* **den,** lair, set, burrow, warren, hole; retreat, shelter, hideout, hideaway.

earthenware ▶ noun *her original line of earthenware* **pottery,** stoneware; china, porcelain; pots, crockery.

earthly ▶ adjective **1** *the earthly environment* **terrestrial,** telluric.
ANTONYMS extraterrestrial.
2 *the promise of earthly delights* **worldly,** temporal, mortal, human; material; carnal, fleshly, bodily, physical, corporeal, sensual.
ANTONYMS spiritual, heavenly.
3 informal *there is no earthly explanation for this* **feasible,** possible, likely, conceivable, imaginable.

earthy ▶ adjective **1** *an earthy smell* **soil-like,** dirtlike.
2 *she was a simple, earthy girl* **down-to-earth,** unsophisticated, unrefined, simple, plain, unpretentious, natural.
3 *Emma's earthy language* **bawdy,** ribald, off-color, racy, rude, vulgar, lewd, crude, foul, coarse, uncouth, unseemly, indelicate, indecent, obscene; informal blue, locker-room, barnyard.

ease ▶ noun **1** *he defeated them all with ease* **effortlessness,** no trouble, simplicity; deftness, adroitness, proficiency, mastery.
ANTONYMS difficulty.
2 *his ease of manner* **naturalness,** casualness, informality, amiability, affability; unconcern, composure, nonchalance, insouciance.
ANTONYMS stiffness, formality.
3 *he couldn't find any ease* **peace,** calm, tranquility, serenity; repose, restfulness, quiet, security, comfort.
ANTONYMS trouble, disturbance.
4 *a life of ease* **affluence,** wealth, prosperity, luxury, plenty; comfort, contentment, enjoyment, well-being.
ANTONYMS poverty, hardship.
▶ verb **1** *the alcohol eased his pain* **relieve,** alleviate, mitigate, soothe, palliate, moderate, dull, deaden, numb; reduce, lighten, diminish.
ANTONYMS aggravate.
2 *the rain **eased off*** **abate,** subside, die down, let up, slack off, diminish, lessen, peter out, relent, come to an end.
ANTONYMS worsen.
3 *work helped to ease her mind* **calm,** pacify, soothe, comfort, console, quieten; hearten, gladden, uplift, encourage.
4 *we want to ease their adjustment* **facilitate,** expedite, assist, help, aid, advance, further, forward, simplify.
ANTONYMS hinder.
5 *he eased out the cork* **guide,** maneuver, inch, edge; slide, slip, squeeze.
– PHRASES **at ease/at one's ease** *she felt completely at ease in their mountain retreat* **relaxed,** calm, serene, tranquil, unworried, contented, content, happy; comfortable.

easy ▶ adjective **1** *the task was very easy* **uncomplicated,** undemanding, unchallenging, effortless, painless, trouble-free, facile, simple, straightforward, elementary; informal easy as pie, a piece of cake, child's play, kids' stuff, a cinch, no sweat, a breeze, smooth sailing, duck soup, a snap.
ANTONYMS difficult, challenging.
2 *easy babies* **docile,** manageable, amenable, tractable, compliant, pliant, acquiescent, obliging, cooperative, easygoing.
ANTONYMS difficult, demanding.
3 *an easy target* **vulnerable,** susceptible, defenseless; naive, gullible, trusting.
ANTONYMS streetwise, savvy.
4 *Dave's easy manner* **natural,** casual, informal, unceremonious, unreserved, uninhibited, unaffected, easygoing, amiable, affable, genial, good-humored; carefree, nonchalant, unconcerned, laid-back.
ANTONYMS formal.
5 *an easy life* **calm,** tranquil, serene, quiet, peaceful, untroubled, contented, relaxed, comfortable, secure, safe; informal cushy.
ANTONYMS stressful, chaotic.
6 *an easy pace* **leisurely,** unhurried, comfortable, undemanding, easygoing, gentle, sedate, moderate, steady.
ANTONYMS demanding.
7 informal *people think she's easy* **promiscuous,** unchaste, loose, wanton, abandoned, licentious, debauched; informal sluttish, slutty, whorish.
ANTONYMS chaste.

easygoing ▶ adjective *Fred was easygoing and a pleasure to work with* **relaxed,** even-tempered, placid, mellow, mild, happy-go-lucky, carefree, free and easy, nonchalant, insouciant, imperturbable; amiable, considerate, undemanding, patient, tolerant, lenient, broad-minded, understanding; good-natured, pleasant, agreeable; informal laid-back, unflappable, Type-B, low-maintenance.
ANTONYMS tense, intolerant.

eat ▶ verb **1** *we ate a hearty breakfast* **consume,** devour, ingest, partake of; gobble (up/down), bolt (down), wolf (down); swallow, chew, munch, chomp; informal guzzle, nosh, put away, chow down on, tuck into, demolish, dispose of, polish off, pig out on, scarf (down).
2 *we ate at a local restaurant* **have a meal,** consume food, feed, snack; breakfast, lunch, dine; feast, banquet; informal graze, nosh; dated sup.

3 *acidic water can **eat away at** pipes* **erode,** corrode, wear away/down/through, burn through, consume, dissolve, disintegrate, crumble, decay; damage, destroy.

eavesdrop ▶ verb *sorry, I refuse to **eavesdrop on** Kenny for you* **listen in on,** spy on; monitor, tap, wiretap, record, overhear; informal snoop on, bug.

ebb ▶ verb **1** *the tide ebbed* **recede,** go out, retreat, flow back, fall back/away, subside.
ANTONYMS come in.
2 *his courage began to ebb* **diminish,** dwindle, wane, fade away, peter out, decline, flag, let up, decrease, weaken, disappear.
ANTONYMS increase, intensify.
▶ noun **1** *the ebb of the tide* **receding,** retreat, subsiding.
2 *the ebb of the fighting* **abatement,** subsiding, easing, dying down, de-escalation, decrease, decline, diminution.

ebony ▶ adjective *his ebony eyes* **black,** jet-black, pitch-black, coal-black, sable, inky, sooty, raven, dark.

ebullience ▶ noun *the director's ebullience inspires the cast* **exuberance,** buoyancy, cheerfulness, cheeriness, merriment, jollity, sunniness, jauntiness, lightheartedness, high spirits, elation, euphoria, jubilation; animation, sparkle, vivacity, enthusiasm, perkiness; informal chirpiness, bounciness, pep.

ebullient ▶ adjective *in an ebullient mood* **exuberant,** buoyant, cheerful, joyful, cheery, merry, jolly, sunny, jaunty, lighthearted, elated; animated, sparkling, vivacious, irrepressible; informal bubbly, bouncy, peppy, upbeat, chirpy, smiley, full of beans; dated gay.
ANTONYMS depressed.

eccentric ▶ adjective *eccentric behavior* **unconventional,** uncommon, abnormal, irregular, aberrant, anomalous, odd, queer, strange, peculiar, weird, bizarre, outlandish, freakish, extraordinary; idiosyncratic, quirky, nonconformist, outré; informal way out, offbeat, freaky, oddball, wacky, kooky.
ANTONYMS conventional.
▶ noun *he was something of an eccentric* **oddity,** odd fellow, character, individualist, individual, free spirit; misfit; informal oddball, odd duck, weirdo, freak, nut, head case, crank, wacko, kook, screwball, crackpot.

eccentricity ▶ noun *Sidney's eccentricity was more charming than alarming* **unconventionality,** singularity, oddness, strangeness, weirdness, quirkiness, freakishness; peculiarity, foible, idiosyncrasy, caprice, whimsy, quirk; informal nuttiness, screwiness, freakiness, kookiness.

ecclesiastic ▶ noun *a high ecclesiastic* See CLERGY.

echelon ▶ noun *he reached the upper echelons of government* **level,** rank, grade, step, rung, tier, position, order.

echo ▶ noun **1** *a faint echo of my shout* **reverberation,** reflection, ringing, repetition, repeat.
2 *the scene she described was an echo of the photograph* **duplicate,** copy, replica, imitation, mirror image, double, match, parallel; informal look-alike, spitting image, dead ringer.
3 *a faint echo of their love* **trace,** vestige, remnant, ghost, shadow, memory, recollection, remembrance; reminder, sign, mark, token, souvenir, indication, suggestion, hint; evidence.
▶ verb **1** *his laughter echoed around the room* **reverberate,** resonate, resound, reflect, ring, vibrate.
2 *Bill echoed Rex's words* **repeat,** restate, reiterate; copy, imitate, parrot, mimic; reproduce, recite, quote, regurgitate; informal recap.

eclectic ▶ adjective *an eclectic mix of party music* **wide-ranging,** broad-based, extensive, comprehensive, encyclopedic; varied, diverse, catholic, all-embracing, multifaceted, multifarious, heterogeneous, miscellaneous, assorted.

eclipse ▶ noun **1** *the eclipse of the sun* **blotting out,** blocking, covering, obscuring, concealing, darkening; Astronomy occultation.
2 *the eclipse of the empire* **decline,** fall, failure, decay, deterioration, degeneration, weakening, collapse.
▶ verb **1** *the sun was eclipsed by the moon* **blot out,** block, cover, obscure, hide, conceal, obliterate, darken; shade; Astronomy occult.
2 *the system was eclipsed by new methods* **outshine,** overshadow, surpass, exceed, outclass, outstrip, outdo, top, trump, transcend, upstage.

economic ▶ adjective **1** *economic reform* **financial,** monetary, budgetary, fiscal; commercial.
2 *an economic alternative to carpeting* **cheap,** inexpensive, low-cost, economical, cut-rate, discount, bargain.
ANTONYMS expensive.

economical ▶ adjective **1** *an economical car* **cheap,** inexpensive, low-cost, budget, economy, economic; cut-rate, discount, bargain.
ANTONYMS expensive.
2 *a very economical shopper* **thrifty,** provident, prudent, sensible, frugal, sparing, abstemious; mean, parsimonious, penny-pinching, miserly, stingy.
ANTONYMS spendthrift.

CHOOSE THE RIGHT WORD

economical, frugal, miserly, parsimonious, provident, sparing, thrifty

If you don't like to spend money unnecessarily, you may simply be **economical**, which means that you manage your finances wisely and avoid any unnecessary expenses. If you're **thrifty**, you're both industrious and clever in managing your resources (*a thrifty shopper who never leaves home without her coupons*). **Frugal**, on the other hand, means that you tend to be sparing with money—sometimes getting a little carried away in your efforts—by avoiding any form of luxury or lavishness (*too frugal to take a taxi, even at night*). If you're **sparing**, you exercise such restraint in your spending that you sometimes deprive yourself (*sparing to *the point where she allowed herself only one new item of clothing a season*). If you're **provident**, however, you're focused on providing for the future (*never one to be provident, she spent her allowance the day she received it*). **Miserly** and **parsimonious** are both used to describe frugality in its most extreme form. But while being *frugal* might be considered a virtue, being *parsimonious* is usually considered to be a fault or even a vice (*they could have been generous with their wealth, but they chose to lead a parsimonious life*). And no one wants to be called *miserly*, which implies being stingy out of greed rather than need (*so miserly that he reveled in his riches while those around him were starving*).

economize ▶ verb *they economized by growing their own vegetables* **save (money),** cut costs; cut back, make cutbacks, retrench, budget, make economies, be thrifty, be frugal, scrimp, cut corners, tighten one's belt, watch the/one's pennies.

economy ▶ noun **1** *the nation's economy* **wealth,** (financial) resources; financial system, financial management.
2 *one can combine good living with economy* **thrift,** thriftiness, providence, prudence, careful budgeting, economizing, saving, scrimping, restraint, frugality, abstemiousness.
ANTONYMS extravagance.

ecstasy ▶ noun *the ecstasy of loving him* **rapture,** bliss, elation, euphoria, transports, rhapsodies; joy, jubilation, exultation. See note at **RAPTURE**.
ANTONYMS misery.

ecstatic ▶ adjective *the news of Sophie's safe return made them ecstatic* **enraptured,** elated, in raptures, euphoric, rapturous, joyful, overjoyed, blissful; on cloud nine, in seventh heaven, beside oneself with joy, jumping for joy, delighted, thrilled, exultant; informal over the moon, on top of the world, blissed out.

eddy ▶ noun *small eddies at the river's edge* **swirl,** whirlpool, vortex, maelstrom.
▶ verb *cold air eddied around her* **swirl,** whirl, spiral, wind, circulate, twist; flow, ripple, stream, surge, billow.

edge ▶ noun **1** *the edge of the lake* **border,** boundary, extremity, fringe, margin, side; lip, rim, brim, brink, verge; perimeter, circumference, periphery, limits, bounds. See note at **BORDER**.
ANTONYMS middle.
2 *she had an edge in her voice* **sharpness,** severity, bite, sting, asperity, acerbity, acidity, trenchancy; sarcasm, acrimony, malice, spite, venom.
ANTONYMS kindness.
3 *they have an edge over their rivals* **advantage,** lead, head start, the whip hand, the upper hand; superiority, dominance, ascendancy, supremacy, primacy; informal inside track.
ANTONYMS disadvantage.
▶ verb **1** *poplars edged the orchard* **border,** fringe, verge, skirt; surround, enclose, encircle, circle, encompass, bound.
2 *a nightie edged with lace* **trim,** pipe, band, decorate, finish; border, fringe; bind, hem.
3 *he edged closer to the fire* **creep,** inch, work one's way, pick one's way, ease oneself; sidle, steal, slink.
– PHRASES **on edge** *they were always on edge when Uncle Herman visited* See **EDGY** (sense 1).

edgy ▶ adjective **1** *everyone was edgy as the deadline approached* **tense,** nervous, on edge, anxious, apprehensive, uneasy, unsettled; twitchy, jumpy, keyed up, restive, skittish, neurotic, insecure; irritable, touchy, tetchy, testy, crotchety, prickly; informal uptight, wired, snappy, strung out.
ANTONYMS calm.
2 *an edgy new novel* **cutting-edge,** on-the-edge, fringe, avant-garde, innovative, original, offbeat; gritty.
ANTONYMS conventional.

edible ▶ adjective *these berries may not be edible* **safe to eat,** fit for human consumption, wholesome, good to eat; consumable, digestible, palatable; formal comestible.

edict ▶ noun *rules established by government edict* **decree,** order, command, commandment, mandate, proclamation, pronouncement, dictate, fiat, promulgation; law, statute, act, bill, ruling, injunction; formal ordinance.

edification ▶ noun formal *I read Latin for my own personal edification* **education,** instruction, tuition, teaching, training, tutelage, guidance; enlightenment, cultivation, information; improvement, development.

USAGE

edification

In the phrase *for your edification* (= for your moral or intellectual instruction), the word *edification* is sometimes misused to mean "for your enjoyment" or the like—e.g.:

- "Dennis has come to the Tishomingo Lodge and Casino to perform daredevil dives for the edification [read *thrill*] of the casino guests." (*Rocky Mountain News* [Denver]; Feb. 15, 2002.)
- "Everyone says vaguely snotty things about each other and hidden cameras record, for our edification [read *titillation*], sundry couples' first kisses." (*Daily News of Los Angeles*; June 2, 2002.)
- "Quinn and his best friend Creedy (Gerard Butler) reenact the climactic light-saber battle between Luke Skywalker and Darth Vader for the edification [read *enjoyment*] of the local children." (*Austin American-Statesman*; July 12, 2002.) — **BG**

edifice ▶ noun *the imposing new edifice on Whitfield Street* **building,** structure, construction, erection, pile, complex; property, development, premises.

edify ▶ verb formal *students who have no desire to be edified should leave my classroom and take up thumb-twiddling* **educate,** instruct, teach, school, tutor, train, guide; enlighten, inform, cultivate, develop, improve, better.

edit ▶ verb **1** *she edited the text* **correct,** check, copyedit, improve, emend, polish; modify, adapt, revise, rewrite, reword, rework, redraft; shorten, condense, cut, abridge; informal clean up, blue-pencil.
2 *this volume was edited by a consultant* **select,** choose, assemble, organize, put together.
3 *he edited the school newspaper* **be the editor of,** direct, run, manage, head, lead, supervise, oversee, preside over; informal be the boss of.

edition ▶ noun *the latest edition includes candid photos from the peace rally* **issue,** number, volume, impression, publication; version, revision.

educate ▶ verb *it's nearly impossible to educate children who hate being in school* **teach,** school, tutor, instruct, coach, train, drill; guide, inform, enlighten; inculcate, indoctrinate; formal edify.

educated ▶ adjective *her assistant was an educated and creative young man* **informed,** literate, schooled, tutored, well-read, learned, knowledgeable, enlightened; intellectual, academic, erudite, scholarly, cultivated, cultured; dated lettered.

education ▶ noun **1** *the education of young children* **teaching,** schooling, tuition, tutoring, instruction, coaching, training, tutelage, guidance; indoctrination, inculcation, enlightenment; formal edification.
2 *a woman of some education* **learning,** knowledge, literacy, scholarship, enlightenment.

educational ▶ adjective **1** *a stuffy educational establishment* **academic,** scholastic, school, learning, teaching, pedagogic, instructional.
2 *an educational experience* **instructive,** instructional, educative, informative, illuminating, pedagogic, enlightening, didactic, heuristic; formal edifying.

educator ▶ noun *Mr. Chips is one of the most beloved educators in fiction* **teacher,** tutor, instructor, schoolteacher; educationalist, educationist; lecturer, professor; guide, mentor, guru; formal pedagogue; dated schoolmaster, schoolmistress, schoolmarm; archaic schoolman.

eerie ▶ adjective *eerie sounds from the swamp* **uncanny,** sinister, ghostly, unnatural, unearthly, supernatural, otherworldly; strange, abnormal, odd, weird, freakish; creepy, scary, spooky, freaky, frightening; bone-chilling, spine-chilling, hair-raising, blood-curdling, terrifying.

efface ▶ verb **1** *the chalk drawings were effaced by the rain* **erase,** eradicate, expunge, blot out, rub out, wipe out, remove, eliminate; delete, cancel, obliterate.
2 *he attempted to **efface himself*** **make oneself inconspicuous,** keep out of sight, keep out of the limelight, lie low, keep a low profile, withdraw (oneself).

effect ▶ noun **1** *the effect of these changes* **result,** consequence, upshot, outcome, repercussions, ramifications; end result, conclusion, culmination, corollary, concomitant, aftermath; fruit(s), product, by-product, payoff; Medicine sequela.
ANTONYMS cause.
2 *the effect of the drug* **impact,** action, effectiveness, influence; power, potency, strength; success; formal efficacy.
3 *the new rules come into effect tomorrow* **force,** operation, enforcement, implementation, effectiveness; validity, lawfulness, legality, legitimacy.
4 *some words to that effect* **sense,** meaning, theme, drift, import, intent, intention, tenor, significance, message; gist, essence, spirit.
5 (**effects**) *the dead man's effects* **belongings,** possessions, goods, worldly goods, chattels, goods and chattels; property, paraphernalia; informal gear, tackle, things, stuff.
▶ verb *they effected many changes* **achieve,** accomplish, carry out, realize, manage, bring off, execute, conduct, engineer, perform, do, perpetrate, discharge, complete, consummate; cause, bring about, create, produce, make; provoke, occasion, generate, engender, actuate, initiate; formal effectuate.
– PHRASES **in effect** *the battle had, in effect, already been won* **really,** in reality, in truth, in fact, in actual fact, effectively, essentially, in essence, practically, to all intents and purposes, all but, as good as, more or less, almost, nearly, just about; informal pretty much; literary well-nigh, nigh on. **take effect 1** *these measures will take effect in May* **come into force,** come into operation, become operative, begin, become valid, become law, apply, be applied. **2** *the drug started to take effect* **work,** act, be effective, produce results.

effective ▶ adjective **1** *an effective treatment* **successful,** effectual, potent, powerful; helpful, beneficial, advantageous, valuable, useful; formal efficacious.
ANTONYMS ineffective, weak.
2 *a more effective argument* **convincing,** compelling, strong, forceful, potent, weighty, sound, valid; impressive, persuasive, plausible, credible, authoritative; logical, reasonable, lucid, coherent, cogent, eloquent; formal efficacious.
ANTONYMS weak.
3 *the new law will become effective next week* **operative,** in force, in effect; valid, official, lawful, legal, binding; Law effectual.
ANTONYMS invalid.
4 *Korea was under effective Japanese control* **virtual,** practical, essential, actual, implicit, tacit.
ANTONYMS theoretical.

CHOOSE THE RIGHT WORD

effective, effectual, efficacious, efficient

All of these adjectives mean producing or capable of producing a result, but they are not interchangeable. Use **effective** when you want to describe something that produces a definite effect or result (*an effective speaker who was able to rally the crowd's support*) and **efficacious** when it produces the desired effect or result (*an efficacious remedy that cured her almost immediately*). If something produces the desired effect or result in a decisive manner, use **effectual** (*an effectual recommendation that got him the job*), an adjective that is often employed when looking back after an event is over (*an effectual strategy that finally turned the tide in their favor*). Reserve the use of **efficient** for when you want to imply skill and economy of energy in producing the desired result (*so efficient in her management of the company that layoffs were not necessary*). When applied to people, *efficient* means capable or competent (*an efficient homemaker*) and places less emphasis on the achievement of results and more on the skills involved.

effectiveness ▶ noun *we were impressed by the effectiveness of the nontoxic pesticide* **success,** productiveness, potency, power; benefit, advantage, value, virtue, usefulness; formal efficacy.

effectual ▶ adjective **1** *effectual political action* **effective,** successful, productive, constructive; worthwhile, helpful, beneficial, advantageous, valuable, useful; formal efficacious. See note at EFFECTIVE.
2 Law *an effectual document* **valid,** authentic, bona fide, genuine, official; lawful, legal, legitimate, binding, legally binding, contractual.

effeminate ▶ adjective *an effeminate bartender* **womanish,** effete, foppish, unmanly, feminine; informal camp, campy, flaming.
ANTONYMS manly.

effervescence ▶ noun **1** *wines of uniform effervescence* **fizz,** fizziness, sparkle, gassiness, carbonation, aeration, bubbliness.
2 *his cheeky effervescence* **vivacity,** liveliness, animation, high spirits, ebullience, exuberance, buoyancy, sparkle, gaiety, jollity, cheerfulness, perkiness, breeziness, enthusiasm, irrepressibility, vitality, zest, energy, dynamism, pep, bounce, spunk.

effervescent ▶ adjective **1** *an effervescent drink* **fizzy,** sparkling, carbonated, aerated, gassy, bubbly.
ANTONYMS flat, still.
2 *effervescent young people* **vivacious,** lively, animated, high-spirited, bubbly, ebullient, buoyant, sparkling, scintillating, lighthearted, jaunty, happy, jolly, cheery, cheerful, perky, sunny, enthusiastic, irrepressible, vital, zestful, energetic, dynamic; informal bright-eyed and bushy-tailed, peppy, bouncy, upbeat, chirpy, full of beans.
ANTONYMS depressed.

effete ▶ adjective **1** *effete trendies* **affected,** pretentious, precious, mannered, overrefined; ineffectual; informal la-di-da.
ANTONYMS unpretentious.
2 *an effete young man* **effeminate,** unmanly, girlish, feminine; soft, timid, cowardly, lily-livered, spineless, pusillanimous; informal sissy, wimpish, wimpy.
ANTONYMS manly.
3 *the fabric of society is effete* **weak,** enfeebled, enervated, worn out, exhausted, finished, drained, spent, powerless, ineffectual.
ANTONYMS powerful.

efficacious ▶ adjective formal *a change in diet may be quite efficacious* **effective,** effectual, successful, productive, constructive, potent; helpful, beneficial, advantageous, valuable, useful. See note at EFFECTIVE.

efficacy ▶ noun formal *the efficacy of prescription drugs* **effectiveness,** success, productiveness, potency, power; benefit, advantage, value, virtue, usefulness.

efficiency ▶ noun **1** *we need to make changes to improve efficiency* **organization,** order, orderliness, regulation, coherence; productivity, effectiveness.
2 *I compliment you on your efficiency* **competence,** capability, ability, proficiency, adeptness, expertise, professionalism, skill, effectiveness.

efficient ▶ adjective **1** *efficient techniques* **organized,** methodical, systematic, logical, orderly, businesslike, streamlined, productive, effective, cost-effective, labor-saving. See note at EFFECTIVE.
ANTONYMS disorganized.
2 *an efficient secretary* **competent,** capable, able, proficient, adept, skillful, skilled, effective, productive, organized, businesslike.
ANTONYMS incompetent.

effigy ▶ noun *protestors threw water-balloon "bombs" at an effigy of the president* **statue,** statuette, sculpture, model, dummy, figurine; likeness, image; bust.

effluent ▶ noun *the effluent from papermaking contains may contaminants* (**liquid**) **waste,** sewage, waste water, effluvium, outflow, discharge, emission.

effort ▶ noun **1** *they made an effort to work together* **attempt,** try, endeavor; informal crack, shot, stab; formal essay.
2 *his score was a fine effort* **achievement,** accomplishment, attainment, result, feat; undertaking, enterprise, work; triumph, success, coup.
3 *the job requires little effort* **exertion,** energy, work, endeavor, application, labor, power, muscle, toil, strain; informal sweat, elbow grease.

effortless ▶ adjective *he makes the most complex dance moves look effortless* **easy,** undemanding, unchallenging, painless, simple, uncomplicated, straightforward, elementary; fluent, natural; informal as easy as pie, child's play, kids' stuff, a cinch, no sweat, a breeze, duck soup, a snap.
ANTONYMS difficult.

effrontery ▶ noun *Stearns had the effrontery to counter the admiral's directive* **impudence,** impertinence, cheek, insolence, cockiness, audacity, temerity, presumption, nerve, gall, shamelessness, impoliteness, disrespect, bad manners; informal brass, face, chutzpah, sauce, sass. See note at TEMERITY.

effusion ▶ noun **1** *an effusion of poisonous gas* **outflow,** outpouring, rush, current, flood, deluge, emission, discharge, emanation; spurt, surge, jet, stream, torrent, gush, flow.
2 *reporters' flamboyant effusions* **outburst,** outpouring, gushing, rhapsody; wordiness, verbiage.

effusive ▸ adjective *effusive compliments* **gushing,** gushy, unrestrained, extravagant, fulsome, demonstrative, lavish, enthusiastic, lyrical; expansive, wordy, verbose, over the top. See note at SENTIMENTAL.
ANTONYMS restrained.

egg ▸ noun *the eggs are suspended in a gelatinous mass* **ovum**; gamete, germ cell; (**eggs**) roe, spawn, seed.
– PHRASES **egg someone on** *Earl didn't really want to enter the talent contest, but his friends egged him on* **urge,** goad, incite, provoke, push, drive, prod, prompt, induce, impel, spur on; encourage, exhort, motivate, galvanize.

egghead ▸ noun informal *Frances fits right in with all the chess-club eggheads* **intellectual,** thinker, academic, scholar, sage; bookworm, highbrow; expert, genius, mastermind; informal brain, whiz, brainiac, rocket scientist.
ANTONYMS dunce.

ego ▸ noun *the defeat was a bruise to his ego* **self-esteem,** self-importance, self-worth, self-respect, self-image, self-confidence.

egotism, egoism ▸ noun *Darla's egotism will always thwart her chances for a lasting relationship* **self-centeredness,** egomania, egocentricity, self-interest, selfishness, self-seeking, self-serving, self-regard, self-love, narcissism, self-admiration, vanity, conceit, self-importance; boastfulness. See also note at PRIDE.

> CHOOSE THE RIGHT WORD
>
> **egotism, conceit, egoism, narcissism, solipsism, vanity**
>
> Is the handsome, arrogant, successful politician who thinks the world revolves around him an egoist or an egotist? **Egotism** is a negative term that combines extreme self-preoccupation with a tendency to show off or attract attention, while **egoism** is a more neutral term for those who are preoccupied with their own needs and interests but do not necessarily consider themselves superior (*the egoism of teenagers is well-documented*). There is nothing neutral about **conceit**, which carries strong connotations of superiority and a failure to see oneself realistically (*he was so rich and powerful that conceit came easily*). **Vanity**, on the other hand, is not based so much on feelings of superiority as it is on a love for oneself and a craving for the admiration of others (*his vanity drove him to cosmetic surgery*). **Narcissism** and **solipsism** were once considered technical terms drawn from psychology and philosophy, respectively, but nowadays they are also in the general language. *Narcissism* means self-love and preoccupation with one's physical or mental attributes (*the beautiful young actress had a reputation for narcissism*), while *solipsism* refers to someone who is completely wrapped up in his or her own concerns (*the solipsism of the theoretical mathematician*).

egotist, egoist ▸ noun *boxing is a sport that breeds egotists* **self-seeker,** egocentric, egomaniac, narcissist; boaster, braggart; informal show-off, big head, showboat.

egotistic, egoistic ▸ adjective *Archie's egotistic lifestyle has alienated many people over the years* **self-centered,** selfish, egocentric, egomaniacal, self-interested, self-seeking, self-absorbed, narcissistic, vain, conceited, self-important; boastful.

egregious ▸ adjective *an egregious error of judgment* **shocking,** appalling, terrible, awful, horrendous, frightful, atrocious, abominable, abhorrent, outrageous; monstrous, heinous, dire, unspeakable, shameful, unforgivable, intolerable, dreadful; formal grievous.
ANTONYMS marvelous.

egress ▸ noun **1** *the egress from the gallery was blocked* **exit,** way out, escape route.
ANTONYMS entrance.
2 *a means of egress* **departure,** exit, withdrawal, retreat, exodus; escape.
ANTONYMS entry.

ejaculate ▸ verb **1** *the male ejaculates* **emit semen,** climax, have an orgasm, orgasm; informal come.
2 dated *"What?" he ejaculated* **exclaim,** cry out, call out, yell, blurt out, come out with.

ejaculation ▸ noun **1** *the ejaculation of fluid* **emission,** ejection, discharge, release, expulsion.
2 *premature ejaculation* **emission of semen,** climax, orgasm.
3 dated *the conversation consisted of ejaculations* **exclamation,** interjection; call, shout, yell.

eject ▸ verb **1** *the volcano ejected ash* **emit,** spew out, discharge, give off, send out, belch, vent; expel, release, disgorge, spout, vomit, throw up.
2 *the pilot had time to eject* **bail out,** escape, get out.
3 *they were ejected from the hall* **expel,** throw out, turn out, cast out, remove, oust; evict, banish; informal kick out, boot out, chuck out, give someone the bum's rush.
ANTONYMS admit.
4 *he was ejected from his post* **dismiss,** remove, discharge, oust, expel, ax, throw out, force out, drive out; informal sack, fire, send packing, boot out, kick out, chuck out, give someone their marching orders, show someone the door.
ANTONYMS appoint.

> CHOOSE THE RIGHT WORD
>
> **eject, dismiss, evict, expel, oust**
>
> Want to get rid of someone? You can **eject** him or her, which means to throw or cast out (*he was ejected from the meeting room*). If you hope the person never comes back, use **expel**, a verb that suggests driving someone out of a country, an organization, etc., for all time (*to be expelled from school*); it can also imply the use of voluntary force (*to expel air from the lungs*). If you exercise force or the power of law to get rid of someone or something, **oust** is the correct verb (*ousted after less than two years in office*). If as a property owner you are turning someone out of a house or a place of business, you'll want to **evict** the person (*she was evicted for

not paying the rent). **Dismiss** is by far the mildest of these terms, suggesting that you are rejecting or refusing to consider someone or something (*to dismiss a legal case*). It is also commonly used of loss of employment (*dismissed from his job for excessive tardiness*).

ejection ▶ noun **1** *the ejection of electrons* **emission,** discharge, expulsion, release; elimination.
2 *their ejection from the grounds* **expulsion,** removal; eviction, banishment, exile.
3 *his ejection from office* **dismissal,** removal, discharge, expulsion.

eke ▶ verb *I had to* **eke out** *my remaining funds* **husband,** use sparingly, be thrifty with, be frugal with, be sparing with, use economically; informal go easy on.
ANTONYMS squander.
– PHRASES **eke out a living** *they barely eked out a living* **subsist,** survive, get by, scrape by, make ends meet, keep body and soul together, keep the wolf from the door, keep one's head above water.

elaborate ▶ adjective **1** *an elaborate plan* **complicated,** complex, intricate, involved; detailed, painstaking, careful; tortuous, convoluted, serpentine, Byzantine.
ANTONYMS simple, plain.
2 *an elaborate plasterwork ceiling* **ornate,** decorated, embellished, adorned, ornamented, fancy, fussy, busy, ostentatious, extravagant, showy, baroque, rococo, florid; informal fancy-schmancy.
ANTONYMS simple, plain.
▶ verb *both sides refused to* **elaborate on** *their reasons* **expand on,** enlarge on, add to, flesh out, put flesh on the bones of, add detail to, expatiate on; develop, fill out, embellish, embroider, enhance, amplify.

elapse ▶ verb *how much time has elapsed?* **pass,** go by/past, wear on, slip by/away/past, roll by/past, slide by/past, steal by/past, tick by/past.

elastic ▶ adjective **1** *elastic material* **stretchy,** elasticized, stretchable, springy, flexible, pliant, pliable, supple, yielding, plastic, resilient. See note at FLEXIBLE.
ANTONYMS rigid.
2 *an elastic concept of nationality* **adaptable,** flexible, adjustable, accommodating, variable, fluid, versatile.
ANTONYMS inflexible.
▶ noun *buying elastics for her hair* **rubber band,** elastic band, scrunchie.

elasticity ▶ noun **1** *the skin's natural elasticity* **stretchiness,** flexibility, pliancy, suppleness, plasticity, resilience, springiness, give.
2 *the elasticity of the term* **adaptability,** flexibility, adjustability, fluidity, versatility.

elated ▶ adjective *Sally and Marv were elated at the idea of becoming grandparents* **thrilled,** delighted, overjoyed, ecstatic, euphoric, very happy, joyous, gleeful, jubilant, beside oneself, exultant, rapturous, in raptures, walking on air, on cloud nine, in seventh heaven, jumping for joy, in transports of delight; informal on top of the world, over the moon, on a high, tickled pink.
ANTONYMS miserable.

elation ▶ noun *the declaration of peace is indeed cause for our greatest elation* **euphoria,** ecstasy, happiness, delight, transports of delight, joy, joyousness, glee, jubilation, exultation, bliss, rapture.

elbow ▶ verb *he elbowed his way through the crowd* **push,** shove, force, shoulder, jostle, barge, muscle, bulldoze.

elbow room ▶ noun *the committee desires more elbow room within the confines of the organization* **room to maneuver,** room, space, breathing space, personal space, scope, opportunity, freedom, play, free rein, license, latitude, leeway.

elder ▶ adjective *his elder brother* **older,** senior, big.
▶ noun *the native elders* **leader,** senior figure, patriarch, father.

elderly ▶ adjective *her elderly mother* **aged,** old, advanced in years, aging, long in the tooth, past one's prime; gray-haired, grizzled, hoary; in one's dotage, decrepit, doddering, doddery, senescent; informal getting on, past it, over the hill, no spring chicken.
ANTONYMS youthful.
▶ noun (**the elderly**) *health care for the elderly* **old people,** the aged, senior citizens; geriatrics, seniors; retired people, retirees, golden agers; informal oldsters, geezers.

elect ▶ verb **1** *a new president was elected* **vote for, vote in,** return, cast one's vote for; choose, pick, select.
2 *she elected to stay behind* **choose,** decide, opt, vote.
▶ adjective *the president-elect* **future,** -to-be, designate, chosen, elected, coming, next, appointed.
▶ noun (**the elect**) *it is not the elect who need better health care and safer schools* **the chosen,** the elite, the favored; the crème de la crème.

election ▶ noun *announcing the results of the election* **ballot,** vote, popular vote, ballot box; poll(s); acclamation; primary.

elector ▶ noun *my thanks to the faithful electors who brought me to this place* **voter,** member of the electorate, constituent.

electric ▶ adjective **1** *an electric kettle* **electric-powered,** electrically operated, battery-operated.
2 *the atmosphere was electric* **exciting,** charged, electrifying, thrilling, heady, dramatic, intoxicating, dynamic, stimulating, galvanizing, rousing, stirring, moving; tense, knife-edge, explosive, volatile.

electrify ▶ verb *lecturers who electrify their students* **excite,** thrill, stimulate, arouse, rouse, inspire, stir (up), exhilarate, intoxicate, galvanize, move, fire (with enthusiasm), fire someone's imagination, invigorate, animate; startle, jolt, shock, light a fire under; informal give someone a thrill, give someone a charge.

elegance ▶ noun **1** *he was attracted by her elegance* **style,** stylishness, grace, gracefulness, taste, tastefulness, sophistication; refinement, dignity, beauty, poise, charm, culture; suaveness, urbanity, panache.

2 *the elegance of the idea* **neatness,** simplicity; ingenuity, cleverness, inventiveness.

elegant ▶ adjective **1** *an elegant black outfit* **stylish,** graceful, tasteful, sophisticated, classic, chic, smart, fashionable, modish; refined, dignified, poised, beautiful, lovely, charming, artistic, aesthetic; cultivated, polished, cultured; dashing, debonair, suave, urbane.
ANTONYMS gauche.
2 *an elegant solution* **neat,** simple, effective; ingenious, clever, deft, intelligent, inventive.
ANTONYMS messy, unwieldy.

elegiac ▶ adjective *an elegiac piece for small orchestra* **mournful,** melancholic, melancholy, plaintive, sorrowful, sad, lamenting, doleful; funereal, dirgelike; nostalgic, valedictory, poignant; literary dolorous.
ANTONYMS cheerful.

elegy ▶ noun *an elegy for his father* **lament,** requiem, threnody, dirge; literary plaint; Irish keen.

element ▶ noun **1** *an essential element of the game* **component,** constituent, part, section, portion, piece, segment, bit; aspect, factor, feature, facet, ingredient, strand, detail, point; member, unit, module, item.
2 *there is an element of truth in this stereotype* **trace,** touch, hint, smattering, soupçon.
3 (**elements**) *the elements of political science* **basics,** essentials, principles, first principles; foundations, fundamentals, rudiments; informal nuts and bolts, ABCs.
4 (**elements**) *I braved the elements* **weather,** climate, meteorological conditions, atmospheric conditions; wind, rain, snow.

elemental ▶ adjective **1** *the elemental principles of accounting* **basic,** primary, fundamental, essential, root, underlying; rudimentary.
2 *elemental forces* **natural,** atmospheric, meteorological, environmental, climatic.

elementary ▶ adjective **1** *an elementary astronomy course* **basic,** rudimentary, fundamental; preparatory, introductory, initiatory, entry-level; informal 101.
ANTONYMS advanced.
2 *a lot of the work is elementary* **easy,** simple, straightforward, uncomplicated, undemanding, painless, child's play, plain sailing; informal as easy as pie, as easy as ABC, a piece of cake, no sweat, kids' stuff.
ANTONYMS complicated, difficult.

elephantine ▶ adjective *a tropical plant with elephantine leaves* **enormous,** huge, gigantic, very big, massive, giant, immense, tremendous, colossal, mammoth, gargantuan, vast, prodigious, monumental, titanic; hulking, bulky, heavy, weighty, ponderous, lumbering; informal jumbo, whopping, humongous, monster, ginormous.
ANTONYMS tiny.

elevate ▶ verb **1** *we need a breeze to elevate the kite* **raise,** lift (up), raise up/aloft, upraise; hoist, hike up, haul up.
ANTONYMS lower.
2 *he was elevated to senior writer* **promote,** upgrade, advance, move up, raise, prefer; ennoble, exalt, aggrandize; informal move up the ladder.
ANTONYMS demote.

elevated ▶ adjective **1** *an elevated highway* **raised,** upraised, high up, aloft; overhead.
2 *elevated language* **lofty,** grand, exalted, fine, sublime; inflated, pompous, bombastic, orotund.
ANTONYMS lowly, base.
3 *the gentry's elevated status* **high,** higher, high-ranking, of high standing, lofty, superior, exalted, eminent; grand, noble.
ANTONYMS lowly, humble.

elevation ▶ noun **1** *his elevation to the directorship* **promotion,** upgrading, advancement, advance, preferment, aggrandizement; ennoblement; informal step up the ladder.
2 *15,000–30,000 feet in elevation* **altitude,** height.
3 *elevations in excess of 8,000 feet* **height,** hill, mountain, mount; formal eminence.
4 *elevation of thought* **grandeur,** greatness, nobility, loftiness, majesty, sublimity.

elf ▶ noun *elves inhabit the great hollow trees* **pixie,** fairy, sprite, imp, brownie; dwarf, gnome, goblin, hobgoblin; leprechaun, puck, troll.

elfin ▶ adjective *her elfin little brother charmed all the aunts and uncles* **elflike,** elfish, elvish, pixielike; puckish, impish, playful, mischievous; dainty, delicate, small, petite, slight, little, tiny, diminutive.

elicit ▶ verb *your sarcastic remarks will no doubt elicit a negative response* **obtain,** draw out, extract, bring out, evoke, call forth, bring forth, induce, prompt, generate, engender, trigger, provoke; formal educe.

elite ▶ noun *hobnobbing with Southport's elite* **best,** pick, cream, crème de la crème, flower, nonpareil, elect; high society, jet set, beautiful people, beau monde, haut monde, glitterati; aristocracy, nobility, upper class.
ANTONYMS dregs.

elixir ▶ noun *a homemade elixir purported to enhance virility* **potion,** concoction, brew, philter, decoction, mixture; medicine, tincture; extract, essence, concentrate, distillate, distillation; literary draft.

elliptical ▶ adjective **1** *an elliptical shape* **oval,** egg-shaped, elliptic, ovate, ovoid, oviform, ellipsoidal.
2 *elliptical phraseology* **cryptic,** abstruse, ambiguous, obscure, oblique, Delphic; terse, concise, succinct, compact, economic, laconic, sparing, abridged.

elocution ▶ noun *the producers brought in a teacher to help with her elocution* **pronunciation,** enunciation, articulation, diction, speech, intonation, vocalization, modulation; phrasing, delivery, public speaking.

elongate ▶ verb **1** *an exercise that elongates the muscles* **lengthen,** extend, stretch (out).
ANTONYMS shorten.
2 *the high notes were elongated* **prolong,** protract, draw out, sustain.
ANTONYMS shorten.

eloquence ▶ noun *the eloquence of his sermons* **fluency,** articulateness, expressiveness, silver tongue, persuasiveness, forcefulness, power, potency, effectiveness; oratory, rhetoric, grandiloquence, magniloquence; informal gift of the gab, way with words.

eloquent ▶ adjective **1** *an eloquent speaker* **fluent,** articulate, expressive, silver-tongued; persuasive, strong, forceful, powerful, potent, well-expressed, effective, lucid, vivid, graphic; smooth-tongued, glib.
ANTONYMS inarticulate.
2 *her glance was more eloquent than words* **expressive,** meaningful, suggestive, revealing, telling, significant, indicative.

elsewhere ▶ adverb *the negatives are stored in one place, and the prints are stored elsewhere* **somewhere else,** in/at/to another place, in/at/to a different place, hence; not here, not present, absent, away, abroad, out.
ANTONYMS here.

elucidate ▶ verb *Sherwood's diaries may help elucidate his motives* **explain,** make clear, illuminate, throw/shed light on, clarify, clear up, sort out, unravel, spell out; interpret, explicate; gloss. See note at CLARIFY.
ANTONYMS confuse.

elucidation ▶ noun *the manual provides elucidation useful to the beginner* **explanation,** clarification, illumination; interpretation, explication; gloss.

elude ▶ verb *Holbrook eluded the police for several weeks* **evade,** avoid, get away from, dodge, escape from, run from, run away from; lose, shake off, give the slip to, slip away from, throw off the scent; informal slip through someone's fingers, slip through the net.

elusive ▶ adjective **1** *her elusive husband* **difficult to find**; evasive, slippery; informal always on the move.
2 *an elusive quality* **indefinable,** intangible, impalpable, ambiguous.

Elysium ▶ noun Greek Mythology *human souls conveyed to Elysium* **heaven,** paradise, the Elysian fields; eternity, the afterlife, the next world, the hereafter; Scandinavian Mythology Valhalla; Classical Mythology the Islands of the Blessed; Arthurian Legend Avalon.

emaciated ▶ adjective *emaciated bodies* **thin,** skeletal, bony, gaunt, wasted; scrawny, skinny, scraggy, skin and bones, rawboned, sticklike, waiflike; starved, underfed, undernourished, underweight, half-starved; cadaverous, shriveled, shrunken, withered; informal anorexic, like a bag of bones.
ANTONYMS fat.

emanate ▶ verb **1** *warmth emanated from the fireplace* **issue,** spread, radiate, be sent forth/out.
2 *the proposals emanated from a committee* **originate,** stem, derive, proceed, spring, issue, emerge, flow, come.
3 *he emanated an air of power* **exude,** emit, radiate, give off/out, send out/forth.

emanation ▶ noun **1** *an emanation of his tortured personality* **product,** consequence, result, fruit.
2 *radon gas emanation* **discharge,** emission, radiation, effusion, outflow, outpouring, flow, leak; technical efflux.

emancipate ▶ verb *the young Cowles emancipated his father's serfs* **free,** liberate, set free, release, deliver, discharge; unchain, unfetter, unshackle, untie, unyoke; rare disenthrall.
ANTONYMS enslave.

emasculate ▶ verb *the opposition emasculated the committee's proposal* **weaken,** enfeeble, debilitate, erode, undermine, cripple; remove the sting from, pull the teeth out of; informal water down.

embalm ▶ verb **1** *his body had been embalmed* **preserve,** mummify, lay out.
2 *the poem ought to embalm his memory* **preserve,** conserve, enshrine, immortalize.

embargo ▶ noun *an embargo on oil sales* **ban,** bar, prohibition, stoppage, interdict, proscription, veto, moratorium; restriction, restraint, block, barrier, impediment, obstruction; boycott.
▶ verb *arms sales were embargoed* **ban,** bar, prohibit, stop, interdict, debar, proscribe, outlaw; restrict, restrain, block, obstruct; boycott.
ANTONYMS allow.

embark ▶ verb **1** *the passengers were not allowed to embark until 4:30* **board ship,** go on board, go aboard; informal hop on, jump on.
2 *he **embarked on** a new career* **begin,** start, commence, undertake, set about, take up, turn one's hand to, get down to; enter into, venture into, launch into, plunge into, engage in, settle down to; informal get cracking on, get going on, have a go/crack/shot at.

embarrass ▶ verb *his parents would show up drunk and embarrass him* **mortify,** shame, put someone to shame, humiliate, abash, chagrin, make uncomfortable, make self-conscious; discomfit, disconcert, discompose, upset, distress; informal show up, discombobulate.

embarrassed ▶ adjective *the officer's flashlight caught a pair of embarrassed teens in the back seat* **mortified,** red-faced, blushing, abashed, shamed, ashamed, shamefaced, humiliated, chagrined, awkward, self-conscious, uncomfortable, sheepish; discomfited, disconcerted, upset, discomposed, flustered, agitated, distressed; shy, bashful, tongue-tied; informal with egg on one's face, wishing the earth would swallow one up.

embarrassing ▶ adjective *many embarrassing moments have been preserved on videotape* **humiliating,** shaming, shameful, mortifying, ignominious; awkward, uncomfortable, cringeworthy, compromising; disconcerting, discomfiting, upsetting, distressing.

embarrassment ▶ noun **1** *he was scarlet with embarrassment* **mortification,** humiliation, shame, shamefacedness, chagrin, awkwardness, self-consciousness, sheepishness, discomfort, discomfiture, discomposure, agitation, distress; shyness, bashfulness.
2 *his current financial embarrassment* **difficulty,** predicament, plight, problem, mess, imbroglio; informal bind, jam, pickle, fix, scrape.
3 *an embarrassment of riches* **surplus,** excess, overabundance, superabundance, glut, surfeit, superfluity; abundance, profusion, plethora.

embassy ▸ noun 1 *the Italian embassy* **consulate,** legation.
2 historical *the king sent an embassy to the rebels* **envoy,** representative, delegate, emissary; delegation, deputation, legation, mission, diplomatic mission.

embed, imbed ▸ verb *rhinestones are then embedded in the leather trim* **implant,** plant, set, fix, lodge, root, insert, place; sink, drive, hammer, ram.

embellish ▸ verb 1 *weapons embellished with precious metal* **decorate,** adorn, ornament; beautify, enhance, grace; trim, garnish, gild; deck, bedeck, festoon, emblazon; informal tart up, pimp; literary bejewel, bedizen.
2 *the legend was embellished in later retellings* **elaborate,** embroider, expand on, exaggerate.

embellishment ▸ noun 1 *architectural embellishments* **decoration,** ornamentation, adornment; beautification, enhancement, trimming, trim, garnishing, gilding.
2 *we wanted the truth, not romantic embellishments* **elaboration,** addition, exaggeration.

embezzle ▸ verb *he's accused of embezzling donated funds* **misappropriate,** steal, thieve, pilfer, purloin, appropriate, defraud someone of, siphon off, pocket, help oneself to; abstract; informal rob, rip off, skim, line one's pockets with, pinch.

embezzlement ▸ noun *four corporate managers were indicted for embezzlement* **misappropriation,** theft, stealing, robbery, thieving, pilfering, purloining, pilferage, appropriation, swindling; fraud, larceny.

emblazon ▸ verb 1 *shirts emblazoned with the company name* **adorn,** decorate, ornament, embellish; inscribe.
2 *a flag with a hammer and sickle emblazoned on it* **display,** depict, show.

emblem ▸ noun *their emblem is an eagle perched atop a cannon* **symbol,** representation, token, image, figure, mark, sign; crest, badge, device, insignia, stamp, seal, heraldic device, coat of arms, shield; logo, trademark, brand.

CHOOSE THE RIGHT WORD

emblem, attribute, image, sign, symbol, token, type

When it comes to representing or embodying the invisible or intangible, you can't beat a **symbol**. It applies to anything that serves as an outward sign of something immaterial or spiritual (*the cross as a symbol of salvation; the crown as a symbol of monarchy*), although the association between the symbol and what it represents does not have to be based on tradition or convention and may, in fact, be quite arbitrary (*the annual gathering at the cemetery became a symbol of the family's long and tragic history*). An **emblem** is a visual symbol or pictorial device that represents the character or history of a family, a nation, or an office (*the eagle is an emblem of the United States*). It is very close in meaning to **attribute**, which is an object that is conventionally associated with either an individual, a group, or an abstraction (*the spiked wheel as an attribute of St. Catherine; the scales as an attribute of Justice*). An **image** is also a visual representation or embodiment, but in a much broader sense (*veins popping, he was the image of the angry father*). **Sign** is often used in place of *symbol* to refer to a simple representation of an agreed-upon meaning (*the upraised fist as a sign of victory; the white flag as a sign of surrender*), but a *symbol* usually embodies a wider range of meanings, while a *sign* can be any object, event, or gesture from which information can be deduced (*her faltering voice was a sign of her nervousness*). A **token**, on the other hand, is something offered as a symbol or reminder (*he gave her his class ring as a token of his devotion*) and a **type**, particularly in a religious context, is a symbol or representation of something not present (*Jerusalem as the type of heaven; the paschal lamb as the type of Christ*).

embodiment ▸ noun *the embodiment of the hippie culture* **personification,** incarnation, realization, manifestation, avatar, expression, representation, actualization, symbol, symbolization, materialization; paradigm, epitome, paragon, soul, model; type, essence, quintessence, exemplification, example, exemplar, ideal; formal reification.

embody ▸ verb 1 *he embodies the spirit of industrial capitalism* **personify,** realize, manifest, symbolize, represent, express, concretize, incarnate, epitomize, stand for, typify, exemplify; formal reify, hypostatize.
2 *the changes embodied in the gun control legislation* **incorporate,** include, contain, encompass; assimilate, consolidate, integrate, organize, systematize; combine.

embolden ▸ verb *emboldened by the brandy, he walked over to her table* **fortify,** make brave/braver, encourage, hearten, strengthen, brace, stiffen the resolve of, lift the morale of; rouse, stir, stimulate, cheer, rally, fire, animate, inspirit, invigorate; informal buck up. See note at ENCOURAGE.
ANTONYMS dishearten.

embrace ▸ verb 1 *he embraced her warmly* **hug,** take/hold in one's arms, hold, cuddle, clasp to one's bosom, clasp, squeeze, clutch; caress; enfold, enclasp, encircle, envelop, entwine oneself around; informal canoodle, clinch.
2 *most states have embraced the concept* **welcome,** welcome with open arms, accept, take up, take to one's heart, adopt; espouse, support, back, champion.
3 *the faculty embraces a wide range of departments* **include,** take in, comprise, contain, incorporate, encompass, cover, involve, embody, subsume, comprehend.
▸ noun *a fond embrace* **hug,** cuddle, squeeze, clinch, caress, clasp; bear hug.

embroider ▸ verb 1 *a cushion embroidered with a pattern of golden keys* **sew,** stitch; decorate, adorn, ornament, embellish.
2 *she embroidered her stories with colorful detail*

elaborate, embellish, enlarge on, exaggerate, touch up, dress up, gild, color; informal jazz up.

embroidery ▶ **noun 1** *the girls were taught embroidery* **needlework,** needlepoint, needlecraft, sewing, tatting, crewel work, tapestry.
2 *fanciful embroidery of the facts* **elaboration,** embellishment, adornment, ornamentation, coloring, enhancement; exaggeration, overstatement, hyperbole.

embryonic ▶ **adjective 1** *an embryonic chick* **fetal,** unborn, unhatched; in utero.
2 *an embryonic prodemocracy movement* **rudimentary,** undeveloped, unformed, immature, incomplete, incipient, inchoate; fledgling, budding, nascent, emerging, developing, early, germinal.
ANTONYMS mature.

emend ▶ **verb** *the editors select letters for publication and may emend content at their own discretion* **correct,** rectify, repair, fix; improve, enhance, polish, refine, amend; edit, rewrite, revise, copyedit, redraft, recast, rephrase, reword, rework, alter, change, modify; rare redact.

emerge ▶ **verb 1** *a policeman emerged from the alley* **come out,** appear, come into view, become visible, surface, materialize, manifest oneself, issue, come forth.
2 *several unexpected facts emerged* **become known,** become apparent, be revealed, come to light, come out, turn up, transpire, unfold, prove to be the case.

emergence ▶ **noun** *the emergence of a new generation* **appearance,** arrival, coming, materialization; advent, inception, dawn, birth, origination, start, development, rise.

emergency ▶ **noun 1** *a military emergency* **crisis,** urgent situation, extremity, exigency; accident, disaster, catastrophe, calamity; difficulty, plight, predicament, danger.
2 *get her down to emergency right away* emergency room, ER.
▶ **adjective 1** *an emergency meeting* **urgent,** crisis; impromptu, extraordinary.
2 *emergency supplies* **reserve,** standby, backup, fallback, in reserve.

emergent ▶ **adjective** *an emergent democracy* **emerging,** developing, rising, dawning, budding, embryonic, infant, fledgling, nascent, incipient, inchoate.

emigrate ▶ **verb** *her Swedish ancestors emigrated in 1901* **move abroad,** move overseas, leave one's country, migrate; relocate, resettle; defect.
ANTONYMS immigrate.

emigration ▶ **noun** *the main incentive for emigration was the promise of higher wages* **moving abroad,** moving overseas, expatriation, migration; exodus, diaspora; relocation, resettling; defection.

eminence ▶ **noun 1** *his eminence as a scientist* **fame,** celebrity, illustriousness, distinction, renown, preeminence, notability, greatness, prestige, importance, reputation, repute, note; prominence, superiority, stature, standing.
2 *various legal eminences* **important person,** dignitary, luminary, worthy, grandee, notable, notability, personage, leading light, VIP; informal somebody, someone, big shot, big gun, heavyweight.
3 formal *the hotel's eminence above the sea* **elevation,** height, rise.

eminent ▶ **adjective 1** *an eminent man of letters* **illustrious,** distinguished, renowned, esteemed, preeminent, notable, noteworthy, great, prestigious, important, influential, affluential, outstanding, noted, of note; famous, celebrated, prominent, well-known, lionized, acclaimed, exalted, revered, august, venerable.
ANTONYMS unknown.
2 *the eminent reasonableness of their claims* **obvious,** clear, conspicuous, marked, singular, signal; total, complete, utter, absolute, thorough, perfect, downright, sheer.

eminently ▶ **adverb** *this vehicle is eminently suitable for rough terrain* **very,** greatly, highly, exceedingly, extremely, particularly, exceptionally, supremely, uniquely; obviously, clearly, conspicuously, markedly, singularly, signally, outstandingly, strikingly, notably, surpassingly; totally, completely, utterly, absolutely, thoroughly, perfectly, downright.

emissary ▶ **noun** *the president sent emissaries to several African countries* **envoy,** ambassador, delegate, attaché, consul, plenipotentiary; agent, representative, deputy; messenger, courier; nuncio.

emission ▶ **noun** *controlling the emission of carbon dioxide* **discharge,** release, outpouring, outflow, leak, excretion, secretion, ejection; emanation, radiation, effusion, ejaculation, disgorgement, issuance.

emit ▶ **verb 1** *the hydrocarbons emitted from vehicle exhausts* **discharge,** release, give out/off, pour out, send forth, throw out, void, vent, issue; leak, ooze, excrete, disgorge, secrete, eject, ejaculate; spout, belch, spew out; emanate, radiate, exude.
ANTONYMS absorb.
2 *he emitted a loud cry* **utter,** voice, let out, produce, give vent to, come out with, vocalize.

emolument ▶ **noun** formal *his name alone is worth the emolument they're willing to offer* **salary,** pay, payment, wage(s), earnings, allowance, stipend, honorarium, reward, premium; fee, charge, consideration; income, profit, gain, return.

emotion ▶ **noun 1** *she was good at hiding her emotions* **feeling,** sentiment; reaction, response.
2 *overcome by emotion, she turned away* **passion,** strength of feeling, warmth of feeling.
3 *responses based purely on emotion* **instinct,** intuition, gut feeling; sentiment, the heart.

CHOOSE THE RIGHT WORD

emotion, affect, feeling, passion, sentiment

A **feeling** can be almost any subjective reaction or state—pleasant or unpleasant, strong or mild, positive or negative—that is characterized by an emotional response (*a feeling of insecurity; a feeling of pleasure*).

An **emotion** is a very intense feeling, which often involves a physical as well as a mental response and implies outward expression or agitation (*to be overcome with emotion*). **Passion** suggests a powerful or overwhelming emotion, with connotations of sexual love (*their passion remained undiminished after 30 years of marriage*) or intense anger (*a passion for revenge*). There is more intellect and less feeling in **sentiment**, which is often applied to an emotion inspired by an idea (*political sentiments; antiwar sentiments*). *Sentiment* also suggests a refined or slightly artificial feeling (*a speech marked by sentiment rather than passion*). **Affect** is a formal psychological term that refers to an observed emotional state (*heavily sedated, he spoke without affect*).

emotional ▶ **adjective 1** *an emotional young man* **passionate,** hot-blooded, ardent, fervent, excitable, temperamental, melodramatic, tempestuous; demonstrative, responsive, tender, loving, feeling, sentimental, sensitive.
ANTONYMS cold, apathetic.
2 *he paid an emotional tribute to his wife* **poignant,** moving, touching, affecting, powerful, stirring, emotive, heart-rending, heartwarming, impassioned, dramatic; haunting, pathetic, sentimental; informal tear-jerking.
ANTONYMS unfeeling.
3 *during the speech we all became a little emotional* **tearful,** teary-eyed, sad, choked up, weepy; formal literary lachrymose.
ANTONYMS dry-eyed.
4 *their emotional needs are often ignored* **spiritual,** inner, psychological, psychic, of the heart.
ANTONYMS material.

emotionless ▶ **adjective** *emotionless faces* **unemotional,** unfeeling, dispassionate, passionless, unexpressive, inexpressive, cool, cold, cold-blooded, impassive, indifferent, detached, remote, aloof; toneless, flat, dead, expressionless, blank, wooden, stony, deadpan, vacant, poker-faced.

emotive ▶ **adjective 1** *a highly emotive book* See EMOTIONAL (sense 2).
2 *an emotive issue* **controversial,** contentious, inflammatory; sensitive, delicate, difficult, problematic, touchy, awkward, prickly, ticklish.

empathize ▶ **verb** *John could empathize with the survivors* **identify with,** sympathize with, be in sympathy with, understand, share the feelings of, be in tune with; be on the same wavelength as, talk the same language as; relate to, feel for, have insight into; informal put oneself in someone else's shoes.

emperor ▶ **noun** *the emperor of Japan* **ruler,** sovereign, king, monarch, potentate; historical czar, kaiser, mikado, khan.

emphasis ▶ **noun 1** *the curriculum gave more emphasis to reading and writing* **prominence,** importance, significance, value; stress, weight, accent, attention, priority, preeminence, urgency, force.
2 *the emphasis is on the word "little"* **stress,** accent, accentuation, weight, prominence; beat; Prosody ictus.

emphasize ▶ **verb** *the profile emphasizes Orgento's dedication to feeding the hungry* **stress,** underline, highlight, focus attention on, point up, lay stress on, draw attention to, spotlight, foreground, play up, make a point of; bring to the fore, insist on, belabor; accent, accentuate, underscore; informal press home, rub it in.
ANTONYMS understate.

emphatic ▶ **adjective 1** *an emphatic denial* **vehement,** firm, wholehearted, forceful, forcible, energetic, vigorous, direct, assertive, insistent; certain, definite, out-and-out, one hundred percent; decided, determined, categorical, unqualified, unconditional, unequivocal, unambiguous, absolute, explicit, downright, outright, clear.
ANTONYMS hesitant, tentative.
2 *an emphatic victory* **conclusive,** decisive, decided, unmistakable; resounding, telling; informal thundering.
ANTONYMS narrow.

empire ▶ **noun 1** *the Ottoman Empire* **kingdom,** realm, domain, territory, imperium; commonwealth; power, world power, superpower.
2 *a worldwide shipping empire* **organization,** corporation, multinational, conglomerate, consortium, company, business, firm, operation.
3 *his dream of empire* **power,** rule, ascendancy, supremacy, command, control, authority, sway, dominance, domination, dominion.

employ ▶ **verb 1** *she employed a chauffeur* **hire,** engage, recruit, take on, secure the services of, sign up, sign, put on the payroll, enroll, appoint; retain, contract; indenture, apprentice.
ANTONYMS dismiss.
2 *Julio was employed in carving a stone figure* **occupy,** engage, involve, keep busy, tie up; absorb, engross, immerse.
3 *the team employed subtle psychological tactics* **use,** utilize, make use of, avail oneself of; apply, exercise, practice, put into practice, exert, bring into play, bring to bear; draw on, resort to, turn to, have recourse to.

employed ▶ **adjective** *it is a myth that most employed people have adequate health insurance for their families* **working,** in work, in employment, holding down a job; earning, wage-earning, waged, breadwinning.

employee ▶ **noun** *each employee receives a Thanksgiving turkey | the slowdown has been a hard blow to our employees* **worker,** member of staff, staffer; blue-collar worker, white-collar worker, laborer, hand, hired hand; wage earner; informal desk jockey; (**employees**) personnel, staff, workforce, human resources.

employer ▶ **noun 1** *his employer gave him a glowing reference* **manager,** boss, proprietor, director, chief executive, chief, president, head man, head woman; informal boss man, skipper; padrone.
2 *the largest private-sector employer in Ohio* **company,** firm, business, organization, manufacturer.

employment ▶ noun **1** *she found employment as a clerk* **work,** service, labor; a job, a post, a position, a situation, an occupation, a profession, a trade, a line of work, a calling, a vocation, a craft, a pursuit; archaic employ.
2 *the employment of children* **hiring,** hire, engagement, taking on; apprenticing.
3 *the employment of nuclear weapons* **use,** utilization, application, exercise.

emporium ▶ noun *a furniture emporium* **store,** shop, outlet, retail outlet, superstore, megastore, department store, chain store, supermarket; establishment.

empower ▶ verb **1** *the act empowered police to arrest dissenters* **authorize,** entitle, permit, allow, license, sanction, warrant, commission, delegate, qualify, enable, equip.
ANTONYMS forbid.
2 *movements to empower the poor* **emancipate,** unshackle, set free, liberate.
ANTONYMS enslave.

emptiness ▶ noun *she had filled an emptiness in his life* **void,** vacuum, empty space, vacuity, gap, vacancy, hole, lack.

empty ▶ adjective **1** *an empty house* **vacant,** unoccupied, uninhabited, untenanted, bare, desolate, deserted, abandoned; clear, free.
ANTONYMS full.
2 *an empty threat* **meaningless,** hollow, idle, vain, futile, worthless, useless, nugatory, insubstantial, ineffective, ineffectual.
ANTONYMS meaningful, serious.
3 *without her, my life is empty* **futile,** pointless, purposeless, worthless, meaningless, valueless, of no value, useless, of no use, aimless, senseless, hollow, barren, insignificant, inconsequential, trivial.
ANTONYMS worthwhile.
4 *his eyes were empty* **blank,** expressionless, vacant, deadpan, wooden, stony, impassive, absent, glazed, fixed, lifeless, emotionless, unresponsive.
ANTONYMS expressive.
▶ verb **1** *I emptied the dishwasher* **unload,** unpack, void; clear, evacuate.
ANTONYMS fill, load.
2 *he emptied out the contents of the case* **remove,** take out, extract, tip out, pour out, dump out, drain.

empty-headed ▶ adjective *they treat her like some empty-headed bimbo* **stupid,** foolish, silly, unintelligent, idiotic, brainless, witless, vacuous, stunned, vapid, featherbrained, birdbrained, harebrained, scatterbrained, thoughtless, imbecilic; informal halfwitted, dumb, dim, airheaded, brain-dead, dippy, dizzy, dopey, flaky, soft in the head, slow on the uptake, ditzy, dumb-ass.
ANTONYMS intelligent.

enable ▶ verb *the brace will enable you to walk more steadily* **allow,** permit, let, give the means, equip, empower, make able, fit; make possible, facilitate; authorize, entitle, qualify; formal capacitate.
ANTONYMS prevent.

enact ▶ verb **1** *the charter was enacted in 1982* **pass,** make law, legislate; approve, ratify, sanction, authorize; impose, lay down, bring down.
ANTONYMS repeal.
2 *members of the church enacted the Nativity* **act out,** act, perform, appear in, stage, mount, put on, present.

enactment ▶ noun **1** *the enactment of a Bill of Rights* **passing**; ratification, sanction, approval, authorization; imposition.
2 *congressional enactments* **act,** law, bylaw, ruling, rule, regulation, statute, measure; formal ordinance; (**enactments**) legislation.

enamored ▶ adjective *she was secretly **enamored** of the prince* **in love with,** infatuated with, besotted with, smitten with, captivated by, enchanted by, fascinated by, bewitched by, beguiled by; keen on, taken with; informal mad about, crazy about, wild about, bowled over by, stuck on, hot for, sweet on, carrying a torch for, moonstruck by; literary ensorcelled by.

encampment ▶ noun *Dolan and Martini reached the encampment only minutes before daybreak* **camp,** military camp, bivouac, cantonment; campsite, camping ground; tents.

encapsulate ▶ verb **1** *their conclusions are encapsulated in one sentence* **summarize,** sum up, give the gist of, put in a nutshell; capture, express.
2 *seeds encapsulated in resin* **enclose,** encase, contain, envelop, enfold, sheathe, cocoon, surround.

enchant ▶ verb *these tales are sure to enchant your little ones | mermaids enchanted the sailors* **captivate,** charm, delight, enrapture, entrance, enthrall, beguile, bewitch, spellbind, fascinate, hypnotize, mesmerize, rivet, grip, transfix; rare ensorcell; informal bowl someone over.
ANTONYMS bore.

enchanter ▶ noun *an evil enchanter named Norg* **wizard,** witch, sorcerer, warlock, magician, necromancer, magus; witch doctor, medicine man, shaman; archaic mage; rare thaumaturge.

enchanting ▶ adjective *an enchanting ballerina* **captivating,** charming, delightful, bewitching, beguiling, adorable, lovely, attractive, appealing, engaging, winning, fetching, winsome, alluring, disarming, seductive, irresistible, fascinating; dated taking.

enchantment ▶ noun **1** *a race of giants skilled in enchantment* **magic,** witchcraft, sorcery, wizardry, necromancy; charms, spells, incantations, mojo; rare thaumaturgy.
2 *the enchantment of the garden by moonlight* **allure,** delight, charm, beauty, attractiveness, appeal, fascination, irresistibility, magnetism, pull, draw, lure.
3 *being with him was sheer enchantment* **bliss,** ecstasy, heaven, rapture, joy.

enchantress ▶ noun *the enchantress put a curse on all the young men of Underwood Village* **witch,** sorceress, magician, fairy; Circe, siren.

encircle ▶ verb *"... and the smoke, it encircled his head like a wreath"* **surround,** enclose, circle, girdle, ring, encompass; close in, shut in, fence in, wall in, hem in, confine; literary gird, engirdle. See note at CIRCUMSCRIBE.

enclose ▶ verb **1** *tall trees enclosed the campsite* **surround,** circle, ring, girdle, encompass, encircle; confine, close in, shut in, corral,

fence in, wall in, hedge in, hem in; literary gird, engirdle. See note at CIRCUMSCRIBE.
2 *please enclose a stamped addressed envelope* **include,** insert, put in; send.

enclosure ▶ **noun** *they drove the donkeys into the enclosure* **paddock,** fold, pen, compound, stockade, ring, yard; sty, coop, corral.

encompass ▶ **verb 1** *the apartment buildings encompass common recreational grounds, complete with swimming pool and tennis court* **surround,** enclose, encircle, circumscribe, bound, border; literary gird, engird; rare compass. See note at CIRCUMSCRIBE.
2 *the debates encompassed a vast range of subjects* **cover,** embrace, include, incorporate, take in, contain, comprise, involve, deal with, range across; formal comprehend.

encounter ▶ **verb 1** *I encountered a teacher I used to know* **meet,** meet by chance, run into, come across/upon, stumble across/on/upon, chance on/upon, happen on/upon; informal bump into.
2 *we encountered a slight problem* **experience,** hit, run into, come up against, face, be faced with, confront.
▶ **noun 1** *an unexpected encounter* **meeting,** chance meeting.
2 *a violent encounter between police and demonstrators* **battle,** fight, clash, confrontation, struggle, skirmish, engagement; informal run-in, set-to, scrap.

encourage ▶ **verb 1** *the players were encouraged by the crowd's response* **hearten,** cheer, buoy up, uplift, inspire, motivate, spur on, stir, stir up, fire up, stimulate, invigorate, vitalize, revitalize, embolden, fortify, rally; informal buck up, pep up, give a shot in the arm to.
ANTONYMS discourage.
2 *she had encouraged him to go* **persuade,** coax, urge, press, push, pressure, pressurize, prod, goad, egg on, prompt, influence, sway; informal put ideas into one's head.
ANTONYMS dissuade.
3 *the municipal government must encourage local businesses* **support,** back, champion, promote, further, foster, nurture, cultivate, strengthen, stimulate; help, assist, aid, boost, fuel.
ANTONYMS hinder.

CHOOSE THE RIGHT WORD

encourage, embolden, foster, hearten, inspire, instigate, stimulate

To **encourage** is to give active help or to raise confidence to the point where one dares to do what is difficult (*encouraged by her teacher, she set her sights on attending Harvard*). **Embolden** also entails giving confidence or boldness, but it implies overcoming reluctance or shyness (*success as a public speaker emboldened her to enter politics*). To **hearten** is to put one's heart into or to renew someone's spirit (*heartened by the news of his recovery*), and to **inspire** is to infuse with confidence, resolution, or enthusiasm (*inspired by her mother's example, she started exercising regularly*). To **foster** is to encourage by nurturing or extending aid (*to foster the growth of small businesses by offering low-interest loans*); in some contexts, *foster* suggests an unwise or controversial kind of help (*to foster rebellion among local farmers*). **Instigate** also implies that what is being encouraged is not necessarily desirable (*to instigate a fight*), while **stimulate** is a more neutral term meaning to rouse to action or effort (*to stimulate the growth of crops; to stimulate an interest in literature*).

encouragement ▶ **noun 1** *she needed a bit of encouragement* **heartening,** cheering up, inspiration, motivation, stimulation, fortification; support, morale-boosting, a boost, a shot in the arm.
2 *they required no encouragement to get back to work* **persuasion,** coaxing, urging, pep talk, pressure, prodding, prompting; spur, goad, inducement, incentive, bait, motive; informal carrot.
3 *the encouragement of foreign investment* **support,** backing, championship, championing, sponsoring, promotion, furtherance, furthering, fostering, nurture, cultivation; help, assistance, boosterism.

encroach ▶ **verb** *she didn't want to* ***encroach on*** *his privacy* **intrude on,** trespass on, impinge on, obtrude on, impose oneself on, invade, infiltrate, interrupt, infringe on, violate, interfere with, disturb; informal horn in on, muscle in on; archaic entrench on.

encroachment ▶ **noun** *the encroachment on their territory* **intrusion on,** trespass on, invasion of, infiltration of, incursion into, appropriation of; infringement of, impingement on.

encumber ▶ **verb 1** *her movements were encumbered by her heavy skirts* **hamper,** hinder, obstruct, impede, cramp, inhibit, restrict, limit, constrain, restrain, bog down, retard, slow (down); inconvenience, disadvantage, handicap. See note at HINDER.
2 *they are encumbered with debt* **burden,** load, weigh down, saddle; overwhelm, tax, stress, strain, overload, overburden.

encumbrance ▶ **noun 1** *he soon found the old equipment a great encumbrance* **hindrance,** obstruction, obstacle, impediment, constraint, handicap, inconvenience, nuisance, disadvantage, drawback; literary trammel; archaic cumber.
2 *she knew she was an encumbrance to him* **burden,** responsibility, obligation, liability, weight, load, stress, strain, pressure, trouble, worry; millstone, albatross, cross to bear; informal ball and chain.

encyclopedic ▶ **adjective** *his encyclopedic knowledge of food* **comprehensive,** complete, thorough, thoroughgoing, full, exhaustive, in-depth, wide-ranging, all-inclusive, all-embracing, all-encompassing, universal, vast; formal compendious.

end ▶ **noun 1** *the end of the road* **extremity,**

furthermost part, limit; margin, edge, border, boundary, periphery; point, tip, tail end, tag end, terminus.
ANTONYMS beginning, middle.
2 *the end of the novel* **conclusion,** termination, ending, finish, close, resolution, climax, finale, culmination, denouement; epilogue, coda, peroration.
ANTONYMS beginning.
3 *wealth is a means and not an end in itself* **aim,** goal, purpose, objective, object, holy grail, target; intention, intent, design, motive; aspiration, wish, desire, ambition.
4 *the commercial end of the business* **aspect,** side, section, area, field, part, share, portion, segment, province.
5 *his end might come at any time* **death,** dying, demise, passing, expiry, quietus; doom, extinction, annihilation, extermination, destruction; downfall, ruin, ruination, Waterloo; informal curtains; formal decease.
ANTONYMS birth.
▶ **verb 1** *the show **ended with** a wedding scene* **finish with,** conclude with, terminate with, come to an end with, draw to a close with, close with, stop with, cease with; culminate in, climax with, build up to, lead up to, come to a head with.
ANTONYMS begin, start.
2 *she ended their relationship* **break off,** call off, bring to an end, put an end to, stop, finish, terminate, discontinue, curtail; dissolve, cancel, annul; informal can, ax.
ANTONYMS begin.

endanger ▶ **verb** *the pollutants endanger the fish* **imperil,** jeopardize, risk, put at risk, put in danger, expose to danger; threaten, pose a threat to, be a danger to, be detrimental to, damage, injure, harm; archaic peril.

endearing ▶ **adjective** *the baby ducklings are endearing* **lovable,** adorable, cute, sweet, dear, delightful, lovely, charming, appealing, attractive, engaging, winning, captivating, enchanting, beguiling, winsome.

endearment ▶ **noun 1** *his murmured endearments* **term of affection,** term of endearment, pet name; (**endearments**) sweet nothings, sweet talk.
2 *he spoke to her without endearment* **affection,** fondness, tenderness, feeling, sentiment, warmth, love, liking, care.

endeavor ▶ **verb** *the company endeavored to expand its activities* **try,** attempt, seek, undertake, aspire, aim, set out; strive, struggle, labor, toil, work, exert oneself, apply oneself, do one's best, do one's utmost, give one's all, be at pains; informal have a go, have a shot, have a stab, give something one's best shot, do one's damnedest, go all out, bend over backwards; formal essay.
▶ **noun 1** *an endeavor to build a more buoyant economy* **attempt,** try, bid, effort, venture; informal go, crack, shot, stab; formal essay.
2 *several days of endeavor* **effort,** exertion, striving, struggling, laboring, toil, struggle, labor, hard work, application, industry; pains; informal sweat, 'blood, sweat, and tears', elbow grease; literary travail.
3 *an extremely unwise endeavor* **undertaking,** enterprise, venture, exercise, activity, exploit, deed, act, action, move; scheme, plan, project; informal caper.

ending ▶ **noun** *a happy ending* **end,** finish, close, closing, conclusion, resolution, summing-up, windup, denouement, finale; cessation, stopping, termination, discontinuation.
ANTONYMS beginning.

endless ▶ **adjective 1** *a woman with endless energy* **unlimited,** limitless, infinite, inexhaustible, boundless, unbounded, untold, immeasurable, measureless, incalculable; abundant, abounding, great; bottomless, ceaseless, unceasing, unending, without end, everlasting, constant, continuous, continual, interminable, unfading, unfailing, perpetual, eternal, enduring, lasting. See note at **ETERNAL**.
ANTONYMS limited, transient.
2 *as children we played endless games* **countless,** innumerable, untold, legion, numberless, unnumbered, numerous, very many, manifold, multitudinous, multifarious; a great number of, infinite numbers of, a multitude of; informal umpteen, no end of, loads of, stacks of, heaps of, masses of, oodles of, scads of, zillions of, gazillions of; literary myriad, divers.
ANTONYMS few.

endorse ▶ **verb 1** *endorse a product* **support,** back, agree with, approve (of), favor, subscribe to, recommend, champion, stick up for, uphold, affirm, sanction; informal throw one's weight behind, okay. See note at **APPROVE**.
ANTONYMS oppose.
2 *endorse a check* **countersign,** sign, autograph, authenticate; rare chirographate.

endorsement ▶ **noun** *the proposal won their overwhelming endorsement* **support,** backing, approval, seal of approval, agreement, recommendation, championship, patronage, affirmation, sanction; informal buy-in.

endow ▶ **verb 1** *the CEO endowed a hospital for sick kids* **finance,** fund, pay for, provide for, subsidize, support financially, put up the money for; establish, found, set up, institute.
2 *nature endowed fish with gills* **provide,** supply, furnish, equip, invest, favor, bless, grace, gift; give, bestow; literary endue.

endowment ▶ **noun 1** *the endowment of a Chair of Botany* **funding,** financing, subsidizing; establishment, foundation, institution.
2 *her will contained a generous endowment* **bequest,** legacy, inheritance; gift, present, grant, award, donation, contribution, subsidy, settlement; formal benefaction.
3 *his natural endowments* **quality,** characteristic, feature, attribute, facility, faculty, ability, talent, gift, strength, aptitude, capability, capacity.

endurance ▶ **noun 1** *she pushed him beyond the limit of his endurance* **toleration,** tolerance, sufferance, forbearance, patience, acceptance, resignation, stoicism.
2 *the race is a test of endurance* **stamina,** staying power, fortitude, perseverance, persistence, tenacity, doggedness, grit, indefatigability, resolution, determination; formal pertinacity.

endure ▶ verb **1** *he endured years of pain* **undergo,** go through, live through, experience, meet, encounter; cope with, deal with, face, suffer, tolerate, put up with, brave, bear, withstand, sustain, weather; Brit. thole.
2 *I cannot endure such behavior* **tolerate,** bear, put up with, suffer, take, abide; informal hack, stand for, stomach, swallow, hold with; formal brook.
3 *our love will endure forever* **last,** live, live on, go on, survive, abide, continue, persist, persevere, remain, stay.
ANTONYMS fade.

enduring ▶ adjective *our enduring faith* **lasting,** long-lasting, abiding, durable, continuing, persisting, eternal, perennial, permanent, unending, everlasting; constant, stable, steady, steadfast, fixed, firm, unwavering, unfaltering, unchanging; literary amaranthine.
ANTONYMS short-lived.

enemy ▶ noun *he and his brother have been enemies for years | the enemy would strike at dawn* **opponent,** adversary, foe, rival, antagonist, combatant, challenger, competitor, opposer; (**the enemy**) the opposition, the competition, the other side, the opposing side.
ANTONYMS ally, friend.

energetic ▶ adjective **1** *an energetic teacher* **active,** lively, dynamic, zestful, spirited, animated, vital, vibrant, bouncy, bubbly, exuberant, ebullient, perky, frisky, sprightly, tireless, indefatigable, enthusiastic; informal peppy, feisty, full of beans, bright-eyed and bushy-tailed.
ANTONYMS lethargic, inactive.
2 *energetic exercises* **vigorous,** strenuous, brisk; hard, arduous, demanding, taxing, tough, rigorous.
ANTONYMS gentle.
3 *an energetic advertising campaign* **forceful,** vigorous, high-powered, all-out, determined, bold, powerful, potent; intensive, hard-hitting, pulling no punches, aggressive, high-octane; informal punchy, in-your-face.
ANTONYMS halfhearted.

energize ▶ verb **1** *people are energized by his ideas* **enliven,** liven up, animate, vitalize, invigorate, perk up, excite, electrify, stimulate, stir up, fire up, rouse, motivate, move, drive, spur on, encourage, galvanize; informal pep up, buck up, jump-start, kick-start, give a shot in the arm to, turbocharge.
2 *floor sensors energized by standing passengers* **activate,** trigger, trip, operate, actuate, switch on, turn on, start, start up, power.

energy ▶ noun *a good night's sleep will restore their energy* **vitality,** vigor, life, liveliness, animation, vivacity, spirit, spiritedness, verve, enthusiasm, zest, vibrancy, spark, sparkle, effervescence, ebullience, exuberance, buoyancy, sprightliness; strength, stamina, forcefulness, power, dynamism, drive; fire, passion, ardor, zeal; informal zip, zing, pep, pizzazz, punch, bounce, oomph, moxie, mojo, go, get-up-and-go, vim and vigor, feistiness.

enervate ▶ verb *the hot weather enervated her* **exhaust,** tire, fatigue, weary, wear out, devitalize, drain, sap, weaken, enfeeble, debilitate, incapacitate, prostrate; informal knock out, do in, shatter.
ANTONYMS invigorate.

enfold ▶ verb **1** *the summit was enfolded in white cloud* **envelop,** engulf, sheathe, swathe, swaddle, cocoon, shroud, veil, cloak, drape, cover; surround, enclose, encase, encircle; literary enshroud, mantle.
2 *he enfolded her in his arms* **clasp,** hold, fold, wrap, squeeze, clutch, gather; embrace, hug, cuddle; literary embosom.

enforce ▶ verb **1** *the sheriff enforced the law* **impose,** apply, administer, implement, bring to bear, discharge, execute, prosecute.
2 *they cannot enforce cooperation between the parties* **force,** compel, coerce, exact, extort; archaic constrain.

enforced ▶ adjective *an enforced break from work* **compulsory,** obligatory, mandatory, involuntary, forced, imposed, required, requisite, stipulated, prescribed, contractual, binding, necessary, unavoidable, inescapable.
ANTONYMS voluntary.

enfranchise ▶ verb **1** *women were enfranchised in Manitoba in 1916* **give the vote to,** give suffrage to, grant suffrage to.
2 historical *he enfranchised his slaves* **emancipate,** liberate, free, set free, release; unchain, unyoke, unfetter, unshackle.

engage ▶ verb **1** *tasks that engage children's interest* **capture,** catch, arrest, grab, snag, draw, attract, gain, win, hold, grip, captivate, engross, absorb, occupy.
ANTONYMS lose.
2 *he engaged a landscaper to do the job* **employ,** hire, recruit, take on, secure the services of, put on the payroll, enroll, appoint.
ANTONYMS dismiss.
3 *he engaged to pay them $10,000* **contract,** promise, agree, pledge, vow, covenant, commit oneself, bind oneself, undertake, enter into an agreement.
4 *the chance to* **engage in** *many social activities* **participate in,** take part in, join in, become involved in, go in for, partake in/of, share in, play a part/role in; have a hand in, be a party to, enter into.
5 *infantry units engaged the enemy* **fight,** do battle with, wage war on/against, attack, take on, set upon, clash with, skirmish with; encounter, meet.
6 *he engaged the gears* **interlock,** interconnect, mesh, intermesh, fit together, join, join together, unite, connect, couple.
ANTONYMS disengage.

engaged ▶ adjective **1** *he's otherwise engaged* **busy,** occupied, unavailable; informal tied up. See note at BUSY.
ANTONYMS free, unoccupied.
2 *she's engaged to an American guy* **betrothed,** promised in marriage, pledged in marriage; attached; informal spoken for; literary affianced; archaic plighted, espoused.
ANTONYMS unattached.

engagement ▶ noun **1** *they broke off their engagement* **marriage contract**; dated betrothal; archaic espousal.
2 *a social engagement* **appointment,** meeting,

arrangement, commitment; date, assignation, rendezvous; literary tryst.
3 *the first engagement of the war* **battle,** fight, clash, confrontation, encounter, conflict, skirmish; warfare, action, combat, hostilities; informal dogfight.

engaging ▸ **adjective 1** *an engaging young person* **charming,** appealing, attractive, pretty, delightful, lovely, pleasing, pleasant, agreeable, likable, winsome, enchanting, captivating.
ANTONYMS unappealing.
2 *an engaging story* **interesting,** engrossing, gripping, involving, absorbing, fascinating.
ANTONYMS boring.

engender ▸ **verb 1** *his works engendered considerable controversy* **cause,** be the cause of, give rise to, bring about, occasion, lead to, result in, produce, create, generate, arouse, rouse, inspire, provoke, prompt, kindle, trigger, spark, stir up, whip up, induce, incite, instigate, foment; literary beget, enkindle.
2 archaic *he engendered six children* **father,** sire, bring into the world, spawn, breed; literary beget.

engine ▸ **noun 1** *a power-generating engine* **motor,** machine, mechanism; jet, turbojet, turboprop, turbofan, turbine, generator.
2 *the main engine of change* **cause,** agent, instrument, originator, initiator, generator.
3 historical *engines of war* **device,** contraption, apparatus, machine, appliance, mechanism, implement, instrument, tool.

engineer ▸ **noun 1** *a structural engineer* designer, planner, builder.
2 *the ship's engineer* **operator,** driver, controller.
3 *the prime engineer of the approach* **originator,** deviser, designer, architect, inventor, developer, creator; mastermind.
▸ **verb** *he engineered a takeover deal* **bring about,** arrange, pull off, bring off, contrive, maneuver, manipulate, negotiate, organize, orchestrate, choreograph, mount, stage, mastermind, originate, manage, stage-manage, coordinate, control, superintend, direct, conduct; informal wangle.

engrave ▸ **verb 1** *my name was engraved on the ring* **carve,** inscribe, cut (in), incise, chisel, chase, score, notch, etch, imprint, impress.
2 *the image was engraved in his memory* **fix,** set, imprint, stamp, brand, impress, embed, etch.

engraving ▸ **noun** *an engraving of a clipper ship* **etching,** print, impression, lithograph; plate, dry point, woodcut, linocut.

engross ▸ **verb** *Poppa's stories will engross them* **absorb,** engage, rivet, grip, hold, interest, involve, occupy, preoccupy; fascinate, captivate, enthrall, intrigue.

engrossed ▸ **adjective** *Leopold is engrossed in his stamp collection* **absorbed in,** involved in, interested in, engaged in, occupied by/with, preoccupied by/with, immersed in, caught up in, riveted by, gripped by, rapt in, fascinated by/with, intent on, captivated by, enthralled by/with, intrigued by/with.

engrossing ▸ **adjective** *an engrossing murder mystery* **absorbing,** interesting, riveting, gripping, captivating, compelling, fascinating, intriguing, enthralling, engaging; informal unputdownable.

engulf ▸ **verb** *waves engulfed the sand castles* **inundate,** flood, deluge, immerse, swamp, swallow up, submerge; bury, envelop, overwhelm.

enhance ▸ **verb** *background music will enhance the mood* **increase,** add to, intensify, heighten, magnify, amplify, inflate, strengthen, build up, supplement, augment, boost, raise, lift, elevate, exalt; improve, enrich, complement.
ANTONYMS diminish.

enigma ▸ **noun** *how it works is an enigma to me* **mystery,** puzzle, riddle, conundrum, paradox, problem, quandary; a closed book; informal poser. See note at RIDDLE.

enigmatic ▸ **adjective** *she smiled that enigmatic smile again* **mysterious,** inscrutable, puzzling, mystifying, baffling, perplexing, impenetrable, unfathomable, sphinxlike, Delphic, oracular; cryptic, elliptical, ambiguous, equivocal, paradoxical, obscure, oblique, secret. See note at DOUBTFUL.

enjoin ▸ **verb** *I enjoin you to admit your mistake* **urge,** encourage, admonish, press; instruct, direct, require, order, command, tell, call on, demand, charge; formal adjure; literary bid. See note at PROHIBIT.

enjoy ▸ **verb 1** *he enjoys playing the piano* **like,** love, be fond of, be entertained by, take pleasure in, be keen on, delight in, appreciate, relish, revel in, adore, lap up, savor, luxuriate in, bask in; informal get a kick out of, get a thrill out of, dig.
ANTONYMS dislike, hate.
2 *she had always enjoyed good health* **benefit from,** have the benefit of; be blessed with, be favored with, be endowed with, be possessed of, possess, own, boast.
ANTONYMS dislike, lack.
– PHRASES **enjoy oneself** *she travels just to enjoy herself* **have fun,** have a good time, have the time of one's life; make merry, celebrate, revel, disport; informal party, love life, have a ball, have a whale of a time, whoop it up, let one's hair down.

enjoyable ▸ **adjective** *a most enjoyable movie* **entertaining,** amusing, agreeable, pleasurable, diverting, engaging, delightful, to one's liking, pleasant, congenial, convivial, lovely, fine, good, great, delicious, delectable, satisfying, gratifying; marvelous, wonderful, magnificent, splendid; informal super, fantastic, fabulous, fab, terrific, magic, killer. See note at PLEASANT.

enjoyment ▸ **noun** *he has brought enjoyment to millions* **pleasure,** fun, entertainment, amusement, diversion, recreation, relaxation; delight, happiness, merriment, joy, gaiety, jollity; satisfaction, gratification, liking, relish, gusto; humorous delectation.

enlarge ▸ **verb 1** *they enlarged the scope of their research* **extend,** expand, grow, add to, amplify, augment, magnify, build up, supplement; widen, broaden, stretch, lengthen; elongate, deepen, thicken.
ANTONYMS reduce.
2 *the lymph glands had enlarged* **swell,** distend,

bloat, bulge, dilate, tumefy, blow up, puff up, balloon.
ANTONYMS shrink.
3 *he **enlarged on** this subject* **elaborate on,** expand on, add to, build on, flesh out, add detail to, expatiate on; develop, fill out, embellish, embroider.

enlargement ▶ noun *the enlargement of the park* **expansion,** extension, growth, amplification, augmentation, addition, magnification, widening, broadening, lengthening; elongation, deepening, thickening; swelling, distension, dilation.

enlighten ▶ verb *please enlighten us about the latest developments* **inform,** tell, make aware, open someone's eyes, notify, illuminate, apprise, brief, update, bring up to date; disabuse, set straight; informal put in the picture, clue in, fill in, put wise, bring up to speed.

enlightened ▶ adjective *without a free press there cannot be an enlightened people* **informed,** well-informed, aware, sophisticated, advanced, developed, liberal, open-minded, broad-minded, educated, knowledgeable, wise; civilized, refined, cultured, cultivated.
ANTONYMS benighted.

enlightenment ▶ noun *sharing her musical enlightenment with her children* **insight,** understanding, awareness, wisdom, education, learning, knowledge; illumination, awakening, instruction, teaching; sophistication, advancement, development, open-mindedness, broad-mindedness; culture, refinement, cultivation, civilization.

enlist ▶ verb **1** *he **enlisted in** the scouts* **join up with,** join, enroll in, sign up for, volunteer for.
2 *he was enlisted in the army* **recruit,** call up, enroll, sign up; conscript; draft, induct; archaic levy.
3 *he enlisted the help of a friend* **obtain,** engage, secure, win, get, procure.

enliven ▶ verb **1** *a meeting enlivened by her wit and vivacity* **liven up,** spice up, add spice to, ginger up, vitalize, leaven; informal perk up, pep up. See note at QUICKEN.
2 *the visit had enlivened my mother* **cheer up,** brighten up, liven up, raise someone's spirits, uplift, gladden, buoy up, animate, vivify, vitalize, invigorate, restore, revive, refresh, rejuvenate, stimulate, rouse, boost, exhilarate, light a fire under; informal perk up, buck up, pep up.

en masse ▶ adverb *the angry audience walked out en masse* **(all) together,** as a group, as one, en bloc, as a whole, wholesale; unanimously, with one voice.

enmity ▶ noun *a world free from enmity between nations and races* **hostility,** animosity, antagonism, friction, antipathy, animus, acrimony, bitterness, rancor, resentment, aversion, ill feeling, bad feeling, ill will, bad blood, hatred, hate, loathing, odium; malice, spite, spitefulness, venom, malevolence.
ANTONYMS friendship.

ennoble ▶ verb *the original vision of the modern Olympic Games was to ennoble and strengthen sports* **dignify,** honor, exalt, elevate, raise, enhance, add dignity to, distinguish; magnify, glorify, aggrandize.
ANTONYMS demean.

ennui ▶ noun *an ennui bred of long familiarity* **boredom,** tedium, listlessness, lethargy, lassitude, languor, weariness, enervation; malaise, dissatisfaction, melancholy, depression, world-weariness, Weltschmerz.

enormity ▶ noun **1** *the enormity of the task* **immensity,** hugeness; size, extent, magnitude, greatness.
2 *the enormity of his crimes* **wickedness,** evil, vileness, baseness, depravity; outrageousness, monstrousness, hideousness, heinousness, horror, atrocity; villainy, cruelty, inhumanity, mercilessness, brutality, savagery, viciousness.
3 *the enormities of the regime* **outrage,** horror, evil, atrocity, barbarity, abomination, monstrosity, obscenity, iniquity; crime, sin, violation, wrong, offense, disgrace, injustice, abuse.

> USAGE
> **enormity**
> This word is imprecisely used to mean 'great size,' as in *it is difficult to comprehend the enormity of the continent,* but the original and preferred meaning is 'extreme wickedness,' as in *the enormity of the mass murders.* To indicate enormous size, the words *enormousness, immensity, vastness, hugeness,* etc., are preferable.

enormous ▶ adjective *enormous waves battered the shore* **huge,** vast, immense, gigantic, very big, great, giant, massive, colossal, mammoth, tremendous, mighty, monumental, epic, prodigious, mountainous, king-size(d), economy-size(d), titanic, towering, elephantine, gargantuan, Brobdingnagian; informal mega, monster, whopping, humongous, jumbo, astronomical, ginormous.
ANTONYMS tiny.

enormously ▶ adverb **1** *an enormously important factor* **very,** extremely, really, exceedingly, exceptionally, tremendously, immensely, hugely; singularly, particularly, eminently; informal terrifically, awfully, seriously, desperately, ultra, damn, damned, darn, darned; real, mighty.
ANTONYMS slightly, moderately.
2 *prices vary enormously* **considerably,** greatly, widely, very much, a great deal, a lot.
ANTONYMS slightly, not at all.

enough ▶ adjective *they had enough food* **sufficient,** adequate, ample, the necessary; informal plenty of.
ANTONYMS insufficient.
▶ pronoun *there's enough for everyone* **sufficient,** plenty, a sufficient amount, an adequate amount, as much as necessary; a sufficiency, an ample supply; one's fill.

enrage ▶ verb *the scheme is bound to enrage union members* **anger,** infuriate, incense, madden, inflame; antagonize, provoke, exasperate; informal drive mad/crazy, drive up the wall, make someone see red, make someone's blood boil,

make someone's hackles rise, get someone's back up, get someone's dander up; informal tick off, piss off, burn up.
ANTONYMS placate.

enraged ▶ adjective *an enraged mob* **furious,** infuriated, very angry, irate, incensed, raging, incandescent, fuming, ranting, raving, seething, beside oneself; informal mad, hopping mad, wild, livid, boiling, apoplectic, hot under the collar, on the warpath, foaming at the mouth, steamed up, fit to be tied, pissed off, PO'd; literary wrathful.
ANTONYMS calm.

enrapture ▶ verb *enraptured by the music* **delight,** enchant, captivate, charm, enthrall, entrance, bewitch, beguile, transport, thrill, excite, exhilarate, intoxicate, take someone's breath away; informal bowl over, blow someone's mind; literary ravish.

enrich ▶ verb *enrich the soil with nitrogen* **enhance,** improve, better, add to, augment; supplement, complement; boost, elevate, raise, lift, refine.
ANTONYMS spoil.

enroll ▶ verb **1** *they both* ***enrolled for*** *the course* **register for,** sign up/on for, put one's name down for, apply for, volunteer for; enter, join.
2 *280 new members were enrolled* **accept,** admit, take on, register, sign on/up, recruit, engage; impanel.

en route ▶ adverb *he was en route from Delaware to Illinois* **on the way,** in transit, during the journey, along/on the road, on the move; coming, going, proceeding, traveling.

ensconce ▶ verb *Agnes ensconced herself in their bedroom* **settle,** install, plant, position, seat, sit; establish, nestle; hide away, tuck away; informal park, plonk.

ensemble ▶ noun **1** *a Bulgarian folk ensemble* **group,** band; company, troupe, cast, chorus, corps; informal combo.
2 *the buildings present a charming provincial ensemble* **whole,** entity, unit, body, set, combination, composite, package; sum, total, totality, entirety, aggregate.
3 *a pink and black ensemble* **outfit,** costume, suit; separates, coordinates; informal getup.

enshrine ▶ verb *the following rights should be enshrined in the treaty* **preserve,** entrench, set down, lay down, set in stone, embody, incorporate, contain, include, treasure, immortalize, cherish.

enshroud ▶ verb literary *gray clouds enshrouded the city* **envelop,** veil, shroud, swathe, cloak, cloud, enfold, surround, bury; cover, conceal, obscure, blot out, hide, mask; literary mantle.

ensign ▶ noun *the ship flew a Greek ensign* **flag,** standard, color(s), banner, pennant, pennon, streamer, banderole.

ensnare ▶ verb *the larvae construct pits to ensnare their prey* **capture,** catch, trap, entrap, snare, net; entangle, embroil, enmesh.

ensue ▶ verb *Evelyn showed up unexpectedly and a fierce argument ensued* **result,** follow, develop, proceed, succeed, emerge, stem, arise, derive, issue; occur, happen, take place, come next/after, transpire, supervene; formal eventuate; literary come to pass, befall.

ensure ▶ verb **1** *ensure that the surface is completely clean* **make sure,** make certain, see to it; check, confirm, establish, verify.
2 *legislation to ensure equal opportunities for all* **secure,** guarantee, assure, certify, safeguard, set the seal on, clinch, entrench.

entail ▶ verb *first, we'll need to know exactly what the job entails* **involve,** necessitate, require, need, demand, call for; mean, imply; cause, produce, result in, lead to, give rise to, occasion.

entangle ▶ verb **1** *their parachutes became entangled* **twist,** intertwine, entwine, tangle, ravel, snarl, knot, coil, mat.
2 *the fish are easily entangled in fine nets* **catch,** capture, trap, snare, ensnare, entrap, enmesh.
3 *he was entangled in a lawsuit* **involve,** implicate, embroil, mix up, catch up, bog down, mire.

entanglement ▶ noun **1** *their entanglement in the war* **involvement,** embroilment.
2 *romantic entanglements* **affair,** relationship, love affair, romance, amour, fling, dalliance, liaison, involvement, intrigue; complication.

enter ▶ verb **1** *police entered the house from the side* **go in/into,** come in/into, get in/into, set foot in, cross the threshold of, gain access to, infiltrate, access.
ANTONYMS leave.
2 *a bullet entered his chest* **penetrate,** pierce, puncture, perforate; literary transpierce.
ANTONYMS leave.
3 *he entered politics in 1979* **get involved in,** join, throw oneself into, engage in, embark on, take up; participate in, take part in, play a part/role in, contribute to.
ANTONYMS leave.
4 *the planning entered a new phase* **reach,** move into, get to, begin, start, commence.
ANTONYMS finish.
5 *they entered the military at eighteen* **join,** become a member of, enroll in/for, enlist in, volunteer for, sign up for; take up.
ANTONYMS leave.
6 *she entered a cooking competition* **sign on/up for,** put one's name down for, register for, enroll in/for, go in for; compete in, take part in, participate in.
7 *the cashier entered the details in a ledger* **record,** write, set down, put down, take down, note, jot down; put on record, minute, register, log.
ANTONYMS erase.
8 *please enter your password* **key (in),** type (in).
9 Law *he entered a plea of guilty* **submit,** register, lodge, record, file, put forward, present.
ANTONYMS withdraw.

enterprise ▶ noun **1** *a joint enterprise* **undertaking,** endeavor, venture, exercise, activity, operation, task, business, proceeding; project, scheme, plan, program, campaign.
2 *we want candidates with enterprise* **initiative,** resourcefulness, imagination, entrepreneurialism, ingenuity, inventiveness, originality, creativity; quick-wittedness, cleverness; enthusiasm, dynamism, drive, ambition, energy; boldness, daring, courage, leadership; informal gumption, get-up-and-go, oomph.

3 *a profit-making enterprise* **business,** company, firm, venture, organization, operation, concern, corporation, establishment, partnership; informal outfit, setup.

enterprising ▶ adjective *an enterprising farmer is now charging visitors* **resourceful,** entrepreneurial, imaginative, ingenious, inventive, creative; quick-witted, clever, bright, sharp, sharp-witted; enthusiastic, dynamic, proactive, ambitious, energetic; bold, daring, courageous, adventurous; informal go-ahead, take-charge, self-motivated.
ANTONYMS unimaginative.

entertain ▶ verb **1** *she wrote plays to entertain them* **amuse,** divert, delight, please, charm, cheer, interest; informal bring the house down; engage, occupy, absorb, engross.
ANTONYMS bore.
2 *he entertains foreign visitors* **receive,** host, play host/hostess to, invite (around/round/over), throw a party for; wine and dine, feast, cater for, feed, treat, welcome, féte.
3 *we don't entertain much* **receive guests,** have people around/round/over, have company, throw/have a party.
4 *I would never entertain such an idea* **consider,** give consideration to, contemplate, think about, give thought to; countenance, tolerate, support; formal brook.
ANTONYMS reject.

entertainer ▶ noun *a family of entertainers* **performer,** artiste, artist.

entertaining ▶ adjective *Ben is an entertaining companion* **delightful,** enjoyable, diverting, amusing, pleasing, agreeable, appealing, engaging, interesting, fascinating, absorbing, compelling; humorous, funny, comical; informal fun.

entertainment ▶ noun **1** *he reads for entertainment* **amusement,** pleasure, leisure, recreation, relaxation, fun, enjoyment, interest, diversion.
2 *an entertainment for the emperor* **show,** performance, presentation, production, extravaganza, spectacle, pageant.

enthrall ▶ verb *the exhibit of Calder's early mobiles enthralled us* **captivate,** charm, enchant, bewitch, fascinate, beguile, entrance, delight; win, ensnare, absorb, engross, rivet, grip, transfix, hypnotize, mesmerize, spellbind.
ANTONYMS bore.

enthralling ▶ adjective *her travel journals are enthralling* **fascinating,** entrancing, enchanting, bewitching, captivating, charming, beguiling, delightful; absorbing, engrossing, compelling, riveting, gripping, exciting, spellbinding; informal unputdownable.

enthuse ▶ verb **1** *I enthused about the idea* **rave about,** be enthusiastic about, gush over, wax lyrical about, be effusive about, get all worked up about, rhapsodize about; praise to the skies, extol; informal go wild/mad/crazy about/over/for, ballyhoo.
2 *he enthuses people* **motivate,** inspire, stimulate, encourage, spur (on), galvanize, rouse, excite, stir (up), fire; rare inspirit.

> USAGE
> **enthuse**
> The verb *enthuse* is a back-formation from the noun *enthusiasm* and, like many verbs formed from nouns in this way, it is regarded by traditionalists as unacceptable. *Enthuse* has been in the language for more than 150 years, but, before using the word in formal writing, be aware that readers familiar with its Greek meaning may find casual usage misguided or irritating. *Enthusiasm* derives from a word originally meaning 'to become inspired or possessed by a god' (*en* 'in' + *theos* 'god'). From the traditionalist point of view, *inspired* or *excited* is preferable to *enthused*.

enthusiasm ▶ noun **1** *she worked with enthusiasm* **eagerness,** keenness, ardor, fervor, passion, zeal, zest, gusto, energy, verve, vigor, vehemence, fire, spirit, avidity; wholeheartedness, commitment, willingness, devotion, earnestness; informal get-up-and-go.
ANTONYMS apathy, half-heartedness.
2 *he responded to the proposal with enthusiasm* **interest,** admiration, approval, support, encouragement.
ANTONYMS apathy, disinterest.
3 *they put their enthusiasms to good use* **interest,** passion, obsession, mania; inclination, preference, penchant, predilection, fancy; pastime, hobby, recreation, pursuit.

enthusiast ▶ noun *a railroad enthusiast* **fan,** devotee, aficionado, lover, admirer, follower; expert, connoisseur, authority, pundit; informal buff, bum, freak, fanatic, nut, fiend, addict, maniac; geek, eager beaver. See note at ZEALOT.

enthusiastic ▶ adjective *an enthusiastic supporter of Latin American baseball* **eager,** keen, avid, ardent, fervent, passionate, ebullient, zealous, vehement; excited, wholehearted, committed, devoted, fanatical, earnest; informal hog-wild, can-do, gung-ho, rah-rah, psyched. See note at EAGER.

entice ▶ verb *he tried to entice us by promising a screen test at his studio* **tempt,** lure, allure, attract, appeal to; invite, persuade, convince, beguile, coax, woo, court; seduce, lead on; informal sweet-talk. See note at TEMPT.

enticement ▶ noun *on my budget, I have to resist the enticement of colorful packaging and clever advertising* **lure,** temptation, allure, attraction, appeal, draw, pull, bait; charm, seduction, fascination; informal come-on.

entire ▶ adjective **1** *I devoted my entire life to him* **whole,** complete, total, full; undivided.
ANTONYMS partial.
2 *only one of the vases is entire* **intact,** unbroken, undamaged, unimpaired, unscathed, unspoiled, perfect, in one piece.
ANTONYMS partial, broken.
3 *they are in entire agreement* **absolute,** total, utter, out-and-out, thorough, wholehearted; unqualified, unreserved, outright.
ANTONYMS partial, qualified.

entirely ▶ adverb **1** *that's entirely out of the*

question **absolutely,** completely, totally, wholly, utterly, quite; altogether, in every respect, thoroughly, downright, one hundred percent.
2 *a gift entirely for charitable purposes* **solely,** only, exclusively, purely, merely, just, alone.

entirety ▶ **noun** *I'll give you ten bucks for the entirety* **whole,** total, aggregate, totality, sum total.
ANTONYMS part.
– PHRASES **in its entirety** *we heard his miserable life story, in its entirety* **completely,** entirely, totally, fully, wholly; in every respect, in every way, one hundred percent, all the way, every inch, to the hilt, to the core.

entitle ▶ **verb 1** *this pass entitles you to visit the museum* **qualify,** make eligible, authorize, allow, permit; enable, empower.
2 *a chapter entitled "Comedy and Tragedy"* **title,** name, call, label, head, designate, dub; formal denominate.

entity ▶ **noun 1** *a single entity* **being,** creature, individual, organism, life form; person; body, object, article, thing.
2 *the distinction between entity and nonentity* **existence,** being; life, living, animation; substance, essence, reality, actuality.

entourage ▶ **noun** *the king's entourage* **retinue,** escort, cortège, train, suite; court, staff, bodyguard(s); attendants, companions, retainers; informal posse.

entrails ▶ **plural noun** *the entrails are removed by the butcher* **intestines,** bowels, guts, viscera, internal organs, vital organs; offal; informal insides, innards.

entrance[1] ▶ **noun 1** *the main entrance* **entry,** way in, entryway, entranceway, access, approach; door, portal, gate; opening, mouth; entrance hall, foyer, lobby, porch.
ANTONYMS exit.
2 *the entrance of Mrs. Salter* **appearance,** arrival, entry, ingress, coming.
ANTONYMS exit, departure.
3 *he was refused entrance* **admission,** admittance, entry, right of entry, access, ingress.

entrance[2] ▶ **verb 1** *I was entranced by her beauty* **enchant,** bewitch, beguile, captivate, mesmerize, hypnotize, spellbind; enthrall, engross, absorb, fascinate; stun, stupefy, overpower, electrify; charm, dazzle, delight; informal bowl over, knock out.
2 *Orpheus entranced the wild beasts* **cast a spell on,** bewitch, hex, spellbind, hypnotize, mesmerize.

entrant ▶ **noun 1** *university entrants* **new member,** new arrival, beginner, newcomer, freshman, recruit; novice, neophyte, tenderfoot; informal rookie, newbie, greenhorn.
2 *a prize will be awarded to the best entrant* **competitor,** contestant, contender, participant; candidate, applicant.

entrap ▶ **verb 1** *fishing lines can entrap wildlife* **trap,** snare, snag, ensnare, entangle, enmesh; catch, capture.
2 *he was entrapped by an undercover policeman* **entice,** lure, inveigle; bait, decoy, trap; lead on, trick, deceive, dupe, hoodwink, sting; informal set up, frame.

entreat ▶ **verb** *my lord, I entreat you to believe me* **implore,** beg, plead with, pray, ask, request; bid, enjoin, appeal to, call on, petition, solicit, importune; literary beseech. See note at BEG.

entreaty ▶ **noun** *he ignored Gert's entreaties* **plea,** appeal, request, petition; suit, application, claim; solicitation, supplication; prayer.

entrench ▶ **verb** *they set up lopsided rules in order to entrench their power* **establish,** settle, lodge, set, root, install, plant, embed, seat; enshrine; informal dig (oneself) in.

entrenched ▶ **adjective** *they tend to cling to entrenched attitudes* **ingrained,** established, confirmed, fixed, firm, deep-seated, deep-rooted; unshakable, indelible, ineradicable, inexorable.

entrepreneur ▶ **noun** *a newsletter for young entrepreneurs* **businessman/businesswoman,** enterpriser, speculator, tycoon, magnate, mogul; dealer, trader; promoter, impresario; informal wheeler-dealer, whiz kid, mover and shaker, go-getter, high flyer, hustler, idea man/person.

entrust ▶ **verb 1** *he was entrusted with the task* **charge,** invest, endow; burden, encumber, saddle.
2 *the powers* **entrusted to** *the treasury department* **assign to,** confer on, bestow on, vest in, consign to; delegate to, depute to, devolve to; give to, grant to, vouchsafe to.
3 *she entrusted them to the hospital* **hand over,** give custody of, turn over, commit, consign, deliver; formal commend.

entry ▶ **noun 1** *my moment of entry* **appearance,** arrival, entrance, ingress, coming.
ANTONYMS departure, exit.
2 *the entry to the building* See ENTRANCE[1] (sense 1).
3 *he was refused entry* **admission,** admittance, entrance, access, ingress.
4 *entries in the cash book* **item,** record, note, listing; memo, memorandum; account.
5 *data entry* **recording,** archiving, logging, documentation, capture, keying.
6 *we must pick a winner from the entries* **contestant,** competitor, contender, entrant, participant; candidate, applicant; submission, entry form, application.

entwine ▶ **verb** *her hair was entwined with ropes of pearls* **wind around,** twist around, coil around; weave, intertwine, interlace, interweave; entangle, tangle; twine, braid, plait, wreathe, knit.

enumerate ▶ **verb 1** *he enumerated four objectives* **list,** itemize, set out, give; cite, name, specify, identify, spell out, detail, particularize.
2 *they enumerated voters* **calculate,** compute, count, add up, tally, total, number, quantify; reckon, work out, tot up.

enunciate ▶ **verb 1** *she enunciated each word slowly* **pronounce,** articulate; say, speak, utter, voice, vocalize, sound.
2 *a document enunciating the policy* **express,** state, put into words, declare, profess, set forth, assert, affirm; put forward, air, proclaim.

envelop ▶ **verb** *enveloped in a blanket, safe in his mother's arms* **surround,** cover, enfold, engulf, encircle, encompass, cocoon, sheathe, swathe, enclose; cloak, screen, shield, veil, shroud. See note at CIRCUMSCRIBE.

envelope ▶ noun *she tore open the envelope* **wrapper,** wrapping, sleeve, cover, covering, casing, package.

enviable ▶ adjective *of the three candidates, St. Clair has the enviable advantage of experience* **desirable,** desired, favored, sought-after, admirable, covetable, attractive; fortunate, lucky; informal to die for.

envious ▶ adjective *she felt envious of her friend's beauty* **jealous,** covetous, desirous; grudging, begrudging, resentful; bitter. See note at JEALOUS.

environment ▶ noun **1** *birds from many environments* **habitat,** territory, domain; surroundings, environs, conditions.
2 *the hospital environment* **situation, setting,** milieu, background, backdrop, scene, location; context, framework; sphere, world, realm; ambience, atmosphere.
3 (**the environment**) *the impact of pesticides on the environment* **the natural world,** nature, the earth, the planet, the ecosystem, the biosphere, Mother Nature; wildlife, flora and fauna, the countryside.

environmentalist ▶ noun *environmentalists and industrialists must unite to save the world's forests* **conservationist,** preservationist, ecologist, nature lover; informal tree hugger, green, greenie.

environs ▶ plural noun *the environs of Milwaukee* **surroundings,** surrounding area, vicinity, purlieu; locality, neighborhood, district, region; precincts.

envisage ▶ verb *can you envisage the factories of the future?* **imagine,** contemplate, visualize, envision, picture; conceive of, think of; foresee.

envoy ▶ noun *a UN envoy has visited the home of Myanmar's opposition leader* **ambassador,** emissary, diplomat, consul, attaché, chargé d'affaires, plenipotentiary; nuncio; representative, delegate, proxy, surrogate, liaison, spokesperson; agent, intermediary, mediator; informal go-between; historical legate.

envy ▶ noun **1** *a pang of envy* **jealousy,** covetousness; resentment, bitterness, discontent; the green-eyed monster.
2 *the firm is the envy of Europe* **finest,** best, pride, top, cream, jewel, flower, leading light, the crème de la crème.
▶ verb **1** *I admired and envied her* **be envious of,** be jealous of; begrudge, be resentful of.
2 *we envied her lifestyle* **covet,** desire, aspire to, wish for, want, long for, yearn for, hanker after, crave.

ephemeral ▶ adjective *last year's ephemeral fashions* **transitory,** transient, fleeting, passing, short-lived, momentary, brief, short; temporary, impermanent, short-term; fly-by-night. See note at TEMPORARY.
ANTONYMS permanent.

epic ▶ noun **1** *the epics of Homer* **heroic poem;** story, saga, legend, romance, chronicle, myth, fable, tale.
2 *a big Hollywood epic* long film; informal blockbuster.
▶ adjective **1** *a traditional epic poem* **heroic,** long, grand, monumental, Homeric, Miltonian.
2 *their epic journey* **ambitious,** heroic, grand, great, Herculean; very long, monumental; adventurous.

epicure ▶ noun *this Caribbean island will help you meet your own inner epicure* **gourmet,** gastronome, gourmand, connoisseur; informal foodie.

epicurean ▶ noun *a generous, life-loving epicurean* **hedonist,** sensualist, pleasure-seeker, sybarite, voluptuary, bon vivant, bon viveur; epicure, gourmet, gastronome, connoisseur, gourmand.
▶ adjective *epicurean excesses* **hedonistic,** sensualist, pleasure-seeking, self-indulgent, good-time, sybaritic, voluptuary, lotus-eating; decadent, unrestrained, extravagant, intemperate, immoderate; gluttonous, gourmandizing. See note at SENSUOUS.

epidemic ▶ noun **1** *an epidemic of typhoid* **outbreak,** plague, pandemic, epizootic.
2 *an epidemic of violence in elementary schools* **spate,** rash, wave, eruption, outbreak, craze; flood, torrent; upsurge, upturn, increase, growth, rise.
▶ adjective *the craze is now epidemic* **rife,** rampant, widespread, wide-ranging, extensive, pervasive; global, universal, ubiquitous; endemic, pandemic, epizootic.

CHOOSE THE RIGHT WORD

epidemic, endemic, pandemic

A disease that quickly and severely affects a large number of people and then subsides is an **epidemic**: *throughout the Middle Ages, successive epidemics of the plague killed millions. Epidemic* is also used as an adjective: *she studied the causes of epidemic cholera.* A disease that is continually present in an area and affects a relatively small number of people is **endemic**: *malaria is endemic in* (or *to*) *hot, moist climates.* A **pandemic** is a widespread epidemic that may affect entire continents or even the world: *the pandemic of 1918 ushered in a period of frequent epidemics of gradually diminishing severity.* Thus, from an epidemiologist's point of view, the Black Death in Europe and AIDS in sub-Saharan Africa are pandemics rather than epidemics.

epigram ▶ noun *a collection of humorous epigrams from old gravestones* **witticism,** quip, jest, pun, bon mot; saying, maxim, adage, aphorism, apophthegm, epigraph; informal one-liner, wisecrack, (old) chestnut. See note at SAYING.

epigrammatic ▶ adjective *her epigrammatic verses* **concise,** succinct, pithy, aphoristic; incisive, short and sweet; witty, clever, quick-witted, piquant, sharp, gnomic, laconic; informal snappy.
ANTONYMS expansive.

epilogue ▶ noun *the book is summarized in the epilogue* **afterword,** postscript, PS, coda, codicil, appendix, tailpiece, supplement, addendum, postlude, rider, back matter; conclusion.
ANTONYMS prologue.

episode ▶ noun **1** *the best episode of his career* **incident,** event, occurrence, happening; occasion, experience, adventure, exploit; matter, affair, thing; interlude, chapter.
2 *the final episode of the series* **installment,** chapter, passage; part, portion, section, component; program, show.
3 *an episode of illness* **period,** spell, bout, attack, phase; informal patch.

episodic ▶ adjective **1** *episodic wheezing* **intermittent,** sporadic, periodic, fitful, irregular, spasmodic, occasional.
ANTONYMS continuous.
2 *an episodic account of the war* **in episodes,** in installments, in sections, in parts.

epistle ▶ noun formal *the historical backdrop of St. Paul's epistles* **letter,** missive, communication, dispatch, note, line; news, correspondence.

epitaph ▶ noun *the epitaphs on their tombstones* **elegy,** commemoration, obituary; inscription, legend.

epithet ▶ noun *Rome befits its epithet "the Eternal City"* **sobriquet,** nickname, byname, title, name, label, tag; description, designation; informal moniker, handle; formal appellation, denomination.

epitome ▶ noun *the sanatorium there is the epitome of Modernist hospital design* **personification,** embodiment, incarnation, paragon; essence, quintessence, archetype, paradigm; exemplar, model, soul, example; height.

epitomize ▶ verb *a nation that has come to epitomize socialism* **embody,** encapsulate, typify, exemplify, represent, manifest, symbolize, illustrate, sum up; personify; formal reify.

epoch ▶ noun *England's Tudor epoch* **era,** age, period, time, span, stage; eon.

equable ▶ adjective **1** *an equable man* **even-tempered,** calm, composed, collected, self-possessed, relaxed, easygoing; nonchalant, insouciant, mellow, mild, tranquil, placid, stable, levelheaded; imperturbable, unexcitable, untroubled, well-balanced, serene; informal unflappable, together, laid-back.
ANTONYMS temperamental, excitable.
2 *an equable climate* **stable,** constant, uniform, unvarying, consistent, unchanging, changeless; moderate, temperate.
ANTONYMS uneven, extreme.

equal ▶ adjective **1** *lines of equal length* **identical,** uniform, alike, like, the same, equivalent; matching, even, comparable, similar, corresponding. See note at **SAME**.
ANTONYMS different.
2 *fares* ***equal to*** *a month's wages* **equivalent to,** identical to, amounting to; proportionate to; commensurate with, on a par with.
ANTONYMS more than, less than.
3 *equal treatment before the law* **unbiased,** impartial, nonpartisan, fair, just, equitable; unprejudiced, nondiscriminatory, egalitarian; neutral, objective, disinterested.
ANTONYMS discriminatory.
4 *an equal contest* **evenly matched,** even, balanced, level; on a par, on an equal footing; informal fifty-fifty, neck and neck.
ANTONYMS uneven.
▶ noun *they did not treat him as their equal* **equivalent,** peer, fellow, coequal, like; counterpart, match, parallel.
▶ verb **1** *two plus two equals four* **be equal to,** be equivalent to, be the same as; come to, amount to, make, total, add up to.
2 *he equaled the world record* **match,** reach, parallel, be level with, measure up to.
3 *the fable equals that of any other poet* **be as good as,** be a match for, measure up to, equate with; be in the same league as, rival, compete with.
– PHRASES **equal to** *trust me, I am equal to the task* **capable of,** fit for, up to, good enough for, strong enough for; suitable for, suited to, appropriate for.

equality ▶ noun **1** *we promote equality for women* **fairness,** equal rights, equal opportunities, equity, egalitarianism; impartiality, evenhandedness; justice.
2 *equality between supply and demand* **parity,** similarity, comparability, correspondence; likeness, resemblance; uniformity, evenness, balance, equilibrium, consistency, homogeneity, agreement, congruence, symmetry.

equalize ▶ verb *attempts to equalize their earnings* **make equal,** make even, even out/up, level, regularize, standardize, balance, square, match; bring into line.

equanimity ▶ noun *she confronted the daily crises with equanimity* **composure,** calm, level-headedness, self-possession, coolheadedness, presence of mind; serenity, tranquility, phlegm, imperturbability, equilibrium; poise, assurance, self-confidence, aplomb, sangfroid, nerve; informal cool.
ANTONYMS anxiety.

equate ▶ verb **1** *he equates criticism with treachery* **identify,** compare, liken, associate, connect, link, relate, class, bracket.
2 *the rent equates to $24 per square foot* **correspond,** be equivalent, amount; equal.
3 *moves to equate supply and demand* **equalize,** balance, even out/up, level, square, tally, match; make equal, make even, make equivalent.

equation ▶ noun **1** *a quadratic equation* **mathematical problem,** sum, calculation, question.
2 *the equation of success with riches* **identification,** association, connection, matching; equivalence, correspondence, agreement, comparison.
3 *other factors came into the equation* **situation,** problem, case, question; quandary, predicament.

equatorial ▶ adjective *equatorial regions* **tropical,** hot, humid, sultry.
ANTONYMS polar.

equestrian ▶ adjective *an equestrian statue* **on horseback,** mounted, riding.
▶ noun *tracks for equestrians* **rider,** horseback rider, horseman, horsewoman, jockey.

equilibrium ▶ noun 1 *the equilibrium of the economy* **balance,** symmetry, equipoise, parity, equality; stability.
ANTONYMS imbalance.
2 *his equilibrium was never shaken* **composure,** calm, equanimity, sangfroid; level-headedness, coolheadedness, imperturbability, poise, presence of mind; self-possession, self-command; impassivity, placidity, tranquility, serenity; informal cool.
ANTONYMS nervousness, agitation.

equip ▶ verb 1 *the boat was equipped with a flare gun* **provide,** furnish, supply, issue, stock, provision, arm, endow, rig.
2 *the course will equip them for the workplace* **prepare,** qualify, suit, train, ready.

equipment ▶ noun *taking inventory of our equipment* **apparatus,** paraphernalia, articles, appliances, impedimenta; tools, utensils, implements, instruments, hardware, gadgets, gadgetry; stuff, things; kit, tackle, rig; resources, supplies; trappings, appurtenances, accouterments; informal gear; dated equipage; Military matériel, baggage.

equitable ▶ adjective *a plan to distribute the burden of taxes in an equitable way* **fair,** just, impartial, evenhanded, unbiased, unprejudiced, egalitarian; disinterested, objective, neutral, nonpartisan, open-minded; informal fair and square.
ANTONYMS unfair.

equity ▶ noun 1 *the equity of Finnish society* **fairness,** justness, impartiality, egalitarianism; objectivity, balance, open-mindedness.
2 *he owns 25% of the equity in the property* **value,** worth; ownership, rights, proprietorship.

equivalence ▶ noun *equivalence of birth and death rates in human populations is rare* **equality,** sameness, interchangeability, comparability, correspondence; uniformity, similarity, likeness, nearness.

equivalent ▶ adjective *a degree or equivalent qualification* **equal,** identical; similar, comparable, corresponding, analogous, homologous, commensurate, parallel, synonymous; approximate, near. See note at SAME.
▶ noun *the program is the digital equivalent of modeling clay* **counterpart,** parallel, alternative, match, analog, twin, clone, opposite number; equal, peer; version; rare coequal.

equivocal ▶ adjective *an equivocal statement* **ambiguous,** indefinite, noncommittal, vague, imprecise, inexact, inexplicit, hazy; unclear, cryptic, enigmatic, pettifogging; ambivalent, uncertain, unsure, indecisive. See note at DOUBTFUL.
ANTONYMS definite.

equivocate ▶ verb *you have equivocated too often in the past* **prevaricate,** be evasive, be noncommittal, be vague, be ambiguous, dodge the question, beat around the bush, hedge; vacillate, shilly-shally, waver; temporize, hesitate, stall, hem and haw; informal pussyfoot around, sit on the fence; rare tergiversate. See note at LIE[1].

era ▶ noun *the Roosevelt era* **epoch,** age, period, phase, time, span, eon; generation.

eradicate ▶ verb *a total of three monthly applications will eradicate the termites* **eliminate,** get rid of, remove, obliterate; exterminate, destroy, annihilate, kill, wipe out; abolish, stamp out, extinguish, quash; erase, efface, excise, expunge, expel; informal zap, nuke, wave goodbye to. See note at DESTROY.

erase ▶ verb 1 *they erased his name from all lists* **delete,** rub out, wipe off, blot out, cancel; efface, expunge, excise, remove, obliterate, eliminate, cut.
2 *the old differences in style were erased* **destroy,** wipe out, obliterate, eradicate, abolish, stamp out, quash.

erect ▶ adjective 1 *she held her body erect* **upright,** straight, vertical, perpendicular; standing.
ANTONYMS bent, flaccid.
2 *an erect penis* **engorged,** enlarged, swollen, tumescent; hard, stiff, rigid.
ANTONYMS limp.
3 *the dog's fur was erect* **bristling,** standing on end, upright.
ANTONYMS flat.
▶ verb *erecting a new barn* **build,** construct, put up; assemble, put together, fabricate.
ANTONYMS demolish, dismantle.

erection ▶ noun 1 *the erection of a house* **construction,** building, assembly, fabrication, elevation.
2 *a bleak concrete erection* **building,** structure, edifice, construction, pile.
3 *a normal erection* **erect penis,** phallus; tumescence; vulgar slang boner, hard-on.

erode ▶ verb *waves and weather are seriously eroding the north side of the island* **wear away/down,** abrade, grind down, crumble; weather; eat away at, dissolve, corrode, rot, decay; undermine, weaken, deteriorate, destroy.

erosion ▶ noun *erosion has dramatically affected the topography here over the past two hundred years* **wearing away,** abrasion, attrition; weathering; dissolution, corrosion, decay; deterioration, disintegration, destruction.

erotic ▶ adjective *erotic literature* **sexy,** sexually arousing, sexually stimulating, titillating, suggestive; pornographic, sexually explicit, lewd, smutty, hard-core, soft-core, dirty, racy, risqué, ribald, naughty; sexual, sensual, amatory; seductive, alluring, tantalizing; informal blue, X-rated, steamy, raunchy, bootylicious; euphemistic adult.

err ▶ verb *the judge had erred in not allowing new evidence* **make a mistake,** be wrong, be in error, be mistaken, blunder, fumble, be incorrect, miscalculate, get it wrong; sin, lapse; informal slip up, screw up, foul up, goof, make a boo-boo, drop the ball, bark up the wrong tree.

errand ▶ noun *one of my errands is to stop at the pharmacy for batteries* **task,** job, chore, assignment; collection, delivery; mission, undertaking.

errant ▶ adjective 1 *the errant officers were suspended* **offending,** guilty, culpable, misbehaving, delinquent, lawbreaking; troublesome, unruly, wayward, disobedient.
ANTONYMS innocent, law-abiding.
2 archaic *a knight errant* **traveling,** wandering,

itinerant, roaming, roving, voyaging.
ANTONYMS sedentary.

erratic ▶ adjective *the test results were too erratic for useful analysis* **unpredictable,** inconsistent, changeable, variable, inconstant, irregular, fitful, unstable, turbulent, unsettled, changing, varying, fluctuating, mutable; unreliable, undependable, volatile, spasmodic, mercurial, capricious, fickle, temperamental, moody.
ANTONYMS consistent.

erring ▶ adjective *the jury agreed that the erring party should pay full restitution* **offending,** guilty, culpable, misbehaving, errant, delinquent, lawbreaking, aberrant, deviant.

erroneous ▶ adjective *an erroneous accusation* **wrong,** incorrect, mistaken, in error, inaccurate, untrue, false, fallacious; unsound, specious, faulty, flawed; informal way out, full of holes.
ANTONYMS correct.

error ▶ noun *leaving the door unlocked was my error* **mistake,** inaccuracy, miscalculation, blunder, oversight; fallacy, misconception, delusion; misprint, erratum; informal slip-up, boo-boo, goof. See note at **MISTAKE**.
– PHRASES **in error** *millions of tax dollars were collected in error* **wrongly,** by mistake, mistakenly, incorrectly; accidentally, by accident, inadvertently, unintentionally, by chance.

ersatz ▶ adjective *ersatz coffee* **artificial,** substitute, imitation, synthetic, fake, false, faux, mock, simulated; pseudo, sham, bogus, spurious, counterfeit; manufactured, man-made; informal phony, wannabe. See note at **SPURIOUS**.
ANTONYMS genuine.

erudite ▶ adjective *our erudite cousin, Norma* **learned,** scholarly, educated, knowledgeable, well-read, well-informed, intellectual; intelligent, clever, academic, literary; bookish, highbrow, sophisticated, cerebral; informal brainy; dated lettered. See note at **KNOWLEDGE**.
ANTONYMS ignorant.

erupt ▶ verb **1** *the volcano erupted* **emit lava,** become active, flare up; explode.
2 *fighting erupted* **break out,** flare up, start suddenly; ensue, arise, happen.
3 *a boil erupted on her temple* **appear,** break out, flare up, come to a head, suppurate, emerge.

eruption ▶ noun **1** *a volcanic eruption* **discharge,** ejection, emission; explosion.
2 *an eruption of violence* **outbreak,** flare-up, upsurge, outburst, explosion; wave, spate.
3 *a skin eruption* **rash,** outbreak, breakout, inflammation.

escalate ▶ verb **1** *prices have escalated* **increase rapidly,** soar, rocket, shoot up, mount, spiral, climb, go up, inflate; informal go through the ceiling, go through the roof, skyrocket.
ANTONYMS plunge.
2 *the dispute escalated* **grow,** develop, mushroom, increase, heighten, intensify, accelerate.
ANTONYMS shrink.

escapade ▶ noun *famous for his flying escapades* **exploit,** stunt, caper, antic(s), spree, shenanigans, hijinks; adventure, venture, mission; deed, feat, trial, experience; incident, occurrence, event.

escape ▶ verb **1** *he escaped from prison* **run away/off,** get out, break out, break free, make a break for it, bolt, flee, take flight, make off, take off, abscond, take to one's heels, make one's getaway, make a run for it; disappear, vanish, slip away, sneak away; informal cut and run, skedaddle, vamoose, fly the coop, take French leave, go on the lam.
2 *he escaped his pursuers* **get away from,** escape from, elude, avoid, dodge, shake off; informal give someone the slip.
3 *they escaped injury* **avoid,** evade, dodge, elude, miss, cheat, sidestep, circumvent, steer clear of; informal duck.
4 *lethal gas escaped* **leak (out),** seep (out), discharge, emanate, issue, flow (out), pour (out), gush (out), spurt (out), spew (out).
▶ noun **1** *his escape from prison* **getaway,** breakout, jailbreak, bolt, flight; disappearance, vanishing act.
2 *a narrow escape from death* **avoidance of,** evasion of, circumvention of.
3 *a gas escape* **leak,** leakage, spill, seepage, discharge, effusion, emanation, outflow, outpouring; gush, stream, spurt.
4 *an escape from boredom* **distraction,** diversion.

escapism ▶ noun *romance novels offer a form of escapism that many people thoroughly enjoy* **fantasy,** fantasizing, daydreaming, daydreams, reverie; imagination, flight(s) of fancy, pipe dreams, wishful thinking, woolgathering; informal pie in the sky.
ANTONYMS realism.

eschew ▶ verb *he firmly eschewed political involvement* **abstain from,** refrain from, give up, forgo, shun, renounce, steer clear of, have nothing to do with, fight shy of; relinquish, reject, disavow, abandon, spurn, wash one's hands of, drop; informal kick, pack in; formal forswear, abjure.

escort ▶ noun **1** *a police escort* **guard,** bodyguard, protector, minder, attendant, chaperone; entourage, retinue, cortège; protection, defense, convoy.
2 *her escort for the evening* **companion,** partner; informal date; formal attendant.
3 *an agency dealing with escorts* **paid companion,** hostess; geisha; gigolo.
▶ verb *he escorted her down the aisle* **conduct,** accompany, guide, lead, usher, shepherd, bring, take; drive, walk.

esoteric ▶ adjective *in attendance were more than 50 antiques dealers brimming with esoteric knowledge* **abstruse,** obscure, arcane, recherché, rarefied, recondite, abstract; enigmatic, inscrutable, cryptic, Delphic; complex, complicated, incomprehensible, opaque, impenetrable, mysterious.

especial ▶ adjective **1** *especial care is required* **particular,** special, extra special, superior, exceptional, extraordinary; unusual, out of the ordinary, uncommon, remarkable, singular.
2 *her especial brand of charm* **distinctive,** individual, special, particular, distinct, peculiar,

personal, own, unique, specific.

especially ▶ adverb **1** *complaints poured in, especially from Toronto* **mainly,** mostly, chiefly, principally, largely; substantially, particularly, primarily, generally, usually, typically.
2 *a committee especially for the purpose* **expressly,** specially, specifically, exclusively, just, particularly, explicitly.
3 *he is especially talented* **exceptionally,** particularly, specially, very, extremely, singularly, strikingly, distinctly, unusually, extraordinarily, uncommonly, uniquely, remarkably, outstandingly, really; informal seriously, majorly.

espionage ▶ noun *an American pilot suspected of espionage* **spying,** infiltration; eavesdropping, surveillance, reconnaissance, intelligence, undercover work.

espousal ▶ noun *Will's recent espousal of neo-Nazism has distressed his family and perplexed his friends* **adoption,** embracing, acceptance; support, championship, encouragement, defense; sponsorship, promotion, endorsement, advocacy, approval.

espouse ▶ verb *do you espouse the political beliefs of your parents?* **adopt,** embrace, take up, accept, welcome; support, back, champion, favor, prefer, encourage; promote, endorse, advocate.
ANTONYMS reject.

espy ▶ verb literary *he espied a niche up in the rocks* **catch sight of,** glimpse, see, spot, spy, notice, observe, discern, pick out, detect; literary behold.

essay ▶ noun **1** *he wrote an essay* **article,** composition, study, paper, dissertation, thesis, discourse, treatise, disquisition, monograph; commentary, critique, theme.
2 formal *his first essay in telecommunications* **attempt,** effort, endeavor, try, venture, trial, experiment, undertaking.

essence ▶ noun **1** *the very essence of economics* **quintessence,** soul, spirit, nature; core, heart, crux, nucleus, substance; principle, fundamental quality, sum and substance, warp and woof, reality, actuality; informal nitty-gritty.
2 *essence of ginger* **extract,** concentrate, distillate, elixir, decoction, juice, tincture; scent, perfume, oil.
– PHRASES **in essence** *in essence, his essays are the products of an indoctrinated young mind* **essentially,** basically, fundamentally, primarily, principally, chiefly, predominantly, substantially; above all, first and foremost; effectively, virtually, to all intents and purposes; intrinsically, inherently. **of the essence** *absolute secrecy is of the essence* See **ESSENTIAL** (sense 1 of the adjective).

essential ▶ adjective **1** *it is essential to remove the paint* **crucial,** necessary, key, vital, indispensable, important, all-important, of the essence, critical, imperative, mandatory, compulsory, obligatory; urgent, pressing, paramount, preeminent, high-priority, nonnegotiable; informal must-have. See note at **NECESSARY.**
ANTONYMS unimportant, optional.
2 *the essential simplicity of his style* **basic,** inherent, fundamental, quintessential, intrinsic, underlying, characteristic, innate, primary, elementary, elemental; central, pivotal, vital. See note at **INHERENT.**
ANTONYMS secondary.
▶ noun **1** *an essential for broadcasters* **necessity,** prerequisite, requisite, requirement, need; condition, precondition, stipulation; sine qua non; informal must, must-have.
2 *the essentials of the job* **fundamentals,** basics, rudiments, first principles, foundations, bedrock; essence, basis, core, kernel, crux, sine qua non; informal nitty-gritty, brass tacks, nuts and bolts, meat and potatoes.

establish ▶ verb **1** *they established an office in Moscow* **set up,** start, initiate, institute, form, found, create, inaugurate; build, construct, install.
2 *evidence to establish his guilt* **prove,** demonstrate, show, indicate, signal, exhibit, manifest, attest to, evidence, determine, confirm, verify, certify, substantiate.

established ▶ adjective **1** *established practice* **accepted,** traditional, orthodox, habitual, set, fixed, official; usual, customary, common, normal, general, prevailing, accustomed, familiar, expected, routine, typical, conventional, standard.
2 *an established composer* **well-known,** recognized, esteemed, respected, famous, prominent, noted, renowned.

establishment ▶ noun **1** *the establishment of a democracy* **foundation,** institution, formation, inception, creation, installation; inauguration, start, initiation.
2 *a dressmaking establishment* **business,** firm, company, concern, enterprise, venture, organization, operation; factory, plant, store, shop, office, practice; informal outfit, setup.
3 *educational establishments* **institution,** place, premises, foundation, institute.
4 (**the Establishment**) *they dare to poke fun at the Establishment* **the authorities,** the powers that be, the system, the ruling class; the hierarchy, the oligarchy; informal Big Brother.

estate ▶ noun **1** *the Knowltons' estate* **property,** grounds, garden(s), park, parkland, land(s), landholding, manor, territory; historical seigneury.
2 *a coffee estate* **plantation,** farm, holding; forest, vineyard; ranch.
3 *he left an estate worth $610,000* **assets,** capital, wealth, riches, holdings, fortune; property, effects, possessions, belongings; Law goods and chattels.

esteem ▶ noun *she was held in high esteem* **respect,** admiration, acclaim, approbation, appreciation, favor, recognition, honor, reverence; estimation, regard, opinion.
▶ verb **1** *such ceramics are highly esteemed* **respect, admire,** value, regard, acclaim, appreciate, like, prize, treasure, favor, revere.
2 formal *I would esteem it a favor if you could speak to him* See **DEEM.**

CHOOSE THE RIGHT WORD

esteem, admire, appreciate, prize, regard, respect

If you're a classical music aficionado, you might **appreciate** a good symphony orchestra, **admire** someone who plays the oboe, and **esteem** the works of Beethoven above all other classical composers. All three of these verbs are concerned with recognizing the worth of something, but in order to *appreciate* it, you have to understand it well enough to judge it critically. If you *admire* something, you appreciate its superiority (*to admire a pianist's performance*), while *esteem* goes one step further, implying that your admiration is of the highest degree (*a musician esteemed throughout the music world*). You **prize** what you value highly or cherish, especially if it is a possession (*she prized her Stradivarius violin*), while **regard** is a more neutral term meaning to look at or to have a certain mental view of something, either favorable or unfavorable (*to regard him as a great musician; to regard her as a ruthless competitor*). To **respect** is to have a deferential regard for someone or something because of its worth or value (*to respect the conductor's interpretation of the music*).

estimate ▶ verb **1** *estimate the cost* **calculate roughly,** approximate, guess; evaluate, judge, gauge, reckon, rate, determine; informal guesstimate, ballpark.
2 *we estimate it to be worth $50,000* **consider,** believe, reckon, deem, judge, rate, gauge.
▶ noun **1** *an estimate of the cost* **rough calculation,** approximation, estimation, rough guess; costing, quotation, valuation, evaluation; informal guesstimate.
2 *his estimate of Paul's integrity* **evaluation,** estimation, judgment, rating, appraisal, opinion, view.

estimation ▶ noun **1** *an estimation of economic growth* **estimate,** approximation, rough calculation, rough guess, evaluation; informal guesstimate, ballpark figure.
2 *she rated highly in Janice's estimation* **assessment,** evaluation, judgment, perception; esteem, opinion, view.

estrange ▶ verb *it is sheer stupidity to estrange a potential sponsor* **alienate,** antagonize, turn away, drive away, distance; sever, set at odds with; drive a wedge between (oneself and).

estrangement ▶ noun *the estrangement between Vita and her family* **alienation,** antagonism, antipathy, disaffection, hostility, unfriendliness; variance, difference; parting, separation, divorce, breakup, split, breach, schism; informal splitsville. See note at SOLITUDE.

estuary ▶ noun *we paddled down the estuary, observing herons and ospreys* **(river) mouth,** delta; archaic embouchure, debouchure, debouchment, discharge, disemboguement.

et cetera ▶ adverb *they make their own linguini, fettuccini, ziti, lasagna, et cetera* **and so on,** and so forth, and the rest, and/or the like, and suchlike, among others, et al., etc.; informal and what have you, and whatnot, and on and on, yadda yadda yadda.

etch ▶ verb *the metal is etched with a dilute acid* **engrave,** carve, inscribe, incise, chase, score, print, mark.

etching ▶ noun *Picasso's etchings were often relatively large and bold* **engraving,** print, impression, block, plate; woodcut, linocut.

eternal ▶ adjective **1** *eternal happiness* **everlasting,** never-ending, endless, perpetual, undying, immortal, abiding, permanent, enduring, infinite, boundless, timeless; amaranthine.
ANTONYMS transient.
2 *eternal vigilance* **constant,** continual, continuous, perpetual, persistent, sustained, unremitting, relentless, unrelieved, uninterrupted, unbroken, never-ending, nonstop, around/round-the-clock, endless, ceaseless.
ANTONYMS intermittent.

CHOOSE THE RIGHT WORD

eternal, endless, everlasting, interminable, never-ending, unending

There are some things in life that seem to exist beyond the boundaries of time. **Endless** is the most informal and has the broadest scope of all these adjectives. It can mean without end in time (*an endless argument*) or space (*the endless universe*), and it implies never stopping, or going on continuously as if in a circle (*to consult an endless succession of doctors*). **Unending** is a less formal word used to describe something that endures or has no end, and it can be used either in an approving sense (*unending devotion*) or a disapproving one (*unending conflict*). **Never-ending** is a more emphatic term than *unending*; it, too, can be used in either a positive or a negative sense (*a never-ending delight; a never-ending source of embarrassment*). In contrast, **interminable** is almost always used in a disapproving or negative sense for something that lasts a long time (*interminable delays in construction*). **Everlasting** refers to something that will continue to exist once it is created, while **eternal** implies that it has always existed and will continue to exist in the future. In Christian theology, for example, believers in the *eternal* God look forward to *everlasting* life.

eternally ▶ adverb **1** *I shall be eternally grateful* **forever,** permanently, perpetually, (for) evermore, for ever and ever, for eternity, in perpetuity, enduringly; forevermore; informal until the cows come home; archaic for aye.
2 *the drummer is eternally complaining* **constantly,** continually, continuously, always, all the time, persistently, repeatedly, regularly; day and night, night and day, nonstop; endlessly, incessantly, perpetually; interminably, relentlessly; informal 24-7.

eternity ▶ noun **1** *the memory will remain for eternity* **ever,** all time, perpetuity.
2 Theology *souls destined for eternity* **the afterlife,** everlasting life, life after death, the hereafter,

the afterworld, the next world; heaven, paradise, immortality.
3 informal *I waited an eternity for you* **a long time,** an age, ages, a lifetime; hours, years, eons; forever; informal donkey's years, a month of Sundays, a coon's age.

ethereal ▶ adjective *melodic phrases of ethereal beauty* **delicate,** exquisite, dainty, elegant, graceful; fragile, airy, fine, subtle; unearthly.
ANTONYMS substantial, earthly.

ethical ▶ adjective **1** *an ethical dilemma* **moral,** social, behavioral. See note at **MORAL**.
2 *an ethical investment policy* **moral,** right-minded, principled, irreproachable; righteous, high-minded, virtuous, good, morally correct; clean, lawful, just, honorable, reputable, respectable, noble, worthy; praiseworthy, commendable, admirable, laudable; whiter than white, saintly, impeccable, politically correct; informal squeaky clean, PC.

ethics ▶ plural noun *your so-called newspaper is clearly not burdened by a sense of ethics* **moral code,** morals, morality, values, rights and wrongs, principles, ideals, standards (of behavior), value system, virtues, dictates of conscience.

ethnic ▶ adjective *a wide spectrum of ethnic groups* **racial,** race-related, ethnological; cultural, national, tribal, ancestral, traditional.

ethos ▶ noun *responsibility for the ethos of the school* **spirit,** character, atmosphere, climate, mood, feeling, tenor, essence; disposition, rationale, morality, moral code, value system, principles, standards, ethics.

etiquette ▶ noun *the article includes tips on etiquette* **protocol,** manners, accepted behavior, rules of conduct, decorum, good form; courtesy, propriety, formalities, niceties, punctilios; custom, convention; Computing netiquette; informal the done thing; formal politesse.

eulogize ▶ verb *the police eulogized the positive effect of speed cameras* **extol,** acclaim, sing the praises of, praise to the skies, wax lyrical about, rhapsodize about, rave about, enthuse about, ballyhoo, hype. See note at **PRAISE**.
ANTONYMS criticize.

eulogy ▶ noun *a graveside eulogy* **accolade,** panegyric, paean, tribute, compliment, commendation; praise, acclaim; plaudits, bouquets; formal encomium.
ANTONYMS attack.

euphemism ▶ noun *'influential person' is the local euphemism for underworld don* **polite term,** indirect term, circumlocution, substitute, alternative, understatement, genteelism.

euphemistic ▶ adjective *the textbooks reportedly use the euphemistic term 'advance' instead of 'invade' to describe Japan's takeover of the Korean Peninsula* **polite,** substitute, mild, understated, indirect, neutral, evasive; diplomatic, inoffensive, genteel; periphrastic, circumlocutory, mealy-mouthed.

euphonious ▶ adjective *the euphonious chorus of songbirds* **pleasant-sounding,** sweet-sounding, mellow, mellifluous, dulcet, sweet, honeyed, lyrical, silvery, golden, lilting, soothing; harmonious, melodious; informal easy on the ear.
ANTONYMS cacophonous.

euphoria ▶ noun *the euphoria of victory* **elation,** happiness, joy, delight, glee; excitement, exhilaration, jubilation, exultation; ecstasy, bliss, rapture. See note at **RAPTURE**.
ANTONYMS misery.

euphoric ▶ adjective *they received a euphoric welcome* **elated,** happy, joyful, delighted, gleeful; excited, exhilarated, jubilant, exultant; ecstatic, blissful, rapturous, transported, on cloud nine, in seventh heaven; informal on top of the world, over the moon, on a high.

euthanasia ▶ noun *both veterinarians recommended euthanasia as the most merciful procedure* **mercy killing,** assisted suicide; rare quietus.

evacuate ▶ verb **1** *local residents were evacuated* **remove,** clear, move out, take away, shift.
2 *they evacuated the bombed town* **leave,** vacate, abandon, desert, move out of, quit, withdraw from, retreat from, decamp from, flee, depart from, escape from.
3 *police evacuated the area* **clear,** empty.
4 *patients couldn't evacuate their bowels* **empty (out),** void, open, move, purge; defecate.
5 *he evacuated the contents of his stomach* **expel,** eject, discharge, excrete, void, empty (out), vomit up.

evade ▶ verb **1** *they evaded the guards* **elude,** avoid, dodge, escape (from), steer clear of, keep at arm's length, sidestep; lose, leave behind, shake off; informal give someone the slip.
ANTONYMS confront, run into.
2 *he evaded the question* **avoid,** dodge, sidestep, bypass, shirk, hedge, skirt around, fudge, be evasive about; informal duck.
ANTONYMS face.

evaluate ▶ verb *the house was most recently evaluated in 2002* **assess,** judge, gauge, rate, estimate, appraise, analyze, examine, get the measure of; informal size up, check out.

evaluation ▶ noun *proper evaluation of the results is critical* **assessment,** appraisal, judgment, gauging, rating, estimation, consideration; analysis, examination, test, review.

evanescent ▶ adjective literary *operating on an evanescent budget* **vanishing,** fading, evaporating, melting away, disappearing; ephemeral, fleeting, short-lived, short-term, transitory, transient, fugitive, temporary. See note at **TEMPORARY**.
ANTONYMS permanent.

evangelical ▶ adjective **1** *evangelical Christianity* **scriptural,** biblical; fundamentalist.
2 *an evangelical preacher* **evangelistic,** evangelizing, missionary, crusading, proselytizing; informal Bible-thumping.

evangelist ▶ noun *he was born into a family of Pentecostal evangelists* **preacher,** missionary, gospeler, proselytizer, crusader; informal Bible-thumper.

evangelistic ▶ adjective See **EVANGELICAL** (sense 2).

evangelize ▶ verb *his calling is to evangelize the downtrodden in these poor neighborhoods | evangelizing in the West Indies* **convert,**

proselytize, redeem, save, preach to, recruit; act as a missionary, missionize, crusade, campaign.

evaporate ▶ verb **1** *the water evaporated* **vaporize,** become vapor, volatilize; dry up.
ANTONYMS condense.
2 *the rock salt is washed and evaporated* **dry out,** dehydrate, desiccate, dehumidify.
ANTONYMS wet.
3 *the feeling has evaporated* **end,** pass, pass away, fizzle out, peter out, wear off, vanish, fade, disappear, dissolve, melt away.
ANTONYMS materialize.

evasion ▶ noun **1** *the evasion of immigration control* **avoidance,** elusion, circumvention, dodging, sidestepping.
2 *she grew tired of all the evasion* **prevarication,** evasiveness, beating around the bush, hedging, pussyfooting, hemming and hawing, equivocation, vagueness, temporization; rare tergiversation.

evasive ▶ adjective *the judge was infuriated by the defendant's evasive answers* **equivocal,** prevaricating, elusive, ambiguous, noncommittal, vague, inexplicit, unclear; roundabout, indirect; informal cagey, shifty, slippery.

eve ▶ noun **1** *the eve of the election* **day before,** evening before, night before; period (just) before.
2 literary *a winter's eve* **evening,** night; end of day, close of day; twilight, dusk, sunset, sundown, nightfall; literary eventide, evenfall, gloaming.
ANTONYMS morning.

even ▶ adjective **1** *an even surface* **flat,** smooth, uniform, featureless; unbroken, undamaged; level, plane.
ANTONYMS bumpy.
2 *an even temperature* **uniform,** constant, steady, stable, consistent, unvarying, unchanging, regular.
ANTONYMS variable, irregular.
3 *they all have an even chance* **equal,** the same, identical, like, alike, similar, comparable, parallel.
ANTONYMS unequal.
4 *the score was even* **tied,** drawn, level, all square, balanced; neck and neck; informal even-steven.
ANTONYMS unequal.
5 *an even disposition* **even-tempered,** balanced, stable, equable, placid, calm, composed, poised, cool, relaxed, easy, imperturbable, unexcitable, unruffled, untroubled; informal together, laid-back, unflappable.
ANTONYMS excitable, moody.
▶ verb **1** *the canal bottom was* ***evened out*** **flatten,** level (off/out), smooth (off/out), plane; make uniform, make regular.
2 ***even up*** *the portions* **equalize,** make equal, balance, square; standardize, regularize, homogenize.
▶ adverb **1** *it got even colder* **still,** yet, more, all the more.
2 *even the best hitters missed the ball* **surprisingly,** unexpectedly, paradoxically.
3 *she is afraid, even ashamed, to ask for help* **indeed,** you could say, veritably, in truth, actually, or rather; dated nay.
4 *she could not even afford food* **not so much as,** hardly, barely, scarcely.
– PHRASES **even as** *we laugh even as we empathize with his discomfort* **while,** whilst, as, just as, at the very time that, during the time that. **even so** *I feel better, but the doubts persist even so* **nevertheless,** nonetheless, all the same, just the same, anyway, anyhow, still, yet, however, notwithstanding, despite that, in spite of that, for all that, be that as it may, in any event, at any rate; informal anyhoo, anyways. **get even** *he thinks he's struck the final blow, but I'll get even* **have one's revenge,** avenge oneself, take vengeance, even the score, settle the score, hit back, give as good as one gets, pay someone back, repay someone, reciprocate, retaliate, take reprisals, exact retribution; give someone their just deserts; informal give someone a taste of their own medicine, settle someone's hash; literary be revenged.

evenhanded ▶ adjective *for reasons we have yet to analyze, our older teachers are far more evenhanded than the younger ones* **fair,** just, equitable, impartial, unbiased, unprejudiced, nonpartisan, nondiscriminatory; disinterested, detached, objective, neutral.
ANTONYMS biased.

evening ▶ noun *they met in town nearly every evening* **night,** late afternoon, end of day, close of day; twilight, dusk, nightfall, sunset, sundown; literary eve, eventide, evenfall, gloaming.

event ▶ noun **1** *an annual event* **occurrence,** happening, proceeding, incident, affair, circumstance, occasion, phenomenon; function, gathering; informal bash.
2 *the team lost the event* **competition,** contest, tournament, round, heat, match, fixture; race, game, bout.
– PHRASES **in any event** *we may not join you for dinner, but in any event we'll see you at the theater* **regardless,** whatever happens, come what may, no matter what, at any rate, in any case, anyhow, anyway, even so, still, nevertheless, nonetheless; informal anyways, anyhoo. **in the event** *in the event, they squabbled and the plan fell through* **as it turned out,** as it happened, in the end; as a result, as a consequence.

eventful ▶ adjective *a long and eventful day* **busy,** action-packed, full, lively, active, hectic, strenuous; momentous, significant, important, historic, consequential, fateful.
ANTONYMS dull.

eventual ▶ adjective *the eventual outcome of the competition* **final,** ultimate, concluding, closing, end; resulting, ensuing, consequent, subsequent.

eventuality ▶ noun *it is impossible to anticipate every eventuality* **event,** incident, occurrence, happening, development, phenomenon, situation, circumstance, case, contingency, chance, likelihood, possibility, probability; outcome, result.

eventually ▶ adverb *the culprit will be caught eventually* **in the end,** in due course, by and by, in time, after some time, after a bit, finally, at last, over the long haul; ultimately, in the long run, at the end of the day, one day, some day, sometime, at some point, sooner or later.

eventuate ▶ verb formal **1** *you never know what might eventuate* See HAPPEN (sense 1).
2 *the fight* ***eventuated in*** *his death* **result in,** end in, lead to, give rise to, bring about, cause.

ever ▶ adverb **1** *the best I've ever done* **at any time,** at any point, on any occasion, under any circumstances, on any account; up till now, until now.
2 *he was ever the optimist* **always,** forever, eternally, until hell freezes over, until the cows come home.
3 *an ever increasing rate of crime* **continually,** constantly, always, endlessly, perpetually, incessantly, unremittingly.
4 *will she ever learn?* **at all,** in any way.

everlasting ▶ adjective **1** *everlasting love* **eternal,** endless, never-ending, perpetual, undying, abiding, enduring, infinite, boundless, timeless. See note at ETERNAL.
ANTONYMS transient.
2 *his everlasting complaints* **constant,** continual, continuous, persistent, relentless, unrelieved, uninterrupted, unabating, endless, interminable, never-ending, nonstop, incessant.
ANTONYMS occasional.

every ▶ adjective **1** *he exercised every day* **each,** each and every, every single.
2 *we make every effort to satisfy our clients* **all possible,** the utmost.

everyday ▶ adjective **1** *the everyday demands of a baby* **daily,** day-to-day, quotidian.
2 *everyday drugs like acetaminophen* **commonplace,** ordinary, common, usual, regular, familiar, conventional, run-of-the-mill, standard, stock; household, domestic; informal garden variety.
ANTONYMS unusual.

everything ▶ pronoun *everything is half price* **each item,** each thing, every single thing, the lot, the whole lot; all; informal the whole kit and caboodle, the whole shebang, the whole schmear, the whole ball of wax, the whole nine yards.
ANTONYMS nothing.

everywhere ▶ adverb *fast-food restaurants are found everywhere* **all over,** all around, ubiquitously, in every nook and cranny, far and wide, near and far, high and low, 'here, there, and everywhere'; throughout the land, the world over, worldwide, globally; informal all over the place, everyplace, all over the map.
ANTONYMS nowhere.

evict ▶ verb *Leonard took no pleasure in evicting tenants* **expel,** eject, oust, remove, dislodge, turn out, throw out, drive out; dispossess, expropriate; informal chuck out, kick out, boot out, bounce, give someone the (old) heave-ho, throw someone out on their ear, give someone the bum's rush, give someone their walking papers. See note at EJECT.

eviction ▶ noun *a notice of eviction was left in the mailbox* **expulsion,** ejection, ousting, removal, dislodgment, displacement, banishment; dispossession, expropriation; Law ouster.

evidence ▶ noun **1** *they found evidence of his plotting* **proof,** confirmation, verification, substantiation, corroboration, affirmation, attestation.
2 *the court accepted her evidence* **testimony,** statement, attestation, declaration, avowal, submission, claim, contention, allegation; Law deposition, representation, affidavit.
3 *evidence of a struggle* **signs,** indications, pointers, marks, traces, suggestions, hints; manifestation.
▶ verb *the rise of racism is evidenced here* **indicate,** show, reveal, display, exhibit, manifest; testify to, confirm, prove, substantiate, endorse, bear out; formal evince.
ANTONYMS disprove.
– PHRASES **in evidence** *team spirit was in evidence* **noticeable,** conspicuous, obvious, perceptible, visible, on view, on display, plain to see; palpable, tangible, unmistakable, undisguised, prominent, striking, glaring; informal as plain as the nose on your face, sticking out like a sore thumb, staring someone in the face.

evident ▶ adjective *the fact that he loves his family is evident* **obvious,** apparent, noticeable, conspicuous, perceptible, visible, discernible, clear, clear-cut, plain, manifest, patent; palpable, tangible, distinct, pronounced, marked, striking, glaring, blatant; unmistakable, indisputable; informal as plain as the nose on your face, sticking out like a sore thumb, as clear as day.

evidently ▶ adverb **1** *he was evidently dismayed* **obviously,** clearly, plainly, visibly, manifestly, patently, distinctly, markedly; unmistakably, undeniably, undoubtedly.
2 *evidently, she believed herself superior* **seemingly,** apparently, as far as one can tell, from all appearances, on the face of it; it seems (that), it appears (that).

evil ▶ adjective **1** *an evil deed* **wicked,** bad, wrong, immoral, sinful, foul, vile, dishonorable, corrupt, iniquitous, depraved, reprobate, villainous, nefarious, vicious, malicious; malevolent, sinister, demonic, devilish, diabolical, fiendish, dark; monstrous, shocking, despicable, atrocious, heinous, odious, contemptible, horrible, execrable; informal lowdown, dirty.
ANTONYMS good, virtuous.
2 *an evil spirit* **cruel,** mischievous, pernicious, malignant, malign, baleful, vicious; destructive, harmful, hurtful, injurious, detrimental, deleterious, inimical, bad, ruinous.
ANTONYMS good, beneficial.
3 *an evil smell* **unpleasant,** disagreeable, nasty, horrible, foul, disgusting, filthy, vile, noxious.
ANTONYMS pleasant.
▶ noun **1** *the evil in our midst* **wickedness,** bad, badness, wrongdoing, sin, ill, immorality, vice, iniquity, degeneracy, corruption, depravity, villainy, nefariousness, malevolence; devil; formal turpitude.
2 *nothing but evil would ensue* **harm,** pain, misery, sorrow, suffering, trouble, disaster, misfortune, catastrophe, affliction, woe, hardship.
3 *the evils of war* **abomination,** atrocity,

obscenity, outrage, enormity, crime, monstrosity, barbarity.

evince ▶ verb formal *his letters evince the excitement he felt* **reveal,** show, make plain, manifest, indicate, display, exhibit, demonstrate, evidence, attest to; convey, communicate, proclaim, bespeak; informal ooze.
ANTONYMS conceal.

evocative ▶ adjective *evocative photos from our childhood* **reminiscent,** suggestive, redolent; expressive, vivid, graphic, powerful, haunting, moving, poignant.

evoke ▶ verb *the music evoked some forgotten memories* **bring to mind,** put one in mind of, conjure up, summon (up), invoke, elicit, induce, kindle, stimulate, stir up, awaken, arouse, call forth; recall, echo, capture.

evolution ▶ noun **1** *the evolution of Bolshevism* **development,** advancement, growth, rise, progress, expansion, unfolding; transformation, adaptation, modification, revision.
2 *his interest in evolution* **Darwinism,** natural selection.

evolve ▶ verb *our little tea party evolved into an all-night bash* **develop,** progress, advance; mature, grow, expand, spread; alter, change, transform, adapt, metamorphose; humorous transmogrify.

exacerbate ▶ verb *each party blames the other for exacerbating the problem* **aggravate,** worsen, inflame, compound; intensify, increase, heighten, magnify, add to, amplify, augment; informal add fuel to the fire/flames.
ANTONYMS reduce.

exact ▶ adjective **1** *an exact description* **precise,** accurate, correct, faithful, close, true; literal, strict, faultless, perfect, impeccable; explicit, detailed, minute, meticulous, thorough; informal on the nail, on the mark, bang on, on the money, on the button.
ANTONYMS inaccurate.
2 *an exact manager* **careful,** meticulous, painstaking, punctilious, conscientious, scrupulous, exacting; methodical, organized, orderly.
ANTONYMS careless.
▶ verb **1** *she exacted high standards from them* **demand,** require, insist on, request, impose, expect; extract, compel, force, squeeze.
2 *they exacted a terrible vengeance on him* **inflict,** impose, administer, apply.

exacting ▶ adjective **1** *an exacting training routine* **demanding,** stringent, testing, challenging, onerous, arduous, laborious, taxing, grueling, punishing, hard, tough.
ANTONYMS easy.
2 *an exacting boss* **strict,** stern, severe, firm, demanding, tough, harsh; inflexible, uncompromising, unyielding, unsparing; informal persnickety.
ANTONYMS easygoing.

exactly ▶ adverb **1** *it's exactly as I expected it to be* **precisely,** entirely, absolutely, completely, totally, just, quite, in every way, in every respect, one hundred percent, every inch; informal to a T, on the money.
2 *write the quotation out exactly* **accurately,** precisely, correctly, unerringly, faultlessly, perfectly; verbatim, word for word, letter for letter, to the letter, faithfully.
▶ exclamation *"She escaped?" "Exactly."* **precisely,** yes, that's right, just so, quite so, quite, indeed, absolutely; informal you got it.
– PHRASES **not exactly** *I'm not exactly a spring chicken* **by no means,** not at all, in no way, certainly not; not really.

exaggerate ▶ verb *the conflict was exaggerated by the media* **overstate,** overemphasize, overestimate, magnify, amplify, aggrandize, inflate; embellish, embroider, elaborate, overplay, dramatize; hyperbolize, stretch the truth; informal lay it on thick, make a mountain out of a molehill, blow out of all proportion, blow up, make a big thing of.
ANTONYMS understate.

exaggerated ▶ adjective *an exaggerated account of my exploits* **overstated,** inflated, magnified, amplified, aggrandized, excessive; hyperbolic, elaborate, overdone, overplayed, overblown, overdramatized, melodramatic, sensational; informal over the top.

exaggeration ▶ noun *his testimony was a laughable mix of contradiction and exaggeration* **overstatement,** overemphasis, magnification, amplification, aggrandizement; dramatization, elaboration, embellishment, embroidery, hyperbole, overkill, gilding the lily.

exalt ▶ verb **1** *they exalted their hero* **extol,** praise, acclaim, esteem; pay homage to, revere, venerate, worship, lionize, idolize, look up to; informal put on a pedestal, laud.
ANTONYMS disparage, despise.
2 *this power exalts the peasant* **elevate,** promote, raise, advance, upgrade, ennoble, dignify, aggrandize.
ANTONYMS lower.
3 *his works exalt the emotions* **uplift,** elevate, inspire, excite, stimulate, enliven, exhilarate.
ANTONYMS depress.

exaltation ▶ noun **1** *a heart full of exaltation* **elation,** joy, rapture, ecstasy, bliss, happiness, delight, gladness.
2 *their exaltation of Shakespeare* **praise,** acclamation, reverence, veneration, worship, adoration, idolization, lionization.

exalted ▶ adjective **1** *his exalted office* **high,** high-ranking, elevated, superior, lofty, eminent, prestigious, illustrious, distinguished, esteemed.
2 *his exalted aims* **noble,** lofty, high-minded, elevated; inflated, pretentious.
3 *she felt spiritually exalted* **elated,** exultant, jubilant, joyful, rapturous, ecstatic, blissful, transported, happy, exuberant, exhilarated; informal high.

exam ▶ noun See EXAMINATION (sense 3).

examination ▶ noun **1** *artifacts spread out for examination* **scrutiny,** inspection, perusal, study, investigation, consideration, analysis, appraisal, evaluation.
2 *a medical examination* **inspection,** checkup, assessment, appraisal; probe, test, scan; informal once-over, overhaul.

3 *a school examination* **test,** exam, quiz, assessment; oral, midterm, final; paper, term paper.
4 Law *the examination of witnesses* **interrogation,** questioning, cross-examination, inquisition.

examine ▶ **verb 1** *they examined the bank records* **inspect,** scrutinize, investigate, look at, study, scan, sift (through), probe, appraise, analyze, review, survey; informal check out.
2 *students were examined after a year* **test,** quiz, question; assess, appraise.
3 Law *name the witnesses to be examined* **interrogate,** question, quiz, cross-examine; catechize, give the third degree to, probe, sound out; informal grill, pump.

example ▶ **noun 1** *a fine example of Chinese porcelain* **specimen,** sample, exemplar, exemplification, instance, case, illustration, case in point.
2 *we must follow their example* **precedent,** lead, model, pattern, exemplar, ideal, standard, template, paradigm; role model, object lesson. See note at **MODEL**.
3 *he was hanged as an example to others* **warning,** caution, lesson, deterrent, admonition; moral.
– PHRASES **for example** *why not, for example, assemble art from studio clutter?* **for instance,** e.g., by way of illustration, such as, as, like; in particular, case in point, namely, viz., to wit.

exasperate ▶ **verb** *her bratty children exasperate their teachers* **infuriate,** incense, anger, annoy, irritate, madden, enrage, antagonize, provoke, irk, vex, get on someone's nerves, ruffle someone's feathers, rub the wrong way; informal aggravate, rile, bug, needle, get someone's back up, get someone's goat, tee off, tick off.
ANTONYMS please.

exasperation ▶ **noun** *she provoked exasperation among her colleagues* **irritation,** annoyance, vexation, anger, fury, rage, ill humor, crossness, testiness, tetchiness; disgruntlement, discontent, displeasure, chagrin; informal aggravation.

excavate ▶ **verb 1** *she excavated a narrow tunnel* **dig,** dig out, bore, hollow out, scoop out; burrow, tunnel, sink, gouge.
2 *numerous artifacts have been excavated* **unearth,** dig up, uncover, reveal; disinter, exhume.

excavation ▶ **noun 1** *the excavation of a grave* **unearthing,** digging up; disinterment, exhumation.
2 *the excavation of a moat* **digging,** hollowing out, boring, channeling.
3 *implements found in the excavations* **hole,** pit, trench, trough; archaeological site.

exceed ▶ **verb 1** *the cost will exceed $400* **be more than,** be greater than, be over, go beyond, overreach, top.
2 *Brazil exceeds the U.S. in fertile land* **surpass,** outdo, outstrip, outshine, outclass, transcend, top, cap, beat, excel, better, eclipse, overshadow; informal best, leave standing, be head and shoulders above.

exceedingly ▶ **adverb** *an exceedingly comfortable home* **extremely,** exceptionally, especially, tremendously, very, really, truly, awfully, seriously, totally, completely; formal most; informal mega, ultra, real, mighty; archaic exceeding.

excel ▶ **verb 1** *he excelled at football* **shine,** be excellent, be outstanding, be skillful, be talented, be preeminent, reign supreme; stand out, be the best, be unparalleled, be unequaled, be second to none, be unsurpassed.
2 *she excelled him in her work* **surpass,** outdo, outshine, outclass, outstrip, beat, top, transcend, exceed, better, pass, eclipse, overshadow; informal best, be head and shoulders above, be a cut above.

excellence ▶ **noun** *a center of medical excellence* **distinction,** quality, superiority, brilliance, greatness, merit, caliber, eminence, preeminence, supremacy; skill, talent, virtuosity, accomplishment, mastery.

excellent ▶ **adjective** *a cruise ship with excellent accommodations* **very good,** superb, outstanding, exceptional, marvelous, wonderful, magnificent; preeminent, perfect, matchless, unbeatable, peerless, supreme, prime, first-rate, first-class, superlative, splendid, fine, beautiful, exemplary; informal A1, ace, great, terrific, tremendous, fantastic, fabulous, splendiferous, fab, top-notch, dandy, divine, blue-ribbon, blue-chip, bang-up, skookum, class, awesome, magic, wicked, mean, cool, out of this world, hunky-dory, A-OK, brilliant, killer.
ANTONYMS inferior, poor.

except ▶ **preposition** *every day except Monday* **excluding,** not including, excepting, omitting, not counting, but, besides, apart from, aside from, barring, bar, other than, saving; with the exception of, save for; informal outside of.
ANTONYMS including.
▶ **verb** *lawyers are all crooks, present company excepted* **exclude,** omit, leave out, count out, disregard; exempt.
ANTONYMS include.

exception ▶ **noun** *this case is an exception* **anomaly,** irregularity, deviation, special case, isolated example, peculiarity, abnormality, oddity; misfit, aberration; informal freak; bad apple.
– PHRASES **take exception to** *Lydia took exception to their criticism of her husband* **object to,** take offense at, take umbrage at, demur at, disagree with; resent, argue against, protest against, oppose, complain about, shudder at; informal kick up a fuss about, raise a stink about. **with the exception of** *all of the sopranos, with the exception of Dia, will wear black dresses with red sashes* See **EXCEPT** (preposition).

exceptionable ▶ **adjective** formal See **OBJECTIONABLE**.

exceptional ▶ **adjective 1** *the drought was exceptional* **unusual,** uncommon, abnormal, atypical, extraordinary, out of the ordinary, rare, unprecedented, unexpected, surprising; strange, odd, freakish, anomalous, peculiar, weird; informal freaky, something else.
ANTONYMS normal, usual.

2 *her exceptional ability* **outstanding,** extraordinary, remarkable, special, excellent, phenomenal, prodigious; unequaled, unparalleled, unsurpassed, peerless, matchless, nonpareil, first-rate, first-class; informal A1, top-notch.
ANTONYMS average.

excerpt ▶ **noun** *an excerpt from the poem* **extract,** part, section, piece, portion, snippet, clip, bit, sample; reading, citation, quotation, quote, line, passage.
▶ **verb** *a portion of her play was excerpted for the magazine* **quote,** extract, cite.

excess ▶ **noun 1** *an excess of calcium* **surplus,** surfeit, overabundance, superabundance, superfluity, glut.
ANTONYMS lack, dearth.
2 *the excess is turned into fat* **remainder,** rest, residue; leftovers, remnants; surplus, extra, difference.
3 *a life of excess* **overindulgence,** intemperance, immoderation, profligacy, lavishness, extravagance, decadence, self-indulgence.
ANTONYMS moderation, restraint.
▶ **adjective** *excess skin oils* **surplus,** superfluous, redundant, unwanted, unneeded, excessive; extra.
– PHRASES **in excess of** *the book sold in excess of 10,000 copies* **more than,** over, above, upwards of, beyond.

excessive ▶ **adjective 1** *excessive alcohol consumption* **immoderate,** intemperate, imprudent, overindulgent, unrestrained, uncontrolled, lavish, extravagant; superfluous.
2 *the cost is excessive* **exorbitant,** extortionate, unreasonable, outrageous, undue, uncalled for, extreme, inordinate, unwarranted, disproportionate, too much, de trop; informal over the top.

excessively ▶ **adverb** *her father had excessively high standards* **inordinately,** unduly, unnecessarily, unreasonably, ridiculously, overly; very, extremely, exceedingly, exceptionally, impossibly; immoderately, intemperately; ad nauseam.

exchange ▶ **noun 1** *the exchange of ideas* **interchange,** trade, trading, swapping, traffic, trafficking.
2 *a broker on the exchange* **stock exchange,** money market; bourse.
3 *an acrimonious exchange* **conversation,** dialogue, talk, discussion, chat; debate, argument, altercation, row; formal confabulation, colloquy.
▶ **verb** *we exchanged shirts* **trade,** swap, switch, change, interchange.
– PHRASES **exchange blows** *they exchanged blows out in the parking lot* **fight,** brawl, scuffle, tussle; informal scrap, have a set-to. **exchange words** *the children would tearfully listen from upstairs when their parents exchanged words* **argue,** quarrel, squabble, have an argument, have a disagreement.

excise[1] ▶ **noun** *the excise on liquor* **duty,** tax, levy, tariff.

excise[2] ▶ **verb 1** *the tumors were excised* **cut out/off/away,** take out, extract, remove; technical resect.
2 *all unnecessary detail should be excised* **delete,** cross out/through, strike out, score out, cancel, put a line through; erase, scratch; informal ditch, nix, kill; Printing dele.

excitable ▶ **adjective** *the horses are very excitable* **temperamental,** mercurial, volatile, emotional, sensitive, high-strung, unstable, nervous, tense, edgy, jumpy, twitchy, uneasy, neurotic; informal uptight, wired.
ANTONYMS placid.

excite ▶ **verb 1** *the prospect of a vacation excited me* **thrill,** exhilarate, animate, enliven, rouse, stir, stimulate, galvanize, electrify, inspirit; informal buck up, pep up, give someone a buzz, give someone a kick, give someone a charge.
ANTONYMS bore, depress.
2 *she wore a chiffon nightgown to excite him* **arouse,** arouse sexually, stimulate, titillate, inflame; informal turn someone on, get someone going.
ANTONYMS turn off.
3 *his clothes excited envy* **provoke,** stir up, rouse, arouse, kindle, trigger (off), spark (off), incite, cause; literary enkindle.

excited ▶ **adjective 1** *they were excited about the prospect* **thrilled,** exhilarated, animated, enlivened, electrified; enraptured, intoxicated, feverish, adrenalized, enthusiastic; informal high, high as a kite, fired up, aflutter, psyched.
2 *excited lovers* **aroused,** sexually aroused, stimulated, titillated, inflamed; informal turned on, hot, horny, sexed up.

excitement ▶ **noun 1** *the excitement of seeing a leopard in the wild* **thrill,** pleasure, delight, joy; informal kick, buzz, charge, high.
2 *excitement in her eyes* **exhilaration,** elation, animation, enthusiasm, eagerness, anticipation, feverishness; informal pep, vim, zing.
3 *their excitement was mutual* **arousal,** sexual arousal, passion, stimulation, titillation.

exciting ▶ **adjective 1** *an exciting story* **thrilling,** exhilarating, action-packed, stirring, rousing, stimulating, intoxicating, electrifying, invigorating; gripping, compelling, powerful, dramatic.
2 *an exciting encounter with her lover* **arousing,** sexually arousing, stimulating, sexually stimulating, titillating, erotic, sexual, sexy; informal raunchy, steamy.

exclaim ▶ **verb** *"Well, I never!" she exclaimed* **cry out,** cry, declare, blurt out; call, call out, shout, yell; dated ejaculate.

exclamation ▶ **noun** *an exclamation of amazement* **cry,** call, shout, yell, interjection.

exclude ▶ **verb 1** *women were excluded from many scientific societies* **keep out,** deny access to, shut out, debar, disbar, bar, ban, prohibit, ostracized.
ANTONYMS admit, accept.
2 *the clause excluded any judicial review* **eliminate,** rule out, preclude, foreclose; formal except.
ANTONYMS allow for.
3 *the price excludes postage* **be exclusive of,** not include.
ANTONYMS include.
4 *he excluded his own name from the list* **leave**

out/off, omit, miss out.
ANTONYMS include.

exclusive ▶ adjective 1 *an exclusive club* **select,** chic, high-class, elite, fashionable, stylish, elegant, premier, grade A; expensive, upscale, upmarket, high-toned; informal posh, ritzy, classy, tony.
2 *a room for your exclusive use* **sole,** unshared, unique, only, individual, personal, private.
ANTONYMS partial.
3 *prices **exclusive of** sales tax* **not including,** excluding, leaving out, omitting, excepting.
ANTONYMS inclusive.
4 *mutually exclusive alternatives* **incompatible,** irreconcilable.
▶ noun *a six-page exclusive* **scoop,** exposé, special.

excoriate ▶ verb 1 Medicine *the skin had been excoriated* **abrade,** rub away, rub raw, scrape, scratch, chafe; strip away, skin.
2 formal *he was excoriated in the press* See CRITICIZE.

excrement ▶ noun *cleaning up the ferrets' excrement* **feces,** excreta, stools, droppings; waste matter, ordure, dung; informal poop, poo, dirt, turds, caca.

excrescence ▶ noun 1 *an excrescence on his leg* **growth,** lump, swelling, nodule, outgrowth.
2 *the new buildings were an excrescence* **eyesore,** blot on the landscape, monstrosity.

excrete ▶ verb *waste products are excreted from the body* **expel,** pass, void, discharge, eject, evacuate; defecate, urinate.
ANTONYMS ingest.

excruciating ▶ adjective *excruciating pain* **agonizing,** severe, acute, intense, violent, racking, searing, piercing, stabbing, raging; unbearable, unendurable; informal splitting, killing.

excursion ▶ noun *a lovely excursion to Nassau* **trip,** outing, jaunt, expedition, journey, tour; day trip, day out, side trip, drive, run, ride; informal junket, spin, sortie. See note at JOURNEY.

excusable ▶ adjective *it's an excusable mistake* **forgivable,** pardonable, defensible, justifiable; venial.
ANTONYMS unforgivable.

excuse ▶ verb 1 *eventually she excused him* **forgive,** pardon, absolve, exonerate, acquit; informal let someone off (the hook); formal exculpate.
ANTONYMS punish, blame.
2 *such conduct can never be excused* **justify,** defend, condone, vindicate; forgive, overlook, disregard, ignore, tolerate, sanction.
ANTONYMS condemn.
3 *she has been excused from her duties* **let off,** release, relieve, exempt, absolve, free.
▶ noun 1 *that's no excuse for stealing* **justification,** defense, reason, explanation, mitigating circumstances, mitigation, vindication.
2 *an excuse to get away* **pretext,** ostensible reason, pretense; informal story, alibi.
3 informal *that pathetic **excuse for a man!*** **travesty of,** poor specimen of; informal apology for.

execrable ▶ adjective *an execrable piece of work* **appalling,** atrocious, lamentable, egregious, awful, dreadful, terrible; disgusting, deplorable, disgraceful, frightful, reprehensible, abhorrent, loathsome, odious, hateful, vile, abysmal, lousy, godawful.
ANTONYMS admirable.

execute ▶ verb 1 *he was convicted and executed* **put to death,** kill; hang, behead, guillotine, electrocute, send to the (electric) chair, shoot, put before a firing squad; informal string up, fry. See note at KILL.
2 *the corporation executed a series of financial deals* **carry out,** accomplish, bring off/about, achieve, complete, engineer, conduct; informal pull off; formal effectuate.
3 *a well-executed act* **perform,** present, render; stage.

execution ▶ noun 1 *the execution of the plan* **implementation,** carrying out, accomplishment, bringing off/about, engineering, attainment, realization.
2 *the execution of the play* **performance,** presentation, rendition, rendering, staging.
3 *thousands were sentenced to execution* **capital punishment,** the death penalty; the gibbet, the gallows, the noose, the rope, the scaffold, the guillotine, the firing squad, the electric chair, the chair.

executioner ▶ noun *today he meets his executioner* **hangman**; historical headsman.

executive ▶ adjective *executive powers* **administrative,** decision-making, managerial; lawmaking.
▶ noun 1 *top-level bank executives* **chief,** head, director, senior official, senior manager, CEO, chief executive officer; informal boss, exec, suit, big cheese.
2 *the executive has increased in number* **administration,** management, directorate; government, legislative body.

exegesis ▶ noun *the exegesis of ancient texts* **interpretation,** explanation, exposition, explication.

exemplar ▶ noun *Luciano is an exemplar of decorum* **epitome,** perfect example, paragon, ideal, exemplification, textbook example, embodiment, essence, quintessence; paradigm, model, role model, template.

exemplary ▶ adjective 1 *her exemplary behavior* **perfect,** ideal, model, faultless, flawless, impeccable, irreproachable; excellent, outstanding, admirable, commendable, laudable, above/beyond reproach; textbook.
ANTONYMS deplorable.
2 *exemplary jail sentences* **deterrent,** cautionary, warning, admonitory; rare monitory.
3 *her works are exemplary of cutting-edge feminism* **representative,** illustrative, characteristic, typical.

exemplify ▶ verb 1 *this story exemplifies current trends* **typify,** epitomize, be a typical example of, represent, be representative of, symbolize.
2 *he exemplified his point with an anecdote* **illustrate,** give an example of, demonstrate.

exempt ▶ adjective *they are **exempt from** all charges* **free from,** not liable to, not subject to, exempted from, excepted from, excused of/from, absolved of.

ANTONYMS subject to.
▶ verb *he had been exempted from military service* **excuse,** free, release, exclude from, give/grant immunity, spare, absolve from; informal let off (the hook), grandfather. See note at ABSOLVE.

exemption ▶ noun *exemption from the road tax* **immunity,** exception, dispensation, indemnity, exclusion, freedom, release, relief, absolution.

exercise ▶ noun 1 *exercise improves your heart* **physical activity,** a workout, working out; gymnastics, sports, games, physical education, physical training, aerobics, body conditioning, calisthenics; informal phys ed.
2 *here are some French translation exercises* **task,** piece of work, problem, assignment, activity; Music étude.
3 *the exercise of professional skill* **use,** utilization, employment; practice, application.
4 (**exercises**) *military exercises* **maneuvers,** operations; war games.
▶ verb 1 *she exercised every day* **work out,** do exercises, train; informal pump iron.
2 *he must learn to exercise patience* **use,** employ, make use of, utilize; practice, apply.

exert ▶ verb 1 *he exerted considerable pressure on me* **bring to bear,** apply, exercise, employ, use, utilize, deploy.
2 *Geoff had been* ***exerting himself*** **strive,** try hard, make an/every effort, endeavor, do one's best, do one's utmost, give one's all, push oneself, drive oneself, work hard; informal go all out, pull out all the stops, bend/lean over backwards, do one's damnedest, do one's darnedest, move heaven and earth, bust one's chops.

exertion ▶ noun 1 *she was panting with exertion* **effort,** strain, struggle, toil, endeavor, hard work, labor; literary travail.
2 *the exertion of pressure* **use,** application, exercise, employment, utilization.

exhaust ▶ verb 1 *the effort had exhausted him* **tire out,** wear out, overtire, fatigue, weary, tire, drain, run someone into the ground; informal do in, take it out of one, wipe out, knock out, burn out, poop, tucker out.
ANTONYMS invigorate, refresh.
2 *the country has exhausted its reserves* **use up,** run through, go through, consume, finish, deplete, spend, empty, drain, run out of; informal blow.
ANTONYMS replenish.
3 *we've exhausted the subject* **treat thoroughly,** say all there is to say about, do to death, overwork.

exhausted ▶ adjective 1 *I worked until I was exhausted* **tired out,** worn out, weary, dead-tired, dog-tired, bone-tired, ready to drop, drained, fatigued, enervated; informal beat, done in, all in, bushed, zonked, bagged, knocked out, wiped out, burned out, pooped, tuckered out, tapped out, fried, whipped. See note at TIRED.
2 *exhausted reserves* **used up,** consumed, finished, spent, depleted; empty, drained.

exhausting ▶ adjective *an exhausting day of moving furniture* **tiring,** wearying, taxing, fatiguing, wearing, enervating, draining; arduous, strenuous, onerous, demanding, grueling; informal killing, murderous.

exhaustion ▶ noun 1 *sheer exhaustion forced Mona to give up* **extreme tiredness,** overtiredness, fatigue, weariness, burnout.
2 *the exhaustion of fuel reserves* **consumption,** depletion, using up, expenditure; draining, emptying.

exhaustive ▶ adjective *an exhaustive study of Icelandic history* **comprehensive,** all-inclusive, complete, full, full-scale, encyclopedic, sweeping, thorough, in-depth; detailed, meticulous, painstaking.
ANTONYMS perfunctory.

exhibit ▶ verb 1 *the paintings were exhibited at the Wadsworth* **put on display/show,** display, show, put on public view, showcase; set out, lay out, array, arrange.
2 *Luke exhibited signs of jealousy* **show,** reveal, display, manifest; express, indicate, demonstrate, present; formal evince.
▶ noun 1 *exhibit A is a handwritten letter* **object,** item, piece, showpiece; display; evidence.
2 *people flocked to the exhibit* See EXHIBITION (sense 1).

exhibition ▶ noun 1 *an exhibition of Inuit sculpture* **(public) display,** show, showing, presentation, demonstration, exposition, showcase, exhibit.
2 *a convincing exhibition of concern* **display,** show, demonstration, manifestation, expression.

exhilarate ▶ verb *the fireworks display exhilarated us* **thrill,** excite, intoxicate, elate, delight, enliven, animate, invigorate, energize, vitalize, stimulate; informal give someone a thrill, give someone a buzz, give someone a charge.

exhilaration ▶ noun *a feeling of exhilaration* **elation,** euphoria, exultation, exaltation, joy, happiness, delight, joyousness, jubilation, rapture, ecstasy, bliss.

exhort ▶ verb *the president exhorted state legislatures to beef up educational standards and help put welfare recipients to work* **urge,** encourage, call on, enjoin, charge, press; bid, appeal to, entreat, implore, beg; formal adjure; literary beseech. See note at INCITE.

exhortation ▶ noun 1 *no amount of exhortation had any effect* **urging,** encouragement, persuasion, pressure; warning.
2 *the government's exhortations to voters* **entreaty,** appeal, call, charge, injunction; admonition, warning.

exhume ▶ verb *the district attorney is requesting that Baker's body be exhumed* **disinter,** dig up, unearth.
ANTONYMS bury.

exigency ▶ noun 1 *the exigencies of the continuing war* **need,** demand, requirement, necessity.
2 *financial exigency* **urgency,** crisis, difficulty, pressure.

exiguous ▶ adjective formal *Bob Cratchit's exiguous wages* **meager,** inadequate, insufficient, small, scanty, paltry, negligible, modest, deficient, miserly, niggardly, beggarly; informal measly, stingy, piddling.
ANTONYMS ample, generous.

exile ▶ noun 1 *his exile from the land of his*

birth **banishment,** expulsion, expatriation, deportation.
2 *political exiles* **émigré,** expatriate; displaced person, refugee, deportee; informal expat; historical DP.
▶ verb *he was exiled from his country* **expel,** banish, expatriate, deport, drive out, throw out, outlaw.

exist ▶ verb 1 *animals existing in the distant past* **live,** be alive, be living; be; happen.
2 *the liberal climate that existed during his presidency* **prevail,** occur, be found, be in existence; be the case.
3 *she had to exist on a low income* **survive,** subsist, live, support oneself; manage, make do, get by, scrape by, make ends meet.

existence ▶ noun 1 *the industry's continued existence* **actuality,** being, existing, reality; survival, continuation.
2 *her suburban existence* **way of life,** way of living, life, lifestyle.
– PHRASES **in existence** *there are millions of unidentified species in existence* See EXISTENT.

existent ▶ adjective *species that are no longer existent* **in existence,** alive, existing, living, extant; surviving, remaining, undestroyed.

exit ▶ noun 1 *the fire exit* **way out,** door, egress, escape route; doorway, gate, gateway, portal.
ANTONYMS entrance.
2 *take the second exit* **turning,** turnoff, turn, junction.
3 *his sudden exit* **departure,** leaving, withdrawal, going, decamping, retreat; flight, exodus, escape.
ANTONYMS arrival.
▶ verb *the doctor had just exited* **leave,** go (out), depart, withdraw, retreat.
ANTONYMS enter.

exodus ▶ noun *the exodus of refugees from Albania* **mass departure,** withdrawal, evacuation, leaving; migration, emigration; flight, escape, fleeing.

exonerate ▶ verb 1 *the inquiry exonerated them* **absolve,** clear, acquit, find innocent, discharge; formal exculpate. See note at ABSOLVE.
ANTONYMS charge, convict.
2 *Pope Clement V exonerated the king from his oath* **release,** discharge, free, liberate; excuse, exempt, except, dispense; informal let off.
ANTONYMS hold to.

exorbitant ▶ adjective *exorbitant interest rates* **extortionate,** excessively high, excessive, prohibitive, outrageous, unreasonable, inflated, unconscionable, huge, enormous; informal steep, stiff, sky-high, over the top, rip-off.
ANTONYMS reasonable.

exotic ▶ adjective 1 *exotic birds* **foreign,** nonnative, tropical; introduced, imported.
ANTONYMS native.
2 *exotic places* **foreign,** faraway, far-off, far-flung, distant.
ANTONYMS familiar, nearby.
3 *Carlotta's exotic appearance* **striking,** colorful, eye-catching, flamboyant; unusual, unconventional, out of the ordinary, foreign-looking, extravagant, outlandish, orchidaceous; informal offbeat, off the wall.
ANTONYMS conventional.

expand ▶ verb 1 *metals expand when heated* **increase in size,** become larger, enlarge; swell, dilate, inflate; lengthen, stretch, thicken, fill out.
ANTONYMS shrink, contract.
2 *the company is expanding* **grow,** become/make larger, become/make bigger, increase in size, increase in scope, upsize; extend, augment, broaden, widen, develop, diversify, build up; branch out, spread, proliferate.
ANTONYMS shrink, scale down.
3 *the senator* ***expanded on*** *the proposals* **elaborate on,** enlarge on, go into detail about, flesh out, develop, expatiate on.
4 *she learned to expand and flourish among new acquaintances* **relax,** unbend, become relaxed, grow friendlier, loosen up.
ANTONYMS tense up, clam up.

expanse ▶ noun *an expanse of wheat and barley* **area,** stretch, sweep, tract, swathe, belt, region; sea, carpet, blanket, sheet.

expansion ▶ noun 1 *expansion and contraction of blood vessels* **enlargement,** increase in size, swelling, dilation; lengthening, elongation, stretching, thickening.
ANTONYMS contraction.
2 *the expansion of the company* **growth,** increase in size, enlargement, extension, development; spread, proliferation, multiplication.
ANTONYMS reduction in size.
3 *an expansion of a lecture given last year* **elaboration,** enlargement, amplification, development.
ANTONYMS abridgment, summary.

expansive ▶ adjective 1 *expansive grassland* **extensive,** sweeping, rolling.
2 *expansive coverage* **wide-ranging,** extensive, broad, wide, comprehensive, thorough, full-scale.
3 *Bethany became engagingly expansive* **communicative,** forthcoming, sociable, friendly, outgoing, affable, chatty, talkative, garrulous, effusive, loquacious, voluble.

expatiate ▶ verb *he expatiated on the topic of volunteerism* **speak/write at length,** go into detail, expound, dwell, dilate, expand, enlarge, elaborate; formal perorate.

expatriate ▶ noun *expatriates working overseas* **emigrant,** nonnative, émigré, migrant; informal expat.
ANTONYMS national.
▶ adjective *expatriate workers* **emigrant,** living abroad, nonnative, foreign, émigré; informal expat.
ANTONYMS indigenous, native.
▶ verb *he was expatriated* **exile,** deport, banish, expel.
ANTONYMS repatriate.

expect ▶ verb 1 *I expect she'll be late* **suppose,** presume, think, believe, imagine, assume, surmise; informal guess, reckon, figure.
2 *a 10 percent rise was expected* **anticipate,** await, look for, hope for, look forward to; contemplate, bargain for/on, bank on; predict, forecast, envisage, envision.
3 *we expect total loyalty* **require,** ask for, call

for, want, insist on, demand.

expectancy ▶ noun 1 *feverish expectancy* **anticipation,** expectation, eagerness, excitement.
2 *life expectancy* **likelihood,** probability, outlook, prospect.

expectant ▶ adjective 1 *expectant fans* **eager,** excited, psyched, agog, waiting with bated breath, hopeful; in suspense, on tenterhooks.
2 *an expectant mother* **pregnant**; informal expecting, with a bun in the oven; chiefly Brit. informal preggers; technical gravid; dated in the family way; archaic with child.

expectation ▶ noun 1 *her expectations were unrealistic* **supposition,** assumption, presumption, conjecture, surmise, calculation, prediction, hope.
2 *tense with expectation* **anticipation,** expectancy, eagerness, excitement, suspense.

expecting ▶ adjective informal See EXPECTANT (sense 2).

expedient ▶ adjective *a politically expedient strategy* **convenient,** advantageous, in one's own interests, useful, of use, beneficial, of benefit, helpful; practical, pragmatic, politic, prudent, wise, judicious, sensible.
▶ noun *a temporary expedient* **measure,** means, method, stratagem, scheme, plan, move, tactic, maneuver, device, contrivance, ploy, machination, dodge.

expedite ▶ verb *our legal assistants can help expedite the paperwork* **speed up,** accelerate, hurry, hasten, step up, quicken, precipitate, dispatch; advance, facilitate, ease, make easier, further, promote, aid, push through, urge on, boost, stimulate, spur on, help along, catalyze, fast-track.
ANTONYMS delay.

expedition ▶ noun 1 *an expedition to the South Pole* **journey,** voyage, tour, odyssey; exploration, safari, trek, hike. See note at JOURNEY.
2 informal *a shopping expedition* **trip,** excursion, outing, jaunt.
3 *all members of the expedition* **group,** team, party, crew, band, squad.

expeditious ▶ adjective *an expeditious review* **speedy,** swift, quick, rapid, fast, brisk, efficient; prompt, punctual, immediate, instant; literary fleet.
ANTONYMS slow.

expel ▶ verb 1 *the opposition leader was expelled from her party* **throw out,** eject, bar, ban, debar, drum out, oust, remove, get rid of, dismiss; Military cashier; informal chuck out, sling out, kick out, boot out, give someone the bum's rush. See note at EJECT.
ANTONYMS admit.
2 *he was expelled from the country* **banish,** exile, deport, evict, expatriate, drive out, throw out.
3 *Dolly expelled a hiss* **let out,** discharge, eject, issue, send forth.

expend ▶ verb 1 *they had already expended $75,000* **spend,** pay out, disburse, dole out, get through, waste, fritter (away), dissipate; informal fork out, dish out, shell out, lay out, cough up, blow, splurge, ante up.
ANTONYMS save, conserve.
2 *children expend a lot of energy* **use up,** use, utilize, consume, eat up, deplete, get through, burn through.
ANTONYMS conserve.

expendable ▶ adjective 1 *an accountant decided Mathers was expendable* **dispensable,** replaceable, nonessential, inessential, unnecessary, noncore, unneeded, not required, superfluous, disposable.
ANTONYMS indispensable, essential.
2 *an expendable satellite launcher* **disposable,** throwaway, single-use.

expenditure ▶ noun 1 *the expenditure of funds* **spending,** paying out, outlay, use, disbursement, doling out, waste, wasting, frittering (away), dissipation.
ANTONYMS saving, conservation.
2 *reducing public expenditure* **costs,** spending, payments, expenses, overheads.
ANTONYMS income.

expense ▶ noun 1 *the expense of entertaining* **cost,** price, charge, outlay, fee, tariff, levy, payment; informal humorous damage.
2 (**expenses**) *regular expenses* **overhead,** costs, outlay, expenditure(s), charges, bills, payment(s); incidentals.
3 *tax cuts come at the expense of social programs* **sacrifice,** cost, loss.

expensive ▶ adjective *an expensive meal* **costly,** high-priced, dear; overpriced, exorbitant, extortionate; informal steep, pricey, costing an arm and a leg, big-ticket, costing the earth.
ANTONYMS cheap, economical.

experience ▶ noun 1 *qualifications and experience* **skill,** knowledge, practical knowledge, understanding; background, record, history; maturity, worldliness, sophistication; informal know-how.
2 *an enjoyable experience* **incident,** occurrence, event, happening, episode; adventure, exploit, escapade.
3 *his first **experience of** business* **involvement in,** participation in, contact with, acquaintance with, exposure to, observation of, awareness of, insight into.
▶ verb *some policemen experience harassment* **undergo,** encounter, meet, come into contact with, come across, come up against, face, be faced with.

experienced ▶ adjective 1 *an experienced pilot* **knowledgeable,** skillful, skilled, expert, accomplished, adept, adroit, master, consummate; proficient, trained, competent, capable, well trained, well versed; seasoned, practiced, mature, veteran.
ANTONYMS novice.
2 *she deluded herself that she was experienced* **worldly wise,** worldly, sophisticated, suave, urbane, mature, knowing; informal streetwise, street smart.
ANTONYMS naive.

experiment ▶ noun 1 *carrying out experiments* **test,** investigation, trial, examination, observation; assessment, evaluation, appraisal, analysis, study.
2 *these results have been established by experiment* **research,** experimentation,

observation, analysis, testing.
▶ verb *they experimented with new ideas* **conduct experiments,** carry out trials/tests, conduct research; test, trial, do tests on, try out, assess, appraise, evaluate.

experimental ▶ adjective **1** *the experimental stage* **exploratory,** investigational, trial, test, pilot; speculative, conjectural, hypothetical, tentative, preliminary, untested, untried.
2 *experimental music* **innovative,** innovatory, new, original, radical, avant-garde, cutting-edge, alternative, unorthodox, unconventional; informal way-out.

expert ▶ noun *she is an art expert* **specialist,** authority, pundit; adept, maestro, virtuoso, master, past master, wizard; connoisseur, aficionado; informal ace, buff, pro, techie, whiz, hotshot, maven, crackerjack.
▶ adjective *an expert chess player* **skillful,** skilled, adept, accomplished, talented, fine; master, masterly, brilliant, virtuoso, magnificent, outstanding, great, exceptional, excellent, first-class, first-rate, superb; proficient, good, able, capable, experienced, practiced, knowledgeable; informal ace, crack, mean.
ANTONYMS incompetent.

expertise ▶ noun *a high level of expertise in psychiatry is required* **skill,** skillfulness, expertness, prowess, proficiency, competence; knowledge, mastery, ability, aptitude, facility, capability; informal know-how.

expiate ▶ verb *the desire to expiate his sins* **atone for,** make amends for, make up for, do penance for, pay for, redress, redeem, offset, make good.

expire ▶ verb **1** *my contract has expired* **run out,** become invalid, become void, lapse; **end,** finish, stop, come to an end, terminate.
2 *the spot where he expired* **die,** pass away/on, breathe one's last; informal kick the bucket, bite the dust, croak, buy it, buy the farm; dated depart this life.
3 technical *the breath is then expired* **breathe out,** exhale, blow out, expel.

explain ▶ verb **1** *a technician explained the procedure* **describe,** give an explanation of, make clear, make intelligible, spell out, put into words; elucidate, expound, explicate, clarify, throw/shed light on; gloss, interpret. See note at CLARIFY.
2 *nothing could explain his newfound wealth* **account for,** give an explanation for, give a reason for; justify, give a justification for, give an excuse for, vindicate, legitimize.

explanation ▶ noun **1** *an explanation of the ideas contained in the essay* **clarification,** simplification; description, report, statement; elucidation, exposition, expounding, explication; gloss, interpretation, commentary, exegesis.
2 *I owe you an explanation* **account,** reason; justification, excuse, alibi, defense, vindication, story, answers.

explanatory ▶ adjective *write two or three explanatory paragraphs* **explaining,** descriptive, describing, illustrative, interpretive, instructive, expository.

expletive ▶ noun *she let out an expletive and slammed the phone down* **swear word,** obscenity, profanity, oath, curse, four-letter word, dirty word; informal cuss word, cuss; formal imprecation; (**expletives**) bad language, foul language, strong language, swearing.

explicable ▶ adjective *it is our understanding of history that makes the present more explicable* **explainable,** understandable, comprehensible, accountable, intelligible, interpretable.

explicate ▶ verb *I'm not sure anyone could fully explicate the works of Joyce* **explain,** make explicit, clarify, make plain/clear, spell out, untangle; interpret, translate, elucidate, expound, illuminate, throw light on. See note at CLARIFY.

explicit ▶ adjective **1** *explicit instructions* **clear,** plain, straightforward, crystal clear, easily understandable; precise, exact, specific, unequivocal, unambiguous; detailed, comprehensive, exhaustive.
ANTONYMS vague.
2 *sexually explicit material* **graphic,** uncensored, candid, full-frontal, hard-core.

explode ▶ verb **1** *a bomb has exploded* **blow up,** detonate, go off, burst (apart), fly apart, erupt.
2 *exploding the first atomic device* **detonate,** set off, let off, discharge.
ANTONYMS disarm, defuse.
3 *he exploded in anger* **lose one's temper,** blow up, get angry, become enraged, get mad; informal fly off the handle, hit the roof, blow one's cool/top/stack, go wild, go bananas, go ballistic, see red, go off the deep end, go crackers, go postal.
4 *the city's population is exploding* **increase suddenly/rapidly,** mushroom, snowball, escalate, multiply, burgeon, rocket, skyrocket.
5 *exploding the myths about men* **disprove,** refute, invalidate, negate, discredit, debunk, dispel, belie, give the lie to; informal poke holes in, blow out of the water; formal confute.
ANTONYMS confirm.

exploit ▶ verb **1** *we should exploit this new technology* **utilize,** harness, use, make use of, turn/put to good use, make the most of, capitalize on, benefit from; informal cash in on.
2 *exploiting the workers* **take advantage of,** abuse, impose on, treat unfairly, misuse, ill-treat; informal walk (all) over, take for a ride, rip off.
▶ noun *his exploits brought him notoriety* **feat,** deed, act, adventure, stunt, escapade; achievement, accomplishment, attainment; informal lark, caper.

exploration ▶ noun **1** *the exploration of space* **investigation,** study, survey, research, inspection, examination, scrutiny, observation; consideration, analysis, review.
2 *explorations into the mountains* **expedition,** trip, journey, voyage; archaic peregrination; (**explorations**) travels.

exploratory ▶ adjective *exploratory surgery* **investigative,** investigational, explorative, probing, fact-finding; experimental, trial, tentative, test, preliminary, provisional.

explore ▶ verb **1** *they explored all the possibilities* **investigate,** look into, consider; examine,

research, survey, scrutinize, study, review, go over with a fine-tooth comb; informal check out.
2 *a rare chance to explore the Galapagos Islands* **travel over/in/through,** tour, range over; survey, take a look at, inspect, investigate, reconnoiter, wander through.

explorer ▶ **noun** *the street is named after Peary, the Arctic explorer* **traveler,** discoverer, voyager, adventurer; surveyor, scout, prospector.

explosion ▶ **noun 1** *Edward heard the explosion* **detonation,** eruption, blowing up; bang, blast, boom, kaboom.
2 *an explosion of anger* **outburst,** flare-up, outbreak, eruption, storm, rush, surge; fit, paroxysm, attack.
3 *the explosion of human populations* **sudden/rapid increase,** mushrooming, snowballing, escalation, multiplication, burgeoning, rocketing, skyrocketing.

explosive ▶ **adjective 1** *explosive gases* **volatile,** inflammable, flammable, combustible, incendiary.
2 *Biff's explosive temper* **fiery,** stormy, violent, volatile, angry, passionate, tempestuous, turbulent, touchy, irascible, hotheaded, short-tempered.
3 *an explosive situation* **tense,** charged, highly charged, overwrought; dangerous, perilous, hazardous, sensitive, delicate, unstable, volatile.
4 *explosive population growth* **sudden,** dramatic, rapid; mushrooming, snowballing, escalating, rocketing, skyrocketing, accelerating.
▶ **noun** *stocks of explosives* **bomb,** incendiary (device).

exponent ▶ **noun** *the new premier is an exponent of free trade* **advocate,** supporter, proponent, upholder, backer, defender, champion; promoter, propagandist, campaigner, fighter, crusader, enthusiast, apologist; informal cheerleader, booster.
ANTONYMS critic, opponent.

export ▶ **verb 1** *exporting raw materials* **sell overseas/abroad,** send overseas/abroad, ship overseas/abroad, market overseas/abroad, trade internationally.
ANTONYMS import.
2 *she is trying to export her ideas to Japan* **transmit,** spread, disseminate, circulate, communicate, pass on; literary bruit about/abroad.

expose ▶ **verb 1** *at low tide, the sands are exposed* **reveal,** uncover, lay bare.
ANTONYMS cover.
2 *he was* **exposed to** *asbestos* **make vulnerable to,** subject to, lay open to, put at risk of/from, put in jeopardy of/from.
ANTONYMS protect.
3 *they were* **exposed to** *liberal ideas* **introduce to,** bring into contact with, make aware of, familiarize with, acquaint with.
ANTONYMS keep away.
4 *he was exposed as a liar* **uncover,** reveal, unveil, unmask, detect, find out; discover, bring to light, bring into the open, make known; denounce, condemn; informal spill the beans on, blow the whistle on.

exposed ▶ **adjective** *an exposed hillside* **unprotected,** unsheltered, open to the elements/weather; vulnerable, defenseless, undefended.
ANTONYMS sheltered.

exposition ▶ **noun 1** *a lucid exposition* **explanation,** description, elucidation, explication, interpretation; account, commentary, appraisal, assessment, discussion, exegesis.
2 *the exposition will feature 200 exhibits* **exhibition,** fair, trade fair, trade show, show, expo, display, presentation, demonstration, exhibit.

expository ▶ **adjective** *expository dialogue* **explanatory,** descriptive, describing, explicatory, explicative, interpretative, exegetical.

expostulate ▶ **verb** *Jim* **expostulated with** *the teacher's opinion to no avail* **remonstrate with,** disagree with, argue with, take issue with, protest against, reason against, express disagreement with, raise objections to, rail against.

exposure ▶ **noun 1** *the exposure of the lizard's vivid blue tongue* **revealing,** revelation, uncovering, baring, laying bare.
2 *exposure to harmful chemicals* **subjection,** vulnerability, laying open.
3 *suffering from exposure* **hypothermia,** cold, frostbite.
4 ***exposure to*** *great literature* **introduction to,** experience of/with, contact with, familiarity with, acquaintance with, awareness of.
5 *the exposure of a banking scandal* **uncovering,** revelation, disclosure, unveiling, unmasking, discovery, detection; denunciation, condemnation.
6 *we're getting a lot of exposure* **publicity,** coverage, publicizing, advertising, public interest/attention, media interest/attention, ink; informal hype, face time.
7 *a southern exposure* **outlook,** aspect, view; position, setting, location.

expound ▶ **verb 1** *he expounded his theories* **present,** put forward, set forth, propose, propound; explain, give an explanation of, detail, spell out, describe.
2 *a treatise expounding Chomsky's theories* **explain,** interpret, explicate, elucidate; comment on, give a commentary on.
– PHRASES **expound on** *he expounded on the virtues of books* **elaborate on,** expand on, expatiate on, discuss at length.

express[1] ▶ **verb 1** *community leaders expressed their anger* **communicate,** convey, indicate, show, demonstrate, reveal, make manifest, put across/over, get across/over; articulate, put into words, utter, voice, give voice to; state, assert, proclaim, profess, air, make public, give vent to; formal evince.
2 *all the juice is expressed* **squeeze out,** press out, extract.
– PHRASES **express oneself** *he had difficulty expressing himself* **communicate one's thoughts/opinions/views,** put thoughts into words, speak one's mind, say what's on one's mind.

express[2] ▶ **adjective** *an express bus* **rapid,** swift,

fast, quick, speedy, high-speed; nonstop, direct.
ANTONYMS slow, local.

expression ▶ noun **1** *the free expression of opposition views* **utterance,** uttering, voicing, pronouncement, declaration, articulation, assertion, setting forth; dissemination, circulation, communication, spreading, promulgation.
2 *an expression of sympathy* **indication,** demonstration, show, exhibition, token; communication, illustration, revelation.
3 *an expression of harassed fatigue* **look,** appearance, air, manner, countenance, mien.
4 *a timeworn expression* **idiom,** phrase, idiomatic expression; proverb, saying, adage, maxim, axiom, aphorism, saw, motto, platitude, cliché.
5 *these pieces are very different in expression* **emotion,** feeling, spirit, passion, intensity; style, intonation, tone.
6 *essential oils obtained by expression* **squeezing,** pressing, extraction, extracting.

expressionless ▶ adjective **1** *his face was expressionless* **inscrutable,** deadpan, poker-faced; blank, vacant, emotionless, unemotional, inexpressive; glazed, stony, wooden, impassive.
ANTONYMS expressive.
2 *a flat, expressionless tone* **dull,** dry, toneless, monotonous, boring, tedious, flat, wooden, unmodulated, unvarying, devoid of feeling/emotion.
ANTONYMS interesting, lively.

expressive ▶ adjective **1** *an expressive shrug* **eloquent,** meaningful, demonstrative, suggestive.
ANTONYMS expressionless.
2 *an expressive song* **emotional,** full of emotion/feeling, passionate, poignant, moving, stirring, evocative, powerful, emotionally charged.
ANTONYMS unemotional.
3 *his diction is very expressive of his upbringing* **indicative,** demonstrative, revealing.

expressly ▶ adverb **1** *he was expressly forbidden to discuss the matter* **explicitly,** clearly, directly, plainly, distinctly, unambiguously, unequivocally; absolutely; specifically, categorically, pointedly, emphatically.
2 *a machine expressly built for spraying paint* **solely,** specifically, particularly, specially, exclusively, just, only, explicitly.

expropriate ▶ verb *legislation to expropriate land from absentee landlords* **seize,** take away, take over, take, appropriate, take possession of, requisition, commandeer, claim, acquire, sequestrate, confiscate; Law distrain.

expulsion ▶ noun **1** *expulsion from the party* **removal,** debarment, dismissal, exclusion, discharge, ejection, drumming out.
ANTONYMS admission.
2 *the expulsion of bodily wastes* **discharge,** ejection, excretion, voiding, evacuation, elimination, passing.

expunge ▶ verb *a moment that cannot be expunged from his memory* **erase,** remove, delete, rub out, wipe out, efface; cross out, strike out, blot out, destroy, obliterate, scratch, eradicate, eliminate, deep-six.

expurgate ▶ verb *a book that had been expurgated for use in schools* **censor,** bowdlerize, blue-pencil, cut, edit; clean up, sanitize, make acceptable, make palatable, water down, tame.

exquisite ▶ adjective **1** *exquisite antique glass* **beautiful,** lovely, elegant, fine; magnificent, superb, excellent, wonderful, ornate, well-crafted, well-made, perfect; delicate, fragile, dainty, subtle.
2 *exquisite taste* **discriminating,** discerning, sensitive, selective, fastidious; refined, cultivated, cultured, educated.
3 *exquisite agony* **intense,** acute, keen, piercing, sharp, severe, racking, excruciating, agonizing, harrowing, searing; unbearable, unendurable.

extant ▶ adjective *extant manuscripts* **still existing,** in existence, existent, surviving, remaining, undestroyed.

extempore ▶ adjective *an extempore speech* **impromptu,** spontaneous, unscripted, ad lib, extemporary, extemporaneous; improvised, unrehearsed, unplanned, unprepared, off the top of one's head; informal off-the-cuff; formal ad libitum.
ANTONYMS rehearsed.
▶ adverb *he was speaking extempore* **spontaneously,** extemporaneously, ad lib, without preparation, without rehearsal, off the top of one's head; informal off the cuff; formal ad libitum.

extemporize ▶ verb *jazz musicians extemporize freely* **improvise,** ad lib, play it by ear, think on one's feet; informal wing it, fly by the seat of one's pants.

extend ▶ verb **1** *he attempted to extend his dominions* **expand,** enlarge, increase, make larger, make bigger; lengthen, widen, broaden.
ANTONYMS reduce, shrink.
2 *the garden extends down to the road* **continue,** carry on, run on, stretch (out), reach, lead.
3 *we have extended our range of services* **widen,** expand, broaden; augment, supplement, increase, add to, enhance, develop.
ANTONYMS narrow.
4 *extending the life of the charter* **prolong,** lengthen, increase; stretch out, protract, spin out, string out.
ANTONYMS shorten.
5 *extend your arms and legs* **stretch out,** spread out, reach out, straighten out.
6 *he extended a hand in greeting* **hold out,** reach out, hold forth; offer, give, outstretch, proffer.
7 *we wish to extend our thanks to Mr. Bayes* **offer,** proffer, give, grant, bestow, accord.
– PHRASES **extend to** *her tolerance did not always extend to her staff* **include,** take in, incorporate, encompass.

extended ▶ adjective *an extended legal battle* **prolonged,** protracted, long-lasting, long-drawn-out, spun out, long, dragged out, strung out, lengthy; informal marathon.

extension ▶ noun **1** *they are planning a new extension* **addition,** adjunct, annex, wing, supplementary building, ell, add-on, bump-out.
2 *an extension of knowledge* **expansion,** increase, enlargement, widening, broadening, deepening; augmentation, enhancement,

development, growth, continuation.
3 *an extension of opening hours* **prolongation,** lengthening, increase.
4 *I need an extension on my essay* **postponement,** more/extra time, deferral, delay.

extensive ▶ adjective **1** *a mansion with extensive grounds* **large,** large-scale, sizable, substantial, considerable, ample, expansive, great, vast.
2 *extensive knowledge* **comprehensive,** thorough, exhaustive; broad, wide, wide-ranging, catholic, eclectic.

extent ▶ noun **1** *two acres in extent* **area,** size, expanse, length; proportions, dimensions.
2 *the full extent of her father's illness* **degree,** scale, level, magnitude, scope; size, breadth, width, reach, range.

extenuating ▶ adjective *a just decision must allow for extenuating circumstances* **mitigating,** excusing, exonerative, palliative, justifying, justificatory, vindicating; formal exculpatory.

exterior ▶ adjective *the exterior walls* **outer,** outside, outermost, outward, external.
ANTONYMS interior.
▶ noun *the exterior of the building* **outside,** outer surface, external surface, outward appearance, facade.

exterminate ▶ verb *they were hired to exterminate the carpenter ants* **kill,** put to death, take/end the life of, dispatch; slaughter, butcher, massacre, wipe out, eliminate, eradicate, annihilate; murder, assassinate, execute, slay; informal do away with, bump off, do in, take out, blow away, ice, rub out, waste. See note at DESTROY.

external ▶ adjective **1** *an external wall* **outer,** outside, outermost, outward, exterior.
ANTONYMS internal.
2 *an external examiner* **outside,** independent, nonresident, from elsewhere.
ANTONYMS in-house.

extinct ▶ adjective **1** *an extinct species* **vanished,** lost, died out, no longer existing, no longer extant, wiped out, destroyed, gone.
ANTONYMS extant.
2 *an extinct volcano* **inactive.**
ANTONYMS dormant.

extinction ▶ noun *efforts to save the California condor from extinction* **dying out,** disappearance, vanishing; extermination, destruction, elimination, eradication, annihilation.

extinguish ▶ verb **1** *the fire was extinguished* **douse,** put out, stamp out, smother, beat out.
ANTONYMS light.
2 *all hope was extinguished* **destroy,** end, finish off, put an end to, bring to an end, terminate, remove, annihilate, wipe out, erase, eliminate, eradicate, obliterate; informal take out, rub out.
ANTONYMS start up.

extol ▶ verb *nutritionists extol the virtues of fiber* **praise enthusiastically,** go into raptures about/over, wax lyrical about, sing the praises of, praise to the skies, acclaim, exalt, eulogize, adulate, rhapsodize over, rave about, enthuse about/over; informal go wild about, go on about, ballyhoo; formal laud; archaic panegyrize. See note at PRAISE.
ANTONYMS criticize.

extort ▶ verb *he was convicted of extorting money from local residents* **force,** extract, exact, wring, wrest, screw, squeeze, obtain by threat(s), blackmail someone for; informal put the bite on someone for; soak, rook.

extortion ▶ noun *arrested on a charge of extortion* **blackmail,** shakedown; formal exaction.

extortionate ▶ adjective *extortionate prices* **exorbitant,** excessively high, excessive, outrageous, unreasonable, inordinate, inflated, exacting, harsh, severe, oppressive; informal over the top; grasping, bloodsucking, avaricious, greedy, money-grubbing.

extra ▶ adjective *extra income* **additional,** more, added, supplementary, further, auxiliary, ancillary, subsidiary, secondary, bonus.
▶ adverb **1** *working extra hard* **exceptionally,** particularly, specially, especially, very, extremely; unusually, extraordinarily, uncommonly, remarkably, outstandingly, amazingly, incredibly, really, awfully, terribly; informal seriously, mucho, majorly.
2 *we charge extra for cheese* **in addition,** additionally, as well, also, too, besides, on top (of that); archaic withal.
▶ noun **1** *an optional extra* **addition,** supplement, adjunct, addendum, add-on, bonus.
2 *a group of tourists were hired as extras for the scene on the bus* **walk-on,** supernumerary, spear carrier.

extract ▶ verb **1** *he extracted the videocassette* **take out,** draw out, pull out, remove, withdraw; free, release, extricate.
ANTONYMS insert.
2 *extracting money* **wrest,** exact, wring, screw, squeeze, obtain by force, obtain by threat(s), extort, blackmail someone for; informal put the bite on someone for.
3 *the roots are crushed to extract the juice* **squeeze out,** express, press out, obtain.
ANTONYMS add, infuse.
4 *the figures are extracted from the report* **excerpt,** select, reproduce, copy, take; Computing download.
ANTONYMS insert.
5 *ideas extracted from a variety of theories* **derive,** develop, evolve, deduce, infer, obtain; formal educe.
▶ noun **1** *an extract from his article* **excerpt,** passage, citation, quotation; Computing download; (**excerpts**) analects.
2 *an extract of the ginseng root* **decoction,** distillation, distillate, abstraction, concentrate, essence, juice.

extraction ▶ noun **1** *the extraction of gallstones* **removal,** taking out, drawing out, pulling out, withdrawal; freeing, release, extrication.
ANTONYMS insertion.
2 *the extraction of grape juice* **squeezing,** expressing, pressing, obtaining.
3 *a man of Irish extraction* **descent,** ancestry, parentage, ancestors, family, antecedents; lineage, line, origin, derivation, birth; genealogy, heredity, stock, pedigree, blood, bloodline; roots, origins; rare filiation, stirps.

extradite ▶ verb *the Russians extradited him to*

Germany **deport,** send, ship, deliver, hand over; repatriate.

extradition ▶ noun *detainees awaiting extradition* **deportation,** repatriation, expulsion.

extraneous ▶ adjective **1** *extraneous considerations* **irrelevant,** immaterial, beside the point, unrelated, unconnected, inapposite, inapplicable, superfluous.
2 *extraneous noise* **external,** outside, exterior.

extraordinary ▶ adjective **1** *an extraordinary coincidence* **remarkable,** exceptional, amazing, astonishing, astounding, sensational, stunning, incredible, unbelievable, phenomenal; striking, outstanding, momentous, impressive, singular, memorable, unforgettable, unique, noteworthy; out of the ordinary, unusual, uncommon, rare, surprising; informal fantastic, terrific, tremendous, stupendous, awesome; literary wondrous.
2 *extraordinary speed* **very great,** tremendous, enormous, immense, prodigious, stupendous, monumental.

extravagance ▶ noun **1** *a fit of extravagance* **profligacy,** improvidence, wastefulness, prodigality, lavishness.
2 *the costliest brand is an extravagance* **luxury,** indulgence, self-indulgence, treat, extra, nonessential.
3 *the extravagance of the decor* **ornateness,** elaborateness, embellishment, ornamentation; ostentation, overelaborateness, excessiveness, exaggeration, outrageousness, immoderation, excess.

extravagant ▶ adjective **1** *an extravagant lifestyle* **spendthrift,** profligate, improvident, wasteful, prodigal, lavish.
ANTONYMS thrifty.
2 *extravagant gifts* **expensive,** costly, lavish, high-priced, high-cost; valuable, precious; informal pricey, costing the earth.
ANTONYMS cheap.
3 *extravagant prices* **exorbitant,** extortionate, excessive, high, unreasonable.
ANTONYMS reasonable, low.
4 *extravagant praise* **excessive,** immoderate, exaggerated, gushing, unrestrained, effusive, fulsome. See note at PROFUSE.
ANTONYMS moderate.
5 *decorated in an extravagant style* **ornate,** elaborate, decorated, ornamented, fancy; overelaborate, gaudy, garish, ostentatious, exaggerated, baroque, rococo; informal lavish, flashy, glitzy.
ANTONYMS plain.

extravaganza ▶ noun *a star-studded extravaganza to raise funds for AIDS research* **spectacular,** display, spectacle, show, pageant, gala; blowout, barn-burner.

extreme ▶ adjective **1** *extreme danger* **utmost,** very great, greatest, greatest possible, maximum, maximal, highest, supreme, great, acute, enormous, severe, high, exceptional, extraordinary.
ANTONYMS slight.
2 *extreme measures* **drastic,** serious, desperate, dire, radical, far-reaching, momentous, consequential, impactful; heavy, sharp, severe, austere, harsh, tough, strict, rigorous, oppressive, draconian.
ANTONYMS mild.
3 *extreme views* **radical,** extremist, immoderate, fanatical, revolutionary, rebel, subversive, militant, far-right, far-left.
ANTONYMS moderate.
4 *extreme sports* **dangerous,** hazardous, risky, high-risk, adventurous.
ANTONYMS tame, safe.
5 *the extreme north* **furthest,** farthest, furthermost, far, very, utmost; archaic outmost.
ANTONYMS near.
▶ noun **1** *the two extremes* **opposite,** antithesis, side of the coin, (opposite) pole, antipode.
2 *this attitude is taken to its extreme in the following quote* **limit,** extremity, highest/greatest degree, maximum, height, top, zenith, peak, ne plus ultra.
– PHRASES **in the extreme** *David was generous in the extreme* See EXTREMELY.

extremely ▶ adverb *even on the hottest days, the caverns are extremely cold* **very,** exceedingly, exceptionally, especially, extraordinarily, in the extreme, tremendously, immensely, vastly, hugely, intensely, acutely, singularly, uncommonly, unusually, decidedly, particularly, supremely, highly, remarkably, really, truly, mightily; informal terrifically, awfully, terribly, devilishly, majorly, seriously, mega, ultra, damn, damned, ever so, real, mighty, awful, way, darned, gosh-darn; archaic exceeding.
ANTONYMS slightly, barely.

extremist ▶ noun *the attack was carried out by a group of right-wing extremists* **fanatic,** radical, zealot, fundamentalist, hard-liner, militant, activist; informal ultra. See note at ZEALOT.
ANTONYMS moderate.

extremity ▶ noun **1** *the eastern extremity* **limit,** end, edge, side, farthest point, boundary, border, frontier; perimeter, periphery, margin; literary bourn, marge.
2 *she lost feeling in her extremities* **fingers and toes,** hands and feet, limbs.
3 *the extremity of the violence* **intensity,** magnitude, acuteness, ferocity, vehemence, fierceness, violence, severity, seriousness, strength, power, powerfulness, vigor, force, forcefulness.
4 *in extremity he will send for her* **dire straits,** trouble, difficulty, hard times, hardship, adversity, misfortune, distress; (a) crisis, an emergency, (a) disaster, (a) catastrophe, calamity; a predicament, a plight, mess, a dilemma; informal a fix, a pickle, a jam, a spot, a bind, a hole, a sticky situation, hot water, deep water.

extricate ▶ verb *there's always someone who can extricate these wealthy little brats from their run-ins with the law* **extract,** free, release, disentangle, get out, remove, withdraw, disengage; informal get someone/oneself off the hook.

extrinsic ▶ adjective *climate, geography, and other extrinsic factors* **external,** extraneous, exterior, outside, outward.
ANTONYMS intrinsic.

extrovert ▶ noun *like many extroverts, he was*

unhappy inside **outgoing person,** sociable person, socializer, life of the party.
ANTONYMS introvert.

▶ **adjective** *Raj's extrovert personality* **outgoing,** extroverted, sociable, gregarious, genial, affable, friendly, unreserved.
ANTONYMS introverted.

extrude ▶ **verb** *machines extrude the plastics that become jars and bottles* **force out,** thrust out, express, eject, expel, release, emit.

exuberant ▶ **adjective 1** *exuberant guests dancing on the terrace* **ebullient,** buoyant, cheerful, jaunty, lighthearted, high-spirited, exhilarated, excited, elated, exultant, euphoric, joyful, cheery, merry, jubilant, vivacious, enthusiastic, irrepressible, energetic, animated, full of life, lively, vigorous, adrenalized; informal bubbly, bouncy, chipper, chirpy, full of beans; literary blithe.
ANTONYMS gloomy.
2 *an exuberant welcome* **effusive,** extravagant, fulsome, expansive, gushing, gushy, demonstrative.
ANTONYMS restrained.
3 *an exuberant coating of mosses* **luxuriant,** lush, rich, dense, thick, abundant, profuse, plentiful, prolific.
ANTONYMS meager.

exude ▶ **verb 1** *milkweed exudes a milky sap* **give off/out,** discharge, release, emit, issue; ooze, weep, secrete, excrete.
2 *slime exudes from the fungus* **ooze,** seep, issue, escape, discharge, flow, leak.
3 *he exuded self-confidence* **emanate,** radiate, ooze, emit; display, show, evince, exhibit, manifest, transmit, embody.

exult ▶ **verb 1** *her opponents exulted when she left* **rejoice,** be joyful, be happy, be delighted, be elated, be ecstatic, be overjoyed, be jubilant, be rapturous, be in raptures, be thrilled, jump for joy, be on cloud nine, be in seventh heaven; celebrate, cheer; informal be over the moon, be on top of the world; literary joy; archaic jubilate.
ANTONYMS sorrow.
2 *he exulted in his triumph* **rejoice at/in,** take delight in, find/take pleasure in, find joy in, enjoy, revel in, glory in, delight in, relish, savor; be/feel proud of, congratulate oneself on.
ANTONYMS sorrow.

exultant ▶ **adjective** *the exultant winners waved to the crowd* **jubilant,** thrilled, triumphant, delighted, exhilarated, happy, overjoyed, joyous, joyful, gleeful, excited, rejoicing, ecstatic, euphoric, elated, rapturous, in raptures, enraptured, on cloud nine, in seventh heaven; rare exilient; informal over the moon, jumping for joy.

exultation ▶ **noun** *a gold medalist filled with exultation* **jubilation,** rejoicing, happiness, pleasure, joy, gladness, delight, glee, elation, cheer, euphoria, exhilaration, delirium, ecstasy, rapture, exuberance.

eye ▶ **noun 1** *he rubbed his eyes* **eyeball;** informal peeper, baby blues; literary or humorous orb.
2 *sharp eyes* **eyesight,** vision, sight, powers of observation, perception, visual perception.
3 *an eye for a bargain* **appreciation,** awareness, alertness, perception, consciousness, feeling, instinct, intuition, nose.
4 *his thoughtful eye* **watch,** observance, gaze, stare, regard; observation, surveillance, vigilance, contemplation, scrutiny.
5 (**eyes**) *to desert was despicable in their eyes* **opinion,** thinking, way of thinking, mind, view, viewpoint, point of view, attitude, standpoint, perspective, belief, judgment, assessment, analysis, estimation.
6 *the eye of a needle* **hole,** opening, aperture, eyelet, slit, slot.
7 *the eye of the storm* **center,** middle, heart, core, hub, thick.

▶ **verb** *I saw him intently eyeing that antique car* **look at,** observe, view, gaze at, stare at, regard, contemplate, survey, scrutinize, consider, glance at; watch, keep an eye on, keep under observation; ogle, leer at, make eyes at; informal have/take a gander at, check out, size up, eyeball; literary behold.

– PHRASES **lay/set/clap eyes on** informal *have you ever laid your eyes on a more beautiful sailboat?* **see,** observe, notice, spot, spy, catch sight of, glimpse, catch/get a glimpse of; literary behold, espy, descry. **see eye to eye** *even best friends can't expect to see eye to eye on everything* **agree,** concur, be in agreement, be of the same mind/opinion, be in accord, think as one; be on the same wavelength, get on/along.

eye-catching ▶ **adjective** *eye-catching designs adorn each door* **striking,** arresting, impactful, conspicuous, dramatic, impressive, spectacular, breathtaking, dazzling, amazing, stunning, sensational, remarkable, distinctive, unusual, out of the ordinary.

eyesight ▶ **noun** *my eyesight is perfect* **sight,** vision, faculty of sight, ability to see, visual perception, perception.

eyesore ▶ **noun** *what's left of the old factory is a danger and an eyesore* **monstrosity,** blot (on the landscape), mess, scar, blight, disfigurement, blemish, ugly sight.

eyewitness ▶ **noun** *several eyewitnesses were questioned by the police* **observer,** onlooker, witness, bystander, spectator, watcher, viewer, passerby, gawker; literary beholder.

Ff

fable ▶ noun **1** *the fable of the wary fox* **moral tale,** tale, parable, allegory.
2 *the fables of ancient Greece* **myth,** legend, saga, epic, folk tale, folk story, fairy tale, mythos, folklore, mythology. See note at FICTION.

fabric ▶ noun **1** *the finest silk fabric* **cloth,** material, textile, tissue.
2 *the fabric of society* **structure,** infrastructure, framework, frame, form, composition, construction, foundations, warp and woof.

fabricate ▶ verb **1** *he fabricated research data* **falsify,** fake, counterfeit, cook; invent, make up. See note at LIE[1].
2 *fabricating a pack of lies* **concoct,** make up, dream up, invent, trump up; informal cook up.
3 *you will have to fabricate an exhaust system* **make,** create, manufacture, produce; construct, build, assemble, put together, form, fashion.

fabulous ▶ adjective **1** *fabulous wealth* **tremendous,** stupendous, prodigious, phenomenal, remarkable, exceptional; astounding, amazing, fantastic, breathtaking, staggering, unthinkable, unimaginable, incredible, unbelievable, unheard of, untold, undreamed of, beyond one's wildest dreams; informal mind-boggling, mind-blowing, jaw-dropping.
2 informal *we had a fabulous time* See EXCELLENT.
3 *a fabulous horselike beast* **mythical,** legendary, mythic, mythological, fabled, folkloric, fairy-tale; fictitious, imaginary, imagined, made up.

face ▶ noun **1** *a beautiful face* **countenance,** physiognomy, features; informal mug; puss; literary visage; archaic front.
2 *her face grew sad* **(facial) expression,** look, appearance, air, manner, bearing, countenance, mien.
3 *he made a face at the sourness of the drink* **grimace,** scowl, wry face, wince, frown, glower, pout, moue.
4 *a cube has six faces* **side,** aspect, flank, surface, plane, facet, wall, elevation.
5 *a watch face* **dial,** display.
6 *changing the face of the industry* **appearance,** outward appearance, aspect, nature, image.
7 *he put on a brave face* **front,** show, display, act, appearance, facade, exterior, mask, masquerade, pretense, pose, veneer.
8 *criticism should never cause the recipient to lose face* **respect,** honor, esteem, regard, admiration, approbation, acclaim, approval, favor, appreciation, popularity, prestige, standing, status, dignity; self-respect, self-esteem.
▶ verb **1** *the hotel faces the sea* **look out on,** front on to, look toward, be facing, look over/across, overlook, give on to, be opposite (to).
2 *you'll just have to face the facts* **accept,** become reconciled to, get used to, become accustomed to, adjust to, acclimatize oneself to; learn to live with, cope with, deal with, come to terms with, become resigned to.
3 *he faces a humiliating rejection* **be confronted by,** be faced with, encounter, experience, come into contact with, come up against.
4 *the problems facing our police force* **beset,** worry, distress, trouble, bother, confront; harass, oppress, vex, irritate, exasperate, strain, stress, tax; torment, plague, blight, bedevil, curse; formal discommode.
5 *he faced the challenge boldly* **brave,** face up to, encounter, meet, meet head-on, confront; oppose, resist, withstand.
6 *a wall faced with stucco* **cover,** clad, veneer, overlay, surface, dress, put a facing on, laminate, coat, line.
– PHRASES **face to face** *the two men stood face to face* **facing (each other),** opposite (each other), across from each other. **on the face of it** *on the face on it, the peace talks are going quite well* **ostensibly,** to all appearances, to all intents and purposes, at first glance, on the surface, superficially; apparently, seemingly, outwardly, it seems (that), it would seem (that), it appears (that), it would appear (that), as far as one can see/tell, by all accounts.

facet ▶ noun **1** *the many facets of the gem* **surface,** face, side, plane.
2 *other facets of his character* **aspect,** feature, side, dimension, characteristic, detail, point, ingredient, strand; component, constituent, element.

facetious ▶ adjective *unfortunately, they took my facetious remarks seriously* **flippant,** flip, glib, frivolous, tongue-in-cheek, ironic, sardonic, joking, jokey, jocular, playful, sportive, teasing, mischievous; witty, amusing, funny, droll, comic, comical, lighthearted, jocose.
ANTONYMS serious.

facile ▶ adjective **1** *a facile explanation* **simplistic,** superficial, oversimplified; shallow, glib, jejune, naive; dime-store.
2 *he achieved a facile victory* **effortless,** easy, undemanding, unexacting, painless, trouble-free.

USAGE

facile

Always meaning "easy" in one sense or another, *facile* may connote either proficiency or shallowness. The writer must achieve clarity through context. Sometimes the word connotes the ease that comes with artistic mastery—e.g.: "Nicolai Dobrev played the jester, a noble baritone with a facile instrument." (*Boston Herald*; Mar. 30, 2002.) More often, it connotes triteness or oversimplification—e.g.: "But most mental health experts say closure is no holy grail, only rendered so by people seeking facile solutions to complex problems." (*Christian Science Monitor*; Mar. 28, 2002.) — **BG**

facilitate ▶ verb *private funding has facilitated our research* **make easy/easier,** ease, make possible, make smooth/smoother, smooth the way for; enable, assist, help (along), aid, oil the wheels of, expedite, speed up, accelerate, forward, advance, promote, further, encourage, catalyze, be a catalyst for.
ANTONYMS impede.

facility ▶ noun **1** *parking facilities* **provision,** space, means, potential, equipment.
2 *the facilities consisted of an old wooden outhouse* **washroom,** toilet, restroom, bathroom.
3 *a wealth of local facilities* **amenity,** resource, service, advantage, convenience, benefit.
4 *a medical facility* **establishment,** center, place, station, location, premises, site, post, base; informal joint, outfit, setup.
5 *his facility for drawing* **aptitude,** talent, gift, flair, bent, skill, knack, genius; ability, proficiency, competence, capability, capacity, faculty; expertness, adeptness, prowess, mastery, artistry.

facing ▶ noun **1** *green velvet facings* **covering,** trimming, lining, interfacing.
2 *brick facing on a concrete core* **siding,** facade, cladding, veneer, skin, surface, front, coating, covering, dressing, overlay, lamination, plating.

facsimile ▶ noun *a facsimile of the manuscript* **copy,** reproduction, duplicate, photocopy, replica, likeness, print, reprint, printout, offprint, fax; trademark Xerox; dated carbon copy, photostat, mimeograph.
ANTONYMS original.

fact ▶ noun **1** *it is a fact that the water is polluted* **reality,** actuality, certainty; truth, verity, gospel.
ANTONYMS lie, fiction.
2 *every fact was double-checked* **detail,** piece of information, particular, item, specific, element, point, factor, feature, characteristic, ingredient, circumstance, aspect, facet; (**facts**) information.
3 *an accessory after the fact* **event,** happening, occurrence, incident, act, deed.
– PHRASES **in fact** *Mr. Hartmann was in fact present at the time of the shooting* **actually,** in actuality, in actual fact, really, in reality, in point of fact, as a matter of fact, as it happens, in truth, to tell the truth; archaic in sooth, verily.

faction ▶ noun **1** *a faction of the party* **clique,** coterie, caucus, cabal, bloc, camp, group, grouping, sector, section, wing, arm, branch, set; ginger group, pressure group.
2 *the council was split by faction* **infighting,** dissension, dissent, dispute, discord, strife, conflict, friction, argument, disagreement, controversy, quarreling, wrangling, bickering, squabbling, disharmony, disunity, schism.

factious ▶ adjective *factious parties have weakened the movement* **divided,** split, schismatic, discordant, conflicting, argumentative, disagreeing, disputatious, quarreling, quarrelsome, clashing, warring, at loggerheads, at odds, rebellious, mutinous.
ANTONYMS harmonious.

factor ▶ noun *this had been a key factor in his decision to withdraw* **element,** part, component, ingredient, strand, constituent, point, detail, item, feature, facet, aspect, characteristic, consideration, influence, circumstance.

factory ▶ noun *jobs in the factories were getting harder to find* **plant,** works, yard, mill, workshop, shop; informal sweatshop.

factotum ▶ noun *back then, these wealthy college boys made sure their personal factotums were just a whistle away* **handyman,** jack of all trades; assistant, man Friday, gal/girl Friday; gofer; informal Mr./Ms. Fix-It.

factual ▶ adjective *a factual report from the chairman* **truthful,** true, accurate, authentic, historical, genuine, fact-based; true-to-life, correct, exact, honest, faithful, literal, verbatim, word for word, well-documented, unbiased, objective, unvarnished; formal veridical.
ANTONYMS fictitious.

faculty ▶ noun **1** *the faculty of speech* **power,** capability, capacity, facility, wherewithal, means; (**faculties**) senses, wits, reason, intelligence.
2 *an unusual faculty for unearthing contributors* **ability,** proficiency, competence, capability, potential, capacity, facility; aptitude, talent, gift, flair, bent, skill, knack, genius; expertise, expertness, adeptness, adroitness, dexterity, prowess, mastery, artistry.
3 *conflict between students and faculty* **staff,** teachers, professors, instructors.
4 *the arts faculty* **department,** school, division, section.

fad ▶ noun *when I was a kid, no fad was more apparent than the coonskin cap* **craze,** vogue, trend, fashion, mode, enthusiasm, passion, obsession, mania, rage, compulsion, fixation, fetish, fancy, whim, fascination; informal thing.

fade ▶ verb **1** *the paintwork has faded* **become pale,** become bleached, become washed out, lose color, discolor; grow dull, grow dim, lose luster.
ANTONYMS brighten.
2 *sunlight had faded the picture* **bleach,** wash out, make pale, blanch, whiten.
ANTONYMS brighten, enhance.
3 *remove the flower heads as they fade* **wither,** wilt, droop, shrivel, die.
4 *the afternoon light began to fade* **dim,** grow dim, grow faint, fail, dwindle, die away, wane, disappear, vanish, decline, melt away; literary evanesce.
ANTONYMS increase.
5 *a traditional culture that was **fading away*** **decline,** die out, diminish, deteriorate, decay, crumble, collapse, fail, fall, sink, slump, go

downhill; informal go to pot, go to the dogs; archaic retrograde.
ANTONYMS thrive.

fail ▸ verb 1 *the enterprise had failed* **be unsuccessful,** not succeed, fall through, fall flat, collapse, founder, backfire, meet with disaster, come to nothing, come to naught; informal flop, bomb.
ANTONYMS succeed.
2 *he has failed the final French examination* **be unsuccessful in,** not pass; not make the grade on; informal **flunk,** botch, blow, screw up, bungle.
ANTONYMS pass.
3 *at his lowest point, his friends failed him* **let down,** disappoint; desert, abandon, betray, be disloyal to; literary forsake.
ANTONYMS support.
4 *the crops failed* **die,** wither; be deficient, be insufficient, be inadequate.
ANTONYMS thrive.
5 *daylight failed* **fade,** dim, die away, wane, disappear, vanish.
6 *the ventilation system failed* **break down,** break, stop working, cut out, crash; malfunction, go wrong, develop a fault; informal conk out, go on the blink, go on the fritz.
ANTONYMS work.
7 *Joe's health was failing* **deteriorate,** degenerate, decline, fade, wane, ebb.
ANTONYMS improving.
8 *900 businesses are failing a week* **collapse,** crash, go under, go bankrupt, go into receivership, go into liquidation, cease trading; informal fold, flop, go bust, go broke, go belly-up.
ANTONYMS thrive.
– PHRASES **without fail** *without fail, Carlos leaves for lunch at 12:05 every day* **without exception,** unfailingly, regularly, invariably, predictably, conscientiously, religiously, whatever happened.

failing ▸ noun *Deborah accepted him despite his failings* **fault,** shortcoming, weakness, imperfection, defect, flaw, frailty, foible, idiosyncrasy, vice.
ANTONYMS strength.
▸ preposition *failing financial assistance, you will be bankrupt* **in the absence of,** lacking, barring, absent, without.

failure ▸ noun 1 *the failure of the assassination attempt* **lack of success,** nonfulfillment, defeat, collapse, foundering.
ANTONYMS success.
2 *all his schemes had been a failure* **fiasco,** debacle, catastrophe, disaster; informal flop, megaflop, washout, dead loss, snafu, clinker, dud, no-go.
ANTONYMS success.
3 *she was regarded as a failure* **loser,** underachiever, ne'er-do-well, disappointment; informal no-hoper, dead loss, dud, write-off.
ANTONYMS success.
4 *his failure in duty* **negligence,** dereliction; omission, oversight.
5 *a crop failure* **inadequacy,** insufficiency, deficiency, dearth, scarcity, shortfall.
6 *the failure of the camera* **breaking down,** breakdown, malfunction; crash.
7 *company failures* **collapse,** crash, bankruptcy, insolvency, liquidation, closure.
ANTONYMS success.

faint ▸ adjective 1 *a faint mark* **indistinct,** vague, unclear, indefinite, ill-defined, imperceptible, unobtrusive; pale, light, faded.
ANTONYMS clear.
2 *a faint cry* **quiet,** muted, muffled, stifled; feeble, weak, whispered, murmured, indistinct; low, soft, gentle.
ANTONYMS loud.
3 *a faint possibility* **slight,** slender, slim, small, tiny, negligible, remote, vague, unlikely, improbable; informal minuscule.
ANTONYMS great.
4 *faint praise* **unenthusiastic,** halfhearted, weak, feeble.
ANTONYMS strong.
5 *I suddenly felt faint* **dizzy,** giddy, lightheaded, unsteady; informal woozy.
▸ verb *she thought he would faint* **pass out,** lose consciousness, black out, keel over, swoon; informal flake out, conk out, zonk out, go out like a light.
▸ noun *a dead faint* **blackout,** fainting fit, loss of consciousness, swoon; Medicine syncope.

faint-hearted ▸ adjective *come now, my faint-hearted friend, I'll get you to safety* **timid,** timorous, nervous, easily scared, fearful, afraid; cowardly, craven, spineless, pusillanimous, lily-livered; informal chicken, chicken-hearted, yellow-bellied, gutless, sissy, wimpy, wimpish.
ANTONYMS brave.

faintly ▸ adverb 1 *Maria called his name faintly* **indistinctly,** softly, gently, weakly; in a whisper, in a murmur, in a low voice.
ANTONYMS loudly.
2 *he looked faintly bewildered* **slightly,** vaguely, somewhat, quite, fairly, rather, a little, a bit, a touch, a shade; informal sort of, kind of, kinda.
ANTONYMS extremely.

fair[1] ▸ adjective 1 *the courts were generally fair* **just,** equitable, honest, upright, honorable, trustworthy; impartial, unbiased, unprejudiced, nonpartisan, neutral, evenhanded; lawful, legal, legitimate; informal legit, on the level; on the up and up.
ANTONYMS unjust, biased.
2 *fair weather* **fine,** dry, bright, clear, sunny, cloudless; warm, balmy, clement, benign, pleasant.
ANTONYMS inclement.
3 *fair winds* **favorable,** advantageous, benign; on one's side, in one's favor.
ANTONYMS unfavorable.
4 *fair hair* **blond/blonde,** yellowish, golden, flaxen, light, light brown, ash blond.
ANTONYMS dark.
5 *Hermione's fair skin* **pale,** light, light-colored, white, creamy.
ANTONYMS dark.
6 archaic *the fair maiden's heart* See **BEAUTIFUL**.
7 *the restaurant was fair* **reasonable,** passable, tolerable, satisfactory, acceptable, respectable, decent, all right, good enough, pretty good, not bad, average, middling; informal OK, so-so, 'comme ci, comme ça'.
– PHRASES **fair and square** *face it, I beat you fair and square* **honestly,** fairly, without cheating,

without foul play, by the book; lawfully, legally, legitimately; informal on the level, on the up and up.

fair² ▶ noun 1 *a country fair* **carnival,** festival, exhibition; midway.
2 *an antiques fair* **market,** bazaar, flea market, exchange, sale; dated emporium.
3 *a new art fair* **exhibition,** exhibit, display, show, presentation, exposition.

fairly ▶ adverb 1 *all students were treated fairly* **justly,** equitably, impartially, without bias, without prejudice, evenhandedly; lawfully, legally, legitimately, by the book; equally, the same.
2 *the pipes are in fairly good condition* **reasonably,** passably, tolerably, adequately, moderately, quite, relatively, comparatively; informal pretty, kind of, kinda, sort of.

fair-minded ▶ adjective *all you can do now is pray for a fair-minded jury* **fair,** just, evenhanded, equitable, impartial, nonpartisan, unbiased, unprejudiced; honest, honorable, trustworthy, upright, decent; informal on the level; on the up and up.

fairy ▶ noun *we were gleefully certain that little fairies inhabited our woods* **sprite,** pixie, elf, imp, brownie, puck, leprechaun; literary faerie, fay.

fairy tale, fairy story ▶ noun 1 *the movie was inspired by a fairy tale* **folk tale,** folk story, traditional story, myth, legend, fantasy, fable.
2 informal *she accused him of telling fairy tales* **lie,** white lie, fib, half-truth, untruth, falsehood, tall tale, story, fabrication, invention, fiction; informal whopper, cock-and-bull story.

faith ▶ noun 1 *he justified his boss's faith in him* **trust,** belief, confidence, conviction; optimism, hopefulness, hope.
ANTONYMS mistrust.
2 *she gave her life for her faith* **religion,** church, sect, denomination, (religious) persuasion, (religious) belief, ideology, creed, teaching, doctrine.
– PHRASES **break faith with** *our own chairman has broken faith with this organization* **be disloyal to,** be unfaithful to, be untrue to, betray, play someone false, break one's promise to, fail, let down; double-cross, deceive, cheat, stab in the back. **keep faith with** *Mrs. Grimes has always kept faith with everyone in my department* **be loyal to,** be faithful to, be true to, stand by, stick by, keep one's promise to.

faithful ▶ adjective 1 *his faithful assistant* **loyal,** constant, true, devoted, true-blue, unswerving, staunch, steadfast, dedicated, committed; trusty, trustworthy, dependable, reliable. See note at RESOLUTE.
ANTONYMS traitorous, unreliable.
2 *a faithful copy* **accurate,** precise, exact, errorless, unerring, faultless, true, close, strict; realistic, authentic; informal on the mark, bang on, on the money.
ANTONYMS inaccurate.

faithless ▶ adjective 1 *her faithless lover* **unfaithful,** disloyal, inconstant, false, untrue, adulterous, traitorous; fickle, flighty, untrustworthy, unreliable, undependable; deceitful, two-faced, double-crossing; informal cheating, two-timing, backstabbing; literary perfidious.
2 *a faithless society* **unbelieving,** nonbelieving, irreligious, disbelieving, agnostic, atheistic; pagan, heathen.

fake ▶ noun 1 *the sculpture was a fake* **forgery,** counterfeit, copy, pirate(d) copy, sham, fraud, hoax, imitation, mock-up, dummy, reproduction; informal phony, rip-off, knockoff, dupe.
2 *that doctor is a fake* **charlatan,** fraud, fraudster, mountebank, sham, quack, humbug, impostor, hoaxer, cheat, trickster; informal phony, con man, con artist, scam artist. See note at QUACK.
▶ adjective 1 *fake $50 bills* **counterfeit,** forged, fraudulent, sham, imitation, pirate(d), false, bogus; invalid, inauthentic; informal phony, dud.
ANTONYMS genuine.
2 *fake diamonds* **imitation,** artificial, synthetic, simulated, reproduction, replica, ersatz, faux, man-made, dummy, false, mock, bogus; informal pretend, phony, pseudo.
ANTONYMS genuine.
3 *a fake accent* **feigned,** faked, put-on, assumed, invented, affected, pseudo; unconvincing, artificial, mock; informal phony.
ANTONYMS authentic.
▶ verb 1 *the certificate was faked* **forge,** counterfeit, falsify, mock up, copy, pirate, reproduce, replicate; doctor, alter, tamper with.
2 *she faked a yawn* **feign,** pretend, simulate, put on, affect.

fall ▶ verb 1 *bombs began to fall* **drop,** descend, come down, go down; plummet, plunge, sink, dive, tumble; cascade.
ANTONYMS rise.
2 *he tripped and fell* **topple over,** tumble over, keel over, fall down/over, go head over heels, go headlong, collapse, take a spill, pitch forward; trip, stumble, slip; informal come a cropper.
ANTONYMS get up.
3 *the river began to fall* **subside,** recede, ebb, flow back, fall away, go down, sink.
ANTONYMS rise, flood.
4 *inflation will fall* **decrease,** decline, diminish, fall off, drop off, lessen, dwindle; plummet, plunge, slump, sink; depreciate, cheapen, devalue; informal go through the floor, nosedive, take a header, crash.
ANTONYMS rise, increase.
5 *the Mogul empire fell* **decline,** deteriorate, degenerate, go downhill, go to rack and ruin; decay, wither, fade, fail; informal go to the dogs, go to pot, go down the toilet.
ANTONYMS rise, flood, increase, flourish.
6 *those who fell in the war* **die,** perish, lose one's life, be killed, be slain, be lost, meet one's death; informal bite the dust, croak, buy it, buy the farm.
ANTONYMS flourish.
7 *the town* **fell to** *the barbarians* **surrender to,** yield to, submit to, give in to, capitulate to, succumb to; be taken by, be defeated by, be conquered by, be overwhelmed by.
ANTONYMS resist.
8 *Easter fell on April 11th* **occur,** take place, happen, come about; arise; literary come to pass.

9 *night fell* **come,** arrive, appear, arise, materialize.
10 *she fell ill* **become,** grow, get, turn.
11 *more tasks may fall to him* **be the responsibility of,** be the duty of, be borne by, be one's job; come someone's way.
▶ **noun 1** *an accidental fall* **tumble,** trip, spill, topple, slip; collapse; informal nosedive, header, cropper.
2 *a fall in sales* **decline,** falloff, drop, decrease, cut, dip, reduction, downswing; plummet, plunge, slump; informal nosedive, crash.
ANTONYMS increase.
3 *the fall of the Roman Empire* **downfall,** collapse, ruin, ruination, failure, decline, deterioration, degeneration; destruction, overthrow, demise.
ANTONYMS increase, rise, ascent.
4 *the fall of the city* **surrender,** capitulation, yielding, submission; defeat.
ANTONYMS rise.
5 *a steep fall down to the ocean* **descent,** declivity, slope, slant, incline, downgrade.
ANTONYMS ascent.
6 *the fall of man* **sin,** wrongdoing, transgression, error, offense, lapse, fall from grace, original sin.
7 (**falls**) *rafting trips below the falls* **waterfall,** cascade, cataract; rapids, white water.
– PHRASES **fall apart** *the old teacup fell apart in my hands* **fall to pieces,** fall to bits, come apart (at the seams); disintegrate, fragment, break up, break apart, crumble, decay, perish; informal bust. **fall asleep** *I almost fell asleep at work* **doze off,** drop off, go to sleep; informal nod off, go off, drift off, crash, conk out, go out like a light, sack out. **fall away** *the ground here falls away abruptly* **slope down,** slope, slant down, go down, drop, drop away, descend, dip, sink, plunge. **fall back** *the troops were ordered to fall back* **retreat,** withdraw, back off, draw back, pull back, pull away, move away. **fall back on** *I can always fall back on my career in landscaping* **resort to,** turn to, look to, call on, have recourse to; rely on, depend on, lean on. **fall behind 1** *the other walkers fell behind* **lag,** lag behind, trail, trail behind, be left behind, drop back, bring up the rear; straggle, dally, dawdle, hang back. **2** *they fell behind on their payments* **get into debt,** get into arrears, default, be in the red. **fall for 1** *she fell for John* **fall in love with,** become infatuated with, lose one's heart to, take a fancy to, be smitten with/by, be attracted to; informal have the hots for. **2** *she won't fall for that trick* **be deceived by,** be duped by, be fooled by, be taken in by, believe, trust, be convinced by; informal go for, buy, swallow (hook, line, and sinker). **fall in 1** *the roof fell in* **collapse,** cave in, crash in, fall down; give way, crumble, disintegrate. **2** *the soldiers fell in* **get in formation,** get in line, line up, take one's position. **3** *he fell in with a bad crowd* **get involved,** take up, join up, go around, make friends; informal hang, hang out. **fall off** See FALL (sense 4 of the verb). **fall on** *the army fell on the rebels* **attack,** assail, assault, fly at, set about, set upon; pounce upon, ambush, surprise, rush, storm, charge; informal jump, lay into, have a go at. **fall out** *let's not fall out over something so silly* **quarrel,** argue, row, fight, squabble, bicker, have words, disagree, be at odds, clash, wrangle, cross swords, lock horns, be at loggerheads, be at each other's throats; informal scrap. **fall short** *we sincerely hope that our fund-raising efforts will not fall short* **be deficient,** be inadequate, be insufficient, be wanting, be lacking, disappoint; informal not come up to scratch, not come up to snuff. **fall short of** *the results fell short of what was expected* **fail to meet,** fail to reach, fail to live up to. **fall through** *the deal fell through* **fail,** be unsuccessful, come to nothing, miscarry, abort, go awry, collapse, founder, come to grief; informal fizzle out, flop, fold, come a cropper, go over like a lead balloon.

fallacious ▶ **adjective** *we almost printed his fallacious information* **erroneous,** false, untrue, wrong, incorrect, flawed, inaccurate, mistaken, misinformed, misguided; specious, spurious, bogus, fictitious, fabricated, made up; groundless, unfounded, ill-founded, unproven, unsupported, uncorroborated; informal phony, full of holes.
ANTONYMS correct.

fallacy ▶ **noun** *the fallacy that the sun moves round the earth* **misconception,** misbelief, delusion, mistaken impression, error, misapprehension, misinterpretation, misconstruction, mistake; untruth, inconsistency, myth.

fallen ▶ **adjective 1** *fallen heroes* **dead,** perished, killed, slain, slaughtered, murdered; lost, late, lamented, departed, gone; formal deceased.
2 dated *fallen women* **immoral,** loose, promiscuous, unchaste, sinful, impure, sullied, tainted, dishonored, ruined.

fallible ▶ **adjective** *what good is a fallible security system?* **error-prone,** errant, liable to err, open to error; imperfect, flawed, weak.

fallow ▶ **adjective 1** *fallow farmland* **uncultivated,** unplowed, untilled, unplanted, unsown; unused, dormant, resting, empty, bare.
ANTONYMS cultivated.
2 *a fallow trading period* **inactive,** dormant, quiet, slack, slow, stagnant; barren, unproductive.
ANTONYMS busy.

false ▶ **adjective 1** *a false report* **incorrect,** untrue, wrong, erroneous, fallacious, flawed, distorted, inaccurate, imprecise; untruthful, fictitious, concocted, fabricated, invented, made up, trumped up, unfounded, spurious; counterfeit, forged, fraudulent.
ANTONYMS correct, truthful.
2 *a false friend* **faithless,** unfaithful, disloyal, untrue, inconstant, treacherous, traitorous, two-faced, double-crossing, deceitful, dishonest, duplicitous, untrustworthy, unreliable; untruthful; informal cheating, two-timing, backstabbing; literary perfidious.
ANTONYMS faithful.
3 *false pearls* See FAKE (sense 2 of the adjective).

falsehood ▶ **noun 1** *a downright falsehood* **lie,** untruth, fib, falsification, fabrication, invention, fiction, story, cock-and-bull story, flight of fancy; half truth; informal tall story, tall

tale, fairy tale, whopper. See note at FICTION.
ANTONYMS truth.
2 *he accused me of falsehood* **lying,** mendacity, untruthfulness, fibbing, fabrication, invention, perjury, telling stories; deceit, deception, pretense, artifice, double-crossing, treachery; literary perfidy.
ANTONYMS honesty.

falsify ▶ verb **1** *she falsified the accounts* **forge,** fake, counterfeit, fabricate; alter, change, doctor, tamper with, fudge, manipulate, adulterate, corrupt, misrepresent, misreport, distort, warp, embellish, embroider; informal cook.
2 *the theory is falsified by the evidence* **disprove,** refute, debunk, negate, negative, invalidate, contradict, controvert, confound, demolish, discredit; informal poke holes in, blow out of the water; formal confute.

falter ▶ verb **1** *the government faltered* **hesitate,** delay, drag one's feet, stall; waver, vacillate, waffle, be indecisive, be irresolute, blow hot and cold, hem and haw; informal sit on the fence, dilly-dally, shilly-shally.
2 *she faltered over his name* **stammer,** stutter, stumble; hesitate, flounder.
3 *the economy was faltering* **struggle,** stumble, flounder, founder, be in difficulty.

fame ▶ noun *a designer of international fame* **renown,** celebrity, stardom, popularity, prominence; note, distinction, esteem, importance, account, consequence, greatness, eminence, prestige, stature, repute; notoriety, infamy.
ANTONYMS obscurity.

familiar ▶ adjective **1** *a familiar task* **well-known,** recognized, accustomed; common, commonplace, everyday, day-to-day, ordinary, habitual, usual, customary, routine, standard, stock, mundane, run-of-the-mill; literary wonted.
2 *are you **familiar with** the subject?* **acquainted with,** conversant with, versed in, knowledgeable of, well-informed in/of; skilled in, proficient in; at home with, no stranger to, au fait with, au courant with; informal up on, in the know about.
3 *a familiar atmosphere* **informal,** casual, relaxed, easy, comfortable; friendly, unceremonious, unreserved, open, natural, unpretentious.
ANTONYMS formal.
4 *he is too familiar with the teachers* **presumptuous,** overfamiliar, disrespectful, forward, bold, impudent, impertinent.
ANTONYMS formal.

familiarity ▶ noun **1** *her familiarity with Asian politics* **acquaintance with,** awareness of, experience with/of, insight into, knowledge of, understanding of, comprehension of, grasp of, skill in, proficiency in.
2 *she was affronted by his familiarity* **presumption,** overfamiliarity, presumptuousness, forwardness, boldness, audacity, cheek, impudence, impertinence, disrespect; liberties.
3 *our familiarity allows us to tease one another* **closeness,** intimacy, attachment, affinity, friendliness, friendship, amity; informal chumminess.

familiarize ▶ verb *let me familiarize you with our new phone setup* **make conversant with,** make familiar with, acquaint with; accustom to, habituate to, instruct in, teach in, educate in, school in, prime in, introduce to; brief in/about; informal put in the picture about/with, give the lowdown on, fill in on, get up to speed on/with.

family ▶ noun **1** *I met his family* **relatives,** relations, kin, next of kin, kinsfolk, kindred, one's (own) flesh and blood, nearest and dearest, people, connections; extended family, in-laws; clan, tribe; informal folks.
2 *he had the right kind of family* **ancestry,** parentage, pedigree, genealogy, background, family tree, descent, lineage, bloodline, blood, extraction, stock; forebears, forefathers, antecedents, roots, origins.
3 *she is married with a family* **children,** little ones, youngsters; offspring, progeny, descendants, scions, heirs; a brood; Law issue; informal kids, kiddies, tots.
4 *the warbler family* **taxonomic group,** order, class, genus, species; stock, strain, line; Zoology phylum.

famine ▶ noun *a nation threatened by famine* **food shortages,** scarcity of food; starvation, malnutrition.
ANTONYMS plenty.

famished ▶ adjective *the hikers were famished by the time they reached camp* **ravenous,** hungry, starving, starved, empty, unfed; informal peckish.
ANTONYMS full.

famous ▶ adjective *an exhibit featuring the artwork of famous actors* **well known,** prominent, famed, popular; renowned, noted, eminent, distinguished, esteemed, celebrated, respected; of distinction, of repute; illustrious, acclaimed, great, legendary, lionized; having one's name in lights; notorious, infamous.
ANTONYMS unknown.

fan[1] ▶ noun *a ceiling fan* **ventilator,** blower, air conditioner.
▶ verb **1** *she fanned her face* **cool,** aerate, ventilate; freshen, refresh.
2 *they fanned public fears* **intensify,** increase, agitate, inflame, exacerbate; stimulate, stir up, whip up, fuel, kindle, spark, arouse.
3 *the police squad **fanned out*** **spread (out),** branch (out); outspread.

fan[2] ▶ noun *a basketball fan* **enthusiast,** devotee, admirer, lover; supporter, follower, disciple, adherent, zealot; expert, connoisseur, aficionado; informal buff, bum, fiend, freak, nut, addict, junkie, fanatic, groupie.

fanatic ▶ noun **1** *a religious fanatic* **zealot,** extremist, militant, dogmatist, devotee, adherent; sectarian, bigot, partisan, radical, diehard; informal maniac. See note at ZEALOT.
2 informal *a hockey fanatic* See FAN[2].

fanatical ▶ adjective **1** *they are fanatical about their faith* **zealous,** extremist, extreme, militant, dogmatic, radical, diehard; intolerant, single-minded, blinkered, inflexible, uncompromising, hardcore.
2 *he was fanatical about tidiness* **enthusiastic,** eager, keen, overkeen, fervent, ardent,

passionate; obsessive, obsessed, fixated, compulsive; informal wild, gung-ho, nuts, crazy, hog-wild.

fanciful ▶ adjective **1** *a fanciful story* **fantastic,** far-fetched, unbelievable, extravagant; ridiculous, absurd, preposterous; imaginary, made-up, make-believe, mythical, fabulous; informal tall, hard to swallow.
ANTONYMS literal.
2 *a fanciful girl* **imaginative,** inventive; whimsical, impractical, dreamy, quixotic; out of touch with reality, in a world of one's own.
ANTONYMS down-to-earthl.
3 *a fanciful building* **ornate,** exotic, fancy, imaginative, extravagant, fantastic; curious, bizarre, eccentric, unusual.
ANTONYMS practical.

fancy ▶ verb **1** *she fancied him* See LIKE[1] (sense 1).
2 *I fancied I could see lights* **think,** imagine, believe, be of the opinion, be under the impression; reckon.
▶ adjective *fancy clothes* **elaborate,** ornate, ornamental, decorative, adorned, embellished, intricate; ostentatious, showy, flamboyant; luxurious, lavish, extravagant, expensive; informal flashy, jazzy, ritzy, snazzy, posh, classy; fancy-schmancy.
ANTONYMS plain.
▶ noun *she took a fancy to you* **liking,** taste, inclination; urge, wish, whim, impulse, notion, whimsy, hankering, craving; informal yen, itch.

fanfare ▶ noun **1** *a fanfare announced her arrival* **trumpet call,** flourish, fanfaronade; archaic trump.
2 *the project was greeted with great fanfare* **fuss,** commotion, show, display, ostentation, flashiness, pageantry, splendor; informal ballyhoo, hype, pizzazz, razzle-dazzle, glitz.

fantastic ▶ adjective **1** *a fantastic car* **marvelous,** wonderful, sensational, outstanding, superb, super, excellent, first-rate, first-class, dazzling, out of this world, breathtaking; informal great, terrific, fabulous, ace, magic, cool, wicked, awesome, brilliant, killer.
ANTONYMS ordinary.
2 *a fantastic notion* **fanciful,** extravagant, extraordinary, irrational, wild, absurd, far-fetched, nonsensical, incredible, unbelievable, unthinkable, implausible, improbable, unlikely, doubtful, dubious; strange, peculiar, odd, queer, weird, eccentric, whimsical, capricious; visionary, romantic; informal crazy, cockeyed, off the wall.
ANTONYMS rational.
3 *fantastic shapes* **strange,** weird, bizarre, outlandish, queer, peculiar, grotesque, freakish, surreal, exotic; elaborate, ornate, intricate.
ANTONYMS ordinary.
4 *his fantastic accuracy* **tremendous,** remarkable, great, terrific, impressive, outstanding, phenomenal.

fantasy ▶ noun **1** *a mix of fantasy and realism* **imagination,** fancy, invention, make-believe; creativity, vision; daydreaming, reverie.
ANTONYMS realism, truth.
2 *his fantasy about being famous* **dream,** daydream, pipe dream, fanciful notion, wish; fond hope, chimera, delusion, illusion; informal pie in the sky.

far ▶ adverb **1** *we walked far that afternoon* **a long way,** a great distance, a good way; afar.
2 *her charm far outweighs any flaws* **much,** considerably, markedly, immeasurably, greatly, significantly, substantially, appreciably, noticeably; to a great extent, by a long way, by far, by a mile, easily.
ANTONYMS slightly.
▶ adjective **1** *far places* **distant,** faraway, far-off, remote, out of the way, far-flung, outlying.
ANTONYMS near, neighboring.
2 *the far side of the campus* **further,** more distant; opposite.
ANTONYMS near.
– PHRASES **by far** *this is by far the best essay we've read today* **by a great amount,** by a good deal, by a long way, by a mile, far and away; undoubtedly, without doubt, without question, positively, absolutely, easily; significantly, substantially, appreciably, much. **far and near** *people came from far and near in hopes of witnessing a miracle* **everywhere,** 'here, there, and everywhere', far and wide, all over (the world), throughout the land, worldwide; informal all over the place; all over the map. **far from** *staff were far from happy* **not,** not at all, nowhere near; the opposite of, the antithesis of, anything but. **go far** *we always knew that Rudy would go far* **be successful,** succeed, prosper, flourish, thrive, get on, get on in the world, make good, set the world on fire; informal make a name for oneself, make one's mark, go places, do all right for oneself, find a place in the sun. **go too far** *one of these days, you're going to go too far and they're going to haul you away* **go to extremes,** go overboard, overdo it, go over the top, not know when to stop. **so far 1** *nobody has noticed so far* **up to this point,** up to now, as yet, thus far, hitherto, up to the present, to date.
2 *his liberalism only extends so far* **to a certain extent,** up to a point, to a degree, within reason, within limits.

farce ▶ noun **1** *the stories approach farce* **slapstick comedy,** slapstick, burlesque, vaudeville, buffoonery.
ANTONYMS tragedy.
2 *the trial was a farce* **mockery,** travesty, absurdity, sham, pretense, masquerade, charade, joke, waste of time; informal shambles.

farcical ▶ adjective **1** *the idea is farcical* **ridiculous,** preposterous, ludicrous, absurd, laughable, risible, nonsensical; senseless, pointless, useless; silly, foolish, idiotic, stupid, harebrained, cockamamie; informal crazy, daft.
2 *farcical goings-on* **madcap,** zany, slapstick, comic, comical, clownish, amusing; hilarious, uproarious; informal wacky.

fare ▶ noun **1** *we paid the fare* **ticket price**; price, cost, charge, fee, toll, tariff; transport cost.
2 *the taxi picked up a fare* **passenger,** traveler, customer.
3 *they eat simple fare* **food,** meals, sustenance, nourishment, nutriment, foodstuffs, provender, eatables, provisions; cooking, cuisine; diet; informal grub, nosh, eats, chow; formal comestibles, victuals.

4 *typical Hollywood fare* **offering(s),** wares; menu.

▶ verb *how are you faring?* **get on,** get along, cope, manage, do, muddle through/along, survive; informal make out.

farewell ▶ exclamation *farewell, New York* **goodbye,** so long, bye, bye-bye, see you (later), cheers; adieu, au revoir, ciao, adios, sayonara; bon voyage; informal dated toodle-oo.

▶ noun *an emotional farewell* **goodbye,** valediction, adieu; leave-taking, parting, departure; send-off.

far-fetched ▶ adjective *a far-fetched story about alien abduction* **improbable,** unlikely, implausible, unconvincing, dubious, doubtful, incredible, unbelievable, unthinkable; contrived, fanciful, unrealistic, ridiculous, absurd, preposterous; informal hard to swallow, fishy.

farm ▶ noun *a farm of 100 acres* **ranch,** farmstead, plantation, estate, family farm, dairy farm, hobby farm; farmland, market garden.

▶ verb 1 *he farmed locally* **work the land,** be a farmer, cultivate the land; rear livestock.
2 *they farm the land* **cultivate,** till, work, plow, dig, plant.
3 *the family farms sheep* **breed,** rear, keep, raise, tend.

– PHRASES **farm something out** *we farmed out the warehouse construction to another firm* **contract out,** outsource, subcontract, delegate.

farmer ▶ noun *the independent Tennessee farmers have been hurt by this careless legislation* **agriculturist,** agronomist, rancher, smallholder, peasant; farmhand; historical habitant, grazier.

farming ▶ noun *her family's been in farming since the 1700s* **agriculture,** cultivation, ranching, land management, farm management; husbandry; agronomy, agribusiness.

farsighted ▶ adjective *reaping the benefits of her farsighted investments* **prescient,** visionary, percipient, shrewd, discerning, judicious, canny, prudent.

farther ▶ adverb *he'd like to live even farther from the city* **further,** farther away, further away, more remote, more distant, more removed.

▶ adjective *the farther side of the field* **more distant,** more remote, remoter, farther away/off, further, further (away/off); far, other, opposite.

farthest ▶ adjective *the farthest island in the chain is uninhabited* **most distant,** most remote, remotest, farthest away, furthest, furthest away, farthermost, furthermost; (most) outlying, (most) outer, outermost, extreme, uttermost, ultimate; archaic outmost.
ANTONYMS nearest.

▶ adverb *Charlie threw his discus the farthest* **most distant,** farthest away, furthest, furthest away, at/for the greatest distance.

fascinate ▶ verb *the space program fascinates me* **interest,** captivate, engross, absorb, enchant, enthrall, entrance, transfix, rivet, mesmerize, engage, compel; lure, tempt, entice, draw; charm, attract, intrigue, divert, entertain.
ANTONYMS bore.

fascinating ▶ adjective *the book is a fascinating study of Southern schools during the Civil War* **interesting,** captivating, engrossing, absorbing, enchanting, enthralling, spellbinding, riveting, engaging, compelling, compulsive, gripping, thrilling; alluring, tempting, irresistible; charming, attractive, intriguing, diverting, entertaining.

fascination ▶ noun *crime and criminals are topics of endless fascination* **interest,** preoccupation, passion, obsession, compulsion; allure, lure, charm, attraction, intrigue, appeal, pull, draw.

fashion ▶ noun 1 *the fashion for tight clothes* **vogue,** trend, craze, rage, mania, fad; style, look; tendency, convention, custom, practice; informal thing.
2 *the world of fashion* **clothes,** clothing design, couture; the garment industry; informal the rag trade.
3 *it needs to be run in a sensible fashion* **manner,** way, method, mode, style; system, approach.

▶ verb *the model was fashioned from lead* **construct,** build, make, manufacture, fabricate, tailor, contrive; cast, shape, form, mold, sculpt; forge, hew.

– PHRASES **after a fashion** *the arrangement worked after a fashion* **to a certain extent,** in a way, somehow, somehow or other, in a manner of speaking, in its way. **in fashion** *are these hideous shoes really in fashion?* **fashionable,** in vogue, up-to-date, up-to-the-minute, all the rage, chic, à la mode; informal trendy, with it, cool, in, the in thing, hot, big, hip, happening, now, sharp, groovy, tony, fly. **out of fashion** *sorry, Dad, that necktie is completely out of fashion* **unfashionable,** dated, old-fashioned, out of date, outdated, outmoded, behind the times; unstylish, untrendy, unpopular, passé, démodé; informal old hat, out, square, uncool.

fashionable ▶ adjective *a fashionable spa in Newport* **in vogue,** voguish, in fashion, popular, up-to-date, up-to-the-minute, modern, all the rage, du jour, modish, à la mode, trendsetting; stylish, chic; informal trendy, classy, with it, cool, in, hot, big, hip, happening, now, snazzy, spiffy, tony, fly.

fast[1] ▶ adjective 1 *a fast pace* **speedy,** quick, swift, rapid; fast-moving, fast-paced, high-speed, turbo, sporty; accelerated, express, blistering, breakneck, pell-mell; hasty, hurried; informal nippy, zippy, blinding, supersonic; literary fleet.
ANTONYMS slow.
2 *he held the door fast* **secure,** fastened, tight, firm, closed, shut; immovable, unbudgeable.
ANTONYMS loose.
3 *a fast color* **indelible,** lasting, permanent, stable.
ANTONYMS temporary.
4 *fast friends* **loyal,** devoted, faithful, firm, steadfast, staunch, true, bosom, inseparable; constant, enduring, unswerving.
5 *a fast woman* **promiscuous,** licentious, dissolute, debauched, impure, unchaste, wanton, abandoned, of easy virtue; sluttish, whorish; intemperate, immoderate, shameless, sinful, immoral; informal easy; dated loose.
ANTONYMS chaste.

▶ adverb 1 *she drove fast* **quickly,** rapidly, swiftly,

speedily, briskly, at speed, at full tilt; hastily, hurriedly, in a hurry, posthaste, pell-mell; like a shot, like a flash, on the double, at the speed of light; informal lickety-split, PDQ (pretty damn quick), nippily, like (greased) lightning, hell-bent for leather, like mad, like the wind, like a bat out of hell; literary apace.
ANTONYMS slowly.
2 *his wheels were stuck fast* **securely,** firmly, immovably, fixedly.
3 *he's fast asleep* **deeply,** sound, completely.
4 *she lived fast and dangerously* **wildly,** dissolutely, intemperately, immoderately, recklessly, self-indulgently, extravagantly.

fast² ▶ **verb** *we must fast and pray* **eat nothing,** abstain from food, refrain from eating, go without food, go hungry, starve oneself; go on a hunger strike.
ANTONYMS eat.
▶ **noun** *a five-day fast* **period of fasting,** period of abstinence; hunger strike; diet.
ANTONYMS feast.

fasten ▶ **verb 1** *he fastened the door* **bolt,** lock, secure, make fast, chain, seal.
ANTONYMS unlock.
2 *they fastened splints to his leg* **attach,** fix, affix, clip, pin, tack; stick, bond, join.
ANTONYMS remove.
3 *he fastened his horse to a tree* **tie,** tie up, bind, tether, truss, fetter, lash, hitch, anchor, strap, rope.
ANTONYMS untie.
4 *the dress fastens at the front* **button (up),** zip (up), do up, close.
ANTONYMS undo.
5 *his gaze fastened on me* **focus,** fix, be riveted, concentrate, zero in, zoom in, direct at.
6 *blame had been* ***fastened on*** *the underling* **ascribe to,** attribute to, assign to, chalk up to; pin on, lay at the door of.
7 *critics* ***fastened on*** *the end of the report* **single out,** concentrate on, focus on, pick out, fix on, seize on.

fastidious ▶ **adjective** *he was fastidious about personal hygiene* **scrupulous,** punctilious, painstaking, meticulous; perfectionist, fussy, finicky, overparticular; critical, overcritical, hypercritical, hard to please, exacting, demanding; informal persnickety, nitpicking, choosy, picky, anal.
ANTONYMS lax.

fat ▶ **adjective 1** *a fat man* **plump,** stout, overweight, large, chubby, portly, flabby, paunchy, potbellied, beer-bellied, meaty, of ample proportions, heavyset; obese, corpulent, fleshy, gross; informal plus-sized, big-boned, tubby, roly-poly, well-upholstered, beefy, porky, blubbery, chunky, pudgy.
ANTONYMS thin, skinny.
2 *fat bacon* **fatty,** greasy, oily, oleaginous; formal pinguid.
ANTONYMS lean.
3 *a fat book* **thick,** big, chunky, bulky, substantial, voluminous; long.
ANTONYMS thin.
4 informal *a fat salary* **large,** substantial, sizable, considerable; generous, lucrative.
ANTONYMS small.
▶ **noun 1** *exercises to burn away the fat* **fatty tissue,** adipose tissue, cellulite; blubber; flab; informal spare tire, love handles.
2 *eggs fried in sizzling fat* **cooking oil,** grease; lard, suet, butter, margarine.

fatal ▶ **adjective 1** *a fatal disease* **deadly,** lethal, mortal, death-dealing; terminal, incurable, untreatable, inoperable, malignant; literary deathly.
ANTONYMS harmless, superficial.
2 *a fatal mistake* **disastrous,** devastating, ruinous, catastrophic, calamitous, dire; costly; formal grievous.
ANTONYMS harmless, beneficial.

fatalism ▶ **noun** *Paulette's fatalism made her come across as pretty morose* **passive acceptance,** resignation, stoicism, acceptance of the inevitable; pessimism, defeatism, negativism, negative thinking, doom and gloom; predeterminism.

fatality ▶ **noun** *news of this fatality has spread quickly* **death,** casualty, mortality, victim; fatal accident.

fate ▶ **noun 1** *what has fate in store for me?* **destiny,** providence, the stars, chance, luck, serendipity, fortune, kismet, karma.
2 *my fate was in their hands* **future,** destiny, outcome, end, lot.
3 *a similar fate would befall other killers* **death,** demise, end; retribution, sentence.
4 Mythology **(the Fates)** *the Fates will decide* the weird sisters; the Parcae, the Moirai, the Norns; 'Clotho, Lachesis, and Atropos'.
▶ **verb (be fated)** *his daughter was fated to face the same problem* **be predestined,** be preordained, be destined, be meant, be doomed; be sure, be certain, be bound, be guaranteed.

fateful ▶ **adjective 1** *that fateful day* **decisive,** critical, crucial, pivotal; momentous, important, key, significant, historic, portentous; informal earth-shattering, earth-shaking. See note at **OMINOUS.**
ANTONYMS unimportant, trivial.
2 *their fateful defeat in 1812* **disastrous,** ruinous, calamitous, devastating, tragic, terrible.

father ▶ **noun 1** *his mother and father* **dad;** daddy, pop, pa, dada, papa; old man, patriarch, paterfamilias.
2 literary *the religion of my fathers* **ancestor,** forefather, forebear, predecessor, antecedent, progenitor, primogenitor.
ANTONYMS descendant.
3 *the father of democracy* **originator,** initiator, founder, inventor, creator, maker, author, architect.
4 *the city fathers* **leader,** elder, patriarch, official.
5 (Father) *our heavenly Father* **God,** Lord, Lord God.
6 (often **Father**) *ask the father to pray for you* **priest,** pastor, parson, clergyman, cleric, minister, preacher; informal reverend, padre.
▶ **verb parent,** be the father of, bring into the world, spawn, sire, breed; literary beget; archaic engender.

fatherland ▶ **noun** *returning to his fatherland after forty years* **native land,** native country, homeland, mother country, motherland, land of one's birth.

fatherly ▶ adjective *she appreciated his fatherly advice* **paternal,** fatherlike; protective, supportive, encouraging, affectionate, caring, sympathetic, indulgent.

fathom ▶ verb **1** *Charlotte tried to fathom her cat's expression* **understand,** comprehend, work out, make sense of, grasp, divine, puzzle out, get to the bottom of; interpret, decipher, decode; informal make head(s) or tail(s) of, crack. **2** *fathoming the ocean* **measure the depth of,** sound, plumb.

fatigue ▶ noun **tiredness,** weariness, sleepiness, drowsiness, exhaustion, enervation, languor, lethargy, torpor, prostration.
ANTONYMS energy.
▶ verb *the troops were fatigued* **tire (out),** exhaust, wear out, drain, weary, wash out, overtire, prostrate, enervate; informal knock out, take it out of, do in, poop, bush, wear to a frazzle. See note at **TIRED**.
ANTONYMS invigorate.

fatness ▶ noun *persons with varying degrees of fatness were chosen for the stress tests* **plumpness,** stoutness, heaviness, chubbiness, portliness, rotundity, flabbiness, paunchiness; obesity, corpulence; informal tubbiness, pudginess.
ANTONYMS thinness.

fatten ▶ verb **1** *fattening livestock* **make fat/fatter,** feed (up), build up.
2 *we're sending her home to **fatten up*** **put on weight,** gain weight, get heavier, grow fatter, fill out.
ANTONYMS lose weight, slim down.

fatty ▶ adjective *avoid fatty foods* **greasy,** oily, fat, oleaginous; high-fat.
ANTONYMS lean.

fatuous ▶ adjective *the irritation of fatuous questions* **silly,** foolish, stupid, inane, idiotic, vacuous, asinine; pointless, senseless, ridiculous, ludicrous, absurd; informal dumb, daft.
ANTONYMS sensible.

fault ▶ noun **1** *he has his faults* **defect,** failing, imperfection, flaw, blemish, shortcoming, weakness, frailty, foible, vice.
ANTONYMS merit, strength.
2 *engineers have located the fault* **defect,** flaw, imperfection, bug; error, mistake, inaccuracy; informal glitch, gremlin.
3 *it was not my fault* **responsibility,** liability, culpability, blameworthiness, guilt.
4 *don't blame one child for another's faults* **misdeed,** wrongdoing, offense, misdemeanor, misconduct, indiscretion, peccadillo, transgression; informal no-no. See note at **SIN**.
▶ verb *you couldn't fault any of the players* **find fault with,** criticize, attack, censure, condemn, reproach; complain about, quibble about, moan about; informal knock, slam, gripe about, beef about, pick holes in.
– PHRASES **at fault** *no one is at fault* **to blame,** blameworthy, culpable; responsible, guilty, in the wrong. **to a fault** *Katherine is very giving, sometimes to a fault* **excessively,** unduly, immoderately, overly, needlessly.

CHOOSE THE RIGHT WORD

fault, blemish, defect, failing, flaw, foible, shortcoming

No one is perfect. But when it comes to cataloguing your own imperfections, it's best to start with your **foibles**—the slight weaknesses or eccentricities for which you will be most quickly forgiven. You also have a good chance of being forgiven for your **shortcomings**, which are not necessarily damaging to others (*his ardent devotion to his dog was a shortcoming that was readily overlooked*). **Failing** suggests a more severe shortcoming, usually with more serious consequences (*chronic tardiness was one of her failings*), but a *failing* can also be a weakness of character that you're not responsible for and perhaps not even aware of (*pride is a common failing among those who have met with great success early in life*). **Fault** also implies failure—but not necessarily a serious failure—to reach moral perfection (*his major fault was his outspokenness*). While *fault* usually indicates something inherent in your nature rather than external to it, a **flaw** can be either superficial (*a flaw in his otherwise immaculate appearance*) or profound (*a personality flaw that made her impossible to work with*), and it can refer to things as well as people (*a flaw in the table's finish*). A **blemish** is usually a physical flaw (*a facial blemish*), although it can be anything that disfigures or mars the perfection of someone or something (*a blemish on her otherwise spotless academic record*). You can get rid of a blemish and even overcome your shortcomings, but a **defect** is a flaw so serious that you may never be able to get rid of it (*a defect in his hearing*).

fault-finding ▶ noun *he came to expect nothing but fault-finding from his wife* **criticism,** captiousness, caviling, quibbling; complaining, grumbling, carping, moaning; informal nitpicking, griping, grousing, bellyaching.
ANTONYMS praise.

faultless ▶ adjective *speaking faultless English* **perfect,** flawless, without fault, error-free, impeccable, accurate, precise, exact, correct, exemplary.
ANTONYMS flawed.

faulty ▶ adjective **1** *a faulty electric blanket* **malfunctioning,** broken, damaged, defective, not working, out of order; informal on the blink, acting up, kaput, bust, busted, on the fritz.
ANTONYMS working.
2 *her logic is faulty* **defective,** flawed, unsound, inaccurate, incorrect, erroneous, fallacious, wrong.
ANTONYMS sound.

faux pas ▶ noun *excuse my faux pas* **mistake,** blunder, gaffe, indiscretion, impropriety, solecism, barbarism; informal boo-boo, blooper. See note at **MISTAKE**.

favor ▶ noun **1** *will you do me a favor?* **service,**

good turn, good deed, kindness, act of kindness, courtesy.
ANTONYMS disservice.
2 *she looked on him with favor* **approval,** approbation, goodwill, kindness, benevolence.
ANTONYMS disapproval.
3 *they showed favor to one of the players* **favoritism,** bias, partiality, partisanship.
4 *you shall receive the king's favor* **patronage,** backing, support, assistance.
▶ **verb 1** *she favors the modest option* **prefer,** lean toward, opt for, tend toward, be in favor of; approve (of), advocate, support.
ANTONYMS oppose.
2 *he favors his son over his daughter* **treat partially,** be biased toward, prefer.
3 *the conditions favored the other team* **benefit,** advantage, help, assist, aid, be of service to, do a favor for.
ANTONYMS hinder.
4 *he favored Lucy with a smile* **oblige,** honor, gratify, humor, indulge.
– PHRASES **in favor of** *we're in favor of a strike* **on the side of,** pro, (all) for, giving support to, approving of, sympathetic to.

favorable ▶ **adjective 1** *a favorable assessment of his ability* **approving,** commendatory, complimentary, flattering, glowing, enthusiastic; good, pleasing, positive; informal rave.
ANTONYMS critical.
2 *conditions are favorable* **advantageous,** beneficial, in one's favor, good, right, suitable, fitting, appropriate; propitious, auspicious, promising, encouraging.
ANTONYMS disadvantageous.
3 *a favorable reply* **positive,** affirmative, assenting, agreeing, approving; encouraging, reassuring.
ANTONYMS negative.

favorite ▶ **adjective** *his favorite aunt* **best-loved,** most-liked, favored, dearest; preferred, chosen, choice.
▶ **noun 1** *Brutus was Caesar's favorite* **(first) choice,** pick, preference, pet, darling, the apple of one's eye; informal blue-eyed boy/girl, golden boy/girl, fair-haired boy/girl.
2 *the favorite in the first race* **expected winner,** probable winner, odds-on favorite, top seed, top pick, front runner.

favoritism ▶ **noun** *we want one rule for everyone and no favoritism* **partiality,** partisanship, preferential treatment, favor, prejudice, bias, inequality, unfairness, discrimination.

fawn ▶ **verb** *they were fawning over the president* **be obsequious to,** be sycophantic to, curry favor with, flatter, play up to, crawl to, ingratiate oneself with, dance attendance on; informal suck up to, be all over, brown-nose, toady.

fawning ▶ **adjective** *her fawning personal staff* **obsequious,** servile, sycophantic, flattering, ingratiating, unctuous, oleaginous, groveling, crawling; informal bootlicking, smarmy, sucky, brown-nosing, toadying.

fear ▶ **noun 1** *he felt fear at entering the house* **terror,** fright, fearfulness, horror, alarm, panic, agitation, trepidation, dread, consternation, dismay, distress; anxiety, worry, angst, unease, uneasiness, apprehension, apprehensiveness, nervousness, nerves, perturbation, foreboding; informal the creeps, the shivers, the willies, the heebie-jeebies, jitteriness, twitchiness, butterflies (in the stomach).
2 *she overcame her fears* **phobia,** aversion, antipathy, dread, bugbear, nightmare, horror, terror; anxiety, neurosis; informal hang-up.
3 *there's no fear of my leaving you alone* **likelihood,** likeliness, prospect, possibility, chance, probability; risk, danger.
▶ **verb 1** *she feared her husband* **be afraid of,** be fearful of, be scared of, be apprehensive of, dread, live in fear of, be terrified of; be anxious about, worry about, feel apprehensive about.
2 *he fears heights* **have a phobia about,** have a horror of, take fright at.
3 *he feared to tell them* **be too afraid,** be too scared, hesitate, dare not.
4 *they* ***feared for*** *his health* **worry about,** feel anxious about, feel concerned about, have anxieties about.
5 *all who fear the Lord* **stand in awe of,** revere, reverence, venerate, respect.
6 *I fear that you may be right* **suspect,** have a (sneaking) suspicion, be inclined to think, be afraid, have a hunch, think it likely.

fearful ▶ **adjective 1** *they are fearful of being overheard* **afraid,** frightened, scared (stiff), scared to death, terrified, petrified; alarmed, panicky, nervous, tense, apprehensive, uneasy, worried (sick), anxious; informal jittery, jumpy.
2 *the guards were fearful* **nervous,** trembling, quaking, cowed, daunted; timid, timorous, faint-hearted; informal jittery, jumpy, twitchy, trepidatious, keyed up, in a cold sweat, a bundle of nerves; informal spooked.
3 *a fearful accident* **horrific,** terrible, dreadful, awful, appalling, frightful, ghastly, horrible, horrifying, horrendous, terribly bad, shocking, atrocious, abominable, hideous, monstrous, gruesome.

fearfully ▶ **adverb** *she opened the door fearfully* **apprehensively,** uneasily, nervously, timidly, timorously, hesitantly, with one's heart in one's mouth.

fearless ▶ **adjective** *fearless warriors* **bold,** brave, courageous, intrepid, valiant, valorous, gallant, plucky, lionhearted, heroic, daring, audacious, indomitable, doughty; unafraid, undaunted, unflinching; informal gutsy, spunky, ballsy, feisty.
ANTONYMS timid, cowardly.

fearsome ▶ **adjective** *the crocodile's teeth were a fearsome sight* **frightening,** scary, horrifying, terrifying, menacing, chilling, spine-chilling, hair-raising, alarming, unnerving, daunting, formidable, forbidding, dismaying, disquieting, disturbing.

feasible ▶ **adjective** *a feasible solution* **practicable,** practical, workable, achievable, attainable, realizable, viable, realistic, sensible, reasonable, within reason; suitable, possible, expedient; informal doable.
ANTONYMS impractical.

feast ▶ **noun 1** *a wedding feast* **banquet,** celebration meal, lavish dinner; entertainment; revels, festivities; informal blowout, spread.
2 *the feast of St. Stephen* **(religious) festival,**

feast day, saint's day, holy day, holiday.
3 *a feast for the eyes* **treat,** delight, joy, pleasure.
▶ **verb 1** *they **feasted on** lobster* **gorge on,** dine on, eat one's fill of, overindulge in, binge on; eat, devour, consume, partake of; informal stuff one's face with, stuff oneself with, pig out on, chow down on.
2 *they feasted the returning heroes* **hold a banquet for,** throw a party for, wine and dine, entertain lavishly, regale, treat, fête.

feat ▶ **noun** *his gaining access to the imperial palace was no small feat* **achievement,** accomplishment, attainment, coup, triumph; undertaking, enterprise, venture, operation, exercise, endeavor, effort, performance, exploit.

feather ▶ **noun** *the size and markings of this feather would indicate a barred owl* **plume,** quill, flight feather, tail feather; Ornithology covert, plumule; (**feathers**) plumage, feathering, down.

feature ▶ **noun 1** *a typical feature of French music* **characteristic,** attribute, quality, property, trait, hallmark, trademark; aspect, facet, factor, ingredient, component, element, theme; peculiarity, idiosyncrasy, quirk.
2 *her delicate features* **face,** countenance, physiognomy; informal mug, kisser; puss, pan; literary visage, lineaments.
3 *she made a feature of her garden sculptures* **centerpiece,** (special) attraction, highlight, focal point, focus (of attention).
4 *she writes features at the newspaper* **article,** piece, item, report, story, column, review, commentary, write-up.
5 *tonight's feature stars Clint Eastwood* **movie,** film; main show, main event; informal flick, pic.
▶ **verb 1** *PBS is featuring a week of live concerts* **present,** promote, make a feature of, give prominence to, focus attention on, spotlight, highlight.
2 *she is to feature in a major advertising campaign* **star,** appear, participate, play a part.

feces ▶ **plural noun** *the feces were examined for parasites* **excrement,** bodily waste, waste matter, ordure, dung, manure; excreta, stools, droppings; dirt, filth, muck, mess, night soil; informal poop, pooh, doo-doo, turds, poo, caca.

fecund ▶ **adjective** *the fecund wheat fields* **fertile,** fruitful, productive, high-yielding; rich, lush, flourishing, thriving. See note at FERTILE.
ANTONYMS barren.

federation ▶ **noun** *a federation of Protestant denominations* **confederation,** confederacy, league; combination, alliance, coalition, union, syndicate, guild, consortium, partnership, cooperative, association, amalgamation; informal federacy.

fee ▶ **noun** *for the quality of work, I think the fee was reasonable* **payment,** wage, salary, allowance; price, cost, charge, tariff, rate, amount, sum, figure; (**fees**) remuneration, dues, earnings, pay; formal emolument.

feeble ▶ **adjective 1** *he was very old and feeble* **weak,** weakly, weakened, frail, infirm, delicate, sickly, ailing, unwell, poorly, enfeebled, enervated, debilitated, incapacitated, decrepit, etiolated. See note at WEAK.
ANTONYMS strong.
2 *a feeble argument* **ineffective,** ineffectual, inadequate, unconvincing, implausible, unsatisfactory, poor, weak, flimsy.
ANTONYMS effective.
3 *he's too feeble to stand up to his boss* **cowardly,** craven, faint-hearted, spineless, spiritless, lily-livered, chinless; timid, timorous, fearful, unassertive, weak, ineffectual, wishy-washy; informal wimpy, sissy, sissified, gutless, chicken.
ANTONYMS forceful, brave.
4 *a feeble light* **faint,** dim, weak, pale, soft, subdued, muted.
ANTONYMS strong.

feeble-minded ▶ **adjective** *he's not as feeble-minded as he pretends to be* **stupid,** idiotic, imbecilic, foolish, witless, doltish, empty-headed, vacuous; informal halfwitted, moronic, dumb, dim, dopey, dippy; daft.
ANTONYMS clever.

feed ▶ **verb 1** *feed the kids* **give food to,** provide (food) for, cater for, cook for.
2 *feed the baby* **nurse,** breast-feed, suckle; bottle-feed.
3 *too many cows feeding in a small area* **graze,** browse, crop, pasture; eat, consume food, chow down.
4 *the birds **feed on** a varied diet* **live on/off,** exist on, subsist on, eat, consume.
5 *feeding one's self-esteem* **strengthen,** fortify, support, bolster, reinforce, boost, fuel, encourage.
6 *she fed secrets to the Russians* **supply,** provide, give, deliver, furnish, issue, pass on.
▶ **noun** *feed for goats and sheep* **fodder,** food, forage, pasturage, herbage, provender; formal comestibles.

feel ▶ **verb 1** *she felt the fabric* **touch,** stroke, caress, fondle, finger, thumb, handle.
2 *she felt a breeze on her back* **perceive,** sense, detect, discern, notice, be aware of, be conscious of.
3 *you will not feel any pain* **experience,** undergo, go through, bear, endure, suffer.
4 *he felt his way toward the door* **grope,** fumble, scrabble, pick.
5 *feel the temperature of the water* **test,** try (out), check, assess.
6 *he feels that he should go to the meeting* **believe,** think, consider (it right), be of the opinion, hold, maintain, judge; informal reckon, figure.
7 *I feel that he is only biding his time* **sense,** have a (funny) feeling, get the impression, have a hunch, intuit.
8 *the air feels damp* **seem,** appear, strike one as.
▶ **noun 1** *the divers worked by feel* (**sense of**) **touch,** tactile sense, feeling (one's way).
2 *the feel of the paper* **texture,** surface, finish; weight, thickness, consistency, quality.
3 *the feel of a room* **atmosphere,** ambience, aura, mood, feeling, air, impression, character, tenor, spirit, flavor; informal vibrations, vibes.
4 *a feel for languages* **aptitude,** knack, flair, bent, talent, gift, faculty, ability.
– PHRASES **feel for** *tell your mother we certainly feel for her* **sympathize with,** be sorry for, pity, feel pity for, feel sympathy for, feel compassion

for, be moved by; commiserate with, condole with. **feel like** *I feel like some lemon meringue pie* **want,** would like, wish for, desire, fancy, feel in need of, long for; informal yen for, be dying for.

feeler ▶ **noun 1** *the fish has two feelers on its head* **antenna,** tentacle, tactile/sensory organ; Zoology antennule.
2 *the committee put out feelers* **tentative inquiry/proposal,** advance, approach, overture, probe.

feeling ▶ **noun 1** *assess the fabric by feeling* **(sense of) touch,** feel, tactile sense, using one's hands.
2 *a feeling of nausea* **sensation,** sense, consciousness.
3 *I had a feeling that I would win* **suspicion,** sneaking suspicion, notion, inkling, hunch, funny feeling, feeling in one's bones, fancy, idea; presentiment, premonition; informal gut feeling.
4 *the strength of her feeling* **love,** affection, fondness, tenderness, warmth, warmness, emotion, sentiment; passion, ardor, desire. See note at **EMOTION**.
5 *a rush of feeling* **compassion,** sympathy, empathy, fellow feeling, concern, solicitude, solicitousness, tenderness, love; pity, sorrow, commiseration.
6 *he had hurt her feelings* **sensibilities,** sensitivities, self-esteem, pride.
7 *my feeling is that it is true* **opinion,** belief, view, impression, intuition, instinct, hunch, estimation, guess.
8 *a feeling of peace* **atmosphere,** ambience, aura, air, feel, mood, impression, spirit, quality, flavor; informal vibrations, vibes.
▶ **adjective** *a feeling man* **sensitive,** warm, warmhearted, tender, tenderhearted, caring, sympathetic, kind, compassionate, understanding, thoughtful.

feign ▶ **verb 1** *she lay still and feigned sleep* **simulate,** fake, sham, affect, give the appearance of, make a pretense of.
2 *he's not really ill, he's only feigning* **pretend,** put it on, fake, sham, bluff, masquerade, play-act; informal kid.

felicitations ▶ **plural noun** *on the occasion of your marriage, felicitations from us all* **congratulations,** good wishes, best wishes, regards, kind regards, blessings, compliments, respects.

felicitous ▶ **adjective 1** *his nickname was particularly felicitous* **apt,** well-chosen, fitting, suitable, appropriate, apposite, pertinent, germane, relevant.
ANTONYMS inappropriate.
2 *the room's only felicitous feature* **favorable,** advantageous, good, pleasing.
ANTONYMS unfortunate.

feline ▶ **adjective** *she moved with feline grace* **catlike,** graceful, sleek, sinuous.
▶ **noun** *her pet feline* **cat,** kitten; informal puss, pussy (cat), kitty (cat); archaic grimalkin.

fell ▶ **verb 1** *all the dead sycamores had to be felled* **cut down,** chop down, hack down, saw down, clear.
2 *she felled him with one punch* **knock down/over,** knock to the ground, strike down, bring down, bring to the ground, prostrate; knock out, knock unconscious; informal deck, floor, flatten, down, lay out, KO.

fellow ▶ **noun 1** informal *he's a decent sort of fellow* **man,** boy; person, individual, soul; informal guy, character, customer, joe, devil, bastard, chap, dude, hombre; dated dog.
2 *he exchanged glances with his fellows* **companion,** friend, comrade, partner, associate, coworker, colleague; peer, equal, contemporary, confrère; informal chum, pal, buddy.
– PHRASES **fellow feeling** *the fellow feeling he had for his jilted brother came from recent experience* **sympathy,** empathy, feeling, compassion, care, concern, solicitude, solicitousness, warmth, tenderness, (brotherly) love; pity, sorrow, commiseration.

fellowship ▶ **noun 1** *a community bound together in fellowship* **companionship,** companionability, sociability, comradeship, camaraderie, friendship, mutual support; togetherness, solidarity; informal chumminess.
2 *the church fellowship* **association,** society, club, league, union, guild, affiliation, alliance, fraternity, confraternity, brotherhood, sorority, sodality, benevolent society.

female ▶ **adjective** *female attributes* **feminine,** womanly, ladylike.
ANTONYMS male.
▶ **noun** *the author was a female* See **WOMAN** (sense 1).

feminine ▶ **adjective 1** *a very feminine young woman* **womanly,** ladylike; girlish; soft, delicate, gentle, graceful; informal girly.
ANTONYMS masculine.
2 *he seemed slightly feminine* **effeminate,** womanish, unmanly, effete, epicene; informal sissy, sissified, wimpy.
ANTONYMS manly.

fence ▶ **noun 1** *a gap in the fence* **barrier,** fencing, enclosure, barricade, stockade, palisade, fenceline; railing.
2 informal *a fence dealing mainly in jewelry* **receiver (of stolen goods),** dealer.
▶ **verb 1** *they fenced off many acres* **enclose,** surround, circumscribe, encircle, circle, encompass; archaic compass.
2 *he* ***fenced in*** *his chickens* **confine,** pen in, coop up, shut in/up, separate off; enclose, surround, corral.
3 *she fences as a hobby* **sword-fight**; duel.
– PHRASES **(sitting) on the fence** informal *voters tend to shy away from candidates who are on the fence* **undecided,** uncommitted, uncertain, unsure, vacillating, wavering, dithering, hesitant, doubtful, ambivalent, of two minds, in a quandary, hemming and hawing, wishy-washy; neutral, impartial, nonpartisan.

fend ▶ **verb** *they were unable to* ***fend off*** *the invasion* **ward off,** head off, stave off, hold off, repel, repulse, resist, fight off, defend oneself against, prevent, stop, block, intercept, hold back.
– PHRASES **fend for oneself** *the children were forced to fend for themselves* **take care of oneself,** look after oneself, provide for oneself, manage (by oneself), cope alone, stand on one's

own two feet.

ferment ▶ verb **1** *the beer continues to ferment* **undergo fermentation,** brew; effervesce, fizz, foam, froth.
2 *an environment that ferments disorder* **cause,** bring about, give rise to, generate, engender, spawn, instigate, provoke, incite, excite, stir up, whip up, foment; literary beget, enkindle.
▶ noun *a ferment of revolutionary upheaval* **fever,** furor, frenzy, tumult, storm, rumpus; turmoil, upheaval, unrest, disquiet, uproar, agitation, turbulence, disruption, confusion, disorder, chaos, mayhem; informal hoo-ha, to-do.

ferocious ▶ adjective **1** *ferocious animals* **fierce,** savage, wild, predatory, aggressive, dangerous.
ANTONYMS gentle, tame.
2 *a ferocious attack* **brutal,** vicious, violent, bloody, barbaric, savage, sadistic, ruthless, cruel, merciless, heartless, bloodthirsty, murderous; literary fell.
ANTONYMS gentle.
3 informal *a ferocious headache* **intense,** strong, powerful, fierce, severe, extreme, acute, unbearable, raging; informal hellish.
ANTONYMS mild.

ferret ▶ verb **1** *she ferreted in her handbag* **rummage,** feel around, grope around, forage around, fish around/about, poke around/about; search through, hunt through, rifle through.
2 *ferreting out misdemeanors* **unearth,** uncover, discover, detect, search out, bring to light, track down, dig up, root out, nose out, snoop around for.

ferry ▶ noun *the Block Island ferry from New London* **passenger boat,** passenger ship, ferry boat, car ferry; ship, boat, vessel; historical packet, packet boat.
▶ verb *the new cars were ferried to the island* **transport,** convey, carry, ship, run, take, bring, shuttle.

fertile ▶ adjective **1** *the soil is fertile* **fecund,** fruitful, productive, high-yielding, rich, lush.
2 *fertile couples* **able to conceive,** able to have children; technical fecund.
ANTONYMS barren.
3 *a fertile brain* **imaginative,** inventive, innovative, creative, visionary, original, ingenious; productive, prolific.
ANTONYMS unimaginative.

> CHOOSE THE RIGHT WORD
>
> **fertile, fecund, fruitful, prolific**
>
> A **fertile** woman is one who has the power to produce offspring, just as *fertile* soil produces crops and a *fertile* imagination produces ideas. This adjective pertains to anything in which seeds (or thoughts) can take root and grow. A woman with ten children might be described as **fecund**, which means that she is not only capable of producing many offspring but has actually done it. A woman can be *fertile*, in other words, without necessarily being *fecund*. **Fruitful**, whose meaning is very close to that of *fecund* when used to describe plants and may replace *fertile* in reference to soil or land, pertains specifically to something that promotes fertility or fecundity (*a fruitful downpour*). It can also apply in a broader sense to anything that bears or promotes results (*a fruitful idea; a fruitful discussion*). While it's one thing to call a woman with a large family *fecund*, **prolific** is more usually applied to animals or plants in the literal sense of fertility, and suggests reproducing in great quantity or with rapidity. Figuratively, prolific is often used of highly productive creative efforts (*a prolific author with 40 titles published*).

fertilize ▶ verb **1** *the field was fertilized* **feed,** mulch, compost, green manure, manure, dress, top-dress, add fertilizer to.
2 *these orchids are fertilized by insects* **pollinate,** cross-pollinate, cross-fertilize, fecundate.

fertilizer ▶ noun *we use only organic fertilizer* **manure,** plant food, compost, dressing, top dressing, dung.

fervent ▶ adjective *a fervent prayer* **impassioned,** passionate, intense, vehement, ardent, sincere, fervid, heartfelt; enthusiastic, zealous, fanatical, hardcore, wholehearted, avid, eager, keen, committed, dedicated, devout; literary perfervid. See note at EAGER.
ANTONYMS apathetic.

fervid ▶ adjective *fervid protestations of love* **fervent,** ardent, passionate, impassioned, intense, vehement, wholehearted, heartfelt, sincere, earnest; literary perfervid.

fervor ▶ noun *even the smallest of tasks he tackled with fervor* **passion,** ardor, intensity, zeal, vehemence, emotion, warmth, earnestness, avidity, eagerness, keenness, enthusiasm, excitement, animation, vigor, energy, fire, spirit, zest, fervency.
ANTONYMS apathy.

fester ▶ verb **1** *his deep wound festered* **suppurate,** become septic, become infected, form pus, weep; Medicine be purulent; archaic rankle.
2 *the garbage festered* **rot,** molder, decay, decompose, putrefy, go bad, spoil, deteriorate.
3 *their resentment festered* **rankle,** eat away, gnaw away, brew, smolder.

festival ▶ noun **1** *the town's fall festival* **fair,** carnival, fiesta, jamboree, celebrations, festivities, fest.
2 *fasting precedes the festival* **holy day,** feast day, saint's day, commemoration, day of observance.

festive ▶ adjective *a festive mood* **jolly,** merry, joyous, joyful, happy, jovial, lighthearted, cheerful, jubilant, convivial, high-spirited, mirthful, uproarious; celebratory, holiday, carnival; Christmassy; archaic festal.

festivity ▶ noun **1** (**festivities**) *food plays an important part in the festivities* **celebration,** festival, entertainment, party, jamboree; merrymaking, feasting, revelry, jollification; revels, fun and games; informal bash.
2 *the festivity of Opening Day* **jubilation,** merriment, gaiety, cheerfulness, cheer, joyfulness, jollity, conviviality, high spirits, revelry.

festoon ▶ noun *festoons of paper flowers* **garland,** chain, lei, swathe, swag, loop.
▶ verb *the room was festooned with streamers* **decorate,** adorn, ornament, trim, deck (out), hang, loop, drape, swathe, garland, wreathe, bedeck; informal do up/out, get up, trick out; literary bedizen.

fetch ▶ verb **1** *he went to fetch a doctor* **(go and) get,** go for, call for, summon, pick up, collect, bring, carry, convey, transport.
2 *the land could fetch a million dollars* **sell for,** bring in, raise, realize, yield, make, command, cost, be priced at; informal go for, set one back, pull in.

fetching ▶ adjective *give this note to the fetching young lady in the blue dress* **attractive,** appealing, sweet, pretty, good-looking, lovely, delightful, charming, prepossessing, captivating, enchanting, irresistible; Scottish bonny; informal divine, heavenly; killer; archaic comely, fair.

fetish ▶ noun **1** *he developed a bodybuilding fetish* **fixation,** obsession, compulsion, mania; weakness, fancy, fascination, fad; informal thing, hang-up.
2 *an African fetish* **juju,** talisman, charm, amulet; totem, idol, image, effigy.

fetter ▶ verb **1** *the captive was fettered* **shackle,** manacle, handcuff, clap in irons, put in chains, chain (up); informal cuff; literary enfetter.
2 *these obligations fetter the company's powers* **restrict,** restrain, constrain, limit; hinder, hamper, impede, obstruct, hamstring, inhibit, check, curb, trammel; informal hog-tie.

fetters ▶ plural noun *bound by fetters of iron* **shackles,** manacles, handcuffs, irons, leg irons, chains, restraints; informal cuffs, bracelets; historical bilboes.

fettle ▶ noun *my, you certainly are in fine fettle* **shape,** trim, fitness, physical fitness, health, state of health; condition, form, repair, state of repair, order, working order.

fetus ▶ noun *an ultrasonic photo of the fetus* **embryo,** unborn baby/child.

feud ▶ noun *tribal feuds* **vendetta,** conflict; rivalry, hostility, enmity, strife, discord; quarrel, argument, falling out. See note at QUARREL.
▶ verb *he feuded with his teammates* **quarrel,** fight, argue, bicker, squabble, fall out, dispute, clash, differ, be at odds; informal scrap.

fever ▶ noun **1** *he developed a fever* **feverishness,** high temperature, febrility; Medicine pyrexia; informal **temperature.**
2 *a fever of excitement* **ferment,** frenzy, furor; ecstasy, rapture.
3 *Stanley Cup fever* **excitement,** frenzy, agitation, passion.

feverish ▶ adjective **1** *she's really feverish* **febrile,** fevered, hot, burning; informal having a temperature.
2 *feverish excitement* **frenzied,** frenetic, hectic, agitated, excited, restless, nervous, worked up, overwrought, frantic, furious, hysterical, wild, uncontrolled, unrestrained.

few ▶ adjective **1** *police are revealing few details* **not many,** hardly any, scarcely any; a small number of, a small amount of, one or two, a handful of; little. See note at LESS.
ANTONYMS many.
2 *comforts here are few* **scarce,** scant, meager, insufficient, in short supply; thin on the ground, few and far between, infrequent, uncommon, rare; negligible.
ANTONYMS plentiful.
▶ pronoun **(a few)** *there weren't many biscuits, but we saved you a few* **a small number,** a handful, one or two, a couple, two or three; not many, hardly any.

fiasco ▶ noun *the picnic was a fiasco* **failure,** disaster, catastrophe, debacle, shambles, farce, mess, wreck; informal flop, washout, snafu.
ANTONYMS success.

fib ▶ noun *you're telling a fib* **lie,** untruth, falsehood, made-up story, invention, fabrication, deception, (piece of) fiction; (little) white lie, half-truth; informal tall story/tale, whopper. See note at LIE[1].
ANTONYMS truth.

fiber ▶ noun **1** *fibers from the murderer's sweater* **thread,** strand, filament; technical fibril.
2 *natural fibers* **material,** cloth, fabric.
3 *fiber in the diet* **roughage,** bulk.

fickle ▶ adjective *the fickle Loretta has a different boyfriend every month* **capricious,** changeable, variable, volatile, mercurial; inconstant, undependable, unsteady, unfaithful, faithless, flighty, giddy, skittish; fair-weather; technical labile; literary mutable.
ANTONYMS constant.

fiction ▶ noun **1** *the popularity of South American fiction* **novels,** stories, (creative) writing, (prose) literature; informal lit.
2 *the president dismissed the allegation as absolute fiction* **fabrication,** invention, lies, fibs, untruth, falsehood, fantasy, nonsense.
ANTONYMS fact.

CHOOSE THE RIGHT WORD

fiction, deception, fable, fabrication, falsehood, figment

If a young child tells you there is a dinosaur under his bed, you might assume that his story is a **fiction**, but it is probably a **figment**. A *fiction* is a story that is invented either to entertain or to deceive (*her excuse was ingenious, but it was pure fiction*), while *figment* suggests the operation of fancy or imagination (*a figment of his imagination*). If a child hides his sandwich under the sofa cushions and tells you that a dinosaur ate it, this would be a **fabrication**, which is a story that is intended to deceive. Unlike a *figment*, which is mostly imagined, a *fabrication* is a false but thoughtfully constructed story in which some truth is often interwoven (*the city's safety record was a fabrication designed to lure tourists downtown*). A **falsehood** is basically a lie—a statement or story that one knows to be false but tells with intent to deceive (*a deliberate falsehood about where the money had come from*). A **deception**, on the other hand, is an act that deceives but not always intentionally (*a foolish deception designed to prevent her parents from worrying*). A **fable** is a fictitious story that deals with events or situations that are clearly fantastic, impossible, or incredible. It often gives animals or inanimate objects the power to speak and conveys a lesson of practical wisdom, as in *Aesop's Fables*.

fictional ▶ adjective *fictional characters* **fictitious,** fictive, invented, imaginary, made up, make-believe, unreal, fabricated, mythical.
ANTONYMS real.

fictitious ▶ adjective 1 *a fictitious name* **false,** fake, fabricated, sham; bogus, spurious, assumed, affected, adopted, feigned, invented, made up; informal pretend, phony.
ANTONYMS genuine.
2 *a fictitious character* See FICTIONAL.

fiddle informal ▶ noun *she played the fiddle* **violin,** viola.
▶ verb 1 *he fiddled with a coaster* **fidget,** play, toy, twiddle, fuss, fool about/around; finger, thumb, handle; informal mess around/about.
2 *he fiddled with the dials* **adjust,** tinker, play around, meddle, interfere.
3 *fiddling the figures* **falsify,** manipulate, massage, rig, distort, misrepresent, doctor, alter, tamper with, interfere with; informal fix, flimflam, cook (the books).

fidelity ▶ noun 1 *fidelity to her husband* **faithfulness,** loyalty, constancy; trueheartedness, trustworthiness, dependability, reliability; formal troth.
ANTONYMS infidelity, disloyalty.
2 *fidelity to your king* **loyalty,** allegiance, obedience; historical homage, fealty.
ANTONYMS disloyalty.
3 *the fidelity of the reproduction* **accuracy,** exactness, precision, preciseness, correctness; strictness, closeness, faithfulness, authenticity.
ANTONYMS inaccuracy.

fidget ▶ verb 1 *the audience began to fidget* **move restlessly,** wriggle, squirm, twitch, jiggle, shuffle, be agitated; informal be jittery.
2 *she fidgeted with her scarf* **play,** fuss, toy, twiddle, fool around; informal fiddle, mess around.
▶ noun 1 *his convulsive fidgets* **twitch,** wriggle, squirm, jiggle, shuffle, tic, spasm.
2 *what a fidget you are!* **flibbertigibbet,** restless person, bundle of nerves.

fidgety ▶ adjective *why is the dog so fidgety?* **restless,** restive, on edge, uneasy, antsy, nervous, keyed up, anxious, agitated; informal jittery, twitchy.

field ▶ noun 1 *a large plowed field* **meadow,** pasture, paddock, grassland, pastureland; literary lea, sward; archaic glebe.
2 *a soccer field* **playing field,** ground, sports field; Brit. pitch.
3 *the field of biotechnology* **area,** sphere, discipline, province, department, domain, sector, branch, subject; informal bailiwick.
4 *your field of vision* **scope,** range, sweep, reach, extent.
5 *she is well ahead of the field* **competitors,** entrants, competition; applicants, candidates, possibles.
▶ verb 1 *she fielded the ball* **catch,** stop, retrieve; return, throw back.
2 *they can field an army of about one million* **deploy,** position, range, dispose.
3 *he fielded some awkward questions* **deal with,** handle, cope with, answer, reply to, respond to.
▶ adjective 1 *field experience* **practical,** hands-on, applied, experiential, empirical.
ANTONYMS theoretical.
2 *field artillery* **mobile,** portable, transportable, movable, maneuverable, light.

fiend ▶ noun 1 *a fiend had taken possession of him* **demon,** devil, evil spirit; informal spook.
2 *a fiend bent on global evildoing* **villain,** beast, brute, barbarian, monster, ogre, sadist, evildoer, swine.
3 informal *a drug fiend* **addict,** abuser, user; informal junkie, —head, —freak.
4 informal *a fitness fiend* **enthusiast,** maniac; devotee, fan, lover, fanatic, addict, buff, freak, nut.

fiendish ▶ adjective 1 *a fiendish torturer* **wicked,** cruel, vicious, evil, malevolent, villainous; brutal, savage, barbaric, barbarous, inhuman, murderous, ruthless, merciless; dated dastardly.
2 *a fiendish plot* **cunning,** clever, ingenious, crafty, canny, wily, devious, shrewd; informal sneaky.
3 *a fiendish puzzle* **difficult,** complex, challenging, complicated, intricate, involved, knotty, thorny, tricky.

fierce ▶ adjective 1 *a fierce black mastiff* **ferocious,** savage, vicious, aggressive.
ANTONYMS gentle.
2 *fierce competition* **aggressive,** cutthroat, competitive; keen, intense, strong, relentless.
ANTONYMS mild.
3 *fierce, murderous jealousy* **intense,** powerful, vehement, passionate, impassioned, fervent, fervid, ardent.
ANTONYMS mild.
4 *a fierce wind* **powerful,** strong, violent, forceful; stormy, blustery, gusty, tempestuous.
ANTONYMS gentle, mild.
5 *a fierce pain* **severe,** extreme, intense, acute, awful, dreadful; excruciating, agonizing, piercing.
ANTONYMS mild.

fight ▶ verb 1 *two men were fighting* **brawl,** exchange blows, attack each other, assault each other, hit each other, punch each other; struggle, grapple, wrestle; informal scrap, have a set-to, roughhouse, engage in fisticuffs.
2 *they fought in the First World War* (**do**) **battle,** go to war, take up arms, be a soldier; engage, meet, clash, skirmish.
3 *a war fought for freedom* **engage in,** wage, conduct, prosecute, undertake.
4 *they are always fighting* **quarrel,** argue, bicker, squabble, fall out, have a fight, have a row, wrangle, be at odds, disagree, differ, have words, bandy words, be at each other's throats, be at loggerheads; informal scrap.
5 *fighting against wage reductions* **campaign,** strive, battle, struggle, contend, crusade, agitate, lobby, push, press.
6 *they will fight the decision* **oppose,** contest, contend with, confront, challenge, combat,

dispute, quarrel with, argue against/with, strive against, struggle against.
7 *Tyler fought the urge to stick his tongue out* **repress,** restrain, suppress, stifle, smother, hold back, fight back, keep in check, curb, control, rein in, choke back; informal keep the lid on.
▶ **noun 1** *a fight outside a club* **brawl,** fracas, melee, rumpus, skirmish, sparring match, struggle, scuffle, altercation, clash, disturbance; fisticuffs; informal scrap, set-to, donnybrook.
2 *a heavyweight fight* **boxing match,** bout, match.
3 *Japan's fight against Russia* **battle,** engagement, clash, conflict, struggle; war, campaign, crusade, action, hostilities.
4 *a fight with my girlfriend* **argument,** quarrel, squabble, row, wrangle, disagreement, falling-out, contretemps, altercation, dispute; informal tiff, spat, scrap, cat fight, blowup.
5 *their fight for control of the company* **struggle,** battle, campaign, push, effort.
6 *she had no fight left in her* **will to resist,** resistance, spirit, courage, pluck, pluckiness, grit, strength, backbone, determination, resolution, resolve, resoluteness, aggression, aggressiveness; informal guts, spunk, moxie.
– PHRASES **fight back 1** *if the enemy attacks, we will fight back* **retaliate,** counterattack, strike back, hit back, respond, reciprocate, return fire, give tit for tat. **2** *Russ fought back tears* See FIGHT (sense 7 of the verb). **fight off** *they tried in vain to fight off the swarming locusts* **repel,** repulse, beat off/back, ward off, fend off, keep/hold at bay, drive away/back, force back.

fighter ▶ **noun 1** *a guerrilla fighter* **soldier,** fighting man/woman, warrior, combatant, serviceman, servicewoman, trooper, mercenary; archaic man-at-arms.
2 *the fighter was knocked to the ground* **boxer,** pugilist, prizefighter; wrestler.
3 *enemy fighters* **warplane,** armed aircraft.

figurative ▶ **adjective** *the example given was meant to be figurative* **metaphorical,** nonliteral, symbolic, allegorical, representative, emblematic.
ANTONYMS literal.

figure ▶ **noun 1** *the production figure* **statistic,** number, quantity, amount, level, total, sum; (**figures**) data, information.
2 *the second figure was 9* **digit,** numeral, numerical symbol.
3 *he can't put a figure on it* **price,** cost, amount, value, valuation.
4 (**figures**) *I'm good with figures* **arithmetic,** mathematics, math, calculations, computation, numbers.
5 *her petite figure* **physique,** build, frame, body, proportions, shape, form.
6 *a dark figure emerged* **silhouette,** outline, shape, form.
7 *a figure of authority* **person,** personage, individual, man, woman, character, personality; representative, embodiment, personification, epitome.
8 *life-size figures* **human representation,** effigy, model, statue.
9 *geometrical figures* **shape,** pattern, design, motif.
10 *see figure 4* **diagram,** illustration, drawing, picture, plate.
▶ **verb 1** *a beast figuring in Egyptian legend* **feature,** appear, be featured, be mentioned, be referred to, have prominence, crop up.
2 *a way to figure the values* **calculate,** work out, total, reckon, compute, determine, assess, put a figure on, crunch the numbers, tot up.
3 informal *I figured that I didn't have a chance* **suppose,** think, believe, consider, expect, take it, suspect, sense; assume, dare say, conclude, take it as read, presume, deduce, infer, extrapolate, gather, guess.
4 *"Charlotte's late." "That figures."* **make sense,** seem reasonable, stand to reason, be to be expected, be logical, follow, ring true.
– PHRASES **figure on** *they figured on paying about $100* **plan on,** count on, rely on, bank on, bargain on, depend on, pin one's hopes on; anticipate, expect to (be). **figure out** *he tried to figure out how to switch on the lamp* **work out,** fathom, puzzle out, decipher, ascertain, make sense of, think through, get to the bottom of; understand, comprehend, see, grasp, get the hang of, get the drift of; informal crack; Brit. informal twig.

figurehead ▶ **noun 1** *the president was just a figurehead* **titular head,** nominal leader, leader in name only, front man, cipher, token, mouthpiece, puppet, instrument.
2 *the figurehead on the ship* **carving,** bust, sculpture, image, statue.

filament ▶ **noun** *the fragile filament inside the bulb* **fiber,** thread, strand; technical fibril.

file[1] ▶ **noun 1** *he opened the file* **folder,** portfolio, binder, document case.
2 *we have files on all the major companies* **dossier,** document, record, report; data, information, documentation, annals, archives.
3 *the computer file was searched* **data,** document, text.
4 *the director needed updating on the Uecker file* **dossier,** department, front.
▶ **verb 1** *file the documents correctly* **categorize,** classify, organize, put in place/order, order, arrange, catalog, record, store, archive.
2 *Debbie has filed for divorce* **apply,** register, ask.
3 *two women have filed a civil suit against him* **bring,** press, lodge, place; formal prefer.

file[2] ▶ **noun** *a file of boys* **line,** column, row, string, chain, procession, queue.
▶ **verb** *we filed out into the parking lot* **walk in a line,** march, parade, troop.

file[3] ▶ **verb** *she filed her nails* **smooth,** buff, rub (down), polish, shape; scrape, abrade, rasp, sandpaper.

filigree ▶ **noun** *decorated with gold filigree* **tracery,** fretwork, latticework, scrollwork, lacework, quilling.

fill ▶ **verb 1** *he filled a bowl with cereal* **make full,** fill up, fill to the brim, top up, charge.
ANTONYMS empty.
2 *guests filled the parlor* **crowd into,** throng, pack (into), occupy, squeeze into, cram (into); overcrowd, overfill.
3 *he was filling his shelves* **stock,** pack, load,

supply, replenish, restock, refill.
4 *fill all the holes with a spackling compound* **block up,** stop (up), plug, seal, caulk.
ANTONYMS unblock.
5 *the perfume filled the room* **pervade,** permeate, suffuse, be diffused through, penetrate, infuse, perfuse.
6 *he was going to fill a government post* **occupy,** hold, take up; informal hold down.
7 *we had just filled a big order* **carry out,** complete, fulfill, execute, discharge.
– PHRASES **fill in** *while Mr. Grant is on vacation, Luis will be filling in* **substitute,** deputize, stand in, cover, take over, act as stand-in, take the place of; informal sub, step into someone's shoes/boots, pinch-hit. **fill in on** *when we get home, you can fill us in on the details* **inform of,** advise of, tell about, acquaint with, apprise of, brief on, update with; informal put in the picture about, bring up to speed on. **fill something in/out** *fill in these forms | he filled out the questionnaire* **complete,** answer. **fill out** *the puppies will begin to fill out once they start getting proper nutrition* **grow fatter,** become plumper, flesh out, put on weight, gain weight, get heavier.

film ▶ **noun 1** *a film of sweat* **layer,** coat, coating, covering, cover, sheet, patina, overlay.
2 *Emma was watching a film* **movie,** picture, feature film, motion picture; informal flick, pic; dated moving picture, talkie.
3 *she would like to work in film* **movies,** cinema, pictures, the motion picture industry.
▶ **verb 1** *he immediately filmed the next scene* **record (on film),** shoot, capture on film, video.
2 *his eyes had* ***filmed over*** **cloud (over),** mist (over), haze (over); become blurred, blur; archaic blear.

filmy ▶ **adjective** *a filmy black blouse* **diaphanous,** transparent, see-through, translucent, sheer, gossamer; delicate, fine, light, thin, silky.
ANTONYMS thick, opaque.

filter ▶ **noun** *a carbon filter* **strainer,** sifter; riddle; gauze, netting.
▶ **verb 1** *the farmers filter the water* **sieve,** strain, sift, filtrate, clarify, purify, refine, treat.
2 *the rain had filtered through her jacket* **seep,** percolate, leak, trickle, ooze.

filth ▶ **noun 1** *stagnant pools of filth* **dirt,** muck, grime, mud, mire, sludge, slime, ooze; excrement, excreta, dung, manure, ordure, sewage; rubbish, refuse, dross; pollution, contamination, filthiness, uncleanness, foulness, nastiness, garbage, crud, grunge, gunge, trash.
2 *I felt sick after reading that filth* **pornography,** pornographic literature/films, dirty books, smut, obscenity, indecency; informal porn, porno.

filthy ▶ **adjective 1** *the room was filthy* **dirty,** grimy, muddy, slimy, unclean, mucky; foul, squalid, sordid, nasty, soiled, sullied; polluted, contaminated, unhygienic, unsanitary; informal cruddy, grungy; literary besmirched; formal feculent.
ANTONYMS clean.
2 *his face was filthy* **unwashed,** unclean, dirty, grimy, smeared, grubby, muddy, mucky, black, blackened, stained; literary begrimed.
ANTONYMS clean.
3 *filthy jokes* **obscene,** indecent, dirty, smutty, rude, improper, coarse, bawdy, vulgar, lewd, racy, raw, off-color, earthy, barnyard, locker-room, ribald, risqué, "adult", pornographic, explicit; informal blue, porn, porno, X-rated.
ANTONYMS clean, polite.
4 *you filthy brute!* **despicable,** contemptible, nasty, low, base, mean, vile, obnoxious; informal dirty (rotten), lowdown, no-good.
5 *he was in a filthy mood* **bad,** foul, bad-tempered, ill-tempered, irritable, grumpy, grouchy, cross, fractious, peevish; informal cranky, ornery.
ANTONYMS good.
▶ **adverb** *filthy rich* **very,** extremely, tremendously, immensely, remarkably, excessively, exceedingly; informal stinking, awfully, terribly, seriously, mega, majorly, ultra, damn.

final ▶ **adjective 1** *the final year of study* **last,** closing, concluding, finishing, end, terminating, ultimate, eventual.
ANTONYMS first.
2 *their decisions are final* **irrevocable,** unalterable, absolute, conclusive, irrefutable, incontrovertible, indisputable, unchallengeable, binding.
ANTONYMS provisional.
▶ **noun** *the Stanley Cup final* **decider,** clincher, final game/match.
ANTONYMS qualifier.

finale ▶ **noun** *the show's spectacular finale* **climax,** culmination; end, ending, finish, close, conclusion, termination; denouement, last act, final scene.
ANTONYMS beginning.

finality ▶ **noun** *an answer delivered with finality* **conclusiveness,** decisiveness, decision, definiteness, definitiveness, certainty, certitude; irrevocability, irrefutability.

finalize ▶ **verb** *they had yet to finalize a peace treaty* **conclude,** complete, clinch, settle, work out, secure, wrap up, wind up, put the finishing touches to; reach an agreement on, agree on, come to terms on; informal sew up.

finally ▶ **adverb 1** *she finally got her man to the altar* **eventually,** ultimately, in the end, after a long time, at (long) last; in the long run, in the fullness of time.
2 *finally, wrap the ribbon around the edge* **lastly,** last, in conclusion, to conclude, to end.
3 *this should finally dispel that common misconception* **conclusively,** irrevocably, decisively, definitively, for ever, for good, once and for all.

finance ▶ **noun 1** *he knows about finance* **financial affairs,** money matters, fiscal matters, economics, money management, commerce, business, investment.
2 *short-term finance* **funds,** assets, money, capital, resources, cash, reserves, revenue, income; funding, backing, sponsorship.
▶ **verb** *the project was financed by grants* **fund,** pay for, back, capitalize, endow, subsidize, invest in; underwrite, guarantee, sponsor, support, bankroll.

financial ▶ **adjective** *our financial picture has improved* **monetary,** money, economic, pecuniary, fiscal, banking, commercial, business, investment.

> CHOOSE THE RIGHT WORD
>
> **financial, monetary, pecuniary, fiscal**
>
> What's the difference between a **financial** crisis and a **fiscal** one? It all depends on who's having trouble with money and the scale of the difficulties. *Financial* usually applies to money matters involving large sums or transactions of considerable importance (*the auction was a financial success*). *Fiscal* refers specifically to the financial affairs of a government, organization, or corporation (*the end of the company's fiscal year*), while **pecuniary** refers to money matters of a more personal or practical nature and is preferred to *financial* when money is being discussed on a smaller scale (*pecuniary motives, pecuniary assistance, pecuniary difficulties*). Of all these words, **monetary** refers most directly to money as such and is often used when discussing the coinage, distribution, and circulation of money (*the European Monetary System; the monetary unit of a country*).

find ▶ **verb 1** *I found the book I wanted* **locate,** spot, pinpoint, unearth, obtain; search out, nose out, track down, root out; come across/upon, run across/into, chance on, light on, happen on, stumble on, encounter; informal bump into; literary espy.
2 *they say they've found a cure for rabies* **discover,** invent, come up with, hit on.
3 *the police found her purse* **retrieve,** recover, get back, regain, repossess.
ANTONYMS lose.
4 *I hope you find peace* **obtain,** acquire, get, procure, come by, secure, gain, earn, achieve, attain.
5 *I found the courage to speak* **summon (up),** gather, muster (up), screw up, call up.
6 *caffeine* ***is found*** *in coffee and tea* **be (present),** occur, exist, be existent, appear.
7 *you'll find that it's a lively area* **discover,** become aware, realize, observe, notice, note, perceive, learn.
8 *I find their decision strange* **consider,** think, believe to be, feel to be, look on as, view as, see as, judge, deem, regard as.
9 *he was found guilty* **judge,** adjudge, adjudicate, deem, rule, declare, pronounce.
10 *her barb found its mark* **arrive at,** reach, attain, achieve; hit, strike.
▶ **noun 1** *an archaeological find* **discovery,** acquisition, asset.
2 *this table is a real find* **good buy,** bargain; godsend, boon.
– PHRASES **find out** *let us know what you find out about the theft* **discover,** become aware, learn, detect, discern, perceive, observe, notice, note, get/come to know, realize; bring to light, reveal, expose, unearth, disclose; informal figure out, cotton on, catch on, get wise (to), savvy; Brit. informal twig.

finding ▶ **noun 1** *the finding of the leak* **discovery,** location, locating, detection, detecting, uncovering.
2 *the tribunal's findings* **conclusion,** decision, verdict, pronouncement, judgment, ruling, rule, decree, order, recommendation, resolve; Law determination.

fine¹ ▶ **adjective 1** *fine wines* **excellent,** first-class, first-rate, great, exceptional, outstanding, quality, superior, splendid, magnificent, exquisite, choice, select, prime, supreme, superb, wonderful, superlative, of high quality, second to none; informal A1, top-notch, blue-ribbon, blue-chip, splendiferous.
ANTONYMS poor.
2 *a fine citizen* **worthy,** admirable, praiseworthy, laudable, estimable, upright, upstanding, respectable.
3 *the initiative is fine, but it's not enough on its own* **all right,** acceptable, suitable, good (enough), passable, satisfactory, adequate, reasonable, tolerable; informal OK.
ANTONYMS unsatisfactory.
4 *I feel fine* **in good health,** well, healthy, all right, (fighting) fit, as fit as a fiddle, blooming, thriving, in good shape, in good condition, in fine fettle; informal OK, in the pink.
ANTONYMS ill.
5 *a fine day* **fair,** dry, bright, clear, sunny, without a cloud in the sky, warm, balmy, summery.
ANTONYMS inclement.
6 *a fine old house* **impressive,** imposing, striking, splendid, grand, majestic, magnificent, stately.
7 *fine clothes* **elegant,** stylish, expensive, smart, chic, fashionable; fancy, sumptuous, lavish, opulent; informal flashy, swanky, ritzy, plush.
8 *a fine mind* **keen,** quick, alert, sharp, bright, brilliant, astute, clever, intelligent, perspicacious.
ANTONYMS slow.
9 *fine china* **delicate,** fragile, dainty.
ANTONYMS coarse.
10 *fine hair* **thin,** light, delicate, wispy, flyaway.
ANTONYMS thick.
11 *a fine point* **sharp,** keen, acute, sharpened, razor-sharp.
ANTONYMS thick, blunt.
12 *fine material* **sheer,** light, lightweight, thin, flimsy; diaphanous, filmy, gossamer, silky, transparent, translucent, see-through.
ANTONYMS thick, coarse.
13 *fine sand* **fine-grained,** powdery, powdered, dusty, ground, crushed; technical comminuted.
ANTONYMS coarse.
14 *fine detailed work* **intricate,** delicate, detailed, elaborate, dainty, meticulous.
15 *a fine distinction* **subtle,** ultra-fine, nice, hair-splitting, nitpicking.
16 *people's finer feelings* **elevated,** lofty, exalted, noble; refined, sensitive, cultivated, cultured, civilized, sophisticated.
ANTONYMS coarse.
17 *fine taste* **discerning,** discriminating, refined, cultivated, cultured, critical.
ANTONYMS vulgar.
▶ **adverb** informal *you're doing fine* **well,** all right,

not badly, satisfactorily, adequately, nicely, tolerably; informal OK, good.
ANTONYMS badly.

fine² ▶ noun *heavy fines* (**financial**) **penalty,** sanction, fee, charge.
▶ verb *they were fined for breaking environmental laws* **penalize,** impose a fine on, charge.

finery ▶ noun *all dressed up in her finery* **regalia,** best clothes, best, Sunday best; informal glad rags.

finesse ▶ noun 1 *masterly finesse* **skill,** skillfulness, expertise, subtlety, flair, panache, élan, polish, artistry, virtuosity, mastery.
2 *a modicum of finesse* **tact,** tactfulness, discretion, diplomacy, delicacy, sensitivity, perceptiveness, savoir faire.
3 *a clever finesse* **winning move,** trick, stratagem, ruse, maneuver, artifice, machination.

finger ▶ noun *he wagged his finger at the cat* **digit,** thumb, index finger, forefinger; informal pinkie.
▶ verb 1 *she fingered her brooch uneasily* **touch,** feel, handle, stroke, rub, caress, fondle, toy with, play (around) with, fiddle with.
2 *no one fingered the culprit* **identify,** recognize, pick out, spot; inform on, point the finger at; informal rat on, squeal on, tell on, blow the whistle on, snitch on.

finicky ▶ adjective *their fancy words and finicky manners* **fussy,** fastidious, punctilious, overparticular, difficult, exacting, demanding; informal picky, choosy, persnickety; archaic nice.

finish ▶ verb 1 *Mrs. Porter had just finished the task* **complete,** end, conclude, stop, cease, terminate, bring to a conclusion/end/close, wind up; crown, cap, round off, put the finishing touches to; accomplish, discharge, carry out, do, get done, fulfill; informal wrap up, sew up, polish off.
ANTONYMS start.
2 *Sarah has finished school* **leave,** give up, drop; stop, discontinue, have done with, complete; informal pack in, quit.
ANTONYMS begin, continue.
3 *Hitch finished his dinner* **consume,** eat, devour, drink, finish off, polish off, gulp (down); use (up), exhaust, empty, drain, get through, run through; informal down.
ANTONYMS start.
4 *the program has finished* **end,** come to an end, stop, conclude, come to a conclusion/end/close, cease.
ANTONYMS start, begin.
5 *some items were finished in a black lacquer* **varnish,** lacquer, veneer, coat, stain, wax, shellac, enamel, glaze.
▶ noun 1 *the finish of filming* **end,** ending, completion, conclusion, close, closing, cessation, termination; final part/stage, finale, denouement; informal sewing up, polishing off.
ANTONYMS start, beginning.
2 *a gallop to the finish* **finishing line,** finishing post, tape.
3 *an antiquated paint finish* **veneer,** lacquer, lamination, glaze, coating, covering; surface, texture.
– PHRASES **finish off** 1 *the executioners finished them off* **kill,** take/end the life of, execute, terminate, exterminate, liquidate, get rid of; informal wipe out, do in, bump off, take out, dispose of, do away with, ice, rub out, waste.
2 *financial difficulties finished off the business* **overwhelm,** overcome, defeat, get the better of, worst, bring down; informal drive to the wall, best.

finished ▶ adjective 1 *the finished job* **completed,** concluded, terminated, over (and done with), at an end; accomplished, executed, discharged, fulfilled, done; informal wrapped up, sewn up, polished off; formal effectuated.
ANTONYMS incomplete.
2 *a finished performance* **accomplished,** polished, flawless, faultless, perfect; expert, proficient, masterly, impeccable, virtuoso, skillful, skilled, professional.
ANTONYMS crude, unpolished.
3 *he was finished* **ruined,** defeated, beaten, wrecked, doomed, bankrupt, broken; informal washed up, through.

finite ▶ adjective *there is a finite amount of water in the system* **limited,** restricted, determinate, fixed.

fire ▶ noun 1 *a fire broke out* **blaze,** conflagration, inferno; flames, burning, combustion; forest fire, wildfire, brush fire.
2 *he lacked fire* **dynamism,** energy, vigor, animation, vitality, vibrancy, exuberance, zest, élan; passion, ardor, zeal, spirit, verve, vivacity, vivaciousness; enthusiasm, eagerness, gusto, fervor, fervency; informal pep, vim, go, get-up-and-go, oomph.
3 *rapid machine-gun fire* **gunfire,** firing, flak, bombardment.
4 *they directed their fire at the state legislature* **criticism,** censure, condemnation, denunciation, opprobrium, admonishments, brickbats; hostility, antagonism, animosity; informal flak.
▶ verb 1 *howitzers firing shells* **launch,** shoot, discharge, let fly with.
2 *someone fired a gun* **shoot,** discharge, let off, set off.
3 informal *he was fired* **dismiss,** discharge, give someone their notice, lay off, let go, get rid of, ax, cashier; informal sack, give someone the sack, boot out, give someone the boot, give someone their marching orders, pink-slip; Brit. make redundant.
4 *the engine fired* **start,** get started, get going.
5 *the stories fired my imagination* **stimulate,** stir up, excite, awaken, arouse, rouse, inflame, animate, inspire, motivate.
– PHRASES **catch fire** *it was amazing that neither of the adjoining buildings caught fire* **ignite,** catch light, burst into flames, go up in flames.
on fire 1 *the restaurant was on fire* **burning,** alight, ablaze, blazing, aflame, in flames; literary afire. 2 *she was on fire with passion* **ardent,** passionate, fervent, excited, eager, enthusiastic.

firebrand ▶ noun *a group of political firebrands* **radical,** revolutionary, agitator, rabble-rouser, incendiary, subversive, troublemaker.

fireproof ▶ adjective *fireproof coveralls* **nonflammable,** incombustible, fire resistant, flame resistant, flame retardant, heatproof.
ANTONYMS inflammable.

fireworks ▶ plural noun 1 *there are fireworks*

after every Friday night game **pyrotechnics,** firecrackers.
2 *his stubbornness has produced some fireworks* **uproar,** trouble, mayhem, fuss; tantrums, hysterics.

firm[1] ▶ **adjective 1** *the ground is fairly firm* **hard,** solid, unyielding, resistant; solidified, hardened, compacted, compressed, dense, stiff, rigid, frozen, set.
ANTONYMS soft, yielding.
2 *firm foundations* **secure,** secured, stable, steady, strong, fixed, fast, set, taut, tight; immovable, irremovable, stationary, motionless.
ANTONYMS unstable.
3 *a firm handshake* **strong,** vigorous, sturdy, forceful.
ANTONYMS limp.
4 *I was very firm about what I wanted | a firm supporter* **resolute,** determined, decided, resolved, steadfast; adamant, emphatic, insistent, single-minded, in earnest, wholehearted; unfaltering, unwavering, unflinching, unswerving, unbending; hardline, committed, dyed-in-the-wool.
ANTONYMS irresolute.
5 *firm friends* **close,** good, intimate, inseparable, dear, special, fast; constant, devoted, loving, faithful, long-standing, steady, steadfast, rock-steady.
ANTONYMS distant.
6 *firm plans* **definite,** fixed, settled, decided, established, confirmed, agreed; unalterable, unchangeable, irreversible.
ANTONYMS indefinite.

firm[2] ▶ **noun** *an accounting firm* **company,** business, concern, enterprise, organization, corporation, conglomerate, office, bureau, agency, consortium; informal outfit, setup.

firmament ▶ **noun** literary *gazing up to the firmament* **the sky,** heaven; the heavens, the skies; literary the empyrean, the welkin.

first ▶ **adjective 1** *the first chapter* **earliest,** initial, opening, introductory.
ANTONYMS last, closing.
2 *first principles* **fundamental,** basic, rudimentary, primary; key, cardinal, central, chief, vital, essential.
3 *our first priority* **foremost,** principal, highest, greatest, paramount, top, uppermost, prime, chief, leading, main, major; overriding, predominant, prevailing, central, core, dominant; informal number-one.
ANTONYMS last.
4 *first prize* **top,** best, prime, premier, winner's, winning.
▶ **adverb 1** *the room they had first entered* **at first,** to begin with, first of all, at the outset, initially.
2 *she would eat first* **before anything else,** first and foremost, now.
3 *she wouldn't go—she'd die first!* **in preference,** sooner, rather.
▶ **noun** *it was a first for both of us* **novelty,** new experience; unknown territory.

first-hand ▶ **adjective** *her first-hand experience in grant writing* **direct,** immediate, personal, hands-on, experiential, empirical, evidence-based, eye-witness.
ANTONYMS vicarious, indirect.

first-rate ▶ **adjective** *they have done a first-rate job* **top-quality,** high-quality, top-grade, first-class, second to none, fine; superlative, excellent, superb, outstanding, exceptional, exemplary, marvelous, magnificent, splendid; informal top-notch, blue-ribbon, blue-chip, ace, A1, super, great, terrific, tremendous, bang-up, skookum, fantastic, killer.

fiscal ▶ **adjective** *figures for the past fiscal year show a trend of improvement* budgetary; financial, economic, monetary, money. See note at FINANCIAL.

fish ▶ **verb 1** *we can fish in Putnam's Pond* **go fishing,** angle, angle, cast, trawl, troll, seine.
2 *she fished for her purse* **search,** delve, look, hunt; grope, fumble, ferret (about/around), root around/about, rummage (around/about).
3 *I'm not* ***fishing for*** *compliments* **try to get,** seek to obtain, solicit, angle for, aim for, hope for, cast around/about for, be after.
– PHRASES **fish out** *I fished my earring out of the cake batter* **pull out,** haul out, remove, extricate, extract, retrieve; rescue from, save from.

fisherman ▶ **noun** *a favorite vacation spot for fishermen* **angler,** fisher, fisheries worker.

fishy ▶ **adjective 1** *a fishy smell* **fishlike,** piscine.
2 *round fishy eyes* **expressionless,** inexpressive, vacant, lackluster, glassy.
3 informal *there was something fishy going on* **suspicious,** questionable, dubious, doubtful, suspect; odd, queer, peculiar, strange; informal funny, shady, crooked, sketchy.

fission ▶ **noun** *the radioactive materials absorb neutrons and undergo fission* **splitting,** division, dividing, rupture, breaking, severance.
ANTONYMS fusion.

fissure ▶ **noun** *the flood was blamed on an unreported fissure in the dam* **opening,** crevice, crack, cleft, breach, crevasse, chasm; break, fracture, fault, rift, rupture, split.

fit[1] ▶ **adjective 1** *fit for human habitation | he is a fit subject for such a book* **suitable,** good enough; relevant, pertinent, apt, appropriate, suited, apposite, fitting; archaic meet.
ANTONYMS unsuitable.
2 *is he fit to look after a child?* **competent,** able, capable; ready, prepared, qualified, trained, equipped.
ANTONYMS incapable.
3 informal *you look fit to commit murder!* **ready,** prepared, all set, in a fit state, likely, about; informal psyched up.
4 *he looked tanned and fit* **healthy,** well, in good health, in (good) shape, in (good) trim, in good condition, fighting fit, as fit as a fiddle; athletic, muscular, well-built, strong, robust, hale and hearty, in the pink.
ANTONYMS unwell.
▶ **verb 1** *have your carpets fitted professionally* **lay,** position, place, put in place/position, fix.
2 *cameras fitted with a backlight button* **equip,** provide, supply, fit out, furnish.
3 *concrete slabs were* ***fitted together*** **join,** connect, put together, piece together, attach, unite, link (together), slot together.

4 *a sentence that fits her crimes* **match,** suit, be appropriate to, correspond to, tally with, go with, accord with, correlate to, be congruous with, be congruent with, be consonant with.
5 *an MA fits you for a professional career* **qualify,** prepare, make ready, train, groom.
▶ **noun** *the degree of fit between a school's philosophy and practice* **correlation,** correspondence, agreement, consistency, equivalence, match, similarity, compatibility, concurrence.
– PHRASES **fit in** *he never fit in with the academic crowd* **conform,** be in harmony, blend in, be in line, be assimilated into.

fit² ▶ **noun 1** *an epileptic fit* **convulsion,** spasm, paroxysm, seizure, attack; Medicine ictus.
2 *a fit of the giggles* **outbreak,** outburst, attack, bout, spell.
3 *my mother would have a fit if she knew* **tantrum,** fit of temper, outburst of anger/rage, frenzy; informal blowout, hissy fit, conniption (fit).
– PHRASES **in/by fits and starts** *she writes in fits and starts yet manages to complete a new book almost every year* **spasmodically,** intermittently, sporadically, erratically, irregularly, fitfully, haphazardly.

fitful ▶ **adjective** *a fitful night's sleep* **intermittent,** sporadic, spasmodic, broken, disturbed, disrupted, patchy, irregular, uneven, unsettled; informal herky-jerky.

fitness ▶ **noun 1** *marathon running requires tremendous fitness* **good health,** strength, robustness, vigor, athleticism, toughness, physical fitness, muscularity; good condition, good shape, well-being.
2 *his fitness for active service* **suitability,** capability, competence, ability, aptitude; readiness, preparedness, eligibility.

fitted ▶ **adjective** *a fitted sheet* **shaped,** contoured, fitting tightly, fitting well.

fitting ▶ **noun 1** *bathroom fittings* **furnishings,** furniture, fixtures, equipment, appointments, appurtenances.
2 *the fitting of catalytic converters* **installation,** installing, putting in, fixing.
▶ **adjective** *a fitting conclusion* **apt,** appropriate, suitable, apposite; fit, proper, right, seemly, correct; archaic meet.
ANTONYMS unsuitable.

fix ▶ **verb 1** *he fixed my washing machine* **repair,** mend, put right, put to rights, get working, restore (to working order); overhaul, service, renovate, recondition.
2 *signs were fixed to utility poles* **fasten,** attach, affix, secure; join, connect, couple, link; install, implant, embed; stick, glue, pin, nail, screw, bolt, clamp, clip.
3 *his words are fixed in my memory* **stick,** lodge, embed, burned, branded.
4 *his eyes were fixed on the ground* **focus,** direct, level, point, train.
5 informal *Laura was fixing her hair* **arrange,** put in order, adjust; style, groom, comb, brush; informal do.
6 informal *Chris will fix supper* **prepare,** cook, make, get; informal rustle up, whip up.
7 *let's fix a date for the meeting* **decide on,** select, choose, resolve on; determine, settle, set, arrange, establish, allot; designate, name, appoint, specify.
8 *chemicals are used to fix the dye* **make permanent,** make fast, set.
9 informal *the fight was fixed* **rig,** arrange fraudulently; tamper with, influence; informal fiddle.
10 informal *don't tell anybody, or I'll fix you!* **get one's revenge on,** avenge oneself on, get even with, get back at, take reprisals against, punish, deal with; sort someone out.
11 *the cat has been fixed* **castrate,** neuter, geld, spay, desex, sterilize; informal doctor, alter.
▶ **noun** informal **1** *they are in a bit of a fix* **predicament,** plight, difficulty, awkward situation, corner, tight spot; mess, mare's nest, dire straits; informal pickle, jam, hole, scrape, bind, sticky situation.
2 *he needed his fix* **dose;** informal hit.
3 *a quick fix for the coal industry* **solution,** answer, resolution, way out, remedy, cure, placebo; informal magic bullet, band-aid solution.
4 *the result was a complete fix* **fraud,** swindle, trick, charade, sham; informal setup, fiddle.
– PHRASES **fix up** informal *we need to get Dolly fixed up with a job* **provide,** supply, furnish.

fixation ▶ **noun** *his sports fixation has gotten intolerable* **obsession,** preoccupation, mania, addiction, compulsion; informal thing, bug, craze, fad.

fixture ▶ **noun 1** *fixtures and fittings* **fixed appliance,** installation, unit.
2 *she's a fixture at the bar* **resident,** lifer, permanent feature; informal part of the furniture.

fizz ▶ **verb** *the soda really fizzes when you first open the bottle* **effervesce,** sparkle, bubble, froth; literary spume.
▶ **noun 1** *the fizz in champagne* **effervescence,** sparkle, fizziness, bubbles, bubbliness, gassiness, carbonation, froth.
2 informal *their set is a little lacking in fizz* **ebullience,** exuberance, liveliness, life, vivacity, animation, vigor, energy, verve, dash, spirit, sparkle, zest, fire; informal pizzazz, pep, zip, oomph.
3 *the fizz of the static* **crackle,** crackling, buzz, buzzing, hiss, hissing, white noise; literary susurration.

fizzle ▶ **verb** *the loudspeaker fizzled* **crackle,** buzz, hiss, fizz, crepitate.
▶ **noun 1** *electric fizzle* See FIZZ (sense 3 of the noun).
2 *the whole thing turned out to be a fizzle* **failure,** fiasco, debacle, disaster; informal flop, washout, letdown, dead loss, snafu.
– PHRASES **fizzle out** *the viewers' enthusiasm pretty much fizzled out after the first season* **peter out,** die off, ease off, cool off, flatline; tail off, wither away, wind down.

fizzy ▶ **adjective** *fizzy root beer* **effervescent,** sparkling, carbonated, gassy, bubbly, frothy; spumante, frizzante.
ANTONYMS still, flat.

flabbergast ▶ **verb** informal See ASTONISH.

flabby ▶ **adjective 1** *his flabby stomach* **soft,** loose, flaccid, slack, untoned, drooping, sagging.
ANTONYMS firm.

2 *a flabby child* **fat,** fleshy, overweight, plump, chubby, portly, rotund, broad in the beam, of ample proportions, obese, corpulent; informal tubby, roly-poly, well-upholstered.
ANTONYMS thin.

flaccid ▶ **adjective 1** *a flaccid muscle* **soft,** loose, flabby, slack, lax; drooping, sagging.
ANTONYMS firm.
2 *his play seemed flaccid* **lackluster,** lifeless, listless, uninspiring, unanimated, tame, dull, vapid.
ANTONYMS spirited.

flag[1] ▶ **noun** *he raised the flag* **banner,** standard, ensign, pennant, banderole, streamer, jack, gonfalon; colors; Stars and Stripes, Old Glory, Union Jack; Jolly Roger; Canadian Red Ensign, Maple Leaf.
▶ **verb** *flag the misspelled words* **indicate,** identify, point out, mark, label, tag, highlight.
– PHRASES **flag down** *we had no luck flagging down a cab* **hail,** wave down, signal to stop, stop, halt.

flag[2] ▶ **verb 1** *they were flagging toward the finish* **tire,** grow tired/weary, weaken, grow weak, wilt, droop, fade, run out of steam.
ANTONYMS revive.
2 *my energy flags in the afternoon* **fade,** decline, wane, ebb, diminish, decrease, lessen, dwindle; wither, melt away, peter out, die away/down.
ANTONYMS increase.

flagrant ▶ **adjective** *it was a flagrant distortion of the facts* **blatant,** glaring, obvious, overt, conspicuous, barefaced, shameless, brazen, undisguised, unconcealed; outrageous, scandalous, shocking, disgraceful, dreadful, terrible, gross.

flagstone ▶ **noun** *the landscapers unearthed a beautiful flagstone walkway, perhaps laid a hundred years ago* **paving slab,** paving stone, slab, flag.

flail ▶ **verb 1** *he fell headlong, his arms flailing* **wave,** swing, thrash about, flap about.
2 *I was flailing about in the water* **flounder,** struggle, thrash, writhe, splash.
3 *he flailed their shoulders with his cane* **thrash,** beat, strike, flog, whip, lash, scourge, cane; informal wallop, whack.

flair ▶ **noun 1** *a flair for publicity* **aptitude,** talent, gift, instinct, (natural) ability, facility, skill, bent, feel, knack.
2 *she dressed with flair* **style,** stylishness, panache, dash, élan, poise, elegance; taste, good taste, discernment, discrimination; informal class, pizzazz.

flake[1] ▶ **noun 1** *flakes of pastry* **sliver,** wafer, shaving, paring; chip, scale; fragment, scrap, shred; technical lamina.
2 informal *Geoff can be such a flake* **ditz,** space cadet, airhead, fool, scatterbrain.
▶ **verb** *the paint was flaking* **peel (off),** chip, blister, come off (in layers).

flake[2] ▶ **verb**
– PHRASES **flake out** informal *she flaked out in her chair* **fall asleep,** go to sleep, drop off; collapse, faint, pass out, lose consciousness, black out, swoon; informal conk out, nod off, sack out.

flamboyant ▶ **adjective 1** *her flamboyant personality* **exuberant,** confident, lively, animated, vibrant, vivacious.
ANTONYMS modest, restrained.
2 *a flamboyant cravat* **colorful,** brightly colored, bright, vibrant, vivid; dazzling, eye-catching, bold; showy, ostentatious, gaudy, garish, lurid, loud; informal jazzy, flashy.
ANTONYMS dull, restrained.
3 *a flamboyant architectural style* **elaborate,** ornate, fancy; baroque, rococo.
ANTONYMS simple.

flame ▶ **noun 1** (**flames**) *a sheet of flames* **fire,** blaze, conflagration, inferno.
2 (**flames**) *the flames of her anger* **passion,** warmth, ardor, fervor, fervency, fire, intensity.
3 informal *an old flame* **sweetheart,** boyfriend, girlfriend, lover, partner; informal beau; dated steady.
▶ **verb 1** *logs crackled and flamed* **burn,** blaze, be ablaze, be alight, be on fire, be in flames, be aflame.
2 *Erica's cheeks flamed* **become red,** go red, blush, flush, redden, grow pink/crimson/scarlet, color, glow.
– PHRASES **in flames** *the cabin was in flames* **on fire,** burning, alight, flaming, blazing, ignited; literary afire.

flame-proof ▶ **adjective** *flame-proof gloves* **nonflammable,** noninflammable, flame-resistant, fire-resistant, flame-retardant.
ANTONYMS flammable.

flaming ▶ **adjective 1** *a flaming bonfire* **blazing,** ablaze, burning, on fire, in flames, aflame; literary afire.
2 *flaming hair* **bright,** brilliant, vivid; red, reddish-orange, ginger, titian.
3 *a flaming altercation* **furious,** violent, vehement, frenzied, angry, passionate.
4 *in a flaming temper* **furious,** enraged, fuming, seething, incensed, infuriated, angry, raging, livid; literary wrathful.

flank ▶ **noun 1** *the horse's flanks* **side,** haunch, quarter, thigh.
2 *the southern flank of the army* **side,** wing.
▶ **verb** *the garden is flanked by two rivers* **edge,** bound, line, border, fringe.

flap ▶ **verb 1** *the mallards flapped their wings* **beat,** flutter, agitate, wave, wag, swing.
2 *the flag flapped in the breeze* **flutter,** fly, blow, swing, sway, ripple, stir.
▶ **noun 1** *pockets with buttoned flaps* **fold,** overlap, covering.
2 *a few flaps of the wing* **flutter,** fluttering, beat, beating, waving.
3 informal *I'm in a desperate flap* **panic,** fluster, state, dither, twitter, stew, tizzy.
4 informal *she created a flap with her controversial statement* **fuss,** commotion, stir, hubbub, storm, uproar; controversy, brouhaha, furor; informal to-do, ballyhoo, hoo-ha.

flare ▶ **noun 1** *the flare of the match* **blaze,** flash, dazzle, burst, flicker.
2 *a flare set off by the crew* **distress signal,** rocket, beacon, light, signal.
3 *a flare of anger* **burst,** rush, eruption, explosion, spasm, access.
▶ **verb 1** *the wick flared* **blaze,** flash, flare up, flame, burn; glow, flicker.

2 *her nostrils flared* **spread,** broaden, widen; dilate.

– PHRASES **flare up 1** *the wooden houses flared up like matchsticks* **burn,** blaze, go up in flames. **2** *his injury has flared up again* **recur,** reoccur, reappear; break out, start suddenly, erupt. **3** *I flared up at him* **lose one's temper,** become enraged, fly into a temper, go berserk; informal blow one's top, fly off the handle, go mad, go bananas, hit the roof, go off the deep end, flip out, explode, have a fit, go crackers, flip one's wig, blow one's stack, go ballistic, go postal, have a conniption fit.

flash ▶ **verb 1** *a torch flashed* **light up,** shine, flare, blaze, gleam, glint, sparkle, burn; blink, wink, flicker, shimmer, twinkle, glimmer, glisten, scintillate; literary glister, coruscate. **2** informal *he was flashing his money around* **show off,** flaunt, flourish, display, parade. **3** informal *he flashed at me* **expose oneself**. **4** *racing cars flashed past* **zoom,** streak, tear, shoot, dash, dart, fly, whistle, hurtle, careen, rush, bolt, race, speed, career, whiz, whoosh, buzz; informal belt, zap, bomb; barrel.
▶ **noun 1** *a flash of light* **flare,** blaze, burst; gleam, glint, sparkle, flicker, shimmer, twinkle, glimmer. **2** *a basic uniform with no flashes* **emblem,** insignia, badge; stripe, bar, chevron, brevet, wings. **3** *a sudden flash of inspiration* **burst,** outburst, wave, rush, surge, flush.
▶ **adjective** informal *a flash sports car* See FLASHY.
– PHRASES **in/like a flash** *the police were there in a flash* **instantly,** suddenly, abruptly, immediately, all of a sudden; quickly, rapidly, swiftly, speedily; in an instant/moment, in a (split) second, in a trice, in the blink of an eye; informal in a jiff, in a jiffy.

flashy ▶ **adjective** informal *a flashy outfit for the dance number* **ostentatious,** flamboyant, showy, conspicuous, extravagant, expensive; vulgar, tasteless, brash, lurid, garish, loud, gaudy; informal snazzy, fancy, swanky, flash, jazzy, glitzy.
ANTONYMS understated.

flask ▶ **noun** *a flask of warm brandy* **bottle,** container; hip flask, vacuum flask; trademark Thermos.

flat ▶ **adjective 1** *a flat surface* **level,** horizontal; smooth, even, uniform, regular, plane.
ANTONYMS vertical, uneven.
2 *the sea was flat* **calm,** still, pacific, tranquil, glassy, undisturbed, without waves, like a millpond.
ANTONYMS choppy.
3 *a flat wooden box* **shallow,** low-sided.
ANTONYMS deep.
4 *flat sandals* **low,** low-heeled, without heels.
5 *the teacher's flat voice* **monotonous,** toneless, droning, boring, dull, tedious, uninteresting, unexciting, soporific; bland, dreary, colorless, featureless, emotionless, expressionless, lifeless, spiritless, lackluster, plain-vanilla.
ANTONYMS exciting, emotional.
6 *he felt too flat to get out of bed* **depressed,** dejected, dispirited, despondent, downhearted, disheartened, low, low-spirited, down, unhappy, blue; without energy, enervated, sapped, weary, tired out, worn out, exhausted, drained; informal down in the dumps.
ANTONYMS cheerful, energized.
7 *the market was flat* **slow,** inactive, sluggish, slack, quiet, depressed.
ANTONYMS busy.
8 *a flat tire* **deflated,** punctured, burst.
ANTONYMS inflated.
9 *a flat fee* **fixed,** set, regular, unchanging, unvarying, invariable.
10 *a flat denial* **outright,** direct, absolute, definite, positive, straight, plain, explicit; firm, resolute, adamant, assertive, emphatic, categorical, unconditional, unqualified, unequivocal.
▶ **adverb 1** *she lay down flat on the floor* **stretched out,** outstretched, spread-eagle, sprawling, prone, supine, prostrate, recumbent. **2** informal *she turned me down flat* **outright,** absolutely, firmly, resolutely, adamantly, emphatically, insistently, categorically, unconditionally, unequivocally.
▶ **noun** (**flats**) *they race their bikes across the flats* **tidal flats,** mud flats, tideland, intertidal area.
– PHRASES **flat out** *I'd been working flat out* **hard,** as hard as possible, for all one's worth, to the limit, all out; at full speed, as fast as possible, at full tilt, full bore, full throttle, in high gear; informal like crazy, like mad, like the wind, firing on all cylinders, like a bat out of hell.

flatten ▶ **verb 1** *Flynn flattened the crumpled paper* **make flat,** make even, smooth (out/off), level (out/off). **2** *the cows flattened the grass* **compress,** press down, crush, squash, compact, trample; informal smoosh. **3** *tornadoes can flatten buildings in seconds* **demolish,** raze (to the ground), tear down, knock down, destroy, wreck, devastate, obliterate; informal total. **4** informal *Griff flattened him with a single punch* **knock down/over,** knock to the ground, fell, prostrate; informal floor, deck.

flatter ▶ **verb 1** *it amused him to flatter her* **compliment,** praise, express admiration for, say nice things about, fawn over; cajole, humor, flannel, blarney; informal sweet-talk, soft-soap, brown-nose, butter up, play up to, slobber over; formal laud.
ANTONYMS insult.
2 *I was flattered to be asked* **honor,** gratify, please, delight; informal tickle pink.
ANTONYMS offend.
3 *a hairstyle that flattered her* **suit,** become, look good on, go well with; informal do something for.
ANTONYMS clash with.

flattering ▶ **adjective 1** *flattering remarks* **complimentary,** praising, favorable, commending, admiring, applauding, appreciative, good; fulsome, honeyed, sugary, cajoling, silver-tongued, honey-tongued; fawning, oily, obsequious, ingratiating, servile, sycophantic; informal sweet-talking, soft-soaping, crawling, bootlicking; formal encomiastic. **2** *it was very flattering to be nominated* **pleasing,** gratifying, honoring, gladdening.

3 *her most flattering dress* **becoming,** enhancing.

flattery ▶ **noun** *she's simply not vain enough to fall for your flattery* **praise,** adulation, compliments, blandishments, honeyed words; fawning, blarney, cajolery; formal encomium; informal sweet talk, soft soap, snow job, buttering up, toadying.

flatulence ▶ **noun 1** *medications that help with flatulence* **(intestinal) gas,** wind; informal farting, tooting; formal flatus.
2 *the flatulence of his latest recordings* **pomposity,** pompousness, pretension, pretentiousness, grandiloquence, bombast, turgidity.

flaunt ▶ **verb** *he flaunts his young wife as if she were the prize heifer at the county fair* **show off,** display ostentatiously, make a (great) show of, put on show/display, parade; brag about, crow about, vaunt; informal flash.

> USAGE
>
> **flaunt, flout**
>
> Confusion about these terms is so distressingly common that some dictionaries have thrown in the towel and now treat *flaunt* as a synonym of *flout*. *Flout* means "contravene or disregard; treat with contempt." *Flaunt* means "show off or parade something in an ostentatious manner," but is often incorrectly used for *flout*, perhaps because it is misunderstood as a telescoped version of *flout* and *taunt*—e.g.: "In Washington, the White House issued a statement that deplored the Nigerian Government's 'flaunting [read *flouting*] of even the most basic international norms and universal standards of human rights.' " (*New York Times*; Nov. 11, 1995.)
>
> Of course, *flaunt* is more often used correctly—e.g.: "He donates millions to religious and charitable groups, yet flaunts his own wealth." (*Fortune*; Aug. 18, 1997.) *Flout*, meanwhile, almost never causes a problem. Here it's correctly used: "A record rider turnout, fueled by the mayor's earlier pledge to end the escort and crack down on cyclists flouting traffic laws, poured into the streets on an improvised route." (*San Francisco Examiner*; Aug. 3, 1997.) But the rare mistake of misusing *flout* for *flaunt* does sometimes occur—e.g.: "Mr. Talton was soon joined by almost two dozen other conservative Republicans who filed en masse into the clerk's office to flout [read *flaunt*] their disapproval for their colleague and fellow party member." (*Dallas Morning News*; May 25, 2000.)
>
> One federal appellate judge who misused *flaunt* for *flout* in a published opinion—only to be corrected by judges who later quoted him—appealed to *Webster's Third New International Dictionary of the English Language*, which accepts as standard any usage that can be documented with any frequency. The judge then attempted to justify his error and pledged to persist in it. Seeking refuge in a nonprescriptive dictionary, however, merely ignores the all-important distinction between formal contexts, in which strict standards of usage must apply, and informal contexts, in which venial faults of grammar or usage may, if we are lucky, go unnoticed (or unmentioned).
> **— BG**

flavor ▶ **noun 1** *the flavor of prosciutto* **taste,** savor, tang.
2 *cilantro gives a distinctive flavor to the sauce* **flavoring,** seasoning, tastiness, tang, relish, bite, piquancy, pungency, spice, spiciness, zest; informal zing, zip.
3 *a strong international flavor* **character,** quality, feel, feeling, ambience, atmosphere, aura, air, mood, tone; spirit, essence, nature.
4 *this excerpt will give a flavor of the report* **impression,** suggestion, hint, taste.
▶ **verb** *spices for flavoring food* **add flavor to,** add flavoring to, season, spice (up), add piquancy to, ginger up, enrich; informal pep up.
– PHRASES **flavor of the month** informal *sure, it's great to be flavor of the month, but where will you be a year from now?* **all the rage,** the latest thing, the fashion, in vogue; a one-hit wonder; informal hot, in.

flavoring ▶ **noun 1** *this cheese is often combined with other flavorings* **seasoning,** spice, herb, additive; condiment, dressing.
2 *vanilla flavoring* **extract,** flavor, essence, concentrate, distillate.

flaw ▶ **noun** *the reactor's design flaw | a flaw in his character* **defect,** blemish, fault, imperfection, deficiency, weakness, weak spot/point/link, inadequacy, shortcoming, limitation, failing, foible; literary hamartia; Computing bug; informal glitch. See note at FAULT.
ANTONYMS strength.

flawless ▶ **adjective** *a flawless performance* **perfect,** unblemished, unmarked, unimpaired; whole, intact, sound, unbroken, undamaged, mint, pristine; impeccable, immaculate, consummate, accurate, correct, faultless, error-free, unerring; exemplary, model, ideal, copybook; Theology inerrant.
ANTONYMS flawed.

fleck ▶ **noun** *flecks of pale blue* **spot,** mark, dot, speck, speckle, freckle, patch, smudge, streak, blotch, dab; informal splotch; rare macula.
▶ **verb** *the deer's flanks were flecked with white* **spot,** mark, dot, speckle, bespeckle, freckle, stipple, stud, bestud, blotch, mottle, streak, splash, spatter, bespatter, scatter, sprinkle; informal splotch.

flee ▶ **verb 1** *she fled to her room* **run (away/off),** run for it, make a run for it, dash, take flight, be gone, make off, take off, take to one's heels, make a break for it, bolt, beat a (hasty) retreat, make a quick exit, make one's getaway, escape; informal beat it, clear off/out, vamoose, skedaddle, split, leg it, turn tail, scram, light out, cut out, peel out; archaic fly.
2 *they fled the country* **run away from,** leave hastily, escape from; informal skip; archaic fly.

fleece ▶ noun *a sheep's fleece* **wool,** coat.
▶ verb informal *we were fleeced by a scalper* See SWINDLE (verb).

fleecy ▶ adjective *a fleecy robe* **fluffy,** woolly, downy, soft, fuzzy, furry, velvety, shaggy; technical floccose, pilose.
ANTONYMS coarse.

fleet[1] ▶ noun *the fleet set sail* **navy,** naval force, (naval) task force, armada, flotilla, squadron, convoy.

fleet[2] ▶ adjective literary *as fleet as a greyhound* **nimble,** agile, lithe, lissome, acrobatic, supple, light-footed, light on one's feet, spry, sprightly; quick, fast, swift, rapid, speedy, brisk, smart; informal zippy, twinkle-toed.

fleeting ▶ adjective *ours was a fleeting romance* **brief,** short, short-lived, quick, momentary, cursory, transient, ephemeral, fugitive, passing, transitory; literary evanescent. See note at TEMPORARY.
ANTONYMS lasting.

flesh ▶ noun **1** *you need more flesh on your bones* **muscle,** meat, tissue, brawn; informal beef.
2 *she carries too much flesh* **fat,** weight; Anatomy adipose tissue; informal blubber, flab.
3 *a fruit with juicy flesh* **pulp,** soft part, marrow, meat.
4 *the pleasures of the flesh* **the body,** human nature, physicality, carnality, animality; sensuality, sexuality.
– PHRASES **one's (own) flesh and blood** *how can you deny your own flesh and blood?* **family,** relative(s), relation(s), blood relation(s), kin, kinsfolk, kinsman, kinsmen, kinswoman, kinswomen, kindred, nearest and dearest, people; informal folks. **flesh out 1** *he really fleshed out for his latest movie role* **put on weight,** gain weight, get heavier, grow fat/fatter, fatten up, get fat, fill out. **2** *the story line should be fleshed out a bit* **expand (on),** elaborate on, add to, build on, add flesh to, put flesh on (the bones of), add detail to, expatiate on, supplement, reinforce, augment, fill out, enlarge on. **in the flesh** *look, it's him, in the flesh* **in person,** before one's (very) eyes, in front of one; in real life, live; physically, bodily, in bodily/human form, incarnate.

flex ▶ verb **1** *you must flex your elbow* **bend,** crook, hook, cock, angle, double up.
ANTONYMS straighten.
2 *Rachel flexed her cramped muscles* **tighten,** tauten, tense (up), tension, contract.
ANTONYMS relax.

flexible ▶ adjective **1** *flexible tubing* **pliable,** supple, bendable, pliant, plastic; elastic, stretchy, whippy, springy, resilient, bouncy; informal bendy.
ANTONYMS rigid.
2 *a flexible arrangement* **adaptable,** adjustable, variable, versatile, open-ended, open, free.
ANTONYMS inflexible.
3 *the need to be flexible toward tenants* **accommodating,** amenable, willing to compromise, cooperative, tolerant, easygoing.
ANTONYMS intransigent.

> CHOOSE THE RIGHT WORD
>
> **flexible, elastic, limber, pliable, pliant, resilient, supple**
>
> If you can bend over and touch your toes, you are **flexible**. But a dancer or gymnast is **limber**, an adjective that specifically applies to a body that has been brought into condition through training (*to stay limber, she did yoga every day*). *Flexible* applies to whatever can be bent without breaking, whether or not it returns to its original shape (*a flexible plastic hose; a flexible electrical conduit*); it does not necessarily refer, as *limber* does, to the human body. Unlike *flexible*, **resilient** implies the ability to spring back into shape after being bent or compressed, or to recover one's health or spirits quickly (*so young and resilient that she was back at work in a week*). **Elastic** is usually applied to substances or materials that are easy to stretch or expand and that quickly recover their shape or size (*pants with an elastic waist*), while **supple** is applied to whatever is easily bent, twisted, or folded without breaking or cracking (*a soft, supple leather*). When applied to the human body, *supple* suggests the ability to move effortlessly. **Pliant** and **pliable** may be used to describe either people or things that are easily bent or manipulated. *Pliant* suggests a tendency to bend without force or pressure from the outside, while *pliable* suggests the use of force or submission to another's will. A *pliant* person is merely adaptable, but a *pliable* person is easy to influence and eager to please.

flick ▶ noun *a flick of the wrist* **jerk,** snap, flip, whisk.
▶ verb **1** *he flicked the switch* **click,** snap, flip, jerk.
2 *the horse flicked its tail* **swish,** twitch, wave, wag, waggle, shake.
– PHRASES **flick through** *flick through the pages and try to find a hairstyle you like* **thumb (through),** leaf through, flip through, skim through, scan, look through, browse through, dip into, glance at/through, peruse, run one's eye over.

flicker ▶ verb **1** *the lights flickered* **glimmer,** glint, flare, dance, gutter; twinkle, sparkle, blink, wink, flash, scintillate; literary glister, coruscate.
2 *his eyelids flickered* **flutter,** quiver, tremble, shiver, shudder, spasm, jerk, twitch.

flight ▶ noun **1** *the history of flight* **aviation,** flying, air transport, aerial navigation, aeronautics.
2 *a flight to Rome* **airplane/plane trip,** air trip, trip/journey by air.
3 *the flight of a baseball* **trajectory,** path through the air, track, orbit.
4 *a flight of birds* **flock,** skein, covey, swarm, cloud.
5 *his headlong flight from home* **escape,** getaway, hasty departure, exit, exodus, decamping, breakout, bolt, disappearance.

6 a flight of stairs **staircase,** set of steps, set of stairs.

– PHRASES **put someone to flight** *the king's infantry put our demoralized militia to flight* **chase away/off,** drive back/away/off/out, scatter (to the four winds), disperse, repel, repulse, rout, stampede, scare off; informal send packing. **take flight** *the cowards took flight as the enemy approached* **flee,** run (away/off), run for it, make a run for it, be gone, make off, take off, take to one's heels, make a break for it, bolt, beat a (hasty) retreat, make a quick exit, make one's getaway, escape; informal beat it, clear off/out, vamoose, skedaddle, split, leg it, turn tail, scram, light out, bug out, cut out, peel out; archaic fly.

flighty ▶ adjective *his flighty sister has changed her college major four times* **fickle,** inconstant, mercurial, whimsical, capricious, skittish, volatile, impulsive; irresponsible, giddy, reckless, wild, careless, thoughtless.
ANTONYMS steady, responsible.

flimsy ▶ adjective **1** *a flimsy building* **insubstantial,** fragile, breakable, frail, shaky, unstable, wobbly, tottery, rickety, ramshackle, makeshift; jerry-built, badly built, shoddy, chintzy, gimcrack.
ANTONYMS sturdy.
2 *a flimsy garment* **thin,** light, fine, filmy, floaty, diaphanous, sheer, delicate, insubstantial, wispy, gossamer, gauzy.
ANTONYMS thick.
3 *flimsy evidence* **weak,** feeble, poor, inadequate, insufficient, thin, unsubstantial, unconvincing, implausible, unsatisfactory.
ANTONYMS sound.

flinch ▶ verb **1** *he flinched at the noise* **wince,** start, shudder, quiver, jerk, shy. See note at WINCE.
2 *she never **flinched from** her duty* **shrink from,** recoil from, shy away from, swerve from, demur from; dodge, evade, avoid, duck, balk at, jib at, quail at, fight shy of.

fling ▶ verb *he flung the ax into the river* **throw,** toss, sling, hurl, cast, pitch, lob; informal chuck, heave.
▶ noun **1** *a birthday fling* **good time,** spree, bit of fun, night on the town; fun and games, revels, larks; informal binge.
2 *she had a brief fling with him* **affair,** love affair, relationship, romance, affaire (de cœur), amour, flirtation, dalliance, liaison, entanglement, involvement, attachment.

flip ▶ verb **1** *the wave **flipped** the dinghy **over** | the plane flipped on to its back* **overturn,** turn over, tip over, roll (over), upturn, capsize; upend, invert, knock over; keel over, topple over, turn turtle; archaic overset.
2 *he flipped the key through the air* **throw,** flick, toss, fling, sling, pitch, cast, spin, lob; informal chuck; dated shy.
3 *I flipped the transmitter switch* **flick,** click, snap.

– PHRASES **flip through** *mindlessly flipping through the magazine* **thumb (through),** leaf through, flick through, skim through, scan, look through, browse through, glance at/through, peruse, run one's eye over.

flippant ▶ adjective *a flippant remark* **frivolous,** facetious, tongue-in-cheek; disrespectful, irreverent, cheeky, impudent, impertinent; informal flip, waggish.
ANTONYMS serious, respectful.

flirt ▶ verb **1** *it amused him to **flirt with** her* **trifle with,** toy with, tease, lead on.
2 *those conservatives who **flirted with** fascism* **dabble in,** toy with, trifle with, amuse oneself with, play with, tinker with, dip into, scratch the surface of.
3 *he is **flirting with** danger* **court,** risk, not fear, invite.
▶ noun *Anna was quite a flirt* **tease,** trifler, philanderer, coquette, heartbreaker.

flirtatious ▶ adjective *her blatantly flirtatious manner* **coquettish,** flirty, kittenish, teasing.

float ▶ verb **1** *oil floats on water* **stay afloat,** stay on the surface, be buoyant, be buoyed up.
ANTONYMS sink.
2 *the balloon floated in the air* **hover,** levitate, be suspended, hang, defy gravity.
3 *a cloud floated across the moon* **drift,** glide, sail, slip, slide, waft.
ANTONYMS rush.
4 *they have just floated that idea* **suggest,** put forward, come up with, submit, moot, propose, advance, test the popularity of; informal run something up the flagpole (to see who salutes).
ANTONYMS withdraw.

floating ▶ adjective **1** *floating seaweed* **buoyant,** on the surface, afloat, drifting.
ANTONYMS sunken.
2 *floating helium balloons* **hovering,** levitating, suspended, hanging, defying gravity.
ANTONYMS grounded.
3 *floating voters* **uncommitted,** undecided, of two minds, torn, split, uncertain, unsure, wavering, vacillating, indecisive, blowing hot and cold, undeclared; informal sitting on the fence.
ANTONYMS committed.
4 *a floating population* **unsettled,** transient, temporary, variable, fluctuating; migrant, wandering, nomadic, on the move, migratory, traveling, drifting, roving, roaming, itinerant, vagabond.
ANTONYMS settled.
5 *a floating exchange rate* **variable,** changeable, changing, fluid, fluctuating.
ANTONYMS fixed.

flock ▶ noun **1** *a flock of sheep* **herd,** drove.
2 *a flock of birds* **flight,** congregation, covey, clutch.
3 *flocks of people* **crowd,** throng, horde, mob, rabble, mass, multitude, host, army, pack, swarm, sea; informal gaggle.
▶ verb **1** *people flocked around the star* **gather,** collect, congregate, assemble, converge, mass, crowd, throng, cluster, swarm.
2 *tourists flock to the place* **stream,** go in large numbers, swarm, crowd, troop.

flog ▶ verb *the thief was flogged* **whip,** scourge, flagellate, lash, birch, switch, cane, thrash, beat; tan someone's hide.

flood ▶ noun **1** *a flood warning* **inundation,** swamping, deluge, high water; torrent, overflow, flash flood, freshet, spate.

2 *a flood of tears* **outpouring,** torrent, rush, stream, gush, surge, cascade.
3 *a flood of complaints* **succession,** series, string, chain; barrage, volley, battery; avalanche, torrent, stream, tide, spate, storm, shower, cascade.
ANTONYMS trickle.
▶ **verb 1** *the whole town was flooded* **inundate,** swamp, deluge, immerse, submerge, drown, engulf.
2 *the river could flood* **overflow,** burst its banks, brim over, run over.
3 *imports are flooding the domestic market* **glut,** swamp, saturate, oversupply.
4 *refugees flooded in* **pour,** stream, flow, surge, swarm, pile, crowd.
ANTONYMS trickle.

floor ▶ **noun 1** *he sat on the floor* **ground,** flooring.
2 *the second floor* **story,** level, deck, tier.
▶ **verb 1** *he floored his attacker* **knock down,** knock over, bring down, fell, prostrate; informal lay out.
2 informal *the question floored him* **baffle,** defeat, confound, perplex, puzzle, mystify; informal beat, flummox, stump, fox.

flop ▶ **verb 1** *he flopped into a chair* **collapse,** slump, crumple, subside, sink, drop.
2 *his hair flopped over his eyes* **hang** (**down**), dangle, droop, sag, loll.
3 informal *the play flopped* **be unsuccessful,** fail, not work, fall flat, founder, misfire, backfire, be a disappointment, do badly, lose money, be a disaster; informal bomb, tank, flame out, come a cropper, bite the dust, blow up in someone's face.
ANTONYMS succeed.
▶ **noun** informal *the play was a flop* **failure,** disaster, debacle, catastrophe, loser; informal washout, also-ran, dog, lemon, nonstarter, clinker, turkey.
ANTONYMS success.

florid ▶ **adjective 1** *a florid complexion* **ruddy,** red, red-faced, rosy, rosy-cheeked, pink; flushed, blushing, high-colored; archaic sanguine.
ANTONYMS pale.
2 *florid plasterwork* **ornate,** fancy, elaborate, embellished, curlicued, extravagant, flamboyant, baroque, rococo, fussy, busy.
ANTONYMS plain.
3 *florid prose* **flowery,** flamboyant, high-flown, high-sounding, grandiloquent, ornate, fancy, bombastic, elaborate, turgid, pleonastic; informal highfalutin; rare fustian.
ANTONYMS plain.

flotsam ▶ **noun** *search and salvage crews are gathering flotsam by the boatfuls* **wreckage,** cargo, remains; debris, detritus, waste, dross, refuse, scrap, trash, garbage, rubbish; informal dreck, junk.

flounder ▶ **verb 1** *people were floundering in the water* **struggle,** thrash, flail, twist and turn, splash, stagger, stumble, reel, lurch, blunder, squirm, writhe.
2 *she floundered, not knowing quite what to say* **struggle,** be out of one's depth, have difficulty, be confounded, be confused; informal scratch one's head, be flummoxed, be clueless, be foxed, be fazed, be floored, be beaten.
3 *more firms are floundering* **struggle financially,** be in dire straits, face financial ruin, be in difficulties, face bankruptcy/insolvency, founder.
ANTONYMS prosper.

flourish ▶ **verb 1** *ferns flourish in the shade* **grow,** thrive, prosper, do well, burgeon, increase, multiply, proliferate; spring up, shoot up, bloom, blossom, bear fruit, burst forth, run riot.
ANTONYMS die, wither.
2 *the arts flourished* **thrive,** prosper, bloom, be in good health, be vigorous, be in its heyday; progress, make progress, advance, make headway, develop, improve; evolve, make strides, move forward (in leaps and bounds), expand; informal be in the pink, go places, go great guns, get somewhere.
ANTONYMS decline.
3 *he flourished the sword at them* **brandish,** wave, shake, wield; swing, twirl, swish; display, exhibit, flaunt, show off.

flout ▶ **verb** *countless retailers flout the law by selling cigarettes to children* **defy,** refuse to obey, disobey, break, violate, fail to comply with, fail to observe, contravene, infringe, breach, commit a breach of, transgress against; ignore, disregard. See note at **FLAUNT**.
ANTONYMS observe.

flow ▶ **verb 1** *the water flowed down the channel* **run,** course, glide, drift, circulate; trickle, seep, ooze, dribble, drip, drizzle, spill; stream, swirl, surge, sweep, gush, cascade, pour, roll, rush.
2 *many questions flow from today's announcement* **result,** proceed, arise, follow, ensue, derive, stem, accrue; originate, emanate, spring, emerge; be caused by, be brought about by, be produced by, be consequent on.
▶ **noun** *a good flow of water* **movement,** motion, current, flux, circulation; trickle, ooze, percolation, drip; stream, swirl, surge, gush, rush, spate, tide.

flower ▶ **noun 1** *blue flowers* **bloom,** blossom, floweret, floret.
2 *the flower of the nation's youth* **best,** finest, pick, choice, cream, crème de la crème, elite.
ANTONYMS dregs.

flowery ▶ **adjective 1** *flowery fabrics* **floral,** flower-patterned.
2 *flowery language* **florid,** flamboyant, ornate, fancy, convoluted; high-flown, high-sounding, magniloquent, grandiloquent, baroque, orotund, overblown, pleonastic; informal highfalutin, purple, fancy-dancy, fancy-schmancy; rare fustian.
ANTONYMS plain.

flowing ▶ **adjective 1** *long flowing hair* **loose,** free, unconfined, draping.
ANTONYMS stiff, curly.
2 *the new model will have soft, flowing lines* **sleek,** streamlined, aerodynamic, smooth, clean; elegant, graceful; technical faired.
ANTONYMS jagged.
3 *he writes in an easy, flowing style* **fluent,** fluid, free-flowing, effortless, easy, natural, smooth.
ANTONYMS stilted, halting.

fluctuate ▶ **verb** *profits fluctuate from month to month* **vary,** change, differ, shift, alter, waver, swing, oscillate, alternate, rise and fall, go up and down, seesaw, yo-yo, be unstable.

fluctuation ▶ noun *a natural fluctuation in temperature* **variation,** change, shift, alteration, swing, movement, oscillation, alternation, rise and fall, seesawing, yo-yoing, instability, unsteadiness.
ANTONYMS stability.

flue ▶ noun *periodically check the flue for obstructions* **duct,** tube, shaft, vent, pipe, passage, channel, conduit; funnel, chimney, smokestack.

fluent ▶ adjective 1 *a fluent campaign speech* **articulate,** eloquent, expressive, communicative, coherent, cogent, illuminating, vivid, well-written/spoken.
ANTONYMS inarticulate.
2 *fluent in French* **articulate**; (**be fluent in**) have a (good) command of.
3 *a very fluent running style* **free-flowing,** smooth, effortless, easy, natural, fluid; graceful, elegant; regular, rhythmic.
ANTONYMS jerky.

fluff ▶ noun 1 *fluff on her sleeve* **fuzz,** lint, dust, dustballs, dust bunnies.
2 informal *he only made a few fluffs* **mistake,** error, slip, misstep, flub, slip of the tongue; wrong note, slip-up; formal lapsus linguae.
▶ verb informal *he fluffed an easy shot | he fluffed his only line* **fumble,** make a mess of, bungle, miss, deliver badly, muddle up, forget; informal mess up, make a hash of, botch, foul up, screw up, flub, goof up.
ANTONYMS succeed in.

fluffy ▶ adjective *the gloves have a fluffy lining* **fleecy,** woolly, fuzzy, hairy, feathery, downy, furry; soft.
ANTONYMS rough.

fluid ▶ noun *the fluid seeps up the tube* **liquid,** watery substance, solution.
ANTONYMS solid.
▶ adjective 1 *a fluid substance* **free-flowing**; liquid, liquefied, melted, molten, runny, running.
ANTONYMS solid.
2 *his plans were still fluid* **adaptable,** flexible, adjustable, open-ended, open, open to change, changeable, variable.
ANTONYMS firm.
3 *the fluid state of affairs* **fluctuating,** changeable, subject/likely to change, shifting, ever-shifting, inconstant; unstable, unsettled, turbulent, volatile, mercurial, protean.
ANTONYMS static.
4 *he stood up in one fluid movement* **smooth,** fluent, flowing, effortless, easy, continuous, seamless; graceful, elegant.
ANTONYMS jerky.

fluke ▶ noun *what a nice fluke, finding you here* **chance,** coincidence, accident, twist of fate; piece of luck, stroke of good luck/fortune, serendipity.

flunky ▶ noun 1 *a flunky brought us drinks* **servant,** lackey, steward, butler, footman, valet, attendant, page.
2 *government flunkies searched his offices* **minion,** lackey, hireling, subordinate, underling, servant; creature, instrument, cat's paw; informal stooge, gofer.

flurry ▶ noun 1 *snow flurries* **swirl,** whirl, eddy, billow, shower, gust.
2 *a flurry of activity* **burst,** outbreak, spurt, fit, spell, bout, rash, eruption; fuss, stir, bustle, hubbub, commotion, disturbance, furor; informal to-do, flap.
3 *a flurry of imports* **spate,** wave, flood, deluge, torrent, stream, tide, avalanche; series, succession, string, outbreak, rash, explosion, run, rush.
ANTONYMS dearth, trickle.

flush[1] ▶ verb 1 *Shane flushed in embarrassment* **blush,** redden, go pink, go red, go crimson, go scarlet, color (up).
ANTONYMS pale.
2 *fruit helps to flush toxins from the body* **rinse,** wash, sluice, swill, cleanse, clean.
3 *they flushed out the snipers* **drive,** chase, force, dislodge, expel, frighten, scare.
▶ noun 1 *a flush crept over her face* **blush,** reddening, high color, color, rosiness, pinkness, ruddiness, bloom.
ANTONYMS paleness.
2 *the flush of youth* **bloom,** glow, freshness, radiance, vigor, rush.

flush[2] ▶ adjective informal 1 *the company was flush with cash* **well supplied with,** well provided with, well stocked with, replete with, overflowing with, bursting with, brimming with, loaded with, overloaded with, teeming with, stuffed with, swarming with, thick with, solid with; full of, abounding in, rich in, abundant in; informal awash with, jam-packed with, chock-full of.
ANTONYMS bereft.
2 *the years when cash was flush* **plentiful,** abundant, in abundance, copious, ample, profuse, superabundant; informal galore; literary plenteous, bounteous. See note at WEALTHY.
ANTONYMS lacking, low.

flushed ▶ adjective 1 *flushed faces* **red,** pink, ruddy, glowing, reddish, pinkish, rosy, florid, high-colored, healthy-looking, aglow, burning, feverish; blushing, red-faced, embarrassed, shamefaced.
ANTONYMS pale.
2 *flushed with success* **elated,** excited, thrilled, exhilarated, happy, delighted, overjoyed, joyous, gleeful, jubilant, exultant, ecstatic, euphoric, rapturous; informal blissed out, over the moon, high, on a high.
ANTONYMS dismayed.

fluster ▶ verb *she was flustered by his presence* **unsettle,** make nervous, unnerve, agitate, ruffle, upset, bother, put on edge, disquiet, disturb, worry, perturb, disconcert, confuse, throw off balance, confound; informal rattle, faze, put into a flap, throw into a tizzy, discombobulate.
ANTONYMS calm.
▶ noun *I was in a terrible fluster* **state of agitation,** state of anxiety, nervous state, panic, frenzy, fret; informal dither, flap, tizz, tizzy, twitter, state, sweat.
ANTONYMS state of calm.

flutter ▶ verb 1 *butterflies fluttered around* **flit,** hover, flitter, dance.

2 *a tern was fluttering its wings* **flap,** move up and down, beat, quiver, agitate, vibrate, whiffle.
3 *she fluttered her eyelashes* **flicker,** bat.
4 *flags fluttered* **flap,** wave, ripple, undulate, quiver; fly.
5 *her heart fluttered* **beat weakly,** beat irregularly, palpitate, miss/skip a beat, quiver, go pit-a-pat; Medicine exhibit arrhythmia.
▶ **noun 1** *the flutter of wings* **beating,** flapping, quivering, agitation, vibrating.
2 *a flutter of dark eyelashes* **flicker,** bat.
3 *the flutter of the flags* **flapping,** waving, rippling.
4 *a flutter of nervousness* **tremor,** wave, rush, surge, flash, stab, flush, tremble, quiver, shiver, frisson, chill, thrill, tingle, shudder, ripple, flicker.

fly ▶ **verb 1** *a bird flew overhead* **travel through the air,** wing its way, wing, glide, soar, wheel; hover, hang; take wing, take to the air, mount.
2 *they flew to Paris* **travel by airplane/plane,** travel by air, jet.
3 *military planes flew in food supplies* **transport by airplane/plane,** transport by air, airlift, lift, jet.
4 *he could fly a plane* **pilot,** operate, control, maneuver, steer.
5 *the ship was flying a red flag* **display,** show, exhibit, bear; have hoisted, have run up.
6 *flags flew in the town* **flutter,** flap, wave.
7 *doesn't time fly?* **go quickly,** fly by/past, pass swiftly, slip past, rush past.
8 *the runners flew by* See **SPEED** (sense 1 of the verb).
9 archaic *the beaten army had to fly* See **FLEE** (sense 1).
– PHRASES **fly at** *he flew at Rodriguez with fire in his eyes* **attack,** assault, pounce on, set upon, set about, let fly at, turn on, round on, lash out at, hit out at, fall on; informal lay into, tear into, lace into, sail into, pitch into, let someone have it, jump, have a go at, light into. **let fly** See **LET**.

flying ▶ **adjective 1** *a flying beetle* **winged; airborne,** in the air, in flight.
2 *a flying visit* **brief,** short, lightning, fleeting, hasty, rushed, hurried, quick, whistle-stop, cursory, perfunctory; informal quickie.
ANTONYMS long.

foam ▶ **noun** *the foam on the waves* **froth,** spume, surf; fizz, effervescence, bubbles, head; lather, suds.
▶ **verb** *the water foamed* **froth,** spume; fizz, effervesce, bubble; lather; ferment, rise; boil, seethe, simmer.

focus ▶ **noun 1** *schools are a focus of community life* **center,** focal point, central point, center of attention, hub, pivot, nucleus, heart, cornerstone, linchpin, cynosure.
2 *the focus is on helping people* **emphasis,** accent, priority, attention, concentration.
3 *the main focus of this chapter* **subject,** theme, concern, subject matter, topic, issue, thesis, point, thread; substance, essence, gist, matter.
4 *the resulting light beams are brought to a focus at the eyepiece* **focal point,** point of convergence.
▶ **verb 1** *she focused her binoculars on the tower* **bring into focus**; aim, point, turn.
2 *the investigation will* ***focus on*** *areas of social need* **concentrate on,** center on, zero in on, zoom in on; address itself to, pay attention to, pinpoint, revolve around, have as its starting point.
– PHRASES **in focus** *submit only those snapshots that are in focus* **sharp,** crisp, distinct, clear, well-defined, well focused. **out of focus** *the shots are slightly out of focus, which gives them an eerie quality* **blurred,** unfocused, indistinct, blurry, fuzzy, hazy, misty, cloudy, lacking definition, nebulous.

foe ▶ **noun** *a well-armed foe* **enemy,** adversary, opponent, rival, antagonist, combatant, challenger, competitor, opposer, opposition, competition, other side.
ANTONYMS friend.

fog ▶ **noun** *we can't set sail in this fog* **mist,** smog, murk, haze, ice fog; archaic sea smoke; literary brume, fume.
▶ **verb 1** *the windshield* ***fogged up*** | *his breath fogged the glass* **steam up,** mist over, cloud over, film over, make/become misty.
ANTONYMS clear.
2 *his brain was fogged with sleep* **muddle,** daze, stupefy, fuddle, befuddle, bewilder, confuse, befog; literary bedim, becloud.

foggy ▶ **adjective 1** *the weather was foggy* **misty,** smoggy, hazy, murky.
ANTONYMS clear.
2 *she was foggy with sleep* | *a foggy memory* **muddled,** fuddled, befuddled, confused, at sea, bewildered, dazed, stupefied, numb, groggy, fuzzy, bleary; dark, dim, hazy, shadowy, cloudy, blurred, obscure, vague, indistinct, unclear; informal dopey, woolly, woozy, out of it.
ANTONYMS lucid.

foible ▶ **noun** *tolerating each other's foibles* **weakness,** failing, shortcoming, flaw, imperfection, blemish, fault, defect, limitation; quirk, kink, idiosyncrasy, eccentricity, peculiarity. See note at **FAULT**.
ANTONYMS strength.

foil[1] ▶ **verb** *their escape attempt was foiled* **thwart,** frustrate, counter, balk, impede, obstruct, hamper, euchre, hinder, snooker, cripple, scotch, derail, scupper, scuttle, smash; stop, block, prevent, defeat; informal do for, put paid to, stymie, cook someone's goose. See note at **THWART**.
ANTONYMS assist.

foil[2] ▶ **noun** *Abbott was the perfect foil to Costello* **contrast,** complement, antithesis, relief.

foist ▶ **verb** *why are you trying to* ***foist*** *your crummy old furniture* ***on me?*** **impose on,** force on, thrust on, offload on, unload on, dump on, palm off on; pass off on; saddle someone with, land someone with.

fold[1] ▶ **verb 1** *I folded the cloth* **double (over/up),** crease, turn under/up/over, bend; tuck, gather, pleat.
2 *fold the cream into the chocolate mixture* **mix,** blend, stir gently, incorporate.
3 *he folded her in his arms* **enfold,** wrap, envelop; take, gather, clasp, squeeze, clutch; embrace, hug, cuddle, cradle.
4 *the firm folded last year* **fail,** collapse,

founder; go bankrupt, become insolvent, cease trading, go into receivership, go into liquidation, be closed (down), be shut (down); informal crash, go bust, go broke, go under, go belly up.

▶ **noun** *there was a fold in the paper* **crease,** wrinkle, crinkle, pucker, furrow; pleat, gather.

fold[2] ▶ **noun 1** *the sheep were in their fold* **enclosure,** pen, paddock, pound, compound, ring, corral; sheepfold.
2 *they welcomed Joe back into the fold* **community,** group, body, company, mass, flock, congregation, assembly.

folder ▶ **noun** *it's the blue folder labeled "Taxes"* **file,** binder, portfolio, envelope, sleeve, wallet.

foliage ▶ **noun** *the plant is grown for its striking foliage* **leaves,** leafage; greenery, vegetation, verdure.

folk ▶ **noun** informal **1** *the local folk* **people,** individuals, 'men, women, and children', (living) souls, mortals; citizenry, inhabitants, residents, populace, population; formal denizens.
2 *my folks came from the north* **parents, relatives,** relations, blood relations, family, nearest and dearest, people, kinsfolk, kinsmen, kinswomen, kin, kith and kin, kindred, flesh and blood.

folklore ▶ **noun** *Adrian is fascinated by the local folklore* **mythology,** lore, oral history, tradition, folk tradition; legends, fables, myths, folk tales, folk stories, old wives' tales; mythos.

follow ▶ **verb 1** *we'll let the others follow* **come behind,** come after, go behind, go after, walk behind.
ANTONYMS lead.
2 *he was expected to follow his father in the business* **succeed,** replace, take the place of, take over from; informal step into someone's shoes, fill someone's shoes/boots.
3 *people used to **follow** the band **around*** **accompany,** go along with, go around with, travel with, escort, attend, trail around with, string along with; informal tag along with.
ANTONYMS lead.
4 *the KGB followed her everywhere* **shadow,** trail, stalk, track, dog, hound; informal tail.
5 *follow the instructions* **obey,** comply with, conform to, adhere to, stick to, keep to, hew to, act in accordance with, abide by, observe, heed, pay attention to.
ANTONYMS flout.
6 *penalties may **follow from** such behaviour* **result from,** arise from, be a consequence of, be caused by, be brought about by, be a result of, come after, develop from, ensue from, emanate from, issue from, proceed from, spring from, flow from, originate from, stem from.
ANTONYMS lead to.
7 *I couldn't follow what he said* **understand,** comprehend, apprehend, take in, grasp, fathom, appreciate, see; informal make head(s) or tail(s) of, get, figure out, savvy, wrap/get one's head around, wrap/get one's mind around, get the drift of.
ANTONYMS misunderstand.
8 *she followed her mentor in her poetic style* **imitate,** copy, mimic, ape, reproduce, mirror, echo; emulate, take as a pattern, take as an example, take as a model, adopt the style of, model oneself on, take a leaf out of someone's book.
9 *he follows the Pacers* **be a fan of,** be a supporter of, support, be a follower of, be an admirer of, be a devotee of, be devoted to.
ANTONYMS dislike.
– PHRASES **follow through** *they lack the resources to follow the project through* **complete,** bring to completion, see something through; continue with, carry on with, keep on with, keep going with, stay with; informal stick something out. **follow up** *I've got a hunch and I'm going to follow it up* **investigate,** research, look into, dig into, delve into, make inquiries into, inquire about, ask questions about, pursue, chase up; informal check out, scope out.

follower ▶ **noun 1** *the president's closest followers* **acolyte,** assistant, attendant, companion; henchman, minion, lackey, servant; informal hanger-on, sidekick.
ANTONYMS leader.
2 *a follower of Christ* **disciple,** apostle, supporter, defender, champion; believer, true believer, worshiper.
ANTONYMS opponent.
3 *followers of winter sports* **fan,** enthusiast, admirer, devotee, lover, supporter, adherent.

following ▶ **noun** *his devoted following* **admirers,** supporters, backers, fans, adherents, devotees, advocates, patrons, public, audience, circle, retinue, train.
ANTONYMS opposition.
▶ **adjective 1** *the following day* **next,** ensuing, succeeding, subsequent.
ANTONYMS preceding.
2 *the following questions* below, further on; these; formal hereunder, hereinafter.
ANTONYMS preceding, aforementioned.

folly ▶ **noun** *the folly of youth* **foolishness,** foolhardiness, stupidity, idiocy, lunacy, madness, rashness, recklessness, imprudence, injudiciousness, irresponsibility, thoughtlessness, indiscretion; informal craziness.
ANTONYMS wisdom.

foment ▶ **verb** *accused of fomenting civil unrest* **instigate,** incite, provoke, agitate, excite, stir up, whip up, encourage, urge, fan the flames of. See note at INCITE.

fond ▶ **adjective 1** *she was **fond of** dancing* **keen on,** partial to, addicted to, enthusiastic about, passionate about; attached to, attracted to, enamored of, in love with, having a soft spot for; informal into, hooked on, gone on, sweet on, struck on.
ANTONYMS indifferent.
2 *her fond husband* **adoring,** devoted, doting, loving, caring, affectionate, warm, tender, kind, attentive, uxorious.
ANTONYMS unfeeling.
3 *a fond hope* **unrealistic,** naive, foolish, overoptimistic, deluded, delusory, absurd, vain, Panglossian.
ANTONYMS realistic.

fondle ▶ **verb** *gently fondling the puppies | the sight of a woman quietly fondling her lover* **caress,** stroke, pat, pet, finger, tickle, play with; maul, molest; informal paw, grope, feel up, touch up, cop a feel of.

fondness ▶ noun 1 *they look at each other with such fondness* **affection,** love, liking, warmth, tenderness, kindness, devotion, endearment, attachment, friendliness.
ANTONYMS hatred.
2 *a fondness for spicy food* **liking,** love, taste, partiality, keenness, inclination, penchant, predilection, relish, passion, appetite; weakness, soft spot; informal thing, yen, jones.
ANTONYMS dislike.

food ▶ noun 1 *French food* **nourishment,** sustenance, nutriment, fare; bread, daily bread; cooking, cuisine; foodstuffs, edibles, provender, refreshments, meals, provisions, rations; solids; informal eats, eatables, nosh, grub, chow; formal comestibles; literary viands; dated victuals; archaic commons, meat, aliment.
2 *food for the cattle* **fodder,** feed, provender, forage.

fool ▶ noun 1 *you've acted like a complete fool* **idiot,** ass, blockhead, dunce, dolt, ignoramus, imbecile, cretin, dullard, simpleton, moron, clod; informal nitwit, halfwit, dope, ninny, nincompoop, chump, dimwit, dingbat, dipstick, goober, coot, goon, dumbo, dummy, ditz, dumdum, fathead, numbskull, numbnuts, dunderhead, thickhead, airhead, flake, lamebrain, zombie, nerd, peabrain, birdbrain, jughead, jerk, donkey, twit, goat, dork, twerp, schmuck, bozo, boob, turkey, schlep, chowderhead, dumbhead, goofball, goof, goofus, galoot, lummox, klutz, putz, schlemiel, sap, meatball, dumb cluck.
2 *she made a fool of me* **laughingstock,** dupe, butt, gull, cat's paw; informal stooge, sucker, fall guy, sap.
3 historical *the fool in King James's court* **jester,** court jester, clown, buffoon, joker, zany.
▶ verb 1 *he'd been fooled by a mere child* **deceive,** trick, hoax, dupe, take in, mislead, delude, hoodwink, sucker, bluff, gull; swindle, defraud, cheat, double-cross; informal con, bamboozle, pull a fast one on, take for a ride, pull the wool over someone's eyes, put one over on, have on, diddle, fiddle, sting, shaft, snooker, stiff, euchre, hornswoggle; literary cozen.
2 *I'm not fooling, I promise* **pretend,** make believe, feign, put on an act, act, sham, fake; joke, jest; informal kid; have someone on.
– PHRASES **fool around 1** *someone's been fooling around with the controls* **fiddle,** play (around), toy, trifle, meddle, tamper, interfere, monkey (around); informal mess (around). **2** informal *my husband's been fooling around* **philander,** womanize, flirt, have an affair, commit adultery, cheat; informal play around, mess around, carry on, play the field, sleep around.

foolery ▶ noun *the foolery in this dormitory has gotten out of hand* **clowning,** fooling, tomfoolery, buffoonery, silliness, foolishness, stupidity, idiocy; antics, capers; informal larks, shenanigans, didoes; archaic harlequinade.

foolhardy ▶ adjective *their foolhardy plans* **reckless,** rash, irresponsible, impulsive, hotheaded, impetuous, bullheaded, daredevil, devil-may-care, madcap, harebrained, precipitate, hasty, overhasty; literary temerarious. See note at TEMERITY.
ANTONYMS prudent.

foolish ▶ adjective *don't let your foolish impulses get you into trouble* **stupid,** silly, idiotic, witless, brainless, mindless, unintelligent, thoughtless, half-baked, imprudent, incautious, injudicious, unwise; ill-advised, ill-considered, impolitic, rash, reckless, foolhardy, daft; informal dumb, dim, dimwitted, halfwitted, thick, harebrained, crack-brained, crackpot, pea-brained, wooden-headed, dumb-ass, chowderheaded. See note at ABSURD.
ANTONYMS sensible, wise.

foolishness ▶ noun *I regretted my foolishness* **folly,** stupidity, idiocy, imbecility, silliness, inanity, thoughtlessness, imprudence, injudiciousness, lack of foresight, lack of sense, irresponsibility, indiscretion, foolhardiness, rashness, recklessness.
ANTONYMS sense, wisdom.

foolproof ▶ adjective *a foolproof security system* **infallible,** dependable, reliable, trustworthy, certain, sure, guaranteed, safe, sound, tried and tested; watertight, airtight, flawless, perfect; informal sure-fire, idiot-proof, goof-proof; formal efficacious.
ANTONYMS flawed.

foot ▶ noun 1 (**feet**) *my feet hurt* informal tootsies, dogs, boats; Brit. informal trotters.
2 *the animal's foot* paw, hoof, pad; Brit. trotter.
3 *the foot of the hill* **bottom,** base, lowest part; end; foundation.
– PHRASES **foot the bill** informal *as usual, the taxpayers will have to foot the bill* **pay (the bill),** settle up; informal pick up the tab, pick up the check, cough up (the money/dough), fork out (the money/dough), shell out (the money/dough).

footing ▶ noun 1 *Natalie lost her footing* **foothold,** toehold, grip, purchase.
2 *a solid financial footing* **basis,** base, foundation.
3 *on an equal footing* **standing,** status, position; condition, arrangement, basis; relationship, terms.

footstep ▶ noun 1 *he heard a footstep* **footfall,** step, tread, stomp, stamp.
2 *footsteps in the sand* **footprint,** footmark, mark, impression; (**footsteps**) track(s), spoor.

fop ▶ noun *he was known as quite a fop in the old neighborhood, always dressed to the nines and whistling a cheery tune* **dandy,** man about town, poseur; informal snappy dresser, trendoid, hipster; archaic coxcomb, popinjay.

forage ▶ verb *Colonel Kendricks sent out a small party to forage for provisions* **hunt,** search, look, rummage around, ferret, root about/around, nose around/about, scavenge.
▶ noun 1 *forage for the horses* **fodder,** feed, food, provender.
2 *a nightly forage for food* **hunt,** search, look, quest, rummage, scavenge.

forbear ▶ verb *can you* ***forbear from*** *drinking?* **refrain from,** abstain from, desist from, keep from, restrain oneself from, stop oneself from, hold back from, withhold from; resist the

temptation to (be); eschew, avoid, decline to (be).
ANTONYMS persist.

forbearance ▶ noun *we are proud of the forbearance you have demonstrated during these difficult weeks* **tolerance,** patience, resignation, endurance, fortitude, stoicism; leniency, clemency, indulgence; restraint, self-restraint, self-control. See note at ABSTINENCE.

forbid ▶ verb *the law forbids gender discrimination* **prohibit,** ban, outlaw, make illegal, veto, proscribe, disallow, embargo, bar, debar, interdict; Law enjoin, restrain. See also note at PROHIBIT.
ANTONYMS permit.

forbidding ▶ adjective **1** *a forbidding manner* **hostile,** unwelcoming, unfriendly, off-putting, unsympathetic, unapproachable, grim, stern, hard, tough, frosty.
ANTONYMS friendly.
2 *the dark castle looked forbidding* **threatening,** ominous, menacing, sinister, brooding, daunting, formidable, fearsome, frightening, chilling, disturbing, disquieting. See note at OMINOUS.
ANTONYMS inviting.

force ▶ noun **1** *he pushed with all his force* **strength,** power, energy, might, effort, exertion; impact, pressure, weight, impetus.
ANTONYMS weakness.
2 *they used force to achieve their aims* **coercion,** compulsion, constraint, duress, oppression, harassment, intimidation, threats; informal arm-twisting, bullying tactics.
3 *the force of the argument* **cogency,** potency, weight, effectiveness, soundness, validity, strength, power, significance, influence, authority; informal punch; formal efficacy.
ANTONYMS weakness.
4 *a force for good* **agency,** power, influence, instrument, vehicle, means.
5 *a peace-keeping force* **body,** body of people, group, outfit, party, team; detachment, unit, squad; informal bunch.
▶ verb **1** *he was forced to pay* **compel,** coerce, make, constrain, oblige, impel, drive, pressurize, pressure, press, push, press-gang, bully, dragoon, bludgeon; informal put the screws on, lean on, twist someone's arm. See note at COMPEL.
2 *the door had to be forced* **break open,** burst open, knock down, smash down, kick in.
3 *water was forced through a hole* **propel,** push, thrust, shove, drive, press, pump.
4 *they forced a confession out of the kids* **extract,** elicit, exact, extort, wrest, wring, drag, screw, squeeze.
– PHRASES **in force 1** *the law is now in force* **effective,** in operation, operative, operational, in action, valid. **2** *her fans were out in force* **in great numbers,** in hordes, in full strength.

forced ▶ adjective **1** *forced entry* **violent,** forcible.
2 *forced repatriation* **enforced,** forcible, compulsory, obligatory, mandatory, involuntary, imposed, required, stipulated, dictated, ordained, prescribed.
ANTONYMS voluntary.
3 *a forced smile* **strained,** unnatural, artificial, false, feigned, simulated, contrived, labored, stilted, studied, mannered, affected, unconvincing, insincere, hollow; informal phony, pretend, put on.
ANTONYMS natural.

forceful ▶ adjective **1** *a forceful personality* **dynamic,** energetic, assertive, authoritative, vigorous, powerful, strong, pushy, driving, determined, insistent, commanding, dominant, domineering; informal bossy, in-your-face, go-ahead, feisty.
ANTONYMS weak, submissive.
2 *a forceful argument* **cogent,** convincing, compelling, strong, powerful, potent, weighty, effective, well-founded, telling, persuasive, irresistible, eloquent, coherent.
ANTONYMS weak, unconvincing.

forcible ▶ adjective **1** *forcible entry* **forced,** violent.
2 *forcible repatriation* See FORCED (sense 2).

forebear ▶ noun *his forebears had been pioneers* **ancestor,** forefather, antecedent, progenitor, primogenitor.
ANTONYMS descendant.

forebode ▶ verb literary *the scarlet sky forebodes the visitation of mischief* **presage,** augur, portend, herald, warn of, forewarn of, foreshadow, be an omen of, indicate, signify, signal, promise, threaten, spell, denote; literary betoken, foretoken. See note at OMINOUS.

foreboding ▶ noun **1** *a feeling of foreboding* **apprehension,** anxiety, trepidation, disquiet, unease, uneasiness, misgiving, suspicion, worry, fear, fearfulness, dread, alarm; informal the willies, the heebie-jeebies, the jitters, the creeps.
ANTONYMS calm.
2 *their forebodings proved justified* **premonition,** presentiment, bad feeling, sneaking suspicion, funny feeling, intuition; archaic presage.

forecast ▶ verb *they forecast record profits* **predict,** prophesy, prognosticate, foretell, foresee, forewarn of. See note at PREDICT.
▶ noun *a gloomy forecast* **prediction,** prophecy, forewarning, prognostication, augury, divination, prognosis.

forefather ▶ noun See FOREBEAR.

forefront ▶ noun *her first CD propelled her to the forefront of the music scene* **vanguard,** van, spearhead, head, lead, front, fore, front line, cutting edge, avant-garde.
ANTONYMS rear, background.

foregoing ▶ adjective *the foregoing circumstances are no longer applicable to this argument* **preceding,** aforesaid, aforementioned, previously mentioned, earlier, above; previous, prior, antecedent.
ANTONYMS following.

foregone ▶ adjective
– PHRASES **a foregone conclusion** *a rental increase is a foregone conclusion* **certainty,** inevitability, matter of course, predictable result; informal sure thing, no-brainer.

foreground ▶ noun **1** *the foreground of the picture* **front,** fore.
2 *in the foreground of the political drama* **forefront,** vanguard, van, spearhead, head,

lead, front, fore, front line, cutting edge.

foreign ▶ adjective 1 *foreign branches of American banks* **overseas,** exotic, distant, external, alien, nonnative.
ANTONYMS domestic, native.
2 *the concept is very foreign to us* **unfamiliar,** unknown, unheard of, strange, alien; novel, new.
ANTONYMS familiar.

foreigner ▶ noun *her unease with foreigners* **alien,** nonnative, stranger, outsider; immigrant, landed immigrant, refugee, settler, newcomer.
ANTONYMS native.

foreman, forewoman ▶ noun *report any injury to the foreman* **supervisor,** overseer, superintendent, team leader; foreperson; captain; ramrod, straw boss.

foremost ▶ adjective *the foremost impressionist of his age* **leading,** principal, premier, prime, top, top-level, greatest, best, supreme, preeminent, outstanding, most important, most prominent, most influential, most illustrious, most notable; ranking, number-one, star.
ANTONYMS minor.

forerunner ▶ noun 1 *archosaurs were the forerunners of dinosaurs* **predecessor,** precursor, antecedent, ancestor, forebear; prototype.
ANTONYMS descendant.
2 *a headache may be the forerunner of other complaints* **prelude,** herald, harbinger, precursor, sign, signal, indication, warning.

foresee ▶ verb *I foresee much good fortune in your future* **anticipate,** predict, forecast, expect, envisage, envision, see; foretell, prophesy, prognosticate; literary foreknow.

foreshadow ▶ verb *those things that foreshadow war are sadly upon us* **signal,** indicate, signify, mean, be a sign of, suggest, herald, be a harbinger of, warn of, portend, prefigure, presage, promise, point to, anticipate; informal spell; literary forebode, foretoken, betoken, adumbrate; archaic foreshow. See note at PREDICT.

foresight ▶ noun *my lack of foresight has cost me dearly* **forethought,** planning, farsightedness, vision, anticipation, prudence, care, caution, precaution, readiness, preparedness.
ANTONYMS hindsight.

forest ▶ noun *the cooling shade of the forest* **wood**(s), woodland, timberland, trees, bush, plantation; jungle, rain forest, pinewood; archaic greenwood; taiga, boreal forest, Carolinian forest, Acadian forest.

forestall ▶ verb *they were unable to forestall Roosevelt's reelection* **preempt,** get in before; anticipate, second-guess; nip in the bud, thwart, frustrate, foil, stave off, ward off, fend off, avert, preclude, obviate, prevent; informal beat someone to it.

forestry ▶ noun *a college degree in forestry* **forest management,** tree growing, agroforestry; technical arboriculture, silviculture, dendrology.

foretell ▶ verb 1 *the locals can foretell a storm* **predict,** forecast, prophesy, prognosticate; foresee, anticipate, envisage, envision, see. See note at PREDICT.
2 *dreams can foretell the future* **indicate,** foreshadow, prefigure, anticipate, warn of, point to, signal, portend, augur, presage, be an omen of; literary forebode, foretoken, betoken; archaic foreshow.

forethought ▶ noun *without forethought, you'll just keep stumbling through life* **anticipation,** planning, forward planning, provision, precaution, prudence, care, caution; foresight, farsightedness, vision.
ANTONYMS impulse, recklessness.

forever ▶ adverb 1 *their love would last forever* **for always,** evermore, for ever and ever, for good, for all time, until the end of time, until hell freezes over, eternally, forevermore, perpetually, in perpetuity; informal until the cows come home, until kingdom come; archaic for aye.
2 *he was forever banging into things* **always,** continually, constantly, perpetually, incessantly, endlessly, persistently, repeatedly, regularly; nonstop, day and night, 'morning, noon, and night'; all the time, the entire time; informal 24–7.
ANTONYMS never, occasionally.

forewarn ▶ verb *the building would have been torched if the authorities had not been forewarned* **warn,** warn in advance, give advance warning, give fair warning, give notice, apprise, inform; alert, caution, put someone on their guard; informal tip off.

foreword ▶ noun *he wrote the foreword to one of her books* **preface,** introduction, prologue, preamble; informal intro, lead-in; formal exordium, prolegomenon, proem.
ANTONYMS conclusion.

forfeit ▶ verb *latecomers will forfeit their places* **lose,** be deprived of, surrender, relinquish, sacrifice, give up, yield, renounce, forgo; informal pass up, lose out on.
ANTONYMS retain.
▶ noun *they are liable to a forfeit* **penalty,** sanction, punishment, penance; fine; confiscation, loss, relinquishment, forfeiture, surrender; Law sequestration.

forge[1] ▶ verb 1 *smiths forged swords* **hammer out,** beat into shape, fashion.
2 *they forged a partnership* **build,** construct, form, create, establish, set up.
3 *he forged her signature* **fake,** falsify, counterfeit, copy, imitate, reproduce, replicate, simulate.

forge[2] ▶ verb *they forged through swamps* **advance steadily,** advance gradually, press on, push on, soldier on, march on, push forward, make progress, make headway.
– PHRASES **forge ahead** *Jack's horse forged ahead and took the lead* **advance rapidly,** progress quickly, make rapid progress, increase speed.

forgery ▶ noun 1 *guilty of forgery* **counterfeiting,** falsification, faking, copying, pirating.
2 *the painting was a forgery* **fake,** counterfeit, fraud, sham, imitation, replica, copy, pirate copy; informal phony.

forget ▶ verb 1 *he forgot where he was* **fail to remember,** fail to recall, fail to think of; informal disremember.
ANTONYMS remember.
2 *I never forget my briefcase* **leave behind,** fail

to take/bring.
3 *I forgot to close the door* **neglect,** fail, omit.
4 *you can forget that idea* **stop thinking about,** put out of one's mind, shut out, blank out, pay no heed to, not worry about, ignore, overlook, take no notice of; abandon, say goodbye to, deep-six.

forgetful ▶ **adjective 1** *I'm so forgetful these days* **absentminded,** amnesic, amnesiac, vague, disorganized, dreamy, abstracted; informal scatterbrained, having a mind/memory like a sieve.
ANTONYMS reliable.
2 *forgetful of the time* **heedless of,** careless of, unmindful of; inattentive to, negligent about, oblivious to, unconcerned about, indifferent to, not bothered about.
ANTONYMS heedful.

forgetfulness ▶ **noun 1** *his excuse was forgetfulness* **absentmindedness,** amnesia, poor memory, a lapse of memory, vagueness, abstraction; informal scattiness.
ANTONYMS reliability.
2 *a forgetfulness of duty* **neglect,** heedlessness, carelessness, disregard; inattention, obliviousness, lack of concern, indifference.
ANTONYMS heed.

forgive ▶ **verb 1** *she would not forgive him* **pardon,** excuse, exonerate, absolve; make allowances for, feel no resentment toward, feel no malice toward, harbor no grudge against, bury the hatchet with; let bygones be bygones; informal let off (the hook); formal exculpate. See note at **ABSOLVE**.
ANTONYMS blame, resent.
2 *you must forgive his rude conduct* **excuse,** overlook, disregard, ignore, pass over, make allowances for, allow; turn a blind eye to, turn a deaf ear to, wink at, indulge, tolerate.
ANTONYMS punish.

forgiveness ▶ **noun** *we beg your forgiveness* **pardon,** absolution, exoneration, remission, dispensation, indulgence, clemency, mercy; reprieve, amnesty; archaic shrift.
ANTONYMS mercilessness, punishment.

forgiving ▶ **adjective** *Cromwell was not renowned for his forgiving nature* **merciful,** lenient, compassionate, magnanimous, humane, softhearted, forbearing, tolerant, indulgent, understanding.
ANTONYMS merciless, vindictive.

forgo, forego ▶ **verb** *we had to forgo our trip to Wyoming* **do without,** go without, give up, waive, renounce, surrender, relinquish, part with, drop, sacrifice, abstain from, refrain from, eschew, cut out; informal swear off; formal forswear, abjure.
ANTONYMS keep.

forgotten ▶ **adjective** *Vivaldi's operas are largely forgotten* **unremembered,** out of mind, past recollection, beyond/past recall, consigned to oblivion; left behind; neglected, overlooked, ignored, disregarded, unrecognized.
ANTONYMS remembered.

fork ▶ **verb** *the road forks at the south end of the lake* **split,** branch (off), divide, subdivide, separate, part, diverge, go in different directions, bifurcate; technical divaricate, ramify.

forked ▶ **adjective** *the hawk's distinctive forked tail* **split,** branching, branched, bifurcate(d), Y-shaped, V-shaped, pronged, divided; technical divaricate.
ANTONYMS straight.

forlorn ▶ **adjective 1** *he sounded forlorn* **unhappy,** sad, miserable, sorrowful, dejected, despondent, disconsolate, wretched, abject, down, downcast, dispirited, downhearted, crestfallen, depressed, melancholy, gloomy, glum, mournful, despairing, doleful, woebegone; informal blue, down in/at the mouth, down in the dumps; rare lachrymose.
ANTONYMS happy.
2 *a forlorn garden* **desolate,** deserted, abandoned, forsaken, forgotten, neglected.
ANTONYMS cared for.
3 *a forlorn attempt* **hopeless,** vain, with no chance of success; useless, futile, pointless, purposeless, unavailing, nugatory; archaic bootless.
ANTONYMS hopeful, sure-fire.

form ▶ **noun 1** *the general form of the landscape | form is less important than content* **shape,** configuration, formation, structure, construction, arrangement, appearance, exterior, outline, format, layout, design.
2 *the human form* **body,** shape, figure, stature, build, frame, physique, anatomy; informal vital statistics.
3 *the infection takes different forms* **manifestation,** appearance, embodiment, incarnation, semblance, shape, guise.
4 *sponsorship is a form of advertising* **kind,** sort, type, class, classification, category, variety, genre, brand, style; species, genus, family.
5 *put the mixture into a form* **mold,** cast, shape, matrix, die.
6 *what is the form here?* **etiquette,** social practice, custom, usage, use, modus operandi, habit, wont, protocol, procedure, rules, convention, tradition, fashion, style; formal praxis.
7 *you have to fill in a form* **questionnaire,** document, coupon, paper, sheet.
8 *in top form* **fitness,** condition, fettle, shape, trim, health.
▶ **verb 1** *the pads are formed from mild steel* **make,** construct, build, manufacture, fabricate, assemble, put together; create, produce, concoct, devise, contrive, frame, fashion, shape.
2 *he formed a plan* **formulate,** devise, conceive, work out, think up, lay, draw up, put together, produce, fashion, concoct, forge, hatch, incubate, develop; informal dream up.
3 *they plan to form a company* **set up,** establish, found, launch, float, create, bring into being, institute, start (up), get going, initiate, bring about, inaugurate.
ANTONYMS dissolve.
4 *a mist was forming* **materialize,** come into being/existence, crystallize, emerge, spring up, develop; take shape, appear, loom, show up, become visible.
ANTONYMS disappear.
5 *the horse may form bad habits* **acquire,** develop, get, pick up, contract, slip into, get into.

ANTONYMS avoid, break.
6 *the warriors formed themselves into a diamond pattern* **arrange,** draw up, line up, assemble, organize, sort, order, range, array, dispose, marshal, deploy.
7 *the parts of society form an integrated whole* **constitute,** make, make up, compose, add up to.
8 *the city formed a natural meeting point* **constitute,** serve as, act as, function as, perform the function of, do duty for, make.
9 *teachers form the minds of children* **develop,** mold, shape, train, teach, instruct, educate, school, drill, discipline, prime, prepare, guide, direct, inform, enlighten, inculcate, indoctrinate, edify.
– PHRASES **good form** *it is not good form to leave visitors on their own* **good manners,** manners, polite behavior, correct behavior, convention, etiquette, protocol; informal the done thing.

formal ▶ **adjective 1** *a formal dinner* **ceremonial,** ceremonious, ritualistic, ritual, conventional, traditional; stately, courtly, solemn, dignified; elaborate, ornate, dressy; black-tie.
ANTONYMS informal.
2 *a very formal manner* **aloof,** reserved, remote, detached, unapproachable; stiff, prim, stuffy, staid, ceremonious, correct, proper, decorous, conventional, precise, exact, punctilious, unbending, inflexible, straitlaced; informal buttoned-down, standoffish.
ANTONYMS informal, casual.
3 *a formal garden* **symmetrical,** regular, orderly, arranged, methodical, systematic.
ANTONYMS informal.
4 *formal permission* **official,** legal, authorized, approved, validated, certified, endorsed, documented, sanctioned, licensed, recognized, authoritative.
ANTONYMS informal, unofficial.
5 *formal education* **conventional,** mainstream; school, institutional.
ANTONYMS informal.

CHOOSE THE RIGHT WORD

formal, ceremonial, ceremonious, pompous, proper, punctilious

Formal suggests a suit-and-tie approach to certain situations—reserved, conventional, obeying all the rules (*an engraved invitation to a formal dinner requiring black tie or evening gown*). **Proper**, in this regard, implies scrupulously correct behavior that observes rules of etiquette (*the proper way to serve a guest; the proper spoon for dessert*). **Punctilious** behavior observes all the proper formalities (a *"punctilio"* is a detail or fine point), but may verge on the annoying (*her punctilious attention to the correct placement of silverware made setting the table an ordeal*). Someone (usually a man) who likes to show off just how *formal* and *proper* he can be runs the risk of becoming the most dreaded dinner guest of all: the **pompous** ass. *Pompous* individuals may derive more than the normal amount of pleasure from participating in **ceremonial** acts or events, which are those performed according to set rules, but **ceremonious** suggests a less negative and more ritualized approach to formality (*the Japanese woman could not have been more ceremonious than when she was carrying out the ceremonial serving of tea*).

formality ▶ **noun 1** *the formality of the occasion* **ceremony,** ceremoniousness, ritual, conventionality, red tape, protocol, decorum; stateliness, courtliness, solemnity.
ANTONYMS informality.
2 *his formality was off-putting* **aloofness,** reserve, remoteness, detachment, unapproachability; stiffness, primness, stuffiness, staidness, correctness, decorum, punctiliousness, inflexibility; informal standoffishness.
ANTONYMS informality.
3 (**formalities**) *we keep the formalities to a minimum* **official procedure,** bureaucracy, red tape, paperwork.
4 *the medical examination is just a formality* **routine,** routine practice, normal procedure.

formation ▶ **noun 1** *the formation of the island's sand ridges* **emergence,** coming into being, genesis, development, evolution, shaping, origination.
ANTONYMS destruction, disappearance.
2 *the formation of a new government* **establishment,** setting up, start, initiation, institution, foundation, inception, creation, inauguration, launch, flotation.
ANTONYMS dissolution.
3 *the aircraft were flying in tight formation* **configuration,** arrangement, pattern, array, alignment, positioning, disposition, order.

formative ▶ **adjective 1** *at a formative stage* **developmental,** developing, growing, malleable, impressionable, susceptible.
2 *a formative influence* **determining,** controlling, influential, guiding, decisive, forming, shaping, determinative.

former ▶ **adjective 1** *the former bishop* **one-time,** erstwhile, sometime, ex-, late; **previous,** foregoing, preceding, earlier, prior, past, last.
ANTONYMS future, next.
2 *in former times* **earlier,** old, past, bygone, olden, long-ago, gone by, long past, of old; literary of yore.
ANTONYMS future, present.
3 *the former of the two* **first-mentioned,** first.
ANTONYMS latter.

formerly ▶ **adverb** *this is Mr. Kane, formerly of Kane Industries* **previously,** earlier, before, until now/then, hitherto, née, once, once upon a time, at one time, in the past; formal heretofore.

formidable ▶ **adjective 1** *a formidable curved dagger* **intimidating,** forbidding, daunting, disturbing, alarming, frightening, disquieting, brooding, awesome, fearsome, ominous, foreboding, sinister, menacing, threatening, dangerous.
ANTONYMS pleasant-looking, comforting.
2 *a formidable task* **onerous,** arduous, taxing, difficult, hard, heavy, laborious, burdensome, strenuous, back-breaking, uphill, Herculean,

monumental, colossal; demanding, tough, challenging, exacting; formal exigent; archaic toilsome.
ANTONYMS easy.
3 *a formidable pianist* **capable,** able, proficient, adept, adroit, accomplished, seasoned, skillful, skilled, gifted, talented, masterly, virtuoso, expert, knowledgeable, qualified; impressive, powerful, mighty, terrific, tremendous, great, complete, redoubtable; informal mean, wicked, deadly, nifty, crack, ace, magic, crackerjack.
ANTONYMS weak.

formula ▶ **noun 1** *a legal formula* **form of words,** set expression, phrase, saying, aphorism.
2 *a peace formula* **recipe,** prescription, blueprint, plan, method, procedure, technique, system; template.
3 *a formula for removing grease* **preparation,** concoction, mixture, compound, creation, substance.

formulate ▶ **verb 1** *the miners formulated a plan* **devise,** conceive, work out, think up, lay, draw up, put together, form, produce, fashion, concoct, contrive, forge, hatch, prepare, develop; informal dream up.
2 *this is how Marx formulated his question* **express,** phrase, word, put into words, frame, couch, put, articulate, convey, say, state, utter.

fornication ▶ **noun** formal *the nuns warned us about the spiritual price one pays for fornication* **extramarital sex,** extramarital relations, adultery, infidelity, unfaithfulness, cuckoldry; premarital sex; informal hanky-panky.

forsake ▶ **verb** literary **1** *he forsook his wife* **abandon,** desert, leave, leave high and dry, turn one's back on, cast aside, break (up) with; jilt, strand, leave stranded, leave in the lurch, throw over; informal walk out on, run out on, dump, ditch, can.
ANTONYMS return to, stay with.
2 *I won't forsake my vegetarian principles* **renounce,** abandon, relinquish, dispense with, disclaim, disown, disavow, discard, wash one's hands of; give up, drop, jettison, do away with, ax; informal ditch, scrap, scrub, junk; formal forswear.
ANTONYMS keep (to).

forswear ▶ **verb** formal *we are formally forswearing the use of chemical weapons* **renounce,** relinquish, reject, forgo, disavow, abandon, deny, repudiate, give up, wash one's hands of; eschew, abstain from, refrain from; informal kick, pack in, quit, swear off; Law disaffirm; literary forsake; formal abjure, abnegate.
ANTONYMS adhere to, persist with, take up.

fort ▶ **noun** *dozens of settlers in the area sought refuge within the confines of the fort* **fortress,** castle, citadel, blockhouse, stronghold, redoubt, fortification, bastion; fastness.

forte ▶ **noun** *acting had always been her forte* **strength,** strong point, specialty, strong suit, talent, special ability, skill, bent, gift, métier; informal thing.
ANTONYMS weakness.

forth ▶ **adverb 1** *smoke billowed forth* **out,** outside, away, off, ahead, forward, into view; into existence.
2 *from that day forth* **onward,** onwards, on, forward; for ever, into eternity; until now.

forthcoming ▶ **adjective 1** *forthcoming events* **imminent,** impending, coming, upcoming, approaching, future; close, (close) at hand, in store, in the wind, in the air, in the offing, in the pipeline, on the horizon, on the way, on us, about to happen.
ANTONYMS past, current.
2 *no reply was forthcoming* **available,** ready, at hand, accessible, obtainable, at someone's disposal, obtained, given, vouchsafed to someone; informal up for grabs, on tap.
ANTONYMS unavailable.
3 *he was not very forthcoming about himself* **communicative,** talkative, chatty, loquacious, vocal; expansive, expressive, unreserved, uninhibited, outgoing, frank, open, candid; informal gabby.
ANTONYMS uncommunicative.

forthright ▶ **adjective** *a forthright statement to the press about her involvement in the cover-up* **frank,** direct, straightforward, honest, candid, open, sincere, outspoken, straight, blunt, plain-spoken, no-nonsense, downright, bluff, matter-of-fact, to the point; informal upfront.
ANTONYMS secretive, evasive.

forthwith ▶ **adverb** *all hostages are to be released forthwith* **immediately,** at once, instantly, directly, right away, straightaway, posthaste, without delay, without hesitation; quickly, speedily, promptly; informal pronto.
ANTONYMS sometime.

fortification ▶ **noun** *fortifications loomed ominously along the high banks of the river* **rampart,** wall, defense, bulwark, palisade, stockade, redoubt, earthwork, bastion, parapet, barricade.

fortify ▶ **verb 1** *the knights fortified their citadel* **build defenses around,** strengthen, secure, protect.
ANTONYMS weaken, expose.
2 *the wall had been fortified* **strengthen,** reinforce, toughen, consolidate, bolster, shore up, brace, buttress.
ANTONYMS weaken.
3 *I'll have a drink to fortify me* **invigorate,** strengthen, energize, enliven, liven up, animate, vitalize, rejuvenate, restore, revive, refresh; informal pep up, buck up, give a shot in the arm to.
ANTONYMS sedate, subdue.

fortitude ▶ **noun courage,** bravery, endurance, resilience, mettle, moral fiber, strength of mind, strength of character, strong-mindedness, backbone, spirit, grit, true grit, doughtiness, steadfastness; informal guts. See note at **COURAGE.**
ANTONYMS faint-heartedness.

fortress ▶ **noun** *the fortress fell into the hands of the French* **fort,** castle, citadel, blockhouse, stronghold, redoubt, fortification, bastion; fastness.

fortuitous ▶ **adjective 1** *a fortuitous resemblance* **chance,** adventitious, unexpected, unanticipated, unpredictable, unforeseen, unlooked-for, serendipitous, casual, incidental, coincidental, random, accidental, inadvertent,

unintentional, unintended, unplanned, unpremeditated. See note at **ACCIDENTAL**.
ANTONYMS predictable.
2 *the Red Wings were saved by a fortuitous rebound* **lucky,** fluky, fortunate, providential, advantageous, timely, opportune, serendipitous, heaven-sent.
ANTONYMS unlucky.

> USAGE
> **fortuitous**
> The traditional, etymological meaning of *fortuitous* is 'happening by chance': a *fortuitous meeting* is a chance meeting, which might turn out to be either a good thing or a bad thing. In modern uses, however, *fortuitous* tends more often to be used to refer to fortunate outcomes, and the word has become more or less a synonym for 'lucky' or 'fortunate.' This use is frowned upon as being not etymologically correct and is best avoided except in informal contexts.

fortunate ▶ adjective **1** *he was fortunate that the punishment was so slight* **lucky,** favored, blessed, blessed with good luck, in luck, having a charmed life, charmed; informal sitting pretty.
ANTONYMS unfortunate.
2 *in a fortunate position* **favorable,** advantageous, providential, auspicious, welcome, heaven-sent, beneficial, propitious, fortuitous, opportune, happy, felicitous.
ANTONYMS unfavorable.
3 *the society gives generously to less fortunate people* **wealthy,** rich, affluent, prosperous, well off, moneyed, well-to-do, well-heeled, opulent, comfortable; favored, privileged.
ANTONYMS underprivileged.

fortune ▶ noun **1** *fortune favored him* **chance,** accident, coincidence, serendipity, destiny, fortuity, providence, happenstance.
2 *a change of fortune* **luck,** fate, destiny, predestination, the stars, serendipity, karma, kismet, lot.
3 (**fortunes**) *an upswing in the team's fortunes* **circumstances,** state of affairs, condition, position, situation; plight, predicament.
4 *he made his fortune in steel* **wealth,** riches, substance, property, assets, resources, means, possessions, treasure, estate.
5 informal *this dress cost* ***a fortune*** **a huge amount,** a vast sum, a king's ransom, millions, billions; informal a small fortune, a mint, a bundle, a pile, a wad, an arm and a leg, a pretty penny, a tidy sum, big money, big bucks, gazillions, megabucks, top dollar.
ANTONYMS pittance.

fortune teller ▶ noun *for two bucks you could get a reading from a gypsy fortune teller* **clairvoyant,** crystal-gazer, psychic, prophet, seer, oracle, soothsayer, augur, diviner, sibyl; palmist, palm-reader.

forum ▶ noun **1** *forums were held for staff to air grievances* **meeting,** assembly, gathering, rally, conference, seminar, convention, symposium, colloquium, caucus; informal get-together; formal colloquy.
2 *a forum for discussion* **setting,** place, scene, context, stage, framework, backdrop; medium, means, apparatus, auspices.
3 *the Roman forum* **public meeting place,** marketplace, agora.

forward ▶ adverb **1** *the traffic moved forward* **ahead,** forward, onward, onwards, on, further.
2 *the winner stepped forward* **toward the front,** out, forth, into view.
3 *from that day forward* **onward,** onwards, on, forth; for ever, into eternity; until now.
▶ adjective **1** *in a forward direction* **moving forward,** moving forward, moving ahead, onward, advancing, progressing, progressive.
ANTONYMS backward.
2 *the fortress served as the Austrian army's forward base against the Russians* **front,** advance, foremost, head, leading, frontal.
ANTONYMS rear.
3 *forward planning* **future,** forward-looking, for the future, prospective.
4 *the girls seemed very forward* **bold, brazen,** brazen-faced, barefaced, brash, shameless, immodest, audacious, daring, presumptuous, familiar, overfamiliar, pert; informal fresh.
ANTONYMS shy.
▶ verb **1** *my mother forwarded me your email* **send on,** mail on, redirect, re-address, pass on.
2 *the goods were forwarded by sea* **send,** dispatch, transmit, carry, convey, deliver, ship.

forward-looking ▶ adjective *the forward-looking countries of Europe forged ahead* **progressive,** enlightened, dynamic, pushing, bold, enterprising, ambitious, pioneering, innovative, modern, avant-garde, positive, reforming, radical; informal go-ahead, go-getting.
ANTONYMS backward-looking.

forwards ▶ adverb See **FORWARD** (adverb).

fossil ▶ noun *we could detect fossils in the cornerstone of the building* **petrified remains,** petrified impression, remnant, relic.

foster ▶ verb **1** *he fostered the arts* **encourage,** promote, further, stimulate, advance, forward, cultivate, nurture, strengthen, enrich; help, aid, abet, assist, contribute to, support, back, be a patron of. See note at **ENCOURAGE**.
ANTONYMS neglect, suppress.
2 *they started fostering children* **bring up,** rear, raise, care for, take care of, look after, nurture, provide for; mother, parent.

foul ▶ adjective **1** *a foul stench* **disgusting,** revolting, repulsive, repugnant, abhorrent, loathsome, offensive, sickening, nauseating, nauseous, stomach-churning, stomach-turning, distasteful, obnoxious, objectionable, odious, noxious, vomitous; informal ghastly, gruesome, gross, putrid, yucky, skanky, beastly; literary miasmic, noisome, mephitic.
ANTONYMS fragrant.
2 *a pile of foul laundry* **dirty,** filthy, mucky, grimy, grubby, muddy, muddied, unclean, unwashed; squalid, sordid, soiled, sullied, scummy; rotten, defiled, decaying, putrid, putrefied, smelly, fetid; informal cruddy, yucky, icky; rare feculent.
ANTONYMS clean.
3 *he had been foul to her* **unkind,** malicious, mean, nasty, unpleasant, unfriendly, spiteful,

cruel, vicious, base, malevolent, despicable, contemptible; informal horrible, horrid, rotten; beastly.
ANTONYMS pleasant, kind.
4 *foul weather* **inclement,** unpleasant, disagreeable, bad; rough, stormy, squally, gusty, windy, blustery, wild, blowy, rainy, wet.
ANTONYMS fair.
5 *foul drinking water* **contaminated,** polluted, infected, tainted, impure, filthy, dirty, unclean; rare feculent.
ANTONYMS clean.
6 *a foul deed* **evil,** wicked, bad, wrong, immoral, sinful, vile, dishonorable, corrupt, iniquitous, depraved, villainous, nefarious, vicious, malicious; malevolent, sinister, demonic, devilish, diabolical, fiendish, dark; monstrous, shocking, despicable, atrocious, heinous, odious, contemptible, horrible, execrable; informal lowdown, dirty.
ANTONYMS righteous.
7 *foul language* **vulgar,** crude, coarse, filthy, dirty, obscene, indecent, indelicate, naughty, lewd, smutty, ribald, salacious, scatological, offensive, abusive.
ANTONYMS mild.
8 *a foul tackle* **illegal**; unfair, unsporting, unsportsmanlike, below the belt, dirty.
ANTONYMS fair.
▶ **verb 1** *the river had been fouled with waste* **dirty,** infect, pollute, contaminate, poison, taint, sully, soil, stain, blacken, muddy, splash, spatter, smear, blight, defile, make filthy.
ANTONYMS clean up.
2 *the vessel had fouled her nets* **tangle up,** entangle, snarl, catch, entwine, enmesh, twist.
ANTONYMS disentangle.

found ▶ **verb 1** *she founded her company in 2002* **establish,** set up, start (up), begin, get going, institute, inaugurate, launch, float, form, create, bring into being, originate, develop.
ANTONYMS dissolve, liquidate.
2 *they founded a new city* **build,** construct, erect, put up; plan, lay plans for.
ANTONYMS abandon, demolish.
– PHRASES **be founded on** *our relationship must be founded on trust* **be based on,** be built on, be constructed on; be grounded in, be rooted in; rest, hinge, depend.

foundation ▶ **noun 1** *the foundations of a building* **footing,** foot, base, substructure, infrastructure, underpinning; bottom, bedrock, substratum.
2 *the report has a scientific foundation* **basis,** starting point, base, point of departure, beginning, premise; principles, fundamentals, rudiments; cornerstone, core, heart, thrust, essence, kernel.
3 *there was no foundation for the claim* **justification,** grounds, defense, reason, rationale, cause, basis, motive, excuse, call, pretext, provocation.
4 *an educational foundation* **endowed institution,** charitable body, funding agency, source of funds, endowment.

founder[1] ▶ **noun** *the founder of modern physics* **originator,** creator, (founding) father, prime mover, architect, engineer, designer, developer, pioneer, author, planner, inventor, mastermind; literary begetter.

founder[2] ▶ **verb 1** *the ship foundered* **sink,** go to the bottom, go down, be lost at sea.
2 *the scheme foundered* **fail,** be unsuccessful, not succeed, fall flat, fall through, collapse, backfire, meet with disaster, come to nothing, come to naught; informal flatline, flop, bomb.
ANTONYMS succeed.
3 *their horses foundered in the river* **stumble,** trip, trip up, lose one's balance, lose/miss one's footing, slip, stagger, lurch, totter, fall, tumble, topple, sprawl, collapse.

foundling ▶ **noun** *it was during the Depression that Mrs. Aronson took in eight little foundlings and raised them as her own* **abandoned infant,** waif, stray, orphan, outcast.

fountain ▶ **noun 1** *a fountain of water* **jet,** spray, spout, spurt, well, fount, cascade.
2 *a fountain of knowledge* **source,** fount, font, well; reservoir, fund, mass, mine.

foyer ▶ **noun** *you may hang your coats in the foyer* **entrance hall,** hall, hallway, entrance, entry, entranceway, entryway, porch, reception area, atrium, concourse, lobby, narthex.

fracas ▶ **noun** *the fracas in the alley drew the attention of a passing patrol car* **disturbance,** brawl, melee, rumpus, skirmish, struggle, scuffle, scrum, clash, fisticuffs, altercation; informal scrap, dust-up, set-to, donnybrook.

fraction ▶ **noun 1** *a fraction of the population* **part,** subdivision, division, portion, segment, slice, section, sector; proportion, percentage, ratio, measure.
ANTONYMS whole.
2 *only a fraction of the collection* **tiny part,** fragment, snippet, snatch, smattering, selection. See note at FRAGMENT.
3 *he moved a fraction closer* **tiny amount,** little, bit, touch, soupçon, trifle, mite, shade, jot; informal smidgen, smidge, tad.

fractious ▶ **adjective 1** *fractious children* **grumpy,** bad-tempered, irascible, irritable, crotchety, grouchy, cantankerous, short-tempered, tetchy, testy, curmudgeonly, ill-tempered, ill-humored, peevish, cross, waspish, crabby, crusty, prickly, touchy; informal snappish, cranky, ornery.
ANTONYMS contented, affable.
2 *the fractious opposition party* **wayward,** unruly, uncontrollable, unmanageable, out of hand, obstreperous, difficult, headstrong, recalcitrant, intractable; disobedient, insubordinate, disruptive, disorderly, undisciplined; contrary, willful; formal refractory; archaic contumacious.
ANTONYMS dutiful.

fracture ▶ **noun 1** *the risk of vertebral fracture* **breaking,** breakage, cracking, fragmentation, splintering, rupture.
2 *tiny fractures in the rock* **crack,** split, fissure, crevice, break, rupture, breach, rift, cleft, chink, interstice; crazing.
▶ **verb** *the glass fractured* **break,** crack, shatter, splinter, split, rupture; informal bust.

fragile ▶ **adjective 1** *fragile porcelain* **breakable,** easily broken; delicate, dainty, fine, flimsy;

eggshell; formal frangible.
ANTONYMS durable, robust.
2 *the fragile cease-fire* **tenuous,** shaky, insecure, unreliable, vulnerable, flimsy.
ANTONYMS durable.
3 *she is still very fragile* **weak,** delicate, frail, debilitated; ill, unwell, ailing, poorly, sickly, infirm, enfeebled.
ANTONYMS strong.

fragment ▶ noun **1** *meteorite fragments* **piece,** bit, particle, speck; chip, shard, sliver, splinter; shaving, paring, snippet, scrap, flake, shred, wisp, morsel.
2 *a fragment of conversation* **snatch,** snippet, scrap, bit.
▶ verb *explosions caused the granite to fragment* **break up,** break, break into pieces, crack open/apart, shatter, splinter, fracture; disintegrate, fall to pieces, fall apart.

CHOOSE THE RIGHT WORD

fragment, fraction, part, piece, portion, section, segment

The whole is equal to the sum of its **parts**—*part* being a general term for any of the components of a whole. But how did the whole come apart? **Fragment** suggests that breakage has occurred (*fragments of pottery*) and often refers to a brittle substance such as glass or pottery. **Segment** suggests that the whole has been separated along natural or pre-existing lines of division (*a segment of an orange*), and **section** suggests a substantial and clearly separate *part* that fits closely with other parts to form the whole (*a section of a bookcase*). **Fraction** usually suggests a less substantial but still clearly delineated *part* (*a fraction of her income*), and a **portion** is a *part* that has been allotted or assigned to someone (*her portion of the program*). Finally, the very frequently used **piece** is any *part* that is separate from the whole.

fragrance ▶ noun **1** *the fragrance of spring flowers* **sweet smell,** scent, perfume, bouquet; aroma, redolence, nose. See note at SMELL.
2 *a bottle of fragrance* **perfume,** scent, eau de toilette, toilet water; eau de cologne, cologne; aftershave.

fragrant ▶ adjective *an infusion of fragrant herbs* **sweet-scented,** sweet-smelling, scented, perfumed, aromatic, odoriferous, odiferous, perfumy; literary redolent.
ANTONYMS smelly.

frail ▶ adjective **1** *a frail old lady* **weak,** delicate, feeble, enfeebled, debilitated; infirm, ill, ailing, unwell, sickly, poorly, in poor health. See note at WEAK.
ANTONYMS strong, fit.
2 *a frail structure* **fragile,** breakable, easily damaged, delicate, flimsy, insubstantial, unsteady, unstable, rickety; formal frangible.
ANTONYMS sturdy, robust.

frailty ▶ noun **1** *the frailty of old age* **infirmity,** weakness, enfeeblement, debility; fragility, delicacy; ill health, sickliness.
ANTONYMS strength.
2 *his many frailties* **weakness,** fallibility; weak point, flaw, imperfection, defect, failing, fault, shortcoming, deficiency, inadequacy, limitation.
ANTONYMS strength.

frame ▶ noun **1** *a tubular metal frame* **framework,** structure, substructure, skeleton, chassis, shell, casing, body, bodywork; support, scaffolding, foundation, infrastructure.
2 *his tall, slender frame* **body,** figure, form, shape, physique, build, size, proportions.
3 *a picture frame* **setting,** mount, mounting.
▶ verb **1** *he had the picture framed* **mount,** set in a frame.
2 *the legislators who frame the regulations* **formulate,** draw up, draft, plan, shape, compose, put together, form, devise, create, establish, conceive, think up, originate; informal dream up.
– PHRASES **frame of mind** *what was your frame of mind at the time just preceding the accident?* **mood,** state of mind, humor, temper, disposition.

frame-up ▶ noun informal *he spent six years behind bars, the victim of a clever frame-up* **conspiracy,** plot; trick, trap, entrapment; informal put-up job, setup.

framework ▶ noun **1** *a metal framework* **frame,** substructure, infrastructure, structure, skeleton, chassis, shell, body, bodywork; support, scaffolding, foundation.
2 *the framework of society* **structure,** shape, fabric, order, scheme, system, organization, construction, configuration, composition, warp and woof; informal makeup.

franchise ▶ noun **1** *the extension of the franchise to women* **suffrage,** the vote, the right to vote, voting rights, enfranchisement.
2 *the company lost its TV franchise* **warrant,** charter, license, permit, authorization, permission, sanction, privilege.

frank ▶ adjective **1** *he was quite frank with me* **candid,** direct, forthright, plain, plain-spoken, straight, straightforward, explicit, to the point, matter-of-fact; open, honest, truthful, sincere; outspoken, bluff, blunt, unsparing, not afraid to call a spade a spade; informal upfront.
ANTONYMS evasive.
2 *she looked at the child with frank admiration* **open,** undisguised, unconcealed, naked, unmistakable, clear, obvious, transparent, patent, manifest, evident, perceptible, palpable; blatant, barefaced, flagrant.
ANTONYMS concealed.

frankly ▶ adverb **1** *frankly, I couldn't care less* **to be frank,** to be honest, to tell you the truth, to be truthful, in all honesty, as it happens.
2 *he stated the case quite frankly* **candidly,** directly, plainly, straightforwardly, forthrightly, openly, honestly, without beating about the bush, without mincing one's words, without prevarication, point-blank; bluntly, outspokenly, with no holds barred.

frantic ▶ adjective *the families of the missing passengers were frantic* **panic-stricken,** panicky, beside oneself, at one's wits' end, distraught, overwrought, worked up, agitated, distressed; frenzied, wild, frenetic, fraught, feverish, hysterical, desperate; informal in a state, in a tizzy,

wound up, het up, in a flap, tearing one's hair out.
ANTONYMS calm.

fraternity ▶ noun 1 *a spirit of fraternity* **brotherhood,** fellowship, kinship, friendship, (mutual) support, solidarity, community, union, togetherness; sisterhood.
2 *the teaching fraternity* **profession,** body of workers; band, group, set, circle.
3 *a college fraternity* **society,** club, association; group, set.

fraternize ▶ verb *the musicians were told not to fraternize with the dancers* **associate,** mix, consort, socialize, keep company, rub elbows; informal hang around, hang out, run around, hobnob, be thick with.

fraud ▶ noun 1 *he was arrested for fraud* **fraudulence,** cheating, swindling, embezzlement, deceit, deception, double-dealing, chicanery, sharp practice.
2 *social insurance frauds* **swindle,** racket, deception, trick, cheat, hoax; informal scam, con, rip-off, sting, gyp, fiddle, bunco, hustle, grift.
3 *they exposed him as a fraud* **impostor,** fake, sham, charlatan, quack, mountebank; swindler, gonif, snake oil salesman, fraudster, racketeer, cheat, confidence trickster; informal phony, con man, con artist, scam artist.

fraudulent ▶ adjective *a fraudulent stock transaction* **dishonest,** cheating, swindling, corrupt, criminal, illegal, unlawful, illicit; deceitful, double-dealing, duplicitous, dishonorable, unscrupulous, unprincipled; informal crooked, shady, dirty.
ANTONYMS honest.

fraught ▶ adjective 1 *their world is* ***fraught with*** *danger* **full of,** filled with, rife with; attended by, accompanied by.
2 *she sounded a bit fraught* **anxious,** worried, stressed, upset, distraught, overwrought, worked up, antsy, agitated, distressed, distracted, desperate, frantic, panic-stricken, panic-struck, panicky; beside oneself, at one's wits' end, at the end of one's tether/rope; informal wound up, in a state, in a flap, in a cold sweat, tearing one's hair out, having kittens.

fray ▶ verb 1 *cheap fabric soon frays* **unravel,** wear, wear thin, wear out/through, become worn.
2 *her nerves were frayed* **strain,** tax, overtax, put on edge.

freak ▶ noun 1 *a genetically engineered freak* **aberration,** abnormality, irregularity, oddity; monster, monstrosity, mutant; freak of nature.
2 *the accident was a complete freak* **anomaly,** aberration, rarity, oddity, unusual occurrence; fluke, twist of fate.
3 informal *they were dismissed as a bunch of freaks* **oddity,** eccentric, misfit; crank, lunatic; informal oddball, weirdo, nutcase, nut, fruit loop, wacko, kook.
4 informal *a fitness freak* **enthusiast,** fan, devotee, lover, aficionado; informal fiend, nut, fanatic, addict, maniac.
▶ adjective *a freak storm | a freak result* **unusual,** anomalous, aberrant, atypical, unrepresentative, irregular, fluky, exceptional, unaccountable, bizarre, queer, peculiar, odd, freakish; unpredictable, unforeseeable, unexpected, unanticipated, surprising; rare, singular, isolated.
ANTONYMS normal.
▶ verb informal *he* ***freaked out*** **go crazy,** go mad, go out of one's mind, go to pieces, crack, snap, lose control; panic, become hysterical; informal lose it, lose one's cool, crack up, go ape, go postal.

free ▶ adjective 1 *admission is free* **without charge,** free of charge, for nothing; complimentary, gratis; informal for free, on the house.
2 *she was* ***free of*** *any pressures* **unencumbered by,** unaffected by, clear of, without, rid of; exempt from, not liable to, safe from, immune to, excused from; informal sans, minus.
3 *I'm free this afternoon* **unoccupied,** not busy, available, between appointments; off duty, off work, off; on vacation, on leave; at leisure, with time on one's hands, with time to spare.
ANTONYMS busy, occupied, unavailable.
4 *the bathroom's free now* **vacant,** empty, available, unoccupied, not taken, not in use.
ANTONYMS occupied.
5 *a citizen of a free nation* **independent,** self-governing, self-governed, self-ruling, self-determining, nonaligned, sovereign, autonomous; democratic.
ANTONYMS dependent.
6 *the killer is still free* **on the loose,** at liberty, at large; loose, unconfined, unbound, untied, unchained, untethered, unshackled, unfettered, unrestrained.
ANTONYMS captive.
7 *you are free to leave* **allowed,** permitted; **able,** in a position to.
ANTONYMS unable.
8 *the free flow of water* **unimpeded,** unobstructed, unrestricted, unhampered, clear, open, unblocked.
ANTONYMS obstructed.
9 *she was free with her money* **generous,** liberal, openhanded, unstinting, bountiful; lavish, extravagant, prodigal.
ANTONYMS mean.
10 *his free and hearty manner* **frank,** open, candid, direct, plain-spoken; unrestrained, unconstrained, free and easy, uninhibited.
▶ verb 1 *three of the hostages were freed* **release,** set free, let go, liberate, discharge, deliver; set loose, let loose, turn loose, untie, unchain, unfetter, unshackle, unleash; literary disenthrall.
ANTONYMS confine, lock up.
2 *the victims were freed by firefighters* **extricate,** release, get out, pull out, pull free; rescue, set free.
ANTONYMS trap.
3 *they wish to be freed from all legal ties* **exempt,** except, excuse, relieve, unburden, disburden.
– PHRASES **free and easy** *the restaurant's free and easy atmosphere* **easygoing,** relaxed, casual, informal, unceremonious, unforced, natural, open, spontaneous, uninhibited, friendly; tolerant, liberal; informal laid-back. **a free hand** *he was allowed a free hand in appointing new staff* **free rein,** carte blanche, freedom, liberty, license, latitude, leeway, a blank check.

freedom ▶ noun 1 *a desperate bid for freedom* **liberty,** liberation, release, deliverance,

delivery, discharge; literary **disenthrallment**; historical manumission. See note at LIBERTY.
ANTONYMS captivity.
2 *revolution was the only path to freedom* **independence**, self-government, self-determination, self-rule, home rule, sovereignty, nonalignment, autonomy; democracy.
ANTONYMS dependence.
3 *freedom from local political accountability* **exemption**, immunity, dispensation; impunity.
ANTONYMS liability.
4 *freedom to choose your course of treatment* **right**, entitlement, privilege, prerogative; scope, latitude, leeway, flexibility, space, breathing space, room, elbow room; license, leave, free rein, a free hand, carte blanche, a blank check.
ANTONYMS restriction.

freeze ▶ verb **1** *the stream had frozen* **ice over**, ice up, solidify.
ANTONYMS thaw, melt.
2 *my fingers froze* become frozen, become frostbitten.
ANTONYMS thaw, warm up.
3 *the campers stifled in summer and froze in winter* **be very cold**, be numb with cold, turn blue with cold, shiver, be chilled to the bone/marrow.
ANTONYMS overheat.
4 *she froze in horror* **stop dead**, stop in one's tracks, stop, stand (stock) still, go rigid, become motionless, become paralyzed.
ANTONYMS run away.
5 *the price of gasoline was frozen* **fix**, hold, peg, set; limit, restrict, cap, confine, regulate; hold/keep down.
ANTONYMS change.
– PHRASES **freeze out** informal *she was frozen out by her husband's relatives* **exclude**, leave out, shut out, cut out, ignore, ostracize, spurn, snub, shun, turn one's back on, cold-shoulder, give someone the cold shoulder, leave out in the cold.

freezing ▶ adjective **1** *a freezing wind* **bitter**, bitterly cold, icy, chill, frosty, glacial, wintry, subzero, hypothermic; raw, biting, piercing, bone-chilling, penetrating, cutting, numbing; arctic, polar, Siberian.
ANTONYMS balmy.
2 *you must be freezing* **frozen**, extremely cold, numb with cold, chilled to the bone/marrow, frozen stiff, shivery, shivering; informal frozen to death.
ANTONYMS hot.

freight ▶ noun **1** *freight carried by rail* **goods**, cargo, load, consignment, delivery, shipment; merchandise.
2 *our reliance on air freight* **transportation**, transport, conveyance, carriage, portage, haulage.

frenzied ▶ adjective *frenzied holiday shoppers* **frantic**, wild, frenetic, hectic, fraught, feverish, fevered, mad, crazed, manic, intense, furious, uncontrolled, out of control.
ANTONYMS calm.

frenzy ▶ noun **1** *the crowd whipped itself into a state of frenzy* **hysteria**, madness, mania, delirium, feverishness, fever, wildness, agitation, turmoil, tumult; wild excitement, euphoria, elation, ecstasy.
2 *a frenzy of anger* **fit**, paroxysm, spasm, bout.

frequency ▶ noun *the frequency of errors* **rate of occurrence**, incidence, amount, commonness, prevalence; Statistics **distribution**.

frequent ▶ adjective **1** *frequent bouts of chest infection* **recurrent**, recurring, repeated, periodic, continual, one after another, successive; many, numerous, lots of, several.
ANTONYMS few.
2 *a frequent business traveler* **habitual**, regular.
ANTONYMS occasional.
▶ verb *he frequented chic nightclubs* **visit**, patronize, spend time in, visit regularly, be a regular visitor to, haunt; informal hang out at.

frequenter ▶ noun *a frequenter of Ed's Bar and Grill* **habitué of**, patron of, regular at, regular visitor to, regular customer at/of, regular client of, familiar face at.

frequently ▶ adverb *he frequently attends church* **regularly**, often, very often, all the time, habitually, customarily, routinely; many times, a lot, many a time, lots of times, again and again, time and again, over and over again, repeatedly, recurrently, continually, oftentimes; literary oft, ofttimes.

fresh ▶ adjective **1** *fresh fruit* **newly picked**, garden-fresh, crisp, unwilted; raw, natural, unprocessed.
ANTONYMS stale, processed.
2 *a fresh sheet of paper* **clean**, blank, empty, clear, white; unused, new, pristine, unmarked, untouched.
ANTONYMS used.
3 *a fresh approach* **new**, recent, latest, up-to-date, modern, modernistic, ultra-modern, newfangled; original, novel, different, innovative, unusual, unconventional, unorthodox; radical, revolutionary; informal offbeat.
ANTONYMS old.
4 *fresh recruits* **young**, youthful; new, inexperienced, naive, untrained, unqualified, untried, raw; informal wet behind the ears.
ANTONYMS experienced.
5 *he felt fresh and happy to be alive* **refreshed**, rested, restored, revived; (as) fresh as a daisy, energetic, vigorous, invigorated, full of vim and vigor, lively, vibrant, spry, sprightly, bright, alert, perky; informal full of beans, raring to go, bright-eyed and bushy-tailed, chirpy, chipper.
ANTONYMS tired.
6 *her fresh complexion* **healthy**, healthy-looking, clear, bright, youthful, blooming, glowing, unblemished; fair, rosy, rosy-cheeked, pink, ruddy.
ANTONYMS healthy.
7 *the night air was fresh* **cool**, crisp, refreshing, invigorating, tonic; pure, clean, clear, uncontaminated, untainted.
ANTONYMS stale, stifling.
8 *a fresh wind* **chilly**, chill, cool, cold, brisk, bracing, invigorating; strong; informal nippy.
ANTONYMS sultry, warm.
9 informal *don't get fresh with me* **impudent**, sassy, saucy, brazen, shameless, forward, bold,

cheeky, impertinent, insolent, presumptuous, disrespectful, rude, pert, (as) bold as brass; informal lippy, mouthy.
ANTONYMS polite.

freshen ▸ verb 1 *this will freshen your breath* **refresh,** deodorize, cleanse; revitalize, restore.
2 *she went to* ***freshen up*** *before dinner* **wash,** wash up, bathe, shower; tidy oneself (up), spruce oneself up, smarten oneself up, groom oneself, primp oneself; informal titivate oneself, doll oneself up; formal humorous perform one's ablutions.
3 *the waitress freshened their coffee* **refill,** top up, fill up, replenish.

fret ▸ verb 1 *she was fretting about Jonathan* **worry,** be anxious, feel uneasy, be distressed, be upset, upset oneself, concern oneself; agonize, sigh, pine, brood, eat one's heart out.
2 *his absence began to fret her* **trouble,** bother, concern, perturb, disturb, disquiet, disconcert, distress, upset, alarm, panic, agitate; informal eat away at.

fretful ▸ adjective *the long wait in traffic was making us fretful* **distressed,** upset, miserable, unsettled, uneasy, ill at ease, uncomfortable, edgy, agitated, worked up, tense, stressed, restive, fidgety, antsy; querulous, irritable, cross, fractious, peevish, petulant, out of sorts, bad-tempered, irascible, grumpy, crotchety, captious, testy, tetchy, cranky, het up, uptight, twitchy, crabby.

friction ▸ noun 1 *a lubrication system that reduces friction* **abrasion,** rubbing, chafing, grating, rasping, scraping; resistance, drag.
2 *there was considerable friction between father and son* **discord,** strife, conflict, disagreement, dissension, dissent, infighting, opposition, contention, dispute, disputation, arguing, argument, quarreling, bickering, squabbling, wrangling, fighting, feuding, rivalry; hostility, animosity, antipathy, enmity, antagonism, resentment, acrimony, bitterness, bad feeling, ill feeling, ill will, bad blood.
ANTONYMS harmony.

friend ▸ noun 1 *a close friend* **companion,** soul mate, intimate, confidante, confidant, familiar, alter ego, second self, playmate, playfellow, classmate, schoolmate, workmate; ally, associate; sister, brother; best friend, kindred spirit, bosom buddy, bosom friend; informal pal, chum, sidekick, crony, main man, mate, buddy, bud, amigo, compadre, homeboy, homegirl, homie; archaic compeer.
ANTONYMS enemy.
2 *the friends of the National Ballet* **patron,** backer, supporter, benefactor, benefactress, sponsor; well-wisher, defender, champion; informal angel.

friendless ▸ adjective *caring for those who are poor and friendless* **alone,** all alone, by oneself, solitary, lonely, with no one to turn to, lone, without friends, companionless, unbefriended, unpopular, unwanted, unloved, abandoned, rejected, forsaken, shunned, spurned, forlorn, lonesome.
ANTONYMS popular.

friendliness ▸ noun *her host's friendliness* **affability,** amiability, geniality, congeniality, bonhomie, cordiality, good nature, good humor, warmth, affection, demonstrativeness, conviviality, joviality, companionability, sociability, gregariousness, camaraderie, neighborliness, hospitableness, approachability, accessibility, openness, kindness, kindliness, sympathy, amenability, benevolence.

friendly ▸ adjective 1 *a friendly woman* **affable,** amiable, genial, congenial, cordial, warm, affectionate, demonstrative, convivial, companionable, sociable, gregarious, outgoing, comradely, neighborly, hospitable, approachable, easy to get on with, accessible, communicative, open, unreserved, easygoing, good-natured, kindly, benign, amenable, agreeable, obliging, sympathetic, well-disposed, benevolent; informal chummy, buddy-buddy.
2 *friendly conversation* **amicable,** congenial, cordial, pleasant, easy, relaxed, casual, informal, unceremonious; close, intimate, familiar.
ANTONYMS hostile.
3 *a friendly wind swept the boat to the shore* **favorable,** advantageous, helpful; lucky, providential.
ANTONYMS unfavorable.
4 *a kid-friendly hotel* **compatible,** suited, adapted, appropriate.

friendship ▸ noun 1 *lasting friendships* **relationship,** close relationship, attachment, mutual attachment, association, bond, tie, link, union.
2 *old ties of love and friendship* **amity,** camaraderie, friendliness, comradeship, companionship, fellowship, fellow feeling, closeness, affinity, rapport, understanding, harmony, unity; intimacy, mutual affection.
ANTONYMS enmity.

fright ▸ noun 1 *she was paralyzed with fright* **fear,** fearfulness, terror, horror, alarm, panic, dread, trepidation, dismay, nervousness, apprehension, apprehensiveness, perturbation, disquiet; informal jitteriness, twitchiness.
2 *the experience gave everyone* ***a fright*** **a scare,** a shock, a surprise, a turn, a jolt, a start; the shivers, the shakes; informal the jitters, the heebie-jeebies, the willies, the creeps, a cold sweat, butterflies (in one's stomach).
3 informal *she looked an absolute fright* **ugly sight,** eyesore, monstrosity; informal mess, sight, state, blot on the landscape.

frighten ▸ verb *the fighting in the streets frightened us* **scare,** startle, alarm, terrify, petrify, shock, chill, panic, shake, disturb, dismay, unnerve, unman, intimidate, terrorize, cow, daunt; strike terror into, put the fear of God into, chill someone to the bone/marrow, make someone's blood run cold; informal scare the living daylights out of, scare stiff, scare someone out of their wits, scare witless, scare to death, scare the pants off, spook, make someone's hair stand on end, make someone jump out of their skin, give someone the heebie-jeebies, make someone's hair curl, scare the bejesus out of; archaic affright.

frightful ▸ adjective *the house was in a frightful mess* **horrible,** horrific, ghastly, horrendous, serious, awful, dreadful, terrible, nasty, grim, dire, unspeakable; alarming, shocking, terrifying, harrowing, appalling, fearful; hideous, gruesome, grisly; informal horrid; formal grievous.

frigid ▶ adjective **1** *a frigid January night* **very cold,** bitterly cold, bitter, freezing, frozen, frosty, icy, gelid, chilly, chill, wintry, bleak, subzero, arctic, Siberian, bone-chilling, polar, glacial, hypothermic; informal nippy.
ANTONYMS hot, tropical.
2 *frigid politeness* **stiff,** formal, stony, wooden, unemotional, passionless, unfeeling, indifferent, unresponsive, unenthusiastic, austere, distant, aloof, remote, reserved, unapproachable; frosty, cold, icy, cool, unsmiling, forbidding, unfriendly, unwelcoming, hostile; informal offish, standoffish.
ANTONYMS friendly.

frill ▶ noun **1** *a full skirt with a wide frill* **ruffle,** flounce, ruff, furbelow, jabot, peplum, ruche, ruching, fringe; archaic purfle.
2 *a comfortable apartment with no-frills* **ostentation,** ornamentation, decoration, embellishment, fanciness, fuss, chi-chi, gilding, excess; trimmings, extras, additions, nonessentials, luxuries, extravagances, superfluities.

fringe ▶ noun **1** *the city's northern fringe* **perimeter,** periphery, border, borderline, margin, rim, outer edge, edge, extremity, limit; outer limits, limits, borders, bounds, outskirts; literary marge.
ANTONYMS middle.
2 *the curtains with the yellow fringe* **edging,** edge, border, trimming, frill, flounce, ruffle; tassels; archaic purfle.
▶ adjective *fringe theater* **unconventional,** unorthodox, alternative, avant-garde, experimental, innovative, left-field, innovatory, radical, extreme; peripheral; off-off Broadway; informal offbeat, way out.
ANTONYMS mainstream.
▶ verb **1** *a robe of gold, fringed with black velvet* **trim,** edge, hem, border, bind, braid; decorate, adorn, ornament, embellish, finish; archaic purfle.
2 *the lake is fringed by a belt of trees* **border,** edge, bound, skirt, line, surround, enclose, encircle, circle, girdle, encompass, ring; literary gird.

frisk ▶ verb **1** *the spaniels frisked around my ankles* **frolic,** gambol, cavort, caper, scamper, skip, dance, romp, trip, prance, leap, spring, hop, jump, bounce.
2 *the officer frisked him* **search,** check, inspect.

frisky ▶ adjective *frisky squirrels* **lively,** bouncy, bubbly, perky, active, energetic, animated, zestful, full of vim and vigor; playful, coltish, skittish, spirited, high-spirited, in high spirits, exuberant; informal full of beans, zippy, peppy, bright-eyed and bushy-tailed; literary frolicsome.

fritter ▶ verb *he frittered away his inheritance* **squander,** waste, misuse, misspend, dissipate; overspend, spend like water, be prodigal with, run through, get through; informal blow, splurge, pour/throw down the drain.
ANTONYMS save.

frivolity ▶ noun *everyone needs a little frivolity now and again* **lightheartedness,** levity, joking, jocularity, gaiety, fun, frivolousness, silliness, foolishness, flightiness, skittishness; superficiality, shallowness, flippancy, vacuity, empty-headedness.

frivolous ▶ adjective **1** *a frivolous girl* **skittish,** flighty, giddy, silly, foolish, superficial, shallow, irresponsible, thoughtless, featherbrained, empty-headed, peabrained, birdbrained, vacuous, vapid; informal dizzy, dippy, ditzy, flaky.
ANTONYMS sensible, serious.
2 *frivolous remarks* **flippant,** glib, facetious, joking, jokey, lighthearted; fatuous, inane, senseless, thoughtless; informal flip.
ANTONYMS serious.
3 *new rules to stop frivolous lawsuits* **time-wasting,** pointless, trivial, trifling, minor, petty, insignificant, unimportant.
ANTONYMS important.

frolic ▶ verb *children frolicked on the sand* **play,** amuse oneself, romp, disport oneself, frisk, gambol, cavort, caper, cut capers, scamper, skip, dance, prance, leap about, jump about; dated sport.
▶ noun *the youngsters enjoyed their frolic* **antic,** caper, game, romp, escapade; (**frolics**) fun, fun and games, hijinks, merrymaking, amusement, skylarking.

front ▶ noun **1** *the front of the boat* **fore,** foremost part, forepart, anterior, forefront, nose, head; bow, prow; foreground.
ANTONYMS rear, back.
2 *the store's front* **frontage,** face, facing, facade; window.
3 *the battlefield surgeons who work at the front* **front line,** firing line, vanguard, van; trenches.
4 *the front of the line* **head,** beginning, start, top, lead.
ANTONYMS back.
5 *she kept up a brave front* **appearance,** air, face, manner, demeanor, bearing, pose, exterior, veneer, (outward) show, act, pretense, affectation.
6 *the shop was a front for his real business* **cover,** cover-up, false front, blind, disguise, facade, mask, cloak, screen, smokescreen, camouflage.
▶ adjective *the front runners* **leading,** lead, first, foremost; in first place.
ANTONYMS last.
▶ verb *the houses* ***fronted on*** *a reservoir* **overlook,** look out on/over, face (toward), lie opposite (to); have a view of, command a view of.
– PHRASES **in front** *it looks as if Carson is now in front* **ahead,** to/at the fore, at the head, up ahead, in the vanguard, in the van, in the lead, leading, coming first; informal up front.

frontier ▶ noun *the lakes sit astride the U.S.-Canadian frontier* **border,** boundary, borderline, dividing line, demarcation line; perimeter, limit, edge, rim, bounds.

frost ▶ noun **1** *bushes covered with frost* **ice crystals,** ice, rime, verglas; hoarfrost, ground frost, black frost; informal Jack Frost; archaic hoar.
2 *there was frost in his tone* **coldness,** coolness, frostiness, ice, iciness, frigidity; hostility, unfriendliness, stiffness, aloofness; informal standoffishness.

frosty ▶ adjective **1** *a frosty morning* **freezing,** cold, icy-cold, bitter, bitterly cold, chill, wintry,

frigid, glacial, hypothermic, arctic; frozen, icy, gelid; informal nippy; literary rimy.
2 *her frosty gaze* **cold,** frigid, icy, glacial, unfriendly, inhospitable, unwelcoming, forbidding, hostile, stony, stern, steely, hard.

froth ▶ noun *the froth on top of his beer* **foam,** head; bubbles, frothiness, fizz, effervescence; lather, suds; scum; literary spume.
▶ verb *the liquid frothed up* **bubble,** fizz, effervesce, foam, lather; churn, seethe; literary spume.

frothy ▶ adjective 1 *a frothy liquid* **foaming,** foamy, bubbling, bubbly, fizzy, sparkling, effervescent, gassy, carbonated; sudsy; literary spumy.
2 *a frothy daytime show* **lightweight,** light, superficial, shallow, slight, insubstantial; trivial, trifling, frivolous.

frown ▶ verb 1 *she frowned at him* **scowl,** glower, glare, lower, make a face, look daggers, give someone a black look; knit/furrow one's brows; informal give someone a dirty look.
ANTONYMS smile.
2 *public displays of affection were frowned on* **disapprove of,** view with disfavor, dislike, look askance at, not take kindly to, take a dim view of, take exception to, object to, have a low opinion of.

frozen ▶ adjective 1 *the frozen ground* **icy,** ice-covered, ice-bound, frosty, frosted, gelid; frozen solid, hard, (as) hard as iron; literary rimy.
ANTONYMS thawed.
2 *his hands were frozen* **freezing,** icy, very cold, chilled to the bone/marrow, numb, numbed, frozen stiff, frostbitten; informal frozen to death.
ANTONYMS hot, boiling.

frugal ▶ adjective 1 *a hard-working, frugal woman* **thrifty,** economical, careful, cautious, prudent, provident, unwasteful, sparing, scrimping; abstemious, abstinent, austere, self-denying, ascetic, monkish, spartan; parsimonious, miserly, niggardly, cheeseparing, penny-pinching, close-fisted; informal tightfisted, tight, stingy. See note at ECONOMICAL.
ANTONYMS extravagant.
2 *their frugal breakfast* **meager,** scanty, scant, paltry, skimpy; plain, simple, spartan, inexpensive, cheap, economical.
ANTONYMS lavish.

fruitful ▶ adjective 1 *a fruitful tree* **fertile,** fecund, prolific, high-yielding; fruit-bearing, fruiting. See note at FERTILE.
ANTONYMS barren.
2 *fruitful discussions* **productive,** constructive, useful, of use, worthwhile, helpful, beneficial, valuable, rewarding, profitable, advantageous, gainful, successful, effective, effectual, well-spent.
ANTONYMS futile.

fruition ▶ noun *when the project comes to its fruition, you will be favorably impressed* **fulfillment,** realization, actualization, materialization, achievement, attainment, accomplishment, resolution; success, completion, consummation, conclusion, close, finish, perfection, maturity, maturation, ripening, ripeness; implementation, execution, performance.

fruitless ▶ adjective *fruitless negotiations* **futile,** vain, in vain, to no avail, to no effect, idle; pointless, useless, worthless, wasted, hollow; ineffectual, ineffective, inefficacious; unproductive, unrewarding, frustrating, profitless, unsuccessful, unavailing, barren, for naught; abortive; archaic bootless.
ANTONYMS productive.

frustrate ▶ verb 1 *his plans were frustrated* **thwart,** defeat, foil, block, stop, put a stop to, counter, spoil, check, balk, disappoint, forestall, dash, scotch, quash, crush, derail, snooker; obstruct, impede, hamper, hinder, hamstring, stand in the way of; informal stymie, foul up, screw up, put the kibosh on, do for; informal scuttle.
ANTONYMS help, facilitate.
2 *the delays frustrated her* **exasperate,** infuriate, annoy, anger, vex, irritate, irk, try someone's patience; disappoint, discontent, dissatisfy, discourage, dishearten, dispirit; informal aggravate, bug, miff.
ANTONYMS please.

frustration ▶ noun 1 *he clenched his fists in frustration* **exasperation,** annoyance, anger, vexation, irritation; disappointment, dissatisfaction, discontentment, discontent; informal aggravation.
2 *the frustration of her attempts to introduce changes* **thwarting,** defeat, prevention, foiling, blocking, spoiling, circumvention, forestalling, disappointment, derailment; obstruction, hampering, hindering; failure, collapse.

fuddy-duddy ▶ noun informal *stop being such a fuddy-duddy and listen to the kids' music* (**old**) **fogey,** conservative, traditionalist, conformist; fossil, dinosaur, troglodyte, mossback, museum piece, stick-in-the-mud, square, stuffed shirt, dodo.

fudge ▶ verb 1 *the mayor tried to fudge the issue* **evade,** avoid, dodge, skirt, duck, gloss over; hedge on, prevaricate about, vacillate on, be noncommittal on, stall on, beat around the bush about, equivocate on, hem and haw on; informal cop out on, sit on the fence about; rare tergiversate about.
2 *the government has been fudging figures* **adjust,** manipulate, massage, put a spin on, juggle, misrepresent, misreport, bend; tamper with, tinker with, interfere with, doctor, falsify, distort; informal cook, fiddle with.

fuel ▶ noun 1 *the car ran out of fuel* **gas,** gasoline, diesel, petroleum, propane; power source; Brit. petrol.
2 *she added more fuel to the fire* **firewood,** wood, kindling, logs; coal, coke, anthracite; oil, kerosene, propane, lighter fluid; heat source.
3 *we all need fuel to keep our bodies going* **nourishment,** food, sustenance, nutriment, nutrition.
4 *his antics added fuel to the opposition's cause* **encouragement,** ammunition, stimulus, incentive; provocation, goading.
▶ verb 1 *power stations fueled by low-grade coal* **power,** fire, charge.
2 *the rumors fueled anxiety among opposition* **fan,** feed, stoke up, inflame, intensify, stimulate, encourage, provoke, incite, whip up;

sustain, keep alive.

fugitive ▶ noun *a hunted fugitive* **escapee,** runaway, deserter, absconder; refugee.

▶ adjective 1 *a fugitive criminal* **escaped,** runaway, on the run, on the loose, at large; wanted; informal AWOL, on the lam.
2 *the fugitive nature of life* **fleeting,** transient, transitory, ephemeral, fading, momentary, short-lived, short, brief, passing, impermanent, here today and gone tomorrow; literary evanescent.

fulfill ▶ verb 1 *she fulfilled a lifelong ambition to visit Israel* **achieve,** attain, realize, actualize, make happen, succeed in, bring to completion, bring to fruition, satisfy.
2 *she failed to fulfill her duties* **carry out,** perform, accomplish, execute, do, discharge, conduct; complete, finish, conclude, perfect.
3 *they fulfilled the criteria* **meet,** satisfy, comply with, conform to, fill, answer.

fulfilled ▶ adjective *the new job has me feeling fulfilled* **satisfied,** content, contented, happy, pleased; serene, placid, untroubled, at ease, at peace.
ANTONYMS discontented.

full ▶ adjective 1 *her glass was full* **filled,** filled up, filled to capacity, filled to the brim, brimming, brimful.
ANTONYMS empty.
2 *streets full of people* **crowded with,** packed with, crammed with, congested with; teeming with, swarming with, thick with, thronged with, overcrowded with, overrun with; abounding with, bursting with, overflowing with; informal jam-packed with, wall-to-wall with, stuffed with, chockablock with, chock-full of, bursting at the seams with, packed to the gunwales with, awash with.
ANTONYMS empty.
3 *all the seats were full* **occupied,** taken, in use, unavailable.
ANTONYMS empty, unoccupied.
4 *I'm full* **replete,** full up, satisfied, well-fed, sated, satiated, surfeited; gorged, glutted; informal stuffed.
ANTONYMS hungry.
5 *she'd had a full life* **eventful,** interesting, exciting, lively, action-packed, busy, energetic, active.
ANTONYMS uneventful.
6 *a full list of available facilities* **comprehensive,** thorough, exhaustive, all-inclusive, all-encompassing, all-embracing, in depth; complete, entire, whole, unabridged, uncut.
ANTONYMS selective, incomplete.
7 *a fire engine driven at full speed* **maximum,** top, greatest, highest.
ANTONYMS low.
8 *she had a full figure* **plump,** well-rounded, rounded, buxom, shapely, ample, curvaceous, voluptuous, womanly, Junoesque; informal busty, curvy, well-upholstered, well-endowed, zaftig.
ANTONYMS thin.
9 *a full skirt* **loose-fitting,** loose, baggy, voluminous, roomy, capacious, billowing.
ANTONYMS tight, tight-fitting.
10 *his full baritone voice* **resonant,** rich, sonorous, deep, vibrant, full-bodied, strong, fruity, clear.
ANTONYMS thin.
11 *the full flavor of a Bordeaux* **rich,** intense, full-bodied, strong, deep.
ANTONYMS watery, thin.

▶ adverb 1 *she looked full into his face* **directly,** right, straight, squarely, square, dead, point-blank; informal bang, plumb.
2 *you knew full well I was leaving* **very,** perfectly, quite; informal darn, damn, damned, darned; chiefly Brit. bloody.

– PHRASES **in full** *my letter was published in full* **in its entirety,** in toto, in total, unabridged, uncut. **to the full** *live your life to the full* **fully,** thoroughly, completely, to the utmost, to the limit, to the maximum, for all one's worth.

full-grown ▶ adjective *how full-grown men can act so childishly is beyond me* **adult,** mature, grown-up, of age; fully grown, fully developed, fully fledged, in one's prime, in full bloom, ripe.
ANTONYMS infant.

fullness ▶ noun 1 *the fullness of the information they provide* **comprehensiveness,** completeness, thoroughness, exhaustiveness, all-inclusiveness.
2 *the fullness of her body* **plumpness,** roundedness, roundness, shapeliness, curvaceousness, voluptuousness, womanliness; informal curviness.
3 *the recording has a fullness and warmth* **resonance,** richness, intensity, depth, vibrancy, strength, clarity, three-dimensionality.

– PHRASES **in the fullness of time** *in the fullness of time, Ricardo would realize they were right* **in due course,** when the time is ripe, eventually, in time, in time to come, one day, some day, sooner or later; ultimately, finally, in the end.

full-scale ▶ adjective 1 *a full-scale model* **full-size,** life-size.
ANTONYMS small-scale.
2 *a full-scale public inquiry* **thorough,** comprehensive, extensive, exhaustive, complete, all-out, all-encompassing, all-inclusive, all-embracing, thoroughgoing, wide-ranging, sweeping, in-depth, far-reaching.
ANTONYMS partial.

fully ▶ adverb 1 *I fully agree with him* **completely,** entirely, wholly, totally, quite, utterly, perfectly, altogether, thoroughly, in all respects, in every respect, without reservation, without exception, to the hilt.
ANTONYMS partly, nearly.
2 *fully two minutes must have passed* **at least,** no less than, no fewer than, easily, without exaggeration.
ANTONYMS nearly.

fulminate ▶ verb *homeowners fulminated against the tax hikes* **protest,** rail against, rage about, rant about, thunder about, storm about, vociferate against, declaim, inveigh against, speak out against, make/take a stand against; denounce, decry, condemn, criticize, censure, disparage, attack, execrate; informal mouth off about; formal excoriate.

fulmination ▶ noun *the fulminations of media moralists* **protest,** objection, complaint, rant, tirade, diatribe, harangue, invective, railing, obloquy; denunciation, condemnation, criticism, censure, attack, broadside, brickbats; formal excoriation; literary philippic.

fulsome ▶ adjective *he paid fulsome tribute to his secretary* **excessive,** extravagant, overdone, immoderate, inordinate, over-appreciative, flattering, adulatory, fawning, unctuous, ingratiating, cloying, saccharine; enthusiastic, effusive, rapturous, glowing, gushing, profuse, generous, lavish; informal over the top, smarmy.

fumble ▶ verb **1** *she fumbled for her keys* **grope,** fish, search blindly, scrabble around.
2 *he fumbled about in the dark* **stumble,** blunder, flounder, lumber, stagger, totter, lurch; (**fumble about/around**) feel one's way, grope one's way.
3 *the quarterback fumbled the ball* **miss,** drop, mishandle, bobble.
4 *she fumbled her lines* **mess up,** make a mess of, bungle, mismanage, mishandle, spoil; informal make a hash of, fluff, botch, muff, flub.
▶ noun *a fumble from the goaltender* **slip,** mistake, error, gaffe; informal slip-up, boo-boo.

fume ▶ noun (**fumes**) **1** *a fire giving off toxic fumes* **smoke,** vapor, gas, effluvium; exhaust; pollution.
2 *stale wine fumes* **smell,** odor, stink, reek, stench, fetor, funk; literary miasma.
▶ verb **1** *fragments of lava were fuming and sizzling* **emit smoke,** emit gas, smoke; archaic reek.
2 *Elsa was still fuming at his arrogance* **be furious,** be enraged, be very angry, seethe, be livid, be incensed, boil, be beside oneself, spit; rage, rant and rave; informal be hot under the collar, foam at the mouth, see red.

fumigate ▶ verb *the prisoners' quarters are fumigated once a month* **disinfect,** purify, sterilize, sanitize, decontaminate, cleanse, clean out.
ANTONYMS soil.

fun ▶ noun **1** *I joined in with the fun | did you have fun?* **enjoyment,** entertainment, amusement, pleasure; jollification, merrymaking; recreation, diversion, leisure, relaxation; a good time, a great time; informal R and R (rest and recreation), a ball.
ANTONYMS boredom.
2 *she's full of fun* **merriment,** cheerfulness, cheeriness, jollity, joviality, jocularity, high spirits, gaiety, mirth, laughter, hilarity, glee, gladness, lightheartedness, levity.
ANTONYMS misery.
3 *he became a figure of fun* **ridicule,** derision, mockery, laughter, scorn, contempt, jeering, sneering, jibing, teasing, taunting.
ANTONYMS respect.
▶ adjective informal *a fun evening* **enjoyable,** entertaining, amusing, diverting, pleasurable, pleasing, agreeable, interesting.
– PHRASES **in fun** *the teasing was all in fun* **playful,** in jest, as a joke, tongue in cheek, lighthearted, for a laugh. **make fun of** *the kids who made fun of Marty were total jerks* **tease,** poke fun at, ridicule, mock, laugh at, taunt, jeer at, scoff at, deride; parody, lampoon, caricature, satirize; informal rib, kid, have on, pull someone's leg, send up, rag on, razz.

> USAGE
> **fun**
> The use of *fun* as an adjective meaning 'enjoyable,' as in *we had a fun evening,* is not fully accepted in standard English and should only be used in informal contexts. There are signs, however, that this situation is changing, given the recent appearance in American English of comparative and superlative forms *funner* and *funnest,* formed as if *fun* were a normal adjective. The adjectival forms *funner* and *funnest* have not 'arrived' in all the dictionaries, however, and if employed at all, they should be used sparingly and not in formal written English.

function ▶ noun **1** *the main function of the machine* **purpose,** task, use, role.
2 *my function was to select and train the recruits* **responsibility,** duty, role, concern, province, activity, assignment, obligation, charge; task, job, mission, undertaking, commission; capacity, post, situation, office, occupation, employment, business.
3 *a function attended by local dignitaries* **social event,** party, social occasion, affair, gathering, reception, soirée, jamboree, gala, meet-and-greet; informal do, bash, shindig.
▶ verb **1** *the electrical system had ceased to function* **work,** go, run, be in working/running order, operate, be operative.
2 *the museum* ***functions as*** *an educational center* **act as,** serve as, operate as; perform as, work as, play the role of, do duty as.

functional ▶ adjective **1** *a small functional kitchen* **practical,** useful, utilitarian, utility, workaday, serviceable; minimalist, plain, simple, basic, modest, unadorned, unostentatious, no-frills, without frills; impersonal, characterless, soulless, institutional, clinical.
2 *the machine is now fully functional* **working,** in working order, functioning, in service, in use; going, running, operative, operating, in operation, in commission, in action; informal up and running.

functionary ▶ noun *a Capitol Hill functionary* **official,** officeholder, public servant, civil servant, bureaucrat, administrator, apparatchik; informal bean counter.

fund ▶ noun **1** *an emergency fund for refugees* **collection,** kitty, reserve, pool, purse; endowment, foundation, trust, grant, investment; savings, nest egg; informal stash.
2 (**funds**) *I was very short of funds* **money,** cash, ready money; wealth, means, assets, resources, savings, capital, reserves, the wherewithal; informal dough, bread, loot.
3 *his fund of stories* **stock,** store, supply, accumulation, collection, bank, pool; mine, reservoir, storehouse, treasury, treasure house, hoard, repository; informal pork barrel.
▶ verb *the agency was funded by a federal grant* **finance,** pay for, back, capitalize, sponsor,

put up the money for, subsidize, underwrite, endow, support, maintain; informal foot the bill for, pick up the tab for, bankroll, stake.

fundamental ▶ adjective *fundamental principles* **basic,** underlying, core, foundational, rudimentary, elemental, elementary, basal, root; primary, prime, cardinal, first, principal, chief, key, central, vital, essential, important, indispensable, necessary, crucial, pivotal, critical; structural, organic, constitutional, inherent, intrinsic.
ANTONYMS secondary, unimportant.

fundamentally ▶ adverb *she was, fundamentally, a good person* **essentially,** in essence, basically, at heart, at bottom, deep down, au fond; primarily, above all, first and foremost, first of all; informal at the end of the day, when all is said and done, when you get right down to it.

fundamentals ▶ plural noun *the fundamentals of the job* **basics,** essentials, rudiments, foundations, basic principles, first principles, preliminaries; crux, crux of the matter, heart of the matter, essence, core, heart, base, bedrock; informal nuts and bolts, nitty-gritty, brass tacks, ABC, meat and potatoes.

funeral ▶ noun **1** *he'd attended a funeral* **burial,** interment, entombment, committal, inhumation, laying to rest; cremation; obsequies, last offices, memorial service; archaic sepulture.
2 informal *ignore my advice if you like—it's your funeral* **responsibility,** problem, worry, concern, business, affair; informal headache.

funereal ▶ adjective **1** *the funereal atmosphere* **somber,** gloomy, mournful, melancholy, lugubrious, sepulchral, miserable, doleful, woeful, sad, sorrowful, cheerless, joyless, bleak, dismal, depressing, dreary; grave, solemn, serious; literary dolorous.
ANTONYMS cheerful.
2 *funereal colors* **dark,** black, drab.

fungus ▶ noun *the fungus will flourish in a dark, moist environment* **mushroom,** toadstool; mold, mildew, rust; Biology saprophyte.

funny ▶ adjective **1** *a funny movie | these guys are really funny* **amusing,** humorous, witty, comic, comical, droll, facetious, jocular, jokey; hilarious, hysterical, riotous, uproarious; entertaining, diverting, sparkling, scintillating; silly, farcical, slapstick; informal side-splitting, rib-tickling, laugh-a-minute, wacky, zany, off the wall, a scream, rich, priceless; informal dated killing.
ANTONYMS serious, unamusing.
2 *a funny coincidence* **strange,** peculiar, odd, queer, weird, bizarre, curious, freakish, freak, quirky; mysterious, mystifying, puzzling, perplexing; unusual, uncommon, anomalous, irregular, abnormal, exceptional, singular, out of the ordinary, extraordinary.
3 *there's something funny about him* **suspicious,** suspect, dubious, untrustworthy, questionable; informal shady, sketchy, fishy.
ANTONYMS trustworthy.

furious ▶ adjective **1** *she was furious when she learned about it* **enraged,** infuriated, very angry, irate, incensed, raging, incandescent, fuming, ranting, raving, seething, beside oneself, outraged; informal mad, hopping mad, wild, livid, boiling, apoplectic, hot under the collar, on the warpath, foaming at the mouth, steamed up, fit to be tied; literary wrathful.
ANTONYMS calm.
2 *a furious debate* **heated,** hot, passionate, fiery, "lively"; fierce, vehement, violent, wild, unrestrained, tumultuous, turbulent, tempestuous, stormy.
ANTONYMS calm.

furnish ▶ verb **1** *the bedrooms are elegantly furnished* **fit out,** provide with furniture, appoint, outfit.
2 *grooms furnished us with horses for our journey* **supply,** provide, equip, provision, issue, kit out, present, give, offer, afford, purvey, bestow; informal fix up.

furniture ▶ noun *most of the bedroom furniture is mahogany* **furnishings,** fittings, movables, appointments, effects; Law chattels; informal stuff, things.

furor ▶ noun *her memoirs caused a furor* **commotion,** uproar, outcry, fuss, upset, brouhaha, foofaraw, palaver, pother, tempest, agitation, pandemonium, disturbance, hubbub, rumpus, tumult, turmoil; stir, excitement; informal song and dance, to-do, hoo-ha, hullabaloo, ballyhoo, flap, stink.

furrow ▶ noun **1** *furrows in a plowed field* **groove,** trench, rut, trough, channel, hollow.
2 *the furrows on either side of her mouth* **wrinkle,** line, crease, crinkle, crow's foot, corrugation.
▶ verb *his brow furrowed* **wrinkle,** crease, line, crinkle, pucker, screw up, scrunch up, corrugate.

further ▶ adverb **1** *further information* **additional,** more, extra, supplementary, supplemental, other; new, fresh.
2 *further, it gave him an excellent excuse not to attend* See FURTHERMORE.
3 *she's transferring to a school further from home* See FARTHER.
▶ adjective *the further end of the hall* See FARTHER.
▶ verb *an attempt to further his career* **promote,** advance, forward, develop, facilitate, aid, assist, help, help along, lend a hand to, abet; expedite, hasten, speed up, catalyze, accelerate, step up, spur on, oil the wheels of, give a push to, boost, encourage, cultivate, nurture, foster.
ANTONYMS impede.

furtherance ▶ noun *the furtherance of his business interests* **promotion,** furthering, advancement, forwarding, development, facilitation, aiding, assisting, helping, abetting; hastening, acceleration, boosting, encouragement, cultivation, nurturing, fostering.
ANTONYMS hindrance.

furthermore ▶ adverb *furthermore, you'll have access to a better library* **moreover,** further, what's more, also, additionally, in addition, besides, as well, too, to boot, on top of that, over and above that, into the bargain, by the same token; archaic withal.

furthest ▶ adjective *the furthest car on the left is mine* See FARTHEST.
▶ adverb *Lynda had to walk the furthest* See FARTHEST.

furtive ▶ adjective *they met in seedy dives to craft their furtive plans* **secretive,** secret, surreptitious, clandestine, hidden, covert, conspiratorial, cloak-and-dagger, backroom, backstairs, sly, sneaky, under-the-table; sidelong, sideways, oblique, indirect; informal hush-hush, shifty. See note at SECRET.
ANTONYMS open.

fury ▶ noun **1** *she exploded with fury* **rage,** anger, wrath, outrage, spleen, temper; crossness, indignation, umbrage, annoyance, exasperation; literary ire, choler.
ANTONYMS good humor.
2 *the fury of the storm* **fierceness,** ferocity, violence, turbulence, tempestuousness, savagery; severity, intensity, vehemence, force, forcefulness, power, strength.
ANTONYMS mildness.
3 *she turned on her mother like a fury* **virago,** hellcat, termagant, spitfire, vixen, shrew, harridan, dragon, gorgon; (**Furies**) Greek Mythology Eumenides.

fuse ▶ verb **1** *a band that fuses rap with rock* **combine,** amalgamate, put together, join, unite, marry, blend, merge, meld, mingle, integrate, intermix, intermingle, synthesize; coalesce, compound, alloy; technical admix; literary commingle.
ANTONYMS separate.
2 *metal fused to a base of colored glass* **bond,** stick, bind, weld, solder; melt, smelt.
ANTONYMS disconnect.

fuss ▶ noun **1** *what's all the fuss about?* **ado,** excitement, agitation, pother, stir, commotion, confusion, disturbance, brouhaha, uproar, furor, palaver, foofaraw, tempest in a teapot, much ado about nothing; bother, fluster, flurry, bustle; informal hoo-ha, to-do, ballyhoo, song and dance, performance, pantomime.
2 *they settled in with very little fuss* **bother,** trouble, inconvenience, effort, exertion, labor; informal hassle.
3 *he didn't put up a fuss* **protest,** complaint, objection, grumble, grouse; informal gripe.
▶ verb *he was still* ***fussing over*** *his clothes* **worry about,** fret about, be anxious about, be agitated about, make a big thing out of; informal flap about, be in a tizzy over/about, be in a stew over/about.

fussy ▶ adjective **1** *he's very fussy about what he eats* **finicky,** particular, overparticular, fastidious, discriminating, selective, dainty; hard to please, difficult, exacting, demanding; faddish; informal persnickety, choosy, picky.
2 *a fussy, frilly bridal gown* **overelaborate,** overdecorated, ornate, fancy, overdone; busy, cluttered.

futile ▶ adjective *they piled on thousands of sandbags in a futile attempt to hold back the river* **fruitless,** vain, pointless, useless, ineffectual, ineffective, inefficacious, to no effect, of no use, in vain, to no avail, unavailing; unsuccessful, failed, thwarted; unproductive, barren, unprofitable, abortive; impotent, hollow, empty, forlorn, idle, hopeless; archaic bootless.
ANTONYMS useful.

futility ▶ noun *the futility of his actions* **fruitlessness,** pointlessness, uselessness, vanity, ineffectiveness, inefficacy; failure, barrenness, unprofitability; impotence, hollowness, emptiness, forlornness, hopelessness.

future ▶ noun **1** *his plans for* ***the future*** **the time to come,** the time ahead; what lies ahead, (the) coming times.
ANTONYMS past.
2 *she knew her future lay in acting* **destiny,** fate, fortune; prospects, expectations, chances.
▶ adjective **1** *a future date* **later,** to come, following, ensuing, succeeding, subsequent, coming.
2 *his future wife* **to be,** destined; intended, planned, prospective.
– PHRASES **in future** *in future, let's bring plenty of extra batteries* **from now on,** after this, in the future, from this day forward, hence, henceforward, subsequently, in time to come, down the road; formal hereafter.

fuzzy ▶ adjective **1** *her fuzzy hair* **frizzy,** fluffy, woolly; downy, soft.
2 *a fuzzy picture* **blurry,** blurred, indistinct, unclear, bleary, misty, distorted, out of focus, unfocused, lacking definition, nebulous; ill-defined, indefinite, vague, hazy, imprecise, inexact, loose, woolly.
3 *my mind was fuzzy* **confused,** muddled, addled, fuddled, befuddled, groggy, disoriented, disorientated, mixed up, fazed, foggy, dizzy, stupefied, benumbed.

Gg

gad ▶ verb informal *she's been **gadding about** in Europe* **gallivant about,** traipse around, flit around, run around, travel around, roam (about/around).

gadabout ▶ noun informal *Marc and Patty linked up with some other gadabouts in Paris* **pleasure-seeker**; traveler, globetrotter, wanderer, drifter.

gadget ▶ noun *Everett had to buy every new gadget on the market* **appliance,** apparatus, instrument, implement, tool, utensil, contrivance, contraption, machine, mechanism, device, labor-saving device, convenience, invention; informal gizmo, widget.

gaffe ▶ noun *I made some real gaffes at work* **blunder,** mistake, error, slip, faux pas, indiscretion, impropriety, miscalculation, gaucherie, solecism; informal slip-up, howler, boo-boo, fluff, flub, blooper, goof.

gag[1] ▶ verb **1** *a dirty rag was used to gag her mouth* **smother,** block, plug, stifle, stop up, muffle.
2 *the government tried to gag its critics* **silence,** muzzle, mute, muffle, suppress, stifle; censor, curb, check, restrain, fetter, shackle, restrict.
3 *the stench made her gag* **retch,** heave, dry-heave.
▶ noun *his scream was muffled by the gag* **muzzle,** tie, restraint.

gag[2] ▶ noun informal *a film full of lame gags* **joke,** jest, witticism, quip, pun, play on words, double entendre; practical joke, stunt, lark; informal crack, wisecrack, one-liner.

gaiety ▶ noun **1** *the gaiety of Susannah's youth had been supplanted by the cares of widowhood* **cheerfulness,** lightheartedness, happiness, merriment, glee, gladness, joy, joie de vivre, joyfulness, joyousness, delight, high spirits, good spirits, good humor, cheeriness, jollity, mirth, joviality, exuberance, elation; liveliness, vivacity, animation, effervescence, sprightliness, zest, zestfulness; informal chirpiness, bounce, pep; literary blitheness.
ANTONYMS misery.
2 *the hotel restaurant was a scene of gaiety* **merrymaking,** festivity, fun, fun and games, frolics, revelry, jollification, celebration, pleasure; informal partying; dated sport.

gain ▶ verb **1** *he gained a scholarship to the college* **obtain,** get, secure, acquire, come by, procure, attain, achieve, earn, win, garner, capture, clinch, pick up, carry off, reap; informal land, net, bag, scoop, wangle, swing, walk away/off with. See note at GET.
ANTONYMS lose.
2 *they stood to gain from the deal* **profit,** make money, reap benefits, benefit, do well; informal make a killing.
ANTONYMS lose.
3 *the dog gained weight* **put on,** increase in.
ANTONYMS lose.
4 *the others were **gaining on** us* **catch up with/on,** catch someone up, catch, close (in) on, near.
5 *we finally gained the ridge* **reach,** arrive at, get to, come to, make, attain, set foot on; informal hit, wind up at.
▶ noun **1** *his gain from the deal* **profit,** advantage, benefit, reward; percentage, takings, yield, return, winnings, receipts, proceeds, dividend, interest; informal pickings, cut, take, divvy, slice, piece of the pie.
ANTONYMS loss.
2 *a price gain of 7.5 percent* **increase,** rise, increment, augmentation, addition.
ANTONYMS decrease.
– PHRASES **gain time** *the district attorney had run out of plausible ways to gain time* **play for time,** stall, procrastinate, delay, temporize, hold back, hang back, hang fire, dally, drag one's feet.

gainful ▶ adjective *a gainful investment* **profitable,** paid, well-paid, remunerative, lucrative, moneymaking; rewarding, fruitful, worthwhile, useful, productive, constructive, beneficial, advantageous, valuable.

gainsay ▶ verb formal *it was difficult to gainsay his claim* **deny,** dispute, disagree with, argue with, dissent from, contradict, repudiate, challenge, oppose, contest, counter, controvert, rebut.
ANTONYMS confirm.

gait ▶ noun *there was a new liveliness to her gait* **walk,** step, stride, pace, tread, bearing, carriage; formal comportment.

gala ▶ noun *the annual summer gala* **fête,** fair, festival, carnival, pageant, jubilee, jamboree, party, garden party, celebration; festivities.
▶ adjective *a gala occasion* **festive,** celebratory, merry, joyous, joyful; diverting, entertaining, enjoyable, spectacular.

galaxy ▶ noun *the search for life in other galaxies* **star system,** solar system, constellation; stars, heavens.

gale ▶ noun **1** *a howling gale* See STORM (sense 1 of the noun).
2 *gales of laughter* **peal,** howl, hoot, shriek, scream, roar; outburst, burst, fit, paroxysm, explosion.

gall[1] ▶ noun **1** *she had the gall to ask for money* **effrontery,** impudence, impertinence, cheek, cheekiness, insolence, audacity, temerity, presumption, cockiness, nerve, shamelessness,

disrespect, bad manners; informal face, chutzpah; sauce, sass. See note at TEMERITY.
2 *scholarly gall was poured on this work* **bitterness,** resentment, rancor, bile, spleen, malice, spite, spitefulness, malignity, venom, vitriol, poison.

gall² ▶ noun **1** *this was a gall that she frequently had to endure* **irritation,** irritant, annoyance, vexation, nuisance, provocation, bother, torment, plague, thorn in one's side/flesh; informal aggravation, bore, headache, hassle, pain, pain in the neck, pain in the butt.
2 *a bay horse with a gall on its side* **sore,** ulcer, ulceration; abrasion, scrape, scratch, graze, chafe.
▶ verb *it galled him that he had to wake early* **irritate,** annoy, vex, anger, infuriate, exasperate, irk, pique, nettle, put out, displease, antagonize, get on someone's nerves, make someone's hackles rise, rub the wrong way; informal aggravate, peeve, miff, rile, needle, get (to), bug, get someone's goat, get/put someone's back up, get someone's dander up, drive mad/crazy, drive round/around the bend, drive up the wall, tee off, tick off, rankle.

gallant ▶ adjective **1** *his gallant countrymen* **brave,** courageous, valiant, valorous, bold, plucky, daring, fearless, intrepid, heroic, lionhearted, stouthearted, doughty, mettlesome, dauntless, undaunted, unflinching, unafraid; informal gutsy, spunky.
ANTONYMS cowardly.
2 *her gallant companion* **chivalrous,** princely, gentlemanly, honorable, courteous, polite, mannerly, attentive, respectful, gracious, considerate, thoughtful.
ANTONYMS discourteous.

gallantry ▶ noun **1** *he received medals for gallantry* **bravery,** courage, courageousness, valor, pluck, pluckiness, nerve, daring, boldness, fearlessness, dauntlessness, intrepidity, heroism, mettle, grit, stoutheartedness; informal guts, spunk, moxie.
2 *she acknowledged his selfless gallantry* **chivalry,** chivalrousness, gentlemanliness, courtesy, courteousness, politeness, good manners, attentiveness, graciousness, respectfulness, respect.

galling ▶ adjective *his hypocrisy was galling* **annoying,** irritating, vexing, vexatious, infuriating, maddening, irksome, provoking, exasperating, trying, tiresome, troublesome, bothersome, displeasing, disagreeable; informal aggravating.

gallivant ▶ verb *my days of gallivanting are long past* **flit,** jaunt, run; roam, wander, travel, rove; informal gad.

gallop ▶ verb *Paul galloped across the clearing* **rush,** race, run, sprint, bolt, dart, dash, career, charge, shoot, hurtle, careen, hare, fly, speed, zoom, streak; informal tear, belt, pelt, scoot, zip, whip, hotfoot it, hightail it, bomb, barrel.
ANTONYMS amble.

gallows ▶ plural noun **1** *the wooden gallows* **gibbet,** scaffold, gallows tree.
2 *they were condemned to **the gallows*** **hanging,** being hanged, the noose, the rope, the gibbet, the scaffold, execution.

galore ▶ adjective *up in the attic were old trunks and hatboxes galore* **aplenty,** in abundance, in profusion, in great quantities, in large numbers, by the dozen; to spare; everywhere, all over (the place); informal by the truckload.

galvanize ▶ verb *the reverend's words galvanized our group into action* **jolt,** shock, startle, impel, stir, spur, prod, urge, motivate, stimulate, electrify, excite, rouse, arouse, awaken; invigorate, fire, animate, vitalize, energize, exhilarate, thrill, catalyze, inspire, light a fire under; informal give someone a shot in the arm.

gambit ▶ noun *the most ambitious financial gambit in history* **stratagem,** scheme, plan, tactic, maneuver, move, course/line of action, device; machination, ruse, trick, ploy, wangle.

gamble ▶ verb **1** *he started to gamble more often* **bet,** place/lay a bet on something, stake money on something, back the horses, game; informal play the ponies.
2 *investors are gambling that the British pound will fall* **take a chance,** take a risk; informal stick one's neck out, go out on a limb.
▶ noun **1** *his grandfather enjoyed a gamble* **bet,** wager, speculation; game of chance.
2 *I took a gamble and it paid off* **risk,** chance, hazard, shot in the dark, leap of faith; pig in a poke, pot luck; rare salto.

gambol ▶ verb *lambs gamboled in the pasture* **frolic,** frisk, cavort, caper, skip, dance, romp, prance, leap, hop, jump, spring, bound, bounce; play; dated sport.

game ▶ noun **1** *Andrew and his friends invented a new game* **pastime,** diversion, entertainment, amusement, distraction, divertissement, recreation, sport, activity.
2 *the team hasn't lost a game all season* **match,** contest, tournament, meet; final, playoff.
3 *I spoiled his little game* **scheme,** plot, ploy, stratagem, strategy, gambit, tactics; trick, device, maneuver, wile, dodge, ruse, machination, contrivance, subterfuge; prank, practical joke; informal scam; archaic shift.
4 *she lived off fish and game* **wild animals,** wild fowl, big game.
▶ adjective **1** *they weren't game enough to join in* **brave,** courageous, plucky, bold, daring, intrepid, valiant, stouthearted, mettlesome; fearless, dauntless, undaunted, unflinching; informal gutsy, spunky.
2 *I need a bit of help—are you game?* **willing,** prepared, ready, disposed, of a mind; eager, keen, enthusiastic, up for it.
▶ verb *they were drinking and gaming all evening* **gamble,** bet, place/lay bets.

gamut ▶ noun *the complete gamut of human emotion* **range,** spectrum, span, scope, sweep, compass, area, breadth, reach, extent, catalog, scale; variety. See note at RANGE.

gang ▶ noun **1** *a gang of tough-looking boys* **band,** group, crowd, pack, horde, throng, mob, herd, swarm, troop, cluster; company, gathering; informal posse, bunch, gaggle, load.
2 informal *Shania was one of our gang* **circle,** social circle, social set, group, clique, in-crowd, coterie, cabal, lot, ring; informal crew, rat pack.
3 *a gang of workmen* **crew,** team, group, squad, shift, detachment, unit.
▶ verb *they all **ganged up** to put me down* **conspire,**

cooperate, collude, work together, act together, combine, join forces, team up, get together, unite, ally.

gangster ▶ noun *Prohibition was a boon era for gangsters* **hoodlum,** gang member, racketeer, robber, ruffian, thug, tough, villain, lawbreaker, criminal; gunman; Mafioso; informal mobster, crook, lowlife, hit man, hood; dated desperado.

gap ▶ noun **1** *a gap in the shutters* **opening,** aperture, space, breach, chink, slit, slot, vent, crack, crevice, cranny, cavity, hole, orifice, interstice, perforation, break, fracture, rift, rent, fissure, cleft, divide.
2 *a gap between meetings* **pause,** intermission, interval, interlude, break, breathing space, breather, respite, hiatus, recess.
3 *a gap in our records* **omission,** blank, lacuna, void, vacuity.
4 *the gap between rich and poor* **chasm,** gulf, rift, split, separation, breach; contrast, difference, disparity, divergence, imbalance.

gape ▶ verb **1** *she gaped at him in astonishment* **stare,** stare open-mouthed, stare in wonder, goggle, gaze, ogle; informal rubberneck, gawk.
2 *a padded coat that gaped at every seam* **open wide,** open up, yawn; part, split.

garb ▶ noun *men and women in riding garb* **clothes,** clothing, garments, attire, dress, costume, outfit, wear, uniform, livery, regalia; informal gear, getup, togs, duds; formal apparel; archaic raiment, habiliment, vestments.
▶ verb *both men were garbed in black* **dress,** clothe, attire, fit out, turn out, deck (out), costume, robe; informal get up; archaic apparel.

garbage ▶ noun **1** *the garbage is taken to landfill sites* **trash,** rubbish, refuse, waste, detritus, litter, junk, scrap; scraps, leftovers, remains, slops; informal crap.
2 *most of what he says is garbage* **nonsense,** balderdash, claptrap, twaddle, blather; dross, rubbish; informal hogwash, baloney, tripe, jive, bilge, bull, crap, bunk, poppycock, piffle, bunkum.

garble ▶ verb *the message was garbled in transmission* **mix up,** muddle, jumble, confuse, obscure, distort, scramble; misstate, misquote, misreport, misrepresent, mistranslate, misinterpret, misconstrue, twist.

gargantuan ▶ adjective *a gargantuan wedding cake* **huge,** enormous, vast, gigantic, very big, giant, massive, colossal, mammoth, immense, mighty, monumental, mountainous, titanic, towering, tremendous, elephantine, king-size(d), economy-size(d), prodigious; informal mega, monster, whopping, humongous, jumbo, ginormous.
ANTONYMS tiny.

garish ▶ adjective *garish party decorations* **gaudy,** lurid, loud, harsh, glaring, violent, showy, glittering, brassy, brash; tasteless, in bad taste, tawdry, vulgar, unattractive, bilious; informal flash, flashy, tacky, tinselly, neon.
ANTONYMS drab.

garland ▶ noun *a garland of flowers* **festoon,** lei, wreath, ring, circle, swag; coronet, crown, coronal, chaplet, fillet.
▶ verb *gardens garlanded with colored lights* **festoon,** wreathe, swathe, hang; adorn, ornament, embellish, decorate, deck, trim, dress, bedeck, array; literary bedizen.

garment ▶ noun *the brown tweed is a lovely garment | all of her garments seem to be red* **item of clothing,** article of clothing; informal getup; (**garments**) clothes, clothing, dress, garb, outfit, costume, attire; informal gear, togs, duds, threads; formal apparel.

garner ▶ verb *Edward garnered ideas from his travels* **gather,** collect, accumulate, amass, assemble, reap.

garnish ▶ verb *garnish the dish with chopped parsley* **decorate,** adorn, ornament, trim, dress, embellish; enhance, grace, beautify, prettify, add the finishing touch to.
▶ noun *keep a few sprigs for a garnish* **decoration,** adornment, trim, trimming, ornament, ornamentation, embellishment, enhancement, finishing touch; Cooking chiffonade.

garret ▶ noun *there were two straw beds in the garret* **loft,** attic, mansard.

garrison ▶ noun **1** *the enemy garrison had been burned alive* **troops,** militia, soldiers, forces; armed force, military detachment, unit, platoon, brigade, squadron, battalion, corps.
2 *forces from three garrisons* **fortress,** fort, fortification, stronghold, citadel, camp, encampment, cantonment, command post, base, station; barracks.
▶ verb **1** *French infantry garrisoned the town* **defend,** guard, protect, barricade, shield, secure; man, occupy.
2 *troops were garrisoned in various regions* **station,** post, put on duty, deploy, assign, install; base, site, place, position; billet.

garrulous ▶ adjective **1** *a garrulous old man* **talkative,** loquacious, voluble, verbose, chatty, chattering, gossipy; effusive, expansive, forthcoming, conversational, communicative; informal mouthy, gabby, gassy, windy, having the gift of the gab, motormouthed. See note at TALKATIVE.
ANTONYMS taciturn, reticent.
2 *his garrulous reminiscences* **long-winded,** wordy, verbose, prolix, long, lengthy, rambling, wandering, maundering, meandering, digressive, diffuse, discursive; gossipy, chatty; informal windy, gassy.
ANTONYMS concise.

gash ▶ noun *a gash on his forehead* **laceration,** cut, wound, injury, slash, tear, incision; slit, split, rip, rent; scratch, scrape, graze, abrasion; Medicine lesion.
▶ verb *he gashed his hand on some broken glass* **lacerate,** cut (open), wound, injure, hurt, slash, tear, gouge, puncture, slit, split, rend; scratch, scrape, graze, abrade.

gasp ▶ verb **1** *I gasped in surprise* **catch one's breath,** draw in one's breath, gulp; exclaim, cry (out).
2 *she collapsed on the ground, gasping* **pant,** puff, wheeze, breathe hard, choke, fight for breath.
▶ noun *a gasp of dismay* **gulp**; exclamation, cry; sharp inhalation.

gastric ▶ adjective *gastric pain* **stomach,** intestinal, enteric, duodenal, celiac, abdominal, ventral.

gate ▶ noun *they barged through the gate without stopping* **gateway,** doorway, entrance, entryway; exit, egress, opening; door, portal; barrier, turnstile.

gather ▶ verb **1** *we gathered in the hotel lobby* **congregate,** assemble, meet, collect, come/get together, convene, muster, rally, converge; cluster together, crowd, mass, flock together. ANTONYMS scatter.
2 *she **gathered** her family **together*** **summon,** call together, bring together, assemble, convene, rally, round up, muster, marshal. ANTONYMS disperse.
3 *knickknacks he had gathered over the years* **collect,** accumulate, amass, garner, accrue; store, stockpile, hoard, put away/by, lay by/in; informal stash away, squirrel away.
4 *they gathered corn from the fields* **harvest,** reap, crop; pick, pluck; collect.
5 *the show soon gathered a fanatical following* **attract,** draw, pull, pull in, collect, pick up.
6 *I gather that environmentalism is the hot issue* **understand,** be given to understand, believe, be led to believe, think, conclude, deduce, infer, assume, take it, surmise, fancy; hear, hear tell, learn, discover.
7 *he gathered her to his chest* **clasp,** clutch, pull, embrace, enfold, hold, hug, cuddle, squeeze; literary embosom.
8 *his tunic was gathered at the waist* **pleat,** shirr, pucker, tuck, fold, ruffle.

CHOOSE THE RIGHT WORD

gather, assemble, collect, congregate, convene, marshal, muster

Gather is the most general of these terms meaning to come or bring together. It implies bringing widely scattered things or people to one place but with no particular arrangement (*to gather shells at the beach; to gather the family in the living room*). **Collect**, on the other hand, implies both selectivity (*to collect evidence for the trial*) and organization (*to collect butterflies as a hobby*). To *gather* one's thoughts means to bring them together because they have been previously scattered; to *collect* one's thoughts is to organize them. **Assemble** pertains to objects or people who are brought together for a purpose (*to assemble data for a report; to assemble Congress so that legislation will be passed*), while **congregate** may be more spontaneous, done as a free choice (*people congregated in front of the palace, hoping to catch a glimpse of the queen*). **Convene** is a formal word meaning to *assemble* or meet in a body (*to convene an international conference on the subject of global warming*). **Marshal** and **muster** are usually thought of as military terms. *Muster* implies bringing together the parts or units of a force (*troops mustered for inspection*), and *marshal* suggests a very orderly and purposeful arrangement (*to marshal the allied forces along the battle front*).

gathering ▶ noun **1** *she rose to address the gathering* **assembly,** meeting, convention, rally, turnout, congress, convocation, conclave, council, synod, forum; congregation, audience, crowd, group, throng, mass, multitude; informal get-together; formal concourse.
2 *the gathering of data for a future book* **collecting,** collection, garnering, amassing, compilation, accumulation, accrual, cumulation, building up.

gauche ▶ adjective *Rose was embarrassed by her gauche relatives* **awkward,** gawky, inelegant, graceless, ungraceful, ungainly, maladroit, klutzy, inept; lacking in social grace(s), unsophisticated, uncultured, uncultivated, unrefined, raw, inexperienced, unworldly. ANTONYMS elegant, sophisticated.

gaudy ▶ adjective *the motel rooms were clean but howlingly gaudy* **garish,** lurid, loud, overbright, glaring, harsh, violent, showy, glittering, brassy, ostentatious; tasteless, in bad taste, tawdry, vulgar, unattractive, bilious; informal flash, flashy, tacky, kitsch, kitschy. ANTONYMS drab, tasteful.

gauge ▶ noun **1** *the temperature gauge* **measuring device,** measuring instrument, meter, measure; indicator, dial, scale, display.
2 *exports are an important gauge of economic activity* **measure,** indicator, barometer, point of reference, guide, guideline, touchstone, yardstick, benchmark, criterion, test, litmus test.
3 *guitar strings of a different gauge* **size,** diameter, thickness, width, breadth; measure, capacity, magnitude; bore, caliber.
▶ verb **1** *astronomers can gauge the star's intrinsic brightness* **measure,** calculate, compute, work out, determine, ascertain; count, weigh, quantify, put a figure on, pin down.
2 *it is difficult to gauge how effective the ban was* **assess,** evaluate, determine, estimate, form an opinion of, appraise, get the measure of, judge, guess; informal guesstimate, size up.

gaunt ▶ adjective **1** *a gaunt, graying man* **haggard,** drawn, thin, lean, skinny, spindly, spare, bony, angular, rawboned, pinched, hollow-cheeked, scrawny, scraggy, as thin as a rail, cadaverous, skeletal, emaciated, skin-and-bones; wasted, withered, etiolated; informal like a bag of bones; dated spindle-shanked. See note at THIN. ANTONYMS plump.
2 *the gaunt ruin of the dark tower* **bleak,** stark, desolate, bare, gloomy, dismal, somber, grim, stern, harsh, forbidding, uninviting, cheerless. ANTONYMS cheerful.

gawk ▶ verb informal *I somehow managed not to gawk at his gorgeous roommate* **gape,** goggle, gaze, ogle, stare, stare open-mouthed; informal rubberneck.

gawky ▶ adjective *how can you convince a fourteen-year-old boy that he will not always be so gawky?* **awkward,** ungainly, gangling, maladroit, clumsy, klutzy, inelegant, uncoordinated, graceless, ungraceful; unconfident, unsophisticated. ANTONYMS graceful.

gay ▶ adjective **1** *gay men and women* **homosexual,** lesbian; informal queer.
2 dated *her children were all chubby and gay* See

CHEERFUL (sense 1).
▶ noun See **HOMOSEXUAL**.

USAGE

gay

Gay meaning 'homosexual,' dating back to the 1930s (if not earlier), became established in the 1960s as the term preferred by homosexual men to describe themselves. It is now the standard accepted term throughout the English-speaking world. As a result, the centuries-old other senses of *gay* meaning either 'carefree' or 'bright and showy,' once common in speech and literature, are much less frequent. The word *gay* cannot be readily used unselfconsciously today in these older senses without sounding old-fashioned or arousing a sense of double entendre, despite concerted attempts by some to keep them alive.

Gay in its modern sense typically refers to men (*lesbian* being the standard term for homosexual women), but in some contexts it can be used of both men and women.

gaze ▶ verb *he gazed at her* **stare at,** look fixedly at, gape at, goggle at, eye, look at, study, scrutinize, take a good look at; ogle, leer at; informal gawk at, rubberneck, eyeball.
▶ noun *her piercing gaze* **stare,** fixed look, gape; regard, inspection, scrutiny.

gazette ▶ noun *it's in this week's gazette* **newspaper,** paper, journal, periodical, organ, newsletter, bulletin; informal rag.

gear ▶ noun informal **1** *his fishing gear* **equipment,** apparatus, paraphernalia, articles, appliances, impedimenta; tools, utensils, implements, instruments, gadgets; stuff, things; kit, rig, tackle, odds and ends, bits and pieces, trappings, appurtenances, accoutrements, regalia; archaic equipage.
2 *I'll go back to the hotel and pick up my gear* **belongings,** possessions, effects, personal effects, property, paraphernalia, odds and ends, bits and pieces, bags, baggage, luggage; Law chattels; informal things, stuff.
3 *police in riot gear* **clothes,** clothing, garments, outfits, attire, garb; dress, wear; informal togs, duds, getup, threads; formal apparel.

gelatinous ▶ adjective *stir over low heat until the mixture becomes gelatinous* **jellylike,** glutinous, viscous, viscid, mucilaginous, sticky, gluey, gummy, slimy; informal gooey, gunky.

geld ▶ verb *Mitch selects the horses that are to be gelded* **castrate,** neuter, fix, alter, desex, doctor.

gem ▶ noun **1** *rubies and other gems* **jewel,** gemstone, stone, precious stone, semiprecious stone; solitaire, cabochon; archaic bijou.
2 *the gem of the collection* **best,** finest, pride, prize, treasure, flower, pearl, jewel in the crown; pick, choice, cream, the crème de la crème, elite, acme; informal one in a million, bee's knees.

genealogy ▶ noun *our genealogy has been difficult to determine* **lineage,** line, line of descent, family tree, bloodline; pedigree, ancestry, extraction, heritage, parentage, birth, family, dynasty, house, stock, blood, roots.

general ▶ adjective **1** *this is suitable for general use* **widespread,** common, extensive, universal, wide, popular, public, mainstream; established, conventional, traditional, orthodox, accepted. See note at **UNIVERSAL**.
ANTONYMS restricted.
2 *a general pay increase* **comprehensive,** overall, across the board, blanket, umbrella, mass, wholesale, sweeping, broad-ranging, inclusive, companywide; universal, global, worldwide, nationwide.
ANTONYMS localized.
3 *general knowledge* **miscellaneous,** mixed, assorted, diversified, composite, heterogeneous, eclectic.
ANTONYMS specialist.
4 *the general practice* **usual,** customary, habitual, traditional, normal, conventional, typical, standard, regular; familiar, accepted, prevailing, routine, run-of-the-mill, established, everyday, ordinary, common.
ANTONYMS exceptional.
5 *a general description* **broad,** imprecise, inexact, rough, loose, approximate, unspecific, vague, woolly, indefinite; informal ballpark.
ANTONYMS detailed.

generality ▶ noun **1** *the debate has moved on from generalities* **generalization,** general statement, general principle, sweeping statement; abstraction, extrapolation.
ANTONYMS specific.
2 *the generality of this principle* **universality,** comprehensiveness, all-inclusiveness, broadness.

generally ▶ adverb **1** *summers were generally hot* **normally,** in general, as a rule, by and large, more often than not, almost always, mainly, mostly, for the most part, predominantly, on the whole; usually, habitually, customarily, typically, ordinarily, commonly.
2 *popular opinion veers generally to the left* **overall,** in general terms, generally speaking, all in all, broadly, on average, basically, effectively.
3 *the method was generally accepted* **widely,** commonly, extensively, universally, popularly.

generate ▶ verb **1** *moves to generate extra business* **cause,** give rise to, lead to, result in, bring about, create, make, produce, engender, spawn, precipitate, prompt, provoke, trigger, spark off, stir up, induce, promote, foster.
2 *captive animals may not generate offspring* **procreate,** breed, reproduce, father offspring, sire offspring, mother offspring, spawn offspring, create offspring, produce offspring, have offspring; literary beget offspring; archaic engender offspring.

generation ▶ noun **1** *people of the same generation* **age,** age group, peer group.
2 (**generations**) *generations ago* **ages,** years, eons, a long time, an eternity; informal donkey's years.
3 *the next generation of computers* **crop,** batch, wave, range.
4 *the generation of novel ideas* **creation,** production, initiation, origination, inception, inspiration.
5 *human generation* **procreation,** reproduction, breeding; creation.

generic ▶ adjective **1** *a generic classification for similar offenses* **general,** common, collective, nonspecific, inclusive, all-encompassing, broad, comprehensive, blanket, umbrella. See note at **UNIVERSAL**.
ANTONYMS specific.
2 *generic drugs are cheaper than brand-name ones* **unbranded,** nonproprietary, no-name.
ANTONYMS specific.

generosity ▶ noun **1** *the generosity of our host* **liberality,** lavishness, magnanimity, munificence, openhandedness, free-handedness, unselfishness; kindness, benevolence, altruism, charity, big-heartedness, goodness; literary bounteousness.
2 *the generosity of the food portions* **abundance,** plentifulness, copiousness, lavishness, liberality, largeness.

generous ▶ adjective **1** *she is generous with money* **liberal,** lavish, magnanimous, munificent, giving, openhanded, free-handed, bountiful, unselfish, ungrudging, free, indulgent, prodigal; literary bounteous.
ANTONYMS mean, stingy.
2 *it was generous of them to offer* **magnanimous,** kind, benevolent, altruistic, charitable, noble, big-hearted, honorable, good; unselfish, self-sacrificing.
ANTONYMS mean, selfish.
3 *a generous amount of fabric* **lavish,** plentiful, copious, ample, liberal, large, great, abundant, profuse, bumper, opulent, prolific; informal galore; literary bounteous, plenteous.
ANTONYMS meager.

genesis ▶ noun **1** *the hatred had its genesis in something dark* **origin,** source, root, beginning, start.
2 *the genesis of his neurosis* **formation,** development, evolution, emergence, inception, origination, creation, formulation, propagation.

genial ▶ adjective *my genial colleagues* **friendly,** affable, cordial, amiable, warm, easygoing, approachable, sympathetic; good-natured, good-humored, cheerful; neighborly, hospitable, companionable, comradely, sociable, convivial, outgoing, gregarious; informal chummy.
ANTONYMS unfriendly.

genius ▶ noun **1** *the world knew of his genius* **brilliance,** intelligence, intellect, ability, cleverness, brains, erudition, wisdom, fine mind; artistry, flair.
ANTONYMS stupidity.
2 *she has a genius for organization* **talent,** gift, flair, aptitude, facility, knack, bent, ability, expertise, capacity, faculty; strength, forte, brilliance, skill, artistry.
3 *he is a genius* **brilliant person,** gifted person, mastermind, Einstein, intellectual, great intellect, brain, mind; prodigy; informal egghead, bright spark, brainiac, rocket scientist.
ANTONYMS dunce.

genre ▶ noun *historical fiction is my favorite genre of literature* **category,** class, classification, group, set, list; type, sort, kind, breed, variety, style, model, school, stamp, cast, ilk.

genteel ▶ adjective *she never quite fit in with Harold's genteel family* **refined,** respectable, decorous, mannerly, well-mannered, courteous, polite, proper, correct, seemly; well-bred, cultured, sophisticated, ladylike, gentlemanly, dignified, gracious; affected. See note at **URBANE**.
ANTONYMS uncouth.

gentility ▶ noun *an air of old-fashioned gentility* **refinement,** distinction, breeding, sophistication; respectability, punctiliousness, decorum, good manners, politeness, civility, courtesy, graciousness, correctness; affectation, ostentation.

gentle ▶ adjective **1** *his manner was gentle* **kind,** tender, sympathetic, considerate, understanding, compassionate, benevolent, good-natured; humane, lenient, merciful, clement; mild, placid, serene, sweet-tempered.
ANTONYMS brutal.
2 *a gentle breeze* **light,** soft.
ANTONYMS strong.
3 *a gentle slope* **gradual,** slight, easy.
ANTONYMS steep.
4 archaic *a woman of gentle birth* See **NOBLE** (sense 1 of the adjective).

gentlemanly ▶ adjective *gentlemanly manners came naturally to him* **chivalrous,** gallant, honorable, noble, courteous, civil, mannerly, polite, gracious, considerate, thoughtful; well-bred, cultivated, cultured, refined, suave, urbane.
ANTONYMS rude.

genuine ▶ adjective **1** *a genuine Picasso* **authentic,** real, actual, original, bona fide, true, veritable; attested, undisputed; informal the real McCoy, honest-to-goodness, honest-to-God, the real thing, kosher.
ANTONYMS bogus.
2 *a genuine person* **sincere,** honest, truthful, straightforward, direct, frank, candid, open; artless, natural, unaffected; informal straight, upfront, on the level, on the up and up.
ANTONYMS insincere.

CHOOSE THE RIGHT WORD

genuine, actual, authentic, bona fide, legitimate, veritable

A car salesperson might claim that the seats of that pricey sedan you're considering are made from **genuine** leather, a word that applies to anything that is really what it is claimed or represented to be. If you're in the market for a Model T Ford, however, you'll want to make sure that the car is **authentic**, which emphasizes formal proof or documentation that an object is what it is claimed to be. Use **bona fide** when sincerity is involved (*a bona fide offer*), and **legitimate** when you mean lawful or in accordance with established rules, principles, and standards (*a legitimate business*). **Veritable** implies correspondence with the truth but not necessarily a literal or strict correspondence with reality (*a veritable supermarket for car-buyers*). How will it feel to drive that Mercedes out of the showroom? You won't know until you're the **actual** owner of the car—a word that means existing in fact rather than in the imagination.

genus ▶ noun **1** Biology *a large genus of plants* **subdivision,** division, group, subfamily.
2 *a new genus of music* **type,** sort, kind, genre, style, variety, category, class; breed, brand, family, stamp, cast, ilk.

germ ▶ noun **1** *this detergent kills germs* **microbe,** microorganism, bacillus, bacterium, virus; informal bug.
2 *a fertilized germ* **embryo,** bud; seed, spore, ovule; egg, ovum.
3 *the germ of an idea* **start,** beginning(s), seed, embryo, bud, root, rudiment; origin, source, potential; core, nucleus, kernel, essence.

germane ▶ adjective *your question is not germane to the topic at hand* **relevant,** pertinent, applicable, apposite, material; apropos, appropriate, apt, fitting, suitable; connected, related, akin.
ANTONYMS irrelevant.

germinate ▶ verb **1** *the grain is allowed to germinate* **sprout,** shoot (up), bud; develop, grow, spring up; dated vegetate.
2 *the idea began to germinate* **develop,** take root, grow, incubate, emerge, evolve, mature, expand, advance, progress.

gestation ▶ noun **1** *a gestation of thirty days* **pregnancy,** incubation; development, maturation.
2 *the law underwent a period of gestation* **development,** evolution, formation, emergence, origination.

gesticulate ▶ verb *they frantically gesticulated to get someone's attention* **gesture,** signal, motion, wave, sign.

gesture ▶ noun **1** *a gesture of surrender* **signal,** sign, motion, indication, gesticulation; show.
2 *a symbolic gesture* **action,** act, deed, move.
▶ verb *he gestured to her* **signal,** motion, gesticulate, wave, indicate, give a sign.

get ▶ verb **1** *where did you get that hat?* **acquire,** obtain, come by, receive, gain, earn, win, come into, take possession of, be given; buy, purchase, procure, secure; gather, collect, pick up, hook, net, land; achieve, attain; informal get one's hands on, get one's mitts on, get hold of, grab, bag, score.
ANTONYMS give.
2 *I got your letter* **receive,** be sent, be in receipt of, be given.
ANTONYMS send.
3 *your tea's getting cold* **become,** grow, turn, go.
4 *get the children from school* **fetch,** collect, go for, call for, pick up, bring, deliver, convey, ferry, transport.
ANTONYMS leave.
5 *the chairman gets $650,000 a year* **earn,** be paid, take home, bring in, make, receive, collect, gross; informal pocket, bank, rake in, net, bag.
6 *have the police got their man?* **apprehend,** catch, arrest, capture, seize; take prisoner, take into custody, detain, put in jail, put behind bars, imprison, incarcerate; informal collar, grab, nab, nail, run in, pinch, bust, pick up, pull in.
7 *I got a taxi* **travel by/on/in;** take, catch, use.
8 *she got the flu* **succumb to,** develop, come/go down with, get sick with, fall victim to, be struck down with, be afflicted by/with; become infected with, catch, contract, fall ill with, be taken ill with.
9 *I got a pain in my arm* **experience,** suffer, be afflicted with, sustain, feel, have.
10 *I got him on the radio* **contact,** get in touch with, communicate with, make contact with, reach; phone, call, radio; speak to, talk to; informal get hold of.
11 *I didn't get what he said* **hear,** discern, distinguish, make out, perceive, follow, take in.
12 *I don't get the joke* **understand,** comprehend, grasp, see, fathom, follow, perceive, apprehend, unravel, decipher; informal get the drift of, catch on to, latch on to, figure out.
13 *we got there early* **arrive,** reach, come, make it, turn up, appear, come on the scene, approach, enter, present oneself, come along, materialize, show one's face; informal show (up), roll in/up, blow in.
14 *we got her to go* **persuade,** induce, prevail on/upon, influence.
15 *I'd like to get to meet him* **contrive,** arrange, find a way, manage; informal work it, fix it.
16 *I'll get supper* **prepare,** get ready, cook, make, assemble, muster, concoct; informal fix, rustle up.
17 informal *I'll get him for that* **take revenge on,** exact/wreak revenge on, get one's revenge on, avenge oneself on, take vengeance on, get even with, pay back, get back at, exact retribution on, give someone their just deserts.
18 *you really got me with that third question* **baffle,** perplex, puzzle, bewilder, mystify, bemuse, confuse, confound; informal flummox, faze, stump, beat, fox, discombobulate.
19 *what gets me is how neurotic she is* **annoy,** irritate, exasperate, anger, irk, vex, provoke, incense, infuriate, madden, try someone's patience, ruffle someone's feathers; informal aggravate, peeve, miff, rile, get to, needle, get someone's back up, get on someone's nerves, get someone's goat, drive mad, make someone see red, tee off, tick off.

– PHRASES **get about** *he uses a wheelchair to get about* **move about,** move around, travel. **get across** *a photo will help you get the message across* **communicate,** impart, convey, transmit, make clear, express. **get ahead** *the desire to get ahead* **prosper,** flourish, thrive, do well; succeed, make it, advance, get on in the world, go up in the world, make good, become rich; informal go places, get somewhere, make the big time. **get along 1** *can't you try to get along with his family?* **be friendly,** be compatible, get on; agree, see eye to eye, concur, be in accord; informal hit it off, be on the same wavelength. **2** *she was getting along well at school* **fare,** manage, progress, advance, get on, get by, do, cope; succeed. **get around** *Toby really gets around* **travel,** circulate, socialize, do the rounds. **get at 1** *it's difficult to get at the pipes* **access,** get to, reach, touch. **2** *she had been got at by enemy agents* **corrupt,** suborn, influence, bribe, buy off, pay off; informal fix, square. **3** informal *what are you getting at?* **imply,** suggest, intimate, insinuate, hint, mean, drive at, allude to. **get away** *the prisoners got away* **escape,** run away/off, break out, break free, break loose, bolt, flee, take flight, make off, take off, decamp, abscond, make a run for it; slip away, sneak away; informal cut and run, skedaddle, do a disappearing act. **get away with** *he's been getting away with every kind of wrongdoing since he was three* **escape blame for,** escape punishment for. **get back 1** *they should get back before dawn* **return,** come home, come back. **2** *she got her gloves back from the lost and found* **retrieve,** regain, win back, recover, recoup, reclaim, repossess, recapture, redeem; find (again), trace. **get back at** *she wasted years of her life thinking about getting back at her ex-husband* **take revenge on,** exact/wreak revenge on, avenge oneself on, take vengeance on, get even with, pay back, retaliate on/against, exact retribution on, give someone their just deserts. **get by** *he had just enough money to get by* **manage,** cope, survive, exist, subsist, muddle through/along, scrape by, make ends meet, make do, keep the wolf from the door; informal make out. **get down** *her poetry always gets me down* **depress,** sadden, make unhappy, make gloomy, dispirit, dishearten, demoralize, discourage, crush, weigh down, oppress; upset, distress; informal give someone the blues, make someone fed up. **get off 1** *Sally got off the bus* **step off,** alight (from), dismount (from), descend (from), disembark (from), leave, exit. **2** informal *he was arrested but got off* **escape punishment,** be acquitted, be absolved, be cleared, be exonerated. **get on 1** *we got on the train* **board,** enter, step aboard, climb on, mount, ascend, catch; informal hop on, jump on. **2** *how are you getting on?* **fare,** manage, progress, get along, do, cope, get by, survive, muddle through/along; succeed, prosper; informal make out. **get on with** *she got on with her job* **continue (with),** proceed with, go ahead with, carry on with, go on with, press on with, persist with/in, persevere with; keep at; informal stick with/at. **get out** *the news got out* **become known,** become common knowledge, come to light, emerge, transpire; come out, be uncovered, be revealed, be divulged, be disseminated, be disclosed, be reported, be released, leak out. **get out of** *how do you plan to get out of this mess?* **evade,** dodge, shirk, avoid, escape, sidestep; informal duck (out of), wriggle out of, cop out of. **get over 1** *I just got over the flu* **recover from,** recuperate from, get better after, shrug off, survive. **2** *we tried to get over this problem* **overcome,** surmount, get the better of, master, find an/the answer to, get a grip on, deal with, cope with, sort out, take care of, crack, rise above; informal lick. **get together 1** *get together the best writers* **collect,** gather, assemble, bring together, rally, muster, marshal, congregate, convene, amass; formal convoke. **2** *we must get together soon* **meet,** meet up, rendezvous, see each other, socialize. **get up** *he seldom gets up before noon* **get out of bed,** rise, stir, rouse oneself; informal surface; formal arise.

CHOOSE THE RIGHT WORD

get, acquire, attain, gain, obtain, procure, secure

Get is a very broad term meaning to come into possession of. You can *get* something by fetching it (*get some groceries*), by receiving it (*get a birthday gift*), by earning it (*get interest on a bank loan*), or by any of a dozen other familiar means. It is such a common, over-used word that many writers try to substitute **obtain** for it whenever possible, perhaps because it sounds less colloquial. But it can also sound pretentious (*all employees were required to obtain an annual physical exam*) and should be reserved for contexts where the emphasis is on seeking something out (*to obtain blood samples*). **Acquire** often suggests a continued, sustained, or cumulative acquisition (*to acquire poise as one matures*), but it can also hint at deviousness (*to acquire the keys to the safe*). Use **procure** if you want to emphasize the effort involved in bringing something to pass (*procure a mediated divorce settlement*) or if you want to imply maneuvering to possess something (*procure a reserved parking space*). But beware: *Procure* is so often used to describe the act of obtaining partners to gratify the lust of others (*to procure a prostitute*) that it has acquired somewhat unsavory overtones. **Gain** also implies effort, usually in *getting* something advantageous or profitable (*gain entry, gain victory*). In a similar vein, **secure** underscores the difficulty involved in bringing something to pass and the desire to place it beyond danger (*secure a permanent peace; secure a lifeline*). **Attain** should be reserved for achieving a high goal or desirable result (*If she attains the summit of Mt. Everest, she will secure for herself a place in mountaineering history*).

getaway ▸ **noun** *he made his getaway in broad daylight* **escape,** breakout, bolt for freedom, flight; disappearance, vanishing act.

get-together ▸ **noun** *a friendly get-together at Pete's house* **party,** meeting, gathering, social event, social; informal do, bash.

getup ▸ **noun** informal *check out Stacey's wild getup* **outfit,** clothes, costume, ensemble, suit, clothing, dress, attire, garments, garb; informal gear, togs, duds, threads; formal apparel.

get-up-and-go ▸ **noun** informal *your grandfather has more get-up-and-go than you do* **drive,** initiative, enterprise, enthusiasm, eagerness, ambition, motivation, dynamism, energy, gusto, vim, vigor, vitality, verve, fire, fervor, zeal, commitment, spirit; informal gumption, oomph, pep.

ANTONYMS apathy.

ghastly ▸ **adjective 1** *a ghastly stabbing* **terrible,** horrible, grim, awful, dire; frightening, terrifying, horrifying, alarming; distressing, shocking, appalling, harrowing; dreadful, frightful, horrendous, monstrous, gruesome, grisly; informal gut-wrenching.

ANTONYMS pleasant.

2 informal *a ghastly building* **unpleasant,** objectionable, disagreeable, distasteful, awful, terrible, dreadful, detestable, insufferable, vile; informal horrible, horrid.

ANTONYMS charming.

3 *a ghastly pallor* **pale,** white, pallid, pasty, wan, bloodless, peaked, ashen, gray, waxy, blanched, drained, pinched, green, sickly, ghostly, ghostlike; informal like death warmed over.
ANTONYMS ruddy, healthy.

ghost ▶ **noun 1** *his ghost haunts the crypt* **specter,** phantom, wraith, spirit, presence; apparition; informal spook.
2 *the ghost of a smile* **trace,** hint, suggestion, impression, suspicion, tinge; glimmer, semblance, shadow, whisper.

ghostly ▶ **adjective** *a ghostly vision at the end of the hallway* **spectral,** ghostlike, phantom, wraithlike, phantasmal, phantasmic; unearthly, unnatural, supernatural; insubstantial, shadowy; eerie, weird, uncanny; frightening, spine-chilling, hair-raising, blood-curdling, bone-chilling, terrifying, chilling, sinister; informal creepy, scary, spooky.

giant ▶ **noun** *the mythical giant of the forest* **colossus,** behemoth, Brobdingnagian, mammoth, monster, leviathan, titan; giantess; informal jumbo, whopper.
ANTONYMS dwarf.
▶ **adjective** *a giant balloon* **huge,** colossal, massive, enormous, gigantic, very big, mammoth, vast, immense, monumental, mountainous, titanic, towering, elephantine, king-size(d), economy-size(d), gargantuan, Brobdingnagian; substantial, hefty; informal mega, monster, whopping, humongous, jumbo, hulking, bumper, ginormous.
ANTONYMS miniature.

gibberish ▶ **noun** *am I going deaf, or is she speaking gibberish?* **nonsense,** garbage, balderdash, blather, rubbish; informal drivel, gobbledygook, mumbo-jumbo, tripe, hogwash, baloney, bilge, bull, bunk, guff, eyewash, piffle, twaddle, poppycock.

giddy ▶ **adjective 1** *just one beer would make him feel giddy* **dizzy,** lightheaded, faint, weak, vertiginous; unsteady, shaky, wobbly; informal woozy.
ANTONYMS steady.
2 *she was young and giddy* **flighty,** silly, frivolous, skittish, irresponsible, flippant, whimsical, capricious; featherbrained, scatty, thoughtless, heedless, carefree; informal dippy, ditzy, flaky.
ANTONYMS sensible.

gift ▶ **noun 1** *he gave the staff a gift* **present,** handout, donation, offering, bestowal, bonus, award, endowment; tip, gratuity; largesse; informal freebie, perk; formal benefaction. See note at **PRESENT**[3].
2 *Marlin possessed a gift for interior design* **talent,** flair, aptitude, facility, knack, bent, ability, expertise, capacity, capability, faculty; endowment, strength, genius, brilliance, skill, artistry.
▶ **verb** *he gifted a composition to the orchestra* **present,** give, bestow, confer, donate, endow, award, accord, grant; hand over, make over.

gifted ▶ **adjective** *a gifted young percussionist* **talented,** skillful, skilled, accomplished, expert, consummate, master(ly), virtuoso, first-rate, able, apt, adept, proficient; intelligent, clever, bright, brilliant; precocious; informal crack, top-notch, ace.
ANTONYMS inept.

gigantic ▶ **adjective** *the new houses on Long Hill Road are gigantic* **huge,** enormous, vast, extensive, very big, very large, giant, massive, colossal, mammoth, immense, monumental, mountainous, titanic, towering, elephantine, king-size(d), economy-size(d), gargantuan; informal mega, monster, whopping, humongous, jumbo, hulking, bumper, ginormous.
ANTONYMS tiny.

giggle ▶ **noun & verb** *she suppressed a giggle | he giggled at the picture* **titter,** snigger, snicker, tee-hee, chuckle, chortle, laugh.

gigolo ▶ **noun** *she was mortified to learn her husband had been a gigolo in LA when he was twenty-something* **playboy,** escort, male escort, paid escort; lover; informal toy boy.

gild ▶ **verb 1** *she gilded the picture frame* **gold-plate;** cover with gold, paint gold.
2 *he tends to gild the truth* **elaborate,** embellish, embroider; camouflage, disguise, dress up, color, exaggerate, expand on; informal jazz up.

gimcrack ▶ **adjective** *they lived in gimcrack villas you'd be afraid to sneeze in* **shoddy,** jerry-built, flimsy, insubstantial, thrown together, makeshift; inferior, poor-quality, second-rate, cheap, cheapjack; tawdry, kitsch, kitschy, chintzy, trashy, dime-store; informal tacky, junky, cheapo, schlocky.

gimmick ▶ **noun** *the trivia contest was a gimmick to sell more newspapers* **publicity stunt,** contrivance, scheme, stratagem, ploy; informal shtick.

gingerly ▶ **adverb** *he stepped gingerly on to the ice* **cautiously,** carefully, with care, warily, charily, circumspectly, delicately; heedfully, watchfully, vigilantly, attentively; hesitantly, timidly.
ANTONYMS recklessly.

gird ▶ **verb 1** *the island was girded by rocks* **surround,** enclose, encircle, circle, encompass, border, bound, edge, skirt, fringe; close in, confine.
2 *they girded themselves for war* **prepare,** get ready, gear up; nerve, steel, galvanize, brace, fortify; informal psych oneself up.

girdle ▶ **noun 1** *her stockings were held up by her girdle* **corset,** panty girdle, corselet, foundation garment; truss.
2 *a diamond-studded girdle* **belt,** sash, cummerbund, waistband, strap, band, girth, cord.
▶ **verb** *a garden girdled the house* **surround,** enclose, encircle, circle, encompass, circumscribe, border, bound, skirt, edge; literary gird.

girl ▶ **noun 1** *a five-year-old girl* **female child,** daughter; schoolgirl; Scottish lass, lassie. See also **CHILD**.
2 *he settled down with a nice girl* **young woman,** young lady, miss, mademoiselle; Scottish lass, lassie; informal chick, gal, grrrl, babe; literary maid, damsel, ingénue.
3 *his girl left him* **girlfriend**.

girth ▶ **noun 1** *a tree ten feet in girth* **circumference,** perimeter; width, breadth.
2 *he tied the towel around his girth* **stomach,** midriff, middle, abdomen, belly, gut; informal tummy, tum.
3 *a horse's girth* cinch.

gist ▶ noun *the gist of her essay is an indictment of the religious right* **essence,** substance, central theme, heart of the matter, nub, kernel, marrow, meat, burden, crux; thrust, drift, sense, meaning, significance, import; informal nitty-gritty.

give ▶ verb **1** *she gave them $2000* **present with,** provide with, supply with, furnish with, let someone have; hand (over to), offer, proffer; award, grant (to), bestow on/upon, accord, confer on, make over to; donate to, contribute to.
ANTONYMS receive, take.
2 *can I give him a message?* **convey to,** pass on to, impart to, communicate to, transmit to; send, deliver (to), relay to; tell (to).
3 *a baby given into their care* **entrust,** commit, consign, assign; formal commend.
4 *she gave her life for them* **sacrifice,** give up, relinquish; devote, dedicate.
5 *he gave her time to think* **allow,** permit, grant, accord; offer.
6 *this leaflet gives our opening times* **show,** display, set out, indicate, detail, list.
7 *they gave no further trouble* **cause,** make, create, occasion.
8 *garlic gives flavor* **produce,** yield, afford, impart, lend.
9 *she gave a party* **organize,** arrange, throw, host, hold, have, provide.
10 *Dominic gave a bow* **perform,** execute, make, do.
11 *she gave a shout* **utter,** let out, emit, produce, make.
12 *he gave Larry a beating* **administer,** deliver, deal, inflict, impose.
13 *the door gave* **give way,** cave in, collapse, break, fall apart; bend, buckle.
▶ noun informal *there isn't enough give in the jacket* **elasticity,** flexibility, stretch, stretchiness; slack, play.
– PHRASES **give away 1** *he refused to believe that his own sister had given him away* **betray,** inform on; informal rat on, blow the whistle on, sell down the river, rat out, finger.
2 *his face gave little away* **reveal,** disclose, divulge, let slip, leak, let out.
3 *Kellie gave away all of her possessions* **donate,** make a gift of, confer, contribute, will, bequeath; distribute; sacrifice; get rid of, dispose of, relent, throw in the towel/sponge.
give in *in the end, Dolan was forced to give in* **capitulate,** concede defeat, admit defeat, give up, surrender, yield, submit, back down, give way, defer, relent, throw in the towel.
give off *the lantern gives off a powerful glow* **emit,** produce, send out, throw out; discharge, release, exude, vent. **give out 1** *the gas reserves have finally given out* **run out,** be used up, be consumed, be exhausted, be depleted; fail, flag; dry up. **2** *thousands of leaflets were given out* **distribute,** issue, hand out, pass around, dispense; dole out, dish out, mete out; allocate, allot. **give up** *when did you give up drinking?* **stop,** cease, discontinue, desist from, abstain from, cut out, renounce, forgo; resign from, stand down from; informal quit, kick, swear off, leave off, pack in, lay off.

> CHOOSE THE RIGHT WORD
>
> **give, afford, award, bestow, confer, donate, grant**
>
> You **give** a birthday present, **grant** a favor, **bestow** charity, and **confer** an honor. While all of these verbs mean to convey something or transfer it from one's own possession to that of another, the circumstances surrounding that transfer dictate which word is the best one. *Give* is the most general, meaning to pass over, deliver, or transmit something (*give him encouragement*). *Grant* implies that a request or desire has been expressed, and that the receiver is dependent on the giver's discretion (*grant permission for the trip*). **Award** suggests that the giver is in some sense a judge, and that the thing given is deserved (*award a scholarship*), while *bestow* implies that something is given as a gift and may imply condescension on the part of the giver (*bestow a large sum of money on a needy charity*). To *confer* is to give an honor, a privilege, or a favor; it implies that the giver is a superior (*confer a knighthood; confer a college degree*). **Donate** implies that the giving is to a public cause or charity (*donate a painting to the local art museum*), and to **afford** is to give or bestow as a natural consequence (*the window afforded a fine view of the mountains*).

giver ▶ noun *Lynette threw her indolent nephews out of the house, vowing that her days as the "family giver" were over* **donor,** contributor, donator, benefactor, benefactress, provider; supporter, backer, patron, sponsor, subscriber.

glacial ▶ adjective **1** *glacial conditions* **freezing,** cold, icy, ice-cold, subzero, frozen, gelid, wintry; arctic, polar, Siberian, hypothermic; bitter, biting, raw; literary chill.
ANTONYMS tropical, hot.
2 *Beverly's tone was glacial* **unfriendly,** hostile, unwelcoming; frosty, icy, cold, chilly.
ANTONYMS warm, friendly.
3 *they proceeded at a glacial pace* **slow,** lugubrious, unhurried, leisurely, steady, sedate, slow-moving, plodding, dawdling, sluggish, sluggardly, lead-footed.
ANTONYMS fast, brisk.

glad ▶ adjective **1** *I'm really glad you're coming* **pleased,** happy, delighted, thrilled, overjoyed, elated, gleeful; gratified, grateful, thankful; informal tickled pink, over the moon.
ANTONYMS dismayed, annoyed.
2 *I'd be glad to help* **willing,** eager, happy, pleased, delighted; ready, prepared.
ANTONYMS unwilling, reluctant.
3 *glad tidings* **pleasing,** welcome, happy, joyful, cheering, heartening, gratifying.
ANTONYMS unwelcome, distressing.

gladden ▶ verb *it gladdens us to see you so happy* **delight,** please, make happy, elate; cheer, cheer up, hearten, buoy up, give someone a lift, uplift; gratify; informal tickle someone pink, buck up.
ANTONYMS sadden.

gladly ▶ adverb *we gladly accepted the senator's*

invitation **with pleasure,** happily, cheerfully; willingly, readily, eagerly, freely, ungrudgingly; archaic fain, lief.

glamorous ▶ adjective **1** *a glamorous woman* **beautiful,** attractive, lovely, bewitching, enchanting, beguiling; elegant, chic, stylish, fashionable; charming, charismatic, appealing, alluring, seductive; informal classy, glam.
ANTONYMS dowdy, drab.
2 *a glamorous lifestyle* **exciting,** thrilling, stimulating; dazzling, glittering, glossy, colorful, exotic; informal ritzy, glitzy, jet-setting.
ANTONYMS boring, dull.

glamour ▶ noun **1** *she had undeniable glamour* **beauty,** allure, attractiveness; elegance, chic, style; charisma, charm, magnetism, desirability.
2 *the glamour of show business* **allure,** attraction, fascination, charm, magic, romance, mystique, exoticism, spell; excitement, thrill; glitter, bright lights; informal glitz, glam, tinsel.

glance ▶ verb **1** *Rachel glanced at him* **look briefly,** look quickly, peek, peep; glimpse; informal have a gander.
2 *I* ***glanced through*** *the report* **read quickly,** scan, skim through, leaf through, flip through, thumb through, browse (through); dip into.
3 *a bullet* ***glanced off*** *the ice* **ricochet off,** rebound off, be deflected off, bounce off; graze, clip.
4 *sunlight glanced off her hair* **reflect,** flash, gleam, glint, glitter, glisten, glimmer, shimmer.
▶ noun *a glance at his watch* **peek,** peep, brief look, quick look, glimpse; informal gander.
– PHRASES **at first glance** *at first glance, the plastic stemware could have been mistaken for crystal* **on the face of it,** on the surface, at first sight, to the casual eye, to all appearances; apparently, seemingly, outwardly, superficially, it would seem, it appears, as far as one can see/tell, by all accounts.

glare ▶ verb **1** *she glared at him* **scowl,** glower, stare angrily, look daggers, frown, lower, give someone a black look, look threateningly; informal give someone a dirty look.
2 *the sun glared out of the sky* **blaze,** beam, shine brightly, be dazzling, be blinding.
▶ noun **1** *a cold glare* **scowl,** glower, angry stare, frown, black look, threatening look; informal dirty look.
2 *the harsh glare of the lights* **blaze,** dazzle, shine, beam; radiance, brilliance, luminescence.

glaring ▶ adjective **1** *glaring lights* **dazzling,** blinding, blazing, strong, bright, harsh.
ANTONYMS soft, dim.
2 *a glaring omission* **obvious,** conspicuous, unmistakable, inescapable, unmissable, striking; flagrant, blatant, outrageous, gross; overt, patent, transparent, manifest; informal standing/sticking out like a sore thumb.
ANTONYMS inconspicuous, minor.

glass ▶ noun **1** *a glass of water* **tumbler,** drinking vessel; goblet, flute, schooner, chalice.
2 *we sell china and glass* **glassware,** stemware, crystal, crystalware.

glasses ▶ plural noun *Hale looks older in his glasses* **eyeglasses,** eyewear, spectacles; informal specs; bifocals.

glassy ▶ adjective **1** *the glassy surface of the lake* **smooth,** mirrorlike, gleaming, shiny, glossy, polished, vitreous; slippery, icy; clear, transparent, translucent; calm, still, flat.
ANTONYMS rough.
2 *a glassy stare* **expressionless,** glazed, blank, vacant, fixed, motionless; emotionless, impassive, lifeless, wooden, vacuous.
ANTONYMS expressive.

glaze ▶ verb **1** *the pots are glazed when dry* **varnish,** enamel, lacquer, japan, shellac, paint; gloss.
2 *pastry glazed with caramel* **cover,** coat; ice, frost.
3 *his eyes glazed over* **become glassy,** go blank; mist over, film over.
▶ noun **1** *pottery with a blue glaze* **varnish,** enamel, lacquer, finish, coating; luster, shine, gloss.
2 *a cake with an apricot glaze* **coating,** topping; icing, frosting.

gleam ▶ verb *the new silver tea service positively gleams* **shine,** glimmer, glint, glitter, shimmer, sparkle, twinkle, flicker, wink, glisten, flash; literary glister.
▶ noun **1** *a gleam of light* **glimmer,** glint, shimmer, twinkle, sparkle, flicker, flash; beam, ray, shaft.
2 *the gleam of brass* **shine,** luster, gloss, sheen; glint, glitter, glimmer, sparkle; brilliance, radiance, glow; literary glister.
3 *a gleam of hope* **glimmer,** flicker, ray, spark, trace, suggestion, hint, sign.

glee ▶ noun *Agnes clapped her hands together with glee* **delight,** pleasure, happiness, joy, gladness, elation, euphoria; amusement, mirth, merriment; excitement, gaiety, exuberance; relish, triumph, jubilation, satisfaction, gratification.
ANTONYMS disappointment.

gleeful ▶ adjective *the gleeful bunch over there must have been rooting for the Patriots* **delighted,** pleased, joyful, happy, glad, overjoyed, elated, euphoric; amused, mirthful, merry, exuberant; jubilant; informal over the moon.

glib ▶ adjective *glib phrases rolled off his tongue* **slick,** pat, fast-talking, smooth-talking; disingenuous, insincere, facile, shallow, superficial, flippant; smooth, silver-tongued, urbane; informal flip, sweet-talking. See note at TALKATIVE.
ANTONYMS sincere.

glide ▶ verb **1** *a gondola glided past* **slide,** slip, sail, float, drift, flow; coast, freewheel, roll; skim, skate.
2 *seagulls gliding over the waves* **soar,** wheel, plane; fly.
3 *he glided out of the door* **slip,** steal, slink.

glimmer ▶ verb *moonlight glimmered on the lawn* **gleam,** shine, glint, flicker, shimmer, glisten, glow, twinkle, sparkle, glitter, wink, flash; literary glister.
▶ noun **1** *a glimmer of light* **gleam,** glint, flicker, shimmer, glow, twinkle, sparkle, flash, ray.
2 *a glimmer of hope* **gleam,** flicker, ray, trace, sign, suggestion, hint.

glimpse ▶ noun *a glimpse of her face* **brief look,** quick look; glance, peek, peep; sight, sighting.
▶ verb *he glimpsed a figure* **catch sight of,** notice, discern, spot, spy, sight, pick out, make out; literary espy, descry.

glint ▶ verb *the diamond glinted* **shine,** gleam,

catch the light, glitter, sparkle, twinkle, wink, glimmer, shimmer, glisten, flash; literary glister.
▶ noun *the glint of the silver* **glitter,** gleam, sparkle, twinkle, glimmer, flash.

glisten ▶ verb *the sea glistened in the morning light* **shine,** sparkle, twinkle, glint, glitter, glimmer, shimmer, wink, flash; literary glister.

glitter ▶ verb *crystal glittered in the candlelight* **shine,** sparkle, twinkle, glint, gleam, shimmer, glimmer, wink, flash, catch the light; literary glister.
▶ noun 1 *the glitter of light on the water* **sparkle,** twinkle, glint, gleam, shimmer, glimmer, flicker, flash; brilliance, luminescence.
2 *the glitter of show business* **glamour,** excitement, thrills, attraction, appeal; dazzle; informal razzle-dazzle, razzmatazz, glitz, ritziness.

gloat ▶ verb *Richard's been gloating ever since he won the lottery* **delight,** relish, take great pleasure, revel, rejoice, glory, exult, triumph, crow; boast, brag, be smug, congratulate oneself, preen oneself, pat oneself on the back; rub one's hands together; informal rub it in.

global ▶ adjective 1 *the global economy* **worldwide,** international, world, intercontinental.
2 *a global view of the problem* **comprehensive,** overall, general, all-inclusive, all-encompassing, encyclopedic, universal, blanket; broad, far-reaching, extensive, sweeping.

globe ▶ noun 1 *every corner of the globe* **world,** earth, planet.
2 *the sun is a globe* **sphere,** orb, ball, spheroid, round.

globule ▶ noun *a globule of gravy on the tablecloth* **droplet,** drop, bead, tear, ball, bubble, pearl; informal blob, glob.

gloom ▶ noun 1 *she peered into the gloom* **darkness,** dark, dimness, blackness, murkiness, shadows, shade; dusk, twilight, gloaming.
ANTONYMS light.
2 *his gloom deepened* **despondency,** depression, dejection, melancholy, melancholia, downheartedness, unhappiness, sadness, glumness, gloominess, misery, sorrow, woe, wretchedness; despair, pessimism, hopelessness; informal the blues, the dumps.
ANTONYMS happiness.

gloomy ▶ adjective 1 *a gloomy room* **dark,** shadowy, sunless, dim, somber, dingy, dismal, dreary, murky, unwelcoming, cheerless, comfortless, funereal; literary Stygian.
ANTONYMS bright, sunny.
2 *Joanna looked gloomy* **despondent,** downcast, downhearted, dejected, dispirited, disheartened, discouraged, demoralized, crestfallen; depressed, desolate, low, sad, unhappy, glum, melancholy, miserable, woebegone, mournful, forlorn, morose; informal blue, down in/at the mouth, down in the dumps; literary dolorous.
ANTONYMS happy, cheerful.
3 *gloomy forecasts about the economy* **pessimistic,** depressing, downbeat, disheartening, disappointing; unfavorable, bleak, bad, black, somber, grim, cheerless, hopeless.
ANTONYMS upbeat, optimistic.

glorify ▶ verb 1 *they gather to glorify God* **praise,** extol, exalt, worship, revere, reverence, venerate, pay homage to, honor, adore, thank, give thanks to; formal laud; archaic magnify.
2 *a poem to glorify the memory of the dead* **ennoble,** exalt, elevate, dignify, enhance, augment, promote; praise, celebrate, honor, extol, lionize, acclaim, applaud, hail; glamorize, idealize, romanticize, enshrine, immortalize; formal laud.
ANTONYMS dishonor.

glorious ▶ adjective 1 *a glorious victory* **illustrious,** celebrated, famous, acclaimed, distinguished, honored; outstanding, great, magnificent, noble, triumphant.
ANTONYMS undistinguished.
2 *glorious views* **wonderful,** marvelous, magnificent, superb, sublime, spectacular, lovely, fine, delightful; informal super, great, stunning, fantastic, terrific, tremendous, sensational, heavenly, divine, gorgeous, fabulous, fab, awesome, ace, killer; literary wondrous, beauteous.
ANTONYMS miserable, horrid.

glory ▶ noun 1 *a sport that won him glory* **renown,** fame, prestige, honor, distinction, kudos, eminence, acclaim, praise; celebrity, recognition, reputation; informal bouquets.
ANTONYMS shame, obscurity.
2 *glory to the Lord* **praise,** worship, adoration, veneration, honor, reverence, exaltation, homage, thanksgiving, thanks.
3 *a house restored to its former glory* **magnificence,** splendor, resplendence, grandeur, majesty, greatness, nobility; opulence, beauty, elegance.
ANTONYMS lowliness, modesty.
4 *the glories of Vermont* **wonder,** beauty, delight, marvel, phenomenon; sight, spectacle.
▶ verb *we **gloried in** our independence* **take pleasure in,** revel in, rejoice in, delight in; relish, savor; congratulate oneself on, be proud of, boast about, bask in; informal get a kick out of, get a thrill out of.

gloss[1] ▶ noun 1 *the gloss of her hair* **shine,** sheen, luster, gleam, patina, brilliance, shimmer. See note at POLISH.
2 *beneath the gloss of success* **facade,** veneer, surface, show, camouflage, disguise, mask, smokescreen; window dressing.
▶ verb 1 *she glossed her lips* **make glossy,** shine; glaze, polish, burnish.
2 *he tried to **gloss over** his problems* **conceal,** cover up, hide, disguise, mask, veil; shrug off, brush aside, play down, minimize, understate, make light of; informal brush under the carpet.

gloss[2] ▶ noun *glosses in the margin* **explanation,** interpretation, exegesis, explication, elucidation; annotation, note, footnote, commentary, comment, rubric; translation, definition; historical scholium.
▶ verb *difficult words are glossed in a footnote* **explain,** interpret, explicate, define, elucidate; annotate; translate, paraphrase.

glossy ▶ adjective 1 *a glossy wooden floor* **shiny,** gleaming, lustrous, brilliant, shimmering, glistening, satiny, sheeny, smooth, glassy; polished, lacquered, glazed.

ANTONYMS dull, lusterless.
2 *a glossy magazine* **expensive,** high-quality; stylish, fashionable, glamorous; attractive, artistic, upmarket; informal classy, ritzy, glitzy.
ANTONYMS downmarket, cheap.

glow ▶ verb 1 *lights glowed from the windows* **shine,** radiate, gleam, glimmer, flicker, flare; luminesce.
2 *a fire glowed in the hearth* **radiate heat,** smolder, burn.
3 *she glowed with embarrassment* **flush,** blush, redden, color (up), go pink, go scarlet; burn.
4 *she glowed with pride* **tingle,** thrill; beam.
▶ noun 1 *the glow of the fire* **radiance,** light, shine, gleam, glimmer, incandescence, luminescence; warmth, heat.
2 *a glow spread over her face* **flush,** blush, rosiness, pinkness, redness, high color; bloom, radiance.
ANTONYMS pallor.
3 *a warm glow deep inside her* **happiness,** contentment, pleasure, satisfaction.

glower ▶ verb *she glowered at him* **scowl,** glare, look daggers, frown, lower, give someone a black look; informal give someone a dirty look.
▶ noun *the glower on his face* **scowl,** glare, frown, black look; informal dirty look.

glowing ▶ adjective 1 *glowing coals* **bright,** shining, radiant, glimmering, flickering, twinkling, incandescent, luminous, luminescent; lit (up), lighted, illuminated, ablaze; aglow, smoldering.
2 *his glowing cheeks* **rosy,** pink, red, flushed, blushing; radiant, blooming, ruddy, florid; hot, burning.
3 *glowing colors* **vivid,** vibrant, bright, brilliant, rich, intense, strong, radiant, warm.
4 *a glowing report* **complimentary,** favorable, enthusiastic, positive, commendatory, admiring, lionizing, rapturous, rhapsodic, adulatory; fulsome; informal rave.

glue ▶ noun *a tube of glue* **adhesive,** fixative, gum, paste, cement; epoxy, epoxy resin, size, sizing, mucilage, stickum.
▶ verb 1 *the planks were glued together* **stick,** gum, paste; affix, fix, cement, bond.
2 informal *she* ***is glued to*** *the television* **be riveted to,** be gripped by, be hypnotized by, be mesmerized by.

glum ▶ adjective *Gary sure looks glum today* **gloomy,** downcast, downhearted, dejected, despondent, crestfallen, disheartened; depressed, desolate, unhappy, doleful, melancholy, miserable, woebegone, mournful, forlorn, in the doldrums, morose; informal blue, down in/at the mouth, in a blue funk, down in the dumps.
ANTONYMS cheerful.

CHOOSE THE RIGHT WORD

glum, doleful, dour, lugubrious, melancholy, saturnine, sullen

All happy people are alike, to paraphrase Tolstoy, but each unhappy person is unhappy in his or her own way. A **sullen** person is gloomy, untalkative, and ill-humored by nature; a **glum** person is usually silent because of low spirits or depressing circumstances (*to be glum in the face of a plummeting stock market*). **Melancholy** suggests a more or less chronic sadness (*her melancholy was the result of an unhappy childhood*), while a person who is **saturnine** has a forbiddingly gloomy and taciturn nature (*his request was met with a saturnine and scornful silence*). **Dour** refers to a grim and bitter outlook or disposition (*a dour old woman who never smiled*), and **doleful** implies a mournful sadness (*the child's doleful expression as his parents left*). Someone or something described as **lugubrious** is mournful or gloomy in an affected or exaggerated way (*lugubrious songs about lost love*).

glut ▶ noun *a glut of cars* **surplus,** excess, surfeit, superfluity, overabundance, superabundance, oversupply, plethora.
ANTONYMS dearth.
▶ verb *the factories are glutted* **overload,** cram, cram full, overfill, oversupply, saturate, flood, inundate, deluge, swamp, congest; informal stuff.

glutinous ▶ adjective *a glutinous white liquid* **sticky,** viscous, viscid, tacky, gluey, gummy, treacly; adhesive; informal gooey, cloggy, gloppy.

glutton ▶ noun *I can barely stomach being at the same table with that glutton* **gourmand,** overeater, big eater, gorger, gobbler; informal pig, greedy pig, guzzler.

gluttonous ▶ adjective *doesn't anyone ever feed those gluttonous children?* **greedy,** gourmandizing, voracious, insatiable, wolfish; informal piggish, piggy. See note at GREEDY.

gluttony ▶ noun *the gluttony you displayed last evening was reprehensible* **greed,** greediness, overeating, gourmandism, gourmandizing, voracity, insatiability; informal piggishness.

gnarled ▶ adjective 1 *a gnarled tree trunk* **knobbly,** knotty, knotted, gnarly, lumpy, bumpy, nodular; twisted, bent, crooked, distorted, contorted.
2 *gnarled hands* **twisted,** bent, misshapen; arthritic; rough, wrinkled, wizened.

gnash ▶ verb *she wailed and gnashed her teeth* **grind,** grate, rasp, grit; archaic gristbite.

gnaw ▶ verb 1 *the dog gnawed at a bone* **chew,** chomp, champ, bite, munch, crunch; nibble.
2 *the pressures are* ***gnawing away at*** *their independence* **erode,** wear away, wear down, eat away (at); consume, devour.
3 *the doubts* ***gnawed at*** *her* **nag,** plague, torment, torture, trouble, distress, worry, haunt, oppress, burden, hang over, bother, fret; niggle at.

go ▶ verb 1 *he's gone into town* **move,** proceed, make one's way, advance, progress, pass; walk, travel, journey; literary betake oneself.
2 *the road goes to Michigan Avenue* **extend,** stretch, reach; lead.
3 *the money will go to charity* **be given,** be donated, be granted, be presented, be awarded; be devoted; be handed (over).
4 *it's time to go* **leave,** depart, go away, withdraw, absent oneself, make an exit, exit; set off, start out, get underway, be on one's way; decamp, retreat, retire, make off, clear out, run off, run away, flee, make a move; informal make

tracks, push off, beat it, take off, skedaddle, scram, split, scoot.
ANTONYMS arrive, come.
5 *how quickly the years go by* **pass,** elapse, slip by/past, roll by/past, tick away; fly by/past.
6 *a golden age that has gone for good* **disappear,** vanish, be no more, cease to exist, come to an end, be over, run its course, fade away; finish, end, cease.
ANTONYMS return.
7 *when your money is gone, you'll come crawling back* **be used up,** be spent, be exhausted, be consumed, be drained, be depleted.
8 *I'd like to see my grandchildren before I go* **die,** pass away, pass on, lose one's life, expire, breathe one's last, perish, go to meet one's maker; informal give up the ghost, kick the bucket, croak, buy it, bite the big one, buy the farm, check out; archaic decease, depart this life.
9 *the bridge went suddenly* **collapse,** give way, fall down, cave in, crumble, disintegrate.
10 *his hair had gone gray* **become,** get, turn, grow.
11 *he heard the bell go* **make a sound,** sound, reverberate, resound; ring, chime, peal, toll, clang.
12 *everything went well* **turn out,** work out, develop, come out; result, end (up); informal pan out.
13 *those colors don't go* **match,** be harmonious, harmonize, blend, be suited, be complementary, coordinate, be compatible.
ANTONYMS clash.
14 *my car won't go* **function,** work, run, operate.
15 *where does the cutlery go?* **belong,** be kept.
16 *this all goes to prove my point* **contribute,** help, serve; incline, tend.
▶ **noun 1** *her second go* **attempt,** try, effort, bid, endeavor; informal shot, stab, crack, bash, whirl, whack; formal essay.
2 *he has plenty of go in him* **energy,** vigor, vitality, life, liveliness, spirit, verve, enthusiasm, zest, vibrancy, sparkle; stamina, dynamism, drive, push, determination; informal pep, punch, oomph, get-up-and-go.
– PHRASES **go about** *Ruth went about with her housework* **set about,** begin, embark on, start, commence, address oneself to, get down to, get to work on, get going on, undertake; approach, tackle, attack; informal get cracking on/with. **go along with** *I'm willing to go along with that idea* **agree to/with,** fall in with, comply with, cooperate with, acquiesce in, assent to, follow; submit to, yield to, defer to. **go around 1** *the wheels were going around* **spin,** revolve, turn, rotate, whirl. **2** *a nasty rumor is going around* **be spread,** be circulated, be put about, circulate, be broadcast. **go away** See GO (sense 4 of the verb). **go back on** *she went back on her promise* **renege on,** break, fail to honor, default on, repudiate, retract; do an about-face; informal cop out (of). **go by** *we have to go by his decision* **obey,** abide by, comply with, keep to, conform to, follow, heed, defer to, respect. **go down 1** *the ship went down* **sink,** founder, go under. **2** *interest rates are going down* **decrease,** get lower, fall, drop, decline; plummet, plunge, slump. **3** informal *they went down in the first round* **lose,** be beaten, be defeated. **4** *his name will go down in history* **be remembered,** be recorded, be commemorated, be immortalized. **go far** *stick with your aunts' company and you'll go far* **be successful,** succeed, be a success, do well, get on, get somewhere, get ahead, make good; informal make a name for oneself, make one's mark. **go for 1** *I went for the tuna* **choose,** pick, opt for, select, decide on, settle on. **2** *the dog went for her* **attack,** assault, hit, strike, beat up, assail, set upon, rush at, lash out at; informal lay into, rough up, have a go at, beat up on. **3** *she goes for younger men* **be attracted to,** like, fancy; prefer, favor, choose; informal have a thing about. **go in for** *until I got to San Juan, I'd never gone in for water sports* **take part in,** participate in, engage in, get involved in, join in, enter into, undertake; practice, pursue; espouse, adopt, embrace. **go into** *you should have gone into the subject more thoroughly* **investigate,** examine, inquire into, look into, research, probe, explore, delve into; consider, review, analyze. **go off** *the bomb went off* **explode,** detonate, blow up. **go on 1** *the lecture went on for hours* **last,** continue, carry on, run on, proceed; endure, persist; take. **2** *she went on about her cruise* **talk at length,** ramble, rattle on, chatter, prattle, blather, twitter; informal gab, yak, yabber, yatter, run off at the mouth, mouth off. **3** *I'm not sure what went on* **happen,** take place, occur, transpire; informal go down; literary come to pass, betide. **go out 1** *the lights went out* **be turned off,** be extinguished; stop burning. **2** *he's going out with Kate* **see,** date, take out, be someone's boyfriend/girlfriend, be involved with; informal go steady with, go with; dated court, woo, step out with. **go over 1** *go over the figures* **examine,** study, scrutinize, inspect, look at/over, scan, check; analyze, appraise, review. **2** *we are going over our lines* **rehearse,** practice, read through, run through. **go through 1** *the terrible things she has gone through* **undergo,** experience, face, suffer, be subjected to, live through, endure, brave, bear, tolerate, withstand, put up with, cope with, weather. **2** *she went through hundreds of dollars* **spend,** use up, run through, get through, expend, deplete, burn up; waste, squander, fritter away. **3** *she went through Sue's bag* **search,** look through, hunt through, rummage in/through, rifle through. **4** *I have to go through the report* **examine,** study, scrutinize, inspect, look over, scan, check; analyze, appraise, review. **5** *the deal has gone through* **be completed,** be concluded, be brought off; be approved, be signed, be rubber-stamped, be given the green light. **go under** *another local restaurant has gone under* **go bankrupt,** be shut (down), go into receivership, go into liquidation, become insolvent, be liquidated, cease trading; fail; informal go broke, go belly up, fold. **go without 1** *I went without breakfast* **abstain from,** refrain from, forgo, do without, deny oneself. **2** *the children did not go without* **be deprived,** be in want, go short, go hungry, be in need.

goad ▶ noun 1 *he applied his goad to the cows* **prod,** spike, staff, crook, rod.
2 *a goad to political change* **stimulus,** incentive, encouragement, inducement, fillip, spur, prod, prompt, catalyst; motive, motivation.
▶ verb *we were goaded into action* **provoke,** spur, prod, egg on, hound, badger, incite, rouse, stir, move, stimulate, motivate, prompt, induce, encourage, urge, inspire; impel, pressure, dragoon.

go-ahead informal ▶ noun *they gave the go-ahead for the scheme* **permission,** consent, leave, license, dispensation, warrant, clearance; authorization, assent, agreement, approval, endorsement, sanction, blessing, nod; informal thumbs up, OK, green light.
▶ adjective *go-ahead companies* **enterprising,** resourceful, innovative, ingenious, original, creative; progressive, pioneering, modern, forward-looking, enlightened; enthusiastic, ambitious, entrepreneurial, high-powered; bold, daring, audacious, adventurous, dynamic; informal go-getting.

goal ▶ noun *I never numbered wealth as one of my goals* **objective,** aim, end, target, design, intention, intent, plan, purpose; (holy) grail; ambition, aspiration, wish, dream, brass ring, desire, hope.

goat ▶ noun 1 *a herd of goats* billy goat, nanny goat, kid.
2 *be careful of that old goat* **lecher,** libertine, womanizer, seducer, Don Juan, Casanova, Lothario, Romeo; pervert, debauchee, rake; informal lech, dirty old man, ladykiller, wolf.

gobble ▶ verb *must you gobble your food so? | he* ***gobbled down*** *every last crumb | the dogs* ***gobbled up*** *their kibble* **eat greedily, eat hungrily,** guzzle, bolt, gulp (down), devour, wolf (down), gorge (oneself) on; informal tuck into, put away, pack away, demolish, polish off, shovel in/down, stuff one's face with, pig out on; informal scoff (down/up), scarf (down/up), inhale; rare gluttonize, gourmandize, ingurgitate.

gobbledygook, gobbledegook ▶ noun informal *a letter full of legal gobbledygook* **gibberish,** claptrap, nonsense, rubbish, balderdash, blather, garbage; informal mumbo-jumbo, drivel, tripe, hogwash, baloney, bilge, bull, bunk, guff, eyewash, piffle, twaddle, poppycock, phooey, hooey.

go-between ▶ noun *history will recognize his skills as a go-between* **intermediary,** middleman, agent, broker, liaison, contact; negotiator, interceder, intercessor, mediator.

goblet ▶ noun *the goblets go on the right* **wine glass,** water glass, chalice; glass, tumbler, cup, beaker.

goblin ▶ noun *the goblins of Yekov would make their surreptitious jaunts into town every third moon* **hobgoblin,** gnome, dwarf, troll, imp, elf, brownie, fairy, pixie, leprechaun.

god ▶ noun 1 **(God)** *a gift from God* **the Lord,** the Almighty, the Creator, the Maker, the Godhead; Allah, Jehovah, Yahweh; (God) the Father, (God) the Son, the Holy Ghost/Spirit, the Holy Trinity; the Great Spirit, Gitchi Manitou; humorous the Man Upstairs.
2 *sacrifices to appease the gods* **deity,** goddess, divine being, celestial being, divinity, immortal, avatar.
3 *wooden gods* **idol,** graven image, icon, totem, talisman, fetish, juju.

godforsaken ▶ adjective *this godforsaken town holds no future for you* **wretched,** miserable, dreary, dismal, depressing, grim, cheerless, bleak, desolate, gloomy; deserted, neglected, isolated, remote, backward.
ANTONYMS charming.

godless ▶ adjective 1 *a godless society* **atheistic,** unbelieving, agnostic, skeptical, heretical, faithless, irreligious, ungodly, unholy, impious, profane; infidel, heathen, idolatrous, pagan; satanic, devilish.
ANTONYMS religious.
2 *godless pleasures* **immoral,** wicked, sinful, wrong, evil, bad, iniquitous, corrupt; irreligious, sacrilegious, profane, blasphemous, impious; depraved, degenerate, debauched, perverted, decadent; impure.
ANTONYMS virtuous.

godlike ▶ adjective *the godlike giants of Roman mythology* **divine,** godly, superhuman; angelic, seraphic; spiritual, heavenly, celestial; sacred, holy, saintly.

godly ▶ adjective *their claims of a godly agenda do not jibe with their hateful activities* **religious,** devout, pious, reverent, believing, God-fearing, saintly, holy, prayerful, spiritual, churchgoing.

godsend ▶ noun *the state subsidies have been a godsend to our preschool center* **boon,** blessing, bonus, plus, benefit, advantage, help, aid, asset; stroke of luck, windfall, manna (from heaven).
ANTONYMS curse.

goings-on ▶ plural noun *the goings-on at his Hollywood parties have become legendary* **events,** happenings, affairs, business; mischief, misbehavior, misconduct, funny business; informal monkey business, hanky-panky, shenanigans.

gold ▶ noun 1 *she won the gold* **gold medal,** first prize.
2 *he struck gold* **pay dirt,** the jackpot, the bull's-eye.

golden ▶ adjective 1 *her golden hair* **blond/blonde,** yellow, fair, flaxen, tow-colored.
ANTONYMS dark, raven.
2 *a golden time* **successful,** prosperous, flourishing, thriving; favorable, providential, lucky, fortunate; happy, joyful, glorious.
ANTONYMS unsuccessful, unhappy.
3 *a golden opportunity* **excellent,** fine, superb, splendid; special, unique; favorable, opportune, promising, bright, full of promise; advantageous, profitable, valuable, providential.
4 *the golden girl of tennis* **favorite,** favored, popular, admired, beloved, pet; acclaimed, applauded, praised; brilliant, consummate, gifted; informal blue-eyed; formal lauded.

good ▶ adjective 1 *a good product* **fine,** superior, quality; excellent, superb, outstanding, magnificent, exceptional, marvelous, wonderful, first-rate, first-class, sterling; satisfactory, acceptable, not bad, all right; informal great, OK, A1, jake, hunky-dory, ace, terrific,

fantastic, fabulous, fab, top-notch, blue-chip, blue-ribbon, bang-up, killer, class, awesome, wicked; smashing, brilliant.
ANTONYMS bad.
2 *a good person* **virtuous,** righteous, upright, upstanding, moral, ethical, high-minded, principled; exemplary, law-abiding, irreproachable, blameless, guiltless, unimpeachable, honorable, scrupulous, reputable, decent, respectable, noble, trustworthy; meritorious, praiseworthy, admirable; whiter than white, saintly, saintlike, angelic; informal squeaky clean.
ANTONYMS wicked.
3 *the children are good at school* **well-behaved,** obedient, dutiful, polite, courteous, respectful, deferential, compliant.
ANTONYMS naughty.
4 *a good thing to do* **right,** correct, proper, decorous, seemly; appropriate, fitting, apt, suitable; convenient, expedient, favorable, opportune, felicitous, timely; archaic meet.
5 *a good driver* **capable,** able, proficient, adept, adroit, accomplished, skillful, skilled, talented, masterly, virtuoso, expert; informal great, mean, wicked, nifty, ace, crackerjack.
ANTONYMS inept.
6 *a good friend* **close,** intimate, dear, bosom, special, best, firm, valued, treasured; loving, devoted, loyal, faithful, constant, reliable, dependable, trustworthy, trusty, true, unfailing, staunch.
7 *the dogs are in good condition* **healthy,** fine, sound, tip-top, hale and hearty, fit, robust, sturdy, strong, vigorous.
ANTONYMS poor, ill.
8 *a good time was had by all* **enjoyable,** pleasant, agreeable, pleasurable, delightful, great, nice, lovely; amusing, diverting, jolly, merry, lively; informal super, fantastic, fabulous, fab, terrific, grand, brilliant, killer, peachy, ducky.
ANTONYMS unpleasant, terrible.
9 *it was good of you to come* **kind,** kindhearted, good-hearted, thoughtful, generous, charitable, magnanimous, gracious; altruistic, unselfish, selfless.
ANTONYMS unkind, thoughtless.
10 *a good time to call* **convenient,** suitable, appropriate, fitting, fit; opportune, timely, favorable, advantageous, expedient, felicitous, happy, providential.
ANTONYMS inconvenient.
11 *bananas are good for you* **wholesome,** healthy, healthful, nourishing, nutritious, nutritional, beneficial, salubrious.
ANTONYMS bad, unhealthy.
12 *are these eggs good?* **edible,** safe to eat, fit for human consumption; fresh, wholesome, consumable; formal comestible.
ANTONYMS bad, inedible.
13 *good food* **delicious,** tasty, mouthwatering, appetizing, flavorful, delectable, toothsome, palatable; succulent, luscious; informal scrumptious, delish, yummy, lip-smacking, finger-licking, nummy, melt-in-your-mouth.
14 *a good reason* **valid,** genuine, authentic, legitimate, sound, bona fide; convincing, persuasive, telling, potent, cogent, compelling.
ANTONYMS unconvincing.
15 *we waited a good hour* **whole,** full, entire, complete, solid.
16 *a good number of them* **considerable,** sizable, substantial, appreciable, significant; goodly, fair, reasonable; plentiful, abundant, great, large, generous; informal tidy.
ANTONYMS small.
17 *wear your good clothes* **best,** finest, nicest; special, party, Sunday, formal, dressy, smart, smartest.
ANTONYMS casual, everyday.
18 *good weather* **fine,** fair, dry; bright, clear, sunny, cloudless; calm, windless; warm, mild, balmy, clement, pleasant, nice.
ANTONYMS bad, inclement.
▶ **noun 1** *issues of good and evil* **virtue,** righteousness, goodness, morality, integrity, rectitude; honesty, truth, honor, probity; propriety, worthiness, merit; blamelessness, purity.
ANTONYMS wickedness.
2 *it's all for your good* **benefit,** advantage, profit, gain, interest, welfare, well-being; enjoyment, comfort, ease, convenience; help, aid, assistance, service; behalf.
ANTONYMS disadvantage.
▶ **exclamation** *good, that's settled* **fine,** very well, all right, right, all right then, yes, agreed; informal okay, OK, okey-dokey.
– PHRASES **for good** *those days are gone for good* **forever,** permanently, for always, evermore, forevermore, for ever and ever, for eternity, never to return, forevermore; informal for keeps, until the cows come home, until hell freezes over; archaic for aye. **make good 1** *if I don't get away from my family, I'll never make good* **succeed,** be successful, be a success, do well, get ahead, reach the top; prosper, flourish, thrive; informal make it, make the grade, make a name for oneself, make one's mark, get somewhere, arrive. **2** *he promised to make good any damage* **repair,** mend, fix, put right, see to; restore, remedy, rectify. **3** *they made good their escape* **effect,** conduct, perform, implement, execute, carry out; achieve, accomplish, succeed in, realize, attain, engineer, bring about, bring off. **4** *he will make good his promise* **fulfill,** carry out, implement, discharge, honor, redeem; keep, observe, abide by, comply with, stick to, heed, follow, be bound by, live up to, stand by, adhere to.

goodbye ▶ **exclamation** *Goodbye! See you all next year!* **farewell,** adieu, au revoir, ciao, adios; bye, bye-bye, so long, see you later, see you, sayonara; bon voyage; cheers; informal toodle-oo.
ANTONYMS hello.
▶ **noun** (often **goodbyes**) *we said our goodbyes at the door* **parting,** leave-taking, send-off.

good-for-nothing ▶ **adjective** *a good-for-nothing bum* **useless,** worthless, incompetent, inefficient, inept, ne'er-do-well; lazy, idle, slothful, indolent, shiftless; informal no-good, lousy.
ANTONYMS worthy.
▶ **noun** *lazy good-for-nothings* **ne'er-do-well,** layabout, do-nothing, idler, loafer, lounger, sluggard, shirker, underachiever; informal slacker, lazybones, couch potato.

good-humored ▶ **adjective** *Disney insisted on*

hiring only the most good-humored of personnel **genial,** affable, cordial, friendly, amiable, easygoing, approachable, good-natured, cheerful, cheery; companionable, comradely, sociable, convivial; informal chummy.
ANTONYMS grumpy.

good-looking ▶ adjective *a good-looking couple* **attractive,** beautiful, pretty, handsome, lovely, stunning, striking, arresting, gorgeous, prepossessing, fetching, captivating, bewitching, beguiling, engaging, charming, enchanting, appealing, delightful; sexy, seductive, alluring, tantalizing, irresistible, ravishing, desirable; Scottish bonny; informal hot, easy on the eye, drop-dead gorgeous, cute, foxy, bodacious; literary beauteous; archaic comely, fair.
ANTONYMS ugly.

goodly ▶ adjective *I'll bet he paid a goodly sum for that car* **large,** largish, sizable, substantial, considerable, respectable, significant, decent, generous, handsome; informal tidy, serious.
ANTONYMS paltry.

good-natured ▶ adjective *the crowd was rowdy but good-natured* **warmhearted,** friendly, amiable; neighborly, benevolent, kind, kindhearted, generous, unselfish, considerate, thoughtful, obliging, helpful, supportive, charitable; understanding, sympathetic, easygoing, accommodating.
ANTONYMS malicious.

goodness ▶ noun **1** *she must have seen some goodness in him* **virtue,** good, righteousness, morality, integrity, rectitude; honesty, truth, truthfulness, honor, probity; propriety, decency, respectability, nobility, worthiness, worth, merit, trustworthiness; blamelessness, purity.
2 *the neighbor's goodness toward us* **kindness,** kindliness, tenderheartedness, humanity, mildness, benevolence, graciousness; tenderness, warmth, affection, love, goodwill; sympathy, compassion, care, concern, understanding, tolerance, generosity, charity, leniency, clemency, magnanimity.
3 *slow cooking retains the food's goodness* **nutritional value,** nutrients, wholesomeness, nourishment.

CHOOSE THE RIGHT WORD

goodness, morality, probity, rectitude, virtue

Of all these words denoting moral excellence, **goodness** is the broadest in meaning. It describes an excellence so well established that it is thought of as inherent or innate and is associated with kindness, generosity, helpfulness, and sincerity (*she has more goodness in her little finger than most people have in their whole body*). **Morality**, on the other hand, is moral excellence based on a code of ethical conduct or religious teaching (*his behavior was kept in line by fear of punishment rather than morality*). Although it is often used as a synonym for *goodness*, **virtue** suggests moral excellence that is acquired rather than innate and that is consciously or steadfastly maintained, often in spite of temptations or evil influences (*her virtue was as unassailable as her noble character*). **Rectitude** is used to describe strict adherence to the rules of just or right behavior and carries strong connotations of sternness and self-discipline (*he had a reputation for rectitude and insisted on absolute truthfulness*). **Probity** describes an honesty or integrity that has been tried and proved (*as mayor, she displayed a probity that was rare in a politician*).

goods ▶ plural noun **1** *he dispatched the goods* **merchandise,** wares, stock, commodities, produce, products, articles; imports, exports.
2 *the dead woman's goods* **property,** possessions, worldly possessions, effects, chattels, valuables; informal things, stuff, junk, gear, bits and pieces.

goodwill ▶ noun *your acts of goodwill have not gone unnoticed* **benevolence,** compassion, goodness, kindness, consideration, charity; cooperation, collaboration; friendliness, amity, thoughtfulness, decency, sympathy, understanding, neighborliness.
ANTONYMS hostility.

gorge ▶ noun *the river runs through a gorge* **ravine,** canyon, gully, defile, couloir; chasm, gulf; gulch, coulee.
▶ verb **1** *they gorged themselves on cake* **stuff,** cram, fill; glut, satiate, overindulge, overfill; informal pig out.
2 *vultures **gorged on** the flesh* **devour,** guzzle, gobble, gulp (down), wolf (down); informal demolish, polish off, scoff (down), down, stuff one's face with; scarf (down/up).

gorgeous ▶ adjective **1** *a gorgeous woman* See GOOD-LOOKING.
2 *a gorgeous view* **spectacular,** splendid, superb, wonderful, grand, impressive, awe-inspiring, awesome, amazing, stunning, breathtaking, incredible; informal sensational, fabulous, fantastic.
3 *gorgeous uniforms* **resplendent,** magnificent, sumptuous, luxurious, elegant, opulent; dazzling, brilliant.
ANTONYMS drab.

gory ▶ adjective **1** *a gory ritual slaughter* **grisly,** gruesome, violent, bloody, brutal, savage; ghastly, frightful, horrid, fearful, hideous, macabre, horrible, horrific; shocking, appalling, monstrous, unspeakable; informal blood-and-guts.
2 *gory pieces of flesh* **bloody,** bloodstained, bloodsoaked.

gospel ▶ noun **1** (**the Gospel**) *the Gospel according to John* **Christian teaching,** Christian doctrine, Christ's teaching; the word of God, the good news, the New Testament.
2 *don't treat this as gospel* **the truth**; fact, actual fact, reality, actuality, factuality, the case, a certainty.
3 *her gospel of nonviolence* **doctrine,** dogma, teaching, principle, ethic, creed, credo, ideology, ideal; belief, tenet, canon.

gossamer ▶ noun *her dress swirled like gossamer* **cobwebs**; silk, gauze, chiffon.
▶ adjective *a gossamer veil* **gauzy,** gossamery, fine, diaphanous, delicate, filmy, floaty, chiffony, cobwebby, wispy, thin, light, insubstantial, flimsy; translucent, transparent, see-through, sheer.

gossip ▶ noun 1 *tell me all the gossip* **rumor**(s), tittle-tattle, whispers, canards, tidbits; scandal, hearsay; informal dirt, buzz, scuttlebutt.
2 *she's such a gossip* **scandalmonger,** gossipmonger, tattler, busybody, muckraker, flibbertigibbet.
▶ verb *she gossiped about Dean's wife* **spread rumors,** spread gossip, talk, whisper, tell tales, tittle-tattle, tattle; informal dish the dirt.

govern ▶ verb 1 *he governs the province* **rule,** preside over, reign over, control, be in charge of, command, lead, dominate; run, head, administer, manage, regulate, oversee, supervise; informal be in the driver's seat of.
2 *the rules governing social behavior* **determine,** decide, control, regulate, direct, rule, dictate, shape; affect, influence, sway, act on, mold, modify, impact on.

government ▶ noun 1 *the government announced further cuts* **administration,** executive, regime, authority, powers that be, directorate, council, leadership; cabinet, ministry; informal feds; (**the government**) Washington.
2 *her job was the government of the district* **rule,** governing, running, leadership, control, administration, regulation, management, supervision.

gown ▶ noun *a blue gown with seed pearls on the bodice* **dress,** evening gown, prom dress, prom gown, wedding gown; frock, shift; robe, dressing gown.

grab ▶ verb 1 *Jessica grabbed his arm* **seize,** grasp, snatch, take hold of, grip, clasp, clutch; take; informal glom on to.
2 informal *I'll grab another drink* **get,** acquire, obtain; buy, purchase, procure; secure, snap up; gather, collect, garner; achieve, attain; informal get one's hands on, get one's mitts on, get hold of, bag, score, nab.
▶ noun *she made a grab for his gun* **lunge,** snatch.
– PHRASES **up for grabs** informal *dozens of prizes are up for grabs* **available,** obtainable, to be had, for the taking; for sale, on the market; informal for the asking, on tap, gettable.

grace ▶ noun 1 *the grace of a ballerina* **elegance,** poise, gracefulness, finesse; suppleness, agility, nimbleness, light-footedness.
ANTONYMS inelegance, stiffness.
2 *he at least had the grace to look sheepish* **courtesy,** decency, (good) manners, politeness, decorum, respect, tact.
ANTONYMS effrontery.
3 *she fell from grace* **favor,** approval, approbation, acceptance, esteem, regard, respect; goodwill.
ANTONYMS disfavor.
4 *he lived there by grace of the king* **favor,** goodwill, generosity, kindness, indulgence; formal benefaction.
5 *they have five days' grace to decide* **deferment,** deferral, postponement, suspension, adjournment, delay, pause; respite, stay, moratorium, reprieve.
6 *who would like to say this evening's grace?* **blessing,** prayer of thanks, thanksgiving, benediction.
▶ verb 1 *the occasion was graced by the president* **dignify,** distinguish, honor, favor; enhance, ennoble, glorify, elevate, aggrandize, upgrade.
2 *a mosaic graced the floor* **adorn,** embellish, decorate, ornament, enhance; beautify, prettify, enrich, bedeck.

graceful ▶ adjective *our dancers must be both muscular and graceful* **elegant,** fluid, fluent, natural, neat; agile, supple, nimble, light-footed.

gracious ▶ adjective 1 *a gracious hostess* **courteous,** polite, civil, chivalrous, well-mannered, mannerly, decorous; tactful, diplomatic; kind, benevolent, considerate, thoughtful, obliging, accommodating, indulgent, magnanimous; friendly, amiable, cordial, hospitable.
ANTONYMS rude.
2 *gracious colonial buildings* **elegant,** stylish, tasteful, graceful; comfortable, luxurious, sumptuous, opulent, grand, high-class; informal swanky, plush.
ANTONYMS shabby, crude.
3 *God's gracious intervention* **merciful,** compassionate, kind; forgiving, lenient, clement, forbearing, humane, tenderhearted, sympathetic; indulgent, generous, magnanimous, benign, benevolent.
ANTONYMS cruel.

grade ▶ noun 1 *a higher grade of steel* **category,** set, class, classification, grouping, group, bracket.
2 *his job is of the lowest grade* **rank,** level, echelon, standing, position, class, status, order; step, rung, stratum, tier.
3 *she got the best grades in the class* **mark,** score; assessment, evaluation, appraisal.
4 *he's in grade 5* **year**; class.
5 *a steep grade* See **GRADIENT**.
▶ verb 1 *eggs are graded by size* **classify,** class, categorize, bracket, sort, group, arrange, pigeonhole; rank, evaluate, rate, value.
2 *the essays have been graded* **score,** mark, assess, judge, evaluate, appraise.
3 *the colors grade into one another* **blend,** shade, merge, pass.
– PHRASES **make the grade** informal *he lacked the experience to make the grade* **qualify,** be up to scratch, come up to standard, pass, pass muster, measure up; succeed, win through; informal be up to snuff, cut it, cut the mustard.

gradient ▶ noun 1 *the gradient of Miller's Hill Road is less steep than it was fifty years ago* **slope,** incline, hill, rise, ramp, bank; declivity, grade.
2 *the gradient of the line* **steepness,** angle, slant, slope, inclination.

gradual ▶ adjective 1 *a gradual transition* **slow,** measured, unhurried, cautious; piecemeal, step-by-step, progressive, continuous, systematic, steady.
ANTONYMS abrupt, sudden.
2 *a gradual slope* **gentle,** moderate, slight, easy.
ANTONYMS steep.

gradually ▶ adverb *the icicles gradually got longer throughout the day | gradually add the flour mixture* **slowly,** slowly but surely, cautiously, gently, gingerly; piecemeal, little by little, bit by bit, inch by inch, by degrees; progressively, systematically; regularly, steadily.

graduate ▶ verb 1 *he wants to teach when he graduates* **get one's diploma,** get one's degree,

pass one's exams, complete/finish one's studies.
2 *she wants to graduate to serious drama* **progress,** advance, move up.
3 *a thermometer graduated in Fahrenheit* **calibrate,** mark off, measure out, grade.

graft[1] ▶ **noun 1** *grafts may die from lack of water* **scion,** cutting, shoot, offshoot, bud, sprout, sprig.
2 *a skin graft* **transplant,** implant.
▶ **verb 1** *graft a bud onto the stem* **affix,** join, insert, splice.
2 *tissue is grafted on to the cornea* **transplant,** implant.
3 *a mansion grafted on to a farmhouse* **attach,** add, join.

graft[2] ▶ **noun** *sweeping measures to curb official graft* **corruption,** bribery, dishonesty, deceit, fraud, unlawful practices, illegal means, payola; informal palm-greasing, hush money, kickbacks, crookedness.
ANTONYMS honesty.

grain ▶ **noun 1** *the local farmers grow grain* **cereal,** cereal crops.
2 *a grain of wheat* **kernel,** seed, grist.
3 *grains of sand* **granule,** particle, speck, mote, mite; bit, piece; scrap, crumb, fragment, morsel.
4 *a grain of truth* **trace,** hint, tinge, suggestion, shadow; bit, soupçon; scintilla, ounce, iota, jot, whit, scrap, shred; informal smidgen, smidge, tad.
5 *the grain of the lumber* **texture,** surface, finish; weave, pattern.

grand ▶ **adjective 1** *a grand hotel* **magnificent,** imposing, impressive, awe-inspiring, splendid, resplendent, majestic, monumental; palatial, stately, large; luxurious, sumptuous, lavish, opulent, upmarket, upscale; informal fancy, posh, plush, classy, swanky, five-star.
ANTONYMS inferior, unimpressive.
2 *a grand scheme* **ambitious,** bold, epic, big, extravagant.
3 *a grand old lady* **august,** distinguished, illustrious, eminent, esteemed, honored, venerable, dignified, respectable; preeminent, prominent, notable, renowned, celebrated, famous; aristocratic, noble, regal, blue-blooded, high-born, patrician; informal upper-crust.
ANTONYMS ordinary, humble.
4 *a grand total of $2,000* **complete,** comprehensive, all-inclusive, inclusive; final.
ANTONYMS partial.
5 *the grand staircase* **main,** principal, central, prime; biggest, largest.
ANTONYMS minor, secondary.
6 informal *you're doing a grand job* **excellent,** very good, marvelous, first-class, first-rate, wonderful, outstanding, sterling, fine, splendid, superb, terrific, fabulous, great; informal super, ace, killer; smashing, brilliant.
ANTONYMS poor.
▶ **noun** informal *a check for ten grand* **thousand dollars;** informal thou, K/Ks; G/Gs, gee/gees.

grandeur ▶ **noun** *the grandeur of the Rockies | the grandeur of a royal wedding* **splendor,** magnificence, impressiveness, glory, resplendence, majesty, greatness; stateliness, pomp, ceremony.

grandfather ▶ **noun 1** *his grandfather lives here* informal granddad, grandad, grandpa, gramps, grampy, granddaddy, grandaddy, poppa.
2 *the grandfather of modern liberalism* **founder,** inventor, originator, creator, initiator; father, founding father, pioneer.
3 *our pioneering grandfathers* **forefather,** forebear, ancestor, progenitor, antecedent.
▶ **verb** *federal funding was eliminated for these air-polluting road projects, but a loophole has grandfathered the previously funded projects* **exempt,** excuse, free, exclude, grant immunity to, spare, absolve; informal let off (the hook).

grandiloquent ▶ **adjective** *grandiloquent speeches* **pompous,** bombastic, magniloquent, pretentious, ostentatious, high-flown, orotund, florid, flowery; overwrought, overblown, overdone; informal highfalutin, purple.
ANTONYMS understated.

grandiose ▶ **adjective 1** *the court's grandiose facade* **magnificent,** impressive, grand, imposing, awe-inspiring, splendid, resplendent, majestic, glorious, elaborate; palatial, stately, luxurious, opulent; informal plush, swanky, flash.
ANTONYMS humble, unimpressive.
2 *a grandiose plan* **ambitious,** bold, overambitious, extravagant, high-flown, flamboyant; informal over the top.
ANTONYMS humble, modest.

grandmother ▶ **noun** informal grandma, gramma, granny, grannie, gran, nana.

grant ▶ **verb 1** *he granted them leave of absence* **allow,** accord, permit, afford, vouchsafe.
ANTONYMS refuse.
2 *he granted them $20,000* **give,** award, bestow on, confer on, present with, provide with, endow with, supply with. See note at GIVE.
3 *I grant that the difference is not absolute* **admit,** accept, concede, yield, allow, appreciate, recognize, acknowledge, confess; agree.
ANTONYMS deny.
▶ **noun** *a grant from the council* **endowment,** subvention, award, donation, bursary, allowance, subsidy, contribution, handout, allocation, gift; scholarship.

granule ▶ **noun** *minute granules of gold* **grain,** particle, fragment, bit, crumb, morsel, mote, speck.

graph ▶ **noun** *use graphs to analyze your data* **chart,** diagram; bar chart, pie chart, histogram, scatter diagram.
▶ **verb** *we graphed the new prices* **plot,** trace, draw up, delineate.

graphic ▶ **adjective 1** *a graphic representation of language* **visual,** symbolic, pictorial, illustrative, diagrammatic; drawn, written.
2 *a graphic account of the war* **vivid,** explicit, expressive, detailed; uninhibited, powerful, colorful, rich, lurid, shocking; realistic, descriptive, illustrative; telling, effective.
ANTONYMS vague.
▶ **noun** Computing *this printer's good enough for graphics* **picture,** illustration, image; diagram, graph, chart; (**graphics**) art, visual art.

CHOOSE THE RIGHT WORD

graphic, pictorial, picturesque, vivid

A photograph of a car accident on the front page of a newspaper might be described as

graphic, while a photograph of a mountain village would be called **picturesque**. Both adjectives are used to describe things that have visual impact or that produce a strong, clear impression, but *graphic* means having the power to evoke a strikingly lifelike representation, whether it is in pictures or in words (*the driving instructor gave them a graphic description of what happens in a 50-mph head-on collision*). **Vivid** is a more general term suggesting something that is felt, seen, heard, or apprehended with a sense of intense reality (*the vivid colors of the landscape; a vivid memory of the horrors of war*). Something that is **pictorial** aims to present a vivid picture (*a pictorial writing style*), while **picturesque** usually applies to scenes, pictures, etc. that are visually striking because they are panoramic, quaint, or unusual (*from a distance the village looked picturesque, but up close it was seen to be rundown*).

grapple ▶ verb **1** *the policemen grappled with him* **wrestle,** struggle, tussle; brawl, fight, scuffle, battle.
2 *he grappled his prey* **seize,** grab, catch, catch hold of, take hold of, grasp.
3 *she is **grappling with** her problems* **tackle,** confront, face, deal with, cope with, come to grips with; apply oneself to, devote oneself to.

grasp ▶ verb **1** *she grasped his hands* **grip,** clutch, clasp, hold, clench; catch, seize, grab, snatch, latch on to.
ANTONYMS release.
2 *everybody grasped the important points* **understand,** comprehend, follow, take in, perceive, see, apprehend, assimilate, absorb; informal get, catch on to, figure out, get one's head around, take on board.
3 *he grasped the opportunity* **take advantage of,** act on; seize, leap at, snatch, jump at, pounce on.
ANTONYMS miss, overlook.
▶ noun **1** *his grasp on her hand* **grip,** hold; clutch, clasp, clench.
2 *his domineering mother's grasp* **control,** power, clutches, command, domination, rule, tyranny.
3 *a prize lay within their grasp* **reach,** scope, power, limits, range; sights.
4 *your grasp of history* **understanding,** comprehension, perception, apprehension, awareness, grip, knowledge; mastery, command.

grate ▶ verb **1** *she grated the cheese* **shred,** pulverize, mince, grind, granulate, crush, crumble.
2 *her bones grated together* **grind,** rub, rasp, scrape, jar, grit, creak.
3 *the tune is beginning to grate* **irritate,** set someone's teeth on edge, jar; annoy, nettle, chafe, fret; informal aggravate, get on someone's nerves, get under someone's skin, get someone's goat.

grateful ▶ adjective *we were all grateful to Rita* **thankful,** appreciative; indebted, obliged, obligated, in someone's debt, beholden.

gratify ▶ verb **1** *it gratified him to be seen with her* **please,** gladden, make happy, delight, make someone feel good, satisfy; informal tickle pink, buck up. See note at PLEASANT.
ANTONYMS displease.
2 *he gratified her desires* **satisfy,** fulfill, indulge, comply with, pander to, cater to, give in to, satiate, feed, accommodate.
ANTONYMS frustrate.

grating ▶ adjective **1** *the chair made a grating noise* **scraping,** scratching, grinding, rasping, jarring.
2 *a grating voice* **harsh,** raucous, strident, piercing, shrill, screechy; discordant, cacophonous; hoarse, rough, gravelly.
ANTONYMS harmonious, pleasing.
3 *it's written in grating language* **irritating,** annoying, infuriating, irksome, maddening, displeasing, tiresome; jarring, unsuitable, inappropriate; informal aggravating.
ANTONYMS pleasing, appropriate.

gratis ▶ adverb *the room was provided gratis, courtesy of the casino* **free,** free of charge, without charge, for nothing, at no cost, gratuitously; informal on the house, for free.

gratitude ▶ noun *Chip was miffed by his nephew's lack of gratitude* **gratefulness,** thankfulness, thanks, appreciation, indebtedness; recognition, acknowledgment, credit.

gratuitous ▶ adjective *there was one moment of nudity in the movie, and it was ridiculously gratuitous* **unjustified,** uncalled for, unwarranted, unprovoked, undue; indefensible, unjustifiable; needless, unnecessary, inessential, unmerited, groundless, senseless, wanton, indiscriminate; excessive, immoderate, inordinate, inappropriate.
ANTONYMS necessary.

gratuity ▶ noun *I'm not allowed to accept this gratuity* **tip,** gift, present, donation, reward, handout; bonus, extra; baksheesh. See note at PRESENT[3].

grave[1] ▶ noun *she left flowers at his grave* **burial site,** gravesite, cemetery plot, tomb, sepulcher, vault, burial chamber, mausoleum, crypt; last resting place.

grave[2] ▶ adjective **1** *a grave matter* **serious,** important, weighty, profound, significant, momentous; critical, acute, urgent, pressing; dire, terrible, awful, dreadful; formal exigent.
ANTONYMS trivial.
2 *Jackie looked grave* **solemn,** serious, sober, unsmiling, grim, somber; severe, stern, dour.
ANTONYMS cheerful.

graveyard ▶ noun *he visits the graveyard every Sunday* **cemetery,** burial ground, burying ground, necropolis, columbarium, memorial park/garden; informal boneyard; historical potter's field.

gravitate ▶ verb *take her to a bar, and she automatically gravitates to the lowlifes* **move,** head, drift, be drawn, be attracted; tend, lean, incline.

gravity ▶ noun **1** *the gravity of the situation* **seriousness,** importance, significance, weight, consequence, magnitude; acuteness, urgency, exigence; awfulness, dreadfulness; formal moment.
2 *the gravity of his demeanor* **solemnity,** seriousness, somberness, sobriety, soberness, severity, grimness, humorlessness, dourness; gloominess.

gray ▶ adjective **1** *a gray suit* silvery, silver-gray,

gunmetal, slate, charcoal, smoky.
2 *his gray hair* **white,** silver, hoary.
3 *a gray day* **cloudy,** overcast, dull, sunless, gloomy, dreary, dismal, somber, bleak, murky.
ANTONYMS sunny, bright.
4 *her face looked gray* **ashen,** wan, pale, pasty, pallid, colorless, bloodless, white, waxen; sickly, peaked, drained, drawn, deathly.
ANTONYMS ruddy.
5 *the gray daily routine* **characterless,** colorless, nondescript, insipid, jejune, unremarkable, flat, bland, dry, stale; dull, uninteresting, boring, tedious, monotonous, monochrome.
ANTONYMS lively.
6 *their policy regarding unmarried couples is a gray area* **ambiguous,** unclear, uncertain, doubtful, indefinite, indistinct, indeterminate, debatable, open to question.
ANTONYMS black and white, certain.
▸ **verb** *the population grayed* **age,** grow old, mature.

graze[1] ▸ **verb** *the deer grazed* **feed,** eat, nibble, browse.

graze[2] ▸ **verb 1** *she grazed her knuckles on the box* **scrape,** abrade, skin, scratch, chafe, bark, scuff, rasp; cut, nick.
2 *his shot grazed the far post* **touch,** brush, shave, skim, kiss, scrape, clip, glance off.
▸ **noun** *grazes on the skin* **scratch,** scrape, abrasion, cut; Medicine trauma.

greasy ▸ **adjective 1** *a plate of greasy food* **fatty,** oily, buttery, oleaginous; formal pinguid.
ANTONYMS lean.
2 *greasy hair* **oily**.
ANTONYMS dry.
3 *the pole was very greasy* **slippery,** slick, slimy, slithery, oily; informal slippy.
ANTONYMS dry.
4 *a greasy little man* **ingratiating,** obsequious, sycophantic, fawning, toadying, groveling; effusive, gushing, gushy; unctuous, oily; informal smarmy, slimy, bootlicking.

great ▸ **adjective 1** *they showed great interest* **considerable,** substantial, significant, appreciable, special, serious; exceptional, extraordinary.
ANTONYMS little.
2 *a great expanse of water* **large,** big, extensive, expansive, broad, wide, sizable, ample; vast, immense, huge, enormous, massive; informal humongous, whopping, ginormous.
ANTONYMS small.
3 *you great fool!* **absolute,** total, utter, out-and-out, downright, thoroughgoing, complete; perfect, positive, prize, sheer, arrant, unqualified, consummate, veritable.
4 *great writers* **prominent,** eminent, important, distinguished, illustrious, celebrated, honored, acclaimed, admired, esteemed, revered, renowned, notable, famous, famed, well-known; leading, top, major, principal, first-rate, matchless, peerless, star.
ANTONYMS minor.
5 *the great navies in world history* **powerful,** dominant, influential, strong, potent, formidable, redoubtable; leading, important, foremost, major, chief, principal.
ANTONYMS minor.
6 *a great castle* **magnificent,** imposing, impressive, awe-inspiring, grand, splendid, majestic, sumptuous, resplendent.
ANTONYMS modest.
7 *a great sportsman* **expert,** skillful, skilled, adept, accomplished, talented, fine, masterly, master, brilliant, virtuoso, marvelous, outstanding, first-class, superb; informal crack, ace, A1, class.
ANTONYMS poor.
8 *a great fan of rugby* **enthusiastic,** eager, keen, zealous, devoted, ardent, fanatical, passionate, dedicated, committed.
ANTONYMS unenthusiastic.
9 *we had a great time* **enjoyable,** delightful, lovely, pleasant, congenial; exciting, thrilling; excellent, marvelous, wonderful, fine, splendid, very good; informal terrific, fantastic, fabulous, splendiferous, fab, super, grand, cool, hunky-dory, killer, swell.
ANTONYMS bad.

greatly ▸ **adverb** *your donations are greatly appreciated* **very much,** considerably, substantially, appreciably, significantly, markedly, sizably, seriously, materially, profoundly; enormously, vastly, immensely, tremendously, mightily, abundantly, extremely, exceedingly; informal plenty, majorly.
ANTONYMS slightly.

greatness ▸ **noun 1** *a child destined for greatness* **eminence,** distinction, illustriousness, repute, high standing; importance, significance; celebrity, fame, prominence, renown.
2 *her greatness as a writer* **genius,** prowess, talent, expertise, mastery, artistry, virtuosity, skill, proficiency; flair, finesse; caliber, distinction.

greedy ▸ **adjective 1** *a greedy eater* **gluttonous,** ravenous, voracious, intemperate, self-indulgent, insatiable, wolfish; informal piggish, piggy.
2 *a greedy capitalist* **avaricious,** acquisitive, covetous, grasping, materialistic, mercenary, possessive; informal money-grubbing, money-grabbing, grabby.
3 *she is greedy for an award* **eager,** avid, hungry, craving, longing, yearning, hankering; impatient, anxious; informal dying, itching.

CHOOSE THE RIGHT WORD

greedy, acquisitive, covetous, avaricious, rapacious, gluttonous

The desire for money and the things it can buy is often associated with Americans. But not all Americans are **greedy**, which implies an insatiable desire to possess or acquire something, beyond what one needs or deserves (*greedy for profits*). Someone who is *greedy* for food might be called **gluttonous**, which emphasizes consumption as well as desire (*a gluttonous appetite for sweets*), but *greedy* is a derogatory term only when the object of longing is itself evil or when it cannot be possessed without harm to oneself or others (*a reporter greedy for information*). A *greedy* child may grow up to be an **avaricious** adult, which implies a fanatical greediness for money or other valuables. **Rapacious** is an even stronger term, with an emphasis on taking things by force (*so rapacious in his desire for land that he forced dozens of families from their homes*). **Acquisitive**, on the other hand, is a more neutral word suggesting a willingness to exert effort in acquiring things (*an acquisitive woman who filled her house with antiques and artwork*), and not necessarily material things (*a probing, acquisitive mind*). **Covetous**, in contrast to *acquisitive*, implies an intense desire for something as opposed to the act of acquiring or possessing it. It is often associated with the Ten Commandments (*Thou shalt not covet thy neighbor's wife*) and suggests a longing for something that rightfully belongs to another.

green ▶ adjective **1** *a green scarf* viridescent; olive, jade, pea green, emerald (green), lime (green), sea green; literary virescent, glaucous.
2 *a green island* **verdant,** grassy, leafy, verdurous.
ANTONYMS barren.
3 (**Green**) *he promotes Green issues* **environmental,** ecological, conservation, ecocentric, eco-.
4 *a green alternative to diesel* **environmentally friendly,** nonpolluting, ecological; ozone-friendly.
ANTONYMS polluting.
5 *green bananas* **unripe,** immature.
ANTONYMS ripe.
6 *green firewood* **unseasoned,** not aged; pliable, supple.
ANTONYMS seasoned, dry.
7 *the new lieutenant was green* **inexperienced,** unversed, callow, immature; new, raw, unseasoned, untried; inexpert, untrained, unqualified, ignorant; simple, unsophisticated, unpolished; naive, innocent, ingenuous, credulous, gullible, unworldly; informal wet behind the ears, born yesterday.
ANTONYMS experienced.
8 *he went green* **pale,** wan, pallid, ashen, ashen-faced, pasty, pasty-faced, gray, whitish, washed out, blanched, drained, pinched, sallow; sickly, nauseous, ill, sick, unhealthy.
ANTONYMS ruddy.
▶ noun **1** *a canopy of green over the road* **foliage,** greenery, plants, leaves, leafage, vegetation.
2 *a village green* **park,** common, grassy area, lawn, sward.
3 *eat your greens* **vegetables,** leafy vegetables, salad; informal veggies.
4 (**Green**) *Greens are against multinationals* **environmentalist,** conservationist, preservationist, nature lover, eco-activist; informal derogatory tree hugger, greenie.

green light ▶ noun *he was given the green light to implement his proposals* **authorization,** permission, approval, assent, consent, sanction; leave, clearance, warranty, agreement, imprimatur, one's blessing, the seal/stamp of approval, the rubber stamp, the nod; authority, license, dispensation, empowerment, freedom, liberty; informal the OK, the go-ahead, the thumbs up, the say-so.
ANTONYMS the red light, refusal.

greet ▶ verb **1** *sh e greeted Hank cheerily* **say hello to,** address, salute, hail; welcome, meet, receive.
2 *the decision was greeted with outrage* **receive,** acknowledge, respond to, react to, take.

greeting ▶ noun **1** *he shouted a greeting* **hello,** salute, salutation, address; welcome; acknowledgment.
ANTONYMS farewell.
2 (**greetings**) *birthday greetings* **best wishes,** good wishes, congratulations, felicitations; compliments, regards, respects.

gregarious ▶ adjective **1** *he was fun-loving and gregarious* **sociable,** company-loving, convivial, companionable, outgoing, friendly, affable, amiable, genial, warm, comradely; informal chummy.
ANTONYMS unsociable.
2 *gregarious fish* **social,** living in groups.

grief ▶ noun **1** *he was overcome with grief* **sorrow,** misery, sadness, anguish, pain, distress, heartache, heartbreak, agony, torment, affliction, suffering, woe, desolation, dejection, despair; mourning, mournfulness, bereavement, lamentation; literary dolor, dole.
ANTONYMS joy.
2 informal *the police gave me a lot of grief* **trouble,** annoyance, bother, irritation, vexation, harassment; informal aggravation, hassle.

grievance ▶ noun **1** *social and economic grievances* **injustice,** wrong, injury, ill, unfairness; affront, insult, indignity.
2 *students voiced their grievances* **complaint,** criticism, objection, grumble, grouse; ill feeling, bad feeling, resentment, bitterness, pique; informal gripe; Brit. whinge, moan, grouch, niggle, beef, bone to pick.

grieve ▶ verb **1** *she grieved for her father* **mourn,** lament, sorrow, be sorrowful; cry, sob, weep, shed tears, weep and wail, beat one's breast. See note at MOURN.
ANTONYMS rejoice.
2 *it grieved me to leave her* **sadden,** upset, distress, pain, hurt, wound, break someone's heart, make someone's heart bleed.
ANTONYMS please.

grievous formal ▶ adjective **1** *his death was a grievous blow* **serious,** severe, grave, bad, critical, dreadful, terrible, awful, crushing, calamitous; painful, agonizing, traumatic, wounding, damaging, injurious; sharp, acute.
ANTONYMS slight, trivial.
2 *a grievous sin* **heinous,** grave, deplorable, shocking, appalling, atrocious, gross, dreadful, egregious, iniquitous.
ANTONYMS venial, trivial.

grim ▶ adjective **1** *his grim expression* **stern,** forbidding, uninviting, unsmiling, dour, formidable, harsh, steely, flinty, stony; cross, churlish, surly, sour, ill-tempered; fierce, ferocious, threatening, menacing, implacable, ruthless, merciless.
ANTONYMS amiable, pleasant.
2 *grim humor* **black,** dark, mirthless, bleak, cynical.
ANTONYMS lighthearted.
3 *the asylum holds some grim secrets* **dreadful,** dire, ghastly, horrible, horrendous, horrid,

terrible, awful, appalling, frightful, shocking, unspeakable, grisly, gruesome, hideous, macabre; depressing, distressing, upsetting, worrying, unpleasant.
4 *a grim little hovel* **bleak,** dreary, dismal, dingy, wretched, miserable, depressing, cheerless, comfortless, joyless, gloomy, uninviting; informal godawful.
ANTONYMS cheery.
5 *grim determination* **resolute,** determined, firm, decided, steadfast, dead set; obstinate, stubborn, obdurate, unyielding, intractable, uncompromising, unshakable, unrelenting, relentless, dogged, tenacious.
ANTONYMS irresolute.

grimace ▶ **noun** *his mouth twisted into a grimace* **scowl,** frown, sneer; face.
▶ **verb** *Nina grimaced at Joe* **scowl,** frown, sneer, glower, lower; make a face, make faces.
ANTONYMS smile.

grime ▶ **noun** *her skirt was smeared with grime* **dirt,** filth, grunge, mud, mire, smut, soot, dust; informal muck, crud, gunge.
▶ **verb** *concrete grimed by diesel exhaust* **blacken,** dirty, stain, soil; literary begrime, besmirch.

grimy ▶ **adjective** *grimy old rags* **dirty,** grubby, grungy, mucky, soiled, stained, smeared, filthy, smutty, sooty, dusty, muddy; informal yucky, cruddy; literary besmirched, begrimed.
ANTONYMS clean.

grin ▶ **verb** *Liam grinned at us* **smile,** smile broadly, beam, smile from ear to ear, grin like a Cheshire cat; smirk; informal be all smiles.
▶ **noun** *a silly grin* **smile,** broad smile; smirk. See note at **SMILE**.
ANTONYMS frown, scowl.

grind ▶ **verb 1** *the sandstone is ground into powder* **crush,** pound, pulverize, mill, granulate, crumble, smash, press; technical triturate, comminute.
2 *a knife being ground on a wheel* **sharpen,** whet, hone, file, strop; smooth, polish, sand, sandpaper.
3 *one tectonic plate grinds against another* **rub,** grate, scrape, rasp.
▶ **noun** *the daily grind* **drudgery,** toil, hard work, labor, exertion, chores, slog; informal sweat; literary travail. See note at **LABOR**.
– PHRASES **grind out** *the composing department grinds out hundreds of pages a day* **produce,** generate, crank out, turn out; informal churn out.

grip ▶ **verb 1** *she gripped the edge of the table* **grasp,** clutch, hold, clasp, take hold of, clench, grab, seize, cling to; squeeze, press; informal glom on to.
ANTONYMS release, hold lightly.
2 *Harry was gripped by a sneezing fit* **afflict,** affect, take over, beset, rack, convulse.
3 *we were gripped by the drama* **engross,** enthrall, absorb, rivet, spellbind, hold spellbound, bewitch, fascinate, hold, mesmerize, enrapture; interest.
ANTONYMS bore, repel.
▶ **noun 1** *a tight grip* **grasp,** hold.
2 *the wheels lost their grip on the road* **traction,** purchase, friction, adhesion, resistance.
3 *he was in the grip of an obsession* **control,** power, hold, stranglehold, chokehold, clutches, command, mastery, influence.
4 *I had a pretty good grip on the situation* **understanding of,** comprehension of, grasp of, command of, perception of, awareness of, apprehension of, conception of; formal cognizance of.
5 *a leather grip* **travel bag,** traveling bag, suitcase, bag, overnight bag, flight bag.
– PHRASES **come to grips with** *you need to come to grips with the divorce* **deal with,** cope with, handle, grasp, tackle, undertake, take on, grapple with, face, face up to, confront.

gripe informal ▶ **verb** *he's always griping about something* **complain,** grumble, grouse, protest, whine, bleat; informal moan, bellyache, beef, bitch, kvetch; Brit. whinge, kvetch.
▶ **noun** *employees' gripes* **complaint,** grumble, grouse, grievance, objection; cavil, quibble, niggle; informal moan, beef, kvetch; Brit. whinge.

gripping ▶ **adjective** *a gripping spy novel* **engrossing,** enthralling, absorbing, riveting, captivating, spellbinding, bewitching, fascinating, compulsive, compelling, mesmerizing; thrilling, exciting, action-packed, dramatic, stimulating; informal unputdownable, page-turning.
ANTONYMS boring.

grisly ▶ **adjective** *the grisly details of the crime* **gruesome,** ghastly, frightful, horrid, horrifying, fearful, hideous, macabre, spine-chilling, horrible, horrendous, grim, awful, dire, dreadful, terrible, horrific, shocking, appalling, abominable, loathsome, abhorrent, odious, monstrous, unspeakable, disgusting, repulsive, repugnant, revolting, repellent, sickening; informal gross.

grit ▶ **noun 1** *the grit from the paths* **sand,** dust, dirt; gravel, pebbles, stones.
2 *just the grit we're looking for in a candidate* **courage,** bravery, pluck, mettle, backbone, spirit, strength of character, strength of will, moral fiber, steel, nerve, fortitude, toughness, hardiness, resolve, resolution, determination, tenacity, perseverance, endurance; informal guts, spunk.
▶ **verb** *Gina gritted her teeth* **clench,** clamp together, shut tightly; grind, gnash.

gritty ▶ **adjective 1** *a gritty floor* **sandy,** gravelly, pebbly, stony; powdery, dusty.
2 *a gritty performance* **courageous,** brave, plucky, mettlesome, stouthearted, valiant, bold, spirited, intrepid, tough, determined, resolute, purposeful, dogged, tenacious; informal gutsy, spunky, feisty.
3 *a gritty look at urban life* **realistic,** uncompromising, tough, true-to-life, unidealized, graphic, sordid.

groan ▶ **verb 1** *she groaned and rubbed her stomach* **moan,** whimper, cry, call out.
2 *they were groaning about the management* **complain,** grumble, grouse; informal moan, niggle, beef, bellyache, bitch, gripe.
3 *the old wooden door groaned* **creak,** squeak; grate, rasp.
▶ **noun 1** *a groan of anguish* **moan,** cry, whimper.
2 *their moans and groans* **complaint,** grumble, grouse, objection, protest, grievance; informal grouch, moan, beef, gripe.

3 *the groan of the elevator* **creaking,** creak, squeak, grating, grinding.

groggy ▶ adjective *the sedative made him groggy* **dazed,** stupefied, in a stupor, befuddled, fuddled, dizzy, disoriented, disorientated, punch-drunk, shaky, unsteady, wobbly, weak, faint, muzzy; informal dopey, woozy, not with it.

groom ▶ verb 1 *she groomed her pony* **curry,** brush, comb, clean, rub down.
2 *his dark hair was carefully groomed* **brush,** comb, arrange, do; tidy, spruce up, smarten up, preen, primp; informal fix.
3 *they were groomed for stardom* **prepare,** prime, ready, condition, tailor; coach, train, instruct, drill, teach, school.
▶ noun 1 *a groom took his horse* **stable hand,** stableman, stable boy, stable girl; historical equerry.
2 *the bride and groom* **bridegroom**; newly married man, newlywed.

groove ▶ noun *water trickled down the grooves* **furrow,** channel, trench, trough, canal, gouge, hollow, indentation, rut, gutter, cutting, cut, fissure; Carpentry rabbet.

grope ▶ verb 1 *she groped for her glasses* **fumble,** scrabble, fish, ferret, rummage, feel, search, hunt.
2 informal *one of the men started groping her* **fondle,** touch; informal paw, maul, feel up, touch up.

gross ▶ adjective 1 *the child was pale and gross* **obese,** corpulent, overweight, fat, big, large, fleshy, flabby, portly, bloated; informal porky, pudgy, tubby, blubbery, roly-poly.
ANTONYMS slender.
2 *men of gross natures* **boorish,** coarse, vulgar, loutish, oafish, thuggish, brutish, philistine, uncouth, crass, common, unrefined, unsophisticated, uncultured, uncultivated; informal cloddish.
ANTONYMS refined.
3 informal *the place smelled gross* **disgusting,** repellent, repulsive, abhorrent, loathsome, foul, nasty, obnoxious, sickening, nauseating, stomach-churning, unpalatable; vomitous; informal yucky, icky, gut-churning.
ANTONYMS pleasant, lovely.
4 *a gross distortion of the truth* **flagrant,** blatant, glaring, obvious, overt, naked, barefaced, shameless, brazen, audacious, undisguised, unconcealed, patent, transparent, manifest, palpable; out and out, utter, complete.
ANTONYMS minor.
5 *their gross income* **total,** whole, entire, complete, full, overall, combined, aggregate; before deductions, before tax, pretax.
ANTONYMS net.
▶ verb *she grosses over a million dollars a year* **earn,** make, bring in, take, get, receive, collect; informal rake in.

grotesque ▶ adjective 1 *a grotesque creature* **malformed,** deformed, misshapen, misproportioned, distorted, twisted, gnarled, mangled, mutilated; ugly, unsightly, monstrous, hideous, freakish, unnatural, abnormal, strange, odd, peculiar; informal weird, freaky.
ANTONYMS normal.
2 *grotesque mismanagement of funds* **outrageous,** monstrous, shocking, appalling, preposterous; ridiculous, ludicrous, farcical, unbelievable, incredible.

ground ▶ noun 1 *she collapsed on the ground* **floor,** earth, terra firma; flooring; informal deck.
2 *the soggy ground* **earth,** soil, dirt, clay, loam, turf, clod, sod; land, terrain.
3 (**grounds**) *the mansion's grounds* **estate,** lawn(s), yard(s), gardens, park, parkland, land, acres, property, surroundings, holding, territory; archaic demesne.
4 (**grounds**) *grounds for dismissal* **reason,** cause, basis, base, foundation, justification, rationale, argument, premise, occasion, excuse, pretext, motive, motivation.
5 (**grounds**) *coffee grounds* **sediment,** precipitate, settlings, dregs, lees, deposit, residue.
▶ verb 1 *the boat grounded on a sandbar* **run aground,** run ashore, beach, land.
2 *an assertion grounded on results of several studies* **base,** found, establish, root, build, construct, form.
3 *they were grounded in classics and history* **instruct,** coach, teach, tutor, educate, school, train, drill, prime, prepare; familiarize with, acquaint with.
– PHRASES **hold one's ground** *he tried to dissuade me with his negative remarks, but I held my ground* **stand firm,** stand fast, make a stand, stick to one's guns, dig in one's heels.
gain ground *we failed to gain ground in that last campaign* **advance,** progress, make headway; catch up, close in.

groundless ▶ adjective *groundless accusations* **baseless,** without basis, without foundation, ill-founded, unfounded, unsupported, uncorroborated, unproven, empty, idle, unsubstantiated, unwarranted, unjustified, unjustifiable, without cause, without reason, without justification, unreasonable, irrational, illogical, misguided.

groundwork ▶ noun *their predecessors did all the groundwork and got none of the credit* **preliminary work,** preliminaries, preparations, spadework, legwork, donkey work; planning, arrangements, organization, homework; basics, essentials, fundamentals, underpinning, foundation.

group ▶ noun 1 *the exhibits were divided into three distinct groups* **category,** class, classification, grouping, set, lot, batch, bracket, type, sort, kind, variety, family, species, genus, breed; grade, grading, rank, status.
2 *a group of tourists* **crowd,** party, body, band, company, gathering, congregation, assembly, collection, cluster, flock, pack, troop, gang; informal bunch, pile.
3 *a coup attempt by a group within the legislature* **faction,** division, section, clique, coterie, circle, set, ring, camp, bloc, caucus, cabal, fringe movement, splinter group.
4 *the women's group* **association,** club, society, league, guild, circle, union, sorority, fraternity.
5 *a small group of trees* **cluster,** knot, collection, mass, clump.
6 *a local singing group* **band,** ensemble, act; informal combo, outfit.
▶ verb 1 *patients were grouped according to their*

symptoms **categorize,** classify, class, catalog, sort, bracket, pigeonhole, grade, rate, rank; prioritize, triage.
2 *extra chairs were grouped around the table* **place,** arrange, assemble, organize, range, line up, dispose.
3 *the two parties* ***grouped together*** **unite,** join together/up, team up, gang up, join forces, get together, ally, form an alliance, affiliate, combine, marry, merge, pool resources; collaborate, work together, pull together, cooperate.

grouse ▶ **verb** *she groused about the food* **grumble,** complain, protest, whine, bleat, carp, cavil, make a fuss; informal moan, bellyache, gripe, beef, bitch, grouch, sound off, kvetch.
▶ **noun** *our biggest grouse was about the noise* **grumble,** complaint, grievance, objection, cavil, quibble; informal moan, beef, gripe, grouch.

grovel ▶ **verb 1** *George groveled at his feet, begging for mercy* **prostrate oneself,** lie, kneel, cringe.
2 *she was not going to* ***grovel to him*** **be obsequious to,** fawn on, kowtow to, bow and scrape to, toady to, truckle to, abase oneself to, humble oneself to; curry favor with, flatter, dance attendance on, make up to, play up to, ingratiate oneself with; informal crawl to, suck up to, lick someone's boots.

grow ▶ **verb 1** *the boys had grown* **get bigger,** get taller, get larger, increase in size.
ANTONYMS shrink.
2 *sales and profits continue to grow* **increase,** swell, multiply, snowball, mushroom, balloon, build up, mount up, pile up; informal skyrocket.
ANTONYMS decline.
3 *flowers grew among the rocks* **sprout,** germinate, shoot up, spring up, develop, bud, burst forth, bloom, flourish, thrive, burgeon.
4 *he grew vegetables* **cultivate,** produce, propagate, raise, rear, nurture, tend; farm.
5 *the family business grew* **expand,** extend, develop, progress, make progress; flourish, thrive, burgeon, prosper, succeed, boom.
ANTONYMS fail, decline.
6 *the modern fable grew from an ancient myth* **originate,** stem, spring, arise, emerge, issue; develop, evolve.
7 *Leonora grew bored* **become,** get, turn, begin to feel.

growl ▶ **verb** *why is your dog growling at us?* **snarl,** bark, yap, bay.

grown-up ▶ **noun** *she wanted to be treated like a grown-up* **adult,** (grown) woman, (grown) man, mature woman, mature man.
ANTONYMS child.
▶ **adjective** *she has two grown-up daughters* **adult,** mature, of age; fully grown, full-grown, fully developed.

growth ▶ **noun 1** *population growth* **increase,** expansion, augmentation, proliferation, multiplication, enlargement, mushrooming, snowballing, rise, escalation, buildup.
ANTONYMS decrease.
2 *the growth of plants* **development,** maturation, growing, germination, sprouting; blooming.
ANTONYMS withering.
3 *the marked growth of local enterprises* **expansion,** extension, development, progress, advance, advancement, headway, spread; rise, success, boom, upturn, upswing.
ANTONYMS failure, decline.
4 *a growth on his jaw* **tumor,** malignancy, cancer; lump, excrescence, outgrowth, swelling, nodule; cyst, polyp.

grub ▶ **noun 1** *a small black grub* **larva**; maggot; caterpillar.
2 informal *we'll grab some grub on the way* See FOOD (sense 1).
▶ **verb 1** *they* ***grubbed up*** *the weeds* **dig up,** unearth, uproot, root up/out, pull up/out, tear out.
2 *he began grubbing around in the trash* **rummage,** search, hunt, delve, dig, scrabble, ferret, root, rifle, fish, poke.

grubby ▶ **adjective** *his grubby work clothes* **dirty,** grimy, filthy, mucky, unwashed, stained, soiled, smeared, spotted, muddy, dusty, sooty; unhygienic, unsanitary; informal cruddy, yucky; literary befouled, begrimed.
ANTONYMS clean.

grudge ▶ **noun** *a former employee with a grudge* **grievance,** resentment, bitterness, rancor, pique, umbrage, dissatisfaction, disgruntlement, bad feelings, hard feelings, ill feelings, ill will, animosity, antipathy, antagonism, enmity, animus; informal a chip on one's shoulder.
▶ **verb** *he grudges the time the meetings use up* **begrudge,** resent, feel aggrieved about, be resentful of, mind, object to, take exception to, take umbrage at.

grueling ▶ **adjective** *a grueling hike through the snow* **exhausting,** tiring, fatiguing, wearying, taxing, draining, debilitating; demanding, exacting, difficult, hard, arduous, strenuous, laborious, back-breaking, harsh, severe, stiff, stressful, punishing, crippling; informal killing, murderous, hellish.

gruesome ▶ **adjective** *Arnie's gruesome Halloween mask frightened the little kids* **grisly,** ghastly, frightful, horrid, horrifying, hideous, horrible, horrendous, grim, awful, dire, dreadful, terrible, horrific, shocking, appalling, disgusting, repulsive, repugnant, revolting, repellent, sickening; loathsome, abhorrent, odious, monstrous, unspeakable; informal sick, gross.
ANTONYMS pleasant.

gruff ▶ **adjective 1** *a gruff reply | his gruff exterior* **abrupt,** brusque, curt, short, blunt, bluff, no-nonsense; laconic, taciturn; surly, churlish, grumpy, crotchety, curmudgeonly, crabby, cross, bad-tempered, short-tempered, ill-natured, crusty, tetchy, bearish, ungracious, unceremonious; informal grouchy. See note at BRUSQUE.
ANTONYMS friendly, courteous.
2 *a gruff voice* **rough,** guttural, throaty, gravelly, husky, croaking, rasping, raspy, growly, hoarse, harsh; low, thick.
ANTONYMS mellow, soft.

grumble ▶ **verb** *they grumbled about the disruption* **complain,** grouse, whine, mutter, bleat, carp, cavil, protest, make a fuss; informal moan, bellyache, beef, bitch, grouch, sound off, gripe, kvetch; Brit. whinge.

▶ **noun** *his customers' grumbles* **complaint,** grievance, protest, cavil, quibble, criticism, grouse; informal grouch, moan, beef, bitch, gripe.

grumpy ▶ **adjective** *she can be quite grumpy in the morning* **bad-tempered,** crabby, ill-tempered, short-tempered, crotchety, tetchy, testy, waspish, prickly, touchy, irritable, irascible, crusty, cantankerous, curmudgeonly, bearish, surly, ill-natured, churlish, ill-humored, peevish, pettish, cross, fractious, disagreeable, snappish; informal grouchy, snappy, cranky, shirty, ornery.
ANTONYMS good-humored.

guarantee ▶ **noun 1** *all repairs have a one-year guarantee* **warranty.**
2 *a guarantee that the hospital will stay open* **promise,** assurance, word (of honor), pledge, vow, oath, bond, commitment, covenant.
3 *banks usually demand **a guarantee** for loans* **collateral,** security, surety, a guaranty, earnest.

▶ **verb 1** *he agreed to guarantee the loan* **underwrite,** put up collateral for.
2 *can you guarantee that he wasn't involved?* **promise,** swear, swear to the fact, pledge, vow, undertake, give one's word, give an assurance, give an undertaking, take an oath.

guard ▶ **verb 1** *infantry guarded the barricaded bridge* **protect,** stand guard over, watch over, keep an eye on; cover, patrol, police, defend, shield, safeguard, keep safe, secure.
2 *the prisoners were guarded by armed men* **keep under surveillance,** keep under guard, keep watch over, mind.
3 *forest wardens must **guard against** poachers* **beware of,** keep watch for, be alert to, keep an eye out for, be on the lookout for, be on the alert for.

▶ **noun 1** *border guards* **sentry,** sentinel, security guard, watchman, night watchman; protector, defender, guardian; lookout, watch; garrison.
2 *her prison guard* **warden,** warder, keeper; jailer; informal screw; archaic turnkey.
3 *he let his guard slip and they escaped* **vigilance,** vigil, watch, surveillance, watchfulness, caution, heed, attention, care, wariness.
4 *a metal guard* **safety guard,** safety device, protective device, shield, screen, fender; bumper, buffer.

– PHRASES **off (one's) guard** *the explosion from the furnace room caught everyone off guard* **unprepared,** unready, inattentive, unwary, with one's defenses down, cold, unsuspecting; informal napping, asleep at the wheel. **on one's guard** *homeowners should be on their guard* **vigilant,** alert, on the alert, wary, watchful, cautious, careful, heedful, chary, circumspect, on the lookout, on the qui vive, on one's toes, prepared, ready, wide awake, attentive, observant, keeping one's eyes peeled.

guarded ▶ **adjective** *they showed guarded enthusiasm for the proposal* **cautious,** careful, circumspect, wary, chary, on one's guard, reluctant, reticent, noncommittal, restrained, reserved; informal buttoned-up, cagey.

guardian ▶ **noun** *Linwood has been my guardian since I was three* **protector,** defender, preserver, custodian, warden, guard, keeper; conservator, curator, caretaker, steward, trustee.

guerrilla ▶ **noun** *the communications canter was raided by leftist guerrillas from the north* **freedom fighter,** irregular, member of the resistance, partisan; rebel, radical, revolutionary, revolutionist; terrorist.

guess ▶ **verb 1** *he guessed she was about 40* **estimate,** hazard a guess, reckon, gauge, judge, calculate; hypothesize, postulate, predict, speculate, conjecture, surmise; informal guesstimate.
2 informal *I guess I owe you an apology* **suppose,** think, imagine, expect, suspect, dare say; informal reckon, figure.

▶ **noun** *my guess was right* **hypothesis,** theory, prediction, postulation, conjecture, surmise, estimate, belief, opinion, reckoning, judgment, supposition, speculation, suspicion, impression, feeling; informal guesstimate, shot in the dark.

guesswork ▶ **noun** *the educated guesswork we rely on in our research* **guessing,** conjecture, surmise, supposition, assumptions, presumptions, speculation, hypothesizing, theorizing, prediction; approximations, rough calculations; hunches; informal guesstimates, ballpark figures.

guest ▶ **noun 1** *I have two guests coming to dinner* **visitor,** house guest, caller; company; archaic visitant.
ANTONYMS host.
2 *hotel guests* **patron,** client, visitor, boarder, lodger, roomer.
ANTONYMS host, landlord, landlady.

▶ **adjective** *a guest speaker* **invited,** featured, special.

guidance ▶ **noun 1** *she looked to her father for guidance* **advice,** counsel, direction, instruction, enlightenment, information; recommendations, suggestions, tips, hints, pointers, guidelines.
2 *work continued under the guidance of a project supervisor* **direction,** control, leadership, management, supervision, superintendence, charge; handling, conduct, running, overseeing.

guide ▶ **noun 1** *our guide took us back to the hotel* **escort,** attendant, tour guide, docent, cicerone; usher, chaperone; historical dragoman.
2 *she is an inspiration and a guide* **adviser/advisor,** mentor, counselor; guru.
3 *the light acted as a guide for shipping* **pointer,** marker, indicator, signpost, mark, landmark; guiding light, sign, signal, beacon.
4 *the techniques outlined are meant as a guide* **model,** pattern, blueprint, template, example, exemplar; standard, touchstone, measure, benchmark, yardstick, gauge.
5 *a pocket guide to the Aleutians* **guidebook.**

▶ **verb 1** *he guided her to her seat* **lead,** conduct, show, show the way, usher, shepherd, direct, steer, pilot, escort, accompany, attend; see, take, help, assist.
2 *the chairperson must guide the meeting* **direct,** steer, control, manage, command, lead, conduct, run, be in charge of, have control of, pilot, govern, preside over, superintend, supervise, oversee; handle, regulate.
3 *he was always there to guide me* **advise,** counsel, give advice to, direct, give direction to.

guideline ▶ noun *the zoning commission's strict guidelines* **recommendation,** instruction, direction, suggestion, advice; regulation, rule, principle, guiding principle; standard, criterion, measure, gauge, yardstick, benchmark, touchstone; procedure, parameter.

guild ▶ noun *the copper craftsmen have formed a guild* **association,** society, union, league, organization, company, cooperative, fellowship, club, order, lodge, brotherhood, fraternity, sisterhood, sorority.

guile ▶ noun *Georgia was the only one among us not taken in by Owen's guile* **cunning,** craftiness, craft, artfulness, art, artifice, wiliness, slyness, deviousness; wiles, ploys, schemes, stratagems, maneuvers, tricks, subterfuges, ruses; deception, deceit, duplicity, underhandedness, double-dealing, trickery.
ANTONYMS honesty.

guileless ▶ adjective *how can you take advantage of someone so sweet and guileless?* **artless,** ingenuous, naive, open, genuine, natural, simple, childlike, innocent, unsophisticated, unworldly, unsuspicious, trustful, trusting; honest, truthful, sincere, straightforward.
ANTONYMS scheming.

guilt ▶ noun **1** *the proof of his guilt* **culpability,** guiltiness, blameworthiness; wrongdoing, wrong, criminality, misconduct, sin.
ANTONYMS innocence.
2 *a terrible feeling of guilt* **self-reproach,** self-condemnation, shame, a guilty conscience, pangs of conscience; remorse, remorsefulness, regret, contrition, contriteness, compunction.
ANTONYMS innocence.

guiltless ▶ adjective *the victims here are these guiltless children* **innocent,** blameless, not to blame, without fault, above reproach, above suspicion, in the clear, unimpeachable, irreproachable, faultless, sinless, spotless, immaculate, unsullied, uncorrupted, undefiled, untainted, unblemished, untarnished, impeccable; informal squeaky clean, whiter than white, as pure as the driven snow.
ANTONYMS guilty.

guilty ▶ adjective **1** *the guilty party* **culpable,** to blame, at fault, in the wrong, blameworthy, responsible; erring, errant, delinquent, offending, sinful, criminal; archaic peccant.
ANTONYMS innocent.
2 *I still feel guilty about it* **ashamed,** guilt-ridden, conscience-stricken, remorseful, sorry, contrite, repentant, penitent, regretful, rueful, abashed, shamefaced, sheepish, hangdog; in sackcloth and ashes.
ANTONYMS unrepentant.

guise ▶ noun **1** *the god appeared in the guise of a swan* **likeness,** outward appearance, appearance, semblance, form, shape, image; disguise.
2 *additional payments were made under the guise of consulting fees* **pretense,** disguise, front, facade, cover, blind, screen, smokescreen.

gulf ▶ noun **1** *our ship sailed into the gulf* **inlet,** bay, bight, cove, fjord, estuary, sound.
2 *the ice gave way and a gulf widened slowly* **hole,** crevasse, fissure, cleft, split, rift, pit, cavity, chasm, abyss, void; ravine, gorge, canyon, gully.
3 *a growing gulf between rich and poor* **divide,** division, separation, gap, breach, rift, split, chasm, abyss; difference, contrast, polarity.

gullet ▶ noun *the bird's gullet* **esophagus,** throat, maw, pharynx; crop, craw; archaic throttle, gorge.

gullible ▶ adjective *he was a swindler who preyed on gullible elderly widows* **credulous,** naive, overtrusting, overtrustful, easily deceived, easily taken in, exploitable, dupable, impressionable, unsuspecting, unsuspicious, unwary, ingenuous, innocent, inexperienced, unworldly, green; informal wet behind the ears, born yesterday.
ANTONYMS suspicious.

> CHOOSE THE RIGHT WORD
>
> **gullible, callow, credulous, ingenuous, naive, trusting, unsophisticated**
>
> Some people will believe anything. Those who are truly **gullible** are the easiest to deceive, which is why they so often make fools of themselves. Those who are merely **credulous** might be a little too quick to believe something, but they usually aren't stupid enough to act on it. **Trusting** suggests the same willingness to believe (*a trusting child*), but it isn't necessarily a bad way to be (*a person so trusting he completely disarmed his enemies*). No one likes to be called **naive** because it implies a lack of street smarts (*she's so naive she'd accept a ride from a stranger*), but when applied to things other than people, it can describe a simplicity and absence of artificiality that is quite charming (*the naive style in which nineteenth-century American portraits were often painted*). Most people would rather be thought of as **ingenuous**, meaning straightforward and sincere (*an ingenuous confession of the truth*), because it implies the simplicity of a child without the negative overtones. **Callow**, however, comes down a little more heavily on the side of immaturity and almost always goes hand-in-hand with youth. Whether young or old, someone who is **unsophisticated** suffers from a lack of experience.

gully ▶ noun **1** *a steep icy gully* **ravine,** canyon, gorge, pass, defile, couloir, gulch, coulee, draw.
2 *water runs from the drainpipe into a gully* **channel,** conduit, trench, ditch, drain, culvert, cut, gutter.

gulp ▶ verb **1** *she gulped her juice* **swallow,** guzzle (down), quaff, swill down, down; informal swig, knock back, chug, chugalug.
ANTONYMS sip.
2 *he* ***gulped down*** *the rest of his meal* **gobble (down),** guzzle (down), devour, bolt down, wolf down; informal put away, demolish, polish off, shovel in/down, scoff (down).
ANTONYMS nibble.
3 *Lisa* ***gulped back*** *her tears* **choke back,** fight back, hold back/in, suppress, stifle, smother.
▶ noun *a gulp of cold beer* **mouthful,** swallow,

draft; informal swig.

gum ▶ **noun** *photographs stuck down with gum* **glue,** adhesive, fixative, paste, epoxy, epoxy resin, mucilage.

▶ **verb** *the receipts were gummed into a book* **stick,** glue, paste; fix, affix, attach, fasten.

– PHRASES **gum up** *check to see if the valves are gummed up* **clog (up),** choke (up), stop up, plug; obstruct; informal bung up, gunge up; technical occlude.

gumption ▶ **noun** informal *we never thought Clarence would have the gumption to stand up to the committee—and actually get what he wanted* **initiative,** resourcefulness, enterprise, ingenuity, imagination; astuteness, shrewdness, acumen, sense, common sense, wit, mother wit, practicality; spirit, backbone, pluck, mettle, nerve, courage, wherewithal; informal getup-and-go, spunk, oomph, moxie, savvy, horse sense, (street) smarts.

gun ▶ **noun** *the illegal trafficking of drugs and guns* **firearm,** pistol, revolver, rifle, shotgun, carbine, automatic, handgun, semiautomatic, machine gun, Uzi; weapon; informal piece, gat, heater.

gunman ▶ **noun** *a lone gunman apparently hid in the stairwell for several hours* **armed robber,** gangster, terrorist; sniper, gunfighter; assassin, murderer, killer; informal hit man, hired gun, gunslinger, mobster, shootist, hood.

gurgle ▶ **verb** *the water swirled and gurgled* **babble,** burble, tinkle, bubble, ripple, murmur, purl, splash; literary plash.

▶ **noun** *the gurgle of a small brook* **babbling,** tinkling, bubbling, rippling, trickling, murmur, murmuring, purling, splashing; literary plashing.

guru ▶ **noun 1** *a Hindu guru and mystic* **spiritual teacher,** teacher, tutor, sage, mentor, spiritual leader, leader, master; Hinduism swami, maharishi.
ANTONYMS disciple.
2 *a management guru* **expert,** authority, pundit, leading light, master, specialist; informal whiz.
ANTONYMS amateur.

gush ▶ **verb 1** *water gushed through the weir* **surge,** burst, spout, spurt, jet, stream, rush, pour, spill, well out, cascade, flood; flow, run, issue.
2 *everyone gushed about the script* **enthuse,** rave, be enthusiastic, be effusive, rhapsodize, go into raptures, wax lyrical, praise to the skies; informal go mad, go wild, go crazy.

▶ **noun** *a gush of water* **surge,** stream, spurt, jet, spout, outpouring, outflow, burst, rush, cascade, flood, torrent; technical efflux.

gust ▶ **noun 1** *a sudden gust of wind* **flurry,** blast, puff, blow, rush; squall.
2 *gusts of laughter* **outburst,** burst, eruption, fit, paroxysm; gale, peal, howl, hoot, shriek, roar.

▶ **verb** *wind gusted around the chimneys* **blow,** bluster, flurry, roar.

gusto ▶ **noun** *neighbors remembered the slain soldier as a friendly kid who played sports with gusto* **enthusiasm,** relish, appetite, enjoyment, delight, glee, pleasure, satisfaction, appreciation, liking; zest, zeal, fervor, verve, keenness, avidity.
ANTONYMS apathy, distaste.

gut ▶ **noun 1** *he had an ache in his gut* **stomach,** belly, abdomen, solar plexus; intestines, bowels; informal tummy, tum, insides, innards.
2 *fish heads and guts* **entrails;** intestines, viscera; offal; gurry; informal insides, innards.
3 informal **(guts)** *Nicola had the guts to say what she felt* **courage,** bravery, backbone, nerve, pluck, spirit, boldness, audacity, daring, grit, fearlessness, feistiness, toughness, determination; informal spunk, moxie. See note at **COURAGE.**

▶ **adjective** informal *a gut feeling* **instinctive,** instinctual, intuitive, deep-seated; knee-jerk, automatic, involuntary, spontaneous, unthinking, visceral.

▶ **verb 1** *clean, scale, and gut the trout* **remove the guts from,** disembowel, draw; formal eviscerate.
2 *the church was gutted by fire* **devastate,** destroy, demolish, wipe out, lay waste, ravage, consume, ruin, wreck.

gutter ▶ **noun** *gutters clogged with leaves* **drain,** sluice, sluiceway, culvert, spillway, sewer; channel, conduit, pipe; rain gutter; trough, trench, ditch, furrow, cut.

guttural ▶ **adjective** *the man who called had a guttural voice* **throaty,** husky, gruff, gravelly, growly, growling, croaky, croaking, harsh, rough, rasping, raspy; deep, low, thick.

guy ▶ **noun** informal *he's a handsome guy* **man,** fellow, gentleman; youth, boy; informal lad, fella, gent, chap, dude, joe, Joe Blow, Joe Schmo, hombre.

guzzle ▶ **verb** *she guzzled down the orange juice* **gulp down,** swallow, quaff, down, swill; informal knock back, swig, slug.

gypsy ▶ **noun** *a caravan of gypsies* **Romany,** Rom, traveler, nomad, rover, roamer, wanderer.

gyrate ▶ **verb** *the disk gyrates atop an aluminum pole* **rotate,** revolve, wheel, turn around, whirl, circle, pirouette, twirl, swirl, spin, swivel.

Hh

habit ▶ noun 1 *it was his habit to go for a run every morning* **custom,** practice, routine, wont, pattern, convention, way, norm, tradition, matter of course, rule, usage.
2 *her many irritating habits* **mannerism,** way, quirk, foible, trick, trait, idiosyncrasy, peculiarity, singularity, oddity, eccentricity, feature; tendency, propensity, inclination, bent, proclivity, disposition, predisposition.
3 *his cocaine habit* **addiction,** dependence, dependency, craving, fixation, compulsion, obsession, weakness; informal monkey on one's back.
4 *a monk's habit* **garment**(s), dress, garb, clothes, clothing, attire, outfit, costume; informal gear; formal apparel.
– PHRASES **habit of mind** *a scientific habit of mind* **disposition,** temperament, character, nature, makeup, constitution, frame of mind, bent. **in the habit of** *they were in the habit of phoning each other daily* **accustomed to,** used to, given to, wont to, inclined to.

habitable ▶ adjective *it's not the Ritz, but it's habitable* **fit to live in,** inhabitable, fit to occupy, in good repair, livable; formal tenantable.

habitat ▶ noun *the habitat of the spotted turtle has been greatly diminished* **natural environment,** natural surroundings, home, domain, haunt; formal habitation.

habitation ▶ noun 1 *a house fit for human habitation* **occupancy,** occupation, residence, residency, living in, tenancy.
2 formal *his main habitation* **residence,** place of residence, house, home, seat, lodging place, billet, quarters, living quarters, rooms, accommodations; informal pad, digs; formal dwelling, dwelling place, abode, domicile.

habitual ▶ adjective 1 *her father's habitual complaints* **constant,** persistent, continual, continuous, perpetual, nonstop, recurrent, repeated, frequent; interminable, incessant, ceaseless, endless, never-ending; informal eternal.
ANTONYMS occasional, infrequent.
2 *habitual drinkers* **inveterate,** confirmed, compulsive, obsessive, incorrigible, hardened, ingrained, dyed-in-the-wool, chronic, regular; addicted; informal pathological.
ANTONYMS occasional.
3 *his habitual secretiveness* **customary,** accustomed, regular, usual, normal, set, fixed, established, routine, common, ordinary, familiar, traditional, typical, general, characteristic, standard, time-honored; literary wonted.
ANTONYMS unaccustomed.

habituate ▶ verb *poverty had habituated their children to a life of hopelessness* **accustom,** make used, familiarize, adapt, adjust, attune, acclimatize, acculturate, condition; inure, harden; acclimate.

hack[1] ▶ verb *Stuart hacked the padlock off* **cut,** chop, hew, lop, saw; slash.
– PHRASES **hack it** informal *he tried to run his own commercial fishing outfit, but he couldn't hack it* **cope,** manage, get on/by, carry on, come through, muddle along/through; stand it, tolerate it, bear it, endure it, put up with it; informal handle it, abide it, stick it out.

hack[2] ▶ noun 1 *a tabloid hack* **journalist,** reporter, newspaperman, newspaperwoman, writer; informal journo, scribbler; archaic penny-a-liner.
2 *office hacks* **drudge,** menial, menial worker, factotum; informal gofer.

hackles ▶ plural noun
– PHRASES **make someone's hackles rise** *Julie's compulsive criticizing made her sister's hackles rise* **annoy,** irritate, exasperate, anger, incense, infuriate, irk, nettle, vex, put out, provoke, gall, antagonize, get on someone's nerves, ruffle someone's feathers, rankle with; rub the wrong way; informal aggravate, peeve, needle, rile, make someone see red, make someone's blood boil, get someone's back up, get someone's goat, get someone's dander up, bug, tee off, tick off, burn up.

hackneyed ▶ adjective *your hackneyed arguments fail to persuade anyone* **overused,** overdone, overworked, worn out, timeworn, platitudinous, vapid, stale, tired, threadbare; trite, banal, hack, clichéd, hoary, commonplace, common, ordinary, stock, conventional, stereotyped, predictable; unimaginative, unoriginal, uninspired, prosaic, dull, boring, pedestrian, run-of-the-mill, boilerplate, routine; informal old hat, cheesy, corny, played out.
ANTONYMS original.

hag ▶ noun *we'd all heard tales of a wizened hag who lived alone on the far side of the mountain* **crone,** old woman, gorgon; informal witch, crow, cow, old bag.

haggard ▶ adjective *he looked terrible, all pale and haggard* **drawn,** tired, exhausted, drained, careworn, unwell, unhealthy, spent, washed out, run-down; gaunt, pinched, peaked, hollow-cheeked, hollow-eyed, thin, emaciated, wasted, cadaverous; pale, wan, gray, ashen.
ANTONYMS healthy.

haggle ▶ verb *John spent nearly every Saturday morning haggling at flea markets and garage* *sales* **barter,** bargain, negotiate, dicker, quibble, wrangle; beat someone down, drive a hard bargain.

hail[1] ▶ **verb 1** *a friend hailed him from the upper deck* **call out to,** shout to, address; greet, say hello to, salute.
2 *he hailed a cab* **flag down,** wave down, signal to.
3 *critics hailed the film as a masterpiece* **acclaim,** praise, applaud, rave about, extol, eulogize, hymn, lionize, sing the praises of, make much of, glorify, cheer, salute, toast, ballyhoo; formal laud.
4 *Rick* ***hails from*** *Australia* **come from,** be from, be a native of, have one's roots in.

hail[2] ▶ **noun** *a hail of bullets* **barrage,** volley, shower, rain, torrent, burst, stream, storm, avalanche, onslaught; bombardment, cannonade, battery, blast, salvo; historical broadside.
▶ **verb** *tons of dust hailed down on us* **beat,** shower, rain, fall, pour; pelt, pepper, batter, bombard, assail.

hair ▶ **noun 1** *her thick black hair* **locks,** curls, ringlets, mane, mop; shock of hair, head of hair; tresses.
2 *I like your hair* **hairstyle,** haircut, cut, coiffure; informal hairdo, do, coif.
3 *a dog with short, blue-gray hair* **fur,** wool; coat, fleece, pelt; mane.
– PHRASES **a hair's breadth** *she won by a hair's breadth* **the narrowest of margins,** a narrow margin, the skin of one's teeth, a split second, a nose, a whisker. **let one's hair down** informal *even the chairman of the board has to let his hair down once in a while* **enjoy oneself,** have a good time, have fun, make merry, let oneself go; informal have a ball, whoop it up, paint the town red, live it up, have a whale of a time, let it all hang out. **make someone's hair stand on end** *the truth about Corrine would make your hair stand on end* **horrify,** shock, appall, scandalize, stun; make someone's blood run cold; informal make someone's hair curl, turn someone's hair white. **split hairs** *you missed the point because you were so busy splitting hairs* **quibble,** cavil, carp, niggle; informal nitpick; archaic pettifog.

hair-raising ▶ **adjective** *the hair-raising stories we would tell around the campfire* **terrifying,** frightening, petrifying, alarming, chilling, horrifying, shocking, spine-chilling, blood-curdling, bone-chilling, white-knuckle, fearsome, nightmarish; eerie, sinister, weird, ghostly, unearthly; eldritch; informal hairy, spooky, scary, creepy.

hairy ▶ **adjective 1** *animals with hairy coats* **shaggy,** bushy, long-haired; woolly, furry, fleecy, fuzzy; Botany & Zoology pilose.
2 *his hairy face* **bearded,** bewhiskered, mustachioed; unshaven, stubbly, bristly; formal hirsute.
3 informal *a hairy situation* **risky,** dangerous, perilous, hazardous, touch-and-go; tricky, ticklish, difficult, awkward; informal dicey, sticky.

halcyon ▶ **adjective** *the halcyon days of our youth* **happy,** golden, idyllic, carefree, blissful, joyful, joyous, contented; flourishing, thriving, prosperous, successful; serene, calm, tranquil, peaceful. See note at CALM.

hale ▶ **adjective** *fair weather and a hale crew* **healthy,** fit, fighting fit, well, in good health, bursting with health, in fine fettle, strong, robust, vigorous, hardy, sturdy, hearty, lusty, able-bodied; informal in the pink, as right as rain.
ANTONYMS unwell.

half ▶ **adjective** *a half grapefruit* **halved,** bisected, divided in two.
ANTONYMS whole.
▶ **adverb 1** *the chicken is half cooked* **partially,** partly, incompletely, inadequately, insufficiently; in part, part, slightly.
ANTONYMS fully, completely.
2 *I'm half inclined to believe you* **to a certain extent/degree,** to some extent/degree, (up) to a point, in part, partly, in some measure.
ANTONYMS fully.
▶ **noun** *the first half of the show* **portion,** section, part, period; 50 percent.

half-baked ▶ **adjective 1** *half-baked theories* **ill-conceived,** hare-brained, cockamamie, ill-judged, impractical, unrealistic, unworkable, ridiculous, absurd; informal crazy, crackpot, cockeyed.
ANTONYMS sensible.
2 *her half-baked nephew* **foolish,** stupid, silly, idiotic, simpleminded, feebleminded, empty-headed, featherbrained, featherheaded, brainless, witless, unintelligent, ignorant; informal dim, dopey, dumb, thick, halfwitted, dimwitted, birdbrained, dozy.
ANTONYMS sensible.

half-hearted ▶ **adjective** *the half-hearted applause was not exactly encouraging* **unenthusiastic,** cool, lukewarm, tepid, apathetic, indifferent, uninterested, unconcerned, languid, listless; perfunctory, cursory, superficial, desultory, feeble, lackluster.
ANTONYMS enthusiastic.

halfway ▶ **adjective** *the halfway point* **midway,** middle, mid, central, center, intermediate; Anatomy medial, mesial.
▶ **adverb 1** *he started running down the passage and then stopped halfway* **midway,** in the middle, in the center; partway, part of the way.
2 *she seemed halfway friendly* **to some extent/degree,** in some measure, relatively, comparatively, moderately, somewhat, (up) to a point; just about, almost, nearly.
– PHRASES **meet someone halfway** *I was willing to meet him halfway* **compromise,** come to terms, reach an agreement, make a deal, make concessions, find the middle ground, strike a balance; give and take.

halfwit ▶ **noun** informal See FOOL (sense 1 of the noun).

halfwitted ▶ **adjective** informal See STUPID (sense 1).

hall ▶ **noun 1** *hang your coat in the hall* **entrance hall,** hallway, entry, entrance, lobby, foyer, vestibule; atrium, concourse; passageway, passage, corridor, entryway.
2 *we booked a hall for the wedding* **banquet hall,** community center, assembly room, meeting room, chamber; auditorium, concert hall, theater.

hallmark ▶ **noun 1** *the hallmark on silver* **assay**

mark, official mark, stamp of authenticity.
2 *tiny bubbles are the hallmark of fine champagnes* **mark,** distinctive feature, characteristic, sign, sure sign, telltale sign, badge, stamp, trademark, indication, indicator, calling card.

hallucinate ▶ verb *the fever made her hallucinate* **have hallucinations,** see things, be delirious, fantasize; informal trip, see pink elephants.

hallucination ▶ noun *are you sure that what you saw wasn't a hallucination?* **delusion,** illusion, figment of the imagination, vision, apparition, mirage, chimera, fantasy; (**hallucinations**) delirium, phantasmagoria; informal trip, pink elephants.

halo ▶ noun *a stunning depiction of the angel's halo* **ring of light,** nimbus, aureole, glory, crown of light, corona; technical halation; rare gloriole.

halt ▶ verb **1** *Jen halted and turned around* **stop,** come to a halt, come to a stop, come to a standstill; pull up, draw up.
ANTONYMS start, go.
2 *a further strike has halted production* **stop,** bring to a stop, put a stop to, bring to an end, put an end to, terminate, end, wind up; suspend, break off, arrest; impede, check, curb, stem, block, stall, hold back; informal pull the plug on, put the kibosh on.
ANTONYMS start, continue.
▶ noun **1** *the car drew to a halt* **stop,** standstill.
2 *a halt in production* **stoppage,** stopping, discontinuation, break, suspension, pause, interval, interruption, hiatus; cessation, termination, close, end.

halting ▶ adjective **1** *a halting conversation | halting English* **hesitant,** faltering, hesitating, stumbling, stammering, stuttering; broken, imperfect.
ANTONYMS fluent.
2 *his halting gait* **unsteady,** awkward, faltering, stumbling, limping, hobbling.
ANTONYMS steady, nimble.

hammer ▶ noun *a hammer and chisel* mallet, beetle, gavel, sledgehammer, jackhammer.
▶ verb **1** *the alloy is hammered into a circular shape* **beat,** forge, shape, form, mold, fashion, make.
2 *Sally **hammered at** the door* **batter,** pummel, beat, bang, pound; strike, hit, knock on, thump on; cudgel, bludgeon, club; informal bash, wallop, clobber, whack, thwack.
3 *they **hammered away at** their nonsmoking campaign* **work hard at,** labor at, slog away at, plod away at, grind away at, slave away at, work like a dog on, put one's nose to the grindstone for; persist with, persevere with, press on with; informal stick at, plug away at, work one's tail off on/for, soldier on with.
4 *antiracism had been **hammered into** her* **drum into,** instill in, inculcate into, knock into, drive into; drive home to, impress upon; ingrain into.
5 informal *we've hammered them twice this season* See **TROUNCE**.
– PHRASES **hammer out** *the committee sat for three hours hammering out a new budget* **thrash out,** work out, agree on, sort out, decide on, bring about, effect, produce, broker, negotiate, reach an agreement on.

hamper¹ ▶ noun *a picnic hamper* **basket,** pannier, wickerwork basket; box, container.

hamper² ▶ verb *the search was hampered by fog* **hinder,** obstruct, impede, inhibit, retard, balk, thwart, foil, curb, delay, set back, slow down, hobble, hold up, interfere with; restrict, constrain, trammel, block, check, curtail, frustrate, cramp, bridle, handicap, cripple, hamstring, shackle, fetter; informal stymie, hog-tie, throw a (monkey) wrench in the works of. See note at **HINDER**.
ANTONYMS help.

hamstring ▶ verb **1** *cattle were killed or hamstrung* **cripple,** lame, disable, incapacitate.
2 *he felt hamstrung by the regulations* See **HAMPER²**.

hand ▶ noun **1** *big, strong hands* palm, fist; informal paw, mitt, duke, hook, meathook.
2 *the clock's second hand* **pointer,** indicator, needle, arrow, marker.
3 (**hands**) *the frontier posts remained in government hands* **control,** power, charge, authority; command, responsibility, guardianship, management, care, supervision, jurisdiction; possession, keeping, custody; clutches, grasp, thrall; disposal; informal say-so.
4 *let me give you **a hand*** **help,** a helping hand, assistance, aid, support, succor, relief; a good turn, a favor.
5 *a document written in his own hand* **handwriting,** writing, script, calligraphy.
6 *a ranch hand* **worker,** workman, laborer, operative, hired hand, roustabout, peon; cowboy.
▶ verb *she handed each of us an envelope* **pass,** give, let someone have; throw, toss; present to.
– PHRASES **at hand** *the time for courage is at hand* **imminent,** approaching, coming, about to happen, on the horizon; impending.
big hand informal *her fans gave her a big hand* **round of applause,** clap, handclap, ovation, standing ovation; applause, handclapping.
close at hand *keep the manual close at hand* **readily available,** available, handy, to hand, within reach, accessible, close, close by, near, nearby, at the ready, at one's fingertips, at one's disposal, convenient; informal get-at-able.
hand down *this bracelet has been handed down from four generations* **pass on,** pass down; bequeath, will, leave, make over, give, gift, transfer; Law demise, devise. **hand in glove** *working hand in glove with their former adversaries* **in close collaboration,** in close association, in close cooperation, very closely, in partnership, in league, in collusion; informal in cahoots, in bed. **hand out** *volunteers were asked to hand out pamphlets* **distribute,** give out, pass out/around, dole out, dish out, deal out, mete out, issue, dispense; allocate, allot, apportion, disburse; circulate, disseminate.
hand over *they handed over the stolen goods to the authorities* **yield,** give, give up, pass, grant, entrust, surrender, relinquish, cede, turn over, deliver up, forfeit, sacrifice. **hands down** *we won hands down* **easily,** effortlessly, with ease, with no trouble, without effort; informal by a mile, no sweat. **try one's hand at** *I regret that I never tried my hand at waterskiing* **have a go at,**

make an attempt at, have a shot at; attempt, try, try out, give something a try; informal have a stab at, give something a whirl; formal essay.

handbag ▶ noun *a leather handbag* **purse,** bag, shoulder bag, clutch purse, evening bag; pocketbook; historical reticule.

handbill ▶ noun *annoyed by the handbills on our windshield* **notice,** advertisement, flyer, leaflet, circular, handout, pamphlet, brochure, fact sheet; informal ad.

handbook ▶ noun *the handbook explains our late-fee policy* **manual,** instructions, instruction manual, how-to guide; almanac, companion, directory, compendium; guide, guidebook, vade mecum.

handcuff ▶ verb *police officers handcuffed the individual* **manacle,** shackle, fetter; restrain, clap/put someone in irons; informal cuff.

handcuffs ▶ plural noun *when her lawyer came, Paula was still in handcuffs* **manacles,** shackles, irons, fetters, bonds, restraints; informal cuffs, bracelets.

handful ▶ noun **1** ***a handful of*** *bad apples* **a few,** a small number of, a small amount of, a small quantity of, one or two, some, not many, a scattering of, a trickle of.
2 informal *the child is a real handful* **nuisance,** problem, bother, irritant, thorn in someone's flesh/side; informal pest, headache, pain, pain in the neck, pain in the butt.

handicap ▶ noun **1** *a visual handicap* **disability,** physical abnormality, mental abnormality, defect, impairment, affliction, deficiency, dysfunction.
2 *a handicap to the competitiveness of the industry* **impediment,** hindrance, obstacle, barrier, bar, obstruction, encumbrance, constraint, restriction, check, block, curb; disadvantage, drawback, stumbling block, difficulty, shortcoming, limitation; ball and chain, albatross, millstone (around someone's neck), burden, liability; literary trammel.
ANTONYMS benefit, advantage.
▶ verb *lack of funding handicapped the research* **hamper,** impede, hinder, impair, hamstring; restrict, check, obstruct, block, curb, bridle, hold back, constrain, trammel, limit, encumber; informal stymie.
ANTONYMS help, advance.

handiwork ▶ noun *the jewelry is the handiwork of Chinese smiths* **creation,** product, work, achievement; handicraft, craft, craftwork.

handle ▶ verb **1** *the equipment must be handled with care* **hold,** pick up, grasp, grip, lift; feel, touch, finger; informal paw.
2 *a car that is easy to handle* **control,** drive, steer, operate, maneuver, manipulate.
3 *she handled the problems well* **deal with,** manage, tackle, take care of, take charge of, attend to, see to, sort out, apply oneself to, take in hand; respond to, field.
4 *the advertising company that is handling the account* **administer,** manage, control, conduct, direct, guide, supervise, oversee, be in charge of, take care of, look after.
5 *the traders handled goods manufactured in the Rhineland* **trade in,** deal in, buy, sell, supply, peddle, traffic in, purvey, hawk, tout, market.
▶ noun *the knife's handle* **haft,** shank, stock, shaft, grip, handgrip, hilt, helve, butt; knob.

handout ▶ noun **1** (**handouts**) *she existed on handouts* **charity,** aid, benefit, financial support, donations, subsidies, welfare; historical alms.
2 *a photocopied handout* **leaflet,** pamphlet, brochure, fact sheet; handbill, flyer, notice, circular.

hand-picked ▶ adjective *six hand-picked contestants will be flown to Ireland for the finals* **specially chosen,** selected, invited; select, elite; choice.

handsome ▶ adjective **1** *a handsome man* **good-looking,** attractive, striking, gorgeous; informal hunky, drop-dead gorgeous, hot, cute.
ANTONYMS ugly.
2 *a handsome woman of 30* **striking,** imposing, prepossessing, elegant, stately, dignified, statuesque, good-looking, attractive, personable.
ANTONYMS plain.
3 *a handsome profit* **substantial,** considerable, sizable, princely, large, big, ample, bumper; informal tidy, whopping, not to be sneezed at, ginormous.
ANTONYMS meager.

handwriting ▶ noun *barely legible handwriting* **writing,** script, hand, pen; penmanship, calligraphy, chirography; informal scrawl, scribble, chicken scratch.

handy ▶ adjective **1** *a handy reference tool* **useful,** convenient, practical, easy-to-use, well-designed, user-friendly, user-oriented, helpful, functional, serviceable.
ANTONYMS inconvenient.
2 *keep your credit card handy* **readily available,** available, at hand, near at hand, within reach, accessible, ready, close, close by, near, nearby, at the ready, at one's fingertips; informal get-at-able.
3 *he's handy with a needle and thread* **skillful,** skilled, dexterous, deft, nimble-fingered, adroit, able, adept, proficient, capable; good with one's hands; informal nifty.
ANTONYMS inept.

hang ▶ verb **1** *lights hung from the trees* **be suspended,** dangle, hang down, be pendent, swing, sway.
2 *hang the pictures at eye level* **put up,** fix, attach, affix, fasten, post, display, suspend, pin up, nail up.
3 *the room was hung with streamers* **decorate,** adorn, drape, festoon, deck out, trick out, bedeck, array, garland, swathe, cover, ornament; literary bedizen.
4 *he was hanged for murder* **string up,** send to the gallows.
5 *a pall of smoke hung over the city* **hover,** float, drift, be suspended.
– PHRASES **hang around** informal **1** *they spent their time hanging around in bars* **loiter,** linger, wait around, waste time, kill time, mark time, while away the/one's time, cool one's heels, twiddle one's thumbs; frequent, be a regular visitor to, haunt; informal hang out in. **2** *she's hanging around with a gang of marketing types* **associate,** mix, keep company, socialize,

fraternize, consort, rub elbows; informal hang out, run around, be thick, hobnob. **hang on 1** *he hung on to her coat* **hold on to,** hold fast to, grip, clutch, grasp, hold tightly to, cling to. **2** *her future hung on their decision* **depend on,** be dependent on, turn on, hinge on, rest on, be contingent on, be determined by, be decided by. **3** *I'll hang on as long as I can* **persevere,** hold out, hold on, go on, carry on, keep on, keep going, keep at it, continue, persist, stay with it, struggle on, plod on; informal soldier on, stick to/at it, stick it out, hang in there. **4** informal *hang on, let me think* **wait,** wait a minute, wait a second, hold on, stop; hold the line/phone; informal hold your horses, sit tight, wait a sec. **hang over someone** *the threat of budget cuts is hanging over us* **be imminent,** threaten, be close, be impending, impend, loom, be on the horizon.

hangdog ▶ **adjective** *his hangdog expression betrayed his alleged confidence* **shamefaced,** sheepish, abashed, ashamed, guilty-looking, abject, cowed, dejected, downcast, crestfallen, woebegone, disconsolate.
ANTONYMS unabashed.

hanger-on ▶ **noun** *here comes Mr. Bigshot and his creepy hangers-on* **follower,** flunky, toady, camp follower, sycophant, parasite, leech, bottom feeder; henchman, minion, lackey, vassal; acolyte; cohort; informal groupie, sponger, freeloader, passenger, sidekick.

hang-up ▶ **noun** *Louie has a hang-up about dirty windows* **neurosis,** phobia, preoccupation, fixation, obsession, idée fixe; inhibition, mental block, psychological block, block, difficulty; informal complex, thing, bee in one's bonnet.

hank ▶ **noun** *a hank of yarn* **coil,** skein, length, roll, loop, twist, piece; lock, ringlet, curl.

hanker ▶ **verb** *I hanker to go home* **yearn,** long, crave, desire, wish, want, hunger, thirst, lust, ache, pant, be eager, be desperate, be eating one's heart out; fancy, pine; informal be dying, have a yen, itch.

hankering ▶ **noun** *I had a sudden hankering for a BLT* **longing,** yearning, craving, desire, wish, hunger, thirst, urge, ache, lust, appetite, fancy; informal yen, itch; archaic appetency.
ANTONYMS aversion.

haphazard ▶ **adjective** *Shelley's haphazard piles of laundry* **random,** unplanned, unsystematic, unmethodical, disorganized, disorderly, irregular, indiscriminate, chaotic, hit-and-miss, arbitrary, aimless, careless, casual, slapdash, slipshod; chance, accidental; informal higgledy-piggledy.

hapless ▶ **adjective** *the hapless victims of exploitation* **unfortunate,** unlucky, luckless, out of luck, ill-starred, ill-fated, jinxed, cursed, doomed; unhappy, forlorn, wretched, miserable, woebegone; informal down on one's luck; literary star-crossed.
ANTONYMS lucky.

happen ▶ **verb 1** *remember what happened last time he was here* **occur,** take place, come about; ensue, result, transpire, materialize, arise, crop up, come up, present itself, supervene; informal go down; formal eventuate; literary come to pass, betide.
2 *I wonder what happened to Joe?* **become of;** literary befall, betide.
3 *they happened to be in* **chance,** have the good/bad luck.
4 *she happened on a blue jay's nest* **discover,** find, find by chance, come across, chance on, stumble on, hit on.

> CHOOSE THE RIGHT WORD
>
> **happen, befall, occur, transpire**
>
> When things **happen**, they come to pass either for a reason or by chance (*it happened the day after school started; she happened upon the scene of the accident*), but the verb is more frequently associated with chance (*it happened to be raining when we got there*). **Occur** can also refer either to something that comes to pass either accidentally or as planned, but it should only be used interchangeably with *happen* when the subject is a definite or actual event (*the tragedy occurred last winter*). Unlike *happen, occur* also carries the implication of something that presents itself to sight or mind (*it never occurred to me that he was lying*). **Transpire** is a more formal (and some would say undesirable) word meaning to *happen* or *occur*, and it conveys the sense that something has leaked out or become known (*he told her exactly what had transpired while she was away*). While things that *happen, occur,* or *transpire* can be either positive or negative, when something **befalls** it is usually unpleasant (*he had no inkling of the disaster that would befall him when he got home*).

happening ▶ **noun** *bizarre happenings* **occurrence,** event, incident, proceeding, affair, doing, circumstance, phenomenon, episode, experience, occasion, development, eventuality.
▶ **adjective** informal *a happening nightspot* **fashionable,** modern, popular, new, latest, up-to-date, up-to-the-minute, in fashion, in vogue, le dernier cri; informal trendy, funky, hot, cool, with it, hip, in, big, now, groovy.
ANTONYMS old-fashioned.

happily ▶ **adverb 1** *he smiled happily* **contentedly,** cheerfully, cheerily, merrily, delightedly, joyfully, joyously, gaily, gleefully.
2 *I will happily do as you ask* **gladly,** willingly, readily, freely, cheerfully, ungrudgingly, with pleasure; archaic fain.
3 *happily, we are living in enlightened times* **fortunately,** luckily, thankfully, mercifully, by good luck, by good fortune, as luck would have it; thank goodness, thank God, thank heavens, thank the Lord.

happiness ▶ **noun** *trying to rediscover the happiness we once knew* **pleasure,** contentment, satisfaction, cheerfulness, merriment, gaiety, joy, joyfulness, joviality, jollity, glee, delight, good spirits, lightheartedness, well-being, enjoyment; exuberance, exhilaration, elation, ecstasy, jubilation, rapture, bliss, blissfulness, euphoria, transports of delight.

happy ▶ adjective **1** *Melissa looked happy and excited* **cheerful,** cheery, merry, joyful, jovial, jolly, jocular, gleeful, carefree, untroubled, delighted, smiling, beaming, grinning, in good spirits, in a good mood, lighthearted, pleased, contented, content, satisfied, gratified, buoyant, radiant, sunny, blithe, joyous, beatific; thrilled, elated, exhilarated, ecstatic, blissful, euphoric, overjoyed, exultant, rapturous, in seventh heaven, on cloud nine, walking on air, jumping for joy, jubilant; informal chirpy, over the moon, on top of the world, tickled pink, on a high, as happy as a clam; formal jocund.
ANTONYMS sad.
2 *we will be happy to advise you* **glad,** pleased, delighted; willing, ready, disposed.
ANTONYMS unwilling.
3 *a happy coincidence* **fortunate,** lucky, favorable, advantageous, opportune, timely, well-timed, convenient.
ANTONYMS unfortunate.

happy-go-lucky ▶ adjective *what's wrong with letting your children be happy-go-lucky?* **easygoing,** carefree, casual, free and easy, devil-may-care, blithe, nonchalant, insouciant, blasé, unconcerned, untroubled, unworried, lighthearted, laid-back.
ANTONYMS anxious.

harangue ▶ noun *a ten-minute harangue* **tirade,** diatribe, lecture, polemic, rant, fulmination, broadside, attack, onslaught; criticism, condemnation, censure, admonition, sermon; declamation, speech; informal blast; literary philippic.
▶ verb *he harangued his erstwhile colleagues* **rant at,** hold forth to, lecture, shout at; berate, criticize, attack; informal sound off at, mouth off to.

harass ▶ verb **1** *tenants who harass their neighbors* **persecute,** intimidate, hound, harry, plague, torment, bully, bedevil; pester, bother, worry, disturb, trouble, provoke, stress; informal hassle, bug, ride, give someone a hard time, get on someone's case.
2 *they were sent to harass the enemy flanks* **harry,** attack, beleaguer, set upon, assail.

harassed ▶ adjective *the job left her totally harassed* **stressed,** stressed out, strained, worn out, hard-pressed, careworn, worried, troubled, beleaguered, under pressure, at the end of one's tether, at the end of one's rope; informal hassled.
ANTONYMS carefree.

harbinger ▶ noun *I long to see the robins, crocuses, and other harbingers of spring* **herald,** sign, indication, signal, portent, omen, augury, forewarning, presage; forerunner, precursor, messenger; literary foretoken.

harbor ▶ noun **1** *a picturesque harbor* **port,** dock, haven, marina; mooring, moorage, anchorage; waterfront.
2 *a safe harbor for me* **refuge,** haven, safe haven, shelter, sanctuary, retreat, place of safety, port in a storm.
▶ verb **1** *he is harboring a dangerous criminal* **shelter,** conceal, hide, shield, protect, give sanctuary to; take in, put up, accommodate, house.
2 *Rose had harbored a grudge against him* **bear,** nurse, nurture, cherish, entertain, foster, hold on to, cling to.

hard ▶ adjective **1** *hard ground* **firm,** solid, rigid, stiff, resistant, unbreakable, inflexible, impenetrable, unyielding, solidified, hardened, compact, compacted, dense, close-packed, compressed; steely, tough, strong, stony, rocklike, flinty, as hard as stone; frozen; literary adamantine.
ANTONYMS soft.
2 *hard physical work* **arduous,** strenuous, tiring, fatiguing, exhausting, wearying, back-breaking, grueling, heavy, laborious; difficult, taxing, exacting, testing, challenging, demanding, punishing, tough, formidable, onerous, rigorous, uphill, Herculean; informal murderous, killing, hellish; formal exigent; archaic toilsome.
ANTONYMS easy.
3 *hard workers* **diligent,** hard-working, industrious, sedulous, assiduous, conscientious, energetic, keen, enthusiastic, zealous, earnest, persevering, persistent, unflagging, untiring, indefatigable; studious.
ANTONYMS lazy.
4 *a hard problem* **difficult,** puzzling, perplexing, baffling, bewildering, mystifying, knotty, thorny, problematic, complicated, complex, intricate, involved; insoluble, unfathomable, impenetrable, incomprehensible, unanswerable.
ANTONYMS simple.
5 *times are hard* **harsh,** grim, difficult, bad, bleak, dire, tough, austere, unpleasant, uncomfortable, straitened, spartan; dark, distressing, painful, awful.
ANTONYMS comfortable.
6 *a hard taskmaster* **strict,** harsh, firm, severe, stern, tough, rigorous, demanding, exacting; callous, unkind, unsympathetic, cold, heartless, hard-hearted, unfeeling; intransigent, unbending, uncompromising, inflexible, implacable, stubborn, obdurate, unyielding, unrelenting, unsparing, grim, ruthless, merciless, pitiless, cruel; standing no nonsense, ruling with a rod of iron.
ANTONYMS kind, easygoing.
7 *a hard winter* **bitterly cold,** cold, bitter, harsh, severe, bleak, freezing, icy, icy-cold, arctic.
ANTONYMS mild.
8 *a hard blow* **forceful,** heavy, strong, sharp, smart, violent, powerful, vigorous, mighty, hefty, tremendous.
ANTONYMS light, gentle.
9 *hard facts* **reliable,** definite, true, confirmed, substantiated, undeniable, indisputable, unquestionable, verifiable.
ANTONYMS unverified, questionable.
10 *hard cider* **alcoholic,** strong, intoxicating, potent; formal spirituous.
ANTONYMS nonalcoholic.
11 *hard drugs* **addictive,** habit-forming; strong, harmful.
▶ adverb **1** *George pushed the door hard* **forcefully,** forcibly, roughly, powerfully, strongly, heavily, sharply, vigorously, energetically, with all one's might, with might and main.

ANTONYMS gently.
2 *they worked hard* **diligently,** industriously, assiduously, conscientiously, sedulously, busily, enthusiastically, energetically, doggedly, steadily; informal like mad, like crazy.
3 *this prosperity has been hard won* **with difficulty,** with effort, after a struggle, painfully, laboriously.
ANTONYMS easily.
4 *her death hit him hard* **severely,** badly, acutely, deeply, keenly, seriously, profoundly, gravely; formal grievously.
ANTONYMS slightly.
5 *it was raining hard* **heavily,** strongly, in torrents, in sheets; steadily; informal cats and dogs, buckets.
ANTONYMS lightly.
6 *my mother looked hard at me* **closely,** attentively, intently, critically, carefully, keenly, searchingly, earnestly, sharply.
ANTONYMS casually.
– PHRASES **hard and fast** *get used to it—the curfew here is hard and fast* **definite,** fixed, set, strict, rigid, binding, clear-cut, cast-iron, ironclad; inflexible, immutable, unchangeable, incontestable. **hard by close to,** right by, beside, near (to), nearby, not far from, a stone's throw from, on the doorstep of; informal within spitting distance of, 'a hop, skip, and jump away from'. **hard feelings** *I had no idea that our separation had left him with such hard feelings* **resentment,** animosity, ill feeling, ill will, bitterness, bad blood, resentfulness, rancor, malice, acrimony, antagonism, antipathy, animus, friction, anger, hostility, hate, hatred. **hard up** informal *this administration ignores the families that are hard up* **poor,** short of money, badly off, impoverished, impecunious, in reduced circumstances, unable to make ends meet; penniless, destitute, poverty-stricken; informal broke, strapped for cash, strapped.

CHOOSE THE RIGHT WORD

hard, arduous, difficult, laborious, trying

For the student who doesn't read well, homework is **hard** work, which means that it demands great physical or mental effort. An English assignment to write an essay might be particularly **difficult**, meaning that it not only requires effort but skill. Where *hard* suggests toil, *difficult* emphasizes complexity (*a difficult math problem*). Memorizing long lists of vocabulary words would be **laborious**, which is even more restrictive than *hard* and suggests prolonged, wearisome toil with no suggestion of the skill required and no reference to the complexity of the task. Reading *War and Peace*, however, would be an **arduous** task, because it would require a persistent effort over a long period of time. A school assignment may be *difficult*, but is usually not *arduous*; that is, it may require skill rather than perseverance. It may also be *arduous* without being particularly *difficult*, as when a student is asked to write "I will not throw spitballs" five hundred times. A student who is new to a school may find it especially **trying**, which implies that it taxes the individual's patience, skill, or capabilities.

hard-bitten ▶ adjective *a hard-bitten FBI agent* **hardened,** tough, cynical, unsentimental, hardheaded, case-hardened, as tough as nails; informal hard-nosed, hard-edged, hard-boiled.
ANTONYMS sentimental.

hard-boiled ▶ adjective informal See HARD-BITTEN.

hard-core ▶ adjective *hard-core socialists* **diehard,** staunch, dedicated, committed, steadfast, dyed-in-the-wool, long-standing; hardline, extreme, entrenched, radical, intransigent, uncompromising, rigid.

harden ▶ verb **1** *this glue will harden in four hours* **solidify,** set, congeal, clot, coagulate, stiffen, thicken, cake, cure, inspissate; freeze, crystallize; ossify, calcify, petrify.
ANTONYMS liquefy.
2 *their suffering had hardened them* **toughen,** desensitize, inure, case-harden, harden someone's heart; deaden, numb, benumb, anesthetize; brutalize.
ANTONYMS soften.

hardened ▶ adjective **1** *he was hardened to the violence he had seen* **inured,** desensitized, deadened; accustomed, habituated, acclimatized, used.
2 *a hardened criminal* **inveterate,** seasoned, habitual, chronic, compulsive, confirmed, dyed-in-the-wool; incorrigible, incurable, irredeemable, unregenerate.

hardheaded ▶ adjective *a hardheaded jurist* **unsentimental,** practical, pragmatic, businesslike, realistic, sensible, rational, clear-thinking, coolheaded, down-to-earth, matter-of-fact, no-nonsense, with both feet on the ground; tough, hard-bitten; shrewd, astute, sharp, sharp-witted; informal hard-nosed, hard-edged, hard-boiled.
ANTONYMS idealistic, sentimental.

hard-hearted ▶ adjective *he's not nearly as hard-hearted as he pretends to be* **unfeeling,** heartless, cold, hard, callous, unsympathetic, uncaring, unloving, unconcerned, indifferent, unmoved, unkind, uncharitable, unemotional, cold-hearted, cold-blooded, mean-spirited, stony-hearted, having a heart of stone, as hard as nails, cruel.
ANTONYMS compassionate.

hard-hitting ▶ adjective *a hard-hitting ad campaign* **uncompromising,** blunt, forthright, frank, honest, direct, tough; critical, unsparing, strongly worded, straight-talking, pulling no punches, not mincing one's words, not beating around/about the bush.

hardiness ▶ noun *in New England, you should select plants for their hardiness* **robustness,** strength, toughness, ruggedness, sturdiness, resilience, stamina, vigor; healthiness, good health.
ANTONYMS frailty.

hardline ▶ adjective *one of the president's key hardline allies* **uncompromising,** strict, extreme, tough, diehard, immoderate,

inflexible, intransigent, firm, intractable, unyielding, undeviating, unwavering, single-minded, not giving an inch; rare indurate.
ANTONYMS moderate, flexible.

hardly ▶ adverb *we hardly know each other* **scarcely,** barely, only just, slightly.

hard-pressed ▶ adjective **1** *the hard-pressed infantry* **under attack,** hotly pursued, harried.
2 *the hard-pressed construction industry* **in difficulties,** under pressure, troubled, beleaguered, harassed, with one's back to/against the wall, in a tight corner, in a tight spot, between a rock and a hard place; overburdened, overworked, overloaded, stressed-out; informal up against it.

hardship ▶ noun *by age six, she was a refugee and no stranger to hardship* **privation,** deprivation, destitution, poverty, austerity, penury, want, need, neediness, impecuniousness; misfortune, distress, suffering, affliction, trouble, pain, misery, wretchedness, tribulation, adversity, trials, trials and tribulations, dire straits; literary travails.
ANTONYMS prosperity, ease.

hard-working ▶ adjective *even the hard-working employees got stiffed at bonus time* **diligent,** industrious, conscientious, assiduous, sedulous, painstaking, persevering, unflagging, untiring, tireless, indefatigable, studious; keen, enthusiastic, zealous, busy, with one's shoulder to the wheel, with one's nose to the grindstone.
ANTONYMS lazy.

hardy ▶ adjective *our tiny frail baby has grown into a strapping hardy man* **robust,** healthy, fit, strong, sturdy, tough, rugged, hearty, lusty, vigorous, hale and hearty, fit as a fiddle, fighting fit, in fine fettle, in good health, in good condition; dated stalwart.
ANTONYMS delicate.

hare-brained ▶ adjective **1** *a hare-brained scheme* **ill-judged,** rash, foolish, foolhardy, reckless, madcap, wild, silly, stupid, ridiculous, absurd, idiotic, asinine, imprudent, impracticable, unworkable, unrealistic, unconsidered, half-baked, ill-thought-out, ill-advised, ill-conceived; informal crackpot, cockeyed, crazy, daft.
ANTONYMS sensible.
2 *a hare-brained kid* **foolish,** silly, idiotic, unintelligent, empty-headed, scatterbrained, featherbrained, birdbrained, peabrained, brainless, giddy; informal dippy, dizzy, flaky, dopey, dotty, airheaded.
ANTONYMS intelligent.

hark ▶ verb literary *hark, I hear a warning note* **listen,** lend an ear, pay attention, attend, mark; archaic hearken, give ear.
– PHRASES **hark back to** *why hark back to such unpleasant memories?* **recall,** call to mind, bring to mind, look back on, evoke, put one in mind of.

harlequin ▶ noun historical *the gaily garbed harlequins of his court* **jester,** joker, merry-andrew.
▶ adjective *a harlequin pattern* **multicolored,** many-colored, colorful, parti-colored, varicolored, many-hued, rainbow, variegated, jazzy, kaleidoscopic, psychedelic, polychromatic, checkered; archaic motley.

harlot ▶ noun archaic *stay off that street, unless you want to be mistaken for a harlot* **prostitute,** whore, fille de joie, call girl; promiscuous woman; informal hooker, hustler, tramp; dated streetwalker, hussy, lady of the evening, tart, pro, member of the oldest profession, scarlet woman, loose woman, fallen woman, cocotte, wanton; archaic strumpet, courtesan, trollop, doxy, trull.

harm ▶ noun **1** *the voltage is not sufficient to cause harm* **injury,** hurt, pain, trauma; damage, impairment, mischief.
ANTONYMS benefit.
2 *I can't see any harm in it* **evil,** wrong, ill, wickedness, iniquity, sin.
ANTONYMS good.
▶ verb **1** *he's never harmed anybody in his life* **injure,** hurt, wound, lay a finger on, maltreat, mistreat, misuse, ill-treat, ill-use, abuse, molest.
2 *this could harm her Olympic prospects* **damage,** hurt, spoil, mar, do mischief to, impair.

harmful ▶ adjective *the harmful rays of the sun* **damaging,** injurious, detrimental, dangerous, deleterious, unfavorable, negative, disadvantageous, unhealthy, unwholesome, hurtful, baleful, destructive; noxious, hazardous, poisonous, toxic, deadly, lethal; bad, evil, malign, malignant, malevolent, corrupting, subversive, pernicious.
ANTONYMS beneficial.

harmless ▶ adjective **1** *a harmless substance* **safe,** innocuous, benign, gentle, mild, wholesome, nontoxic, nonpoisonous, nonirritant, nonirritating, hypoallergenic; nonaddictive.
ANTONYMS dangerous, toxic.
2 *he seems harmless enough* **inoffensive,** innocuous, unobjectionable, unexceptionable.
ANTONYMS objectionable.

harmonious ▶ adjective **1** *harmonious music* **tuneful,** melodious, melodic, sweet-sounding, mellifluous, dulcet, lyrical; euphonious, euphonic, harmonic, polyphonic; informal easy on the ear.
ANTONYMS discordant.
2 *their harmonious relationship* **friendly,** amicable, cordial, amiable, congenial, easy, peaceful, peaceable, cooperative; compatible, sympathetic, united, attuned, in harmony, in rapport, in tune, in accord, of one mind, seeing eye to eye.
ANTONYMS hostile.
3 *a harmonious blend of traditional and modern* **congruous,** coordinated, balanced, in proportion, compatible, well-matched, well-balanced; literary consilient.
ANTONYMS incongruous.

harmonize ▶ verb **1** *colors that harmonize in a pleasing way* **coordinate,** go together, match, blend, mix, balance; be compatible, be harmonious, suit each other.
ANTONYMS clash.
2 *a plan to harmonize tax laws across the country* **coordinate,** systematize, correlate, integrate, synchronize, make consistent, homogenize, bring in line, bring in tune.

harmony ▶ noun **1** *musical harmony* **euphony,** polyphony; tunefulness, melodiousness,

mellifluousness.
ANTONYMS dissonance.
2 *the harmony of the whole structure* **balance,** symmetry, congruity, consonance, coordination, compatibility.
ANTONYMS incongruity.
3 *the villagers live together in harmony* **accord,** agreement, peace, peacefulness, amity, amicability, friendship, fellowship, cooperation, understanding, consensus, unity, sympathy, rapport, like-mindedness; unison, union, concert, oneness, synthesis; formal concord.
ANTONYMS disagreement.

harness ▶ **noun** *a horse's harness* **tack,** tackle, equipment; trappings; yoke; archaic equipage.
▶ **verb 1** *he harnessed his horse* **hitch up,** put in harness, yoke, couple.
2 *attempts to harness solar energy* **control,** exploit, utilize, use, employ, make use of, put to use; channel, mobilize, apply, capitalize on.

harp ▶ **verb**
– PHRASES **harp on about** *the way she harps on about his shortcomings, it's a wonder he can stand to be with her* **keep on about,** go on about, keep talking about, dwell on, make an issue of; labor the point of.

harridan ▶ **noun** *Steve tried to scare us with stories of the evil harridan Miss Duffy, who in reality was the sweetest teacher in Coolidge Elementary* **shrew,** termagant, virago, harpy, vixen, nag, hag, crone, dragon, ogress; fishwife, hellcat, she-devil, gorgon; martinet, tartar; informal old bag, old bat, battle-ax, witch; archaic scold.

harrowing ▶ **adjective** *a harrowing experience for the hostages* **distressing,** distressful, traumatic, upsetting; shocking, disturbing, painful, haunting, appalling, horrifying.

harry ▶ **verb 1** *they harried the retreating enemy* **attack,** assail, assault; charge, rush, strike, set upon; bombard, shell, strafe.
2 *the government was harried by a new lobby* **harass,** hound, bedevil, torment, pester, bother, worry, badger, nag, plague; informal hassle, bug, lean on, give someone a hard time.

harsh ▶ **adjective 1** *a harsh voice* **grating,** jarring, rasping, strident, raucous, brassy, discordant, unharmonious, unmelodious; screeching, shrill; rough, coarse, hoarse, gruff, croaky.
ANTONYMS soft, dulcet.
2 *harsh colors* **glaring,** bright, dazzling; loud, garish, gaudy, lurid, bold.
ANTONYMS subdued.
3 *his harsh rule over them* **cruel,** savage, barbarous, despotic, dictatorial, tyrannical, tyrannous; ruthless, merciless, pitiless, relentless, unmerciful; severe, strict, intolerant, illiberal, iron-fisted; hard-hearted, heartless, unkind, inhuman, inhumane.
ANTONYMS kind, enlightened.
4 *they took harsh measures to end the crisis* **severe,** stringent, draconian, firm, stiff, hard, stern, rigorous, grim, uncompromising; punitive, cruel, brutal.
ANTONYMS lenient.
5 *harsh words* **rude,** discourteous, uncivil, impolite; unfriendly, sharp, bitter, abusive, unkind, disparaging; abrupt, brusque, curt, gruff, short, surly, offhand.
ANTONYMS friendly.
6 *harsh conditions* **austere,** grim, spartan, hard, comfortless, inhospitable, stark, bleak, desolate.
ANTONYMS comfortable.
7 *a harsh winter* **hard,** severe, cold, bitter, bleak, freezing, icy; arctic, polar, Siberian.
ANTONYMS balmy, mild.
8 *harsh detergents* **abrasive,** strong, caustic; coarse, rough.
ANTONYMS gentle, mild.

harum-scarum ▶ **adjective** *the rules were too restrictive for a couple of harum-scarum teens like Bella and Maud* **reckless,** impetuous, impulsive, imprudent, rash, wild; daredevil, madcap, hotheaded, hare-brained, foolhardy, incautious, careless, heedless; informal devil-may-care; literary temerarious. See note at SUPERFICIAL.
ANTONYMS cautious.

harvest ▶ **noun 1** *we all helped with the harvest* **harvesting,** reaping, picking, collecting.
2 *a poor harvest* **yield,** crop, vintage; fruits, produce.
3 *the experiment yielded a meager harvest* **return,** result, fruits; product, output, effect; consequence.
▶ **verb 1** *he harvested the wheat* **gather (in),** bring in, reap, pick, collect.
2 *she harvested many honors* **acquire,** obtain, gain, get, earn; accumulate, amass, gather, collect; informal land, net, bag, rake in, scoop up.

hash ▶ **noun** *a whole hash of excuses* **mixture,** assortment, variety, array, mix, miscellany, selection, medley, mishmash, ragbag, gallimaufry, potpourri, hodgepodge.
– PHRASES **make a hash of** informal *he was sorry to have made such a hash of the travel arrangements* **bungle,** fluff, flub, mess up, make a mess of; mismanage, mishandle, ruin, wreck; botch, muff, muck up, foul up, screw up, blow.

hassle ▶ **noun** informal **1** *parking is such a hassle* **inconvenience,** bother, nuisance, problem, trouble, struggle, difficulty, annoyance, irritation, thorn in one's side/flesh, fuss; informal aggravation, stress, headache, pain, pain in the neck.
2 *she got into a hassle with that guy* See QUARREL (noun).
▶ **verb** *they were hassling him to pay up* **harass,** pester, nag, keep on at, badger, hound, harry, bother, torment, plague; informal bug, give someone a hard time, get on someone's case, breathe down someone's neck.

haste ▶ **noun** *working with feverish haste* **speed,** hastiness, hurriedness, swiftness, rapidity, quickness, briskness; formal expedition.
ANTONYMS delay.
– PHRASES **in haste** *the curtains look as if they were hung in haste* **quickly,** rapidly, fast, speedily, with urgency, in a rush, in a hurry.

hasten ▶ **verb 1** *we hastened back home* **hurry,** rush, dash, race, fly, shoot; scurry, scramble, dart, bolt, sprint, run, gallop; go fast, go quickly, go like lightning, go hell-bent for leather; informal tear, scoot, zip, zoom, belt, hotfoot it, bomb, hightail, barrel; dated make haste.
ANTONYMS dawdle, crawl.

2 *chemicals can hasten aging* **speed up,** accelerate, quicken, precipitate, advance, hurry on, step up, spur on, catalyze; facilitate, aid, assist, boost.
ANTONYMS slow down, delay.

hasty ▶ **adjective 1** *hasty steps* **quick,** hurried, fast, swift, rapid, speedy, brisk; literary fleet.
ANTONYMS slow.
2 *hasty decisions* **rash,** impetuous, impulsive, reckless, precipitate, spur-of-the-moment, premature, unconsidered, unthinking; literary temerarious.
ANTONYMS considered.

hat ▶ **noun** *please remove your hat* **cap,** beret, bonnet.

hatch ▶ **verb 1** *the duck hatched her eggs* **incubate,** brood.
2 *the plot that you* ***hatched up*** *last night* **devise,** conceive, concoct, brew, invent, plan, design, formulate; think up, dream up; informal cook up.

hatchet ▶ **noun** *a small hatchet with an oak handle* **ax,** tomahawk, cleaver, mattock.

hate ▶ **verb 1** *they hate each other* **loathe,** detest, despise, dislike, abhor, execrate; be repelled by, be unable to bear/stand, find intolerable, recoil from, shrink from; formal abominate.
ANTONYMS love.
2 *I hate to bother you* **be sorry,** be reluctant, be loath, be unwilling, be disinclined; regret, dislike.
▶ **noun 1** *feelings of hate* **hatred,** loathing, detestation, dislike, distaste, abhorrence, abomination, execration, aversion; hostility, enmity, animosity, antipathy, revulsion, disgust, contempt, odium.
ANTONYMS love.
2 *a hate of mine is filling in forms* **peeve,** pet peeve, bugbear, bane, bête noire, bogey, aversion, thorn in one's flesh/side, bugaboo.
ANTONYMS love.

hateful ▶ **adjective** *his hateful letters were presented as evidence* **detestable,** horrible, horrid, unpleasant, awful, nasty, disagreeable, despicable, objectionable, insufferable, revolting, loathsome, abhorrent, abominable, execrable, odious, disgusting, distasteful, obnoxious, offensive, vile, heinous, ghastly, beastly, godawful.
ANTONYMS delightful.

hatred ▶ **noun** *he finally overcame the hatred he felt for his unfaithful wife* **loathing,** hate, detestation, dislike, distaste, abhorrence, abomination, execration; aversion, hostility, ill will, ill feeling, enmity, animosity, antipathy; revulsion, disgust, contempt, odium.

haughty ▶ **adjective** *he is both haughty and disdainful* **proud,** arrogant, vain, conceited, snobbish, superior, self-important, pompous, supercilious, condescending, patronizing; scornful, contemptuous, disdainful; full of oneself, above oneself; informal stuck-up, snooty, hoity-toity, uppity, uppish, big-headed, high and mighty, la-di-da.
ANTONYMS humble.

haul ▶ **verb 1** *she hauled the basket along* **drag,** pull, tug, heave, lug, hump, draw, tow; informal yank.
2 *a contract to haul coal* **transport,** convey, carry, ship, ferry, move.
▶ **noun** *the thieves abandoned their haul* **booty,** loot, plunder; spoils, stolen goods, ill-gotten gains; informal swag, boodle.

haunt ▶ **verb 1** *a ghost haunts this house* **appear in,** materialize in; visit.
2 *he haunts street markets* **frequent,** patronize, visit regularly; loiter in, linger in; informal hang out in.
3 *the sight haunted me for years* **torment,** disturb, trouble, worry, plague, burden, beset, beleaguer; prey on, weigh on, gnaw at, nag at, weigh heavily on, obsess; informal bug.
▶ **noun** *a favorite haunt of artists* **hangout,** stomping ground, stamping ground, meeting place; territory, domain, resort, retreat, spot.

haunting ▶ **adjective** *the haunting background music* **evocative,** emotive, affecting, moving, touching, stirring, powerful; poignant, nostalgic, wistful, elegiac; memorable, indelible, unforgettable.

have ▶ **verb 1** *he had a new car* **possess,** own, be in possession of, be the owner of; be blessed with, boast, enjoy; keep, retain, hold, occupy.
2 *the apartment has five rooms* **comprise,** consist of, contain, include, incorporate, be composed of, be made up of; encompass; formal comprehend.
3 *they had dinner together* **eat,** consume, devour, partake of; drink, imbibe, quaff; informal demolish, dispose of, put away, scoff (down), scarf (down/up).
4 *she had a letter from Mark* **receive,** get, be given, be sent, obtain, acquire, come by, take receipt of.
ANTONYMS send, give.
5 *we've decided to have a party* **organize,** arrange, hold, give, host, throw, put on, lay on, set up, fix up.
6 *she's going to have a baby* **give birth to,** bear, be delivered of, bring into the world, produce; informal drop; archaic beget.
7 *we are having guests for dinner* **entertain,** be host to, cater for, receive; invite over, ask over/around, wine and dine; accommodate, put up.
8 *he had trouble finding the restaurant* **experience,** encounter, face, meet, find, run into, go through, undergo.
9 *I have a headache* **be suffering from,** be afflicted by, be affected by, be troubled with.
10 *I had a good time* **experience**; enjoy.
11 *many of them have doubts* **harbor,** entertain, feel, nurse, nurture, sustain, maintain.
12 *he had little patience* **manifest,** show, display, exhibit, demonstrate.
13 *she had them line up according to height* **make,** ask to, request to, get to, tell to, require to, induce to, prevail upon to; order to, command to, direct to, force to.
14 *I can't have you insulting me* **tolerate,** endure, bear, support, accept, put up with, go along with, take, countenance; permit to, allow to; informal stand, abide, stomach; formal brook.
15 *I* ***have to*** *get up at six* **must,** be obliged to, be required to, be compelled to, be forced to, be bound to.

16 informal *I'd been had* **trick,** fool, deceive, cheat, dupe, take in, hoodwink, swindle; informal con, diddle, rip off, shaft, hose, sucker, snooker.

– PHRASES **have had it** informal **1** *they admit that they've had it* **have no chance,** have no hope, have failed, be finished, be defeated, have lost; informal have flopped, have come a cropper, have bought the farm. **2** *if you tell anyone, you've had it* **be in trouble,** be in for a scolding; informal be in hot water, be in deep doo-doo, be toast, be dead meat. **have on** *she had a blue dress on* **be wearing,** be dressed in, be clothed in, be attired in, be decked out in, be robed in.

haven ▶ **noun 1** *a safe haven* **refuge,** retreat, shelter, sanctuary, asylum; port in a storm, oasis, sanctum.
2 *they stopped in a small haven* **anchorage,** harbor, harborage, port, moorage, mooring; cove, inlet, bay.

haversack ▶ **noun** *they looked like little soldiers with their khaki haversacks* **knapsack,** backpack, rucksack, pack.

havoc ▶ **noun 1** *the hurricane caused havoc* **devastation,** destruction, damage, desolation, ruination, ruin; disaster, catastrophe.
2 *hyperactive children create havoc* **disorder,** chaos, disruption, mayhem, bedlam, pandemonium, turmoil, tumult, uproar; commotion, furor, a three-ring circus; informal hullabaloo.

hawk ▶ **noun** *every October we meet at Dobbs' Hill to watch the red-tailed hawks*

hay ▶ **noun** *soon the barns will be filled with hay* **forage,** dried grass, silage, fodder, straw, herbage.

– PHRASES **make hay while the sun shines** *Jack was a firm believer in making hay while the sun shines* **make the most of an opportunity,** take advantage of something, strike while the iron is hot, seize the day, carpe diem.

haywire ▶ **adjective** informal *the binding machine has gone haywire | by midnight, the negotiations were completely haywire* **out of control,** erratic, faulty, malfunctioning, out of order; chaotic, confused, disorganized, disordered, topsy-turvy; informal on the blink, on the fritz.

hazard ▶ **noun 1** *the hazards of radiation* **danger,** risk, peril, threat, menace; problem, pitfall.
2 literary *the laws of hazard* **chance,** probability, fortuity, luck, fate, destiny, fortune, providence.
▶ **verb 1** *he hazarded a guess* **venture,** advance, put forward, volunteer, float; conjecture, speculate, surmise; formal opine.
2 *it's too risky to hazard money on* **risk,** jeopardize, gamble, stake, bet, chance; endanger, imperil.

hazardous ▶ **adjective** *a hazardous construction site* **risky,** dangerous, unsafe, perilous, precarious, fraught with danger; unpredictable, uncertain, chancy, high-risk, insecure, touch-and-go; informal dicey, hairy.
ANTONYMS safe, certain.

haze ▶ **noun 1** *a thick haze on the sea* **mist,** fog, cloud; smoke, vapor, steam.
2 *a haze of euphoria* **blur,** daze, confusion, muddle, befuddlement.

hazy ▶ **adjective 1** *a hazy day* **misty,** foggy, cloudy, overcast; smoggy, murky.
2 *hazy memories* **vague,** indistinct, unclear, faint, dim, nebulous, shadowy, blurred, fuzzy, confused.

head ▶ **noun 1** *she scratched her head thoughtfully* skull, cranium, crown; informal nut, noodle, noggin, dome.
2 *he had to use his head* **brain**(s), brainpower, intellect, intelligence; wit(s), wisdom, mind, sense, reasoning, common sense; informal savvy, gray matter, smarts.
3 *she had a good head for business* **aptitude,** faculty, talent, gift, capacity, ability; mind, brain.
4 *the head of the church* **leader,** chief, controller, governor, superintendent, commander, captain; director, manager; principal, president, premier; chieftain, headman, sachem; CEO; informal boss, boss man, kingpin, top dog, Mr. Big, skipper, ringleader, numero uno, head honcho, big kahuna.
5 *the head of the line* **front,** beginning, start, fore, forefront; top.
6 *the head of the river* **source,** origin, headspring, headwater; literary wellspring.
7 *beer with a head* **froth,** foam, bubbles, spume, fizz, effervescence; suds.
▶ **adjective** *the head waiter* **chief,** principal, leading, main, first, foremost, prime, premier, senior, top, highest, supreme, superior, top-ranking, ranking.
ANTONYMS subordinate.
▶ **verb 1** *the procession was headed by the mayor* **lead,** be at the front of; be first, lead the way.
2 *Dr. Jones heads a research team* **command,** control, lead, run, manage, direct, supervise, superintend, oversee, preside over, rule, govern, captain; informal be the boss of.
3 *she was* ***heading for*** *the exit* **move toward,** make for, aim for, go in the direction of, be bound for, make a beeline for; set out for, start out for.

– PHRASES **at the head of** *Stasha will now be at the head of the department* **in charge of,** controlling, commanding, leading, managing, running, directing, supervising, overseeing; at the wheel of, at the helm of. **come to a head** *the violence came to a head after two civilians were killed* **reach a crisis,** come to a climax, reach a critical point, reach a crossroads. **go to someone's head 1** *the wine has gone to my head* **intoxicate someone,** befuddle someone, make someone drunk; informal make someone woozy; formal inebriate someone. **2** *her victory went to her head* **make someone conceited,** make someone full of themselves, turn someone's head, puff someone up. **head off 1** *he went to head off the cars* **intercept,** divert, deflect, redirect, reroute, draw away, turn away. **2** *they headed off a confrontation* **forestall,** avert, ward off, fend off, stave off, hold off, nip in the bud, keep at bay; prevent, avoid, stop. **keep one's head** *Richie kept his head throughout the confrontation* **keep/stay calm,** keep one's self-control, maintain one's composure; informal keep one's cool, keep one's shirt on, keep it together, cool one's jets. **lose one's head** *you cannot lose* *your head in the courtroom* **lose control,** lose one's composure, lose one's equilibrium, go to pieces; panic, get flustered, get confused, get hysterical; informal lose one's cool, freak out, crack up.

headache ▶ noun **1** *I've got a headache* **pain in the head,** migraine; neuralgia; informal head.
2 informal *their behavior was a headache for the teacher* **nuisance,** trouble, problem, bother, bugbear, pest, worry, inconvenience, vexation, irritant, thorn in one's side; informal aggravation, hassle, pain (in the neck).

heading ▶ noun **1** *chapter headings* **title,** caption, legend, subtitle, subheading, rubric, headline.
2 *this topic falls under four main headings* **category,** division, classification, class, section, group, grouping, subject, topic.

headlong ▶ adverb **1** *he fell headlong into the tent* **head first,** on one's head.
ANTONYMS feet first.
2 *she rushed headlong to join the craze* **without thinking,** without forethought, precipitously, impetuously, rashly, recklessly, carelessly, heedlessly, hastily, head first.
ANTONYMS cautiously.
▶ adjective *a headlong dash* **breakneck,** whirlwind; reckless, precipitate, precipitous, hasty, careless, heedless, head-first.
ANTONYMS cautious.

head-on ▶ adjective **1** *a head-on collision* **direct,** full on.
2 *a head-on confrontation* **direct,** face to face, personal; informal eyeball to eyeball.

headquarters ▶ plural noun *the report was immediately dispatched to headquarters* **the head office,** the main office, HQ, the base, the nerve center, the war room, mission control, the command post.

headstone ▶ noun *the heavy salt air up here is erosive to these old headstones* **gravestone,** tombstone, stone, grave marker, monument, memorial.

headstrong ▶ adjective *our middle child is the most headstrong* **willful,** strong-willed, stubborn, obstinate, unyielding, obdurate; contrary, perverse, wayward, unruly; formal refractory.
ANTONYMS tractable.

headway ▶ noun
– PHRASES **make headway** *critics charge that the ground troops are making no headway in their purported mission* **make progress,** progress, make strides, gain ground, advance, proceed, move, get ahead, come along, take shape.

heady ▶ adjective **1** *heady wine* **potent,** intoxicating, strong; alcoholic, vinous; formal spirituous.
ANTONYMS nonalcoholic.
2 *the heady days of my youth* **exhilarating,** exciting, thrilling, stimulating, invigorating, electrifying, rousing; informal mind-blowing.
ANTONYMS boring.

heal ▶ verb **1** *he heals sick people* **make better,** make well, cure, treat, restore to health.
ANTONYMS make worse.
2 *his knee had healed* **get better,** get well, be cured, recover, mend, improve.
ANTONYMS get worse.
3 *time will heal the pain of grief* **alleviate,** ease, assuage, palliate, relieve, help, lessen, mitigate, attenuate, allay.
ANTONYMS aggravate.
4 *we tried to heal the rift* **put right,** set right, repair, remedy, resolve, correct, settle; conciliate, reconcile, harmonize; informal patch up.
ANTONYMS worsen.

health ▶ noun **1** *he was restored to health* **well-being,** healthiness, fitness, good condition, good shape, fine fettle; strength, vigor, wellness.
ANTONYMS illness.
2 *bad health forced him to retire* **physical state,** physical shape, condition, constitution.

healthy ▶ adjective **1** *a healthy baby* **well,** in good health, fine, fit, in good trim, in good shape, in fine fettle, in tip-top shape; blooming, thriving, hardy, robust, strong, vigorous, fighting fit, fit as a fiddle, the picture of health; informal OK, in the pink, right as rain.
ANTONYMS ill.
2 *a healthy diet* **health-giving,** healthful, good for one; wholesome, nutritious, nourishing; beneficial, salubrious.
ANTONYMS unwholesome.

heap ▶ noun **1** *a heap of boxes* **pile,** stack, mound, mountain, mass, quantity, load, lot, jumble; collection, accumulation, assemblage, store, hoard.
2 informal *we have* ***heaps of room*** | ***a heap of*** *troubles* **a lot of,** a fair amount of, much, plenty of, a good deal of, a great deal of, an abundance of, a wealth of, a profusion of; (a great) many, a large number of, numerous, scores of; informal hundreds of, thousands of, millions of, a load of, loads of, a pile of, piles of, oodles of, stacks of, lots of, masses of, scads of, reams of, oceans of, miles of, tons of, zillions of.
▶ verb *she heaped logs on the fire* **pile up,** pile, stack up, stack, make a mound of; assemble, collect.
– PHRASES **heap on/upon** *they heaped praise on her* **shower on,** lavish on, load on; bestow on, confer on, give, grant, vouchsafe, favor with.

hear ▶ verb **1** *she can't hear* **perceive sound**; have hearing.
2 *she could hear men's voices* **perceive,** make out, discern, catch, get, apprehend; overhear.
3 *I heard that radio show* **listen to,** catch.
4 *they heard that I had moved* **be informed,** be told, find out, discover, learn, gather, glean, ascertain, get word, get wind.
5 *a jury heard the case* **try,** judge; adjudicate (on), adjudge, pass judgment on.
6 *I totally hear what you're saying* **acknowledge,** understand, sympathize with, recognize, get, perceive.

hearing ▶ noun **1** *the wolf's acute hearing* **ability to hear,** auditory perception, sense of hearing, aural faculty.
2 *she moved out of hearing* **earshot,** hearing distance, hearing range, auditory range.
3 *I had a fair hearing* **chance to speak,** opportunity to be heard; interview, audience.

4 *he gave evidence at the hearing* **trial,** court case, inquiry, inquest, tribunal; investigation, inquisition.

hearsay ▶ noun *that's all hearsay, and I don't care to listen to such tripe* **rumor,** gossip, tittle-tattle, idle talk; stories, tales; informal the grapevine, scuttlebutt, loose lips.

heart ▶ noun **1** *my heart stopped beating* informal ticker.
2 *he poured out his heart* **emotions,** feelings, sentiments; soul; love, affection, passion.
3 *she has no heart* **compassion,** sympathy, humanity, feeling(s), fellow feeling, tenderness, softness, empathy, understanding; kindness, goodwill.
4 *they may lose heart* **enthusiasm,** keenness, eagerness, spirit, determination, resolve, purpose, courage, nerve, willpower, fortitude; informal guts, spunk.
5 *the heart of the city* **center,** middle, hub, core, nucleus, eye, bosom.
ANTONYMS edge.
6 *the heart of the matter* **essence,** crux, core, nub, root, gist, meat, marrow, pith, substance, kernel; informal nitty-gritty.
ANTONYMS peripherals.
– PHRASES **after one's own heart** *Lucie was always a girl after my own heart* **like-minded,** of the same mind, kindred, compatible, congenial, sharing one's tastes; informal on the same wavelength. **at heart** *he's a good kid at heart* **deep down,** basically, fundamentally, essentially, in essence, intrinsically; really, actually, truly, in fact; informal when you get right down to it. **by heart** *I know the lyrics by heart* **from memory,** down pat, by rote, word for word, verbatim, word-perfect. **do one's heart good** *it does my heart good to see the children getting along* **cheer one (up),** please one, gladden one, make one happy, delight one, hearten one, gratify one, make one feel good, give one a lift; informal tickle someone pink. **eat one's heart out** *Adam will eat his heart out when he hears about Julia's engagement* **pine,** long, ache, brood, mope, fret, sigh, sorrow, yearn, agonize; grieve, mourn, lament. **from the bottom of one's heart** *everything in that poem I meant from the bottom of my heart* **sincerely,** earnestly, fervently, passionately, truly, genuinely, heartily, with all sincerity. **give/lose one's heart to** *so, which young lady have you given your heart to this week?* **fall in love with,** fall for, be smitten by; informal fall head over heels for, be swept off one's feet by, develop a crush on. **have a change of heart** *it seems that the Smiths have had a change of heart about selling their house* **change one's mind,** flip-flop, change one's tune, have second thoughts, have a rethink, think again, think twice; informal get cold feet, do a U-turn, pull a U-ey. **have a heart** *come on, have a heart and let Sandy keep the puppy* **be compassionate,** be kind, be merciful, be lenient, be sympathetic, be considerate, have mercy. **heart and soul** *the volunteers were into the campaign heart and soul* **wholeheartedly,** enthusiastically, eagerly, zealously; absolutely, completely, entirely, fully, utterly, to the hilt, one hundred percent. **take heart** *your cards and letters helped us to take heart* **be encouraged,** be heartened, be comforted; cheer up, brighten up, perk up, liven up, revive. **with one's heart in one's mouth** *she slowly made her way down the dark cellar stairs with her heart in her mouth* **in alarm,** in fear, fearfully, apprehensively, on edge, with trepidation, in suspense, in a cold sweat, with bated breath, on tenterhooks; informal with butterflies in one's stomach, in a state, in a stew, in a sweat.

heartache ▶ noun *a life of heartache* **anguish,** grief, suffering, distress, unhappiness, misery, sorrow, sadness, heartbreak, via dolorosa, pain, hurt, agony, angst, despondency, despair, woe, desolation.
ANTONYMS happiness.

heartbreaking ▶ adjective *heartbreaking news from the doctor* **distressing,** upsetting, disturbing, heart-rending, sad, tragic, painful, traumatic, agonizing, harrowing; pitiful, poignant, plaintive, moving, tearjerker, tearjerking, gut-wrenching.
ANTONYMS comforting.

heartbroken ▶ adjective *the disqualified gymnasts were heartbroken* **anguished,** devastated, broken-hearted, heavy-hearted, grieving, grief-stricken, inconsolable, crushed, shattered, desolate, despairing; upset, distressed, miserable, sorrowful, sad, downcast, disconsolate, crestfallen, despondent; informal down in the dumps.

heartburn ▶ noun *the chest pains may indicate something more serious than heartburn* **indigestion,** dyspepsia, acid reflux, pyrosis.

hearten ▶ verb *the letter from Daphne will hearten him* **cheer (up),** encourage, raise someone's spirits, boost, buoy up, perk up, inspirit, uplift, elate; comfort, reassure; informal buck up, pep up. See note at ENCOURAGE.

heartfelt ▶ adjective *her heartfelt confession* **sincere,** genuine, from the heart; earnest, profound, deep, wholehearted, ardent, fervent, passionate, enthusiastic, eager; honest, bona fide.
ANTONYMS insincere.

heartily ▶ adverb **1** *we heartily welcome the changes* **wholeheartedly,** sincerely, genuinely, warmly, profoundly, with all one's heart; eagerly, enthusiastically, earnestly, ardently.
2 *they were heartily sick of her* **very,** extremely, thoroughly, completely, absolutely, really, exceedingly, immensely, most, downright, quite, seriously; informal real, mighty.

heartless ▶ adjective *Amelia had known more than her share of heartless men* **unfeeling,** unsympathetic, unkind, uncaring, unconcerned, insensitive, inconsiderate, hard-hearted, stony-hearted, cold-hearted, mean-spirited; cold, callous, cruel, merciless, pitiless, inhuman.
ANTONYMS compassionate.

heart-rending ▶ adjective *their heart-rending testimonies had the audience in tears* **distressing,** upsetting, disturbing, heartbreaking, sad, tragic, painful, traumatic, harrowing; pitiful, poignant, plaintive, moving, tearjerker, tearjerking, gut-wrenching.

heartsick ▶ adjective literary *we were heartsick when we read the story of his misfortune* despondent, dejected, depressed, desolate, downcast, forlorn, unhappy, sad, upset, miserable, wretched, woebegone, inconsolable, grieving, grief-stricken, heavy-hearted, broken-hearted.

heart-to-heart ▶ adjective *a heart-to-heart chat* **intimate,** personal, man-to-man, woman-to-woman; candid, honest, truthful, sincere.
▶ noun *they had a long heart-to-heart* **private conversation,** tête-à-tête, one-to-one, chat, talk, word; informal confab.

heartwarming ▶ adjective *tonight's heartwarming episode reunites Dan's family for a memorable Thanksgiving* **touching,** moving, heartening, stirring, uplifting, pleasing, cheering, gladdening, encouraging, gratifying.
ANTONYMS distressing.

hearty ▶ adjective **1** *a hearty character* **exuberant,** jovial, ebullient, cheerful, uninhibited, effusive, lively, loud, animated, vivacious, energetic, spirited, dynamic, enthusiastic, eager; warm, cordial, friendly, affable, amiable, good natured.
ANTONYMS introverted.
2 *hearty congratulations* **wholehearted,** heartfelt, sincere, genuine, real, true; earnest, fervent, ardent, enthusiastic.
ANTONYMS halfhearted.
3 *a hearty woman of sixty-five* **robust,** healthy, hardy, fit, flourishing, blooming, fighting fit, fit as a fiddle; vigorous, sturdy, strong; informal full of vim.
ANTONYMS frail.
4 *a hearty meal* **substantial,** large, ample, sizable, filling, generous, square, solid; healthy.
ANTONYMS light.

heat ▶ noun **1** *a plant sensitive to heat* **warmth,** hotness, warmness, high temperature; hot weather, warm weather, sultriness, mugginess, humidity; heat wave, hot spell.
ANTONYMS cold.
2 *he took the heat out of the dispute* **passion,** intensity, vehemence, warmth, fervor, fervency; enthusiasm, excitement, agitation; anger, fury.
ANTONYMS apathy.
3 *a female bear in heat* **estrus,** season, sexual receptivity.
▶ verb **1** *the food was heated* **warm,** warm up, heat up, make hot, make warm; reheat, cook, microwave; informal nuke, zap.
ANTONYMS cool, chill.
2 *the pipes expand as they* ***heat up*** **become hot,** become warm, get hotter, get warmer, increase in temperature.
ANTONYMS cool (down).
3 *he calmed down as quickly as he had* ***heated up*** **become impassioned,** become excited, become animated; get angry, become enraged.

heated ▶ adjective **1** *a heated swimming pool* **warm,** hot; thermal.
2 *a heated argument* **vehement,** passionate, impassioned, animated, spirited, lively, intense, fiery; angry, bitter, furious, fierce, stormy, tempestuous.
3 *Robert grew heated as he spoke of the risks* **excited,** animated, inflamed, worked up, wound up, keyed up; informal het up, in a state.

heathen ▶ noun **1** *the evangelist preached to the heathens* **pagan,** infidel, idolater, heretic, unbeliever, disbeliever, nonbeliever, atheist, agnostic, skeptic; archaic paynim.
ANTONYMS believer.
2 *heathens who spoil good whiskey with ice* **philistine,** boor, oaf, ignoramus, lout, yahoo, vulgarian, plebeian; informal pleb, peasant.
▶ adjective *a heathen practice* **pagan,** infidel, idolatrous, heathenish; unbelieving, nonbelieving, atheistic, agnostic, heretical, faithless, godless, irreligious, ungodly, unholy; barbarian, barbarous, uncivilized, uncultured, primitive, ignorant, philistine.

heave ▶ verb **1** *she heaved the sofa backward* **haul,** pull, lug, drag, draw, tug, heft; informal hump, yank.
2 informal *she heaved a brick at him* **throw,** fling, cast, toss, hurl, lob, pitch; informal chuck, sling.
3 *he heaved a sigh of relief* **let out,** breathe, give, sigh; emit, utter.
4 *the sea heaved* **rise and fall,** roll, swell, surge, churn, seethe, swirl.
5 *she heaved into the sink* **retch,** gag; vomit, be sick, get sick; informal throw up, puke, hurl, spew, barf, upchuck, ralph.

heaven ▶ noun **1** *the good will have a place in heaven* **paradise,** nirvana, Zion; the hereafter, the next world, the next life, Elysium, the Elysian Fields, Valhalla; literary the empyrean.
ANTONYMS hell, purgatory.
2 *a good book is my idea of heaven* **bliss,** ecstasy, rapture, contentment, happiness, delight, joy, seventh heaven; paradise, Utopia, nirvana.
ANTONYMS misery.
3 (**the heavens**) *he observed the heavens* **the sky,** the skies, the upper atmosphere, the stratosphere, space; literary the firmament, the vault of heaven, the blue, the (wild/wide) blue yonder, the welkin, the empyrean, the azure, the upper regions, the sphere, the celestial sphere.
– PHRASES **in seventh heaven** *we're all in seventh heaven with this new swimming pool* **ecstatic,** euphoric, thrilled, elated, delighted, overjoyed, on cloud nine, walking on air, jubilant, rapturous, jumping for joy, transported, delirious, blissful; informal over the moon, on top of the world, on a high, tickled pink, as happy as a clam. **move heaven and earth** *I'm going to get this promotion, even if I have to move heaven and earth to do it* **try one's hardest,** do one's best, do one's utmost, do all one can, give one's all, spare no effort, put oneself out; strive, exert oneself, work hard; informal bend over backwards, do one's damnedest, pull out all the stops, go all out, bust a gut.

heavenly ▶ adjective **1** *heavenly choirs* **divine,** holy, celestial, supernal; angelic, seraphic, cherubic; literary empyrean.
ANTONYMS mortal, infernal.
2 *heavenly constellations* **celestial,** cosmic, stellar, astral; planetary; extraterrestrial, superterrestrial.
ANTONYMS terrestrial, earthly.
3 informal *a heavenly morning* **delightful,** wonderful, glorious, perfect, excellent, sublime, idyllic, first-class, first-rate; blissful,

pleasurable, enjoyable; exquisite, beautiful, lovely, gorgeous, enchanting; informal divine, super, great, fantastic, fabulous, terrific.
ANTONYMS dreadful.

heavily ▶ adverb **1** *Dad walked heavily* **laboriously,** slowly, ponderously, woodenly, stiffly; with difficulty, painfully, awkwardly, clumsily.
ANTONYMS easily, quickly.
2 *we were heavily defeated* **decisively,** conclusively, roundly, soundly; utterly, completely, thoroughly.
ANTONYMS narrowly.
3 *he drank heavily* **excessively,** to excess, immoderately, copiously, inordinately, intemperately, a great deal, too much, overmuch.
ANTONYMS moderately.
4 *the area is heavily planted with trees* **densely,** closely, thickly.
ANTONYMS lightly, sparsely.
5 *I became heavily involved in politics* **deeply,** very, extremely, greatly, exceedingly, tremendously, profoundly; informal seriously, ever so.

heavy ▶ adjective **1** *a heavy box* **weighty,** hefty, substantial, ponderous; solid, dense, leaden; burdensome; informal hulking, weighing a ton.
ANTONYMS light.
2 *a heavy man* **overweight,** fat, obese, corpulent, large, bulky, stout, stocky, portly, plump, paunchy, fleshy; informal hulking, tubby, beefy, porky, pudgy.
ANTONYMS thin.
3 *a heavy blow to the head* **forceful,** hard, strong, violent, powerful, vigorous, mighty, hefty, sharp, smart, severe.
ANTONYMS gentle.
4 *a gardener did the heavy work for me* **arduous,** hard, physical, laborious, difficult, strenuous, demanding, tough, onerous, back-breaking, grueling; archaic toilsome.
ANTONYMS easy.
5 *a heavy burden of responsibility* **onerous,** burdensome, demanding, challenging, difficult, formidable, weighty; worrisome, stressful, trying, crushing, oppressive.
ANTONYMS undemanding, moderate.
6 *heavy fog* **dense,** thick, soupy, murky, impenetrable.
ANTONYMS light, wispy.
7 *a heavy sky* **overcast,** cloudy, clouded, gray, dull, gloomy, murky, dark, black, stormy, leaden, lowering.
ANTONYMS sunny, bright.
8 *heavy rain* **torrential,** relentless, copious, teeming, severe.
ANTONYMS light, intermittent.
9 *heavy soil* **clayey,** muddy, sticky, wet.
ANTONYMS friable, dry.
10 *a heavy fine* **sizable,** hefty, substantial, colossal, big, considerable; stiff; informal tidy, whopping, steep, astronomical.
ANTONYMS small.
11 *heavy seas* **tempestuous,** turbulent, rough, wild, stormy, choppy, squally.
ANTONYMS calm.
12 *heavy fighting* **intense,** fierce, vigorous, relentless, all-out, severe, serious.
ANTONYMS halfhearted.
13 *a heavy drinker* **immoderate,** excessive, intemperate, overindulgent, unrestrained, uncontrolled.
ANTONYMS moderate.
14 *a heavy meal* **substantial,** filling, hearty, large, big, ample, sizable, generous, square, solid.
ANTONYMS light.
15 *their diet is **heavy on** vegetables* **abounding in,** abundant in, lavish with, profuse with, unstinting with, using a lot of.
ANTONYMS light on.
16 *he felt heavy and very tired* **lethargic,** listless, sluggish, torpid, languid, apathetic, logy.
ANTONYMS energetic, animated.
17 *a heavy heart* **sad,** sorrowful, melancholy, gloomy, downcast, downhearted, heartbroken, dejected, disconsolate, demoralized, despondent, depressed, crestfallen, desolate, down; informal blue; literary dolorous.
ANTONYMS cheerful.
18 *these poems are rather heavy* **tedious,** difficult, dull, dry, serious, heavy going, dreary, boring, turgid, uninteresting.
19 *branches heavy with blossoms* **laden,** loaded, covered, filled, groaning, bursting, teeming, abounding.
20 *a heavy crop* **bountiful,** plentiful, abundant, large, bumper, rich, copious, considerable, sizable, profuse; informal whopping; literary plenteous.
ANTONYMS meager.
21 *he has heavy features* **coarse,** rough, rough-hewn, unrefined; rugged, craggy.
ANTONYMS delicate.

CHOOSE THE RIGHT WORD

heavy, burdensome, cumbersome, massive, ponderous, weighty

Trying to move a refrigerator out of a third-floor apartment is difficult because it is **cumbersome**, which means that it is so heavy and bulky that it becomes unwieldy or awkward to handle. Cartons filled with books, on the other hand, are merely **heavy**, which implies greater density and compactness than the average load. A huge oak dining table might be described as **massive**, which stresses largeness and solidity rather than weight, while something that is **ponderous** is too large or too *massive* to move, or to be moved quickly (*a ponderous printing press*). Most of these terms can be used figuratively as well. *Heavy*, for example, connotes a pressing down on the mind, spirits, or senses (*heavy with fatigue; a heavy heart*) and *ponderous* implies a dull and labored quality (*a novel too ponderous to read*). **Burdensome**, which refers to something that is not only *heavy* but must be carried or supported, is even more likely to be used in an abstract way to describe something that is difficult but can, with effort, be managed (*a burdensome task*). Both a package and a problem may be described as **weighty**, meaning actually (as opposed to relatively) heavy; but it is more commonly used to mean very important or momentous (*weighty matters to discuss*).

heavy-handed ▶ adjective **1** *they are heavy-handed with the equipment* **clumsy,** awkward, maladroit, unhandy, inept, unskillful; informal ham-handed, ham-fisted, all thumbs.
ANTONYMS dexterous.
2 *heavy-handed policing* **insensitive,** oppressive, overbearing, high-handed, harsh, stern, severe, tyrannical, despotic, ruthless, merciless; tactless, undiplomatic, inept.
ANTONYMS sensitive.

heckle ▶ verb *he was heckled by the drunk in the back of the room* **jeer,** taunt, jibe at, shout down, boo, hiss, harass; informal give someone a hard time.
ANTONYMS cheer.

hectic ▶ adjective *the trip to the airport was hectic* **frantic,** frenetic, frenzied, feverish, manic, busy, active, fast and furious, fast-paced; lively, brisk, bustling, buzzing, abuzz.
ANTONYMS leisurely.

hedge ▶ noun **1** *high hedges* **hedgerow,** bushes; windbreak.
2 *an excellent hedge against a fall in the dollar* **safeguard,** protection, shield, screen, guard, buffer, cushion; insurance, security.
3 *his analysis is full of hedges* **equivocation,** evasion, fudge, quibble, qualification; temporizing, uncertainty, prevarication, vagueness.
▶ verb **1** *fields hedged with forsythia* **surround,** enclose, encircle, ring, border, edge, bound.
2 *she was **hedged in** by her limited education* **confine,** restrict, limit, hinder, obstruct, impede, constrain, trap; hem in.
3 *he hedged at every new question* **prevaricate,** equivocate, vacillate, quibble, hesitate, stall, dodge the issue, be noncommittal, be evasive, be vague, beat around the bush, pussyfoot around, mince one's words; hem and haw; informal sit on the fence, duck the question.
4 *the company hedged its position on the market* **safeguard,** protect, shield, guard, cushion; cover, insure.

heed ▶ verb *heed the warnings* **pay attention to,** take notice of, take note of, pay heed to, attend to, listen to; bear in mind, be mindful of, mind, mark, consider, take into account, follow, obey, adhere to, abide by, observe, take to heart, be alert to.
ANTONYMS disregard.
▶ noun *he paid no heed* **attention,** notice, note, regard; consideration, thought, care.

heedful ▶ adjective *the governor is about to deliver a statement regarding the hurricane, and it is imperative that everyone is heedful* **attentive,** careful, mindful, cautious, prudent, circumspect; alert, aware, wary, chary, watchful, vigilant, on guard, on the alert.

heedless ▶ adjective *the evacuation warnings were clear, but he was heedless and didn't get out in time* **unmindful,** taking no notice, paying no heed, unheeding, disregardful, neglectful, oblivious, inattentive, blind, deaf; incautious, imprudent, rash, reckless, foolhardy, improvident, unwary.

heel[1] ▶ noun **1** *shoes with low heels* wedge, stiletto.
2 *the heel of a loaf* **tail end,** end, crust, remnant, remainder, remains.
3 informal *you're such a heel to have left Liz at the altar* **scoundrel,** rogue, rascal, reprobate, miscreant; informal beast, rat, louse, swine, snake, scumbag, scumbucket, scuzzball, sleazeball, sleazebag, stinker.

heel[2] ▶ verb *the ship heeled to starboard* **lean over,** list, careen, tilt, tip, incline, keel over.

heft ▶ verb *Doug helped us heft the kegs up into the truck* **lift,** lift up, raise, raise up, heave, hoist, haul; carry, lug, tote; informal cart, hump, schlep.
▶ noun *the heft of the urn surprised us* **weight,** heaviness, bulk.

hefty ▶ adjective **1** *a hefty young man* **burly,** heavy, sturdy, strapping, bulky, brawny, husky, strong, muscular, large, big, solid, well-built; portly, stout; informal hulking, hunky, beefy.
ANTONYMS slight, gaunt.
2 *a hefty kick* **powerful,** violent, hard, forceful, heavy, mighty.
ANTONYMS feeble.
3 *hefty loads of lumber* **heavy,** weighty, bulky, big, large, substantial, massive, ponderous; unwieldy, cumbersome, burdensome, hulking.
ANTONYMS light.
4 *a hefty fine* **substantial,** sizable, considerable, stiff, extortionate, large, excessive; informal steep, astronomical, whopping.
ANTONYMS paltry, small.

height ▶ noun **1** *the height of the wall* **size,** tallness, extent upward, vertical measurement, elevation, stature, altitude.
ANTONYMS width.
2 *the mountain heights* **summit,** top, peak, crest, crown, tip, cap, pinnacle, apex, brow, ridge.
ANTONYMS base.
3 *the height of their fame* **highest point,** crowning moment, peak, acme, zenith, apogee, pinnacle, climax, high-water mark.
ANTONYMS nadir.
4 *the height of bad manners* **epitome,** acme, zenith, quintessence, very limit; ultimate, utmost; ne plus ultra.
5 (**heights**) *he is terrified of heights* **high places,** high ground; precipices, cliffs.

heighten ▶ verb **1** *the roof had to be heightened* **raise,** make higher, lift (up), elevate.
ANTONYMS lower.
2 *her pleasure was heightened by guilt* **intensify,** increase, enhance, add to, augment, boost, strengthen, deepen, magnify, amplify, aggravate, reinforce.
ANTONYMS reduce.

heinous ▶ adjective *heinous crimes* **odious,** wicked, evil, atrocious, monstrous, abominable, detestable, contemptible, reprehensible, despicable, egregious, horrific, terrible, awful, abhorrent, loathsome, hideous, unspeakable, execrable; iniquitous, villainous, beyond the pale.
ANTONYMS admirable.

helix ▶ noun *the teacher's crude drawing of a DNA double helix* **spiral,** coil, corkscrew, curl, curlicue, twist, gyre, whorl, convolution; technical volute, volution.

hell ▶ noun **1** *they feared hell* **the netherworld,** the Inferno, the infernal regions, the abyss; eternal damnation, perdition; hellfire, fire and brimstone; Hades, Sheol, Acheron, Gehenna, Tophet; literary the pit.
ANTONYMS heaven.
2 *he made her life hell* **a misery,** torture, agony, a torment, a nightmare, an ordeal; anguish, wretchedness, woe.
ANTONYMS paradise.
– PHRASES **give someone hell** informal **1** *when I found out, I gave him hell* **reprimand severely,** rebuke, admonish, chastise, castigate, chide, upbraid, reprove, scold, berate, remonstrate with, reprehend, take to task, lambaste; read the riot act, give a piece of one's mind, rake/haul over the coals; informal tell off, dress down, give an earful, give a roasting, rap over the knuckles, let have it, bawl out, come down hard on, lay into, blast, chew out. **2** *she gave me hell when I was her assistant* **harass,** hound, plague, harry, bother, trouble, bully, intimidate, pick on, victimize, terrorize; informal hassle, give a hard time. **raise hell** informal **1** *they were hollering and raising hell* **cause a disturbance,** cause a commotion, be noisy, run riot, run wild, go on the rampage, be out of control; informal raise the roof. **2** *he raised hell with the planners* **remonstrate,** expostulate, be angry, be furious; argue; informal kick up a fuss, raise a stink.

hellish ▶ adjective **1** *the hellish face of Death* **infernal,** Hadean, chthonic; diabolical, fiendish, satanic, demonic; evil, wicked.
ANTONYMS angelic.
2 informal *a hellish week* **horrible,** rotten, awful, terrible, dreadful, ghastly, horrid, vile, foul, appalling, atrocious, horrendous, frightful; difficult, unpleasant, nasty, disagreeable; stressful, taxing, tough, hard, frustrating, fraught, traumatic, grueling; informal murderous, lousy; beastly, hellacious.
ANTONYMS wonderful.

helm ▶ noun *he took the helm* **tiller,** wheel; steering gear, rudder.
– PHRASES **at the helm** *Judith will be at the helm while I am in New Jersey* **in charge,** in command, in control, responsible, in authority, at the wheel, in the driver's seat, in the saddle, holding the reins, running the show, calling the shots.

help ▶ verb **1** *can you help me please?* **assist,** aid, lend a (helping) hand to, give assistance to, come to the aid of; be of service to, be of use to; do someone a favor, do someone a service, do someone a good turn, bail someone out, come to someone's/the rescue, give someone a leg up; informal get someone out of a tight spot, save someone's bacon, save someone's skin.
ANTONYMS hinder.
2 *this credit card helps cancer research* **support,** contribute to, give money to, donate to; promote, boost, back; further the interests of, bankroll.
ANTONYMS impede.
3 *sore throats are helped by lozenges* **relieve,** soothe, ease, alleviate, make better, improve, assuage, lessen; remedy, cure, heal.
ANTONYMS worsen.
▶ noun **1** *I'll take help wherever I can find it | this may be of help to you* **assistance,** aid, a helping hand, support, succor, advice, guidance; benefit, use, advantage, service, comfort; informal a shot in the arm.
2 *he sought help for his eczema* **relief,** alleviation, improvement, assuagement, healing; a remedy, a cure, a restorative.
3 *they treated the help badly* **domestic worker,** domestic servant, cleaner, cleaning lady, housekeeper, maid, hired help, helper.
▶ exclamation *we heard the faint cries of "Help!" in the distance* **SOS,** mayday.
– PHRASES **cannot help** *he could not help laughing* **be unable to stop,** be unable to refrain from, be unable to keep from. **help oneself to** *Tara helped herself to one of the photo albums that we left on the table* **steal,** take, appropriate, borrow, liberate, pocket, lift, purloin, commandeer; informal swipe, nab, filch, walk off with, run off with, pinch.

helper ▶ noun *the teachers' helpers are treated to a picnic lunch at the end of each school year* **assistant,** aide, helpmate, helpmeet, deputy, auxiliary, second, right-hand man/woman, attendant, acolyte; coworker, workmate, teammate, associate, colleague, partner; informal sidekick.

helpful ▶ adjective **1** *the staff are helpful* **obliging,** eager to please, kind, accommodating, supportive, cooperative; sympathetic, boosterish, neighborly, charitable.
ANTONYMS unsympathetic, unobliging.
2 *we found your comments helpful* **useful,** of use, beneficial, valuable, profitable, advantageous, fruitful, worthwhile, constructive; informative, instructive.
ANTONYMS useless.
3 *a helpful new tool* **handy,** useful, convenient, practical, easy-to-use, functional, serviceable; informal neat, nifty.
ANTONYMS inconvenient.

helping ▶ noun *the helpings are very generous* **portion,** serving, piece, slice, share, ration, allocation; informal dollop.

helpless ▶ adjective *the cubs are born blind and helpless* **dependent,** incapable, powerless, impotent, weak; defenseless, vulnerable, exposed, unprotected, open to attack; paralyzed, disabled.
ANTONYMS independent.

helpmate, helpmeet ▶ noun *he thanked his wife of twenty years for being his helpmate and best friend* **helper,** assistant, attendant; supporter, friend, companion; spouse, partner, life partner, mate, husband, wife.

helter-skelter ▶ adverb *they ran helter-skelter down the hill* **headlong,** pell-mell, hotfoot, posthaste, hastily, hurriedly, at full tilt, hell-bent for leather; recklessly, precipitately, heedlessly, wildly; informal like a bat out of hell, like the wind, like greased lightning, lickety-split.

▶ adjective *a helter-skelter collection of houses* **disordered,** disorderly, chaotic, muddled, jumbled, untidy, haphazard, disorganized, topsy-turvy; informal higgledy-piggledy.
ANTONYMS orderly.

hem ▶ noun *the hem of her dress* **edge,** edging, border, trim, trimming.
– PHRASES **hem in 1** *a bay hemmed in by pine trees* **surround,** border, edge, encircle, circle, ring, enclose, skirt, fringe, encompass, corral. **2** *we were hemmed in by the rules* **restrict,** confine, trap, hedge in, fence in; constrain, restrain, limit, curb, check. **hem and haw** *they hem and haw every time we ask for an explanation* **hesitate,** dither, vacillate, be indecisive, equivocate, waver; informal blow hot and cold, shilly-shally.

hence ▶ adverb *the amount of traffic—and hence the amount of pollution—will be reduced* **consequently,** as a consequence, for this reason, therefore, ergo, thus, so, accordingly, as a result, because of that, that being so.

henceforth, henceforward ▶ adverb *henceforth, we will accept only photo IDs* **from now on,** as of now, in (the) future, hence, subsequently, from this day on, from this day forth; formal hereafter.

henchman ▶ noun *he leaves all the dirty work to his henchmen* **right-hand man,** assistant, aide, helper; underling, minion, man Friday, lackey, flunky, stooge; bodyguard; informal sidekick, crony, heavy, goon.

henpecked ▶ adjective *the prosecution characterized him as a henpecked husband who finally snapped* **browbeaten,** downtrodden, bullied, dominated, subjugated, oppressed, intimidated; meek, timid, cringing, long-suffering; informal under someone's thumb.
ANTONYMS domineering.

herald ▶ noun **1** historical *a herald announced the armistice* **messenger,** courier; proclaimer, announcer, crier.
2 *the first herald of spring* **harbinger,** sign, indicator, indication, signal, prelude, portent, omen; forerunner, precursor; literary foretoken.
▶ verb **1** *shouts heralded their approach* **proclaim,** announce, broadcast, publicize, declare, trumpet, blazon, advertise.
2 *the speech heralded a policy change* **signal,** indicate, announce, spell, presage, augur, portend, promise, foretell; usher in, pave the way for, be a harbinger of; literary foretoken, betoken.

Herculean ▶ adjective **1** *a Herculean task* **arduous,** grueling, laborious, back-breaking, onerous, strenuous, difficult, formidable, hard, tough, huge, massive, uphill; demanding, exhausting, taxing; archaic toilsome.
ANTONYMS easy.
2 *his Herculean build* **strong,** muscular, muscly, powerful, robust, solid, strapping, brawny, burly; informal hunky, beefy, hulking.
ANTONYMS puny.

herd ▶ noun **1** *a herd of cows* drove, flock, pack, fold; group, collection.
2 *a herd of actors* **crowd,** group, bunch, horde, mob, host, pack, multitude, throng, swarm, company.
3 *they consider themselves above the herd* **common people,** masses, rank and file, crowd, commonality, plebeians; hoi polloi, mob, proletariat, rabble, riffraff, great unwashed; informal proles, plebs.
▶ verb **1** *we herded the sheep into the pen* **drive,** shepherd, guide; round up, gather, collect, corral.
2 *we all herded into the room* **crowd,** pack, flock; cluster, huddle.
3 *they herd reindeer* **tend,** look after, keep, watch (over), mind, guard.

here ▶ adverb **1** *they lived here* **at/in this place,** at/in this spot, at/in this location.
2 *I am here now* **present,** in attendance, attending, at hand; available.
ANTONYMS absent.
3 *come here tomorrow* **to this place,** to this spot, to this location, over here, nearer, closer; literary hither.
4 *here is your opportunity* **now,** at this moment, at this point, at this point in time, at this juncture, at this stage.
– PHRASES **here and there 1** *clumps of crabgrass here and there* **in various places,** in different places; at random. **2** *they darted here and there* **back and forth,** around, about, to and fro, hither and thither, in all directions.

hereafter ▶ adverb formal *nothing I say hereafter is intended to offend* **from now on,** after this, as of now, from this moment forth, from this day forth, from this day forward, subsequently, in (the) future, hence, henceforth, henceforward; formal hereinafter.
▶ noun (**the hereafter**) *our preparation for the hereafter* **life after death,** the afterlife, the afterworld, the next world; eternity, heaven, paradise.

hereditary ▶ adjective **1** *a hereditary right* **inherited**; bequeathed, willed, handed-down, passed-down, passed-on, transferred; ancestral, family, familial.
2 *a hereditary disease* **genetic,** congenital, inborn, inherited, inbred, innate; in the family, in the blood, in the genes.

heredity ▶ noun *heredity is a major factor in the diagnosis of many conditions* **congenital traits,** genetic makeup, genes; ancestry, descent, extraction, parentage.

heresy ▶ noun *an age in which scientists were often accused of heresy* **dissension,** dissent, nonconformity, heterodoxy, unorthodoxy, apostasy, blasphemy, freethinking; agnosticism, atheism, nonbelief; idolatry, paganism.

heretic ▶ noun *heretics were banished or put to death* **dissenter,** nonconformist, apostate, freethinker, iconoclast; agnostic, atheist, nonbeliever, unbeliever, idolater, idolatress, pagan, heathen; archaic paynim.
ANTONYMS conformist, believer.

heritage ▶ noun **1** *they stole his heritage* **inheritance,** birthright, patrimony; legacy, bequest.
2 *Hawaii's cultural heritage* **tradition,** history, past, background; culture, customs.
3 *his Greek heritage* **ancestry,** lineage, descent,

extraction, parentage, roots, background, heredity.

hermit ▶ **noun** *just because I prefer to live alone doesn't make me a hermit* **recluse,** solitary, loner, ascetic, marabout, troglodyte; historical anchorite, anchoress; archaic eremite.

hero ▶ **noun 1** *the heroes of Guadalcanal* **brave person,** brave man/woman, man/woman of courage, man/woman of the hour, lionheart, warrior, knight; champion, victor, conqueror.
ANTONYMS coward, loser.
2 *a football hero* **star,** superstar, megastar, idol, celebrity, luminary; ideal, paragon, shining example, demigod; favorite, darling; informal celeb.
ANTONYMS unknown, nobody.
3 *the hero of the film* **(male) protagonist,** principal (male) character, principal (male) role, main character, title character, starring role, star part; (male) lead, lead actor, leading man.
ANTONYMS villain, supporting character, supporting role.

heroic ▶ **adjective** *firefighters perform heroic acts every single day* **brave,** courageous, valiant, valorous, lionhearted, superhuman, intrepid, bold, fearless, daring, audacious; unafraid, undaunted, dauntless, doughty, plucky, manly, stout-hearted, mettlesome; gallant, chivalrous, noble; informal gutsy, spunky, ballsy.

heroine ▶ **noun 1** *she's a heroine—she saved my baby | the heroines of the air corps* **brave woman,** hero, woman of courage, woman of the hour; victor, winner, conqueror.
ANTONYMS coward, loser.
2 *the literary heroine of Moscow* **star,** superstar, megastar, idol, celebrity, luminary; ideal, paragon, shining example; favorite, darling, queen; informal celeb.
ANTONYMS unknown, nobody.
3 *the film's heroine* **(female) protagonist,** principal (female) character, principal (female) role, main character, title character; (female) lead, lead actress, leading lady; prima donna, diva.
ANTONYMS villain, supporting character, supporting role.

heroism ▶ **noun** *an award for his heroism* **bravery,** courage, valor, intrepidity, boldness, daring, audacity, fearlessness, dauntlessness, pluck, stout-heartedness, lionheartedness; backbone, spine, grit, spirit, mettle; gallantry, chivalry; informal guts, spunk, balls, cojones, moxie.

hero-worship ▶ **noun** *the hero-worship of his fans soon became unsettling to him* **idolization,** adulation, admiration, lionization, idealization, worship, adoration, veneration.

hesitancy ▶ **noun** See HESITATION.

hesitant ▶ **adjective 1** *she is hesitant about buying* **uncertain,** undecided, unsure, doubtful, dubious, skeptical; tentative, nervous, reluctant, gun-shy; indecisive, irresolute, hesitating, dithering, vacillating, wavering, waffling, blowing hot and cold; ambivalent, of two minds, hemming and hawing; informal iffy.
ANTONYMS certain, decisive.
2 *a hesitant child* **lacking confidence,** diffident, timid, shy, bashful, insecure, tentative.
ANTONYMS confident.

hesitate ▶ **verb 1** *she hesitated, unsure of what to say* **pause,** delay, wait, shilly-shally, dither, stall, temporize; be of two minds, be uncertain, be unsure, be doubtful, be indecisive, hedge, equivocate, fluctuate, vacillate, waver, waffle, have second thoughts, think twice; informal dilly-dally, blow hot and cold, get cold feet, hem and haw.
2 *don't hesitate to contact me* **be reluctant,** be unwilling, be disinclined, scruple; have misgivings about, have qualms about, shrink from, demur from, think twice about, balk at; informal miss a beat.

hesitation ▶ **noun** *she answered without hesitation* **hesitancy,** uncertainty, unsureness, doubt, doubtfulness, dubiousness; irresolution, irresoluteness, indecision, indecisiveness, hesitance; equivocation, vacillation, waffling, wavering, second thoughts; dithering, stalling, dawdling, temporization, delay; reluctance, disinclination, unease, ambivalence; informal cold feet; formal dubiety.

hew ▶ **verb 1** *the logs are freshly hewn* **chop,** hack, cut, lop, ax, cleave, split; fell.
2 *steps had been hewn into the rock wall* **cut,** carve, chisel, shape, fashion, sculpt.

heyday ▶ **noun** *during his heyday, he was quite the matinee idol* **prime,** peak, height, pinnacle, summit, apex, acme, zenith, climax, high point; day, time, bloom, flowering; prime of life, salad days, halcyon days, glory days.

hiatus ▶ **noun** *the spring hiatus gave us time to rethink our next project* **pause,** break, gap, lacuna, interval, intermission, interlude, interruption, suspension, lull, respite, time out, time off, recess; informal breather, letup.

hibernate ▶ **verb 1** *bears hibernate in winter* **lie dormant,** lie torpid, sleep; overwinter.
2 *he wanted to hibernate in front of a fire for the night* **hole up,** escape, withdraw, retreat, cocoon.

hidden ▶ **adjective 1** *a hidden camera* **concealed,** secret, undercover, invisible, unseen, out of sight, closeted, covert; secluded, tucked away; camouflaged, disguised, masked, cloaked.
ANTONYMS visible.
2 *a hidden meaning* **obscure,** unclear, veiled, clouded, shrouded, concealed; cryptic, mysterious, secret, abstruse, arcane; ulterior, deep, subliminal, coded.
ANTONYMS clear, obvious.

hide[1] ▶ **verb 1** *he hid the money* **conceal,** secrete, put out of sight; camouflage; lock up, stow away, tuck away, squirrel away, cache; informal stash.
ANTONYMS flaunt, expose.
2 *they hid in an air vent* **conceal oneself,** sequester oneself, hide out, take cover, keep out of sight; lie low, go underground; informal hole up.
3 *clouds hid the moon* **obscure,** block out, blot out, obstruct, cloud, shroud, veil, blanket, envelop, eclipse.
ANTONYMS reveal.

4 *he could not hide his dislike* **conceal,** keep secret, cover up, keep quiet about, hush up, bottle up, suppress, curtain, bury; disguise, dissemble, mask, camouflage; informal keep under one's hat, keep a/the lid on.
ANTONYMS disclose.

hide² ▶ noun *the hide should be tanned quickly* **skin,** pelt, coat; leather.

hideaway ▶ noun *the cabin in Maine is our hideaway* **retreat,** refuge, hiding place, hideout, den, bolt-hole, shelter, sanctuary, sanctum; hermitage, secret place.

hidebound ▶ adjective *hidebound traditionalists* **conservative,** reactionary, conventional, orthodox; fundamentalist, diehard, hardline, dyed-in-the-wool, set in one's ways, unyielding, inflexible; narrow-minded, small-minded, intolerant, uncompromising, rigid; prejudiced, bigoted.
ANTONYMS liberal.

hideous ▶ adjective *the scenes were too hideous to watch* **ugly,** repulsive, repellent, unsightly, revolting, gruesome, grotesque, monstrous, ghastly; informal as ugly as sin; awful, terrible, appalling, dreadful, frightful, horrible, horrendous, horrific, horrifying, shocking, sickening, unspeakable, abhorrent, heinous, abominable, foul, vile, odious, execrable.
ANTONYMS beautiful, pleasant.

hideout ▶ noun *the gang had a hideout up in the mountains* **hiding place,** hideaway, retreat, refuge, shelter, safe house, sanctuary, sanctum.

hierarchy ▶ noun *in the corporate hierarchy, Curt is about six levels below the CEO* **pecking order,** order, ranking, chain of command, grading, gradation, ladder, scale, range.

high ▶ adjective **1** *a high mountain* **tall,** lofty, towering, soaring, elevated, giant, big; multistory, high-rise.
ANTONYMS short, low.
2 *a high position in the government* **high-ranking,** high-level, leading, top, top-level, prominent, preeminent, foremost, senior; influential, powerful, important, elevated, prime, premier, exalted, ranking; informal top-notch, chief.
ANTONYMS low-ranking, lowly.
3 *high principles* **high-minded,** noble, lofty, moral, ethical, honorable, exalted, admirable, upright, honest, virtuous, righteous.
ANTONYMS amoral.
4 *high prices* **inflated,** excessive, unreasonable, expensive, costly, exorbitant, extortionate, prohibitive, dear; informal steep, stiff, pricey.
ANTONYMS reasonable, low.
5 *high winds* **strong,** powerful, violent, intense, extreme, forceful; **blustery,** gusty, stiff, squally, tempestuous, turbulent, howling, roaring.
ANTONYMS light, calm.
6 *the high life* **luxurious,** lavish, extravagant, grand, opulent; sybaritic, hedonistic, epicurean, decadent; upmarket, upscale; informal fancy, classy, swanky.
ANTONYMS abstemious.
7 *I have a high opinion of you* **favorable,** good, positive, approving, admiring, complimentary, commendatory, flattering, glowing, adulatory, rapturous.
ANTONYMS unfavorable.
8 *a high note | his high voice* **high-pitched,** high-frequency; soprano, treble, falsetto, shrill, sharp, piercing, penetrating.
ANTONYMS low, low-pitched, deep.
9 informal *they were high before they even got to the party* **intoxicated,** inebriated, drugged, on drugs, stupefied, befuddled, delirious, hallucinating; informal **stoned,** wired, hopped up, high as a kite, tripping, hyped up, doped up, coked, spaced out, wasted, wrecked.
ANTONYMS sober, straight.
10 *high in fiber* **elevated in,** rich in, ample in, loaded with, plentiful in, full of; informal chock-full of, jam-packed with.
ANTONYMS deficient.
▶ noun *prices were at a rare high* **high level,** high point, peak, high-water mark; pinnacle, zenith, acme, height.
ANTONYMS low.
▶ adverb *a jet flew high overhead* **at great height,** high up, far up, way up, at altitude; in the air, in the sky, on high, aloft, overhead.
ANTONYMS low.
– PHRASES **high and dry** *we track down these guys who have left their wives and children high and dry* **destitute,** helpless, in the lurch, in difficulties; abandoned, stranded, marooned. **high and low** *I searched high and low for my keys* **everywhere,** all over, all around, far and wide, 'here, there, and everywhere', extensively, thoroughly, widely, in every nook and cranny; informal all over the place, all over the map. **high and mighty** informal *he feels high and mighty just because he was lucky enough to keep his job* **self-important,** condescending, patronizing, pompous, disdainful, supercilious, superior, snobbish, snobby, haughty, conceited, above oneself; informal stuck-up, puffed up, snooty, hoity-toity, la-di-da, uppity, full of oneself, too big for one's britches/boots. **on a high** informal *she was obviously on a high after Joey proposed* **ecstatic,** euphoric, exhilarated, delirious, elated, ebullient, thrilled, overjoyed, beside oneself, walking on air, on cloud nine, in seventh heaven, jumping for joy, in raptures, in high spirits, exultant, jubilant; excited, overexcited; informal blissed out, over the moon, on top of the world.

high-born ▶ adjective *her high-born father had given up his inheritance to marry a lowly seamstress* **noble,** aristocratic, well-born, titled, patrician, blue-blooded, upper-class, genteel; informal upper-crust, top-drawer; archaic gentle.
ANTONYMS lowly.

highbrow ▶ adjective *his work has a highbrow following* **intellectual,** scholarly, bookish, well-read, literary, cultured, academic, educated, lettered, sophisticated, erudite, learned, cerebral; informal brainy, egghead, inkhorn.
ANTONYMS lowbrow.
▶ noun *highbrows who hate rap music* **intellectual,** scholar, academic, bluestocking, bookish person, thinker; informal egghead, brain, bookworm, brainiac.

high-class ▶ adjective *the casino's high-class hotel* **superior,** upper-class, first-rate; excellent, select, elite, choice, premier, top, top-flight;

luxurious, deluxe, upscale, high-quality, top-quality, upmarket; informal top-notch, blue-ribbon, five-star, top-drawer, A1, ritzy, tony, classy, posh.

highfalutin ▶ adjective informal See PRETENTIOUS.

high-flown ▶ adjective *one of his high-flown ideas finally panned out* **grand,** extravagant, elaborate, flowery, lofty, ornate, overblown, overdone, overwrought, grandiloquent, magniloquent, grandiose, orotund, inflated, high-sounding; affected, pretentious, bombastic, pompous, turgid; informal windy, purple, highfalutin, la-di-da.
ANTONYMS plain.

high-handed ▶ adjective *I'll not be subordinate to any high-handed individual, male or female* **imperious,** arbitrary, peremptory, arrogant, haughty, domineering, supercilious, pushy, overbearing, heavy-handed, lordly, magisterial; inflexible, rigid; autocratic, authoritarian, dictatorial, tyrannical; informal bossy, high and mighty.
ANTONYMS modest.

highland ▶ noun *Peru's Andean highland* **uplands,** highlands, mountains, hills, heights, moors; upland, tableland, plateau.

highlight ▶ noun *the highlight of his career* **high point,** best part, climax, peak, pinnacle, height, acme, zenith, summit, crowning moment, high-water mark, centerpiece.
ANTONYMS nadir.
▶ verb *he has highlighted shortcomings in the plan* **spotlight,** call attention to, point out, single out, focus on, underline, feature, play up, show up, bring out, accentuate, accent, give prominence to, zero in on, stress, emphasize.

highly ▶ adverb **1** *a highly dangerous substance* **very,** extremely, exceedingly, particularly, most, really, thoroughly, decidedly, distinctly, exceptionally, immensely, greatly, inordinately, singularly, extraordinarily; informal awfully, terribly, majorly, seriously, supremely, desperately, hugely, ultra, oh-so, damn, damned; real, mighty, awful; dated frightfully.
ANTONYMS slightly.
2 *he was highly regarded* **favorably,** well, appreciatively, admiringly, approvingly, positively, glowingly, enthusiastically.
ANTONYMS unfavorably.

high-minded ▶ adjective *high-minded civil libertarians* **high-principled,** principled, honorable, moral, upright, upstanding, right-minded, noble, good, honest, decent, ethical, righteous, virtuous, worthy, idealistic.
ANTONYMS unprincipled.

high-powered ▶ adjective *high-powered career women* **dynamic,** ambitious, energetic, assertive, enterprising, vigorous; forceful, powerful, potent, aggressive; informal go-getting, high-octane.

high-pressure ▶ adjective **1** *high-pressure sales tactics* **forceful,** insistent, persistent, pushy; intensive, high-powered, aggressive, coercive, compelling, not taking no for an answer.
2 *a high-pressure job* **demanding,** stressful, nerve-racking, tense, pressured.

high-priced ▶ adjective *high-priced luxury cars* **expensive,** costly, dear, big-ticket, high-end; overpriced, exorbitant, extortionate; informal pricey, steep, stiff.

high-sounding ▶ adjective See HIGH-FLOWN.

high-spirited ▶ adjective *a high-spirited horse* **lively,** spirited, full of fun, fun-loving, animated, zestful, bouncy, bubbly, sparkling, vivacious, buoyant, cheerful, joyful, exuberant, ebullient, jaunty, irrepressible; informal chirpy, peppy, full of beans; literary frolicsome.

high spirits ▶ plural noun *the high spirits of these young competitors is indeed infectious* **liveliness,** vitality, spirit, zest, energy, bounce, sparkle, vivacity, buoyancy, cheerfulness, good humor, joy, joyfulness, exuberance, ebullience, joie de vivre; informal pep, zing.

high-strung ▶ adjective *a high-strung woman answered the phone and started accusing me of harassing her* **nervous,** excitable, agitated, temperamental, sensitive, unstable; brittle, on edge, edgy, jumpy, jittery, restless, anxious, tense, stressed, overwrought, neurotic; informal worked up, uptight, twitchy, wired, wound up, het up, strung out.
ANTONYMS easygoing.

hijack ▶ verb *two flight attendants thwarted Girard's attempt to hijack the plane* **commandeer,** seize, take over, take control; skyjack, carjack; appropriate, expropriate, confiscate, co-opt.

hike ▶ noun *a five-mile hike* **walk,** trek, tramp, trudge, slog, footslog, march; ramble.
▶ verb *they hiked across the island* **walk,** trek, tramp, tromp, trudge, slog, footslog, march; ramble, rove, traipse; informal hoof it, leg it.
– PHRASES **hike up 1** *Roy hiked up his trousers* **hitch up,** pull up, hoist, lift, raise; informal yank up. **2** *they hiked up the price* **increase,** raise, up, put up, boost up, mark up, push up, inflate; informal jack up, bump up.

hilarious ▶ adjective *the final scene is hilarious* **very funny,** hysterically funny, hysterical, uproarious, riotous, rollicking, farcical, rib-tickling; humorous, comic, amusing, entertaining, jocular, jovial, laughable; informal side-splitting, gut-busting, knee-slapping, thigh-slapping, priceless, a scream, a hoot.

hilarity ▶ noun *we always enjoy a great deal of hilarity when we get together* **amusement,** mirth, laughter, merriment, lightheartedness, levity, fun, humor, jocularity, jollity, gaiety, delight, glee, exuberance, high spirits; comedy.

hill ▶ noun **1** *the top of the hill* **high ground,** prominence, hillock, foothill, hillside, rise, mound, mount, knoll, butte, hummock, mesa; bank, bluff, ridge, slope, incline, gradient; (**hills**) heights, highland(s), downs, elevation; Geology drumlin; formal eminence.
2 *a hill of garbage* **heap,** pile, stack, mound, mountain, mass.

hillock ▶ noun *the lovely green hillocks in the distance* **mound,** small hill, prominence, elevation, rise, knoll, hummock, hump, dune; bank, ridge, knob; formal eminence.

hilt ▶ noun *the hilt of his sword* **handle,** haft, handgrip, grip, shaft, shank, helve.

– PHRASES **to the hilt** *we will support our leaders to the hilt* **completely,** fully, wholly, totally, absolutely, entirely, utterly, unreservedly, unconditionally, in every respect, in all respects, one hundred percent, every inch, to the full, to the maximum extent, all the way, body and soul, heart and soul.

hind ▶ adjective *the left hind leg* **back,** rear, hinder, hindmost, posterior; dorsal.
ANTONYMS fore, front.

hinder ▶ verb *budget cuts have hindered our progress* **hamper,** obstruct, impede, inhibit, retard, balk, prevent, thwart, foil, curb, delay, arrest, interfere with, set back, slow down, hobble, hold back, hold up, stop, halt; restrict, restrain, constrain, block, check, curtail, frustrate, cramp, handicap, cripple, hamstring; informal stymie, throw a wrench in the works. See note at **PROHIBIT**.
ANTONYMS facilitate.

CHOOSE THE RIGHT WORD

encumber, hamper, hinder, impede, obstruct, prevent

If you're about to set off on a cross-country trip by car and wake up to find that a foot of snow has fallen overnight, it would be correct to say that the weather has **hindered** you. But if you're trying to drive through a snowstorm and are forced to creep along at a snail's pace behind a snowplow, it would be correct to say you were **impeded**. To *hinder* is to delay or hold something back, especially something that is under way or is about to start (*she entered college but was hindered by poor study habits*); it connotes a thwarting of progress, either deliberate or accidental. *Impede*, on the other hand, means to slow the progress of someone or something by a deliberate act; it implies that the obstacles are more serious and suggests that movement or progress is so slow that it is painful or frustrating (*the shoes were so tight they impeded his circulation*). Both **hamper** and **encumber** involve hindering by outside forces. To *hamper* is to impede by placing restraints on someone or something so as to make action difficult (*hampered by family responsibilities*), while *encumber* means to hinder by the placing of a burden (*encumbered with several heavy suitcases*). To **obstruct** is to place obstacles in the way, often bringing progress or movement to a complete halt (*obstruct traffic; obstruct justice*). **Prevent** suggests precautionary or restraining measures (*the police prevented him from entering the burning building*) and is also used to describe a nonhuman agency or cause that hinders something (*the snow prevented us from leaving that day*).

hindrance ▶ noun *bad weather was the primary hindrance to our rescue efforts* **impediment,** obstacle, barrier, bar, obstruction, handicap, block, hurdle, restraint, restriction, limitation, encumbrance, interference; complication, delay, drawback, setback, difficulty, inconvenience, snag, catch, hitch, check, stumbling block; informal fly in the ointment, hiccup, wrench in the works.
ANTONYMS help.

hinge ▶ verb *our future hinges on the election* **depend on,** hang on, rest on, turn on, center on, pivot on, be contingent on, be dependent on, be conditional on; be determined by, be decided by, revolve around.

hint ▶ noun **1** *a hint that he would leave* **clue,** inkling, suggestion, indication, indicator, sign, signal, pointer, intimation, insinuation, innuendo, mention, whisper.
2 *handy hints about painting* **tip,** suggestion, pointer, clue, guideline, recommendation; advice, help; informal how-to.
3 *a hint of mint* **trace,** touch, suspicion, suggestion, dash, soupçon, tinge, modicum, whiff, taste, undertone; informal smidgen, tad, speck.
▶ verb *what are you hinting at?* **imply,** insinuate, intimate, suggest, indicate, signal; allude to, refer to, drive at, mean; informal get at.

hippie ▶ noun *yesterday's hippies are today's ad execs* **flower child,** Bohemian, beatnik, long-hair, free spirit, nonconformist, dropout.

hire ▶ verb **1** *they hire labor in line with demand* **employ,** engage, recruit, appoint, take on, sign up, enroll, commission, enlist, contract.
ANTONYMS dismiss, lay off.
2 *we hired a car* **rent,** lease, charter, let, sublet.

hiss ▶ verb **1** *the escaping gas hissed* **fizz,** fizzle, whistle, wheeze; rare sibilate.
2 *the audience hissed* **jeer,** catcall, boo, heckle, whistle, hoot; scoff, jibe.
▶ noun **1** *the hiss of the steam* **fizz,** fizzing, whistle, hissing, sibilance, wheeze, pfft; rare sibilation.
2 *the speaker received hisses* **jeer,** catcall, boo, whistle; abuse, scoffing, taunting, derision.

historic ▶ adjective *the historic first flight at Kitty Hawk* **significant,** notable, important, momentous, consequential, memorable, newsworthy, unforgettable, remarkable; famous, famed, celebrated, renowned, legendary; landmark, sensational, groundbreaking, epoch-making, red-letter, earth-shattering.
ANTONYMS insignificant.

USAGE

historic, historical

Historical, meaning "of or relating to or occurring in history," is called upon for use far more frequently than historic. *Historic* means "historically significant" *the Alamo is a historic building*. An event that makes history is historic; momentous happenings or developments are historic—e.g.: "The Supreme Court's historic decision about whether mentally competent, dying patients and their doctors have the right to hasten death won't be known for months." (*USA Today,* Jan. 10, 1997.) A documented fact, event, or development—perhaps having no great importance—is *historical.* E.g.: "Despite the historical data, some people just don't feel comfortable knowing their loan's rate can drift up 5 or 6 points." (*Chicago Sun-Times*, Jan. 24, 1997). Examples of *historic* used incorrectly for *historical* could easily run for several pages—e.g.: "The Sunday Trading Act, which formally became law yesterday, removes historic [read *historical*] anomalies of the kind that allowed shopkeepers to sell pornographic magazines but not Bibles on the Sabbath, and instant but not ground coffee." (*Times* (London), Aug. 27, 1994.) "The odds are now on a further easing of monetary policy and there is a good historic [read *historical*] correlation between falling interest rates and a rising stock market." (*Financial Times*, June 13, 1996.) "Rape is also an historic [read a *historical*] soldiers' sport." (*Harper's Magazine*, Jan. 2003.) The far less common mistake is misusing *historical* for *historic*—e.g.: "Gary Pinkel didn't know what to expect after Toledo and Nevada found themselves going into a historical [read *historic*] overtime in the Las Vegas Bowl." (*Austin Am.-Statesman*, Dec. 16, 1995.) — **BG**

historical ▶ adjective **1** *historical evidence* **documented,** recorded, chronicled, archival; authentic, factual, actual, true.
ANTONYMS mythical, legendary.
2 *historical figures* **past,** bygone, ancient, old, former; literary of yore. See note at **HISTORIC**.
ANTONYMS contemporary.

history ▶ noun **1** *my interest in history* **the past,** former times, historical events, the olden days, the old days, bygone days, long ago, yesterday, antiquity; literary days of yore, yesteryear.
2 *a history of the Boxer Rebellion* **chronicle,** archive, record, diary, report, narrative, account, study, tale, story, saga; memoir.
3 *she gave details of her history* **background,** past, life story, biography, experiences, backstory; antecedents.

hit ▶ verb **1** *she hit her child* **strike,** slap, smack, spank, cuff, punch, thump, swat; beat, thrash, batter, pound, pummel, box someone's ears; whip, flog, cane; informal whack, wallop, bash, bop, clout, clip, clobber, sock, swipe, crown, beat the living daylights out of, knock someone around, belt, tan, lay into, let someone have it, deck, floor, slug; literary smite.
2 *a car hit the barrier* **crash into,** run into, smash into, smack into, knock into, bump into, plow into, collide with, meet head-on, impact.
3 informal *spending will hit $180 million* **reach,** touch, arrive at, rise to, climb to.
4 *it hit me that I had forgotten* **occur to,** strike, dawn on, come to; enter one's head, cross one's mind, come to mind, spring to one's mind.
▶ noun **1** *he received a hit from behind* **blow,** thump, punch, knock, bang, cuff, slap, smack, spank, tap, crack, stroke, welt, karate chop; impact, collision, bump, crash; informal whack, thwack, wallop, bash, belt, clout, sock, swipe, clip, slug.
2 *he directed many big hits* **success,** box-office success, sellout, winner, triumph, sensation; best seller; informal smash, smash hit, megahit, knockout, crowd-pleaser, chart-topper, chart-buster, wow, biggie, number one.
ANTONYMS failure.
– PHRASES **hit back** *if you're gonna come after me with lies and innuendo, I'm gonna hit back* **retaliate,** respond, reply, react, counter, defend oneself. **hit hard** *the tragedy hit her hard* **devastate,** affect badly, hurt, harm, leave a mark on; upset, shatter, crush, shock, overwhelm, traumatize. **hit home** *the documentary on teen suicide painfully hit home* **have the intended effect,** strike home, hit the mark, register, be understood, get through, sink in. **hit it off** informal *Mark and Mika hit it off almost immediately* **get on well,** get along, get on, be friends, be friendly, be compatible, be well matched, feel a rapport, see eye to eye, take to each other, warm to each other; informal click, get on like a house on fire, be on the same wavelength. **hit on/upon 1** *he hit on the truth | Cagney hit upon a great idea for the finale* **discover,** come up with, think of, conceive of, dream up, work out, invent, create, devise, design, pioneer; uncover, stumble on, happen upon, chance on, light on, come upon.
2 *he tried to hit on me* **flirt with,** show interest in, make eyes at, come on to, make advances to/toward.

hitch ▶ verb **1** *Tom hitched the pony to his cart* **harness,** yoke, couple, fasten, connect, attach, tether, tie.
2 *she hitched the blanket around her* **pull,** jerk, tug, hike, lift, raise, yank, shift.
3 informal *they hitched a ride* informal **thumb,** hitchhike.
▶ noun *it went without a hitch* **problem,** difficulty, snag, catch, setback, hindrance, obstacle, obstruction, complication, impediment, stumbling block, barrier; holdup, interruption, delay; informal headache, glitch, hiccup.

hither ▶ adverb literary See **HERE** (sense 3).

hitherto ▶ adverb *hitherto a part of French West Africa, Benin achieved independence in 1960* **previously,** formerly, earlier, before, beforehand; so far, thus far, to date, as yet, until now, until then, till now, till then, up to now, up to then; formal heretofore.

hit-or-miss, hit-and-miss ▶ adjective *even his approach to finding a job is hit-or-miss* **erratic,** haphazard, disorganized, undisciplined, unmethodical, uneven; careless, slapdash, slipshod, casual, cursory, lackadaisical, random, aimless, undirected, indiscriminate; informal sloppy.
ANTONYMS meticulous.

hoard ▶ noun *a secret hoard of gold* **cache,** stockpile, stock, store, collection, supply, reserve, reservoir, fund, accumulation; treasury, treasure house, treasure trove; informal stash.
▶ verb *they hoarded rations* **stockpile,** store, store up, stock up on, put aside, put by, lay by, lay up, set aside, stow away, buy up; cache, amass, collect, save, gather, garner, accumulate, squirrel away, put aside for a rainy day; informal stash away, salt away.
ANTONYMS squander.

hoarse ▶ adjective *voices hoarse from shouting* **rough,** harsh, throaty, gruff, husky, growly, gravelly, grating, scratchy, raspy, rasping, raucous, croaky, croaking, with a frog in one's

throat.
ANTONYMS mellow, clear.

hoary ▶ adjective 1 *hoary cobwebs* **grayish-white,** gray, white, snowy, silver, silvery; frosty; literary rimy.
2 *a hoary old man* **gray-haired,** white-haired, silver-haired, grizzled; elderly, aged, old, ancient, venerable; informal over the hill.
ANTONYMS young.

hoax ▶ noun *the Piltdown man was perhaps the most successful hoax of the twentieth century* **practical joke,** joke, jest, prank, trick; ruse, deception, fraud, bluff, confidence trick; informal con, spoof, scam, setup.

hobble ▶ verb *Luke hobbled into the post office* **limp,** walk with difficulty, walk lamely, move unsteadily, walk haltingly; shamble, totter, dodder, stagger, falter, stumble, lurch.

hobby ▶ noun *writing poetry is just one of my hobbies* **pastime,** leisure activity, leisure pursuit; sideline, side interest, diversion, avocation; recreation, entertainment, amusement.

hobgoblin ▶ noun *he believed there were hobgoblins under his bed* **goblin,** imp, sprite, elf, brownie, pixie, puck, leprechaun, gnome; bogey, bugbear, bogeyman.

hobnob ▶ verb informal *she sought out every opportunity to hobnob with the rich and famous* **associate,** mix, fraternize, socialize, keep company, spend time, go around, mingle, consort, network, rub shoulders, rub elbows; informal hang around/out, be thick, schmooze.

hocus-pocus ▶ noun 1 *a little hocus-pocus and—presto!—the tiger disappears* **magic,** sleight of hand, conjuring, witchcraft, wizardry, sorcery; deception, sham, devilry, trickery; informal scam.
2 *she dismissed it as so much hocus-pocus* **nonsense,** rubbish, garbage, balderdash, malarkey, baloney, bunk, hogwash, bull, hokum.

hodgepodge ▶ noun *a rambling hodgepodge of Chinese modern and art deco* **mixture,** mix, mixed bag, assortment, random collection, conglomeration, jumble, ragbag, grab bag, miscellany, medley, salmagundi, potpourri, patchwork, pastiche; mélange, mishmash, hash, confusion, farrago, gallimaufry. See note at JUMBLE.

hog ▶ noun *a prize-winning hog* **pig,** sow, swine, porker, piglet, boar; informal piggy.
▶ verb informal *he hogged the limelight* **monopolize,** dominate, take over, corner, control.
ANTONYMS share.

hogwash ▶ noun informal See NONSENSE (sense 1 of the noun).

hoi polloi ▶ noun *in days long past, the royal family would not have deigned to commune with the hoi polloi* **masses,** common people, populace, public, multitude, rank and file, lower order(s), plebeians, proletariat; mob, herd, rabble, riffraff, great unwashed; informal plebs, proles; historical third estate.

hoist ▶ verb *we hoisted the mainsail* **raise,** raise up, lift, lift, haul up, heave up, jack up, hike up, winch up, pull up, heft up, upraise, uplift, elevate, erect.
ANTONYMS lower.
▶ noun *a mechanical hoist* **lifting gear,** crane, winch, block and tackle, pulley, windlass, derrick; Nautical sheerlegs.

hold ▶ verb 1 *she held a suitcase* **clasp,** clutch, grasp, grip, clench, cling to, hold on to; carry, bear.
ANTONYMS release, let go of.
2 *I wanted to hold her* **embrace,** hug, clasp, cradle, enfold, squeeze, fold in one's arms, cling to.
3 *do you hold a degree?* **possess,** have, own, bear, carry, have to one's name.
4 *the branch held my weight* **support,** bear, carry, take, keep up, sustain, prop up, shore up.
5 *the police were holding him* **detain,** hold in custody, imprison, lock up, put behind bars, put in prison, put in jail, incarcerate, keep under lock and key, confine, constrain, intern, impound; informal put away.
ANTONYMS release, let go.
6 *try to hold the audience's attention* **maintain,** keep, occupy, engross, absorb, interest, captivate, fascinate, enthrall, rivet, mesmerize, transfix; engage, catch, capture, arrest.
ANTONYMS lose.
7 *he held a senior post* **occupy,** have, fill; informal hold down.
8 *the tank holds 250 gallons* **take,** contain, accommodate, fit; have a capacity of, have room for.
9 *the court held that there was no evidence* **maintain,** consider, take the view, believe, think, feel, deem, be of the opinion; judge, rule, decide; informal reckon; formal opine, esteem.
10 *let's hope the good weather holds* **persist,** continue, carry on, go on, hold out, keep up, last, endure, stay, remain.
ANTONYMS end.
11 *the offer still holds* **be available,** be valid, hold good, stand, apply, remain, exist, be the case, be in force, be in effect.
12 *they held a meeting* **convene,** call, summon; conduct, have, organize, run; formal convoke.
ANTONYMS disband.
13 *hold your fire* **stop,** halt, restrain, check, cease, discontinue; informal break off, give up; hold back, suppress, repress, refrain from using, stifle, withhold.
ANTONYMS resume.
▶ noun 1 *she kept a hold on my hand* **grip,** grasp, clasp, clutch.
2 *Tom had a hold over his father* **influence,** power, control, dominance, authority, command, leverage, sway, mastery, dominion.
3 *the military tightened their hold on the capital* **control,** grip, power, stranglehold, chokehold, dominion, authority.
– PHRASES **get hold of** informal *I'll try to get hold of Stevenson this evening* **contact,** get in touch with, communicate with, make contact with, reach, notify; phone, call, speak to, talk to.
hold back 1 *if you feel like singing, don't hold back* **hesitate,** pause, stop oneself, restrain oneself, desist, forbear. **2** *Jane held back her tears* **suppress,** fight back, choke back, stifle, smother, subdue, rein in, repress, curb, control, keep a tight rein on; informal keep a lid on. **3** *don't hold anything back from me*

withhold, hide, conceal, keep secret, keep hidden, keep quiet about, keep to oneself, hush up; informal sit on, keep under one's hat. **4** *you'll never make it in music if you keep letting your parents hold you back* **hinder,** hamper, impede, obstruct, inhibit, hobble, check, curb, block, thwart, balk, hamstring, restrain, frustrate, stand in someone's way. **hold dear** *she holds this house dear* **cherish,** treasure, prize, appreciate, adore, value highly, care for/about; informal put on a pedestal. **hold down 1** *they will hold down inflation* **keep down,** keep low, freeze, fix. **2** informal *she held down two jobs* **occupy,** have, do, fill. **3** *the people can be held down only so long* **oppress,** repress, suppress, subdue, subjugate, keep down, keep under, tyrannize, dominate. **hold forth** *he was holding forth on the qualities of good wine* **speak at length,** talk at length, go on, sound off; declaim, spout, pontificate, orate, preach, sermonize; informal speechify, drone on. **hold off 1** *the rain held off* **stay away,** keep off, not come, delay. **2** *we held off the swarms of ants as long as we could* **resist,** repel, repulse, rebuff, parry, deflect, fend off, stave off, ward off, keep at bay. **hold on 1** *hold on, I'll be right there* **wait,** wait a minute, just a moment, just a second; stay here, stay put; hold the line; informal just a sec, hang on, sit tight, hold your horses. **2** *if only they could hold on just a little longer* **keep going,** persevere, survive, last, continue, struggle on, carry on, go on, hold out, see it through, stay the course; informal soldier on, stick it out, hang in there. **hold on to 1** *he held on to the chair* **clutch,** hang on to, clasp, grasp, grip, cling to. **2** *they can't hold on to their staff* **retain,** keep, hang on to. **hold one's own** See **OWN**. **hold out 1** *the small band of weary soldiers held out until reinforcements arrived* **persist,** last, remain; persevere, continue. **2** *Celia held out her hands* **extend,** proffer, offer, present; outstretch, reach out, stretch out, put out. **hold over** *the family gathering was held over until late January* **postpone,** put off, put back, delay, defer, suspend, shelve, put over, table, take a rain check on; informal put on ice, put on the back burner, put in cold storage, mothball. **hold up 1** *the argument doesn't hold up* **be convincing,** be logical, hold water, bear examination, be sound. **2** *they held up the trophy* **display,** hold aloft, exhibit, show (off), flourish, brandish; informal flash. **3** *concrete pillars hold up the bridge* **support,** bear, carry, take, keep up, prop up, shore up, buttress. **4** *our flight was held up for hours* **delay,** detain, make late, set back, keep back, retard, slow up. **5** *a lack of cash has held up progress* **obstruct,** impede, hinder, hamper, inhibit, arrest, balk, thwart, curb, hamstring, frustrate, foil, interfere with, stop; informal stymie, hog-tie. **6** *two gunmen held up the bank* **rob**; informal stick up. **hold water** See **WATER**. **with no holds barred** *you can tell us everything that happened, with no holds barred* **candidly,** honestly, frankly, directly, openly, bluntly; informal point-blank, without mincing one's words.

holder ▶ **noun 1** *a knife holder* **container,** receptacle, case, casing, cover, covering, housing, sheath; stand, rest, rack. **2** *are you the holder of a major credit card?* **bearer,** owner, possessor, keeper; custodian.

holdup ▶ **noun 1** *I ran into a series of holdups* **delay,** setback, hitch, snag, obstruction, difficulty, problem, trouble, stumbling block; informal tie-up, logjam; traffic jam, gridlock, bottleneck, roadblock; snarl-up, glitch, hiccup. **2** *a bank holdup* **robbery,** raid, armed robbery, armed raid; theft, burglary, mugging; informal stickup, heist.

hole ▶ **noun 1** *a hole in the roof* **opening,** aperture, gap, space, orifice, vent, chink, breach, break; crack, leak, rift, rupture; puncture, perforation, cut, split, gash, slit, rent, tear, crevice, fissure.
2 *a hole in the ground* **pit,** ditch, trench, cavity, crater, depression, indentation, hollow; well, borehole, excavation, dugout; cave, cavern, pothole.
3 *the gopher's hole* **burrow,** lair, den, earth, set; retreat, shelter.
4 *there are holes in their argument* **flaw,** fault, defect, weakness, shortcoming, inconsistency, discrepancy, loophole; error, mistake.
5 informal *I was living in a real hole* **hovel,** slum, shack; informal dump, dive, pigsty, hole in the wall, rathole, sty.
6 informal *she has dug herself into a hole* **predicament,** difficult situation, awkward situation, corner, tight corner, quandary, dilemma; crisis, emergency, difficulty, trouble, plight, dire straits, imbroglio; informal fix, jam, mess, bind, scrape, spot, tight spot, pickle, sticky situation, can of worms, hot water.
– PHRASES **hole up 1** *the bears hole up in winter* **hibernate,** lie dormant. **2** informal *the snipers holed up in a farmhouse* **hide (out),** conceal oneself, secrete oneself, shelter, take cover, lie low. **poke holes in** informal *it was pretty easy to poke holes in Dr. Delvecchio's theories* **find fault with,** pick apart, deconstruct, query, quibble with; deflate, puncture. **in the hole** *the diner was in the hole within six months after Abdul's sons took over* **in debt,** in arrears, in deficit, overdrawn, behind; informal in the red.

holiday ▶ **noun 1** *Presidents' Day is a federal holiday* **day of observance,** festival, feast day, féte, fiesta, celebration, anniversary, jubilee; saint's day, holy day.
2 chiefly Brit. *Sara and Lou's ten-day holiday* **vacation,** break, rest, respite, recess; time off, time out, leave, furlough, sabbatical; trip, tour, journey, voyage; informal getaway; formal sojourn.

holier-than-thou ▶ **adjective** *you will never sell your opinions to me with that holier-than-thou attitude* **sanctimonious,** self-righteous, smug, self-satisfied; priggish, pious, pietistic, Pharisaic.
ANTONYMS humble.

hollow ▶ **adjective 1** *each fiber has a hollow core* **empty,** void, unfilled, vacant.
ANTONYMS solid.

2 *hollow cheeks* **sunken,** gaunt, deep-set, concave, depressed, indented; rare incurvate.
3 *a hollow sound* **dull,** low, flat, toneless, expressionless; muffled, muted.
4 *a hollow victory* **meaningless,** empty, valueless, worthless, useless, pyrrhic, nugatory, futile, fruitless, profitless, pointless.
ANTONYMS worthwhile.
5 *a hollow promise* **insincere,** hypocritical, feigned, false, sham, deceitful, cynical, spurious, untrue, two-faced; informal phony, pretend.
ANTONYMS sincere.
▶ **noun 1** *a hollow under the tree* **hole,** pit, cavity, crater, trough, bowl, cave, cavern; depression, indentation, dip, dent; niche, nook, cranny, recess.
2 *the village lay in a hollow* **valley,** vale, dale, basin, glen; literary dell.
▶ **verb** *a tunnel hollowed out of a mountain* **gouge,** scoop, dig, shovel, cut; excavate, channel.

holocaust ▶ **noun** *fears of a nuclear holocaust* **cataclysm,** disaster, catastrophe; destruction, devastation, annihilation; massacre, slaughter, mass murder, extermination, extirpation, carnage, butchery; genocide, ethnic cleansing, pogrom.

holy ▶ **adjective 1** *holy men* **saintly,** godly, saintlike, pious, pietistic, religious, devout, God-fearing, spiritual; righteous, good, virtuous, angelic, sinless, pure, numinous, beatific; canonized, beatified, ordained. See note at DIVINE.
ANTONYMS sinful, irreligious.
2 *a Jewish holy place* **sacred,** consecrated, hallowed, sanctified, sacrosanct, venerated, revered, divine, religious, blessed, dedicated.
ANTONYMS cursed.

home ▶ **noun 1** *they fled their homes* **residence,** place of residence, house, apartment, flat, bungalow, cottage; accommodations, property, quarters, rooms, lodgings; a roof over one's head; address, place; informal pad, digs; hearth, nest; formal domicile, abode, dwelling, dwelling place, habitation.
2 *an Italian stonemason far from his home* See HOMELAND.
3 *a home for the elderly* **institution,** nursing home, retirement home, rest home; children's home; hospice, shelter, refuge, retreat, asylum, hostel, halfway house.
4 *the home of fine wines* **origin,** source, cradle, fount, fountainhead.
▶ **adjective 1** *the home market* **domestic,** internal, local, national, interior.
ANTONYMS foreign, international.
2 *home movies | the sale of home produce* **homemade,** homegrown, family.
– PHRASES **at home 1** *I was at home all day* **in,** in one's house, present, available, indoors, inside, here. **2** *she felt very much at home* **at ease,** comfortable, relaxed, content; in one's element, on one's own turf. **3** *he is at home with mathematics* **confident with,** conversant with, proficient in; used to, familiar with, au fait with, au courant with, skilled in, experienced in, well versed in. **bring home to someone** *Sylvia's overdose brought home to them the fragility of their own lives* **make someone realize,** make someone understand, make someone aware, make clear to someone; drive home to someone, impress upon someone, draw attention to, focus attention on, underline, highlight, spotlight, emphasize, stress; informal clue someone in to. **hit home** See HIT HOME at HIT. **home free** *when the inspector at the third checkpoint nodded at Mitchell, I knew we were home free | I passed the final flag with so much stamina that I knew I was home free* **safe,** secure, out of danger, off the hook; assured of success, the winner, victorious; informal golden. **home in on** *the reporters immediately wanted to home in on his broken engagement* **focus on,** concentrate on, zero in on, center on, fix on; highlight, spotlight, target, underline, pinpoint, track, zoom in on. **nothing to write home about** informal *the amusement park was enjoyable enough, but nothing to write home about* **unexceptional,** mediocre, ordinary, commonplace, indifferent, average, middle-of-the-road, run-of-the-mill, garden variety; boring, mundane, humdrum, ho-hum; tolerable, passable, adequate, fair; informal OK, so-so, 'comme ci, comme ça', plain-vanilla, no great shakes, not so hot.

homeland ▶ **noun** *she left her homeland to settle in Japan with her husband's family* **native land,** country of origin, home, birthplace, hometown; roots, fatherland, motherland, mother country, land of one's fathers; the old country.

homeless ▶ **adjective** *homeless people* **of no fixed address,** without a roof over one's head, on the streets, vagrant, displaced, dispossessed, destitute, down-and-out.
▶ **noun** *charities for the homeless* **people of no fixed address,** vagrants, down-and-outs, street people, tramps, vagabonds, itinerants, transients, migrants, derelicts, drifters, hoboes; informal bag ladies, bums.

homely ▶ **adjective** *she's rather homely* **unattractive,** plain, unprepossessing, unlovely, ill-favored, ugly; informal not much to look at.
ANTONYMS attractive.

homeowner ▶ **noun** *homeowners in the Scotch Hill section have drafted a petition against the proposed landfill on Fuller Drive* **owner,** householder, resident, occupant, proprietor.

homespun ▶ **adjective** *homespun rural philosophy* **unsophisticated,** plain, simple, basic, unpolished, unrefined, rustic, folksy; coarse, rough, crude, rudimentary, bush-league.
ANTONYMS sophisticated.

homicidal ▶ **adjective** *his homicidal tendencies went undetected for years* **murderous,** violent, brutal, savage, ferocious, vicious, bloody, bloodthirsty, barbarous, barbaric; deadly, lethal, mortal; literary fell; archaic sanguinary.

homicide ▶ **noun** *we're investigating a homicide that took place in this building* **murder,** killing, slaughter, butchery, massacre; assassination, execution, extermination; patricide, matricide, infanticide; literary slaying.

homily ▶ **noun** *a guest preacher delivered today's homily* **sermon,** lecture, discourse, address, lesson, talk, speech, oration.

homogeneous ▶ adjective *should the members of a society become so homogeneous that any trace of cultural diversity vanishes?* **uniform,** identical, unvaried, consistent, indistinguishable, homologous, homogenized; alike, similar, the same, much the same, all of a piece, melting-pot.
ANTONYMS different.

homogenize ▶ verb *my job is to homogenize all you precious little 'individuals' into one fighting machine* **make uniform,** make similar, standardize, unite, integrate, fuse, merge, blend, meld, coalesce, amalgamate, combine.
ANTONYMS diversify.

homosexual ▶ adjective *we decided to march with our homosexual friends* **gay,** lesbian, homoerotic, same-sex; informal queer, camp, pink, lavender, homo; literary Uranian. See note at **GAY**.
ANTONYMS heterosexual.
▶ noun *she has a serious crush on William, who, unfortunately for her, is a homosexual* **gay,** lesbian; informal queer, queen, dyke, butch, femme; literary Uranian.
ANTONYMS heterosexual.

honest ▶ adjective **1** *an honest man* **upright,** honorable, moral, ethical, principled, righteous, right-minded, respectable; virtuous, good, decent, fair, law-abiding, high-minded, upstanding, incorruptible, truthful, trustworthy, reliable, conscientious, scrupulous, reputable; informal on the level, trusty.
ANTONYMS unscrupulous, dishonest.
2 *I haven't been honest with you* **truthful,** sincere, candid, frank, open, forthright, ingenuous, straight; straightforward, plain-speaking, matter-of-fact; informal upfront, aboveboard, on the level.
ANTONYMS insincere.
3 *an honest mistake* **genuine,** true, bona fide, legitimate; informal legit, honest-to-goodness.

honestly ▶ adverb **1** *he earned the money honestly* **fairly,** lawfully, legally, legitimately, honorably, decently, ethically, in good faith, by the book; openly, on the level, aboveboard.
2 *we honestly believe this is for the best* **sincerely,** genuinely, truthfully, truly, wholeheartedly; really, frankly, actually, seriously, to be honest, to tell you the truth, to be frank, in all honesty, in all sincerity; informal Scout's honor.
▶ exclamation *Honestly! I don't know what to do with you!* **for heaven's sake,** for goodness' sake, for Pete's sake, really, sheesh, jeepers.

honesty ▶ noun **1** *I can attest to his honesty* **integrity,** uprightness, honorableness, honor, morality, morals, ethics, principles, high principles, righteousness, right-mindedness; virtue, goodness, probity, high-mindedness, fairness, incorruptibility, truthfulness, trustworthiness, reliability, dependability, rectitude.
2 *they spoke with honesty about their fears* **sincerity,** candor, frankness, directness, bluntness, truthfulness, truth, openness, straightforwardness.

honor ▶ noun **1** *a man of honor* **integrity,** honesty, uprightness, ethics, morals, morality, principles, high principles, righteousness, high-mindedness; virtue, goodness, decency, probity, character, good character, scrupulousness, worth, fairness, justness, trustworthiness, reliability, dependability.
ANTONYMS unscrupulousness, dishonor.
2 *a mark of honor* **distinction,** recognition, privilege, glory, kudos, cachet, prestige, merit, credit; importance, illustriousness, notability; respect, esteem, approbation.
ANTONYMS disgrace.
3 *our honor is at stake* **reputation,** name, good name, good credit, character, esteem, repute, image, standing, stature, status, popularity.
4 *he was welcomed with honor* **acclaim,** acclamation, applause, accolades, adoration, tributes, compliments, salutes, bouquets; homage, praise, veneration, glory, reverence, adulation, exaltation; dated laud.
ANTONYMS contempt.
5 *she had the honor of meeting the first lady* **privilege,** pleasure, pride, joy; compliment, favor, distinction.
ANTONYMS shame.
6 *military honors* **accolade,** award, reward, prize, decoration, distinction, medal, ribbon, star, laurel.
7 dated *she died defending her honor* **chastity,** virginity, maidenhead, purity, innocence, modesty; archaic virtue, maidenhood.
▶ verb **1** *we should honor our parents* **esteem,** respect, admire, defer to, look up to; appreciate, value, cherish, adore; reverence, revere, venerate, worship; informal put on a pedestal.
ANTONYMS disrespect.
2 *they were honored at a special ceremony* **applaud,** acclaim, praise, salute, recognize, celebrate, commemorate, commend, hail, lionize, exalt, eulogize, pay homage to, pay tribute to, sing the praises of; formal laud.
ANTONYMS disgrace, criticize.
3 *he honored the contract* **fulfill,** observe, keep, obey, heed, follow, carry out, discharge, implement, execute, effect; keep to, abide by, adhere to, comply with, conform to, be true to, live up to.
ANTONYMS disobey.

CHOOSE THE RIGHT WORD

honor, deference, homage, obeisance, reverence

The Ten Commandments instruct us to "**Honor** thy father and mother." But what does *honor* entail? While all of these nouns describe the respect or esteem that one shows to another, *honor* implies acknowledgment of a person's right to such respect (*honor one's ancestors; honor the dead*). **Homage** is honor with praise or tributes added, and it connotes a more worshipful attitude (*pay homage to the king*). **Reverence** combines profound respect with love or devotion (*he treated his wife with reverence*), while **deference** suggests courteous regard for a superior, often by yielding to the person's status or wishes (*show deference to one's elders*). **Obeisance** is a show of honor or reverence by an act or gesture of submission or humility, such as a bow or a curtsy (*the schoolchildren were instructed to pay obeisance when the Queen arrived*).

honorable ▶ adjective 1 *an honorable man* **honest,** moral, ethical, principled, righteous, right-minded; decent, respectable, estimable, virtuous, good, upstanding, upright, worthy, noble, fair, just, truthful, trustworthy, law-abiding, reliable, reputable, creditable, dependable. See note at **MORAL**.
ANTONYMS crooked.
2 *an honorable career* **illustrious,** distinguished, eminent, great, glorious, renowned, acclaimed, prestigious, noble, creditable, admirable.
ANTONYMS deplorable.

honorarium ▶ noun *each technical adviser receives an annual honorarium of $500* **fee,** payment, consideration, allowance, stipend; remuneration, pay, expenses, compensation, recompense, reward; formal emolument.

honorary ▶ adjective *she has received honorary diplomas from eleven colleges and universities worldwide* **titular,** symbolic, in name only, ceremonial, nominal, unofficial, token.

hood ▶ noun *they wore sunglasses and hoods to disguise themselves* **head covering,** cowl, snood, headscarf, amice.

hoodlum ▶ noun *he was roughed up by a bunch of hoodlums* **thug,** lout, delinquent, vandal, ruffian, hooligan, lowlife; gangster, crook, mobster, criminal; informal tough, bruiser, goon, hood, punk, rowdy.

hoodwink ▶ verb *Jimmy was hoodwinked by his own brother* **deceive,** trick, dupe, outwit, fool, delude, inveigle, cheat, take in, hoax, mislead, lead on, defraud, double-cross, swindle, gull, scam; informal con, bamboozle, hornswoggle, fleece, do, have, sting, gyp, shaft, rip off, lead up the garden path, pull a fast one on, put one over on, take for a ride, pull the wool over someone's eyes, sucker, snooker; literary cozen.

hook ▶ noun 1 *she hung her jacket on the hook* **peg,** coat rack.
2 *the dress has six hooks* **fastener,** fastening, catch, clasp, hasp, clip, pin.
3 *I had a fish on the end of my hook* **fishhook,** barb, gaff, snare, snag.
4 *a right hook to the chin* **punch,** blow, hit, cuff, thump, smack; informal belt, bop, sock, clout, whack, wallop, slug; informal boff.
▶ verb 1 *they hooked baskets onto the ladder* **attach,** hitch, fasten, fix, secure, clasp.
2 *he hooked his thumbs in his belt* **curl,** bend, crook, loop, curve.
3 *he hooked a 24-pound pike* **catch,** land, net, take; bag, snare, trap.
– PHRASES **by hook or by crook** *I'll get to Hollywood by hook or by crook* **by any means,** somehow (or other), no matter how, in one way or another, by fair means or foul. **hook, line, and sinker** *they believed her phony alibi hook, line, and sinker* **completely,** totally, utterly, entirely, wholly, absolutely, through and through, one hundred percent, 'lock, stock, and barrel'. **off the hook** informal *Mr. Lee paid the fine, so now Tammy is off the hook* **out of trouble,** in the clear, free, home free; acquitted, cleared, reprieved, exonerated, absolved; informal let off.

hooked ▶ adjective 1 *a hooked nose* **curved,** hook-shaped, hooklike, aquiline, angular, bent, crooked.
ANTONYMS straight.
2 informal *he is **hooked on** reality TV* **keen on,** enthusiastic about, addicted to, obsessed with, infatuated with, fixated on, fanatical about; informal mad about, crazy about, wild about, nuts about.
3 *she had the audience hooked* **captivated,** enthralled, entranced, bewitched, charmed.
ANTONYMS indifferent.

hooligan ▶ noun *I want you to stop hanging around with those hooligans* **troublemaker,** delinquent, juvenile delinquent, mischief-maker, vandal; rowdy, ruffian, yahoo.

hoop ▶ noun *a simple gold hoop* **ring,** band, circle, circlet, bracelet, (hoop) earring, loop; technical annulus.

hoot ▶ noun 1 *the hoot of an owl* **screech,** shriek, call, cry.
2 *hoots of derision* **shout,** yell, cry, snort, howl, shriek, whoop, whistle; boo, hiss, jeer, catcall.
3 informal *the party was a hoot* **good time,** scream, laugh, blast, riot, giggle, barrel of laughs; dated caution.
▶ verb 1 *an owl hooted* **screech,** shriek, cry, call.
2 *they hooted in disgust* **shout,** yell, cry, howl, shriek, whistle; boo, hiss, jeer, heckle, catcall.
– PHRASES **give a hoot** informal *obviously you don't give a hoot about clean air* **care,** be concerned, mind, be interested, be bothered, trouble oneself about; informal give a damn.

hop ▶ verb 1 *he hopped over the fence* **jump,** bound, spring, bounce, leap, vault.
2 informal *she hopped over the Atlantic* **go,** dash; travel, journey; jet, fly; informal pop, whip, nip.
▶ noun 1 *the rabbit had a hop around* **jump,** bound, bounce, leap, spring.
2 informal *a short hop by taxi* **journey,** distance, ride, drive, run, trip, jaunt; flight; informal hop, skip, and a jump.

hope ▶ noun 1 *I had high hopes* **aspiration,** desire, wish, expectation, ambition, aim, goal, plan, design; dream, daydream, pipe dream.
2 *a life filled with hope* **hopefulness,** optimism, expectation, expectancy; confidence, faith, trust, belief, conviction, assurance; promise, possibility.
ANTONYMS pessimism.
3 *have we any hope of winning?* **chance,** prospect, likelihood, probability, possibility; informal shot.
▶ verb 1 *he's **hoping for** a medal* **expect,** anticipate, look for, be hopeful of, pin one's hopes on, want; wish for, long for, dream of.
2 *we're hoping to address the issue* **aim,** intend, be looking, have the intention, have in mind, plan, aspire.

hopeful ▶ adjective 1 *he remained hopeful* **optimistic,** full of hope, confident, positive, buoyant, sanguine, expectant, bullish, cheerful, lighthearted; informal upbeat.

2 *hopeful signs* **promising,** encouraging, heartening, inspiring, reassuring, auspicious, favorable, optimistic, propitious, bright, rosy.
▶ **noun** *the Democratic hopeful for 2004* **candidate,** aspirant, prospect, possibility; nominee, competitor, contender; informal up-and-comer.

hopefully ▶ **adverb 1** *he rode on hopefully* **optimistically,** full of hope, confidently, buoyantly, sanguinely; expectantly.
2 *hopefully it will finish soon* **if all goes well,** God willing, with luck, with any luck; most likely, probably; conceivably, feasibly; informal knock on wood, fingers crossed.

USAGE

hopefully

Four points about this word: First, it was widely condemned from the 1960s to the 1980s. Briefly, the objections are that (1) *hopefully* properly means "in a hopeful manner" and shouldn't be used in the radically different sense "I hope" or "it is to be hoped"; (2) if the extended sense is accepted, the original sense will be forever lost; and (3) in constructions such as "Hopefully, it won't rain this afternoon," the writer illogically ascribes an emotion (*hopefulness*) to a nonperson. *Hopefully* isn't analogous to *curiously* (= it is a curious fact that), *fortunately* (= it is a fortunate thing that), and *sadly* (= it is a sad fact that). How so? Unlike all those other sentence adverbs, *hopefully* can't be resolved into any longer expression involving the word *hopeful*—but only *hope* (e.g., *it is to be hoped that* or *I hope that*).

Second, whatever the merits of those arguments, the battle is now over. *Hopefully* is now a part of American English, and it has all but lost its traditional meaning—e.g.: "Hopefully, one day we will all grow older." (*San Diego Union-Tribune*; Nov. 26, 1997.) Sometimes, the word is genuinely ambiguous (if the original meaning is considered still alive)—e.g.: "Dave Krieg will take the snaps and, hopefully, hand off to RB Garrison Hearst." (*USA Today*; Sept. 1, 1995.) (Is Krieg hoping for the best when Hearst runs? Or is the writer hoping that Krieg won't pass the football or hand off to another running back?) Indeed, the original meaning of *hopefully* is alive, even if moribund—e.g.: "Officials recently have pointed hopefully to signs of increased usage of the garage." (*Boston Globe*; Oct. 9, 1994.)

Third, some stalwarts continue to condemn the word, so that anyone using it in the new sense is likely to have a credibility problem with some readers—e.g.

- "Professor Michael Dummett, an Oxford logician, condemns the new usage of *hopefully* because only a person can be hopeful, and in many such cases there is nobody around in the sentence to be hopeful." (*Daily Telegraph* [UK]; Dec. 11, 1996.)
- "Although various adverbs may be used to modify entire clauses, *hopefully* isn't among them—yet. I only hope I won't have to concede that it is until I'm an old, old woman." (Barbara Wallraff, *Word Court*; 2000.)

Fourth, though the controversy swirling around this word has subsided, any use of it is likely to distract some readers. Avoid it in all senses if you're concerned with your credibility: if you use it in the traditional way, many readers will think it odd; if you use it in the newish way, a few readers will tacitly tut-tut you.

Throughout the late twentieth century, the common wisdom was that the use of *hopefully* as a sentence adverb had begun sometime around the early 1930s. Then, in 1999, a lexicographic scholar named Fred Shapiro, using computer-assisted research, traced it back to Cotton Mather's 1702 book, *Magnalia Christi Americana*, in this sentence: "Chronical diseases, which evidently threaten his Life, might hopefully be relieved by his removal." The evidence then skips to 1851, then to the 1930s. **— BG**

hopeless ▶ **adjective 1** *she felt weary and hopeless* **despairing,** desperate, wretched, forlorn, pessimistic, defeatist, resigned; dejected, downhearted, despondent, demoralized; archaic woebegone.
2 *a hopeless case* **irremediable,** beyond hope, lost, beyond repair, irreparable, irreversible; helpless, incurable; impossible, no-win, unwinnable, futile, unworkable, impracticable, useless; archaic bootless.
3 *Joseph was hopeless at tennis* **bad,** awful, terrible, dreadful, horrible, atrocious; inferior, incompetent, inadequate, unskilled; informal pathetic, useless, lousy, rotten.
4 *a hopeless romantic* **incurable,** incorrigible, chronic, compulsive; complete, utter, absolute, total, out-and-out; inveterate, confirmed, established, dyed-in-the-wool.

horde ▶ **noun** *a horde of fans stormed the playing field* **crowd,** mob, pack, gang, group, troop, army, legion, swarm, mass, herd, rabble; throng, multitude, host, band, flock, drove, press, crush; informal crew, tribe, pile.

horizon ▶ **noun 1** *the sun rose above the horizon* **skyline.**
2 *she wanted to broaden her horizons* **outlook,** perspective, perception; range of experience, range of interests, scope, prospect, ambit, compass, orbit.
– PHRASES **on the horizon** *a better life for us is on the horizon* **imminent,** impending, due, close, near, approaching, coming, forthcoming, at hand, on the way, about to happen, upon us, in the offing, in the pipeline, in the air, in the wings, in the cards, just around the corner, coming down the pike; brewing, looming, threatening, menacing.

horizontal ▶ **adjective 1** *a horizontal surface* level, flat, plane, smooth, even; straight, parallel.
ANTONYMS vertical.
2 *she was horizontal on the bed* **flat,** supine,

prone, prostrate, recumbent.
ANTONYMS upright.
3 *a horizontal move* **lateral,** sideways.

horrendous ▶ **adjective** See HORRIBLE.

horrible ▶ **adjective 1** *a horrible murder* **dreadful,** awful, terrible, shocking, appalling, horrifying, horrific, horrendous, horrid, hideous, grisly, ghastly, gruesome, gory, harrowing, heinous, vile, unspeakable; nightmarish, macabre, spine-chilling, blood-curdling; loathsome, monstrous, abhorrent, hateful, hellish, execrable, abominable, atrocious, sickening, foul.
ANTONYMS pleasant, agreeable.
2 informal *a horrible little man* **nasty,** horrid, disagreeable, unpleasant, detestable, awful, dreadful, terrible, appalling, horrendous, foul, repulsive, repugnant, repellent, ghastly; obnoxious, hateful, odious, hideous, objectionable, insufferable, vile, loathsome, abhorrent; informal frightful, godawful.
ANTONYMS pleasant, agreeable.

horrid ▶ **adjective** See HORRIBLE.

horrify ▶ **verb 1** *she horrified us with ghastly tales* **frighten,** scare, terrify, petrify, paralyze, alarm, panic, terrorize, fill with fear, scare someone out of their wits, frighten the living daylights out of, make someone's hair stand on end, make someone's blood run cold, give someone the creeps; informal scare the pants off, spook; archaic affright.
2 *he was horrified by her remarks* **shock,** appall, outrage, scandalize, offend; disgust, revolt, nauseate, sicken.

horror ▶ **noun 1** *children screamed in horror* **terror,** fear, fright, alarm, panic; dread, trepidation.
ANTONYMS delight.
2 *to her horror she found herself alone* **dismay,** consternation, perturbation, alarm, distress; disgust, outrage, shock.
ANTONYMS satisfaction.
3 *the horror of the tragedy* **awfulness,** frightfulness, savagery, barbarity, hideousness; atrocity, outrage.
4 informal *he's a little horror* **rascal,** devil, imp, monkey; informal terror, scamp, scalawag, tyke, varmint.
5 informal *her new dress is a horror* **eyesore,** monstrosity, abomination, blot, disgrace, mess, sight.
ANTONYMS beauty.

horse ▶ **noun** *Nadine boards and grooms horses* **equine,** mount, charger, cob, nag; pony; foal, yearling, colt, stallion, gelding, mare, filly; bronco; dated stepper; archaic steed.
– PHRASES **horse around** informal *they knew better than to horse around when their father came home* **fool around,** play, have fun, clown around, monkey around.

horseplay ▶ **noun** *the brothers' horseplay was not looked on too kindly by Aunt Smitty* **tomfoolery,** fooling around, roughhousing, clowning, buffoonery, fun; pranks, antics, hijinks; informal shenanigans, monkey business.

horse sense ▶ **noun** informal See COMMON SENSE.

horticulture ▶ **noun** *your gardener apparently knows very little about horticulture* **gardening,** landscaping, cultivation; floriculture, arboriculture, agriculture.

hosanna ▶ **noun** *the people's hosannas greeted him as he rode into the city* **shout of praise,** alleluia, hurrah, hurray, hooray, cheer, paean.

hose ▶ **noun 1** *a flexible green hose* See PIPE (sense 1 of the noun).
2 *some new black dress hose* See HOSIERY.

hosiery ▶ **noun** *rinsing out some hosiery* **stockings,** tights, nylons, hose, pantyhose, leotards; socks.

hospitable ▶ **adjective** *my hospitable in-laws* **welcoming,** friendly, congenial, genial, sociable, convivial, cordial, courteous; gracious, well-disposed, amenable, helpful, obliging, accommodating, neighborly, warm, kind, generous, bountiful.

hospital ▶ **noun** *the hospitals were overwhelmed with cases of influenza* **infirmary,** medical center, health center, clinic, sanatorium, hospice; Military field hospital; dated asylum.

hospitality ▶ **noun** *we found nothing but hospitality among the local inhabitants* **friendliness,** hospitableness, warm reception, welcome, helpfulness, neighborliness, warmth, kindness, congeniality, geniality, cordiality, courtesy, amenability, generosity, entertainment, catering, food.

host[1] ▶ **noun 1** *the host greeted the guests* **party-giver,** hostess, entertainer.
ANTONYMS guest.
2 *the host of a TV series* **presenter,** anchor, anchorman, anchorwoman, announcer, master of ceremonies, ringmaster; informal emcee.
▶ **verb 1** *Diane hosted a dinner party* **give,** have, hold, throw, put on, provide, arrange, organize.
2 *Jack hosted the show* **present,** introduce, front, anchor, announce; informal emcee.
3 *she hosted her colleagues from overseas* **entertain,** play host/hostess to; receive, welcome; take in, house, provide accommodations for, put up.

host[2] ▶ **noun 1** *a host of memories* **multitude,** lot, abundance, wealth, profusion; informal load, heap, mass, pile, ton, number; literary myriad.
2 *a host of movie stars* **crowd,** throng, group, flock, herd, swarm, horde, mob, army, legion, pack, tribe, troop; assemblage, congregation, gathering.

hostage ▶ **noun** *all of the hostages were released unharmed* **captive,** prisoner, inmate, detainee, internee; victim, abductee, prey; human shield, pawn, instrument.

hostile ▶ **adjective 1** *a hostile attack* **unfriendly,** unkind, bitter, unsympathetic, malicious, vicious, rancorous, venomous, poisonous, virulent; antagonistic, aggressive, confrontational, belligerent, truculent, vitriolic; bellicose, pugnacious, warlike.
ANTONYMS friendly, mild.
2 *hostile conditions* **unfavorable,** adverse, bad, harsh, grim, hard, tough, brutal, fierce, inhospitable, forbidding, menacing, threatening.
ANTONYMS favorable.
3 *they are hostile to the idea* **opposed to,** averse to, antagonistic to, ill-disposed to, disapproving

of, unsympathetic to, antipathetic to; opposing, against, inimical to; informal anti, down on.

> CHOOSE THE RIGHT WORD
>
> **hostile, adverse, bellicose, belligerent, inimical**
>
> Few people have trouble recognizing hostility when confronted with it. Someone who is **hostile** displays an attitude of intense ill will and acts like an enemy (*the audience grew hostile after waiting an hour for the show to start*). Both **bellicose** and **belligerent** imply a readiness or eagerness to fight, but the former is used to describe a state of mind or temper (*after drinking all night, he was in a bellicose mood*), while the latter is normally used to describe someone who is actively engaged in hostilities (*the belligerent brothers were at it again*). While *hostile* and *belligerent* usually apply to people, **adverse** and **inimical** are used describe tendencies or influences. *Inimical* means having an antagonistic tendency (*remarks that were inimical to everything she believed in*), and *adverse* means turned toward something in opposition (*an adverse wind; under adverse circumstances*). Unlike *hostile, adverse* and *inimical* need not connote the involvement of human feeling.

hostility ▶ **noun 1** *he glared at her with hostility* **antagonism,** unfriendliness, enmity, malevolence, malice, unkindness, rancor, venom, hatred, loathing; resentment, animosity, antipathy, acrimony, ill will, ill feeling; aggression, belligerence.
2 *their hostility to the present regime* **opposition,** antagonism, aversion, resistance, dissidence.
3 (**hostilities**) *a cessation of hostilities* **fighting,** conflict, armed conflict, combat, aggression, warfare, war, bloodshed, violence.

hot ▶ **adjective 1** *hot food* **heated,** piping hot, sizzling, steaming, roasting, boiling (hot), searing, scorching, scalding, burning, red-hot.
ANTONYMS cold, chilled.
2 *a hot day* **very warm,** balmy, summery, tropical, scorching, broiling, searing, blistering; sweltering, torrid, sultry, humid, muggy, close, boiling, baking, roasting.
ANTONYMS cold, chilly.
3 *she felt very hot* **feverish,** fevered, febrile; burning, flushed, sweaty; rare pyretic.
4 *a hot chili* **spicy,** spiced, highly seasoned, peppery, fiery, strong; piquant, pungent, aromatic, zesty.
ANTONYMS mild.
5 *hot competition* **fierce,** intense, keen, competitive, cutthroat, dog-eat-dog, ruthless, aggressive, strong.
ANTONYMS weak.
6 informal *hot gossip* **new,** fresh, recent, late, up to date, up-to-the-minute; just out, hot off the press(es), real-time.
ANTONYMS old, stale.
7 informal *this band is hot* **popular,** in demand, sought-after, in favor; fashionable, in vogue, all the rage; informal big, in, now, hip, trendy, cool.
ANTONYMS out of fashion, unpopular.
8 *she thought Mark was hot* **good-looking,** sexy, attractive, gorgeous, handsome, beautiful; archaic comely, fair.
ANTONYMS unappealing.
9 *hot goods* **stolen,** illegally obtained, purloined, pilfered, illegal, illicit, unlawful; smuggled, fenced, bootleg, contraband.
ANTONYMS lawful.
10 *her dancing made him hot* **aroused,** sexually aroused, excited, stimulated, titillated, inflamed; informal turned on, hot to trot.
ANTONYMS frigid.
– PHRASES **blow hot and cold** *when it comes to her romantic interest in him, she blows hot and cold* **vacillate,** dither, shilly-shally, waver, be indecisive, change one's mind, be undecided, be uncertain, be unsure, hem and haw. **hot and heavy** *isn't it a bit too soon for them to be so hot and heavy with each other?* intense, ardent, passionate, fervid. **have the hots for** *Liza admits that she has the hots for Ryan* be (sexually) attracted to, desire, lust after; informal have a crush on, have a thing for, be crazy about. **hot on the heels/trail of** *the marketing mavens are hot on the heels of this latest craze* **close behind,** directly after, right after, straight after, hard on the heels of, following closely. **hot under the collar** informal See ANGRY (sense 1).

hotbed ▶ **noun** *a hotbed of crime* **breeding ground,** den, nest, stronghold, flash point, cradle, seedbed.

hot-blooded ▶ **adjective** *he's not exactly the hot-blooded Latin lover I thought he'd be* **passionate,** amorous, amatory, ardent, fervid, lustful, libidinous, lecherous, sexy, virile; informal horny.
ANTONYMS cold.

hotel ▶ **noun** *we booked separate rooms at the hotel* **inn,** motel, boarding house, guest house, bed and breakfast, B&B, hostel, lodge, accommodations, lodging.

hotfoot ▶ **verb**
– PHRASES **hotfoot it** informal *we'd better hotfoot it to the airport* **hurry,** dash, run, rush, race, sprint, bolt, dart, career, careen, charge, shoot, hurtle, fly, speed, zoom, streak; informal tear, belt, scoot, clip, leg it, go like a bat out of hell, bomb, hightail it; archaic hie.

hotheaded ▶ **adjective** *Desi could camp it up as the hotheaded Cuban bandleader* **impetuous,** impulsive, headstrong, reckless, rash, irresponsible, foolhardy, madcap, devil-may-care; excitable, volatile, explosive, fiery, hot-tempered, quick-tempered, unruly.

hothouse ▶ **noun 1** *tomatoes grew in the hothouse* **greenhouse,** conservatory.
2 *society was becoming a hothouse of narcissism* **breeding ground,** hotbed, seedbed.
▶ **adjective** *the school has a hothouse atmosphere* **intense,** oppressive, stifling; overprotected, sheltered, insular, isolated, shielded; sensitive.

hound ▶ **noun** *take the hounds out for a run* **dog,** hunting dog, canine, mongrel, cur; informal doggy, pooch, mutt, pup.
▶ **verb 1** *she was hounded by the press* **pursue,** chase, follow, shadow, be hot on someone's heels, hunt (down), stalk, track, trail, tail, dog;

harass, hassle, persecute, harry, pester, bother, badger, torment, bedevil; informal bug, give someone a hard time, devil.
2 *they hounded him out of office* **force,** drive, pressure, pressurize, push, urge, coerce, impel, dragoon, strong-arm; nag, bully, browbeat; informal bulldoze, railroad, hustle.

house ▶ **noun 1** *a new development with 200 houses* **residence,** home, place of residence; homestead; a roof over one's head; formal habitation, dwelling (place), abode, domicile.
2 *you'll wake the whole house!* **household,** family, occupants; clan, tribe; informal brood.
3 *the house of Windsor* **family,** clan, tribe; dynasty, line, bloodline, lineage, ancestry, family tree.
4 *a printing house* **firm,** business, company, corporation, enterprise, establishment, institution, organization, operation; informal outfit, setup.
5 *the country's upper house* **legislative assembly,** legislative body, legislature, chamber, council, congress, senate, parliament, diet.
6 *the house applauded* **audience,** crowd, spectators, viewers, listeners; assembly, congregation.
7 *they filled the house* theater, auditorium, amphitheater, hall, gallery, stalls.
▶ **verb 1** *they can house twelve employees* **accommodate,** provide accommodations for, give someone a roof over their head, lodge, quarter, board, billet, take in, sleep, put up; harbor, shelter.
2 *this panel houses the main switch* **contain,** hold, store; cover, protect, enclose.
– PHRASES **on the house** informal *drinks are on the house* **free,** free of charge, without charge, at no cost, for nothing, gratis; complimentary; informal for free, comp.

household ▶ **noun** *the household was asleep* **family,** house, occupants, residents, ménage; clan, tribe; informal brood.
▶ **adjective** *household goods* **domestic,** family; everyday, ordinary, common, commonplace, regular, practical, workaday.

housing ▶ **noun 1** *they invested in housing* **houses,** homes, residences, apartment buildings, condominiums; accommodations, lodging, living quarters, shelter; formal dwellings, dwelling places, habitations.
2 *the housing for the antenna* **casing,** covering, case, cover, holder, sheath, jacket, shell, carapace, capsule.

hovel ▶ **noun** *living in the most dismal hovels* **shack,** slum, chantey, hut; informal dump, hole, dive, pigsty.

hover ▶ **verb 1** *helicopters hovered overhead* **be suspended,** be poised, hang, levitate, float; fly.
2 *she hovered anxiously nearby* **linger,** loiter, wait (around); informal hang around/about, stick around.

however ▶ **adverb 1** *however, gaining weight is not inevitable* **nevertheless,** nonetheless, but, still, yet, though, although, even so, for all that, despite that, in spite of that; anyway, anyhow, be that as it may, all the same, having said that, notwithstanding; informal still and all.
2 *however you look at it* **in whatever way,** regardless of how, no matter how.

howl ▶ **noun 1** *the howl of a wolf* **baying,** howling, bay, cry, yowl, bark, yelp.
2 *a howl of anguish* **wail,** cry, yell, yelp, yowl; bellow, roar, shout, shriek, scream, screech.
▶ **verb 1** *dogs howled in the distance* **bay,** cry, yowl, bark, yelp.
2 *a baby started to howl* **wail,** cry, yell, yowl, bawl, bellow, shriek, scream, screech, caterwaul; informal holler.
3 *the movie was so funny, we just howled* **laugh,** guffaw, roar; be doubled up, split one's sides; informal crack up, be in stitches, be rolling in the aisles, be on the floor.

hub ▶ **noun 1** *the hub of the wheel* **pivot,** axis, fulcrum, center, middle.
2 *the hub of family life* **center,** core, heart, middle, focus, focal point, central point, nucleus, kernel, nerve center, polestar.
ANTONYMS periphery.

huddle ▶ **verb 1** *they huddled together* **crowd,** cluster, gather, bunch, throng, flock, herd, collect, group, congregate, mass; press, pack, squeeze.
ANTONYMS disperse.
2 *he huddled beneath the sheets* **curl up,** snuggle, nestle, hunch up.
▶ **noun 1** *a huddle of passengers* **crowd,** cluster, bunch, knot, group, throng, flock, press, pack; collection, assemblage; informal gaggle.
2 *the team went into a huddle* **consultation,** discussion, debate, talk, parley, meeting, conference; informal confab, powwow.

hue ▶ **noun** *a lovely hue of lilac* **color,** shade, tone, tint, tinge.

huff ▶ **noun** *he ran out in a huff* **bad mood,** fit of pique, temper, tantrum, rage; informal snit, state, grump, hissy fit.

hug ▶ **verb 1** *they hugged each other* **embrace,** cuddle, squeeze, clasp, clutch, cradle, cling to, hold close, hold tight, take/fold someone in one's arms, clasp someone to one's bosom.
2 *our route hugged the coastline* **follow closely,** keep close to, stay near to, follow the course of.
3 *we hugged the comforting thought* **cling to,** hold on to, cherish, hold dear; harbor, nurse, foster, retain, keep in mind.
▶ **noun** *there were hugs as we left* **embrace,** cuddle, squeeze, bear hug, clasp, hold, clinch.

huge ▶ **adjective** *a huge battleship* **enormous,** vast, immense, large, big, great, massive, colossal, prodigious, gigantic, gargantuan, mammoth, monumental; giant, towering, elephantine, mountainous, monstrous, titanic; epic, Herculean, Brobdingnagian; informal jumbo, mega, monster, king-size(d), economy-size(d), oversize(d), super-size(d), whopping, humongous, honking, hulking, astronomical, cosmic, ginormous.
ANTONYMS tiny.

hulk ▶ **noun 1** *the rusting hulks of ships* **wreck,** shipwreck, wreckage, ruin, derelict; shell, skeleton, hull.
2 *a great hulk of a man* **giant,** lump, blob, clod; oaf; informal clodhopper, ape, gorilla, lummox, lubber.

hulking ▶ adjective informal *a hulking black dog lumbered down the stairs* **large,** big, heavy, sturdy, burly, brawny, hefty, strapping; bulky, weighty, massive, ponderous; clumsy, awkward, ungainly, lumbering, lumpish, oafish; informal beefy, clunky, clodhopping.
ANTONYMS small.

hull ▶ noun 1 *the ship's hull* **framework,** body, shell, frame, skeleton, structure; fuselage.
2 *seed hulls* **shell,** husk, pod, case, covering, integument, calyx, shuck; Botany pericarp, legume.

hullabaloo ▶ noun informal *the hullabaloo outside the police station attracted reporters by the dozen* **fuss,** commotion, hue and cry, uproar, outcry, clamor, storm, furor, hubbub, ruckus, brouhaha; pandemonium, mayhem, tumult, turmoil, hurly-burly, rumpus, palaver; informal hoo-ha, to-do, song and dance, stink.

hum ▶ verb 1 *the engine was humming* **purr,** drone, murmur, buzz, thrum, whine, whir, throb, vibrate, rumble.
2 *she hummed a tune* sing, croon, murmur, drone.
3 *the workshops are humming* **be busy,** be active, be lively, buzz, bustle, be a hive of activity, throb, pulsate; informal be happening.
▶ noun *a low hum of conversation* **murmur,** drone, purr, buzz, mumble.

human ▶ adjective 1 *they're only human* **mortal,** flesh and blood; fallible, weak, frail, imperfect, vulnerable, susceptible, erring, error-prone; physical, bodily, fleshly.
2 *the human side of politics* **compassionate,** humane, kind, considerate, understanding, sympathetic, tolerant; approachable, accessible.
3 *in human form* **anthropomorphic,** anthropoid, humanoid, hominid.
▶ noun *the link between humans and animals* **person,** human being, personage, mortal, member of the human race; man, woman; individual, soul, living soul, being; Homo sapiens; earthling.

humane ▶ adjective *the humane treatment of animals* **compassionate,** kind, considerate, understanding, sympathetic, tolerant; lenient, forbearing, forgiving, merciful, mild, gentle, tender, clement, benign, humanitarian, benevolent, charitable; warmhearted, tenderhearted, softhearted.
ANTONYMS cruel.

humanitarian ▶ adjective 1 *a humanitarian act* **compassionate,** humane; unselfish, altruistic, generous, magnanimous, benevolent, merciful, kind, sympathetic.
ANTONYMS selfish.
2 *a humanitarian organization* **charitable,** philanthropic, public-spirited, socially concerned, welfare; rare eleemosynary.
▶ noun *Mrs. Roosevelt would be most gratified to be remembered as a humanitarian* **philanthropist,** altruist, benefactor, patron, social reformer, good Samaritan; do-gooder; archaic philanthrope.

humanities ▶ plural noun *if higher education becomes any more driven by corporate objectives, the humanities will be grappling for survival* **arts,** liberal arts, literature, philosophy; classics, classical studies, classical literature.

humanity ▶ noun 1 *humanity evolved from the apes* **humankind,** mankind, man, people, human beings, humans, the human race, mortals; Homo sapiens.
2 *the humanity of Christ* **human nature,** humanness, mortality.
3 *he praised them for their humanity* **compassion,** brotherly love, fraternity, fellow feeling, philanthropy, humaneness, kindness, consideration, understanding, sympathy, tolerance; leniency, mercy, mercifulness, clemency, pity, tenderness; benevolence, charity, goodness, magnanimity, generosity.

humble ▶ adjective 1 *her bearing was humble* **meek,** deferential, respectful, submissive, diffident, self-effacing, unassertive; unpresuming, modest, unassuming, self-deprecating; subdued, chastened.
ANTONYMS proud, overbearing.
2 *a humble background* **lowly,** working-class, lower-class, poor, undistinguished, mean, modest, ignoble, low-born, plebeian, underprivileged; common, ordinary, simple, inferior, unremarkable, insignificant, inconsequential.
ANTONYMS noble.
3 *my humble abode* **modest,** plain, simple, ordinary, unostentatious, unpretentious.
ANTONYMS grand.
▶ verb *he had to humble himself to ask for my help* **humiliate,** abase, demean, lower, degrade, debase; mortify, shame, abash; informal cut down to size, deflate, make eat humble pie, take down a peg or two, settle someone's hash, make eat crow.

CHOOSE THE RIGHT WORD

humble, abase, debase, degrade, demean, humiliate

While all of these verbs mean to lower in one's own estimation or in the eyes of others, there are subtle distinctions among them. **Humble** and **humiliate** sound similar, but *humiliate* emphasizes shame and the loss of self-respect and usually takes place in public (*humiliated by her tearful outburst*), while *humble* is a milder term implying a lowering of one's pride or rank (*to humble the arrogant professor by pointing out his mistake*). **Abase** suggests groveling or a sense of inferiority and is usually used reflexively (*got down on his knees and abased himself before the king*), while **demean** is more likely to imply a loss of dignity or social standing (*refused to demean herself by marrying a common laborer*). When used to describe things, **debase** means a deterioration in the quality or value of something (*a currency debased by the country's political turmoil*), but in reference to people it connotes a weakening of moral standards or character (*debased himself by accepting bribes*). **Degrade** is even stronger, suggesting the destruction of a person's character through degenerate or shameful behavior (*degraded by long association with criminals*).

humdrum ▶ adjective *they were quite wrong in assuming that the lighthouse keeper led a lonely and humdrum life* **mundane,** dull, dreary, boring, tedious, monotonous, prosaic; unexciting, uninteresting, uneventful, unvaried, repetitive, unremarkable; routine, ordinary, everyday, day-to-day, workaday, quotidian, run-of-the-mill, commonplace, garden variety, pedestrian; informal plain-vanilla, ho-hum.
ANTONYMS remarkable, exciting.

humidity ▶ noun *a climate of warm temperatures and high humidity* **mugginess,** humidness, closeness, sultriness, stickiness, steaminess, airlessness, stuffiness, clamminess; dampness, damp, dankness, moisture, moistness, wetness, dewiness.
ANTONYMS freshness, aridity.

humiliate ▶ verb *he was humiliated in front of the whole school* **embarrass,** mortify, humble, shame, put to shame, disgrace, chagrin; discomfit, chasten, abash, deflate, crush, squash; abase, debase, demean, degrade, lower; belittle, cause to feel small, cause to lose face; informal show up, put down, cut down to size, take down (a peg or two), put someone in their place, make someone eat crow. See note at HUMBLE.

humiliation ▶ noun *the humiliation of having been left at the altar* **embarrassment,** mortification, shame, indignity, ignominy, disgrace, discomfiture, dishonor, degradation, discredit, belittlement, opprobrium; loss of face; informal blow to one's pride/ego, slap in the face, kick in the teeth, comedown.
ANTONYMS honor.

humility ▶ noun *he accepted the award with sincere humility* **modesty,** humbleness, meekness, diffidence, unassertiveness; lack of pride, lack of vanity; servility, submissiveness.
ANTONYMS pride.

humor ▶ noun 1 *the humor of the film* **comedy,** comical aspect, funny side, fun, amusement, funniness, hilarity, jocularity; absurdity, ludicrousness, drollness; satire, irony, farce.
2 *the stories are spiced up with humor* **jokes,** joking, jests, jesting, quips, witticisms, bon mots, funny remarks, puns, sallies, badinage; wit, wittiness, funniness, comedy, drollery; informal gags, wisecracks, cracks, kidding, waggishness, one-liners. See note at WIT.
3 *his good humor was infectious* **mood,** temper, disposition, temperament, nature, state of mind, frame of mind; spirits.
▶ verb *she was always humoring him* **indulge,** accommodate, pander to, cater to, yield to, give way to, give in to, go along with; pamper, spoil, baby, overindulge, mollify, placate, gratify, satisfy.

humorist ▶ noun *the sports editor was looking for a humorist to write a brief daily column during the course of the Olympic Games* **comic writer,** wit, wag; comic, funny man/woman, comedian, comedienne, stand-up comic, joker, jester, clown, wisecracker; informal cutup.

humorous ▶ adjective *a humorous account of our expedition* **amusing,** funny, comic, comical, entertaining, diverting, witty, jocular, jocose, lighthearted, tongue-in-cheek, wry, facetious, laughable, risible; hilarious, uproarious, riotous, zany, farcical, droll; informal priceless, side-splitting, gut-busting, rib-tickling, knee-slapping, thigh-slapping.
ANTONYMS serious.

hump ▶ noun *the hump made her look old and slouchy* **protuberance,** prominence, lump, bump, knob, protrusion, projection, bulge, swelling, hunch; growth, outgrowth.

hunch ▶ verb 1 *he hunched his shoulders* **arch,** curve, hump, bend, bow.
ANTONYMS straighten.
2 *I **hunched up** as small as I could* **crouch,** huddle, curl; hunker down, bend, stoop, slouch, squat, duck.
ANTONYMS stretch (out).
▶ noun 1 *the hunch on his back* **protuberance,** hump, lump, bump, knob, protrusion, prominence, bulge, swelling; growth, outgrowth.
2 *my hunch is that he'll be back* **feeling,** feeling in one's bones, guess, suspicion, impression, conjecture, inkling, idea, sense, notion, fancy, intuition, premonition, presentiment; informal gut feeling, gut instinct.

hunger ▶ noun 1 *she was faint with hunger* **lack of food,** hungriness, ravenousness, emptiness; starvation, malnutrition, famine, malnourishment, undernourishment.
2 *a hunger for news* **desire,** craving, longing, yearning, hankering, appetite, thirst; want, need; informal itch, yen.
– PHRASES **hunger after/for** *all actors hunger after such a role* **desire,** crave, covet; long for, yearn for, pine for, ache for, hanker after, thirst for, lust for; want, need; informal have a yen for, itch for, be dying for.

hungry ▶ adjective 1 *I was really hungry* **ravenous,** empty, in need of food, hollow, faint from/with hunger; starving, starved, famished; malnourished, undernourished, underfed; informal peckish, able to eat a horse; archaic esurient.
ANTONYMS full.
2 *they are hungry for success* **eager,** keen, avid, longing, yearning, aching, pining, greedy, covetous; craving, hankering; informal itching, dying, hot.
ANTONYMS indifferent.

hunk ▶ noun 1 *a hunk of bread* **chunk,** piece, wedge, block, slab, lump, square; gobbet.
2 informal *he's such a hunk* **good-looking man,** heartthrob, macho man; informal babe, stud, studmuffin, dreamboat, (male) specimen, looker, beefcake, chick magnet, babe magnet, he-man, hottie.

hunt ▶ verb 1 *they hunted deer* **chase,** stalk, pursue, course, run down; track, trail, follow, hound, shadow; informal tail.
2 *police are **hunting for** her* **search for,** look for, look high and low for, scour the area for, sweep the area for, comb the area for; seek, try to find; scout around, rummage around/about, root around/about, fish around/about.
▶ noun 1 *the thrill of the hunt* **chase,** pursuit.
2 *police have stepped up their hunt* **search,** look, quest, manhunt.

hurdle ▸ noun **1** *his leg hit a hurdle* **fence,** jump, barrier, barricade, bar, railing, rail.
2 *the final hurdle to overcome* **obstacle,** difficulty, problem, barrier, bar, snag, stumbling block, impediment, obstruction, complication, hindrance, hitch; informal headache, hiccup, glitch, fly in the ointment, wrench in the works.

hurl ▸ verb **1** *he hurled an eraser at her head* **throw,** toss, fling, pitch, cast, lob, bowl, launch, catapult; project, propel, let fly, fire; informal chuck, heave, sling, peg; dated shy.
2 informal *she felt like she was going to hurl* See VOMIT.

hurricane ▸ noun See STORM (sense 1 of the noun).

hurried ▸ adjective **1** *a hurried greeting* **quick,** fast, swift, rapid, speedy, brisk, hasty, abrupt; cursory, perfunctory, brief, short, fleeting, flying, passing, superficial, slapdash.
ANTONYMS slow, leisurely.
2 *a hurried decision* **hasty,** rushed, speedy, quick, expeditious; impetuous, impulsive, precipitate, precipitous, rash, incautious, imprudent, spur-of-the-moment.
ANTONYMS considered.

hurry ▸ verb **1** *hurry or you'll be late* **be quick,** hurry up, hurry it up, hasten, speed up, speed it up, press on, push on; run, dash, rush, race, fly; scurry, scramble, scuttle, sprint; informal get a move on, move it, step on it, get cracking, get moving, shake a leg, hightail it, tear, zip, zoom, hotfoot it, leg it, get the lead out; dated make haste; archaic hie.
ANTONYMS dawdle, move slowly.
2 *she hurried him out* **hustle,** hasten, push, urge, drive, spur, goad, prod.
▸ noun *in all the hurry, we forgot* **rush,** haste, flurry, hustle and bustle, confusion, commotion, hubbub, turmoil; race, scramble, scurry.

hurt ▸ verb **1** *my back hurts* **be painful,** be sore, be tender, cause pain, cause discomfort; ache, smart, sting, burn, throb; informal be killing (one).
2 *Dad hurt his leg* **injure,** wound, damage, abuse, disable, incapacitate, maim, mutilate, wrench; bruise, cut, gash, graze, scrape, scratch, lacerate.
ANTONYMS heal.
3 *his words hurt her* **distress,** pain, wound, sting, upset, sadden, devastate, grieve, mortify; cut to the quick.
ANTONYMS please, comfort.
4 *high interest rates are hurting the economy* **harm,** damage, be detrimental to, weaken, blight, impede, jeopardize, undermine, ruin, wreck, sabotage, cripple.
ANTONYMS improve, benefit.
▸ noun *she apologized for the hurt she had caused* **distress,** pain, suffering, injury, grief, misery, anguish, agony, trauma, woe, upset, sadness, sorrow; harm, damage, trouble.
ANTONYMS joy.
▸ adjective **1** *my hurt hand* **injured,** wounded, bruised, grazed, cut, gashed, battered, sore, painful, aching, smarting, throbbing.
ANTONYMS healed.
2 *Anne's hurt expression* **pained,** injured, distressed, anguished, upset, sad, mortified, offended; informal miffed, peeved, sore.
ANTONYMS pleased.

hurtful ▸ adjective *the effects of hurtful remarks may last a lifetime* **upsetting,** distressing, wounding, painful, injurious; unkind, cruel, nasty, mean, malicious, spiteful, vindictive; cutting, barbed, poisonous; informal catty, bitchy.

husband ▸ noun *Chris's husband is a South American businessman* **spouse,** partner, life partner, mate, consort, man, helpmate, helpmeet; groom, bridegroom; informal hubby, old man, better half, other half, significant other.

husbandry ▸ noun **1** *farmers have new methods of husbandry* **farm management,** land management, farming, agriculture, agronomy; cultivation; animal husbandry, ranching.
2 *the careful husbandry of their resources* **conservation,** management; economy, thrift, thriftiness, frugality.

hush ▸ verb *will somebody please hush those kids in the back row?* **silence,** quiet, quiet down, shush; soothe, calm, pacify; gag, muzzle, muffle, mute; informal shut up.
▸ exclamation *someone's coming, everybody hush!* **be quiet,** keep quiet, quiet, quiet down, be silent, stop talking, hold your tongue; informal shut up, shh, hush up, shut your mouth, shut your face, shut your trap, button your lip, pipe down, put a sock in it, give it a rest, save it, not another word.
▸ noun *a hush descended* **silence,** quiet, quietness; stillness, peace, peacefulness, calm, lull, tranquility.
ANTONYMS noise.
– PHRASES **hush up** *management took steps to hush up the dangers* **keep secret,** conceal, hide, suppress, cover up, keep quiet about; obscure, veil, sweep under the carpet; informal sit on, keep under one's hat.

hush-hush ▸ adjective informal See SECRET (sense 1 of the adjective).

husk ▸ noun *the husk of the coconut* **shell,** hull, pod, case, covering, integument, shuck; Botany pericarp, legume.

husky ▸ adjective **1** *a husky voice* **throaty,** gruff, gravelly, hoarse, croaky, rough, guttural, harsh, rasping, raspy; deep.
ANTONYMS shrill, soft.
2 *Paddy was a husky guy* **strong,** muscular, muscly, muscle-bound, big, brawny, hefty, burly, hulking, strapping, thickset, solid, powerful, heavy, robust, sturdy, stalwart, blocky, Herculean, well-built; informal beefy, hunky; literary thewy.
ANTONYMS puny.

hussy ▸ noun *in this farcical version, Juliet is portrayed as a shameless hussy* **minx,** coquette, tease, seductress, Lolita, Jezebel; slut, harlot, loose woman; informal floozy, tart, vamp, tramp; dated trollop; archaic jade, strumpet.

hustle ▸ verb **1** *I was hustled away* **manhandle,** push, shove, thrust, frogmarch, whisk, bundle.
2 *we'll have to hustle to catch the bus* rush, hurry, be quick, hasten; speed up, press on; informal get a move on, step on it, get moving, get

cracking, shake a leg.
3 *if you want it, you'll have to hustle for it* **work,** work hard, strive, endeavor, apply oneself, exert oneself; informal pull out all the stops.
4 informal *don't be hustled into joining some cause you don't believe in* **coerce,** force, compel, pressure, pressurize, badger, pester, hound, harass, nag, harry, urge, goad, prod, spur; browbeat, bulldoze, bludgeon, steamroller, strong-arm; informal railroad, fast-talk.
– PHRASES **hustle and bustle** *I need the hustle and bustle of the city* **activity,** bustle, tumult, hubbub, action, liveliness, animation, excitement, agitation, commotion, flurry, whirl; informal ballyhoo, hoo-ha, hullabaloo.

hut ▶ noun *we spent two nights in a rustic little hut near the village* **shack,** chantey, cabin, log cabin, shelter, shed, lean-to, hovel; hovel; cabana.

hybrid ▶ noun *a hybrid between a brown and an albino mouse* **cross,** cross-breed, mixed breed, half-breed, half-blood; mixture, blend, amalgamation, combination, composite, compound, fusion.
▶ adjective *a hybrid organization* **composite,** cross-bred, interbred, mongrel; heterogeneous, mixed, blended, compound, amalgamated, hyphenated.

hygiene ▶ noun *they teach preschoolers the fundamentals of personal hygiene* **cleanliness,** sanitation, sterility, purity, disinfection; public health, environmental health.

hygienic ▶ adjective *keeping the kitchen hygienic* **sanitary,** clean, germ-free, disinfected, sterilized, sterile, antiseptic, aseptic, unpolluted, uncontaminated, salubrious, healthy, wholesome, purified; informal squeaky clean. See note at **SANITARY**.
ANTONYMS unsanitary.

hymn ▶ noun *singing the old familiar hymns* **religious song,** song of praise, anthem, canticle, chorale, psalm, paean, carol; spiritual.

hype informal ▶ noun *her work relies on hype and headlines* **publicity,** advertising, promotion, marketing, exposure; informal ballyhoo, promo.
▶ verb *a stunt to hype a new product* **publicize,** advertise, promote, push, boost, merchandise, build up; informal plug.

hyperbole ▶ noun *the media hyperbole that accompanied their championship series* **exaggeration,** overstatement, magnification, embroidery, embellishment, excess, overkill, rhetoric; informal purple prose, puffery.
ANTONYMS understatement.

hypnotic ▶ adjective *hypnotic music* **mesmerizing,** mesmeric, spellbinding, entrancing, bewitching, irresistible, magnetic, compelling, enthralling, captivating, charming; soporific, sleep-inducing, sedative, numbing; Medicine stupefacient.

hypnotize ▶ verb **1** *he had been hypnotized as a stunt* **mesmerize,** put into a trance.
2 *they were hypnotized by the dancers* **entrance,** mesmerize, spellbind, enthrall, transfix, captivate, bewitch, charm, enrapture, grip, rivet, absorb, fascinate, magnetize.

hypocrisy ▶ noun *must politics be the perennial benchmark of hypocrisy?* **dissimulation,** false virtue, cant, posturing, affectation, speciousness, empty talk, insincerity, falseness, deceit, dishonesty, mendacity, pretense, duplicity; sanctimoniousness, sanctimony, pietism, piousness; informal phoniness, fraud.
ANTONYMS sincerity.

hypocrite ▶ noun *I've been made to feel inadequate my whole life by someone who turns out to be a total hypocrite* **pretender,** dissembler, deceiver, liar, pietist, sanctimonious person, plaster saint; informal phony, fraud, sham, fake.

hypothesis ▶ noun *his 'steady state' hypothesis of the origin of the universe* **theory,** theorem, thesis, conjecture, supposition, postulation, postulate, proposition, premise, assumption; notion, concept, idea, possibility.

hypothetical ▶ adjective *the scenario I suggested was strictly hypothetical* **theoretical,** speculative, conjectured, conjectural, notional, suppositional, supposed, putative, assumed; academic.
ANTONYMS actual.

hysteria ▶ noun *his fictional account of an alien invasion caused not-so-fictional hysteria among the radio audience* **frenzy,** feverishness, hysterics, fit of madness, derangement, mania, delirium; panic, alarm, distress.
ANTONYMS calm.

hysterical ▶ adjective **1** *Janet became hysterical* **overwrought,** overemotional, out of control, frenzied, frantic, wild, feverish, crazed; beside oneself, driven to distraction, distraught, agitated, berserk, manic, delirious, unhinged, deranged, out of one's mind, raving; informal in a state.
2 informal *her attempts to dance were hysterical* **hilarious,** uproarious, very funny, very amusing, comical, farcical; informal hysterically funny, priceless, side-splitting, rib-tickling, gut-busting, knee-slapping, thigh-slapping, a scream, a hoot, a barrel of laughs; dated killing.

Ii

ice ▶ noun **1** *a roof covered with ice* **frozen water,** icicles; black ice, frost, rime, glaze.
2 *the ice in her voice* **coldness,** coolness, frost, frostiness, iciness; hostility, unfriendliness; stiffness, aloofness.
ANTONYMS warmth, friendliness.
▶ verb **1** *the lake has iced over* **freeze, freeze over,** turn into ice, harden, solidify; archaic glaciate.
ANTONYMS thaw.
2 *she had iced the cake* **frost,** cover with icing, glaze.
– PHRASES **on ice** informal See PENDING (sense 1 of the adjective). **on thin ice** *I may be on thin ice with my theory* **in a risky situation,** at risk, in peril, imperiled, living dangerously, living on the edge.

icing ▶ noun *a cake with pink icing* **glaze,** frosting, topping, fondant, piping.

icon ▶ noun **1** *an icon of the Blessed Virgin* **image,** idol, portrait, picture, representation, likeness, symbol, sign; figure, statue.
2 *he became a teen icon* **idol,** paragon, hero, heroine; celebrity, superstar, star; favorite, darling.

icy ▶ adjective **1** *icy roads* **frozen,** frozen over, iced over, frosty, frosted, ice-bound, ice-covered, iced up; slippery; literary rimy.
2 *an icy wind* **freezing,** cold, chill, chilly, chilling, nippy, frigid, frosty, biting, cutting, bitter, raw, arctic, wintry, glacial, Siberian, hypothermic, polar, gelid.
ANTONYMS hot, warm.
3 *an icy voice* **unfriendly,** hostile, forbidding, unwelcoming, inhospitable; cold, cool, chilly, frigid, frosty, glacial, gelid; haughty, stern, hard.
ANTONYMS friendly.

idea ▶ noun **1** *the idea of death scares her* **concept,** notion, conception, thought; image, visualization; hypothesis, postulation.
2 *our idea is to open a new shop* **plan,** scheme, design, proposal, proposition, suggestion, brainchild, vision; aim, intention, purpose, objective, object, goal, target.
3 *Liz had other ideas on the subject* **thought,** theory, view, opinion, feeling, belief, attitude, conclusion; informal take.
4 *I had an idea that it might happen* **sense,** feeling, suspicion, inkling, hunch, clue, theory, notion, impression; dated fancy.
5 *I get the idea* **meaning,** significance, sense, import, essence, gist, drift; point, aim, intention, purport, implication; design, motive.
6 *an idea of the cost* **estimate,** estimation, approximation, guess, conjecture, rough calculation; informal guesstimate.

CHOOSE THE RIGHT WORD

idea, concept, conception, impression, notion, thought

If you have an **idea** it might refer to something perceived through the senses (*I had no idea it was so cold out*), to something visualized (*the idea of a joyous family outing*), or to something that is the product of the imagination (*a great idea for raising money*). *Idea* is a comprehensive word that applies to almost any aspect of mental activity. A **thought**, on the other hand, is an idea that is the result of meditation, reasoning, or some other intellectual activity (*she hadn't given much thought to the possibility of losing*). A **notion** is a vague or capricious idea, often without any sound basis (*he had a notion that he could get there by hitchhiking*). A widely held idea of what something is or should be is a **concept** (*the concept of loyalty was beyond him*), while a **conception** is a concept that is held by an individual or small group and that is often colored by imagination and feeling (*her conception of marriage as a romantic ideal*). An idea that is triggered by something external is an **impression**, a word that suggests a half-formed mental picture or superficial view (*he made a good impression; she had the impression that everything would be taken care of*).

ideal ▶ adjective **1** *ideal flying weather* **perfect,** best possible, consummate, supreme, excellent, flawless, faultless, exemplary, classic, model, ultimate, quintessential.
ANTONYMS bad.
2 *an ideal concept* **abstract,** theoretical, conceptual, notional; hypothetical, speculative, conjectural, suppositional.
ANTONYMS concrete.
3 *an ideal world* **unattainable,** unachievable, impracticable, chimerical; unreal, fictitious, hypothetical, theoretical, ivory-towered, imaginary, illusory, idealized, idyllic, visionary, Utopian, fairy-tale.
ANTONYMS attainable, real.
▶ noun **1** *no woman could be the ideal he imagined for himself* **perfection,** paragon, epitome, shining example, ne plus ultra, nonpareil, dream.
2 *an ideal to aim at* **model,** pattern, exemplar,

standard, example, paradigm, archetype, prototype; yardstick, lodestar. See note at MODEL.
3 *a liberal ideal* **principle,** standard, value, belief, conviction, persuasion; (**ideals**) morals, morality, ethics, ideology, creed.

idealist ▶ noun *the title character is a liberal idealist set up to lose a senatorial election* **Utopian,** visionary, wishful thinker, pipe-dreamer, fantasist, romantic, dreamer, daydreamer, stargazer; Walter Mitty, Don Quixote; rare fantast.

idealistic ▶ adjective *some say I'm drawing a wildly idealistic portrait of what the Church can become* **Utopian,** visionary, romantic, quixotic, dreamy, unrealistic, impractical, starry-eyed; fanciful; informal with one's head in the clouds; chiefly Brit. informal airy-fairy.

ideally ▶ adverb *ideally, it would be a good thing to provide rehabilitation* **in a perfect world**; preferably, if possible, by choice, by preference, as a matter of choice, rather; all things being equal, theoretically, hypothetically, in theory, in principle, on paper.

identical ▶ adjective **1** *wearing identical badges* **indistinguishable,** (exactly) the same, uniform, twin, duplicate, interchangeable, synonymous, undifferentiated, homogeneous, of a piece, cut from the same cloth; alike, like, matching, like (two) peas in a pod; similar.
ANTONYMS different, unlike.
2 *I used the identical technique* **same,** very same, selfsame, very, one and the same; aforementioned, aforesaid, aforenamed, above, above-stated; foregoing, preceding.
ANTONYMS different.

identification ▶ noun **1** *the identification of the suspect* **recognition,** singling out, pinpointing, naming; discerning, distinguishing; informal fingering.
2 *early identification of problems* **determination,** establishment, ascertainment, discovery, diagnosis, divination; verification, confirmation.
3 *may I see your identification?* **ID,** (identity/identification) papers, bona fides, documents, credentials; ID card, identity card, pass, badge, warrant, license, permit, passport.
4 *the identification of Nonconformity with Victorian values* **association,** link, linkage, connection, tie, interconnection, interrelation, interdependence.
5 *his identification with the music is evident* **empathy,** rapport, relationship, fellow feeling, sympathetic cord.

identify ▶ verb **1** *the driver was identified by two witnesses* **recognize,** single out, pick out, spot, point out, pinpoint, put one's finger on, put a name to, name, know; discern, distinguish; remember, recall, recollect; informal finger; formal espy.
2 *I identified four problem areas* **determine,** establish, ascertain, make out, diagnose, discern, distinguish; verify, confirm; informal figure out, get a fix on, peg.
3 *they identify professional sports with wealth and glamour* **associate,** link, connect, relate, bracket, couple; mention in the same breath as, put side by side with.
4 *Peter identifies with the hero* **empathize with,** be in tune with, have a rapport with, feel at one with, sympathize with; be on the same wavelength as, speak the same language as; understand, relate to, feel for.

identity ▶ noun **1** *the identity of the owner* **name,** ID; specification.
2 *she was afraid of losing her identity* **individuality,** self, selfhood; personality, character, originality, distinctiveness, differentness, singularity, uniqueness.
3 *a case of mistaken identity* **identification,** recognition, naming, singling out.

ideology ▶ noun *the party has to jettison outdated ideology and give up its stranglehold on power* **beliefs,** ideas, ideals, principles, ethics, morals; doctrine, creed, credo, faith, teaching, theory, philosophy; tenets, canon(s); conviction(s), persuasion; informal ism.

idiocy ▶ noun *a seventeenth-century antidote to idiocy was to rub the forehead with beaver testicles* **stupidity,** folly, foolishness, foolhardiness, ignorance; madness, insanity, lunacy, nonsense; silliness, brainlessness, thoughtlessness, senselessness, irresponsibility, imprudence, ineptitude, inanity, absurdity, ludicrousness, fatuousness; informal craziness.
ANTONYMS sense.

idiom ▶ noun *these musicians all work in the gospel idiom* **language,** mode of expression, turn of phrase, style, speech, locution, diction, usage, phraseology, phrasing, phrase, vocabulary, terminology, parlance, jargon, argot, cant, patter, tongue, vernacular; informal lingo.

idiosyncrasy ▶ noun *traveling with her own fruitcake is one of the queen's idiosyncrasies | Fenway's Green Monster is perhaps the most recognizable ballpark idiosyncrasy* **peculiarity,** oddity, eccentricity, mannerism, trait, singularity, quirk, tic, whim, vagary, caprice, kink; fetish, foible, crotchet, habit, characteristic; individuality; unorthodoxy, unconventionality.

idiot ▶ noun informal *that idiot was driving way too fast* **fool,** ass, halfwit, dunce, dolt, ignoramus, cretin, moron, imbecile, simpleton; informal dope, ninny, nincompoop, chump, dimwit, dumbo, dummy, dum-dum, loon, dork, sap, jackass, blockhead, jughead, bonehead, knucklehead, fathead, numbskull, numbnuts, dumb-ass, doofus, clod, dunderhead, ditz, lummox, dipstick, thickhead, meathead, meatball, woodenhead, airhead, pinhead, lamebrain, peabrain, birdbrain, jerk, nerd, donkey, nitwit, twit, boob, twerp, schmuck, bozo, turkey, chowderhead, dingbat.
ANTONYMS genius.

idiotic ▶ adjective *her latest comedy is fanciful without being idiotic* **stupid,** silly, foolish, witless, brainless, mindless, thoughtless, unintelligent; imprudent, unwise, ill-advised, ill-considered, half-baked, foolhardy; absurd, senseless, pointless, nonsensical, inane, fatuous, ridiculous; informal dumb, dim, dimwitted, halfwitted, dopey, hare-brained, pea-brained, wooden-headed, thickheaded, dumb-ass.

idle ▶ adjective **1** *an idle person* **lazy,** indolent, slothful, work-shy, shiftless, inactive, sluggish, lethargic, listless; slack, lax, lackadaisical, good-for-nothing; rare otiose.
ANTONYMS industrious.
2 *being idle won't pay the bills* **unemployed,** jobless, out-of-work, redundant, between jobs, workless, unwaged, unoccupied.
ANTONYMS employed.
3 *they left the machine idle* **inactive,** unused, unoccupied, unemployed, disused; not in use, out of use, out of action, inoperative, nonfunctioning, out of service.
ANTONYMS working.
4 *their idle hours* **unoccupied,** spare, empty, vacant, unfilled, available.
ANTONYMS busy, full.
5 *idle remarks* **frivolous,** trivial, trifling, vain, minor, petty, lightweight, shallow, superficial, insignificant, unimportant, worthless, paltry, niggling, peripheral, inane, fatuous; unnecessary, time-wasting.
ANTONYMS meaningful, serious.
6 *idle threats* **empty,** meaningless, pointless, worthless, vain, hollow, insubstantial, futile, ineffective, ineffectual; groundless, baseless.
ANTONYMS serious.
▶ verb **1** *Lily idled on the window seat* **do nothing,** be inactive, vegetate, take it easy, mark time, twiddle one's thumbs, kill time, languish, laze, lounge, loll, loaf, loiter; informal hang around, veg out, bum around, lollygag. See note at LOITER.
2 *he let the engine idle* **run in neutral,** run.

idol ▶ noun **1** *idols deemed sacrilegious were summarily destroyed* **icon,** representation of a god, image, effigy, statue, figure, figurine, fetish, totem; graven image, false god, golden calf.
2 *a teen idol* **hero, heroine,** star, superstar, icon, celebrity; favorite, darling, pet, beloved; informal pinup, heartthrob, dreamboat, golden boy/girl.

idolatry ▶ noun *the prophets railed against idolatry* **idolization,** fetishization, fetishism, idol worship, adulation, adoration, reverence, veneration, glorification, lionization, hero-worshiping.

idolize ▶ verb *the kids idolize their fighter-pilot father* **hero-worship,** worship, revere, venerate, deify, lionize; stand in awe of, reverence, look up to, admire, adore, exalt; informal put on a pedestal. See note at REVERE.

if ▶ conjunction **1** *if the rain holds off, we can walk* **on (the) condition that,** provided (that), providing (that), presuming (that), supposing (that), assuming (that), as long as, given that, in the event that.
2 *if I miss curfew, she lays down the law* **whenever,** every time.
3 *a useful, if unintended innovation* **although,** albeit, but, yet, while; even though, despite being; chiefly Brit. whilst.
▶ noun *there is one if in all this* **uncertainty,** doubt; condition, stipulation, provision, proviso, constraint, precondition, requirement, specification, restriction.

iffy ▶ adjective informal **1** *an iffy neighborhood* **dubious,** doubtful, questionable, shaky; substandard, second-rate, inferior; sketchy.
2 *the date was a bit iffy* **uncertain,** undecided, unsettled, unsure, unresolved, in doubt, dubious, ambivalent; informal up in the air, borderline.

ignite ▶ verb **1** *he escaped moments before the gas ignited* **catch fire,** burst into flames, combust; be set off, explode.
ANTONYMS go out.
2 *his cigarette ignited the blanket* **light,** set fire to, set on fire, set alight, kindle, spark, touch off; informal set/put a match to.
ANTONYMS extinguish.
3 *the campaign failed to ignite voter interest* **arouse,** kindle, trigger, spark, instigate, excite, provoke, stimulate, animate, stir up, whip up, rally, jump-start, incite, fuel.
ANTONYMS dampen.

ignominious ▶ adjective *he made an ignominious exit after 21 months in power* **humiliating,** undignified, embarrassing, mortifying; ignoble, inglorious; disgraceful, shameful, dishonorable, discreditable.
ANTONYMS glorious.

ignominy ▶ noun *the Braves face the ignominy of losing three straight games to the league's worst team* **shame,** humiliation, embarrassment, mortification; disgrace, dishonor, discredit, degradation, scandal, infamy, indignity, ignobility, loss of face.
ANTONYMS honor.

ignorance ▶ noun **1** *our ignorance of foreign affairs* **incomprehension of,** unawareness of, unconsciousness of, unfamiliarity with, inexperience with, lack of knowledge about, lack of information about; informal cluelessness about.
ANTONYMS understanding, familiarity.
2 *both ignorance and poverty contribute to the growing problem of forced child labor* **lack of knowledge,** lack of education, unenlightenment, illiteracy; lack of intelligence, stupidity, foolishness, idiocy.
ANTONYMS knowledge, education.

ignorant ▶ adjective **1** *the plight of these ignorant children should be an international concern* **uneducated,** unknowledgeable, untaught, unschooled, untutored, untrained, illiterate, unlettered, unlearned, unread, uninformed, unenlightened, benighted; inexperienced, unworldly, unsophisticated.
ANTONYMS educated.
2 *they were **ignorant of** working-class life* **without knowledge of,** unaware of, unconscious of, oblivious to, incognizant of, unfamiliar with, unacquainted with, uninformed about, ill-informed about, unenlightened about, unconversant with, inexperienced in/with, naive about, green about; informal in the dark about, clueless about.
ANTONYMS knowledgeable.

CHOOSE THE RIGHT WORD

ignorant, illiterate, uneducated, uninformed, unlearned, unlettered, untutored

Someone who knows nothing about growing things might be called **ignorant** by a farmer who never went to high school but has spent his life in the fields. Although all of these adjectives refer to a lack of knowledge, *ignorant* refers to a lack of knowledge in general (*a foolish, ignorant person*) or to a lack of knowledge of some particular subject (*ignorant of the fine points of financial management*). A professor of art history might refer to someone who doesn't know how to look at a painting as **uneducated** or **untutored**, both of which refer to a lack of formal education in schools (*she was very bright but basically uneducated, and completely untutored in the fine arts*). Someone who cannot read or write is **illiterate**, a term that may also denote a failure to display civility or cultivated behavior (*the professor routinely referred to his students as illiterate louts*). Someone who is **unlettered** lacks a knowledge of fine literature (*a scientist who was highly trained but unlettered*); it also implies being able to read and write, but with no skill in either of these areas. **Unlearned** is similar to *ignorant* in that it refers to a lack of learning in general or in a specific subject (*an unlearned man who managed to become a millionaire*), but it does not carry the same negative connotations. **Uninformed** refers to a lack of definite information or data. For example, one can be highly intelligent and well educated but still *uninformed* about the latest developments in earthquake prediction.

ignore ▶ verb **1** *he ignored the customers* **disregard,** take no notice of, pay no attention to, pay no heed to; turn a blind eye to, turn a deaf ear to, tune out. See note at **NEGLECT**.
ANTONYMS pay attention to.
2 *he was ignored by the journalists* **snub,** slight, spurn, shun, disdain, look right through, pass over, look past; informal give someone the brush-off, give someone the cold shoulder.
ANTONYMS acknowledge.
3 *doctors ignored her husband's instructions* **set aside,** pay no attention to, take no account of; break, contravene, fail to comply with, fail to observe, disregard, disobey, breach, defy, flout; informal pooh-pooh.
ANTONYMS obey.

ill ▶ adjective **1** *she was feeling rather ill* **unwell,** sick, not (very) well, ailing, poorly, sickly, peaked, indisposed, infirm; out of sorts, not oneself, bad, off, in a bad way, far gone; bedridden, valetudinarian; queasy, nauseous, nauseated; informal under the weather, laid up, rotten, crummy, lousy, pukey, dizzy, woozy, green around the gills, like death warmed over.
ANTONYMS well, healthy.
2 *the ill effects of smoking* **harmful,** damaging, detrimental, deleterious, adverse, injurious, hurtful, destructive, pernicious, dangerous; unhealthy, unwholesome, poisonous, noxious; literary malefic, maleficent.
ANTONYMS good, beneficial.
3 *ill feelings had divided them for years* **hostile,** antagonistic, acrimonious, inimical, antipathetic; unfriendly, unsympathetic, unkind; resentful, spiteful, malicious, vindictive, malevolent, bitter.
ANTONYMS friendly, warm.
4 *an ill omen* **unlucky,** adverse, unfavorable, unfortunate, unpropitious, inauspicious, unpromising, infelicitous, ominous, sinister; literary direful.
ANTONYMS auspicious.
5 *ill manners* **rude,** discourteous, impolite, improper; impertinent, insolent, impudent, uncivil, disrespectful; informal ignorant.
ANTONYMS good, polite.
6 *the ill management of the front office* **bad,** poor, incompetent, unsatisfactory, inadequate, inexpert, deficient.
ANTONYMS good, competent.
▶ noun **1** (**ills**) *the ills of society* **problems,** troubles, evils, difficulties, misfortunes, trials, tribulations; worries, anxieties, concerns; informal headaches, hassles; archaic travails.
2 *he wished them no ill* **harm,** hurt, injury, damage, pain, trouble, misfortune, suffering, distress.
3 (**ills**) *the body's ills* **illnesses,** ailments, disorders, complaints, afflictions, sicknesses, diseases, maladies, infirmities.
▶ adverb **1** *such behavior ill becomes a chief executive* **poorly,** badly, imperfectly.
ANTONYMS well.
2 *the look on her face boded ill for her opponents* **unfavorably,** adversely, badly, inauspiciously.
ANTONYMS well, auspiciously.
3 *he can ill afford the loss of income* **barely,** scarcely, hardly, only just, (only) with difficulty, just possibly.
ANTONYMS easily.
4 *we are ill prepared for another flood* **inadequately,** unsatisfactorily, insufficiently, imperfectly, poorly, badly.
ANTONYMS well, satisfactorily.
– PHRASES **ill at ease** *Ritchie was cautioned not to appear ill at ease in the courtroom* **awkward,** uneasy, uncomfortable, embarrassed, self-conscious, out of place, inhibited, gauche; restless, restive, fidgety, discomfited, worried, anxious, on edge, edgy, nervous, tense, high-strung; informal twitchy, jittery, discombobulated, antsy. **speak ill of** *we never heard him once speak ill of his ex-wife* **denigrate,** disparage, criticize, be critical of, speak badly of, be malicious about, blacken the name of, run down, insult, abuse, attack, revile, malign, vilify, slur; informal badmouth, dis, bitch about, slag; formal derogate; rare asperse.

ill-advised ▶ adjective *an ill-advised business venture* **unwise,** injudicious, misguided, imprudent, ill-considered, ill-judged, impolitic; foolhardy, foolish, hare-brained, rash, reckless, irresponsible; informal crazy, idiotic, crackpot, madcap.
ANTONYMS wise, judicious.

ill-bred ▶ adjective See **ILL-MANNERED**.

ill-defined ▶ adjective *an ill-defined property line* | *the ill-defined messages in his art* **vague,** indistinct, unclear, imprecise, nebulous, shadowy, obscure; blurred, fuzzy, hazy, woolly.

ill-disposed ▶ adjective *the court may be*

ill-disposed to foreign companies **hostile to,** antagonistic to, unfriendly to, unsympathetic to, antipathetic to, inimical to, unfavorable to, adverse to, averse to, at odds with; informal anti, down on.
ANTONYMS friendly.

illegal ▸ adjective *illegal campaign contributions* **unlawful,** illicit, illegitimate, criminal, felonious; unlicensed, unauthorized, unsanctioned; outlawed, banned, forbidden, prohibited, proscribed, taboo; contraband, black-market, bootleg; Law malfeasant; informal crooked, shady, sketchy.
ANTONYMS lawful, legitimate.

illegible ▸ adjective *nearly a billion prescriptions are rechecked each year because of physicians' illegible handwriting* **unreadable,** indecipherable, unintelligible, incomprehensible, hieroglyphic; scrawled, scribbled, crabbed, cramped.

illegitimate ▸ adjective **1** *illegitimate share trading* **illegal,** unlawful, illicit, criminal, felonious; unlicensed, unauthorized, unsanctioned; prohibited, outlawed, banned, forbidden, proscribed; fraudulent, corrupt, dishonest; Law malfeasant; informal crooked, shady.
ANTONYMS legal, lawful.
2 dated *her illegitimate children* **born out of wedlock,** bastard, unfathered; archaic natural, misbegotten; (**illegitimate child**) love child.
ANTONYMS legitimate.

ill-fated ▸ adjective *an ill-fated rebellion* **doomed,** blighted, damned, cursed, accursed, ill-starred, unlucky, hapless, jinxed; disastrous, unfortunate; literary star-crossed.

ill-favored ▸ adjective *he was particularly ill-favored after a night of drunken debauchery* **unattractive,** plain, ugly, homely, unprepossessing, displeasing; informal not much to look at.
ANTONYMS attractive.

illicit ▸ adjective **1** *illicit drugs* **illegal,** unlawful, illegitimate, criminal, felonious; outlawed, banned, forbidden, prohibited, proscribed; unlicensed, unauthorized, unsanctioned; contraband, black-market, bootleg; Law malfeasant.
ANTONYMS lawful, legal.
2 *an illicit love affair* **taboo,** forbidden, impermissible, unacceptable, adulterous; secret, clandestine, furtive.
ANTONYMS aboveboard.

illiteracy ▸ noun **1** *for these villagers, poverty and illiteracy go hand in hand* **inability to read or write.**
2 *technological illiteracy* **ignorance,** unawareness, inexperience, unenlightenment, lack of knowledge, lack of education; informal cluelessness; literary nescience.

illiterate ▸ adjective **1** *an illiterate peasant* **unable to read or write,** unlettered.
2 *too many voters are politically illiterate* **ignorant,** unknowledgeable, unenlightened, uneducated, unschooled, untaught, untutored, untrained, uninstructed, uninformed, unread, unlearned; informal clueless; literary nescient. See note at IGNORANT.

ill-judged ▸ adjective See ILL-ADVISED.

ill-mannered ▸ adjective *we never encountered the ill-mannered locals you had warned us about* **bad-mannered,** discourteous, rude, impolite, uncivil, abusive, disagreeable; insolent, impertinent, impudent, cheeky, presumptuous, audacious, disrespectful; badly behaved, ill-behaved, boorish, loutish, oafish, uncouth, uncivilized, unmannered, ill-bred, vulgar, crass; informal ignorant. See note at RUDE.
ANTONYMS polite.

ill-natured ▸ adjective *Cinderella's ill-natured stepsisters* **mean,** nasty, spiteful, malicious, disagreeable; poisonous, venomous, bitter; ill-tempered, bad-tempered, moody, irritable, irascible, surly, sullen, peevish, petulant, fractious, cross, crabbed, crabby, tetchy, testy, grouchy, waspish; informal bitchy.
ANTONYMS good-natured, sweet.

illness ▸ noun *more than fifty students have been diagnosed with the same illness* **sickness,** disease, ailment, complaint, disorder, malady, affliction, indisposition; ill health, poor health, infirmity; infection, virus; informal bug; dated contagion.
ANTONYMS good health.

illogical ▸ adjective *it is illogical to assume that there will never be a cure for Parkinson's disease* **irrational,** unreasonable, unsound, unreasoned, unjustifiable, groundless, unfounded; incorrect, erroneous, invalid, spurious, faulty, flawed, fallacious, unscientific; specious, sophistic, casuistic; absurd, preposterous, untenable; informal full of holes, off the wall.
ANTONYMS logical.

ill-starred ▸ adjective See ILL-FATED.

ill-tempered ▸ adjective *retirement didn't suit Uncle Luke, who soon became sullen and ill-tempered* **bad-tempered,** short-tempered, quick-tempered, ill-humored, moody; in a (bad) mood, cross, irritable, irascible, tetchy, testy, crotchety, touchy, cantankerous, curmudgeonly, peevish, fractious, waspish, prickly, pettish; grumpy, grouchy, crabbed, crabby, disagreeable, splenetic, dyspeptic, choleric; informal snappish, snippy, short-fused, on a short fuse, soreheaded, cranky, ornery, bitchy.

ill-timed ▸ adjective *our ill-timed vacation landed us in the worst-hit area during the hurricane* **untimely,** mistimed, badly timed; premature, hasty; inconvenient, inopportune; in, unsuitable, malapropos; unfavorable, unfortunate.
ANTONYMS timely, opportune.

illuminate ▸ verb **1** *the bundle was illuminated by the torch* **light** (**up**), lighten, throw light on, brighten, shine on, irradiate; literary illumine, illume, enlighten.
ANTONYMS darken.
2 *the manuscripts were illuminated* **decorate,** illustrate, embellish, adorn, ornament.
3 *documents often illuminate people's thought processes* **clarify,** elucidate, explain, reveal, shed light on, give insight into, demystify; exemplify, illustrate; informal spell out.
ANTONYMS confuse, conceal.

illuminating ▶ adjective *the lectures have been interesting as well as illuminating* **informative,** enlightening, explanatory, instructive, instructional, edifying, helpful, educational, revealing; informal tell-all.

illumination ▶ noun **1** *a floodlight provided illumination* **light,** lighting, radiance, gleam, glow, glare; shining, gleaming, glowing; brilliance, luminescence; literary illumining, irradiance, lucency, lambency, effulgence, refulgence.
ANTONYMS darkness.
2 *the illumination of a manuscript* **decoration,** illustration, embellishment, adornment, ornamentation.
3 *these books give illumination on the subject* **clarification,** elucidation, explanation, revelation, explication.
4 *it was an era of great illumination* **enlightenment,** insight, understanding, awareness; learning, education, edification.
ANTONYMS ignorance.

illusion ▶ noun **1** *he had destroyed her illusions* **delusion,** misapprehension, misconception, false impression; fantasy, fancy, dream, chimera; fool's paradise, self-deception.
2 *the lighting increases the illusion of depth* **appearance,** impression, semblance; misperception, false appearance; rare simulacrum.
3 *it's just an illusion* **mirage,** hallucination, apparition, figment of the imagination, trick of the light, trompe l'oeil; deception, trick, smoke and mirrors.
4 *Houdini's amazing illusions* (**magic**) **trick,** conjuring trick; (**illusions**) magic, conjuring, sleight of hand, legerdemain.

illustrate ▶ verb **1** *the photographs that illustrate the book* **decorate,** adorn, ornament, accompany, embellish; add pictures/drawings to, provide artwork for.
2 *this can be illustrated through a brief example* **explain,** explicate, elucidate, clarify, make plain, demonstrate, show, emphasize; informal get across.
3 *his sense of humor was illustrated by his screen saver* **exemplify,** typify, epitomize, show, demonstrate, display, represent, encapsulate.

illustration ▶ noun **1** *the illustrations in children's books* **picture,** drawing, sketch, figure, image, plate, print, artwork; visual aid.
2 *by way of illustration* **exemplification,** demonstration, showing; example, typical case, case in point, object lesson, analogy.

illustrative ▶ adjective *the parables are wonderfully illustrative* **exemplifying,** explanatory, elucidative, explicative, expository, exegetical; demonstrative, descriptive, representative, indicative, emblematic, symbolic, typical; rare evincive.

illustrious ▶ adjective *the book falls short of its illustrious cinematic predecessor* **eminent,** distinguished, acclaimed, notable, noteworthy, prominent, preeminent, foremost, leading, important, influential; renowned, famous, famed, well-known, celebrated, legendary; esteemed, honored, respected, venerable, august, highly regarded, well-thought-of, of distinction; brilliant, glorious, stellar.
ANTONYMS lackluster, unknown.

ill will ▶ noun *the ill will between the two families predates anyone's memory* **animosity,** hostility, enmity, acrimony, animus, hatred, hate, loathing, antipathy; ill feeling, bad feeling, bad blood, antagonism, unfriendliness, dislike; spite, spitefulness, resentment, hard feelings, bitterness, malice, rancor; informal grudge, friction.
ANTONYMS goodwill.

image ▶ noun **1** *an image of St. Bartholomew* **likeness,** resemblance; depiction, portrayal, representation; statue, statuette, sculpture, bust, effigy; painting, picture, portrait, drawing, sketch.
2 *images of the planet Neptune* **picture,** photograph, snapshot, photo.
3 *he contemplated his image in the mirror* **reflection,** mirror image, likeness.
4 *the image of this country as democratic* **conception,** impression, idea, perception, notion; mental picture, vision; character, reputation; appearance, semblance. See note at **EMBLEM**.
5 *biblical images* **simile,** metaphor, metonymy; figure of speech, trope, turn of phrase; imagery.
6 *his heartthrob image* **public perception,** persona, profile, reputation, stature, standing; face, front, facade, mask, guise.
7 *I'm the image of my grandfather* **double,** living image, look-alike, clone, copy, twin, duplicate, exact likeness, mirror image, doppelgänger; informal spitting image, dead ringer, carbon copy; archaic similitude.
8 *a graven image* **idol,** icon, fetish, totem.
▶ verb *she imaged imposing castles* **envisage,** envision, imagine, picture, see in one's mind's eye.

imaginable ▶ adjective *they did everything imaginable to save the farm* **thinkable,** conceivable, supposable, believable, credible, creditable; possible, plausible, feasible, tenable, within reason, under the sun.

imaginary ▶ adjective *his imaginary friends* **unreal,** nonexistent, fictional, fictitious, pretend, make-believe, mythical, mythological, fabulous, fanciful, storybook, fantastic; made-up, dreamed-up, invented, concocted, fancied; illusory, illusive, a figment of one's imagination; archaic visionary.
ANTONYMS real, actual.

imagination ▶ noun **1** *a vivid imagination* **creative power,** fancy, vision; informal mind's eye.
2 *you need imagination in dealing with these problems* **creativity,** imaginativeness, creativeness; vision, inspiration, inventiveness, invention, resourcefulness, ingenuity; originality, innovation, innovativeness.
3 *the album captured the public's imagination* **interest,** fascination, attention, passion, curiosity.

imaginative ▶ adjective *imaginative writers | an imaginative solution* **creative,** visionary, inspired, inventive, resourceful, ingenious; original, innovative, innovatory, unorthodox, unconventional; fanciful, whimsical, fantastic; informal offbeat, off the wall, zany. See note at **CREATIVE**.

imagine ▶ verb **1** *imagine sitting through five hours of steady air turbulence* **visualize,** envisage, envision, picture, see in the mind's eye; dream up, think up/of, conjure up, conceive, conceptualize; formal ideate.
2 *I imagine he was at home* **assume,** presume, expect, take it, presuppose; suppose, think (it likely), dare say, surmise, believe, be of the view, figure; informal guess, reckon; formal opine.

imbecile ▶ noun See FOOL (sense 1 of the noun).

imbed ▶ verb See EMBED.

imbibe ▶ verb formal **1** *they'd imbibed too much whiskey* **drink,** consume, quaff, guzzle, gulp (down); informal knock back, down, swill, chug.
2 *he had imbibed liberally* **drink (alcohol),** take strong drink, tipple; informal booze, knock a few back, hit the bottle, bend one's elbow.
3 *imbibing local history* **assimilate,** absorb, soak up, take in, drink in, digest, learn, acquire, grasp, pick up, familiarize oneself with.

imbroglio ▶ noun *the company may not survive another legal imbroglio* **complicated situation,** complication, problem, difficulty, predicament, trouble, confusion, quandary, entanglement, muddle, mess, quagmire, morass, sticky situation; informal bind, jam, pickle, fix, corner, hole, scrape.

imbue ▶ verb *the painting has become deeply imbued with the idea of Basque separatism* **permeate,** saturate, diffuse, suffuse, pervade, bathe, drench, steep; impregnate, inject, inculcate, ingrain, instill, invest, inspire, breathe; fill.

imitate ▶ verb **1** *other artists have imitated her style* **emulate,** copy, model oneself on, follow, echo, parrot; informal rip off, knock off, pirate.
2 *he imitated several politicians superbly* **mimic,** do an impression of, impersonate, ape; parody, caricature, burlesque, travesty; informal take off, send up, make like, mock; formal personate.

CHOOSE THE RIGHT WORD

imitate, ape, copy, impersonate, mimic, mock

A young girl might **imitate** her mother by answering the phone in exactly the same tone of voice, while a teenager who deliberately *imitates* the way her mother talks for the purpose of irritating her would more accurately be said to **mimic** her. *Imitate* implies following something as an example or model (*he imitated the playing style of his music teacher*), while *mimic* suggests imitating someone's mannerisms for fun or ridicule (*they liked to mimic the teacher's southern drawl*). To **copy** is to imitate or reproduce something as closely as possible (*he copied the style of dress and speech used by the other gang members*). When someone assumes another person's appearance or mannerisms, sometimes for the purpose of perpetrating a fraud, he or she is said to **impersonate** (*arrested for impersonating a police officer; a comedian well known for impersonating political figures*). **Ape** and **mock** both imply an unflattering imitation. Someone who mimics in a contemptuous way is said to *ape* (*he entertained everyone in the office by aping the boss's phone conversations with his wife*), while someone who imitates with the intention of belittling or irritating is said to *mock* (*the students openly mocked their teacher's attempt to have a serious discussion about sex*).

imitation ▶ noun **1** *an imitation of a sailor's hat* **copy,** simulation, reproduction, replica; counterfeit, forgery, rip off.
2 *learning by imitation* **emulation,** copying, echoing, parroting.
3 *a perfect imitation of Elvis* **impersonation,** impression, parody, mockery, caricature, burlesque, travesty, lampoon, pastiche; mimicry, mimicking, imitating, aping; informal send-up, takeoff, spoof.
▶ adjective *imitation ivory* **artificial,** synthetic, simulated, man-made, manufactured, ersatz, substitute; mock, sham, fake, faux, bogus, knockoff, pseudo, phony.
ANTONYMS real, genuine.

imitative ▶ adjective **1** *imitative crime* **similar,** like, mimicking; informal copycat, me-too.
2 *I found the film empty and imitative* **derivative,** unoriginal, unimaginative, uninspired, uninventive, plagiarized, plagiaristic, slavish; clichéd, hackneyed, stale, trite, banal, rehashed; informal cribbed, old hat.
ANTONYMS original.

imitator ▶ noun *she has many imitators* **copier,** emulator, follower, mimic, plagiarist, ape, parrot; informal copycat.

immaculate ▶ adjective **1** *an immaculate white shirt* **clean,** spotless, ultraclean, pristine, unsoiled, unstained, unsullied; shining, shiny, gleaming; neat, tidy, spick-and-span; informal squeaky clean, as clean as a whistle.
ANTONYMS dirty.
2 *a guitar in immaculate condition* **perfect,** pristine, mint, as good as new; flawless, faultless, unblemished, unspoiled, undamaged; excellent, impeccable; informal tip-top, A1.
ANTONYMS worn, damaged.
3 *his immaculate service record* **unblemished,** spotless, impeccable, unsullied, undefiled, untarnished, stainless; pure, virtuous, incorrupt, above reproach; informal squeaky clean, as pure as the driven snow.
ANTONYMS defiled, reproachable.

immaterial ▶ adjective **1** *the difference in our ages was immaterial* **irrelevant,** unimportant, inconsequential, insignificant, of no matter/consequence, of little account, beside the point, neither here nor there.
ANTONYMS significant, important.
2 *the immaterial soul* **intangible,** incorporeal, bodiless, disembodied, impalpable, ethereal, insubstantial, metaphysical; spiritual, unearthly, supernatural.
ANTONYMS tangible, physical.

immature ▶ adjective **1** *an immature Stilton cheese* **unripe,** not mature, premature, unmellowed; undeveloped, unformed,

unfinished, raw, embryonic.
ANTONYMS ripe.
2 *an extremely immature girl* **childish,** babyish, infantile, juvenile, adolescent, puerile, sophomoric, jejune, callow, green, tender, young, inexperienced, unsophisticated, unworldly, naive; informal wet behind the ears. See note at **YOUTHFUL**.
ANTONYMS mature, worldly.

immeasurable ▶ adjective *the immeasurable riches provided to us by nature* **incalculable,** inestimable, innumerable, untold; limitless, boundless, unbounded, unlimited, illimitable, infinite, countless, never-ending, interminable, endless, inexhaustible; vast, immense, extensive, great, abundant; informal no end of; literary myriad.

immediate ▶ adjective **1** *the UN called for immediate action* **instant,** instantaneous, swift, prompt, fast, speedy, rapid, brisk, quick, expeditious; sudden, hurried, hasty, precipitate; informal snappy.
ANTONYMS delayed, gradual.
2 *their immediate concerns* **current,** present, existing, actual; urgent, pressing, exigent.
ANTONYMS past, future.
3 *the immediate past* **recent,** not long past, just gone, latest.
ANTONYMS remote.
4 *our immediate neighbors* **nearest,** near, close, closest, next-door; adjacent, adjoining, contiguous.
ANTONYMS distant.
5 *the immediate cause of death* **direct,** primary.
ANTONYMS indirect.

immediately ▶ adverb **1** *it was necessary to make a decision immediately* **straightaway,** at once, right away, instantly, now, directly, promptly, forthwith, this/that (very) minute, this/that instant, there and then, then and there, on the spot, here and now, without delay, without further ado, posthaste; quickly, as fast as possible, speedily, as soon as possible; informal ASAP, pronto, double-quick, on the double, PDQ, in/like a flash, like a shot, tout de suite; humorous toot sweet; archaic forthright.
2 *I sat immediately behind him* **directly,** right, exactly, precisely, squarely, just, dead; informal smack dab.

immemorial ▶ adjective *immemorial customs* **ancient,** (very) old, age-old, antediluvian, timeless, archaic, venerable, long-standing, timeworn, time-honored, tried and true; traditional; literary of yore.

immense ▶ adjective *an immense brick church | immense jars of mayonnaise* **huge,** vast, massive, enormous, gigantic, colossal, great, very large/big, monumental, towering, tremendous; giant, elephantine, monstrous, mammoth, titanic, king-size(d), economy-size(d); informal mega, monster, whopping, humongous, jumbo, astronomical, cosmic, ginormous, Brobdingnagian.
ANTONYMS tiny.

immerse ▶ verb **1** *litmus paper turns red on being immersed in acid* **submerge,** dip, dunk, duck, sink, plunge; soak, drench, saturate, marinate, wet, douse, souse, steep.
2 *Elliot was immersed in his work* **absorb in,** engross in, occupy by/with, engage in, involve in/with, bury in, swamp with, lose oneself in; busy with, preoccupy with, fixate on/upon.

immigrant ▶ noun *they will convene to discuss the civil liberties of immigrants* **newcomer,** settler, migrant, emigrant; nonnative, foreigner, alien, outsider; expatriate; informal expat.
ANTONYMS native.

imminent ▶ adjective *a cease-fire was imminent* **impending,** close (at hand), near, (fast) approaching, coming, forthcoming, on the way, in the offing, in the pipeline, on the horizon, in the air, just around the corner, coming down the pike, expected, anticipated, brewing, looming, threatening, menacing; informal in the cards.

immobile ▶ adjective **1** *she sat immobile for a long time* **motionless,** without moving, still, stock-still, static, stationary; rooted to the spot, rigid, frozen, transfixed, like a statue, not moving a muscle.
ANTONYMS moving.
2 *I dreaded being immobile* **unable to move,** immobilized; paralyzed, crippled.
ANTONYMS mobile.

immobilize ▶ verb *the virus has immobilized the House's internal communication system | it is important to immobilize the injured part of the body* **put out of action,** disable, make inoperative, inactivate, deactivate, paralyze, freeze, cripple; bring to a standstill, halt, stop; restrain, stabilize.

immoderate ▶ adjective *immoderate spending* **excessive,** heavy, intemperate, unrestrained, unrestricted, uncontrolled, unlimited, unbridled, uncurbed, overindulgent, imprudent, reckless; undue, inordinate, unreasonable, unjustified, unwarranted, uncalled for, outrageous; extravagant, lavish, exorbitant, prodigal, profligate, wanton, dissipated.

immodest ▶ adjective *the deputy minister complained that the dance was too immodest for the memorial ceremony* **indecorous,** improper, indecent, indelicate, immoral; forward, bold, brazen, impudent, shameless, loose, wanton; informal fresh, cheeky, saucy, brassy.

immoral ▶ adjective *the legality of the fugitive slave laws does not alter the fact that they were deeply immoral* **unethical,** bad, morally wrong, wrongful, wicked, evil, foul, unprincipled, unscrupulous, dishonorable, dishonest, unconscionable, iniquitous, disreputable, corrupt, depraved, vile, villainous, nefarious, base, miscreant; sinful, godless, impure, unchaste, unvirtuous, shameless, degenerate, debased, debauched, dissolute, reprobate, lewd, obscene, perverse, perverted; licentious, wanton, promiscuous, loose; informal shady, lowdown, crooked, sleazy.
ANTONYMS ethical, chaste.

immorality ▶ noun *he charged that the overseas press was prone to lies and immorality* **wickedness,** immoral behavior, badness, evil, vileness, corruption, dishonesty, dishonorableness; sinfulness, ungodliness, unchastity, sin, depravity, villainy, vice, degeneracy, debauchery, dissolution, perversion, lewdness, obscenity, wantonness, promiscuity; informal shadiness, crookedness; formal turpitude.

immortal ▶ adjective **1** *our souls are immortal* **undying,** deathless, eternal, everlasting, never-ending, endless, lasting, enduring, ceaseless; imperishable, indestructible, inextinguishable, immutable, perpetual, permanent, unfading.
2 *an immortal children's classic* **timeless,** perennial, classic, time-honored, enduring; famous, famed, renowned, legendary, great, eminent, outstanding, acclaimed, celebrated.
▶ noun **1** *Greek temples of the immortals* **god, goddess,** deity, divine being, supreme being, divinity.
2 *one of the immortals of literature* **great,** hero, legend, god, celebrity, star, Olympian.

immortality ▶ noun **1** *the immortality of the gods* **eternal life,** everlasting life, deathlessness; indestructibility, imperishability.
2 *the book has achieved immortality* **timelessness,** legendary status, lasting fame/renown.

immortalize ▶ verb *the battle was immortalized by Pushkin* **commemorate,** memorialize, eternalize; celebrate, deify, exalt, glorify; eulogize, pay tribute to, honor, salute.

immovable ▶ adjective **1** *lock your bike to something immovable* **fixed,** secure, stable, moored, anchored, rooted, braced, set firm, set fast; stuck, jammed, stiff, unbudgeable, four-square.
ANTONYMS mobile.
2 *there he was, silent and immovable* **motionless,** unmoving, immobile, stationary, still, stock-still, not moving a muscle, rooted to the spot; transfixed, paralyzed, frozen.
ANTONYMS moving, in motion.
3 *she was immovable in her loyalties* **steadfast,** unwavering, unswerving, resolute, determined, firm, unshakable, adamant, unfailing, dogged, tenacious, inflexible, unyielding, unbending, uncompromising, obdurate, obstinate, iron-willed; informal rock-steady, diehard.
ANTONYMS fickle, unsure.

immune ▶ adjective *they are **immune to** hepatitis B | this company seems to be **immune to** fluctuations in the economy* **resistant to,** not subject to, not liable to, unsusceptible to, not vulnerable to; protected from, safe from, secure against, not in danger of; impervious to, invulnerable to, unaffected by.
ANTONYMS susceptible.

immunity ▶ noun **1** *an **immunity to** malaria* **resistance to,** nonsusceptibility to; ability to fight off, protection against, defenses against; immunization against, inoculation against.
2 *immunity from prosecution* **exemption,** exception, freedom, release, dispensation, amnesty.
3 *diplomatic immunity* **indemnity,** privilege, prerogative, right, liberty, license; legal exemption, impunity, protection.

immunize ▶ verb *have these children been **immunized against** rubella?* **vaccinate against,** inoculate against; protect from, safeguard against.

imp ▶ noun **1** *our neighborhood imps are, for the most part, harmless* **rascal,** monkey, devil, troublemaker, urchin; informal scamp, brat, monster, horror, terror, tyke, whippersnapper, hellion, varmint, rapscallion; archaic scapegrace.
2 *this trickster of Indian myth is an inscrutable imp possessed of satanic charisma* **hobgoblin,** goblin, elf, sprite, pixie, brownie, fairy, puck; demon, little devil; archaic bugbear.

impact ▶ noun **1** *the force of the impact* **collision,** crash, smash, bump, bang, knock.
2 *the job losses will have a major impact* **effect,** influence, significance, meaning; consequences, repercussions, ramifications, reverberations.
▶ verb **1** *a comet impacted the earth sixty million years ago* **crash into,** smash into, collide with, hit, strike, ram, smack into, bang into, slam into.
2 *high interest rates have impacted retail spending* **affect,** influence, have an effect on, make an impression on; hit, touch, change, alter, modify, transform, shape.

> USAGE
> **impact**
> *Impact* has traditionally been only a noun. In recent years, however, it has undergone a semantic shift that has allowed it to act as a verb. Such use has become widespread (and also widely condemned by stylists)—e.g.: "The researchers concluded that this low level of intensity may have impacted [read *affected*] the results." (*Tampa Tribune*; July 17, 1997.) This use of the word would be perfectly acceptable if *impact* were performing any function not as ably performed by *affect* or *influence*. If *affect* as a verb is not sufficiently straightforward in context, then the careful writer might use *have an impact on*, which, though longer, is probably better than the jarring impact of *impacted*. Reserve *impact* for noun uses and *impacted* for wisdom teeth.
> Interestingly, *impact* as a verb might have arisen partly in response to widespread diffidence about the spelling of *affect* (often confused with *effect*). — **BG**

impair ▶ verb *sagging eyelid skin can impair eyesight* **have a negative effect on,** damage, harm, diminish, reduce, weaken, lessen, decrease, impede, hinder, hobble; undermine, compromise; formal vitiate.
ANTONYMS improve, enhance.

impale ▶ verb *her knife impaled the counter like a javelin* **stick,** skewer, spear, spike, transfix, harpoon; pierce, stab, run through; literary transpierce.

impalpable ▶ adjective *his skin was sallow and his pulse impalpable | impalpable clouds* **intangible,** insubstantial, incorporeal, immaterial; indefinable, elusive, imperceptible, indescribable.

impart ▶ verb **1** *she had news to impart* **communicate,** pass on, convey, transmit, relay,

relate, recount, tell, make known, make public, report, announce, proclaim, herald, spread, disseminate, circulate, promulgate, broadcast; disclose, reveal, divulge; informal let on about, blab, blurt.
2 *the picture imparts some color to the drab office* **give,** bestow, confer, grant, lend, afford, provide, supply.

impartial ▶ **adjective** *can the United Nations be trusted as an impartial arbiter of world affairs?* **unbiased,** unprejudiced, neutral, nonpartisan, nondiscriminatory, disinterested, detached, dispassionate, objective, open-minded, equitable, evenhanded, fair, fair-minded, just; without favoritism, without fear or favor.
ANTONYMS biased, partisan.

impassable ▶ **adjective** *the farm-to-market roads were impassable* **unpassable,** unnavigable, untraversable, impenetrable; closed, blocked, barricaded; dense, thick, blind.

impasse ▶ **noun** *an impasse in the peace talks poses new challenges* **deadlock,** dead end, stalemate, standoff; standstill, halt, stoppage, stop; informal Catch-22.

impassioned ▶ **adjective** *an impassioned commentary about the state of American politics* **emotional,** heartfelt, wholehearted, earnest, sincere, fervent, ardent, passionate, fervid, intense, burning; vehement, zealous, heated; literary perfervid.

impatience ▶ **noun 1** *he was shifting in his seat with impatience* **restlessness,** restiveness, agitation, nervousness, anxiety; eagerness, keenness; informal jitteriness.
2 *a burst of impatience* **irritability,** testiness, tetchiness, irascibility, querulousness, peevishness, petulance, frustration, exasperation, annoyance, pique.

impatient ▶ **adjective 1** *Elaine grew impatient* **restless,** restive, agitated, nervous, anxious, tense, ill at ease, edgy, jumpy, keyed up; informal twitchy, jittery, uptight, high-strung.
ANTONYMS calm, indifferent.
2 *they are impatient to get back home* **anxious,** eager, keen, yearning, longing, aching, agog; informal itching, dying, raring, gung-ho, straining at the leash.
ANTONYMS reluctant.
3 *why must you be so impatient with the children?* **irritated,** annoyed, angry, testy, tetchy, snappy, cross, querulous, peevish, piqued, short-tempered; abrupt, curt, brusque, terse, short; informal peeved.
ANTONYMS even-tempered, pleased.

impeach ▶ **verb 1** *there were two attempts to impeach Andrew Johnson* **indict,** charge, accuse, lay charges against, arraign, take to court, put on trial, prosecute.
2 *the headlines impeached their clean image* **challenge,** question, disparage, criticize, call into question, raise doubts about, cast aspersions on.
ANTONYMS confirm.

impeccable ▶ **adjective** *the lieutenant's record is impeccable* **flawless,** faultless, unblemished, spotless, immaculate, stainless, perfect, exemplary; sinless, irreproachable, blameless, guiltless; informal squeaky clean.
ANTONYMS imperfect, sinful.

impecunious ▶ **adjective** *she left Evansville to escape the solicitations of her impecunious relatives* **penniless,** poor, impoverished, indigent, insolvent, hard up, poverty-stricken, needy, destitute; in straitened circumstances, unable to make ends meet; informal (flat) broke, strapped (for cash); formal penurious.
ANTONYMS wealthy.

impede ▶ **verb** *your efforts to impede our progress will be unsuccessful* **hinder,** obstruct, hamper, hold back/up, delay, interfere with, disrupt, retard, slow (down), hobble, cripple; block, check, stop, scupper, scuttle, thwart, frustrate, balk, foil, derail; informal stymie, throw a (monkey) wrench in the works of; dated cumber. See note at **HINDER**.
ANTONYMS facilitate.

impediment ▶ **noun 1** *an impediment to economic improvement* **hindrance,** obstruction, obstacle, barrier, bar, block, handicap, check, curb, restriction, limitation; setback, difficulty, snag, hitch, hurdle, stumbling block; informal fly in the ointment, hiccup, (monkey) wrench in the works, glitch; archaic cumber.
2 *a speech impediment* **defect**; stammer, stutter, lisp.

impel ▶ **verb 1** *financial difficulties impelled her to seek work* **force,** compel, constrain, oblige, require, make, urge, exhort, press, pressurize, drive, push, spur, prod, goad, incite, prompt, persuade.
2 *vital energies impel him in unforeseen directions* **propel,** drive, move, get going, get moving.

impending ▶ **adjective** *a smarter grid could warn of impending blackouts* **imminent,** close (at hand), near, nearing, approaching, coming, forthcoming, upcoming, to come, on the way, about to happen, in store, in the offing, on the horizon, in the air/wind, brewing, looming, threatening, menacing; informal coming down the pike, in the cards.

impenetrable ▶ **adjective 1** *impenetrable armor* **impervious,** impermeable, indestructible, solid, thick, unyielding; impregnable, inviolable, invulnerable, unassailable, unpierceable; informal bulletproof.
ANTONYMS permeable, vulnerable.
2 *a dark, impenetrable forest* **impassable,** unpassable, inaccessible, unnavigable, untraversable; dense, thick, overgrown; archaic thickset.
ANTONYMS sparse, accessible.
3 *an impenetrable clique* **exclusive,** closed, secretive, secret, private; restrictive, restricted, limited.
ANTONYMS open.
4 *impenetrable statistics* **incomprehensible,** unfathomable, inexplicable, unintelligible, inscrutable, unclear, baffling, bewildering, puzzling, perplexing, enigmatic, cryptic, confusing, abstruse, opaque; complex, complicated, difficult.
ANTONYMS clear.

impenitent ▶ **adjective** *the hardness of their impenitent hearts* **unrepentant,** unrepenting, uncontrite, remorseless, unashamed, unapologetic, unabashed.

imperative ▶ adjective **1** *it is imperative that you find him* **vitally important,** of vital importance, all-important, vital, crucial, critical, essential, necessary, indispensable, urgent; compulsory, obligatory, mandatory.
ANTONYMS unimportant, optional.
2 *the imperative note in her voice* **peremptory,** commanding, imperious, authoritative, masterful, dictatorial, magisterial, assertive, firm, insistent.
ANTONYMS submissive.

imperceptible ▶ adjective *the imperceptible shift of constellations | an imperceptible rustle of cellophane* **unnoticeable,** undetectable, indistinguishable, indiscernible, invisible, inaudible, inappreciable, impalpable, unobtrusive, inconspicuous, unseen; slight, small, tiny, minute, microscopic, infinitesimal, subtle, faint, fine, negligible, inconsequential; indistinct, unclear, obscure, vague, indefinite, hard to make out.
ANTONYMS noticeable, obvious.

imperfect ▶ adjective **1** *the goods were returned as imperfect* **faulty,** flawed, defective, shoddy, unsound, inferior, second-rate, below standard, substandard; damaged, blemished, torn, broken, cracked, scratched; informal not up to snuff, not up to scratch, crummy, lousy.
ANTONYMS flawless.
2 *an imperfect form of the manuscript* **incomplete,** unfinished, half-done; unpolished, unrefined, rough.
ANTONYMS complete.
3 *she spoke imperfect Arabic* **broken,** faltering, halting, hesitant, rudimentary, limited.
ANTONYMS flawless, fluent.

imperfection ▶ noun **1** *the glass is free from imperfections* **defect,** fault, flaw, deformity, discoloration, disfigurement; crack, scratch, chip, nick, pit, dent; blemish, stain, spot, mark, streak.
ANTONYMS strength.
2 *he was aware of his imperfections* **flaw,** fault, failing, deficiency, weakness, vice, weak point, fallibility, shortcoming, foible, inadequacy, frailty, limitation, chink in one's armor.
ANTONYMS perfection.
3 *the imperfection of the fossil record* **incompleteness,** patchiness, deficiency; roughness, crudeness.
ANTONYMS completeness.

imperial ▶ adjective **1** *imperial banners* **royal,** regal, monarchical, sovereign, kingly, queenly, princely.
2 *her imperial bearing* **majestic,** grand, august, dignified, proud, stately, noble, aristocratic, regal; magnificent, imposing, impressive.
3 *our customers thought we were imperial* See IMPERIOUS.

imperil ▶ verb *technology can affect and possibly imperil civilization* **endanger,** jeopardize, risk, put in danger, put in jeopardy, expose to danger, hazard; threaten, pose a threat to; archaic peril.

imperious ▶ adjective *Black tells stories of imperious judges and duplicitous witnesses* **peremptory,** high-handed, commanding, imperial, overbearing, overweening, domineering, authoritarian, dictatorial, autocratic, authoritative, lordly, assertive, bossy, arrogant, haughty, presumptuous; informal pushy, high and mighty.

impermanent ▶ adjective *the methods they're proposing for reforestation are risky and impermanent* **temporary,** transient, transitory, passing, fleeting, momentary, ephemeral, fugitive; short-lived, brief, here today and gone tomorrow; literary evanescent.

impersonal ▶ adjective **1** *an impersonal judgment* **neutral,** unbiased, nonpartisan, unprejudiced, objective, detached, disinterested, dispassionate, without favoritism.
ANTONYMS biased.
2 *their impersonal relationships extended even to their own wives and children* **aloof,** distant, remote, reserved, withdrawn, unemotional, unsentimental, dispassionate, cold, cool, indifferent, unconcerned; formal, stiff, businesslike; informal starchy, standoffish, wooden.
ANTONYMS emotional, warm.

impersonate ▶ verb *impersonating the boss during a meeting was not your smartest move* **imitate,** mimic, do an impression of, ape, copy, parrot; parody, caricature, burlesque, travesty, satirize, lampoon; masquerade as, pose as, pass oneself off as; informal take off, send up, make like; formal personate. See note at IMITATE.

impersonation ▶ noun *the president seemed genuinely amused by the impersonations of the first family* **impression,** imitation; parody, caricature, burlesque, travesty, lampoon, pastiche; informal takeoff, send-up; formal personation.

impertinence ▶ noun *I'll refrain from answering with the impertinence your question deserves* **rudeness,** insolence, impoliteness, bad manners, discourtesy, disrespect, incivility; impudence, cheek, cheekiness, audacity, presumption, temerity, effrontery, nerve, gall, boldness, cockiness, brazenness; informal brass, sauce, sass, sassiness, chutzpah, lip, back-talk, guff; archaic assumption.

impertinent ▶ adjective *impertinent remarks* **rude,** insolent, impolite, ill-mannered, bad-mannered, uncivil, discourteous, disrespectful; impudent, cheeky, audacious, bold, brazen, brash, presumptuous, forward; tactless, undiplomatic; informal saucy, pert, sassy, smart-alecky.
ANTONYMS polite.

CHOOSE THE RIGHT WORD

impertinent, impudent, insolent, intrusive, meddlesome, obtrusive

All of these adjectives mean exceeding the bounds of propriety; the easiest way to distinguish **impertinent** from the others is to think of its root: *impertinent* behavior is not pertinent—in other words, it is inappropriate or or out of place. The *impertinent* individual has a tendency to be rude or presumptuous toward those who are entitled to deference or respect (*it was an impertinent question to ask a woman who had just lost her husband*). The **intrusive** person is unduly curious about other people's affairs (*her constant questions about the state of their marriage were intrusive and unwelcome*), while **obtrusive** implies objectionable actions rather than an objectionable disposition. The *obtrusive* person has a tendency to thrust himself or herself into a position where he or she is conspicuous and apt to do more harm than good (*they tried to keep him out of the meeting because his presence would be obtrusive*). To be **meddlesome** is to have a prying or inquisitive nature and a tendency to interfere in an annoying way in other people's affairs (*a meddlesome neighbor*). **Impudent** and **insolent** are much stronger words for inappropriate behavior. Young people are often accused of being *impudent*, which means to be *impertinent* in a bold and shameless way (*an impudent young man who had a lot to learn about tact*). Anyone who is guilty of insulting and contemptuously arrogant behavior might be called *insolent* (*he was so insolent to the arresting officer that he was handcuffed*).

imperturbable ▶ adjective *the guide dogs are trained to be imperturbable* **self-possessed,** composed, calm, cool, and collected, coolheaded, self-controlled, serene, relaxed, unexcitable, even-tempered, placid, phlegmatic; unperturbed, unflustered, unruffled; informal unflappable, unfazed, nonplussed, laid-back; rare equanimous.
ANTONYMS excitable, edgy.

impervious ▶ adjective **1** *he seemed **impervious to** the chill wind* **unaffected by,** untouched by, immune to, invulnerable to, insusceptible to, resistant to, indifferent to, heedless of, insensible to, unconscious of, oblivious to; proof against.
2 *an impervious rain jacket* **impermeable,** impenetrable, impregnable, waterproof, watertight, water-resistant, repellent; (hermetically) sealed, zip-locked.
ANTONYMS permeable.

impetuous ▶ adjective **1** *an impetuous decision* **impulsive,** rash, hasty, overhasty, reckless, heedless, careless, foolhardy, bullheaded, headstrong, incautious, imprudent, injudicious, ill-considered, unthought-out; spontaneous, impromptu, spur-of-the-moment, precipitate, precipitous, hurried, rushed; informal devil-may-care, harum-scarum, hotheaded. See note at **TEMERITY.**
ANTONYMS considered, cautious.
2 *an impetuous flow of water* **torrential,** powerful, forceful, vigorous, violent, raging, relentless, uncontrolled; rapid, fast, fast-flowing, swift.
ANTONYMS sluggish.

impetus ▶ noun **1** *the flywheel lost all its impetus* **momentum,** propulsion, impulsion, motive force, driving force, drive, thrust; energy, force, power, push, strength.
2 *the sales force were given fresh impetus* **motivation,** stimulus, incitement, incentive, inducement, inspiration, encouragement, boost, fillip, springboard; informal a shot in the arm.

impiety ▶ noun **1** *a world of impiety and immorality* **godlessness,** ungodliness, unholiness, irreligion, irreverence, sinfulness, sin, vice, transgression, wrongdoing, immorality, unrighteousness, blasphemy, sacrilege; apostasy, atheism, agnosticism, paganism, heathenism, nonbelief, unbelief.
ANTONYMS holiness.
2 *not even motherhood was immune to impiety* **irreverence,** disrespect, impertinence, insolence, mockery, derision.
ANTONYMS reverence.

impinge ▶ verb **1** *these issues **impinge on** all of us* **affect,** have an effect on, touch, have a bearing on, influence, have/make an impact on, leave a mark on.
2 *the proposed highway would **impinge on** parkland* **encroach on,** intrude on, infringe (on), invade, trespass on, obtrude, cut through, interfere with; violate; informal horn in on.

impious ▶ adjective *the impious magistrate of the Sung dynasty* **godless,** ungodly, unholy, irreligious, sinful, wicked, immoral, unrighteous, sacrilegious, heretical, profane, blasphemous, irreverent; apostate, atheistic, agnostic, pagan, heathen, faithless, nonbelieving, unbelieving; rare nullifidian.

impish ▶ adjective **1** *he takes an impish delight in shocking the press* **mischievous,** naughty, wicked, devilish, rascally, roguish, playful, sportive; mischief-making, full of mischief.
2 *an impish grin* **elfin,** elflike, pixieish, puckish; mischievous, roguish, sly.

implacable ▶ adjective *the computer hacker has become the new implacable foe* **unappeasable,** unforgiving, unsparing; inexorable, intransigent, inflexible, unyielding, unbending, uncompromising, unrelenting, relentless, ruthless, remorseless, merciless, heartless, pitiless, cruel, hard, harsh, stern, tough, iron-fisted.

implant ▶ verb **1** *the microchip is implanted under the skin* **insert,** embed, bury, lodge, place; graft.
2 *he implanted the idea in my mind* **instill,** inculcate, insinuate, introduce, inject, plant, sow, root, lodge.
▶ noun *a silicone implant* **transplant,** graft, implantation, insert.

implausible ▶ adjective *a swift conclusion to the negotiations is implausible | another one of his implausible excuses* **unlikely,** improbable, questionable, doubtful, debatable; unrealistic, unconvincing, far-fetched, incredible, unbelievable, unimaginable, inconceivable, fantastic, fanciful, ridiculous, absurd, preposterous, outrageous; informal hard to swallow, cock and bull.
ANTONYMS convincing.

implement ▶ noun *garden implements* **tool,** utensil, instrument, device, apparatus, gadget, contraption, appliance, machine, contrivance; informal gizmo; (**implements**) equipment, kit,

tackle, accoutrements, paraphernalia. See note at TOOL.
▶ verb *the cost of implementing the new law* **execute,** apply, put into effect, put into action, put into practice, carry out/through, perform, enact; fulfill, discharge, accomplish, bring about, achieve, realize, actualize, phase in; formal effectuate.

implicate ▶ verb **1** *he had been implicated in a financial scandal* **incriminate,** compromise; involve, connect, link, embroil, enmesh, ensnare, entangle; archaic inculpate; informal finger.
2 *viruses are **implicated in** the development of cancer* **involve in,** concern with, associate with, connect to/with.

implication ▶ noun **1** *he was smarting at their implication* **suggestion,** insinuation, innuendo, hint, intimation, imputation.
2 *important political implications* **consequence,** result, ramification, repercussion, reverberation, effect, significance.
3 *his implication in the murder case* **incrimination,** involvement, connection, entanglement, association; dated inculpation.

implicit ▶ adjective **1** *implicit assumptions* **implied,** hinted at, suggested, insinuated; unspoken, unexpressed, undeclared, unstated, tacit, unacknowledged, taken for granted; inherent, latent, underlying, inbuilt, incorporated; understood, inferred, deducible.
ANTONYMS explicit.
2 *an implicit trust in human nature* **absolute,** complete, total, wholehearted, perfect, utter; unqualified, unconditional, categorical; unshakable, unquestioning, firm, steadfast.
ANTONYMS limited.

implicitly ▶ adverb *a man in whom they implicitly believed* **completely,** absolutely, totally, wholeheartedly, utterly, unconditionally, unreservedly, without reservation.

implied ▶ adjective See IMPLICIT.

implore ▶ verb *his mother implored him to continue studying* **plead with,** beg, entreat, beseech, appeal to, ask, request, call on; exhort, urge, enjoin, press, push, petition, bid, importune; supplicate. See note at BEG.

imply ▶ verb **1** *are you implying he is mad?* **insinuate,** suggest, hint (at), intimate, say indirectly, indicate, give someone to understand, convey the impression, signal. See note at INFER.
2 *the forecasted traffic increase implies more roads* **involve,** entail; mean, point to, signify, indicate, signal, connote, denote; necessitate, require, presuppose.

impolite ▶ adjective *Devon was consistently impolite, always interrupting and making the most doltish remarks* **rude,** bad-mannered, ill-mannered, discourteous, uncivil, disrespectful, inconsiderate, boorish, churlish, ill-bred, ungentlemanly, unladylike, ungracious; insolent, impudent, impertinent, cheeky; loutish, rough, crude, vulgar, indelicate, indecorous, tactless, gauche, uncouth; informal ignorant, lippy, saucy; archaic contumelious.
ANTONYMS polite, well-mannered.

impolitic ▶ adjective *it was impolitic of you to alienate the very people who could finance our program* **imprudent,** unwise, injudicious, incautious, irresponsible; ill-judged, ill-advised, misguided, rash, reckless, foolhardy, foolish, shortsighted; undiplomatic, tactless, thoughtless.
ANTONYMS prudent, wise.

import ▶ verb **1** *Greenland imports just about everything that is consumed* **buy from abroad,** bring in, ship in.
ANTONYMS export.
2 *practices imported from the business world* **derive,** obtain, take, extract, glean; informal steal, crib, filch.
▶ noun **1** *a tax on **imports*** **imported goods,** foreign goods, imported merchandise, foreign merchandise, imported commodities, foreign commodities.
2 *the import of foreign books* **importation,** importing, introduction, bringing in, bringing from abroad, shipping in.
3 *a matter of great import* **importance,** significance, consequence, momentousness, magnitude, substance, weight, note, gravity, seriousness; formal moment.
ANTONYMS insignificance.
4 *the full import of her words* **meaning,** sense, essence, gist, drift, purport, connotation, message, thrust, point, substance, implication.

importance ▶ noun **1** *the signing of the treaty was an event of immense importance* **significance,** momentousness, import, consequence, note, noteworthiness, substance; seriousness, gravity, weightiness, urgency.
2 *she had a fine sense of her own importance* **power,** influence, authority, sway, weight, impact, dominance; prominence, eminence, preeminence, prestige, notability, worth, stature; informal clout, pull.

important ▶ adjective **1** *an important meeting* **significant,** consequential, momentous, of great import, major; critical, crucial, vital, pivotal, decisive, urgent, historic; serious, grave, weighty, material, impactful; formal of great moment.
ANTONYMS trivial.
2 *the important thing is that you do well in your exams* **main,** chief, principal, key, major, salient, prime, foremost, paramount, overriding, crucial, vital, critical, essential, significant; central, fundamental; informal number-one.
ANTONYMS inessential.
3 *the school was important to the community* **of value,** valuable, (highly) prized, beneficial, necessary, essential, indispensable, vital; of concern, of interest, relevant, pertinent.
ANTONYMS irrelevant, of no concern.
4 *he was an important man* **powerful,** influential, of influence, well-connected, high-ranking, high-powered; prominent, eminent, preeminent, notable, noteworthy, of note; distinguished, esteemed, respected, prestigious, celebrated, famous, great; informal affluential, major league.
ANTONYMS insignificant.

importune ▶ verb *he importuned her for some spare change* **beg,** beseech, entreat, implore, plead with, appeal to, call on, lobby; harass, pester, press, badger, bother, nag, harry; informal hassle, bug. See note at **BEG**.

impose ▶ verb **1** *he imposed his ideas on the art director* **foist,** force, inflict, press, urge; informal saddle someone with, land someone with.
2 *new taxes will be imposed* **levy,** charge, apply, enforce; set, establish, institute, introduce, bring into effect.
3 *it was never my intention to* ***impose on*** *you* **take advantage of,** exploit, take liberties with, treat unfairly; bother, trouble, disturb, inconvenience, put out, put to trouble, be a burden on; informal walk all over.

imposing ▶ adjective *an imposing mansion* **impressive,** striking, arresting, eye-catching, impactful, dramatic, spectacular, stunning, awesome, awe-inspiring, formidable, splendid, grand, grandiose, majestic, stately, august.
ANTONYMS modest.

imposition ▶ noun **1** *the imposition of an alien culture* **imposing,** foisting, forcing, inflicting.
2 *the imposition of tax on consumables* **levying,** charging, application, applying, enforcement, enforcing, enjoining; setting, establishment, introduction, institution.
3 *it would be no imposition* **burden,** encumbrance, strain, bother, worry; informal hassle, drag.

impossible ▶ adjective **1** *gale-force winds made fishing impossible* **not possible,** out of the question, unfeasible, impractical, impracticable, nonviable, unworkable; unthinkable, unimaginable, inconceivable, absurd.
ANTONYMS easy.
2 *an impossible dream* **unattainable,** unachievable, unobtainable, unwinnable, hopeless, impractical, implausible, far-fetched, outrageous, preposterous, ridiculous, absurd, impracticable, unworkable, futile.
ANTONYMS attainable.
3 informal *an impossible customer* **unreasonable,** objectionable, difficult, awkward; intolerable, unbearable, unendurable; exasperating, maddening, infuriating, irritating; informal high maintenance.
ANTONYMS bearable.

imposture ▶ noun *Barton's imposture was recognized as such only after he had fled town* **misrepresentation,** pretense, deceit, deception, trickery, artifice, subterfuge, feint; hoax, trick, ruse, dodge; informal con, scam, flimflam.

impotent ▶ adjective **1** *the legal sanctions are impotent* **powerless,** ineffective, ineffectual, inadequate, weak, feeble, useless, worthless, futile; literary impuissant.
ANTONYMS powerful, effective.
2 *natural forces that humans are impotent to control* **unable,** incapable, powerless, helpless.
ANTONYMS able.

impound ▶ verb **1** *officials began impounding documents* **confiscate,** take possession of, seize, commandeer, expropriate, requisition, sequester, sequestrate; Law distrain.
2 *the cattle were impounded* **pen in,** shut up/in, fence in, enclose, cage, confine, corral.
3 *criminals impounded in prison* **lock up,** incarcerate, imprison, confine, intern, immure, hold captive, hold prisoner.

impoverished ▶ adjective **1** *an impoverished peasant farmer* **poor,** poverty-stricken, penniless, destitute, indigent, impecunious, needy, beggared, beggarly, pauperized, down-and-out, bankrupt, ruined, insolvent; informal (flat) broke, hard up, dirt poor, on skid row; formal penurious.
ANTONYMS rich, wealthy.
2 *the soil is impoverished* **weakened,** exhausted, drained, sapped, depleted, spent; barren, unproductive, unfertile, unfruitful.
ANTONYMS rich, fertile.

impracticable ▶ adjective *a repeat autopsy would be impracticable* **unworkable,** unfeasible, nonviable, unachievable, unattainable, unrealizable; impractical, impossible.
ANTONYMS workable, feasible.

impractical ▶ adjective **1** *an impractical suggestion* **unrealistic,** unworkable, unfeasible, nonviable, impracticable; ill-thought-out, impossible, absurd, wild; informal cockeyed, crackpot, crazy.
ANTONYMS practical, sensible.
2 *impractical white ankle boots* **unsuitable,** not sensible, inappropriate, unserviceable.
ANTONYMS practical, sensible.
3 *an impractical scholar* **idealistic,** unrealistic, romantic, dreamy, fanciful, quixotic; informal ivory-tower, blue-sky, starry-eyed; chiefly Brit. informal airy-fairy.
ANTONYMS practical, down-to-earth.

imprecation ▶ noun See **CURSE** (sense 1 of the noun), **CURSE** (sense 4 of the noun).

imprecise ▶ adjective **1** *a rather imprecise definition* **vague,** loose, indefinite, inexplicit, indistinct, nonspecific, unspecific, sweeping, broad, general; hazy, fuzzy, woolly, sketchy, nebulous, ambiguous, equivocal, uncertain; informal loosey-goosey.
ANTONYMS narrow.
2 *an imprecise estimate* **inexact,** approximate, estimated, rough, ballpark.
ANTONYMS exact.

impregnable ▶ adjective **1** *the fortress is impregnable* **invulnerable,** impenetrable, unassailable, inviolable, secure, strong, well fortified, well defended; invincible, unconquerable, unbeatable, indestructible.
ANTONYMS vulnerable.
2 *he displayed a calm, impregnable certainty* **unassailable,** unbeatable, undefeatable, unshakable, invincible, unconquerable, invulnerable.
ANTONYMS shaky, vulnerable.

impregnate ▶ verb **1** *a pad impregnated with natural oils* **infuse,** soak, steep, saturate, drench; permeate, pervade, suffuse, imbue.
2 *the woman he had impregnated* **make/get pregnant,** inseminate, fertilize; informal get/put in the family way; vulgar slang knock up; informal dated get into trouble; archaic fecundate, get with child.

impresario ▶ noun *a theatrical impresario* **organizer,** (stage) manager, producer; promoter, publicist, showman; director, conductor, maestro.

impress ▶ verb **1** *Hazel had impressed him*

make an impression on, have an impact on, influence, affect, move, stir, rouse, excite, inspire; dazzle, awe, overawe, take someone's breath away, amaze, astonish; informal grab, blow someone away, stick in someone's mind.
ANTONYMS disappoint.
2 *goldsmiths impressed his likeness on medallions* **imprint,** print, stamp, mark, emboss, punch.
3 *you must **impress upon** her the need to save* **emphasize to,** stress to, bring home to, instill in, inculcate into, drum into.

impression ▸ **noun 1** *he got the impression that she was hiding something* **feeling,** feeling in one's bones, sense, fancy, (sneaking) suspicion, inkling, premonition, intuition, presentiment, hunch; notion, idea, funny feeling, gut feeling.
2 *a favorable impression* **opinion,** view, image, picture, perception, judgment, verdict, estimation. See note at **IDEA**.
3 *school made a profound impression on me* **impact,** effect, influence.
4 *the cap had left a circular impression* **indentation,** dent, mark, outline, imprint.
5 *he did a good impression of their science teacher* **impersonation,** imitation; parody, caricature, burlesque, travesty, lampoon; informal takeoff, send-up, spoof; formal personation.
6 *an artist's impression of the gardens* **representation,** portrayal, depiction, rendition, interpretation, picture, drawing.

impressionable ▸ **adjective** *his music has anxious parents concerned about what impressionable children may hear and think* **easily influenced,** suggestible, susceptible, persuadable, pliable, malleable, pliant, trusting, naive, innocent, wide-eyed, credulous, gullible.

impressive ▸ **adjective 1** *an impressive building* **magnificent,** majestic, imposing, splendid, spectacular, grand, awe-inspiring, striking, stunning, breathtaking, impactful; informal mind-blowing, jaw-dropping.
ANTONYMS ordinary.
2 *it was an impressive performance* **admirable,** masterly, accomplished, expert, skilled, skillful, consummate; excellent, outstanding, first-class, first-rate, fine, superb; informal awesome, great, mean, nifty, ace, crackerjack, bang-up.
ANTONYMS mediocre.

imprint ▸ **verb 1** *patterns can be imprinted in the clay* **stamp,** print, impress, mark, emboss, brand, inscribe, etch.
2 *the image was imprinted into his mind* **fix,** establish, stick, lodge, implant, plant, embed, instill, impress, inculcate.
▸ **noun 1** *her feet left imprints on the floor* **impression,** print, mark, indentation.
2 *colonialism has left its imprint* **impact,** lasting effect, influence, impression, mark, trace.

imprison ▸ **verb** *we expect to imprison another two dozen individuals by the end of this month alone* **incarcerate,** send to prison, jail, lock up, put away, intern, detain, hold prisoner, hold captive; confine, shut up, cage; informal put behind bars.
ANTONYMS free, release.

improbable ▸ **adjective 1** *it seemed improbable that the hot weather would continue* **unlikely,** doubtful, dubious, debatable, questionable, uncertain; unthinkable, inconceivable, unimaginable, incredible; informal iffy.
ANTONYMS certain.
2 *an improbable explanation* **unconvincing,** unbelievable, incredible, ridiculous, absurd, preposterous, outrageous; far-fetched, fantastic, fanciful.
ANTONYMS believable.

impromptu ▸ **adjective** *an impromptu lecture* **unrehearsed,** unprepared, unscripted, extempore, extemporized, extemporaneous, improvised, spontaneous, unplanned; informal off-the-cuff, offhand, spur-of-the-moment, ad-lib. See note at **SPONTANEOUS**.
ANTONYMS prepared, rehearsed.
▸ **adverb** *they played the song impromptu* **extempore,** spontaneously, extemporaneously, without preparation, without rehearsal; informal off the cuff, off the top of one's head, on the spur of the moment, ad lib.

improper ▸ **adjective 1** *it is improper for policemen to accept gifts* **inappropriate,** unacceptable, unsuitable, unprofessional, irregular; unethical, corrupt, immoral, dishonest, dishonorable.
ANTONYMS appropriate, acceptable.
2 *it was improper for young ladies to drive a young man home* **unseemly,** indecorous, unfitting, unbecoming, undignified, unladylike, ungentlemanly; indecent, immodest, immoral; scandalous, shocking, offensive.
ANTONYMS proper, fitting.
3 *improper limericks* **indecent,** risqué, off color, indelicate, naughty, suggestive, smutty, vulgar, crude, obscene; informal raunchy, steamy, blue, X-rated.
ANTONYMS decent.
4 *improper installation will affect performance* **incorrect,** wrong, inaccurate, erroneous, mistaken.
ANTONYMS correct.

impropriety ▸ **noun 1** *a suggestion of impropriety* **wrongdoing,** misconduct, dishonesty, corruption, unscrupulousness, unprofessionalism, irregularity; unseemliness, indecorousness, indelicacy, indecency, immorality.
2 *fiscal improprieties* **transgression,** misdemeanor, offense, misdeed, misconduct, crime; indiscretion, mistake, peccadillo, solecism; archaic trespass.

improve ▸ **verb 1** *ways to improve the service* **make better,** better, ameliorate, upgrade, update, refine, enhance, boost, build on, raise, polish, fix (up), amend; informal tweak; formal meliorate.
ANTONYMS worsen.
2 *communications improved during the eighteenth century* **get better,** advance, progress, develop; make headway, make progress, pick up, look up.
ANTONYMS deteriorate.
3 *the dose is not repeated if patient improves* **recover,** get better, recuperate, gain strength, rally, revive, get back on one's feet, get over something; be on the road to recovery, be on the mend; informal turn the corner, take a turn for the better, bounce back.

ANTONYMS deteriorate.
4 *resources are needed to improve the offer* **increase,** make larger, raise, augment, enhance, boost, supplement, top up; informal up, hike up, bump up, soup up, beef up.
ANTONYMS decrease, diminish.
– PHRASES **improve on** *how could anyone improve on his brilliant analysis?* **surpass,** better, do better than, outdo, exceed, beat, top, cap.

improvement ▶ noun *identifying the areas most in need of improvement | passengers will notice many new improvements* **advance,** development, upgrade, refinement, renovation, enhancement, advancement, upgrading, amelioration, betterment; boost, lift, rise, augmentation, raising, step up; rally, recovery, upswing, upturn.

improvident ▶ adjective *one consequence of a healthy economy may be a generation of improvident youth* **spendthrift,** thriftless, wasteful, prodigal, profligate, extravagant, lavish, free-spending, immoderate, excessive; imprudent, irresponsible, careless, reckless, heedless.
ANTONYMS thrifty, conservative.

improvise ▶ verb **1** *she was improvising in front of the cameras* **extemporize,** ad lib, speak impromptu; informal speak off the cuff, speak off the top of one's head, wing it; jam, scat.
2 *she improvised a playhouse for the kids* **contrive,** devise, throw together, cobble together, rig up; informal whip up, rustle up.

improvised ▶ adjective **1** *an improvised speech* **impromptu,** unrehearsed, unprepared, unscripted, extempore, extemporized, spontaneous, unplanned; informal off-the-cuff, ad-libbed, spur-of-the-moment. See note at SPONTANEOUS.
ANTONYMS prepared, rehearsed.
2 *an improvised shelter* **makeshift,** thrown together, cobbled together, rough and ready, crude, make-do, temporary, jerry-built, jury-rigged, slapdash.

imprudent ▶ adjective *a series of imprudent marriages* **unwise,** injudicious, incautious, indiscreet, misguided, ill-advised, ill-judged; thoughtless, unthinking, improvident, irresponsible, shortsighted, foolish; rash, reckless, heedless.
ANTONYMS sensible.

impudence ▶ noun *her irrepressible impudence landed her in the principal's office about a million times* **impertinence,** insolence, effrontery, audacity, cheek, cheekiness, cockiness, brazenness, brass, boldness; presumption, presumptuousness, disrespect, flippancy, bumptiousness, brashness; rudeness, impoliteness, ill manners, gall; informal chutzpah, nerve, sauce, sass, sassiness.

impudent ▶ adjective *the oblivious couple and their impudent children were asked to leave* **impertinent,** insolent, cheeky, cocky, brazen, bold, audacious; presumptuous, forward, disrespectful, insubordinate, bumptious, brash; rude, impolite, ill-mannered, discourteous, ill-bred; informal saucy, lippy, sassy, brassy, smart-alecky; archaic contumelious. See note at IMPERTINENT.
ANTONYMS polite.

impugn ▶ verb *are you impugning my judgment?* **call into question,** challenge, question, dispute, query, take issue with.

impulse ▶ noun **1** *she had an impulse to run and hide* **urge,** instinct, drive, compulsion, itch; whim, desire, fancy, notion, inclination, temptation.
2 *passions provide the main impulse of poetry* **inspiration,** stimulation, stimulus, incitement, motivation, encouragement, incentive, spur, catalyst, impetus, thrust.
3 *impulses from the spinal cord to the muscles* **pulse,** current, wave, signal.
– PHRASES **on (an) impulse** *I agreed to bungee-jump on an impulse | they claimed the robbery was not planned, that they did it on impulse* **impulsively,** spontaneously, on the spur of the moment, without forethought, without premeditation.

impulsive ▶ adjective **1** *he had an impulsive nature* **impetuous,** spontaneous, hasty, passionate, emotional, uninhibited; rash, reckless, careless, imprudent, foolhardy, unwise, madcap, devil-may-care, daredevil.
ANTONYMS cautious.
2 *an impulsive decision* **impromptu,** snap, spontaneous, unpremeditated, spur-of-the-moment, extemporaneous; impetuous, precipitate, hasty, rash; sudden, ill-considered, ill-thought-out, whimsical. See note at SPONTANEOUS.
ANTONYMS premeditated.

impunity ▶ noun *the lawsuit attempts to fight the impunity that these military officials have enjoyed for too long* **immunity,** indemnity, exemption (from punishment), freedom from liability, nonliability, license; amnesty, dispensation, reprieve, pardon, exoneration; stay of execution; privilege, favoritism, special treatment, carte blanche.
ANTONYMS liability.
– PHRASES **with impunity** *they boldly break laws at will, and do so with impunity* **without punishment,** with no ill consequences, scot-free, unpunished.

impure ▶ adjective **1** *impure gold* **adulterated,** mixed, combined, blended, alloyed; technical admixed.
ANTONYMS pure.
2 *the water was impure* **contaminated,** polluted, tainted, unwholesome, poisoned; dirty, filthy, foul, unclean, defiled; unhygienic, unsanitary; literary befouled.
ANTONYMS clean.
3 *impure thoughts* **immoral,** sinful, wrongful, wicked; unchaste, lustful, lecherous, lewd, lascivious, prurient, obscene, indecent, ribald, risqué, improper, crude, coarse, debased, degenerate; formal concupiscent.
ANTONYMS chaste.

impurity ▶ noun **1** *the impurity of the cast iron* **adulteration,** debasement, degradation, corruption; contamination, pollution.
2 *the impurities in beer* **contaminant,** pollutant, foreign body, foreign matter; dross, dirt, filth.
3 *sin and impurity* **immorality,** sin, sinfulness,

wickedness; unchastity, lustfulness, lechery, lecherousness, lewdness, lasciviousness, prurience, obscenity, dirtiness, crudeness, indecency, ribaldry, impropriety, vulgarity, depravity, coarseness; formal concupiscence.

impute ▶ verb *the worst of these mistakes have been unfairly* ***imputed to*** *him* **attribute to,** ascribe to, assign to, credit to; connect with, associate with.

in ▶ preposition **1** *she was hiding in the closet* **inside,** within, in the middle of; surrounded by, enclosed by.
2 *he was covered in mud* **with,** by.
3 *he put a candy in his mouth* **into,** inside.
4 *they met in 1921* **during,** in the course of, over.
5 *I'll see you in half an hour* **after,** at the end of, following; within, in less than, in under.
▶ adverb **1** *his mom walked in* **inside,** indoors, into the room, into the house/building.
2 *the tide's in* **high,** at its highest level, rising.
▶ adjective **1** *no one is in* **present,** (at) home; inside, indoors, in the house/room.
2 informal *sculpted beards are in* **fashionable,** in fashion, in vogue, popular, stylish, modern, modish, chic, à la mode, de rigueur, trendy, cool, all the rage, du jour, with it, the in thing, hip, hot.
ANTONYMS unfashionable, unpopular.
– PHRASES **in for** *we're probably in for some rain* **due for,** in line for; expecting, about to undergo/receive. **in for it** *when Dad gets home, you're gonna be in for it* **in trouble,** about to be punished; informal in hot/deep water. **in on** *we were never in on the whole story* **privy to,** aware of, acquainted with, informed about/of, apprised of; informal wise to, in the know about, hip to. **ins and outs** informal *no one expects you to learn all the ins and outs on your first day of work* **details,** particulars, facts, features, characteristics, nuts and bolts; informal nitty gritty. **in with** *her principal mission was to get in with as many senior executives as possible* **in favor with,** popular with, friendly with, friends with, on good terms with; liked by, admired by, accepted by.

inability ▶ noun *the state's inability to build a credible case against him* **lack of ability,** incapability, incapacity, powerlessness, impotence, helplessness; incompetence, ineptitude, unfitness, inefficacy.

inaccessible ▶ adjective **1** *inaccessible woodlands* **unreachable,** out of reach, unapproachable; cutoff, isolated, remote, insular, in the back of beyond, out of the way, lonely, solitary, godforsaken.
2 *the book was elitist and inaccessible* **incomprehensible,** impenetrable, inscrutable, baffling; obscure, esoteric, abstruse, recondite, arcane; elitist, exclusive, pretentious.
3 *the lecturer was inaccessible to students* **unapproachable,** aloof, distant, unfriendly, standoffish.

inaccuracy ▶ noun **1** *the inaccuracy of recent opinion polls* **incorrectness,** inexactness, imprecision, erroneousness, mistakenness, fallaciousness, faultiness.
ANTONYMS correctness.
2 *the article contained a number of inaccuracies* **error,** mistake, fallacy, slip, slip-up, oversight, fault, blunder, gaffe; erratum, solecism; informal howler, typo, blooper, goof.

inaccurate ▶ adjective *inaccurate reports* **inexact,** imprecise, incorrect, wrong, erroneous, careless, faulty, imperfect, flawed, defective, unsound, unreliable; fallacious, false, mistaken, untrue; informal wide of the mark.

inactive ▶ adjective **1** *I was terribly inactive over the holidays* **idle,** indolent, lazy, lifeless, slothful, lethargic, inert, sluggish, unenergetic, listless, torpid, sedentary.
2 *the computer is currently inactive* **inoperative,** nonfunctioning, idle; not working, out of service, unused, not in use; dormant.

inadequacy ▶ noun **1** *the inadequacy of available resources* **insufficiency,** deficiency, deficit, scarcity, sparseness, dearth, paucity, shortage, want, lack, undersupply; paltriness, meagerness.
ANTONYMS abundance, surplus.
2 *her feelings of personal inadequacy* **incompetence,** incapability, unfitness, ineffectiveness, inefficiency, inefficacy, inexpertness, ineptness, uselessness, impotence, powerlessness; inferiority, mediocrity.
ANTONYMS competence.
3 *the inadequacies of the present system* **shortcoming,** defect, fault, failing, weakness, weak point, limitation, flaw, imperfection.
ANTONYMS strength.

inadequate ▶ adjective **1** *inadequate water supplies* **insufficient,** deficient, poor, scant, scanty, scarce, sparse, in short supply; paltry, meager, niggardly, beggarly, limited; informal measly, pathetic; formal exiguous.
ANTONYMS sufficient.
2 *an inadequate typist* **incompetent,** incapable, unsatisfactory, unfit, unacceptable, ineffective, ineffectual, inefficient, unskillful, inexpert, inept, amateurish, substandard, poor, useless, inferior; informal not up to scratch, not up to snuff, no great shakes, lame, shabby.
ANTONYMS competent.

inadmissible ▶ adjective *inadmissible evidence* **unallowable,** not allowed, invalid, unacceptable, impermissible, disallowed, forbidden, prohibited, precluded.

inadvertent ▶ adjective *an inadvertent omission* **unintentional,** unintended, accidental, unpremeditated, unplanned, innocent, uncalculated, unconscious, unthinking, unwitting, involuntary; careless, negligent.
ANTONYMS deliberate.

inadvisable ▶ adjective *traveling to the village is inadvisable for the president at this time* **unwise,** ill-advised, imprudent, ill-judged, ill-considered, injudicious, impolitic, foolish, misguided; Medicine contraindicated.
ANTONYMS wise, shrewd.

inalienable ▶ adjective *the preservation of inalienable rights* **inviolable,** absolute, sacrosanct; untransferable, nontransferable, nonnegotiable; Law indefeasible.

inane ▶ adjective *another one of Craig's inane*

schemes **silly,** foolish, stupid, fatuous, idiotic, ridiculous, ludicrous, absurd, senseless, asinine, frivolous, vapid; childish, puerile; informal dumb, moronic, ditzy, daft.
ANTONYMS sensible.

inanimate ▶ adjective *in the dream sequence, several of the inanimate objects in his bedroom come to life* **lifeless,** insentient, without life, inorganic; dead, defunct.
ANTONYMS living.

inapplicable ▶ adjective *they argued that executive privilege was simply inapplicable in the face of the grand jury subpoena* **irrelevant,** immaterial, not germane, not pertinent, unrelated, unconnected, extraneous, beside the point; unsuitable, inapposite; formal impertinent.
ANTONYMS relevant.

inappropriate ▶ adjective *children's access to the Internet may expose them to inappropriate material* **unsuitable,** unfitting, unseemly, unbecoming, unbefitting, improper, impolite; incongruous, out of place/keeping, inapposite, inapt, infelicitous, ill-suited; ill-judged, ill-advised; informal out of order/line; formal malapropos.
ANTONYMS suitable.

inapt ▶ adjective See INAPPROPRIATE.

inarticulate ▶ adjective **1** *an inarticulate young man* **tongue-tied,** lost for words, unable to express oneself.
ANTONYMS silver-tongued.
2 *an inarticulate reply* **unintelligible,** incomprehensible, incoherent, unclear, indistinct, mumbled, muffled.
ANTONYMS fluent.
3 *inarticulate rage* **unspoken,** silent, unexpressed, wordless, speechless, unvoiced.
ANTONYMS vocal.

inattentive ▶ adjective **1** *an inattentive student* **distracted,** lacking concentration, preoccupied, absentminded, daydreaming, dreamy, abstracted, distrait; informal miles away, spaced out.
ANTONYMS alert.
2 *inattentive service* See NEGLIGENT.

inaudible ▶ adjective *inaudible voices* **unheard,** out of earshot; indistinct, imperceptible, faint, muted, soft, low, muffled, whispered, muttered, murmured, mumbled; silent, soundless, noiseless, hushed; ultrasonic.

inaugural ▶ adjective *the inaugural meeting of the Geographic Society* **opening,** first, launching, initial, introductory, initiatory, maiden.
ANTONYMS final.

inaugurate ▶ verb **1** *he inaugurated a new trade policy* **initiate,** begin, start, commence, institute, launch, start off, get going, get underway, set in motion, get off the ground, establish, found, lay the foundations of; bring in, usher in, introduce; informal kick off.
2 *the new president will be inaugurated in January* **admit to office,** install, instate, swear in; invest, ordain; crown, enthrone.
3 *the library was inaugurated on Jefferson's birthday* **open,** declare open, unveil; dedicate, consecrate.

inauspicious ▶ adjective *after an inauspicious start, the Giants ended the season in first place* **unpromising,** unpropitious, unfavorable, unfortunate, infelicitous, unlucky, ill-omened, ominous; discouraging, disheartening, bleak.
ANTONYMS promising.

inborn ▶ adjective *inborn allergic reactions* **innate,** congenital, connate, instinctive, inherent, natural, inbred, inherited, hereditary, in one's genes. See note at INHERENT.

incalculable ▶ adjective *artifacts of incalculable value | incalculable losses* **inestimable,** untold, indeterminable, immeasurable, incomputable; infinite, endless, limitless, boundless, measureless; enormous, immense, huge, vast, innumerable, countless.

incandescent ▶ adjective **1** *incandescent fragments of lava* **white-hot,** red-hot, burning, fiery, blazing, ablaze, aflame; glowing, aglow, radiant, bright, brilliant, luminous, sparkling; literary fervid, lucent; rare igneous.
2 *an incandescent speech* **passionate,** ardent, fervent, fervid, intense, impassioned, spirited, fiery.

incantation ▶ noun *I was more amused than entranced by the flickering candles and spooky incantations* **chant,** invocation, conjuration, magic spell/formula, charm, hex, enchantment, mojo; intonation, recitation.

incapable ▶ adjective **1** *the job should never have been assigned to an incapable crew* **incompetent,** inept, inadequate, lacking ability, not good enough, leaving much to be desired, inexpert, unskillful, ineffective, ineffectual, inefficacious, feeble, unfit, unqualified, unequal to the task; informal not up to it, not up to snuff, useless, hopeless.
ANTONYMS competent.
2 *he was judged to be mentally incapable* **incapacitated,** incompetent, helpless, powerless, impotent.
ANTONYMS competent.
3 *they are incapable of supporting themselves* **unable to (be),** not capable of, lacking the ability to (be), not equipped to (be), lacking the experience to (be).
ANTONYMS able.

incapacitated ▶ adjective *Ivan did not expect to be incapacitated for more than a few days* **disabled,** debilitated, indisposed, unfit, impaired; immobilized, paralyzed, out of action, out of commission, hors de combat; informal laid up.
ANTONYMS fit.

incapacity ▶ noun *the doctors were baffled by the severity of her physical incapacity* **disability,** incapability, inability, debility, impairment, indisposition; impotence, powerlessness, helplessness; incompetence, inadequacy, ineffectiveness.
ANTONYMS capability.

incarcerate ▶ verb *she returned to the site where she had been incarcerated nearly fifty years earlier* **imprison,** put in prison, send to prison, jail, lock up, put under lock and key, put away, intern, confine, detain, hold, immure, put in chains, hold prisoner, hold captive; informal put behind bars.

ANTONYMS release, set free.

incarceration ▶ noun *eight years of incarceration* **imprisonment,** internment, confinement, detention, custody, captivity, restraint; informal time; archaic durance, duress.

incarnate ▶ adjective *the chairman has been labeled "evil incarnate" by various conservationists* **in human form,** in the flesh, in physical form, in bodily form, made flesh; corporeal, physical, fleshly, embodied, personified.

incarnation ▶ noun 1 *the incarnation of artistic genius* **embodiment,** personification, exemplification, type, epitome; manifestation, bodily form, avatar.
2 *a previous incarnation* **lifetime,** life, existence.

incautious ▶ adjective *my uncle's history of incautious behavior is hardly a secret* **rash,** unwise, careless, heedless, thoughtless, reckless, unthinking, imprudent, misguided, ill-advised, ill-judged, injudicious, impolitic, unguarded, foolhardy, foolish.
ANTONYMS circumspect.

incendiary ▶ adjective 1 *an incendiary bomb* **combustible,** flammable, inflammable.
2 *an incendiary speech* **inflammatory,** rabble-rousing, provocative, seditious, subversive; contentious, controversial.
▶ noun *a political incendiary* **agitator,** demagogue, rabble-rouser, firebrand, troublemaker, agent provocateur, revolutionary, insurgent, subversive.

incense ▶ verb See **ENRAGE.**

incentive ▶ noun *only financial incentives will curb the polluting activities of major industries* **inducement,** motivation, motive, reason, stimulus, stimulant, spur, impetus, encouragement, impulse; incitement, goad, provocation; attraction, lure, bait; informal carrot, sweetener, come-on.
ANTONYMS deterrent.

inception ▶ noun *the airline plans to file for bankruptcy, seven years after its inception* **beginning,** commencement, start, birth, dawn, genesis, origin, outset; establishment, institution, foundation, founding, formation, initiation, setting up, origination, constitution, inauguration, opening, debut, day one; informal kickoff. See note at **ORIGIN.**
ANTONYMS end.

incessant ▶ adjective *their dog's incessant barking* **ceaseless,** unceasing, constant, continual, unabating, interminable, endless, unending, never-ending, everlasting, eternal, perpetual, continuous, nonstop, around/round-the-clock, uninterrupted, unbroken, unremitting, persistent, relentless, unrelenting, unrelieved, sustained.
ANTONYMS intermittent, occasional.

incidence ▶ noun *an increased incidence of heart disease* **occurrence,** prevalence; rate, frequency; amount, degree, extent.

incident ▶ noun 1 *incidents in his youth* **event,** occurrence, episode, experience, happening, occasion, proceeding, eventuality, affair, business; adventure, exploit, escapade; matter, circumstance, fact, development.
2 *police were investigating the incident* **disturbance,** fracas, melee, commotion, rumpus, scene; fight, skirmish, clash, brawl, free-for-all, encounter, conflict, ruckus, confrontation, altercation, contretemps; informal ruction.
3 *the journey was not without incident* **excitement,** adventure, drama; danger, peril.

incidental ▶ adjective 1 *incidental details* **less important,** secondary, subsidiary; minor, peripheral, background, nonessential, inessential, unimportant, insignificant, inconsequential, tangential, extrinsic, extraneous, superfluous.
ANTONYMS essential, crucial.
2 *an incidental discovery* **chance,** accidental, by chance, by accident, random; fortuitous, serendipitous, adventitious, coincidental, unlooked-for, unexpected, fluky. See note at **ACCIDENTAL.**
ANTONYMS deliberate.
3 *the risks* ***incidental to*** *the job* **connected with,** related to, associated with, accompanying, attending, attendant on, concomitant to/with.
ANTONYMS unrelated.

incidentally ▶ adverb 1 *incidentally, I haven't had a reply yet* **by the way,** by the by, by the bye, in passing, en passant, speaking of which; parenthetically; informal BTW, as it happens.
2 *the infection was discovered incidentally* **by chance,** by accident, accidentally, fortuitously, by a fluke, by happenstance; coincidentally, by coincidence.

incinerate ▶ verb *we would incinerate our household trash in a barrel in the backyard* **burn,** reduce to ashes, consume by fire, carbonize; cremate.

incipient ▶ adjective *the system detects incipient problems early* **developing,** growing, emerging, emergent, dawning, just beginning, inceptive, initial, inchoate; nascent, embryonic, fledgling, in its infancy, germinal.
ANTONYMS full-blown.

incision ▶ noun 1 *a surgical incision* **cut,** opening, slit.
2 *incisions on the marble* **notch,** carving, etching, engraving, inscription, score; nick, scratch, scarification.

incisive ▶ adjective *an incisive commentator* **penetrating,** acute, sharp, sharp-witted, razor-sharp, keen, astute, trenchant, shrewd, piercing, cutting, perceptive, insightful, percipient, perspicacious, discerning, analytical, clever, smart, quick; concise, succinct, pithy, to the point, brief, crisp, clear, effective; informal punchy, heads-up, on the ball; rare sapient.
ANTONYMS rambling, vague.

incite ▶ verb 1 *we're hoping that last night's incident will not incite altercations in the stadium today* **stir up,** whip up, encourage, fan the flames of, stoke up, fuel, kindle, ignite, inflame, stimulate, instigate, provoke, excite, arouse, awaken, inspire, engender, trigger, spark off, ferment, foment; literary enkindle.
ANTONYMS suppress.
2 *she incited him to commit murder* **egg on,** encourage, urge, goad, provoke, spur on, drive,

stimulate, push, prod, prompt, induce, impel; arouse, rouse, excite, inflame, sting, prick; informal put up to.
ANTONYMS discourage, deter.

CHOOSE THE RIGHT WORD

incite, arouse, exhort, foment, instigate, provoke

The best way to start a riot is to **incite** one, which means to urge or stimulate to action, either in a favorable or an unfavorable sense. If you **instigate** an action, however, it implies that you are responsible for initiating it and that the purpose is probably a negative or evil one (*the man who instigated the assassination plot*). **Foment** suggests agitation or incitement over an extended period of time (*foment a discussion; foment the rebellion that leads to war*). An instigator, in other words, is someone who initiates the idea, while a fomenter is someone who keeps it alive. You can **provoke** a riot in the same way that you instigate one, but the emphasis here is on spontaneity rather than on conscious design (*her statement provoked an outcry from animal rights activists*). To **arouse** is to awaken a feeling or elicit a response (*my presence in the junkyard aroused suspicion*), or to open people's eyes to a situation (*we attempted to arouse public awareness*). But once you've aroused people, you may have to **exhort** them, meaning to urge or persuade them, by appealing to their sympathy or conscience, to take constructive action.

incivility ▶ noun *several cadets were reprimanded for incivility* **rudeness,** discourtesy, impoliteness, bad manners, disrespect, boorishness, ungraciousness; insolence, impertinence, impudence.
ANTONYMS politeness.

inclement ▶ adjective *inclement weather* **cold,** chilly, bleak, wintry, freezing, snowy, icy; wet, rainy, drizzly, damp; stormy, blustery, wild, rough, squally, windy; unpleasant, bad, foul, nasty, brutal, severe, extreme, harsh.
ANTONYMS fine, sunny.

inclination ▶ noun **1** *his political inclination* **tendency,** propensity, proclivity, leaning, predisposition, disposition, predilection, desire, wish, impulse, bent, bias; liking, affection, penchant, partiality, preference, appetite, fancy, interest, affinity; stomach, taste; informal yen.
ANTONYMS aversion.
2 *an inclination of his head* **bowing,** bow, bending, nod, nodding, lowering.

incline ▶ verb **1** *his prejudice inclines him to overlook obvious facts* **predispose,** lead, make, make of a mind, dispose, prejudice, bias; prompt, induce, influence, sway; persuade, convince.
2 *I* ***incline to*** *the opposite view* **prefer,** favor, go for; tend to, lean to, swing to, veer to, gravitate to, be drawn to.
3 *he inclined his head* **bend,** bow, nod, bob, lower, dip.
▶ noun *a steep incline* **slope,** gradient, pitch, ramp, bank, ascent, rise, upslope, dip, descent, declivity, downslope; hill, grade, downgrade.

include ▶ verb **1** *activities include sports and drama* **incorporate,** comprise, encompass, cover, embrace, involve, take in, number, contain; consist of, be made up of, be composed of; formal comprehend.
ANTONYMS exclude.
2 *don't forget to include the cost of repairs* **allow for,** count, take into account, take into consideration.
ANTONYMS omit, leave out.

CHOOSE THE RIGHT WORD

include, comprise

Include has a broader meaning than **comprise**. In the sentence *the accommodations comprise two bedrooms, bathroom, kitchen, and living room*, the word **comprise** implies that there are no accommodations other than those listed. **Include** can be used in this way too, but it is also used in a nonrestrictive way, implying that there may be other things not specifically mentioned that are part of the same category, as in *the price includes a special welcome pack*. Careful writers will avoid superfluous uses of "including . . . and more," commonly found in advertising. The 'and more' is superfluous because **including** or **includes** implies that there is more than what is listed.

inclusive ▶ adjective *an inclusive travel package* **all-inclusive,** with everything included, comprehensive, in toto; overall, full, all-around, umbrella, blanket, across-the-board, catch-all, all-encompassing.

incognito ▶ adverb & adjective *you'll be traveling incognito* **under an assumed name,** under a false name, in disguise, disguised, under cover, in plain clothes, camouflaged, unidentified; secretly, anonymously.

incoherent ▶ adjective **1** *a long, incoherent speech* **unclear,** confused, unintelligible, incomprehensible, hard to follow, disjointed, disconnected, disordered, mixed up, garbled, jumbled, scrambled, muddled; rambling, wandering, disorganized, illogical; inarticulate, mumbling, slurred.
ANTONYMS intelligible.
2 *she was incoherent and shivering* **delirious,** raving, babbling, hysterical, irrational.
ANTONYMS lucid.

income ▶ noun *annual income* **earnings,** salary, pay, remuneration, wages, stipend; revenue, receipts, takings, profits, gains, proceeds, turnover, yield, dividend, means, take; formal emolument.
ANTONYMS expenditure.

incoming ▶ adjective **1** *the incoming train* **arriving,** entering; approaching, coming (in), inbound.
ANTONYMS outgoing.

2 *the incoming president* **newly elected,** newly appointed, succeeding, new, next, future; elect, to-be, designate.
ANTONYMS outgoing.

incomparable ▶ adjective *the incomparable Maggie Smith is once again the deputy headmistress of Hogwarts* **without equal,** beyond compare, unparalleled, matchless, peerless, unmatched, without parallel, beyond comparison, second to none, in a class of its/one's own, unequaled, unrivaled, inimitable, nonpareil, par excellence; transcendent, superlative, surpassing, unsurpassed, unsurpassable, supreme, top, best, outstanding, consummate, singular, unique, rare, perfect; informal one-in-a-million; formal unexampled.
ANTONYMS ordinary, commonplace.

incompatible ▶ adjective **1** *she and her husband are totally incompatible* **unsuited,** mismatched, ill-matched; worlds apart, poles apart, like night and day.
ANTONYMS well-matched, suited.
2 *incompatible economic objectives* **irreconcilable,** conflicting, opposed, opposing, opposite, contradictory, antagonistic, antipathetic; clashing, inharmonious, discordant; mutually exclusive; poles apart, worlds apart, night and day.
ANTONYMS compatible, complementary.
3 *his theory was **incompatible with** that of his predecessor* **inconsistent with,** at odds with, out of keeping with, at variance with, inconsonant with, different to, divergent from, contrary to, in conflict with, in opposition to, antithetical to, (diametrically) opposed to, counter to, irreconcilable with.
ANTONYMS consistent.

incompetent ▶ adjective *not only are the staff overpaid, they're incompetent* **inept,** unskillful, unskilled, inexpert, amateurish, unprofessional, bungling, blundering, clumsy, inadequate, substandard, inferior, ineffective, deficient, inefficient, ineffectual, wanting, lacking, leaving much to be desired; incapable, unfit, unqualified; informal useless, pathetic, ham-fisted, not up to it, not up to scratch, bush league.

incomplete ▶ adjective **1** *the project is still incomplete* **unfinished,** uncompleted, partial, half-finished, half-done, half-completed.
2 *inaccurate or incomplete information* **deficient,** insufficient, imperfect, defective, partial, patchy, sketchy, fragmentary, fragmented.

incomprehensible ▶ adjective *the patient's muttering was incomprehensible | the judge ruled that the original contract was too incomprehensible to be binding* **unintelligible,** impossible to understand, impenetrable, unclear, indecipherable, inscrutable, beyond one's comprehension, beyond one, beyond one's grasp, complicated, complex, involved, baffling, bewildering, mystifying, unfathomable, puzzling, cryptic, confusing, perplexing; abstruse, esoteric, recondite, arcane, mysterious, Delphic; informal over one's head, all Greek.
ANTONYMS intelligible, clear.

inconceivable ▶ adjective *even his oldest rivals thought the charges of treason against him were inconceivable* **unbelievable,** beyond belief, incredible, unthinkable, unimaginable, extremely unlikely; impossible, beyond the bounds of possibility, out of the question, preposterous, ridiculous, ludicrous, absurd, incomprehensible; informal hard to swallow.
ANTONYMS likely.

inconclusive ▶ adjective *the defendant was confident that the evidence would be inconclusive* **indecisive,** proving nothing; indefinite, indeterminate, unresolved, unproved, unsettled, still open to question/doubt, debatable, unconfirmed; moot; vague, ambiguous; informal up in the air, left hanging.

incongruous ▶ adjective **1** *the women visiting the mission looked incongruous in their smart hats and fur coats* **out of place,** out of keeping, inappropriate, unsuitable, unsuited; wrong, strange, odd, curious, queer, absurd, bizarre.
ANTONYMS appropriate.
2 *an incongruous collection of objects* **ill-matched,** ill-assorted, mismatched, unharmonious, discordant, dissonant, conflicting, clashing, jarring, incompatible, different, dissimilar, contrasting, disparate.
ANTONYMS harmonious.

inconsequential ▶ adjective *their efforts to save the Bixner Building were ultimately inconsequential* **insignificant,** unimportant, of little/no consequence, neither here nor there, incidental, inessential, nonessential, immaterial, irrelevant; negligible, inappreciable, inconsiderable, slight, minor, trivial, trifling, petty, paltry, measly; informal piddling, piffling.
ANTONYMS significant, important, of great consequence.

inconsiderate ▶ adjective *she reproached her son for being routinely inconsiderate to his wife* **thoughtless,** unthinking, insensitive, selfish, self-centered, unsympathetic, uncaring, heedless, unmindful, unkind, uncharitable, ungracious, impolite, discourteous, rude, disrespectful; tactless, undiplomatic, indiscreet, indelicate.
ANTONYMS thoughtful.

inconsistent ▶ adjective **1** *his inconsistent behavior* **erratic,** changeable, unpredictable, variable, varying, changing, inconstant, unstable, irregular, fluctuating, unsteady, unsettled, uneven; self-contradictory, contradictory, paradoxical; capricious, fickle, flighty, whimsical, unreliable, mercurial, volatile, blowing hot and cold, ever-changing, chameleonlike; technical labile.
2 *he had done nothing **inconsistent with** his morality* **incompatible with,** conflicting with, in conflict with, at odds with, at variance with, differing from, contrary to, in opposition to, (diametrically) opposed to, irreconcilable with, out of keeping with, out of step with; antithetical to.

inconsolable ▶ adjective *those left homeless by the fire were inconsolable* **heartbroken,** broken-hearted, grief-stricken, beside oneself with grief, devastated, wretched, sick at heart, desolate, despairing, distraught, comfortless; miserable, unhappy, sad; literary heartsick.

inconspicuous ▶ adjective *the flaw in the carpeting is inconspicuous | wearing inconspicuous street clothes, he escaped through the crowd* **unobtrusive,** unnoticeable, unremarkable, unspectacular, unostentatious, undistinguished, unexceptional, modest, unassuming, discreet, hidden, concealed; unseen, in the background, low-profile.
ANTONYMS noticeable.

inconstant ▶ adjective *an inconstant friend* **fickle,** faithless, unfaithful, false, wayward, unreliable, untrustworthy, capricious, volatile, flighty, unpredictable, erratic, blowing hot and cold; changeable, mutable, mercurial, variable, irregular; informal cheating, two-timing.
ANTONYMS faithful.

incontestable ▶ adjective See INCONTROVERTIBLE.

incontinent ▶ adjective *incontinent hysteria* **unrestrained,** lacking self-restraint, uncontrolled, unbridled, unchecked, unfettered; uncontrollable, ungovernable.
ANTONYMS restrained.

incontrovertible ▶ adjective *he realizes that his forensic findings are not incontrovertible* **indisputable,** incontestable, undeniable, irrefutable, unassailable, beyond dispute, unquestionable, beyond question, indubitable, beyond doubt, unarguable, undebatable; certain, sure, definite, definitive, proven, decisive, conclusive, demonstrable, emphatic, categorical, airtight, watertight.
ANTONYMS questionable.

inconvenience ▶ noun **1** *we apologize for any inconvenience caused by the delay* **trouble,** bother, problems, disruption, difficulty, disturbance; vexation, irritation, annoyance; informal aggravation, hassle.
2 *his early arrival was clearly an inconvenience* **nuisance,** trouble, bother, problem, vexation, worry, trial, bind, bane, irritant, thorn in someone's side; informal headache, pain, pain in the neck, pain in the butt, drag, aggravation, hassle.
▶ verb *I don't want to inconvenience you* **trouble,** bother, put out, put to any trouble, disturb, impose on, burden, incommode; informal hassle, plague; formal discommode.

inconvenient ▶ adjective *symptoms can range from merely inconvenient to downright life-changing* **awkward,** difficult, inopportune, untimely, ill-timed, unsuitable, inappropriate, unfortunate; tiresome, troublesome, irritating, annoying, vexing, bothersome; informal aggravating.

incorporate ▶ verb **1** *the region was incorporated into Moldavian territory* **absorb,** include, subsume, assimilate, integrate, take in, swallow up.
2 *the model incorporates some advanced features* **include,** contain, comprise, embody, embrace, build in, encompass.
3 *literary references were incorporated with photographs* **blend,** mix, mingle, meld; combine, unite, join.

incorrect ▶ adjective **1** *an incorrect answer* **wrong,** erroneous, in error, mistaken, inaccurate, imprecise, wide of the mark, off target; untrue, false, fallacious; informal out, way out.
2 *incorrect behavior* **inappropriate,** wrong, unsuitable, inapt, inapposite; ill-advised, ill-considered, ill-judged, injudicious, unacceptable, unfitting, out of keeping, improper, unseemly, unbecoming, indecorous; informal out of line, out of order.

incorrigible ▶ adjective *an incorrigible flirt* **inveterate,** habitual, confirmed, hardened, dyed-in-the-wool, incurable, chronic, irredeemable, hopeless, beyond hope; impenitent, unrepentant, unapologetic, unashamed; bad, naughty, terrible.
ANTONYMS repentant.

incorruptible ▶ adjective **1** *an incorruptible man* **honest,** honorable, trustworthy, principled, high-principled, unbribable, moral, ethical, good, virtuous.
ANTONYMS venal.
2 *an incorruptible substance* **imperishable,** indestructible, indissoluble, enduring, everlasting.
ANTONYMS perishable.

increase ▶ verb **1** *demand is likely to increase* **grow,** get bigger, get larger, enlarge, expand, swell; rise, climb, escalate, soar, surge, rocket, shoot up, spiral; intensify, strengthen, extend, heighten, stretch, spread, widen; multiply, snowball, mushroom, proliferate, balloon, build up, mount up, pile up, accrue, accumulate; literary wax.
ANTONYMS decrease.
2 *higher expectations will increase user demand* **add to,** make larger, make bigger, augment, supplement, top up, build up, extend, raise, swell, inflate; magnify, maximize, intensify, strengthen, heighten, amplify; informal up, jack up, hike up, bump up, torque up, crank up.
ANTONYMS reduce.
▶ noun *the increase in size | an increase in demand* **growth,** rise, enlargement, expansion, extension, multiplication, elevation, inflation; increment, addition, augmentation; magnification, intensification, amplification, climb, escalation, surge, upsurge, upswing, spiral, spurt; informal hike.
ANTONYMS decrease, reduction.

increasingly ▶ adverb *the regime became increasingly draconian* **more and more,** progressively, to an increasing extent, ever more.

incredible ▶ adjective **1** *I find his story incredible* **unbelievable,** beyond belief, hard to believe, unconvincing, far-fetched, implausible, improbable, highly unlikely, dubious, doubtful; inconceivable, unthinkable, unimaginable, impossible; informal hard to swallow, cock-and-bull.
2 *an incredible feat of engineering* **magnificent,** wonderful, marvelous, spectacular, remarkable, phenomenal, prodigious, breathtaking, extraordinary, unbelievable, amazing, stunning, astounding, astonishing, awe-inspiring, staggering, formidable, impressive, supreme, great, awesome, superhuman; informal fantastic,

terrific, tremendous, stupendous, mind-boggling, mind-blowing, jaw-dropping, out of this world, far-out; literary wondrous.

incredulous ▸ adjective *we were incredulous when the congressman was not more forthcoming in his first broadcast interview about the case* **disbelieving,** skeptical, unbelieving, distrustful, mistrustful, suspicious, doubtful, dubious, unconvinced; cynical.

increment ▸ noun *the three-percent increment is unlikely to make much difference to the price* **increase,** addition, supplement, gain, augmentation, accretion, addendum; enlargement, enhancement, boost; informal hike.
ANTONYMS reduction.

incriminate ▸ verb *no witnesses to last night's shooting have incriminated this man* **implicate,** involve, enmesh; blame, accuse, denounce, inform against, point the finger at; entrap; informal frame, set up, stick/pin the blame on, rat on; archaic inculpate.

inculcate ▸ verb *the beliefs inculcated in him by his father* **instill in,** implant in, fix in, impress in, imprint in; hammer into, drum into, drive into, drill into.

incumbent ▸ adjective **1** *it is* ***incumbent on*** *you to tell them* **necessary for one to,** essential that, required that, imperative that; compulsory for one to, binding on one to, mandatory that.
2 *the incumbent president* **current,** present, in office, in power; reigning.
▸ noun *the first incumbent of the post* **holder,** bearer, occupant.

incur ▸ verb *it is astonishing how many expenses they incurred in just one evening | these actions are likely to incur the coach's wrath* **bring upon oneself,** expose oneself to, lay oneself open to; run up; attract, invite, earn, arouse, cause, give rise to, be liable/subject to, meet with, sustain, experience, contract.

incurable ▸ adjective **1** *an incurable illness* **untreatable,** inoperable, irremediable; terminal, fatal, mortal; chronic.
2 *an incurable romantic* **inveterate,** dyed-in-the-wool, confirmed, established, long-established, long-standing, absolute, complete, utter, thorough, out-and-out, through and through; unashamed, unapologetic, unrepentant, incorrigible, hopeless.

incursion ▸ noun *an enemy* ***incursion into*** *our camp left nine dead* **attack on,** assault on, raid on, invasion of, storming of, overrunning of, foray into, blitz on, sortie into, sally into/against, advance on/into, push into, thrust into, infiltration of.
ANTONYMS retreat.

indebted ▸ adjective *nations we assumed would be indebted to us have turned a blind eye* **beholden,** under an obligation, obliged, obligated, grateful, thankful, in debt, owing a debt of gratitude.

indecent ▸ adjective **1** *indecent photographs* **obscene,** dirty, filthy, rude, coarse, naughty, vulgar, gross, crude, lewd, salacious, improper, smutty, off-color; pornographic, offensive, prurient, sordid, scatological; ribald, risqué, racy; informal porn, porno, X-rated, XXX, raunchy, blue; euphemistic adult.
2 *they left the dinner table with indecent haste* **unseemly,** improper, indecorous, unceremonious, indelicate, unbecoming, ungentlemanly, unladylike, unfitting, unbefitting; untoward, unsuitable, inappropriate; in bad taste, tasteless, unacceptable, offensive, crass.

indecipherable ▸ adjective *indecipherable handwriting* **illegible,** unreadable, hard to read, unintelligible, unclear; scribbled, scrawled, hieroglyphic, cramped, crabbed.

indecision ▸ noun *many an opportunity has been lost to indecision* **indecisiveness,** irresolution, hesitancy, hesitation, tentativeness; ambivalence, doubt, doubtfulness, uncertainty, incertitude; vacillation, wavering, equivocation, second thoughts; shilly-shallying, dithering, temporizing, hemming and hawing, dilly-dallying, sitting on the fence; formal dubiety.

indecisive ▸ adjective **1** *an indecisive result* **inconclusive,** proving nothing, settling nothing, open, indeterminate, undecided, unsettled, borderline, indefinite, unclear, ambiguous, vague; informal up in the air.
2 *an indecisive leader* **irresolute,** hesitant, tentative, weak; vacillating, equivocating, dithering, wavering, faltering; ambivalent, divided, blowing hot and cold, of two minds, in a dilemma, in a quandary, torn; doubtful, unsure, uncertain; undecided, uncommitted; informal iffy, sitting on the fence, wishy-washy, shilly-shallying, waffling, waffly.

indecorous ▸ adjective *they swaggered in sporting wild hair and the most indecorous attire* **improper,** unseemly, unbecoming, undignified, immodest, indelicate, indecent, unladylike, ungentlemanly; inappropriate, incorrect, unsuitable, undesirable, unfitting, in bad taste, ill-bred, vulgar.

indeed ▸ adverb **1** *there was, indeed, quite a furor* **as expected,** to be sure; in fact, in point of fact, as a matter of fact, in truth, actually, as it happens/happened, if truth be told, admittedly; archaic in sooth.
2 *"May I join you?" "Yes, indeed."* **certainly,** assuredly, of course, naturally, without (a) doubt, without question, by all means, yes; informal you bet, I'll say; informal indeedy.
3 *you are indeed clever* **very,** extremely, exceedingly, tremendously, immensely, singularly, decidedly, particularly, remarkably, really.

indefatigable ▸ adjective *the indefatigable celebrity spoke at eight different colleges* **tireless,** untiring, unflagging, unwearied; determined, tenacious, dogged, single-minded, assiduous, industrious, hard-working, unswerving, unfaltering, unwavering, unshakable, resolute, indomitable; persistent, relentless, unremitting.

indefensible ▸ adjective *Smith admitted that her remarks about Collins were indefensible* **inexcusable,** unjustifiable, unjustified, unpardonable, unforgivable; uncalled for, unprovoked, gratuitous, unreasonable, unnecessary; insupportable, unacceptable, unwarranted, unwarrantable; flawed, wrong, untenable, unsustainable.

indefinable ▶ adjective *the flavor is indefinable* **hard to define,** hard to describe, indescribable, inexpressible, nameless; vague, obscure, nebulous, impalpable, intangible, elusive.

indefinite ▶ adjective **1** *an indefinite period* **indeterminate,** unspecified, unlimited, unrestricted, undecided, undetermined, undefined, unfixed, unsettled, unknown, uncertain; limitless, infinite, endless, immeasurable.
ANTONYMS fixed, limited.
2 *an indefinite idea* **vague,** ill-defined, unclear, imprecise, inexact, loose, general, nebulous, fuzzy, hazy, obscure, ambiguous, equivocal.
ANTONYMS clear.

indelible ▶ adjective *indelible memories* **ineradicable,** permanent, lasting, ingrained, persisting, enduring, unfading, unforgettable, haunting, never to be forgotten.

indelicate ▶ adjective **1** *an indelicate question* **insensitive,** tactless, inconsiderate, undiplomatic, impolitic.
ANTONYMS tactful.
2 *an indelicate sense of humor* **vulgar,** rude, crude, tasteless, bawdy, racy, risqué, ribald, earthy, indecent, improper, naughty, indecorous, off-color, dirty, smutty, raunchy.
ANTONYMS polite, clean.

indemnity ▶ noun **1** *indemnity against loss* **insurance,** assurance, protection, security, indemnification, surety, guarantee, warranty, safeguard.
2 *the company was paid $100,000 in indemnity* **compensation,** reimbursement, recompense, repayment, restitution, payment, redress, reparation(s), damages.
3 *legislative indemnity* **salary,** wages, pay, remuneration, earnings.

indent ▶ verb *the shoreline is indented by marshes, harbors, and tidal inlets* **notch,** make an indentation in, nick; depress, impress, mark, imprint; scallop, groove, furrow.
▶ noun See INDENTATION.

indentation ▶ noun *the indentation in the side of the refrigerator is barely visible* **hollow,** depression, dip, dent, indent, cavity, concavity, pit, trough; dimple, cleft; nick, notch, groove; impression, imprint, mark; recess, bay, inlet, cove.

indenture ▶ noun *the validity of the indenture was in question* **contract,** agreement, compact, deal, covenant, bond.
▶ verb *Taylor was indentured by the age of twelve* **bind,** contract, employ, apprentice; Law article.

independence ▶ noun **1** *the struggle for national independence* **self-government,** self-rule, home rule, separation, self-determination, sovereignty, autonomy, freedom, liberty.
2 *he valued his independence* **self-sufficiency,** self-reliance, autonomy, freedom, liberty. See note at LIBERTY.
3 *financial independence* **freedom,** comfort, ease.

independent ▶ adjective **1** *an independent country* **self-governing,** self-ruling, self-determining, sovereign, autonomous, free, nonaligned.
ANTONYMS subservient, dependent.
2 *two independent groups of biologists verified the results* **separate,** different, unconnected, unrelated, dissociated, discrete.
ANTONYMS connected.
3 *independent schools* **private,** private-sector, non-state-run, fee-paying; privatized, denationalized.
ANTONYMS public, state-run.
4 *her grown-up, independent children* **self-sufficient,** self-supporting, self-reliant, standing on one's own two feet.
ANTONYMS dependent.
5 *independent advice* **impartial,** unbiased, unprejudiced, neutral, disinterested, uninvolved, uncommitted, detached, dispassionate, objective, nonpartisan, nondiscriminatory.
ANTONYMS biased.
6 *an independent spirit* **freethinking,** free, individualistic; unconventional, maverick, bold, unconstrained, unfettered, untrammeled.
ANTONYMS orthodox, constrained.

indescribable ▶ adjective *indescribable joy* **inexpressible,** indefinable, beyond words/description, ineffable, incommunicable; unutterable, unspeakable.

indestructible ▶ adjective *indestructible plastics* **unbreakable,** shatterproof, durable; lasting, enduring, everlasting, perennial, deathless, undying, immortal, inextinguishable, imperishable; informal heavy-duty, industrial-strength; literary adamantine.
ANTONYMS fragile, breakable.

indeterminate ▶ adjective **1** *an indeterminate period of time* **undetermined,** uncertain, unknown, unspecified, unstipulated, indefinite, unfixed.
ANTONYMS known.
2 *some indeterminate figures* **vague,** indefinite, unspecific, unclear, nebulous, indistinct; amorphous, shapeless, formless; hazy, faint, fuzzy, shadowy, dim.
ANTONYMS definite, clear.

index ▶ noun **1** *the library's subject index* **list,** listing, inventory, catalog, register, directory.
2 *literature is an index to its time* **guide,** sign, indication, indicator, gauge, measure, signal, mark, evidence, symptom, token; clue, hint.
▶ verb *he indexed his sources* **list,** catalog, make an inventory of, itemize, inventory, record.

indicate ▶ verb **1** *sales indicate a growing market* **point to,** be a sign of, be evidence of, evidence, demonstrate, show, testify to, bespeak, be a symptom of, be symptomatic of, denote, connote, mark, signal, signify, suggest, imply; manifest, reveal, betray, display, reflect, represent; formal evince; literary betoken.
2 *the president indicated his willingness to use force* **state,** declare, make known, communicate, announce, mention, express, reveal, divulge, disclose; put it on record; admit.
3 *please indicate your preferences on the form* **specify,** designate, mark, stipulate; show.
4 *he indicated the direction we needed to go* **point to,** point out, gesture toward.

indication ▸ noun *there was no indication of injury* **sign,** signal, indicator, symptom, mark, manifestation, demonstration, show, evidence, attestation, proof; pointer, guide, hint, clue, intimation, omen, augury, portent, warning, forewarning. See note at SIGN.

indicative ▸ adjective *the results are indicative of a possible warming trend* **symptomatic,** expressive, suggestive, representative, emblematic, symbolic; typical, characteristic.

indicator ▸ noun *the test is used as an indicator of performance* **measure,** gauge, barometer, guide, index, mark, sign, signal, symptom; bellwether, herald, hint; standard, touchstone, yardstick, benchmark, criterion, point of reference, guideline, test, litmus test.

indict ▸ verb *the teenager was* ***indicted for*** *second-degree robbery* **charge with,** accuse of, arraign for, take to court for, put on trial for, bring to trial for, prosecute for; cite for, impeach for.
ANTONYMS acquit.

indifference ▸ noun **1** *his apparent indifference infuriated her* **lack of concern,** unconcern, disinterest, lack of interest, lack of enthusiasm, apathy, nonchalance, insouciance; boredom, unresponsiveness, impassivity, dispassion, detachment, coolness.
2 *a matter of indifference* **unimportance,** insignificance, irrelevance, inconsequentiality.

indifferent ▸ adjective **1** *an indifferent shrug* **unconcerned,** uninterested, uncaring, casual, nonchalant, offhand, uninvolved, unenthusiastic, apathetic, lukewarm, phlegmatic, blasé, insouciant; unimpressed, bored, unmoved, unresponsive, impassive, dispassionate, detached, cool.
ANTONYMS heedful, caring.
2 *an indifferent performance* **mediocre,** ordinary, average, middling, middle-of-the-road, uninspired, undistinguished, unexceptional, unexciting, unremarkable, run-of-the-mill, pedestrian, prosaic, lackluster, forgettable, amateur, amateurish; informal OK, so-so, 'comme ci, comme ça', fair-to-middling, no great shakes, bush-league.
ANTONYMS brilliant.

indigenous ▸ adjective *indigenous species* **native,** original, aboriginal, autochthonous; local, domestic, homegrown; earliest, first. See note at NATIVE.

indigent ▸ adjective *indigent families* **poor,** impecunious, destitute, penniless, impoverished, insolvent, poverty-stricken; needy, in need, hard up, disadvantaged, badly off; informal (flat) broke, strapped (for cash), on skid row, down-and-out; formal penurious.
ANTONYMS rich.
▸ noun *a shelter for the city's indigents* **vagrant,** homeless person, down-and-out, beggar, pauper, derelict, have-not; informal bum.

indigestion ▸ noun *my indigestion was probably caused by the fried shrimp* **dyspepsia,** heartburn, hyperacidity, stomachache; upset stomach; informal bellyache, tummy ache, collywobbles; technical pyrosis.

indignant ▸ adjective *after the shabby way you've treated me, why shouldn't I be indignant?* **aggrieved,** resentful, affronted, disgruntled, displeased, cross, angry, mad, annoyed, offended, exasperated, irritated, piqued, nettled, in high dudgeon, chagrined; informal peeved, vexed, irked, put out, miffed, aggravated, riled, in a huff, huffy, ticked off, sore.

indignation ▸ noun *she was filled with indignation at having been blamed unjustly* **resentment,** umbrage, affront, disgruntlement, displeasure, anger, outrage, annoyance, irritation, exasperation, vexation, offense, pique; informal aggravation; literary ire.

indignity ▸ noun *the indignity of being dumped by one's wife* **shame,** humiliation, loss of self-respect, loss of pride, loss of face, embarrassment, mortification, ignominy; disgrace, dishonor, stigma, discredit; affront, insult, abuse, mistreatment, injury, offense, injustice, slight, snub, discourtesy, disrespect; informal slap in the face, kick in the teeth.

indirect ▸ adjective **1** *an indirect effect* **incidental,** accidental, unintended, unintentional, secondary, subordinate, ancillary, concomitant.
2 *the indirect route* **roundabout,** circuitous, wandering, meandering, serpentine, winding, tortuous, zigzag.
3 *an indirect answer* **oblique,** inexplicit, implicit, implied, allusive, mealy-mouthed; backhanded.

indirectly ▸ adverb **1** *we're all affected, if only indirectly* **incidentally,** secondarily, concomitantly, consequentially, contingently, accidentally.
2 *I heard about it indirectly* **secondhand,** at second hand, from others, in a roundabout way; informal through the grapevine.
3 *he referred to the subject indirectly* **obliquely,** by implication, allusively, by hinting.

indiscernible ▸ adjective See IMPERCEPTIBLE.

indiscreet ▸ adjective *indiscreet office romances* **imprudent,** unwise, impolitic, injudicious, incautious, irresponsible, ill-judged, ill-advised, misguided, ill-considered, careless, thoughtless, rash, unwary, hasty, reckless, precipitate, impulsive, foolhardy, foolish, shortsighted; undiplomatic, indelicate, tactless, insensitive; untimely, infelicitous; immodest, indecorous, unseemly, improper.

indiscretion ▸ noun **1** *he was prone to indiscretion* **imprudence,** injudiciousness, incaution, irresponsibility; carelessness, rashness, recklessness, impulsiveness, foolhardiness, foolishness, folly; tactlessness, thoughtlessness, insensitivity; humorous foot-in-mouth disease.
2 *his past indiscretions* **blunder,** lapse, gaffe, mistake, faux pas, error, slip, impropriety; misdemeanor, transgression, peccadillo, solecism, misdeed; informal slip-up. See note at SIN.

indiscriminate ▸ adjective *their choice of furnishings is appallingly indiscriminate* **nonselective,** unselective, undiscriminating, uncritical, aimless, hit-or-miss, haphazard,

random, arbitrary, unsystematic, undirected; wholesale, general, sweeping, blanket; thoughtless, unthinking, inconsiderate, casual, careless.
ANTONYMS selective.

indispensable ▶ adjective *the volunteers' help has been indispensable* **essential,** necessary, all-important, of the utmost importance, of the essence, vital, must-have, crucial, key, needed, required, requisite, imperative; invaluable. See note at NECESSARY.
ANTONYMS superfluous.

indisposed ▶ adjective 1 *my wife is indisposed* **ill,** unwell, sick, on the sick list, poorly, ailing, not (very) well, out of sorts, out of action, hors de combat; informal under the weather, laid up.
ANTONYMS well.
2 *she was indisposed to help him* **reluctant,** unwilling, disinclined, loath, unprepared, not disposed, not keen.
ANTONYMS willing.

indisposition ▶ noun See ILLNESS.

indisputable ▶ adjective *the photographs are what really made the facts indisputable* **incontrovertible,** incontestable, undeniable, irrefutable, beyond dispute, unassailable, unquestionable, beyond question, indubitable, not in doubt, beyond doubt, beyond a shadow of a doubt, unarguable, airtight, watertight; unequivocal, unmistakable, certain, sure, definite, definitive, proven, decisive, conclusive, demonstrable, self-evident, clear, clear-cut, plain, obvious, manifest, patent, palpable.
ANTONYMS questionable.

indistinct ▶ adjective 1 *the distant shoreline was indistinct* **blurred,** out of focus, fuzzy, hazy, misty, foggy, cloudy, shadowy, dim, nebulous; unclear, obscure, vague, faint, indistinguishable, indiscernible, barely perceptible, hard to see, hard to make out.
ANTONYMS clear.
2 *the last two digits are indistinct* **indecipherable,** illegible, unreadable, hard to read.
ANTONYMS legible.
3 *indistinct sounds* **muffled,** muted, low, quiet, soft, faint, inaudible, hard to hear; muttered, mumbled.
ANTONYMS audible, clear.

indistinguishable ▶ adjective 1 *the two girls were indistinguishable* **identical,** difficult to tell apart, like (two) peas in a pod, like Tweedledum and Tweedledee, very similar, two of a kind.
ANTONYMS dissimilar.
2 *the image had become indistinguishable | the voices are indistinguishable* **unintelligible,** incomprehensible, hard to make out, indistinct, unclear; inaudible.
ANTONYMS clear.

individual ▶ adjective 1 *exhibitions devoted to individual artists* **single,** separate, discrete, independent, solo; sole, lone, solitary, isolated.
2 *the fashion world was eager to be rocked by her individual style* **characteristic,** distinctive, distinct, typical, particular, peculiar, personal, personalized, special; original, unique, exclusive, singular, idiosyncratic, different, unusual, novel, unorthodox, atypical, out of the ordinary, one of a kind.
▶ noun 1 *Ed was never a particularly happy individual* **person,** human being, mortal, soul, creature; man, boy, woman, girl; character, personage; informal type, sort, customer, guy.
2 *the anthology is dedicated to the math professor who most encouraged her to be an individual* **individualist,** free spirit, nonconformist, original, eccentric, character, maverick, rare bird, something else.

individualistic ▶ adjective *an individualistic approach to symphonic composition* **unconventional,** unorthodox, atypical, singular, unique, original, nonconformist, independent, individual, freethinking; eccentric, maverick, strange, odd, peculiar, quirky, queer, idiosyncratic; informal off-the-wall.

individuality ▶ noun *the need to assert our individuality* **distinctiveness,** distinction, uniqueness, originality, singularity, particularity, peculiarity, differentness, separateness; personality, character, identity, self, ego.

individually ▶ adverb *the applications will be reviewed individually* **one at a time,** one by one, singly, separately, severally, independently, apart.
ANTONYMS together.

indoctrinate ▶ verb *armed with an evil political agenda, they set out to indoctrinate the nation's idealistic youth* **brainwash,** propagandize, proselytize, inculcate, instill, reeducate, persuade, convince, condition, program, mold, discipline; instruct, teach, train, school, drill.

indolent ▶ adjective *those who choose to remain aimless and indolent will never benefit from our self-help programs* **lazy,** idle, slothful, loafing, do-nothing, sluggardly, shiftless, lackadaisical, languid, inactive, inert, sluggish, lethargic, torpid; slack, good-for-nothing, feckless.
ANTONYMS industrious, energetic.

indomitable ▶ adjective *the indomitable spirit of this team* **invincible,** unconquerable, unbeatable, unassailable, invulnerable, unshakable, unsinkable; indefatigable, unyielding, unbending, stalwart, stout-hearted, lionhearted, strong-willed, strong-minded, steadfast, staunch, resolute, firm, determined, intransigent, inflexible, adamant; unflinching, courageous, brave, valiant, heroic, intrepid, fearless, plucky, gritty.
ANTONYMS submissive.

indubitable ▶ adjective *indubitable testimony* **unquestionable,** undoubtable, indisputable, unarguable, undebatable, incontestable, undeniable, irrefutable, incontrovertible, unmistakable, unequivocal, certain, sure, positive, definite, absolute, conclusive, watertight, ironclad; beyond doubt, beyond the shadow of a doubt, beyond dispute, beyond question, not in question, not in doubt; informal sure as shootin'.
ANTONYMS doubtful.

induce ▶ verb 1 *the pickets induced many workers to stay away* **persuade,** convince, prevail upon,

get, make, prompt, move, inspire, influence, encourage, motivate; coax into, wheedle into, cajole into, talk into, prod into; informal twist someone's arm.
ANTONYMS dissuade.
2 *how to induce hypnosis* **bring about,** cause, produce, effect, create, give rise to, generate, instigate, engender, occasion, set in motion, lead to, result in, trigger, whip up, stir up, kindle, arouse, rouse, foster, promote, encourage; literary beget, enkindle; rare effectuate.
ANTONYMS prevent.

inducement ▶ **noun** *customers responded best to such inducements as rebates and low interest rates* **incentive,** encouragement, attraction, temptation, stimulus, bait, lure, pull, draw, spur, goad, impetus, motive, motivation, provocation; bribe, reward; informal carrot, come-on, sweetener.
ANTONYMS deterrent.

indulge ▶ **verb 1** *Seth indulged his passion for vintage stemware* **satisfy,** gratify, fulfill, feed, accommodate; yield to, give in to, give way to.
2 *she seldom* ***indulged in*** *sentimentality* **wallow in,** give oneself up to, give way to, yield to, abandon oneself to, give free rein to; luxuriate in, revel in, lose oneself in.
3 *she did not indulge her children* **pamper,** spoil, overindulge, coddle, mollycoddle, cosset, baby, spoon-feed, pander to, wait on hand and foot, cater to someone's every whim, kill with kindness.
– PHRASES **indulge oneself** *it's healthy to indulge yourself once in a while* **treat oneself,** give oneself a treat; go on a spree; informal go to town, splurge.

indulgence ▶ **noun 1** *the indulgence of all his desires* **satisfaction,** gratification, fulfillment, satiation, appeasement; accommodation; slaking, quenching.
ANTONYMS denial, withholding.
2 *excessive indulgence contributed to his ill health* **self-gratification,** self-indulgence, overindulgence, intemperance, immoderation, excess, excessiveness, lack of restraint, extravagance, decadence; rare sybaritism.
ANTONYMS moderation, restraint.
3 *they viewed vacations as an indulgence* **extravagance,** luxury, treat, nonessential, extra, frill.
ANTONYMS necessity.
4 *his mother's indulgence made him ungovernable* **pampering,** coddling, mollycoddling, spoiling, cosseting, babying.
ANTONYMS strictness.
5 *I ask for your indulgence* **tolerance,** forbearance, understanding, kindness, compassion, sympathy, forgiveness, leniency, mercy, clemency, liberality.
ANTONYMS severity, harshness.

indulgent ▶ **adjective** *the children took advantage of their indulgent sitter* **permissive,** easygoing, liberal, tolerant, forgiving, forbearing, lenient, kind, kindly, generous, softhearted, compassionate, understanding, sympathetic; fond, doting, soft; compliant, obliging, accommodating. See note at **LENIENT**.
ANTONYMS strict.

industrial ▶ **adjective 1** *industrial areas of the city* **manufacturing,** factory; commercial, business, trade.
2 *industrial plastic* **heavy-duty,** durable, strong, tough, rugged.

industrialist ▶ **noun** *nineteenth-century industrialists* **manufacturer,** factory owner; captain of industry, big businessman, magnate, tycoon, capitalist, financier.

industrious ▶ **adjective** *the industrious immigrants who founded our town in 1826* **hard-working,** diligent, assiduous, conscientious, steady, painstaking, sedulous, persevering, unflagging, untiring, tireless, indefatigable, studious; busy, as busy as a bee, active, bustling, energetic, on the go, vigorous, determined, dynamic, zealous, productive; with one's shoulder to the wheel, with one's nose to the grindstone. See note at **BUSY**.
ANTONYMS indolent.

industry ▶ **noun 1** *Canadian industry* **manufacturing,** production; construction.
2 *the publishing industry* **business,** trade, field, line (of business); informal racket.
3 *the kitchen was a hive of industry* **activity,** busyness, energy, vigor, productiveness; hard work, industriousness, diligence, application, dedication.
ANTONYMS inactivity.

inebriated ▶ **adjective** *an apparently inebriated boater stunned diners at a waterfront restaurant when he docked his craft in the buff* **drunk,** intoxicated, inebriate, impaired, drunken, tipsy, under the influence; informal plastered, smashed, bombed, sloshed, sozzled, sauced, lubricated, well-oiled, wrecked, juiced, blasted, stinko, blitzed, half-cut, fried, gassed, polluted, tanked (up), soaked, out of one's head/skull, loaded, trashed, buzzed, befuddled, besotted, pickled, pixilated, canned, cockeyed, blotto, blind drunk, roaring drunk, dead drunk, punch-drunk, ripped, stewed, tight, the worse for wear, far gone, pie-eyed, three sheets to the wind; vulgar slang shit-faced; Brit. informal bladdered, lashed; informal, dated in one's cups, merry; literary crapulous. See note at **DRUNK**.
ANTONYMS sober.

inedible ▶ **adjective** *the stew looked fabulous but it was inedible* **uneatable,** indigestible, unsavory, unpalatable, unappetizing, unwholesome; stale, rotten, off, bad, unfit to eat.

ineffable ▶ **adjective 1** *the ineffable, surging joy of the Beatles* **indescribable,** inexpressible, beyond words, beyond description, begging description; indefinable, unutterable, untold, unimaginable; overwhelming, breathtaking, awesome, marvelous, wonderful, staggering, amazing.
2 *the ineffable name of God* **unutterable,** not to be uttered, not to be spoken, unmentionable, forbidden, taboo.

ineffective ▶ **adjective 1** *an ineffective scheme* **unsuccessful,** unproductive, fruitless, unprofitable, abortive, futile, purposeless, useless, worthless, ineffectual, inefficient, inefficacious, inadequate; feeble, inept, lame; archaic bootless.
2 *an ineffective president* **ineffectual,**

inefficient, inefficacious, unsuccessful, powerless, impotent, lame-duck; inadequate, incompetent, incapable, unfit, inept, bungling, weak, poor; informal useless, hopeless.

ineffectual ▶ **adjective** See INEFFECTIVE (sense 1), INEFFECTIVE (sense 2).

inefficient ▶ **adjective 1** *an inefficient worker* **ineffective,** ineffectual, unproductive, incompetent, inept, incapable, unfit, unskillful, inexpert, amateurish, unprofessional; disorganized, unprepared; negligent, lax, sloppy, slack, careless; informal lousy, useless, good-for-nothing.
2 *inefficient processes* **uneconomical,** wasteful, unproductive, time-wasting, slow; deficient, disorganized, unsystematic.

inelegant ▶ **adjective 1** *an inelegant laugh* **unrefined,** uncouth, unsophisticated, unpolished, uncultivated; ill-bred, coarse, vulgar, rude, impolite, unmannerly, tasteless.
ANTONYMS refined.
2 *an inelegant maneuver* **graceless,** ungraceful, ungainly, uncoordinated, awkward, clumsy, lumbering; inept, unskillful, inexpert; informal having two left feet, clunky.
ANTONYMS graceful.

ineligible ▶ **adjective** *the aforementioned agencies will be ineligible to participate in any federally funded assistance program* **unqualified,** unsuitable, unacceptable, undesirable, inappropriate, unworthy; ruled out, disqualified, disentitled; Law incompetent.
ANTONYMS qualified.

inept ▶ **adjective** *his mother could pitch a wicked fastball, but she was completely inept in the kitchen* **incompetent,** unskillful, unskilled, inexpert, amateurish; clumsy, awkward, maladroit, bungling, blundering; unproductive, unsuccessful, ineffectual, not up to scratch; informal ham-handed, ham-fisted, butterfingered, klutzy, all thumbs.
ANTONYMS competent.

inequality ▶ **noun** *the opposition spoke out against the inequality in their country* **imbalance,** inequity, inconsistency, variation, variability; divergence, polarity, disparity, discrepancy, dissimilarity, difference; bias, prejudice, discrimination, unfairness.

inequitable ▶ **adjective** *inequitable salaries for similar positions* **unfair,** unjust, unequal, uneven, unbalanced, one-sided, discriminatory, preferential, biased, partisan, partial, prejudiced.
ANTONYMS fair.

inequity ▶ **noun** *the inequity of the law* **unfairness,** injustice, unjustness, discrimination, partisanship, partiality, favoritism, bias, prejudice.

inert ▶ **adjective** *forces that once drove the economy have become inert* **unmoving,** motionless, immobile, inanimate, still, stationary, static; dormant, sleeping; unconscious, comatose, lifeless, insensible, insensate, insentient; idle, inactive, sluggish, lethargic, indolent, stagnant, listless, torpid.
ANTONYMS active.

inertia ▶ **noun** *by the nature of its own inertia, the coal industry has remained an unshakab constant* **inactivity,** inaction, inertness; unchanged state, stationary condition, stasi

inescapable ▶ **adjective** *meeting the future in-laws is inescapable* **unavoidable,** inevitab ineluctable, inexorable; assured, sure, certai guaranteed; necessary, required, compulsor mandatory; rare ineludible.
ANTONYMS avoidable.

inestimable ▶ **adjective** *inestimable damage* **immeasurable,** incalculable, innumerable, unfathomable, indeterminable, measureless, countless, untold; limitless, boundless, unlimited, infinite, endless, inexhaustible; informal no end of; literary myriad.
ANTONYMS little.

inevitable ▶ **adjective** *at this point, war is inevitable* **unavoidable,** inescapable, inexorable, ineluctable; assured, certain, sure, fixed; fated, destined, predestined, predetermined; rare ineludible.
ANTONYMS uncertain.

inexact ▶ **adjective** *inexact diagnostic practices* **imprecise,** inaccurate, approximate, rough, crude, general, vague, fuzzy, ill-defined; informa off-base, ballpark.

inexcusable ▶ **adjective** *our report found inexcusable national security weaknesses* **indefensible,** unjustifiable, unwarranted, unpardonable, unforgivable; blameworthy, censurable, reprehensible, deplorable, unconscionable, disgraceful, unacceptable, unreasonable.

inexhaustible ▶ **adjective 1** *her patience is inexhaustible* **unlimited,** limitless, illimitable, infinite, boundless, endless, never-ending, unfailing, everlasting; immeasurable, incalculable, inestimable, untold; copious, abundant, plentiful, bottomless.
ANTONYMS limited.
2 *the dancers were inexhaustible* **tireless,** indefatigable, untiring, unwearied, unwearying, unfaltering, unflagging, unremitting, persevering, persistent, dogged.
ANTONYMS weary, lacking stamina.

inexorable ▶ **adjective 1** *the inexorable advance of science* **relentless,** unstoppable, inescapable, inevitable, unavoidable, irrevocable, unalterable; persistent, continuous, nonstop, steady, interminable, incessant, unceasing, unremitting, unrelenting.
2 *inexorable creditors* **intransigent,** unbending, unyielding, inflexible, adamant, obdurate, immovable, unshakable; implacable, unappeasable, severe, hard, unforgiving, unsparing, uncompromising, ruthless, relentless, pitiless, merciless.

inexpensive ▶ **adjective** *inexpensive wine* **cheap,** low-priced, low-cost, modest, economical, competitive, affordable, reasonable, budget, bargain, cut-rate, reduced, discounted, discount, rock-bottom, giveaway, downmarket, low-end; informal bargain-basement, dirt cheap.

inexperienced ▶ **adjective** *she's inexperienced, but we expect her to become an excellent teacher* **unseasoned,** unpracticed, untrained, unschooled, unqualified, unskilled, amateur;

ignorant, unversed, inexpert; ill-equipped, ill-prepared; naive, unsophisticated, callow, immature, green, unworldly; informal wet behind the ears.

inexpert ▶ adjective *inexpert installation spoils the windows irreparably* **unskilled,** unskillful, amateur, amateurish, unprofessional, inexperienced; inept, incompetent, maladroit, uncoordinated, clumsy, bungling, blundering; informal ham-handed, ham-fisted, butterfingered.

inexplicable ▶ adjective *these inexplicable acts of vandalism have left the community stunned* **unaccountable,** unexplainable, incomprehensible, unfathomable, impenetrable, insoluble; baffling, puzzling, perplexing, mystifying, bewildering, confusing; mysterious, strange.
ANTONYMS understandable.

inexpressible ▶ adjective *my grief is inexpressible* **indescribable,** indefinable, unutterable, unspeakable, ineffable, beyond words, nameless; unimaginable, inconceivable, unthinkable, untold.

inexpressive ▶ adjective *a room of inexpressive faces* **expressionless,** impassive, emotionless; inscrutable, unreadable, blank, vacant, glazed, glassy, lifeless, deadpan, wooden, stony; poker-faced, straight-faced.

inextinguishable ▶ adjective *his inextinguishable passion for literature* **irrepressible,** unquenchable, indestructible, undying, immortal, imperishable, unfailing, unceasing, ceaseless, enduring, everlasting, eternal, persistent.

inextricable ▶ adjective **1** *our lives are inextricable* **inseparable,** indivisible, entangled, tangled, mixed up.
2 *an inextricable situation* **inescapable,** unavoidable, ineluctable.

infallible ▶ adjective **1** *an infallible sense of timing* **unerring,** unfailing, faultless, flawless, impeccable, perfect, precise, accurate, meticulous, scrupulous.
2 *an infallible remedy* **unfailing,** unerring, guaranteed, dependable, trustworthy, reliable, sure, certain, safe, foolproof, effective; informal sure-fire; formal efficacious.

infamous ▶ adjective **1** *an infamous train robber* **notorious,** disreputable; legendary, fabled, famed.
ANTONYMS reputable.
2 *infamous misconduct* **abominable,** outrageous, shocking, shameful, disgraceful, dishonorable, discreditable, contemptible, unworthy; monstrous, atrocious, nefarious, appalling, dreadful, terrible, heinous, egregious, detestable, despicable, loathsome, hateful, vile, unspeakable, unforgivable, iniquitous, scandalous; informal dirty, filthy, lowdown.
ANTONYMS honorable.

infancy ▶ noun **1** *his twin died in infancy* **babyhood,** early childhood.
2 *music video was in its infancy* **beginnings,** early days, early stages; seeds, roots; start, commencement, rise, emergence, genesis, dawn, birth, inception.
ANTONYMS end.

infant ▶ noun *a fretful infant* **baby,** newborn, young child, (tiny) tot, little one, papoose; Medicine neonate; informal tiny; literary babe, babe in arms, suckling.
▶ adjective *an infant stage* **developing,** emergent, emerging, embryonic, nascent, incipient, new, fledgling, budding, up-and-coming.

infantile ▶ adjective *it's time you outgrew your infantile behavior* **childish,** babyish, immature, puerile, juvenile, adolescent, jejune; silly, inane, fatuous.

infantry ▶ noun *the infantry, as usual, took the worst of the battle* **infantrymen,** foot soldiers, foot guards; the ranks; informal GIs; cannon fodder; Military slang grunts; historical footmen.

infatuated ▶ adjective *Kyle was hopelessly infatuated with his cousin's girlfriend* **besotted with,** in love with, head over heels about, obsessed with, taken with, lovesick for, moonstruck over; enamored of, attracted to, devoted to, captivated by, enthralled by, enchanted by, bewitched by, under the spell of; informal smitten with, sweet on, keen on, hot for, gone on, hung up on, mad about, crazy about, nuts about, stuck on, carrying a torch for.

infect ▶ verb **1** *he didn't want to infect others with his chicken pox* **pass infection to,** spread disease to, contaminate.
2 *nitrates were infecting rivers* **contaminate,** pollute, taint, foul, dirty, blight, damage, ruin; poison.
3 *his high spirits infected everyone* **affect,** influence, have an impact on, touch; excite, inspire, stimulate, animate.

infection ▶ noun *a treatable skin infection* **disease,** virus; disorder, condition, affliction, complaint, illness, ailment, sickness, infirmity; contamination, poison, septicemia, suppuration; informal bug; dated contagion; Medicine sepsis.

infectious ▶ adjective **1** *infectious disease* **communicable,** transmittable, transferable, spreadable, contagious; epidemic; informal catching; dated infective.
2 *her laughter is infectious* **irresistible,** compelling, persuasive, contagious, catching.

infer ▶ verb *is it really possible to infer that a crime was committed, given this flimsy evidence?* **deduce,** conclude, conjecture, surmise, reason, interpret; gather, understand, presume, assume, take it, extrapolate; read between the lines, figure (out); informal reckon.

USAGE

infer

Properly used, *infer* means "deduce; reason from premises to a conclusion"—e.g.: "We get no sense of the man himself from this book except what we can infer from the biographical facts that Mr. Magida presents." (*New York Times*; Aug. 18, 1996.)

Writers frequently misuse *infer* when *imply* (= hint at; suggest) would be the correct word—e.g.: "And no team is, of course, inferring [read *implying*] that Dallas isn't

talented." (*New York Times*; Jan. 12, 1996.) Remember: a speaker or writer *implies* something without putting it expressly. A listener or reader *infers* beyond what has been literally expressed. Or, as Theodore Bernstein put it, "The *implier* is the pitcher; the *inferrer* is the catcher." (*The Careful Writer*; 1965.) Stylists agree that the important distinction between these words deserves to be maintained. — **BG**

inference ▶ noun *there should be no inference drawn from the fact that he chooses not to be a witness* **deduction,** conclusion, reasoning, conjecture, speculation, guess, presumption, assumption, supposition, reckoning, extrapolation.

inferior ▶ adjective **1** *poorer people were thought to be innately inferior* **second-class,** lesser, lower in status, lower-ranking, subordinate, second-fiddle, junior, minor; subservient, lowly, humble, menial, beneath one.
ANTONYMS superior.
2 *inferior accommodations* **second-rate,** substandard, low-quality, low-grade, downmarket, bush-league, unsatisfactory, shoddy, deficient; poor, bad, awful, dreadful, wretched; informal crummy, scuzzy, rotten, lousy, third-rate, tinpot, rinky-dink.
ANTONYMS luxury.
▶ noun *how dare she treat him as an inferior?* **subordinate,** junior, underling, minion, menial, peon.
ANTONYMS superior.

infernal ▶ adjective **1** *the infernal regions* **hellish,** nether, subterranean, underworld, chthonic, Tartarean; satanic, devilish, diabolical, fiendish, demonic.
2 informal *an infernal nuisance* **damnable,** wretched, confounded; annoying, irritating, infuriating, irksome, detestable, exasperating; informal damned, damn, blasted, blessed, pesky, aggravating; informal dated cursed.

infertile ▶ adjective **1** *infertile soil* **barren,** unfruitful, unproductive; sterile, impoverished, arid.
2 *she was infertile* **sterile,** barren; childless, unable to procreate/reproduce, impotent; Medicine infecund.

infest ▶ verb *without follow-up treatment, a new horde of ants will infest the building* **overrun,** spread through, invade, infiltrate, pervade, permeate, inundate, overwhelm; beset, plague, swarm.

infidel ▶ noun *a holy war against the infidels* **unbeliever,** disbeliever, nonbeliever, agnostic, atheist; heathen, pagan, idolater, heretic, freethinker, dissenter, nonconformist; archaic paynim; rare nullifidian.

infidelity ▶ noun *even after reconciliation, she could not forgive his infidelity* **unfaithfulness,** adultery, cuckoldry, disloyalty, extramarital sex; deceit, falseness; affair, liaison, fling, amour; informal fooling/playing around, cheating, two-timing, hanky-panky; formal fornication.
ANTONYMS faithfulness.

infiltrate ▶ verb *spies were prepared to infiltrate the enemy camp* **insinuate oneself into,** worm one's way into, sneak into, slip into, get into, invade, penetrate, enter; permeate, pervade, seep into/through, soak into.

infinite ▶ adjective **1** *the universe is infinite* **boundless,** unbounded, unlimited, limitless, never-ending, interminable; immeasurable, fathomless, imponderable; extensive, vast; immense, great, huge, enormous.
ANTONYMS limited, small.
2 *infinite resources* **countless,** uncountable, inestimable, innumerable, numberless, immeasurable, incalculable, untold, myriad.
ANTONYMS limited.

infinitesimal ▶ adjective *these infinitesimal organisms can cause monstrously huge problems* **minute,** tiny, minuscule, very small; microscopic, imperceptible, indiscernible; informal teeny, wee, teeny-weeny, itsy-bitsy, little-bitty.
ANTONYMS enormous.

infinity ▶ noun **1** *the infinity of space* **endlessness,** infinitude, infiniteness, boundlessness, limitlessness; vastness, immensity.
2 *an infinity of accessories* **infinite number,** great number; abundance, profusion, host, multitude, mass, wealth; informal heap, stack.

infirm ▶ adjective *how long has he been so infirm?* **frail,** weak, feeble, debilitated, decrepit, disabled; ill, unwell, sick, sickly, indisposed, ailing. See note at WEAK.
ANTONYMS healthy.

infirmity ▶ noun *the family would never openly discuss their aunt's infirmity* **illness,** malady, ailment, disease, disorder, sickness, affliction, complaint, indisposition, frailty, weakness; disability, impairment.

inflame ▶ verb **1** *his opinions inflamed his rival* **enrage,** incense, anger, madden, infuriate, exasperate, provoke, antagonize, rile; informal make someone see red, make someone's blood boil.
ANTONYMS placate.
2 *the case inflamed passions against the pit bull* **incite,** arouse, rouse, provoke, stir up, whip up, kindle, ignite, touch off, foment, inspire, stimulate, agitate.
ANTONYMS calm, dampen.
3 *he inflamed an already tense situation* **aggravate,** exacerbate, intensify, worsen, compound.
ANTONYMS soothe.

inflamed ▶ adjective **1** *the cut became inflamed* **swollen,** puffed up; red; raw, sore, painful, tender; infected, septic.
2 *inflamed feelings* **angry,** infuriated, furious, enraged; excited, aroused, stimulated, titillated.

inflammation ▶ noun *apply ice to the inflammation* **swelling,** puffiness; redness; rawness, soreness, tenderness; infection, festering, suppuration, septicity.

inflammatory ▶ adjective *neither senator condemned the inflammatory language that had been used* **provocative,** incendiary, inflaming, inciting, agitating, stirring, rousing, provoking, fomenting, rabble-rousing, seditious, subversive, mutinous; fiery, passionate; controversial, contentious.

inflate ▶ verb 1 *she inflated the mattress* **blow up,** fill up, fill with air, aerate, pump up; dilate, distend, swell.
ANTONYMS deflate.
2 *the demand inflated prices* **increase,** raise, boost, escalate, put up; informal hike up, jack up, bump up, boost (up).
ANTONYMS decrease, depress.
3 *the figures were inflated by the press* **exaggerate,** magnify, overplay, overstate, enhance, embellish, increase, amplify, augment.
ANTONYMS play down, understate, soft-pedal.

inflated ▶ adjective 1 *an inflated balloon* **blown up,** aerated, filled, puffed up/out, pumped up; distended, expanded, engorged, swollen.
2 *inflated prices* **high,** sky-high, excessive, unreasonable, prohibitive, outrageous, exorbitant, extortionate; informal steep, stiff, pricey.
3 *an inflated opinion of himself* **exaggerated,** magnified, aggrandized, immoderate, overblown, overstated.
4 *inflated language* **high-flown,** extravagant, exaggerated, elaborate, flowery, ornate, overblown, overwrought, grandiloquent, magniloquent, lofty, grandiose; affected, pretentious, bombastic, tumid; informal windy, highfalutin.

inflection ▶ noun *when I read my lines, he'd gently correct my pronunciation and inflection* **stress,** cadence, rhythm, accent, intonation, pitch, emphasis, modulation, lilt, tone.

inflexible ▶ adjective 1 *his inflexible attitude* **stubborn,** obstinate, obdurate, intractable, intransigent, unbending, immovable, unaccommodating; hidebound, single-minded, pigheaded, mulish, uncompromising, adamant, firm, resolute, diehard, dyed-in-the-wool; formal refractory.
ANTONYMS accommodating, flexible.
2 *inflexible rules* **unalterable,** unchangeable, immutable, unvarying; firm, fixed, set, established, entrenched, hard and fast, carved in stone; stringent, strict, hardline, ironclad.
ANTONYMS flexible.
3 *inflexible plastic* **rigid,** stiff, unyielding, unbending, unbendable; hard, firm, inelastic.
ANTONYMS pliable, flexible.

inflict ▶ verb 1 *he **inflicted** an injury **on** James* **administer to,** deliver to, deal out to, dispense to, mete out to; impose on, exact on, wreak on; cause to, give to; informal dish out to.
2 *I won't inflict myself on you any longer* **impose,** force, thrust, foist; saddle someone with, burden someone with.

influence ▶ noun 1 *the influence of parents on their children* **effect,** impact; control, sway, hold, power, authority, mastery, domination, supremacy; guidance, direction; pressure.
2 *a bad **influence on** young girls* **example to,** (role) model for, guide for, inspiration to.
3 *political influence* **power,** authority, sway, leverage, weight, pull, standing, prestige, stature, rank; informal clout, muscle, teeth.
▶ verb 1 *bosses can influence our careers* **affect,** have an impact on, impact, determine, guide, control, shape, govern, decide; change, alter, transform.
2 *an attempt to influence the jury* **sway,** bias, prejudice, suborn; pressure, coerce; dragoon, intimidate, browbeat, brainwash; informal twist someone's arm, lean on, put ideas into one's head.

influential ▶ adjective 1 *an influential leader* **powerful,** dominant, controlling, strong, authoritative, persuasive; important, affluential, prominent, distinguished, eminent.
ANTONYMS unimportant, impotent.
2 *she was influential in shaping his career* **instrumental,** significant, important, crucial, pivotal.
ANTONYMS insignificant.

influx ▶ noun 1 *an influx of tourists* **inundation,** rush, stream, flood, incursion; invasion, intrusion.
2 *influxes of river water* **inflow,** inrush, flood, inundation.

inform ▶ verb 1 *she informed him that she was ill* **tell,** notify, apprise, advise, impart to, communicate to, let someone know; brief, prime, enlighten, send word to, give/supply information to; informal fill someone in, clue someone in.
2 *he **informed on** two of the suspects* **denounce,** give away, betray, incriminate, inculpate, report, finger; sell out, stab in the back; informal rat on/out, squeal on, tell on, blab on, tattle on, blow the whistle on, sell down the river, snitch on.
3 *the articles were informed by feminism* **suffuse,** pervade, permeate, infuse, imbue, inspire; characterize.

informal ▶ adjective 1 *an informal chat* **unofficial,** casual, relaxed, easygoing, unceremonious; open, friendly, intimate; simple, unpretentious, easy; informal unstuffy, laid-back, chummy.
ANTONYMS official, formal.
2 *informal language* **colloquial,** vernacular, idiomatic, demotic, popular; familiar, everyday, unofficial; simple, natural, unpretentious; informal slangy, chatty, folksy.
ANTONYMS literary, formal.
3 *informal clothes* **casual,** relaxed, comfortable, everyday, sloppy, leisure; informal comfy, cazh.
ANTONYMS formal.

information ▶ noun *we'll give you the latest information* **details,** particulars, facts, figures, statistics, data; knowledge, intelligence; instruction, advice, guidance, direction, counsel, enlightenment; news, word; informal info, lowdown, dope, dirt, inside story, scoop, poop. See note at KNOWLEDGE.

informative ▶ adjective *he hosts TV's most informative game show* **instructive,** instructional, illuminating, enlightening, revealing, explanatory; factual, educational, educative, edifying, didactic; informal newsy.

informed ▶ adjective *our informed listeners tell us we've reported the wrong concert dates* **knowledgeable,** enlightened, literate, educated; sophisticated, cultured; briefed, versed, up to date, up to speed, in the know, au courant, au fait; informal hip, in the loop.

ANTONYMS ignorant.

informer ▸ noun *an informer for the CIA* **informant,** betrayer, traitor, Judas, double-crosser, collaborator, spy, double agent, fifth columnist, infiltrator, plant, tattletale; informal rat, squealer, whistle-blower, snake in the grass, snitch, fink, stool pigeon, stoolie, canary.

infraction ▸ noun *leaving the grounds before noon is an infraction of the rules | Hurley has been cited for another infraction* **violation,** contravention, breach, transgression, infringement, offense; neglect, dereliction, noncompliance; Law contumacy.

infrequent ▸ adjective *her infrequent visits* **rare,** uncommon, unusual, exceptional, few (and far between), as rare/scarce as hen's teeth; unaccustomed, unwonted; isolated, scarce, scattered; sporadic, irregular, intermittent, seldom; informal once in a blue moon.
ANTONYMS common.

infringe ▸ verb **1** *the statute infringed constitutionally guaranteed rights* **contravene,** violate, transgress, break, breach; disobey, defy, flout, fly in the face of; disregard, ignore, neglect; go beyond, overstep, exceed; Law infract.
ANTONYMS obey, comply with.
2 *the surveillance* ***infringed on*** *his rights* **restrict,** limit, curb, check, encroach on; undermine, erode, diminish, weaken, impair, damage, compromise.
ANTONYMS preserve.

infuriate ▸ verb *the governor's veto is likely to infuriate child-care providers statewide* **enrage,** incense, anger, inflame; exasperate, antagonize, provoke, rile, annoy, irritate, aggravate, madden, nettle, gall, irk, vex, get on someone's nerves, try someone's patience, rankle; informal make someone see red, get someone's back up, make someone's blood boil, needle, ride, tick off, tee off, piss off, PO, wind up, get to, bug.
ANTONYMS please, humor.

infuriating ▸ adjective *it's infuriating that they leave that dog outside to bark all day* **exasperating,** maddening, annoying, irritating, irksome, vexatious, trying, tiresome; informal aggravating, pesky, infernal.

ingenious ▸ adjective *an ingenious economist | the kids in her science class have devised an ingenious machine for sorting recyclables* **inventive,** creative, imaginative, original, innovative, pioneering, resourceful, enterprising, inspired; clever, intelligent, smart, brilliant, masterly, talented, gifted, skillful; astute, sharp-witted, quick-witted, shrewd; elaborate, sophisticated. See note at **CREATIVE**.

ingenuous ▸ adjective *she had never before met a grown man so ingenuous* **naive,** innocent, simple, childlike, trusting, unwary; unsuspicious, unworldly, wide-eyed, inexperienced, green; open, sincere, honest, frank, candid, forthright, artless, guileless, genuine, upfront. See note at **GULLIBLE**.
ANTONYMS artful.

inglorious ▸ adjective *her association with the blackmailers brought an inglorious end to an otherwise brilliant career* **shameful,** dishonorable, ignominious, discreditable, disgraceful, scandalous; humiliating, mortifying, demeaning, ignoble, undignified, wretched, shabby.

ingrained, engrained ▸ adjective **1** *ingrained attitudes* **entrenched,** established, deep-rooted, deep-seated, fixed, firm, unshakable, ineradicable; inveterate, dyed-in-the-wool, abiding, enduring, stubborn. See note at **INHERENT**.
ANTONYMS transient.
2 *ingrained dirt* **ground-in,** fixed, implanted, embedded; permanent, indelible, ineradicable.
ANTONYMS superficial.

ingratiate ▸ verb
– PHRASES **ingratiate oneself** *he has* ***ingratiated himself*** *with the premier by running ideological education campaigns* **curry favor with,** cultivate, win over, get in good with; toady to, grovel to, fawn over, kowtow to, play up to, pander to, flatter, court, wheedle, schmooze; informal suck up to, lick someone's boots, butter up, brown-nose.

ingratiating ▸ adjective *a forced and ingratiating smile* **sycophantic,** toadying, fawning, unctuous, obsequious; flattering, insincere; smooth-tongued, slick; greasy, oily, saccharine; informal smarmy, slimy.

ingratitude ▸ noun *these sanctions have sent a message of ingratitude to the many honest and hard-working officers* **ungratefulness,** thanklessness, lack of appreciation, nonrecognition.

ingredient ▸ noun *crystallized iodine is a legal ingredient of an illegal drug* **constituent,** component, element; part, piece, bit, strand, portion, unit, feature, aspect, attribute; (**ingredients**) contents, makings.

ingress ▸ noun *two doors offer ingress to the station* **entry,** entrance, entryway, entrée, access, admittance, admission; way in, approach, passage.
ANTONYMS exit.

inhabit ▸ verb *outside of the research team, humans do not inhabit this island* **live in/on,** occupy; settle (in/on), people, populate, colonize; dwell in/on, reside in/on, tenant, lodge in/on, have one's home in/on; formal be domiciled in/on, abide in/on.

inhabitant ▸ noun *the inhabitants have organized a protest* **resident,** occupant, occupier, dweller, squatter, settler; local, native; formal denizen; (**inhabitants**) population, populace, people, public, community, citizenry, townsfolk, townspeople.

inhale ▸ verb *inhale deeply | we'd rather not inhale your cigar smoke* **breathe in,** inspire, draw in, suck in, take in, sniff in, drink in.

inharmonious ▸ adjective **1** *inharmonious sounds* **unmelodious,** discordant, unharmonious, unmusical, dissonant, off-key; grating, harsh, cacophonous; rare absonant.
ANTONYMS musical.
2 *once you've endured a dinner with her family you will never again think that your relatives are inharmonious* **antagonistic,** argumentative, quarrelsome, captious, disputatious,

belligerent, confrontational, combative.
ANTONYMS congenial.

inherent ▶ adjective *inherent traits* **intrinsic,** innate, immanent, built-in, indwelling, inborn, ingrained, deep-rooted; essential, fundamental, basic, structural, organic; natural, instinctive, instinctual, congenital, native.
ANTONYMS acquired.

CHOOSE THE RIGHT WORD

inherent, congenital, essential, inborn, ingrained, innate, intrinsic

A quality that is **inherent** is a permanent part of a person's nature or essence (*an inherent tendency to fight back*). If it is **ingrained**, it is deeply wrought into his or her substance or character (*ingrained prejudice against women*). **Inborn** and **innate** are nearly synonymous, sharing the basic sense of existing at the time of birth, but *innate* is usually preferred in an abstract or philosophical context (*innate defects; innate ideas*), while *inborn* is reserved for human characteristics that are so deep-seated they seem to have been there from birth (*an inborn aptitude for the piano*). **Congenital** also means from the time of one's birth, but it is primarily used in medical contexts and refers to problems or defects (*congenital color-blindness; a congenital tendency toward schizophrenia*). **Intrinsic** and **essential** are broader terms that can apply to things as well as people. Something that is *essential* is part of the essence or constitution of something (*an essential ingredient; essential revisions in the text*), while an *intrinsic* quality is one that belongs naturally to a person or thing (*her intrinsic fairness; an intrinsic weakness in the design*).

inherit ▶ verb **1** *she inherited his farm* **become heir to,** come into/by, be bequeathed, be left, be willed, receive; Law be devised.
2 *Richard inherited the title* **succeed to,** assume, take over, come into; formal accede to.

inheritance ▶ noun **1** *a comfortable inheritance* **legacy,** bequest, endowment, bestowal, provision; birthright, heritage, patrimony; Law devise.
2 *his* ***inheritance of*** *the title* **succession to,** accession to, assumption of, elevation to.

inhibit ▶ verb **1** *the obstacles that inhibit change* **impede,** hinder, hamper, hold back, discourage, interfere with, obstruct, slow down, retard; curb, check, suppress, restrict, fetter, cramp, frustrate, stifle, prevent, block, thwart, foil, stop, halt. See note at THWART.
ANTONYMS encourage, allow.
2 *she feels inhibited from taking part* **prevent,** disallow, exclude, forbid, prohibit, preclude, ban, bar, interdict.
ANTONYMS encourage.

inhibited ▶ adjective *witnesses should not be inhibited to reveal what they know | she was so inhibited that most people thought she was cold and unfeeling* **shy,** reticent, reserved, self-conscious, diffident, bashful, coy; wary, reluctant, hesitant, insecure, unconfident, unassertive, timid; withdrawn, repressed, constrained, undemonstrative; informal uptight, anal-retentive.

inhibition ▶ noun **1** *they overcame their inhibitions* **shyness,** reticence, self-consciousness, reserve, diffidence; wariness, hesitancy, hesitation, insecurity; timidity; repression, reservation; psychological block; informal hang-up.
2 *writing without inhibition* **hindrance,** hampering, discouragement, obstruction, impediment, suppression, repression, restriction, restraint, constraint, cramping, stifling, prevention; curb, check, bar, barrier.

inhospitable ▶ adjective **1** *the inhospitable landscape* **uninviting,** unwelcoming; bleak, forbidding, cheerless, hostile, savage, wild, harsh, inimical; uninhabitable, barren, bare, austere, desolate, stark, spartan.
ANTONYMS welcoming, cheery.
2 *forgive me if I seem inhospitable* **unwelcoming,** unfriendly, unsociable, antisocial, unneighborly, uncongenial; aloof, cool, cold, frosty, distant, remote, indifferent, uncivil, discourteous, ungracious; ungenerous, unkind, unsympathetic; informal standoffish.
ANTONYMS welcomng, warm, friendly.

inhuman ▶ adjective **1** *inhuman treatment* **cruel,** harsh, inhumane, brutal, callous, sadistic, severe, savage, vicious, barbaric; monstrous, heinous, egregious; merciless, ruthless, pitiless, remorseless, cold-blooded, heartless, hard-hearted, dastardly; unkind, inconsiderate, unfeeling, uncaring; informal beastly.
ANTONYMS humane.
2 *he ran at an inhuman pace* **superhuman,** unearthly, extraordinary, phenomenal, exceptional, incredible, unbelievable.

inhumane ▶ adjective See INHUMAN (sense 1).

inimical ▶ adjective *an inimical gaze | policies inimical to democracy* **harmful,** injurious, detrimental, deleterious, prejudicial, damaging, hurtful, destructive, ruinous, pernicious; antagonistic, contrary, antipathetic, unfavorable, adverse, opposed; hostile, unkind, unsympathetic, unfriendly, ill-disposed, malevolent; unwelcoming, cold, frosty; literary malefic. See note at HOSTILE.
ANTONYMS friendly, favorable.

inimitable ▶ adjective *after years of trying to imitate Hitchcock, I finally accepted the fact that the master is inimitable* **incomparable,** unparalleled, unrivaled, peerless, matchless, unequaled, unsurpassable, superlative, supreme, perfect, beyond compare, second to none, in a class of one's own; unique, distinctive, individual, sui generis; formal unexampled.

iniquity ▶ noun **1** *many runaways become the pawns of these merchants of iniquity* **wickedness,** sinfulness, immorality, impropriety; vice, evil, sin; villainy, criminality; odiousness, atrocity, egregiousness; outrage, monstrosity, obscenity, reprehensibility; formal turpitude.
ANTONYMS morality, virtue.

2 *I will forgive their iniquity* **sin,** crime, transgression, wrongdoing, wrong, violation, offense, vice.
ANTONYMS goodness, virtue.

initial ▶ adjective *the initial stages* **beginning,** opening, commencing, starting, inceptive, embryonic, fledgling; first, early, primary, preliminary, elementary, foundational, preparatory; introductory, inaugural.
ANTONYMS final.
▶ verb *he initialed the warrant* **put one's initials on,** initialize, sign, ink, countersign, autograph, endorse, inscribe, witness, verify.

initially ▶ adverb *initially, we thought it might be pilot error* **at first,** at the start, at the outset, in/at the beginning, to begin with, to start with, originally.

initiate ▶ verb **1** *the government initiated the scheme* **begin,** start (off), commence; institute, inaugurate, launch, instigate, establish, set up, start the ball rolling on; originate, pioneer; informal kick off, spark.
ANTONYMS finish.
2 *he was initiated into a cult* **admit,** induct, install, incorporate, enlist, enroll, recruit, sign up, swear in; ordain, invest.
ANTONYMS expel.
3 *she was **initiated into** the business of publishing* **teach about,** instruct in, tutor in, school in, prime in, ground in; familiarize with, acquaint with; indoctrinate; informal show someone the ropes in/within.
▶ noun *the initiates were put through the customary opening-day paces* **novice,** starter, beginner, newcomer; student, pupil, learner, trainee, apprentice; recruit, new recruit, raw recruit, tyro, neophyte; postulant, novitiate; informal rookie, newbie, new kid (on the block), greenhorn.

initiation ▶ noun **1** *the initiation of the program* **beginning,** starting, commencement; institution, inauguration, launch, opening, instigation, actuation, origination, devising, inception; establishment, setting up; informal kickoff.
ANTONYMS finish.
2 *a rite of initiation into the tribe* **induction,** introduction, admission, admittance, installation, incorporation, ordination, investiture, enlistment, enrollment, recruitment; baptism.
ANTONYMS expulsion.

initiative ▶ noun **1** *employers are looking for people with initiative* **self-motivation,** resourcefulness, inventiveness, imagination, ingenuity, originality, creativity, enterprise; drive, dynamism, ambition, motivation, spirit, energy, vision; informal get-up-and-go, pep, moxie, spunk, gumption.
2 *a recent initiative on recycling* **plan,** scheme, strategy, stratagem, measure, proposal, step, action, approach.

inject ▶ verb **1** *he injected a painkiller* **administer,** introduce; informal shoot (up), mainline.
2 *a pump injects air into the valve* **insert,** introduce, feed, push, force, shoot. See note at INSERT.
3 *he injected new life into the team* **introduce,** instill, infuse, imbue, breathe.
4 *she injected a note of realism into the debate* **interject,** interpose, throw in, add, contribute.

injection ▶ noun **1** *every time I go to the doctor's, I seem to be due for another injection* **inoculation,** vaccination, immunization, booster (shot); informal jab, shot, needle, hypo, fix.
2 *her injection of humor into the discussion was a godsend* **introduction,** infusion, instilling, imbuing, inculcation.

injudicious ▶ adjective *he now regrets his injudicious comments* **imprudent,** unwise, inadvisable, ill-advised, misguided; ill-considered, ill-judged, incautious, hasty, rash; inappropriate, impolitic, inexpedient; foolish, foolhardy, hare-brained.
ANTONYMS prudent.

injunction ▶ noun *the injunction prevents Sunday trading* **order,** ruling, directive, command, instruction; decree, edict, dictum, dictate, fiat, mandate, writ; warning, caution, admonition.

injure ▶ verb **1** *he injured his foot* **hurt,** wound, damage, harm; cripple, lame, disable; maim, mutilate, deform, mangle, break.
2 *his comments injured her reputation* **damage,** mar, impair, spoil, ruin, blight, blemish, tarnish, blacken.
3 dated *my actions have injured no one* **wrong,** abuse, do an injustice to, offend against, maltreat, mistreat, ill-use.

injured ▶ adjective **1** *his injured arm* **hurt,** wounded, damaged, sore, bruised; crippled, lame, disabled; maimed, mutilated, deformed, mangled, broken, fractured.
ANTONYMS healthy.
2 *the injured party* **wronged,** offended, maltreated, mistreated, ill-used, harmed; defamed, maligned, insulted, dishonored.
ANTONYMS offending.
3 *an injured tone* **upset,** hurt, wounded, offended, reproachful, pained, aggrieved; displeased, unhappy, put out, disgruntled, cut to the quick.
ANTONYMS healthy, offending.

injurious ▶ adjective *the searing summer sun could prove injurious | an injurious story* **harmful,** damaging, deleterious, detrimental, hurtful, baleful; disadvantageous, unfavorable, undesirable, adverse, inimical, unhealthy, pernicious; insulting, libelous, wrongful; literary malefic.

injury ▶ noun **1** *minor injuries* **wound,** bruise, cut, gash, laceration, scratch, graze, abrasion, contusion, lesion; Medicine trauma.
2 *they escaped without injury* **harm,** hurt, damage, pain, suffering, impairment, affliction; disfigurement.
3 *the injury to her feelings* **offense,** abuse; affront, insult, slight, snub, indignity, slap in the face; wrong, wrongdoing, injustice.

injustice ▶ noun **1** *the injustice of the world* **unfairness,** unjustness, inequity, corruption; cruelty, tyranny, repression, exploitation; bias, prejudice, discrimination, intolerance.
2 *his sacking was an injustice* **wrong,** offense,

crime, sin, misdeed, outrage, atrocity, scandal, disgrace, affront; informal raw deal.

inkling ▶ noun *I had no inkling of their intentions* **idea,** notion, sense, impression, conception, suggestion, indication, whisper, glimmer; (sneaking) suspicion, fancy, hunch, feeling; hint, clue, intimation, sign; informal the foggiest (idea), the faintest (idea).

inky ▶ adjective 1 *the inky darkness* **black,** jet-black, pitch-black; sable, ebony, dark, raven; literary Stygian.
2 *inky fingers* **ink-stained,** stained, blotchy, smudged.

inlaid ▶ adjective *an inlaid design of glass beads in the tile | an inlaid floor* **inset,** set, studded, lined, paneled, laid; ornamented, decorated; mosaic, intarsia, marquetry.

inland ▶ adjective 1 *inland areas* **interior,** inshore, central, internal, upcountry, upriver; landlocked.
ANTONYMS coastal.
2 *inland trade* **domestic,** internal, home, local; national, provincial.
ANTONYMS international.
▶ adverb *the goods were carried inland* **upcountry,** upriver, inshore, to the interior.

inlet ▶ noun 1 *we drifted toward a marshy inlet* **cove,** bay, bight, estuary, fjord, sound, armlet, salt chuck.
2 *a fresh-air inlet* **vent,** flue, shaft, duct, channel, passage, pipe, pipeline, opening.

inmate ▶ noun 1 *at least two dozen inmates were treated for minor injuries following the prison fire* **prisoner,** convict, captive, detainee, internee; informal jailbird, con, yardbird, lifer.
2 *from our treehouse we would watch the inmates of Twin Oaks Hospital tending to their pretty little gardens* **patient,** in-patient; convalescent; resident, inhabitant, occupant.

inn ▶ noun *the inn where Longfellow stayed* **hotel,** guest house, lodge, bed and breakfast, B&B, hostel; tavern, bar, hostelry, taproom, pub, public house, watering hole; French auberge; dated alehouse.

innate ▶ adjective *an innate talent for woodworking* **inborn,** inbred, inherent, indwelling, natural, intrinsic, instinctive, intuitive, unlearned; hereditary, inherited, in the blood, in the family; inbuilt, deep-rooted, deep-seated, hard-wired, connate. See note at INHERENT.
ANTONYMS acquired.

inner ▶ adjective 1 *the inner gates* **internal,** interior, inside, inmost, innermost.
ANTONYMS external.
2 *the premier's inner circle* **privileged,** restricted, exclusive, private, confidential, intimate.
3 *inner feelings* **hidden,** secret, deep, underlying, unapparent; veiled, unrevealed.
ANTONYMS apparent.
4 *one's inner life* **mental,** intellectual, psychological, spiritual, emotional.

innkeeper ▶ noun *relatively few innkeepers maintain a constant Internet connection* **landlord,** landlady, hotelier, hotel owner, proprietor, manager, host, hostess; licensee, barkeeper, barkeep; publican, restaurateur.

innocence ▶ noun 1 *he protested his innocence* **guiltlessness,** blamelessness, irreproachability.
2 *the innocence of Sleeping Beauty is beyond the comprehension of these young girls* **virginity,** chastity, chasteness, purity; integrity, morality, decency; dated honor; archaic virtue.
3 *she took advantage of his innocence* **naiveté,** ingenuousness, credulity, inexperience, gullibility, simplicity, unworldliness, guilelessness, greenness.

innocent ▶ adjective 1 *he was entirely innocent* **guiltless,** blameless, in the clear, unimpeachable, irreproachable, above suspicion, faultless; honorable, honest, upright, law-abiding; informal squeaky clean.
ANTONYMS guilty.
2 *innocent fun* **harmless,** benign, innocuous, safe, inoffensive.
ANTONYMS harmful.
3 *Alcott's depiction of innocent girls* **virtuous,** pure, moral, decent, righteous, upright, wholesome; demure, modest, chaste, virginal; impeccable, spotless, sinless, unsullied, incorrupt, undefiled; informal squeaky clean, lily-white, pure as the driven snow.
ANTONYMS sinful.
4 *she is **innocent of** guile* **free from,** without, lacking (in), clear of, ignorant of, unaware of, untouched by.
5 *at the innocent age of twelve* **naive,** ingenuous, trusting, credulous, unsuspicious, unwary, unguarded; impressionable, gullible, easily led; inexperienced, unworldly, unsophisticated, green; simple, artless, guileless, wide-eyed; informal wet behind the ears, born yesterday.
ANTONYMS worldly, seasoned.
▶ noun *an innocent in a strange land* **ingénue,** unworldly person; child, baby, babe; novice; informal greenhorn; literary babe in arms.

> USAGE
> **innocent**
> *Innocent* properly means 'harmless,' but it has long been extended in general language to mean 'not guilty.' The jury (or judge) in a criminal trial does not, strictly speaking, find a defendant 'innocent.' Rather, a defendant may be *guilty* or *not guilty* of the charges brought. In common use, however, owing perhaps to the concept of the *presumption of innocence*, which instructs a jury to consider a defendant free of wrongdoing until proven guilty on the basis of evidence, *not guilty* and *innocent* have come to be thought of as synonymous.

innocuous ▶ adjective 1 *an innocuous fungus* **harmless,** safe, nontoxic, innocent; edible, eatable.
ANTONYMS harmful, toxic.
2 *an innocuous comment* **inoffensive,** unobjectionable, unexceptionable, harmless, mild, tame, anodyne, soft-focus.
ANTONYMS offensive.

innovation ▶ noun *no appliance manufacturer*

can survive without an ongoing commitment to innovation **change,** alteration, revolution, upheaval, transformation, metamorphosis, breakthrough; new measures, new methods, modernization, novelty, newness; creativity, originality, ingenuity, inspiration, inventiveness; informal a shake up.

innuendo ▶ **noun** *his innuendoes were usually just thinly veiled sexual remarks* **insinuation,** suggestion, intimation, implication, hint, overtone, undertone, allusion, reference; aspersion, slur.

innumerable ▶ **adjective** *innumerable letters and telegrams flooded the courtroom during the trial* **countless,** untold, legion, without number, numberless, unnumbered, multitudinous, incalculable, limitless; informal umpteen, a slew of, no end of, loads of, stacks of, heaps of, masses of, oodles of, zillions of, gazillions of; literary myriad.
ANTONYMS few.

inoculation ▶ **noun** *the school nurse has no record of your child's most recent inoculation* **immunization,** vaccination, vaccine; injection, booster; informal jab, shot, hypo, needle.

inoffensive ▶ **adjective** *many people are challenging your contention that these were inoffensive remarks* **harmless,** innocuous, unobjectionable, unexceptionable; nonviolent, nonaggressive, mild, peaceful, peaceable, gentle; tame, innocent.

inoperative ▶ **adjective 1** *the fan is inoperative* **defective,** out of order, out of service, down, unserviceable, unusable, inoperable, bust/busted, out of action, shot, broken, faulty, on the blink, on the fritz, out of commission, acting up, kaput.
ANTONYMS working.
2 *the contract is inoperative* **void,** null and void, invalid, ineffective, nonviable; canceled, revoked, terminated; worthless, valueless, unproductive, abortive.
ANTONYMS valid.

inopportune ▶ **adjective** *the embassy's decision to release that statement was unfortunate and inopportune* **inappropriate,** unsuitable, malapropos, unfavorable, unfortunate, infelicitous, inexpedient; untimely, ill-timed, ill-chosen, unseasonable; awkward, difficult, inconvenient, disruptive.
ANTONYMS appropriate.

inordinate ▶ **adjective** *don't you think this is an inordinate amount of luggage for one weekend?* **excessive,** undue, unreasonable, unjustifiable, unwarrantable, disproportionate, unwarranted, unnecessary, needless, uncalled for, gratuitous, exorbitant, extreme; outrageous, immoderate, extravagant, intemperate; informal over the top.
ANTONYMS moderate, conservative.

inquest ▶ **noun** See INQUIRY (sense 2).

inquire ▶ **verb 1** *I inquired about part-time training courses* **ask,** make inquiries, question someone, request/solicit information.
2 *the commission will* ***inquire into*** *the state of health care* **investigate,** conduct an inquiry into/about/regarding, probe, look into; research, examine, explore, delve into, study; informal check out.

inquiring ▶ See INQUISITIVE.

inquiry ▶ **noun 1** *an inquiry about our location* **question,** query.
2 *an inquiry into alleged security leaks* **investigation,** probe, examination, review, analysis, exploration; inquest, hearing.

inquisition ▶ **noun** *what started as a few friendly questions soon turned into a not-so-friendly inquisition* **interrogation,** questioning, quizzing, cross-examination; investigation, inquiry, inquest, hearing; informal grilling; Law examination.

inquisitive ▶ **adjective** *we laughed when Brian said his sister was studying journalism—she was always such an inquisitive little pest* **curious,** interested, intrigued, prying, spying, eavesdropping, intrusive, busybody, meddlesome, snooping; inquiring, questioning, probing, searching; informal nosy, Nosy Parker, snoopy.
ANTONYMS uninterested.

insane ▶ **adjective 1** *she was declared insane* **mentally ill,** mentally disordered, of unsound mind, certifiable; psychotic, schizophrenic, bipolar; mad, deranged, demented, out of one's mind, non compos mentis, unhinged, unbalanced, unstable, disturbed, crazed; informal crazy, (stark) raving mad, not all there, bushed, bonkers, cracked, psycho, batty, cuckoo, loony, loopy, loco, nuts, screwy, bananas, crackers, wacko, off one's rocker, out of one's tree, around the bend, mad as a hatter, buggy.
ANTONYMS sane.
2 *insane laughter* **maniacal,** psychotic, crazed, hysterical.
ANTONYMS normal.
3 *an insane suggestion* **foolish,** idiotic, stupid, silly, senseless, nonsensical, absurd, ridiculous, ludicrous, lunatic, preposterous, fatuous, inane, asinine, hare-brained, half-baked; impracticable, implausible, irrational, illogical; informal crazy, mad, cockeyed, daft.
ANTONYMS sensible.
4 *I just looked at next week's schedule, and now I'm completely insane* **mad,** crazy; angry, furious, annoyed; informal aggravated, foaming at the mouth, hot under the collar.
ANTONYMS calm, contented.

insanity ▶ **noun 1** *insanity runs in her family* **mental illness,** madness, dementia; lunacy, instability; mania, psychosis; informal craziness.
2 *it would be insanity to take this loan* **folly,** foolishness, madness, idiocy, stupidity, lunacy, silliness; informal craziness.

insatiable ▶ **adjective** *an insatiable appetite for expensive jewelry* **unquenchable,** unappeasable, uncontrollable; voracious, gluttonous, greedy, hungry, ravenous, wolfish; avid, eager, keen; informal piggy; literary insatiate.

inscribe ▶ **verb 1** *his name was inscribed above the door* **carve,** write, engrave, etch, cut, incise; imprint, stamp, impress, mark.
2 *a book inscribed to him by the author* **dedicate,** address, name, sign.

inscription ▶ **noun 1** *the inscription on the sarcophagus* **engraving,** etching; wording,

writing, lettering, legend, epitaph, epigraph.
2 *the book had an inscription* **dedication,** message; signature, autograph.

inscrutable ▶ adjective *he was a financial genius with inscrutable motives* **enigmatic,** mysterious, unreadable, inexplicable, unexplainable, incomprehensible, impenetrable, unfathomable, unknowable; opaque, abstruse, arcane, obscure, cryptic.
ANTONYMS transparent.

insecure ▶ adjective **1** *an insecure young man* **unconfident,** uncertain, unsure, doubtful, hesitant, self-conscious, unassertive, diffident, unforthcoming, shy, timid, retiring, timorous, inhibited, introverted; anxious, fearful, worried; informal mousy.
ANTONYMS confident.
2 *an insecure railing* **unstable,** rickety, rocky, wobbly, shaky, unsteady, precarious; weak, flimsy, unsound, unsafe; informal jerry-built.
ANTONYMS stable.

insecurity ▶ noun **1** *he hid his insecurity* **lack of confidence,** self-doubt, diffidence, unassertiveness, timidity, uncertainty, nervousness, inhibition; anxiety, worry, unease.
2 *the insecurity of our situation* **vulnerability,** defenselessness, peril, danger; instability, fragility, frailty, shakiness, unreliability.

insensible ▶ adjective **1** *she was insensible on the floor* **unconscious,** insensate, senseless, insentient, inert, comatose, knocked out, passed out, blacked out; stunned, numb, numbed; informal out (cold), down for the count, out of it, zonked out, dead to the world.
ANTONYMS conscious.
2 *he was **insensible to** the risks* **unaware of,** ignorant of, unconscious of, unmindful of, oblivious to, incognizant of; indifferent to, impervious to, deaf to, blind to, unaffected by; informal in the dark about.
ANTONYMS aware.
3 *he showed insensible disregard* **insensitive,** dispassionate, cool, emotionless, unfeeling, unconcerned, detached, indifferent, hardened, tough, callous; informal hard-boiled.
ANTONYMS sensitive.

insensitive ▶ adjective **1** *an insensitive bully* **heartless,** unfeeling, inconsiderate, thoughtless, thick-skinned; hard-hearted, cold-blooded, uncaring, unconcerned, unsympathetic, unkind, callous, cruel, merciless, pitiless.
ANTONYMS compassionate.
2 *he was **insensitive to** her feelings* **impervious to,** oblivious to, unaware of, unresponsive to, indifferent to, unaffected by, unmoved by, untouched by; informal in the dark about.

inseparable ▶ adjective **1** *inseparable friends* **devoted,** bosom, close, fast, firm, good, best, intimate, faithful; informal as thick as thieves, joined at the hip.
2 *the laws are inseparable* **indivisible,** indissoluble, inextricable, entangled; (one and) the same.

insert ▶ verb **1** *he inserted a tape in the machine* **put,** place, push, thrust, slide, slip, load, fit, slot, lodge, install; informal pop, stick.
ANTONYMS extract, take out.
2 *she inserted a clause* **enter,** introduce, add, incorporate, interpolate, interpose, interject.
ANTONYMS remove.
▶ noun *the newspaper carried an insert* **enclosure,** insertion, supplement; circular, advertisement, pamphlet, leaflet; informal ad.

> CHOOSE THE RIGHT WORD
>
> **insert, inject, interject, interpolate, introduce, mediate**
>
> If you want to put something in a fixed place between or among other things, you can **insert** it (*insert a new paragraph in an essay; insert photographs in the text of a book*). If it's a liquid, you'll probably want to **inject** it (*inject the flu vaccine*), although to inject can also mean to add something new or different (*inject some humor into an otherwise dreary speech*). If it's a person, you should **introduce** him or her, which suggests placing the individual in the midst of a group so as to become part of it. You can also introduce things (*introduce a new subject into the curriculum*), but if the thing you're introducing is extraneous or lacks authorization, you may have to **interpolate** it (*interpolate editorial comments*). If you have remarks, statements, or questions to introduce in an abrupt or forced manner, you'll have to **interject** them (*in the midst of his speech, she interjected what she felt were important details*). If you interject too often, however, you risk offending the speaker and may have to ask someone to **mediate**, which means to settle a dispute or bring about a compromise by taking a stand midway between extremes.

inside ▶ noun **1** *the inside of a volcano* **interior,** inner part; center, core, middle, heart.
ANTONYMS exterior.
2 informal *my insides are aching* **stomach,** gut, internal organs, bowels, intestines; informal belly, tummy, guts, innards, viscera.
▶ adjective **1** *his inside pocket* **inner,** interior, internal, innermost.
ANTONYMS outer.
2 *inside information* **confidential,** classified, restricted, privileged, private, secret, exclusive; informal hush-hush.
ANTONYMS public.
▶ adverb **1** *she ushered me inside* **indoors,** within, in.
2 *how do you feel inside?* **inwardly,** within, secretly, privately, deep down, at heart, emotionally, intuitively, instinctively.
3 informal *if I get caught again I'll be back inside* **in prison,** in jail, in custody; locked up, imprisoned, incarcerated; informal behind bars, doing time.

insidious ▶ adjective *the insidious bond between big money and political decisions* **stealthy,** subtle, surreptitious, cunning, crafty, treacherous, artful, sly, wily, shifty, underhanded, indirect; informal sneaky.

insight ▶ noun **1** *your insight has been invaluable* **intuition,** discernment, perception, awareness,

understanding, comprehension, apprehension, appreciation, penetration, acumen, perspicacity, judgment, acuity; vision, wisdom, prescience; informal savvy.
2 *an insight into the government* **understanding of,** appreciation of, revelation about; introduction to; informal eye-opener about.

insignia ▶ noun *I thought from the insignia that he was at least a colonel* **badge,** crest, emblem, symbol, sign, device, mark, seal, logo, colors.

insignificant ▶ adjective *the raises the kitchen staff received were insignificant* **unimportant,** trivial, trifling, negligible, inconsequential, of no account, inconsiderable; nugatory, paltry, petty, insubstantial, frivolous, pointless, worthless, meaningless, irrelevant, immaterial, peripheral; informal piddling.

insincere ▶ adjective *voters respond favorably to even the most insincere campaign promises, as long as they hear just what they want* **false,** fake, hollow, artificial, feigned, pretended, put-on, inauthentic; disingenuous, hypocritical, cynical, deceitful, deceptive, duplicitous, double-dealing, two-faced, lying, untruthful, mendacious; informal phony, pretend.

insinuate ▶ verb *he insinuated that she lied* **imply,** suggest, hint, intimate, indicate, let it be known, give someone to understand; informal make out.
– PHRASES **insinuate oneself into** *he is trying to insinuate himself into their family* **worm one's way into,** ingratiate oneself with, curry favor with; foist oneself on, introduce oneself into, edge one's way into, insert oneself into; infiltrate, invade, sneak into, maneuver oneself into, intrude on, impinge on; informal muscle in on.

insinuation ▶ noun *she made many unkind insinuations regarding his parental ability* **implication,** inference, suggestion, hint, intimation, connotation, innuendo, reference, allusion, indication, undertone, overtone; aspersion, slur, allegation.

insipid ▶ adjective **1** *insipid coffee* **tasteless,** flavorless, bland, weak, wishy-washy; unappetizing, unpalatable.
ANTONYMS tasty.
2 *insipid pictures* **unimaginative,** uninspired, uninspiring, characterless, flat, uninteresting, lackluster, dull, drab, boring, dry, humdrum, ho-hum, monochrome, tedious, run-of-the-mill, commonplace, pedestrian, trite, tired, hackneyed, stale, lame, wishy-washy, colorless, anemic, lifeless.
ANTONYMS interesting, imaginative.

insist ▶ verb **1** *she insisted that they pay up* **demand,** command, require, dictate; urge, exhort.
2 *he insisted that he knew nothing* **maintain,** assert, hold, contend, argue, protest, claim, vow, swear, declare, stress, repeat, reiterate; formal aver.
– PHRASES **insist on** *she insisted on her children's going to college* **be set on,** be intent on, persist in, stand firm about, stand one's ground about, be resolute about, be emphatic about, be adamant about, not take no for an answer about; informal stick to one's guns about.

insistent ▶ adjective **1** *Tony's insistent questioning* **persistent,** determined, adamant, importunate, tenacious, unyielding, dogged, unrelenting, tireless, inexorable; demanding, pushy, forceful, urgent; clamorous, vociferous; emphatic, firm, assertive.
2 *the insistent rattle of the fan* **incessant,** constant, unremitting, repetitive; obtrusive, intrusive, loud.

insolent ▶ adjective *Dan is an inveterate wise guy who can't help making insolent cracks as he narrates the tale* **impertinent,** impudent, cheeky, ill-mannered, bad mannered, unmannerly, rude, impolite, uncivil, discourteous, disrespectful, insubordinate, contemptuous; audacious, bold, cocky, brazen; insulting, abusive; informal fresh, lippy, saucy, pert, sassy, smart-alecky; archaic contumelious. See note at IMPERTINENT.
ANTONYMS polite.

insoluble ▶ adjective **1** *some problems are insoluble* **unsolvable,** unanswerable, unresolvable; unfathomable, impenetrable, unexplainable, inscrutable, inexplicable.
2 *these minerals are insoluble in water* **indissoluble,** incapable of dissolving.

insolvency ▶ noun See BANKRUPTCY.

insolvent ▶ adjective *even his family never suspected that he was insolvent* **bankrupt,** ruined, wiped out, in receivership; penniless, poor, impoverished, impecunious, destitute, without a penny (to one's name), in debt, in arrears; informal bust, (flat) broke, belly up, in the red, hard up, strapped (for cash), cleaned out; formal penurious.

insomnia ▶ noun *I've tried every wild remedy for insomnia, including cinnamon baths and standing on my head* **sleeplessness,** wakefulness, restlessness, inability to sleep.

insouciant ▶ adjective *only outwardly did he possess an insouciant attitude about the disease* **nonchalant,** untroubled, unworried, unruffled, unconcerned, indifferent, blasé, heedless, careless; relaxed, calm, equable, serene, composed, easy, easygoing, carefree, free and easy, happy-go-lucky, lighthearted, airy, blithe, mellow; informal cool, laid-back, slaphappy.

inspect ▶ verb *by all means, inspect any part of the house you wish* **examine,** check, scrutinize, investigate, vet, test, monitor, survey, study, look over, peruse, scan, explore, probe; assess, appraise, review, audit; informal check out, give something a/the once-over.

inspection ▶ noun *on further inspection, we detected a slight crack in the pipe* **examination,** checkup, survey, scrutiny, probe, exploration, observation, investigation; assessment, appraisal, review, evaluation; informal once-over, going-over, look-see.

inspector ▶ noun *the inspector's report is due here by noon* **examiner,** scrutineer, investigator, surveyor, assessor, appraiser, reviewer, analyst; observer, overseer, supervisor, monitor, watchdog, ombudsman; auditor.

inspiration ▶ noun **1** *her work is a real inspiration to others* **guiding light,** example, model, muse, motivation, encouragement,

influence, spur, stimulus, lift, boost, incentive, impulse, catalyst.
2 *his work lacks inspiration* **creativity,** inventiveness, innovation, ingenuity, genius, imagination, originality; artistry, insight, vision; finesse, flair.
3 *she had a sudden inspiration* **bright idea,** revelation, flash; informal brainwave, brainstorm, eureka moment.

inspire ▶ verb **1** *the landscape inspired him to write* **stimulate,** motivate, encourage, influence, rouse, move, stir, energize, galvanize, incite; animate, fire, excite, spark, inspirit, incentivize, affect. See note at ENCOURAGE.
2 *the film inspired a musical* **give rise to,** lead to, bring about, cause, prompt, spawn, engender; literary beget.
3 *Charles inspired awe in her* **arouse,** awaken, prompt, induce, ignite, trigger, kindle, produce, bring out; literary enkindle.

inspired ▶ adjective *toe-tapping melodies and inspired lyrics* **outstanding,** wonderful, marvelous, excellent, magnificent, fine, exceptional, first-class, first-rate, virtuoso, supreme, superlative, brilliant; innovative, ingenious, imaginative, original; informal tremendous, superb, super, ace, wicked, awesome, out of this world.
ANTONYMS dull, poor.

instability ▶ noun **1** *the instability of political life* **unreliability,** uncertainty, unpredictability, insecurity, riskiness; impermanence, inconstancy, changeability, variability, fluctuation, mutability, transience.
ANTONYMS certainty, steadiness.
2 *emotional instability* **volatility,** unpredictability, variability, capriciousness, flightiness, fickleness, changeability, vacillation.
ANTONYMS steadiness.
3 *the instability of the foundations* **unsteadiness,** unsoundness, shakiness, frailty, fragility, weakness.
ANTONYMS soundness.

install ▶ verb **1** *a photocopier was installed in the office* **put,** position, place, locate, situate, station, site, lodge; insert.
ANTONYMS remove.
2 *the college installs its new president this afternoon* **swear in,** induct, instate, inaugurate, invest; appoint; ordain, consecrate, anoint; enthrone, crown.
ANTONYMS remove.
3 *she installed herself behind the table* **ensconce,** establish, position, settle, seat, lodge, plant; sit (down); informal plonk, park.
4 *you'll need to install new software* **load,** store.

installment ▶ noun **1** *I pay monthly installments* **part payment**; deferred payment, premium.
2 *a story published in installments* **part,** portion, section, segment, bit; chapter, episode, volume, issue.

instance ▶ noun *an instance of racism* **example,** exemplar, occasion, occurrence, case; illustration.
▶ verb *they instanced the previous case as an example* **cite,** quote, refer to, mention, allude to, give; specify, name, identify, draw attention to, put forward, offer, advance.

instant ▶ adjective **1** *instant access to your money* **immediate,** instantaneous, on-the-spot, prompt, swift, speedy, rapid, quick, express, lightning; sudden, precipitate, abrupt; informal snappy, PDQ, pretty damn/darn quick.
ANTONYMS delayed.
2 *instant meals* **preprepared,** precooked, ready-made, ready-mixed, heat-and-serve, fast; microwaveable.
▶ noun **1** *come here this instant!* **moment,** minute, second; juncture, point.
2 *it all happened in an instant* **moment,** minute, trice, (split) second, wink/blink/twinkling of an eye, flash, no time (at all), heartbeat; informal sec, jiffy, jiff, snap.

instantaneous ▶ adjective *it doesn't have the instantaneous delivery aspect of the Internet but you'll get much higher resolution* **immediate,** instant, on-the-spot, prompt, swift, speedy, rapid, quick, express, expeditious, lightning; sudden, hurried, precipitate; informal snappy, PDQ, pretty damn/darn quick; literary fleet.
ANTONYMS delayed.

instead ▶ adverb *instead, let's take the train* **as an alternative,** alternatively, alternately; on second thought, all things being equal.
– PHRASES **instead of** *I'll have the blue instead of the yellow, please* **as an alternative to,** as a substitute for, as a replacement for, in place of, in lieu of, in preference to; rather than, as opposed to, as against, as contrasted with, before.

instigate ▶ verb **1** *the committee instigated formal proceedings* **set in motion,** get underway, get off the ground, start, commence, begin, initiate, launch, institute, set up, inaugurate, establish, organize; actuate, generate, bring about; start the ball rolling on, kick off. See note at ENCOURAGE.
ANTONYMS halt.
2 *the liberal clergy is instigating a movement of political reform* **incite,** encourage, urge, provoke, goad, spur (on), initiate, stimulate, push (for), prompt, induce; arouse, rouse, inflame, excite, stir up; informal root on. See note at INCITE.
ANTONYMS dissuade, quell.

instigation ▶ noun **1** *it was primarily Aaron's instigation that brought the festival into being* **prompting,** suggestion, recommendation; request, entreaty, demand, insistence; wish, desire, persuasion; formal instance.
2 *foreign instigation is suspected to be at the root of this disturbance* **incitement,** initiation, provocation, stirring up, fomentation, inducement, encouragement.

instigator ▶ noun *the instigators behind the crime wave* **initiator,** prime mover, motivator, architect, designer, planner, inventor, mastermind, originator, author, creator, agent; founder, pioneer, founding father; agitator, fomenter, troublemaker, ringleader, rabble-rouser.

instill ▶ verb **1** *we instill vigilance in our children* **inculcate,** implant, ingrain, impress, imprint, introduce; engender, produce, generate, induce,

inspire, promote, foster; drum (into), drill (into).
2 *he instilled Monet with a love of nature* **imbue,** inspire, infuse, inculcate, inject; indoctrinate; teach.

instinct ▶ noun **1** *some instinct told me to be careful* **natural tendency,** inherent tendency, inclination, urge, drive, compulsion, need; intuition, feeling, hunch, sixth sense, insight; nose.
2 *his instinct for music* **talent,** gift, ability, aptitude, faculty, skill, flair, feel, genius, knack, bent.

instinctive ▶ adjective *an instinctive understanding of machinery | an instinctive urge to scream* **intuitive,** natural, instinctual, innate, inborn, inherent; unconscious, subconscious, intuitional; automatic, reflex, knee-jerk, mechanical, spontaneous, involuntary, impulsive; informal gut, second nature.
ANTONYMS learned, voluntary.

institute ▶ noun See INSTITUTION (sense 1).
▶ verb *the company has asked us to institute the new hiring policies before December 31* **initiate,** set in motion, get underway, get off the ground, get going, start, commence, begin, launch; set up, inaugurate, found, establish, organize, generate, bring about; start the ball rolling on; informal kick off.
ANTONYMS end.

institution ▶ noun **1** *an academic institution* **establishment,** organization, institute, foundation, center; academy, school, college, university; society, association, body, guild, federation, consortium.
2 *how much do we know about the quality of medical care in these institutions?* **hospital, nursing home,** retirement home, old-age home, old folks' home, (residential) home; asylum, mental institution; sanatorium.
3 *the institution of marriage* **practice,** custom, convention, tradition, habit; phenomenon, fact; system, policy; idea, notion, concept, principle.
4 *the institution of legal proceedings* **initiation,** instigation, launch, start, commencement, beginning, inauguration, generation, origination.

institutional ▶ adjective **1** *an institutional framework for discussions* **organized,** established, bureaucratic, conventional, procedural, prescribed, set, routine, formal, systematic, systematized, methodical, businesslike, orderly, coherent, structured, regulated.
2 *the rooms are rather institutional* **impersonal,** formal, regimented, uniform, unvaried, monotonous; insipid, bland, uninteresting, dull; unappealing, uninviting, unattractive, unwelcoming, dreary, drab, colorless; stark, spartan, bare, clinical, sterile, austere.

instruct ▶ verb **1** *the union instructed them to strike* **order,** direct, command, tell, enjoin, require, call on, mandate, charge; literary bid.
2 *do not attempt to operate the binder until you've been thoroughly instructed* **teach,** school, coach, train, enlighten, inform, educate, tutor, guide, prepare, prime.
3 *the judge instructed the jury to consider all of the facts* **inform,** tell, notify, apprise, advise, brief, prime; informal fill someone in, clue someone in.

instruction ▶ noun **1** *my instructions are to be obeyed at all times* **order,** command, directive, direction, decree, edict, injunction, mandate, dictate, commandment, bidding; requirement, stipulation; informal marching orders; literary behest.
2 (**instructions**) *read the instructions* **directions,** key, rubric, specification, how-tos; handbook, manual, guide, tutorial.
3 *most of the instruction we received was combat-related* **teaching,** coaching, schooling, education, tutelage, tuition; lessons, classes, lectures; training, preparation, grounding, guidance.

instructive ▶ adjective *the manual is not sufficiently instructive* **informative,** instructional, informational, illuminating, enlightening, explanatory; educational, educative, edifying, didactic, pedagogic, heuristic; improving, moralistic, homiletic; useful, helpful.

instructor ▶ noun *Heilbrun was briefly an instructor at Brooklyn College* **teacher,** schoolteacher, educator, professor; mentor, tutor; coach, trainer; adviser, counselor, guide; formal pedagogue.

instrument ▶ noun **1** *a wound made with a sharp instrument* **implement,** tool, utensil; device, apparatus, contrivance, gadget. See note at TOOL.
2 *check all the cockpit instruments* **measuring device,** gauge, meter; indicator, dial, display; avionics.
3 *Tony tuned his instruments* **musical instrument.**
4 *drama can be an instrument of learning* **agent,** agency, cause, channel, medium, means, mechanism, vehicle, organ.
5 *he is a mere instrument* **pawn,** puppet, creature, dupe, cog; tool, cat's paw; informal stooge.

instrumental ▶ adjective *the space program has always been instrumental in our efforts to make medical advances* **involved,** active, influential, contributory; helpful, useful, of service; significant, important, crucial, critical, essential, pivotal, key; (**be instrumental in**) play a part in, contribute to, be a factor in, have a hand in; add to, help, promote, advance, further; be conducive to, lead to, cause.

insubordinate ▶ adjective *she defended her insubordinate behavior by exposing corruption in high places* **disobedient,** unruly, wayward, errant, badly behaved, disorderly, undisciplined, delinquent, troublesome, rebellious, defiant, recalcitrant, uncooperative, willful, intractable, unmanageable, uncontrollable; awkward, difficult, perverse, contrary; disrespectful, cheeky.
ANTONYMS obedient.

insubordination ▶ noun *one quickly learns at West Point that insubordination is a serious matter* **disobedience,** unruliness, indiscipline, bad behavior, misbehavior, misconduct, delinquency, insolence; rebellion, defiance, mutiny, revolt; recalcitrance, willfulness, awkwardness, perversity; informal acting-up; Law contumacy.

insubstantial ▶ adjective 1 *an insubstantial structure* **flimsy,** fragile, breakable, weak, frail, slight, unstable, shaky, wobbly, rickety, ramshackle, jerry-built.
ANTONYMS sturdy.
2 *insubstantial evidence* **weak,** flimsy, feeble, poor, inadequate, insufficient, tenuous, insignificant, unconvincing, implausible, unsatisfactory, paltry.
ANTONYMS sound.
3 *insubstantial visions* **intangible,** impalpable, untouchable, discarnate, unsubstantial, incorporeal; imaginary, unreal, illusory, spectral, ghostlike, vaporous, immaterial.
ANTONYMS tangible.
4 *an insubstantial amount* **small,** negligible, inconsequential, inconsiderable, trifling, measly; informal piddling.
ANTONYMS ample, generous.

insufferable ▶ adjective 1 *the heat was insufferable* **intolerable,** unbearable, unendurable, insupportable, unacceptable, oppressive, overwhelming, overpowering; informal too much.
ANTONYMS bearable.
2 *his win made him insufferable* **conceited,** arrogant, boastful, cocky, cocksure, full of oneself, self-important, swaggering; vain, puffed up, self-satisfied, self-congratulatory, smug; informal bigheaded, too big for one's britches, too big for one's boots; literary vainglorious.
ANTONYMS modest.

insufficient ▶ adjective *the emergency lighting is insufficient | insufficient funds* **inadequate,** deficient, poor, scant, scanty; not enough, too little, too few, too small; scarce, sparse, in short supply, lacking, wanting; paltry, meager, niggardly; incomplete, restricted, limited; informal measly, pathetic, piddling.

insular ▶ adjective 1 *insular attitudes* **narrow-minded,** small-minded, inward-looking, parochial, provincial, small-town, shortsighted, hidebound, blinkered; set in one's ways, inflexible, rigid, entrenched; illiberal, intolerant, prejudiced, bigoted, biased, partisan, xenophobic; informal redneck.
ANTONYMS broad-minded, tolerant.
2 *an insular existence* **isolated,** inaccessible, cutoff, segregated, detached, solitary, lonely, hermitic.
ANTONYMS cosmopolitan.

insulate ▶ verb 1 *pipes must be insulated* **wrap,** sheathe, cover, coat, encase, enclose, envelop; heatproof, soundproof; pad, cushion.
2 *they were insulated from the impact of the war* **protect,** save, shield, shelter, screen, cushion, buffer, cocoon; isolate, segregate, sequester, detach, cut off.

insult ▶ verb *he insulted my wife* **abuse,** be rude to, slight, disparage, discredit, libel, slander, malign, defame, denigrate, cast aspersions on, call someone names, put someone down; offend, affront, hurt, humiliate, wound; informal badmouth, dis; formal derogate, calumniate; rare asperse.
ANTONYMS compliment.
▶ noun *he hurled insults at us* **abusive remark,** jibe, affront, slight, barb, slur, indignity; injury, libel, slander, defamation; abuse, disparagement, aspersions; informal dig, crack, put-down, slap in the face, kick in the teeth, cheap shot, low blow.

insulting ▶ adjective *once you send that insulting message, there's no taking it back* **abusive,** rude, offensive, disparaging, belittling, derogatory, deprecatory, disrespectful, uncomplimentary, pejorative; disdainful, derisive, scornful, contemptuous; defamatory, slanderous, libelous, scurrilous, blasphemous; informal bitchy, catty, snide. See note at OFFENSIVE.

insupportable ▶ adjective 1 *his arrogance was insupportable* **intolerable,** insufferable, unbearable, unendurable; oppressive, overwhelming, overpowering; informal too much.
ANTONYMS bearable.
2 *this view is insupportable* **unjustifiable,** indefensible, inexcusable, unwarrantable, unreasonable, untenable; unjustified, baseless, groundless, unfounded, unsupported, unsubstantiated, unconfirmed, uncorroborated, invalid; implausible, weak, flawed, specious, defective.
ANTONYMS defensible, justified.

insurance ▶ noun 1 *insurance for his new car* **indemnity,** indemnification, assurance, (financial) protection, security, coverage.
2 *insurance against a third world war* **protection,** defense, safeguard, security, hedge, precaution, provision, surety; immunity; guarantee, warranty; informal backstop.

insure ▶ verb *the high cost of insuring a teenage driver* **provide insurance for,** indemnify, cover, assure, protect, underwrite; guarantee, warrant.

insurgent ▶ adjective *insurgent forces* **rebellious,** rebel, revolutionary, mutinous, insurrectionist; renegade, seditious, subversive.
ANTONYMS loyal.
▶ noun *the insurgents are gaining popularity* **rebel,** revolutionary, revolutionist, mutineer, insurrectionist, agitator, subversive, renegade, incendiary; guerrilla, freedom fighter, anarchist, terrorist.
ANTONYMS loyalist.

insurmountable ▶ adjective *I refuse to believe that any of the problems mentioned here today are insurmountable* **insuperable,** unconquerable, invincible, unassailable; overwhelming, hopeless, impossible.

insurrection ▶ noun *the suspects all escaped after a prison insurrection* **rebellion,** revolt, uprising, mutiny, revolution, insurgence, riot, sedition, subversion; civil disorder, unrest, anarchy; coup (d'état).

intact ▶ adjective *we expect to find the house intact when we get back* **whole,** entire, complete, unbroken, undamaged, unimpaired, faultless, flawless, unscathed, untouched, unspoiled, unblemished, unmarked, perfect, pristine, inviolate, undefiled, unsullied, virgin, in one piece; sound, solid.
ANTONYMS damaged.

intangible ▶ adjective 1 *the shadows were more*

intangible than usual as they shifted with each quavering bough and passing cloud **impalpable,** untouchable, incorporeal, discarnate, abstract; ethereal, insubstantial, immaterial, airy; ghostly, spectral, unearthly, supernatural.
2 *team spirit may be intangible, but we wouldn't have gotten to the finals without it* **indefinable,** indescribable, inexpressible, nameless; vague, obscure, abstract, unclear, indefinite, undefined, subtle, elusive.

integral ▶ **adjective 1** *an integral part of human behavior* **essential,** fundamental, basic, intrinsic, inherent, constitutive, innate, structural; vital, necessary, requisite.
ANTONYMS peripheral, incidental.
2 *the dryer has integral cord storage* **built-in,** integrated, incorporated, included.
ANTONYMS peripheral.
3 *an integral approach to learning* **unified,** integrated, comprehensive, composite, combined, aggregate; complete, whole.
ANTONYMS partial, fragmented.

integrate ▶ **verb** *reserve forces will be more closely integrated with the regular forces* **combine,** amalgamate, merge, unite, fuse, blend, mingle, coalesce, consolidate, meld, intermingle, mix; incorporate, unify, assimilate, homogenize; desegregate.
ANTONYMS separate.

integrated ▶ **adjective 1** *an integrated package of services* **unified,** united, consolidated, amalgamated, combined, merged, fused, homogeneous, assimilated, cohesive, complete; Brit. joined-up.
2 *an integrated school* **desegregated,** nonsegregated, unsegregated, mixed, multicultural.

integrity ▶ **noun 1** *I never doubted his integrity* **honesty,** probity, rectitude, honor, good character, principle(s), ethics, morals, righteousness, morality, virtue, decency, fairness, scrupulousness, sincerity, truthfulness, trustworthiness.
ANTONYMS dishonesty.
2 *the integrity of the federation* **unity,** unification, coherence, cohesion, togetherness, solidarity.
ANTONYMS division.
3 *the structural integrity of the aircraft* **soundness,** strength, sturdiness, solidity, durability, stability, stoutness, toughness.
ANTONYMS fragility.

intellect ▶ **noun 1** *a film that appeals to one's intellect* **mind,** brain(s), intelligence, reason, understanding, thought, brainpower, sense, judgment, wisdom, wits; informal gray matter, IQ, brain cells, smarts.
2 *one of the finest intellects* **thinker,** intellectual, sage; mind, brain.

intellectual ▶ **adjective 1** *her intellectual capacity* **mental,** cerebral, cognitive, psychological; rational, abstract, conceptual, theoretical, analytical, logical; academic.
ANTONYMS physical.
2 *an intellectual man* **intelligent,** clever, academic, educated, well-read, lettered, erudite, cerebral, learned, knowledgeable, literary, bookish, highbrow, scholarly, studious, enlightened, sophisticated, cultured, donnish; informal brainy.
ANTONYMS stupid.
▶ **noun** *"The Simpsons" is among the most revered TV shows among intellectuals* **highbrow,** learned person, academic, bookworm, man/woman of letters, bluestocking; thinker, brain, scholar, genius, Einstein, polymath, mastermind; informal egghead, brains, brainiac, rocket scientist.
ANTONYMS dunce.

intelligence ▶ **noun 1** *a man of great intelligence* **intellectual capacity,** mental capacity, intellect, mind, brain(s), IQ, brainpower, judgment, reasoning, understanding, comprehension; acumen, wit, sense, insight, perception, penetration, discernment, smartness, canniness, astuteness, intuition, acuity, cleverness, brilliance, ability; informal braininess.
2 *we're awaiting the latest intelligence from our operatives* **information,** facts, details, particulars, data, knowledge, reports, inside story; informal info, dope, skinny, lowdown.
3 *intelligence operation* **information gathering,** surveillance, observation, reconnaissance, spying, espionage, infiltration, ELINT, humint; informal recon.

intelligent ▶ **adjective 1** *an intelligent writer* **clever,** bright, brilliant, quick-witted, quick on the uptake, smart, canny, astute, intuitive, insightful, perceptive, perspicacious, discerning; knowledgeable; able, gifted, talented; informal brainy.
2 *an intelligent being* **rational,** higher-order, capable of thought.

intelligentsia ▶ **plural noun** *this antidemocratic system is supported by the political intelligentsia who call themselves democratic, even progressive* **intellectuals,** intelligent people, academics, scholars, literati, cognoscenti, illuminati, highbrows, thinkers, brains; intelligent; informal eggheads.
ANTONYMS masses.

intelligible ▶ **adjective** *finally, an owner's manual that's actually intelligible* **comprehensible,** understandable; accessible, digestible, user-friendly, penetrable, fathomable; lucid, clear, coherent, plain, simple, explicit, precise, unambiguous, self-explanatory; formal exoteric.

intemperate ▶ **adjective** *a man of intemperate taste may soon find himself with little left to taste* **immoderate,** excessive, undue, inordinate, extreme, unrestrained, uncontrolled; self-indulgent, overindulgent, extravagant, lavish, prodigal, profligate; imprudent, reckless, wild; dissolute, debauched, wanton, dissipated.
ANTONYMS moderate.

intend ▶ **verb** *I intend to lease a car | what does Mark intend to do about the broken gate?* **plan,** mean, have in mind, have the intention, aim, propose; aspire, hope, expect, be resolved, be determined; want, wish; contemplate, think of, envisage, envision; design, earmark, designate, set aside; formal purpose.

> CHOOSE THE RIGHT WORD
>
> **intend, aim, design, mean, plan, propose, purpose**
>
> If you **intend** to do something, you may or may not be serious about getting it done (*I intend to clean out the garage some day*) but at least you have a goal in mind. Although **mean** can also imply either a firm resolve (*I mean to go, with or without her permission*) or a vague intention (*I've been meaning to write her for weeks*), it is a less formal word that usually connotes a certain lack of determination or a weak resolve. **Plan**, like *mean* and *intend*, may imply a vague goal (*I plan to tour China some day*), but it is often used to suggest that you're taking active steps (*I plan to leave as soon as I finish packing*). **Aim** indicates that you have an actual goal or purpose in mind and that you're putting some effort behind it (*I aim to be the first woman president*), without the hint of failure conveyed by *mean*. If you **propose** to do something, you declare your intention ahead of time (*I propose that we set up a meeting next week*), and if you **purpose** to do it, you are even more determined to achieve your goal (*I purpose to write a three-volume history of baseball in America*). **Design** suggests forethought in devising a plan (*design a strategy that will keep everyone happy*).

intense ▶ adjective **1** *intense heat* **extreme,** great, acute, fierce, severe, high; exceptional, extraordinary; harsh, strong, powerful, potent, overpowering, vigorous; informal serious.
ANTONYMS mild.
2 *a very intense young man* **passionate,** impassioned, ardent, fervent, zealous, vehement, fiery, emotional; earnest, eager, animated, spirited, vigorous, energetic, fanatical, committed.
ANTONYMS apathetic.

> CHOOSE THE RIGHT WORD
>
> **intense, intensive**
>
> **Intense** and **intensive** are similar in meaning, but they differ in emphasis. **Intense** tends to relate to subjective responses—emotions and how we feel—while **intensive** tends to relate to objective descriptions. Thus *an intensive course* simply describes the type of course: one that is designed to cover a lot of ground in a short time. On the other hand, in *the course was intense*, the word **intense** describes how someone felt about the course.

intensify ▶ verb *leaders here are fearful that yesterday's bombing will intensify the fighting north of the city* **escalate,** increase, step up, boost, raise, strengthen, augment, reinforce; pick up, build up, heighten, deepen, extend, expand, amplify, magnify; aggravate, exacerbate, worsen, inflame, compound.
ANTONYMS abate, lessen.

intensity ▶ noun **1** *the intensity of the sun* **strength,** power, potency, force; severity, ferocity, vehemence, fierceness, harshness; magnitude, greatness, acuteness, extremity.
2 *many here today remember the intensity in Dr. King's voice* **passion,** ardor, fervor, fervency, zeal, vehemence, fire, heat, emotion; eagerness, animation, spirit, vigor, strength, energy; fanaticism.
ANTONYMS apathy, indifference.

intensive ▶ adjective *an intensive search of the area | an intensive course in Russian* **thorough,** thoroughgoing, in-depth, rigorous, exhaustive; all-inclusive, comprehensive, all-embracing, all-encompassing, complete, full; vigorous, strenuous; concentrated, condensed, accelerated; detailed, minute, close, meticulous, scrupulous, painstaking, methodical, careful. See note at INTENSE.
ANTONYMS cursory, superficial.

intent ▶ noun *he tried to figure out his father's intent* **aim,** intention, purpose, objective, object, goal, target; design, plan, scheme; wish, desire, ambition, idea, aspiration.
▶ adjective **1** *he was **intent on** proving his point* **bent on,** set on, insistent on, hell-bent on; committed to, obsessive about, obsessed with, fanatical about, fixated on; determined to; anxious to, resolved to, impatient to.
2 *an intent expression* **attentive,** absorbed, engrossed, fascinated, enthralled, rapt, riveted; focused, earnest, concentrating, intense, studious, preoccupied; alert, watchful.
– PHRASES **for/to all intents and purposes** *if you sublet your apartment, realize that you are—for all intents and purposes—a landlord* **in effect,** effectively, in essence, essentially, virtually, practically; more or less, just about, all but, as good as, in all but name, almost, nearly; informal pretty much, pretty well; literary nigh on.

intention ▶ noun **1** *it is his intention to be leader* See INTENT (noun).
2 *he managed, without intention, to upset me* **intent,** intentionality, deliberateness, design, calculation, meaning; premeditation, forethought, preplanning; Law malice aforethought.

intentional ▶ adjective *intentional contamination of our food supply is a real threat* **deliberate,** calculated, conscious, intended, planned, meant, studied, knowing, willful, purposeful, purposive, done on purpose, premeditated, preplanned, preconceived; rare witting.

intentionally ▶ adverb *she would never intentionally hurt anyone* **deliberately,** on purpose, purposely, purposefully, by design, knowingly, wittingly, consciously; premeditatedly, calculatedly, in cold blood, willfully, wantonly; Law with malice aforethought.
ANTONYMS accidentally.

inter ▶ verb See BURY (sense 1).

intercede ▶ verb *a third party was called in to intercede* **mediate,** intermediate, arbitrate, conciliate, negotiate, moderate; intervene, interpose, step in, act; plead, petition, advocate.

intercept ▸ verb *the ball was intercepted | a nearby Coast Guard cutter was able to intercept the gunrunners before they reached the harbor* **stop,** head off, cut off; catch, seize, grab, snatch; obstruct, impede, interrupt, block, check, detain; ambush, challenge, waylay.

intercession ▸ noun *the hostages were released after intercession by trained negotiators* **mediation,** intermediation, arbitration, conciliation, negotiation; intervention, involvement; pleading, petition, entreaty, agency; diplomacy.

interchange ▸ verb *the watch comes with five different straps, which can be interchanged to match your outfit* **substitute,** transpose, switch, alternate; exchange, swap, trade; reverse, invert, replace.

▸ noun 1 *the interchange of ideas* **exchange,** trade, swap, barter, give and take, traffic, reciprocation, reciprocity; archaic truck.

2 *a highway interchange* **junction,** intersection, crossing; overpass, exit (ramp), cloverleaf.

interchangeable ▸ adjective *the attachments for these two vacuum cleaners are interchangeable* **similar,** identical, indistinguishable, alike, the same, uniform, twin, undifferentiated; corresponding, commensurate, equivalent, synonymous, comparable, equal; transposable.

intercourse ▸ noun 1 *social intercourse* **dealings,** relations, relationships, association, connections, contact; interchange, communication, communion, correspondence; negotiations, bargaining, transactions; trade, traffic, commerce; informal doings, truck.

2 *she did not consent to intercourse* **sexual intercourse,** sex, lovemaking, sexual relations, intimacy, coupling, mating, copulation, penetration; informal nookie, whoopee; technical coitus, coition; formal fornication; dated carnal knowledge.

interdict ▸ noun *they breached an interdict* **prohibition,** ban, bar, veto, proscription, interdiction, embargo, moratorium, injunction.
ANTONYMS permission.

▸ verb 1 *they interdicted foreign commerce* **prohibit,** forbid, ban, bar, veto, proscribe, embargo, disallow, debar, outlaw; stop, suppress; Law enjoin. See note at PROHIBIT.
ANTONYMS permit.

2 *efforts to interdict the flow of heroin* **intercept,** stop, head off, cut off; obstruct, impede, block; detain.
ANTONYMS facilitate.

interest ▸ noun 1 *we listened with interest* **attentiveness,** attention, absorption; heed, regard, notice; curiosity, inquisitiveness; enjoyment, delight, enthusiasm.
ANTONYMS boredom.

2 *places of interest* **attraction,** appeal, fascination, charm, beauty, allure.
ANTONYMS repulsion.

3 *this will be of interest to those involved* **concern,** consequence, importance, import, significance, note, relevance, value, weight; formal moment.
ANTONYMS irrelevance.

4 *her interests include reading* **hobby,** pastime, leisure pursuit, recreation, diversion, amusement; passion, enthusiasm; informal thing, bag, cup of tea.

5 *a financial interest in the firm* **stake,** share, claim, investment, stock, equity; involvement, concern.

6 *what is your interest in the case?* **involvement,** partiality, partisanship, preference, loyalty; bias, prejudice.

7 *his attorney guarded his interests* **concern,** business, affair.

8 *her savings earned interest* **dividends,** profits, returns; a percentage.

▸ verb 1 *a topic that interests you* **appeal to,** be of interest to, attract, intrigue, fascinate; absorb, engross, rivet, grip, captivate; amuse, divert, entertain; arouse one's curiosity, whet one's appetite; informal float someone's boat, tickle someone's fancy.
ANTONYMS bore.

2 *can I* ***interest*** *you* ***in*** *a drink?* persuade to have, tempt to have; sell.

– PHRASES **in someone's best interests** *there was bitter disagreement over which treatment would be in their father's best interests* **of (the most) benefit to,** to the advantage of; for the sake of, for the benefit of.

interested ▸ adjective 1 *an interested crowd* **attentive,** intent, absorbed, engrossed, fascinated, riveted, gripped, captivated, rapt, agog; intrigued, inquisitive, curious; keen, eager; informal all ears, nosy, snoopy.
ANTONYMS uninterested, bored.

2 *the government consulted with interested groups* **concerned,** involved, affected, connected, related.
ANTONYMS uninvolved.

3 *no interested party can judge the contest* **partisan,** partial, biased, prejudiced, preferential.
ANTONYMS disinterested, nonpartisan.

interesting ▸ adjective *a dramatic look inside the classroom that makes for some interesting television* **absorbing,** engrossing, fascinating, riveting, gripping, compelling, compulsive, captivating, engaging, enthralling; appealing, attractive; amusing, entertaining, stimulating, thought-provoking, diverting, intriguing.
ANTONYMS boring.

interfere ▸ verb 1 *we don't let emotion* ***interfere with*** *our duty* **impede,** obstruct, stand in the way of, hinder, inhibit, restrict, constrain, hamper, handicap, cramp, check, block; disturb, disrupt, influence, impinge on, affect, confuse.

2 *she tried not to* ***interfere in*** *his life* **butt into,** barge into, pry into, intrude into, intervene in, get involved in, encroach on, impinge on; meddle in, tamper with; informal poke one's nose into, horn in on, muscle in on, stick one's oar in.

interference ▸ noun 1 *they resent state interference* **intrusion,** intervention, intercession, involvement, trespass, meddling, prying; informal butting in.

2 *radio interference* **disruption,** disturbance, distortion, static.

interim ▸ noun *in the interim they did more research* **meantime,** meanwhile, intervening time; interlude, interval.

▶ **adjective** *an interim advisory body* **provisional,** temporary, pro tem, stopgap, short-term, fill-in, caretaker, acting, transitional, makeshift, improvised, impromptu.
ANTONYMS permanent.

interior ▶ **adjective 1** *the house has interior paneling* **inside,** inner, internal, intramural.
ANTONYMS exterior.
2 *the interior waterways of British Columbia* **inland,** inshore, noncoastal, inner, innermost, central, upcountry, upland.
ANTONYMS outer.
3 *an interior monologue* **inner,** mental, spiritual, psychological; private, personal, intimate, secret.
▶ **noun 1** *the yacht's interior* **inside,** inner part, inner area, depths, recesses, bowels, belly; center, core, heart, nucleus; informal innards.
ANTONYMS exterior, outside.
2 *the interior of the province* **center,** heartland, hinterland, backcountry, bush.
ANTONYMS borderland.

interject ▶ **verb 1** *may I interject a comment?* **interpose,** introduce, throw in, interpolate, add, insert. See note at INSERT.
2 *please refrain from interjecting during each speaker's two-minute introductory remarks* **interrupt,** intervene, cut in, break in, butt in, chime in; have one's say; informal put one's oar in, put one's two cents in.

interloper ▶ **noun** *we were made to feel more like interlopers than vacationers* **intruder,** encroacher, trespasser, invader, infiltrator; uninvited guest; outsider, stranger, alien; informal gatecrasher, buttinsky.

interlude ▶ **noun** *the scene in the hospital room was a welcome interlude in this relentlessly high-paced adventure* **interval,** intermission, break, recess, pause, respite, rest, breathing space, halt, gap, stop, stoppage, hiatus, lull; informal breather, time out.

intermediary ▶ **noun** *the deal was concluded through an intermediary* **mediator,** go-between, negotiator, intervenor, intercessor, arbitrator, arbiter, conciliator, peacemaker; middleman, broker.

intermediate ▶ **adjective** *an intermediate stage in the cell's development* **in-between,** middle, mid, midway, halfway, median, medial, intermediary, intervening, transitional.

interment ▶ **noun** See BURIAL.

> USAGE
>
> **interment, internment**
>
> *Interment* = burial (*interment will take place just after the funeral service*). *Internment* = detention, esp. of aliens in wartime (*the internment of Japanese Americans during World War II*). *Interment* is sometimes, especially in obituaries, confounded with *internment*—e.g.: "Graveside ceremony and internment [read *interment*] will be at Hillside Cemetery in Peekskill immediately following." (*Times Union* [Albany]; Aug. 22, 2000.)

interminable ▶ **adjective** *the interminable silence was finally broken by the plaints of her crying infant* (**seemingly**) **endless,** never-ending, unending, nonstop, everlasting, ceaseless, unceasing, incessant, constant, continual, uninterrupted, sustained; monotonous, tedious, long-winded, overlong, rambling. See note at ETERNAL.

intermingle ▶ **verb** *marinating overnight allows the flavors to intermingle* **mix,** intermix, mingle, blend, fuse, merge, combine, amalgamate, integrate, unite; rare commix, admix; literary commingle.

intermission ▶ **noun** *refreshments are available during the intermission* **interval,** interlude, halftime, entr'acte, break, recess, pause, rest, respite, breathing space, lull, gap, stop, stoppage, halt, hiatus; cessation, suspension; informal breather, time out.

intermittent ▶ **adjective** *intermittent bursts of gunfire* **sporadic,** irregular, fitful, spasmodic, broken, fragmentary, discontinuous, isolated, random, patchy, scattered; occasional, infrequent, periodic, episodic, on and off; informal herky-jerky.
ANTONYMS continuous.

intern ▶ **verb 1** *the refugees were interned in camps* **confine,** detain, hold (captive), lock up, imprison, incarcerate, impound, jail; informal put away.
2 *she's interning with an accounting firm* **apprentice,** train; Law article.
▶ **noun** *an intern at a local firm* **trainee,** apprentice, probationer, (summer) student, novice, beginner.

internal ▶ **adjective 1** *the internal structure of the building* **inner,** interior, inside, intramural; central.
ANTONYMS external.
2 *Canada's internal affairs* **domestic,** home, interior, civil, local; national, federal, provincial, state.
ANTONYMS foreign.
3 *an internal battle with herself* **mental,** psychological, emotional; personal, private, secret, hidden.

international ▶ **adjective** *international business concerns* **global,** worldwide, intercontinental, universal; multinational.
ANTONYMS national, local.

interpolate ▶ **verb** *language models can be interpolated online* **insert,** interpose, interject, enter, add, incorporate, inset, put, introduce. See note at INSERT.

interpose ▶ **verb 1** *he interposed himself between the girls* **insinuate,** insert, place, put.
2 *I must interpose a note of caution* **introduce,** insert, interject, add, put in; informal slip in.
3 *they interposed to uphold the truce* **intervene,** intercede, step in, involve oneself; interfere, intrude, butt in, cut in, meddle; informal barge in, horn in, muscle in.

interpret ▶ **verb 1** *the rabbis interpret the Jewish laws* **explain,** elucidate, expound, explicate, clarify, illuminate, shed light on. See note at CLARIFY.
2 *the remark was interpreted as an invitation*

understand, construe, take (to mean), see, regard.
3 *the symbols are difficult to interpret* **decipher,** decode, unscramble, make intelligible; understand, comprehend, make sense of, figure out; informal crack.
4 *he interpreted the role of Hamlet* **perform,** act, play, render, depict, portray.

interpretation ▶ **noun 1** *the interpretation of the Bible's teachings* **explanation,** elucidation, expounding, exposition, explication, exegesis, clarification.
2 *they argued over interpretation* **meaning,** understanding, construal, connotation, explanation, inference.
3 *the interpretation of experimental findings* **analysis,** evaluation, review, study, examination.
4 *his interpretation of the sonata* **rendition,** rendering, execution, presentation, performance, portrayal.

interpreter ▶ **noun 1** *he spoke through an interpreter | interpreters were brought in to read the German messages* **translator,** transcriber, transliterator.
2 *a fine interpreter of this role* **performer,** presenter, exponent; singer, player, actor, dancer.
3 *interpreters of Soviet history* **analyst,** evaluator, reviewer, critic.

interrogate ▶ **verb** *the suspects were interrogated in separate rooms* **question,** cross-question, cross-examine, quiz, catechize; interview, examine, debrief, give someone the third degree; informal pump, grill.

interrogation ▶ **noun** *he was taken to the police station for interrogation* **questioning,** cross-questioning, cross-examination, quizzing; interview, debriefing, inquiry, the third degree; informal grilling; Law examination.

interrupt ▶ **verb 1** *she opened her mouth to interrupt* **cut in (on),** break in (on), barge in (on), intervene (in), put one's oar in, put one's two cents in, interject; informal butt in (on), chime in (with).
2 *the band had to interrupt their tour* **suspend,** adjourn, discontinue, break off, put on hold; stop, halt, cease, end, bring to an end/close; informal put on ice, put on the back burner.
3 *the coastal plain is* ***interrupted by*** *large lagoons* **break (up) by,** punctuate by/with; pepper with, strew with, dot with, scatter with, sprinkle with.
4 *their view was interrupted by houses* **obstruct,** impede, block, restrict, hamper.

interruption ▶ **noun 1** *he was not pleased at her interruption* **cutting in,** barging in, intervention, intrusion; informal butting in.
2 *an interruption of the power supply* **discontinuation,** breaking off, suspension, disruption, stopping, stoppage, halting, cessation.
3 *an interruption in her career* **interval,** interlude, break, pause, gap, hiatus.

intersect ▶ **verb 1** *the lines intersect at right angles* **cross,** crisscross; technical decussate.
2 *the cornfield is intersected by a track* **bisect,** divide, cut in two/half, cut across/through, crosscut; cross, traverse.

intersection ▶ **noun 1** *the intersection of two lines* **crossing,** crisscrossing; meeting.
2 *the driver stopped at an intersection* **junction,** interchange, crossroads, corner, cloverleaf.

intersperse ▶ **verb 1** *giant poppies were interspersed among the rocks* **scatter,** disperse, spread, strew, dot, sprinkle, pepper.
2 *the beech trees are interspersed with pines* **intermix,** mix, mingle, diversified, punctuate.

intertwine ▶ **verb** *a wreath of laurel, intertwined with daffodils* **entwine,** interweave, interlace, twist, braid, plait, splice, knit, weave, mesh.

interval ▶ **noun 1** *Baldwin made two speeches in the interval* **interim,** interlude, intervening time, intervening period, meantime, meanwhile.
2 *short intervals between contractions* **stretch,** period, time, spell; break, pause, gap.
3 *intervals of still water* **opening,** distance, span, space, area.

intervene ▶ **verb 1** *had the war not intervened, they might have married* **occur,** happen, take place, arise, crop up, come about; literary come to pass, befall, betide.
2 *she intervened in the dispute* **intercede,** involve oneself, get involved, interpose oneself, step in; mediate, referee; interfere, intrude, meddle, interrupt.

interview ▶ **noun** *all applicants will be called for an interview* **meeting,** discussion, conference, examination, interrogation; audience, talk, dialogue, exchange, conversation.
▶ **verb** *we interviewed seventy subjects for the survey* **talk to,** have a discussion with, have a dialogue with; question, interrogate, cross-examine, meet with; poll, canvass, survey, sound out; informal grill, pump; Law examine.

interviewer ▶ **noun** *her first stint as an interviewer was for her fifth-grade newsletter* **questioner,** interrogator, examiner, assessor, appraiser; journalist, reporter.

interweave ▶ **verb 1** *the threads are interwoven* **intertwine,** entwine, interlace, splice, braid, plait; twist together, weave together, wind together; Nautical marry.
2 *their fates were interwoven* **interlink,** link, connect; intermix, mix, merge, blend, interlock, bind together, knit together, fuse.

intestinal ▶ **adjective** *he was treated for an intestinal complaint* **enteric,** gastro-enteric, duodenal, celiac, gastric, ventral, stomach, abdominal.

intestines ▶ **plural noun** *the intestines are used in pet foods* **gut,** guts, entrails, viscera; informal insides, innards.

intimacy ▶ **noun 1** *the sisters reestablished their old intimacy* **closeness,** togetherness, affinity, rapport, attachment, familiarity, friendliness, friendship, amity, affection, warmth, confidence; informal chumminess.
2 *the memory of their intimacy* **sexual relations,** (sexual) intercourse, sex, lovemaking; dated carnal knowledge; formal copulation, (sexual) congress; technical coitus.

intimate[1] ▶ **adjective 1** *an intimate friend of Picasso's* **close,** bosom, dear, cherished, faithful,

devoted, fast, firm, familiar; informal chummy.
ANTONYMS distant.
2 *an intimate atmosphere* **friendly,** warm, welcoming, hospitable, relaxed, informal; cozy, comfortable, snug; informal comfy.
ANTONYMS formal, cold.
3 *intimate thoughts* **personal,** private, confidential, secret; innermost, inner, inward, deep, deepest; unspoken, undisclosed.
4 *an intimate knowledge of the music industry* **detailed,** thorough, exhaustive, deep, in-depth, profound; direct, personal, immediate, firsthand; informal up-close-and-personal.
ANTONYMS sketchy, superficial.
5 *intimate relations* **sexual,** carnal, romantic, amorous, amatory.
ANTONYMS nonsexual, platonic.
▶ **noun** *his circle of intimates* **close friend,** best friend, bosom friend, confidant, confidante; informal chum, pal, crony, buddy, bosom buddy, bud; chiefly Brit. informal mate.

intimate[2] ▶ **verb 1** *he intimated to the committee his decision to retire* **announce,** state, proclaim, declare, make known, make public, publicize, disclose, reveal, divulge, set forth.
2 *her feelings were subtly intimated* **imply,** suggest, hint at, insinuate, indicate, signal, allude to, refer to, convey; informal get at, drive at.

intimation ▶ **noun** *the first intimation of trouble came when the police began going door to door* **suggestion,** hint, indication, sign, signal, inkling, suspicion, impression; clue, undertone, whisper, wind; communication, notification, notice, warning.

intimidate ▶ **verb** *he sent his goons to intimidate the local merchants* **frighten,** menace, terrify, scare, terrorize, cow, dragoon, subdue; **threaten,** browbeat, bully, pressure, harass, harry, hassle, hound, torment, tyrannize, persecute; informal lean on, push around, bulldoze, railroad, twist someone's arm, strong-arm.

intolerable ▶ **adjective** *the drilling noise had become intolerable* **unbearable,** insufferable, unsupportable, insupportable, unendurable, beyond endurance, too much to bear; unacceptable; informal too much.
ANTONYMS bearable.

intolerance ▶ **1** *clearly she had not inherited her parents' racial intolerance* **bigotry,** narrow-mindedness, small-mindedness, illiberality, parochialism, provincialism; prejudice, bias, partisanship, partiality, discrimination; injustice, inequality. See note at BIAS.
2 *lactose intolerance* **sensitivity,** hypersensitivity; allergy.

intolerant ▶ **adjective 1** *intolerant in religious matters* **bigoted,** narrow-minded, small-minded, parochial, provincial, illiberal; prejudiced, biased, partial, partisan, discriminatory.
2 *foods to which you are intolerant* **allergic,** sensitive, hypersensitive.

intonation ▶ **noun 1** *she read with the wrong intonation* **inflection,** pitch, tone, timbre, cadence, lilt, rise and fall, modulation, speech pattern; accentuation, accent, emphasis, stress.
2 *the intonation of hymns* **chanting,** intoning, incantation, recitation, singing.

intoxicate ▶ **verb 1** *one glass of wine intoxicated him* **inebriate,** make drunk, make someone's head spin, befuddle, go to someone's head; informal make someone woozy.
2 *she became intoxicated by sci-fi literature at age ten* **exhilarate,** thrill, elate, delight, captivate, enthrall, entrance, enrapture, excite, stir, rouse, invigorate, inspire, fire with enthusiasm, electrify, transport; informal give someone a buzz, give someone a kick, give someone a thrill, bowl over.

intoxicated ▶ **adjective** *several passengers later said they suspected the driver of being intoxicated* **drunk,** inebriated, inebriate, impaired, drunken, tipsy, under the influence; informal plastered, smashed, bombed, sloshed, sozzled, hammered, sauced, lubricated, well-oiled, wrecked, juiced, blasted, stinko, blitzed, half-cut, fried, gassed, polluted, pissed, tanked (up), soaked, out of one's head, out of one's skull, loaded, trashed, buzzed, befuddled, hopped up, besotted, pickled, pixilated, canned, cockeyed, wasted, blotto, blind drunk, roaring drunk, dead drunk, punch-drunk, ripped, stewed, tight, high, merry, the worse for wear, far gone, pie-eyed, in one's cups, three sheets to the wind; Brit. informal bladdered, lashed; literary crapulous. See note at DRUNK.
ANTONYMS sober.

intoxicating ▶ **adjective 1** *intoxicating drink* **alcoholic,** strong, hard, fortified, potent, stiff, intoxicant; formal spirituous.
ANTONYMS nonalcoholic.
2 *an intoxicating sense of freedom* **heady,** exhilarating, thrilling, exciting, rousing, stirring, stimulating, invigorating, electrifying; strong, powerful, potent; informal mind-blowing.

intractable ▶ **adjective 1** *intractable problems* **unmanageable,** uncontrollable, difficult, awkward, troublesome, demanding, burdensome.
ANTONYMS manageable.
2 *an intractable man* **stubborn,** obstinate, obdurate, inflexible, headstrong, willful, unbending, unyielding, uncompromising, unaccommodating, uncooperative, difficult, awkward, perverse, contrary, pigheaded, stiff-necked. See note at STUBBORN.
ANTONYMS compliant.

intransigent ▶ **adjective** *leaders on both sides have grown increasingly intransigent* **uncompromising,** inflexible, unbending, unyielding, diehard, unshakable, unwavering, resolute, rigid, unaccommodating, uncooperative, stubborn, obstinate, obdurate, pigheaded, single-minded, iron-willed, stiff-necked.
ANTONYMS compliant.

intrepid ▶ **adjective** *our intrepid leader inspired us to forge ahead* **fearless,** unafraid, undaunted, unflinching, unshrinking, bold, daring, gallant, audacious, adventurous, heroic, dynamic, spirited, indomitable; brave, courageous, valiant, valorous, stouthearted, stalwart, plucky, doughty; informal gutsy, spunky, ballsy. See note at BOLD.
ANTONYMS timid.

intricate ▶ adjective *intricate designs etched into the glass | an intricate plot* **complex,** complicated, convoluted, tangled, entangled, twisted; elaborate, ornate, detailed, baroque, delicate; involuted; bewildering, confusing, perplexing, labyrinthine, Byzantine; informal fiddly.

intrigue ▶ verb *her answer intrigued him* **interest,** be of interest to, fascinate, arouse someone's curiosity, arouse someone's interest, pique someone's curiosity, pique someone's interest, attract.
▶ noun 1 *political intrigue* **secret plan,** plotting, plot, conspiracy, collusion, conniving, scheme, scheming, stratagem, machination, trickery, double-dealing, underhandedness, subterfuge; informal dirty tricks. See note at PLOT.
2 *Rick's intrigue with his brother's wife caused the family immeasurable grief* **(love) affair,** affair of the heart, liaison, amour, fling, flirtation, dalliance, tryst; adultery, infidelity, unfaithfulness, indiscretion; informal fooling around, playing around, hanky-panky.

intriguing ▶ adjective *intriguing stories* **interesting,** fascinating, absorbing, compelling, gripping, riveting, captivating, engaging, enthralling, enchanting, attractive, appealing.

intrinsic ▶ adjective *an intrinsic eye for fashion* **inherent,** innate, inborn, inbred, congenital, connate, natural; deep-rooted, deep-seated, indelible, ineradicable, ingrained; integral, basic, fundamental, essential; built-in. See note at INHERENT.

introduce ▶ verb 1 *she has introduced a new system* **institute,** initiate, launch, inaugurate, establish, found; bring in, usher in, set in motion, start, begin, commence, get going, get underway, originate, pioneer, kick off.
2 *she introduced new legislation* **propose,** put forward, suggest, bring to the table, submit; set forth, raise, broach, bring up, mention, air, float; informal run something up the flagpole.
3 *she introduced Lindsey to the young man* **present (formally),** make known, acquaint with.
4 *introducing nitrogen into canned beer* **insert,** inject, put, force, shoot, feed. See note at INSERT.
5 *she introduced a note of severity into her voice* **instill,** infuse, inject, add, insert.
6 *Clayton introduces the program each week* **announce,** present, give an introduction to; start off, begin, open.

introduction ▶ noun 1 *the introduction of democratic reforms* **institution,** establishment, initiation, launch, inauguration, foundation; start, commencement, debut, inception, origination.
ANTONYMS abolition.
2 *an* ***introduction to*** *the king* **(formal) presentation to**; meeting with, audience with.
3 *the book's introduction* **foreword,** preface, preamble, prologue, prelude; opening (statement), beginning; informal intro, lead-in, prelims; formal proem, prolegomenon.
ANTONYMS afterword.
4 ***an introduction to*** *hothouse gardening* **a primer of,** a basic explanation of, a brief account of; the basics of, the rudiments of, the fundamentals of.
5 *freshmen would soon experience the traditional* ***introduction to*** *school life* **initiation into,** induction into, inauguration into, baptism into.

introductory ▶ adjective 1 *the introductory chapter* **opening,** initial, starting, initiatory, first; prefatory, preliminary, leadoff.
ANTONYMS final.
2 *an introductory course* **elementary,** basic, rudimentary, primary; initiatory, preparatory, entry-level, survey; informal 101.
ANTONYMS advanced.

introspective ▶ adjective *an introspective poet* **inward-looking,** self-analyzing, introverted, introvert, brooding; contemplative, thoughtful, pensive, meditative, reflective; informal navel-gazing.

introverted ▶ adjective *his introverted parents were uncomfortable with the rowdy friends he brought home from college* **shy,** reserved, withdrawn, reticent, diffident, retiring, quiet; introspective, introvert, inward-looking, self-absorbed; pensive, contemplative, thoughtful, meditative, reflective.
ANTONYMS extroverted.

intrude ▶ verb *there will never be a consensus on just how entitled the press is to* ***intrude on*** *the lives of celebs* **encroach on,** impinge on, interfere in, trespass on/upon, infringe on, obtrude on/into, invade, violate, disturb, disrupt, interrupt; meddle in, barge in on; informal horn in on, muscle in on, poke one's nose into.

intruder ▶ noun *the intruder turned out to be a raccoon in the garage* **trespasser,** interloper, invader, infiltrator; burglar, housebreaker, thief, prowler.

intrusion ▶ noun *victims of illegal computer intrusion* **encroachment,** invasion, incursion, intervention, infringement, impingement; disturbance, disruption, interruption.

intrusive ▶ adjective *an intrusive journalist* **intruding,** invasive, obtrusive, unwelcome, pushy; meddlesome, prying, impertinent, interfering; informal nosy, snoopy. See note at IMPERTINENT.

intuition ▶ noun 1 *he works according to intuition* **instinct,** intuitiveness; sixth sense, clairvoyance, second sight.
2 *this confirms an intuition I had* **hunch,** feeling (in one's bones), inkling, (sneaking) suspicion, idea, sense, notion; premonition, presentiment; informal gut feeling, gut instinct.

intuitive ▶ adjective *an intuitive grasp of the truth* **instinctive,** instinctual; innate, inborn, inherent, natural, congenital; unconscious, subconscious, right-brained, involuntary, visceral; informal gut.

inundate ▶ verb 1 *a flood inundated the temple* **flood,** deluge, overrun, swamp, drown, submerge, engulf.
2 *we have been inundated with complaints* **overwhelm,** overrun, overload, bog down, swamp, besiege, snow under, bombard, glut.

inure ▶ verb *they had become inured to poverty* **harden,** toughen, season, temper, condition;

accustom, habituate, familiarize, acclimatize, adjust, adapt, desensitize.
ANTONYMS sensitize.

invade ▶ verb 1 *the army invaded the town* **occupy,** conquer, capture, seize, take (over), annex, win, gain, secure; march into, storm.
ANTONYMS withdraw from.
2 *someone had invaded our privacy* **intrude on,** violate, encroach on, infringe on, trespass on, obtrude on, disturb, disrupt; informal horn in on, muscle in on, barge in on.
ANTONYMS respect.
3 *every summer, tourists invaded the beach* **overrun,** swarm, overwhelm, inundate.

invader ▶ noun *invaders surprised them at dawn* **attacker,** aggressor, raider, marauder; occupier, conqueror; intruder, interloper.

invalid[1] ▶ noun *a home for invalids* **ill person,** sick person, valetudinarian; patient, convalescent, shut-in.
▶ adjective *her invalid husband* **ill,** sick, sickly, ailing, unwell, infirm, in poor health, indisposed; incapacitated, bedridden, housebound, frail, feeble, weak, debilitated.
ANTONYMS healthy.

invalid[2] ▶ adjective 1 *the law was invalid* (**legally**) **void,** null and void, unenforceable, not binding, illegitimate, inapplicable.
ANTONYMS binding.
2 *the theory is invalid* **false,** untrue, inaccurate, faulty, fallacious, spurious, unconvincing, unsound, weak, wrong, wide of the mark, off target; untenable, baseless, ill-founded, groundless; informal full of holes.
ANTONYMS true.

invalidate ▶ verb 1 *the court invalidated the statute* **render invalid,** void, nullify, annul, negate, cancel, disallow, overturn, overrule; informal nix. See note at **VOID**.
2 *this case invalidates the general argument* **disprove,** refute, contradict, negate, belie, discredit, debunk; weaken, undermine, explode; informal poke holes in; formal confute.

invaluable ▶ adjective *an invaluable member of the organization* **indispensable,** crucial, critical, key, vital, necessary, irreplaceable, all-important; immeasurable, incalculable, inestimable, priceless.
ANTONYMS dispensable.

invariably ▶ adverb *we say we'll order light, but we invariably end up with platters of fried food* **always,** on every occasion, at all times, without fail, without exception; everywhere, in all places, in all cases, in all instances; regularly, consistently, repeatedly, habitually, unfailingly, religiously; constantly, steadily.
ANTONYMS sometimes, never.

invasion ▶ noun 1 *the invasion of the island* **occupation,** capture, seizure, annexation, annexing, takeover; storming, incursion, attack, assault.
ANTONYMS withdrawal.
2 *an invasion of tourists* **influx,** inundation, flood, rush, torrent, deluge, avalanche, juggernaut.
3 *an invasion of my privacy* **violation,** infringement, interruption, intrusion, encroachment, disturbance, disruption, breach.
ANTONYMS respect.

invective ▶ noun *the invective that spewed from his lips left everyone speechless* **abuse,** insults, expletives, swear words, swearing, curses, foul language, foul language, vituperation; denunciation, censure, vilification, revilement, reproach, castigation, recrimination; informal tongue-lashing, trash talk; formal obloquy, contumely.
ANTONYMS praise.

inveigh ▶ verb *he was one of the few Wall Streeters willing to* ***inveigh against*** *corporate greed* **fulminate against,** declaim against, protest (against), rail against/at, rage at, remonstrate against; denounce, censure, condemn, decry, criticize; disparage, denigrate, run down, abuse, vituperate, vilify, impugn; informal sound off about, blast, dis, slam.
ANTONYMS support.

inveigle ▶ verb *planted in colleges throughout the country are brainwashed members whose only mission is to inveigle unsuspecting students into the cult* **entice,** tempt, lure, seduce, beguile; wheedle, cajole, coax, persuade; informal sweet-talk, soft-soap, con, sucker, snow. See note at **TEMPT**.

invent ▶ verb 1 *Louis Braille invented an alphabet for the blind* **originate,** create, design, devise, contrive, develop, innovate; conceive, think up, dream up, come up with, pioneer; coin.
2 *they invented the story for a laugh* **make up,** fabricate, concoct, hatch, dream up, conjure up; informal cook up.

invention ▶ noun 1 *the invention of the telescope* **origination,** creation, innovation, devising, development, design.
2 *medieval inventions* **innovation,** creation, design, contraption, contrivance, construction, device, gadget; informal brainchild.
3 *she played with taste and invention* **inventiveness,** originality, creativity, imagination, inspiration.
4 *the story was a total invention* **fabrication,** concoction, (piece of) fiction, story, tale; lie, untruth, falsehood, fib, myth, fantasy, make-believe; informal tall tale, cock-and-bull story.

inventive ▶ adjective *a well-intentioned and fairly inventive kids' movie* **creative,** original, innovative, imaginative, ingenious, resourceful; unusual, fresh, novel, new, newfangled; experimental, avant-garde, groundbreaking, revolutionary, unorthodox, unconventional. See note at **CREATIVE**.
ANTONYMS unimaginative, hackneyed.

inventor ▶ noun *the inventor of the separating zipper* **originator,** creator, innovator; designer, deviser, developer, maker, producer; author, architect; pioneer, mastermind, father, progenitor.

inventory ▶ noun *an inventory of all their belongings | our inventory of leaf rakes is low* **list,** listing, catalog, record, register, checklist, log, archive; stock, supply, store.
▶ verb *I inventoried his collection of music boxes* **list,** catalog, record, register, log, document.

inverse ▶ adjective *inverse snobbery* See **REVERSE**

(sense 2 of the adjective).
▶ noun *alkalinity is the inverse of acidity* See OPPOSITE (noun).

invert ▶ verb *the crew inverted the mast* **turn upside down,** upend, upturn, turn around/about, turn inside out, turn back to front, transpose, reverse, flip (over).

invest ▶ verb 1 *he invested in a soap company* **put money into,** provide capital for, fund, back, finance, subsidize, bankroll, underwrite; buy into, buy shares in; informal grubstake.
2 *they invested $18 million* **spend,** expend, put in, venture, speculate, risk; informal lay out.
3 *they invested in a new car* **purchase,** buy, procure.
4 *the scene was invested with magic* **imbue,** infuse, charge, steep, suffuse, permeate, pervade.
5 *the powers invested in the bishop* **vest in,** confer on, bestow on, grant to, entrust to, put in the hands of.

investigate ▶ verb *police are still investigating this apparent murder* **inquire into,** look into, go into, probe, explore, scrutinize, conduct an investigation into, make inquiries about; inspect, analyze, study, examine, consider, research; informal check out, suss out, scope out, dig, get to the bottom of.

investigation ▶ noun *we cannot determine the cause of the fire without further investigation* **examination,** inquiry, study, inspection, exploration, consideration, analysis, appraisal; research, scrutiny, perusal; probe, review, (background) check, survey.

investigator ▶ noun *investigators searching the ship on Monday found a cache of weapons* **inspector,** examiner, inquirer, inquisitor, explorer, analyzer; researcher, fact-finder, scrutineer, prober, searcher, auditor; detective.

investiture ▶ noun *the investiture of archbishops* **inauguration,** appointment, installation, initiation, swearing in; ordination, consecration, crowning, enthronement.

investment ▶ noun 1 *some tips for responsible investment* **investing,** speculation; funding, backing, financing, underwriting; buying shares.
2 *it's a good investment* **venture,** speculation, risk, gamble; asset, acquisition, holding, possession; informal grubstake.
3 *an investment of $305,000* **stake,** share, money/capital invested.
4 *a substantial investment of time* **contribution,** surrender, loss, forfeiture, sacrifice.

inveterate ▶ adjective 1 *an inveterate gambler* **confirmed,** hardened, incorrigible, addicted, habitual, compulsive, obsessive; informal pathological, chronic.
2 *an inveterate liberal* **staunch,** steadfast, committed, devoted, dedicated, dyed-in-the-wool, out-and-out, diehard, hard-core.
3 *inveterate corruption* **ingrained,** deep-seated, deep-rooted, entrenched, congenital, ineradicable, incurable.

invidious ▶ adjective 1 *that put her in an invidious position* **unpleasant,** awkward, difficult; undesirable, unenviable; odious, hateful, detestable.
ANTONYMS pleasant.
2 *an invidious comparison* **unfair,** unjust, iniquitous, unwarranted; deleterious, detrimental, discriminatory.
ANTONYMS fair.

invigorate ▶ verb *invigorated by the chilly autumn air | the need to invigorate the peace process in the Middle East* **revitalize,** energize, refresh, revive, vivify, brace, rejuvenate, enliven, liven up, perk up, wake up, animate, galvanize, fortify, stimulate, rouse, exhilarate; informal buck up, pep up, breathe new life into. See note at QUICKEN.
ANTONYMS tire.

invincible ▶ adjective *invincible superheroes* **invulnerable,** indestructible, unconquerable, unbeatable, indomitable, unassailable; impregnable, inviolable; informal bulletproof.
ANTONYMS vulnerable.

inviolable ▶ adjective See INALIENABLE.

inviolate ▶ adjective *the insignia of the Red Cross was regarded as virtually inviolate* **untouchable,** inviolable, safe from harm; **untouched,** undamaged, unhurt, unharmed, unscathed; unspoiled, unflawed, unsullied, unstained, undefiled, unprofaned, perfect, pristine, pure; intact, unbroken, whole, entire, complete.

invisible ▶ adjective *when the glue dries, it is invisible* **unable to be seen,** not visible; undetectable, indiscernible, inconspicuous, imperceptible; unseen, unnoticed, unobserved, hidden, veiled, obscured, out of sight.

invitation ▶ noun 1 *an invitation to dinner* **request to attend,** call, summons; offer; card, note; informal invite.
2 *an open door is an invitation to a thief* **encouragement,** provocation, temptation, lure, magnet, bait, enticement, attraction, allure; informal come-on.

invite ▶ verb 1 *they invited us to Sunday brunch* **ask,** summon, have someone over, request someone's company, request the pleasure of someone's company.
2 *we invite your comments* **ask for,** request, call for, appeal for, solicit, seek, summon.
3 *airing such views invites trouble* **provoke,** induce, cause, create, generate, engender, foster, encourage, lead to; incite, elicit, bring on oneself, arouse, call forth.

inviting ▶ adjective *the inviting aromas wafting from her kitchen* **tempting,** enticing, alluring, beguiling; attractive, appealing, pleasant, agreeable, delightful; appetizing, mouthwatering; fascinating, enchanting, entrancing, captivating, intriguing, irresistible, seductive.
ANTONYMS repellent.

invoice ▶ noun *an invoice for the goods* **bill,** account, statement (of charges), check; informal tab; archaic reckoning.
▶ verb *we'll invoice you for the damage* **bill,** charge, send an invoice/bill to.

invoke ▶ verb 1 *he invoked his statutory rights* **cite,** refer to, adduce, instance; resort to, have recourse to, turn to.

2 *I invoked the Madonna* **appeal to,** pray to, call on, supplicate, entreat, solicit, beg, implore; literary beseech.
3 *invoking spirits* **summon,** call (up), conjure (up).

involuntary ▶ adjective *an involuntary urge* **spontaneous,** instinctive, unconscious, unintentional, uncontrollable; reflex, automatic; informal knee-jerk.
ANTONYMS deliberate.

involve ▶ verb **1** *the inspection involved a lot of work* **require,** necessitate, demand, call for; entail, mean, imply, presuppose.
ANTONYMS preclude.
2 *I try to involve everyone in key decisions* **include,** count in, bring in, take into account, take note of; incorporate, encompass, touch on, embrace, comprehend, cover.
ANTONYMS exclude.

involved ▶ adjective **1** *social workers involved in the case* **associated with,** connected with, concerned in/with.
ANTONYMS unconnected.
2 *he had been involved in drug dealing* **implicated,** incriminated, inculpated, embroiled, entangled, caught up; informal mixed up.
3 *a long and involved story* **complicated,** intricate, complex, elaborate; convoluted, impenetrable, unfathomable.
ANTONYMS straightforward.
4 *very involved with the organization* **engrossed in,** absorbed in, immersed in, caught up in, preoccupied by, busy with, engaged in/with, intent on.
ANTONYMS uninterested.

invulnerable ▶ adjective *she plays a character as invulnerable as Superman* **impervious,** insusceptible, immune; indestructible, impenetrable, impregnable, unassailable, inviolable, invincible, secure; proof (against); informal bulletproof.

inward ▶ adjective **1** *an inward curve* **toward the inside,** going in; concave.
ANTONYMS outward.
2 *an inward smile* **internal,** inner, interior, innermost; private, personal, hidden, secret, veiled, masked, concealed, unexpressed.
ANTONYMS external.
▶ adverb *the door opened inward* **inside,** into the interior, inwards, within.

inwardly ▶ adverb *inwardly, George blamed himself* **inside,** internally, within, deep down (inside), in one's heart (of hearts); privately, secretly, confidentially; literary inly.

iota ▶ noun *nothing she said made an iota of difference* **bit,** speck, mite, scrap, shred, ounce, scintilla, atom, jot, grain, whit, trace; informal smidgen, smidge, tad; archaic scruple.

irascible ▶ adjective *this hot weather has put everyone in an irascible mood* **irritable,** quick-tempered, short-tempered, hot-tempered, testy, touchy, tetchy, edgy, crabby, petulant, waspish, dyspeptic, snappish; cross, surly, crusty, grouchy, grumpy, cranky, cantankerous, curmudgeonly, ill-natured, peevish, querulous, fractious; informal prickly, snippy.
ANTONYMS even-tempered, good-natured.

irate ▶ adjective *several irate customers demanded a full refund* **angry,** furious, infuriated, incensed, enraged, fuming, seething, cross, mad, livid; raging, ranting, raving, in a frenzy, beside oneself, outraged, up in arms; indignant, exasperated, annoyed, irritated, irked, vexed, piqued, choleric; informal foaming at the mouth, hot under the collar, seeing red, cheesed off, hopping mad, PO'd, fit to be tied; literary wrathful; archaic wroth.
ANTONYMS calm, contented.

ire ▶ noun literary *the plans provoked the ire of conservationists* **anger,** rage, fury, wrath, outrage, temper, crossness, spleen; annoyance, exasperation, irritation, displeasure, indignation, vexation, chagrin, pique; literary choler.

iridescent ▶ adjective *an iridescent film of oil on the puddle* **opalescent,** nacreous; shimmering, luminous, glittering, sparkling, dazzling, shining, gleaming, glowing, lustrous, scintillating; kaleidoscopic, rainbow-colored, multicolored; literary glistering, coruscating, effulgent, scintillant.

irk ▶ verb *clearly, the prosecutor's opening questions irked him* **irritate,** annoy, gall, pique, nettle, exasperate, try someone's patience; anger, infuriate, madden, incense, get on someone's nerves; antagonize, provoke; informal get someone's dander up, ruffle someone's feathers, make someone's hackles rise; rub the wrong way, get (someone's goat), get/put someone's back up, make someone's blood boil, peeve, miff, frost, rile, aggravate, needle, get to, bug, drive mad/crazy, tee off, tick off, piss off, PO, rankle, ride, drive up the wall, make someone see red.
ANTONYMS please.

irksome ▶ adjective *the irksome babbling of the couple upstairs* **irritating,** annoying, vexing, vexatious, galling, exasperating, disagreeable; tiresome, wearisome, tedious, trying, troublesome, bothersome, nettlesome, obnoxious, awkward, difficult, boring, uninteresting; infuriating, maddening; informal infernal.

iron ▶ noun **1** *a ship built of iron* metal, pig iron, cast iron, wrought iron.
2 (**irons**) *they were clapped in irons* **manacles,** shackles, fetters, chains, handcuffs; informal bracelets, cuffs.
▶ adjective **1** *an iron law of politics* **inflexible,** unbreakable, absolute, unconditional, categorical, incontrovertible, infallible.
ANTONYMS flexible.
2 *an iron will* **uncompromising,** unrelenting, unyielding, unbending, resolute, resolved, determined, firm, rigid, steadfast, unwavering, steely; literary adamantine.
ANTONYMS flexible.
– PHRASES **iron out** *it's time we iron out our differences* **resolve,** straighten out, sort out, smooth out, clear up, settle, put right, solve, remedy, rectify, fix, mend, eliminate, eradicate, erase, get rid of; harmonize, reconcile.

ironic ▶ adjective **1** *Edward's tone was ironic* **sarcastic,** sardonic, cynical, mocking, satirical,

caustic, wry.
ANTONYMS sincere.
2 *it's ironic that a former illiterate is now a successful writer* **paradoxical,** incongruous.
ANTONYMS logical.

irony ▶ noun **1** *that note of irony in her voice* **sarcasm,** causticity, cynicism, mockery, satire, sardonicism. See note at WIT.
ANTONYMS sincerity.
2 *the irony of the situation* **paradox,** incongruity, incongruousness.
ANTONYMS logic.

irradiate ▶ verb **1** *her smile irradiated the room* **illuminate,** light (up), cast light upon, brighten, shine on; literary illumine, illume.
2 *irradiated with gamma rays* **radiate,** charge, blast, shoot; infuse, permeate, saturate, flood; informal zap, nuke.

irrational ▶ adjective *an irrational fear of insects* **unreasonable,** illogical, groundless, baseless, unfounded, unjustifiable; absurd, ridiculous, ludicrous, preposterous, silly, foolish, senseless.
ANTONYMS reasonable, logical.

irreconcilable ▶ adjective **1** *irreconcilable views about religion* **incompatible,** at odds, at variance, conflicting, clashing, antagonistic, mutually exclusive, diametrically opposed; disparate, poles apart.
ANTONYMS compatible, similar.
2 *irreconcilable enemies* **implacable,** unappeasable, uncompromising, inflexible; mortal, bitter, deadly, sworn, out-and-out.

irrefutable ▶ adjective *irrefutable evidence* **indisputable,** undeniable, unquestionable, incontrovertible, incontestable, beyond question, beyond doubt, conclusive, definite, definitive, decisive, certain, positive, sure; informal sure as shootin'.

irregular ▶ adjective **1** *irregular features | an irregular coastline* **asymmetrical,** nonuniform, uneven, crooked, misshapen, lopsided, twisted; unusual, peculiar, strange, bizarre; jagged, ragged, serrated, indented.
ANTONYMS straight.
2 *irregular surfaces* **rough,** bumpy, uneven, pitted, rutted; lumpy, knobbly, gnarled.
ANTONYMS smooth.
3 *an irregular heartbeat* **inconsistent,** unsteady, uneven, fitful, patchy, variable, varying, changeable, changing, inconstant, erratic, unstable, unsettled, spasmodic, intermittent, fluctuating; informal herky-jerky.
ANTONYMS steady.
4 *irregular financial dealings* **against the rules,** out of order, improper, illegitimate, unscrupulous, unethical, unprofessional, unacceptable; informal shady.
ANTONYMS aboveboard.
5 *irregular clothing* **flawed,** damaged, imperfect, discarded, rejected, throwaway.

irregularity ▶ noun **1** *the irregularity of the coastline* **asymmetry,** nonuniformity, unevenness, crookedness, lopsidedness; jaggedness, raggedness, indentation.
2 *the irregularity of the surface* **roughness,** bumpiness, unevenness; lumpiness.
3 *irregularity in the fabric* **flaw,** damage, imperfection; blemish, mark, spot, stain.
4 *the irregularity of the bus service* **inconsistency,** unsteadiness, unevenness, fitfulness, patchiness, instability, variability, changeableness, fluctuation, unpredictability, unreliability.
5 *financial irregularities* **impropriety,** wrongdoing, misconduct, dishonesty, corruption, immorality; informal shadiness, crookedness, dodginess.
6 *the staff noted any irregularity in operation* **abnormality,** unusualness, strangeness, oddness, singularity, anomaly, deviation, aberration, peculiarity, idiosyncrasy.

irrelevant ▶ adjective *the judge ruled that the victim's use of drugs was irrelevant* **beside the point,** immaterial, not pertinent, not germane, off the subject, unconnected, unrelated, peripheral, extraneous, inapposite, inapplicable; unimportant, inconsequential, insignificant, trivial; formal impertinent.

irreligious ▶ adjective *it was a great miscalculation to assess America as an irreligious society* **atheistic,** unbelieving, nonbelieving, agnostic, heretical, faithless, godless, ungodly, impious, profane, infidel, barbarian, heathen, pagan; secular, humanist.
ANTONYMS pious, God-fearing.

irreparable ▶ adjective *irreparable damage to the landing module* **irreversible,** irrevocable, irrecoverable, unrepairable, beyond repair, unrectifiable; hopeless.
ANTONYMS repairable.

irreplaceable ▶ adjective *an irreplaceable set of engraved wine glasses* **unique,** invaluable, priceless, unrepeatable, one-of-a-kind, incomparable, unparalleled; treasured, prized, cherished.

irrepressible ▶ adjective **1** *the desire for freedom is irrepressible* **inextinguishable,** unquenchable, uncontainable, uncontrollable, indestructible, undying, everlasting.
2 *his irrepressible personality* **ebullient,** exuberant, buoyant, sunny, breezy, jaunty, lighthearted, high-spirited, vivacious, animated, full of life, lively; informal bubbly, bouncy, peppy, chipper.

irreproachable ▶ adjective *her irreproachable character* **impeccable,** above/beyond reproach, blameless, faultless, flawless, unblemished, untarnished, spotless, immaculate, exemplary, model, outstanding, exceptional, admirable, perfect; informal squeaky clean; trademark Teflon.
ANTONYMS reprehensible.

irresistible ▶ adjective **1** *irresistible snakeskin stilettos | his irresistible smile* **enticing,** tempting, alluring, inviting, seductive; attractive, desirable, fetching, glamorous, appealing, delightful; ravishing, captivating, beguiling, tantalizing, enchanting, charming, fascinating, magnetic.
ANTONYMS undesirable, off-putting.
2 *an irresistible impulse to scream* **uncontrollable,** overwhelming, overpowering, compelling, compulsive, irrepressible, ungovernable, besetting; unavoidable, inexorable, unpreventable, inescapable, driving, potent, forceful, urgent, imperative; obsessive.

ANTONYMS controllable.

irresolute ▶ adjective *once again, faced with an important issue, this legislative body sits irresolute and utterly useless* **indecisive,** hesitant, vacillating, equivocating, dithering, wavering, shilly-shallying; ambivalent, blowing hot and cold, of two minds, hemming and hawing, in a dilemma, in a quandary, torn; doubtful, in doubt, unsure, uncertain, undecided, wishy-washy; informal sitting on the fence.
ANTONYMS decisive.

irrespective ▶ adjective *each member has one vote, **irrespective of** the number of shares held* **regardless of,** without regard to/for, notwithstanding, whatever, no matter what, without consideration of.

irresponsible ▶ adjective *such irresponsible behavior is unthinkable for a man your age* **reckless,** rash, careless, thoughtless, foolhardy, foolish, impetuous, impulsive, devil-may-care, delinquent, derelict, negligent, hare-brained; unreliable, undependable, untrustworthy, flighty, immature.
ANTONYMS sensible.

irreverent ▶ adjective *no one was amused by his irreverent joke-telling* **disrespectful,** disdainful, scornful, contemptuous, derisive, disparaging; impertinent, impudent, cheeky, saucy, flippant, rude, discourteous.
ANTONYMS respectful.

irreversible ▶ adjective *irreversible damage* **irreparable,** beyond repair, irremediable, irrevocable, permanent; unalterable, unchangeable, immutable, carved in stone; Law peremptory.
ANTONYMS temporary.

irrevocable ▶ adjective *an irrevocable commitment* **irreversible,** unalterable, unchangeable, immutable, final, binding, permanent, carved in stone; Law peremptory.
ANTONYMS temporary.

irritable ▶ adjective *being out of work made him irritable* **bad-tempered,** short-tempered, irascible, tetchy, testy, touchy, grumpy, grouchy, moody, crotchety, in a (bad) mood, cantankerous, bilious, curmudgeonly, ill-tempered, annoyed, cross, ill-humored, peevish, fractious, pettish, crabby, bitchy, waspish, prickly, splenetic, dyspeptic, choleric; informal cranky, ornery, shirty, on a short fuse, soreheaded.
ANTONYMS easygoing.

irritate ▶ verb **1** *they seem to enjoy irritating me* **annoy,** vex, make angry, make cross, anger, exasperate, irk, gall, pique, nettle, put out, antagonize, get on someone's nerves, try someone's patience, ruffle someone's feathers, make someone's hackles rise; infuriate, madden, provoke, pester, rub the wrong way; informal aggravate, hassle, miff, rile, needle, get to, bug, get in someone's hair, get under someone's skin, get someone's dander up, rattle someone's cage, get/put someone's back up, drive mad/crazy, drive someone around the bend, drive up the wall, drive bananas, tee off, tick off, burn up, rankle, ride. See note at AGGRAVATE.
ANTONYMS pacify.
2 *paint fumes irritate my throat* **inflame,** aggravate; pain, hurt; chafe, abrade, scratch, rasp; rare excoriate.
ANTONYMS soothe.

irritating ▶ adjective *a slow Web site is irritating to your customers* **annoying,** infuriating, exasperating, maddening, trying, tiresome, vexing, vexatious, obnoxious, irksome, nagging, niggling, galling, grating, aggravating, pestilential.

irritation ▶ noun **1** *she tried not to show her irritation* **annoyance,** exasperation, vexation, indignation, impatience, crossness, displeasure, chagrin, pique; anger, rage, fury, wrath, aggravation; literary ire.
ANTONYMS delight.
2 *I realize my presence is an irritation for you* **irritant,** annoyance, thorn in someone's side/flesh, bother, trial, torment, plague, inconvenience, nuisance, aggravation, pain (in the neck), headache, burr under someone's saddle.
ANTONYMS pleasure.

island ▶ noun *she lived on an island* **isle,** islet; atoll; (**islands**) archipelago.
▶ verb *he was islanded from the problems of real life* **isolate,** cloister, seclude; separate, detach, cut off.

isolate ▶ verb **1** *the police isolated the area* **cordon off,** seal off, close off, fence off.
2 *doctors isolated the patients* separate, set/keep apart, segregate, detach, cut off, shut away, keep in solitude, quarantine, cloister, seclude, sequester.
ANTONYMS integrate.
3 *I have isolated the problem* **identify,** single out, pick out, point out, spot, recognize, distinguish, pinpoint, locate.

isolated ▶ adjective **1** *isolated communities* **remote,** out of the way, outlying, off the beaten track/path, secluded, lonely, godforsaken, far-flung, inaccessible, cutoff, incommunicado, in the backwoods, in the back of beyond, in the back concessions, in the boonies/boondocks, in the middle of nowhere, in the sticks, in the tall timbers, in the hinterland.
ANTONYMS accessible.
2 *he lived an isolated existence* **solitary,** lonely, companionless, friendless; secluded, cloistered, segregated, unsociable, reclusive, hermitic, lonesome.
ANTONYMS sociable.
3 *an isolated incident* **unique,** lone, solitary; unusual, uncommon, exceptional, anomalous, abnormal, untypical, atypical, freak.
ANTONYMS common, everyday.

issue ▶ noun **1** *the committee discussed the issue* **matter,** matter in question, question, point, point at issue, affair, case, subject, topic; problem, bone of contention.
2 *the issue of a special stamp* **issuing,** publication, publishing, printing; circulation, distribution.
3 *the latest issue of our magazine* **edition,** number, copy, installment, volume, publication.
4 Law *she died without issue* **offspring,**

descendants, heirs, successors, children, progeny, family; archaic seed, fruit (of one's loins).

5 *an issue of water* **discharge,** emission, release, outflow, outflowing, secretion, emanation, exudation, effluence; technical efflux.

▶ **verb 1** *the mayor issued a statement* **send out,** put out, release, deliver, publish, announce, pronounce, broadcast, communicate, circulate, distribute, disseminate, transmit.

2 *the students were issued with new uniforms* **supply,** provide, furnish, arm, equip, fit out, rig out; Brit. kit out; informal fix up.

3 *the smell of onion issued from the kitchen* **emanate,** emerge, exude, flow (out/forth), pour (out/forth); be emitted.

4 *large profits might* ***issue from*** *the deal* **result from,** follow, ensue from, stem from, spring (forth) from, arise from, proceed from, come (forth) from; be the result of, be brought on/about by, be produced by.

– PHRASES **at issue** *at issue here is what constitutes 'art'* **in question,** in dispute, under discussion, under consideration, for debate.

take issue with *we'll get nowhere if you have to take issue with everything that anybody says* **disagree with,** be in dispute with, be in contention with, be at variance with, be at odds with, argue with, quarrel with; challenge, dispute, (call into) question.

itch ▶ **noun 1** *I have an itch on my back* tingling, irritation, prickle, prickling, tickle, tickling, itchiness.

2 informal *the itch to travel* **longing,** yearning, craving, ache, hunger, thirst, keenness, urge, hankering; wish, fancy, desire; informal yen.

▶ **verb 1** *my scar really itches* tingle, prickle, tickle, be irritated, be itchy.

2 informal *he itched to help her* **long,** yearn, ache, burn, crave, hunger, thirst, be eager, be desperate; want, wish, desire, pine, fancy; informal have a yen, be dying.

item ▶ **noun 1** *an item of farm equipment | the main item in a moose's diet* **thing,** article, object, artifact, piece, product; element, constituent, component, ingredient.

2 *a news item* **report,** story, account, article, piece, write-up, bulletin, feature.

3 *I hear they are an item* **couple,** twosome, partners, lovers; informal thing.

itemize ▶ **verb** *they itemized thirty-two design flaws in the reactor type* **list,** catalog, inventory, record, document, register, detail, specify, identify; enumerate, number.

itinerant ▶ **adjective** *itinerant traders* **traveling,** peripatetic, wandering, roving, roaming, touring, saddlebag, nomadic, gypsy, migrant, vagrant, vagabond, of no fixed address.

▶ **noun** *an encampment of itinerants* **traveler,** wanderer, roamer, rover, nomad, gypsy, migrant, transient, drifter, vagabond, hobo, vagrant, tramp.

itinerary ▶ **noun** *the old stone chapel should be on every visitor's itinerary* **travel plan,** schedule, timetable, agenda, program, tour; (planned) route.

Jj

jab ▶ verb *he jabbed the officer with his finger* **poke,** prod, dig, nudge, butt, ram; thrust, stab, push.
▶ noun **1** *a jab in the ribs* **poke,** prod, dig, nudge, butt; thrust, stab, push.
2 *felled by a left jab* **punch,** blow, hit, whack, smack, cuff.
3 *exchanging verbal jabs* **insult,** cutting remark, barb; informal dig, put-down.

jabber ▶ verb *they jabbered nonstop* **prattle,** babble, chatter, twitter, prate, yap, gabble, rattle on, blather; informal yak, yammer, yabber, yatter, blab, blabber.
▶ noun *stop your jabber!* **prattle,** babble, chatter, chattering, twitter, twittering, gabble, blather; informal yabbering, yatter, blabber.

jack ▶ noun *a phone jack* **socket,** outlet, plug, connection.
– PHRASES **jack something up 1** *they jacked up the car* **raise,** hoist, lift (up), winch up, lever up, hitch up, elevate. **2** informal *they may need to jack up interest rates* **increase,** raise, up, mark up; informal hike (up), bump up, boost.

jackpot ▶ noun *this week's lottery jackpot* **top prize,** first prize; pool, kitty, pot, gold mine, bonanza.
– PHRASES **hit the jackpot** informal *Ingalls may have hit the jackpot with this latest novel* **strike it rich,** strike gold, succeed; informal clean up, hit the big time, score.

jaded ▶ adjective *a taste exotic enough for the most jaded palate | the uninspired writing of a jaded journalist* **surfeited,** sated, satiated, glutted; dulled, blunted, deadened, inured; **tired,** weary, wearied; unmoved, blasé, apathetic.
ANTONYMS fresh.

jagged ▶ adjective *don't give your dog a jagged bone* **spiky,** barbed, ragged, rough, uneven, irregular, broken; jaggy, snaggy; serrated, sawtooth, sawtoothed, indented.
ANTONYMS smooth.

jail ▶ noun *he was thrown into the local jail* **prison,** penitentiary, penal institution, lockup, detention center, jailhouse, stockade, correctional facility, reformatory, reform school; informal clink, slammer, big house, jug, brig, can, pen, hoosegow, cooler, cage, slam, pokey.
▶ verb *she was jailed for killing her husband* **imprison,** put in prison, send to prison, incarcerate, lock up, put away, intern, detain, hold (prisoner/captive), put into detention, put behind bars, put inside.
ANTONYMS acquit, release.

jailer ▶ noun *one day a careless jailer left his keys in the door* **warden,** prison officer, guard; captor; informal screw.

jam¹ ▶ verb **1** *he jammed a finger in each ear* **stuff,** shove, force, ram, thrust, press, push, stick, squeeze, cram.
2 *hundreds of people jammed into the hall* **crowd,** pack, pile, press, squeeze, squish, cram, wedge; throng, mob, occupy, fill, overcrowd, obstruct, block, congest.
3 *the rudder had jammed* **stick,** become stuck, catch, seize (up), become trapped.
4 *dust can jam the mechanism* **immobilize,** paralyze, disable, cripple, put out of action, bring to a standstill; clog.
5 *we were just jamming and his amp blew* **improvise,** play (music), extemporize, ad lib.
▶ noun **1** *a traffic jam* **congestion,** holdup, bottleneck, gridlock, backup, tie-up, snarl-up.
2 informal *we are in a real jam* **predicament,** plight, tricky situation, difficulty, problem, quandary, dilemma, muddle, mess, imbroglio, mare's nest, dire straits; informal pickle, stew, fix, hole, scrape, bind, tangle, spot, tight spot, corner, tight corner, hot/deep water, can of worms.

jam² ▶ noun *raspberry jam* **preserve,** conserve, jelly, marmalade, fruit spread, compote, (fruit) butter.

jamboree ▶ noun *the community's annual jamboree* **rally,** gathering, convention, conference; festival, fête, fiesta, gala, carnival, celebration; informal bash, shindig, hoedown.

jangle ▶ verb *keys jangled at his waist* **clank,** clink, jingle, tinkle.
▶ noun *the jangle of his chains* **clank,** clanking, clink, clinking, jangling, jingle, jingling, tintinnabulation.

janitor ▶ noun *the janitor's supply closet* **custodian,** caretaker, cleaner, maintenance man/worker, superintendent.

jar¹ ▶ noun *a jar of honey* **(glass) container,** pot, crock, receptacle, cookie jar, mason jar, ginger jar.

jar² ▶ verb **1** *each step jarred my whole body* **jolt,** jerk, shake, shock, concuss, rattle, vibrate.
2 *the play's symbolism jarred with the realism of its setting* **clash,** conflict, contrast, be incompatible, be at variance, be at odds, be inconsistent, be discordant.

jargon ▶ noun *the brochure is written in legal jargon* **specialized language,** slang, cant, idiom, argot, patter; informal -speak, -ese, -babble, newspeak, journalese, bureaucratese, technobabble, psychobabble; double-talk, doublespeak; gibberish, gobbledygook, blather. See note at **DIALECT**.

jaundiced ▶ **adjective** *a jaundiced view of the world* **bitter,** resentful, cynical, soured, disenchanted, disillusioned, disappointed, pessimistic, skeptical, distrustful, suspicious, misanthropic; envious, jealous.

jaunt ▶ **noun** *a jaunt around Manhattan* **trip,** pleasure trip, outing, excursion, day trip, day out; tour, drive, ride, run; informal spin. See note at **JOURNEY**.

jaunty ▶ **adjective** *Kevin looked pretty jaunty for the awards show | a jaunty musical score* **cheerful,** cheery, happy, merry, jolly, joyful; lively, perky, bright, buoyant, bubbly, bouncy, breezy, in good spirits, exuberant, ebullient; carefree, blithe, airy, lighthearted, nonchalant, insouciant, happy-go-lucky; informal bright-eyed and bushy-tailed, chirpy.
ANTONYMS depressed, serious.

jaw ▶ **noun 1** *a broken jaw* **jawbone,** lower/upper jaw, jowl; Anatomy mandible, maxilla.
2 (**jaws**) *the wolf held the rat in its jaws* **mouth,** maw, muzzle; teeth, fangs; informal chops.

jazz ▶ **noun** *their band plays mostly jazz* **swing,** bebop, big band, boogie woogie.
– PHRASES **jazz up** informal *let's jazz up this boring decor* **enliven,** liven up, brighten up, make more interesting/exciting, add (some) color to, ginger up, spice up; informal perk up, pep up.

jazzy ▶ **adjective** *that's one jazzy bedspread* **funky,** hip, vibrant, lively, spirited, bold, exciting, flamboyant, showy, gaudy, flashy; bright, colorful, brightly colored, striking, impactful, eye-catching, vivid.
ANTONYMS dull.

jealous ▶ **adjective 1** *he was jealous of his sister's popularity* **envious,** covetous, desirous; resentful, grudging, begrudging, green (with envy).
ANTONYMS proud, admiring.
2 *a jealous lover* **suspicious,** distrustful, mistrustful, doubting, insecure, anxious; possessive, overprotective.
ANTONYMS trusting.
3 *they are very jealous of their rights* **protective,** vigilant, watchful, heedful, mindful, careful, solicitous.
ANTONYMS careless.

CHOOSE THE RIGHT WORD

jealous, covetous, envious

Envious implies wanting something that belongs to another and to which one has no particular right or claim (*envious of her good fortune*). **Jealous** may refer to a strong feeling of envy (*it is hard not to be jealous of a man with a job like his*), or it may imply an intense effort to hold on to what one possesses (*jealous of what little time she has to herself*); it is often associated with distrust, suspicion, anger, and other negative emotions (*a jealous wife*). Someone who is **covetous** has fallen prey to an inordinate or wrongful desire, usually for a person or thing that rightfully belongs to another. In other words, a young man might be *jealous* of the other men who flirt with his girlfriend, while they might be *envious* of her obvious preference for him. But the young man had better not be *covetous* of his neighbor's wife.

jealousy ▶ **noun 1** *he was consumed with jealousy* **envy,** covetousness; resentment, resentfulness, bitterness, spite; informal the green-eyed monster.
2 *the jealousy of his long-suffering wife* **suspicion,** suspiciousness, distrust, mistrust, insecurity, anxiety; possessiveness, overprotectiveness.

jeans ▶ **plural noun** See note on **JEANS** below.

jeer ▶ **verb** *the demonstrators **jeered at** the police* **taunt,** mock, scoff at, ridicule, sneer at, deride, insult, abuse, heckle, catcall at, boo, whistle at, jibe at, hiss at.
ANTONYMS cheer.
▶ **noun** *the jeers of the crowd* **taunt,** sneer, insult, shout, jibe, boo, hiss, catcall; derision, teasing, scoffing, abuse, scorn, heckling, catcalling; informal raspberry, Bronx cheer.
ANTONYMS applause.

jell, gel ▶ **verb 1** *leave the mixture to jell* **set,** stiffen, solidify, thicken, harden; cake, congeal, jellify, coagulate, clot.
2 *things started to jell very quickly* **take shape,** fall into place, come together, take form, work out; crystallize.

jeopardize ▶ **verb** *accused of jeopardizing the health of their children* **threaten,** endanger, imperil, risk, put at risk, put in danger/jeopardy; hazard, stake; leave vulnerable; compromise, be a danger to, pose a threat to.
ANTONYMS safeguard.

jeopardy ▶ **noun** *the peace talks are **in jeopardy*** **in danger,** in peril; at risk.
ANTONYMS safety, security.

jerk ▶ **noun 1** *she gave the reins a jerk* **yank,** tug, pull, wrench, tweak, twitch.
2 *the elevator stopped with a jerk* **jolt,** lurch, bump, start, jar, bang, bounce, shake, shock.
3 informal *I showed up for the party on the wrong night and felt like a complete jerk* See **FOOL** (sense 1 of the noun).
4 informal *I called Tim a jerk for screaming at her in public* See **BASTARD** (sense 2 of the noun).
▶ **verb 1** *she jerked her arm free* **yank,** tug, pull, wrench, wrest, drag, pluck, snatch, seize, rip, tear.
2 *the car jerked along* **jolt,** lurch, bump, rattle, bounce, shake, jounce.

jerky ▶ **adjective** *it was a very jerky ride* **convulsive,** spasmodic, fitful, twitchy, shaky; **jolting,** lurching, bumpy, bouncy, jarring.
ANTONYMS smooth.

jerry-built ▶ **adjective** *we entered our jerry-built monstrosity in the raft race and won second prize* **shoddy,** makeshift, badly built, gimcrack, flimsy, insubstantial, rickety, ramshackle, crude, chintzy; inferior, poor-quality, second-rate, third-rate, tinpot, low-grade.
ANTONYMS sturdy.

jest ▶ **verb** *I think he's jesting* fool around, play a practical joke, tease, kid, pull someone's leg, pull/jerk/yank someone's chain, have someone on; fun; joke, quip, gag, tell jokes, crack jokes; informal wisecrack.

▶ **noun** *jests were bandied about freely* **joke,** witticism, funny remark, gag, quip, sally, pun; crack, wisecrack, one-liner.

– PHRASES **in jest** *those sarcastic remarks were made in jest* **in fun,** as a joke, tongue in cheek, playfully, jokingly, facetiously, frivolously, for a laugh.

jester ▶ **noun 1** historical *a court jester* **fool,** court fool, court jester, clown, harlequin, pantaloon; archaic buffoon, merry-andrew.
2 *the class jester* **joker,** clown, comedian, comic, humorist, wag, wit, prankster, jokester, trickster, buffoon; informal card, hoot, scream, laugh, wisecracker, barrel of laughs, smart-ass, smart aleck.

jet[1] ▶ **noun 1** *a jet of water* **stream,** spurt, squirt, spray, spout; gush, rush, surge, burst.
2 *an executive jet* **jet plane,** jetliner; aircraft, plane, jumbo jet.

jet[2] ▶ **adjective** *her glossy jet hair* **black,** jet-black, pitch-black, ink-black, ebony, raven, sable, sooty.

jettison ▶ **verb 1** *six aircraft jettisoned their loads* **dump,** drop, ditch, discharge, throw out, unload, throw overboard.
2 *he jettisoned his unwanted papers | the scheme was jettisoned* **discard,** dispose of, throw away/out, get rid of; reject, scrap, abandon, drop; informal chuck (out), dump, ditch, ax, trash, junk, deep-six.
ANTONYMS keep, retain.

jetty ▶ **noun** *we'd walk out on the jetty at low tide to look for starfish* **pier,** landing stage, landing, quay, wharf, dock; breakwater, mole, groin, dike, dockominium, levee.

jewel ▶ **noun 1** *priceless jewels* **gem,** gemstone, (precious) stone, brilliant; baguette; informal sparkler, rock; archaic bijou.
2 *the jewel of his collection* **finest example/specimen,** showpiece, pride (and joy), cream, crème de la crème, jewel in the crown, masterpiece, nonpareil, glory, prize, boast, pick, ne plus ultra.

jewelry ▶ **noun** *a locked box for her jewelry* **jewels,** gems, gemstones, precious stones; costume jewelry, trinkets; informal bling; archaic bijoux.

jiffy, jiff ▶ **noun**
– PHRASES **in a jiffy/jiff** informal *I'll be there in a jiffy* **(very) soon,** in a second, in a minute, in a moment, momentarily, in a trice, in a flash, shortly, any second, any minute (now), in no time (at all), directly; informal in a sec, in a snap, in two shakes (of a lamb's tail), in a wink, in a twinkle; archaic anon.

jilt ▶ **verb** *do you think she's jilted him?* **leave,** walk out on, throw over, finish with, break up with, spurn, chuck, ditch, dump, drop, run out on, give someone the old heave-ho; literary forsake.

jingle ▶ **noun 1** *the jingle of money* **clink,** chink, tinkle, jangle, ding-a-ling, ring, ding, ping, chime, tintinnabulation.
2 *advertising jingles* **slogan,** catchphrase; ditty, song, rhyme, tune.

▶ **verb** *the keys jingled* **clink,** chink, tinkle, jangle, ring, ding, ping, chime.

jingoism ▶ **noun** *a newspaper known for its jingoism* **extreme patriotism,** chauvinism, extreme nationalism, xenophobia, flag-waving; hawkishness, militarism, belligerence, bellicosity. See note at CHAUVINISM.

jinx ▶ **noun** *after years of bad luck they finally broke the jinx* **curse,** spell, malediction; evil eye, black magic, voodoo, bad luck, hex.

▶ **verb** *the family is jinxed* **curse,** cast a spell on, put the evil eye on, hex.

jittery ▶ **adjective** informal *the company's accounting troubles left stock investors jittery* **nervous,** on edge, edgy, tense, anxious, agitated, ill at ease, uneasy, keyed up, overwrought, jumpy, on tenterhooks, worried, apprehensive; informal with butterflies in one's stomach, twitchy, uptight, het up, in a tizzy, spooky, squirrelly, antsy, trepidatious.
ANTONYMS calm.

job ▶ **noun 1** *my job involves a lot of traveling* **occupation,** profession, trade, position, career, work, line of work, livelihood, post, situation, appointment, métier, craft; vocation, calling; vacancy, opening; humorous McJob.
2 *this job will take three months* **task,** piece of work, assignment, project; chore, errand; undertaking, venture, operation, enterprise, business.
3 *it's your job to protect her* **responsibility,** duty, charge, task; role, function, mission; informal department.
4 informal *a bank job* **robbery,** theft, holdup, burglary, break-in; informal stickup, heist.

jobless ▶ **adjective** *as of today, Young is among the jobless* **unemployed,** out-of-work, out of a job, between jobs, laid off, unwaged, on the dole; Brit. redundant.
ANTONYMS employed.

jockey ▶ **noun** *the legendary jockey won his first horse race when he was 17* **rider,** horseman, horsewoman, equestrian.

▶ **verb** *on the eve of the primary, both men jockeyed for position* **maneuver,** ease, edge, work, steer; compete, contend, vie; struggle, fight, scramble, jostle.

jocular ▶ **adjective** *my jocular uncle* **humorous,** funny, witty, comic, comical, amusing, droll, waggish, jokey, hilarious, facetious, tongue-in-cheek, teasing, playful; lighthearted, jovial, cheerful, cheery, merry; formal jocose, ludic.
ANTONYMS solemn.

jocund ▶ **adjective** formal See CHEERFUL (sense 1).

jog ▶ **verb 1** *he jogged along the road* **run slowly,** trot, lope, dog-trot; dated jog-trot.
2 *something jogged her memory* **stimulate,** prompt, stir, activate, refresh; prod, jar, nudge.

▶ **noun 1** *he set off at a jog* **run,** trot, lope, dog-trot; dated jog trot.
2 *a jog in the road* **bend,** turn, curve, corner, zigzag, kink, dogleg.

join ▶ **verb 1** *we joined a bunch of sticks together* **fasten,** attach, tie, bind, couple, connect, unite, link, yoke, weld, fuse, glue.
2 *the two clubs have joined together* **combine,** amalgamate, merge, join forces, unify, unite.

3 *we joined them in their venture* **team up with,** band together with, cooperate with, collaborate with.
4 *she joined the volleyball team* **sign up with,** enlist in, enroll in, enter, become a member of, be part of.
5 *where the Ottawa River joins the St. Lawrence* **meet,** reach, abut, touch, adjoin, border on, connect with.

CHOOSE THE RIGHT WORD

join, combine, conjoin, connect, consolidate, unite

It is possible for an individual to **join** an investment club, to **consolidate** his or her financial resources, and to **combine** a background in economics with a strong interest in retirement planning. All of these words mean to bring together or to attach two or more things. *Join* is the general term for bringing into contact or conjunction two discrete things (*join two pieces of wood; join one's friends in celebration*), while **conjoin** emphasizes both the separateness of the things that are joined and the unity that results (*her innate brilliance, conjoined with a genuine eagerness to learn, made her the ideal candidate for the job*). In contrast, to *combine* is to mix or mingle things together, often to the point where they merge with one another (*combine the ingredients for a cake*). *Consolidate* also implies a merger of distinct and separate elements, but the emphasis here is on achieving greater compactness, strength, or efficiency (*consolidate their furnishings and buy a new house together*). **Connect** implies a loose or obvious attachment of things to each other, but with each thing's identity or physical separateness preserved (*the two families were connected by blood; she connected the computer to the printer*). In a physical context, it differs from *join* in that it implies an intervening element that permits movement; in other words, the bones are *connected* by ligaments, but bricks are *joined* by mortar. When things are joined or combined so closely that they form a single thing, they are said to **unite** (*the parties were united in their support of the new law*).

joint ▶ **noun 1** *cracks in the joint* **juncture,** junction, join, intersection, confluence, nexus, link, linkage, connection; weld, seam; Anatomy commissure.
2 *the hip joint* ball-and-socket joint, hinge joint, articulation.
3 informal *a classy joint* **establishment,** restaurant, bar, club, nightclub, place; hole, dump, dive. See also BAR (sense 4 of the noun).
4 informal *he rolled a joint* marijuana cigarette, cannabis cigarette; informal reefer, doobie, roach, jay, blunt, spliff.
▶ **adjective** *matters of joint interest | a joint effort* **common,** shared, communal, collective; mutual, cooperative, collaborative, concerted, combined, united, bilateral, multilateral.
ANTONYMS separate.

jointly ▶ **adverb** *Hitachi and NEC will jointly develop business software* **together,** in partnership, in cooperation, cooperatively, in conjunction, in collaboration, in concert, as one, in combination, mutually; in league, in alliance; in collusion.

joke ▶ **noun 1** *they were telling jokes* **funny story,** jest, witticism, quip; pun, play on words; informal gag, wisecrack, crack, one-liner, rib-tickler, knee-slapper, thigh-slapper, punchline, groaner.
2 *playing stupid jokes* **trick,** practical joke, prank, lark, stunt, hoax, jape; informal spoof.
3 informal *he soon became a joke to us* **laughingstock,** object of ridicule, stooge, butt; Brit. informal Aunt Sally.
4 informal *the present system is a joke* **farce,** travesty, waste of time.
▶ **verb 1** *she laughed and joked with the guests* **tell jokes,** crack jokes; jest, banter, quip; informal wisecrack, josh.
2 *they didn't realize you were only joking* **fool,** fool around, play a trick, play a practical joke, tease; informal kid, fun, pull (someone's leg), pull/jerk/yank someone's chain, make a monkey out of someone, put someone on.

joker ▶ **noun** *he was such a joker that he was often not taken seriously* **humorist,** comedian, comedienne, comic, wit, clown, card, jokester, jester, wisecracker, wag; prankster, practical joker, hoaxer, trickster.

jolly ▶ **adjective** *he returned in a jolly mood* **cheerful,** happy, cheery, good-humored, jovial, merry, sunny, joyful, joyous, lighthearted, in high spirits, bubbly, exuberant, ebullient, gleeful, mirthful, genial, affable, fun-loving; informal chipper, chirpy, perky, bright-eyed and bushy-tailed, hail-fellow-well-met; formal jocund, jocose; dated gay; literary blithe.
ANTONYMS miserable.
▶ **noun (jollies)** *people who get their jollies reading the tabloids* **pleasure,** thrill, enjoyment, excitement, titillation; informal kicks.

jolt ▶ **verb 1** *the train jolted the passengers to one side* **push,** thrust, jar, bump, knock, bang; shake, joggle, jog.
2 *the car jolted along* **bump,** bounce, jerk, rattle, lurch, shudder, jounce; Brit. judder.
3 *she was jolted out of her reverie* **startle,** surprise, shock, stun, shake, take aback; astonish, astound, amaze, stagger, stop someone in their tracks; informal rock, floor.
▶ **noun 1** *a series of sickening jolts* **bump,** bounce, shake, jerk, lurch.
2 *he woke up with a jolt* **start,** jerk, jump.
3 *the sight of the dagger gave him a jolt* **fright,** the fright of one's life, shock, scare, surprise; wake-up call.

jostle ▶ **verb 1** *jostled by the crowd* **bump into/against,** knock into/against, bang into, collide with, plow into, jolt; **push,** shove, elbow, mob, shoulder; informal barrel into, bulldoze.
2 *media empires jostle to catch the eye of Asian readers and viewers* **struggle,** vie, jockey, scramble, crowd one another.

jot ▶ **verb** *I've jotted down a few details* **write down,** note down, make a note of, take down, put on paper; scribble, scrawl.

▶ **noun** *not a jot of evidence* **iota,** scrap, shred, whit, grain, crumb, ounce, (little) bit, jot or tittle, speck, atom, particle, scintilla, trace, hint; informal smidgen, tad.

journal ▶ **noun 1** *a medical journal* **periodical,** magazine, gazette, digest, review, newsletter, bulletin; newspaper, paper, tabloid, broadsheet; daily, weekly, monthly, quarterly.
2 *he keeps a journal* **diary,** daily record, daybook, log, logbook, chronicle.

journalism ▶ **noun** *a career in journalism* **the press,** the fourth estate; **reporting,** news writing, news broadcasting, news coverage, reportage, feature writing, photojournalism, sensationalism, the newspaper business; articles, reports, features, pieces, stories.

journalist ▶ **noun** *another journalist has been wounded in Bosnia* **reporter,** correspondent, columnist, writer, commentator, reviewer; investigative journalist, photojournalist, newspaperman, newspaperwoman, newsman, newswoman, newshound, newshawk, hack, stringer.

journey ▶ **noun** *their journey around the world* **trip,** expedition, excursion, tour, trek, voyage, junket, cruise, ride, drive, jaunt; crossing, passage, flight; travels, wandering, globe-trotting; odyssey, pilgrimage; peregrination.
▶ **verb** *they journeyed south* **travel,** go, voyage, sail, cruise, fly, hike, trek, ride, drive, make one's way; take/go on a trip, go on an expedition, tour, rove, roam.

CHOOSE THE RIGHT WORD

journey, excursion, expedition, jaunt, pilgrimage, trip, voyage

While all of these nouns refer to a course of travel to a particular place, usually for a specific purpose, there is a big difference between a **jaunt** to the nearest beach and an **expedition** to the rainforest. While a **trip** may be either long or short, for business or pleasure, and taken at either a rushed or a leisurely pace (*a ski trip; a trip to Europe*), a **journey** suggests that a considerable amount of time and distance will be covered and that the travel will take place over land (*a journey into the Australian outback*). A long trip by water or through air or space is a **voyage** (*a voyage to the Galapagos Islands; a voyage to Mars*), while a short, casual trip for pleasure or recreation is a *jaunt* (*a jaunt to the local shopping mall*). **Excursion** also applies to a brief pleasure trip, usually no more than a day in length, that returns to the place where it began (*an afternoon excursion to the zoo*). Unlike the rest of these nouns, *expedition* and **pilgrimage** apply to *journeys* that are undertaken for a specific purpose. An *expedition* is usually made by an organized group or company (*a scientific expedition; an expedition to locate new sources of oil*), while a *pilgrimage* is a journey to a place that has religious or emotional significance (*the Muslims' annual pilgrimage to Mecca; a pilgrimage to the place where her father died*).

jovial ▶ **adjective** *his jovial manner* **cheerful,** jolly, happy, cheery, good-humored, convivial, genial, good-natured, friendly, amiable, affable, sociable, outgoing; smiling, merry, sunny, joyful, joyous, high-spirited, exuberant; chipper, chirpy, perky, bright-eyed and bushy-tailed, hail-fellow-well-met; formal jocund, jocose; dated gay; literary blithe.
ANTONYMS miserable.

joy ▶ **noun 1** *whoops of joy* **delight,** great pleasure, joyfulness, jubilation, triumph, exultation, rejoicing, happiness, gladness, glee, exhilaration, exuberance, elation, euphoria, bliss, ecstasy, rapture; enjoyment, felicity, joie de vivre, jouissance; literary jocundity.
ANTONYMS misery.
2 *it was a joy to be with her* **pleasure,** source of pleasure, delight, treat, thrill.
ANTONYMS trial.

joyful ▶ **adjective 1** *his joyful mood* **cheerful,** happy, jolly, merry, sunny, joyous, lighthearted, in good spirits, bubbly, exuberant, ebullient, cheery, smiling, mirthful, radiant; jubilant, overjoyed, thrilled, ecstatic, euphoric, blissful, on cloud nine, elated, delighted, gleeful; jovial, genial, good-humored; informal chipper, chirpy, peppy, over the moon, on top of the world, upbeat; dated gay; formal jocund; literary blithe.
ANTONYMS sad, miserable.
2 *joyful news* **pleasing,** happy, good, cheering, gladdening, welcome, heartwarming.
ANTONYMS distressing.
3 *a joyful occasion* **happy,** cheerful, merry, jolly, festive, joyous.
ANTONYMS sad, depressing.

joyless ▶ **adjective 1** *a joyless man* **gloomy,** melancholy, morose, lugubrious, glum, somber, saturnine, sullen, dour, humorless.
ANTONYMS cheerful.
2 *a joyless room* **depressing,** cheerless, gloomy, dreary, bleak, dispiriting, drab, dismal, desolate, austere, somber; unwelcoming, uninviting, inhospitable; literary drear.
ANTONYMS cheerful, welcoming.

joyous ▶ **adjective** See JOYFUL (sense 1), JOYFUL (sense 3).

jubilant ▶ **adjective** *a jubilant crowd* **overjoyed,** exultant, triumphant, joyful, rejoicing, exuberant, elated, thrilled, gleeful, euphoric, ecstatic, enraptured, in raptures, walking on air, in seventh heaven, on cloud nine; informal over the moon, on top of the world, tickled pink, on a high.
ANTONYMS despondent.

jubilation ▶ **noun** *we couldn't conceal our jubilation* **exultation,** joy, joyousness, elation, euphoria, rejoicing, ecstasy, rapture, glee, gleefulness, exuberance.

jubilee ▶ **noun** *Queen Elizabeth II's golden jubilee* **anniversary,** commemoration; celebration, festival, jamboree; festivities, revelry.

judge ▶ **noun 1** *the judge sentenced him to five years* **justice,** magistrate, sheriff, jurist.
2 *a panel of judges will select the winner* **adjudicator,** arbiter, arbitrator, assessor, evaluator, referee, ombudsman, ombudsperson, appraiser, examiner, moderator, mediator.

▶ verb 1 *we judged that it was too late to proceed* **form the opinion,** conclude, decide; consider, believe, think, deem, view; deduce, gather, infer, gauge, estimate, guess, surmise, conjecture; regard as, look on as, take to be, rate as, class as; informal reckon, figure.
2 *the case was judged by a tribunal* **try,** hear; adjudicate, decide, give a ruling on, give a verdict on.
3 *she was judged innocent of murder* **adjudge,** pronounce, decree, rule, find.
4 *the competition will be judged by last year's winner* **adjudicate,** arbitrate, mediate, moderate.
5 *entries were judged by a panel of experts* **assess,** appraise, evaluate; examine, review.

judgment ▶ noun 1 *his temper could affect his judgment* **discernment,** acumen, shrewdness, astuteness, sense, common sense, perception, perspicacity, percipience, acuity, discrimination, reckoning, wisdom, wit, judiciousness, prudence, canniness, sharpness, sharp-wittedness, powers of reasoning, reason, logic; savvy, horse sense, street smarts, gumption.
2 *a court judgment* **verdict,** decision, adjudication, ruling, pronouncement, decree, finding; sentence.
3 *critical judgment* **assessment,** evaluation, appraisal; review, analysis, criticism, critique.
– PHRASES **against one's better judgment** *I paid the asking price, against my better judgment* **reluctantly,** unwillingly, grudgingly.

judicial ▶ adjective *a judicial inquiry* **legal,** juridical, judicatory; official.

judicious ▶ adjective *following a judicious course of action* **wise,** sensible, prudent, politic, shrewd, astute, canny, sagacious, commonsensical, sound, well-advised, discerning, percipient, intelligent, smart; informal heads-up.
ANTONYMS ill-advised.

jug ▶ noun *a jug of cider* **pitcher,** carafe, flask, flagon, bottle, decanter, ewer, crock, jar, urn; historical amphora.

juggle ▶ verb 1 *juggling three part-time jobs* **handle,** manage, deal with, multitask.
2 *the auditors suspect that the books had been juggled* **tamper with,** manipulate, falsify, alter, rig; informal fudge, fix, doctor, cook.

juice ▶ noun 1 *the juice from two lemons* **liquid,** fluid, sap; extract; nectar.
2 informal *he ran out of juice on the last lap* **energy,** power, stamina, steam.

juicy ▶ adjective 1 *a juicy peach* **succulent,** tender, moist; ripe; archaic mellow.
ANTONYMS dry.
2 informal *juicy gossip* **sensational,** very interesting, fascinating, lurid; scandalous, racy, risqué, spicy; informal hot.
ANTONYMS dull.
3 informal *juicy profits | a juicy role* **substantial,** large, sizable, generous; profitable, lucrative, remunerative; **desirable,** appealing, attractive; informal tidy, whopping, to die for.
ANTONYMS insignificant, undesirable.

jumble ▶ noun *a jumble of books and toys* **untidy heap,** clutter, muddle, mess, confusion, disarray, tangle, imbroglio; **hodgepodge,** mishmash, miscellany, motley collection, mixed bag, medley, jambalaya, farrago, gallimaufry.
▶ verb *the photographs are all* ***jumbled up*** **mix up,** muddle up, disarrange, disorganize, disorder, put in disarray.

CHOOSE THE RIGHT WORD

jumble, confusion, conglomeration, disarray, farrago, hodgepodge, mélange, muddle

Confusion is a very broad term, applying to any indiscriminate mixing or mingling that makes it difficult to distinguish individual elements or parts (*a confusion of languages*). The typical teenager's bedroom is usually a **jumble** of books, papers, clothing, CDs, and soda cans—the word suggests physical disorder and a mixture of dissimilar things. If the disorder exists on a figurative level, it is usually called a **hodgepodge** (*a hodgepodge of ideas, opinions, and quotations, with a few facts thrown in for good measure*). **Conglomeration** refers to a collection of dissimilar things, but with a suggestion that the collection is random or inappropriate (*a conglomeration of decorating styles*). A **mélange** can be a mixture of foods (*add peppers or zucchini to the mélange*), but it can also be used in a derogatory way (*an error-filled mélange of pseudoscience, religion, and fanciful ideas*). A **farrago** is an irrational or confused mixture of elements and is usually worse than a *conglomeration* (*a farrago of doubts, fears, hopes, and desires*), while a **muddle** is less serious and suggests confused thinking and lack of organization (*their bank records were in a complete muddle*). **Disarray** implies disarrangement and is most appropriately used when order or discipline has been lost (*his unexpected appearance threw the meeting into disarray*).

jumbo ▶ adjective informal See HUGE.

jump ▶ verb 1 *the cat jumped off his lap | Flora began to jump around* **leap,** spring, bound, hop; skip, caper, dance, prance, frolic, cavort.
2 *he jumped the fence* **vault (over),** leap over, clear, sail over, hop over, hurdle.
3 *pretax profits jumped* **rise,** go up, shoot up, soar, surge, climb, increase; informal skyrocket.
4 *the noise made her jump* **start,** jerk, jolt, flinch, recoil; informal jump out of one's skin.
5 *Polly* ***jumped at*** *the chance* **accept eagerly,** leap at, welcome with open arms, seize on, snap up, grab, pounce on.
6 *the place was jumping* **rock,** hop, buzz, be lively, be wild.
7 *two guys jumped him in the alley* **assault,** assail, set upon, mug, attack, pounce on.
▶ noun 1 *a short jump across the ditch* **leap,** spring, vault, bound, hop.
2 *a jump in profits* **rise,** leap, increase, upsurge, upswing, upturn; informal hike.
3 *I woke up with a jump* **start,** jerk, involuntary

movement, spasm.

– PHRASES **jump the gun** informal *several radio stations have jumped the gun by announcing winners long before the polls have closed in certain districts* **act prematurely,** act too soon, be too/overly hasty, be precipitate, be rash; informal be ahead of oneself. **jump to it** informal *this year, students will really have to jump to it if they hope to get a hot meal before the kitchen closes* **hurry up,** get a move on, be quick; informal get cracking, shake a leg, look lively, look sharp, get the lead out; dated make haste.

jumpy ▶ **adjective 1** informal *he was tired and jumpy* **nervous,** on edge, edgy, tense, anxious, ill at ease, uneasy, restless, fidgety, keyed up, overwrought, on tenterhooks; informal a bundle of nerves, jittery, uptight, het up, in a tizzy; strung out; squirrelly, antsy.
ANTONYMS calm, relaxed.
2 *jumpy black-and-white footage* **jerky,** jolting, lurching, bumpy, jarring; fitful, convulsive.

junction ▶ **noun 1** *the junction between the roof and the wall* **joint,** intersection, join, bond, seam, connection, juncture; Anatomy commissure.
2 *the junction of the two rivers* **confluence,** convergence, meeting point, juncture.
3 *turn right at the next junction* **intersection,** crossroads, crossing, interchange; turn, turnoff, exit; traffic circle, cloverleaf.

juncture ▶ **noun 1** *at this juncture, I am unable to tell you* **point,** point in time, time, moment, moment in time; period, occasion, phase.
2 *the juncture of the pipes* See JUNCTION (sense 1).
3 *the juncture of the rivers* See JUNCTION (sense 2).

jungle ▶ **noun 1** *the Amazon jungle* **tropical forest,** (tropical) rain forest, wilderness.
2 *the jungle of bureaucracy* **complexity,** confusion, complication, chaos, mess; labyrinth, maze, tangle, web.

junior ▶ **adjective 1** *the junior members of the family* **younger,** youngest.
ANTONYMS senior, older.
2 *a junior position in the firm* **low-ranking,** lower-ranking, entry-level, subordinate, lesser, lower, minor, secondary.
ANTONYMS senior, higher-ranking.

junk informal ▶ **noun** *an attic full of junk* **rubbish,** clutter, odds and ends, bric-a-brac, bits and pieces; garbage, trash, refuse, litter, scrap, waste, debris, detritus, dross; informal crap.
▶ **verb** *time to junk the old pickup* **throw away/out,** discard, get rid of, dispose of, scrap, toss out, jettison; informal chuck, dump, ditch, deep-six, trash.

junket ▶ **noun** informal *the company sponsored a New Year's Eve gambling junket* **excursion,** outing, spree, trip, jaunt; celebration, party, jamboree, feast, festivity; informal bash, shindig.

jurisdiction ▶ **noun 1** *an area under French jurisdiction* **authority,** control, power, dominion, rule, administration, command, sway, leadership, sovereignty, hegemony.
2 *foreign jurisdictions* **territory,** region, province, district, area, domain, realm.

CHOOSE THE RIGHT WORD

jurisdiction, authority, command, dominion, power, sovereignty, sway

The **authority** of our elected officials refers to their *power* (often conferred by rank or office) to give orders, require obedience, or make decisions. Their authority is normally limited by their **jurisdiction**, which is a legally predetermined division of a larger whole, within which someone has a right to rule or decide (*the matter was beyond his jurisdiction*). The president of the United States has more **power** than any other American official, which means that he has the ability to exert force or control over something. He does not, however, have the *authority* to make laws on his own. As commander in chief, he does have **command** over the nation's armed forces, implying that he has the kind of authority that can enforce obedience. Back in the days when Great Britain had **dominion**, or supreme authority, over the American colonies, it was the king of England who held **sway** over this country's economic and political life—an old-fashioned word that stresses the sweeping scope of one's power. But his **sovereignty**, which emphasizes absolute or autonomous rule over something considered as a whole, was eventually challenged. The rest, as they say, is history.

just ▶ **adjective 1** *a just and democratic society* **fair,** fair-minded, equitable, evenhanded, impartial, unbiased, objective, neutral, disinterested, unprejudiced, open-minded, nonpartisan; honorable, upright, decent, honest, righteous, moral, virtuous, principled.
ANTONYMS unfair.
2 *a just reward* **deserved,** well deserved, well earned, earned, merited; rightful, due, fitting, appropriate, suitable; formal condign; archaic meet.
ANTONYMS undeserved.
3 *just criticism* **valid,** sound, well-founded, justified, justifiable, warranted, legitimate.
ANTONYMS unfair, wrongful.
▶ **adverb 1** *I just saw him* **a moment ago,** a second ago, a short time ago, very recently, not long ago.
2 *she's just right for him* **exactly,** precisely, absolutely, completely, totally, entirely, perfectly, utterly, wholly, thoroughly, in all respects; informal to a T, dead.
3 *we just made it* **narrowly,** only just, by a hair's breadth; barely, scarcely, hardly; informal by the skin of one's teeth, by a whisker.
4 *she's just a child* **only,** merely, simply, but, nothing but, no more than.
5 *the color's just fantastic* **really,** absolutely, completely, positively, entirely, totally, quite; indeed, truly.

– PHRASES **just about** informal *that's just about all I can eat at one meal* **nearly,** almost, practically, all but, virtually, as good as, more or less, to all intents and purposes; informal pretty much; literary well-nigh, nigh on.

justice ▶ noun **1** *I appealed to his sense of justice* **fairness,** justness, fair play, fair-mindedness, equity, evenhandedness, impartiality, objectivity, neutrality, disinterestedness, honesty, righteousness, morals, morality.
2 *they were determined to exact justice* **punishment,** judgment, retribution, compensation, just deserts.
3 *an order made by the justices* **judge,** magistrate, jurist.
– PHRASES **do justice to** *the movie didn't do justice to the book* **consider fairly,** be worthy of.

justifiable ▶ adjective *justifiable criticism* **valid,** legitimate, warranted, well-founded, justified, just, reasonable; defensible, tenable, supportable, acceptable.
ANTONYMS indefensible.

justification ▶ noun *there's no justification for their rudeness* **grounds,** reason, basis, rationale, premise, rationalization, vindication, explanation; defense, argument, apologia, apology, case.

justify ▶ verb **1** *directors must justify the expenditure* **give grounds for,** give reasons for, give a justification for, explain, give an explanation for, account for; defend, answer for, vindicate.
2 *the situation justified further investigation* **warrant,** be good reason for, be a justification for.

justly ▶ adverb **1** *he is justly proud of his achievement* **justifiably,** with (good) reason, legitimately, rightly, rightfully, deservedly.
ANTONYMS unjustifiably.
2 *they were treated justly* **fairly,** with fairness, equitably, evenhandedly, impartially, without bias, objectively, without prejudice, fairly and squarely.
ANTONYMS unfairly.

jut ▶ verb *the face of the cliff is sheer, except for one shelf of rock that* ***juts out*** **stick out,** project, protrude, bulge out, overhang.

juvenile ▶ adjective **1** *juvenile offenders* **young,** teenage, adolescent, boyish, girlish, junior, pubescent, prepubescent, youthful. See note at YOUTHFUL.
ANTONYMS adult.
2 *juvenile behavior* **childish,** immature, puerile, infantile, babyish; jejune, inexperienced, callow, green, unsophisticated, sophomoric, naive, foolish, silly.
ANTONYMS mature.
▶ noun *two juveniles fled the scene* **young person,** youngster, child, teenager, adolescent, youth, boy/girl, minor, junior; informal kid, punk.
ANTONYMS adult.

juxtapose ▶ verb *the exhibit juxtaposes works by Van Gogh and Gauguin* **place side by side,** set side by side, collocate, mix; compare, contrast.

Kk

kaleidoscopic ▸ adjective **1** *kaleidoscopic swirls in the puddles* **multicolored,** many-colored, multicolor, many-hued, variegated, particolored, varicolored, psychedelic, rainbow, polychromatic.
ANTONYMS monochrome.
2 *the kaleidoscopic political landscape* **ever-changing,** changeable, shifting, fluid, protean, variable, inconstant, fluctuating, unpredictable, impermanent.
ANTONYMS fixed, constant.

keel ▸ noun & verb
– PHRASES **on an even keel** *finally, the relationship seems to be on an even keel* **steady,** on track, on course, untroubled. **keel over 1** *the boat keeled over* **capsize,** turn turtle, turn upside down, founder; overturn, turn over, flip (over), tip over. **2** *the slightest activity made him keel over* **collapse,** faint, pass out, black out, lose consciousness, swoon.

keen ▸ adjective **1** *his publishers were keen to capitalize on his success* **eager,** anxious, intent, impatient, determined, ambitious, champing at the bit; informal raring, itching, dying. See note at EAGER.
ANTONYMS reluctant.
2 *a keen birdwatcher* **enthusiastic,** avid, eager, ardent, passionate, fervent, impassioned; conscientious, committed, dedicated, zealous.
ANTONYMS apathetic, halfhearted.
3 *they are* **keen on** *horses | a girl he was* **keen on** **enthusiastic about,** interested in, passionate about; attracted to, fond of, taken with, smitten with, enamored of, infatuated with; informal struck on, hot on/for, mad about, crazy about, nuts about.
ANTONYMS indifferent, unenthusiastic.
4 *a keen cutting edge* **sharp,** sharpened, honed, razor-sharp.
ANTONYMS blunt.
5 *keen eyesight* **acute,** sharp, discerning, sensitive, perceptive, clear.
ANTONYMS weak.
6 *a keen mind* **acute,** penetrating, astute, incisive, sharp, perceptive, piercing, razor-sharp, perspicacious, shrewd, discerning, clever, intelligent, brilliant, bright, smart, wise, canny, percipient, insightful.
ANTONYMS dull, stupid.
7 *a keen wind* **cold,** icy, freezing, harsh, raw, bitter; penetrating, piercing, biting.
ANTONYMS gentle.
8 *a keen sense of duty* **intense,** acute, fierce, passionate, burning, fervent, ardent, strong, powerful.

CHOOSE THE RIGHT WORD

keen, acute, astute, penetrating, perspicacious, sharp, shrewd

A knife can be **sharp**, even **keen**, but it can't be **astute**. While *keen* and *sharp* mean having a fine point or edge, they also pertain to mental agility and perceptiveness. You might describe someone as having a *keen* mind, which suggests the ability to grapple with complex problems, or to observe details and see them as part of a larger pattern (*a keen appreciation of what victory would mean for the Democratic Party*) or a *keen* wit, which suggests an incisive or stimulating sense of humor. Someone who is *sharp* has an alert and rational mind, but is not necessarily well grounded in a particular field and may in some cases be cunning or devious (*sharp enough to see how the situation might be turned to her advantage*). An **astute** mind, in contrast, is one that has a thorough and profound understanding of a given subject or field (*an astute understanding of the legal principles involved*). Like *sharp*, **shrewd** implies both practicality and cleverness, but with an undercurrent of self-interest (*a shrewd salesperson*). **Acute** is close in meaning to *keen*, but with more emphasis on sensitivity and the ability to make subtle distinctions (*an acute sense of smell*). While a keen mind might see only superficial details, a **penetrating** mind would focus on underlying causes (*a penetrating analysis of the plan's feasibility*). **Perspicacious** is the most formal of these terms, meaning both perceptive and discerning (*a perspicacious remark; perspicacious judgment*).

keep ▸ verb **1** *you should keep all the old forms* **retain,** hold on to, keep hold of, retain possession of, keep possession of, not part with; save, store, conserve, put aside, set aside; informal hang on to, stash away.
ANTONYMS throw away, lose.
2 *I tried to keep calm* **remain,** continue to be, stay, carry on being, persist in being.
3 *he keeps talking about the Super Bowl* **persist in,** keep on, carry on, continue, do something constantly.
ANTONYMS stop, give up.
4 *I won't keep you long* **detain,** keep waiting, delay, hold up, retard, slow down.
5 *most people kept the rules | he had to keep his*

promise **comply with,** obey, observe, conform to, abide by, adhere to, stick to, heed, follow; fulfill, carry out, act on, make good, honor, keep to, stand by.
ANTONYMS disobey, break.
6 *keeping the old traditions* **preserve,** keep alive/up, keep going, carry on, perpetuate, maintain, uphold, sustain.
ANTONYMS discard, abandon.
7 *that's where we keep the linen* **store,** house, stow, put (away), place, deposit.
8 *she keeps rabbits* **breed,** rear, raise, farm; own, have as a pet.
9 *God keep you | keep them from harm* **look after,** care for, take care of, mind, watch over; **preserve,** protect, keep safe, shield, shelter, safeguard, defend, guard.
ANTONYMS neglect, endanger.
10 *she kept their whereabouts from us* **keep secret,** keep hidden, hide, conceal, withhold.
11 *worry kept her from sleeping* **prevent,** stop, restrain, hold back.
ANTONYMS enable, allow.
▶ **noun** *money to pay for his keep* **maintenance,** upkeep, sustenance, board, room and board, lodging, food, livelihood.
– PHRASES **keep at** *she's determined to keep at her studies until she passes the bar exam* **persevere with/in/at,** persist in/with, keep going with, carry on with, press on with, work away at, continue with; informal stick at, plug away at, hammer away at. **keep something back 1** *she kept back some of the money* **reserve,** keep in reserve, put aside/by, set aside; retain, hold back, hold on to, not part with; informal stash away. **2** *she kept back the details* **withhold,** keep secret, keep hidden, conceal, suppress, keep quiet about. **3** *she could hardly keep back her tears* **suppress,** stifle, choke back, fight back, hold back/in, repress, keep in check, contain, smother, swallow, bite back. **keep from** *it's hard to keep from smoking* **refrain from,** stop oneself, restrain oneself from, prevent oneself from, forbear from, avoid. **keep off 1** *we ask that you please keep off the playing field* **stay off,** not enter, keep away from, stay away from, not trespass on. **2** *Maud tried to keep off political subjects* **avoid,** steer clear of, stay away from, evade, dodge, sidestep, bypass, skirt around; informal duck. **3** *you should keep off alcohol* **abstain from,** do without, refrain from, give up, forgo, not touch; informal swear off; formal forswear. **keep on** *they kept on working | despite our exhaustion, we agreed to keep on* **continue,** go on, carry on, persist in, persevere in; soldier on, struggle on, keep going. **keep something up** *keep up the good work* **continue (with),** keep on with, keep going with, carry on with, persist with, persevere with. **keep up with** *she walked fast to keep up with them* **keep pace with,** keep abreast of; match, equal.

keeper ▶ **noun** *Gregor is the keeper of the tennis courts and adjacent grounds* **guardian,** custodian, curator, administrator, overseer, steward, caretaker.

keeping ▶ **noun**
– PHRASES **in keeping with** *in keeping with the patriotic theme, we've asked the band to conclude with a Sousa medley* **consistent with,** in harmony with, in accord with, in agreement with, in line with, in character with, compatible with; appropriate to, befitting, suitable for.

keepsake ▶ **noun** *a box with concert programs, pressed corsages, and other keepsakes* **memento,** souvenir, reminder, remembrance, token; party favor, bomboniere.

keg ▶ **noun** *the beer is delivered in kegs* **barrel,** cask, vat, butt, tun, hogshead; historical firkin.

kernel ▶ **noun 1** *the kernel of a nut* **seed,** grain, core; nut.
2 *the kernel of the argument* **essence,** core, heart, essentials, quintessence, fundamentals, basics, nub, gist, substance; informal nitty-gritty.
3 *a kernel of truth* **nucleus,** germ, grain, nugget.

key ▶ **noun 1** *I put my key in the lock* **door key,** latchkey, pass key, master key.
2 *the key to the mystery | the key to success* **answer,** clue, solution, explanation; basis, foundation, requisite, precondition, means, way, route, path, passport, secret, formula.
▶ **adjective** *a key figure* **crucial,** central, essential, indispensable, pivotal, critical, dominant, vital, principal, prime, primary, chief, major, leading, main, important, significant.
ANTONYMS peripheral.

keynote ▶ **noun** *the keynote of this year's conference is 'Adequate and Affordable Health Care'* **theme,** salient point, gist, substance, burden, tenor, pith, marrow, essence, heart, core, basis, essential feature/element, crux.

keystone ▶ **noun** *the keystone of the government's policy* **foundation,** basis, linchpin, cornerstone, base, principle, guiding principle, core, heart, center, crux, fundament.

kibosh ▶ **noun**
– PHRASES **put the kibosh on** informal *inclement weather can put the kibosh on a promising vintage* **put a stop to,** stop, halt, put an end to, quash, block, cancel, scotch, thwart, prevent, suppress; informal stymie; scuttle.

kick ▶ **verb 1** *she kicked the ball over the fence* **boot,** punt, drop-kick; informal hoof.
2 informal *he was struggling to kick his drug habit* **give up,** break, abandon, end, stop, cease, desist from, renounce; informal shake, pack in, leave off, quit.
▶ **noun 1** *that kick landed the ball across the street* **blow with the foot,** punt; informal boot.
2 informal *I get a kick out of driving a race car* **thrill,** excitement, stimulation, tingle; fun, enjoyment, amusement, pleasure, gratification; informal buzz, high, rush, charge.
3 informal *a drink with a powerful kick* **potency,** stimulant effect, strength, power; tang, zest, bite, piquancy, edge, pungency; informal punch.
4 informal *a health kick* **craze,** enthusiasm, obsession, mania, passion; fashion, vogue, trend; informal fad.
– PHRASES **kick someone/something around** informal **1** *I'm tired of getting kicked around* **abuse,** mistreat, maltreat, push around, trample on, take for granted; informal boss around, walk all over. **2** *they began to kick around some ideas* **discuss,** talk over, debate, thrash out, consider,

toy with, play with. **kick back** informal *I just wanna kick back and watch some TV* **relax,** unwind, take it easy, rest, slow down, let up, ease up/off, sit back, chill (out), hang loose. **kick off** informal *we'll kick off with a brief description of how a timeshare works | they kicked off the ceremony with a parade of cadets* **start,** commence, begin, get going, get off the ground, get underway; open, start off, set in motion, launch, initiate, introduce, inaugurate, usher in. **kick someone out** informal *most of us were given one-week suspensions from school, but Andy and Olivia were actually kicked out* **expel,** eject, banish, exile, throw out, oust, evict, get rid of, ax; dismiss, discharge; informal chuck (out), send packing, boot out, give someone their marching orders, give someone their walking papers, give someone the gate, give someone the (old) heave-ho, sack, bounce, fire, give someone the bum's rush.

kickoff ▶ **noun** informal *breakfast on the boat was a great kickoff to the weekend* **beginning,** start, commencement, launch, outset, opening.

kid[1] ▶ **noun** informal *they have three kids* **child,** youngster, little one, baby, toddler, tot, infant, boy/girl, young person, minor, juvenile, adolescent, teenager, youth, stripling; offspring, son/daughter; informal kiddie, shaver, young 'un, rug rat, ankle-biter, munchkin, whippersnapper; derogatory brat; literary babe.

kid[2] ▶ **verb** informal **1** *I'm not kidding | stop kidding me* **joke,** tease, jest, chaff, be facetious, fool around, pull (someone's) leg, pull/jerk/yank someone's (chain), have (someone) on, rib.
2 *don't kid yourself* **delude,** deceive, fool, trick, hoodwink, hoax, beguile, dupe, gull; informal con, pull the wool over (someone's) eyes.

kidnap ▶ **verb** *they attempted to kidnap the president's child* **abduct,** carry off, capture, seize, snatch, take hostage.

kill ▶ **verb 1** *gangs killed twenty-seven people* **murder,** take/end the life of, assassinate, eliminate, terminate, dispatch, finish off, put to death, execute; slaughter, butcher, massacre, wipe out, annihilate, exterminate, mow down, shoot down, cut down, cut to pieces; informal bump off, polish off, do away with, do in, knock off, take out, croak, stiff, blow away, liquidate, dispose of, ice, snuff, rub out, waste, whack, smoke; euphemistic neutralize; literary slay.
2 *this would kill all hopes of progress* **destroy,** put an end to, end, extinguish, dash, quash, ruin, wreck, shatter, smash, crush, scotch, thwart; informal put the kibosh on, stymie, scuttle.
3 *we had to kill several hours at the airport* **while away,** fill (up), occupy, pass, spend, waste.
4 informal *you must rest or you'll kill yourself* **exhaust,** wear out, tire out, overtax, overtire, fatigue, weary, sap, drain, enervate, knock out.
5 informal *my feet were killing me* **hurt,** cause pain to, torture, torment, cause discomfort to; be painful, be sore, be uncomfortable.
6 *a shot to kill the pain* **alleviate,** assuage, soothe, allay, dull, blunt, deaden, stifle, suppress, subdue.
7 informal *an opposition attempt to kill the bill* **veto,** defeat, vote down, rule against, reject, throw out, overrule, overturn, put a stop to, quash, squash.
8 informal *Noel killed the engine* **turn off,** switch off, stop, shut off/down, cut.
▶ **noun 1** *the hunter's kill* **prey,** quarry, victim, bag.
2 *the wolf was moving in for the kill* **death blow,** killing, dispatch, finish, end, coup de grâce.

CHOOSE THE RIGHT WORD

kill, assassinate, dispatch, execute, massacre, murder, slaughter, slay

When it comes to depriving someone or something of life, the options are seemingly endless. To **kill** is the most general term, meaning to cause the death of a person, animal, or plant, with no reference to the manner of killing, the agent, or the cause (*killed in a car accident*). Even inanimate things may be killed (*Congress killed the project when they vetoed the bill*). To **slay** is to kill deliberately and violently; it is used more often in written than in spoken English (*a novel about a presidential candidate who is slain by his opponent*). **Murder** implies a malicious and premeditated killing of one person by another (*a gruesome murder carried out by the son-in-law*), while **assassinate** implies that a politically important person has been murdered, often by someone hired to do the job (*assassinate the head of the guerrilla forces*). Someone who is put to death by a legal or military process is said to be **executed** (*execute by lethal injection*), but if someone is killed primarily to get rid or him or her, the appropriate verb is **dispatch**, which also suggests speed or promptness (*after delivering the secret documents, the informer was dispatched*). While **slaughter** is usually associated with the killing of animals for food, it can also apply to a mass killing of humans (*the slaughter of innocent civilians provoked a worldwide outcry*). **Massacre** also refers to the brutal murder of large numbers of people, but it is used more specifically to indicate the wholesale destruction of a relatively defenseless group of people (*the massacre of Bethlehem's male children by King Herod*).

killer ▶ **noun 1** *police are searching for the killer* **murderer,** assassin, slaughterer, butcher, serial killer, gunman; executioner, hit man, cutthroat; literary slayer; dated homicide.
2 *a major killer* **cause of death,** fatal illness, deadly illness, threat to life, scourge.

killing ▶ **noun** *a brutal killing* **murder,** assassination, homicide, manslaughter, elimination, putting to death, execution; slaughter, massacre, butchery, carnage, bloodshed, extermination, annihilation; literary slaying.
▶ **adjective 1** *a killing blow* **deadly,** lethal, fatal,

mortal, death-dealing; murderous, homicidal; literary deathly.
2 informal *a killing schedule* **exhausting,** grueling, punishing, taxing, draining, wearing, prostrating, crushing, tiring, fatiguing, debilitating, enervating, arduous, tough, demanding, onerous, strenuous, rigorous; informal murderous.
– PHRASES **make a killing** informal *Tess made a killing in real estate* **make a large profit,** make a/one's fortune, make money, rake it in, clean up, cash in, make a pretty penny, make big bucks.

killjoy ▶ noun *uh-oh, here comes that killjoy Walter* **spoilsport,** wet blanket, damper, party pooper; prophet of doom.

kilter ▶ noun
– PHRASES **out of kilter** *jet lag has left me completely out of kilter* **awry,** off balance, unbalanced, out of order, disordered, confused, muddled, disoriented, out of tune, out of whack, out of step; humorous discombobulated.

kin ▶ noun *their own kin* **relatives,** relations, family (members), kindred, kith and kin; flesh and blood, nearest and dearest; kinsfolk, kinsmen, kinswomen, people; informal folks.

kind ▶ adjective *she is such a kind and caring person* **kindly,** good-natured, kindhearted, warmhearted, caring, affectionate, loving, warm; considerate, helpful, thoughtful, obliging, unselfish, selfless, altruistic, good, attentive; compassionate, sympathetic, understanding, big-hearted, benevolent, benign, friendly, neighborly, hospitable, well-meaning, public-spirited.
ANTONYMS inconsiderate, mean.
▶ noun **1** *all kinds of gifts | the kinds of bird that could be seen* **sort,** type, variety, style, form, class, category, genre; genus, species, race, breed; flavor.
2 *they were different in kind | the first of its kind* **character,** nature, essence, quality, disposition, makeup; type, style, stamp, manner, description, mold, cast, temperament, ilk, stripe.
– PHRASES **kind of** informal *it was kind of spicy* **rather,** quite, fairly; somewhat, a little, slightly, a shade; informal pretty, sort of; a bit, kinda, a touch, a tad.

kindle ▶ verb **1** *he kindled a fire* **light,** ignite, set alight, set light to, set fire to, put a match to.
ANTONYMS extinguish, douse.
2 *the Beatles kindled my interest in music* **rouse,** arouse, wake, awake, awaken; stimulate, inspire, stir (up), excite, evoke, provoke, fire, inflame, trigger, activate, spark off; literary waken, enkindle.

kindly ▶ adjective *a kindly old lady* **benevolent,** kind, kindhearted, warm-hearted, generous, gentle, warm, good-natured, compassionate, caring, loving, benign, well meaning; helpful, thoughtful, considerate, good-hearted, nice, friendly, neighborly.
ANTONYMS unkind, cruel.
▶ adverb **1** *she spoke kindly* **benevolently,** good-naturedly, warmly, affectionately, tenderly, lovingly, compassionately; considerately, thoughtfully, helpfully, obligingly, generously, selflessly, unselfishly, sympathetically.
ANTONYMS unkindly, harshly.
2 *kindly explain what you mean* **please,** if you please, if you wouldn't mind; archaic prithee, pray.

kindness ▶ noun *he thanked her for her kindness* **kindliness,** kindheartedness, warmheartedness, affection, warmth, gentleness, concern, care; consideration, helpfulness, thoughtfulness, unselfishness, selflessness, altruism, compassion, sympathy, understanding, big-heartedness, benevolence, benignity, friendliness, hospitality, neighborliness; generosity, magnanimity, charitableness.

kindred ▶ noun *his mother's kindred* **family,** relatives, relations, kin, kith and kin, one's own flesh and blood; kinsfolk, kinsmen/kinswomen, people; informal folks.
▶ adjective **1** *industrial relations and kindred subjects* **related,** allied, connected, comparable, similar, like, parallel, associated, analogous.
ANTONYMS unrelated.
2 *a kindred spirit* **like-minded,** in sympathy, in harmony, in tune, of one mind, akin, similar, like, compatible; informal on the same wavelength.
ANTONYMS unsympathetic, alien.

king ▶ noun **1** *the king of France* **monarch,** sovereign, ruler, crowned head, Crown, emperor, prince, potentate, lord.
2 informal *the king of country music* **star,** leading light, luminary, superstar, giant, master; informal supremo, megastar.

kingdom ▶ noun **1** *his kingdom stretched to the sea* **realm,** domain, dominion, country, empire, principality, duchy, land, nation, state, sovereign state, province, territory.
2 *the third floor was Henderson's little kingdom* **domain,** province, realm, sphere, dominion, territory, arena, zone.
3 *the plant kingdom* **division,** category, classification, grouping, group.

kink ▶ noun **1** *your fishing line should have no kinks in it* **curl,** twist, twirl, loop, crinkle; knot, tangle, entanglement.
2 *there are still some kinks to iron out* **flaw,** defect, imperfection, problem, complication, hitch, snag, shortcoming, weakness; informal hiccup, glitch.
3 *a kink in my neck* **crick,** stiffness, pinch, knot.

kinky ▶ adjective **1** informal *kinky underwear* **provocative,** sexy, erotic, titillating, naughty, indecent, immodest.
2 informal *a kinky relationship* **perverse,** abnormal, deviant, unconventional, unnatural, degenerate, depraved, perverted; informal pervy.
3 *Catriona's long kinky hair* **curly,** crimped, curled, curling, frizzy, frizzed, wavy.

kinship ▶ noun **1** *the value of kinship in society* **family ties,** blood ties, common ancestry, consanguinity.
2 *she felt kinship with the others* **affinity,** sympathy, rapport, harmony, understanding, empathy, closeness, fellow feeling, bond, compatibility; similarity, likeness, correspondence, concordance.

kiosk ▶ noun *the kiosks along the boardwalk*

booth, stand, stall, concession, counter, newsstand; information booth.

kiss ▶ verb **1** *he kissed her on the lips | they kissed* **give a kiss to,** brush one's lips against, blow a kiss to; informal peck, smooch, canoodle, neck, buss, make out, lock lips; formal/humorous osculate.
2 *allow your foot just to kiss the floor* **brush (against),** caress, touch (gently), stroke, skim over.
▶ noun **1** *a kiss on the cheek | a passionate kiss* **peck,** smack, smooch, buss, French kiss; X; formal/humorous osculation.
2 *the kiss of the flowers against her cheeks* **gentle touch,** caress, brush, stroke.

kit ▶ noun **1** *the sculptor's kit* **equipment,** tools, implements, instruments, gadgets, utensils, appliances, tools of the trade, gear, tackle, hardware, paraphernalia; informal things, stuff, (the) necessaries; Military accoutrements.
2 *a model airplane kit* **set (of parts),** do-it-yourself kit.

knack ▶ noun **1** *a knack for making money* **gift,** talent, flair, genius, instinct, faculty, ability, capability, capacity, aptitude, aptness, bent, forte, facility; **technique,** method, trick, skill, adroitness, art, expertise; (**a knack for**) informal the hang of.
2 *his **knack of** getting injured at the wrong time* **tendency to,** propensity for, habit of, proneness to, aptness to, bent for, liability to, predisposition to, inclination to.

knave ▶ noun archaic See JERK (sense 3 of the noun).

knead ▶ verb *kneading the dough* **pummel,** work, pound, squeeze, shape, mold.

kneel ▶ verb *they knelt to pray* **fall to one's knees,** get down on one's knees, genuflect; historical kowtow.

knell ▶ noun literary **1** *the knell of the ship's bell* **toll,** tolling, dong, resounding, reverberation; death knell; archaic tocsin.
2 *this sounded the knell for the project* **end,** beginning of the end, death knell, death warrant.

knickknack ▶ noun *it's no fun dusting all her knickknacks* **trinket,** novelty, gewgaw, bibelot, ornament, trifle, bauble, gimcrack, curio, tchotchke; memento, souvenir, kickshaw; archaic gaud.

knife ▶ noun *a sharp knife* **cutting tool,** blade, cutter.
▶ verb *the victims had been knifed* **stab,** hack, gash, run through, slash, lacerate, cut, pierce, jab, stick, spike, impale, transfix, bayonet, spear.

knight ▶ noun *knights in armor* **cavalier,** cavalryman, horseman; lord, noble, nobleman; historical chevalier, paladin, banneret.
– PHRASES **knight in shining armor** *she clung to the fantasy of her knight in shining armor* **Sir Galahad,** knight on a white charger/horse/steed, rescuer, savior, champion, hero, liberator, defender, protector, guardian, guardian angel.

knit ▶ verb **1** *he learned to knit in medical school, to keep his fingers nimble* **loop,** weave, interweave, crochet.
2 *disparate regions began to knit as one* **unite,** unify, come together, draw together, become closer, bond, fuse, coalesce, merge, meld, blend.
3 *Marcus knitted his brows* **furrow,** tighten, contract, gather, wrinkle.
▶ noun *silky knits in pretty shades* **knitted garment,** knitwear, woolen; sweater, pullover, jersey, cardigan.

knob ▶ noun **1** *the drake has a black bill with a knob at the base* **lump,** bump, protuberance, protrusion, bulge, swelling, knot, node, nodule, ball, boss.
2 *the knobs on the radio* **dial,** button.
3 *she turned the knob on the door* **doorknob,** handle, door handle.

knock ▶ verb **1** *he knocked on the door* **bang,** tap, rap, thump, pound, hammer; strike, hit, beat.
2 *she knocked her knee on the table* **bump,** bang, hit, strike, crack; injure, hurt, bruise; informal bash, thwack.
3 *he **knocked into** an elderly man* **collide with,** bump into, bang into, be in collision with, run into, crash into, smash into, plow into, bash into.
4 informal *I'm not knocking the company* See CRITICIZE.
▶ noun **1** *a sharp knock at the door* **tap,** rap, rat-tat-tat, knocking, bang, banging, pounding, hammering, drumming, thump, thud.
2 *the casing is tough enough to withstand knocks* **bump,** blow, bang, jolt, jar, shock; collision, crash, smash, impact.
3 informal *this isn't a knock on Dave* See CRITICISM (sense 1).
4 *life's hard knocks* **setback,** reversal, defeat, failure, difficulty, misfortune, bad luck, mishap, blow, disaster, calamity, disappointment, sorrow, trouble, hardship; informal kick in the teeth.
– PHRASES **knock something back** informal *we can watch the game and knock back a few beers* **swallow,** gulp down, drink (up), quaff, guzzle, slug, down, swig, drain, swill (down), toss off, scarf (down). **knock someone/something down** *he deliberately knocked down the display of toilet paper in aisle 3* **fell,** floor, flatten, bring down, knock to the ground; knock over, run over/down; **demolish,** pull down, tear down, destroy; raze (to the ground), level, bulldoze. **knock it off!** informal *it's not funny anymore, so just knock it off!* **stop it**; informal cut it out, give it a rest, pack it in, that's enough, lay off. **knock someone out 1** *I hit him and knocked him out* **knock unconscious,** knock senseless; floor, prostrate, put out cold, KO, kayo. **2** *in the second match, Canada was knocked out* **eliminate,** beat, defeat, vanquish, overwhelm, trounce. **3** informal *walking that far knocked her out* **exhaust,** wear out, tire (out), overtire, fatigue, weary, drain; informal do in, take it out of. **4** informal *the view knocked me out* **overwhelm,** stun, stupefy, amaze, astound, astonish, stagger, take someone's breath away; impress, dazzle, enchant, awe, entrance; informal bowl over, flabbergast, blow away. **knock someone up** vulgar slang *she's not the first girl he's knocked up* **get/make pregnant,** impregnate; informal put in the family way.

knockout ▶ noun **1** *the match was won by a*

knockout **KO,** finishing blow, coup de grâce, stunning blow, kayo, TKO, technical knockout.
2 informal *she's a knockout!* **beauty,** babe, bombshell, vision, dream, hottie, dish, looker, eye-catcher, peach, heartthrob, fox, arm candy.
3 informal *the performance was a knockout* **masterpiece,** sensation, marvel, wonder, triumph, success, feat, coup, master stroke, tour de force; informal humdinger, doozy, stunner.

knoll ▸ **noun** *she walked up the grassy knoll* **mound,** hillock, rise, hummock, hill, hump, bank, ridge, elevation; Geology drumlin.

knot ▸ **noun 1** *make a small knot* **tie,** twist, loop, bow, hitch, half hitch, clove hitch, join, fastening; square knot, reef knot, slip knot, overhand knot, granny knot; tangle, entanglement.
2 *a knot in the wood* **nodule,** gnarl, node; lump, knob, swelling, gall, protuberance, bump, burl.
▸ **verb** *a long blue scarf was knotted around her waist* **tie (up),** fasten, secure, bind, do up.

knotty ▸ **adjective 1** *a knotty legal problem* **complex,** complicated, involved, intricate, convoluted, involuted; difficult, hard, thorny, taxing, awkward, tricky, problematic, troublesome.
ANTONYMS straightforward, simple.
2 *knotty roots* **gnarled,** knotted, knurled, nodular, knobbly, lumpy, bumpy.
3 *a knotty piece of thread* **knotted,** tangled, tangly, twisted, entangled, snarled, matted.

know ▸ **verb 1** *who knows I'm here?* **be aware,** realize, be conscious, be informed; notice, perceive, see, sense, recognize; informal be clued in, savvy.
2 *I think Mary knows his address* **have knowledge of,** be informed of, be apprised of; formal be cognizant of.
3 *you should know the rules beforehand* **be familiar with,** be conversant with, be acquainted with, have knowledge of, be versed in, have mastered, have a grasp of, understand, comprehend; have learned, have memorized, be up to speed on.
4 *I know only a few people here* **be acquainted with,** have met, be familiar with; be friends with, be friendly with, be on good terms with, be close to, be intimate with.
5 *he had known better times* **experience,** go through, live through, undergo, taste.
6 *my brothers don't know a saucepan from a frying pan* **distinguish,** tell (apart), differentiate, discriminate; recognize, pick out, identify.

know-how ▸ **noun** informal *good old American know-how* **knowledge,** expertise, skill, skillfulness, expertness, proficiency, understanding, mastery, technique; ability, capability, competence, capacity, adeptness, dexterity, deftness, aptitude, adroitness, ingenuity, faculty; informal savvy.

knowing ▸ **adjective 1** *a knowing smile* **significant,** meaningful, eloquent, expressive, suggestive; **arch,** sly, mischievous, impish, teasing, playful.
2 *she's a very knowing child* **sophisticated,** worldly, worldly-wise, urbane, experienced; knowledgeable, well-informed, enlightened; shrewd, astute, canny, sharp, wily, perceptive.
3 *a knowing infringement of the rules* **deliberate,** intentional, conscious, calculated, willful, done on purpose, premeditated, planned, preconceived.

knowingly ▸ **adverb** *a civil court jury agreed that the auto maker did not knowingly design a faulty vehicle* **deliberately,** intentionally, consciously, wittingly, on purpose, by design, premeditatedly, willfully.

knowledge ▸ **noun 1** *his knowledge of history* | *technical knowledge* **understanding,** comprehension, grasp, command, mastery; expertise, skill, proficiency, expertness, accomplishment, adeptness, capacity, capability; informal know-how.
ANTONYMS ignorance.
2 *people anxious to display their knowledge* **learning,** erudition, education, scholarship, schooling, wisdom.
ANTONYMS ignorance, illiteracy.
3 *he slipped away without my knowledge* **awareness,** consciousness, realization, cognition, apprehension, perception, appreciation; formal cognizance.
ANTONYMS unawareness.
4 *an intimate* **knowledge of** *the countryside* **familiarity with,** acquaintance with, intimacy with.
5 *inform the police of your knowledge* **information,** facts, intelligence, news, reports; informal info, (the) lowdown.

CHOOSE THE RIGHT WORD

knowledge, erudition, information, learning, pedantry, scholarship, wisdom

How much do you know? **Knowledge** applies to any body of facts gathered by study, observation, or experience, and to the ideas inferred from these facts (*an in-depth knowledge of particle physics; firsthand knowledge about the company*). **Information** may be no more than a collection of data or facts (*information about vacation resorts*) gathered through observation, reading, or hearsay, with no guarantee of their validity (*false information that led to the arrest*). **Scholarship** emphasizes academic knowledge or accomplishment (*a special award for scholarship*), while **learning** is knowledge gained not only by study in schools and universities but by individual research and investigation (*a man of education and learning*), which puts it on a somewhat higher plane. **Erudition** is on a higher plane still, implying bookish knowledge that is beyond the average person's comprehension (*exhibit extraordinary erudition in a doctoral dissertation*). **Pedantry**, on the other hand, is a negative term for a slavish attention to obscure facts or details or an undue display of learning (*the pedantry of modern literary criticism*). You can have extensive *knowledge* of a subject and even exhibit *erudition*, however, without attaining **wisdom**, the superior judgment and understanding that is based on both knowledge and experience.

knowledgeable ▶ adjective **1** *Beryl was a knowledgeable woman* **well-informed,** learned, well-read, educated, well-educated, erudite, scholarly, cultured, cultivated, enlightened.
ANTONYMS ignorant.
2 *he is **knowledgeable about** modern art* **acquainted with,** familiar with, (well) versed in, conversant with, au courant with, au fait with; having a knowledge of, up on, up to date with, up to speed on, abreast of, plugged in to, (well) grounded in.
ANTONYMS ill-informed.

known ▶ adjective **1** *a known criminal* **recognized,** well-known, widely known, noted, celebrated, notable, notorious; acknowledged, self-confessed, declared, overt.
2 *the known world* **familiar,** known about, well-known; studied, investigated.

kowtow ▶ verb **1** *they **kowtowed to** the emperor* **prostrate oneself before,** bow (down) to/before, genuflect to/before, do/make obeisance to/before, fall on one's knees before, kneel before.
2 *she didn't have to **kowtow to** a boss* **grovel to,** be obsequious to, be servile to, be sycophantic to, fawn over/on, cringe to, bow and scrape to, toady to, truckle to, abase oneself before, humble oneself to; curry favor with, dance attendance on, ingratiate oneself with, suck up to, kiss up to, brown-nose, lick someone's boots.

kudos ▶ noun *kudos to you for a lifetime of quiet courage and unwavering generosity | much kudos comes with the job* **praise,** glory, honor, status, standing, distinction, fame, celebrity; admiration, respect, esteem, acclaim, prestige, cachet, credit, full marks, props.

Wordfinder

Index

Animals

Amphibians

axolotl
barking frog
bell toad
blind salamander
bullfrog
caecilian/coecilian
cane toad
cave salamander
chorus frog
congo eel/snake
cricket frog
dusky salamander
eft
flying frog
four-toed salamander
frog
giant salamander
giant toad
gopher frog
green frog
green salamander
hellbender
horned toad
hyla
Jefferson salamander
leopard frog
long-tailed salamander
marbled salamander
marine toad
midwife toad
mudpuppy
mud siren
narrow-mouthed frog
natterjack (toad)
newt
Olympic salamander
painted salamander
peeper/spring peeper
pickerel frog
purple salamander
red-backed salamander
red-legged frog
red salamander
robber frog
salamander
siren
slimy salamander
spadefoot toad
spotted frog
spotted salamander
tadpole
tailed toad
Texas salamander
tiger salamander
toad
tree frog
tree salamander
tree toad
two-lined salamander
waterdog
whistling frog
white-lipped frog
wood frog
worm salamander

Birds

blackbird
bluebird
blue jay
bobolink
bobwhite
bunting
cardinal
catbird
chat
chickadee
chuck-will's-widow
cowbird
creeper
crossbill
crow
cuckoo
dickcissel
dove
finch
flicker
flycatcher
gnatcatcher
goldfinch
grackle
grosbeak
hummingbird
junco
kingbird
kingfisher
kinglet
lark
longspur
magpie
martin
meadowlark
mockingbird
nighthawk
nightingale
nightjar
nuthatch
oriole
ovenbird
phoebe
pigeon
pipit
raven
redpoll
redstart
robin
sapsucker
shrike
siskin
skylark
sparrow
starling
swallow
swift
tanager
thrasher
thrush
titmouse
towhee
veery
vireo
warbler
waterthrush
waxwing
wheatear
whippoorwill
woodpecker
wood thrush
wren
yellowthroat

Birds of Prey

accipiter
American eagle
bald eagle
barn owl
barred owl
boreal owl
brown owl
burrowing owl
buteo
buzzard
caracara
chicken hawk
condor
eagle owl
eagle
falcon
falconet
fish eagle
fish hawk
golden eagle
goshawk
great gray owl
great horned owl
gyrfalcon
harpy eagle
harrier
hawk owl
horned owl
kestrel
kite
lammergeier
lanner
marsh harrier
marsh hawk
merlin
northern harrier
osprey
owl
peregrine falcon
pigeon hawk
red-tailed hawk
ringtail
rough-legged hawk
saker
saw-whet owl
screech owl
sea eagle
sharp-shinned hawk
short-eared owl
snowy owl
sparrow hawk
spotted owl
tawny eagle
tawny owl
tiercel

Chickens and Other Ground Birds

Ancona
bantam (chicken)
black grouse
blue grouse
bobwhite
brahma (chicken)
capercaillie
chukar
Cornish (chicken)
fool hen
francolin
grouse
guinea fowl
hazel grouse
Hungarian partridge
leghorn
partridge
peafowl/peacock/peahen
pheasant
Plymouth Rock
prairie chicken
ptarmigan
quail
Rhode Island Red
ringneck
ring-necked pheasant
Rock Cornish (game hen)
rock ptarmigan
ruffed grouse
sage grouse
sharp-tailed grouse
snow partridge
spruce grouse
Sussex
tragopan
turkey
White Rock
willow grouse
willow ptarmigan
Wyandot

Seabirds

See also **Penguins**

ancient murrelet
Arctic tern
Atlantic puffin
auk
auklet
baccalieu bird
bawk
black guillemot
black skimmer
black tern
black-footed albatross
Bonaparte's gull
booby
brown noddy
brown pelican
bull bird
cahow
Cassin's auklet
common murre
cormorant
crow
duck
double-crested cormorant
dovekie
Franklin's gull
frigate bird
fulmar
gannet
glaucous gull
greater shearwater
guillemot
gull
gun-billed tern
herring gull
Iceland gull
jaeger
kittiwake
laughing gull
little auk
little gull
little tern
Manx shearwater
marbled murrelet
mew gull
Mother Carey's chicken
murre
murrelet
noddy

northern fulmar
northern gannet
parasitic jaeger
pelagic cormorant
pelican
petrel
pigeon guillemot
pomarine jaeger
prion
puffin
razorbill
ring-billed gull
roseate tern
Ross's gull
Sabine's gull
sea pigeon
sea swallow
seagull
shag
shearwater
skimmer
skua
sooty shearwater
sooty tern
storm petrel
tern
ticklace
tropicbird
turr
white pelican

Penguins

Adélie penguin
African jackass penguin
blue penguin
chinstrap penguin
emperor penguin
erect-crested penguin
fairy penguin
Fiordland crested penguin
Galapagos penguin
gentoo (penguin)
Humboldt penguin
king penguin
little penguin
macaroni penguin
Magellanic penguin
Peruvian penguin
rockhopper (penguin)
royal penguin
Snares Island penguin
yellow-eyed penguin

Shorebirds

adjutant stork
American egret
avocet
Baird's sandpiper
beach bird
bittern
brolga
cattle egret
coot
crane
curlew
dotterel
dowitcher
dunlin
egret
flamingo
gallinule
godwit
golden plover
great blue heron
great white egret
heron
ibis
jabiru
jacana
killdeer
lapwing
least bittern
limpkin
marabou
moorhen
oystercatcher
pectoral sandpiper
pewit
piping plover
plover
rail
red knot sandpiper
ringed plover
ruff/reeve
sanderling
sandhill crane
sandpiper
snipe
snowy egret
sora
spoonbill
stilt
stint
stork
tattler
turnstone
waterhen
whimbrel
whooping crane
willet
yellowlegs

Waterfowl

Arctic loon
barnacle goose
black duck
black swan
blue goose
brant
bufflehead
Canada goose
canvasback
eared grebe
eider
fulvous whistling duck
gadwall
garganey
goldeneye
gray goose
graylag
harlequin duck
helldiver
hooded merganser
horned grebe
king eider
loon
mallard
mandarin duck
merganser
mottled duck
Muscovy duck
mute swan
oldsquaw
Pacific loon
pied-billed grebe
pintail
red-breasted goose
redhead
red-necked grebe
red-throated loon
ring-necked duck
Ross's goose
ruddy duck
sawbill
scaup
scoter
shoveler
smew
snow goose
surf scoter
teal
trumpeter swan
tundra swan
baldpate
Western grebe
whistling swan
white-fronted goose
white-winged scoter
whooper
wigeon
wood duck
yellow-billed loon

Fish

albacore (tuna)
amberjack
anchovy
angelfish
anglerfish
bacalao
barbel
barracuda
bass
blackfish
blenny
blowfish
bluefish
bonito
bream
brill
brisling
buffalo fish
burbot
butterfish
carp
catfish
char
cod/codfish
conger eel
crappie
cusk
dogfish
dolphinfish
dorado
dory
Dover sole
eel
finnan (haddie)
flounder
fluke
flying fish
fugu
goby
grouper
grunion
grunt
haddock
hake
halibut
herring
John Dory
kingfish
kipper
lamprey
lemon sole
limpet
lox
lutefisk
mackerel
mahimahi
monkfish
moray eel
orange roughy
parrotfish
perch
pilchard
pollack
pompano
rainbow trout
ray
red mullet
red snapper
rockfish
rouget
sablefish
salmon
sand dab
sardine
scrod
sea bass
sea bream
sea trout
shad
shark
skate
smelt
snapper
sole
sprat
striped bass
sturgeon
sunfish
swordfish
tarpon
tilapia
tilefish
torsk
trout
tuna
turbot
wahoo
whitefish
wrasse
yellowtail

Sharks

angel shark
basking shark
blue shark
dogfish
great white shark
hammerhead
mackerel shark
mako
monkfish
nurse shark
porbeagle
requiem shark
shovelhead
thresher shark
tope
whale shark

Insects

ant
alderfly
amberwing
ant lion
aphid
army ant
assassin bug
backswimmer
bee
bedbug
beetle
blackfly
blowfly
bluebottle
boatman
boll weevil
booklouse
borer
botfly
bristletail
bumblebee
butterfly
caddisfly
carpenter ant
carpenter bee
carpet beetle
carrion beetle
chafer
chinch bug
cicada

click beetle
cluster fly
coccid
cockroach
Colorado beetle
corn borer
crane fly
cricket
cuckoo bee
cucumber beetle
damselfly
darner
deathwatch beetle
deerfly
diving beetle
dobsonfly
doodlebug
dragonfly
dung beetle
earwig
elater
emmet
engraver beetle
fire ant
firefly
flea
froghopper
fruit fly
furniture beetle
gall wasp
glowworm
gnat
Goliath beetle
grasshopper
greenbottle
harvester ant
Hercules beetle
honeybee
hornet
horsefly
housefly
ichneumon
Japanese beetle
June bug
katydid
ladybug
leafcutter
leafhopper
lightning bug
locust
louse
mayfly
mealy bug
Mexican bean beetle
mosquito
moth
mud dauber
no-see-um
paper wasp
pismire
potato beetle
praying mantis
rhinoceros beetle
roach
robber fly
rose chafer
rove beetle
sandfly
sawfly
sawyer
scarab beetle
scorpion fly
shadfly
snout beetle
snowflea
spittlebug
springtail
squash bug
stag beetle
stink bug
stonefly
termite
tiger beetle
tsetse fly
walking stick
water beetle
wasp
weevil
white ant
whitefly
yellow jacket

Butterflies

admiral
aguna
alpine
American lady
arctic
azure
banner
beauty
blue
bolla
brushfoot
buckeye
cabbage white
checkered skipper
checkerspot
clearwing
cloudywing
comma
copper
cracker
crescent
daggerwing
Diana
dogface
dotted blue
duskywing
elfin
emperor
flasher
fritillary
giant skipper
glassywing
greenstreak
groundstreak
hairstreak
harvester
heliconian
Julia
lady butterfly
leaf butterfly
leafwing
long dash
longtail
marble
metalmark
Mexican bluewing
milkweed butterfly
mimic
ministreak
monarch
mourning cloak
mulberry wing
orange
orangetip
orion
owl butterfly
painted lady
patch
peacock
pearly eye
pixie
powdered skipper
purple
purplewing
queen
question mark
red admiral
ringlet
roadside skipper
satyr
scallopwing
scrub hairstreak
shoemaker
silverdrop
silverspot
skipper
skipperling
soldier
sootywing
sulfur/sulphur
swallowtail
tortoiseshell
viceroy
white
white admiral
wood nymph
yellow
zebra

Moths

acrea moth
armyworm moth
bagworm moth
black witch
buck moth
bumblebee moth
burnet
carpenter moth
carpet moth
cecropia
clearwing
clothes moth
codling moth
cotton leafworm moth
ctenuchid
cutworm moth
Cynthia
dagger moth
day moth
diamondback moth
dried leaf moth
emperor moth
flannel moth
forester
geometer
grain moth
green cloverworm moth
gypsy moth
handmaid
hawk moth
honey-locust moth
hummingbird moth
imperial moth
Indian meal moth
Io moth
Isabella moth
leopard moth
luna moth
lunate moth
meal moth
Mediterranean flour moth
noctuid
oakworm moth
Pandora moth
pantry moth
pitch twigmoth
plume moth
polyphemus moth
Promethea moth
prominent
regal/royal moth
rosy maple moth
salt marsh moth
satin moth
saturnid
silkworm/silk moth
snout moth
sphinx
tentmaker
three-spotted fillip
tiger moth
tortrix
tussock
underwing
wax moth
yucca moth
Zimmerman pine moth

Mammals

Bears

Alaskan brown bear
American black bear
Asian black bear
black bear
blue bear
brown bear
cave bear (extinct)
cinnamon bear
giant panda
glacier bear
grizzly (bear)
Kodiak bear
Malayan sun bear
panda
polar bear
Siberian brown bear
silvertip grizzly (bear)
sloth bear
sun bear
white bear
yellow bear

Cats

DOMESTIC CATS

Abyssinian
American bobtail
American curl
American shorthair
American wirehair
angora
Balinese
Birman
bobtail
Bombay
British shorthair
Burmese
calico
chartreux
chinchilla (cat)
colorpoint shorthair
Cornish Rex
curl
Devon Rex
Egyptian mau
exotic
ginger
Havana brown
Himalayan
Javanese
Japanese bobtail
Korat
LaPerm
longhair
Maine coon
Manx
marmalade
Norwegian forest cat
ocicat
Oriental
Persian
ragdoll
Rex
Russian Blue
Scottish fold
Selkirk Rex
shorthair
Siamese
Siberian
Singapura
Somali
Sphynx
tabby
Tonkinese
tortoiseshell
Turkish angora
Turkish Van
wirehair

WILD CATS

Bengal tiger
bobcat
Canada lynx
caracal
catamount
cheetah
clouded leopard
cougar
eyra

cat
jaguar
jaguarundi
kodkod
leopard
leopard cat
lion
lynx
margay
mountain lion
ocelot
oncilla
panther
puma
serval
Siberian tiger
snow leopard
tiger
tiger cat
wildcat

Cattle

Aberdeen Angus
African buffalo
Alderney
Ayrshire
banteng
beefalo
bison
Black Angus
Brahman
Brown Swiss
buffalo
Charolais
Chianina
fighting bull
Galloway
gaur
gayal
Guernsey
Hereford
Highland cattle
Holstein
Jersey
kouprey
Limousin
longhorn
musk ox
ox
plains bison
Red Angus
Red Poll
shorthorn
Simmental
Texas longhorn
water buffalo
wood bison
yak
zebu

Deer

axis
barren ground caribou
blacktail
brocket
caribou
chital
elk
fallow deer
moose
mule deer
muley
muntjac
musk deer
Père David's deer
Peary caribou
red deer
reindeer
roe
sika
wapiti
whitetail
woodland caribou

Dogs

DOMESTIC DOGS

affenpinscher
Afghan hound
Airedale (terrier)
Akita
Alaskan malamute
American Eskimo dog
American water spaniel
Anatolian shepherd
Australian shepherd
Australian terrier
basenji
basset hound
beagle
bearded collie
Bedlington terrier
Belgian Malinois
Belgian sheepdog
Belgian Tervuren
Bernese mountain dog
Bichon Frisé
black and tan
Black Russian terrier
bloodhound
bluetick (coonhound)
border collie
border terrier
borzoi
Boston terrier
Bouvier des Flandres
boxer
Briard
Brittany (spaniel)
Brussels griffon
bull terrier
bulldog
bullmastiff
cairn terrier
Canaan dog
Cardigan Welsh corgi
Cavalier King Charles spaniel
Chesapeake Bay retriever
chihuahua
Chinese crested
chow chow
Clumber spaniel
cockapoo
cocker spaniel
collie
coonhound
curly-coated retriever
dachshund
Dalmatian
Dandie Dinmont (terrier)
Doberman (pinscher)
Australian cattle dog
English setter
English springer spaniel
English toy spaniel
field spaniel
Finnish spitz
flat-coated retriever
foxhound
French bulldog
German shepherd dog
German shorthaired pointer
German wirehaired pointer
giant schnauzer
Glen of Imaal terrier
golden retriever
Gordon setter
Great Dane
Great Pyrenees
greater Swiss mountain dog
greyhound
harrier
Havana silk dog/ Havanese
Ibizan hound
Irish setter
Irish terrier
Irish water spaniel
Irish wolfhound
Italian greyhound
Jack Russell terrier
Japanese chin
keeshond
kelpie
Kerry blue (terrier)
Komondor
kuvasz
labradoodle
Labrador retriever
Lakeland terrier
Lhasa apso
Löwchen
Maltese (terrier)
Manchester terrier
mastiff
miniature bull terrier
miniature pinscher
miniature poodle
miniature schnauzer
Neapolitan mastiff
Newfoundland
Norfolk terrier
Norwegian elkhound
Norwich terrier
Old English sheepdog
otterhound
papillon
Pekingese/ Pekinese
Pembroke Welsh corgi
petit basset griffon Vendéen
pharaoh hound
Plott hound
pointer
Polish lowland sheepdog
Pomeranian
Portuguese water dog
pug
puli
redbone (coonhound)
Rhodesian ridgeback
Rottweiler
rough collie
Saluki
Samoyed
schipperke
Scottish deerhound
Scottish terrier
Sealyham terrier
Shar-Pei
Shetland sheepdog
Shiba Inu
Shih Tzu
Siberian husky
silky terrier
Skye terrier
smooth fox terrier
soft-coated wheaten terrier
Spinone (Italiano)
St. Bernard
Staffordshire bull terrier
Staffordshire terrier
staghound
standard poodle
standard schnauzer
Sussex spaniel
teacup poodle
Tibetan spaniel
Tibetan terrier
toy Manchester terrier
toy poodle
vizsla
Weimaraner
Welsh springer spaniel
Welsh terrier
West Highland (white) terrier
whippet
wire fox terrier
wirehaired pointing griffon
Yorkshire terrier

WILD DOGS

Arctic fox
Arctic wolf
brush wolf
coyote
cross fox
dingo
fox
gray wolf
jackal
prairie wolf
red fox
silver fox
swift fox
timber wolf
tundra wolf
wolf

Horses

American saddle horse
Andalusian
Appaloosa
Arabian
Belgian
Canadian
cayuse
Chincoteague pony
Clydesdale
Dartmoor pony
Falabella
Hanoverian
Lipizzaner
Morgan
mustang
Newfoundland pony
palomino
Percheron
polo pony
Quarter Horse
racehorse
Shetland pony
shire horse
Standardbred
Tennessee Walking Horse
thoroughbred
Waler

Marsupials

antechinus
bandicoot
cuscus
dasyure
flying phalanger
honey possum
kangaroo
koala
numbat
opossum/ possum
pademelon
phalanger
pygmy possum
quoll
rat kangaroo
ringtail
Tasmanian devil
wallaby
wombat

Primates

ape
aye-aye
baboon
Barbary ape
bonobo
bush baby

capuchin
chimpanzee
colobus
douroucouli
drill
gelada
gibbon
gorilla
guenon
hamadryas
hanuman (langur)
howler
indri
langur
lemur
loris
macaque
mandrill
mangabey
marmoset
monkey
orangutan
proboscis monkey
rhesus monkey
silverback
spider monkey
squirrel monkey
tamarin
tarsier
titi
vervet
wanderoo

Rodents

agouti
Arctic ground squirrel
bandicoot rat
beaver
black squirrel
brown rat
bushy-tailed wood rat
capybara
cavy
chinchilla
chipmunk
collared lemming
coypu
deer mouse
dormouse
field mouse
flying squirrel
gerbil
golden hamster
gopher
gray squirrel
groundhog
ground squirrel
guinea pig
hamster
hoary marmot
house mouse
jerboa
jumping mouse
kangaroo mouse
kangaroo rat
lemming
marmot
mole rat
mouse
muskrat
Norway rat
paca
pack rat
pocket gopher
porcupine
prairie dog
rat
red squirrel
squirrel
suslik
viscacha
vole
water rat
water vole
woodchuck
woodmouse
wood rat

Seals

bearded seal
bedlamer
blueback
California sea lion
common seal
elephant seal
fur seal
gray seal
harp seal
hooded seal
northern sea lion
ringed seal
sea dog
sea elephant
sea lion
square-flipper seal
walrus
whitecoat

Whales, Dolphins, and Porpoises

beaked whale
beluga
black dolphin
blue whale
bottlenose dolphin
bottlenose whale
bowhead
Burmeister's porpoise
cochito
common dolphin
Dall's porpoise
dusky dolphin
finback (whale)
finless porpoise
grampus
gray whale
harbor porpoise
hourglass dolphin
humpback (whale)
humpbacked dolphin
Irrawaddy dolphin
killer whale
minke (whale)
narwhal
orca
pilot whale
pothead
right whale
right whale dolphin
rorqual
rough-toothed dolphin
sei whale
spectacled porpoise
sperm whale
spinner dolphin
spotted dolphin
strap-toothed whale
striped dolphin
tucuxi
white whale
white-beaked dolphin
white-sided dolphin

Spiders and Other Arachnids

American house spider
ant mimic
argiope
banana spider
barn spider
basilica spider
bird spider
black widow
blue bug
bolas spider
bowl and doily spider
brown dog tick
brown recluse
brown spider
brown widow
castor bean tick
cattle tick
cave spider
cellar spider
chigger
cobweb weaver
combfooted spider
crab spider
cross spider
daddy longlegs
deer tick
dwarf spider
featherlegged spider
filmy dome spider
fishing spider
folding-door spider
funnel weaver
furrow spider
garden spider
giant crab spider
giant hairy hadrurus
golden silk spider
grass spider
hairy mygalomorph
hammock spider
harvest mite
harvestman
itch mite
jumping spider
lattice spider
Lone Star tick
lynx spider
marbled spider
micrathena
mite
northern widow
nursery web spider
ogre-faced spider
orb weaver
orchard spider
pirate spider
platform spider
pseudoscorpion
purseweb spider
rabbit tick
ray spider
red widow
sac spider
scabies mite
schizomid
scorpion
shamrock spider
sheetweb spider
six-eyed crab spider
spider mite
spitting spider
star-bellied spider
sun spider/ scorpion
tarantula
thick-jawed spider
tick
trapdoor spider
triangle spider
velvet mite
vinegarone/ vinegaroon
wandering spider
water mite
whip scorpion
wind scorpion
wolf spider
wood spider
wood tick
yellow vejovis

Mollusks and Crustaceans

Bivalves

bar clam
bay scallop
cherrystone clam
clam
cockle
gaper
geoduck
littleneck
mussel
oyster
pearl oyster
pecten
piddock
quahog
razor clam
scallop
sea scallop
steamer
teredo
zebra mussel

Gastropods

abalone
conch
cowrie
haliotis
limpet
murex
nudibranch
periwinkle
ram's-horn-snail
sea slug
sea snail
slug
snail
volute
whelk
winkle

Cephalopods

cuttlefish
nautilus
octopus
squid

Crustaceans

barnacle
black tiger shrimp
blue crab
brine shrimp
copepod
crab
crawdad
crawfish
crayfish
daphnia
doodlebug
Dungeness crab
fiddler crab
ghost shrimp
hermit crab
king crab
krill
land crab

langouste
langoustine
lobster
Norway lobster
pillbug
prawn
roly-poly
scampi
shrimp
snow crab
soft-shell crab
spider crab
spiny lobster
squill
stone crab
tiger shrimp
trilobite
wood louse

Reptiles

alligator
alligator snapping turtle
basilisk
blindworm
box turtle
caiman
chameleon
chuckwalla
crocodile
diamondback
flying dragon
flying lizard
frill lizard
galliwasp
gecko
gharial
Gila monster
glass lizard
goanna
green turtle
hawksbill
horned toad
iguana
Komodo dragon
leatherback turtle
lizard
loggerhead turtle
monitor lizard
mugger
painted turtle
skink
slow-worm
snapping turtle
terrapin
tortoise
tuatara
turtle

Snakes

adder
anaconda
asp
boa
boa constrictor
bull snake
cobra
constrictor
copperhead
coral snake
cottonmouth
death adder
diamondback
fer-de-lance
garter snake
grass snake
hamadryad
hognose snake
horned viper
king cobra
krait
mamba
massasauga
milk snake
pit viper
puff adder
python
rattlesnake
rock python
sidewinder
spitting cobra
taipan
viper
water moccasin
water snake
whip snake

Dinosaurs

Acanthopholis
Albertosaurus
Allosaurus
Amargasaurus
Ankylosaurus
Apatosaurus
Baryonyx
Brachiosaurus
Brontosaurus
Camarasaurus
Camptosaurus
Carnotaurus
Ceratosaurus
Corythosaurus
Deinonychus
Dilophosaurus
Diplodocus
Dryosaurus
Edmontosaurus
Euoplocephalus
Gallimimus
Gigantosaurus
Homalocephale
Hylaeosaurus
Hypacrosaurus
Iguanodon
Janenschia
Kentrosaurus
Lambeosaurus
Lesothosaurus
Maiasaura
Majungatholis
Mamenchisaurus
Megalosaurus
Megaraptor
Notoceratops
Ornithomimus
Ouranosaurus
Pachycephalosaurus
Parasaurolophus
Plateosaurus
Protarchaeopteryx
Psittacosaurus
Pteranodon
Quaesitosaurus
Riojasaurus
Saichania
Saltopus
Sauropelta
Scelidosaurus
Scipionyx
Sinornithosaurus
Spinosaurus
Stegoceras
Stegosaurus
Styracosaurus
Triceratops
Tröodon
Tyrannosaurus (rex)/T. rex
Ultrasauros
Utahraptor
Velociraptor
Vulcanodon
Wannanosaurus
Xiaosaurus
Yangchuanosuarus
Zigongosaurus

Architecture

Architectural Styles

American Craftsman
art deco
art nouveau
Arts and Crafts
baroque
Bauhaus
beaux-arts
brutalist
Byzantine
Carolingian
Château
Churrigueresque
cinquecento
classical
colonial
Corinthian
Craftsman
Decorated
Doric
Dutch colonial
Early Christian
Early English
Early Renaissance
Edwardian
Elizabethan
Empire
flamboyant
functional
Georgian
Gothic
Gothic Revival
Greco-Roman
Grecian
Greek Revival
International (Style)
Ionic
Islamic
Jacobean
medieval
mission
modernist
Moorish
Moresque
Mozarabic
neoclassical
neo-Gothic
Norman
Palladian
Perpendicular
postmodernist
Prairie (Style)
quattrocento
Queen Anne
Regency
Renaissance
rococo
Roman
Romanesque
Saxon
Spanish colonial
Spanish mission
Tudor
Tudorbethan
Tuscan
vernacular
Victorian Gothic

Apartments

bachelor apartment/pad
bachelorette apartment/pad
efficiency (apartment/ unit)
flat
garden apartment
in-law apartment
loft
maisonette
nanny suite
penthouse
pied-à-terre
studio apartment
suite
walk-up

Houses

adobe house
A-frame
apartment house
attached house
beach house
bi-level
brownstone
bungalow
bunkhouse
cabin
Cape Cod
carriage house
chalet
clapboard house
coach house
colonial
cottage
country house
detached
dormitory
double-wide (trailer)
duplex

farmhouse
frame house
galerie house
garrison house
hacienda
half-timbered house
house trailer
igloo
log cabin
longhouse
maisonette
manor
mansion
mobile home
octagon house
penthouse
prefabricated house/prefab
quadruplex
raised ranch
ranch house
row house
semidetached
solar house
split-level
tepee
townhouse
tract house
trailer
triplex
two-family house
Victorian
wickiup
wigwam

Rooms

anteroom
antechamber
armory
assembly room
attic
back room
ballroom
barroom
basement
bathroom
bedchamber
bedroom
billiard room
birthing room
boardroom
boiler room
boudoir
breakfast nook
cabin
cafeteria
cell
cellar
chamber
changing room
chapel
checkroom
classroom
cloakroom
coatroom
cold room
common room
control room
conference room
conservatory
courtroom
cutting room
darkroom
day room
den
dining room
dormitory
drawing room
dressing room
drying room
dungeon
emergency room
engine room
family room
fitting room
Florida room
foyer
front room
gallery
game room
garret
great room
green room
grotto
guardroom
guest room
gunroom
gymnasium
hall
homeroom
keep
kitchen
kitchenette
ladies' room
larder
laundry room
lavatory
library
living room
lobby
locker room
loft
lounge
lunchroom
maid's room
mailroom
men's room
morning room
mud room
music room
newsroom
nursery
office
operating room
operations room
oratory
panic room
pantry
parlor
playroom
poolroom
powder room
receiving room
recovery room
rec room
refectory
restroom
rotunda
rubber room
rumpus room
salesroom
salon
sauna
schoolroom
scullery
showroom
sickbay
sickroom
sitting room
situation room
smoking room
solarium
staff room
state room
stockroom
storeroom
strongroom
studio
study
suite
sunroom
tack room
taproom
tearoom
throne room
trophy room
utility room
vestiary
vestibule
waiting room
wardroom
war room
washroom
water closet
weight room
wet room
women's room
workroom

Windows

awning window
barred window
bay window
bow window
bull's-eye
casement
Chicago window
cottage window
dormer
double-glazed window
double-hung window
drop window
fanlight
fan window
French window
gable window
hopper casement
jalousie
loop window
Palladian window
picture window
porthole
projected window
ribbon window
rose window
sash window
sidelight
single-hung window
stained glass window
store window
storm window
transom window
Venetian window
wheel window

Art

Art Schools, Styles, and Movements

abstract expressionism
Aesthetic Movement
Art Deco
Art Nouveau
Arts and Crafts
Ashcan
avant-garde
Barbizon
baroque
Bauhaus
Beaux Arts
Blaue Reiter
Bloomsbury Group
classicism
conceptual art
constructivism
cubism
Dada
deconstructivism
De Stijl
expressionism
fauvism
Florentine school
folk art
futurism
Grand Manner
Group of Seven
Impressionism
Jugendstil
magic realism
Mannerism
minimalism
modernism
naive art
naturalism
Nazarenes
neoclassicism
neo-Impressionism
neoplasticism
neo-realism
Neue Sachlichkeit
op art
performance art
photorealism
plein-air painting
pop art
post-Impressionism
postmodernism
Pre-Raphaelitism
primitive art
Purism
realism
Renaissance art
rococo
romanticism
socialist realism
social realism
Sturm und Drang
suprematism
surrealism
symbolism
tenebrism
ukiyo-e

Art Techniques and Media

acrylic painting
action painting
airbrushing
aquatint
batik
brass rubbing
calligraphy
cartooning
ceramics
charcoal
cire perdue
clay
cloisonné
collage
conté
distemper
decoupage
drawing
dry point
enameling
encaustic
engraving
etching
fresco
gouache
grisaille
illumination
impasto
intaglio
intarsia
linocut
lithography
lost wax
marbling
marquetry
mezzotint
montage
mosaic
mural painting
oil painting
painting
pastel
pen and ink
photography
photogravure
photomontage
pointillism
screen printing
sculpture
scumbling
sgraffito
silk-screen printing
sketching
stained glass
stonecutting
tachism
tempera
trompe l'oeil
watercolor
wood carving
woodcutting
wood engraving

Paint Types

acrylic
color wash
distemper
eggshell
emulsion
enamel
gloss
gouache
latex
matte
oil
poster paint
primer
tempera
undercoat
watercolor
whitewash

Clothing

Coats and Jackets

anorak
bed jacket
blanket coat
blazer
bolero
bomber jacket
bush jacket
capote
car coat
cardigan
Chanel jacket
chesterfield
commuter jacket/coat
cutaway
dinner jacket
dolman
double-breasted jacket/coat
doublet
duffle coat
field coat
flight jacket
frock coat
fur coat
greatcoat
happi coat
jean jacket
jibba
lumberjack jacket
Mackinaw
mackintosh
mess jacket
Nehru jacket
Norfolk jacket
overcoat
parka
peacoat
pea jacket
peplum jacket
puffy jacket/coat
raglan
rain jacket
raincoat
redingote
reefer
safari jacket
shell
shirt jacket
single-breasted (jacket/coat)
slicker
sport/sports coat
sport/sports jacket
stadium jacket
storm coat
suit coat
surcoat
surtout
sweater coat
swing coat
tailcoat
topcoat
topper
tuxedo
ulster
whisper jacket
windbreaker
trench coat

Dresses

A-line dress
baby doll
ballgown
caftan
chemise
cheongsam
coat dress
cocktail dress
dirndl
empire dress
evening dress/gown
gown
granny dress
halter dress
housedress
jumper
kimono
little black dress
maternity dress
minidress
Mother Hubbard
muumuu
off-the-shoulder dress
pinafore
princess dress
sack dress
sari
sarong
sheath
shift
shirtdress
shirtwaist
skimmer
slip dress
strapless dress/gown
sundress
tank dress
tea gown
tube dress
tunic
wedding gown

Headgear

alpine hat
balaclava
balmoral
bandanna/bandana
baseball cap
beanie
bearskin
beaver (hat)
beret
bicorne
bird's nest hat
biretta
boater
bonnet
bowler
bucket hat
busby
cap
cap of liberty
chapeau
chauffeur's cap
chef's hat
cloche
cocked hat
coif
coolie hat
coonskin (cap)
cowboy hat
crown
deerstalker
derby
Dolly Varden
dunce cap
Dutch cap
engineer's cap
fedora
fez
forage cap
gangster hat
gaucho hat
glengarry
graduation cap
hard hat
headdress
headscarf
helmet
high hat
homburg
hunting cap
Juliet cap
kaffiyeh
kepi
kerchief
knit cap
leghorn
mantilla
matador's hat
miter
mobcap
mortarboard
nightcap
niqab
opera hat
panama hat
petasus
picture hat
pillbox
pith helmet
porkpie (hat)
sailor hat
sallet

service cap
shako
shovel hat
silk hat
ski cap
skimmer
skullcap
slouch hat
snap-brim
snood
sombrero
sou'wester
Stetson™
stocking cap
stovepipe hat
straw hat
sunbonnet
tam
tam-o'-shanter
tarboosh
tarpaulin
ten-gallon hat
topi
toque
toreador hat
tricorne
trilby
turban
veil
Viking hat/helmet
war bonnet
watch cap
wide-awake
wimple
yarmulke
zucchetto

Pants and Trousers

baggies
bell-bottoms
Bermuda shorts
bicycle shorts
bloomers
blue jeans
breeches
britches
capri pants
cargo pants
chaps
chinos
clamdiggers
cords
corduroys
culottes
cutoffs
dress pants
dungarees
flannels
flares
galligaskins
gauchos
harem pants
hip-huggers
hot pants
jeans
jodhpurs
khakis
knee pants
knickers
lederhosen
leggings
overalls
pajama pants
palazzo pants
pantalets
pantaloons
pedal pushers
rugby pants
shorts
ski pants
slacks
stirrup pants
stretch pants
sweatpants
toreador pants
track pants
trousers
tuxedo pants
walking shorts

Shirts and Tops

blouse
boat-neck shirt
button-down shirt
camisole
cowl-neck shirt
dashiki
dress shirt
golf shirt
halter top
Hawaiian shirt
jersey
kurta
lumberjack shirt
middy
muscle shirt
overblouse
overshirt
Oxford shirt
polo shirt
rugby shirt
shell
sports shirt
sweatshirt
tank top
T-shirt
tube top
turtleneck
twin set

Footwear

aerobic shoes
athletic shoes
ballerinas
ballet flats
ballet slippers
bedroom slippers
Birkenstocks™
boat shoes
booties/bootees
boots
bowling shoes
brogans
brogues
buckskins
buskins
cleats
clodhoppers
clogs
combat boots
cowboy boots
cross-trainers
Cuban heels
deck shoes
Doc Martens
dress shoes
elevator shoes
espadrilles
flip-flops
French heels
galoshes
ghillies
golf shoes
gym shoes
half boots
heels
high heels
high-lows
high-tops
hiking shoes
huaraches
jazz shoes
jellies
jogging shoes
kilties
loafers
Louis heels
low heels
Mary Janes
moccasins
moon boots
mukluks
mules
open-toes
overshoes
oxfords
patent leather
pattens
penny loafers
platform shoes
pumps
running shoes
sabots
saddle shoes
sandals
sling-backs
slip-ons
slippers
sneakers
spectator pumps
spike heels
spikes
square-toed shoes
stacked heels
stiletto heels
tap shoes
tennis shoes
thongs
Top-Siders™
track shoes
training shoes
T-straps
Ugg boots™
walking shoes
wedge heels
wedgies
wellies
wellingtons
white bucks
wing tips
zoris

Skirts

A-line skirt
bias-cut skirt
circle skirt
crinoline
dirndl (skirt)
flared skirt
gored skirt
grass skirt
half-circle skirt
hobble skirt
jeans skirt
kilt
miniskirt
overskirt
petal skirt
petticoat
pleated skirt
poodle skirt
prairie skirt
sheath
tutu
wraparound skirt

Underwear

bikini briefs
bloomers
boxers/boxer shorts
bra
brassiere
briefs
camisole
chemise
corset
girdle
Jockey shorts™
long johns
long underwear
panties
panty girdle
petticoat
shorts
slip
snuggies
sports bra
tanga briefs
tap pants
teddy
thermals/thermal underwear
thong
tighty-whities
underpants
undershirt
undershorts
union suit

Dance

Dances

allemande
bachata
ballet
ballroom
beguine
belly dance
bird dance
bolero
boogaloo
bossa nova
bourrée
breakdance
bunny hop
bus stop
butoh
butterfly
cachucha
cakewalk
cancan
capoeira
carioca
Celtic dance
cha-cha
chaconne
character dance
Charleston
chicken scratch
cinque-pace
clog dance
conga
contra
contredanse
Cossack dance
country dance
courante
cumbia
czardas
dancesport
disco
doppio
drum dance
eightsome reel
fan dance
fandango
farandole
flamenco
folk dance
foxtrot
freak
frug
galliard
galop
gavotte
go-go dance
grass dance
habanera
hamatsa
hand jive
hasapiko
Highland fling
hokey-pokey
hoop dance
hopak
hora
hornpipe
hula
hustle
Irish dance
jazz
jig
jitterbug
jive
Kathak
lambada
ländler
Latin hustle
lavolta
limbo
lindy (hop)
line dance
lion dance
locomotion
Macarena
mambo
mashed potato
mazurka
merengue
minuet
modern dance
monkey
morris dance
mosh
musette
one-step
paso doble
pavane
pogo
polka
polonaise
quadrille
quickstep
rain dance
Red River jig
reel
robot
round dance
roundel
rumba
salsa
samba
saraband
schottische
shimmy
shuffle
skank
slam dance
snake dance
soft shoe
square dance
step dance
stomp
strathspey
striptease
stroll
sun dance
swing
sword dance
syrto
tango
tap dance
tarantella
time warp
turkey trot
tush push
twist
two-step
Virginia reel
waltz
war dance
watusi
whip
zouk

Dance Events

ball
barn dance
cotillion dance
hoedown
homecoming
prom
rave
Sadie Hawkins dance
social
sock hop
tea dance

Ballet Steps and Positions

arabesque
arabesque penchée
à terre
attitude
balancé
ballonné
ballotté
battement
batterie
bourreée
brisé
cabriole
cambré
chaîné
changement de pied
chassé
ciseaux
couru
déboîté
dégagé
demi-plié
demi-pointe
développé
écarté
échappé
emboîté
enchaînement
entrechat
failli
fondu
fouetté
frappé
glissade
glissé
grand battement
grand jeté
jeté
pas allé
pas de basque
pas de bourrée
pas de chat
pas de cheval
petit battement
petit jeté
piqué
pirouette
plié
port de bras
promenade
relevé
retiré
rond de jambe
sauté
saut de basque
sissonne
soubresaut
sous-sous
temps levé
temps lié
tombé
tour en l'air
tour jeté

Drinks

Beers

abbey
ale
alt
altbier
barley wine
Berliner Weisse
Biere de Garde
bitter
bock
brown ale
celery
chili
cream ale
diat pils
doppelbock
Dortmunder
draft
dry
dunkel
Eisbock
faro
franboise
ginger
green
Gueuze
heavy
Hefe
Hell
honey
ice
India Pale Ale
Irish ale
Kölsch
Kriek
Kristall
lager
lambic
light
malt
malt liquor
Märzen
mild

- Muncher
- Munich
- Oktoberfest
- old ale
- oud bruin
- pale ale
- pils
- pilsner
- poire
- porter
- Schwarzbier
- season
- shandy
- special
- Sticke
- stock ale
- stout
- trappist
- Vienna
- weiss
- wheat
- Zwickl

Cocktails and Other Mixed Drinks

- Alabama slammer
- amaretto sour
- American Beauty
- Bellini
- Black Russian
- Bloody Mary
- brandy Alexander
- Bronx cocktail
- Cape Codder
- champagne cocktail
- cosmopolitan
- Cuba libre
- daiquiri
- dirty martini
- fuzzy navel
- Gibson
- gimlet
- gin and tonic
- gin rickey
- grasshopper
- greyhound
- Harvey Wallbanger
- highball
- hot buttered rum
- hot toddy
- Irish coffee
- Jack Rose
- kamikaze
- Kir royale
- lemon drop
- Long Island iced tea
- mai tai
- Manhattan
- margarita
- martini
- merry widow
- mimosa
- mint julep
- mudslide
- negroni
- New York sour
- old-fashioned
- Pimm's cup
- piña colada
- pink lady
- pisco sour
- planter's punch
- red lion
- Rob Roy
- rum runner
- rusty nail
- sangria
- screwdriver
- sea breeze
- shandy
- sidecar
- Singapore sling
- sloe gin fizz
- spritzer
- stinger
- tequila sunrise
- toasted almond
- Tom and Jerry
- Tom Collins
- vodka tonic
- whiskey sour
- White Russian
- yellow bird
- zombie

Coffees

- Altura
- Amatitlan
- Angola
- Antiqua
- Arabica
- Baba Budans
- Barahona
- Blawan
- Blue Java
- Blue Mountain
- Bourbon de Coatepec
- Bourbon Santos
- Brazil
- Bukoba
- Buqisu
- Burundi
- Cameroon
- Casa
- Misael
- Celebes
- Chamba
- Chaqqa
- chicory
- China
- cinnamon roast
- city roast
- Colombia
- Costa Rica
- Cuba
- Cucutas
- Djimmah
- Ecuador
- El Salvador
- espresso
- Ethiopia
- Ethiopia Harrar
- French roast
- Greek
- Guatemala
- Haiti
- Holualoa
- Honduras
- India
- Italian roast
- Ituri
- Ivory Coast
- Jamaica
- Jampit
- Java
- Kalossi
- Kauai
- Kenya
- Kilimanjaro
- Kivu
- Kona
- Kopi Luwak
- La Lucie
- Liberica
- Los Volcanos
- Malabar
- Malawi
- Malaysia
- Mandelhing
- Maui Kaanapali
- Medellin Excelso
- Mexico
- Mocca
- Mocha/Moka
- Moloka'i
- Mysore
- Narino
- Nicaragua
- Oahu
- Oaxaca
- Panama
- Papua New Guinea
- Peaberry
- Puerto Rico
- Reunion
- Robusta
- Rwanda
- Santo Domingo
- Santos
- Sulawesi
- Sumatra
- Tachiras
- Tanzania
- Tarrazu
- Timor
- Turkish
- Uganda
- Venezuela
- Viennese roast
- Vietnam
- Yemen
- Yirgacheffe
- Yunnan
- Zambia
- Zimbabwe

Liqueurs

- absinthe
- advocaat
- amaretto
- anisette
- Baileys™
- Benedictine™
- cassis
- Campari™
- Chambord™
- Chartreuse™
- Cointreau™
- crème de cacao
- crème de cassis
- crème de menthe
- curaçao
- Drambuie™
- Frangelico™
- Galliano™
- Grand Marnier™
- Irish Cream
- Kahlúa™
- kümmel
- Lillet™
- maraschino
- Midori™
- ratafia
- pastis
- Pernod™
- Pimm's™
- Rémy Martin™
- sambuca
- slivovitz
- Southern Comfort™
- Tia Maria™
- triple sec

Liquors

Whiskey

- bourbon
- Canadian whisky/whiskey
- grain whiskey
- Irish whiskey
- Kentucky bourbon
- malt whiskey
- rye
- Scotch whisky/whiskey
- single malt
- sour mash
- usquebaugh

Brandy

- applejack
- Armagnac™
- Calvados™
- cherry brandy
- cognac
- Courvoisier™
- eau-de-vie
- grappa
- kirsch
- marc
- mirabelle

Gin

- Hollands
- London gin
- sloe gin

Rum

- Bacardi™
- cachaca
- demerara (rum)
- tafia

Other Liquors

- aquavit
- arrack
- cachaça
- ouzo
- raki
- sake
- schnapps
- tequila
- vodka

Soft Drinks and Other Nonalcoholic Beverages

- ambrosia
- atole
- batido
- birch beer
- bubble tea
- café au lait

caffè latte
cappuccino
chai
cherry cola
chocolate milk
cider
club soda
Coca-Cola™
coconut milk
coffee
cola
cream soda
Dr. Pepper™
egg cream
eggnog
espresso
flip
float
frappé
fruit juice
fruit punch
ginger ale
ginger beer
grape soda
green tea
guarana
horchata
iced coffee
iced tea
kava
kefir
koumiss
lemonade
lemon-lime
lime rickey
limeade
macchiato
malted
maté
milkshake
mineral water
mochaccino
Mountain Dew™
nectar
orangeade
orange soda
Orangina™
Pepsi™
pop
refresco
ristretto
root beer
Russian tea
sarsaparilla
seltzer
7-UP™
Shirley Temple
slush
smoothie
soy milk
spritzer
tea
tisane
tonic water
Virgin Mary

Teas

Assam
black
black currant
Caravan
Ceylon
chai
chamomile
chrysanthemum
dragon well
Darjeeling
dragon phoenix
Earl Grey
English breakfast
genmai
ginseng
green gunpowder
Gyokuro Asahi
herbal
Hubei
Huo Mountain
infusion
Irish breakfast
jasmine
Kashmiri
Keemun
kukicha
lapsang souchong
matcha
Nilgiri
oolong
pearl
pekoe
peppermint
pinhead
Pu-erh
red
Rooibos
sage
sencha
tisane
white
Yunnan
Zhufeng

Wines and Wine Grapes

Aglianco
Albariño
Alicante Bouschet
Amarone
Amontillado
Ardeche
Arneis
Asti Spumante
Barbaresco
Barbera
Barolo
Barsac
Beaujolais
Beaujolais-Villages
Beaune
blanc de blancs
blanc de noirs
blush
Bordeaux
Bourgogne
Brouilly
Brunello
brut
Bual
Burger
Burgundy
Cabernet
Cabernet Franc
Cabernet Sauvignon
Carignane
Carnelian
Cava
Chablis
Chambertin
Chambourcin
Champagne
Charbono
Eiswein
Chardonnay
Château Pétrus
Chenas
Chenin Blanc
Chianti
Chianti Classico
Chianti Ruffina
Chiroubles
Claret
Classico
Concord
Condrieu
Corvina
Côte de Brouilly
demi sec
Dolcetto
doux
Durif
Eiswein
extra dry
extra sec
Fino
Fleurie
Flor
Flora
Folle Blanche
fortified
Frascati
French Colombard
Frontignac
Fumé Blanc
Gamay
Garnacha
Gattinara
Gewürztraminer
Ghemme
Grand Cru
Graves
Grenache
Grignolino
Haut-Medoc
Hermitage
Heuriger
ice wine
Johannisberg Riesling
Johannisberger
Juliénas
Kabinett
Labrusca
Lambrusco
Liebfraumilch
Madiera
Málaga
Malbec
Malmsey
Malvasia
Malvasia Blanca
Malvoisie
Manzanilla
Margaux
Marichal Foch
Marsanne
Mataro
Médoc
Melon
Meritage™
Merlot
Meursault
Monastrell
Montepulciano
Montilla
Montrachet
Morgon
Moscato
Moselle
Moulin-à-Vent
Mourvedre
Mousseux
Muscadel
Muscadelle
Muscadet
Muscadine
Muscat
Muscatel
Nebbiolo
Negra Mole
Negro Amaro
Niersteiner
nonvintage
off-dry
Oloroso
Orvieto
Palomino
Pauillac
Pedro Ximénez
Petite Syrah
Petite Verdot
Piesporter
Pinot
Pinot Bianco
Pinot Blanc
Pinot Grigio
Pinot Gris
Pinot Noir
Pinotage
Pomerol
port
Pouilly-Fuissé
Pouilly-Fumé
Premier Cru
Prosecco
Régnié
Retsina
Rhenish
Riesling
Rioja
Riserva
Rosé
Roussanne
Ruby Port
Saint-Amour
Saint-Émilion
Saint-Estèphe
sake
Sancerre
Sangiovese
Sauternes
Sauvignon Blanc
Scheurebe
sec
sekt
Sémillon
semisweet
Sercial
sherry
Shiraz
Soave
Solera
Souzao
Spätlese
Spumante
Sylvaner
Symphony
Syrah
table wine
Taurasi
Tavel
Tawny Port
Tempranillo
Toscana
Traminer
Trebbiano
Trockenbeeren-auslese
Valpolicella
Vendange
Verdelho
Verdicchio
Vermouth
Vernaccia
vin de pays
vin de table
vin ordinaire
vinho verde
vino
Vino Nobile
vintage
Vintage Port
Viognier
Vouvray
White Zinfandel
Zinfandel

Fashion

Fabrics

acetate
acid-washed
acrylic
alpaca
angora
astrakhan
baize
barathea
batik
batiste
bengaline
bombazine
bouclé
broadcloth
brocade
buckram
buckskin
bunting
burlap
calico
cambric
camel hair
canvas
cashmere
cavalry twill
challis
chambray
charmeuse
chenille
chiffon
chino
chintz
ciré
cloqué
corduroy
cotton
crash
crepe
cretonne
crinoline
crushed velvet
Dacron
damask
denim
dimity
drill
drugget
duck
duffel
dupioni
faille
felt
fishnet
flannel
flannelette
fleece
foulard
gabardine
gauze
gingham
Gore-Tex™
grasscloth
grenadine
grosgrain
gunny
Harris tweed
herringbone
hopsack
horsehair
huckaback
ikat
jaconet
jacquard
jean
jersey
kente
kersey
khaddar
khaki
knit
lace
lamé
lawn
leatherette
leno
linen
loden
Lurex™
Lycra™
mackintosh
madras
melton
merino
mohair
moiré
muslin
nainsook
nankeen
Naugahyde™
nylon
oilcloth
organdy
organza
Orlon™
ottoman
oxford cloth
paisley
panne
pashmina
peachskin
peau de soie
percale
piqué
plaid
plissé
plush
polar fleece
polycotton
polyester
pongee
poplin
ramie
rayon
sateen
satin
saxony
seersucker
serge
shantung
sharkskin
silk
spandex
suede
swansdown
taffeta
tartan
tattersall
terrycloth
ticking
toile
toweling
tricot
tulle
tweed
twill
Ultrasuede™
veiling
velour
velvet
velveteen
vicuña
Viyella™
voile
webbing
whipcord
wool
worsted

Fabric Patterns

argyle
basketweave
bird's-eye
Black Watch
broken check
check
diaper
dogtooth
Fair Isle
figured
geometric
glen plaid
houndstooth
herringbone
labyrinth
moire
oblique
paisley
parquet
pinstripe
plaid
pointillé
polka dot
stripe
tartan
tattersall
tiling
twill
waffle
zigzag

Gemstones

agate
alexandrite
almandine
amber
amethyst
aquamarine
beryl
bloodstone
carbuncle
carnelian
cat's-eye
chalcedony
chrysoberyl
chrysoprase
citrine
corundum
demantoid
diamond
emerald
fire opal
garnet
girasol
hyacinth
jacinth
jade
jasper
jet
lapis lazuli
malachite
marcasite
moss agate
olivine
onyx
opal
pearl
peridot
pyrope
rose quartz
ruby
sapphire
sardonyx
smoky quartz
sunstone
tiger's eye
topaz
tourmaline
turquoise
zircon

Hairstyles

Afro
beehive
blunt cut
bob
body wave
bouffant
bowl cut
braids
brush cut
bun
buzz/buzz cut
chignon
cornrows
crewcut
DA/duck's ass
dreadlocks
ducktail
feathercut
flat-top
French braid
French twist
marcel (wave)
Mohawk
mullet
pageboy
perm
permanent wave
pigtails
pixie cut
pompadour
ponytail
razor cut
ringlets
shag
shingle
spike
updo

Jewelry

- ankle bracelet
- anklet
- armlet
- bangle
- beads
- bracelet
- brooch
- cameo
- carcanet
- chain
- chandelier earrings
- charm
- charm bracelet
- choker
- circlet
- clip
- clip-on earrings
- collar
- coronet
- cuff earring
- cufflinks
- cultured pearls
- dangle earrings
- ear cuff
- eardrops
- earrings
- engagement ring
- estate jewelry
- eternity ring
- fibula
- fob
- French-hook earrings
- freshwater pearls
- girandole
- hoop earrings
- ID bracelet
- lavalier
- lever-back earrings
- locket
- mood ring
- necklace
- nose ring
- pendant
- pin
- powerbeads
- ring
- scarfpin
- signet ring
- solitaire
- stickpin
- stud earrings
- studs
- teardrop earrings
- tiara
- tie pin
- toe ring
- torc/torque
- torsade
- wedding band/ring
- wristlet
- wristwatch

Knitting and Crocheting Terms

- afghan stitch
- Aran
- argyle
- back loop
- bind off
- block
- bobble
- bobbin
- casting on
- casting off
- cable needle
- cable stitch
- chain
- circular needle
- crochet hook
- cross
- double crochet
- double-knit
- drop a stitch
- eyelet
- Fair Isle
- fisherman's knit
- front loop
- garter stitch
- gauge
- intarsia
- knit stitch
- knitwise
- moss stitch
- pick up
- picot
- purl stitch
- purlwise
- ribbing
- seed stitch
- selvage stitch
- shaker knit
- single crochet
- slip stitch
- stockinette
- triple crochet
- twist
- wrap yarn
- yarn
- yarn over

Leathers

- alligator
- buckskin
- buff
- calfskin
- capeskin
- chamois
- chrome leather
- cordovan
- cowhide
- crocodile
- deerskin
- doeskin
- full-grain leather
- goatskin
- grain leather
- kid
- kidskin
- lambskin
- Levant morocco
- mocha
- morocco
- nappa/napa
- Nubuck™
- oxhide
- patent leather
- pigskin
- rawhide
- Russia leather
- sealskin
- shagreen
- shammy
- sheepskin
- snakeskin
- suede
- whitleather

Imitation Leathers

- Broncohide™
- DuraSuede™
- leatherette
- leatherlike vinyl
- Naugahyde™
- pleather

Sewing and Needlework Terms

- appliqué
- backstitch
- Bargallo
- bar tack
- basting
- binding
- blanket stitch
- blind stitch
- bobbin
- braid
- broderie anglaise
- buttonhole stitch
- casing
- catch stitch
- chain stitch
- crewel work
- cross-stitch
- cutwork
- darning
- drawn work
- dressmaker
- embroidery
- fagoting
- fancywork
- feather stitch
- fell
- floss
- French knot
- French seam
- gros point
- handstitch
- hemming
- hemstitch
- herringbone stitch
- lock stitch
- loop stitch
- mending
- mitering
- needlepoint
- overcasting
- overhand
- oversewing
- overstitch
- patchwork
- petit point
- pin tuck
- pleating
- presser foot
- quilting
- running stitch
- saddle stitch
- satin stitch
- seam
- seamstress
- selvage
- serger
- serging
- sewing silk
- shirring
- slip stitch
- smocking
- stay stitching
- stitch
- straight stitch
- tack
- tent stitch
- thimble
- thread
- topstitch
- trapunto
- tucking
- tufting
- twist
- whipstitch

Food

Beans and Peas

- adzuki/azuki/aduki bean
- anasazi bean
- asparagus bean
- bambara bean
- black bean
- black turtle bean
- black-eyed pea
- broad bean
- butter bean
- butterfly pea
- cajan pea
- cannellini bean
- carob bean
- castor bean
- chickpea
- cluster bean
- congo bean
- copper bean
- cowpea
- dhal/dal
- English pea
- fava bean
- field bean
- field pea
- flageolet
- garbanzo bean
- garden pea
- Great Northern (white) bean
- green bean
- green pea
- haricot
- haricot vert

horsebean
hyacinth bean
jack bean
kidney bean
lablab
lentil
lima bean
marrowfat pea
mung bean
navy bean
northern (white) bean
pigeon pea
pink bean
pinto bean
protein pea
pulse
purple bean
red bean
rice bean
runner bean
scarlet runner
snap bean
snap pea
snow pea
soybean
split pea
string bean
sugar pea
sugar snap pea
Swedish brown bean
tepary bean
velvet bean
wax bean
white bean
winged bean
yam bean
yard-long bean
yellow pea

Breads, Rolls, and Pancakes

anadama
bagel
baguette
bannock
bara brith
Barbari bread
barmbrack
batter bread
beaten biscuit
bialy
biscuit
black bread
blueberry pancake
Boston brown bread
breadstick
brioche
brown bread
bun
buttermilk biscuit
challah
chapati
ciabatta
cinnamon raisin bread
cinnamon bun/roll
cob
corn dodger
cornbread
cornet
Cornish split
corn pone
cottage loaf
craquelin
crepe
crescent roll
crispbread
croissant
crumpet
dosa
English muffin
farmhouse bread
ficelle
flapjack
flatbread
focaccia
frangipane
French bread
fry bread
gordita
griddle cake
grissini
hoecake
hot cross bun
hotcake
hush puppy
injera
Irish soda bread
Italian bread
Jewish rye (bread)
johnnycake
Kaiser roll
lavash
matzo
monkey bread
muffin
nan
oatcake
oatmeal bread
onion roll
pain au levain
pancake
pan de sal
pane francese
panettone
pappadum
paratha
Parker House roll
pistolette
pita (bread)
poori
popover
Portuguese roll
potato bread
pretzel
Pugliese bread
pull-apart bread
Pullman bread
pumpernickel
raisin bread
roti
Russian rye (bread)
rye (bread)
Sally Lunn
salt-rising bread
salt stick
schnecken
scone
seven-grain bread
sourdough bread
sticky bun
Swedish pancake
taralli
tea bread
tortilla
waffle
white bread
whole wheat bread
zephyr bun

Cereal Grains and Products

amaranth
barley
bran
buckwheat
bulgur
corn
couscous
farina
flaxseed
grits
groats
hominy
kamut
kasha
maize
malt
masa
millet
oat bran
oats
polenta
quinoa
rice
rye
semolina
sorghum
spelt
tapioca
teff
triticale
wheat
wheat germ
wild rice

Cheeses

American
asadero
Asiago
Beaufort
Bel Paese™
bleu/blue
Bonbel™
Boursin
brick
Brie
Caerphilly
Camembert
cheddar
Cheshire
chèvre
colby
Cotija
cottage cheese
cream cheese
Danish blue
Edam
Emmental
farmer cheese
feta
fontina
fresh mozzarella
fromage blanc
goat cheese
Gorgonzola
Gouda
Gruyère
havarti
Humboldt Fog™
jack cheese
Jarlsberg™
Laughing Cow™
Limburger
mascarpone
Monterey jack
mozzarella
Muenster/Munster
Neufchâtel
panir/paneer
Parmesan
Parmigiano Reggiano
Passendale
pecorino
pepper jack
Port-Salut
pot cheese
provolone
quark
queso fresco
Red Hawk™
ricotta
Romano
Roquefort™
Stilton
string cheese
Swiss
Taleggio
Tilsit

Cooking Methods and Food Preparation

bake
barbecue
bard
baste
batter
beat
blacken
blanch
blend
boil
boil down
bone
braise
bread
broil
brown
bruise
butterfly
can
candy
caramelize
carbonado
casserole
char broil
chop
clarify
clean
coat
coddle
concentrate
cream
crisp
crust
crystallize
cube
curdle
cure
cut in
deep fry
deglaze
degrease
dehydrate
desiccate
devein
devil
dice
draw
dredge
dress
drizzle
dry
dry-roast
dunk
dust
eviscerate
fillet
flake
flambé
float
flute

foam
fold
force
form
freeze-dry
frizzle
froth
fry
garnish
glaze
grate
grill
grind
hard-boil
hash
hull
julienne
knead
lard
macerate
marinate
mash
melt
mince
mix
mold
nap
pack
pan-broil
pan-fry
parboil
pare
pickle
pipe
plump
poach
pot
pound
preserve
pressure-cook
pureé
raise
reconstitute
reduce
refresh
render
rice
ripen
roast
roll
salt
sauté
scald
scallop
score
scramble
sear
shirr
shock
shred
sift
simmer
slice
smoke
smother
soak
soft-boil
souse
steam
steep
stew
stir
stir-fry
stuff
sweat
temper
thread
toast
toss
whip
whisk
zest

Cooking Types and Styles

al dente
al forno
Alfredo
alla Taormina
alla vodka
almondine
amandine
anglaise
argenteuil
au bleu
au fromage
au gratin
au jus
au naturel
bérnaise
Bolognese
bourguignon
cacciatore
carbonara
chiffonade
clamart
country fried
Crécy
creole
curried
dauphine
en brochette
en croûte
en papillote
espagnole
escabeche
estragon
étouffée
farci
flambé
Florentine
forestière
fra diavolo
francese
Frenched
fricassee
garni
gratiné
grecque
hollandaise
indienne
jardinière
jerk
julienne
lyonnaise
marinara
marinière
masala
medium
medium rare
meunière
nesselrode
Newburg
niçoise
normande
parmigiana
périgord
parmentier
piccata
pilaf
Pittsburgh style
Provençale
puttanesca
ranchero
rare
relleno
ripieno
roulade
scallopine
stroganoff
subgum
sunny side up
tandoori
tempura
tikka
Véronique
vindaloo

Desserts and Other Sweets

Cakes

angel food cake
baba au rhum
babka
Battenberg cake
Black Forest cake
bûche de Noël
Bundt cake
carrot cake
cassata
coffee cake
crumb cake
cupcake
dacquoise
devil's food cake
Dobos torte
Dundee cake
financier
fruitcake
galette des rois
gateau
genoise
German chocolate cake
gingerbread
honey cake
hummingbird cake
ice cream cake
jelly roll
kuchen
Kugelhopf
lady finger
lemon chiffon cake
Lord Baltimore cake
Madeira cake
madeleine
mooncake
panforte
petit four
plum pudding
pound cake
red velvet cake
rum baba
Sachertorte
savarin
simnel cake
spice cake
sponge cake
stollen
strawberry shortcake
tea cake
tea ring
tiramisù
torte
tres leches
upside-down cake
vasilopita
wedding cake
whoopie pie

Candy and Candied Treats

angel's hair
barfi
bark
barley sugar
boiled sweet
bonbon
bubble gum
buckeye
bullseye
burnt peanut
buttermint
butterscotch
candied fruit
candied nut
candied peel
candied violet
candy apple
candy buttons
candy cane
caramel
caramel apple
caramel corn
chewing gum
chocolate
chocolate-covered cherry
comfit
cotton candy
divinity
dragée
fondant
frangipane
friandise
fruit paste
fruit slice
fudge
ganache
gianduia
gobstopper
gulab jamun
gum ball
gumdrop
gummy bear, worm, etc.
halvah
haystack
heavenly hash
horehound
jawbreaker
Jordan almond
kiss
lemon drop
licorice
Life Saver™
lollipop
lozenge
macaroon
malted milk ball
maple sugar
marchpane
marron glacé
marshmallow
marzipan
meringue
mint
mostarda di frutta
nonpareil
nougat
nougatine
Nutella™
opera cream
pastille
pâte de fruits
peanut brittle
peanut butter cup
pecan log
penuche
peppermint patty
praline
pulled candy
ratafia
red hot
rock candy
rum ball
s'more
saltwater taffy
sesame brittle
stroopballetje
Swedish fish
taffy
toffee
torrone
truffle
Turkish delight
turtle

Cookies

amaretti
animal cracker
arrowroot cookie
biscotti
black and white cookie
blondie
brandy snap
brownie
butter cookie
chew
chocolate chip cookie
crescent cookie
crinkle
crisp
date bar
fig bar
Fig Newton™
florentine
fortune cookie

Garibaldi
gingersnap
Girl Scout cookie
graham cracker
hamantashen
haystack cookie
hermit
icebox cookie
jumble cookie
kolacky
koulourakia
kringle
krumkake
lace cookie
langue de chat
lebkuchen
lemon bar
Lorna Doone™
macaroon
Mallomar™
mandelbrot
meltaway
meringue
Mexican wedding cookie
molasses cookie
mostaccioli
oatmeal raisin cookie
Oreo™
peanut butter cookie
pecan sandie
pepparkakor
petit beurre
pfeffernüsse
pinwheel
pizzelle
ratafia
Rice Krispie Treat™
rugelach
rusk
sand tart
sandwich cookie
shortbread
slice-and-bake cookie
snickerdoodle
speculoo
spice cookie
springerle
spritz
sugar cookie
sugar wafer
tassie
thumbprint cookie
Toll House cookie™
tuile
vanilla wafer

Frozen Desserts

baked Alaska
banana split
bombe
fro-yo
frozen yogurt
granita
ice cream
Italian ice
kulfi
semifreddo
sherbet
sorbet
spumoni
tortoni

Pastries, Doughnuts, and Deep-Fried Treats

almond horn
apple turnover
baklava
bear claw
beignet
Berliner
bismark
buñuelo
cannolo/cannoli
cherry turnover
chiacchiere
chrusciki
churro
cream puff
crepes Suzette
croquembouche
cruller
csoroge
dango
danish
eclair
elephant ear
farsangi fank
feuilletee
fillozes
French cruller
fried ice cream
fritter
funnel cake
glazed doughnut
jalebi
jelly doughnut
kringle
laddu
long john
loukoumas
maple bar/log
mille-feuille
Napoleon
oliebol
paczek/paczki
pain au chocolat
pampushky
profiterole
sata andagi
sfogliatelle
shisky
streusel
strudel
sufganiyah
Swedish braid
zeppola

Pies, Tarts, and Cobblers

apple cobbler
apple crisp
apple crumble
apple pandowdy
apple pie
banana cream pie
Banbury tart
bitter tart
blackberry cobbler
black bottom pie
blueberry buckle
blueberry pie
Boston cream pie
brown Betty
buttermilk pie
cheesecake
cherry cobbler
cherry crisp
cherry pie
chess pie
chocolate cream pie
coconut cream pie
French silk pie
grasshopper pie
jam tart
key lime pie
lemon chiffon pie
lemon meringue pie
millionaire pie
mincemeat pie
Mississippi mud pie
moon pie
onion tart
pasteis de nata
peach cobbler
peach pie
pecan pie
pumpkin pie
ricotta pie
shoofly pie
strawberry rhubarb pie
sweet potato pie
tarte au sucre
tarte Tatin

Puddings and Custards

banana pudding
Bavarian cream
bavarois
blancmange
bread pudding
butterscoth pudding
Charlotte Russe
chocolate pudding
Christmas pudding
clafoutis
crème brûlée
crème caramel
egg custard
flan
floating island
flummery
fool
Indian pudding
instant pudding
mousse
panna cotta
parfait
persimmon pudding
plum pudding
pot de crème
rice pudding
roly poly
snow pudding
spotted dick
suet pudding
syllabub
tapioca pudding
toffee pudding
trifle
vanilla pudding
zabaglione
zuppa inglese

Other Desserts

ambrosia
bananas Foster
cherries in the snow
cherries jubilee
chocolate fondue
chocolate souffle
compote
pavlova
peach Melba
poached pear

Fruits

abiu
achocha
akebia
akee/ackee
ambarella
ananas
apricot
atemoya
avocado
azarole
bael
banana
banana flower
baobab
Barbados cherry
barberry
beach plum
bearberry
bergamot
bignay
bilberry
bilimbi
biriba
blackberry
blackberry jam fruit
blood orange
blueberry
Brazilian cherry
breadfruit
buffaloberry
cabelluda
calamansi
cantaloupe
carambola
casaba
chayote
cherimoya
cherry
Chinese wolfberry
chokecherry
cherry plum
citron
clementine
cloudberry
coconut
corossolier
cranberry
Crenshaw melon
crowberry
currant
damson
date
dewberry
durian
eggfruit
elderberry
feijoa
fig
gamboge
gooseberry
grape
grapefruit
greengage
ground cherry
guava
hackberry
honeydew (melon)
huckleberry
ilama
jaboticaba
jackfruit
jujube
kiwi fruit
kumquat
langsat
lemon
lime
longan
loquat
lychee
mamey
mameyito
mandarin
mango
mangosteen
medlar
melon
monstera
mountain apple
moya
mulberry
muskmelon
mysore raspberry
naranjilla
nectarine
noni
orange
papaw
papaya
passion fruit
peach
peanut butter fruit
pear
pepino
persimmon
pineapple
pitahaya
plantain

plum
pomegranate
pomelo
prickly pear
prune
pummelo
quince
rambutan
raspberry
rhubarb
rollinia
rose apple
salak
salmonberry
santol
sapodilla
sapote
satsuma
serviceberry
soursop
spanspek
squashberry
star fruit
starapple
strawberry
Surinam cherry
tamarillo
tamarind
Ugli™ fruit
wampee
water apple
watermelon
wax jambu
whortleberry
winter melon
yuzu

Apples

Ambrosia
Baldwin
Ben Davis
Blenheim Orange
Braeburn
Cameo
Cortland
crab apple
Crispin
Criterion
Delicious
Discovery
Empire
Esopus Spitzenburg
Fortune
Fuji
Gala
Ginger Gold
Golden Delicious
Golden Russet
Granny Smith
Gravenstein
Greening
Haralson
Honeycrisp
Idared/Ida Red
Jerseymac
Jonagold
Jonamac
Jonathan
Lady
Liberty
Lodi
Macoun
McIntosh
Monarch
Mutsu
Northern Spy
Paula Red
Pearmain
Pink Lady™
Pink Pearl
pippin
Rambo
Red Delicious
Rhode Island Greening
Rome
russet
Spartan
Stayman
Sturmer (pippin)
sugar apple
Sundowner
Sunrise
sweetsop
Tydeman
Winesap
Winter Banana
Yellow Transparent
York

Berries

akala
aronia berry
barberry
bearberry
bilberry
black currant
black raspberry
blackberry
blueberry
boysenberry
buffalo berry
candleberry
cape gooseberry
checkerberry
Chinese wolfberry
chokeberry
chokecherry
cloudberry
cowberry
cranberry
crowberry
darrowberry
dewberry
elderberry
fraise des bois
golden raspberry
gooseberry
grapes
hackberry
huckleberry
hurtleberry
jostaberry
juneberry
juniper berry
kiwi
lingonberry
loganberry
maidenhair berry
marionberry
marlberry
mayhaw
mulberry
nectarberry
olallieberry
passionberry
raspberry
red currant
salmonberry
saskatoon berry
serviceberry
silvanberry
squashberry
strawberry
tayberry
thimbleberry
tummelberry
white currant
whortleberry
wild blueberry
wild strawberry
wineberry
youngberry

Herbs See also **Spices**

basil
bay leaf
bee balm
black cohosh
boldo leaf
borage
bouquet garni
burdock
burnet
calamint
calendula
capers
catnip
chervil
Chinese parsley
chives
cicely
cilantro
coriander
costmary
cress
curry leaf
dandelion
dill
fennel
fenugreek
feverfew
fines herbes
horehound
hyssop
Kaffir lime leaf
laurel leaf
lavender
lemon balm
lemon basil
lemon verbena
lemongrass
lovage
marjoram
Mexican pepperleaf
mint
mugwort
myrtle
oregano
pandanus/pandan leaf
parsley
pennyroyal
peppermint
perilla
ramson
rice paddy herb
rocket
rosemary
rue
sage
savory
saw leaf
shiso
sorrel
sweet basil
tarragon
Thai basil
thyme
wormwood
yarrow

Meals

bag lunch
banquet
barbecue
blue plate special
box lunch
breakfast
brunch
buffet
clambake
continental breakfast
cookout
dinner
feast
high tea
lunch
luncheon
picnic
potluck (supper/dinner)
power lunch
prix fixe
rijsttafel
salad bar
smorgasbord
supper
table d'hôte
takeout
tea
wienie/wiener roast

Meat See also **Sausages**

Types of Meat

alligator
antelope
armadillo
bear
beaver
beefalo
bison
boar
buffalo
caiman
capon
caribou
cervena
chicken
Cornish hen
duck
elk
emu
fowl
frog legs
game
goat
goose
grouse
guinea fowl
hare
kangaroo
kid
lamb
llama
moose
muscovy duck
musk ox
muskrat
mutton
ostrich
partridge
pheasant
pigeon
pork
poultry
poussin
pullet
rabbit
raccoon
rattlesnake
snail
squab
squirrel
turkey
turtle
veal
venison
wild boar
wild turkey
wood pigeon
yak

Cuts of Meat

American leg
arm roast
arm steak
baby back rib
back fat
back rib
bacon
baron
belly
blade
blade Boston
blade chop
blade loin
Boston shoulder
braciola
brains
breast
brisket
burger
butt
butterfly
butterfly chop
Canadian bacon
cap steak
caul
center loin
center rib
charcuterie
charqui
chateaubriand
chitterlings
chop
chuck
chuck blade roast
club steak
cold cut
corned beef
country style rib
cross rib roast
crosscut shank
crown roast
cubed steak
culotte steak
cushion shoulder
cutlet
Delmonico
drumstick
eye of round
fatback
filet
filet mignon
fillet
flank
flanken
flitch
foie gras
fore shank
frenched leg
gammon
gizzards
ground chuck
ground round
ground sirloin
ham
hamburger
heart
heel of round
hindshank
hock
jowl
Kansas City strip
kidney
knuckles
lard
leg of lamb
liver
loin
lung
marrow
medallion
mountain oyster
neck
neck slice
New York sirloin
noisette
numbles
offal
oxtail
paillard
pastrami
picnic meat
pig tail
pig's foot
pin bone sirloin
plate
porterhouse
pot roast
prairie oyster
prosciutto
rack
rib
rib chop
rib eye
rib roast
rib tip
riblet
roast
rolled leg
rolled roast
round bone sirloin
rump
saddle
Salisbury steak
salt pork
sandwich steak
shank
shell steak
shin
short loin
short rib
shortplate
shoulder
sirloin
sirloin chop
sirloin tip
skirt steak
slab bacon
sparerib
Spencer steak
spleen
square shoulder
St. Louis style rib
standing rib roast
steak
steamboat round
stew meat
stomach
strip steak
suet
sweetbread
Swiss steak
T-bone
tenderloin
testicle
thigh
tongue
top loin
top sirloin
tournedo
triangle steak
tripe
tri-tip
umbles
veal
wedge bone sirloin
wing

Noodles

bean thread
cellophane noodles
chasoba
chow fun
dang myun
e-fu
egg noodles
farfel
glass noodles
gooksu
harusame
Hokkien
kreplach
lo mein
mei fun
mung bean noodles
naeng myun
pirogi
ramen
rice noodles
rice sheet
rice stick
rice vermicelli
Sevian
shirataki
soba
somen
spaetzle
udon
wheat noodles
won ton

Nuts and Seeds

acorn
almond
areca nut
beechnut
betel nut
black walnut
Brazil (nut)
breadnut
bunya nut
butternut
candlenut
cashew (nut)
chestnut
chinquapin/chinkapin
cobnut
coco de mer
coconut
cohune/cahoun (nut)
cola/kola nut
corozo
English walnut
filbert
gingko nut
hazelnut
hickory nut
horse chestnut
litchi (nut)
macadamia (nut)
nutmeg
peanut
pecan
pignoli
pignut
pine nut
piñon/pinyon (nut)
pistachio (nut)
pumpkin seed
sesame seed
souari nut
Spanish peanut
sunflower seed
walnut

Pasta

acomo pepe
anelli
angel hair
bavette
bavettine
bucatini
campanelle
cannaroni
cannelloni
capelli d'Angelo
capellini
cappelletti
casarecci
cavatappi
cavatelli
conchiglie
conchiglioni
coralli
creste di galli
ditali
ditalini
eliche
elicodali
farfalle
fedelini
fettucce
fettuccine
fettucelle
fideo
fischietti
fusilli
fusilli col buco
garganelli
gemelli
gigantoni
gigli
gnocchetti
gnocchi
gramigna
grattugiata
igomiti
lasagne
linguine
lumache
lumaconi
macaroni
macceroni
mafalda
malloreddus
maltagliati
manicotti
margherite
margheritine
maruzze
maruzzelle
mezze penne
midollini
millerighe
mostaccioli
occhi di lupo
orecchiette
orsetti
orzo
pansotti
pappardelle
pastina
penne
pennette
perciatelli
pezzoccheri
pipe rigate
pipette rigate
quadrefiore
quadrettini
quadrucci
radiatore
ravioli
riccioli
rigatoni
riso
rotelle
rotini
ruote
sedani rigati
sedanini rigati
seme di mellone
spaghetti
spaghettini
spiralini
stelle

stellini
strozzapreti
tagliarini
tagliatelle
tagliolini
tonnarelli
torchio
tortellini
tortelloni
tortiglioni
trenne
trennette
tripolini
troffiette
tubetti
vermicelli
ziti

Savory Pies and Turnovers

bisteeya
borek
boureki
bridie
calzone
Cornish pasty
dumpling
empanada
Hot Pocket™
knish
momo
pierogi
pork pie
pot pie
pot sticker
quesadilla
quiche lorraine
runza
sambusac
samosa
shepherd's pie
sopaipilla
spanakopita
steak and kidney pie
stromboli
timbale
tiropita
tourtiere
vol-au-vent

Sandwiches

arepa
bagel
baguette
barbecue beef
BLT
boat
bologna
burrito
California club
calzone
canapé
chicken salad
chilaquile
chili dog
chimichanga
club
Coney Island
corn dog
corned beef
Cornish pasty
crepe
croissant
croque madame
croque monsieur
Cuban
cucumber
Dagwood
deviled ham
eggplant parmigiana
egg salad
empanada
enchilada
fajita
finger
flauta
fluffernutter
focaccia
french dip
fried peanut butter and banana
gordita
grilled cheese
grinder
gyro
ham and cheese
hamburger
hero
hoagie
hobo
hot brown
hot dog
hot pastrami
meat loaf
meatball
Monte Cristo
muffuletta
open-faced
oyster loaf
pan bagnat
panino
PB & J
peanut butter and jelly
Philly cheese steak
pig in a blanket
pinwheel
pistolette
pita pocket
poor boy
pocket
pulled pork
quesadilla
Rachel
Reuben
roast beef
sausage and pepper(s)
shawarma
sloppy joe
smoked salmon
steak
stromboli
sub
submarine
taco
tea
tongue
torpedo
torta
triple-decker
tuna melt
tuna salad
watercress
wedge
Welsh rarebit/rabbit
Western
wrap

Sauces, Condiments, and Dressings

alfredo
applesauce
arrabbiata
avgolemono
balsamic vinaigrette
barbecue sauce
Béarnaise
béchamel
beurre blanc
blue/bleu cheese dressing
bolognese
bourguignon
brandy butter
bread sauce
carbonara
chili sauce
chutney
coulis
cream sauce
crème anglaise
custard
dip
dressing
duxelles
finishing sauce
fish sauce
French dressing
gravy
guacamole
hard sauce
hoisin sauce
hollandaise
horseradish
hot sauce
hummus
Italian dressing
jus
ketchup
marinara
mayonnaise
mint sauce
mole
mornay
mousseline
mustard
nam pla
nuoc mam
oyster sauce
pesto
piccalilli
piri piri
pistou
plum sauce
poppyseed dressing
ranch dressing
relish
remoulade
Roquefort dressing
rouille
Russian dressing
salad dressing
salsa
salsa verde
sweet and sour sauce
tartar sauce (sauce tartare)
skordalia
soy sauce
Tabasco™
tahini
tamari
tapenade
teriyaki
Thousand Island dressing
velouté
vinaigrette
white sauce
Worcestershire sauce

Sausages and Hot Dogs

andouille
banger
bierwurst
blood sausage
black pudding
bratwurst
bologna
chili dog
chorizo
chub
cooked salami
corn dog
frankfurter
Genoa salami
hard salami
kielbasa
knackwurst
kolbassa
korv
kubasa
liverwurst
Polish sausage
salami
saveloy
summer sausage
wiener
wurst

Soups

alphabet soup
bird's nest soup
bisque
borscht
bouillon
broth
burgoo
callaloo
chicken noodle soup
chowder
cock-a-leekie
congee
consommé
corn chowder
egg drop soup
gazpacho
gumbo
hot and sour soup
Manhattan clam chowder
minestrone
miso soup
mock turtle soup
mulligatawny
New England clam chowder
oxtail
pea soup
pistou
pot-au-feu
potage
Scotch broth
shchi

stracciatella
tomato soup
turtle soup
vichyssoise
wonton soup
zuppa

Spices See also **Herbs**

achiote
ajwain
allspice
angelica
anise
aniseed
annatto
arrowroot
asafetida
benne seed
berbere
black pepper
cacao
caraway seed
cardamom
cassia
cayenne (pepper)
celery seed
chicory
chili pepper
chili powder
cinnamon
cloves
coriander
cubeb
cumin
curry powder
dill seed
dukka
epazote
epices fines
fennel seed
fenugreek (seed)
filé
fingerroot
finochio
galangal
garam masala
garlic powder
ginger
grains of paradise
green peppercorn
horseradish
juniper
licorice
mace
mahaleb
mastic
mustard seed
nigella
nutmeg
paprika
pepper
pepper flakes
pickling spice
pimento
pomegranate
poppy seed
ras el hanout
red pepper
safflower
saffron
sansho
sassafras
sesame seed
Sichuan pepper
St John's bread
star anise
sumac
tonka bean
turmeric
valerian
vanilla
wasabi
white pepper
zahtar
zedoary

Stews and Casseroles

adobo
baked ziti
beef bourgignon
beef en daube
beef pilaf
beef stew
beef stroganoff
blanquette de veau
bobotie
bouillabaisse
Brunswick stew
burgoo
callaloo
carne guisada
cassoulet
chicken and dumplings
chicken cacciatore
chicken Marengo
chicken paprika
chili
cholent
chop suey
choucroute garni
cioppino
colcannon
coquilles St. Jacques
curry
dhal
daube
eggplant parmigiana
fricassee
frikadeller
ful medames
goulash
groundnut stew
gumbo
hasenpfeffer
hunter's stew
Irish stew
jager-eintopf
jambalaya
kedgeree
kugel
lamb stew
lasagna/lasagne
lobscouse
lobster Newburg
macaroni and cheese
matelote
Mongolian hot pot
moussaka
mulligatawny
olla podrida
oyster stew
paella
peperonata
pepper pot
potage
pot-au-feu
ragout
ratatouille
rendang
Swedish meatballs
tikka
tuna casserole
vindaloo
waterzooi

Sugars

beet sugar
birch sugar
blackstrap molasses
brown sugar
cane sugar
caramel
confectioners' sugar
corn syrup
cube sugar
dark brown sugar
demerara (sugar)
dextrose
fructose
galactose
golden syrup
granulated sugar
gur
honey
icing
jaggery
lactose
loaf sugar
maltose
manna
maple sugar
molasses
muscovado (sugar)
palm sugar
panela
piloncillo
powdered sugar
preserving sugar
raw sugar
sorghum
spun sugar
sucrose
superfine sugar
treacle
turbinado sugar

Sushi

aji (horse mackerel)
ama-ebi (raw shrimp)
anago (sea eel)
awabi (abalone)
ebi (boiled shrimp)
hamachi (yellowtail)
hamaguri (clam)
hamo (sea eel)
hirame (flounder)
hokkigai (surf clam)
hotategai (scallop)
ika (squid)
ikura (salmon roe)
kaibashira (scallop)
kajiki (swordfish)
kani (crab or surimi)
karei (flatfish)
katsuo (bonito)
kazunoko (herring roe)
maguro (tuna)
masago (smelt roe)
masu (trout)
mekajiki (swordfish)
mirugai (surf clam)
saba (mackerel)
sake (salmon)
sawara (Spanish mackerel)
suzuki (sea bass)
tai (sea bream)
tairagai (razor-shell clam)
tako (octopus)
tamago (sweet egg omelet)
tobiko (flying fish roe)
toro (fatty tuna)
unagi (freshwater eel)
uni (sea urchin roe)

Vegetables See also **Beans and Peas**

acorn squash
agave
ancho pepper
artichoke
arugula
ash gourd
asparagus
avocado
bamboo shoot
banana pepper
banana squash
bean sprout
beet
beet green
bell pepper
bibb lettuce
bitter gourd
bok choy
Boston lettuce
bottle gourd
brinjal
broccoflower
broccoli
broccoli rabe

broccolini
Brussels sprout
burdock
butternut squash
cabbage
caper
carrot
cassava
celeriac
celery
chard
cherry pepper
cherry tomato
chicory
chili pepper
Chinese cabbage
collard green
colocasia
corn
corn on the cob
cress
cubanelle pepper
cucumber
daikon
dandelion green
delicata squash
edamame
eggplant
endive
epazote
escarole
fenugreek
fiddlehead
frisée
galangal
gherkin
ginger root
gourd
grape tomato
Habanero pepper
horseradish
Hubbard squash
iceberg lettuce
jalapeño pepper
Jerusalem artichoke
jicama
kabocha squash
kale
kencur
kohlrabi
leek
lotus root
mache
marrow
mesclun
mizuna
mung bean
mushroom
mustard green
napa cabbage
nopal
okra
onion
parsnip
pasilla pepper
plantain
potato
pumpkin
purslane
radicchio
radish
ramp
rhubarb
ridge gourd
romaine (lettuce)
rutabaga
salsify
scallion
sea kale
Serrano pepper
shallot
snake gourd
sorrel
spaghetti squash
spinach
spring onion
summer squash
sweet potato
Swiss chard
taro
Thai chili pepper
tomatillo
tomato
turnip
wakame
water chestnut
watercress
winter melon
yam
yellow squash
zucchini

Furniture

Furniture Types and Styles

American Classical
Art Deco
Art Nouveau
Bauhaus
Biedermeier
Cape Dutch
Chippendale
Colonial
Danish Modern
Early American
Eastlake
Empire
Federal
Gothic Revival
Hepplewhite
Jacobean
Louis XIV
Louis XV
Louis XVI
Mission
Modern
Pilgrim
Queen Anne
Regency
reproduction
Rococo
Scandinavian
Shaker
Sheraton
Tudor
Victorian
William & Mary

Chairs

Adirondack chair
armchair
barber chair
Barcalounger™
barstool
Boston rocker
butterfly chair
cane chair
captain's chair
dentist's chair
dining chair
chaise longue
deck chair
director's chair
easy chair
fiddleback (chair)
fighting chair
folding chair
high chair
ladder-back (chair)
lawn chair
lounge chair
Morris chair
press-back
recliner
rocker
rocking chair
sidechair
stacking chair
stool
straight-backed chair
swivel chair
task chair
Windsor chair
wing chair

Sofas and Couches

button-back sofa
camelback sofa
canapé
chaise longue
chesterfield
davenport
daybed
divan
futon
loveseat
pullout
settee
sleeper
sofa bed
studio couch
tête-à-tête

Games

Card Games

baccarat
bezique
blackjack
bridge
canasta
cassino/casino
chemin de fer
contract bridge
cooncan
crazy eights
cribbage
duplicate bridge
écarté
euchre
fan-tan
faro
five hundred
forty-five
gin rummy
go fish
hearts
monte
napoleon
old maid
pinochle
piquet
pitch
poker
rouge-et-noir
rummy
setback
skat
slapjack
solitaire
solo
spades
stud poker
three-card monte
twenty-one
UNO™
war
whist

Poker Games

all for one/one for all
anaconda
auction
baseball
Canadian stud
Chicago
Cincinnati
cowpie
double-draw
English stud
five-card draw
follow the queen
guts

have a heart
Howdy Doody
jacks to open, trips to win
Lame Brain Pete
Mexican stud
Omaha hold 'em
second hand high
seven-card stud
spit in the ocean
Texas hold 'em
trees

Poker Hands

royal flush
straight flush
four of a kind
full house
flush
straight
three of a kind
two pairs
one pair
high card

Children's Games

blindman's bluff/buff
catch
cat's cradle
charades
cops and robbers
cowboys and Indians
dodge ball
double dutch
duck, duck, goose
follow-the-leader
four square
freeze tag
hangman
hide-and-seek
hopscotch
jacks
kickball
kick the can
leapfrog
marbles
monkey in the middle
musical chairs
pin the tail on the donkey
red light, green light
Red Rover
ring-around-the-rosie
Simon Says
spud
tag
telephone
tetherball
tic-tac-toe
tiddlywinks
tug of war
twenty questions
Twister™

Table Games and Board Games

air hockey
backgammon
bagatelle
Battleship™
billiards
bingo
Boggle™
Candyland™
checkers
chess
Chinese checkers
Chutes and Ladders™
Clue™
dominoes
foosball
go
jigsaw puzzle
kriegspiel
Life™
Monopoly™
Operation™
pachisi/Parcheesi™
pickup sticks
pinball
pool
Risk™
Rummy Kub™
Scrabble™
Sorry!™
table-top hockey
Trivial Pursuit™
Yahtzee™

Geography

Layers of the Earth's Atmosphere

exosphere
ionosphere
mesosphere
ozone layer
stratosphere
thermosphere
troposphere

Cloud Types and Formations

altocumulus
altostratus
anabatic
anvil
arch/arcus
back-sheared
banner
billow
bow
calvus
cap cloud
capillatus
castellanus/castellatus
chinook
cirrocumulus
cirrostratus
cirrus
cloudlet
congestus
contrail
cumuliform
cumulonimbus
cumulus
duplicatus
fall streaks
fibratus
flanking line
floccus
Foehn wall
fog
fractus
fumulus
funnel cloud
humilis
incus
intortus
iridescent
lacunosus
lenticularis
luminous
mackerel sky
mamma/mammatus
mare's tails
mediocris
mesoscale
mother-of-pearl
mushroom
nacreous
nebulosus
nimbostratus
nimbus
noctilucent
opacus
orographic
pannus
perlucidus
pileus
praecipitatio
pyrocumulus
radiatus
rain cloud
scud cloud
spissatus
storm cloud
stratiformus
stratocumulus
stratus
streamer
thundercloud
thunderhead
translucidas
tuba
uncinus
undulatus
veil cloud
velum
vertebratus
virga
wall cloud
wave cloud

Constellations

Andromeda
Antlia: the Air Pump
Apus: Bird of Paradise
Aquarius: the Water Bearer/Carrier
Aquila: the Eagle
Ara: the Altar
Aries: the Ram
Auriga: the Charioteer
Boötes: the Herdsman
Caelum: the Chisel
Camelopardalis: the Giraffe
Cancer: the Crab
Canes Venatici: the Hunting Dogs
Canis Major: the Big Dog
Canis Minor: the Little Dog
Capricornus: the Goat
Carina: the Ship's Keel
Cassiopeia
Centaurus: the Centaur
Cepheus: Cepheus
Cetus: the Whale
Chamaeleon: the Chameleon
Circinus: the Compass
Columba: the Dove
Coma Berenices: Berenice's Hair
Corona Australis: the Southern Crown
Coronas Borealis: the Northern Crown
Corvus: the Crow/Raven

Crater: the Cup
Crux: the Cross
Cygnus: the Swan
Delphinus: the Dolphin
Dorado: the Goldfish/Swordfish
Draco: the Dragon
Equuleus: the Little Horse
Eridanus: the River
Eridanus Fornax: the Furnace
Gemini: the Twins
Grus: the Crane
Hercules
Horologium: the Clock
Hydra: the Sea Monster
Hydrus: the Sea Serpent
Indus: the Indian
Lacerta: the Lizard
Leo: the Lion
Leo Minor: the Little Lion
Lepus: the Hare
Libra: the Scales/Balance
Lupus: the Wolf
Lynx: the Lynx
Lyra: the Harp/Lyre
Mensa: the Table
Microscopium: the Microscope
Monoceros: the Unicorn
Musca: the Fly
Norma: the Rule
Octans: the Octant
Ophiuchus: the Serpent Bearer
Orion: the Hunter
Pavo: the Peacock
Pegasus: the Flying Horse
Perseus
Phoenix: the Firebird
Pictor: the Easel
Pisces: the Fishes
Piscis Austrinus: the Southern Fish
Puppis: the Ship's Stern or Poop Deck
Pyxis: the Ship's Compass
Reticulum: the Net
Sagitta: the Arrow
Sagittarius: the Archer
Scorpius: the Scorpion
Sculptor: the Sculptor
Scutum: the Shield
Serpens Caput: the Serpent
Sextans: the Sextant
Taurus: the Bull
Telescopium: the Telescope
Triangulum: the Triangle
Triangulum Australe: the Southern Triangle
Tucana: the Toucan
Ursa Major: the Great Bear
Ursa Minor: the Little Bear
Vela: the Sails
Virgo: the Virgin
Volans: the Flying Fish
Vulpecula: the Little Fox

Meteor Showers (and approx. peak date)

Quadrantids (January 4)
April Lyrids (April 22)
Eta Aquarids (May 5)
June Lyrids (June 16)
June Boötids (June 27)
South Delta Aquarids (July 27)
Perseids (August 12)
Draconids (October 8)
Orionids (October 22)
Taurids (November 4)
Leonids (November 17)
Geminids (December 14)
Ursids (December 23)

Rocks

Metamorphic

amphibolite
blueschist
eclogite
epidiorite
epidosite
gneiss
granulite
hornfels
lazurite
marble
mica schist
mylonite
phyllite
psammite
pyroxenite
quartzite
schist
serpentinite
slate
verdite

Sedimentary

arenite
argillite
breccia
chalk
chert
claystone
coal
conglomerate
diatomite
dolomite
flint
ironstone
limestone
marl
mudstone
oil shale
oolite
pholphorite
pisolite
radiolarite
rag
rudite
sandstone
shale
siltstone
tillite

Igneous

andesite
anorthosite
aplite
basalt
diorite
dolerite
dunite
elvan
felsite
gabbro
granite
greenstone
kimberlite
lamprophyre
lava
monzonite
obsidian
ophiolite
pegmatite
peridotite
phonolite
picrite
porphyry
pumice
rhyolite
syenite
tephrite
tonalite
trachyte
trap rock
tuff
variolite
vitrophyre

Snow Types and Conditions

blizzard
blowing snow
corn snow
drift
dusting
flurry/flurries
freezing rain
frozen granular snow
hard-packed snow
icy snow
lake effect
loose granular snow
machine-groomed snow
névé
packed powder
packing snow
powder
skiff
sleet
slush
snow devil
snow squall
snowstorm
soft-packed snow
wet granular snow
wet-packed snow
wet snow
whiteout
windblown snow

Language

Accents

acute (´)
breve (˘)
caron/háček (ˇ)
cedilla (¸)
circumflex (^)
dieresis/umlaut (¨)
grave (`)
macron (¯)
ogonek (˛)
tilde (˜)

Letters of Correspondence

acknowledgment letter
acceptance letter
air letter
billet-doux
bread-and-butter letter
business letter
chain letter
circular
cover letter
dead letter
Dear John letter
dunning letter
e-mail/email
fan letter
form letter
letter of credit
letter of intent
letter of introduction
letter of recommendation
letter of thanks
love letter
mash letter
memo
memorandum
newsletter
open letter
poison-pen letter
rejection letter
thank-you note

Poetic Forms, Meters, and Feet

alexandrine
anapest
aubade
ballad
ballade
blank verse
choriamb
choriambic
dactyl
dactylic
decasyllable
dimeter
dirge
disyllable
dithyramb
dramatic monologue
eclogue
elegy
encomium
epic
epigram
epithalamium
epode
epyllion
free verse
georgic
ghazal
haiku
heptameter
heroic
hexameter
iamb
iambic
idyll
lay
limerick
lyric
madrigal
monody
ode
pastoral
pentameter
Petrarchan sonnet
prothalamion
rondeau
roundel
roundelay
saga
sapphics
satire
sestina
sonnet
spondee
tanka
tetrameter
threnody
trimeter
triolet
trochaics
trochee
virelay

Rhetorical Devices

allusion
amplification
anacoluthon
anadiplosis
analogy
anaphora
antanagoge
anthimeria
antimetabole
antiphrasis
antithesis
apophasis
aporia
aposiopesis
apostrophe
appositive
assonance
asyndeton
catachresis
chiasmus
climax
conduplicatio
diacope
dirimens copulatio
distinctio
dystmesis
ellipsis
enthymeme
enumeratio
epanalepsis
epimone
epistrophe
epithet
epizeuxis
eponym
exemplum
expletive
hendiadys
hyperbaton
hyperbole
hypocorisma
hypophora
hypotaxis
hysteron proteron
kenning
litotes
malapropism
meiosis
meronym
metabasis
metanoia
metaphor
metonymy
onomatopoeia
oxymoron
paralipsis
parallelism
parataxis
parenthesis
paronomasia
personification
pleonasm
polysyndeton
procatalepsis
prosopopoeia
rhetorical question
scesis onomaton
sententia
simile
syllepsis
symploce
syncope
synecdoche
tmesis
trope
understatement
zeugma

Stories

adventure story
allegory
bedtime story
black comedy
cliffhanger
cock-and-bull story
comedy
conte
crime story
detective story
epic
exemplum
fable
farce
fairy tale
fantasy
fish story
folk tale
ghost story
gothic novel
historical novel
horror story
just-so story
legend
morality tale
mystery
myth
parable
romance
saga
shaggy-dog story
short story
tearjerker
thriller
tragedy
traveler's tale
true story
urban myth

Medicine

Physical Illnesses and Conditions

acid reflux disease
acne
ague
AIDS (acquired immune deficiency syndrome)
allergy
alopecia
altitude sickness
Alzheimer's disease
amyotrophic lateral sclerosis
anaphylaxis
anemia
angina
ankylosing spondylitis
ankylosis
anthrax
appendicitis
arc eye
arteriosclerosis
arthritis
asbestosis
asthma
ataxia
atherosclerosis
athlete's foot
avian flu
Bell's palsy
bends
beriberi
bilharzia
bird flu
blackwater fever
blastoma
blood poisoning
botulism
Bright's disease
Broca's aphasia
bronchitis
brucellosis
bubonic plague
Burkitt's lymphoma
bursitis
cachexia
cancer
carcinoma
cardiomyopathy
carditis
carpal tunnel syndrome (CTS)
cataract
celiac disease
cerebral palsy
chickenpox
cholera
chorea
chronic fatigue syndrome (CFS)
chronic obstructive pulmonary disease (COPD)
cirrhosis
colic
colitis
common cold
consumption
coronary heart disease
cowpox
Creutzfeldt–Jakob disease (CJD)
Crohn's disease
croup
crypto-sporidiosis
cyanosis
cystic fibrosis (CF)
cystitis
decompression sickness
deep-vein thrombosis (DVT)
dengue
dermatitis
dermatosis
diabetes
diabetes mellitus
diarrhea
diphtheria
diverticular disease
double pneumonia
Down syndrome
Duchenne muscular dystrophy (DMD)
Dupuytren's contracture
dysentery
Ebola fever
eclampsia
economy-class syndrome
eczema
edema
elephantiasis
emphysema
encephalitis
endocarditis
endometriosis
endometritis
enteritis
epilepsy
Epstein-Barr virus (EBV)
equine encephalitis
ergotism
erysipelas
fetal alcohol syndrome
fever
fibrositis
filariasis
flu
flux
food poisoning
frozen shoulder
gangrene
gastric flu
gastritis
gastro-enteritis
German measles
gigantism
gingivitis
glandular fever
glaucoma
glue ear
glycemia
goiter
gonorrhea
gout
Graves' disease
Gulf War syndrome
Guillain–Barré syndrome
Hansen's disease
Hashimoto's disease
hay fever
heartburn
heat stroke
helminthiasis
hemophilia
hepatitis A/B/C
hepatoma
hernia
herpes
herpes simplex
hives
Hodgkin's disease
hookworm
Huntington's disease
hydrocephalus
hydrophobia
hypertension
hypoglycemia
hypothermia
hypoxia
impetigo
infantile paralysis
influenza
iritis
irritable bowel syndrome (IBS)
ischemia
jaundice
juvenile diabetes
Kaposi's sarcoma
ketosis
kwashiorkor
laryngitis
Lassa fever
lead poisoning
legionella
legionnaires' disease
leishmaniasis
leprosy
leptospirosis
leukemia
listeria
listeriosis
Lou Gehrig's disease
lupus
lupus vulgaris
Lyme disease
lymphoma
malaria
mastitis
measles
melanoma
meningitis
mercury poisoning
mesothelioma
methicillin-resistant *Staphylococcus aureus* (MRSA)
motor neuron disease
mountain sickness
multiple sclerosis (MS)
mumps
muscular dystrophy
myalgic encephalo-myelitis (ME)
myasthenia gravis
myocarditis
narcolepsy
necrotizing fasciitis
nephritis
neuropathy
new variant Creutzfeldt–Jakob disease (nvCJD)
non-Hodgkin's lymphoma
nonspecific urethritis
ophthalmia
orchitis
osteoarthritis
osteomyelitis
osteoporosis
otitis media
Paget's disease
pancreatitis
paratyphoid
Parkinson's disease
parotitis
pellagra
pelvic inflammatory disease
pericarditis
peritonitis
pernicious anemia
pertussis
phlebitis
pinkeye
plague
pleurisy
pleuro-pneumonia
pneumoconiosis
pneumo-cystitis carinii pneumonia (PCP)
pneumonia
poliomyelitis
porphyria
prickly heat
pruritus
psittacosis
psoriasis
puerperal fever
pulmonary fibrosis
pulmonary emphysema
pyemia
pyrexia
pyrosis
quinsy
rabies
radiation sickness
repetitive strain injury (RSI)
restless leg syndrome
retinitis
retinopathy
Reye's syndrome
rheumatic fever
rheumatism
rheumatoid arthritis
rhinitis
rickets
ringworm
Rocky Mountain spotted fever
roseola
rubella
St. Vitus's dance
salmonella
sarcoma
scabies
scarlet fever
schizophrenia
sciatica
scleritis
scleroderma
sclerosis
scrofula
scurvy
sepsis
septicemia
severe acute respiratory syndrome (SARS)
sexually trans-mitted disease (STD)
shingles
sick building syndrome (SBS)

sickle-cell anemia/disease
silicosis
sinusitis
sleeping sickness
smallpox
Spanish flu
spastic colon
spina bifida
spondylosis
strabismus
sudden infant death syndrome (SIDS)
sunstroke
Sydenham's chorea
synovitis
syphilis
Tay-Sachs disease
tendinitis
tenosynovitis
tetanus
thrombosis
thrush
tonsillitis
Tourette's syndrome
toxemia
toxic shock syndrome
toxocariasis
toxoplasmosis
trench foot
trichinosis
trypanosomiasis
tuberculosis (TB)
tularemia
typhoid
typhus
undulant fever
urethritis
urticaria
vaginismus
venereal disease (VD)
viremia
virus
vitiligo
Weil's disease
West Nile virus
whooping cough
yaws
yellow fever

Psychiatric Illnesses and Conditions

agoraphobia
amnesia
anorexia nervosa
anxiety disorder
Asperger's syndrome
attention deficit hyperactivity disorder (ADHD)
autism
bipolar disorder
body dysmorphic disorder
bulimia nervosa
catatonia
combat fatigue
de Clerambault's syndrome
delirium
delusion
dementia
depression
dissociative identity disorder
dysphoria
dysthymia
eating disorder
erotomania
false memory syndrome
gender dysphoria
gender identity disorder
hebephrenia
hyperactivity
hyperkinesis
hypomania
insomnia
kleptomania
Korsakoff's syndrome
manic depression
megalomania
multiple-personality disorder
Munchausen's syndrome
Munchausen's syndrome by proxy
narcissism
neurosis
obsessive–compulsive disorder (OCD)
panic disorder
paramnesia
paranoia
paraphilia
pica
postpartum depression
post-traumatic stress disorder (PTSD)
psychosis
schizo-affective disorder
schizophrenia
seasonal affective disorder (SAD)
shell shock

Doctors

allergist
anesthetist
cardiologist
chiropractor
clinician
consulting physician
dentist
dermatologist
endocrinologist
family doctor
gastro-enterologist
general practitioner
geriatrician
gynecologist
hematologist
immunologist
internist
naturopath
neonatologist
neurologist
neurosurgeon
obstetrician
oncologist
ophthalmologist
optometrist
orthodontist
orthopedist
osteopath
otolaryngologist
pathologist
pediatrician
plastic surgeon
podiatrist
proctologist
psychiatrist
radiologist
rheumatologist
surgeon
urologist

Forms of Medication

balsam
cachet
caplet
capsule
cream
drip
drops
enema
gargle
hypodermic
inhalant
injectable
intravenous
lotion
lozenge
nasal spray
nebulizer
ointment
pastille
pill
poultice
powder
rub
salve
suppository
tablet

Music

Types of Music See also **Types of Jazz**

a cappella
acid house
acid rock
alternative
barbershop
bluegrass
blues
calypso
chant
choral
country
country and western
dancehall
death metal
disco
easy listening
electronica
emo
flamenco
folk
funk
gangsta
gospel
Goth
grunge
hard rock
heavy metal
hip hop
industrial
jazz
jungle
klezmer
Latin/Latin American
Latino
mariachi
Motown
New Age
new country
new wave
opera
pop
progressive rock
punk
rap
reggae
rhythm and blues
rock
rockabilly
rock and roll
salsa
ska
soul
technofunk
thrash metal
trance
trip hop
world music
zydeco

Types of Jazz

acid
Afro-Cuban
avant-garde
barrelhouse
bebop
big band
boogie-woogie
bop
cool
Dixieland
electronic
free
fusion
gutbucket
gypsy
hard bop
harmolodics
hot
jive
mainstream
manouche
modal
modern
New Orleans
nu
progressive
ragtime
stomp
swing

Musical Directions

a cappella (unaccompanied)
accelerando/accel. (accelerating)
adagio (slowly)
ad libitum/ad lib. (at will)
al fine (to the end)
allargando (broadening)
allegretto (fairly lively)
allegro (lively)
al segno (as far as the sign)
andante (moderately slow)
andantino (slightly faster than andante)
arco (with the bow)
assai (very)
a tempo (in the original tempo)
bis (repeat)
con brio (with vigor)
con moto (with movement)
crescendo/cresc. (becoming louder)
da capo/DC (from the beginning)
dal segno/DS (from the sign)
decrescendo/decresc. (becoming quieter)
diminuendo/dim. (becoming quieter)
dolce (sweetly)
fine (end)
forte/f (loudly)
forte piano (loudly then immediately softly)
fortissimo/ff (very loudly)
glissando (sliding)
larghetto (fairly slowly)
largo (very slowly)
legato (tied/smoothly)
lento (slowly)
maestoso (majestically)
marcato/marc. (accented)
meno (less)
meno mosso (less quickly)
mezzo (half)
mezzo forte/mf (fairly loudly)
mezzo piano/mp (fairly softly)
moderato (at a moderate pace)
molto (very)
mosso (fast and with animation)
moto (motion)
non troppo (not too much)
obbligato (not to be omitted)
ped. (pedal)
pianissimo/pp (very softly)
piano/p (softly)
più (more)
pizzicato/pizz. (plucked)
poco (a little)
rallentando/rall. (slowing down)
ritardando/rit. (slowing down)
ritenuto (suddenly more slowly)
scherzando (playfully)
segno (sign)
sempre (always/throughout)
sforzando/sf/sfz (strongly accented)
smorzando (dying away)
sordino (with a mute)
sostenuto/sost. (sustained)
sotto voce (in an undertone)
staccato/stacc. (detached)
tacet (voice/instrument remains silent)
tenuto/ten. (held)
troppo (too much)
tutti (all players/singers)
vivace (lively)

Brass Instruments

althorn
baritone
bugle
cornet
euphonium
flugelhorn
French horn
helicon
horn
mellophone
sackbut
saxhorn
serpent
slide trombone
sousaphone
trombone
trumpet
tuba
Wagner tuba

Keyboard Instruments

baby grand
calliope
carillon
celesta/celeste
clavichord
clavier
fortepiano
grand piano
harmonium
harpsichord
melodeon
organ
piano
pianoforte
pianola
pipe organ
player piano
spinet
synthesizer
virginals

Percussion Instruments

anvil
bass drum
bells
bongo (drum)
chimes
conga drum
crescent
cymbals/crash cymbals
drums
glockenspiel
gong
kettledrum
maracas
marimba
snare drum
steel drum
tambourine
timpani
traps
triangle
vibraharp
vibraphone
xylophone

Stringed Instruments

acoustic guitar
aeolian harp
balalaika
bandura
banjo
bass guitar
bass viol
bouzouki
cello
Celtic harp
cimbalom
cittern
classical guitar
contrabass
double bass
dulcimer
fiddle
gittern
guitar
harp
hurdy-gurdy
kora
koto
electric guitar
lute
lyre
mandolin
rebec
samisen
sarangi

sarod
sitar
string bass
tamboura
theorbo
trigon
twelve-string guitar
ukulele
veena
viol
viola
viola d'amore
viola da braccio
viola da gamba
violin
violoncello
Welsh harp
zither

Wind Instruments

alto saxophone
bagpipes
bass clarinet
basset horn
bassoon
clarinet
cor anglais
didgeridoo
English horn/cor anglais
flute
harmonica
kazoo
oboe
ocarina
panpipes
pennywhistle
piccolo
recorder
soprano saxophone
tenor saxophone
tin whistle

Orchestral Instruments

bass clarinet
bass drum
bassoon
celesta/celeste
cello
chimes
clarinet
contrabassoon
cymbals/crash cymbals
double bass
English horn/cor anglais
flute
French horn
glockenspiel
gong
harp
kettledrum
oboe
piano
piccolo
snare drum
string bass
tam-tam
tambourine
timpani
triangle
trombone
trumpet
tuba/bass tuba
tubular bells
viola
violoncello
violin
xylophone

Plants

Flowering Plants and Shrubs

Aaron's rod
abelia
acacia
acanthus
aconite
adder's tongue
African daisy
African violet
agapanthus
agave
agrimony
aloe
alstroemeria
alyssum
amaranth
amaryllis
anemone
angelica
angel's trumpet
aquilegia
arabis
arnica
arrowgrass
arrowhead
arum lily
asphodel
aspidistra
aster
astilbe
astrantia
aubretia
avens
azalea
baby's breath
bachelor's buttons
balsam
baneberry
banksia
barberry
bearberry
bedstraw
bee balm
begonia
belladonna
bellflower
bells of Ireland
bergamot
betony
bilberry
bindweed
bird of paradise
bird's-foot trefoil
black-eyed Susan
blackthorn
bladderwort
blazing star
bloodroot
bleeding heart
bluebell
bluebonnet
blue flag
bluet
bog asphodel
bog rosemary
boneset
borage
bougainvillea
bramble
broom
bryony
buckeye
buddleia
bugbane
bugle
bugleweed
bugloss
bullhead lily
bulrush
burdock
burnet
butter-and-eggs
buttercup
butterfly bush
butterfly weed
butterwort
cabbage rose
cactus
calceolaria
calendula
camellia
campanula
campion
candytuft
canna lily
Canterbury bell
Cape primrose
cardinal flower
carnation
catnip
cattail
cattleya
ceanothus
celandine
celosia
centaury
chamomile
checkerberry
chervil
chickweed
chicory
chinaberry
Chinese lantern
chives
choisya
chokeberry
cholla
Christmas cactus
Christmas rose
chrysanthemum
cicely
cinchona
cinquefoil
clarkia
clematis
cleome
cloudberry
clove pink
clover
cockscomb
coltsfoot
columbine
comfrey
coneflower
convolvulus
coreopsis
cornflower
corydalis
cosmos
cotoneaster
cow parsley
cow parsnip
cowslip
cranesbill
crocus
crowberry
crowfoot
crown vetch
cuckoopint
cuckooflower
cyclamen
daffodil
dahlia
daisy
damask rose
dame's rocket
dandelion
daphne
daylily
deadly nightshade
delphinium
Devil's paintbrush
dewdrop
dianthus
dill
dittany
dock
dogbane
dog rose
dog violet
duckweed
Dutchman's breeches
echinacea
edelweiss
eglantine
elder
evening primrose
eyebright
feverfew
figwort
flax
fleabane
fool's parsley
forget-me-not
forsythia
four-o'clock
foxglove
frangipani
fraxinella
freesia
fritillary
fuchsia
furze
gaillardia
gardenia
gazania
gentian
geranium
gerbera
germander
gill-over-the-ground
gillyflower
ginseng
gladiolus
globeflower
glory-of-the-snow
gloxinia

goat's beard
goldenrod
golden glow
gomphrena
gorse
grape hyacinth
grass of Parnassus
groundsel
guelder rose
gypsophila
harebell
hawkbit
hawksbeard
hawkweed
hawthorn
heartsease
heather
helianthemum
helianthus
heliotrope
hellebore
helleborine
hemlock
henbit
hepatica
heuchera
hibiscus
hogweed
holly
hollyhock
honesty
honeysuckle
hop
hosta
hyacinth
hydrangea
hyssop
ice plant
impatiens
Indian paintbrush
Indian pipe
indigo
iris
jacaranda
jack-in-the-pulpit
Jacob's ladder
japonica
jasmine
Jerusalem artichoke
jessamine
jewelweed
jimsonweed
Joe Pye weed
Johnny jump up
jonquil
juneberry
kalanchoe
kale
kalmia
kerria
kingcup
knapweed
knotgrass
Labrador tea
laburnum
lady's mantle
lady's slipper
larkspur
lavatera
lavender
lemon balm
leopard lily
lilac
lily
lily of the valley
lobelia
loosestrife
lords and ladies
lotus
lovage
love-in-a-mist
love-lies-bleeding
lungwort
lupine
lychnis
madder
madonna lily
magnolia
mahonia
mallow
Maltese cross
mandrake
marguerite
marigold
marsh marigold
marshwort
May apple
mayflower
mayweed
meadow rue
meadow saffron
meadowsweet
Michaelmas daisy
mignonette
milfoil
milkweed
milkwort
mimosa
mint
mistletoe
mock orange
money plant
monkey flower
monkshood
montbretia
moonflower
morning glory
moss pink
motherwort
mullein
musk rose
myrtle
narcissus
nasturtium
nemesia
nettle
nicotiana
nigella
night-scented stock
nightshade
old man's beard
oleander
orchid
orchis
ox-eye daisy
oxlip
oyster plant
pansy
Parma violet
parsley
partidgeberry
pasqueflower
passion flower
pelargonium
pennyroyal
penstemon
peony
peppermint
periwinkle
petunia
peyote
phacelia
phlox
pickerelweed
pimpernel
pinesap
pink
pitcher plant
plantain
plumbago
poinsettia
pokeweed
polyanthus
poppy
portulaca
potentilla
prickly pear
prickly poppy
primrose
primula
privet
pulsatilla
purslane
pussytoes
pyracantha
pyrethrum
Queen Anne's lace
ragweed
ragwort
rampion
ramsons
rape
red-hot poker
rhododendron
rock rose
rose
rosebay willowherb
rose mallow
rose of Sharon
rudbeckia
safflower
saguaro
St. John's wort
salpiglossis
salvia
samphire
sandwort
sarsaparilla
saxifrage
scabious
scarlet pimpernel
scilla
sea lavender
sedum
sego lily
shamrock
shasta daisy
shepherd's purse
skullcap
skunk cabbage
snapdragon
snowdrop
snowflake
soapwort
Solomon's seal
sorrel
sowthistle
speedwell
spider flower
spider plant
spiderwort
spikenard
spiraea
spurge
spurrey
squill
star of Bethlehem
starwort
statice
stitchwort
stock
stonecrop
storksbill
strawflower
streptocarpus
sundew
sunflower
sweetbrier
sweet cicely
sweet pea
sweet rocket
sweet william
syringa
tansy
tea rose
teasel
thistle
thorn apple
thrift
tickseed
tiger lily
tithonia
toadflax
torenia
tormentil
touch-me-not
tradescantia
trailing arbutus
traveler's joy
trefoil
trillium
trout lily
trumpet creeper
tuberose
tulip
valerian
Venus flytrap
verbena
veronica
vervain
vetch
viburnum
viola
violet
viper's bugloss
wakerobin
wallflower
water lily
willow herb
windflower
winter jasmine
wintergreen
wisteria
witch hazel
wolfsbane
wood anemone
wood avens
woodruff
wood sorrel
woody nightshade
wormwood
yarrow
yerba buena
yucca
zinnia

Trees and Shrubs

acacia
acer
akee
alder
allspice
almond
angelica
anise
annatto
apple
apricot
araucaria
arbor vitae
ash
aspen
avocado
azalea
bald cypress
balm of Gilead
balsa
balsam fir
bamboo
banksia
banyan
baobab
basswood
bayberry
bay tree
bearberry
beech
bergamot
bilberry
birch
blackthorn
bluegum
bodhi tree
bottlebrush
bottle tree
bo tree
box
box elder
breadfruit
bristlecone pine
broom
buckeye
buckthorn
bullace
bur oak
burning bush
butternut
buttonbush
cacao
calabash
camellia
camphor tree
candelabra tree
candleberry
candlenut
carambola
carob
cashew
cassava
cassia
catalpa
catawba
cedar

cherimoya
cherry
cherry plum
chestnut
chinaberry
chinquapin (oak)
chokeberry
chokecherry
cinnamon
citron
clove
coco de mer
coconut palm
coffee
cola
copper beech
coral tree
cork oak
cottonwood
crab apple
cranberry
crowberry
currant
curry leaf
custard apple
cypress
damson
dewberry
dogwood
Douglas fir
dragon tree
ebony
elder
elderberry
elm
eucalyptus
euonymus
false acacia
ficus
fig
filbert
fir
firethorn
flame tree
frangipani
Fraser fir
fuchsia
gallberry
ginkgo
gooseberry
gorse
grapefruit
greenbrier
greengage
guaiacum
guava
guelder rose
gum tree
hackberry
haw
hawthorn
hazel
hemlock
hickory
holly
holly oak
holm oak
honey locust
honeysuckle
hoptree
hornbeam
horse chestnut
huckleberry
hydrangea
ilex
inkberry
ironbark
ironwood
jacaranda
jackfruit
jack pine
japonica
jasmine
jojoba
Joshua tree
jujube
juneberry
juniper
kalmia
kapok
kermes oak
kola
kumquat
laburnum
lacquer tree
larch
laurel
lemon
lilac
lime
linden
liquidambar
live oak
locust
lodgepole pine
logwood
Lombardy poplar
loquat
lychee
macadamia
macrocarpa
magnolia
mahogany
maidenhair tree
mandarin
mango
mangosteen
mangrove
maple
mastic
maté
mimosa
mock orange
mockernut
monkey puzzle
mossy cup (oak)
mountain ash
mountain laurel
mulberry
myrtle
nectarine
Norway spruce
nutmeg
nux vomica
oak
oleaster
olive
Osage orange
osier
pagoda tree
palm
palmetto
palmyra
papaya
paper mulberry
paperbark
pawpaw
peach
pear
pecan
pedunculate oak
persimmon
pignut
pine
pin oak
pinyon
pipsissewa
pistachio
pitch pine
plane
plum
pomegranate
pomelo
ponderosa pine
poplar
privet
pussy willow
quassia
quince
rain tree
redbud
red cedar
redwood
rhododendron
robinia
rose of sharon
rosewood
rowan
royal palm
rubber plant
rubber tree
sallow
sandalwood
sapele
sapodilla
sassafras
satinwood
Scotch pine
sequoia
serviceberry
service tree
shadblow
shadbush
shagbark hickory
silverberry
silver birch
Sitka spruce
slippery elm
smoke tree
snowball bush
snowberry
soapberry
sourgum
sourwood
spicebush
spindle
spirea
spruce
star anise
stinkwood
stone pine
storax
sugar maple
sumac
sweet gum
sycamore
syringa
tallow tree
tamarack
tamarind
tamarisk
tangerine
tea
teaberry
teak
tea tree
thuja
tree of heaven
trumpet creeper
tulip tree
tulipwood
tupelo
umbrella tree
viburnum
walnut
wattle
weeping willow
wellingtonia
whitebeam
willow
wisteria
witch hazel
wych elm
yew
ylang-ylang
yucca

Flower Parts

androecium
anther
bract
calyx
capitulum
carpel
catkin
corolla
corymb
cyme
filament
floret
glume
gynoecium
involucre
nectary
ovary
ovule
palea
panicle
pedicel
peduncle
perianth
petal
placenta
pollen
rachis
receptacle
sepal
spadix
spathe
spike
spikelet
spur
stamen
stigma
style
tassel
tepal
torus
umbel
whorl

Religion and Mythology

Books of the Bible

Old Testament

Genesis
Exodus
Leviticus
Numbers
Deuteronomy
Joshua
Judges
Ruth
1 Samuel
2 Samuel
1 Kings
2 Kings
1 Chronicles
2 Chronicles
Ezra
Nehemiah
Esther
Job
Psalms
Proverbs
Ecclesiastes
Song of Solomon/ Song of Songs
Isaiah
Jeremiah
Lamentations
Ezekiel
Daniel
Hosea
Joel
Amos
Obadiah

Jonah
Micah
Nahum
Habakkuk
Zephaniah
Haggai
Zechariah
Malachi

Apocrypha

1 Esdras
2 Esdras
Tobit
Judith
Wisdom of Solomon
Ecclesiasticus/Sirach
Baruch
Letter of Jeremiah
Susanna
Bel and the Dragon
Prayer of Manasses
1 Maccabees
2 Maccabees
3 Maccabees

New Testament

Matthew
Mark
Luke
John
Acts of the Apostles
Romans
1 Corinthians
2 Corinthians
Galatians
Ephesians
Philippians
Colossians
1 Thessalonians
2 Thessalonians
1 Timothy
2 Timothy
Titus
Philemon
Hebrews
James
1 Peter
2 Peter
1 John
2 John
3 John
Jude
Revelation

Gods and Goddesses

Egyptian

Amun/Ammon
Anubis
Apis
Bastet
Bes
Hathor
Horus
Isis
Khonsu
Maat
Mut
Nut
Osiris
Ptah
Ra
Sekhmet
Seth
Thoth

Greek

Aeolus
Amphitrite
Aphrodite
Apollo (Phoebus)
Ares
Artemis
Asclepius
Athena
Cronus
Demeter
Dionysus
Eos
Eros
Gaia
Hebe
Hecate
Helios
Hephaestus
Hera
Hermes
Hestia
Hygeia
Hymen
Hypnos
Iris
Momus
Nemesis
Nereus
Oceanus
Orpheus
Pan
Paris
Persephone
Phaethon
Philemon
Pluto
Poseidon
Priapus
Proteus
Selene
Serapis
Tartarus
Tethys
Themis
Tyche
Uranus
Victory
Zeus

Indian/Hindu/Vedic

Agni
Brahma
Ganesha
Ganga
Hanuman
Indra
Kali
Krishna
Kubera
Lakshmi
Parvati
Ram
Saraswati
Shiva
Soma
Surya
Varuna
Vayu
Vishnu
Yama

Mesoamerican

Chalchiuhtlicue
Coatlicue
Huitzilopochtli
Hunab Ku
Huracán
Itzamna
Kukulkán
Mictlantecuhtli
Quetzalcóatl
Teotihuacan
Tezcatlipoca

Middle Eastern

Anshar
Anu
Apsu
Aruru
Assur
Astarte
Baal
Dagan
Ea
Ellil
Ishtar
Ishum
Lahmu
Marduk
Moloch
Mummu
Nanaja
Nergal
Ningal
Ninmah
Ninurta
Nissaba
Qingu
Shamash
Sin
Tammuz
Tiamat

Roman

Aesculapius
Aurora
Bellona
Ceres
Cupid
Diana
Faunus
Flora
Fortuna
Juno
Jupiter
Luna
Maia
Mars
Mercury
Minerva
Mithras
Morpheus
Neptune
Orcus
Saturn
Venus
Vesta
Vulcan

Scandinavian

Aegir
the Aesir
Asgard
Aurvandil
Balder
Bil
Bragi
Eastre/Ostara
Forseti
Frey
Freya
Frigga
Fulla
Gefjon
Heimdall
Hel
Hermod
Hodur
Idun
Loki
Nanna
Niord
the Norns
Odin
Ran
Sif
Skadi
Thor
Tyr
Ull
Vali
the Valkyries
the Vanir
Vidar
the Waves
Ymir

The Nine Muses

Calliope (epic poetry)
Clio (history)
Erato (lyric and love poetry)
Euterpe (music)
Melpomene (tragedy)
Polyhymnia (sacred song and oratory)
Terpsichore (dance and choral song)
Thalia (comedy)
Urania (astronomy)

Spirits and Sprites

angel
apparition
banshee
brownie
cacodemon
daemon/daimon
demon
deva
devil
djinn
dryad
dybbuk
earth mother
eidolon
elf
erlking
eudemon
fairy
familiar spirit
fiend
fay
genie
ghost
ghoul
gnome
goblin
hamadryad
hobgoblin
imp
incubus
jinn/jinni
kachina
kelpie
kobold
leprechaun
manes
manitou
naiad
nature spirit
Nereid
nixie
numen
nymph
oread
phantom
pixie
poltergeist
puca

puck
sea nymph
shade
sidh
specter
succubus
sylph
sylvan
undine
water sprite
wraith

Mythological and Fictional Creatures

abominable snowman
Argus
basilisk
behemoth
Bigfoot
bogie
Cadborosaurus (Caddy)
Cerberus
centaur
Chimera
chupacabra
cockatrice
Cthulhu
Cyclops
devil
dragon
erl-king
Frankenstein
Gorgon
Grendel
griffin
harpy
hippogriff
hobbit
Hydra
kraken
leviathan
Lilith
Loch Ness Monster
loup-garou
lycanthrope
manticore
mermaid
merman
Minotaur
Nessie
Ogopogo
ogre
ogress
orc
Pegasus
phoenix
Sasquatch
satyr
Scylla
sea serpent
sea snake
shape-shifter
siren
Sphinx
thunderbird
Tiamat
troll
Typhon
unicorn
urchin
vampire
werewolf
windigo
witch
yeti

Society

Parties and Social Events

anniversary party
baby shower
bachelor party
ball
banquet
barbecue
barn dance
beach party
beer bash/blast/bust
birthday party
black-tie affair
block party
box social
bridal shower
clambake
class reunion
cocktail party
coffee klatch
cookout
costume party
dance
dance party
dinner party
dinner dance
family reunion
fête champêtre
formal garden party
graduation party
hoedown
holiday party
hootenanny
hop
house party
housewarming
jamboree
jubilee
keg party
lawn party
luau
masquerade (party)
mixer
office party
pajama party
party
patio party
picnic
potluck party
progressive dinner
prom
reception
reunion
roast
semiformal
shower
sleepover
slumber party
social
stag party
Super Bowl party
surprise party
tailgate party
tea party
Tupperware™ party
wedding shower
white-tie affair
wine tasting

Restaurants

auberge
automat
bakery
bar
bar & grill
barbecue
bistro
brasserie
buffet
café
cafeteria
charcuterie
cantina
chophouse
churrascaria
coffee shop
coffeehouse
delicatessen
diner
enoteca
fast food restaurant
gin joint
greasy spoon
lunch counter
luncheonette
malt shop
noodle shop
osteria
oyster bar
paninoteca
patisserie
pizzeria
pub
public house
rathskeller
raw bar
relais
sandwich shop
shabu-shabu
sidewalk café
smorgasbord
snack bar
steakhouse
supper club
sushi bar
sweet shop
tapas bar
taqueria
tavern
tea room
trattoria

Rulers

aga
caesar
caliph
czar
czarina
emir
emperor
empress
kaiser
king
khan
maharajah
mikado
monarch
negus
pharaoh
prince
princess
queen
raja
rani
regent
satrap
shah
sheikh
shogun
sovereign
sultan
tsar
tsarine
viceroy

Schools

academy
Bible school
boarding school
charm school
charter school
cheder
choir school
church school
college
community college
conservatory
convent school
correspondence school
day school
divinity school
elementary school
finishing school
grade school
graduate school
grammar school
high school
juku
junior college

junior high school
kindergarten
law school
library school
lycée
magnet school
middle school
Montessori school
night school
nursery school
parochial school
preparatory school
prep school
preschool
private school
public school
reform school
residential school
secondary school
seminary
senior high school
summer school
Sunday school
teachers' college
technical school
university
vocational school
yeshiva

Sports

acrobatics
aerobatics
aerobics
angling
aquaplaning
archery
badminton
ballooning
base-jumping
BMX
bocce
boxing
bullfighting
bungee jumping
caber tossing
canoeing
canyoning
caving
clay-pigeon shooting
climbing
crew
cross-country running
cycle racing
cycling
darts
deep-sea fishing
dinghy racing
diving
eventing
falconry
fencing
fishing
fly-fishing
fowling
freestyling
game fishing
gliding
greyhound racing
gymkhana
gymnastics
hang-gliding
harness racing
hiking
hockey
horse racing
hot-air ballooning
jet-skiing
kayaking
kiteboarding
kitesurfing
motocross
mountain biking
mountaineering
MX
orienteering
parachuting
paragliding
parapenting
parasailing
parascending
pigeon racing
pistol shooting
powerboat racing
quoits
rafting
riverboarding
rock climbing
rollerskating
rollerblading
rowing
sailing
scuba-diving
sculling
shooting
showjumping
skateboarding
skeet (shooting)
skin-diving
skydiving
snorkeling
spelunking
sprinting
steeplechasing
surfing
swimming
synchronized swimming
track and field
trapshooting
trotting
wakeboarding
walking
waterskiing
weightlifting
whitewater rafting
windsurfing
wrestling
yachting

Ball Games

Association football
Australian Rules football
bandy
baseball
basketball
beach volleyball
billiards
bocce
boule/boules
bowling
bowls
Canadian football
carpetball
court tennis
cricket
croquet
dodgeball
duckpin bowling
field hockey
flag football
foosball™
football
four square
Gaelic football
golf
handball
hockey
hurling
jai alai
kickball
lacrosse
lawn bowling
lawn tennis
miniature golf
netball
ninepins
paddleball
pelota
pétanque
Ping-Pong™
polo
pool
rackets
racquetball
rounders
rugby
rugby league
rugby union
sandlot ball/ baseball
Skee-Ball™
shinty
skittles
snooker
soccer
softball
SPUD
squash
table tennis
tenpin bowling
volleyball
water polo

Gymnastic Events

asymmetric bars
balance beam
balls
clubs
floor exercise
high bar
hoops
horizontal bar
parallel bars
pommel horse
power tumbling
rhythmic (gymnastics)
ribbons
rings
ropes
sports aerobics
teamgym
trampoline
tumbling
uneven bars
vault

Swimming Strokes and Kicks

Australian crawl
backstroke
breaststroke
butterfly (stroke)
crawl
dog paddle
elementary backstroke
freestyle
sidestroke
flutter kick
frog kick
scissor kick
whip kick

Tennis Terms

ace
advantage
alley
backcourt
backhand
ball boy
ball girl
baseline
break
break point
chop
clay court
court
cross-court
deuce
double fault
doubles
drop shot
fault
foot-fault
forecourt
forehand
game
game point
grand slam
grass court
groundstroke
half court
half-volley
let
match point
mixed doubles
net
overhand
passing shot
rally

serve
service break
set
set point
slice
smash
topspin
volley

Track and Field Events

biathlon
cross-country run
decathlon
discus throw
hammer throw
heptathlon
high jump
hurdles
javelin throw
long jump
marathon
modern pentathlon
pole vault
relay
shot put
steeplechase
triathlon
triple jump
walk

Winter Sports

alpine skiing
biathlon
bobsled
cross-country skiing
curling
dogsled racing
downhill skiing
figure skating
free skating
freestyle skiing
giant slalom
heli-skiing
hockey
ice dancing
ice hockey
ice skating
luge
moguls
Nordic combined
skating
skeleton
skiing
skijoring
ski jumping
slalom
snowboarding
speed skating
super-G
tobogganing

Technology

Energy and Fuels

acetylene
agrofuel
anthracite
atomic power
biodiesel
biofuel
biogas
briquette
butane
chemical energy
coal
coal gas
coke
diesel
electricity
electromagnetic energy
firewood
fossil fuel
fuel oil
fusion energy
gas
gasoline
geothermal energy
heat
hydroelectric power
hydrogen
kerosene
leaded gas/gasoline
light
lignite
methane
natural gas
nuclear power
oil
peat
petroleum
propane
renewable energy
solar energy
steam power
tidal power
turf
unleaded petrol
water power
wave power
wind power
wood

Engines

aircraft engine
beam engine
diesel engine
donkey engine
dynamo
electric motor
external-combustion engine
flat-four engine
four-stroke
gas/gasoline engine
gas turbine
generator
heat engine
inboard motor
inline engine
internal-combustion engine
jet engine
linear motor
liquid air cycle engine (LACE)
magneto
oil engine
outboard motor
piston engine
prop jet
pulse detonation engine (PDE)
pulse jet
radial engine
ramjet
rocket engine
rotary engine
scramjet
stationary engine
steam engine
steam turbine
straight-eight
transverse engine
thruster
turbine
turbo diesel
turbofan
turbojet
turboprop
turboshaft
twin-cam engine
two-stroke
V6
V8
V12
Wankel engine

Kitchen Appliances

blender
breadmaker
can opener
cappuccino maker/machine
coffee grinder
coffee maker
coffee pot
convection oven
Crockpot™
deep fryer
dishwasher
double boiler
egg cooker
electric knife
espresso maker/machine
fondue pot
food dehydrator
food processor
freezer
garbage disposal
griddle
hot plate
ice cream maker/freezer
ice maker/machine
juicer
meat slicer
microwave (oven)
mixer
Mixmaster™
pasta maker/machine
percolator
pressure cooker
quesadilla maker
range
refrigerator
rice cooker
slow cooker
steamer
stove
toaster
toaster oven
trash compactor
vacuum sealer
waffle iron
warming tray

Kitchen Tools and Gadgets

baster
butter mold
candy thermometer
can opener
colander
cookie cutter
cookie press
cookie stamp
corer
dicer
egg beater
egg timer
garlic press
grater
jar opener
knife sharpener
mandoline/mandolin
meat tenderizer
meat thermometer
melon baller
pastry blender
peeler
pepper mill/grinder
potato masher
poultry shears
ricer
rolling pin
salad spinner
salt mill/grinder
scale
spatula
strainer
tongs
trivet
turkey baster
whisk
zester

Metals and Alloys

aluminum
antimony
brass
bronze
cast iron
chrome steel
chromium
copper
cupronickel
gold
gunmetal
iron
iridium
lead
magnesium
mercury
nickel
pewter
platinum
silver
solder
stainless steel
steel
tin
titanium
tungsten
uranium
white gold
zinc

Transportation

Boats and Ships

airboat
aircraft carrier
barge
bark/barque
barkentine
bateau
battle cruiser
battleship
bidarka
Boston whaler
brig
brigantine
bulk carrier
bullboat
cabin cruiser
caique
canal boat
canoe
capital ship
caravel
cargo ship
carrack
catamaran
catboat
cigarette boat
clipper
coal ship
cockboat
container ship
coracle
corvette
cruise ship
cruiser
cutter
destroyer
dhow
dinghy
dory
dreadnought
factory ship
felucca
ferry
fishing boat
flatboat
freighter
frigate
galleon
galley
gig
gondola
houseboat
hoy
hydrofoil
hydroplane
iceboat
icebreaker
jet boat
johnboat
jolly
junk
kayak
keelboat
ketch
knockabout
laker
lateen
launch
lifeboat
liner
longboat
merchant ship
motorboat
motorsailer
oil tanker
outboard
outrigger
packet (boat)
paddleboat
passenger ship
pedal boat
pirate ship
pontoon
prahu
pram
punt
riverboat
rowboat
sailboat
sampan
schooner
scow
scull
shell
skiff
skipjack
sloop
smack
steamboat
steamship
sternwheeler
supertanker
tall ship
tanker
tartan
torpedo boat
towboat
trawler
trimaran
tugboat
umiak
water bus
whaleboat
whaler
wherry
windjammer
xebec
yacht
yawl

Cars

buggy
cloth-top
compact
convertible
coupe
cruiser
dragster
electric
four-by-four/4x4
four-door
gas-electric
GTi
hardtop
hatchback
hearse
hot rod
hybrid
jeep
limo/limousine
low-rider
minicar
minivan
off-road vehicle/ORV
patrol car
race car
racing car
ragtop
roadster
runabout
sedan
soft-top
sports car
sport utility vehicle/SUV
station wagon
stretch limo
stock car
subcompact
taxi/taxicab
two-door

Horse-Drawn Carriages, Carts, and Wagons

barouche
brougham
buckboard
buggy
cab
cabriolet
calèche
cariole
carryall
chaise
chariot
chuckwagon
clarence
coach
Conestoga wagon
coupe
covered wagon
curricle
democrat wagon
dogcart
dray
droshky
fiacre
fly
four-in-hand
gig
hackney (carriage)
hansom (cab)
landau
phaeton
post-chaise
stagecoach
stanhope
sulky
surrey
tilbury
trap
troika
victoria
wagonette

Bridges

bascule bridge
cantilever bridge
catwalk
covered bridge
drawbridge
floating bridge
footbridge
lift bridge
pontoon bridge
skew bridge
skybridge
skywalk
suspension bridge
swing bridge
toll bridge
trestle bridge
vertical lift bridge
viaduct

Roads

access road
avenue
back road
beltway
boulevard
broadway
bush road
bylane
bypass
byroad
byway
causeway
circle
cloverleaf
country road
crescent
cul-de-sac
dead-end street
dirt road
drag strip
drive
expressway
feeder road
freeway
frontage road
grid road
highway
interstate
lane
lovers' lane
one-way street
overpass
parkway
pass
post road
ring road
roadway
secondary road
service road
shunpike
side road
speedway
street
surface road
thoroughfare
thruway/throughway
toll road
tote road
trail
turnpike
underpass
walk
walkway

Ll

label ▶ noun 1 *the price is clearly stated on the label* **tag,** ticket, sticker, marker, tab.
2 *a designer label* **brand,** brand name, trade name, trademark, make, logo.
3 *the label the media came up with for me* **designation,** description, tag; name, epithet, nickname, title, sobriquet, pet name, cognomen; formal denomination, appellation.
▶ verb 1 *label each jar with the date* **tag,** put labels on, ticket, mark.
2 *tests labeled him an underachiever* **categorize,** classify, class, describe, designate, identify; mark, stamp, brand, condemn, pigeonhole, stereotype, typecast; call, name, term, dub, nickname.

labor ▶ noun 1 *manual labor* **work,** hard work, toil, exertion, industry, drudgery, effort, menial work; informal slog, grind, sweat, scut work; literary travail, moil.
ANTONYMS rest, leisure.
2 *management and labor need to cooperate* **workers,** employees, workmen, workforce, staff, working people, blue-collar workers, laborers, labor force, proletariat.
ANTONYMS management.
3 *the labors of Hercules* **task,** job, chore, mission, assignment.
4 *a difficult labor* **childbirth,** birth, delivery, nativity; contractions, labor pains; formal parturition; literary travail; dated confinement; archaic lying-in, accouchement, childbed.
▶ verb 1 *a project on which he had labored for many years* **work,** work hard, toil, slave (away), grind away, struggle, strive, exert oneself, work one's fingers to the bone, work like a dog, work like a Trojan; informal slog away, plug away; literary travail, moil.
2 *she labored to unite the party* **strive,** struggle, endeavor, work, try, work hard, try hard, make every effort, do one's best, do one's utmost, do all one can, give one's all, go all out, fight, put oneself out, apply oneself, exert oneself; informal bend/lean/fall over backwards, pull out all the stops, bust a gut, bust one's chops.
3 *there is no need to labor the point* **overemphasize,** belabor, overstress, overdo, strain, overplay, make too much of, exaggerate, dwell on, harp on.
4 *Rex was **laboring under** a misapprehension* **suffer from,** be a victim of, be deceived by, be misled by.

CHOOSE THE RIGHT WORD

labor, drudgery, grind, toil, travail, work

Most people have to **work** for a living, meaning that they have to exert themselves mentally or physically in return for a paycheck. But *work* is not always performed by humans (*a machine that works like a charm*). **Labor** is not only human but usually physical work (*the labor required to build a stone wall*), although it can also apply to intellectual work of unusual difficulty (*the labor involved in writing a symphony*). Anyone who has been forced to perform **drudgery** knows that it is the most unpleasant, uninspiring, and monotonous kind of labor (*a forklift that eliminates the drudgery of stacking boxes; the drudgery of compiling a phone book*). A **grind** is even more intense and unrelenting than drudgery, emphasizing work that is performed under pressure in a dehumanizing way (*the daily grind of classroom teaching*). **Toil** suggests labor that is prolonged and very tiring (*farmers who toil endlessly in the fields*), but not necessarily physical (*mothers who toil to teach their children manners*). Those who **travail** endure pain, anguish, or suffering (*his hours of travail ended in heartbreak*).

labored ▶ adjective 1 *labored breathing* **strained,** difficult, forced, laborious.
2 *his labored alibi only hurt his defense* **contrived,** strained, stilted, forced, stiff, unnatural, artificial, overdone, ponderous, overelaborate, laborious, unconvincing, overwrought.

laborer ▶ noun *auto-industry laborers* **workman,** worker, working man/woman, manual worker, unskilled worker, day laborer, blue-collar worker, hired hand, hand, peon, roustabout, drudge, menial; informal grunt; archaic mechanic, cottier.

laborious ▶ adjective 1 *a laborious job* **arduous,** hard, heavy, difficult, strenuous, grueling, punishing, exacting, tough, onerous, burdensome, back-breaking, labor-intensive, trying, challenging; tiring, fatiguing, exhausting, wearying, wearing, taxing, demanding, wearisome, tedious, boring, time-consuming; archaic toilsome. See note at HARD.
ANTONYMS easy.
2 *Doug's laborious writing style* **labored,** strained, forced, contrived, affected, stiff, stilted, unnatural, artificial, overwrought, heavy, ponderous, convoluted.
ANTONYMS natural, effortless.

labyrinth ▶ noun 1 *a labyrinth of little streets* **maze,** warren, network, complex, web, entanglement.

2 *the labyrinth of conflicting regulations* **tangle,** web, morass, jungle, confusion, entanglement, convolution; jumble, mishmash.

labyrinthine ▶ adjective 1 *labyrinthine corridors* **mazelike,** winding, twisting, serpentine, meandering, wandering, rambling.
2 *a labyrinthine system* **complicated,** intricate, complex, involved, tortuous, convoluted, involuted, tangled, elaborate; confusing, puzzling, mystifying, bewildering, baffling.

lace ▶ noun 1 *a dress trimmed with white lace* **openwork,** lacework, tatting; passementerie, needlepoint (lace), filet, bobbin lace, pillow lace, torchon lace, needle lace, point lace, Battenberg lace, Chantilly lace, Mechlin lace, Valenciennes.
2 *brown shoes with laces* **shoelace,** bootlace, shoestring, lacing, tie.
▶ verb 1 *he* ***laced up*** *his running shoes* **fasten,** do up, tie up, secure, knot.
ANTONYMS untie.
2 *he laced his fingers into mine* **entwine,** intertwine, twine, entangle, interweave, link; braid, plait.
3 *tea laced with rum* **flavor,** mix (in), blend, fortify, strengthen, stiffen, season, spice (up), enrich, liven up; doctor, adulterate; informal spike.
4 *her brown hair was laced with gray* **streak,** stripe, striate, line.
– PHRASES **lace into** informal 1 *Danny laced into him* See **BEAT SOMEONE UP**. 2 *the newspaper laced into the prime minister* See **CRITICIZE**.

lacerate ▶ verb *the nail has lacerated his left arm* **cut (open),** gash, slash, tear, rip, rend, shred; score, scratch, scrape, graze; wound, injure, hurt.

laceration ▶ noun *a bleeding laceration* **gash,** cut, wound, injury, tear, slash; scratch, scrape, abrasion, graze.

lachrymose ▶ adjective See **TEARFUL** (sense 1).

lack ▶ noun *a lack of cash* **absence,** want, need, deficiency, dearth, insufficiency, shortage, shortfall, scarcity, paucity, unavailability, deficit.
ANTONYMS abundance.
▶ verb *they lack sufficient resources* **be without,** be in need of, need, be lacking, require, want, be short of, be deficient in, be bereft of, be low on, be pressed for, have insufficient; informal be strapped for.
ANTONYMS have, possess.

CHOOSE THE RIGHT WORD

lack, absence, dearth, privation, shortage, want

To suffer from a **lack** of food means to be partially or totally without it; to be in **want** of food also implies a lack, but with an emphasis on the essential or desirable nature of what is lacking; for example, you may experience a complete *lack* of pain following surgery, but you would be in *want* of medication if pain were suddenly to occur. **Absence**, on the other hand, refers to the complete nonexistence of something or someone. A *lack* of dairy products in your diet implies that you're not getting enough; an *absence* of dairy products implies that you're not getting any at all. If the scarcity or lack of something makes it costly, or if something is in distressingly low supply, the correct word is **dearth** (*a dearth of water in the desert; a dearth of nylon stockings during World War II*). A **shortage** of something is a partial insufficiency of an established, required, or accustomed amount (*a shortage of fresh oranges after the late-season frost*), while **privation** is the negative state or absence of a corresponding positive (*they suffered from hunger, cold, and other privations*).

lackadaisical ▶ adjective *I was lackadaisical about my training* **lethargic,** apathetic, listless, sluggish, spiritless, passionless; careless, lazy, lax, unenthusiastic, halfhearted, lukewarm, indifferent, unconcerned, casual, offhand, blasé, insouciant, relaxed; informal laid-back, easygoing, couldn't-care-less.
ANTONYMS enthusiastic.

lackey ▶ noun 1 *lackeys helped them from their carriage* **servant,** flunky, footman, manservant, valet, steward, butler, attendant, houseboy, domestic; archaic scullion.
2 *one of the manager's lackeys* **toady,** flunky, sycophant, flatterer, minion, hanger-on, lickspittle, brown-noser, spaniel, pawn, underling, stooge; informal yes-man, trained seal, bootlicker, doormat, drudge, peon.

lackluster ▶ adjective *a lackluster performance* **uninspired,** uninspiring, unimaginative, dull, humdrum, colorless, characterless, bland, dead, insipid, vapid, flat, dry, lifeless, tame, prosaic, spiritless, lusterless; boring, monotonous, dreary, tedious; informal blah.
ANTONYMS inspired.

laconic ▶ adjective 1 *his laconic comment* **brief,** concise, terse, succinct, short, pithy. See note at **TERSE**.
ANTONYMS verbose.
2 *their laconic press agent* **taciturn,** uncommunicative, reticent, quiet, reserved, silent, unforthcoming, brief.
ANTONYMS loquacious.

lad ▶ noun informal *a lad of eight* **boy,** schoolboy, youth, youngster, juvenile, stripling; informal kid, whippersnapper; derogatory brat. See also **CHILD**.

ladder ▶ noun 1 *she climbed down the ladder* **steps,** set of steps; rope ladder, stepladder, extension ladder.
2 *the academic ladder* **hierarchy,** scale, grading, ranking, pecking order.

laden ▶ adjective *a tray laden with plates* **loaded,** burdened, weighed down, encumbered, overloaded, piled high, fully charged; full, filled, packed, stuffed, crammed; informal chock-full, chockablock.

ladle ▶ verb *he was* ***ladling out*** *the contents of the pot* **spoon out,** scoop out, dish up/out, serve.
▶ noun *a soup ladle* **spoon,** scoop, dipper.

lady ▶ noun 1 *several ladies were present* **woman,** female; informal dame; derogatory broad; literary maid,

damsel; archaic wench.
2 *lords and ladies* **noblewoman,** duchess, countess, peeress, viscountess, baroness; archaic gentlewoman.

ladylike ▶ adjective *as ladylike as Audrey Hepburn* **genteel,** polite, refined, well-bred, cultivated, polished, decorous, proper, respectable, seemly, well-mannered, cultured, sophisticated, elegant, modest; feminine, womanly.
ANTONYMS coarse.

lag ▶ verb *I'm sorry to be **lagging behind*** **fall behind,** straggle, fall back, trail (behind), hang back, not keep pace, bring up the rear; dawdle, dilly-dally. See note at LOITER.
ANTONYMS keep up.

laggard ▶ noun *there'll be no laggards on my watch* **straggler,** loiterer, lingerer, dawdler, sluggard, snail, idler, loafer; informal lazybones, slacker, slowpoke, foot-dragger.

lagoon ▶ noun *swimming in the moonlit lagoon* **bay,** inland sea, lake, bight, pool.

laid-back ▶ adjective informal *you must try to be more laid-back* **relaxed,** easygoing, free and easy, casual, nonchalant, unexcitable, imperturbable, unruffled, blasé, cool, equable, even-tempered, low-maintenance, insouciant, calm, unperturbed, unflustered, unflappable, unworried, unconcerned, unbothered; leisurely, unhurried, Type-B; stoical, phlegmatic, tolerant.
ANTONYMS uptight.

lair ▶ noun **1** *the lair of a large python* **den,** burrow, hole, tunnel, cave.
2 *a villain's lair* **hideout,** hiding place, hideaway, refuge, sanctuary, haven, shelter, retreat.

laissez-faire ▶ noun *an agenda that embraces the concept of laissez-faire* **free enterprise,** free trade, nonintervention, free-market capitalism, market forces.
▶ adjective *he has argued for a laissez-faire policy regarding the Internet | a laissez-faire approach to parenting* **noninterventionist,** noninterventional, noninterfering; uninvolved, indifferent; lax, loose, permissive, nonrestrictive, liberal, libertarian; informal hands-off.

lake ▶ noun *the frozen lake* **pond,** pool, tarn, reservoir, slough, lagoon, water, waterhole, watering hole, inland sea; oxbow (lake), pothole (lake), glacial lake; Scottish loch; literary mere.

lambaste ▶ verb *the coach was lambasted in the media* **criticize,** chastise, censure, take to task, harangue, rail at, rant at, fulminate against; upbraid, scold, reprimand, rebuke, castigate, chide, reprove, admonish, berate; informal lay into, tear into, give someone a dressing-down, dress down, give someone what for, give someone a tongue-lashing, tell off, bawl out, chew out; formal excoriate.

lame ▶ adjective **1** *the mare was lame* **limping,** hobbling; crippled, disabled, incapacitated; dated game.
ANTONYMS able-bodied.
2 *a lame excuse* **feeble,** weak, thin, flimsy, poor, sorry; unconvincing, implausible, unlikely.
ANTONYMS convincing.

lament ▶ noun **1** *the widow's laments* **wail,** wailing, lamentation, moan, moaning, weeping, crying, sob, sobbing, keening; jeremiad; complaint.
2 *a lament for the dead* **dirge,** requiem, elegy, threnody, monody; keen.
▶ verb **1** *the mourners lamented* **mourn,** grieve, sorrow, wail, weep, cry, sob, keen, beat one's breast. See note at MOURN.
ANTONYMS celebrate, rejoice.
2 *he lamented the modernization of the buildings* **bemoan,** bewail, complain about, deplore, rue; protest against, object to, oppose, fulminate against, inveigh against, denounce.

lamentable ▶ adjective *lamentable living conditions* **deplorable,** regrettable, sad, terrible, awful, wretched, woeful, dire, disastrous, grave, appalling, dreadful, pitiful, shameful, sorrowful, unfortunate.
ANTONYMS wonderful.

lamentation ▶ noun *the survivors' lamentation* **weeping,** wailing, crying, sobbing, moaning, lament, keening, grieving, mourning.

lamp ▶ noun *we had plenty of illumination from our lamps* **light,** lantern; floor lamp, table lamp, bedside lamp, banker's lamp, gooseneck lamp; chandelier; candelabra; trademark Tiffany lamp; floodlight, spotlight, strobe light, arc lamp; fluorescent lamp, track lights; lava lamp; sunlamp; flashlight; streetlight, streetlamp; Chinese lantern, Japanese lantern; storm lantern, hurricane lamp, oil lamp, kerosene lamp; trademark Coleman lamp.

lampoon ▶ verb *he was mercilessly lampooned* **satirize,** mock, ridicule, make fun of, caricature, burlesque, parody, tease; informal roast, send up.
▶ noun *a lampoon of student life* **satire,** burlesque, parody, skit, caricature, impersonation, travesty, mockery; informal send-up, takeoff, spoof. See note at CARICATURE.

lance ▶ noun *a knight with a lance* **spear,** pike, javelin; harpoon.

land ▶ noun **1** *publicly owned land* **grounds,** fields, terrain, territory, open space; property, landholding, acres, acreage, lands, real estate, realty, estate; historical demesne.
2 *fertile land* **soil,** earth, loam, topsoil, humus; tillage.
3 *many people are leaving **the land*** **the countryside,** the country, rural areas, farmland, agricultural land.
4 *Tunisia is a land of variety* **country,** nation, nation state, state, realm, kingdom, province; region, area, domain.
5 *the lookout sighted land to the east* **terra firma,** dry land; coast, coastline, shore.
ANTONYMS sea.
▶ verb **1** *Canadian troops landed at Juno Beach* **disembark,** go ashore, debark, alight, get off.
ANTONYMS embark.
2 *our ship landed at New London* **dock,** moor, berth, put in, anchor, drop anchor.
ANTONYMS set sail.
3 *their plane landed in Chicago* **touch down,** make a landing, come in to land, come down.
ANTONYMS take off.
4 *a bird landed on the branch* **perch,** settle, come to rest, alight.
ANTONYMS fly off.

5 informal *Nick landed the job of editor* **obtain,** get, acquire, secure, be appointed to, gain, net, win, achieve, attain, carry off; informal bag.
6 informal *Joanne's drug habit* ***landed*** *her in big trouble* **bring,** lead to, drive to, cause to be in.
7 informal *he landed a left hook that staggered Curry* **inflict,** deal, deliver, administer, dispense, score, mete out.

landmark ▶ noun 1 *the cliff is a landmark for hikers* **marker,** mark, indicator, beacon, cairn.
2 *one of Arizona's most famous landmarks* **monument,** distinctive feature, prominent feature.
3 *the ruling was hailed as a landmark* **turning point,** milestone, watershed, critical point, benchmark.
▶ adjective *a landmark decision* **precedent-setting,** normative, consequential, historic.

landscape ▶ noun *the landscape of Tahiti* **scenery,** countryside, topography, country, terrain; outlook, view, vista, prospect, aspect, panorama, perspective, sweep.

landslide ▶ noun 1 *floods and landslides* **rockslide,** mudslide; avalanche.
2 *the Democrats enjoyed a landslide* **decisive victory,** overwhelming majority, triumph, sweep.

lane ▶ noun 1 *country lanes* **road,** street, byroad, byway, alley, alleyway, back alley, back lane, track.
2 *bicycle lanes* | *a three-lane highway* **track,** way, course; road division; express lane.

language ▶ noun 1 *the structure of language* **speech,** writing, communication, conversation, speaking, talking, talk, discourse; words, vocabulary.
2 *the English language* **tongue,** mother tongue, native tongue; dialect, patois, slang, idiom, jargon, argot, cant; informal lingo.
3 *the booklet is written in simple, everyday language* **wording,** phrasing, phraseology, style, vocabulary, terminology, expressions, turns of phrase, parlance, form/mode of expression, usages, locutions, choice of words, idiolect; informal lingo.

languid ▶ adjective 1 *a languid wave of the hand* **relaxed,** unhurried, languorous, slow; listless, lethargic, sluggish, lazy, idle, indolent, apathetic; informal laid-back.
ANTONYMS energetic.
2 *languid days in the sun* **leisurely,** languorous, relaxed, restful, lazy.
ANTONYMS action-packed.
3 *she was pale and languid* **sickly,** weak, faint, feeble, frail, delicate; tired, weary, fatigued.
ANTONYMS vigorous.

languish ▶ verb 1 *the plants languished and died* **weaken,** deteriorate, decline; wither, droop, wilt, fade, waste away; informal go downhill.
ANTONYMS thrive, flourish.
2 *the general is now languishing in prison* **waste away,** rot, be abandoned, be neglected, be forgotten, suffer, experience hardship.

languor ▶ noun 1 *the sultry languor that was stealing over her* **lassitude,** lethargy, listlessness, torpor, fatigue, weariness, sleepiness, drowsiness; laziness, idleness, indolence, inertia, sluggishness, apathy.
ANTONYMS vigor.
2 *the languor of a hot day* **stillness,** tranquility, calm, calmness; oppressiveness, heaviness.

lap[1] ▶ noun *Liam sat on Santa's lap* **knee,** knees, thighs.

lap[2] ▶ noun *a race of eight laps* **circuit,** leg, circle, revolution, round; length.
▶ verb 1 *she lapped the other runners* **overtake,** outstrip, leave behind, pass, go past; catch up with; informal leapfrog.
2 literary *he was lapped in blankets* **wrap,** swathe, envelop, enfold, swaddle.

lap[3] ▶ verb 1 *waves lapped against the sea wall* **splash,** wash, swish, slosh, break, beat, strike, dash, roll; literary plash.
2 *the dog lapped water out of a puddle* **drink,** lick up, swallow, slurp, gulp.
– PHRASES **lap something up** *he was lapping up the accolades* **relish,** revel in, savor, delight in, glory in, enjoy.

lapse ▶ noun 1 *a lapse of concentration* **failure,** failing, slip, error, mistake, blunder, fault, omission, hiccup; informal slip-up.
2 *his lapse into petty crime* **decline,** fall, falling, slipping, drop, deterioration, degeneration, backsliding, regression, retrogression, descent, sinking, slide.
3 *a lapse of time* **interval,** gap, pause, interlude, lull, hiatus, break.
▶ verb 1 *our membership has lapsed* **expire,** become void, become invalid, run out.
2 *she lapsed into self-pity* **revert,** relapse; drift, slide, slip, sink; deteriorate, decline, fall, degenerate, backslide, regress, retrogress.

lapsed ▶ adjective 1 *a lapsed Catholic* **nonpracticing,** backsliding, apostate; former.
ANTONYMS practicing.
2 *a lapsed membership* **expired,** void, invalid, out of date.
ANTONYMS valid.

larceny ▶ noun *his police record included two counts of larceny* **theft,** stealing, robbery, pilfering, thieving; burglary, housebreaking, breaking and entering; informal filching, swiping, pinching; formal peculation.

large ▶ adjective 1 *a large house* | *large numbers of people* **big,** great, huge, sizable, substantial, immense, enormous, colossal, massive, mammoth, vast, prodigious, tremendous, gigantic, giant, monumental, stupendous, gargantuan, elephantine, titanic, mountainous, monstrous; towering, tall, high; mighty, voluminous; king-size(d), economy-size(d), family-size(d), man-size(d), giant-size(d); informal jumbo, whopping, mega, humongous, monster, astronomical, ginormous.
ANTONYMS small.
2 *a large man* **big,** burly, heavy, tall, bulky, thickset, chunky, strapping, hulking, hefty, muscular, brawny, solid, powerful, sturdy, strong, rugged; full-figured, buxom; fat, plump, overweight, chubby, stout, meaty, fleshy, portly, rotund, flabby, paunchy, obese, corpulent; informal hunky, roly-poly, beefy, tubby, well-upholstered, pudgy, well-fed, big-boned, corn-fed.
ANTONYMS small, thin.

3 *a large supply of wool* **abundant,** copious, plentiful, ample, liberal, generous, lavish, bountiful, bumper, boundless, good, considerable, superabundant; literary plenteous.
ANTONYMS meager.
4 *the measure has large economic implications* **wide-reaching,** far-reaching, wide, sweeping, large-scale, broad, extensive, comprehensive, exhaustive.
ANTONYMS trivial.
– PHRASES **at large 1** *fourteen criminals are still at large* **at liberty,** free, loose, on the loose, on the run, fugitive, on the lam. **2** *society at large* **as a whole,** generally, in general. **by and large** *the children, by and large, treated him well* **on the whole,** generally, in general, all things considered, all in all, for the most part, in the main, as a rule, overall, almost always, mainly, mostly; on average, on balance.

largely ▶ **adverb** *the population in this district is largely of retirement age* **mostly,** mainly, to a large/great extent, chiefly, predominantly, primarily, principally, for the most part, in the main; usually, typically, commonly.

large-scale ▶ **adjective** *a large-scale program* **extensive,** wide-ranging, far-reaching, exhaustive, comprehensive; mass, nationwide, global.

largesse ▶ **noun 1** *Bob took advantage of his friend's largesse* **generosity,** liberality, munificence, bounty, bountifulness, beneficence, altruism, charity, philanthropy, magnanimity, benevolence, charitableness, openhandedness, kindness, big-heartedness; formal benefaction.
ANTONYMS stinginess.
2 *distributing largesse to the locals* **gifts,** presents, handouts, grants, aid; patronage, sponsorship, backing, help; alms. See note at PRESENT[3].

lark ▶ **noun** informal *we were just having a bit of a lark* **fun,** good fun, amusement, a laugh, a joke; an escapade, a prank, a trick, a jape, a practical joke.

lascivious ▶ **adjective** *his lascivious jokes are not funny* **lecherous,** lewd, lustful, licentious, libidinous, salacious, lubricious, prurient, dirty, smutty, naughty, indecent, ribald; informal blue; formal concupiscent.

lash ▶ **verb 1** *he lashed the beast repeatedly* **whip,** flog, flagellate, beat, thrash, horsewhip, scourge, birch, belt, strap, cane, switch; strike, hit; informal wallop, whack, tan (someone's hide), larrup, whale.
2 *rain lashed the windowpanes* **beat against,** dash against, pound, batter, strike, hit, knock.
3 *the tiger began to lash its tail* **swish,** flick, twitch, whip.
4 *two boats were lashed together* **fasten,** bind, tie (up), tether, hitch, knot, rope, make fast.
▶ **noun 1** *he brought the lash down upon the prisoner's back* **whip,** horsewhip, scourge, thong, flail, strap, birch, cane, switch; historical cat-o'-nine-tails, cat, knout.
2 *twenty lashes* **stroke,** blow, hit, strike, welt, thwack; archaic stripe.
– PHRASES **lash out at** *the president lashed out at the opposition* **criticize,** chastise, censure, attack, condemn, denounce, lambaste, rail at/against, harangue, pillory; berate, upbraid, rebuke, reproach; informal lay into, tear into, blast; formal castigate.

last[1] ▶ **adjective 1** *the last woman in line* **rearmost,** hindmost, endmost, at the end, at the back, furthest (back), final, ultimate.
ANTONYMS first, leading.
2 *Rembrandt spent his last years in Amsterdam* **closing,** concluding, final, ending, end, terminal; later, latter.
ANTONYMS initial, early.
3 *I'd be the last person to say anything against him* **least likely,** most unlikely, most improbable; least suitable, most unsuitable, most inappropriate, least appropriate.
ANTONYMS first, most likely.
4 *we met last year* **the previous,** the preceding; the prior, the former.
ANTONYMS next.
5 *this was his last chance* **final,** only remaining.
▶ **adverb** *the entrant arriving last is eliminated* **at the end,** at/in the rear.
▶ **noun** *the most important business was left to the last* **end,** ending, finish, close, conclusion, finale, termination.
ANTONYMS beginning.
– PHRASES **at last** *at last, the rain stopped* **finally,** at long last, after a long time, in the end, eventually, ultimately, in (the fullness of) time. **last word 1** *that's my last word* **final decision,** definitive statement, conclusive comment. **2** *she was determined to have the last word* **concluding remark,** final say, closing statement. **3** *the last word in luxury and efficiency* **best,** peak, acme, epitome, latest; pinnacle, apex, apogee, ultimate, height, zenith, nonpareil, crème de la crème; archaic nonsuch. **last hurrah** *Sunday's performance was Shelley's last hurrah* **swan song,** grand finale, finale, curtain call.

last[2] ▶ **verb 1** *the hearing lasted for six days* **continue,** go on, carry on, keep on, keep going, proceed; stay, remain, persist.
2 *how long will he last as manager?* **survive,** endure, hold on, hold out, keep going, persevere; informal stick it out, hang on.
3 *the car is built to last* **endure,** wear well, stand up, bear up; informal go the distance.

last-ditch ▶ **adjective** *a last-ditch effort to save the old church* **last-minute,** last-chance, eleventh-hour, last-resort, desperate, do-or-die, last-gasp, final.

lasting ▶ **adjective** *a lasting friendship* **enduring,** long-lasting, long-lived, abiding, continuing, long-term, surviving, persisting, permanent; durable, constant, stable, established, secure, long-standing; unchanging, irreversible, immutable, eternal, undying, everlasting, unending, never-ending, unfading, changeless, indestructible, unceasing, unwavering, unfaltering.
ANTONYMS ephemeral.

lastly ▶ **adverb** *lastly, I would like to thank my parents* **finally,** in conclusion, to conclude, to sum up, to end, last, ultimately.
ANTONYMS firstly.

latch ▸ noun *he lifted the latch* **fastening,** catch, fastener, clasp, lock.
▸ verb *Jess latched the back door* **fasten,** secure, make fast, lock.

late ▸ adjective 1 *the train was late* **behind schedule,** behind time, behindhand; tardy, running late, overdue, belated, delayed.
ANTONYMS punctual, early.
2 *her late husband* **dead,** departed, lamented, passed on/away, deceased.
ANTONYMS alive, existing.
▸ adverb 1 *she had arrived late* **behind schedule,** behind time, behindhand, belatedly, tardily, at the last minute, at the buzzer.
ANTONYMS early.
2 *I was working late* **after hours,** after office hours, overtime.
3 *don't stay out late* **late at night**; informal till all hours.
– PHRASES **of late** *he's not felt well of late* See LATELY.

lately ▸ adverb *we haven't seen much of you lately* **recently,** of late, latterly, in recent times, in the past few days, in the last couple of weeks.

latent ▸ adjective *his latent skills* **dormant,** untapped, unused, undiscovered, hidden, concealed, underlying, invisible, unseen, undeveloped, unrealized, unfulfilled, potential.

CHOOSE THE RIGHT WORD

latent, abeyant, dormant, quiescent, potential

All of these words refer to what is not currently observable or showing signs of activity. A **latent** talent is one that has not yet manifested itself, while **potential** suggests a talent that exists in an undeveloped state (*a potential concert violinist*). A child may have certain *latent* qualities of which his or her parents are unaware; but teachers are usually quick to spot a *potential* artist or poet in the classroom. **Dormant** and **quiescent** are less frequently associated with people and more often associated with things. A volcano might be described as *dormant,* which applies to anything that is currently inactive but has been active in the past and is capable of becoming active again in the future. *Dormant* carries the connotation of sleeping (*plants that are dormant in the winter*), while *quiescent* means motionless (*a quiescent sea*), emphasizing inactivity without referring to past or future activity. **Abeyant**, like *dormant*, means suspended or temporarily inactive, but it is most commonly used as a noun (*personal rights and privileges kept in abeyance until the danger had passed*).

later ▸ adjective *a later chapter* **subsequent,** following, succeeding, future, upcoming, to come, ensuing, next; formal posterior; archaic after.
ANTONYMS earlier.
▸ adverb 1 *later, the film rights were sold* **subsequently,** eventually, then, next, later on, after this/that, afterward, at a later date, in the future, in due course, by and by, in a while, in time.
2 *two days later a letter arrived* **afterward,** later on, after, after that, subsequently, following; formal thereafter.

lateral ▸ adjective 1 *lateral movements* **sideways,** sidewise, sideward, edgewise, edgeways, oblique, horizontal.
2 *lateral thinking* **unorthodox,** inventive, creative, imaginative, original, innovative, nonlinear.

latest ▸ adjective 1 *latest reports from the coast indicate intensifying winds* **most recent,** newest, just released, up-to-the-minute.
2 *the latest Paris designs* **newest,** just out, fresh, freshest, up-to-date, state-of-the-art, au courant, dernier cri, current, modern, contemporary, fashionable, in fashion, in vogue; newfangled; informal in, with it, trendy, hip, hot, big, funky, happening, cool.
ANTONYMS old, unfashionable.

lather ▸ noun *rich, soapy lather* **foam,** froth, suds, soapsuds; bubbles; literary spume.
– PHRASES **in a lather** *Hannah is in a lather over the chemistry exam* **agitated,** flustered, distressed, worked up, strung out, keyed up, in a state, in a tizzy, in a dither, in a twitter, upset.

latitude ▸ noun 1 *Toronto and Nice are on the same latitude* **parallel**.
ANTONYMS longitude.
2 *he gave them a lot of latitude* **freedom,** scope, leeway, space, breathing space, flexibility, liberty, independence, free rein, license, room to maneuver, elbow room, wiggle room, freedom of action. See note at RANGE.
ANTONYMS restriction.

latter ▸ adjective 1 *the latter stages of development* **later,** closing, end, concluding, final; latest, most recent.
ANTONYMS initial.
2 *Russia chose the latter option* **last-mentioned,** second, last, later.
ANTONYMS former.

latter-day ▸ adjective *a latter-day puritan* **modern,** present-day, current, contemporary.

lattice ▸ noun *the ivy-covered lattice* **grid,** latticework, fretwork, open framework, openwork, trellis, trelliswork, espalier, grille, network, mesh.

laud ▸ verb *a single lauded by the music press* **praise,** extol, hail, applaud, acclaim, commend, sing the praises of, speak highly of, pay tribute to, lionize, eulogize, rhapsodize over/about; informal rave about; archaic magnify, panegyrize. See note at PRAISE.
ANTONYMS criticize.

laudable ▸ adjective *thanked for their laudable contributions of time and talent* **praiseworthy,** commendable, admirable, meritorious, worthy, deserving, creditable, estimable.
ANTONYMS shameful.

laudatory ▸ adjective *a laudatory front-page endorsement* **complimentary,** praising, congratulatory, extolling, adulatory, commendatory, approbatory, flattering, celebratory, eulogizing, panegyrical; informal glowing; formal encomiastic.

ANTONYMS disparaging.

laugh ▸ verb **1** *Norma started to laugh excitedly* **chuckle,** chortle, guffaw, cackle, giggle, titter, twitter, snigger, snicker, yuk, tee-hee, burst out laughing, roar/hoot/howl with laughter, crack up, dissolve into laughter, split one's sides, be (rolling) on the floor, be doubled up, be killing oneself (laughing); informal be in stitches, be rolling in the aisles.

2 *people **laughed at** his theories* **ridicule,** mock, deride, scoff at, jeer at, sneer at, jibe at, make fun of, poke fun at, scorn; lampoon, satirize, parody; dismiss; informal send up, pooh-pooh.

▸ noun **1** *he gave a short laugh* **chuckle,** chortle, guffaw, giggle, titter, twitter, tee-hee, snigger, snicker, yuk, roar/hoot/howl of laughter, belly laugh, horse laugh.

2 informal *he was a laugh* **joker,** jokester, wag, wit, clown, jester, prankster, character; informal card, hoot, scream, riot, gas, barrel of laughs.

3 informal *I entered the contest for a laugh* **joke,** prank, jest, escapade, caper, practical joke; informal hoot, lark.

– PHRASES **laugh something off** *you have to just laugh off their stupid remarks* **dismiss,** make a joke of, make light of, shrug off, brush aside, scoff at; informal pooh-pooh.

laughable ▸ adjective **1** *the government's new education policy is laughable* **ridiculous,** ludicrous, absurd, risible, preposterous; foolish, silly, idiotic, stupid, asinine, nonsensical, crazy, insane, outrageous, harebrained, cockamamie; informal cockeyed, daffy.

2 *if it weren't so tragic, it'd be laughable* **amusing,** funny, humorous, hilarious, uproarious, comical, comic, farcical.

laughingstock ▸ noun *their new airport has been called the laughingstock of world air travel* **butt,** dupe, spectacle, figure of fun, stooge, fall guy.

laughter ▸ noun *the sound of laughter* **laughing,** chuckling, chortling, guffawing, giggling, tittering, twittering, cackling, sniggering; informal hysterics.

launch ▸ verb **1** *they've launched the shuttle | the rocket has launched* **send into orbit,** blast off, take off, lift off.

2 *he launched the boat* **set afloat,** put to sea, put into the water.

3 *a chair was launched at him* **throw,** hurl, fling, pitch, lob, let fly; fire, shoot; informal chuck, heave, sling.

4 *the government launched a new campaign* **set in motion,** get going, get underway, start, commence, begin, embark on, initiate, inaugurate, set up, organize, introduce, bring into being; informal kick off, roll out.

5 *he **launched into** a tirade* **start,** commence, burst into.

launder ▸ verb *the linens are laundered each Thursday* **wash,** wash and iron, clean; dry-clean.

laundry ▸ noun **1** *a big pile of laundry* **washing,** wash, dirty clothes.

2 *the facilities include a laundry* **laundry room,** launderette; trademark Laundromat; cleaners, dry cleaners.

laurels ▸ plural noun *enjoying all the laurels befitting such an accomplished young woman* **honors,** tributes, praise, plaudits, accolades, kudos, acclaim, acclamation, credit, glory, honor, distinction, fame, renown, prestige, recognition.

lavatory ▸ noun See BATHROOM.

lavish ▸ adjective **1** *lavish parties* **sumptuous,** luxurious, costly, expensive, opulent, grand, splendid, rich, fancy, posh; informal fancy-schmancy.

ANTONYMS meager.

2 *lavish hospitality* **generous,** liberal, bountiful, openhanded, unstinting, unsparing, free, munificent, extravagant, prodigal.

ANTONYMS frugal.

3 *lavish amounts of champagne* **abundant,** copious, plentiful, liberal, prolific, generous; literary plenteous. See note at PROFUSE.

ANTONYMS scant.

▸ verb *she lavished money on her children* **give freely to,** spend generously on, bestow on, heap on, shower with.

law ▸ noun **1** *a new law was passed* **regulation,** statute, enactment, act, bill, decree, edict, bylaw, rule, ruling, ordinance, dictum, command, order, directive, pronouncement, proclamation, dictate, fiat.

2 *a career in law* **the legal profession,** the bar.

3 informal *on the run from the law* See POLICE (noun).

4 *the laws of the game* **rule,** regulation, principle, convention, instruction, guideline.

5 *a moral law* **principle,** rule, precept, directive, injunction, commandment, belief, creed, credo, maxim, tenet, doctrine, canon.

law-abiding ▸ adjective *law-abiding citizens* **honest,** righteous, honorable, upright, upstanding, good, decent, virtuous, moral, dutiful, obedient, compliant.

ANTONYMS criminal.

lawbreaker ▸ noun *to her dying day, Bobbie never believed that her son was a lawbreaker* **criminal,** offender, wrongdoer, malefactor, evildoer, transgressor, miscreant; villain, rogue, ruffian, felon; Law malfeasant; informal crook, con, jailbird, hood; archaic miscreant.

lawful ▸ adjective *the lawful seizure of weapons* **legitimate,** legal, licit, just, permissible, permitted, allowable, allowed, rightful, sanctioned, authorized, warranted, within the law; informal legit.

ANTONYMS illegal, criminal.

lawless ▸ adjective *a lawless country* **ungovernable,** unruly, disruptive, anarchic, disorderly, rebellious, insubordinate, riotous, mutinous; uncivilized, wild.

ANTONYMS orderly.

lawsuit ▸ noun *the actor is now involved in a lawsuit against his former business manager* **legal action,** suit, case, action, legal proceedings, judicial proceedings, proceedings, litigation, trial, legal dispute, legal contest.

lawyer ▸ noun *all the lawyers are confident that the case will be dismissed* **attorney,** counsel, counselor, legal practitioner, legal professional, legal adviser, member of the bar, litigator, advocate; chiefly Brit. barrister, solicitor; informal ambulance chaser, mouthpiece, legal eagle, legal beagle.

lax ▶ adjective *lax discipline in schools* **slack,** slipshod, negligent, remiss, careless, heedless, unmindful, slapdash, offhand, casual; easygoing, lenient, permissive, liberal, indulgent, overindulgent; informal sloppy. See note at LENIENT.
ANTONYMS strict.

lay[1] ▶ verb **1** *Curtis laid the newspaper on the table* **put,** place, set, put down, set down, deposit, rest, situate, locate, position; informal stick, dump, park, plunk.
2 *the act laid the foundation for the new system* **set in place,** put in place, set out; set up, establish.
3 *I'll lay money that Michelle will be there* **bet,** wager, gamble, stake, risk, hazard, venture; (**lay money**) give odds, speculate.
4 *they are going to lay charges* **bring,** press, bring forward, lodge, register, place, file.
5 *she* ***laid*** *the blame* ***on*** *Maxwell* **assign to,** attribute to, ascribe to, allot to, attach to; (**lay the blame on**) hold someone accountable, hold someone responsible, find guilty.
6 *we* ***laid out*** *plans for the next voyage* **devise,** arrange, make, make ready, prepare, work out, hatch, design, plan, scheme, plot, conceive, put together, draw up, produce, develop, concoct, formulate, cook up.
7 *this will lay responsibility on the court* **impose,** apply, entrust, vest, place, put; inflict, encumber, saddle, charge, burden.
8 *we laid the trap and waited* **set,** prepare, devise, bait. See note at LIE[2].
– PHRASES **lay something aside 1** *farmers laying aside areas for conservation* **put aside,** put to one side, keep, save. **2** *developers must lay aside their conservatism* **abandon,** cast aside, set aside, reject, renounce, repudiate, disregard, forget, discard; literary forsake. **lay something bare** *his private life has been laid bare* **reveal,** disclose, divulge, show, expose, exhibit, uncover, unveil, unmask, make known, make public. **lay something down 1** *he laid down his glass* **put down,** set down, place down, deposit, rest; informal plunk down. **2** *they were forced to lay down their weapons* **relinquish,** surrender, give up, yield, cede. **3** *the ground rules have been laid down* **formulate,** stipulate, set down, draw up, frame; prescribe, ordain, dictate, decree; enact, pass, decide, determine, impose, codify. **lay down the law** *too many parents have relinquished their right to lay down the law* **be dogmatic,** be in charge (of the rules), set the rules, be domineering, be the boss, call the shots. **lay eyes on** informal *something clicked the first time they laid eyes on each other* **see,** spot, observe, regard, view, catch sight of, set eyes on; literary behold, espy, descry. **lay hands on** *wait till I lay my hands on you!* **catch,** lay/get hold of, get one's hands on, seize, grab, grasp, capture. **lay into** informal **1** *the general's henchmen were encouraged to publicly lay into dissenters* See ASSAULT (sense 1 of the verb). **2** *he laid into her with a string of insults* See CRITICIZE. **lay it on thick** informal *oh, brother, can he lay it on thick when he wants to impress a girl* **exaggerate,** overdo it, embellish the truth; flatter, praise, soft-soap, pile it on, sweet-talk. **lay off** informal **1** *I have to lay off beer* **give up,** abstain from, desist from, cut out. **2** *I lay off work at 5* **quit,** pack in, leave off, stop. **3** *lay off, you big jerk!* **back off,** give it a rest, enough already, shut up, stop it. **4** *three more couriers were laid off today* **dismiss,** let go, discharge, give notice to, release; informal sack, fire, ax, give someone their marching orders, pink-slip, give someone the boot, give someone the (old) heave-ho. **lay out 1** *Robyn laid the plans out on the desk* **spread out,** set out, display, exhibit. **2** *a paper laying out our priorities* **outline,** sketch out, rough out, detail, draw up, formulate, work out, frame, draft. **3** informal *he had to lay out $70* See PAY (sense 2 of the verb). **lay waste to** *any further testing at this site will lay waste to an irreplaceable ecosystem* **devastate,** wipe out, destroy, demolish, annihilate, raze, ruin, wreck, level, flatten, ravage, pillage, sack, despoil.

> USAGE
> **lay**
> The verb *lay* means, broadly, 'put something down': *they are going to lay the carpet*. The past tense and the past participle of *lay* is *laid*: *they laid the groundwork; she had laid careful plans*.
> The verb *lie*, on the other hand, means 'assume a horizontal or resting position': *why don't you lie on the floor?*
> In practice, many speakers inadvertently get the *lay* forms and the *lie* forms into a tangle of right and wrong usage. Here are some examples of typical incorrect usage: *have you been laying on the sofa all day?* (should be *lying*); *he lay the books on the table* (should be *laid*); *I had laid in this position so long, my arm was stiff* (should be *lain*).

lay[2] ▶ adjective **1** *a lay preacher* **nonclerical,** nonordained, secular, temporal.
2 *a lay audience* **nonprofessional,** amateur, nonspecialist, nontechnical, untrained, unqualified.

layabout ▶ noun *I want Carmen and the rest of these layabouts out of here by noon* **idler,** loafer, slacker, lazybones, lounger, flâneur, shirker, sluggard, laggard, slugabed, malingerer, good-for-nothing; informal lazybones, couch potato; literary wastrel.

layoff ▶ noun *a companywide layoff* **dismissal,** discharge; informal sacking, firing; downsizing; the sack, the boot, the ax.
ANTONYMS recruitment.

layout ▶ noun **1** *the layout of the house* **arrangement,** geography, design, organization; plan, map; blueprint.
2 *the magazine's layout* **design,** arrangement, presentation, style, format; structure, organization, composition, configuration.

layperson ▶ noun **1** *a prayer book for laypeople* **unordained person,** member of the congregation, layman, laywoman, member of

the laity.
2 *engineering sounds highly specialized to the layperson* **layman,** nonexpert, nonprofessional, amateur, nonspecialist, dilettante.

laze ▶ verb *lazing by the river* **relax,** unwind, idle, do nothing, loaf (around/about), lounge (around/about), loll (around/about), lie (around/about), take it easy; informal hang around, veg (out), bum (around).

lazy ▶ adjective *the lazy volunteers were sent home* **idle,** indolent, slothful, work-shy, shiftless, inactive, sluggish, lethargic; remiss, negligent, slack, lax, lackadaisical.
ANTONYMS industrious.

lead[1] ▶ verb **1** *Michelle led them into the house* **guide,** conduct, show, show the way, lead the way, usher, escort, steer, pilot, shepherd; accompany, see, take.
ANTONYMS follow.
2 *he led us to believe they were lying* **cause,** induce, prompt, move, persuade, influence, drive, condition, make; incline, dispose, predispose.
3 *this might* **lead to** *job losses* **result in,** cause, bring on/about, give rise to, be the cause of, make happen, create, produce; occasion, effect, generate, contribute to, promote; provoke, stir up, spark off, arouse, foment, instigate; involve, necessitate, entail; formal effectuate.
ANTONYMS prevent.
4 *he led a march to the city center* **be at the head of,** be at the front of, head, spearhead; precede.
ANTONYMS follow.
5 *she led a coalition of radicals* **be the leader of,** be the head of, preside over, head, command, govern, rule, be in charge of, be in command of, be in control of, run, control, direct, be at the helm of; administer, organize, manage; reign over, be in power over; informal head up.
ANTONYMS serve in.
6 *the Bengals were leading at halftime* **be ahead,** be winning, be (out) in front, be in the lead, be first, be on top.
ANTONYMS trail.
7 *the champion was leading the field* **be at the front of,** be first in, be ahead of, head; outrun, outstrip, outpace, leave behind, draw away from; outdo, outclass, beat; informal leave standing.
ANTONYMS trail.
8 *I just want to lead a normal life* **experience,** have, live, spend.
▶ noun **1** *I was in* **the lead** *early on* **the leading position,** first place, the van, the vanguard; ahead, in front, winning.
2 *they took the lead in the personal computer market* **first position,** forefront, primacy, dominance, superiority, ascendancy; preeminence, supremacy, advantage, upper hand, whip hand.
3 *playing the lead* **leading role,** star/starring role, title role, principal part; principal character, male lead, female lead, leading man, leading lady.
4 *a Labrador on a lead* **leash,** tether, rope, chain, cord.
5 *detectives were following up a new lead* **clue,** hint, tip, tip-off, suggestion, indication, sign, pointer.
▶ adjective *the lead position* **leading,** first, top, foremost, front, head; chief, principal, main, premier.
– PHRASES **lead something off** *let's lead off the meeting with a few words from Mr. Diaz* **begin,** start (off), commence, open; informal kick off. **lead someone on** *were you leading her on with that talk about marriage?* **deceive,** mislead, delude, hoodwink, dupe, trick, fool, pull the wool over someone's eyes; informal string along, lead up the garden path, take for a ride, fleece, inveigle, hornswoggle, scam. **lead the way**
1 *he led the way to the kitchen* **guide someone,** conduct someone, show someone the way.
2 *our corporation is leading the way in new technologies* **take the initiative,** break (new) ground, blaze a trail, prepare the way, be at the forefront. **lead up to** *perhaps these informal meetings will lead up to a more formal relationship* **prepare the way for,** pave the way for, lay the groundwork for, set the scene for, work up/around to.

lead[2] ▶ noun informal *get that lead down to forensics immediately* **bullet,** slug, pellet; shot, buckshot, ammunition.
– PHRASES **get the lead out** *come on you guys—get the lead out!* **hurry up,** get a move on, be quick; informal get cracking, shake a leg, look lively, look sharp; dated make haste.

leaden ▶ adjective **1** *he moved on leaden feet* **sluggish,** heavy, lumbering, slow, burdensome, cumbersome.
2 *leaden prose* **boring,** dull, unimaginative, uninspired, monotonous, heavy, labored, wooden, lifeless, plodding; depressing.
3 *a leaden sky* **gray,** grayish, black, dark; cloudy, gloomy, overcast, dull, sunless, oppressive, threatening; literary tenebrous.

leader ▶ noun **1** *the leader of the Democratic Party | world leaders have agreed to meet in Geneva* **chief,** head, principal; commander, captain; superior, headman; chairman, chairwoman, chairperson, chair; (managing) director, CEO, manager, superintendent, supervisor, overseer, administrator, employer, master, mistress; president, premier, governor; ruler, monarch, king, queen, sovereign, emperor; informal boss, skipper, number one, numero uno, honcho, sachem, padrone.
ANTONYMS follower, supporter.
2 *the uncontested leader in genetic engineering* **pioneer,** front runner, world leader, world-beater, innovator, trailblazer, groundbreaker, trendsetter, torchbearer, pathfinder.

leadership ▶ noun **1** *firm leadership* **guidance,** direction, control, management, superintendence, supervision; organization, government.
2 *the leadership of the Rainbow Coalition* **directorship,** governorship, governance, administration, captaincy, control, ascendancy, supremacy, rule, command, power, dominion, influence.

leading ▶ adjective **1** *he played the leading role* **main,** chief, major, prime, most significant, most important, principal, foremost, key, central, focal, preeminent, paramount,

dominant, essential.
ANTONYMS subordinate, secondary.
2 *the nation's leading steel companies* **most important,** most powerful, affluential, foremost, chief, preeminent, outstanding, dominant, most influential.
ANTONYMS minor, secondary.
3 *last season's leading scorer* **top,** highest, best, first; front, lead; unparalleled, matchless, star.
ANTONYMS worst, last.

leaf ▶ **noun 1** *sycamore leaves* **leaflet,** frond, blade, needle; Botany cotyledon, blade, bract.
2 *a leaf in a book* **page,** sheet, folio.
▶ **verb** *he **leafed through** the documents* **flip through,** thumb through, flick through, skim through/over, browse through, glance through/over, riffle through, rifle through; scan, run one's eye over, peruse.
– PHRASES **turn over a new leaf** *how many released prisoners actually turn over a new leaf?* **reform,** improve, mend one's ways, make a fresh start, change for the better; informal go straight.

leaflet ▶ **noun** *leaflets about fire prevention* **pamphlet,** booklet, brochure, handbill, circular, flyer, fact sheet, handout, bulletin.

league ▶ **noun 1** *a league of nations* **alliance,** confederation, confederacy, federation, union, association, coalition, consortium, affiliation, guild, cooperative, partnership, fellowship, syndicate.
2 *the best team in the league* **big league(s),** major league(s), minor league(s), American League, National League, intramural league, Little League, bush league.
3 *the store is not in the same league* **class,** group, circle, category, level.
▶ **verb** *they **leagued together** with other companies* **ally,** join forces, join together, unite, band together, affiliate, combine, amalgamate, confederate, team up, join up.
– PHRASES **in league with** *in league with the drug cartel* **collaborating with,** cooperating with, in alliance with, allied with, conspiring with, hand in glove with; informal in cahoots with, in bed with.

leak ▶ **verb 1** *oil leaking from the tanker* **seep (out),** escape, ooze (out), secrete, bleed, emanate, issue, drip, dribble, drain; discharge, exude.
2 *civil servants leaked information to the press* **disclose,** divulge, reveal, make public, tell, impart, pass on, relate, communicate, expose, broadcast, publish, release, let slip, bring into the open; informal blab; (**leak news/information**) let the cat out of the bag, spill the beans.
▶ **noun 1** *check that there are no leaks in the pipe* **hole,** opening, aperture, puncture, perforation, gash, slit, nick, rent, break, crack, fissure, rupture.
2 *a gas leak* **discharge,** leakage, seepage, drip, escape.
3 *leaks to the media* **disclosure,** revelation, exposé, leakage, tip-off.

lean[1] ▶ **verb 1** *Polly **leaned against** the door* **rest on/against,** recline on/against, be supported by.
2 *trees leaning in the wind* **slant,** incline, bend, tilt, be at an angle, slope, tip, list.
3 *he **leans toward** existentialist philosophy* **tend toward,** incline toward, gravitate toward; have a preference for, have a penchant for, be partial to, have a liking for, have an affinity with.
4 *a strong shoulder to **lean on*** **depend on,** be dependent on, rely on, count on, bank on, have faith in, trust (in).
5 informal *he **leaned on** me to change my mind* **intimidate,** coerce, browbeat, bully, threaten, put pressure on, harass, hassle; informal twist someone's arm, put the screws on, hold a gun to someone's head.

lean[2] ▶ **adjective 1** *a tall, lean man* **slim,** thin, slender, spare, wiry, lanky, skinny. See note at THIN.
ANTONYMS fat.
2 *a lean harvest* **meager,** sparse, poor, mean, inadequate, insufficient, paltry, scanty, deficient, insubstantial.
ANTONYMS plentiful, abundant.
3 *lean times* **hard,** bad, difficult, tough, impoverished, poverty-stricken.
ANTONYMS prosperous.

leaning ▶ **noun** *my leaning is definitely toward a more liberal agenda* **inclination,** tendency, bent, proclivity, propensity, penchant, predisposition, predilection, partiality, preference, bias, attraction, liking, fondness, taste; informal yen.

leap ▶ **verb 1** *he **leaped over** the gate* **jump over,** jump, vault over, vault, spring over, bound over, hop (over), hurdle, leapfrog, clear.
2 *Claudia leapt to her feet* **spring,** jump, jump up, hop, bound.
3 *we leapt into the car* **rush,** hurry, hasten.
4 *she **leaped at** the chance* **accept eagerly,** grasp (with both hands), grab, take advantage of, seize (on), jump at.
5 *don't **leap to** conclusions* **form hastily,** reach hurriedly; hurry to, hasten to, jump to, rush to.
6 *profits leapt in January* **increase rapidly,** soar, rocket, skyrocket, shoot up, escalate.
▶ **noun 1** *an easy leap* **jump,** vault, spring, bound, hop, skip.
2 *a leap of 33%* **sudden rise,** surge, upsurge, upswing, upturn.
– PHRASES **by/in leaps and bounds** *his health has improved by leaps and bounds* **rapidly,** swiftly, quickly, speedily.

learn ▶ **verb 1** *learning a foreign language* **acquire a knowledge of,** acquire skill in, become competent in, become proficient in, grasp, master, take in, absorb, assimilate, digest, familiarize oneself with; study, read up on, be taught, have lessons in; informal get the hang of, bone up on.
2 *she learned the poem in just a few minutes* **memorize,** learn by heart, commit to memory, get down pat; archaic con.
3 *he learned that the school would shortly be closing* **discover,** find out, become aware, be informed, hear, hear tell; gather, understand, ascertain, establish; informal get wind of the fact, get wise to the fact; Brit. informal suss out.

learned ▶ **adjective** *he was by far the most learned man in their community* **scholarly,** erudite, well-educated, knowledgeable, well-read, well-informed, lettered, cultured, intellectual, academic, literary, bookish, highbrow, studious;

informal brainy.
ANTONYMS ignorant.

learner ▶ noun See NOVICE (sense 1).

learning ▶ noun **1** *a center of learning* **study,** studying, education, schooling, tuition, teaching, academic work; research.
2 *the astonishing range of his learning* **scholarship,** knowledge, education, erudition, intellect, enlightenment, illumination, edification, book learning, information, understanding, wisdom. See note at KNOWLEDGE.
ANTONYMS ignorance.

lease ▶ noun *a 15-year lease* **rental agreement,** leasehold, charter; rental, tenancy, tenure, period of occupancy.
▶ verb **1** *the film crew leased a large hangar* **rent,** charter.
2 *they leased the mill to a reputable family* **rent,** rent out, let, let out; sublet, sublease.

leash ▶ noun *keep your dog on a leash* **lead,** tether, rope, chain, restraint.
▶ verb **1** *she leashed the dog* **put a/the leash on,** put a/the lead on, tether, tie up, secure, restrain.
2 *the fury in her face was barely leashed* **curb,** control, keep under control, check, restrain, hold back, suppress, rein in.
– PHRASES **straining at the leash** *thousands of young actors are straining at the leash just for the chance to audition* **eager,** impatient, anxious, enthusiastic; informal itching, dying.

leathery ▶ adjective **1** *leathery skin* **rough,** rugged, leathered, hard, hardened, wrinkled, furrowed, lined, weather-beaten, callous, gnarled.
2 *a leathery cut of beef* **tough,** hard, gristly, chewy, stringy, rubbery.

leave[1] ▶ verb **1** *I left the hotel* **depart from,** go away from, go from, withdraw from, retire from, take oneself off from, exit from, take one's leave of, pull out of, be gone from, decamp from, disappear from, vacate, absent oneself from; say one's farewells/goodbyes to, quit; informal push off from, shove off from, clear out/off of, cut and run from, split, vamoose from, scoot from.
ANTONYMS arrive, stay.
2 *the next morning we left for Taipei* **set off,** head, make; set sail.
3 *he's left his wife* **abandon,** desert, cast aside, jilt, throw over; informal dump, ditch, drop, walk/run out on; literary forsake.
ANTONYMS stay with.
4 *he left his job in November* **quit,** resign from, retire from, step down from, withdraw from, pull out of, give up; pack it in, call it quits.
5 *she left her purse on a bus* **leave behind,** forget, lose, mislay.
6 *I thought I'd leave it to the experts* **entrust,** hand over, pass on, refer; delegate.
7 *he left her $100,000* **bequeath,** will, endow, hand down to, make over to.
8 *the speech left some feelings of disappointment* **cause,** produce, generate, give rise to.
– PHRASES **leave someone/something out**
1 *Adam left out the address* **omit,** fail to include, overlook, forget; skip, miss. **2** *when the roster for Game 2 was drawn up, Harvey was left out* **exclude,** omit, pass over; eliminate, cut, drop.

leave[2] ▶ noun **1** *the judge granted leave to appeal* **permission,** consent, authorization, sanction, warrant, dispensation, approval, clearance, blessing, assent, license; informal the go-ahead, the green light, the OK, the rubber stamp, the nod.
2 *he was on leave* **vacation,** break, time off, holiday, furlough, sabbatical, leave of absence.
– PHRASES **take one's leave of** *he took his leave of us* **bid farewell to,** say goodbye to.

leaven ▶ verb **1** *yeast leavens the bread* **raise,** make rise, puff up, expand.
2 *formal proceedings leavened by humor* **permeate,** infuse, pervade, imbue, suffuse, transform; enliven, liven up, invigorate, energize, electrify, ginger up, season, spice (up), perk up, brighten up, lighten, lift; informal buck up, pep up.

lecher ▶ noun *her blind date turned out to be a lecher* **lecherous man,** libertine, womanizer, debauchee, rake, roué, profligate, wanton; Don Juan, Casanova, Lothario, Romeo; informal lech, dirty old man, (old) goat, wolf, skirt-chaser; archaic fornicator.

lecherous ▶ adjective *the lecherous creep who lives in our building* **lustful,** licentious, lascivious, libidinous, prurient, lewd, salacious, lubricious, debauched, dissolute, wanton, dissipated, degenerate, depraved, dirty, filthy; formal concupiscent.
ANTONYMS chaste.

lecture ▶ noun **1** *a lecture on children's literature* **speech,** talk, address, discourse, disquisition, presentation, oration, lesson.
2 *Dave got a lecture about his daydreaming* **scolding,** chiding, reprimand, rebuke, reproof, reproach, upbraiding, berating, admonishment, sermon; informal dressing-down, talking-to, tongue-lashing, roasting; formal castigation.
▶ verb **1** *lecturing on the dangers of drugs* **give a lecture,** give a talk, talk, make a speech, speak, give an address, discourse, hold forth, declaim, expatiate; informal spout, sound off.
2 *she lectures at Colgate University* **teach,** give instruction, give lessons.
3 *she was lectured for her gossiping* **scold,** chide, reprimand, rebuke, reprove, reproach, upbraid, berate, chastise, admonish, lambaste, rake/haul over the coals, take to task; informal give someone a dressing-down, give someone a talking-to, tell off, bawl out; formal castigate.

lecturer ▶ noun *a guest lecturer from Yale* **university teacher,** college teacher, professor, tutor, educator; academic, academician, preceptor; formal pedagogue.

ledge ▶ noun *a collection of teapots on the ledge* | *a rock ledge* **shelf,** sill, mantel, mantelpiece, shelving; projection, protrusion, overhang, ridge, prominence.

ledger ▶ noun *a sales ledger* **book,** account book, record book, register, log, accounts; records, books; balance sheet, financial statement.

lee ▶ noun *the lee of the wall* **shelter,** protection, cover, refuge, safety, security.

leech ▶ noun *the welfare system is supposed to*

help the needy, not to feed the leeches **parasite,** bloodsucker; informal scrounger, sponger, bottom feeder, freeloader.

leer ▶ verb *Henry* ***leered at*** *her* **ogle,** look lasciviously at, look suggestively at, eye, check out; informal give someone a/the once-over, lust after/over.

▶ noun *a sly leer* **lecherous look,** lascivious look, ogle; informal the once-over, the eye.

leery ▶ adjective *be leery of these slick salesmen* **wary,** cautious, careful, guarded, chary, suspicious, distrustful; worried, anxious, apprehensive, hesitant, uncertain.

leeway ▶ noun *enforcement officials now have more leeway in prosecuting offenders* **freedom,** scope, latitude, space, room, liberty, flexibility, license, free hand, free rein.

left ▶ adjective *it's in my left pocket | move to the left side* **left-hand,** sinistral; Nautical port, larboard; Heraldry sinister.
ANTONYMS right, starboard.

left-handed ▶ adjective **1** *a left-handed golfer* sinistral; informal southpaw.
ANTONYMS right-handed.
2 *a left-handed compliment* **backhanded,** ambiguous, equivocal, double-edged; dubious, ironic, sardonic, insincere, hypocritical.
ANTONYMS forthright.

leftover ▶ noun **1** *a leftover from the 60s* **residue,** survivor, vestige, legacy, throwback.
2 (**leftovers**) *put the leftovers in the fridge* **uneaten food,** leavings, remainder, scraps, remnants, remains; excess, surplus.

▶ adjective *leftover food* **remaining,** left, uneaten, unconsumed; excess, surplus, superfluous, unused, unwanted, spare.

leg ▶ noun **1** *Lee broke his leg* **lower limb,** limb, shank; informal pin.
2 *the first leg of a European tour* **part,** stage, portion, segment, section, phase, stretch, lap.

– PHRASES **give someone a leg up** *we all want to give our kids a leg up in the world* **help/assist someone,** give someone assistance, lend someone a helping hand, give someone a boost. **leg it** informal See RUN (sense 1 of the verb). **on its/one's last legs** *the barn is on its last legs* **dilapidated,** worn out, rickety, about to fall apart, about to become obsolete; failing, dying, terminal, on one's deathbed. **pull someone's leg** *is Julie really sick or is she just pulling my leg?* **tease someone,** make fun of someone, tease, joke, make fun, fool, jest, joke with someone, play a (practical) joke on someone, play a trick on someone, make a monkey out of someone; hoax someone, fool someone, deceive someone, lead someone on, hoodwink someone, dupe someone, beguile someone, gull someone; informal kid someone, have someone on, rib someone, take someone for a ride, put someone on. **stretch one's legs** *we always like to stretch our legs after dinner* **go for a walk,** take a stroll, walk, stroll, move about, get some exercise.

legacy ▶ noun **1** *a legacy from a great aunt* **bequest,** inheritance, heritage, endowment, gift, patrimony, settlement, birthright; formal benefaction.
2 *a legacy of the residential schools* **consequence,** effect, upshot, spin-off, repercussion, aftermath, by-product, result.

legal ▶ adjective *the legal sale of alcoholic beverages* **lawful,** legitimate, licit, within the law, legalized, valid; permissible, permitted, allowable, allowed, aboveboard, admissible, acceptable; authorized, sanctioned, licensed, constitutional; informal legit.
ANTONYMS criminal.

legalize ▶ verb *where do you stand on legalizing marijuana?* **make legal,** decriminalize, legitimize, legitimate, permit, allow, authorize, sanction, license, validate; regularize, normalize; informal OK.
ANTONYMS prohibit.

legatee ▶ noun See BENEFICIARY.

legend ▶ noun **1** *Arthurian legends* **myth,** saga, epic, tale, story, folk tale, folk story, fairy tale, fable, mythos, folklore, lore, mythology, fantasy, oral history, folk tradition; urban myth.
2 *film legends* **celebrity,** star, superstar, icon, phenomenon, luminary, leading light, giant; informal celeb, megastar.

legendary ▶ adjective **1** *legendary knights* **fabled,** heroic, traditional, fairy-tale, storybook, mythical, mythological.
ANTONYMS factual, historical.
2 *a legendary figure in sports* **famous,** celebrated, famed, renowned, acclaimed, illustrious, esteemed, honored, exalted, venerable, well-known, popular, prominent, distinguished, great, eminent, preeminent, high-profile; formal lauded.

legerdemain ▶ noun **1** *stage magicians practicing legerdemain* **sleight of hand,** conjuring, magic, wizardry; formal prestidigitation; rare thaumaturgy.
2 *a piece of management legerdemain* **trickery,** cunning, artfulness, craftiness, chicanery, skulduggery, deceit, deception, artifice.

legible ▶ adjective *large, legible handwriting* **readable,** easy to read, easily deciphered, clear, plain, neat, decipherable, intelligible.

legion ▶ noun **1** *a military legion* **brigade,** regiment, battalion, company, troop, division, squadron, squad, platoon, phalanx, unit, force.
2 *the legions of TV cameras* **horde,** throng, multitude, host, crowd, mass, mob, gang, swarm, flock, herd, score, army, pack.

▶ adjective *her fans are legion* **numerous,** countless, innumerable, incalculable, many, abundant, plentiful; literary myriad.

legislate ▶ verb *we urge Congress to legislate against human cloning* **make laws,** pass laws, enact laws, formulate laws; authorize, decree, order, sanction.

legislation ▶ noun *pushing for stronger gun legislation* **law(s),** body of laws, rules, rulings, regulations, acts, bills, statutes, enactments, ordinances.

legislative ▶ adjective *a legislative assembly* **lawmaking,** judicial, juridical, parliamentary, governmental, policy-making.

legislator ▶ noun *let your legislators know how you feel about the state income tax* **lawmaker,** lawgiver; representative, congressman, congresswoman, senator; parliamentarian.

legitimate ▸ adjective **1** *the only form of legitimate gambling* **legal,** lawful, licit, legalized, authorized, permitted, permissible, allowable, allowed, admissible, sanctioned, approved, licensed, statutory, constitutional; informal legit, street legal.
ANTONYMS illegal.
2 *the legitimate heir* **rightful,** lawful, genuine, authentic, real, true, proper, authorized, sanctioned, acknowledged, recognized. See note at **GENUINE**.
ANTONYMS false, fraudulent.
3 *legitimate grounds for doubt* **valid,** sound, well-founded, justifiable, reasonable, sensible, just, fair, bona fide.
ANTONYMS illegal.

legitimize ▸ verb *this revised constitution will legitimize citizens' rights to hold private property* **validate,** legitimate, permit, authorize, sanction, license, condone, justify, endorse, support; legalize.
ANTONYMS outlaw.

leisure ▸ noun *the balance between leisure and work* **free time,** spare time, time off; recreation, relaxation, inactivity, pleasure; informal R and R, downtime.
ANTONYMS work.
– PHRASES **at your leisure** *Form A may be completed at your leisure* **at your convenience,** when it suits you, in your own (good/sweet) time, without haste, unhurriedly.

leisurely ▸ adjective *a leisurely stroll through town* **unhurried,** relaxed, easy, gentle, sedate, comfortable, restful, undemanding, slow, lazy.
ANTONYMS hurried.

lend ▸ verb **1** *I'll lend you my towel* **loan,** let someone use; advance.
ANTONYMS borrow.
2 *these examples lend weight to his assertions* **add,** impart, give, bestow, confer, provide, supply, furnish, contribute.
ANTONYMS detract.
– PHRASES **lend an ear** *when Travers gets up to speak, I hope you'll lend an ear* **listen,** pay attention, take notice, be attentive, concentrate, heed, pay heed; informal be all ears; archaic hearken. **lend a hand** *I'm here to lend a hand with the harvest* **help,** help out, give a helping hand, assist, give assistance, make a contribution, do one's bit; informal pitch in. **lend itself to** *the terrain lends itself to downhill skiing* **be suitable for,** be suited to, be appropriate for, be applicable for.

length ▸ noun **1** *a length of three or four yards | the whole length of the valley* **extent,** distance, linear measure, span, reach; area, expanse, stretch, range, scope.
2 *a considerable length of time* **period,** duration, stretch, span.
3 *a length of blue silk* **piece,** swatch, measure.
4 *the press criticized the length of her speech* **lengthiness,** extent, prolixity, wordiness, verbosity, long-windedness.
– PHRASES **at length 1** *the preacher spoke at length* **for a long time,** for ages, for hours, interminably, endlessly, ceaselessly, unendingly. **2** *Everett was questioned at length* **thoroughly,** fully, in detail, in depth, comprehensively, exhaustively, extensively. **3** *his search led him, at length, to Seattle* **after a long time,** eventually, in time, finally, at last, at long last, in the end, ultimately.

lengthen ▸ verb *he lengthened his stride to keep up | as the spring days lengthen* **elongate,** make longer, extend, prolong, protract, stretch out, drag out; expand, widen, broaden, enlarge; grow/get longer, draw out.
ANTONYMS shorten.

lengthy ▸ adjective **1** *a lengthy civil war* **long,** very long, long-lasting, prolonged, extended; informal marathon.
ANTONYMS short.
2 *lengthy discussions* **protracted,** overlong, long-drawn-out; verbose, wordy, prolix, long-winded; tedious, boring, interminable.
ANTONYMS brief.

lenient ▸ adjective *Brother Andrew was a lenient teacher* **merciful,** clement, forgiving, forbearing, tolerant, charitable, humane, indulgent, easygoing, magnanimous, sympathetic, compassionate, mild. See note at **MERCY**.
ANTONYMS severe.

CHOOSE THE RIGHT WORD

lenient, forbearing, indulgent, lax, merciful, permissive

Not all parents approach discipline in the same way. Someone who is **lenient** is willing to lower his or her standards of strictness when it comes to imposing discipline (*the principal was lenient with the students who had been caught playing hooky*). A parent who is **forbearing** struggles against giving in to negative feelings and is therefore able to abstain from hasty or ill-tempered actions, no matter what the provocation (*her father's forbearing attitude meant that she escaped with only a lecture*). **Indulgent** goes beyond forbearing and suggests catering to someone's whims (*an indulgent parent who seldom denied her child anything*). **Lax** is a negative kind of leniency involving laziness or indifference (*a lax mother who never imposed a curfew*), while **merciful** suggests a relaxing of standards on the basis of compassion (*a merciful mother who understood her daughter's anger*). To be **permissive** is also to be extremely lenient—an approach that connotes tolerance to the point of passivity (*the children's utter disregard for the rules was the result of their permissive upbringing*).

lesbian ▸ noun *the title character is a nineteen-year-old lesbian* **homosexual woman,** gay woman; informal butch, femme; offensive dyke, bulldyke, queer.
ANTONYMS heterosexual, straight woman.
▸ adjective *a long-term lesbian partnership* **homosexual,** gay, same-sex; Sapphic, homoerotic; informal butch; offensive dykey, queer.
ANTONYMS straight.

lesion ▶ **noun** *symptoms include clusters of red lesions* **wound,** injury, bruise, abrasion, contusion; ulcer, ulceration, sore, running sore, abscess; Medicine trauma.

less ▶ **pronoun** *the fare is **less than** $1* **a smaller amount than,** not so/as much as, under, below.
ANTONYMS more.
▶ **adjective** *there was less noise now* **not so much,** smaller, slighter, shorter, reduced; fewer.
▶ **adverb** *we must use the car less* **to a lesser degree,** to a smaller extent, not so/as much.
▶ **preposition** *figure the list price less 10 percent* **minus,** subtracting, excepting, without.
ANTONYMS plus.

> USAGE
>
> **less, fewer**
>
> Strictly, *less* applies to singular nouns (*less tonic water, please*) or units of measure (*less than six ounces of epoxy*). *Fewer* applies to plural nouns (*fewer guests arrived than expected*) or numbers of things (*we have three fewer members this year*). The exception in using *fewer* occurs when count nouns essentially function as mass nouns because the units are so very numerous or they aren't considered discrete items (the idea of individual units becomes meaningless). Hence *less* is used correctly with time and money: one isn't, ordinarily, talking about the number of years or the number of dollars but rather the amount of time or the amount of money—e.g.:
>
> - "On that mantra, Larry Clark has built a $45 million-a-year company in less than five years." (*Arizona Business Gazette*; Nov. 30, 1995.)
> - "Okay, how about $50 a month for such an apartment—less than two dollars a day?" (*Village Voice*; Apr. 29, 1997.)
>
> *Fewer*, in fact, is incorrect when intended to refer to a period of time—e.g.: "You can run from sea level to the sky and back to earth in as fast as 45 minutes (so far), but even today, going round-trip in fewer [read *less*] than 60 minutes carries a special cachet." (*Anchorage Daily News*; June 29, 1997.) But if the units of time are thought of as wholes, and not by fractions, then *fewer* is called for (*fewer days abroad; fewer weeks spent apart*). Hence we say *less documentation* but *fewer documents*; *less whispering* but *fewer remarks*; *less of a burden* but *fewer burdens*; *less fattening* but *fewer calories*.
>
> Fastidious writers and editors preserve the old distinction. But the loose usage crops up often—e.g.: "You will have less [read *fewer*] people to call and haunt about paying for their outfits and buying their accessories." (*Boston Herald* [magazine]; Oct. 19, 1997.) The linguistic hegemony by which *less* has encroached on *fewer*'s territory is probably now irreversible. What has clinched this development is something as mundane as the express checkout lines in supermarkets. They're typically bedecked with signs cautioning, "15 items or less." These signs are all but ubiquitous in the United States. But the occasional more literate supermarket owner uses a different sign: "15 or fewer items."
>
> Finally, even with the strict usage, it's sometimes a close call whether a thing is a mass noun or a count noun, and hence whether *less* or *fewer* is proper. Take, for example, a percentage: should it be "less than 10% of the homeowners were there" or "fewer than 10% of the homeowners were there"? One could argue that a percentage is something counted (i.e., 10 out of 100), and thus requires *fewer*. One could also argue that a percentage is a collective mass noun (akin, e.g., to money), and thus requires *less*. The latter is the better argument because most percentages aren't whole numbers anyway. And even if it were a toss-up between the two theories, it's sound to choose *less*, which is less formal in tone than *fewer*.
>
> If, in strict usage, *less* applies to singular nouns and *fewer* to plural nouns, the choice is clear: "one less golfer on the course," not "one fewer golfer." This is tricky only because *less* is being applied to a singular count noun, whereas it usually applies to a mass noun. Lyricist Hal David got it right in "One Less Bell to Answer" (1970). Nearly a quarter of the time, however, writers use *one fewer*, an awkward and unidiomatic phrase. One can't help thinking that this is a kind of hypercorrection induced by underanalysis of the *less*-vs.-*fewer* question.
>
> *Lesser*, like *less*, refers to quantity, but is confined to use as an adjective before a singular noun and following an article (*the lesser crime*) or alone before a plural noun (*lesser athletes*), thus performing a function no longer idiomatically possible with less. Dating from the thirteenth century, this formal usage allows *lesser* to act as an antonym of *greater*. **— BG**

lessen ▶ **verb 1** *the new law did little to lessen the stigma* **reduce,** make less/smaller, minimize, decrease; allay, assuage, alleviate, attenuate, palliate, ease, dull, deaden, blunt, moderate, mitigate, dampen, soften, tone down, dilute, weaken.
ANTONYMS increase.
2 *the pain began to lessen* **grow less,** grow smaller, decrease, diminish, decline, subside, abate; fade, die down/off, let up, ease off, tail off, drop (off/away), fall, dwindle, ebb, wane, recede.
ANTONYMS increase.
3 *his behavior lessened him in their eyes* **diminish,** degrade, discredit, devalue, belittle.
ANTONYMS aggrandize.

lesser ▶ **adjective 1** *a lesser offense* **less important,** minor, secondary, subsidiary, marginal, ancillary, auxiliary, supplementary, peripheral; inferior, insignificant, unimportant, petty.
ANTONYMS greater, primary.

2 *you look down at us lesser mortals* **subordinate,** minor, inferior, second-class, subservient, lowly, humble.
ANTONYMS superior.

lesson ▶ noun **1** *a math lesson* **class,** session, seminar, tutorial, lecture, period, period of instruction/teaching.
2 (**lessons**) *they should be industrious at their lessons* **exercises,** assignments, schoolwork, homework, study.
3 *reading the lesson in church* **Bible reading,** scripture, text, reading, passage.
4 *Stuart's accident should be a lesson to all parents* **warning,** deterrent, caution; example, exemplar, message, moral.

let ▶ verb **1** *let him sleep for now* **allow to,** permit to, give permission to, give leave to, authorize to, sanction to, grant the right to, license to, empower to, enable to, entitle to; archaic suffer to.
ANTONYMS prevent, prohibit.
2 *Wilcox opened the door to let her through* **allow to go,** permit to pass; make way for.
– PHRASES **let someone down** *I'm afraid I've let the team down* **fail,** fail to support, disappoint, disillusion; abandon, desert, leave stranded, leave in the lurch. **let something down** *Maryann let down the hem on her mother's old prom dress* **lengthen,** make longer. **let fly 1** *he let fly with a brick* **hurl,** fling, throw, propel, pitch, lob, toss, launch; shoot, fire, blast; informal chuck, sling, heave. **2** *she let fly at Geoffrey* **lose one's temper with,** lash out at, scold, chastise, chide, rant at, inveigh against, rail against; explode at, burst out at, let someone have it; formal excoriate. **let go** *don't let go of the steering wheel* **release,** release one's hold on, loose/loosen one's hold on, relinquish; archaic unhand. **let someone go** *they let half of the warehouse crew go* **dismiss,** discharge, lay off, give notice to; informal sack, fire, ax, give someone their marching orders, send packing, give someone the boot, give someone the (old) heave-ho, can, pink-slip. **let someone in** *they seemed reluctant to let me in* **allow to enter,** allow in, admit, open the door to; receive, welcome, greet. **let someone in on something** *we can't let you in on the details just yet* **include in,** count in on, admit in on, allow to share in, let participate in, inform about, tell about. **let someone off 1** informal *I'll let you off this time* **pardon,** forgive, grant an amnesty to; deal leniently with, be merciful to, have mercy on; acquit, absolve, exonerate, clear, vindicate; informal let someone off the hook; formal exculpate. **2** *he let me off work* **excuse from,** exempt from, spare from. **let on** informal **1** *I never let on that I felt anxious* **reveal,** make known, tell, disclose, mention, divulge, let slip, give away, make public; blab; informal let the cat out of the bag, give the game away. **2** *he let on that he'd won* **pretend,** feign, affect, make out, make believe, simulate. **let something out 1** *I let out a cry of triumph* **utter,** emit, give, give vent to, produce, issue, express, voice, release. **2** *she let out that he'd given her a lift home* **reveal,** make known, tell, disclose, mention, divulge, let slip, give away, let it be known, blurt out. **let someone out** *they let me out of the hospital on Monday* **release,** liberate, (set) free, let go, discharge; set/turn loose, allow to leave. **let up** informal**1** *the rain has let up* **abate,** lessen, decrease, diminish, subside, relent, slacken, die down/off, ease (off), tail off; ebb, wane, dwindle, fade; stop, cease, finish. **2** *you never let up, do you?* **relax,** ease up/off, slow down; pause, break (off), take a break, rest, stop; informal take a breather. **3** *I promise I'll let up on him* **treat less severely,** be more lenient with, be kinder to; informal go easy on.

letdown ▶ noun *the movie was a big letdown after reading the book* **disappointment,** anticlimax, comedown, nonevent, fiasco, setback, blow, disadvantage; informal washout.

lethal ▶ adjective *a lethal dose of arsenic* **fatal,** deadly, mortal, death-dealing, life-threatening, murderous, killing; poisonous, toxic, noxious, venomous; dangerous, destructive, harmful, pernicious; literary deathly, nocuous.
ANTONYMS harmless, safe.

lethargic ▶ adjective *feeling depressed and lethargic* **sluggish,** inert, inactive, slow, torpid, lifeless; languid, listless, lazy, idle, indolent, shiftless, slothful, apathetic, weary, tired, fatigued.

lethargy ▶ noun *the lethargy may be related to his latest medication* **sluggishness,** inertia, inactivity, inaction, slowness, torpor, torpidity, lifelessness, listlessness, languor, laziness, idleness, indolence, shiftlessness, sloth, apathy, passivity, weariness, tiredness, lassitude, fatigue, inanition; literary hebetude.
ANTONYMS vigor, energy.

letter ▶ noun **1** *capital letters* **alphabetical character,** character, sign, symbol, mark, figure, rune; Linguistics grapheme.
2 *he wrote Len a letter* **written message,** message, written communication, communication, note, line, missive, dispatch; correspondence, news, information, intelligence, word; post, mail; formal epistle.
3 (**letters**) *a man of letters* **learning,** scholarship, erudition, education, knowledge; intellect, intelligence, enlightenment, wisdom, sagacity, culture.
– PHRASES **to the letter** *he followed her instructions to the letter* **strictly,** precisely, exactly, accurately, closely, faithfully, religiously, punctiliously, literally, verbatim, in every detail.

lettered ▶ adjective *in colonial Brattleboro, this household of lettered young women was quite a curiosity* **learned,** erudite, academic, educated, well-educated, well-read, widely read, knowledgeable, intellectual, well-schooled, enlightened, cultured, cultivated, scholarly, bookish, highbrow, studious, cerebral.
ANTONYMS ill-educated.

letup ▶ noun informal *there can be no letup in the war against drugs* **abatement,** lessening, decrease, diminishing, diminution, decline, relenting, remission, slackening, weakening, relaxation, dying down, easing off, tailing off, dropping away/off; respite, break, breather, interval, hiatus, suspension, cessation, stop, pause.

level ▶ adjective **1** *a smooth and level surface* **flat,** smooth, even, uniform, plane, flush, plumb.
ANTONYMS uneven, bumpy.
2 *he kept his voice level* **unchanging,** steady, unvarying, even, uniform, regular, constant, invariable, unaltering; calm, unemotional, composed, equable, unruffled, serene, tranquil.
ANTONYMS shaky, unsteady.
3 *his eyes were* ***level with*** *hers* **aligned with,** on the same level as, on a level with, at the same height as, in line with.
ANTONYMS uneven, above, below.
▶ noun **1** *she is at a managerial level* **rank,** standing, status, position; echelon, degree, grade, gradation, stage, standard, rung; class, stratum, group, grouping, set, classification.
2 *a high level of unemployment* **quantity, amount,** extent, measure, degree, volume, size, magnitude, intensity, proportion.
3 *the level of water is rising* **height,** altitude, elevation.
4 *the sixth level* **floor,** story, deck.
▶ verb **1** *tilt the pan to level the mixture* **make level,** level out/off, make even, even out, make flat, flatten, smooth, smooth out, make uniform.
2 *bulldozers leveled the building* **raze,** demolish, flatten, topple, destroy; tear down, knock down, pull down, bulldoze.
3 *he leveled his opponent with a single blow* **knock down,** lay out, flatten, floor, fell; knock out; informal KO, kayo.
4 *Carl leveled the playing field* **equalize,** make equal, equal, even, even up, make level.
5 *he leveled his pistol at me* **aim,** point, direct, train, focus, turn, sight.
6 informal *I knew you'd* ***level with*** *me* **be frank with,** be open with, be honest with, be aboveboard with, tell the truth to, tell all to, hide nothing from, be straightforward with, be upfront with; informal come clean with, set the record straight with.
– PHRASES **on the level** informal *Urbana is such a smooth talker, we never know for sure if she's on the level* **genuine,** straight, honest, aboveboard, fair, true, sincere, straightforward, trustworthy; informal upfront, on the up and up.

levelheaded ▶ adjective *how did those nitwits end up with such levelheaded children?* **sensible,** practical, realistic, prudent, pragmatic, wise, reasonable, rational, mature, judicious, sound, sober, businesslike, no-nonsense, composed, calm, 'calm, cool, and collected', confident, well-balanced, equable, coolheaded, self-possessed, having one's feet on the ground; informal unflappable, together, grounded.
ANTONYMS excitable, foolish.

lever ▶ noun **1** *you can insert a lever and pry the rail off* **crowbar,** bar, jimmy.
2 *he pulled the lever* **handle,** grip, pull, switch.
▶ verb *he levered the door open* **pry,** prize, force, wrench, pull, wrest, heave; informal jimmy.

leverage ▶ noun **1** *the long handles provide increased leverage* **grip,** purchase, hold; support, anchorage, force, strength.
2 *the union's leverage at the bargaining table* **influence,** power, authority, weight, sway, pull, control, say, dominance, advantage, pressure; informal clout, muscle, teeth, bargaining chip.

levitate ▶ verb *the spaceship slowly levitated over the cornfield* **float,** rise, rise into the air, hover, be suspended, glide, hang, fly, soar up.

levity ▶ noun *without some occasional levity, the working environment is no better than a sweatshop* **lightheartedness,** high spirits, vivacity, liveliness, cheerfulness, cheeriness, humor, gaiety, fun, jocularity, hilarity, frivolity, amusement, mirth, laughter, merriment, glee, comedy, wit, wittiness, jollity, joviality.
ANTONYMS seriousness.

levy ▶ verb *the government's right to levy taxes* **impose,** charge, exact, raise, collect; rare mulct.
▶ noun **1** *the levy of taxes* **imposition,** raising, collection; formal exaction.
2 *the levy on alcohol* **tax,** tariff, toll, excise, duty, imposition, impost; rare mulct.

lewd ▶ adjective **1** *a lewd old man* **lecherous,** lustful, licentious, lascivious, dirty, prurient, salacious, lubricious, libidinous; debauched, depraved, degenerate, decadent, dissipated, dissolute, perverted, wanton; formal concupiscent; archaic lickerish.
ANTONYMS chaste.
2 *a lewd song* **vulgar,** crude, smutty, dirty, filthy, obscene, pornographic, coarse, off-color, unseemly, indecent, salacious; rude, racy, risqué, naughty, bawdy, ribald; informal **blue,** raunchy, X-rated, XXX, porno; euphemistic **adult.**
ANTONYMS clean.

liability ▶ noun **1** *journalists' liability for defamation* **accountability,** responsibility, legal responsibility, answerability; blame, culpability, guilt, fault.
ANTONYMS immunity.
2 *they have big liabilities* **financial obligations,** debts, arrears, dues.
ANTONYMS asset.
3 *she was proving to be a liability* **hindrance,** encumbrance, burden, handicap, nuisance, inconvenience; obstacle, impediment, disadvantage, weakness, weak link, shortcoming; millstone around one's neck, albatross, Achilles heel.
ANTONYMS advantage, asset.

liable ▶ adjective **1** *they are liable for negligence* **responsible,** legally responsible, accountable, answerable, chargeable, blameworthy, at fault, culpable, guilty. See note at **RESPONSIBLE.**
2 *my income is liable to fluctuate wildly* **likely,** inclined, tending, disposed, apt, predisposed, prone, given.
3 *areas* ***liable to*** *flooding* **exposed to,** prone to, subject to, susceptible to, vulnerable to, in danger of, at risk of.

liaison ▶ noun **1** *Dave was my liaison with the district manager* **intermediary,** mediator, middleman, contact, link, connection, go-between, representative, agent.
2 *a secret liaison* **love affair,** affair, relationship, romance, attachment, fling, amour, romantic entanglement, entanglement, tryst; informal hanky-panky.

liar ▶ noun *even in a court of law, Jeff was a*

shameless liar **deceiver,** fibber, perjurer, false witness, fabricator, equivocator; fabulist; informal storyteller.

libation ▶ **noun 1** *they pour libations into the holy well* **liquid offering,** offering, tribute, oblation.
2 humorous *would you like a libation?* **(alcoholic) drink,** beverage, liquid refreshment; dram, draft, nip, shot; informal tipple, nightcap, pick-me-up; archaic potation.

libel ▶ **noun** *she sued two newspapers for libel* **defamation,** defamation of character, character assassination, calumny, misrepresentation, scandalmongering; aspersions, denigration, vilification, disparagement, derogation, insult, slander, malicious gossip; lie, slur, smear, untruth, false report; informal mudslinging, bad-mouthing.
▶ **verb** *she alleged the magazine had libeled her* **defame,** malign, slander, blacken someone's name, sully someone's reputation, speak ill/evil of, traduce, smear, cast aspersions on, drag someone's name through the mud, besmirch, tarnish, taint, tell lies about, stain, impugn someone's character/integrity, vilify, denigrate, disparage, run down, stigmatize, discredit, slur; informal dis, bad-mouth; formal derogate, calumniate. See note at **MALIGN**.

liberal ▶ **adjective 1** *the values of a liberal society* **tolerant,** unprejudiced, unbigoted, broad-minded, open-minded, enlightened; permissive, free, free and easy, easygoing, libertarian, indulgent, lenient.
ANTONYMS narrow-minded, bigoted.
2 *a liberal social agenda* **progressive,** advanced, modern, forward-looking, forward-thinking, progressivist, enlightened, reformist, radical.
ANTONYMS reactionary, conservative.
3 *a liberal education* **wide-ranging,** broad-based, general.
4 *a liberal interpretation of divorce laws* **flexible,** broad, loose, rough, free, general, nonliteral, nonspecific, imprecise, vague, indefinite.
ANTONYMS strict, to the letter.
5 *a liberal coating of paint* **abundant,** copious, ample, plentiful, generous, lavish, luxuriant, profuse, considerable, prolific, rich; literary plenteous.
ANTONYMS scant.
6 *they were liberal with their cash* **generous,** openhanded, unsparing, unstinting, ungrudging, lavish, free, munificent, bountiful, beneficent, benevolent, bighearted, philanthropic, charitable, altruistic, unselfish; literary bounteous.
ANTONYMS careful, miserly.

liberate ▶ **verb 1** *they liberated the prisoners* **set free,** free, release, let out, let go, set/let loose, save, rescue; emancipate, enfranchise.
ANTONYMS imprison, enslave.
2 *he liberated a trinket from her jewelry box* **steal,** take; informal swipe, nab, pinch, borrow.

libertine ▶ **noun** *an unrepentant libertine* **philanderer,** playboy, rake, roué, Don Juan, Lothario, Casanova, Romeo; lecher, seducer, womanizer, adulterer, debauchee, profligate, wanton; informal skirt-chaser, ladykiller, lech, wolf; formal fornicator.

liberty ▶ **noun 1** *personal liberty* **freedom,** independence, free rein, license, self-determination, free will, latitude.
ANTONYMS constraint, slavery.
2 *the fight for liberty* **independence,** freedom, autonomy, sovereignty, self-government, self-rule, self-determination; civil liberties, human rights.
ANTONYMS tyranny.
3 *the liberty to go where you please* **right,** birthright, prerogative, entitlement, privilege, permission, sanction, authorization, authority, license, power.
ANTONYMS constraint.
– PHRASES **at liberty 1** *he was at liberty for three months* **free,** on the loose, loose, at large, unconfined; escaped, out, on the lam.
2 *you are at liberty to leave* **free,** permitted, allowed, authorized, able, entitled, eligible.
take liberties with *I'd appreciate it if you would refrain from taking liberties with me* **act with familiarity toward,** show disrespect to/toward, act with impropriety with/toward, act indecorously with, be impudent with, act with impertinence to/toward; take advantage of, exploit.
– PHRASES **take the liberty** *may I take the liberty to order champagne?* **presume,** venture, be so bold as.

CHOOSE THE RIGHT WORD

liberty, freedom, independence, license, permission

The Fourth of July is the day on which Americans commemorate their nation's **independence**, a word that implies the ability to stand alone, without being sustained by anything else. While *independence* is usually associated with countries or nations, **freedom** and **liberty** more often apply to individuals. But unlike *freedom*, which implies an absence of restraint or compulsion (*the freedom to speak openly*), *liberty* implies the power to choose among alternatives rather than merely being unrestrained (*the liberty to select their own form of government*). *Freedom* can also apply to many different types of oppressive influences (*freedom from interruption; freedom to leave the room at any time*), while *liberty* often connotes deliverance or release (*he gave the slaves their liberty*). **License** may imply the *liberty* to disobey rules or regulations imposed on others, especially when there is an advantage to be gained in doing so (*poetic license*). But more often it refers to an abuse of *liberty* or the power to do whatever one pleases (*a license to sell drugs*). **Permission** is an even broader term than *license*, suggesting the capacity to act without interference or censure, usually with some degree of approval or authority (*permission to be absent from his post*).

libidinous ▶ **adjective** *libidinous impulses* **lustful,** lecherous, lascivious, lewd, carnal, salacious, prurient, licentious, libertine, lubricious, dissolute, debauched, depraved, degenerate, decadent, dissipated, wanton, promiscuous; informal wolfish; formal concupiscent.

libido ▶ noun *alcohol may impair your libido* **sex drive,** sexual appetite; sexual desire, desire, passion, sensuality, sexuality, lust, lustfulness; informal horniness; formal concupiscence.

license ▶ noun **1** *a driver's license* **permit,** certificate, document, documentation, authorization, warrant; certification, credentials; pass, papers.
2 *you have license to make changes* **permission,** authority, right, a free hand, leave, authorization, entitlement, privilege, prerogative; liberty, freedom, power, latitude, scope, free rein, carte blanche, a blank check, the go-ahead. See note at LIBERTY.
3 *poetic license* **disregard for the facts,** inventiveness, invention, creativity, imagination, fancy, freedom, looseness.
▶ verb *we're licensed to sell beer* **permit,** allow, authorize, grant/give authority, grant/give permission, grant/give a license; certify, empower, entitle, enable, give approval, let, qualify, sanction; informal rubber stamp.
ANTONYMS ban.

licentious ▶ adjective *a book that exaggerates the licentious behavior of the rich and famous* **dissolute,** dissipated, debauched, degenerate, immoral, naughty, wanton, decadent, depraved, sinful, corrupt; lustful, lecherous, lascivious, libidinous, prurient, lubricious, lewd, promiscuous, lickerish; formal concupiscent.
ANTONYMS moral.

licit ▶ adjective See LEGITIMATE (sense 1).

lick ▶ verb **1** *the spaniel licked his face* **pass one's tongue over,** touch with one's tongue, tongue; lap.
2 informal *they licked the home team 3–0* See DEFEAT (sense 1 of the verb).
3 informal *we've got that problem licked* **overcome,** get the better of, find an answer/solution to, conquer, beat, control, master, curb, check.
▶ noun informal **1** *a lick of paint* **dab,** bit, drop, dash, spot, touch, splash; informal smidgen.
2 *a guitar lick* **short solo,** riff, line, theme.
– PHRASES **lick someone's boots/shoes** *nobody licks the boss's boots with more finesse than Little Miss* **suck up to,** toady to, be servile to, be obsequious to, fawn over, flatter, butter up, ingratiate oneself with, brown-nose with/to.

licking ▶ noun informal **1** *the Mariners took a licking* **defeat,** beating, trouncing, thrashing; informal hiding, pasting, hammering, drubbing, shellacking.
2 *Ray got the worst licking of his life* **thrashing,** beating, flogging, whipping; informal walloping, hiding, pasting, whaling.

lid ▶ noun *the lid of a saucepan* **cover,** top, cap, covering.
– PHRASES **put a lid on it** *hey, chatterbox, put a lid on it* **stop talking, be quiet,** hold your tongue; informal shut up, hush up, shut your mouth, shut your face, shut your trap, button your lip, pipe down, put a sock in it, give it a rest, save it, not another word. **blow the lid off** informal *intelligence officials have blown the lid off the so-called crusade against corruption* **expose,** reveal, make known, make public, bring into the open, disclose, divulge; informal spill the beans, blab.

lie[1] ▶ noun *loyalty had made him tell lies* **untruth,** falsehood, fib, fabrication, deception, invention, fiction, piece of fiction, falsification; (little) white lie, half-truth, exaggeration; informal tall tale, whopper, taradiddle.
ANTONYMS truth.
▶ verb *he lied to the police* **tell an untruth,** tell a lie, fib, dissemble, dissimulate, misinform, mislead, tell a white lie, perjure oneself, commit perjury, prevaricate; informal lie through one's teeth, stretch the truth; formal forswear oneself.

CHOOSE THE RIGHT WORD

lie, equivocate, fabricate, fib, prevaricate, rationalize

If your spouse asks you whether you remembered to mail the tax forms and you say "Yes," even though you know they're still sitting on the passenger seat of your car, you're telling a **lie**, which is a deliberately false statement. If you launch into a lengthy explanation of the day's frustrations and setbacks, the correct word would be **prevaricate**, which is to quibble, dodge the point, or confuse the issue so as to avoid telling the truth. If you tell your spouse that you would have mailed the taxes, but then you started thinking about an important deduction you might be entitled to take and decided it would be unwise to mail them without looking into it, you're **rationalizing**, which is to come up with reasons that put your own behavior in the most favorable possible light. If you say that there was an accident in front of the post office that prevented you from finding a parking space and there really wasn't, **fabricate** is the correct verb, meaning that you've invented a false story or excuse without the harsh connotations of *lie* (*she fabricated an elaborate story about how they got lost on their way home*). **Equivocate** implies saying one thing and meaning another; it usually suggests the use of words that have more than one meaning, or whose ambiguity may be misleading. For example, if your spouse says, "Did you take care of the taxes today?" you might equivocate by saying "Yes," you took care of them—meaning that you finished completing the forms and sealing them in the envelope, but that you didn't actually get them to the post office. To **fib** is to tell a falsehood about something unimportant; it is often used as a euphemism for *lie* (*a child who fibs about eating his vegetables*).

lie[2] ▶ verb **1** *he was lying on a bed* **recline,** lie down, lie back, be recumbent, be prostrate, be supine, be prone, be stretched out, sprawl, rest, repose, lounge, loll.
ANTONYMS stand.

2 *her handbag lay on a chair* **be placed,** be situated, be positioned, rest.
3 *lying on the border of Switzerland and Austria* **be situated,** be located, be placed, be found, be sited.
4 *the difficulty lies in building real quality into the products* **consist,** be inherent, be present, be contained, exist, reside.
– PHRASES **lie heavy on** *keeping these secrets from her family lies heavy on her* **trouble,** worry, bother, torment, oppress, nag, prey on one's mind, plague, niggle at, gnaw at, haunt; informal bug. **lie low** *his family will have to lie low until the trial is over* **hide,** go into hiding, conceal oneself, keep out of sight, go underground, hide out; informal hole up. See note at LAY[1].

> USAGE
> **lie**
> In the sense of telling an untruth, the verb is inflected *lie, lied, lied.*
> The more troublesome inflections belong to the senses of reclining, being placed, and being situated: *lie, lay, lain.* A murderer may *lie in wait.* Yesterday he *lay in wait.* And for several days he *has lain in wait*—e.g.: "The Ramseys say an intruder may have lay [read *lain*] in wait for hours before killing the 6-year-old beauty queen." (*Austin American-Statesman*; Mar. 18, 2000.) — **BG**

life ▶ noun 1 *the joy of giving life to a child* **existence,** being, living, animation; sentience, creation, viability.
ANTONYMS death, nonexistence.
2 *threats to life on the planet* **living things,** living beings, living creatures, the living; human/animal/plant life, fauna, flora, ecosystems; human beings, humanity, humankind, mankind, man.
3 *an easy life* **way of life,** lifestyle, situation, fate, lot.
4 *the last nine months of his life* **lifetime,** life span, days, time on earth, existence.
5 *he is full of life* **vivacity,** animation, liveliness, vitality, verve, high spirits, exuberance, zest, buoyancy, enthusiasm, energy, vigor, dynamism, élan, gusto, brio, bounce, spirit, fire; movement; informal oomph, pizzazz, pep, zing, zip, vim.
6 *the life of the party* **moving spirit,** vital spirit, spirit, life force, lifeblood, heart, soul.
7 *more than 1,500 lives were lost in the accident* **person,** human being, individual, soul.
8 *I really wanted a new car, but that's life* **the way of the world,** the way things go, the human condition; fate, destiny, providence, kismet, karma, fortune, luck, chance; informal the way the cookie crumbles, the breaks.
– PHRASES **come to life 1** *the kids are finally coming to life* **become active,** come alive, wake up, awaken, arouse, rouse, stir; literary waken.
2 *the carved angel suddenly came to life* **become animate,** come alive. **for dear life** *we held on to the rope for dear life* **desperately,** with all one's might, for all one is worth, as fast/hard as possible, like the devil. **give one's life 1** *he would give his life for her* **die for,** lay down one's life for, sacrifice oneself for, offer one's life for, die to save. **2** *he gave his life to the company* **dedicate oneself,** devote oneself, give oneself, surrender oneself.

life-and-death ▶ adjective *a life-and-death decision* **vital,** of vital importance, crucial, critical, urgent, pressing, pivotal, momentous, important, all-important, key, serious, grave, significant; informal earth-shattering; formal of great moment.
ANTONYMS trivial.

lifeblood ▶ noun *for most of these islands, the lifeblood is tourism* **life force,** life, essential constituent, driving force, vital spark, inspiration, stimulus, essence, crux, heart, soul, core.

lifeless ▶ adjective 1 *a lifeless body* **dead,** departed, perished, gone, no more, passed on/away, stiff, cold, (as) dead as a doornail; formal deceased; rare demised.
ANTONYMS alive.
2 *a lifeless rag doll* **inanimate,** without life, inert, insentient.
ANTONYMS animate.
3 *a lifeless landscape* **barren,** sterile, bare, desolate, stark, arid, infertile, uncultivated, uninhabited; bleak, colorless, characterless, soulless.
4 *a lifeless performance* **lackluster,** spiritless, apathetic, torpid, lethargic; dull, monotonous, boring, tedious, dreary, unexciting, expressionless, emotionless, colorless, characterless.
ANTONYMS vibrant, lively.

lifelike ▶ adjective *the doll is so lifelike* **realistic,** true to life, representational, faithful, exact, precise, detailed, vivid, graphic, natural, naturalistic; Art kitchen-sink.
ANTONYMS unrealistic.

lifelong ▶ adjective *a lifelong commitment* **lasting,** long-lasting, long-term, constant, stable, established, steady, enduring, permanent.
ANTONYMS ephemeral.

lifestyle ▶ noun *their privileged lifestyle* **way of life,** way of living, life, situation, fate, lot; conduct, behavior, customs, culture, habits, ways, mores; Anthropology lifeway.

lifetime ▶ noun 1 *he did a lot in his lifetime* **life span,** life, days, duration of life, one's time (on earth), existence, one's career.
2 *it would take* ***a lifetime*** **all one's life,** a very long time, an eternity, years (on end), eons; informal ages (and ages), an age.

lift ▶ verb 1 *lift the pack onto your back* **raise,** hoist, heave, haul up, heft, raise up/aloft, elevate, hold high; pick up, grab, take up, scoop up, snatch up; winch up, jack up, lever up; informal hump; literary upheave.
ANTONYMS drop, put down.
2 *the news lifted his spirits* **boost,** raise, buoy up, elevate, cheer up, perk up, uplift, brighten up, gladden, encourage, stimulate, revive; informal buck up.
ANTONYMS subdue.

3 *the fog had lifted* **clear,** rise, disperse, dissipate, disappear, vanish, dissolve.
ANTONYMS appear.
4 *the ban has been lifted* **cancel,** remove, withdraw, revoke, rescind, annul, void, discontinue, end, stop, terminate.
ANTONYMS establish, impose.
5 *he lifted his voice* **amplify,** raise, make louder, increase.
ANTONYMS soften, quiet.
6 informal *he lifted sections from a 1986 article* **plagiarize,** pirate, copy, reproduce, poach, steal; informal crib, rip off, pinch.
7 informal *she lifted a wallet* See STEAL (sense 1 of the verb).
▶ **noun 1** *give me a lift up* **push,** boost, hoist, heave, thrust, shove.
2 *he gave me* ***a lift*** *to the airport* **a ride,** a drive, transportation.
3 *that goal will give his confidence a real lift* **boost,** fillip, stimulus, impetus, encouragement, spur, push; improvement, enhancement; informal shot in the arm, pick-me-up.
– PHRASES **lift off** *the helicopters lifted off at 1030 hours* **take off,** become airborne, take to the air, take wing; be launched, blast off, rise.

light[1] ▶ **noun 1** *the light of candles* **illumination,** brightness, luminescence, luminosity, shining, gleaming, gleam, brilliance, radiance, luster, glowing, glow, blaze, glare, dazzle; sunlight, moonlight, starlight, lamplight, firelight; ray of light, beam of light; literary effulgence, refulgence, lambency.
ANTONYMS darkness.
2 *there was a light on in the hall* **lamp,** wall light; headlight, headlamp, sidelight; streetlight, floodlight; lantern; flashlight.
3 *have you got a light?* **match,** (cigarette) lighter.
4 *we'll wait for the light* **daylight,** daylight hours, daytime, day; dawn, morning, daybreak, sunrise; natural light, sunlight.
ANTONYMS darkness, nighttime.
5 *he saw the problem in a different light* **aspect,** angle, slant, approach, interpretation, viewpoint, standpoint, context, hue, complexion.
6 *light dawned on Loretta* **understanding,** enlightenment, illumination, comprehension, insight, awareness, knowledge.
ANTONYMS ignorance.
7 *an eminent legal light* **expert,** authority, master, leader, guru, leading light, luminary.
▶ **verb** *Alan lit the kindling* **set alight,** set light to, set burning, set on fire, set fire to, put/set a match to, ignite, kindle, spark (off).
ANTONYMS extinguish.
▶ **adjective 1** *a light, cheerful room* **bright,** full of light, well-lit, well-illuminated, sunny.
ANTONYMS dark, gloomy.
2 *light shades of blue and rose* **light-colored,** light-toned, pale, pale-colored, pastel.
ANTONYMS dark, deep.
3 *light hair* **fair,** light-colored, blond/blonde, golden, flaxen.
ANTONYMS dark, brunette.
– PHRASES **bring something to light** *the surprise inspection brought some incriminating evidence to light* **reveal,** disclose, expose, uncover, unearth, dig up/out, bring to notice, identify.
come to light *a fact important to this case has just come to light* **be discovered,** be uncovered, be unearthed, come out, become known, become apparent, appear, materialize, emerge.
in (the) light of *in light of this new information, there is no reason to continue our questioning* **taking into consideration,** taking into account, considering, bearing in mind, taking note of, in view of. **light into** informal **1** *we started lighting into our attackers* See SET ON/UPON at SET[1].
2 *my father lit into me for being late* See SCOLD (verb). **light on/upon** *we'd almost given up when we lit upon this article about Mathew's murder trial* **come across,** chance on/upon, hit on/upon, happen on/upon, stumble on/upon/across, find, discover, uncover, come up with.
light up 1 *the dashboard lit up* **become bright,** brighten, lighten, shine, gleam, flare, blaze, glint, sparkle, shimmer, glisten, scintillate.
2 *he lit up outside the bar* **start smoking,** light a cigarette. **light something up 1** *a flare lit up the night sky* **make bright,** brighten, illuminate, lighten, throw/cast light on, shine on, irradiate; literary illumine, illume. **2** *her enthusiasm lit up her face* **animate,** irradiate, brighten, cheer up, enliven. **throw/cast/shed (some) light on** *perhaps I can shed some light on this problem* **explain,** elucidate, clarify, clear up, interpret.
out like a light *after a day at the beach, these kids will be out like a light by eight o'clock* **asleep,** unconscious, comatose; informal out cold, dead to the world.

light[2] ▶ **adjective 1** *it's light enough to carry* **easy to lift,** not heavy, lightweight; easy to carry, portable.
ANTONYMS heavy.
2 *a light cotton robe* **flimsy,** lightweight, insubstantial, thin; delicate, floaty, gauzy, gossamer, diaphanous.
ANTONYMS heavy, thick.
3 *she is light on her feet* **nimble,** agile, lithe, limber, lissome, graceful; light-footed, fleet-footed, quick, quick-moving, spry, sprightly; informal twinkle-toed; literary fleet, lightsome.
ANTONYMS clumsy.
4 *a light soil* **friable,** sandy, easily dug, workable, crumbly, loose.
ANTONYMS dense, heavy.
5 *a light dinner* **small,** modest, simple, easily digested; informal low-cal.
ANTONYMS heavy, rich.
6 *light duties* **easy,** simple, undemanding, untaxing; informal cushy.
ANTONYMS hard, burdensome.
7 *his eyes gleamed with light mockery* **gentle,** mild, moderate, slight; playful, lighthearted.
ANTONYMS serious.
8 *light reading* **entertaining,** lightweight, diverting, undemanding, frivolous, superficial, trivial.
ANTONYMS serious, deep.
9 *a light heart* **carefree,** lighthearted, cheerful, cheery, happy, merry, jolly, blithe, bright, sunny; buoyant, bubbly, jaunty, bouncy, breezy, optimistic, positive, upbeat, ebullient; dated gay.
10 *this is no light matter* **unimportant,** insignificant, trivial, trifling, petty, inconsequential, superficial.

ANTONYMS serious, important.
11 *light footsteps* **gentle,** delicate, soft, dainty; faint, indistinct.
ANTONYMS heavy.
12 *her head felt light* **dizzy,** giddy, lightheaded, faint, vertiginous; informal woozy.

lighten[1] ▶ verb **1** *the first touch of dawn lightened the sky* **make lighter,** make brighter, brighten, light up, illuminate, throw/cast light on, shine on, irradiate; literary illumine, illume.
ANTONYMS darken.
2 *he used lemon juice to lighten his hair* **whiten,** make whiter, bleach, blanch, make paler.
ANTONYMS darken.

lighten[2] ▶ verb **1** *lightening the burden of taxation* **make lighter,** lessen, reduce, decrease, diminish, ease; alleviate, mitigate, allay, relieve, palliate, assuage.
ANTONYMS increase, intensify.
2 *his smile lightened her spirits* **cheer (up),** brighten, gladden, hearten, perk up, lift, enliven, boost, buoy (up), uplift, revive, restore, revitalize.
ANTONYMS depress.

light-fingered ▶ adjective *our light-fingered cashier* **thieving,** stealing, pilfering, shoplifting, dishonest; informal sticky-fingered, crooked.
ANTONYMS honest.

lightheaded ▶ adjective *sit down if you're feeling lightheaded* **dizzy,** giddy, faint, light in the head, vertiginous, reeling; informal woozy.

lighthearted ▶ adjective *a lighthearted musical* **carefree,** cheerful, cheery, happy, merry, glad, playful, jolly, jovial, joyful, gleeful, ebullient, high-spirited, lively, blithe, bright, sunny, buoyant, vivacious, bubbly, jaunty, bouncy, breezy; entertaining, amusing, diverting; informal chirpy, upbeat; dated gay.
ANTONYMS miserable.

lightly ▶ adverb **1** *Hermione kissed him lightly on the cheek* **softly,** gently, faintly, delicately.
ANTONYMS hard, heavily.
2 *season very lightly with paprika* **sparingly,** slightly, sparsely, moderately, delicately.
ANTONYMS intensely, abundantly.
3 *he has gotten off lightly* **without severe punishment,** easily, leniently, mildly.
ANTONYMS severely.
4 *her views are not to be dismissed lightly* **carelessly,** airily, heedlessly, without consideration, indifferently, unthinkingly, thoughtlessly, uncaringly, flippantly, breezily, frivolously.
ANTONYMS seriously.

lightweight ▶ adjective **1** *a lightweight jacket* **thin,** light, flimsy, insubstantial; summery.
ANTONYMS heavy, thick.
2 *lightweight entertainment* **trivial,** insubstantial, superficial, shallow, unintellectual, undemanding, frivolous; of little merit/value; informal Mickey Mouse.
ANTONYMS profound.
▶ noun *he's no lightweight* **amateur,** second-rater, unimportant person, insignificant person, nobody, nonentity, no-name, small fry.

like[1] ▶ verb **1** *I like Tony* **be fond of,** be attached to, have a soft spot for, have a liking for, have regard for, think well of, admire, respect, esteem; be attracted to, fancy, find attractive, be keen on, be taken with; be infatuated with, carry a torch for; informal be crazy about, have a crush on, have a thing for, have the hots for, dig, take a shine to.
ANTONYMS hate.
2 *she likes gardening* **enjoy,** have a taste for, have a preference for, have a liking for, be partial to, find/take pleasure in, be keen on, find agreeable, have a penchant for, have a passion for, find enjoyable; appreciate, love, adore, relish; informal have a thing about, be into, be mad about, be hooked on, get a kick out of.
ANTONYMS hate.
3 *feel free to say what you like* **choose,** please, wish, want, see fit, think fit, care to, will.
4 *how would she like it if someone did that to her?* **feel about,** regard, think about, consider.

like[2] ▶ preposition **1** *you're just like a teacher* **similar to,** the same as, identical to.
2 *the figure landed like a cat* **in the same way as,** in the same manner as, in the manner of, in a similar way to.
3 *cities like Joplin* **such as,** for example, for instance; in particular, namely.
4 *he sounded mean, which isn't like him* **characteristic of,** typical of, in character with.
▶ noun *we'll never see his like again* **equal,** match, equivalent, counterpart, twin, parallel; rare compeer.
▶ adjective *a like situation* **similar,** much the same, comparable, corresponding, resembling, alike, analogous, parallel, equivalent, cognate, related, kindred; identical, same, matching.
ANTONYMS dissimilar.

likelihood ▶ noun *the likelihood of getting a fair trial in this court is slim | smoking greatly increases the likelihood of lung disease* **probability,** chance, prospect, possibility, likeliness, odds, feasibility; risk, threat, danger; hope, promise.

likely ▶ adjective **1** *it seemed likely that a scandal would break* **probable,** distinctly possible, to be expected, odds-on, possible, plausible, imaginable; expected, anticipated, predictable, predicted, foreseeable; informal in the cards.
ANTONYMS improbable, impossible.
2 *a likely explanation* **plausible,** reasonable, feasible, acceptable, believable, credible, tenable, conceivable.
ANTONYMS incredible, unbelievable.
3 *a likely story!* **unlikely,** implausible, unbelievable, incredible, untenable, unacceptable, inconceivable.
ANTONYMS believable.
4 *a likely place for a picnic* **suitable,** appropriate, apposite, fit, fitting, acceptable, right; promising, hopeful.
▶ adverb *he was likely dead* **probably,** in all probability, presumably, no doubt, doubtlessly; informal (as) like as not, chances are.

likeness ▶ noun **1** *her likeness to Anne is quite uncanny* **resemblance,** similarity, similitude, correspondence.
ANTONYMS dissimilarity.
2 *she appeared in the likeness of a ghost*

semblance, guise, appearance, outward form, form, shape, image.
3 *a likeness of the president* **representation,** image, depiction, portrayal; picture, drawing, sketch, painting, portrait, photograph, study; statue, sculpture.

CHOOSE THE RIGHT WORD
likeness, affinity, analogy, resemblance, similarity, similitude
Two sisters who are only a year apart in age and who are very similar to each other in terms of appearance and personality would be said to bear a **likeness** to one another. **Similarity** applies to people or things that are merely somewhat alike (*there was a similarity between the two women, both of whom were raised in the Midwest*), while **resemblance** suggests a similarity only in appearance or in superficial or external ways (*with their short hair and blue eyes, they bore a strong resemblance to each other*). **Affinity** adds to *resemblance* a natural kinship, temperamental sympathy, common experience, or some other relationship (*she has an affinity for young children*). **Similitude** is a more literary word meaning *likeness* or *similarity* in reference to abstract things (*a similitude of the truth*). An **analogy** is a comparison of things that are basically unlike but share certain attributes or circumstances (*he drew an analogy between the human heart and a bicycle pump*).

likewise ▶ adverb **1** *an ambush was out of the question, likewise poison* **also,** in addition, too, as well, to boot; besides, moreover, furthermore.
2 *encourage your family and friends to do likewise* **the same,** similarly, correspondingly, in the same way, in similar fashion.

liking ▶ noun *his liking for fine wine* **fondness for,** love of, affection for, penchant for, attachment to; enjoyment of, appreciation of, taste for, passion for; preference for, partiality to, predilection to; desire for, fancy for.

lilt ▶ noun *the lilt of her Scottish accent* **cadence,** rise and fall, inflection, intonation, rhythm, swing, beat, pulse, tempo.

limb ▶ noun **1** *his sore limbs* **arm, leg,** appendage; archaic member.
2 *the limbs of the tree* **branch,** bough, offshoot, shoot.
– PHRASES **go out on a limb** *the government would not go out on a limb* **be put in a precarious position,** become vulnerable, be put in a risky situation; informal be sticking one's neck out.

limber ▶ adjective *I have to practice to keep myself limber* **lithe,** supple, nimble, lissome, flexible, fit, agile, acrobatic, loose-jointed, loose-limbed. See note at FLEXIBLE.
ANTONYMS stiff.
– PHRASES **limber up** *limbering up for the marathon* **warm up,** loosen up, get into condition, get into shape, practice, train, stretch.

limbo ▶ noun
– PHRASES **in limbo** *our mortgage approval is in limbo* **in abeyance,** unattended to, unfinished; suspended, deferred, postponed, put off, pending, on ice, in cold storage; unresolved, undetermined, up in the air, uncertain; informal on the back burner, on hold, treading water, in the balance.

limelight ▶ noun *she was once again enjoying the limelight* **focus of attention,** public attention, public interest, media attention, public eye, glare of publicity, prominence, spotlight; center stage.
ANTONYMS obscurity.

limit ▶ noun **1** *the city limits* **boundary,** border, bound, frontier, edge, demarcation line; perimeter, outside, confine, periphery, margin, rim.
2 *a limit of 4,500 people* **maximum,** ceiling, limitation, upper limit; restriction, check, control, restraint.
3 *resources are stretched to the limit* **utmost,** breaking point, greatest extent.
4 informal *I've reached **my limit**!* **one's/the breaking point,** the last straw; informal the end, it, one's wits' end, one's/the max.
▶ verb *the pressure to limit costs* **restrict,** curb, cap, check, hold in check, restrain, put a brake on, freeze, regulate, control, govern, delimit.
– PHRASES **off limits** *access to their mother's workshop was strictly off limits* **out of bounds,** forbidden, banned, restricted, unacceptable, taboo.

limitation ▶ noun **1** *a limitation on the number of guests* **restriction,** curb, restraint, control, check; bar, barrier, block, deterrent.
ANTONYMS increase.
2 *he is aware of his own limitations* **imperfection,** flaw, defect, failing, shortcoming, weak point, deficiency, failure, frailty, weakness, foible.
ANTONYMS strength.

limited ▶ adjective **1** *limited resources* **restricted,** finite, little, tight, slight, in short supply, short; meager, scanty, sparse, few, insubstantial, deficient, inadequate, insufficient, paltry, poor, minimal.
ANTONYMS ample, boundless.
2 *the limited powers of the council* **restricted,** curbed, checked, controlled, restrained, delimited, rangebound, qualified.
ANTONYMS absolute.

limitless ▶ adjective *a seemingly limitless supply of free software* **boundless,** unbounded, unlimited, illimitable; infinite, endless, never-ending, unending, everlasting, untold, immeasurable, bottomless, fathomless; unceasing, interminable, inexhaustible, constant, perpetual.

limp[1] ▶ verb *she limped out of the house* **hobble,** walk with a limp, walk lamely, walk unevenly, walk haltingly, hitch, falter, stumble, lurch.
▶ noun *walking with **a limp*** **lameness,** a hobble, an uneven gait; Medicine claudication.

limp[2] ▶ adjective **1** *a limp handshake* **soft,** flaccid,

loose, slack, lax; floppy, drooping, droopy, sagging.
ANTONYMS firm.
2 *we were all limp with exhaustion* **tired,** fatigued, weary, exhausted, worn out; lethargic, listless, spiritless, weak.
ANTONYMS energetic.

limpid ▶ **adjective 1** *a limpid pool* **clear,** transparent, glassy, crystal clear, crystalline, translucent, pellucid, unclouded.
ANTONYMS opaque.
2 *his limpid prose* **lucid,** clear, plain, understandable, intelligible, comprehensible, coherent, explicit, unambiguous, simple, vivid, sharp, crystal clear; formal perspicuous.
ANTONYMS unintelligible.

line[1] ▶ **noun 1** *he drew a line through the name* **dash,** rule, bar, score; underline, underscore, stroke, slash; technical stria, striation.
2 *there were lines around her eyes* **wrinkle,** furrow, crease, groove, crinkle, crow's foot, laugh line.
3 (usu. **lines**) *the classic lines of the exterior* **contour,** outline, configuration, shape, figure, delineation, profile.
4 *the line between Canada and the United States* **boundary,** boundary line, limit, border, borderline, demarcation line, dividing line, edge, margin, perimeter, frontier.
5 (usu. **lines**) *behind enemy lines* **position,** formation, defense, fieldwork, front (line); trenches.
6 *he put the wash on the line* **clothesline**; cord, rope, string, cable, wire, thread, twine, strand.
7 *they waited in a line* **row,** file, lineup, queue.
8 *a line of figures* **column,** row.
9 *a long line of bad decisions* **series,** sequence, succession, chain, string, set, cycle.
10 *a line of flight* **course,** route, track, path, way, run.
11 *they took a very tough line with the industry | the party line* **course of action,** course, procedure, technique, tactic, tack; policy, practice, approach, plan, program, position, stance, philosophy.
12 *her own line of thought* **course,** direction, drift, tack, tendency, trend.
13 informal *he fed me a line* **story,** piece of fiction, fabrication; informal spiel.
14 (**lines**) *he couldn't remember his lines* **words,** part, script, speech.
15 *my line is engineering* **line of work,** work, line of business, business, field, trade, occupation, employment, profession, job, career, specialty, forte, province, department, sphere, area, area of expertise.
16 *a new line of cologne* **brand,** kind, sort, type, variety, make.
17 *a noble line* **ancestry,** family, parentage, birth, descent, lineage, extraction, genealogy, roots, origin, background; stock, bloodline, pedigree.
18 *the opening line of the poem* **sentence,** phrase, clause, utterance; passage, extract, quotation, quote, citation.
19 *I should drop Ralph a line* **note,** letter, card, postcard, email, message, communication, missive, memorandum; correspondence, word; informal memo; formal epistle.
▶ **verb 1** *her face was lined with age* **furrow,** wrinkle, crease, pucker, mark with lines.
2 *the driveway was lined by poplars* **border,** edge, fringe, bound, rim.
– PHRASES **draw the line at** *we draw the line at keg parties* **stop short of/at,** refuse to accept, balk at; object to, take issue with, take exception to. **in line 1** *they stood in line for food* **in a row,** in a file, in a lineup; chiefly Brit. in a queue. **2** *the advertisements are in line with the editorial style* **in agreement,** in accord, in accordance, in harmony, in step, in compliance. **3** *he stood in line with the target* **in alignment,** aligned, level, at the same height; side by side. **4** *the referee kept him in line* **under control,** in order, in check. **in line for** *Laine is in line for a senior position* **a candidate for,** in the running for, on the short list for, being considered for. **get a line on** *were you able to get a line on their upcoming projects?* **learn something about,** find out about, be informed about, hear about, hear tell about. **lay it on the line** *go ahead, lay it on the line, I can take it* **speak frankly,** speak honestly, be direct, pull no punches, be blunt, not mince one's words, call a spade a spade; informal give it to someone straight. **line up 1** *line up for inspection* **form a line,** get into rows/columns, fall in; chiefly Brit. queue up; Military dress. **2** *they lined them up against the wall* **arrange in lines,** put in rows, arrange in columns, align, range; Military dress. **3** *we've lined up an all-star cast* **assemble,** put together, organize, prepare, arrange, prearrange, fix up; book, schedule. **on the line** *a firefighter's life is on the line every day* **at risk,** in danger, in jeopardy, endangered, imperiled. **toe the line** *the choice is yours: toe the line or pack your bags* **conform,** obey the rules, observe the rules, comply with the rules, abide by the rules, follow the rules; informal play by the rules.

line[2] ▶ **verb** *they lined the handbags with a quilted rayon* **put a lining in,** interline, face, back, pad.
– PHRASES **line one's pockets** informal *he had lined his pockets with campaign funds* **make money,** accept bribes, embezzle money; informal feather one's nest, graft, grift, be on the make.

lineage ▶ **noun** *tracing his paternal lineage* **ancestry,** family, parentage, birth, descent, line, extraction, derivation, genealogy, roots, origin, background; stock, bloodline, breeding, pedigree.

lineup ▶ **noun 1** *a star-studded lineup* **list of performers,** cast, company, bill, program, schedule.
2 *the Oilers' lineup* **list of players,** roster, team, squad, side.

linger ▶ **verb 1** *the crowd lingered for a long time* **wait around,** stay, remain, wait, stay put; loiter, dawdle, dally, take one's time; informal stick around, hang around, hang on; archaic tarry.
ANTONYMS leave.
2 *the infection can linger for many years* **persist,** continue, remain, stay, endure, carry on, last, keep on/up.
ANTONYMS vanish, disappear.

lingerie ▶ **noun** *fine silk lingerie* **women's**

underwear, underclothes, underclothing, undergarments, foundation garments; nightwear, nightclothes; informal undies, underthings.

lingering ▶ adjective **1** *lingering doubts* **remaining**, surviving, persisting, abiding, nagging, niggling.
2 *a slow, lingering death* **protracted**, prolonged, long-drawn-out, long-lasting.

lingo ▶ noun informal *he quickly picked up the musicians' lingo* **language**, tongue, dialect; jargon, terminology, slang, argot, cant, patter; informal -ese, -speak, mumbo-jumbo. See note at DIALECT.

link ▶ noun **1** *a chain of steel links* **loop**, ring, connection, connector, coupling, joint.
2 *the links between transport and the environment* **connection**, relationship, association, linkage, tie-up.
3 *their links with the labor movement* **bond**, tie, attachment, connection, relationship, association, affiliation.
4 *he was an important link in our operation* **component**, constituent, element, part, piece.
▶ verb **1** *four boxes were linked together* **join**, connect, fasten, attach, bind, unite, combine, amalgamate; clamp, secure, fix, tie, couple, yoke, hitch.
2 *the evidence linking him with the murder* **associate**, connect, relate, join, bracket.

lionhearted ▶ adjective *the lionhearted champion of freedom* **brave**, courageous, valiant, gallant, intrepid, valorous, fearless, bold, daring; stouthearted, stalwart, heroic, doughty, plucky, manly; informal gutsy, spunky, ballsy.
ANTONYMS cowardly.

lionize ▶ verb *popular myths have lionized a man who was in fact little more than a petty thief* **celebrate**, fête, glorify, honor, exalt, acclaim, admire, praise, extol, applaud, hail, venerate, eulogize; formal laud.
ANTONYMS vilify.

lip ▶ noun **1** *the lip of the crater* **edge**, rim, brim, border, verge, brink.
2 informal *don't give me any lip!* **insolence**, impertinence, impudence, cheek, cheekiness, rudeness, audacity, effrontery, disrespect; informal mouth, back-talk, guff, sauce.
– PHRASES **bite one's lip** *I wanted to say something about that hideous dress, but I bit my lip* **keep quiet**, keep one's mouth shut, say nothing, bite one's tongue. **keep a stiff upper lip** *in my neighborhood, you learned early to keep a stiff upper lip when life ain't all sweetness and roses* **keep control of oneself**, not show emotion, appear unaffected; informal keep one's cool.

liquid ▶ adjective **1** *liquid fuels* **fluid**, liquefied; melted, molten, thawed, dissolved; Chemistry hydrous.
ANTONYMS solid, gaseous.
2 *her liquid eyes* **clear**, limpid, crystal clear, crystalline, pellucid, unclouded, bright.
ANTONYMS cloudy, opaque.
3 *liquid sounds* **pure**, clear, mellifluous, dulcet, mellow, sweet, sweet-sounding, soft, melodious, harmonious.
ANTONYMS disharmonious, cacophonous.
4 *liquid assets* **convertible**, disposable, usable, spendable.
ANTONYMS tied up, unavailable.
▶ noun *a vat of liquid* **fluid**, moisture; liquor, solution, juice.

liquidate ▶ verb **1** *the company was liquidated* **close down**, wind up, put into liquidation, dissolve, disband.
2 *he liquidated his share portfolio* **convert to cash**, convert, cash in, sell off, sell up.
3 *liquidating the public debt* **pay off**, pay, pay in full, settle, clear, discharge, square, honor.
4 informal *they were liquidated in bloody purges* See KILL (sense 1 of the verb).

liquor ▶ noun **1** *he liked his liquor* **alcohol**, spirits, drink, alcoholic drink, intoxicating liquor, intoxicant; informal grog, firewater, rotgut, the hard stuff, the bottle, hooch, moonshine; juice, the sauce.
2 *strain the liquor into the sauce* **stock**, broth, bouillon, juice, liquid.

list[1] ▶ noun *a list of the world's wealthiest people* **catalog**, inventory, record, register, roll, file, index, directory, listing, checklist, enumeration.
▶ verb *the accounts are listed alphabetically* **record**, register, make a list of, enter; itemize, enumerate, catalog, file, log, categorize, inventory; classify, group, sort, rank, alphabetize, index.

list[2] ▶ verb *the boat listed to one side* **lean**, lean over, tilt, tip, heel, heel over, keel over, careen, cant, pitch, incline, slant, slope, bank.

listen ▶ verb **1** *are you listening?* **hear**, pay attention, be attentive, attend, concentrate; keep one's ears open, prick up one's ears; informal be all ears, lend an ear; literary hark; archaic hearken.
2 *policy-makers should* **listen to** *popular opinion* **pay attention to**, take heed of, heed, take notice of, take note of, mind, mark, bear in mind, take into consideration, take into account, tune in to.
– PHRASES **listen in** *she handed him a note that said that the police were listening in* **eavesdrop**, spy, overhear, tap, wiretap, bug, monitor.

listless ▶ adjective *this heat makes me listless | a listless performance* **lethargic**, enervated, spiritless, lifeless, languid, languorous, inactive, inert, sluggish, torpid.
ANTONYMS energetic.

litany ▶ noun **1** *reciting the litany* **prayer**, invocation, supplication, devotion; archaic orison.
2 *a litany of complaints* **recital**, recitation, enumeration; list, listing, catalog, inventory.

literacy ▶ noun *testing for literacy* **ability to read and write**, reading/writing proficiency; learning, book learning, education, scholarship, schooling.

literal ▶ adjective **1** *the literal sense of the word "dreadful"* **strict**, factual, plain, simple, exact, straightforward; unembellished, undistorted; objective, correct, true, accurate, genuine, authentic.
ANTONYMS figurative.
2 *a literal translation* **word-for-word**, verbatim, letter-for-letter; exact, precise, faithful, close, strict, accurate.

ANTONYMS loose.

literary ▶ adjective **1** *literary works* **written,** poetic, artistic, dramatic.
2 *her literary friends* **scholarly,** learned, intellectual, cultured, erudite, bookish, highbrow, bluestocking, lettered, academic, cultivated; well-read, widely read, educated, well-educated.
3 *literary language* **formal,** written, poetic, dramatic; elaborate, ornate, flowery; inkhorn.

literate ▶ adjective **1** *many of the workers were not literate* **able to read/write,** educated, schooled.
ANTONYMS illiterate.
2 *her literate friends* **educated,** well-educated, well-read, widely read, scholarly, learned, knowledgeable, lettered, cultured, cultivated, sophisticated, well-informed.
ANTONYMS ignorant.
3 *he was computer literate* **knowledgeable,** well-versed, savvy, smart, conversant, competent; informal up on, up to speed on.
ANTONYMS ignorant.

literature ▶ noun **1** *English literature* **written works,** writings, writing, creative writing, literary texts, compositions; informal lit.
2 *the literature on prototype theory* **publications,** published writings, texts, reports, studies.
3 *election literature* **printed matter,** brochures, leaflets, pamphlets, circulars, flyers, handouts, handbills, bulletins, fact sheets, publicity, propaganda, notices.

lithe ▶ adjective *lithe dancers* **agile,** graceful, supple, limber, lithesome, loose-limbed, nimble, deft, flexible, lissome, slender, slim, willowy.
ANTONYMS clumsy.

litigation ▶ noun *his attorneys advised him to avoid the litigation that his friends were suggesting* **legal proceedings,** legal action, lawsuit, legal dispute, legal case, case, suit, prosecution, indictment.

litter ▶ noun **1** *never drop litter* **garbage,** refuse, junk, waste, debris, scraps, leavings, fragments, detritus, trash, rubbish.
2 *the litter of papers around her* **clutter,** jumble, muddle, mess, heap, disorder, untidiness, confusion, disarray; informal shambles.
3 *a litter of kittens* **brood,** family.
4 *she was carried on a litter* **sedan chair,** palanquin; stretcher.
▶ verb **1** *clothes littered the floor* **make untidy,** mess up, make a mess of, clutter up, be strewn about, be scattered about; informal make a shambles of.
2 *a paper littered with quotes* **fill,** pack, load, clutter.

little ▶ adjective **1** *a little writing desk* **small,** small-scale, compact; mini, miniature, tiny, minute, minuscule; toy, baby, pocket, undersized, dwarf, midget, wee; informal teeny-weeny, teensy-weensy, itsy-bitsy, itty-bitty, little-bitty, half-pint, vest-pocket, li'l, micro. See note at SMALL.
ANTONYMS big, large.
2 *a little man* **short,** small, slight, petite, diminutive, tiny; elfin, dwarfish, midget, pygmy, Lilliputian; informal teeny-weeny, pint-sized, peewee.
ANTONYMS big, large.
3 *my little sister* **young,** younger, junior, small, baby, infant.
ANTONYMS big, elder.
4 *I was a bodyguard for a little while* **brief,** short, short-lived; fleeting, momentary, transitory, transient; fast, quick, hasty, cursory.
ANTONYMS long.
5 *a few little problems* **minor,** unimportant, insignificant, trivial, trifling, petty, paltry, inconsequential, nugatory; informal dinky, piddling.
ANTONYMS important, significant.
6 *they have little political influence* **hardly any,** not much, slight, scant, limited, restricted, modest, little or/to no, minimal, negligible.
ANTONYMS considerable.
7 *you little sneak* **contemptible,** mean, spiteful, petty, small-minded.
▶ adverb **1** *he is little known as a singer | they little thought* **hardly,** barely, scarcely, not much, not at all, slightly, only slightly.
ANTONYMS well.
2 *his art has been little seen in Canada* **rarely,** seldom, infrequently, hardly, hardly ever, scarcely, scarcely ever, not much.
ANTONYMS often.
– PHRASES **a little 1** *add a little vinegar* **some,** a small amount of, a bit of, a touch of, a soupçon of, a dash of, a taste of, a spot of; a shade of, a suggestion of, a trace of, a hint of, a suspicion of; a dribble of, a splash of, a pinch of, a sprinkling of, a speck of; informal a smidgen of, a tad of. **2** *after a little, Oliver came in* **a short time,** a little while, a bit, an interval, a short period; a minute, a moment, a second, an instant; informal a sec, a mo, a jiffy. **3** *this reminds me a little of the Adriatic* **slightly,** faintly, remotely, vaguely; somewhat, a little bit, to some degree. **little by little** *little by little, the house fell into disrepair* **gradually,** slowly, by degrees, by stages, step by step, bit by bit, progressively; subtly, imperceptibly.

liturgy ▶ noun *the Anglican liturgy* **ritual,** worship, service, ceremony, rite, observance, celebration, sacrament; tradition, custom, practice, rubric; formal ordinance.

live[1] ▶ verb **1** *the greatest mathematician who ever lived* **exist,** be alive, be, have life; breathe, draw breath, walk the earth.
ANTONYMS die, be dead.
2 *I live in Arkansas* **reside in,** have one's home in, have one's residence in, be settled in; be housed in, lodge in; inhabit, occupy, populate; formal dwell in, be domiciled in.
3 *they lived quietly* **pass/spend one's life,** have a lifestyle; behave, conduct oneself; formal comport oneself.
4 *she had lived a difficult life* **experience,** spend, pass, lead, have, go through, undergo.
5 *Fred lived by his wits* **survive,** make a living, earn one's living, eke out a living; subsist, support oneself, sustain oneself, make ends meet, keep body and soul together.
6 *you should get out there and live* **enjoy oneself,** enjoy life, have fun, live life to the full/fullest.

– PHRASES **live it up** informal *they're living it up in Hawaii* **live extravagantly,** live in the lap of luxury, live in clover; carouse, revel, enjoy oneself, have a good time, go on a spree; informal party, paint the town red, have a ball, live high on/off the hog; archaic wassail. **live off/on** *the gulls live off discarded fish* **subsist on,** feed on/off, eat, consume.

live² ▶ **adjective 1** *live bait* **living,** alive, having life, breathing, animate, sentient.
ANTONYMS dead, inanimate.
2 *a live performance* **in the flesh,** personal, in person, not recorded.
ANTONYMS recorded.
3 *a live wire* **electrified,** charged, powered, active; informal hot.
ANTONYMS inactive.
4 *live coals* **hot,** glowing, red hot, aglow; burning, alight, flaming, aflame, blazing, ignited, on fire; literary afire.
5 *a live grenade* **unexploded,** explosive, active; unstable, volatile.
ANTONYMS inactive.
– PHRASES **live wire** informal *that Goldie is a real live wire* **energetic person;** informal fireball, human dynamo, powerhouse, life of the party.

livelihood ▶ **noun** *thousands of people relied on that one factory for their livelihood* **income,** source of income, means of support, living, subsistence, keep, maintenance, sustenance, nourishment, daily bread; job, work, employment, occupation, vocation; informal bread and butter.

lively ▶ **adjective 1** *a lively young woman* **energetic,** active, animated, dynamic, full of life, outgoing, spirited, high-spirited, vivacious, enthusiastic, vibrant, buoyant, exuberant, effervescent, cheerful; bouncy, bubbly, perky, sparkling, zestful; informal full of beans, chirpy, chipper, peppy.
ANTONYMS listless, lifeless.
2 *a lively bar* **busy,** crowded, bustling, buzzing; vibrant, boisterous, jolly, festive; informal buzzy, hopping.
ANTONYMS quiet, dead.
3 *a lively debate* **heated,** vigorous, animated, spirited, enthusiastic, forceful; exciting, interesting, memorable.
ANTONYMS lifeless, dull.
4 *a lively portrait of the local community* **vivid,** colorful, striking, graphic, bold, strong.
ANTONYMS lifeless, dull.

liven ▶ **verb**
– PHRASES **liven up** *we livened up when Edie arrived* **brighten up,** cheer up, perk up, revive, rally, pick up, bounce back; informal buck up. **liven someone/something up** *the new sofa livens up the whole room* **brighten up,** cheer up, enliven, animate, raise someone's spirits, perk up, spice up, make lively, wake up, invigorate, revive, refresh, vivify, galvanize, stimulate, stir up, get going; informal buck up, pep up.

livid ▶ **adjective 1** informal *Mom was absolutely livid* See FURIOUS (sense 1).
2 *a livid bruise* **purplish,** bluish, dark, discolored, purple, grayish-blue; bruised; angry, black and blue. See note at PALE².

living ▶ **noun 1** *she cleaned floors for a living* **livelihood,** (source of) income, means of support, subsistence, keep, maintenance, sustenance, nourishment, daily bread; job, work, employment, occupation, vocation; informal bread and butter.
2 *healthy living* **way of life,** lifestyle, way of living, life; conduct, behavior, activities, habits.
▶ **adjective 1** *living organisms* **alive,** live, having life, animate, sentient; breathing, existing, existent; informal alive and kicking. See note at ALIVE.
ANTONYMS dead, extinct.
2 *a living language* **current,** contemporary, present; in use, active, surviving, extant, persisting, remaining, existing, in existence.
ANTONYMS dead, extinct.
3 *a living hell* **complete,** total, utter, absolute, real, veritable, perfect, out-and-out, downright.

living room ▶ **noun** *there is no phone in the living room* **sitting room,** front room, family room, living area, great room, den, lounge.

load ▶ **noun 1** *he has a load to deliver* **cargo,** freight, a consignment, a delivery, a shipment, goods, merchandise; a pack, a bundle, a parcel; a truckload, a shipload, a boatload, a vanload.
2 informal *I bought a load of clothes* **a lot of,** a great deal of, a large amount/quantity of, an abundance of, a wealth of, a mountain of; many, plenty of; informal a heap of, a mass of, a pile of, a stack of, a ton of, lots of, heaps of, masses of, piles of, stacks of, tons of.
3 *a heavy teaching load* **commitment,** responsibility, duty, obligation, charge, burden; trouble, worry, strain, pressure.
▶ **verb 1** *we quickly loaded the van* **fill,** fill up, pack, charge, stock, stack, lade.
2 *Larry loaded boxes into the jeep* **pack,** stow, store, stack, bundle; place, deposit, put away.
3 *loading the committee with responsibilities* **burden,** weigh down, saddle, charge; overburden, overwhelm, encumber, tax, strain, trouble, worry.
4 *Richard loaded Marshal with honors* **reward,** ply, regale, shower.
5 *he loaded a gun* **prime,** charge, prepare to fire/use.
6 *load the cassette into the camcorder* **insert,** put, place, slot.
7 *the dice are loaded against him* **bias,** rig, fix; weight.

loaded ▶ **adjective 1** *a loaded freight train* **full,** filled, laden, packed, stuffed, crammed, brimming, stacked; informal chock-full, chockablock.
2 *a loaded gun* **primed,** charged, armed, ready to fire.
3 informal *they have no money worries, they're loaded* See RICH (sense 1).
4 informal *he came home from the party loaded* See INTOXICATED.
5 *loaded dice* **biased,** rigged, fixed; juiced; weighted.
6 *a loaded question* **charged,** sensitive, delicate.

loaf ▶ **verb** *he was just loafing all day at the beach* **laze,** lounge, loll, idle, waste time; informal hang around, bum around, futz around.

loan ▶ **noun** *a loan of $7,000* **credit,** advance; mortgage, overdraft; lending, moneylending.

▶ verb 1 *he loaned me his car* **lend,** advance, give credit; give on loan, lease, charter.
2 *the majority of exhibits have been loaned* **borrow,** receive/take on loan.

loath ▶ adjective *they were loath to take risks* **reluctant,** unwilling, disinclined, ill-disposed; averse, opposed, resistant.
ANTONYMS willing.

loathe ▶ verb *I loathe their so-called music* **hate,** detest, abhor, execrate, have a strong aversion to, feel repugnance toward, not be able to bear/stand, be repelled by. See note at DESPISE.
ANTONYMS love.

loathing ▶ noun *the loathing she feels for Karyn is understandable* **hatred,** hate, detestation, abhorrence, abomination, execration, odium; antipathy, dislike, hostility, animosity, ill feeling, bad feeling, malice, animus, enmity, aversion; repugnance.

loathsome ▶ adjective *his first wife was a loathsome creature* **hateful,** detestable, abhorrent, repulsive, odious, repugnant, repellent, disgusting, revolting, sickening, abominable, despicable, contemptible, reprehensible, execrable, damnable; vile, horrible, hideous, nasty, obnoxious, gross, foul, horrid; informal yucky.

lob ▶ verb *they lobbed grenades onto the gun platform* **throw,** toss, fling, pitch, hurl, pelt, sling, launch, propel; informal chuck, heave.

lobby ▶ noun 1 *the hotel lobby* **entrance hall,** hallway, entrance, hall, vestibule, foyer, reception area.
2 *the antigun lobby* **special interest group,** interest group, pressure group; movement, campaign, crusade; lobbyists, supporters; faction, camp.
▶ verb 1 *readers are urged to lobby their legislators* **seek to influence,** try to persuade, bring pressure to bear on, importune, sway; petition, solicit, appeal to, pressurize.
2 *a group **lobbying for** better rail services* **campaign for,** crusade for, press for, push for, ask for, call for, demand; promote, advocate, champion.

local ▶ adjective 1 *local government* **community,** district, neighborhood, regional, city, town, municipal, county.
ANTONYMS national, global.
2 *a local restaurant* **neighborhood,** nearby, near, at hand, close by; accessible, handy, convenient.
3 *a local infection* **confined,** restricted, contained, localized.
ANTONYMS general, widespread.
▶ noun *complaints from the locals* **local person,** native, inhabitant, resident.
ANTONYMS outsider.

locale ▶ noun *the advantages of living in a rural locale* **place,** site, spot, area; position, location, setting, scene, venue, background, backdrop, environment; neighborhood, district, region, locality.

localize ▶ verb *our efforts to localize the conflict* **limit,** restrict, confine, contain, circumscribe, concentrate, delimit.
ANTONYMS generalize.

locate ▶ verb 1 *help me locate this photograph* **find,** discover, pinpoint, detect, track down, unearth, sniff out, smoke out, search out, ferret out, uncover.
2 *a company located near Pittsburgh* **situate,** site, position, place, base; put, build, establish, found; station, install, settle.

location ▶ noun *we've found the perfect location for our family reunion* **position,** place, situation, site, locality, locale, spot, whereabouts, point; scene, setting, area, environment; bearings, orientation; venue, address; technical locus.

lock ▶ noun *the lock on the door* **bolt,** catch, fastener, clasp, bar, hasp, latch.
▶ verb 1 *he locked the door* **bolt,** fasten, bar, secure, seal; padlock, latch, chain.
ANTONYMS unlock, open.
2 *they locked arms* **join,** interlock, intertwine, link, mesh, engage, unite, connect, yoke, mate; couple.
ANTONYMS separate, divide.
3 *the wheels locked* **become stuck,** stick, jam, become/make immovable, become/make rigid.
4 *he locked her in an embrace* **clasp,** grasp, embrace, hug, squeeze, clench.
– PHRASES **lock horns** *he's locked horns with every boss he's ever had* **argue,** quarrel, fight, disagree, squabble, bicker. **lock lips** informal *I saw you locking lips with Quinn* **kiss;** informal smooch, peck, neck, canoodle, make out. **lock someone out of** *we were locked out of the conference* **keep out of,** shut out of/from, refuse entrance to, deny admittance to; exclude from, bar from, debar from, ban from. **lock someone up** *take him away and lock him up* **imprison,** jail, incarcerate, send to prison, put behind bars, put under lock and key, put in chains, clap in irons, cage, pen, coop up; informal put away, put inside.

lockup ▶ noun *Eileen spent the night in lockup | the lockup in this town is a historical landmark* **jail,** prison, cell, detention center, jailhouse, penitentiary; informal slammer, jug, can, brig, clink, big house, cooler, hoosegow, cage, pen, pokey.

locomotion ▶ noun *the lemur's amusingly agile locomotion* **movement,** motion, moving; travel, traveling; mobility, motility; walking, running; progress, progression, passage; formal perambulation.

lodge ▶ noun 1 *a hunting lodge* **house,** cottage, cabin, chalet.
2 *we'll eat up at the lodge* **main hall,** main building, dining hall.
3 *a beaver's lodge* **den,** lair, hole, set; retreat, haunt, shelter.
4 *a Masonic lodge* **hall,** clubhouse, meeting room.
5 *the porter's lodge* **gatehouse,** cottage.
▶ verb 1 *William lodged at our house* **reside,** board, stay, live, rent rooms, be put up, be quartered, room; formal dwell, be domiciled, sojourn; archaic abide.
2 *they were lodged at an inn* **accommodate,** put up, take in, house, board, billet, quarter, shelter.
3 *we lodged a complaint* **submit,** register, enter, put forward, advance, lay, present, tender, proffer, put on record, record, file.

4 *the bullet lodged in his back* **become fixed,** embed itself, become embedded, become implanted, get/become stuck, stick, catch, become caught, wedge.

lodging ▸ noun *the lodging provided at the farm was charming* **accommodations,** rooms, chambers, living quarters, place to stay, a roof over one's head, housing, shelter; informal digs, pad, nest; formal abode, residence, dwelling, dwelling place, habitation.

lofty ▸ adjective **1** *a lofty tower* **tall,** high, giant, towering, soaring, skyscraping.
ANTONYMS low, short.
2 *lofty ideals* **noble,** exalted, high, high-minded, worthy, grand, fine, elevated, sublime.
ANTONYMS base, lowly.
3 *lofty disdain* **haughty,** arrogant, disdainful, supercilious, condescending, scornful, patronizing, contemptuous, self-important, conceited, snobbish; aloof, standoffish; informal stuck-up, snooty, snotty, hoity-toity.
ANTONYMS modest.

log ▸ noun **1** *a fallen log* **branch,** trunk; piece of wood; (**logs**) timber, firewood.
2 *a log of phone calls* **record,** register, logbook, journal, diary, minutes, chronicle, daybook, record book, ledger, account, tally.
▸ verb **1** *all complaints are logged* **register,** record, make a note of, note down, write down, jot down, put in writing, enter, file.
2 *the pilot had logged 95 hours* **attain,** achieve, chalk up, make, do, go.
3 *he was injured while logging* **cut down trees,** chop down trees, fell trees, clear cut, harvest trees.
– PHRASES **log in** *just go to our Web site and log in* **sign in,** register, enter, log on.

logic ▸ noun **1** *this case appears to defy all logic* **reason,** judgment, logical thought, rationality, wisdom, sense, good sense, common sense, sanity; informal horse sense.
2 *the logic of their argument* **reasoning,** line of reasoning, rationale, argument, argumentation.

logical ▸ adjective **1** *information displayed in a logical fashion* **reasoned,** well-reasoned, reasonable, rational, left-brained, sound, cogent, well-thought-out, valid; coherent, clear, well-organized, systematic, orderly, methodical, analytical, consistent, objective.
ANTONYMS illogical, irrational.
2 *the logical outcome* **natural,** reasonable, sensible, understandable; predictable, unsurprising, only to be expected, most likely, likeliest, obvious.
ANTONYMS unlikely, surprising.

logistics ▸ plural noun *the logistics of deploying forces in mountainous country* **organization,** planning, plans, management, arrangement, administration, orchestration, coordination, execution, handling, running.

logo ▸ noun *a sweatshirt with the company logo* **emblem,** trademark, brand, device, figure, symbol, design, sign, mark; insignia, crest, seal.

loiter ▸ verb **1** *he loitered at bus stops* **linger,** wait, skulk; loaf, lounge, idle, laze, waste time, lollygag; informal hang around; archaic tarry.
2 *they loitered along the river bank* **dawdle,** dally, stroll, amble, saunter, meander, drift, putter, take one's time; informal dilly-dally, mosey.

> CHOOSE THE RIGHT WORD
>
> **loiter, dally, dawdle, idle, lag**
>
> Someone who hangs around downtown after the stores are closed and appears to be deliberately wasting time is said to **loiter**, a verb that connotes improper or sinister motives (*the police warned the boys not to loiter*). To **dawdle** is to pass time leisurely or to pursue something halfheartedly (*dawdle in a stationery shop; dawdle over a sinkful of dishes*). Someone who **dallies** dawdles in a particularly pleasurable and relaxed way, with connotations of amorous activity (*he dallied with his girlfriend when he should have been delivering papers*). **Idle** suggests that the person makes a habit of avoiding work or activity (*idle away the hours of a hot summer day*), while **lag** suggests falling behind or failing to maintain a desirable rate of progress (*she lagged several yards behind her classmates as they walked to the museum*).

loll ▸ verb **1** *he lolled in an armchair* **lounge,** sprawl, drape oneself, stretch oneself; slouch, slump; laze, luxuriate, put one's feet up, lean back, sit back, recline, relax, take it easy, take a load off.
2 *her head lolled to one side* **hang down,** hang loosely, hang, droop, dangle, sag, drop, flop.

lone ▸ adjective *a lone police officer* **solitary,** single, solo, unaccompanied, unescorted, alone, by oneself/itself, sole, companionless; detached, isolated.

lonely ▸ adjective **1** *I felt very lonely* **isolated,** alone, lonesome, friendless, with no one to turn to, forsaken, abandoned, rejected, unloved, unwanted, outcast; gloomy, sad, depressed, desolate, forlorn, cheerless, down, blue.
ANTONYMS popular.
2 *the lonely life of a writer* **solitary,** unaccompanied, lone, by oneself/itself, companionless.
ANTONYMS sociable.
3 *a lonely road* **deserted,** uninhabited, unfrequented, unpopulated, desolate, isolated, remote, out of the way, secluded, off the beaten track/path, in the back of beyond, godforsaken; informal in the middle of nowhere.
ANTONYMS populous, crowded.

loner ▸ noun *a loner from parts unknown* **recluse,** introvert, lone wolf, hermit, solitary, misanthrope, outsider; historical anchorite.

long[1] ▸ adjective *a long silence* **lengthy,** extended, prolonged, extensive, protracted, long-lasting, long-drawn-out, drawn-out, spun out, dragged out, seemingly endless, lingering, interminable.
ANTONYMS short, brief.
– PHRASES **before long** *we'll be in Kentucky before long* **soon,** shortly, presently, in the near future, in a little while, by and by, in a minute, in a moment, in a second; informal anon, in a jiffy; dated directly; literary ere long.

long² ▶ verb *I longed for a vacation* **yearn for,** pine for, ache for, hanker for/after, hunger for, thirst for, itch for, be eager for, be desperate for; crave, dream of, set one's heart on; informal have a yen for, be dying for.

longing ▶ noun *a longing for the countryside* **yearning,** pining, craving, ache, burning, hunger, thirst, hankering; informal yen, itch.
▶ adjective *a longing look* **yearning,** pining, craving, hungry, thirsty, hankering, wistful, covetous.

long-lasting ▶ adjective *our long-lasting friendship* **enduring,** lasting, abiding, long-lived, long-running, long-established, long-standing, lifelong, deep-rooted, time-honored, traditional, permanent.
ANTONYMS short-lived, ephemeral.

long-standing ▶ adjective *a long-standing business partnership* **well-established,** long-established; time-honored, traditional, age-old; abiding, enduring, long-lived, surviving, persistent, prevailing, perennial, deep-rooted, long-term, confirmed.
ANTONYMS new, recent.

long-suffering ▶ adjective *her long-suffering parents* **patient,** forbearing, tolerant, uncomplaining, stoic, stoical, resigned; easygoing, indulgent, charitable, accommodating, forgiving, understanding.
ANTONYMS impatient, complaining.

long-winded ▶ adjective *long-winded speeches* **verbose,** wordy, lengthy, long, overlong, prolix, prolonged, protracted, long-drawn-out, interminable; discursive, diffuse, rambling, tortuous, meandering, repetitious, maundering; informal windy.
ANTONYMS concise, succinct, laconic.

look ▶ verb **1** *Mrs. Wright **looked at** him* **glance at,** gaze at, stare at, gape at, peer at; peep at, peek, take a look at; watch, observe, view, regard, examine, inspect, eye, scan, scrutinize, survey, study, contemplate, consider, take in, ogle; informal take a gander at, rubberneck, goggle, give someone/something a/the once-over, get a load of, eyeball; literary behold.
ANTONYMS ignore.
2 *her room **looked out on** Broadway* **command a view of,** face, overlook, front.
3 *they looked shocked* **seem,** seem to be, appear, appear to be, have the appearance/air of being, give the impression of being, give every appearance/indication of being, strike someone as being.
▶ noun **1** *here's the latest analysis—let's give it a look* **glance,** view, examination, study, inspection, observation, scan, survey, peep, peek, glimpse, gaze, stare; informal eyeful, gander, look-see, once-over, squint.
2 *the look on her face* **expression,** mien.
3 *that rustic look* **appearance,** air, aspect, bearing, cast, manner, mien, demeanor, facade, impression, effect.
4 *this year's look* **fashion,** style, vogue, mode.
– PHRASES **look after** *Janie looks after our goats and llamas* **take care of,** care for, attend to, minister to, tend, mind, keep an eye on, keep safe, be responsible for, protect; nurse, babysit, house-sit. **look back on** *those songs really make me look back on my college days* **reflect on,** think back to, remember, recall, reminisce about, harken back to. **look down on** *we never understood why Papa looked down on the Italian families in our building* **disdain,** scorn, regard with contempt, look down one's nose at, sneer at, despise. **look for** *he's looking for a book about begonias* **search for,** hunt for, try to find, seek, try to track down, forage for, scout out, quest for/after. **look forward to** *I look forward to Rebecca's call* **await with pleasure,** eagerly anticipate, lick one's lips over, be unable to wait for, count the days until. **look into** *they promised to look into our complaints* **investigate,** inquire into, ask questions about, go into, probe, explore, follow up, research, study, examine; informal check out, give something a/the once-over, scope out. **look like** *in his overcoat he looks like an undertaker* **resemble,** bear a resemblance to, look similar to, take after, have the look of, have the appearance of, remind one of, make one think of; informal be the spitting image of, be a dead ringer for. **look on/upon** *people he looked on as friends took advantage of him* **regard,** consider, think of, deem, judge, see, view, count, reckon. **look out** *you'll get burned if you don't look out* **beware,** watch out, be on (one's) guard, be alert, be wary, be vigilant, be careful, take care, be cautious, pay attention, take heed, keep one's eyes open/peeled, keep an eye out; watch your step. **look something over** *he looked over the engineer's reports* **inspect,** examine, scan, cast an eye over, take stock of, vet, view, look through, peruse, read through, check out; informal give something a/the once-over, eyeball. **look to 1** *we must look to the future* **consider,** think about, turn one's thoughts to, focus on, take heed of, pay attention to, attend to, address, mind, heed. **2** *they look to the government for help* **turn to,** resort to, have recourse to, fall back on, rely on. **look up 1** *things are looking up* **improve,** get better, pick up, come along/on, progress, make progress, make headway, perk up, rally, take a turn for the better. **2** *she looked up his number* **search for,** look for, try to find. **look someone up** informal *I'll look you up next time I'm in Tacoma* **go to visit,** pay a visit to, call on, go to see, look in on, visit with, go see; informal drop in on, drop by, pop by. **look up to** *some of the more self-centered ballplayers resent the responsibility of having thousands of kids look up to them* **admire,** have a high opinion of, think highly of, hold in high regard, regard highly, rate highly, respect, esteem, value, venerate.

look-alike ▶ noun *a contest to see who is the most convincing Alfred E. Neuman look-alike* **double,** twin, clone, duplicate, exact likeness, replica, copy, facsimile, doppelgänger; informal spitting image, dead ringer.

lookout ▶ noun **1** *he saw the smoke from the lookout* **observation post,** lookout point, lookout station, lookout tower, watchtower.
2 *a scenic lookout* **view,** vista, prospect, panorama, scene, aspect, outlook.
3 *he agreed to act as lookout* **watchman,** watch, guard, sentry, sentinel.
– PHRASES **be on the lookout/keep a lookout**

be on the lookout for enemy aircraft **keep watch,** keep an eye out, keep one's eyes peeled, keep a vigil, be alert, be vigilant, be on the qui vive.

loom ▸ verb **1** *ghostly shapes loomed out of the fog* **emerge,** appear, come into view, take shape, materialize, reveal itself.
2 *the church loomed above him* **soar,** tower, rise, rear up; overhang, overshadow, dominate.
3 *without reforms, disaster looms* **be imminent,** be on the horizon, impend, threaten, brew, be just around the corner, be in the air/wind.
– PHRASES **loom large** *the impending cutbacks loom large* **dominate,** be important, be significant, be of consequence; count, matter.

loop ▸ noun *a loop of rope* **coil,** hoop, ring, circle, noose, oval, spiral, curl, bend, curve, arc, twirl, whorl, twist, hook, helix, convolution.
▸ verb **1** *Dave looped rope around their hands* **coil,** wind, twist, snake, wreathe, spiral, curve, bend, turn.
2 *he looped the cables together* **fasten,** tie, join, connect, knot, bind.

loophole ▸ noun *a loophole in the regulations* **means of evasion,** means of avoidance; window, gap, opening.

loose ▸ adjective **1** *a loose floorboard* **not fixed in place,** not secure, unsecured, unattached; detached, unfastened, untied; wobbly, unsteady, movable.
ANTONYMS secure, tight.
2 *she wore her hair loose* **untied,** unpinned, unbound, hanging free, down, flowing.
3 *there's a wolf loose* **free,** at large, at liberty, on the loose, escaped; unconfined, untied, unchained, untethered, stray.
ANTONYMS secure.
4 *a loose interpretation* **vague,** indefinite, inexact, imprecise, approximate; broad, general, rough; liberal; informal ballpark.
ANTONYMS literal, narrow.
5 *a loose jacket* **baggy,** generously cut, slack, roomy; oversized, shapeless, sagging, saggy, sloppy.
ANTONYMS tight, form-fitting.
6 dated *a loose woman* **promiscuous,** of easy virtue, fast, wanton, unchaste, immoral; licentious, dissolute; dated fallen.
ANTONYMS chaste.
7 *loose talk* **indiscreet,** unguarded, free, gossipy, gossiping.
ANTONYMS discreet, guarded.
▸ verb **1** *loose the dogs* **free,** set free, unloose, turn loose, set loose, let loose, let go, release; untie, unchain, unfasten, unleash.
ANTONYMS confine.
2 *the fingers loosed their hold* **relax,** slacken, loosen; weaken, lessen, reduce, diminish, moderate.
ANTONYMS tighten.
– PHRASES **at loose ends** *ever since the factory closed, Don has been at loose ends* **with nothing to do,** unoccupied, unemployed, at leisure, idle, adrift, with time to kill; bored, twiddling one's thumbs, hanging/kicking around. **on the loose** *an inmate from Wickham Hall is on the loose* **free,** at liberty, at large, escaped; on the run, fugitive, wanted; informal on the lam.

loose-limbed ▸ adjective *loose-limbed gymnasts* **supple,** limber, lithe, lissome, willowy; agile, nimble, flexible.

loosen ▸ verb **1** *loosen the clothesline | you simply loosen two screws* **make slack,** slacken, unstick; **unfasten,** detach, release, disconnect, undo, unclasp, unlatch, unbolt.
ANTONYMS tighten.
2 *her fingers loosened* **become slack,** slacken, become loose, let go, ease; work loose, work free.
ANTONYMS tighten.
3 *Philip loosened his grip* **weaken,** relax, slacken, loose, lessen, reduce, moderate, diminish.
ANTONYMS tighten.
– PHRASES **loosen up** *you need to loosen up* **relax,** unwind, ease up, calm down; informal lighten up, go easy, chill out, take a chill pill, kick back.

loot ▸ noun *a bag full of loot* **booty,** spoils, plunder, stolen goods, contraband, pillage; informal swag, hot goods, ill-gotten gains, take.
▸ verb *troops looted the cathedral* **plunder,** pillage, despoil, ransack, sack, raid, rifle, rob, burgle, burglarize.

lop ▸ verb *they've **lopped off** the dead branches* **cut (off),** chop off, hack off, saw off, hew (off), ax; prune, sever, clip, trim, snip (off), dock, crop.

lopsided ▸ adjective *my gingerbread house is lopsided* **crooked,** askew, awry, off-center, uneven, out of line, asymmetrical, tilted, at an angle, aslant, slanting; off-balance, off-kilter; informal cockeyed.
ANTONYMS even, level, balanced.

loquacious ▸ adjective *a loquacious little boy* **talkative,** voluble, communicative, expansive, garrulous, unreserved, chatty, gossipy, gossiping; informal having the gift of gab, gabby, gassy, motormouthed, talky, windy. See note at TALKATIVE.
ANTONYMS reticent, taciturn.

lord ▸ noun **1** *the lord of the manor* **master,** ruler, leader, chief, superior, monarch, sovereign, king, emperor, prince, governor, commander, suzerain, liege, liege lord.
ANTONYMS servant, inferior.
2 *let us pray to **the Lord*** **God,** the Father, the Almighty, the Creator; Jehovah, Adonai, Yahweh, Elohim, Allah; Jesus Christ, the Messiah, the Savior, the Son of God, the Redeemer, the Lamb of God, the Prince of Peace, the King of Kings; informal the Man Upstairs.
3 *a press lord* **magnate,** tycoon, mogul, captain, baron, king; industrialist, proprietor; informal big shot, (head) honcho; derogatory fat cat.
– PHRASES **lord it over someone** *in our schooldays, you used to lord it over us* **order about/around,** dictate to, domineer, ride roughshod over, pull rank on, tyrannize, have under one's thumb; informal boss around, walk all over, push around; throw one's weight around.

lore ▸ noun **1** *Arthurian lore* **mythology,** myths, legends, stories, traditions, folklore, fables, oral tradition, mythos.
2 *baseball lore* **knowledge,** learning, wisdom; informal know-how.

lose ▸ verb **1** *I've lost my watch* **mislay,** misplace,

be unable to find, lose track of, leave (behind), fail to keep/retain, fail to keep sight of.
ANTONYMS find.
2 *he's lost a lot of blood* **be deprived of,** suffer the loss of; no longer have.
ANTONYMS keep, regain.
3 *he lost his pursuers* **escape from,** evade, elude, dodge, avoid, give someone the slip, shake off, throw off, throw off the scent; leave behind, outdistance, outstrip, outrun.
4 *they lost their way* **stray from,** wander from, depart from, go astray from, fail to keep to.
5 *you've lost your chance* **miss,** waste, squander, fail to grasp, fail to take advantage of, let pass, neglect, forfeit; informal pass up, lose out on.
ANTONYMS seize.
6 *they always lose at lacrosse* **be defeated,** be beaten, suffer defeat, be the loser, be conquered, be vanquished, be trounced; informal go down, take a licking, be bested.
ANTONYMS win.
7 *you can lose the phony accent* **discard,** get rid of, dispose of, dump, jettison, throw out, drop.
– PHRASES **lose out** *if we don't act soon, we'll lose out* **be deprived of an opportunity,** fail to benefit, be disadvantaged, be the loser. **lose out on** *the town has lost out on a tourist opportunity* **be unable to take advantage of,** fail to benefit from; informal miss out on.

loser ▶ noun 1 *the loser still gets the silver medal* **defeated person,** also-ran, runner-up.
ANTONYMS winner.
2 informal *he's a complete loser* **failure,** underachiever, ne'er-do-well, write-off, has-been; **misfit,** freak, unpopular person; informal geek, dweeb, nerd, hoser; flop, no-hoper, washout, lemon.
ANTONYMS success.

loss ▶ noun 1 *the loss of the documents* **mislaying,** misplacement, forgetting.
ANTONYMS recovery, finding.
2 *loss of earnings* **deprivation,** disappearance, privation, forfeiture, diminution, erosion, reduction, depletion.
3 *the loss of her husband* **death,** dying, demise, passing (away/on), end; formal decease; archaic expiry.
4 (**losses**) *Canadian losses in the war* **casualties,** fatalities, victims; dead; missing; death toll, number killed/dead.
5 *a loss of $15,000* **deficit,** debit, debt, indebtedness, deficiency.
ANTONYMS gain, profit.
– PHRASES **at a loss** *I'm at a loss about what just happened* **baffled,** nonplussed, mystified, puzzled, perplexed, bewildered, bemused, at sixes and sevens, confused, dumbfounded, stumped, stuck, blank; informal clueless, flummoxed, bamboozled, fazed, floored, beaten, discombobulated.

lost ▶ adjective 1 *her lost keys* **missing,** mislaid, misplaced, vanished, disappeared, gone missing, gone astray, forgotten, nowhere to be found; absent, not present, strayed; irretrievable, unrecoverable.
2 *I think we're lost* **off course,** off track, disorientated, having lost one's bearings, going around in circles, adrift, at sea, astray.
3 *a lost opportunity* **missed,** forfeited, neglected, wasted, squandered, gone by the boards; informal down the drain.
4 *lost traditions* **bygone,** past, former, one-time, previous, old, olden, departed, vanished, forgotten, consigned to oblivion, extinct, dead, gone.
5 *lost species and habitats* **extinct,** died out, defunct, vanished, gone; **destroyed,** wiped out, ruined, wrecked, exterminated, eradicated.
6 *a lost cause* **hopeless,** beyond hope, futile, forlorn, failed, beyond remedy, beyond recovery.
7 *lost souls* **damned,** fallen, irredeemable, irreclaimable, irretrievable, past hope, past praying for, condemned, cursed, doomed; literary accursed.
ANTONYMS saved.
8 *lost in thought* **engrossed,** absorbed, rapt, immersed, deep, intent, engaged, wrapped up.

lot ▶ pronoun *lots of friends* | *a lot of money* **a large amount,** a fair amount, a good/great deal, a great quantity, quantities, an abundance, a wealth, a profusion, plenty, a mass; a large number, a considerable number, scores; informal hundreds, thousands, millions, billions, gazillions, loads, masses, heaps, a pile, a stack, piles, oodles, stacks, scads, reams, wads, pots, oceans, a mountain, mountains, miles, tons, zillions, gobs, a bunch, a bucketload, a shedload; (**lots of/a lot of**) many, a great many, numerous, more —— than one can shake a stick at.
ANTONYMS a little, not much, a few, not many..
▶ noun 1 *the books were auctioned in lots* **item,** article; batch, set, collection, group, bundle, quantity, assortment, parcel.
2 *his lot in life* **fate,** destiny, fortune, doom; situation, circumstances, state, condition, position, plight, predicament.
3 *playing ball in a vacant lot* **patch of ground,** piece of ground, plot, area, tract, parcel, plat.
▶ adverb *I work in pastels a lot* **a great deal,** a good deal, to a great extent, much; often, frequently, regularly.
ANTONYMS a little.
– PHRASES **draw/cast lots** *we drew lots to see who gets to drive* **toss/flip a coin,** draw straws, throw/roll (the) dice. **throw in one's lot with** *he threw in his lot with the conspirators* **join forces with,** join up with, form an alliance with, ally with, align oneself with, link up with, make common cause with.

lotion ▶ noun *scented hand lotion* **ointment,** cream, salve, balm, rub, emollient, moisturizer, lubricant, gel, unguent, liniment, embrocation.

lottery ▶ noun 1 *play the lottery* **raffle,** drawing, prize drawing, sweepstake(s), lotto.
2 *life is a lottery* **gamble,** speculation, venture, risk, game of chance, matter of luck; informal crapshoot.

loud ▶ adjective 1 *loud music* **noisy,** blaring, booming, deafening, roaring, thunderous, thundering, ear-splitting, ear-piercing, piercing; carrying, clearly audible; lusty, powerful, forceful, stentorian; Music forte, fortissimo.
ANTONYMS quiet, soft.
2 *loud complaints* **vociferous,** clamorous, insistent, vehement, emphatic, urgent.

ANTONYMS gentle.
3 *a loud T-shirt* **garish,** gaudy, flamboyant, lurid, glaring, showy, ostentatious; vulgar, tasteless; informal flash, flashy, kitsch, kitschy, tacky.
ANTONYMS sober, tasteful.

loudmouth ▶ **noun** informal *coworkers characterize him as an egocentric loudmouth* **braggart,** boaster, bragger, blusterer, swaggerer; informal blabbermouth, big mouth, blowhard, show-off.

loudspeaker ▶ **noun** *a message came over the loudspeaker* **public address system,** PA (system), intercom; **speaker,** monitor, woofer, tweeter; megaphone; informal squawk box.

lounge ▶ **verb** *he just lounges in his room* **laze,** lie, loll, lie back, lean back, recline, stretch oneself, drape oneself, relax, rest, repose, take it easy, put one's feet up, unwind, luxuriate; sprawl, slump, slouch, flop; loaf, idle, do nothing; informal take a load off, kick back.
▶ **noun 1** *a hotel lounge* **bar,** pub, club, barroom, taproom.
2 *an airport lounge* **waiting area,** reception room.
3 *she sat in the lounge* **living room,** sitting room, front room, salon, family room; dated parlor, drawing room.

lousy informal ▶ **adjective 1** *a lousy film* See AWFUL (sense 2).
2 *the lousy, double-crossing snake!* See DESPICABLE.
3 *I felt lousy* See ILL (sense 1 of the adjective).
– PHRASES **be lousy with** *the restaurant was lousy with screaming little brats* See CRAWL (sense 3).

lout ▶ **noun** *drunken louts* **ruffian,** hooligan, thug, boor, barbarian, oaf, hoodlum, rowdy, lubber; informal tough, roughneck, bruiser, yahoo, lug, knuckle-dragger.
ANTONYMS gentleman.

lovable ▶ **adjective** *lovable baby gorillas* **adorable,** dear, sweet, cute, charming, darling, lovely, likable, delightful, captivating, enchanting, engaging, bewitching, pleasing, appealing, winsome, winning, fetching, endearing.
ANTONYMS hateful, loathsome.

love ▶ **noun 1** *his friendship with Helen grew into love* **deep affection,** fondness, tenderness, warmth, intimacy, attachment, endearment; devotion, adoration, doting, idolization, worship; passion, ardor, desire, lust, yearning, infatuation, besottedness.
ANTONYMS hatred.
2 *her love for fashion | a love of good food* **liking of/for,** enjoyment of, appreciation of/for, taste for, delight for/in, relish of, passion for, zeal for, appetite for, zest for, enthusiasm for, keenness for, fondness for, soft spot for, weakness for, bent for, proclivity for, inclination for, disposition for, partiality for, predilection for, penchant for.
3 *their love for their fellow human beings* **compassion,** care, caring, regard, solicitude, concern, friendliness, friendship, kindness, charity, goodwill, sympathy, kindliness, altruism, unselfishness, philanthropy, benevolence, fellow feeling, humanity.
4 *he was her one true love* **beloved,** loved one, love of one's life, dear, dearest, dear one, darling, sweetheart, sweet, angel, honey; lover, inamorato, inamorata, amour; archaic paramour.
5 *their love will survive* **relationship,** love affair, romance, liaison, affair of the heart, amour.
6 *my mother sends her love* **best wishes,** regards, good wishes, greetings, kind/kindest regards.
▶ **verb 1** *she loves him* **care very much for,** feel deep affection for, hold very dear, adore, think the world of, be devoted to, dote on, idolize, worship; be in love with, be infatuated with, be smitten with, be besotted with; informal be mad/crazy/nuts/wild about, have a crush on, carry a torch for.
ANTONYMS hate.
2 *Laura loved painting* **like very much,** delight in, enjoy greatly, have a passion for, take great pleasure in, derive great pleasure from, relish, savor; have a weakness for, be partial to, have a soft spot for, have a taste for, be taken with; informal get a kick out of, have a thing about, be mad/crazy/nuts/wild about, be hooked on, get off on.
ANTONYMS hate.
– PHRASES **fall in love with** *she didn't mean to fall in love with him* **become infatuated with,** give/lose one's heart to; informal fall for, be bowled over by, be swept off one's feet by, develop a crush on. **in love with** *he's in love with Gillian* **infatuated with,** besotted with, enamored of, smitten with, consumed with desire for; captivated by, bewitched by, enthralled by, entranced by, moonstruck by; devoted to, doting on; informal mad/crazy/nuts/wild about.

lovelorn ▶ **adjective** *my lovelorn son thinks the world has come to an end* **lovesick**; pining, languishing; spurned, jilted, rejected, forsaken.

lovely ▶ **adjective 1** *a lovely young woman* **beautiful,** pretty, attractive, good-looking, appealing, handsome, adorable, exquisite, sweet, personable, charming; enchanting, engaging, winsome, seductive, sexy, gorgeous, alluring, ravishing, glamorous; informal tasty, knockout, stunning, drop-dead gorgeous; killer, cute, foxy, hot; formal beauteous; archaic comely, fair.
ANTONYMS ugly, hideous.
2 *a lovely view* **scenic,** picturesque, pleasing, easy on the eye; magnificent, stunning, splendid.
3 informal *we had a lovely day* **delightful,** very pleasant, very nice, very agreeable, marvelous, wonderful, sublime, superb, magical; informal terrific, fabulous, heavenly, divine, amazing, glorious.
ANTONYMS horrible.

lover ▶ **noun 1** *she had a secret lover* **boyfriend, girlfriend,** beloved, love, darling, sweetheart, inamorata, inamorato; mistress; partner, significant other, main squeeze; informal bit on the side, toy boy, boy toy; dated ladylove, beau; archaic swain, concubine, paramour.
2 *a dog lover* **devotee,** admirer, fan, enthusiast, aficionado; informal buff, freak, nut, junkie.

loving ▶ **adjective** *her loving husband* **affectionate,** fond, devoted, adoring, doting,

solicitous, demonstrative; caring, tender, warm, warmhearted, close; amorous, ardent, passionate, amatory.
ANTONYMS cold, cruel.

low ▶ adjective **1** *a low fence* **short,** small, little; squat, stubby, stunted, dwarf; shallow.
ANTONYMS high.
2 *low prices* **cheap,** economical, moderate, reasonable, modest, bargain, budget, bargain-basement, rock-bottom, cut-rate.
ANTONYMS high, expensive.
3 *supplies were low* **scarce,** scanty, scant, skimpy, meager, sparse, few, little, paltry; reduced, depleted, diminished.
ANTONYMS plentiful, abundant.
4 *low quality* **inferior,** substandard, poor, bad, low-grade, low-end, below par, second-rate, unsatisfactory, deficient, defective, shoddy.
ANTONYMS high, superior.
5 *of low birth* **humble,** lowly, low-ranking, plebeian, proletarian, peasant, poor; common, ordinary.
ANTONYMS superior, noble.
6 *low expectations* **unambitious,** unaspiring, modest.
ANTONYMS high, ambitious.
7 *a low opinion* **unfavorable,** poor, bad, adverse, negative.
ANTONYMS high, favorable, good.
8 *a low blow* See LOWDOWN (adjective).
9 *low humor* **uncouth,** uncultured, unsophisticated, rough, rough-hewn, unrefined, tasteless, crass, common, vulgar, coarse, crude.
ANTONYMS high, exalted.
10 *a low voice* **quiet,** soft, faint, gentle, muted, subdued, muffled, hushed, quieted, whispered, stifled.
ANTONYMS loud.
11 *a low note* **bass,** baritone, low-pitched, deep, rumbling, booming, sonorous.
12 *she was feeling low* **depressed,** dejected, despondent, downhearted, downcast, low-spirited, down, morose, miserable, dismal, heavy-hearted, mournful, forlorn, woebegone, gloomy, glum, crestfallen, dispirited; without energy, enervated, flat, sapped, weary; informal down in/at the mouth, down in the dumps, blue.
ANTONYMS cheerful.
▶ noun *the dollar fell to an all-time low* **nadir,** low point, lowest point, lowest level, minimum, depth, rock bottom.
ANTONYMS high, zenith.

lowdown informal ▶ adjective *a lowdown trick* **unfair,** mean, despicable, reprehensible, contemptible, lamentable, disgusting, shameful, low, cheap, underhanded, foul, unworthy, shabby, base, dishonorable, unprincipled, sordid; informal rotten, dirty; beastly; dated dastardly.
ANTONYMS kind, honorable.
▶ noun *he gave us the lowdown* **facts,** information, story, intelligence, news, inside story; informal info, rundown, score, scoop, word, dope, dirt, poop, skinny.

lower ▶ adjective **1** *the lower house of Parliament* **subordinate,** inferior, lesser, junior, minor, secondary, lower-level, subsidiary, subservient.
ANTONYMS upper, senior.
2 *her lower lip* **bottom,** bottommost, nether, under; underneath, further down, beneath.
ANTONYMS upper, higher, top.
3 *a lower price* **cheaper,** reduced, cut, slashed.
ANTONYMS higher, increased.
▶ verb **1** *she lowered the mask* **move down,** let down, take down, haul down, drop, let fall.
ANTONYMS raise, lift up.
2 *lower your voice* **soften,** modulate, quiet, hush, tone down, muffle, turn down, mute.
ANTONYMS raise, intensify.
3 *they are lowering their prices* **reduce,** decrease, lessen, bring down, mark down, cut, slash, ax, diminish, curtail, prune, pare (down).
ANTONYMS increase.
4 *the water level lowered* **subside,** fall (off), recede, ebb, wane; abate, die down, let up, moderate, diminish, lessen.
5 *don't lower yourself to their level* **degrade,** debase, demean, abase, humiliate, downgrade, discredit, shame, dishonor, disgrace; belittle, cheapen, devalue; (**lower oneself**) stoop, sink, descend.
ANTONYMS boost.

low-grade ▶ adjective *low-grade building materials* **poor-quality,** inferior, substandard, second-rate; shoddy, cheap, reject, trashy, gimcrack, chintzy, rubbishy; informal two-bit, schlocky, bum, cheapjack.
ANTONYMS top-quality, first-class.

low-key ▶ adjective *she conducted a low-key campaign* **restrained,** modest, understated, muted, subtle, quiet, low-profile, inconspicuous, unostentatious, unobtrusive, discreet, toned-down; casual, informal, mellow, laid-back.
ANTONYMS ostentatious, obtrusive.

lowly ▶ adjective *that's right Mrs. Tynesdale, I used to be your lowly stable boy* **humble,** low, low-born, low-ranking, plebeian, proletarian; common, ordinary, plain, average, modest, simple; inferior, ignoble, subordinate, obscure.
ANTONYMS aristocratic, exalted.

loyal ▶ adjective *she was loyal to her country* **faithful,** true, devoted; constant, steadfast, staunch, dependable, reliable, trusted, trustworthy, trusty, dutiful, dedicated, unchanging, unwavering, unswerving; patriotic.
ANTONYMS treacherous.

loyalty ▶ noun *my grandparents never doubted each other's loyalty* **allegiance,** faithfulness, obedience, adherence, homage, devotion; steadfastness, staunchness, trueheartedness, dependability, reliability, trustworthiness, duty, dedication, commitment; patriotism; historical fealty.
ANTONYMS treachery.

lubricant ▶ noun *tubes of lubricant* **grease,** oil, lubrication, emollient, lotion, unguent; informal lube.

lubricate ▶ verb *lubricating the hinges* **oil, grease**; wax, polish; facilitate, smooth, ease; informal lube.

lucid ▶ adjective **1** *a lucid description* **intelligible,** comprehensible, understandable, cogent, coherent, articulate; clear, transparent;

plain, simple, vivid, sharp, straightforward, unambiguous; formal perspicuous.
ANTONYMS confusing, ambiguous.
2 *he was not lucid enough to explain* **rational,** sane, in one's right mind, in possession of one's faculties, compos mentis, able to think clearly, balanced, clearheaded, sober, sensible; informal all there. See note at **SENSIBLE**.
ANTONYMS muddled, confused.

luck ▶ **noun 1** *with luck you'll make it* **good fortune,** good luck; a fluke, a stroke of luck; informal a lucky break.
ANTONYMS bad luck, misfortune.
2 *I wish you luck* **success,** prosperity, good fortune, good luck.
ANTONYMS failure, misfortune.
3 *it is a matter of luck whether it hits or misses* **fortune,** fate, destiny, Lady Luck, lot, the stars, karma, kismet; fortuity, serendipity; chance, accident, a twist of fate.
– PHRASES **in luck** *you're in luck, there's one blue sweater left in your size* **fortunate,** lucky, blessed with good luck, born under a lucky star; successful, having a charmed life. **out of luck** *sorry, you're out of luck—the bus left just five minutes ago* **unfortunate,** unlucky, luckless, hapless, unsuccessful, cursed, jinxed, ill-fated; informal down on one's luck; literary star-crossed.

luckily ▶ **adverb** *luckily, we took the Great Elms Bridge, which was not flooded over* **fortunately,** happily, providentially, opportunely, by good fortune, as luck would have it, propitiously; mercifully, thankfully.
ANTONYMS unfortunately.

luckless ▶ **adjective** *his luckless father died penniless and alone* **unlucky,** unfortunate, unsuccessful, hapless, out of luck, cursed, jinxed, doomed, ill-fated; informal down on one's luck, losingest; literary star-crossed.
ANTONYMS lucky.

lucky ▶ **adjective 1** *the lucky winner* **fortunate,** in luck, blessed, favored, born under a lucky star, charmed; successful, prosperous.
ANTONYMS unfortunate.
2 *a lucky escape* **providential,** fortunate, advantageous, timely, opportune, serendipitous, expedient, heaven-sent, auspicious; chance, fortuitous, fluky, accidental.
ANTONYMS untimely.

lucrative ▶ **adjective** *a lucrative business* **profitable,** profit-making, gainful, remunerative, moneymaking, paying, high-income, well-paid, bankable; rewarding, worthwhile; thriving, flourishing, successful, booming.
ANTONYMS unprofitable.

ludicrous ▶ **adjective** *a ludicrous idea* **absurd,** ridiculous, farcical, laughable, risible, preposterous, foolish, mad, insane, idiotic, stupid, inane, silly, asinine, nonsensical; informal crazy. See note at **ABSURD**.
ANTONYMS sensible.

lug ▶ **verb** *she lugged her groceries to the door* **carry,** lift, bear, tote, heave, hoist, shoulder; haul, drag, tug, tow, transport, move, convey, shift; informal hump, schlep.
▶ **noun** informal *you big lug!* See **OAF**.

luggage ▶ **noun** *a rack for the luggage* **baggage;** bags, suitcases, cases, trunks. See also **BAG** (sense 2 of the noun).

lugubrious ▶ **adjective** *lugubrious hymns | their lugubrious aunt* **mournful,** gloomy, sad, unhappy, doleful, glum, melancholy, woeful, miserable, woebegone, forlorn, somber, solemn, serious, sorrowful, morose, dour, cheerless, joyless, dismal; funereal, sepulchral; informal down in/at the mouth; literary dolorous. See note at **GLUM**.
ANTONYMS cheerful.

lukewarm ▶ **adjective 1** *lukewarm coffee* **tepid,** slightly warm, warmish, at room temperature, chambré.
ANTONYMS hot, cold.
2 *a lukewarm response* **indifferent,** cool, halfhearted, apathetic, unenthusiastic, tepid, perfunctory, noncommittal, lackadaisical; informal laid-back, unenthused, couldn't-care-less.
ANTONYMS enthusiastic.

lull ▶ **verb 1** *the sound of the bells lulled us to sleep* **soothe,** calm, hush; rock.
ANTONYMS waken, agitate.
2 *his honeyed words lulled their suspicions* **assuage,** allay, ease, alleviate, soothe, quiet, quieted; reduce, diminish; quell, banish, dispel.
ANTONYMS aggravate.
3 *they lulled us into a false sense of security* **deceive,** dupe, trick, fool, hoodwink.
▶ **noun 1** *a lull in the fighting* **pause,** respite, interval, break, hiatus, suspension, interlude, intermission, breathing space; informal letup, breather.
2 *the lull before the storm* **calm,** stillness, quiet, tranquility, peace, silence, hush.
ANTONYMS activity.

lullaby ▶ **noun** *Mother's sweet lullabies* **cradle song,** berceuse.

lumber ▶ **verb** *elephants lumbered past* **lurch,** stumble, trundle, shamble, shuffle, waddle; trudge, clump, stump, plod, tramp, tromp; informal galumph.
▶ **noun** *a truckload of quality lumber* **timber,** wood, boards, planks.

lumbering ▶ **adjective** *he was a lumbering bear of a man* **clumsy,** awkward, heavy-footed, slow, blundering, bumbling, inept, maladroit, uncoordinated, ungainly, ungraceful, gauche, lumpish, hulking, ponderous; informal clodhopping.
ANTONYMS nimble, agile.

luminary ▶ **noun** *the luminaries of the art world* **leading light,** guiding light, inspiration, role model, hero, heroine, leader, expert, master; lion, legend, celebrity, personality, great, giant; informal bigwig, rainmaker, VIP.
ANTONYMS nobody.

luminous ▶ **adjective** *the luminous face of the alarm clock* **shining,** bright, brilliant, radiant, dazzling, glowing, gleaming, scintillating, lustrous; luminescent, phosphorescent, fluorescent, incandescent. See note at **BRIGHT**.
ANTONYMS dark.

lump[1] ▶ **noun 1** *a lump of coal* **chunk,** hunk, piece, mass, block, wedge, slab, cake, nugget, ball, brick, cube, pat, knob, clod, gobbet, dollop,

wad; informal glob, gob.
2 *a lump on his head* **swelling,** bump, bulge, protuberance, protrusion, growth, outgrowth, nodule, hump; goose egg.
3 (**lumps**) *take your lumps* **hard knocks,** defeats, losses.
▶ **verb** *it is out of ignorance that they **lump together** all modern artists* **combine,** put together, group, bunch, aggregate, unite, pool, merge, collect, throw together, consider together.

lump² ▶ **verb** informal *like it or lump it* **put up with,** bear, endure, suffer, take, tolerate, accept.

lunacy ▶ **noun 1** *originality demands a degree of lunacy* **insanity,** madness, mental illness, dementia, mania, psychosis; informal craziness.
ANTONYMS sanity.
2 *the lunacy of gambling* **folly,** foolishness, stupidity, silliness, idiocy, madness, recklessness, foolhardiness, imprudence, irresponsibility; informal craziness.
ANTONYMS sense, prudence.

lunatic ▶ **noun** *he drives like a lunatic* **maniac,** madman, madwoman, imbecile, psychopath, psychotic; fool, idiot; eccentric; informal loony, nut, nutcase, head case, psycho, moron, screwball, crackpot, fruitcake, fruit loop, loon.
▶ **adjective 1** *a lunatic prisoner* See MAD (sense 1).
2 *a lunatic idea* See MAD (sense 3).

lunch ▶ **noun** *my usual lunch includes soup and a sandwich* **midday meal,** luncheon, brunch, light meal, snack.
– PHRASES **out to lunch** *some of these therapists are more out to lunch than their patients* **crazy,** out of one's mind, mad; out of touch, out of it, unaware, absentminded; cuckoo, batty, flaky, spacey, nutty, wingy, off one's rocker.

lunge ▶ **noun** *Darren made a lunge at his attacker* **thrust,** jab, stab, dive, rush, charge.
▶ **verb** *he lunged at Finn with a knife* **thrust,** dive, spring, launch oneself, rush, make a grab.

lurch ▶ **verb 1** *he lurched into the kitchen* **stagger,** stumble, wobble, sway, reel, roll, weave, pitch, totter, blunder.
2 *the ship lurched* **sway,** reel, list, heel, rock, roll, pitch, toss, jerk, shake, flounder, swerve, teeter.
– PHRASES **leave someone in the lurch** *Wally talked us into taking part in the protest, and then he just left us in the lurch* **leave in trouble,** let down, leave stranded, leave high and dry, abandon, desert.

lure ▶ **verb** *consumers are frequently lured into debt* **tempt,** entice, attract, induce, coax, persuade, inveigle, allure, seduce, win over, cajole, beguile, bewitch, ensnare. See note at TEMPT.
ANTONYMS deter, put off.
▶ **noun** *the lure of the stage* **temptation,** enticement, attraction, pull, draw, appeal; inducement, allurement, fascination, interest, magnet; informal come-on.

lurid ▶ **adjective 1** *lurid colors* **bright,** brilliant, vivid, glaring, shocking, fluorescent, flaming, dazzling, intense; gaudy, loud, showy, bold, garish, tacky.
ANTONYMS muted, subtle.
2 *the lurid details* **sensational,** sensationalist, exaggerated, overdramatized, colorful; salacious, graphic, explicit, unrestrained, prurient, shocking; gruesome, gory, grisly; informal juicy, full-frontal.
ANTONYMS discreet, restrained.

lurk ▶ **verb** *is someone lurking in the bushes?* **skulk,** loiter, lie in wait, lie low, hide, conceal oneself, take cover, keep out of sight.

luscious ▶ **adjective 1** *luscious fruit* **delicious,** succulent, lush, juicy, mouthwatering, lip-smacking, sweet, tasty, appetizing; informal scrumptious, yummy, nummy; literary ambrosial.
ANTONYMS unappetizing.
2 *a luscious well-tanned beauty* **sexy,** sexually attractive, nubile, ravishing, gorgeous, seductive, alluring, sultry, beautiful, stunning; informal drop-dead gorgeous, hot, curvy, foxy, cute.
ANTONYMS plain, scrawny.

lush ▶ **adjective 1** *lush vegetation* **luxuriant,** rich, abundant, profuse, exuberant, riotous, prolific, vigorous; dense, thick, rank, rampant; informal jungly. See note at PROFUSE.
ANTONYMS barren, meager.
2 *a lush, ripe peach* **succulent,** luscious, juicy, soft, tender, ripe.
ANTONYMS shriveled.
3 *a lush apartment* **luxurious,** deluxe, sumptuous, palatial, opulent, lavish, elaborate, extravagant, fancy; informal plush, ritzy, posh, swanky, swank.
ANTONYMS austere.

lust ▶ **noun 1** *his lust for her* **sexual desire,** sexual appetite, sexual longing, ardor, desire, passion; libido, sex drive, sexuality, biological urge; lechery, lasciviousness, concupiscence; informal horniness, the hots, randiness.
2 *a lust for power* **greed,** desire, craving, covetousness, eagerness, avidity, cupidity, longing, yearning, hunger, thirst, appetite, hankering.
ANTONYMS aversion.
▶ **verb 1** *he **lusted after** his employer's wife* **desire,** be consumed with desire for, find sexually attractive, crave, covet, ache for, burn for; informal have the hots for, fancy, have a thing about/for, drool over.
2 *she **lusted after** adventure* **crave,** desire, covet, want, wish for, long for, yearn for, dream of, hanker for, hanker after, hunger for, thirst for, ache for.
ANTONYMS dread, avoid.

luster ▶ **noun 1** *her hair lost its luster* **sheen,** gloss, shine, glow, gleam, shimmer, burnish, polish, patina. See note at POLISH.
ANTONYMS dullness.
2 *the luster of the Milky Way* **brilliance,** brightness, radiance, sparkle, dazzle, flash, glitter, glint, gleam, luminosity, luminescence.

lustful ▶ **adjective** *a lustful look* **lecherous,** lascivious, libidinous, licentious, salacious, goatish; wanton, unchaste, impure, naughty, immodest, indecent, dirty, prurient; passionate, sensual, sexy, erotic; informal horny, randy, raunchy, lusty; formal concupiscent.
ANTONYMS chaste, pure.

lustrous ▶ **adjective** *lustrous black hair* **shiny,**

shining, satiny, glossy, gleaming, shimmering, burnished, polished; radiant, bright, brilliant, luminous; dazzling, sparkling, glistening, twinkling. See note at **BRIGHT**.
ANTONYMS dull.

lusty ▶ adjective **1** *a lusty baby* **healthy,** strong, fit, vigorous, robust, hale and hearty, energetic; rugged, sturdy, muscular, muscly, strapping, hefty, husky, burly, powerful; informal beefy; dated stalwart.
ANTONYMS feeble, weak.
2 *lusty singing* **loud,** vigorous, hearty, strong, powerful, forceful.
ANTONYMS feeble, weak.
3 informal *lusty young men* See **LUSTFUL**.

luxuriant ▶ adjective *luxuriant vegetation* **lush,** rich, abundant, profuse, exuberant, riotous, prolific, vigorous; dense, thick, rank, rampant; informal jungly. See note at **PROFUSE**.
ANTONYMS barren, sparse.

luxuriate ▶ verb *luxuriating in a bubble bath* **revel,** bask, delight, take pleasure, wallow; (**luxuriate in**) enjoy, relish, savor, appreciate; informal get a kick out of, get a thrill out of.
ANTONYMS dislike.

luxurious ▶ adjective **1** *a luxurious hotel* **opulent,** sumptuous, deluxe, rich, grand, palatial, splendid, magnificent, well appointed, extravagant, fancy, upscale, upmarket, five-star; informal plush, posh, classy, ritzy, swanky, swank.
ANTONYMS poor, austere, spartan.
2 *a luxurious lifestyle* **self-indulgent,** sensual, pleasure-loving, pleasure-seeking, epicurean, hedonistic, sybaritic. See note at **SENSUOUS**.
ANTONYMS abstemious.

luxury ▶ noun **1** *we'll live in luxury* **opulence,** luxuriousness, sumptuousness, grandeur, magnificence, splendor, lavishness, the lap of luxury, a bed of roses, (the land of) milk and honey; informal the life of Riley.
ANTONYMS austerity, poverty.
2 *a TV is his only luxury* **indulgence,** extravagance, self-indulgence, nonessential, treat, extra, frill.
ANTONYMS necessity.

lying ▶ noun *she was no good at lying* **untruthfulness,** fabrication, fibbing, perjury, white lies; falseness, falsity, dishonesty, mendacity, telling stories, invention, misrepresentation, deceit, duplicity; literary perfidy.
ANTONYMS honesty.
▶ adjective *he was a lying womanizer* **untruthful,** false, dishonest, mendacious, deceitful, deceiving, duplicitous, double-dealing, two-faced; literary perfidious.
ANTONYMS truthful.

lynch ▶ verb *DeLuca was lynched by Yardley's mob* **execute illegally,** hang, kill; informal string up.

lyrical ▶ adjective **1** *lyrical love poetry* **expressive,** emotional, deeply felt, personal, subjective, passionate, lyric.
2 *she was lyrical about her success* **enthusiastic,** rhapsodic, effusive, rapturous, ecstatic, euphoric, carried away.
ANTONYMS unenthusiastic.

lyrics ▶ plural noun *Cole Porter wrote the music and lyrics* **words,** libretto, book, text, lines.

Mm

macabre ▶ adjective **1** *a macabre ritual* **gruesome,** grisly, grim, gory, morbid, ghastly, unearthly, grotesque, hideous, horrific, shocking, dreadful, loathsome, repugnant, repulsive, sickening.
2 *a macabre joke* **black,** weird, unhealthy; informal sick.

mace ▶ noun *the thug wielded a mace* **club,** cudgel, stick, staff, shillelagh, bludgeon, truncheon, nightstick, billy club, blackjack.

Machiavellian ▶ adjective *their Machiavellian plot to inherit their aunt's estate* **devious,** cunning, crafty, artful, wily, sly, scheming, treacherous, two-faced, tricky, double-dealing, unscrupulous, deceitful, dishonest; literary perfidious; informal foxy.
ANTONYMS straightforward, ingenuous.

machinations ▶ plural noun *they were always wary of the machinations of rival gangs* **scheming,** schemes, plotting, plots, intrigues, conspiracies, ruses, tricks, wiles, stratagems, tactics, maneuvering. See note at PLOT.

machine ▶ noun **1** *a threshing machine* **apparatus,** appliance, device, contraption, contrivance, mechanism, engine, gadget, tool.
2 *an efficient publicity machine* **organization,** system, structure, arrangement, machinery; informal setup.
3 *he's an eating machine* **powerhouse,** human dynamo; wonder, phenomenon, sensation; automaton.

machinery ▶ noun **1** *printing machinery* **equipment,** apparatus, hardware, gear, tackle, plant; mechanism; instruments, tools; gadgetry, technology.
2 *the machinery of government* **workings,** organization, system, structure, administration, institution; informal setup.

machismo ▶ noun *don't be struttin' your machismo around here, buster* (**aggressive**) **masculinity,** toughness, male chauvinism, sexism, virility, manliness; bravado; informal testosterone, macho.

mad ▶ adjective **1** *he felt he was going mad* **insane,** mentally ill, certifiable, deranged, demented, of unsound mind, out of one's mind, not in one's right mind, sick in the head, crazy, crazed, lunatic, non compos mentis, unhinged, disturbed, raving, psychotic, psychopathic, schizophrenic, bipolar, mad as a hatter, mad as a March hare; informal **crazy,** mental, off one's nut, nuts, nutty, nutty as a fruitcake, nutso, off one's rocker, not right in the head, round/around the bend, (stark) raving mad, bats, batty, buggy, bonkers, dotty, cuckoo, cracked, loopy, loony, bananas, loco, screwy, schizoid, psycho, touched, gaga, not all there, not right upstairs, crackers, out of one's tree, meshuga, wacko, gonzo; (**be mad**) have a screw loose, have bats in the/one's belfry; (**go mad**) lose one's reason, lose one's mind, take leave of one's senses, lose one's marbles, crack up.
ANTONYMS sane.
2 *I'm still mad at him* | *don't get mad* **angry,** furious, infuriated, irate, raging, enraged, fuming, incensed, seeing red, beside oneself; informal livid, sore; literary wrathful; (**get mad**) lose one's temper, get in a rage, rant and rave; informal explode, go off the deep end, go ape, flip, flip out, flip one's wig.
ANTONYMS unruffled, calm.
3 *some mad scheme* **foolish,** insane, stupid, lunatic, foolhardy, idiotic, senseless, absurd, impractical, silly, inane, asinine, wild, unwise, imprudent; informal crazy, crackpot, crack-brained, daft.
ANTONYMS sensible.
4 informal *he's **mad about** jazz* **enthusiastic about,** passionate about; ardent about, fervent about, avid about, fanatical about; devoted to, infatuated with, in love with, hot for; informal crazy about, nuts about, wild about, hooked on, gone on, nutso about.
ANTONYMS indifferent.
5 *it was a mad dash to get ready* **frenzied,** frantic, frenetic, feverish, wild, hectic, manic.
– PHRASES **like mad** informal **1** *I ran like mad* **fast,** quickly, rapidly, speedily, hastily, hurriedly.
2 *he had to fight like mad* **energetically,** enthusiastically, madly, furiously, with a will, for all one is worth, passionately, intensely, ardently, fervently; informal like crazy, hammer and tongs.

madcap ▶ adjective **1** *a madcap scheme* **reckless,** rash, foolhardy, foolish, harebrained, wild, hasty, imprudent, ill-advised; informal crazy, crackpot, crack-brained.
2 *a madcap comedy* **zany,** eccentric, unconventional.
▶ noun *she was a boisterous madcap* **eccentric,** crank, madman/madwoman, maniac, lunatic; oddity, character; informal crackpot, oddball, weirdo, loony, nut, fruit loop, screwball, loon.

madden ▶ verb **1** *what maddens people most is his vagueness* **infuriate,** exasperate, irritate; incense, anger, enrage, provoke, upset, agitate, vex, irk, make someone's hackles rise, make someone see red; informal aggravate, make someone's blood boil, make livid, get someone's goat, get someone's back up, tee off, tick off, steam someone up.

2 *they were maddened with pain* **drive mad,** drive insane, derange, unhinge, unbalance; informal drive round/around the bend.

made-up ▶ adjective 1 *a made-up story* **invented,** fabricated, trumped up, concocted, fictitious, fictional, false, untrue, specious, spurious, bogus, apocryphal, imaginary, mythical.
2 *she was made up for the evening* **wearing makeup**; informal dolled up, decked out.

madhouse ▶ noun informal 1 *his father is shut up in a madhouse* **mental hospital,** mental institution, psychiatric hospital, asylum; informal nuthouse, funny farm, loony bin; dated lunatic asylum.
2 *when we arrived, it was a madhouse* **bedlam,** mayhem, chaos, pandemonium, an uproar, turmoil, disorder, madness, all hell broken loose, a (three-ring) circus, a zoo.

madly ▶ adverb 1 *she was smiling madly* **insanely,** deliriously, wildly, like a lunatic; informal crazily.
ANTONYMS sanely.
2 *madly snapping pictures* **fast,** furiously, hurriedly, quickly, speedily, hastily, energetically; informal like mad, like crazy.
ANTONYMS slowly.
3 informal *she was madly in love with him* **intensely,** fervently, wildly, unrestrainedly, to distraction.
ANTONYMS slightly.
4 informal *a madly eccentric pair* **very,** extremely, really, exceedingly, exceptionally, remarkably, extraordinarily, immensely, tremendously, wildly, hugely; informal awfully, terribly, terrifically, fantastically.
ANTONYMS slightly.

madman, madwoman ▶ noun *there was a madman on the loose* **lunatic,** maniac, psychotic, psychopath, sociopath; informal loony, nut, nutcase, fruit loop, head case, psycho, screwball, loon.

madness ▶ noun 1 *today madness is called mental illness* **insanity,** mental illness, dementia, derangement; lunacy, instability; mania, psychosis; informal craziness.
ANTONYMS sanity.
2 *it would be madness to do otherwise* **folly,** foolishness, idiocy, stupidity, insanity, lunacy, silliness; informal craziness.
ANTONYMS common sense, good sense.
3 *it's absolute madness in here* **bedlam,** mayhem, chaos, pandemonium, craziness, uproar, turmoil, disorder, all hell broken loose, (three-ring) circus.
ANTONYMS calm.

maelstrom ▶ noun 1 *a maelstrom in the sea* **whirlpool,** vortex, eddy, swirl; literary Charybdis.
2 *the maelstrom of war* **turbulence,** tumult, turmoil, disorder, disarray, chaos, confusion, upheaval, pandemonium, bedlam, whirlwind.

maestro ▶ noun 1 *blues maestro Eric Clapton* **virtuoso,** master, expert, genius, wizard, prodigy; informal ace, whiz, pro, hotshot.
ANTONYMS novice, beginner.
2 *the maestro took the podium* **conductor,** (music) director.

magazine ▶ noun *a monthly fashion magazine* **journal,** periodical, serial, supplement, quarterly, monthly, weekly, news magazine; informal glossy, mag, zine, fanzine.

magenta ▶ adjective *the blouse is white with magenta pinstripes* **reddish-purple,** purplish-red, crimson, plum, carmine red, fuchsia; literary incarnadine.

magic ▶ noun 1 *do you believe in magic?* **sorcery,** witchcraft, wizardry, necromancy, enchantment, the supernatural, occultism, the occult, black magic, the black arts, voodoo, hoodoo, mojo, shamanism; charm, hex, spell, jinx.
2 *he does magic at children's parties* **conjuring tricks,** sleight of hand, legerdemain, illusion, prestidigitation.
3 *the magic of the stage* **allure,** attraction, excitement, fascination, charm, glamour.
4 *her dancing is pure magic* **skill,** brilliance, ability, accomplishment, adeptness, adroitness, deftness, dexterity, aptitude, expertise, art, finesse, talent.
▶ adjective 1 *a magic spell* **supernatural,** enchanted, occult.
2 *a magic place* **fascinating,** captivating, charming, glamorous, magical, enchanting, entrancing, spellbinding, magnetic, irresistible, hypnotic.
3 informal *we were magic together* **marvelous,** wonderful, excellent, admirable; informal terrific, fabulous, brilliant.

magician ▶ noun 1 *she imagined she was a magician* **sorcerer,** sorceress, witch, wizard, warlock, enchanter, enchantress, necromancer, shaman.
2 *Houdini was a great magician* **conjuror,** illusionist, prestidigitator.
3 *he is a magician on the ice* **genius,** marvel, wizard.

magisterial ▶ adjective 1 *a magisterial pronouncement* **authoritative,** masterful, assured, lordly, commanding, assertive.
ANTONYMS humble.
2 *his magisterial style of questioning* **domineering,** dictatorial, autocratic, imperious, overbearing, peremptory, high-handed, arrogant, supercilious, patronizing; informal bossy.
ANTONYMS hesitant, tentative.

magnanimous ▶ adjective *her magnanimous contributions to the art world* **generous,** charitable, benevolent, beneficent, big-hearted, handsome, princely, altruistic, philanthropic, unselfish, chivalrous, noble; forgiving, merciful, lenient, indulgent, clement.
ANTONYMS mean-spirited, selfish.

magnate ▶ noun *the industrial magnates of the nineteenth century* **tycoon,** mogul, captain of industry, baron, lord, king, magnifico; industrialist, proprietor; informal big shot, big cheese, (head) honcho; derogatory fat cat.

magnet ▶ noun 1 *you can test if it's steel by using a magnet* **lodestone**; electromagnet, solenoid.
2 *a magnet for tourists* **attraction,** focus, draw, lure, mecca.

magnetic ▶ adjective *a magnetic personality* **alluring,** attractive, fascinating, captivating, enchanting, enthralling, appealing, charming, prepossessing, engaging, entrancing, seductive, inviting, irresistible, charismatic.

magnetism ▶ noun *the sheer magnetism of his physical presence* **allure,** attraction, fascination, appeal, draw, drawing power, pull, charm, enchantment, seductiveness, magic, spell, charisma.

magnification ▶ noun *the fine lines are visible only under magnification* **enlargement,** enhancement, increase, augmentation, extension, expansion, amplification, intensification, inflation.
ANTONYMS reduction.

magnificence ▶ noun *the magnificence of Broadway* **splendor,** grandeur, impressiveness, glory, majesty, nobility, pomp, stateliness, elegance, sumptuousness, opulence, luxury, lavishness, richness, brilliance, dazzle, skill, virtuosity.
ANTONYMS modesty, tawdriness, weakness.

magnificent ▶ adjective **1** *a magnificent view of the mountains* **splendid,** spectacular, impressive, striking, glorious, superb, majestic, awesome, awe-inspiring, breathtaking.
ANTONYMS uninspiring.
2 *a magnificent apartment overlooking the lake* **sumptuous,** resplendent, grand, impressive, imposing, monumental, palatial, stately, opulent, luxurious, lavish, rich, dazzling, beautiful, elegant; informal splendiferous, ritzy, posh, swanky.
ANTONYMS modest, tawdry, cheap.
3 *a magnificent performance* **masterly,** skillful, virtuoso, brilliant.
ANTONYMS poor, weak.

magnify ▶ verb **1** *the lens magnifies the image* **enlarge,** boost, enhance, maximize, increase, augment, extend, expand, amplify, intensify; informal blow up.
ANTONYMS reduce.
2 *they magnified the problem* **exaggerate,** overstate, overemphasize, overplay, dramatize, color, embroider, embellish, inflate, make a mountain out of (a molehill); informal blow up (out of all proportion), make a big thing out of.
ANTONYMS minimize, understate.

magnitude ▶ noun **1** *the magnitude of the task* **immensity,** vastness, hugeness, enormity; size, extent, expanse, greatness, largeness, bigness.
ANTONYMS smallness.
2 *events of tragic magnitude* **importance,** import, significance, weight, consequence, mark, notability, note; formal moment.
ANTONYMS triviality.
– PHRASES **of the first magnitude** *we are witnessing a historic event of the first magnitude* **of the utmost importance,** of the greatest significance, very important, of great consequence; formal of great moment.

maid ▶ noun **1** *the maid cleared the table* **female servant,** maidservant, housemaid, domestic, housekeeper; help, cleaner, cleaning woman/lady; dated parlormaid, lady's maid, chambermaid.
2 literary *a village maid and her swain* **girl,** young woman, young lady, lass, miss, ingenue; literary maiden, damsel, nymph; archaic wench.

maiden ▶ noun literary *a pretty young maiden* See MAID (sense 2).
▶ adjective **1** *a maiden aunt* **unmarried,** spinster, unwed, unwedded, single, husbandless, celibate.
2 *a maiden voyage* **first,** initial, inaugural, introductory, initiatory, virgin.

mail ▶ noun *the mail arrived* letters, correspondence; postal system, postal service, post office; delivery, collection; email; chiefly Brit. post; informal snail mail.
▶ verb *we mailed the card* **send,** dispatch, post, direct, forward, redirect, ship, express, courier; email.

maim ▶ verb *a dog maimed by a coyote* **injure,** wound, cripple, disable, incapacitate, impair, mar, mutilate, lacerate, disfigure, deform, mangle.

main ▶ adjective *the main item* **principal,** chief, head, leading, foremost, most important, major, ruling, dominant, central, focal, key, prime, master, premier, primary, first, first-line, fundamental, supreme, predominant, (most) prominent, preeminent, paramount, overriding, cardinal, crucial, critical, pivotal, salient, elemental, essential, staple.
ANTONYMS subsidiary, minor.
▶ noun *a burst water main* **pipe,** channel, duct, conduit.
– PHRASES **in the main** *in the main, we want the menu to offer a nice selection of kosher alternatives* See MAINLY.

mainly ▶ adverb *the people on the island are mainly tourists* **mostly,** for the most part, in the main, on the whole, largely, by and large, to a large extent, predominantly, chiefly, principally, primarily; generally, usually, typically, commonly, on average, as a rule, almost always.

mainspring ▶ noun *the mainspring of anticommunism* **motive,** motivation, impetus, driving force, incentive, impulse, prime mover, reason, fountain, fount, wellspring, root, generator.

mainstay ▶ noun *agriculture is the mainstay of their economy* **central component,** central figure, centerpiece, prop, linchpin, cornerstone, pillar, bulwark, buttress, chief support, backbone, anchor, foundation, base, staple.

maintain ▶ verb **1** *they wanted to maintain peace* **preserve,** conserve, keep, retain, keep going, keep alive, keep up, prolong, perpetuate, sustain, carry on, continue.
ANTONYMS break (off), discontinue.
2 *the association maintains its private roads* **keep in good condition,** keep in (good) repair, keep up, service, care for, take good care of, look after.
ANTONYMS neglect.
3 *the cost of maintaining a dog* **support,** provide for, keep, sustain; nurture, feed, nourish.
ANTONYMS neglect.
4 *he always maintained his innocence | he maintains that he is innocent* **insist (on),** declare, assert, protest, affirm, avow, profess, claim, allege, contend, argue, swear (to), hold to; formal aver.
ANTONYMS deny.

maintenance ▶ noun **1** *the maintenance of*

peace **preservation,** conservation, keeping, prolongation, perpetuation, carrying on, continuation, continuance.
ANTONYMS breakdown, discontinuation.
2 *car maintenance* **upkeep,** service, servicing, repair(s), care.
ANTONYMS neglect.
3 *the maintenance of his children* **support,** keeping, upkeep, sustenance; nurture, feeding, nourishment.
ANTONYMS neglect.
4 *absent fathers are forced to pay maintenance* **financial support,** child support, alimony, provision; keep, subsistence, living expenses.

majestic ▶ adjective *the majestic Rocky Mountains | his father's majestic presence* **stately,** dignified, distinguished, solemn, magnificent, grand, splendid, resplendent, glorious, sumptuous, impressive, august, noble, awe-inspiring, monumental, palatial; statuesque, Olympian, imposing, marvelous, sonorous, resounding, heroic.
ANTONYMS modest, wretched.

major ▶ adjective **1** *the major North American writers* **greatest,** best, finest, most important, chief, main, prime, principal, capital, cardinal, leading, star, foremost, outstanding, first-rate, preeminent, arch-; informal major league, big league.
ANTONYMS minor.
2 *an issue of major importance* **crucial,** vital, great, considerable, paramount, utmost, prime; informal serious.
ANTONYMS little.
3 *a major factor* **important,** big, significant, weighty, crucial, key, sweeping, substantial.
ANTONYMS trivial.
4 *major surgery* **serious,** radical, complicated, difficult.
ANTONYMS minor.

majority ▶ noun **1** *the majority of cases* **larger part/number,** greater part/number, best/better part, most, more than half; plurality, bulk, mass, weight, (main) body, preponderance, predominance, generality, lion's share.
ANTONYMS minority.
2 *a majority in the election* **(winning) margin,** superiority of numbers/votes; landslide.
3 *my youngest child has reached majority* **legal age,** adulthood, manhood/womanhood, maturity; age of consent, coming of age.

> USAGE
> **majority**
> Strictly speaking, *majority* should be used with countable nouns to mean 'the greater number': *the majority of cases.* The use of *majority* with uncountable nouns to mean 'the greatest part' (*I spent the majority of the day reading*), although common in informal contexts, is not considered good standard English.

make ▶ verb **1** *he makes models* **construct,** build, assemble, put together, manufacture, produce, fabricate, create, form, fashion, model.
ANTONYMS destroy.
2 *I didn't want to go but she made me* **force,** compel, coerce, press, drive, pressure, oblige, require; have someone do something, prevail on, dragoon, bludgeon, strong-arm, impel, constrain; informal railroad.
3 *don't make such a noise* **cause,** create, give rise to, produce, bring about, generate, engender, occasion, effect, set up, establish, institute, found, develop, originate; literary beget.
4 *she made a little bow* **perform,** execute, give, do, accomplish, achieve, bring off, carry out, effect.
5 *they made him chairman* **appoint,** designate, name, nominate, select, elect, vote in, install; induct, institute, invest, ordain.
6 *he had made a will* **formulate,** frame, draw up, devise, make out, prepare, compile, compose, put together; draft, write, pen.
7 *I've made a mistake* **perpetrate,** commit, be responsible for, be guilty of, be to blame for.
8 *he's made a lot of money* **acquire,** obtain, gain, get, realize, secure, win, earn; gross, net, clear; bring in, take (in), rake in.
ANTONYMS lose.
9 *he made dinner* **prepare,** get ready, put together, concoct, cook, dish up, throw together, whip up, brew; informal fix.
10 *we've got to make a decision* **reach,** come to, settle on, determine on, conclude.
11 *she made a short announcement* **utter,** give, deliver, give voice to, enunciate, recite, pronounce.
12 *the sofa makes a good bed* **be,** act as, serve as, function as, constitute, do duty for.
13 *he'll make the team* **gain a place in,** get into, gain access to, enter; achieve, attain.
14 *he just made his train* **catch,** get, arrive/be in time for, arrive at, reach; get to.
ANTONYMS miss.
▶ noun **1** *what make is the car?* **brand,** marque, label.
2 *a man of a different make from his brother* **character,** nature, temperament, temper, disposition, kidney, mold, stamp.
– PHRASES **make as if/though** *he made as if to run away* **feign,** pretend, make a show/pretense of, affect, feint, make out. **make believe** *we encourage the children to make believe* **pretend,** fantasize, daydream, build castles in the air, dream, imagine, play-act, play. **make do** *we have precious little but we make do | we'll have to make do with just one income* **scrape by,** get by, manage, cope, survive, muddle through, improvise, make ends meet, keep the wolf from the door, keep one's head above water; informal make out; (**make do with**) make the best of, get by on, put up with. **make for 1** *she made for the door* **go for/toward,** head for/toward, aim for, make one's way toward, move toward, direct one's steps toward, steer a course toward, be bound for, make a beeline for. **2** *constant arguing doesn't make for a happy marriage* **contribute to,** be conducive to, produce, promote, facilitate, foster. **make it 1** *he'll never make it as a singer* **succeed,** be a success, distinguish oneself, get ahead, make good; informal make the grade, arrive. **2** *she's very ill—is she going to make it?* **survive,**

come through, pull through, get better, recover. **make love** See HAVE SEX WITH. **make off with** *they made off with all the wedding gifts* **take,** steal, purloin, pilfer, abscond with, run away/off with, carry off, snatch; kidnap, abduct; informal walk away/off with, swipe, filch, nab, lift, "liberate", "borrow", snitch, pinch; heist. **make out** informal **1** *how did you make out?* **get on/along,** fare, do, proceed, go, progress, manage, survive, cope, get by. **2** *I could just make out a figure in the distance* **see,** discern, distinguish, perceive, pick out, detect, observe, recognize; literary descry, espy. **3** *he couldn't make out what she was saying* **understand,** comprehend, follow, grasp, fathom, work out, make sense of, interpret, decipher, make head(s) or tail(s) of, get, get the drift of, catch. **4** *she made out that he was violent* **allege,** claim, assert, declare, maintain, affirm, suggest, imply, hint, insinuate, indicate, intimate, impute; formal aver. **5** *he made out a receipt for $20* **write out,** fill out, fill in, complete, draw up. **6** *they made out in the back seat* **kiss,** neck, caress, pet; informal smooch, canoodle, fool around. **make over** *Grandpa made over the deed to Uncle Marc* **transfer,** sign over, turn over, hand over/on/down, give, leave, bequeath, bestow, pass on, assign, consign, entrust; Law devolve. **make up 1** *let's kiss and make up* **be friends again,** bury the hatchet, declare a truce, make peace, forgive and forget, shake hands, become reconciled, settle one's differences, mend fences, call it quits. **2** *exports make up 42% of earnings* **constitute,** form, compose, account for. **3** *Gina brought a friend to make up a foursome* **complete,** round off/out, finish. **4** *the pharmacist made up the prescription* **prepare,** mix, concoct, put together. **5** *he made up an excuse* **invent,** fabricate, concoct, dream up, think up, hatch, trump up; devise, manufacture, formulate, coin; informal cook up. **6** *she made up her face* **apply makeup/cosmetics to,** powder; (**make oneself up**) informal put on one's face, do/paint one's face, apply one's war paint, doll oneself up. **make up for 1** *she tried to make up for what she'd said* **atone for,** make amends for, compensate for, make recompense for, make reparation for, make redress for, make restitution for, expiate. **2** *job satisfaction can make up for low pay* **offset,** counterbalance, counteract, compensate for; balance, neutralize, cancel out, even up, redeem. **make up one's mind** *you need to make up your mind about the job offer* **decide,** come to a decision, make/reach a decision; settle on a plan of action, come to a conclusion, reach a conclusion; determine, resolve. **make way** *make way for the paramedics* **move aside,** clear the way, make a space, make room, stand back.

make-believe ▶ noun *that was sheer make-believe* **fantasy,** pretense, daydreaming, imagination, invention, fancy, dream, fabrication, play-acting, dreaming in technicolor, charade, masquerade, dress-up.
ANTONYMS reality.
▶ adjective *make-believe adventures* **imaginary,** imagined, made-up, fantasy, dreamed-up, fanciful, fictitious, fictive, feigned, fake, mock, sham, simulated; informal pretend, phony.
ANTONYMS real, actual.

maker ▶ noun *the makers of fine furniture* **creator,** manufacturer, constructor, builder, producer, fabricator, inventor, architect, designer.

makeshift ▶ adjective *we stayed dry under some makeshift shelter* **temporary,** provisional, interim, stopgap, make-do, standby, rough and ready, improvised, ad hoc, extempore, jury-rigged, jerry-built, thrown together, cobbled together.
ANTONYMS permanent.

makeup ▶ noun **1** *she used excessive makeup* **cosmetics,** maquillage; greasepaint, face paint; informal war paint.
2 *the cellular makeup of plants* **composition,** constitution, structure, configuration, arrangement, organization, formation.
3 *jealousy isn't part of his makeup* **character,** nature, temperament, personality, disposition, mentality, persona, psyche; informal what makes someone tick.

making ▶ noun **1** *the making of cars* **manufacture,** mass-production, building, construction, assembly, production, creation, putting together, fabrication, forming, molding, forging.
ANTONYMS destruction.
2 (**makings**) *she has the makings of a champion* **qualities,** characteristics, ingredients; potential, promise, capacity, capability; essentials, essence, beginnings, rudiments, basics, stuff.
– PHRASES **in the making** *a hero in the making* **budding,** up and coming, emergent, developing, nascent, potential, promising, incipient.

maladjusted ▶ adjective *a home for maladjusted kids* **disturbed,** unstable, neurotic, unbalanced, unhinged, dysfunctional; informal mixed up, screwed up, messed up.
ANTONYMS normal, stable.

maladroit ▶ adjective *the judge reprimanded him for his maladroit handling of the case* **bungling,** awkward, inept, clumsy, bumbling, incompetent, unskillful, heavy-handed, gauche, tactless, inconsiderate, undiplomatic, impolitic; informal ham-fisted, all thumbs, klutzy.
ANTONYMS adroit, skillful.

malady ▶ noun *every time we visit Jerry, he has a new malady* **illness,** sickness, disease, infection, ailment, disorder, complaint, indisposition, affliction, infirmity, syndrome; informal bug, virus.

malaise ▶ noun *he showed no sign of emerging from his grief and malaise* **unhappiness,** uneasiness, unease, discomfort, melancholy, depression, despondency, dejection, angst, ennui; lassitude, listlessness, languor, weariness; indisposition, ailment, infirmity, illness, sickness, disease.
ANTONYMS comfort, well-being.

malapropism ▶ noun *she's famous for her hilarious malapropisms* **wrong word,** solecism, misuse, misapplication, infelicity, slip of the tongue, Freudian slip, blunder.

malcontent ▶ noun *a group of malcontents* **troublemaker,** mischief-maker, agitator, dissident, rebel, rabble-rouser; discontent, complainer, grumbler, moaner, whiner; informal grouch, grump, bellyacher, kvetch, squeaky wheel.

▶ adjective *a malcontent employee* See DISCONTENTED.

male ▶ adjective *it's his male jealousy, which is nearly always unfounded* **masculine,** virile, manly, macho; red-blooded.
ANTONYMS female.

▶ noun *two males walked past* See MAN (sense 1 of the noun).

CHOOSE THE RIGHT WORD

male, manful, manly, mannish, masculine, virile

We speak of a **male** ancestor, a **masculine** scent, and a **manly** activity, but only of women as **mannish**. While all of these adjectives apply to what is characteristic of the male of the species (particularly the human species), *male* can refer to plants or animals as well as human beings and is used to describe whatever is biologically distinguished from the female sex (*an all-male choir; a male cat; a male holly bush*). *Masculine* refers to the qualities, characteristics, and behaviors associated with or thought to be appropriate to men and boys (*a masculine handshake*). *Manly* emphasizes the desirable qualities that a culture associates with a mature man, such as courage and independence (*the manly virtues; the manly sport of football*). **Manful** differs from *manly* primarily in its emphasis on sturdiness and resoluteness (*a manful effort to hold back tears*). **Virile** is a stronger word than *masculine* or *manly* and is applied only to mature men; it suggests the vigor, muscularity, and forcefulness—and especially the sexual potency—associated with mature manhood (*a virile man who looked like Charlton Heston in his youth*).

malediction ▶ noun *the maledictions of the evil doctor* **curse,** damnation, oath; spell, hex, jinx; formal imprecation; literary anathema; archaic execration.
ANTONYMS blessing.

malefactor ▶ noun *she is studying the psychological profiles of three teenage malefactors* **wrongdoer,** miscreant, offender, criminal, culprit, villain, lawbreaker, felon, evildoer, delinquent, hooligan, hoodlum; sinner, transgressor; informal crook, thug; archaic trespasser.

malevolent ▶ adjective *a malevolent glare* **malicious,** hostile, evil-minded, baleful, evil-intentioned, venomous, evil, malign, malignant, rancorous, vicious, vindictive, vengeful; literary malefic, maleficent.
ANTONYMS benevolent.

malformed ▶ adjective *a mythical island of malformed creatures* **deformed,** misshapen, misproportioned, ill-proportioned, disfigured, distorted, crooked, contorted, twisted, warped; abnormal, grotesque, dysmorphic, monstrous.
ANTONYMS perfect, normal, healthy.

malfunction ▶ verb *the computer has malfunctioned* **crash,** go wrong, break down, fail, stop working, go down; informal conk out, go kaput, blow up, act up.

▶ noun *a computer malfunction* **crash,** breakdown, fault, failure, bug; informal glitch.

malice ▶ noun *she had intended no malice toward him* **spite,** malevolence, ill will, vindictiveness, vengefulness, revenge, malignity, evil intentions, animus, enmity, rancor; informal bitchiness, cattiness; literary maleficence.
ANTONYMS benevolence.

malicious ▶ adjective *their malicious cousin Charles would mysteriously disappear at sea* **spiteful,** malevolent, evil-intentioned, vindictive, vengeful, malign, mean, nasty, hurtful, mischievous, wounding, cruel, unkind; informal bitchy, catty; literary malefic, maleficent.
ANTONYMS benevolent.

malign ▶ adjective *a malign influence* **harmful,** evil, bad, baleful, hostile, inimical, destructive, malignant, injurious; literary malefic, maleficent.
ANTONYMS beneficial.

▶ verb *he maligned an innocent man* **defame,** slander, libel, blacken someone's name/character, smear, vilify, speak ill of, cast aspersions on, run down, traduce, denigrate, disparage, slur, abuse, revile; informal badmouth, dis, knock; formal derogate, calumniate.
ANTONYMS praise.

CHOOSE THE RIGHT WORD

malign, calumniate, defame, libel, slander, vilify

Do you want to ruin someone's life? You can **malign** someone, which is to say or write something evil without necessarily lying (*she was maligned for her past association with radical causes*). To **calumniate** is to make false and malicious statements about someone; the word often implies that you have seriously damaged that person's good name (*after leaving his job, he spent most of his time calumniating and ridiculing his former boss*). To **defame** is to cause actual injury to someone's good name or reputation (*he defamed her by accusing her of being a spy*). If you don't mind risking a lawsuit, you can **libel** the person, which is to write or print something that defames him or her (*the tabloid libeled the celebrity and ended up paying the price*). **Slander**, which is to defame someone orally, is seldom a basis for court action but can nevertheless cause injury to someone's reputation (*after a loud and very public argument, she accused him of slandering her*). If all else fails, you can **vilify** the person, which is to engage in abusive name-calling (*even though he was found innocent by the jury, he was vilified by his neighbors*).

malignant ▶ adjective **1** *a malignant disease* **virulent,** very infectious, invasive, uncontrollable, dangerous, deadly, fatal, incurable, life-threatening.
ANTONYMS curable.
2 *a malignant growth* **cancerous**; technical metastatic.
ANTONYMS benign.
3 *a malignant thought* **spiteful,** malicious, malevolent, evil-intentioned, vindictive, vengeful, malign, mean, nasty, hurtful, mischievous, wounding, cruel, unkind; informal bitchy, catty; literary malefic, maleficent.
ANTONYMS benevolent.

malinger ▶ verb *he was put on report for malingering* **pretend to be ill,** feign (an) illness, fake (an) illness; shirk; informal goof off.

mall ▶ noun *we met at the mall to get our ears pierced* **shopping center,** (shopping) plaza, shopping complex, strip mall, mini-mall, galleria, megamall, marketplace.

malleable ▶ adjective **1** *a malleable substance* **pliable,** ductile, plastic, pliant, soft, workable.
ANTONYMS hard.
2 *a malleable young woman* **easily influenced,** suggestible, susceptible, impressionable, pliable, amenable, compliant, tractable; biddable, complaisant, manipulable, persuadable, like putty in someone's hands.
ANTONYMS intractable.

malnutrition ▶ noun *the malnutrition of millions around the world is shameful* **undernourishment,** malnourishment, poor diet, inadequate diet, unhealthy diet, lack of food; hunger, starvation.

malodorous ▶ adjective *several tenants in the building had complained about the malodorous apartment on the second floor* **foul-smelling,** evil-smelling, fetid, smelly, stinking (to high heaven), reeking, rank, high, putrid, noxious; informal stinky, funky; literary noisome, mephitic.
ANTONYMS fragrant.

malpractice ▶ noun *her foot surgeon was found guilty of malpractice* **wrongdoing,** (professional) misconduct, breach of ethics, unprofessionalism, unethical behavior; negligence, carelessness, incompetence.

maltreat ▶ verb See MISTREAT.

mammoth ▶ adjective *a crisis of mammoth proportions* **huge,** enormous, gigantic, giant, colossal, massive, vast, immense, mighty, stupendous, monumental, Herculean, epic, prodigious, mountainous, monstrous, titanic, towering, elephantine, king-size(d), economy-size(d), gargantuan, Brobdingnagian; informal mega, monster, whopping, honking, humongous, bumper, jumbo, astronomical, ginormous.
ANTONYMS tiny.

man ▶ noun **1** *a handsome man* **male,** adult male, gentleman; informal guy, fellow, fella, joe, geezer, gent, bloke, chap, dude, hombre; **(men)** menfolk.
2 *all men are mortal* **human being,** human, person, mortal, individual, personage, soul.
3 *the evolution of man* **the human race,** the human species, *Homo sapiens*, humankind, humanity, human beings, humans, people, mankind.
4 *the men voted to go on strike* **worker,** workman, laborer, hand, blue-collar worker; staff.
5 *have you met her new man?* **boyfriend,** partner, husband, spouse, lover, admirer, fiancé; common-law husband, live-in lover, significant other, main squeeze; informal toy boy, sugar daddy, intended; dated beau, steady, young man.
▶ verb **1** *the office is manned from 9 to 5* **staff,** crew, occupy, people.
2 *firefighters manned the pumps* **operate,** work, use, utilize.
– PHRASES **man to man** *can we speak man to man?* **frankly,** openly, honestly, directly, candidly, plainly, forthrightly, without beating about the bush; woman to woman. **to a man** *the squad volunteered, to a man, to work another full shift in the rescue mission* **without exception,** with no exceptions, bar none, one and all, everyone, each and every one, unanimously, as one.

> USAGE
> **man**
> Traditionally, the word *man* has been used to refer not only to adult males but also to human beings in general, regardless of sex. There is a historical explanation for this: in Old English, the principal sense of *man* was 'a human being,' and the words *wer* and *wif* were used to refer specifically to 'a male person' and 'a female person,' respectively. Subsequently, *man* replaced *wer* as the normal term for 'a male person,' but the older sense 'a human being' remained in use.
> In the second half of the twentieth century, the generic use of *man* to refer to 'human beings in general' (*reptiles were here long before man appeared on the earth*) became problematic; the use is now often regarded as sexist or old-fashioned. In some contexts, terms such as *the human race* or *humankind* may be used instead of *man* or *mankind*.

manacles ▶ plural noun *he claimed there were no manacles that could hold him* **handcuffs,** shackles, chains, irons, fetters, restraints, bonds; informal cuffs, bracelets.

manage ▶ verb **1** *she manages a staff of 80 people* **be in charge of,** run, be head of, head, direct, control, preside over, lead, govern, rule, command, superintend, supervise, oversee, administer, organize, conduct, handle, guide, be at the helm of; informal head up.
2 *he managed a smile* **accomplish,** achieve, do, carry out, perform, undertake, bring about/off, effect, finish; succeed in, contrive, engineer.
3 *will you be able to manage without him?* **cope,** get along/on, make do, be/fare/do all right, carry on, survive, get by, muddle through/along, fend for oneself, shift for oneself, make ends meet, weather the storm; informal make out, hack it.
4 *she can't manage that horse* **control,** handle,

master; cope with, deal with.

manageable ▶ adjective **1** *a manageable amount of work* **achievable,** doable, practicable, possible, feasible, reasonable, attainable, viable.
ANTONYMS impractical, impossible.
2 *a manageable child* **compliant,** tractable, pliant, pliable, malleable, biddable, docile, amenable, governable, controllable, accommodating, acquiescent, complaisant, yielding.
ANTONYMS unmanageable.
3 *a manageable program* **user-friendly,** easy to use, handy.
ANTONYMS unwieldy.

management ▶ noun **1** *he's responsible for the management of the firm* **administration,** running, managing, organization; charge, care, direction, leadership, control, governing, governance, ruling, command, superintendence, supervision, overseeing, conduct, handling, guidance, operation.
2 *workers are disputing with management* **managers,** employers, directors, board of directors, board, directorate, executives, administrators, administration; owners, proprietors; informal bosses, top brass.

manager ▶ noun **1** *the plant manager* **executive,** head of department, supervisor, principal, administrator, head, director, managing director, CEO, employer, superintendent, foreman, forewoman, overseer; proprietor; informal boss, chief, head honcho.
2 *the band's manager* **organizer,** controller, comptroller; impresario.

mandate ▶ noun **1** *they won a mandate to form the government* **authority,** approval, acceptance, ratification, endorsement, sanction, authorization.
2 *a mandate from the UN* **instruction,** directive, decree, command, order, injunction, edict, charge, commission, bidding, ruling, fiat; formal ordinance.
▶ verb **1** *catalytic converters were mandated in 1975* **make mandatory,** legislate, authorize, require by law; designate.
2 *they were mandated to strike* **instruct,** order, direct, command, tell, require, charge, call on.

mandatory ▶ adjective *a high school diploma is mandatory* **obligatory,** compulsory, binding, required, requisite, necessary, essential, imperative.
ANTONYMS optional.

maneuver ▶ verb **1** *I maneuvered the car into the space* **steer,** guide, drive, negotiate, navigate, pilot, direct, manipulate, move, work, jockey.
2 *he maneuvered things to suit himself* **manipulate,** contrive, manage, engineer, devise, plan, fix, organize, arrange, set up, orchestrate, choreograph, stage-manage; informal wangle.
3 *he began maneuvering for the party leadership* **intrigue,** plot, scheme, plan, lay plans, conspire, pull strings.
▶ noun **1** *a tricky parking maneuver* **operation,** exercise, activity, move, movement, action.
2 *diplomatic maneuvers* **stratagem,** tactic, gambit, ploy, trick, dodge, ruse, plan, scheme, operation, device, plot, machination, artifice, subterfuge, intrigue.
3 (**maneuvers**) *military maneuvers* **training exercises,** exercises, war games, operations.

manger ▶ noun *they laid fresh hay in the manger* **trough,** feeding trough, feeder, crib.

mangle ▶ verb **1** *the bodies were mangled beyond recognition* **mutilate,** maim, disfigure, damage, injure, crush; hack, cut up, lacerate, tear apart, butcher, maul.
2 *he's mangling the English language* **spoil,** ruin, mar, mutilate, make a mess of, wreck; informal murder, make a hash of, butcher.

mangy ▶ adjective **1** *a mangy cat* **scabby,** scaly, scabrous, diseased.
2 *a mangy old armchair* **scruffy,** moth-eaten, shabby, worn; dirty, squalid, sleazy, seedy, flea-bitten; informal tatty, raggedy-ass, the worse for wear, scuzzy.

manhandle ▶ verb **1** *tourists were manhandled by the protestors* **push,** shove, jostle, hustle; maltreat, ill-treat, mistreat, maul, molest; informal paw, rough up, roust.
2 *we manhandled the piano down the stairs* **heave,** haul, push, shove; pull, tug, drag, lug, carry, lift, maneuver; informal hump.

manhood ▶ noun **1** *the transition from boyhood to manhood* **maturity,** sexual maturity, adulthood.
2 *an insult to his manhood* **virility,** manliness, machismo, masculinity, maleness; mettle, spirit, strength, fortitude, determination, bravery, courage, intrepidity, valor, heroism, boldness.

mania ▶ noun **1** *fits of mania* **madness,** derangement, dementia, insanity, lunacy, psychosis, mental illness; delirium, frenzy, hysteria, raving, wildness.
2 *his mania for gadgets* **obsession,** compulsion, fixation, fetish, fascination, preoccupation, infatuation, passion, enthusiasm, desire, urge, craving; craze, fad, rage; informal thing, yen.

maniac ▶ noun **1** *a homicidal maniac* **lunatic,** madman, madwoman, psychopath; informal loony, fruitcake, nutcase, nut, fruit loop, psycho, mental case, head case, sicko, screwball, crazy, loon.
2 informal *a techno maniac* **enthusiast,** fan, devotee, aficionado; informal freak, fiend, fanatic, nut, buff, bum, addict.

manifest ▶ verb **1** *she manifested signs of depression* **display,** show, exhibit, demonstrate, betray, present, reveal; formal evince.
ANTONYMS hide.
2 *his positive potential is **manifested by** his art* **be evidence of,** be a sign of, indicate, show, attest to, reflect, bespeak, prove, establish, evidence, substantiate, corroborate, confirm; literary betoken.
ANTONYMS mask.
▶ adjective *his manifest lack of interest* **obvious,** clear, plain, apparent, evident, patent, palpable, distinct, definite, blatant, overt, glaring, barefaced, explicit, transparent, conspicuous, undisguised, unmistakable, noticeable, perceptible, visible, recognizable.
ANTONYMS secret.

manifestation ▶ noun **1** *the manifestation of anxiety* **display,** demonstration, show, exhibition, presentation.

2 *manifestations of global warming* **sign,** indication, evidence, token, symptom, testimony, proof, substantiation, mark, reflection, example, instance. See note at SIGN.
3 *a supernatural manifestation* **apparition,** appearance, materialization, visitation.

manifesto ▶ noun *a party manifesto that would change the course of world politics* **policy statement,** mission statement, platform, (little) red book, program, declaration, proclamation, pronouncement, announcement.

manifold ▶ adjective *the problems are manifold* **many,** numerous, multiple, multifarious, legion, diverse, various, several, varied, different, miscellaneous, assorted, sundry; literary myriad, divers.

manipulate ▶ verb **1** *he manipulated some knobs and levers* **operate,** work; turn, pull.
2 *she manipulated the muscles of his back* **massage,** rub, knead, feel, palpate.
3 *the government tried to manipulate the situation* **control,** influence, use/turn to one's advantage, exploit, maneuver, engineer, steer, direct, gerrymander; twist someone around one's little finger.
4 *they accused him of manipulating the data* **falsify,** rig, distort, alter, change, doctor, massage, juggle, tamper with, tinker with, interfere with, misrepresent; informal cook, fiddle with.

manipulator ▶ noun *a ruthless political manipulator* **exploiter,** user, maneuverer, conniver, puppet master, wheeler-dealer; informal operator.

mankind ▶ noun *for the good of all mankind* **the human race,** man, humanity, human beings, humans, Homo sapiens, humankind, people, men and women.

manly ▶ adjective **1** *his manly physique* **virile,** masculine, strong, muscular, muscly, strapping, well-built, sturdy, robust, rugged, tough, powerful, brawny, red-blooded, vigorous; informal hunky. See note at MALE.
ANTONYMS effeminate.
2 *their manly deeds* **brave,** courageous, bold, valiant, valorous, fearless, plucky, macho, manful, intrepid, daring, heroic, lionhearted, gallant, chivalrous, swashbuckling, adventurous, stouthearted, dauntless, doughty, resolute, determined, stalwart; informal gutsy, spunky, ballsy.
ANTONYMS cowardly.

man-made ▶ adjective *man-made fabrics* **artificial,** synthetic, manufactured, fabricated; imitation, ersatz, simulated, mock, fake, phony, counterfeit, plastic.
ANTONYMS natural, real.

manner ▶ noun **1** *it was dealt with in a very efficient manner* **way,** fashion, mode, means, method, system, style, approach, technique, procedure, process, methodology, modus operandi, form.
2 *what manner of creature is it?* **kind,** sort, type, variety, nature, breed, brand, stamp, class, category, genre, order.
3 *her rather unfriendly manner* **demeanor,** air, aspect, attitude, bearing, cast, behavior, conduct; mien; formal comportment.
4 (**manners**) *aristocratic manners* **customs,** habits, ways, practices, conventions, usages.
5 (**manners**) *it's bad manners to stare* **behavior,** conduct, way of behaving; form.
6 (**manners**) *you ought to teach him some manners* **correct behavior,** etiquette, social graces, good form, protocol, politeness, decorum, propriety, gentility, civility, Ps and Qs.

mannered ▶ adjective *his highly mannered style of prose* **affected,** pretentious, unnatural, artificial, contrived, stilted, stiff, forced, put-on, theatrical, precious, stagy, camp; informal pseudo.
ANTONYMS natural.

mannerism ▶ noun *he disliked what he considered upper-class mannerisms* **idiosyncrasy,** quirk, oddity, foible, trait, peculiarity, habit, characteristic, tic.

mannish ▶ adjective *she adopted a mannish appearance for the stage* **unfeminine,** unwomanly, masculine, unladylike, Amazonian; informal butch. See note at MALE.
ANTONYMS feminine, girlish.

mansion ▶ noun *a tour of Beverly Hills mansions* **stately home,** hall, manor, manor house, country house; informal palace; formal residence.
ANTONYMS hovel.

manslaughter ▶ noun *the jury will decide if she is guilty of manslaughter* **killing,** murder, homicide, assassination; literary slaying.

mantle ▶ noun **1** *a dark green velvet mantle* **cloak,** cape, shawl, wrap, stole; historical pelisse.
2 *a thick mantle of snow* **covering,** layer, blanket, sheet, veil, curtain, canopy, cover, cloak, pall, shroud.
3 *the mantle of leadership* **role,** burden, onus, duty, responsibility.
▶ verb *heavy mists mantled the forest* **cover,** envelop, veil, cloak, curtain, shroud, swathe, wrap, blanket, conceal, hide, disguise, mask, obscure, surround, clothe; literary enshroud.

manual ▶ adjective **1** *manual work* **done with one's hands,** by hand, laboring, physical, blue-collar.
2 *a manual drill* **hand-operated,** hand, nonelectric, nonautomatic.
▶ noun *a training manual* **handbook,** instruction book, instructions, guide, how-to book, companion, ABC, primer, guidebook, A to Z; informal bible.

manufacture ▶ verb **1** *the company manufactures laser printers* **make,** produce, mass-produce, build, construct, assemble, put together, create, fabricate, turn out, process, engineer.
2 *a story manufactured by the press* **make up,** invent, fabricate, concoct, hatch, dream up, think up, trump up, devise, formulate, frame, contrive; informal cook up.
▶ noun *the manufacture of aircraft engines* **production,** making, manufacturing, mass-production, construction, building, assembly, creation, fabrication, prefabrication, processing.

manufacturer ▶ noun *local manufacturers are important sources of tax revenue* **maker,** producer, builder, constructor, creator; factory owner, industrialist, captain of industry.

manure ▶ noun *spread composted manure over the strawberry plants* **dung,** muck, excrement, droppings, ordure, guano, cow pats; fertilizer; informal cow chips, road apples, horse apples, buffalo chips, cow-pies, cow patties, cow flops; turds, scat.

many ▶ adjective **1** *many animals were killed* **numerous,** a great/good deal of, a lot of, plenty of, countless, innumerable, scores of, crowds of, droves of, an army of, a horde of, a multitude of, a multiplicity of, multitudinous, multiple, untold; several, various, sundry, diverse, assorted, multifarious; copious, abundant, profuse, an abundance of, a profusion of; informal lots of, umpteen, loads of, masses of, stacks of, scads of, heaps of, piles of, bags of, tons of, oodles of, dozens of, hundreds of, thousands of, millions of, billions of, zillions of, gazillions of, a slew of, a boatload of, more —— than one can shake a stick at; literary myriad, divers.
ANTONYMS few.
2 *sacrificing the individual for the sake of the many* **people,** common people, masses, multitude, populace, public, rank and file; informal hoi polloi, common herd, mob, proletariat, riffraff, great unwashed, proles.
ANTONYMS few.

map ▶ noun *we'll never find their house without a map* **plan,** chart, cartogram, survey, plat, plot; road map, street map, guide; atlas, globe; relief map, contour map; Mercator projection, Peters projection.
▶ verb *the region was mapped from the air* **chart,** plot, delineate, draw, depict, portray.
– PHRASES **map out** *he mapped out the plan for our campaign* **outline,** set out, lay out, sketch out, trace out, rough out, block out, delineate, detail, draw up, formulate, work out, frame, draft, plan, plot out, arrange, design, program.

mar ▶ verb **1** *an ugly scar marred his features* **spoil,** impair, disfigure, detract from, blemish, scar; mutilate, deface, deform.
ANTONYMS enhance.
2 *the celebrations were marred by violence* **spoil,** ruin, impair, damage, wreck; harm, hurt, blight, taint, tarnish, sully, stain, pollute; informal foul up; formal vitiate.

marauder ▶ noun *they placed chains across the river to keep out marauders* **raider,** plunderer, pillager, looter, robber, pirate, freebooter, bandit, highwayman, rustler; literary brigand; archaic buccaneer, corsair, reaver.

march ▶ verb **1** *the men marched past* **stride,** walk, troop, step, pace, tread; footslog, slog, tramp, tromp, hike, trudge; parade, file, process.
2 *she marched in without even knocking* **stride,** strut, stalk, flounce, storm, stomp, sweep.
3 *time marches on* **advance,** progress, move on, roll on.
▶ noun **1** *a long march* **hike,** trek, tramp, slog, footslog, walk; route march, forced march.
2 *police in riot gear charged the march* **parade,** procession, cortège; demonstration, protest.
3 *the march of technology* **progress,** advance, progression, development, evolution; passage.

margin ▶ noun **1** *the margin of the lake* **edge,** side, verge, border, perimeter, brink, brim, rim, fringe, boundary, limits, periphery, bound, extremity; literary bourn, skirt. See note at BORDER.
2 *there's no margin for error* **leeway,** latitude, scope, room, room to maneuver, space, allowance, extra, surplus.
3 *they won by a narrow margin* **gap,** majority, amount, difference.

marginal ▶ adjective **1** *the difference is marginal* **slight,** small, tiny, minute, insignificant, minimal, negligible.
2 *a marginal case* **borderline,** disputable, questionable, doubtful.

marijuana ▶ noun *the illegal cultivation of marijuana* **cannabis,** hashish, hemp, sinsemilla; informal **pot,** dope, grass, weed, Mary Jane, bud, hash, bhang, kef, ganja, locoweed; reefer, doob, spliff, toke, roach.

marinate ▶ verb *marinate the ribs in a mixture of beer, honey, and orange rind* **steep,** soak, souse, immerse, marinade, bathe.

marine ▶ adjective **1** *marine plants* **seawater,** sea, saltwater, oceanic; aquatic; technical pelagic.
2 *a marine vessel* **maritime,** nautical, naval; seafaring, seagoing, oceangoing.

mariner ▶ noun *an old mariner from Gloucester* **sailor,** seaman, seafarer; informal sea dog, salt, bluejacket; Brit. matelot.

marital ▶ adjective *Fred was unable to cope with Leah's desire to dissolve their marital bond* **matrimonial,** married, wedded, conjugal, nuptial, marriage, wedding; spousal; literary connubial.

maritime ▶ adjective **1** *maritime law* **naval,** marine, nautical; seafaring, seagoing, sea, oceangoing.
2 *maritime regions* **coastal,** seaside, littoral.

mark ▶ noun **1** *a dirty mark* **blemish,** streak, spot, fleck, dot, blot, stain, smear, speck, speckle, blotch, smudge, smut, fingermark, fingerprint; bruise, discoloration; birthmark; informal splotch; technical stigma.
2 *a punctuation mark* **symbol,** sign, character; diacritic.
3 *books bearing the mark of a well-known bookseller* **logo,** seal, stamp, imprint, symbol, emblem, device, insignia, badge, brand, trademark, monogram, hallmark, logotype, watermark.
4 *unemployment passed the three million mark* **point,** level, stage, degree.
5 *a mark of respect* **sign,** token, symbol, indication, badge, emblem; symptom, evidence, proof.
6 *the war left its mark on him* **impression,** imprint, traces; effect, impact, influence.
7 *the mark of a civilized society* **characteristic,** feature, trait, attribute, quality, hallmark, calling card, badge, stamp, property, indicator.
8 *he got good marks for math* **grade,** grading, rating, score, percentage.
9 *the bullet missed its mark* **target,** goal, aim, bull's-eye; objective, object, end.
▶ verb **1** *be careful not to mark the woodwork* **discolor,** stain, smear, smudge, streak, blotch, blemish; dirty, pockmark, bruise; informal splotch; literary smirch.

2 *her possessions were clearly marked* **put one's name on,** name, initial, label, identify; hallmark, watermark, brand.
3 *I've marked the relevant passages* **indicate,** label, flag, tick, check off, highlight; show, identify, designate, delineate, denote, specify.
4 *a festival to mark the town's 200th anniversary* **celebrate,** observe, recognize, acknowledge, keep, honor, solemnize, pay tribute to, salute, commemorate, remember, memorialize.
5 *the incidents marked a new phase in their campaign* **represent,** signify, be a sign of, indicate, herald.
6 *his style is marked by simplicity and concision* **characterize,** distinguish, identify, typify, brand, signalize, stamp.
7 *I have a pile of essays to mark* **assess,** evaluate, grade, appraise, correct.
8 *it'll cause trouble, you mark my words!* **take heed of,** heed, listen to, take note of, pay attention to, attend to, note, mind, bear in mind, take into consideration.
– PHRASES **make one's mark** *she intends to make her mark in Hollywood* **be successful,** distinguish oneself, succeed, be a success, prosper, get ahead, make good; informal make it, make the grade. **mark down** *the prices will be marked down after Christmas* **reduce,** decrease, lower, cut, put down, discount; informal slash. **mark up** *they were accused of marking up the cost before offering a discount* **increase,** raise, up, put up, hike (up), escalate; informal jack up. **quick off the mark** *an elite force that was more quick off the mark than any fighting element in the sector* **alert,** quick, quick-witted, bright, clever, perceptive, sharp, sharp-witted, observant, wide awake, on one's toes; informal on the ball, quick on the uptake. **wide of the mark** *his answer was wide of the mark* **inaccurate,** incorrect, wrong, erroneous, off target, out, mistaken, misguided, misinformed.

marked ▶ adjective *we see a marked improvement in Sally's grades* **noticeable,** pronounced, decided, distinct, striking, clear, glaring, blatant, unmistakable, obvious, plain, manifest, patent, palpable, prominent, signal, significant, conspicuous, notable, recognizable, identifiable, distinguishable, discernible, apparent, evident; written all over one.
ANTONYMS imperceptible.

market ▶ noun **1** *I'll get some sugar when I'm at the market* **grocery store,** supermarket, store, convenience store; farmers' market.
2 *browsing through old postcards at the antiques market* **marketplace,** mart, flea market, bazaar, fair; archaic emporium.
3 *there's no market for such goods* **demand,** call, want, desire, need, requirement.
4 *the market is sluggish* **stock market,** trading, trade, business, commerce, buying and selling, dealing.
▶ verb *the product was marketed worldwide* **sell,** retail, vend, merchandise, trade, peddle, hawk; advertise, promote.
– PHRASES **on the market** *these are the finest pearls on the market today* **on sale,** (up) for sale, available, obtainable, on the block.

maroon ▶ verb *schoolboys marooned on a desert island* **strand,** cast away, cast ashore, shipwreck; abandon, leave behind, leave, leave in the lurch, desert, forsake; informal leave high and dry.

marriage ▶ noun **1** *a proposal of marriage* **(holy) matrimony,** wedlock; civil union.
2 *the marriage took place at St. Margaret's* **wedding,** wedding ceremony, marriage ceremony, nuptials, union.
ANTONYMS divorce, separation.
3 *a marriage of jazz, pop, and gospel* **union,** alliance, fusion, mixture, mix, blend, amalgamation, combination, merger.
ANTONYMS separation.

married ▶ adjective **1** *a married couple* **wedded,** wed; informal spliced, hitched, coupled.
ANTONYMS single.
2 *married bliss* **marital,** matrimonial, conjugal, nuptial; Law spousal; literary connubial.

marry ▶ verb **1** *the couple married last year* **get/be married,** wed, be wed, become man and wife; informal tie the knot, walk down the aisle, take the plunge, get spliced, get hitched, say "I do"; dated plight/pledge one's troth.
2 *John wanted to marry her* **wed**; informal make an honest woman of; archaic espouse.
ANTONYMS divorce.
3 *the show marries poetry with art* **join,** unite, combine, fuse, mix, blend, merge, amalgamate, link, connect, couple, knit, yoke.
ANTONYMS separate.

marsh ▶ noun *a pair of great blue herons made regular visits to the marsh* **swamp,** marshland, bog, peat bog, muskeg, swampland, morass, mire, moor, quagmire, slough, fen, fenland, wetland, bayou.

marshal ▶ verb **1** *they marshaled an army* **assemble,** gather (together), collect, muster, call together, draw up, line up, align, array, organize, group, arrange, deploy, position, order, dispose; mobilize, rally, round up. See note at GATHER.
2 *guests were marshaled to their seats* **usher,** guide, escort, conduct, lead, shepherd, steer, take.

martial ▶ adjective *their martial exploits* **military,** soldierly, soldier-like, army, naval; warlike, fighting, combative, bellicose, hawkish, pugnacious, militaristic.

martyrdom ▶ noun *the martyrdom of Peter* **death,** suffering, torture, torment, persecution, agony, ordeal; killing, sacrifice, self-sacrifice, crucifixion, immolation, burning, auto-da-fé; Christianity Passion.

marvel ▶ verb *she marveled at their courage* **be amazed,** be astonished, be surprised, be awed, stand in awe, wonder; stare, gape, goggle, not believe one's eyes/ears, be dumbfounded; informal be flabbergasted.
▶ noun *he's a marvel* **wonder,** miracle, sensation, spectacle, phenomenon; informal something else, something to shout about.

marvelous ▶ adjective **1** *his solo climb was marvelous* **amazing,** astounding, astonishing, awesome, breathtaking, sensational, remarkable, spectacular, stupendous, staggering, stunning; phenomenal, prodigious, miraculous, extraordinary, incredible,

unbelievable; literary wondrous.
ANTONYMS commonplace.
2 *marvelous weather* **excellent,** splendid, wonderful, magnificent, superb, glorious, sublime, lovely, delightful, too good to be true; informal super, great, amazing, fantastic, terrific, tremendous, sensational, heavenly, divine, gorgeous, grand, fabulous, fab, marvy, awesome, to die for, magic, ace, killer, wicked, mind-blowing, jaw-dropping, far out, out of this world; smashing, brilliant, boss; informal dated swell, dreamy.
ANTONYMS awful.

masculine ▶ **adjective 1** *a masculine trait* **male,** man's, men's; male-oriented. See note at **MALE**.
ANTONYMS feminine.
2 *a powerfully masculine man* **virile,** macho, manly, muscular, muscly, strong, strapping, well built, rugged, robust, brawny, powerful, red-blooded, vigorous; informal hunky, testosteronic.
ANTONYMS weak, effeminate.
3 *a rather masculine woman* **mannish,** boyish, unfeminine, unwomanly, Amazonian; informal butch.

masculinity ▶ **noun** *he's the picture of masculinity* **virility,** manliness, maleness, machismo, vigor, strength, muscularity, ruggedness, robustness; informal testosterone.

mash ▶ **verb** *mash the potatoes* **smash,** crush, purée, cream, pulp, squash, pound, beat, rice.
▶ **noun** *first pound the garlic to a mash* **pulp,** purée, mush, paste.

mask ▶ **noun 1** *she wore a mask to conceal her face* **disguise,** false face; historical domino, visor.
2 *he dropped his mask of good humor* **pretense,** semblance, veil, screen, front, false front, facade, veneer, blind, disguise, guise, concealment, cover, cover-up, cloak, camouflage.
▶ **verb** *poplar trees masked the factory* **hide,** conceal, disguise, cover up, obscure, screen, cloak, camouflage, veil.

Mass ▶ **noun** *we attended the six o'clock Mass* **Eucharist,** Holy Communion, Communion, service, liturgy.

mass ▶ **noun 1** *a soggy mass of fallen leaves* **pile,** heap; accumulation, aggregation, accretion, concretion, buildup; informal batch, wad.
2 *a mass of cyclists* **crowd,** horde, large group, throng, host, troop, army, herd, flock, drove, swarm, mob, pack, press, crush, flood, multitude.
3 *the mass of our students are licensed drivers* **majority,** greater part/number, best/better part, major part, bulk, main body, lion's share; (**the mass**) most.
4 (**masses**) *bringing the news to the masses* **common people,** populace, public, people, rank and file, crowd, third estate; derogatory hoi polloi, mob, proletariat, common herd, great unwashed.
5 informal *a mass of food* See **LOT** (sense 1 of the noun).
▶ **adjective** *mass hysteria* **widespread,** general, wholesale, universal, large-scale, extensive, pandemic.
▶ **verb** *they began massing troops in the region* **assemble,** marshal, gather together, muster, round up, mobilize, rally.

massacre ▶ **noun 1** *a cold-blooded massacre of innocent civilians* **slaughter,** wholesale/mass slaughter, indiscriminate killing, mass murder, mass execution, annihilation, liquidation, decimation, extermination; carnage, butchery, bloodbath, bloodletting, pogrom, genocide, ethnic cleansing, holocaust, night of the long knives; literary slaying.
2 informal *the game was an 8–0 massacre* See **ROUT** (sense 2 of the noun).
▶ **verb 1** *thousands were brutally massacred* **slaughter,** butcher, murder, kill, annihilate, exterminate, execute, liquidate, eliminate, decimate, wipe out, mow down, cut down, put to the sword, put to death; literary slay. See note at **KILL**.
2 informal *they were massacred in the final round* See **TROUNCE**.

massage ▶ **noun** *her physical therapy includes massage* **rub,** rubdown, rubbing, kneading, palpation, manipulation, pummeling; body rub, back rub; shiatsu, reflexology, acupressure, hydromassage, Swedish massage, osteopathy; effleurage, tapotement.
▶ **verb 1** *he massaged her tired muscles* **rub,** knead, palpate, manipulate, pummel, work.
2 *the statistics have been massaged* **alter,** tamper with, manipulate, doctor, falsify, juggle, fiddle with, tinker with, distort, change, rig, interfere with, misrepresent; informal fix, cook, fiddle.

massive ▶ **adjective** *a massive iceberg* **huge,** enormous, vast, immense, large, big, mighty, great, colossal, tremendous, prodigious, gigantic, gargantuan, mammoth, monstrous, monumental, giant, towering, elephantine, mountainous, titanic; epic, Herculean, Brobdingnagian; informal monster, jumbo, mega, whopping, humongous, hulking, honking, bumper, astronomical, ginormous. See note at **HEAVY**.
ANTONYMS tiny.

mast ▶ **noun 1** *a ship's mast* **spar,** boom, yard, gaff, foremast, mainmast, topmast, mizzen mast, mizzen, royal mast.
2 *the mast on top of the building* **flagpole,** flagstaff, pole, post, rod, upright; aerial, transmitter, pylon.

master ▶ **noun 1** historical *he acceded to his master's wishes* **lord,** overlord, lord and master, ruler, sovereign, monarch, liege (lord), suzerain.
ANTONYMS servant, underling.
2 *the dog's master* **owner,** keeper.
3 *a chess master* **expert,** adept, genius, past master, maestro, virtuoso, professional, doyen, authority, champion; informal ace, pro, wizard, whiz, hotshot, maven, crackerjack.
ANTONYMS novice, amateur.
4 *the master of the ship* **captain,** commander; informal skipper.
5 *their spiritual master* **guru,** teacher, leader, guide, mentor; rabbi, swami, Maharishi.
ANTONYMS acolyte, disciple.
▶ **verb 1** *I managed to master my fears* **overcome,** conquer, beat, quell, quash, suppress, control, overpower, triumph over, subdue, vanquish, subjugate, prevail over, govern, curb, check, bridle, tame, defeat, get the better of, get a grip

on, get over; informal lick.
2 *it took ages to master the technique* **learn,** become proficient in, know inside out, know (frontward and) backwards; pick up, grasp, understand; informal get the hang of.
▶ **adjective 1** *a master craftsman* **expert,** adept, proficient, skilled, skillful, deft, dexterous, adroit, practiced, experienced, masterly, accomplished, complete, demon, brilliant; informal crack, ace, mean, crackerjack.
2 *the master bedroom* **principal,** main, chief; biggest.

masterful ▶ **adjective 1** *a masterful man* **commanding,** powerful, imposing, magisterial, lordly, authoritative; dominating, domineering, overbearing, overweening, imperious.
ANTONYMS weak.
2 *their masterful handling of the situation* **expert,** adept, clever, masterly, skillful, skilled, adroit, proficient, deft, dexterous, accomplished, polished, consummate; informal crack, ace.
ANTONYMS inept.

CHOOSE THE RIGHT WORD

masterful, masterly

Masterful and **masterly** overlap in meaning and are sometimes confused. **Masterful** can mean 'domineering,' but it also means 'very skillful, masterly.' Note, however, that **masterful** used in this 'masterly' sense generally describes a person (*he has limited talent, but he's masterful at exploiting it*), while **masterly** usually describes an achievement or action (*that was a masterly response to our opponents' arguments*).

masterly ▶ **adjective** See note at MASTERFUL.

mastermind ▶ **verb** *he masterminded the whole campaign* **plan,** control, direct, be in charge of, run, conduct, organize, arrange, preside over, orchestrate, stage-manage, engineer, manage, coordinate; conceive, devise, originate, initiate, think up, frame, hatch, come up with; informal be the brains behind.
▶ **noun** *the mastermind behind the project* **genius,** mind, intellect, author, architect, organizer, originator, prime mover, initiator, inventor; informal brain, brains, ideas man.

masterpiece ▶ **noun** *Vivaldi's masterpiece* **pièce de résistance,** chef-d'œuvre, masterwork, magnum opus, finest/best work, tour de force.

mastery ▶ **noun 1** *her mastery of the language* **proficiency,** ability, capability; knowledge, understanding, comprehension, familiarity, command, grasp, grip.
2 *they played with tactical mastery* **skill,** skillfulness, expertise, dexterity, finesse, adroitness, virtuosity, prowess, deftness, proficiency; informal know-how.
3 *man's mastery over nature* **control,** domination, command, ascendancy, supremacy, preeminence, superiority; triumph, victory, the upper hand, the whip hand, rule, government, power, sway, authority, jurisdiction, dominion, sovereignty.

masticate ▶ **verb** *strong jaws enable them to masticate the bones of their prey* **chew,** munch, champ, chomp, crunch, eat; formal manducate.

mat ▶ **noun 1** *the fat cat sat on the mat* **rug,** runner, carpet, doormat, welcome mat, bath mat, hearth rug, floor cloth; dhurrie, numdah; kilim, flokati, tatami.
2 *he placed his glass on the mat* **coaster,** placemat, table mat.
3 *a thick mat of hair* **mass,** tangle, knot, mop, thatch, shock, mane.
▶ **verb** *his hair was matted with blood* **tangle,** entangle, knot, snarl up.

match ▶ **noun 1** *we won the match* **contest,** competition, game, tournament, event, trial, test, meet, matchup; bout, fight; derby; playoff, replay, rematch, engagement; Scottish & Canadian bonspiel.
2 *he was no match for the champion* **equal,** rival, equivalent, peer, counterpart; formal compeer.
3 *the vase was an exact match of the one she already owned* **look-alike,** double, twin, duplicate, mate, fellow, companion, counterpart; replica, copy; informal spitting image, dead ringer.
4 *a love match* **marriage,** betrothal, relationship, partnership, union.
▶ **verb 1** *the curtains matched the duvet cover* **go with,** coordinate with, complement, suit; be the same as, be similar to.
2 *did their statements match?* **correspond,** be in agreement, tally, agree, match up, coincide, accord, conform, square.
3 *no one can match him at chess* **equal,** be a match for, measure up to, compare with, parallel, be in the same league as, be on a par with, touch, keep pace with, keep up with, emulate, rival, vie with, compete with, contend with; informal hold a candle to.

matching ▶ **adjective** *red suede boots with a matching handbag | pick the two matching blocks from the pile* **corresponding,** equivalent, parallel, analogous; coordinating, complementary; paired, twin, identical, like, like (two) peas in a pod, alike.
ANTONYMS different, clashing.

matchless ▶ **adjective** *her sister's matchless beauty* **incomparable,** unrivaled, inimitable, beyond compare/comparison, unparalleled, unequaled, without equal, peerless, second to none, unsurpassed, unsurpassable, nonpareil, unique, consummate, perfect, rare, transcendent, surpassing; formal unexampled.

mate ▶ **noun 1** *she's finally found her ideal mate* **partner,** life partner, husband, wife, spouse, lover, live-in lover, significant other, companion, helpmate, helpmeet, consort; informal better half, other half, main squeeze, hubby, missus, missis, old lady, old man.
2 *this sock has lost its mate* **match,** fellow, twin, companion, other half, equivalent.
3 informal *he's gone out with his mates* See CHUM.
▶ **verb** *pandas rarely mate in captivity* **breed,** couple, copulate.

material ▶ **noun 1** *the decomposition of organic material* **matter,** substance, stuff, medium.
2 *the materials for a new building* **constituent,** raw material, element, component.
3 (**materials**) *cleaning materials* **things,** items,

articles, stuff, necessaries.
4 *curtain material* **fabric,** cloth, textiles.
5 *material for a magazine article* **information,** data, facts, facts and figures, statistics, evidence, details, particulars, background, notes; informal info, dope, lowdown.
▶ **adjective 1** *the material world* **physical,** corporeal, tangible, nonspiritual, mundane, worldly, earthly, secular, temporal, concrete, real, solid, substantial.
ANTONYMS spiritual, abstract.
2 *she was too fond of material comforts* **sensual,** physical, carnal, corporal, fleshly, bodily, creature.
ANTONYMS intellectual, aesthetic.
3 *information that could be material to the inquiry* **relevant,** pertinent, important, applicable, germane; apropos, to the point; vital, essential, key.
ANTONYMS immaterial, irrelevant.
4 *the storms caused material damage* **significant,** major, important.
ANTONYMS insignificant.

materialize ▶ **verb 1** *the forecasted rain did not materialize* **happen,** occur, come about, take place, come into being, transpire; informal come off; formal eventuate; literary come to pass.
2 *Harry materialized at the door* **appear,** turn up, arrive, make/put in an appearance, present oneself/itself, emerge, surface, reveal oneself/itself, show one's face, pop up; informal show up.

maternal ▶ **adjective 1** *her maternal instincts* **motherly,** protective, caring, nurturing, loving, devoted, affectionate, fond, warm, tender, gentle, kind, kindly, comforting.
2 *his maternal grandparents* **on one's mother's side**; dated on the distaff side.

mathematical ▶ **adjective 1** *mathematical symbols* **arithmetical,** numerical; statistical, algebraic, geometric, trigonometric.
2 *mathematical precision* **rigorous,** meticulous, scrupulous, punctilious, scientific, strict, precise, exact, accurate, pinpoint, correct, careful, unerring.

matrimonial ▶ **adjective** See MARITAL.

matrimony ▶ **noun** *the sacrament of holy matrimony* **marriage,** wedlock, union; nuptials; civil union.
ANTONYMS divorce.

matted ▶ **adjective** *the cat's matted fur* **tangled,** tangly, knotted, knotty, tousled, disheveled, uncombed, unkempt; informal ratty, mussy.

matter ▶ **noun 1** *decaying vegetable matter* **material,** substance, stuff.
2 *the heart of the matter* **affair,** business, proceeding, situation, circumstance, event, happening, occurrence, incident, episode, experience; subject, topic, issue, question, point, point at issue, case, concern.
3 *it is of little matter now* **importance,** consequence, significance, note, import, weight; formal moment.
4 *what's the matter?* **problem,** trouble, difficulty, complication; upset, worry.
5 *the matter of the book* **content,** subject matter, text, argument, substance.
▶ **verb** *it doesn't matter what you wear* **be important,** make any/a difference, be of importance, be of consequence, be relevant, count; informal cut any ice.
– PHRASES **as a matter of fact** *as a matter of fact, I was the one who sent the flowers* **actually,** in (actual) fact, in point of fact, as it happens, really, believe it or not, in reality, in truth, to tell the truth. **no matter** *I ordered a blue tablecloth, but no matter, the green one looks just fine* **it doesn't matter,** it makes no difference, it's not important, never mind, don't worry about it.

matter-of-fact ▶ **adjective** *Desmond is too creative and fanciful to fit in with such matter-of-fact people* **unemotional,** practical, down-to-earth, sensible, realistic, rational, sober, unsentimental, pragmatic, businesslike, commonsensical, levelheaded, hardheaded, no-nonsense, factual, literal, straightforward, straight-out, plain, unembellished, unvarnished, unadorned; unimaginative, prosaic.

mature ▶ **adjective 1** *a mature woman* **adult,** grown-up, grown, fully grown, full-grown, of age, fully developed, in one's prime, middle-aged.
ANTONYMS adolescent.
2 *he's very mature for his age* **sensible,** responsible, adult, levelheaded, reliable, dependable; wise, discriminating, shrewd, sophisticated.
ANTONYMS childish.
3 *mature cheese* **ripe,** ripened, mellow; ready to eat/drink.
ANTONYMS fresh, unripe.
4 *on mature reflection, he decided not to go* **careful,** thorough, deep, considered.
ANTONYMS impulsive, unthinking.
▶ **verb 1** *kittens mature when they are about a year old* **be fully grown,** be full-grown; come of age, reach adulthood, reach maturity.
2 *he's matured since he left home* **grow up,** become more sensible, become more adult; blossom.
3 *leave the cheese to mature* **ripen,** mellow; age.
4 *their friendship didn't have time to mature* **develop,** grow, evolve, bloom, blossom, flourish, thrive.

CHOOSE THE RIGHT WORD

mature, age, develop, mellow, ripen

Most of us would prefer to **mature** rather than simply **age**. *Mature* implies gaining wisdom, experience, or sophistication as well as adulthood; when applied to other living things, it indicates fullness of growth and readiness for normal functioning (*a mature crop of strawberries*). To *age*, on the other hand, is to undergo the changes that result from the passage of time, often with an emphasis on the negative or destructive changes that accompany growing old (*the tragedy aged him five years*). **Develop** is like *mature* in that it means to undergo a series of positive changes to attain perfection or effectiveness, but it can refer to a part as well as a whole organism (*the kitten's eyesight had begun to develop at three weeks*). **Ripen** is a less formal word meaning to *mature*, but it usually applies to fruit (*the apples ripened in the sun*). **Mellow** suggests the tempering or moderation of harshness that comes with time or experience. With its connotations of warmth, mildness, and sweetness, it is a more positive word than *mature* or *age* (*to mellow as one gets older*).

maturity ▶ noun 1 *her progress from childhood to maturity* **adulthood,** majority, coming-of-age, manhood, womanhood.
2 *he displayed a maturity beyond his years* **responsibility,** sense, levelheadedness; wisdom, discrimination, shrewdness, sophistication.

maudlin ▶ adjective 1 *maudlin self-pity* **sentimental,** oversentimental, emotional, overemotional, tearful, lachrymose; informal weepy, misty-eyed. See note at SENTIMENTAL.
2 *a maudlin ballad* **mawkish,** sentimental, oversweet, oversentimental; informal tearjerker, tearjerking, mushy, slushy, sloppy, schmaltzy, cheesy, corny, soppy, cornball, three-hankie.

maul ▶ verb 1 *he had been mauled by a lion* **savage,** attack, tear to pieces, lacerate, claw, scratch.
2 *the customers are not allowed to maul our dancers* **molest,** feel, fondle, manhandle; informal grope, paw.
3 informal *his book was mauled by the critics* See CRITICIZE.

mausoleum ▶ noun *the Dirkson family mausoleum dates back to 1878* **tomb,** sepulcher, crypt, vault, charnel house, burial chamber, catacomb.

maverick ▶ noun *Torrey was the maverick in the family, the only one who valued freedom over an inheritance* **individualist,** nonconformist, free spirit, unorthodox person, original, eccentric; rebel, dissenter, dissident, enfant terrible; informal cowboy, loose cannon.
ANTONYMS conformist.

mawkish ▶ adjective *he keeps sending her these mawkish greeting cards* **sentimental,** oversentimental, maudlin, cloying, sickly, saccharine, sugary, oversweet, syrupy, nauseating; informal mushy, slushy, sloppy, schmaltzy, weepy, cutesy, lovey-dovey, cheesy, corny, soppy, cornball, hokey, tearjerker, tearjerking, three-hankie. See note at SENTIMENTAL.

maxim ▶ noun *the maxim "you can't cheat an honest man" is posted on the wall above his desk* **saying,** adage, aphorism, proverb, motto, saw, axiom, dictum, precept, epigram; truism, cliché. See note at SAYING.

maximum ▶ adjective *the maximum amount* **greatest,** highest, biggest, largest, top, topmost, most, utmost, maximal.
ANTONYMS minimum.
▶ noun *production levels are near their maximum* **upper limit,** limit, utmost, uttermost, greatest, most, extremity, peak, height, ceiling, top, apex; informal max.
ANTONYMS minimum.

maybe ▶ adverb *maybe the bus will be on time today* **perhaps,** possibly, conceivably, it could be (that), it is possible (that), for all one knows; literary peradventure, perchance.

mayhem ▶ noun *no one would confess to how the mayhem started* **chaos,** disorder, havoc, bedlam, pandemonium, tumult, uproar, turmoil, commotion, all hell broken loose, maelstrom, trouble, disturbance, confusion, riot, anarchy, violence, insanity, madness; informal madhouse.

maze ▶ noun *the mainland's city streets were a baffling maze to the islanders* **labyrinth,** complex network, warren; web, tangle, jungle, snarl; puzzle.

meadow ▶ noun *Holsteins and Guernseys grazed lazily in the meadows along Route 24* **field,** paddock; pasture, pastureland, prairie; literary lea, mead.

meager ▶ adjective 1 *their meager earnings* **inadequate,** scanty, scant, paltry, limited, restricted, modest, insufficient, sparse, deficient, negligible, skimpy, slender, poor, miserable, pitiful, puny, miserly, niggardly, beggarly; informal measly, stingy, pathetic, piddling; formal exiguous.
ANTONYMS abundant.
2 *a tall, meager man* **thin,** lean, skinny, spare, scrawny, gangling, gangly, spindly, stringy, bony, rawboned, gaunt, underweight, underfed, undernourished, emaciated, skeletal.
ANTONYMS fat.

meal ▶ noun *each meal on the cruise ship was spectacular* **snack;** informal bite (to eat), spread, blowout, feed; formal repast, collation; literary refection.

mean[1] ▶ verb 1 *flashing lights mean the road is blocked* **signify,** convey, denote, designate, indicate, connote, show, express, spell out; stand for, represent, symbolize; imply, suggest, intimate, hint at, insinuate, drive at, refer to, allude to, point to; literary betoken.
2 *she didn't mean to break it* **intend,** aim, plan, design, have in mind, contemplate, purpose, propose, set out, aspire, desire, want, wish, expect. See note at INTEND.
3 *he was hit by a bullet meant for a soldier* **intend,** design; destine, predestine.
4 *the closures will mean a rise in unemployment* **entail,** involve, necessitate, lead to, result in, give rise to, bring about, cause, engender, produce.
5 *this means a lot to me* **matter,** be important, be significant.
6 *a red sky in the morning usually means rain* **presage,** portend, foretell, augur, promise, foreshadow, herald, signal, bode; literary betoken.

mean[2] ▶ adjective 1 *a mean trick* **unkind,** nasty, unpleasant, spiteful, malicious, unfair, cruel, shabby, foul, despicable, contemptible, obnoxious, vile, odious, loathsome, base, low; informal horrible, horrid, hateful, rotten, lowdown; beastly.
ANTONYMS kind.
2 *he's too mean to leave a tip* **miserly,** niggardly, close-fisted, parsimonious, penny-pinching, cheeseparing, Scroogelike; informal tightfisted, stingy, tight, mingy, money-grubbing, cheap; formal penurious.

ANTONYMS generous, munificent.
3 *the truth was obvious to even the meanest intelligence* **inferior,** poor, limited, restricted.
4 *their mean origins* **lowly,** humble, ordinary, low, low-born, modest, common, base, proletarian, plebeian, obscure, ignoble, undistinguished; archaic baseborn.
ANTONYMS noble.
5 informal *he's a mean cook* See **EXCELLENT**.

mean[3] ▶ **noun** *a mean between frugality and miserliness* **middle course,** middle way, midpoint, happy medium, golden mean, compromise, balance; median, norm, average.
▶ **adjective** *the mean temperature* **average,** median, middle, medial, medium, normal, standard.

meander ▶ **verb 1** *the river meandered gently* **zigzag,** wind, twist, turn, curve, curl, bend, snake.
2 *we meandered along the path* **stroll,** saunter, amble, wander, ramble, drift, maunder; informal mosey, tootle, toodle.

meandering ▶ **adjective 1** *a meandering stream* **winding,** windy, zigzag, zigzagging, twisting, turning, curving, serpentine, sinuous, twisty.
ANTONYMS straight.
2 *meandering reminiscences* **rambling,** maundering, circuitous, roundabout, digressive, discursive, indirect, tortuous, convoluted.
ANTONYMS succinct.

meaning ▶ **noun 1** *the meaning of his remark* **significance,** sense, signification, import, gist, thrust, drift, implication, tenor, message, essence, substance, purport, intention.
2 *the word has several different meanings* **definition,** sense, explanation, denotation, connotation, interpretation, nuance.
3 *my life has no meaning* **value,** validity, worth, consequence, account, use, usefulness, significance, point.
4 *his smile was full of meaning* **expressiveness,** significance, eloquence, implications, insinuations.
▶ **adjective** *a meaning look* See **MEANINGFUL** (sense 3).

meaningful ▶ **adjective 1** *a meaningful remark* **significant,** relevant, important, consequential, telling, material, valid, worthwhile.
ANTONYMS inconsequential.
2 *a meaningful relationship* **sincere,** deep, serious, in earnest, significant, important.
3 *a meaningful glance* **expressive,** eloquent, pointed, significant, meaning; pregnant, speaking, telltale, revealing, suggestive, charged, loaded.

meaningless ▶ **adjective 1** *a jumble of meaningless words* **unintelligible,** incomprehensible, incoherent.
2 *she felt her life was meaningless* **futile,** pointless, aimless, empty, hollow, blank, vain, purposeless, valueless, useless, of no use, worthless, senseless, trivial, trifling, unimportant, insignificant, inconsequential.
ANTONYMS worthwhile.

means ▶ **plural noun 1** *the best means to achieve your goal* **method,** way, manner, mode, measure, technique, expedient, agency, medium, instrument, channel, vehicle, avenue, course, process, procedure.
2 *she doesn't have the means to support herself* **money,** resources, capital, income, finance, funds, cash, wherewithal, assets; informal dough, bread, moola.
3 *a man of means* **wealth,** riches, affluence, substance, fortune, property, money, capital.
– PHRASES **by all means** *by all means you must have dinner with us* **of course,** certainly, definitely, surely, absolutely, with pleasure; informal sure thing. **by means of** *the load was raised by means of a crane* **using,** utilizing, employing, through, with the help of; as a result of, by dint of, by way of, by virtue of. **by no means** *the result is by no means certain* **not at all,** in no way, not in the least, not in the slightest, not the least bit, not by a long shot, certainly not, absolutely not, definitely not, on no account, under no circumstances; informal no way.

meantime ▶ **noun**
– PHRASES **in the meantime** See **MEANWHILE** (sense 1).

meanwhile ▶ **adverb 1** *meanwhile, I'll stay here* **for now,** for the moment, for the present, for the time being, meantime, in the meantime, in the interim, in the interval.
2 *cook for a further half hour; meanwhile, make the stuffing* **at the same time,** simultaneously, concurrently.

measurable ▶ **adjective 1** *a measurable amount* **quantifiable,** computable.
2 *a measurable improvement* **appreciable,** noticeable, significant, visible, perceptible, definite, obvious.

measure ▶ **verb 1** *they measured the length of the room* **calculate,** compute, count, meter, quantify, weigh, size, evaluate, assess, gauge, plumb, determine.
2 *she did not need to* ***measure*** *herself* ***against*** *some ideal* **compare with,** pit against, set against, test against, judge by.
▶ **noun 1** *cost-cutting measures* **action,** act, course (of action), deed, proceeding, procedure, step, means, expedient; maneuver, initiative, program, operation.
2 *the House passed the measure* **statute,** act, bill, law, legislation.
3 *the original dimensions were in metric measure* **system,** standard, units, scale.
4 *a measure of egg white* **quantity,** amount, portion.
5 *the students retain* ***a measure*** *of independence* **a certain amount,** an amount, a certain degree, a degree; some.
6 *sales are the measure of the company's success* **yardstick,** test, standard, barometer, touchstone, litmus test, criterion, benchmark.
– PHRASES **beyond measure** *it irritates him beyond measure that she is always right* **immensely,** extremely, vastly, greatly, excessively, immeasurably, incalculably, infinitely. **for good measure** *she added a couple of chili peppers for good measure* **as a bonus,** as an extra, into the bargain, to boot, in addition, besides, as well. **get/have the measure of** *she wants to get the measure of Kate before they meet at the Olympics* **evaluate,** assess, gauge,

judge, understand, fathom, read, be wise to, see through; informal have someone's number.

measure up *he was cut from the Corps because he just couldn't measure up* **pass muster,** match up, come up to standard, fit/fill the bill, be acceptable; informal come up to scratch, make the grade, cut the mustard, be up to snuff.

measure up to *we didn't measure up to their standards* **meet,** come up to, equal, match, bear comparison with, be on a level with; achieve, satisfy, fulfill.

measured ▶ adjective **1** *his measured steps* **regular,** steady, even, rhythmic, rhythmical, unfaltering; slow, dignified, stately, sedate, leisurely, unhurried.

2 *his measured tones* **thoughtful,** careful, carefully chosen, studied, calculated, planned, considered, deliberate, restrained.

measurement ▶ noun **1** *measurement of the effect is difficult* **quantification,** computation, calculation, mensuration; evaluation, assessment, gauging.

2 *all measurements are given in metric units* **size,** dimension, proportions, magnitude, amplitude; mass, bulk, volume, capacity, extent; value, amount, quantity, area, length, height, depth, weight, width, range.

meat ▶ noun **1** *you need to cut down on your consumption of meat* **flesh,** animal flesh.

2 archaic *meat and drink* **food,** nourishment, sustenance, provisions, rations, fare, foodstuff(s), provender, daily bread; informal grub, eats, chow, nosh; formal comestibles; dated victuals; literary viands.

3 *the meat of the matter* **substance,** pith, marrow, heart, kernel, core, nucleus, nub, essence, essentials, gist, fundamentals, basics; informal nitty-gritty.

meaty ▶ adjective **1** *a tall, meaty man* **beefy,** brawny, burly, muscular, muscly, powerful, sturdy, strapping, well-built, solidly built, thickset; fleshy, stout.

2 *a good, meaty story* **interesting,** thought-provoking, three-dimensional, stimulating; substantial, satisfying, meaningful, deep, profound.

mechanical ▶ adjective **1** *a mechanical device* **mechanized,** machine-driven, automated, automatic, power-driven, robotic.

ANTONYMS manual.

2 *a mechanical response* **automatic,** unthinking, unconscious, robotic, involuntary, reflex, knee-jerk, gut, habitual, routine, unemotional, unfeeling, lifeless; perfunctory, cursory, careless, casual.

ANTONYMS conscious.

mechanism ▶ noun **1** *an electrical mechanism* **machine,** piece of machinery, appliance, apparatus, device, instrument, contraption, gadget; informal gizmo.

2 *the train's safety mechanism* **machinery,** workings, works, movement, action, gears, components.

3 *a formal mechanism for citizens to lodge complaints* **procedure,** process, system, operation, method, technique, means, medium, agency, channel.

meddle ▶ verb **1** *don't meddle in my affairs* **interfere in/with,** butt in/into, intrude on/into, intervene in, pry into; informal poke one's nose in, horn in on, muscle in on, snoop into, stick one's oar in, kibitz in.

2 *someone had been meddling with her things* **fiddle,** interfere, tamper, tinker, fool around.

meddlesome ▶ adjective *my meddlesome neighbor is peering out the window at us* **interfering,** meddling, intrusive, prying, busybody; informal nosy. See note at IMPERTINENT.

mediate ▶ verb **1** *the UN tried to mediate between the two countries* **arbitrate,** conciliate, moderate, act as peacemaker, make peace; intervene, step in, intercede, act as an intermediary, liaise.

2 *a tribunal was set up to mediate disputes* **resolve,** settle, arbitrate in, umpire, reconcile, referee; mend, clear up; informal patch up. See note at INSERT.

3 *he attempted to mediate a solution to the conflict* **negotiate,** bring about, effect; formal effectuate.

mediation ▶ noun *mediation between victims and offenders* **arbitration,** conciliation, reconciliation, intervention, intercession, good offices; negotiation, shuttle diplomacy.

mediator ▶ noun *the mediator in their salary dispute* **arbitrator,** arbiter, negotiator, conciliator, peacemaker, go-between, middleman, intermediary, moderator, intervenor, intercessor, broker, honest broker, liaison officer; umpire, referee, adjudicator, judge.

medicinal ▶ adjective *an infusion of medicinal herbs* **curative,** healing, remedial, therapeutic, restorative, corrective, health-giving; medical.

medicine ▶ noun *take your medicine* **medication,** medicament, drug, prescription, pharmaceutical, dose, treatment, remedy, cure; nostrum, panacea, cure-all; informal meds; archaic physic.

medieval ▶ adjective **1** *medieval times* **of the Middle Ages,** of the Dark Ages, Dark-Age; Gothic.

ANTONYMS modern.

2 informal *his attitudes are positively medieval* **primitive,** antiquated, archaic, antique, antediluvian, old-fashioned, out of date, outdated, outmoded, anachronistic, passé, obsolete; informal horse-and-buggy.

ANTONYMS modern.

mediocre ▶ adjective *a mediocre performance* **ordinary,** average, middling, middle-of-the-road, uninspired, undistinguished, indifferent, unexceptional, unexciting, unremarkable, run-of-the-mill, pedestrian, prosaic, lackluster, forgettable, amateur, amateurish; informal OK, so-so, 'comme ci, comme ça', plain-vanilla, fair-to-middling, no great shakes, not up to much, bush-league.

ANTONYMS excellent.

meditate ▶ verb *please allow me more time to meditate* **contemplate,** think, consider, ponder, muse, reflect, deliberate, ruminate, chew the cud, brood, mull something over; be in a brown study, be deep/lost in thought, debate with oneself; pray; informal put on one's thinking cap;

formal cogitate.

meditation ▶ noun *cultivating the presence of God through meditation* **contemplation,** thought, thinking, musing, pondering, consideration, reflection, deliberation, rumination, brooding, reverie, brown study, concentration; prayer; formal cogitation.

medium ▶ noun **1** *using technology as a medium for job creation | radio was the first great medium of mass communication* **means,** method, way, form, agency, avenue, channel, vehicle, organ, instrument, mechanism.
2 *organisms growing in their natural medium* **habitat,** element, environment, surroundings, milieu, setting, conditions.
3 *she consulted a medium* **spiritualist,** spiritist, necromancer, channeler; fortune teller, clairvoyant, psychic.
4 *a happy medium* **middle way,** middle course, middle ground, middle, mean, median, midpoint; compromise, golden mean.
▶ adjective *medium height* **average,** middling, medium-sized, middle-sized, moderate, normal, standard.

medley ▶ noun *a medley of Beatles songs | a vegetable medley* **assortment,** miscellany, mixture, mélange, variety, mixed bag, grab bag, mix, collection, selection, potpourri, patchwork, bricolage; motley collection, ragbag, gallimaufry, mishmash, jumble, hodgepodge, salmagundi.

meek ▶ adjective *they called her Miss Mouse because she was so meek* **submissive,** yielding, obedient, compliant, tame, biddable, tractable, acquiescent, deferential, timid, unprotesting, unresisting, like a lamb to the slaughter; quiet, mild, gentle, docile, lamblike, shy, diffident, unassuming, self-effacing.
ANTONYMS assertive.

meet ▶ verb **1** *I met an old friend on the train* **encounter,** meet up with, come face to face with, run into, run across, come across/upon, chance on, happen on, stumble across/on; informal bump into.
2 *she first met Paul at a party* **get to know,** be introduced to, make the acquaintance of.
3 *the committee met on Saturday* **assemble,** gather, come together, get together, congregate, convene.
4 *the place where three roads meet* **converge,** connect, touch, link up, intersect, cross, join.
5 *she met death bravely* **face,** encounter, undergo, experience, go through, suffer, endure, bear; cope with, handle.
6 *the announcement was met with widespread hostility* **greet,** receive, answer, treat.
7 *he does not meet the job's requirements* **fulfill,** satisfy, fill, measure up to, match (up to), conform to, come up to, comply with, answer.
8 *shipowners would meet the cost of oil spills* **pay,** settle, clear, honor, discharge, pay off, square.
▶ noun *a track meet* **event,** tournament, game, match, contest, competition.
– PHRASES **meet someone halfway** See **HALFWAY**.

meeting ▶ noun **1** *he stood up to address the meeting* **gathering,** assembly, conference, congregation, convention, summit, forum, convocation, conclave, council, rally, caucus; informal get-together.
2 *she demanded a meeting with the councilman* **consultation,** audience, interview.
3 *he intrigued her on their first meeting* **encounter,** contact; appointment, assignation, rendezvous; literary tryst.
4 *the meeting of land and sea* **convergence,** coming together, confluence, conjunction, union, junction, abutment; intersection, T-junction, crossing.

melancholy ▶ adjective *a melancholy expression* **sad,** sorrowful, unhappy, desolate, mournful, lugubrious, gloomy, despondent, dejected, depressed, downhearted, downcast, disconsolate, glum, miserable, wretched, dismal, morose, woeful, woebegone, doleful, joyless, heavy-hearted; informal down in the dumps, down in/at the mouth, blue; literary atrabilious. See note at **GLUM**.
ANTONYMS cheerful.
▶ noun *a feeling of melancholy* **sadness,** sorrow, unhappiness, woe, desolation, melancholia, dejection, depression, despondency, cafard, gloom, gloominess, misery; informal the dumps, the blues.

melee ▶ noun *people were trampled in the melee* **fracas,** disturbance, rumpus, tumult, commotion, ruckus, disorder, fray; brawl, fight, scuffle, struggle, skirmish, scrimmage, free-for-all, tussle; informal scrap, set-to, ruction, slugfest.

mellifluous ▶ adjective *mellifluous dinner music* **sweet-sounding,** dulcet, honeyed, mellow, soft, liquid, silvery, soothing, rich, smooth, euphonious, harmonious, tuneful, musical.
ANTONYMS cacophonous.

mellow ▶ adjective **1** *a mellow mood* **genial,** affable, amiable, good-humored, good-natured, amicable, pleasant, relaxed, easygoing, low-maintenance, placid; jovial, jolly, cheerful, happy, merry.
2 *the mellow tone of his voice* **dulcet,** sweet-sounding, tuneful, melodious, mellifluous; soft, smooth, warm, full, rich.
3 *a mellow wine* **full-bodied,** mature, well matured, full-flavored, rich, smooth. See note at **MATURE**.
– PHRASES **mellow out** *you need to mellow out* **relax,** unwind, loosen up, de-stress, slow down, take it easy; informal chill (out), take a (chill) pill, decompress.

melodious ▶ adjective *the pleasure of hearing her melodious singing voice* **tuneful,** melodic, musical, mellifluous, dulcet, sweet-sounding, silvery, harmonious, euphonious, lyrical; informal easy on the ear.
ANTONYMS discordant.

melodramatic ▶ adjective *the early soap operas of radio days were exceedingly melodramatic* **exaggerated,** histrionic, overdramatic, overdone, operatic, sensationalized, overemotional, overwrought, sentimental, extravagant; theatrical, stagy, actressy; informal hammy.

melody ▶ noun *familiar melodies* **tune,** air, strain, theme, song, refrain, piece of music; informal ditty.

melt ▶ verb 1 *the snow was beginning to melt* **thaw,** liquefy, defrost, soften, dissolve, deliquesce.
2 *his smile melted her heart* **soften,** disarm, touch, affect, move.
3 *his anger **melted away*** **vanish,** disappear, fade away, dissolve, evaporate; literary evanesce.

member ▶ noun 1 *a member of the club* **subscriber,** associate, affiliate, life member, card-carrying member.
2 *a member of a mathematical set* **constituent,** element, component, part, portion, piece, unit.
3 archaic *many victims had injured members* **limb,** organ; arm, leg, appendage.

membrane ▶ noun *the sensitive membranes in the mouth* **layer,** sheet, skin, film, tissue, integument, overlay; technical pellicle.

memento ▶ noun *she kept the painted clamshell as a memento from our trip to Cape Cod* **souvenir,** keepsake, reminder, remembrance, token, memorial, bomboniere; trophy, relic.

memoir ▶ noun 1 *a touching memoir of her childhood* **account,** history, record, chronicle, narrative, story, portrayal, depiction, sketch, portrait, profile, biography, monograph.
2 (**memoirs**) *he published his memoirs in 1955* **autobiography,** life story, memories, recollections, reminiscences; journal, diary.

memorable ▶ adjective *thank you for making our visit so memorable | a memorable theme song* **unforgettable,** indelible, catchy, haunting; momentous, significant, historic, notable, noteworthy, important, consequential, remarkable, special, signal, outstanding, extraordinary, striking, vivid, arresting, impressive, distinctive, distinguished, famous, celebrated, renowned, illustrious, glorious.

memorandum ▶ noun *a memorandum from the general* **message,** communication, note, email, letter, missive, directive; reminder, aide-mémoire; informal memo.

memorial ▶ noun 1 *the war memorial* **monument,** cenotaph, mausoleum; statue, plaque, cairn; shrine; tombstone, gravestone, headstone.
2 *the festival is a memorial to his life's work* **tribute,** testimonial; remembrance, memento.
▶ adjective *a memorial service* **commemorative,** remembrance, commemorating.

memorize ▶ verb *we have to memorize a poem in French* **commit to memory,** remember, learn by heart, get off by heart, learn, learn by rote, become word-perfect in, get something down pat; archaic con.

memory ▶ noun 1 *she is losing her memory* **ability to remember,** powers of recall.
2 *happy memories of her young days* **recollection,** remembrance, reminiscence; impression.
3 *the town built a statue in memory of him* **commemoration,** remembrance; honor, tribute, recognition, respect.
4 *a computer's memory* **memory bank,** store, cache, disk, RAM, ROM, hard drive.

menace ▶ noun 1 *an atmosphere full of menace* **threat,** ominousness, intimidation, warning, ill omen.
2 *a menace to urban society* **danger,** peril, risk, hazard, threat; jeopardy.
3 *that dog is a menace* **nuisance,** pest, annoyance, plague, torment, terror, troublemaker, mischief-maker, thorn in someone's side/flesh.
▶ verb 1 *gorillas are still menaced by poaching* **threaten,** be a danger to, put at risk, jeopardize, imperil.
2 *a gang of skinheads menaced local residents* **intimidate,** threaten, terrorize, frighten, scare, terrify.

menacing ▶ adjective *a menacing driver forced me to take the nearest exit* **threatening,** ominous, intimidating, frightening, terrifying, alarming, forbidding, black, thunderous, glowering, unfriendly, hostile, sinister, baleful, warning; formal minatory.
ANTONYMS friendly.

mend ▶ verb 1 *workmen were mending faulty cabling* **repair,** fix, put back together, piece together, restore; sew (up), stitch, darn, patch, cobble; rehabilitate, renew, renovate; informal patch up.
ANTONYMS break, worsen.
2 *they mended their quarrel* **put/set right,** set straight, straighten out, sort out, rectify, remedy, cure, right, resolve, square, settle, put to rights, correct, retrieve, improve, make better.
ANTONYMS break, worsen.

mendacious ▶ adjective *politicians and their mendacious spin doctors* **lying,** untruthful, dishonest, deceitful, false, dissembling, insincere, disingenuous, hypocritical, fraudulent, double-dealing, two-faced, two-timing, duplicitous, perjured; untrue, fictitious, falsified, fabricated, fallacious, invented, made up; informal full of crap; literary perfidious.
ANTONYMS truthful.

mendicant ▶ noun See **BEGGAR**.

menial ▶ adjective *a menial job* **unskilled,** lowly, humble, low-status, inferior, degrading; routine, humdrum, boring, dull.
▶ noun *they were treated like menials* **servant,** drudge, minion, joe-boy, factotum, lackey, hired hand; informal wage slave, gofer, peon, grunt; archaic scullion.

menstruation ▶ noun *tribal ceremonies regarding menstruation* **period,** menses, menorrhea, menstrual cycle; menarche; informal one's/that time of the month; informal dated the curse.

mental ▶ adjective 1 *mental faculties* **intellectual,** cerebral, brain, rational, cognitive.
ANTONYMS physical.
2 *a mental disorder* **psychiatric,** psychological, psychogenic.
3 informal *he's completely mental* See **MAD** (sense 1).

mentality ▶ noun 1 *I can't understand the mentality of these people* **way of thinking,** mind set, cast of mind, frame of mind, turn of mind, mind, psychology, mental attitude, outlook, disposition, makeup.
2 *a person of limited mentality* **intellect,** intellectual capabilities, intelligence, IQ,

(powers of) reasoning, rationality; informal brains, smarts.

mentally ▶ adverb *mentally, I was prepared to deal with the situation* **in one's mind,** in one's head, inwardly, intellectually, cognitively.

mention ▶ verb 1 *don't mention the war* **allude to,** refer to, touch on/upon; bring up, raise, broach, introduce, moot.
2 *Jim mentioned that he'd met them before* **state,** say, indicate, let someone know, disclose, divulge, reveal.
3 *I'll gladly mention your work to my friends* **recommend,** commend, put in a good word for, speak well of.
▶ noun 1 *he made no* ***mention of*** *your request* **reference to,** allusion to, remark of/about/regarding, statement about/regarding, announcement of, indication of.
2 *my book got a mention on the show* **recommendation,** commendation, a good word.
– PHRASES **don't mention it** *"Sorry for being late." "Oh, don't mention it."* **don't apologize,** it doesn't matter, it makes no difference, it's not important, never mind, don't worry. **not to mention** *if the party's canceled, we'll have to notify the guests, not to mention the caterers* **in addition to,** as well as; not counting, not including, to say nothing of, aside from, besides.

mentor ▶ noun 1 *his political mentors* **adviser,** guide, guru, counselor, consultant; confidant(e).
2 *regular meetings between mentor and trainee* **trainer,** teacher, tutor, instructor.

mercantile ▶ adjective *her grandfather had invested in several mercantile interests at the turn of the century* **commercial,** trade, trading, business, merchant, sales.

mercenary ▶ adjective 1 *mercenary self-interest* **money-oriented,** grasping, greedy, acquisitive, avaricious, covetous, bribable, venal, materialistic; informal money-grubbing.
2 *mercenary soldiers* **hired,** paid, bought, professional.
▶ noun *a group of mercenaries* **soldier of fortune,** professional soldier, hired soldier, gunman; informal hired gun; historical condottiere.

merchandise ▶ noun *a wide range of merchandise* **goods,** wares, stock, commodities, lines, produce, products.
▶ verb *a new product that can be easily merchandised* **promote,** market, sell, retail; advertise, publicize, push; informal plug.

merchant ▶ noun *a tea merchant from Bombay* **trader,** dealer, wholesaler, broker, agent, seller, buyer, buyer and seller, vendor, distributor, peddler, retailer, shopkeeper, storekeeper.

merciful ▶ adjective 1 *God is merciful* **forgiving,** compassionate, clement, pitying, forbearing, lenient, humane, mild, kind, softhearted, tenderhearted, gracious, sympathetic, humanitarian, liberal, tolerant, indulgent, generous, magnanimous, benign, benevolent. See note at LENIENT.
ANTONYMS cruel.
2 *a merciful silence fell* **welcome,** blessed.
– PHRASES **be merciful to** *the judge was inclined to be merciful to first offenders* **have mercy on,** have pity on, show mercy to, spare, pardon, forgive, be lenient to; informal go/be easy on, let off.

merciless ▶ adjective *the merciless Cossacks who invaded Siberia* **ruthless,** remorseless, pitiless, unforgiving, unsparing, implacable, inexorable, relentless, unremitting, inflexible, inhumane, inhuman, unsympathetic, unfeeling, intolerant, rigid, severe, cold-blooded, hard-hearted, stony-hearted, heartless, harsh, callous, cruel, brutal, barbarous, cutthroat.
ANTONYMS compassionate.

mercurial ▶ adjective *a mercurial temperament* **volatile,** capricious, temperamental, excitable, fickle, changeable, unpredictable, variable, protean, mutable, erratic, quicksilver, inconstant, inconsistent, unstable, unsteady, fluctuating, ever-changing, moody, flighty, wayward, whimsical, impulsive; technical labile.
ANTONYMS stable.

mercy ▶ noun 1 *he showed no mercy to the others* **leniency,** clemency, compassion, grace, pity, charity, forgiveness, forbearance, quarter, humanity; soft-heartedness, tenderheartedness, kindness, sympathy, liberality, indulgence, tolerance, generosity, magnanimity, beneficence.
ANTONYMS ruthlessness, cruelty.
2 *we must be thankful for small mercies* **blessing,** godsend, boon, favor, piece/stroke of luck, windfall.
– PHRASES **at the mercy of 1** *they found themselves at the mercy of the tyrant* **in the power of,** under/in the control of, in the clutches of, subject to. **2** *he was at the mercy of the elements* **defenseless against,** vulnerable to, exposed to, susceptible to, prey to, (wide) open to.

CHOOSE THE RIGHT WORD

mercy, benevolence, charity, clemency, compassion, leniency

If you want to win friends and influence people, it's best to start with **benevolence,** a general term for goodwill and kindness (*a grandfather's benevolence*). **Charity** is even better, suggesting generous giving (*the baker gave him bread out of charity*) but also meaning tolerance and understanding of others (*she viewed his selfish behavior with charity*). **Compassion** is a feeling of sympathy or sorrow for someone else's misfortune (*he has shown compassion for the homeless*), and often includes showing **mercy**. Aside from its religious overtones, *mercy* means compassion or kindness in our treatment of others, especially those who have offended us or who deserve punishment (*mercy toward the pickpocket*). **Clemency** is mercy shown by someone whose duty or function it is to administer justice or punish offenses (*the judge granted clemency*), while **leniency** emphasizes gentleness, softness, or lack of severity, even if it isn't quite deserved (*a father's leniency in punishing his young son*).

mere ▸ adjective *it costs a mere $11.00* **no more than,** just, only, merely; no better than; a paltry, a measly, an insignificant, an ordinary, a minor, a little, a piddling, a piffling.

merge ▸ verb **1** *the company merged with a firm based in Peoria* **join (together),** join forces, amalgamate, unite, affiliate, team up, link (up).
ANTONYMS separate.
2 *the two organizations were merged* **amalgamate,** bring together, join, consolidate, conflate, unite, unify, combine, incorporate, integrate, link (up), knit, yoke.
ANTONYMS separate.
3 *the two colors merged* **mingle,** blend, fuse, mix, intermix, intermingle, coalesce; literary commingle.

merger ▸ noun *a pending merger between two Russian oil companies* **amalgamation,** combination, union, fusion, coalition, affiliation, unification, incorporation, consolidation, link-up, alliance.
ANTONYMS split.

merit ▸ noun **1** *composers of outstanding merit* **excellence,** quality, caliber, worth, worthiness, credit, value, distinction, eminence.
ANTONYMS inferiority.
2 *the merits of the scheme* **good point,** strong point, advantage, benefit, value, asset, plus.
ANTONYMS fault, disadvantage.
▸ verb *the accusation did not merit a response* **deserve,** earn, be deserving of, warrant, rate, justify, be worthy of, be worth, be entitled to, have a right to, have a claim to/on.

meritorious ▸ adjective *an award for meritorious conduct* **praiseworthy,** laudable, commendable, admirable, estimable, creditable, worthy, deserving, excellent, exemplary, good.
ANTONYMS discreditable.

merriment ▸ noun *we got caught up in the merriment of the occasion* **high spirits,** high-spiritedness, exuberance, cheerfulness, gaiety, fun, effervescence, verve, buoyancy, levity, zest, liveliness, cheer, joy, joyfulness, joyousness, jolliness, jollity, happiness, gladness, jocularity, conviviality, festivity, merrymaking, revelry, mirth, glee, gleefulness, laughter, hilarity, lightheartedness, amusement, pleasure.
ANTONYMS misery.

merry ▸ adjective *merry throngs of students* **cheerful,** cheery, in high spirits, high-spirited, bright, sunny, smiling, lighthearted, buoyant, lively, carefree, without a care in the world, joyful, joyous, jolly, convivial, festive, mirthful, gleeful, happy, glad, laughing; informal chirpy; formal jocund; dated gay; literary blithe.
ANTONYMS miserable.
– PHRASES **make merry** *I'm afraid we may have made merry a bit too long last night* **have fun,** have a good time, enjoy oneself, have a party, celebrate, carouse, feast, 'eat, drink, and be merry', revel, roister; informal party, have a ball.

mesh ▸ noun *wire mesh* **netting,** net, network; web, webbing, lattice, latticework.
▸ verb **1** *one gear meshes with the other* **engage,** connect, lock, interlock.
2 *our ideas just do not mesh* **harmonize,** fit together, match, dovetail.

mesmerize ▸ verb *the dancers mesmerized us* **enthrall,** hold spellbound, entrance, dazzle, bedazzle, bewitch, charm, captivate, enchant, fascinate, transfix, grip, hypnotize.

mess ▸ noun **1** *please clear up the mess* **untidiness,** disorder, disarray, clutter, shambles, jumble, muddle, chaos.
2 *don't step in the dog mess* **excrement,** muck, feces, excreta.
3 *I've got to get out of this mess* **plight,** predicament, tight spot/corner, difficulty, trouble, quandary, dilemma, problem, muddle, mix-up, imbroglio; informal jam, fix, pickle, stew, scrape.
– PHRASES **make a mess of** *he made a mess of the project* **mismanage,** mishandle, bungle, fluff, spoil, ruin, wreck; informal mess up, botch, make a hash of, foul up. **mess around** *don't mess around with any of the equipment* **fool around,** fiddle about/around, play around; fidget, toy, trifle, tamper, tinker, interfere, meddle, monkey (around/about). **mess up** *he messed up my kitchen* **dirty**; clutter up, disarrange, jumble, dishevel, rumple; informal muss up; literary befoul.

message ▸ noun **1** *are there any messages for me?* **communication,** piece of information, news, note, memorandum, memo, email, letter, missive, report, bulletin, communiqué, dispatch.
2 *the message of his teaching* **meaning,** sense, import, idea; point, thrust, gist, essence, content, subject (matter), substance, implication, drift, lesson.
– PHRASES **get the message** informal *what do I have to say to make you get the message?* **understand,** get the point, comprehend; informal catch on, get the picture.

messenger ▸ noun *the messenger arrived by motorcycle* **courier,** runner, envoy, emissary, agent, go-between, message-bearer; postman, letter carrier, mailman; historical **herald**; archaic legate.

messy ▸ adjective **1** *messy oil spills | messy hair* **dirty,** filthy, grubby, soiled, grimy; mucky, muddy, slimy, sticky, sullied, spotted, stained, smeared, smudged; disheveled, scruffy, unkempt, rumpled, matted, tousled, bedraggled, tangled; informal yucky, grungy.
ANTONYMS clean.
2 *a messy kitchen* **disorderly,** disordered, in a muddle, chaotic, confused, disorganized, in disarray, disarranged; untidy, cluttered, in a jumble; informal like a bomb's hit it, shambolic.
ANTONYMS orderly, tidy.
3 *a messy legal battle* **complex,** intricate, tangled, confused, convoluted; unpleasant, nasty, bitter, acrimonious.
ANTONYMS straightforward, amicable.

metallic ▸ adjective **1** *a metallic sound* **tinny,** jangling, jingling; grating, harsh, jarring, dissonant.
2 *metallic paint* **metalized,** burnished; shiny, glossy, lustrous.

metamorphosis ▸ noun *his amazing metamorphosis from gawky hayseed to sexy pop star* **transformation,** mutation, transmutation, change, alteration, conversion, modification, remodeling, reconstruction; humorous transmogrification; formal transubstantiation.

metaphor ▶ noun *the profusion of metaphors in her everyday speech has gotten pretty tiresome* **figure of speech,** image, trope, analogy, comparison, symbol, word painting/picture.

mete ▶ verb
– PHRASES **mete out** *they were instructed to mete out harsh punishment* **dispense,** hand out, allocate, allot, apportion, issue, deal out, dole out, dish out, assign, administer.

meteoric ▶ adjective *her meteoric rise to fame* **rapid,** lightning, swift, fast, quick, speedy, accelerated, instant, sudden, spectacular, dazzling, brilliant.
ANTONYMS gradual.

method ▶ noun **1** *they use very old-fashioned methods* **procedure,** technique, system, practice, routine, modus operandi, process; strategy, tactic, plan.
2 *there's a method to his madness* **order,** orderliness, organization, structure, form, system, logic, planning, design, sense.
ANTONYMS disorder.

methodical ▶ adjective *a methodical approach to the evaluation* **orderly,** well-ordered, well-organized, (well) planned, efficient, businesslike, systematic, structured, logical, analytic, disciplined; meticulous, punctilious.

meticulous ▶ adjective *the etchers give meticulous attention to each piece* **careful,** conscientious, diligent, scrupulous, punctilious, painstaking, accurate; thorough, studious, rigorous, detailed, perfectionist, fastidious, methodical, particular.
ANTONYMS careless.

metropolis ▶ noun *their trip to the booming metropolis made them eager to return to their little house in the sticks* **capital (city),** chief town, county town; big city, conurbation, megalopolis, megacity.

mettle ▶ noun **1** *a man of mettle* **spirit,** fortitude, strength of character, moral fiber, steel, determination, resolve, resolution, backbone, grit, true grit, courage, courageousness, bravery, valor, fearlessness, daring; informal guts, spunk, balls.
2 *Frazer was of a very different mettle* **caliber,** character, disposition, nature, temperament, personality, makeup, stamp.

microscopic ▶ adjective *microscopic fibers found in the suspect's car* **tiny,** very small, minute, infinitesimal, minuscule; little, micro, diminutive; informal teeny, weeny, teeny-weeny, teensy-weensy, itsy-bitsy, little-bitty; Scottish wee.
ANTONYMS huge.

midday ▶ noun *the bells chime at midday* **noon,** twelve noon, high noon, noontide, noonday.
ANTONYMS midnight.

middle ▶ noun **1** *a shallow dish with a spike in the middle* **center,** midpoint, halfway point, dead center, focus, hub; eye, heart, core, kernel.
ANTONYMS outside.
2 *he had a towel around his middle* **midriff,** waist, belly, stomach, abdomen; informal tummy, tum, gut.
▶ adjective **1** *the middle point* **central,** mid, mean, medium, medial, median, midway, halfway.
2 *the middle level* **intermediate,** intermediary.

middleman ▶ noun *I'd rather avoid the middleman and buy direct from the manufacturer* **intermediary,** intercessor, go-between, liaison, mediator; dealer, broker, agent, factor, wholesaler, distributor.

middling ▶ adjective *a town of the middling kind, neither rich nor poor* **average,** standard, normal, middle-of-the-road; moderate, ordinary, commonplace, everyday, workaday, tolerable, passable; run-of-the-mill, fair, mediocre, undistinguished, unexceptional, unremarkable; informal OK, so-so, 'comme ci, comme ça', fair-to-middling, plain-vanilla.

midget ▶ noun *the inhabitants must have been midgets* **small person,** dwarf, homunculus, Lilliputian, gnome, pygmy; informal shrimp.
▶ adjective **1** *a story about midget matadors* **diminutive,** dwarfish, petite, very small, pygmy; informal pint-sized, peewee.
ANTONYMS giant.
2 *a midget camera* **miniature,** pocket, dwarf, baby, mini.
ANTONYMS giant.

midnight ▶ noun *we'll meet under the clock tower at midnight* **twelve midnight,** the middle of the night, the witching hour.
ANTONYMS midday.

midst ▶ noun literary *in the midst of the confusion, one strong and sturdy voice broke through and was heard* **middle,** center, heart, core, midpoint, kernel, nub; depth(s), thick; (**in the midst of**) in the course of, halfway through, at the heart/core of.
– PHRASES **in our midst** *there is a hero in our midst* **among us,** in our group, with us.

midway ▶ adverb *he was explaining what happened and then just stopped midway* **halfway,** in the middle, at the midpoint, in the center; part-way, at some point.

mien ▶ noun *a scowling mien that did nothing to boost our confidence* **appearance,** look, expression, countenance, aura, demeanor, attitude, air, manner, bearing; formal comportment.

might ▶ noun *she hit him with all her might* **strength,** force, power, vigor, energy, brawn, powerfulness, forcefulness.

mighty ▶ adjective **1** *a mighty blow* **powerful,** forceful, violent, vigorous, hefty, thunderous.
ANTONYMS feeble.
2 *a mighty warrior* **fearsome,** ferocious; big, tough, robust, muscular, strapping.
ANTONYMS puny, tiny.
3 *mighty industrial countries* **dominant,** influential, strong, powerful, important, predominant.
ANTONYMS insignificant.
4 *mighty oak trees* **huge,** enormous, massive, gigantic, big, large, giant, colossal, mammoth, immense; informal monster, whopping, humongous, jumbo(-sized), ginormous.
ANTONYMS tiny.
▶ adverb informal *I'm mighty pleased to see you* **extremely,** exceedingly, enormously, immensely, tremendously, hugely, mightily,

very (much); informal awfully, majorly, mega, plumb, right; informal dated frightfully.

migrant ▶ noun *they exploited the Puerto Rican migrants who toiled in their orchards for dismal wages* **immigrant, emigrant**; nomad, itinerant, traveler, vagrant, transient, rover, wanderer, drifter.

▶ adjective *migrant workers* **traveling,** wandering, drifting, nomadic, roving, roaming, itinerant, vagrant, transient.

migrate ▶ verb 1 *cities grew rapidly as rural populations migrated in search of jobs* **relocate,** resettle, move (house); immigrate; emigrate, go abroad, go overseas, pull up stakes; dated remove.
2 *wildebeest migrate across the Serengeti* **roam,** wander, drift, rove, travel (around).

migratory ▶ adjective *a winter haven for migratory species* **migrant,** migrating, moving, traveling.

mild ▶ adjective 1 *a mild tone of voice* **gentle,** tender, softhearted, tenderhearted, sensitive, sympathetic, warm, placid, calm, tranquil, serene, peaceable, good-natured, mild-mannered, amiable, affable, genial, easygoing.
ANTONYMS harsh.
2 *a mild punishment* **lenient,** light; compassionate, merciful, humane.
ANTONYMS harsh, cruel.
3 *he was eyeing her with mild interest* **slight,** faint, vague, minimal, nominal, moderate, token, feeble.
ANTONYMS strong.
4 *mild weather* **warm,** balmy, temperate, clement.
ANTONYMS cold, severe.
5 *a mild curry* **bland,** insipid, tame.
ANTONYMS spicy, piquant.

milieu ▶ noun *the political milieu in New England* **environment,** sphere, background, backdrop, setting, context, atmosphere; location, conditions, surroundings, environs; informal stomping grounds, stamping grounds, turf.

militant ▶ adjective *militant supporters* **aggressive,** violent, belligerent, bellicose, vigorous, forceful, active, fierce, combative, pugnacious; radical, extremist, extreme, zealous, fanatical.

▶ noun *the demands of the militants* **activist,** extremist, radical, young turk, zealot.

military ▶ adjective *military activity* **fighting,** service, army, armed, defense, martial.
ANTONYMS civilian.

▶ noun *the military took power* **(armed) forces,** services, militia; army, navy, air force, marines.

militate ▶ verb *his resentment of others in the company* ***militates against*** *his own chances for advancement* **tend to prevent,** work against, hinder, discourage, prejudice, be detrimental to.

milk ▶ verb 1 *Pam was milking the cows* **draw milk from,** express milk from.
2 *milk a little of the liquid* **draw off,** siphon (off), pump off, tap, drain, extract.
3 *milking rich clients* **exploit,** take advantage of, cash in on, suck dry; informal bleed, squeeze, fleece.

milky ▶ adjective *a milky complexion* **pale,** white, milk-white, whitish, off-white, cream, creamy, chalky, pearly, nacreous, ivory, alabaster; cloudy, frosted, opaque.
ANTONYMS swarthy.

mill ▶ noun 1 *a steel mill* **factory,** (processing) plant, works, workshop, shop, foundry.
2 *a pepper mill* **grinder,** crusher, quern.

▶ verb *the wheat is milled into flour* **grind,** pulverize, powder, granulate, pound, crush, press; technical comminute, triturate.

– PHRASES **mill around/about** *people were milling about in the streets* **throng,** swarm, crowd.

millstone ▶ noun *a lifetime of lying and stealing had become the very millstone that would crush him* **burden,** encumbrance, dead weight, cross to bear, albatross, load; duty, responsibility, obligation, liability, misfortune.

mime ▶ noun *a mime of someone fencing* **pantomime,** charade, dumb show.

▶ verb *she mimed picking up a phone* **act out,** pantomime, gesture, simulate, represent.

mimic ▶ verb 1 *she mimicked his accent* **imitate,** copy, impersonate, do an impression of, ape, caricature, parody, lampoon, burlesque, parrot; informal send up, take off, spoof. See note at **IMITATE**.
2 *most hoverflies mimic wasps* **resemble,** look like, have the appearance of, simulate; informal make like.

▶ noun *he was a superb mimic* **impersonator,** impressionist, imitator, parodist, caricaturist, lampooner, lampoonist; informal copycat; archaic ape.

mince ▶ verb 1 *mince the meat and onions* **grind,** chop up, cut up, dice, hash, chop fine.
2 *she minced out of the room* **walk affectedly**; informal sashay, flounce, strut.

– PHRASES **not mince (one's) words** *I'll not mince words: you need to stick to this exercise program or you're looking at serious health problems* **talk straight,** not beat around the bush, call a spade a spade, speak straight from the heart, pull no punches, not put too fine a point on it, tell it like it is, talk turkey.

mincing ▶ adjective *no one dared to laugh at the young master's mincing walk* **affected,** dainty, effeminate, pretentious, dandified, foppish; informal camp.

mind ▶ noun 1 *expand your mind* **brain,** intelligence, intellect, intellectual capabilities, brains, brainpower, wits, understanding, reasoning, judgment, sense, head; informal gray matter, brain cells, smarts.
2 *he kept his mind on the job* **attention,** thoughts, concentration, attentiveness.
3 *the tragedy affected her mind* **sanity,** mental faculties, senses, wits, reason, reasoning, judgment; informal marbles.
4 *Justin's words stuck in her mind* **memory,** recollection.
5 *the country's great minds* **intellect,** thinker, brain, scholar, academic.
6 *I've a mind to complain* **inclination,** desire, wish, urge, notion, fancy, intention, will.
7 *we're of the same mind* **opinion,** way of thinking, outlook, attitude, view, viewpoint, point of view.

▶ verb 1 *do you mind if I smoke?* **care,** object, be bothered, be annoyed, be upset, take offense, disapprove, dislike it, look askance; informal give a damn, give a hoot.
2 *mind the step!* **be careful of,** watch out for, look out for, beware of, be on one's guard for, be wary of.
3 ***mind you*** *wipe your feet* **be/make sure (that) you,** see (that) you; remember to, don't forget to.
4 *her husband was minding the baby* **look after,** take care of, keep an eye on, attend to, care for, tend, babysit.
5 *mind what your mother says* **pay attention to,** heed, pay heed to, attend to, take note/notice of, note, mark, listen to, be mindful of; obey, follow, comply with.
– PHRASES **be of two minds** *I am of two minds about going to law school* **be undecided,** be uncertain, be unsure, hesitate, waver, vacillate, hem and haw; informal dilly-dally, shilly-shally. **bear/keep in mind** *just bear in mind that I've never used a Mac* **remember,** note, be mindful of, take note of; formal take cognizance of. **cross one's mind** *did it ever cross your mind that he just doesn't want to go?* **occur to one,** enter one's mind/head, strike one, hit one, dawn on one. **give someone a piece of one's mind** *I'd really like to give that lying Patterson a piece of my mind* See **REPRIMAND** (verb). **have in mind** *now, for the curtains, do you have a specific pattern in mind?* **think of,** contemplate; intend, plan, propose, desire, want, wish. **never mind 1** *never mind the cost* **don't bother about,** don't worry about, disregard, forget. **2** *never mind, it's all right now* **don't apologize,** forget it, don't worry about it, it doesn't matter. **out of one's mind 1** *you must be out of your mind!* See **MAD** (sense 1). **2** *I've been out of my mind with worry* **frantic,** beside oneself, distraught, in a frenzy. **put someone in mind of** *the view here puts me in mind of Amsterdam* **remind of,** recall, conjure up, suggest; **resemble,** look like. **to my mind** *to my mind, this is a clear case of blackmail* **in my opinion,** in my view, as I see it, in my estimation, in my book, if you ask me.

mindful ▶ adjective *with mindful steps we slowly made our way down the gorge* **aware,** conscious, sensible, alive, alert, acquainted, heedful, wary, chary; informal wise, hip; formal cognizant, regardful.
ANTONYMS heedless.

mindless ▶ adjective 1 *a mindless idiot* **stupid,** idiotic, brainless, imbecilic, imbecile, asinine, witless, foolish, empty-headed, slow-witted, obtuse, featherbrained, doltish; informal dumb, pig-ignorant, brain-dead, cretinous, moronic, thick, birdbrained, pea-brained, dopey, dim, halfwitted, dippy, fat-headed, boneheaded, chowderheaded.
2 *mindless acts of vandalism* **unthinking,** thoughtless, senseless, gratuitous, wanton, indiscriminate, unreasoning.
3 *a mindless task* **mechanical,** automatic, routine; tedious, boring, monotonous, brainless, mind-numbing.
– PHRASES **mindless of** *the birds flock to the feeders, mindless of the humans nearby* **indifferent to,** heedless of, unaware of, unmindful of, careless of, blind to.

mine ▶ noun 1 *a coal mine* **pit,** excavation, quarry, workings, diggings; strip mine, open-pit mine, placer (mine), hardrock mine.
2 *a mine of information* **rich source,** repository, store, storehouse, reservoir, gold mine, treasure house, treasury, reserve, fund, wealth, stock.
3 *he was killed by a mine* **explosive,** land mine, limpet mine, magnetic mine, depth charge.
▶ verb 1 *the iron ore was mined from shallow pits* **quarry,** excavate, dig (up), extract, remove; strip-mine, pan.
2 *medical data was mined for relevant statistics* **search,** delve into, scour, scan, read through, survey.
3 *the entrance to the harbor had been mined* **defend with mines,** lay with mines.

miner ▶ noun *the trapped miners were rescued* **digger,** collier, gold panner; dated sourdough.

mingle ▶ verb 1 *fact and fiction are skillfully mingled in his novels* **mix,** blend, intermingle, intermix, interweave, interlace, combine, merge, fuse, unite, join, amalgamate, meld, mesh; literary commingle.
ANTONYMS separate, be separated.
2 *wedding guests mingled in the lobby* **socialize,** circulate, fraternize, get together, associate with others; informal hobnob, rub elbows.
ANTONYMS separate, part.

miniature ▶ adjective *a miniature railroad* **small-scale,** mini; tiny, little, small, minute, baby, toy, pocket, dwarf, pygmy, minuscule, diminutive, vest-pocket; informal teeny, teeny-weeny, teensy, teensy-weensy, itsy-bitsy, eensy, eensy-weensy; Scottish wee. See note at **SMALL.**
ANTONYMS giant.

minimal ▶ adjective *with minimal care, you can have a beautiful terrarium* **very little,** minimum, the least (possible); nominal, token, negligible.
ANTONYMS maximum.

minimize ▶ verb 1 *the aim is to minimize costs* **keep down,** keep at/to a minimum, reduce, decrease, cut down, lessen, curtail, diminish, prune; informal slash.
ANTONYMS maximize, increase.
2 *we should not minimize his contribution* **belittle,** make light of, play down, underestimate, underrate, downplay, undervalue, understate; informal pooh-pooh; archaic hold cheap.
ANTONYMS exaggerate.

minimum ▶ noun *costs will be kept to the minimum* **lowest level,** lower limit, bottom level, rock bottom, nadir; least, lowest, slightest.
ANTONYMS maximum.
▶ adjective *the minimum amount of effort* **minimal,** least, smallest, least possible, slightest, lowest, minutest.

minion ▶ noun *if working for you means being your minion, I'm not the person you're looking for* **underling,** henchman, flunky, lackey, hanger-on, follower, servant, hireling, vassal, stooge, toady, sycophant; informal yes-man, trained seal, bootlicker, brown-noser, suck-up.

minister ▶ noun 1 *our minister visited me in the hospital* **clergyman,** clergywoman, cleric, ecclesiastic, pastor, vicar, rector, priest, parson, deacon, father, man/woman of the cloth, man/woman of God, churchman, churchwoman; curate, chaplain; informal reverend, padre, Holy Joe, sky pilot.
2 *a government minister* **member of the government,** cabinet minister, secretary of state, undersecretary.
3 *the Canadian minister in Egypt* **ambassador,** chargé d'affaires, plenipotentiary, envoy, emissary, diplomat, consul, representative; archaic legate.
▶ verb *doctors were* ***ministering to*** *the injured* **tend to,** care for, take care of, look after, nurse, treat, attend to, see to, administer to, help, assist.

ministry ▶ noun 1 *he's training for the ministry* **holy orders,** the priesthood, the cloth, the church.
2 *the ministry of Jesus* **teaching,** preaching, evangelism.
3 *the ministry for foreign affairs* (**government**) **department,** bureau, agency, office.

minor ▶ adjective 1 *a minor problem* **slight,** small; unimportant, insignificant, inconsequential, inconsiderable, subsidiary, negligible, trivial, trifling, paltry, petty, nickel-and-dime; informal piffling, piddling.
ANTONYMS major.
2 *a minor poet* **little known,** unknown, lesser, unimportant, insignificant, obscure, minor-league; informal small-time, two-bit.
ANTONYMS important.
▶ noun *the heir to the throne was a minor* **child,** infant, youth, adolescent, teenager, boy, girl; informal kid, kiddie.
ANTONYMS adult.

minstrel ▶ noun historical *a band of gay minstrels* **musician,** singer, balladeer, poet; historical troubadour, jongleur; literary bard.

mint ▶ noun informal *the bank made* ***a mint*** *out of the deal* **a vast sum of money,** a king's ransom, millions, billions; informal a (small) fortune, a tidy sum, a bundle, a pile, big money, big bucks, megabucks.
▶ adjective *in mint condition* **brand new,** pristine, perfect, immaculate, unblemished, undamaged, unmarked, unused, first-class, excellent.
▶ verb 1 *the shilling was minted in 1742* **coin,** stamp, strike, cast, forge, manufacture.
2 *the slogan had been freshly minted* **create,** invent, make up, think up, dream up, coin.

minute[1] ▶ noun 1 *it'll only take a minute* **moment,** short time, little while, second, instant; informal sec, jiff, jiffy, flash.
2 *at that minute, Tony walked in* **point,** point in time, moment, instant, juncture.
3 (**minutes**) *their objection was noted in the minutes* **record**(s), proceedings, log, notes; transcript, summary, résumé.
– PHRASES **in a minute** *the biscuits will be done in a minute* **very soon,** in a moment, in a second, in an instant, in a trice, shortly, any minute (now), in a short time, in (less than) no time, before long, momentarily; informal anon, in two shakes, in a snap; literary ere long. **this minute** *you get in here this minute!* **at once,** immediately, directly, this second, instantly, straightaway, right now, right away, forthwith; informal pronto, straight off, right off, tout de suite. **up-to-the-minute** *stay tuned for up-to-the-minute fashion tips* **latest,** newest, up-to-date, modern, fashionable, smart, chic, stylish, all the rage, in vogue, hip; informal trendy, with it, in, styling, phat. **wait a minute** *if you'll just wait a minute, I'm sure we can get to the bottom of this* **be patient,** wait a moment/second, hold on; informal hang on, hold your horses.

minute[2] ▶ adjective 1 *minute particles* See TINY.
2 *a minute chance of success* **negligible,** slight, infinitesimal, minimal, insignificant, inappreciable. See note at SMALL.
ANTONYMS significant.
3 *minute detail* **exhaustive,** painstaking, meticulous, rigorous, scrupulous, punctilious, detailed, precise, accurate.
ANTONYMS cursory.

minutiae ▶ plural noun *the captain cannot be concerned with the minutiae of shipboard life* **details,** niceties, finer points, particulars, trivia, trivialities.

miracle ▶ noun *his recovery was a blessed miracle* **wonder,** marvel, sensation, phenomenon, supernatural phenomenon, mystery.

miraculous ▶ adjective 1 *the miraculous help of St. Blaise* **supernatural,** preternatural, inexplicable, unaccountable, magical.
2 *a miraculous escape* **amazing,** astounding, remarkable, extraordinary, incredible, unbelievable, sensational, marvelous, phenomenal; informal mind-boggling, mind-blowing, out of this world.

mirage ▶ noun *could it be that her face was just a mirage?* **optical illusion,** hallucination, phantasmagoria, apparition, fantasy, chimera, vision, figment of the/one's imagination; literary phantasm.

mire ▶ noun 1 *it's a mire out there* **swamp,** bog, morass, quagmire, slough; swampland, wetland, marshland.
2 *they were stuck in the mire* **mud,** slime, dirt, filth, muck.
3 *struggling to pull the country out of the mire* **mess,** difficulty, plight, predicament, tight spot, trouble, quandary, muddle; informal jam, fix, pickle, hot water.
▶ verb 1 *Frank's horse got mired in a bog* **bog down,** sink (down).
2 *he has become mired in lawsuits* **entangle,** tangle up, embroil, catch up, mix up, involve.

mirror ▶ noun 1 *a quick look in the mirror* reflecting surface; full-length mirror, hand mirror, side mirror, rear-view mirror; chiefly Brit. looking glass, glass.
2 *his life was a mirror of her own* **reflection,** twin, replica, copy, match, parallel.
▶ verb *her music mirrored the mood of desperation* **reflect,** match, reproduce, imitate, simulate, copy, mimic, echo, parallel, correspond to.

mirth ▶ noun *we could not hold back our mirth* **merriment,** high spirits, cheerfulness, cheeriness, hilarity, glee, laughter, gaiety,

buoyancy, blitheness, euphoria, exhilaration, lightheartedness, joviality, joy, joyfulness, joyousness.
ANTONYMS misery.

misadventure ▶ noun *their journey to the Olympics began as one misadventure after another* **accident,** problem, difficulty, misfortune, mishap; setback, reversal (of fortune), stroke of bad luck, blow, contretemps; failure, disaster, tragedy, calamity, woe, trial, tribulation, catastrophe.

misapprehend ▶ verb *I fear you have misapprehended my intentions* **misunderstand,** misinterpret, misconstrue, misconceive, mistake, misread, get the wrong idea about, take something the wrong way.

misappropriate ▶ verb *he confessed to having misappropriated millions from his clients* **embezzle,** expropriate, steal, thieve, pilfer, pocket, help oneself to, make off with; informal swipe, filch, rip off, snitch, pinch.

misbegotten ▶ adjective **1** *a misbegotten scheme* **ill-conceived,** ill-advised, badly planned, badly thought-out, harebrained.
2 *you misbegotten scoundrel!* **contemptible,** despicable, wretched, miserable, confounded; informal infernal, damned; dated cursed, accursed.
3 archaic *misbegotten children* See ILLEGITIMATE (sense 2).

misbehave ▶ verb *our parents would never let us misbehave in public* **behave badly,** be misbehaved, be naughty, be disobedient, disobey, get up to mischief, get up to no good; be bad-mannered, be rude; informal carry on, act up.

miscalculate ▶ verb *please recheck the bill, as I believe you've miscalculated* **misjudge,** make a mistake (about), calculate wrongly, estimate wrongly, overestimate, underestimate, overvalue, undervalue; misconstrue, misinterpret, misunderstand; go wrong, err, be wide of the mark.

miscarriage ▶ noun **1** *she's had a miscarriage* **stillbirth,** spontaneous abortion.
2 *the miscarriage of the project* **failure,** foundering, ruin, ruination, collapse, breakdown, thwarting, frustration, undoing, nonfulfillment, mismanagement.

miscarry ▶ verb **1** *the shock caused her to miscarry* **lose one's baby,** have a miscarriage, abort, have a spontaneous abortion.
2 *our plan miscarried* **go wrong,** go awry, go amiss, be unsuccessful, be ruined, fail, misfire, abort, founder, come to nothing, fall through, fall flat; informal flop, go up in smoke.
ANTONYMS succeed.

miscellaneous ▶ adjective *he does miscellaneous jobs around the studio* **various,** varied, different, assorted, mixed, sundry, diverse, disparate; diversified, motley, multifarious, ragtag, heterogeneous, eclectic, odd; literary divers.

miscellany ▶ noun *amid the miscellany on these shelves are some rare treasures* **assortment,** mixture, mélange, blend, variety, mixed bag, grab bag, mix, medley, diversity, assemblage, potpourri, pastiche, mishmash, ragbag, salmagundi, gallimaufry, hodgepodge, hash; selection, collection, anthology, treasury.

mischief ▶ noun **1** *the boys are always getting into mischief* **naughtiness,** bad behavior, misbehavior, mischievousness, misconduct, disobedience; pranks, tricks, capers, nonsense, devilry, funny business; informal monkey business, shenanigans, carryings-on.
2 *the mischief in her eyes* **impishness,** roguishness, devilment.

mischievous ▶ adjective **1** *a mischievous child* **naughty,** badly behaved, misbehaving, disobedient, troublesome, full of mischief; rascally, roguish.
ANTONYMS well-behaved.
2 *a mischievous smile* **playful,** teasing, wicked, impish, roguish, arch.

misconception ▶ noun *a popular misconception about science* **misapprehension,** misunderstanding, mistake, error, misinterpretation, misconstruction, misreading, misjudgment, misbelief, miscalculation, false impression, illusion, fallacy, delusion.

misconduct ▶ noun **1** *allegations of misconduct* **wrongdoing,** unlawfulness, lawlessness, crime, felony, criminality, sin, sinfulness; unethical behavior, unprofessionalism, malpractice, negligence, impropriety.
2 *he was reprimanded for his misconduct* **misbehavior,** bad behavior, misdeeds, misdemeanors, disorderly conduct, mischief, naughtiness, rudeness.

misconstrue ▶ verb *Pete's shyness is misconstrued as unfriendliness* **misunderstand,** misinterpret, misconceive, misapprehend, mistake, misread; be mistaken about, get the wrong idea about, get it/someone wrong.

miscreant ▶ noun *the South Street playground has been taken over by a pack of drug-dealing miscreants* **criminal,** culprit, wrongdoer, malefactor, offender, villain, lawbreaker, evildoer, delinquent, hoodlum, reprobate; Law malfeasant.

misdeed ▶ noun See MISDEMEANOR.

misdemeanor ▶ noun *he turned a blind eye to his son's misdemeanors* **wrongdoing,** evil deed, crime, felony; misdeed, misconduct, offense, error, peccadillo, transgression, sin; informal no-no; archaic trespass, misdoing.

miser ▶ noun *one wonders how happy a miser could ever be* **penny-pincher,** Scrooge, pinchpenny; informal skinflint, money-grubber, cheapskate, tightwad, piker.
ANTONYMS spendthrift.

miserable ▶ adjective **1** *I'm too miserable to eat* **unhappy,** sad, sorrowful, dejected, depressed, downcast, downhearted, down, despondent, disconsolate, wretched, glum, gloomy, dismal, melancholy, woebegone, doleful, forlorn, heartbroken; informal blue, down in/at the mouth, down in the dumps.
ANTONYMS happy, contented.
2 *their miserable surroundings* **dreary,** dismal, gloomy, drab, wretched, depressing, grim, cheerless, bleak, desolate; poor, shabby, squalid, seedy, dilapidated; informal flea-bitten.
ANTONYMS luxurious.

3 *miserable weather* **unpleasant,** disagreeable, depressing; wet, rainy, stormy; informal rotten.
ANTONYMS glorious, lovely.
4 *a miserable old grouch* **grumpy,** sullen, gloomy, bad-tempered, ill-tempered, ill-natured, dour, surly, sour, glum, moody, unsociable, saturnine, lugubrious, irritable, churlish, cantankerous, crotchety, cross, crabby, cranky, grouchy, testy, peevish, crusty, waspish.
ANTONYMS cheerful, good-natured.
5 *miserable wages* **inadequate,** meager, scanty, paltry, small, poor, pitiful, niggardly; informal measly, stingy, pathetic; formal exiguous.
ANTONYMS generous, adequate.
6 *all that fuss about a few miserable dollars* **wretched,** confounded; informal blithering, blessed, damned, blasted; dated accursed.

miserly ▶ adjective **1** *his miserly uncle* **mean,** niggardly, close-fisted, parsimonious, penny-pinching, cheeseparing, Scroogelike; informal tightfisted, stingy, tight, mingy, money-grubbing, cheap; formal penurious. See note at ECONOMICAL.
ANTONYMS generous.
2 *the prize is a miserly $300* See MEAGER (sense 1).

misery ▶ noun **1** *periods of intense misery* **unhappiness,** distress, wretchedness, suffering, anguish, anxiety, angst, torment, pain, grief, heartache, heartbreak, despair, despondency, dejection, depression, desolation, gloom, melancholy, melancholia, woe, sadness, sorrow; informal the dumps, the blues; literary dolor.
ANTONYMS contentment, pleasure.
2 *the miseries of war* **affliction,** misfortune, difficulty, problem, ordeal, trouble, hardship, deprivation; pain, sorrow, trial, tribulation, woe.

misfire ▶ verb *the plan had misfired* **go wrong,** go awry, be unsuccessful, fail, founder, fall through, fall flat; backfire; informal flop, go up in smoke.

misfit ▶ noun *they prided themselves on being the class misfits* **nonconformist,** eccentric, maverick, individualist, square peg in a round hole; informal oddball, odd duck, weirdo, freak, screwball.

misfortune ▶ noun *the loss of their home in the flood was only the first of several misfortunes* **problem,** difficulty, setback, trouble, adversity, stroke of bad luck, reversal (of fortune), misadventure, mishap, blow, failure, accident, disaster, catastrophe; sorrow, misery, woe, trial, tribulation, tragedy.

misgiving ▶ noun *we finally gave our consent to the marriage, but we still had misgivings* **qualm,** doubt, reservation; suspicion; (**misgivings**) distrust, mistrust, lack of confidence, second thoughts; trepidation, skepticism, unease, uneasiness, anxiety, apprehension, disquiet. See note at QUALMS.

misguided ▶ adjective **1** *the policy is misguided* **erroneous,** fallacious, unsound, misplaced, misconceived, ill-advised, ill-considered, ill-judged, ill-founded, inappropriate, unwise, injudicious, imprudent.
2 *you are quite misguided* **misinformed,** misled, wrong, mistaken, deluded, confused; informal off base.

mishandle ▶ verb **1** *the officer mishandled the situation* **bungle,** fumble, make a mess of, mismanage, spoil, ruin, wreck; informal **botch,** make a hash of, mess up, screw up, fluff.
2 *he mishandled his dog* **bully,** persecute, ill-treat, mistreat, maltreat, manhandle, abuse, knock around, hit, beat; informal beat up.
3 *the equipment could be dangerous if mishandled* **misuse,** abuse, handle/treat roughly.

mishap ▶ noun *even a minor mishap can have serious consequences* **accident,** trouble, problem, difficulty, setback, adversity, misfortune, blow; failure, disaster, tragedy, catastrophe, calamity, mischance, misadventure.

mishmash ▶ noun *a mishmash of colors and patterns* **jumble,** confusion, ragbag, patchwork, farrago, assortment, medley, miscellany, mixture, mélange, blend, mix, potpourri, conglomeration, bricolage, gallimaufry, salmagundi, hodgepodge, hash.

misinform ▶ verb *we're sorry to tell you that you've been deliberately misinformed* **mislead,** misguide, give wrong information, delude, take in, deceive, lie to, hoodwink; informal lead up the garden path, take for a ride, give someone a bum steer.

misinterpret ▶ verb *his proposal was misinterpreted* **misunderstand,** misconceive, misconstrue, misapprehend, mistake, misread; confuse, be mistaken, get the wrong idea, take amiss.

misjudge ▶ verb *she misjudged her opponent's stamina* **get the wrong idea about,** get wrong, judge incorrectly, estimate wrongly, be wrong about, miscalculate, misread; overestimate, underestimate, overvalue, undervalue, underrate.

mislay ▶ verb *I've mislaid my keys* **lose,** misplace, put in the wrong place, be unable to find, forget the whereabouts of.
ANTONYMS find.

mislead ▶ verb *Caroline deliberately misled her* **deceive,** delude, take in, lie to, fool, hoodwink, throw off the scent, pull the wool over someone's eyes, misguide, misinform, give wrong information to; informal lead up the garden path, take for a ride, give someone a bum steer.

misleading ▶ adjective *a leaflet full of misleading statements* **deceptive,** confusing, deceiving, equivocal, ambiguous, fallacious, specious, spurious, false.

mismanage ▶ verb *the accountant had mismanaged their personal finances* **bungle,** make a mess of, mishandle, spoil, ruin, wreck; informal botch, make a hash of, mess up, screw up, fluff.

misogynist ▶ noun *he apparently deserved his reputation as a misogynist* **woman-hater**; antifeminist, (male) chauvinist, sexist; informal male chauvinist pig.

misplace ▶ verb *he had misplaced the tickets* **lose,** mislay, put in the wrong place, be unable to find, forget the whereabouts of.
ANTONYMS find.

misprint ▶ noun *the book is full of misprints*

mistake, error, typographical error, erratum; informal typo.

misquote ▶ verb *my original statement has been misquoted* **misreport,** misrepresent, misstate, take/quote out of context, distort, twist, slant, bias, put a spin on, falsify.

misrepresent ▶ verb *you are misrepresenting the views of the government* **give a false account,** misreport, misquote, quote/take out of context, misinterpret, put a spin on, skew, warp, falsify, distort, misstate, exaggerate.

miss[1] ▶ verb **1** *the shot missed her by inches* **fail to hit,** be/go wide of, fall short of.
ANTONYMS hit.
2 *Mandy missed the ball* **fail to catch,** drop, fumble, bobble, fluff, flub, mishandle, screw up.
ANTONYMS catch.
3 *I've missed my bus* **be too late for,** fail to catch/get.
ANTONYMS catch.
4 *I missed what you said* **fail to hear,** mishear.
5 *you can't miss the station* **fail to see/notice,** overlook.
ANTONYMS see, notice.
6 *she never missed a class* **fail to attend,** be absent from, play truant from, cut, skip.
ANTONYMS attend.
7 *don't miss this exciting opportunity!* **let slip,** fail to take advantage of, let go, let pass, pass up.
8 *I left early to miss rush hour* **avoid,** beat, evade, escape, dodge, sidestep, elude, circumvent, steer clear of, find a way around, bypass.
9 *she missed him when he was away* **pine for,** yearn for, ache for, long for, long to see.
▶ noun *one hit and three misses* **failure,** omission, slip, blunder, error, mistake.

miss[2] ▶ noun *a lovely miss* **young woman,** young lady, girl, schoolgirl, missy; Scottish lass, lassie; French mademoiselle; informal girlie, chick, doll, gal; literary maiden, maid, damsel; archaic wench.

misshapen ▶ adjective *his misshapen feet* **deformed,** malformed, distorted, crooked, twisted, warped, out of shape, bent, asymmetrical, irregular, misproportioned, ill-proportioned, disfigured, dysmorphic, grotesque.

missing ▶ adjective **1** *his wallet is missing* **lost,** mislaid, misplaced, absent, gone (astray), gone AWOL, unaccounted for; disappeared, vanished.
ANTONYMS at hand.
2 *passion was missing from her life* **absent,** not present, lacking, wanting.
ANTONYMS present.

mission ▶ noun **1** *a mercy mission to Africa* **assignment,** commission, expedition, journey, trip, undertaking, operation; task, job, labor, work, duty, charge, trust.
2 *her mission in life* **vocation,** calling, goal, aim, quest, purpose, function, life's work.
3 *a trade mission* **delegation,** deputation, commission, legation.
4 *a teacher in a mission* **missionary post,** missionary station, missionary school.
5 *a bombing mission* **sortie,** operation, raid.

missionary ▶ noun *he died in Manila, where he had been a missionary* **evangelist,** apostle, proselytizer, preacher, minister, priest; historical black robe.

missive ▶ noun *take this missive to Lieutenant Baxter* **message,** communication, letter, word, note, email, memorandum, line, communiqué, dispatch, news; informal memo; formal epistle; literary tidings.

misspent ▶ adjective *our misspent youth* **wasted,** dissipated, squandered, thrown away, frittered away, misused, misapplied.

mist ▶ noun *the mist was clearing* **haze,** fog, smog, murk, cloud, drizzle.

mistake ▶ noun *I assumed it had been a mistake* **error,** fault, inaccuracy, omission, slip, blunder, miscalculation, misunderstanding, oversight, misinterpretation, gaffe, faux pas, solecism; informal slip-up, boo-boo, blooper, boner, goof, flub.
▶ verb **1** *did I mistake your meaning?* **misunderstand,** misinterpret, get wrong, misconstrue, misread.
2 *children often* **mistake** *vitamin pills* **for** *candies* **confuse with,** mix up with, take for, misinterpret as.
– PHRASES **be mistaken** *I'm afraid you are mistaken—I've never been here before* **be wrong,** be in error, be under a misapprehension, be misinformed, be misguided; informal be barking up the wrong tree. **make a mistake** *he admits he's made a mistake* **go wrong,** err, make an error, blunder, miscalculate; informal slip up, make a boo-boo, drop the ball, goof (up).

CHOOSE THE RIGHT WORD

mistake, blooper, blunder, error, faux pas, goof, slip

It would be a **mistake** to argue with your boss the day before he or she evaluates your performance, but to forget an important step in an assigned task would be an **error**. Although these nouns are used interchangeably in many contexts, a *mistake* is usually caused by poor judgment or a disregard of rules or principles (*it was a mistake not to tell the truth at the outset*), while an *error* implies an unintentional deviation from standards of accuracy or right conduct (*a mathematical error*). A **blunder** is a careless, stupid, or blatant mistake involving behavior or judgment; it suggests awkwardness or ignorance on the part of the person who makes it (*his blunder that ruined the evening*). A **slip** is a minor and usually accidental mistake that is the result of haste or carelessness (*her slip of the tongue spoiled the surprise*), while a **faux pas** (which means "false step" in French) is an embarrassing breach of etiquette (*it was a faux pas to have meat at the table when so many of the guests were vegetarians*). **Goofs** and **bloopers** are humorous mistakes. A *blooper* is usually a mix-up in speech, while to *goof* is to make a careless error that is honestly admitted (*she shrugged her shoulders and said, "I goofed!"*).

mistaken ▶ adjective *they were acting on mistaken information* **wrong,** erroneous, inaccurate, incorrect, false, fallacious, unfounded, misguided, misinformed.
ANTONYMS correct.

mistakenly ▶ adverb **1** *she mistakenly assumed that she knew him* **wrongly,** in error, erroneously, incorrectly, falsely, fallaciously, inaccurately.
ANTONYMS correctly.
2 *Matt mistakenly opened the letter* **by accident,** accidentally, inadvertently, unintentionally, unwittingly, unconsciously, by mistake.
ANTONYMS intentionally.

mistreat ▶ verb *he's in prison for mistreating his children* **ill-treat,** maltreat, abuse, knock about/around, hit, beat, strike, molest, injure, harm, hurt; misuse, mishandle; informal beat up, rough up, mess up, kick around.

mistress ▶ noun *her husband's mistress turned out to be one of her friends* **lover,** girlfriend, kept woman; courtesan, concubine, hetaera; informal the other woman; archaic paramour.

mistrust ▶ verb **1** *I mistrust his motives* **be suspicious of,** be mistrustful of, be distrustful of, be skeptical of, be wary of, be chary of, distrust, have doubts about, have misgivings about, have reservations about, suspect.
2 *don't mistrust your impulses* **question,** challenge, doubt, have no confidence in, have no faith in.
▶ noun **1** *mistrust of foreigners was widespread* **suspicion,** distrust, doubt, misgivings, wariness.
2 *their mistrust of David's competence* **questioning,** lack of confidence in, lack of faith in, doubt about.

mistrustful ▶ adjective *Sheila's unlikely stories made him even more mistrustful* **suspicious,** chary, wary, distrustful, doubtful, dubious, uneasy, skeptical, leery.

misty ▶ adjective **1** *misty weather* **hazy,** foggy, cloudy; smoggy.
ANTONYMS clear.
2 *a misty outline* **blurry,** fuzzy, blurred, clouded, dim, indistinct, unclear, vague.
ANTONYMS sharp, distinct.
3 *misty memories* **vague,** unclear, indefinite, hazy, nebulous.
ANTONYMS clear.

misunderstand ▶ verb *she misunderstood his motives* **misapprehend,** misinterpret, misconstrue, misconceive, mistake, misread; be mistaken, get the wrong idea, receive a false impression; informal be barking up the wrong tree, miss the boat.

misunderstanding ▶ noun **1** *a fundamental misunderstanding of juvenile crime* **misinterpretation,** misconstruction, misreading, misapprehension, misconception, the wrong idea, false impression.
2 *we have had some misunderstandings* **disagreement,** difference (of opinion), dispute, falling-out, quarrel, argument, altercation, squabble, wrangle, row, clash; informal spat, scrap, tiff, rhubarb.

misuse ▶ verb **1** *misusing public funds* **put to wrong use,** misemploy, embezzle, use fraudulently; abuse, squander, waste.
2 *she had been misused by her husband* See MISTREAT.
▶ noun **1** *a misuse of company assets* **wrong use,** embezzlement, fraud; squandering, waste.
2 *the misuse of drugs* **illegal use,** abuse.

mitigate ▶ verb *the worst symptoms have been mitigated* **alleviate,** reduce, diminish, lessen, weaken, lighten, attenuate, take the edge off, allay, ease, assuage, palliate, relieve, tone down. See note at ALLEVIATE.
ANTONYMS aggravate.

mitigating ▶ adjective *if not for mitigating circumstances, he would have been convicted* **extenuating,** justificatory, justifying, vindicating, qualifying; face-saving; formal exculpatory.

mix ▶ verb **1** *mix all the ingredients together* **blend,** mix up, mingle, combine, put together, jumble; fuse, unite, unify, join, amalgamate, incorporate, meld, marry, coalesce, homogenize, intermingle, intermix; technical admix; literary commingle.
ANTONYMS separate.
2 *she mixes with all sorts* **associate,** socialize, fraternize, keep company, consort; mingle, circulate, rub elbows; informal hang out/around, hobnob, network.
3 *we just don't mix* **be compatible,** get along/on, be in harmony, see eye to eye, agree; informal hit it off, click, be on the same wavelength.
▶ noun *a mix of ancient and modern* **mixture,** blend, mingling, combination, compound, fusion, alloy, union, amalgamation; medley, mélange, collection, selection, assortment, variety, mixed bag, grab bag, miscellany, potpourri, jumble, ragbag, patchwork, bricolage, farrago, gallimaufry, salmagundi, hodgepodge.
– PHRASES **mix up 1** *mix up the ingredients* See MIX (sense 1 of the verb). **2** *I mixed up the dates* **confuse,** get confused, muddle (up), get muddled up, mistake. **mixed up in** *how did she get mixed up in a car-theft ring?* **involved in,** embroiled in, caught up in.

mixed ▶ adjective **1** *a mixed collection* **assorted,** varied, variegated, miscellaneous, disparate, diverse, diversified, motley, sundry, jumbled, heterogeneous.
ANTONYMS homogeneous.
2 *mixed breeds* **hybrid,** cross-bred, interbred, mongrel, half-caste.
ANTONYMS pure.
3 *mixed reactions* **ambivalent,** equivocal, contradictory, conflicting, confused, muddled.
ANTONYMS unequivocal.

mixed up ▶ adjective informal *sorry, I'm still a little mixed up* **confused,** befuddled, bemused, bewildered, muddled; disturbed, neurotic, unbalanced; informal hung up, messed up, at sea.

mixer ▶ noun **1** *a kitchen mixer* **blender,** food processor, beater; churn.
2 *he attended a mixer* **gathering,** social, function, get-together, meet-and-greet.

mixture ▶ noun **1** *the pudding mixture* **blend,** mix, brew, combination, concoction; composition, compound, alloy, amalgam.

2 *a strange mixture of people* **assortment,** miscellany, medley, mélange, blend, variety, mixed bag, grab bag, mix, diversity, collection, selection, potpourri, mishmash, ragbag, patchwork, bricolage, farrago, gallimaufry, salmagundi, hodgepodge, hash.
3 *genetically, the animal is a mixture* **cross,** cross-breed, mongrel, hybrid, half-breed, half-caste.

mix-up ▶ noun *there was some sort of mix-up in the birth records* **confusion,** muddle, misunderstanding, mistake, error; informal screw-up.

moan ▶ noun **1** *moans of pain* **groan,** wail, whimper, sob, cry.
2 *the moan of the wind* **sigh,** murmur, sough.
3 informal *there were moans about the delay* **complaint,** complaining, grouse, grousing, grumble, grumbling, whine, whining, carping; informal gripe, griping, grouching, bellyaching, bitching, beef, beefing.
▶ verb **1** *he moaned in agony* **groan,** wail, whimper, sob, cry.
2 *the wind moaned in the trees* **sigh,** murmur, sough.
3 informal *you're always moaning about the weather* **complain,** grouse, grumble, whine, carp; informal gripe, grouch, bellyache, bitch, beef, kvetch.

mob ▶ noun **1** *troops dispersed the mob* **crowd,** horde, multitude, rabble, mass, throng, group, gang, gathering, assemblage.
2 (**Mob**) *he was hiding from the Mob* **Mafia,** Cosa Nostra, Camorra.
3 *the mob was excluded from political life* **common people,** masses, rank and file, commonality, third estate, plebeians, proletariat; hoi polloi, lower classes, rabble, riffraff, great unwashed; informal proles, plebs.
▶ verb **1** *the band's lead singer was mobbed when he visited Vancouver* **surround,** swarm, besiege, jostle.
2 *reporters mobbed her hotel* **crowd (into),** fill, pack, throng, press into, squeeze into.

mobile ▶ adjective **1** *both patients are mobile* **able to move (around),** moving, walking; Zoology motile; Medicine ambulant.
ANTONYMS motionless.
2 *a mobile library* **traveling,** transportable, portable, movable; itinerant, peripatetic.
ANTONYMS stationary.
3 *highly mobile young people* **adaptable,** flexible, versatile, adjustable.
ANTONYMS static.

mobilize ▶ verb **1** *the government mobilized the troops* **marshal,** deploy, muster, rally, call up, assemble, mass, organize, prepare.
2 *mobilizing support for the party* **generate,** arouse, awaken, excite, incite, provoke, foment, prompt, stimulate, stir up, galvanize, encourage, inspire, whip up; literary enkindle.

mock ▶ verb **1** *they mocked her accent* **ridicule,** jeer at, sneer at, deride, scorn, make fun of, laugh at, scoff at, tease, taunt; informal josh, rag on, pull/jerk/yank someone's chain.
2 *they mocked the way he speaks* **parody,** ape, take off, satirize, lampoon, imitate, impersonate, mimic; informal send up. See note at IMITATE.
▶ adjective *mock leather* **imitation,** artificial, man-made, simulated, synthetic, ersatz, fake, reproduction, dummy, sham, false, faux, spurious, bogus, counterfeit, inauthentic, pseudo; informal pretend, phony.
ANTONYMS genuine.

mockery ▶ noun **1** *the mockery in his voice* **ridicule,** derision, jeering, sneering, contempt, scorn, scoffing, teasing, taunting, sarcasm.
2 *the trial was a mockery* **travesty,** charade, farce, parody.

model ▶ noun **1** *a working model* **replica,** copy, representation, mock-up, dummy, imitation, duplicate, reproduction, facsimile.
2 *the Canadian model of health care* **prototype,** stereotype, archetype, type, version; mold, template, framework, pattern, design, blueprint.
3 *she was a model of patience* **ideal,** paragon, perfect example/specimen; perfection, acme, epitome, nonpareil, crème de la crème.
4 *a runway model* **fashion model,** supermodel, mannequin.
5 *an artist's model* **subject,** poser, sitter.
6 *the latest model of car* **version,** type, design, variety, kind, sort.
▶ adjective **1** *model trains* **replica, toy,** miniature, dummy, imitation, duplicate, reproduction, facsimile.
2 *model farms* **prototypical,** prototypal, archetypal.
3 *a model teacher* **ideal,** perfect, exemplary, classic, flawless, faultless.

CHOOSE THE RIGHT WORD

model, archetype, example, ideal, paradigm, pattern, prototype

Most parents try to set a good **example** for their children, although they may end up setting a bad one. An *example*, in other words, is a precedent for imitation, either good or bad. Most parents would do better to provide a **model** for their children, which refers to a person or thing that is to be followed or imitated because of its excellence in conduct or character. *Model* also connotes a physical shape to be copied closely (*a ship's model, a model airplane*). Not all children regard their parents as an **ideal** to which they aspire, a word that suggests an imagined perfection or a standard based upon a set of desirable qualities (*the ideal gentleman; the ideal of what an artist should be*); but young people's lives often end up following the **pattern** established by their parents, meaning that their lives follow the same basic configuration or design. While **prototype** and **archetype** are often used interchangeably, they really mean quite different things. An *archetype* is a perfect and unchanging form that existing things or people can approach but never duplicate (*the archetype of a mother*), while a *prototype* is an early, usually unrefined version of something that later versions reflect but may depart from (*a prototype* for a hydrogen-fueled car). **Paradigm** can refer to an example that serves as a model, but today its use is primarily confined to a grammatical context, where it means a set giving all the various forms of a word, such as the conjugation of a verb.

moderate ▶ adjective **1** *moderate success* **average,** modest, medium, middling, ordinary, common, commonplace, everyday, workaday; tolerable, passable, adequate, fair; mediocre, indifferent, unexceptional, unremarkable, run-of-the-mill; informal OK, so-so, 'comme ci, comme ça', fair-to-middling, plain-vanilla, no great shakes, not up to much.
ANTONYMS great, massive.
2 *moderate prices* **reasonable,** acceptable; inexpensive, low, fair, modest.
ANTONYMS outrageous, unreasonable.
3 *moderate views* **middle-of-the-road,** nonextreme, nonradical, centrist.
ANTONYMS extreme.
4 *moderate behavior* **restrained,** controlled, sober; tolerant, lenient.
ANTONYMS unreasonable.
▶ verb **1** *the wind has moderated somewhat* **die down,** abate, let up, calm down, lessen, decrease, diminish; recede, weaken, subside.
ANTONYMS increase.
2 *you can help to moderate her anger* **curb,** control, check, temper, restrain, subdue; repress, tame, lessen, decrease, lower, reduce, diminish, alleviate, allay, appease, assuage, ease, soothe, calm, tone down.
ANTONYMS exacerbate, aggravate.
3 *the panel was moderated by one of the writers* **chair,** take the chair of, preside over.

moderately ▶ adverb *a moderately successful farmer* **somewhat,** quite, rather, fairly, reasonably, comparatively, relatively, to some extent; tolerably, passably, adequately; informal pretty.

moderation ▶ noun **1** *he urged them to show moderation* **self-restraint,** restraint, self-control, self-discipline; temperance, leniency, fairness. See note at ABSTINENCE.
2 *a moderation of their confrontational style* **relaxation,** easing (off), reduction, abatement, weakening, slackening, tempering, softening, diminution, diminishing, lessening; decline, modulation, modification, mitigation, allaying; informal letup.
– PHRASES **in moderation** *I quit drinking because I wasn't able to drink in moderation* **in moderate quantities/amounts,** within (sensible) limits; moderately.

modern ▶ adjective **1** *modern times* **present-day,** contemporary, present, current, twenty-first-century, latter-day, modern-day, recent.
ANTONYMS past.
2 *her clothes are very modern* **fashionable,** in fashion, in style, in vogue, up to date, all the rage, trend-setting, stylish, styling/stylin', voguish, modish, chic, à la mode; the latest, new, newest, newfangled, modernistic, advanced; informal trendy, cool, in, with it, now, hip, phat, happening, kicky, tony, fly.
ANTONYMS out of date, old-fashioned.

modernize ▶ verb **1** *they are modernizing their manufacturing facilities* **update,** bring up to date, streamline, overhaul; renovate, remodel, refashion, revamp.
2 *we must modernize to survive* **get up to date,** move with the times, innovate; informal get in the swim, get with it, go with the flow.

modest ▶ adjective **1** *she was modest about her poetry* **self-effacing,** self-deprecating, humble, unpretentious, unassuming, unostentatious; shy, bashful, self-conscious, diffident, reserved, reticent, coy.
ANTONYMS conceited, boastful.
2 *modest success* **moderate,** fair, limited, tolerable, passable, adequate, satisfactory, acceptable, unexceptional.
ANTONYMS great, runaway.
3 *a modest house* **small,** ordinary, simple, plain, humble, inexpensive, unostentatious, unpretentious.
ANTONYMS grandiose, grand.
4 *her modest dress* **decorous,** decent, seemly, demure, proper.
ANTONYMS flamboyant.

modesty ▶ noun **1** *Hannah's modesty cloaks many talents* **self-effacement,** humility, unpretentiousness; shyness, bashfulness, self-consciousness, reserve, reticence, timidity.
2 *the modesty of his aspirations* **limited scope,** moderation.
3 *the modesty of his home* **unpretentiousness,** simplicity, plainness.

modicum ▶ noun *I'd like to leave while I still have a modicum of my self-respect* **small amount,** particle, speck, fragment, scrap, crumb, grain, morsel, shred, dash, drop, pinch, soupçon, jot, iota, whit, atom, smattering, scintilla, hint, suggestion, tinge; informal smidgen, tad.

modification ▶ noun **1** *the design is undergoing modification* **alteration,** adjustment, change, adaptation, refinement, revision.
2 *some minor modifications were made* **revision,** refinement, improvement, amendment, adaptation, adjustment, change, alteration.
3 *the modification of his views* **softening,** moderation, tempering, qualification.

modify ▶ verb **1** *their economic policy has been modified* **alter,** change, adjust, adapt, amend, revise, reshape, refashion, restyle, revamp, rework, remodel, refine; informal tweak, doctor.
2 *he modified his more extreme views* **moderate,** revise, temper, soften, tone down, qualify.

modulate ▶ verb **1** *the cells modulate the body's response* **regulate,** adjust, set, modify, moderate.
2 *she modulated her voice* **adjust,** change the tone of, temper, soften.

mogul ▶ noun *Hollywood movie moguls* **magnate,** tycoon, VIP, notable, personage, baron, captain, king, lord, grandee, nabob; informal bigwig, big shot, big cheese, top dog, top banana, big kahuna, big enchilada.

moist ▶ adjective **1** *the air was moist* **damp,** dampish, steamy, humid, muggy, clammy, dank, wet, wettish, soggy, sweaty, sticky.
ANTONYMS dry.
2 *a moist fruitcake* **succulent,** juicy, soft.

ANTONYMS dry.
3 *her eyes grew moist* **tearful,** watery, misty, dewy.

moisten ▶ verb *they moisten the towels with almond-scented hot water* **dampen,** wet, damp, water, humidify; literary bedew.

moisture ▶ noun *too much moisture is bad for the tiny seedlings* **wetness,** wet, water, liquid, condensation, dew, steam, vapor, dampness, damp, humidity, clamminess, mugginess, dankness, wateriness.

mold ▶ noun *walls stained with mold* **mildew,** fungus, dry rot, must, moldiness, mustiness.

moldy ▶ adjective *everything in the cellar was moldy* **mildewed,** mildewy, musty, moldering, fusty; decaying, decayed, rotting, rotten, bad, spoiled, far gone, decomposing.

mole ▶ noun **1** *the mole on his left cheek* **mark,** birthmark, freckle, blotch, spot, blemish, beauty spot, beauty mark.
2 *an undercover mole* **spy,** agent, secret agent, undercover agent, operative, plant, infiltrator, sleeper, informant, informer; informal spook; archaic intelligencer.

molest ▶ verb **1** *the crowd molested the police* **harass,** harry, hassle, pester, bother, annoy, beset, persecute, torment; informal roust.
2 *he molested a ten-year-old boy* **(sexually) abuse,** (sexually) assault, interfere with, rape, violate; informal grope, paw, fondle; literary ravish. See note at **ATTACK**.

mollify ▶ verb **1** *they tried to mollify the protesters* **appease,** placate, pacify, conciliate, soothe, calm (down). See note at **PACIFY**.
ANTONYMS enrage.
2 *mollifying the fears of the public* **allay,** assuage, alleviate, mitigate, ease, reduce, moderate, temper, tone down, soften; informal blunt.
ANTONYMS inflame.

mollycoddle ▶ verb *his parents mollycoddle him* **pamper,** cosset, coddle, spoil, indulge, overindulge, pet, baby, nanny, wait on hand and foot.

moment ▶ noun **1** *he thought for a moment* **little while,** short time, bit, minute, instant, second, split second; informal sec.
2 *the moment they met* **point (in time),** time, hour.
3 formal *issues of little moment* **importance,** import, significance, consequence, note, weight, concern, interest.
– PHRASES **in a moment** *the show will start in a moment* **very soon,** in a minute, in a second, in a trice, shortly, any minute (now), in the twinkling of an eye, in (less than) no time, in no time at all, momentarily; informal in a jiff, in a jiffy, in two shakes (of a lamb's tail), in the blink of an eye, in a snap, in a heartbeat, in a flash; literary ere long.

momentarily ▶ adverb **1** *he paused momentarily* **briefly,** fleetingly, for a moment, for a second, for an instant.
2 *my husband will be here momentarily* See **IN A MOMENT**.

momentary ▶ adjective *a momentary lapse in power* **brief,** short, short-lived, fleeting, passing, transient, transitory, ephemeral; literary evanescent.
ANTONYMS lengthy.

momentous ▶ adjective *a momentous decision* **important,** significant, historic, portentous, critical, crucial, life-and-death, decisive, pivotal, consequential, of consequence, far-reaching, impactful, earth-shattering, earth-shaking; formal of moment.
ANTONYMS insignificant.

momentum ▶ noun *we gained momentum going down the Killingworth hill* **impetus,** energy, force, power, strength, thrust, speed, velocity.

monarch ▶ noun *Elizabeth II has been Britain's reigning monarch since 1952* **sovereign,** ruler, the Crown, crowned head, potentate; king, queen, emperor, empress, prince, princess.

monastery ▶ noun *the monastery was temporarily occupied by Nazis* **religious community**; friary, abbey, priory, nunnery, cloister, convent.

monastic ▶ adjective **1** *a monastic community* **cloistered,** cloistral, claustral.
2 *a monastic existence* **austere,** ascetic, simple, solitary, monkish, celibate, quiet, cloistered, sequestered, secluded, reclusive, hermitlike, hermitic, incommunicado.

monetary ▶ adjective *her sharp monetary instincts got us through the recession in very good shape* **financial,** fiscal, pecuniary, money, cash, economic, budgetary. See note at **FINANCIAL**.

money ▶ noun **1** *have you got money for the train fare?* **cash,** hard cash, ready money; the means, the wherewithal, funds, capital, finances, (filthy) lucre; coins, change, specie, silver, currency, bills, (bank) notes; informal dough, bread, bucks, loot, greenbacks, moola, dinero, shekels, mazuma; archaic pelf.
2 *she married him for his money* **wealth,** riches, fortune, affluence, assets, liquid assets, resources, means.
3 *the money here is better* **pay,** salary, wages, remuneration; formal emolument.
– PHRASES **for my money** *for my money, they are the better team* **in my opinion,** to my mind, in my view, as I see it, personally, in my estimation, in my judgment, if you ask me. **in the money** informal *we're finally in the money* See **MONEYED**.

moneyed ▶ adjective *she's got two brothers—one is broke and the other is moneyed* **rich,** wealthy, affluent, well-to-do, well off, prosperous, in clover, opulent, of means, of substance; informal in the money, rolling in it, loaded, stinking/filthy rich, well-heeled, made of money.
ANTONYMS poor.

money-making ▶ adjective *it wasn't the money-making enterprise we had hoped it would be* **profitable,** profit-making, remunerative, lucrative, successful, financially rewarding.
ANTONYMS loss-making.

mongrel ▶ noun *a curly-tailed mongrel* **cross-breed,** cross, mixed breed, half-breed; cur, mutt; informal Heinz 57.
▶ adjective *a mongrel bitch* **cross-bred,** of mixed breed, half-breed, interbred, mixed.

ANTONYMS pedigree.

monitor ▶ noun **1** *a fetal monitor* **detector,** scanner, recorder; listening device; security camera.
2 *UN monitors* **observer,** watchdog, overseer, supervisor.
3 *a computer monitor* **screen,** video display terminal, VDT.
▶ verb *his movements were closely monitored* **observe,** watch, track, keep an eye on, keep under observation, keep watch on, keep under surveillance, record, note, oversee; informal keep tabs on.

monk ▶ noun *the monks teach a class in organic gardening* brother, religious, cenobite, contemplative, mendicant; friar; abbot, prior; novice, oblate, postulant; lama, marabout.

monkey ▶ noun **1** *the monkeys scampered up the trees* **simian,** primate, ape.
2 *you little monkey!* See RASCAL.
– PHRASES **make a monkey (out) of** *she made a monkey out of Clark in front of his friends* **make someone look foolish,** make a fool of, make a laughingstock of, ridicule, make fun of, poke fun at. **monkey with** *don't monkey with those switches* **tamper with,** fiddle with, interfere with, meddle with, tinker with, play with; informal mess with.

monkey business ▶ noun informal *they better not try any monkey business when Ms. Bergdahl is around* **mischief,** misbehavior, mischievousness, devilry, devilment, tomfoolery; dishonesty, trickery, chicanery, skulduggery; informal shenanigans, funny business, hanky-panky, monkeyshines.

monologue ▶ noun *Letterman's nightly monologue* **soliloquy,** speech, address, lecture, sermon, homily; formal oration.

monopolize ▶ verb **1** *the company has monopolized the market* **corner,** control, take over, gain control/dominance over; archaic engross.
2 *he monopolized the conversation* **dominate,** take over; informal hog.
3 *she monopolized the guest of honor* **take up all the attention of,** keep to oneself; informal tie up.

monotonous ▶ adjective **1** *a monotonous job* **tedious,** boring, dull, uninteresting, unexciting, wearisome, tiresome, repetitive, repetitious, unvarying, unchanging, unvaried, humdrum, ho-hum, routine, mechanical, mind-numbing, soul-destroying; colorless, featureless, dreary; informal deadly, samey, dullsville.
ANTONYMS interesting.
2 *a monotonous voice* **toneless,** flat, uninflected, soporific.

monotony ▶ noun **1** *the monotony of everyday life* **tedium,** tediousness, lack of variety, dullness, boredom, repetitiveness, uniformity, routineness, wearisomeness, tiresomeness; lack of excitement, uneventfulness, dreariness, colorlessness, featurelessness; informal deadliness.
2 *the monotony of her voice* **tonelessness,** flatness.

monster ▶ noun **1** *legendary sea monsters* **fabulous creature,** mythical creature.
2 *her husband is a monster* **brute,** fiend, beast, devil, demon, barbarian, savage, animal; informal swine, pig.
3 *the boy's a little monster* **rascal,** imp, monkey, wretch, devil; informal horror, scamp, scalawag, tyke, varmint, hellion; archaic scapegrace, rapscallion.
4 *he's a monster of a man* **giant,** mammoth, colossus, leviathan, titan; informal jumbo.
▶ adjective informal *a monster truck* See HUGE.

monstrosity ▶ noun **1** *a concrete monstrosity* **eyesore,** blot on the landscape, excrescence, horror.
2 *a biological monstrosity* **mutant,** mutation, freak (of nature), monster, abortion.

monstrous ▶ adjective **1** *a monstrous creature* **grotesque,** hideous, ugly, ghastly, gruesome, horrible, horrific, horrifying, grisly, disgusting, repulsive, repellent, dreadful, frightening, terrifying, malformed, misshapen.
ANTONYMS lovely.
2 *a monstrous tidal wave* See HUGE.
3 *monstrous acts of violence* **appalling,** heinous, egregious, evil, wicked, abominable, terrible, horrible, dreadful, vile, outrageous, shocking, disgraceful; unspeakable, despicable, vicious, savage, barbaric, barbarous, inhuman, beastly.
ANTONYMS admirable, good.

monument ▶ noun **1** *a stone monument* **memorial,** statue, pillar, column, obelisk, cross; cenotaph, tomb, mausoleum, shrine.
2 *a monument was placed over the grave* **gravestone,** headstone, tombstone, grave marker, plaque.
3 *a monument to a past era of aviation* **testament,** record, reminder, remembrance, memorial, commemoration.

monumental ▶ adjective **1** *a monumental task* **huge,** great, enormous, gigantic, massive, colossal, mammoth, immense, tremendous, mighty, stupendous.
2 *a monumental error in judgment* **terrible,** dreadful, awful, colossal, staggering, huge, enormous, unforgivable, egregious.
3 *her monumental achievement* **impressive,** striking, outstanding, remarkable, magnificent, majestic, stupendous, ambitious, large-scale, grand, awe-inspiring, important, significant, distinguished, memorable, immortal.

mood ▶ noun **1** *she's in a good mood* **frame/state of mind,** humor, temper; disposition, spirit, tenor.
2 *he's obviously in **a mood*** **a bad mood,** a (bad) temper, a sulk, a fit of pique; low spirits, the doldrums, the blues, a blue funk; informal the dumps.
3 *the mood of the film* **atmosphere,** feeling, spirit, ambience, aura, character, tenor, flavor, feel, tone.
– PHRASES **in the mood** *I don't like to go to the casino unless I'm in the mood* **in the right frame of mind,** wanting to, inclined to, disposed to, minded to, eager to, willing to.

moody ▶ adjective *how can she live with that moody man?* **temperamental,** emotional, volatile, capricious, changeable, mercurial; sullen, sulky, morose, glum, depressed, dejected, despondent, doleful, dour, sour, saturnine, manic-depressive; informal blue, down

in the dumps, down in/at the mouth.
ANTONYMS even-tempered, cheerful.

moon ▶ noun *viewing the eclipse of the moon* **satellite.**
▶ verb 1 *stop* ***mooning about*** *waste time,* loaf, idle, mope; informal lollygag.
2 *he's mooning over her photograph* **mope,** pine, brood, daydream, fantasize, be in a reverie.
– PHRASES **many moons ago** informal *we stayed at that hotel many moons ago* **a long time ago,** ages ago, years ago. **once in a blue moon** informal *Donnie brings me flowers once in a blue moon* **hardly ever,** scarcely ever, rarely, very seldom. **over the moon** informal *I'm over the moon just thinking about our upcoming cruise* See ECSTATIC.

moor ▶ verb *a boat was moored to the quay* **tie up,** secure, make fast, fix firmly, anchor, berth, dock.

moot ▶ adjective *a moot point* **debatable,** open to discussion/question, arguable, questionable, at issue, open to doubt, disputable, controversial, contentious, disputed, unresolved, unsettled, up in the air.
▶ verb *the idea was first mooted in the 1930s* **raise,** bring up, broach, mention, put forward, introduce, advance, propose, suggest.

mop ▶ noun *her tousled mop of hair* **shock,** mane, tangle, mass.
▶ verb *a man was mopping the floor* **wash,** clean, wipe, swab.
– PHRASES **mop up 1** *I mopped up the spilled coffee* **wipe up,** clean up, sponge up. **2** *troops mopped up the last pockets of resistance* **finish off,** deal with, dispose of, take care of, clear up, eliminate.

mope ▶ verb 1 *it's no use moping* **brood,** sulk, be miserable, be despondent, pine, eat one's heart out, fret, grieve; informal be down in the dumps, be down in/at the mouth; literary repine.
2 *she was moping about the house* **languish,** moon, idle, loaf; informal lollygag.

moral ▶ adjective 1 *moral issues* **ethical,** social, having to do with right and wrong.
2 *a moral man* **virtuous,** good, righteous, upright, upstanding, high-minded, principled, honorable, honest, just, noble, incorruptible, scrupulous, respectable, decent, clean-living, law-abiding.
ANTONYMS dishonorable.
3 *moral support* **psychological,** emotional, mental.
▶ noun 1 *the moral of the story* **lesson,** message, meaning, significance, signification, import, point, teaching.
2 *he has no morals* **moral code,** code of ethics, (moral) values, principles, standards, (sense of) morality, scruples.

CHOOSE THE RIGHT WORD

moral, ethical, honorable, righteous, sanctimonious, virtuous

You can be an **ethical** person without necessarily being a **moral** one, since *ethical* implies conformity with a code of fair and honest behavior, particularly in business or in a profession (*an ethical legislator who didn't believe in cutting deals*), while *moral* refers to generally accepted standards of goodness and rightness in character and conduct—especially sexual conduct (*the moral values she'd learned from her mother*). In the same way, you can be **honorable** without necessarily being **virtuous**, since *honorable* suggests dealing with others in a decent and ethical manner, while *virtuous* implies the possession of moral excellence in character (*many honorable businesspeople fail to live a virtuous private life*). **Righteous** is similar in meaning to **virtuous** but also implies freedom from guilt or blame (*righteous anger*); when the righteous person is also somewhat intolerant and narrow-minded, *self-righteous* might be a better adjective. Someone who makes a hypocritical show of being righteous is often described as **sanctimonious**—in other words, acting like a saint without having a saintly character.

morale ▶ noun *morale in the company has been high* **confidence,** self-confidence, self-esteem, spirit(s), team spirit, enthusiasm.

morality ▶ noun 1 *the morality of nuclear weapons* **ethics,** rights and wrongs, ethicality.
2 *a sharp decline in morality* **virtue,** goodness, good behavior, righteousness, rectitude, uprightness; morals, principles, honesty, integrity, propriety, honor, justice, decency; ethics, standards/principles of behavior, mores, standards. See note at GOODNESS.

morass ▶ noun 1 *the muddy morass* **quagmire,** swamp, bog, marsh, muskeg, mire, marshland, wetland, slough, moor.
2 *a morass of paperwork* **confusion,** chaos, muddle, tangle, entanglement, imbroglio, jumble, clutter; informal logjam.

moratorium ▶ noun *a moratorium on nuclear testing* **embargo,** ban, prohibition, suspension, postponement, stay, stoppage, halt, freeze, standstill, respite.

morbid ▶ adjective 1 *a morbid fascination with contemporary warfare* **ghoulish,** macabre, unhealthy, gruesome, unwholesome; abnormal, aberrant, disturbing, worrisome; informal sick, weird.
ANTONYMS wholesome.
2 *I felt decidedly morbid* **gloomy,** glum, melancholy, morose, dismal, somber, doleful, despondent, dejected, sad, depressed, downcast, down, disconsolate, miserable, unhappy, downhearted, dispirited, low; informal blue, down in the dumps, down in/at the mouth.
ANTONYMS cheerful.

mordant ▶ adjective *a mordant sense of humor* **caustic,** trenchant, biting, cutting, acerbic, sardonic, sarcastic, scathing, acid, sharp, keen; critical, bitter, virulent, vitriolic.

more ▶ adjective *I could do with some more clothes* **additional,** further, added, extra, increased, new, other, supplementary.
ANTONYMS less, fewer.
▶ adverb 1 *he was able to concentrate more on his writing* **to a greater extent,** further, some more, better.

2 *he was rich, and more, he was handsome* See MOREOVER.

▶ pronoun *we're going to need more* **extra,** an additional amount, an additional amount, an addition, an increase.
ANTONYMS less, fewer.

– PHRASES **more or less** *the jar holds more or less 18 pickles* **approximately,** roughly, nearly, almost, close to, about, of/on the order of, in the region of.

moreover ▶ adverb *Lindsey is going to the wedding, and moreover, she'll be singing at the reception* **besides,** furthermore, what's more, in addition, also, as well, too, to boot, additionally, on top of that, into the bargain, more, likewise; archaic withal.

moribund ▶ adjective **1** *the patient was moribund* **dying,** expiring, terminal, on one's deathbed, near death, at death's door, not long for this world.
ANTONYMS thriving, recovering.
2 *the moribund shipbuilding industry* **declining,** in decline, waning, dying, stagnating, stagnant, crumbling, on its last legs.
ANTONYMS flourishing.

morning ▶ noun **1** *I've got a meeting this morning* **before noon,** before lunch/lunchtime, this a.m.; literary this morn, this forenoon.
2 *morning is on its way* **dawn,** daybreak, sunrise, first light, sunup; literary dayspring, dawning, aurora, cock crow.

– PHRASES **morning, noon, and night** *she stayed at his bedside morning, noon, and night* **all the time,** without a break, constantly, continually, incessantly, ceaselessly, perpetually, unceasingly; informal 24–7.

moron ▶ noun *what moron left ice cream on the stove?* **fool,** idiot, ass, blockhead, dunce, dolt, ignoramus, imbecile, cretin, dullard, simpleton, clod; informal nitwit, halfwit, dope, ninny, nincompoop, chump, dimwit, dingbat, dipstick, goober, coot, goon, dumbo, dummy, ditz, dumdum, fathead, numbskull, numbnuts, dunderhead, thickhead, airhead, flake, lamebrain, zombie, nerd, peabrain, birdbrain, jughead, jerk, donkey, twit, goat, dork, twerp, schmuck, bozo, boob, turkey, schlep, chowderhead, dumbhead, goofball, goof, goofus, galoot, lummox, klutz, putz, schlemiel, sap, meatball, dumb cluck.
ANTONYMS genius.

morose ▶ adjective *Louis sat alone, looking morose* **sullen,** sulky, gloomy, bad-tempered, ill-tempered, dour, surly, sour, glum, moody, ill-humored, melancholy, melancholic, brooding, broody, doleful, miserable, depressed, dejected, despondent, downcast, unhappy, low, down, grumpy, irritable, churlish, cantankerous, crotchety, cross, crabby, cranky, grouchy, testy, snappish, peevish, crusty; informal blue, down in the dumps, down in/at the mouth.
ANTONYMS cheerful.

morsel ▶ noun *we sampled morsels of their splendid desserts* **mouthful,** bite, nibble, bit, soupçon, taste, spoonful, forkful, sliver, drop, dollop, spot, gobbet, tidbit.

mortal ▶ adjective **1** *mortal remains | all men are mortal* **perishable,** physical, bodily, corporeal, fleshly, earthly; human, impermanent, transient, ephemeral.
2 *a mortal blow* **deadly,** fatal, lethal, death-dealing, murderous, terminal.
3 *mortal enemies* **irreconcilable,** deadly, sworn, bitter, out-and-out, implacable.
4 *a mortal sin* **unpardonable,** unforgivable.
ANTONYMS venial.
5 *living in mortal fear* **extreme,** (very) great, terrible, awful, dreadful, intense, severe, grave, dire, unbearable.

▶ noun *we are mere mortals* **human being,** human, person, man/woman; earthling.

mortality ▶ noun **1** *a sense of his own mortality* **impermanence,** transience, ephemerality, perishability; humanity; corporeality.
2 *the causes of mortality* **death,** loss of life, dying.

mortify ▶ verb **1** *I'd be mortified if my friends found out* **embarrass,** humiliate, chagrin, discomfit, shame, abash, horrify, appall.
2 *he was mortified at being excluded* **hurt,** wound, affront, offend, put out, pique, irk, annoy, vex; informal rile.
3 *mortifying the flesh* **subdue,** suppress, subjugate, control; discipline, chasten, punish.

mortuary ▶ noun *flowers were sent to the mortuary* **funeral parlor,** funeral home; morgue.

most ▶ pronoun *most of the guests brought gifts* **nearly all,** almost all, the greatest part/number, the majority, the bulk, the preponderance.
ANTONYMS little, few.

– PHRASES **for the most part** See MOSTLY (sense 1), MOSTLY (sense 2).

mostly ▶ adverb **1** *the other passengers were mostly businessmen* **mainly,** for the most part, on the whole, in the main, largely, chiefly, predominantly, principally, primarily.
2 *I mostly wear jeans* **usually,** generally, in general, for the most part, as a rule, ordinarily, normally, customarily, typically, most of the time, almost always, on average, on balance.

mother ▶ noun **1** *I will ask my mother* **female parent,** materfamilias, matriarch; informal mom, mommy, ma, mama; old lady, old woman; chiefly Brit. informal mum, mummy.
2 *the foal's mother* **dam.**
3 *necessity is the mother of invention* **source,** origin, genesis, fountainhead, inspiration, stimulus; literary wellspring.
4 informal *a mother of a storm* **humdinger,** dilly, doozy, lulu, whopper.

▶ verb **1** *she mothered her husband* **look after,** care for, take care of, nurse, protect, tend, raise, rear; pamper, coddle, cosset, fuss over.
ANTONYMS neglect.
2 *she mothered two sets of twins* **give birth to,** have, bear, produce, birth; archaic be brought to bed of.

▶ adjective *my mother tongue* **native,** first, original; ancestral.

motherly ▶ adjective *thanks for your motherly advice* **maternal,** maternalistic, protective, caring, loving, devoted, affectionate, fond, warm, tender, gentle, kind, kindly, understanding, compassionate.

motion ▶ noun **1** *the rocking motion of the boat | a planet's motion around the sun* **movement,** moving, locomotion, rise and fall, shifting; progress, passage, passing, transit, course, travel, traveling.
2 *a motion of the hand* **gesture,** movement, signal, sign, indication; wave, nod, gesticulation.
3 *the motion failed to obtain a majority* **proposal,** proposition, recommendation, suggestion.
▶ verb *he motioned her to sit down* **gesture,** signal, direct, indicate; wave, beckon, nod, gesticulate.
– PHRASES **in motion** *remain seated while the bus is in motion* **moving,** on the move, going, traveling, running, functioning, operational.
set/put in motion *they have set in motion a formal review of the law* **start,** commence, begin, activate, initiate, launch, get underway, get going, get off the ground; trigger off, set off, spark off, generate, cause.

motionless ▶ adjective *the leaves were motionless in the still night air* **unmoving,** still, stationary, stock-still, immobile, static, not moving a muscle, rooted to the spot, transfixed, paralyzed, frozen.
ANTONYMS moving.

motivate ▶ verb **1** *she was primarily motivated by the desire for profit* **prompt,** drive, move, inspire, stimulate, influence, activate, impel, push, propel, spur (on).
2 *it's the teacher's job to motivate the child* **inspire,** stimulate, encourage, spur (on), excite, inspirit, incentivize, fire with enthusiasm.

motivation ▶ noun **1** *his motivation was financial* **motive,** motivating force, incentive, stimulus, stimulation, inspiration, inducement, incitement, spur, reason; informal carrot.
2 *keep up the staff's motivation* **enthusiasm,** drive, ambition, initiative, determination, enterprise; informal get-up-and-go.

motive ▶ noun **1** *the motive for the attack* **reason,** motivation, motivating force, rationale, grounds, cause, basis, object, purpose, intention; incentive, inducement, incitement, lure, inspiration, stimulus, stimulation, spur.
2 *religious motives in art* **motif,** theme, idea, concept, subject, topic, leitmotif.
▶ adjective *motive power* **kinetic,** driving, impelling, propelling, propulsive, motor.

motley ▶ adjective *a motley collection of vintage fabrics* **miscellaneous,** disparate, diverse, assorted, varied, diversified, heterogeneous; informal ragtag, raggle-taggle.
ANTONYMS homogeneous.

mottled ▶ adjective *mottled horses* **blotchy,** blotched, spotted, spotty, speckled, streaked, streaky, marbled, flecked, freckled, dappled, stippled; piebald, skewbald, brindled, brindle, pinto, calico; informal splotchy.

motto ▶ noun *the town's motto is "Tolerance and Prosperity"* **maxim,** saying, proverb, aphorism, adage, saw, axiom, apophthegm, formula, expression, phrase, dictum, precept; slogan, catchphrase, mantra; truism, cliché, platitude.

mound ▶ noun **1** *a mound of leaves* **heap,** pile, stack, mountain; mass, accumulation, assemblage.
2 *high on the mound* **hillock,** hill, knoll, rise, hummock, hump, embankment, bank, ridge, elevation; Geology drumlin.
▶ verb *mound up the rice on a serving plate* **pile (up),** heap (up).

mount ▶ verb **1** *he mounted the stairs* **go up,** ascend, climb (up), scale.
ANTONYMS descend.
2 *the committee mounted the platform* **climb on to,** jump on to, clamber on to, get on to.
3 *they mounted their horses* **get astride,** bestride, get on to, hop on to.
4 *the museum is mounting an exhibition* **(put on) display,** exhibit, present, install; organize, put on, stage.
5 *the company mounted a takeover bid* **organize,** stage, prepare, arrange, set up; launch, set in motion, initiate.
6 *their losses mounted rapidly* **increase,** grow, rise, escalate, soar, spiral, shoot up, rocket, climb, accumulate, build up, multiply.
ANTONYMS decrease, diminish.
7 *cameras were mounted above the door* **install,** place, fix, set, put up, put in position.

mountain ▶ noun **1** *a range of mountains* **peak,** height, mount, prominence, summit, pinnacle, alp; (**mountains**) range, sierra, cordillera, massif.
2 *a mountain of work* **a great deal,** a lot; a profusion, an abundance, a quantity, a backlog; informal a heap, a pile, a stack, a slew, lots, loads, heaps, piles, tons, masses; gobs.
– PHRASES **move mountains 1** *faith can move mountains* **perform miracles,** work/do wonders. **2** *his fans move mountains to attend his performances* **make every effort,** pull out all the stops, do one's utmost/best; informal bend/lean over backwards.

mountainous ▶ adjective **1** *a mountainous region* **hilly,** craggy, rocky, alpine; upland, highland.
ANTONYMS flat.
2 *mountainous waves* **huge,** enormous, gigantic, massive, giant, colossal, immense, tremendous, mighty; informal whopping, humongous, ginormous.
ANTONYMS tiny.

mourn ▶ verb **1** *Isobel mourned her husband* **grieve for,** sorrow over, lament for, weep for.
2 *he mourned the loss of the beautiful buildings* **deplore,** bewail, bemoan, rue, regret.

CHOOSE THE RIGHT WORD

mourn, bemoan, grieve, lament, rue, sorrow

Not everyone exhibits unhappiness in the same way. **Grieve** is the strongest of these verbs, implying deep mental anguish or suffering, often endured alone and in silence (*she grieved for years over the loss of her baby*). **Mourn** is more formal and often more public; although it implies deep emotion felt over a period of time, that emotion may be more ceremonial than sincere (*the people mourned the loss of their *leader*). **Lament** comes from a Latin word meaning to wail or weep, and it therefore suggests a vocal or verbal expression of loss (*The shrieking women lamented their husbands' deaths*). **Bemoan** also suggests suppressed or inarticulate sounds of *grief*, often expressing regret or disapproval (*to bemoan one's fate*). **Sorrow** combines deep sadness with regret and often pertains to a less tragic loss than *grieve* or *mourn* (*sorrow over a lost love*), while **rue** has even stronger connotations of regret and repentance (*she rued the day she was born*).

mournful ▶ adjective *mournful music* **sad,** sorrowful, doleful, melancholy, melancholic, woeful, grief-stricken, miserable, unhappy, heartbroken, broken-hearted, gloomy, dismal, desolate, dejected, despondent, depressed, downcast, disconsolate, woebegone, forlorn, rueful, lugubrious, joyless, cheerless; literary dolorous.
ANTONYMS cheerful.

mourning ▶ noun **1** *a period of mourning* **grief,** grieving, sorrowing, lamentation, lament, keening, wailing, weeping.
2 *she was dressed in mourning* **black (clothes),** (widow's) weeds; archaic sables.

mousy ▶ adjective **1** *mousy hair* **lightish brown,** brownish, brownish-gray, dun-colored; dull, lackluster.
2 *a small, mousy woman* **timid,** quiet, fearful, timorous, shy, self-effacing, diffident, unassertive, unforthcoming, withdrawn, introverted, introvert.

mouth ▶ noun **1** *open your mouth* **lips,** jaws; maw, muzzle; informal trap, chops, kisser, puss.
2 *the mouth of the cave* **entrance,** opening, entry, way in, access, ingress.
3 *the mouth of the bottle* **opening,** rim, lip.
4 *the mouth of the river* **outfall,** outlet, debouchment; estuary.
5 informal *don't give me any mouth* **impudence,** insolence, impertinence, effrontery, presumption, presumptuousness, rudeness, disrespect, cheek, cheekiness; informal lip, sauce, sass, sassiness, back talk.
▶ verb **1** *he mouthed platitudes* **utter,** speak, say; pronounce, enunciate, articulate, voice, express; say insincerely, say for form's sake, pay lip service to.
2 *he mouthed the words to the song* **lip-synch.**
– PHRASES **down in/at the mouth** informal See UNHAPPY (sense 1). **keep one's mouth shut** informal *just keep your mouth shut and no one will get hurt* **say nothing,** keep quiet, not breathe a word, not tell a soul; informal keep mum, not let the cat out of the bag. **mouth off** informal **1** *he was mouthing off about politics again* **rant,** spout, declaim, sound off. **2** *the students mouthed off to their teacher* **talk insolently,** be disrespectful.

mouthful ▶ noun **1** *a mouthful of pizza* **bite,** nibble, taste, bit, piece; spoonful, forkful.
2 *a mouthful of beer* **sip,** swallow, drop, gulp, slug; informal swig.
3 *"sesquipedalian" is a bit of a mouthful* **tongue-twister,** long word, difficult word.

mouthpiece ▶ noun **1** *the flute's mouthpiece* **embouchure.**
2 *a mouthpiece for the government* **spokesperson,** spokesman, spokeswoman, speaker, agent, representative, propagandist, voice; organ, channel, vehicle, instrument.

movable ▶ adjective **1** *movable objects* **portable,** transportable, transferable; mobile.
2 *movable dates* **variable,** changeable, alterable.
ANTONYMS fixed.

move ▶ verb **1** *she moved to the door | don't move!* **go,** walk, proceed, progress, advance; budge, stir, shift, change position.
2 *he moved the chair closer to the fire* **carry,** transport, transfer, shift.
3 *things were moving too fast* **(make) progress,** make headway, advance, develop.
4 *he urged the council to move quickly* **take action,** act, take steps, do something, take measures; informal get moving.
5 *she's moved to Rotterdam* **relocate,** move away, change one's address, leave, go away, go down the road, decamp, pull up stakes.
6 *I was deeply moved by the story* **affect,** touch, impress, shake, upset, disturb, make an impression on.
7 *she was moved to act* **inspire,** prompt, stimulate, motivate, provoke, influence, rouse, induce, incite.
8 *they are not prepared to move on this issue* **change,** budge, shift one's ground, change one's tune, change one's mind, have second thoughts; make a U-turn, do an about-face.
9 *she moves in the art world* **circulate,** mix, socialize, keep company, associate; informal hang out/around.
10 *I move that we adjourn* **propose,** submit, suggest, advocate, recommend, urge.
▶ noun **1** *his eyes followed her every move* **movement,** motion, action; gesture, gesticulation.
2 *his recent move to Sarasota* **relocation,** change of address, transfer, posting.
3 *the latest move in the war against drugs* **initiative,** step, action, act, measure, maneuver, tactic, stratagem.
4 *it's your move* **turn,** go; opportunity, chance.
– PHRASES **get a move on** informal *c'mon guys, let's get a move on* **hurry up,** speed (it) up, move faster; informal get cracking, get moving, step on it, shake a leg, hop to it; dated make haste. **make a move** *waiting for the other side to make a move* **do something,** take action, act, take the initiative; informal get moving. **on the move** **1** *she's always on the move* **traveling,** in transit, moving, journeying, on the road; informal on the go. **2** *the economy is on the move* **progressing,** making progress, advancing, developing.

movement ▶ noun **1** *Rachel made a sudden movement | there was almost no movement* **motion,** move; gesture, gesticulation, sign, signal; action, activity.
2 *the movement of supplies* **transportation,** shift, shifting, conveyance, moving, transfer.
3 *the labor movement* **political group,** party, faction, wing, lobby, camp.
4 *a movement to declare war on poverty*

campaign, crusade, drive, push.
5 *there have been movements in the financial markets* **development,** change, fluctuation, variation.
6 *the movement toward equality* **trend,** tendency, drift, swing.
7 *some movement will be made by the end of the month* **progress,** progression, advance.
8 *a symphony in three movements* **part,** section, division.

moving ▶ adjective 1 *moving parts* | *a moving train* **in motion,** operating, operational, working, going, on the move, active; movable, mobile.
ANTONYMS fixed, stationary.
2 *a moving book* **affecting,** touching, poignant, heartwarming, heart-rending, emotional, disturbing; inspiring, inspirational, stimulating, stirring.

> CHOOSE THE RIGHT WORD
> **moving, affecting, pathetic, poignant, touching**
> A movie about the Holocaust might be described as **moving**, since it arouses emotions or strong feelings, particularly feelings of pathos. A movie about a young girl's devotion to her dog might more accurately be described as **touching**, which means arousing tenderness or compassion, while a movie dealing with a young girl's first experience with love would be **poignant**, since it pierces one's heart or keenly affects one's sensibilities. While *poignant* implies a bittersweet response that combines pity and longing or other contradictory emotions, **pathetic** means simply moving one to pity (*a pathetic scene in which the dog struggled to save his drowning mistress*). Almost any well-made film can be **affecting**, a more general term that suggests moving one to tears or some other display of feeling (*the affecting story of a daughter's search for her birth mother*).

mow ▶ verb *she had mown the lawn* **cut (down),** trim; crop, clip, prune, manicure.
– PHRASES **mow down** *they were ordered to mow down the student protestors* **kill,** run down, gun down, shoot down, cut down, cut to pieces, butcher, slaughter, massacre, annihilate, wipe out; informal blow away.

much ▶ adjective *did you get much help?* **a lot of,** a great/good deal of, a great/large amount of, plenty of, ample, copious, abundant, plentiful, considerable; informal lots of, loads of, heaps of, masses of, tons of, piles of, mucho.
ANTONYMS little.
▶ adverb 1 *it didn't hurt much* **greatly,** to a great extent/degree, a great deal, a lot, considerably, appreciably.
2 *does he come here much?* **often,** frequently, many times, repeatedly, regularly, habitually, routinely, usually, normally, commonly; informal a lot.
▶ pronoun *he did much for our team* **a lot,** a great/good deal, plenty; informal lots, loads, heaps, masses.

muck ▶ noun 1 *I'll just clean off the muck* **dirt,** grime, filth, mud, slime, mess; informal crud, gunk, grunge, gunge, guck, glop.
2 *spreading muck on the fields* **dung,** manure, ordure, excrement, excreta, droppings, feces, sewage, sludge, biosolids; informal cow chips, horse apples.

mud ▶ noun *we trekked through the mud* **mire,** sludge, ooze, silt, clay, dirt, soil.
– PHRASES **as clear as mud** *her lectures are as clear as mud* **unclear,** unintelligible, opaque, unfathomable, incomprehensible, baffling, perplexing, inscrutable.

muddle ▶ verb 1 *you've muddled things up* **confuse,** mix up, jumble (up), disarrange, disorganize, disorder, disturb, mess up.
2 *she became muddled* **bewilder,** confuse, bemuse, perplex, puzzle, baffle, mystify.
▶ noun 1 *the files are in a muddle* **mess,** confusion, jumble, tangle, mishmash, chaos, disorder, disarray, disorganization, imbroglio, hodgepodge. See note at JUMBLE.
2 *a bureaucratic muddle* **bungle,** mix-up, misunderstanding; informal foul-up, snafu.
– PHRASES **muddle along/through** *don't worry, we'll muddle through* **cope,** manage, get by/along, scrape by/along, make do.

muddy ▶ adjective 1 *muddy ground* **waterlogged,** boggy, marshy, swampy, squishy, mucky, slimy, spongy, wet, soft, heavy; archaic quaggy.
2 *muddy shoes* **mud-caked,** muddied, dirty, filthy, mucky, grimy, soiled; literary begrimed.
ANTONYMS clean.
3 *muddy water* **murky,** cloudy, muddied, turbid, riled.
ANTONYMS clear.
4 *a muddy pink* **dingy,** dirty, drab, dull, sludgy.
▶ verb 1 *don't muddy your boots* **make muddy,** dirty, soil, spatter, bespatter; literary besmirch, begrime.
2 *these results muddy the situation* **make unclear,** obscure, confuse, obfuscate, blur, cloud, befog.
ANTONYMS clarify.

muffle ▶ verb 1 *everyone was muffled up in coats* **wrap (up),** swathe, enfold, envelop, cloak.
2 *the sound of their footsteps was muffled* **deaden,** dull, dampen, mute, soften, quiet, tone down, mask, stifle, smother.

muffled ▶ adjective *we thought we heard muffled voices* **indistinct,** faint, muted, dull, soft, stifled, smothered.
ANTONYMS loud.

mug ▶ noun 1 *a china mug* **cup,** glass; stein, flagon, tankard; archaic stoup.
2 informal *her ugly mug* See FACE (sense 1 of the noun).
▶ verb informal *he was mugged by three youths* **assault,** attack, set upon, beat up, rob; informal jump, rough up, lay into, do over.

muggy ▶ adjective *a muggy August afternoon* **humid,** close, sultry, sticky, oppressive, airless, stifling, suffocating, stuffy, clammy, damp, heavy.
ANTONYMS fresh.

mull ▶ verb
– PHRASES **mull over** *I'll have to mull it over before making a final decision* **ponder,** consider, think over/about, reflect on, contemplate, turn over in one's mind, chew over, cogitate on, give some thought to.

multifarious ▶ adjective *our multifarious ethnic traditions* **diverse,** many, numerous, various, varied, diversified, multiple, multitudinous, multiplex, manifold, multifaceted, different, heterogeneous, miscellaneous, assorted; literary myriad, divers.
ANTONYMS homogeneous.

multiple ▶ adjective *words with multiple meanings* **numerous,** many, various, different, diverse, several, manifold, multifarious, multitudinous; literary myriad, divers.
ANTONYMS single.

multiply ▶ verb **1** *their difficulties seem to be multiplying* **increase,** grow, become more numerous, accumulate, proliferate, mount up, mushroom, snowball.
ANTONYMS decrease.
2 *the rabbits have multiplied* **breed,** reproduce, procreate.

multitude ▶ noun **1** *a multitude of birds* **a lot,** a great/large number, a great/large quantity, a host, a horde, a mass, a swarm, an abundance, a profusion; scores, quantities, droves; informal a slew, lots, loads, masses, stacks, heaps, piles, tons, dozens, hundreds, thousands, millions, gazillions.
2 *Father Philip addressed the multitude* **crowd,** gathering, assembly, congregation, flock, throng, horde, mob; formal concourse.
3 *political power in the hands of the multitude* **common people,** people, populace, masses, rank and file, commonality, plebeians; hoi polloi, mob, proletariat, common herd; informal great unwashed, rabble, proles, plebs.

munch ▶ verb *the rustle we heard turned out to be giraffes munching leaves* **chew,** champ, chomp, masticate, crunch, eat, gnaw, nibble, snack, chow down on.

mundane ▶ adjective **1** *her mundane life* **humdrum,** dull, boring, tedious, monotonous, tiresome, wearisome, unexciting, uninteresting, uneventful, unvarying, unremarkable, repetitive, repetitious, routine, ordinary, everyday, day-to-day, run-of-the-mill, commonplace, workaday; informal plain-vanilla, ho-hum.
ANTONYMS extraordinary, imaginative.
2 *the mundane world* **earthly,** worldly, terrestrial, material, temporal, secular, areligious; literary sublunary.
ANTONYMS spiritual.

municipal ▶ adjective *land use is controlled by the municipal authorities* **civic,** civil, metropolitan, urban, city, town, borough.
ANTONYMS rural.

munificent ▶ adjective *a munificent bequest* **generous,** bountiful, openhanded, magnanimous, philanthropic, princely, handsome, lavish, liberal, charitable, big-hearted, beneficent; literary bounteous.
ANTONYMS mean.

murder ▶ noun **1** *a brutal murder* **killing,** homicide, assassination, liquidation, extermination, execution, slaughter, butchery, massacre; manslaughter; literary slaying.
2 informal *driving there was murder* **hell,** hell on earth, a nightmare, an ordeal, a trial, misery, torture, agony.
▶ verb **1** *someone tried to murder him* **kill,** put to death, assassinate, execute, liquidate, eliminate, dispatch, butcher, slaughter, massacre, wipe out; informal bump off, do in, do away with, knock off, blow away, blow someone's brains out, take out, dispose of, ice, rub out, smoke, waste; literary slay. See note at KILL.
2 informal *Anna was murdering a Mozart sonata* See MANGLE (sense 2).
3 informal *he murdered his opponent* See TROUNCE.

murderer, murderess ▶ noun *the murderer was finally brought to justice* **killer,** assassin, serial killer, butcher, slaughterer; informal hit man, gunman, hired gun; literary slayer.

murderous ▶ adjective **1** *a murderous attack* **homicidal,** brutal, violent, savage, ferocious, fierce, vicious, bloodthirsty, barbarous, barbaric; fatal, lethal, deadly, mortal, death-dealing; archaic sanguinary.
2 informal *a murderous schedule* **arduous,** grueling, strenuous, punishing, onerous, exhausting, taxing, difficult, rigorous; informal killing, hellish.

murky ▶ adjective **1** *a murky winter afternoon* **dark,** gloomy, gray, leaden, dull, dim, overcast, cloudy, clouded, sunless, dismal, dreary, bleak; literary tenebrous.
ANTONYMS bright, sunny.
2 *murky water* **dirty,** muddy, cloudy, turbid, riled, roily.
ANTONYMS clear.
3 *her murky past* **questionable,** suspicious, suspect, dubious, dark, mysterious, secret; informal shady, sketchy.
ANTONYMS spotless, innocent.

murmur ▶ noun **1** *his voice was a murmur* **whisper,** undertone, mutter, mumble.
2 *they left without a murmur* **complaint,** grumble, grouse; informal gripe, moan.
3 *the murmur of bees* **hum,** humming, buzz, buzzing, thrum, thrumming, drone; sigh, rustle; literary susurration, murmuration.
▶ verb **1** *he heard them murmuring in the hall* **mutter,** mumble, whisper, talk under one's breath, speak softly.
2 *no one murmured at the delay* **complain,** mutter, grumble, grouse; informal gripe, moan.
3 *the wind was murmuring through the trees* **rustle,** sigh; burble, purl; literary whisper.

muscle ▶ noun **1** *he had muscle but no brains* **strength,** power, muscularity, brawn, burliness; informal beef, beefiness; literary thew.
2 *financial muscle* **influence,** power, strength, might, force, forcefulness, weight; informal clout.
– PHRASES **muscle in on** informal *we don't like people muscling in on our private affairs* **interfere with,** force one's way into, impose oneself on, encroach on; informal horn in on, barge in on.

muscular ▶ adjective **1** *muscular tissue* **fibrous,** sinewy.
2 *he's very muscular* **strong,** brawny, muscly,

sinewy, powerfully built, well muscled, hard-bodied, burly, strapping, sturdy, powerful, athletic; Physiology mesomorphic; informal hunky, beefy, muscle-bound; literary thewy.
3 *a muscular economy* **vigorous,** robust, strong, powerful, dynamic, potent, active.

muse ▶ **noun** *the poet's muse* **inspiration,** creative influence, stimulus; formal afflatus.

mushroom ▶ **noun** *the mushrooms thrive in this warm wet weather* **fungus,** button mushroom, cep, chanterelle, cremini, enoki, field mushroom, honey mushroom, horse mushroom, matsutake, morel, oyster mushroom, pine mushroom, porcini, portobello, shiitake, death cap, bolete.
▶ **verb** *ecotourism mushroomed in the 1980s* **proliferate,** grow/develop rapidly, burgeon, spread, increase, expand, boom, explode, snowball, rocket, skyrocket; thrive, flourish, prosper.
ANTONYMS contract.

musical ▶ **adjective** *musical poetry* **tuneful,** melodic, melodious, harmonious, sweet-sounding, sweet, mellifluous, euphonious, euphonic.
ANTONYMS discordant.

musing ▶ **noun** *in my musing of late, I have decided that I need more purpose in my life* **meditation,** thinking, contemplation, deliberation, pondering, reflection, rumination, introspection, daydreaming, reverie, dreaming, preoccupation, brooding; formal cogitation.

muss ▶ **verb** informal *don't be mussing your hair before the photo shoot* **ruffle,** tousle, dishevel, rumple, mess up, make a mess of, disarrange, make untidy.

must[1] ▶ **verb** *I must go* **ought to,** should, have (got) to, need to, be obliged to, be required to, be compelled to.
▶ **noun** informal *this video is **a must*** **not to be missed,** very good; a necessity, essential, a requirement, a requisite.

must[2] ▶ **noun** *a smell of must* **mold,** mustiness, moldiness, mildew, fustiness, decay, rot.

muster ▶ **verb 1** *they mustered 50,000 troops* **assemble,** mobilize, rally, raise, summon, gather (together), mass, collect, convene, call up, call to arms, recruit, conscript, draft; archaic levy. See note at **GATHER**.
2 *reporters mustered outside her house* **congregate,** assemble, gather together, come together, collect together, convene, mass, rally.
3 *she mustered her courage* **summon (up),** screw up, call up, rally.
▶ **noun** *the colonel called a muster* **roll call,** assembly, rally, meeting, gathering, assemblage, congregation, convention; parade, review.
– PHRASES **pass muster** *as far as Dean's parents are concerned, I'll never pass muster* **be good enough,** come up to standard, come up to scratch, measure up, be acceptable/adequate, fill/fit the bill; informal make the grade, come/be up to snuff.

musty ▶ **adjective 1** *the room smelled musty* **moldy,** stale, fusty, damp, dank, mildewy, smelly, stuffy, airless, unventilated; informal funky.
ANTONYMS fresh, fragrant.
2 *the play seemed musty* **unoriginal,** uninspired, unimaginative, hackneyed, stale, flat, tired, banal, trite, clichéd, old-fashioned, outdated; informal old hat.
ANTONYMS fresh.

mutable ▶ **adjective** *the mutable nature of fashion* **changeable,** variable, varying, fluctuating, shifting, inconsistent, unpredictable, inconstant, fickle, uneven, unstable, protean; literary fluctuant.
ANTONYMS invariable.

mutation ▶ **noun 1** *cells that have undergone mutation* **alteration,** change, variation, modification, transformation, metamorphosis, transmutation; humorous transmogrification.
2 *a genetic mutation* **mutant,** freak (of nature), deviant, monstrosity, monster, anomaly.

mute ▶ **adjective 1** *she remained mute* **silent,** speechless, dumb, unspeaking, tight-lipped, taciturn; informal mum, tongue-tied.
ANTONYMS voluble, talkative.
2 *a mute appeal* **wordless,** silent, dumb, unspoken, unvoiced, unexpressed.
ANTONYMS spoken.
3 *the forest was mute* **quiet,** silent, hushed.
ANTONYMS noisy.
4 *he was deaf and mute* **dumb,** unable to speak; Medicine aphasic.
▶ **verb 1** *the noise was muted by the heavy curtains* **deaden,** muffle, dampen, soften, quiet, hush; stifle, smother, suppress.
ANTONYMS amplify.
2 *Bruce muted his criticisms* **restrain,** soften, tone down, moderate, temper.
ANTONYMS intensify.

muted ▶ **adjective 1** *the muted hum of traffic* **muffled,** faint, indistinct, quiet, soft, low.
2 *muted colors* **subdued,** pastel, delicate, subtle, understated, restrained.

mutilate ▶ **verb 1** *the bodies had been mutilated* **mangle,** maim, disfigure, butcher, dismember; cripple.
2 *the painting was mutilated* **vandalize,** damage, deface, ruin, spoil, destroy, wreck, violate, desecrate; informal trash.

mutinous ▶ **adjective** *your mutinous scheme has failed* **rebellious,** insubordinate, subversive, seditious, insurgent, insurrectionary, rebel, riotous.

mutiny ▶ **noun** *there was a mutiny over wages* **insurrection,** rebellion, revolt, riot, uprising, insurgence, insubordination. See note at **UPRISING**.
▶ **verb** *thousands of soldiers mutinied* **rise up,** rebel, revolt, riot, disobey/defy authority, be insubordinate.

mutter ▶ **verb 1** *a group of men stood muttering* **talk under one's breath,** murmur, mumble, whisper, speak in an undertone.
2 *the players muttered about the salary freezes* **grumble,** complain, grouse, carp, whine; informal moan, gripe, beef, whinge, kvetch.

muzzle ▶ **noun 1** *the dog's velvety muzzle* **snout,** nose, mouth, maw.
2 *the muzzle of a gun* **barrel,** end.
▶ **verb** *attempts to muzzle the media* **gag,** silence,

censor, stifle, restrain, check, curb, fetter.

myopic ▶ adjective **1** *a myopic patient* **nearsighted**; chiefly Brit. shortsighted.
ANTONYMS farsighted.
2 *the government's myopic attitude* **unimaginative,** uncreative, unadventurous, narrow-minded, small-minded, short-term, shortsighted.
ANTONYMS farsighted.

myriad ▶ noun literary *a myriad of insects* **a multitude,** a large/great number, a large/great quantity, scores, quantities, a mass, a host, droves, a horde; informal lots, loads, masses, stacks, scads, tons, hundreds, thousands, millions, gazillions.
▶ adjective *the myriad lights of the city* **innumerable,** countless, infinite, numberless, untold, unnumbered, immeasurable, multitudinous, numerous; literary divers.

mysterious ▶ adjective **1** *he vanished in mysterious circumstances* **puzzling,** strange, peculiar, curious, funny, queer, odd, weird, bizarre, mystifying, inexplicable, baffling, perplexing, incomprehensible, unexplainable, unfathomable.
ANTONYMS straightforward.
2 *he was being very mysterious* **enigmatic,** inscrutable, secretive, reticent, evasive, furtive, surreptitious.
ANTONYMS straightforward, open.

mystery ▶ noun **1** *his death remains a mystery* **puzzle,** enigma, conundrum, riddle, secret, problem, unsolved problem. See note at RIDDLE.
2 *her past is shrouded in mystery* **secrecy,** obscurity, uncertainty, mystique.
3 *reading a classic mystery* **thriller,** murder mystery, detective story/novel, murder story, crime novel; informal whodunit.

mystify ▶ verb *Houdini mystified his audiences* **bewilder,** puzzle, perplex, baffle, confuse, confound, bemuse, bedazzle, throw; informal flummox, stump, bamboozle, fox.

myth ▶ noun **1** *ancient Greek myths* **folk tale,** folk story, legend, tale, story, fable, saga, mythos, lore, folklore, mythology.
2 *the myths surrounding childbirth* **misconception,** fallacy, false notion, old wives' tale, fairy tale/story, fiction; informal tall tale, cock-and-bull story, urban myth/legend.

mythical ▶ adjective **1** *mythical beasts* **legendary,** mythological, fabled, fabulous, folkloric, fairy-tale, storybook; fantastical, imaginary, imagined, fictitious, storied.
2 *her mythical child* **imaginary,** fictitious, make-believe, fantasy, invented, made-up, nonexistent; informal pretend.

mythology ▶ noun *no ancient culture is without its mythology* **myth(s),** legend(s), folklore, folk tales, folk stories, lore, tradition.

Nn

nadir ▶ noun *the nadir of his career* **lowest point,** lowest level, all-time low, bottom, rock-bottom; informal pits.
ANTONYMS zenith.

nag[1] ▶ verb **1** *she's constantly nagging me* **harass,** badger, give someone a hard time, hound, harry, criticize, carp, find fault with, keep on at, grumble at, go on at; henpeck; informal hassle, get on someone's case, ride.
2 *this has been nagging me for weeks* **trouble,** worry, bother, plague, torment, niggle, prey on one's mind; annoy, irritate; informal bug, aggravate.
▶ noun *don't be such a nag* **shrew,** harpy, termagant, harridan; archaic scold.

nag[2] ▶ noun *she rode the nag into town* **worn-out horse,** old horse, hack; informal plug; archaic jade.

nagging ▶ adjective **1** *his nagging wife* **shrewish,** complaining, grumbling, fault-finding, scolding, carping, criticizing.
2 *a nagging pain* **persistent,** continuous, niggling, unrelenting, unremitting, unabating.

nail ▶ noun **1** *fastened with nails* **tack,** spike, pin, rivet; finishing nail, roofing nail, hobnail, brad.
2 *polishing her nails* **fingernail,** thumbnail, toenail.
▶ verb **1** *a board was nailed to the wall* **fasten,** attach, fix, affix, secure, tack, hammer, pin.
2 informal *he nailed the suspect* **catch,** capture, apprehend, arrest, seize; informal collar, nab, pull in, pick up.
3 *she nailed that somersault* **perform well,** succeed in, execute, complete, bring about/off; informal land, pull off, score.
– PHRASES **hard as nails** *he regretted having been a father who always acted as if he were hard as nails* **callous,** hard-hearted, heartless, unfeeling, unsympathetic, uncaring, insensitive, unsentimental, hard-bitten, tough, lacking compassion. **hit the nail on the head** *when Arthur said that Donna couldn't be trusted, he really hit the nail on the head* **get it right,** get it, guess correctly, speak (the) truth.

naked ▶ adjective **1** *naked sunbathers* **nude,** bare, in the nude, stark naked, having nothing on, stripped, unclothed, undressed; informal without a stitch on, in one's birthday suit, in the buff, in the raw, in the altogether, buck-naked, butt-naked, mother-naked.
ANTONYMS clothed, dressed.
2 *a naked flame* **unprotected,** uncovered, exposed, unguarded.
ANTONYMS covered.
3 *the naked branches of the trees* **bare,** barren, denuded, stripped, uncovered.
4 *I felt naked and exposed* **vulnerable,** helpless, weak, powerless, defenseless, exposed, open to attack.
5 *the naked truth | naked hostility* **undisguised,** plain, unadorned, unvarnished, unqualified, stark, bald; overt, obvious, open, patent, evident, apparent, manifest, unmistakable, blatant.

> CHOOSE THE RIGHT WORD
>
> **naked, bald, bare, barren, nude**
>
> Someone who isn't wearing any clothes is **naked**; this adjective is usually associated with revealing a part or all of the body (*her naked shoulder; a naked man ran from the burning building*). A *naked* person who appears in a painting or photograph is called a **nude**, a euphemistic but more socially acceptable term referring to the unclothed human body. **Bare** can describe the branches of a tree as well as human limbs; it implies the absence of the conventional or appropriate covering (*a bare wooden floor; bare legs; four bare walls*). **Bald** also suggests a lack of covering, but it refers particularly to a lack of natural covering, especially hair (*a bald head*). **Barren** implies a lack of vegetation, and it also connotes destitution and fruitlessness (*a barren wasteland devoid of life*). A *bald* artist might paint a *nude* woman whose *bare* arms are extended against a *barren* winter landscape.

namby-pamby ▶ adjective *her new boyfriend is the essence of virility—nothing like that namby-pamby guy she used to date* **weak,** feeble, spineless, effeminate, effete; ineffectual; informal wimpy, sissy.

name ▶ noun **1** *her name's Emma* designation, honorific, title, tag, epithet, label; informal moniker, handle; formal denomination, appellation.
2 *the top names in the fashion industry* **celebrity,** star, superstar, VIP, leading light, big name, luminary; expert, authority; informal celeb, somebody, megastar, big shot, bigwig, big gun, great, giant.
3 *the good name of the firm* **reputation,** character, repute, standing, stature, esteem, prestige, cachet, kudos; renown, popularity, notability, distinction.
▶ verb **1** *they named the baby Phoebe* **call,** give a name to, dub; label, style, term, title, entitle; baptize, christen; formal denominate.

2 *he named the woman in the photograph* **identify,** specify.
3 *he has named his successor* **choose,** select, pick, decide on, nominate, designate.

nameless ▶ **adjective 1** *a nameless photographer* **unnamed,** unidentified, anonymous, incognito, unspecified, unacknowledged, uncredited; unknown, unsung, uncelebrated.
2 *nameless fears* **unspeakable,** unutterable, inexpressible, indescribable; indefinable, vague, unspecified.

namely ▶ **adverb** *I want to go someplace warm, namely Aruba* **that is,** that is to say, in other words, to be specific, specifically, viz., to wit.

nap[1] ▶ **verb** *they were napping on the sofa* **doze,** sleep, sleep lightly, take a nap, catnap, rest, take a siesta; informal snooze, catch forty winks, get some shut-eye, catch some Zs, catch a few Zs.
▶ **noun** *a nap will make you feel better* **(some) sleep,** a little sleep, a catnap, a siesta, a doze, a lie-down, (a/some) rest, a little rest; informal a snooze, forty winks, (some) shut-eye, a little shut-eye, (some) beauty sleep/rest, a little beauty sleep/rest, a power nap.
– PHRASES **catch someone napping** *the teacher had warned us to be ever prepared, but the unannounced test caught most of us napping* **catch off guard,** catch unawares, surprise, take by surprise, catch out, find unprepared; informal catch someone with their pants down.

nap[2] ▶ **noun** *the nap of the velvet* **pile,** fibers, threads, weave, surface, grain.

narcissism ▶ **noun** *his emotional development was hindered by his mother's narcissism* **vanity,** self-love, self-admiration, self-absorption, self-obsession, conceit, self-centeredness, self-regard, egotism, egoism. See note at EGOTISM.
ANTONYMS modesty.

narcissistic ▶ **adjective** *she was never happy in the narcissistic life that her press agent and manager had crafted for her* **vain,** self-loving, self-admiring, self-absorbed, self-obsessed, conceited, self-centered, self-regarding, egotistic, egotistical, egoistic; informal full of oneself.

narcotic ▶ **noun** *addicted to narcotics* **soporific (drug),** opiate, sleeping pill; painkiller, pain reliever, analgesic, anodyne, palliative, anesthetic; tranquilizer, sedative; informal downer, dope; Medicine stupefacient.
▶ **adjective** *a narcotic sleeping pill* **soporific,** sleep-inducing, opiate; painkilling, pain-relieving, analgesic, anodyne, anesthetic, tranquilizing, sedative; Medicine stupefacient.

narrate ▶ **verb** *the story is narrated by an English butler* **tell,** relate, recount, describe, chronicle, give a report of, report; voice-over.

narrative ▶ **noun** *an interesting narrative about her year in Bolivia* **account,** chronicle, history, description, record, report, story.

narrator ▶ **noun 1** *the narrator of "The Arabian Nights"* **storyteller,** teller of tales, relater, chronicler, raconteur, anecdotalist.
ANTONYMS listener, audience.
2 *the film's narrator* **voice-over,** commentator, speaker.

narrow ▶ **adjective 1** *the path became narrow* **small,** tapered, tapering, narrowing; archaic strait.
ANTONYMS wide, broad.
2 *her narrow waist* **slender,** slim, slight, spare, attenuated, thin.
ANTONYMS broad.
3 *a narrow space* **confined,** cramped, tight, restricted, limited, constricted.
ANTONYMS spacious.
4 *a narrow range of products* **limited,** restricted, circumscribed, small, inadequate, insufficient, deficient.
ANTONYMS wide, broad.
5 *a narrow view of the world* See NARROW-MINDED.
6 *nationalism in the narrowest sense of the word* **strict,** literal, exact, precise.
ANTONYMS broad.
7 *a narrow escape* **by a very small margin,** close, near, by a hair's breadth; informal by a whisker.
▶ **verb** *the path narrowed | narrowing the gap between rich and poor* **get/become/make narrower,** get/become/make smaller, taper, diminish, decrease, reduce, contract, shrink, constrict; archaic straiten.

narrowly ▶ **adverb 1** *one bullet narrowly missed him* **only just,** just, barely, scarcely, hardly, by a hair's breadth; informal by a whisker.
2 *she looked at me narrowly* **closely,** carefully, searchingly, attentively.

narrow-minded ▶ **adjective** *our school has no place for such narrow-minded teaching* **intolerant,** illiberal, reactionary, conservative, parochial, provincial, insular, small-minded, petty, blinkered, inward-looking, narrow, hidebound, prejudiced, bigoted; informal redneck. See note at BIAS.
ANTONYMS tolerant.

narrows ▶ **plural noun** *these narrows were first navigated in the sixteenth century* **strait(s),** sound, channel, waterway, passage, sea passage, neck.

nascent ▶ **adjective** *the nascent economic recovery* **just beginning,** budding, developing, growing, embryonic, incipient, young, fledgling, evolving, emergent, dawning, burgeoning.

nastiness ▶ **noun 1** *my mother tried to shut herself off from all the nastiness of life* **unpleasantness,** disagreeableness, offensiveness, vileness, foulness.
2 *her uncharacteristic nastiness* **unkindness,** unpleasantness, unfriendliness, disagreeableness, rudeness, churlishness, spitefulness, maliciousness, meanness, ill temper, ill nature, viciousness, malevolence; informal bitchiness, cattiness.

nasty ▶ **adjective 1** *a nasty smell* **unpleasant,** disagreeable, disgusting, distasteful, awful, dreadful, horrible, terrible, vile, foul, abominable, frightful, loathsome, revolting, repulsive, odious, sickening, nauseating, repellent, repugnant, horrendous, appalling, atrocious, offensive, objectionable, obnoxious, unsavory, unappetizing, off-putting; noxious, foul-smelling, smelly, stinking, rank, fetid, malodorous, mephitic; informal ghastly, horrid, gruesome, diabolical, yucky, skanky, godawful,

gross, beastly, lousy, funky; literary miasmal, noisome.
ANTONYMS pleasant, delightful.
2 *the weather turned nasty* **unpleasant,** disagreeable, foul, filthy, inclement; wet, stormy, cold, blustery, blizzardy.
ANTONYMS sunny, pleasant.
3 *she can be really nasty* **unkind,** unpleasant, unfriendly, disagreeable, rude, churlish, spiteful, malicious, mean, ill-tempered, ill-natured, vicious, malevolent, obnoxious, hateful, hurtful; informal bitchy, catty.
ANTONYMS nice, charming.
4 *a nasty accident | a nasty cut* **serious,** dangerous, bad, awful, dreadful, terrible, severe; painful, ugly.
ANTONYMS minor, slight.
5 *she had the nasty habit of appearing unannounced* **annoying,** irritating, infuriating, disagreeable, unpleasant, maddening, exasperating.
6 *they wrote nasty things on the wall* **obscene,** indecent, offensive, crude, rude, dirty, filthy, vulgar, foul, gross, disgusting, pornographic, smutty, lewd; informal sick, X-rated.
ANTONYMS polite, decent.

nation ▶ **noun** *an independent nation* **country,** sovereign state, state, land, realm, kingdom, republic; fatherland, motherland; people, race.

national ▶ **adjective 1** *national politics* **state,** public, federal, governmental; civic, civil, domestic, internal.
ANTONYMS local, international.
2 *a national strike* See NATIONWIDE.
▶ **noun** *a Canadian national* **citizen,** subject, native; voter.

nationalism ▶ **noun** *their extreme nationalism was frightening* **patriotism,** patriotic sentiment, flag-waving, xenophobia, chauvinism, jingoism. See note at CHAUVINISM.

nationality ▶ **noun 1** *what is your nationality?* **citizenship.**
2 *all the main nationalities of Ethiopia* **ethnic group,** ethnic minority, tribe, clan, race, nation.

nationwide ▶ **adjective** *a nationwide talent search* **national,** countrywide, general, widespread, extensive.
ANTONYMS local.

native ▶ **noun** *a native of Rome, New York* **inhabitant,** resident, local; citizen, national; aborigine, autochthon; formal dweller.
ANTONYMS foreigner.
▶ **adjective 1** *the native peoples* **indigenous,** original, first, earliest, aboriginal, autochthonous.
ANTONYMS immigrant.
2 *native produce | native plants* **domestic,** homegrown, homemade, local; indigenous.
ANTONYMS imported.
3 *a native instinct for politics* **innate,** inherent, inborn, instinctive, intuitive, natural; hereditary, inherited, congenital, inbred, connate.
ANTONYMS acquired.
4 *her native tongue* **mother,** vernacular, first.

CHOOSE THE RIGHT WORD

native, aboriginal, endemic, indigenous

A **native** New Yorker is probably not **indigenous**, although both words apply to persons or things that belong to or are associated with a particular place by birth or origin. *Native* means born or produced in a specific region or country (*native plants; native dances*), but it can also apply to persons or things that were introduced from elsewhere some time ago—which is the case with most New Yorkers who consider themselves natives. *Indigenous*, on the other hand, is more restricted in meaning; it applies only to someone or something that is not only native but was not introduced from elsewhere (*the pumpkin is indigenous to America*). Generally speaking, *native* applies to individual organisms, while *indigenous* applies to races or species. Something that is **endemic** is prevalent in a particular region because of special conditions there that favor its growth or existence (*heather is endemic in the Scottish Highlands; malaria is endemic in Central America*). There are no longer any **aboriginal** New Yorkers, a word that refers to the earliest known inhabitants of a place or to ancient peoples who have no known ancestors and have inhabited a region since its earliest historical time. Australia is known for its *aboriginal* culture, which was preserved for centuries through geographical isolation.

natty ▶ **adjective** informal *he's looking pretty darn natty in that new suit* **smart,** stylish, fashionable, dapper, debonair, dashing, spruced up, well-dressed, chic, elegant, trim; informal snazzy, trendy, snappy, nifty, sassy, spiffy, fly, kicky, styling/stylin', sharp.
ANTONYMS scruffy.

natural ▶ **adjective 1** *a natural occurrence* **normal,** ordinary, everyday, usual, regular, common, commonplace, typical, routine, standard, established, customary, accustomed, habitual. See note at NORMAL.
ANTONYMS abnormal, exceptional.
2 *natural produce* **unprocessed,** organic, pure, wholesome, unrefined, pesticide-free, additive-free.
ANTONYMS artificial, refined.
3 *Alex is a natural leader* **born,** naturally gifted, untaught.
4 *his natural instincts* **innate,** inborn, inherent, native, instinctive, intuitive; hereditary, inherited, inbred, congenital, connate.
ANTONYMS acquired.
5 *she seemed very natural* **unaffected,** spontaneous, uninhibited, relaxed, unselfconscious, genuine, open, artless, guileless, ingenuous, unpretentious, without airs.
ANTONYMS self-conscious, false, affected.
6 *it was quite natural to think that* **reasonable,** logical, understandable, (only) to be expected,

predictable.
ANTONYMS unreasonable.

naturalist ▶ noun *the wildlife preserve employs a team of naturalists from around the world* **natural historian,** life scientist, wildlife expert; biologist, botanist, zoologist, ornithologist, entomologist, ecologist.

naturalistic ▶ adjective *her sculptures are so naturalistic they seem to breathe* **realistic,** real-life, true-to-life, lifelike, graphic, representational, faithful, photographic.
ANTONYMS abstract.

naturalize ▶ verb **1** *he was naturalized in 1950* **grant citizenship to,** make a citizen, enfranchise, give a passport to.
2 *they naturalized new species of grass and wildflowers* **establish,** introduce, acclimatize, domesticate; acclimate.

naturally ▶ adverb **1** *he's naturally shy* **by nature,** by character, inherently, innately, congenitally.
2 *try to act naturally* **normally,** in a natural manner/way, unaffectedly, spontaneously, genuinely, unpretentiously; informal natural.
ANTONYMS self-consciously.
3 *naturally, they wanted everything kept quiet* **of course,** as might be expected, needless to say; obviously, clearly, it goes without saying.
ANTONYMS surprisingly.

nature ▶ noun **1** *the beauty of nature* **the natural world,** Mother Nature, Mother Earth, the environment; wildlife, flora and fauna, the countryside; the universe, the cosmos.
2 *such crimes are, by their very nature, difficult to hide* **essence,** inherent/basic/essential qualities, inherent/basic/essential features, character, complexion.
3 *it was not in her nature to argue* **character,** personality, disposition, temperament, makeup, psyche, constitution.
4 *experiments of a similar nature* **kind,** sort, type, variety, category, ilk, class, species, genre, style, cast, order, kidney, mold, stamp, stripe.

naughty ▶ adjective **1** *a naughty boy* **badly behaved,** disobedient, bad, misbehaved, misbehaving, wayward, defiant, unruly, insubordinate, willful, delinquent, undisciplined, uncontrollable, ill-mannered, ungovernable, unbiddable, disorderly, disruptive, fractious, recalcitrant, wild, wicked, obstreperous, difficult, troublesome, awkward, contrary, perverse, incorrigible; mischievous, playful, impish, roguish, rascally; informal bratty; formal refractory.
ANTONYMS well-behaved.
2 *naughty jokes* **indecent,** risqué, rude, racy, ribald, bawdy, suggestive, improper, indelicate, indecorous; vulgar, dirty, filthy, smutty, crude, coarse, obscene, lewd, pornographic; informal raunchy, saucy; euphemistic adult.
ANTONYMS decent.

nausea ▶ noun **1** *symptoms include nausea and headaches* **sickness,** biliousness, queasiness; vomiting, retching, gagging; upset stomach; travel-sickness, seasickness, carsickness, airsickness.
2 *it induces a feeling of nausea* **disgust,** revulsion, repugnance, repulsion, distaste, aversion, loathing, abhorrence.

nauseous ▶ adjective *the food made her feel nauseous* **sick,** nauseated, queasy, bilious, green around the gills, ill, unwell; seasick, carsick, airsick, travel-sick; informal barfy; rare qualmish.

nautical ▶ adjective *a library of nautical history and literature* **maritime,** marine, naval, seafaring; boating, sailing.

navel ▶ noun **1** *one's navel can be hollow or projecting* informal belly button; Anatomy umbilicus.
2 *the navel of Byzantine culture* **center,** central point, hub, focal point, focus, nucleus, heart, core; literary omphalos.

navigable ▶ adjective *after October, these waters are not navigable by ordinary craft* **passable,** negotiable, traversable; clear, open, unobstructed, unblocked.

navigate ▶ verb **1** *he navigated the yacht across the Atlantic* **steer,** pilot, guide, direct, helm, captain; Nautical con; informal skipper.
2 *the upper reaches are dangerous to navigate* **sail across/over,** sail, travel/journey/voyage across/over, cross, traverse, negotiate, pass.
3 *I'll drive—you can navigate* **map-read,** give directions, plan the route.

navigator ▶ noun *he had learned to be an able navigator by the time he was twelve* **helmsman,** steersman, pilot, guide, wheelman.

navy ▶ noun **1** *a 600-ship navy* **fleet,** flotilla, armada, naval force.
2 *a navy blazer* **navy blue,** dark blue, midnight blue, indigo.

near ▶ adverb **1** *her children live near* **nearby**.
2 *near perfect conditions* **almost,** just about, nearly, practically, virtually; literary well-nigh.
▶ preposition *a hotel near the seafront* **close to,** close by, a short distance from, in the vicinity of, in the neighborhood of, within reach of, a stone's throw away from; informal within spitting distance of.
▶ adjective **1** *the nearest house* **close,** nearby, close/near at hand, at hand, a stone's throw away, within reach, accessible, handy, convenient; informal within spitting distance.
ANTONYMS far.
2 *the final judgment is near* **imminent,** in the offing, close/near at hand, at hand, (just) around the corner, impending, looming.
ANTONYMS remote, distant.
3 *a near relation* **closely related,** close, related.
ANTONYMS distant.
4 *a near escape* **narrow,** close, by a hair's breadth; informal by a whisker.
▶ verb **1** *by dawn we were nearing Moscow* **approach,** draw near/nearer to, get close/closer to, advance toward, close in on.
2 *the death toll is nearing 3,000* **verge on,** border on, approach.

nearly ▶ adverb *it was nearly midnight* **almost,** just about, about, more or less, practically, virtually, all but, as good as, not far off, to all intents and purposes; not quite; informal pretty much, pretty well; literary well-nigh.

nearsighted ▶ adjective *I'm too nearsighted to go without my glasses* **myopic;** informal as blind as a bat; archaic purblind.
ANTONYMS farsighted.

neat ▶ adjective **1** *the bedroom was neat and clean* **tidy**, orderly, well-ordered, in (good) order, shipshape, in apple-pie order, spick-and-span, uncluttered, straight, trim.
ANTONYMS untidy.
2 *he's very neat* **smart**, dapper, trim, well-groomed, well-turned-out, spruce; informal natty.
ANTONYMS shabby.
3 *her neat script* **well-formed**, regular, precise, elegant, well-proportioned.
4 *this neat little gadget* **compact**, well designed, handy.
5 *his neat footwork* **skillful**, deft, dexterous, adroit, adept, expert; informal nifty.
ANTONYMS clumsy.
6 *a neat solution* **clever**, ingenious, inventive.
7 *neat gin* **undiluted**, straight, unmixed; informal straight up.
8 informal *we had a really neat time* See **WONDERFUL**.

neatly ▶ adverb **1** *neatly arranged papers* **tidily**, methodically, systematically; smartly, sprucely.
2 *the point was neatly put* **cleverly**, aptly, elegantly.
3 *a neatly executed turn* **skillfully**, deftly, adroitly, adeptly, expertly.

nebulous ▶ adjective **1** *the figure was nebulous* **indistinct**, indefinite, unclear, vague, hazy, cloudy, fuzzy, misty, blurred, blurry, foggy; faint, shadowy, obscure, formless, amorphous.
ANTONYMS clear.
2 *nebulous ideas* **vague**, ill-defined, unclear, hazy, uncertain, indefinite, indeterminate, imprecise, unformed, muddled, confused, ambiguous.
ANTONYMS well-defined.

necessarily ▶ adverb *an increase in fees does not necessarily guarantee a balanced budget* **as a consequence**, as a result, automatically, as a matter of course, certainly, surely, definitely, incontrovertibly, undoubtedly, inevitably, unavoidably, inescapably, ineluctably, of necessity; formal perforce.

necessary ▶ adjective **1** *parental permission is necessary* **obligatory**, requisite, required, compulsory, mandatory, imperative, needed, de rigueur; essential, indispensable, vital.
2 *a necessary consequence* **inevitable**, unavoidable, inescapable, inexorable, ineluctable; predetermined, preordained.

CHOOSE THE RIGHT WORD

necessary, essential, indispensable, requisite

Food is **essential** to human life, which means that we must have it to survive. *Essential* can also apply to something that makes up the *essence*, or necessary qualities or attributes, of a thing (*a good safecracker is essential to our plan*). Clothing is **indispensable** in Northern climates, which means that it cannot be done without if the specified or implied purpose—in this case, survival—is to be achieved. **Necessary** applies to something without which a condition cannot be fulfilled (*cooperation was necessary to gather the harvest*), although it generally implies a pressing need rather than absolute indispensability. **Requisite** refers to that which is required by the circumstances (*the requisite skills for a botanist*) and generally describes a requirement that is imposed from the outside rather than an inherent need.

necessitate ▶ verb *the additional enrollment necessitates an additional staff person* **make necessary**, entail, involve, mean, require, demand, call for, be grounds for, warrant, constrain, force. See note at **COMPEL**.

necessitous ▶ adjective *distributing milk to necessitous mothers* **needy**, poor, short of money, disadvantaged, underprivileged, in straitened circumstances, impoverished, poverty-stricken, penniless, impecunious, destitute, pauperized, indigent, without a cent to one's name; informal hard up; formal penurious.
ANTONYMS wealthy.

necessity ▶ noun **1** *the microwave is now regarded as a necessity* **essential**, indispensable item, requisite, prerequisite, necessary, basic, sine qua non, desideratum; informal must-have.
2 *political necessity forced him to resign* **force of circumstance**, obligation, need, call, exigency; force majeure.
3 *the necessity of growing old* **inevitability**, certainty, inescapability, inexorability, ineluctability.
4 *necessity made them steal* **poverty**, need, neediness, want, deprivation, privation, penury, destitution, indigence.
– PHRASES **of necessity** *the renovations will, of necessity, require a more aggressive fund-raising campaign* **necessarily**, inevitably, unavoidably, inescapably, ineluctably; as a matter of course, naturally, automatically, certainly, surely, definitely, incontrovertibly, undoubtedly; formal perforce.

necromancer ▶ noun *a convention of spiritualists and necromancers* **sorcerer**, sorceress, (black) magician, wizard, warlock, witch, enchantress, occultist, diviner; spiritualist, medium; rare thaumaturge, thaumaturgist.

necromancy ▶ noun *he had been a practitioner of necromancy in some small village in Central America* **sorcery**, (black) magic, witchcraft, witchery, wizardry, the occult, occultism, voodoo, hoodoo; divination; spiritualism.

necropolis ▶ noun *overlooking the woeful sea is the home to many a lost soldier, a rolling green necropolis* **cemetery**, graveyard, churchyard, burial ground; informal boneyard; historical potter's field, God's acre.

need ▶ verb **1** *do you need money?* **require**, be in need of, have need of, want; be crying out for, be desperate for; demand, call for, necessitate, entail, involve; lack, be without, be short of.
2 *you needn't come* **have to**, be obliged to, be compelled to.
3 *she needed him so much* **yearn for**, pine for, long for, desire, miss.
▶ noun **1** *there's no need to apologize* **necessity**, obligation, requirement, call, demand.
2 *basic human needs* **requirement**, essential,

necessity, want, requisite, prerequisite, demand, desideratum.
3 *their need was particularly pressing* **neediness,** want, poverty, deprivation, privation, hardship, destitution, indigence.
4 *my hour of need* **difficulty,** trouble, distress; crisis, emergency, urgency, extremity.
– PHRASES **in need** *these children are in need* **needy,** necessitous, deprived, disadvantaged, underprivileged, poor, impoverished, poverty-stricken, destitute, impecunious, indigent; formal penurious.

needful ▶ adjective formal *we'll do whatever is needful* **necessary,** needed, required, requisite; essential, imperative, vital, indispensable.

needle ▶ noun **1** *a needle and thread* **bodkin.**
2 *the virus is transmitted via needles* hypodermic needle, syringe; informal hypo.
3 *the needle on the meter* **indicator,** pointer, marker, arrow, hand.
4 *put the needle on the record* **stylus.**
▶ verb informal *he needled her too much* **goad,** provoke, bait, taunt, pester, harass, prick, prod, sting, tease; **irritate,** annoy, anger, vex, irk, nettle, pique, exasperate, infuriate, get on someone's nerves, rub the wrong way, ruffle someone's feathers, try someone's patience; informal aggravate, rile, niggle, get in someone's hair, hassle, get to, bug, miff, peeve, get/put someone's back up, get under someone's skin, get at, ride.

needless ▶ adjective *needless details* **unnecessary,** inessential, nonessential, unneeded, undesired, unwanted, uncalled for; gratuitous, pointless; dispensable, expendable, superfluous, redundant, excessive, supererogatory.
ANTONYMS necessary.
– PHRASES **needless to say** *needless to say, we are grateful for any and all donations* **of course,** as one would expect, not unexpectedly, it goes without saying, obviously, naturally; informal natch.

needlework ▶ noun *some of the surgeons keep their fingers nimble with needlework* **sewing,** stitching, embroidery, needlepoint, needlecraft, tapestry, crewel (work).

needy ▶ adjective *collecting food and blankets for needy families* **poor,** deprived, disadvantaged, underprivileged, necessitous, in need, needful, hard up, in straitened circumstances, poverty-stricken, indigent, impoverished, pauperized, destitute, impecunious, penniless, moneyless; informal broke, strapped (for cash), busted; formal penurious.
ANTONYMS wealthy.

ne'er-do-well ▶ noun *I don't want to end up a ne'er-do-well like my old man* **good-for-nothing,** layabout, loafer, idler, shirker, sluggard, slugabed, drone; informal lazybones, bum; archaic wastrel.

nefarious ▶ adjective *the nefarious long-lost brother returns to steal Iris's inheritance* **wicked,** evil, sinful, iniquitous, egregious, heinous, atrocious, vile, foul, abominable, odious, depraved, monstrous, fiendish, diabolical, unspeakable, despicable; villainous, criminal, corrupt, illegal, unlawful; dated dastardly.
ANTONYMS good.

negate ▶ verb **1** *they negated the court's ruling* **invalidate,** nullify, neutralize, cancel; undo, reverse, annul, void, revoke, rescind, repeal, retract, countermand, overrule, overturn; informal nix; formal abrogate. See note at VOID.
ANTONYMS validate, confirm.
2 *he has never successfully negated Henderson's central theory* **disprove,** prove wrong, prove false, refute, debunk, discredit, invalidate; informal poke holes in; formal confute.
ANTONYMS confirm.

negation ▶ noun **1** *negation of the findings* **denial,** contradiction, repudiation, refutation, rebuttal; nullification, cancellation, revocation, repeal, retraction; formal abrogation.
2 *evil is not just the negation of goodness* **opposite,** reverse, antithesis, contrary, inverse, converse; absence, want.

negative ▶ adjective **1** *a negative reply* **opposing,** opposed, contrary, anti-, dissenting, saying "no", in the negative.
ANTONYMS positive, affirmative.
2 *stop being so negative* **pessimistic,** defeatist, gloomy, cynical, fatalistic, dismissive, antipathetic, critical; unenthusiastic, uninterested, unresponsive.
ANTONYMS positive, optimistic.
3 *a negative effect on the economy* **harmful,** bad, adverse, damaging, detrimental, unfavorable, disadvantageous.
ANTONYMS good, favorable.
▶ noun *he murmured a negative* **"no",** refusal, rejection, veto; dissension, contradiction; denial; informal thumbs-down.

neglect ▶ verb **1** *she neglected the children* **fail to look after,** leave alone, abandon, desert; literary forsake.
ANTONYMS cherish, look after.
2 *he's neglecting his work* **pay no attention to,** let slide, not attend to, be remiss about, be lax about, leave undone, shirk.
ANTONYMS concentrate on.
3 *don't neglect our advice* **disregard,** ignore, pay no attention to, take no notice of, pay no heed to, overlook; disdain, scorn, spurn.
ANTONYMS heed.
4 *I neglected to inform her* **fail,** omit, forget.
ANTONYMS remember.
▶ noun **1** *the place had an air of neglect* **disrepair,** dilapidation, deterioration, shabbiness, disuse, abandonment; rare desuetude.
2 *her doctor was guilty of neglect* **negligence,** dereliction of duty, carelessness, heedlessness, unconcern, laxity, slackness, irresponsibility; formal delinquency.
ANTONYMS care.
3 *the neglect of women's concerns* **disregard of/for,** ignoring of, overlooking of; inattention to, indifference to, heedlessness to.
ANTONYMS attention.

CHOOSE THE RIGHT WORD

neglect, disregard, ignore, overlook, slight

One of the most common reasons why people fail to arrive at work on time is that they **neglect** to set their alarm clocks, a verb that implies a failure to carry out some expected or required action, either intentionally or through carelessness. Some people, of course, choose to **disregard** their employer's rules pertaining to tardiness, which implies a voluntary, and sometimes deliberate, inattention. Others hear the alarm go off and simply **ignore** it, which suggests not only a deliberate decision to **disregard** something but a stubborn refusal to face the facts. No doubt they hope their employers will **overlook** their frequent late arrivals, which implies a failure to see or to take action, which can be either intentional or due to haste or lack of care (*to overlook minor errors*). But they also hope no one will **slight** them for their conduct when it comes to handing out raises and promotions, which means to **disregard** or **neglect** in a disdainful way.

neglected ▶ adjective **1** *neglected animals* **uncared for,** abandoned; mistreated, maltreated; literary forsaken.
2 *a neglected cottage* **derelict,** dilapidated, tumbledown, ramshackle, untended.
3 *a neglected masterpiece of prose* **disregarded,** forgotten, overlooked, ignored, unrecognized, unnoticed, unsung, underestimated, undervalued, unappreciated.

neglectful ▶ adjective See NEGLIGENT.

negligent ▶ adjective *a negligent safety inspector* **neglectful,** remiss, careless, lax, irresponsible, inattentive, heedless, thoughtless, unmindful, forgetful; slack, sloppy, derelict; formal delinquent.
ANTONYMS dutiful.

negligible ▶ adjective *the defects are negligible* **trivial,** trifling, insignificant, unimportant, minor, inconsequential; minimal, small, slight, inappreciable, infinitesimal, nugatory, petty; paltry, inadequate, insufficient, meager, pitiful; informal minuscule, piddling, measly; formal exiguous.
ANTONYMS significant.

negotiable ▶ adjective **1** *salary is negotiable* **open to discussion,** discussable, flexible, open to modification; unsettled, undecided.
2 *the pathway was negotiable* **passable,** navigable, crossable, traversable; clear, unblocked, unobstructed.
3 *negotiable checks* **transferable;** valid.

negotiate ▶ verb **1** *she refused to negotiate* **discuss terms,** talk, consult, parley, confer, debate; compromise; mediate, intercede, arbitrate, moderate, conciliate; bargain, haggle.
2 *he negotiated a new contract* **arrange,** broker, work out, thrash out, agree on; settle, clinch, conclude, pull off, bring off, transact; informal sort out, swing.
3 *I negotiated the obstacles* **get around,** get past, get over, clear, cross; surmount, overcome, deal with, cope with.

negotiation ▶ noun **1** (**negotiations**) *the negotiations resume next week* **discussion(s),** talks, deliberations; conference, debate, dialogue, consultation; mediation, arbitration, conciliation.
2 *the negotiation of the deal* **arrangement,** brokering; settlement, conclusion, completion, transaction.

negotiator ▶ noun *they brought in an impartial negotiator to help settle the dispute* **mediator,** arbitrator, arbiter, moderator, go-between, middleman, intermediary, intercessor, intervener, conciliator; representative, spokesperson, broker, bargainer.

neighborhood ▶ noun **1** *a quiet neighborhood* **district,** area, locality, locale, quarter, community; part, region, zone; informal neck of the woods, hood, nabe, stomping ground, stamping ground.
2 *in the neighborhood of Greensboro* **vicinity,** environs, purlieus, precincts, vicinage.
– PHRASES **in the neighborhood of** *a new roof will be in the neighborhood of $4,000* **approximately,** about, around, roughly, in the region of, of/on the order of, nearly, almost, close to, just about, practically, there or thereabouts, circa.

neighboring ▶ adjective *the owner of the neighboring property* **adjacent,** adjoining, bordering, connecting, abutting; proximate, near, close, close/near at hand, next-door, nearby, in the vicinity.
ANTONYMS remote.

nemesis ▶ noun **1** *they were beaten in the final by their nemesis* **archrival,** adversary, foe, opponent, arch enemy.
2 *this could be the bank's nemesis* **downfall,** undoing, ruin, ruination, destruction, Waterloo.
3 *the nemesis that his crime deserved* **retribution,** vengeance, punishment, just deserts; fate, destiny.

neologism ▶ noun *the delightful neologisms of Lewis Carroll* **new word,** new expression, new term, new phrase, coinage; made-up word, nonce word.

neophyte ▶ noun **1** *a neophyte of the monastery* **novice,** novitiate; postulant, catechumen.
2 *cooking classes are offered to neophytes* **beginner,** learner, novice, newcomer; initiate, tyro, fledgling; trainee, apprentice, probationer, tenderfoot; informal rookie, newbie, greenhorn. See note at NOVICE.

ne plus ultra ▶ noun *the ne plus ultra of jazz pianists* **last word,** ultimate, perfect example, height, acme, zenith, epitome, quintessence.

nepotism ▶ noun *hiring my daughter was not nepotism—it was just good business* **favoritism,** preferential treatment, the old boy network, looking after one's own, bias, partiality, partisanship.
ANTONYMS impartiality.

nerve ▶ noun **1** *the nerves that transmit pain* **nerve fiber,** neuron, axon, dendrite.
2 *the match will be a test of nerve* **confidence,** assurance, coolheadedness, self-possession; courage, bravery, pluck, boldness, intrepidity, fearlessness, daring; determination, willpower, spirit, backbone, fortitude, intestinal fortitude, mettle, grit, true grit, stout-heartedness; informal

guts, spunk, moxie. See note at COURAGE.
3 *he had the nerve to ask her out again* **audacity,** cheek, effrontery, gall, temerity, presumption, boldness, brazenness, impudence, impertinence, arrogance, cockiness; informal face, front, chutzpah.
4 *pre-wedding nerves* **anxiety,** tension, nervousness, stress, worry, cold feet, apprehension; informal butterflies (in one's stomach), the jitters, the shakes, the heebie-jeebies.
– PHRASES **get on someone's nerves** *her squeaky voice gets on my nerves* **irritate,** annoy, irk, anger, bother, vex, provoke, displease, exasperate, infuriate, gall, pique, needle, ruffle someone's feathers, try someone's patience; jar on, grate on, rankle; rub the wrong way; informal aggravate, get to, bug, miff, peeve, rile, nettle, get someone's goat, tick off.

nerve-racking ▶ adjective *it's the waiting that's the most nerve-racking* **stressful,** anxious, worrying, fraught, nail-biting, tense, difficult, trying, worrisome, daunting, frightening; informal scary, hairy.

nervous ▶ adjective **1** *a nervous woman* **high-strung,** anxious, edgy, tense, excitable, jumpy, skittish, brittle, neurotic; timid, mousy, shy, fearful.
ANTONYMS relaxed, calm.
2 *he was so nervous he couldn't eat* **anxious,** worried, apprehensive, on edge, edgy, tense, stressed, agitated, uneasy, restless, worked up, keyed up, overwrought, jumpy; fearful, frightened, scared, shaky, in a cold sweat, gun-shy; informal with butterflies in one's stomach, trepidatious, jittery, twitchy, in a state, uptight, wired, in a flap, het up, strung out, having kittens.
ANTONYMS relaxed, calm.
3 *a nervous disorder* **neurological,** neural.

nervous breakdown ▶ noun *the boss's nervous breakdown almost destroyed the company* **mental collapse,** breakdown, collapse, crisis, trauma; nervous exhaustion, mental illness; informal crack-up.

nervousness ▶ noun *she began chattering out of nervousness* **anxiety,** edginess, tension, agitation, stress, worry, apprehension, uneasiness, disquiet, fear, trepidation, perturbation, alarm; informal butterflies (in one's stomach), the jitters, the willies, the heebie-jeebies, the shakes.

nervy ▶ adjective *it was a nervy move* **audacious,** impudent, brazen, cheeky, bold, plucky; informal gutsy, spunky, ballsy.

nest ▶ noun **1** *the birds built a nest* **roost,** aerie.
2 *the animals disperse rapidly from the nest* **lair,** den, burrow.
3 *a cozy love nest* **hideaway,** hideout, retreat, shelter, refuge, den.
4 *a nest of intrigue* **hotbed,** den, breeding ground, cradle.

nest egg ▶ noun *her nest egg wasn't much, but it was enough to keep the wolves from the door* **savings,** life savings, cache, funds, reserve.

nestle ▶ verb *the little ones nestled under the cozy quilt with their mother* **snuggle,** cuddle, huddle, nuzzle, settle, burrow.

Net ▶ noun *their first communication was through the Net* **the Internet,** the World Wide Web, the Web; dated cyberspace, the information superhighway, the infobahn.

net[1] ▶ noun **1** *fishermen mending their nets* **fishing net,** dragnet, drift net, trawl (net), landing net, gill net, cast net, seine.
2 *a dress of green net* **netting,** meshwork, webbing, tulle, fishnet, openwork, lace, latticework.
3 *he managed to escape the net* **trap,** snare.
▶ verb *they netted big criminals* **catch,** capture, trap, entrap, snare, ensnare, bag, hook, land; informal nab, collar.

net[2] ▶ adjective **1** *net earnings* **after tax,** after deductions, take-home, final; informal bottom line.
ANTONYMS gross.
2 *the net result* **final,** end, ultimate, closing; overall, actual, effective.
▶ verb *she netted $50,000* **earn,** make, get, gain, obtain, acquire, accumulate, clear, take home, bring in, pocket, realize, be paid; informal rake in.

nether ▶ adjective *the nether regions* **lower,** low, bottom, bottommost, under, basal; underground.
ANTONYMS upper.

nettle ▶ verb *I try not to be nettled by her, but it isn't easy* **irritate,** annoy, irk, gall, vex, anger, exasperate, infuriate, provoke; upset, displease, offend, affront, pique, get on someone's nerves, try someone's patience, ruffle someone's feathers; rub the wrong way, rankle; informal peeve, aggravate, miff, rile, needle, get to, bug, get someone's goat, tick off.

network ▶ noun **1** *a network of arteries* **web,** lattice, net, matrix, mesh, crisscross, grid, reticulum, reticulation; Anatomy plexus.
2 *a network of lanes* **maze,** labyrinth, warren, tangle.
3 *a network of friends* **system,** complex, nexus, web, webwork.

neurosis ▶ noun *has he been diagnosed with an actual neurosis?* **mental illness,** mental disorder, psychological disorder; psychoneurosis, psychopathy; obsession, phobia, fixation; Medicine neuroticism.

neurotic ▶ adjective **1** Medicine *neurotic patients* **mentally ill,** mentally disturbed, unstable, unbalanced, maladjusted; psychopathic, phobic, obsessive–compulsive.
ANTONYMS stable, well balanced.
2 *a neurotic, self-obsessed woman* **overanxious,** oversensitive, nervous, tense, high-strung, strung-out, paranoid; obsessive, fixated, hysterical, overwrought, worked-up, irrational, twitchy.
ANTONYMS laid-back, calm.

neuter ▶ adjective *the traumatic abuses of his childhood left him feeling more neuter than masculine* **asexual,** sexless, unsexed; androgynous, epicene.
▶ verb *have your pets neutered* **sterilize,** castrate, spay, geld, fix, desex, alter, doctor; archaic emasculate.

neutral ▶ adjective **1** *a neutral judge* **impartial,** unbiased, unprejudiced, objective, open-minded,

nonpartisan, disinterested, dispassionate, detached, impersonal, unemotional, indifferent, uncommitted.
ANTONYMS biased, partisan.
2 *Switzerland remained neutral* **unaligned,** nonaligned, unaffiliated, unallied, uninvolved; noncombatant.
ANTONYMS partisan, combatant.
3 *a neutral topic of conversation* **inoffensive,** bland, unobjectionable, unexceptionable, anodyne, unremarkable, ordinary, commonplace; safe, harmless, innocuous.
ANTONYMS provocative, offensive.
4 *a neutral background* **pale,** light; beige, cream, taupe, oatmeal, ecru, buff, fawn, gray; colorless, uncolored, achromatic; indeterminate, insipid, nondescript, dull, drab.
ANTONYMS bright, colorful.

neutralize ▶ **verb** *if the internal dissension is not neutralized, we have no hope of moving forward* **counteract,** offset, counterbalance, balance, counterpoise, countervail, compensate for, make up for; cancel out, nullify, negate; equalize.

never ▶ **adverb 1** *his room is never tidy* **not ever,** at no time, not at any time, not once; literary ne'er.
ANTONYMS always.
2 *she will never agree to it* **not at all,** certainly not, not for a moment, under no circumstances, on no account, nevermore; informal no way, not on your life, not in a million years, when pigs fly, when hell freezes over.
ANTONYMS certainly, definitely.

never-ending ▶ **adjective** *never-ending noise* **incessant,** continuous, unceasing, ceaseless, constant, continual, perpetual, uninterrupted, unbroken, steady, unremitting, relentless, persistent, interminable, nonstop, endless, unending, everlasting, eternal. See note at **ETERNAL.**

nevertheless ▶ **adverb** *nevertheless, it makes sense to take a few precautions* **nonetheless,** even so, however, but, still, yet, though; in spite of that, despite that, be that as it may, for all that, that said, just the same, all the same; notwithstanding, regardless, anyway, anyhow, still and all.

new ▶ **adjective 1** *new technology* **recently developed,** up to date, latest, current, state-of-the-art, contemporary, advanced, recent, modern, cutting-edge, leading-edge.
ANTONYMS old, existing.
2 *new ideas* **novel,** original, fresh, imaginative, creative, experimental; contemporary, modernist, up to date; newfangled, ultramodern, avant-garde, futuristic; informal way out, far out.
ANTONYMS old-fashioned, hackneyed.
3 *is your boat new?* **unused,** brand new, pristine, fresh, in mint condition.
ANTONYMS old, secondhand.
4 *we have to find a new approach* **different,** another, alternative; unfamiliar, unknown, strange; unaccustomed, untried.
ANTONYMS present.
5 *they had a new classroom built* **additional,** extra, supplementary, further, another, fresh.
ANTONYMS existing.
6 *I came back a new woman* **reinvigorated,** restored, revived, improved, refreshed, regenerated, reborn.

newborn ▶ **adjective** *newborn babies* **just born,** recently born.
▶ **noun** *the bacteria are dangerous to newborns* **young baby,** tiny baby, infant; Medicine neonate.

newcomer ▶ **noun 1** *a newcomer to the village* **(new) arrival,** immigrant, settler; stranger, outsider, foreigner, alien; informal johnny-come-lately, new kid on the block.
2 *photography tips for the newcomer* **beginner,** novice, learner; trainee, apprentice, tyro, initiate, neophyte, tenderfoot; informal rookie, newbie, greenhorn.

newfangled ▶ **adjective** *newfangled digital technology* **new,** the latest, modern, ultramodern, up-to-the-minute, state-of-the-art, advanced, contemporary, new-generation; informal trendy, flash.
ANTONYMS dated.

newly ▶ **adverb** *a newly discovered species of moth* **recently,** just, only just, lately, freshly; not long ago, a short time ago, only now, of late; new-.

news ▶ **noun** *they were stunned by the news of his death* **report,** announcement, story, account; article, news flash, newscast, headlines, press release, communication, communiqué, bulletin; message, dispatch, statement, intelligence; disclosure, revelation, word, talk, gossip; informal scoop; literary tidings.

newspaper ▶ **noun** *the front-page story in today's newspaper* **paper,** journal, gazette, tabloid, broadsheet, local (paper), daily (paper), weekly (paper); scandal sheet; informal rag, tab.

next ▶ **adjective 1** *the next chapter* **following,** succeeding, upcoming, to come.
ANTONYMS previous, preceding.
2 *the next house in the street* **neighboring,** adjacent, adjoining, next-door, bordering, connected, attached; closest, nearest.
▶ **adverb** *where shall we go next?* **then,** after, afterward, afterwards, after this/that, following that/this, later, subsequently; formal thereafter, thereupon.
ANTONYMS before.
– PHRASES **next to** *she sat down next to a window* **beside,** by, alongside, by the side of, next door to, adjacent to, side by side with; close to, near, neighboring, adjoining.

nibble ▶ **verb 1** *they nibbled at mangoes* **take small bites from,** pick at, gnaw at, peck at, snack on; toy with; taste, sample; informal graze on.
2 *the mouse nibbled his finger* **peck,** nip, bite.
▶ **noun 1** *the fish enjoyed a nibble on the lettuce* **bite,** gnaw, chew; taste.
2 *a few nibbles before dinner* **morsel,** mouthful, bite; snack, tidbit, canapé, hors d'oeuvre.

nice ▶ **adjective 1** *have a nice time* **enjoyable,** pleasant, agreeable, good, satisfying, gratifying, delightful, marvelous; entertaining, amusing, diverting, lovely, great.
ANTONYMS unpleasant.
2 *a nice landlord* **pleasant,** likable, agreeable, personable, congenial, amiable, affable, genial, friendly, charming, delightful, engaging;

sympathetic, simpatico, compassionate, good.
ANTONYMS nasty.
3 *nice manners* **polite,** courteous, civil, refined, polished, genteel, elegant.
ANTONYMS unrefined, rough.
4 *that's a rather nice distinction* **subtle,** fine, delicate, minute, precise, strict, close; careful, meticulous, scrupulous.
ANTONYMS approximate, rough.
5 *it's a nice day* **fine,** pleasant, agreeable; dry, sunny, warm, mild.
ANTONYMS stormy, nasty.

USAGE

nice

Nice originally had a number of meanings, including 'fine, subtle, discriminating' (*they are not very nice in regard to the company they keep*); 'refined in taste, hard to please, fastidious' (*for company so nice, the finest caterers would be engaged*); and 'precise, strict' (*she has a nice sense of decorum*). The popular overuse of *nice* to mean 'pleasant, agreeable, satisfactory' has rendered the word trite: *we had a very nice time; this is a nice room; he's a nice boy.*

nicety ▶ **noun 1** *legal niceties* **subtlety,** fine point, nuance, refinement, detail.
2 *great nicety of control* **precision,** accuracy, exactness, meticulousness.

niche ▶ **noun 1** *a niche in the wall* **recess,** alcove, nook, cranny, hollow, bay, cavity, cubbyhole, pigeonhole.
2 *he found his niche in life* **ideal position,** place, function, vocation, calling, métier, job.

nickname ▶ **noun** *"Bambi" is the nickname my sister gave me when I was a baby* **sobriquet,** byname, tag, label, epithet, cognomen; pet name, diminutive, endearment; informal moniker; formal appellation.

nifty ▶ **adjective** informal **1** *nifty camerawork* **skillful,** deft, agile, capable.
ANTONYMS clumsy.
2 *a nifty little gadget* **useful,** handy, practical.
3 *a nifty suit* **fashionable,** stylish, smart.

niggardly ▶ **adjective 1** *a niggardly person* **cheap,** mean, miserly, parsimonious, close-fisted, penny-pinching, cheeseparing, grasping, ungenerous, illiberal; informal stingy, tight, tightfisted.
ANTONYMS generous.
2 *niggardly rations* **meager,** inadequate, scanty, scant, skimpy, paltry, sparse, insufficient, deficient, short, lean, small, slender, poor, miserable, pitiful, puny; informal measly, stingy, pathetic, piddling.
ANTONYMS lavish, abundant.

niggle ▶ **verb 1** *his behavior does niggle me* **irritate,** annoy, bother, provoke, exasperate, upset, gall, irk, rankle with; informal rile, get to, bug.
2 *he niggles about the prices* **complain,** quibble, nitpick, fuss, carp, cavil, grumble, gripe, grouse, moan.
▶ **noun** *niggles about the lack of equipment* **quibble,** trivial complaint, criticism, grumble, grouse, cavil; informal gripe, moan, beef.

night ▶ **noun** *they did all their dirty dealing during the night* nighttime; hours of darkness, darkness, dark; nightfall, sunset.
ANTONYMS day.
– PHRASES **night and day** *wartime factories ran night and day* **all the time,** around/round the clock, 'morning, noon, and night', 'day in, day out', ceaselessly, endlessly, incessantly, unceasingly, interminably, constantly, perpetually, continually, relentlessly; informal 24–7.

nightfall ▶ **noun** *we lock the doors at nightfall* **sunset,** sundown, dusk, twilight, evening, close of day, dark; literary eventide.
ANTONYMS dawn.

nightly ▶ **adjective 1** *nightly raids* **every night,** each night, night after night.
2 *his nightly wanderings* **nocturnal,** nighttime.
▶ **adverb** *a band plays there nightly* **every night,** each night, night after night.

nightmare ▶ **noun 1** *she woke from a nightmare* **bad dream,** night terrors; archaic incubus.
2 *the journey was a nightmare* **ordeal,** trial, torment, horror, hell, misery, agony, torture, murder; curse, bane.

nihilism ▶ **noun** *she could not accept Bacon's nihilism, his insistence that man is a futile being* **skepticism,** negativity, cynicism, pessimism; disbelief, unbelief, agnosticism, atheism.

nil ▶ **noun** *our chances of getting there on time were nil* **nothing,** none; zero, O, naught/nought; Tennis love; informal zilch, zip, nada, a goose egg, nix; dated cipher.

nimble ▶ **adjective 1** *he was nimble on his feet* **agile,** sprightly, light, spry, lively, quick, graceful, lithe, limber; skillful, deft, dexterous, adroit; informal nippy, twinkle-toed; literary lightsome.
ANTONYMS clumsy.
2 *a nimble mind* **quick-witted,** quick, alert, lively, wide awake, observant, astute, adroit, perceptive, penetrating, discerning, shrewd, sharp; intelligent, bright, smart, clever, brilliant; informal brainy, quick on the uptake.
ANTONYMS dull.

nip ▶ **verb** *the child nipped her* **bite,** nibble, peck; pinch, tweak, squeeze, grip.
▶ **noun** *a nip in the air* **chill,** biting cold, iciness.
– PHRASES **nip something in the bud** *before your children start spending most of their free time in front of the television or computer, nip it in the bud* **cut short,** curtail, check, curb, thwart, frustrate, stop, halt, arrest, stifle, obstruct, block, squash, quash, subdue, crack down on, stamp out; informal put the kibosh on.

nipple ▶ **noun** *the mother dog's nipples* **teat;** informal tit; Anatomy mamilla.

nippy ▶ **adjective** *it's a bit nippy in here* **cold,** chilly, icy, bitter, raw.
ANTONYMS warm.

nirvana ▶ **noun** *there are no shortcuts to nirvana* **paradise,** heaven; bliss, ecstasy, joy, peace, serenity, tranquility; enlightenment.
ANTONYMS hell.

nitpicking ▶ **adjective** informal See **PEDANTIC**.

nitty-gritty ▶ **noun** informal *now let's get to the nitty-gritty of managing your own business* **basics,** essentials, fundamentals, substance, quintessence, heart of the matter; nub, crux, gist, meat, kernel, marrow; informal brass tacks, bottom line; nuts and bolts.

nitwit ▶ **noun** informal See IDIOT.

no ▶ **exclamation** *no, I will not go on a date with your cousin Ralph* **absolutely not,** most certainly not, of course not, under no circumstances, by no means, not at all, negative, never, not really; informal nope, uh-uh, nah, not on your life, no way, no way José, ixnay; archaic nay.
ANTONYMS yes.

nobility ▶ **noun 1** *a member of the nobility* **aristocracy,** aristocrats, peerage, peers (of the realm), lords, nobles, noblemen, noblewomen, patricians; informal aristos.
2 *the nobility of his deed* **virtue,** goodness, honor, decency, integrity; magnanimity, generosity, selflessness.

noble ▶ **adjective 1** *a noble family* **aristocratic,** patrician, blue-blooded, high-born, titled; archaic gentle.
ANTONYMS humble.
2 *a noble cause* **righteous,** virtuous, good, honorable, upright, decent, worthy, moral, ethical, reputable; magnanimous, unselfish, generous.
ANTONYMS dishonorable.
3 *a noble pine forest* **magnificent,** splendid, grand, stately, imposing, dignified, proud, striking, impressive, majestic, glorious, awesome, monumental, statuesque, regal, imperial.
ANTONYMS unimpressive.
▶ **noun** *Scottish nobles* **aristocrat,** nobleman, noblewoman, lord, lady, peer, peeress, peer of the realm, patrician; informal aristo.

nod ▶ **verb 1** *she nodded her head* **incline,** bob, bow, dip.
2 *he nodded to me to start* **signal,** gesture, gesticulate, motion, sign, indicate.
▶ **noun 1** *she gave a nod to the manager* **signal,** indication, sign, cue; gesture.
2 *a quick nod of his head* **inclination,** bob, bow, dip.
3 *Halifax will get the nod as host city* **approval,** selection, sanction, endorsement; informal OK, A-OK, green light, thumbs up.
– PHRASES **nod off** *give me a pillow and I'll nod off right this second* **fall asleep,** go to sleep, doze off, drop off; informal drift off, go out like a light, sack out, drift into the arms of Morpheus.

node ▶ **noun** *the node of the branches* **junction,** intersection, interchange, fork, confluence, convergence, crossing.

noise ▶ **noun** *I have a headache from all the noise* **sound,** din, hubbub, clamor, racket, uproar, tumult, commotion, pandemonium, babel; informal hullabaloo.
ANTONYMS silence.

noisome ▶ **adjective** See ODIOUS.

noisy ▶ **adjective 1** *a noisy crowd* **rowdy,** clamorous, boisterous, turbulent, uproarious, riotous, rambunctious, rackety; chattering, talkative, vociferous, shouting, screaming.
ANTONYMS quiet.
2 *noisy music* **loud,** fortissimo, blaring, booming, overloud, deafening, thunderous, tumultuous, clamorous, ear-splitting, piercing, strident, cacophonous, raucous.
ANTONYMS soft.

nomad ▶ **noun** *a photojournalist who lived with a clan of nomads for six months* **itinerant,** traveler, migrant, wanderer, roamer, rover; gypsy, Bedouin; transient, drifter, vagabond, vagrant, tramp.

nominal ▶ **adjective 1** *the nominal head of the campaign* **in name only,** titular, formal, official; theoretical, supposed, ostensible, so-called.
ANTONYMS real.
2 *a nominal rent* **token,** symbolic; tiny, minute, minimal, small, insignificant, trifling; informal minuscule, piddling, piffling.
ANTONYMS considerable.

nominate ▶ **verb 1** *you may nominate a candidate* **propose,** recommend, suggest, name, put forward, present, submit.
2 *he nominated his assistant* **appoint,** select, choose, elect, commission, designate, name, delegate.

nonbeliever ▶ **noun** *her family condemned her for marrying a nonbeliever* **unbeliever,** disbeliever, skeptic, doubter, doubting Thomas, cynic, nihilist; atheist, agnostic, freethinker; infidel, pagan, heathen.

nonce ▶ **noun**
– PHRASES **for the nonce** *for the nonce, I'll be the acting chairman* **for the time being,** temporarily, pro tem, for now, for the moment, for the interim, for a while, for the present, in the meantime; provisionally.

nonchalant ▶ **adjective** *she acts nonchalant, but I think she's quite nervous* **calm,** composed, unconcerned, cool, 'calm, cool, and collected', cool as a cucumber; indifferent, blasé, dispassionate, apathetic, casual, insouciant; informal laid-back.
ANTONYMS anxious.

noncommittal ▶ **adjective** *please advise your client that this court expects something more substantial than a string of noncommittal responses* **evasive,** equivocal, guarded, circumspect, reserved; discreet, uncommunicative, tactful, diplomatic, vague; informal cagey.
– PHRASES **be noncommittal** *he was noncommittal about their chances of success* **equivocate,** give nothing away, dodge the issue, sidestep the issue, hedge, pussyfoot around, beat around the bush, temporize, shilly-shally, vacillate, waver; hem and haw; informal duck the question, sit on the fence.

non compos mentis ▶ **adjective** See INSANE (sense 1).

nonconformist ▶ **noun** *our college has the reputation of being a haven for nonconformists* **dissenter,** dissentient, protester, rebel, renegade, schismatic; freethinker, apostate, heretic; individualist, free spirit, maverick, eccentric, original, deviant, misfit, dropout, outsider, Bohemian.

nondescript ▶ adjective *he was of average height and build, and even his clothes were nondescript* **undistinguished,** unremarkable, unexceptional, featureless, characterless, faceless, unmemorable, lackluster; ordinary, commonplace, average, run-of-the-mill, mundane, garden-variety; uninteresting, uninspiring, colorless, bland, dull.
ANTONYMS distinctive.

none ▶ pronoun **1** *I saw none of the fish that you saw* **not one,** not a (single) one.
ANTONYMS all.
2 *none of this concerns me* **no part,** not a bit, not any.
ANTONYMS all.
3 *none can know better than you* **not one,** no one, nobody, not a soul, not a single person, no man.
ANTONYMS all.
– PHRASES **none the ——** *we were left none the wiser* **not at all,** not a bit, not the slightest bit, in no way, by no means any.

nonentity ▶ noun *the tragedy is that, even after all the therapy we can provide, many of these kids will continue to be the nonentities that they've been taught to be* **nobody,** unimportant person, zero, nonperson, no-name, nothing, small fry, mediocrity; informal no-hoper, loser.
ANTONYMS celebrity.

nonessential ▶ adjective *nonessential items such as colognes and cosmetics are not permitted* **unnecessary,** inessential, unessential, noncore, needless, unneeded, superfluous, uncalled for, redundant, dispensable, expendable, unimportant, extraneous.

nonetheless ▶ adverb *I doubt you have much to add—nonetheless, we want to hear your side of the story* **nevertheless,** even so, however, but, still, yet, though; in spite of that, despite that, be that as it may, for all that, that said, just the same, all the same; notwithstanding, regardless, anyway, anyhow, still and all.

nonexistent ▶ adjective *studio honchos would feed the press stories of the nonexistent guy-girl romances of their homosexual stars* **imaginary,** imagined, unreal, fictional, fictitious, made up, invented, fanciful; fantastic, mythical; illusory, hallucinatory, chimerical, notional, shadowy, insubstantial; missing, absent; literary illusive.
ANTONYMS real.

nonintervention ▶ noun *a policy of nonintervention is not appropriate when the fundamental freedoms of others are in jeopardy and their very lives at risk* **laissez-faire,** nonparticipation, noninterference, inaction, passivity, neutrality; live and let live.

nonobservance ▶ noun *we take the nonobservance of curfew very seriously* **infringement,** breach, violation, contravention, transgression, noncompliance, infraction; dereliction, neglect.

nonpareil ▶ adjective *a nonpareil storyteller* **incomparable,** matchless, unrivaled, unparalleled, unequaled, peerless, beyond compare, second to none, unsurpassed, unbeatable, inimitable; unique, consummate, superlative, supreme; formal unexampled.
ANTONYMS mediocre.
▶ noun *without a doubt, theirs is the nonpareil* **best,** finest, crème de la crème, peak of perfection, elite, jewel in the crown, ne plus ultra, paragon; archaic nonesuch.

nonsense ▶ noun **1** *that's a lot of damn nonsense* **rubbish,** gibberish, claptrap, balderdash, blarney; informal hogwash, baloney, rot, moonshine, garbage, jive, tripe, drivel, bilge, bull, guff, bunk, bosh, BS, eyewash, piffle, poppycock, phooey, hooey, malarkey, hokum, twaddle, gobbledygook, codswallop, flapdoodle, hot air; dated bunkum, tommyrot; vulgar slang bullshit, crap.
ANTONYMS (good) sense.
2 *she stands no nonsense* **mischief,** naughtiness, bad behavior, misbehavior, misconduct, misdemeanor; pranks, tricks, clowning, buffoonery, funny business; informal tomfoolery, monkey business, shenanigans, hanky-panky.
ANTONYMS good behavior.
3 *they dismissed the concept as nonsense* **absurdity,** folly, stupidity, ludicrousness, inanity, foolishness, idiocy, insanity, madness.
ANTONYMS (good) sense, wisdom.
▶ exclamation *"Nonsense!" she retorted* **rubbish,** balderdash; informal no way, get out of here, get real, phooey, puh-leeze, hooey, poppycock, come off it, like hell; dated pshaw.

> CHOOSE THE RIGHT WORD
>
> **nonsense, bull, bunk, drivel, poppycock, twaddle**
>
> If you write or speak in an obscure, senseless, or unintelligible manner, you'll probably be accused of producing **nonsense**. It is the most general of these nouns and may refer to behavior as well as to what is said (*the demonstrators were told in no uncertain terms to stop this nonsense or leave the room*). **Twaddle** refers to silly, empty utterances from people who know nothing about a subject but who write or talk about it anyway (*I was sick of her twaddle about the dangers of electromagnetic fields*). **Bunk** (short for bunkum) applies to an utterance that strikes the popular fancy even though it is lacking in worth or substance (*the speech, which received enthusiastic applause, was pure bunk*). **Poppycock** applies to nonsense that is full of complex, confused, or clichéd ideas (*the report was a strange combination of logical thinking and outright poppycock*). **Bull** is a slang term for deceitful and often boastful writing or speech (*he gave them a line of bull*). Perhaps the most insulting of these terms is **drivel**, which implies a steady flow of inane, idle, or nonsensical speech or writing similar to what might be expected from a very young child or an idiot (*his first novel was full of romantic drivel*).

nonsensical ▶ adjective **1** *her nonsensical way of talking* **meaningless,** senseless, illogical.
ANTONYMS logical, rational.
2 *a nonsensical generalization* **foolish,** insane, stupid, idiotic, illogical, irrational, senseless,

absurd, silly, inane, harebrained, ridiculous, ludicrous, preposterous; informal crazy, crackpot, nutty; daft.
ANTONYMS sane, sensible.

nonstop ▶ adjective *nonstop entertainment* **continuous,** constant, continual, perpetual, incessant, unceasing, ceaseless, endless, uninterrupted, round-the-clock; unremitting, relentless, persistent, never-ending.
ANTONYMS occasional.
▶ adverb *we worked nonstop* **continuously,** continually, incessantly, unceasingly, ceaselessly, all the time, constantly, perpetually, around/round the clock, day and night, steadily, relentlessly, persistently; informal 24–7.
ANTONYMS occasionally.

nook ▶ noun *the children's library has cozy nooks for quiet reading* **recess,** corner, alcove, niche, cranny, bay, inglenook, cavity, cubbyhole, pigeonhole; opening, gap, aperture; hideaway, hiding place, hideout, shelter.

noon ▶ noun *the bank closes at noon* **midday,** twelve o'clock, twelve hundred hours, twelve noon, high noon, noon hour, noonday; literary noontime, noontide.

no one ▶ pronoun *no one shed a tear when he was fired* **nobody,** not a soul, not anyone, not a single person, never a one, none.

norm ▶ noun 1 *norms of diplomatic behavior* **convention,** standard; criterion, yardstick, benchmark, touchstone, rule, formula, pattern, guide, guideline, model, exemplar.
2 *such teams are now* ***the norm*** **standard,** usual, the rule; normal, typical, average, unexceptional, par for the course, expected.

normal ▶ adjective 1 *they issue books in the normal way* **usual,** standard, ordinary, customary, conventional, habitual, accustomed, expected, wonted; typical, stock, common, everyday, regular, routine, established, set, fixed, traditional, time-honored.
ANTONYMS unusual.
2 *a normal couple* **ordinary,** average, typical, run-of-the-mill, middle-of-the-road, common, conventional, mainstream, unremarkable, unexceptional, garden-variety, a dime a dozen.

CHOOSE THE RIGHT WORD

normal, average, natural, ordinary, regular, typical, usual

Most of us want to be regarded as **normal**, an adjective that implies conformity with established norms or standards and is the opposite of abnormal (*a normal body temperature; normal intelligence*). **Regular**, like *normal*, is usually preferred to its opposite (irregular) and implies conformity to prescribed standards or established patterns (*their regular monthly meeting; a regular guy*), but *normal* carries stronger connotations of conformity within prescribed limits and sometimes allows for a wider range of differences. Few of us think of ourselves as **ordinary**, a term used to describe what is commonplace or unexceptional (*an ordinary person wearing ordinary clothes*), although many people are ordinary in some ways and extraordinary in others. **Average** also implies conformity with what is regarded as normal or ordinary (*a woman of average height*), although it tends to emphasize the middle ground and to exclude both positive and negative extremes. **Typical** applies to persons or things possessing the representative characteristics of a type or class (*a typical teenager*). Someone or something described as **natural** behaves or operates in accordance with an inherent nature or character (*his fears were natural for one so young*), while **usual** applies to that which conforms to common or ordinary use or occurrence (*we paid the usual price*).

normality ▶ noun *after a season of elections, it takes some time to return to normality* **normalcy,** business as usual, the daily round; routine, order, regularity.

normally ▶ adverb 1 *she wanted to walk normally* **naturally,** conventionally, ordinarily; as usual, as normal.
2 *normally we'd keep quiet about this* **usually,** ordinarily, as a rule, generally, in general, mostly, for the most part, by and large, mainly, most of the time, on the whole; typically, customarily, traditionally.

north ▶ adjective *the north winds can be brutal* **northern,** northerly, polar, Arctic, boreal.

nose ▶ noun 1 *a punch on the nose* **snout,** muzzle, proboscis, trunk; informal beak, snoot, schnoz, schnozzola, sniffer, honker.
2 *a nose for scandal* **instinct,** feeling, sixth sense, intuition, insight, perception.
3 *wine with a fruity nose* **smell,** bouquet, aroma, fragrance, perfume, scent, odor.
4 *the plane's nose dipped* **nose cone,** bow, prow, front end.
▶ verb 1 *the dog nosed the ball* **nuzzle,** nudge, push.
2 *she's* ***nosing into*** *my business* **pry into,** inquire about/into, poke around/about, interfere in/with, meddle in/with; be a busybody about, stick/poke one's nose in/into; informal be nosy about, snoop around/into.
3 *he nosed the car into the traffic* **ease,** inch, edge, move, maneuver, steer, guide.
– PHRASES **by a nose** *Harris won the third race by a nose* **just,** only just, barely, narrowly, by a hair's breadth, by the skin of one's teeth, by a whisker. **nose around/about** *you check the bedrooms and we'll nose around the kitchen* **investigate,** explore, ferret around/through, rummage around/through, search; delve into, peer into; prowl around; informal snoop around/about. **nose out** *a team of trained dogs help us to nose out the armed passengers* **detect,** find, discover, bring to light, track down, dig up, ferret out, root out, uncover, unearth, sniff out. **on the nose** informal *the plane landed at 7:15 on the nose* **exactly,** precisely, sharp, on the dot, on the button, promptly, prompt, dead on, bang on.

nosedive ▶ noun 1 *the plane went into a nosedive* **dive,** descent, drop, plunge, plummet, fall.
ANTONYMS climb.

2 informal *the dollar took a nosedive* **fall,** drop, plunge, plummet, tumble, decline, slump; informal crash.

▶ **verb 1** *the device nosedived to earth* **dive,** plunge, pitch, drop, plummet.

2 informal *costs have nosedived* **fall,** take a header, drop, sink, plunge, plummet, tumble, slump, go down, decline; informal crash.

ANTONYMS soar, rise.

nosh informal ▶ **noun** *all kinds of nosh* See FOOD (sense 1).

▶ **verb** *they noshed on smoked salmon* See EAT (sense 1).

nostalgia ▶ **noun** *a nostalgia for traditional values* **reminiscence,** remembrance, recollection; wistfulness, regret, sentimentality; homesickness.

nostalgic ▶ **adjective** *music that evokes nostalgic memories of our youth* **wistful,** evocative, romantic, sentimental; dewy-eyed, misty-eyed, maudlin; homesick.

nostrum ▶ **noun 1** *they have to prove their nostrums work* **medicine,** patent medicine, potion, elixir, panacea, cure-all, wonder drug, quack remedy; informal magic bullet.

2 *right-wing nostrums* **magic formula,** recipe for success, remedy, cure, prescription, answer.

nosy ▶ **adjective** informal *the nosy guy next door is always peeking out through the curtains* **prying,** inquisitive, curious, spying, eavesdropping, intrusive; informal snooping, snoopy.

notable ▶ **adjective 1** *notable examples of workmanship* **noteworthy,** remarkable, outstanding, important, significant, momentous, memorable; marked, striking, impressive; uncommon, unusual, special, exceptional, signal.

ANTONYMS unremarkable, insignificant.

2 *a notable author* **prominent,** important, well-known, famous, affluential, famed, noted, distinguished, great, eminent, illustrious, respected, esteemed, renowned, celebrated, acclaimed, influential, prestigious, of note.

ANTONYMS obscure, unknown.

▶ **noun** *movie stars and other notables* **celebrity,** public figure, VIP, personage, notability, dignitary, worthy, luminary; star, superstar, icon, name, big name; informal celeb, somebody, bigwig, big shot, big cheese, big fish, megastar, big kahuna, high muckamuck.

ANTONYMS nonentity, no-name.

notably ▶ **adverb** *these are notably short-lived birds* **remarkably,** especially, specially, very, extremely, exceptionally, singularly, particularly, peculiarly, distinctly, significantly, unusually, extraordinarily, strikingly, uncommonly, incredibly, really, decidedly, surprisingly, conspicuously; in particular, primarily, principally.

notation ▶ **noun 1** *algebraic notation* **symbols,** alphabet, syllabary, script; code, cipher, hieroglyphics.

2 *notations in the margin* **annotation,** jotting, comment, footnote, entry, memo, gloss, explanation.

notch ▶ **noun 1** *a notch in the end of the arrow* **nick,** cut, incision, score, scratch, slit, slot, groove, cleft, indentation.

2 *her opinion of Nick dropped a notch* **degree,** level, rung, point, mark, measure, grade.

▶ **verb** *notch the plank* **nick,** cut, score, incise, carve, scratch, slit, gouge, groove, furrow.

note ▶ **noun 1** *a note in her diary* **record,** entry, item, notation, jotting, memorandum, reminder, aide-mémoire; informal memo.

2 (**notes**) *his notes were read at the next meeting* **minutes,** records, details; report, account, commentary, transcript, proceedings, transactions; synopsis, summary, outline.

3 *notes in the margins* **annotation,** footnote, commentary, comment; marginalia, exegesis.

4 *he dropped me a note* **message,** communication, letter, line; formal epistle, missive.

5 *this note is legal tender* **bill**; banknote; (**notes**) paper money.

6 *this is worthy of note* **attention,** consideration, notice, heed, observation, regard.

7 *a composer of note* **distinction,** importance, eminence, prestige, fame, celebrity, acclaim, renown, repute, stature, standing, consequence, account.

8 *a note of hopelessness in her voice* **tone,** intonation, inflection, sound; hint, indication, sign, element, suggestion.

▶ **verb 1** *we will note your suggestion* **bear in mind,** be mindful of, consider, observe, heed, take notice of, pay attention to, take in.

2 *the letter noted the ministers' concern* **mention,** refer to, touch on, indicate, point out, make known, state.

3 *note the date in your diary* **write down,** put down, jot down, take down, inscribe, enter, mark, record, register, pencil (in).

notebook ▶ **noun** *a new notebook for French class* **notepad,** scratch pad, exercise book, workbook, memo pad, tablet, writing tablet; register, logbook, log, diary, daybook, journal, record.

noted ▶ **adjective** *a noted authority on the boll weevil* **renowned,** well-known, famous, famed, prominent, celebrated; notable, of note, important, eminent, distinguished, illustrious, acclaimed, esteemed; of distinction, of repute.

ANTONYMS unknown.

noteworthy ▶ **adjective** *her work in the field of anthropology is noteworthy* **notable,** interesting, significant, important; remarkable, impressive, striking, outstanding, memorable, unique, special; unusual, extraordinary, singular, rare.

ANTONYMS unexceptional.

nothing ▶ **pronoun 1** *all my efforts add up to nothing* **not a thing,** not anything, nil, zero, naught/nought; informal zilch, zip, nada, diddly-squat, squat.

ANTONYMS something.

2 *forget it—it's nothing* **a trifling matter,** a trifle; neither here nor there; informal no big deal.

3 *he treats her as a nothing* **nobody,** unimportant person, nonentity, no-name, nonperson.

ANTONYMS celebrity.

4 *the share value fell to nothing* **zero,** naught/nought, O; Tennis love.

– PHRASES **be/have nothing to do with 1** *it has nothing to do with you* **be unconnected with,** be unrelated to, not concern; be irrelevant to, be inapplicable to, be inapposite to. **2** *I'll have nothing to do with him* **avoid,** shun, ignore, have no contact with, steer clear of, give a wide berth to. **for nothing 1** *she hosted the show for nothing* **free,** free of charge, gratis, without charge, at no cost; informal for free, on the house. **2** *all this trouble for nothing* **in vain,** to no avail, to no purpose, with no result, needlessly, pointlessly. **nothing but** *he's nothing but a nuisance* **merely,** only, just, solely, simply, purely, no more than.

nothingness ▶ **noun 1** *the nothingness of death* **oblivion,** nullity, blankness; void, vacuum; rare nihility.
2 *the nothingness of it all overwhelmed him* **unimportance,** insignificance, triviality, pointlessness, uselessness, worthlessness.

notice ▶ **noun 1** *nothing escaped his notice* **attention,** observation, awareness, consciousness, perception; regard, consideration, scrutiny; watchfulness, vigilance, attentiveness.
2 *a notice on the wall* **poster,** bill, handbill, advertisement, announcement, bulletin; flyer, leaflet, pamphlet; sign, card; informal ad.
3 *show times may change without notice* **notification,** warning, advance warning, announcement; information, news, communication, word.
4 *I handed in my notice* **resignation.**
5 *the play got bad notices* **review,** write-up, critique, criticism.
▶ **verb** *I noticed that the door was open* **observe,** perceive, note, see, discern, detect, spot, distinguish, mark, remark, descry; literary behold.
ANTONYMS overlook.
– PHRASES **take no notice of** *he took no notice of anything I said* **ignore,** pay no attention to, disregard, pay no heed to, take no account of, brush aside, shrug off, turn a blind eye to, pass over, let go, overlook; look the other way (from).

noticeable ▶ **adjective** *a fresh coat of paint will make a noticeable difference* **distinct,** evident, obvious, apparent, manifest, patent, plain, clear, marked, conspicuous, front-and-center, unmistakable, undeniable, pronounced, prominent, striking, arresting; perceptible, discernible, detectable, observable, visible, appreciable.

CHOOSE THE RIGHT WORD

noticeable, conspicuous, outstanding, prominent, remarkable, striking

A scratch on someone's face might be **noticeable**, while a scar that runs from cheekbone to chin would be **conspicuous**. When it comes to describing the things that attract our attention, *noticeable* means readily noticed or unlikely to escape observation (*a noticeable facial tic; a noticeable aversion to cocktail parties*), while *conspicuous* implies that the eye (or mind) cannot miss it (*her absence was conspicuous*). Use **prominent** when you want to describe something that literally or figuratively stands out from its background (*a prominent nose; a prominent position on the committee*). It can also apply to persons or things that stand out so clearly they are generally known or recognized (*a prominent citizen*). Someone or something that is **outstanding** rises above or beyond others and is usually superior to them (*an outstanding student*). **Remarkable** applies to anything that is noticeable because it is extraordinary or exceptional (*remarkable blue eyes*). **Striking** is an even stronger word, used to describe something so out of the ordinary that it makes a deep and powerful impression on the observer's mind or vision (*a striking young woman over six feet tall*).

notification ▶ **noun 1** *the notification of the victim's wife* **informing,** telling, alerting, filling in.
2 *she received notification that he was on the way* **information,** word, advice, news, intelligence; communication, message; literary tidings.

notify ▶ **verb** *we will notify you as soon as possible* **inform,** tell, advise, brief, apprise, let someone know, put in the picture, fill in; alert, warn.

notion ▶ **noun 1** *he had a notion that something was wrong* **idea,** belief, conviction, opinion, view, thought, impression, perception; hypothesis, theory; feeling, funny feeling, suspicion, sneaking suspicion, hunch. See note at IDEA.
2 *Claire had no notion of what he meant* **understanding,** idea, awareness, knowledge, clue, inkling.
3 *he got a notion to return* **impulse,** inclination, whim, desire, wish; dated fancy.

notional ▶ **adjective** *the notional line between East and West* **hypothetical,** theoretical, speculative, conjectural, suppositional, putative, conceptual; imaginary, fanciful, unreal, illusory.
ANTONYMS actual.

notoriety ▶ **noun** *his undeserved notoriety* **infamy,** disrepute, ill repute, bad name, dishonor, discredit; dated ill fame.

notorious ▶ **adjective** *a notorious gunman of the Old West* **infamous,** scandalous; well known, famous, famed, legendary.

notwithstanding ▶ **preposition** *notwithstanding his workload, he is a dedicated father* **despite,** in spite of, regardless of, for all.
▶ **adverb** *she is bright and ambitious—notwithstanding, she is now jobless* **nevertheless,** nonetheless, even so, all the same, in spite of this, despite this, however, still, yet, that said, just the same, anyway, in any event, at any rate.
▶ **conjunction** ***notwithstanding that*** *the rain was torrential, they played on* **although,** even though, though, in spite of the fact that, despite the fact that.

nourish ▶ **verb 1** *patients must be well nourished*

feed, provide for, sustain, maintain.
2 *we nourish the talents of children* **encourage,** promote, foster, nurture, cultivate, stimulate, boost, advance, assist, help, aid, strengthen, enrich.
3 *the hopes Emma nourished* **cherish,** nurture, foster, harbor, nurse, entertain, maintain, hold, have.

nourishing ▶ adjective *a nourishing snack* **nutritious,** nutritive, wholesome, good for one, healthy, health-giving, healthful, beneficial, sustaining.
ANTONYMS unhealthy.

nourishment ▶ noun **food,** sustenance, nutriment, nutrition, subsistence, provisions, provender, fare; informal grub, nosh, chow, eats, scoff, chuck; formal comestibles; dated victuals.

nouveau riche ▶ plural noun *we appeal to the nouveau riche for much of our funding* new rich, parvenus, arrivistes, upstarts, social climbers, vulgarians.

novel[1] ▶ noun *curl up with a good novel* **book,** paperback, hardcover; **story,** tale, narrative, romance, roman à clef; piece of fiction; best seller, blockbuster; potboiler, pulp (fiction).

novel[2] ▶ adjective *a novel way of making money* **new,** original, unusual, unfamiliar, unconventional, unorthodox; different, fresh, imaginative, innovative, innovatory, inventive, modern, neoteric, avant-garde, pioneering, groundbreaking, revolutionary; rare, unique, singular, unprecedented; experimental, untested, untried; strange, exotic, newfangled.
ANTONYMS traditional.

novelist ▶ noun *Kafka was a Czech novelist who wrote in German* **writer,** author, fictionist, man/woman of letters, scribe; informal penman, scribbler.

novelty ▶ noun **1** *the novelty of our approach* **originality,** newness, freshness, unconventionality, unfamiliarity; difference, imaginativeness, creativity, innovation, modernity.
2 *we sell seasonal novelties* **knickknack,** trinket, bauble, toy, trifle, gewgaw, gimcrack, ornament, kickshaw.

novice ▶ noun **1** *a five-day course for novices* **beginner,** learner, neophyte, newcomer, initiate, tyro, fledgling; apprentice, trainee, probationer, student, pupil, tenderfoot; informal rookie, newbie, greenhorn.
ANTONYMS expert, veteran.
2 *a novice who was never ordained* **neophyte,** novitiate; postulant, proselyte, catechumen.

> CHOOSE THE RIGHT WORD
>
> **novice, apprentice, beginner, neophyte, probationer**
>
> All of these nouns are used to describe someone who has not yet acquired the skills and experience needed to qualify for a trade, a career, a profession, or a sphere of life. **Beginner** is the most general and informal term, used to describe someone who has begun to acquire the necessary skills but has not yet mastered them (*violin lessons for beginners*). An **apprentice** is also a beginner, usually a young person, who is serving under a more experienced master or teacher to learn the skills of a trade or profession (*an apprentice to one of the great Renaissance painters*); in a broad sense, *apprentice* refers to any beginner whose efforts are unpolished. **Novice** implies that the person lacks training and experience (*a novice when it came to writing fiction*), while **neophyte** is a less negative term, suggesting that the person is eagerly learning the ways, methods, or principles of something (*he was a neophyte at this type of sailing*). A **probationer** is a beginner who is undergoing a trial period, during which he or she must prove an aptitude for a certain type of work or life (*she was a lowly probationer, with no privileges or status*).

novitiate ▶ noun **1** *his novitiate lasts a year* **probationary period,** probation, trial period, test period, apprenticeship, training period, traineeship, training, initiation.
2 *two young novitiates* **novice,** neophyte; postulant, proselyte, catechumen.

now ▶ adverb **1** *I'm extremely busy now* **at the moment,** at present, at the present (time/moment), at this moment in time, currently, presently.
2 *television is now the main source of news* **nowadays,** today, these days, in this day and age; in the present climate.
3 *you must leave now* **at once,** straightaway, right away, right now, this minute, this instant, immediately, instantly, directly, without further ado, promptly, without delay, as soon as possible; informal pronto, straight off, ASAP.
– PHRASES **as of now** *as of now, cigarettes are banned in this house* **from this time on,** from now on, henceforth, from this day forward, in (the) future; formal hereafter. **for now** *for now, we'll just have salad* **for the time being,** for the moment, for the present, for the meantime, for the nonce. **not now** *I promise I will, but not now* **later,** later on, sometime, one day, some day, one of these days, sooner or later, in due course, by and by, eventually, ultimately. **(every) now and again** *now and again, we like to visit the gallery* **occasionally,** now and then, from time to time, sometimes, every so often, at times, on occasion(s), (every) once in a while; periodically, once in a blue moon.

nowadays ▶ adverb *nowadays, it seems as if everyone is obsessed with staying young* **these days,** today, at the present time, in these times, in this day and age, now, currently, at the moment, at present, at this moment in time; in the present climate, presently.

noxious ▶ adjective *noxious fumes* **poisonous,** toxic, deadly, harmful, dangerous, pernicious, damaging, destructive; unpleasant, nasty, disgusting, awful, dreadful, horrible, terrible; vile, revolting, foul, nauseating, appalling, offensive; malodorous, fetid, putrid; informal ghastly, horrid; literary noisome.
ANTONYMS innocuous.

nuance ▸ noun *the nuances of light are very effective* **fine distinction,** subtle difference; shade, shading, gradation, variation, degree; subtlety, nicety, overtone.

nucleus ▸ noun *the nucleus of the international banking world* **core,** center, central part, heart, nub, hub, middle, eye, focus, focal point, pivot, crux.

nude ▸ adjective *nude sunbathers* **naked,** stark naked, bare, unclothed, undressed, disrobed, stripped, unclad, au naturel, without a stitch on, in one's birthday suit, in the raw, in the altogether, in the buff; informal buck-naked, butt-naked, mother-naked. See note at NAKED.
ANTONYMS clothed.

nudge ▸ verb **1** *he nudged Ben* **poke,** elbow, dig, prod, jog, jab.
2 *the canoe nudged a bank* **touch,** bump (against), push (against), run into.
3 *we nudged them into action* **prompt,** encourage, stimulate, prod, galvanize.
4 *unemployment was nudging 3,000,000* **approach,** near, come close to, be verging on, border on.
▸ noun **1** *Maggie gave him a nudge* **poke,** prod, jog, jab, push, dig (in the ribs).
2 *after a nudge, she remembered Lillian* **reminder,** prompt, prompting, prod, encouragement.

nudity ▸ noun *there was one brief moment of nudity* **nakedness,** bareness, state of undress, undress; informal one's birthday suit.

nugget ▸ noun *a nugget of gold | doughy nuggets in the stew* **lump,** nub, chunk, piece, hunk, wad, gobbet; informal gob.

nuisance ▸ noun *I find these long journeys a nuisance* **annoyance,** inconvenience, bore, bother, irritation, problem, trouble, trial, burden; pest, plague, thorn in one's side/flesh; informal pain, pain in the neck, hassle, bind, drag, chore, aggravation, headache, nudnik.
ANTONYMS blessing.

null ▸ adjective *their marriage was declared null* **invalid,** null and void, void; annulled, nullified, canceled, revoked.
ANTONYMS valid.

nullify ▸ verb **1** *they nullified the legislation* **annul,** render null and void, void, invalidate; repeal, reverse, rescind, revoke, disallow, cancel, abolish; countermand, do away with, terminate, quash; Law vacate; formal abrogate. See note at VOID.
ANTONYMS ratify.
2 *the costs would nullify any tax relief* **cancel out,** neutralize, negate, negative.

numb ▸ adjective *his fingers were numb* **without sensation,** without feeling, numbed, benumbed, desensitized, insensible, senseless, unfeeling; anesthetized; dazed, stunned, stupefied, paralyzed, immobilized, frozen.
ANTONYMS sensitive.
▸ verb *the cold numbed her senses* **deaden,** benumb, desensitize, dull; anesthetize; daze, stupefy, paralyze, immobilize, freeze.
ANTONYMS sensitize.

number ▸ noun **1** *a whole number* **numeral,** integer, figure, digit; character, symbol; decimal, unit; cardinal number, ordinal number.
2 *a large number of complaints* **amount,** quantity; total, aggregate, tally; quota.
3 *the wedding of one of their number* **group,** company, crowd, circle, party, band, crew, set, gang.
4 *the band performed another number* **song,** piece (of music), tune, track; routine, sketch, dance, act.
▸ verb **1** *visitors numbered more than two million* **add up to,** amount to, total, come to.
2 *he numbers the fleet at a thousand* **calculate,** count, total, compute, reckon, tally; assess, tot up; formal enumerate.
3 *each paragraph is numbered* **assign a number to,** mark with a number; itemize, enumerate.
4 *he numbers her among his friends* **include,** count, reckon, deem.
5 *his days are numbered* **limit,** restrict, fix.
– PHRASES **a number of** *she's collected a number of ashtrays* **several,** various, quite a few, sundry. **without number** *the nights I've worried about those kids is without number* **countless,** innumerable, unlimited, endless, limitless, untold, numberless, uncountable, uncounted; numerous, many, multiple, manifold, legion.

numberless ▸ adjective *there are numberless questions to be answered* **innumerable,** countless, unlimited, endless, limitless, untold, uncountable, uncounted; numerous, many, multiple, manifold, legion; informal more —— than one can shake a stick at; literary myriad.

numbing ▸ adjective **1** *menthol has a numbing effect* **desensitizing,** deadening, benumbing, anesthetic, anesthetizing; paralyzing.
2 *numbing cold* **freezing,** raw, bitter, biting, arctic, icy.
3 *numbing boredom* **stupefying,** mind-numbing, boring, stultifying, soul-destroying; soporific.

numeral ▸ noun *your password should have at least one numeral* **number,** integer, figure, digit; character, symbol, unit.

numerous ▸ adjective *numerous studies have been published on the subject* **many,** very many, a lot of, scores of, countless, numberless, innumerable; several, quite a few, various; plenty of, copious, a quantity of, an abundance of, a profusion of, a multitude of; frequent; informal umpteen, lots of, loads of, masses of, stacks of, heaps of, bags of, tons of, oodles of, hundreds of, thousands of, millions of, gazillions of, more —— than one can shake a stick at; literary myriad.
ANTONYMS few.

nuncio ▸ noun *Father Mike was in a dither over the nuncio's visit* **(papal) ambassador,** legate, envoy, messenger.

nuptial ▸ adjective *our nuptial vows* **matrimonial,** marital, marriage, wedding, conjugal, bridal; married, wedded; literary connubial; Law spousal.

nuptials ▸ plural noun *we attended the young duke's nuptials* **wedding,** wedding ceremony, marriage, union; archaic espousal.

nurse ▸ noun **1** *skilled nurses* **caregiver,** RN, LPN, nurse practitioner, physician's assistant, health

care worker; informal Florence Nightingale.
2 *she had been his nurse in childhood* **nanny,** nursemaid, governess, au pair, babysitter; wet nurse.
▶ verb **1** *they nursed smallpox patients* **care for,** take care of, look after, tend, minister to.
2 *I nursed my sore finger* **treat,** medicate, tend; dress, bandage, soothe, doctor.
3 *Rosa was nursing her baby* **breast-feed,** suckle, feed; wet-nurse.
4 *they nursed old grievances* **harbor,** foster, entertain, bear, have, hold (on to), cherish, cling to, retain.

nurture ▶ verb **1** *she nurtured her children into adulthood* **bring up,** care for, take care of, look after, tend, rear, raise, support, foster; parent, mother.
ANTONYMS neglect.
2 *we nurtured these plants* **cultivate,** grow, keep, tend.
3 *he nurtured my love of art* **encourage,** promote, stimulate, develop, foster, cultivate, boost, contribute to, assist, help, abet, strengthen, fuel.
ANTONYMS hinder.
▶ noun **1** *we are what nature and nurture have made us* **upbringing,** rearing, raising, child care; training, education.
ANTONYMS nature.
2 *the nurture of ideas* **encouragement,** promotion, fostering, development, cultivation.

nut ▶ noun **1** *nuts in their shells* **kernel,** nutmeat.
2 informal *some nut arrived at the office* **maniac,** lunatic, madman, madwoman; eccentric; informal loony, nutcase, fruitcake, fruit loop, head case, crank, crackpot, weirdo, screwball, crazy, dingbat, loon.
3 informal *a health nut* **enthusiast,** fan, devotee, aficionado; informal freak, fiend, fanatic, addict, buff, bum.
– PHRASES **off one's nut** informal See MAD (sense 1).

nutrition ▶ noun *the child was not receiving adequate nutrition* **nourishment,** nutriment, nutrients, sustenance, food; informal grub, chow, nosh; literary viands; dated victuals.

nutritious ▶ adjective *a nutritious fruit drink* **nourishing,** good for one, full of nutrients, nutritive, nutritional, wholesome, healthy, healthful, beneficial, sustaining.

nuts ▶ adjective informal **1** *they thought we were nuts* See MAD (sense 1).
2 *he's nuts about her* **infatuated with,** devoted to, in love with, smitten with, enamored of, hot for, keen on; informal mad about, crazy about, nutty about, wild about, hooked on, gone on.

nuts and bolts ▶ plural noun *the nuts and bolts of running an airline* **practical details,** fundamentals, basics, practicalities, essentials, mechanics, rudiments, ABCs; informal nitty-gritty, ins and outs, brass tacks, meat and potatoes.

nuzzle ▶ verb **1** *the horse nuzzled at her pocket* **nudge,** nose, prod, push, root.
2 *she nuzzled up to her boyfriend* **snuggle up to,** cuddle up to, nestle close to, embrace, hug.

nymph ▶ noun **1** *a nymph with winged sandals* **sprite,** sylph, spirit.
2 literary *a slender nymph with brown eyes* **girl,** belle, nymphet, sylph, ingénue; young woman, young lady; Scottish lass; literary maid, maiden, damsel.

Oo

oaf ▶ noun *the oaf upstairs with his television on full blast* **lout,** boor, barbarian, Neanderthal, churl, bumpkin, yokel; **fool,** dolt, dullard; informal idiot, imbecile, moron, halfwit, cretin, ass, jackass, goon, yahoo, ape, baboon, clod, blockhead, meathead, meatball, bonehead, knucklehead, chucklehead, lamebrain, palooka, lug, bozo, boob, chowderhead, lummox, klutz, goofus, doofus, dork, turkey, dingbat; Brit. informal twit, nerk, git, yob; archaic lubber.

oafish ▶ adjective *his oafish brother* **stupid,** foolish, idiotic, cretinous; **ungainly,** loutish, awkward, clumsy, lumbering, apelike, cloddish, Neanderthal, uncouth, uncultured, boorish, rough, coarse, brutish, ill-mannered, unrefined, rough-hewn; informal blockheaded, moronic, boneheaded, halfwitted, lamebrained, thickheaded; archaic lubberly.

oasis ▶ noun **1** *an oasis near Cairo* **watering hole,** watering place, waterhole, spring.
2 *the park is an oasis filled with half a million flowers and thousands of lights* **refuge,** haven, retreat, sanctuary, sanctum, shelter, harbor, asylum.

oath ▶ noun **1** *an oath of allegiance* **vow,** pledge, sworn statement, promise, avowal, affirmation, word, word of honor, bond, guarantee; formal troth.
2 *he uttered a stream of oaths* **swear word,** profanity, expletive, four-letter word, dirty word, obscenity, vulgarity, curse, malediction, blasphemy; informal cuss, cuss word; formal imprecation.

obdurate ▶ adjective *the brass were also obdurate in their opposition to having women in any combat positions* **stubborn,** obstinate, intransigent, inflexible, unyielding, unbending, pigheaded, bullheaded, mulish, stiff-necked; headstrong, unshakable, intractable, unpersuadable, immovable, inexorable, uncompromising, iron-willed, adamant, firm, determined. See note at STUBBORN.
ANTONYMS malleable, tractable.

obedience ▶ noun *the party leadership wants blind obedience to their policies* **compliance,** acquiescence, tractability, amenability; **dutifulness,** duty, deference, observance of the law/rules; **submissiveness,** submission, conformity, docility, tameness, subservience, obsequiousness, servility.
ANTONYMS disobedience, rebellion.

obedient ▶ adjective *obviously, you want an obedient dog for security work* **compliant,** acquiescent, tractable, amenable; **dutiful,** good, law-abiding, deferential, respectful, duteous, well trained, well disciplined, manageable, governable; **docile,** tame, biddable, meek, passive, submissive, unresisting, yielding; malleable, pliable, pliant, subservient, obsequious, servile.
ANTONYMS disobedient, rebellious.

CHOOSE THE RIGHT WORD

obedient; biddable; docile; dutiful; compliant

Children and animals may be expected to obey, but nowadays **obedient** is seldom used to describe adult human beings without a suggestion that they are allowing someone else to assume too great a degree of authority (*are we to believe that Cinderella became the prince's demure, obedient wife?*). The critical note is stronger in **biddable**. A biddable person is excessively meek and ready to obey any instruction, without questioning either its wisdom or the authority of the person giving it (*he could barely think for herself, having been so biddable to his domineering parents*). **Docile** (from Latin *docilis* 'teachable') has similar implications, but in addition to unquestioning obedience it suggests a general reluctance to complain or rebel, even where such behavior would be justified (*employers depended on the regime for a cheap and docile workforce*). **Dutiful** may evoke a sneer, suggesting the virtuous, yet dull (*his dutiful niece spent most of her life caring for him*) or the perfunctory fulfillment of an obligation (*a dutiful postcard to his mother*). One of the oldest (and still living) meanings of **compliant** is 'reshaping under pressure' (*conversion of the gel to a much less compliant glass*). This helps to explain the principal modern sense of the adjective, '(excessively) disposed to agree with others or obey rules' (*compliant legislators loyally followed party policy*). In the computer age a further sense, 'technically compatible,' has developed (*the system is Windows compliant*).

obeisance ▶ noun **1** *he made a very formal, elaborate gesture of obeisance* **respect,** homage, worship, adoration, reverence, veneration, honor, submission, deference. See note at HONOR.
2 *he made a half-bow, half-curtsy, a sort of unisex obeisance* **bow,** curtsy, bob, genuflection,

salaam; historical kowtow.

obelisk ▶ noun *an obelisk marks the mass grave where Custer was buried* **pillar,** column, needle, shaft, monolith, monument.

obese ▶ adjective *a physician would describe her as a young obese white female* **fat,** overweight, corpulent, gross, stout, fleshy, heavy, portly, plump, paunchy, potbellied, beer-bellied, broad in the beam, bulky, bloated, flabby, Falstaffian; informal porky, roly-poly, blubbery, pudgy, well-upholstered.
ANTONYMS thin, skinny, emaciated.

obesity ▶ noun *businesses are developing programs to fight workers' obesity* **fatness,** corpulence, stoutness, portliness, plumpness, chubbiness, rotundity, flabbiness, grossness.
ANTONYMS thinness, emaciation.

obey ▶ verb **1** *I was honor-bound to obey* **do what someone says,** carry out someone's orders; **submit to,** defer to, bow to, yield to, give in to.
2 *he refused to obey the order* **carry out,** perform, act on, execute, discharge, implement, fulfill.
3 *NRA activists point out that criminals don't obey gun laws* **comply with,** adhere to, observe, abide by, act in accordance with, conform to, respect, follow, keep to, stick to.
4 *she wants me to just obey and shut up* **follow orders,** do as one's told, play it by the book, toe the line.
ANTONYMS disobey, defy, ignore.

obfuscate ▶ verb **1** *mere rationalizations to obfuscate rather than clarify the real issue* **obscure,** confuse, make unclear, blur, muddle, complicate, muddy, cloud, befog.
ANTONYMS clarify.
2 *her work became more and more obfuscated by mathematics and jargon* **bewilder,** mystify, puzzle, perplex, confuse, baffle, confound, bemuse, befuddle, nonplus; informal flummox.

obituary ▶ noun *the local paper ran a full-page obituary* **death notice,** eulogy; informal obit; rare necrology.

object ▶ noun **1** *wooden objects* **thing,** article, item, device, gadget, entity; informal doodad, thingamajig, thingamabob, whatsit, whatchamacallit, thingy, doohickey, dingus.
2 *he spent five years as the object of a frenzied manhunt* **target,** butt, focus, recipient, victim.
3 *the object was to let everyone have a voice in the decision* **objective,** aim, goal, target, purpose, end, plan; ambition, design, intent, intention, point, idea.
▶ verb *people attending the meeting* ***objected to*** *nearly every element of the new ordinance* **protest (against),** lodge a protest against, oppose, raise objections to, express disapproval of, take exception to, take issue with, take a stand against, argue against, quarrel with, condemn, draw the line at, demur at, disapprove of, mind, complain about, cavil at, quibble about; beg to differ with; informal kick up a fuss/stink about, kvetch about.
ANTONYMS approve, accept.

objection ▶ noun *he lodged an official objection with the town council* **protest,** protestation, demur, demurral, demurrer, complaint, expostulation, grievance, cavil, quibble; **opposition,** argument, counterargument, disagreement, disapproval, dissent; informal gripe, beef.

objectionable ▶ adjective *there is restricted access to objectionable material* **unpleasant,** offensive, disagreeable, distasteful, displeasing, off-putting, undesirable, obnoxious, unacceptable; **nasty,** disgusting, awful, terrible, dreadful, frightful, horrid, appalling, insufferable, intolerable, odious, vile, foul, unsavory, repulsive, repellent, repugnant, revolting, abhorrent, loathsome, hateful, detestable, reprehensible, deplorable; informal ghastly, horrible, beastly; formal exceptionable, rebarbative.
ANTONYMS pleasant, agreeable.

objective ▶ adjective **1** *I was hoping to get an objective and pragmatic report* **impartial,** unbiased, unprejudiced, nonpartisan, disinterested, neutral, uninvolved, evenhanded, equitable, fair, fair-minded, just, open-minded, dispassionate, detached, neutral.
ANTONYMS biased, partial, prejudiced.
2 *eight objective measurements to track student performance* **factual,** actual, real, empirical, evidence-based, verifiable.
ANTONYMS subjective.
▶ noun *you can't achieve your objectives unless people understand them* **aim,** intention, purpose, target, goal, intent, object, end; idea, point, design, plan, ambition, aspiration, desire, hope.

objectively ▶ adverb *encourage people to look at the information objectively and see how it will affect them* **impartially,** without bias, without prejudice, evenhandedly, dispassionately, detachedly, equitably, fairly, justly, open-mindedly, with an open mind.
ANTONYMS one-sidedly, with prejudice.

objectivity ▶ noun *the quest for total objectivity is unrealistic* **impartiality,** absence/lack of bias, absence/lack of prejudice, fairness, fair-mindedness, neutrality, evenhandedness, justice, open-mindedness, disinterest, detachment, dispassion, neutrality.

obligate ▶ verb *signing the agreement does not obligate you to stay through the end of the program* **oblige,** compel, commit, bind, require, constrain, force, impel.

obligation ▶ noun **1** *no obligation may be placed upon you without your consent* **duty,** commitment, responsibility, moral imperative; **function,** task, job, assignment, commission, burden, charge, onus, liability, accountability, requirement, debt; literary trust.
2 *he felt an obligation to tip well* **duty,** compulsion, indebtedness; duress, necessity, pressure, constraint.
– PHRASES **under (an) obligation** *the district attorney is under obligation to investigate | they don't understand that they are under obligation to intervene* **beholden,** obliged, in someone's debt, indebted, obligated, compelled, duty-bound, honor-bound.

obligatory ▶ adjective *top hat and tails are obligatory for men* **compulsory,** mandatory, prescribed, required, demanded, statutory, enforced, binding, incumbent; requisite,

necessary, imperative, unavoidable, inescapable, essential.
ANTONYMS optional, voluntary.

oblige ▶ verb **1** *it was impractical to oblige taxis to carry infant seats* **require,** compel, bind, constrain, obligate, leave with no option but, force. See note at COMPEL.
2 *she was kind enough to oblige* **do someone a favor,** accommodate, help, assist, serve; indulge, humor, gratify someone's wishes.

obliging ▶ adjective *he was obliging enough to carry all the bags* **helpful,** accommodating, willing, cooperative, considerate, complaisant, agreeable, amenable, generous, kind, neighborly, hospitable, friendly, pleasant, good-natured, amiable, gracious, unselfish, civil, courteous, polite, decent.
ANTONYMS inconsiderate, uncooperative.

oblique ▶ adjective **1** *an oblique line* **slanting,** slanted, sloping, at an angle, angled, diagonal, aslant, slant, slantwise, skew, askew, cater-cornered, kitty-corner.
ANTONYMS straight.
2 *an oblique reference to an inside joke* **indirect,** inexplicit, roundabout, circuitous, circumlocutory, implicit, implied, elliptical, evasive, backhanded.
ANTONYMS direct, explicit.
3 *an oblique glance* **sidelong,** sideways, furtive, covert, sly, surreptitious.

obliquely ▶ adverb **1** *the rope ran obliquely from the top of one wall to the base of the other* **diagonally,** at an angle, slantwise, sideways, sidelong, aslant.
2 *she was an embarrassment, someone who could only be spoken of obliquely* **indirectly,** in a roundabout way, not in so many words, circuitously, evasively.

obliterate ▶ verb **1** *I briefly contemplated trying to obliterate the logo with nail polish remover* **erase,** eradicate, expunge, efface, wipe out, blot out, rub out, block out, remove all traces of.
2 *I want to see the super-turtle obliterate an entire Japanese district in under a minute* **destroy,** wipe out, annihilate, demolish, eliminate, decimate, liquidate, wipe off the face of the earth, wipe off the map; informal zap, nuke.
ANTONYMS create.
3 *she slapped her puff over her face, trying to obliterate it with powder* **obscure,** hide, conceal, blot out, block (out), cover, screen.

oblivion ▶ noun **1** *they drank themselves into oblivion* **unconsciousness,** insensibility, a stupor, stupefaction, senselessness; a coma, a blackout; literary the waters of Lethe.
ANTONYMS consciousness.
2 *luckily, he was able to rescue that design from oblivion* **obscurity,** limbo, anonymity, nonexistence, nothingness, neglect, disregard.
ANTONYMS fame.

oblivious ▶ adjective *oblivious to the conversation around the table | utterly and happily* ***oblivious of*** *the effect he was having upon his audience* **unaware of,** unconscious of, heedless of, unmindful of, insensible of/to, unheeding of, ignorant of, incognizant of, blind to, deaf to, unsuspecting of, unobservant of; **insensitive to,** unconcerned with, impervious to, unaffected by, indifferent to; informal clueless.
ANTONYMS aware, conscious, sensitive.

obloquy ▶ noun **1** *he was able to control the press of New York City, so as to hold me up to obloquy* **vilification,** opprobrium, vituperation, condemnation, denunciation, abuse, criticism, censure, defamation, denigration, calumny, insults; informal flak; formal castigation, excoriation; archaic contumely.
ANTONYMS praise.
2 *there is no moral obloquy connected with getting drunk in Japan* **disgrace,** dishonor, shame, discredit, stigma, humiliation, loss of face, ignominy, odium, opprobrium, disfavor, disrepute, ill repute, infamy, stain, notoriety, scandal.
ANTONYMS honor.

obnoxious ▶ adjective **1** *the gasoline-powered pump made an obnoxious racket* **unpleasant,** disagreeable, nasty, distasteful, offensive, objectionable, unsavory, unpalatable, off-putting, awful, terrible, dreadful, frightful, revolting, repulsive, repellent, repugnant, disgusting, odious, vile, foul, abhorrent, loathsome, nauseating, sickening, hateful, insufferable, intolerable, detestable, abominable, despicable, contemptible; informal horrible, horrid, ghastly, gross, putrid, yucky, godawful, beastly, skanky; literary noisome.
ANTONYMS delightful, fragrant.
2 *I prayed I could express myself without being obnoxious* **annoying,** tiresome, irritating; overbearing, bumptious; unpleasant, nasty; informal bratty, pesky.
ANTONYMS pleasant, charming.

obscene ▶ adjective **1** *a vengeful lover sent obscene photos of his former girlfriend to her new partner* **pornographic, indecent,** smutty, salacious, dirty, filthy, X-rated, explicit, lewd, rude, vulgar, coarse, crude, offensive, immoral, improper, impure, off-color, degenerate, depraved, debauched; lubricious, risqué, erotic, carnal, lascivious, licentious, bawdy; scatological, profane; informal blue, porn, porno, skin; euphemistic adult.
ANTONYMS pure, clean, decent.
2 *I was watching obscene amounts of daytime TV* **shocking,** scandalous, vile, foul, atrocious, outrageous, heinous, odious, abhorrent, abominable, disgusting, hideous, repugnant, offensive, objectionable, repulsive, revolting, repellent, loathsome, nauseating, sickening, awful, dreadful, terrible, frightful.

obscenity ▶ noun **1** *the over-the-top obscenity of the musical interludes* **indecency,** immorality, impropriety, salaciousness, smuttiness, smut, lewdness, impurity, crudeness, vulgarity, dirtiness, dirt, filth, coarseness, crudity; profanity; eroticism, carnality, lasciviousness, licentiousness.
2 *he attacked, first with obscenities, and then with fists* **expletive,** swear word, oath, profanity, curse, four-letter word, dirty word, blasphemy; informal cuss, cuss word; formal imprecation.
3 *they claimed that nearly a third of UN member states practiced human rights obscenities* **atrocity,** (act of) brutality, (act of) cruelty, (act

of) savagery, (act of) inhumanity, crime, evil.

obscure ▶ adjective **1** *the truth is that many aspects of a war's outcome remain obscure for years* **unclear,** uncertain, unknown, in doubt, doubtful, dubious, mysterious, hazy, vague, indeterminate, concealed, hidden.
ANTONYMS clear, obvious.
2 *obscure references to Proust* **abstruse,** recondite, arcane, esoteric; mystifying, puzzling, perplexing, baffling, ambiguous, cryptic, enigmatic, Delphic, oracular, oblique, opaque, elliptical, unintelligible, incomprehensible, impenetrable, unfathomable; informal as clear as mud.
ANTONYMS clear, plain.
3 *rumors from open-mouth radio shows and obscure web sites* **little known,** unknown, unheard of, unnoticed, undistinguished, unimportant, insignificant, inconsequential, minor, lowly; nameless, anonymous; unsung, unrecognized, forgotten.
ANTONYMS famous, renowned.
4 *an obscure shape* **indistinct,** faint, vague, nebulous, ill-defined, unclear, blurred, blurry, misty, hazy; dark, dim, shadowy; literary tenebrous; archaic caliginous.
ANTONYMS distinct.
▶ verb **1** *a shy and abject manner obscured her prettiness* **hide,** conceal, cover, veil, shroud, screen, mask, cloak, cast a shadow over, shadow, block (out), obliterate, eclipse, darken; literary bedim, enshroud.
ANTONYMS reveal.
2 *human rights are often obscured by the shadow of politics* **confuse,** complicate, obfuscate, cloud, blur, muddy; muddy the waters of; literary befog, becloud.
ANTONYMS illuminate, clarify.

CHOOSE THE RIGHT WORD

obscure; abstruse; recondite

Obscureis the general term for something that is unclear or not easy to understand; **abstruse** and **recondite** are more formal terms. **Obscure** often expresses dissatisfaction at one's inability to identify something (*the causation of his mental disorder is obscure*), or, more critically, refers to something that's not sufficiently clearly expressed (*the law is too obscure to interpret correctly; we find it difficult to address your obscure complaints*). A reference to, say, "an obscure congressman" is a dismissive comment, suggesting that this is someone not only little known but perhaps deservedly so. **Abstruse** is more precise in its meaning—'difficult to understand'—and usually implies that the subject would be puzzling to most anyone (*reading her essays, one wonders if even she can understand her abstruse philosophy*). **Recondite** denotes topics that are known and understood by only a few experts: *recondite though their theme may be, they demonstrate that it is not without relevance*. There is often a critical suggestion that difficulty or obscurity has been deliberately sought out or magnified.

obscurity ▶ noun **1** *the novel plots Carlotta's rise from obscurity to stardom* **insignificance,** inconspicuousness, unimportance, anonymity; limbo, twilight, oblivion.
ANTONYMS fame.
2 *small-minded intellectuals who had accused him of obscurity* **incomprehensibility,** impenetrability, unintelligibility, opacity; abstruseness, arcaneness, esotericism.
ANTONYMS clarity.
3 *there may be obscurities but no answerless riddles* **enigma,** puzzle, mystery, ambiguity.

obsequies ▶ plural noun *they left the sad obsequies to my men* **funeral rites,** funeral service, funeral, burial, interment, entombment, inhumation, last offices; formal exequies; archaic sepulture.

obsequious ▶ adjective *an elderly gentlemen surrounded by obsequious heirs* **servile,** ingratiating, sycophantic, fawning, unctuous, oily, oleaginous, groveling, cringing, subservient, submissive, slavish; informal brown-nosing, bootlicking, smarmy; vulgar slang ass-kissing.
ANTONYMS domineering.

CHOOSE THE RIGHT WORD

obsequious, servile, slavish, subservient

If you want to get ahead with your boss, you might trying being **obsequious,** which suggests an attitude of inferiority that may or may not be genuine, but that is assumed in order to placate a superior in hopes of getting what one wants (*a "goody two shoes" whose obsequious behavior made everyone in the class cringe*). While **subservient** may connote similar behavior, it is more often applied to those who are genuinely subordinate or dependent and act accordingly (*a timid, subservient child who was terrified of making a mistake*). **Servile** is a stronger and more negative term, suggesting a cringing submissiveness (*the dog's servile obedience to her master*). **Slavish**, suggesting the status or attitude of a slave, is often used to describe strict adherence to a set of rules or a code of conduct (*a slavish adherence to the rules of etiquette*).

observable ▶ adjective *that will certainly cause an observable change in the instrument reading* **noticeable,** visible, perceptible, perceivable, detectable, conspicuous, distinguishable, discernible, recognizable, evident, apparent, manifest, obvious, patent, palpable, overt, clear, distinct, plain, unmistakable.
ANTONYMS hidden.

observance ▶ noun **1** *elders responsible for the correct observance of sacred rites* **compliance with,** adherence to, accordance with, respect for, observation of, obedience to; keeping of, obeying of, fulfillment of, following of, honoring of; archaic abidance by.
ANTONYMS disregard.
2 *a Catholic calendar of saints' days and religious*

observances **rite,** ritual, ceremony, ceremonial, celebration, practice, service, office, festival, tradition, custom, convention, formality, form; formal praxis.

observant ▶ adjective **1** *the farmer whose weather eye has been usurped by the radio has become less observant* **alert,** sharp-eyed, sharp, eagle-eyed, hawk-eyed, having eyes like a hawk, watchful, heedful, aware; on the lookout, on the qui vive, on guard, attentive, vigilant, having one's eyes open/peeled; informal beady-eyed, not missing a trick, on the ball.
ANTONYMS inattentive.
2 *observant Jews* **practicing,** obedient, conforming, conformist; law-abiding, orthodox, devout.

observation ▶ noun **1** *the patient has been brought in for observation | whatever the reason, many people are irrationally afraid of snakes, and this makes for poor observation* **monitoring,** watching, scrutiny, examination, inspection, survey, surveillance, consideration, study, review.
2 *who was the recipient of that flattering observation?* **remark,** comment, statement, utterance, pronouncement, declaration; **opinion,** impression, thought, reflection; Law obiter dictum.
3 *the* ***observation of*** *the law* **observance of,** compliance with, adherence to, respect for, obedience to, keeping of, obeying of, heeding of.

observe ▶ verb **1** *every time he looked at her now, he observed something new | other behavioral problems have been observed in our patient population* **notice,** see, note, perceive, discern, detect, spot; literary espy, descry, behold.
ANTONYMS overlook.
2 *I may not even observe them unawares* **watch,** look at, eye, contemplate, view, witness, survey, regard, keep an eye on, scrutinize, keep under observation, keep (a) watch on, keep under surveillance, monitor, check out, keep a weather eye on, keep tabs on, spy on; informal eyeball.
3 *she'd observed that the Christmas tree looked underdecorated* **remark,** comment, say, mention, note, declare, announce, state, pronounce; formal opine.
4 *both countries agreed to observe the cease-fire* **comply with,** abide by, keep, obey, adhere to, heed, honor, be heedful of, respect, follow, consent to, acquiesce in, accept, fulfill.
ANTONYMS disregard, ignore.
5 *this year he observed the anniversary at a ceremony on the South Lawn* **commemorate,** mark, keep, memorialize, solemnize, remember, recognize, celebrate.

observer ▶ noun **1** *a casual observer might not have noticed* **spectator,** onlooker, watcher, looker-on, fly on the wall, viewer, witness, eyewitness, bystander; informal **rubberneck**; literary beholder.
2 *industry observers expect the deal to be finalized today* **commentator,** reporter; monitor.

obsess ▶ verb *being thin is obsessing her* **preoccupy,** be uppermost in someone's mind, prey on someone's mind, prey on, possess, haunt, consume, plague, torment, hound, bedevil, beset, take control of, control, take over, have a hold on, rule, eat up, have a grip on, grip.
– PHRASES **be obsessed** *he* ***was obsessed with*** *his roommate's sister | I* ***am obsessed by*** *a desire to win* **be fixated on/upon,** be preoccupied with, be possessed by, be consumed with/by (thoughts of), have an obsession with; be infatuated with, be besotted with, be smitten with; informal have a thing about/for, be hung up about/on, have it bad for.

obsession ▶ noun *that new car has become his obsession* **fixation,** ruling/consuming passion, passion, mania, idée fixe, compulsion, preoccupation, infatuation, addiction, fetish, craze, hobbyhorse; phobia, complex, neurosis; informal a bee in one's bonnet, hang-up, thing.

obsessive ▶ adjective *her obsessive behavior includes relentless tidying* **all-consuming,** consuming, compulsive, controlling, obsessional, fanatic, fanatical, neurotic, excessive, overkeen, besetting, tormenting, inescapable, pathological.

obsolescent ▶ adjective *much of the business etiquette our parents knew is obsolescent* **dying out,** on the decline, declining, waning, on the wane, disappearing, past its prime, aging, moribund, on its last legs, old-fashioned, outmoded, downlevel, on the way out; obsolete, outdated, out of date, behind the times.

obsolete ▶ adjective *most of the machinery in their Somerville plant is obsolete | obsolete hairstyles* **outdated,** out of date, outmoded, old-fashioned, démodé, passé, out of fashion; no longer in use, disused, fallen into disuse, behind the times, superannuated, outworn, antiquated, antediluvian, anachronistic, discontinued, old, dated, archaic, ancient, fossilized, extinct, defunct, dead, bygone, out; informal prehistoric. See note at **OLD**.
ANTONYMS cutting-edge, the latest, modern.

obstacle ▶ noun *blindness is not the worst obstacle I've had to overcome* **barrier,** hurdle, stumbling block, obstruction, bar, block, impediment, hindrance, snag, catch, drawback, hitch, handicap, deterrent, complication, difficulty, problem, disadvantage, curb, check; informal fly in the ointment, monkey wrench (in the works).
ANTONYMS advantage, aid.

obstinacy ▶ noun *Zach's obstinacy contributed to his unfavorable performance evaluation* **stubbornness,** inflexibility, intransigence, intractability, obduracy, mulishness, pigheadedness, willfulness, contrariness, perversity, recalcitrance, refractoriness, implacability, rigidity, uncooperativeness; persistence, tenacity, tenaciousness, pertinacity, doggedness, single-mindedness.
ANTONYMS flexibility.

obstinate ▶ adjective *it's unusual for two such obstinate people to have a happy marriage* **stubborn,** unyielding, inflexible, unbending, intransigent, intractable, obdurate, mulish, bullheaded, stubborn as a mule, pigheaded, self-willed, strong-willed, headstrong, willful, contrary, perverse, recalcitrant, refractory,

uncooperative, unmanageable, stiff-necked, rigid, uncompromising, implacable, unrelenting, immovable, unshakable; persistent, tenacious, pertinacious, dogged, single-minded. See note at **STUBBORN**.
ANTONYMS compliant.

obstreperous ▶ adjective *the hotel manager was accustomed to dealing with obstreperous guests* **unruly,** unmanageable, disorderly, undisciplined, uncontrollable, rowdy, disruptive, truculent, difficult, refractory, rebellious, mutinous, riotous, out of control, wild, turbulent, uproarious, boisterous; noisy, loud, clamorous, raucous, vociferous; informal rambunctious. See note at **VOCIFEROUS**.
ANTONYMS quiet, restrained.

obstruct ▶ verb **1** *ensure that the air vents are not obstructed* **block (up),** clog (up), get in the way of, jam (up), cut off, shut off, bung up, choke, dam up; barricade, bar; technical occlude.
ANTONYMS clear.
2 *he was charged with obstructing traffic* **hold up,** bring to a standstill, stop, halt, block.
3 *fears that the regime would obstruct the distribution of food* **impede,** hinder, interfere with, hamper, hobble, block, interrupt, hold up, stand in the way of, frustrate, thwart, balk, inhibit, hamstring, sabotage; slow down, retard, delay, stonewall, stall, stop, halt, stay, restrict, limit, curb, put a brake on, bridle; informal stymie. See note at **HINDER**.
ANTONYMS facilitate, further.

obstruction ▶ noun *wealthy property owners have created one obstruction after another to undermine the low-income housing project* **obstacle,** barrier, stumbling block, hurdle, bar, block, impediment, hindrance, snag, difficulty, catch, drawback, hitch, handicap, deterrent, curb, check, restriction; blockage, stoppage, congestion, bottleneck, holdup, jam; Medicine occlusion; informal fly in the ointment, monkey wrench (in the works).

obstructive ▶ adjective *he pursued his dreams of being a musician despite the efforts of his obstructive parents* **unhelpful,** uncooperative, unsupportive, awkward, difficult, unaccommodating, disobliging, perverse, contrary; archaic froward, contrarious.
ANTONYMS helpful, supportive.

obtain ▶ verb **1** *the newspaper obtained a copy of the letter* **get,** acquire, come by, secure, procure, come into the possession of, pick up, be given; gain, earn, achieve, attain; informal get hold of, get/lay one's hands on, get one's mitts on, land, net. See note at **GET**.
ANTONYMS relinquish, lose.
2 formal *rules obtaining in other jurisdictions* **prevail,** be in force, apply, exist, be in use, be in effect, stand, hold, be the case.

obtainable ▶ adjective *use dried herbs only when fresh ones are not obtainable* **available,** to be had, in circulation, on the market, in season, at one's disposal, at hand, attainable, procurable, accessible, realizable, gettable; informal up for grabs, on tap, get-at-able.

obtrusive ▶ adjective *a car dealership on this stretch of road would be too obtrusive | she wears the most obtrusive outfits* **conspicuous,** prominent, noticeable, obvious, unmistakable; intrusive, out of place; bold, loud, showy, gaudy, garish, flashy; informal sticking/standing out like a sore thumb. See note at **IMPERTINENT**.
ANTONYMS unobtrusive, inconspicuous.

obtuse ▶ adjective *he frustrated his teachers by pretending to be obtuse* **stupid,** slow-witted, slow, dull-witted, unintelligent, ignorant, simpleminded, witless; insensitive, imperceptive, uncomprehending; informal dim, dimwitted, dense, dumb, slow on the uptake, halfwitted, brain-dead, moronic, cretinous, thick, dopey, lamebrained, dumb-ass, dead from the neck up, boneheaded, chowderheaded. See note at **STUPID**.
ANTONYMS clever, astute.

obvious ▶ adjective *it's obvious that they don't get along | her intentions are obvious* **clear,** crystal clear, plain, plain to see, evident, apparent, manifest, patent, conspicuous, pronounced, transparent, palpable, prominent, marked, decided, distinct, noticeable, unmissable, perceptible, visible, discernible; unmistakable, indisputable, self-evident, incontrovertible, incontestable, undeniable, beyond doubt, beyond question, as clear as day, staring someone in the face; overt, open, undisguised, unconcealed, frank, glaring, blatant, written all over someone; informal as plain as the nose on one's face, sticking/standing out like a sore thumb, right under one's nose.
ANTONYMS imperceptible, obscure.

obviously ▶ adverb *they were obviously thrilled to hear your good news | obviously, I had forgotten her name* **clearly,** evidently, plainly, patently, visibly, discernibly, manifestly, noticeably; unmistakably, undeniably, incontrovertibly, demonstrably, unquestionably, indubitably, undoubtedly, without doubt, doubtless; of course, naturally, needless to say, it goes without saying. See note at **CLEARLY**.
ANTONYMS perhaps.

occasion ▶ noun **1** *a previous occasion* **time,** instance, moment, juncture, point; event, occurrence, affair, incident, episode, experience; situation, case, circumstance.
2 *a family occasion* **social event,** event, affair, function, celebration, party, get-together, gathering; informal do, bash.
3 *I doubt if the occasion will arise* **opportunity,** right moment, opportune time, chance, opening, window.
4 *it's the first time I've had occasion to complain* **reason,** cause, call, grounds, justification, need, motive, inducement.
▶ verb *her situation occasioned a good deal of sympathy* **cause,** give rise to, bring about, result in, lead to, prompt, elicit, call forth, evoke, make for, produce, create, arouse, generate, engender, precipitate, provoke, stir up, inspire, spark (off), trigger; literary beget.
– PHRASES **on occasion** See **OCCASIONALLY**.

occasional ▶ adjective *the admiral made occasional appearances on board our ship* **infrequent,** intermittent, irregular, sporadic, odd, random; periodic; uncommon, rare, isolated, few and far between, sometime.
ANTONYMS regular, frequent.

occasionally ▶ **adverb** *I occasionally have wine with dinner* **sometimes,** from time to time, (every) now and then, (every) now and again, at times, every so often, (every) once in a while, on occasion; periodically, at intervals; irregularly, sporadically, infrequently, intermittently, on and off, off and on.
ANTONYMS often, frequently.

occult ▶ **noun** *his interest in the occult* **the supernatural,** the paranormal, supernaturalism, magic, black magic, witchcraft, sorcery, necromancy, wizardry, the black arts, occultism, diabolism, devil worship, devilry, voodoo, hoodoo, white magic, witchery, mysticism; rare theurgy.
▶ **adjective 1** *occult powers* **supernatural,** magic, magical, mystical, mystic, psychic, preternatural, paranormal, transcendental; Kabbalistic, hermetic.
2 *the typically occult language of the time* **esoteric,** arcane, recondite, abstruse, secret; obscure, incomprehensible, impenetrable, puzzling, perplexing, mystifying, mysterious, enigmatic.

occupancy ▶ **noun** *our occupancy is temporary* **occupation,** tenancy, tenure, residence, residency, inhabitation, habitation, living, lease, holding, possession; formal dwelling.

occupant ▶ **noun 1** *the occupants of the houses* **resident,** inhabitant, owner, householder, tenant, renter, leaseholder, lessee; addressee, occupier; formal dweller.
2 *the first occupant of the post* **incumbent,** holder.

occupation ▶ **noun 1** *his father's occupation* **job,** profession, work, line of work, trade, employment, position, post, situation, business, career, field, métier, vocation, calling, craft.
2 *her leisure occupations* **pastime,** activity, hobby, pursuit, interest, entertainment, recreation, amusement, diversion, divertissement.
3 *a property suitable for occupation by seniors* **residence,** residency, habitation, inhabitation, occupancy, tenancy, tenure, lease, living in, possession; formal dwelling.
4 *the Roman occupation of Britain* **conquest,** capture, invasion, seizure, takeover, annexation, overrunning, subjugation, subjection, appropriation; **colonization,** rule, control, possession, suzerainty.

occupational ▶ **adjective** *occupational hazards | occupational choices* **job-related,** work, professional, vocational, employment, business, career.

occupied ▶ **adjective 1** *tasks that kept her occupied all day* **busy,** engaged, working, at work, active; immersed, preoccupied, absorbed, engrossed; informal tied up, wrapped up, hard at it.
ANTONYMS idle.
2 *all the tables were occupied* **in use,** full, engaged, taken, unavailable.
ANTONYMS available, empty, free.
3 *only two of the apartments are occupied* **inhabited,** lived-in, tenanted, settled.
ANTONYMS vacant, empty.

occupy ▶ **verb 1** *Carol occupied the basement apartment* **live in,** inhabit, be the tenant of, lodge in; move into, take up residence in, make one's home in; people, populate, settle; formal reside in, dwell in.
2 *two windows occupied almost the whole of the end wall* **take up,** fill, fill up, cover, use up.
3 *he occupies a senior post at the firm* **hold,** fill, be in, have, hold down.
4 *I need something to occupy my mind* **engage,** busy, employ, distract, absorb, engross, preoccupy, hold, interest, involve, entertain, amuse, divert.
5 *the region was occupied by Soviet troops* **capture,** seize, take possession of, conquer; invade, overrun; take over, garrison, hold, annex, subjugate, colonize.

occur ▶ **verb 1** *the accident occurred at about 3:30* **happen,** take place, come about, transpire, materialize, arise, crop up; informal go down; literary come to pass, befall, betide; formal eventuate. See note at HAPPEN.
2 *the disease occurs chiefly in tropical climates* **be found,** be present, exist, appear, prevail, present itself, manifest itself, turn up.
3 *an idea occurred to her* **enter one's head/mind,** cross one's mind, come to mind, spring to mind, strike one, hit one, dawn on one, suggest itself, present itself.

occurrence ▶ **noun 1** *vandalism used to be a rare occurrence* **event,** incident, happening, phenomenon, affair, matter, circumstance.
2 *the occurrence of cancer increases with age* **existence,** instance, appearance, manifestation, materialization, development; frequency, incidence, rate, prevalence; Statistics distribution.

odd ▶ **adjective 1** *an odd man* **strange,** peculiar, weird, queer, funny, bizarre, abnormal, eccentric, unusual, unconventional, outlandish, quirky, zany; informal wacky, kooky, screwy, freaky, oddball, offbeat, off the wall, out there.
ANTONYMS normal, conventional.
2 *quite a few odd things had happened* **strange,** unusual, peculiar, funny, curious, bizarre, weird, uncanny, queer, outré, unexpected, unfamiliar, abnormal, atypical, anomalous, different, out of the ordinary, out of the way, exceptional, rare, extraordinary, remarkable, puzzling, mystifying, mysterious, perplexing, baffling, unaccountable, uncommon, irregular, singular, deviant, aberrant, freak, freakish; informal fishy, freaky.
ANTONYMS ordinary, usual.
3 *we have the odd drink together | he does odd jobs for friends* **occasional,** casual, irregular, isolated, random, sporadic, periodic; miscellaneous, various, varied, sundry.
ANTONYMS regular, scheduled.
4 *odd socks* **mismatched,** unmatched, unpaired; single, lone, solitary, extra, surplus, leftover, remaining.
5 *when you've got an odd ten minutes, stop by my office* **spare,** free, available, unoccupied; between appointments, between engagements.
– PHRASES **odd man out** *no matter what our group planned to do over school vacations, Cassidy was always odd man out* **outsider,** exception, oddity, nonconformist, maverick, individualist, misfit, fish out of water, square peg in a round hole.

oddity ▶ noun **1** *she was regarded as a bit of an oddity* **eccentric,** misfit, square peg in a round hole, maverick, nonconformist, odd one, rare bird, crank; informal character, oddball, weirdo, crackpot, nut, freak, screwball, kook, queer/odd fish, queer/odd duck.
ANTONYMS conformist, average Joe.
2 *his work remains an oddity in some respects* **anomaly,** aberration, curiosity, rarity.
3 *there was a real oddity about their artwork* **strangeness,** peculiarity, oddness, weirdness, bizarreness, eccentricity, queerness, unconventionality, outlandishness; informal wackiness, kookiness.
4 *the oddities of human nature* **peculiarity,** idiosyncrasy, eccentricity, quirk, irregularity, twist.

odds ▶ plural noun **1** *odds are that he is no longer alive* **the likelihood is,** the probability is, chances are, there's a good chance.
2 *the odds are in our favor | against all odds* **advantage,** edge; superiority, supremacy, ascendancy.
– PHRASES **at odds 1** *Duncan and Eliza have been at odds all week* **in conflict,** in disagreement, on bad terms, at cross purposes, at loggerheads, quarreling, arguing, on the outs, at daggers drawn, at each other's throats. **2** *your behavior is **at odds with** the interests of the company* **at variance with,** not in keeping with, out of keeping with, out of line with, in opposition to, conflicting with, contrary to, incompatible with, inconsistent with, irreconcilable with. **odds and ends bits and pieces,** bits, pieces, stuff, paraphernalia, things, sundries, miscellanea, bric-a-brac, knickknacks, oddments, junk.

odious ▶ adjective *the odious procedures of the military government | the dumpsite was especially odious in summer* **revolting,** repulsive, repellent, repugnant, disgusting, offensive, objectionable, vile, foul, abhorrent, loathsome, nauseating, sickening, hateful, detestable, execrable, abominable, monstrous, appalling, reprehensible, deplorable, insufferable, intolerable, despicable, contemptible, unspeakable, atrocious, awful, terrible, dreadful, frightful, obnoxious, unsavory, unpalatable, unpleasant, disagreeable, nasty, noisome, distasteful; informal ghastly, horrible, horrid, gross, godawful; beastly.
ANTONYMS delightful, pleasant.

odium ▶ noun *during the trial, he sensed his family's distrust and odium* **disgust,** abhorrence, repugnance, revulsion, loathing, detestation, hatred, hate, obloquy, dislike, distaste, disfavor, antipathy, animosity, animus, enmity, hostility, contempt; disgrace, shame, opprobrium, discredit, dishonor.
ANTONYMS approval.

odor ▶ noun **1** *an odor of sweat* **smell,** stench, stink, reek, whiff, fetor; informal funk; literary miasma.
2 *the pleasing odor of fresh-roasted coffee* **aroma,** smell, scent, fragrance, bouquet, perfume. See note at SMELL.
3 *an odor of suspicion* **atmosphere,** air, aura, quality, flavor, savor, hint, suggestion, impression, whiff.

odyssey ▶ noun *Magellan's great odyssey | the book details her odyssey from housewife to world leader* **journey,** voyage, trek, travels, quest, crusade, pilgrimage, wandering, journeying; archaic peregrination.

off ▶ adverb **1** *Kate's off today* **away,** absent, out, unavailable, not at work, off duty, on leave, on vacation; free, at leisure; Brit. on holiday.
ANTONYMS in, at work, working.
2 *the game's off* **canceled,** postponed, called off, shelved.
ANTONYMS on.
▶ adjective **1** *the fish was a bit off* **rotten,** bad, stale, moldy, sour, rancid, turned, spoiled, putrid, putrescent; (of beer) skunky.
ANTONYMS fresh.
2 informal *I felt decidedly off* **unwell,** ill, out of sorts, not oneself, sick, indisposed, bad; informal under the weather, not up to par, lousy, crummy; vulgar slang crappy.
ANTONYMS well.
– PHRASES **off and on** *I still play tennis, but only off and on* **periodically,** at intervals, on and off, (every) once in a while, every so often, (every) now and then/again, from time to time, occasionally, sometimes, intermittently, irregularly.

offbeat ▶ adjective informal *an offbeat suggestion | offbeat clothes* **unconventional,** unorthodox, unusual, eccentric, idiosyncratic, outré, strange, bizarre, weird, peculiar, odd, freakish, outlandish, out of the ordinary, Bohemian, alternative, zany, quirky; informal wacky, freaky, way-out, off the wall, kooky, oddball.
ANTONYMS conventional, ordinary.

off-color ▶ adjective *off-color jokes* **smutty,** dirty, rude, crude, filthy, suggestive, indecent, indelicate, risqué, racy, bawdy, naughty, blue, vulgar, ribald, broad, salacious, coarse, obscene; informal raunchy; euphemistic adult.

offend ▶ verb **1** *I'm sorry if I offended him* **hurt someone's feelings,** give offense to, affront, displease, upset, distress, hurt, wound; annoy, anger, exasperate, irritate, vex, pique, gall, irk, nettle, ruffle someone's feathers, tread on someone's toes; rub the wrong way; informal rile, rattle, peeve, needle, miff, put someone's nose out of joint, put someone's back up; vulgar slang piss off.
2 *the smell of cigarette smoke offended him* **displease,** be distasteful to, be disagreeable to, be offensive to, disgust, repel, revolt, sicken, nauseate, be repugnant to; informal turn off, gross out.
ANTONYMS please, delight.
3 *criminals who offend again and again* **break the law,** commit a crime, do wrong, sin, go astray, transgress; archaic trespass.

offended ▶ adjective *he was offended because she had forgotten their anniversary* **upset, insulted,** affronted, aggrieved, displeased, hurt, wounded, disgruntled, put out, annoyed, angry, cross, exasperated, indignant, irritated, piqued, vexed, irked, stung, galled, nettled, resentful, in a huff, huffy, in high dudgeon; informal riled, miffed, peeved, aggravated, sore, teed off,

ticked off; vulgar slang pissed off.
ANTONYMS pleased.

offender ▶ noun *my client is not the offender in this case* **wrongdoer, criminal,** lawbreaker, miscreant, malefactor, felon, delinquent, culprit, guilty party, outlaw, sinner, transgressor; Law malfeasant.

offense ▶ noun **1** *he denied having committed any offense* **crime,** illegal/unlawful act, misdemeanor, breach of the law, felony, wrongdoing, wrong, misdeed, peccadillo, sin, transgression, infringement; Law malfeasance; informal no-no; archaic trespass; rare malefaction. See note at SIN.
2 *an offense to basic justice* **affront,** slap in the face, insult, outrage, violation, slight.
3 *I do not want to cause offense* **annoyance,** anger, resentment, indignation, irritation, exasperation, wrath, displeasure, hard/bad/ill feelings, disgruntlement, pique, vexation, animosity, antipathy.
4 *planning our next offense* **attack,** offensive, assault, onslaught, invasion, incursion, foray, sortie.
– PHRASES **take offense** *his jokes were very insulting, and many of us took offense* **be/feel offended,** take exception, take something personally, feel affronted, be/feel resentful, take something amiss, take umbrage, be/get/feel upset, be/get/feel annoyed, be/get/feel angry, get into a huff.

offensive ▶ adjective **1** *offensive remarks* **insulting,** insolent, derogatory, disrespectful, hurtful, wounding, abusive; annoying, exasperating, irritating, galling, provocative, outrageous; rude, impertinent, discourteous, uncivil, impolite; crude, vulgar, coarse, improper, indecent; formal exceptionable.
ANTONYMS complimentary, polite, courteous.
2 *an offensive smell* **unpleasant,** disagreeable, nasty, distasteful, displeasing, objectionable, off-putting, awful, terrible, dreadful, frightful, obnoxious, abominable, disgusting, repulsive, repellent, repugnant, revolting, abhorrent, loathsome, detestable, odious, vile, foul, sickening, nauseating; informal ghastly, horrible, horrid, gross, putrid, godawful, beastly; literary noisome, mephitic.
ANTONYMS pleasant, delightful.
3 *an offensive air strike* **hostile,** attacking, aggressive, invading, incursive, combative, belligerent, on the attack.
ANTONYMS defensive.
▶ noun *a military offensive* **attack,** assault, onslaught, drive, invasion, push, thrust, charge, sortie, sally, foray, raid, incursion, offense, blitz, campaign.
– PHRASES **take the offensive** *our fleet will take the offensive within the next 48 hours* **launch an attack,** begin to attack, attack first, strike the first blow.

CHOOSE THE RIGHT WORD

offensive, abhorrent, abominable, detestable, odious, repugnant

Looking for just the right word to express your dislike, distaste, disgust, or aversion to something? **Offensive** is a relatively mild adjective, used to describe anyone or anything that is unpleasant or disagreeable (*she found his remarks offensive; the offensive sight of garbage piled in the alley*). If you want to express strong dislike for someone or something that deserves to be disliked, use **detestable** (*a detestable man who never had a kind word for anyone*). If something is so offensive that it provokes a physical as well as a moral or intellectual response, use **odious** (*the odious treatment of women during the war in Bosnia*), and if you instinctively draw back from it, use **repugnant** (*the very thought of piercing one's nose was repugnant to her*). If your repugnance is extreme, go one step further and use **abhorrent** (*an abhorrent act that could not go unpunished*). Persons and things that are truly loathsome or terrifying can be called **abominable** (*an abominable act of desecration; the abominable snowman*), although this word is often used as an overstatement to mean "awful" (*abominable taste in clothes*).

offer ▶ verb **1** *Chris offered another suggestion* **put forward,** proffer, provide, give, present, come up with, suggest, extend, recommend, propose, advance, submit, tender, render.
ANTONYMS withdraw, withhold.
2 *she offered to help | if you're looking for assistance, I'm offering* **volunteer,** volunteer one's services, be at someone's disposal, be at someone's service, make oneself available, step/come forward.
3 *the product is offered at a competitive price* **put up for sale,** put on the market, sell, market, make available, put under the gavel/hammer; Law vend.
4 *he offered $200* **bid,** tender, put in a bid of, put in an offer of.
5 *a job offering good career prospects* **provide,** afford, supply, give, furnish, present, purvey, hold out.
6 *she offered no resistance* **attempt,** try, give, show, express; formal essay.
7 *birds were offered to the gods* **sacrifice,** offer up, immolate, give.
▶ noun **1** *a job offer | offers of help* **proposal,** proposition, suggestion, submission, approach, overture; literary proffer.
2 *the highest offer* **bid,** tender, bidding price.

offering ▶ noun **1** *you may place offerings in the basket* **contribution,** donation, gift, present, handout, charity; formal benefaction; historical alms.
2 *many offerings were made to the goddess* **sacrifice,** oblation, burnt offering, immolation, libation; peace offering, sin offering; Hinduism prasad, puja; Judaism Omer.

offhand ▶ adjective *an offhand manner* **casual,** careless, uninterested, unconcerned, indifferent, cool, nonchalant, blasé, aloof, insouciant, cavalier, glib, perfunctory, cursory, unceremonious, ungracious, dismissive, discourteous, uncivil, impolite, terse, abrupt, curt; informal couldn't-care-less, take-it-or-leave-it.
▶ adverb *I can't think of a better answer offhand* **on**

the spur of the moment, without preparation, without consideration, extempore, impromptu, ad lib; extemporaneously, spontaneously; Latin ad libitum; informal off the cuff, off the top of one's head, just like that. See note at SPONTANEOUS.

office ▶ noun 1 *her office on Union Street* **place of work,** place of business, workplace; headquarters, base; workroom, studio, workspace, cubicle.
2 *the newspaper's Paris office* **branch,** division, section, bureau, department; agency.
3 *he assumed the office of mayor* **post,** position, appointment, job, occupation, role, situation, station, function, capacity.
4 *he was saved by the good **offices** of his uncle* **assistance,** help, aid, services, intervention, intercession, mediation, agency, support, backing, patronage, auspices, aegis.
5 *the offices of a nurse* **duty,** job, task, chore, obligation, assignment, responsibility, charge, commission.

officer ▶ noun 1 *an officer in the army* **military officer,** commissioned officer, noncommissioned officer, NCO, commanding officer, CO.
2 *all the officers in this precinct carry guns* **police officer,** policeman, policewoman, officer of the law, law-enforcement officer/agent, peace officer, patrolman, trooper; informal cop, copper, flatfoot.
3 *the officers of the society* **official,** officeholder, committee member, board member; public servant, administrator, executive, functionary, bureaucrat; derogatory apparatchik.
4 *officers of the court* **representative,** deputy, agent, envoy.

official ▶ adjective 1 *an official inquiry* **authorized,** approved, validated, authenticated, certified, accredited, endorsed, sanctioned, licensed, recognized, accepted, legitimate, legal, lawful, valid, bona fide, proper, ex cathedra; informal kosher.
ANTONYMS unofficial, unauthorized.
2 *an official function* **ceremonial,** formal, solemn, ceremonious; bureaucratic; informal stuffed-shirt.
ANTONYMS informal.
▶ noun *a union official* **officer,** officeholder, administrator, executive, appointee, functionary; bureaucrat, mandarin; representative, agent; derogatory apparatchik.

officiate ▶ verb 1 *he officiated the game* **preside over,** be in charge of, take charge of, direct, head (up); oversee, superintend, supervise, conduct, run; referee, umpire, judge, adjudicate; emcee.
2 *Father Buckley **officiated at** the wedding service* **conduct,** perform, celebrate, solemnize.

officious ▶ adjective *I try to avoid their officious salesclerks* **self-important,** bumptious, self-assertive, overbearing, overzealous, domineering, opinionated, interfering, intrusive, meddlesome, meddling; informal pushy, bossy.
ANTONYMS self-effacing.

offing ▶ noun
– PHRASES **in the offing** *I knew that a significant change in my life was in the offing* **on the way,** coming (soon), (close) at hand, near, imminent, in prospect, on the horizon, in the wings, just around the corner, in the air, in the wind, brewing, upcoming, forthcoming; bound to happen, likely to happen; informal in the cards, coming down the pike.

offload ▶ verb 1 *the cargo was being offloaded* **unload,** remove, empty (out), tip (out); archaic unlade.
2 *he offloaded 5,000 shares* **dispose of,** dump, jettison, get rid of, transfer, shift; palm off, foist; Brit. fob off.

off-putting ▶ adjective 1 *an off-putting aroma* **unpleasant,** unappealing, uninviting, unattractive, disagreeable, repellent, offensive, distasteful, unsavory, unpalatable, unappetizing, objectionable, nasty, disgusting; informal horrid, horrible.
2 *her manner was off-putting* **uninviting,** discouraging, disheartening, demoralizing, dispiriting, daunting, disconcerting, unnerving, unsettling; formal rebarbative.

offset ▶ verb *we were not able to offset our losses over the last quarter* **counterbalance,** balance (out), cancel (out), even out/up, counteract, countervail, neutralize, compensate for, make up for, make good, redeem, indemnify; atone for, make amends for, make restitution for.

offshoot ▶ noun 1 *the plant's offshoots* **side shoot,** shoot, sucker, tendril, runner, scion, slip, offset, stolon; twig, branch, bough, limb.
2 *an offshoot of Cromwell's line* **descendant,** scion, relation.
3 *rap music began as an underground offshoot of disco* **outcome,** result, (side) effect, corollary, consequence, upshot, product, by-product, spin-off, development, outgrowth, fallout.
4 *the company now controls several offshoots* **subsidiary,** branch, adjunct, derivative.

offspring ▶ noun (usually as plural) *his offspring gathered to mourn his passing* **children,** sons and daughters, progeny, family, youngsters, babies, brood; descendants, heirs, successors, scions; Law issue; informal kids; derogatory spawn; archaic fruit of one's loins.

often ▶ adverb *we go there often* **frequently,** many times, many a time, on many/numerous occasions, a lot, as often as not, repeatedly, again and again, time and (time) again; all the time, regularly, routinely, usually, habitually, commonly, generally, in many cases/instances, ordinarily, oftentimes, recurrently; informal lots; literary oft, ofttimes.
ANTONYMS seldom, never.

ogle ▶ verb *he never disguised his desire to ogle the young ladies* **leer at,** stare at, eye, make eyes at, check out; informal give someone the once-over, lech after, undress with one's eyes.

oil ▶ noun 1 *make sure the car has enough oil | we heat our house with oil* **lubricant,** lubrication, grease; crude, crude oil, fuel oil, petroleum; informal black gold; humorous Texas tea.
2 *brown the beef in hot oil* **cooking oil,** vegetable oil; corn oil, olive oil, sunflower oil, safflower oil, canola oil, peanut oil.
3 *add some oil to the bath water* bath oil, essential oil, baby oil, scented oil, suntan oil.

▶ verb *I'll oil that gate for you* **lubricate,** grease, smear/cover/rub with oil; informal lube.

oily ▶ adjective **1** *oily substances* **greasy,** oleaginous, unctuous; technical sebaceous; formal pinguid.
2 *oily food* **greasy,** fatty, buttery, swimming in oil/fat.
3 *he's an oily character* **unctuous,** ingratiating, fawning, smooth-talking, fulsome, flattering, obsequious, sycophantic, oleaginous; informal smarmy, slimy.

ointment ▶ noun *apply the ointment twice a day* **lotion,** cream, salve, liniment, rub, gel, balm, emollient, unguent; formal embrocation; technical humectant; proprietary Vaseline.

old ▶ adjective **1** *old ladies* **elderly,** aged, older, senior, advanced in years, up in years; venerable; in one's dotage, long in the tooth, gray-haired, grizzled, hoary; past one's prime, not as young as one was, ancient, decrepit, doddering, doddery, not long for this world, senescent, senile, superannuated; informal getting on, past it, over the hill, no spring chicken.
ANTONYMS young.
2 *that old barn is an eyesore* **dilapidated,** broken-down, beat-up, run-down, tumbledown, ramshackle, decaying, crumbling, disintegrating.
ANTONYMS new, modern.
3 *old clothes | an old sofa* **worn,** worn out, shabby, threadbare, holey, torn, frayed, patched, tattered, moth-eaten, ragged; old-fashioned, out of date, outmoded, démodé; castoff, hand-me-down; informal tatty.
ANTONYMS new, fashionable.
4 *a collector of old cars | the city's old architecture* **antique,** historic, vintage, classic; veteran.
ANTONYMS new, modern.
5 *she's old for her years* **mature,** wise, sensible, experienced, worldly-wise, knowledgeable.
ANTONYMS young, inexperienced.
6 *in the old days* **bygone,** past, former, olden, of old, previous, early, earlier, earliest; medieval, ancient, classical, primeval, primordial, prehistoric, antediluvian.
ANTONYMS modern, recent.
7 *the same old phrases* **hackneyed,** hack, banal, trite, overused, overworked, tired, worn out, stale, clichéd, platitudinous, unimaginative, pedestrian, stock, conventional; out of date, outdated, old-fashioned, outmoded, archaic, obsolete, antiquated, hoary; informal old hat, corny, played out.
ANTONYMS fresh, innovative.
8 *an old girlfriend* **former,** previous, ex-, one-time, erstwhile, once, then; formal quondam.
ANTONYMS new.
9 *the town has held tight to its old ways* **time-honored,** old-time, long-established, age-old; **familiar,** established; customary, usual, routine, habitual; historic, folk, ancestral, old-world.
ANTONYMS modern, progressive.
– PHRASES **old age** *I was not prepared to deal with my father's old age* **declining years,** advanced years, age, agedness, oldness, winter/autumn of one's life, senescence, senility, dotage. **old person** *the old people in this community deserve our support* **senior citizen,** senior, elder, retiree, geriatric, dotard, golden ager; crone; Methuselah; septuagenarian, octogenarian, nonagenarian, centenarian; informal old-timer, oldie, oldster, codger.

> CHOOSE THE RIGHT WORD
>
> **old, aged, ancient, antediluvian, antiquated, archaic, obsolete**
>
> Almost no one likes to be thought of as **old**, which means having been in existence or use for a relatively long time (*an old washing machine*). But those who are **aged**, indicating a longer life span than *old* and usually referring to persons of very advanced years, are often proud of the fact that they have outlived most of their peers. Children may exaggerate and regard their parents as **ancient**, which means dating back to the remote past, often specifically the time before the end of the Roman Empire (*ancient history*), and their attitudes as **antediluvian**, which literally means dating back to the period before the biblical Great Flood and Noah's ark (*an antediluvian transportation system*). Some people seem older than they really are, simply because their ideas are **antiquated**, which means out of vogue or no longer practiced (*antiquated ideas about dating*). Things rather than people are usually described as **archaic**, which means having the characteristics of an earlier, sometimes primitive, period (*archaic words like "thou" and "thine"*). **Obsolete** also refers to things, implying that they have gone out of use or need to be replaced by something newer (*an obsolete textbook; a machine that will be obsolete within the decade*).

old-fashioned ▶ adjective *an old-fashioned hairstyle | old-fashioned thinking* **out of date,** outdated, dated, out of fashion, outmoded, unfashionable, passé, démodé, frumpy; outworn, old, old-time, behind the times, archaic, obsolescent, downlevel, obsolete, ancient, antiquated, superannuated, defunct; medieval, prehistoric, antediluvian, old-fogeyish, old-fangled, conservative, backward-looking, quaint, anachronistic, fusty, moth-eaten, old-world, olde-worlde; informal old hat, square, not with it; horse-and-buggy, clunky, mossy.
ANTONYMS modern, fashionable.

old-time ▶ adjective *we danced to Grandfather's old-time music | it's an old-time tradition* **old-style,** former, past, bygone, old-fashioned, historic; traditional, folk, ancestral, classical, old-world, quaint.
ANTONYMS modern.

omen ▶ noun *the torrential rains on day one of their journey were an omen of things to come* **portent,** sign, signal, token, forewarning, warning, foreshadowing, prediction, forecast, prophecy, harbinger, augury, auspice, presage; straw in the wind, (hand)writing on the wall, indication, hint; literary foretoken. See note at SIGN.

ominous ▶ adjective *ominous clouds* **threatening,** menacing, baleful, forbidding, sinister, inauspicious, unpropitious, unfavorable, unpromising; portentous, foreboding, fateful, premonitory; black, dark, gloomy; formal minatory; literary direful; rare minacious.
ANTONYMS promising, auspicious.

CHOOSE THE RIGHT WORD

ominous, fateful, forbidding, foreboding, portentous, premonitory

A sky filled with low, dark clouds might look **ominous**, but it probably wouldn't be considered **portentous**, even though the root words *omen* and *portent* are nearly synonymous. What is *ominous* is usually threatening and may imply impending disaster (*an ominous silence*), while *portentous* is more often used to describe something that provokes awe or amazement (*a portentous show of military strength*) or a very important outcome (*a portentous moment for the American people*). Like *ominous*, **foreboding** implies that something evil is coming (*foreboding words that sent shivers through us*), while **forbidding** suggests an unfriendly or threatening appearance (*a dark, forbidding castle*). **Fateful** and **premonitory** are less frightening words. What is *fateful* appears to have been inevitable or decreed by fate, with an emphasis on decisive importance (*a fateful meeting with her ex-boyfriend; a battle that would prove fateful*). Anything that serves to warn beforehand is **premonitory**, whether or not the warning concerns something negative (*a premonitory dream about her father's death; a premonitory feeling about the exam*).

omission ▶ noun **1** *we have read the report, and there seem to be several omissions* **exclusion,** leaving out, exception; deletion, cut, excision, elimination, erasure; gap, blank, absence; oversight.
ANTONYMS inclusion.
2 *the damage was not caused by any omission on behalf of the carrier* **negligence,** neglect, neglectfulness, dereliction, forgetfulness, oversight, default, lapse, failure.
ANTONYMS conscientiousness.

omit ▶ verb **1** *they omitted his name from the list* **leave out,** exclude, leave off, fail to mention, miss, pass over; take out, drop, cut, delete, eliminate, erase, rub out, cross out, expunge, strike out.
ANTONYMS include.
2 *I omitted to mention our guest lecturer* **forget,** neglect, fail; leave undone, overlook, ignore, skip.
ANTONYMS remember.

omnipotence ▶ noun *the omnipotence of God* **all-powerfulness,** almightiness, supremacy, preeminence, supreme power, absolute power, unlimited power; invincibility.
ANTONYMS powerlessness.

omnipotent ▶ adjective *the worship of omnipotent deities* **all-powerful,** almighty, supreme, preeminent, most high; invincible, unconquerable.

omnipresent ▶ adjective *she was omnipresent in her children's lives long after her death* **ubiquitous,** all-pervasive, everywhere; boundless, infinite; rife, pervasive, prevalent, far-reaching.

omniscient ▶ adjective *he thought I was some kind of omniscient guru* **all-knowing,** all-wise, all-seeing.

omnivorous ▶ adjective **1** *most duck species are omnivorous* **able to eat anything,** having a mixed/varied diet; rare omnivorant.
2 *an omnivorous reader* **of varied tastes,** undiscriminating, indiscriminate, unselective.

on ▶ preposition **1** *your purse is on the hood of my car* **resting on,** supported by, resting atop, touching the (upper) surface of.
ANTONYMS under, underneath.
2 *put the cushion on the chair* **so as to be resting on,** on to, onto, to the (upper) surface.
▶ adjective *the computer's on* **functioning,** in operation, working, in use, operating.
ANTONYMS off.
▶ adverb *the professor droned on* See **ON AND ON** below.
– PHRASES **on and off** *they've been dating, on and off, for years* See **OFF AND ON** at **OFF**.
on and on *after a few drinks, he blabbers on and on* **for a long time,** for ages, for hours, at (great) length, incessantly, ceaselessly, constantly, continuously, continually, endlessly, unendingly, eternally, forever, interminably, unremittingly, relentlessly, indefatigably, without letup, without a pause/break, without cease.

once ▶ adverb **1** *I spoke to him only once* **on one occasion,** one time, one single time.
ANTONYMS twice, many times, often.
2 *he did not once help* **ever,** at any time, on any occasion, at all, under any circumstances, on any account.
3 *they were friends once* **formerly,** previously, in the past, at one time, at one point, once upon a time, time was when, in days/times gone by, in times past, in the (good) old days, long ago; archaic sometime, erstwhile, whilom; literary in days/times of yore, of yore.
ANTONYMS now, currently.
▶ conjunction *he'll be all right once she's gone* **as soon as,** when, after, the instant, the second, the minute, the moment.
– PHRASES **at once 1** *you must leave at once* **immediately,** right away, right now, this instant, this second, this minute, this moment, now, straightaway, instantly, directly, forthwith, promptly, without delay, without hesitation, without further ado; quickly, as fast as possible, as soon as possible, ASAP, speedily; informal like a shot, in a flash, pronto, in two shakes (of a lamb's tail). **2** *all the guests arrived at once* **at the same time,** at one and the same time, (all) together, simultaneously; as

a group, in unison, in concert, in chorus. **once and for all** *I've made up my mind, once and for all* **conclusively,** decisively, finally, positively, definitely, definitively, absolutely, irrevocably; for good, for always, forever, permanently; informal for keeps. **once in a while** *we go hiking once in a while* **occasionally,** from time to time, (every) now and then/again, every so often, on occasion, at times, sometimes, off and on, at intervals, periodically, sporadically, intermittently.

oncoming ▶ adjective *the lights from the oncoming traffic | bracing for the oncoming storm* **approaching,** advancing, nearing, onrushing; forthcoming, on the way, imminent, impending, looming, gathering, (close) at hand, about to happen, to come.

one ▶ cardinal number **1** *each one is loosely wrapped* **unit,** item; technical monad.
2 *only one person came* **a single,** a solitary, a sole, a lone.
3 *her one concern was her daughter* **only,** single, solitary, sole, exclusive.
4 *they have now become one* **united,** a unit, unitary, amalgamated, consolidated, integrated, combined, incorporated, allied, affiliated, linked, joined, unified, in league, in partnership; wedded, married.
5 *I'll get my big break one day* **some,** any.
▶ pronoun *one never knows what tomorrow may bring* See note **ONE** below.

> USAGE
> **one**
> *One* is used as a pronoun to mean 'anyone' or 'I (or me) and people in general,' as in *one must try one's best*. In modern English, it is generally used only in formal and written contexts. In informal and spoken contexts, the normal alternative is *you*, as in *you must try your best*.
> Until quite recently, sentences in which *one* is followed by *his* or *him* were considered perfectly correct: *one must try his best*. These uses are now held to be less than perfectly grammatical (and possibly sexist as well).

onerous ▶ adjective *the job had become onerous* **burdensome,** arduous, strenuous, difficult, hard, severe, heavy, back-breaking, oppressive, weighty, uphill, formidable, laborious, Herculean, exhausting, tiring, taxing, demanding, punishing, grueling, exacting, wearing, wearisome, fatiguing; archaic toilsome.
ANTONYMS effortless, easy.

oneself ▶ pronoun
– PHRASES **by oneself** See **BY**.

one-sided ▶ adjective **1** *a one-sided account* **biased,** prejudiced, partisan, partial, preferential, discriminatory, slanted, colored, inequitable, unfair, unjust.
ANTONYMS impartial, fair-minded.
2 *a one-sided game* **unequal,** uneven, unbalanced, lopsided.

one-time ▶ adjective *a one-time Little League coach* **former,** ex-, old, previous, sometime, erstwhile; lapsed; formal quondam.

ongoing ▶ adjective **1** *negotiations are ongoing* **in progress,** under way, going on, continuing, taking place, proceeding, progressing, advancing; unfinished.
ANTONYMS stalled, finished.
2 *an ongoing struggle* **continuous,** continuing, uninterrupted, unbroken, nonstop, constant, around/round-the-clock, ceaseless, unceasing, unending, endless, never-ending, unremitting, relentless, unfaltering.
ANTONYMS intermittent.

onlooker ▶ noun *onlookers lined the streets* **eyewitness,** witness, observer, looker-on, fly on the wall, spectator, watcher, viewer, bystander; sightseer; informal rubberneck; literary beholder.

only ▶ adverb **1** *there was only enough for two* **at most,** at best, (only) just, no/not more than; barely, scarcely, hardly, narrowly.
2 *she works only on one painting at a time* **exclusively,** solely, to the exclusion of everything else.
3 *you're only saying that* **merely,** simply, just.
▶ adjective *their only son* **sole,** single, one (and only), solitary, lone, unique; exclusive.

> USAGE
> **only**
> In normal, everyday English, the tendency is to place the word *only* as early as possible in the sentence, generally just before the verb, and the result is rarely ambiguous. Misunderstandings are possible, however, and grammarians have debated the matter for more than two hundred years. Advice varies, but in general, ambiguity is less likely if *only* is placed as close as is naturally possible to the word(s) to be modified or emphasized.
> The wording *Bill ate only the salad* explains that the salad was the sole item that Bill ate. There is no doubt what the statement means. The clear implication is that Bill did not eat the ham, the dessert, or anything else that may have been available.
> The wording *Bill only ate the salad* almost certainly means the same thing, but in a literal sense, there is indeed some doubt. The linking of *only* with *ate* could imply that what Bill did to the salad was simply eat it; he did not prepare it, or spill it, or throw it across the room, or anything else that one could imagine doing to a salad.
> In normal conversation, the second statement would probably not be so misunderstood, but, especially when writing, it's never a mistake to favor the less ambiguous wording.

onomatopoeic ▶ adjective *several words that describe sounds are onomatopoeic, like 'hiss' and 'buzz'* **imitative,** echoic.

onset ▶ noun *they foolishly ignored the onset of his aggressive behavior* **start,** beginning,

commencement, arrival, (first) appearance, inception, emergence, day one, outbreak, dawn, genesis.
ANTONYMS end.

onslaught ▶ noun *the battalion's onslaught was relentless* **assault,** attack, offensive, advance, charge, onrush, rush, storming, sortie, sally, raid, descent, incursion, invasion, foray, push, thrust, drive, blitz, bombardment, barrage, salvo; historical broadside.

onus ▶ noun *the onus of single parenting* **burden,** responsibility, liability, obligation, duty, weight, load, charge, mantle, encumbrance; cross to bear, millstone round one's neck, albatross.

ooze ▶ verb **1** *blood oozed from the wound* **seep,** discharge, flow, exude, trickle, drip, dribble, issue, filter, percolate, escape, leak, drain, empty, bleed, sweat, well; Medicine extravasate.
2 *she was positively oozing charm* **exude,** gush, drip, pour forth, emanate, radiate.
▶ noun **1** *the ooze of blood* **seepage,** seeping, discharge, flow, exudation, trickle, drip, dribble, percolation, escape, leak, leakage, drainage; secretion, excretion; Medicine extravasation.
2 *the ooze on the ocean floor* **mud,** slime, alluvium, silt, mire, sludge, muck, deposit.

opacity ▶ noun **1** *analyzing the opacity of their drinking water* **cloudiness,** nontransparency, opaqueness, filminess, blurriness, blurredness, blur, haziness, haze.
ANTONYMS transparency, translucence, clarity.
2 *the opacity of his arguments* **obscurity,** lack of clarity, abstruseness, unclearness, unintelligibility, density, incomprehensibility.
ANTONYMS clarity.

opalescent ▶ adjective *opalescent sequins* **iridescent,** prismatic, rainbowlike, kaleidoscopic, multicolored, many-hued, lustrous, shimmering, glittering, sparkling, variegated, scintillating, shot, moiré, opaline, milky, pearly, nacreous.

opaque ▶ adjective **1** *opaque glass* **nontransparent,** cloudy, filmy, blurred, smeared, smeary, misty, hazy; dirty, muddy, muddied, grimy.
ANTONYMS transparent, translucent, clear.
2 *the technical jargon was opaque to him* **obscure,** unclear, mysterious, puzzling, perplexing, baffling, mystifying, confusing, unfathomable, incomprehensible, unintelligible, ambiguous, Delphic, impenetrable, oblique, enigmatic, cryptic, hazy, foggy; informal as clear as mud.
ANTONYMS clear.

open ▶ adjective **1** *the door's open* **not shut,** not closed, unlocked, unbolted, unlatched, off the latch, unfastened, unsecured; ajar, gaping, wide open, yawning.
ANTONYMS closed, shut.
2 *a blue silk shirt, open at the neck* **unfastened,** not done up, undone, loose; unbuttoned, unzipped, unbuckled, untied, unlaced.
3 *the main roads are open* **clear,** passable, navigable, unblocked, unobstructed.
ANTONYMS blocked, impassable.
4 *open countryside | open spaces* **unenclosed,** rolling, sweeping, extensive, wide open, unfenced, exposed, unsheltered; spacious, airy, uncrowded, uncluttered; undeveloped, unbuilt-up.
ANTONYMS enclosed, developed.
5 *a map was open beside him* **spread out,** unfolded, unfurled, unrolled; extended, stretched out.
ANTONYMS closed (up), folded.
6 *the bank wasn't open* **open for business,** open to the public.
ANTONYMS closed.
7 *the position is still open* **available,** vacant, free, unfilled; informal up for grabs.
ANTONYMS unavailable, filled.
8 *the system is **open to abuse*** **vulnerable to,** subject to, susceptible to, liable to, exposed to, an easy target for, at risk of, permitting of.
ANTONYMS immune.
9 *she was open about her feelings* **frank,** candid, honest, forthcoming, communicative, forthright, direct, unreserved, plain-spoken, outspoken, straightforward, blunt, not afraid to call a spade a spade; informal **upfront**; archaic free-spoken.
ANTONYMS secretive, withdrawn.
10 *open hostility* **overt,** obvious, patent, manifest, palpable, conspicuous, plain, undisguised, unconcealed, clear, apparent, evident; blatant, flagrant, barefaced, brazen.
ANTONYMS concealed.
11 *the case is still open* **unresolved,** undecided, unsettled, yet to be settled, up in the air; open to debate, open for discussion, arguable, debatable, moot.
ANTONYMS resolved, concluded.
12 *an open mind* **impartial,** unbiased, unprejudiced, objective, disinterested, nonpartisan, nondiscriminatory, neutral, dispassionate, detached.
ANTONYMS biased, one-sided.
13 *I'm open to suggestions* **receptive,** amenable, willing to listen, ready to listen, responsive.
14 *what other options are open to us?* **available,** accessible, on hand, obtainable.
15 *an open meeting* **public,** general, unrestricted, nonexclusive, nonrestrictive.
ANTONYMS private.
▶ verb **1** *she opened the front door* **unfasten,** unlatch, unlock, unbolt, unbar; throw wide.
ANTONYMS close, shut.
2 *Katherine opened the parcel* **unwrap,** undo, untie, unseal.
ANTONYMS wrap, seal.
3 *shall I open another bottle?* **uncork,** broach, crack (open).
ANTONYMS seal, cork.
4 *Adam opened the map* **spread out,** unfold, unfurl, unroll, straighten out; extend, stretch out.
ANTONYMS close, fold up.
5 *he opened his heart to her* **reveal,** uncover, expose, lay bare, bare, pour out, disclose, divulge.
6 *we're hoping to open next month* **open for business,** start trading, set up shop; informal hang out one's shingle.
7 *Valerie opened the meeting* **begin,** start, commence, initiate, set in motion, launch, get going, get underway, get the ball rolling, get off the ground; inaugurate; informal kick off, get the

show on the road.
ANTONYMS conclude, end.
8 *the lounge* ***opens on to*** *a balcony* **give access to,** lead to, be connected to, communicate with; face, overlook, command a view of.

open-air ▶ adjective *an open-air market* **outdoor,** out-of-doors, outside, alfresco, al fresco.
ANTONYMS indoor.

openhanded ▶ adjective *it was a much-appreciated openhanded contribution* **generous,** magnanimous, charitable, benevolent, beneficent, munificent, bountiful, liberal, unstinting; altruistic, philanthropic; literary bounteous.
ANTONYMS tightfisted, stingy.

opening ▶ noun 1 *an opening in the center of the roof* **hole,** gap, aperture, orifice, vent; peephole; split, crack, fissure, cleft, crevice, chink, slit; perforation; Anatomy foramen.
2 *the opening in the wall* **doorway,** gateway, portal, entrance, (means of) entry, entryway, way in, (means of) access; way out, exit, egress.
3 *their defensive lapse gave Torrez the opening he needed* **opportunity,** chance, window (of opportunity), possibility; informal (lucky) break, shot.
4 *an opening in the sales department* **vacancy,** position, job, opportunity.
5 *the opening of the session* **beginning,** start, commencement, outset, inception; introduction, prefatory remarks, opening statement; informal kickoff; formal proem.
ANTONYMS close, closure.
6 *a gallery opening* **opening ceremony,** official opening, launch, inauguration; opening night, premiere, first showing, first night; vernissage.

openly ▶ adverb 1 *drugs were openly on sale* **publicly,** for all to see, blatantly, flagrantly, brazenly, boldly, overtly, in full view; shamelessly, immodestly, wantonly.
ANTONYMS secretly, covertly.
2 *the senator spoke openly of his drinking problems* **frankly,** candidly, explicitly, honestly, sincerely, forthrightly, straightforwardly, bluntly, without constraint, without holding back, straight from the shoulder, straight from the hip.
ANTONYMS allusively, indirectly.

open-minded ▶ adjective 1 *open-minded attitudes* **unbiased,** unprejudiced, nonpartisan, neutral, nonjudgmental, nondiscriminatory; objective, dispassionate, disinterested; tolerant, liberal, permissive, broad-minded.
ANTONYMS prejudiced, judgmental.
2 *it was a progressive school that appealed to parents who were open-minded* **receptive,** open to suggestions, open to new ideas, amenable, flexible, willing to change.
ANTONYMS narrow-minded.

operate ▶ verb 1 *he can operate the machine* **work,** run, make go, use, utilize, handle, control, manage; drive, steer, maneuver.
2 *the machine ceased to operate* **function,** work, go, run, be in working/running order, be operative.
ANTONYMS break down.
3 *the way the law operates in practice* **take effect,** act, apply, be applied, function.
4 *he operated the mine until 1931* **direct,** control, manage, run, govern, administer, superintend, head (up), supervise, oversee, preside over, be in control/charge of.
5 *doctors decided to operate* **perform surgery,** do an operation; informal put under the knife.

operation ▶ noun 1 *the slide bars ensure smooth operation* **functioning,** working, running, performance, action.
2 *the operation of the factory* **management,** running, control, direction, governing, administration, supervision.
3 *a cardiologist from Atlanta will perform the operation* **surgery,** surgical procedure.
4 *a military operation* **action,** activity, exercise, undertaking, enterprise, maneuver, campaign.
5 *their mining operation in Pennsylvania* **business,** enterprise, company, organization, firm, concern; informal outfit, setup.
– PHRASES **in operation** *only one of the automatic doors was in operation* See **OPERATIONAL.**

operational ▶ adjective *the new conveyor belts will be operational by tomorrow* **up and running,** running, working, functioning, operative, in operation, in use, in action; in working order, workable, serviceable, functional, usable, ready for action.
ANTONYMS out of order, broken.

operative ▶ adjective 1 *this piece of legislation is not yet operative* **in force,** in operation, in effect, valid.
ANTONYMS invalid.
2 *most of our antique machinery is operative* See **OPERATIONAL.**
3 *when I say 'perhaps I'll go,' the operative word is 'perhaps'* **key,** significant, relevant, applicable, pertinent, apposite, germane, crucial, critical, pivotal, central, essential.
ANTONYMS irrelevant.
▶ noun 1 *the operatives clean the machines* **machinist,** (machine) operator, mechanic, engineer, worker, workman, blue-collar worker.
2 *an operative of the CIA* **agent,** secret agent, undercover agent, spy, mole, plant, double agent; informal spook; archaic intelligencer.
3 *we hired our own operatives* **detective,** private detective, investigator, private investigator, sleuth; informal private eye, bloodhound; informal dated gumshoe, dick, private dick.

operator ▶ noun 1 *a machine operator* **machinist,** mechanic, operative, engineer, driver, worker.
2 *a tour operator* **contractor,** entrepreneur, promoter, arranger, fixer, dealer, outfitter, expediter.
3 informal *a ruthless operator* **manipulator,** maneuverer, mover and shaker, wheeler-dealer, hustler, wirepuller.

opiate ▶ noun *she refused to take the prescribed opiates* **drug,** narcotic, sedative, tranquilizer, depressant, soporific, anesthetic, painkiller, analgesic, anodyne; morphine, opium, codeine; informal dope; Medicine stupefacient.

opinion ▶ noun *she did not share her husband's opinion* **belief,** judgment, thought(s), (way of) thinking, mind, (point of) view, viewpoint, outlook, attitude, stance, position, perspective, persuasion, standpoint; sentiment, conception, conviction.

– PHRASES **a matter of opinion** *whether his art is worthy of an exhibition is a matter of opinion* **debatable,** open to question, open to debate, a moot point, up to the individual. **be of the opinion** *we are of the opinion that his poetry lacks insight* **believe,** think, consider, maintain, reckon, estimate, feel, have a/the feeling, contend, be convinced; informal allow; formal opine. **in my opinion** *in my opinion, the green tiles clash with the yellow walls* **as I see it,** to my mind, (according) to my way of thinking, personally, in my estimation, if you ask me, for my money, in my book.

CHOOSE THE RIGHT WORD

opinion, belief, conviction, persuasion, sentiment, view

When you give your **opinion** on something, you offer a conclusion or a judgment that, although it may be open to question, seems true or probable to you at the time (*she was known for her strong opinions on women in the workplace*). A **view** is an opinion that is affected by your personal feelings or biases (*his views on life were essentially optimistic*), while a **sentiment** is a more or less settled opinion that may still be colored by emotion (*her sentiments on aging were shared by many other women approaching fifty*). A **belief** differs from an opinion or a view in that it is not necessarily the creation of the person who holds it; the emphasis here is on the mental acceptance of an idea, a proposition, or a doctrine and on the assurance of its truth (*religious beliefs; his belief in the power of the body to heal itself*). A **conviction** is a firmly-held and unshakable belief whose truth is not doubted (*she could not be swayed in her convictions*), while a **persuasion** (in this sense) is a strong belief that is unshakable because you want to believe that it's true rather than because there is evidence proving it so (*she was of the persuasion that he was innocent*).

opinionated ▶ adjective *she got tired of listening to her opinionated boyfriend* **dogmatic,** of fixed views, dictatorial, pontifical, domineering, pompous, self-important, arrogant; inflexible, uncompromising, prejudiced, bigoted.
ANTONYMS open-minded, flexible.

opponent ▶ noun **1** *his political opponent* **rival,** adversary, opposer, (the) opposition, fellow contestant, (fellow) competitor, enemy, antagonist, combatant, contender, challenger; literary foe.
ANTONYMS ally, partner.
2 *an opponent of the reforms* **opposer,** objector, dissenter, dissident.
ANTONYMS supporter.

opportune ▶ adjective *it seemed like the most opportune occasion to make our announcement* **auspicious,** propitious, favorable, advantageous, golden, felicitous; timely, convenient, suitable, appropriate, apt, fitting. See note at TIMELY.
ANTONYMS inopportune, disadvantageous.

opportunism ▶ noun *she scaled the ladder of success with hard work and opportunism* **expediency,** pragmatism, exploitation, Machiavellianism, maneuvering; pushing (all) the right buttons, striking while the iron is hot, making hay while the sun shines.

opportunity ▶ noun *this is your opportunity to move on | don't miss another opportunity* **chance,** lucky chance, favorable time/occasion/moment, time, right set of circumstances, occasion, moment, opening, option, window (of opportunity), turn, go, possibility; informal shot, break, new lease on life.

oppose ▶ verb *most voters opposed the new school budget* **be against,** object to, be hostile to, be in opposition to, disagree with, dislike, disapprove of; resist, take a stand against, put up a fight against, stand up to, fight, challenge; take issue with, dispute, argue with/against, quarrel with; informal be anti-; formal gainsay; rare controvert.
ANTONYMS support.

opposing ▶ adjective **1** *two opposing points of view* **conflicting,** contrasting, opposite, incompatible, irreconcilable, contradictory, antithetical, differing, different, dissimilar, clashing, at variance, at odds, divergent, opposed, poles apart, polar.
ANTONYMS similar, in agreement, identical.
2 *opposing sides in the war* **rival,** opposite, enemy, antagonistic.
ANTONYMS allied.
3 *the opposing page* **opposite,** facing.

opposite ▶ adjective **1** *the opposite page* **facing,** opposing, reverse.
2 *opposite views* **conflicting,** contrasting, incompatible, irreconcilable, antithetical, contradictory, clashing, contrary, at variance, at odds, different, differing, divergent, dissimilar, unalike, disagreeing, opposed, opposing, poles apart, polar.
ANTONYMS similar, same, identical.
3 *opposite sides in a war* **rival,** opposing, enemy.
ANTONYMS same.
▶ preposition *they sit opposite one another* **facing,** face to face with, across from; informal eyeball to eyeball with; archaic fronting.
▶ noun *the opposite was also true* **reverse,** converse, antithesis, contrary, inverse, obverse, antipode; the other side of the coin; informal flip side.

CHOOSE THE RIGHT WORD

opposite; contradictory; antithetical; contrary; reverse

All of these adjectives are usually applied to abstractions and are used to describe ideas, statements, qualities, forces, etc., that are so far apart as to seem irreconcilable. **Opposite** refers to ideas or things that are symmetrically opposed in position, direction, or character—in other words, that are set against each other in such a way that the contrast or conflict between them is highlighted (*they sat opposite one another* at the table). **Contradictory** goes a little further, implying that if one of two opposing statements, propositions, or principles is true, the other must be false (*he assured us the fee would be under $500; his partner gave us contradictory information, saying costs could go as high as $800*). Two contradictory elements are mutually exclusive; for example, *alive* and *dead* are contradictory terms because logically they cannot be applied to the same thing. **Antithetical** implies that the two things being contrasted are diametrically opposed—as far apart or as different from each other as is possible (*they debated the antithetical theories of creationism and evolution*). **Contrary** adds connotations of conflict or antagonism (*the group's discussion was hindered by his contrary remarks*). **Reverse** applies to that which moves or faces in the opposite direction (*he scribbled something on the reverse side of her business card*).

opposition ▶ noun **1** *the proposal met with opposition* **resistance,** hostility, antagonism, enmity, antipathy, objection, dissent, disapproval, criticism, demurral; defiance, noncompliance, obstruction.
2 *they beat the opposition* **opponents,** opposing side, other side, other team, competition, opposers, rivals, adversaries; enemies; literary foes.
3 *the opposition between the public and the private domains* **conflict,** clash, disparity, antithesis, polarity.

oppress ▶ verb **1** *the invaders oppressed the people* **persecute,** abuse, maltreat, ill-treat, tyrannize, crush, repress, suppress, subjugate, subdue, keep down, grind down, ride roughshod over, rule with an iron fist/hand.
2 *the darkness of winter oppressed her* **depress,** make gloomy, make despondent, weigh down, weigh heavily on, cast down, dampen someone's spirits, dispirit, dishearten, discourage, sadden, get down, bring down; archaic deject.

oppressed ▶ adjective *talk of a revolution spread rapidly among the oppressed masses* **persecuted,** downtrodden, abused, maltreated, ill-treated, subjugated, tyrannized, repressed, subdued, crushed, browbeaten; disadvantaged, underprivileged.

oppression ▶ noun *the young people in this country have known nothing but oppression* **persecution,** abuse, maltreatment, ill-treatment, tyranny, despotism, repression, suppression, subjection, subjugation; cruelty, brutality, injustice, hardship, suffering, misery.
ANTONYMS freedom, democracy.

oppressive ▶ adjective **1** *an oppressive dictatorship* **harsh,** cruel, brutal, repressive, tyrannical, tyrannous, iron-fisted, autocratic, dictatorial, despotic, undemocratic; ruthless, merciless, pitiless, draconian.
ANTONYMS lenient, humane.
2 *an oppressive sense of despair* **overwhelming,** overpowering, unbearable, unendurable, intolerable, burdensome.
3 *it was gray and oppressive* **muggy,** close, heavy, hot, humid, sticky, steamy, airless, stuffy, stifling, suffocating, sultry.
ANTONYMS airy, fresh.

oppressor ▶ noun *the rebels overthrew their oppressors in a bloody coup* **persecutor,** tyrant, despot, autocrat, dictator, subjugator, tormentor, slave driver, taskmaster.

opprobrium ▶ noun **1** *the government endured months of opprobrium* **vilification,** abuse, vituperation, condemnation, criticism, censure, denunciation, defamation, denigration, castigation, disparagement, obloquy, derogation, slander, calumny, execration, lambasting, bad press, invective, libel, character assassination; informal flak, mudslinging, bad-mouthing, tongue-lashing; formal excoriation; archaic contumely; rare objurgation.
ANTONYMS praise.
2 *the opprobrium of being associated with thugs* **disgrace,** shame, dishonor, stigma, humiliation, discredit, loss of face, ignominy, obloquy, disrepute, infamy, notoriety, scandal; rare disesteem.
ANTONYMS honor.

opt ▶ verb **1** *I always **opt for** the better quality* **choose,** select, pick (out), decide on, go for, settle on, take.
2 *she's opted to stay in Richmond* **choose,** elect, decide, make/reach the decision, make up one's mind.

optimistic ▶ adjective **1** *she felt optimistic about the future* **hopeful,** confident, positive, cheerful, cheery, sanguine, bright, buoyant, full of hope, bullish, Panglossian, Pollyannaish; informal upbeat; dated of good cheer.
ANTONYMS pessimistic, hopeless.
2 *the forecast is optimistic* **encouraging,** promising, hopeful, reassuring, favorable, auspicious, propitious.
ANTONYMS ominous, gloomy.

optimum ▶ adjective *the team is in optimum health | this is the optimum gas-to-oil ratio* **(the) best,** (the) best of, (the) most favorable, (the) most advantageous, ideal, perfect, prime, optimal, model; top, (the) finest, peak, excellent; informal tip-top, top-notch, A1.

option ▶ noun **1** *leave quietly or be forcibly removed—it's your option* **choice,** alternative, recourse, course of action; power to choose, right to choose.
2 *there are three options: beef, chicken, fish* **choice,** selection, alternative, possibility, way to go; informal bet.

optional ▶ adjective *in senior year, phys ed is optional* **voluntary,** discretionary, not required, elective, noncompulsory, nonmandatory; Law permissive; rare discretional.
ANTONYMS compulsory, mandatory, required.

opulence ▶ noun **1** *the opulence of the room* **luxuriousness,** sumptuousness, lavishness, richness, luxury, luxuriance, splendor, magnificence, grandeur, splendidness; informal plushness, classiness, ritziness, poshness, swankiness.
ANTONYMS simplicity, restraint.
2 *a display of opulence* **wealth,** affluence, wealthiness, richness, riches, prosperity, money.
ANTONYMS poverty.

opulent ▶ adjective 1 *his opulent home* **luxurious,** sumptuous, palatial, lavish, lavishly appointed, rich, splendid, magnificent, grand, grandiose, fancy; informal plush, classy, ritzy, posh, swanky, swank.
ANTONYMS spartan, stark, ascetic.
2 *an opulent family* **wealthy,** rich, affluent, well off, well-to-do, moneyed, prosperous, of means, of substance; informal well-heeled, rolling in money/dough, rolling in it, loaded, stinking/filthy rich, made of money, in clover, (living) on easy street; dated in the chips. See note at WEALTHY.
ANTONYMS penniless, poor, impoverished.
3 *her opulent red hair* **copious,** abundant, profuse, prolific, plentiful, luxuriant; literary plenteous.
ANTONYMS sparse, thin.

opus ▶ noun *her latest opus is a critical success* **composition,** work, work of art, oeuvre, piece, creation.

oracle ▶ noun 1 *the oracle of Apollo* **prophet, prophetess,** sibyl, seer, augur, prognosticator, diviner, soothsayer, fortune teller, sage.
2 *our oracle on Africa* **authority,** expert, specialist, pundit, mentor, adviser, guru.

oracular ▶ adjective 1 *his every utterance was given oracular significance* **prophetic,** prophetical, sibylline, predictive, prescient, prognostic, divinatory, augural.
2 *oracular responses* **enigmatic,** cryptic, abstruse, unclear, obscure, confusing, mystifying, baffling, puzzling, perplexing, mysterious, arcane; ambiguous, equivocal, Delphic.
ANTONYMS clear, unambiguous.

oral ▶ adjective *an oral agreement* **spoken,** verbal, unwritten, vocal, uttered, said, by mouth, viva voce.
ANTONYMS written.
▶ noun *studying for French orals* **oral examination;** Brit. viva, viva voce.

oration ▶ noun *an oration given in memory of McKinley* **speech,** address, lecture, talk, homily, sermon, discourse, declamation, valedictory, salutatory; informal spiel; rare allocution.

orator ▶ noun *Patrick Henry, the great orator* **speaker,** public speaker, speech-maker, lecturer, declaimer, rhetorician, rhetor.

oratorical ▶ adjective *he imitated the oratorical style of Churchill* **rhetorical,** grandiloquent, magniloquent, high-flown, orotund, bombastic, grandiose, pompous, pretentious, overblown, declamatory, turgid, flowery, florid, Ciceronian; informal silver-tongued; rare euphuistic, fustian.
ANTONYMS plain-spoken, simple.

orb ▶ noun *the hallway features a display of luminous orbs suspended at various lengths from the ceiling* **sphere,** globe, ball; spheroid, spherule; circle.

orbit ▶ noun 1 *the monthly orbit of the Moon* **course,** path, circuit, track, trajectory, rotation, revolution, circle; rare circumgyration.
2 *the problem comes outside our orbit* **sphere,** sphere of influence, area of activity, range, scope, ambit, compass, jurisdiction, authority, domain, realm, province, territory, turf; informal bailiwick.
▶ verb *Mercury orbits the Sun* **revolve around,** circle around, go around, travel around.

orchestrate ▶ verb 1 *the piece was orchestrated by Mozart* **arrange,** adapt, score.
2 *orchestrating a campaign of civil disobedience* **organize,** arrange, plan, set up, bring about, mobilize, mount, stage, stage-manage, mastermind, coordinate, direct, engineer, choreograph.

ordain ▶ verb 1 *the Church voted to ordain women* **confer holy orders on,** appoint, anoint, consecrate, install, invest, induct.
2 *the path ordained by fate* **predetermine,** predestine, preordain, destine, determine, prescribe, designate, will.
3 *she ordained that anyone found hunting in the forest must pay a fine* **decree,** rule, order, command, enjoin, lay/set down, establish, dictate, legislate, prescribe, pronounce.

ordeal ▶ noun *the hostages survived the ordeal* **unpleasant experience,** painful experience, trial, tribulation, nightmare, trauma, hell (on earth), misery, trouble, difficulty, torture, torment, agony.

order ▶ noun 1 *alphabetical order* **sequence,** arrangement, organization, disposition, system, series, succession; grouping, classification, categorization, codification, systematization.
2 *his tidy desk demonstrates his sense of order* **tidiness,** neatness, orderliness, organization, method, system; symmetry, uniformity, regularity; routine.
ANTONYMS chaos, disarray.
3 *the police were needed to keep order* **peace,** control, law (and order), lawfulness, discipline, calm, (peace and) quiet, peacefulness, peaceableness.
4 *the equipment was in good order* **condition,** state, repair, shape.
5 *I had to obey her orders* **command,** instruction, directive, direction, decree, edict, injunction, mandate, dictate, commandment, rescript; law, rule, regulation, diktat; demand, bidding, requirement, stipulation; informal say-so; formal ordinance; literary behest.
ANTONYMS suggestion.
6 *the company has won the order* **commission,** contract, purchase order, request, requisition; booking, reservation.
ANTONYMS chaos.
7 *the lower orders of society* **class,** level, rank, grade, degree, position, category; dated station.
8 *the established social order* **(class) system,** hierarchy, pecking order, grading, ranking, scale.
9 *the higher orders of insects* **taxonomic group,** class, family, species, breed; taxon.
10 *a religious order* **community,** brotherhood, sisterhood, organization, association, society, fellowship, fraternity, confraternity, congregation, sodality, lodge, guild, league, union, club; sect.
11 *skills of a very high order* **type,** kind, sort, nature, variety; quality, caliber, standard.
▶ verb 1 *he ordered me to return* **instruct,** command, direct, enjoin, tell, require, charge; formal adjure; literary bid. **2** *the judge ordered that*

their assets be confiscated **decree,** ordain, rule, legislate, dictate, prescribe. **3** *you can order your tickets by phone* **request,** apply for, place an order for; book, reserve; formal bespeak. **4** *the messages are ordered chronologically* **organize,** put in order, arrange, sort out, marshal, dispose, lay out; group, classify, categorize, catalog, codify, systematize, systemize.

– PHRASES **in order 1** *list the dates in order* **in sequence,** in series.
2 *he found everything in order* **tidy,** neat, orderly, straight, trim, shipshape, in apple-pie order; in position, in place.
3 *I think it's in order for me to take the credit* **appropriate,** fitting, suitable, acceptable, (all) right, permissible, permitted, allowable; informal okay. **order about/around** *what makes him think he can just waltz in and start ordering us about?* **tell what to do,** give orders to, dictate to; lay down the law to; informal boss around, push around. **out of order** *the elevator's out of order* **not working,** not in working order, not functioning, broken, broken-down, out of service, out of commission, faulty, defective, inoperative; down; informal conked out, bust, busted, (gone) kaput, on the fritz, on the blink, out of whack.

orderly ▶ **adjective 1** *an orderly room* **neat,** tidy, well-ordered, in order, trim, in apple-pie order, spick-and-span, shipshape.
ANTONYMS untidy, messy.
2 *the orderly presentation of information* **(well) organized,** efficient, methodical, systematic, meticulous, punctilious; coherent, structured, logical, well-planned, well regulated, systematized.
ANTONYMS disorganized.
3 *the crowd was orderly* **well-behaved,** law-abiding, disciplined, peaceful, peaceable, nonviolent.
ANTONYMS unruly.

ordinarily ▶ **adverb** *he ordinarily worked from home* **usually,** normally, as a (general) rule, generally, in general, for the most part, mainly, mostly, most of the time, typically, habitually, commonly, routinely.

ordinary ▶ **adjective 1** *the ordinary course of events* **usual,** normal, standard, typical, common, customary, habitual, everyday, regular, routine, day-to-day. See note at **NORMAL**.
ANTONYMS abnormal.
2 *my life seemed very ordinary* **average,** normal, run-of-the-mill, standard, typical, middle-of-the-road, conventional, unremarkable, unexceptional, workaday, undistinguished, nondescript, colorless, commonplace, humdrum, mundane, unmemorable, pedestrian, prosaic, quotidian, uninteresting, uneventful, dull, boring, bland, suburban, hackneyed, garden-variety; informal plain-vanilla, nothing to write home about, no great shakes.
ANTONYMS unusual, exceptional.

– PHRASES **out of the ordinary** *nothing out of the ordinary happened* **unusual,** exceptional, remarkable, extraordinary, unexpected, surprising, unaccustomed, unfamiliar, abnormal, atypical, different, special, exciting, memorable, noteworthy, unique, singular, outstanding; unconventional, unorthodox, strange, peculiar, odd, queer, curious, bizarre, outlandish; informal offbeat.

organ ▶ **noun 1** *the internal organs* **body part,** biological structure.
2 *the official organ of the teachers' union* **newspaper,** paper, journal, periodical, magazine, newsletter, gazette, publication, mouthpiece; informal rag.

organic ▶ **adjective 1** *organic matter* **living,** live, animate, biological, biotic.
2 *organic vegetables* **pesticide-free,** additive-free, natural.
3 *the love scenes were an organic part of the drama* **essential,** fundamental, integral, intrinsic, vital, indispensable, inherent.
4 *a society is an organic whole* **structured,** organized, coherent, integrated, coordinated, ordered, harmonious.

organism ▶ **noun 1** *fish and other organisms* **living thing,** being, creature, animal, plant, life form.
2 *a complex political organism* **structure,** system, organization, entity.

organization ▶ **noun 1** *the organization of conferences* **planning,** arrangement, coordination, administration, organizing, running, management.
2 *the overall organization of the book* **structure,** arrangement, plan, pattern, order, form, format, framework, composition, constitution.
3 *his lack of organization* **efficiency,** order, orderliness, planning.
4 *a large international organization* **company,** firm, corporation, institution, group, consortium, conglomerate, agency, association, society; informal outfit.

organize ▶ **verb 1** *organizing and disseminating information* **(put in) order,** arrange, sort (out), assemble, marshal, put straight, group, classify, collocate, categorize, catalog, codify, systematize, systemize; rare methodize.
2 *they organized a search party* **make arrangements for,** arrange, coordinate, sort out, put together, fix up, set up, orchestrate, take care of, see to/about, deal with, manage, conduct, administrate, mobilize; schedule, timetable, program; formal concert.

orgy ▶ **noun 1** *a drunken orgy* **wild party,** debauch, carousal, carouse, revel, revelry; informal binge, jag, bender, love-in, toot; literary bacchanal; archaic wassail.
2 *an orgy of violence* **bout,** excess, spree, surfeit; informal binge.

orientation ▶ **noun 1** *the orientation of the radar station* **positioning,** location, position, situation, placement, alignment.
2 *his orientation to his new way of life* **adaptation,** adjustment, acclimatization.
3 *broadly Marxist in orientation* **attitude,** inclination.
4 *freshman orientation begins the week before school starts* **induction,** training, initiation, briefing.

orifice ▶ **noun** *the orifice must be kept free from debris* **opening,** hole, aperture, slot, slit, cleft.

origin ▶ **noun 1** *the origin of life* **beginning,**

start, commencement, origination, genesis, birth, dawning, dawn, emergence, creation, birthplace, cradle; source, basis, cause, root(s); formal radix.
2 *the Latin origin of the word* **source,** derivation, root(s), provenance, etymology.
3 *her Scottish origin* **descent,** ancestry, parentage, pedigree, lineage, line (of descent), heritage, birth, extraction, family, stock, blood, bloodline.

CHOOSE THE RIGHT WORD

origin, inception, provenance, root, source

The **origin** of something is the point from which it starts or sets out, or the person or thing from which it is ultimately derived (*the origin of the custom of carving pumpkins at Halloween; the origin of a word*). It often applies to causes that were in operation before the thing itself was brought into being. **Source**, on the other hand, applies to that which provides a first and continuous supply (*the source of the river; an ongoing source of inspiration and encouragement*). **Root**, more often than *source*, applies to what is regarded as the first or final cause of something; it suggests an origin so fundamental as to be the ultimate cause from which something stems (*the love of money is the root of all evil*). **Inception** refers specifically to the beginning of an undertaking, project, institution, or practice (*she was in charge of the organization from its inception*). **Provenance** is similarly restricted in meaning, referring to the specific place, or sometimes the race or people, from which something is derived or by whom it was invented or constructed (*in digging, they uncovered an artifact of unknown provenance*).

original ▶ adjective **1** *the original inhabitants* **indigenous,** native, aboriginal, autochthonous; first, earliest, early.
2 *original Rembrandts* **authentic,** genuine, actual, true, bona fide; informal kosher.
3 *the film is highly original* **innovative,** creative, imaginative, inventive; new, novel, fresh, refreshing; unusual, unconventional, unorthodox, groundbreaking, pioneering, avant-garde, cutting-edge, unique, distinctive. See note at CREATIVE.
▶ noun **1** *a copy of the original* **archetype,** prototype, source, master.
2 *he really is an original* **individualist,** individual, eccentric, nonconformist, free spirit, maverick; informal character, oddball.

originality ▶ noun *their animated short won an award for its originality* **inventiveness,** ingenuity, creativeness, creativity, innovation, novelty, freshness, imagination, imaginativeness, individuality, unconventionality, uniqueness, distinctiveness.

originally ▶ adverb *the conference was originally scheduled for November* (**at**) **first,** in/at the beginning, to begin with, initially, in the first place, at the outset.

originate ▶ verb **1** *the disease originates in Africa* **arise,** have its origin, begin, start, stem, spring, emerge, emanate.
2 *Tom originated the idea* **invent,** create, initiate, devise, think up, dream up, conceive, formulate, form, develop, generate, engender, produce, mastermind, pioneer; literary beget.

originator ▶ noun *the originator of the Dixie cup* **inventor,** creator, architect, author, father, mother, initiator, innovator, founder, pioneer, mastermind; literary begetter.

ornament ▶ noun **1** *small tables covered with ornaments* **knickknack,** trinket, bauble, bibelot, gewgaw, gimcrack, furbelow; informal whatnot, doodad, tchotchke.
2 *the dress had no ornament at all* **decoration,** adornment, embellishment, ornamentation, trimming, accessories.
▶ verb *the room was highly ornamented* **decorate,** adorn, embellish, trim, bedeck, deck (out), festoon; literary bedizen.

ornamental ▶ adjective *the ornamental trim above the doors gives the room a dramatic lift* **decorative,** fancy, ornate, ornamented.

ornate ▶ adjective **1** *an ornate mirror* **elaborate,** decorated, embellished, adorned, ornamented, fancy, fussy, ostentatious, showy; informal flash, flashy.
ANTONYMS unadorned.
2 *ornate language* **elaborate,** flowery, florid; grandiose, pompous, pretentious, high-flown, orotund, magniloquent, grandiloquent, rhetorical, oratorical, bombastic, overwrought, overblown; informal highfalutin, purple.
ANTONYMS plain, simple.

orotund ▶ adjective **1** *an orotund singing voice* **deep,** sonorous, strong, powerful, full, rich, resonant, loud, booming.
2 *the orotund rhetoric of his prose* **pompous,** pretentious, affected, fulsome, grandiose, ornate, overblown, flowery, florid, high-flown, magniloquent, grandiloquent, rhetorical, oratorical; informal highfalutin, purple.

orthodox ▶ adjective **1** *orthodox views* **conventional,** mainstream, conformist, (well) established, traditional, traditionalist, prevalent, popular, conservative, unoriginal.
ANTONYMS unconventional.
2 *an orthodox Hindu* **conservative,** traditional, observant, devout, strict.

orthodoxy ▶ noun **1** *a pillar of orthodoxy* **conventionality,** conventionalism, conformism, conservatism, traditionalism, conformity.
2 *Christian orthodoxies* **doctrine,** belief, conviction, creed, dogma, credo, theory, tenet, teaching.

oscillate ▶ verb **1** *the pendulum started to oscillate* **swing,** swing back and forth, swing to and fro, sway; informal wigwag.
2 *oscillating between fear and bravery* **waver,** swing, fluctuate, alternate, seesaw, yo-yo, sway, vacillate, waffle, hover; informal wobble.

oscillation ▶ noun **1** *the oscillation of the pendulum* **swinging,** swinging to and fro, swing, swaying.
2 *his oscillation between commerce and art*

wavering, swinging, fluctuation, seesawing, yo-yoing, vacillation.

ossify ▶ verb **1** *the cartilage may ossify* **turn into bone,** become bony, calcify, harden, solidify, rigidify, petrify.
2 *the old political institutions have ossified* **become inflexible,** become rigid, fossilize, calcify, rigidify, stagnate.

ostensible ▶ adjective *the ostensible star is Lana Turner, but it's Juanita Moore who makes the movie click* **apparent,** outward, superficial, professed, supposed, alleged, purported.
ANTONYMS genuine.

> CHOOSE THE RIGHT WORD
> **ostensible, apparent, illusory, seeming**
> The **apparent** reason for something is not necessarily the real reason. In this sense the word applies to what appears only on the surface, not to what is borne out by scientific investigation or an examination of the relevant facts and circumstances (*the apparent cause was only an illusion*). The **ostensible** reason for something is the reason that is expressed, declared, or avowed; but it implies that the truth is being concealed (*the ostensible purpose of the meeting was to give the two men a chance to get acquainted*). **Seeming** usually refers to the character of the thing observed rather than to a defect in the observation; it implies even more doubt than either *apparent* or *ostensible* (*her seeming innocence fooled no one*). That which is **illusory** is always deceptive; it has a character or appearance that doesn't really exist (*an illusory beauty that faded quickly in the bright light*).

ostensibly ▶ adverb *it is ostensibly a book about football* **apparently,** seemingly, on the face of it, to all intents and purposes, outwardly, superficially, allegedly, supposedly, purportedly.

ostentation ▶ noun *most car buyers are looking for a lot more than ostentation* **showiness,** show, pretentiousness, vulgarity, conspicuousness, display, flamboyance, gaudiness, brashness, extravagance, ornateness, exhibitionism; informal flashiness, glitz, glitziness, ritziness.

ostentatious ▶ adjective *an ostentatious display of wealth* **showy,** pretentious, conspicuous, flamboyant, gaudy, brash, vulgar, loud, extravagant, fancy, ornate, overelaborate; informal flash, flashy, splashy, over the top, glitzy, ritzy, superfly.
ANTONYMS restrained.

ostracize ▶ verb *they were ostracized by their fellow workers* **exclude,** shun, spurn, cold-shoulder, reject, shut out, avoid, ignore, snub, cut dead, keep at arm's length, leave out in the cold; blackball, blacklist; informal freeze out.
ANTONYMS welcome.

other ▶ adjective **1** *these homes use other fuels* **alternative,** different, dissimilar, disparate, distinct, separate, contrasting.
2 *are there any other questions?* **more,** further, additional, extra, added, supplementary.

otherwise ▶ adverb **1** *hurry up, otherwise we'll be late* **or,** or else, if not.
2 *she's exhausted, but otherwise she's fine* **in other respects,** apart from that.
3 *he could not have acted otherwise* **in any other way,** differently.

ounce ▶ noun *it took every ounce of courage for her to board the plane* **particle,** scrap, bit, speck, iota, whit, jot, trace, atom, shred, crumb, fragment, grain, drop, soupçon, spot; informal smidgen.

oust ▶ verb *armed forces ousted the new coalition government* **drive out,** expel, force out, throw out, remove (from office/power), eject, get rid of, depose, dethrone, topple, unseat, overthrow, bring down, overturn, dismiss, dislodge, displace; informal boot out, kick out. See note at EJECT.

out ▶ adjective & adverb **1** *she's out at the moment* **not here,** not at home, not in, (gone) away, elsewhere, absent.
ANTONYMS in.
2 *the secret was out* **revealed,** (out) in the open, common knowledge, public knowledge, known, disclosed, divulged.
ANTONYMS unknown.
3 *the roses are out* **in flower,** flowering, in (full) bloom, blooming, in blossom, blossoming, open.
4 *the book should be out soon* **available,** for sale, obtainable, in stores, published, in print.
5 *the fire was nearly out* **extinguished,** no longer alight.
6 informal *grunge is out* **unfashionable,** out of fashion, dated, outdated, passé; informal old hat, old school, not with it.
ANTONYMS fashionable.
7 *smoking and drinking are out* **forbidden,** not permitted, not allowed, proscribed, taboo, unacceptable.
ANTONYMS permitted, OK.
▶ verb informal *it was not our intention to out him* **expose,** unmask.
– PHRASES **out cold** *one swift punch from Max, and Parnell was out cold* **unconscious,** knocked out, down/out for the count; informal KO'd, kayoed.

out-and-out ▶ adjective *he's an out-and-out chauvinist* **utter,** downright, thoroughgoing, absolute, complete, thorough, total, unmitigated, outright, full-bore, real, perfect, consummate.
ANTONYMS partial.

outbreak ▶ noun **1** *the latest outbreak of hostility* **eruption,** flare-up, upsurge, groundswell, outburst, rash, wave, spate, flood, explosion, burst, flurry.
2 *on the outbreak of war* **start,** beginning, commencement, onset, outset.

outburst ▶ noun *a wild outburst of applause* **eruption,** explosion, burst, outbreak, flare-up, access, rush, flood, storm, outpouring, surge, upsurge, outflowing.

outcast ▶ noun *his corrupt practices as an attorney had made him an outcast in the community* **pariah,** persona non grata, reject, black sheep, outsider, leper.

outclass ▶ verb *even in her freshman year, Taurasi outclassed most everyone on the team* **surpass,** be superior to, be better than, outshine, overshadow, eclipse, outdo, outplay, outmaneuver, outstrip, get the better of, upstage; top, cap, beat, defeat, exceed; informal be a cut above, be head and shoulders above, run rings around.

outcome ▶ noun *the future of the industry could hinge on the outcome of next month's election* **result,** end result, consequence, net result, upshot, aftereffect, aftermath, conclusion, issue, end, end product.

outcry ▶ noun 1 *an outcry of passion* **shout,** exclamation, cry, yell, howl, roar, scream; informal holler.
2 *public outcry* **protest(s),** protestation(s), complaints, objections, furor, fuss, commotion, uproar, outbursts, opposition, dissent; informal hullabaloo, ballyhoo, ructions, stink.

outdated ▶ adjective *an outdated filing system* **old-fashioned,** out of date, outmoded, out of fashion, unfashionable, dated, passé, old, behind the times, behindhand, obsolete, antiquated; informal out, old hat, square, not with it, horse-and-buggy, clunky.
ANTONYMS modern.

outdistance ▶ verb 1 *the hare outdistanced the fox* **outrun,** outstrip, outpace, leave behind, get (further) ahead of; overtake, pass.
2 *the mill outdistanced all its rivals* **surpass,** outshine, outclass, outdo, exceed, transcend, top, cap, beat, better, leave behind; informal leave standing.

outdo ▶ verb *every year, Hank and Oscar try to outdo each other in the triathlon* **surpass,** outshine, overshadow, eclipse, outclass, outmaneuver, get the better of, put in the shade, upstage; exceed, transcend, top, cap, beat, better, leave behind, get ahead of; informal be a cut above, be head and shoulders above, run rings around.

outdoor ▶ adjective *outdoor activities* **open-air,** outdoors, outside, alfresco, field.
ANTONYMS indoor.

outer ▶ adjective 1 *the outer layer* **outside,** outermost, outward, exterior, external, surface.
2 *outer areas of the city* **outlying,** distant, remote, faraway, furthest, peripheral; suburban.
ANTONYMS inner.

outfit ▶ noun 1 *a new outfit* **costume,** suit, uniform, ensemble, attire, clothes, clothing, dress, garb; informal getup, gear, togs, threads; formal apparel; archaic habit, raiment.
2 *a studio lighting outfit* **kit,** equipment, tools, implements, tackle, apparatus, paraphernalia, things, stuff.
3 *a local manufacturing outfit* **organization,** setup, enterprise, company, firm, business; group, band, body, team.
▶ verb *enough swords to outfit an army* **equip,** kit out, fit out/up, rig out, supply, arm; dress, attire, clothe, deck out; archaic apparel, invest, habit.

outfitter ▶ noun 1 *our outfitters planned the canoe route* **supplier,** grubstaker; guide.
2 *the studio has dozens of outfitters at its disposal* **clothier,** tailor, couturier, costumer, dressmaker, seamstress; dated modiste.

outflow ▶ noun *the outflow of waste materials is monitored continuously* **discharge,** outflowing, outpouring, rush, flood, deluge, issue, spurt, jet, cascade, stream, torrent, gush, outburst; flow, flux; technical efflux.

outgoing ▶ adjective 1 *outgoing children* **extrovert,** uninhibited, unreserved, demonstrative, affectionate, warm, friendly, genial, cordial, affable, easygoing, sociable, convivial, lively, gregarious; communicative, responsive, open, forthcoming, frank.
ANTONYMS introverted.
2 *the outgoing president* **departing,** retiring, leaving.
ANTONYMS incoming.

outing ▶ noun 1 *family outings* **(pleasure) trip,** excursion, jaunt, expedition, day out, (mystery) tour, drive, ride, run; informal junket, spin.
2 informal *the outing of public figures* **exposure,** unmasking, revelation.

outlandish ▶ adjective *he gives the most outlandish excuses* **weird,** queer, far out, quirky, zany, eccentric, idiosyncratic, unconventional, unorthodox, funny, bizarre, unusual, singular, extraordinary, strange, unfamiliar, peculiar, odd, curious; informal offbeat, off the wall, way-out, wacky, freaky, kooky, kinky, oddball, in left field.
ANTONYMS ordinary.

outlaw ▶ noun *bands of outlaws* **fugitive,** (wanted) criminal, public enemy, outcast, exile, pariah; bandit, robber; dated desperado.
▶ verb 1 *they voted to outlaw the grizzly hunt* **ban,** bar, prohibit, forbid, veto, make illegal, proscribe, interdict.
ANTONYMS permit.
2 *she feared she would be outlawed* **banish,** exile, expel.

outlay ▶ noun *the initial outlay of funds was within their means* **expenditure,** expenses, spending, cost, price, payment, investment.
ANTONYMS profit.

outlet ▶ noun 1 *a power outlet* **socket,** receptacle, power bar, power source.
2 *the outlet of the drain* **vent,** way out, egress; outfall, opening, channel, conduit, duct.
3 *an outlet for farm produce* **store,** market, marketplace, shop, source.
4 *an outlet for their creative energies* **means of expression,** (means of) release, vent, avenue, channel.

outline ▶ noun 1 *the outline of the building* **silhouette,** profile, shape, contours, form, line, delineation; diagram, sketch; literary lineaments.
2 *an outline of expenditure for each department* **rough idea,** thumbnail sketch, (quick) rundown, summary, synopsis, résumé, précis; essence, main/key points, gist, (bare) bones, draft, sketch.
▶ verb 1 *the plane was outlined against the sky* **silhouette,** define, demarcate; sketch, delineate, trace.
2 *she outlined the plan briefly* **rough out,** sketch out, draft, give a rough idea of, summarize, précis.

outlook ▶ noun 1 *the two men were wholly*

different in outlook **point of view,** viewpoint, views, opinion, (way of) thinking, perspective, attitude, standpoint, stance, frame of mind.
2 *the outlook for the economy* **prospects,** expectations, hopes, future, lookout.
3 *a lovely open outlook* **view,** vista, prospect, panorama, scene, aspect.

outlying ▶ adjective *people in the outlying areas had little interest in the politics of the city* **distant,** remote, outer, out of the way, faraway, extrasolar, far-flung, inaccessible, off the beaten track/path.

outmoded ▶ adjective *the fax machine we got three years ago is already outmoded* **out of date,** old-fashioned, out of fashion, outdated, dated, behind the times, antiquated, obsolete, passé, unstylish, untrendy, uncool; informal old hat, old school.

out of date ▶ adjective **1** *this design is out of date* **old-fashioned,** outmoded, out of fashion, unfashionable, frumpish, frumpy, outdated, dated, old, passé, behind the times, behindhand, obsolete, antiquated; informal out, old hat, square, not with it, horse-and-buggy, clunky.
ANTONYMS fashionable, modern.
2 *many of the facts are out of date* **superseded,** obsolete, expired, lapsed, invalid, (null and) void.
ANTONYMS current.

out-of-the-way ▶ adjective *an out-of-the-way campsite* **outlying,** distant, remote, faraway, far-flung, isolated, lonely, godforsaken, inaccessible, off the beaten track/path.
ANTONYMS accessible.

out of work ▶ adjective *I'm an actor, currently out of work* **unemployed,** jobless, out of a job; redundant, laid off, on welfare, on the dole; euphemistic between jobs.

outpouring ▶ noun *the defendant received an outpouring of public support* **outflow,** outflowing, rush, flood, deluge, discharge, issue, spurt, jet, cascade, stream, torrent, gush, outburst, niagara, flow, flux; technical efflux.

output ▶ noun *our output always increases at the end of summer* **production,** amount/quantity produced, yield, gross domestic product, works, writings.

outrage ▶ noun **1** *widespread public outrage* **indignation,** fury, anger, rage, disapproval, wrath, resentment.
2 *it is an outrage* **scandal,** offense, insult, injustice, disgrace.
3 *the bomb outrage* **atrocity,** act of violence/wickedness, crime, wrong, barbarism, inhumane act.
▶ verb *his remarks outraged his parishioners* **enrage,** infuriate, incense, anger, scandalize, offend, give offense to, affront, shock, horrify, disgust, appall.

outrageous ▶ adjective **1** *outrageous acts of cruelty* **shocking,** disgraceful, scandalous, atrocious, appalling, monstrous, heinous; evil, wicked, abominable, terrible, horrendous, dreadful, foul, nauseating, sickening, vile, nasty, odious, loathsome, unspeakable; beastly.
2 *the politician's outrageous promises* **far-fetched,** (highly) unlikely, doubtful, dubious, questionable, implausible, unconvincing, unbelievable, incredible, preposterous, extravagant, excessive.
3 *outrageous clothes* **eye-catching,** flamboyant, showy, gaudy, ostentatious; shameless, brazen, shocking; informal saucy, flashy.

outright ▶ adverb **1** *he rejected the proposal outright* **completely,** entirely, wholly, fully, totally, categorically, absolutely, utterly, flatly, unreservedly, in every respect.
2 *I told her outright* **explicitly,** directly, forthrightly, openly, frankly, candidly, honestly, sincerely, bluntly, plainly, in plain language, truthfully, to someone's face, straight from the shoulder, straight up, in no uncertain terms.
3 *they were killed outright* **instantly,** instantaneously, immediately, at once, straightaway, then and there, on the spot.
4 *paintings have to be bought outright* **all at once,** in one go.
▶ adjective **1** *an outright lie* **out-and-out,** absolute, complete, downright, utter, sheer, categorical, unqualified, unmitigated, unconditional.
2 *the outright winner* **definite,** unequivocal, clear, unqualified, incontestable, unmistakable.

outset ▶ noun *at the outset, we had nothing but problems* **start,** starting point, beginning, commencement, dawn, birth, origin, inception, opening, launch, inauguration; informal the word go.
ANTONYMS end.

outshine ▶ verb *watching Nadia outshine the other gymnasts was a thrill for viewers around the world* **surpass,** overshadow, eclipse, outclass, put in the shade, upstage, exceed, transcend, top, cap, beat, better; informal be a cut above, be head and shoulders above, run rings around.

outside ▶ noun *the outside of the building* **outer/external surface,** exterior, outer side/layer, case, skin, shell, covering, facade.
▶ adjective **1** *outside lights* **exterior,** external, outer, outdoor, out-of-doors.
2 *outside contractors* **independent,** hired, temporary, freelance, casual, external, extramural.
3 *an outside chance* **slight,** slender, slim, small, tiny, faint, negligible, remote, vague.
▶ adverb *they went outside | shall we eat outside?* **outdoors,** out of doors, alfresco.
ANTONYMS inside.

outsider ▶ noun *after six years, I still feel like an outsider in this town* **stranger,** visitor, nonmember; foreigner, alien, immigrant, emigrant, émigré; newcomer, parvenu.

outskirts ▶ plural noun *they live in the outskirts of Youngstown* **outlying districts,** edges, fringes, suburbs, suburbia, bedroom community, commutershed; purlieus, borders, environs.

outsmart ▶ verb *buyers and sellers attempt to outsmart each other* **outwit,** outmaneuver, outplay, steal a march on, trick, get the better of; informal outfox, pull a fast one on, put one over on.

outspoken ▶ adjective *an outspoken critic of the administration* **forthright,** direct, candid, frank, straightforward, honest, open, plain-spoken; blunt, abrupt, bluff, brusque.

outstanding ▶ adjective **1** *an outstanding painter* **excellent,** marvelous, magnificent, superb, fine, wonderful, superlative, exceptional, first-class, first-rate; informal great, terrific, tremendous, super, amazing, fantastic, sensational, fabulous, ace, neat, killer, crack, A1, mean, awesome, bang-up, skookum, out of this world; smashing, brilliant.
ANTONYMS mediocre.
2 *the outstanding decorative element in this presentation* **remarkable,** extraordinary, exceptional, striking, eye-catching, arresting, impressive, distinctive, unforgettable, memorable, special, momentous, significant, notable, noteworthy; informal out of this world. See note at **NOTICEABLE.**
ANTONYMS unexceptional.
3 *how much work is still outstanding?* **to be done,** undone, unattended to, unfinished, incomplete, remaining, pending, ongoing.
ANTONYMS finished.
4 *outstanding debts* **unpaid,** unsettled, owing, past due, owed, to be paid, payable, due, overdue, undischarged, delinquent.
ANTONYMS paid.

outward ▶ adjective *his outward demeanor hides the pain he feels inside* **external,** outer, outside, exterior; surface, superficial, seeming, apparent, ostensible.
ANTONYMS inward.

outwardly ▶ adverb *outwardly, these two products are just about identical* **externally,** on the surface, superficially, on the face of it, to all intents and purposes, apparently, ostensibly, seemingly.

outweigh ▶ verb *the costs outweigh the benefits* **be greater than,** exceed, be superior to, prevail over, have the edge on/over, override, supersede, offset, cancel out, (more than) make up for, outbalance, compensate for.

outwit ▶ verb *the murderers always thought they could outwit Columbo, but of course they couldn't* **outsmart,** outmaneuver, outplay, steal a march on, trick, gull, get the better of, euchre; informal outfox, pull a fast one on, put one over on.

oval ▶ adjective *an oval mirror* **egg-shaped,** ovoid, ovate, oviform, elliptical.

ovation ▶ noun *what performer doesn't appreciate an ovation from the crowd?* **round of applause,** applause, hand-clapping, clapping, cheering, cheers, bravos, acclaim, acclamation, tribute, standing ovation; informal (big) hand.

oven ▶ noun *the roast is in the oven* **(kitchen) stove,** microwave (**oven**), (kitchen) range; roaster; kiln.

over ▶ preposition **1** *there will be clouds over most of the state* **above,** on top of, higher (up) than, atop, covering.
ANTONYMS under.
2 *he walked over the grass* **across,** around, throughout.
3 *over 200,000 people live in the area* **more than,** above, in excess of, upwards of.
4 *lengthy discussions over what to do next* **on the subject of,** about, concerning, apropos of, with reference to, regarding, relating to, in connection with, vis-à-vis.
▶ adverb **1** *a flock of geese flew over* **overhead,** on high, above, past, by.
2 *the relationship is over* **at an end,** finished, concluded, terminated, ended, no more, a thing of the past; informal kaput.
3 *he had some money left over* **remaining,** unused, surplus, in excess, in addition.
– PHRASES **over and above** *we will not pay any costs over and above the original quote* **in addition to,** on top of, plus, as well as, besides, along with. **over and over** *he tells the same jokes over and over* **repeatedly,** again and again, over and over again, time and (time) again, many times over, frequently, constantly, continually, persistently, ad nauseam.

overact ▶ verb *during dramatic scenes, she has a tendency to overact* **exaggerate,** overdo it, overplay it; informal ham it up, camp it up.

overall ▶ adjective *the overall cost* **all-inclusive,** general, comprehensive, universal, all-embracing, gross, net, final, inclusive, total; wholesale, complete, across the board, global, worldwide.
▶ adverb *overall, things have improved* **generally (speaking),** broadly, in general, altogether, all in all, on balance, on average, for the most part, in the main, on the whole, by and large, to a large extent.

overawe ▶ verb *Jane was overawed by her landlady* **intimidate,** daunt, cow, disconcert, unnerve, subdue, dismay, frighten, alarm, scare, terrify; informal psych out.

overbearing ▶ adjective *his overbearing wife* **domineering,** dominating, autocratic, tyrannical, despotic, oppressive, high-handed, bullying; informal bossy.

overblown ▶ adjective *an overblown piece of writing* **overwritten,** florid, grandiose, pompous, overelaborate, flowery, overwrought, pretentious, high-flown, turgid, grandiloquent, magniloquent, orotund; informal highfalutin.

overcast ▶ adjective *she feared it was bad luck to be married on an overcast day* **cloudy,** clouded (over), sunless, darkened, dark, gray, black, leaden, heavy, dull, murky, dismal, dreary.
ANTONYMS bright.

overcharge ▶ verb **1** *clients are being overcharged* **swindle,** charge too much, cheat, defraud, fleece, short-change; informal rip off, sting, screw, rob, diddle, have, rook, gouge.
2 *the decoration is overcharged* **overstate,** overdo, exaggerate, overembroider, overembellish; overwrite, overdraw.

overcome ▶ verb **1** *we overcame the home team* **defeat,** beat, conquer, trounce, thrash, rout, vanquish, overwhelm, overpower, get the better of, triumph over, prevail over, win over/against, outdo, outclass, worst, crush; informal drub, slaughter, clobber, hammer, lick, best, crucify, demolish, wipe the floor with, make mincemeat of, blow out of the water, take to the cleaners, shellac, skunk.
2 *they overcame their fear of flying* **get the better of,** prevail over, control, get/bring under control, master, conquer, defeat, beat; get over, get a grip on, curb, subdue; informal lick, best.
▶ adjective *I was overcome* **overwhelmed,** emotional, moved, affected, speechless.

overconfident ▶ adjective *her downfall came through being overconfident* **cocksure,** cocky, smug, conceited, self-assured, brash, blustering, overbearing, presumptuous, heading for a fall, riding for a fall; informal too big for one's britches/boots.

overcritical ▶ adjective *overcritical parents* **fault-finding,** hypercritical, captious, carping, caviling, quibbling, hair-splitting, overparticular; fussy, finicky, fastidious, pedantic, overscrupulous, punctilious; informal nitpicking, persnickety.

overcrowded ▶ adjective *an overcrowded bus* **overfull,** overflowing, full to overflowing/bursting, crammed full, congested, overpopulated, overpeopled, crowded, swarming, teeming; informal bursting/bulging at the seams, full to the gunwales, jam-packed.
ANTONYMS empty.

overdo ▶ verb **1** *she overdoes the love scenes* **exaggerate,** overstate, overemphasize, overplay, go overboard with, overdramatize; informal ham up, camp up.
ANTONYMS understate.
2 *don't overdo the desserts* **overindulge in,** have/use/eat/drink too much of, have/use/eat/drink to excess.
3 *they overdid the beef* **overcook,** burn.
– PHRASES **overdo it** *on your first day of an exercise program, you mustn't overdo it* **work too hard,** overwork, do too much, burn the candle at both ends, overtax oneself, drive/push oneself too hard, work/run oneself into the ground, wear oneself out, bite off more than one can chew, strain oneself; informal kill oneself, knock oneself out.

overdone ▶ adjective **1** *the flattery was overdone* **excessive,** too much, undue, immoderate, inordinate, disproportionate, inflated, overstated, overworked, exaggerated, overemphasized, overenthusiastic, overeffusive; informal a bit much, over the top.
ANTONYMS understated.
2 *overdone food* **overcooked,** dried out, burnt.
ANTONYMS underdone.

overdue ▶ adjective **1** *the ship is overdue* **late,** behind schedule, behind time, delayed, unpunctual.
ANTONYMS early, punctual.
2 *overdue payments* **unpaid,** unsettled, owing, owed, payable, due, outstanding, undischarged, delinquent.

overeat ▶ verb *it's hard not to overeat at one of their buffets* **eat too much,** be greedy, gorge (oneself), overindulge (oneself), feast, gourmandize, gluttonize; informal binge, make a pig of oneself, pig out, have eyes bigger than one's stomach.
ANTONYMS starve.

overemphasize ▶ verb *the importance of regularly testing your smoke alarms cannot be overemphasized* **place/lay too much emphasis on,** overstress, place/lay too much stress on, exaggerate, make too much of, overplay, overdo, overdramatize; informal make a big thing about/of, blow up out of all proportion.
ANTONYMS understate, play down.

overflow ▶ verb *cream had overflowed the edges of the shallow dish* **spill over,** flow over, brim over, well over, pour forth, stream forth, flood.
▶ noun **1** *an overflow from the tank* **overspill,** spill, spillage, flood.
2 *to accommodate the overflow, five more offices were built* **surplus,** excess, additional people/things, extra people/things, remainder, overspill.

overhang ▶ verb *above the garage door overhangs a massive cluster of icicles* **stick out (over),** stand out (over), extend (over), project (over), protrude (over), jut out (over), bulge out (over), hang over.

overhaul ▶ verb *I've been overhauling the engine* **service,** maintain, repair, mend, fix up, rebuild, renovate, recondition, refit, refurbish; informal do up, patch up.

overhead ▶ adverb *a burst of thunder erupted overhead* **(up) above,** high up, (up) in the sky, on high, above/over one's head.
ANTONYMS below.
▶ adjective *overhead lines* **aerial,** elevated, raised, suspended.
ANTONYMS underground.
▶ noun *subtract your overhead from the gross income* **(running) costs,** operating costs, fixed costs, expenses.

overindulge ▶ verb **1** *we overindulged at Christmas* **drink/eat too much,** overeat, overdrink, be greedy, be intemperate, overdo it, drink/eat to excess, gorge (oneself), feast, gourmandize, gluttonize; informal binge, stuff oneself, go overboard, make a pig of oneself, pig out.
ANTONYMS abstain.
2 *his mother had overindulged him* **spoil,** give in to, indulge, humor, pander to, pamper, mollycoddle, baby.

overjoyed ▶ adjective *we're just overjoyed to be grandparents* **ecstatic,** euphoric, thrilled, elated, delighted, on cloud nine, in seventh heaven, jubilant, rapturous, jumping for joy, delirious, blissful, in raptures, as pleased as punch; informal over the moon, on top of the world, tickled pink, as happy as a clam.
ANTONYMS unhappy.

overlay ▶ verb *the area was overlaid with marble* **cover,** face, surface, veneer, inlay, laminate, plaster; coat, varnish, glaze.
▶ noun *an overlay of fiberglass* **covering,** cover, layer, face, surface, veneer, lamination; coat, varnish, glaze, wash.

overload ▶ verb **1** *avoid overloading the ship* **overburden,** put too much in, overcharge, weigh down.
2 *don't overload the wiring* **strain,** overtax, overwork, overuse, swamp, oversupply, overwhelm.
▶ noun *there was an overload of demands* **excess,** overabundance, superabundance, profusion, glut, surfeit, surplus, superfluity; avalanche, deluge, flood.

overlook ▶ verb **1** *he overlooked the mistake* **fail to notice,** fail to spot, miss.
2 *his work has been overlooked* **disregard,** neglect, ignore, pay no attention/heed to, pass over, forget. See note at NEGLECT.
3 *she was almost willing to overlook his faults*

ignore, not take into consideration, disregard, take no notice of, make allowances for, turn a blind eye to, excuse, pardon, forgive.
4 *the breakfast room overlooks the garden* **have a view of,** look over/across, look on to, look out on/over, give on to, command a view of.

overly ▶ adverb *the guitars here are not overly expensive* **unduly,** excessively, inordinately, too; wildly, absurdly, ridiculously, outrageously, unreasonably, exorbitantly, impossibly.

overpower ▶ verb **1** *the prisoners might overpower the crew* **gain control over,** overwhelm, prevail over, get the better of, outdo, gain mastery over, overthrow, overturn, subdue, suppress, subjugate, repress, bring someone to their knees, conquer, defeat, triumph over, worst, trounce; informal thrash, lick, best, clobber, wipe the floor with.
2 *he was overpowered by grief* **overcome,** overwhelm, move, stir, affect, touch, stun, shake, devastate, take aback, leave speechless; informal bowl over.

overpowering ▶ adjective **1** *overpowering disappointment* **overwhelming,** oppressive, unbearable, unendurable, intolerable, shattering.
2 *an overpowering smell* **stifling,** suffocating, strong, pungent, powerful; nauseating, offensive, acrid, fetid, mephitic.
3 *overpowering evidence* **irrefutable,** undeniable, indisputable, incontestable, incontrovertible, compelling, conclusive.

overrate ▶ verb *I think his music is overrated* **overestimate,** overvalue, think too much of, attach too much importance to, praise too highly.
ANTONYMS underestimate.

overreach ▶ verb
– PHRASES **overreach oneself** *he waited for his opponents to overreach themselves* **try to do too much,** overestimate one's ability, overdo it, overstretch oneself, wear/burn oneself out, bite off more than one can chew.

overreact ▶ verb *before you overreact, let's just calmly discuss this* **react disproportionately,** act irrationally, lose one's sense of proportion, blow something up out of all proportion, make a mountain out of a molehill.

override ▶ verb **1** *the court could not override her decision* **disallow,** overrule, countermand, veto, quash, overturn, overthrow; cancel, reverse, rescind, revoke, repeal, annul, nullify, invalidate, negate, void; Law vacate; formal abrogate.
2 *the government can override all opposition* **disregard,** pay no heed to, take no account of, turn a deaf ear to, ignore, ride roughshod over.
3 *a positive attitude will override any negative thoughts* **outweigh,** supersede, take priority over, take precedence over, offset, cancel out, (more than) make up for, outbalance, compensate for.

overriding ▶ adjective *safety was the overriding consideration* **deciding,** decisive, most important, of greatest importance, of greatest significance, uppermost, top, first (and foremost), highest, preeminent, predominant, principal, primary, paramount, chief, main, major, foremost, central, key, focal, pivotal; informal number-one.

overrule ▶ verb *this ban was overruled by a federal court* **countermand,** cancel, reverse, rescind, repeal, revoke, retract, disallow, override, veto, quash, overturn, overthrow, annul, nullify, invalidate, negate, void; Law vacate; formal abrogate; archaic recall.

overrun ▶ verb **1** *guerrillas overran the barracks* **invade,** storm, occupy, swarm into, surge into, inundate, overwhelm.
2 *the talks overran the deadline* **exceed,** go beyond/over, run over.

overseer ▶ noun *they finally brought in an overseer that knew how to deal with the workers* **supervisor,** foreman, forewoman, team leader, controller, (line) manager, manageress, head (of department), superintendent, captain; informal boss, chief, straw boss.

overshadow ▶ verb **1** *a massive hill overshadows the town* **cast a shadow over,** shade, darken, conceal, obscure, screen; dominate, overlook.
2 *this feeling of tragedy overshadowed his story* **cast gloom over,** blight, take the edge off, mar, spoil, ruin.
3 *he was overshadowed by his brilliant elder brother* **outshine,** eclipse, surpass, exceed, be superior to, outclass, outstrip, outdo, upstage; informal be head and shoulders above.

oversight ▶ noun **1** *a stupid oversight* **mistake,** error, omission, lapse, slip, blunder; informal slip-up, boo-boo, goof, flub.
2 *the omission was due to oversight* **carelessness,** inattention, negligence, forgetfulness, laxity.

overt ▶ adjective *an overt attempt to sidestep the truth* **undisguised,** unconcealed, plain (to see), clear, apparent, conspicuous, obvious, noticeable, manifest, patent, open, blatant.
ANTONYMS covert.

overtake ▶ verb **1** *a green car overtook the taxi* **pass,** go past/by, get/pull ahead of, leave behind, outdistance, outstrip.
2 *tourism overtook lumber as the main revenue source* **outstrip,** surpass, overshadow, eclipse, outshine, outclass; dwarf, put in the shade, exceed, top, cap.
3 *the calamity that overtook us* **befall,** happen to, come upon, hit, strike, overwhelm, overcome, be visited on; literary betide.

overthrow ▶ verb **1** *the president was overthrown* **remove (from office/power),** bring down, topple, depose, oust, displace, unseat, dethrone.
2 *an attempt to overthrow military rule* **put an end to,** defeat, conquer.
▶ noun **1** *the overthrow of the general* **removal (from office/power),** downfall, fall, toppling, deposition, ousting, displacement, supplanting, unseating.
2 *the overthrow of capitalism* **ending,** defeat, displacement, fall, collapse, downfall, demise.

overtone ▶ noun *there were overtones of flirtatious mischief in her letter* **connotation,** hidden meaning, implication, association, undercurrent, undertone, echo, vibrations, hint, suggestion, insinuation, intimation, suspicion, feeling, nuance.

overture ▶ noun 1 *the overture to "Don Giovanni"* **prelude,** introduction, opening, introductory movement.
2 *the overture to a long debate* **preliminary,** prelude, introduction, lead-in, precursor, start, beginning.
3 *peace overtures* (**opening**) **move,** approach, advances, feeler, signal, proposal, proposition.

overturn ▶ verb 1 *the boat overturned* **capsize,** turn turtle, keel over, tip over, topple over, turn over, flip; Nautical pitchpole.
2 *I overturned the stool* **upset,** tip over, topple over, turn over, knock over, upend.
3 *the Supreme Court may overturn this ruling* **cancel,** reverse, rescind, repeal, revoke, retract, countermand, disallow, override, overrule, veto, quash, overthrow, annul, nullify, invalidate, negate, void; Law vacate; formal abrogate; archaic recall.

overweening ▶ adjective *that overweening attitude of his makes my skin crawl* **overconfident,** conceited, cocksure, cocky, smug, haughty, supercilious, lofty, patronizing, arrogant, proud, vain, self-important, imperious, overbearing; informal high and mighty, uppish.
ANTONYMS unassuming.

overweight ▶ adjective *the growing number of overweight children is a legitimate health crisis* **fat,** obese, stout, full-figured, corpulent, gross, fleshy, plump, portly, chubby, rotund, paunchy, potbellied, flabby, well-upholstered, broad in the beam; informal porky, tubby, blubbery, pudgy.
ANTONYMS skinny.

overwhelm ▶ verb 1 *advancing sand dunes could overwhelm the village* **swamp,** submerge, engulf, bury, deluge, flood, inundate.
2 *Canada overwhelmed the U.S. in the hockey final* **defeat** (**utterly/heavily**), trounce, rout, beat (hollow), conquer, vanquish, be victorious over, triumph over, worst, overcome, overthrow, crush; informal thrash, steamroller, lick, best, massacre, clobber, wipe the floor with.
3 *she was overwhelmed by a sense of tragedy* **overcome,** move, stir, affect, touch, strike, dumbfound, shake, devastate, floor, leave speechless; informal bowl over, snow under.

overwhelming ▶ adjective 1 *an overwhelming number of players were unavailable* **very large,** enormous, immense, inordinate, massive, huge.
2 *the overwhelming desire to laugh* **very strong,** forceful, uncontrollable, irrepressible, irresistible, overpowering, compelling.

overwork ▶ verb 1 *we should not overwork* **work too hard,** work/run oneself into the ground, wear oneself to a shadow, work one's fingers to the bone, burn the candle at both ends, overtax oneself, burn oneself out, do too much, overdo it, strain oneself, overload oneself, drive/push oneself too hard; informal kill oneself, knock oneself out.
2 *my colleagues did not overwork me* **drive** (**too hard**), exploit, drive into the ground, tax, overtax, overburden, put upon, impose on.

overworked ▶ adjective 1 *overworked staff* **stressed** (**out**), stress-ridden, overtaxed, overburdened, overloaded, exhausted, worn out, burned out.
ANTONYMS relaxed.
2 *an overworked phrase* **hackneyed,** overused, worn out, tired, played out, cliché́d, threadbare, stale, trite, banal, stock, unoriginal.
ANTONYMS original.

overwrought ▶ adjective 1 *she was too overwrought to listen* **tense,** agitated, nervous, on edge, edgy, keyed up, worked up, high-strung, neurotic, overexcited, beside oneself, distracted, distraught, frantic, hysterical; informal in a state, in a tizzy, uptight, wound up, het up, strung out.
ANTONYMS calm.
2 *the painting is overwrought* **overelaborate,** overornate, overblown, overdone, contrived, overworked, strained.
ANTONYMS understated.

owe ▶ verb *I don't want to owe anyone* **be in debt to,** be indebted to, be in arrears to, be under an obligation to.

owing ▶ adjective *the rent was owing* **unpaid,** to be paid, payable, due, past due, overdue, undischarged, owed, outstanding, in arrears, delinquent.
ANTONYMS paid.
– PHRASES **owing to** *owing to the severity of the weather, tonight's concert will be postponed until next Tuesday* **because of,** as a result of, on account of, due to, as a consequence of, thanks to, in view of, by dint of; formal by reason of.

own ▶ adjective *he has his own reasons* **personal,** individual, particular, private, personalized, unique.
▶ verb 1 *I own this house* **be the owner of,** possess, be the possessor of, have in one's possession, have (to one's name).
2 *she had to own that she agreed* **admit,** concede, grant, accept, acknowledge, agree, confess.
– PHRASES **hold one's own** *developing countries must start to hold their own in world markets* **stand firm,** stand one's ground, keep one's end up, keep one's head above water, compete, survive, cope, get on/along. **on one's own 1** *I live on my own* (**all**) **alone,** (all) by oneself, solitary, unaccompanied, companionless; informal by one's lonesome. **2** *she works well on her own* **unaided,** unassisted, without help, without assistance, (all) by oneself, independently. **own up to** *in the long run, it's always better to own up to your mistakes* **confess,** admit to, admit the guilt of, accept blame/responsibility for, tell the truth about, make a clean breast of; informal come clean about.

owner ▶ noun *the owner is no longer interested in selling* **possessor,** holder, proprietor/proprietress, homeowner, landowner, freeholder, landlord, landlady.

ownership ▶ noun *there is no question of ownership* **possession,** right of possession, freehold, proprietorship, proprietary rights, title.

ox ▶ noun *a team of oxen* **bull,** bullock, steer; Farming beef.

Pp

pace ▶ **noun 1** *he stepped back a pace* **step,** stride.
2 *a slow, steady pace* **gait,** stride, walk, march.
3 *he drove home at a furious pace* **speed,** rate, velocity; informal clip, lick.
▶ **verb** *she paced up and down* **walk,** stride, tread, march, pound, patrol.

pacific ▶ **adjective 1** *a pacific community* **peace-loving,** peaceable, pacifist, nonviolent, nonaggressive, nonbelligerent, unwarlike.
ANTONYMS aggressive, belligerent.
2 *their pacific intentions* **conciliatory,** peacemaking, placatory, propitiatory, appeasing, mollifying, mediatory, dovish; formal irenic.
ANTONYMS warmongering.
3 *pacific waters* **calm,** still, smooth, tranquil, placid, waveless, unruffled, like a millpond.
ANTONYMS stormy.

pacifist ▶ **noun** *you know, even pacifists can support their nation's armed forces* **peace-lover,** conscientious objector, passive resister, peacemaker, peace-monger, dove.
ANTONYMS warmonger.

pacify ▶ **verb** *go out there and try to pacify the passengers* **placate,** appease, calm (down), conciliate, propitiate, assuage, mollify, soothe.
ANTONYMS enrage.

CHOOSE THE RIGHT WORD

pacify, appease, conciliate, mollify, placate, propitiate

You might try to **pacify** a crying baby, to **appease** a demanding boss, to **mollify** a friend whose feelings have been hurt, and to **placate** an angry crowd. While all of these verbs have something to do with quieting people who are upset, excited, or disturbed, each involves taking a slightly different approach. *Pacify* suggests soothing or calming (*the mother made soft cooing noises in an attempt to pacify her child*). *Appease* implies that you've given in to someone's demands or made concessions in order to please (*she said she would visit his mother just to appease him*), while *mollify* stresses minimizing anger or hurt feelings by taking positive action (*her flattery failed to mollify him*). *Placate* suggests changing a hostile or angry attitude to a friendly or favorable one, usually with a more complete or long-lasting effect than *appease* (*they were able to placate their enemies by offering to support them*). You can **propitiate** a superior or someone who has the power to injure you by allaying or forestalling their anger (*they were able to propitiate the trustees by holding a dinner party in their honor*). **Conciliate** implies the use of arbitration or compromise to settle a dispute or to win someone over (*the company made every effort to conciliate its angry competitor*).

pack ▶ **noun 1** *a pack of cigarettes* **packet,** container, package, box, carton, parcel.
2 *with a pack on his back* **backpack,** knapsack, rucksack, day pack, kit bag, bag.
3 *a pack of youngsters* **crowd,** mob, group, band, troupe, troop, party, set, clique, gang, rabble, horde, herd, throng, huddle, mass, assembly, gathering, host; informal crew, bunch.
▶ **verb 1** *she helped pack the picnic basket* **fill (up),** put things in, load.
2 *they packed their belongings* **stow,** put away, store, box up.
3 *the glasses were packed in straw* **wrap (up),** package, parcel, swathe, swaddle, encase, enfold, envelop, bundle.
4 *Christmas shoppers packed the store* **throng,** crowd (into), fill (to overflowing), cram, jam, squash into, squeeze into.
5 *pack the cloth against the wall* **compress,** press, squash, squeeze, jam, tamp.
– PHRASES **pack off** informal *we packed our youngest son off to college just last week* **send off,** dispatch, bundle off. **pack up 1** *pack up your toys now* **put away,** tidy up/away, clear up/away. **2** informal *it's time to pack up* **stop,** call it a day, finish, cease; informal knock off, quit, pack it in.

package ▶ **noun 1** *the delivery of a package* **parcel,** packet, container, box.
2 *a complete package of services* **collection,** bundle, combination.
▶ **verb** *goods packaged in recyclable materials* **wrap (up),** gift-wrap; pack (up), parcel (up), box, encase.

packaging ▶ **noun** *the outer packaging is crucial to consumer appeal* **wrapping,** wrappers, packing, covering.

packed ▶ **adjective** *the actors peeked from behind the curtain to see a packed house* **crowded,** full, filled (to capacity), crammed, jammed, solid, overcrowded, overfull, teeming, seething, swarming; informal jam-packed, chock-full, standing room only, chockablock, full to the gunwales, bursting/bulging at the seams.

packet ▶ **noun** *a small packet of jelly beans* **pack,** carton, (cardboard) box, container, case, package.

pact ▶ noun *the pact was signed at the site of the surrender* **agreement,** treaty, entente, protocol, deal, settlement, concordat, accord; armistice, truce; formal concord.

pad[1] ▶ noun **1** *a pad over the eye* piece of cotton, dressing, pack, padding, wadding, wad.
2 *a seat pad* **cushion,** pillow.
3 *making notes on a pad* **notebook,** notepad, writing pad, memo pad, sketch pad, steno pad, sketchbook, scratch pad.
▶ verb *a quilted jacket padded with goose down* **stuff,** fill, pack, wad.
– PHRASES **pad out** *don't pad out your answer to make it seem impressive* **expand unnecessarily,** fill out, amplify, increase, flesh out, lengthen, spin out, overdo, elaborate.

pad[2] ▶ verb *he padded along toward the bedroom* **walk quietly,** tread warily, creep, tiptoe, steal, pussyfoot.

padding ▶ noun **1** *padding around the ankle* **wadding,** cushioning, stuffing, packing, filling, lining.
2 *a concise style with no padding* **verbiage,** verbosity, wordiness, prolixity, filler.

paddle[1] ▶ noun *use the paddles to row ashore* **oar,** scull, blade.
▶ verb *we paddled around the bay* **row gently,** pull, scull, canoe, kayak.

paddle[2] ▶ verb *children were paddling in the water* **splash about,** wade; dabble.

paddock ▶ noun *the horses got out of the paddock* **field,** meadow, pasture; pen, pound, corral.

padlock ▶ verb *padlock the shed* **lock (up),** fasten, secure.

padre ▶ noun *many of the soldiers requested time with the padre before shipping out* **chaplain,** priest, minister, pastor, father, parson, clergyman, cleric, ecclesiastic, man of the cloth, churchman, vicar, rector, curate, preacher; informal reverend, Holy Joe, sky pilot.

paean ▶ noun *a great paean of triumph* **song of praise,** hymn, alleluia; plaudit, glorification, eulogy, tribute, panegyric, accolade, acclamation; formal encomium.

pagan ▶ noun *pagans worshiped the sun* **heathen,** infidel, idolater, idolatress; archaic paynim.
▶ adjective *the pagan festival* **heathen,** ungodly, irreligious, infidel, idolatrous.

page[1] ▶ noun **1** *a book of 672 pages* **folio,** sheet, side, leaf.
2 *a glorious page in her life* **period,** time, stage, phase, epoch, era, chapter; episode, event.

page[2] ▶ noun *she worked as a page at the state legislature* **messenger,** errand boy/girl.
▶ verb *could you please page Mr. Johnson?* **call (for),** summon, send for, buzz.

pageant ▶ noun *people dress up their dogs in wild costumes for the annual pageant* **parade,** procession, cavalcade, tableau (vivant); spectacle, extravaganza, show.

pageantry ▶ noun *the pageantry of a royal wedding* **spectacle,** display, ceremony, magnificence, pomp, splendor, grandeur, show; informal razzle-dazzle, razzmatazz.

pain ▶ noun **1** *she endured great pain* **suffering,** agony, torture, torment, discomfort.
2 *a pain in the stomach* **ache,** aching, soreness, throb, throbbing, sting, stinging, twinge, shooting pain, stab, pang, cramps; discomfort, irritation, tenderness.
3 *the pain of losing a loved one* **sorrow,** grief, heartache, heartbreak, sadness, unhappiness, distress, desolation, misery, wretchedness, despair; agony, torment, torture, via dolorosa.
4 informal *that child is a pain* See NUISANCE.
5 (pains) *he took great pains to hide his feelings* **care,** effort, bother, trouble.
▶ verb **1** *her foot is still **paining her*** **hurt,** cause pain, be painful, be sore, be tender, ache, throb, sting, twinge, cause discomfort; informal kill one.
2 *the memory pains her* **sadden,** grieve, distress, trouble, perturb, oppress, cause anguish to.

pained ▶ adjective *it troubles us to see you so pained* **upset,** hurt, wounded, injured, insulted, offended, aggrieved, displeased, disgruntled, annoyed, angered, angry, cross, indignant, irritated, resentful; informal riled, miffed, aggravated, peeved, teed off, ticked off, sore.

painful ▶ adjective **1** *a painful arm* **sore,** hurting, tender, aching, throbbing, angry.
2 *a painful experience* **disagreeable,** unpleasant, nasty, bitter, distressing, upsetting, traumatic, miserable, sad, heartbreaking, agonizing, harrowing.

painkiller ▶ noun *these painkillers will make you drowsy* **analgesic,** pain reliever, anodyne, anesthetic, narcotic; palliative.

painless ▶ adjective **1** *any killing of animals should be painless* **without pain,** pain-free.
ANTONYMS painful.
2 *getting rid of him proved to be painless* **easy,** trouble-free, effortless, simple, plain sailing; informal as easy as pie, a piece of cake, child's play, a cinch.
ANTONYMS difficult.

painstaking ▶ adjective *painting these window frames is painstaking work* **careful,** meticulous, thorough, assiduous, sedulous, attentive, diligent, industrious, conscientious, punctilious, scrupulous, rigorous, particular; pedantic, fussy.
ANTONYMS slapdash.

paint ▶ noun *a gallon of white paint* **coloring,** colorant, tint, dye, stain, pigment, color.
▶ verb **1** *paint the ceiling* **color,** apply paint to, decorate, whitewash, emulsion, gloss, spray-paint, airbrush.
2 *painting slogans on a wall* **daub,** smear, spray-paint, airbrush.
3 *Rembrandt painted his mother* **portray,** picture, paint a picture of, depict, represent.
4 *you paint a very stark picture of the suffering* **tell,** recount, outline, sketch, describe, depict, evoke, conjure up.
– PHRASES **paint the town red** informal *we're taking the train into Albany, and we're gonna paint the town red* **celebrate,** carouse, enjoy oneself, have a good/wild time, have a party; informal go out on the town, whoop it up, make whoopee, live it up, party, have a ball.

painting ▶ noun *his paintings are so charming in their simplicity* **picture,** illustration, portrayal, depiction, representation, image, artwork; oil (painting), watercolor, canvas.

pair ▸ **noun 1** *a pair of gloves* **set (of two),** matching set, two of a kind.
2 *the pair were arrested* **two,** couple, duo, brace, twosome, duplet; twins.
3 *a pair of lines* **couplet**; Prosody distich.
4 *the happy pair* **couple,** man/husband and wife.
▸ **verb** *a cardigan paired with a matching skirt* **match,** put together, couple, twin.
– PHRASES **pair off/up** *Rachel paired up with Tommy* **get together,** team up, form a couple, make a twosome, hook up, marry.

pal ▸ **noun** informal *my best pal* See FRIEND (sense 1).

palace ▸ **noun** *tourists are not allowed in the east wing of the palace* **royal/official residence,** castle, chateau, mansion, stately home, schloss.

palatable ▸ **adjective 1** *palatable meals* **edible,** eatable, digestible, tasty, appetizing, flavorful; formal comestible.
ANTONYMS tasteless, insipid.
2 *the truth is not always palatable* **pleasant,** acceptable, pleasing, agreeable, to one's liking.
ANTONYMS disagreeable, unpleasant.

palate ▸ **noun 1** *the tea burned her palate* **roof of the mouth,** hard/soft palate.
2 *menus to suit the tourist palate* **(sense of) taste,** appetite, stomach.
3 *wine with a peachy palate* **flavor,** savor, taste.

palatial ▸ **adjective** *a palatial estate on Long Island* **luxurious,** deluxe, magnificent, sumptuous, splendid, grand, opulent, lavish, stately, regal; fancy, upscale, upmarket; informal plush, swanky, posh, ritzy, swish.
ANTONYMS modest.

palaver ▸ **noun** informal *holy cow, what a palaver we caused in the girls' dormitory!* **fuss,** commotion, trouble, rigmarole, folderol; informal song and dance, performance, to-do, carrying-on, hoo-ha, hullabaloo, ballyhoo.

pale¹ ▸ **noun 1** *the pales of a fence* **stake,** post, pole, picket, upright.
2 *outside the pale of decency* **boundary,** confines, bounds, limits.
– PHRASES **beyond the pale** *his behavior was beyond the pale* **unacceptable,** unseemly, improper, unsuitable, unreasonable, unforgivable, intolerable, disgraceful, deplorable, outrageous, scandalous, shocking; informal not on, out of line; formal exceptionable.

pale² ▸ **adjective 1** *she looked pale and drawn* **white,** pallid, pasty, wan, colorless, anemic, bloodless, washed out, peaked, ashen, gray, whitish, white-faced, whey-faced, drained, sickly, sallow, as white as a sheet, deathly pale; milky, creamy, cream, ivory, milk-white, alabaster; informal like death warmed over.
ANTONYMS rosy, flushed.
2 *pale colors* **light,** light-colored, pastel, muted, subtle, soft; faded, bleached, washed out.
3 *the pale light of morning* **dim,** faint, weak, feeble.
ANTONYMS dark, bright.
4 *a pale imitation* **feeble,** weak, insipid, bland, poor, inadequate; uninspired, unimaginative, lackluster, spiritless, lifeless; informal pathetic.
▸ **verb 1** *his face paled* **go/turn white,** grow/turn pale, blanch, lose color.
2 *everything else pales by comparison* **decrease in importance,** lose significance, pale into insignificance, fade into the background.

> CHOOSE THE RIGHT WORD
>
> **pale, ashen, livid, pallid, wan**
>
> Someone of fair complexion who usually stays indoors and spends little time in the sun is apt to be **pale**, referring to an unusually white or colorless complexion; one can also become *pale* out of fear or illness. Someone who has lost color from being ill or under stress may be described as **pallid**, which suggests a paleness that is the result of some abnormal condition (*she appeared pallid when she left the police station*). **Wan** also connotes an unhealthy condition or sickly paleness (*her wan face smiled at him from the hospital bed*). Someone who is **ashen** has skin the pale grayish color of ashes (*ashen with fear*), while **livid** can mean either bluish to describe loss of normal coloring (*the livid face of a drowned corpse*) or reddish or flushed (*livid with rage*).

pall¹ ▸ **noun 1** *a rich velvet pall* **funeral cloth,** coffin covering.
2 *a pall of black smoke* **cloud,** covering, cloak, veil, shroud, layer, blanket.
– PHRASES **cast a pall over** *the bad news from home cast a pall over our honeymoon* **spoil,** cast a shadow over, overshadow, cloud, put a damper on.

pall² ▸ **verb** *the high life was beginning to pall* **become/grow tedious,** become/grow boring, lose its/their interest, lose attraction, wear off; weary, sicken, nauseate; irritate, irk.

palliate ▸ **verb 1** *the treatment works by palliating symptoms* **alleviate,** ease, relieve, soothe, take the edge off, assuage, moderate, temper, diminish, decrease, blunt, deaden.
2 *there is no way to palliate his dirty deed* **disguise,** hide, gloss over, conceal, cover (up), camouflage, mask; excuse, justify, extenuate, mitigate.

pallid ▸ **adjective 1** *a pallid child* **pale,** white, pasty, wan, colorless, anemic, washed out, peaked, whey-faced, ashen, gray, whitish, drained, sickly, sallow; informal like death warmed over. See note at PALE².
2 *pallid watercolors* **insipid,** uninspired, colorless, uninteresting, unexciting, unimaginative, lifeless, spiritless, sterile, bland.

pallor ▸ **noun** *her dark hair accentuated her pallor* **paleness,** pallidness, lack of color, wanness, ashen hue, pastiness, grayness, sickliness, sallowness.

palm ▸ **noun & verb**
– PHRASES **grease someone's palm** informal *my Uncle would grease the commissioner's palm on Tuesday, and on Wednesday his speakeasy would be serving up booze by the barrel* **bribe,** buy (off), corrupt, suborn, give an inducement to; informal give a sweetener to. **have someone in the palm of one's hand** *can't you see that Dorrey has you in the palm of her hand?*

have control over, have influence over, have someone eating out of one's hand, have someone on a string, have someone in one's hip pocket, have someone wrapped around one's finger. **palm off** *you're not going to palm off that rusty old truck on me* **foist,** fob off, get rid of, dispose of, unload.

palpable ▶ adjective **1** *a palpable bump* **tangible,** touchable, noticeable, detectable. See note at TANGIBLE.
ANTONYMS imperceptible.
2 *his reluctance was palpable* **perceptible,** perceivable, visible, noticeable, discernible, detectable, observable, tangible, unmistakable, transparent, self-evident; obvious, clear, plain (to see), evident, apparent, manifest, staring one in the face, written all over someone.
ANTONYMS imperceptible.

> USAGE
> **palpable**
> *Palpable* (literally, "touchable") = tangible; apparent. There is nothing wrong with using this word in figurative senses (*palpable weaknesses in the argument*), as it has been used since at least the fifteenth century. What is nonsensical, however, is to say that the *level* of frustration, tension, etc., is *palpable*—e.g.: "When they share a scene, the energy level is palpable [read *the energy is palpable*]." (*Daily News* [New York]; Sept. 24, 2002.) — **BG**

palpitate ▶ verb **1** *her heart began to palpitate* **beat rapidly,** pound, throb, pulsate, pulse, thud, thump, hammer, race.
2 *palpitating with terror* **tremble,** quiver, quake, shake (like a leaf).

paltry ▶ adjective **1** *a paltry sum of money* **small,** meager, trifling, insignificant, negligible, inadequate, insufficient, derisory, pitiful, pathetic, miserable, niggardly, beggarly; informal measly, piddling; formal exiguous.
ANTONYMS considerable.
2 *naval glory struck him as paltry* **worthless,** petty, trivial, unimportant, insignificant, inconsequential, of little account.
ANTONYMS important.

pamper ▶ verb *Trevor's big sister pampered him* **spoil,** indulge, overindulge, cosset, mollycoddle, coddle, baby, wait on someone hand and foot.

pamphlet ▶ noun *there's some interesting information in this pamphlet* **brochure,** leaflet, booklet, circular, flyer, fact sheet, handbill, mailer, folder.

pan[1] ▶ noun **1** *a heavy pan* **saucepan,** skillet, frying pan, pot, wok.
2 *salt pans* **hollow,** pit, depression, dip, crater, concavity.
▶ verb **1** informal *the movie was panned by the critics* See CRITICIZE.
2 *prospectors panned for gold* **sift,** search, look.
– PHRASES **pan out 1** *Bob's idea hadn't panned out* **succeed,** be successful, work (out), turn out well, come to fruition. **2** *the deal panned out badly* **turn out,** work out, end (up), come out, fall out, evolve; formal eventuate.

pan[2] ▶ verb *the camera panned to the building* **swing (around),** sweep, move, turn, circle.

panacea ▶ noun *a panacea for the country's economic problems* **universal cure,** cure-all, cure for all ills, universal remedy, elixir, wonder drug; informal magic bullet.

panache ▶ noun *the chorus line lacks panache* **flamboyance,** confidence, self-assurance, style, flair, élan, dash, verve, zest, spirit, brio, éclat, vivacity, gusto, liveliness, vitality, energy; informal pizzazz, oomph, zip, zing.

pancake ▶ noun *a short stack of pancakes with maple syrup* hotcake, flapjack, griddle cake, crepe, blintz; latke, potato pancake.

pandemic ▶ adjective *the disease is pandemic in Africa* **widespread,** prevalent, pervasive, rife, rampant. See note at EPIDEMIC.

pandemonium ▶ noun *we heard a bang and then there was complete pandemonium* **bedlam,** chaos, mayhem, uproar, turmoil, tumult, commotion, confusion, anarchy, furor, hubbub, rumpus; informal hullabaloo, hoopla.
ANTONYMS peace.

pander ▶ verb
– PHRASES **pander to** *David was always there to pander to her every whim* **indulge,** gratify, satisfy, cater to, give in to, accommodate, comply with.

panegyric ▶ noun *the panegyric she delivered in Syd's memory brought tears to our eyes* **eulogy,** speech of praise, paean, accolade, tribute.

pang ▶ noun **1** *hunger pangs* **pain,** sharp pain, shooting pain, twinge, stab, spasm.
2 *a pang of remorse* **qualm,** twinge, prick.

panic ▶ noun *a wave of panic* **alarm,** anxiety, nervousness, fear, fright, trepidation, dread, terror, agitation, hysteria, consternation, perturbation, dismay, apprehension; informal flap, fluster, cold sweat, funk, tizzy, swivet.
ANTONYMS calm.
▶ verb **1** *there's no need to panic* **be alarmed,** be scared, be nervous, be afraid, take fright, be agitated, be hysterical, lose one's nerve, get overwrought, get worked up; informal flap, get in a flap, lose one's cool, get into a tizzy, freak out, get in a stew, have kittens.
2 *talk of love panicked her* **frighten,** alarm, scare, unnerve; informal throw into a tizzy, freak out.

panoply ▶ noun **1** *the full panoply of U.S. military might* **array,** range, collection.
2 *all the panoply of religious liturgy* **trappings,** regalia; splendor, spectacle, ceremony, ritual.

panorama ▶ noun **1** *he surveyed the panorama* **view,** wide view, scenic view, vista, prospect, scene, scenery, landscape, seascape.
2 *a panorama of the art scene* **overview,** survey, review, presentation, appraisal.

panoramic ▶ adjective **1** *a panoramic view* **sweeping,** wide, extensive, scenic, commanding.
2 *a panoramic look at the twentieth century* **wide-ranging,** extensive, broad, far-reaching, comprehensive, all-embracing.

pant ▶ verb **1** *he was panting as they reached the top* **breathe heavily,** breathe hard, puff, huff and puff, gasp, wheeze.
2 *it makes you* ***pant for*** *more* **yearn for,** long for, crave, hanker after/for, ache for, hunger for, thirst for, be hungry for, be thirsty for, wish for, desire, want; informal itch for, be dying for.

pants ▶ plural noun *a cashmere sweater with khaki pants* **trousers,** slacks, britches; (blue) jeans, bell-bottoms.

pap ▶ noun **1** *a plateful of tasteless pap* **soft food,** mush, slop, pulp, purée, mash; trademark Pablum; informal goo, goop, glop, gook.
2 *commercial pap* **trivia,** pulp (fiction), garbage, rubbish, nonsense; informal dreck, drivel, trash, twaddle, pablum.

paper ▶ noun **1** *a sheet of paper* writing paper, notepaper, vellum.
2 *the local paper* **newspaper,** journal, gazette, periodical; tabloid, broadsheet, daily, weekly, evening paper; informal rag, tab.
3 *the paper was peeling off the walls* **wallpaper,** wallcovering.
4 *a three-hour paper* **exam,** examination, test, quiz.
5 *she has just published a paper* **essay,** article, monograph, thesis, work, dissertation, treatise, study, report, analysis, tract, critique, exegesis, review, term paper, theme.
6 (**papers**) *personal papers* **documents,** certificates, letters, files, deeds, records, archives, paperwork, documentation; Law muniments.
7 (**papers**) *they asked us for our papers* **identification papers/documents,** identity card, ID, credentials.
▶ verb *we papered the walls* **wallpaper,** hang wallpaper on.
– PHRASES **on paper 1** *he put his thoughts on paper* **in writing,** in black and white, in print. **2** *the combatants were evenly matched on paper* **in theory,** theoretically, supposedly.

papery ▶ adjective *papery leaves* **thin,** paper-thin, flimsy, delicate, insubstantial, light, lightweight.

par ▶ noun
– PHRASES **below par 1** *their performances have been below par* **substandard,** inferior, not up to scratch, subpar, under par, below average, second-rate, mediocre, poor, undistinguished; informal not up to snuff, bush-league. **2** *I'm feeling below par* **slightly unwell,** not (very) well, not oneself, out of sorts; ill, unwell, poorly, washed out, run-down, peaked, off; informal under the weather, not up to snuff, lousy, rough. **on a par with** *his voice is on a par with Tony Bennett* **as good as,** comparable with, in the same class/league as, equivalent to, equal to, on a level with, of the same standard as. **par for the course** *long hours are par for the course in catering* **normal,** typical, standard, usual, what one would expect. **up to par** *students whose grades are up to par* **good enough,** up to the mark, satisfactory, acceptable, adequate, up to scratch; informal up to snuff.

parable ▶ noun *the parable of the prodigal son* **allegory,** moral story/tale, fable, exemplum.

parade ▶ noun **1** *a Memorial Day parade* **procession,** march, cavalcade, motorcade, spectacle, display, pageant; review, dress parade, tattoo; march past.
2 *she made a great parade of doing the housework* **exhibition,** show, display, performance, spectacle, fuss; informal hoo-ha, to-do.
▶ verb **1** *the teams paraded through the city* **march,** process, file, troop.
2 *she paraded up and down* **strut,** swagger, stride.
3 *he was keen to parade his knowledge* **display,** exhibit, make a show of, flaunt, show (off), demonstrate.

paradigm ▶ noun *why should your sets of values be the paradigm for the rest of us?* **model,** pattern, example, exemplar, template, standard, prototype, archetype. See note at MODEL.

paradise ▶ noun **1** *the souls in paradise* **heaven,** the kingdom of heaven, the heavenly kingdom, Elysium, the Elysian Fields, Valhalla, Avalon.
ANTONYMS hell.
2 *Adam and Eve's expulsion from Paradise* **the Garden of Eden,** Eden.
3 *a tropical paradise* **Utopia,** Shangri-La, heaven, idyll, nirvana.
4 *this is sheer paradise!* **bliss,** heaven, ecstasy, delight, joy, happiness, nirvana, heaven on earth.
ANTONYMS hell.

paradox ▶ noun *the paradox of war is that you have to kill people in order to stop people from killing each other* **contradiction,** contradiction in terms, self-contradiction, inconsistency, incongruity; oxymoron; conflict, anomaly; enigma, puzzle, mystery, conundrum. See note at RIDDLE.

paradoxical ▶ adjective *I admit it seems paradoxical for a pacifist such as myself to be in favor of this military action* **contradictory,** self-contradictory, inconsistent, incongruous, anomalous; illogical, puzzling, baffling, incomprehensible, inexplicable.

paragon ▶ noun *a paragon of cheerfulness* | *your cook is a paragon* **perfect example,** shining example, model, epitome, archetype, ideal, exemplar, nonpareil, embodiment, personification, quintessence, apotheosis, acme; jewel, gem, angel, treasure; informal one in a million, the tops; archaic a nonesuch.

paragraph ▶ noun **1** *the concluding paragraph* **section,** subdivision, part, subsection, division, portion, segment, passage.
2 *a paragraph in the newspaper* **report,** article, item, sidebar, piece, write-up, mention.

parallel ▶ adjective **1** *parallel lines* **side by side,** aligned, collateral, equidistant.
2 *parallel careers* **similar,** analogous, comparable, corresponding, like, of a kind, akin, related, equivalent, matching, homologous.
3 *a parallel universe* **coexisting,** coexistent, concurrent; contemporaneous, simultaneous, synchronous.
ANTONYMS divergent.
▶ noun **1** *an exact parallel* **counterpart,** analog, equivalent, likeness, match, twin, duplicate, mirror.
2 *there is an interesting parallel between these*

figures **similarity,** likeness, resemblance, analogy, correspondence, equivalence, correlation, relation, symmetry, parity.
▸ verb 1 *his experiences parallel mine* **resemble,** be similar to, be like, bear a resemblance to; correspond to, be analogous to, be comparable/equivalent to, equate with/to, correlate with, imitate, echo, remind one of, duplicate, mirror, follow, match.
2 *her performance has never been paralleled* **equal,** match, rival, emulate.

paralysis ▸ noun 1 *the disease can cause paralysis* **immobility,** powerlessness, incapacity, debilitation; Medicine paraplegia, quadriplegia, tetraplegia, monoplegia, hemiplegia, diplegia, paresis, paraparesis.
2 *complete paralysis of the ports* **shutdown,** immobilization, stoppage.

paralytic ▸ adjective *her hands became paralytic* **paralyzed,** crippled, disabled, incapacitated, powerless, immobilized, useless.

paralyze ▸ verb 1 *both of his legs were paralyzed* **disable,** cripple, immobilize, incapacitate, debilitate; formal torpefy.
2 *Sally was paralyzed by the sight of him* **immobilize,** transfix, become rooted to the spot, freeze, stun, render motionless.
3 *the capital was paralyzed by a general strike* **bring to a standstill,** immobilize, bring to a (grinding) halt, freeze, cripple, disable.

parameter ▸ noun *the parameters of the debate* **framework,** variable, limit, boundary, limitation, restriction, criterion, guideline.

paramount ▸ adjective *the safety of the staff is paramount* **most important,** of greatest/prime importance; uppermost, supreme, chief, overriding, predominant, foremost, prime, primary, principal, highest, main, key, central, leading, major, top; informal number-one.

paramour ▸ noun archaic *he was in love with his father's paramour* **lover,** significant other, inamorata; mistress, girlfriend, kept woman, other woman; boyfriend, main squeeze, other man, inamorato; informal toy boy, sugar daddy; archaic concubine, courtesan.

paranoid ▸ adjective *all the layoffs in my department have made me paranoid* **oversuspicious,** paranoiac, suspicious, mistrustful, fearful, insecure.

parapet ▸ noun 1 *Marian leaned over the parapet* **balustrade,** barrier, wall.
2 *the sandbags making up the parapet* **barricade,** rampart, bulwark, bank, embankment, fortification, defense, earthwork, breastwork, bastion.

paraphernalia ▸ plural noun *they have a ton of camping paraphernalia* **equipment,** stuff, things, apparatus, kit, implements, tools, utensils, material(s), appliances, accoutrements, appurtenances, odds and ends, bits and pieces; informal gear.

paraphrase ▸ verb *paraphrasing literary texts* **reword,** rephrase, put/express in other words, rewrite, gloss.
▸ noun *this paraphrase of Frye's words* **rewording,** rephrasing, rewriting, rewrite, rendition, rendering, gloss.

parasite ▸ noun *she longed to be free of the parasites in her family* **hanger-on,** cadger, leech, passenger; informal bloodsucker, sponger, bottom feeder, scrounger, freeloader, mooch.

parcel ▸ noun 1 *a parcel of clothes* **package,** packet; pack, bundle, box, case, bale.
2 *a parcel of land* **plot,** piece, patch, tract, allotment, lot, plat.
▸ verb 1 *she parceled up the papers* **pack (up),** package, wrap (up), gift-wrap, tie up, bundle up.
2 ***parceling out** commercial farmland* **divide up,** portion out, distribute, share out, allocate, allot, apportion, hand out, dole out, dish out; informal divvy up.

parched ▸ adjective 1 *the parched earth* **(bone) dry,** dried up/out, arid, desiccated, dehydrated, baked, burned, scorched; withered, shriveled. See note at DRY.
2 informal *I'm parched* **thirsty,** longing for a drink, dry, dehydrated.

pardon ▸ noun 1 *pardon for your sins* **forgiveness,** absolution, clemency, mercy, leniency, remission.
2 *he offered them a full pardon* **reprieve,** free pardon, amnesty, exoneration, release, acquittal, discharge; formal exculpation.
▸ verb 1 *I know she will pardon me* **forgive,** absolve, have mercy on; excuse, condone, overlook.
ANTONYMS blame.
2 *they were subsequently pardoned* **exonerate,** acquit, amnesty; reprieve, release, free; informal let off; formal exculpate. See note at ABSOLVE.
ANTONYMS punish.
▸ exclamation *Pardon?* **what did you say,** what, what's that, pardon me, I beg your pardon, sorry, excuse me; informal come again, say what.

pardonable ▸ adjective *a pardonable offense* **excusable,** forgivable, condonable, understandable, minor, venial, slight.
ANTONYMS inexcusable.

parent ▸ noun *you'll need the signed consent of a parent* **mother, father,** birth/biological parent, progenitor; adoptive parent, foster-parent, step-parent, guardian; literary begetter.
▸ verb *those who parent young children* **raise,** bring up, look after, take care of, rear.

parentage ▸ noun *Deedham was bound by tradition to marry only a woman of the finest parentage* **origins,** extraction, birth, family, ancestry, lineage, heritage, pedigree, descent, blood, stock, roots.

pariah ▸ noun *they were treated as social pariahs* **outcast,** persona non grata, black sheep, leper, undesirable, unperson, nonperson.

parish ▸ noun 1 *the municipal council of the parish of Oka* **district,** community.
2 *the story scandalized the parish* **parishioners,** churchgoers, congregation, fold, flock, community.

parity ▸ noun *we strive for a parity of wages* **equality,** equivalence, uniformity, consistency, correspondence, congruity, levelness, unity, coequality.

park ▸ noun 1 *we were playing in the park* **playground,** play area, public garden, garden(s), green.

2 *a new national park* **parkland,** wilderness area, protected area, nature reserve, game reserve.

▶ **verb 1** *she parked her car* **leave,** position; stop, pull up, pull over.

2 informal *park your bag by the door* **put (down),** place, deposit, leave, stick, shove, dump; informal plonk.

– PHRASES **park oneself** informal *park yourself there and we'll be with you in a moment* **sit down,** seat oneself, settle (oneself), install oneself; informal plunk oneself.

parlance ▶ **noun** *for the character of Lyndsay-Ann, she uses her most annoying Valley Girl parlance* **jargon,** language, phraseology, talk, speech, argot, patois, cant; informal lingo, -ese, -speak.

parliament ▶ **noun** *the Russian parliament* **legislature,** legislative assembly, congress, senate, (upper/lower) house, (upper/lower) chamber, diet, assembly.

parliamentary ▶ **adjective** *parliamentary assemblies* **legislative,** lawmaking, governmental, congressional, senatorial, democratic, elected, representative.

parochial ▶ **adjective** *she was constantly challenging their parochial approach to education* **narrow-minded,** small-minded, provincial, narrow, small-town, conservative, illiberal, intolerant; informal jerkwater. See note at **BIAS**.

ANTONYMS broad-minded.

parody ▶ **noun 1** *a parody of the Gothic novel* **satire,** burlesque, lampoon, pastiche, caricature, imitation, mockery; informal spoof, takeoff, send-up. See note at **CARICATURE**.

2 *a parody of the truth* **distortion,** travesty, caricature, misrepresentation, perversion, corruption, debasement.

▶ **verb** *parodying schoolgirl fiction* **satirize,** burlesque, lampoon, caricature, mimic, imitate, ape, copy, make fun of, travesty, take off; informal send up.

paroxysm ▶ **noun** *paroxysms of coughing* **spasm,** attack, fit, burst, bout, convulsion, seizure, outburst, eruption, explosion, access.

parrot ▶ **verb** *they parroted slogans without appreciating their significance* **repeat (mindlessly),** repeat mechanically, echo.

parry ▶ **verb 1** *Alfonso parried the blow* **ward off,** fend off; deflect, hold off, block, counter, repel, repulse.

2 *I parried her constant questions* **evade,** sidestep, avoid, dodge, answer evasively, field, fend off.

parsimonious ▶ **adjective** *Lou's parsimonious mother was horrified by his lavish spending* **cheap,** miserly, mean, niggardly, close-fisted, close, penny-pinching, ungenerous, Scroogelike; informal tightfisted, cheeseparing, tight, stingy, mingy; formal penurious. See note at **ECONOMICAL**.

ANTONYMS generous.

parsimony ▶ **noun** *the parsimony of her grandparents had embittered her against the elderly* **cheapness,** miserliness, meanness, parsimoniousness, niggardliness, close-fistedness, closeness, penny-pinching; informal stinginess, minginess, tightness, tightfistedness, cheeseparing; formal penuriousness.

parson ▶ **noun** *the new parson brings a youthful joy to the pulpit* **vicar,** rector, clergyman, cleric, chaplain, pastor, curate, man of the cloth, ecclesiastic, minister, priest, preacher; informal reverend, padre.

part ▶ **noun 1** *the last part of the cake | a large part of their life* **bit,** slice, chunk, lump, hunk, wedge, fragment, scrap, piece; portion, proportion, percentage, fraction. See note at **FRAGMENT**.

ANTONYMS whole.

2 *car parts* **component,** bit, constituent, element, module.

3 *body parts* **part of the body,** organ, limb, member.

4 *the third part of the book* **section,** division, volume, chapter, act, scene, installment.

5 *another part of the country* **district,** neighborhood, quarter, section, area, region.

6 *the part of Juliet* **(theatrical) role,** character, persona.

7 *she's learning her part* **lines,** words, script, speech; libretto, lyrics, score.

8 *he was jailed for his part in the affair* **involvement,** role, function, hand, work, responsibility, capacity, position, participation, contribution; informal bit.

▶ **verb 1** *the curtains parted* **separate,** divide (in two), split (in two), move apart.

ANTONYMS join.

2 *we parted on bad terms* **leave,** take one's leave, say goodbye/farewell, say one's goodbyes/farewells, go one's (separate) ways, split, go away, depart.

ANTONYMS meet.

▶ **adjective** *a part payment* **incomplete,** partial, half, semi-, limited, inadequate, insufficient, unfinished.

ANTONYMS complete.

▶ **adverb** *it is part finished* **to a certain extent/degree,** to some extent/degree, partly, partially, in part, half, relatively, comparatively, (up) to a point, somewhat; not totally, not entirely, (very) nearly, almost, just about, all but.

ANTONYMS completely.

– PHRASES **for the most part** See **MOSTLY**. **in part** *the water damage is due in part to the clogged gutters* **to a certain extent/degree,** to some extent/degree, partly, partially, slightly, in some measure, (up) to a point. **on the part of** *there is increased interest in these coins on the part of collectors* **(made/done) by,** carried out by, caused by, from. **part with** *Danielle could not part with her stuffed animals* **give up/away,** relinquish, forgo, surrender, hand over, deliver up, dispose of. **take part** *anyone who cares to can take part* **participate,** join in, get involved, enter, play a part/role, be a participant, contribute, have a hand, help, assist, lend a hand; informal get in on the act. **take part in** *all students must take part in the CPR course before the end of junior year* **participate in,** engage in, join in, get involved in, share in, play a part/role in, be a participant in, contribute to, be associated with, have a hand in.

partake ▶ verb **1** *only senior officers are allowed to* ***partake in*** *the negotiations* **participate in,** take part in, engage in, join in, enter into, get involved in, share in, contribute to, play a part in, have a hand in, sit in on.
ANTONYMS be excluded from, sit out.
2 *those averse to sushi can* ***partake of*** *the hot buffet* **consume,** have, eat, drink, take, ingest, devour; informal wolf down, polish off, tuck into.
ANTONYMS forgo, abstain from.
3 *the lyric essay* ***partakes of*** *the poem in its distillation of ideas and musicality of language* **have the qualities/attributes of,** suggest, evoke, be characterized by, hint at, manifest, evince.

partial ▶ adjective **1** *a partial recovery* **incomplete,** limited, qualified, imperfect, fragmentary, unfinished.
ANTONYMS complete, total.
2 *a very partial view of the situation* **biased,** prejudiced, partisan, one-sided, slanted, skewed, colored, unbalanced.
ANTONYMS unbiased.
– PHRASES **be partial to** *I'm partial to hotdogs and beer* **like,** love, enjoy, have a liking for, be fond of, be keen on, have a soft spot for, have a taste for, have a penchant for; informal adore, be mad about/for, have a thing about, be crazy about, be nutty about, cotton to.

partiality ▶ noun **1** *his partiality toward their cause* **bias,** prejudice, favoritism, favor, partisanship. See note at **BIAS**.
2 *her partiality for brandy* **liking,** love, fondness, taste, soft spot, predilection, penchant, passion.

partially ▶ adverb *the plan was only partially successful* **to a limited extent/degree,** to a certain extent/degree, partly, in part, not totally, not entirely, relatively, moderately, (up) to a point, somewhat, comparatively, slightly.

participant ▶ noun *the first 100 participants to sign up will get a free T-shirt* **participator,** contributor, party, member; entrant, competitor, player, contestant, candidate.

participate ▶ verb *at least he's willing to* ***participate in*** *town events* **take part in,** engage in, join in, get involved in, share in, play a part/role in, be a participant in, partake in, have a hand in, be associated with; cooperate in, help (out) with, assist in, lend a hand with/to.

participation ▶ noun *your participation is appreciated* **involvement,** part, contribution, association.

particle ▶ noun **1** *minute particles of rock* **(tiny) bit,** (tiny) piece, speck, spot, fleck; fragment, sliver, splinter.
2 *he never showed a particle of sympathy* **iota,** jot, whit, bit, scrap, shred, crumb, drop, hint, touch, trace, suggestion, whisper, suspicion, scintilla; informal smidgen.

particular ▶ adjective **1** *a particular group of companies* **specific,** certain, distinct, separate, discrete, definite, precise; single, individual.
ANTONYMS general.
2 *an issue of particular importance* **(extra) special,** especial, exceptional, unusual, singular, uncommon, notable, noteworthy, remarkable, unique; formal peculiar.
ANTONYMS ordinary.
3 *he was particular about what he ate* **fussy,** fastidious, finicky, meticulous, punctilious, discriminating, selective, painstaking, exacting, demanding; informal persnickety, choosy, picky.
ANTONYMS careless.
▶ noun *the same in every particular* **detail,** item, point, specific, element, aspect, respect, regard, particularity, fact, feature.
– PHRASES **in particular 1** *nothing in particular* **specific,** special. **2** *the poor, in particular, were hit by rising prices* **particularly,** specifically, especially, specially.

particularize ▶ verb *the indictment particularized several incidents* **specify,** detail, itemize, list, enumerate, spell out, cite, stipulate, instance.

particularly ▶ adverb **1** *the acoustics are particularly good* **especially,** specially, very, extremely, exceptionally, singularly, peculiarly, unusually, extraordinarily, remarkably, outstandingly, amazingly, incredibly, really, seriously.
2 *he particularly asked that I should help you* **specifically,** explicitly, expressly, in particular, especially, specially.

parting ▶ noun **1** *an emotional parting* **farewell,** leave-taking, goodbye, adieu, departure; valediction.
2 *they kept their parting quiet* **separation,** breakup, split, divorce, rift, estrangement; informal splitsville.
3 *the parting of the Red Sea* **division,** dividing, separation, separating, splitting, breaking up/apart, partition, partitioning.
▶ adjective *a parting kiss* **farewell,** goodbye, last, final, valedictory.

partisan ▶ noun **1** *conservative partisans* **supporter,** follower, adherent, devotee, champion; fanatic, fan, enthusiast, stalwart, zealot, booster.
2 *the partisans opened fire from the woods* **guerrilla,** freedom fighter, resistance fighter, underground fighter, irregular (soldier).
▶ adjective *partisan attitudes* **biased,** prejudiced, one-sided, discriminatory, colored, partial, interested, sectarian, factional.
ANTONYMS unbiased.

partition ▶ noun **1** *the 1905 partition of Bengal* **dividing up,** partitioning, separation, division, dividing, subdivision, splitting (up), breaking up, breakup.
2 *room partitions* **screen,** (room) divider, (dividing) wall, barrier, panel.
▶ verb **1** *the resolution partitioned Poland* **divide (up),** subdivide, separate, split (up), break up; share (out), parcel out.
2 *the huge hall was partitioned* **subdivide,** divide (up); separate (off), section off, screen off.

partly ▶ adverb *I admit I am partly responsible* **to a certain extent/degree,** to some extent/degree, in part, partially, a little, somewhat, not totally, not entirely, relatively, moderately, (up) to a point, in some measure, slightly.
ANTONYMS completely.

partner ▶ noun **1** *business partners* **colleague,** associate, coworker, fellow worker,

collaborator, comrade, teammate; archaic compeer.
2 *his partner in crime* **accomplice,** confederate, accessory, collaborator, fellow conspirator, helper; informal sidekick.
3 *your relationship with your partner* **spouse,** husband, wife, consort, life partner; lover, girlfriend, boyfriend, fiancé, fiancée, significant other, live-in lover, common-law husband/wife, man, woman, mate; informal hubby, missus, old man, old lady/woman, better half, intended, other half, main squeeze.

partnership ▶ **noun 1** *close partnership* **cooperation,** association, collaboration, coalition, alliance, union, affiliation, relationship, connection.
2 *thriving partnerships* **company,** firm, business, corporation, organization, association, consortium, syndicate.

parturition ▶ **noun** formal *even today, in many parts of the world, mortality associated with parturition is alarmingly high* **childbirth,** birth, delivery, birthing, labor; archaic confinement, travail.

party ▶ **noun 1** *150 people attended the party* **(social) gathering,** (social) function, get-together, affair, celebration, festivity, reception, at-home; frolic, soirée, carousal, carouse, fete; informal bash, shindig, rave, do, shebang, bop, hop, blast, wingding.
2 *a party of German tourists* **group,** company, body, gang, band, crowd, pack, contingent; informal bunch, crew, load.
3 *the left-wing parties* **faction,** political party, group, grouping, cabal, junta, bloc, camp, caucus.
4 *don't mention a certain party* **person,** individual, somebody, someone.
▶ **verb** informal *let's party!* **celebrate,** have fun, enjoy oneself, have a party, have a good/wild time, go on a spree, rave it up, carouse, make merry; informal go out on the town, paint the town red, whoop it up, let one's hair down, make whoopee, live it up, have a ball.
– PHRASES **be a party to** *he refused to be a party to their vandalism* **get involved in/with,** be associated with, be a participant in.

parvenu ▶ **noun** *make way for our newest little hotshot parvenu* **upstart,** social climber, arriviste.

pass[1] ▶ **verb 1** *the traffic passing through the village* **go,** proceed, move, progress, make one's way, travel.
ANTONYMS stop.
2 *a car passed him* **overtake,** go past/by, pull ahead of, overhaul, leave behind; informal leapfrog.
3 *time passed* **elapse,** go by/past, advance, wear on, roll by, tick by.
4 *he passed the time writing letters* **occupy,** spend, fill, use (up), employ, while away.
5 *pass me the salt* **hand (over),** give, reach.
6 *Max passed the ball back* **kick,** hit, throw, lob.
7 *her estate passed to her grandson* **be transferred,** go, be left, be bequeathed, be handed down/on, be passed on; Law devolve.
8 *his death passed almost unnoticed* **happen,** occur, take place, come about, transpire, come and go; literary befall.
9 *the storm passed* **abate,** fade (away), come to an end, blow over, run its course, die out, finish, end, cease, subside.
10 *nature's complexity passes all human understanding* **surpass,** exceed, transcend.
11 *he passed the exam* **be successful in,** succeed in, gain a pass in, get through; informal sail through, scrape through.
ANTONYMS fail.
12 *the senate passed the bill* **approve,** vote for, accept, ratify, adopt, agree to, authorize, endorse, legalize, enact; informal OK.
ANTONYMS reject.
13 *she could not let that comment pass* **go (unnoticed),** stand, go unremarked, go undisputed.
14 *we should not pass judgment* **declare,** pronounce, utter, express, deliver, issue.
15 *passing urine* **discharge,** excrete, evacuate, expel, emit, release.
▶ **noun 1** *you must show your pass* **permit,** warrant, authorization, license.
2 *a perfectly executed pass* **kick,** hit, throw, cross, lateral (pass).
– PHRASES **come to pass** literary *it came to pass that Dorothy left Roberto* **happen,** come about, occur, transpire, arise; literary befall. **make a pass at** *are you accusing Mr. Allen of making a pass at you?* **make (sexual) advances to,** proposition; informal come on to, make a play for, hit on, make time with, put the make on. **pass away/on** See DIE (sense 1). **pass as/for** *I really think you could pass for an attorney* **be mistaken for,** be taken for, be accepted as. **pass off** *he tried to pass her off as his daughter* **misrepresent,** falsely represent; disguise. **pass out** *this heat could make anyone pass out* **faint,** lose consciousness, black out. **pass over** *many a great movie has been passed over by the Academy* **disregard,** overlook, ignore, pay no attention to, let pass, gloss over, take no notice of, pay no heed to, turn a blind eye to. **pass up** *I should never have passed up my chance to go to Rome* **turn down,** reject, refuse, decline, give up, forgo, let pass, miss (out on); informal give something a miss.

pass[2] ▶ **noun** *a pass through the mountains* **route,** way, road, passage, cut, gap, notch.

passable ▶ **adjective 1** *the beer was passable* **adequate,** all right, fairly good, acceptable, satisfactory, moderately good, not (too) bad, average, tolerable, fair; mediocre, middling, ordinary, indifferent, unremarkable, unexceptional; informal OK, so-so, 'comme ci, comme ça', nothing to write home about.
2 *the road is still passable* **navigable,** traversable, negotiable, unblocked, unobstructed, open, clear.

passage ▶ **noun 1** *their passage through the country* **transit,** progress, passing, movement, motion, traveling.
2 *the passage of time* **passing,** advance, course, march.
3 *a passage from the embassy* **safe conduct,** warrant, visa; admission, access.
4 *the overnight passage* **voyage,** crossing, trip, journey.
5 *clearing a passage to the front door*

way (**through**), route, path.
6 *a passage to the kitchen* **passageway**.
7 *the nasal passages* **duct,** orifice, opening, channel; inlet, outlet.
8 *the passage to democracy* **transition,** development, progress, move, change, shift.
9 *the passage of the bill* **enactment,** passing, ratification, royal assent, approval, adoption, authorization, legalization.
10 *a passage from "Macbeth"* **extract,** excerpt, quotation, quote, citation, reading, piece, selection.

passenger ▶ **noun** *rail passengers* **traveler,** commuter, fare, rider.

passerby ▶ **noun** *several passersby confirmed his description of the collision* **bystander,** eyewitness, witness.

passing ▶ **adjective 1** *of passing interest* **fleeting,** transient, transitory, ephemeral, brief, short-lived, temporary, momentary; literary evanescent.
2 *a passing glance* **hasty,** rapid, hurried, brief, quick; cursory, superficial, casual, perfunctory.
▶ **noun 1** *the passing of time* **passage,** course, progress, advance.
2 *Jack's passing* **death,** demise, passing away/on, end, loss, quietus; formal decease.
3 *the passing of the new bill* **enactment,** ratification, approval, adoption, authorization, legalization, endorsement.
– PHRASES **in passing** *in passing, let me add that the new membership directory will be available on Thursday* **incidentally,** by the by/way, en passant.

passion ▶ **noun 1** *the passion of activists* **fervor,** ardor, enthusiasm, eagerness, zeal, zealousness, vigor, fire, fieriness, energy, fervency, animation, spirit, spiritedness, fanaticism.
ANTONYMS apathy.
2 *he worked himself up into a passion* (**blind**) **rage,** fit of anger/temper, temper, towering rage, tantrum, fury, frenzy. See note at EMOTION.
3 *hot with passion* **love,** (sexual) desire, lust, ardor, infatuation, lasciviousness, lustfulness.
4 *his passion for football* **enthusiasm,** love, mania, fascination, obsession, fanaticism, fixation, compulsion, appetite, addiction; informal thing.
5 *French literature is my passion* **obsession,** preoccupation, craze, mania, hobbyhorse.
6 *the Passion of Christ* **crucifixion,** suffering, agony, martyrdom.

passionate ▶ **adjective 1** *a passionate entreaty* **intense,** impassioned, ardent, fervent, vehement, heated, emotional, heartfelt, eager, excited, animated, adrenalized, spirited, energetic, fervid, frenzied, fiery, wild, consuming, violent; literary perfervid.
ANTONYMS apathetic.
2 *Elizabeth is **passionate about** sports* **very keen on,** very enthusiastic about, addicted to; informal mad about, crazy about, hooked on, nuts about, nutso for.
3 *a passionate kiss* **amorous,** ardent, hot-blooded, aroused, loving, sexy, sensual, erotic, lustful; informal steamy, hot, red-hot, turned on.
ANTONYMS cold.
4 *a passionate woman* **excitable,** emotional, fiery, volatile, mercurial, quick-tempered, high-strung, impulsive, temperamental.
ANTONYMS phlegmatic.

passionless ▶ **adjective** *a room full of passionless faces* **unemotional,** cold, cold-blooded, emotionless, frigid, cool, unfeeling, unloving, unresponsive, undemonstrative, impassive.

passive ▶ **adjective 1** *a passive role* **inactive,** nonactive, nonparticipative, uninvolved.
2 *passive victims* **submissive,** acquiescent, unresisting, unassertive, compliant, pliant, obedient, docile, tractable, malleable, pliable.
ANTONYMS active, assertive.
3 *the woman's face was passive* **emotionless,** impassive, unemotional, unmoved, dispassionate, passionless, detached, unresponsive, undemonstrative, apathetic, phlegmatic.

passport ▶ **noun** *qualifications are the passport to success* **key,** path, way, route, avenue, door, doorway.

past ▶ **adjective 1** *memories of times past* **gone (by),** over (and done with), no more, done, bygone, former, (of) old, olden, long-ago; literary of yore.
2 *the past few months* **last,** recent, preceding.
3 *a past chairman* **previous,** former, foregoing, erstwhile, one-time, sometime, ex-; formal quondam.
ANTONYMS present, future.
▶ **noun** *details about her past* **history,** background, life (story).
▶ **preposition 1** *she walked past the café* **in front of,** by.
2 *he's past retirement age* **beyond,** in excess of.
▶ **adverb** *they hurried past* **along,** by, on.
– PHRASES **in the past** *in the past, they did not allow women to sit in the bar* **formerly,** previously, in days/years/times gone by, in former times, in the (good) old days, in days of old, in olden times, once (upon a time); literary in days of yore, in yesteryear.

paste ▶ **noun 1** *blend the ingredients to a paste* **purée,** pulp, mush, mash, blend.
2 *wallpaper paste* **adhesive,** glue, gum, fixative, mucilage.
▶ **verb** *a notice was pasted on the door* **glue,** stick, gum, fix, affix.

pastel ▶ **adjective** *we softened the look of the room with pastel paints and fabrics* **pale,** soft, light, light-colored, muted, subtle, subdued, soft-hued.
ANTONYMS dark, bright.

pastiche ▶ **noun 1** *a pastiche of literary models* **mixture,** blend, medley, mélange, miscellany, mixed bag, potpourri, mix, compound, composite, collection, assortment, conglomeration, jumble, ragbag, hodgepodge.
2 *a pastiche of eighteenth-century style* **imitation,** parody; informal takeoff.

pastime ▶ **noun** *two of my favorite pastimes are softball and street hockey* **hobby,** leisure activity/pursuit, sport, game, recreation, amusement, diversion, avocation, entertainment, interest, sideline.

past master ▶ **noun** *when it comes to interior design, Sheri is a past master* **expert,** master, wizard, genius, old hand, veteran, maestro, connoisseur, authority, grandmaster; informal ace, pro, star, hotshot, maven, crackerjack.

pastor ▶ noun *our pastor is taking a group to Guatemala to help with disaster relief* **minister,** clergyman, priest, parson, cleric, chaplain, padre, ecclesiastic, man of the cloth, churchman, vicar, rector, curate, preacher, imam; informal reverend.

pastoral ▶ adjective **1** *a pastoral scene* **rural,** country, countryside, rustic, agricultural, bucolic; literary sylvan, Arcadian.
ANTONYMS urban.
2 *his pastoral duties* **priestly,** clerical, ecclesiastical, ministerial.

pastry ▶ noun **1** *breakfast pastries* **cake,** doughnut, croissant, cruller, Danish (pastry), eclair, tart, tartlet, pie.
2 *two layers of pastry* **crust,** piecrust, croute.

pasture ▶ noun *the cows are in the pasture* **grazing land,** grassland, grass, pastureland, pasturage; Brit. ley; meadow, field; literary lea, mead, greensward.

pat[1] ▶ verb *Brian patted her on the shoulder* **tap,** slap lightly, clap, touch.
▶ noun **1** *a pat on the cheek* **tap,** light blow, clap, touch.
2 *a pat of butter* **piece,** dab, lump, portion, knob, mass, gobbet, ball, curl.
– PHRASES **pat on the back** *Lenny's fellow students were eager to pat him on the back for his amazing test scores* **congratulate,** praise, take one's hat off to; commend, compliment, applaud, acclaim.

pat[2] ▶ adjective *pat answers* **glib,** simplistic, facile, unconvincing.
▶ adverb *his reply came rather pat* **opportunely,** conveniently, at just/exactly the right moment, expediently, favorably, appropriately, fittingly, auspiciously, providentially, felicitously, propitiously.
– PHRASES **down pat** *the understudy knew Lori's lines down pat* **word-perfect,** by heart, by rote, by memory. **get down pat** *I have to get these lyrics down pat within the next two hours* **memorize,** commit to memory, remember, learn by heart, learn (by rote).

patch ▶ noun **1** *a patch over one eye* **cover,** eye patch, covering, pad.
2 *a reddish patch on her wrist* **blotch,** mark, spot, smudge, speckle, smear, stain, streak, blemish; informal splotch.
3 *a patch of ground* **plot,** area, piece, strip, tract, parcel; bed, allotment, lot, plat.
4 informal *they are going through a difficult patch* **period,** time, spell, phase, stretch.
▶ verb *her jeans were neatly patched* **mend,** repair, put a patch on, sew (up), stitch (up).
– PHRASES **patch up** informal **1** *the houses were being patched up* **repair,** mend, fix hastily, do a makeshift repair on. **2** *he's trying to patch things up with his wife* **reconcile,** make up, settle, remedy, put to rights, rectify, clear up, set right, make good, resolve, square.

patchwork ▶ noun *the exhibit is essentially a patchwork of the students' favorite pieces* **assortment,** miscellany, mixture, mélange, medley, blend, mixed bag, mix, collection, selection, assemblage, combination, potpourri, jumble, mishmash, bricolage, ragbag, hodgepodge.

patchy ▶ adjective **1** *their education has been patchy* **uneven,** varying, variable, intermittent, fitful, sporadic, erratic, irregular, haphazard, hit-and-miss.
ANTONYMS uniform.
2 *patchy evidence* **fragmentary,** inadequate, insufficient, rudimentary, limited, sketchy.
ANTONYMS comprehensive.

patent ▶ noun *there is a patent on the drug* **copyright,** license, legal protection, registered trademark.
▶ adjective **1** *patent nonsense* **obvious,** clear, plain, evident, manifest, self-evident, transparent, overt, conspicuous, blatant, downright, barefaced, flagrant, undisguised, unconcealed, unmistakable.
2 *patent medicines* **proprietary,** patented, licensed, branded.

paternal ▶ adjective **1** *his face showed paternal concern* **fatherly,** fatherlike, patriarchal; protective, solicitous, compassionate, sympathetic.
2 *his paternal grandfather* **on one's father's side,** patrilineal.
ANTONYMS maternal.

paternity ▶ noun *the blood tests are used to determine paternity* **fatherhood.**

path ▶ noun **1** *a path down to the beach* **trail,** pathway, walkway, track, footpath, trackway, bridleway, bridle path, portage trail, lane, alley, alleyway, passage, passageway; sidewalk, bikeway.
2 *journalists blocked his path* **route,** way, course; direction, bearing, line; orbit, trajectory.
3 *the best path toward a settlement* **course of action,** route, road, avenue, line, approach, tack, strategy, tactic.

pathetic ▶ adjective **1** *a pathetic groan* **pitiful,** pitiable, piteous, moving, touching, poignant, plaintive, distressing, upsetting, heartbreaking, heart-rending, harrowing, wretched, forlorn. See note at MOVING.
2 informal *a pathetic excuse* **feeble,** woeful, sorry, poor, pitiful, lamentable, deplorable, contemptible, inadequate, paltry, insufficient, insubstantial, unsatisfactory.

pathological ▶ adjective **1** *a pathological condition* **morbid,** diseased.
2 informal *a pathological liar* **compulsive,** obsessive, inveterate, habitual, persistent, chronic, hardened, confirmed.

pathos ▶ noun *the pathos of Antoine's predicament* **poignancy,** tragedy, sadness, pitifulness, piteousness, pitiableness.

patience ▶ noun **1** *she tried everyone's patience* **forbearance,** tolerance, restraint, self-restraint, stoicism; calmness, composure, equanimity, serenity, tranquility, imperturbability, phlegm, understanding, indulgence.
2 *a task requiring patience* **perseverance,** persistence, endurance, tenacity, assiduity, application, staying power, doggedness, determination, resolve, resolution,

resoluteness.

patient ▶ adjective **1** *I must ask you to be patient* **forbearing,** uncomplaining, tolerant, resigned, stoical; calm, composed, even-tempered, imperturbable, unexcitable, accommodating, understanding, indulgent; informal unflappable, cool.
2 *a good deal of patient work* **persevering,** persistent, tenacious, indefatigable, dogged, determined, resolved, resolute, single-minded; formal pertinacious.
▶ noun *a doctor's patient* **sick person,** case; invalid, convalescent, outpatient, in-patient.

patio ▶ noun *we had cocktails on the patio* **terrace,** sundeck, deck; courtyard.

patois ▶ noun *he recognized the patois of New Orleans in her speech* **vernacular,** (local) dialect, regional language; jargon, argot, cant; informal (local) lingo.

patrician ▶ noun *the great patricians of the British Empire* **aristocrat,** grandee, noble, nobleman, noblewoman, lord, lady, peer, peeress; blue blood.
▶ adjective *patrician families* **aristocratic,** noble, titled, blue-blooded, high-born, upper-class, landowning; informal upper-crust; archaic gentle.

patriot ▶ noun *would a true patriot abandon a comrade?* **nationalist,** loyalist; chauvinist, jingoist, flag-waver.

patriotic ▶ adjective *a patriotic show of support* **nationalist,** nationalistic, loyalist, loyal; chauvinistic, jingoistic, flag-waving.
ANTONYMS traitorous.

patrol ▶ noun **1** *an all-night patrol to protect the witness* **vigil,** guard, watch, monitoring, policing, patroling.
2 *the patrol stopped a suspect* **security guard,** sentry, sentinel, patrolman; scout, scouting party.
▶ verb *a security guard was patroling the neighborhood* **keep guard (on),** guard, keep watch (on); police, make the rounds (of); stand guard (over), keep a vigil (on), defend, safeguard.

patron ▶ noun **1** *a patron of the arts* **sponsor,** backer, financier, benefactor, benefactress, contributor, subscriber, donor; philanthropist, promoter, friend, supporter; informal angel.
2 *club patrons* **customer,** client, frequenter, consumer, user, visitor, guest; informal regular, habitué.

patronage ▶ noun **1** *art patronage* **sponsorship,** backing, funding, financing, promotion, assistance, support.
2 *political patronage* **power of appointment,** favoritism, nepotism, preferential treatment, cronyism, pork-barreling.
3 *thank you for your patronage* **custom,** trade, business.

patronize ▶ verb **1** *don't patronize me!* **treat condescendingly,** condescend to, look down on, talk down to, put down, treat like a child, treat with disdain.
2 *they patronized local merchants* **do business with,** buy from, shop at, be a customer of, be a client of, deal with, trade with, frequent, support.
3 *he patronized a national museum* **sponsor,** back, fund, finance, be a patron of, support, champion.

patronizing ▶ adjective *your patronizing mother just told me how "adequate" my dress is* **condescending,** disdainful, supercilious, superior, imperious, scornful, contemptuous; informal uppity, high and mighty.

patter[1] ▶ verb **1** *raindrops pattered against the window* **go pitter-patter,** tap, drum, beat, pound, rat-a-tat, go pit-a-pat, thrum.
2 *she pattered across the floor* **scurry,** scuttle, skip, trip.
▶ noun *the patter of rain* **pitter-patter,** tapping, pattering, drumming, beat, beating, pounding, rat-a-tat, pit-a-pat, clack, thrum, thrumming.

patter[2] ▶ noun **1** *this witty patter* **prattle,** prating, blather, blither, drivel, chatter, jabber, babble; informal yabbering, yatter; archaic twaddle.
2 *the salesman's patter* **(sales) pitch,** sales talk; informal line, spiel.
3 *the local patter* **speech,** language, parlance, dialect; informal lingo.
▶ verb *she pattered on incessantly* **prattle,** prate, blather, drivel, chatter, jabber, babble; informal yabber, yatter.

pattern ▶ noun **1** *the pattern on the wallpaper* **design,** decoration, motif, marking, ornament, ornamentation.
2 *the patterns of ant behavior* **system,** order, arrangement, form, method, structure, scheme, plan, format, framework.
3 *this would set the pattern for a generation* **model,** example, criterion, standard, basis, point of reference, gauge, norm, yardstick, touchstone, benchmark; blueprint, archetype, prototype. See note at MODEL.
4 *textile patterns* **sample,** specimen, swatch.
▶ verb *someone else is patterning my life* **shape,** influence, model, fashion, mold, style, determine, control.

patterned ▶ adjective *patterned glassware* **decorated,** ornamented, fancy, adorned, embellished.
ANTONYMS plain.

paucity ▶ noun *the police cannot act with such a paucity of evidence* **scarcity,** sparseness, sparsity, dearth, shortage, poverty, insufficiency, deficiency, lack, want.
ANTONYMS abundance.

paunch ▶ noun *I love everything about him, even his cute little paunch* **potbelly,** beer belly, beer gut, spare tire, pot.

pauper ▶ noun *the story of a lowly pauper who rises to the top of a major crime syndicate* **poor person,** indigent, down-and-out; informal have-not.

pause ▶ noun *a pause in the conversation* **stop,** cessation, break, halt, interruption, check, lull, respite, breathing space, discontinuation, hiatus, gap, interlude; adjournment, suspension, rest, wait, hesitation; informal letup, breather.
▶ verb *Hannah paused for a moment* **stop,** cease, halt, discontinue, break off, take a break; adjourn, rest, wait, hesitate, falter, waver; informal take a breather, take five.

pave ▶ verb
– PHRASES **pave the way for** *a document that could pave the way for legislation* **prepare (the way) for,** make preparations for, get ready for, lay the foundations for, herald, precede.

paw ▶ noun *protect their paws from frostbite* **foot,** forepaw, hind paw.
▶ verb **1** *their offspring were pawing each other* **handle roughly,** pull, grab, maul, manhandle.
2 *some Casanova tried to paw her* **fondle,** feel, maul, molest; informal grope, feel up, goose.

pawn ▶ verb *he pawned his watch* **pledge,** put in pawn, give as security, use as collateral; informal hock, put in hock.
▶ noun *a pawn in the battle for the throne* **puppet,** dupe, hostage, tool, cat's paw, instrument.

pay ▶ verb **1** *I want to pay him for his work* **reward,** reimburse, recompense, give payment to, remunerate.
2 *Tom must pay a few more dollars* **spend,** expend, pay out, dish out, disburse; informal lay out, shell out, fork out, cough up; ante up, pony up.
3 *he paid his debts* **discharge,** settle, pay off, clear, liquidate.
4 *hard work will pay dividends* **yield,** return, produce.
5 *he made the buses pay* **be profitable,** make money, make a profit.
6 *it doesn't pay to get involved* **be advantageous,** be of advantage, be beneficial, benefit.
7 *paying compliments* **bestow,** grant, give, offer.
8 *he will pay for his mistakes* **suffer,** suffer the consequences, be punished, atone, pay the penalty/price.
▶ noun *equal pay for women* **salary,** wages, payment; earnings, remuneration, reimbursement, income, revenue; formal emolument(s).
– PHRASES **pay back 1** *she has sworn to pay him back for his philandering* **get one's revenge on,** be revenged on, avenge oneself on, get back at, get even with, settle accounts with, exact retribution on. **2** *they eventually paid back the money* **repay,** pay off, give back, return, reimburse, refund. **pay for** *I'll pay for dinner* **fund,** finance, defray the cost of, settle up for, treat someone to; informal foot the bill for, shell out for, fork out for, cough up for, ante up for, pony up for. **pay off 1** *he was busted for trying to pay off a cop* **bribe,** suborn, buy (off); informal grease someone's palm. **2** *she paid off the car loan in less than a year* **pay (in full),** settle, discharge, clear, liquidate. **3** *his hard work paid off* **meet with success,** be successful, be effective, get results. **pay out** *how much did you have to pay out for that bike?* **spend,** expend, dish out, put up, part with, hand over; informal shell out, fork out/up, lay out, cough up. **pay up** *you have one more week to pay up* **make payment,** settle up, pay (in full); informal cough up.

payable ▶ adjective *a notice of payable taxes* **due,** owed, owing, outstanding, unpaid, overdue, in arrears, delinquent.

payment ▶ noun **1** *discounts for early payment* **remittance,** settlement, discharge, clearance, liquidation.
2 *monthly payments* **installment,** premium.
3 *extra payment for good performance* **salary,** wages, pay, earnings, fee(s), remuneration, reimbursement, income; formal emolument(s).

peace ▶ noun **1** *can't a man get any peace around here?* **tranquility,** calm, restfulness, peace and quiet, peacefulness, quiet, quietness; privacy, solitude.
ANTONYMS noise.
2 *peace of mind* **serenity,** peacefulness, tranquility, equanimity, calm, calmness, composure, ease, contentment, contentedness.
ANTONYMS agitation, distress.
3 *we pray for peace* **law and order,** lawfulness, order, peacefulness, peaceableness, harmony, nonviolence; formal concord.
ANTONYMS conflict.
4 *a lasting peace* **treaty,** truce, cease-fire, armistice, cessation/suspension of hostilities.
ANTONYMS war.

peaceable ▶ adjective **1** *a peaceable man* **peace-loving,** nonviolent, nonaggressive, easygoing, placid, gentle, inoffensive, good-natured, even-tempered, amiable, amicable, friendly, affable, genial, pacific, dovelike, dovish, unwarlike, pacifist; formal irenic.
ANTONYMS aggressive, belligerent.
2 *a peaceable society* **peaceful,** strife-free, harmonious; law-abiding, disciplined, orderly, civilized.
ANTONYMS unruly, warring.

peaceful ▶ adjective **1** *everything was quiet and peaceful* **tranquil,** calm, restful, quiet, still, relaxing, soothing, undisturbed, untroubled, private, secluded. See note at **CALM**.
ANTONYMS noisy, bustling.
2 *his peaceful mood* **serene,** calm, tranquil, composed, placid, at ease, untroubled, unworried, content.
ANTONYMS agitated.
3 *peaceful relations* **harmonious,** at peace, peaceable, on good terms, amicable, friendly, cordial, nonviolent.
ANTONYMS hostile.

peacemaker ▶ noun *she was regarded as the great peacemaker of her people* **arbitrator,** arbiter, mediator, negotiator, conciliator, go-between, intermediary, pacifier, appeaser, peace-monger, pacifist, peace-lover, dove; informal peacenik.

peak ▶ noun **1** *the peaks of the mountains* **summit,** top, crest, pinnacle, apex, crown, cap.
2 *the highest peak* **mountain,** hill, height, mount, alp.
3 *the peak of a cap* **brim,** visor.
4 *the peak of his career* **height,** high point/spot, pinnacle, summit, top, climax, culmination, apex, zenith, crowning point, acme, capstone, apogee, prime, heyday.
▶ verb *conservative support has peaked* **reach its height,** climax, reach a climax, come to a head.
▶ adjective *peak loads* **maximum,** top, greatest, highest; ultimate, best, optimum.

peaked ▶ adjective *Marjorie, my dear, you look so peaked* **pale,** pasty, wan, drained, washed out, drawn, pallid, anemic, ashen, gray, pinched, sickly, sallow, ill, unwell, poorly, indisposed, run down, off; informal under the weather, rough, lousy.

peal ▶ noun 1 *a peal of bells* **chime,** carillon, ring, ringing, tintinnabulation.
2 *peals of laughter* **shriek,** shout, scream, howl, gale, fit, roar, hoot.
3 *a peal of thunder* **rumble,** roar, boom, crash, clap, crack.
▶ verb 1 *the bell pealed* **ring (out),** chime (out), clang, sound, ding, jingle.
2 *the thunder pealed* **rumble,** roar, boom, crash, resound.

peasant ▶ noun 1 *peasants working the land* **agricultural worker,** small farmer, rustic, swain, villein, serf, campesino; historical habitant.
2 informal *you peasants!* See BOOR.

peccadillo ▶ noun *I'm sure we can overlook a few peccadilloes* **misdemeanor,** petty offense, indiscretion, lapse, misdeed.

peck ▶ verb 1 *the cockerel pecked my heel* **bite,** nip, strike, hit, tap, rap, jab.
2 *he pecked her on the cheek* **kiss,** give a peck.
3 informal *she* ***pecked at*** *her food* **nibble (at),** pick at, take very small bites from, toy with, play with.

peculiar ▶ adjective 1 *something peculiar began to happen* **strange,** unusual, odd, funny, curious, bizarre, weird, queer, unexpected, unfamiliar, abnormal, atypical, anomalous, out of the ordinary; exceptional, extraordinary, remarkable; puzzling, mystifying, mysterious, perplexing, baffling; suspicious, eerie, uncanny, unnatural; informal freaky, fishy, creepy, spooky.
ANTONYMS ordinary.
2 *peculiar behavior* **bizarre,** eccentric, strange, odd, weird, queer, funny, unusual, abnormal, idiosyncratic, unconventional, outlandish, quirky; informal wacky, freakish, oddball, offbeat, off the wall, wacko.
3 *mannerisms* ***peculiar to*** *the islanders* **characteristic of,** typical of, representative of, indicative of, suggestive of, exclusive to, unique to.
4 *their own peculiar contribution* **distinctive,** characteristic, distinct, individual, special, idiosyncratic, unique, personal.

peculiarity ▶ noun 1 *a legal peculiarity* **oddity,** anomaly, abnormality.
2 *a physical peculiarity* **idiosyncrasy,** mannerism, quirk, foible.
3 *one of the peculiarities of the city* **characteristic,** feature, (essential) quality, property, trait, attribute, hallmark, trademark.
4 *the peculiarity of this notion* **strangeness,** oddness, bizarreness, weirdness, queerness, unexpectedness, unfamiliarity, incongruity.
5 *there is a certain peculiarity about her appearance* **outlandishness,** bizarreness, unconventionality, idiosyncrasy, weirdness, oddness, eccentricity, unusualness, abnormality, queerness, strangeness, quirkiness; informal wackiness, freakiness.

pecuniary ▶ adjective *free from pecuniary anxieties* **financial,** monetary, money, fiscal, economic. See note at FINANCIAL.

pedagogic ▶ adjective *Dr. Snow encouraged me in my pedagogic endeavors* **educational,** educative, pedagogical, teaching, instructional, instructive, didactic; academic, scholastic.

pedagogue formal ▶ noun *her thirty-two years as a most beloved pedagogue* **teacher,** schoolteacher, schoolmaster, schoolmistress, master, mistress, tutor; lecturer, academic, don, professor, instructor, educator, educationist, educationalist.

pedant ▶ noun *pedants insist that the twenty-first century starts with 2001* **dogmatist,** purist, literalist, formalist, doctrinaire, perfectionist; quibbler, hair-splitter, casuist, sophist; informal nitpicker.

pedantic ▶ adjective *a pedantic interpretation of the rules* **overscrupulous,** scrupulous, precise, exact, perfectionist, punctilious, meticulous, fussy, fastidious, finicky; dogmatic, purist, literalist, literalistic, formalist; casuistic, casuistical, sophistic, sophistical; captious, hair-splitting, quibbling; informal nitpicking, persnickety.

pedantry ▶ noun *the pedantry in her argument has upset the flow of our discussion* **dogmatism,** purism, literalism, formalism; overscrupulousness, scrupulousness, perfectionism, fastidiousness, punctiliousness, meticulousness; captiousness, quibbling, hair-splitting, casuistry, sophistry; informal nitpicking. See note at KNOWLEDGE.

peddle ▶ verb 1 *they are peddling water filters* **sell,** sell from door to door, hawk, tout, vend; trade (in), deal in, traffic in.
2 *peddling unorthodox views* **advocate,** champion, preach, put forward, proclaim, propound, promote, promulgate.

pedestal ▶ noun *a bust on a pedestal* **plinth,** base, support, mounting, stand, foundation, pillar, column, pier; Architecture socle.
– PHRASES **put on a pedestal** *if you put me on a pedestal, I'll eventually disappoint you* **idealize,** lionize, look up to, respect, hold in high regard, think highly of, admire, esteem, revere, worship.

pedestrian ▶ noun *accidents involving pedestrians* **walker,** person on foot; (**pedestrians**) foot traffic.
ANTONYMS driver.
▶ adjective *pedestrian lives* **dull,** boring, tedious, monotonous, uneventful, unremarkable, tiresome, wearisome, uninspired, unimaginative, unexciting, uninteresting; unvarying, unvaried, repetitive, routine, commonplace, workaday; ordinary, everyday, run-of-the-mill, mundane, humdrum; informal plain-vanilla.
ANTONYMS exciting.

pedigree ▶ noun *a long pedigree* **ancestry,** descent, lineage, line (of descent), genealogy, family tree, extraction, derivation, origin(s), heritage, parentage, bloodline, background, roots.
▶ adjective *a pedigree cat* **pure-bred,** thoroughbred, pure-blooded.

peek ▶ verb 1 *Hermione peeked from behind the curtains* **(have a) peep,** have a peek, spy, take a sly/stealthy look, sneak a look/peek; informal take a gander.
2 *the deer's antlers* ***peeked out*** *from the trees* **appear (slowly/partly),** show, come into

view/sight, become visible, emerge, peep (out).
▶ **noun** *a peek at the map* **secret look,** sly look, stealthy look, sneaky look, peep, glance, glimpse, hurried/quick look; informal gander, squint.

peel ▶ **verb 1** *peel and core the fruit* **pare,** skin, take the skin/rind off; hull, shell, husk, shuck; technical decorticate.
2 *use a long knife to peel the veneer* **trim (off),** peel off, pare, strip (off), shave (off), remove.
3 *the wallpaper was peeling* **flake (off),** peel off, come off in layers/strips.
▶ **noun** *orange peel* **rind,** skin, covering, zest; hull, pod, integument, shuck.
– PHRASES **keep one's eyes peeled** *keep your eyes peeled for a light blue Pontiac* **keep a (sharp) lookout,** look out, keep one's eyes open, keep watch, be watchful, be alert, be on the alert, be on the qui vive, be on guard.

peep[1] ▶ **verb 1** *I peeped through the keyhole* **look quickly,** cast a brief look, take a secret look, sneak a look, (have a) peek, glance; informal take a gander.
2 *the moon peeped through the clouds* **appear (slowly/partly),** show, come into view/sight, become visible, emerge, peek, peer out.
▶ **noun** *I'll just take a peep at it* **quick look,** brief look, (sneak) peek, glance; informal gander, squint.

peep[2] ▶ **noun 1** *I heard a quiet peep* **cheep,** chirp, chirrup, tweet, twitter, chirr, warble.
2 *there's been not a peep out of the children* **sound,** noise, cry, word.
3 *the painting was sold without a peep* **complaint,** grumble, mutter, murmur, grouse, objection, protest, protestation; informal moan, gripe, grouch.

peephole ▶ **noun** *just take a look through this peephole* **opening,** gap, cleft, slit, crack, chink, keyhole, knothole, squint.

peer[1] ▶ **verb** *he peered at the manuscript* **look closely,** try to see, narrow one's eyes, screw up one's eyes, squint.

peer[2] ▶ **noun 1** *his academic peers* **equal,** coequal, fellow, confrère; contemporary; formal compeer.
2 *hereditary peers* **aristocrat,** lord, lady, peer of the realm, peeress, noble, nobleman, noblewoman, titled man/woman, patrician; duke/duchess, marquess/marchioness, earl/countess, viscount/viscountess, baron/baroness, marquis/marquise, count.

peerage ▶ **noun** *she claims to be related to British peerage* **aristocracy,** nobility, peers and peeresses, lords and ladies, patriciate; the House of Lords, the Lords.

peerless ▶ **adjective** *a peerless performance* **incomparable,** matchless, unrivaled, inimitable, beyond compare/comparison, unparalleled, unequaled, without equal, second to none, unsurpassed, unsurpassable, nonpareil; unique, consummate, perfect, rare, transcendent, surpassing; formal unexampled.

peeve ▶ **verb** informal *it seems that everything I do peeves her* **irritate,** annoy, vex, anger, exasperate, irk, gall, pique, nettle, put out, get on someone's nerves, try someone's patience, ruffle someone's feathers; rub the wrong way; informal aggravate, rile, needle, get to, bug, get someone's goat, get/put someone's back up, tee off, tick off.

peevish ▶ **adjective** *he was embarrassed by his mother's peevish disposition* **irritable,** fractious, fretful, cross, petulant, querulous, pettish, crabby, crotchety, cantankerous, curmudgeonly, sullen, grumpy, bad-tempered, short-tempered, touchy, testy, tetchy, snappish, irascible, waspish, prickly, crusty, dyspeptic, splenetic, choleric; informal cranky, ornery.
ANTONYMS good-humored.

peg ▶ **noun** *the joints are secured by pegs* **pin,** nail, dowel, skewer, spike, rivet, brad, screw, bolt, hook, spigot; Mountaineering piton; Golf tee.
▶ **verb 1** *the tarp is pegged to the ground* **fix,** pin, attach, fasten, secure, make fast.
2 *we decided to peg our prices* **hold down,** keep down, fix, set, hold, freeze.
– PHRASES **take down a peg or two** *wouldn't I just love to take that Mr. Bigshot down a peg or two* **humble,** humiliate, mortify, bring down, shame, embarrass, abash, put someone in their place, chasten, subdue, squash, deflate, make someone eat humble pie; informal show up, settle someone's hash, cut down to size, make someone eat crow.

pejorative ▶ **adjective** *his remarks were considered too pejorative for daytime radio* **disparaging,** derogatory, denigratory, deprecatory, defamatory, slanderous, libelous, abusive, insulting, slighting; informal bitchy.
ANTONYMS complimentary.

pellet ▶ **noun 1** *a pellet of mud* **little ball,** little piece.
2 *pellet wounds* **bullet,** shot, lead shot, buckshot, slug.
3 *rabbit pellets* **excrement,** excreta, droppings, feces, dung, turd.

pell-mell ▶ **adverb 1** *people streamed pell-mell from the building* **helter-skelter,** headlong, (at) full tilt, hotfoot, posthaste, hurriedly, hastily, recklessly, precipitately.
2 *the sacks' contents were thrown pell-mell to the ground* **untidily,** anyhow, in disarray, in a mess, in a muddle; informal all over the place, every which way, any old how, all over the map, all over the lot.

pellucid ▶ **adjective 1** *the pellucid waters* **translucent,** transparent, clear, crystal clear, crystalline, glassy, limpid, unclouded, gin-clear.
2 *pellucid prose* **lucid,** limpid, clear, crystal clear, articulate; coherent, comprehensible, understandable, intelligible, straightforward, simple, clean, well-constructed; formal perspicuous.

pelt[1] ▶ **verb 1** *they pelted him with snowballs* **bombard,** shower, attack, assail, pepper.
2 *they said we'd get some showers, but it's really pelting down* **pour (down),** come down, teem (down), stream down, rain cats and dogs, rain hard.
3 informal *they pelted into the factory* **dash,** run, race, rush, sprint, bolt, dart, career, charge, shoot, hurtle, career, fly, speed, zoom, streak; hasten, hurry; informal tear, belt, hotfoot it, scoot, leg it, go like a bat out of hell, bomb, hightail it.

pelt[2] ▶ noun *an animal's pelt* **skin,** hide, fleece, coat, fur.

pen[1] ▶ noun *you'll need a pen and paper* ballpoint (pen), fountain pen, rollerball; felt tip (pen); highlighter, marker (pen).
▶ verb *she penned a number of articles* **write,** compose, draft, dash off; write down, jot down, set down, take down, scribble.

pen[2] ▶ noun *a sheep pen* **enclosure,** fold, sheepfold, pound, compound, stockade; sty, coop, corral.
▶ verb *the hostages had been penned up in a basement* **confine,** coop (up), cage, shut in, box up/in, lock up/in, trap, imprison, incarcerate, immure.

penal ▶ adjective **1** *a penal institution* **disciplinary,** punitive, corrective, correctional.
2 *penal rates of interest* **exorbitant,** extortionate, excessive, outrageous, preposterous, unreasonable, inflated, sky-high.

penalize ▶ verb **1** *if you break the rules you will be penalized* **punish,** discipline, inflict a penalty on.
ANTONYMS reward.
2 *people with certain medical conditions would be penalized* **handicap,** disadvantage, put at a disadvantage, cause to suffer.
ANTONYMS favor.

penalty ▶ noun **1** *increased penalties for dumping oil at sea* **punishment,** sanction, punitive action, retribution; fine, forfeit, sentence; penance; formal mulct.
ANTONYMS reward.
2 *a game full of penalties* **foul,** infraction.
3 *the penalties of old age* **disadvantage,** difficulty, drawback, handicap, downside, minus; trial, tribulation, bane, affliction, burden, trouble.
ANTONYMS advantage.

penance ▶ noun *true penance requires honest self-examination* **atonement,** expiation, self-punishment, self-mortification, self-abasement, amends; punishment, penalty.

penchant ▶ noun *I have a penchant for small dogs* **liking,** fondness, preference, taste, relish, appetite, partiality, soft spot, love, passion, desire, fancy, whim, weakness, inclination, bent, bias, proclivity, predilection, predisposition.

pencil ▶ noun **1** *a sharpened pencil* **lead pencil,** mechanical pencil, colored pencil; grease pencil; eyebrow pencil, lip pencil.
2 *a pencil of light* **beam,** ray, shaft, finger, gleam.
▶ verb **1** *he penciled his name inside the cover* **write,** write down, jot down, scribble, note, take down.
2 *pencil a line along the top of the molding* **draw,** trace, sketch.

pendant ▶ noun *she wore an antique gold pendant around her neck* **necklace,** locket, medallion.

pendent ▶ adjective *the tree's pendent catkins* **hanging,** suspended, dangling, pendulous, pensile, pendant, drooping, droopy, trailing.

pending ▶ adjective **1** *nine cases were still pending* **unresolved,** undecided, unsettled, awaiting decision/action, undetermined, open, hanging fire, (up) in the air, on ice, ongoing, outstanding, not done, unfinished, incomplete; informal on the back burner.
2 *with a general election pending* **imminent,** impending, about to happen, forthcoming, upcoming, on the way, coming, approaching, looming, gathering, near, nearing, close, close at hand, in the offing, to come.
▶ preposition *they were released on bail pending an appeal* **awaiting,** until, till, until there is/are.

penetrate ▶ verb **1** *the knife penetrated his lungs* **pierce,** puncture, make a hole in, perforate, stab, prick, gore, spike.
2 *they penetrated the enemy territory* **infiltrate,** slip into, sneak into, insinuate oneself into.
3 *fear penetrated her bones* **permeate,** pervade, fill, spread throughout, suffuse, seep through.
4 *he seemed to have penetrated the mysteries of nature* **understand,** comprehend, apprehend, fathom, grasp, perceive, discern, get to the bottom of, solve, resolve, make sense of, interpret, puzzle out, work out, unravel, decipher, make head(s) or tail(s) of; informal crack, get, figure out.
5 *her words finally penetrated* **register,** sink in, be understood, be comprehended, become clear, fall into place; informal click.

penetrating ▶ adjective **1** *a penetrating wind* **piercing,** cutting, biting, stinging, keen, sharp, harsh, raw, freezing, chill, wintry, cold. See note at KEEN.
ANTONYMS mild, gentle.
2 *a penetrating voice* **shrill,** strident, piercing, carrying, loud, high, high-pitched, piping, ear-splitting, screechy, intrusive.
ANTONYMS mellow, soft.
3 *a penetrating smell* **pungent,** pervasive, strong, powerful, sharp, acrid; heady, aromatic.
ANTONYMS mild.
4 *her penetrating gaze* **observant,** searching, intent, alert, shrewd, perceptive, probing, piercing, sharp, keen.
5 *a penetrating analysis* **perceptive,** insightful, keen, sharp, sharp-witted, intelligent, clever, smart, incisive, piercing, razor-edged, trenchant, astute, shrewd, clear, acute, percipient, perspicacious, discerning, sensitive, thoughtful, deep, profound.
ANTONYMS dull.

penetration ▶ noun **1** *skin penetration by infective larvae* **perforation,** piercing, puncturing, puncture, stabbing, pricking.
2 *remarks of great penetration* **insight,** discernment, perception, perceptiveness, intelligence, sharp-wittedness, cleverness, incisiveness, keenness, sharpness, trenchancy, astuteness, shrewdness, acuteness, clarity, acuity, percipience, perspicacity, discrimination, sensitivity, thoughtfulness, profundity; formal perspicuity.

penitence ▶ noun *the writer prays to God in penitence* **repentance,** contrition, regret, remorse, remorsefulness, ruefulness, sorrow, sorrowfulness, pangs of conscience, self-reproach, shame, guilt, compunction; archaic rue.

penitent ▶ adjective *she stood there looking like a penitent child* **repentant,** contrite, remorseful, sorry, apologetic, regretful, conscience-stricken,

rueful, ashamed, shamefaced, abject, in sackcloth and ashes.
ANTONYMS unrepentant.

pen name ▶ **noun** *her pen name was Annabelle Lord* **pseudonym,** nom de plume, assumed name, alias, professional name.

pennant ▶ **noun** *pennants fly from the towers* **flag,** standard, ensign, color(s), banner, banderole, guidon; Nautical burgee.

penniless ▶ **adjective** *Van Gogh died penniless* **destitute,** poverty-stricken, impoverished, poor, indigent, impecunious, in penury, moneyless, necessitous, needy, bankrupt, insolvent, without a cent (to one's name), without a sou; informal (flat) broke, cleaned out, strapped for cash, bust; formal penurious.
ANTONYMS wealthy.

penny ▶ **noun**
– PHRASES **a pretty penny** informal *I bet that boat cost you a pretty penny* **a lot of money,** millions, billions, a king's ransom; informal a (small) fortune, lots/heaps of money, a mint, a killing, a bundle, a tidy sum, big money, big bucks, an arm and a leg.

penny-pinching ▶ **adjective** *Zane's penny-pinching aunt gave him five dollars as a wedding gift* **mean,** miserly, niggardly, parsimonious, close-fisted, cheeseparing, grasping, Scroogelike; informal stingy, mingy, tight, tightfisted, money-grubbing; formal penurious; archaic near.
ANTONYMS generous.

pension ▶ **noun** *I doubt I can live on my pension* **retirement (benefits),** superannuation; Social Security; allowance, benefit, support, welfare.

pensive ▶ **adjective** *sorry to interrupt your pensive mood, but we've got to leave* **thoughtful,** reflective, contemplative, musing, meditative, introspective, ruminative, absorbed, preoccupied, deep/lost in thought, in a brown study, brooding; formal cogitative.

pent-up ▶ **adjective** *pent-up anger will eventually explode* **repressed,** suppressed, stifled, smothered, restrained, confined, bottled up, held in/back, unvented, kept in check, curbed, bridled.

penurious ▶ **adjective** formal **1** *a penurious student* **poor,** poor as a church mouse, poverty-stricken, destitute, necessitous, impecunious, impoverished, indigent, needy, in need/want, badly off, in reduced/straitened circumstances, hard up, unable to make ends meet, penniless, without a cent (to one's name), without a sou; informal (flat) broke, strapped for cash.
ANTONYMS wealthy.
2 *a penurious old skinflint* **mean,** miserly, niggardly, parsimonious, penny-pinching, close-fisted, Scroogelike; informal stingy, mingy, tight, tightfisted, money-grubbing; archaic near.
ANTONYMS generous.

penury ▶ **noun** *Dylan was oblivious to his brother's wretched state of penury* **extreme poverty,** destitution, pennilessness, impecuniousness, impoverishment, indigence, pauperism, privation, beggary.

people ▶ **plural noun 1** *crowds of people* **human beings,** persons, individuals, humans, mortals, (living) souls, personages, 'men, women, and children'; informal folks.
2 *the American people* **citizens,** subjects, electors, voters, taxpayers, residents, inhabitants, (general) public, citizenry, nation, population, populace.
3 *a man of the people* **common people,** proletariat, masses, populace, rank and file, commonality, third estate, plebeians; derogatory hoi polloi, common herd, great unwashed, proles, plebs.
4 *her people don't live far away* **family,** parents, relatives, relations, folks, kinsmen, kin, kith and kin, kinsfolk, flesh and blood, nearest and dearest.
5 (**singular noun**) *the peoples of Africa* **race,** (ethnic) group, tribe, clan.
▶ **verb** *the Beothuk who once peopled Newfoundland* **populate,** settle (in), colonize, inhabit, live in, occupy; formal reside in, be domiciled in, dwell in.

pep informal ▶ **noun** *a performance full of pep* **dynamism,** life, energy, spirit, liveliness, animation, bounce, sparkle, effervescence, verve, spiritedness, ebullience, high spirits, enthusiasm, vitality, vivacity, fire, dash, panache, élan, zest, exuberance, vigor, gusto, brio; informal feistiness, get-up-and-go, oomph, pizzazz, vim.
– PHRASES **pep up** *why don't we pep up this gathering with some tunes?* **enliven,** animate, liven up, put some/new life into, invigorate, vitalize, revitalize, vivify, ginger up, energize, galvanize, put some spark into, stimulate, get something going, perk up; brighten up, cheer up; informal buck up.

pepper ▶ **verb 1** *salt and pepper the potatoes* **add pepper to,** season, flavor.
2 *stars peppered the desert skies* **sprinkle,** fleck, dot, spot, stipple; cover, fill.
3 *a burst of bullets peppered the tank* **bombard,** pelt, shower, rain down on, attack, assail, batter, strafe, rake, blitz, hit.

peppery ▶ **adjective 1** *a peppery sauce* **spicy,** spiced, peppered, hot, highly seasoned, piquant, pungent, sharp.
ANTONYMS mild, bland.
2 *a peppery old man* **irritable,** cantankerous, irascible, bad-tempered, ill-tempered, grumpy, grouchy, crotchety, short-tempered, tetchy, testy, crusty, crabby, curmudgeonly, peevish, cross, fractious, pettish, prickly, waspish; informal ornery, snappish, cranky.
ANTONYMS affable.

perceive ▶ **verb 1** *I immediately perceived the flaws in her story* **discern,** recognize, become aware of, see, distinguish, realize, grasp, understand, take in, make out, find, identify, hit on, comprehend, apprehend, appreciate, sense, divine; informal figure out; Brit. informal twig; formal become cognizant of.
2 *she perceived a twitch in his nose whenever he lied* **see,** discern, detect, catch sight of, spot, observe, notice.
3 *she was perceived as too negative* **regard,** look on, view, consider, think of, judge, deem, adjudge.

perceptible ▶ **adjective** *I am sure that the flaw in* *the upholstery is perceptible only to you, my dear* **noticeable,** perceivable, detectable, discernible, visible, observable, recognizable, appreciable; obvious, apparent, evident, manifest, patent, clear, distinct, plain, conspicuous. See note at TANGIBLE.

perception ▶ noun **1** *our perception of our own limitations* **recognition,** awareness, consciousness, appreciation, realization, knowledge, grasp, understanding, comprehension, apprehension; formal cognizance.
2 *popular perceptions of old age* **impression,** idea, conception, notion, thought, belief, judgment, estimation.
3 *he talks with great perception* **insight,** perceptiveness, percipience, perspicacity, understanding, sharpness, sharp-wittedness, intelligence, intuition, cleverness, incisiveness, trenchancy, astuteness, shrewdness, acuteness, acuity, discernment, sensitivity, penetration, thoughtfulness, profundity; formal perspicuity.

perceptive ▶ adjective *children are usually more perceptive than their parents think* **insightful,** discerning, sensitive, intuitive, observant; piercing, penetrating, percipient, perspicacious, penetrative, clear-sighted, farsighted, intelligent, clever, canny, keen, sharp, sharp-witted, astute, shrewd, quick, smart, acute, discriminating; informal on the ball, right-brained, heads-up, with it.
ANTONYMS obtuse.

perch ▶ noun *the chicken's perch* **pole,** rod, branch, roost, rest, resting place.
▶ verb **1** *three swallows perched on the telegraph wire* **roost,** sit, rest; alight, settle, land, come to rest.
2 *she perched her glasses on her nose* **put,** place, set, rest, balance.
3 *the church **is perched** on a hill* **be located,** be situated, be positioned, be sited, stand.

perchance ▶ adverb literary *perchance we shall meet again* **maybe,** perhaps, possibly, for all one knows, it could be, it's possible, conceivably; literary peradventure.

percipient ▶ adjective See PERCEPTIVE.

percolate ▶ verb **1** *water percolated through the soil* **filter,** drain, drip, ooze, seep, trickle, dribble, leak, leach.
2 *these views began to percolate through society as a whole* **spread,** be disseminated, filter, pass; permeate, pervade.
3 *he put some coffee on to percolate* **brew;** informal perk.

perdition ▶ noun *I hope that lawyer goes to perdition!* **damnation,** eternal punishment; hell, hellfire, doom.

peremptory ▶ adjective **1** *a peremptory reply* **brusque,** imperious, high-handed, brisk, abrupt, summary, commanding, dictatorial, autocratic, overbearing, dogmatic, arrogant, overweening, lordly, magisterial, authoritarian; emphatic, firm, insistent; informal bossy.
2 *a peremptory order of the court* **irreversible,** binding, absolute, final, conclusive, decisive, definitive, categorical, irrefutable, incontrovertible; Law unappealable.

perennial ▶ adjective *the perennial fascination with crime* **abiding,** enduring, lasting, everlasting, perpetual, eternal, continuing, unending, unceasing, never-ending, endless, undying, ceaseless, persisting, permanent, constant, continual, unfailing, unchanging, never-changing.

perfect ▶ adjective **1** *she strove to be the perfect wife* **ideal,** model, without fault, faultless, flawless, consummate, quintessential, exemplary, best, ultimate, copybook; unrivaled, unequaled, matchless, unparalleled, beyond compare, without equal, second to none, too good to be true, Utopian, incomparable, nonpareil, peerless, inimitable, unexcelled, unsurpassed, unsurpassable.
2 *a classic Les Paul guitar in perfect condition* **flawless,** mint, as good as new, pristine, impeccable, immaculate, superb, superlative, optimum, prime, optimal, peak, excellent, faultless, as sound as a bell, unspoiled, unblemished, undamaged, spotless, unmarred; informal tip-top, A1.
3 *a perfect copy* **exact,** precise, accurate, faithful, correct, unerring, inerrant, right, true, strict; informal on the money.
4 *the perfect Christmas present for golfers* **ideal,** just right, right, appropriate, fitting, fit, suitable, apt, made to order, tailor-made; very.
5 *she felt like a perfect idiot* **absolute,** complete, total, real, out-and-out, thorough, thoroughgoing, downright, utter, sheer, arrant, unmitigated, unqualified, veritable, in every respect, unalloyed.
▶ verb *he's busy perfecting his bowling technique* **improve,** better, polish (up), hone, refine, put the finishing/final touches to, brush up, fine-tune.

perfection ▶ noun **1** *the perfection of her technique* **improvement,** betterment, refinement, refining, honing.
2 *for him, she was still perfection* **the ideal,** a paragon, the ne plus ultra, a nonpareil, the crème de la crème, the last word, the ultimate, the best; informal one in a million, the tops, da bomb; dated informal the bee's knees, the cat's meow/pajamas/whiskers.

perfectionist ▶ noun *the just-so placement of every little figurine and throw pillow immediately gave him away as a perfectionist* **purist,** stickler for perfection, idealist; pedant.

perfectly ▶ adverb **1** *a perfectly cooked meal* **faultlessly,** superbly, superlatively, excellently, flawlessly, to perfection, without fault, ideally, inimitably, incomparably, impeccably, immaculately, exquisitely, consummately; informal like a dream, to a T.
2 *I think we understand each other perfectly* **absolutely,** utterly, completely, altogether, entirely, wholly, totally, thoroughly, fully, in every respect.
3 *you know perfectly well that is not what I meant* **very,** quite, full; informal damn, damned, darned, bloody.

perfidious ▶ adjective literary *a perfidious lover* **treacherous,** duplicitous, deceitful, disloyal, faithless, unfaithful, traitorous, treasonous, false, false-hearted, double-dealing, two-faced, untrustworthy.

ANTONYMS faithful.

perfidy ▶ **noun** literary *the perfidy of her husband* **treachery,** duplicity, deceit, deceitfulness, disloyalty, infidelity, faithlessness, unfaithfulness, betrayal, treason, double-dealing, untrustworthiness, breach of trust; literary perfidiousness.

perforate ▶ **verb** *a shell fragment perforated his left lung* **pierce,** penetrate, enter, puncture, prick, bore through, riddle.

perform ▶ **verb 1** *I have my duties to perform* **carry out,** do, execute, discharge, bring about, bring off, accomplish, achieve, fulfill, complete, conduct, effect, dispatch, work, implement; informal pull off; formal effectuate; archaic acquit oneself of.
ANTONYMS neglect.
2 *a car that performs well at low speeds* **function,** work, operate, run, go, respond, behave, act, acquit oneself/itself.
3 *the play has been performed in San Francisco* **stage,** put on, present, mount, enact, act, produce.
4 *the band performed live in Central Park* **appear,** play, be on stage, sing, dance, act.

performance ▶ **noun 1** *the evening performance* **show,** production, showing, presentation, staging; concert, recital; informal gig.
2 *their performance of Mozart's concerto in E flat* **rendition,** rendering, interpretation, reading, playing, acting, representation.
3 *the continual performance of a single task* **carrying out,** execution, discharge, accomplishment, completion, fulfillment, dispatch, implementation; formal effectuation.
4 *the performance of the processor* **functioning,** working, operation, running, behavior, capabilities, capability, capacity, power, potential.
5 informal *he made a great performance of telling her about it* **fuss,** production, palaver, scene, business, pantomime; informal song and dance, big deal, to-do, hoo-ha.

performer ▶ **noun** *he began his career as a bit performer in B movies* **actor, actress,** thespian, artiste, artist, entertainer, trouper, player, musician, singer, dancer, comic, comedian, comedienne.

perfume ▶ **noun 1** *a bottle of perfume* **fragrance,** scent, eau de toilette, toilet water, eau de cologne, cologne, aftershave.
2 *the heady perfume of lilacs* **smell,** scent, fragrance, aroma, bouquet, redolence. See note at **SMELL**.

perfunctory ▶ **adjective** *a perfunctory review* **cursory,** desultory, quick, brief, hasty, hurried, rapid, fleeting, token, casual, superficial, careless, halfhearted, sketchy, mechanical, automatic, routine, offhand, inattentive.
ANTONYMS careful, thorough.

perhaps ▶ **adverb** *perhaps they'll get married* **maybe,** for all one knows, it could be, it may be, it's possible, possibly, conceivably; literary peradventure, perchance.

peril ▶ **noun** *a situation fraught with peril* **danger,** jeopardy, risk, hazard, insecurity, uncertainty, menace, threat, perilousness; pitfall, problem.

perilous ▶ **adjective** *a perilous journey through the mountains* **dangerous,** fraught with danger, hazardous, risky, unsafe, treacherous; precarious, vulnerable, uncertain, insecure, exposed, at risk, in jeopardy, in danger, touch-and-go; informal dicey.
ANTONYMS safe.

perimeter ▶ **noun 1** *the perimeter of a circle* **circumference,** outside, outer edge.
2 *the perimeter of the vast estate* **boundary,** border, limits, bounds, confines, edge, margin, fringe(s), periphery, borderline, verge; literary bourn, marge.

period ▶ **noun 1** *a six-week period* **time,** spell, interval, stretch, term, span, phase, bout, run, duration, chapter, stage; while, patch.
2 *the postwar period* **era,** age, epoch, time, days, years; Geology eon.
3 *a double math period* **lesson,** class, session.
4 *women who suffer from painful periods* **menstruation,** menstrual flow, menses; informal the curse, time of the month, monthlies.

periodic ▶ **adjective** *Michael made periodic visits to the hospital* **regular,** periodical, at fixed intervals, recurrent, recurring, repeated, cyclical, cyclic, seasonal; occasional, infrequent, intermittent, sporadic, spasmodic, odd.

periodical ▶ **noun** *he wrote for two periodicals* **journal,** publication, magazine, newspaper, paper, review, digest, gazette, newsletter, organ, quarterly, annual, weekly; informal mag, glossy.

peripatetic ▶ **adjective** *I could never get used to her peripatetic lifestyle* **nomadic,** itinerant, traveling, wandering, roving, roaming, migrant, migratory, unsettled.

peripheral ▶ **adjective 1** *the city's peripheral subdivisions* **outlying,** outer, on the edge/outskirts, surrounding.
2 *peripheral issues* **secondary,** subsidiary, incidental, tangential, marginal, minor, unimportant, lesser, inessential, nonessential, immaterial, ancillary.
ANTONYMS central.

periphery ▶ **noun** *rambling estates on the periphery of the city* **edge,** outer edge, margin, fringe, boundary, border, perimeter, rim, verge, borderline; outskirts, outer limits/reaches, bounds; literary bourn, marge.
ANTONYMS center.

periphrastic ▶ **adjective** *the periphrastic nature of legal syntax* **circumlocutory,** circuitous, roundabout, indirect, tautological, pleonastic, prolix, verbose, wordy, long-winded, rambling, wandering, tortuous, diffuse.

perish ▶ **verb 1** *millions of soldiers perished* **die,** lose one's life, be killed, fall, expire, meet one's death, be lost, lay down one's life, breathe one's last, pass away, go the way of all flesh, give up the ghost, go to glory, meet one's maker, cross the great divide; informal kick the bucket, turn up one's toes, shuffle off this mortal coil, buy it, croak, bite the big one, buy the farm; archaic decease, depart this life.
2 *must these hopes perish so soon?* **come to an end,** die (away), disappear, vanish, fade, dissolve, evaporate, melt away, wither.
3 *the rubber had perished* **go bad,** go off,

spoil, rot, go moldy, molder, putrefy, decay, decompose.

perjure ▶ verb
– PHRASES **perjure oneself** *he made the regrettable mistake of perjuring himself* **lie under oath,** lie, commit perjury, give false evidence/testimony; formal forswear oneself, be forsworn.

perjury ▶ noun *she was found guilty of perjury* **lying under oath,** giving false evidence/testimony, making false statements, willful falsehood.

perk[1] ▶
– PHRASES **perk up 1** *you seem to have perked up* **cheer up,** brighten up, liven up, take heart; informal buck up. **2** *the economy has been slow to perk up* **recover,** rally, improve, revive, take a turn for the better, look up, pick up, bounce back. **3** *you could do with something to perk you up* **cheer up,** liven up, brighten up, raise someone's spirits, give someone a boost/lift, revitalize, invigorate, energize, enliven, ginger up, put new life/heart into, put some spark into, rejuvenate, refresh, vitalize; informal buck up, pep up.

perk[2] ▶ noun *a job with a lot of perks* **fringe benefit,** additional benefit, benefit, advantage, bonus, extra, plus; informal freebie; formal perquisite.

permanence ▶ noun *the permanence of their relationship gives them a mutual sense of security* **stability,** durability, permanency, fixity, fixedness, changelessness, immutability, endurance, constancy, continuity, immortality, indestructibility, perpetuity, endlessness.

permanent ▶ adjective **1** *permanent brain damage* **lasting,** enduring, indefinite, continuing, perpetual, everlasting, eternal, abiding, constant, irreparable, irreversible, lifelong, indissoluble, indelible, standing, perennial, unending, endless, never-ending, immutable, undying, imperishable, indestructible, ineradicable; literary sempiternal, perdurable.
ANTONYMS temporary.
2 *a permanent job* **long-term,** stable, secure, durable.
ANTONYMS temporary.

permanently ▶ adverb **1** *the attack left her permanently disabled* **for all time,** forever, forevermore, for good, for always, for ever and ever, (for) evermore, until hell freezes over, in perpetuity, indelibly, immutably, until the end of time; informal for keeps, until the cows come home, until kingdom come; archaic for aye.
2 *I was permanently hungry* **continually,** constantly, perpetually, always.

permeate ▶ verb **1** *the delicious smell permeated the entire apartment* **pervade,** spread through, fill, filter through, diffuse through, imbue, penetrate, pass through, percolate through, perfuse, charge, suffuse, steep, impregnate, inform.
2 *these resins are able to permeate the timber* **soak through,** penetrate, seep through, saturate, transfuse, percolate through, leach through.

permissible ▶ adjective *permissible levels of atmospheric pollution* **permitted,** allowable, allowed, acceptable, legal, lawful, legitimate, admissible, licit, authorized, sanctioned, tolerated; informal legit, OK.
ANTONYMS forbidden.

permission ▶ noun *so, do I have permission to use the car?* **authorization,** consent, leave, authority, sanction, license, dispensation, assent, acquiescence, agreement, approval, seal/stamp of approval, approbation, endorsement, blessing, imprimatur, clearance, allowance, tolerance, sufferance, empowerment; informal the go-ahead, the thumbs up, the OK, the green light, say-so. See note at **LIBERTY**.

permissive ▶ adjective *our parents were far less permissive than we are* **liberal,** broad-minded, open-minded, free, free and easy, easygoing, live-and-let-live, latitudinarian, laissez-faire, libertarian, tolerant, forbearing, indulgent, lenient; overindulgent, lax, soft. See note at **LENIENT**.
ANTONYMS intolerant, strict.

permit ▶ verb *I cannot permit you to leave | I cannot permit your leaving* **allow,** authorize, give someone permission, sanction, grant, give someone the right, license, empower, enable, entitle, qualify; give one's blessing to, give the nod to; consent to, assent to, acquiesce in, agree to, tolerate, countenance; legalize, legitimate; informal give the go-ahead to, give the thumbs up to, OK, give the OK to, give the green light to; formal accede to; archaic suffer; (**permit someone to**) let.
ANTONYMS ban, forbid.
▶ noun *I need to see your permit* **authorization,** license, pass, ticket, warrant, document, certification; passport, visa.

permutation ▶ noun *all the possible permutations were explored* **arrangement,** order, grouping, organization, disposition, sorting, configuration, presentation, selection.

pernicious ▶ adjective *a pernicious influence on society* **harmful,** damaging, destructive, injurious, hurtful, detrimental, deleterious, dangerous, adverse, inimical, unhealthy, unfavorable, bad, evil, baleful, wicked, malign, malevolent, malignant, noxious, poisonous, corrupting; literary maleficent.
ANTONYMS beneficial.

perpendicular ▶ adjective **1** *the perpendicular stones* **upright,** vertical, erect, plumb, straight (up and down), on end, standing, upended.
ANTONYMS horizontal.
2 *lines perpendicular to each other* **at right angles,** at 90 degrees.
3 *the perpendicular hillside* **steep,** sheer, precipitous, abrupt, bluff, vertiginous.

perpetrate ▶ verb *they perpetrated a series of armed robberies* **commit,** carry out, perform, execute, do, effect, bring about, accomplish; be guilty of, be to blame for, be responsible for, inflict, wreak; informal pull off; formal effectuate.

perpetual ▶ adjective **1** *deep caves in perpetual darkness* **everlasting,** never-ending, eternal, permanent, unending, endless, without

end, lasting, long-lasting, constant, abiding, enduring, perennial, timeless, ageless, deathless, undying, immortal; unfailing, unchanging, never-changing, changeless, unfading; rare sempiternal, perdurable.
ANTONYMS transitory, temporary.
2 *a perpetual state of fear* **constant**, permanent, uninterrupted, continuous, unremitting, unending, unceasing, persistent, unbroken.
ANTONYMS intermittent.
3 *her mother's perpetual nagging* **interminable**, incessant, ceaseless, endless, without respite, relentless, unrelenting, persistent, continual, continuous, nonstop, never-ending, recurrent, repeated, unremitting, sustained, around/round-the-clock, chronic, unabating; informal eternal.

perpetuate ▶ verb *must you perpetuate these stupid myths?* **keep alive**, keep going, preserve, conserve, sustain, maintain, continue, extend, carry on, keep up, prolong; immortalize, commemorate, memorialize, eternalize.

perpetuity ▶ noun
– PHRASES **in perpetuity** *the archive will be preserved in perpetuity as a unified collection* **forever**, forevermore, permanently, for always, for good, perpetually, for ever and ever, for all time, until the end of time, until hell freezes over, eternally, for eternity, everlastingly; informal for keeps; archaic for aye.

perplex ▶ verb *the bizarre notes left at each of these crime scenes perplexed us* **puzzle**, baffle, mystify, bemuse, bewilder, confound, confuse, disconcert, dumbfound, throw, throw/catch off balance, exercise, worry; informal flummox, be all Greek to, stump, bamboozle, floor, beat, faze, fox; informal discombobulate.

perplexing ▶ adjective *he was famous for solving the most perplexing cases* **puzzling**, baffling, mystifying, mysterious, bewildering, confusing, disconcerting, worrying, unaccountable, difficult to understand, beyond one, paradoxical, peculiar, funny, strange, weird, odd.

perplexity ▶ noun 1 *he scratched his head in perplexity* **confusion**, bewilderment, puzzlement, bafflement, incomprehension, mystification, bemusement; informal bamboozlement, discombobulation.
2 *the perplexities of international relations* **complexity**, complication, intricacy, problem, difficulty, mystery, puzzle, enigma, paradox.

perquisite ▶ noun formal See PERK².

persecute ▶ verb 1 *they were persecuted for their religious beliefs* **oppress**, abuse, victimize, ill-treat, mistreat, maltreat, tyrannize, torment, torture; martyr.
2 *she was persecuted by the press* **harass**, hound, plague, badger, harry, intimidate, pick on, pester, bother, devil, bully, victimize, terrorize; informal hassle, give someone a hard time, get on someone's case.

perseverance ▶ noun *in a competitive environment, perseverance is an invaluable asset* **persistence**, tenacity, determination, staying power, indefatigability, steadfastness, purposefulness; patience, endurance, application, diligence, dedication, commitment, doggedness, assiduity, tirelessness, stamina; intransigence, obstinacy; informal stick-to-it-iveness; formal pertinacity.

persevere ▶ verb *she will persevere regardless of the obstacles* **persist**, continue, carry on, go on, keep on, keep going, struggle on, hammer away, be persistent, be determined, see/follow something through, keep at it, press on/ahead, not take no for an answer, be tenacious, stand one's ground, stand fast/firm, hold on, go the distance, stay the course, plod on, stop at nothing, leave no stone unturned; informal soldier on, hang on, plug away, stick to one's guns, stick it out, hang in there.
ANTONYMS give up.

persist ▶ verb 1 *Corbett persisted with his questioning* See PERSEVERE.
2 *if dry weather persists, water the lawn thoroughly* **continue**, hold, carry on, last, keep on, keep up, remain, linger, stay, endure.

persistence ▶ noun See PERSEVERANCE.

persistent ▶ adjective 1 *a very persistent man* **tenacious**, persevering, determined, resolute, purposeful, dogged, single-minded, tireless, indefatigable, patient, unflagging, untiring, insistent, importunate, relentless, unrelenting; stubborn, intransigent, obstinate, obdurate; formal pertinacious.
ANTONYMS irresolute.
2 *persistent rain* **constant**, continuous, continuing, continual, nonstop, never-ending, steady, uninterrupted, unbroken, interminable, incessant, unceasing, endless, unending, perpetual, unremitting, unrelenting, relentless, unrelieved, sustained.
ANTONYMS occasional, intermittent.
3 *a persistent cough* **chronic**, permanent, nagging, frequent; repeated, habitual.

persnickety ▶ adjective informal *my persnickety boss makes us disinfect the drawers in the cash register every night* **fussy**, difficult to please, difficult, finicky, overfastidious, fastidious, overparticular, particular, faddish, punctilious, hair-splitting, critical, overcritical; informal nitpicking, choosy, picky.
ANTONYMS easygoing.

person ▶ noun *that person over there is the one who called the police* **human being**, individual, man/woman, child, human, being, (living) soul, mortal, creature; personage, character, customer; informal type, sort, cookie; informal dated body, dog; archaic wight.
– PHRASES **in person** *I hope to talk to you in person before I leave Cleveland* **physically**, in the flesh, in propria persona, personally; oneself; informal as large as life.

persona ▶ noun *her stage persona is nothing like the real Muriel* **image**, face, public face, character, personality, identity, self; front, facade, guise, exterior, role, part.

personable ▶ adjective *I was blessed with the most personable in-laws* **pleasant**, agreeable, likable, nice, amiable, affable, charming, congenial, genial, simpatico, engaging, pleasing; attractive, presentable, good-looking, nice-looking, pretty, appealing; Scottish bonny.
ANTONYMS disagreeable, unattractive.

personage ▶ noun *we always have a table for a personage such as yourself* **important person,** VIP, luminary, celebrity, personality, name, famous name, household name, public figure, star, leading light, dignitary, notable, notability, worthy, panjandrum; person; informal celeb, somebody, big shot, big wheel, big kahuna, big cheese.

personal ▶ adjective **1** *a highly personal style* **distinctive,** characteristic, unique, individual, one's own, particular, peculiar, idiosyncratic, individualized, personalized.
ANTONYMS public, general.
2 *a personal appearance* **in person,** in the flesh, actual, live, physical.
3 *his personal life* **private,** intimate; confidential, secret.
4 *a personal friend* **intimate,** close, dear, great, bosom.
5 *I have personal knowledge of the family* **direct,** empirical, firsthand, immediate, experiential.
6 *personal remarks* **derogatory,** ad hominem; disparaging, belittling, insulting, critical, rude, slighting, disrespectful, offensive, pejorative.

personality ▶ noun **1** *her cheerful personality* **character,** nature, disposition, temperament, makeup, persona, psyche.
2 *she had loads of personality* **charisma,** magnetism, strength/force of personality, character, charm, presence.
3 *a famous personality* **celebrity,** VIP, star, superstar, name, famous name, household name, big name, somebody, leading light, luminary, notable, personage, notability; informal celeb.

personalize ▶ verb **1** *products that can be personalized to your requirements* **customize,** individualize.
2 *attempts to personalize God* **personify,** humanize, anthropomorphize.

personally ▶ adverb **1** *I'd like to thank you personally* **in person,** oneself.
2 *personally, I think it's a good idea* **for my part,** for myself, to my way of thinking, to my mind, in my estimation, as far as I am concerned, in my view/opinion, from my point of view, from where I stand, as I see it, if you ask me, my sense is, for my money, in my book; privately.
– PHRASES **take personally** *please don't take this personally, but I think the trim should be a shade darker* **take offense,** take something amiss, be offended, be upset, be affronted, take umbrage, take exception, feel insulted, feel hurt.

personification ▶ noun *Foote is the personification of heroism* **embodiment,** incarnation, epitome, quintessence, essence, type, symbol, soul, model, exemplification, exemplar, image, representation.

personify ▶ verb *the picture on the label should personify good, wholesome American cooking* **epitomize,** embody, hypostatize, typify, exemplify, represent, symbolize, stand for, be the incarnation of, body forth, put a face on.

personnel ▶ noun *sales personnel* **staff,** employees, workforce, workers, labor force, human resources, manpower, wage labor; informal liveware.

perspective ▶ noun **1** *her perspective on things had changed* **outlook,** view, viewpoint, point of view, POV, standpoint, position, stand, stance, angle, slant, attitude, frame of mind, frame of reference, approach, way of looking, interpretation.
2 *a perspective of the whole valley* **view,** vista, panorama, prospect, bird's-eye view, outlook, aspect.

perspicacious ▶ adjective *his perspicacious advisers recommended caution* **discerning,** shrewd, perceptive, astute, penetrating, observant, percipient, sharp-witted, sharp, smart, alert, clear-sighted, farsighted, acute, clever, canny, intelligent, insightful, wise, sage, sensitive, intuitive, understanding, aware, discriminating; informal on the ball, heads-up, with it. See note at KEEN.
ANTONYMS stupid.

perspiration ▶ noun *you should avoid products that prevent normal perspiration* **sweat,** moisture; Medicine diaphoresis.

perspire ▶ verb *it's natural to perspire under these hot lights* **sweat,** be dripping/pouring with sweat, glow.

persuade ▶ verb **1** *he tried to persuade her to come with him* **prevail on,** coax, convince, get, induce, win over, bring around, coerce, influence, sway, inveigle, entice, tempt, lure, cajole, wheedle; Law procure; informal sweet-talk, twist someone's arm; (**persuade someone to**) make. See note at CONVINCE.
ANTONYMS dissuade, deter.
2 *a shortage of money persuaded them to abandon the scheme* **cause,** lead, move, dispose, incline.

persuasion ▶ noun **1** *Monica needed plenty of persuasion* **coaxing,** persuading, coercion, inducement, convincing, blandishment, encouragement, urging, inveiglement, cajolery, enticement, wheedling; informal sweet-talking, arm-twisting; formal suasion.
2 *various political and religious persuasions* **group,** grouping, sect, denomination, party, camp, side, faction, affiliation, school of thought, belief, creed, credo, faith, philosophy. See note at OPINION.

persuasive ▶ adjective *her argument is quite persuasive* **convincing,** cogent, compelling, potent, forceful, powerful, eloquent, impressive, influential, sound, valid, strong, effective, winning, telling; plausible, credible.
ANTONYMS unconvincing.

pert ▶ adjective **1** *a pert little hat* **jaunty,** neat, chic, trim, stylish, smart, perky, rakish; informal natty, sassy.
2 *a young girl with a pert manner* **impudent,** impertinent, cheeky, irreverent, forward, insolent, disrespectful, flippant, familiar, presumptuous, bold, as bold as brass, brazen; informal fresh, saucy, sassy.

pertain ▶ verb **1** *developments* ***pertaining to*** *the economy* **concern,** relate to, be related to, be connected with, be relevant to, regard, apply to, be pertinent to, refer to, have a bearing on, appertain to, bear on, affect, involve, touch on.
2 *the stock and assets* ***pertaining to*** *the business*

belong to, be a part of, be included in.
3 *the economic situation that pertained at that time* **exist,** be the order of the day, be the case, prevail; formal obtain.

pertinacious ▶ **adjective** formal *they were quite pertinacious in their demands* **determined,** tenacious, persistent, persevering, purposeful, resolute, dogged, indefatigable, insistent, single-minded, unrelenting, relentless, tireless, unshakable; stubborn, obstinate, inflexible, unbending. See note at **STUBBORN**.
ANTONYMS irresolute, tentative.

pertinent ▶ **adjective** *he asked a lot of pertinent questions* **relevant,** to the point, apposite, appropriate, suitable, fitting, fit, apt, applicable, material, germane, to the purpose, apropos; formal ad rem.
ANTONYMS irrelevant.

perturb ▶ **verb** *David's appearance perturbs his parents* **worry,** upset, unsettle, disturb, concern, trouble, disquiet; disconcert, discomfit, unnerve, alarm, bother, distress, dismay, gnaw at, agitate, fluster, ruffle, discountenance; informal rattle, throw.
ANTONYMS reassure.

perturbed ▶ **adjective** *our pets are perturbed by all the construction going on next door* **upset,** worried, unsettled, disturbed, concerned, troubled, anxious, ill at ease, uneasy, disquieted, fretful; disconcerted, discomposed, distressed, unnerved, alarmed, bothered, dismayed, agitated, flustered, ruffled, shaken, discountenanced; informal twitchy, rattled, fazed, unstrung; discombobulated.
ANTONYMS calm.

peruse ▶ **verb** *perusing the racing forms* **read,** study, scrutinize, inspect, examine, wade through, look through; browse through, leaf through, scan, run one's eye over, glance through, flick through, skim through, thumb through, dip into.

pervade ▶ **verb** *the smell of floor polish pervaded the house* **permeate,** spread through, fill, suffuse, be diffused through, imbue, penetrate, filter through, percolate through, infuse, perfuse, flow through; charge, steep, saturate, impregnate, inform.

pervasive ▶ **adjective** *the low-carb craze is pervasive* **prevalent,** pervading, permeating, extensive, ubiquitous, omnipresent, universal, rife, widespread, general.

perverse ▶ **adjective 1** *he is being deliberately perverse* **awkward,** contrary, difficult, unreasonable, uncooperative, unhelpful, obstructive, disobliging, recalcitrant, stubborn, obstinate, obdurate, mulish, pigheaded, bullheaded; formal refractory. See note at **STUBBORN**.
ANTONYMS accommodating, cooperative.
2 *a verdict that is manifestly perverse* **illogical,** irrational, unreasonable, wrong, wrong-headed.
ANTONYMS reasonable.
3 *an evil life dedicated to perverse pleasure* **perverted,** depraved, unnatural, abnormal, deviant, degenerate, immoral, warped, twisted, corrupt; wicked, base, evil; informal kinky, sick, pervy. See note at **DEPRAVED**.

perversion ▶ **noun 1** *a twisted perversion of the truth* **distortion,** misrepresentation, falsification, travesty, misinterpretation, misconstruction, twisting, corruption, subversion, misuse, misapplication, debasement.
2 *sexual perversion* **deviance,** abnormality; depravity, degeneracy, debauchery, corruption, vice, wickedness, immorality.

perversity ▶ **noun 1** *out of sheer perversity, he refused* **contrariness,** awkwardness, recalcitrance, stubbornness, obstinacy, obduracy, mulishness, pigheadedness; formal refractoriness.
2 *the perversity of the decision* **unreasonableness,** irrationality, illogicality, wrong-headedness.

pervert ▶ **verb 1** *people who attempt to pervert the rules* **distort,** corrupt, subvert, twist, bend, abuse, misapply, misuse, misrepresent, misinterpret, falsify.
2 *men can be perverted by power* **corrupt,** lead astray, debase, warp, pollute, poison, deprave, debauch.
▶ **noun** *a sexual pervert* **deviant,** degenerate; informal perv, dirty old man, sicko.

perverted ▶ **adjective** *I don't want to hear any more of your perverted stories* **unnatural,** deviant, warped, corrupt, twisted, abnormal, unhealthy, depraved, perverse, aberrant, immoral, debauched, debased, degenerate, evil, wicked, vile, amoral, wrong, bad; informal sick, sicko, kinky, pervy.

pessimism ▶ **noun** *Felicia has apparently drawn him out of his pessimism* **defeatism,** negativity, doom and gloom, gloominess, miserablism, cynicism, fatalism; hopelessness, depression, despair, despondency, angst.

pessimist ▶ **noun** *pessimists have been predicting the doom of the planet for thousands of years* **defeatist,** fatalist, prophet of doom, cynic, doomsayer, doomster, Cassandra; skeptic, doubter, doubting Thomas; misery, miserablist, killjoy, Job's comforter; informal doom (and gloom) merchant, wet blanket, Chicken Little, gloomy Gus.
ANTONYMS optimist, Pollyanna.

pessimistic ▶ **adjective** *a pessimistic outlook on life* **gloomy,** negative, defeatist, downbeat, cynical, bleak, fatalistic, dark, black, despairing, despondent, depressed, hopeless; suspicious, distrustful, doubting.
ANTONYMS optimistic.

pest ▶ **noun** *Dan is dating the girl he used to think was such a pest* **nuisance,** annoyance, irritation, irritant, thorn in one's flesh/side, vexation, trial, the bane of one's life, menace, trouble, problem, worry, bother; informal pain (in the neck), aggravation, headache, nudnik.

pester ▶ **verb** *is there someplace I can study where no one will pester me?* **badger,** hound, harass, plague, annoy, bother, trouble, keep after, persecute, torment, bedevil, harry, worry, beleaguer, nag, hassle, bug, devil, get on someone's case.

pestilence ▶ **noun** archaic See **PLAGUE** (sense 1 of the noun).

pet ▶ **noun** *the teacher's pet* **favorite,** darling, the

apple of one's eye; informal fair-haired boy/girl.
▶ adjective 1 *a pet lamb* **tame,** domesticated, domestic, housebroken, house-trained.
2 *his pet theory* **favorite,** favored, cherished, dear to one's heart; particular, special, personal.
▶ verb 1 *the cats came to be petted* **stroke,** caress, fondle, pat.
2 *she had always been petted by her parents* **pamper,** spoil, mollycoddle, coddle, cosset, baby, indulge, overindulge.
3 *couples were petting in their cars* **kiss and cuddle,** kiss, cuddle, embrace, caress; informal make out, canoodle, neck, smooch, get it on.
– PHRASES **pet name** *'Cuddles' is a pet name John gave to me years ago* **affectionate name,** term of endearment, endearment, nickname, diminutive; rare hypocoristic.

peter ▶ verb
– PHRASES **peter out** *our enthusiasm eventually petered out* **fizzle out,** fade (away), die away/out, dwindle, diminish, taper off, tail off, trail away/off, wane, ebb, melt away, evaporate, disappear, come to an end, subside.

petition ▶ noun 1 *more than 1,000 people signed the petition* **appeal,** round robin.
2 *petitions to the king* **entreaty,** supplication, plea, prayer, appeal, request, invocation, suit; archaic orison.
▶ verb *they petitioned the governor to revoke the decision* **appeal to,** request, ask, call on, entreat, beg, implore, plead with, apply to, press, urge; formal adjure; literary beseech. See note at **BEG**.

petrify ▶ verb *the thought of speaking in public petrified her* **terrify,** horrify, frighten, scare, scare/frighten to death, scare/frighten the living daylights out of, scare/frighten the life out of, strike terror into, put the fear of God into; paralyze, transfix; informal scare the pants off, scare the bejesus out of.

petty ▶ adjective 1 *petty regulations* **trivial,** trifling, minor, small, unimportant, insignificant, inconsequential, inconsiderable, negligible, paltry, footling, pettifogging; informal piffling, piddling, fiddling.
ANTONYMS important, serious.
2 *a petty form of revenge* **small-minded,** mean, ungenerous, shabby, spiteful.
ANTONYMS magnanimous.

petulant ▶ adjective *he's as petulant as a spoiled child* **peevish,** bad-tempered, querulous, pettish, fretful, cross, irritable, sulky, snappish, crotchety, touchy, tetchy, testy, fractious, grumpy, disgruntled, crabby; informal grouchy, cranky.
ANTONYMS good-humored.

phantom ▶ noun 1 *a phantom who haunts lonely roads* **ghost,** apparition, spirit, specter, wraith; informal spook; literary phantasm, shade.
2 *the phantoms of an overactive imagination* **delusion,** figment of the imagination, hallucination, illusion, chimera, vision, mirage.

phase ▶ noun 1 *the final phase of the campaign* **stage,** period, chapter, episode, part, step, point, time, juncture.
2 *he's going through a difficult phase* **period,** stage, time, spell, patch.
3 *the phases of the moon* **aspect,** shape, form, appearance, state, condition.
– PHRASES **phase in** *compliance with the new regulations will be phased in over a six-month period* **introduce gradually,** begin to use, ease in. **phase out** *we're going to phase out the cash-rebate program* **withdraw gradually,** discontinue, stop using, run down, wind down.

phenomenal ▶ adjective *sales growth has been nothing short of phenomenal* **remarkable,** exceptional, extraordinary, amazing, astonishing, astounding, sensational, stunning, incredible, unbelievable; marvelous, magnificent, wonderful, outstanding, singular, out of the ordinary, unusual, unprecedented; informal fantastic, terrific, tremendous, stupendous, awesome, out of this world; literary wondrous.
ANTONYMS ordinary.

phenomenon ▶ noun 1 *a rare phenomenon* **occurrence,** event, happening, fact, situation, circumstance, experience, case, incident, episode.
2 *the band was a pop phenomenon* **marvel,** sensation, wonder, prodigy, miracle, rarity, nonpareil; informal humdinger, phenom, stunner, doozy, ripsnorter.

philander ▶ verb *he had no time or inclination to philander* **womanize,** have affairs, flirt; informal play around, carry on, play the field, sleep around, fool around.

philanderer ▶ noun *everyone warned me he was a philanderer* **womanizer,** Casanova, Don Juan, Lothario, flirt, ladies' man, playboy, rake, roué; informal stud, skirt-chaser, ladykiller, wolf.

philanthropic ▶ adjective *a philanthropic millionaire* **charitable,** generous, benevolent, humanitarian, public-spirited, altruistic, magnanimous, munificent, openhanded, bountiful, liberal, generous to a fault, beneficent, caring, compassionate, unselfish, kind, kind-hearted, bighearted; formal eleemosynary.
ANTONYMS selfish, mean.

philanthropist ▶ noun *the trust was funded by an anonymous philanthropist* **benefactor,** benefactress, patron, patroness, donor, contributor, sponsor, backer, helper, good Samaritan; do-gooder, Lady Bountiful; historical almsgiver.

philanthropy ▶ noun *a family noted for its philanthropy* **benevolence,** generosity, humanitarianism, public-spiritedness, altruism, social conscience, charity, charitableness, brotherly love, fellow feeling, magnanimity, munificence, liberality, largesse, openhandedness, bountifulness, beneficence, unselfishness, humanity, kindness, kindheartedness, compassion; historical almsgiving.

philippic ▶ noun literary *no publisher wanted to touch his scathing philippic* **tirade,** diatribe, harangue, lecture, attack, onslaught, denunciation, rant, polemic, broadside, fulmination, condemnation, criticism, censure; informal blast.

philistine ▶ adjective *a romantic visionary, persecuted by a philistine establishment* **uncultured,** lowbrow, anti-intellectual, uncultivated, uncivilized, uneducated, unenlightened, commercial, materialist, bourgeois; ignorant, crass, boorish, barbarian.

philosopher ▶ noun *when I was young, I failed to appreciate what an insightful philosopher my father was* **thinker,** theorist, theorizer, theoretician, metaphysicist, metaphysician; scholar, intellectual, sage, wise man.

philosophical ▶ adjective **1** *a philosophical question* **theoretical,** metaphysical.
2 *a philosophical mood* **thoughtful,** reflective, pensive, meditative, contemplative, introspective, ruminative; formal cogitative.
3 *he was philosophical about losing the contract* **calm,** composed, cool, collected, 'calm, cool, and collected', self-possessed, serene, tranquil, stoical, impassive, dispassionate, phlegmatic, unperturbed, imperturbable, unruffled, patient, forbearing, long-suffering, resigned, rational, realistic.

philosophy ▶ noun **1** *the philosophy of Aristotle* **thinking,** thought, reasoning.
2 *her political philosophy* **beliefs,** credo, convictions, ideology, ideas, thinking, notions, theories, doctrine, tenets, principles, views, school of thought; informal ism.

phlegmatic ▶ adjective *I come from a very demonstrative, emotional Italian family—I can't remember one phlegmatic moment from my childhood* **calm,** cool, composed, 'calm, cool, and collected', controlled, serene, tranquil, placid, impassive, imperturbable, unruffled, dispassionate, philosophical; stolid, dull, bland, unemotional, lifeless; informal unflappable.
ANTONYMS excitable.

phobia ▶ noun *fear of spiders is just one of his many phobias* **fear,** irrational fear, obsessive fear, dread, horror, terror, hatred, loathing, detestation, aversion, antipathy, revulsion; complex, neurosis; informal thing, hang-up.

phone ▶ noun *she tried to reach you on your phone* **telephone,** cell phone, cell, car phone, cordless phone, speakerphone; extension; informal blower, horn.
▶ verb *I'll phone you later* **telephone,** call, give someone a call; informal call up, give someone a buzz, get someone on the horn/blower.

phony informal ▶ adjective *a phony address* **bogus,** false, fake, fraudulent, spurious; counterfeit, forged, feigned; pseudo, imitation, sham, man-made, mock, ersatz, synthetic, artificial; simulated, pretended, contrived, affected, insincere, inauthentic; informal pretend, put-on.
ANTONYMS authentic.
▶ noun **1** *he's nothing but a phony* **impostor,** sham, fake, fraud, charlatan; informal con artist.
2 *the diamond's a phony* **fake,** imitation, counterfeit, forgery.

photocopy ▶ noun *we kept a photocopy for our records* **copy,** facsimile, duplicate, reproduction; trademark Xerox.

photograph ▶ noun *a photograph of her father* **picture,** photo, snapshot, shot, image, likeness, print, slide, transparency, still, enlargement, snap; informal mug shot, head shot.
▶ verb *she was photographed leaving the castle* **take someone's picture/photo,** snap, shoot, film.

photographic ▶ adjective **1** *a photographic record* **pictorial,** in photographs; cinematic, filmic.
2 *a photographic memory* **detailed,** graphic, exact, precise, accurate, vivid, picture-perfect.

phrase ▶ noun *familiar words and phrases* **expression,** group of words, construction, locution, term, turn of phrase; idiom, idiomatic expression; saying, tag.
▶ verb *how could I phrase the question?* **express,** put into words, put, word, style, formulate, couch, frame, articulate, verbalize.

phraseology ▶ noun *no phraseology is more endearing than that of Miss Sallie* **wording,** choice of words, phrasing, way of speaking/writing, usage, idiom, diction, parlance, words, language, vocabulary, terminology; jargon; informal lingo, -speak, -ese.

physical ▶ adjective **1** *physical pleasure* **bodily,** corporeal, corporal, somatic; carnal, fleshly, nonspiritual.
ANTONYMS mental, spiritual.
2 *hard physical work* **manual,** laboring, labor-intensive, blue-collar.
ANTONYMS intellectual, clerical.
3 *the physical universe* **material,** concrete, tangible, palpable, solid, substantial, real, actual, visible.
ANTONYMS intangible, abstract.

physician ▶ noun *consult your physician first* **doctor,** doctor of medicine, MD, medical practitioner, general practitioner, GP, clinician, family doctor; specialist, consultant; informal doc, quack, medic, medico; intern, resident; informal dated sawbones.

physique ▶ noun *the physique of an athlete* **body,** build, figure, frame, anatomy, shape, form, proportions; muscles, musculature; informal vital statistics, bod.

pick ▶ verb **1** *I got a job picking apples* **harvest,** gather (in), collect, pluck; literary cull.
2 *pick the time that suits you best* **choose,** select, pick out, single out, take, opt for, elect, decide on, settle on, fix on, sift out, sort out; name, nominate.
3 *Beth* **picked at** *her food* **nibble (at),** toy with, play with, eat like a bird.
4 *people were picking guitars and singing* **strum,** twang, thrum, pluck.
5 *he tried to pick a fight* **provoke,** start, cause, incite, stir up, whip up, instigate, prompt, bring about.
▶ noun **1** *take your pick* **choice,** selection, option, decision; preference, favorite.
2 *the pick of the crop* **best,** finest, top, choice, choicest, prime, cream, flower, prize, pearl, gem, jewel, jewel in the crown, crème de la crème, elite.
– PHRASES **pick on** *why don't you pick on somebody your own size?* **bully,** victimize, tyrannize, torment, persecute, criticize, harass, hound, taunt, tease; informal get at, have it in for, be down on, needle. **pick out 1** *one painting was picked out for special mention* **choose,** select, single out, opt for, decide on, elect, settle on, fix on, sift out, sort out; name, nominate.
2 *she picked out Jessica in the crowd* **see,**

make out, distinguish, discern, spot, perceive, detect, notice, recognize, identify, catch sight of, glimpse; literary espy, behold, descry. **pick up 1** *business has really picked up* **improve,** recover, be on the road to recovery, rally, make a comeback, bounce back, perk up, look up, take a turn for the better, turn the/a corner, be on the mend, make headway, make progress. **2** *they teach you the proper way to pick up heavy boxes* **lift**, take up, raise, hoist, scoop up, gather up, snatch up. **3** *I'll pick you up after lunch* **fetch,** collect, call for. **4** informal *she was picked up by the police* **arrest**, apprehend, detain, take into custody, seize; informal nab, run in, bust. **5** *we picked it up at a thrift store* **find,** discover, come across, stumble across, happen on, chance on; acquire, obtain, come by, get, procure; purchase, buy; informal get hold of, get/lay one's hands on, get one's mitts on, bag, land. **6** *she picked up a virus* **catch,** contract, get, come down with. **7** *he told us the bits of gossip he'd picked up* **hear,** hear tell, get wind of, be told, learn; glean, garner. **8** *we're picking up a distress signal* **receive,** detect, get, hear.

picket ▶ **noun 1** *forty pickets were arrested* **striker,** demonstrator, protester, objector, picketer.
2 *fences made of cedar pickets* **stake,** post, paling; upright, stanchion, piling.
▶ **verb** *over 200 people picketed the factory* **demonstrate at,** protest at, strike at, form a picket at, man the picket line at; blockade, shut off.

pickle ▶ **noun** informal *they got into a real pickle over this one* **plight**, predicament, mess, difficulty, trouble, dire/desperate straits, problem, quandary; informal tight corner, tight spot, jam, fix, scrape, bind, hole, hot water, fine kettle of fish.
▶ **verb** *fish pickled in brine* **preserve,** souse, marinate, conserve.

pick-me-up ▶ **noun 1** *a drink that's a good pick-me-up* **tonic,** restorative, energizer, stimulant, refresher, reviver; informal bracer; Medicine analeptic.
2 *his winning goal was a perfect pick-me-up* **boost,** boost to the spirits, fillip, stimulant, stimulus; informal shot in the arm.

pickpocket ▶ **noun** *a crowded outdoor event is a pickpocket's playground* **thief,** petty thief, purse-snatcher, sneak thief; archaic cutpurse.

picnic ▶ **noun 1** *a picnic on the beach* **outdoor meal,** alfresco meal, cookout, barbecue.
2 informal *working for him was no picnic* **easy task/job,** child's play, five-finger exercise, gift, walkover; informal piece of cake, cinch, breeze, kids' stuff, cakewalk, pushover, duck soup.

pictorial ▶ **adjective** *a pictorial essay on desegregation* **illustrated,** in pictures, in picture form, in photographs, photographic, graphic. See note at **GRAPHIC**.

picture ▶ **noun 1** *pictures in an art gallery* **painting, drawing,** sketch, oil painting, watercolor, print, canvas, portrait, portrayal, illustration, artwork, depiction, likeness, representation, image, icon, miniature, landscape; fresco, mural, wall painting; informal oil.
2 *we were told not to take pictures* **photograph,** photo, snap, snapshot, shot, print, slide, transparency, exposure, still, enlargement.
3 *do you have a picture of what your ideal home might look like?* **concept,** idea, impression, view, (mental) image, vision, visualization, notion.
4 *the picture of health* **personification,** embodiment, epitome, essence, quintessence, perfect example, soul, model.
5 *an all-star Hollywood picture* **movie,** film, motion picture, feature film; informal flick; dated moving picture.
▶ **verb 1** *he was pictured with his guests* **photograph,** take a photograph/photo of, snap, shoot, film.
2 *in the drawing they were pictured against a snowy background* **paint, draw,** sketch, depict, delineate, portray, show, illustrate.
3 *Anne still pictured Richard as he had been* **visualize,** see in one's mind's eye, conjure up a picture/image of, imagine, see, evoke.
– PHRASES **put in the picture** *please come in and sit down, and we'll put you in the picture* **inform,** fill in, explain the situation/circumstances to, bring up to date, update, brief, keep posted, clue in, bring up to speed.

picturesque ▶ **adjective 1** *a picturesque village* **attractive,** pretty, beautiful, lovely, scenic, charming, quaint, pleasing, delightful, picture-perfect.
ANTONYMS ugly, drab.
2 *a picturesque description* **vivid,** graphic, colorful, impressive, striking. See note at **GRAPHIC**.
ANTONYMS dull.

piddling ▶ **adjective** informal *I'm tired of your piddling complaints* **trivial,** trifling, petty, footling, slight, small, insignificant, unimportant, inconsequential, inconsiderable, negligible; meager, inadequate, insufficient, paltry, scant, scanty, derisory, pitiful, miserable, puny, niggardly, beggarly, mere; informal measly, pathetic, piffling, mingy, nickel-and-dime.

pie ▶ **noun** *the enticing aroma of fresh-baked pies* **pastry,** tart, turnover.
– PHRASES **pie in the sky** informal *they thought her dream of fame was just pie in the sky* **false hope,** illusion, delusion, fantasy, pipe dream, daydream, a castle in the air, a castle in Spain.

piebald ▶ **adjective** See **PIED**.

piece ▶ **noun 1** *a piece of cheese | a piece of wood* **bit,** slice, chunk, segment, section, lump, hunk, wedge, slab, block, cake, bar, cube, stick, length; offcut, sample, fragment, sliver, splinter, wafer, chip, crumb, scrap, remnant, shred, shard, snippet; mouthful, morsel. See note at **FRAGMENT**.
2 *the pieces of a clock* **component,** part, bit, section, segment, constituent, element; unit, module.
3 *a piece of furniture* **item,** article, specimen.
4 *a piece of the profit* **share,** portion, slice, quota, part, bit, percentage, amount, quantity, ration, fraction, division; informal cut.

5 *pieces from his private collection* **work (of art),** creation, production; composition, opus.
6 *the reporter who wrote the piece* **article,** item, story, report, essay, study, review, composition, column.
7 *the pieces on a game board* **token,** counter, man, disk, chip, marker.
– PHRASES **in one piece 1** *the camera was still in one piece* **unbroken,** entire, whole, intact, undamaged, unharmed. **2** *I'll bring her back in one piece* **unhurt,** uninjured, unscathed, safe, safe and sound. **in pieces** *the vase was in pieces* **broken,** in bits, shattered, smashed, in smithereens; informal bust, busted. **go/fall to pieces** *he went to pieces when his wife died* **have a breakdown,** break down, go out of one's mind, lose control, lose one's head, fall apart; informal crack up, lose it, come/fall apart at the seams, freak, freak out.

piecemeal ▶ **adverb** *the reforms were implemented piecemeal* **a little at a time,** piece by piece, bit by bit, gradually, slowly, in stages, in steps, step by step, little by little, by degrees, in/by fits and starts.

pied ▶ **adjective** *a lovely little pied pony* **particolored,** multicolored, variegated, black and white, brown and white, piebald, skewbald, dappled, brindle, spotted, mottled, speckled, flecked, pinto, calico, tabby.

pier ▶ **noun 1** *a boat was tied to the pier* **jetty,** quay, wharf, dock, levee, landing, landing stage.
2 *the piers of the bridge* **support,** cutwater, pile, piling, abutment, buttress, stanchion, prop, stay, upright, pillar, post, column.

pierce ▶ **verb 1** *the metal pierced his flesh* **penetrate,** puncture, perforate, prick, lance; stab, spike, stick, impale, transfix, bore through, drill through.
2 *his anguish pierced her very soul* **hurt,** wound, pain, sting, sear, grieve, distress, upset, trouble, harrow, afflict; affect, move.

piercing ▶ **adjective 1** *a piercing shriek* **shrill,** earsplitting, high-pitched, penetrating, strident, loud.
2 *the piercing wind* **bitter,** biting, cutting, penetrating, sharp, keen, stinging, raw; freezing, frigid, glacial, arctic, chill.
3 *a piercing pain* **intense,** excruciating, agonizing, sharp, stabbing, shooting, stinging, severe, extreme, fierce, searing, racking.
4 *his piercing gaze* **searching,** probing, penetrating, penetrative, shrewd, sharp, keen.
5 *his piercing intelligence* **perceptive,** percipient, perspicacious, penetrating, discerning, discriminating, intelligent, quick-witted, sharp, sharp-witted, shrewd, insightful, keen, acute, astute, clever, smart, incisive, razor-edged, trenchant.

piety ▶ **noun** *the piety of a saint* **devoutness,** devotion, piousness, religion, holiness, godliness, saintliness; veneration, reverence, faith, religious duty, spirituality, religious zeal, fervor; pietism, religiosity.

pig ▶ **noun 1** *a herd of pigs* **hog,** boar, sow, porker, swine, piglet; children's word piggy.
2 informal *he's such a pig, he'll eat us out of house and home* **glutton**; informal hog, greedy guts.

pigeonhole ▶ **verb 1** *they were pigeonholed as an indie guitar band* **categorize,** compartmentalize, classify, characterize, label, brand, tag, typecast, ghettoize, designate.
2 *the plan was pigeonholed last year* **postpone,** put off, put back, defer, shelve, hold over, put to one side, put on ice, mothball, put in cold storage; informal put on the back burner.

pigheaded ▶ **adjective** *you pigheaded old fool* **obstinate,** stubborn (as a mule), mulish, bullheaded, obdurate, headstrong, self-willed, willful, perverse, contrary, recalcitrant, stiff-necked; uncooperative, inflexible, uncompromising, intractable, intransigent, unyielding, bloody-minded; formal refractory.

pigment ▶ **noun** *a chestnut brown pigment* **coloring matter,** coloring, colorant, color, tint, dye, dyestuff.

pile[1] ▶ **noun 1** *a pile of stones* **heap,** stack, mound, pyramid, mass, quantity; collection, accumulation, assemblage, store, stockpile, hoard.
2 informal *I've got a pile of work to do* **great deal,** lot, large quantity/amount, mountain; abundance, cornucopia; informal load, heap, mass, slew, ocean, stack, ton.
3 informal *he'd made his pile in the fur trade* **fortune,** millions, billions; informal small fortune, bundle, wad.
▶ **verb 1** *she* **piled up** *the plates* **heap (up),** stack (up).
2 *he piled his plate with fried eggs* **load,** heap, fill (up), lade, stack, charge, stock.
3 *our debts were piling up* **increase,** grow, mount up, escalate, soar, spiral, leap up, shoot up, rocket, climb, accumulate, accrue, build up, multiply.
4 *we piled into the car* **crowd,** climb, pack, squeeze, push, shove.
– PHRASES **pile it on** informal *if you pile it on like that, no one will believe you* **exaggerate,** overstate the case, make a mountain out of a molehill, overdo it, overplay it, overdramatize; informal lay it on thick.

pile[2] ▶ **noun** *a wall supported by timber piles* **post,** stake, pillar, column, support, foundation, piling, abutment, pier, cutwater, buttress, stanchion, upright.

pile[3] ▶ **noun** *a carpet with a short pile* **nap,** fibers, threads.

pileup ▶ **noun** *a terrible pileup on I-95* **crash,** multiple crash, collision, multiple collision, smash, accident, road accident, wreck; informal smash-up.

pilfer ▶ **verb** *the gun was part of a cache pilfered from the air force* **steal,** thieve, take, snatch, purloin, loot; informal swipe, rob, nab, rip off, lift, "liberate", "borrow", filch, snaffle; pinch, heist.

pilgrim ▶ **noun** *the destination of these weary pilgrims* worshiper, devotee, believer; traveler, crusader; literary wayfarer; historical palmer.

pilgrimage ▶ **noun** *an annual pilgrimage to the Holy City* **religious journey,** religious expedition, hajj, crusade, mission. See note at **JOURNEY**.

pill ▶ **noun** *take one pill at bedtime* **tablet,** capsule, caplet, cap, gelcap, pellet, lozenge, pastille, horse pill; Veterinary Medicine bolus.

pillage ▶ verb 1 *the abbey was pillaged* **ransack,** rob, plunder, despoil, raid, loot; sack, devastate, lay waste, ravage, rape. See note at RAVAGE.
2 *columns pillaged from an ancient town* **steal,** pilfer, thieve, take, snatch, purloin, loot; informal swipe, rob, nab, rip off, lift, "liberate", "borrow", filch, snaffle, pinch, heist.
▶ noun *the rebels were intent on pillage* **robbery,** robbing, raiding, plunder, looting, sacking, rape, marauding; literary rapine.

pillar ▶ noun 1 *stone pillars* **column,** post, support, upright, baluster, pier, pile, pilaster, stanchion, prop, newel; obelisk, monolith.
2 *a pillar of the community* **stalwart,** mainstay, bastion, rock; leading light, worthy, backbone, support, upholder, champion, tower of strength.

pillory ▶ noun *offenders were put in the pillory* **stocks.**
▶ verb 1 *he was pilloried by the press* **attack,** criticize, censure, condemn, denigrate, lambaste, savage, stigmatize, denounce; informal knock, slam, pan, bash, crucify, hammer, pummel; formal excoriate.
2 *they were pilloried at school* **ridicule,** jeer at, sneer at, deride, mock, scorn, make fun of, poke fun at, laugh at, scoff at, tease, taunt; informal rib, josh, razz.

pillow ▶ noun *his head rested on the pillow* **cushion,** bolster, pad; headrest.
▶ verb *she pillowed her head on folded arms* **cushion,** cradle, rest, lay, support.

pilot ▶ noun 1 *a fighter pilot* **airman/airwoman,** flyer; captain, commander, co-pilot, wingman, first officer, bush pilot; informal skipper; dated aviator, aviatrix, aeronaut.
2 *a harbor pilot* **navigator,** helmsman, steersman, coxswain.
3 *a pilot for his new TV series* **trial episode;** sample, experiment, trial run.
▶ adjective *a pilot project* **experimental,** exploratory, trial, test, sample, speculative; preliminary.
▶ verb 1 *he piloted the jet to safety* **navigate,** guide, maneuver, steer, control, direct, captain, shepherd; fly, drive; sail; informal skipper.
2 *the questionnaire has been piloted* **test,** trial, try out; assess, investigate, examine, appraise, evaluate.

pimple ▶ noun *the last thing you want on prom night is a pimple* **zit,** pustule, bleb, boil, swelling, eruption, blackhead, whitehead, carbuncle, blister, spot; technical comedo, papule; (**pimples**) acne, bad skin.

pin ▶ noun 1 *fasten the hem with a pin* **tack,** safety pin, nail, staple, fastener.
2 *a broken pin in the machine* **bolt,** peg, rivet, dowel, screw.
3 *souvenir pins* **badge,** brooch.
▶ verb 1 *she pinned the brooch to her dress* **attach,** fasten, affix, fix, tack, clip; join, secure.
2 *they pinned him to the ground* **hold,** press, hold fast, hold down; restrain, pinion, immobilize.
3 *they* ***pinned*** *the crime* ***on*** *him* **blame for,** hold responsible for, attribute to, impute to, ascribe to; lay something at someone's door; informal stick on.
– PHRASES **pin down 1** *our troops can pin down the enemy* **confine, trap,** hem in, corner, close in, shut in, hedge in, pen in, restrain, entangle, enmesh, immobilize. **2** *she tried to pin him down to a plan* **constrain,** make someone commit themselves, pressure, tie down, nail down. **3** *it evoked a memory but he couldn't pin it down* **define,** put one's finger on, put into words, express, name, specify, identify, pinpoint, place.

pinch ▶ verb 1 *he pinched my arm* **tweak,** nip, squeeze, grasp.
2 *my new shoes pinch my toes* **hurt,** pain; squeeze, crush, cramp; be uncomfortable.
3 *I scraped and pinched to afford it* **economize,** scrimp (and save), be sparing, be frugal, cut back, tighten one's belt, retrench; informal be stingy, be tight.
4 informal *you pinched his baseball cards* **steal,** thieve, take, snatch, pilfer, purloin, loot; informal swipe, rob, nab, lift, "liberate", "borrow", filch, heist.
▶ noun 1 *he gave her arm a pinch* **tweak,** nip, squeeze.
2 *a pinch of salt* **bit,** touch, dash, spot, trace, soupçon, speck, taste; informal smidgen, tad.
– PHRASES **feel the pinch** *many of our customers are feeling the pinch* **suffer hardship,** be short of money, be poor, be impoverished. **in a pinch** *there's room for four adults, five in a pinch* **if necessary,** if need be, in an emergency, just possibly, with difficulty.

pinched ▶ adjective *their pinched faces* **strained,** stressed, fraught, tense, taut; tired, worn, drained, sapped; wan, peaked, pale, gray, blanched; thin, drawn, haggard, gaunt.
ANTONYMS healthy.

pine ▶ verb 1 *I am* ***pining away*** *from love* **languish,** decline, weaken, waste away, wilt, wither, fade, sicken, droop; brood, mope, moon.
2 *he was pining for his son* **yearn,** long, ache, sigh, hunger, languish; miss, mourn, lament, grieve over, shed tears for, bemoan, rue, eat one's heart out over; informal itch.

pinion ▶ verb *the hostages were pinioned to each other* **hold down,** pin down, restrain, hold fast, immobilize; tie, bind, truss (up), shackle, fetter, hobble, manacle, handcuff; informal cuff.

pink ▶ adjective *the meat should be slightly pink* **rose,** rosy, rosé, pale red, salmon, coral; flushed, blushing.
▶ noun informal *she's in the pink of condition* **prime,** perfection, best, finest, height; utmost, greatest, apex, zenith, acme, bloom.
– PHRASES **in the pink** informal *I'm finally in the pink again* **in good health,** very healthy, very well, hale and hearty; blooming, flourishing, thriving, vigorous, strong, lusty, robust, in fine fettle, (as) fit as a fiddle, in excellent shape.

pinnacle ▶ noun 1 *pinnacles of rock* **peak,** needle, crag, tor, aiguille, hoodoo; summit, crest, apex, tip.
2 *the pinnacles of the clock tower* **turret,** minaret, spire, finial, mirador.
3 *the pinnacle of the sport* **highest level,** peak, height, high point, top, capstone, apex, zenith, apogee, acme.

ANTONYMS nadir.

pinpoint ▶ noun *a pinpoint of light* **point,** spot, speck, dot, speckle.

▶ adjective *pinpoint accuracy* **precise,** strict, exact, meticulous, scrupulous, punctilious, accurate, careful.

▶ verb *pinpoint the cause of the trouble* **identify,** determine, distinguish, discover, find, locate, detect, track down, spot, diagnose, recognize, pin down, home in on, put one's finger on.

pioneer ▶ noun 1 *the pioneers of the Wild West* **settler,** colonist, colonizer, frontiersman, frontierswoman, explorer, trailblazer, bushwhacker.
2 *an aviation pioneer* **developer,** innovator, trailblazer, groundbreaker, spearhead; founder, founding father, architect, creator.

▶ verb *he pioneered the sale of insurance* **introduce,** develop, evolve, launch, instigate, initiate, spearhead, institute, establish, found, be the father/mother of, originate, set in motion, create; lay the groundwork, prepare the way, blaze a trail, break new ground.

pious ▶ adjective 1 *a pious family* **religious,** devout, God-fearing, churchgoing, spiritual, prayerful, holy, godly, saintly, dedicated, reverent, dutiful, righteous.
ANTONYMS irreligious.
2 *pious platitudes* **sanctimonious,** hypocritical, insincere, self-righteous, holier-than-thou, pietistic, churchy; informal goody-goody.
ANTONYMS sincere.
3 *a pious hope* **forlorn,** vain, doomed, hopeless, desperate; unlikely, unrealistic.

pipe ▶ noun 1 *a water pipe* **tube,** conduit, hose, main, duct, line, channel, pipeline, drain; tubing, piping, siphon.
2 *he smokes a pipe* **brier (pipe),** meerschaum, chibouk; hookah, narghile, bong, churchwarden.
3 *she was playing a pipe* **whistle,** pennywhistle, tin whistle, flute, recorder, fife; chanter.
4 *regimental pipes and drums* **bagpipes,** uillean pipes; pan pipes.

▶ verb 1 *the beer is piped into barrels* **siphon,** feed, channel, run, convey.
2 *television shows piped in from New York* **transmit,** feed, patch.
3 *he heard a tune being piped* **play on a pipe,** tootle, whistle; literary flute.
4 *a curlew piped* **chirp,** cheep, chirrup, twitter, warble, trill, peep, sing, shrill.

– PHRASES **pipe down** informal *we had to ask that couple in the first row to pipe down* **be quiet,** be silent, hush, stop talking, hold one's tongue, settle down; informal shut up, shut one's mouth, zip it, button it, button one's lip, put a sock in it.

pipe dream ▶ noun *for most aspiring actors, that starring role is just a pipe dream* **fantasy,** false hope, illusion, delusion, daydream, chimera; castle in the air, castle in Spain; informal pie in the sky.

pipeline ▶ noun *a gas pipeline* **pipe,** conduit, main, line, duct, tube.

– PHRASES **in the pipeline** *word of a layoff is in the pipeline* **on the way,** coming, forthcoming, upcoming, imminent, about to happen, near, close, brewing, in the offing, in the wind.

piquant ▶ adjective 1 *a piquant sauce* **spicy,** tangy, peppery, hot; tasty, flavorful, appetizing, savory; pungent, sharp, tart, zesty, strong, salty.
ANTONYMS bland.
2 *a piquant story* **intriguing,** stimulating, interesting, fascinating, colorful, exciting, lively; spicy, provocative, racy; informal juicy.
ANTONYMS dull.

pique ▶ noun *a fit of pique* **irritation,** annoyance, resentment, anger, displeasure, indignation, petulance, ill humor, vexation, exasperation, disgruntlement, discontent; offense, umbrage.

▶ verb 1 *his curiosity was piqued* **stimulate,** arouse, rouse, provoke, whet, awaken, excite, kindle, stir, galvanize.
2 *she was piqued by his neglect* **irritate,** annoy, bother, vex, displease, upset, offend, affront, anger, exasperate, infuriate, gall, irk, nettle; informal peeve, aggravate, miff, rile, bug, needle, get someone's back up, get someone's goat, tick off, tee off.

piracy ▶ noun 1 *piracy on the high seas* **freebooting,** robbery at sea; archaic buccaneering.
2 *software piracy* **illegal copying,** plagiarism, copyright infringement, bootlegging.

pirate ▶ noun 1 *pirates boarded the ship* **freebooter,** marauder, raider; historical privateer; archaic buccaneer, corsair.
2 *software pirates* **copyright infringer,** plagiarist, plagiarizer.

▶ verb *designers may pirate good ideas* **steal,** plagiarize, poach, copy illegally, reproduce illegally, appropriate, bootleg; Computing download illegally; informal crib, lift, rip off, pinch.

pit[1] ▶ noun 1 *a pit in the ground* **hole,** ditch, trench, trough, hollow, excavation, cavity, crater, pothole; shaft, mineshaft, sump.
2 *pit closures* **coal mine,** colliery, quarry.
3 *the pits in her skin* **pockmark,** pock, hollow, indentation, depression, dent, dimple.

▶ verb 1 *his skin had been pitted by acne* **mark,** pockmark, scar, blemish, disfigure.
2 *raindrops pitted the bare earth* **make holes in,** make hollows in, dent, indent.

– PHRASES **pit against** *it's your chance to pit your wits against the world champions* **set against,** match against, put in opposition to, put in competition with; compete with, contend with, vie with, wrestle with. **the pits** informal *this place is really the pits* **hell,** the worst, the lowest of the low, a nightmare; rock-bottom, extremely bad, awful, terrible, dreadful, deplorable; informal appalling, lousy, abysmal.

pit[2] ▶ noun *cherry pits* **stone,** pip, seed.

pitch[1] ▶ noun 1 *her voice rose in pitch* **tone,** timbre, key, modulation, frequency.
2 *the pitch of the roof* **gradient,** slope, slant, angle, steepness, tilt, incline, inclination.
3 *her anger reached such a pitch that she screamed* **level,** intensity, point, degree, height, extent.
4 *a pitch of the ball* **throw,** fling, hurl, toss, lob; delivery; informal heave.
5 *his sales pitch* **patter,** talk; informal spiel, line.

▶ verb 1 *she pitched the crumpled note into the fire* **throw,** toss, fling, hurl, cast, lob, flip, propel,

bowl; informal chuck, sling, heave, peg.
2 *he pitched overboard* **fall,** tumble, topple, plunge, plummet.
3 *they pitched their tents* **put up,** set up, erect, raise.
4 *the boat pitched* **lurch,** toss (about), plunge, roll, reel, sway, rock, keel, list, wallow, labor.
– PHRASES **make a pitch for** *we made a pitch for the Loman account, but we lost in the bidding* **try to obtain,** try to acquire, try to get, bid for, make a bid for. **pitch in** *if we all pitch in, we can be out of here in thirty minutes* **help (out),** assist, lend a hand, join in, participate, contribute, do one's bit, chip in, cooperate, collaborate.

pitch[2] ▶ **noun** *cement coated with pitch* bitumen, asphalt, tar.

pitch-black ▶ **adjective** *we ventured into the pitch-black tunnel* **black,** dark, pitch-dark, inky, jet-black, coal-black, jet, ebony; starless, moonless; literary Stygian.

pitcher ▶ **noun** *a pitcher of beer* **jug,** ewer, jar; creamer.

piteous ▶ **adjective** *a piteous cry* **sad,** pitiful, pitiable, pathetic, heart-rending, heartbreaking, moving, touching; plaintive, poignant, forlorn; poor, wretched, miserable.

pitfall ▶ **noun** *home schooling has its pitfalls* **hazard,** danger, risk, peril, difficulty, catch, snag, stumbling block, drawback.

pith ▶ **noun 1** *the pith of the argument* **essence,** main point, fundamentals, heart, substance, nub, core, quintessence, crux, gist, meat, kernel, marrow, burden; informal nitty-gritty.
2 *he writes with pith and exactitude* **succinctness,** conciseness, concision, pithiness, brevity; cogency, weight, depth, force.

pithy ▶ **adjective** *pithy comments* **succinct,** terse, concise, compact, short (and sweet), brief, condensed, to the point, epigrammatic, crisp, thumbnail; significant, meaningful, expressive, telling; formal compendious. See note at TERSE.
ANTONYMS verbose.

pitiful ▶ **adjective 1** *a child in a pitiful state* **distressing,** sad, piteous, pitiable, pathetic, heart-rending, heartbreaking, moving, touching, tearjerking; plaintive, poignant, forlorn; poor, sorry, wretched, abject, miserable.
2 *a pitiful $500 a month* **paltry,** miserable, meager, insufficient, trifling, negligible, pitiable, derisory; informal pathetic, measly, piddling, mingy.
3 *his performance was pitiful* **woeful,** deplorable, awful, terrible, lamentable, hopeless, poor, bad, feeble, pitiable, dreadful, inadequate, below par, laughable; informal pathetic, useless, appalling, lousy, abysmal, dire.

pitiless ▶ **adjective** *a pitiless executioner* **merciless,** unmerciful, unpitying, ruthless, cruel, heartless, remorseless, hard-hearted, cold-hearted, harsh, callous, severe, unsparing, unforgiving, unfeeling, uncaring, unsympathetic, uncharitable, brutal, inhuman, inhumane, barbaric, sadistic.
ANTONYMS merciful.

pittance ▶ **noun** *the musicians were paid a pittance* **a tiny amount,** next to nothing, very little; informal peanuts, chicken feed, slave wages, chump change.

pity ▶ **noun 1** *a voice full of pity* **compassion,** commiseration, condolence, sympathy, fellow feeling, understanding; sorrow, regret, sadness.
ANTONYMS indifference, cruelty.
2 *it's a pity he never had children* **shame,** sad thing, bad luck, misfortune; informal crime, bummer, sin.
▶ **verb** *they pitied me* **feel sorry for,** feel for, sympathize with, empathize with, commiserate with, take pity on, be moved by, grieve for.
– PHRASES **take pity on** *a better person would take pity on them* **feel sorry for,** relent, be compassionate toward, be sympathetic toward, have mercy on, help (out), put someone out of their misery. **what a pity!** *Cameron lost by less than a tenth of a second? What a pity!* **how sad,** what a shame, too bad, tant pis, oh dear, bummer.

pivot ▶ **noun 1** *the machine turns on a pivot* **fulcrum,** axis, axle, swivel; pin, shaft, hub, spindle, hinge, kingpin, gudgeon.
2 *the pivot of government policy* **center,** focus, hub, heart, nucleus, crux, keystone, cornerstone, linchpin, kingpin.
▶ **verb 1** *the panel pivots inward* **rotate,** turn, swivel, revolve, spin.
2 *it all pivoted on his response* **depend,** hinge, turn, center, hang, rely, rest; revolve around.

pixie ▶ **noun** *Loolah was a mischievous little pixie* **elf,** fairy, sprite, imp, brownie, puck, leprechaun; literary faerie, fay.

placard ▶ **noun** *placards with antiwar slogans* **notice,** poster, sign, bill, advertisement; banner; informal ad.

placate ▶ **verb** *John did his best to placate her* **pacify,** calm, appease, mollify, soothe, win over, conciliate, propitiate, make peace with, humor. See note at PACIFY.
ANTONYMS provoke.

place ▶ **noun 1** *an ideal place for dinner* **location,** site, spot, setting, position, situation, area, region, locale; venue; technical locus.
2 *foreign places* **country,** state, area, region, town, city; locality, district; literary clime.
3 *a place of her own* **home,** house, flat, apartment; accommodations, property, pied-à-terre; rooms, quarters; informal pad, digs; formal residence, abode, dwelling (place), domicile, habitation.
4 *if I were in your place, I'd sell now* **situation,** position, circumstances; informal shoes.
5 *a place was reserved for her* **seat,** chair, space.
6 *I offered him a place in the company* **job,** position, post, appointment, situation, office; employment.
7 *I know my place* **status,** position, standing, rank, niche; dated estate, station.
8 *it was not her place to sort it out* **responsibility,** duty, job, task, role, function, concern, affair, charge; right, privilege, prerogative.
▶ **verb 1** *books were placed on the table* **put (down),** set (down), lay, deposit, position, plant, rest, stand, station, situate, leave; informal stick, dump, park, plonk, pop, plunk.

2 *the trust you placed in me* **put,** lay, set, invest.
3 *a survey placed the company sixth* **rank,** order, grade, class, classify, categorize; put, set, assign.
4 *Joe couldn't quite place her* **identify,** recognize, remember, put a name to, pin down; locate, pinpoint.
5 *we were* ***placed with*** *foster parents* house with, billet to; allocate to, assign to, appoint to.
– PHRASES **in the first place** *in the first place, you're not old enough* **initially,** at first, at the start, at the outset, in/at the beginning, in the first instance, to begin with, to start with, originally. **in place 1** *the veil was held in place by pearls* **in position,** in situ. **2** *the plans are in place* **ready,** set up, all set, established, arranged, in order. **in place of** *in place of fresh flowers, use sprays of dried lavender* **instead of,** rather than, as a substitute for, as a replacement for, in exchange for, in lieu of; in someone's stead. **out of place 1** *she never had a hair out of place* **out of position,** out of order, in disarray, disarranged, in a mess, messy, topsy-turvy, muddled. **2** *he said something out of place* **inappropriate,** unsuitable, unseemly, improper, untoward, out of keeping, unbecoming, wrong. **3** *she seemed out of place at the literary parties* **incongruous,** out of one's element, like a fish out of water; uncomfortable, uneasy. **put someone in their place** *Marsha's father-in-law finally spoke up and put that hateful woman in her place* **humiliate,** take down a peg or two, deflate, crush, squash, humble; informal cut down to size, settle someone's hash, make someone eat crow. **take place** *the site where the crash took place* **happen,** occur, come about, transpire, crop up, materialize, arise, go down; literary come to pass, befall, betide. **take the place of** *I know I'll never be able to take the place of your father* **replace,** stand in for, substitute for, act for, fill in for, cover for, relieve.

placid ▶ adjective **1** *she's normally very placid* **even-tempered,** calm, tranquil, equable, unexcitable, serene, mild, 'calm, cool, and collected', composed, self-possessed, poised, easygoing, levelheaded, steady, unruffled, unperturbed, phlegmatic; informal unflappable. See note at CALM.
ANTONYMS excitable.
2 *a placid village* **quiet,** calm, tranquil, still, peaceful, undisturbed, restful, sleepy.
ANTONYMS bustling.

plagiarize ▶ verb *he was fined for plagiarizing a song* **copy,** infringe the copyright of, pirate, steal, poach, appropriate; Computing download illegally; informal rip off, crib, "borrow", pinch.

plague ▶ noun **1** *they died of the plague* **bubonic plague,** pneumonic plague, Black Death; disease, sickness, epidemic; dated contagion; archaic pestilence.
2 *a plague of fleas* **infestation,** epidemic, invasion, swarm, multitude, host.
3 *theft is the plague of restaurants* **bane,** curse, scourge, affliction, blight.
▶ verb **1** *he was plagued by poor health* **afflict,** bedevil, torment, trouble, beset, dog, curse.
2 *he plagued her with questions* **pester,** harass, badger, bother, torment, persecute, bedevil, harry, hound, trouble, irritate, nag, annoy, vex, molest; informal hassle, bug, aggravate, devil.

plain ▶ adjective **1** *it was plain that something was wrong* **obvious,** clear, crystal clear, evident, apparent, manifest, patent; discernible, perceptible, noticeable, recognizable, unmistakable, transparent; pronounced, marked, striking, conspicuous, self-evident, indisputable; writ large; informal standing/sticking out like a sore thumb.
2 *plain English* **intelligible,** comprehensible, clear, understandable, coherent, uncomplicated, lucid, unambiguous, simple, straightforward, user-friendly; formal perspicuous.
ANTONYMS obscure, unclear.
3 *plain speaking* **candid,** frank, outspoken, forthright, direct, honest, truthful, blunt, bald, explicit, unequivocal; informal upfront.
4 *a plain dress* **simple,** ordinary, unadorned, unembellished, unornamented, unostentatious, unfussy, basic, modest, unsophisticated, without frills, homespun; restrained, muted; everyday, workaday.
ANTONYMS elaborate, fancy.
5 *a plain girl* **homely,** unattractive, unprepossessing, ugly, ill-favored, unlovely, ordinary; informal not much to look at.
ANTONYMS attractive.
6 *it was plain bad luck* **sheer,** pure, downright, out-and-out, unmitigated.
▶ adverb *this is just plain stupid* **downright,** utterly, absolutely, completely, totally, really, thoroughly, positively, simply, unquestionably, undeniably; informal plumb.
▶ noun *the endless grassy plains* **grassland,** prairie, flatland, lowland, pasture, meadowland, savanna, steppe; tableland, tundra, pampas, veld.

plain-spoken ▶ adjective *he's not being rude, he's just plain-spoken* **candid,** frank, outspoken, forthright, direct, honest, truthful, open, blunt, straightforward, explicit, unequivocal, unambiguous, not afraid to call a spade a spade, tell-it-like-it-is; informal upfront.
ANTONYMS evasive.

plaintive ▶ adjective *a plaintive cry* **mournful,** sad, wistful, doleful, pathetic, pitiful, piteous, melancholy, sorrowful, unhappy, wretched, woeful, forlorn, woebegone; literary dolorous.

plan ▶ noun **1** *a plan for raising money* **procedure,** scheme, strategy, idea, proposal, proposition, suggestion; project, program, system, method, stratagem, formula, recipe; way, means, measure, tactic.
2 *her plan was to win a medal* **intention,** aim, idea, intent, objective, object, goal, target, ambition.
3 *plans for the clubhouse* **blueprint,** drawing, diagram, sketch, layout; illustration, representation.
▶ verb **1** *plan your route in advance* **organize,** arrange, work out, design, outline, map out, prepare, schedule, formulate, frame, develop, devise, concoct; plot, scheme, hatch, brew, slate.
2 *he plans to buy a house* **intend,** aim, propose, mean, hope, want, wish, desire, envisage; formal purpose. See note at INTEND.
3 *I'm planning a new garden* **design,** draw up,

sketch out, map out.

plane[1] ▶ noun 1 *a horizontal plane* **flat surface,** level surface; horizontal.
2 *a higher plane of achievement* **level,** degree, standard, stratum; position, rung, echelon.
▶ adjective *a plane surface* **flat,** level, horizontal, even; smooth, regular, uniform; technical planar.
▶ verb 1 *seagulls planed overhead* **soar,** glide, float, drift, wheel.
2 *boats planed across the water* **skim,** glide.

plane[2] ▶ noun *the plane took off* **aircraft,** airplane, airliner, jet, jumbo jet, jetliner, bush plane, float plane, seaplane, crop duster, water bomber; dated flying machine.

plant ▶ noun 1 *garden plants* flower, vegetable, herb, shrub, weed; (**plants**) vegetation, greenery, flora, herbage, verdure.
2 *the plant commenced production* **factory,** works, foundry, mill, workshop, shop.
3 *a CIA plant* **spy,** informant, informer, agent, secret agent, mole, infiltrator, operative; informal spook.
▶ verb 1 *plant the seeds this autumn* **sow,** scatter, seed; bed out, transplant.
2 *he planted his feet on the ground* **place,** put, set, position, situate, settle; informal plonk.
3 *she planted the idea in his mind* **instill,** implant, impress, imprint, put, place, introduce, fix, establish, lodge.
4 *letters were planted to embarrass them* **hide,** conceal, secrete.

plaque ▶ noun *a plaque in her honor was placed on the door to the auditorium* **plate,** tablet, panel, sign, cartouche, brass.

plaster ▶ noun 1 *the plaster covering the bricks* **plasterwork,** stucco, pargeting.
2 *a statuette made of plaster* **plaster of Paris,** gypsum.
▶ verb 1 *bread plastered with butter* **cover thickly,** smother, spread, smear, cake, coat, slather.
2 *his hair was* ***plastered down*** *with sweat* **flatten (down),** smooth down, slick down.

plastic ▶ adjective 1 *at high temperatures the rocks become plastic* **malleable,** moldable, pliable, pliant, ductile, flexible, soft, workable, bendable; informal bendy.
ANTONYMS rigid.
2 *the plastic minds of children* **impressionable,** malleable, receptive, pliable, pliant, flexible; compliant, tractable, biddable, persuadable, susceptible, manipulable.
ANTONYMS intractable.
3 *a plastic smile* **artificial,** false, fake, superficial, pseudo, bogus, unnatural, insincere; informal phony, pretend.
ANTONYMS genuine.

plate ▶ noun 1 *a dinner plate* **dish,** platter, salver, paten, charger; historical trencher.
2 *a plate of spaghetti* **plateful,** helping, portion, serving.
3 *steel plates* **panel,** sheet, layer, pane, slab.
4 *a brass plate on the door* **plaque,** sign, tablet, cartouche.
5 *the book has color plates* **picture,** print, illustration, photograph, photo.
▶ verb *the roof was plated with steel* **cover,** coat, overlay, laminate, veneer; electroplate, galvanize, gild.

plateau ▶ noun 1 *a windswept plateau* **upland,** tableland, plain, mesa, highland, coteau.
2 *prices reached a plateau* quiescent period; letup, respite, lull.

platform ▶ noun 1 *he made a speech from the platform* **stage,** dais, rostrum, podium, soapbox.
2 *the party's platform* **policy,** program, party line, manifesto, plan, principles, objectives, aims.

platitude ▶ noun *boring us with his platitudes* **cliché,** truism, commonplace, banality, old chestnut, bromide, inanity, banal/trite/hackneyed/stock phrase.

platitudinous ▶ adjective *platitudinous political sound bites* **hackneyed,** overworked, overused, clichéd, banal, trite, commonplace, well-worn, stale, tired, unoriginal; informal corny, old hat.
ANTONYMS original.

platonic ▶ adjective *the roommates' platonic relationship* **nonsexual,** nonphysical, chaste; intellectual, friendly.
ANTONYMS sexual.

platoon ▶ noun *our platoon lost 200 men on that mission* **unit,** patrol, troop, squad, squadron, team, company, corps, outfit, detachment, contingent.

platter ▶ noun *a platter of broiled oysters* **plate,** dish, salver, paten, tray; historical trencher.

plaudits ▶ plural noun *the mayor won plaudits for his aggressive campaign against crime* **praise,** acclaim, commendation, congratulations, accolades, compliments, cheers, applause, tributes, bouquets; a pat on the back; informal a (big) hand.
ANTONYMS criticism.

plausible ▶ adjective *a plausible explanation* **credible,** reasonable, believable, likely, feasible, tenable, possible, conceivable, imaginable; convincing, persuasive, cogent, sound, rational, logical, thinkable. See note at **BELIEVABLE**.
ANTONYMS unlikely.

play ▶ verb 1 *Aidan and Robert were playing with their toys* **amuse oneself,** entertain oneself, enjoy oneself, have fun; relax, occupy oneself, divert oneself; frolic, frisk, romp, caper; informal mess around.
2 *I used to play hockey* **take part in,** participate in, be involved in, compete in, do.
3 *St. Joseph's plays Boston on Sunday* **compete against,** take on, challenge, vie with, face, go up against.
4 *he was to play Macbeth* **act (the part of),** take the role of, appear as, portray, depict, impersonate, represent, render, perform, enact; formal personate.
5 *get your guitar and let's play* **perform,** make music, jam.
6 *Bryanna played a note on the flute* **make,** produce, reproduce; blow, toot; plunk, bang out; sound.
7 *the sunlight played on the water* **dance,** flit, ripple, touch; sparkle, glint.
▶ noun 1 *a balance between work and play* **amusement,** entertainment, relaxation, recreation, diversion, distraction, leisure; enjoyment, pleasure, fun, games, fun and games; horseplay, merrymaking, revelry; informal living it up.

2 *a Shakespearean play* **drama,** theatrical work; screenplay, comedy, tragedy; production, performance, show, sketch.
3 *a new tool came into play* **action,** activity, operation, working, function; interaction, interplay.
4 *there is foul play afoot* **behavior,** goings-on, activity, action, deed.
5 *there was a little play in the rope* **movement,** slack, give; room to maneuver, scope, latitude.
– PHRASES **play around** informal *he's been playing around for years* **womanize,** philander, have affairs, flirt; informal carry on, mess around, play the field, sleep around, fool around. **play at being** *she just plays at being the caring one* **pretend to be,** pass oneself off as, masquerade as, profess to be, pose as, impersonate; fake, feign, simulate, affect; informal make like. **play ball** informal *if you play ball, I can help you* **co-operate,** collaborate, play the game, help, lend a hand, assist, contribute; informal pitch in. **play down** *officials tried to play down the extent of the damage* **make light of,** make little of, gloss over, de-emphasize, downplay, understate; soft-pedal, tone down, diminish, trivialize, underrate, underestimate, undervalue; disparage, belittle, scoff at, sneer at, shrug off; informal pooh-pooh. **play for time** *all his opponents accused him of playing for time in order to pull an election-year coup* **stall,** temporize, delay, hold back, hang fire, procrastinate, drag one's feet. **play it by ear** *when a guest doesn't show up for live radio, you learn quickly how to play it by ear* **improvise,** extemporize, ad lib; informal wing it. **play on** *they play on our fears* **exploit,** take advantage of, use, turn to (one's) account, profit by, capitalize on, trade on, milk, abuse. **play the fool** *by the time she was ten, Ronnie knew it was her God-given job to play the fool* **clown around,** fool around, mess around, monkey around, joke; informal horse around. **play the game** *you find out early on who's willing to play the game, and that's the kind of person this company holds on to* **play fair,** be fair, play by the rules, conform, be a good sport, toe the line. **play up** *his agents really play up the story of his rise from poverty* **emphasize,** accentuate, call attention to, point up, underline, highlight, spotlight, foreground, feature, stress, accent. **play up to** *wannabes who play up to the boss* **ingratiate oneself with,** curry favor with, court, fawn over, make up to, toady to, crawl to, pander to, flatter; informal soft-soap, suck up to, butter up, lick someone's boots.

playboy ▶ **noun** *he claims his days as a playboy are over* **socialite,** pleasure-seeker, sybarite; ladies' man, womanizer, philanderer, wolf, rake, roué; informal ladykiller.

player ▶ **noun 1** *a tournament for young players* **participant,** contestant, competitor, contender; sportsman/woman, athlete.
2 *the players in the orchestra* **musician,** performer, instrumentalist, soloist, virtuoso.
3 *the players at the Shaw Festival* **actor,** actress, performer, thespian, entertainer, artist/artiste, trouper.

playful ▶ **adjective 1** *a playful mood* **frisky,** jolly, lively, full of fun, frolicsome, sportive, high-spirited, exuberant, perky; mischievous, impish, clownish, kittenish, rascally, tricksy; informal full of beans; formal ludic.
ANTONYMS solemn.
2 *a playful remark* **lighthearted,** in jest, joking, jokey, teasing, humorous, jocular, good-natured, tongue-in-cheek, facetious, frivolous, flippant, arch; informal waggish.
ANTONYMS serious.

playground ▶ **noun** *they need more supervision on the playground* **play area,** park, playing field, recreation ground.

playwright ▶ **noun** *we're reading the works of Simon and other modern playwrights* **dramatist,** dramaturge, scriptwriter, screenwriter, writer, scenarist; tragedian.

plea ▶ **noun 1** *a plea for aid* **appeal,** entreaty, supplication, petition, request, call, suit, solicitation.
2 *her plea of a headache was unconvincing* **claim,** explanation, defense, justification; excuse, pretext.

plead ▶ **verb 1** *he pleaded with her to stay* **beg,** implore, entreat, appeal to, supplicate, importune, petition, request, ask, call on; literary beseech. See note at BEG.
2 *she pleaded ignorance* **claim,** use as an excuse, assert, allege, argue, state.

pleasant ▶ **adjective 1** *a pleasant evening* **enjoyable,** pleasurable, nice, agreeable, pleasing, satisfying, gratifying, good; entertaining, amusing, delightful, charming; fine, balmy; informal lovely, great.
2 *the staff are pleasant* **friendly,** agreeable, amiable, nice, genial, cordial, likable, amicable, good-humored, good-natured, personable; hospitable, approachable, gracious, courteous, polite, obliging, helpful, considerate; charming, lovely, delightful, sweet, sympathetic, simpatico.
ANTONYMS disagreeable.

CHOOSE THE RIGHT WORD

pleasant, agreeable, attractive, congenial, enjoyable, gratifying, pleasing

One might have a **pleasant** smile and a **pleasing** personality, since the former suggests something that is naturally appealing while the latter suggests a conscious attempt to please. Something that is **enjoyable** is able to give enjoyment or pleasure (*a thoroughly enjoyable evening*), while **agreeable** describes something that is in harmony with one's personal mood or wishes (*an agreeable afternoon spent relaxing in the sun*). **Gratifying** is more intense, suggesting that deeper expectations or needs have been met (*the awards ceremony was particularly gratifying for parents*). Something that is **attractive** gives pleasure because of its appearance or manner (*an attractive house in a wooded setting*), while **congenial** has more to do with compatibility (*a congenial couple*).

pleasantry ▶ noun **1** *we exchanged pleasantries* **banter,** badinage; polite remark, casual remark.
2 *he laughed at his own pleasantry* **joke,** witticism, quip, jest, gag, bon mot; informal wisecrack, crack.

please ▶ verb **1** *he'd do anything to please her* **make happy,** give pleasure to, make someone feel good; delight, charm, amuse, entertain; satisfy, gratify, humor, oblige, content, suit.
ANTONYMS annoy.
2 *do as you please* **like,** want, wish, desire, see fit, think fit, choose, will, prefer.
▶ adverb *please sit down* **if you please,** if you wouldn't mind, if you would be so good; kindly, pray; archaic prithee.

pleased ▶ adjective *Edward seemed really pleased to see me* **happy,** glad, delighted, gratified, grateful, thankful, content, contented, satisfied; thrilled, elated, overjoyed; informal over the moon, tickled pink, on cloud nine.
ANTONYMS unhappy.

pleasing ▶ adjective **1** *a pleasing day* **nice,** agreeable, pleasant, pleasurable, satisfying, gratifying, good, enjoyable, entertaining, amusing, delightful; informal lovely, great; Brit. informal cushty. See note at PLEASANT.
2 *her pleasing manner* **friendly,** amiable, pleasant, agreeable, affable, nice, genial, likable, good-humored, charming, engaging, delightful; informal lovely, simpatico.

pleasure ▶ noun **1** *she smiled with pleasure* **happiness,** delight, joy, gladness, glee, satisfaction, gratification, contentment, enjoyment, amusement.
2 *his greatest pleasures in life* **joy,** amusement, diversion, recreation, pastime; treat, thrill.
3 *don't mix business and pleasure* **enjoyment,** fun, entertainment; recreation, leisure, relaxation; informal jollies.
4 *a life of pleasure* **hedonism,** indulgence, self-indulgence, self-gratification, lotus-eating.
5 *what's your pleasure?* **wish,** desire, preference, will, inclination, choice.
– PHRASES **take pleasure in** *we're still healthy enough to take pleasure in our retirement years* **enjoy,** delight in, love, like, adore, appreciate, relish, savor, revel in, glory in; informal get a kick out of, get a thrill out of. **with pleasure** *certainly I can give you a ride, with pleasure* **gladly,** willingly, happily, readily; by all means, of course; archaic fain.

plebeian ▶ noun *plebeians and gentry lived together* **proletarian,** commoner, working-class person, worker; peasant; informal pleb, prole.
ANTONYMS aristocrat.
▶ adjective **1** *people of plebeian descent* **lower-class,** working-class, proletarian, common, peasant; mean, humble, lowly.
ANTONYMS noble.
2 *plebeian tastes* **uncultured,** uncultivated, unrefined, lowbrow, philistine, uneducated; coarse, uncouth, common, vulgar.
ANTONYMS refined.

pledge ▶ noun **1** *his election pledge* **promise,** undertaking, vow, word, word of honor, commitment, assurance, oath, guarantee.
2 *he gave it as a pledge to a creditor* **surety,** bond, security, collateral, guarantee, deposit.
3 *a pledge of my sincerity* **token,** symbol, sign, earnest, mark, testimony, proof, evidence.
▶ verb **1** *he pledged to root out corruption* **promise,** vow, swear, undertake, engage, commit oneself, declare, affirm, avow.
2 *they pledged $10 million* **promise (to give),** donate, contribute, give, put up.
3 *his home is pledged as security against the loan* **mortgage,** put up as collateral, guarantee, pawn.

plentiful ▶ adjective *a plentiful supply of food* **abundant,** copious, ample, profuse, rich, lavish, generous, bountiful, large, great, bumper, superabundant, inexhaustible, prolific; informal galore; literary plenteous. See note at PREVALENT.
ANTONYMS scarce.

plenty ▶ noun *times of plenty* **prosperity,** affluence, wealth, opulence, comfort, luxury; plentifulness, abundance; literary plenteousness.
▶ pronoun *there are* ***plenty of*** *books* **a lot of,** many, a great deal of, enough (and to spare), no lack of, sufficient, a wealth of; informal loads of, lots of, heaps of, stacks of, masses of, tons of, oodles of, scads of, a slew of, a bucketload of.

plethora ▶ noun *a plethora of opinion polls* **excess,** overabundance, superabundance, surplus, glut, superfluity, surfeit, profusion; (**a plethora of**) too many, too much, enough and to spare; informal more —— than one can shake a stick at.
ANTONYMS dearth.

USAGE

plethora

According to the *Oxford English Dictionary* (OED) and most other dictionaries, this word refers (and has always referred) to an overabundance, an overfullness, or an excess. The phrase *a plethora of* is essentially a highfalutin equivalent of *too many*—e.g.: "Our electoral politics now is beset with a plethora of [read *too many*] players and a confusing clutter of messages." (*Brookings Review*; Jan. 1, 2002.) But sometimes, when not preceded by the indefinite article, the word is genuinely useful—e.g.: "Critics say the plethora of scrip circulating in Argentina risks running out of control." (*Wall Street Journal*; Dec. 26, 2001.)

Unfortunately, through misunderstanding of the word's true sense, many writers use it as if it were equivalent to *plenty* or *many*. This meaning is unrecorded in the OED and in most other dictionaries. And it represents an unfortunate degeneration of sense—e.g.:

- "Buffalo may seem like a boring city, but we've managed to produce a plethora [read *plenty*] of famous people, the Goo Goo Dolls, Ani Difranco, David Boreanaz and now, Chad Murray." (*Buffalo News*; Jan. 8, 2002.)
- "The old policies did not anticipate a plethora [read *series* or *group* or *lot*] of suicide bombers." (*Orlando Sentinel*; Jan. 10, 2002.) (One suicide bomber is too many—so plethora doesn't work.)

Phrases such as *a whole plethora of* are likewise ill-considered—e.g.: "Then, once you get to the airport ticket counter, there's a whole plethora [read *a whole range* or *a wide variety*] of biometric identifiers you could use to tie the background checks you've done to the individuals who present themselves at the ticket counter." (*Boston Globe*; Jan. 6, 2002.)

The word is pronounced /**pleth**-er-uh/, not /pluh-**thor**-uh/. — **BG**

pliable ▶ adjective **1** *leather is pliable* **flexible,** pliant, bendable, elastic, supple, malleable, workable, plastic, springy, ductile; informal bendy. See note at FLEXIBLE.
ANTONYMS rigid.
2 *pliable teenage minds* **malleable,** impressionable, flexible, adaptable, pliant, compliant, biddable, tractable, yielding, amenable, susceptible, suggestible, persuadable, manipulable, receptive.
ANTONYMS obdurate.

plight ▶ noun *the plight of the homeless* **predicament,** quandary, difficult situation, dire straits, trouble, difficulty, extremity, bind; informal dilemma, tight corner, tight spot, hole, pickle, jam, fix.

plod ▶ verb **1** *Mom plodded wearily upstairs* **trudge,** walk heavily, clump, stomp, tramp, tromp, lumber, slog.
2 *I have to plod through the whole book* **wade,** plow, trawl, toil, labor; informal slog.

plot ▶ noun **1** *a plot to overthrow him* **conspiracy,** intrigue, secret plan; machinations.
2 *the plot of her novel* **story line,** story, scenario, action, thread; formal diegesis.
3 *a three-acre plot* **piece of ground,** patch, area, tract, acreage, allotment, lot, plat, homesite.
▶ verb **1** *he plotted their downfall* **plan,** scheme, arrange, organize, hatch, concoct, devise, dream up; informal cook up.
2 *his brother was plotting against him* **conspire,** scheme, intrigue, collude, connive, machinate.
3 *the fifty-three sites were plotted* **mark,** chart, map, represent, graph.

CHOOSE THE RIGHT WORD

plot, cabal, conspiracy, intrigue, machination

If you come up with a secret plan to do something, especially with evil or mischievous intent, it's called a **plot** (*a plot to seize control of the company*). If you get other people or groups involved in your plot, it's called a **conspiracy** (*a conspiracy to overthrow the government*). **Cabal** usually applies to a small group of political conspirators (*a cabal of right-wing extremists*), while **machination** (usually plural) suggests deceit and cunning in devising a plot intended to harm someone (*the machinations of the would-be assassins*). An **intrigue** involves more complicated scheming or maneuvering than a plot and often employs underhanded methods in an attempt to gain one's own ends (*she had a passion for intrigue, particularly where romance was involved*).

plow ▶ verb **1** *the fields were plowed* **till,** furrow, harrow, cultivate, work, break up.
2 *the streets haven't been plowed yet* **clear** (**of snow**), shovel.
3 *the car plowed into a telephone pole* **crash,** smash, career, plunge, bulldoze, hurtle, careen, cannon, run, drive, barrel.
4 *they plowed through deep snow* **trudge,** plod, toil, wade; informal slog.

ploy ▶ noun *perhaps this had been a ploy to revive her husband's fading interest* **ruse,** tactic, move, device, stratagem, scheme, trick, gambit, plan, maneuver, dodge, subterfuge, wile.

pluck ▶ verb **1** *he plucked a thread from his lapel* **remove,** pick (off), pull (off/out), extract, take (off).
2 *she* ***plucked at*** *his T-shirt* **pull** (**at**), tug (at), clutch (at), snatch (at), grab, catch (at), tweak, jerk; informal yank.
3 *the turkeys have been plucked* **deplume,** remove the feathers from.
4 *Jen plucked the guitar strings* **strum,** pick, plunk, thrum, twang; play pizzicato.
▶ noun *saying those things to her took a lot of pluck* **courage,** bravery, nerve, backbone, spine, daring, spirit, intrepidity, fearlessness, mettle, grit, true grit, determination, fortitude, resolve, stout-heartedness, dauntlessness, valor, heroism, audacity; informal guts, spunk, gumption, moxie. See note at COURAGE.

plucky ▶ adjective *these plucky young players are still about the game, not about the money* **brave,** courageous, bold, daring, fearless, intrepid, spirited, game, valiant, valorous, stouthearted, dauntless, resolute, determined, undaunted, unflinching, audacious, unafraid, doughty, mettlesome; informal gutsy, spunky.
ANTONYMS timid.

plug ▶ noun **1** *she pulled out the plug* **stopper,** bung, cork, seal, spile.
2 *a plug of tobacco* **wad,** quid, twist, chew, cake, stick.
3 informal *a plug for her new book* **advertisement,** promotion, commercial, recommendation, mention, good word; informal hype, push, puff piece, ad, boost, ballyhoo.
▶ verb **1** *plug the holes* **stop** (**up**), seal (up/off), close (up/off), cork, stopper, bung, block (up/off), fill (up).
2 informal *she plugged her new film* **publicize,** promote, advertise, mention, bang the drum for, draw attention to; informal hype (up), push, puff.
3 informal *don't move or I'll plug you* **shoot,** gun down; informal blast, fill/pump full of lead.
– PHRASES **plug away** informal *he plugged away at his novel, unaware of the day or the time* **toil,** labor, slave away, soldier on, persevere, persist, keep on; informal slog away, beaver away.

plum ▶ adjective informal *a plum job* **excellent,** very good, wonderful, marvelous, choice, first-class; informal great, terrific, cushy.

plumb ▶ verb *an attempt to plumb her psyche* **explore,** probe, delve into, search, examine, investigate, fathom, penetrate, understand.
▶ adverb **1** informal *it went plumb through the screen* **right,** exactly, precisely, directly, dead, straight; informal bang.
2 informal *I plumb forgot* **completely,** absolutely,

downright, totally, quite, thoroughly.
3 *the bell hangs plumb* **vertically,** perpendicularly, straight down.
▶ **adjective** *a plumb drop* **vertical,** perpendicular, straight.
– PHRASES **plumb the depth of** *she had plumbed the depths of depravity* **find,** experience the extremes of, reach the lowest point of; reach rock bottom of.

plummet ▶ **verb 1** *the plane plummeted to the ground* **plunge,** nosedive, dive, drop, fall, descend, hurtle.
2 *share prices plummeted* **fall steeply,** plunge, tumble, drop rapidly, go down, slump; informal crash, nosedive.

plump ▶ **adjective** *a plump child* **chubby,** fat, stout, rotund, well padded, ample, full-figured, pillowy, round, chunky, portly, overweight, fleshy, paunchy, bulky, corpulent; rare pulvinate; informal tubby, roly-poly, pudgy, beefy, porky, zaftig, corn-fed.
ANTONYMS thin.

plunder ▶ **verb 1** *they plundered the countryside* **pillage,** loot, rob, raid, ransack, despoil, strip, ravage, lay waste, devastate, sack, rape. See note at RAVAGE.
2 *money plundered from pension funds* **steal,** purloin, thieve, seize, pillage; embezzle.
▶ **noun 1** *the plunder of the villages* **looting,** pillaging, plundering, raiding, ransacking, devastation, sacking; literary rapine.
2 *the army took huge quantities of plunder* **booty,** loot, stolen goods, spoils, ill-gotten gains; informal swag.

plunge ▶ **verb 1** *Joy plunged into the sea* **dive,** jump, throw oneself, launch oneself.
2 *the aircraft plunged to the ground* **plummet,** nosedive, drop, fall, pitch, tumble, descend, dive-bomb.
3 *the car plunged down an alley* **charge,** hurtle, career, plow, cannon, tear; informal barrel.
4 *oil prices plunged* **fall sharply,** plummet, drop, go down, tumble, slump; informal crash, nosedive.
5 *he plunged the dagger into her back* **thrust,** jab, stab, sink, stick, ram, drive, push, shove, force.
6 *plunge the pears into boiling water* **immerse,** submerge, dip, dunk.
7 *the room was plunged into darkness* **throw,** cast, pitch.
▶ **noun 1** *a plunge into the deep end* **dive,** jump, nosedive, fall, pitch, drop, plummet, descent.
2 *a plunge in profits* **fall,** drop, slump; informal nosedive, crash.
– PHRASES **take the plunge** *she decided to take the plunge and headed for Hollywood* **commit oneself,** go for it, do the deed, throw caution to the wind(s), risk it; informal jump in at the deep end, go for broke.

plus ▶ **preposition 1** *three plus three makes six* **and,** added to.
ANTONYMS minus.
2 *he wrote four novels plus various poems* **as well as,** together with, along with, in addition to, and, not to mention, besides.
▶ **noun** *one of the pluses of the job* **advantage,** good point, asset, pro, (fringe) benefit, bonus, extra, attraction; informal perk; formal perquisite.
ANTONYMS disadvantage.

plush ▶ **adjective** informal *the car's plush interior* **luxurious,** luxury, deluxe, sumptuous, palatial, lavish, opulent, magnificent, lush, rich, expensive, fancy, grand, upscale, upmarket; informal posh, ritzy, swanky, classy, swank.
ANTONYMS austere.

plutocrat ▶ **noun** *champagne-swilling plutocrats* **rich person,** magnate, millionaire, billionaire, multimillionaire; nouveau riche; informal fat cat, moneybags.

ply ▶ **verb 1** *the gondolier plied his oar* **use,** wield, work, manipulate, handle, operate, utilize, employ.
2 *he plied a profitable trade* **engage in,** carry on, pursue, conduct, practice; archaic prosecute.
3 *ferries ply between all lake resorts* **go regularly,** travel, shuttle, go back and forth.
4 *she plied me with chocolate chip cookies* **provide,** supply, lavish, shower, regale.
5 *he plied her with questions* **bombard,** assail, beset, pester, plague, harass, importune; informal hassle, devil.

poach ▶ **verb 1** *he's been poaching salmon* **hunt illegally,** catch illegally, jacklight, jack; steal.
2 *workers were poached by other firms* **steal,** appropriate, purloin, take, lure away; informal nab, swipe, pinch.

pocket ▶ **noun 1** *a bag with two pockets* **pouch,** compartment.
2 *these donors have deep pockets* **means,** budget, resources, finances, funds, money, wherewithal, pocketbook.
3 *pockets of disaffection* **area,** patch, region, isolated area, island, cluster, center.
▶ **adjective** *a pocket dictionary* **small,** little, miniature, mini, compact, concise, abridged, portable, vest-pocket.
▶ **verb** *he pocketed $900,000 of their money* **steal,** take, appropriate, thieve, purloin, misappropriate, embezzle; informal filch, swipe, pinch.

pod ▶ **noun** *the seeds are formed inside a pod* **shell,** husk, hull, case; shuck; Botany pericarp, capsule.

podium ▶ **noun** *he was a natural-born speaker, in his glory up at the podium* **platform,** stage, dais, rostrum, stand, soapbox.

poem ▶ **noun** *Lydia saved every poem that Marshall wrote that year* **verse,** rhyme, piece of poetry, song.

poet ▶ **noun** *she has the soul of a poet* **writer of poetry,** versifier, rhymester, rhymer, sonneteer, lyricist, lyrist; laureate; literary bard; derogatory poetaster; historical troubadour, balladeer.

poetic ▶ **adjective 1** *poetic compositions* **poetical,** verse, metrical, lyrical, lyric, elegiac.
2 *poetic language* **expressive,** figurative, symbolic, flowery, artistic, elegant, fine, beautiful; sensitive, imaginative, creative.

poetry ▶ **noun** *a book of very good poetry* **poems,** verse, versification, metrical composition, rhymes, balladry; archaic poesy.

pogrom ▶ **noun** *how is that every civilized nation has not formally denounced this pogrom?* **massacre,** slaughter, mass murder, annihilation, extermination, decimation, carnage, bloodbath, bloodletting, butchery, genocide, holocaust, purge, ethnic cleansing.

poignancy ▶ noun *his imminent death gave his words a special poignancy* **pathos,** pitifulness, piteousness, sadness, sorrow, mournfulness, wretchedness, misery, tragedy.

poignant ▶ adjective *they read aloud the poignant letters written by the victims' children* **touching,** moving, sad, affecting, pitiful, piteous, pathetic, sorrowful, mournful, wretched, miserable, distressing, heart-rending, tearjerking, plaintive, tragic. See note at MOVING.

point[1] ▶ noun 1 *the point of a needle* **tip,** (sharp) end, extremity; prong, spike, tine, nib, barb.
2 *points of light* **pinpoint,** dot, spot, speck, fleck.
3 *a meeting point* **place,** position, location, site, spot, area.
4 *this point in her life* **time,** stage, juncture, period, phase.
5 *the tension had reached such a high point* **level,** degree, stage, pitch, extent.
6 *an important point* **detail,** item, fact, thing, argument, consideration, factor, element; subject, issue, topic, question, matter.
7 *get to the point* **heart of the matter,** most important part, essence, nub, keynote, core, pith, crux; meaning, significance, gist, substance, thrust, bottom line, burden, relevance; informal brass tacks, nitty-gritty.
8 *what's the point of this?* **purpose,** aim, object, objective, goal, intention; use, sense, value, advantage.
9 *he had his good points* **attribute,** characteristic, feature, trait, quality, property, aspect, side.
▶ verb 1 *she pointed the gun at him* **aim,** direct, level, train.
2 *the evidence **pointed to** his guilt* **indicate,** suggest, evidence, signal, signify, denote, bespeak, reveal, manifest.
– PHRASES **beside the point** *those accusations are beside the point* **irrelevant,** immaterial, unimportant, neither here nor there, inconsequential, incidental, out of place, unconnected, peripheral, tangential, extraneous. **in point of fact** *in point of fact, all three of these gentlemen have immaculate service records* **in fact,** as a matter of fact, actually, in actual fact, really, in reality, as it happens, in truth. **make a point of** *she made a point of letting us know she was recently divorced* **make an effort to,** go out of one's way to, put emphasis on. **on the point of** *we were on the point of quitting, but something kept us going* **(just) about to (be),** on the verge of, on the brink of, going to (be), all set to (be). **point of view** *we have different points of view* **opinion,** view, belief, attitude, feeling, sentiment, thoughts; position, perspective, viewpoint, standpoint, outlook. **point out** *the flaws in the plan have already been pointed out* **identify,** show, designate, draw attention to, indicate, specify, detail, mention. **point up** *it's as if he deliberately points up every negative aspect of our work* **emphasize,** highlight, draw attention to, accentuate, underline, spotlight, foreground, put emphasis on, stress, play up, accent, bring to the fore. **to the point** *his observations were concise and to the point* **relevant,** pertinent, apposite, germane, applicable, apropos, appropriate, apt, fitting, suitable, material; formal ad rem. **up to a point** *I agree with you, but only up to a point* **partly,** to some extent, to a certain degree, in part, somewhat, partially.

point[2] ▶ noun *the ship rounded the point* **promontory,** headland, foreland, cape, spit, peninsula, bluff, ness, horn.

point-blank ▶ adverb 1 *he fired the pistol point-blank* **at close range,** close up, close to.
2 *she couldn't say it point-blank* **bluntly,** directly, straight, frankly, candidly, openly, explicitly, unequivocally, unambiguously, plainly, flatly, categorically, outright.
▶ adjective *a point-blank refusal* **blunt,** direct, straight, straightforward, frank, candid, forthright, explicit, unequivocal, plain, clear, flat, decisive, unqualified, categorical, outright.

pointed ▶ adjective 1 *a pointed stick* **sharp,** tapering, tapered, conical, jagged, spiky, spiked, barbed; informal pointy.
2 *a pointed remark* **cutting,** trenchant, biting, incisive, acerbic, caustic, scathing, venomous, sarcastic; informal snarky.

pointer ▶ noun 1 *the pointer moved to 100 mph* **indicator,** needle, arrow, hand.
2 *he used a pointer on the chart* **stick,** rod, cane; cursor.
3 *a pointer to the outcome of the election* **indication,** indicator, clue, hint, sign, signal, evidence, intimation, inkling, suggestion.
4 *I can give you a few pointers* **tip,** hint, suggestion, guideline, recommendation.

pointless ▶ adjective *our attempts to help Ryan were pointless* **senseless,** futile, hopeless, fruitless, useless, needless, in vain, unavailing, aimless, idle, worthless, valueless; absurd, insane, stupid, silly, foolish.
ANTONYMS valuable.

poise ▶ noun 1 *poise and good deportment* **grace,** gracefulness, elegance, balance, control.
2 *in spite of the setback she retained her poise* **composure,** equanimity, self-possession, aplomb, presence of mind, self-assurance, self-control, nerve, calm, sangfroid, dignity; informal cool, unflappability.
▶ verb 1 *she was poised on one foot* **balance,** hold (oneself) steady, be suspended, remain motionless, hang, hover.
2 *he was poised for action* **prepare oneself,** ready oneself, brace oneself, gear oneself up, stand by.

poison ▶ noun 1 *a deadly poison* **toxin,** toxicant, venom; archaic bane.
2 *Marianne would spread her poison* **malice,** ill will, hate, malevolence, bitterness, spite, spitefulness, venom, acrimony, rancor; bad influence, cancer, corruption, pollution.
▶ verb 1 *her mother poisoned her* **give poison to;** murder.
2 *a blackmailer poisoning pet food* **contaminate,** put poison in, envenom, adulterate, spike, lace, doctor.
3 *the Amazon is being poisoned* **pollute,** contaminate, taint, blight, spoil; literary befoul.
4 *they poisoned his mind* **prejudice,** bias, jaundice, embitter, sour, envenom, warp, corrupt, subvert.

poisonous ▸ **adjective 1** *a poisonous snake* **venomous,** deadly.
ANTONYMS harmless.
2 *a poisonous chemical* **toxic,** noxious, deadly, fatal, lethal, mortal, death-dealing.
ANTONYMS harmless, nontoxic.
3 *a poisonous glance* **malicious,** malevolent, hostile, vicious, spiteful, bitter, venomous, vindictive, vitriolic, rancorous, malign, pernicious, mean, nasty; informal bitchy, catty.
ANTONYMS benevolent.

poke ▸ **verb 1** *she poked him in the ribs* **prod,** jab, dig, nudge, butt, shove, jolt, stab, stick.
2 *leave the cable* ***poking out*** **stick out,** jut out, protrude, project, extend.
▸ **noun** *give him a poke* **prod,** jab, dig, elbow, nudge, shove, stab.
– PHRASES **poke around/about** *we were just poking around some antique shops* **search,** hunt, rummage (around), forage, grub, root about/around, scavenge, nose around, ferret (about/around); sift through, rifle through, scour, comb, probe. **poke fun at** *I never meant to poke fun at you* **mock,** make fun of, ridicule, laugh at, jeer at, sneer at, deride, scorn, scoff at, pillory, lampoon, tease, taunt, chaff, jibe at; informal send up, kid, rib, goof on. **poke one's nose into** *maybe Barry should stop poking his nose into other people's lives* **pry into,** interfere in, intrude on, butt into, meddle with; informal snoop into.

poky ▸ **adjective** *his poky old horse* See **SLOW** (sense 1 of the adjective).

polar ▸ **adjective 1** *polar regions* **Arctic,** Antarctic, circumpolar, Nearctic.
2 *polar conditions* **cold,** freezing, icy, glacial, chilly, gelid, hypothermic.
3 *polar opposites* **opposite,** opposed, dichotomous, extreme, contrary, contradictory, antithetical.

polarity ▸ **noun** *the marked polarity of their political positions* **difference,** dichotomy, separation, opposition, contradiction, antithesis, antagonism.

pole[1] ▸ **noun** *gulls like to perch atop the poles* **post,** pillar; telephone pole, utility pole; stanchion, paling, stake, stick, support, prop, batten, bar, rail, rod, beam; staff, stave, cane, baton.

pole[2] ▸ **noun** *points of view at opposite poles* **extremity,** extreme, limit, antipode.
– PHRASES **poles apart** *it would seem that our priorities are poles apart* **completely different,** directly opposed, antithetical, incompatible, irreconcilable, worlds apart, at opposite extremes.

police ▸ **noun** *we phoned the police as soon as we heard the collision* **police force,** police officers, policemen, policewomen, officers of the law, law officers, authorities, constabulary; informal cops, fuzz, law, long arm of the law, boys/men in blue; coppers, force, heat.
▸ **verb 1** *we must police the area* **guard,** watch over, protect, defend, patrol; control, regulate.
2 *the regulations will be policed by the ministry* **enforce,** regulate, oversee, supervise, monitor, observe, check.

policy ▸ **noun 1** *government policy* **plans,** strategy, stratagem, approach, code, system, guidelines, theory; line, position, stance, attitude.
2 *it's good policy to listen to your elders* **practice,** custom, idea, procedure, conduct, convention.

polish ▸ **verb 1** *I polished his shoes* **shine,** wax, buff, rub up/down; gloss, burnish; varnish, oil, glaze, lacquer, japan, shellac.
2 ***polish up*** *your essay* **perfect,** refine, improve, hone, enhance; brush up, revise, edit, correct, rewrite, go over, touch up; informal clean up.
▸ **noun 1** *furniture polish* **wax,** glaze, varnish; lacquer, japan, shellac.
2 *a good surface polish* **shine,** gloss, luster, sheen, sparkle, patina, finish.
3 *his polish made him stand out* **sophistication,** refinement, urbanity, suaveness, elegance, style, grace, finesse, cultivation, civility, gentility, breeding, courtesy, (good) manners; informal class.
– PHRASES **polish off** informal **1** *he polished off an apple pie* **eat,** finish, consume, devour, guzzle, wolf down, down, bolt; drink up, drain, quaff, gulp (down), binge on, gorge on; informal stuff oneself with, put away, scoff, shovel down, pig out on, swill, knock back, scarf (down/up). **2** *the enemy tried to polish him off* **destroy,** finish off, dispatch, do away with, eliminate, kill, liquidate; informal bump off, knock off, do in, take out, dispose of; rub out. **3** *I'll polish off the last few pages* **complete,** finish, deal with, accomplish, discharge, do; end, conclude, close, finalize, round off, wind up; informal wrap up, sew up.

> CHOOSE THE RIGHT WORD
>
> **polish, gloss, luster, sheen**
>
> All of these words refer to a smooth, shining, or bright surface that reflects light. If this surface is produced by rubbing or friction, the correct word is **polish** (*the car's mirrorlike polish was the result of regular waxing and buffing*). **Gloss,** on the other hand, suggests the hard smoothness associated with lacquered, varnished, or enameled surfaces (*a high-gloss paint*). **Luster** is associated with the light reflected from the surfaces of certain materials, such as silk or pearl (*a green stone with a brilliant luster*). **Sheen** describes a glistening or radiant brightness that is also associated with specific materials (*her hair had a rich, velvety sheen*).

polished ▸ **adjective 1** *a polished table* **shiny,** glossy, gleaming, lustrous, glassy; waxed, buffed, burnished; varnished, glazed, lacquered, japanned, shellacked.
ANTONYMS dull, tarnished.
2 *a polished performance* **expert,** accomplished, masterly, masterful, skillful, adept, adroit, dexterous; impeccable, flawless, perfect, consummate, exquisite, outstanding, excellent, superb, superlative, first-rate, fine; informal ace.
ANTONYMS inexpert.
3 *polished manners* **refined,** cultivated, civilized, well-bred, polite, courteous, genteel, decorous, respectable, urbane, suave, sophisticated.

ANTONYMS gauche.

polite ▶ adjective **1** *a very polite girl* **well-mannered,** civil, courteous, mannerly, respectful, deferential, well-behaved, well-bred, gentlemanly, ladylike, genteel, gracious, urbane; tactful, diplomatic.
ANTONYMS rude.
2 *polite society* **civilized,** refined, cultured, sophisticated, genteel, courtly.
ANTONYMS uncivilized.

politic ▶ adjective *I do not think it politic to express my reservations* **wise,** prudent, sensible, judicious, canny, sagacious, shrewd, astute; recommended, advantageous, beneficial, profitable, desirable, advisable; appropriate, suitable, fitting, apt.
ANTONYMS unwise.

political ▶ adjective **1** *the political affairs of the nation* **governmental,** government, constitutional, ministerial, parliamentary, diplomatic, legislative, administrative, bureaucratic; public, civic, state.
2 *he's a political man* **politically active,** party; militant, factional, partisan.

politician ▶ noun *campaigning politicians make more promises than they can keep* **legislator,** elected official, statesman, stateswoman, public servant; senator, congressman, congresswoman; informal politico, pol.

politics ▶ noun **1** *a career in politics* **government,** affairs of state, public affairs; diplomacy.
2 *she studies politics* **political science,** civics, statecraft.
3 *what are his politics?* **political views,** political leanings, party politics.
4 *office politics* **power struggle,** machinations, maneuvering, opportunism, realpolitik.

poll ▶ noun **1** *a second-round poll* **vote,** ballot, show of hands, referendum, plebiscite; election.
2 *the poll was unduly low* **voting figures,** vote, returns, count, tally.
3 *a poll to investigate holiday choices* **survey,** opinion poll, straw poll, canvass, market research, census.
▶ verb **1** *most of those polled supported the vice president* **canvass,** survey, ask, question, interview, ballot.
2 *she polled 119 votes* **get,** gain, register, record, return.

pollute ▶ verb **1** *fish farms will pollute the lake* **contaminate,** adulterate, taint, poison, foul, dirty, soil, infect; literary befoul.
ANTONYMS purify.
2 *propaganda polluted this nation* **corrupt,** poison, warp, pervert, deprave, defile, blight, sully; literary besmirch.

> CHOOSE THE RIGHT WORD
>
> **pollute, adulterate, contaminate, defile, taint**
>
> When a factory pours harmful chemicals or wastes into the air or water, it is said to **pollute** the environment. But *pollute* may also refer to impairing the purity, integrity, or effectiveness of something (*a campaign polluted by allegations of sexual impropriety*). To **contaminate** is to spread harmful or undesirable impurities throughout something; unlike *pollute*, which suggests visible or noticeable impurities, **contaminate** is preferred where the change is unsuspected or not immediately noticeable (*milk contaminated by radioactive fallout from a nuclear plant accident*). **Adulterate** often refers to food products to which harmful, low-quality, or low-cost substances have been added in order to defraud the consumer (*cereal adulterated with sawdust*), although this word can apply to any mixture to which the inferior or harmful element is added deliberately and in the hope that no one will notice (*a report adulterated with false statistics*). To **defile** is to pollute something that should be kept pure or sacred (*a church defiled by vandals*), while **taint** implies that a trace of something toxic or corrupt has been introduced (*he contracted the disease from a tainted blood transfusion; the book is tainted by gratuitous violence*).

pollution ▶ noun **1** *air and water pollution* **contamination,** adulteration, impurity; dirt, filth, toxins, infection; smog.
2 *the pollution of young minds* **corruption,** defilement, poisoning, warping, depravation, sullying, violation.

pomp ▶ noun *the pomp of a royal wedding* **ceremony,** ceremonial, solemnity, ritual, display, spectacle, pageantry; show, showiness, ostentation, splendor, grandeur, magnificence, majesty, stateliness, glory, opulence, brilliance, drama, resplendence, splendidness; informal razzmatazz.

pompous ▶ adjective *pompous officials* **self-important,** imperious, overbearing, domineering, magisterial, pontifical, sententious, grandiose, affected, pretentious, puffed up, arrogant, vain, haughty, proud, conceited, egotistic, supercilious, condescending, patronizing; informal snooty, uppity, uppish. See note at FORMAL.
ANTONYMS modest.

pond ▶ noun *snowy egrets visit our pond* **pool,** waterhole, lake, tarn, reservoir, slough, beaver pond, lagoon.

ponder ▶ verb *she had time to* ***ponder over*** *the incident* **think about,** contemplate, consider, review, reflect on, mull over, meditate on, muse on, deliberate about, cogitate on, dwell on, brood on, ruminate on, chew over, puzzle over, turn over in one's mind.

ponderous ▶ adjective **1** *a ponderous dance* **clumsy,** heavy, awkward, lumbering, slow, cumbersome, ungainly, graceless, uncoordinated, blundering; informal clodhopping, clunky. See note at HEAVY.
ANTONYMS light, graceful.
2 *his ponderous sentences* **labored,** laborious, awkward, clumsy, forced, stilted, unnatural, artificial; stodgy, lifeless, plodding, pedestrian, boring, dull, tedious, monotonous; overelaborate, convoluted, windy.
ANTONYMS lively.

pontificate ▶ verb *he pontificated about life and art* **hold forth,** expound, declaim, preach, lay down the law, sound off, dogmatize, sermonize, moralize, lecture; informal preachify, mouth off.

pooh-pooh ▶ verb informal *an idea pooh-poohed by the scientific community* **dismiss,** reject, spurn, rebuff, wave aside, disregard, discount; play down, make light of, belittle, deride, mock, scorn, scoff at, sneer at.

pool[1] ▶ noun **1** *pools of water* **puddle,** pond, slough; literary plash.
2 *the hotel has a pool* **swimming pool,** baths, lap pool, natatorium.

pool[2] ▶ noun **1** *a pool of skilled labor* **supply,** reserve(s), reservoir, fund; store, stock, accumulation, cache.
2 *a pool of money for emergencies* **fund,** reserve, kitty, pot, bank, purse.
3 *the office hockey pool* **lottery,** bet.
▶ verb *they pooled their skills* **combine,** amalgamate, group, join, unite, merge; fuse, conglomerate, integrate; share.

poor ▶ adjective **1** *a poor family* **poverty-stricken,** penniless, moneyless, impoverished, low-income, necessitous, impecunious, indigent, needy, destitute, pauperized, unable to make ends meet, without a sou; insolvent, in debt, without a cent (to one's name); informal (flat) broke, hard up, cleaned out, strapped; formal penurious.
ANTONYMS rich, wealthy.
2 *poor workmanship* **substandard,** below par, bad, deficient, defective, faulty, imperfect, inferior; appalling, abysmal, atrocious, awful, terrible, dreadful, unsatisfactory, second-rate, third-rate, tinpot, shoddy, crude, lamentable, deplorable, inadequate, unacceptable; informal crummy, lame, crappy, dismal, bum, rotten.
ANTONYMS superior.
3 *a poor crop* **meager,** scanty, scant, paltry, disappointing, limited, reduced, modest, insufficient, inadequate, sparse, spare, deficient, insubstantial, skimpy, short, small, lean, slender; informal measly, stingy, pathetic, piddling; formal exiguous.
ANTONYMS satisfactory, good.
4 *poor soil* **unproductive,** barren, unyielding, unfruitful; arid, sterile.
ANTONYMS fertile, productive.
5 *the waters are* ***poor in*** *nutrients* **deficient in,** lacking in, wanting in, weak in; short of, low on.
6 *you poor thing!* **unfortunate,** unlucky, luckless, unhappy, hapless, ill-fated, ill-starred, pitiable, pitiful, wretched.
ANTONYMS lucky.

poorly ▶ adverb *the text is poorly written* **badly,** deficiently, defectively, imperfectly, incompetently; appallingly, abysmally, atrociously, awfully, dreadfully; crudely, shoddily, inadequately.
▶ adjective *she felt poorly* **ill,** unwell, not (very) well, ailing, indisposed, out of sorts, under/below par, peaked; sick, queasy, nauseous; off; informal under the weather, funny, peculiar, lousy, rough.

pop ▶ verb **1** *champagne corks popped* **go bang,** go off; crack, snap, burst, explode.
2 *I'm just popping home* **go**; drop in, stop by, visit.
3 *pop a lid over the pot* **put,** place, slip, slide, stick, set, lay, install, position, arrange.
▶ noun **1** *the balloons burst with a pop* **bang,** crack, snap; explosion, report.
2 informal *a bottle of pop* **soft drink,** soda, carbonated drink.
– PHRASES **pop up** *you never know when a new problem is going to pop up* **appear (suddenly),** occur (suddenly), arrive, materialize, come along, happen, emerge, arise, crop up, turn up, present itself, come to light; informal show up.

populace ▶ noun *when the populace wants to, it can change the course of history* **population,** inhabitants, residents, natives; community, country, (general) public, people, nation; common people, man/woman in the street, masses, multitude, rank and file, commonalty, commonality, third estate, plebeians, proletariat; informal proles, plebs; formal denizens; derogatory hoi polloi, common herd, rabble, riffraff; (**the populace**) Joe Public, John Q. Public.

popular ▶ adjective **1** *the most popular restaurant in town* **well-liked,** favored, sought-after, in demand, desired, wanted; commercial, marketable, fashionable, trendy, in vogue, all the rage, hot; informal in, cool, big.
2 *popular science* **nonspecialist,** nontechnical, amateur, lay person's, general, middle-of-the-road; accessible, simplified, plain, simple, easy, straightforward, understandable; mass-market, middlebrow, lowbrow, pop.
ANTONYMS highbrow.
3 *popular opinion* **widespread,** general, common, current, prevalent, prevailing, standard, stock; ordinary, usual, accepted, established, acknowledged, conventional, orthodox.
4 *a popular movement for independence* **mass,** general, communal, collective, social, collaborative, group, civil, public.

popularize ▶ verb **1** *tobacco was popularized by Sir Walter Raleigh* **make popular,** make fashionable; market, publicize; informal hype.
2 *he popularized the subject* **simplify,** make accessible, give mass-market appeal to, universalize, vulgarize.
3 *the report popularized the unfounded notion* **give currency to,** spread, propagate, give credence to.

popularly ▶ adverb **1** *old age is popularly associated with illness* **widely,** generally, universally, commonly, usually, customarily, habitually, conventionally, traditionally, as a rule.
2 *the bar was popularly known as "the May"* **informally,** unofficially; by lay people.
3 *the president is popularly elected* **democratically,** by the people.

populate ▶ verb **1** *the town is populated by 40,000 people* **inhabit,** occupy, people; live in, reside in.
2 *an attempt to populate the island* **settle,** colonize, people, occupy, move into, make one's home in.

population ▶ noun *a new social agenda for the population of these emerging nations* **inhabitants,** residents, people, citizens, citizenry, public, community, populace, society, body politic, natives, occupants; formal denizens.

populous ▶ adjective *a populous island* **densely populated,** heavily populated, congested, crowded, packed, jammed, crammed, teeming, swarming, seething, crawling; informal jam-packed.
ANTONYMS deserted.

porch ▶ noun *the chair would be ideal for a porch or patio* **vestibule,** foyer, entrance (hall), entry, portico, lobby; veranda, terrace; stoop; Architecture lanai, tambour, narthex.

pore[1] ▶ noun *pores in the skin* **opening,** orifice, aperture, hole, outlet, inlet, vent; Biology stoma, foramen.

pore[2] ▶ verb *they* ***pored over*** *the map* **study,** read intently, peruse, scrutinize, scan, examine, go over.

pornographic ▶ adjective *pornographic magazines* **obscene,** indecent, crude, lewd, dirty, vulgar, smutty, filthy; erotic, titillating, arousing, suggestive, sexy, risqué; off-color, adult, X-rated, hard-core, soft-core; informal porn, porno, blue, skin.
ANTONYMS wholesome.

pornography ▶ noun *selling pornography to minors* erotica, pornographic material, dirty books; smut, filth, vice; informal (hard/soft) porn, porno, girlie magazines, skin flicks.

porous ▶ adjective *porous fibers* **permeable,** penetrable, pervious, cellular, holey; absorbent, absorptive, spongy.
ANTONYMS impermeable.

port ▶ noun **1** *the German port of Kiel* **seaport.**
2 *shells exploded down by the port* **harbor,** dock(s), haven, marina; anchorage, moorage, harborage, roads.

portable ▶ adjective *a portable tape recorder* **transportable,** movable, mobile, travel; lightweight, compact, handy, convenient.

portend ▶ verb *the sight of a dead bird was believed to portend tragedy* **presage,** augur, foreshadow, foretell, prophesy; be a sign, warn, be an omen, indicate, herald, signal, bode, promise, threaten, signify, spell, denote; literary betoken, foretoken, forebode.

portent ▶ noun **1** *a portent of things to come* **omen,** sign, signal, token, forewarning, warning, foreshadowing, prediction, forecast, prophecy, harbinger, augury, auspice, presage; writing on the wall, indication, hint; literary foretoken.
2 *the word carries terrifying portent* **significance,** importance, import, consequence, meaning, weight; formal moment.

portentous ▶ adjective **1** *portentous signs* **ominous,** warning, premonitory, threatening, menacing, ill-omened, foreboding, inauspicious, unfavorable. See note at OMINOUS.
2 *portentous dialogue* **pompous,** bombastic, self-important, pontifical, solemn, sonorous, grandiloquent.

porter ▶ noun *a porter helped with the bags* **carrier,** baggage clerk, redcap.

portion ▶ noun **1** *the upper portion of the chimney* **part,** piece, bit, section, segment. See note at FRAGMENT.
2 *her portion of the allowance* **share,** slice, quota, quantum, part, percentage, amount, quantity, ration, fraction, division, allocation, measure; informal cut.
3 *a portion of cake* **helping,** serving, amount, quantity; plateful, bowlful; slice, piece, chunk, wedge, slab, hunk.
4 archaic *poverty was certain to be his portion* See DESTINY (sense 1).
▶ verb *she* ***portioned out*** *the food* **share out,** allocate, allot, apportion; distribute, hand out, deal out, dole out, give out, dispense, mete out; informal divvy up.

portly ▶ adjective *a portly gentleman showed us the way to the dining room* **stout,** plump, fat, overweight, heavy, corpulent, fleshy, paunchy, potbellied, well padded, rotund, stocky, heavyset, bulky; informal tubby, roly-poly, beefy, porky, pudgy; informal corn-fed.
ANTONYMS slim.

portrait ▶ noun **1** *a portrait of the first lady* **painting,** picture, drawing, sketch, likeness, image, study, miniature; informal oil; formal portraiture.
2 *a vivid portrait of Italy* **description,** portrayal, representation, depiction, impression, account; sketch, vignette, profile.

portray ▶ verb **1** *she portrays the older architecture of her province* **paint,** draw, sketch, picture, depict, represent, illustrate, render.
2 *the Newfoundland portrayed by Proulx* **describe,** depict, characterize, represent, present, delineate, evoke, tell of.
3 *the actor portrays a spy* **play,** act the part of, take the role of, represent, appear as; formal personate.

portrayal ▶ noun **1** *a portrayal of a parrot* **painting,** picture, portrait, drawing, sketch, representation, depiction, study.
2 *her portrayal of adolescence* **description,** representation, characterization, depiction, evocation.
3 *Brando's* ***portrayal of*** *Corleone* **performance as,** representation of, interpretation of, rendering of, reading of; formal personation of.

pose ▶ verb **1** *pollution poses a threat to health* **constitute,** present, create, cause, produce, be.
2 *the question posed earlier* **raise,** ask, put, set, submit, advance, propose, suggest, moot.
3 *she posed for the artist* **model,** sit.
4 *he posed her on the sofa* **position,** place, put, arrange, dispose, locate, situate.
5 *I wonder what poor sucker she's posing for tonight* **behave affectedly,** strike a pose, posture, attitudinize, put on airs; informal show off.
▶ noun **1** *a sexy pose* **posture,** position, stance, attitude, bearing.
2 *her pose of aggrieved innocence* **pretense,** act, affectation, facade, show, front, display, masquerade, posture.
– PHRASES **pose as** *they pay us to pose as the celebrities we resemble* **pretend to be,** impersonate, pass oneself off as, masquerade as, profess to be, represent oneself as; formal personate.

poser ▶ noun *this situation's a bit of a poser*

difficult question, vexed question, awkward problem, tough one, puzzle, mystery, conundrum, puzzler, enigma, riddle; informal dilemma, toughie, stumper.

posh ▶ adjective *a posh hotel* **smart,** stylish, fancy, high-class, fashionable, chic, luxurious, luxury, deluxe, exclusive, opulent, lavish, grand, showy, upscale, upmarket; informal classy, swanky, snazzy, plush, ritzy, flash, la-di-da, fancy-dancy, fancy-schmancy, swank, tony.

position ▶ noun **1** *the aircraft's position* **location,** place, situation, spot, site, locality, setting, area; whereabouts, bearings, orientation; technical locus.
2 *a standing position* **posture,** stance, attitude, pose.
3 *our financial position* **situation,** state, condition, circumstances; predicament, plight, strait(s).
4 *the two parties jockeyed for position* **advantage,** the upper hand, the edge, the whip hand, primacy; informal the catbird seat.
5 *their position in society* **status,** place, level, rank, standing; stature, prestige, influence, reputation, importance, consequence, class; dated station.
6 *a secretarial position* **job,** post, situation, appointment, role, occupation, employment; office, capacity, duty, function; opening, vacancy, placement.
7 *the government's position on the matter* **viewpoint,** opinion, outlook, attitude, stand, standpoint, stance, perspective, approach, slant, thinking, policy, feelings.
▶ verb *he positioned a chair between them* **put,** place, locate, situate, set, site, stand, station; plant, stick, install; arrange, dispose; informal park.

positive ▶ adjective **1** *a positive response* **affirmative,** favorable, good, approving, enthusiastic, supportive, encouraging.
ANTONYMS negative.
2 *do something positive* **constructive,** practical, useful, productive, helpful, worthwhile, beneficial, effective.
3 *she seems a lot more positive* **optimistic,** hopeful, confident, cheerful, sanguine, buoyant; informal upbeat.
ANTONYMS pessimistic.
4 *positive economic signs* **favorable,** good, promising, encouraging, heartening, propitious, auspicious.
ANTONYMS negative, unfavorable.
5 *positive proof* **definite,** conclusive, certain, categorical, unequivocal, incontrovertible, indisputable, undeniable, unmistakable, irrefutable, reliable, concrete, tangible, clear-cut, explicit, firm, decisive, real, actual.
ANTONYMS doubtful.
6 *I'm positive he's coming back* **certain,** sure, convinced, confident, satisfied, assured.
ANTONYMS uncertain, unsure.

positively ▶ adverb **1** *I could not positively identify the voice* **confidently,** definitely, emphatically, categorically, with certainty, conclusively, unquestionably, undoubtedly, indisputably, unmistakably, assuredly.
2 *he was positively livid* **absolutely,** really, downright, thoroughly, completely, utterly, totally, extremely, fairly; informal plain.

possess ▶ verb **1** *the only hat she possessed* **own,** have (to one's name), hold.
2 *he does not possess a sense of humor* **have,** be blessed with, be endowed with; enjoy, boast.
3 *a supernatural force possessed him* **take control of,** take over, control, dominate, influence; bewitch, enchant, enthrall.
4 *she was possessed by a need to talk to him* **obsess,** haunt, preoccupy, consume; eat someone up, prey on someone's mind.

possessed ▶ adjective *he was like a man possessed* **mad,** demented, insane, crazed, berserk, out of one's mind; bewitched, enchanted, haunted, under a spell.

possession ▶ noun **1** *the estate came into their possession* **ownership,** control, hands, keeping, care, custody, charge, hold, title, guardianship.
2 *her possession of the premises* **occupancy,** occupation, tenure, holding, tenancy.
3 (**possessions**) *she packed her possessions* **belongings,** things, property, (worldly) goods, (personal) effects, assets, chattels, movables, valuables; stuff, bits and pieces; luggage, baggage; informal gear, junk.
4 *colonial possessions* **colony,** dependency, territory, holding, protectorate.
– PHRASES **take possession of** *they were under orders to take possession of the house and all of its contents* **seize,** appropriate, impound, expropriate, sequestrate, sequester, confiscate; take, get, acquire, obtain, procure, possess oneself of, get hold of, get one's hands on; capture, commandeer, requisition; Law distrain; informal get one's mitts on.

possessive ▶ adjective **1** *he was very possessive* **proprietorial,** overprotective, controlling, dominating, jealous, clingy.
2 *kids are possessive of their own property* **covetous,** selfish, unwilling to share; grasping, greedy, acquisitive, grabby.

possibility ▶ noun **1** *there is a possibility that he might be alive* **chance,** likelihood, probability, hope; risk, hazard, danger, fear.
2 *they discussed the possibility of launching a new project* **feasibility,** practicability, chances, odds, probability.
3 *buying a smaller house is one possibility* **option,** alternative, choice, course of action, solution.
4 (**possibilities**) *the idea has distinct possibilities* **potential,** promise, prospects.

possible ▶ adjective **1** *it's not possible to check the figures* **feasible,** practicable, practical, viable, within the bounds/realms of possibility, attainable, achievable, workable; informal doable.
2 *a possible reason for his disappearance* **conceivable,** plausible, imaginable, believable, likely, potential, probable, credible.
ANTONYMS unlikely.
3 *a possible future leader* **potential,** prospective, likely, probable.

possibly ▶ adverb **1** *possibly he took the boy with him* **perhaps,** maybe, it is possible, for all one knows, very likely; literary peradventure, perchance, mayhap.
2 *you can't possibly refuse* **conceivably,** under any circumstances, by any means.

3 *could you possibly help me?* **please,** kindly, be so good as to.

post[1] ▶ **noun** *wooden posts* **pole,** stake, upright, longer, shaft, prop, support, picket, strut, pillar, pale, paling, stanchion; historical puncheon.
▶ **verb 1** *the notice posted on the wall* **affix,** attach, fasten, display, pin (up), put up, stick (up), tack (up).
2 *the group posted a net profit* **announce,** report, make known, publish.

post[2] ▶ **noun** *our federally regulated post* **mail,** postal service; airmail, surface mail, registered mail.
▶ **verb 1** *post the order form today* **mail,** send (off), put in the mail.
2 *post the transaction in the second column* **record,** write in, enter, register.
– PHRASES **keep posted** *we have no more news at this moment, but we'll keep you posted* **keep informed,** keep up to date, keep in the picture, keep briefed, update, fill in; informal keep up to speed.

post[3] ▶ **noun 1** *there were seventy candidates for the post* **job,** position, appointment, situation, place; vacancy, opening.
2 *back to your posts!* **(assigned) position,** station, observation post.
▶ **verb 1** *he'd been **posted to** Berlin* **send to,** assign to a post in/at, dispatch to.
2 *armed guards were posted beside the exit* **put on duty,** station, position, situate, locate.

poster ▶ **noun** *they put up posters all over town* **notice,** placard, bill, sign, advertisement, playbill.

posterity ▶ **noun** *the names of those who died are recorded for posterity* **future generations,** the future.

post-mortem ▶ **noun 1** *the hospital carried out a postmortem* **autopsy,** postmortem examination, necropsy.
2 *a postmortem of her failed relationship* **analysis,** evaluation, assessment, appraisal, examination, review.

postpone ▶ **verb** *sorry, we'll have to postpone the relay race* **put off/back,** delay, defer, reschedule, adjourn, shelve, put over, take a rain check on; informal put on ice, put on the back burner; rare remit.
ANTONYMS bring forward.

> CHOOSE THE RIGHT WORD
>
> **postpone, adjourn, defer, delay, suspend**
>
> All of these verbs have to do with putting things off. **Defer** is the broadest in meaning; it suggests putting something off until a later time (*defer payment; defer a discussion*). If you **postpone** an event or activity, you put it off intentionally, usually until a definite time in the future (*we postponed the party until the next weekend*). If you **adjourn** an activity, you postpone its completion until another day or place; *adjourn* is usually associated with meetings or other formal gatherings that are brought to an end and then resumed (*the judge adjourned the hearing until the following morning*). If you **delay** something, you postpone it because of obstacles (*delayed by severe thunderstorms and highway flooding*) or because you are reluctant to do it (*delay going to the dentist*). **Suspend** suggests stopping an activity for a while, usually for a reason (*forced to suspend work on the bridge until the holiday weekend was over*).

postponement ▶ **noun** *a further postponement of the trial* **deferral,** deferment, delay, putting off/back, rescheduling, adjournment, shelving.

postscript ▶ **noun 1** *a handwritten postscript* **afterthought,** PS, additional remark.
2 *he added postscripts of his own* **addendum,** supplement, appendix, codicil, afterword, addition.

postulate ▶ **verb** *a theory postulated by a respected scientist* **put forward,** suggest, advance, posit, hypothesize, propose; assume, presuppose, presume, take for granted.

posture ▶ **noun 1** *a kneeling posture* **position,** pose, attitude, stance.
2 *good posture* **bearing,** carriage, stance, comportment.
3 *the unions adopted a militant posture* **attitude,** stance, standpoint, point of view, opinion, position, frame of mind.
▶ **verb** *Keith postured, flexing his biceps* **pose,** strike an attitude, strut.

potency ▶ **noun 1** *the potency of his words* **forcefulness,** force, effectiveness, persuasiveness, cogency, influence, strength, authoritativeness, authority, power, powerfulness; literary puissance.
2 *the potency of the drugs* **strength,** powerfulness, power, effectiveness; formal efficacy; efficaciousness.

potent ▶ **adjective 1** *a potent political force* **powerful,** strong, mighty, formidable, influential, dominant, forceful; literary puissant.
ANTONYMS weak.
2 *a potent argument* **forceful,** convincing, cogent, compelling, persuasive, powerful, strong.
3 *a potent drug* **strong,** powerful, effective; formal efficacious.
ANTONYMS weak.

potentate ▶ **noun** *diplomatic missions to foreign potentates* **ruler,** monarch, sovereign, king, queen, emperor, empress, sultan, shah, raja, pharaoh.

potential ▶ **adjective** *a potential source of conflict* **possible,** likely, prospective, future, probable; latent, inherent, undeveloped. See note at **LATENT.**
▶ **noun** *economic potential* **possibilities,** potentiality, prospects; promise, capability, capacity.

potion ▶ **noun** *people paid good money to sample her so-called magic potions* **concoction,** mixture, brew, elixir, philter, drink, decoction; medicine, tonic; literary draft.

potpourri ▶ **noun** *the book is a potpourri of curious animal stories* **mixture,** assortment, collection, selection, assemblage, medley, miscellany, mix, mélange, variety, mixed bag, patchwork, bricolage; ragbag, mishmash, salmagundi, jumble, farrago, hodgepodge, gallimaufry.

pottery ▶ noun *a collection of antique pottery* **china,** crockery, ceramics, earthenware, stoneware.

pouch ▶ noun **1** *a leather pouch* **bag,** purse, sack, sac, pocket.
2 *a kangaroo's pouch* marsupium.

pounce ▶ verb *two men* ***pounced on*** *him* **jump on,** spring on, leap on, dive on, lunge at, fall on, set on, attack suddenly; informal jump, mug.
▶ noun *a sudden pounce* **leap,** spring, jump, dive, lunge, bound.

pound[1] ▶ verb **1** *the two men pounded him with their fists* **beat,** strike, hit, batter, thump, pummel, punch, rain blows on, belabor, hammer, thrash, set on, tear into; informal bash, clobber, wallop, beat the living daylights out of, whack, thwack, lay into, pitch into, light into, whale.
2 *waves pounded the seafront* **beat against,** crash against, batter, dash against, lash, buffet.
3 *gunships pounded the capital* **bombard,** bomb, shell, fire on; archaic cannonade.
4 *pound the cloves with salt* **crush,** grind, pulverize, mill, mash, pulp; technical triturate.
5 *I heard him pounding along the gangway* **walk/run heavily,** stomp, lumber, clomp, clump, tramp, tromp, trudge.
6 *her heart was pounding* **throb,** thump, thud, hammer, pulse, race, go pit-a-pat; literary pant, thrill.

pound[2] ▶ noun *a dog pound* **enclosure,** compound, pen, yard, corral.

pour ▶ verb **1** *blood was pouring from his nose* **stream,** flow, run, gush, course, jet, spurt, surge, spill.
2 *Amy poured wine into his glass* **tip,** let flow, splash, spill, decant; informal slosh, slop.
3 *it was pouring when we set out* **rain heavily/hard,** teem down, pelt down, come down in torrents/sheets, rain cats and dogs.
4 *people poured off the train* **throng,** crowd, swarm, stream, flood.

pout ▶ verb *Crystal pouted sullenly* **look petulant,** pull a face, look sulky.
▶ noun *a childish pout* **petulant expression,** sulky expression, moue.

poverty ▶ noun **1** *abject poverty* **penury,** destitution, pauperism, pauperdom, beggary, indigence, pennilessness, impoverishment, neediness, need, hardship, impecuniousness.
ANTONYMS wealth.
2 *the poverty of choice* **scarcity,** deficiency, dearth, shortage, paucity, insufficiency, absence, lack.
ANTONYMS abundance.
3 *the poverty of her imagination* **inferiority,** mediocrity, poorness, sterility.

powder ▶ noun *the residue was a pinkish powder* **dust,** fine particles; talcum powder, talc.
▶ verb **1** *she powdered her face* **dust,** sprinkle/cover with powder.
2 *the grains are powdered* **crush,** grind, pulverize, pound, mill; technical comminute.
3 *powdered milk* dry, freeze-dry; technical lyophilize.

powdery ▶ adjective *a powdery substance floated through the air* **fine,** dry, fine-grained, powder-like, dusty, chalky, floury, sandy, crumbly, friable.

power ▶ noun **1** *the power of speech* **ability,** capacity, capability, potential, faculty, competence.
ANTONYMS inability.
2 *the unions wield enormous power* **control,** authority, influence, dominance, mastery, domination, dominion, sway, weight, leverage; informal clout, teeth, drag; literary puissance. See note at JURISDICTION.
3 *police have the power to stop and search* **authority,** right, authorization, warrant, license.
4 *a major international power* **state,** country, nation.
5 *he hit the ball with as much power as he could* **strength,** powerfulness, might, force, forcefulness, vigor, energy; brawn, muscle; informal punch; literary thew.
6 *the power of his arguments* **forcefulness,** powerfulness, potency, strength, force, cogency, persuasiveness.
ANTONYMS impotence, weakness.
7 *the new engine has more power* **driving force,** horsepower, h.p., acceleration; informal oomph.
8 *generating power from waste* **energy,** electrical power.
9 informal *the time off did him* ***a power of*** *good* **a great deal of,** a lot of, much; informal lots of, loads of.
– PHRASES **have someone in/under one's power** *I doubt that Roger will ever have Etta under his power* **have control over,** have influence over, have under one's thumb, have at one's mercy, have in one's clutches, have in the palm of one's hand, have someone wrapped around one's little finger, have in one's hip pocket; informal have over a barrel. **the powers that be** *the powers that be did nothing to defuse the situation* **the authorities,** the people in charge, the government.

powerful ▶ adjective **1** *powerful shoulders* **strong,** muscular, muscly, sturdy, strapping, robust, brawny, burly, athletic, manly, well built, solid; informal beefy, hunky; dated stalwart; literary stark, thewy.
ANTONYMS weak.
2 *a powerful drink* **intoxicating,** hard, strong, stiff, industrial-strength; formal spirituous.
3 *a powerful blow* **violent,** forceful, hard, mighty.
ANTONYMS gentle.
4 *he felt a powerful desire to kiss her* **intense,** keen, fierce, passionate, ardent, burning, strong, irresistible, overpowering, overwhelming.
5 *a powerful nation* **influential,** strong, important, dominant, commanding, potent, forceful, formidable; literary puissant.
ANTONYMS weak, powerless.
6 *a powerful critique* **cogent,** compelling, convincing, persuasive, forceful; dramatic, graphic, vivid, moving.

ANTONYMS ineffective.

powerless ▶ adjective *the outgoing administrators are essentially powerless* **impotent,** helpless, ineffectual, ineffective, useless, defenseless, vulnerable; lame-duck; literary impuissant.

practicable ▶ adjective *what we need is a practicable solution* **realistic,** feasible, possible, within the bounds/realms of possibility, viable, reasonable, sensible, workable, achievable; informal doable.

practical ▶ adjective **1** *practical experience* **empirical,** hands-on, actual, active, applied, heuristic, experiential, evidence-based.
ANTONYMS theoretical.
2 *there are no practical alternatives* **feasible,** practicable, realistic, viable, workable, possible, reasonable, sensible; informal doable.
3 *practical clothes* **functional,** sensible, utilitarian, workaday.
4 *try to be more practical* **realistic,** sensible, down-to-earth, businesslike, commonsensical, grounded, hardheaded, no-nonsense; informal hard-nosed.
5 *a practical certainty* **virtual,** effective, near.

practically ▶ adverb **1** *the theater was practically empty* **almost,** (very) nearly, virtually, just about, all but, more or less, as good as, to all intents and purposes, verging on, bordering on; informal pretty near, pretty well; literary well-nigh.
2 *"You can't afford it," he pointed out practically* **realistically,** sensibly, reasonably.

practice ▶ verb **1** *he practiced the songs every day* **rehearse,** run through, go over/through, work on/at; polish, perfect.
2 *the performers were practicing* **train,** rehearse, prepare, go through one's paces.
3 *we still practice these rituals today* **carry out,** perform, observe.
4 *she practices medicine* **work at,** pursue a career in.
▶ noun **1** *the practice of hypnosis* **application,** exercise, use, operation, implementation, execution.
2 *common practice* **custom,** procedure, policy, convention, tradition; formal praxis.
3 *it takes lots of practice | the team's final practice* **training,** rehearsal, repetition, preparation; practice session, dummy run, run-through; informal dry run.
4 *the practice of medicine* **profession,** career, business, work.
5 *a small legal practice* **business,** firm, office, company; informal outfit.
– PHRASES **in practice** *it seemed like a good idea, but in practice it just didn't work* **in reality,** realistically, practically. **out of practice** *considering how out of practice she was, Elizabeth did very well on the balance beam* **rusty,** unpracticed. **put into practice** *it's time you put your teaching degree into practice* **use,** make use of, put to use, utilize, apply.

practiced ▶ adjective *a practiced judge of character* **expert,** experienced, seasoned, skilled, skillful, accomplished, proficient, talented, able, adept, consummate, master, masterly; informal crack, ace, mean, crackerjack.

pragmatic ▶ adjective *she remains pragmatic in the most emotional circumstances* **practical,** matter-of-fact, sensible, down-to-earth, commonsensical, businesslike, having both/one's feet on the ground, hardheaded, no-nonsense; informal hard-nosed.
ANTONYMS impractical.

praise ▶ verb **1** *the police praised Pauline for her courage* **commend,** express admiration for, applaud, pay tribute to, speak highly of, eulogize, compliment, congratulate, sing the praises of, rave about, go into raptures about, heap praise on, wax lyrical about, make much of, pat on the back, take one's hat off to, lionize, admire, hail, ballyhoo; formal laud.
ANTONYMS criticize, condemn.
2 *we praise God* **worship,** glorify, honor, exalt, adore, pay tribute to, give thanks to, venerate, reverence; formal laud; archaic magnify.
▶ noun **1** *your praise means a great deal to us* **approval,** acclaim, admiration, approbation, acclamation, plaudits, congratulations, commendation; tribute, accolade, compliment, a pat on the back, eulogy, panegyric; formal encomium.
2 *give praise to God* **honor,** thanks, glory, worship, devotion, adoration, reverence.

CHOOSE THE RIGHT WORD

acclaim, commend, eulogize, extol, laud

If your dog sits when you tell him to sit, you'll want to **praise** him for his obedience. *Praise* is a general term for expressing approval, esteem, or commendation that usually suggests the judgment of a superior (*the teacher's praise for her students*). If a salesperson goes out of his way to help you, you may want to **commend** him to his superior, which is a more formal, public way of praising someone, either verbally or in writing. If you're watching a performance and want to express your approval verbally or with applause, **acclaim** is the verb you're looking for. **Laud** and **extol** suggest the highest of praise, although *laud* may imply that the praise is excessive (*the accomplishments for which she was lauded were really nothing out of the ordinary*). *Extol*, which comes from the Latin meaning to raise up, suggests that you're trying to magnify whatever or whomever you're praising (*to extol her virtues so that everyone would vote for her*). If you want to praise someone who has died recently, you will **eulogize** him or her, which means to speak or write your praise for a special occasion, such as a funeral.

praiseworthy ▶ adjective *it was a praiseworthy effort* **commendable,** admirable, laudable, worthy (of admiration), meritorious, estimable, exemplary.

prance ▶ verb *prancing around in his underpants* **cavort,** dance, jig, trip, caper, jump, leap, spring, bound, skip, hop, frisk, romp, frolic.

prank ▶ noun *it was just a stupid and childish prank* **(practical) joke,** trick, piece of mischief, escapade, stunt, caper, jape, game, hoax, antic; informal lark.

prattle ▶ verb *he prattled on for ages* See CHAT (verb).
▶ noun *childish prattle* See CHATTER (noun).

pray ▶ verb **1** *let us pray* **say one's prayers,** make one's devotions, offer a prayer/prayers.
2 *she prayed God to forgive her* **invoke,** call on, implore, appeal to, entreat, beg, petition, supplicate; literary beseech.

prayer ▶ noun **1** *the priest's murmured prayers* **invocation,** intercession, devotion; archaic orison.
2 *a quick prayer that she wouldn't bump into him* **appeal,** plea, entreaty, petition, supplication, invocation.
– PHRASES **not have a prayer** informal *everyone thought this Minnesota team didn't have a prayer against Duke* **have no hope,** have/stand no chance, not have/stand (the ghost of) a chance; informal not have a hope in hell.

preach ▶ verb **1** *he preached to a large congregation* **give/deliver a sermon,** sermonize, address, speak.
2 *preaching the gospel* **proclaim,** teach, spread, propagate, expound.
3 *they preach toleration* **advocate,** recommend, advise, urge, teach, counsel.
4 *who are you to preach at me?* **moralize,** sermonize, pontificate, lecture, harangue; informal preachify.

preacher ▶ noun *the preacher counsels young couples about marital concerns* **minister,** parson, clergyman, clergywoman, member of the clergy, priest, imam, rabbi, man/woman of the cloth, man/woman of God, cleric, churchman, churchwoman, evangelist; informal reverend, padre, Holy Joe, sky pilot.

preaching ▶ noun *I ain't got no use for your preaching* **religious teaching,** message, sermons; informal Bible-thumping.

preamble ▶ noun *we memorized the preamble to the Constitution* **introduction,** preface, prologue; foreword, prelude, front matter; informal intro, lead-in; formal exordium, proem, prolegomenon.

precarious ▶ adjective *those steps look a bit precarious* **uncertain,** insecure, unpredictable, risky, parlous, hazardous, dangerous, unsafe; unsettled, unstable, unsteady, shaky; informal dicey, chancy, iffy.
ANTONYMS safe.

precaution ▶ noun *the guard rails are just a precaution* **safeguard,** preventative/preventive measure, safety measure, contingency (plan), insurance.

precede ▶ verb **1** *commercials preceded the movie* **go/come before,** lead (up) to, pave/prepare the way for, herald, introduce, usher in.
ANTONYMS follow.
2 *Catherine preceded him into the studio* **go ahead of,** go in front of, go before, go first, lead the way.
3 *he preceded the book with a poem* **preface,** introduce, begin, open.

precedence ▶ noun *quarrels over precedence* **priority,** rank, seniority, superiority, primacy, preeminence, eminence.
– PHRASES **take precedence over** *the children's needs take precedence over all the other concerns* **take priority over,** outweigh, prevail over, come before.

precedent ▶ noun *there are few precedents for this type of legislation* **model,** exemplar, example, pattern, previous case, prior instance/example; paradigm, criterion, yardstick, standard.

preceding ▶ adjective *refer to the preceding chart* **foregoing,** previous, prior, former, precedent, earlier, above, aforementioned, antecedent; formal anterior, prevenient.

precept ▶ noun **1** *the precepts of Orthodox Judaism* **principle,** rule, tenet, canon, doctrine, command, order, decree, dictate, dictum, injunction, commandment; Judaism mitzvah; formal prescript.
2 *precepts that her grandmother used to quote* **maxim,** saying, adage, axiom, aphorism, apophthegm.

precinct ▶ noun **1** *a pedestrian precinct* **area,** zone, sector.
2 (**precincts**) *within the precincts of the city* **bounds,** boundaries, limits, confines.
3 *the cathedral precinct* **enclosure,** close, court.
4 *the friendliest cop of the 20th precinct* **division.**

precious ▶ adjective **1** *precious works of art* **valuable,** costly, expensive; invaluable, priceless, beyond price.
2 *her most precious possession* **valued,** cherished, treasured, prized, favorite, dear, dearest, beloved, darling, adored, loved, special.
3 *his precious manners* **affected,** overrefined, pretentious; informal la-di-da.

precipice ▶ noun *it's amazing how these goats can scale such a precipice* **cliff face,** cliff, steep cliff, rock face, sheer drop, height, crag, bluff, escarpment, scarp; literary steep.

precipitate ▶ verb **1** *the incident precipitated a crisis* **bring about/on,** cause, lead to, give rise to, instigate, trigger, spark, touch off, provoke, hasten, accelerate, expedite.
2 *they were precipitated down the mountain* **hurl,** catapult, throw, plunge, launch, fling, propel.
▶ adjective **1** *their actions were precipitate* **hasty,** overhasty, rash, hurried, rushed; impetuous, impulsive, spur-of-the-moment, precipitous, incautious, imprudent, injudicious, ill-advised, reckless, harum-scarum; informal previous; literary temerarious.
2 *a precipitate decline* See PRECIPITOUS (sense 2).

precipitous ▶ adjective **1** *a precipitous drop* **steep,** sheer, perpendicular, abrupt, sharp, vertical.
2 *his fall from power was precipitous* **sudden,** rapid, swift, abrupt, headlong, speedy, quick, fast, precipitate.
3 *she was too precipitous* See PRECIPITATE (sense 1 of the adjective).

precise ▶ adjective **1** *precise measurements* **exact,** accurate, correct, specific, detailed, explicit, unambiguous, definite.
ANTONYMS inaccurate.
2 *at that precise moment the car stopped* **exact,**

particular, very, specific.
3 *the attention to detail is very precise* **meticulous,** careful, exact, scrupulous, punctilious, conscientious, particular, methodical, strict, rigorous.
ANTONYMS careless.

precisely ▶ adverb **1** *at 2 o'clock precisely* **exactly,** sharp, promptly, prompt, dead on, on the stroke of; informal on the button, on the dot, on the nose.
2 *precisely the kind of man I am looking for* **exactly,** absolutely, just, in all respects; informal to a T.
3 *fertilization can be timed precisely* **accurately,** exactly; clearly, distinctly, strictly.
4 *"So it's all done?" "Precisely."* **yes,** exactly, absolutely, (that's) right, quite so, indubitably, definitely; informal you bet, I'll say.

precision ▶ noun *tools crafted with precision* **exactness,** exactitude, accuracy, correctness, preciseness; care, carefulness, meticulousness, scrupulousness, punctiliousness, methodicalness, rigor, rigorousness.

preclude ▶ verb *his difficulties preclude him from leading a normal life* **prevent,** make it impossible for, rule out, stop, prohibit, debar, bar, hinder, impede, inhibit, exclude. See note at PROHIBIT.

precocious ▶ adjective *some of the boys were extremely precocious* **advanced for one's age,** forward, mature, gifted, talented, clever, intelligent, quick; informal smart.
ANTONYMS backward.

preconception ▶ noun *it will be difficult to find jurors who have no preconceptions about this case* **preconceived idea/notion,** presupposition, assumption, presumption, prejudgment; prejudice.

precondition ▶ noun *one of the preconditions is a spotless driving record* **prerequisite,** (necessary/essential) condition, requirement, necessity, essential, imperative, sine qua non; informal must.

precursor ▶ noun **1** *a three-stringed precursor of the guitar* **forerunner,** predecessor, forefather, father, antecedent, ancestor, forebear.
2 *a precursor of disasters to come* **harbinger,** herald, sign, indication, portent, omen.

predatory ▶ adjective **1** *predatory birds* **predacious,** carnivorous, hunting, raptorial; of prey.
2 *a predatory gleam in his eyes* **exploitative,** wolfish, rapacious, vulturine, vulturous.

predecessor ▶ noun **1** *the senator's predecessor* **forerunner,** precursor, antecedent.
ANTONYMS successor.
2 *our Victorian predecessors* **ancestor,** forefather, forebear, antecedent.
ANTONYMS descendant.

predetermined ▶ adjective **1** *a predetermined budget* **prearranged,** established in advance, preset, set, fixed, agreed.
2 *our predetermined fate* **predestined,** preordained.

predicament ▶ noun *how did you ever get yourself into such a predicament* **difficult situation,** mess, difficulty, plight, quandary, muddle, mare's nest; informal hole, fix, jam, pickle, scrape, bind, tight spot/corner, dilemma, can of worms.

predict ▶ verb *no one can predict the outcome* **forecast,** foretell, foresee, prophesy, anticipate, tell in advance, envision, envisage; literary previse; archaic augur, presage.

CHOOSE THE RIGHT WORD

predict, augur, divine, forecast, foreshadow, foretell, prognosticate, prophesy

While all of these words refer to telling something before it happens, **predict** is the most commonly used and applies to the widest variety of situations. It can mean anything from hazarding a guess (*they predicted he'd never survive the year*) to making an astute inference based on facts or statistical evidence (*predict that the Republicans would win the election*). When a meteorologist tells us whether it will rain or snow tomorrow, he or she is said to **forecast** the weather, a word that means *predict* but is used particularly in the context of weather and other phenomena that cannot be predicted easily by the general public (*statistics forecast an influx of women into the labor force*). **Divine** and **foreshadow** mean to suggest the future rather than to predict it, especially by giving or evaluating subtle hints or clues. To *divine* something is to perceive it through intuition or insight (*to divine in the current economic situation the disaster that lay ahead*), while *foreshadow* can apply to anyone or anything that gives an indication of what is to come (*her abrupt departure that night foreshadowed the breakdown in their relationship*). **Foretell,** like *foreshadow,* can refer to the clue rather than the person who gives it and is often used in reference to the past (*evidence that foretold the young girl's violent end*). **Augur** means to foreshadow a favorable or unfavorable outcome for something (*the turnout on opening night augured well for the play's success*). **Prophesy** connotes either inspired or mystical knowledge of the future and suggests more authoritative wisdom than *augur* (*a baseball fan for decades, he prophesied the young batter's rise to stardom*). Although anyone who has inside information or knowledge of signs and symptoms can **prognosticate**, it is usually a doctor who does so by looking at the symptoms of a disease to predict its future outcome.

predictable ▶ adjective *Guido's reaction was predictable* **foreseeable,** (only) to be expected, anticipated, foreseen, unsurprising; informal inevitable.

prediction ▶ noun *seven months later, his prediction came true* **forecast,** prophecy, prognosis, prognostication, augury; projection, conjecture, guess.

predilection ▶ noun **liking,** fondness, preference, partiality, taste, penchant,

weakness, soft spot, fancy, inclination, leaning, bias, propensity, bent, proclivity, predisposition, appetite.
ANTONYMS dislike.

predispose ▶ verb **1** *lack of exercise may predispose an individual to high blood pressure* **make susceptible,** make liable, make prone, make vulnerable, put at risk of.
2 *attitudes which predispose people to behave badly* **lead,** influence, sway, induce, prompt, dispose; bias, prejudice.

predisposed ▶ adjective **inclined,** prepared, ready, of a mind, disposed, minded, willing.

predisposition ▶ noun **1** *a predisposition to heart disease* **susceptibility,** proneness, tendency, liability, inclination, disposition, vulnerability.
2 *their political predispositions* **preference,** predilection, inclination, leaning.

predominance ▶ noun **1** *the predominance of women caregivers* **prevalence,** dominance, preponderance.
2 *the superpower's military predominance* **supremacy,** mastery, control, power, ascendancy, dominance, preeminence, superiority.

predominant ▶ adjective **1** *our predominant objectives* **main,** chief, principal, most important, primary, prime, central, leading, foremost, key, paramount; informal number-one.
2 *the predominant political forces* **controlling,** dominant, predominating, more/most powerful, preeminent, ascendant, superior, in the ascendancy.
ANTONYMS subsidiary.

predominate ▶ verb **1** *small-scale producers predominate* **be in the majority,** preponderate, be predominant, prevail, be most prominent.
2 *private interest predominates over the public good* **prevail,** dominate, be dominant, carry most weight; override, outweigh.

preeminence ▶ noun **superiority,** supremacy, greatness, excellence, distinction, prominence, predominance, eminence, importance, prestige, stature, fame, renown, celebrity.

preeminent ▶ adjective **greatest,** leading, foremost, best, finest, chief, outstanding, excellent, distinguished, prominent, eminent, important, top, famous, renowned, celebrated, illustrious, supreme, marquee.
ANTONYMS undistinguished.

preempt ▶ verb **1** *his action may have preempted war* **forestall,** prevent.
2 *many tables were already preempted by family parties* **commandeer,** occupy, seize, arrogate, appropriate, take over, secure, reserve.

preen ▶ verb **1** *the robin preened its feathers* **clean,** tidy, groom, smooth, arrange; archaic plume.
2 *she preened before the mirror* **admire oneself,** primp oneself, groom oneself, spruce oneself up; informal titivate oneself, doll oneself up, gussy oneself up.

preface ▶ noun *the preface to the novel* **introduction,** foreword, preamble, prologue, prelude; front matter; informal prelims, intro, lead-in; formal exordium, proem, prolegomenon.
▶ verb *the chapter is prefaced by a poem* **precede,** introduce, begin, open, start.

prefatory ▶ adjective *prefatory text* **introductory,** preliminary, opening, initial, preparatory, initiatory, precursory.
ANTONYMS closing.

prefer ▶ verb **1** *I prefer white wine to red* **like better,** would rather (have), would sooner (have), favor, be more partial to; choose, select, pick, opt for, go for.
2 formal *do you want to prefer charges?* **bring,** press, file, lodge, lay.
3 archaic *he was preferred to the post* **promote,** upgrade, raise, elevate.

preferable ▶ adjective *Dom sleeps on a foam pillow, but for me goose down is preferable* **better,** best, more desirable, more suitable, advantageous, superior, preferred, recommended.

preferably ▶ adverb *we'd like a table by the window, preferably nonsmoking* **ideally,** if possible, for preference, from choice.

preference ▶ noun **1** *her preference for boys' games* **liking,** partiality, predilection, proclivity, fondness, taste, inclination, leaning, bias, bent, penchant, predisposition.
2 *my preference is rock music* **favorite,** (first) choice, selection; informal cup of tea, thing, druthers.
3 *preference will be given to applicants speaking Japanese* **priority,** favor, precedence, preferential treatment.
– PHRASES **in preference to** *the thief chose their home in preference to others* **rather than,** instead of, in place of, sooner than.

preferential ▶ adjective *we were not expecting this preferential treatment* **special,** better, privileged, superior, favorable; partial, discriminatory, partisan, biased.

pregnancy ▶ noun *how far along is she in the pregnancy?* gestation; rare parturiency, gravidity.

pregnant ▶ adjective **1** *she is pregnant* **expecting a baby,** expectant, carrying a child; informal expecting, in the family way, with a bun in the oven, knocked up; informal preggie; informal dated in trouble; archaic with child; technical parturient, gravid.
2 *a ceremony pregnant with religious significance* **filled,** charged, heavy; full of.
3 *a pregnant pause* **meaningful,** significant, suggestive, expressive, charged.

prehistoric ▶ adjective **1** *prehistoric times* **primitive,** primeval, primordial, primal, ancient, early, antediluvian.
2 *the special effects look prehistoric* **out of date,** outdated, outmoded, old-fashioned, passé, antiquated, archaic, behind the times, primitive; antediluvian; informal horse-and-buggy, clunky.
ANTONYMS modern.

prejudice ▶ noun **1** *male prejudices about women* **preconceived idea,** preconception, prejudgment.
2 *they are motivated by prejudice* **bigotry,** bias, partisanship, partiality, intolerance, discrimination, unfairness, inequality. See note at BIAS.

3 *without prejudice to the interests of others* **detriment,** harm, damage, injury, hurt, loss.
▶ **verb 1** *the article could prejudice the jury* **bias,** influence, sway, predispose, make biased, make partial, color.
2 *this could prejudice his chances of victory* **damage,** be detrimental to, be prejudicial to, injure, harm, hurt, spoil, impair, undermine, hinder, compromise.

prejudiced ▶ **adjective** *his prejudiced views* **biased,** bigoted, discriminatory, partisan, intolerant, narrow-minded, unfair, unjust, inequitable, colored.
ANTONYMS impartial.

prejudicial ▶ **adjective** *disclosure of the information would be prejudicial* **detrimental,** damaging, injurious, harmful, disadvantageous, hurtful, deleterious.
ANTONYMS beneficial.

preliminary ▶ **adjective** *the discussions are still at a preliminary stage* **preparatory,** introductory, initial, opening, prefatory, precursory; early, exploratory.
ANTONYMS final.
▶ **noun 1** (**preliminaries**) *he began without any preliminaries* **introduction,** preamble, opening/prefatory remarks, formalities.
2 *a preliminary to the resumption of war* **prelude,** preparation, preparatory measure, preliminary action.
– PHRASES **preliminary to** *the geese gather in estuaries, preliminary to their flight southward* **in preparation for,** before, in advance of, prior to, preparatory to.

prelude ▶ **noun 1** *the cease-fire was a prelude to peace negotiations* **preliminary,** overture, opening, preparation, introduction, start, commencement, beginning, lead-in, precursor.
2 *an orchestral prelude* **overture,** introductory movement, introduction, opening.
3 *the passage forms a prelude to Part III* **introduction,** preface, prologue, foreword, preamble; informal intro, lead-in; formal exordium, proem, prolegomenon.

premature ▶ **adjective 1** *his premature death* **untimely,** (too) early, unseasonable, before time.
ANTONYMS overdue.
2 *a premature baby* **preterm.**
ANTONYMS overdue.
3 *such a step would be premature* **rash,** ill-considered, overhasty, hasty, precipitate, precipitous, impulsive, impetuous, inopportune; informal previous.

premeditated ▶ **adjective** *the premeditated murder of Lady Boswell* **planned,** intentional, deliberate, preplanned, calculated, cold-blooded, conscious, prearranged.
ANTONYMS spontaneous.

premier ▶ **adjective** *a premier chef* **leading,** foremost, chief, principal, head, top-ranking, top, prime, primary, first, highest, preeminent, nonpareil, senior, outstanding, master, ranking; informal top-notch, blue-ribbon, blue-chip.
▶ **noun** *the Nova Scotian premier* **leader,** head of government, government leader; president, chancellor, prime minister, PM.

premiere ▶ **noun** *tickets for a Broadway premiere* **first performance,** first night, opening night.

premise ▶ **noun** *the premise that human life consists of a series of choices* **proposition,** assumption, hypothesis, thesis, presupposition, postulation, postulate, supposition, presumption, surmise, conjecture, speculation, assertion, belief.
▶ **verb** *they premised that the cosmos is indestructible* **postulate,** hypothesize, conjecture, posit, theorize, suppose, presuppose, surmise, assume.

premises ▶ **plural noun** *he was asked to leave the premises* **building(s),** property, site, office.

premium ▶ **noun 1** *monthly premiums of $30* **(regular) payment,** installment.
2 *you must pay a premium for organic fruit* **surcharge,** additional payment, extra amount.
3 *a foreign service premium* **bonus,** extra; incentive, inducement; informal perk; formal perquisite.
– PHRASES **at a premium** *back then, sugar was at a premium* **scarce,** in great demand, hard to come by, in short supply, thin on the ground.
put/place a premium on 1 *I place a high premium on our relationship* **value greatly,** attach great/special importance to, set great store by, put a high value on. **2** *the high price of oil put a premium on the coal industry* **make valuable,** make invaluable, make important.

premonition ▶ **noun** *we've learned to take her premonitions seriously* **foreboding,** presentiment, intuition, (funny) feeling, hunch, suspicion, feeling in one's bones; misgiving, apprehension, fear; archaic presage. See note at **OMINOUS**.

preoccupation ▶ **noun 1** *an air of preoccupation* **pensiveness,** concentration, engrossment, absorption, self-absorption, musing, thinking, deep thought, brown study, brooding; abstraction, absentmindedness, distraction, forgetfulness, inattentiveness, woolgathering, daydreaming.
2 *their main preoccupation was feeding their family* **obsession,** concern; passion, enthusiasm, hobbyhorse.

preoccupied ▶ **adjective 1** *officials preoccupied with their careers* **obsessed,** concerned, absorbed, engrossed, intent, involved, wrapped up.
2 *she looked preoccupied* **lost/deep in thought,** in a brown study, pensive, absentminded, distracted, abstracted.

preoccupy ▶ **verb** *the issues that preoccupy environmentalists* **engross,** concern, absorb, take up someone's attention, distract, obsess, occupy, prey on someone's mind.

preparation ▶ **noun 1** *the preparation of contingency plans* **devising,** putting together, drawing up, construction, composition, production, getting ready, development.
2 (**preparations**) *preparations for the party* **arrangements,** planning, plans, preparatory measures.
3 *preparation for exams* **instruction,** teaching, coaching, training, tutoring, drilling, priming.

4 *a preparation to kill off mites* **mixture,** compound, concoction, solution, tincture, medicine, potion, cream, ointment, lotion.

preparatory ▶ adjective *preparatory work* **preliminary,** initial, introductory, prefatory, opening, preparative, precursory.
– PHRASES **preparatory to** *we locked all the doors and windows preparatory to leaving* **in preparation for,** before, prior to, preliminary to.

prepare ▶ verb **1** *I want you to prepare a report* **make/get ready,** put together, draw up, produce, arrange, assemble, construct, compose, formulate.
2 *the meal was easy to prepare* **cook,** make, get, put together, concoct; informal fix, rustle up.
3 *preparing for war* **get ready,** make preparations, arrange things, make provision, get everything set.
4 *athletes preparing for the Olympics* **train,** get into shape, practice, get ready.
5 *I must prepare for my exams* **study,** review.
6 *this course prepares students for their exams* **instruct,** coach, train, tutor, drill, prime.
7 *prepare yourself for a shock* **brace,** make ready, tense, steel, steady.

prepared ▶ adjective **1** *he needs to be prepared for the worst* **ready,** (all) set, equipped, primed; waiting, on hand, poised, in position.
2 *I'm not prepared to cut the price* **willing,** ready, disposed, predisposed, (favorably) inclined, of a mind, minded.

preponderance ▶ noun **1** *the preponderance of women among older people* **prevalence,** predominance, dominance.
2 *the preponderance of the evidence* **bulk,** majority, larger part, best/better part.
3 *the preponderance of the unions* **predominance,** dominance, ascendancy, supremacy, power.

prepossessing ▶ adjective *his prepossessing wife turned heads wherever they went* **attractive,** beautiful, pretty, handsome, good-looking, fetching, charming, delightful, enchanting, captivating; archaic fair.
ANTONYMS ugly.

preposterous ▶ adjective *at these sessions, no ideas are too preposterous to throw on the table* **absurd,** ridiculous, foolish, stupid, ludicrous, farcical, laughable, comical, risible, nonsensical, senseless, insane; outrageous, monstrous; informal crazy. See note at **ABSURD**.
ANTONYMS sensible.

prerequisite ▶ noun *a prerequisite for the course* **(necessary) condition,** precondition, essential, requirement, requisite, necessity, sine qua non; informal must.
▶ adjective *the prerequisite qualifications* **necessary,** required, called for, essential, requisite, obligatory, compulsory.
ANTONYMS unnecessary.

prerogative ▶ noun *it's my prerogative to hold on to the farm* **entitlement,** right, privilege, advantage, due, birthright.

presage ▶ verb *the owl's hooting presages death* **portend,** augur, foreshadow, foretell, prophesy, be an omen of, herald, be a sign of, be the harbinger of, warn of, be a presage of, signal, bode, promise, threaten; literary betoken, foretoken, forebode.
▶ noun *a somber presage of his final illness* **omen,** sign, indication, portent, warning, forewarning, harbinger, augury, prophecy, foretoken.

prescribe ▶ verb **1** *the doctor prescribed antibiotics* **write a prescription for,** authorize.
2 *traditional values prescribe a life of domesticity* **advise,** recommend, advocate, suggest, endorse, champion, promote.
3 *rules prescribing your duty* **stipulate,** lay down, dictate, specify, determine, establish, fix.

prescription ▶ noun **1** *the doctor wrote a prescription* **instruction,** authorization; informal scrip; archaic recipe.
2 *he fetched the prescription from the drug store* **medicine,** drugs, medication.
3 *a painless prescription for improvement* **method,** measure; recommendation, suggestion, recipe, formula.

presence ▶ noun **1** *the presence of a train was indicated electrically* **existence,** being there.
ANTONYMS absence.
2 *I requested the presence of a nurse* **attendance,** appearance; company, companionship.
ANTONYMS absence.
3 *a woman of great presence* **aura,** charisma, (strength/force of) personality; poise, self-assurance, self-confidence.
4 *she felt a presence in the castle* **ghost,** spirit, specter, phantom, apparition, supernatural being; informal spook; literary shade.
– PHRASES **presence of mind** *I didn't have the presence of mind to read his license plate* **composure,** equanimity, self-possession, levelheadedness, self-assurance, calmness, sangfroid, imperturbability; alertness, quick-wittedness; informal cool, unflappability.

present[1] ▶ adjective **1** *a doctor must be present at the ringside* **in attendance,** here, there, near, nearby, (close/near) at hand, available.
ANTONYMS absent.
2 *organic compounds are present in the waste* **in existence,** existing, existent.
ANTONYMS absent.
3 *the present economic climate* **current,** present-day, existing.
ANTONYMS past, future.
▶ noun *forget the past and think about the present* **now,** today, the present time/moment, the here and now.
ANTONYMS past, future.
– PHRASES **at present** *at present, we are offering free installation* **at the moment,** just now, right now, at the present time, currently, at this moment in time. **for the present** *he can stay in the guest room, but only for the present* **for the time being,** for now, for the moment, for a while, temporarily, pro tem.

present[2] ▶ verb **1** *the president presented a check to the winner* **hand over/out,** give (out), confer, bestow, award, grant, accord.
2 *the committee presented its report* **submit,** set forth, put forward, proffer, offer, tender, table.
3 *may I present my wife?* **introduce,** make known, acquaint someone with.
4 *I called to present my warmest compliments*

offer, give, express.
5 *they presented their new product last month* **demonstrate,** show, put on show/display, exhibit, display, launch, unveil.
6 *presenting good quality opera* **stage,** put on, produce, perform.
7 *she presents a TV show* **host,** introduce, be the presenter of, emcee.
8 *the authorities present him as a common criminal* **represent,** describe, portray, depict.
– PHRASES **present oneself/itself 1** *he presented himself at ten* **be present,** make an appearance, appear, turn up, arrive. **2** *an opportunity that presented itself* **occur,** arise, happen, come about/up, appear, crop up, turn up.

present[3] ▶ noun *a birthday present* **gift,** donation, offering, contribution; informal freebie; formal benefaction.

CHOOSE THE RIGHT WORD

present, bonus, donation, gift, gratuity, lagniappe, largesse

What's the difference between a birthday **present** and a Christmas **gift**? Both words refer to something given as an expression of friendship, affection, esteem, etc. But *gift* is a more formal term, suggesting something of monetary value that is formally bestowed on an individual, group, or institution (*a gift to the university*). *Present,* on the other hand, implies something of less value that is an expression of goodwill (*a housewarming present; a present for the teacher*). **Largesse** is a somewhat pompous term for a very generous gift that is conferred in an ostentatious or condescending way, often on many recipients (*the king's largesse; the largesse of our government*). A **gratuity** is associated with tipping and other forms of voluntary compensation for special attention or service above and beyond what is included in a charge (*known for her generous gratuities, the duchess enjoyed watching the waiters compete with each other to serve her*), while a **lagniappe** is a Southern word, used chiefly in Louisiana and southeast Texas, for either a gratuity or a small gift given to a customer along with a purchase. If you give money or anything else as a gift to a philanthropic, charitable, or religious organization, it is known as a **donation** (*donations for the poor*). But if your employer gives you money at the end of the year in addition to your regular salary, it isn't a Christmas gift; it's a Christmas **bonus**.

presentable ▶ adjective **1** *I'm making the place look presentable* **tidy,** neat, straight, clean, spick-and-span, in good order, shipshape.
2 *make yourself presentable* **nicely dressed,** tidily dressed, smartly dressed, tidy, well-groomed, trim, spruce; informal natty.
3 *presentable videos* **fairly good,** passable, all right, satisfactory, moderately good, not (too) bad, average, fair; informal OK.

presentation ▶ noun **1** *the presentation of his certificate* **awarding,** presenting, giving, handing over/out, bestowal, granting, award.
2 *the presentation of food* **appearance,** arrangement, packaging, disposition, display, layout.
3 *the presentation of new proposals* **submission,** proffering, offering, tendering, advancing, proposal, suggestion, mooting, tabling.
4 *a sales presentation* **demonstration,** talk, lecture, address, speech, show, exhibition, display, introduction, launch, launching, unveiling.
5 *a presentation of his latest play* **staging,** production, performance, mounting, showing.

presentiment ▶ noun *a presentiment of disaster* **premonition,** foreboding, intuition, (funny) feeling, hunch, feeling in one's bones, sixth sense; archaic presage.

presently ▶ adverb **1** *I shall see you presently* **soon,** shortly, directly, quite soon, in a short time, in a little while, at any moment/minute/second, in next to no time, before long, momentarily; informal pretty soon, any moment now, in a jiffy, in two shakes of a lamb's tail; literary ere long.
2 *he is presently abroad* **currently,** at present, at the/this moment, at the present moment/time, now, nowadays, these days.

preservation ▶ noun **1** *wood preservation* **conservation,** protection, care.
2 *the preservation of the status quo* **continuation,** conservation, maintenance, upholding, sustaining, perpetuation.
3 *the preservation of food* **conserving,** bottling, canning, freezing, drying; curing, smoking, pickling.

preserve ▶ verb **1** *oil helps preserve wood* **conserve,** protect, maintain, care for, look after.
2 *they wish to preserve the status quo* **continue (with),** conserve, keep going, maintain, uphold, sustain, perpetuate.
3 *preserving him from harassment* **guard,** protect, keep, defend, safeguard, shelter, shield.
4 *spices enable us to preserve food* **conserve,** bottle, can, freeze, dry, freeze-dry; cure, smoke, pickle.
▶ noun **1 (preserves)** *strawberry preserves* **jam,** jelly, marmalade, conserve, fruit spread.
2 *the preserve of an educated middle-class* **domain,** area, field, sphere, orbit, realm, province, territory; informal turf, bailiwick.
3 *a game preserve* **sanctuary,** (game) reserve, reservation, protected area.

preside ▶ verb *Dorothy* ***presides at*** *the meeting* **chair,** be chairman/chairwoman/chairperson of/at, officiate (at), conduct, lead.
– PHRASES **preside over** *the chief financial officer should preside over these budget talks* **be in charge of,** be responsible for, be at the head/helm of, head, be head of, manage, administer, be in control of, control, direct, lead, govern, rule, command, supervise, oversee; informal head up, be boss of, be in the driver's seat of/at, be in the saddle of/at.

president ▶ noun **1** *the president's second inaugural address* **head of state,** chief executive, premier, prime minister.
2 *the president of the society* **head,** chief,

director, leader, governor, principal, master; informal prez.
3 *the president of the company* **chairman, chairwoman,** chief executive (officer), CEO; owner, managing director.

press ▶ **verb 1** *press the paper down firmly* **push (down),** press down, depress, hold down, force, thrust, squeeze, compress.
2 *his shirt was pressed* **smooth (out),** iron, remove creases from.
3 *we pressed the grapes* **crush,** squeeze, squash, mash, pulp, pound, pulverize, macerate.
4 *she pressed the child to her bosom* **clasp,** hold close, hug, cuddle, squeeze, clutch, grasp, embrace.
5 *she pressed his hand* **squeeze,** grip, clutch.
6 *the crowd pressed around* **cluster,** gather, converge, congregate, flock, swarm, throng, crowd.
7 *the government pressed its claim* **plead,** urge, advance insistently, present, submit, put forward.
8 *they pressed him to agree* **urge,** put pressure on, force, push, coerce, dragoon, steamroller, browbeat; informal lean on, put the screws on, twist someone's arm, railroad, bulldoze.
9 *they pressed for a ban on the ivory trade* **call,** ask, advocate, clamor, push, campaign, demand, lobby.
▶ **noun 1** *a small literary press* **publishing house,** publisher; printing house/company; printing press.
2 *the freedom of* ***the press*** **the media,** the newspapers, the papers, the news media, the fourth estate; journalists, reporters, newspapermen/newspaperwomen, newsmen/newswomen, pressmen; informal journos, newshounds, newsies.
3 *the company had some bad press* **(press) reports,** press coverage, press articles, (press) reviews, media attention.
– PHRASES **be pressed for** *you shouldn't schedule an interview when you are pressed for time* **have too little,** be short of, have insufficient, lack, be lacking (in), be deficient in, need, be/stand in need of; informal be strapped for. **press on** *the team regrouped and pressed on* **proceed,** keep going, continue, carry on, make progress, make headway, press ahead, forge on/ahead, soldier on, push on, keep on, struggle on, persevere, keep at it, stay with it, stick with it, plod on, plug away.

pressing ▶ **adjective 1** *a pressing problem* **urgent,** critical, crucial, acute, desperate, serious, grave, life-and-death.
2 *a pressing engagement* **important,** high-priority, critical, crucial, compelling, inescapable. See note at CRUCIAL.

pressure ▶ **noun 1** *confined gas exerts a constant pressure* **physical force,** load, stress, thrust; compression, weight.
2 *they put pressure on us to borrow money* **coercion,** force, compulsion, constraint, duress; pestering, harassment, nagging, badgering, intimidation, arm-twisting, persuasion.
3 *she had a lot of pressure from work* **strain,** stress, tension, trouble, difficulty; informal hassle.
▶ **verb** *they pressured him into resigning* **coerce,** pressure, put pressure on, press, push, persuade, force, bulldoze, hound, harass, nag, harry, badger, goad, pester, browbeat, bully, bludgeon, intimidate, dragoon, twist someone's arm, strong-arm; informal railroad, lean on, hustle.

prestige ▶ **noun** *she missed the prestige of the job, but not the ungodly hours of work* **status,** standing, stature, reputation, repute, regard, fame, note, renown, honor, esteem, celebrity, importance, prominence, influence, eminence; kudos, cachet; informal clout.

prestigious ▶ **adjective 1** *prestigious journals* **reputable,** distinguished, respected, esteemed, eminent, august, highly regarded, well-thought-of, acclaimed, authoritative, celebrated, illustrious, leading, renowned.
ANTONYMS obscure.
2 *a prestigious job* **impressive,** important, prominent, high-ranking, influential, affluential, powerful, glamorous; well paid, expensive, upmarket.
ANTONYMS minor.

presumably ▶ **adverb** *presumably, they'll want an ocean view* **I presume,** I expect, I assume, I take it, I suppose, I imagine, I dare say, I guess, in all probability, probably, in all likelihood, as likely as not, doubtless, undoubtedly, no doubt.

presume ▶ **verb 1** *I presumed that it had once been an attic* **assume,** suppose, dare say, imagine, take it, expect, believe, think, surmise, guess, judge, conjecture, speculate, postulate, presuppose.
2 *let me presume to give you some advice* **venture,** dare, have the audacity/effrontery, be so bold as.
– PHRASES **presume on** *he was careful not to presume on their friendship* **take (unfair) advantage of,** exploit, take liberties with; count on, bank on, place reliance on.

presumption ▶ **noun 1** *this presumption may be easily rebutted* **assumption,** supposition, presupposition, belief, guess, judgment, surmise, conjecture, speculation, hypothesis, postulation, inference, deduction, conclusion.
2 *he apologized for his presumption* **brazenness,** audacity, boldness, audaciousness, temerity, arrogance, presumptuousness, forwardness; cockiness, insolence, impudence, bumptiousness, impertinence, effrontery, cheek, cheekiness; rudeness, impoliteness, disrespect, familiarity; informal nerve, chutzpah, sass, sassiness; archaic assumption.

presumptive ▶ **adjective 1** *a presumptive diagnosis* **conjectural,** speculative, tentative; theoretical, unproven, unconfirmed.
2 *the heir presumptive* **probable,** likely, prospective, assumed, supposed, expected.

presumptuous ▶ **adjective** *that was quite a presumptuous remark* **brazen,** overconfident, arrogant, bold, audacious, forward, familiar, impertinent, insolent, impudent, cocky; cheeky, rude, impolite, uncivil, bumptious; informal sassy. See note at BOLD.

presuppose ▶ **verb 1** *this presupposes the existence of a policy-making group* **require,** necessitate, imply, entail, mean, involve, assume.

2 *I had presupposed that theme parks make people happy* **presume,** assume, take it for granted, take it as read, suppose, surmise, think, accept, consider.

presupposition ▶ noun *the presupposition that all enzymes are proteins* **presumption,** assumption, preconception, supposition, hypothesis, surmise, thesis, theory, premise, belief, postulation.

pretend ▶ verb **1** *they just pretend to listen* **make as if,** profess, affect; dissimulate, dissemble, put it on, put on a false front, go through the motions, sham, fake it.
2 *I'll* ***pretend to be*** *the dragon* **put on an act as,** make believe one is, play at being, act (the part of), play-act (the part of), impersonate.
3 *it was useless to pretend innocence* **feign,** sham, fake, simulate, put on, counterfeit, affect.
4 *he cannot* ***pretend to*** *sophistication* **claim,** lay claim to, purport to have, profess to have.
▶ adjective informal *a pretend conversation* **imaginary,** imagined, pretended, make-believe, made-up, fantasy, fantasized, dreamed-up, unreal, invented, fictitious, mythical, feigned, fake, mock, sham, simulated, artificial, ersatz, false, pseudo; informal phony.

pretended ▶ adjective *pretended tears* **fake,** faked, affected, assumed, professed, spurious, mock, imitation, simulated, make-believe, pseudo, sham, false, bogus; informal pretend, phony.

pretender ▶ noun *a pretender to the throne* **claimant,** aspirant.

pretense ▶ noun **1** *cease this pretense* **make-believe,** putting on an act, acting, dissembling, shamming, faking, feigning, simulation, dissimulation, play-acting, posturing; deception, deceit, deceitfulness, fraud, fraudulence, duplicity, subterfuge, trickery, dishonesty, hypocrisy, falsity, lying, mendacity.
ANTONYMS honesty.
2 *he made a pretense of being unconcerned* (**false**) **show,** semblance, affectation, (false) appearance, outward appearance, impression, (false) front, guise, facade, display.
3 *she had dropped any pretense to faith* **claim,** profession.
4 *he was absolutely without pretense* **pretentiousness,** display, ostentation, affectation, showiness, posturing, humbug.

pretension ▶ noun **1** *the author has no pretension to exhaustive coverage* **aspiration,** claim, assertion, pretense, profession.
2 *she spoke without pretension* **pretentiousness,** affectation, ostentation, artificiality, airs, posing, posturing, show, flashiness; pomposity, pompousness, grandiosity, grandiloquence, magniloquence.

pretentious ▶ adjective *Clytemnestra is a pretentious name for a dog* **affected,** ostentatious, showy; overambitious, pompous, artificial, inflated, overblown, high-sounding, flowery, grandiose, elaborate, extravagant, flamboyant, ornate, grandiloquent, magniloquent, sophomoric; informal flashy, highfalutin, la-di-da, pseudo.

preternatural ▶ adjective *autumn had arrived with preternatural speed* **extraordinary,** exceptional, unusual, uncommon, singular, unprecedented, remarkable, phenomenal, abnormal, inexplicable, unaccountable; strange, mysterious, fantastic.

pretext ▶ noun *he used the pretext of looking for his dog to come into our yard* **excuse,** false excuse, ostensible reason, alleged reason; guise, ploy, pretense, ruse.

pretty ▶ adjective *a pretty child* **attractive,** lovely, good-looking, nice-looking, personable, fetching, prepossessing, appealing, charming, delightful, cute, as pretty as a picture; Scottish bonny; informal easy on the eye; literary beauteous; archaic fair, comely.
ANTONYMS plain, ugly.
▶ adverb *a pretty large sum* **quite,** rather, somewhat, fairly, reasonably, comparatively, relatively.
▶ verb *she's* ***prettying*** *herself* ***up*** **beautify,** make attractive, make pretty, prettify, adorn, ornament, smarten; informal do oneself up, titivate.

prevail ▶ verb **1** *common sense will prevail* **win,** win out/through, triumph, be victorious, carry the day, come out on top, succeed, prove superior, conquer, overcome; rule, reign.
2 *the conditions that prevailed in the 1950s* **exist,** be in existence, be present, be the case, occur, be prevalent, be current, be the order of the day, be customary, be common, be widespread, be in force/effect; formal obtain.
– PHRASES **prevail on/upon** *they prevailed upon me to emcee their charity affair* **persuade,** induce, coax, convince, get, urge, pressure, coerce; informal sweet-talk, soft-soap.

prevailing ▶ adjective *prevailing attitudes* **current,** existing, prevalent, usual, common, general, widespread. See note at PREVALENT.

prevalence ▶ noun *the prevalence of smoking among teenagers* **commonness,** currency, widespread presence, generality, popularity, pervasiveness, universality, extensiveness; rampancy, rifeness.

prevalent ▶ adjective *opposition to the war is prevalent* **widespread,** prevailing, frequent, usual, common, current, popular, general, universal; endemic, rampant, rife.
ANTONYMS rare.

CHOOSE THE RIGHT WORD

prevalent, prevailing, abundant, plentiful, rife, copious, common

Wildflowers might be **prevalent** in the mountains during the spring months, but a particular type of wildflower might be the **prevailing** one. *Prevalent*, in other words, implies widespread occurrence or acceptance in a particular place or time (*a prevalent belief during the nineteenth century*), while *prevailing* suggests that something exists in such quantity that it surpasses or leads all others in acceptance, usage, or belief (*the prevailing theory about the evolution of man*). Wildflowers might also be **abundant** in the valleys—a word that, unlike *prevalent* and *prevailing*, is largely restricted to observations about a place and may suggest oversupply (*an abundant harvest; indications of decay were abundant*). **Plentiful**, on the other hand, refers to a large or full supply without the connotations of oversupply (*a country where jobs were plentiful*). If wildflowers are **rife**, it means that they are not only *prevalent* but spreading rapidly (*speculation was rife among the soldiers*); if they're **copious**, it means they are being produced in such quantity that they constitute a rich or flowing abundance (*weep copious tears*). What often happens, with wildflowers as well as with other beautiful things, is that they become so abundant they are regarded as **common**, a word meaning usual or ordinary (*the common cold*). Like *prevalent, common* can apply to a time as well as a place (*an expression common during the Depression*). But neither *abundant* nor *common* connotes dominance as clearly as *prevalent* does.

prevaricate ▶ **verb** *you have prevaricated so often through this testimony that the truth has become unrecognizable* **be evasive,** beat around the bush, hedge, fence, shilly-shally, dodge (the issue), sidestep (the issue), equivocate, waffle; temporize, stall (for time); hem and haw; rare tergiversate. See note at LIE[1].

prevent ▶ **verb** *how can any one agency prevent drug trafficking?* **stop,** put a stop to, avert, nip in the bud, fend off, stave off, ward off; hinder, impede, hamper, obstruct, balk, foil, thwart, forestall, counteract, inhibit, curb, restrain, preclude, preempt; disallow, prohibit, forbid, proscribe, exclude, debar, bar; literary stay. See note at HINDER.
ANTONYMS allow.

previous ▶ **adjective** *the previous commissioner retired after more than 40 years of service* **foregoing,** preceding, antecedent; old, earlier, prior, former, ex-, past, last, sometime, one-time, erstwhile; formal quondam, anterior.
ANTONYMS next.
– PHRASES **previous to** *previous to this, everything was fine* **before,** prior to, until, leading up to, up to, earlier than, preceding; formal anterior to.

previously ▶ **adverb** *previously, only the outermost doors were locked at night* **formerly,** earlier, earlier on, before, hitherto, once, at one time, in the past, in days gone by, in times gone by, in bygone days, in times past, in former times; in advance, already, beforehand; formal heretofore.

prey ▶ **noun 1** *the lions killed their prey* **quarry,** kill.
ANTONYMS predator, hunter.
2 *she was Julia's easy prey* **victim,** target, dupe, gull; informal sucker, soft touch, pushover, patsy, sap, schlemiel.
– PHRASES **prey on 1** *certain larvae prey on aphids* **hunt,** catch; eat, feed on, live on/off.
2 *they prey on the elderly* **exploit,** victimize, pick on, take advantage of; trick, swindle, cheat, hoodwink, fleece; informal con. **3** *the problem preyed on his mind* **oppress,** weigh on, weigh heavily on, lie heavy on, gnaw at; trouble, worry, beset, disturb, distress, haunt, nag, torment, plague, obsess.

price ▶ **noun 1** *the purchase price* **cost,** charge, fee, fare, levy, amount, sum; outlay, expense, expenditure; valuation, quotation, estimate, asking price; informal humorous damage.
2 *spinsterhood was the price of her career* **consequence,** result, cost, penalty, sacrifice; downside, snag, drawback, disadvantage, minus.
3 *he had a price on his head* **reward,** bounty, premium.
▶ **verb** *we priced each ticket is at $5.00* **fix/set the price of,** value, rate, cost; estimate.

priceless ▶ **adjective 1** *priceless works of art* **invaluable,** of incalculable value/worth, of immeasurable value/worth, beyond price; irreplaceable, incomparable, unparalleled.
ANTONYMS worthless, cheap.
2 informal *that's priceless!* See HILARIOUS.

prick ▶ **verb 1** *prick the potatoes with a fork* **pierce,** puncture, make/put a hole in, stab, perforate, nick, jab.
2 *her conscience pricked her* **trouble,** worry, distress, perturb, disturb, cause someone anguish, afflict, torment, plague, prey on, gnaw at.
3 *ambition pricked him on to greater effort* **goad,** prod, incite, provoke, urge, spur, stimulate, encourage, inspire, motivate, push, propel, impel.
4 *the horse* **pricked up** *its ears* **raise,** erect.
▶ **noun 1** *it felt like the prick of a pin* **jab,** sting, pinprick, prickle, stab.
2 *the prick of tears behind her eyelids* **sting,** stinging, smart, smarting, burning.
3 *the prick of conscience* **pang,** twinge, stab.
– PHRASES **prick up one's ears** *we pricked up our ears when he mentioned the Christmas bonuses* **listen carefully,** pay attention, become attentive, begin to take notice, attend; informal be all ears.

prickle ▶ **noun 1** *the cactus is covered with prickles* **thorn,** needle, barb, spike, point, spine.
2 *Willie felt a cold prickle of fear* **tingle,** tingling, tingling sensation, prickling sensation, chill, thrill; Medicine paresthesia.
▶ **verb** *its tiny spikes prickled his skin* **sting,** prick.

prickly ▶ **adjective 1** *a prickly hedgehog* **spiky,** spiked, thorny, barbed, spiny; briery, brambly; rough, scratchy; technical spiculate, spicular, aculeate, spinose.
2 *my skin feels prickly* **tingly,** tingling, prickling.
3 *a prickly character* See IRRITABLE.
4 *the prickly question of the refugees* **problematic,** awkward, ticklish, tricky, delicate, sensitive, difficult, knotty, thorny, irksome, tough, troublesome, bothersome, vexatious.

pride ▶ **noun 1** *their triumphs were a source of pride* **self-esteem,** dignity, honor, self-respect, self-worth, self-regard, pride in oneself.
ANTONYMS shame.
2 *take pride in a good job well done* **pleasure,** joy, delight, gratification, fulfillment,

satisfaction, a sense of achievement.
3 *he refused her offer out of pride* **arrogance,** vanity, self-importance, hubris, conceit, conceitedness, self-love, self-adulation, self-admiration, narcissism, egotism, superciliousness, haughtiness, snobbery, snobbishness; informal big-headedness; literary vainglory.
ANTONYMS modesty, humility.
4 *the bull is the pride of the herd* **best,** finest, top, cream, pick, choice, prize, glory, jewel in the crown.
ANTONYMS dregs.
5 *the rose-covered trellis was the pride of the gardener* **source of satisfaction,** pride and joy, treasured possession, joy, delight.
– PHRASES **pride oneself on** *Lucas prides himself on his knowledge of wine* **be proud of,** be proud of oneself for, take pride in, take satisfaction in, congratulate oneself on, pat oneself on the back for.

CHOOSE THE RIGHT WORD

pride, arrogance, conceit, egotism, self-esteem, vainglory, vanity

If you take **pride** in yourself or your accomplishments, it means that you believe in your own worth, merit, or superiority—whether or not that belief is justified (*she took pride in her accomplishments*). When your opinion of yourself is exaggerated, you're showing **conceit**, a word that combines *pride* with self-obsession. If you like to be noticed and admired for your appearance or achievements, you're revealing your **vanity**, and if you show off or boast about your accomplishments, you're likely to be accused of **vainglory**, a somewhat literary term for a self-important display of power, skill, or influence. **Arrogance** is an overbearing pride combined with disdain for others (*his arrogance led him to assume that everyone else would obey his orders*), while **egotism** implies self-centeredness or an excessive preoccupation with yourself (*blinded by egotism to the suffering of others*). While no one wants to be accused of *arrogance* or *egotism*, there's a lot to be said for **self-esteem**, which may suggest undue pride but is more often used to describe a healthy belief in oneself and respect for one's worth as a person (*she suffered from low self-esteem*).

priest ▶ noun *he requested to see a priest* See CLERGY.
prig ▶ noun *the notion that librarians are typically prigs is ridiculous* **prude,** puritan, killjoy; informal goody-goody, goody two-shoes.
priggish ▶ adjective *Miss Sinclair couldn't possibly have been as priggish as she seemed way back then* **self-righteous,** moralistic, holier-than-thou, sanctimonious, prudish, puritanical, prim, straitlaced, stuffy, prissy, governessy, narrow-minded; informal goody-goody, starchy.
ANTONYMS broad-minded.
prim ▶ adjective *Reverend Cooke had two prim little maids for daughters and one wild little hellion for a son* **demure,** proper, prim and proper, formal, stuffy, straitlaced, prudish; governessy, prissy, priggish, puritanical; informal starchy.
prima donna ▶ noun **1** *this solo was added to give the prima donna another aria* **leading soprano,** leading lady, diva, star, opera star, principal singer.
2 *a city council filled with prima donnas* **ego,** self-important person, his nibs, temperamental person, princess, diva, pooh-bah.
primarily ▶ adverb **1** *the bishop was primarily a leader of the local community* **first and foremost,** first, firstly, essentially, in essence, fundamentally, principally, predominantly, basically.
2 *such work is undertaken primarily for large institutions* **mostly,** for the most part, chiefly, mainly, in the main, on the whole, largely, to a large extent, especially, generally, usually, typically, commonly, as a rule.
primary ▶ adjective **1** *our primary role* **main,** chief, key, prime, central, principal, foremost, first, first-line, most important, predominant, paramount; informal number-one.
ANTONYMS secondary, subordinate.
2 *the primary cause* **original,** earliest, initial, first; essential, fundamental, basic.
ANTONYMS secondary.
prime[1] ▶ adjective **1** *his prime reason for leaving* **main,** chief, key, primary, central, principal, foremost, first, most important, paramount, major; informal number-one.
ANTONYMS secondary, subordinate.
2 *the prime cause of flooding* **fundamental,** basic, essential, primary, central.
ANTONYMS secondary.
3 *prime agricultural land* **top-quality,** top, best, first-class, first-rate, grade A, superior, supreme, choice, select, finest; excellent, superb, fine; informal tip-top, A1, top-notch, blue-ribbon.
ANTONYMS inferior.
4 *a prime example* **archetypal,** prototypical, typical, classic, excellent, characteristic, quintessential.
▶ noun *he is in his prime* **heyday,** best days, best years, prime of one's life; youth, salad days; peak, pinnacle, zenith.
prime[2] ▶ verb **1** *he primed the gun* **prepare,** load, get ready.
2 *Lucy had primed him carefully* **brief,** fill in, prepare, put in the picture, inform, advise, instruct, coach, drill; informal clue in, give someone the lowdown.
primeval ▶ adjective **1** *primeval forest* **ancient,** earliest, first, prehistoric, antediluvian, primordial; pristine, original, virgin.
2 *primeval fears* **instinctive,** primitive, basic, primal, primordial, intuitive, inborn, innate, inherent.
primitive ▶ adjective **1** *primitive times* **ancient,** earliest, first, prehistoric, antediluvian, primordial, primeval, primal.
ANTONYMS modern, recent.
2 *primitive peoples* **uncivilized,** barbarian, barbaric, barbarous, savage, ignorant, uncultivated.

ANTONYMS civilized.
3 *primitive tools* **crude,** simple, rough, rough and ready, basic, rudimentary, unrefined, unsophisticated, rude, makeshift.
ANTONYMS sophisticated, advanced.
4 *primitive art* **simple,** natural, unsophisticated, unaffected, undeveloped, unpretentious.
ANTONYMS sophisticated, refined.

primp ▶ **verb** *students are encouraged to primp just before the photo session* **groom,** tidy, arrange, brush, comb; smarten (up), spruce up; informal titivate, doll up, tart up, gussy up.

prince ▶ **noun** *the young prince was the object of much media attention* **ruler,** sovereign, monarch, king, princeling; crown prince; emir, sheikh, sultan, maharaja, raja.

princely ▶ **adjective 1** *princely buildings* See SPLENDID (sense 1).
2 *a princely sum* See HANDSOME (sense 3).

principal ▶ **adjective** *the principal cause of poor air quality* **main,** chief, primary, leading, foremost, first, first-line, most important, predominant, dominant, (most) prominent; key, crucial, vital, essential, basic, prime, central, focal; premier, paramount, major, overriding, cardinal, preeminent, uppermost, highest, top, topmost; informal number-one.
ANTONYMS minor.
▶ **noun 1** *the principal of the firm* **chief,** chief executive (officer), CEO, president, chairman, chairwoman, director, managing director, manager, head; informal boss.
2 *the school's principal* **headmaster, headmistress;** dean, rector, chancellor, president, provost.
3 *a principal in a soap opera* **leading actor/actress,** leading player/performer/dancer, leading role, lead, star.
4 *repayment of the principal* **capital (sum),** debt, loan.

> USAGE
>
> **principal, principle**
>
> These two words, though often confused and used incorrectly and interchangeably, share no common definitions. Generally, it's enough to remember that *principal* (= chief, primary, most important) is usually an adjective and that *principle* (= a truth, rule, doctrine, or course of action) is virtually always a noun. Although *principle* is not a verb, we have *principled* as an adjective. But *principal* is sometimes a noun—an elliptical form of *principal official* (*Morgan is principal of the elementary school*) or *principal investment* (*principal and interest*).
>
> Substituting *principal* for *principle* is a fairly common blunder—e.g.: "The Ways and Means bill approved today, after more than a month of deliberation and voting, preserves two of the central principals [read *principles*] put forth by the President: universal coverage and the requirement that employers assume 80 percent of its cost for their workers." (*New York Times*; July 1, 1994.)
>
> Substituting *principle* for *principal* is perhaps even more common—e.g.: "Audio CDs are a principle [read *principal*] source of material for making music with samples." (*Electronic Musician*; June 1994.) — **BG**

principally ▶ **adverb** *the decline is principally due to overfishing* **mainly,** mostly, chiefly, for the most part, in the main, on the whole, largely, to a large extent, predominantly, basically, primarily.

principle ▶ **noun 1** *elementary principles* **truth,** proposition, concept, idea, theory, assumption, fundamental, essential, ground rule.
2 *the principle of laissez-faire* **doctrine,** belief, creed, credo, (golden) rule, criterion, tenet, code, ethic, dictum, canon, law.
3 *a woman of principle | sticking to one's principles* **morals,** morality, (code of) ethics, beliefs, ideals, standards; integrity, uprightness, righteousness, virtue, probity, (sense of) honor, decency, conscience, scruples. See note at PRINCIPAL.
– PHRASES **in principle 1** *there is no reason, in principle, why we couldn't work together* **in theory,** theoretically, on paper. **2** *he has accepted the idea in principle* **in general,** in essence, on the whole, in the main.

print ▶ **verb 1** *the newspaper is printed just after midnight* **send to press,** set in print, run off, reprint.
2 *patterns were printed on the cloth* **imprint,** impress, stamp, mark.
3 *they printed 30,000 copies* **publish,** issue, release, circulate.
4 *the incident is printed on her memory* **register,** record, impress, imprint, engrave, etch, stamp, mark.
▶ **noun 1** *small print* **type,** printing, letters, lettering, characters, type size, typeface, font.
2 *prints of his left hand* **impression,** fingerprint, footprint.
3 *Rockwell prints are on sale in the lobby* **picture,** design, engraving, etching, lithograph, linocut, woodcut.
4 *prints and negatives* **photograph,** photo, snapshot, picture, still.
5 *soft floral prints* **printed cloth/fabric,** patterned cloth/fabric, chintz.
– PHRASES **in print** *I noticed on Amazon.com that the book is still in print* **published,** printed, available in bookstores. **out of print** *they will help you track down editions that are out of print* **no longer available,** unavailable, unobtainable, discontinued.

prior ▶ **adjective** *by prior arrangement* **earlier,** previous, preceding, foregoing, antecedent, advance; formal anterior.
ANTONYMS subsequent.
– PHRASES **prior to** *prior to bedtime, set the clocks back an hour* **before,** until, till, up to, previous to, earlier than, preceding, leading up to; formal anterior to.

priority ▶ **noun 1** *safety is our priority* **prime concern,** most important consideration, primary issue.
2 *giving priority to elementary schools* **precedence,** greater importance, preference,

preeminence, predominance, primacy, first place.
3 *traffic in the right lane has priority* **right of way.**

priory ▶ noun *the sisters of this priory are famous for their spinning and weaving* **religious house,** abbey, cloister; monastery, friary; convent, nunnery.

prison ▶ noun *the prisons upstate are just as crowded* **jail,** lockup, penal institution, detention center, jailhouse, penitentiary, correctional facility; informal clink, slammer, hoosegow, the big house, stir, jug, brig, can, pen, cooler, pokey, slam; (**be in prison**) informal be inside, be behind bars, do time.

prisoner ▶ noun **1** *a prisoner serving a life sentence* **convict,** detainee, inmate; informal jailbird, con, lifer, yardbird.
2 *the army took many prisoners* **captive,** internee, prisoner of war, POW.

pristine ▶ adjective *Lurene's clothes are always so pristine* **immaculate,** perfect, in mint condition, as new, unspoiled, spotless, flawless, clean, fresh, new, virgin, pure, unused.
ANTONYMS dirty, spoiled.

privacy ▶ noun *protecting one's privacy* **seclusion,** solitude, isolation, freedom from disturbance, freedom from interference.

private ▶ adjective **1** *his private plane* **personal,** own, individual, special, exclusive, privately owned.
ANTONYMS public.
2 *private talks* **confidential,** secret, classified, unofficial, off the record, closet, in camera; backstage, privileged, one-on-one, tête-à-tête, sub rosa.
ANTONYMS public, open.
3 *private thoughts* **intimate,** personal, secret; innermost, undisclosed, unspoken, unvoiced.
4 *a very private man* **reserved,** introvert, introverted, self-contained, reticent, discreet, uncommunicative, unforthcoming, retiring, unsociable, withdrawn, solitary, reclusive, hermitic.
ANTONYMS extrovert, extroverted.
5 *they found a private place in which to talk* **secluded,** solitary, undisturbed, concealed, hidden, remote, isolated, out of the way, sequestered.
ANTONYMS busy, crowded.
6 *we can be private here* **undisturbed,** uninterrupted; alone, by ourselves.
7 *the governor attended in a private capacity* **unofficial,** personal.
ANTONYMS official.
8 *private industry* **independent**; privatized, denationalized; commercial, private-enterprise.
ANTONYMS public, nationalized.
▶ noun *a private in the army* **private soldier,** common soldier; trooper; sapper, gunner; enlisted personnel; informal GI.
– PHRASES **in private** *I'll tell you later, in private* **in secret,** secretly, privately, behind closed doors, in camera; in confidence, confidentially, between ourselves, entre nous, off the record; formal sub rosa.

privately ▶ adverb **1** *we must talk privately* **in secret,** secretly, in private, behind closed doors, in camera; in confidence, confidentially, between ourselves, entre nous, off the record; formal sub rosa.
ANTONYMS publicly.
2 *privately, I am glad* **secretly,** inwardly, deep down, personally, unofficially.
3 *he lived very privately* **out of the public eye,** out of public view, in seclusion, in solitude, alone.

privation ▶ noun *years of rationing and privation* **deprivation,** hardship, destitution, impoverishment, want, need, neediness, austerity. See note at LACK.
ANTONYMS plenty, luxury.

privilege ▶ noun **1** *senior students have certain privileges* **advantage,** benefit; prerogative, entitlement, right; concession, freedom, liberty.
2 *it was a privilege to meet her* **honor,** pleasure.
3 *congressional privilege* **immunity,** exemption, dispensation.

privileged ▶ adjective **1** *a privileged background* **wealthy,** rich, affluent, prosperous; **lucky,** fortunate, elite, favored; (socially) advantaged.
ANTONYMS underprivileged, disadvantaged.
2 *privileged information* **confidential,** private, secret, restricted, classified, not for publication, off the record, inside; informal hush-hush.
ANTONYMS public.
3 *these foreign diplomats are privileged* **immune (from prosecution),** protected, exempt, excepted.
ANTONYMS liable.

privy ▶ adjective *he was not privy to the discussions* **in the know about,** acquainted with, in on, informed of, advised of, apprised of; informal wise to; formal cognizant of.
▶ noun dated *he went out to the privy* See BATHROOM.

prize ▶ noun **1** *an art prize* **award,** reward, premium, purse; trophy, medal; honor, accolade, crown, laurels, palm.
2 (**prizes**) *the prizes of war* **spoils,** booty, plunder, loot, pickings.
▶ adjective **1** *a prize bull* **champion,** award-winning, prize-winning, winning, top, best.
ANTONYMS second-rate.
2 *a prize example* **outstanding,** excellent, superlative, superb, supreme, very good, prime, fine, magnificent, marvelous, wonderful; informal great, terrific, tremendous, fantastic.
3 *a prize idiot* **complete,** utter, total, absolute, real, perfect, veritable.
▶ verb *many collectors prize his work* **value,** set great store by, rate highly, attach great importance to, esteem, hold in high regard, think highly of, treasure, cherish. See note at ESTEEM.

prized ▶ adjective *his prized sheepdog* **treasured,** precious, cherished, much loved, beloved, valued, esteemed, highly regarded.

probability ▶ noun **1** *the probability of winning* **likelihood,** prospect, expectation, chance, chances, odds.
2 *relegation is a distinct probability* **probable event,** prospect, possibility, good/fair/reasonable bet.

probable ▶ adjective *a recurrence of the symptoms is probable* **likely,** most likely,

odds-on, expected, anticipated, predictable, foreseeable, ten to one; informal in the cards, a good/fair/reasonable bet.
ANTONYMS unlikely.

probably ▸ adverb *I knew I would probably never see her again* **in all likelihood,** in all probability, as likely as not, (very/most) likely, ten to one, the chances are, doubtless, no doubt; archaic like enough.

probation ▸ noun *during your probation it is imperative that you miss no scheduled meetings* **trial period,** test period, experimental period, trial. See note at **NOVICE**.

probe ▸ noun *a probe into the air crash* **investigation,** inquiry, examination, inquest, exploration, study, analysis.
▸ verb **1** *alien hands probed his body* **examine,** feel, feel around, explore, prod, poke, check.
2 *police probed the tragedy* **investigate,** inquire into, look into, study, examine, scrutinize, go into, carry out an inquest into.

problem ▸ noun **1** *they ran into a problem* **difficulty,** trouble, worry, complication, difficult situation; snag, hitch, drawback, stumbling block, obstacle, hurdle, hiccup, setback, catch; predicament, plight; misfortune, mishap, misadventure; dilemma, quandary; informal headache, nightmare.
2 *I don't want to be a problem* **nuisance,** bother, pest, irritant, thorn in one's side/flesh, vexation; informal drag, pain, pain in the neck.
3 *mathematical problems* **puzzle,** question, poser, enigma, riddle, conundrum; informal teaser, brainteaser.
▸ adjective *a problem child* **troublesome,** difficult, unmanageable, unruly, disobedient, uncontrollable, recalcitrant, delinquent.
ANTONYMS well-behaved, manageable.

problematic ▸ adjective *the pest control in this building has gotten very problematic* **difficult,** hard, taxing, troublesome, tricky, awkward, controversial, ticklish, complicated, complex, knotty, thorny, prickly, vexed; informal sticky. See note at **DOUBTFUL**.
ANTONYMS easy, simple, straightforward.

procedure ▸ noun *once we establish a procedure, it must be followed* **course of action,** plan of action, action plan, policy, series of steps, method, system, strategy, way, approach, formula, mechanism, methodology, MO, modus operandi, technique; routine, drill, practice, operation.

proceed ▸ verb **1** *she was uncertain how to proceed* **begin,** make a start, get going, move, set something in motion; **take action,** act, go on, go ahead, make progress, make headway.
ANTONYMS stop.
2 *he proceeded down the road* **go,** make one's way, advance, move, progress, carry on, press on, push on.
ANTONYMS stop.
3 *we should proceed with the talks* **go ahead,** carry on, go on, continue, keep on, get on, get ahead; (**proceed with**) pursue, prosecute.
4 *there is not enough evidence to **proceed against him*** **take someone to court,** start/take proceedings against, start an action against, make a case against, sue.
5 *all power proceeds from God* **originate,** spring, stem, come, derive, arise, issue, flow, emanate.

proceedings ▸ plural noun **1** *the evening's proceedings are underway* **events,** activities, happenings, goings-on, doings.
2 *they published the proceedings of the meeting* **report,** transactions, minutes, account, record(s); annals, archives.
3 *legal proceedings* **legal action,** court/judicial proceedings, litigation; lawsuit, case, prosecution.

proceeds ▸ plural noun *most of the proceeds go to pay salaries* **profits,** earnings, receipts, returns, takings, take, income, revenue, royalty; Sports gate (money/receipts).

process ▸ noun **1** *investigation is a long process* **procedure,** operation, action, activity, exercise, affair, business, job, task, undertaking.
2 *a new canning process* **method,** system, technique, means, practice, way, approach, methodology.
▸ verb *applications are processed rapidly* **deal with,** attend to, see to, sort out, handle, take care of, action.
– PHRASES **in the process of** *we're in the process of updating our files* **in the middle of,** in the course of, in the midst of, in the throes of, busy with, occupied in/with, taken up with/by, involved in.

procession ▸ noun *a procession of marching bands* **parade,** march, march past, cavalcade, motorcade, cortège; column, file, train.

proclaim ▸ verb **1** *messengers proclaimed the good news* **declare,** announce, pronounce, state, make known, give out, advertise, publish, broadcast, promulgate, trumpet, blazon. See note at **ANNOUNCE**.
2 *the men proclaimed their innocence* **assert,** declare, profess, maintain, protest.
3 *she proclaimed herself president* **declare,** pronounce, announce.
4 *cheap paint soon proclaims its cheapness* **demonstrate,** indicate, show, reveal, manifest, betray, testify to, signify.

proclamation ▸ noun *the Church issued a proclamation denouncing the movie* **declaration,** announcement, pronouncement, statement, notification, publication, broadcast, promulgation, blazoning; assertion, profession, protestation; **decree,** order, edict, ruling.

proclivity ▸ noun *his sexual proclivities are none of your business* **inclination,** tendency, leaning, disposition, proneness, propensity, bent, bias, penchant, predisposition; predilection, partiality, liking, preference, taste, fondness, weakness.

procrastinate ▸ verb *fear of failure often causes people to procrastinate* **delay,** put off doing something, postpone action, defer action, be dilatory, use delaying tactics, stall, temporize, drag one's feet/heels, take one's time, play for time, play a waiting game.

procure ▸ verb **1** *he managed to procure a coat* **obtain,** acquire, get, find, come by, secure, pick up; buy, purchase, engage; informal get hold of, get one's hands on. See note at **GET**.
2 *the police found that he was procuring* **pimp.**

prod ▶ verb 1 *Cassie prodded him in the chest* **poke,** jab, dig, elbow, butt, stab.
2 *they hoped to prod the government into action* **spur,** stimulate, stir, rouse, prompt, drive, galvanize; persuade, urge, chivvy; incite, goad, egg on, provoke.
▶ noun 1 *a prod in the ribs* **poke,** jab, dig, elbow, butt, thrust.
2 *they need a prod to get them to act* **stimulus,** push, prompt, reminder, spur; incitement, goad.

prodigal ▶ adjective 1 *prodigal habits die hard* **wasteful,** extravagant, spendthrift, profligate, improvident, imprudent.
ANTONYMS thrifty.
2 *a composer who is prodigal with his talents* **generous,** lavish, liberal, unstinting, unsparing; literary bounteous.
ANTONYMS mean.
3 *a dessert prodigal with whipped cream* **abounding in,** abundant in, rich in, covered in, awash with, slathered with. See note at PROFUSE.
ANTONYMS deficient.

prodigious ▶ adjective *prodigious quantities of food* **enormous,** huge, colossal, immense, vast, great, massive, gigantic, mammoth, tremendous, inordinate, monumental; amazing, astonishing, astounding, staggering, stunning, remarkable, phenomenal, terrific, miraculous, impressive, striking, startling, sensational, spectacular, extraordinary, exceptional, breathtaking, incredible; informal humongous, stupendous, fantastic, fabulous, mega, awesome, ginormous; literary wondrous.
ANTONYMS small, unexceptional.

prodigy ▶ noun 1 *a seven-year-old prodigy* **genius,** mastermind, virtuoso, wunderkind, wonder child, boy wonder, girl wonder; informal whiz kid, whiz, wizard.
2 *Germany seemed a prodigy of industrial discipline* **model,** classic example, paragon, paradigm, epitome, exemplar, archetype.

produce ▶ verb 1 *the company produces furniture* **manufacture,** make, construct, build, fabricate, put together, assemble, turn out, create; mass-produce; informal churn out.
2 *the vineyards produce excellent wines* **yield,** grow, give, supply, provide, furnish, bear, bring forth.
3 *she produced ten puppies* **give birth to,** bear, deliver, bring forth, bring into the world.
4 *he produced five novels* **create,** originate, fashion, turn out; compose, write, pen; paint.
5 *she produced an ID card* **pull out,** extract, fish out; present, offer, proffer, show.
6 *no evidence was produced* **present,** offer, provide, furnish, advance, put forward, bring forward, come up with.
7 *that will produce a reaction* **give rise to,** bring about, cause, occasion, generate, engender, lead to, result in, effect, induce, set off; provoke, precipitate, breed, spark off, trigger; literary beget.
8 *James produced the play* **stage,** put on, mount, present.
▶ noun *fresh produce* **food,** foodstuff(s), products; harvest, crops, fruit, vegetables, greens.

producer ▶ noun 1 *a car producer* **manufacturer,** maker, builder, constructor, fabricator.
2 *coffee producers* **grower,** farmer.
3 *the producer of the show* **impresario,** manager, administrator, promoter, regisseur.

product ▶ noun 1 *a household product* **artifact,** commodity, manufactured article; creation, invention; (**products**) goods, wares, merchandise, produce.
2 *his skill is a product of experience* **result,** consequence, outcome, effect, upshot, fruit, by-product, spin-off.

production ▶ noun 1 *the production of washing machines* **manufacture,** making, construction, building, fabrication, assembly, creation; mass-production.
2 *the production of literary works* **creation,** origination, fashioning; composition, writing.
3 *literary productions* **work,** opus, creation; publication, composition, piece; work of art, painting, picture; Law intellectual property.
4 *agricultural production* **output,** yield; productivity.
5 *admission only on production of a ticket* **presentation,** proffering, showing.
6 *a theater production* **performance,** staging, presentation, show, piece, play.

productive ▶ adjective 1 *a productive artist* **prolific,** inventive, creative; energetic.
2 *productive talks* **useful,** constructive, profitable, fruitful, gainful, valuable, effective, worthwhile, helpful.
3 *productive land* **fertile,** fruitful, rich, fecund.
ANTONYMS sterile, barren.

productivity ▶ noun 1 *workers have boosted productivity* **efficiency,** work rate; output, yield, production.
2 *the productivity of the soil* **fruitfulness,** fertility, richness, fecundity.
ANTONYMS sterility, barrenness.

profane ▶ adjective 1 *subjects both sacred and profane* **secular,** lay, nonreligious, temporal; formal laic.
ANTONYMS religious, sacred.
2 *a profane man* **irreverent,** irreligious, ungodly, godless, unbelieving, impious, disrespectful, sacrilegious.
ANTONYMS reverent.
3 *profane language* **obscene,** blasphemous, indecent, foul, vulgar, crude, filthy, dirty, smutty, coarse, rude, offensive, indecorous.
ANTONYMS decorous.
▶ verb *invaders profaned our sacred temples* **desecrate,** violate, defile, treat sacrilegiously.

profanity ▶ noun 1 *he hissed a profanity | an outburst of profanity* **oath,** swear word, expletive, curse, obscenity, four-letter word, dirty word; blasphemy, swearing, foul language, bad language, cursing; informal cuss, cuss word; formal imprecation; archaic execration.
2 *some traditional festivals were tainted with profanity* **sacrilege,** blasphemy, irreligion, ungodliness, impiety, irreverence, disrespect.

profess ▶ verb 1 *he professed his love* **declare,** announce, proclaim, assert, state, affirm, avow, maintain, protest; formal aver.
2 *she professed to loathe publicity* **claim,** pretend, purport, affect; make out; informal let on.
3 *the emperor professed Christianity* **affirm one's faith in,** affirm one's allegiance to, avow,

confess.

professed ▶ adjective **1** *his professed ambition* **claimed,** supposed, ostensible, self-styled, apparent, pretended, purported.
2 *a professed libertarian* **declared,** self-acknowledged, self-confessed, confessed, sworn, avowed, confirmed.

profession ▶ noun **1** *his chosen profession of teaching* **career,** occupation, calling, vocation, métier, line (of work), walk of life, job, business, trade, craft; informal racket.
2 *a profession of allegiance* **declaration,** affirmation, statement, announcement, proclamation, assertion, avowal, vow, claim, protestation; formal averment.

professional ▶ adjective **1** *people in professional occupations* **white-collar,** nonmanual.
ANTONYMS blue-collar.
2 *a professional rugby player* **paid,** salaried.
ANTONYMS amateur.
3 *a thoroughly professional performance* **expert,** accomplished, skillful, masterly, masterful, fine, polished, skilled, proficient, competent, able, experienced, practiced, trained, seasoned, businesslike, deft; informal ace, crack, top-notch.
ANTONYMS amateurish.
4 *not a professional way to behave* **appropriate,** fitting, proper, honorable, ethical, correct, comme il faut.
ANTONYMS inappropriate, unethical.
▶ noun **1** *affluent young professionals* **white-collar worker,** office worker.
ANTONYMS blue-collar worker.
2 *his first season as a professional* **professional player,** paid player, salaried player; informal pro.
ANTONYMS amateur.
3 *she was a real professional on stage* **expert,** virtuoso, old hand, master, maestro, past master; informal pro, ace, wizard, whiz, hotshot, maven, crackerjack.
ANTONYMS amateur.

professor ▶ noun *a number of our professors were Rhodes scholars* **prof,** tenured faculty member, dean, full/assistant/associate professor, instructor, lecturer, doctor, scholar, academic.

proffer ▶ verb *he proffered his resignation* **offer,** tender, submit, extend, volunteer, suggest, propose, put forward; hold out.
ANTONYMS refuse, withdraw.

proficiency ▶ noun *her proficiency was obvious to anyone who sailed with her* **skill,** expertise, experience, accomplishment, competence, mastery, prowess, professionalism, deftness, adroitness, dexterity, finesse, ability, facility; informal know-how.
ANTONYMS incompetence.

proficient ▶ adjective *a proficient equestrian* **skilled,** skillful, expert, experienced, accomplished, competent, masterly, adept, adroit, deft, dexterous, able, professional, consummate, complete, master; informal crack, ace, mean.
ANTONYMS incompetent.

profile ▶ noun **1** *his handsome profile* **side view,** outline, silhouette, contour, shape, form, figure, lines.
2 *she wrote a profile of the organization* **description,** account, study, portrait, portrayal, depiction, rundown, sketch, outline.
▶ verb *he was profiled in the local paper* **describe,** write about, give an account of, portray, depict, sketch, outline.
– PHRASES **keep a low profile** *in matters concerning his family, he managed to keep a low profile* **lie low,** keep quiet, keep out of the public eye, avoid publicity, keep out of sight.

profit ▶ noun **1** *the firm made a profit* **(financial) gain,** return(s), yield, proceeds, earnings, winnings, surplus, excess; informal pay dirt, bottom line.
ANTONYMS loss.
2 *we could gain no profit by continuing* **advantage,** benefit, value, use, good, avail; informal mileage.
ANTONYMS disadvantage.
▶ verb **1** *this company must not profit from its wrongdoing* **make money,** make a profit; informal rake it in, clean up, make a killing, make a bundle, make big bucks, make a fast/quick buck.
ANTONYMS lose.
2 *how will that profit us?* **benefit,** be beneficial to, be of benefit to, be advantageous to, be of advantage to, be of use to, be of value to, do someone good, help, be of service to, serve, assist, aid.
ANTONYMS disadvantage.
– PHRASES **profit by/from** *if you're smart, you'll profit from their mistakes* **benefit from,** take advantage of, derive benefit from, capitalize on, make the most of, turn to one's advantage, put to good use, do well out of, exploit, gain from; informal cash in on.

profitable ▶ adjective **1** *a profitable company* **moneymaking,** profit-making, commercial, successful, solvent, in the black, gainful, remunerative, financially rewarding, paying, lucrative, bankable.
ANTONYMS loss-making.
2 *profitable study* **beneficial,** useful, advantageous, valuable, productive, worthwhile; rewarding, fruitful, illuminating, informative, well-spent.
ANTONYMS fruitless, useless.

profligate ▶ adjective **1** *profligate local authorities* **wasteful,** extravagant, spendthrift, improvident, prodigal.
ANTONYMS thrifty, frugal.
2 *a profligate lifestyle* **dissolute,** degenerate, dissipated, debauched, corrupt, depraved; **promiscuous,** loose, wanton, licentious, libertine, decadent, abandoned, fast; **sybaritic,** voluptuary.
ANTONYMS moral, upright.
▶ noun *he was an out-and-out profligate* **libertine,** debauchee, degenerate, dissolute, roué, rake, sybarite, voluptuary.

profound ▶ adjective **1** *profound relief* **heartfelt,** intense, keen, great, extreme, acute, severe, sincere, earnest, deep, deep-seated, overpowering, overwhelming, fervent, ardent.
ANTONYMS superficial, mild.
2 *profound silence* **complete,** utter, total, absolute.
3 *a profound change* **far-reaching,**

radical, extensive, sweeping, exhaustive, thoroughgoing.
ANTONYMS slight.
4 *a profound analysis* **wise,** learned, clever, intelligent, scholarly, sage, erudite, discerning, penetrating, perceptive, astute, thoughtful, insightful, percipient, perspicacious; rare sapient.
ANTONYMS superficial.
5 *profound truths* **complex,** abstract, deep, weighty, difficult, abstruse, recondite, esoteric.
ANTONYMS simple.

profoundly ▶ **adverb 1** *she was profoundly grateful that none of her colleagues could see her* **extremely,** very, deeply, exceedingly, greatly, immensely, enormously, tremendously, intensely, heartily, keenly, acutely, painfully, from the bottom of one's heart, downright, thoroughly, sincerely, so; informal awfully, terribly, seriously, majorly, oh-so, mighty.
2 *he spoke profoundly on the subject* **penetratingly,** discerningly, wisely, sagaciously, thoughtfully, philosophically, weightily, seriously, learnedly, eruditely.

profuse ▶ **adjective 1** *profuse apologies* **copious,** prolific, abundant, liberal, unstinting, fulsome, effusive, extravagant, lavish, gushing; informal over the top, gushy.
2 *profuse blooms* **luxuriant,** plentiful, copious, abundant, lush, rich, exuberant, riotous, teeming, rank, rampant; informal jungly.
ANTONYMS meager, sparse.

> CHOOSE THE RIGHT WORD
>
> **profuse, extravagant, lavish, lush, luxuriant, prodigal**
>
> Something that is **profuse** is poured out or given freely, often to the point of exaggeration or excess (*profuse apologies*). **Extravagant** also suggests unreasonable excess, but with an emphasis on wasteful spending (*her gift was much too extravagant for the occasion*). Someone who is **prodigal** is so recklessly extravagant that his or her resources will ultimately be exhausted (*the prodigal heir to the family fortune*). Another way to end up impoverished is through **lavish** spending, a word that combines extravagance with generosity or a lack of moderation (*lavish praise; lavish furnishings*). While *lavish, extravagant* and *prodigal* are often used to describe human behavior, **lush** and **luxuriant** normally refer to things. What is *luxuriant* is produced in great quantity, suggesting that it is not only profuse but gorgeous (*luxuriant auburn hair*). Something described as *lush* is not only luxuriant but has reached a peak of perfection (*the lush summer grass*).

profusion ▶ **noun** *a profusion of crocuses covered the front lawn* **abundance,** mass, host, cornucopia, riot, superabundance; informal sea, wealth; formal plenitude.

progeny ▶ **noun** *genetic traits passed on from parent to progeny* **offspring,** young, babies, children, sons and daughters, family, brood; **descendants,** heirs, scions; Law issue; archaic seed, fruit of one's loins.

program ▶ **noun 1** *our program for the day* **schedule,** agenda, calendar, timetable; order of events, lineup.
2 *the government's reform program* **plan of action,** series of measures, strategy, scheme.
3 *a television program* **broadcast,** production, show, presentation, transmission, performance, telecast.
4 *a program of study* **course,** syllabus, curriculum.
5 *a theater program* **guide,** list of performers, cast list, playbill.
▶ **verb** *they programmed the day well* **arrange,** organize, schedule, plan, map out, timetable, line up, slate.

progress ▶ **noun 1** *boulders made progress difficult* **forward movement,** advance, going, progression, headway, passage.
2 *scientific progress* **development,** advance, advancement, headway, step(s) forward; improvement, betterment, growth.
▶ **verb 1** *they progressed slowly down the road* **go,** make one's way, move, move forward, go forward, proceed, advance, go on, continue, make headway, work one's way.
2 *the school has progressed rapidly* **develop,** make progress, advance, make headway, take steps forward, move on, get on, gain ground; improve, get better, come on, come along, make strides; thrive, prosper, blossom, flourish; informal be getting there.
ANTONYMS regress.
– PHRASES **in progress** *the game was already in progress* **underway,** going on, ongoing, happening, occurring, taking place, proceeding, continuing; unfinished, in the works.

progression ▶ **noun 1** *progression to the next stage* **progress,** advancement, movement, passage, march; development, evolution, growth.
2 *a progression of peaks on the graph* **succession,** series, sequence, string, stream, chain, concatenation, train, row, cycle.

progressive ▶ **adjective 1** *progressive deterioration* **continuing,** continuous, increasing, growing, developing, ongoing, accelerating, escalating; gradual, step-by-step, cumulative.
2 *progressive views* **modern,** liberal, advanced, forward-thinking, enlightened, enterprising, innovative, pioneering, dynamic, bold, avant-garde, reforming, reformist, radical; informal go-ahead.
ANTONYMS conservative, reactionary.
▶ **noun** *he is very much a progressive* **innovator,** reformer, reformist, liberal, libertarian.

prohibit ▶ **verb 1** *state law prohibits gambling* **forbid,** ban, bar, interdict, proscribe, make illegal, embargo, outlaw, disallow, veto; Law enjoin.
ANTONYMS permit, authorize.
2 *a cash shortage prohibited the visit* **prevent,** stop, rule out, preclude, make impossible.
ANTONYMS facilitate, allow.

CHOOSE THE RIGHT WORD

prohibit, ban, disallow, enjoin, forbid, hinder, interdict, preclude

There are a number of ways to prevent something from happening. You can **prohibit** it, which assumes that you have legal or other authority and are willing to back up your prohibition with force (*prohibit smoking*); or you can simply **forbid** it and hope that you've got the necessary clout (*forbid teenagers to stay out after midnight*). **Ban** carries a little more weight—both legal and moral—and **interdict** suggests that church or civil authorities are behind the idea. To **enjoin** (in this sense) is to prohibit by legal injunction (*the truckers were enjoined from striking*), which practically guarantees that you'll get what you want. A government or some other authority may **disallow** an act it might otherwise have permitted (*the IRS disallowed the deduction*), but anyone with a little gumption can **hinder** an activity by putting obstacles in its path (*hinder the thief's getaway by tripping him on his way out the door*). Of course, the easiest way to prohibit something is to **preclude** it, which means stopping it before it even gets started.

prohibition ▶ noun **1** *the prohibition of marijuana* **banning,** forbidding, prohibiting, barring, debarment, vetoing, proscription, interdiction, outlawing.
2 *a prohibition was imposed* **ban,** bar, interdict, veto, embargo, injunction, moratorium.

prohibitive ▶ adjective **1** *prohibitive costs* **exorbitant,** excessively high, sky-high, overinflated; out of the question, beyond one's means; extortionate, unreasonable; informal steep, criminal.
2 *prohibitive regulations* **proscriptive,** prohibitory, restrictive, repressive.

project ▶ noun **1** *an engineering project* **plan,** program, enterprise, undertaking, venture; proposal, idea, concept, scheme.
2 *a history project* **assignment,** piece of work, piece of research, task.
▶ verb **1** *profits are projected to rise* **forecast,** predict, expect, estimate, calculate, reckon.
2 *his projected book* **intend,** plan, propose, devise, design, outline.
3 *balconies projected over the lake* **stick out,** jut (out), protrude, extend, stand out, bulge out, poke out, thrust out, cantilever. See note at **BULGE**.
4 *seeds are projected from the tree* **propel,** discharge, launch, throw, cast, fling, hurl, shoot.
5 *the sun projected his shadow on the wall* **cast,** throw, send, shed, shine.
6 *she tried to project a calm image* **convey,** put across, put over, communicate, present, promote.

projectile ▶ noun *the cyclone sent pieces of the house flying like wild projectiles* **missile,** rocket, bullets.

projection ▶ noun **1** *a sales projection* **forecast,** prediction, prognosis, outlook, expectation, estimate.
2 *tiny projections on the cliff face* **protuberance,** protrusion, prominence, eminence, outcrop, outgrowth, jut, jag, snag; overhang, ledge, shelf.

proletariat ▶ noun *the voice of the proletariat* **the workers,** working-class people, wage earners, the working classes, the common people, the lower classes, the masses, the rank and file, the third estate, the plebeians; derogatory the hoi polloi, the plebs, the proles, the great unwashed, the mob, the rabble.
ANTONYMS aristocracy.

proliferate ▶ verb *stories of her trial proliferated* **increase rapidly,** grow rapidly, multiply, rocket, mushroom, snowball, burgeon, run riot.
ANTONYMS decrease, dwindle.

prolific ▶ adjective **1** *a prolific crop of tomatoes* **plentiful,** abundant, bountiful, profuse, copious, luxuriant, rich, lush; fruitful, fecund; literary plenteous, bounteous.
2 *a prolific composer* **productive,** creative, inventive, fertile. See note at **FERTILE**.

prolix ▶ adjective *his prolix speeches* **long-winded,** verbose, wordy, pleonastic, discursive, rambling, long-drawn-out, overlong, lengthy, protracted, interminable; informal windy, waffly.

prologue ▶ noun *Davis wrote the prologue to her brother's autobiography* **introduction,** foreword, preface, preamble, prelude; informal intro, lead-in; formal exordium, proem, prolegomenon.
ANTONYMS epilogue.

prolong ▶ verb *your bickering just prolongs these negotiations* **lengthen,** extend, draw out, drag out, protract, spin out, stretch out, string out, elongate; carry on, continue, keep up, perpetuate.
ANTONYMS shorten.

prominence ▶ noun **1** *his rise to prominence* **fame,** celebrity, eminence, preeminence, importance, distinction, greatness, note, notability, prestige, stature, standing, position, rank.
2 *the press gave prominence to the reports* **good coverage,** importance, precedence, weight, a high profile, top billing.
3 *a rocky prominence* **hillock,** hill, hummock, mound; outcrop, crag, spur, rise; ridge, arête; peak, pinnacle; promontory, cliff, headland.

prominent ▶ adjective **1** *a prominent surgeon* **important,** well-known, leading, eminent, distinguished, notable, noteworthy, noted, illustrious, celebrated, famous, renowned, acclaimed, famed, influential, affluential, major-league.
ANTONYMS unimportant, unknown.
2 *prominent cheekbones* **protuberant,** protruding, projecting, jutting (out), standing out, sticking out, proud, bulging, bulbous.
3 *a prominent feature of the landscape* **conspicuous,** noticeable, easily seen, obvious, front-and-center, unmistakable, eye-catching, impactful, pronounced, salient, striking, dominant; obtrusive. See note at **NOTICEABLE**.
ANTONYMS inconspicuous.

promiscuity ▶ noun *the promiscuity associated*

with the sixties and seventies **licentiousness,** wantonness, immorality; informal sleeping around, sluttishness, whorishness; dated looseness.
ANTONYMS chastity, virtue.

promiscuous ▶ **adjective 1** *a promiscuous teenager* **licentious,** sexually indiscriminate, wanton, immoral, fast; informal easy, swinging, sluttish, whorish, bed-hopping; dated loose, fallen.
ANTONYMS chaste, virtuous.
2 *promiscuous reading* **indiscriminate,** undiscriminating, unselective, random, haphazard, irresponsible, unthinking, unconsidered.
ANTONYMS selective.

promise ▶ **noun 1** *you broke your promise* **word (of honor),** assurance, pledge, vow, guarantee, oath, bond, undertaking, agreement, commitment, contract, covenant.
2 *he shows promise* **potential,** ability, aptitude, capability, capacity.
3 *the promise of fine weather* **indication,** hint, suggestion, sign.
▶ **verb 1** *she promised to go* **give one's word,** swear, pledge, vow, undertake, guarantee, contract, engage, give an assurance, commit oneself, bind oneself, swear/take an oath, covenant; archaic plight.
2 *the skies promised sunshine* **indicate,** lead one to expect, point to, denote, signify, be a sign of, be evidence of, give hope of, bespeak, presage, augur, herald, bode, portend; literary betoken, foretoken, forebode.

promising ▶ **adjective 1** *a promising start* **good,** encouraging, favorable, hopeful, full of promise, auspicious, propitious, bright, rosy, heartening, reassuring.
ANTONYMS unfavorable.
2 *a promising actor* **with potential,** budding, up-and-coming, rising, coming, in the making.

promontory ▶ **noun** *a lone beacon shone from the promontory* **headland,** point, cape, head, foreland, horn, bill, peninsula.

promote ▶ **verb 1** *she's been promoted at work* **upgrade,** give promotion to, elevate, advance, move up; humorous kick upstairs; archaic prefer.
ANTONYMS demote.
2 *an organization promoting justice* **encourage,** advocate, further, advance, assist, aid, help, contribute to, foster, nurture, develop, boost, stimulate, forward, work for.
ANTONYMS obstruct.
3 *she is promoting her new film* **advertise,** publicize, give publicity to, beat/bang the drum for, market, merchandise; informal push, plug, hype, boost, ballyhoo.
ANTONYMS play down.

promotion ▶ **noun 1** *her promotion at work* **upgrading,** preferment, elevation, advancement, step up (the ladder).
2 *the promotion of justice* **encouragement,** advocacy, furtherance, furthering, advancement, assistance, aid, help, contribution to, fostering, boosting, stimulation, boosterism.
3 *the promotion of her new film* **advertising,** publicizing, marketing; publicity, campaign, propaganda; informal hard sell, blitz, plug, hype, ballyhoo.

prompt ▶ **verb 1** *curiosity prompted him to look* **induce,** make, move, motivate, lead, dispose, persuade, incline, encourage, stimulate, prod, impel, spur on, inspire.
ANTONYMS discourage.
2 *the statement prompted a hostile reaction* **give rise to,** bring about, cause, occasion, result in, lead to, elicit, produce, bring on, engender, induce, precipitate, trigger, spark off, provoke.
ANTONYMS restrain.
3 *the actors needed prompting* **remind,** cue, feed, help out; jog someone's memory.
▶ **adjective** *a prompt reply* **quick,** swift, rapid, speedy, fast, direct, immediate, instant, expeditious, early, punctual, in good time, on time, timely.
ANTONYMS slow, late.
▶ **noun** *the actor stopped, and Julia supplied a prompt* **reminder,** cue, feed.

promptly ▶ **adverb 1** *William arrived promptly at 7:30* **punctually,** on time; informal bang on, on the button, on the dot, on the nose.
ANTONYMS late.
2 *I expect the matter to be dealt with promptly* **without delay,** straightaway, right away, at once, immediately, now, as soon as possible; **quickly,** swiftly, rapidly, speedily, fast, expeditiously, momentarily; informal pronto, ASAP, PDQ, pretty damn quick.
ANTONYMS slowly.

promulgate ▶ **verb 1** *they promulgated their own views* **make known,** make public, publicize, spread, communicate, propagate, disseminate, broadcast, promote, preach; literary bruit abroad. See note at ANNOUNCE.
2 *the law was promulgated in 1942* **put into effect,** enact, implement, enforce.

prone ▶ **adjective 1** *untreated wood is prone to rotting | prone to disease* **susceptible,** vulnerable, subject, open, liable, given, predisposed, likely, disposed, inclined, apt; at risk of.
ANTONYMS resistant, immune.
2 *his prone body* **(lying) face down,** face downward, on one's stomach/front; **lying flat/down,** horizontal, prostrate.
ANTONYMS upright.

prong ▶ **noun** *sharpening the prongs of the pitchfork* **tine,** spike, point, tip, projection.

pronounce ▶ **verb 1** *his name is difficult to pronounce* **say,** enunciate, articulate, utter, voice, sound, vocalize, get one's tongue around.
2 *the doctor pronounced that I had a virus* **announce,** proclaim, declare, affirm, assert; judge, rule, decree.

pronounced ▶ **adjective** *a pronounced German accent* **noticeable,** marked, strong, conspicuous, striking, distinct, prominent, unmistakable, obvious, recognizable, identifiable.
ANTONYMS slight.

pronouncement ▶ **noun** *we awaited an official pronouncement from Washington* **announcement,** proclamation, declaration, assertion; judgment, ruling, decree; formal ordinance.

pronunciation ▶ **noun** *the pronunciation of difficult words* **accent,** manner of speaking, speech, diction, delivery, elocution, intonation; articulation, enunciation, voicing, vocalization, sounding.

proof ▶ noun **1** *proof of ownership* **evidence,** verification, corroboration, authentication, confirmation, certification, documentation, validation, attestation, substantiation.
2 *the proofs of a book* **page proof,** galley proof, galley.
▶ adjective *no system is **proof against** theft* **resistant to,** immune from, unaffected by, invulnerable to, impenetrable by, impervious to, repellent to.

prop ▶ noun **1** *the roof is held up by props* **pole,** post, support, upright, brace, buttress, stay, strut, stanchion, shore, pier, pillar, pile, piling, bolster, truss, column.
2 *a prop for the economy* **mainstay,** pillar, anchor, backbone, support, foundation, cornerstone.
▶ verb **1** *she propped her bike against the wall* **lean,** rest, stand, balance, steady.
2 *this post is **propping** the wall **up*** **hold up,** shore up, bolster up, buttress, support, brace, underpin.
3 *they **prop up** failing industries* **subsidize,** underwrite, fund, finance.

propaganda ▶ noun *a so-called documentary that was really socialist propaganda* **information,** promotion, advertising, publicity, spin; disinformation, counter-information; historical agitprop; informal info, hype, plugging; puff piece; the big lie.

propagate ▶ verb **1** *an easy plant to propagate* **breed,** grow, cultivate.
2 *these shrubs propagate easily* **reproduce,** multiply, proliferate, increase, spread, self-seed, self-sow.
3 *they propagated socialist ideas* **spread,** disseminate, communicate, make known, promulgate, circulate, broadcast, publicize, proclaim, preach, promote; literary bruit abroad.

propel ▶ verb **1** *a boat propelled by oars* **move,** power, push, drive.
2 *he propelled the ball into the air* **throw,** thrust, toss, fling, hurl, launch, pitch, project, send, shoot.
3 *confusion propelled her into action* **spur,** drive, prompt, precipitate, catapult, motivate, force, impel.

propensity ▶ noun *his propensity for giving long speeches* **tendency,** inclination, predisposition, proneness, proclivity, readiness, liability, disposition, leaning, weakness.

proper ▶ adjective **1** *he's not a proper scientist* **real,** genuine, actual, true, bona fide; informal kosher.
ANTONYMS fake.
2 *the proper channels* **right,** correct, accepted, orthodox, conventional, established, official, formal, regular, acceptable, appropriate, de rigueur; archaic meet.
ANTONYMS inappropriate, wrong.
3 *they were terribly proper* **respectable,** decorous, seemly, decent, refined, ladylike, gentlemanly, genteel; formal, conventional, correct, comme il faut, orthodox, polite, punctilious. See note at FORMAL.
ANTONYMS unconventional.

property ▶ noun **1** *lost property* **possessions,** belongings, things, effects, stuff, gear, chattels, movables; resources, assets, valuables, fortune, capital, riches, wealth; Law personalty, goods and chattels.
2 *private property* **building(s),** premises, house(s), land, estates, realty, real estate.
3 *healing properties* **quality,** attribute, characteristic, feature, power, trait, mark, hallmark.

prophecy ▶ noun **1** *her prophecy is coming true* **prediction,** forecast, prognostication, prognosis, divination, augury.
2 *the gift of prophecy* **divination,** fortune-telling, crystal-gazing, prediction, second sight, prognostication, augury, soothsaying.

prophesy ▶ verb *did those mystical sages ever prophesy anything other than calamity?* **predict,** foretell, forecast, foresee, forewarn of, prognosticate. See note at PREDICT.

prophet, prophetess ▶ noun *the queen was disturbed by the prophet's interpretation of her dreams* **seer,** soothsayer, fortune teller, clairvoyant, diviner; oracle, augur, sibyl.
– PHRASES **prophet of doom** *if you want to listen to these prophets of doom, you may as well cash it in today* **pessimist,** doom-monger, doomsayer, doomster, Cassandra, Jeremiah; informal Chicken Little.

prophetic ▶ adjective *his words proved prophetic—within a week he was dead* **prescient,** predictive, far-seeing, prognostic, divinatory, sibylline, apocalyptic; rare vatic.

prophylactic ▶ adjective *prophylactic measures* **preventive,** preventative, precautionary, protective, inhibitory.
▶ noun **1** *a prophylactic against malaria* **preventive measure,** precaution, safeguard, safety measure; preventive medicine.
2 *prophylactic dispensers in public washrooms* See CONDOM.

prophylaxis ▶ noun *our dental insurance covers twice-yearly prophylaxis* **preventive treatment,** prevention, protection, precaution.

propitiate ▶ verb *my attempts to propitiate you are useless* **appease,** placate, mollify, pacify, make peace with, conciliate, make amends to, soothe, calm. See note at PACIFY.
ANTONYMS provoke.

propitious ▶ adjective *the timing for such a meeting seemed propitious* **favorable,** auspicious, promising, providential, advantageous, optimistic, bright, rosy, heaven-sent, hopeful; opportune, timely. See note at TIMELY.
ANTONYMS inauspicious, unfortunate.

proponent ▶ noun *a proponent of the youth basketball program* **advocate,** champion, supporter, backer, promoter, protagonist, campaigner, booster, cheerleader.

proportion ▶ noun **1** *a small proportion of the land* **part,** portion, amount, quantity, bit, piece, percentage, fraction, section, segment, share.
2 *the proportion of water to alcohol* **ratio,** distribution, relative amount/number; relationship.
3 *the drawing is out of proportion* **balance,**

symmetry, harmony, correspondence, correlation, agreement.
4 (**proportions**) *men of huge proportions* **size,** dimensions, magnitude, measurements; mass, volume, bulk; expanse, extent, width, breadth.

proportional ▶ adjective *a proportional increase in wages* **corresponding,** proportionate, comparable, in proportion, pro rata, commensurate, equivalent, consistent, relative, analogous.
ANTONYMS disproportionate.

proposal ▶ noun 1 *the proposal was rejected* **plan,** idea, scheme, project, program, manifesto, motion, proposition, suggestion, submission, trial balloon.
2 *the proposal of a new constitution* **putting forward,** proposing, suggesting, submitting.
ANTONYMS withdrawal.

propose ▶ verb 1 *he proposed a solution* **put forward,** suggest, submit, advance, offer, present, move, come up with, lodge, table, nominate.
ANTONYMS withdraw.
2 *do you propose to go?* **intend,** mean, plan, have in mind/view, resolve, aim, purpose, think of, aspire, want. See note at INTEND.
3 *you've proposed to her!* **ask someone to marry you,** make an offer of marriage, offer marriage; informal pop the question; dated ask for someone's hand in marriage.

proposition ▶ noun 1 *the analysis derives from one proposition* **theory,** hypothesis, thesis, argument, premise, principle, theorem, concept, idea, statement.
2 *a business proposition* **proposal,** scheme, plan, project, idea, program, bid.
3 *doing it for real is a very different proposition* **task,** job, undertaking, venture, activity, affair, problem.
▶ verb *he never dared proposition her* **propose sex with,** make sexual advances to, make an indecent proposal to, make an improper suggestion to; informal hit on.

propound ▶ verb *exactly what solution are you propounding?* **put forward,** advance, offer, proffer, present, set forth, submit, tender, suggest, introduce, postulate, propose, pose, posit; advocate, promote, peddle, spread.

proprietor, proprietress ▶ noun *the proprietor is thinking about selling this bar* **owner,** possessor, holder, master/mistress; landowner, landlord/landlady; innkeeper, hotel-keeper, hotelier, storekeeper.

propriety ▶ noun 1 *she behaves with the utmost propriety* **decorum,** respectability, decency, correctness, protocol, appropriateness, suitability, good manners, courtesy, politeness, rectitude, morality, civility, modesty, demureness; sobriety, refinement, discretion.
ANTONYMS indecorum.
2 (**proprieties**) *he was careful to preserve the proprieties in public* **etiquette,** convention(s), social grace(s), niceties, one's Ps and Qs, protocol, standards, civilities, formalities, accepted behavior, good form, the done thing, the thing to do, punctilio.

propulsion ▶ noun *these birds use their wings for propulsion under water* **thrust,** motive force, impetus, impulse, drive, driving force, actuation, push, pressure, power.

prosaic ▶ adjective *a prosaic lecture that had us fighting to stay awake* **ordinary,** everyday, commonplace, conventional, straightforward, routine, run-of-the-mill, by-the-numbers, workaday; **unimaginative,** uninspired, uninspiring, matter-of-fact, dull, dry, dreary, tedious, boring, humdrum, mundane, pedestrian, tame, plodding; bland, insipid, banal, trite, literal, factual, unpoetic, unemotional, unsentimental.
ANTONYMS interesting, imaginative, inspired.

proscribe ▶ verb 1 *gambling was proscribed* **forbid,** prohibit, ban, bar, interdict, make illegal, embargo, outlaw, disallow, veto; Law enjoin.
ANTONYMS allow, permit.
2 *the book was proscribed by the Church* **condemn,** denounce, attack, criticize, censure, damn, reject, taboo.
ANTONYMS authorize, accept.

proscription ▶ noun 1 *the proscription of alcohol* **banning,** forbidding, prohibition, prohibiting, barring, debarment, vetoing, interdiction, outlawing.
ANTONYMS allowing.
2 *a proscription was imposed* **ban,** prohibition, bar, interdict, veto, embargo, moratorium.
ANTONYMS authorization.
3 *the proscription of his literary works* **condemnation,** denunciation, attacking, criticism, censuring, damning, rejection.
ANTONYMS acceptance.

prosecute ▶ verb 1 *they prosecute offenders* **take to court,** bring/institute legal proceedings against, bring an action against, take legal action against, sue, try, impeach, bring to trial, put on trial, put in the dock, bring a suit against, indict, arraign.
ANTONYMS defend, let off, pardon.
2 *they helped him prosecute the war* **pursue,** fight, wage, carry on, conduct, direct, engage in, proceed with, continue (with), keep on with.
ANTONYMS give up.

proselyte ▶ noun *proselytes are not spiritually mature enough to be counseling others in church matters* **convert,** new believer, catechumen.

prospect ▶ noun 1 *there is little prospect of success* **likelihood,** hope, expectation, anticipation, (good/poor) chance, odds, probability, possibility, promise; fear, danger.
2 (**prospects**) *her job prospects* **possibilities,** potential, promise, expectations, outlook.
3 *a daunting prospect* **vision,** thought, idea; task, undertaking.
4 *Jack is an exciting prospect* **candidate,** possibility; informal catch.
5 *there is a pleasant prospect from the lounge* **view,** vista, outlook, perspective, panorama, aspect, scene; picture, spectacle, sight.
▶ verb *they are prospecting for gold* **search,** look, explore, survey, scout, hunt, reconnoiter, examine, inspect.

prospective ▶ adjective *offering incentives to prospective buyers* **potential,** possible, probable, likely, future, eventual, -to-be, soon-to-be, in the making; intending, aspiring, would-be; forthcoming, approaching, coming, imminent.

prospectus ▶ **noun** *nowhere in your prospectus do you list actual costs* **brochure,** pamphlet, description, particulars, announcement, advertisement; syllabus, curriculum, catalog, program, list, fact sheet, scheme, schedule.

prosper ▶ **verb** *the family business continues to prosper* **flourish,** thrive, do well, bloom, blossom, burgeon, progress, do all right for oneself, get ahead, get on (in the world), be successful; informal go places.
ANTONYMS fail, flounder.

prosperity ▶ **noun** *she deserves all the prosperity she now enjoys* **success,** profitability, affluence, wealth, opulence, luxury, the good life, milk and honey, (good) fortune, ease, plenty, comfort, security, well-being.
ANTONYMS hardship, failure.

prosperous ▶ **adjective** *a prosperous shipping firm* **thriving,** flourishing, successful, strong, vigorous, profitable, lucrative, expanding, booming, burgeoning; **affluent,** wealthy, rich, moneyed, well off, well-to-do, opulent, substantial, in clover; informal on a roll, in the money. See note at **WEALTHY**.
ANTONYMS ailing, poor.

prostitute ▶ **noun** *undercover cops posing as prostitutes* **call girl,** whore; informal **hooker**; working girl, lady of the evening, streetwalker, member of the oldest profession, tart, moll, fille de joie, escort, courtesan, hustler; ho; dated scarlet woman, camp follower, cocotte, strumpet, harlot, trollop, woman of ill repute, wench.
▶ **verb** *they prostituted their art* **betray,** sacrifice, sell, sell out, debase, degrade, demean, devalue, cheapen, lower, shame, misuse, pervert; abandon one's principles (at the expense of).

prostitution ▶ **noun** *they claim that the casino industry only encourages prostitution in the area* **the sex trade,** the sex industry, whoring, streetwalking, sex tourism; informal the oldest profession, hooking, hustling; dated whoredom; archaic harlotry.

prostrate ▶ **adjective 1** *the prostrate figure on the ground* **prone,** lying flat, lying down, stretched out, spread-eagled, sprawling, horizontal, recumbent; rare procumbent.
ANTONYMS upright.
2 *his wife was prostrate with shock* **overwhelmed,** overcome, overpowered, brought to one's knees, stunned, dazed; speechless, helpless.
3 *the fever left me prostrate* **worn out,** exhausted, fatigued, tired out, sapped, dog-tired, spent, drained, debilitated, enervated, laid low; informal dead, dead beat, dead on one's feet, ready to drop, bushed, frazzled, worn to a frazzle, whacked, pooped.
ANTONYMS fresh.
▶ **verb** *she was prostrated by the tragedy* **overwhelm,** overcome, overpower, bring to one's knees, devastate, debilitate, weaken, enfeeble, enervate, lay low, wear out, exhaust, tire out, drain, sap, wash out, take it out of; informal frazzle, do in, poop.
– PHRASES **prostrate oneself** *he prostrated himself on the altar mat* **throw oneself flat/down,** lie down, stretch oneself out; throw oneself (at someone's feet).

protagonist ▶ **noun 1** *the protagonist in the plot* **chief/central/principal/main/leading character,** chief/central/principal/main/leading participant, chief/central/principal/main/leading figure, chief/central/principal/main/leading player, principal, hero/heroine, leading man/lady, title role, lead.
2 *a protagonist of deregulation* **champion,** advocate, upholder, supporter, backer, promoter, proponent, exponent, campaigner, fighter, crusader; apostle, apologist, booster.
ANTONYMS opponent.

protean ▶ **adjective 1** *the protean nature of mental disorders* **ever-changing,** variable, changeable, mutable, kaleidoscopic, inconstant, inconsistent, unstable, shifting, unsettled, fluctuating, fluid, wavering, vacillating, mercurial, volatile; technical labile.
ANTONYMS constant, consistent.
2 *a remarkably protean composer* **versatile,** adaptable, flexible, all-around, multifaceted, multitalented, many-sided.
ANTONYMS limited.

protect ▶ **verb** *they fought to protect their homes and families* **keep safe,** keep from harm, save, safeguard, preserve, defend, shield, cushion, insulate, hedge, shelter, screen, secure, fortify, guard, watch over, look after, take care of, keep; inoculate.
ANTONYMS expose, neglect, attack, harm.

protection ▶ **noun 1** *protection against frost* **defense,** security, shielding, preservation, conservation, safekeeping, safeguarding, safety, sanctuary, shelter, refuge, lee, immunity, insurance, indemnity.
2 *under the protection of the Church* **safekeeping,** care, charge, keeping, protectorship, guidance, aegis, auspices, umbrella, guardianship, support, patronage, championship, providence.
3 *good protection against noise* **barrier,** buffer, shield, screen, hedge, cushion, preventative, armor, refuge, bulwark.

protective ▶ **adjective 1** *protective clothing* **preservative,** protecting, safeguarding, shielding, defensive, safety, precautionary, preventive, preventative.
2 *he felt protective toward the dog* **solicitous,** caring, warm, paternal/maternal, fatherly/motherly, gallant, chivalrous; overprotective, possessive, jealous.

protector ▶ **noun 1** *a protector of the environment* **defender,** preserver, guardian, guard, champion, watchdog, ombudsman, knight in shining armor, guardian angel, patron, chaperone, escort, keeper, custodian, bodyguard, minder; informal hired gun.
2 *ear protectors* **guard,** shield, buffer, cushion, pad, screen.

protest ▶ **noun 1** *he resigned as a protest* **objection,** complaint, exception, disapproval, challenge, dissent, demurral, remonstration, fuss, outcry.
ANTONYMS support, approval.

2 *women staged a protest* **demonstration,** (protest) march, rally; sit-in, occupation; work-to-rule, industrial action, (work) stoppage, strike, walkout, mutiny, picket, boycott.
▶ **verb 1** *residents protested against the plans* **express opposition,** object, dissent, take issue, make/take a stand, put up a fight, kick, take exception, complain, express disapproval, disagree, demur, remonstrate, make a fuss; cry out, speak out, rail, inveigh, fulminate; informal kick up a fuss/stink.
2 *people protested outside the cathedral* **demonstrate,** march, hold a rally, sit in, occupy somewhere; work to rule, take industrial action, stop work, strike, go on strike, walk out, mutiny, picket; boycott something.
3 *he protested his innocence* **insist on,** maintain, assert, affirm, announce, proclaim, declare, profess, contend, argue, claim, vow, swear (to), stress; formal aver.

protestation ▶ **noun 1** *her protestations of innocence* **declaration,** announcement, profession, assertion, insistence, claim, affirmation, assurance, oath, vow.
2 *we helped him despite his protestations* **objection,** protest, exception, complaint, disapproval, opposition, challenge, dissent, demurral, remonstration, fuss, outcry; informal stink.

protester ▶ **noun** *protesters gathers outside of the arena* **demonstrator,** objector, opposer, opponent, complainant, complainer, dissenter, dissident, nonconformist, protest marcher; striker, picket.

protocol ▶ **noun 1** *a stickler for protocol* **etiquette,** conventions, formalities, customs, rules of conduct, procedure, ritual, accepted behavior, propriety, proprieties, one's Ps and Qs, decorum, good form, the done thing, the thing to do, punctilio.
2 *the two countries signed a protocol* **agreement,** treaty, entente, concordat, convention, deal, pact, contract, compact; formal concord.

prototype ▶ **noun 1** *a prototype of the weapon* **original,** first example/model, master, mold, template, framework, mock-up, pattern, sample; **design,** guide, blueprint. See note at **MODEL**.
2 *the prototype of an ideal wife* **paradigm,** typical example, archetype, exemplar, essence.

protract ▶ **verb** *the opposition will try to protract the discussion* **prolong,** lengthen, extend, draw out, drag out, spin out, stretch out, string out, elongate; carry on, continue, keep up, perpetuate.
ANTONYMS curtail, shorten.

protracted ▶ **adjective** *weeks of protracted negotiations* **prolonged,** long-lasting, extended, long-drawn-out, spun out, dragged out, strung out, lengthy, long; informal marathon.
ANTONYMS short.

protrude ▶ **verb** *the emergency lever protrudes from the left side* **stick out,** jut (out), project, extend, stand out, bulge out, poke out, thrust out, cantilever. See note at **BULGE**.

protrusion ▶ **noun 1** *the neck vertebrae have short vertical protrusions* **bump,** lump, knob; protuberance, projection, prominence, swelling, eminence, outcrop, outgrowth, jut, jag, snag; ledge, shelf, ridge.
2 *protrusion of the lips* **sticking out,** jutting, projection, obtrusion, prominence; swelling, bulging.

protuberance ▶ **noun 1** *a protuberance can cause drag* **bump,** lump, knob, projection, protrusion, prominence, swelling, eminence, outcrop, outgrowth, jut, jag, snag; ledge, shelf, ridge.
2 *the protuberance of the incisors* **sticking out,** jutting, projection, obtrusion, prominence; swelling, bulging.

protuberant ▶ **adjective** *his eyes are a little protuberant* **sticking out,** protruding, projecting, prominent, jutting, overhanging, proud, bulging.
ANTONYMS sunken, flush.

proud ▶ **adjective 1** *the proud parents beamed* **pleased,** glad, happy, delighted, joyful, overjoyed, thrilled, satisfied, gratified, content.
ANTONYMS ashamed.
2 *a proud day* **pleasing,** gratifying, satisfying, cheering, heartwarming; happy, good, glorious, memorable, notable, red-letter.
ANTONYMS shameful.
3 *they were poor but proud* **self-respecting,** dignified, noble, worthy; independent.
ANTONYMS humble.
4 *I'm not too proud to admit I'm wrong* **arrogant,** conceited, vain, self-important, full of oneself, puffed up, jumped-up, smug, complacent, disdainful, condescending, scornful, supercilious, snobbish, imperious, pompous, overbearing, bumptious, haughty; informal big-headed, too big for one's britches/boots, high and mighty, stuck-up, Pooterish, uppity, snooty, highfalutin; literary vainglorious; rare hubristic.
ANTONYMS humble, modest.
5 *the proud ships* **magnificent,** splendid, resplendent, grand, noble, stately, imposing, dignified, striking, impressive, majestic, glorious, awe-inspiring, awesome, monumental.
ANTONYMS unimpressive.

prove ▶ **verb 1** *that proves I'm right* **show (to be true),** demonstrate (the truth of), show beyond doubt, manifest, produce proof/evidence; witness to, give substance to, determine, substantiate, corroborate, verify, ratify, validate, authenticate, document, bear out, confirm; formal evince.
ANTONYMS disprove.
2 *the rumor proved to be correct* **turn out,** be found, happen.
– PHRASES **prove oneself** *I was happy to have the chance to prove myself* **demonstrate one's abilities/qualities,** show one's (true) mettle, show what one is made of.

proverb ▶ **noun** *Mama didn't just recite proverbs about decency and good sense, she lived by them* **saying,** adage, saw, maxim, axiom, motto, bon mot, aphorism, apophthegm, epigram, gnome, dictum, precept; words of wisdom. See note at **SAYING**.

proverbial ▶ **adjective** *well, the proverbial bad son has returned at last* **well-known,** famous, famed, renowned, traditional, time-honored, legendary; notorious, infamous.

provide ▶ verb **1** *the foundation will provide funds* **supply,** give, issue, furnish, come up with, dispense, bestow, impart, produce, yield, bring forth, bear, deliver, donate, contribute, pledge, advance, spare, part with, allocate, distribute, allot, put up; informal fork out, lay out, ante up, pony up.
ANTONYMS refuse, withhold.
2 *she was provided with enough tools* **equip,** furnish, issue, supply, outfit; fit out, rig out, arm, provision; informal fix up.
ANTONYMS deprive.
3 *he had to* ***provide for*** *his family* **feed,** nurture, nourish; **support,** maintain, keep, sustain, provide sustenance for, fend for, finance, endow.
ANTONYMS neglect.
4 *the test may provide the answer* **make available,** present, offer, afford, give, add, bring, yield, impart.
5 *we have provided for further restructuring* **prepare,** allow, make provision, be prepared, arrange, get ready, plan, cater.
6 *the banks have to provide against bad debts* **take precautions,** take steps/measures, guard, forearm oneself.
7 *the legislation provides that factories must be kept clean* **stipulate,** lay down, make it a condition, require, order, ordain, demand, prescribe, state, specify.

providence ▶ noun **1** *a life mapped out by providence* **fate,** destiny, nemesis, kismet, God's will, divine intervention, predestination, predetermination, the stars; one's lot (in life); archaic one's portion.
2 *he had a streak of providence* **prudence,** foresight, forethought, farsightedness, judiciousness, shrewdness, circumspection, wisdom, sagacity, common sense; careful budgeting, thrift, economy.

provident ▶ adjective *Kaye was provident enough to be able to buy her first home at age 24* **prudent,** farsighted, judicious, shrewd, circumspect, forearmed, wise, sagacious, sensible; thrifty, economical. See note at **ECONOMICAL**.
ANTONYMS improvident.

province ▶ noun **1** *Canada's westernmost province* **territory,** region, state, department, canton, area, district, sector, zone, division.
2 *that's outside my province* **responsibility,** area of activity, area of interest, knowledge, department, sphere, world, realm, field, domain, territory, orbit, preserve; business, affair, concern; specialty, forte; jurisdiction, authority; informal bailiwick, turf.

provincial ▶ adjective **1** *the provincial government* **regional,** state, territorial, district; sectoral, zonal, cantonal.
ANTONYMS national.
2 *provincial areas* **nonmetropolitan,** small-town, nonurban, outlying, rural, country, rustic, backwoods, backwater; informal one-horse, hick, jerkwater, freshwater.
ANTONYMS national, metropolitan, cosmopolitan.
3 *provincial attitudes* **unsophisticated,** narrow-minded, parochial, small-town, suburban, insular, bush-league, inward-looking, conservative; small-minded, blinkered, bigoted, prejudiced; informal jerkwater, corn-fed. See note at **BIAS**.
ANTONYMS sophisticated, broad-minded.
▶ noun *they were dismissed as provincials* **hillbilly,** (country) bumpkin, country cousin, rustic, yokel, village idiot, peasant, hayseed, hick, rube, redneck.
ANTONYMS sophisticate.

provision ▶ noun **1** *the provision of weapons to guerrillas* **supplying,** supply, providing, giving, presentation, donation; equipping, furnishing.
2 *there has been limited provision for gifted children* **facilities,** services, amenities, resource(s), arrangements; means, funds, benefits, assistance, allowance(s).
3 (**provisions**) *provisions for the trip* **supplies,** food and drink, stores, groceries, foodstuff(s), provender, rations; informal grub, eats, nosh; formal comestibles; literary viands; dated victuals.
4 *he made no provision for the future* **preparations,** plans, arrangements, prearrangement, precautions, contingency.
5 *the provisions of the law* **term,** clause; requirement, specification, stipulation; proviso, condition, qualification, restriction, limitation.

provisional ▶ adjective *a provisional government* **interim,** temporary, pro tem; transitional, changeover, stopgap, short-term, fill-in, acting, caretaker, subject to confirmation; penciled in, working, tentative, contingent.
ANTONYMS permanent, definite.

proviso ▶ noun *he could use the company car, with the proviso that he would pay for routine maintenance* **condition,** stipulation, provision, clause, rider, qualification, restriction, caveat.

provocation ▶ noun **1** *he remained calm despite severe provocation* **goading,** prodding, egging on, incitement, pressure; **annoyance,** irritation, nettling; harassment, plaguing, molestation; teasing, taunting, torment; affront, insults; informal hassle, aggravation.
2 *without provocation, Bill punched Mr. Cartwright* **justification,** excuse, pretext, occasion, call, motivation, motive, cause, grounds, reason, need; formal casus belli.

provocative ▶ adjective **1** *provocative remarks* **annoying,** irritating, exasperating, infuriating, maddening, vexing, galling; insulting, offensive, inflammatory, incendiary, controversial; informal aggravating, in-your-face.
ANTONYMS soothing, calming.
2 *a provocative pose* **sexy,** sexually arousing, sexually exciting, alluring, seductive, suggestive, inviting, tantalizing, titillating; indecent, pornographic, indelicate, immodest, shameless; erotic, sensuous, slinky, coquettish, amorous, flirtatious; informal tarty, come-hither.
ANTONYMS modest, decorous.

provoke ▶ verb **1** *the plan has provoked outrage* **arouse,** produce, evoke, cause, give rise to, occasion, call forth, elicit, induce, excite, spark off, touch off, kindle, generate, engender, instigate, result in, lead to, bring on,

precipitate, prompt, trigger; literary beget.
ANTONYMS allay.
2 *she was provoked into replying* **goad,** spur, prick, sting, prod, egg on, incite, rouse, stir, move, stimulate, motivate, excite, inflame, work/fire up, impel. See note at INCITE.
ANTONYMS deter.
3 *he wouldn't be provoked* **annoy,** anger, incense, enrage, irritate, infuriate, exasperate, madden, nettle, get/take a rise out of, ruffle, ruffle someone's feathers, make someone's hackles rise; harass, harry, plague, molest; tease, taunt, torment; rub the wrong way; informal peeve, aggravate, hassle, miff, needle, rankle, ride, rile, get, bug, make someone's blood boil, get under someone's skin, get in someone's hair, get/put someone's back up, get someone's goat, wind up.
ANTONYMS pacify, appease.

prow ▶ noun *the prow of the skiff* **bow(s),** stem, front, nose, head, cutwater.

prowess ▶ noun **1** *his prowess as a winemaker* **skill,** expertise, mastery, facility, ability, capability, capacity, savoir faire, talent, genius, adeptness, aptitude, dexterity, deftness, competence, accomplishment, proficiency, finesse; informal know-how.
ANTONYMS inability, ineptitude.
2 *the knight's prowess in battle* **courage,** bravery, gallantry, valor, heroism, intrepidity, nerve, pluck, pluckiness, feistiness, boldness, daring, audacity, fearlessness; informal guts, spunk, moxie, grit, sand.
ANTONYMS cowardice.

prowl ▶ verb *they were seen prowling around the docks late at night* **move stealthily,** slink, skulk, steal, nose, pussyfoot, sneak, stalk, creep; informal snoop.

proximity ▶ noun *the proximity to her parents' home was a consideration* **closeness,** nearness, propinquity; accessibility, handiness; archaic vicinity.

proxy ▶ noun *I am here to vote as Mrs. Carlson's proxy* **deputy,** representative, substitute, delegate, agent, surrogate, stand-in, attorney, go-between.

prude ▶ noun *I never knew a boy to be such a prude* **puritan,** prig, killjoy, moralist, pietist; informal goody-goody.

prudence ▶ noun **1** *you have gone beyond the bounds of prudence* **wisdom,** judgment, good judgment, common sense, sense, sagacity, shrewdness, advisability.
ANTONYMS folly, recklessness.
2 *financial prudence* **caution,** care, providence, farsightedness, foresight, forethought, shrewdness, circumspection; thrift, economy.
ANTONYMS extravagance.

prudent ▶ adjective **1** *it is prudent to obtain consent* **wise,** well judged, sensible, politic, judicious, sagacious, sage, shrewd, advisable, well-advised.
ANTONYMS unwise.
2 *a prudent approach to borrowing* **cautious,** careful, provident, farsighted, judicious, shrewd, circumspect; thrifty, economical. See note at ECONOMICAL.
ANTONYMS reckless.

prudish ▶ adjective *it's unusual to find someone so young and yet so prudish* **puritanical,** priggish, prim, prim and proper, moralistic, pietistic, sententious, censorious, straitlaced, Victorian, old-maidish, governessy, fussy, stuffy, strict; informal goody-goody, starchy.
ANTONYMS permissive.

prune ▶ verb **1** *I pruned the roses* **cut back,** trim, thin, pinch back, clip, shear, top, dock.
2 *prune lateral shoots of wisteria* **cut off,** lop (off), chop off, clip, snip (off), nip off, dock.
3 *staff numbers have been pruned* **reduce,** cut (back/down), pare (down), slim down, make reductions in, make cutbacks in, trim, decrease, diminish, downsize, ax, shrink; informal slash.
ANTONYMS increase.

prurient ▶ adjective *she was completely turned off by his prurient remarks* **salacious,** licentious, voyeuristic, lascivious, lecherous, lustful, lewd, libidinous, lubricious; formal concupiscent.

pry ▶ verb *I'm not one to pry, but the goings-on at that house are very suspicious* **inquire impertinently,** be inquisitive, be curious, poke around/about, ferret (about/around), spy, be a busybody; eavesdrop, listen in, tap someone's phone, intrude; informal stick/poke one's nose in/into, be nosy, nose, snoop.
ANTONYMS mind one's own business.

psalm ▶ noun *one of the psalms attributed to King David* **sacred song,** religious song, hymn, song of praise; (**psalms**) psalmody, psalter.

pseudo ▶ adjective *her 'diamonds' are so pseudo* **bogus,** sham, phony, artificial, mock, ersatz, quasi-, fake, false, spurious, deceptive, misleading, assumed, contrived, affected, insincere; informal pretend, put-on.
ANTONYMS genuine.

pseudonym ▶ noun *Geisel was best known by the pseudonym 'Dr. Seuss'* **pen name,** nom de plume, assumed name, false name, alias, professional name, sobriquet, stage name, nom de guerre.

psych ▶ verb informal
– PHRASES **psych someone out** *she's trying to psych me out with that demonic stare of hers* **intimidate,** daunt, browbeat, bully, cow, tyrannize, scare, terrorize, frighten, dishearten, unnerve, subdue; informal bulldoze.
psych oneself up *I've really psyched myself up for the marathon* **nerve oneself,** steel oneself, brace oneself, summon one's courage, prepare oneself, gear oneself up, urge oneself on, gird (up) one's loins.

psyche ▶ noun *getting in touch with your own psyche* **soul,** spirit, (inner) self, ego, true being, inner man/woman, persona, subconscious, mind, intellect; technical anima.
ANTONYMS body.

psychiatrist ▶ noun *he's been seeing a psychiatrist for several years* **psychotherapist,** psychoanalyst; informal shrink, head doctor.

psychic ▶ adjective **1** *psychic powers* **supernatural,** paranormal, otherworldly, supernormal, preternatural, metaphysical, extrasensory, magic, magical, mystical, mystic, occult.
2 *I'm not psychic* **clairvoyant,** telepathic, having

second sight, having a sixth sense.
3 *psychic development* **emotional,** spiritual, inner; cognitive, psychological, intellectual, mental, psychiatric, psychogenic.
ANTONYMS physical.
▶ **noun** *she is a psychic* **clairvoyant,** fortune teller, crystal-gazer; medium, channeler, spiritualist; telepath, mind-reader, palmist, palm-reader.

psychological ▶ **adjective 1** *his psychological state* **mental,** emotional, intellectual, inner, cerebral, brain, rational, cognitive.
2 *her pain was psychological* **(all) in the mind,** psychosomatic, emotional, irrational, subjective, subconscious, unconscious.
ANTONYMS physical.

psychology ▶ **noun 1** *a degree in psychology* **study of the mind,** science of the mind.
2 *the psychology of the motorist* **mindset,** mind, mental processes, thought processes, way of thinking, cast of mind, mentality, persona, psyche, (mental) attitude(s), makeup, character; informal what makes someone tick.

psychopathic ▶ **adjective** See MAD (sense 1).

psychosomatic ▶ **adjective** *psychosomatic illnesses can produce very real physical symptoms* **(all) in the mind,** psychological, irrational, stress-related, stress-induced, subjective, subconscious, unconscious.

pub ▶ **noun** See BAR (sense 4 of the noun).

puberty ▶ **noun** *parents often forget how difficult going through puberty can be* **adolescence,** pubescence, sexual maturity, growing up; youth, young adulthood, the/one's teenage years, the/one's teens, the awkward age; formal juvenescence.

public ▶ **adjective 1** *public affairs* **state,** national, federal, government; constitutional, civic, civil, official, social, municipal, community, communal, local; nationalized.
ANTONYMS private.
2 *by public demand* **popular,** general, common, communal, collective, shared, joint, universal, widespread.
3 *a public figure* **prominent,** well-known, important, leading, eminent, distinguished, notable, noteworthy, noted, celebrated, household, famous, famed, influential, major-league.
ANTONYMS obscure, unknown.
4 *public places* **open (to the public),** communal, accessible to all, available, free, unrestricted, community.
ANTONYMS restricted.
5 *the news became public* **known,** published, publicized, in circulation, exposed, overt, plain, obvious.
ANTONYMS unknown, secret.
▶ **noun 1** *the American public* **people,** citizens, subjects, general public, electors, electorate, voters, taxpayers, residents, inhabitants, citizenry, population, populace, community, society, country, nation, world; everyone.
2 *his adoring public* **audience,** spectators, followers, following, fans, devotees, aficionados, admirers; patrons, clientele, market, consumers, buyers, customers, readers, viewers, listeners.
– PHRASES **in public** *she didn't like it when he would kiss her in public* **publicly,** in full view of people, openly, in the open, for all to see, undisguisedly, blatantly, flagrantly, brazenly, overtly.

publication ▶ **noun 1** *the author of this publication* **book,** volume, title, work, tome, opus; newspaper, paper, magazine, periodical, newsletter, bulletin, journal, report; organ, booklet, chapbook, brochure, catalog; daily, weekly, monthly, quarterly, annual; informal rag, mag, 'zine.
2 *the publication of her new book* **issuing,** announcement, publishing, printing, notification, reporting, declaration, communication, proclamation, broadcasting, publicizing, advertising, distribution, spreading, dissemination, promulgation, issuance, appearance.

publicity ▶ **noun 1** *the blaze of publicity* **public attention,** public interest, public notice, media attention/interest, face time, exposure, glare, limelight.
2 *all this publicity should boost sales* **promotion,** advertising, propaganda; boost, push; informal hype, ballyhoo, puffery, buildup, razzmatazz; plug.

publicize ▶ **verb 1** *I never publicize the fact* **make known,** make public, publish, announce, report, post, communicate, broadcast, issue, put out, distribute, spread, promulgate, disseminate, circulate, air; disclose, reveal, divulge, leak. See note at ANNOUNCE.
ANTONYMS conceal.
2 *she just wants to publicize her book* **advertise,** promote, build up, talk up, push, beat the drum for, boost; informal hype, plug, puff (up).
ANTONYMS suppress.

publish ▶ **verb 1** *we publish novels* **issue,** bring out, produce, print.
2 *he ought to publish his views* **make known,** make public, publicize, announce, report, post, communicate, broadcast, issue, put out, distribute, spread, promulgate, disseminate, circulate, air; disclose, reveal, divulge, leak.

pucker ▶ **verb** *she puckered her forehead* **wrinkle,** crinkle, crease, furrow, crumple, rumple, ruck up, scrunch up, corrugate, ruffle, screw up, shrivel.
▶ **noun** *a pucker in the sewing* **wrinkle,** crinkle, crumple, corrugation, furrow, line, fold.

puckish ▶ **adjective** *he gave her a puckish grin* **mischievous,** naughty, impish, roguish, playful, arch, prankish; informal waggish.

puddle ▶ **noun** *puppies and kids are drawn to puddles the way moths are drawn to light* **pool,** spill, splash; literary plash.

pudgy ▶ **adjective** informal *the toddler's pudgy little hands* **chubby,** plump, fat, stout, rotund, well-padded, ample, round, chunky, portly, overweight, fleshy, paunchy, bulky, corpulent; informal tubby, roly-poly, beefy, porky, blubbery, zaftig, corn-fed.
ANTONYMS thin.

puerile ▶ **adjective** *you're too old for these puerile outbursts* **childish,** immature, infantile, juvenile, babyish; silly, inane, fatuous, jejune, asinine, foolish, petty. See note at YOUTHFUL.

ANTONYMS mature, sensible.

puff ▶ noun 1 *a puff of wind* **gust,** blast, flurry, rush, draft, waft, breeze, breath.
2 *he took a puff at his cigar* informal **drag,** toke.
▶ verb 1 *she walked fast, puffing a little* **breathe heavily,** pant, blow; gasp, fight for breath.
2 *she **puffed on** a cigarette* **smoke,** draw on, suck at/on.
– PHRASES **puff up** *the site of the incision may puff up slightly* **bulge,** swell (up), stick out, distend, tumefy, balloon (up/out), expand, inflate, enlarge.

puffy ▶ adjective *the doctor said his eyes were puffy because of allergies* **swollen,** puffed up, distended, enlarged, inflated, dilated, bloated, engorged, bulging, tumid, tumescent.

pugilist ▶ noun dated *in his neighborhood, guys pretty much had two career choices: drug dealer or pugilist* **boxer,** fighter, prizefighter; informal bruiser, pug.

pugnacious ▶ adjective *this looks like the kind of dive that appeals to pugnacious patrons* **combative,** aggressive, antagonistic, belligerent, bellicose, warlike, quarrelsome, argumentative, contentious, disputatious, hostile, threatening, truculent; fiery, hot-tempered.
ANTONYMS peaceable.

pull ▶ verb 1 *he pulled the box toward him* **tug,** haul, drag, draw, tow, heave, lug, jerk, wrench; informal yank.
ANTONYMS push.
2 *he pulled the bad tooth out* **extract,** take out, remove.
3 *she pulled a muscle* **strain,** sprain, wrench, turn, tear; damage.
4 *race day pulled big crowds* **attract,** draw, bring in, pull in, lure, seduce, entice, tempt, beckon, interest, fascinate.
ANTONYMS repel.
▶ noun 1 *give the chain a pull* **tug,** jerk, heave; informal yank.
2 *she felt the pull of the sea* **attraction,** draw, lure, allurement, enticement, magnetism, temptation, fascination, appeal.
3 *he has a lot of pull in finance* **influence,** sway, power, authority, say, prestige, standing, weight, leverage, muscle, teeth, clout.
– PHRASES **pull apart** *they pulled apart the suitcase looking for hidden drugs* **dismantle,** disassemble, take/pull to pieces, take/pull to bits, take apart, strip down; demolish, destroy, break up. **pull back** *the troops were ordered to pull back* **withdraw,** retreat, fall back, back off; pull out, retire, disengage; flee, turn tail. **pull in** *pull in here, next to the Camaro* **stop,** halt, come to a halt, pull over, pull up, draw up, brake, park. **pull someone's leg** *are we really getting a snowstorm, or are you pulling my leg?* **tease,** fool, play a trick on, rag, pull the wool over someone's eyes; informal kid, rib, take for a ride, have on. **pull off** *they pulled off a daring crime* **achieve,** fulfill, succeed in, accomplish, bring off, carry off, perform, discharge, complete, clinch, fix, effect, engineer. **pull out** *our forces have begun to pull out* **withdraw,** resign, leave, retire, step down, bow out, back out, give up; informal quit. **pull through** *we're all praying that Steve will pull through* **get better,** get well again, improve, recover, rally, come through, recuperate. **pull oneself together** *it's just a movie, pull yourself together* **regain one's composure,** recover, get a grip on oneself, get over it; informal snap out of it, get one's act together, buck up.

pulp ▶ noun 1 *he kneaded it into a pulp* **mush,** mash, paste, purée, pomace, pap, slop, slush, mulch; informal gloop, goo, glop.
2 *the sweet pulp on cocoa seeds* **flesh,** marrow, meat.
▶ verb *pulp the blueberries* **mash,** purée, cream, crush, press, liquidize, liquefy, sieve, squash, pound, macerate, grind, mince.
▶ adjective *pulp fiction* **trashy,** cheap, sensational, lurid, tasteless; informal tacky, rubbishy.

pulsate ▶ verb *the alien pods continued to pulsate, as if at any moment writhing creatures would emerge* **palpitate,** pulse, throb, pump, undulate, surge, heave, rise and fall; beat, thump, drum, thrum; flutter, quiver.

pulse[1] ▶ noun 1 *the pulse in her neck* **heartbeat,** pulsation, pulsing, throbbing, pounding.
2 *the pulse of the train wheels* **rhythm,** beat, tempo, cadence, pounding, thudding, drumming.
3 *pulses of ultrasound* **burst,** blast, spurt, impulse, surge.
▶ verb *music pulsed through the building* **throb,** pulsate, vibrate, beat, pound, thud, thump, drum, thrum, reverberate, echo.

pulse[2] ▶ noun *eat plenty of pulses* **legume,** pea, bean, lentil.

pulverize ▶ verb 1 *the seeds are pulverized into flour* **grind,** crush, pound, powder, mill, crunch, squash, press, pulp, mash, sieve, mince, macerate; technical comminute.
2 informal *he pulverized the opposition* See TROUNCE.

pump ▶ verb 1 *I pumped air out of the tube* **force,** drive, push; suck, draw, tap, siphon, withdraw, expel, extract, bleed, drain.
2 *she **pumped up** the tire* **inflate,** aerate, blow up, fill up; swell, enlarge, distend, expand, dilate, puff up.
3 *blood was pumping from his leg* **spurt,** spout, squirt, jet, surge, spew, gush, stream, flow, pour, spill, well, cascade, run, course.
4 informal *I pumped them for information* **interrogate,** cross-examine, ask, question, quiz, probe, sound out, catechize, give someone the third degree; informal grill.

pun ▶ noun *"you can make your own antifreeze by stealing her blanket" is a pun guaranteed to get some groans* **play on words,** wordplay, double entendre, innuendo, witticism, quip, bon mot.

punch[1] ▶ verb *Diana punched him in the face* **hit,** strike, thump, jab, smash, welt, cuff, clip; batter, buffet, pound, pummel; informal sock, slug, bop, wallop, clobber, bash, whack, thwack, clout, whomp, cold-cock; literary smite.
▶ noun 1 *a punch on the nose* **blow,** hit, knock, thump, box, jab, clip, uppercut, hook; informal sock, slug, bop, wallop, bash, whack, clout, belt, knuckle sandwich; dated buffet.
2 *the soundtrack is full of punch* **vigor,**

liveliness, vitality, drive, strength, zest, verve, enthusiasm; impact, bite, kick; informal oomph, zing, pep.

punch² ▶ verb *he punched her ticket* **make a hole in,** perforate, puncture, pierce, prick, hole, spike, skewer; literary transpierce.

punctilio ▶ noun **1** *a stickler for punctilio* **conformity,** conscientiousness, punctiliousness; etiquette, protocol, conventions, formalities, propriety, decorum, manners, politesse, good form, the done thing.
ANTONYMS informality.
2 *the punctilios of court procedure* **nicety,** detail, fine point, subtlety, nuance, refinement.

punctilious ▶ adjective *his punctilious implementation of orders* **meticulous,** conscientious, diligent, scrupulous, careful, painstaking, rigorous, perfectionist, methodical, particular, strict; fussy, fastidious, finicky, pedantic; informal nitpicking, persnickety. See note at **FORMAL.**
ANTONYMS careless.

punctual ▶ adjective *she liked her guests to be punctual* **on time,** prompt, on schedule, in (good) time; informal on the dot.
ANTONYMS late.

punctuate ▶ verb **1** *how to punctuate direct speech* **add punctuation to,** put punctuation marks in.
2 *slides were used to punctuate the talk* **break up,** interrupt, intersperse, pepper.

puncture ▶ noun **1** *the tire developed a puncture* **hole,** perforation, rupture; cut, slit; leak.
2 *my car has a puncture* **flat tire**; informal flat.
▶ verb **1** *he punctured the child's balloon* **make a hole in,** pierce, rupture, perforate, stab, cut, slit, prick, spike, stick, lance; deflate.
2 *she knows how to puncture his speeches* **put an end to,** cut short, deflate, reduce.

pundit ▶ noun *an economics pundit* **expert,** authority, specialist, doyen(ne), master, guru, sage, savant, maven; informal buff, whiz.

pungent ▶ adjective **1** *a pungent marinade* **strong,** powerful, pervasive, penetrating; sharp, acid, sour, biting, bitter, tart, vinegary, tangy; highly flavored, aromatic, spicy, piquant, peppery, hot.
ANTONYMS bland, mild.
2 *pungent remarks* **caustic,** biting, trenchant, cutting, acerbic, sardonic, sarcastic, scathing, acrimonious, barbed, sharp, tart, incisive, bitter, venomous, waspish.
ANTONYMS bland, mild.

punish ▶ verb **1** *they punished their children* **discipline,** teach someone a lesson; tan someone's hide; informal wallop, come down on (like a ton of bricks).
2 *higher charges would punish the poor* **penalize,** unfairly disadvantage, handicap, hurt, wrong, ill-use, maltreat.

punishing ▶ adjective *a punishing schedule* **arduous,** demanding, taxing, onerous, burdensome, strenuous, rigorous, stressful, trying; hard, difficult, tough, exhausting, tiring, grueling, crippling, relentless; informal killing.
ANTONYMS easy.

punishment ▶ noun **1** *the punishment of the guilty* **penalizing,** punishing, disciplining; retribution; dated chastisement.
2 *the teacher imposed punishments* **penalty,** penance, sanction, sentence, one's just deserts; discipline, correction, vengeance, justice, judgment; informal comeuppance.
3 *both boxers took punishment* **a battering,** a thrashing, a beating, a drubbing.
4 *the ovens take continual punishment* **maltreatment,** mistreatment, abuse, ill-use, manhandling; damage, harm.

punitive ▶ adjective **1** *punitive measures* **penal,** disciplinary, corrective, correctional, retributive.
2 *punitive taxes* **harsh,** severe, stiff, stringent, burdensome, demanding, crushing, crippling; high, sky-high, inflated, exorbitant, extortionate, excessive, inordinate, unreasonable.

puny ▶ adjective **1** *he had been a puny kid* **undersized,** undernourished, underfed, stunted, slight, small, little; weak, feeble, sickly, delicate, frail, fragile; informal weedy, pint-sized.
ANTONYMS sturdy.
2 *puny efforts to save their homes* **pitiful,** pitiable, inadequate, insufficient, derisory, miserable, sorry, meager, paltry, trifling, inconsequential; informal pathetic, measly, piddling; formal exiguous.
ANTONYMS substantial.

pupil ▶ noun **1** *former pupils of the school* **student,** scholar; schoolchild, schoolboy, schoolgirl.
2 *the guru's pupils* **disciple,** follower, student, protégé, apprentice, trainee, novice.

puppet ▶ noun **1** *a show with puppets* **marionette**; hand puppet, finger puppet.
2 *a puppet of the government* **pawn,** tool, instrument, cat's paw, creature, dupe; mouthpiece, minion, stooge.

purchase ▶ verb *we purchased the software* **buy,** pay for, acquire, obtain, pick up, snap up, take, procure; invest in; informal get hold of, score.
ANTONYMS sell.
▶ noun **1** *he's happy with his purchase* **acquisition,** buy, investment, order, bargain; shopping, goods.
ANTONYMS sale.
2 *he could get no purchase on the wall* **grip,** grasp, hold, foothold, toehold, anchorage, attachment, support; resistance, friction, leverage.

pure ▶ adjective **1** *pure gold* **unadulterated,** uncontaminated, unmixed, undiluted, unalloyed, unblended; sterling, solid, refined, one hundred percent; clarified, clear, filtered; flawless, perfect, genuine, real.
ANTONYMS adulterated.
2 *the air is so pure* **clean,** clear, fresh, sparkling, unpolluted, uncontaminated, untainted; wholesome, natural, healthy; sanitary, uninfected, disinfected, germ-free, sterile, sterilized, aseptic.
ANTONYMS dirty, polluted.
3 *pure in body and mind* **virtuous,** moral, ethical, good, righteous, saintly, honorable, reputable, wholesome, clean, honest, upright, upstanding, exemplary, irreproachable; chaste,

virginal, maidenly; decent, worthy, noble, blameless, guiltless, spotless, unsullied, uncorrupted, undefiled; informal squeaky clean.
ANTONYMS immoral.
4 *pure math* **theoretical,** abstract, conceptual, academic, hypothetical, speculative, conjectural.
ANTONYMS practical.
5 *three hours of pure magic* **sheer,** utter, absolute, out-and-out, complete, total, perfect, unmitigated.

purely ▶ **adverb** *the mission of this weekend is purely recreational* **entirely,** completely, absolutely, wholly, exclusively, solely, only, just, merely.

purge ▶ **verb 1** *he purged them of their doubt* **cleanse,** clear, purify, wash, shrive, absolve.
2 *lawbreakers were purged from the army* **remove,** get rid of, expel, eject, exclude, dismiss, sack, oust, eradicate, clear out, weed out.
▶ **noun** *the purge of dissidents* **removal,** expulsion, ejection, exclusion, eviction, dismissal, sacking, ousting, eradication.

purify ▶ **verb 1** *trees help to purify the air* **clean,** cleanse, refine, decontaminate; filter, clarify, clear, freshen, deodorize; sanitize, disinfect, sterilize.
2 *they purify themselves before the ceremony* **purge,** cleanse, unburden, deliver; redeem, shrive, exorcise, sanctify.

purist ▶ **noun** *the quilting purist doesn't want to hear the words "sewing machine"* **pedant,** perfectionist, formalist, literalist, stickler, traditionalist, doctrinaire, quibbler, dogmatist; informal nitpicker.

puritanical ▶ **adjective** *by modern standards, his parents are considered puritanical* **moralistic,** puritan, pietistic, straitlaced, stuffy, prudish, prim, priggish; narrow-minded, sententious, censorious; austere, severe, ascetic, abstemious; informal goody-goody, starchy.
ANTONYMS permissive.

purity ▶ **noun 1** *the purity of our tap water* **cleanness,** clearness, clarity, freshness; sterility, healthiness, safety.
2 *they sought purity in a foul world* **virtue,** morality, goodness, righteousness, saintliness, piety, honor, honesty, integrity, decency, ethicality, impeccability; innocence, chastity.

purport ▶ **verb** *this work purports to be authoritative* **claim to be,** profess to be, pretend to be; appear to be, seem to be; be ostensibly, pose as, impersonate, masquerade as, pass for.
▶ **noun 1** *the purport of his remarks* **gist,** substance, drift, implication, intention, meaning, significance, sense, essence, thrust, message.
2 *the purport of the attack* **intention,** purpose, object, objective, aim, goal, target, end, design, idea.

purpose ▶ **noun 1** *the purpose of his visit* **motive,** motivation, grounds, cause, occasion, reason, point, basis, justification.
2 *their purpose was to subvert the economy* **intention,** aim, object, objective, goal, end, plan, scheme, target; ambition, aspiration.
3 *I cannot see any purpose in it* **advantage,** benefit, good, use, value, merit, worth, profit; informal mileage, percentage.
4 *the original purpose of the porch* **function,** role, use.
5 *they started the game with purpose* **determination,** resolution, resolve, steadfastness, backbone, drive, push, enthusiasm, ambition, motivation, commitment, conviction, dedication; informal get-up-and-go.
▶ **verb** formal *they purposed to reach the summit* **intend,** mean, aim, plan, design, have the intention; decide, resolve, determine, propose, aspire. See note at **INTEND**.
– PHRASES **on purpose** *we'd like to believe that she didn't start the fire on purpose* **deliberately,** intentionally, purposely, by design, willfully, knowingly, consciously, of one's own volition; expressly, specifically, especially, specially.

purposeful ▶ **adjective** *she'll need a more purposeful attitude if she wants to succeed in college* **determined,** resolute, steadfast, single-minded; enthusiastic, motivated, committed, dedicated, persistent, dogged, tenacious, unfaltering, unshakable.
ANTONYMS aimless.

purposely ▶ **adverb** See **ON PURPOSE**.

purse ▶ **noun 1** *a woman's purse* See **HANDBAG**.
2 *the public purse* **fund(s),** kitty, coffers, pool, bank, treasury, exchequer; money, finances, wealth, reserves, cash, capital, assets.
3 *the fight will net him a $75,000 purse* **prize,** reward, award; winnings, stake(s).
▶ **verb** *she pursed her lips* **press together,** compress, tighten, pucker, pout.

pursue ▶ **verb 1** *I pursued him through the garden* **follow,** run after, chase; hunt, stalk, track, trail, shadow, hound, course; informal tail.
ANTONYMS avoid.
2 *pursue the goal of political union* **strive for,** work toward, seek, search for, aim at/for, aspire to.
ANTONYMS eschew.
3 *he had been pursuing her for weeks* **chase,** run after, go after; informal make up to; dated woo, court, romance.
4 *she pursued a political career* **engage in,** be occupied in, practice, follow, prosecute, conduct, ply, take up, undertake, carry on.
ANTONYMS shun.
5 *we will not pursue the matter* **investigate,** research, inquire into, look into, examine, scrutinize, analyze, delve into, probe.

pursuit ▶ **noun 1** *the pursuit of profit* **striving toward,** quest after/for, search for; aim, goal, objective, dream.
2 *a worthwhile pursuit* **activity,** hobby, pastime, diversion, recreation, relaxation, divertissement, amusement; occupation, trade, vocation, business, work, job, employment.

purvey ▶ **verb** *they traveled southward to purvey their furs* **sell,** supply, provide, furnish, cater, retail, deal in, trade, stock, offer; peddle, hawk, traffic in; informal flog.

pus ▶ **noun** *cleanse the wound twice daily until there is no longer any pus* **suppuration,** matter;

discharge, secretion.

push ▶ **verb 1** *she tried to push him away* **shove,** thrust, propel; send, drive, force, prod, poke, nudge, elbow, shoulder; sweep, bundle, hustle, manhandle.
ANTONYMS pull.
2 *she pushed her way into the apartment* **force,** shove, thrust, squeeze, jostle, elbow, shoulder, bundle, hustle; work, inch.
3 *he pushed the panic button* **press,** depress, bear down on, hold down, squeeze; operate, activate.
4 *don't push her to join in* **urge,** press, pressure, force, impel, coerce, nag; prevail on; informal lean on, twist someone's arm, bulldoze.
5 *they push their own products* **advertise,** publicize, promote, bang the drum for; sell, market, merchandise; informal plug, hype (up), puff (up), flog, ballyhoo.
▶ **noun 1** *I felt a push in the back* **shove,** thrust, nudge, ram, bump, jolt, butt, prod, poke.
2 *the enemy's eastward push* **advance,** drive, thrust, charge, attack, assault, onslaught, onrush, offensive, sortie, sally, incursion.
– PHRASES **push around** *she wasn't used to being pushed around* **bully,** domineer, ride roughshod over, trample on, bulldoze, browbeat, tyrannize, intimidate, threaten, victimize, pick on; informal lean on, boss around. **push for** *the workers are pushing for flexible hours* **demand,** call for, request, press for, campaign for, lobby for, speak up for; urge, promote, advocate, champion, espouse. **push off** informal *you're not welcome here, so push off* **go away,** depart, leave, get out; go, get moving, be off (with you), shoo; informal skedaddle, vamoose, split, scram, run along, beat it, get lost, shove off, buzz off, clear off, bug off, take a powder, take a hike; literary begone. **push on** *I decided to push on toward the coast* **press on,** continue one's journey, carry on, advance, proceed, go on, progress, make headway, forge ahead.

pushover ▶ **noun 1** *the teacher was a pushover* **weakling,** feeble opponent, straw man, prey; informal soft touch.
2 *this course is no pushover* **easy task,** walkover, laugher, five-finger exercise, gift; child's play, Mickey Mouse ——; informal piece of cake, picnic, walk in the park, cinch, breeze, duck soup, snap.

pushy ▶ **adjective** *a pushy salesperson* **assertive,** self-assertive, overbearing, domineering, aggressive, forceful, forward, bold, bumptious, officious; thrusting, ambitious, overconfident, cocky; informal bossy.
ANTONYMS submissive.

pusillanimous ▶ **adjective** *with the tough issues facing this city, the last thing we need is another pusillanimous mayor* **timid,** timorous, cowardly, fearful, faint-hearted, lily-livered, spineless, craven, shrinking; informal chicken, gutless, wimpy, wimpish, sissy, yellow, yellow-bellied.
ANTONYMS brave.

pussyfoot ▶ **verb** *when the subject is the prosecution of abusive parents, we can't pussyfoot around* **equivocate,** tergiversate, be evasive, be noncommittal, sidestep the issue, prevaricate, quibble, hedge, waffle, beat around the bush, hem and haw; informal duck the question, sit on the fence, shilly-shally.

pustule ▶ **noun** *an infected pustule that began as an ingrown hair* **pimple,** spot, bleb, boil, swelling, eruption, carbuncle, blister, abscess; informal whitehead, zit, blackhead; technical comedo, papule.

put ▶ **verb 1** *she put the parcel on a chair* **place,** set (down), lay (down), deposit, position, settle; leave, plant; informal stick, dump, park, plonk, plunk, pop.
2 *he didn't want to be* ***put in*** *a category* **assign to,** consign to, allocate to, place in.
3 *don't* ***put*** *the blame* ***on*** *me* **lay on,** pin on, place on, fix on; attribute to, impute to, assign to, allocate to, ascribe to.
4 *the proposals put to the committee* **submit,** present, tender, offer, proffer, advance, suggest, propose, put forward.
5 *she put it bluntly* **express,** word, phrase, frame, formulate, render, convey, couch; state, say, utter.
6 *he put the cost at $8,000* **estimate,** calculate, reckon, gauge, assess, evaluate, value, judge, measure, compute, fix, set, peg; informal guesstimate.
– PHRASES **put about** *the ship put about* **turn around,** tack, come about, change course. **put across/over** *we need to put our message across more clearly* **communicate,** convey, get across/over, explain, make clear, spell out, clarify; get through to someone. **put aside 1** *we've got a bit put aside in the bank* **save,** put by, set aside, deposit, reserve, store, stockpile, hoard, stow, cache; informal salt away, squirrel away, stash away. **2** *they put aside their differences* **disregard,** set aside, ignore, forget, discount, bury. **put away** informal **1** *they put him away for life* **jail,** imprison, put in prison, put behind bars, lock up, incarcerate. **2** *you should be put away!* **certify,** commit, institutionalize, hospitalize, consign to a psychiatric/mental hospital. **3** *I put away some money* See PUT ASIDE (sense 1) above. **4** *she never puts her toys away* **replace,** put back, tidy up, clean up, clear away. **5** informal *he can put away a lot of pies* See EAT (sense 1). **put back** *he put the books back* **replace,** return, restore, put away. **put down 1** informal *she often puts me down* **criticize,** belittle, disparage, deprecate, denigrate, slight, humiliate, shame, crush, squash, deflate; informal show up, cut down to size. **2** *I put him down as shy* **consider to be,** judge to be, reckon to be, take to be; regard as, have down as, take for. **3** *she put her ideas down on paper* **write down,** note down, jot down, take down, set down; list, record, register, log. **4** *they put down the rebellion* **suppress,** check, crush, quash, squash, quell, overthrow, stamp out, repress, subdue. **5** *the horse had to be put down* **destroy,** put to sleep, put out of its misery, put to death, kill, euthanize. **6** *put it down to inexperience* **attribute,** ascribe, chalk up, impute; blame on. **put forward** See PUT (sense 4). **put in for** *I've put in for the promotion* **apply for,** put in an application for, try for; request, seek, ask for. **put off 1** *you shouldn't let his bad attitude put you off* **deter,** discourage, dissuade, daunt, unnerve, intimidate, scare off, repel, repulse;

distract, disturb, divert, sidetrack; informal turn off. **2** *don't put off such important decisions* **postpone,** defer, delay, put back, adjourn, hold over, reschedule, shelve, table; informal put on ice, put on the back burner. **put it on** *she may be really crying, but I think she's putting it on* **pretend,** play-act, make believe, fake it, fool, go through the motions. **put on 1** *she put on jeans* **dress in,** don, pull on, throw on, slip into, change into; informal doll oneself up in. **2** *I put the light on* **switch on,** turn on, activate. **3** *they put on an extra train* **provide,** lay on, supply, make available. **4** *the museum put on an exhibition* **organize,** stage, mount, present, produce. **5** *she put on a funny English accent* **feign,** fake, simulate, mimic, affect, assume. **6** *she put ten dollars on Blue Bonnet to win* **bet,** gamble, stake, wager; place, lay; risk, chance, hazard. **put one over on** informal See **HOODWINK**. **put out 1** *Maria was put out by the slur* **annoy,** anger, irritate, offend, affront, displease, irk, vex, pique, nettle, gall, upset; informal rile, miff, peeve. **2** *I don't want to put you out* **inconvenience,** trouble, bother, impose on, disoblige; informal put on the spot; formal discommode. **3** *firefighters put out the blaze* **extinguish,** quench, douse, smother; blow out, snuff out. **4** *he put out a press release* **issue,** publish, release, bring out, circulate, publicize, post. **put up 1** *we can put him up for a few days* **accommodate,** house, take in, lodge, quarter, billet; give a roof over someone's head. **2** *they put up a candidate* **nominate,** propose, put forward, recommend. **3** *the building was put up 100 years ago* **build,** construct, erect, raise. **4** *she put up a poster* **display,** pin up, stick up, hang up, post. **5** *we put up alternative schemes* **propose,** put forward, present, submit, suggest, tender. **6** *he put up most of the funding* **provide,** supply, furnish, give, contribute, donate, pledge, pay; informal fork out, cough up, shell out, ante up, pony up. **put upon** informal *you allow yourself to be put upon* **take advantage of,** impose on, exploit, use, misuse; informal walk all over. **put up to** informal *was drag racing your idea, or did someone put you up to it?* **persuade to (do),** encourage to (do), urge to (do), egg on to (do), incite to (do), goad into. **put up with** *she put up with his nonsense for two years, and then she kicked him out* **tolerate,** take, stand (for), accept, stomach, swallow, endure, bear, support, take something lying down; informal abide, lump it; formal brook.

putative ▶ adjective *the putative cause of the brain damage was lead poisoning* **supposed,** assumed, presumed; accepted, recognized; commonly regarded, presumptive, alleged, reputed, reported, rumored.

put-down ▶ noun informal *he was still smarting from the put-down* **snub,** slight, affront, rebuff, sneer, disparagement, humiliation, barb, jibe, criticism; informal dig.

puzzle ▶ verb **1** *her decision puzzled me* **perplex,** confuse, bewilder, bemuse, baffle, mystify, confound; informal flummox, faze, stump, beat, discombobulate.
2 *she puzzled over the problem* **think hard about,** mull over, muse over, ponder, contemplate, meditate on, consider, deliberate on, chew over, wonder about.
3 *she tried to* ***puzzle out*** *what he meant* **work out,** understand, comprehend, sort out, reason out, solve, make sense of, make head(s) or tail(s) of, unravel, decipher; informal figure out.
▶ noun *the poem has always been a puzzle* **enigma,** mystery, paradox, conundrum, poser, riddle, problem, quandary; informal stumper. See note at **RIDDLE**.

puzzled ▶ adjective *a puzzled look on her face* **perplexed,** confused, bewildered, bemused, baffled, mystified, confounded, nonplussed, at a loss, at sea; informal flummoxed, stumped, fazed, clueless, discombobulated.

puzzling ▶ adjective *his explanation was rather puzzling* **baffling,** perplexing, bewildering, confusing, complicated, unclear, mysterious, enigmatic, ambiguous, obscure, abstruse, unfathomable, incomprehensible, impenetrable, cryptic.
ANTONYMS clear.

pygmy ▶ noun **1** *a Congo pygmy* **dwarf,** midget, very small person, homunculus, manikin; Lilliputian; informal shrimp.
2 *an intellectual pygmy* **lightweight,** mediocrity, nonentity, nobody, no-name, cipher; small fry; informal pipsqueak, no-hoper, picayune.
ANTONYMS giant.

pyromaniac ▶ noun *the fire marshal has suggested it may be the work of a pyromaniac* **arsonist,** incendiary; informal firebug, pyro, torch.

Qq

quack ▸ noun *a quack selling fake medicines* **swindler,** charlatan, mountebank, trickster, fraud, fraudster, impostor, hoaxer; informal con man, snake oil salesman, shark, grifter.

> CHOOSE THE RIGHT WORD
>
> **quack, charlatan, dissembler, fake, impostor, mountebank**
>
> There are many different ways to describe a **fake**, a colloquial term for anyone who knowingly practices deception or misrepresentation. Someone who sells a special tonic that claims to do everything from curing the common cold to making hair grow on a bald man's head is called a **quack**, a term that refers to any fraudulent practitioner of medicine or law. **Mountebank** sometimes carries implications of quackery, but more often it refers to a self-promoting person who resorts to cheap tricks or undignified efforts to win attention (*political mountebanks*). A **charlatan** is usually a writer, speaker, preacher, professor, or some other "expert" who tries to conceal his or her lack of skill or knowledge by resorting to pretentious displays (*supposedly a leading authority in his field, he turned out to be nothing but a charlatan*). An individual who tries to pass himself or herself off as someone else is an **impostor** (*an impostor who bore a close physical resemblance to the king*), although this term can also refer to anyone who assumes a title or profession that is not his or her own. Although all of these deceivers are out to fool people, it is the **dissembler** who is primarily interested in concealing his or her true motives or evil purpose (*he is a dissembler who weaves a tangled web of lies*).

quaff ▸ verb *they quaffed a few beers before heading home* **drink,** swallow, gulp (down), guzzle, slurp, down, empty; imbibe, partake of, consume; informal kill, swig, swill, slug, knock back, toss off, chug, chugalug, scarf (down).

quagmire ▸ noun **1** *the field became a quagmire* **swamp,** morass, bog, marsh, muskeg, mire, slough; archaic quag.
2 *a judicial quagmire* **muddle,** mix-up, mess, predicament, mare's nest, can of worms, quandary, tangle, imbroglio; trouble, confusion, difficulty; informal sticky situation, pickle, stew, dilemma, fix, bind.

quail ▸ verb *the sound of gunfire made us quail* **cower,** cringe, flinch, shrink, recoil, shy (away), pull back; shiver, tremble, shake, quake, blench.

quaint ▸ adjective **1** *a quaint town* **picturesque,** charming, sweet, attractive, old-fashioned, old-world, cunning; pseudoarchaic olde, olde worlde.
ANTONYMS ugly, modern.
2 *quaint customs* **unusual,** different, out of the ordinary, curious, eccentric, quirky, bizarre, whimsical, unconventional; informal offbeat.
ANTONYMS normal, ordinary.

quake ▸ verb **1** *the ground quaked* **shake,** tremble, quiver, shudder, sway, rock, wobble, move, heave, convulse. See note at SHAKE.
2 *we quaked when we saw the soldiers* **tremble,** shake, quiver, shiver; blench, flinch, shrink, recoil, cower, cringe.

qualification ▸ noun **1** *a teaching qualification* **certificate,** diploma, degree, license, document, warrant; eligibility, acceptability, adequacy; proficiency, skill, ability, capability, aptitude.
2 *I can't accept it without qualification* **modification,** limitation, reservation, stipulation; alteration, amendment, revision, moderation, mitigation; condition, proviso, caveat.

qualified ▸ adjective *qualified mechanics* **certified,** certificated, chartered, credentialed, licensed, professional; trained, fit, competent, accomplished, proficient, skilled, experienced, expert.

qualify ▸ verb **1** *I qualify for free prescriptions* **be eligible for,** meet the requirements for; be entitled to, be permitted.
2 *they qualify as refugees* **count,** be considered, be designated, be eligible.
3 *she qualified as a doctor* **be certified,** be licensed; pass, graduate, make the grade, succeed, pass muster.
4 *the course qualified them to teach* **authorize,** empower, allow, permit, license; equip, prepare, train, educate, teach.
5 *they qualified their findings* **modify,** limit, restrict, make conditional; moderate, temper, modulate, mitigate.

quality ▸ noun **1** *the TV signal is of a poor quality | the quality of life* **standard,** grade, class, caliber, condition, character, nature, form, rank, value, level; sort, type, kind, variety.
2 *work of such quality is rare* **excellence,** superiority, merit, worth, value, virtue, caliber, eminence, distinction, incomparability; talent, skill, virtuosity, craftsmanship.
3 *her good qualities* **feature,** trait, attribute, characteristic, point, aspect, facet, side, property.

▶ adjective *quality furniture* **excellent,** superior, valuable, distinctive, incomparable; well-crafted; informal top-notch.

qualms ▶ plural noun *I have no qualms about overseas travel* **misgivings,** doubts, reservations, second thoughts, worries, concerns, anxiety; hesitation, hesitance, hesitancy, demur, reluctance, disinclination, apprehension, trepidation, unease; scruples, remorse, compunction.

> CHOOSE THE RIGHT WORD
>
> **qualms, compunction, demur, misgiving, scruple**
>
> To have **qualms** is to have an uneasy feeling that you have acted or are about to act against your better judgment (*she had qualms about leaving a nine-year-old in charge of an infant*). **Misgivings** are even stronger, implying a disturbed state of mind because you're no longer confident that what you're doing is right (*his misgivings about letting his 80-year-old mother drive herself home turned out to be justified*). **Compunction** implies a momentary pang of conscience because what you are doing or are about to do is unfair, improper, or wrong (*they showed no compunction in carrying out their devious plans*). **Scruples** suggest a more highly-developed conscience or sense of honor; it implies that you have principles, and that you would be deeply disturbed if you thought you were betraying them (*her scruples would not allow her to participate in what she considered antifeminist activities*). **Demur** connotes hesitation to the point of delay, but the delay is usually caused by objections or indecision rather than a sense of conscience (*they accepted his decision without demur*).

quandary ▶ noun *conflicting appointments left us in a quandary* **predicament,** plight, difficult situation, awkward situation; trouble, muddle, mess, confusion, difficulty, dilemma, mare's nest; informal sticky situation, pickle, hole, stew, fix, bind, jam.

quantity ▶ noun **1** *the quantity of food collected* **amount,** total, aggregate, sum, quota, mass, weight, volume, bulk; quantum, proportion, portion, part.
2 *a quantity of ammunition* **amount,** lot, great deal, good deal, abundance, wealth, profusion; informal pile, ton, load, heap, mass, stack.

quarrel ▶ noun *they had a quarrel about money* **argument,** disagreement, squabble, fight, dispute, wrangle, clash, altercation, feud, contretemps, disputation, falling-out, war of words, shouting match; informal tiff, run-in, hassle, blowup, row.
▶ verb *don't quarrel over it* **argue,** fight, disagree, fall out; differ, be at odds; bicker, squabble, cross swords, lock horns, be at each other's throats; archaic altercate.
– PHRASES **quarrel with** *you can't quarrel with the verdict* **find fault with,** fault, criticize, object to, oppose, take exception to; attack, take issue with, impugn, contradict, dispute, controvert; informal knock; formal gainsay.

> CHOOSE THE RIGHT WORD
>
> **quarrel, altercation, dispute, feud, row, spat, squabble, wrangle**
>
> Family feuds come in a variety of shapes and sizes. A husband and his wife may have a **quarrel**, which suggests a heated verbal argument, with hostility that may persist even after it is over (*it took them almost a week to patch up their quarrel*). Siblings tend to have **squabbles**, which are childlike disputes over trivial matters, although they are by no means confined to childhood (*frequent squabbles over who would pick up the check*). A **spat** is also a petty quarrel, but unlike *squabble*, it suggests an angry outburst followed by a quick ending without hard feelings (*another spat in an otherwise loving relationship*). A **row** is more serious, involving noisy quarreling and the potential for physical violence (*a row that woke the neighbors*). Neighbors are more likely to have an **altercation**, which is usually confined to verbal blows but may involve actual or threatened physical ones (*an altercation over the location of the fence*). A **dispute** is also a verbal argument, but one that is carried on over an extended period of time (*an ongoing dispute over who was responsible for taking out the garbage*). Two families who have been enemies for a long time are probably involved in a **feud**, which suggests a bitter quarrel that lasts for years or even generations (*the feud between the Hatfields and the McCoys*). There is no dignity at all in being involved in a **wrangle**, which is an angry, noisy, and often futile dispute in which both parties are unwilling to listen to the other's point of view.

quarrelsome ▶ adjective *his quarrelsome neighbors* **argumentative,** disputatious, confrontational, captious, pugnacious, combative, antagonistic, contentious, bellicose, belligerent, cantankerous, choleric; informal scrappy.
ANTONYMS peaceable.

quarry ▶ noun *he would not allow his quarry to elude him* **prey,** victim; object, goal, target; kill, game.

quarter ▶ noun **1** *the Italian quarter* **district,** area, region, part, side, neighborhood, precinct, locality, sector, zone; ghetto, community, enclave, Little ——, —— town.
2 *help from an unexpected quarter* **source,** direction, place, location; person.
3 (**quarters**) *the servants' quarters* **accommodations,** lodgings, rooms, chambers; home; informal pad, digs; formal abode, residence, domicile.
4 *the riot squads gave no quarter* **mercy,** leniency, clemency, lenity, compassion, pity, charity, sympathy, tolerance.
▶ verb **1** *they were quartered in a villa* **accommodate,** house, board, lodge, put up, take

in, install, shelter; Military billet.
2 *I quartered the streets* **patrol,** range over, tour, reconnoiter, traverse, survey, scout.

quash ▶ verb **1** *the judge may quash the sentence* **cancel,** reverse, rescind, repeal, revoke, retract, countermand, withdraw, overturn, overrule, veto, annul, nullify, invalidate, negate, void; Law vacate; formal abrogate.
ANTONYMS validate.
2 *we want to quash these rumors* **put an end to,** put a stop to, stamp out, crush, put down, check, curb, nip in the bud, squash, quell, subdue, suppress, extinguish, stifle; informal squelch, put the kibosh on, deep-six.
ANTONYMS bring about.

quasi- ▶ combining form **1** *quasi-scientific theories* **supposedly,** seemingly, apparently, allegedly, ostensibly, on the face of it, on the surface, to all intents and purposes, outwardly, superficially, purportedly, nominally; pseudo-.
2 *a quasi-autonomous organization* **partly,** partially, part, to a certain extent, to some extent, half, relatively, comparatively, (up) to a point; almost, nearly, just about, all but.

quaver ▶ verb *Farnam's voice quavered with emotion* **tremble,** waver, quiver, shake, vibrate, oscillate, fluctuate, falter, warble.

queasy ▶ adjective *just the smell of shellfish makes him queasy* **nauseous,** nauseated, bilious, sick; ill, unwell, poorly, green around the gills.

queen ▶ noun **1** *the queen was crowned* **monarch,** sovereign, ruler, head of state; Her Majesty; king's consort, queen consort.
2 informal *the queen of country music* **doyenne,** star, superstar, leading light, big name, queen bee, prima donna, idol, heroine, favorite, darling, goddess.

queer ▶ adjective **1** *his diction is archaic and queer* **odd,** strange, unusual, funny, peculiar, curious, bizarre, weird, uncanny, freakish, eerie, unnatural; unconventional, unorthodox, unexpected, unfamiliar, abnormal, anomalous, atypical, untypical, out of the ordinary, incongruous, irregular; puzzling, perplexing, baffling, unaccountable; informal fishy, spooky, bizarro, freaky.
ANTONYMS normal.
2 *queer culture* See **GAY** (sense 1 of the adjective).

> USAGE
> **queer**
> The word *queer* was first used to mean 'homosexual' in the early 20th century: it was originally, and often still is, a deliberately offensive and aggressive term when used by heterosexual people. In recent years, however, many gay people have taken the word *queer* and deliberately used it in place of *gay* or *homosexual*, in an attempt, by using the word positively, to deprive it of its negative power. This use of *queer* is now well established and widely used among gay people (esp. as an adjective or noun modifier, as in *queer rights; queer theory*) and at present exists alongside the other, deliberately offensive, use. (This use is similar to the way in which a racial epithet may be used *within* a racial group, but not by outsiders.)

quell ▶ verb **1** *troops quelled the unrest* **put an end to,** put a stop to, end, crush, put down, check, crack down on, curb, nip in the bud, squash, quash, subdue, suppress, overcome; informal squelch.
2 *he quelled his misgivings* **calm,** soothe, pacify, settle, quiet, silence, allay, assuage, mitigate, moderate; literary stay.

quench ▶ verb **1** *they quenched their thirst* **satisfy,** slake, sate, satiate, gratify, relieve, assuage, take the edge off, indulge; lessen, reduce, diminish, check, suppress, extinguish, overcome.
2 *the flames were quenched* **extinguish,** put out, snuff out, smother, douse.

query ▶ noun **1** *we are happy to answer any queries* **question,** inquiry.
2 *there was a query as to who owned the hotel* **doubt,** uncertainty, question, reservation; skepticism.
▶ verb **1** *"Why do that?" queried Isobel* **ask,** inquire, question.
2 *some folk may query his credentials* **question,** call into question, challenge, dispute, cast aspersions on, doubt, have suspicions about, have reservations about.

quest ▶ noun **1** *their quest for her killer* **search,** hunt.
2 *Sir Galahad's quest* **expedition,** journey, voyage, trek, travels, odyssey, adventure, exploration, search; crusade, mission, pilgrimage; informal Holy Grail.
– PHRASES **in quest of** *thousands flocked north in quest of gold* **in search of,** in pursuit of, seeking, looking for, on the lookout for, after.

question ▶ noun **1** *please answer my question* **inquiry,** query; interrogation.
ANTONYMS answer, response.
2 *there is no question that he is ill* **doubt,** dispute, argument, debate, uncertainty, dubiousness, reservation.
ANTONYMS certainty.
3 *the political questions of the day* **issue,** matter, business, problem, concern, topic, theme, case; debate, argument, dispute, controversy.
▶ verb **1** *the lieutenant questions the suspect* **interrogate,** cross-examine, cross-question, quiz, catechize; interview, debrief, examine, give the third degree to; informal grill, pump.
2 *she questioned his motives* **query,** call into question, challenge, dispute, cast aspersions on, doubt, suspect, have suspicions about, have reservations about.
– PHRASES **beyond question 1** *her loyalty is beyond question* **undoubted,** beyond doubt, certain, indubitable, indisputable, incontrovertible, unquestionable, undeniable, clear, patent, manifest. **2** *the results demonstrated this beyond question* **indisputably,** irrefutably, incontestably, incontrovertibly, unquestionably, undeniably, undoubtedly, beyond doubt, without doubt, clearly, patently, obviously. **in question** *the*

matter in question **at issue,** under discussion, under consideration, on the agenda, to be decided. **out of the question** *changing the date of the wedding is out of the question* **impossible,** impracticable, unfeasible, unworkable, inconceivable, unimaginable, unrealizable, unsuitable.

questionable ▸ adjective **1** *the premise to the argument remains questionable* **controversial,** contentious, doubtful, dubious, uncertain, debatable, arguable; unverified, unprovable, unresolved, unconvincing, implausible, improbable; borderline, marginal, moot; informal iffy. See note at DOUBTFUL.
ANTONYMS indisputable, certain.
2 *questionable financial dealings* **suspicious,** suspect, dubious, irregular, odd, strange, murky, dark, unsavory, disreputable; informal funny, fishy, shady, iffy.
ANTONYMS trustworthy.

queue ▸ noun *a long queue of people* **lineup,** line, row, column, file, chain, string; procession, train, cavalcade. See note at CUE.
▸ verb *we queued for ice cream* **line up,** wait in line, form a line, fall in, form a queue, queue up.

quibble ▸ noun *I have just one quibble* **criticism,** objection, complaint, protest, argument, exception, grumble, grouse, cavil; informal beef, gripe, moan.
▸ verb *no one **quibbled with** the title* **object to,** find fault with, complain about, cavil at; split hairs about; criticize, query, fault, pick holes in; informal nitpick; archaic pettifog.

quick ▸ adjective **1** *a quick pace* **fast,** swift, rapid, speedy, high-speed, breakneck, expeditious, brisk, smart; informal zippy; literary fleet.
ANTONYMS slow.
2 *she took a quick trip down memory lane* **hasty,** hurried, cursory, perfunctory, desultory, superficial, summary; brief, short, fleeting, transient, transitory, short-lived, lightning, momentary, whirlwind, whistle-stop.
ANTONYMS careful, long.
3 *a quick end to the recession* **sudden,** instantaneous, immediate, instant, abrupt, precipitate.
ANTONYMS gradual.
4 *she isn't quick enough to advance to the next level* **intelligent,** bright, clever, gifted, able, astute, quick-witted, sharp-witted, smart; observant, alert, sharp, perceptive; informal brainy, on the ball, quick on the uptake.
ANTONYMS dull-witted.

quicken ▸ verb **1** *she quickened her pace* **speed up,** accelerate, step up, hasten, hurry (up).
2 *the film quickened his interest in nature* **stimulate,** excite, arouse, rouse, stir up, activate, galvanize, whet, inspire, kindle; invigorate, revive, revitalize.

> CHOOSE THE RIGHT WORD
>
> **quicken, animate, enliven, invigorate, stimulate, vitalize**
>
> While all of these verbs mean to make alive or lively, **quicken** suggests the rousing or renewal of life, especially life that has been inert or suspended (*she felt the baby quicken during her second trimester of pregnancy*). **Animate** means to impart life, motion, or activity to something that previously lacked such a quality (*a discussion animated by the presence of so many young people*). **Stimulate** means to goad into activity from a state of inertia, inactivity, or lethargy (*the professor's constant questions stimulated her students to do more research*), while **enliven** refers to a stimulating influence that brightens or makes lively what was previously dull, depressed, or torpid (*a sudden change in the weather enlivened the group's activities*). **Invigorate** and **vitalize** both mean to fill with vigor or energy, but the former refers to physical energy (*invigorated by the climb up the mountain*), while the latter implies that energy has been imparted in a nonphysical sense (*to vitalize an otherwise dull meeting*).

quickly ▸ adverb **1** *he walked quickly* **fast,** swiftly, briskly, rapidly, speedily, at the speed of light, at full tilt, as fast as one's legs can carry one, at a gallop, on the double, posthaste; informal PDQ, pretty damn quick, like lightning, like greased lightning, like mad, like blazes, like the wind, lickety-split; literary apace.
2 *you'd better leave quickly* **immediately,** directly, at once, now, straightaway, right away, instantly, forthwith, without delay, without further ado; soon, promptly, early, momentarily; informal like a shot, ASAP, as soon as possible, pronto, straight off.
3 *he quickly inspected it* **briefly,** fleetingly, briskly; hastily, hurriedly, cursorily, perfunctorily, superficially, desultorily.

quick-tempered ▸ adjective *they tend to be impulsive and quick-tempered* **irritable,** irascible, hot-tempered, short-tempered, snappish, fiery, touchy, volatile; cross, crabby, crotchety, cantankerous, grumpy, ill-tempered, bad-tempered, testy, tetchy, prickly, choleric; informal snappy, grouchy, cranky, on a short fuse.
ANTONYMS placid.

quick-witted ▸ adjective *Russell was always the quick-witted one in our circle* **intelligent,** bright, clever, gifted, able, astute, quick, smart, sharp-witted; observant, alert, sharp, perceptive; informal brainy, on the ball, quick on the uptake.
ANTONYMS slow.

quid pro quo ▸ noun *the latest agreement between labor and management is a textbook example of quid pro quo* **exchange,** trade, trade-off, swap, switch, barter, substitute, reciprocation, return; amends, compensation, recompense, restitution, reparation.

quiescent ▸ adjective *the volcano is in a quiescent state* **inactive,** inert, idle, dormant, at rest, inoperative, deactivated, quiet; still, motionless, immobile, passive. See note at LATENT.
ANTONYMS active.

quiet ▸ adjective **1** *the whole pub went quiet* **silent,** still, hushed, noiseless, soundless; mute, dumb, speechless.
ANTONYMS noisy.

2 *a quiet voice* **soft,** low, muted, muffled, faint, indistinct, inaudible, hushed, whispered, suppressed.
ANTONYMS loud.
3 *a quiet village* **peaceful,** sleepy, tranquil, calm, still, restful, undisturbed, untroubled; unfrequented.
ANTONYMS busy, hectic.
4 *can I have a quiet word?* **private,** confidential, secret, discreet, unofficial, off the record, between ourselves.
ANTONYMS public.
5 *quiet colors* **unobtrusive,** restrained, muted, understated, subdued, subtle, low-key; soft, pale, pastel.
ANTONYMS loud.
6 *you can't keep it quiet for long* **secret,** confidential, classified, unrevealed, undisclosed, unknown, under wraps; informal hush-hush, mum; formal sub rosa.
ANTONYMS public.
7 *business is quiet* **slow,** stagnant, slack, sluggish, inactive, idle.
ANTONYMS busy, active.
▶ **noun** *the quiet of the countryside* **peacefulness,** peace, restfulness, calm, tranquility, serenity; silence, quietness, stillness, still, quietude, hush, soundlessness.

quietly ▶ **adverb 1** *she quietly entered the room* **silently,** in silence, noiselessly, soundlessly, inaudibly; mutely.
2 *he spoke quietly* **softly,** in a low voice, in a whisper, in a murmur, under one's breath, in an undertone, sotto voce, gently, faintly, weakly, feebly.
3 *some bonds were sold quietly* **discreetly,** privately, confidentially, secretly, unofficially, off the record.
4 *she is quietly confident* **calmly,** patiently, placidly, serenely.

quilt ▶ **noun** *she flipped the quilt back and rose from bed* **duvet,** cover(s), coverlet, comforter; bedspread; dated counterpane.

quintessence ▶ **noun 1** *it's the quintessence of the modern home* **perfect example,** exemplar, prototype, stereotype, picture, epitome, embodiment, ideal, apotheosis; best, pick, prime, acme, crème de la crème.
2 *brain scientists are investigating the quintessence of intelligence* **essence,** soul, spirit, nature, core, heart, crux, kernel, marrow, substance; informal nitty-gritty; Philosophy quiddity, esse.

quip ▶ **noun** *the quip provoked a smile* **joke,** witty remark, witticism, jest, pun, bon mot, sally, pleasantry; informal one-liner, gag, crack, wisecrack, funny.
▶ **verb** *"I think he got the point," quipped Sean* **joke,** jest, pun, sally; informal wisecrack.

quirk ▶ **noun 1** *they all know his quirks* **idiosyncrasy,** peculiarity, oddity, eccentricity, foible, whim, vagary, caprice, fancy, crotchet, habit, characteristic, trait, fad; informal hang-up.
2 *a quirk of fate* **chance,** fluke, freak, anomaly, twist.

quit ▶ **verb 1** *she quit work at 12:30* **leave,** vacate, exit, depart from, withdraw from; abandon, desert.
2 *he's decided to quit his job* **resign from,** leave, give up, hand in one's notice, stand down from, relinquish, vacate, walk out on, retire from; informal chuck, pack in; pack it in, call it quits.
3 informal *quit living in the past* **give up,** stop, cease, discontinue, drop, break off, abandon, abstain from, desist from, refrain from, avoid, forgo.

quite ▶ **adverb 1** *two quite different types* **completely,** entirely, totally, wholly, absolutely, utterly, thoroughly, altogether.
2 *red hair was quite common in Rita's family* **fairly,** rather, somewhat, slightly, relatively, comparatively, moderately, reasonably, to a certain extent; informal pretty, kind of, kinda, sort of.

quiver ▶ **verb 1** *I quivered with terror* **tremble,** shake, shiver, quaver, quake, shudder. See note at SHIVER.
2 *the bird quivers its wings* **flutter,** flap, beat, agitate, vibrate.
▶ **noun** *a quiver in her voice* **tremor,** tremble, shake, quaver, flutter, fluctuation, waver.

quiz ▶ **noun 1** *there may be a short quiz next class* **exam,** test, pop quiz.
2 *a music quiz on the radio* **competition,** game, game show.
▶ **verb** *a man was being quizzed by police* **question,** interrogate, cross-examine, cross-question, interview, sound out, give someone the third degree; test, examine; informal grill, pump.

quizzical ▶ **adjective** *a quizzical look on her face* **inquiring,** questioning, curious; puzzled, perplexed, baffled, mystified; amused, mocking, teasing.

quota ▶ **noun** *she rarely took her full quota of vacation time* **allocation,** share, allowance, limit, ration, portion, dispensation, slice (of the cake); percentage, commission; proportion, fraction, bit, amount, quantity; informal cut.

quotation ▶ **noun** *a quotation from Jefferson's first inaugural address* **citation,** quote, excerpt, extract, passage, line, paragraph, verse, phrase; reference, allusion.

quote ▶ **verb 1** *he quoted a sentence from the book* **recite,** repeat, reproduce, retell, echo, parrot, iterate; take, extract.
2 *she quoted one case in which a girl died* **cite,** mention, refer to, name, instance, specify, identify; relate, recount; allude to, point out, present, offer, advance.
▶ **noun 1** *a Shakespearean quote* See QUOTATION.
2 *a quote from the contractor* **estimate,** price, bid, costing, charge, figure, tender.

Rr

rabble ▶ noun **1** *a rabble of noisy youths* **mob,** crowd, throng, gang, swarm, horde, pack, mass, group.
2 *rule by the rabble* **common people,** masses, populace, multitude, rank and file, commonality, plebeians, proletariat, peasantry, hoi polloi, lower classes, riffraff; informal great unwashed, proles, plebs.
ANTONYMS nobility.

rabid ▶ adjective **1** *a rabid dog* **rabies-infected,** mad, hydrophobic.
2 *her rabid anti-immigration views | a mecca for rabid shoppers* **extreme,** fanatical, overzealous, extremist, maniacal, passionate, fervent, overkeen, diehard, uncompromising, illiberal; informal gung-ho, foaming at the mouth.
ANTONYMS moderate.

race[1] ▶ noun **1** *Sasha won the race* **contest,** competition, event, heat, trial(s).
2 *the race for naval domination* **competition,** rivalry, contention; quest.
3 *the water in the millrace* **channel,** waterway, millrace, raceway, conduit, sluice, chute, spillway.
▶ verb **1** *he will race in the final* **compete,** contend; run.
2 *Claire raced after him* **hurry,** dash, rush, run, sprint, bolt, dart, gallop, career, charge, shoot, hurtle, careen, hare, fly, speed, scurry; informal tear, take off, belt, pelt, scoot, hotfoot it, leg it, hightail it.
3 *her heart was racing* **pound,** beat rapidly, throb, pulsate, thud, thump, hammer, palpitate, flutter, pitter-patter, go pit-a-pat, quiver, pump.

race[2] ▶ noun **1** *students of many different races* **ethnic group,** racial type, origin, ethnic origin, color.
2 *a bloodthirsty race* **people,** nation.

racial ▶ adjective *racial pride* **ethnic,** ethnological, race-related; cultural, national, tribal.

racism ▶ noun *Aborigines are the main victims of racism is Australia* **racial discrimination,** racialism, racial prejudice, xenophobia, chauvinism, bigotry.

racist ▶ noun *he was exposed as a racist* **racial bigot,** racialist, xenophobe, chauvinist, supremacist.
▶ adjective *a racist society* **(racially) discriminatory,** racialist, prejudiced, bigoted.

rack ▶ noun *put the cake on a wire rack* **frame,** framework, stand, holder, trestle, support, shelf.
▶ verb *she was racked with guilt* **torment,** afflict, torture, agonize, harrow; plague, bedevil, persecute, wrack, trouble, worry.
– PHRASES **on the rack** *these latest allegations are keeping the Church on the rack* **under pressure,** under stress, under a strain, in distress; in trouble, in difficulties, having problems. **rack one's brains** *I've racked my brain, but I still can't think of his name* **think hard,** concentrate, try to remember; informal scratch one's head.

racket ▶ noun **1** *the engine makes such a racket* **noise,** din, hubbub, clamor, uproar, tumult, commotion, rumpus, pandemonium, babel; informal hullabaloo.
2 informal *a gold-smuggling racket* **scheme,** fraud, swindle; informal rip-off, shakedown.

raconteur ▶ noun *an interviewer with his favorite raconteur, Studs Terkel* **storyteller,** teller of tales, spinner of yarns, narrator; rare anecdotist, anecdotalist.

racy ▶ adjective *racy lingerie* **risqué,** suggestive, naughty, sexy, spicy, ribald; indecorous, indecent, immodest, off-color, dirty, rude, smutty, crude, salacious; informal raunchy, blue; euphemistic adult.
ANTONYMS prim.

radiance ▶ noun **1** *the radiance of the sun* **light,** brightness, brilliance, luminosity, beams, rays, illumination, blaze, glow, gleam, luster, glare; luminescence, incandescence.
2 *her face beamed with radiance* **joy,** elation, jubilance, ecstasy, rapture, euphoria, delirium, happiness, delight, pleasure.

radiant ▶ adjective **1** *the radiant moon* **shining,** bright, illuminated, brilliant, gleaming, glowing, ablaze, luminous, luminescent, lustrous, incandescent, dazzling, shimmering, resplendent; archaic splendent. See note at **BRIGHT**.
ANTONYMS dark, dull.
2 *she looked radiant* **joyful,** elated, thrilled, overjoyed, jubilant, rapturous, ecstatic, euphoric, in seventh heaven, on cloud nine, delighted, very happy; informal on top of the world, over the moon.
ANTONYMS gloomy.

radiate ▶ verb **1** *the stars radiate energy* **emit,** give off, give out, discharge, diffuse; shed, cast.
2 *light radiated from the hall* **shine,** beam, emanate.
3 *their faces radiate hope* **display,** show, exhibit; emanate, breathe, be a picture of.
4 *four spokes radiate from the hub* **fan out,** spread out, branch out/off, extend, issue.

radical ▶ adjective **1** *radical reform* **thoroughgoing,** thorough, complete, total, comprehensive, exhaustive, sweeping, far-reaching, wide-ranging, extensive, across the board, profound, major, stringent, rigorous.

ANTONYMS superficial.
2 *radical differences between the two theories* **fundamental,** basic, essential, quintessential; structural, deep-seated, intrinsic, organic, constitutive.
ANTONYMS minor.
3 *a radical political movement* **revolutionary,** progressive, reformist, revisionist, progressivist; extreme, extremist, fanatical, militant, diehard, hard-core.
ANTONYMS reactionary, moderate, conservative.
▶ noun *the arrested man was a radical* **revolutionary,** progressive, reformer, revisionist; militant, zealot, extremist, fanatic, diehard; informal ultra.
ANTONYMS reactionary, moderate, conservative.

raffish ▶ adjective *donning a raffish cap | her raffish, faithless husband* **rakish,** unconventional, Bohemian; devil-may-care, casual, careless; louche, disreputable, dissolute, decadent.

raffle ▶ noun *the winner of our raffle was Doris* **lottery,** lotto, drawing, prize drawing, sweepstake(s).

rag ▶ noun 1 *an oily rag* **cloth,** scrap of cloth; informal schmatte.
2 (**rags**) *a man dressed in rags* **tatters,** torn clothing, old clothes; castoffs, hand-me-downs.

ragamuffin ▶ noun *I always got stuck playing the part of some Dickensian-type ragamuffin* **urchin,** waif, guttersnipe, street kid.

rage ▶ noun 1 *his rage is due to frustration* **fury,** anger, wrath, outrage, indignation, temper, spleen, resentment, pique, annoyance, vexation, displeasure; tantrum, bad mood; literary ire, choler.
2 *the current rage for home improvement* **craze,** passion, fashion, taste, trend, vogue, fad, enthusiasm, obsession, compulsion, fixation, fetish, mania, preoccupation; informal thing.
▶ verb 1 *she raged silently* **be angry,** be furious, be enraged, be incensed, seethe, be beside oneself, rave, storm, fume, spit; informal be livid, be wild, foam at the mouth, have a fit, be steamed up.
2 *he* ***raged against*** *the reforms* **protest about,** complain about, oppose, denounce; fulminate against, storm about, rail against.
3 *a storm was raging* **thunder,** rampage, be violent, be turbulent, be tempestuous.
– PHRASES (**all**) **the rage** *pocket-size digital cameras are all the rage* **popular,** fashionable, in fashion, in vogue, the (latest) thing, in great demand, sought after, le dernier cri; informal in, the in thing, cool, big, trendy, red-hot, hip.

ragged ▶ adjective 1 *ragged jeans* **tattered,** in tatters, torn, ripped, holey, in holes, moth-eaten, frayed, worn, worn out, falling to pieces, threadbare, scruffy, shabby; informal tatty, raggedy-ass.
2 *a ragged child* **shabby,** scruffy, unkempt, dressed in rags.
3 *a ragged coastline* **jagged,** craggy, rugged, uneven, rough, irregular; serrated, sawtooth, sawtoothed, indented; technical crenulate, crenulated.

raging ▶ adjective 1 *a raging mob* **angry,** furious, enraged, incensed, infuriated, irate, fuming, seething, ranting; informal livid, wild; literary wrathful; informal smash-mouth.
2 *raging seas* **stormy,** violent, wild, turbulent, tempestuous.
3 *a raging headache* **excruciating,** agonizing, painful, throbbing, acute, bad.
4 *her raging thirst* **severe,** extreme, great, excessive.

raid ▶ noun 1 *the raid on Dieppe* **attack,** assault, descent, blitz, incursion, sortie; onslaught, storming, charge, offensive, invasion, blitzkrieg.
2 *a police raid* **search**; informal bust, takedown, shakedown.
▶ verb 1 *they raided shipping in the harbor* **attack,** assault, set upon, descend on, swoop on, blitz, assail, storm, rush.
2 *armed men raided the store* **rob,** hold up, break into; plunder, steal from, pillage, loot, ransack, sack; informal stick up, heist.

raider ▶ noun *Kelley and his band of raiders* **robber,** burglar, thief, housebreaker, plunderer, pillager, looter, marauder; attacker, assailant, invader.

rail ▶ verb *he* ***rails against*** *injustice* **protest** (**against**), fulminate against, inveigh against, rage against, speak out against, make a stand against; expostulate about, criticize, denounce, condemn; object to, oppose, complain about, challenge; informal kick up a fuss about.
▶ noun *travel by rail* **train,** locomotive; informal iron horse.

railing ▶ noun *hold on to the railing* **fence,** fencing, rail(s), paling, palisade, balustrade, banister.

raillery ▶ noun *affectionate raillery* **teasing,** mockery, chaff, ragging; banter, badinage; informal leg-pulling, joshing, ribbing, kidding.

rain ▶ noun 1 *the rain had stopped* **rainfall,** precipitation, raindrops, wet weather; drizzle, shower, rainstorm, cloudburst, torrent, downpour, deluge, storm.
2 *a rain of hot ash* **shower,** deluge, flood, torrent, avalanche, flurry; storm, hail.
▶ verb 1 *it rained heavily* **pour,** pour down, come down, pelt down, teem down, beat down, rain cats and dogs; fall, drizzle.
2 *bombs rained on the city* **fall,** hail, drop, shower.

rainy ▶ adjective *rainy weather* **wet,** showery, drizzly, damp, inclement.

raise ▶ verb 1 *he raised a hand in greeting* **lift,** lift up, hold aloft, elevate, uplift, upraise, upthrust; hoist, haul up, hitch up.
ANTONYMS lower.
2 *he raised himself in the bed* **set upright,** set vertical; sit up, stand up.
ANTONYMS lay down, knock over.
3 *they raised prices* **increase,** put up, push up, up, mark up, escalate, inflate; informal hike (up), jack up, bump up.
ANTONYMS lower, reduce.
4 *he raised his voice* **amplify,** louden, magnify, intensify, boost, lift, increase, heighten, augment.
ANTONYMS lower.

5 *they wished to raise a new temple dedicated to the goddess* **build,** construct, erect, assemble, put up.
ANTONYMS raze, demolish.
6 *how will you raise the money?* **get,** obtain, acquire; accumulate, amass, collect, fetch, net, make.
ANTONYMS distribute, spend.
7 *the city raised troops to fight for them* **recruit,** enlist, sign up, conscript, call up, mobilize, rally, assemble, draft.
ANTONYMS demobilize, stand down.
8 *a tax raised on imports* **levy,** impose, exact, demand, charge.
9 *he raised several objections* **bring up,** air, ventilate; present, table, propose, submit, advance, suggest, moot, put forward.
ANTONYMS withdraw, keep quiet about.
10 *the disaster raised doubts about safety* **give rise to,** occasion, cause, produce, engender, elicit, create, result in, lead to, prompt, awaken, arouse, induce, kindle, incite, stir up, trigger, spark off, provoke, instigate, foment, whip up; literary beget.
ANTONYMS allay, end.
11 *most parents try to raise their children well* **bring up,** rear, nurture, look after, care for, provide for, mother, parent, tend, cherish; educate, train.
12 *she raised cattle* **breed,** rear, nurture, keep, tend; grow, farm, cultivate, produce.
13 *he was raised to a captaincy* **promote,** advance, upgrade, elevate, ennoble; informal kick upstairs.
ANTONYMS demote.
▶ **noun** *the workers wanted a raise* pay increase, increment.
– PHRASES **raise hell** informal See HELL.

rake[1] ▶ **verb 1** *he raked the leaves into a pile* **scrape up,** collect, gather.
2 *she raked the gravel* **smooth,** smooth out, level, even out, flatten, comb.
3 *the cat raked his arm with its claws* **scratch,** lacerate, scrape, rasp, graze, grate; Medicine excoriate.
4 *she raked a hand through her hair* **drag,** pull, scrape, tug, comb.
5 *I raked through my pockets* **rummage,** search, hunt, sift, rifle.
6 *machine-gun fire raked the streets* **sweep,** enfilade, pepper, strafe.
– PHRASES **rake something in** informal *his frozen yogurt business is raking in the dough* **earn,** make, get, gain, garner, obtain, acquire, accumulate, bring in, pull in, pocket, realize, fetch, return, yield, raise, net, gross. **rake something up** *I guess I've raked up some bad memories* **remind people of,** recollect, remember, call to mind; drag up, dredge up.

rake[2] ▶ **noun** *he was something of a rake* **playboy,** libertine, profligate; degenerate, roué, debauchee; lecher, seducer, womanizer, philanderer, adulterer, Don Juan, Lothario, Casanova; informal ladykiller, ladies' man, lech.

rakish ▶ **adjective** *Felipe's snap-brimmed hat is always cocked at a rakish angle* **dashing,** debonair, stylish, jaunty, devil-may-care; raffish, disreputable, louche; informal sharp.

rally ▶ **verb 1** *the troops rallied and held their ground* **regroup,** reassemble, re-form, reunite.
ANTONYMS disperse.
2 *he rallied an army* **muster,** marshal, mobilize, raise, call up, recruit, enlist, conscript; assemble, gather, round up, draft; formal convoke.
ANTONYMS demobilize, disband.
3 *team owners rallied to denounce the rumors* **get together,** band together, assemble, join forces, unite, ally, collaborate, cooperate, pull together.
ANTONYMS separate, split up.
4 *share prices rallied* **recover,** improve, get better, pick up, revive, bounce back, perk up, look up, turn a corner.
ANTONYMS deteriorate, slump.
▶ **noun 1** *a rally in support of the strike* **meeting,** mass meeting, gathering, assembly; demonstration, march, protest march, protest.
2 *a rally in oil prices* **recovery,** upturn, improvement, comeback, resurgence.
ANTONYMS slump.

ram ▶ **verb 1** *he rammed his sword into its sheath* **force,** thrust, plunge, stab, push, sink, dig, stick, cram, jam, stuff, pack.
2 *a van rammed the police car* **hit,** strike, crash into, collide with, impact, run into, smash into, smack into, bump (into), butt.

ramble ▶ **verb 1** *we rambled around the village* **walk,** hike, tramp, trek, backpack; wander, stroll, saunter, amble, roam, range, rove, traipse; informal mosey, tootle; formal perambulate.
2 *she does ramble* **chatter,** babble, prattle, prate, blather, jabber, twitter, maunder; informal jaw, gas, gab, yak, yabber.
▶ **noun** *a ramble in the hills* **walk,** hike, trek; wander, stroll, saunter, amble, roam, traipse, jaunt, promenade; informal mosey, tootle; formal perambulation.

rambler ▶ **noun** *for two years, he and his dog were a pair of carefree ramblers* **walker,** hiker, backpacker, wanderer, rover; literary wayfarer.

rambling ▶ **adjective 1** *a rambling speech* **long-winded,** verbose, wordy, prolix; digressive, maundering, roundabout, circuitous, tortuous, circumlocutory; disconnected, disjointed, incoherent.
ANTONYMS concise.
2 *rambling streets* **winding,** twisting, twisty, tortuous, labyrinthine; sprawling.
3 *a rambling rose* **trailing,** creeping, climbing, vining.

ramification ▶ **noun** *the Gulf War of 1991 had ramifications far beyond the Middle East* **consequence,** result, aftermath, outcome, effect, upshot; development, implication; product, byproduct.

ramp ▶ **noun** *they wheeled the appliances down the ramp* **slope,** bank, incline, gradient, tilt; rise, ascent, drop, descent, declivity.

rampage ▶ **verb** *mobs rampaged through the streets* **riot,** run riot, go on the rampage, run amok, go berserk; storm, charge, tear.
– PHRASES **go on the rampage** *the prisoners have gone on a rampage* **riot,** go berserk, get out of control, run amok; informal go postal.

rampant ▶ adjective **1** *rampant inflation* **uncontrolled,** unrestrained, unchecked, unbridled, widespread; out of control, out of hand, rife.
ANTONYMS controlled.
2 *rampant dislike* **vehement,** strong, violent, forceful, intense, passionate, fanatical.
ANTONYMS mild.
3 *rampant vegetation* **luxuriant,** exuberant, lush, rich, riotous, rank, profuse, vigorous; informal jungly.

rampart ▶ noun *the castle's stony ramparts* **defensive wall,** embankment, earthwork, parapet, breastwork, battlement, bulwark, outwork.

ramshackle ▶ adjective *their first home was a ramshackle cottage* **tumbledown,** dilapidated, derelict, decrepit, neglected, run-down, gone to rack and ruin, beat-up, crumbling, decaying; rickety, shaky, unsound.
ANTONYMS sound, sturdy.

rancid ▶ adjective *rancid bacon* **sour,** stale, overstored, turned, rank, putrid, foul, rotten, bad, off; gamy, high, fetid, stinking, malodorous, foul-smelling; literary noisome.
ANTONYMS fresh.

rancor ▶ noun *partisans on both sides have created much rancor* **bitterness,** spite, hate, hatred, resentment, malice, ill will, malevolence, animosity, antipathy, enmity, hostility, acrimony, venom, vitriol.

rancorous ▶ adjective *California's rancorous recall campaign* **bitter,** spiteful, hateful, resentful, acrimonious, malicious, malevolent, hostile, venomous, vindictive, baleful, vitriolic, vengeful, pernicious, mean, nasty; informal bitchy, catty. See note at **VINDICTIVE**.
ANTONYMS amicable.

random ▶ adjective *random spot checks* **unsystematic,** unmethodical, arbitrary, unplanned, undirected, casual, indiscriminate, nonspecific, haphazard, stray, erratic; chance, accidental.
ANTONYMS systematic.
– PHRASES **at random** *we chose the names at random* **unsystematically,** arbitrarily, randomly, unmethodically, haphazardly.

range ▶ noun **1** *his range of vision* **span,** scope, compass, sweep, extent, area, field, orbit, ambit, horizon, latitude; limits, bounds, confines, parameters.
2 *a range of mountains* **row,** chain, sierra, ridge, massif; line, string, series.
3 *a range of quality foods* **assortment,** variety, diversity, mixture, collection, array, selection, choice.
4 *she put the dish into the range* **stove,** oven.
5 *cows grazed on the open range* **pasture,** pasturage, pastureland, prairie, grass, grassland, grazing land, veld; literary greensward.
▶ verb **1** *interest charges range from 1% to 5%* **vary,** fluctuate, differ; extend, stretch, reach, cover, go, run.
2 *they ranged over the sprawling hills* **roam,** rove, traverse, travel, journey, wander, drift, ramble, meander, stroll, traipse, walk, hike, trek.

CHOOSE THE RIGHT WORD

range, compass, gamut, latitude, reach, scope, sweep

To say that someone has a wide **range** of interests implies that these interests are not only extensive but varied. Another way of expressing the same idea would be to say that the person's interests run the **gamut** from TV quiz shows to nuclear physics, a word that suggests a graduated scale or series running from one extreme to another. **Compass** implies a range of knowledge or activity that falls within very definite limits reminiscent of a circumference (*within the compass of her abilities*), while **sweep** suggests more of an arc-shaped range of motion or activity (*the sweep of the searchlight*) or a continuous extent or stretch (*a broad sweep of lawn*). **Latitude** and **scope** both emphasize the idea of freedom, although *scope* implies great freedom within prescribed limits (*the scope of the investigation*), while *latitude* means freedom from such limits (*she was granted more latitude than usual in interviewing the disaster victims*). Even someone who has a wide *range* of interests and a broad *scope* of authority, however, will sooner or later come up against something that is beyond his or her **reach**, which suggests the furthest limit of effectiveness or influence.

rank[1] ▶ noun **1** *she was elevated to an administrative rank* **position,** level, grade, echelon; class, status, standing; dated station.
2 *a family of rank* **high standing,** blue blood, high birth, nobility, aristocracy; eminence, distinction, prestige; prominence, influence, consequence, power.
3 *a rank of riflemen* **row,** line, file, column, string, train, procession.
▶ verb **1** *this orchid is ranked as endangered* **classify,** class, categorize, rate, grade, bracket, group, pigeonhole, designate; catalog, file, list.
2 *he ranked them in order of experience* **prioritize,** order, organize, arrange, list; triage.
3 *she ranked below the others* **have a rank,** be graded, have a status, be classed, be classified, be categorized; belong.
– PHRASES **rank and file 1** *the officers and the rank and file* **other ranks,** soldiers, NCOs, noncommissioned officers, lower ranks, enlisted personnel; men, troops; informal noncoms. **2** *a speech appealing to the rank and file* **people,** common people, proletariat, masses, populace, commonality, third estate, plebeians; hoi polloi, rabble, riffraff, great unwashed; informal proles, plebs.

rank[2] ▶ adjective **1** *rank vegetation* **abundant,** lush, luxuriant, dense, profuse, vigorous, overgrown; informal jungly.
ANTONYMS sparse.
2 *a rank smell* **offensive,** unpleasant, nasty, revolting, sickening, obnoxious, noxious; foul, fetid, smelly, stinking, reeking, high, off, rancid, putrid, malodorous; literary noisome; Brit.

informal minging, pongy.
ANTONYMS pleasant.
3 *rank stupidity* **downright,** utter, outright, out-and-out, absolute, complete, sheer, arrant, thoroughgoing, unqualified, unmitigated, positive, perfect, patent, pure, total; archaic arrant.

rankle ▶ **verb** *she'd always rankled certain people with her independence and forthrightness* **cause resentment to,** annoy, upset, anger, irritate, offend, affront, displease, provoke, irk, vex, pique, nettle, gall; informal rile, miff, peeve, aggravate, tick off.

ransack ▶ **verb** *Joonie's thugs ransacked Leon's apartment* **plunder,** pillage, raid, rob, loot, sack, strip, despoil; ravage, devastate, turn upside down; scour, rifle, comb, search.

ransom ▶ **noun** *they demanded a huge ransom* **payoff,** payment, sum, price.
▶ **verb** *the girl was ransomed for $4 million* **release,** free, deliver, liberate, rescue; exchange for a ransom, buy the freedom of.

rant ▶ **verb** *she ranted about the unfairness* **fulminate,** go on, hold forth, vociferate, sound off, spout, pontificate, bluster, declaim; shout, yell, bellow; informal mouth off.
▶ **noun** *he went into a rant about them* **tirade,** diatribe, broadside; literary philippic.

rap ▶ **verb 1** *she rapped his fingers with a ruler* **hit,** strike; informal whack, thwack, bash, wallop; literary smite.
2 *I rapped on the door* **knock,** tap, bang, hammer, pound.
▶ **noun 1** *a rap on the knuckles* **blow,** hit, knock, bang, crack; informal whack, thwack, bash, wallop.
2 *a rap at the door* **knock,** tap, rat-tat, bang, hammering, pounding.
– PHRASES **take the rap** informal *why should I take the rap for what Clarence did?* **be punished,** take the blame, suffer, suffer the consequences, pay, pay the price.

rapacious ▶ **adjective** *poor Tom has fallen for a rapacious gold digger* **grasping,** greedy, avaricious, acquisitive, covetous; mercenary, materialistic; insatiable, predatory; informal money-grubbing, grabby. See note at GREEDY.
ANTONYMS generous.

rape ▶ **noun 1** *he was charged with rape* **sexual assault,** sexual abuse, sexual interference; archaic ravishment, defilement.
2 *the rape of the rain forest* **destruction,** violation, ravaging, pillaging, plundering, desecration, defilement, sacking, sack.
▶ **verb 1** *he raped her at knifepoint* **sexually assault,** sexually abuse, violate, force oneself on; literary ravish; archaic defile.
2 *they raped our country* **ravage,** violate, desecrate, defile, plunder, pillage, despoil; lay waste, ransack, sack.

rapid ▶ **adjective** *his rapid rise to stardom* **quick,** fast, swift, speedy, expeditious, express, brisk; lightning, meteoric, whirlwind; sudden, instantaneous, instant, immediate; hurried, hasty, precipitate; informal PDQ, pretty damn quick; literary fleet.
ANTONYMS slow.

rapidly ▶ **adverb** *a new computer worm spread rapidly through the Internet on Tuesday* **quickly,** fast, swiftly, speedily, at the speed of light, posthaste, at full tilt, briskly; hurriedly, hastily, in haste, in a rush, precipitately; informal like a shot, PDQ, pretty damn quick, in a flash, on the double, like a bat out of hell, like lightning, like greased lightning, like mad, like the wind, lickety-split; literary apace.
ANTONYMS slowly.

rapport ▶ **noun** *board members fired him for failing to maintain good rapport with the trustees* **affinity,** close relationship, understanding, mutual understanding, bond, empathy, sympathy, accord.

rapt ▶ **adjective** *a rapt teenage audience* **fascinated,** enthralled, spellbound, captivated, riveted, gripped, mesmerized, enchanted, entranced, bewitched, moonstruck; transported, enraptured, thrilled, ecstatic.
ANTONYMS inattentive.

rapture ▶ **noun** *she gazed at him in rapture* **ecstasy,** bliss, exaltation, euphoria, elation, joy, enchantment, delight, happiness, pleasure.
– PHRASES **go into raptures** *the Cambodian crowd went into raptures over Carreras's rendition of "Some Enchanted Evening"* **enthuse,** rhapsodize, rave, gush, wax lyrical; informal go wild/crazy/mad.

CHOOSE THE RIGHT WORD

rapture, bliss, ecstasy, euphoria, transport

Happiness is one thing; **bliss** is another, suggesting a state of utter joy and contentment (*marital bliss*). **Ecstasy** is even more extreme, describing a trancelike state in which one loses consciousness of one's surroundings (*the ecstasy of young love*). Although **rapture** originally referred to being raised or lifted out of oneself by divine power, nowadays it is used in much the same sense as *ecstasy* to describe an elevated sensation of bliss (*she listened in speechless rapture to her favorite soprano*). **Transport** applies to any powerful emotion by which one is carried away (*a transport of delight*). When happiness is carried to an extreme or crosses over into mania, it is called **euphoria**. *Euphoria* may outwardly resemble *ecstasy* or *rapture*; but upon closer examination, it is usually found to be exaggerated and out of proportion (*the euphoria that came over him whenever he touched alcohol*).

rapturous ▶ **adjective** *Nelson Mandela received a rapturous welcome in London* **ecstatic,** joyful, elated, euphoric, enraptured, on cloud nine, in seventh heaven, transported, enchanted, blissful, happy; enthusiastic, delighted, thrilled, overjoyed, rapt; informal over the moon, on top of the world, blissed out.

rare ▶ **adjective 1** *rare moments of privacy* **infrequent,** scarce, sparse, few and far between, thin on the ground, like gold dust, as scarce as hen's teeth; occasional, limited, odd, isolated, unaccustomed, unwonted.

ANTONYMS common, frequent.
2 *rare stamps* **unusual,** recherché, uncommon, unfamiliar, atypical, singular.
ANTONYMS ordinary, commonplace.
3 *a man of rare talent* **exceptional,** outstanding, unparalleled, peerless, matchless, unique, unrivaled, inimitable, beyond compare, without equal, second to none, unsurpassed; consummate, superior, superlative, first-class; informal A1, top-notch.
ANTONYMS common, everyday.

rarely ▶ adverb *we rarely leave the house in the winter* **seldom,** infrequently, hardly ever, hardly, scarcely, not often; once in a while, now and then, occasionally; informal once in a blue moon.
ANTONYMS often.

rarity ▶ noun **1** *the rarity of earthquakes in Vermont* **infrequency,** rareness, scarcity, unusualness, uncommonness.
2 *this book is a rarity* **collector's item,** rare thing, rare bird, rara avis; wonder, nonpareil, one of a kind; curiosity, oddity.

rascal ▶ noun *the title character is a lovable rascal* **scalawag,** imp, monkey, mischief-maker, wretch; informal scamp, tyke, horror, monster, varmint; archaic rapscallion.

rash[1] ▶ noun **1** *he broke out in **a rash*** **spots,** a breakout, an eruption; hives; Medicine erythema, exanthema, urticaria.
2 *a rash of articles in the press* **series,** succession, spate, wave, flood, deluge, torrent; outbreak, epidemic, flurry.

rash[2] ▶ adjective *a rash decision* **reckless,** impulsive, impetuous, hasty, foolhardy, incautious, precipitate; careless, heedless, thoughtless, imprudent, foolish; ill-advised, injudicious, ill-judged, misguided, harebrained, trigger-happy; literary temerarious. See note at TEMERITY.
ANTONYMS prudent.

rasp ▶ verb **1** *tartar is rasped off the teeth* **scrape,** rub, abrade, grate, grind, sand, file, scratch, scour; Medicine excoriate.
2 *"Help!" he rasped* **croak,** squawk, caw, say hoarsely.

rasping ▶ adjective *the rasping voice on the phone sounded familiar* **harsh,** grating, jarring; raspy, scratchy, hoarse, rough, gravelly, croaky, gruff, husky, throaty, guttural.

rate ▶ noun **1** *a fixed rate of interest* **percentage,** ratio, proportion; scale, standard, level.
2 *an hourly rate of $30* **charge,** price, cost, tariff, fare, levy, toll; fee, remuneration, payment, wage, allowance.
3 *the rate of change* **speed,** pace, tempo, velocity, momentum.
▶ verb **1** *they rated his driving ability* **assess,** evaluate, appraise, judge, estimate, calculate, gauge, measure, adjudge; grade, rank, classify, categorize.
2 *the scheme was rated effective* **consider,** judge, reckon, think, hold, deem, find; regard as, look on as, count as.
3 *he rated only a brief mention* **merit,** deserve, warrant, be worthy of, be deserving of.
– PHRASES **at any rate** *at any rate, we ask that you remember to vote* **in any case,** anyhow, anyway, in any event, nevertheless; whatever happens, come what may, regardless, notwithstanding.

rather ▶ adverb **1** *I would rather stay home* **sooner,** by preference, preferably, by choice.
2 *it's rather complicated* **quite,** a bit, a little, fairly, slightly, somewhat, relatively, to some degree, comparatively; informal pretty, sort of, kind of, kinda.
3 *her true feelings—or rather, lack of feelings* **more precisely,** to be precise, to be exact, strictly speaking.
4 *she seemed sad rather than angry* **more**; as opposed to, instead of.
5 *it was not impulsive, but rather a considered decision* **on the contrary,** au contraire, instead.

ratify ▶ verb *they failed to ratify the amendment* **confirm,** approve, sanction, endorse, agree to, accept, uphold, authorize, formalize, validate, recognize; sign. See note at APPROVE.
ANTONYMS reject.

rating ▶ noun *the hotel's four-star rating* **grade,** grading, classification, ranking, rank, category, designation; assessment, evaluation, appraisal; mark, score.

ratio ▶ noun *the fat ratios in American diets are dangerously askew* **proportion,** comparative number, correlation, relationship, correspondence; percentage, fraction, quotient.

ration ▶ noun **1** *a daily ration of chocolate* **allowance,** allocation, quota, quantum, share, portion, helping; amount, quantity, measure, proportion, percentage.
2 (**rations**) *the garrison ran out of rations* **supplies,** provisions, food, foodstuffs, eatables, edibles, provender; stores; informal grub, eats; formal comestibles; dated victuals.
▶ verb *fuel supplies were rationed* **control,** limit, restrict; conserve.

rational ▶ adjective **1** *a rational approach* **logical,** reasoned, sensible, reasonable, cogent, intelligent, judicious, shrewd, common-sense, commonsensical, sound, prudent; down-to-earth, practical, pragmatic. See note at SENSIBLE.
ANTONYMS illogical.
2 *she was not rational at the time of signing* **sane,** compos mentis, in one's right mind, of sound mind; normal, balanced, grounded, lucid, coherent; informal all there.
ANTONYMS insane.
3 *humans are rational beings* **intelligent,** thinking, reasoning; cerebral, logical, analytical; formal ratiocinative.

rationale ▶ noun *the director outlined the rationale for his plan* **reason**(s), reasoning, thinking, logic, grounds, sense; principle, theory, argument, case; motive, motivation, explanation, justification, excuse; the whys and wherefores.

rationalize ▶ verb **1** *he tried to rationalize his behavior* **justify,** explain, explain away, account for, defend, vindicate, excuse. See note at LIE[1].
2 *an attempt to rationalize the industry* **streamline,** reorganize, modernize, update; trim, hone, simplify, downsize, prune.

rattle ▶ verb **1** *hailstones rattled against the*

window **clatter,** patter; clink, clunk.
2 *he rattled some coins* **jingle,** jangle, clink, tinkle.
3 *the bus rattled along* **jolt,** bump, bounce, jounce, shake.
4 *the government was rattled by the strike* **unnerve,** disconcert, disturb, fluster, shake, perturb, discompose, discomfit, ruffle, throw; informal faze.
▶ **noun 1** *the rattle of the bottles* **clatter,** clank, clink, clang; jingle, jangle.
2 *she gave the baby a rattle* **noisemaker,** shaker, rain stick, maraca.
– PHRASES **rattle something off** *she can rattle off the complete list of Shakespeare's plays* **reel off,** recite, list, fire off, run through, enumerate. **rattle on/away** *rattling on about her grandchildren* **prattle,** babble, chatter, prate, go on, jabber, gibber, ramble; informal gab, yak, yap.

raucous ▶ **adjective 1** *raucous laughter* **harsh,** strident, screeching, piercing, shrill, grating, discordant, dissonant; noisy, loud, cacophonous.
ANTONYMS soft, dulcet.
2 *a raucous party* **rowdy,** noisy, boisterous, roisterous, wild.
ANTONYMS restrained, quiet.

ravage ▶ **verb** *they ravaged the countryside* **lay waste,** devastate, ruin, destroy, wreak havoc on, leave desolate; pillage, plunder, despoil, ransack, sack, loot, rape.

> CHOOSE THE RIGHT WORD
> **ravage, despoil, devastate, pillage, plunder, sack, waste**
> **Ravage**, **pillage**, **sack**, and **plunder** are all verbs associated with the actions of a conquering army during wartime. *Ravage* implies violent destruction, usually in a series of raids or invasions over an extended period of time (*the invading forces ravaged the countryside*). *Plunder* refers to the roving of soldiers through recently conquered territory in search of money and goods (*they plundered the city and left its inhabitants destitute*), while *pillage* describes the act of stripping a conquered city or people of valuables (*churches pillaged by ruthless invaders*). *Sack* is even more extreme than *pillage*, implying not only the seizure of all valuables, but total destruction as well (*the army sacked every village along the coast*). **Despoil** also entails the stripping of valuables, but with less violence than *sack*; it is more common in nonmilitary contexts, where it describes a heedless or inadvertent destruction (*forests despoiled by logging companies*). **Devastate** emphasizes ruin and desolation, whether it happens to buildings, forests, or crops (*fields of corn devastated by flooding*). **Waste** comes close in meaning to *devastate*, but it suggests a less violent or more gradual destruction (*a region of the country wasted by years of drought and periodic fires*).

ravages ▶ **plural noun 1** *the ravages of time* **damaging effects,** ill effects.
2 *the ravages carried out by humanity* **acts of destruction,** destruction, damage, devastation, ruin, havoc, depredation(s).

rave ▶ **verb 1** *he was raving about the fires of hell* **talk wildly,** babble, jabber, talk incoherently.
2 *I raved and swore at them* **rant,** rant and rave, rage, lose one's temper, storm, fulminate, fume; shout, roar, thunder, bellow; informal fly off the handle, blow one's top, hit the roof, flip one's wig.
3 *he* ***raved about*** *her singing* **praise enthusiastically,** go into raptures about/over, wax lyrical about, sing the praises of, rhapsodize over, enthuse about/over, acclaim, eulogize, extol; informal ballyhoo; formal laud; archaic panegyrize.
ANTONYMS criticize.
▶ **noun** informal **1** *the food won raves from the critics* **enthusiastic praise,** lavish praise, a rapturous reception, tribute, plaudits, acclaim.
ANTONYMS criticism.
2 *an all-night rave* See PARTY (sense 1 of the noun).
▶ **adjective** informal *rave reviews* **very enthusiastic,** rapturous, glowing, ecstatic, excellent, highly favorable.

ravenous ▶ **adjective 1** *I'm absolutely ravenous* **very hungry,** starving, famished; rare esurient.
2 *her ravenous appetite* **voracious,** insatiable; greedy, gluttonous; literary insatiate.

ravine ▶ **noun** *the ravine that runs along Hubble Hollow Road* **gorge,** canyon, gully, couloir; chasm, abyss, gulf, gulch, coulee.

raving ▶ **adjective** See MAD (sense 1).

ravings ▶ **plural noun** *the ravings of a madman* **gibberish,** rambling, babbling, wild talk, incoherent talk.

ravish ▶ **verb 1** literary *he tried to ravish her* **rape,** sexually assault/abuse, violate, force oneself on, molest; archaic dishonor, defile.
2 literary *you will be ravished by this wine* **enrapture,** enchant, delight, charm, entrance, enthrall, captivate.
3 archaic *her child was ravished from her breast* **seize,** snatch, carry off/away, steal, abduct.

ravishing ▶ **adjective** *you look utterly ravishing* **very beautiful,** gorgeous, stunning, wonderful, lovely, striking, magnificent, dazzling, radiant, delightful, charming, enchanting; informal amazing, sensational, fantastic, fabulous, terrific, bodacious, hot, red-hot.
ANTONYMS hideous.

raw ▶ **adjective 1** *raw carrot* **uncooked,** fresh.
ANTONYMS cooked.
2 *raw materials* **unprocessed,** untreated, unrefined, crude, natural; unedited, undigested, unprepared.
ANTONYMS refined, processed.
3 *raw recruits* **inexperienced,** new, untrained, untried, untested, unseasoned; callow, immature, green, naive; informal wet behind the ears, raggedy-ass.
ANTONYMS experienced, skilled.
4 *his skin is raw* **sore,** red, painful, tender; abraded, chafed; Medicine excoriated.
5 *a raw morning* **bleak,** cold, chilly, bone-

chilling, freezing, icy, icy-cold, wintry, bitter, biting; informal nippy.
ANTONYMS warm, balmy.
6 *raw emotions* **strong,** intense, passionate, fervent, powerful, violent; undisguised, unconcealed, unrestrained, uninhibited.
7 *raw images of Latin America* **realistic,** unembellished, unvarnished, brutal, harsh, gritty, graphic.
ANTONYMS idealized.
– PHRASES **in the raw** informal *sleeping in the raw* See **NAKED** (sense 1).

ray ▶ **noun 1** *rays of light* **beam,** shaft, streak, stream.
2 *a ray of hope* **glimmer,** flicker, spark, hint, suggestion, sign.

raze ▶ **verb** *the old library will be razed on Saturday* **destroy,** demolish, raze to the ground, tear down, pull down, knock down, level, flatten, bulldoze, wipe out, lay waste. See note at **DESTROY**.

reach ▶ **verb 1** *Travis* ***reached out*** *a hand* **stretch out,** hold out, extend, outstretch, thrust out, stick out.
2 *reach me that book* **pass,** hand, give, let someone have.
3 *soon she reached Helen's house* **arrive at,** get to, come to; end up at; informal make.
4 *the temperature reached 32 degrees* **attain,** get to; rise to, climb to; fall to, sink to, drop to; informal hit.
5 *the leaders reached an agreement* **achieve,** attain, work out, draw up, put together, negotiate, thrash out, hammer out.
6 *I have been trying to reach you all day* **get in touch with,** contact, get through to, get, speak to; informal get hold of.
7 *our concern is to reach more people* **influence,** sway, get (through) to, make an impression on, have an impact on.
▶ **noun 1** *Bobby moved out of her reach* **grasp,** range. See note at **RANGE**.
2 *small goals within your reach* **capabilities,** capacity.
3 *beyond the reach of the law* **jurisdiction,** authority, influence; scope, range, compass, ambit.

react ▶ **verb 1** *how would he react if she told him the truth?* **behave,** act, take it, conduct oneself; respond, reply, answer.
2 *she* ***reacted against*** *the new regulations* **rebel against,** oppose, rise up against.

reaction ▶ **noun 1** *his reaction had bewildered her* **response,** answer, reply, rejoinder, retort, riposte; informal comeback.
2 *a reaction against modernism* **backlash,** counteraction.

reactionary ▶ **adjective** *a reactionary policy* **right-wing,** conservative, rightist, ultraconservative; traditionalist, conventional, old-fashioned, unprogressive; informal redneck.
ANTONYMS progressive.
▶ **noun** *an extreme reactionary* **right-winger,** conservative, rightist; traditionalist, conventionalist, dinosaur.
ANTONYMS radical.

read ▶ **verb 1** *Nadine and Ian were reading the paper by the fireplace* **peruse,** study, scrutinize, look through; pore over, be absorbed in; run one's eye over, cast an eye over, leaf through, scan, flick through, skim through, thumb through.
2 *he read a passage of the letter* **read out/aloud,** recite, declaim.
3 *I can't read my own writing* **decipher,** make out, make sense of, interpret, understand.
4 *her remark could be read as a criticism* **interpret,** take, take to mean, construe, see, understand.
5 *the dial read 70 mph* **indicate,** register, record, display, show.
▶ **noun** *have a read of this* **perusal,** study, scan; look (at), browse (through).
– PHRASES **read something into something** *don't read too much into their statistics* **infer from,** interpolate from, assume from, attribute to; read between the lines. **read up on** *we'll need to read up on Peruvian culture* **study,** brush up on; informal bone up on.

readable ▶ **adjective 1** *the inscription is perfectly readable* **legible,** easy to read, decipherable, clear, intelligible, comprehensible, reader-friendly.
ANTONYMS illegible.
2 *her novels are immensely readable* **enjoyable,** entertaining, interesting, absorbing, engaging, gripping, enthralling, engrossing, stimulating; informal unputdownable.
ANTONYMS boring.

readily ▶ **adverb 1** *Durkin readily offered to drive him* **willingly,** without hesitation, unhesitatingly, ungrudgingly, gladly, happily, eagerly, promptly.
ANTONYMS reluctantly.
2 *the island is readily accessible* **easily,** with ease, without difficulty.
ANTONYMS with difficulty.

readiness ▶ **noun 1** *their readiness to accept change* **willingness,** enthusiasm, eagerness, keenness; promptness, quickness, alacrity.
2 *a state of readiness* **preparedness,** preparation.
3 *the readiness of his reply* **promptness,** quickness, rapidity, swiftness, speed, speediness.
– PHRASES **in readiness** *there were candles in readiness* **ready,** at the ready, available, on hand, accessible, handy; prepared, primed, on standby, standing by, on full alert.

reading ▶ **noun 1** *a cursory reading of the financial pages* **perusal,** study, scan, scanning; browse (through), look (through), glance (through), leaf (through), skim (through).
2 *a man of wide reading* **book learning,** learning, scholarship, education, erudition.
3 *readings from the Bible* **passage,** lesson; section, piece; recital, recitation.
4 *my reading of the situation* **interpretation,** construal, understanding, explanation, analysis.
5 *a meter reading* **record,** figure, indication, measurement.

ready ▶ **adjective 1** *are you ready?* **prepared,** set, all set, organized, primed; informal fit, psyched up, geared up.
2 *everything is ready* **completed,** finished, prepared, organized, done, arranged, fixed, in

readiness.
3 *he's always ready to help* **willing,** prepared, pleased, inclined, disposed, predisposed; eager, keen, happy, glad; informal game.
4 *she looked* ***ready to*** *collapse* **about to,** on the point of, on the verge of, close to, liable to, likely to.
5 *a ready supply of food* **available,** easily available, accessible; handy, close/near at hand, on hand, convenient, within reach, at the ready, near, at one's fingertips.
6 *a ready answer* **prompt,** quick, swift, speedy, fast, immediate, unhesitating; clever, sharp, astute, shrewd, keen, perceptive, discerning.
▶ **verb** *he needed time to ready himself* **prepare,** get/make ready, organize; gear oneself up; informal psych oneself up.
– PHRASES **at the ready** *the fire extinguishers are at the ready* **in position,** poised, ready for use/action, waiting, on deck. **make ready** *making ready for their departure* **prepare,** make preparations, get everything ready, gear up for.

real ▶ **adjective 1** *is she a fictional character or a real person?* **actual,** nonfictional, factual, real-life; historical; material, physical, tangible, concrete, palpable.
ANTONYMS imaginary.
2 *real gold* **genuine,** authentic, bona fide; informal kosher, honest-to-goodness, honest-to-God.
ANTONYMS imaginary, fake.
3 *my real name* **true,** actual.
4 *tears of real grief* **sincere,** genuine, true, unfeigned, heartfelt, unaffected.
ANTONYMS false, feigned.
5 *a real man* **proper,** true; informal regular.
6 *you're a real idiot* **complete,** utter, thorough, absolute, total, prize, perfect.
▶ **adverb** informal *that's real good of you* See VERY (adverb).

realistic ▶ **adjective 1** *you've got to be realistic* **practical,** pragmatic, matter-of-fact, down-to-earth, sensible, commonsensical, grounded; rational, reasonable, levelheaded, clear-sighted, businesslike; informal having both/one's feet on the ground, hard-nosed, no-nonsense.
ANTONYMS idealistic.
2 *a realistic aim* **achievable,** attainable, feasible, practicable, viable, reasonable, sensible, workable; informal doable.
ANTONYMS impracticable.
3 *a realistic portrayal of war* **true to life,** lifelike, truthful, true, faithful, unidealized, real-life, naturalistic, graphic.
ANTONYMS fictional, imaginative.

reality ▶ **noun 1** *distinguishing fantasy from reality* **the real world,** real life, actuality; truth; physical existence.
ANTONYMS fantasy.
2 *the harsh realities of life* **fact,** actuality, truth.
3 *the reality of Steinbeck's detail* **verisimilitude,** authenticity, realism, fidelity, faithfulness.
ANTONYMS idealism.
– PHRASES **in reality** *they got an invitation, but in reality they were not especially welcome* **in fact,** in actual fact, in point of fact, as a matter of fact, actually, really, in truth; in practice; archaic in sooth.

realization ▶ **noun 1** *a growing realization of the danger* **awareness,** understanding, comprehension, consciousness, appreciation, recognition, discernment; formal cognizance.
2 *the realization of our dreams* **fulfillment,** achievement, accomplishment, attainment; formal effectuation.

realize ▶ **verb 1** *he suddenly realized what she meant* **register,** perceive, discern, be/become aware of (the fact that), be/become conscious of (the fact that), notice; understand, grasp, comprehend, see, recognize, work out, fathom, apprehend; informal latch on to, savvy, figure out, get (the message); Brit. suss; formal be/become cognizant of.
2 *they realized their dream* **fulfill,** achieve, accomplish, make a reality, make happen, bring to fruition, bring about/off, carry out/through; formal effectuate.
3 *the company realized significant profits* **make,** clear, gain, earn, return, produce.
4 *the goods realized $3000* **be sold for,** fetch, go for, make, net.
5 *he realized his assets* **cash in,** liquidate, capitalize.

really ▶ **adverb 1** *he is really very wealthy* **in fact,** in actual fact, actually, in reality, in point of fact, as a matter of fact, in truth, to tell the truth; archaic in sooth.
2 *he really likes her* **genuinely,** truly, honestly; undoubtedly, without a doubt, indubitably, certainly, assuredly, unquestionably; archaic verily.
3 *they were really kind to me* **very,** extremely, thoroughly, decidedly, exceptionally, exceedingly, immensely, monumentally, tremendously, uncommonly, unbelievably, remarkably, eminently, extraordinarily, incredibly, most, downright, terrifically, awfully, so, ever so; informal totally, ultra, too —— for words, seriously, real, mighty, awful, plumb, powerful, way.
▶ **exclamation** *"They've split up." "Really?"* **no kidding,** for real, is that so, is that a fact, is that right.

realm ▶ **noun 1** *peace in the realm* **kingdom,** country, land, dominion, nation.
2 *the realm of academia* **domain,** sphere, area, field, world, province, territory.

reap ▶ **verb 1** *the grain has been reaped* **harvest,** garner, gather in, bring in.
2 *reaping the benefits* **receive,** obtain, get, acquire, secure, realize.

rear[1] ▶ **verb 1** *I was reared on a farm* **bring up,** raise, care for, look after, nurture, parent; educate.
2 *he reared cattle* **breed,** raise, keep, farm, ranch.
3 *laboratory-reared plants* **grow,** cultivate.
4 *the bear reared its head* **raise,** lift (up), hold up, uplift.
5 *Mount Logan reared up before them* **rise,** rise up, tower, soar, loom.

rear[2] ▶ **noun 1** *the rear of the building* **back,** back part, hind part, back end; Nautical stern.
ANTONYMS front.
2 *we were standing near the rear of the line* **end,** tail, rear end, back end, tail, tag end.
ANTONYMS front.

3 *he slapped the horse on the rear* See **BUTTOCKS**.
▶ **adjective** *the rear bumper* **back,** end, rearmost; hind, hinder, hindmost; technical posterior.

reason ▶ **noun 1** *the main reason for his decision* **cause,** ground(s), basis, rationale; motive, motivation, purpose, point, aim, intention, objective, goal; explanation, justification, argument, defense, vindication, excuse, pretext.
2 *postmodern voices railing against reason* **rationality,** logic, logical thought, reasoning, cognition; formal ratiocination.
3 *he was losing his reason* **sanity,** mind, mental faculties; senses, wits; informal marbles.
4 *he continues, against reason, to love her* **good sense,** good judgment, common sense, wisdom, sagacity, reasonableness.
▶ **verb 1** *a young child is unable to reason* **think rationally,** think logically, use one's common sense, use one's head/brain; formal cogitate, ratiocinate.
2 *Scott reasoned that Annabel might be ill* **calculate,** come to the conclusion, conclude, reckon, think, judge, deduce, infer, surmise; informal figure.
3 *she tried to* ***reason with*** *her husband* **bring around,** coax, persuade, prevail on, convince, make someone see the light.
– PHRASES **by reason of** formal *by reason of mental illness, Peterson will not be held in contempt of court* **because of,** on account of, as a result of, owing to, due to, by virtue of, thanks to. **reason something out** *we finally reasoned out the cryptic message in chapter twelve* **work out,** think through, make sense of, get to the bottom of, puzzle out; informal figure out. **with reason** *he was anxious, with reason, about his own political survival* **justifiably,** justly, legitimately, rightly, reasonably.

> USAGE
> **reason is because**
> This construction is loose because *reason* implies *because* and vice versa. As Robert W. Burchfield, the distinguished *Oxford English Dictionary* lexicographer, put it: "Though often defended by modern grammarians, the type 'the reason . . . is because' (instead of 'the reason . . . is that') aches with redundancy, and is still as inadmissible in Standard English as it was when H. W. Fowler objected to it in 1926." Points of View 116 (1992). After *reason is,* you'll need a noun phrase, a predicate adjective, or a clause introduced by *that*. The best cure for *reason is because* is to replace *because* with *that*—e.g.: "Marcello (Jean Reno) has one frantic mission in life: to keep anyone from dying in the small Italian village where he lives. The reason is because [read *reason is that*] there are only three plots left in the local cemetery and his terminally ill wife, Roseanna (Mercedes Ruehl), wishes only that she be buried next to their daughter." (*Star-Ledger* [Newark]; June 27, 1997.)
> Variations such as *reason is due to* are no better—e.g.: "It's a challenge for any athlete to come back after four years of inactivity. The challenge is even greater when the reason is due to injury [read *the layoff is due to injury* or *injury is the cause*]." (*Tulsa Tribune & Tulsa World*; May 4, 1997.) — **BG**

reasonable ▶ **adjective 1** *a reasonable man | a reasonable explanation* **sensible,** rational, logical, fair, fair-minded, just, equitable; intelligent, wise, levelheaded, practical, realistic; sound, reasoned, well-reasoned, valid, commonsensical; tenable, plausible, credible, believable.
2 *you must take all reasonable precautions* **within reason,** practicable, sensible; appropriate, suitable.
3 *cars in reasonable condition* **fairly good,** acceptable, satisfactory, average, adequate, fair, all right, tolerable, passable; informal OK.
4 *reasonable prices* **inexpensive,** moderate, low, cheap, budget, bargain, downmarket; competitive.

reasoned ▶ **adjective** *you have drawn a reasoned conclusion* **logical,** rational, well-thought-out, clear, lucid, coherent, cogent, well-expressed, well-presented, considered, sensible.

reasoning ▶ **noun** *it is a neurological disorder that results in impaired memory and reasoning* **thinking,** reason, thought, train of thought, thought process, logic, analysis, interpretation, explanation, rationalization; reasons, rationale, arguments; formal ratiocination.

reassure ▶ **verb** *officials hope to reassure tourists in the wake of these latest storms* **put/set someone's mind at rest,** put someone at ease, encourage, inspirit, hearten, buoy up, cheer up; comfort, soothe.
ANTONYMS alarm.

rebate ▶ **noun** *a 20-percent rebate* **refund,** partial refund, repayment; discount, deduction, reduction, decrease.

rebel ▶ **noun 1** *the rebels took control of the capital* **revolutionary,** insurgent, revolutionist, mutineer, insurrectionist, insurrectionary, guerrilla, terrorist, freedom fighter.
2 *the concept of the artist as a rebel* **nonconformist,** dissenter, dissident, iconoclast, maverick.
▶ **verb 1** *the citizens rebelled* **revolt,** mutiny, riot, rise up, take up arms, stage/mount a rebellion, be insubordinate.
2 *his stomach rebelled at the thought of food* **recoil,** show/feel repugnance.
3 *teenagers* ***rebelling against*** *their parents* **defy,** disobey, refuse to obey, kick against, challenge, oppose, resist.
ANTONYMS obey.
▶ **adjective 1** *rebel troops* **insurgent,** revolutionary, mutinous, rebellious, insurrectionary, insurrectionist, renegade.
2 *rebel clergymen* **rebellious,** defiant, disobedient, insubordinate, subversive, resistant, recalcitrant; nonconformist, maverick, iconoclastic; archaic contumacious.
ANTONYMS compliant, conformist.

rebellion ▶ **noun 1** *troops suppressed the rebellion* **uprising,** revolt, insurrection, mutiny, revolution, insurgence, insurgency; rioting, riot, disorder, unrest. See note at **UPRISING**.

2 *an act of rebellion* **defiance,** disobedience, rebelliousness, insubordination, subversion, subversiveness, resistance.

rebellious ▶ **adjective 1** *rebellious troops* **rebel,** insurgent, mutinous, mutinying, rebelling, rioting, riotous, insurrectionary, insurrectionist, revolutionary.
2 *a rebellious adolescent* **defiant,** disobedient, insubordinate, unruly, mutinous, wayward, obstreperous, recalcitrant, intractable; formal refractory; archaic contumacious.

rebound ▶ **verb 1** *the ball rebounded off the wall* **bounce,** bounce back, spring back, ricochet, boomerang, carom.
2 *finally the dollar rebounded* **recover,** rally, pick up, make a recovery.
3 *Thomas's tactics rebounded on him* **backfire,** boomerang, have unwelcome repercussions; come back to haunt; archaic redound on.

rebuff ▶ **verb** *his offer was rebuffed* **reject,** turn down, spurn, refuse, decline, repudiate; snub, slight, repulse, repel, dismiss, brush off, give someone the cold shoulder; informal give someone the brush-off, give someone the bum's rush, freeze out.
ANTONYMS accept.
▶ **noun** *the rebuff did little to dampen his ardor* **rejection,** snub, slight, repulse; refusal, spurning, cold-shouldering, discouragement; informal brush-off, kick in the teeth, slap in the face.

rebuke ▶ **verb** *she never rebuked him in front of others* **reprimand,** reproach, scold, admonish, reprove, chastise, upbraid, berate, take to task, criticize, censure; informal tell off, give someone a talking-to, give someone a dressing-down, give someone an earful, chew out, ream out; formal castigate.
ANTONYMS praise.
▶ **noun** *Damian was silenced by the rebuke* **reprimand,** reproach, reproof, scolding, admonishment, admonition, upbraiding; informal dressing-down; formal castigation.
ANTONYMS compliment.

CHOOSE THE RIGHT WORD

rebuke, admonish, censure, reprimand, reproach, scold

All of these verbs mean to criticize or express disapproval, but which one you use depends on how upset you are. If you want to go easy on someone, you can **admonish** or **reproach**, both of which indicate mild and sometimes kindly disapproval. To *admonish* is to warn or counsel someone, usually because a duty has been forgotten or might be forgotten in the future (*admonish her about leaving the key in the lock*), while *reproach* also suggests mild criticism aimed at correcting a fault or pattern of misbehavior (*he was reproved for his lack of attention in class*). If you want to express your disapproval formally or in public, use **censure** or **reprimand**. You can *censure* someone either directly or indirectly (*the judge censured the lawyer for violating courtroom procedures; a newspaper article that censured "deadbeat dads"*), while *reprimand* suggests a direct confrontation (*reprimanded by his parole officer for leaving town without reporting his whereabouts*). If you're irritated enough to want to express your disapproval quite harshly and at some length, you can **scold** (*to scold a child for jaywalking*). **Rebuke** is the harshest word of this group, meaning to criticize sharply or sternly, often in the midst of some action (*rebuke a carpenter for walking across an icy roof*).

rebut ▶ **verb** *you will have your opportunity to rebut the allegations* **deny,** contradict, controvert, repudiate, counter, attempt to refute, attempt to discredit; informal poke holes in; formal gainsay.
ANTONYMS confirm.

USAGE

rebut, refute

Rebut means "attempt to refute." *Refute* means "defeat (countervailing arguments)." Thus one who *rebuts* certainly hopes to *refute*; it is immodest to assume, however, that one has *refuted* another's arguments. See also note at refute.

Rebut is sometimes wrongly written *rebutt*.
— BG

recalcitrant ▶ **adjective** *Amy was unprepared to deal with three recalcitrant stepchildren* **uncooperative,** intractable, obstreperous, truculent, insubordinate, defiant, rebellious, willful, wayward, headstrong, self-willed, contrary, perverse, difficult; formal refractory; archaic froward, contumacious.
ANTONYMS amenable.

recall ▶ **verb 1** *he recalled his student days* **remember,** recollect, call to mind; think back on/to, look back on, reminisce about.
ANTONYMS forget.
2 *their exploits recall the days of chivalry* **bring to mind,** call to mind, put one in mind of, call up, conjure up, evoke.
3 *the ambassador was recalled* **summon back,** order back, call back.
ANTONYMS prorogue.
▶ **noun 1** *the recall of the ambassador* **summoning back,** ordering back, calling back.
2 *their recall of dreams* **recollection,** remembrance, memory.

recant ▶ **verb 1** *he was forced to recant his political beliefs* **renounce,** disavow, deny, repudiate, renege on; formal forswear, abjure.
2 *he refused to recant* **change one's mind,** be apostate; rare tergiversate.
3 *he recanted his testimony* **retract,** take back, withdraw, unsay.

USAGE

recant, recount

Recant = publicly repudiate a previous statement, belief, or accusation. *Recount* = narrate a past event, esp. from personal experience. *Recant* sometimes erroneously displaces the similar-sounding *recount*—e.g.: "Dressed in a top hat and tails, Garrett chats with his riders and recants [read *recounts*] tales of Weston's glory days." (*Des Moines Register*; May 19, 2002.) The *Oxford English Dictionary* does give "recount" as one sense of *recant* but labels it obsolete and rare. The most recent example is from 1611.

Recant is best reserved for use with personal statements and public positions (think *cant* = sing). Other words are better suited when the thing taken back is something other than words—e.g.:

- "The state's consumer counsel has asked state regulators to recant [read *reverse*] a recent decision under which she said Yankee Gas ratepayers would bear all of the costs of the company's proposed multimillion-dollar system expansion." (*Hartford Courant*; Feb. 14, 2002.)
- "Why do I feel like I'm listening to a deathbed confession by someone who's been a bastard all his life and suddenly, at the 11th hour, is terrified and wants to recant [read *make up for* or *renounce*?] his evil ways?" (*Daily News Leader* [Staunton, VA]; Mar. 5, 2002.)

Recant may be transitive (as in the first use in the following example) or intransitive (as in the second): "Police have a follow-up interview scheduled with Olowokandi's former girlfriend, Suzanne Ketcham, who says she plans to recant her original statements to them and a representative of the district attorney's special victims unit. 'It's not unusual for victims of domestic abuse to recant,' Nilsson said." (*Los Angeles Times*; Dec. 7, 2001.) — **BG**

recapitulate ▶ verb *I will recapitulate the main points* **summarize,** sum up; restate, repeat, reiterate, go over, review; informal recap.

recede ▶ verb **1** *the floodwaters receded* **retreat,** go back, go down, move back, move away, withdraw, ebb, subside, abate.
ANTONYMS advance, approach.
2 *the lights receded into the distance* **disappear from view,** fade, be lost to view, pass from sight.
3 *fears of violence have receded* **diminish,** lessen, decrease, dwindle, fade, abate, subside, ebb, wane.
ANTONYMS intensify, grow.

receipt ▶ noun **1** *the receipt of a letter* **receiving,** getting, obtaining, gaining; arrival, delivery.
2 *make sure you get a receipt* **proof of purchase,** bill, bill of sale, invoice, sales ticket.
3 *receipts from house sales* **proceeds,** takings, money/payment received, income, revenue, earnings; profits, return(s), financial return(s), take.

receive ▶ verb **1** *Toni received an award | they received $650 in damages* **be given,** be presented with, be awarded, collect, garner; get, obtain, gain, acquire; win, be paid, earn, gross, net.
ANTONYMS give, present.
2 *she received a letter* **be sent,** be in receipt of, accept delivery of, accept.
ANTONYMS send.
3 *Alec received the news on Monday* **be told,** be informed of, be notified of, hear, discover, find out (about), learn; informal get wind of.
4 *he received her suggestion with a complete lack of interest* **hear,** listen to; respond to, react to.
5 *she received a serious injury* **experience,** sustain, undergo, meet with; suffer, bear.
6 *they received their guests* **greet,** welcome, say hello to.
7 *she's not receiving visitors* **entertain,** see.

recent ▶ adjective **1** *recent research* **new,** (the) latest, current, fresh, modern, contemporary, up-to-date, up-to-the-minute.
ANTONYMS old.
2 *his recent visit* **not long past,** occurring recently, just gone.
ANTONYMS former.

recently ▶ adverb *they recently installed a new flagpole* **not long ago,** a short time ago, in the past few days/weeks/months, a little while back; lately, latterly, just now.

receptacle ▶ noun *a receptacle for recycling* **container,** holder, repository; box, tin, bin, can, canister, case, bag.

reception ▶ noun **1** *the reception of the goods* **receipt,** receiving, getting.
2 *the reception of foreign diplomats* **greeting,** welcoming, entertaining.
3 *a chilly reception* **response,** reaction, treatment.
4 *a wedding reception* (**formal**) **party,** function, social occasion, soirée, fête, levee; informal do, bash.

receptive ▶ adjective *a receptive audience* **open-minded,** responsive, amenable, well-disposed, flexible, approachable, accessible; archaic susceptive.
ANTONYMS unresponsive.

recess ▶ noun **1** *two recesses fitted with bookshelves* **alcove,** bay, niche, nook, corner, hollow, oriel.
2 (**recesses**) *the deepest recesses of the castle* **innermost parts/reaches,** remote places, secret places, heart, depths, bowels.
3 *the Christmas recess* **adjournment,** break, interlude, interval, rest; vacation, holiday; informal breather.
▶ verb *let's recess for lunch* **adjourn,** take a recess, stop, pause, break, take a break; informal take five, take a time out.

recession ▶ noun *job losses are symptomatic of the recession* **economic decline,** downturn, depression, slump, slowdown.
ANTONYMS boom.

recipe ▶ noun **1** *a tasty recipe* **cooking instructions/directions**; archaic receipt.
2 *a recipe for success* **means/way of achieving,** prescription, formula, blueprint.

reciprocal ▶ adjective **1** *reciprocal love* **given/felt in return,** requited, reciprocated.
2 *reciprocal obligations and duties* **mutual,** common, shared, joint, corresponding, complementary.

reciprocate ▶ verb **1** *I was happy to reciprocate*

do the same (in return), respond in kind, return the favor.
2 *love that was not reciprocated* **requite,** return, give back; match, equal.

recital ▶ **noun 1** *a piano recital* **concert,** performance, musical performance, solo performance, solo; informal gig.
2 *her recital of Bob's failures* **enumeration,** list, litany, catalog, listing, detailing; account, report, description, recapitulation, recounting.
3 *a recital of the Lord's Prayer* See RECITATION (sense 1).

recitation ▶ **noun 1** *the recitation of his poem* **recital,** saying aloud, declamation, rendering, rendition, delivery, performance.
2 *a recitation of her life story* **account,** description, narration, narrative, story.
3 *songs and recitations* **reading,** passage; poem, verse, monologue.

recite ▶ **verb 1** *he began to recite verses of the Koran* **repeat from memory,** say aloud, declaim, quote, deliver, render.
2 *he stood up and started reciting* **give a recitation,** say a poem.
3 *Sir John recited the facts they knew* **enumerate,** list, detail, reel off; recount, relate, describe, narrate, give an account of, recapitulate, repeat.

reckless ▶ **adjective** *reckless driving* **rash,** careless, thoughtless, heedless, unheeding, hasty, overhasty, precipitate, precipitous, impetuous, impulsive, daredevil, devil-may-care; **irresponsible,** foolhardy, audacious, overadventurous; ill-advised, injudicious, madcap, imprudent, unwise, ill-considered; informal kamikaze; literary temerarious.
ANTONYMS careful.

reckon ▶ **verb 1** *the cost was reckoned at $6,000* **calculate,** compute, peg, work out, put a figure on, figure; count (up), add up, total; chiefly Brit. tot up.
2 *Anselm reckoned Hugh among his friends* **include,** count, consider to be, regard as, look on as.
3 informal *I reckon I can manage that* **believe,** think, be of the opinion/view, be convinced, dare say, imagine, guess, suppose, consider, figure.
4 *it was reckoned a failure* **regard as,** consider, judge, hold to be, think of as; deem, rate, gauge, count.
5 *I* ***reckon to*** *get good value for money* **expect to,** anticipate, hope to, be looking to; count on, rely on, depend on, bank on, figure on.
– PHRASES **to be reckoned with** *the competition is indeed a force to be reckoned with* **important,** of considerable importance, significant; influential, estimable, powerful, strong, potent, formidable, redoubtable. **reckon with 1** *it's her mother you'll have to reckon with* **deal with,** contend with, face, face up to. **2** *they hadn't reckoned with her burning ambition* **take into account,** take into consideration, bargain for/on, anticipate, foresee, be prepared for, consider.

reckoning ▶ **noun 1** *by my reckoning, this comes to $2 million* **calculation,** estimation, count, computation, working out, summation, addition.
2 *by her reckoning, the train was late* **opinion,** view, judgment, evaluation, estimate, estimation.
3 *the terrible reckoning that he deserved* **retribution,** fate, doom, nemesis, punishment.
– PHRASES **day of reckoning** *I promise you, the enemy will remember this as their day of reckoning* **judgment day,** day of retribution, doomsday, D-Day.

reclaim ▶ **verb 1** *traveling expenses can be reclaimed* **get back,** recoup, claim back, recover, regain, retrieve. See note at RECOVER.
2 *Henrietta had reclaimed him from a life of despair* **save,** rescue, redeem; reform.

recline ▶ **verb** *recline on the sofa* **lie,** lie down, lie back, lean back; be recumbent; relax, repose, loll, lounge, sprawl, stretch out; literary couch.

recluse ▶ **noun 1** *a religious recluse* **hermit,** ascetic, eremite, marabout; historical anchorite, anchoress.
2 *a natural recluse* **loner,** solitary, lone wolf, troglodyte; misanthrope; rare solitudinarian, solitarian.

recognition ▶ **noun 1** *there was no sign of recognition on his face* **identification,** recollection, remembrance.
2 *his recognition of his lack of experience* **acknowledgment,** acceptance, admission; realization, awareness, consciousness, knowledge, appreciation; formal cognizance.
3 *the sport has finally received the recognition it deserves* **official approval,** certification, accreditation, endorsement, validation.
4 *you deserve recognition for the tremendous job you are doing* **appreciation,** gratitude, thanks, congratulations, credit, commendation, acclaim, acknowledgment; informal bouquets.

recognize ▶ **verb 1** *Hannah recognized him at once* **identify,** place, know, put a name to; remember, recall, recollect; know by sight.
2 *they recognized Alan's ability* **acknowledge,** accept, admit; realize, be aware of, be conscious of, perceive, discern, appreciate; formal be cognizant of.
3 *psychotherapists who are recognized officially* **approve,** certify, accredit, endorse, sanction, validate.
4 *the board recognized their hard work* **pay tribute to,** show appreciation of/for, appreciate, be grateful for, acclaim, commend.

recoil ▶ **verb 1** *she instinctively recoiled* **draw back,** jump back, pull back; flinch, shy away, shrink (back). See note at WINCE.
2 *he recoiled from the thought* **feel revulsion at,** feel disgust at, be unable to stomach, shrink from, balk at.
3 *her rifle recoiled* **kick (back),** jerk back, spring back.
4 *this will eventually* ***recoil on*** *him* **have an adverse effect on,** rebound on, affect badly, backfire on, boomerang on, come back to haunt; archaic redound on.
▶ **noun** *the recoil of the gun* **kickback,** kick.

recollect ▶ **verb** *we recollected many events from our childhood* **remember,** recall, call to mind, think of; think back to, look back on, reminisce about.

ANTONYMS forget.

recollection ▶ noun *according to my recollection, he was wearing a striped necktie* **memory,** remembrance, impression, reminiscence.

recommend ▶ verb **1** *her former employer recommended her for the post* **advocate,** endorse, commend, suggest, put forward, propose, nominate, put up; speak favorably of, speak well of, put in a good word for, vouch for; informal plug.
2 *the committee recommended a cautious approach* **advise,** counsel, urge, exhort, enjoin, prescribe, argue for, back, support; suggest, advocate, propose.
3 *there was little to recommend her* **have in one's favor,** give an advantage to; informal have going for one.

recommendation ▶ noun **1** *the advisory group's recommendations* **advice,** counsel, guidance, direction, suggestion, proposal.
2 *a personal recommendation* **commendation,** endorsement, good word, favorable mention, testimonial; suggestion, tip; informal plug.
3 *a place whose only recommendation is that it has few traffic problems* **advantage,** good point/feature, benefit, asset, boon, attraction, appeal.

reconcile ▶ verb **1** *the news reconciled us* **reunite,** bring (back) together (again), restore friendly relations between, make peace between; pacify, appease, placate, mollify; formal conciliate.
ANTONYMS estrange, alienate.
2 *her divorced parents have reconciled* **settle one's differences,** make (one's) peace, make up, kiss and make up, bury the hatchet, declare a truce.
ANTONYMS quarrel.
3 *trying to reconcile his religious beliefs with his career* **make compatible,** harmonize, square, make congruent, balance; rare syncretize.
4 *the quarrel was reconciled* **settle,** resolve, sort out, mend, remedy, heal, rectify; informal patch up.
5 *they had to **reconcile themselves to** drastic losses* **accept,** come to accept, resign oneself to, come to terms with, learn to live with, get used to.

reconciliation ▶ noun **1** *the reconciliation of the disputants* **reuniting,** reunion, bringing together (again), conciliation, reconcilement, rapprochement, fence-mending; pacification, appeasement, placating, mollification.
2 *a reconciliation of their differences* **resolution,** settlement, settling, resolving, mending, remedying.
3 *there was little hope of reconciliation* **agreement,** compromise, understanding, peace; formal concord.
4 *the reconciliation of theory with practice* **harmonizing,** harmonization, squaring, balancing.

recondite ▶ adjective *the recondite realms of Semitic philology* **obscure,** abstruse, arcane, esoteric, recherché, profound, difficult, complex, complicated, involved; incomprehensible, unfathomable, impenetrable, cryptic, opaque. See note at OBSCURE.

reconnaissance ▶ noun *unfortunately, our latest reconnaissance has uncovered no new information* **preliminary survey,** survey, exploration, observation, investigation, examination, inspection; patrol, search; reconnoitering; informal recon.

reconnoiter ▶ verb *two of our best pilots were sent in to reconnoiter the area* **survey,** make a reconnaissance of, explore; investigate, examine, scrutinize, inspect, observe, take a look at; patrol; informal check out, scope out, recon.

reconsider ▶ verb *the plaintiff has asked an appeals court to reconsider its decision to order a new trial* **rethink,** review, revise, reexamine, reevaluate, reassess, reappraise; change, alter, modify; have second thoughts, change one's mind.

reconstruct ▶ verb **1** *the building had to be reconstructed* **rebuild,** restore, renovate, recreate, remake, reassemble, remodel, refashion, revamp, recondition, refurbish.
2 *reconstructing the events of that day* **recreate,** build up a picture/impression of, piece together, reenact.

record ▶ noun **1** *written records of the past* **account**(s), document(s), documentation, data, file(s), dossier(s), evidence, report(s); annal(s), archive(s), chronicle(s); minutes, transactions, proceedings, transcript(s); certificate(s), instrument(s), deed(s); register, log, logbook; Law muniment(s).
2 *listening to records* album, vinyl; dated phonograph record, LP, single, forty-five, seventy-eight.
3 *the judge weighed the factor of his good record* **previous conduct/performance,** track record, history, life history, reputation.
4 *she's got armed robbery on her record* **criminal record,** police record; informal rap sheet.
5 *she won the race and set a new record* **best performance,** highest achievement; best time, fastest time; world record.
6 *a lasting record of what they have achieved* **reminder,** memorial, souvenir, memento, remembrance, testament.
▶ adjective *record profits* **record-breaking,** best ever, unsurpassed, unparalleled, unequaled, second to none.
▶ verb **1** *the doctor recorded her blood pressure* **write down,** put in writing, take down, note, make a note of, jot down, put down on paper; document, put on record, enter, register, log; list, catalog.
2 *the thermometer recorded a high temperature* **indicate,** register, show, display.
3 *the team recorded their fourth win* **achieve,** accomplish, chalk up, notch up.
4 *the recital was recorded live* **make a record/recording of,** tape, tape-record; video-record, videotape, video.
– PHRASES **off the record 1** *his comments were off the record* **unofficial,** confidential, in (strict) confidence, not to be made public.
2 *they admitted, off the record, that they had made a mistake* **unofficially,** privately, in

(strict) confidence, confidentially, between ourselves.

recorder ▶ noun **1** *he put a cassette in the recorder* tape recorder, cassette recorder; VCR, videocassette recorder, videotape recorder; DVD recorder, digital recorder.
2 *a recorder of rural life* **record keeper,** archivist, annalist, diarist, chronicler, historian; rare chronologer, chronologist.

recount ▶ verb *Gretchen recounted everything she could remember about what happened that night* **tell,** relate, narrate, give an account of, describe, report, outline, delineate, relay, convey, communicate, impart. See note at RECANT.

recoup ▶ verb *the construction cost was extremely high, but most of that will be recouped through lower operating costs* **get back,** regain, recover, win back, retrieve, redeem. See note at RECOVER.

> USAGE
>
> **recoup, recuperate**
>
> *Recoup*, dating from the fifteenth century as an English word, is a transitive verb with two senses: (1) "get back (lost money, etc.)"; or (2) "pay back (money owed, etc.)." Although sense 2 is older, sense 1 is now predominant. *Recuperate*, dating from the mid-sixteenth century, is almost always an intransitive verb with the sense "get well; regain one's strength after a medical procedure or an illness." The misuse of *recoup* for *recuperate* is not uncommon—e.g.: "Still recouping [read *recuperating*] from foot surgery and planning to strike a long-term performance deal in Las Vegas for early next year, Cassidy kicked back and watched hours of rare footage of the Rats in action." (*Las Vegas Review-Journal*; July 23, 1999.)
>
> A related mistake is the misspelling *recouperate*—e.g.: "Lance Diamond, the godfather of Buffalo soul, is in Mercy Hospital recouperating [read *recuperating*] from a flu-like illness." (*Buffalo News*; Nov. 30, 2000.)
>
> Another error is the misuse of *recuperate* for *recoup*—e.g.:
>
> - "The funeral provider would have to file a civil lawsuit to recuperate [read *recoup*] its money, Yabuno said." (*Press-Enterprise* [Riverside, CA]; July 19, 2000.)
> - "They have demanded a jury trial in the hopes of recuperating [read *recouping*] losses they claim are a result of 'incompetence' by the attorneys they are suing." (*South Bend Tribune*; Aug. 4, 2000.) — **BG**

recourse ▶ noun *surgery may be the only recourse* **option,** possibility, alternative, resort, way out, hope, remedy, choice, expedient.
– PHRASES **have recourse to** *we had recourse to the national committee for additional funding* **resort to,** make use of, avail oneself of, turn to, call on, look to, fall back on.

recover ▶ verb **1** *he's recovering from a heart attack* **recuperate,** get better, convalesce, regain one's strength, get stronger, get back on one's feet; be on the mend, be on the road to recovery, pick up, rally, respond to treatment, improve, heal, pull through, bounce back.
ANTONYMS deteriorate.
2 *later, shares recovered* **rally,** improve, pick up, make a recovery, rebound, bounce back.
3 *the stolen material has been recovered* **retrieve,** regain (possession of), get back, recoup, reclaim, repossess, redeem, recuperate, find (again), track down.
ANTONYMS lose.
4 *gold coins recovered from a wreck* **salvage,** save, rescue, retrieve.
– PHRASES **recover oneself** *as nervous as she was, she convincingly recovered herself* **pull oneself together,** regain one's composure, regain one's self-control; informal get a grip (on oneself).

> CHOOSE THE RIGHT WORD
>
> **recover, reclaim, recoup, regain, restore, retrieve**
>
> If you lose or let go of something and find it either by chance or with effort, you **recover** it (*recover the stolen artwork*). Although it is often used interchangeably with *recover*, **regain** puts more emphasis on the search or effort involved in getting back something you have been deprived of (*regain one's position as chairperson; regain one's eyesight*). **Recoup** refers to the recovery of something similar or equivalent to what has been lost, usually in the form of compensation (*he tried to recoup his gambling losses*). **Reclaim** and **restore** both involve bringing something back to its original condition or to a better or more useful state. *Reclaim* is usually associated with land (*reclaim neglected farmlands*), while *restore* is linked to buildings or objects of art (*restore an eighteenth-century house*). **Retrieve** implies that something has slipped beyond reach, and that a concerted effort or search is required to recover it (*her desperate efforts to retrieve the family dog from the flooded house*).

recovery ▶ noun **1** *her recovery may be slow* **recuperation,** convalescence.
ANTONYMS relapse.
2 *the economy was showing signs of recovery* **improvement,** rallying, picking up, upturn, upswing.
ANTONYMS deterioration.
3 *the recovery of the stolen goods* **retrieval,** regaining, repossession, getting back, reclamation, recouping, redemption, recuperation.
ANTONYMS loss.

recreation ▶ noun **1** *she cycles for recreation* **pleasure,** leisure, relaxation, fun, enjoyment, entertainment, amusement; play, sport; informal R and R; archaic disport.
ANTONYMS work.
2 *his favorite recreations* **pastime,** hobby,

leisure activity.

recrimination ▶ noun *this is not a time for recrimination, but a time to come together in solidarity* **accusation**(s), counteraccusation(s), countercharge(s), counterattack(s), retaliation(s).

recruit ▶ verb **1** *more soldiers were recruited* **enlist,** call up, conscript, draft, muster in; archaic levy.
2 *the king recruited an army* **muster,** form, raise, mobilize.
ANTONYMS disband.
3 *the company is recruiting staff* **hire,** employ, take on; enroll, sign up, engage.
ANTONYMS dismiss.
▶ noun **1** *thousands of recruits were enlisted* **conscript,** new soldier; draftee, yardbird.
2 *top-quality recruits* **new member,** new entrant, newcomer, initiate, beginner, novice, tenderfoot, hire; informal rookie, newbie, greenhorn.

rectify ▶ verb *Perry is willing to do anything to rectify the situation with his estranged grandfather* **correct,** right, put right, put to rights, sort out, deal with, amend, remedy, repair, fix, make good, resolve, settle; informal patch up.

rectitude ▶ noun *not all of his colleagues share his personal frugality and public rectitude* **righteousness,** goodness, virtue, morality, honor, honorableness, integrity, principle, probity, honesty, trustworthiness, uprightness, decency, good character. See note at GOODNESS.

recuperate ▶ verb **1** *Amanda went to Jackson Hole to recuperate* **get better,** recover, convalesce, get well, regain one's strength/ health, get over something.
2 *he recuperated the money* See note at RECOUP.

recur ▶ verb *we don't want the termite infestation to recur* **happen again,** reoccur, occur again, repeat (itself); come back (again), return, reappear, appear again.

recurrent ▶ adjective *a recurrent blood clot in his lung | patriotic feminism is a recurrent theme in her music* **repeated,** recurring, repetitive, periodic, cyclical, seasonal, perennial, regular, frequent; intermittent, sporadic, spasmodic.

recycle ▶ verb *the UPS Store will recycle those annoying styrofoam peanuts* **reuse,** reprocess, reclaim, recover; salvage, save.

red ▶ adjective **1** *a red dress* scarlet, vermilion, crimson, ruby, cherry, cerise, cardinal, carmine, wine, blood-red; coral, cochineal, rose; brick-red, maroon, rufous; reddish; rusty, cinnamon, fulvous; literary damask, vermeil, sanguine.
2 *he was red in the face* **flushed,** reddish, crimson, pink, pinkish, florid, rubicund; ruddy, rosy, glowing; burning, feverish; literary rubescent; archaic sanguine.
3 *his eyes were red* **bloodshot,** sore.
4 *red hair* reddish, auburn, titian, chestnut, carroty, ginger, sandy.
– PHRASES **in the red** *his account is still in the red* **overdrawn,** in debt, in debit, in deficit, in arrears. **see red** informal *when Kate showed up drunk, Julian saw red* **become very angry,** become enraged, lose one's temper; informal go mad, go crazy, go wild, go bananas, hit the roof, fly off the handle, blow one's top, flip out, go ballistic, flip one's wig, blow one's stack.

redden ▶ verb *the sleet reddened our faces | Sean could feel his cheeks redden* **turn red,** go red, make red, blush, flush, color, burn.

redeem ▶ verb **1** *the whimsical artwork redeems the book* **save,** compensate for the defects of, vindicate.
2 *he fully redeemed himself in the next race* **vindicate,** free from blame, absolve.
3 *you cannot redeem their sins* **atone for,** make amends for, make restitution for.
4 *who shall redeem these sinners?* **save,** deliver from sin, convert.
5 *Billy redeemed his drums from the pawnbrokers* **retrieve,** regain, recover, get back, reclaim, repossess; buy back.
6 *this voucher can be redeemed at any branch* **exchange,** give in exchange, cash in, convert, trade in.
7 *they could not redeem their debts* **pay off/back,** clear, discharge, honor.
8 *he made no effort to redeem his promise* **fulfill,** carry out, discharge, make good; keep, keep to, stick to, hold to, adhere to, abide by, honor.

redemption ▶ noun **1** *God's redemption of his people* **saving,** freeing from sin, absolution.
2 *the redemption of their possessions* **retrieval,** recovery, reclamation, repossession, return.
3 *the redemption of credit vouchers* **exchange,** cashing in, conversion.
4 *the redemption of the mortgage* **paying off,** paying back, discharge, clearing, honoring.
5 *the redemption of his obligations* **fulfillment,** carrying out, discharge, performing, honoring, meeting.

redolent ▶ adjective *their pubs bear names redolent of the monarchy* **evocative,** suggestive, reminiscent.

redoubtable ▶ adjective *a redoubtable army commander* **formidable,** awe-inspiring, fearsome, daunting; impressive, commanding, indomitable, invincible, doughty, mighty.

redound ▶ verb formal *such sanctions would not* ***redound to*** *their benefit internationally* **contribute to,** be conducive to, result in, lead to, effect; formal conduce to.

redress ▶ verb **1** *we redressed the problem* **rectify,** correct, right, put to rights, compensate for, amend, remedy, make good, resolve, settle.
2 *we aim to redress the balance* **even up,** regulate, equalize.
▶ noun *your best hope of redress* **compensation,** reparation, restitution, recompense, repayment, indemnity, indemnification, retribution, satisfaction; justice.

reduce ▶ verb **1** *the aim to reduce pollution* **lessen,** make smaller, lower, bring down, decrease, diminish, minimize; shrink, narrow, contract, shorten; ax, cut, cut back/down, make cutbacks in, trim, curtail, slim (down), prune; informal chop.
ANTONYMS increase.
2 *she* ***reduced*** *him* ***to*** *tears* **bring to,** bring to the point of, drive to.
3 *he was reduced to the ranks* **demote,**

downgrade, bring low, lower, lower in rank.
ANTONYMS promote.
4 *Halloween items have been reduced* **discount,** mark down, lower the price of, cut, cut in price, make cheaper, put on sale; informal slash, knock down.
ANTONYMS mark up.
– PHRASES **in reduced circumstances** *Quinlan was shocked to find his brother in reduced circumstances* **impoverished,** broke, in straitened circumstances, ruined, bankrupted; poor, indigent, impecunious, in penury, poverty-stricken, destitute; needy, badly off, hard up; informal without two cents to rub together, strapped for cash; formal penurious.

reduction ▶ noun **1** *a reduction in pollution* **lessening,** lowering, decrease, diminution, fade-out.
2 *a staff reduction* **cutback,** cut, downsizing, scaling down, trimming, pruning, axing, chopping.
3 *a reduction in inflationary pressure* **easing,** lightening, moderation, alleviation.
4 *a reduction in status* **demotion,** downgrading, lowering.
5 *substantial reductions* **discount,** markdown, deduction, cut, price cut.

redundant ▶ adjective *many churches are now redundant* **unnecessary,** not required, inessential, unessential, needless, unneeded, uncalled for; surplus, superfluous.
ANTONYMS essential, necessary.

reel ▶ verb **1** *he reeled as the ship began to roll* **stagger,** lurch, sway, rock, stumble, totter, wobble, falter.
2 *the room reeled* **go round,** go round and round, whirl, spin, revolve, swirl, twirl, turn, swim.
– PHRASES **reel something off** *she can reel off all the U.S. vice presidents in less than a minute* **recite,** rattle off, list rapidly, run through, enumerate, detail, itemize. **reeling from** *we were reeling from the crisis* **shaken by,** stunned by, in shock from, shocked by, taken aback by, staggered by, aghast at, upset by.

refer ▶ verb **1** *he **referred to** errors in the article* **mention,** make reference to, allude to, touch on, speak of/about, talk of/about, write about, comment on, deal with, point out, call attention to.
2 *the matter has been referred to my insurers* **pass,** hand over, hand, send on, transfer, remit, entrust, assign.
3 *these figures **refer to** only the year 2001* **apply to,** be relevant to, concern, relate to, be connected with, pertain to, appertain to, be pertinent to, have a bearing on, cover.
4 *the name **refers to** a native village* **denote,** describe, indicate, mean, signify, designate.
5 *the doctor **referred to** his notes* **consult,** turn to, look at, have recourse to.

referee ▶ noun **1** *the referee blew his whistle* **umpire,** judge, linesman; informal ref, ump.
2 *include the names of two referees* **supporter,** character witness, advocate.
▶ verb **1** *he refereed the game* **umpire,** judge; informal ump.
2 *they asked him to referee in the dispute* **arbitrate,** mediate.

reference ▶ noun **1** *his journal contains many **references to** railroads* **mention of,** allusion to, comment on, remark about.
2 *references are given in the bibliography* **source,** citation, authority, credit; bibliographical data.
3 *reference to a higher court* **referral,** transfer, remission.
4 *a glowing reference* **testimonial,** character reference, recommendation; credentials.
– PHRASES **with reference to** *with reference to your latest request for funding, the directors will submit their final decision on Friday* **apropos to,** with regard to, regarding, with respect to, on the subject of, re; in relation to, relating to, vis-à-vis, in connection with.

referendum ▶ noun *he called for a referendum on the death penalty* **popular vote,** vote, public vote, plebiscite, ballot, poll.

refine ▶ verb **1** *refining our cereal foods* **purify,** process, treat.
2 *helping students to refine their language skills* **improve,** perfect, polish (up), hone, fine-tune.

refined ▶ adjective **1** *refined sugar* **purified,** processed, treated.
ANTONYMS crude.
2 *a refined lady* **cultivated,** cultured, polished, stylish, elegant, sophisticated, urbane; polite, gracious, well-mannered, well-bred, gentlemanly, ladylike, genteel.
ANTONYMS boorish, coarse.
3 *a person of refined taste* **discriminating,** discerning, fastidious, exquisite, impeccable, fine.

refinement ▶ noun **1** *the refinement of sugar* **purification,** refining, processing, treatment, treating.
2 *all writing needs endless refinement* **improvement,** polishing, honing, fine-tuning, touching up, finishing off, revision, editing, reworking.
3 *a woman of refinement* **style,** elegance, finesse, polish, sophistication, urbanity; politeness, grace, graciousness, good manners, good breeding, gentility; cultivation, taste, discrimination.

reflect ▶ verb **1** *the snow reflects light* **send back,** throw back, cast back.
2 *their expressions reflected their feelings* **indicate,** show, display, demonstrate, be evidence of, register, reveal, betray, disclose; express, communicate; formal evince.
3 *he **reflected on** his responsibilities* **think about,** give thought to, consider, give consideration to, review, mull over, contemplate, cogitate about/on, meditate on, muse on, brood on/over, turn over in one's mind; archaic pore on.
– PHRASES **reflect badly on** *stunts like these reflect badly on our school* **discredit,** disgrace, dishonor, shame, put in a bad light, damage, tarnish the reputation of, give a bad name to, bring into disrepute.

reflection ▶ noun **1** *the reflection of light* **sending back,** throwing back, casting back.
2 *her reflection in the pond* **image,** mirror image, likeness.

3 *your hands and nails are a reflection of your well-being* **indication,** display, demonstration, manifestation; expression, evidence.
4 *a sad reflection on society* **slur,** aspersion, imputation, reproach, shame, criticism.
5 *after some reflection, he turned it down* **thought,** thinking, consideration, contemplation, deliberation, pondering, meditation, musing, rumination; formal cogitation.
6 *write down your reflections* **opinion,** thought, view, belief, feeling, idea, impression, conclusion, assessment; comment, observation, remark.

reflex ▶ adjective *sneezing is a reflex action* **instinctive,** automatic, involuntary, reflexive, impulsive, intuitive, spontaneous, unconscious, unconditioned, untaught, unlearned.
ANTONYMS conscious.

reform ▶ verb 1 *a plan to reform the system* **improve,** better, make better, ameliorate, refine; alter, make alterations to, change, adjust, make adjustments to, adapt, amend, revise, reshape, refashion, redesign, restyle, revamp, rebuild, reconstruct, remodel, reorganize.
2 *after his marriage he reformed* **mend one's ways,** change for the better, turn over a new leaf, improve.
▶ noun *the reform of the prison system* **improvement,** amelioration, refinement; alteration, change, adaptation, amendment, revision, reshaping, refashioning, redesigning, restyling, revamp, revamping, renovation, rebuilding, reconstruction, remodeling, reorganizing, reorganization.

refractory ▶ adjective formal *their refractory children* **obstinate,** stubborn, mulish, pigheaded, obdurate, headstrong, self-willed, wayward, willful, perverse, contrary, recalcitrant, obstreperous, disobedient, difficult; informal balky; archaic contumacious, froward.
ANTONYMS obedient.

refrain ▶ verb *the demonstrators have promised to* ***refrain from*** *violent behavior* **abstain from,** desist from, hold back from, stop oneself from, forbear (from), avoid, eschew, shun, renounce; informal swear off; formal forswear, abjure.

refresh ▶ verb 1 *the cool air will refresh me* **reinvigorate,** revitalize, revive, restore, fortify, enliven, perk up, stimulate, freshen, energize, exhilarate, reanimate, wake up, revivify, inspirit; blow away the cobwebs; informal buck up, pep up.
ANTONYMS weary.
2 *let me refresh your memory* **jog,** stimulate, prompt, prod.
3 *I refreshed his glass* **refill,** top up, replenish, recharge.

refreshing ▶ adjective 1 *a refreshing drink* **invigorating,** revitalizing, reviving, restoring, bracing, fortifying, enlivening, inspiriting, stimulating, energizing, exhilarating.
2 *a refreshing change of direction* **welcome,** stimulating, fresh, imaginative, innovative, innovatory.

refrigerate ▶ verb *don't refrigerate the bananas* **keep cold,** cool, cool down, chill; freeze.
ANTONYMS heat.

refuge ▶ noun 1 *homeless people seeking refuge in subway stations* **shelter,** protection, safety, security, asylum, sanctuary.
2 *a refuge for mountain gorillas* **sanctuary,** shelter, place of safety, haven, safe haven, sanctum; retreat, hiding place, hideaway, hideout.

refugee ▶ noun *collecting blankets for the refugees* **émigré,** fugitive, exile, displaced person, asylum seeker; (**refugees**) boat people.

refund ▶ verb 1 *we will refund your money if you're not satisfied* **repay,** give back, return, pay back.
2 *they refunded the subscribers* **reimburse,** compensate, recompense, remunerate, indemnify.
▶ noun *a full refund* **repayment,** reimbursement, rebate.

refurbish ▶ verb *the airfield plans to refurbish its museum* **renovate,** recondition, rehabilitate, revamp, overhaul, restore, renew, redevelop, rebuild, reconstruct; redecorate, spruce up, upgrade, refit, retrofit, bring up to code; informal do up, rehab.

refusal ▶ noun 1 *we had one refusal to our invitation* **nonacceptance,** no, dissent, demurral, negation, turndown; regrets.
2 *you can have first refusal* **option,** choice, opportunity to purchase.
3 *the refusal of a zoning variance* **withholding,** denial, turndown.

refuse[1] ▶ verb 1 *he refused their invitation* **decline,** turn down, say no to; reject, spurn, rebuff, dismiss; send one's regrets; informal pass up.
ANTONYMS accept.
2 *the city refused planning permission* **withhold,** deny, refuse to grant; informal give thumbs down to.
ANTONYMS grant.

refuse[2] ▶ noun *piles of refuse* **garbage,** trash, waste, debris, litter, detritus, dross; dregs, leftovers; informal junk.

regain ▶ verb 1 *government troops regained the capital* **recover,** get back, win back, recoup, retrieve, reclaim, repossess; take back, retake, recapture, reconquer. See note at RECOVER.
2 *they regained dry land* **return to,** get back to, reach again, rejoin.

regal ▶ adjective 1 *a regal feast* See SPLENDID (sense 1).
2 *his regal forebears* **royal,** kingly, queenly, princely.

regale ▶ verb 1 *they were lavishly regaled* **entertain,** wine and dine, fête, feast, serve, feed.
2 *he regaled her with colorful stories* **entertain,** amuse, divert, delight, fascinate, captivate.

regard ▶ verb 1 *we regard these results as encouraging* **consider,** look on, view, see, think of, judge, deem, estimate, assess, reckon, adjudge, rate, gauge.
2 *he regarded her coldly* **look at,** contemplate, eye, gaze at, stare at; watch, observe, view, study, scrutinize; literary behold.
▶ noun 1 *she has no regard for human life*

consideration, care, concern, thought, notice, heed, attention.
2 *doctors are held in high regard* **esteem,** respect, acclaim, admiration, approval, approbation, estimation. See note at **ESTEEM**.
3 (**regards**) *Jamie sends his regards* **best wishes,** good wishes, greetings, kind/kindest regards, felicitations, salutations, respects, compliments, best, love.
4 *his steady regard* **look,** fixed look, gaze, stare; observation, contemplation, study, scrutiny.
5 *in this regard I disagree with you* **respect,** aspect, point, item, particular, detail, specific; matter, issue, topic, question.
– PHRASES **with/in regard to** See **REGARDING**.

> USAGE
> **regard**
> As a noun in *with regard to* and *in regard to*, the singular noun is correct. The plural form (as in with regards to and in regards to) is, to put it charitably, poor usage—e.g.: "Single men and women are overwhelmed and confused by a barrage of information and advice on what to do and what not to do in regards to [read *in regard to*] finding Mr. Right and Ms. Girl-of-My-Dreams." (*Ebony*; Dec. 1997.) The acceptable forms are best used as introductory phrases. But even these may be advantageously replaced by a single word such as *concerning*, *regarding*, or *considering*, or even *in*, *about*, or *for*.
> The plural *regards* is acceptable in this sense only in the phrase *as regards*, a traditional literary idiom (though now a little old-fashioned). But some writers mistakenly use with *regards to*—e.g.: "He became furious at the mere mention of . . . the columnist who accused him recently of 'judicial exhibitionism' with regards to [read *with regard to*] his trade-agreement ruling." (*New York Times*; Sept. 17, 1993.)
> The verb *regard* commonly appears in two combinations. The one phrase, *highly regarded*, is a vague expression of praise; the other, *widely regarded as*, usually leads to words of praise—though it would certainly be possible to say that someone is "widely regarded as beneath contempt." It's a mistake, however, to truncate the latter phrase—to say *widely regarded* in place of *highly regarded*: "Crotty has published four novels since leaving the newspaper, and he's widely regarded [read *highly regarded*] by both fiction writers and journalists." **— BG**

regarding ▶ preposition *the condo commission has called a special meeting regarding pet ownership* **concerning,** as regards, with/in regard to, with respect to, with reference to, relating to, respecting, re, about, apropos, on the subject of, in connection with, vis-à-vis.

regardless ▶ adverb *he decided to go, regardless* **anyway,** anyhow, in any case, nevertheless, nonetheless, despite everything, in spite of everything, even so, all the same, in any event, come what may; informal still and all, irregardless.
– PHRASES **regardless of** *the race will be held on Saturday, regardless of the weather* **irrespective of,** without regard to, without reference to, disregarding, without consideration of, discounting, ignoring, notwithstanding, no matter.

regenerate ▶ verb *Marion's daily walks really seem to regenerate her* **revive,** revitalize, renew, restore, breathe new life into, revivify, rejuvenate, reanimate, resuscitate; informal give a shot in the arm to.

regime ▶ noun **1** *the former Communist regime* **government,** system of government, authorities, rule, authority, control, command, administration, leadership.
2 *a health regime* **system,** arrangement, order, pattern, method, procedure, routine, course, plan, program.

regiment ▶ noun *the regiment was fighting in Europe* **unit,** outfit, force, corps, division, brigade, battalion, squadron, company, platoon.
▶ verb *their life is strictly regimented* **organize,** order, systematize, control, regulate, manage, discipline.

region ▶ noun *the western region of the country* **district,** province, territory, division, area, section, sector, zone, belt, part, quarter; informal parts.
– PHRASES **in the region of** See **APPROXIMATELY**.

regional ▶ adjective **1** *regional variations* **geographical,** territorial; by region.
2 *a regional government* **local,** localized, provincial, district, parochial.
ANTONYMS national.

register ▶ noun **1** *the register of electors* **official list,** listing, roll, roster, index, directory, catalog, inventory.
2 *the parish register* **record,** chronicle, log, logbook, ledger, archive; annals, files.
3 *the lower register of the piano* **range,** reaches; notes, octaves.
▶ verb **1** *I wish to register a complaint* **record,** put on record, enter, file, lodge, write down, put in writing, submit, report, note, log.
2 *it is not too late to register* **enroll,** put one's name down, enlist, sign on, sign up, apply.
3 *the dial registered a speed of 100 mph* **indicate,** read, record, show, display.
4 *her face registered anger* **display,** show, express, exhibit, betray, evidence, reveal, manifest, demonstrate, bespeak; formal evince.
5 *the content of her statement did not register* **make an impression,** get through, sink in, penetrate, have an effect, strike home.

regress ▶ verb *he regressed to his former state of madness* **revert,** retrogress, relapse, lapse, backslide, slip back; deteriorate, decline, worsen, degenerate, get worse; informal go downhill.
ANTONYMS progress.

regret ▶ verb **1** *they came to regret their decision* **be sorry about,** feel contrite about, feel remorse about/for, be remorseful about, rue, repent (of), feel repentant about, be regretful at/about.
ANTONYMS welcome, applaud.
2 *regretting the passing of youth* **mourn,** grieve

for/over, feel grief at, weep over, sigh over, feel sad about, lament, sorrow for, deplore.

▶ noun 1 *both players later expressed regret* **remorse,** sorrow, contrition, contriteness, repentance, penitence, guilt, compunction, remorsefulness, ruefulness.
ANTONYMS satisfaction.
2 (**regrets**) *please give your grandmother my regrets* **apology,** apologies; refusal.
3 *they left with genuine regret* **sadness,** sorrow, disappointment, unhappiness, grief.
ANTONYMS happiness.

regretful ▶ adjective *when your abandoned children grow up, will they care that you claim to be regretful?* **sorry,** remorseful, contrite, repentant, rueful, penitent, conscience-stricken, apologetic, guilt-ridden, ashamed, shamefaced.
ANTONYMS unrepentant.

regrettable ▶ adjective *a regrettable mistake* **undesirable,** unfortunate, unwelcome, sorry, woeful, disappointing; deplorable, lamentable, shameful, disgraceful.

regular ▶ adjective 1 *plant them at regular intervals* **uniform,** even, consistent, constant, unchanging, unvarying, fixed.
ANTONYMS erratic.
2 *a regular beat* **rhythmic,** steady, even, uniform, constant, unchanging, unvarying.
ANTONYMS unsteady.
3 *the subject of regular protests* **frequent,** repeated, continual, recurrent, periodic, constant, perpetual, numerous.
ANTONYMS occasional.
4 *regular methods of business* **established,** conventional, orthodox, proper, official, approved, bona fide, standard, usual, traditional, tried and tested.
ANTONYMS experimental.
5 *a regular procedure* **methodical,** systematic, structured, well-ordered, well-organized, orderly, efficient.
ANTONYMS haphazard.
6 *his regular route to work* **usual,** normal, customary, habitual, routine, typical, accustomed, established. See note at **NORMAL.**
ANTONYMS unusual.

regulate ▶ verb 1 *the flow of the river has been regulated* **control,** adjust, manage.
2 *a new act regulating businesses* **supervise,** police, monitor, check, check up on, be responsible for; control, manage, direct, guide, govern.

regulation ▶ noun 1 *they obey all the regulations* **rule,** ruling, order, directive, act, law, bylaw, statute, edict, canon, pronouncement, dictate, dictum, decree, fiat, command, precept.
2 *the regulation of blood sugar* **adjustment,** control, management, balancing.
3 *the regulation of financial services* **supervision,** policing, superintendence, monitoring, inspection; control, management, ordering.

▶ adjective *regulation dress* **official,** prescribed, set, fixed, mandatory, compulsory, obligatory, de rigueur.
ANTONYMS unofficial.

rehabilitate ▶ verb 1 *efforts to rehabilitate patients* **restore to normality,** reintegrate, readapt; informal rehab.
2 *former dissidents were rehabilitated* **reinstate,** restore, bring back; pardon, absolve, exonerate, forgive; formal exculpate.
3 *rehabilitating vacant housing* **recondition,** restore, renovate, refurbish, revamp, overhaul, redevelop, rebuild, reconstruct; redecorate, spruce up; upgrade, refit, modernize; informal do up, rehab.

rehearsal ▶ noun *our first concert rehearsal is Monday evening* **practice,** practice session, trial performance, read-through, run-through, walk-through; dress rehearsal; informal dry run.

rehearse ▶ verb 1 *I rehearsed the role* **prepare,** practice, read through, run through/over, go over.
2 *he rehearsed the Vienna Philharmonic* **train,** drill, prepare, coach, put someone through their paces.
3 *the document rehearsed all the arguments* **enumerate,** list, itemize, detail, spell out, catalog, recite, rattle off; restate, repeat, reiterate, regurgitate, recapitulate, go over, run through; informal recap.

reign ▶ verb 1 *Robert II reigned for nineteen years* **be king/queen,** be monarch, be sovereign, sit on the throne, wear the crown, rule.
2 *chaos reigned* **prevail,** exist, be present, be the case, occur, be prevalent, be current, be rife, be rampant, be the order of the day, be in force, be in effect; formal obtain.

▶ noun 1 *during Henry's reign* **rule,** sovereignty, monarchy.
2 *his reign as manager* **period in office,** incumbency, managership, leadership. See note at **REIN.**

rein ▶ noun *there is no rein on his behavior* **restraint,** check, curb, constraint, restriction, limitation, control, brake.

▶ verb *they **reined back** costs* **restrain,** check, curb, constrain, hold back/in, keep under control, regulate, restrict, control, curtail, limit.

– PHRASES **free rein** *the sponsors gave the writers free rein* **freedom,** a free hand, leeway, latitude, flexibility, liberty, independence, free play, license, room to maneuver, carte blanche, a blank check. **keep a tight rein on** *he's a coach who likes to keep a tight rein on his players* **exercise strict control over,** regulate, discipline, regiment, keep in line.

USAGE

rein, reign

Like many homophones, these words are frequently mistaken for each other in print—but perhaps no other pair is confused in so many different ways. *Rein in,* not *reign in,* is the correct phrase for "check, restrain." The metaphorical image is of the rider pulling on the reins of the horse to slow down (i.e., "hold your horses")—e.g.: "With every disclosure it becomes clearer that Yeltsin is unwilling or unable to reign in [read *rein in*] his protégé." (*Times Magazine* [London]; Mar. 11, 1995.)

The error also occurs with the noun forms:

one holds the *reins*, not the *reigns*—e.g.:

- "Ron Low has a hold of the Oilers' reigns [read *reins*] for now, but should he not work out, look for former Canucks and Flyers coach Bob McCammon to take over as coach next season." (*Tampa Tribune*; Apr. 16, 1995.)
- "In other cases, the computer recommended keeping tighter reign [read *rein*] on inventory, pressing the vendor for more discounts, or raising prices." (*New York Times*; May, 20, 2001.)

The opposite error (*rein* for *reign*) occurs as well—e.g.:

- "His rein [read *reign*] as Fort Meade's tobacco-chewing, play-calling leader ended abruptly in September 1993." (*Tampa Tribune*; Sept. 1, 1995.)
- "Confusion reined [read *reigned*] when everyone within a five-mile radius was asked to evacuate." (*Houston Chronicle*; Jan. 4, 2003.) — **BG**

reinforce ▶ **verb 1** *troops reinforced the dam* **strengthen,** fortify, bolster up, shore up, buttress, prop up, underpin, brace, support.
2 *reinforcing links between colleges and companies* **strengthen,** fortify, support; cement, boost, promote, encourage, deepen, enrich, enhance, intensify, improve.
3 *the need to reinforce NATO troops* **augment,** increase, add to, supplement, boost, top up.

reinforcement ▶ **noun 1** *the reinforcement of our defenses* **strengthening,** fortification, bolstering, shoring up, buttressing, bracing.
2 *reinforcement of the bomber force* **augmentation,** increase, supplementing, boosting, topping up.
3 *they returned later with reinforcements* **additional troops,** fresh troops, auxiliaries, reserves; support, backup, help.

reiterate ▶ **verb** *he reiterated his concerns* **repeat,** say again, restate, retell, recapitulate, go over (and over), rehearse.

reject ▶ **verb 1** *the loggers rejected the offer* **turn down,** refuse, decline, say no to, spurn; informal give the thumbs down to.
ANTONYMS accept.
2 *Jamie rejected her* **rebuff,** spurn, shun, snub, repudiate, cast off/aside, discard, abandon, desert, turn one's back on, have nothing (more) to do with, wash one's hands of; informal give someone the brush-off; literary forsake.
ANTONYMS welcome.
▶ **noun 1** *a bin of factory rejects* **substandard article,** discard, second.
2 *what a reject!* **failure,** loser, incompetent.

rejection ▶ **noun 1** *a rejection of the offer* **refusal,** declining, turning down, dismissal, spurning.
2 *Madeleine's rejection of him* **repudiation,** rebuff, spurning, abandonment, desertion; informal brush-off; literary forsaking.

rejoice ▶ **verb 1** *they rejoiced when she returned* **be joyful,** be happy, be pleased, be glad, be delighted, be elated, be ecstatic, be euphoric, be overjoyed, be as pleased as punch, be jubilant, be in raptures, be beside oneself with joy, be delirious, be thrilled, be on cloud nine, be in seventh heaven; celebrate, make merry; informal be over the moon, be on top of the world; literary joy; archaic jubilate.
ANTONYMS mourn.
2 *he **rejoiced in** their success* **take delight in,** find/take pleasure in, feel satisfaction in, find joy in, enjoy, revel in, glory in, delight in, relish, savor.

rejoicing ▶ **noun** *news of the war's end unleashed a spectacle of rejoicing in the streets* **happiness,** pleasure, joy, gladness, delight, elation, jubilation, exuberance, exultation, celebration, revelry, merrymaking.

rejoinder ▶ **noun** *what serious rejoinder could I possibly offer when you make such a ludicrous accusation?* **answer,** reply, response, retort, riposte, counter; informal comeback.

relapse ▶ **verb 1** *a few patients relapse* **get ill/worse again,** have/suffer a relapse, deteriorate, degenerate, take a turn for the worse.
ANTONYMS improve.
2 *she relapsed into silence* **revert,** lapse; regress, retrogress, slip back, slide back, degenerate.
▶ **noun 1** *his sister suffered a relapse of leukemia* **deterioration,** turn for the worse, setback.
2 *a relapse into alcoholism* **decline,** lapse, deterioration, degeneration, reversion, regression, retrogression, fall, descent, slide.

relate ▶ **verb 1** *he related many stories* **tell,** recount, narrate, report, chronicle, outline, delineate, retail, recite, repeat, communicate, impart.
2 *suicide rates are **related to** unemployment levels* **connect to/with,** associate with, link to/with, correlate to/with, ally with, couple with.
3 *the charges **relate to** offenses committed in August* **apply to,** be relevant to, concern, pertain to, be pertinent to, have a bearing on, appertain to, involve.
4 *she cannot **relate to** her stepfather* **have a rapport with,** get on (well) with, sympathize with, feel for, identify with, empathize with, understand; informal hit it off with.

related ▶ **adjective 1** *related ideas* **connected,** interconnected, associated, linked, coupled, allied, affiliated, concomitant, corresponding, analogous, kindred, parallel, comparable, homologous, equivalent.
ANTONYMS unconnected.
2 *are you two related?* **of the same family,** kin, akin, kindred; formal cognate, consanguineous.
ANTONYMS unrelated.

relation ▶ **noun 1** *the relation between church and state* **connection,** relationship, association, link, correlation, correspondence, parallel, alliance, bond, interrelation, interconnection.
2 *this had no relation to national security* **relevance,** applicability, reference, pertinence, bearing.
3 *are you a relation of his? | she has relations in Pennsylvania* **relative,** member of the family, kinsman, kinswoman; (**relations**) family, kin, kith and kin, kindred.
4 (**relations**) *improving relations with China* **dealings,** communication, relationship, connections, contact, interaction.

5 *sexual relations* See **SEX** (sense 1).

relationship ▶ **noun 1** *the relationship between diet and diabetes* **connection,** relation, association, link, correlation, correspondence, parallel, alliance, bond, interrelation, interconnection.
2 *evidence of their relationship to Buffalo Bill Cody* **family ties,** family connections, blood ties, blood relationship, kinship, affinity, consanguinity, common ancestry, common lineage.
3 *the end of their relationship* **romance,** (love) affair, love, liaison, amour, partnership.

relative ▶ **adjective 1** *the relative importance of each factor* **comparative,** respective, comparable, correlative, parallel, corresponding.
2 *the food required is relative to body weight* **proportionate,** proportional, in proportion, commensurate, corresponding.
3 *relative ease* **moderate,** reasonable, a fair degree of, considerable, comparative.
▶ **noun** *he's a relative of mine* **relation,** member of someone's/the family, kinsman, kinswoman; (**relatives**) family, kin, kith and kin, kindred, kinsfolk.

relatively ▶ **adverb** *today's puzzle is relatively easy* **comparatively,** by comparison; quite, fairly, reasonably, rather, somewhat, to a (certain) degree, tolerably, passably; informal pretty, kind of, kinda, sort of.

relax ▶ **verb 1** *yoga is helpful in learning to relax* **unwind,** loosen up, ease up/off, slow down, de-stress, unbend, rest, put one's feet up, take it easy; informal unbutton, hang loose, chill, chill out, take a chill pill, take a load off.
ANTONYMS be tense.
2 *a leisurely walk will relax you* **calm,** calm down, unwind, loosen up, make less tense/uptight, soothe, pacify, compose.
3 *he relaxed his grip* **loosen,** loose, slacken, unclench, weaken, lessen.
ANTONYMS tighten.
4 *her muscles relaxed* **become less tense,** loosen, slacken, unknot.
ANTONYMS contract, tighten.
5 *they relaxed the restrictions* **moderate,** modify, temper, ease, ease up on, loosen, lighten, dilute, weaken, reduce, decrease; informal let up on.
ANTONYMS tighten up.

relaxation ▶ **noun 1** *a state of relaxation* **mental repose,** repose, calm, tranquility, peacefulness, loosening up, unwinding.
2 *I just play for relaxation* **recreation,** enjoyment, amusement, entertainment, fun, pleasure, leisure; informal R and R, downtime.
3 *muscle relaxation* **loosening,** slackening.
4 *relaxation of censorship rules* **moderation,** easing, loosening, lightening; alleviation, mitigation, dilution, weakening, reduction; informal letting up.

relay ▶ **noun** *a live relay of the performance* **broadcast,** transmission, showing, podcast, webcast, simulcast.
▶ **verb** *relaying messages through a third party* **pass on,** hand on, transfer, repeat, communicate, send, transmit, disseminate, spread, circulate.

release ▶ **verb 1** *all prisoners were released* **free,** set free, let go/out, allow to leave, liberate, set at liberty; historical manumit.
ANTONYMS imprison.
2 *Burke released the animal* **untie,** undo, loose, let go, unleash, unfetter.
ANTONYMS tie up.
3 *this released staff for other duties* **make available,** free, free up, put at someone's disposal, supply, furnish, provide.
ANTONYMS detain.
4 *she released Stephen from his promise* **excuse,** exempt, discharge, deliver, absolve; informal let off.
5 *police released the news yesterday* **make public,** make known, issue, break, announce, declare, report, reveal, divulge, disclose, publish, broadcast, circulate, communicate, disseminate.
ANTONYMS suppress, withhold.
6 *the film has been released on video* **launch,** put on the market, put on sale, bring out, make available.
▶ **noun 1** *the release of political prisoners* **freeing,** liberation, deliverance, bailout; freedom, liberty.
2 *the release of the news* **issuing,** announcement, declaration, reporting, revealing, divulging, disclosure, publication, communication, dissemination.
3 *a press release* **announcement,** bulletin, news flash, dispatch, proclamation.
4 *the hot new band's latest release* **CD,** album, single, record; video, film; book.

relent ▶ **verb 1** *the government finally relented* **change one's mind,** backpedal, do a U-turn, back down, give way/in, capitulate; become merciful, become lenient, agree to something, allow something, concede something; formal accede.
2 *the rain has relented* **ease off/up,** slacken, let up, abate, drop, die down, lessen, decrease, subside, weaken.

relentless ▶ **adjective 1** *their relentless pursuit of quality* **persistent,** continuing, constant, continual, continuous, nonstop, never-ending, unabating, interminable, incessant, unceasing, endless, unending, unremitting, unrelenting, unrelieved; unfaltering, unflagging, untiring, unwavering, dogged, tenacious, single-minded, tireless, indefatigable; formal pertinacious.
2 *a relentless taskmaster* **harsh,** grim, cruel, severe, strict, remorseless, merciless, pitiless, ruthless, unmerciful, heartless, hard-hearted, unforgiving; inflexible, unbending, uncompromising, obdurate, unyielding.

relevant ▶ **adjective** *the relevant page numbers* **pertinent,** applicable, apposite, material, apropos, to the point, germane; connected, related, linked.

reliable ▶ **adjective 1** *reliable evidence* **dependable,** good, well-founded, authentic, valid, genuine, sound, true.
2 *a reliable friend* **trustworthy,** dependable, good, true, faithful, devoted, steadfast, staunch, constant, loyal, trusty, dedicated, unfailing; truthful, honest.
ANTONYMS untrustworthy.

3 *reliable brakes* **dependable,** safe, fail-safe.
4 *a reliable company* **reputable,** dependable, trustworthy, honest, responsible, established, proven.
ANTONYMS disreputable.

reliance ▶ **noun 1** *reliance on the state* **dependence,** dependency.
2 *reliance on his own judgment* **trust,** confidence, faith, belief, conviction.

relic ▶ **noun 1** *a Viking relic* **artifact,** historical object, ancient object, antiquity, antique.
2 *a saint's relics* **remains,** corpse, bones; Medicine cadaver.

relief ▶ **noun 1** *it was such a relief to share my worries* **reassurance,** consolation, comfort, solace.
2 *the relief of pain* **alleviation,** alleviating, relieving, assuagement, assuaging, palliation, allaying, soothing, easing, lessening, reduction.
ANTONYMS intensification.
3 *relief from her burden* **freedom,** release, liberation, deliverance.
4 *a little light relief* **respite,** amusement, diversion, entertainment, jollity, jollification, recreation.
ANTONYMS solemnity.
5 *bringing relief to the starving* **help,** aid, assistance, succor, sustenance, TLC; charity, gifts, donations.
6 *his relief arrived to take over* **replacement,** substitute, deputy, reserve, cover, stand-in, supply, locum, locum tenens, understudy.
– PHRASES **throw into relief** *we hope these photos will throw into relief the gravity of their plight* **highlight,** spotlight, give prominence to, point up, show up, emphasize, bring out, stress, accent, underline, underscore, accentuate.

relieve ▶ **verb 1** *this helps relieve pain* **alleviate,** mitigate, assuage, ease, dull, reduce, lessen, diminish. See note at ALLEVIATE.
ANTONYMS aggravate.
2 *relieving the boredom* **counteract,** reduce, alleviate, mitigate; interrupt, vary, stop, dispel, prevent.
ANTONYMS exacerbate.
3 *the helpers relieved us* **replace,** take over from, stand in for, fill in for, substitute for, deputize for, cover for.
4 *this relieves the teacher of a heavy load* **free,** set free, release, exempt, excuse, absolve, let off, discharge.

religious ▶ **adjective 1** *a religious person* **devout,** pious, reverent, godly, God-fearing, churchgoing, faithful, devoted, committed.
ANTONYMS atheistic, irreverent.
2 *religious beliefs* **spiritual,** theological, scriptural, doctrinal, ecclesiastical, church, faith-based, churchly, holy, divine, sacred.
ANTONYMS secular.
3 *religious attention to detail* **scrupulous,** conscientious, meticulous, sedulous, punctilious, strict, rigorous, close.
ANTONYMS slapdash.

relinquish ▶ **verb 1** *he relinquished control of the company* **renounce,** give up/away, hand over, let go of.
ANTONYMS retain, keep.
2 *she relinquished her post* **leave,** resign from, stand down from, bow out of, give up; informal quit, chuck.
3 *he relinquished his pipe-smoking* **discontinue,** stop, cease, give up, desist from; informal quit, kick; formal forswear.
ANTONYMS continue.
4 *she relinquished her grip* **let go of,** release, loose, loosen, relax.

CHOOSE THE RIGHT WORD

relinquish, abandon, cede, surrender, waive, yield

Of all these verbs meaning to let go or give up, **relinquish** is the most general. It can imply anything from simply releasing one's grasp (*she relinquished the wheel*) to giving up control or possession reluctantly (*after the defeat, he was forced to relinquish his command*). **Surrender** also implies giving up, but usually after a struggle or show of resistance (*the villagers were forced to surrender to the guerrillas*). **Yield** is a milder synonym for *surrender,* implying some concession, respect, or even affection on the part of the person who is surrendering (*she yielded to her mother's wishes and stayed home*). **Waive** means to give up voluntarily a right or claim to something (*she waived her right to have a lawyer present*), while **cede** is to give up by legal transfer or according to the terms of a treaty (*the French ceded the territory that is now Louisiana*). If one *relinquishes* something finally and completely, often because of weariness or discouragement, the correct word is **abandon** (*they were told to abandon all hope of being rescued*).

relish ▶ **noun 1** *he dug into his food with relish* **enjoyment,** gusto, delight, pleasure, glee, rapture, satisfaction, contentment, appreciation, enthusiasm, appetite; humorous delectation.
ANTONYMS dislike.
2 *a hot relish* **condiment,** sauce, dressing, flavoring, seasoning, dip, chutney, chili sauce.
▶ **verb 1** *she was relishing her moment of glory* **enjoy,** delight in, love, adore, take pleasure in, rejoice in, appreciate, savor, revel in, luxuriate in, glory in.
2 *I don't relish the drive* **look forward to,** fancy, anticipate with pleasure.

reluctance ▶ **noun** *he said he was glad to go, but she sensed his reluctance* **unwillingness,** disinclination; hesitation, wavering, vacillation; doubts, second thoughts, misgivings.

reluctant ▶ **adjective 1** *when it came to trying something new, her parents were usually reluctant* **unwilling,** disinclined, unenthusiastic, resistant, resisting, opposed; hesitant.
ANTONYMS willing, eager.
2 *a reluctant smile* **shy,** bashful, coy, diffident, reserved, timid, timorous.
ANTONYMS eager.
3 *he was* ***reluctant to*** *leave* **loath to,** unwilling to, disinclined to, indisposed to; not in favor of,

against, opposed to.
ANTONYMS willing, eager.

rely ▶ verb **1** *we can rely on his discretion* **depend on,** count on, bank on, place reliance on, reckon on; be confident of, be sure of, believe in, have faith in, trust in; informal swear by, figure on.
2 *we rely on government funding* **be dependent on,** depend on, be unable to manage without.

remain ▶ verb **1** *the problem will remain* **continue to exist,** endure, last, abide, carry on, persist, stay, stay around, prevail, survive, live on.
2 *he remained in the hospital* **stay,** stay behind, stay put, wait, wait around, be left, hang on; informal hang around.
3 *union leaders remain skeptical* **continue to be,** stay, keep, persist in being, carry on being.
4 *the few minutes that remain* **be left,** be left over, be still available, be unused; have not yet passed.

remainder ▶ noun *the remainder of the materials should be itemized on a separate list* **residue,** balance, remaining part/number, rest, others, those left, remnant(s), surplus, extra, excess, overflow; technical residuum.

remains ▶ plural noun **1** *the remains of her drink* **remainder,** residue, remaining part/number, rest, remnant(s); technical residuum.
2 *Roman remains* **antiquities,** relics.
3 *the saint's remains* **corpse,** body, dead body, carcass; bones, skeleton; Medicine cadaver. See note at BODY.

remark ▶ verb **1** *"You're quiet," he remarked* **comment,** say, observe, mention, reflect, state, declare, announce, pronounce, assert; formal opine.
2 *many critics **remarked on** their rapport* **comment on,** mention, refer to, speak of, pass comment on.
3 *she remarked the absence of policemen* **note,** notice, observe, take note of, perceive, discern.
▶ noun **1** *his remarks have been misinterpreted* **comment,** statement, utterance, observation, declaration, pronouncement.
2 *worthy of remark* **attention,** notice, comment, mention, observation, acknowledgment.

remarkable ▶ adjective *a remarkable coincidence* **extraordinary,** exceptional, amazing, astonishing, astounding, marvelous, wonderful, sensational, stunning, incredible, unbelievable, phenomenal, outstanding, momentous; out of the ordinary, unusual, uncommon, surprising; informal fantastic, terrific, tremendous, stupendous, awesome; literary wondrous. See also note at NOTICEABLE.
ANTONYMS ordinary.

remedy ▶ noun **1** *herbal remedies* **treatment,** cure, medicine, medication, medicament, drug; archaic physic.
2 *a remedy for all kinds of problems* **solution,** answer, cure, antidote, curative, nostrum, panacea, cure-all; informal magic bullet.
▶ verb **1** *remedying the situation* **put/set right,** put/set to rights, right, rectify, solve, sort out, straighten out, resolve, correct, repair, mend, make good.
2 *anemia can be remedied by iron pills* **cure,** treat, heal, make better; relieve, ease, alleviate, palliate.

remember ▶ verb **1** *remembering happy times* **recall,** call to mind, recollect, think of; reminisce about, look back on; archaic bethink oneself of.
ANTONYMS forget.
2 *can you remember all that?* **memorize,** commit to memory, retain; learn by heart.
ANTONYMS forget.
3 *you must remember that she's only five* **bear/keep in mind,** be mindful of the fact; take into account, take into consideration.
ANTONYMS overlook.
4 *remember to feed the cat* **be sure,** be certain; mind that you, make sure that you.
ANTONYMS neglect.
5 ***remember me** to Alice* **send one's best wishes,** send one's regards, give one's love, send one's compliments, say hello.
6 *the nation remembered those who gave their lives* **commemorate,** pay tribute to, honor, salute, pay homage to.
7 *she remembered them in her will* **bequeath something to,** leave something to, bestow something on.

remembrance ▶ noun **1** *an expression of remembrance* **recollection,** reminiscence; remembering, recalling, recollecting, reminiscing.
2 *she smiled at the remembrance* **memory,** recollection, reminiscence, thought.
3 *we sold poppies in remembrance* **commemoration,** memory, recognition.
4 *a remembrance of my father* **memento,** reminder, keepsake, souvenir, memorial, token.

remind ▶ verb **1** *I left a note to remind him* **jog someone's memory,** help someone remember, prompt.
2 *the song **reminded me of** my sister* **make one think of,** cause one to remember, put one in mind of, bring/call to mind, evoke.

reminisce ▶ verb *we reminisced about Freddy's first Christmas with us* **remember,** remember with pleasure, cast one's mind back to, look back on, be nostalgic about, recall, recollect, reflect on, call to mind.

reminiscences ▶ plural noun *her reminiscences of a wartime childhood* **memories,** recollections, reflections, remembrances.

reminiscent ▶ adjective *the smell of fresh apple pies was reminiscent of the aromas from Gramma's kitchen in Middlefield* **similar to,** comparable with, evocative of, suggestive of, redolent of.

remiss ▶ adjective *I would be remiss if I did not thank my sister* **negligent,** neglectful, irresponsible, careless, thoughtless, heedless, lax, slack, slipshod, lackadaisical, derelict; informal sloppy; formal delinquent.
ANTONYMS careful.

remission ▶ noun **1** *the remission of all fees* **cancellation,** setting aside, suspension, revocation; formal abrogation.
2 *the cancer is in remission* **respite,** abeyance.
3 *the wind howled without remission* **respite,** lessening, abatement, easing, decrease,

reduction, diminution, dying down, slackening, lull; informal letup.
4 *the remission of sins* **forgiveness,** pardoning, absolution, exoneration; formal exculpation.

remit ▶ verb **1** *the fines were remitted* **cancel,** set aside, suspend, revoke; formal abrogate.
2 *remitting duties to the authorities* **send,** dispatch, forward, hand over; pay.
3 *the case was remitted to the Supreme Court* **pass (on),** refer, send (on), transfer.
4 rare *we remitted all further discussion* **postpone,** defer, put off/back, shelve, delay, suspend, table; informal put on the back burner, put on ice.
5 *remitting their sins* **pardon,** forgive; excuse.

remittance ▶ noun **1** *send the form with your remittance* **payment,** money, fee; check; formal monies.
2 *a monthly remittance* **allowance,** sum of money.

remnant ▶ noun **1** *the remnants of the picnic* **remains,** remainder, leftovers, residue, rest; technical residuum.
2 *remnants of cloth* **scrap,** piece, bit, fragment, shred, offcut, oddment. See note at TRACE.

remonstrate ▶ verb **1** *"I'm not a child!" he remonstrated* **protest,** complain, expostulate; argue with, take issue with.
2 *we remonstrated against this proposal* **object strongly to,** complain vociferously about, protest against, argue against, oppose strongly, make a fuss about, challenge; deplore, condemn, denounce, criticize; informal kick up a fuss/stink about.

remorse ▶ noun *have you no remorse for what you did to your friends?* **contrition,** deep regret, repentance, penitence, guilt, compunction, remorsefulness, ruefulness, contriteness; pangs of conscience, self-condemnation, self-reproach.

remorseful ▶ adjective *remorseful criminals* **sorry,** full of regret, regretful, contrite, repentant, penitent, guilt-ridden, conscience-stricken, guilty, chastened.
ANTONYMS unrepentant.

remote ▶ adjective **1** *areas remote from hospitals* **faraway,** distant, far, far off, far removed, extrasolar.
ANTONYMS close, near.
2 *a remote mountain village* **isolated,** out of the way, off the beaten track/path, secluded, lonely, in the back of beyond, godforsaken, inaccessible, far-flung, in the backwoods, lonesome; informal in the sticks, in the middle of nowhere.
ANTONYMS central.
3 *events* ***remote from*** *modern times* **irrelevant to,** unrelated to, unconnected to, unconcerned with, not pertinent to, immaterial to, unassociated with; foreign to, alien to.
ANTONYMS relevant.
4 *a remote possibility* **unlikely,** improbable, implausible, doubtful, dubious; faint, slight, slim, small, slender.
ANTONYMS likely, strong.
5 *she seems very remote* **aloof,** distant, detached, withdrawn, reserved, uncommunicative, unforthcoming, unapproachable, unresponsive, unfriendly, unsociable, introspective, introverted; informal standoffish.
ANTONYMS friendly, approachable.

removal ▶ noun **1** *the removal of heavy artillery* **taking away,** moving, carrying away.
ANTONYMS installation.
2 *his removal from office* **dismissal,** ejection, expulsion, ousting, displacement, deposition, ouster; informal firing, sacking.
ANTONYMS installation, appointment.
3 *the removal of customs barriers* **withdrawal,** elimination, taking away.
4 *the removal of errors in the copy* **deletion,** elimination, erasing, effacing, obliteration.
5 *the removal of weeds* **uprooting,** eradication.
6 *the removal of old branches from the tree* **cutting off,** chopping off, hacking off.
7 *her removal to the West Coast* **move,** transfer, relocation.
8 *the removal of a rival* **disposal,** elimination, killing, murder, dispatch; informal liquidation.

remove ▶ verb **1** *remove the plug* **detach,** unfasten; pull out, take out, disconnect.
ANTONYMS attach.
2 *she removed the lid* **take off,** undo, unfasten.
ANTONYMS put on.
3 *he removed a twenty from his wallet* **take out,** produce, bring out, get out, pull out, withdraw.
ANTONYMS insert.
4 *police removed boxes of documents* **take away,** carry away, move, transport; confiscate; informal cart off.
ANTONYMS put back, replace.
5 *Sheila removed the mud* **clean off,** wash off, wipe off, rinse off, scrub off, sponge out.
6 *Harry removed his coat* **take off,** pull off, slip out of, peel off; dated doff.
ANTONYMS put on, don.
7 *she was removed from her post* **dismiss,** discharge, dislodge, displace, expel, oust, depose; informal fire, sack, kick out, boot out.
ANTONYMS install, appoint.
8 *tax relief was removed* **withdraw,** abolish, eliminate, get rid of, do away with, stop, cut; informal ax.
ANTONYMS introduce.
9 *Gabriel removed two words* **delete,** erase, rub out, cross out, strike out, obliterate; informal deep-six.
ANTONYMS add.
10 *weeds have to be removed* **uproot,** pull out, eradicate.
11 *removing branches* **cut off,** chop off, lop off, hack off.

remuneration ▶ noun *you will receive adequate remuneration for the work you have done* **payment,** pay, salary, wages; earnings, fee(s), reward, compensation, recompense, reimbursement; formal emolument(s).

remunerative ▶ adjective *a remunerative position in his father's firm* **lucrative,** well-paid, financially rewarding; profitable.

renaissance ▶ noun *the renaissance of Byzantine art* **revival,** renewal, resurrection, reawakening, reemergence, rebirth, reappearance, resurgence, regeneration; formal renascence.

render ▶ verb **1** *her fury rendered her speechless* **make,** cause to be/become, leave.
2 *rendering assistance* **give,** provide, supply, furnish, contribute; offer, proffer.
3 *the invoices rendered by the accountants* **send in,** present, submit.
4 *the jury rendered its verdict* **deliver,** return, hand down, give, announce.
5 *paintings rendered in muted colors* **paint,** draw, depict, portray, represent, execute; literary limn.
6 *she rendered all three verses* **perform,** sing.
7 *the characters are vividly rendered* **act,** perform, play, depict, interpret.
8 *the phrase was rendered into English* **translate,** put, express, rephrase, reword.
9 *the fat can be rendered* **melt down,** clarify.

rendezvous ▶ noun *Eleanor was late for their rendezvous* **meeting,** appointment, assignation; informal date; literary tryst.
▶ verb *the bar where they had agreed to rendezvous* **meet,** come together, gather, assemble.

renegade ▶ noun **1** *he was denounced as a renegade* **traitor,** defector, deserter, turncoat, rebel, mutineer.
2 archaic *a religious renegade* **apostate,** heretic, dissenter.
▶ adjective **1** *renegade troops* **treacherous,** traitorous, disloyal, treasonous, rebel, mutinous.
ANTONYMS loyal.
2 *a renegade monk* **apostate,** heretic, heretical, dissident.

renege ▶ verb *he reneged on his campaign promises* **default on,** fail to honor, go back on, break, back out of, withdraw from, retreat from, welsh on, backtrack on; break one's word/promise about.
ANTONYMS honor.

renounce ▶ verb **1** *Edward renounced his claim to the throne* **give up,** relinquish, abandon, abdicate, surrender, waive, forgo; Law disclaim; formal abnegate.
ANTONYMS assert.
2 *Hungary renounced the agreement* **reject,** refuse to abide by, repudiate.
ANTONYMS abide by, accept.
3 *she renounced her family* **repudiate,** deny, reject, abandon, wash one's hands of, turn one's back on, disown, spurn, shun; literary forsake.
ANTONYMS embrace.
4 *he renounced alcohol* **abstain from,** give up, desist from, refrain from, keep off, eschew; informal quit, pack in, lay off; formal forswear.
ANTONYMS turn to.
– PHRASES **renounce the world** *you can't just renounce the world* **become a recluse,** turn one's back on society, cloister oneself, hide oneself away.

renovate ▶ verb *the hotel has been renovated* **modernize,** restore, refurbish, revamp, recondition, rehabilitate, overhaul, redevelop; update, upgrade, refit, bring something up to code; informal do up, rehab.

renown ▶ noun *born to a family of political renown* **fame,** distinction, eminence, preeminence, prominence, repute, reputation, prestige, acclaim, celebrity, notability.

renowned ▶ adjective *a renowned Indian filmmaker* **famous,** celebrated, famed, eminent, distinguished, acclaimed, illustrious, preeminent, prominent, great, esteemed, of note, of repute, well-known, well-thought-of.
ANTONYMS unknown.

rent[1] ▶ noun *I can't afford to pay the rent* **rental,** fee, lease.
▶ verb **1** *she rented a car* lease, charter.
2 *why don't you **rent it out**?* **let (out),** lease (out), hire (out); sublet, sublease.

rent[2] ▶ noun **1** *the rent in his pants* **rip,** tear, split, hole, slash, slit.
2 *a vast rent in the mountains* **gorge,** chasm, fault, rift, fissure, crevasse.

renunciation ▶ noun **1** *the queen's renunciation of her throne* **relinquishment,** giving up, abandonment, abdication, surrender, waiving, forgoing; Law disclaimer; rare abnegation.
2 *his **renunciation of** luxury* **abstention from,** refraining from, going without, giving up, eschewal of; formal forswearing of.
3 *their renunciation of terrorism* **repudiation,** rejection, abandonment; rare abjuration.

repair[1] ▶ verb **1** *the car was repaired* **mend,** fix (up), put/set right, restore, restore to working order, overhaul, service; informal patch up.
2 *they repaired the costumes* **mend,** darn; informal patch up.
3 *repairing relations with other countries* **put/set right,** mend, fix, straighten out, smooth, improve, warm up; informal patch up.
4 *she sought to repair the wrong she had done* **rectify,** make good, right, put right, correct, make up for, make amends for, make reparation for.
▶ noun **1** *in need of repair* **restoration,** fixing (up), mending, renovation; archaic reparation.
2 *an invisible repair* **mend,** darn.
3 *in good repair* **condition,** working order, state, shape, fettle.
– PHRASES **beyond repair** *the front wheel is beyond repair | their marriage appears to be beyond repair* **irreparable,** irreversible, irretrievable, irremediable, irrecoverable, past hope.

repair[2] ▶ verb formal *we **repaired to** the sitting room* **go to,** head for, adjourn to, wend one's way to; formal remove to; literary betake oneself to.

reparation ▶ noun *the victims are seeking reparation* **amends,** restitution, redress, compensation, recompense, repayment, atonement.

repartee ▶ noun *an evening of wit and repartee* **banter,** badinage, bantering, raillery, witticism(s), ripostes, sallies, quips, joking, jesting; formal persiflage. See note at **WIT**.

repast ▶ noun formal *a sumptuous repast* **meal,** feast, banquet; informal spread, feed, bite, bite to eat; formal collation, refection.

repay ▶ verb **1** *they promised to repay customers who had been cheated* **reimburse,** refund, pay back/off, recompense, compensate, indemnify.
2 *the grants have to be repaid* **pay back,** return, refund, reimburse.
3 *I'd like to repay her generosity* **reciprocate,** return, requite, recompense, reward.

repeal ▶ verb *the Eighteenth Amendment was repealed in 1933* **revoke,** rescind, cancel, reverse, annul, nullify, declare null and void, quash, abolish; Law vacate; formal abrogate; archaic recall.
ANTONYMS enact.
▶ noun *the repeal of the law* **revocation,** rescinding, cancellation, reversal, annulment, nullification, quashing, abolition; formal abrogation; archaic recall.

repeat ▶ verb 1 *she repeated her story* **say again,** restate, reiterate, go/run through again, recapitulate; informal recap.
2 *children can repeat large chunks of text* **recite,** quote, parrot, regurgitate.
3 *Steele was invited to repeat his work* **do again,** redo, replicate, rehash, duplicate.
4 *the episodes were repeated* **rebroadcast,** rerun.
▶ noun 1 *a repeat of the previous year's final* **repetition,** duplication, replication, duplicate, rehash.
2 *repeats of the classic sitcom* **rerun,** rebroadcast.
– PHRASES **repeat itself** **reoccur,** recur, occur again, happen again.

repeated ▶ adjective *his repeated complaints about the noise* **recurrent,** frequent, persistent, continual, incessant, constant; regular, periodic, numerous, many, very many.
ANTONYMS occasional.

repeatedly ▶ adverb *he tried repeatedly to hit that low note* **frequently,** often, again and again, over and over (again), time and (time) again, time after time, many times, many a time; persistently, recurrently, constantly, continually, regularly, oftentimes; literary oft, ofttimes.

repel ▶ verb 1 *the rebels were repelled* **fight off,** repulse, drive back/away, force back, beat back, push back; hold off, ward off, keep at bay; archaic rebut.
2 *the coating will repel water* **be impervious to,** be impermeable to, keep out, resist, be —— proof.
3 *the thought of kissing him repelled me* **revolt,** disgust, repulse, sicken, nauseate, turn someone's stomach, be repulsive, be distasteful, be repugnant; informal turn off, gross out.

repellent ▶ adjective 1 *a repellent stench* **revolting,** repulsive, disgusting, repugnant, sickening, nauseating, stomach-turning, nauseous, vile, nasty, foul, horrible, awful, dreadful, terrible, obnoxious, loathsome, offensive, objectionable; abhorrent, despicable, reprehensible, contemptible, odious, hateful, execrable, vomitous; informal ghastly, horrid, gross, yucky, icky, funky; literary noisome. See note at REPULSIVE.
ANTONYMS delightful.
2 *a repellent coating* **impermeable,** impervious, resistant; -proof.

repent ▶ verb *the senator claims to have repented* **feel remorse,** regret, be sorry, rue, reproach oneself, be ashamed, feel contrite; be penitent, be remorseful, be repentant.

repentance ▶ noun *her lack of repentance angered them* **remorse,** contrition, contriteness, penitence, regret, ruefulness, remorsefulness, shame, guilt.

repentant ▶ adjective *there are two repentant children in there waiting to talk to you* **penitent,** contrite, regretful, rueful, remorseful, apologetic, chastened, ashamed, shamefaced, guilt-ridden.
ANTONYMS impenitent.

repercussion ▶ noun (**repercussions**) *the political repercussions of the scandal* **consequence(s),** result(s), effect(s), outcome; reverberation(s), backlash, aftermath, fallout, tremors.

repetition ▶ noun 1 *the facts bear repetition* **reiteration,** repeating, restatement, retelling.
2 *endless repetition of passages of poetry* **repeating,** echoing, parroting.
3 *a repetition of the scene in the kitchen* **recurrence,** reoccurrence, rerun, repeat; informal déjà vu, instant replay.
4 *the author is guilty of repetition* **repetitiousness,** repetitiveness, redundancy, tautology.

repetitive ▶ adjective *repetitive tasks on the assembly line* **monotonous,** tedious, boring, humdrum, mundane, dreary, tiresome; unvaried, unchanging, unvarying, recurrent, recurring, repeated, repetitious, routine, mechanical, automatic.

replace ▶ verb 1 *Eve replaced the receiver* **put back,** return, restore.
ANTONYMS remove.
2 *a new chairman came in to replace him* **take the place of,** succeed, take over from, supersede; stand in for, substitute for, deputize for, cover for, relieve; informal step into someone's shoes/boots.
3 *she replaced the spoon with a fork* **substitute,** exchange, change, swap.

CHOOSE THE RIGHT WORD

replace, displace, supersede, supplant

When a light bulb burns out, you **replace** it, meaning that you substitute something new or functioning for what is lost, destroyed, or worn out. If something that is obsolete or ineffective is replaced by something that is superior, more up-to-date, or more authoritative, the correct verb is **supersede** (*the computer superseded the electric typewriter*). In contrast, **displace** suggests that someone or something has been ousted or dislodged forcibly, without necessarily implying that it was inferior or ineffective (*a growing number of workers were being displaced by machines*). **Supplant** is more restricted in meaning; it suggests displacement by force, fraud, or innovation (*the democratic government had been supplanted by a power-hungry tyrant*). It can also mean to uproot or wipe out (*the English immigrants gradually supplanted the island's native inhabitants*).

replacement ▶ noun 1 *we have to find a*

replacement **successor**; **substitute,** stand-in, locum, relief, cover.
2 *the wiring was in need of replacement* **renewal,** replacing.

replenish ▶ **verb 1** *she replenished their glasses* **refill,** top up, fill up, recharge, freshen.
ANTONYMS empty.
2 *their supplies were replenished* **restock,** stock up, restore, replace.
ANTONYMS use up, exhaust.

replete ▶ **adjective 1** *the guests were replete* **well-fed,** sated, satiated, full, full up; glutted, gorged; informal stuffed.
2 *a sumptuous environment replete with antiques* **filled,** full, well-stocked, well-supplied, crammed, packed, jammed, teeming, overflowing, bursting; informal jam-packed, chockablock, chock-full.

replica ▶ **noun 1** *is it real or a replica?* **copy,** carbon copy, model, duplicate, reproduction, replication; dummy, imitation, facsimile; informal knockoff.
2 *a replica of her mother* **perfect likeness,** double, look-alike, mirror image, living image, picture, twin, clone, doppelgänger; informal spitting image, dead ringer, ringer.

reply ▶ **verb** *Rachel didn't bother to reply* **answer,** respond, come back, write back, retort, riposte, counter.
▶ **noun** *"Why would we lie?" she replied* **answer,** response, rejoinder, retort, riposte; informal comeback.

report ▶ **verb 1** *the government reported a fall in inflation* **announce,** describe, give an account of, detail, outline, communicate, divulge, disclose, reveal, make public, publish, broadcast, proclaim, publicize.
2 *the newspapers* ***reported on*** *the scandal* **cover,** write about, describe, give details of, commentate on; investigate, look into, inquire into.
3 *I reported him to the police* **inform on,** tattle on; informal tell on, squeal on, rat on.
4 *Juliet reported for duty* **present oneself,** arrive, turn up, clock in, sign in, punch in; informal show up.
▶ **noun 1** *a full report on the meeting* **account,** review, record, description, statement; transactions, proceedings, transcripts, minutes.
2 *reports of drug dealing* **news,** information, word, intelligence; literary tidings.
3 *newspaper reports* **story,** account, article, piece, item, column, feature, bulletin, dispatch.
4 *a school report* **assessment,** report card, evaluation, appraisal.
5 *reports of his imminent resignation* **rumor,** whisper; informal buzz; archaic bruit.
6 *the report of a gun* **bang,** blast, crack, shot, gunshot, explosion, boom.

reporter ▶ **noun** *my client has been instructed not to talk to reporters* **journalist,** correspondent, newspaperman, newspaperwoman, newsman, newswoman, columnist, pressman; informal newshound, hack, stringer, journo, newsie.

repose ▶ **noun 1** *a face in repose* **rest,** relaxation, inactivity; sleep, slumber.
2 *they found true repose* **peace,** peace and quiet, peacefulness, quiet, quietness, calm, tranquility.
3 *he lost his repose* **composure,** serenity, equanimity, poise, self-possession, aplomb.
▶ **verb 1** *the diamond reposed on a bed of velvet* **lie,** rest, be placed, be situated.
2 *the trust he had reposed in her* **put,** place, invest, entrust.
3 *the beds where we reposed* **lie,** lie down, recline, rest, sleep; literary slumber.

repository ▶ **noun** *a repository for nuclear fuel | he's a veritable repository of musical knowledge* **store,** storehouse, depository; reservoir, bank, cache, treasury, fund, mine.

reprehensible ▶ **adjective** *his conduct was reprehensible* **deplorable,** disgraceful, discreditable, despicable, blameworthy, culpable, wrong, bad, shameful, dishonorable, objectionable, opprobrious, repugnant, inexcusable, unforgivable, indefensible, unjustifiable; criminal, sinful, scandalous, iniquitous; formal exceptionable.
ANTONYMS praiseworthy.

represent ▶ **verb 1** *a character representing a single quality* **symbolize,** stand for, personify, epitomize, typify, embody, illustrate.
2 *the initials that represent her qualification* **stand for,** designate, denote; literary betoken.
3 *Hathor is represented as a woman with cow's horns* **depict,** portray, render, picture, delineate, show, illustrate; literary limn.
4 *he represented himself as the owner of the factory* **describe as,** present as, profess to be, claim to be, pass oneself off as, pose as, pretend to be.
5 *aging represents a threat to one's independence* **constitute,** be, amount to, be regarded as.
6 *a panel representing a cross section of the public* **be a typical sample of,** be representative of, typify.
7 *her lawyer represented her in court* **appear for,** act for, speak on behalf of; informal go to bat for.
8 *the governor general represented the royal family* **deputize for,** substitute for, stand in for.
9 formal *I represented the case as I saw it* **point out,** state, present, put forward.

representation ▶ **noun 1** *Rossetti's representation of women* **portrayal,** depiction, delineation, presentation, rendition.
2 *representations of the human form* **likeness,** painting, drawing, picture, illustration, sketch, image, model, figure, figurine, statue, statuette.
3 formal *making representations to the council* **statement,** deposition, allegation, declaration, exposition, report, protestation.

representative ▶ **adjective 1** *a representative sample* **typical,** prototypical, characteristic, illustrative, archetypal.
ANTONYMS atypical.
2 *the red maple leaf is representative of Canada* **symbolic,** emblematic, evocative.
3 *representative government* **elected,** elective, chosen, democratic, popular.
ANTONYMS totalitarian.
▶ **noun 1** *a representative of Greenpeace* **spokesperson,** spokesman, spokeswoman, agent, official, mouthpiece.

2 *one of our representatives will show you our new line of pop-up books* **salesperson,** salesman, saleswoman, agent; informal rep.
3 *the Cambodian representative at the UN* **delegate,** commissioner, ambassador, attaché, envoy, emissary, chargé d'affaires, deputy.
4 *contact your representatives and urge them to protect our wetlands* **legislator,** lawmaker; senator, congressman, congresswoman, member of Congress, alderman, alderwoman, alderperson, selectman, selectwoman, lawmaker; voice.
5 *he acted as his father's representative* **deputy,** substitute, stand-in, proxy.
6 *fossil representatives of lampreys* **example,** specimen, exemplar, exemplification.

repress ▶ **verb 1** *the rebellion was repressed* **suppress,** quell, quash, subdue, put down, crush, extinguish, stamp out, defeat, conquer, rout, overwhelm, contain.
2 *the peasants were repressed* **oppress,** subjugate, keep down, rule with a rod of iron, rule with an iron fist, intimidate, tyrannize, crush.
3 *these emotions may well be repressed* **restrain,** hold back/in, keep back, suppress, keep in check, control, keep under control, curb, stifle, bottle up; informal button up, keep the lid on.

repressed ▶ **adjective 1** *a repressed country* **oppressed,** subjugated, subdued, tyrannized.
ANTONYMS democratic, free.
2 *repressed feelings* **restrained,** suppressed, held back/in, kept in check, stifled, pent up, bottled up, unvented.
ANTONYMS overt, expressed.
3 *emotionally repressed* **inhibited,** frustrated, restrained; informal uptight, hung up.
ANTONYMS relaxed, uninhibited.

repression ▶ **noun 1** *the repression of the protests* **suppression,** quashing, subduing, crushing, stamping out.
2 *political repression* **oppression,** subjugation, suppression, tyranny, despotism, authoritarianism.
3 *the repression of sexual urges* **restraint,** restraining, holding back, keeping back, suppression, keeping in check, control, keeping under control, stifling, bottling up.

repressive ▶ **adjective** *a repressive military regime* **oppressive,** authoritarian, despotic, tyrannical, dictatorial, fascist, autocratic, totalitarian, undemocratic.

reprieve ▶ **verb 1** *less than two hours ago the governor reprieved Edgerton* **grant a stay of execution to,** pardon, spare, grant an amnesty to, amnesty; informal let off, let off the hook.
2 *the project has been reprieved* **save,** rescue; informal take off the hit list.
▶ **noun** *a last-minute reprieve* **stay of execution,** remission, pardon, amnesty; Law continuance.

reprimand ▶ **verb** *was it really necessary to reprimand him in public?* **rebuke,** admonish, chastise, chide, upbraid, reprove, reproach, scold, berate, take to task, lambaste, give someone a piece of one's mind, rake/haul over the coals, lecture, criticize, censure; informal come down on, give someone a talking-to, tell off, dress down, give someone a dressing-down, give someone an earful, give someone a roasting, rap over the knuckles, rap, slap someone's wrist, bawl out, lay into, lace into, blast, give someone what for, chew out, ream out; formal castigate.
ANTONYMS praise.
▶ **noun** *they received a severe reprimand* **rebuke,** reproof, admonishment, admonition, reproach, scolding, upbraiding, censure; informal rap over the knuckles, slap on the wrist, dressing-down, talking-to, earful, roasting, tongue-lashing; formal castigation. See note at REBUKE.
ANTONYMS commendation.

reprisal ▶ **noun** *following the ethnic violence in Nigeria, the fear is of reprisal* **retaliation,** counterattack, comeback; revenge, vengeance, retribution, requital; informal a taste of one's own medicine.

reproach ▶ **verb** *Albert reproached him for being late* See REPRIMAND (verb). See also note at REBUKE.
▶ **noun 1** *an expression of reproach* See REPRIMAND (noun).
2 *this party is a reproach to Canadian politics* **disgrace,** discredit, source of shame, blemish, stain, blot; literary smirch.
– PHRASES **beyond/above reproach** *I never claimed to be above reproach* **perfect,** blameless, above suspicion, without fault, faultless, flawless, irreproachable, exemplary, impeccable, immaculate, unblemished, spotless, untarnished, stainless, unsullied, whiter than white; informal squeaky clean.

reproachful ▶ **adjective** **disapproving,** reproving, critical, censorious, disparaging, withering, accusatory, admonitory.
ANTONYMS approving.

reproduce ▶ **verb 1** *each piece of artwork is reproduced in color* **copy,** duplicate, replicate; photocopy, xerox, print.
2 *this work has not been reproduced in other laboratories* **repeat,** replicate, recreate, redo; simulate, imitate, emulate, mirror, mimic.
3 *some animals reproduce prolifically* **breed,** produce offspring, procreate, propagate, multiply.

reproduction ▶ **noun 1** *color reproduction* **copying,** duplication, duplicating; photocopying, xeroxing, printing.
2 *a reproduction of the original* **print,** copy, reprint, duplicate, facsimile, carbon copy, photocopy; trademark Xerox.
3 *the process of reproduction* **breeding,** procreation, multiplying, propagation.

reproof ▶ **noun** *he muttered reproof* **rebuke,** reprimand, reproach, admonishment, admonition; disapproval, censure, criticism, condemnation; informal dressing down.

reprove ▶ **verb** *was it necessary to reprove Vicki just for dropping a few crumbs?* **reprimand,** rebuke, reproach, scold, admonish, chastise, chide, upbraid, berate, take to task, rake/haul over the coals, criticize, censure; informal tell off, give someone a talking-to, dress down, give someone a dressing-down, give someone an earful, give someone a roasting, rap over the knuckles, slap someone's wrist; formal castigate.

repudiate ▶ verb **1** *she repudiated communism* **reject,** renounce, abandon, give up, turn one's back on, disown, cast off, lay aside; formal forswear, abjure; literary forsake.
ANTONYMS embrace.
2 *Hansen repudiated the allegations* **deny,** contradict, controvert, rebut, dispute, dismiss, brush aside; formal gainsay.
ANTONYMS acknowledge, confirm.
3 *Egypt repudiated the treaty* **cancel,** revoke, rescind, reverse, overrule, overturn, invalidate, nullify; disregard, flout, renege on; Law disaffirm; formal abrogate.
ANTONYMS ratify, abide by.

repugnance ▶ noun *a look of repugnance* **revulsion,** disgust, abhorrence, repulsion, loathing, hatred, detestation, aversion, distaste, antipathy, contempt.

repugnant ▶ adjective **1** *the idea of cannibalism is repugnant* **abhorrent,** revolting, repulsive, repellent, disgusting, offensive, objectionable, cringeworthy, vile, foul, nasty, loathsome, sickening, nauseating, hateful, detestable, execrable, abominable, monstrous, appalling, insufferable, intolerable, unacceptable, contemptible, unsavory, unpalatable; informal ghastly, gross, horrible, horrid; literary noisome. See note at OFFENSIVE.
ANTONYMS attractive, pleasant.
2 formal *the restriction is* ***repugnant to*** *the tenancy* **incompatible with,** in conflict with, contrary to, at variance with, inconsistent with.

repulsive ▶ adjective *their bathroom was repulsive* **revolting,** disgusting, abhorrent, repellent, repugnant, offensive, objectionable, vile, foul, nasty, loathsome, sickening, nauseating, hateful, detestable, execrable, abominable, monstrous, noxious, horrendous, awful, terrible, dreadful, frightful, obnoxious, unsavory, unpleasant, disagreeable, distasteful; ugly, hideous, grotesque; informal ghastly, horrible, horrid, gross; literary noisome; archaic loathly.
ANTONYMS attractive.

CHOOSE THE RIGHT WORD

repulsive, repellent

Repulsive and **repellent** are very close in meaning, but the former, perhaps because of its sound, is felt to express stronger feeling.

reputable ▶ adjective *a reputable talent scout* **well-thought-of,** highly regarded, respected, well-respected, respectable, of (good) repute, prestigious, established; reliable, dependable, trustworthy.
ANTONYMS untrustworthy.

reputation ▶ noun *your careless gossip has ruined my reputation in this town* **name, good name,** character, repute, standing, stature, status, position, renown, esteem, prestige; informal rep, rap.

repute ▶ noun **1** *a woman of ill repute* **reputation,** name, character.
2 *a firm of international repute* **fame,** renown, celebrity, distinction, high standing, stature, prestige.

reputedly ▶ adverb *the Atacoma Desert is reputedly the driest place in the world* **supposedly,** by all accounts, so I'm told, so people say, allegedly.

request ▶ noun **1** *requests for assistance* **appeal,** entreaty, plea, petition, application, demand, call; formal adjuration; literary behest.
2 *Charlotte spoke, at Ursula's request* **bidding,** entreaty, demand, insistence.
3 *indicate your requests on the form* **requirement,** wish, desire; choice.
▶ verb **1** *the government requested military aid* **ask for,** appeal for, call for, seek, solicit, plead for, apply for, demand; formal adjure.
2 *I requested him to help* **call on,** beg, entreat, implore; literary beseech.

require ▶ verb **1** *the child required hospital treatment* **need,** be in need of.
2 *a situation requiring patience* **necessitate,** demand, call for, involve, entail.
3 *unquestioning obedience is required* **demand,** insist on, call for, ask for, expect.
4 *she was required to pay costs* **order,** instruct, command, enjoin, oblige, compel, force.
5 *do you require anything else?* **want,** wish to have, desire; lack, be short of.

required ▶ adjective **1** *required reading* **essential,** vital, indispensable, necessary, compulsory, obligatory, mandatory, prescribed; informal must-have.
ANTONYMS optional.
2 *cut it to the required length* **desired,** preferred, chosen; correct, proper, right.

requirement ▶ noun *good spelling is a requirement of the job* **need,** wish, demand, want, necessity, essential, prerequisite, stipulation.

requisite ▶ adjective *he lacks the requisite skills* **necessary,** required, prerequisite, essential, indispensable, vital. See note at NECESSARY.
ANTONYMS optional.
▶ noun *a requisite for a successful career* **necessity,** essential, essential requirement, prerequisite, precondition, sine qua non; informal must.

requisition ▶ noun **1** *we have submitted our requisition for additional staff* **order,** request, call, application, claim, demand.
2 *the requisition of cultural treasures* **appropriation,** commandeering, seizure, confiscation, expropriation.
▶ verb **1** *their house was requisitioned by the army* **commandeer,** appropriate, take over, take possession of, occupy, seize, confiscate, expropriate.
2 *she requisitioned statements* **request,** order, call for, demand.

rescind ▶ verb *the court can rescind a bankruptcy order* **revoke,** repeal, cancel, reverse, overturn, overrule, annul, nullify, void, invalidate, quash, abolish; Law vacate; formal abrogate.
ANTONYMS enforce.

rescue ▶ verb **1** *an attempt to rescue the hostages* **save,** save from danger, save the life of, come to the aid of; free, set free, release, liberate.
2 *Boyd rescued his papers* **retrieve,** recover, salvage, get back.
▶ noun *the rescue of 10 crewmen* **saving,** rescuing;

release, freeing, liberation, bailout, deliverance, redemption.
– PHRASES **come to someone's rescue** *we were stuck in the elevator until Marty came to our rescue* **help,** assist, lend a helping hand to, lend a hand to, bail out; informal save someone's bacon, save someone's neck, save someone's skin.

research ▶ **noun 1** *medical research* **investigation,** experimentation, testing, analysis, fact-finding, fieldwork, examination, scrutiny.
2 *he continued his research* **experiment(s),** experimentation, test(s), testing, inquiry/inquiries, study/studies.
▶ **verb 1** *the phenomenon has been widely researched* **investigate,** study, inquire into, look into, probe, explore, analyze, examine, scrutinize, review.
2 *I researched all the available material* **study,** read, read up on, sift through, look into; informal check out.

resemblance ▶ **noun** *Sara says they're twins, but I don't see any resemblance* **similarity,** likeness, similitude, correspondence, congruity, congruence, coincidence, conformity, agreement, equivalence, comparability, parallelism, uniformity, sameness. See note at LIKENESS.

resemble ▶ **verb** *cape gooseberries resemble overgrown ground cherries* **look like,** be similar to, be like, bear a resemblance to, remind one of, take after, favor, have the look of; approximate to, smack of, have (all) the hallmarks of, correspond to, echo, mirror, parallel; archaic bear semblance to.

resent ▶ **verb** *she resented the models who got better assignments* **begrudge,** feel aggrieved at/about, feel bitter about, grudge, be annoyed at/about, be resentful of, dislike, take exception to, object to, take amiss, take offense at, take umbrage at, bear/harbor a grudge about.
ANTONYMS welcome.

resentful ▶ **adjective** *constant criticism will make your partner feel resentful* **aggrieved,** indignant, irritated, piqued, put out, in high dudgeon, dissatisfied, disgruntled, discontented, offended, bitter, jaundiced; envious, jealous; brooding; informal miffed, peeved, sore.

resentment ▶ **noun** *his success led to resentment from cities* **bitterness,** indignation, irritation, pique, dissatisfaction, disgruntlement, discontentment, discontent, resentfulness, bad feelings, hard feelings, ill will, acrimony, rancor, animosity, jaundice; envy, jealousy.

reservation ▶ **noun 1** (**reservations**) *grave reservations about traveling abroad* **doubts,** qualms, scruples; misgivings, skepticism, unease, hesitation, objection.
2 *the reservation of the room* **booking,** ordering, securing.
– PHRASES **without reservation** *Mr. McNeill apologized without reservation* **wholeheartedly,** unreservedly, without qualification, fully, completely, totally, entirely, wholly, unconditionally.

reserve ▶ **verb 1** *ask the library to reserve a copy for you* **put to one side,** put aside, set aside, keep, keep back, save, hold, put on hold, keep in reserve, earmark.
2 *he reserved a table* **book,** make a reservation for, order, arrange for, secure; formal bespeak; dated engage.
3 *the management reserves the right to alter the program* **retain,** maintain, keep, hold.
4 *reserve your judgment until you know him better* **defer,** postpone, put off, delay, withhold.
▶ **noun 1** *reserves of gasoline* **stock,** store, supply, stockpile, pool, hoard, cache.
2 *the army is calling up reserves* **reinforcements,** the militia, extras, auxiliaries.
3 *a nature reserve* **national park,** sanctuary, preserve, conservation area, protected area, wildlife park.
4 *it was difficult to get past his reserve* **reticence,** detachment, distance, remoteness, coolness, aloofness, constraint, formality; shyness, diffidence, timidity, taciturnity, inhibition; informal standoffishness.
5 *she trusted him without reserve* **reservation,** qualification, condition, limitation, hesitation, doubt.
▶ **adjective** *a reserve goaltender* **backup,** substitute, stand-in, relief, replacement, fallback, spare, extra.
– PHRASES **in reserve** *we have four generators in reserve* **available,** to/on hand, ready, in readiness, set aside, at one's disposal.

reserved ▶ **adjective 1** *Rodney is rather reserved* **reticent,** quiet, private, uncommunicative, unforthcoming, undemonstrative, unsociable, formal, constrained, cool, aloof, detached, distant, remote, unapproachable, unfriendly, withdrawn, secretive, silent, taciturn; shy, retiring, diffident, timid, self-effacing, inhibited, introverted; informal buttoned-up, standoffish.
ANTONYMS outgoing.
2 *that table is reserved* **booked,** taken, spoken for, prearranged; dated engaged; formal bespoken.
ANTONYMS free.

reservoir ▶ **noun 1** *water pumped from the reservoir* pool, pond; water supply, water tower.
2 *an ink reservoir* **receptacle,** container, holder, repository, tank.
3 *the reservoir of managerial talent* **stock,** store, stockpile, reserve(s), supply, bank, pool, stable, fund.

reside ▶ **verb 1** *most students* ***reside in*** *apartments* **live in,** occupy, inhabit, stay in, lodge in; formal dwell in, be domiciled in.
2 *the paintings reside in an air-conditioned vault* **be situated,** be found, be located, lie.
3 *executive power* ***resides in*** *the president* **be vested in,** be bestowed on, be conferred on, be in the hands of.
4 *the qualities that reside within each individual* **be inherent,** be present, exist.

residence ▶ **noun 1** formal *her private residence* **home,** house, place of residence, address; quarters, lodgings; informal **pad,** digs; formal dwelling, dwelling place, domicile, abode.
2 *the university residence* **dormitory,** dorm.
3 *his place of residence* **occupancy,** habitation, residency; formal abode.

resident ▶ noun *the residents of Ivoryton* **inhabitant,** local, citizen, native; townsfolk, townspeople; householder, homeowner, occupier, tenant; formal denizen.
▶ adjective 1 *is he currently resident in New Brunswick?* **living,** residing, in residence; formal dwelling.
2 *a resident nurse* **live-in,** living in.

residue ▶ noun *the residue of explosives found in the wreckage* **remainder,** remaining part, rest, remnant(s); surplus, extra, excess; remains, leftovers; technical residuum.

resign ▶ verb 1 *the executive director resigned* **leave,** hand in one's notice, give notice, stand down, step down; informal quit, jump ship.
2 *three state senators resigned their seats* **give up,** leave, vacate, stand down from; informal quit, pack in.
3 *he resigned his right to the title* **renounce,** relinquish, give up, abandon, surrender, forgo, cede; Law disclaim; literary forsake.
4 *we* ***resigned ourselves to*** *a long wait* **reconcile oneself to,** become resigned to, come to terms with, accept.

resignation ▶ noun 1 *his resignation from his post* **departure,** leaving, standing down, stepping down; informal quitting.
2 *she handed in her resignation* **notice,** notice to quit, letter of resignation.
3 *he accepted his fate with resignation* **patience,** forbearance, stoicism, fortitude, fatalism, acceptance, acquiescence, compliance, passivity.

resigned ▶ adjective *he gave a resigned sigh* **patient,** long-suffering, uncomplaining, forbearing, stoical, philosophical, fatalistic, acquiescent, compliant, passive, submissive.

resilient ▶ adjective 1 *resilient materials* **flexible,** pliable, supple; durable, hardwearing, stout, strong, sturdy, tough. See note at **FLEXIBLE**.
2 *young and resilient* **strong,** tough, hardy; quick to recover, buoyant, irrepressible.

resist ▶ verb 1 *built to resist cold winters* **withstand,** be proof against, combat, weather, endure, be resistant to, keep out.
ANTONYMS be harmed by, be susceptible to.
2 *they resisted his attempts to change things* **oppose,** fight against, refuse to accept, object to, defy, set one's face against, kick against; obstruct, impede, hinder, block, thwart, frustrate.
ANTONYMS welcome, accept.
3 *I resisted the urge to retort* **refrain from,** abstain from, forbear from, desist from, not give in to, restrain oneself from, stop oneself from.
ANTONYMS succumb to, give in to.
4 *she tried to resist him* **struggle with/against,** fight (against), stand up to, withstand, hold off; fend off, ward off.
ANTONYMS yield to, submit to.
– PHRASES **cannot resist** *I cannot resist a challenge* **love,** adore, relish, have a weakness for, be very keen on, like, delight in, enjoy, take great pleasure in; informal be mad about, get a kick/thrill out of, cannot help wanting.

resistance ▶ noun 1 ***resistance to*** *change* **opposition to,** hostility to, refusal to accept.
2 *a spirited resistance* **opposition,** fight, stand, struggle.
3 *the body's* ***resistance to*** *disease* **ability to fight off,** immunity from, defenses against.
4 *the French resistance* **resistance movement,** freedom fighters, underground, partisans.

resistant ▶ adjective 1 *resistant to water* **impervious to,** unsusceptible to, immune, invulnerable to, proof against, unaffected by.
2 ***resistant to*** *change* **opposed to,** averse to, hostile to, inimical to, against; informal anti.

resolute ▶ adjective *both factions held jittery but resolute hopes for peace* **determined,** purposeful, resolved, adamant, single-minded, firm, unswerving, unwavering, steadfast, staunch, stalwart, unfaltering, unhesitating, persistent, indefatigable, tenacious, strong-willed, unshakable; stubborn, dogged, obstinate, obdurate, inflexible, intransigent, implacable, unyielding, unrelenting; spirited, brave, bold, courageous, plucky, indomitable; informal gutsy, spunky, feisty; formal pertinacious.
ANTONYMS halfhearted.

CHOOSE THE RIGHT WORD

resolute, constant, decisive, determined, faithful, staunch

Any of the above adjectives might apply to you if you take a stand on something and stick to it, or show your loyalty to a person, country, or cause. If you show unswerving loyalty to someone or something you are tied to (as in marriage, friendship, etc.), you would be described as **faithful** (*a faithful wife; a faithful Republican*). **Constant** also implies a firm or steady attachment to someone or something, but with less emphasis on vows, pledges, and obligations; it is the opposite of fickleness rather than of unfaithfulness (*my grandfather's constant confidant*). To be described as **staunch** carries loyalty one step further, implying an unwillingness to be dissuaded or turned aside (*a staunch friend who refused to believe the rumors that were circulating*). To be called **resolute** means that you are both staunch and steadfast, but the emphasis here is on character and a firm adherence to your own goals and purposes rather than to those of others (*resolute in insisting upon her right to be heard*). **Determined** and **decisive** are less forceful words. You can be *decisive* in almost any situation, as long as you have a choice among alternatives and don't hesitate in taking a stand (*decisive as always, she barely glanced at the menu before ordering*). *Determined*, unlike *resolute*, suggests a stubborn will rather than a conscious adherence to goals or principles (*he was determined to be home before the holidays*).

resolution ▶ noun 1 *her resolution not to smoke* **intention,** resolve, decision, intent, aim, plan; commitment, pledge, promise.
2 *the committee passed the resolution* **motion,** proposal, proposition, resolve.
3 *she handled the work with resolution* **determination,** purpose, purposefulness,

resolve, resoluteness, single-mindedness, firmness, firmness of purpose; steadfastness, staunchness, perseverance, persistence, indefatigability, tenacity, tenaciousness, staying power, dedication, commitment; stubbornness, doggedness, obstinacy, obduracy; boldness, spiritedness, braveness, bravery, courage, pluck, grit, courageousness; informal guts, spunk; formal pertinacity. See note at COURAGE.

4 *a satisfactory* ***resolution of*** *the problem* **solution to,** answer to, end to, ending to, settlement of, conclusion to.

resolve ▶ **verb 1** *this matter cannot be resolved overnight* **settle,** sort out, solve, find a solution to, fix, straighten out, deal with, put right, put to rights, rectify; informal hammer out, thrash out, figure out.

2 *Bob resolved not to wait any longer* **determine,** decide, make up one's mind, make a decision.

3 *the committee resolved that the project should proceed* **vote,** pass a resolution, rule, decide formally, agree.

4 *the compounds were resolved into their active constituents* **break down/up,** separate, reduce, divide.

5 *the ability to resolve facts into their legal categories* **analyze,** dissect, break down, categorize.

6 *the gray smudge resolved into a sandy beach* **turn,** change, be transformed, be converted.

▶ **noun 1** *their intimidation merely strengthened his resolve* See RESOLUTION (sense 3).

2 *he made a resolve not to go there again* **decision,** resolution, commitment.

resort ▶ **noun 1** *a seaside resort* **vacation spot,** tourist center, vacationland; retreat; spa; informal tourist trap.

2 *settle the matter without* ***resort to*** *legal proceedings* **recourse to,** turning to, the use of, utilizing.

3 *strike action is our last resort* **expedient,** measure, step, recourse, alternative, option, choice, possibility, hope.

– PHRASES **resort to** *I don't have to resort to such underhanded tricks* **have recourse to,** fall back on, turn to, make use of, use, employ, avail oneself of; stoop to, descend to, sink to.

resound ▶ **verb 1** *the explosion resounded around the silent street* **echo,** re-echo, reverberate, ring out, boom, thunder, rumble.

2 *resounding with the clang of hammers* **reverberate,** echo, re-echo, resonate, ring.

3 *nothing will resound like their earlier achievements* **be acclaimed,** be celebrated, be renowned, be famed, be glorified, be trumpeted.

resounding ▶ **adjective 1** *a resounding voice* **reverberant,** reverberating, resonant, resonating, echoing, ringing, sonorous, deep, full-throated, rich, clear; loud, booming.

2 *a resounding success* **enormous,** huge, very great, tremendous, terrific, colossal; emphatic, decisive, conclusive, outstanding, remarkable, phenomenal.

resource ▶ **noun 1** (**resources**) *use your resources efficiently* **assets,** funds, wealth, money, capital; staff; supplies, materials, raw materials, store(s), stock(s), reserve(s).

2 *your tutor is there as a resource* **facility,** amenity, aid, help, support.

3 *tears were her only resource* **expedient,** resort, course, scheme, stratagem; trick, ruse, device.

4 *a person of resource* **initiative,** resourcefulness, enterprise, ingenuity, inventiveness; talent, ability, capability; informal gumption.

resourceful ▶ **adjective** *a group of resourceful fifth graders came up with a workable plan to overhaul the town's inefficient recycling center* **ingenious,** enterprising, inventive, creative; clever, talented, able, capable; informal clueful. See note at CREATIVE.

respect ▶ **noun 1** *the respect due to a great artist* **esteem,** regard, high opinion, admiration, reverence, deference, honor.

ANTONYMS contempt.

2 *he spoke to her with respect* **due regard,** politeness, courtesy, civility, deference.

ANTONYMS disrespect.

3 *paying one's respects* **regards,** kind regards, compliments, greetings, best/good wishes, felicitations, salutations; archaic remembrances.

4 *the report was accurate in every respect* **aspect,** regard, facet, feature, way, sense, particular, point, detail.

▶ **verb 1** *she is highly respected in the book industry* **esteem,** admire, think highly of, have a high opinion of, hold in high regard, hold in (high) esteem, look up to, revere, reverence, honor. See note at ESTEEM.

ANTONYMS despise.

2 *they respected our privacy* **show consideration for,** have regard for, observe, be mindful of, be heedful of; formal take cognizance of.

ANTONYMS scorn.

3 *her father respected her wishes* **abide by,** comply with, follow, adhere to, conform to, act in accordance with, defer to, obey, observe, keep, keep to.

ANTONYMS disregard, disobey.

– PHRASES **with respect to/in respect of** *with respect to the new town garage, the council has decided to accept contractors' bids through the end of the month* **concerning,** regarding, in/with regard to, with reference to, respecting, re, about, apropos, on the subject of, in connection with, vis-à-vis.

respectable ▶ **adjective 1** *a respectable middle-class background* **reputable,** of good repute, upright, honest, honorable, trustworthy, decent, good, well-bred, clean-living.

ANTONYMS disreputable.

2 *a respectable salary* **fairly good,** decent, fair, reasonable, moderately good; substantial, considerable, sizable.

ANTONYMS paltry.

respective ▶ **adjective** *please return to your respective classrooms* **separate,** personal, own, particular, individual, specific, special, appropriate, different, various.

respite ▶ **noun 1** *a brief respite* **rest,** break, breathing space, interval, intermission, interlude, recess, lull, pause, time out; relief, relaxation, repose; informal breather, letup.

2 *respite from debts* **postponement,** deferment, delay, reprieve; Law continuance.

respond ▶ verb **1** *they do not **respond to** questions* **answer,** reply to, make a response to, make a rejoinder to.
2 *"No," she responded* **say in response,** answer, reply, rejoin, retort, riposte, counter.
3 *they were slow to respond* **react,** make a response, reciprocate, retaliate.

response ▶ noun **1** *his response to the question* **answer,** reply, rejoinder, retort, riposte; informal comeback.
2 *an angry response* **reaction,** reply, retaliation, feedback; informal comeback.

responsibility ▶ noun **1** *it was his responsibility to find witnesses* **duty,** task, function, job, role, business.
2 *they denied responsibility for the bomb attack* **blame,** fault, guilt, culpability, liability.
3 *let's show some social responsibility* **trustworthiness,** common sense, sense, maturity, reliability, dependability.
4 *a job with greater responsibility* **authority,** control, power, leadership.

responsible ▶ adjective **1** *who is **responsible for** the prisons?* **in charge of,** in control of, at the helm of, accountable for, liable for.
2 *if an error's been made, I'm the one who's responsible* **accountable,** answerable, to blame, guilty, culpable, blameworthy, at fault, in the wrong.
3 *a responsible job* **important,** powerful, executive.
4 *he is responsible to the president* **answerable,** accountable.
5 *a responsible tenant* **trustworthy,** sensible, mature, reliable, dependable.

CHOOSE THE RIGHT WORD

responsible, accountable, answerable, liable

Responsible is an adjective that applies to anyone who is in charge of an endeavor or to whom a duty has been delegated, and who is subject to penalty or blame in case of default (*responsible for getting everyone out of the building in the event of a fire*). **Answerable** implies a legal or moral obligation for which one must answer (*the parents were held to be answerable for their children's behavior*). **Accountable** is more positive than *responsible* or *answerable*, suggesting that something has been entrusted to someone who will be called to account for how that trust has been carried out (*She was directly accountable to the department head for the funds that had been allocated to her group*). **Liable** is more restricted in scope than any of the foregoing words; it refers exclusively to the assignment of blame or the payment of monetary damages in the event of a mishap (*because he was responsible for the accident, he was held liable for damages*).

responsive ▶ adjective *several consumers said the company hadn't been **responsive to** their needs* **quick to react to,** reactive to, receptive to, open to suggestions about, amenable to, flexible to, sensitive to, sympathetic to; aware of.

rest¹ ▶ verb **1** *he needed to rest* **relax,** take a rest, ease up/off, let up, slow down, have/take a break, unbend, unwind, recharge one's batteries, be at leisure, take it easy, put one's feet up; lie down, go to bed, have/take a nap, catnap, doze, sleep; informal take five, have/take a breather, catch forty winks, get some shut-eye, take a load off, chill, chill out, catch some Zs.
2 *his hands rested on the rail* **lie,** be laid, repose, be placed, be positioned, be supported by.
3 *she rested her basket on the ground* **support,** prop (up), lean, lay, set, stand, position, place, put.
4 *the film script **rests on** an improbable premise* **be based on,** depend on, be dependent on, rely on, hinge on, turn on, be contingent on, revolve around, center on.
▶ noun **1** *get some rest* **repose,** relaxation, leisure, respite, time off, breathing space, downtime; sleep, nap, doze; informal shut-eye, snooze, lie-down, forty winks.
2 *a short rest from work* **break,** vacation, breathing space, interval, interlude, intermission, time off/out, holiday; informal breather.
3 *she took the poker from its rest* **stand,** base, holder, support, rack, frame, shelf.
4 *passengers queried why the train had come to rest several miles before the next station* **a standstill,** a halt, a stop.

rest² ▶ noun *the rest of the board members are appointees* **remainder,** residue, balance, remaining part/number/quantity, others, those left, remains, remnant(s), surplus, excess; technical residuum.
▶ verb *you may rest assured that he is there* **remain,** continue to be, stay, keep, carry on being.

restful ▶ adjective *a restful cruise* **relaxed,** relaxing, quiet, calm, calming, tranquil, soothing, peaceful, placid, reposeful, leisurely, undisturbed, untroubled.
ANTONYMS exciting.

restitution ▶ noun **1** *restitution of the land seized* **return,** restoration, handing back, surrender.
2 *restitution for the damage caused* **compensation,** recompense, reparation, damages, indemnification, indemnity, reimbursement, repayment, redress, remuneration.

restive ▶ adjective **1** *Edward is getting restive* See RESTLESS (sense 1).
2 *the militants are increasingly restive* **unruly,** disorderly, uncontrollable, unmanageable, willful, recalcitrant, insubordinate; formal refractory; archaic contumacious.

restless ▶ adjective **1** *Maria was restless throughout the meeting* **uneasy,** ill at ease, restive, fidgety, edgy, on edge, tense, worked up, nervous, agitated, anxious, on tenterhooks, keyed up; informal jumpy, jittery, twitchy, uptight, antsy.
2 *a restless night* **sleepless,** wakeful; fitful, broken, disturbed, troubled, unsettled.

restoration ▶ noun **1** *the restoration of*

democracy **reinstatement,** reinstitution, reestablishment, reimposition, return.
2 *the restoration of derelict housing* **repair,** repairing, fixing, mending, whitepainting, refurbishment, reconditioning, rehabilitation, rebuilding, reconstruction, overhaul, redevelopment, renovation; informal rehab.

restore ▶ **verb 1** *the aim to restore democracy* **reinstate,** bring back, reinstitute, reimpose, reinstall, reestablish. See note at RECOVER.
ANTONYMS abolish.
2 *he restored it to its rightful owner* **return,** give back, hand back.
3 *the building has been restored* **repair,** fix, mend, refurbish, recondition, rehabilitate, rebuild, reconstruct, remodel, overhaul, redevelop, renovate; informal do up, rehab.
ANTONYMS neglect.
4 *a good sleep can restore you* **reinvigorate,** revitalize, revive, refresh, energize, fortify, revivify, regenerate, stimulate, freshen.

restrain ▶ **verb 1** *Charles restrained his anger* **control,** keep under control, check, hold/keep in check, curb, suppress, repress, contain, dampen, subdue, smother, choke back, stifle, bottle up, rein back/in; informal keep the lid on.
2 *she could barely restrain herself from swearing* **prevent,** stop, keep, hold back.
3 *that beast ought to be restrained* **tie up,** bind, tether, chain (up), fetter, shackle, manacle, put in irons; informal hog-tie.

restrained ▶ **adjective 1** *Julie was quite restrained* **self-controlled,** self-restrained, not given to excesses, sober, steady, unemotional, undemonstrative.
2 *restrained elegance* **muted,** soft, discreet, subtle, quiet, unobtrusive, unostentatious, understated, tasteful.

restraint ▶ **noun 1** *a restraint on their impulsiveness* **constraint,** check, control, restriction, limitation, curtailment; rein, bridle, brake, damper, impediment, obstacle.
2 *the protestors showed restraint* **self-control,** self-restraint, self-discipline, control, moderation, prudence, judiciousness, abstemiousness.
3 *the room has been decorated with restraint* **subtlety,** understatedness, taste, tastefulness, discretion, discrimination.
4 *a child restraint* **belt,** harness, strap.

restrict ▶ **verb 1** *a busy working life restricted his leisure activities* **limit,** keep within bounds, regulate, control, moderate, cut down.
2 *the cuff supports the ankle without restricting movement* **hinder,** interfere with, impede, hamper, obstruct, block, check, curb, shackle.
3 *he restricted himself to a 15-minute speech* **confine,** limit.

restricted ▶ **adjective 1** *restricted space* **cramped,** confined, constricted, small, narrow, tight.
ANTONYMS roomy.
2 *a restricted calorie intake* **limited,** controlled, regulated, reduced, rangebound.
ANTONYMS unlimited.
3 *a restricted zone* **out of bounds,** off limits, private, exclusive.
ANTONYMS public.
4 *restricted information* **secret,** top secret, classified; informal hush-hush.

restriction ▶ **noun 1** *there is no restriction on the number of places* **limitation,** limit, constraint, control, check, curb; condition, proviso, qualification.
2 *the restriction of personal freedom* **reduction,** limitation, diminution, curtailment.
3 *restriction of movement* **hindrance,** impediment, slowing, reduction, limitation.

result ▶ **noun 1** *stress is the result of overwork* **consequence,** outcome, product, upshot, sequel, effect, reaction, repercussion, ramification, conclusion, culmination.
ANTONYMS cause.
2 *having made the calculation, what is your result?* **answer,** solution; sum, total, product.
3 *exam results* **grade,** score, mark.
4 *the result of the trial* **verdict,** decision, outcome, conclusion, judgment, findings, ruling.
▶ **verb 1** *differences between species could **result from** their habitat* **follow from,** ensue from, develop from, stem from, spring from, arise from, derive from, evolve from, proceed from; occur from, happen from, take place from, come about from; be caused by, be brought about by, be produced by, originate in, be consequent on.
2 *the shooting **resulted in** five deaths* **end in,** culminate in, finish in, terminate in, lead to, prompt, precipitate, trigger; cause, bring about, occasion, effect, give rise to, produce, engender, generate; literary beget.

resume ▶ **verb 1** *the government resumed negotiations* **restart,** recommence, begin again, start again, reopen; renew, return to, continue with, carry on with.
ANTONYMS suspend, abandon.
2 *the priest resumed his kneeling posture* **return to,** come back to, take up again, reoccupy.
ANTONYMS leave.

resurrect ▶ **verb 1** *we believe that Jesus was resurrected* **raise from the dead,** restore to life, revive.
2 *resurrecting his career* **revive,** restore, regenerate, revitalize, breathe new life into, bring back to life, reinvigorate, resuscitate, rejuvenate, stimulate, reestablish, relaunch.

resuscitate ▶ **verb 1** *medics resuscitated him* **bring around,** revive, bring back to consciousness; give CPR (cardiopulmonary resuscitation) to, give the kiss of life to.
2 *measures to resuscitate the economy* **revive,** resurrect, restore, regenerate, revitalize, breathe new life into, reinvigorate, rejuvenate, stimulate.

retain ▶ **verb 1** *the government retained a share in the industries* **keep,** keep possession of, keep hold of, hold on to, hang on to.
ANTONYMS give up.
2 *existing footpaths are to be retained* **maintain,** keep, preserve, conserve.
ANTONYMS discontinue.
3 *some students retain facts easily* **remember,** memorize, keep in one's mind, keep in one's memory, store.
ANTONYMS forget.
4 *we have decided to retain a company lawyer* **employ,** contract, secure the services of, sign

on, put on the payroll, keep on the payroll.
ANTONYMS dismiss.

retainer ▶ noun **1** *they're paid a retainer* **retaining fee,** fee, periodic payment, advance, standing charge.
2 *a faithful retainer* See SERVANT (sense 1).

retaliate ▶ verb *the gang will look for an opportunity to retaliate* **fight back,** hit back, respond, react, reply, reciprocate, counterattack, return like for like, get back at someone, give tit for tat, take reprisals, get even, get one's own back, pay someone back, give someone a taste of their own medicine; have/get/take one's revenge, be revenged, avenge oneself.

retard ▶ verb *the process is retarded by bureaucratic red tape* **delay,** slow down, slow up, hold back, hold up, set back, postpone, put back, detain, decelerate; hinder, hamper, obstruct, inhibit, impede, check, restrain, restrict, trammel; literary stay.
ANTONYMS accelerate.

retch ▶ verb **1** *the sour taste made her retch* **gag,** heave, almost vomit.
2 *he went into the bushes to retch* See VOMIT (sense 1 of the verb).

reticence ▶ noun *security concerns may explain Taylor's reticence* **reserve,** restraint, inhibition, diffidence, shyness; unresponsiveness, quietness, taciturnity, secretiveness.

reticent ▶ adjective *Smith was reticent about his personal affairs* **reserved,** withdrawn, introverted, inhibited, diffident, shy; uncommunicative, unforthcoming, unresponsive, tight-lipped, buttoned-up, quiet, taciturn, silent, guarded, secretive.
ANTONYMS expansive.

retire ▶ verb **1** *he has retired* **give up work,** stop working, stop work; pack it in, call it quits.
2 *we've retired him on full pension* force to retire, give someone the golden handshake/parachute.
3 *Gillian retired to her office* **withdraw,** go away, take oneself off, decamp, shut oneself away; formal repair; literary betake oneself.
4 *their forces retired* **retreat,** withdraw, pull back, fall back, disengage, back off, give ground.
5 *everyone retired early* **go to bed,** call it a day, go to sleep; informal turn in, hit the hay, hit the sack.

retiring ▶ adjective **1** *the retiring president* **departing,** outgoing.
ANTONYMS incoming.
2 *a retiring sort of man* **shy,** diffident, self-effacing, unassuming, unassertive, reserved, reticent, quiet, timid, modest; private, secret, secretive, withdrawn, reclusive, unsociable.
ANTONYMS outgoing.

retract ▶ verb **1** *the sea otter can retract its claws* **pull in,** draw in, pull back.
2 *she retracted her allegation* **take back,** withdraw, recant, disavow, disclaim, repudiate, renounce, reverse, revoke, rescind, go back on, backtrack on, unsay; formal abjure.

retreat ▶ verb **1** *the army retreated* **withdraw,** retire, draw back, pull back/out, fall back, give way, give ground, beat a retreat, beat a hasty retreat.
ANTONYMS advance.
2 *the tide was retreating* **go out,** ebb, recede, fall, go down, wane.
3 *the government had to retreat* **change one's mind,** change one's plans; back down, climb down, do a U-turn, backtrack, backpedal, give in, concede defeat; informal pull a U-ey, do a one-eighty.
▶ noun **1** *the retreat of the army* **withdrawal,** pulling back.
2 *the president's retreat* **about-face,** U-turn; informal one-eighty.
3 *her rural retreat* **refuge,** haven, sanctuary; hideaway, hideout, hiding place, escape.
4 *a period of retreat from the world* **seclusion,** withdrawal, retirement, solitude, isolation, sanctuary.

retrench ▶ verb **1** *we have to retrench* **economize,** cut back, make cutbacks, make savings, make economies, reduce expenditure, be economical, be frugal, tighten one's belt.
2 *services have to be retrenched* **reduce,** cut, cut back, cut down, pare, pare down, slim down, make reductions in, make cutbacks in, trim, prune; shorten, abridge; informal slash.

retribution ▶ noun *officials condemned the suicide bombing and vowed retribution* **punishment,** penalty, one's just deserts; revenge, reprisal, requital, retaliation, vengeance, an eye for an eye (and a tooth for a tooth), tit for tat, lex talionis; redress, reparation, restitution, recompense, repayment, atonement, indemnification, amends.

retrieve ▶ verb **1** *I retrieved the ball from their garden* **get back,** bring back, recover, regain (possession of), recoup, reclaim, repossess, redeem, recuperate. See note at RECOVER.
2 *they were trying to retrieve the situation* **put right,** set right, rectify, remedy, restore, sort out, straighten out, resolve, save.

retrograde ▶ adjective **1** *a retrograde step* **for the worse,** regressive, negative, downhill, unwelcome.
ANTONYMS positive, forward-looking.
2 *retrograde motion* **backward,** backwards, reverse, rearward.
ANTONYMS forward.

retrospect ▶ noun
– PHRASES **in retrospect** *in retrospect, we can see that more guards should have been installed at the front gate* **looking back,** on reflection, on reexamination, in/with hindsight.

return ▶ verb **1** *he returned to Halifax* **go back,** come back, come home.
ANTONYMS depart.
2 *the symptoms returned* **recur,** reoccur, occur again, repeat (itself); reappear, appear again.
ANTONYMS disappear.
3 *he returned the money* **give back,** hand back; pay back, repay.
ANTONYMS keep.
4 *Peter returned the book to the shelf* **restore,** put back, replace, reinstall.
5 *he returned the volley* **hit back,** throw back.
ANTONYMS miss.
6 *she returned his kiss* **reciprocate,** requite, give in return, respond to, repay, give back.
ANTONYMS ignore.

7 *"Later," returned Isabel* **answer,** reply, respond, counter, rejoin, retort, come back.
8 *the jury returned a unanimous verdict* **deliver,** bring in, hand down.
9 *the club returned a profit* **yield,** earn, realize, net, gross, clear.
10 *the swing might result in a leftist party being returned in the next election* **elect,** vote in, choose, select.
▶ **noun 1** *his return to Oregon* **homecoming.**
ANTONYMS departure.
2 *the return of hard times* **recurrence,** reoccurrence, repeat, repetition, reappearance, revival, resurrection, reemergence, resurgence, renaissance.
ANTONYMS disappearance.
3 *I requested the return of my books* **giving back,** handing back, replacement, restoration, reinstatement, restitution.
4 *a quick return on investments* **yield,** profit, gain, revenue, interest, dividend.
5 *a census return* **statement,** report, submission, record, dossier; document, form.
– PHRASES **in return for** *I'm authorized to show you some leniency in return for information about Sawyer* **in exchange for,** as a reward for, as compensation for.

reveal ▶ **verb 1** *the police can't reveal his whereabouts* **divulge,** disclose, tell, let slip, let drop, give away, give out, blurt (out), release, leak; make known, make public, broadcast, publicize, circulate, disseminate; informal let on.
ANTONYMS hide, conceal.
2 *the screen moved back to reveal the new car* **show,** display, exhibit, disclose, uncover, unveil; literary uncloak.
ANTONYMS hide.
3 *the data can reveal a good deal of information* **bring to light,** uncover, lay bare, unearth, expose; formal evince; literary uncloak.

revel ▶ **verb 1** *they reveled all night* **celebrate,** make merry, have a party, carouse, roister, go on a spree; informal party, live it up, whoop it up, make whoopee, rave, paint the town red.
2 *she* ***reveled in*** *the applause* **enjoy,** delight in, love, like, adore, be pleased by, take pleasure in, appreciate, relish, lap up, savor; informal get a kick out of.
▶ **noun** *late-night revels* **celebration,** festivity, jollification, merrymaking, carousing, spree; party, jamboree, hedonism; informal rave, shindig, bash, wingding, blast.

revelation ▶ **noun 1** *revelations about his personal life* **disclosure,** surprising fact, announcement, report; admission, confession.
2 *the revelation of a secret* **divulging,** divulgence, disclosure, disclosing, letting slip, letting drop, giving away, giving out, leaking, leak, betrayal, unveiling, making known, making public, broadcasting, publicizing, dissemination, reporting, report, declaring, declaration.

reveler ▶ **noun** *the New Year's Eve revelers have poured into Times Square in record numbers* **partygoer,** merrymaker, carouser, roisterer; archaic wassailer.

revenge ▶ **noun 1** *she is seeking revenge* **vengeance,** retribution, retaliation, reprisal, requital, recrimination, an eye for an eye (and a tooth for a tooth), redress, satisfaction.
2 *they were filled with revenge* **vengefulness,** vindictiveness, vitriol, spite, spitefulness, malice, maliciousness, malevolence, ill will, animosity, hate, hatred, rancor, bitterness; literary maleficence.
▶ **verb** *he revenged his brother's murder* **avenge,** take/exact revenge for, exact retribution for, take reprisals for, get redress for, get satisfaction for.

revenue ▶ **noun** *this month's revenue is up 5 percent from last month* **income,** takings, receipts, proceeds, earnings, sales; profit(s).
ANTONYMS expenditure.

reverberate ▶ **verb** *Fred's voice reverberated across the room* **resound,** echo, re-echo, resonate, ring, boom, rumble, vibrate.

revere ▶ **verb** *she is revered as a national hero* **respect,** admire, honor, think highly of, esteem, hold in high esteem, hold in high regard, look up to, put on a pedestal, lionize, reverence.
ANTONYMS despise.

CHOOSE THE RIGHT WORD

revere, admire, adore, idolize, venerate, worship

We might **admire** someone who walks a tightrope between two skyscrapers, **idolize** a rock star, **adore** our mothers, and **revere** a person like Martin Luther King, Jr. Each of these verbs conveys the idea of regarding someone or something with respect and honor, but they differ considerably in terms of the feelings they connote. *Admire* suggests a feeling of delight and enthusiastic appreciation (*admire the courage of the mountain climber*), while *adore* implies the tenderness and warmth of unquestioning love (*he adored babies*). *Idolize* is an extreme form of adoration, suggesting a slavish, helpless love, (*he idolized the older quarterback*). We *revere* individuals and institutions that command our respect for their accomplishments or attributes (*he revered his old English professor*). **Venerate** and **worship** are usually found in religious contexts (*venerate saints and worship God*) but both words may be used in other contexts as well. *Venerate* is usually associated with dignity and advanced age (*venerate the old man who had founded the company more than 50 years ago*), while *worship* connotes an excessive and uncritical respect (*the young girls who waited outside the stage door worshiped the ground he walked on*).

reverence ▶ **noun** *reverence for the countryside* **high esteem,** high regard, great respect, acclaim, admiration, appreciation, estimation, favor. See note at HONOR.
ANTONYMS scorn.
▶ **verb** *they reverence modern jazz* See REVERE.

reverent ▶ **adjective** *a reverent silence* **respectful,** reverential, admiring, devoted, devout, dutiful, awed, deferential.

reversal ▶ noun **1** *there was no reversal on this issue* **turnaround,** turnabout, about-face, volte-face, change of heart, U-turn, one-eighty, 180, backtracking; rare tergiversation.
2 *a reversal of roles* **swap,** exchange, change, swapping, interchange.
3 *the reversal of the decision* **alteration,** changing; countermanding, undoing, overturning, overthrow, disallowing, overriding, overruling, veto, vetoing, revocation, repeal, rescinding, annulment, nullification, voiding, invalidation, abrogation.
4 *a very slow July was the only reversal we suffered during the entire fiscal year* **setback,** reverse, upset, failure, misfortune, mishap, disaster, blow, disappointment, adversity, hardship, affliction, vicissitude, defeat; bad luck.

reverse ▶ verb **1** *the car reversed into a lamppost* **back,** back up, drive back/backward, move back/backward.
2 *reverse the bottle in the ice bucket* **turn upside down,** turn over, upend, upturn, invert.
3 *I reversed my jacket* **turn inside out,** turn outside in.
4 *reverse your roles* **swap,** change, change around, exchange, interchange, switch, switch around.
5 *the umpire reversed the decision* **alter,** change; overturn, overthrow, disallow, override, overrule, veto, revoke, repeal, rescind, annul, nullify, void, invalidate; formal abrogate.
▶ adjective **1** *in reverse order* **backward,** reversed, inverted, transposed.
2 *reverse racism* **inverse,** reversed, opposite, converse, contrary, counter, antithetical.
▶ noun **1** *the reverse is the case* **opposite,** contrary, converse, inverse, obverse, antithesis. See note at OPPOSITE.
2 *successes and reverses* See REVERSAL (sense 4).
3 *the reverse of the page* **other side,** reverse side, back, underside, wrong side, verso.

review ▶ noun **1** *the council undertook a review* **analysis,** evaluation, assessment, appraisal, examination, investigation, inquiry, probe, inspection, study.
2 *the rent is due for review* **reconsideration,** reassessment, reevaluation, reappraisal; change, alteration, modification, revision.
3 *book reviews* **criticism,** critique, assessment, evaluation, commentary; informal take.
4 *a scientific review* **journal,** periodical, magazine, publication.
5 *their review of the economy* **survey,** report, study, account, description, statement, overview, analysis.
6 *a military review* **inspection,** parade, tattoo, procession, march past.
▶ verb **1** *I reviewed the evidence* **survey,** study, research, consider, analyze, examine, scrutinize, explore, look into, probe, investigate, inspect, assess, appraise; informal size up.
2 *the referee reviewed his decision* **reconsider,** reexamine, reassess, reevaluate, reappraise, rethink; change, alter, modify, revise.
3 *he reviewed the day* **remember,** recall, reflect on, think through, go over in one's mind, look back on.
4 *reviewing troops* **inspect,** view.
5 *she reviewed the play* **comment on,** evaluate, assess, appraise, judge, critique, criticize.

reviewer ▶ noun *a restaurant reviewer for the local paper* **critic, commentator,** judge, observer, pundit, analyst.

revile ▶ verb *reviled as a traitor* **criticize,** censure, condemn, attack, inveigh against, rail against, castigate, lambaste, denounce; slander, libel, malign, vilify, abuse; informal knock, slam, pan, crucify, roast, tear into, badmouth, dis, pummel; formal excoriate, calumniate. See note at SCOLD.
ANTONYMS praise.

revise ▶ verb **1** *she revised her opinion* **reconsider,** review, reexamine, reassess, reevaluate, reappraise, rethink; change, alter, modify.
2 *the editor revised the text* **amend,** emend, correct, alter, change, edit, rewrite, redraft, rephrase, rework.

revision ▶ noun **1** *a revision of the fifth chapter* **emendation,** correction, alteration, adaptation, editing, rewriting, redrafting.
2 *a new revision* **version,** edition, rewrite.
3 *a major revision of the system* **reconsideration,** review, reexamination, reassessment, reevaluation, reappraisal, rethink; change, alteration, modification.

revival ▶ noun **1** *a revival in the economy* **improvement,** recovery, rallying, picking up, amelioration, turn for the better, upturn, upswing, resurgence.
ANTONYMS downturn.
2 *the revival of traditional crafts* **comeback,** reestablishment, reintroduction, restoration, reappearance, resurrection, regeneration, renaissance, rejuvenation.
ANTONYMS disappearance.

revive ▶ verb **1** *attempts to revive her failed* **resuscitate,** bring around, bring back to consciousness.
2 *the man soon revived* **regain consciousness,** come around, wake up.
3 *a cup of tea revived her* **reinvigorate,** revitalize, refresh, energize, reanimate, resuscitate, revivify, rejuvenate, regenerate, enliven, stimulate.
4 *reviving old traditions* **reintroduce,** reestablish, restore, resurrect, bring back, regenerate, resuscitate, rekindle.

revoke ▶ verb *their liquor license was revoked* **cancel,** repeal, rescind, reverse, annul, nullify, void, invalidate, countermand, retract, withdraw, overrule, override; Law vacate; formal abrogate.

revolt ▶ verb **1** *the people revolted* **rebel,** rise up, rise, take to the streets, riot, mutiny.
2 *the smell revolted him* **disgust,** sicken, nauseate, make nauseous, make someone sick, turn someone's stomach, be repugnant to, be repulsive to, put off, be offensive to, make someone's gorge rise; informal turn off, gross out.
▶ noun *an armed revolt* **rebellion,** revolution, insurrection, mutiny, uprising, riot, rioting, insurgence, seizure of power, coup, coup d'état.

revolting ▶ adjective *a number of revolting items in their refrigerator* **disgusting,** sickening,

nauseating, stomach-turning, stomach-churning, repulsive, repellent, repugnant, appalling, abominable, hideous, horrible, awful, dreadful, terrible, obnoxious, vile, nasty, foul, loathsome, offensive, objectionable, off-putting, distasteful, disagreeable, vomitous; informal ghastly, putrid, horrid, gross, gut-churning, yucky, icky; formal rebarbative; literary noisome; archaic loathly.
ANTONYMS attractive, pleasant, mouthwatering.

revolution ▶ noun **1** *the French aristocracy was ill-prepared to quell a revolution* **rebellion,** revolt, insurrection, mutiny, uprising, riot, rioting, insurgence, seizure of power, coup (d'état). See note at UPRISING.
2 *a revolution in printing techniques* **dramatic change,** radical alteration, sea change, metamorphosis, transformation, innovation, reorganization, restructuring; informal shake-up, shakedown.
3 *one revolution of a wheel* **turn,** single turn, rotation, circle, spin; circuit, lap.
4 *the revolution of the earth* **turning,** rotation, circling; orbit.

revolutionary ▶ adjective **1** *revolutionary troops* **rebellious,** rebel, insurgent, rioting, mutinous, renegade, insurrectionary, insurrectionist, seditious, subversive, extremist.
2 *revolutionary change* **thoroughgoing,** thorough, complete, total, absolute, utter, comprehensive, sweeping, far-reaching, extensive, profound.
3 *a revolutionary kind of wheelchair* **new,** novel, original, unusual, unconventional, unorthodox, newfangled, innovative, modern, state-of-the-art, cutting-edge, futuristic, pioneering.
▶ noun *political revolutionaries* **rebel,** insurgent, revolutionist, mutineer, insurrectionist, agitator, subversive.

revolve ▶ verb **1** *a fan revolved slowly* **go around,** turn around, rotate, spin.
2 *the moon revolves around the earth* **circle,** travel, orbit.
3 *his life* ***revolves around*** *cars* **be concerned with,** be preoccupied with, focus on, center on/around.

revulsion ▶ noun *the violence has sent a wave of revulsion through the community* **disgust,** repulsion, abhorrence, repugnance, nausea, horror, aversion, abomination, distaste.
ANTONYMS delight.

reward ▶ noun *a reward for its safe return* **recompense,** prize, award, honor, decoration, bonus, premium, bounty, present, gift, payment; informal payoff, perk; formal perquisite.
▶ verb *they were well rewarded* **recompense,** pay, remunerate, make something worth someone's while; give an award to.
ANTONYMS punish.

rewarding ▶ adjective *working in Professor Ott's intern program has been a rewarding experience* **satisfying,** gratifying, pleasing, fulfilling, enriching, edifying, beneficial, illuminating, worthwhile, productive, fruitful.

rhetoric ▶ noun **1** *a form of rhetoric* **oratory,** eloquence, command of language, way with words.
2 *empty rhetoric* **bombast,** turgidity, grandiloquence, magniloquence, pomposity, extravagant language, purple prose; wordiness, verbosity, prolixity; informal hot air; rare fustian.

USAGE

rhetoric

Rhetoric = (1) the art of using language persuasively; the rules that help one achieve eloquence; (2) the persuasive use of language; (3) a treatise on persuasive language; (4) prose composition as a school subject. These are the main senses outlined in the *Oxford English Dictionary*. There should probably be added a new sense, related to but distinct from the first sense: (5) the bombastic or disingenuous use of language to manipulate people.

Older books defined *rhetoric* in line with sense 1:

- "Rhetoric is the Art of speaking suitably upon any Subject." (John Kirkby, *A New English Grammar*; 1746.)
- "Rhetoric is the art of adapting discourse, in harmony with its subject and occasion, to the requirements of a reader or hearer." (John F. Genung, *The Working Principles of Rhetoric*; 1902.)

But the slippage toward the pejorative sense 5 began early. In "Some Fruits of Solitude" (1693), William Penn suggested its iniquitous uses: "There is a Truth and Beauty in Rhetorick; but it oftener serves ill Turns than good ones." (Charles W. Eliot, ed., *Harvard Classics*; 1909.) By the twentieth century, some writers with a classical bent were trying hard to reclaim the word—e.g.: "No one who reads [ancient authors] can hold the puerile notions of rhetoric that prevail in our generation. The ancients would have made short work of the cult of the anti-social that lies behind the cult of mystification and the modern hatred of rhetoric. All the great literary ages have exalted the study of rhetoric." (Van Wyck Brooks, *Opinions of Oliver Allston*; 1941.) But T. S. Eliot probably had it right when he acknowledged that the word is essentially ambiguous today—generally pejorative but with flashes of a favorable sense: "The word [*rhetoric*] simply cannot be used as synonymous with bad writing. The meanings which it has been obliged to shoulder have been mostly opprobrious; but if a precise meaning can be found for it this meaning may occasionally represent a virtue." (" 'Rhetoric' and Poetic Drama," in *The Sacred Wood*, 7th ed.; 1950.) — **BG**

rhetorical ▶ adjective **1** *rhetorical devices* **stylistic,** oratorical, linguistic, verbal.
2 *rhetorical hyperbole* **extravagant,** grandiloquent, magniloquent, high-flown, orotund, bombastic, grandiose, pompous, pretentious, overblown, oratorical, turgid,

flowery, florid; informal highfalutin; rare fustian.

rhyme ▶ noun *an amusing rhyme by Ogden Nash* **poem,** piece of poetry, verse; (**rhymes**) poetry, doggerel.

rhythm ▶ noun **1** *the rhythm of the music* **beat,** cadence, tempo, time, pulse, throb, swing.
2 *poetic features such as rhythm* **meter,** measure, stress, accent, cadence.
3 *the rhythm of daily life* **pattern,** flow, tempo.

ribald ▶ adjective See CRUDE (sense 3).

rich ▶ adjective **1** *rich people* **wealthy,** affluent, moneyed, well off, well-to-do, prosperous, opulent, silk-stocking; informal rolling in money, rolling in it, rolling in (the) dough, in the money, loaded, flush, stinking rich, filthy rich, well-heeled, made of money. See note at WEALTHY.
ANTONYMS poor.
2 *rich furnishings* **sumptuous,** opulent, luxurious, luxury, deluxe, lavish, gorgeous, splendid, magnificent, costly, expensive, fancy; informal posh, plush, ritzy, swanky, classy, swank.
ANTONYMS plain, austere.
3 *a garden rich in flowers* **abounding in,** full of, well provided with, well stocked in/with, crammed with, packed with, teeming with, bursting with; informal jam-packed with, chockablock with, chock-full of.
4 *a rich supply of restaurants* **plentiful,** abundant, copious, ample, profuse, lavish, liberal, generous, bountiful; literary plenteous, bounteous.
ANTONYMS poor, meager.
5 *rich soil* **fertile,** productive, fecund, fruitful.
ANTONYMS barren.
6 *a rich sauce* **creamy,** heavy, full-flavored, fatty.
ANTONYMS delicate, light.
7 *a rich wine* **full-bodied,** heavy, fruity.
ANTONYMS light.
8 *rich colors* **strong,** deep, full, intense, vivid, brilliant.
ANTONYMS delicate, pastel.
9 *her rich voice* **sonorous,** full, resonant, deep, clear, mellow, mellifluous, full-throated.
ANTONYMS thin, reedy.

riches ▶ plural noun **1** *his newfound riches* **money,** wealth, funds, cash, (filthy) lucre, wherewithal, means, assets, liquid assets, capital, resources, reserves; opulence, affluence, prosperity; informal dough, bread, loot, shekels, moola, bucks, dinero, jack.
2 *a cache of underwater riches* **resources,** treasure(s), bounty; jewels, gems.

richly ▶ adverb **1** *the richly furnished chamber* **sumptuously,** opulently, luxuriously, lavishly, gorgeously, splendidly, magnificently; informal plushly, ritzily, swankily, classily.
ANTONYMS meanly, shabbily.
2 *the joy she richly deserves* **fully,** thoroughly, in full measure, well, completely, wholly, totally, entirely, absolutely, amply, utterly.

rid ▶ verb *ridding the building of asbestos* **clear,** free, purge, empty, strip.
– PHRASES **get rid of 1** *we must get rid of some stuff* **dispose of,** throw away, throw out, clear out, discard, scrap, dump, jettison, divest oneself of; informal chuck, ditch, junk, trash, deep-six. **2** *the cats got rid of the rats* **destroy,** eliminate, annihilate, obliterate, wipe out, kill.

riddle ▶ noun *an answer to the riddle* **puzzle,** conundrum, brainteaser, problem, unsolved problem, question, poser, enigma, mystery, quandary; informal stumper.

> CHOOSE THE RIGHT WORD
>
> **riddle, conundrum, enigma, mystery, paradox, puzzle**
>
> All of these terms imply something baffling or challenging. A **mystery** is anything that is incomprehensible to human reason, particularly if it invites speculation (*the mystery surrounding her sudden disappearance*). An **enigma** is a statement whose meaning is hidden under obscure or ambiguous allusions, so that we can only guess at its significance; it can also refer to a person of puzzling or contradictory character (*he remained an enigma throughout his long career*). A **riddle** is a mystery involving contradictory statements, with a hidden meaning designed to be guessed at (*the old riddle about how many college graduates it takes to change a light bulb*). **Conundrum** applies specifically to a riddle phrased as a question, the answer to which usually involves a pun or a play on words, such as "What is black and white and read all over?"; *conundrum* can also refer to any puzzling or difficult situation. A **paradox** is a statement that seems self-contradictory or absurd, but in reality expresses a possible truth (*Francis Bacon's well-known paradox, "The most corrected copies are commonly the least correct"*). A **puzzle** is not necessarily a verbal statement, but it presents a problem with a particularly baffling solution or tests one's ingenuity or skill in coming up with a solution (*a crossword puzzle*).

ride ▶ verb **1** *she can ride a horse* **sit on,** mount, bestride; manage, handle, control.
2 *riding through the town on motorbikes* **travel,** move, proceed, make one's way; drive, cycle; trot, canter, gallop.
▶ noun *a ride in the new car* **trip,** journey, drive, run, excursion, outing, jaunt; lift; informal spin.

ridicule ▶ noun *she was subjected to ridicule* **mockery,** derision, laughter, scorn, scoffing, contempt, jeering, sneering, sneers, jibes, jibing, teasing, taunts, taunting, badinage, chaffing, sarcasm, satire; informal kidding, ribbing, joshing, goofing, razzing.
ANTONYMS respect.
▶ verb *his theory was ridiculed* **deride,** mock, laugh at, heap scorn on/upon, jeer at, jibe at, sneer at, treat with contempt, scorn, make fun of, poke fun at, scoff at, satirize, lampoon, burlesque, caricature, parody, tease, taunt, chaff; informal kid, rib, josh, razz.

ridiculous ▶ adjective **1** *she looked ridiculous in her dad's oversized shorts and striped socks* **laughable,** absurd, comical, funny, hilarious, risible, droll, amusing, farcical, silly, ludicrous;

rare derisible.
ANTONYMS serious.
2 *a ridiculous suggestion* **senseless,** silly, foolish, foolhardy, stupid, inane, fatuous, childish, puerile, half-baked, harebrained, cockamamie, ill-thought-out, crackpot, idiotic.
ANTONYMS sensible.
3 *a ridiculous exaggeration* **absurd,** preposterous, ludicrous, risible, laughable, nonsensical, senseless, outrageous. See note at **ABSURD**.
ANTONYMS reasonable.

rife ▶ **adjective 1** *violence is rife* **widespread,** general, common, universal, extensive, ubiquitous, omnipresent, endemic, inescapable, insidious, prevalent. See note at **PREVALENT**.
ANTONYMS scarce, unknown.
2 *the village was rife with gossip* **overflowing,** bursting, alive, teeming, abounding.
ANTONYMS devoid.

riffraff ▶ **noun** *this government considers its citizens riffraff and is quick to silence the mere whispers of dissent* **rabble,** scum, good-for-nothings, undesirables, lowlifes, hoi polloi, the lowest of the low; informal peasants.
ANTONYMS elite.

rifle ▶ **verb 1** *she rifled through her closet* **rummage,** search, hunt, forage.
2 *a thief rifled her home* **burgle,** burglarize, rob, steal from, loot, raid, plunder, ransack.
▶ **noun** *he refused to register the rifle* **firearm,** gun, shotgun, 30-30; trademark Winchester.

rift ▶ **noun 1** *a deep rift in the ice* **crack,** fault, flaw, split, break, breach, fissure, fracture, cleft, crevice, cavity, opening.
2 *the rift between them* **breach,** division, split; quarrel, squabble, disagreement, falling-out, row, argument, dispute, conflict, feud; estrangement; informal spat, scrap.

USAGE

riff, rift

These two are sometimes confused. *Riff* is now largely confined to jazz and pop-music contexts. It refers to a melodic phrase, usually repeated and often played in unison by several instruments; sometimes it's a variation on a tune, and it may be either an accompaniment to a solo or the only melodic element—e.g.: "With guitar riffs so rudimentary they seem to have been made up on the spot, . . . the U.K. sextet played with rude ebullience." (*Chicago Tribune*; Sept. 29, 2000.) The term dates only from the mid-twentieth century—and has little discernible relation to the older, mostly obsolete senses of *riff* (= [1] a string of onions, [2] the diaphragm, or [3] the mange; an itchy rash). That's probably because this particular *riff* seems to have originated as a truncated form of the musical term *refrain*.

Rift arose in Middle English in the sense "a fissure or divide; a split or crack"—the meaning it still carries—e.g.: "Word out of Washington is that Bondra wants to change teams because of a rift with coach Ron Wilson." (*Boston Globe*; Oct. 1, 2000.) Occasionally the term also refers to the rapids formed by rocks protruding from the bed of a stream. It formerly also meant "a burp"—a sense long obsolete.

Although the *Oxford English Dictionary* records two early-seventeenth-century uses of *riff* in the obsolete sense "rift, chink," the modern use of the word in that sense appears to be nothing more than rank word-swapping resulting from sound association—e.g.: "The way he sees it, things aren't bad at all. No riffs [read *rifts*] between him and crew chief Todd Parrott." (*USA Today*; May 26, 2000.) — **BG**

rig ▶ **verb 1** *the boats were rigged with a single sail* **equip,** fit out, supply, furnish, provide, arm.
2 *I **rigged** myself **out** in black* **dress,** clothe, attire, robe, garb, array, deck out, drape, accoutre, outfit, get up, trick out/up; informal doll up; archaic apparel.
3 *he will **rig up** a shelter* **set up,** erect, assemble, build; throw together, cobble together, put together, whip up, improvise, contrive.
▶ **noun 1** *a CB radio rig* **apparatus,** appliance, machine, device, instrument, contraption, system; tackle, gear, kit, outfit.
2 *the rig of a Civil War cavalry officer* **uniform,** costume, ensemble, outfit, livery, attire, clothes, clothing, garments, dress, garb, regalia, trappings; informal getup, gear, togs, kit; formal apparel; archaic raiment, vestments.

right ▶ **adjective 1** *it wouldn't be right to do that* **just,** fair, proper, good, upright, righteous, virtuous, moral, ethical, honorable, honest; lawful, legal.
ANTONYMS wrong, unjust.
2 *Mr. Hubert had the right answer* **correct,** accurate, exact, precise; proper, valid, conventional, established, official, formal.
ANTONYMS wrong, inaccurate.
3 *the right person for the job* **suitable,** appropriate, fitting, correct, proper, desirable, preferable, ideal; archaic meet.
ANTONYMS wrong, unsuitable.
4 *you've come at the right time* **opportune,** advantageous, favorable, propitious, good, lucky, happy, fortunate, providential, felicitous; timely, seasonable, convenient, expedient, suitable, appropriate.
ANTONYMS wrong, inopportune.
5 *he's not right in the head* **sane,** lucid, rational, balanced, together, compos mentis; healthy, well; informal all there.
ANTONYMS non compos mentis, insane.
6 *my right hand* **dextral**.
ANTONYMS left.
▶ **adverb 1** *she was right at the limit of her patience* **completely,** fully, totally, absolutely, utterly, thoroughly, quite.
2 *right in the middle of the village* **exactly,** precisely, directly, immediately, just, squarely, dead; informal bang, smack, plumb, smack dab.
3 *keep going right ahead* **straight,** directly.
ANTONYMS indirectly.
4 informal *he'll be right down* **straight,** immediately, instantly, at once, straightaway, now, right now, this minute, directly, forthwith,

without further ado, promptly, quickly, as soon as possible, ASAP, in short order; informal straight off, PDQ (pretty damn quick), pronto, lickety-split.
ANTONYMS sometime, later.
5 *I think I heard right* **correctly,** accurately, properly, precisely, aright, rightly, perfectly.
ANTONYMS wrong.
6 *make sure you're treated right by the authorities* **well,** properly, justly, fairly, nicely, equitably, impartially, honorably, lawfully, legally, ethically.
ANTONYMS unjustly.
7 *things will turn out right* **well,** for the best, favorably, happily, advantageously, profitably, providentially, luckily, conveniently.
ANTONYMS badly.
▶ **noun 1** *the difference between right and wrong* **goodness,** righteousness, virtue, integrity, rectitude, propriety, morality, truth, honesty, honor, justice, fairness, equity; lawfulness, legality.
ANTONYMS wrong.
2 *you have the right to say no* **entitlement,** prerogative, privilege, advantage, due, birthright, liberty, authority, power, license, permission, dispensation, leave, sanction, freedom; Law historical droit.
▶ **verb 1** *the way to right a capsized dinghy* **set upright,** turn back over.
2 *we must right the situation* **remedy,** put right, rectify, retrieve, fix, resolve, sort out, settle, square; straighten out, correct, repair, mend, redress, make good, ameliorate, better.
– PHRASES **by rights** *by rights, these kids should have been offered a decent education* **properly,** correctly, technically, in fairness; legally, de jure. **in the right** *please explain why you think you're in the right* **justified,** vindicated. **put right** See RIGHT (sense 2 of the verb). **right away** *we'll miss the bus if we don't leave right away* **at once,** straightaway, now, right now, this minute, this very minute, this instant, immediately, instantly, directly, forthwith, without further ado, promptly, quickly, without delay, as soon as possible, ASAP, in short order; informal straight off, PDQ (pretty damn quick), pronto, lickety-split. **within one's rights** *Mr. Barnes is within his rights to dispute the charges to his account* **entitled,** permitted, allowed, at liberty, empowered, authorized, qualified, licensed, justified.

righteous ▶ **adjective 1** *righteous living* **good,** virtuous, upright, upstanding, decent; ethical, principled, moral, high-minded, law-abiding, honest, honorable, blameless, irreproachable, noble; saintly, angelic, pure. See note at MORAL.
ANTONYMS sinful.
2 *righteous anger* **justifiable,** justified, legitimate, defensible, supportable, rightful; admissible, allowable, understandable, excusable, acceptable, reasonable.
ANTONYMS unjustifiable.

rigid ▶ **adjective 1** *a rigid container* **stiff,** hard, firm, inflexible, unbending, unyielding, inelastic.
ANTONYMS flexible.
2 *a rigid routine* **fixed,** set, firm, inflexible, unalterable, unchangeable, immutable, unvarying, invariable, hard and fast, cast-iron, ironclad.
ANTONYMS flexible.
3 *a rigid approach to funding* **strict,** severe, stern, stringent, rigorous, inflexible, uncompromising, intransigent.
ANTONYMS flexible, lenient.

rigor ▶ **noun 1** *a mine operated under conditions of rigor* **strictness,** severity, stringency, toughness, harshness, rigidity, inflexibility, intransigence.
2 *intellectual rigor* **meticulousness,** thoroughness, carefulness, diligence, scrupulousness, exactness, exactitude, precision, accuracy, correctness, strictness.
3 (**rigors**) *the rigors of the journey* **hardship,** harshness, severity, adversity; ordeal, misery, trial; discomfort, inconvenience, privation.

rigorous ▶ **adjective 1** *rigorous attention to detail* **meticulous,** conscientious, punctilious, careful, diligent, attentive, scrupulous, painstaking, exact, precise, accurate, thorough, particular, strict, demanding, exacting; informal persnickety.
ANTONYMS slapdash.
2 *the rigorous enforcement of rules* **strict,** severe, stern, stringent, tough, harsh, rigid, relentless, unsparing, inflexible, draconian, intransigent, uncompromising, exacting.
ANTONYMS lax.
3 *rigorous yachting conditions* **harsh,** severe, bad, bleak, extreme, inclement; unpleasant, disagreeable, foul, nasty, filthy; stormy, wild, tempestuous.
ANTONYMS gentle, mild.

rim ▶ **noun 1** *the rim of her cup* **brim,** edge, lip.
2 *the rim of the crater* **edge,** border, side, margin, brink, fringe, boundary, perimeter, limits, periphery. See note at BORDER.

rind ▶ **noun** *dried lemon rind* **skin,** peel, zest, integument; Botany pericarp.

ring[1] ▶ **noun 1** *the rings around Saturn* **circle,** band, loop, hoop, halo, disk.
2 *she wore a ring* **wedding ring,** wedding band, band.
3 *a circus ring* **arena,** enclosure, field, ground; amphitheater, stadium.
4 *a ring of onlookers* **circle,** group, cluster, bunch, band, throng, crowd, flock, pack.
5 *a spy ring* **gang,** syndicate, cartel, mob, band, circle, organization, association, society, alliance, league, coterie, cabal, cell.
▶ **verb** *police ringed the building* **surround,** circle, encircle, encompass, girdle, enclose, hem in, confine, seal off.

ring[2] ▶ **verb 1** *church bells rang all day* **toll,** sound, peal, chime, clang, bong, ding, jingle, tinkle; literary knell.
2 *the room rang with laughter* **resound,** reverberate, resonate, echo.
▶ **noun** *the ring of a bell* **chime,** toll, peal, clang, clink, ding, jingle, tinkle, tintinnabulation, sound; literary knell.
– PHRASES **ring something in** *our biggest sale of the season will ring in the new year* **herald,** signal, announce, proclaim, usher in, introduce; mark, signify, indicate; literary betoken, knell.

rinse ▶ **verb** *the campers rinsed their socks and hung them near the fire* **wash,** wash out, clean, cleanse, bathe; dip, drench, splash, hose down.

riot ▶ noun **1** *a riot in the capital* **uproar,** commotion, upheaval, disturbance, furor, tumult, melee, scuffle, fracas, fray, brawl, free-for-all; violence, fighting, vandalism, mayhem, turmoil, lawlessness, anarchy, violent protest.
2 *the garden was a riot of color* **mass,** sea, splash, show, exhibition.
▶ verb *the miners rioted* **rampage,** go on the rampage, run riot, fight in the streets, run wild, run amok, go berserk; informal raise hell.
– PHRASES **run riot 1** *the children ran riot* **go on the rampage,** rampage, riot, run amok, go berserk, go out of control; informal raise hell.
2 *the vegetation has run riot* **grow profusely,** spread uncontrolled, grow rapidly, spread like wildfire; burgeon, multiply, rocket, skyrocket.

riotous ▶ adjective **1** *the demonstration turned riotous* **unruly,** rowdy, disorderly, uncontrollable, unmanageable, undisciplined, uproarious, tumultuous; violent, wild, ugly, lawless, anarchic.
ANTONYMS peaceable.
2 *a riotous party* **boisterous,** lively, loud, noisy, unrestrained, uninhibited, uproarious, unruly, rollicking, knockabout; informal rambunctious.
ANTONYMS restrained.

ripe ▶ adjective **1** *a ripe tomato* **mature,** ripened, full grown, ready to eat; luscious, juicy, tender, sweet.
ANTONYMS green.
2 *the dock is ripe for development* **ready,** fit, suitable, right.
ANTONYMS unsuitable, unready.
3 *the ripe old age of ninety* **advanced,** hoary, venerable, old.
4 *the time is ripe for his return* **opportune,** advantageous, favorable, auspicious, propitious, promising, good, right, fortunate, benign, providential, felicitous, seasonable; convenient, suitable, appropriate, apt, fitting.
ANTONYMS unsuitable.

ripen ▶ verb *we let the grapes ripen on the vine* **become ripe,** mature, mellow. See note at MATURE.

riposte ▶ noun *an indignant riposte* **retort,** counter, rejoinder, sally, return, answer, reply, response; informal comeback.
▶ verb *"Heaven help you," riposted Alicia* **retort,** counter, rejoin, return, retaliate, hurl back, answer, reply, respond, come back.

rise ▶ verb **1** *the sun rose* **move up/upwards,** come up, make one's/its way up, arise, ascend, climb, mount, soar.
ANTONYMS fall, descend, set.
2 *the mountains rising above us* **loom,** tower, soar, rise up, rear (up).
3 *prices rose* **go up,** increase, soar, shoot up, surge, leap, jump, rocket, escalate, spiral.
ANTONYMS drop.
4 *living standards have risen* **improve,** get better, advance, go up, soar, shoot up.
ANTONYMS worsen.
5 *her voice rose* **get higher,** grow, increase, become louder, swell, intensify.
ANTONYMS drop.
6 *he rose from his chair* **stand up,** get to one's feet, get up, jump up, leap up; formal arise.
ANTONYMS sit.
7 *she rises at dawn* **get up,** get out of bed, rouse oneself, stir, bestir oneself, be up and about; informal rise and shine, surface; formal arise.
ANTONYMS retire, go to bed.
8 *the court rose at midday* **adjourn,** recess, be suspended, pause, take a break; informal knock off, take five.
ANTONYMS resume, continue.
9 *he rose through the ranks* **make progress,** climb, advance, get on, work one's way, be promoted.
10 *she wouldn't* **rise to** *the bait* **react to,** respond to; take.
11 *on the third day, Christ rose* **come back to life,** be resurrected, revive.
ANTONYMS die.
12 *the dough started to rise* **swell,** expand, enlarge, puff up.
13 *the nation rose against its oppressors* **rebel,** revolt, mutiny, riot, take up arms.
ANTONYMS kowtow.
14 *the river* **rises in** *the mountains* **originate in,** begin in, start in, emerge in/from; issue from, spring from, flow from, emanate from.
15 *her spirits rose* **brighten,** lift, cheer up, improve, pick up; informal buck up.
16 *the ground rose gently* **slope upward,** go uphill, incline, climb.
ANTONYMS drop away, drop.
▶ noun **1** *a price rise* **increase,** hike, leap, upsurge, upswing, climb, escalation.
2 *a rise in standards* **improvement,** amelioration, upturn, leap.
3 *her rise to power* **progress,** climb, promotion, elevation, aggrandizement.
4 *we walked up the rise* **slope,** incline, hillock, hill; formal eminence.

risk ▶ noun **1** *there is a certain amount of risk* **chance,** uncertainty, unpredictability, precariousness, instability, insecurity, perilousness, riskiness.
ANTONYMS safety.
2 *the risk of fire* **possibility,** chance, probability, likelihood, danger, peril, threat, menace, fear, prospect.
ANTONYMS impossibility.
▶ verb **1** *he risked his life to save them* **endanger,** imperil, jeopardize, hazard, gamble, gamble with, chance; put on the line, put in jeopardy.
2 *you risk getting cold and wet* **chance,** stand a chance of.
– PHRASES **at risk** *our soldiers are at risk every day* **in danger,** in peril, in jeopardy, under threat.

risky ▶ adjective *risky sports* **dangerous,** hazardous, perilous, high-risk, fraught with danger, unsafe, insecure, precarious, touch-and-go, treacherous, parlous; uncertain, unpredictable; informal chancy, dicey, hairy.

rite ▶ noun *a religious rite practiced for thousands of years* **ceremony,** ritual, ceremonial; service, sacrament, liturgy, worship, office; act, practice, custom, tradition, convention, institution, procedure.

ritual ▶ noun *an elaborate civic ritual* **ceremony,** rite, ceremonial, observance; service, sacrament, liturgy, worship; act, practice, custom, tradition, convention, formality, procedure, protocol.

▶ **adjective** *a ritual burial* **ceremonial,** ritualistic, prescribed, set, formal; sacramental, liturgical; traditional, conventional.

rival ▶ **noun 1** *his rival for the nomination* **opponent,** challenger, competitor, contender; adversary, antagonist, enemy; literary foe.
ANTONYMS ally.
2 *the tool has no rival* **equal,** match, peer, equivalent, counterpart, like.
▶ **verb** *few countries can rival ours for natural resources* **match,** compare with, compete with, vie with, equal, measure up to, be in the same league as, be on a par with, touch, challenge; informal hold a candle to.
▶ **adjective** *rival candidates* **competing,** opposing, contending.

rivalry ▶ **noun** *a growing rivalry between the two groups* **competitiveness,** competition, contention, vying; opposition, conflict, feuding, antagonism, friction, enmity.

road ▶ **noun 1** *the roads were crowded with traffic* **street,** avenue, boulevard, freeway, highway, parkway, thoroughfare, thruway, turnpike.
2 *a step on the road to recovery* **way,** path, route, course.
– PHRASES **on the road** *the band will be on the road for two months* **on tour,** touring, traveling.

roam ▶ **verb** *he had roamed the countryside for nine years* **wander,** rove, ramble, drift, walk, traipse; range, travel, tramp, traverse, trek; informal cruise, mosey around/about; formal perambulate; archaic peregrinate.

roar ▶ **noun 1** *the roars of the crowd* **shout,** bellow, yell, cry, howl; clamor; informal holler.
2 *the roar of the sea* **boom,** crash, rumble, roll, thundering.
3 *roars of laughter* **guffaw,** howl, hoot, shriek, gale, peal.
▶ **verb 1** *"Get out!" roared Angus* **bellow,** yell, shout, bawl, howl; informal holler.
2 *thunder roared* **boom,** rumble, crash, roll, thunder.
3 *the movie left them roaring* **guffaw,** laugh, hoot; informal split one's sides, be rolling in the aisles, be doubled up, crack up, be in stitches, die laughing.
4 *a motorbike roared past* **speed,** zoom, whiz, flash; belt, tear, zip, bomb.

rob ▶ **verb 1** *the gang robbed the local bank* **burgle,** burglarize, steal from, hold up, break into; raid, loot, plunder, pillage; informal knock off, stick up.
2 *he robbed an old woman* **steal from**; informal mug, jump, roll.
3 *she was robbed of her savings* **cheat (out),** swindle (out), defraud (out); informal do out, con out, fleece (out); informal stiff (out).
4 informal *if you paid $300 for that watch, you were robbed* **overcharge**; informal rip off, sting, have, diddle, gouge.
5 *a dubious call robbed him of his championship title* **deprive,** strip, divest; deny.

robber ▶ **noun** *the robbers fled the scene in a blue Camaro* **burglar,** thief, housebreaker, mugger, shoplifter, purse-snatcher; stealer, pilferer, raider, looter, plunderer, pillager; bandit; pirate; informal crook, yegg, second-story man; literary brigand, highwayman.

robbery ▶ **noun 1** *they were arrested for the robbery* **burglary,** theft, thievery, stealing, breaking and entering, housebreaking, larceny, shoplifting, purse-snatching; embezzlement, fraud; holdup, break-in, raid; informal mugging, stickup, heist.
2 informal *Six bucks? That's robbery!* **a swindle**; informal a rip-off, a gyp, a con, a con job.

robe ▶ **noun 1** *they put on their robes after swimming* **bathrobe,** dressing gown, kimono, housecoat, kaftan, cover-up, wrapper.
2 *she wore a fur-trimmed red robe* **cloak,** wrap, mantle, cape.
3 (robes) *coronation robes* **garb,** regalia, costume, finery; garments, clothes; formal apparel; archaic raiment, habiliments, vestments.
4 (robes) *priestly robes* **vestment,** surplice, cassock, soutane, rochet, alb, dalmatic, chasuble, tunicle, Geneva gown; canonicals.
▶ **verb** *he robed for Mass* **dress,** vest, clothe oneself; formal enrobe.

robot ▶ **noun** *robots can perform certain tasks that are considered hazardous for humans* **automaton,** android, golem; informal bot, droid.

robust ▶ **adjective 1** *a large, robust man* **strong,** vigorous, sturdy, tough, powerful, solid, muscular, sinewy, rugged, hardy, strapping, brawny, burly, husky; healthy, fit, fighting fit, hale and hearty, lusty, in fine fettle; informal beefy, hunky.
ANTONYMS frail, weak.
2 *these knives are robust* **durable,** resilient, tough, hardwearing, long-lasting, sturdy, strong.
ANTONYMS fragile.
3 *a robust commodities market* **strong,** healthy, resilient, invulnerable; productive, profitable.
ANTONYMS vulnerable.
4 *a robust red wine* **strong,** full-bodied, flavorful, rich.
ANTONYMS tasteless, insipid.

rock[1] ▶ **verb 1** *the ship rocked on the water* **move to and fro,** move back and forth, sway, seesaw; roll, pitch, plunge, toss, lurch, reel, list; wobble, oscillate.
2 *the building began to rock* **shake,** vibrate, quake, tremble.
3 *Wall Street was rocked by the news* **stun,** shock, stagger, astonish, startle, surprise, shake, shake up, take aback, throw, unnerve, disconcert.
4 informal *this game totally rocks* **be impressive**; informal kick butt, blow one away, blow one's mind, rock one's world, be cool, be on fire.

rock[2] ▶ **noun 1** *a gully strewn with rocks* **boulder,** stone, pebble.
2 *a castle built on a rock* **crag,** cliff, outcrop.
3 *Toni was the rock on which they relied* **foundation,** cornerstone, support, prop, mainstay; tower of strength, bulwark, anchor.
4 informal *she wore a massive rock on her finger* **diamond,** jewel, precious stone.
– PHRASES **on the rocks** informal **1** *her marriage is on the rocks* **in difficulty,** in trouble, breaking up, over; in tatters, in ruins, ruined. **2** *a Scotch on the rocks* **with ice,** on ice, over ice.

rocket ▶ **noun 1** *guerrillas fired rockets at them* **missile,** projectile.
2 *they lit some colorful rockets* **firework,** firecracker, Roman candle.
▶ **verb 1** *prices have rocketed* **shoot up,** soar, increase, rise, escalate, spiral; informal go through the roof.
ANTONYMS plummet.
2 *they rocketed into the alley* **speed,** zoom, shoot, whiz, career; informal barrel, tear, bomb, hightail it.

rocky[1] ▶ **adjective** *a rocky path* **stony,** pebbly, shingly; rough, bumpy; craggy, mountainous.

rocky[2] ▶ **adjective 1** *that table's rocky* **unsteady,** shaky, unstable, wobbly, tottery, rickety, flimsy.
ANTONYMS steady, stable.
2 *a rocky marriage* **difficult,** problematic, precarious, unstable, unreliable, undependable; informal iffy, up and down.
ANTONYMS solid, stable.

rod ▶ **noun 1** *an iron rod* **bar,** stick, pole, baton, staff; shaft, strut, rail, spoke.
2 *the ceremonial rod* **staff,** mace, scepter.
3 (**the rod**) *instruction was accompanied by the rod* **corporal punishment,** the cane, the lash, the birch; beating, flogging, caning, birching.

rogue ▶ **noun 1** *a rogue without ethics* **scoundrel,** villain, miscreant, reprobate, rascal, good-for-nothing, ne'er-do-well, wretch; informal rat, dog, louse, crook; dated cad; archaic blackguard, picaroon, knave.
2 *your boy's a little rogue* **rascal,** imp, devil, monkey; informal scamp, scalawag, monster, horror, terror, hellion.

role ▶ **noun 1** *a small role in the film* **part**; character, cameo.
2 *his role as class president* **capacity,** position, job, post, office, duty, responsibility, mantle, place; function, part.

roll ▶ **verb 1** *the bottle rolled down the table* **turn round and round,** go round and round, turn over and over, spin, rotate.
2 *waiters rolled in the trolleys* **wheel,** push, trundle.
3 *we rolled past fields* **travel,** go, move, pass, cruise, sweep.
4 *the months* **rolled by pass,** pass by, go by, slip by, fly by, elapse, wear on, march on.
5 *tears rolled down her cheeks* **flow,** run, course, stream, pour, spill, trickle.
6 *the mist rolled in* **billow,** undulate, tumble.
7 *he rolled his handkerchief into a ball* **wind,** coil, fold, curl; twist.
8 ***roll out*** *the pastry* **flatten (out),** level (out); even out.
9 *they rolled about with laughter* **stagger,** lurch, reel, totter, teeter, wobble.
10 *the ship began to roll* **lurch,** toss, rock, pitch, plunge, sway, reel, list, keel.
11 *thunder rolled* **rumble,** reverberate, echo, resound, boom, roar, grumble.
▶ **noun 1** *a roll of wrapping paper* **cylinder,** tube, scroll; bolt.
2 *a roll of film* **reel,** spool.
3 *a roll of $20 bills* **wad,** bundle.
4 *a roll of the dice* **throw,** toss, turn, spin.
5 *crusty rolls* **bread roll,** bun, bagel, hoagie, kaiser roll.
6 *the electoral roll* **list,** register, directory, record, file, index, catalog, inventory; census.
7 *a roll of thunder* **rumble,** reverberation, echo, boom, clap, crack, roar, grumble.
– PHRASES **roll in** informal **1** *money has been rolling in* **pour in,** flood in, flow in. **2** *he rolled in at nine o'clock* **arrive,** turn up, appear, show one's face; informal show up, blow in. **rolling in it** informal See RICH (sense 1). **roll something out** *she rolled out her towel* **unroll,** spread out, unfurl, unfold, open (out), unwind, uncoil. **roll something up** *they rolled up the sleeping bags* **fold (up),** furl, wind up, coil (up), bundle up.

romance ▶ **noun 1** *their romance blossomed* **love,** passion, ardor, adoration, devotion; affection, fondness, attachment.
2 *he's had many romances* **love affair,** relationship, liaison, courtship, attachment; flirtation, dalliance.
3 *an author of historical romances* **love story,** novel; romantic fiction; informal tearjerker, bodice-ripper.
4 *the romance of the Far East* **mystery,** glamour, excitement, exoticism, mystique; appeal, allure, charm.
▶ **verb 1** dated *he was romancing Carolyn* **woo,** chase, pursue; go out with, seduce; informal see, go steady with, date; dated court, make love to.
2 *I am romancing the past* **romanticize,** idealize, paint a rosy picture of.

romantic ▶ **adjective 1** *he's so romantic* **loving,** amorous, passionate, tender, affectionate; informal lovey-dovey.
2 *the book was a bit too romantic for my tastes* **sentimental,** mawkish, saccharine, syrupy; informal mushy, schmaltzy, gooey, treacly, cheesy, corny, sappy, soppy, cornball. See note at SENTIMENTAL.
ANTONYMS unsentimental, gritty.
3 *a romantic setting* **idyllic,** picturesque, fairy-tale; beautiful, lovely, charming, pretty.
4 *romantic notions of life in rural communities* **idealistic,** idealized, romanticized, unrealistic, fanciful, impractical; head-in-the-clouds, starry-eyed, optimistic, hopeful, visionary, Utopian, fairy-tale.
ANTONYMS practical, realistic.
▶ **noun** *an incurable romantic* **idealist,** sentimentalist, romanticist; dreamer, visionary, Utopian, Don Quixote, fantasist, fantasizer; archaic fantast.
ANTONYMS realist.

room ▶ **noun 1** *there isn't much room* **space**; headroom, legroom; area, expanse, extent; informal elbow room.
2 *room for improvement* **capacity,** scope, leeway, latitude, freedom; opportunity, chance.
3 *she wandered around the room* **chamber**.
4 (**rooms**) *he had rooms at the Plaza* **accommodations,** quarters, lodgings; a suite, an apartment, an efficiency unit; informal a pad, digs.
▶ **verb** *she roomed there in September* **board,** lodge, live, stay; be quartered, be housed, be billeted; formal dwell, reside, sojourn.

roomy ▶ **adjective** *a roomy apartment | roomy pants* **spacious,** capacious, sizable, generous, big, large, extensive; voluminous, ample; formal

commodious.
ANTONYMS cramped, tight-fitting.

root ▶ **noun 1** *a plant's roots* rootstock, tuber, rootlet; Botany rhizome, radicle.
2 *the root of the problem* **source,** origin, germ, beginning(s), genesis; cause, reason, basis, foundation, bottom, seat; core, heart, nub, essence; informal ground zero.
3 (**roots**) *he rejected his roots* **origins,** beginnings, family, ancestors, predecessors, heritage; birthplace, homeland. See note at **ORIGIN**.
▶ **verb 1** *has the shoot rooted?* **take root,** grow roots, establish, strike, take.
2 *root the cuttings* **plant,** bed out, sow.
3 *he rooted around in the cupboard* **rummage,** hunt, search, rifle, delve, forage, dig, nose, poke.
– PHRASES **put down roots** *they married and put down roots in Yemen* **settle,** establish oneself, make one's home, set up home. **root and branch 1** *the company's accounting department should be eradicated, root and branch* **completely,** entirely, wholly, totally, thoroughly.
2 *a root-and-branch reform* **complete,** total, thorough, radical. **root for** informal *Mollie roots for the Broncos* **cheer,** cheer on, applaud, support, encourage. **root out 1** *the hedge was rooted out* **uproot,** deracinate, pull up, grub out.
2 *root out corruption* **eradicate,** eliminate, weed out, destroy, wipe out, stamp out, extirpate, abolish, end, put a stop to.
3 *he rooted out a dark secret* **unearth,** dig up, bring to light, uncover, discover, dredge up, ferret out, expose. **take root 1** *leave the plants to take root* **germinate,** sprout, establish, strike, take. **2** *Christianity took root in Persia* **become established,** take hold; develop, thrive, flourish.

rope ▶ **noun** *secure the rope to the post* **cord,** cable, line, hawser; string; lasso, lariat.
▶ **verb** *his feet were roped together* **tie,** bind, lash, truss; secure, moor, fasten, attach; hitch, tether, lasso.
– PHRASES **know the ropes** informal *you'll spend your first day with someone who knows the ropes* **know what to do,** know the routine, know one's way around, know one's stuff, know what's what; be experienced; informal know the drill, know the score, be streetwise. **rope someone in/into** *why did you let Bruce rope you into this deal?* **persuade to join/participate in,** talk into, trap into, inveigle into; enlist in/into, engage in.

roster ▶ **noun** *check to see if your name's on the roster for tomorrow's game* **schedule,** list, listing, register, agenda, calendar, table.

rostrum ▶ **noun** *the speakers will be seated on either side of the rostrum* **dais,** platform, podium, stage; soapbox.

rosy ▶ **adjective 1** *a rosy complexion* **pink,** pinkish, roseate, reddish, peaches-and-cream; glowing, healthy, fresh, radiant, blooming; blushing, flushed; ruddy, high-colored, florid, rubicund; rare rubescent, erubescent.
ANTONYMS pale, sallow.
2 *his future looks rosy* **promising,** optimistic, auspicious, hopeful, encouraging, favorable, bright, golden; informal upbeat.
ANTONYMS dismal, bleak.

rot ▶ **verb 1** *the floorboards rotted* **decay,** decompose, become rotten; disintegrate, crumble, perish.
2 *the meat began to rot* **go bad,** spoil, go off; molder, putrefy, fester.
3 *poor neighborhoods have been left to rot* **deteriorate,** degenerate, decline, decay, go to rack and ruin, go to seed, go downhill; informal go to pot, go to the dogs.
ANTONYMS improve, recover.
▶ **noun 1** *the leaves turned black with rot* **decay,** decomposition, mold, mildew, blight, canker; putrefaction.
2 *traditionalists said the rot had set in* **deterioration,** decline; corruption, cancer.

rotary ▶ **adjective** *rotary blades* **rotating,** rotational, revolving, turning, spinning, gyrating; formal rotatory.

rotate ▶ **verb 1** *the wheels rotate continually* **revolve,** go around, turn, turn around, spin, gyrate, whirl, twirl, swivel, circle, pivot.
2 *many nurses rotate jobs* **alternate,** take turns, change, switch, interchange, exchange, swap; move around.

rotation ▶ **noun 1** *the rotation of the wheels* **revolving,** turning, spinning, gyration, circling.
2 *a rotation of Jupiter* **turn,** revolution, orbit, spin.
3 *each member is chair for six months in rotation* **sequence,** succession; alternation, cycle.

rotten ▶ **adjective 1** *rotten meat* **decaying,** rotting, bad, off, far gone, decomposing, putrid, putrescent, perished, moldy, moldering, mildewy, rancid, festering, fetid; maggoty, wormy.
ANTONYMS fresh.
2 *rotten teeth* **decaying,** decayed, carious, black; disintegrating, crumbling.
3 *he's rotten to the core* **corrupt,** unprincipled, dishonest, dishonorable, unscrupulous, untrustworthy, immoral; villainous, bad, wicked, evil, iniquitous, venal; informal crooked.
ANTONYMS decent, honorable.
4 informal *a rotten thing to do* **nasty,** unkind, unpleasant, obnoxious, vile, contemptible, despicable, shabby, loathsome; spiteful, mean, low, malicious, hateful, hurtful; unfair, uncharitable, uncalled for; informal dirty, lowdown.
ANTONYMS nice, kind.
5 informal *he was a rotten singer* **bad,** poor, dreadful, awful, terrible, frightful, atrocious, hopeless, inadequate, inferior, substandard; informal crummy, pathetic, useless, lousy, appalling, abysmal.
ANTONYMS accomplished, good.
6 informal *she had a rotten time* **unpleasant,** miserable, awful, dreadful, terrible, frightful, bad, horrible; disappointing, regrettable; informal crummy, lousy.
ANTONYMS good, delightful.
7 informal *I feel rotten about it* **guilty,** conscience-stricken, remorseful, ashamed, shamefaced, chastened, contrite, sorry, regretful, repentant, penitent.
8 informal *I felt rotten with that cold* See **ILL** (sense 1 of the adjective).

rotund ▸ adjective **1** *a small, rotund man* **plump,** chubby, fat, stout, portly, dumpy, round, chunky, overweight, heavy, paunchy, ample; flabby, fleshy, bulky, heavyset, corpulent, obese; informal tubby, roly-poly, pudgy, porky, blubbery, zaftig, corn-fed.
ANTONYMS thin.
2 *rotund cauldrons* **round,** bulbous, spherical, spheric.
3 *the tenor's splendidly rotund tones* See ROUND (sense 3 of the adjective).

rough ▸ adjective **1** *rough ground* **uneven,** irregular, bumpy, lumpy, knobbly, stony, rocky, rugged, rutted, pitted, rutty.
ANTONYMS smooth, flat.
2 *the terrier's rough coat* **coarse,** bristly, scratchy, prickly; shaggy, hairy, bushy.
ANTONYMS smooth, sleek.
3 *rough skin* **dry,** leathery, weather-beaten; chapped, calloused, scaly, scabrous.
ANTONYMS smooth.
4 *his voice was rough* **gruff,** hoarse, harsh, rasping, raspy, croaking, croaky, husky, throaty, gravelly, guttural.
ANTONYMS soft.
5 *rough red wine* **sharp,** sharp-tasting, sour, acidic, acid, vinegary, acidulous.
ANTONYMS sweet, mellow.
6 *he gets rough when he's drunk* **violent,** brutal, vicious; **aggressive,** belligerent, pugnacious, thuggish; boisterous, rowdy, disorderly, unruly, riotous.
ANTONYMS gentle, passive.
7 *a machine that can take rough handling* **careless,** clumsy, inept, unskillful.
ANTONYMS careful.
8 *rough manners* **boorish,** loutish, oafish, brutish, coarse, crude, uncouth, vulgar, unrefined, unladylike, ungentlemanly, uncultured; unmannerly, impolite, discourteous, uncivil, ungracious, rude. See note at RUDE.
ANTONYMS cultured, refined, civilized.
9 *rough seas* **turbulent,** stormy, tempestuous, violent, heavy, heaving, choppy.
ANTONYMS calm.
10 informal *I've had a rough time* **difficult,** hard, tough, bad, unpleasant; demanding, arduous.
ANTONYMS easy, pleasant.
11 informal *you were a bit* ***rough on*** *her* **harsh on/to,** hard on, tough on, stern to, severe to, unfair to, unjust to; insensitive to, nasty to, cruel to, unkind to, unsympathetic to, brutal to, heartless to, merciless to.
ANTONYMS gentle, kind.
12 *a rough draft* **preliminary,** hasty, quick, sketchy, cursory, basic, crude, rudimentary, raw, unpolished; incomplete, unfinished.
ANTONYMS finished, perfected.
13 *a rough estimate* **approximate,** inexact, imprecise, vague, estimated, hazy; informal ballpark.
ANTONYMS exact, precise.
14 *the accommodations are rather rough* **plain, basic,** simple, rough and ready, rude, crude, primitive, spartan.
ANTONYMS luxurious.
▸ noun *the artist's initial roughs* **sketch,** draft, outline, mock-up.
▸ verb *rough the surface with sandpaper* **roughen,** make rough.
– PHRASES **rough something out** *we roughed out a few drawings of the monument* **draft,** sketch out, outline, block out, mock up. **rough someone up** informal *a beefy businessman is roughed up by some thugs for his cellphone* **beat up,** attack, assault, knock around/about, batter, manhandle; informal do over, beat the living daylights out of.

rough-and-tumble ▸ adjective *rough-and-tumble play* **disorderly,** unruly, boisterous, rough, riotous, rowdy, knockabout, noisy, loud.
▸ noun *a political rough-and-tumble* **scuffle,** fight, brawl, melee, free-for-all, fracas, rumpus; horseplay; informal scrap, dust-up, shindy, roughhouse.

round ▸ adjective **1** *a round window* **circular,** ring-shaped, disk-shaped, hoop-shaped; spherical, spheroidal, globular, globe-shaped, orb-shaped; cylindrical; bulbous, rounded, rotund; technical annular, discoid.
2 *round cheeks* **plump,** chubby, fat, full.
ANTONYMS thin.
3 *his deep, round voice* **sonorous,** full-bodied, full-toned, rich, deep, mellow, resonant, reverberant; grandiloquent, magniloquent, rotund, orotund; pear-shaped; rare canorous.
ANTONYMS thin, reedy.
4 *a round dozen* **complete,** entire, whole, full.
5 dated *she berated him in round terms* **candid,** frank, direct, honest, truthful, straightforward, plain, blunt, forthright, bald, explicit, unequivocal, unmistakable, categorical.
ANTONYMS evasive.
▸ noun **1** *mold the dough into rounds* **ball,** sphere, globe, orb, circle, disk, ring, hoop; technical annulus.
2 (**rounds**) *a policeman on his rounds* **circuit,** beat, route, tour.
3 *the first round of the tournament* **stage,** level; heat, game, bout, contest; go-round.
4 *an endless round of parties* **succession,** sequence, series, cycle.
5 *the gun fires thirty rounds per second* **bullet,** cartridge, shell, shot.
▸ verb *the ship rounded the point* **go around,** travel around, skirt, circumnavigate, orbit.
– PHRASES **round about** *the campsite is round about two miles from the main road* See AROUND (sense 3 of the preposition). **round the bend** *this time, I think Gordon's really gone round the bend* See MAD (sense 1). **round the clock** See AROUND THE CLOCK. **round off 1** *the square edges were rounded off* **smooth (off),** plane (off), sand (off), blunt. **2** *the party rounded off a successful year* **complete,** finish off, crown, cap, top; conclude, close, end. **round up** *go round up your brothers for dinner* **gather together,** herd together, muster, marshal, rally, assemble, collect, group, corral.

CHOOSE THE RIGHT WORD

round, annular, circular, globular, spherical

What do a bicycle wheel, a basketball, and a barrel of oil have in common? All are considered to be **round**, an adjective that may be applied to anything shaped like a circle, a sphere, or a cylinder. But of these three objects, only a basketball is **spherical**, which means having a round body whose surface is equally distant from the center at all points. Something that is **globular** is shaped like a ball or a globe but is not necessarily a perfect sphere (*globular drops of oil leaking from the seam*). A wheel is **circular**, as is a Frisbee; in fact, anything with a round, flat surface in the shape of a ring or a disk may be described as *circular*—whether or not it corresponds to a perfect circle. But only the rings of a tree can be described as **annular**, a word that usually implies having a series of concentric ringlike forms or structures.

roundabout ▶ adjective **1** *a roundabout route* **circuitous,** indirect, meandering, serpentine, tortuous.
ANTONYMS direct, straight.
2 *I asked in a roundabout sort of way* **indirect,** oblique, circuitous, circumlocutory, periphrastic, digressive, long-winded; evasive.
ANTONYMS direct.

rouse ▶ verb **1** *he roused Ralph at dawn* **wake,** wake up, awaken, arouse; formal waken.
2 *she roused and looked around* **wake up,** awake, awaken, come to, get up, rise, bestir oneself; formal arise.
ANTONYMS go to sleep.
3 *he roused the crowd* **stir up,** excite, galvanize, electrify, stimulate, inspire, inspirit, move, inflame, agitate, goad, provoke; incite, spur on, light a fire under.
ANTONYMS calm.
4 *he's got a temper when he's roused* **provoke,** annoy, anger, infuriate, madden, incense, vex, irk; informal aggravate.
ANTONYMS appease, pacify.
5 *her disappearance roused my suspicions* **arouse,** awaken, prompt, provoke, stimulate, pique, trigger, spark off, touch off, kindle, elicit.
ANTONYMS allay.

rousing ▶ adjective *rousing cheers from the audience* **stirring,** inspiring, exciting, stimulating, moving, electrifying, invigorating, energizing, exhilarating; enthusiastic, vigorous, spirited.

rout ▶ noun **1** *the army's ignominious rout* **retreat,** flight.
2 *the game was a rout for the Marlins* **crushing defeat,** trouncing, annihilation; debacle, fiasco; informal licking, hammering, thrashing, drubbing, massacre.
ANTONYMS victory.
▶ verb **1** *his army was routed* **put to flight,** drive off, scatter; defeat, beat, conquer, vanquish, crush, overpower.
2 *he routed the defending champion* See DEFEAT (sense 1 of the verb).

route ▶ noun *a different route to school* **way,** course, road, path, direction; passage, journey.
▶ verb *inquiries are routed to the relevant desk* **direct,** send, convey, dispatch, forward.

routine ▶ noun **1** *his morning routine* **procedure,** practice, pattern, drill, regimen; program, schedule, plan; formula, method, system; customs, habits; wont.
2 *a stand-up routine* **act,** performance, number, turn, piece; informal spiel, patter, shtick.
▶ adjective *a routine safety inspection* **standard,** regular, customary, normal, usual, ordinary, typical; everyday, common, commonplace, conventional, habitual, wonted.
ANTONYMS unusual.

row[1] ▶ noun **1** *rows of children* **line,** column, file, queue; procession, chain, string, succession.
2 *the middle row of seats* **tier,** line, rank, bank.
– PHRASES **in a row** *three days in a row* **consecutively,** in succession; running, straight.

row[2] informal ▶ noun *the siblings were having a row* **argument,** quarrel, squabble, fight, contretemps, falling-out, disagreement, dispute, clash, altercation, shouting match; informal tiff, set-to, run-in, blowup, spat. See note at QUARREL.

rowdy ▶ adjective *rowdy youths* **unruly,** disorderly, obstreperous, riotous, undisciplined, uncontrollable, ungovernable, disruptive, out of control, rough, wild, lawless; boisterous, uproarious, noisy, loud, clamorous; informal rambunctious.
ANTONYMS peaceful.
▶ noun *the bar was full of rowdies* **ruffian,** troublemaker, lout, hooligan, thug, hoodlum; informal tough, yahoo, punk, knuckle-dragger.

royal ▶ adjective **1** *the royal prerogative* **regal,** kingly, queenly, princely; sovereign, monarchical.
2 *a royal welcome* **excellent,** fine, magnificent, splendid, superb, wonderful, first-rate, first-class; informal fantastic, great, tremendous.
3 informal *she's a royal pain in the neck* **complete,** utter, total, absolute, real, thorough.

rub ▶ verb **1** *Sally rubbed her arm* **massage,** knead; stroke, pat.
2 *he rubbed sunscreen on her back* **apply,** smear, spread, work in.
3 *my shoes rub badly* **chafe,** pinch; hurt, be painful.
▶ noun **1** *she gave his back a rub* **massage,** rubdown.
2 *I gave the countertop a rub* **polish,** wipe, clean.
3 *it's too complicated—that's the rub* **problem,** difficulty, trouble, drawback, hindrance, impediment; snag, hitch, catch.
– PHRASES **rub something down** *Jake and Pauline are in the stable, rubbing down the horses* **clean,** sponge, wash; groom. **rub it in** informal *yes, I screwed up, but you don't have to rub it in* **emphasize it,** stress it, underline it, highlight it; go on (and on) about it, harp on it; informal rub someone's nose in it. **rub off on** *we just don't want his bad habits rubbing off on you* **be transferred to,** be passed on to, be transmitted to, be communicated to; affect, influence. **rub something out** *they promise to rub out your bad credit history* **erase,** delete, remove, efface, obliterate, expunge. **rub elbows** *it's our chance to rub elbows with the company execs* **associate,** mingle, fraternize, socialize, mix, keep company, consort; informal

hang around/out, hobnob. **rub someone the wrong way** *Regina's roommates rub her boyfriend the wrong way* **irritate,** annoy, irk, vex, provoke, displease, exasperate, infuriate, get on someone's nerves, put out, pique, upset, nettle, ruffle someone's feathers, make someone's hackles rise, try someone's patience, grate on; informal aggravate, get, get to, bug, miff, peeve, rile, needle, tick off, tee off, get under someone's skin, get in someone's hair, get/put someone's back up, get someone's goat, rankle, ride.

rubbish ▸ **noun 1** *throw away that rubbish* See **GARBAGE** (sense 1).
2 *she's talking rubbish* **nonsense,** balderdash, gibberish, claptrap, blarney, moonshine, garbage; informal hogwash, baloney, jive, guff, tripe, drivel, bilge, bunk, BS, piffle, poppycock, hooey, twaddle, gobbledygook, flapdoodle; dated bunkum, tommyrot.

ruddy ▸ **adjective** *a ruddy complexion* **rosy,** red, pink, roseate, rubicund; healthy, glowing, fresh; flushed, blushing; florid, high-colored; literary rubescent.
ANTONYMS pale.

rude ▸ **adjective 1** *a rude man | rude remarks* **ill-mannered,** bad-mannered, impolite, discourteous, uncivil, unmannerly, mannerless; impertinent, insolent, impudent, disrespectful, cheeky; churlish, curt, brusque, brash, offhand, short, sharp; offensive, insulting, derogatory, disparaging, abusive; tactless, undiplomatic, uncomplimentary.
ANTONYMS polite, civil.
2 *rude jokes* **vulgar,** coarse, smutty, dirty, filthy, crude, lewd, obscene, off-color, offensive, indelicate, tasteless; risqué, naughty, ribald, bawdy, racy; informal blue; euphemistic adult.
ANTONYMS clean.
3 *a rude awakening* **abrupt,** sudden, sharp, startling; unpleasant, nasty, harsh.
4 dated *a rude cabin* **primitive,** crude, rudimentary, rough, simple, basic, makeshift.
ANTONYMS classy, luxurious.

CHOOSE THE RIGHT WORD

rude, callow, crude, ill-mannered, rough, uncivil, uncouth

Someone who lacks consideration for the feelings of others and who is deliberately insolent is **rude** (*It was rude of you not to introduce me to your friends*). **Ill-mannered** suggests that the person is ignorant of the rules of social behavior rather than deliberately rude (*an ill-mannered child*), while **uncivil** implies disregard for even the most basic rules of social behavior among civilized people (*his uncivil response resulted in his being kicked out of the classroom*). **Rough** is used to describe people who lack polish and refinement (*he was a rough but honest man*), while **crude** is a more negative term for individuals and behavior lacking culture, civility, and tact (*he made a crude gesture*). **Uncouth** describes what seems strange, awkward, or unmannerly rather than rude (*his uncouth behavior at the wedding*). Although individuals of any age may be rude, crude, ill-mannered, or uncouth, **callow** almost always applies to those who are young or immature; it suggests naiveté and lack of sophistication (*he was surprisingly callow for a man of almost 40*).

rudimentary ▸ **adjective 1** *rudimentary carpentry skills* **basic,** elementary, primary, fundamental, essential.
ANTONYMS advanced.
2 *the equipment was rudimentary* **primitive,** crude, simple, unsophisticated, rough, rough and ready, makeshift.
ANTONYMS sophisticated.
3 *a rudimentary thumb* **vestigial,** undeveloped, incomplete; Biology abortive, primitive.
ANTONYMS developed.

rudiments ▸ **plural noun** *the rudiments of sign language* **basics,** fundamentals, essentials, first principles, foundation; informal nuts and bolts, ABCs.

rue ▸ **verb** *she may live to rue this impetuous decision* **regret,** be sorry about, feel remorseful about, repent of, reproach oneself for; deplore, lament, bemoan, bewail. See note at **MOURN**.

rueful ▸ **adjective** *his rueful expression said it all* **regretful,** apologetic, sorry, remorseful, shamefaced, sheepish, abashed, hangdog, contrite, repentant, penitent, conscience-stricken, sorrowful, sad.

ruffian ▸ **noun** *a gang of young ruffians* **thug,** lout, hooligan, hoodlum, vandal, delinquent, rowdy, scoundrel, villain, rogue, bully, brute; informal tough, roughneck, bruiser, heavy, yahoo, knuckle-dragger, goon.

ruffle ▸ **verb 1** *he ruffled her hair* **disarrange,** tousle, dishevel, rumple, disorder, mess up, tangle; informal muss up.
ANTONYMS smooth.
2 *the wind ruffled the water* **ripple,** riffle.
ANTONYMS smooth.
3 *don't let him ruffle you* **annoy,** irritate, vex, nettle, anger, exasperate; disconcert, unnerve, fluster, agitate, harass, upset, disturb, discomfit, put off, perturb, unsettle, bother, worry, trouble; informal rattle, faze, throw, get to, rile, needle, aggravate, bug, peeve.
ANTONYMS calm, soothe.
▸ **noun** *a shirt with ruffles* **frill,** flounce, ruff, ruche, jabot, furbelow.

rugged ▸ **adjective 1** *a rugged path* **rough,** uneven, bumpy, rocky, stony, pitted, jagged, craggy.
ANTONYMS smooth.
2 *a rugged vehicle* **durable,** sturdy, robust, strong, tough, resilient.
ANTONYMS fragile, flimsy.
3 *rugged manly types* **well-built,** burly, strong, muscular, muscly, brawny, strapping, husky, hulking; tough, hardy, robust, sturdy, lusty, solid; informal hunky, beefy.
ANTONYMS frail, scrawny, weedy.
4 *his rugged features* **strong,** craggy, rough-hewn; manly, masculine; irregular, weathered.
ANTONYMS delicate.
5 *the rugged outdoor life* **tough,** harsh, rigorous,

arduous, onerous, exacting, difficult, hard; austere, spartan.
ANTONYMS easy.
6 *the author was captivated by the rugged individualism of these villagers* **uncompromising,** unwavering, unflinching, firm, tenacious, resolute, determined.
ANTONYMS feeble, ineffectual.

ruin ▶ **noun 1** *the buildings were saved from ruin* **disintegration,** decay, disrepair, dilapidation, ruination; destruction, demolition, wreckage.
ANTONYMS preservation, reconstruction.
2 (**ruins**) *the ruins of a church* **remains,** remnants, fragments, relics; rubble, debris, wreckage.
3 *he was careening toward his ruin* **downfall,** collapse, defeat, undoing, failure, breakdown, ruination; Waterloo.
ANTONYMS success, triumph.
4 *local merchants are facing ruin* **bankruptcy,** insolvency, penury, poverty, destitution, impoverishment, indigence; failure.
ANTONYMS success, wealth.
▶ **verb 1** *don't ruin my plans* **wreck,** destroy, spoil, mar, blight, shatter, dash, torpedo, scotch, mess up; sabotage; informal screw up, foul up, put the kibosh on, nix, scupper, scuttle.
ANTONYMS save, restore.
2 *the bank's collapse ruined them all* **bankrupt,** make insolvent, impoverish, pauperize, wipe out, break, cripple, devastate; bring someone to their knees.
3 *a country ruined by civil war* **destroy,** devastate, lay waste, ravage; raze, demolish, wreck, wipe out, flatten.
ANTONYMS repair, rebuild.
– PHRASES **in ruins 1** *the abbey is in ruins* **derelict,** ruined, in disrepair, falling to pieces, dilapidated, tumbledown, ramshackle, decrepit, decaying, ruinous. **2** *his career is in ruins* **destroyed,** ruined, in pieces, over, finished; informal in tatters, on the rocks, done for.

ruinous ▶ **adjective 1** *a ruinous trade war* **disastrous,** devastating, catastrophic, calamitous, crippling, crushing, damaging, destructive, harmful; costly.
2 *ruinous interest rates* **extortionate,** exorbitant, excessive, sky-high, outrageous, inflated; informal criminal, steep.

rule ▶ **noun 1** *health and safety rules* **regulation,** ruling, directive, order, act, law, statute, edict, canon, mandate, command, dictate, decree, fiat, injunction, commandment, stipulation, requirement, guideline, direction; formal ordinance.
2 *lateness was the general rule* **procedure,** practice, protocol, convention, norm, routine, custom, habit, wont; formal praxis.
3 *moderation is the golden rule* **precept,** principle, standard, axiom, truth, maxim.
4 *Punjab came under British rule* **control,** jurisdiction, command, power, dominion; government, administration, sovereignty, leadership, supremacy, authority.
▶ **verb 1** *El Salvador was ruled by Spain* **govern,** preside over, control, lead, dominate, run, head, administer, manage.
2 *Elizabeth has ruled for more than fifty years* **be in power,** be in control, be in command, be in charge, govern; reign, be monarch, be sovereign.
3 *the judge ruled that they be set free* **decree,** order, pronounce, judge, adjudge, ordain; decide, find, determine, resolve, settle.
4 *chaos ruled* **prevail,** predominate, be the order of the day, reign supreme; formal obtain.
– PHRASES **as a rule** *as a rule, we eat in the kitchen* **usually,** generally, in general, normally, ordinarily, customarily, for the most part, on the whole, by and large, in the main, mainly, mostly, commonly, typically. **rule something out** *the gold brocade isn't one of the top choices, but don't yet rule it out* **exclude,** eliminate, disregard; preclude, prohibit, prevent, disallow.

ruler ▶ **noun** *blessings on our fair ruler* **leader,** sovereign, monarch, potentate, king, queen, emperor, empress, prince, princess; crowned head, head of state, president, premier, governor; overlord, chief, chieftain, lord; dictator, autocrat.
ANTONYMS subject.

ruling ▶ **noun** *the judge's ruling* **judgment,** decision, adjudication, finding, verdict; pronouncement, resolution, decree, injunction.
▶ **adjective 1** *the ruling class* **governing,** controlling, commanding, supreme, leading, dominant, ascendant, reigning.
2 *hockey was their ruling passion* **main,** chief, principal, major, prime, dominating, foremost; predominant, central, focal; informal number-one.

ruminate ▶ **verb** *we ruminated on the nature of existence* **think about,** contemplate, consider, meditate on, muse on, mull over, ponder on/over, deliberate about/on, chew on, puzzle over; formal cogitate about.

rummage ▶ **verb** *he rummaged through Stacey's bureau drawers* **search (through),** hunt through, root about/around (in), ferret about/around (in), fish about/around (in), poke around (in), dig through, delve through, go through, explore, sift through, rifle (through).

rumor ▶ **noun** *do you think the talk of her resignation is fact or just rumor? | the latest rumors say they're eloping* **gossip,** hearsay, talk, tittle-tattle, speculation, word; (**rumors**) reports, stories, whispers, canards; informal grapevine, word on the street, buzz, dirt, scuttlebutt, loose lips.

rumple ▶ **verb 1** *the sheet was rumpled* **crumple,** crease, wrinkle, crinkle, scrunch up.
ANTONYMS smooth (out).
2 *Ian rumpled her hair* **ruffle,** disarrange, tousle, dishevel, mess up; informal muss up.
ANTONYMS smooth.

run ▶ **verb 1** *she ran across the road* **sprint,** race, dart, rush, dash, hasten, hurry, scurry, scamper, bolt, fly, gallop, career, charge, shoot, hurtle, speed, zoom, go like lightning, go hell-bent for leather, go like the wind, go like a bat out of hell; jog, trot; informal tear, pelt, scoot, hotfoot it, leg it, belt, zip, whip, bomb, hightail it, barrel.
2 *the robbers turned and ran* **flee,** run away, run off, run for it, take flight, make off, take off, take to one's heels, make a break for it, bolt, make one's getaway, escape; informal beat it, clear

off, clear out, vamoose, skedaddle, split, leg it, scram, light out, take a powder, make tracks.
3 *he ran in the marathon* **compete,** take part, participate.
4 *a shiver ran down my spine* **go,** pass, slide, move, travel.
5 *he ran his eye down the list* **cast,** pass, skim, flick.
6 *the road runs the length of the valley* **extend,** stretch, reach, continue.
7 *water ran from the eaves* **flow,** pour, stream, gush, flood, cascade, roll, course, spill, trickle, drip, dribble, leak.
8 *a bus runs to Sorrento* **travel,** go.
9 *I'll run you home* **drive,** take, bring, ferry, chauffeur, give someone a ride/lift.
10 *he runs a mail-order company* **be in charge of,** manage, direct, control, head, govern, supervise, superintend, oversee; operate, conduct, own.
11 *it's expensive to run a car* **maintain,** keep, own, possess, have; drive.
12 *they ran some tests* **carry out,** do, perform, execute.
13 *he left the engine running* **operate,** function, work, go; idle.
14 *the lease runs for twenty years* **be valid,** last, be in effect, be operative, continue, be effective.
15 *the show ran for two years* **be staged,** be performed, be on, be mounted, be screened.
16 *he ran for president* **be a candidate for,** stand for, be a contender for.
17 *the paper ran the story* **publish,** print, feature, carry, put out, release, issue.
18 *they run drugs* **smuggle,** traffic in, deal in.
19 *they were run out of town* **chase,** drive, hound.
▶ **noun 1** *his morning run* **sprint,** jog, dash, gallop, trot.
2 *she did the school run* **route,** journey; circuit, round, beat.
3 *an unbeaten run of victories* **series,** succession, sequence, string, chain, streak, spell, stretch, spate.
4 *a* ***run on*** *umbrellas* **demand for,** rush on.
5 *they had the* ***run of*** *the house* **free use of,** unrestricted access to.
6 *the usual run of movies* **type,** kind, sort, variety, class.
7 *a dog run* **enclosure,** pen, coop.
8 *a toboggan run* **slope,** track, piste, trail, slide.
9 *a run in her pantyhose* **rip,** tear, snag, hole, pull; Brit. ladder.
– PHRASES **in the long run** *in the long run, the move to Spokane may be a really good thing* **eventually,** in the end, ultimately, when all is said and done, in the fullness of time, over the long haul, at the end of the day. **on the run** *police report that Prentiss has been on the run since early this morning* **on the loose,** at large, loose; running away, fleeing, fugitive; informal AWOL, on the lam. **run across** *we never expected to run across Mrs. Gundlach at the casino* **meet,** meet by chance, come across, run into, chance on/upon, stumble on/upon, happen on/upon; informal bump into. **run after** informal *I have no intention of running after him* **pursue,** chase; make advances to, flirt with; informal come on to, be all over; dated set one's cap for/at. **run along** informal *it's time for you and your pesky little friends to run along* **go away,** be off (with you), shoo; informal scram, buzz off, skedaddle, scat, beat it, get lost, shove off, clear off; literary begone. **run around** informal *that creep's been running around since their honeymoon* **be unfaithful,** have affairs, philander; informal play the field, sleep around, fool around. **run away** *her attacker ran away* See RUN (sense 2 of the verb). **run away with** *she ran away with the championship* **win easily,** win hands down; informal win by a mile. **run down** *obviously, this barn didn't start running down yesterday* **decline,** degenerate, go downhill, go to seed, decay, go to rack and ruin; informal go to pot, go to the dogs. **run someone down 1** *he was run down by a drunk driver* **run over,** knock down, knock over; hit, strike. **2** *she ran him down in front of other people* **criticize,** denigrate, belittle, disparage, deprecate, find fault with; informal put down, knock, badmouth, dis; formal derogate. **run for it** *they saw the cop car and ran for it* See RUN (sense 2 of the verb). **run high** *feelings ran high* **be strong,** be fervent, be passionate, be intense. **run in 1** *heart disease runs in the family* **be common in,** be inherent in. **2** informal *you mean they actually ran him in for littering?* See ARREST (sense 1 of the verb). **run into 1** *a car ran into his van* **collide with,** hit, strike, crash into, smash into, plow into, ram, impact. **2** *I ran into Hugo the other day* See RUN ACROSS. **3** *we ran into a problem* **experience,** encounter, meet with, be faced with, be confronted with. **4** *his debts run into six figures* **reach,** extend to, be as much as. **run low** *supplies were running low* **dwindle,** diminish, become depleted, be used up, be in short supply, be tight. **run off** *the youths ran off* See RUN (sense 2 of the verb). **run off with** *he ran off with her money* See STEAL (sense 1 of the verb). **run something off 1** *would you run off that list for me?* **copy,** photocopy, xerox, duplicate, print, reproduce. **2** *run off some of the excess water* **drain,** bleed, draw off, pump out. **run on 1** *the call ran on for hours* **continue,** go on, carry on, last, keep going, stretch.
2 *your mother does run on* **talk incessantly,** talk a lot, go on, chatter on, ramble on; informal yak, gab, run off at the mouth. **run out 1** *supplies ran out* **be used up,** dry up, be exhausted, be finished, peter out. **2** *her contract ran out* **expire,** end, terminate, finish; lapse. **run out of** *they ran out of their cash* **use up**; be out of, consume, eat up; informal be fresh out of. **run out on** informal *she ran out on her husband* See ABANDON (sense 3 of the verb). **run over 1** *the bathwater ran over* **overflow,** spill over, brim over. **2** *the project ran over budget* **exceed,** go over, overshoot, overreach. **3** *he quickly ran over the story* **recapitulate,** repeat, run through, go over, reiterate, review; look over, read through; informal recap. **run someone over** See RUN SOMEONE DOWN (sense 1). **run the show** informal *Todd always tries to run the show* **be in charge,** be in control, be at the helm, be in the driver's seat, be at the wheel; informal be the boss, call the shots. **run through 1** *they quickly ran through their money* **squander,** spend, fritter

away, dissipate, waste, go through, consume, use up; informal blow. **2** *the attitude that runs through his writing* **pervade,** permeate, suffuse, imbue, inform. **3** *he ran through his notes* See RUN OVER (sense 3). **4** *let's run through scene three* **rehearse,** practice, go over, repeat; informal recap. **run someone through** *they hung an effigy of the former despot and ran it through with sharp sticks* **stab,** pierce, transfix, impale. **run to 1** *the bill ran to $22,000* **amount to,** add up to, total, come to, equal, reach, be as much as. **2** *he was running to fat* **tend to,** become, get, grow.

runaway ▶ **noun** *a teenage runaway* **fugitive,** escapee; refugee; truant; absconder, deserter.
▶ **adjective 1** *a runaway horse* **out of control,** escaped, loose, on the loose.
2 *a runaway victory* **easy,** effortless; informal as easy as pie.
3 *runaway inflation* **rampant,** out of control, unchecked, unbridled.

rundown ▶ **noun** *here's the rundown on the latest digital gear* **summary,** synopsis, précis, run-through, summarization, summation, review, overview, briefing, sketch, outline; informal lowdown, recap.

run-down ▶ **adjective 1** *a run-down area* **dilapidated,** tumbledown, ramshackle, derelict, ruinous, in ruins, crumbling, beat-up; neglected, uncared-for, depressed, seedy, shabby, slummy, squalid, flea-bitten; informal crummy.
2 *she was feeling rather run-down* **unwell,** ill, poorly, unhealthy, peaked; tired, drained, exhausted, fatigued, worn out, below par, washed out; informal under the weather, off; dated seedy.

runner ▶ **noun 1** *the runners were limbering up* sprinter, hurdler, racer, jogger; athlete.
2 *a strawberry runner* **shoot,** offshoot, sprout, tendril; Botany stolon.
3 *he worked as a runner for the mob* **messenger,** courier, errand boy; informal gofer.

running ▶ **noun 1** *his running was particularly fast* **sprinting,** sprint, racing, jogging, jog.
2 *the running of the school* **administration,** management, organization, coordination, orchestration, handling, direction, control, regulation, supervision.
3 *the smooth running of her department* **operation,** working, function, performance.
▶ **adjective 1** *running water* **flowing,** gushing, rushing, moving.
2 *a running argument* **ongoing,** sustained, continuous, rolling, incessant, ceaseless, constant, perpetual; recurrent, recurring.
3 *she was late two days running* **in succession,** in a row, in sequence, consecutively; straight, together.
– PHRASES **in the running for** *he's in the running for a prize* **likely to get,** a candidate for, in line for, on the short list for, up for.

run-of-the-mill ▶ **adjective** *even the car he drives is run-of-the-mill* **ordinary,** average, middle-of-the-road, commonplace, humdrum, mundane, standard, nondescript, characterless, conventional; unremarkable, unexceptional, uninteresting, dull, boring, routine, bland, lackluster, garden-variety; informal nothing to write home about, nothing special, a dime a dozen.
ANTONYMS exceptional.

rupture ▶ **noun 1** *pipeline ruptures* **break,** fracture, crack, breach, burst, split, fissure.
2 *a rupture due to personal differences* **rift,** estrangement, falling-out, breakup, breach, split, separation, parting, division, schism; informal bust-up.
3 *an abdominal rupture* **hernia.**
▶ **verb 1** *the reactor core might rupture* **break,** fracture, crack, breach, burst, split; informal bust.
2 *the problem ruptured their relationships* **sever,** break off, breach, disrupt; literary sunder.

rural ▶ **adjective** *the rural backdrop was filmed in Georgia* **country,** countryside, bucolic, rustic, pastoral; agricultural, agrarian; literary sylvan, georgic.
ANTONYMS urban.

ruse ▶ **noun** *his offer to help with my presentation was just a clever ruse* **ploy,** stratagem, tactic, scheme, trick, gambit, cunning plan, dodge, subterfuge, machination, wile.

rush ▶ **verb 1** *she rushed home* **hurry,** dash, run, race, sprint, bolt, dart, gallop, career, charge, shoot, hurtle, careen, hare, fly, speed, zoom, scurry, scuttle, scamper, hasten; informal tear, belt, pelt, scoot, zip, whip, hotfoot it, leg it, bomb, hightail it.
2 *water rushed along gutters* **flow,** pour, gush, surge, stream, cascade, run, course.
3 *the legislation was rushed through both houses* **push,** hurry, hasten, speed, hustle, press, force.
4 *the mob rushed the police* **attack,** charge, run at, assail, storm.
▶ **noun 1** *Tim made a rush for the exit* **dash,** run, sprint, dart, bolt, charge, scramble, break.
2 *the lunch rush* **hustle and bustle,** commotion, hubbub, stir; busy time.
3 *a last-minute rush for flights* **demand,** clamor, call, request; run on.
4 *he was in no rush to leave* **hurry,** haste, urgency.
5 *a rush of adrenaline* **surge,** flow, flood, spurt, stream; thrill, flash; informal charge, jolt, kick.
6 *a rush of cold air* **gust,** blast, draft.
7 *I made a sudden rush at him* **charge,** onslaught, attack, assault, onrush.
▶ **adjective** *a rush job* **urgent,** high-priority, emergency; hurried, hasty, fast, quick, swift; informal hurry-up.

rushed ▶ **adjective 1** *a rushed divorce* **hasty,** fast, speedy, quick, swift, rapid, hurried.
2 *he was too rushed to enjoy his stay* **pressed for time,** busy, in a hurry, run off one's feet.

rustic ▶ **adjective 1** *a rustic setting* **rural,** country, countryside, countrified, pastoral, bucolic; agricultural, agrarian; literary sylvan, georgic.
ANTONYMS urban.
2 *rustic wooden tables* **plain,** simple, homely, unsophisticated; rough, rude, crude.
ANTONYMS fancy, ornate.
3 *rustic peasants* **unsophisticated,** uncultured, unrefined, simple; artless, unassuming, guileless, naive, ingenuous; coarse, rough, uncouth, boorish; informal hillbilly, hick.
ANTONYMS urbane, cultured, sophisticated.
▶ **noun** *the rustics were carousing* **peasant,**

countryman, countrywoman, bumpkin, yokel, country cousin; informal hillbilly, hayseed, hick; archaic swain, cottier.

rustle ▶ verb **1** *her dress rustled as she moved* **swish,** whoosh, swoosh, whisper, sigh.
2 *he was rustling cattle* **steal,** thieve, take; abduct, kidnap; informal swipe.
▶ noun *the rustle of the leaves* **swish,** whisper, rustling; literary susurration, susurrus.
– PHRASES **rustle something up** informal *I'll rustle up some breakfast for us* **prepare hastily,** throw together, make; informal fix.

rusty ▶ adjective **1** *rusty wire* **rusted,** rust-covered, corroded, oxidized; tarnished, discolored.
2 *rusty hair* **reddish-brown,** rust-colored, chestnut, auburn, tawny, russet, coppery, copper, Titian, red, ginger, gingery.
3 *my French is a little rusty* **out of practice,** below par; unpracticed, deficient, impaired, weak.

rut ▶ noun **1** *the car bumped across the ruts* **furrow,** groove, trough, ditch, hollow, pothole, crater.
2 *he was stuck in a rut* **boring routine,** humdrum existence, habit, dead end.

ruthless ▶ adjective *ruthless killers* **merciless,** pitiless, cruel, heartless, hard-hearted, cold-hearted, cold-blooded, harsh, callous, unmerciful, unforgiving, uncaring, unsympathetic, uncharitable; remorseless, unbending, inflexible, implacable; brutal, inhuman, inhumane, barbarous, barbaric, savage, sadistic, vicious.
ANTONYMS merciful.

Ss

sable ▶ adjective *her long sable hair* **black,** jet-black, pitch-black, ebony, raven, sooty, dusky, inky, coal-black.

sabotage ▶ noun *the fire may have been an act of sabotage* **vandalism,** wrecking, destruction, impairment, incapacitation, damage; subversion, obstruction, disruption, spoiling, undermining; informal a (monkey) wrench in the works.
▶ verb *they were hired to sabotage the competition* **vandalize,** wreck, damage, destroy, cripple, impair, incapacitate; obstruct, disrupt, spoil, ruin, undermine, threaten, subvert.

saccharine ▶ adjective *saccharine love songs* **sentimental,** sickly, mawkish, cloying, sugary, sickening, nauseating; informal mushy, sappy, schmaltzy, weepy, gooey, drippy, cheesy, corny, soppy, cornball.

sack[1] ▶ noun **1** *she carried her supplies in a sack* **bag,** pouch, pack, satchel; knapsack, backpack, rucksack, packsack, day pack, bookbag, tote bag.
2 informal *work hard or you'll get **the sack*** **a dismissal,** a discharge; informal the boot, the ax, the heave-ho, one's marching orders, a pink slip.
3 informal *she stayed in **the sack*** **bed.**
▶ verb informal *she was sacked for stealing* **dismiss,** discharge, lay off, let go, terminate, get rid of; Military cashier; Brit. make redundant; informal fire, give the sack, give someone their marching orders, give someone the boot, show someone the door, send packing, pink-slip.
– PHRASES **hit the sack** informal *I'm hitting the sack early tonight* **go to bed,** retire, go to sleep; informal turn in, hit the hay.

sack[2] ▶ verb *raiders sacked the town for its food supplies* **ravage,** lay waste, devastate, raid, ransack, strip, plunder, despoil, pillage, loot, rob. See note at RAVAGE.

sackcloth ▶ noun *artsy lamps made of castoff materials such as old chicken wire and sackcloth* **hessian,** sacking, hopsack, burlap; gunny.
– PHRASES **in/wearing sackcloth and ashes** *I never thought I'd live to see the day that Josie was wearing sackcloth and ashes* **penitent,** contrite, regretful, sorrowful, rueful, remorseful, apologetic, ashamed, guilt-ridden, chastened, shamefaced, guilty.

sacred ▶ adjective **1** *the priest entered the sacred place* **holy,** hallowed, blessed, consecrated, sanctified, venerated, revered; archaic blest.
2 *sacred music* **religious,** spiritual, devotional, church, ecclesiastical.
ANTONYMS secular, profane.
3 *the hill is sacred to the tribe* **sacrosanct,** inviolable, inviolate, invulnerable, untouchable, protected, defended, secure.

sacrifice ▶ noun **1** *the sacrifice of animals* **ritual slaughter,** offering, oblation, immolation.
2 *the calf was a sacrifice* **(votive) offering,** burnt offering, gift, oblation.
3 *joining a federation may result in the sacrifice of sovereignty* **surrender,** giving up, abandonment, renunciation, forfeiture, relinquishment, resignation, abdication.
▶ verb **1** *two goats were sacrificed* **offer up,** immolate, slaughter.
2 *he sacrificed his principles* **give up,** abandon, surrender, forgo, renounce, forfeit, relinquish, resign, abdicate; betray.

sacrilege ▶ noun *any form of gambling on the church grounds, including bingo and raffles, would be sacrilege* **desecration,** profanity, blasphemy, impiety, irreligion, unholiness, irreverence, disrespect, profanation.
ANTONYMS piety.

sacrilegious ▶ adjective *your vile language is sacrilegious* **profane,** blasphemous, impious, sinful, irreverent, irreligious, unholy, disrespectful.

sad ▶ adjective **1** *we felt sad when we left* **unhappy,** sorrowful, dejected, depressed, downcast, miserable, down, despondent, despairing, disconsolate, desolate, wretched, glum, gloomy, doleful, dismal, melancholy, mournful, woebegone, forlorn, crestfallen, heartbroken, inconsolable; informal blue, down in/at the mouth, down in the dumps, blah.
ANTONYMS happy, cheerful.
2 *they knew her sad story* **tragic,** unhappy, unfortunate, awful, miserable, wretched, sorry, pitiful, pathetic, traumatic, heartbreaking, heart-rending, harrowing.
ANTONYMS cheerful.
3 *a sad state of affairs* **unfortunate,** regrettable, sorry, deplorable, lamentable, pitiful, shameful, disgraceful.
ANTONYMS fortunate.

sadden ▶ verb *of course we all saddened by this tragic news* **depress,** dispirit, deject, dishearten, grieve, desolate, discourage, upset, get down, bring down, break someone's heart.

sadness ▶ noun *our sadness cannot be measured* **unhappiness,** sorrow, dejection, depression, misery, despondency, despair, desolation, wretchedness, gloom, gloominess, dolefulness, melancholy, mournfulness, woe, heartache, grief; informal the blues.

safe ▶ adjective **1** *the jewels are safe in the bank* **secure,** protected, shielded, sheltered, guarded, out of harm's way.

ANTONYMS insecure, at risk.
2 *the lost children are all safe* **unharmed,** unhurt, uninjured, unscathed, all right, well, in one piece, out of danger, home free; informal OK.
ANTONYMS in danger.
3 *a safe place to hide* **secure,** sound, impregnable, unassailable, invulnerable.
ANTONYMS dangerous.
4 *a safe driver* **cautious,** circumspect, prudent, attentive; unadventurous, conservative, unenterprising.
ANTONYMS reckless.
5 *the drug is safe* **harmless,** innocuous, benign, nontoxic, nonpoisonous.
ANTONYMS harmful.
▶ **noun** *I keep the ring in a safe* **strongbox,** safety-deposit box, safe-deposit box, coffer, strongroom, vault.

safeguard ▶ **noun** *a safeguard against terrorism* **protection,** defense, guard, screen, buffer, preventive, precaution, provision, security; surety, cover, insurance, indemnity.
▶ **verb** *the contract will safeguard 1,000 jobs* **protect,** preserve, conserve, save, secure, shield, guard, keep safe.
ANTONYMS jeopardize.

safety ▶ **noun 1** *the safety of the residents* **welfare,** well-being, protection, security.
2 *she worried about the safety of planes* **security,** soundness, dependability, reliability.
3 *we reached the safety of the shore* **shelter,** sanctuary, refuge.

sag ▶ **verb 1** *she sagged in his arms* **sink,** slump, loll, flop, crumple.
2 *the floors all sag* **dip,** droop; bulge, bag.
3 *the markets sagged as the day wore on* **decline,** fall, drop, slump, plummet; informal nosedive.

saga ▶ **noun 1** *Celtic tribal sagas* **epic,** chronicle, legend, folk tale, romance, history, narrative, adventure, myth, fairy story.
2 *the saga of how they met* **long story,** rigmarole; chain of events; informal spiel.

sage ▶ **noun** *the Chinese sage Confucius* **wise man/woman,** learned person, philosopher, thinker, scholar, savant; authority, expert, guru.
▶ **adjective** *some very sage comments* **wise,** learned, clever, intelligent, having/showing great knowledge, knowledgeable, sensible, intellectual, scholarly, sagacious, erudite; discerning, judicious, canny, penetrating, perceptive, acute, astute, shrewd, prudent, politic, thoughtful, insightful, percipient, perspicacious, philosophical, profound, deep.

sail ▶ **noun** *the ship's sails* canvas, sailcloth.
▶ **verb 1** *we sailed across the Atlantic* **voyage,** travel by water, steam, navigate, cruise.
2 *you can learn to sail here* **yacht,** boat, go sailing; crew, helm.
3 *we sail tonight* **set sail,** put to sea, leave port, weigh anchor, shove off.
4 *he is sailing the ship* **steer,** pilot, navigate, con, helm, captain; informal skipper.
5 *clouds were sailing past* **glide,** drift, float, flow, sweep, skim, coast, flit.
6 *a pencil sailed past his ear* **whiz,** speed, streak, shoot, whip, buzz, zoom, flash; fly, wing, soar, zip.
– PHRASES **sail through** *she sailed through the exam* **succeed easily at,** pass easily, romp through, walk through.

sailor ▶ **noun** *his mentor at sea was a well-seasoned sailor named Coates* **seaman,** seafarer, mariner; boatman, yachtsman, hand; informal (old) salt, sea dog, rating, bluejacket; Brit. matelot, shellback.

> USAGE
>
> **sailor, sailer**
>
> A *sailor* is one who sails—always in reference to a person. A *sailer* is a vessel or vehicle that sails, or that moves by the use of a sail—e.g.: "The second part of the project is to launch an operational solar sailer with eight sails to be tested in an 850-km. (528-mi.) circular orbit, also using a Volna rocket." (*Aviation Week & Space Technology*; July 16, 2001.) It isn't unusual to see *sailer* misused for *sailor*—e.g.: "The current exercises involve about 15,000 sailers [read *sailors*] and Marines, and include cruisers and destroyers, with nonexplosive bombs dropped from the air, according to the Associated Press." (*Chicago Sun-Times*; Apr. 30, 2001.) — **BG**

saintly ▶ **adjective** *he was a saintly but somewhat ineffective archbishop* **holy,** godly, pious, religious, devout, spiritual, prayerful; virtuous, righteous, good, moral, innocent, sinless, guiltless, irreproachable, spotless, uncorrupted, pure, angelic.
ANTONYMS ungodly.

sake ▶ **noun 1** *this is simplified for the sake of clarity* **purpose,** reason, aim, end, objective, object, goal, motive.
2 *she had to be brave for her daughter's sake* **benefit,** advantage, good, well-being, welfare, interest, profit.

salacious ▶ **adjective 1** *salacious writing* **pornographic,** obscene, indecent, crude, lewd, vulgar, dirty, filthy; erotic, titillating, arousing, suggestive, sexy, risqué, ribald, smutty, bawdy; X-rated; informal porn, porno, blue, XXX; euphemistic adult.
2 *salacious women* **lustful,** lecherous, licentious, lascivious, libidinous, prurient, lewd; debauched, wanton, loose, fast, impure, unchaste, degenerate, sinful, depraved, promiscuous; informal randy, horny, hot to trot.

salary ▶ **noun** *an annual raise in his salary* **pay,** wages, earnings, payment, remuneration, fee(s), stipend, income; informal take-home; formal emolument.

sale ▶ **noun 1** *the sale of firearms* **selling,** vending; dealing, trading.
ANTONYMS purchase.
2 *they make a sale every minute* **deal,** transaction.
ANTONYMS purchase.
3 *there's a sale on* **markdown,** discount, blowout, clearance (sale), fire sale, liquidation (sale).
– PHRASES **for sale** *is that picture for sale?* **on the market,** on sale, available, purchasable, obtainable.

salient ▶ **adjective** *the most salient point is that the suggested cost is beyond our budget* **important,**

main, principal, major, chief, primary; notable, noteworthy, outstanding, conspicuous, striking, noticeable, obvious, remarkable, prominent, predominant, dominant; key, crucial, vital, essential, pivotal, prime, central, paramount.
ANTONYMS minor.

sallow ▶ adjective *a disturbingly sallow complexion* **yellowish,** jaundiced, pallid, wan, pale, anemic, bloodless, pasty; unhealthy, sickly, washed out; informal like death warmed over; Medicine icteric.

sally ▶ noun **1** *the garrison made a sally against us* **sortie,** charge, foray, thrust, drive, offensive, attack, assault, raid, incursion, invasion, onset, onslaught.
2 *a fruitless sally into the city* **expedition,** excursion, trip, outing, jaunt, visit.
3 *they exchanged amusing sallies* **witticism,** smart remark, quip, barb, pleasantry; joke, pun, jest, bon mot; retort, riposte, counter, rejoinder; informal gag, wisecrack, comeback.

salon ▶ noun **1** *he works in an uptown salon* establishment, premises; boutique, store, shop; beauty parlor, beauty shop, hair salon; nail salon; tanning salon.
2 *the chateau's mirrored salon* **drawing room,** sitting room, living room, lounge; dated parlor.
3 *he showed his artwork in a salon* **exhibition,** (public) display, show, showing, showcase, exhibit.

salt ▶ noun **1** *the potatoes need salt* **sodium chloride,** table salt, NaCl.
2 literary *he added salt to the conversation* **zest,** spice, piquancy, bite, edge; vitality, liveliness, spirit, sparkle; informal zing, punch.
▶ adjective *salt water* **salty,** salted, saline, briny, brackish.
– PHRASES **salt away** informal *Esther salted away most of her allowance* **save,** put aside, put by, set aside, reserve, keep, store, stockpile, hoard, stow away; informal squirrel away, stash away.
with a grain of salt *he's a spinner of tales, so take what he says with a grain of salt* **with reservations,** with misgivings, skeptically, cynically, doubtfully, doubtingly, suspiciously, quizzically, incredulously.

salty ▶ adjective **1** *salty water* **salt,** salted, saline, briny, brackish.
2 *a salty sense of humor* **earthy,** colorful, spicy, racy, risqué, naughty, vulgar, rude; piquant, biting.

salubrious ▶ adjective **1** *I found the climate salubrious* **healthy,** health-giving, healthful, beneficial, wholesome; archaic salutary. See note at SANITARY.
ANTONYMS unhealthy.
2 *a salubrious Sunday afternoon* **pleasant,** agreeable, pleasing, enjoyable, pleasurable, nice, delightful; select, high-class, upscale, upmarket; informal posh, swanky, classy, swank; Brit. informal cushty.
ANTONYMS unpleasant.

salutary ▶ adjective **1** *a salutary lesson on the fragility of nature* **beneficial,** advantageous, good, profitable, productive, helpful, useful, valuable, worthwhile; timely.
2 archaic *the salutary Atlantic air* See SALUBRIOUS (sense 1).

salutation ▶ noun *his cheery salutations are a bit too much for a Monday morning* **greeting,** salute, address, welcome.

salute ▶ noun **1** *he gave the captain a salute* **greeting,** salutation, gesture of respect, obeisance, acknowledgment, welcome, address.
2 *she raised her hands in salute* **tribute,** testimonial, homage, toast, honor, eulogy; celebration, acknowledgment.
▶ verb **1** *he saluted the ambassadors* **greet,** address, hail, welcome, acknowledge, toast; make obeisance to.
2 *we salute a great photographer* **pay tribute to,** pay homage to, honor, celebrate, acknowledge, take one's hat off to.

salvage ▶ verb **1** *an attempt to salvage the vessel* **rescue,** save, recover, retrieve, raise, reclaim.
2 *he tried to salvage his reputation* **retain,** preserve, conserve; regain, recoup, redeem, snatch.
▶ noun **1** *the salvage is taking place off the coast* **rescue,** recovery, reclamation.
2 *she sifted through the salvage* **remains,** debris, wreckage, rubble, remnants, flotsam and jetsam, scrap.

salvation ▶ noun **1** *salvation by way of repentance* **redemption,** deliverance, reclamation.
ANTONYMS damnation.
2 *that conviction was her salvation* **lifeline,** preservation; means of escape, help, saving, savior.

same ▶ adjective **1** *we stayed at **the same** hotel* **identical,** selfsame, very same, one and the same.
ANTONYMS another, different.
2 *they had **the same** symptoms* **matching,** identical, alike, duplicate, carbon copy, twin; indistinguishable, interchangeable, corresponding, equivalent, parallel, like, comparable, similar, congruent, concordant, consonant.
ANTONYMS different, dissimilar.
3 *it happened that same month* **selfsame**; aforesaid, aforementioned.
4 *they provide **the same** menu worldwide* **unchanging,** unvarying, unvaried, invariable, consistent, uniform, regular.
ANTONYMS varying, different.
▶ noun *Louise said the same* **same thing,** aforementioned, aforesaid, above-mentioned.
– PHRASES **all the same 1** *I was frightened all the same* **in spite of everything,** despite that, nevertheless, nonetheless, even so, however, but, still, yet, though, be that as it may, just the same, at the same time, in any event, notwithstanding, regardless, anyway, anyhow; informal still and all. **2** *it's all the same to me* **immaterial,** of no importance, of no consequence, inconsequential, unimportant, of little account, irrelevant, insignificant, trivial, petty.

CHOOSE THE RIGHT WORD

same, equal, equivalent, identical, selfsame, tantamount

All of these adjectives describe something that is not significantly different from something else. **Same** may imply, and **selfsame** always implies, that what is referred to is one thing and not two or more distinct things (*they go to the same restaurant every Friday night; this is the selfsame house in which the family once lived*). In one sense, **identical** is synonymous with *selfsame* (*the identical place where we first met*); but it can also imply exact correspondence in quality, shape, and appearance (*wearing identical raincoats*). **Equivalent** describes things that are interchangeable or that amount to the same thing in value, force, or significance (*the equivalent of a free hotel room at a luxury resort*), while **equal** implies exact correspondence in quantity, value, or size (*equal portions of food*). **Tantamount** is used to describe one of a pair of things, usually intangible, that are in effect equivalent to each other (*her tears were tantamount to a confession of guilt*).

sample ▶ **noun 1** *a sample of the fabric* **specimen,** example, bit, snippet, swatch, representative piece, exemplification; prototype, test piece, dummy, pilot, trial, taste, taster, tester.
2 *a sample of 10,000 people nationwide* **cross section,** variety, sampling, test.
▶ **verb** *we sampled the culinary offerings* **try (out),** taste, test, put to the test, experiment with; appraise, evaluate, test drive; informal check out.
▶ **adjective 1** *the sample group is small* **representative,** illustrative, selected, specimen, test, trial, typical.
2 *a sample copy can be obtained* **specimen,** test, trial, pilot, dummy.

sanctify ▶ **verb 1** *he came to sanctify the site* **consecrate,** bless, make holy, hallow, make sacred, dedicate to God.
2 *they sanctified themselves* **purify,** cleanse, free from sin, absolve, unburden, redeem.
3 *we must not sanctify this outrage* **approve,** sanction, condone, vindicate, endorse, support, back, permit, allow, authorize, legitimize.

sanctimonious ▶ **adjective** *no one wants to hear your sanctimonious hot air* **self-righteous,** holier-than-thou, pious, pietistic, churchy, moralizing, preachy, smug, superior, priggish, hypocritical, insincere; informal goody-goody. See note at MORAL.

sanction ▶ **noun 1** *trade sanctions* **penalty,** punishment, deterrent; punitive action, discipline, restriction; embargo, ban, prohibition, boycott.
ANTONYMS reward.
2 *the scheme has the sanction of the court* **authorization,** consent, leave, permission, authority, warrant, license, dispensation, assent, acquiescence, agreement, approval, approbation, endorsement, accreditation, ratification, validation, blessing, imprimatur; informal go-ahead, OK, green light.
ANTONYMS prohibition.
▶ **verb 1** *the rally was sanctioned by the government* **authorize,** permit, allow, warrant, accredit, license, endorse, approve, accept, back, support; informal OK. See note at APPROVE.
ANTONYMS prohibit.
2 *the penalties available to sanction crime* **punish,** discipline someone for.

sanctity ▶ **noun 1** *the sanctity of St. Francis* **holiness,** godliness, blessedness, saintliness, spirituality, piety, piousness, devoutness, righteousness, goodness, virtue, purity; formal sanctitude.
2 *the sanctity of the family meal* **inviolability**; importance, paramountcy.

sanctuary ▶ **noun 1** *the sanctuary at Delphi* **sanctum.**
2 *the island is our sanctuary* **refuge,** haven, harbor, port in a storm, oasis, shelter, retreat, hideaway, hideout.
3 *he was given sanctuary in the embassy* **safety,** protection, shelter, immunity, asylum.
4 *a bird sanctuary* **reserve,** park, reservation, preserve.

sane ▶ **adjective 1** *the accused is presumed to be sane* **of sound mind,** in one's right mind, compos mentis, lucid, rational, balanced, stable, normal; informal all there, together.
ANTONYMS mad.
2 *it isn't sane to use nuclear weapons* **sensible,** practical, advisable, responsible, realistic, prudent, wise, reasonable, rational, levelheaded, commonsensical, judicious, politic. See note at SENSIBLE.
ANTONYMS foolish.

sang-froid ▶ **noun** *he recovered his usual sangfroid* **composure,** equanimity, self-possession, equilibrium, aplomb, poise, self-assurance, self-control, nerve, calm, presence of mind; informal cool, unflappability.

sanguine ▶ **adjective 1** *he is sanguine about the advance of technology* **optimistic,** bullish, hopeful, buoyant, positive, confident, cheerful, cheery; informal upbeat.
ANTONYMS gloomy.
2 archaic *a sanguine complexion* See FLORID (sense 1).

sanitary ▶ **adjective** *improvements in health are also the result of more sanitary conditions* **hygienic,** clean, antiseptic, aseptic, sterile, uninfected, disinfected, unpolluted, uncontaminated; salubrious, healthy, wholesome.

CHOOSE THE RIGHT WORD

sanitary, antiseptic, healthful, hygienic, salubrious, sterile

Americans thrive on cleanliness and the eradication of germs. They try to keep their homes **sanitary**, a term that goes beyond cleanliness to imply that measures have been taken to guard against infections or disease. They demand that their communities provide schools and workplaces that are **hygienic**—in other words, that adhere to the rules or standards promoting public health. But it would be almost impossible to duplicate the conditions found in a hospital, where everything that comes in contact with patients must be **sterile** or free of germs entirely. Most Americans want to make their environment **healthful**, which means conducive to the health or soundness of the body, but they are not interested in making it **antiseptic**, a word that is similar in meaning to *sterile* but implies preventing infections by destroying germs that are already present (*an antiseptic solution*). Many Americans, as they grow older, choose to move to a more **salubrious** climate, a word that means health-giving and applies primarily to an air quality that is invigorating and that avoids harsh extremes.

sanity ▶ noun **1** *she was losing her sanity* **mental health,** faculties, reason, rationality, saneness, stability, lucidity; sense, wits, mind.
2 *sanity has prevailed* **(common) sense,** wisdom, prudence, judiciousness, rationality, soundness, sensibleness.

sap ▶ noun **1** *sap from the roots of trees* **juice,** secretion, fluid, liquid.
2 *they're full of youthful sap* **vigor,** energy, drive, dynamism, life, spirit, liveliness, sparkle, verve, ebullience, enthusiasm, gusto, vitality, vivacity, fire, zest, zeal, exuberance; informal get-up-and-go, oomph, vim.
▶ verb *they sapped the will of the troops* **erode,** wear away/down, deplete, reduce, lessen, attenuate, undermine, exhaust, drain, bleed.

sarcasm ▶ noun *well, it's easy to see that she got her biting sarcasm from her mother* **derision,** mockery, ridicule, scorn, sneering, scoffing; irony; cynicism. See note at WIT.

sarcastic ▶ adjective *I've had enough of your sarcastic comments* **sardonic,** ironic, ironical; derisive, snide, scornful, contemptuous, mocking, sneering, jeering; caustic, scathing, trenchant, cutting, biting, sharp, acerbic; informal smart-alecky.

sardonic ▶ adjective *his sardonic wit* **mocking,** satirical, sarcastic, ironical, ironic; cynical, scornful, contemptuous, derisive, derisory, sneering, jeering; scathing, caustic, trenchant, cutting, sharp, acerbic.

Satan ▶ noun See DEVIL (sense 1).

satanic ▶ adjective *a series of satanic messages were written on the wall* **diabolical,** fiendish, devilish, demonic, demoniacal, ungodly, hellish, infernal, wicked, evil, sinful, iniquitous, nefarious, vile, foul, abominable, unspeakable, loathsome, monstrous, heinous, hideous, horrible, horrifying, shocking, appalling, dreadful, awful, terrible, ghastly, abhorrent, despicable, damnable.

satellite ▶ noun **1** *the satellite orbited the earth* **space station,** space capsule, spacecraft; communications satellite, weather satellite.
2 *the two small satellites of Mars* **moon,** secondary planet.
3 *Bulgaria was then a Russian satellite* **branch,** colony, protectorate, puppet state, possession, holding; historical fief, vassal; informal offshoot.
▶ adjective *a satellite state* **dependent,** subordinate, subsidiary.

satiate ▶ verb *here, this stew should satiate you* **fill,** satisfy, sate; slake, quench; gorge, stuff, surfeit, glut, cloy, sicken, nauseate.

satire ▶ noun **1** *a satire on Canadian politics* **parody,** burlesque, caricature, lampoon, skit; informal spoof, takeoff, sendup. See note at WIT.
2 *he has become the subject of satire* **mockery,** ridicule, derision, scorn, caricature; irony, sarcasm.

satirical ▶ adjective *satirical essays about American politics* **mocking,** ironic, ironical, satiric, sarcastic, sardonic; caustic, trenchant, mordant, biting, cutting, stinging, acerbic; critical, irreverent, disparaging, disrespectful.

satirize ▶ verb *a comedy troupe that satirized the conservative establishment of the sixties* **mock,** ridicule, deride, make fun of, poke fun at, parody, lampoon, burlesque, caricature, take off; criticize; informal send up.

satisfaction ▶ noun **1** *he derived great satisfaction from his work* **contentment,** pleasure, gratification, fulfillment, enjoyment, happiness, pride; self-satisfaction, smugness, complacency.
2 *the satisfaction of consumer needs* **fulfillment,** gratification; appeasement, assuaging.
3 *investors turned to the courts for satisfaction* **compensation,** recompense, redress, reparation, restitution, repayment, payment, settlement, reimbursement, indemnification, indemnity.

satisfactory ▶ adjective *the work isn't extraordinary, but it is satisfactory* **adequate,** all right, acceptable, good enough, sufficient, reasonable, quite good, competent, fair, decent, average, passable; fine, in order, up to scratch, up to the mark, up to standard, up to par; informal OK, jake, hunky-dory, so-so, 'comme ci, comme ça'.
ANTONYMS inadequate, poor.

satisfied ▶ adjective **1** *a satisfied smile* **pleased,** well pleased, content, contented, happy, proud, triumphant; smug, self-satisfied, pleased with oneself, complacent.
ANTONYMS unhappy.
2 *the pleasure of satisfied desire* **fulfilled,** gratified.
ANTONYMS unfulfilled.
3 *I am satisfied that she understands* **convinced,** certain, sure, positive, persuaded, easy in one's mind.
ANTONYMS unconvinced.

satisfy ▶ verb **1** *a last chance to satisfy his hunger for romance* **fulfill,** gratify, meet, fill; indulge, cater to, pander to; appease, assuage; quench, slake, satiate, sate, take the edge off.
ANTONYMS frustrate.
2 *she satisfied herself that it had been an accident* **convince,** persuade, assure; reassure, put someone's mind at rest.
3 *products that satisfy the criteria* **comply with,** meet, fulfill, answer, conform to; measure up to, come up to; suffice, be good enough, fit/fill the bill.
4 *there was insufficient collateral to satisfy the loan* **repay,** pay (off), settle, make good, discharge, square, liquidate, clear.

saturate ▶ verb **1** *heavy rain saturated the ground* **soak,** drench, waterlog, wet through; souse, steep, douse.

2 *the air was saturated with the stench of incense* **permeate,** suffuse, imbue, pervade, charge, infuse, fill.
3 *the company has saturated the market* **flood,** glut, oversupply, overload.

sauce ▶ noun 1 *a piquant sauce* gravy; relish, condiment, salsa, ketchup; dip, dressing.
2 informal *"I'll have less of your sauce," said Aunt Edie* **impudence,** impertinence, cheek, cheekiness, sauciness, effrontery, forwardness, brazenness; insolence, rudeness, disrespect; informal mouth, lip, sass, sassiness.
3 *Uncle Reg was into the sauce again* **alcohol,** drink, spirits, liquor; informal booze, hooch, hard stuff, firewater, rotgut, moonshine, grog, demon rum, bottle, juice.

saucy ▶ adjective informal 1 *you saucy girl!* **cheeky,** impudent, impertinent, irreverent, forward, disrespectful, bold, as bold as brass, brazen, pert; informal fresh, lippy, mouthy, sassy.
ANTONYMS demure, polite.
2 *the cap sat at a saucy angle* **jaunty,** rakish, sporty, raffish.

saunter ▶ verb *they sauntered back to the car* **stroll,** amble, wander, meander, drift, walk; stretch one's legs, take the air; informal mosey, tootle; formal promenade.

savage ▶ adjective 1 *savage dogs* **ferocious,** fierce; wild, untamed, untamable, undomesticated, feral.
ANTONYMS tame.
2 *a savage assault* **vicious,** brutal, cruel, sadistic, ferocious, fierce, violent, bloody, murderous, homicidal, bloodthirsty; literary fell; archaic sanguinary; informal smash-mouth.
3 *a savage attack on free-trade policy* **fierce,** blistering, scathing, searing, stinging, devastating, mordant, trenchant, caustic, cutting, biting, withering, virulent, vitriolic.
ANTONYMS mild.
4 *a savage race* **primitive,** uncivilized, unenlightened, nonliterate.
ANTONYMS civilized.
5 *a savage landscape* **rugged,** rough, wild, inhospitable, uninhabitable.
6 *a savage blow for the town* **severe,** crushing, devastating, crippling, terrible, awful, dreadful, dire, catastrophic, calamitous, ruinous.
▶ noun 1 *she'd expected mud huts and savages* **barbarian,** wild man, wild woman, primitive.
2 *she described her son's assailants as savages* **brute,** beast, monster, barbarian, sadist, animal.
▶ verb 1 *he was savaged by a dog* **maul,** attack, tear to pieces, lacerate, claw, bite.
2 *critics savaged the film* **criticize severely,** attack, lambaste, condemn, denounce, pillory, revile; informal pan, tear to pieces, hammer, slam, do a hatchet job on, crucify, trash; formal excoriate.

save ▶ verb 1 *the captain was saved by his crew* **rescue,** come to someone's rescue, save someone's life; set free, free, liberate, deliver, extricate; bail out; informal save someone's bacon/neck/skin.
2 *the farmhouse has been saved from demolition* **preserve,** keep safe, keep, protect, safeguard; salvage, retrieve, reclaim, rescue.
3 *start saving money* **put aside,** set aside, put by, put to one side, save up, keep, retain, reserve, conserve, stockpile, store, hoard, save for a rainy day; informal salt away, squirrel away, stash away, hang on to.
4 *asking me first would have saved a lot of trouble* **prevent,** obviate, forestall, spare; stop; avoid, avert.
▶ preposition & conjunction formal *no one needed to know save herself* **except,** apart from, but, other than, besides, aside from, bar, barring, excluding, leaving out, saving; informal outside of.

savior ▶ noun *he was hailed as the country's savior* **rescuer,** liberator, deliverer, emancipator; champion, knight in shining armor, friend in need, good Samaritan.

savoir faire ▶ noun *the French admired Franklin's wit and Jefferson's savoir faire* **social skill,** social grace(s), urbanity, suavity, finesse, sophistication, poise, aplomb, adroitness, polish, style, smoothness, tact, tactfulness, diplomacy, discretion, delicacy, sensitivity; informal savvy.
ANTONYMS gaucheness.

savor ▶ verb 1 *she wanted to savor every moment* **relish,** enjoy (to the full), appreciate, delight in, revel in, luxuriate in, bask in.
2 *such a declaration* **savored of** *immodesty* **suggest,** smack of, have the hallmarks of, seem like, have the air of, show signs of.
▶ noun 1 *the subtle savor of wood smoke* **smell,** aroma, fragrance, scent, perfume, bouquet; **taste,** flavor, tang, smack.
2 *a savor of bitterness seasoned my feelings for him* **trace,** hint, suggestion, touch, smack.
3 *her usual diversions had lost their savor* **piquancy,** interest, attraction, flavor, spice, zest, excitement, enjoyment, shine; informal zing, pizzazz, sparkle.

savory ▶ adjective 1 *sweet or savory dishes* salty, spicy, piquant, tangy.
ANTONYMS sweet.
2 *a rich, savory aroma* **appetizing,** mouthwatering, delicious, delectable, luscious, tasty, flavorful, full of flavor, palatable, toothsome; informal scrumptious, finger-licking, lip-smacking, melt-in-your/the-mouth, yummy.
ANTONYMS unappetizing.
3 *one of the less savory aspects of the affair* **acceptable,** pleasant, respectable, wholesome, honorable, proper, seemly.
ANTONYMS unpleasant, unacceptable.

saw ▶ noun *the old saw about when the going gets tough* **saying,** maxim, proverb, aphorism, axiom, adage, epigram.

say ▶ verb 1 *she felt her stomach flutter as he said her name* **speak,** utter, voice, pronounce, give voice to, vocalize.
2 *"I must go," she said* **declare,** state, announce, remark, observe, mention, comment, note, add; reply, respond, answer, rejoin; informal come out with.
3 *Newall says he's innocent* **claim,** maintain, assert, hold, insist, contend; allege, profess; formal opine, aver.
4 *I can't conjure up the words to say how I feel* **express,** put into words, phrase, articulate, communicate, make known, put/get across, convey, verbalize; reveal, divulge, impart, disclose; imply, suggest.

5 *they sang hymns and said a prayer* **recite,** repeat, utter, deliver, perform, declaim, orate.
6 *the clock said one twenty* **indicate,** show, read.
7 *I'd say it's about five miles* **estimate,** judge, guess, hazard a guess, predict, speculate, surmise, conjecture, venture; informal reckon.
8 *let's say you'd just won a million dollars* **suppose,** assume, imagine, presume, hypothesize, postulate, posit.
▶ **noun 1** *everyone is entitled to their say* **chance to speak,** turn to speak, opinion, view, voice; informal two cents, two cents' worth.
2 *don't I have any say in the matter?* **influence,** sway, weight, voice, input, share, part.
– PHRASES **that is to say** *they're inquiring about Miss Leslie—that is to say, they want to know if she's safe and well* **in other words,** to put it another way; i.e., that is, to wit, viz., namely. **to say the least** *his performance was disappointing to say the least* **to put it mildly,** putting it mildly, without any exaggeration, at the very least.

saying ▶ **noun** *you know the old saying about all work and no play?* **proverb,** maxim, aphorism, axiom, adage, saw, tag, motto, epigram, dictum, expression, phrase, formula; slogan, catchphrase, mantra; platitude, cliché, commonplace, truism, chestnut.
– PHRASES **it goes without saying** *it goes without saying we'll need to rent a car when we get there* **of course,** naturally, needless to say, it's taken for granted, it's understood/assumed, it's taken as read, it's an accepted fact; obviously, self-evidently, manifestly; informal natch.

CHOOSE THE RIGHT WORD

saying, adage, aphorism, apothegm, epigram, epigraph, maxim, proverb

"Once burned, twice shy" is an old **saying** about learning from your mistakes. In fact, *sayings*—a term used to describe any current or habitual expression of wisdom or truth—are a dime a dozen. **Proverbs**—sayings that are well known and often repeated, usually expressing metaphorically a truth based on common sense or practical experience—are just as plentiful (*her favorite proverb was "A stitch in time saves nine"*). An **adage** is a time-honored and widely known proverb, such as "Where's there's smoke, there's fire." A **maxim** offers a rule of conduct or action in the form of a proverb, such as "Neither a borrower nor a lender be." **Epigram** and **epigraph** are often confused, but their meanings are quite separate. An *epigram* is a terse, witty, or satirical statement that often relies on a paradox for its effect (*Oscar Wilde's well-known epigram that "The only way to get rid of temptation is to yield to it"*). An *epigraph,* on the other hand, is a brief quotation used to introduce a piece of writing (*he used a quote from T. S. Eliot as the epigraph to his new novel*). An **aphorism** requires a little more thought than an *epigram,* since it aims to be profound rather than witty (*she'd just finished reading a book of Mark Twain's aphorisms*). An **apothegm** is a pointed and often startling aphorism, such as Samuel Johnson's remark that "Patriotism is the last refuge of a scoundrel.".

scale[1] ▶ **noun 1** *reptiles have scales covering the skin* plate; technical lamella, lamina, squama, scute, scutum.
2 *the disease causes scales on the skin* **flake;** (**scales**) scurf, dandruff; technical furfur.
3 *how can I remove the scale from my tea kettle?* **buildup,** deposit, incrustation.

scale[2] ▶ **noun 1** *the Richter scale* **calibrated system,** calibration, graduated system, system of measurement, measuring system.
2 *we are at opposite ends of the social scale* **hierarchy,** ladder, ranking, pecking order, order, spectrum, progression, succession, sequence, series.
3 *the scale of the map is too small to show details* **ratio,** proportion, relative size.
4 *no one foresaw the scale of the disaster* **extent,** size, scope, magnitude, dimensions, range, breadth, compass, degree, reach, spread, sweep.
▶ **verb** *thieves scaled the fence* **climb,** ascend, go up, clamber up, scramble up, mount, shinny (up); historical escalade.
– PHRASES **scale down** *manufacturing capacity has been scaled down* **reduce,** cut down, cut back, cut, make cutbacks in, decrease, lessen, lower, trim, slim down, prune, curtail. **scale up** *the departments intend to scale up their activities* **increase,** expand, augment, build up, add to; step up, boost, escalate.

scaly ▶ **adjective 1** *the dragon's scaly hide* technical squamous, squamate, squamose, lamellate, lamellar, lamelliform, lamellose.
2 *scaly patches of dead skin* **flaky, dry,** flaking, scurfy, peeling, rough, scabrous, mangy, scabious; technical furfuraceous.

scamp ▶ **noun** informal *he was a scamp in his younger days* **rascal,** monkey, devil, imp, wretch, mischief-maker, troublemaker, prankster, rogue; informal scalawag, horror, monster, terror, holy terror, hellion, varmint, rapscallion; archaic scapegrace.

scamper ▶ **verb** *the boy scampered off | his dogs scampered around the yard* **scurry,** scuttle, dart, run, rush, race, dash, sprint, hurry, hasten, make haste, scoot; romp, skip, frolic, gambol; Brit. scutter.

scan ▶ **verb 1** *Adam scanned the horizon* **scrutinize, examine,** study, inspect, survey, search, scour, sweep, look at, stare at, look someone/something up and down, gaze at, eye, watch; contemplate, regard, take stock of; informal check out, scope (out).
2 *I scanned the pages of his diary* **glance through/over,** look through/over, have a look at, run/cast/pass one's eye over, skim (through), flick through, flip through, leaf through, thumb through, rifle through, read quickly, browse (through).
ANTONYMS pore over.
▶ **noun 1** *a careful scan of the terrain* **inspection,** scrutiny, examination, survey.

2 *a quick scan through the report* **glance,** look, flick, browse, skim.
3 *a brain scan* **examination,** screening, MRI, ultrasound.

scandal ▶ **noun 1** *the sex scandal forced him to resign* (**outrageous**) **wrongdoing,** impropriety, misconduct, immoral behavior, unethical behavior, discreditable behavior, outrageous behavior; shocking incident, shocking series of events; offense, transgression, crime, sin; skeleton in the closet; informal business, affair, -gate.
2 *unmarried motherhood at that time was fraught with scandal* **shame,** dishonor, disgrace, disrepute, discredit, infamy, ignominy, embarrassment; odium, opprobrium, censure, obloquy; stigma.
3 *it's a scandal that the disease is not adequately treated* **disgrace,** outrage, injustice; (crying) shame, pity; affront, insult, reproach.
4 *no scandal is attached to her name* **malicious gossip,** malicious rumor(s), slander, libel, calumny, defamation, aspersions, muckraking, scandalmongering, smear campaign; informal dirt.

scandalize ▶ **verb** *the audience was scandalized by the speaker's racist remarks* **shock,** appall, outrage, horrify, disgust, revolt, repel, sicken; offend, give offense to, affront, insult; cause raised eyebrows.
ANTONYMS impress.

scandalous ▶ **adjective 1** *a scandalous waste of taxpayers' money* **disgraceful,** shocking, outrageous, monstrous, criminal, wicked, sinful, shameful, atrocious, appalling, dreadful, deplorable, reprehensible, inexcusable, intolerable, insupportable, unforgivable, unconscionable, unpardonable; rare egregious.
ANTONYMS acceptable, praiseworthy.
2 *a series of scandalous liaisons* **discreditable,** disreputable, dishonorable, improper, unseemly, sordid.
ANTONYMS proper, seemly.
3 *scandalous rumors* **scurrilous,** malicious, slanderous, libelous, defamatory; rare calumnious, calumniatory, aspersive.

scant ▶ **adjective** *there is only scant evidence to support this hypothesis* **little,** little or no, minimal, hardly (any), limited, negligible, barely sufficient, meager; insufficient, too little, inadequate, deficient; formal exiguous.
ANTONYMS abundant, ample, sufficient.

scanty ▶ **adjective 1** *their scanty wages | details of his life are scanty* **meager,** scant, minimal, limited, modest, restricted, sparse; tiny, small, paltry, negligible, insufficient, inadequate, deficient, too small/little/few, poor, sketchy, thin; scarce, in short supply, few and far between; informal measly, piddling, mingy, pathetic; formal exiguous.
ANTONYMS ample, abundant, plentiful.
2 *scanty clothing* **skimpy,** revealing, short, brief; low, low-cut; indecent.
ANTONYMS modest.

scapegoat ▶ **noun** *find yourself another scapegoat* **whipping boy**; informal fall guy, patsy.

scar ▶ **noun 1** *the scar on his left cheek* **cicatrix,** mark, blemish, disfigurement, discoloration, defacement; pockmark, pock, pit; lesion, stigma; birthmark, nevus; (**scars**) stigmata.
2 *deep psychological scars* **trauma,** damage, injury.
▶ **verb 1** *the leg will heal, but he's likely to be scarred for life* **disfigure,** mark, blemish, discolor; pockmark, pit; stigmatize.
2 *the landscape has been scarred by strip mining* **damage,** spoil, mar, deface, injure; rare disfeature.
3 *she was profoundly scarred by the incident* **traumatize,** damage, injure, wound; distress, disturb, upset.

USAGE

scarify, scorify

Scarify (from *scar*, but pronounced as if from *scare*) means (1) "make superficial marks or incisions in; cut off skin from"; (2) "break up the surface of (the ground) with a spiked machine [a scarifier] for loosening soil or building roads"; or (3) "pain by severe criticism."

Sense 1 is most common—e.g.: "Rub the seed across some sandpaper to weaken the hard seed coat or scarify it with a knife for better germination." (*Virginian-Pilot* [Norfolk]; Apr. 20, 1997.) This sense applies also to body adornment by cutting and scraping—e.g.: "Worse, once piercing becomes commonplace among people like, well, Leslie, the trendsetters up the ante with other forms of body alteration: cutting (scarification as adornment), branding (searing flesh with high heat in artistic patterns) and—please don't eat during this next sentence—tongue splitting, in which the tongue is cleaved nearly in half so as to cause it to fork like a lizard's." (*Washington Post*; Feb. 11, 2003.)

Sense 3 is also fairly common—e.g.: "With a combination of dazzling philosophical acumen and scarifying wit, Stove does for irrationalism in Karl Popper's philosophy . . . what the Romans did for Carthage in the Third Punic War." (*New Criterion*; Mar. 1997.)

An identically pronounced, but separate, *scarify*, based on the root word *scare*, dates from the late 18th century but remains mostly dialectal. It often carries a lighthearted connotation—e.g.: "The cost-of-living index had taken a scarifying new jump of 1.2 percent in February, to an annual rate of 15 percent." (*Newsweek*; Apr. 2, 1979.)

Scorify = reduce to dross or slag. The term surfaces most commonly in cognate forms, such as *scorifier*—e.g.: "Hanging adjacent to the furnace are the specialized tongs for handling crucibles, cupels and the dishlike ceramic containers called scorifiers." (*Bulletin* [Bend, OR]; Apr. 2, 1997.) — **BG**

scarce ▶ **adjective 1** *food was scarce | scarce financial resources* **in short supply,** scant, scanty, meager, sparse, short, hard to find, hard to come by, too little, insufficient, deficient, inadequate, lacking, wanting; at a

premium, paltry, negligible; informal rare/scarce as hen's teeth, rarer/scarcer than hen's teeth, not to be had for love or money; formal exiguous.
ANTONYMS plentiful, abundant.
2 *birds that prefer dense forest are becoming scarce* **rare,** few and far between; uncommon, unusual.
ANTONYMS common.

scarcely ▶ **adverb 1** *she could scarcely hear what he was saying* **hardly,** barely, only just; almost not.
2 *I **scarcely ever** see him* **rarely,** seldom, infrequently, not often, hardly ever, almost never, on rare occasions, every once in a while; informal once in a blue moon.
ANTONYMS often.
3 *this could scarcely be accidental* **surely not,** not, hardly, certainly not, definitely not, not at all, on no account, under no circumstances, by no means, in no way, noway, noways.

scarcity ▶ **noun** *the scarcity of affordable housing* **shortage,** dearth, lack, want, undersupply, insufficiency, paucity, scarceness, scantness, scantiness, meagerness, sparseness, poverty; deficiency, inadequacy; unavailability, absence; rare exiguity, exiguousness.
ANTONYMS abundance, excess, surplus.

scare ▶ **verb** *stop it, you're scaring me* **frighten,** startle, alarm, terrify, petrify, intimidate, terrorize, make afraid, make fearful, fill with fear, give someone a fright, panic, throw into a panic, shock, unnerve, cow; strike terror into, put the fear of God into, chill to the bone/marrow, make someone's blood run cold, scare/frighten to death, scare/frighten someone out of their wits, send into a cold sweat, scare/frighten the living daylights out of, scare/frighten the life out of, scare the hell out of, scare stiff, scare witless, make someone shake in their boots/shoes; informal scare the pants off, make someone's hair stand on end, make someone jump out of their skin, make someone's hair curl, spook, scarify, scare the bejesus out of, scare the bejabbers out of, give someone the heebie-jeebies; vulgar slang scare shitless, scare the shit out of.
ANTONYMS reassure.
▶ **noun** *you gave me a scare—how did you get here?* **fright,** shock, start, turn, jump; informal heart attack.

scared ▶ **adjective** *I've never been so scared in all my life* **frightened,** afraid, fearful, startled, nervous, panicky, alarmed, intimidated; terrified, petrified, terrorized, horrified, unnerved, panic-stricken/-struck, terror-stricken/-struck, horror-stricken/-struck, with one's heart in one's mouth, scared stiff, scared/frightened out of one's wits, scared witless, scared/frightened to death, chilled to the bone/marrow, in a cold sweat; informal spooked, scarified; vulgar slang scared shitless.

scarf ▶ **noun** *she wore a scarf* **muffler,** headscarf, mantilla, stole, tippet; kerchief, neckerchief, bandanna, babushka.
▶ **verb** informal *stop scarfing your food! | we **scarfed down** the entire batch of cookies | I can't believe how fast he **scarfed up** his dinner* **gobble up/down,** eat greedily, eat hungrily, guzzle, bolt, gulp (down), devour, wolf (down), gorge (oneself) on; informal tuck into, put away, pack away, demolish, polish off, shovel in/down, stuff one's face (with), pig out (on); informal scoff (down/up), inhale; rare gluttonize, gourmandize, ingurgitate.
ANTONYMS nibble.

scary ▶ **adjective** informal *that movie is too scary for me* **frightening,** alarming, terrifying, petrifying, hair-raising, spine-chilling, blood-curdling, bone-chilling, chilling, horrifying, nerve-racking, fearsome, unnerving; eerie, sinister; informal creepy, spine-tingling, spooky, hairy.

scathing ▶ **adjective** *another restaurant has fallen victim to one of her scathing reviews* **devastating,** extremely critical, blistering, searing, withering, scorching, fierce, ferocious, savage, severe, stinging, biting, cutting, mordant, trenchant, virulent, caustic, vitriolic, scornful, sharp, bitter, harsh, unsparing; rare mordacious.
ANTONYMS mild, gentle, complimentary.

scatter ▶ **verb 1** *the papers were scattered by the sudden breeze | scatter the seeds as evenly as possible* **throw,** strew, toss, fling; **sprinkle,** spread, distribute, sow, broadcast, disseminate; literary bestrew.
ANTONYMS gather.
2 *the crowd scattered | onlookers were scattered in all directions* **disperse,** break up, disband, separate, move/go in different directions, go separate ways; dissipate, dissolve; drive, send, put to flight, chase.
ANTONYMS assemble.

CHOOSE THE RIGHT WORD

scatter, broadcast, diffuse, dispel, disperse, disseminate, dissipate

If you **scatter** something, you throw it about in different directions, often using force (*the wind scattered leaves around the yard*). **Disperse** implies a scattering that completely breaks up a mass or assemblage and spreads the units far and wide (*the crowd dispersed as soon as the storm arrived; the ships were so widely dispersed that they couldn't see each other*). To **dispel** is to scatter or to drive away something that obscures, confuses, or bothers (*to dispel her fears*), while to **diffuse** is to lessen the intensity of something by spreading it out over a broader area (*the curtains diffused the bright sunlight pouring in the window*). **Dissipate** suggests that something has completely dissolved, disintegrated, or vanished (*early-morning mist dissipated by the sun*). **Broadcast** originally meant to scatter seed, but it is also used figuratively to mean make public (*The news of the president's defeat was broadcast the next morning*). **Disseminate** also means to publish or make public, but it implies a wider audience and usually a longer duration. You can spend a lifetime *disseminating* knowledge, in other words, but you would *broadcast* the news of the birth of your first grandchild.

scatterbrained ▶ adjective *my scatterbrained kids left their jackets on the bus* **absentminded,** forgetful, disorganized; dreamy, with one's head in the clouds, with a mind/memory like a sieve, featherbrained, birdbrained, giddy; informal dizzy, dippy, ditzy, flaky, scatty, not with it, out to lunch.

scavenge ▶ verb *they scavenge for food in the restaurant's trash cans* **forage,** rummage, search, hunt, look, root around/about, grub around/about.

scavenger ▶ *yesterday he ran the company, today he's a homeless scavenger* **forager,** rummager, grubber; historical ragpicker; rare mudlark.

scenario ▶ noun **1** *Walt wrote scenarios for a major Hollywood studio* **plot,** outline, synopsis, story line, framework; screenplay, script, libretto; formal diegesis.
2 *every possible scenario must be explored* **sequence of events,** course of events, chain of events, series of developments, situation.
3 *this film has a more contemporary scenario* **setting,** background, context, scene, milieu.

scene ▶ noun **1** *the scene of the accident* **location,** site, place, position, point, spot; locale, setting, whereabouts; technical locus.
2 *the scene is Montreal, in the late 1890s* **background,** setting, context, milieu, backdrop, mise en scène.
3 *terrible scenes of violence* **incident,** event, episode, happening, moment.
4 *an impressive mountain scene* **view,** vista, outlook, panorama, sight; landscape, scenery; picture, tableau, spectacle.
5 *she created a scene outside the bank* **fuss,** exhibition of oneself, performance, tantrum, outburst, commotion, disturbance, upset, furor, brouhaha, row, contretemps; informal song and dance, to-do.
6 *the political scene | sorry, fishing just isn't my scene* **arena,** stage, sphere, world, milieu, realm, domain; area of interest, field, field of interest, specialty, province, preserve; informal thing.
7 *the last scene of the play* **subdivision,** division, section, segment.
8 *a scene from a Laurel and Hardy movie* **clip,** section, segment, part, sequence.
– PHRASES **behind the scenes** adverb informal *discussions continued behind the scenes* **secretly,** in secret, privately, in private, behind closed doors, surreptitiously, off the record; informal on the quiet, on the QT; formal sub rosa. **behind-the-scenes** adjective *a behind-the-scenes romance* **secret,** private, clandestine, surreptitious; confidential.

scenery ▶ noun **1** *the beautiful scenery of the Rockies* **landscape,** countryside, country, terrain, topography, setting, surroundings, environment; view, vista, panorama; cityscape, townscape, roofscape; riverscape, seascape, waterscape, snowscape.
2 *we all helped with the scenery and costumes* **stage set,** set, mise en scène, backdrop, drop curtain; setting, background, decor.

scenic ▶ adjective *countless miles of Route 1 are still quite scenic* **picturesque,** pretty, pleasing, attractive, lovely, beautiful, charming, pretty as a picture, easy on the eye; impressive, striking, spectacular, breathtaking; panoramic.
ANTONYMS dreary, unattractive.

scent ▶ noun **1** *the scent of freshly cut hay* **smell,** fragrance, aroma, perfume, redolence, savor, odor, whiff; bouquet, nose. See note at SMELL.
2 *that's a lovely scent you're wearing* **perfume,** fragrance, cologne, toilet water.
3 *the hounds picked up the scent of a rabbit* **spoor,** trail, track; Hunting foil, wind.
4 *there was a scent of rain in the air* **hint,** suggestion, trace, whiff.
▶ verb **1** *a shark can scent blood from over half a mile away* **smell,** detect the smell of, get a whiff of.
2 *Rose looked at him, scenting a threat* **sense,** become aware of, detect, discern, perceive, recognize, get wind of.

scented ▶ adjective *a hotel with private saunas and scented sheets* **perfumed,** fragranced, perfumy; sweet-smelling, fragrant, aromatic; rare aromatized.

schedule ▶ noun **1** *we need to draw up a production schedule* **plan,** program, timetable, scheme.
2 *I have a very busy schedule* **timetable,** agenda, diary, calendar, timeline; itinerary.
▶ verb *another meeting was scheduled for April 20* **arrange,** organize, plan, program, timetable, set up, line up, slate.
– PHRASES **behind schedule** *the museum renovations are behind schedule* **late,** running late, overdue, behind time, behind, behindhand.

scheme ▶ noun **1** *crazy fundraising schemes* **plan,** project, plan of action, program, strategy, stratagem, tactic, game plan, course/line of action; system, procedure, design, formula, recipe.
2 *police uncovered a scheme to steal the paintings* **plot,** intrigue, conspiracy; ruse, ploy, stratagem, maneuver, subterfuge; machinations; informal game, racket, con, scam.
3 *the sonnet's rhyme scheme* **arrangement,** system, organization, configuration, pattern, format; technical schema.
▶ verb *he schemed to bring about the collapse of the government* **plot,** hatch a plot, conspire, intrigue, connive, maneuver, plan.

scheming ▶ adjective *he finally saw his scheming wife for what she really was* **cunning,** crafty, calculating, devious, designing, conniving, wily, sly, tricky, artful, guileful, slippery, slick, manipulative, Machiavellian, unscrupulous, disingenuous; duplicitous, deceitful, underhanded, treacherous.
ANTONYMS ingenuous, honest.

schism ▶ noun *the schism between her father and his brother* **division,** split, rift, breach, rupture, break, separation, severance; chasm, gulf; discord, disagreement, dissension.

scholar ▶ noun **1** *a leading biblical scholar* **academic,** intellectual, learned person, man/woman of letters, mind, intellect, savant, polymath, highbrow, bluestocking; authority, expert; informal egghead.
2 archaic *the school had 28 scholars* **student,** pupil, schoolchild, schoolboy, schoolgirl.

scholarly ▸ adjective **1** *an earnest, scholarly man* **learned,** erudite, academic, well-read, widely read, intellectual, literary, lettered, educated, knowledgeable, highbrow; studious, bookish, donnish, bluestocking, cerebral; informal pointy-headed.
ANTONYMS uneducated, illiterate.
2 *a scholarly career* **academic,** scholastic, pedagogic.

scholarship ▸ noun **1** *a center of medieval scholarship* **learning,** book learning, knowledge, erudition, education, letters, culture, academic study, academic achievement. See note at KNOWLEDGE.
2 *a scholarship of $200 per semester* **grant,** award, endowment, payment, bursary.

scholastic ▸ adjective *their scholastic achievements* **academic,** educational, school, scholarly.

school ▸ noun **1** *their children went to the local school* **educational institution**; academy, college, university; seminary; alma mater.
2 *the university's School of Law* **department,** faculty, division.
3 *the Barbizon School* **group,** set, circle; followers, following, disciples, apostles, admirers, devotees, votaries; proponents, adherents.
4 *the school of linguistics associated with his ideas* **way of thinking,** persuasion, creed, credo, doctrine, belief, faith, opinion, point of view; approach, method, style.
5 *a school of fish* shoal; pod, gam.
▸ verb **1** *he was born in Paris and schooled in Lyon* **educate,** teach, instruct.
2 *he schooled her in horsemanship* **train,** teach, tutor, coach, instruct, drill, discipline, direct, guide, prepare, groom; prime, verse.

schooling ▸ noun **1** *his parents paid for his schooling* **education,** teaching, tuition, instruction, tutoring, tutelage; lessons; (book) learning.
2 *the schooling of horses* **training,** coaching, instruction, drill, drilling, discipline, disciplining.

schoolteacher ▸ noun *until 1912, the town had in its employ just one schoolteacher* **teacher,** schoolmaster, schoolmistress, tutor, educationist; informal schoolmarm; formal pedagogue.

science ▸ noun **1** *he teaches science at the high school* physics, chemistry, biology; physical sciences, life sciences.
2 *the science of criminology* **branch of knowledge,** body of knowledge/information, area of study, discipline, field.

scientific ▸ adjective **1** *scientific research* technological, technical; research-based, knowledge-based, empirical.
2 *you need to approach it in a more scientific way* **systematic,** methodical, organized, well-organized, ordered, orderly, meticulous, rigorous; exact, precise, accurate, mathematical; analytical, rational.

scintillating ▸ adjective **1** *a scintillating diamond necklace* **sparkling,** shining, bright, brilliant, gleaming, glittering, twinkling, shimmering, glistening; literary glistering, coruscating.
ANTONYMS dull.
2 *a scintillating performance* **brilliant,** dazzling, exciting, exhilarating, stimulating; sparkling, lively, buzzy, vivacious, vibrant, animated, ebullient, effervescent; witty, clever; literary coruscating.
ANTONYMS dull, boring.

scion ▸ noun **1** *a scion of the tree* **cutting,** graft, slip; shoot, offshoot, twig.
2 *the scion of an aristocratic family* **descendant**; heir, successor; child, offspring; Law issue.

scoff ▸ verb *they scoffed at her article* **mock,** deride, ridicule, sneer at, jeer at, jibe at, taunt, make fun of, poke fun at, laugh at, scorn, laugh to scorn, dismiss, make light of, belittle; informal pooh-pooh.

scold ▸ verb *Mom took Anna away, scolding her for her bad behavior* **rebuke,** reprimand, reproach, reprove, admonish, remonstrate with, chastise, chide, upbraid, berate, take to task, read someone the riot act, give someone a piece of one's mind, rake/haul someone over the coals; informal tell off, dress down, give someone an earful, rap over the knuckles, let someone have it, bawl out, give someone hell, give someone what for, chew out, ream (out), light into; formal castigate.
ANTONYMS praise.
▸ noun archaic *she is turning into a scold* **nag,** shrew, fishwife, harpy, termagant, harridan; complainer, moaner, grumbler; informal kvetch.

CHOOSE THE RIGHT WORD

scold, berate, chide, revile, upbraid, vituperate

A mother might **scold** a child who misbehaves, which means to rebuke in an angry, irritated, and often nagging way, whether or not such treatment is justified. **Chide** is a more formal term than *scold*, and it usually implies disapproval for specific failings (*she was chided by her teacher for using "less" instead of "fewer"*), while **berate** suggests a prolonged scolding, usually aimed at a pattern of behavior or way of life rather than a single misdeed and often combined with scorn or contempt for the person being criticized (*he berated his parents for being too protective and ruining his social life*). **Upbraid** also implies a lengthy expression of displeasure or criticism, but usually with more justification than scold and with an eye toward encouraging better behavior in the future (*the tennis coach upbraided her players for missing so many serves*). **Revile** and **vituperate** are reserved for very strong or even violent displays of anger. To *revile* is to use highly abusive and contemptuous language (*revile one's opponent in the press*), while *vituperate* connotes even more violence in the attack (*the angry hockey players were held apart by their teammates, but they continued to vituperate each other with the foulest possible language*).

scolding ▶ **noun** *I'll be in Mr. Kling's office getting my weekly scolding* **rebuke,** reprimand, reproach, reproof, admonishment, remonstration, lecture, upbraiding; informal talking-to, rap over the knuckles, dressing-down, earful, roasting; formal castigation.

scoop ▶ **noun 1** *a measuring scoop* **spoon,** ladle, dipper; bailer.
2 *a scoop of vanilla ice cream* **spoonful,** ladleful, portion, lump, ball; informal dollop.
3 informal *he got the scoop on the new CEO* **exclusive (story),** inside story, exposé, revelation, information.
▶ **verb 1** *a hole was* ***scooped out*** *in the floor* **hollow out,** gouge out, dig, excavate, cut out.
2 *cut the tomatoes in half and* ***scoop out*** *the flesh* **remove,** take out, spoon out, scrape out.
3 *she* ***scooped up*** *armfuls of clothes* **pick up,** gather up, lift, take up; snatch up, grab.

scope ▶ **noun 1** *the scope of the investigation* **extent,** range, breadth, width, reach, sweep, purview, span, horizon; area, sphere, field, realm, compass, orbit, ambit, terms/field of reference, jurisdiction; confine, limit; gamut. See note at RANGE.
2 *the scope for change is limited by political realities* **opportunity,** freedom, latitude, leeway, capacity, liberty, room (to maneuver), elbow room; possibility, chance.

scorch ▶ **verb 1** *the buildings were scorched by the fire* **burn,** sear, singe, char, blacken, discolor. See note at BURN.
2 *grass scorched by the sun* **dry up,** desiccate, parch, wither, shrivel; burn, bake.

scorching ▶ **adjective 1** *the scorching July sun* **extremely hot,** red-hot, blazing, flaming, fiery, burning, blistering, searing, sweltering, torrid, broiling; informal boiling (hot), baking (hot), sizzling.
ANTONYMS freezing.
2 *scorching criticism* **fierce,** savage, scathing, withering, blistering, searing, devastating, stringent, severe, harsh, stinging, biting, mordant, trenchant, caustic, virulent, vitriolic.
ANTONYMS mild.

score ▶ **noun 1** *the final score was 4–3* **result,** outcome; total, sum total, tally, count.
2 *an IQ score of 161* **rating,** grade, mark, percentage.
3 *I've got a score to settle with you* **grievance,** grudge, complaint; dispute, bone of contention; (**score to settle**) bone to pick, ax to grind.
4 informal *he knew* ***the score*** *before he got here* **the situation,** the position, the facts, the truth of the matter, the (true) state of affairs, the picture, how things stand, the lay of the land; informal what's what, what the deal is/was.
5 (**scores**) *scores of complaints* **a great many,** a lot, a great/good deal, large quantities, plenty; informal lots, umpteen, a slew, loads, masses, stacks, scads, heaps, piles, bags, tons, oodles, dozens, hundreds, thousands, millions, billions, gazillions, a bunch.
▶ **verb 1** *Lou's already scored 13 goals this season* **net,** bag, rack up, chalk up, tally, notch, record; get, gain, achieve, make.
2 informal *his new movie really scored* **be successful,** be a success, triumph, make an impression, go down well; informal be a hit, be a winner, be a sellout.
3 *the piece was scored for flute and violin* **orchestrate,** arrange, set, adapt; write, compose.
4 *score the wood in crisscross patterns* **scratch,** cut, notch, incise, scrape, nick, chip, gouge; mark.
5 informal *he was hoping to score on his date tonight* **get lucky,** have sex, go all the way, do it.
– PHRASES **score points off** *he's obsessed with scoring points off everyone, even his best friends* **get the better of,** gain the advantage over, outdo, best, have the edge over; have the last laugh on, make a fool of, humiliate; informal get/be one up on, get one over on.

scorn ▶ **noun** *he was unable to hide the scorn in his voice* **contempt,** derision, contemptuousness, disdain, derisiveness, mockery, sneering.
ANTONYMS admiration, respect.
▶ **verb 1** *critics scorned the painting* **deride,** hold in contempt, treat with contempt, pour/heap scorn on, look down on, look down one's nose at, disdain, curl one's lip at, mock, scoff at, sneer at, jeer at, laugh at, laugh out of court; disparage, slight; dismiss, thumb one's nose at; informal turn one's nose up at. See note at DESPISE.
ANTONYMS admire, respect.
2 *"I am a woman scorned," she thought* **spurn,** rebuff, reject, ignore, shun, snub.

scornful ▶ **adjective** *his scornful remarks* **contemptuous,** derisive, withering, mocking, scoffing, sneering, jeering, scathing, snide, disparaging, supercilious, disdainful, superior; archaic contumelious.
ANTONYMS admiring, respectful.

scoundrel ▶ **noun** *the lying scoundrel* **rogue,** rascal, miscreant, good-for-nothing, reprobate; cheat, swindler, scam artist, fraudster, trickster, charlatan; informal villain, bastard, beast, son of a bitch, SOB, rat, louse, swine, dog, skunk, heel, snake (in the grass), wretch, scumbag, scumbucket, scuzzball, sleazeball, sleazebag, ratfink; informal dated hound; dated cad; archaic blackguard, knave, varlet, whoreson, picaroon.

scour ▶ **verb** *she scoured the oven and cleaned out the cupboards* **scrub,** rub, clean, wash, cleanse, wipe; polish, buff (up), shine, burnish; abrade.

scourge ▶ **noun 1** historical *he was beaten with a scourge* **whip,** horsewhip, lash, strap, birch, switch, bullwhip, rawhide; historical cat-o'-nine-tails.
2 *inflation was the scourge of the mid-1970s* **affliction,** bane, curse, plague, menace, evil, misfortune, burden, cross to bear; blight, cancer, canker.
ANTONYMS blessing, godsend.
▶ **verb 1** historical *he was publicly scourged* **flog,** whip, beat, horsewhip, lash, flagellate, strap, birch, cane, thrash, belt, leather; informal tan someone's hide, take a strap to.
2 *a disease that scourged North America* **afflict,** plague, torment, torture, curse, oppress, burden, bedevil, beset.

scout ▶ **noun 1** *scouts reported the enemy's position* **lookout,** outrider, advance guard, vanguard; spy.
2 *a lengthy scout around the area*

reconnaissance, reconnoiter; exploration, search, expedition; informal recon.
3 *a scout for a major-league team* **talent spotter,** talent scout; informal bird dog.
▶ verb **1** *I scouted around for some logs* **search,** look, hunt, ferret about/around, root around/about.
2 *a night patrol was sent to* **scout out** *the area* **reconnoiter,** explore, make a reconnaissance of, inspect, investigate, spy out, survey; examine, scan, study, observe; informal check out, case.

scowl ▶ noun *the scowl on his face* **frown,** glower, glare, grimace, black look; informal dirty look.
▶ verb *she* **scowled at** *him* **glower at,** frown at, glare at, grimace at, lower at, look daggers at, give someone a black look; make a face at, pull a face, turn the corners of one's mouth down at, pout at; informal give someone a dirty look.
ANTONYMS smile, grin.

scraggy ▶ adjective *this scraggy mutt just wandered into our yard* **scrawny,** thin, as thin as a rake, skinny, skin-and-bones, gaunt, bony, angular, gawky, rawboned.
ANTONYMS fat.

scramble ▶ verb **1** *we scrambled over the boulders* **clamber,** climb, crawl, claw one's way, scrabble, grope one's way, struggle, shinny.
2 *children scrambled for the scattered coins* **jostle,** scuffle, tussle, struggle, strive, compete, contend, vie, jockey.
3 *the alcohol has scrambled his brains* **muddle,** confuse, mix up, jumble (up), disarrange, disorganize, disorder, disturb, mess up.
▶ noun **1** *a short scramble over the rocks* **clamber,** climb, trek.
2 *I lost Tommy in the scramble for a seat* **tussle,** jostle, scrimmage, scuffle, struggle, free-for-all, competition, contention, vying, jockeying; muddle, confusion, melee.

scrap[1] ▶ noun **1** *a scrap of paper* **fragment,** piece, bit, snippet, shred; offcut, oddment, remnant.
2 *there wasn't a scrap of evidence* **bit,** speck, iota, particle, ounce, whit, jot, atom, shred, scintilla, tittle, jot or tittle; informal smidgen, tad.
3 *he slept in the streets and lived on scraps* **leftovers,** leavings, crumbs, scrapings, remains, remnants, residue, odds and ends, bits and pieces.
4 *the whole thing was made from scrap* **waste,** rubbish, refuse, litter, debris, detritus; flotsam and jetsam, garbage, trash; informal junk.
▶ verb **1** *old cars due to be scrapped* **throw away,** throw out, dispose of, get rid of, toss out, throw on the scrap heap, discard, remove, dispense with, lose, decommission, recycle, break up, demolish; informal chuck, ditch, dump, junk, trash, deep-six.
ANTONYMS keep, preserve.
2 *campaigners called for the plans to be scrapped* **abandon,** drop, abolish, withdraw, throw out, do away with, put an end to, cancel, ax, jettison; informal ditch, dump, junk, can, scrub.
ANTONYMS keep, restore.

scrap[2] ▶ noun informal *he and Joe had several scraps* **quarrel,** argument, row, fight, disagreement, difference of opinion, falling-out, blowup, dispute, squabble, contretemps, clash, altercation, brawl, tussle, conflict, shouting match; informal tiff, set-to, run-in, spat, ruction.
▶ verb *the older boys started scrapping with me* **quarrel,** argue, row, fight, squabble, brawl, bicker, spar, wrangle, lock horns.

scrape ▶ verb **1** *we scraped all the paint off the windows* **abrade,** grate, sand, sandpaper, scour, scratch, rub, file, rasp.
2 *their boots scraped along the floor* **grate,** creak, rasp, grind, scratch.
3 *she scraped her hair back behind her ears* **rake,** drag, pull, tug, draw.
4 *he scraped a hole in the ground* **scoop out,** hollow out, dig (out), excavate, gouge out.
5 *Ellen had scraped her shins on the wall* **graze,** scratch, abrade, scuff, rasp, skin, rub raw, cut, lacerate, bark, chafe; Medicine excoriate.
▶ noun **1** *the scrape of her key in the lock* **grating,** creaking, grinding, rasp, rasping, scratch, scratching.
2 *there was a long scrape on his leg* **graze,** scratch, abrasion, cut, laceration, wound.
3 informal *he's always getting into scrapes* **predicament,** plight, tight corner/spot, ticklish/tricky situation, problem, crisis, mess, muddle; informal jam, fix, stew, bind, hole, hot water, a pretty/fine kettle of fish.
– PHRASES **scrape by** *when the money's not there, you learn how to scrape by* **manage,** cope, survive, muddle through/along, make ends meet, get by/along, make do, keep the wolf from the door, keep one's head above water, eke out a living; informal make out.

scratch ▶ verb **1** *the paint was scratched* **scrape,** abrade, score, scuff.
2 *thorns scratched her skin* **graze,** scrape, abrade, skin, rub raw, cut, lacerate, bark, chafe; wound; Medicine excoriate.
3 *many names had been* **scratched out cross out,** strike out, score out, delete, erase, remove, eliminate, expunge, obliterate.
4 *she was forced to* **scratch from** *the race* **withdraw from,** pull out of, back out of, bow out of, stand down from.
▶ noun **1** *he had two scratches on his cheek* **graze,** scrape, abrasion, cut, laceration, wound.
2 *a scratch on the car door* **scrape,** mark, line, score.
– PHRASES **up to scratch** *my housekeeper's work is nearly always up to scratch* **good enough,** up to the mark, up to standard, up to par, satisfactory, acceptable, adequate, passable, sufficient, all right; informal OK, jake, up to snuff.

scrawl ▶ verb *he scrawled his name at the bottom of the page* **scribble,** write hurriedly, write untidily, dash off.
▶ noun *his writing was a scrawl* **scribble,** chicken scratch, squiggle(s), hieroglyphics.

scrawny ▶ adjective *scrawny teenage girls addicted to dieting* **skinny,** thin, lean, as thin as a rake, skin-and-bones, gaunt, bony, angular, gawky, scraggy, rawboned, anorexic.
ANTONYMS fat.

scream ▶ verb *he screamed in pain* **shriek,** screech, yell, howl, shout, bellow, bawl, cry out, call out, yelp, squeal, wail, squawk; informal holler.
▶ noun **1** *a scream of pain* **shriek,** screech, yell, howl, shout, bellow, bawl, cry, yelp, squeal,

wail, squawk; informal holler.
2 informal *the whole thing's a scream* **laugh,** hoot; informal gas, giggle, riot, laff riot, bundle of fun/laughs, blast.
3 informal *he's an absolute scream* **wit,** hoot, comedian, comic, entertainer, joker, clown, character; informal gas, riot; informal dated caution, card.

screech ▶ **verb** See SCREAM (verb).

screen ▶ **noun 1** *he dressed hurriedly behind the screen* **partition,** (room) divider.
2 *a computer with a 15-inch screen* **display,** monitor, video display terminal, VDT, cathode-ray tube, CRT.
3 *the screen keeps out mosquitoes* **mesh,** net, netting.
4 *the hedge acts as a screen against the wind* **buffer,** protection, shield, shelter, guard, windbreak.
5 *sift the dirt through a screen* **sieve,** riddle, strainer, colander, filter.
▶ **verb 1** *the end of the hall had been screened off* **partition,** divide, separate, curtain.
2 *the cottage was screened by the trees* **conceal,** hide, veil; shield, shelter, shade, protect, guard, safeguard.
3 *the prospective candidates will have to be screened* **vet,** check, check up on, investigate; informal check out.
4 *all donated blood is screened for the virus* **check,** test, examine, investigate.
5 *coal used to be screened by hand* **sieve,** riddle, sift, strain, filter, winnow.
6 *the program is screened on Thursday evenings* **show,** broadcast, transmit, air, televise, telecast, put on the air.

screw ▶ **noun 1** *stainless steel screws* **bolt,** fastener; nail, pin, tack, spike, rivet, brad.
2 *the handle needs a couple of screws to tighten it* **turn,** twist, wrench.
3 *the ship's twin screws* **propeller,** rotor.
▶ **verb 1** *he screwed the lid back on the jar* **tighten,** turn, twist, wind.
2 *the bracket was screwed in place* **fasten,** secure, fix, attach.
3 informal *she intended to screw money out of them* **extort,** force, extract, wrest, wring, squeeze; informal bleed.
4 informal *he realized he had been screwed* **cheat,** trick, deceive, swindle, con, scam, dupe, fool; informal rip off, hose, gyp, bamboozle, stiff.
– PHRASES **put the screws on** informal *you don't pay up and my pal Bruno here will put the screws on you, see?* **pressure,** put pressure on, coerce, browbeat, use strong-arm tactics on, strong-arm; hold a gun to someone's head; informal turn the heat on, lean on, bulldoze. **screw up 1** *Tina screwed up her face in disgust* **wrinkle (up),** pucker, crumple, crease, furrow, contort, distort, twist, purse. **2** informal *they'll screw up the whole economy* **wreck,** ruin, destroy, wreak havoc on, damage, spoil, mar; dash, shatter, scotch, make a mess of, mess up; informal louse up, foul up, put the kibosh on, scupper, scuttle, do for, nix.

scribble ▶ **verb** *he scribbled a few lines on a piece of paper* **scrawl,** write hurriedly, write untidily, scratch, dash off, jot (down); doodle.
▶ **noun** *a page of scribble* **scrawl,** squiggle(s), jottings; doodle, doodlings.

scribe ▶ **noun 1** historical *a medieval scribe* **clerk,** secretary, copyist, transcriber, amanuensis; historical penman, scrivener.
2 informal *a local scribe* **writer,** author, penman; journalist, reporter; informal hack, pencil pusher.

scrimp ▶ **verb** *I used to criticize my mother for the way she would scrimp* **economize,** skimp, scrimp and save, save; be thrifty, be frugal, tighten one's belt, cut back, husband one's resources, watch one's pennies, pinch (the) pennies.

script ▶ **noun 1** *her neat, tidy script* **handwriting,** writing, hand, penmanship, calligraphy.
2 *the script of the play* **text,** screenplay; libretto, score; lines, dialogue, words.

scrounge ▶ **verb** *they were always scrounging food from the tourists* **beg,** borrow, cadge; informal sponge, bum, touch someone for, mooch.

scrounger ▶ **noun** *don't give your money to that scrounger* **beggar,** borrower, parasite, cadger; informal sponger, freeloader, mooch, moocher, bum, bottom feeder, schnorrer.

scrub[1] ▶ **verb 1** *he scrubbed the kitchen floor* **scour,** rub; clean, cleanse, wash, wipe.
2 informal *the plans were scrubbed* See SCRAP[1] (sense 2 of the verb).

scrub[2] ▶ **noun** *there the buildings ended and the scrub began* **brush,** brushwood, scrubland, underbrush, undergrowth, krummholz.

scruffy ▶ **adjective** *dressed in scruffy clothes* **shabby,** worn, down-at-heel, down-at-the-heel(s), ragged, tattered, mangy, dirty; untidy, unkempt, bedraggled, messy, disheveled, ill-groomed; informal tatty, raggedy-ass, the worse for wear, ratty, raggedy, scuzzy.
ANTONYMS smart, tidy.

scrumptious ▶ **adjective** informal *scrumptious desserts* **delicious,** delectable, mouthwatering, tasty, appetizing, rich, savory, flavorful, toothsome; succulent, luscious; informal yummy, lip-smacking, finger-licking, melt-in-your/the-mouth, nummy.
ANTONYMS unpalatable.

scruples ▶ **plural noun** *he had no scruples about eavesdropping* **qualms,** compunction, pangs/twinges of conscience, hesitation, reservations, second thoughts, doubt(s), misgivings, uneasiness, reluctance. See note at QUALMS.

scrupulous ▶ **adjective 1** *scrupulous attention to detail* **careful,** meticulous, painstaking, thorough, assiduous, sedulous, attentive, conscientious, punctilious, searching, close, minute, rigorous, particular, strict.
ANTONYMS careless.
2 *a scrupulous man* **honest,** honorable, upright, upstanding, high-minded, right-minded, moral, ethical, good, virtuous, principled, incorruptible.
ANTONYMS dishonest.

scrutinize ▶ **verb** *it has become necessary for us to scrutinize the behavior of our staff toward the customers* **examine,** inspect, survey, study, look at, peruse; investigate, explore, probe, inquire into, go into, check; informal eyeball.

scrutiny ▶ **noun** *passengers can expect much*

more scrutiny at our terminals **examination,** inspection, survey, study, perusal; investigation, exploration, probe, inquiry; informal going-over.

scuffle ▶ **noun** *there was a scuffle outside the pub* **fight,** struggle, tussle, brawl, fracas, free-for-all, scrimmage; informal scrap, set-to, roughhouse.

▶ **verb** *demonstrators scuffled with police* **fight,** struggle, tussle, exchange blows, come to blows, brawl, clash; informal scrap.

sculpture ▶ **noun** *a bronze sculpture* **model,** carving, statue, statuette, figure, figurine, effigy, bust, head, likeness.

scum ▶ **noun 1** *the water was covered with a thick green scum* **film,** layer, covering, froth; filth, dross, dirt.

2 informal *drug dealers are scum* **despicable people,** the lowest of the low, the dregs of society, vermin, riffraff, lowlifes; informal the scum of the earth, dirt.

scurrilous ▶ **adjective** *such scurrilous language!* **defamatory,** slanderous, libelous, scandalous, insulting, offensive, gross; abusive, vituperative, malicious; informal bitchy.

scurry ▶ **verb** *pedestrians scurried for cover* **hurry,** hasten, run, rush, dash; scamper, scuttle, scramble; Brit. scutter; informal scoot, beetle; dated make haste.

ANTONYMS amble.

▶ **noun** *there was a scurry to get out* **rush,** race, dash, run, hurry; scramble, bustle.

sea ▶ **noun 1** *the sea sparkled in the sun* **ocean;** informal drink, briny, salt chuck; literary deep, main, foam.

2 (**seas**) *the boat overturned in the heavy seas* **waves,** swell, breakers, rollers, combers.

3 *a sea of roofs and turrets* **expanse,** stretch, area, tract, sweep, blanket, sheet, carpet, mass; multitude, host, profusion, abundance.

▶ **adjective** *sea creatures* **marine,** ocean, oceanic; saltwater, seawater; oceangoing, seagoing, seafaring; maritime, naval, nautical; technical pelagic.

– PHRASES **at sea** *most of her calculus lectures left me completely at sea* **confused,** perplexed, puzzled, baffled, mystified, bemused, bewildered, nonplussed, disconcerted, disoriented, dumbfounded, at a loss, at sixes and sevens; informal flummoxed, bamboozled, fazed, discombobulated; archaic mazed.

seal[1] ▶ **noun 1** *the seal around the bathtub* **sealant,** sealer, adhesive, caulk, caulking.

2 *the king put his seal on the letter* **emblem,** symbol, insignia, device, badge, crest, coat of arms, mark, monogram, stamp.

3 *the project cannot begin without the committee's seal* **ratification,** approval, seal of approval, blessing, consent, agreement, permission, sanction, endorsement, clearance.

▶ **verb 1** *she quietly sealed the door behind her* **fasten,** secure, shut, close, lock, bolt.

2 *seal each bottle while it is hot* **stop up,** seal up, make airtight/watertight, cork, stopper, plug.

3 (**seal off**) *police sealed off the block* **close off,** shut off, cordon off, fence off, isolate.

4 *that seals it* **clinch,** secure, settle, conclude, determine, complete, establish, set the seal on, confirm, guarantee; informal sew up.

seal[2] ▶ **noun** *seals were basking in the water* male **bull;** female **cow;** young **calf,** pup, whelp.

seam ▶ **noun 1** *the seam was coming undone* **join,** stitching; Surgery suture.

2 *a seam of coal* **layer,** stratum, vein, lode.

3 *the seams of his face* **wrinkle,** line, crow's foot, furrow, crease, corrugation, crinkle, pucker, groove, ridge.

sear ▶ **verb 1** *the heat of the blast seared his face* **scorch,** burn, singe, char. See note at BURN.

2 *sear the meat before adding the other ingredients* **flash-fry,** seal, brown.

3 *his betrayal had seared her terribly* **hurt,** wound, pain, cut to the quick, sting; distress, grieve, upset, trouble, harrow, torment, torture.

search ▶ **verb 1** (**search for**) *I searched for the key in my handbag* **hunt (for),** look for, seek, forage for, fish around/about for, look high and low for, ferret around/about for, root around/about for, rummage around/about for, cast around/about for.

2 *he searched every room in the house* **look through,** hunt through, explore, scour, rifle through, go through, sift through, comb, go through with a fine-tooth comb; turn upside down, turn inside out, leave no stone unturned in.

3 *the guards searched him for weapons* **examine,** inspect, check, frisk.

▶ **noun** *the police continued their search* **hunt,** look, quest; pursuit, manhunt.

– PHRASES **in search of** *they say they are in search of a silver flask with the monogram "DLR"* **searching for,** hunting for, seeking, looking for, on the lookout for, in pursuit of. **search me** informal *"Where's my toolbox?" "Search me."* **I don't know,** how should I know?, it's a mystery, I haven't a clue, I haven't the least/slightest idea, I've no idea, who knows; informal (I) dunno, don't ask me, I haven't the faintest/foggiest (idea/notion), (it) beats me, you got me.

searching ▶ **adjective** *they asked some very searching questions* **penetrating,** piercing, probing, penetrative, keen, shrewd, sharp, intent.

season ▶ **noun** *the rainy season* **period,** time, time of year, spell, term.

▶ **verb 1** *season the casserole to taste* **flavor,** add flavoring to, add salt (and pepper) to, spice.

2 *his answers were seasoned with wit* **enliven,** leaven, spice (up), liven up; informal pep up.

– PHRASES **in season** *we make gallons of sauce when the local tomatoes are in season* **available,** obtainable, to be had, on the market; plentiful, abundant.

seasonable ▶ **adjective** *the Northeast is enjoying seasonable temperatures* **usual,** expected, predictable, normal for the time of year. See note at TIMELY.

seasoned ▶ **adjective** *seasoned sportscasters* **experienced,** practiced, well versed, knowledgeable, established, habituated, veteran, hardened, battle-scarred, battle-weary.

ANTONYMS inexperienced.

seasoning ▶ **noun** *we use a secret seasoning made from 12 herbs and spices* **flavoring,** salt (and pepper), herbs, spices, condiments.

seat ▶ noun **1** *a wooden seat* **chair,** bench, stool, settle, stall; pew; (**seats**) seating.
2 *the seat of government* **headquarters,** base, center, nerve center, hub, heart; location, site, whereabouts, place.
▶ verb **1** *they seated themselves around the table* **position,** put, place; ensconce, install, settle; informal plonk, park.
2 *the hall seats 500* **have room for,** contain, take, sit, hold, accommodate.

seating ▶ noun *we have seating for 200* **seats,** room, places, chairs, accommodations.

secede ▶ verb *the southern states seceded from the Union, precipitating the Civil War* **withdraw from,** break away from, break with, separate (oneself) from, leave, split with, split off from, disaffiliate from, resign from, pull out of; informal quit.
ANTONYMS join.

secluded ▶ adjective *a secluded little park* **sheltered,** private, concealed, hidden, unfrequented, sequestered, tucked away.
ANTONYMS busy.

seclusion ▶ noun *she enjoys the seclusion of her cabin* **isolation,** solitude, retreat, privacy, retirement, withdrawal, concealment, hiding, secrecy.

second[1] ▶ adjective **1** *the second day of the trial* **next,** following, subsequent, succeeding.
ANTONYMS first, preceding.
2 *he keeps a second pair of glasses in his office* **additional,** extra, alternative, another, spare, backup, fallback, alternate.
ANTONYMS primary.
3 *he was demoted to the second level* **secondary,** lower, subordinate, subsidiary, lesser, inferior.
ANTONYMS first, top.
4 *the conflict could turn into a second Vietnam* **another,** new; repeat of, copy of, carbon copy of.
ANTONYMS original.
▶ noun **1** *Eva had been working as his second* See SECOND-IN-COMMAND.
2 informal (**seconds**) *he enjoyed the pie and asked for seconds* **a second helping,** a further helping, more.
▶ verb *Hooper seconded the motion* **formally support,** give one's support to, vote for, back, approve, endorse.
– PHRASES **second to none** *Lori's cheesecake is second to none* **incomparable,** matchless, unrivaled, inimitable, beyond compare/comparison, unparalleled, without parallel, unequaled, without equal, in a class of its own, peerless, unsurpassed, unsurpassable, nonpareil, unique; perfect, consummate, transcendent, surpassing, superlative, supreme; formal unexampled.

second[2] ▶ noun *I'll only be gone for a second* **moment,** bit, little while, short time, instant, split second, eyeblink, heartbeat; informal sec, jiffy, the blink of an eye.
– PHRASES **in a second** *I can fix that lamp in a second* **very soon,** in a minute, in a moment, in a trice, shortly, any minute (now), in the twinkling of an eye, in (less than) no time, in no time at all, momentarily; informal in a jiffy, in two shakes (of a lamb's tail), in the blink of an eye, in a snap; literary ere long.

second[3] ▶ verb *he was seconded to my department* **assign temporarily,** lend; transfer, move, shift, relocate, assign, reassign, send.

secondary ▶ adjective **1** *a secondary issue* **less important,** subordinate, lesser, minor, peripheral, incidental, ancillary, subsidiary, nonessential, inessential, of little account, unimportant.
ANTONYMS primary.
2 *secondary infections* **accompanying,** attendant, concomitant, consequential, resulting, resultant.
ANTONYMS primary.

second-class ▶ adjective *we were treated like second-class citizens* **second-rate,** second-best, inferior, lesser, unimportant.

secondhand ▶ adjective **1** *secondhand clothes* **used,** old, worn, preowned, handed-down, hand-me-down, castoff; informal preloved.
ANTONYMS new.
2 *secondhand information* **indirect,** derivative; vicarious.
ANTONYMS direct.
▶ adverb *I ignore anything I hear secondhand* **indirectly,** at secondhand; informal on the grapevine.
ANTONYMS directly.

second-in-command ▶ noun *while Reade is recuperating, Dunlop will be my second-in-command* **deputy,** number two, subordinate, right-hand man/woman, second; understudy; informal sidekick, second banana.

secondly ▶ adverb *in the first place you're too young, and secondly it's too dangerous* **furthermore,** also, moreover, likewise; second, in the second place, next; secondarily.

second-rate ▶ adjective *I would never buy second-rate shoes* **inferior,** substandard, low-quality, below par, bad, poor, deficient, defective, faulty, imperfect, shoddy, chintzy, inadequate, insufficient, unacceptable; informal crummy, not up to scratch/snuff, rinky-dink.
ANTONYMS first-rate, excellent.

secrecy ▶ noun **1** *the secrecy of the material* **confidentiality,** classified nature.
2 *a government that thrives on secrecy* **secretiveness,** covertness, furtiveness, surreptitiousness, stealth, stealthiness.

secret ▶ adjective **1** *a secret plan* **confidential,** top secret, classified, undisclosed, unknown, private, under wraps; informal hush-hush; formal sub rosa.
ANTONYMS public, known.
2 *a secret drawer in the table* **hidden,** concealed, disguised; invisible.
ANTONYMS visible.
3 *a secret campaign to infiltrate drug operations on the east coast* **clandestine,** covert, undercover, underground, surreptitious, stealthy, furtive, cloak-and-dagger, hole-and-corner, closet; informal hush-hush.
ANTONYMS overt.
4 *a secret message | a secret code* **cryptic,** encoded, coded; mysterious, abstruse, recondite, arcane, esoteric, Kabbalistic.
ANTONYMS open.

5 *a secret place* **secluded,** private, concealed, hidden, unfrequented, out of the way, tucked away.
ANTONYMS public, known about.
6 *a very secret person* See SECRETIVE.
▶ **noun 1** *he just can't keep a secret* **confidential matter,** confidence, private affair; skeleton in the closet.
2 *the secrets of the universe* **mystery,** enigma, paradox, puzzle, conundrum, poser, riddle.
3 *the secret of their success* **recipe,** (magic) formula, blueprint, key, answer, solution.
– PHRASES **in secret** *they met in secret throughout the month of July* See SECRETLY (sense 1).

CHOOSE THE RIGHT WORD

secret, clandestine, covert, furtive, stealthy, surreptitious, underhanded

While all of these adjectives describe an attempt to do something without attracting attention or observation, **secret** is the most general term, implying that something is being concealed or kept from the knowledge of others (*a secret pact; a secret passageway*). **Covert** suggests that something is being done under cover, or concealed as if with a veil or disguise (*a covert attack; a covert threat*), while **clandestine** suggests that something illicit or immoral is being concealed (*a clandestine meeting between the two lovers*). Someone who is deliberately sneaking around and trying to do something without attracting notice is best described as **stealthy** (*the cat moved toward the bird with a slow, stealthy pace*), and **furtive** connotes even more slyness and watchfulness, as revealed not only by movements but by facial expressions (*a furtive glance; a furtive movement toward the door*). **Surreptitious** connotes guilt on the part of the individual who is acting in a stealthy or furtive manner (*a surreptitious attempt to hide the book before it was noticed*). **Underhanded** is the strongest of these words, implying fraud, deceit, or unfairness (*underhanded business dealings*).

secrete ▶ **verb** *a substance secreted by the prostate gland* **produce,** discharge, emit, excrete, release, send out.
ANTONYMS absorb.

secretive ▶ **adjective** *I trusted you with this because you're the most secretive person I know* **uncommunicative,** secret, unforthcoming, playing one's cards close to one's chest, reticent, reserved, silent, noncommunicative, quiet, tight-lipped, buttoned-up, close-mouthed, taciturn.
ANTONYMS open, communicative.

secretly ▶ **adverb 1** *they met secretly for a year* **in secret,** in private, privately, behind closed doors, in camera, behind the scenes, under cover, under the counter, behind someone's back, furtively, stealthily, on the sly, on the quiet, conspiratorially, covertly, clandestinely, on the side; informal on the QT, off the record, hush-hush; formal sub rosa.
2 *he was secretly jealous of Bartholomew* **privately,** in one's heart (of hearts), deep down.

sect ▶ **noun** *she had been duped into joining a sect of supposed do-gooders* **(religious) cult,** religious group, denomination, persuasion, religious order; splinter group, faction.

sectarian ▶ **adjective** *a sectarian society of white supremacists* **factional,** separatist, partisan, parti pris; doctrinaire, dogmatic, extreme, fanatical, rigid, inflexible, bigoted, hidebound, narrow-minded.
ANTONYMS tolerant, liberal.

section ▶ **noun 1** *the separate sections of a train* **part,** piece, bit, segment, component, division, portion, element, unit, constituent. See note at FRAGMENT.
2 *the last section of the questionnaire* **subdivision,** part, subsection, division, portion, bit, chapter, passage, clause.
3 *the reference section of the library* **department,** area, part, division.
4 *a residential section of the city* See SECTOR (sense 2).

sector ▶ **adjective 1** *every sector of the industry is affected* **part,** branch, arm, division, area, department, field, sphere.
2 *the northeastern sector of the town* **district,** quarter, part, section, zone, region, area, belt.

secular ▶ **adjective** *secular music* **nonreligious,** areligious, lay, temporal, worldly, earthly, profane; formal laic.
ANTONYMS holy, religious.

secure ▶ **adjective 1** *check to ensure that all bolts are secure* **fastened,** fixed, secured, done up; closed, shut, locked.
ANTONYMS loose.
2 *an environment in which children can feel secure* **safe,** protected from harm/danger, out of danger, sheltered, safe and sound, out of harm's way, in a safe place, in safe hands, invulnerable; at ease, unworried, relaxed, happy, confident.
ANTONYMS vulnerable.
3 *a secure investment* **certain,** assured, reliable, dependable, settled, fixed.
ANTONYMS uncertain.
▶ **verb 1** *pins secure the handle to the main body* **fix,** attach, fasten, affix, connect, couple.
2 *the doors had not been properly secured* **fasten,** close, shut, lock, bolt, chain, seal.
3 *he leapt out to secure the boat* **tie up,** moor, make fast; anchor.
4 *they sought to secure the country against attack* **protect,** make safe, fortify, strengthen; undergird.
5 *a written constitution would secure the rights of the individual* **assure,** ensure, guarantee, protect, confirm, establish.
6 *the division secured a major contract* **obtain,** acquire, gain, get, get possession of; informal get hold of, land. See note at GET.

security ▶ **noun 1** *the security of the nation's citizens* **safety,** freedom from danger, protection, invulnerability.
ANTONYMS vulnerability, danger.
2 *he could give her the security she needed* **peace of mind,** feeling of safety, stability, certainty,

happiness, confidence.
ANTONYMS disquiet.
3 *security at the court was tight* **safety measures,** safeguards, surveillance, defense, protection.
4 *additional security for your loan may be required* **guarantee,** collateral, surety, pledge, bond.

sedate[1] ▶ verb *the patient had to be sedated* **tranquilize,** put under sedation, drug.

sedate[2] ▶ adjective **1** *a sedate pace* **slow,** steady, dignified, unhurried, relaxed, measured, leisurely, slow-moving, easy, easygoing, gentle.
ANTONYMS fast.
2 *he had lived a sedate life* **calm,** placid, tranquil, quiet, uneventful; boring, dull.
ANTONYMS exciting.

sedative ▶ adjective *sedative drugs* **tranquilizing,** calming, calmative, relaxing, soporific, narcotic; depressant; Medicine neuroleptic.
▶ noun *the doctor gave him a sedative* **tranquilizer,** calmative, sleeping pill, narcotic, opiate; depressant; informal trank, downer.

sedentary ▶ adjective *a sedentary job* **sitting,** seated, desk-bound, stationary; inactive, lethargic, lazy, idle.
ANTONYMS active.

sediment ▶ noun *the sediment in the coffee pot* **dregs,** lees, precipitate, deposit, grounds; residue, remains; silt, alluvium; technical residuum.

sedition ▶ noun *the on-campus protestors were charged with sedition* **rabble-rousing,** incitement to rebel, subversion, troublemaking, provocation; rebellion, insurrection, mutiny, insurgence, civil disorder.

seditious ▶ adjective *a seditious speech* **rabble-rousing,** provocative, inflammatory, subversive, troublemaking; rebellious, insurrectionist, mutinous, insurgent.

seduce ▶ verb **1** *he took her to his hotel room and tried to seduce her* **persuade to have sex;** euphemistic have one's way with, take advantage of; dated debauch.
2 *she was seduced by the smell of coffee* **attract,** allure, lure, tempt, entice, beguile, inveigle, maneuver. See note at TEMPT.

seductive ▶ adjective *a seductive red dress* **sexy,** alluring, tempting, irresistible, exciting, provocative, sultry, slinky; coquettish, flirtatious; informal vampish, come-hither.

see ▶ verb **1** *he saw her running across the road* **discern,** spot, notice, catch sight of, glimpse, catch/get a glimpse of, make out, pick out, spy, distinguish, detect, perceive, note; informal lay/set eyes on; literary behold, descry, espy.
2 *I saw a documentary about it last week* **watch,** look at, view; catch.
3 *would you like to see the house?* **inspect,** view, look round, tour, survey, examine, scrutinize; informal give something a/the once-over.
4 *I finally saw what she meant* **understand,** grasp, comprehend, follow, take in, realize, appreciate, recognize, work out, get the drift of, perceive, fathom; informal get, latch on to, cotton on to, catch on to, savvy, figure out, get a fix on.
5 *I must go and see what Victor is up to* **find out,** discover, learn, ascertain, determine, establish.
6 *see that no harm comes to him* **ensure,** make sure/certain, see to it, take care, mind.
7 *I see trouble ahead* **foresee,** predict, forecast, prophesy, anticipate, envisage, picture, visualize.
8 *about a year later, I saw him in town* **encounter,** meet, run into/across, come across, stumble on/across, happen on, chance on; informal bump into.
9 *they see each other from time to time* **meet,** meet up with, get together with, socialize with.
10 *you'd better see a doctor* **consult,** confer with, talk to, speak to, have recourse to, call on, call in, turn to, ask.
11 *he's seeing someone else now* **go out with,** date, take out, be involved with; informal go steady with; dated court.
12 *he saw her to her car* **escort,** accompany, show, walk, conduct, lead, take, usher, attend.
– PHRASES **see through 1** *they can see through your dirty little plan* **understand,** get/have the measure of, read like a book; informal be wise to; have someone's number (about). **2** *Marlon saw us through these long, hard months* **sustain,** encourage, buoy up, keep going, support, be a tower of strength to, comfort, help (out), stand by, stick by. **3** *I'm tired of this campaign, but I promised I would see it through* **persevere with,** persist with, continue (with), carry on with, keep at, follow through, stay with; informal stick to, stick it out, hang in there (with/for). **see to** *I'll see to the dogs as soon as we finish lunch* **attend to,** deal with, see about, take care of, look after, sort out, fix, organize, arrange.

seed ▶ noun **1** *apple seeds* pip, stone, kernel; ovule.
2 *each war contains within it the seeds of a fresh war* **genesis,** source, origin, root, starting point, germ, beginnings, potential (for); cause, reason, motivation, motive, grounds.
3 *Abraham and his seed* **descendants,** heirs, successors, scions; offspring, children, sons and daughters, progeny, family; Law issue; derogatory spawn; archaic fruit of someone's loins.
– PHRASES **go/run to seed** *in just two years, this hotel has really gone to seed* **deteriorate,** degenerate, decline, decay, fall into decay, go to rack and ruin, go downhill, molder, rot; informal go to pot, go to the dogs, go down the toilet.

seedy ▶ adjective **1** *the seedy world of prostitution* **sordid,** disreputable, seamy, sleazy, squalid, unwholesome, unsavory.
ANTONYMS high-class.
2 *a seedy roadside diner* **dilapidated,** tumbledown, ramshackle, falling to pieces, decrepit, gone to rack and ruin, run-down, down-at-heel, down-at-the-heel(s), shabby, dingy, slummy, insalubrious, squalid; informal crummy; scuzzy.
ANTONYMS classy.

seek ▶ verb **1** *they sought shelter from the winter snows* **search for,** try to find, look for, be on the lookout for, be after, hunt for, be in quest of.
2 *the company is seeking a judicial review of the decision* **try to obtain,** work toward, be intent on, aim at/for.

3 *he sought help from the police* **ask for,** request, solicit, call for, entreat, beg for, petition for, appeal for, apply for, put in for.
4 *we constantly seek to improve the service* **try,** attempt, endeavor, strive, work, do one's best; formal essay.

seem ▶ verb *they seem friendly* **appear (to be),** have the appearance/air of being, give the impression of being, look, look as though one is, show signs of being, look to be; come across as, strike someone as, sound.

seeming ▶ adjective *his seeming gentility* **apparent,** ostensible, supposed, outward, surface, superficial; pretended, feigned. See note at OSTENSIBLE.
ANTONYMS actual, genuine.

seemly ▶ adjective *we expect more seemly behavior at our dinner table* **decorous,** proper, decent, becoming, fitting, suitable, appropriate, apt, apposite, in good taste, genteel, polite, the done thing, right, correct, acceptable, comme il faut.
ANTONYMS unseemly, unbecoming.

seep ▶ verb *a brown substance is seeping into the basement* **ooze,** trickle, exude, drip, dribble, flow, issue, escape, leak, drain, bleed, filter, percolate, soak.

seer ▶ noun *the woeful predictions of an ancient seer* **soothsayer,** oracle, prophet(ess), augur, prognosticator, diviner, visionary, fortune teller, crystal-gazer, clairvoyant, psychic, medium; literary sibyl.

seesaw ▶ verb *interest rates continue to seesaw* **fluctuate,** swing, go up and down, rise and fall, oscillate, alternate, yo-yo, vary.
▶ noun *the seesaws on the playground* **teeter-totter.**

seethe ▶ verb 1 *the brew seethed* **boil,** bubble, simmer, foam, froth, fizz, effervesce.
2 *the water was seething with fish* **teem,** swarm, boil, swirl, churn, surge.
3 *I seethed at the injustice of it all* **be angry,** be furious, be enraged, be incensed, be beside oneself, boil, simmer, rage, rant, rave, storm, fume, smolder; informal be livid, be wild, foam at the mouth, be steamed up, be hot under the collar.

segment ▶ noun 1 *orange segments* **piece,** bit, section, part, chunk, portion, division, slice; fragment, wedge, lump. See note at FRAGMENT.
2 *all segments of society* **part,** section, sector, division, portion, constituent, element, unit, compartment; branch, wing.
▶ verb *they plan to segment their market share* **divide (up),** subdivide, separate, split, cut up, carve up, slice up, break up; segregate, divorce, partition, section.
ANTONYMS amalgamate.

segregate ▶ verb *routes that will segregate passenger cars from tractor trailers* **separate,** set apart, keep apart, isolate, quarantine, closet; partition, divide, detach, disconnect, sever, dissociate; marginalize, ghettoize.
ANTONYMS amalgamate.

seize ▶ verb 1 *she seized the microphone* **grab,** grasp, snatch, take hold of, get one's hands on; grip, clutch; nab.
ANTONYMS let go of.
2 *rebels seized the air base* **capture,** take, overrun, occupy, conquer, take over.
ANTONYMS relinquish, liberate.
3 *the drugs were seized by customs* **confiscate,** impound, commandeer, requisition, appropriate, expropriate, take away; Law distrain.
ANTONYMS release.
4 *the conspirators have seized his wife* **kidnap,** abduct, take captive, take prisoner, take hostage, hold for ransom; informal snatch.
ANTONYMS ransom, release.
– PHRASES **seize on** *they seized on the opportunity* **take advantage of,** exploit, grasp with both hands, leap at, jump at, pounce on.

seizure ▶ noun 1 *Napoleon's seizure of Spain* **capture,** takeover, annexation, invasion, occupation, colonization.
2 *the seizure of property* **confiscation,** appropriation, expropriation, sequestration; Law distraint.
3 *the seizure of UN staff by rebels* **kidnapping,** kidnap, abduction.
4 *the baby suffered a seizure* **convulsion,** fit, spasm, paroxysm; Medicine ictus; dated apoplexy.

seldom ▶ adverb *we seldom use the dining room* **rarely,** infrequently, hardly (ever), scarcely (ever), almost never; now and then, occasionally, sporadically; informal once in a blue moon.
ANTONYMS often.

select ▶ verb *select the correct tool for the job* **choose,** pick (out), single out, sort out, take; opt for, decide on, settle on, determine, nominate, appoint, elect.
▶ adjective 1 *a select group of players* **choice,** hand-picked, prime, first-rate, first-class, superior, finest, best, top-class, blue-ribbon, supreme, superb, excellent; informal A1, top-notch.
ANTONYMS inferior.
2 *a select clientele* **exclusive,** elite, favored, privileged; wealthy; informal posh.
ANTONYMS common.

selection ▶ noun 1 *Jim made his selection of toys* **choice,** pick; option, preference.
2 *a wide selection of dishes* **range,** array, diversity, variety, assortment, mixture.
3 *a selection of his poems* **anthology,** assortment, collection, assemblage, compilation; miscellany, medley, potpourri.

selective ▶ adjective *he's very selective about his coffee* **discerning,** discriminating, discriminatory, critical, exacting, demanding, particular; fussy, fastidious; informal choosy, persnickety, picky, finicky.

self-assurance ▶ noun *you need to build up your self-assurance* **self-confidence,** confidence, assertiveness, self-reliance, composure, self-possession, presence of mind, aplomb.
ANTONYMS diffidence.

self-centered ▶ adjective *he's too self-centered to care what his children do* **egocentric,** egotistic, egotistical, egomaniacal, self-absorbed, self-obsessed, self-seeking, self-interested, self-serving; narcissistic, vain; inconsiderate, thoughtless; informal looking after number one.

self-confidence ▶ noun *they told Tom he lacked the self-confidence to make it as a singer* **morale,** confidence, self-assurance, assurance, assertiveness, self-reliance, self-possession, composure.

self-conscious ▶ adjective *he gave me a self-conscious grin* **embarrassed,** uncomfortable, uneasy, nervous; unnatural, inhibited, gauche, awkward; modest, shy, diffident, bashful, retiring, shrinking.
ANTONYMS confident.

self-control ▶ noun *I had more self-control when I was younger* **self-discipline,** restraint, self-possession, willpower, composure, coolness; moderation, temperance, abstemiousness; informal cool.

self-denial ▶ noun *it took years of hard work and self-denial* **self-sacrifice,** selflessness, unselfishness; self-discipline, asceticism, self-deprivation, abstemiousness, abstinence, abstention; moderation, temperance.
ANTONYMS self-indulgence.

self-esteem ▶ noun *the best thing I ever did for my self-esteem was to divorce Roger* **self-respect,** pride, dignity, self-regard, faith in oneself; morale, self-confidence, confidence, self-assurance. See note at **PRIDE**.

self-important ▶ adjective *why, you self-important little toad!* **conceited,** arrogant, bumptious, full of oneself, puffed up, pompous, overbearing, opinionated, cocky, presumptuous, sententious, vain, overweening, proud, egotistical; informal snooty, uppity, uppish; literary Pooterish.
ANTONYMS humble.

selfish ▶ adjective *he is just selfish by nature* **egocentric,** egotistic, egotistical, egomaniacal, self-centered, self-absorbed, self-obsessed, self-seeking, self-serving, wrapped up in oneself; inconsiderate, thoughtless, unthinking, uncaring, uncharitable; mean, miserly, grasping, greedy, mercenary, acquisitive, opportunistic; informal looking after number one.
ANTONYMS altruistic.

selfless ▶ adjective *it was very selfless of you to help out your ex-husband like that* **unselfish,** altruistic, self-sacrificing, self-denying; considerate, compassionate, kind, noble, generous, magnanimous, ungrudging, charitable, benevolent, openhanded.
ANTONYMS inconsiderate.

self-possessed ▶ adjective *I'm usually pretty self-possessed during an interview* **assured,** self-assured, calm, cool, composed, at ease, unperturbed, unruffled, confident, self-confident, poised, imperturbable; informal together, unfazed, nonplussed, unflappable.
ANTONYMS unsure.

self-respect ▶ noun *if you had any self-respect, you wouldn't be wasting your life in front of the television* **self-esteem,** self-regard, amour propre, faith in oneself, pride, dignity, morale, self-confidence.

self-righteous ▶ adjective *we listened to Mom because she wasn't as self-righteous as you* **sanctimonious,** holier-than-thou, self-satisfied, smug, priggish, complacent, pious, moralizing, preachy, superior, hypocritical; informal goody-goody.
ANTONYMS humble.

self-sacrifice ▶ noun *the self-sacrifice of these young men and women is indeed admirable* **self-denial,** selflessness, unselfishness; self-discipline, abstinence, asceticism, abnegation, self-deprivation, moderation, austerity, temperance, abstention.

self-satisfied ▶ adjective *she's such a self-satisfied Miss Perfect* **complacent,** self-congratulatory, smug, superior, puffed up, pleased with oneself; informal goody-goody.

self-seeking ▶ adjective *the self-seeking players would get humbled fast by Coach Higgins* **self-interested,** self-serving, selfish; egocentric, egotistic, egotistical, self-obsessed, self-absorbed; inconsiderate, thoughtless, unthinking; informal looking after number one.
ANTONYMS altruistic.

self-styled ▶ adjective *a self-styled poet* **would-be,** so-called, self-appointed, self-titled, professed, self-confessed, soi-disant.

self-willed ▶ adjective *how can you reason with a self-willed teenager?* **willful,** contrary, perverse, uncooperative, wayward, headstrong, stubborn, obstinate, obdurate, pigheaded, mulish, intransigent, recalcitrant, intractable; formal refractory.
ANTONYMS biddable.

sell ▶ verb **1** *they are selling their house* **put up for sale,** offer for sale, put on sale, dispose of, vend, auction (off); trade, barter.
ANTONYMS buy.
2 *he sells cakes* **trade in,** deal in, traffic in, stock, carry, offer for sale, peddle, hawk, retail, market.
3 *the book should sell well* **go,** be bought, be purchased; move, be in demand.
4 *it sells for $79.95* **cost,** be priced at, retail at, go for, be.
5 *he still has to sell his plan to management* **promote**; persuade someone to accept, talk someone into, bring someone around to, win someone over to, win approval for.
– PHRASES **sell down the river** informal *my own friends sold me down the river* **betray,** inform on; be disloyal to, be unfaithful to, double-cross, break faith with, stab in the back, sell out; informal tell on, blow the whistle on, squeal on, finger. **sell out 1** *we have sold out of chocolate* **have none left,** be out of stock, have run out; informal be fresh out, be cleaned out. **2** *the edition sold out quickly* **be bought up,** be depleted, be exhausted. **3** *they say he has sold out as an artist* **abandon one's principles,** prostitute oneself, sell one's soul, betray one's ideals, be untrue to oneself; debase oneself, degrade oneself, demean oneself. **4** *he never thought his own brother would sell him out* See **SELL DOWN THE RIVER** above. **sell short** *she is always selling herself short* **undervalue,** underrate, underestimate, disparage, deprecate, belittle; formal derogate.

seller ▶ noun *the seller does not seem to know*

the real values of his antiques **vendor,** retailer, purveyor, supplier, trader, merchant, dealer; shopkeeper, salesperson, salesman, saleswoman, sales assistant, sales associate, clerk, shop assistant, traveling salesperson, peddler, hawker; auctioneer.

semblance ▶ noun *there remained at least a semblance of discipline* (**outward**) **appearance,** air, show, facade, front, veneer, guise, pretense.

send ▶ verb **1** *they sent a message to HQ* **dispatch,** post, mail, address, consign, direct, forward; transmit, convey, communicate; telephone, phone, broadcast, radio, fax, email; dated telegraph, wire, cable.
ANTONYMS receive.
2 *we sent for a doctor* **call for,** summon, contact; ask for, request, order.
3 *the pump sent out a jet of steam* **propel,** project, eject, deliver, discharge, spout, fire, shoot, release; throw, let fly; informal chuck.

senile ▶ adjective *she's in her nineties, but she's not a bit senile* **doddering,** doddery, decrepit, senescent, declining, infirm, feeble; aged, long in the tooth, in one's dotage; mentally confused, having Alzheimer's (disease), having senile dementia; informal past it, gaga.

senior ▶ adjective **1** *the senior students can get parking permits* **older,** elder.
ANTONYMS junior.
2 *a senior officer* **superior,** higher-ranking, high-ranking, more important; top, chief, ranking.
ANTONYMS junior, subordinate.
3 *Albert Stone, Senior* **Sr.,** the Elder, I.
ANTONYMS Junior, Jr..
▶ noun **1** *Angela is a senior at Cal Tech | the seniors are sponsoring a concert* senior student, fourth-year student; (**seniors**) graduating class.
2 *the quilts are made by a group of seniors at our church* **senior citizen.**

sensation ▶ noun **1** *a sensation of light* **feeling,** sense, awareness, consciousness, perception, impression.
2 *he caused a sensation by donating a million dollars* **commotion,** stir, uproar, furor, scandal, impact; interest, excitement; informal splash, to-do, hullabaloo, hoopla.
3 *the movie became an instant sensation* **triumph,** success, sellout; talking point; informal smash (hit), hit, winner, crowd-pleaser, knockout, blockbuster.

sensational ▶ adjective **1** *a sensational murder trial* **shocking,** scandalous, appalling; amazing, startling, astonishing, staggering; stirring, exciting, thrilling, electrifying, red-hot; fascinating, interesting, noteworthy, significant, remarkable, momentous, historic, newsworthy.
ANTONYMS run-of-the-mill.
2 *sensational stories* **overdramatized,** dramatic, melodramatic, exaggerated, sensationalist, sensationalistic; graphic, explicit, lurid; informal juicy.
ANTONYMS dull, understated.
3 informal *she looked sensational* **gorgeous,** stunning, wonderful, exquisite, lovely, radiant, delightful, charming, enchanting, captivating; striking, spectacular, remarkable, outstanding, arresting, eye-catching; marvelous, superb, excellent, fine, first-class; informal great, terrific, tremendous, super, fantastic, fabulous, fab, heavenly, divine, knockout, hot, red-hot, delectable, scrumptious, awesome, magic, wicked, killer, out of this world, smashing, brilliant.
ANTONYMS unremarkable.

sense ▶ noun **1** *the sense of touch* **sensory faculty,** feeling, sensation, perception; sight, hearing, touch, taste, smell.
2 *a sense of guilt* **feeling,** awareness, sensation, consciousness, recognition.
3 *a sense of humor* **appreciation,** awareness, understanding, comprehension, discernment; informal nose.
4 *she had the sense to press the panic button* **wisdom,** common sense, sagacity, discernment, perception; wit, intelligence, cleverness, shrewdness, judgment, reason, logic, brain(s); informal gumption, horse sense, savvy, (street) smarts.
ANTONYMS stupidity.
5 *I can't see the sense in this* **purpose,** point, reason, object, motive; use, value, advantage, benefit.
6 *the different senses of "well"* **meaning,** definition, import, signification, significance, purport, implication, nuance; drift, gist, thrust, tenor, message.
▶ verb *she sensed their hostility* **discern,** feel, observe, notice, recognize, pick up (on), be aware of, distinguish, make out, identify; comprehend, apprehend, see, appreciate, realize; suspect, have a funny feeling about, have a hunch about, divine, intuit; informal catch on to.

senseless ▶ adjective **1** *they found him senseless on the floor* **unconscious,** stunned, insensible, insensate, comatose, knocked out, out cold, out for the count; numb; informal KO'd, dead to the world, passed out.
ANTONYMS conscious.
2 *a senseless waste* **pointless,** futile, useless, needless, unavailing, in vain, purposeless, meaningless, unprofitable; absurd, foolish, insane, stupid, idiotic, ridiculous, ludicrous, mindless, illogical.
ANTONYMS wise.

sensibility ▶ noun **1** *develop your sensibility* **sensitivity,** finer feelings, delicacy, taste, discrimination, discernment; understanding, insight, empathy, appreciation; feeling, intuition, responsiveness, receptiveness, perceptiveness, awareness.
2 (**sensibilities**) *the wording might offend their sensibilities* (**finer**) **feelings,** emotions, sensitivities, moral sense.

sensible ▶ adjective *isn't this the sensible thing to do? | a sensible young man* **practical,** realistic, responsible, reasonable, commonsensical, rational, logical, sound, balanced, grounded, sober, no-nonsense, pragmatic, levelheaded, thoughtful, down-to-earth, wise, prudent, judicious, sagacious, shrewd. See note at **TANGIBLE**.
ANTONYMS foolish.

> CHOOSE THE RIGHT WORD
>
> **sensible, lucid, rational, sagacious, sane**
>
> A **sensible** person brings an umbrella when rain is forecast. A **rational** one studies the weather map, observes the movement of the clouds across the sky, listens to the forecast on the radio, and then decides whether or not an umbrella is necessary. *Sensible* implies the use of common sense and an appreciation of the value of experience (*a sensible decision not to travel until his injuries had healed*), while *rational* suggests the ability to reason logically and to draw conclusions from inferences (*a rational explanation for why she failed the exam*). **Lucid** and **sane**, like *rational*, are associated with coherent thinking. *Lucid* suggests a mind free of internal pressures or distortions (*lucid intervals during which he was able to recognize his wife and children*), while *sane* indicates freedom from psychosis or mental derangement (*judged to have been sane when she committed the crime*). *Sane* also has a meaning very close to that of *sensible* (*a sane approach to disciplining problem teenagers*). A **sagacious** person is an extremely shrewd one who is both discerning and practical. He or she can look out the window and tell whether it's going to rain by studying the facial expressions of passersby as they glance nervously at the sky.

sensitive ▸ adjective **1** *she's sensitive to changes in temperature* **responsive to,** reactive to, sentient of, sensitized to; aware of, conscious of, alive to; susceptible to, affected by, vulnerable to; attuned to.
ANTONYMS impervious, unresponsive.
2 *sensitive skin* **delicate,** fragile; tender, sore, raw.
ANTONYMS resilient, tough.
3 *the matter needs sensitive handling* **tactful,** careful, thoughtful, diplomatic, delicate, subtle, kid-glove; sympathetic, compassionate, understanding, intuitive, responsive, insightful.
ANTONYMS clumsy.
4 *he's sensitive about his bald patch* **touchy,** oversensitive, hypersensitive, easily offended, easily upset, easily hurt, thin-skinned, defensive; paranoid, neurotic; informal uptight.
ANTONYMS thick-skinned.
5 *a sensitive issue* **difficult,** delicate, tricky, awkward, problematic, ticklish, precarious; controversial, emotive; informal sticky.
ANTONYMS uncontroversial.

sensitivity ▸ noun **1** *the sensitivity of the skin* **responsiveness,** sensitiveness, reactivity; susceptibility, vulnerability.
2 *the job calls for sensitivity* **consideration,** care, thoughtfulness, tact, diplomacy, delicacy, subtlety, finer feelings; understanding, empathy, sensibility, feeling, intuition, responsiveness, receptiveness; perception, discernment, insight; savoir faire.
3 *her sensitivity on the subject of marriage* **touchiness,** oversensitivity, hypersensitivity, defensiveness.
4 *the sensitivity of the issue* **delicacy,** trickiness, awkwardness, ticklishness.

sensual ▸ adjective **1** *sensual pleasure* **physical,** carnal, bodily, fleshly, animal; hedonistic, epicurean, sybaritic, voluptuary. See note at SENSUOUS.
ANTONYMS spiritual.
2 *a beautiful, sensual woman* **sexually attractive,** sexy, voluptuous, sultry, seductive, passionate; sexually arousing, erotic, sexual.
ANTONYMS passionless.

sensuous ▸ adjective **1** *they lived amid sensuous surroundings* **aesthetically pleasing,** gratifying, rich, sumptuous, luxurious; sensory, sensorial.
2 *sensuous lips* **sexually attractive,** sexy, seductive, voluptuous, luscious, lush.

> CHOOSE THE RIGHT WORD
>
> **sensuous, epicurean, luxurious, sensual, sybaritic, voluptuous**
>
> **Sensuous** and **sensual** are often confused. *Sensuous* implies gratification of the senses for the sake of aesthetic pleasure, or delight in the color, sound, or form of something (*a dress made from a soft, sensuous fabric*), while *sensual* implies indulgence of the appetites or gratification of the senses as an end in itself (*he leads a life of sensual excess*). **Luxurious** implies indulgence in sensuous or sensual pleasures, especially those that induce a feeling of physical comfort or satisfaction (*a luxurious satin coverlet*), while **epicurean** refers to taking delight in the pleasures of eating and drinking (*the epicurean life of a king and his courtiers*). To be **voluptuous** is to give oneself up to the pleasures of the senses (*the symphony is voluptuous in its scoring*), but it carries a suggestion of sensual rather than sensuous enjoyment and can refer to a curvaceous and sexually attractive woman (*he was seen with a voluptuous blonde*). **Sybaritic** implies an overrefined luxuriousness, also suggesting indulgence in good food and drink and the presence of things designed to soothe and charm the senses (*he lived alone, in sybaritic splendor*).

sentence ▸ noun *the judge shortened his sentence to nine months* **prison term,** prison sentence; punishment; informal time, stretch, stint.
▸ verb *they were sentenced to death* **pass judgment on,** punish, convict; condemn, doom.

sententious ▸ adjective *your new churchy friends have certainly made you sententious* **moralistic,** moralizing, sanctimonious, self-righteous, pietistic, pious, priggish, judgmental; pompous, pontifical, self-important; informal preachy.

sentiment ▸ noun **1** *the comments echo my own sentiments* **view,** feeling, attitude, thought, opinion, belief. See note at OPINION.
2 *there's no room for sentiment in this sport* **sentimentality,** sentimentalism, mawkishness,

emotionalism; emotion, sensibility, softheartedness, tenderheartedness; informal schmaltz, mush, slushiness, corniness, soppiness, sappiness. See note at **EMOTION**.

sentimental ▶ **adjective 1** *she kept the vase for sentimental reasons* **nostalgic,** tender, emotional, affectionate.
ANTONYMS practical, dispassionate.
2 *the film is too sentimental* **mawkish,** overemotional, cloying, sickly, saccharine, sugary, oversweet; romantic, touching; informal slushy, mushy, weepy, tear-jerking, schmaltzy, lovey-dovey, gooey, drippy, cheesy, corny, cornball, sappy, hokey.
ANTONYMS realistic, gritty.
3 *she is sentimental about animals* **softhearted,** tenderhearted, soft.

CHOOSE THE RIGHT WORD

sentimental, effusive, maudlin, mawkish, mushy, romantic

If you are moved to tears by a situation that does not really warrant such a response, you're likely to be called **sentimental**, an adjective used to describe a willingness to get emotional at the slightest prompting (*a sentimental man who kept his dog's ashes in an urn on the mantel*). **Effusive** applies to excessive or insincere displays of emotion, although it may be used in an approving sense (*effusive in her gratitude for the help she had received*). **Maudlin** derives from the name Mary Magdalene, who was often shown with her eyes swollen from weeping. It implies a lack of self-restraint, particularly in the form of excessive tearfulness. **Mawkish** carries sentimentality a step further, implying emotion so excessive that it provokes loathing or disgust (*mawkish attempts to win the audience over*). Although **romantic** at one time referred to an expression of deep feeling, nowadays it is often used disapprovingly to describe emotion that has little to do with the way things actually are and that is linked to an idealized vision of the way they should be (*she had a romantic notion of what it meant to be a "starving artist"*). **Mushy** suggests both excessive emotion or sentimentality and a contempt for romantic love (*a mushy love story*).

sentry ▶ **noun** *the sentry on the tower signaled to the gatekeeper* **guard,** sentinel, lookout, watch, watchman, patrol.

separate ▶ **adjective 1** *his personal life was separate from his job* **unconnected,** unrelated, different, distinct, discrete; detached, divorced, disconnected, independent, autonomous.
ANTONYMS linked, interdependent.
2 *the infirmary was separate from the school* **set apart,** detached, fenced off, cut off, segregated, isolated; free-standing, self-contained.
ANTONYMS attached.
▶ **verb 1** *they separated two rioting mobs* **split (up),** break up, part, pull apart, divide; literary sunder.
ANTONYMS unite, bring together.
2 *the connectors can be separated* **disconnect,** detach, disengage, uncouple, unyoke, disunite, disjoin; split, divide, sever; disentangle.
ANTONYMS join, connect, combine.
3 *the wall that separates the two properties* **partition,** divide, come between, keep apart; bisect, intersect.
ANTONYMS link, bridge.
4 *the south aisle was* ***separated off*** **isolate,** partition off, section off; close off, shut off, cordon off, fence off, screen off.
5 *they separated at the airport* **part (company),** go their separate ways, split up; say goodbye; disperse, disband, scatter.
ANTONYMS meet.
6 *the road separated* **fork,** divide, branch, bifurcate, diverge.
ANTONYMS merge, converge.
7 *her parents separated* **split up,** break up, part, be estranged, divorce.
ANTONYMS get together, marry.
8 *separate fact from fiction* **isolate,** set apart, segregate; distinguish, differentiate, dissociate; sort out, sift out, filter out, remove, weed out.
9 *those who* ***separate themselves from*** *society* **break away from,** break with, secede from, withdraw from, leave, quit, dissociate oneself from, resign from, drop out of, repudiate, reject.
ANTONYMS join.

separately ▶ **adverb** *I'll have to interview you all separately* **individually,** one by one, one at a time, singly, severally; apart, independently, alone, by oneself, on one's own.

separation ▶ **noun 1** *the separation of the two companies* **disconnection,** detachment, severance, dissociation, disunion, disaffiliation, segregation, partition.
2 *her parents' separation* **breakup,** split, parting (of the ways), estrangement, rift, rupture, breach; divorce; informal splitsville.
3 *the separation between art and life* **distinction,** difference, differentiation, division, dividing line; gulf, gap, chasm.

septic ▶ **adjective** *a septic finger* **infected,** festering, suppurating, pus-filled, putrid, putrefying, poisoned, diseased; Medicine purulent.

sequel ▶ **noun 1** *the film inspired a sequel* **follow-up,** continuation.
2 *the immediate sequel to the coup was an armed uprising* **consequence,** result, upshot, outcome, development, issue, postscript; effect, aftereffect, aftermath, by-product; informal payoff.

sequence ▶ **noun 1** *the sequence of events* **succession,** order, course, series, chain, train, string, progression, chronology, timeline; pattern, flow; formal concatenation.
2 *a sequence from his film* **excerpt,** clip, extract, episode, section.

sequester ▶ **verb 1** *he sequestered himself from the world* **isolate oneself,** hide away, shut oneself away, seclude oneself, cut oneself off, segregate oneself; closet oneself, cloister oneself, withdraw, retire.
2 *the government sequestered his property*

confiscate, seize, sequestrate, take, appropriate, expropriate, impound, commandeer.

seraphic ▶ adjective *a look of seraphic contentment on his face* **blissful,** beatific, sublime, rapturous, ecstatic, joyful, rapt; serene, ethereal; cherubic, saintly, angelic.

serendipity ▶ noun *the consequence of serendipity is sometimes a brilliant discovery* **(happy) chance,** (happy) accident, fluke; luck, good luck, good fortune, fortuity, providence; happy coincidence.

serene ▶ adjective **1** *on the surface she seemed serene* **calm,** composed, tranquil, peaceful, untroubled, relaxed, at ease, unperturbed, unruffled, unworried; placid, equable, centered; informal together, unflappable. See note at CALM.
ANTONYMS agitated.
2 *serene valleys* **peaceful,** tranquil, quiet, still, restful, relaxing, undisturbed.
ANTONYMS turbulent.

series ▶ noun **1** *a series of lectures* **succession,** sequence, string, chain, run, round; spate, wave, rash; set, course, cycle; row, line; formal concatenation.
2 *a new TV series* **serial,** program, show, drama; soap opera; informal soap, sitcom, miniseries.

serious ▶ adjective **1** *a serious expression* **solemn,** earnest, grave, somber, sober, unsmiling, poker-faced, stern, grim, dour, humorless, stony-faced; thoughtful, preoccupied, pensive.
ANTONYMS lighthearted, cheerful.
2 *serious decisions* **important,** significant, consequential, momentous, weighty, far-reaching, major, grave; urgent, pressing, crucial, critical, vital, life-and-death, high-priority.
ANTONYMS unimportant, trivial.
3 *give serious consideration to this* **careful,** detailed, in-depth, deep, profound, meaningful.
ANTONYMS superficial.
4 *a serious play* **intellectual,** highbrow, heavyweight, deep, profound, literary, learned, scholarly; informal heavy.
ANTONYMS lowbrow, light.
5 *serious injuries* **severe,** grave, bad, critical, acute, terrible, dire, dangerous, perilous, parlous; formal grievous.
ANTONYMS minor, negligible.
6 *we're serious about equality* **in earnest,** earnest, sincere, wholehearted, genuine; committed, resolute, determined.
ANTONYMS halfhearted.

seriously ▶ adverb **1** *Faye nodded seriously* **solemnly,** earnestly, gravely, soberly, somberly, sternly, grimly, dourly, humorlessly; pensively, thoughtfully.
2 *she was seriously injured* **severely,** gravely, badly, critically, acutely, dangerously; formal grievously.
3 *do you seriously expect me to come?* **really,** actually, honestly.
4 *seriously, I'm very pleased* **joking aside,** to be serious, honestly, truthfully, truly, I mean it; informal scout's honor.
5 informal *"I've resigned." "Seriously?"* **really?,** is that so?, is that a fact?, you're joking, well I never, go on, you don't say; informal you're kidding.
6 informal *he was seriously rich* See EXTREMELY.

sermon ▶ noun **1** *he preached a sermon* **homily,** address, speech, talk, discourse, oration; lesson.
2 *her mother gave her a sermon on personal hygiene* **lecture,** tirade, harangue, diatribe; speech, disquisition, monologue; reprimand, reproach, reproof, admonishment, admonition, remonstration, criticism; informal talking-to, dressing-down, earful; formal castigation.

serrated ▶ adjective *the serrated edge of the knife* **jagged,** sawtoothed, sawtooth, zigzag, notched, indented, toothed; Botany serrate; technical crenulated.
ANTONYMS smooth.

servant ▶ noun **1** *servants were cleaning the hall* **attendant,** retainer; domestic (worker), (hired) help, cleaner; lackey, flunky, minion; maid, housemaid, footman, page (boy), valet, butler, manservant; housekeeper, steward; drudge, menial, slave, water boy; archaic scullion.
2 *a servant of the people* **helper,** supporter, follower.

serve ▶ verb **1** *they served their masters faithfully* **work for,** be in the service of, be employed by; obey.
2 *this job serves the community* **be of service to,** be of use to, help, assist, aid, make a contribution to, do one's bit for, do something for, benefit.
3 *she **served on** the committee for years* **be a member of,** work on, be on, sit on, have a place on.
4 *he served his apprenticeship in Washington* **carry out,** perform, do, fulfill, complete, discharge; spend.
5 *serve the soup hot* **dish up/out,** give out, distribute; present, provide, supply.
6 *she served another customer* **attend to,** deal with, see to; **assist,** help, look after.
7 *they **served him with** a writ* **present with,** deliver to, give (to), hand over to.
8 *a plate **serving as** an ashtray* **act as,** function as, do the work of, be a substitute for.
9 *these three sizes of brush will serve for most paint jobs* **suffice,** be adequate, be good enough, fit/fill the bill, do, answer, be useful, meet requirements, suit.

service ▶ noun **1** *your conditions of service* **work,** employment, employ, labor.
2 *he has done us a service* **favor,** kindness, good turn, helping hand; **(services) assistance,** help, aid, offices, ministrations.
3 *the food and service were excellent* **waiting,** waitressing, serving, attendance.
4 *products that give reliable service* **use,** usage; functioning.
5 *the service on the Chevy cost $800* tune-up, maintenance check, servicing, overhaul.
6 *a marriage service* **ceremony,** ritual, rite, observance; liturgy, sacrament; formal ordinance.
7 *a range of local services* **amenity,** facility, resource, utility.
8 *soldiers leaving the service* **armed forces,** armed services, military; army, navy, air force, marines, coast guard.
▶ verb *the appliances are serviced regularly* check, go over, maintain, overhaul; repair, mend, recondition.
– PHRASES **be of service** *can I be of service to*

you? **help,** assist, benefit, be of assistance, be beneficial, serve, be useful, be of use, be valuable; do someone a good turn. **out of service** *the candy machine is out of service* **out of order,** broken, broken-down, out of commission, unserviceable, faulty, defective, inoperative, in disrepair; down; informal conked out, bust, kaput, on the blink, on the fritz, acting up, shot.

serviceable ▶ **adjective 1** *a serviceable heating system* **in working order,** working, functioning, functional, operational, operative; usable, workable, viable.
ANTONYMS unusable.
2 *serviceable lace-up shoes* **functional,** utilitarian, sensible, practical; **hardwearing,** durable, tough, robust.
ANTONYMS impractical.

servile ▶ **adjective** *here comes Mr. Archer and his servile assistant, Bradley* **obsequious,** sycophantic, deferential, subservient, fawning, ingratiating, unctuous, groveling, toadyish, slavish, humble, self-abasing; informal slimy, bootlicking, smarmy, sucky. See note at **OBSEQUIOUS.**
ANTONYMS assertive.

serving ▶ **noun** *you should have at least four servings of vegetables* **portion,** helping, plateful, plate, bowlful; amount, quantity, ration.

servitude ▶ **noun** *born into a life of servitude* **slavery,** enslavement, bondage, subjugation, subjection, domination; historical serfdom.
ANTONYMS liberty.

session ▶ **noun 1** *a special session of the committee* **meeting,** sitting; Law assize, assembly, conclave, plenary; hearing; conference, discussion, forum, symposium, caucus.
2 *training sessions* **period,** time, spell, stretch, bout.
3 *the next session on campus begins in August* **academic year,** school year; term, semester.

set[1] ▶ **verb 1** *Beth set the bag on the table* **put (down),** place, lay, deposit, position, settle, leave, stand, plant, posit; informal stick, dump, park, plunk.
2 *the cottage is set on a hill* **be situated,** be located, lie, stand, be sited, be perched.
3 *the fence is set in concrete* **fix,** embed, insert; mount.
4 *a ring set with precious stones* **adorn,** ornament, decorate, embellish; literary bejewel.
5 *I'll go and set the table* **lay,** prepare, arrange.
6 *we set them some easy tasks* **assign,** allocate, give, allot, prescribe.
7 *just set your mind to it* **apply,** address, direct, aim, turn, focus, concentrate.
8 *they set a date for the election* **decide on,** select, choose, arrange, schedule; fix (on), settle on, determine, designate, name, appoint, specify, stipulate.
9 *he set his horse toward her* **direct,** steer, orient, orientate, point, aim, train.
10 *his jump set a national record* **establish,** create, institute.
11 *he set his watch* **adjust,** regulate, synchronize; calibrate; put right, correct; program, activate, turn on.
12 *the adhesive will set in an hour* **solidify,** harden, stiffen, thicken, jell, cake, congeal, coagulate, clot; freeze, crystallize.
ANTONYMS melt.
13 *the sun was setting* **go down,** sink, dip; vanish, disappear.
ANTONYMS rise.
– PHRASES **set about** *Mike set about raising $5,000* **begin,** start, commence, go about, get to work on, get down to, embark on, tackle, address oneself to, undertake. **set against** *you deliberately set me against my family* **alienate from,** estrange from, set at odds; drive a wedge between (one and another), sow dissension between (one and another). **set apart 1** *the orchestral background sets this song apart from the rest* **distinguish,** differentiate, mark out, single out, separate, demarcate. **2** *one pew was set apart from the rest* **isolate,** separate, segregate, put to one side. **set aside 1** *set aside some money each month* **save,** put by, put aside, put away, lay by, keep, reserve; store, stockpile, hoard, stow away, cache, withhold; informal salt away, squirrel away, stash away. **2** *he set aside his cup* **put down,** cast aside, discard, abandon, dispense with. **3** *set aside your differences* **disregard,** put aside, ignore, forget, discount, shrug off, bury. **4** *the Supreme Court set aside the decision* **overrule,** overturn, reverse, revoke, countermand, nullify, annul, cancel, quash, dismiss, reject, repudiate; Law disaffirm; formal abrogate. **set back** *the rains have set back the work on the bridge* **delay,** hold up, hold back, slow down/up, retard, check, decelerate; hinder, impede, hobble, obstruct, hamper, inhibit, frustrate, thwart. **set down 1** *he set down his thoughts* **write down,** put in writing, jot down, note down, make a note of; record, register, log. **2** *we set down some rules* **formulate,** draw up, establish, frame; lay down, determine, fix, stipulate, specify, prescribe, impose, ordain. **3** *I set it down to the fact that he was drunk* **attribute,** put down, ascribe, assign, chalk up; blame on, impute. **set forth** *you have set forth a very credible argument* **present,** describe, set out, detail, delineate, explain, expound; state, declare, announce; submit, offer, put forward, advance, propose, propound. **set free** *the hostages were released just minutes ago* **release,** free, let go, turn loose, let out, liberate, deliver, emancipate. **set in** *bad weather set in* **begin,** start, arrive, come, develop. **set off 1** *they set off for America with nothing but the clothes on their backs* **set out,** start out, sally forth, leave, depart, embark, set sail; informal hit the road. **2** *the bomb was set off* **detonate,** explode, blow up, touch off, trigger; ignite. **3** *it set off a wave of protest* **give rise to,** cause, lead to, set in motion, occasion, bring about, initiate, precipitate, prompt, trigger (off), spark (off), touch off, provoke, incite. **4** *the blue dress set off her auburn hair* **enhance,** bring out, emphasize, show off, throw into relief; complement. **set on/upon** *the relentless Cossacks set upon village after village* **attack,** assail, assault, hit, strike, beat, thrash, pummel, wallop, set about, fall on; informal lay into, lace into, let someone have it, work over,

rough up, knock about/around, have a go at, beat up on, light into. **set one's heart on** *I think she's set her heart on the orange kitten* **want desperately,** wish for, desire, long for, yearn for, hanker after, ache for, hunger for, thirst for, burn for; informal be itching for, be dying for. **set out 1** *he set out early* See SET OFF (sense 1) above. **2** *the gifts were set out on tables* **arrange,** lay out, put out, array, dispose, display, exhibit. **3** *they set out some guidelines* **present,** set forth, detail; state, declare, announce; submit, put forward, advance, propose, propound. **4** *you've done what you set out to do* **aim,** intend, mean, seek; hope, aspire, want. **set up 1** *his father set him up in business* **establish,** finance, fund, back, subsidize. **2** informal *she set him up for Newley's murder* **falsely incriminate,** frame, entrap. **3** *a monument to her memory was set up* **erect,** put up, construct, build, raise, elevate. **4** *she set up her own business* **establish,** start, begin, initiate, institute, found, create. **5** *set up a meeting* **arrange,** organize, fix (up), schedule, timetable, line up. **6** *set up a committee* **establish,** form.

set² ▶ **noun 1** *a set of color postcards* **group,** collection, series; assortment, selection, compendium, batch, number; arrangement, array.
2 *the literary set* **clique,** coterie, circle, crowd, group, crew, band, company, ring, camp, fraternity, school, faction, league; informal gang, bunch.
3 *a chemistry set* **kit,** apparatus, equipment, outfit.
4 *a set of china* **service.**
5 *the set of his shoulders* **posture,** position, cast, attitude; bearing, carriage.
6 *a set for the play* **scenery,** setting, backdrop, flats; mise en scène.
7 *the band played two sets* **session,** time; stretch, bout, round.

set³ ▶ **adjective 1** *a set routine* **fixed,** established, predetermined, hard and fast, prearranged, prescribed, specified, defined; unvarying, unchanging, invariable, unvaried, rigid, inflexible, cast-iron, strict, ironclad, settled, predictable; routine, standard, customary, regular, usual, habitual, accustomed, wonted.
ANTONYMS variable, changing.
2 *she had set ideas* **inflexible,** rigid, fixed, firm, deep-rooted, deep-seated, ingrained, entrenched.
ANTONYMS flexible.
3 *he had a set speech for such occasions* **stock,** standard, routine, rehearsed, well-worn, formulaic, conventional.
ANTONYMS original, fresh.
4 *I was all set for the evening* **ready,** prepared, organized, equipped, primed; informal geared up, psyched up.
ANTONYMS unprepared.
5 *he's* ***set on*** *marrying her* **determined to,** intent on, bent on, hell-bent on, resolute about, insistent about.
ANTONYMS uncertain.
6 *you were dead* ***set against*** *the idea* **opposed to,** averse to, hostile to, resistant to, antipathetic to, unsympathetic to; informal anti.

setback ▶ **noun** *this is a team famous for surmounting every setback that fate sends their way* **problem,** difficulty, hitch, complication, upset, disappointment, misfortune, mishap, reversal; blow, stumbling block, hurdle, hindrance, impediment, obstruction; delay, holdup; informal glitch, hiccup.
ANTONYMS breakthrough.

setting ▶ **noun 1** *a rural setting* **surroundings,** position, situation, environment, background, backdrop, milieu, environs, habitat; spot, place, location, locale, site, scene; area, region, district.
2 *a garnet in a gold setting* **mount,** fixture, surround.

settle ▶ **verb 1** *they settled the dispute* **resolve,** sort out, solve, clear up, end, fix, work out, iron out, straighten out, set right, rectify, remedy, reconcile; informal patch up.
ANTONYMS prolong.
2 *she settled their affairs* **put in order,** sort out, tidy up, arrange, organize, order, clear up.
3 *they* ***settled on*** *a date for the wedding* **decide on,** set, fix, agree on, name, establish, arrange, appoint, designate, assign; choose, select, pick.
4 *she went down to the lobby to settle her bill* **pay,** settle up, square, clear, defray.
5 *they* ***settled for*** *a 4.2% raise* **accept,** agree to, assent to; formal accede to.
6 *he* ***settled in*** *Otsego County* **make one's home in,** set up home in, take up residence in, put down roots in, establish oneself in; live in, move to, emigrate to.
7 *immigrants settled much of Australia* **colonize,** occupy, inhabit, people, populate.
8 *Catherine* ***settled down to*** *her work* **apply oneself to,** get down to, set about, attack; concentrate on, focus on, devote oneself to.
9 *the class wouldn't* ***settle down*** **calm down,** quiet down, be quiet, be still; informal shut up.
10 *a brandy will settle your nerves* **calm,** quiet; Brit. quieten, soothe, pacify, quell; sedate, tranquilize.
ANTONYMS agitate, disturb.
11 *he settled into an armchair* **sit down,** seat oneself, install oneself, ensconce oneself, plant oneself; informal park oneself, plunk oneself.
12 *a butterfly settled on the flower* **land,** come to rest, alight, descend, perch; archaic light.
13 *when the stirring stops, the sediment settles* **sink,** subside, fall, gravitate.
ANTONYMS rise.

settlement ▶ **noun 1** *a pay settlement* **agreement,** deal, arrangement, resolution, bargain, understanding, pact.
2 *the settlement of the dispute* **resolution,** settling, solution, reconciliation.
3 *a frontier settlement* **community,** colony, outpost, encampment, post; village, commune; historical plantation, clearing.
4 *the settlement of the area* **colonization,** settling, populating; historical plantation.
5 *the settlement of their debts* **payment,** discharge, liquidation, clearance.

settler ▶ **noun** *the settlers were ill-prepared for the severe winter ahead* **colonist,** colonizer, frontiersman, frontierswoman, pioneer, bushwhacker; immigrant, newcomer; historical

homesteader.
ANTONYMS native.

set-up ▶ noun **1** *a complicated setup* **system,** structure, organization, arrangement, framework, layout, configuration.
2 *a setup called Film International* **organization,** group, body, agency, association, operation; company, firm; informal outfit.
3 informal *the whole thing was a setup* **trick,** trap; conspiracy; informal put-up job, frame-up.

sever ▶ verb **1** *the head was severed from the body* **cut off,** chop off, detach, disconnect, dissever, separate, part; amputate; literary sunder.
ANTONYMS join, attach.
2 *a knife had severed the artery* **cut (through),** rupture, split, pierce.
3 *they severed diplomatic relations* **break off,** discontinue, suspend, end, terminate, cease, dissolve.
ANTONYMS establish, maintain.

several ▶ adjective **1** *several people* **some,** a number of, a few; various, assorted, sundry, diverse; literary divers.
2 *they sorted out their several responsibilities* **respective,** individual, own, particular, specific; separate, different, disparate, distinct; various.

severe ▶ adjective **1** *severe injuries* **acute,** very bad, serious, grave, critical, dreadful, terrible, awful; dangerous, parlous, life-threatening; formal grievous.
ANTONYMS minor, negligible.
2 *severe storms* **fierce,** violent, strong, powerful, intense; tempestuous, turbulent.
ANTONYMS gentle.
3 *a severe winter* **harsh,** bitter, cold, bleak, freezing, icy, arctic, extreme; informal brutal.
ANTONYMS mild.
4 *a severe headache* **excruciating,** agonizing, intense, dreadful, awful, terrible, unbearable, intolerable; informal splitting, pounding, screaming.
ANTONYMS slight.
5 *a severe test of their stamina* **difficult,** demanding, tough, arduous, formidable, exacting, rigorous, punishing, onerous, grueling.
ANTONYMS easy, simple.
6 *severe criticism* **harsh,** scathing, sharp, strong, fierce, savage, scorching, devastating, trenchant, caustic, biting, withering.
ANTONYMS mild.
7 *severe tax penalties* **extortionate,** excessive, unreasonable, inordinate, outrageous, sky-high, harsh, stiff; punitive.
8 *they received severe treatment* **harsh,** stern, hard, inflexible, uncompromising, unrelenting, merciless, pitiless, ruthless, draconian, oppressive, repressive, punitive; brutal, cruel, savage.
ANTONYMS lenient, lax.
9 *his severe expression* **stern,** dour, grim, forbidding, disapproving, unsmiling, unfriendly, somber, grave, serious, stony, steely; cold, frosty.
ANTONYMS friendly, genial.
10 *a severe style of architecture* **plain,** simple, austere, unadorned, unembellished, unornamented, stark, spartan, ascetic; clinical, uncluttered.
ANTONYMS fancy, ornate.

CHOOSE THE RIGHT WORD
severe, ascetic, austere, stern, strict, unmitigated

A storm, a hairdo, and a punishment may all be described as **severe**, which means harsh or uncompromising, without a hint of softness, mildness, levity, or indulgence. **Austere**, on the other hand, primarily applies to people, their habits, their way of life, and the environments they create; it implies coldness, stark simplicity, and restraint (*an austere room with only a table and chair*). **Ascetic** implies extreme self-denial and self-discipline, in some cases to the point of choosing what is painful or disagreeable (*he had an ascetic approach to life and rejected all creature comforts*). **Strict** literally means bound or stretched tight; in extended use, it means strenuously exact (*a strict curfew; strict obedience*). **Stern** combines harshness and authority with strictness or severity (*a stern judge*). **Unmitigated** means unmodified and unsoftened in any way (*a streak of unmitigated bad luck*).

severely ▶ adjective **1** *he was severely injured* **badly,** seriously, critically; fatally; formal grievously.
2 *she was severely criticized* **sharply,** roundly, soundly, fiercely, savagely.
3 *murderers should be treated more severely* **harshly,** strictly, sternly, rigorously, mercilessly, pitilessly, roughly, sharply; with a rod of iron; brutally, cruelly, savagely.
4 *she looked severely at Harriet* **sternly,** grimly, dourly, disapprovingly; coldly, frostily.
5 *she dressed severely in black* **plainly,** simply, austerely, starkly.

sew ▶ verb *she sewed the seams of the tunic* **stitch,** tack, baste, seam, hem; embroider.
– PHRASES **sew up 1** *the tear was sewn up* **darn,** mend, repair, patch. **2** informal *the company sewed up a deal with IBM* **secure,** clinch, pull off, bring off, settle, conclude, complete, finalize, tie up; informal swing.

sex ▶ noun **1** *they talked about sex* **sexual intercourse,** intercourse, lovemaking, making love, sex act, (sexual) relations; mating, copulation; informal nooky, whoopee, bonking, boinking, boffing, a roll in the hay, quickie; formal fornication; technical coitus, coition; dated carnal knowledge.
2 *teach your children about sex* **the facts of life,** reproduction; informal the birds and the bees.
3 *adults of both sexes* **gender.**
– PHRASES **have sex with** *she had no interest in having sex with Richie* **have sexual intercourse with,** make love to/with, sleep with, go to bed with; mate with, copulate with; seduce; rape; informal do it with, go all the way with, know in the biblical sense; bonk, boink, boff, get it on with; euphemistic be intimate with; literary ravish;

formal fornicate with.

sexuality ▶ noun 1 *she had a powerful sexuality* **sensuality,** sexiness, seductiveness, desirability, eroticism, physicality; sexual appetite, passion, desire, lust.
2 *I'm open about my sexuality* **sexual orientation,** sexual preference, leaning, persuasion; heterosexuality, homosexuality, lesbianism, bisexuality.

sexy ▶ adjective 1 *he's so sexy* **sexually attractive,** seductive, desirable, alluring, toothsome, sensual, sultry, slinky, provocative, tempting, tantalizing; nubile, voluptuous, luscious, lush, hot, beddable, foxy, cute; informal bootylicious.
2 *sexy videos* **erotic,** sexually explicit, arousing, exciting, stimulating, hot, titillating, racy, naughty, risqué, adult, X-rated; rude, pornographic, crude, lewd; informal raunchy, steamy, porno, blue, skin, XXX.
3 *they weren't feeling sexy* **(sexually) aroused,** sexually excited, amorous, lustful, passionate; informal horny, hot, turned on, sexed up.
4 informal *a sexy sales promotion* **exciting,** stimulating, interesting, appealing, intriguing, slick, red-hot.

shabby ▶ adjective 1 *a shabby little bar* **run-down,** down-at-heel, down-at-the-heel(s), scruffy, dilapidated, ramshackle, tumbledown; seedy, slummy, insalubrious, squalid, sordid, flea-bitten; informal crummy, scuzzy, raggedy-ass.
ANTONYMS smart, upmarket.
2 *a shabby gray coat* **scruffy,** old, worn out, threadbare, ragged, frayed, tattered, battered, faded, moth-eaten, mangy; informal tatty, ratty, the worse for wear, raggedy.
ANTONYMS new.
3 *her shabby treatment of Bill* **contemptible,** despicable, dishonorable, discreditable, mean, low, dirty, hateful, shameful, sorry, ignoble, unfair, unworthy, unkind, shoddy, nasty; informal rotten, lowdown; beastly.
ANTONYMS decent, honorable.

shackle ▶ verb 1 *he was shackled to the wall* **chain,** fetter, manacle; secure, tie (up), bind, tether, hobble; put in chains, clap in irons, handcuff.
2 *journalists were shackled by a new law* **restrain,** restrict, limit, constrain, handicap, hamstring, hamper, hinder, impede, obstruct, inhibit, check, curb.

shackles ▶ plural noun 1 *shackles of iron* **chains,** fetters, irons, leg irons, manacles, handcuffs; bonds; informal cuffs, bracelets.
2 *the shackles of bureaucracy* **restrictions,** restraints, constraints, impediments, hindrances, obstacles, barriers, obstructions, checks, curbs; literary trammels.

shade ▶ noun 1 *they sat in the shade* **shadow(s),** shadiness, shelter, cover; cool.
ANTONYMS light, glare.
2 *shades of blue* **color,** hue, tone, tint, tinge.
3 *shades of meaning* **nuance,** gradation, degree, difference, variation, variety; nicety, subtlety; undertone, overtone.
4 *her skirt was* ***a shade*** *too short* **a little,** a bit, a trace, a touch, a modicum, a tinge; slightly, rather, somewhat; informal a tad, a smidgen, a titch, a tinch, a hair.
5 *the window shade* **blind,** curtain, screen, cover, covering; awning, canopy.
6 informal **(shades)** *he was wearing shades* **sunglasses,** dark glasses; proprietary Polaroids, Raybans.
▶ verb 1 *vines shaded the garden* **cast a shadow over,** shadow, shelter, cover, screen; darken.
2 *she* ***shaded in*** *the picture* **darken,** color in, pencil in, block in, fill in; cross-hatch.
3 *the sky shaded from turquoise to blue* **change,** transmute, turn, go; merge, blend, graduate.
– PHRASES **put in the shade** *Candi's clarinet solo puts mine in the shade* **surpass,** outshine, outclass, overshadow, eclipse, transcend, cap, top, outstrip, outdo, put to shame, beat, outperform, upstage; informal run rings around, be a cut above. **shades of** *this weekend has been perfectly romantic—you know, shades of our honeymoon* **echoes of,** a reminder of, memories of, suggestions of, hints of.

shadow ▶ noun 1 *he saw her shadow in the doorway* **silhouette,** outline, shape, contour, profile.
2 **(shadows)** *he emerged from the shadows* **shade,** darkness, twilight; gloom, murkiness.
3 *the shadow of war* **black cloud,** cloud, pall; gloom, blight; threat.
4 *she knew without any shadow of doubt* **trace,** scrap, shred, crumb, iota, scintilla, jot, whit, grain; informal smidgen, smidge, tad.
5 *a shadow of a smile* **trace,** hint, suggestion, suspicion, ghost, glimmer.
6 *he's a shadow of his former self* **inferior version,** poor imitation, apology, travesty; remnant.
7 *the dog became her shadow* **constant companion,** alter ego, second self; close friend, bosom friend; informal Siamese twin, bosom buddy.
▶ verb 1 *the market is shadowed by the church* **overshadow,** shade; darken, dim.
2 *he is shadowing a poacher* **follow,** trail, track, stalk, pursue, hunt; informal tail, keep tabs on.

shadowy ▶ adjective 1 *a shadowy corridor* **dark,** dim, gloomy, murky, crepuscular, shady, shaded; literary tenebrous.
ANTONYMS bright.
2 *a shadowy figure* **indistinct,** hazy, indefinite, vague, nebulous, ill-defined, faint, blurred, blurry, unclear, indistinguishable, unrecognizable; ghostly, spectral, wraithlike.
ANTONYMS clear.

shady ▶ adjective 1 *a shady garden* **shaded,** shadowy, dim, dark; sheltered, screened, shrouded; leafy; literary bosky, tenebrous.
ANTONYMS bright, sunlit.
2 informal *shady deals* **suspicious,** suspect, questionable, dubious, doubtful, disreputable, untrustworthy, dishonest, devious, dishonorable, underhanded, unscrupulous, irregular, unethical; informal fishy, murky.
ANTONYMS reputable, honest.

shaft ▶ noun 1 *the shaft of a golf club* **pole,** shank, stick, rod, staff; handle, hilt, stem.
2 *the shaft of a feather* **quill;** Ornithology rachis.
3 *shafts of sunlight* **ray,** beam, gleam, streak, finger.
4 *a ventilation shaft* mineshaft, tunnel, passage,

pit, adit, downcast, upcast; borehole, bore; duct, well, flue, vent.

▶ verb *I think we've just been shafted* **deceive,** delude, trick, hoodwink, mislead, take in, dupe, fool, double-cross, cheat, defraud, swindle, fleece, catch out, gull, hoax, bamboozle, con, diddle, rook, put one over on, pull a fast one on, pull the wool over someone's eyes, take for a ride, shanghai, flimflam, sucker, snooker.

shaggy ▶ adjective *his shaggy beard* **hairy,** bushy, thick, woolly; tangled, tousled, unkempt, disheveled, untidy, matted; formal hirsute.
ANTONYMS sleek.

shake ▶ verb **1** *the whole building shook* **vibrate,** tremble, quiver, quake, shiver, shudder, jiggle, wobble, rock, sway; convulse.
2 *she shook the bottle* **jiggle,** joggle, agitate.
3 *he shook his stick at them* **brandish,** wave, flourish, swing, wield.
4 *the look in his eyes really shook her* **upset,** distress, disturb, unsettle, disconcert, discompose, disquiet, unnerve, trouble, throw off balance, agitate, fluster; shock, alarm, frighten, scare, worry; informal rattle.
ANTONYMS soothe.
5 *this will shake their confidence* **weaken,** undermine, damage, impair, harm; reduce, diminish, decrease.
ANTONYMS strengthen.

▶ noun **1** *he gave his coat a shake* **jiggle,** joggle.
2 *a shake of his fist* **flourish,** brandish, wave.
3 (**shakes**) *it gives me the shakes* **tremors,** delirium tremens; informal DTs, jitters, the creeps, the shivers, willies, heebie-jeebies, the jim-jams.

– PHRASES **in two shakes (of a lamb's tail)** informal *I'll be there in two shakes* See **IN A MOMENT** at **MOMENT**. **no great shakes** informal *that movie was no great shakes* **not very good,** unexceptional, unmemorable, forgettable, uninspired, uninteresting, indifferent, unimpressive, lackluster; informal nothing to write home about, nothing special. **shake a leg** informal *c'mon, Ruthie, shake a leg* See **HURRY** (sense 1 of the verb). **shake off 1** *I think we shook off that cop* **get away from,** escape, elude, dodge, lose, leave behind, get rid of, give someone the slip, throw off the scent.
2 *she can't seem to shake off this virus* **recover from,** get over; get rid of, free oneself from.
shake up 1 *the accident shook him up* See **SHAKE** (sense 4 of the verb). **2** *plans to shake up the legal profession* **reorganize,** restructure, revolutionize, alter, change, transform, reform, overhaul.

CHOOSE THE RIGHT WORD

shake, quake, quiver, shiver, shudder, tremble

Does a cool breeze make you **shiver**, **quiver**, **shudder**, or **tremble**? All of these verbs describe vibrating, wavering, or oscillating movements that, in living creatures, are often involuntary expressions of strain or discomfort. **Shake**, which refers to abrupt forward-and-backward, side-to-side, or up-and-down movements, is different from the others in that it can be done to a person or object as well as by one (*shake a can of paint; shake visibly while lifting a heavy load*). *Tremble* applies specifically to the slight and rapid shaking motion the human body makes when it is nervous, frightened, or uneasy (*his hands trembled when he picked up the phone*). To *shiver* is to make a similar movement with the entire body, but the cause is usually cold or fear (*shiver in the draft from an open door*). *Quiver* suggests a rapid and almost imperceptible vibration resulting from disturbed or irregular surface tension; it refers more often to things (*the leaves quivered in the breeze*), although people may quiver when they're under emotional tension (*her lower lip quivered and her eyes were downcast*). *Shudder* suggests a more intense shaking, usually in response to something horrible or revolting (*shudder at the thought of eating uncooked meat*). **Quake** implies a violent upheaval or shaking, similar to what occurs during an earthquake (*the boy's heart quaked at his father's approach*).

shaky ▶ adjective **1** *shaky legs* **trembling,** shaking, tremulous, quivering, quivery, unsteady, wobbly, weak; tottering, tottery, teetering, doddery; informal trembly.
ANTONYMS steady.
2 *I feel a bit shaky* **faint,** dizzy, lightheaded, giddy; weak, wobbly, quivery, groggy, muzzy; informal trembly, woozy.
3 *a shaky table* **unsteady,** unstable, wobbly, precarious, rocky, rickety, ramshackle.
ANTONYMS stable.
4 *the evidence is shaky* **unreliable,** untrustworthy, questionable, dubious, doubtful, tenuous, suspect, flimsy, weak, unsound, unsupported, unsubstantiated, unfounded; informal iffy.
ANTONYMS sound.

shallow ▶ adjective *a shallow analysis of contemporary society* **superficial,** facile, simplistic, oversimplified; flimsy, insubstantial, lightweight, empty, trivial, trifling; surface, skin-deep, two-dimensional; frivolous, foolish, silly, Mickey Mouse. See note at **SUPERFICIAL**.
ANTONYMS profound.

sham ▶ noun **1** *his tenderness had been a sham* **pretense,** fake, act, fiction, simulation, fraud, feint, lie, counterfeit; humbug.
2 *the doctor was a sham* **charlatan,** fake, fraud, impostor, pretender; quack, mountebank; informal phony.

▶ adjective *sham togetherness* **fake,** pretended, feigned, simulated, false, artificial, bogus, insincere, contrived, affected, make-believe, fictitious; imitation, mock, counterfeit, fraudulent; informal pretend, put-on, phony, pseudo.
ANTONYMS genuine.

shamble ▶ verb *I hear Mr. Billings shambling down the hall* **shuffle,** drag one's feet, lumber, totter, dodder; hobble, limp.

shambles ▶ plural noun **1** *we have to sort out this shambles* **chaos,** mess, muddle, confusion,

disorder, havoc, mare's nest, dog's breakfast.
2 *the room was a shambles* **mess,** pigsty; informal disaster area.

shame ▶ **noun 1** *her face was scarlet with shame* **humiliation,** mortification, chagrin, ignominy, embarrassment, indignity, discomfort.
ANTONYMS pride.
2 *I felt shame at telling a lie* **guilt,** remorse, contrition, compunction.
ANTONYMS indifference.
3 *he brought shame on the family* **disgrace,** dishonor, discredit, degradation, ignominy, disrepute, infamy, scandal, opprobrium, contempt; dated disesteem.
ANTONYMS glory, honor.
4 *it's a shame she never married* **pity,** misfortune, sad thing; bad luck; informal bummer, crime, sin, crying shame.
▶ **verb 1** *you shamed your family's name* **disgrace,** dishonor, discredit, degrade, debase; stigmatize, taint, sully, tarnish, besmirch, blacken, drag through the mud.
ANTONYMS honor.
2 *he was shamed in public* **humiliate,** mortify, chagrin, embarrass, abash, chasten, humble, take down a peg or two, cut down to size; informal show up, make someone eat crow.
– PHRASES **put to shame** *these new materials put our old plastics to shame* **outshine,** outclass, eclipse, surpass, excel, outstrip, outdo, put in the shade, upstage; informal run rings around.

shamefaced ▶ **adjective** *Giles looked shamefaced* **ashamed,** abashed, sheepish, guilty, conscience-stricken, guilt-ridden, contrite, sorry, remorseful, repentant, penitent, regretful, rueful, apologetic; embarrassed, mortified, red-faced, chagrined, humiliated; informal with one's tail between one's legs.
ANTONYMS unrepentant.

shameful ▶ **adjective 1** *shameful behavior* **disgraceful,** deplorable, despicable, contemptible, dishonorable, discreditable, reprehensible, low, unworthy, ignoble, shabby; shocking, scandalous, outrageous, abominable, atrocious, appalling, vile, odious, heinous, egregious, loathsome, bad; inexcusable, unforgivable; informal lowdown, hateful.
ANTONYMS admirable.
2 *a shameful secret* **embarrassing,** mortifying, humiliating, degrading, ignominious.

shameless ▶ **adjective** *a shameless display of flirtation* **flagrant,** blatant, barefaced, overt, brazen, brash, audacious, outrageous, undisguised, unconcealed, transparent; immodest, indecorous; unabashed, unashamed, unblushing, unrepentant.
ANTONYMS modest.

shape ▶ **noun 1** *the shape of the dining table* **form,** appearance, configuration, formation, structure; figure, build, physique, body; contours, lines, outline, silhouette, profile.
2 *a spirit in the shape of a fox* **guise,** likeness, semblance, form, appearance, image.
3 *you're in pretty good shape* **condition,** health, fettle, order.
▶ **verb 1** *the metal is shaped into tools* **form,** fashion, make, mold, model, cast; sculpt, sculpture, carve, cut, whittle.
2 *attitudes were shaped by his report* **determine,** form, fashion, mold, define, develop; influence, affect.
– PHRASES **shape up** *her work is shaping up nicely* **improve,** get better, progress, show promise; develop, take shape, come on, come along. **take shape** *our remodeling plans were really starting to take shape* **become clear,** become definite, become tangible, crystallize, come together, fall into place.

shapeless ▶ **adjective 1** *shapeless lumps* **formless,** amorphous, unformed, indefinite.
2 *a shapeless dress* **baggy,** saggy, ill-fitting, sacklike, oversized, unshapely, formless.

shapely ▶ **adjective** *the shapely models of the forties* **well-proportioned,** clean-limbed; curvaceous, voluptuous, Junoesque; attractive, sexy; informal curvy, bootylicious; archaic comely.

shard ▶ **noun** *a shard of glass in her heel* **fragment,** sliver, splinter, shiver, chip, piece, bit, particle.

share ▶ **noun** *her share of the profits* **portion,** part, division, quota, quantum, allowance, ration, allocation, measure, due; percentage, commission, dividend; helping, serving; informal cut, slice.
▶ **verb 1** *we share the bills* **split,** divide, go halves on; informal go fifty-fifty on, go Dutch on.
2 *they* ***shared out*** *the bottles of water* **apportion,** divide up, allocate, portion out, ration out, parcel out, measure out; carve up, divvy up.
3 *we all* ***share in*** *the learning process* **participate in,** take part in, play a part in, be involved in, contribute to, have a hand in, partake in.

sharp ▶ **adjective 1** *a sharp knife* **keen,** razor-edged; sharpened, honed. See note at KEEN.
ANTONYMS blunt.
2 *a sharp pain* **excruciating,** agonizing, intense, stabbing, shooting, severe, acute, keen, fierce, searing; exquisite.
3 *a sharp taste* **tangy,** piquant, strong; **acidic,** acid, sour, tart, pungent, acrid, bitter, acidulous.
ANTONYMS mild, mellow, bland.
4 *a sharp cry of pain* **loud,** piercing, shrill, high-pitched, penetrating, harsh, strident, ear-splitting, deafening.
ANTONYMS soft, quiet.
5 *a sharp wind* **cold,** chilly, chill, brisk, keen, penetrating, biting, icy, bitter, freezing, raw; informal nippy, wicked.
ANTONYMS warm, balmy.
6 *sharp words* **harsh,** bitter, cutting, scathing, caustic, barbed, trenchant, acrimonious, acerbic, sarcastic, sardonic, spiteful, venomous, malicious, vitriolic, vicious, hurtful, nasty, cruel, abrasive; informal bitchy, catty.
ANTONYMS amicable, kind.
7 *a sharp sense of loss* **intense,** acute, keen, strong, bitter, fierce, heartfelt, overwhelming.
8 *the lens brings it into sharp focus* **distinct,** clear, crisp; stark, obvious, marked, definite, pronounced.
ANTONYMS blurred, indistinct.
9 *a sharp increase* **sudden,** abrupt, rapid; steep, precipitous.
ANTONYMS gradual.

10 *a sharp corner* **hairpin,** tight.
11 *a sharp drop* **steep,** sheer, abrupt, precipitous, vertical.
ANTONYMS gentle, gradual.
12 *sharp eyes* **keen,** perceptive, observant, acute, beady, hawklike.
ANTONYMS weak.
13 *she was sharp and witty* **perceptive,** percipient, perspicacious, incisive, sensitive, keen, acute, quick-witted, clever, shrewd, canny, astute, intelligent, intuitive, bright, alert, smart, quick off the mark, insightful, knowing; informal on the ball, quick on the uptake, savvy, heads-up.
ANTONYMS slow, dull, stupid.
14 informal *a sharp suit* **smart,** stylish, fashionable, chic, modish, elegant; informal trendy, cool, hip, snazzy, classy, snappy, styling/stylin', natty, nifty, fly, spiffy.
ANTONYMS shabby.
▶ **adverb 1** *nine o'clock sharp* **precisely,** exactly, on the dot; promptly, prompt, punctually, dead on; informal on the nose, on the button.
ANTONYMS roughly.
2 *the recession pulled people up sharp* **abruptly,** suddenly, sharply, unexpectedly.

sharpen ▶ **verb 1** *sharpen the carving knife* **hone,** whet, strop, grind, file.
2 *the players are sharpening their skills* **improve,** brush up, polish up, better, enhance; hone, fine-tune, perfect.

shatter ▶ **verb 1** *the glasses shattered* **smash,** break, splinter, crack, fracture, fragment, disintegrate, shiver; informal bust.
2 *the announcement shattered their hopes* **destroy,** wreck, ruin, dash, crush, devastate, demolish, torpedo, scotch; informal put the kibosh on, scuttle.
3 *we were shattered by the news* **devastate,** shock, stun, daze, traumatize, crush, distress.

shave ▶ **verb 1** *he shaved his beard* **cut off,** snip off; crop, trim, barber.
2 *shave off excess wood* **plane,** pare, whittle, scrape.
3 *they shaved the deficit by 4 percent* **reduce,** cut, lessen, decrease, pare down, shrink.
4 *the shot just shaved my arm* **graze,** brush, touch, glance off, kiss.

sheath ▶ **noun 1** *put the sword in its sheath* **scabbard,** case.
2 *the wire has a plastic sheath* **covering,** cover, case, casing, envelope, sleeve, wrapper, capsule.
3 *a contraceptive sheath* See **CONDOM**.

shed[1] ▶ **noun** *the rabbit lives in the shed* **hut,** lean-to, outhouse, outbuilding; shack; potting shed, woodshed, tool shed, garden shed.

shed[2] ▶ **verb 1** *the trees shed their leaves* **drop,** scatter, spill.
2 *the caterpillar shed its skin* **slough off,** cast off, molt.
3 *we shed our jackets* **take off,** remove, shrug off, discard, doff, climb out of, slip out of, divest oneself of, peel off.
ANTONYMS don.
4 *much blood has been shed* **spill,** discharge.
5 *she shed 20 pounds* **lose,** get rid of, discard.
ANTONYMS put on.
6 *they must shed their illusions* **discard,** get rid of, dispose of, do away with, drop, abandon, jettison, scrap, cast aside, dump, reject, repudiate; informal ditch, junk.
ANTONYMS adopt, keep.
7 *the moon shed a watery light* **cast,** radiate, diffuse, disperse, give out.
– PHRASES **shed tears** *now, now, there's no need to shed tears* **weep,** cry, sob; lament, grieve, mourn; informal blubber, boo-hoo.

sheen ▶ **noun** *we were admiring the sheen of your dog's coat* **shine,** luster, gloss, patina, shininess, burnish, polish, shimmer, brilliance, radiance. See note at **POLISH**.

sheepish ▶ **adjective** *stop looking so sheepish and come on in* **embarrassed,** uncomfortable, hangdog, self-conscious; shamefaced, ashamed, abashed, mortified, chastened, remorseful, contrite, apologetic, rueful, regretful, penitent, repentant.

sheer[1] ▶ **adjective 1** *the sheer audacity of the plan* **utter,** complete, absolute, total, pure, downright, out-and-out, arrant, thorough, thoroughgoing, patent, veritable, unmitigated, plain.
2 *a sheer drop* **precipitous,** steep, vertical, perpendicular, abrupt, bluff, sharp.
ANTONYMS gradual.
3 *a sheer dress* **diaphanous,** gauzy, filmy, floaty, gossamer, thin, translucent, transparent, see-through, insubstantial.
ANTONYMS thick.

sheer[2] ▶ **verb 1** *the boat* ***sheered off*** *from the landing* **swerve,** veer, slew, skew, swing, change course.
2 *her mind* ***sheered away from*** *his image* **turn away from,** flinch from, recoil from, shy away from; avoid.

sheet ▶ **noun 1** (often **sheets**) *she changed the sheets* **bed linen,** linen, bedclothes.
2 *a sheet of ice* **layer,** stratum, covering, blanket, coating, coat, film, skin.
3 *a sheet of glass* **pane,** panel, piece, plate; slab.
4 *she put a fresh sheet in the typewriter* **piece of paper,** leaf, page, folio.
5 *a sheet of water* **expanse,** area, stretch, sweep.

shelf ▶ **noun 1** *the plant on the shelf* **ledge,** sill, bracket, rack; mantelpiece; shelving.
2 *an ocean shelf* **sandbank,** sandbar, bank, bar, reef, shoal.

shell ▶ **noun 1** *a crab shell* **carapace,** exterior; armor; Zoology exoskeleton.
2 *peanut shells* **pod,** husk, hull, casing, case, covering, integument, shuck.
3 *shells passing overhead* **projectile,** bomb, explosive; grenade; bullet, cartridge.
4 *the metal shell of the car* **framework,** frame, chassis, skeleton; hull, exterior.
▶ **verb 1** *they were shelling peas* **hull,** pod, husk, shuck.
2 *rebel artillery shelled the city* **bombard,** fire on, shoot at, attack, bomb, blitz, strafe.
– PHRASES **shell out** informal *how much did you shell out for those shoes?* See **PAY** (sense 2 of the verb).

shelter ▶ **noun 1** *the trees provide shelter for animals* **protection,** cover, screening, shade; safety, security, refuge, sanctuary, asylum.
ANTONYMS exposure.

2 *a shelter for abused women* **sanctuary,** refuge, home, haven, safe house; harbor, port in a storm.

▶ **verb 1** *the hut sheltered him from the wind* **protect,** shield, screen, cover, shade, save, safeguard, preserve, defend, cushion, guard, insulate.
ANTONYMS expose.
2 *the anchorage where the convoy sheltered* **take shelter,** take refuge, seek sanctuary, take cover; informal hole up.

sheltered ▶ **adjective 1** *a sheltered stretch of water* **protected,** screened, shielded, covered; shady; cozy.
2 *she led a sheltered life* **secluded,** cloistered, isolated, protected, withdrawn, sequestered, reclusive; privileged, secure, safe, quiet.

shelve ▶ **verb** *plans to reopen the school have been shelved* **postpone,** put off, delay, defer, put back, reschedule, hold over/off, put to one side, suspend, stay, keep in abeyance, mothball; abandon, drop, give up, stop, cancel, jettison, ax, put over, table, take a rain check on; informal put on ice, put on the back burner, put in cold storage, ditch, dump, junk.
ANTONYMS execute.

shepherd ▶ **noun** *he worked as a shepherd* herdsman, herder, shepherdess, sheepman.

▶ **verb** *we shepherded them away* **usher,** steer, herd, lead, take, escort, guide, conduct, marshal, walk; show, see, chaperone.

shield ▶ **noun 1** *he used his shield to fend off blows* Heraldry escutcheon; historical buckler, target.
2 *a shield against dirt* **protection,** guard, defense, cover, screen, security, shelter, safeguard, protector.

▶ **verb** *he shielded his eyes* **protect,** cover, screen, shade; save, safeguard, preserve, defend, secure, guard; cushion, insulate.
ANTONYMS expose.

shift ▶ **verb 1** *she shifted her position* **change,** alter, adjust, vary; modify, revise, reverse, retract; do a U-turn.
ANTONYMS keep.
2 *the cargo has shifted* **move,** slide, slip, be displaced.
3 *the wind shifted* **veer,** alter, change, turn, swing round.

▶ **noun 1** *the southward shift of people* **movement,** move, transference, transport, transposition, relocation.
2 *a shift in public opinion* **change,** alteration, adjustment, amendment, variation, modification, revision, reversal, retraction, U-turn.
3 *they worked three shifts* **stint,** stretch, spell of work.
4 *the night shift went home* **workers,** crew, gang, team, squad, patrol.

shiftless ▶ **adjective** *he thought the whole family shiftless and dishonest* **lazy,** idle, indolent, slothful, lethargic, lackadaisical; spiritless, apathetic, feckless, good-for-nothing, worthless; unambitious, unenterprising.

shifty ▶ **adjective** informal *he had a shifty look about him* **devious,** evasive, slippery, duplicitous, false, deceitful, underhanded, untrustworthy, dishonest, shady, wily, crafty, tricky, sneaky, treacherous, artful, sly, scheming, snide; informal hinky.
ANTONYMS honest.

shilly-shally ▶ **verb** *we must not tolerate leaders who shilly-shally over matters of national security* **dither,** be indecisive, be irresolute, vacillate, waver, hesitate, blow hot and cold, falter, drag one's feet, hem and haw; informal dilly-dally.

shimmer ▶ **verb** *the lake shimmered* **glint,** glisten, twinkle, sparkle, flash, scintillate, gleam, glow, glimmer, glitter, wink; literary coruscate.

▶ **noun** *the shimmer of lights from the traffic* **glint,** twinkle, sparkle, flash, gleam, glow, glimmer, luster, glitter; literary coruscation.

shine ▶ **verb 1** *the sun shone* **emit light,** beam, radiate, gleam, glow, glint, glimmer, sparkle, twinkle, glitter, glisten, shimmer, flash, flare, glare, fluoresce; literary glister, coruscate.
2 *she shone his shoes* **polish,** burnish, buff, wax, gloss.
3 *they shone at gymnastics* **excel,** be outstanding, be brilliant, be successful, stand out.

▶ **noun 1** *the shine of the moon on her face* **light,** brightness, gleam, glow, glint, glimmer, sparkle, twinkle, glitter, glisten, shimmer, beam, glare, radiance, illumination, luminescence, luminosity, incandescence.
2 *linseed oil restores the shine* **polish,** burnish, gleam, gloss, luster, sheen, patina.

shining ▶ **adjective 1** *a shining expanse of water* **gleaming,** bright, brilliant, illuminated, lustrous, glowing, glinting, sparkling, twinkling, glittering, glistening, shimmering, dazzling, luminous, luminescent, incandescent; literary glistering, coruscating. See note at **BRIGHT**.
2 *a shining face* **glowing,** beaming, radiant, happy.
3 *shining chromium tubes* **shiny,** bright, polished, gleaming, glossy, sheeny, lustrous.
– PHRASES **a shining example** *a shining example of Yankee ingenuity* **paragon,** model, epitome, archetype, ideal, exemplar, nonpareil, paradigm, quintessence, beau ideal, acme, jewel, flower, treasure.

shiny ▶ **adjective** *a shiny red apple* **glossy,** glassy, bright, polished, gleaming, satiny, sheeny, lustrous.
ANTONYMS matte.

shirk ▶ **verb 1** *she didn't shirk any task* **evade,** dodge, avoid, get out of, sidestep, shrink from, shun, skip, miss; neglect; informal duck (out of), cop out of, cut.
2 *no one shirked* **avoid one's duty,** be remiss, be negligent, play truant, swing the lead, slack off; informal goof off, play hooky.

shirker ▶ **noun** *you'll find no shirkers in my crew* **dodger,** truant, absentee, layabout, good-for-nothing, loafer, idler; informal slacker, bum, lazybones.

shiver[1] ▶ **verb** *he was shivering with fear* **tremble,** quiver, shake, shudder, quaver, quake. See note at **SHAKE**.

▶ **noun** *she gave a shiver as the door opened* **tremble,** quiver, shake, shudder, quaver, quake, tremor, twitch.

shiver[2] ▶ noun *shivers of glass* **splinter,** sliver, shard, fragment, chip, shaving, smithereen, particle, bit, piece.
▶ verb *the window shivered into thousands of pieces* **shatter,** splinter, smash, fragment, crack, break.

shivery ▶ adjective *she felt sick and shivery* **trembling,** trembly, quivery, shaky, shuddering, shuddery, quavery, quaking; cold, chilly.

shock[1] ▶ noun 1 *the news came as a shock* **blow,** upset, disturbance; surprise, revelation, a bolt from the blue, thunderbolt, bombshell, rude awakening, eye-opener; informal whammy, wake-up call.
2 *you gave me a shock* **fright,** scare, jolt, start; informal turn.
3 *she was suffering from shock* **trauma,** prostration; collapse, breakdown.
4 *the first shock of the earthquake* **vibration,** reverberation, shake, jolt, jar, jerk; impact, blow.
▶ verb *the murder shocked the nation* **appall,** horrify, outrage, revolt, disgust, nauseate, sicken; traumatize, distress, upset, disturb, disquiet, unsettle; stun, rock, stagger, astound, astonish, amaze, startle, surprise, dumbfound, shake, take aback, throw, unnerve.

shock[2] ▶ noun *a shock of red hair* **mass,** mane, mop, thatch, head, crop, bush, frizz, tangle, cascade, halo.

shocking ▶ adjective *the news from Cambodia was shocking* **appalling,** horrifying, horrific, dreadful, awful, frightful, terrible; scandalous, outrageous, disgraceful, vile, abominable, abhorrent, atrocious; odious, repugnant, disgusting, nauseating, sickening, loathsome; distressing, upsetting, disturbing, disquieting, unsettling; staggering, amazing, astonishing, startling, surprising; informal gut-wrenching.

shoddy ▶ adjective 1 *shoddy goods* **poor-quality,** inferior, second-rate, third-rate, tinpot, cheap, cheapjack, trashy, jerry-built; informal tacky, chintzy, rubbishy, junky, cheapo, cheesy, schlocky.
ANTONYMS quality.
2 *shoddy workmanship* **careless,** slapdash, sloppy, slipshod, crude; negligent, cursory.
ANTONYMS careful.

shoot ▶ verb 1 *they shot him in the street* **gun down,** mow down, hit, wound, injure; put a bullet in, pick off, bag, fell, kill; informal pot, blast, pump full of lead, plug.
2 *they shot at the enemy* **fire,** open fire, aim, snipe, let fly; bombard, shell.
3 *faster than a gun can shoot bullets* **discharge,** fire, launch, loose off, let fly, emit.
4 *a car shot past* **race,** speed, flash, dash, dart, rush, hurtle, careen, streak, whiz, go like lightning, go hell-bent for leather, zoom, charge; career, sweep, fly, wing; informal belt, scoot, scorch, tear, zip, whip, step on it, burn rubber, bomb, hightail it, barrel.
5 *the plant failed to shoot* **sprout,** bud, burgeon, germinate.
6 *the film was shot in Toronto* **film,** photograph, take, snap, capture, record, tape; videotape, video.
▶ noun *nip off the new shoots* **sprout,** bud, offshoot, scion, sucker, spear, runner, tendril, sprig.

shop ▶ noun 1 *a shop selling clothes* **store,** (retail) outlet, boutique, emporium, department store, big box store, supermarket, superstore, chain store, market, mart, minimart, convenience store, trading post.
2 *he works in the machine shop* **workshop,** workroom, plant, factory, works, mill, yard.
▶ verb *he was* ***shopping for*** *spices* **buy,** purchase, get, acquire, obtain, pick up, snap up, procure, stock up on.

shore[1] ▶ noun *he swam out from the shore* **seashore,** lakeshore, lakefront, bayfront, beach, foreshore, sand(s), shoreline, waterside, front, coast, seaboard; literary strand.

shore[2] ▶ verb *we had to* ***shore up*** *the building* **prop up,** hold up, bolster, support, brace, buttress, strengthen, fortify, reinforce, underpin.

short ▶ adjective 1 *a short piece of string* **small,** little, tiny; informal teeny.
ANTONYMS long.
2 *short people* **small,** little, petite, tiny, diminutive, stubby, elfin, dwarfish, midget, pygmy, Lilliputian, minuscule, miniature; informal pint-sized, vertically challenged, teeny, knee-high to a grasshopper; Scottish wee.
ANTONYMS tall.
3 *a short report* **concise,** brief, succinct, compact, summary, economical, crisp, pithy, epigrammatic, laconic, thumbnail, capsule, abridged, abbreviated, condensed, synoptic, summarized, contracted, truncated; formal compendious.
ANTONYMS long, verbose.
4 *a short time* **brief,** momentary, temporary, short-lived, impermanent, cursory, fleeting, passing, fugitive, lightning, transitory, transient, ephemeral, quick.
ANTONYMS long.
5 *money is a bit short* **scarce,** in short supply, scant, meager, sparse, insufficient, deficient, inadequate, lacking, wanting, tight; rare exiguous.
ANTONYMS plentiful.
6 *he was rather short with her* **curt,** sharp, abrupt, blunt, brusque, terse, offhand, gruff, surly, testy, rude, uncivil; informal snappy, snappish.
ANTONYMS patient, courteous.
▶ adverb *she stopped short* **abruptly,** suddenly, sharply, all of a sudden, all at once, unexpectedly, without warning, out of the blue.
– PHRASES **in short** *in short, we want you to leave* **briefly,** in a word, in a nutshell, in précis, in essence, to come to the point; in conclusion, in summary, to sum up. **short of 1** *we are short of nurses* **deficient in,** lacking, wanting, in need of, low on, short on, missing; informal strapped for, pushed for, minus. **2** *short of searching everyone, there is nothing we can do* **apart from,** other than, aside from, besides, except (for), excepting, without, excluding, not counting, save (for).

shortage ▶ noun *the islanders are accustomed to a shortage of fresh water* **scarcity,** sparseness, sparsity, dearth, paucity, poverty, insufficiency,

deficiency, inadequacy, famine, lack, want, deficit, shortfall, rarity. See note at LACK.
ANTONYMS abundance.

shortcoming ▶ noun *after forty years of marriage, he still claimed she had few shortcomings* **defect,** fault, flaw, imperfection, deficiency, limitation, failing, drawback, weakness, weak point, foible, frailty, vice. See note at FAULT.
ANTONYMS strength.

shorten ▶ verb *shorten your essay to a three-paragraph summary | the drapes will have to be shortened* **make shorter,** abbreviate, abridge, condense, précis, synopsize, contract, compress, reduce, shrink, diminish, cut (down); dock, trim, crop, pare down, prune; curtail, truncate.
ANTONYMS extend.

short-lived ▶ adjective *it was a short-lived romance* **brief,** short, momentary, temporary, impermanent, cursory, fleeting, passing, fugitive, lightning, transitory, transient, ephemeral, quick.

shortly ▶ adverb **1** *she will be with you shortly* **soon,** presently, momentarily, in a little while, at any moment, in a minute, in next to no time, before long, by and by; informal anon, any time now, pretty soon, in a jiffy; dated directly.
2 *"I know," he replied shortly* **curtly,** sharply, abruptly, bluntly, brusquely, tersely, gruffly, snappily, testily, rudely.

shortsighted ▶ adjective *shortsighted critics* **narrow-minded,** unimaginative, small-minded, insular, parochial, provincial, improvident.
ANTONYMS farsighted, imaginative.

short-staffed ▶ adjective *we're always short-staffed around the holidays* **understaffed,** short-handed, undermanned, below strength.

short-tempered ▶ adjective *don't get short-tempered with me, pal!* **irritable,** irascible, hot-tempered, quick-tempered, snappish, fiery, touchy, volatile; cross, crabby, crotchety, cantankerous, grumpy, ill-tempered, bad-tempered, testy, tetchy, prickly, choleric; informal snappy, grouchy, cranky, on a short fuse, bitchy.
ANTONYMS placid.

shot ▶ noun **1** *a shot rang out* report of a gun, crack, bang, blast; (**shots**) gunfire.
2 *the cannons have run out of shot* **bullets,** cannonballs, pellets, ammunition.
3 *the winning shot* **stroke,** hit, strike; kick, throw, pitch, lob.
4 *Mike was an excellent shot* **marksman,** markswoman, shooter.
5 *a shot of us on holiday* **photograph,** photo, snap, snapshot, picture, print, slide, still.
6 informal *it's nice to get a shot at driving* **attempt,** try; turn, chance, opportunity; informal go, stab, crack; formal essay.
7 *tetanus shots* **injection,** inoculation, immunization, vaccination, booster; informal jab, needle.
– PHRASES **a shot in the arm** informal *the new sidewalks and landscaping have been a shot in the arm to downtown commerce* **boost,** tonic, stimulus, spur, impetus, encouragement. **a shot in the dark** *my answer was just a shot in the dark* (**wild**) **guess,** surmise, supposition, conjecture, speculation. **like a shot** informal *when they called his name he ran on to the stage like a shot* **without hesitation,** unhesitatingly, eagerly, enthusiastically; immediately, at once, right away/now, straightaway, instantly, instantaneously, without delay; informal in/like a flash. **not by a long shot** *he is not yet out of the woods, not by a long shot* **by no** (**manner of**) **means,** not at all, in no way, certainly not, absolutely not, definitely not.

shoulder ▶ verb **1** *he shouldered the burden* **take on** (**oneself**), undertake, accept, assume; bear, carry.
2 *another kid shouldered him aside* **push,** shove, thrust, jostle, force, bulldoze, elbow.
– PHRASES **give the cold shoulder** *ever since Deke's party, Linnie has been giving me the cold shoulder* **snub,** shun, ignore, rebuff, spurn, ostracize, cut out; informal freeze out. **put one's shoulder to the wheel** *it's time to stop talking and start putting your shoulder to the wheel* **get** (**down**) **to work,** apply oneself, set to work, buckle down, roll up one's sleeves; work hard, be diligent, be industrious, exert oneself. **shoulder to shoulder 1** *the regiment lined up shoulder to shoulder* **side by side,** abreast, alongside (each other). **2** *he fought shoulder to shoulder with the others* **united,** (working) together, jointly, in partnership, in collaboration, in cooperation, side by side, in alliance.

shout ▶ verb *"Help," he shouted* **yell,** cry (out), call (out), roar, howl, bellow, bawl, call at the top of one's voice, clamor, shriek, scream; raise one's voice, vociferate; informal holler.
ANTONYMS whisper.
▶ noun *a shout of pain* **yell,** cry, call, roar, howl, bellow, bawl, clamor, vociferation, shriek, scream; informal holler.

shove ▶ verb **1** *she shoved him back into the chair* **push,** thrust, propel, drive, force, ram, knock, elbow, shoulder; jostle, hustle, manhandle.
2 *she shoved past him* **push** (**one's way**), force one's way, barge (one's way), elbow (one's way), shoulder one's way.
▶ noun *a hefty shove* **push,** thrust, bump, jolt.
– PHRASES **shove off** informal *shove off, you little creep!* **go away,** get out (of my sight); get going, take oneself off, be off (with you), shoo; informal scram, make yourself scarce, be on your way, beat it, get lost, push off, buzz off, clear off, go (and) jump in the lake, bug off, take a hike; literary begone.

shovel ▶ noun *a pick and shovel* **spade.**
▶ verb *shoveling snow* **scoop** (**up**), dig, excavate.

show ▶ verb **1** *the stitches do not show* **be visible,** be seen, be in view, be obvious.
ANTONYMS be invisible.
2 *he wouldn't show the picture* **display,** exhibit, put on show/display, put on view, parade, uncover, reveal.
ANTONYMS conceal.
3 *Frank showed his frustration* **manifest,** exhibit, reveal, convey, communicate, make known; express, proclaim, make plain, make obvious, disclose, betray; formal evince.
ANTONYMS suppress.
4 *I'll show you how to make a daisy chain* **demonstrate to,** explain to, describe to,

illustrate to; teach, instruct, give instructions to.
5 *recent events show this to be true* **prove,** demonstrate, confirm, show beyond doubt; substantiate, corroborate, verify, establish, attest, certify, testify, bear out; formal evince.
6 *a young woman showed them to their seats* **escort,** accompany, take, conduct, lead, usher, guide, direct, steer, shepherd.
7 informal *they never showed* **appear,** arrive, come, get here/there, put in an appearance, materialize, turn up; informal show up.
▶ **noun 1** *a spectacular show of fireworks* **display,** array, exhibition, presentation, exposition, spectacle.
2 *the boat show* **exhibition,** exposition, fair, extravaganza, spectacle, exhibit.
3 *they took in a show* (**theatrical**) **performance,** musical, play, opera, ballet.
4 *she's only doing it for show* **appearance,** display, impression, ostentation, image.
5 *Drew made a show of looking busy* **pretense,** outward appearance, (false) front, guise, semblance, pose, parade.
6 informal *I don't run the show* **undertaking,** affair, operation, proceedings, enterprise, business, venture.
– PHRASES **show off** informal **1** *he likes to show off when we have company* **behave affectedly,** put on airs, put on an act, swagger around, swank, strut, strike an attitude, posture; draw attention to oneself; informal cop an attitude.
2 *that dress really shows off your green eyes* **display,** show to advantage, exhibit, demonstrate, parade, draw attention to, flaunt.
show up 1 *cancers show up on X-rays* **be visible,** be obvious, be seen, be revealed.
2 informal *only two waitresses showed up* See SHOW (sense 7 of the verb). **3** *the sun showed up the shabbiness of the room* **expose,** reveal, make visible, make obvious, highlight. **4** informal *they showed him up in front of his friends* See HUMILIATE.

showdown ▶ **noun** *his girlfriend got into a showdown with his ex-wife* **confrontation,** clash, face-off.

shower ▶ **noun 1** *a shower of rain* (**light**) **fall,** drizzle, sprinkling, misting.
2 *a shower of arrows* **volley,** hail, salvo, bombardment, barrage, fusillade, cannonade.
3 *a shower of awards* **avalanche,** deluge, flood, spate, flurry; profusion, abundance.
▶ **verb 1** *confetti showered down on us* **rain,** fall, hail.
2 *she showered them with gifts* **deluge,** flood, inundate, swamp, engulf; overwhelm, overload, snow under.
3 *showering praise on his cronies* **lavish,** heap, bestow freely.

showing ▶ **noun 1** *another showing of the series* **presentation,** broadcast, airing, televising, screening.
2 *the party's present showing* **performance,** (track) record, results, success, achievement.

show-off ▶ **noun** informal *no one minds that Amy's a show-off because she's just so funny* **exhibitionist,** extrovert, poser, poseur, peacock, swaggerer, self-publicist, braggart; informal showboat, blowhard, grandstander.

showy ▶ **adjective** *they spared no sequins or feathers in what may be the most showy finale ever seen on this stage* **ostentatious,** conspicuous, pretentious, flamboyant, gaudy, garish, brash, vulgar, loud, extravagant, fancy, ornate, overelaborate, kitsch, kitschy; pyrotechnical; informal flash, flashy, glitzy, ritzy, swanky, fancy-dancy, fancy-schmancy.
ANTONYMS restrained.

shred ▶ **noun 1** *her dress was torn to shreds* **tatter,** scrap, strip, ribbon, rag, fragment, sliver, (tiny) bit/piece.
2 *not a shred of evidence* **scrap,** bit, speck, iota, particle, ounce, whit, jot, crumb, morsel, fragment, grain, drop, trace, scintilla, spot; informal smidgen.
▶ **verb** *shredding vegetables* **chop finely,** cut up, tear up, grate, mince, macerate, grind.

shrew ▶ **noun** *my brother has just married a despicable shrew* **virago,** dragon, termagant, fishwife, witch, tartar, hag; informal battle-ax, old bag, old bat; archaic scold.

shrewd ▶ **adjective** *a shrewd businessman would never have been so careless about keeping appointments* **astute,** sharp-witted, sharp, smart, acute, intelligent, clever, canny, perceptive, perspicacious, sagacious, wise; informal on the ball, savvy, heads-up; formal sapient. See note at KEEN.
ANTONYMS stupid.

shrewdness ▶ **noun** *he was never known for his shrewdness, but we never thought he could be that stupid* **astuteness,** sharp-wittedness, acuteness, acumen, acuity, intelligence, cleverness, smartness, wit, canniness, common sense, discernment, insight, understanding, perception, perceptiveness, perspicacity, discrimination, sagacity, sageness; informal horse sense, savvy, (street) smarts; formal sapience.

shriek ▶ **verb** *she shrieked with fear* **scream,** screech, squeal, squawk, roar, howl, shout, yelp; informal holler.
▶ **noun** *a shriek of laughter* **scream,** screech, squeal, squawk, roar, howl, shout, yelp; informal holler.

shrill ▶ **adjective** *that shrill voice gives me a headache* **high-pitched,** piercing, high, sharp, ear-piercing, ear-splitting, penetrating, screeching, shrieking, screechy.

shrine ▶ **noun 1** *the shrine of St. James* **holy place,** temple, church, chapel, tabernacle, sanctuary, sanctum.
2 *a shrine to the Beatles* **memorial,** monument.

shrink ▶ **verb 1** *the number of competitors shrank* **get smaller,** become/grow smaller, contract, diminish, lessen, reduce, decrease, dwindle, decline, fall off, drop off.
ANTONYMS expand, increase.
2 *he **shrank back** against the wall* **draw back,** recoil, back away, retreat, withdraw, cringe, cower, quail.
3 *he doesn't **shrink from** naming names* **recoil from,** shy away from, demur from, flinch from, have scruples about, have misgivings about, have qualms about, be loath to, be reluctant to, be unwilling to, be averse to, fight shy of, be

hesitant to, be afraid to, hesitate to, balk at.

shrivel ▶ verb *the neglected plants shriveled in their pots* **wither,** shrink; wilt; dry up, desiccate, dehydrate, parch, frazzle.

shroud ▶ noun **1** *the shroud of Turin* **winding sheet;** historical cerements.
2 *a shroud of mist | a shroud of secrecy* **covering,** cover, cloak, mantle, blanket, layer, cloud, veil.
▶ verb *a mist shrouded the shore* **cover,** envelop, veil, cloak, blanket, screen, conceal, hide, mask, obscure; literary enshroud.

shrug ▶ verb
– PHRASES **shrug off** *he just shrugged off all of my advice* **disregard,** dismiss, take no notice of, ignore, pay no heed to, play down, make light of.

shudder ▶ verb *she shuddered at the thought* **shake,** shiver, tremble, quiver, vibrate, palpitate. See note at SHAKE.
▶ noun *a shudder racked his body* **shake,** shiver, tremor, tremble, trembling, quiver, quivering, vibration, palpitation, spasm.

shuffle ▶ verb **1** *they shuffled along the passage* **shamble,** drag one's feet, totter, dodder.
2 *she shuffled her feet* **scrape,** drag, scuffle, scuff.
3 *he shuffled the cards* **mix (up),** mingle, rearrange, jumble.

shun ▶ verb *he shunned publicity* **avoid,** evade, eschew, steer clear of, shy away from, fight shy of, keep one's distance from, give a wide berth to, have nothing to do with; snub, give someone the cold shoulder, cold-shoulder, ignore, look right through; reject, rebuff, spurn, ostracize; informal give someone the brush-off, freeze out, give someone the bum's rush, give someone the brush off.
ANTONYMS welcome.

shut ▶ verb *please shut the door* **close,** pull/push to, slam, fasten; put the lid on, bar, lock, secure.
ANTONYMS open, unlock.
– PHRASES **shut down** *the plant is shutting down in August* **cease activity,** close (down), cease operating, cease trading, be shut (down); turn off, switch off; informal fold; power down. **shut in** *shut the goats in for the night* **confine,** enclose, impound, shut up, pen (in/up), fence in, immure, lock up/in, cage, imprison, intern, incarcerate, corral. **shut out 1** *he shut me out of the house* **lock out,** keep out, refuse entrance to. **2** *she shut out the memories* **block,** suppress. **3** *the bamboo shut out the light* **keep out,** block out, screen, veil. **4** *they shut out the Blue Jays in three straight games* **prevent from scoring,** blank. **shut up 1** informal *will you please shut up so we can hear the movie?* **be quiet,** keep quiet, hold one's tongue, keep one's lips sealed; stop talking, quiet (down); informal keep mum, button it, hush up, shut it, shut your face/mouth/trap, put a sock in it, give it a rest, save it. **2** informal *that should shut them up* **quiet (down),** silence, hush, shush, gag, muzzle. **3** *I haven't shut the hens up yet* See SHUT IN above.

shuttle ▶ verb *they provided a bus to shuttle us to the mall* **ply,** run, commute, go/travel back and forth, go/travel to and fro; ferry.

shy ▶ adjective *I was painfully shy* **bashful,** diffident, farouche, timid, sheepish, reserved, reticent, introverted, retiring, self-effacing, withdrawn, timorous, mousy, nervous, insecure, unconfident, inhibited, repressed, self-conscious, embarrassed.
ANTONYMS confident.
– PHRASES **shy away from** *she shied away from success* **flinch at,** demur at, recoil at, hang back from, have scruples about, have misgivings about, have qualms about, be chary of, be diffident toward, be bashful about, fight shy of, balk at.

shyness ▶ noun *Gerald's shyness was often mistaken for disinterest* **bashfulness,** diffidence, sheepishness, reserve, reservedness, introversion, reticence, timidity, timidness, timorousness, mousiness, lack of confidence, self-consciousness, embarrassment, coyness, demureness.

sick ▶ adjective **1** *the children are sick* **ill,** unwell, poorly, ailing, indisposed, not oneself; off; informal laid up, under the weather.
ANTONYMS well, healthy.
2 *he was feeling sick* **nauseous,** nauseated, queasy, bilious, green around/at the gills; seasick, carsick, airsick, travel-sick; informal about to throw up.
3 informal *we're just sick about it* **disappointed,** depressed, dejected, despondent, downcast, unhappy; angry, cross, annoyed, displeased, disgruntled, fed up.
ANTONYMS glad.
4 *I'm sick of this music* **fed up with,** bored with, tired of, weary of.
ANTONYMS fond.
5 informal *a sick joke* **macabre,** black, ghoulish, morbid, perverted, gruesome, sadistic, cruel.
– PHRASES **be sick** *I'm going to be sick* **vomit,** throw up, retch, heave, gag; informal hurl, puke, spew, spit up, barf, upchuck, toss one's cookies.

sicken ▶ verb **1** *the stench sickened him* **cause to feel sick/nauseous,** make sick, turn someone's stomach, revolt, disgust; informal make someone want to throw up, gross out.
2 *she sickened and died* **become ill,** fall ill, be taken ill/sick, catch something.
ANTONYMS recover.

sickening ▶ adjective *ooh, that smell is sickening* **nauseating,** stomach-turning, stomach-churning, repulsive, revolting, disgusting, repellent, repugnant, appalling, obnoxious, nauseous, vile, nasty, foul, loathsome, offensive, objectionable, off-putting, distasteful, obscene, gruesome, grisly, vomitous; informal gross; formal rebarbative.

sickly ▶ adjective **1** *a sickly child* **unhealthy,** in poor health, delicate, frail, weak.
ANTONYMS healthy.
2 *sickly faces* **pale,** wan, pasty, sallow, pallid, ashen, anemic.
ANTONYMS rosy.
3 *a sickly green* **insipid,** pale, light, light-colored, washed out, faded.
ANTONYMS deep.
4 *sickly love songs* **sentimental,** mawkish, cloying, sugary, syrupy, saccharine; informal

mushy, slushy, schmaltzy, weepy, lovey-dovey, corny, cornball, sappy, hokey, three-hankie.

sickness ▶ noun **1** *she was absent because of sickness* **illness,** disease, ailment, complaint, infection, malady, infirmity, indisposition; informal bug, virus.
2 *a wave of sickness* **nausea,** biliousness, queasiness.
3 *he suffers this kind of sickness whenever we travel* **vomiting,** retching, gagging; travel-sickness, seasickness, carsickness, airsickness, motion sickness; informal throwing up, puking, barfing.

side ▶ noun **1** *they were standing on the side of the road* **edge,** border, verge, boundary, margin, fringe(s), flank, bank, perimeter, extremity, periphery, (outer) limit, limits, bounds; literary marge, bourn.
ANTONYMS center.
2 *you're driving on the wrong side of the road* **half,** part; lane.
3 *the east side of the city* **district,** quarter, area, region, part, neighborhood, sector, section, zone, ward.
4 *one side of the paper* **surface,** face, plane.
5 *his side of the argument* **point of view,** viewpoint, perspective, opinion, way of thinking, standpoint, position, outlook, slant, angle.
6 *the losing side in the war* **faction,** camp, bloc, party, wing.
7 *the players on their side* **team,** squad, lineup.
▶ adjective **1** *elaborate side pieces* **lateral,** wing, flanking.
ANTONYMS front.
2 *a side issue* **subordinate,** lesser, lower-level, secondary, minor, peripheral, incidental, ancillary, subsidiary, of little account, extraneous.
ANTONYMS central.
▶ verb *siding with the underdog* See TAKE SOMEONE'S SIDE below.
– PHRASES **side by side** *they worked side by side* **alongside (each other),** beside each other, abreast, shoulder to shoulder, close together; in collaboration, in solidarity. **take someone's side** *I was surprised to see you taking Jack's side* **support,** take someone's part, side with, be on someone's side, stand by, back, give someone one's backing, be loyal to, defend, champion, ally (oneself) with, sympathize with, favor.

sidelong ▶ adjective *a sidelong glance* **indirect,** oblique, sideways, sideward; surreptitious, furtive, covert, sly.
ANTONYMS overt.
▶ adverb *he looked sidelong at her* **indirectly,** obliquely, sideways, out of the corner of one's eye; surreptitiously, furtively, covertly, slyly.

sidestep ▶ verb *he neatly sidestepped the questions about crime* **avoid,** evade, dodge, circumvent, skirt around, bypass; informal duck, pussyfoot around.

sidetrack ▶ verb *I'm easily sidetracked by things going on outside my office window* **distract,** divert, deflect, draw away.

sideways ▶ adverb **1** *I slid off sideways* **to the side,** laterally.
2 *the expansion slots are mounted sideways* **edgewise,** sideward/sidewards, side first, edgeways, end on, broadside.
3 *he looked sideways at her* **obliquely,** indirectly, sidelong; covertly, furtively, surreptitiously, slyly.
▶ adjective **1** *sideways force* **lateral,** sideward, on the side, side to side.
2 *a sideways look* **oblique,** indirect, sidelong; covert, furtive, sly, surreptitious.

siege ▶ noun *the siege of the fort lasted into the morning* **blockade,** encirclement.
ANTONYMS relief.

siesta ▶ noun *he's enjoying a siesta on the terrace* **afternoon sleep,** nap, catnap, doze, rest; informal snooze, lie-down, forty winks, bit of shut-eye.

sieve ▶ noun *use a sieve to strain the mixture* **strainer,** sifter, filter, riddle, screen.
▶ verb **1** *sieve the mixture into a bowl* See SIFT (sense 1).
2 *the coins were sieved from the ash* **separate out,** filter out, sift, sort out, isolate, part, extract, remove.

sift ▶ verb **1** *sift the flour into a large bowl* **sieve,** strain, screen, filter, riddle; archaic bolt.
2 *we **sift out** unsuitable applications* **separate out,** filter out, sort out, put to one side, weed out, get rid of, remove.
3 *investigators are **sifting through** the wreckage* **search through,** look through, examine, inspect, scrutinize, pore over, investigate, analyze, dissect, review.

sigh ▶ verb **1** *she sighed with relief* **breathe out,** exhale; groan, moan.
2 *the wind sighed in the trees* **rustle,** whisper, murmur, sough.
3 *he **sighed for** younger days gone by* **yearn for,** long for, pine for, ache for, grieve for, cry for/over, weep for/over, rue, miss, mourn, lament, hanker for/after.

sight ▶ noun **1** *she has excellent sight* **eyesight,** vision, eyes, faculty of sight, visual perception.
2 *her first sight of it* **view,** glimpse, glance, look.
3 *within sight of the enemy* **range of vision,** field of vision, view.
4 dated *we are all equal in the sight of God* **perception,** judgment, belief, opinion, point of view, view, viewpoint, mind, perspective, standpoint.
5 *historic sights* **landmark,** place of interest, monument, spectacle, view, marvel, wonder.
6 informal *I must look a sight* **eyesore,** spectacle, mess; informal fright.
▶ verb *one of the helicopters sighted wreckage* **glimpse,** catch/get a glimpse of, catch sight of, see, spot, spy, notice, observe; literary espy, descry.
– PHRASES **catch sight of** *we caught sight of a dim flicker of light in the distance* **glimpse,** catch/get a glimpse of, see, spot, spy, make out, pick out, have sight of; literary espy, descry. **set one's sights on** *she set her sights on a teaching career* **aspire to,** aim at/for, try for, strive for/toward, work toward.

sign ▶ noun **1** *a sign of affection* **indication,** signal, symptom, pointer, suggestion, intimation, mark, manifestation, demonstration, token, evidence; literary sigil.
2 *a sign of things to come* **portent,** omen, warning, forewarning, augury, presage;

promise, threat.
3 *at his sign the soldiers followed* **gesture,** signal, wave, gesticulation, cue, nod.
4 *he read the sign on the wall* **notice,** signpost, signboard, warning sign, road sign, traffic sign, guidepost, marquee.
5 *the dancers were daubed with signs* **symbol,** mark, cipher, letter, character, figure, hieroglyph, ideogram, rune, emblem, device, logo. See note at EMBLEM.
▶ **verb 1** *he signed the letter* **write one's name on,** autograph, endorse, initial, countersign, ink; formal subscribe.
2 *the government signed the agreement* **endorse,** validate, certify, authenticate, sanction, authorize; agree to, approve, ratify, adopt, give one's approval to; informal give something the go-ahead, give something the green light, give something the thumbs up.
3 *he signed his name* **write,** inscribe, pen.
4 *we have signed a new player* **recruit,** hire, engage, employ, take on, appoint, sign on/up, enlist.
5 *she signed to Susan to leave* See SIGNAL[1] (sense 1 of the verb).
– PHRASES **sign on/up 1** *I signed up with Will's committee to raise money for the school library* **enlist,** take a job, join (up), enroll, register, volunteer. **2** *the Yankees have signed on a new right fielder* See SIGN (sense 4 of the verb). **sign over** *he signed over the business to his children* **transfer,** make over, hand over, bequeath, pass on, transmit, cede; Law devolve, convey.

CHOOSE THE RIGHT WORD

sign, augury, indication, manifestation, omen, signal, symptom, token

What's the difference between a **sign** and a **signal**? The former (in this sense) is a general term for anything that gives evidence of an event, a mood, a quality of character, a mental or physical state, or a trace of something (*a sign of approaching rain; a sign of good breeding; a sign that someone has entered the house*). While a *sign* may be involuntary or even unconscious, a *signal* is always voluntary and is usually deliberate. A ship that shows signs of distress may or may not be in trouble; but one that sends a distress *signal* is definitely in need of help. **Indication**, like *sign*, is a comprehensive term for anything that serves to indicate or point out (*he gave no indication that he was lying*). A **manifestation** is an outward or perceptible indication of something (*the letter was a manifestation of his guilt*), and a **symptom** is an indication of a diseased condition (*a symptom of pneumonia*). An object that proves the existence of something abstract is called a **token** (*she gave him a locket as a token of her love*). **Omen** and **augury** both pertain to foretelling future events, with *augury* being the general term for a prediction of the future and *omen* being a definite sign foretelling good or evil (*they regarded the stormy weather as a bad omen*).

signal[1] ▶ **noun 1** *a signal to stop* **gesture,** sign, wave, gesticulation, cue, indication, warning, motion.
2 *a clear signal that the company is in trouble* **indication,** sign, symptom, hint, pointer, intimation, clue, demonstration, evidence, proof. See note at SIGN.
3 *the encroaching dark is a signal for people to emerge* **cue,** prompt, impetus, stimulus; informal go-ahead.
▶ **verb 1** *the driver signaled to her to cross* **gesture,** sign, give a sign to, direct, motion; wave, beckon, nod.
2 *they signaled displeasure by refusing to cooperate* **indicate,** show, express, communicate, proclaim, declare.
3 *his death signals the end of an era* **mark,** signify, mean, be a sign of, be evidence of, herald; literary betoken, foretoken.

signal[2] ▶ **adjective** *a signal victory* See SIGNIFICANT (sense 1).

significance ▶ **noun 1** *a matter of considerable significance* **importance,** import, consequence, seriousness, gravity, weight, magnitude, momentousness; formal moment.
2 *the significance of his remarks* **meaning,** sense, signification, import, thrust, drift, gist, implication, message, essence, substance, point.

significant ▶ **adjective 1** *a significant increase* **notable,** noteworthy, worthy of attention, remarkable, important, of importance, of consequence, signal; serious, crucial, weighty, momentous, epoch-making, uncommon, unusual, rare, extraordinary, exceptional, special; formal of moment.
2 *a significant look* **meaningful,** expressive, eloquent, suggestive, knowing, telling.

signify ▶ **verb 1** *this signified a fundamental change* **be evidence of,** be a sign of, mark, signal, mean, spell, be symptomatic of, herald, indicate; literary betoken.
2 *the egg signifies life* **mean,** denote, designate, represent, symbolize, stand for; literary betoken.
3 *signify your agreement by signing below* **express,** indicate, show, proclaim, declare.
4 *the locked door doesn't signify* **mean anything,** be of importance, be important, be significant, be of significance, be of account, count, matter, be relevant.

silence ▶ **noun 1** *the silence of the night* **quietness,** quiet, quietude, still, stillness, hush, tranquility, noiselessness, soundlessness, peacefulness, peace (and quiet).
ANTONYMS sound.
2 *she was reduced to silence* **speechlessness,** wordlessness, dumbness, muteness, taciturnity.
ANTONYMS speech, loquacity.
3 *the politicians kept their silence* **secretiveness,** secrecy, reticence, taciturnity, uncommunicativeness.
ANTONYMS communicativeness.
▶ **verb 1** *he silenced her with a kiss* **quiet,** hush, shush; gag, muzzle, censor.
2 *silencing outside noises* **muffle,** deaden,

soften, mute, smother, dampen, damp down, mask, suppress, reduce.
3 *this would silence their complaints* **stop,** put an end to, put a stop to.

silent ▶ adjective **1** *the night was silent* **completely quiet,** still, hushed, inaudible, noiseless, soundless.
ANTONYMS audible, noisy.
2 *the right to remain silent* **speechless,** quiet, unspeaking, dumb, mute, taciturn, uncommunicative, tight-lipped; informal mum.
ANTONYMS loquacious.
3 *silent thanks* **unspoken,** wordless, unsaid, unexpressed, unvoiced, tacit, implicit, understood.
ANTONYMS spoken.

silhouette ▶ noun *the silhouette of the dome* **outline,** contour(s), profile, form, shape, figure, shadow.
▶ verb *the castle was silhouetted against the sky* **outline,** delineate, define; stand out.

silky ▶ adjective *her long, silky hair* **smooth,** soft, sleek, fine, glossy, satiny, silken.

silly ▶ adjective **1** *don't be so silly* **foolish,** stupid, unintelligent, idiotic, brainless, mindless, witless, imbecilic, doltish; imprudent, thoughtless, rash, reckless, foolhardy, irresponsible; mad, scatterbrained, featherbrained; frivolous, giddy, inane, immature, childish, puerile, empty-headed; informal crazy, dotty, scatty, loopy, wingy, ditzy, screwy, thick, thickheaded, birdbrained, pea-brained, dopey, dim, dimwitted, halfwitted, dippy, blockheaded, boneheaded, lamebrained; daft, chowderheaded; dated tomfool.
ANTONYMS sensible.
2 *that was a silly thing to do* **unwise,** imprudent, thoughtless, foolish, stupid, idiotic, senseless, mindless; rash, reckless, foolhardy, irresponsible, injudicious, misguided, irrational; informal crazy; daft.
ANTONYMS sensible.
3 *he would brood about silly things* **trivial,** trifling, frivolous, footling, petty, small, insignificant, unimportant; informal piffling, piddling, small-bore.
ANTONYMS important.
4 *he drank himself silly* **senseless,** insensible, unconscious, stupid, into a stupor, into senselessness, stupefied.
▶ noun informal *you're such a silly!* See FOOL (sense 1 of the noun).

similar ▶ adjective **1** *you two are very similar* **alike,** (much) the same, indistinguishable, almost identical, homogeneous, homologous; informal much of a muchness.
ANTONYMS different.
2 *northern India and similar areas* **comparable,** like, corresponding, homogeneous, equivalent, analogous.
– PHRASES **be similar to** *other towns were similar to this one* **be like, resemble,** look like, have the appearance of, be much the same as, be comparable to.

similarity ▶ noun *the similarity between John and his daughter* **resemblance,** likeness, sameness, similitude, comparability, correspondence, parallel, equivalence, homogeneity, indistinguishability, uniformity; archaic semblance. See note at LIKENESS.

similarly ▶ adverb *the two vases are similarly flawed at the base* **likewise,** in similar fashion, in like manner, comparably, correspondingly, uniformly, indistinguishably, analogously, homogeneously, equivalently, in the same way, the same, identically.

similitude ▶ noun *Conrad uses a range of constructions that imply similitude* **resemblance,** similarity, likeness, sameness, similar nature, comparability, correspondence, comparison, analogy, parallel, parallelism, equivalence; interchangeability, closeness, nearness, affinity, homogeneity, agreement, indistinguishability, uniformity; community, kinship, relatedness; archaic semblance. See note at LIKENESS.

simmer ▶ verb **1** *the soup was simmering on the stove* **boil gently,** cook gently, bubble, stew.
2 *she was simmering with resentment* **be furious,** be enraged, be angry, be incensed, be infuriated, seethe, fume, brim, smolder; informal be steamed up, be hot under the collar, stew.
– PHRASES **simmer down** *we're not going to discuss this until you simmer down* **become less angry,** cool off/down, be placated, control oneself, become calmer, calm down, become quieter, quiet down; informal chill out, take a chill pill.

simple ▶ adjective **1** *it's really simple* **straightforward,** easy, uncomplicated, uninvolved, effortless, painless, undemanding, elementary, child's play; informal as easy as pie, as easy as ABC, a piece of cake, a cinch, no sweat, a pushover, kids' stuff, a breeze, duck soup, a snap.
ANTONYMS difficult, hard, complicated.
2 *simple language* **clear,** plain, straightforward, intelligible, comprehensible, uncomplicated, accessible; informal user-friendly.
ANTONYMS complex.
3 *a simple white blouse* **plain,** unadorned, undecorated, unembellished, unornamented, unelaborate, basic, unsophisticated, no-frills; classic, understated, uncluttered, restrained.
ANTONYMS fancy, elaborate.
4 *the simple truth* **candid,** frank, honest, sincere, plain, absolute, unqualified, bald, stark, unadorned, unvarnished, unembellished.
5 *simple country people* **unpretentious,** unsophisticated, ordinary, unaffected, unassuming, natural, honest-to-goodness, cracker-barrel.
ANTONYMS pretentious, affected.
6 *he's a bit simple* **having learning difficulties,** having special (educational) needs; of low intelligence, simpleminded, unintelligent, backward, (mentally) retarded.
ANTONYMS gifted.
7 *simple chemical substances* **noncompound,** noncomplex, uncombined, unblended, unalloyed, pure, single.
ANTONYMS compound.

simpleton ▶ noun See FOOL (sense 1 of the noun).

simplicity ▶ noun **1** *the simplicity of the*

recipes **straightforwardness,** ease, easiness, simpleness, effortlessness.
2 *the simplicity of the language* **clarity,** clearness, plainness, simpleness, intelligibility, comprehensibility, understandability, accessibility, straightforwardness.
3 *the building's simplicity* **plainness,** lack/absence of adornment, lack/absence of decoration, austerity, spareness, clean lines.
4 *the simplicity of their lifestyle* **unpretentiousness,** ordinariness, lack of sophistication, lack of affectation, naturalness.

simplify ▶ verb *please simplify your answer* **make simple/simpler,** make easy/easier to understand, make plainer, clarify, make more comprehensible/intelligible; paraphrase.
ANTONYMS complicate.

simplistic ▶ adjective *the proposed solutions are too simplistic* **facile,** superficial, oversimple, oversimplified; shallow, jejune, naive.

simply ▶ adverb **1** *he spoke simply and forcefully* **straightforwardly,** directly, clearly, plainly, intelligibly, lucidly, unambiguously.
2 *she was dressed simply* **plainly,** without adornment, without decoration, without ornament/ornamentation, soberly, unfussily, unelaborately, classically.
3 *they lived simply* **unpretentiously,** modestly, quietly.
4 *they are welcomed simply because they have plenty of money* **merely,** just, purely, solely, only.
5 *Mrs. Marks was simply livid* **utterly,** absolutely, completely, positively, really; informal plain.
6 *it's simply the best thing ever written* **without doubt,** unquestionably, undeniably, incontrovertibly, certainly, categorically.

simulate ▶ verb **1** *they simulated pleasure* **feign,** pretend, fake, sham, affect, put on, give the appearance of.
2 *simulating conditions in space* **imitate,** reproduce, replicate, duplicate, mimic.

simultaneous ▶ adjective *they carried out simultaneous raids at two houses* **concurrent,** happening at the same time, contemporaneous, concomitant, coinciding, coincident, synchronous, synchronized.

simultaneously ▶ adverb *Alison and Frank spoke simultaneously* **at (one and) the same time,** at the same instant/moment, at once, concurrently, concomitantly; (all) together, in unison, in concert, in chorus.

sin ▶ noun **1** *a sin in the eyes of God* **immoral act,** wrong, wrongdoing, act of evil/wickedness, transgression, crime, offense, misdeed, misdemeanor; archaic trespass.
2 *the human capacity for sin* **wickedness,** wrongdoing, wrong, evil, evildoing, sinfulness, immorality, iniquity, vice, crime.
ANTONYMS virtue.
3 informal *they've cut the school music program—it's a sin* **scandal,** crime, disgrace, outrage.
▶ verb *I have sinned* **commit a sin,** commit an offense, transgress, do wrong, commit a crime, break the law, misbehave, go astray; archaic trespass.

CHOOSE THE RIGHT WORD

sin, crime, fault, indiscretion, offense, transgression, vice

If you've ever driven through a red light or chewed with your mouth open, you've committed an **offense**, which is a broad term covering any violation of the law or of standards of propriety and taste. A **sin**, on the other hand, is an act that specifically violates a religious, ethical, or moral standard (*to marry someone of another faith was considered a sin*). **Transgression** is a weightier and more serious word for *sin*, suggesting any violation of an agreed-upon set of rules (*their behavior was clearly a transgression of the terms set forth in the treaty*). A **crime** is any act forbidden by law and punishable upon conviction (*a crime for which he was sentenced to death*). A **vice** has less to do with violating the law and more to do with habits and practices that debase a person's character (*alcohol was her only vice*). **Fault** and **indiscretion** are gentler words, although they may be used as euphemisms for *sin* or *crime*. A *fault* is an unsatisfactory feature in someone's character (*she is exuberant to a fault*), while *indiscretion* refers to an unwise or improper action (*speaking to the media was an indiscretion for which she was chastised*). In recent years, however, *indiscretion* has become a euphemism for such sins as adultery, as if to excuse such behavior by attributing it to a momentary lapse of judgment (*his indiscretions were no secret*).

sincere ▶ adjective **1** *our sincere gratitude* **heartfelt,** wholehearted, profound, deep; genuine, real, unfeigned, unaffected, true, honest, bona fide.
2 *a sincere person* **honest,** genuine, truthful, unhypocritical, straightforward, direct, frank, candid; informal straight, upfront, on the level, on the up and up.

sincerely ▶ adverb *we sincerely hope you'll be better soon* **genuinely,** honestly, really, truly, truthfully, wholeheartedly, earnestly, fervently.

sincerity ▶ noun *there's no reason to doubt her sincerity* **honesty,** genuineness, truthfulness, integrity, probity, trustworthiness; straightforwardness, openness, candor, candidness.

sinewy ▶ adjective *he was tall, blond, and sinewy* **muscular,** muscly, brawny, powerfully built, burly, strapping, sturdy, rugged, strong, powerful, athletic, muscle-bound, hard-bodied; informal hunky, beefy; dated stalwart; literary thewy.
ANTONYMS puny.

sinful ▶ adjective **1** *sinful conduct* **immoral,** wicked, (morally) wrong, wrongful, evil, bad, iniquitous, corrupt, criminal, nefarious, depraved, degenerate.
ANTONYMS virtuous.
2 *a sinful waste of money* **reprehensible,** scandalous, disgraceful, deplorable, shameful, criminal.

ANTONYMS admirable.

sing ▶ **verb 1** *the choir began to sing* croon, carol, trill, chant, intone, chorus; informal belt out.
2 *the birds were singing* **warble,** trill, chirp, chirrup, cheep, peep.
3 *Rudy* ***sang out*** *a greeting* **call (out),** cry (out), shout, yell; informal holler.
4 informal *he's going to sing to the police* **inform (on someone),** confess; informal squeal, rat on someone, blow the whistle on someone, snitch (on someone), narc (on someone), finger someone, fink on someone.

singe ▶ **verb** *the ends of my hair were singed when I leaned over the candle* **scorch,** burn, sear, char. See note at **BURN**.

singer ▶ **noun** *she's the lead singer* **vocalist,** soloist, songster, songstress, cantor, chorister, cantor; informal songbird, siren, diva, chanteuse, chansonnier; literary troubadour, minstrel.

single ▶ **adjective 1** *a single red rose* **one (only),** sole, lone, solitary, by itself/oneself, unaccompanied, alone.
ANTONYMS double.
2 *she wrote down every single word* **individual,** separate, distinct, particular, last.
3 *is she single?* **unmarried,** unwed, unwedded, unattached, free, a bachelor, a spinster; partnerless, husbandless, wifeless; separated, divorced, widowed; informal solo.
ANTONYMS married.
– PHRASES **single out** *her watercolors were singled out by the judges* **select,** pick out, choose, decide on; target, earmark, mark out, separate out, set apart/aside.

single-handed ▶ **adverb** *I installed the alarm single-handed* **by oneself,** alone, on one's own, solo, unaided, unassisted, without help.

single-minded ▶ **adjective** *I got where I am with hard work and single-minded determination* **determined,** committed, unswerving, unwavering, resolute, purposeful, devoted, dedicated, uncompromising, tireless, tenacious, persistent, indefatigable, dogged; formal pertinacious.
ANTONYMS halfhearted.

singly ▶ **adverb** *people, please enter singly into the hallway* **one by one,** one at a time, one after the other, individually, separately, by oneself, on one's own.
ANTONYMS together.

singular ▶ **adjective 1** *the gallery's singular capacity to attract sponsors* **remarkable,** extraordinary, exceptional, outstanding, signal, notable, noteworthy; rare, unique, unparalleled, unprecedented, amazing, astonishing, phenomenal, astounding; informal fantastic, terrific.
2 *why was Betty behaving in so singular a fashion?* **strange,** unusual, odd, peculiar, funny, curious, extraordinary, bizarre, eccentric, weird, queer, unexpected, unfamiliar, abnormal, atypical, unconventional, out of the ordinary, untypical, puzzling, mysterious, perplexing, baffling, unaccountable.

sinister ▶ **adjective 1** *there was a sinister undertone in his words* **menacing,** threatening, ominous, forbidding, baleful, frightening, alarming, disturbing, disquieting, dark, black; formal minatory; literary direful.
2 *a sinister motive* **evil,** wicked, criminal, corrupt, nefarious, villainous, base, vile, malevolent, malicious; informal shady.
ANTONYMS innocent.

sink ▶ **verb 1** *the coffin sank below the waves* **become submerged,** be engulfed, go down, drop, fall, descend.
ANTONYMS float, rise.
2 *the cruise liner sank yesterday* **founder,** go under, submerge.
3 *they sank their ships* **scuttle,** send to the bottom; scupper.
4 *the announcement sank hopes of a recovery* **destroy,** ruin, wreck, put an end to, demolish, smash, shatter, dash; informal put the kibosh on, put paid to; informal scupper; archaic bring to naught.
5 *I sank myself in student life* **immerse,** submerge, plunge, lose, bury.
6 *the plane sank toward the airstrip* **descend,** drop, go down/downward.
ANTONYMS ascend.
7 *the sun was sinking* **set,** go down/downward.
ANTONYMS rise.
8 *Loretta sank into an armchair* **lower oneself,** flop, collapse, fall, drop down, slump; informal plunk oneself.
9 *her voice sank to a whisper* **fall,** drop, become/get quieter, become/get softer.
ANTONYMS rise.
10 *she would never sink to your level* **stoop,** lower oneself, descend.
11 *he was sinking fast* **deteriorate,** decline, fade, grow weak, flag, waste away; be at death's door, be on one's deathbed, be slipping away; informal go downhill, be on one's last legs, be giving up the ghost.
ANTONYMS recover, improve.
12 *sink the pots into the ground* **embed,** insert, drive, plant.
13 *sinking a gold mine* **dig,** excavate, bore, drill.
14 *they sank their life savings into the company* **invest,** venture, risk.
▶ **noun** *he washed himself at the sink* **basin,** wash basin; dated lavabo.
– PHRASES **sink in** *bad news like this often takes time to sink in* **register,** be understood, be comprehended, be grasped, get through.

sinner ▶ **noun** *on a mission to rescue these sinners from the darkness* **wrongdoer,** evildoer, transgressor, miscreant, offender, criminal; archaic trespasser.

sinuous ▶ **adjective 1** *a sinuous river* **winding,** windy, serpentine, curving, twisting, meandering, snaking, zigzag, curling, coiling.
2 *she moved with sinuous grace* **lithe,** supple, agile, graceful, loose-limbed, limber, lissome.

sip ▶ **verb** *Amanda sipped her coffee* **drink (slowly).**
▶ **noun** *a sip of whiskey* **mouthful,** swallow, drink, drop, dram, nip, taste; informal swig.

siren ▶ **noun 1** *a fire engine's siren* **alarm (bell),** warning bell, danger signal; archaic tocsin.
2 *the siren's allure* **seductress,** temptress, tease, femme fatale; flirt, coquette; informal man-eater, home wrecker, vamp.

sit ▶ verb **1** *here, sit on the comfy chair* **take a seat,** seat oneself, be seated, perch, ensconce oneself, plump oneself, flop; informal take the load/weight off one's feet, plunk oneself, take a load off.
ANTONYMS stand.
2 *she sat the package on the table* **put** (**down**), place, set (down), lay, deposit, rest, stand; informal stick, dump, park, plunk.
ANTONYMS lift.
3 *the church sat about 3,000 people* **hold,** seat, have seats for, have space/room for, accommodate.
4 *she sat for Picasso* **pose,** model.
5 *a hotel sitting on the mountain* **be situated,** be located, be sited, stand.
6 *the committee sits on Saturday* **be in session,** meet, be convened.
7 *women jurists* ***sit on*** *the tribunal* **serve on,** have a seat on, be a member of.
8 *his shyness doesn't sit easily with Hollywood tradition* **be harmonious,** go, fit in, harmonize.
9 *Mrs. Hillman will sit for us* **babysit.**
– PHRASES **sit back** *sit back and listen to the music* **relax,** unwind, lie back; informal let it all hang out, veg out, hang loose, chill (out), take a load off. **sit in for** *I'll be sitting in for Tim while he's away* **stand in for,** fill in for, cover for, substitute for; informal sub for. **sit in on** *you're welcome to sit in on any of your son's classes* **attend,** be present at, be an observer at, observe, audit. **sit tight** informal **1** *just sit tight while I call your parents* **stay put,** wait there, remain in one's place. **2** *we're advising our clients to sit tight* **take no action,** wait, hold back, bide one's time; informal hold one's horses.

site ▶ noun *the site of the battle* **location,** place, position, situation, locality, whereabouts; technical locus.
▶ verb *garbage cans sited along the street* **place,** put, position, situate, locate.

situate ▶ verb *the library is situated just west of the town hall* **locate,** site, position, place, station, build.

situation ▶ noun **1** *their financial situation* **circumstances,** (state of) affairs, state, condition.
2 *I'll fill you in on* ***the situation*** **the facts,** how things stand, the lay of the land, what's going on; informal the score, the scoop.
3 *the hotel's pleasant situation* **location,** position, spot, site, setting, environment; technical locus.
4 *he was offered a situation in Canada* **job,** post, position, appointment; employment.

size ▶ noun *the room was of medium size* **dimensions,** measurements, proportions, magnitude, largeness, bigness, area, expanse; breadth, width, length, height, depth; immensity, hugeness, vastness.
▶ verb *the drills are sized in millimeters* **sort,** categorize, classify.
– PHRASES **size up** informal *having sized up the competition, I knew I would win* **assess,** appraise, form an estimate of, take the measure of, judge, take stock of, evaluate.

skeleton ▶ noun **1** *the human skeleton* **bones.**
2 *she was no more than a skeleton* **skin and bone**; informal bag of bones.
3 *a concrete skeleton* **framework,** frame, shell.
4 *the skeleton of a report* **outline,** (rough) draft, abstract, (bare) bones.
▶ adjective *a skeleton staff* **minimum,** minimal, basic; essential.

skeptic ▶ noun **1** *skeptics said the marriage wouldn't last* **cynic,** doubter; pessimist, prophet of doom.
2 *skeptics who have found faith* **agnostic,** atheist, unbeliever, nonbeliever, disbeliever, doubting Thomas.

skeptical ▶ adjective *she was wisely skeptical about his get-rich-quick scheme* **dubious,** doubtful, taking something with a pinch of salt, doubting; cynical, distrustful, mistrustful, suspicious, disbelieving, unconvinced, incredulous, scoffing; pessimistic, defeatist.
ANTONYMS certain, convinced.

skepticism ▶ noun **1** *his ideas were met with skepticism* **doubt,** doubtfulness, a pinch of salt; disbelief, cynicism, distrust, mistrust, suspicion, incredulity; pessimism, defeatism; formal dubiety. See note at **UNCERTAINTY.**
2 *he passed from skepticism to religious belief* **agnosticism,** doubt; atheism, unbelief, nonbelief.

sketch ▶ noun **1** *a sketch of the proposed design* (**preliminary**) **drawing,** outline; diagram, design, plan; informal rough.
2 *she gave a rough sketch of what had happened* **outline,** brief description, rundown, main points, thumbnail sketch, (bare) bones; summary, synopsis, summarization, précis, résumé, wrap-up.
3 *a biographical sketch* **description,** portrait, profile, portrayal, depiction.
4 *a hilarious sketch* **skit,** scene, piece, act, item, routine.
▶ verb **1** *he sketched the garden* **draw,** make a drawing of, draw a picture of, pencil, rough out, outline.
2 *the company* ***sketched out*** *its plans* **describe,** outline, give a brief idea of, rough out; summarize, précis.

sketchy ▶ adjective *we have only a sketchy description of the assailant* **incomplete,** patchy, fragmentary, cursory, perfunctory, scanty, vague, imprecise, imperfect; hurried, hasty.
ANTONYMS detailed.

skill ▶ noun **1** *his skill as a politician* **expertise,** skillfulness, expertness, adeptness, adroitness, deftness, dexterity, ability, prowess, mastery, competence, capability, aptitude, artistry, virtuosity, talent.
ANTONYMS incompetence.
2 *bringing up a family gives you many skills* **accomplishment,** strength, gift.

skilled ▶ adjective *a skilled architect* **experienced,** trained, qualified, credentialed, proficient, practiced, accomplished, expert, skillful, talented, gifted, adept, adroit, deft, dexterous, able, good, competent; informal crack, crackerjack.
ANTONYMS inexperienced.

skillful ▶ adjective *the work of a skillful shoemaker* **expert,** accomplished, skilled, masterly, master, virtuoso, consummate, proficient, talented, gifted, adept, adroit, deft, dexterous, able, good, competent, capable, brilliant, handy; informal mean, wicked, crack, ace, wizard, crackerjack, pro.

skim ▶ verb 1 *skim off the scum* **remove,** cream off, scoop off.
2 *the boat skimmed over the water* **glide,** move lightly, slide, sail, skate, float.
3 *he skimmed the pebble across the water* **throw,** toss, cast, pitch; bounce.
4 *she* ***skimmed through*** *the newspaper* **glance through,** flick through, flip through, leaf through, riffle through, thumb through, read quickly, scan, run one's eye over.
5 *Hannah* ***skimmed over*** *this part of the story* **mention briefly,** pass over quickly, skate over, gloss over.
ANTONYMS elaborate on.

skimp ▶ verb 1 *don't* ***skimp on*** *the quantity* **stint on,** scrimp on, economize on, cut back on, be sparing with, be frugal with, be mean with, be parsimonious with, cut corners with; informal be stingy with, be mingy with, be tight with.
2 *the process cannot be skimped* **do hastily,** do carelessly.

skimpy ▶ adjective 1 *a skimpy black dress* **revealing,** short, low, low-cut; flimsy, thin, see-through, indecent.
2 *my information is rather skimpy* **meager,** scanty, sketchy, limited, paltry, deficient, sparse.

skin ▶ noun 1 *these chemicals could damage the skin* **epidermis,** dermis, derma.
2 *Mary's fair skin* **complexion,** coloring, skin color/tone, pigmentation.
3 *leopard skins* **hide,** pelt, fleece; historical plew; archaic fell.
4 *a banana skin* **peel,** rind, integument.
5 *milk with a skin on it* **film,** layer, membrane.
6 *the plane's skin was damaged* **casing,** exterior.
▶ verb 1 *skin the tomatoes* **peel,** pare, hull; technical decorticate.
2 *he skinned his knee* **graze,** scrape, abrade, bark, rub raw, chafe; Medicine excoriate.
– PHRASES **by the skin of one's teeth** *he won, but only by the skin of his teeth* **(only) just,** narrowly, barely, by a hair's breadth, by a very small margin; informal by a whisker. **get under someone's skin** informal 1 *the children really got under my skin* See IRRITATE (sense 1).
2 *she got under my skin* **obsess,** intrigue, captivate, charm; enthrall, enchant, entrance. **it's no skin off my nose** informal *if you want to go swimming in that icy water, it's no skin off my nose* **I don't care,** I don't mind, I'm not bothered, it doesn't bother me, it doesn't matter to me; informal I don't give a damn, I couldn't/could care less. **skin alive** informal *Dad would skin me alive if I forgot it* **punish severely**; informal murder, come down on (like a ton of bricks), give what for.

skinflint ▶ noun informal *Jodie has the charisma needed to pry those dollar bills from these skinflints' fists* **miser,** penny-pincher, Scrooge, pinchpenny; informal money-grubber, cheapskate, tightwad, piker.

skinny ▶ adjective *his extreme height made him look especially skinny* **thin,** scrawny, scraggy, bony, angular, rawboned, hollow-cheeked, gaunt, as thin as a rake, skin-and-bones, sticklike, emaciated, waiflike, skeletal, pinched, undernourished, underfed; **slim,** lean, slender, rangy; lanky, spindly, gangly, gangling, gawky; informal looking like a bag of bones, anorexic; dated spindle-shanked. See note at THIN.
▶ noun informal *everybody wants to know the skinny on Karen's divorce* **gossip,** (inside) information, intelligence, news, inside story; informal lowdown, info, dope, dirt, scoop, poop.

skip ▶ verb 1 *skipping down the path* **caper,** prance, trip, dance, bound, bounce, gambol, frisk, romp, cavort.
2 *we skipped the boring stuff* **omit,** leave out, miss out, dispense with, pass over, skim over, disregard; informal give something a miss.
3 *I skipped school* **play truant from,** miss, cut; informal play hooky from, ditch.
4 informal *they* ***skipped off*** *again | first chance I get, I'm* ***skipping out*** **run off/away,** take off; informal beat it, clear off, cut and run, light out, cut out.

skirmish ▶ noun 1 *the unit was caught up in a skirmish* **fight,** battle, clash, conflict, encounter, engagement, fray, combat.
2 *there was a skirmish over the budget* **argument,** quarrel, squabble, contretemps, disagreement, difference of opinion, falling-out, dispute, blowup, clash, altercation; informal tiff, spat; row.
▶ verb *they skirmished with enemy soldiers* **fight,** (do) battle with, engage with, close with, combat, clash with.

skirt ▶ verb 1 *he skirted the city* **go around,** walk around, circle.
2 *the fields that skirt the highway* **border,** edge, flank, line, lie alongside.
3 *he carefully skirted the subject* **avoid,** evade, sidestep, dodge, pass over, gloss over; informal duck.

skit ▶ noun *we auditioned by acting out our own three-minute skits* **comedy sketch,** comedy act, parody, pastiche, burlesque, satire; informal spoof, takeoff, sendup.

skittish ▶ adjective *going to the dentist makes me skittish* **nervous,** anxious, on edge, excitable, restive, skittery, jumpy, jittery, high-strung.

skulk ▶ verb *you're right, I think someone is skulking around behind those cars* **lurk,** loiter, hide; creep, sneak, slink, prowl, pussyfoot.

sky ▶ noun *the sun was shining in the sky* the upper atmosphere; literary the heavens, the firmament, the blue, the (wide) blue yonder, the welkin, the azure, the empyrean.
– PHRASES **to the skies** *he praised Lizzie to the skies* **effusively,** profusely, very highly, very enthusiastically, unreservedly, fervently, fulsomely, extravagantly.

slab ▶ noun *slabs of concrete* **piece,** block, hunk, chunk, lump; cake, tablet, brick.

slack ▶ adjective 1 *the rope went slack* **loose,** limp, hanging, flexible.
ANTONYMS tight, taut.
2 *slack skin* **flaccid,** flabby, loose, sagging, saggy.
ANTONYMS taut.
3 *business is slack* **sluggish,** slow, quiet, slow-

moving, flat, depressed, stagnant.
ANTONYMS thriving, busy.
4 *slack accounting procedures* **lax,** negligent, remiss, careless, slapdash, slipshod, lackadaisical, inefficient, casual; informal sloppy, slaphappy.
ANTONYMS diligent.
▶ **noun 1** *the rope had some slack in it* **looseness,** play, give.
2 *foreign demand will help pick up the slack* **surplus,** excess, residue, spare capacity.
3 *a little slack in the daily routine* **lull,** pause, respite, break, hiatus, breathing space; informal letup, breather.
▶ **verb** informal *no slacking!* **idle,** shirk, be lazy, be indolent, waste time, lounge about; informal goof off.
– PHRASES **slack off 1** *the rain has slacked off* **decrease,** subside, let up, ease off, abate, diminish, die down, fall off. **2** *you deserve to slack off a bit* **relax,** take things easy, let up, ease up/off, loosen up, slow down; informal hang loose, chill (out). **slack up** *he doesn't slack up until he gets there* **slow (down),** decelerate, reduce speed.

slacker ▶ **noun** informal *all right, you slackers, let's get this cargo across the river before the sun sets* **layabout,** idler, shirker, malingerer, sluggard, laggard; informal lazybones, bum, goof-off.

slake ▶ **verb** *we longed for a mountain spring to slake our thirst* **quench,** satisfy, sate, satiate, relieve, assuage.

slam ▶ **verb 1** *he slammed the door behind him* **bang,** shut/close with a bang, shut/close noisily, shut/close with force.
2 *the car **slammed into** a post* **crash into,** smash into, collide with, hit, strike, ram, plow into, run into, bump into, impact.
3 informal *he was slammed by the critics* See CRITICIZE.

slander ▶ **noun** *he could sue us for slander* **defamation (of character),** character assassination, calumny, libel; scandalmongering, malicious gossip, disparagement, denigration, aspersions, vilification, traducement, obloquy; lie, slur, smear, false accusation; informal mudslinging, bad-mouthing; archaic contumely.
▶ **verb** *they were accused of slandering the minister* **defame (someone's character),** blacken someone's name, tell lies about, speak ill/evil of, sully someone's reputation, libel, smear, cast aspersions on, spread scandal about, besmirch, tarnish, taint; malign, traduce, vilify, disparage, denigrate, run down, slur; informal badmouth, dis, trash; formal derogate. See note at MALIGN.

slanderous ▶ **adjective** *slanderous accusations* **defamatory,** denigratory, disparaging, libelous, pejorative, false, misrepresentative, scurrilous, scandalous, malicious, abusive, insulting; informal mudslinging.
ANTONYMS complimentary.

slang ▶ **noun** *the street slang was a bit rough for his uptown ears* **informal language,** colloquialisms, patois, argot, cant, jargon. See note at DIALECT.

slant ▶ **verb 1** *the floor was slanting* **slope,** tilt, incline, be at an angle, tip, cant, lean, dip, pitch, shelve, list, bank.
2 *their findings were slanted in our favor* **bias,** distort, twist, skew, weight, give a bias to.
▶ **noun 1** *the slant of the roof* **slope,** incline, tilt, gradient, pitch, angle, cant, camber, inclination.
2 *a feminist slant* **point of view,** viewpoint, standpoint, stance, angle, perspective, approach, view, attitude, position; bias, leaning.

slanting ▶ **adjective** *the slanting angle of the deck* **oblique,** sloping, at an angle, on an incline, inclined, tilting, tilted, slanted, aslant, diagonal, canted, cambered.

slap ▶ **verb 1** *he slapped her hard* **hit,** strike, smack, clout, cuff, thump, punch, spank; informal whack, thwack, wallop, bash, bop, slug, bust; archaic smite.
2 *he slapped down a $10 bill* **fling,** throw, toss, slam, bang; informal plunk.
3 *slap on a coat of paint* **daub,** plaster, spread.
4 informal *they slapped a huge tax on imports* **impose,** levy, put.
▶ **noun** *a slap across the cheek* **smack,** blow, thump, cuff, clout, punch, spank; informal whack, thwack, wallop, clip, bash.
– PHRASES **a slap in the face** *your disloyalty was a brutal slap in the face* **rebuff,** rejection, snub, insult, put-down, humiliation. **a slap on the back** *he was always trying to earn a slap on the back from his stepfather* **congratulations,** commendation, approbation, approval, accolades, compliments, tributes, a pat on the back, praise, acclaim, acclamation. **a slap on the wrist** *the judge let him go free, with nothing more than a slap on the wrist* **reprimand,** rebuke, reproof, scolding, admonishment; informal rap on/over the knuckles, dressing-down.

slapdash ▶ **adjective** *they did a slapdash job on the driveway* **careless,** slipshod, hurried, haphazard, unsystematic, untidy, messy, hit-or-miss, negligent, neglectful, lax; informal sloppy, slaphappy, shambolic. See note at SUPERFICIAL.
ANTONYMS meticulous.

slash ▶ **verb 1** *her tires had been slashed* **cut (open),** gash, slit, split open, lacerate, knife, make an incision in.
2 informal *the company slashed prices* **reduce,** cut, lower, bring down, mark down.
3 informal *they have slashed 10,000 jobs* **get rid of,** ax, cut, shed, make redundant.
▶ **noun 1** *a slash across his arm* **cut,** gash, laceration, slit, incision; wound.
2 *sentence breaks are indicated by slashes* **solidus,** oblique, backslash.

slaughter ▶ **verb 1** *the animals were slaughtered* **kill,** butcher.
2 *innocent civilians are being slaughtered* **massacre,** murder, butcher, kill (off), annihilate, exterminate, liquidate, eliminate, destroy, decimate, wipe out, put to death; literary slay. See note at KILL.
3 informal *their team was slaughtered* See DEFEAT (sense 1 of the verb).
▶ **noun 1** *the slaughter of 20 demonstrators* **massacre,** murdering, (mass) murder, mass killing, mass execution, annihilation, extermination, liquidation, decimation, carnage, butchery, genocide; literary slaying.

2 *a scene of slaughter* **carnage,** bloodshed, bloodletting, bloodbath.
3 informal *their electoral slaughter* See **DEFEAT** (sense 1 of the noun).

slave ▶ **noun 1** *the work was done by slaves* historical serf, vassal, thrall; archaic bondsman, bondswoman.
ANTONYMS freeman, master.
2 *Anna was his willing slave* **drudge,** servant, lackey, minion; informal gofer.
3 *a fashion slave* **devotee,** worshiper, adherent; fan, lover, aficionado; informal fanatic, freak, nut, addict.
▶ **verb** *slaving away for a pittance* **toil,** labor, grind away, sweat, work one's fingers to the bone, work like a Trojan/dog; informal kill oneself, sweat blood, slog away; literary travail; archaic drudge, moil.

slaver ▶ **verb** *her bloodhound loves to slaver on me* **drool,** slobber, dribble, salivate.

slavery ▶ **noun 1** *thousands were sold into slavery* **bondage,** enslavement, servitude, thralldom, thrall, serfdom, vassalage.
ANTONYMS freedom.
2 *this work is sheer slavery* **drudgery,** toil, hard labor, grind; literary travail; archaic moil.

slavish ▶ **adjective 1** *slavish lackeys of the government* **servile,** subservient, fawning, obsequious, sycophantic, toadying, unctuous; informal bootlicking, forelock-tugging. See note at **OBSEQUIOUS**.
2 *slavish copying* **unoriginal,** uninspired, unimaginative, uninventive, imitative.

slay ▶ **verb 1** literary *8,000 men were slain* **kill,** murder, put to death, butcher, cut down, cut to pieces, slaughter, massacre, shoot down, gun down, mow down, eliminate, annihilate, exterminate, liquidate; informal wipe out, bump off, do in. See note at **KILL**.
2 informal *you slay me, you really do* **amuse greatly,** entertain greatly, make someone laugh; informal have people rolling in the aisles, kill, knock dead, be a hit with.

sleek ▶ **adjective 1** *his sleek dark hair* **smooth,** glossy, shiny, shining, lustrous, silken, silky.
2 *the car's sleek lines* **streamlined,** trim, elegant, graceful.
3 *sleek young men in city suits* **well-groomed,** stylish, wealthy-looking, suave, sophisticated, debonair.

sleep ▶ **noun** *go and have a sleep* **nap,** doze, siesta, catnap, beauty sleep; informal snooze, forty winks, bit of shut-eye, power nap; literary slumber.
▶ **verb** *she slept for about an hour* **be asleep,** doze, take a siesta, take a nap, catnap, sleep like a log; informal snooze, catch/snatch forty winks, get some shut-eye, put one's head down, catch some Zs; humorous be in the land of Nod, be in the arms of Morpheus; literary slumber.
ANTONYMS wake up.
– PHRASES **go to sleep** *I'm trying to go to sleep* **fall asleep,** get to sleep; informal drop off, nod off, drift off, crash out, sack out. **put an animal to sleep** *our beloved poodle Maxie had to be put to sleep* **put down,** destroy, euthanize.

sleepiness ▶ **noun** *did you tell the doctor about your chronic sleepiness?* **drowsiness,** tiredness, somnolence, languor, languidness, doziness; lethargy, sluggishness, lassitude, enervation.

sleepless ▶ **adjective** *he lay sleepless until dawn* **wakeful,** restless, without sleep, insomniac; (wide) awake, unsleeping, tossing and turning.

sleepy ▶ **adjective 1** *she felt very sleepy* **drowsy,** tired, somnolent, languid, languorous, heavy-eyed, asleep on one's feet; lethargic, sluggish, enervated, torpid; informal dopey; literary slumberous.
ANTONYMS awake, alert.
2 *the sleepy heat of the afternoon* **soporific,** sleep-inducing, somnolent.
ANTONYMS invigorating.
3 *a sleepy little village* **quiet,** peaceful, tranquil, placid, slow-moving; dull, boring.
ANTONYMS busy, bustling.

slender ▶ **adjective 1** *her tall slender figure* **slim,** lean, willowy, sylphlike, svelte, lissome, graceful; slight, slightly built, thin, skinny. See note at **THIN**.
ANTONYMS plump.
2 *slender evidence* **meager,** limited, slight, scanty, scant, sparse, paltry, insubstantial, insufficient, deficient, negligible; formal exiguous.
ANTONYMS considerable.
3 *we had a slender chance of making it* **faint,** remote, flimsy, tenuous, fragile, slim; unlikely, improbable.
ANTONYMS strong.

sleuth ▶ **noun** informal *I didn't have to be much of a sleuth to catch Irene stealing company funds* (**private**) **detective,** (private) investigator; informal private eye, snoop, shamus, gumshoe, (private) dick, PI.

slice ▶ **noun 1** *a slice of fruitcake* **piece,** portion, slab, sliver, wafer, shaving.
2 *a huge slice of public spending* **share,** part, portion, tranche, piece, proportion, allocation, percentage.
▶ **verb 1** *slice the cheese thinly* **cut** (**up**), shave, carve, julienne, section.
2 *one man had his ear sliced off* **cut off,** sever, chop off, shear off.

slick ▶ **adjective 1** *a slick advertising campaign* **efficient,** smooth, smooth-running, polished, well-organized, well run, streamlined.
2 *his slick use of words* **glib,** smooth, fluent, plausible.
3 *a slick salesman* **suave,** urbane, polished, assured, self-assured, smooth-talking, glib; informal smarmy.
4 *her slick brown hair* **shiny,** glossy, shining, sleek, smooth, oiled.
5 *the sidewalks were slick with rain* **slippery,** wet, greasy; informal slippy.
▶ **verb** *his hair was slicked down* **smooth,** sleek, grease, oil, gel.

slide ▶ **verb 1** *the glass slid across the table* **glide,** move smoothly, slip, slither, skim, skate; skid, slew.
2 *tears slid down her cheeks* **trickle,** run, flow, pour, stream.
3 *four men slid out of the shadows* **creep,** steal, slink, slip, tiptoe, sidle.
4 *the country is sliding into recession* **sink,** fall, drop, descend; decline, degenerate.
▶ **noun 1** *the current slide in house prices* **fall,**

decline, drop, slump, downturn, downswing.
ANTONYMS rise.
2 *a slide show* **transparency**.
– PHRASES **let slide** *I guess I let things slide at the office during my wife's illness* **neglect**, pay little/no attention to, not attend to, be remiss about, let something go downhill.

slight ▶ **adjective 1** *the chance of success is slight* **small**, modest, tiny, minute, inappreciable, negligible, insignificant, minimal, remote, slim, faint; informal minuscule; formal exiguous.
ANTONYMS considerable.
2 *the book is of slight consequence* **minor**, inconsequential, trivial, unimportant, lightweight, superficial, shallow.
ANTONYMS substantial.
3 *Elizabeth's slight figure* **slim**, slender, petite, diminutive, small, delicate, dainty.
ANTONYMS burly.
▶ **verb** *he had been slighted* **insult**, snub, rebuff, repulse, spurn, treat disrespectfully, give someone the cold shoulder, scorn; informal give someone the brush-off, freeze out. See note at NEGLECT.
ANTONYMS respect.
▶ **noun** *an unintended slight* **insult**, affront, snub, rebuff; informal put-down, brush-off, dig.
ANTONYMS compliment.

slighting ▶ **adjective** *one more slighting remark from you and I'm walking out that door* **insulting**, disparaging, derogatory, disrespectful, denigratory, pejorative, abusive, offensive, defamatory, slanderous, scurrilous; disdainful, scornful, contemptuous; archaic contumelious.

slightly ▶ **adverb** *beat the egg whites until they're slightly stiff* **a little**, a bit, somewhat, rather, moderately, to a certain extent, faintly, vaguely, a shade, a touch.
ANTONYMS very.

slim ▶ **adjective 1** *she was tall and slim* **slender**, lean, thin, willowy, sylphlike, svelte, lissome, trim, slight, slightly built.
ANTONYMS plump.
2 *a slim silver bracelet* **narrow**, slender, slimline.
ANTONYMS broad.
3 *a slim chance of escape* **slight**, small, slender, faint, poor, remote, unlikely, improbable.
ANTONYMS strong.
▶ **verb 1** *I'm trying to* ***slim down*** **lose weight**, get thinner, lose some pounds/inches, diet, get into shape, slenderize.
2 *the number of staff had been* ***slimmed down*** **reduce**, cut (down/back), scale down, decrease, diminish, pare down.

slime ▶ **noun** *a greenish slime slowly dripped from the pipe* **ooze**, sludge, muck, mud, mire; informal goo, gunk, gook, gloop, gunge, guck, glop; humorous ectoplasm.

slimy ▶ **adjective 1** *the floor was slimy* **slippery**, greasy, muddy, mucky, sludgy, wet, sticky; informal slippy, gunky, gooey.
2 informal *her slimy press agent* **obsequious**, sycophantic, excessively deferential, subservient, fawning, toadying, ingratiating, unctuous, oily, oleaginous, greasy, toadyish, slavish; informal bootlicking, smarmy, forelock-tugging.

sling ▶ **noun 1** *she had her arm in a sling* **(support) bandage**, support, strap.
2 *armed only with a sling* **catapult**, slingshot.
▶ **verb 1** *a hammock was slung between two trees* **hang**, suspend, string, swing.
2 informal *she slung her jacket on the sofa* See THROW (sense 1 of the verb).

slink ▶ **verb** *it's impossible to slink quietly across these squeaky floors* **creep**, sneak, steal, slip, slide, sidle, tiptoe, pussyfoot.

slip[1] ▶ **verb 1** *she slipped on the ice* **slide**, skid, glide; fall (over), lose one's balance, tumble.
2 *the envelope slipped through Luke's fingers* **fall**, drop, slide.
3 *we slipped out by a back door* **creep**, steal, sneak, slide, sidle, slope, slink, tiptoe.
4 *standards have slipped* **decline**, deteriorate, degenerate, worsen, get worse, fall (off), drop; informal go downhill, go to the dogs, go to pot.
5 *the stock index slipped 30 points* **drop**, go down, sink, slump, decrease, depreciate.
6 *the hours* ***slipped by*** **pass**, elapse, go by/past, roll by/past, fly by/past, tick by/past.
7 *she slipped the map into her pocket* **put**, tuck, shove; informal pop, stick, stuff.
8 *Sarah* ***slipped into*** *a black skirt* **put on**, pull on, don, dress/clothe oneself in; change into.
9 *she* ***slipped out of*** *her clothes* **take off**, remove, pull off, doff, peel off.
10 *he slipped the knot of his tie* **untie**, unfasten, undo.
▶ **noun 1** *a single slip could send them plummeting downward* **false step**, misstep, slide, skid, fall, tumble.
2 *a careless slip* **mistake**, error, blunder, gaffe, slip of the tongue/pen; oversight, omission, lapse, inaccuracy; informal slip-up, boo-boo, howler, goof, blooper. See note at MISTAKE.
3 *a silk slip* **underskirt**, petticoat.
– PHRASES **give someone the slip** informal *we gave Murphy the slip and headed for the docks* **escape from**, get away from, evade, dodge, elude, lose, shake off, throw off (the scent), get clear of. **let something slip** *who let it slip that we were hiding here?* **reveal**, disclose, divulge, let out, give away, blurt out; give the game away; informal let on, blab, let the cat out of the bag, spill the beans. **slip away 1** *they managed to slip away* **escape**, get away, break free; informal fly the coop, take a powder. **2** *she slipped away in her sleep* See DIE (sense 1). **slip up** informal *Hennie slipped up and left the corral open* **make a mistake**, (make a) blunder, get something wrong, make an error, err; informal make a boo-boo, goof up.

slip[2] ▶ **noun** *they took slips from rare plants* **cutting**, graft; scion, shoot, offshoot.
– PHRASES **a slip of a ——** *she's just a slip of a girl* **small**, slender, slim, slight, slightly built, petite, little, tiny, diminutive; informal pint-sized. **slip of paper** *each person takes one slip of paper from the hat* **piece of paper**, scrap of paper, sheet, note; trademark Post-it.

slipper ▶ **noun** *he pulled on his slippers* bedroom slipper, house shoe, slipper sock, moccasin; mule.

slippery ▶ **adjective 1** *the roads are slippery* **icy**,

greasy, oily, glassy, smooth, slimy, wet; informal slippy.
2 *a slippery customer* **evasive,** unreliable, unpredictable; devious, crafty, cunning, unscrupulous, wily, tricky, artful, slick, sly, sneaky, scheming, untrustworthy, deceitful, duplicitous, dishonest, treacherous, two-faced, snide; informal shady, shifty, hinky.

slipshod ▶ adjective *a slipshod sales presentation* **careless,** lackadaisical, slapdash, disorganized, haphazard, hit-or-miss, untidy, messy, unsystematic, unmethodical, casual, negligent, neglectful, remiss, lax, slack; informal sloppy, slaphappy.
ANTONYMS meticulous.

slip-up ▶ noun informal *don't worry, everyone makes a slip-up or two* **mistake,** slip, error, blunder, oversight, omission, gaffe, slip of the tongue/pen, inaccuracy; informal boo-boo, howler, goof, blooper, boner.

slit ▶ noun **1** *three diagonal slits* **cut,** incision, split, slash, gash, laceration.
2 *a slit in the curtains* **opening,** gap, chink, crack, aperture, slot.
▶ verb *he threatened to slit her throat* **cut,** slash, split open, slice open, gash, lacerate, make an incision in.

slither ▶ verb *the garter snake slithered under the shed* **slide,** slip, glide, wriggle, crawl; skid.

sliver ▶ noun *slivers of glass | who wants this last sliver of cheesecake?* **splinter,** shard, shiver, chip, flake, shred, scrap, shaving, paring, piece, fragment.

slobber ▶ verb *ooh, this mutt keeps slobbering on me* **drool,** slaver, dribble, salivate.

slogan ▶ noun *familiar advertising slogans* **catchphrase,** jingle, byword, motto; informal tag line, buzzword, mantra.

slop ▶ verb *water slopped over the edge* **spill,** flow, overflow, run, slosh, splash.

slope ▶ noun **1** *the slope of the roof* **gradient,** incline, angle, slant, inclination, pitch, decline, ascent, declivity, rise, fall, tilt, tip, downslope, upslope, grade, downgrade, upgrade.
2 *a grassy slope* **hill,** hillside, hillock, bank, sidehill, escarpment, scarp; literary steep.
3 *the ski slopes* **piste,** run, trail.
▶ verb *the garden sloped down to a stream* **slant,** incline, tilt; drop away, fall away, decline, descend, shelve, lean; rise, ascend, climb.

sloping ▶ adjective *a sloping floor* **at a slant,** on a slant, at an angle, slanting, slanted, leaning, inclining, inclined, angled, cambered, canted, tilting, tilted, dipping.
ANTONYMS level.

sloppy ▶ adjective **1** *their defense was sloppy* **careless,** slapdash, slipshod, lackadaisical, haphazard, lax, slack, slovenly; informal slaphappy, shambolic.
2 *sloppy T-shirts* **baggy,** loose-fitting, loose, generously cut; shapeless, sacklike, oversized.
3 *a sloppy serving of cereal* **runny,** watery, thin, liquid, semiliquid, mushy, gloppy.
4 *sloppy letters* **sentimental,** mawkish, cloying, saccharine, sugary, syrupy; romantic; informal slushy, schmaltzy, lovey-dovey, soppy, cornball, corny, sappy, hokey, three-hankie.

slot ▶ noun **1** *he slid a coin into the slot* **aperture,** slit, crack, hole, opening.
2 *I have an early time slot* **spot,** time, period, niche, space; informal window.
▶ verb *he slotted a cassette into the machine* **insert,** put, place, slide, slip.

sloth ▶ noun *who is responsible for the sloth of this department?* **laziness,** idleness, indolence, slothfulness, inactivity, inertia, sluggishness, shiftlessness, apathy, acedia, listlessness, lassitude, lethargy, languor, torpidity; literary hebetude.
ANTONYMS industriousness.

slothful ▶ adjective *fatigue made him slothful* **lazy,** idle, indolent, inactive, sluggish, apathetic, lethargic, listless, languid, torpid; archaic otiose.

slouch ▶ verb **1** *sit up straight—don't slouch!* **slump,** hunch; loll, droop.
2 *he just slouched, pretending to work* **lounge,** loaf, laze, loll, idle, do nothing.
▶ noun *she's no slouch* **incompetent,** amateur, bumbler, bungler.

slovenly ▶ adjective **1** *his slovenly appearance* **scruffy,** untidy, messy, unkempt, ill-groomed, slatternly, disheveled, bedraggled, tousled, rumpled, frowzy; informal slobbish, slobby, raggedy, scuzzy.
ANTONYMS tidy.
2 *his work is slovenly* **careless,** slapdash, slipshod, haphazard, hit-or-miss, untidy, messy, negligent, lax, lackadaisical, slack; informal sloppy, slaphappy.
ANTONYMS careful.

slow ▶ adjective **1** *their slow walk home | the donkey was annoyingly slow* **unhurried,** leisurely, steady, sedate, slow-moving, downtempo, plodding, dawdling, sluggish, sluggardly, lead-footed, poky.
ANTONYMS fast.
2 *a slow process* **long-drawn-out,** time-consuming, lengthy, protracted, prolonged, gradual.
ANTONYMS brief, short.
3 *he can be so slow* **obtuse,** stupid, unperceptive, insensitive, bovine, stolid, slow-witted, dull-witted, unintelligent, doltish, witless; informal dense, dim, dimwitted, thick, slow on the uptake, dumb, dopey, boneheaded, chowderheaded. See note at **STUPID**.
ANTONYMS astute, bright.
4 *they were slow to voice their opinions* **reluctant,** unwilling, disinclined, loath, hesitant, afraid, chary, shy.
5 *the slow season* **sluggish,** slack, quiet, inactive, flat, depressed, stagnant, dead.
ANTONYMS busy, hectic.
6 *a slow movie* **dull,** boring, uninteresting, unexciting, uneventful, tedious, tiresome, wearisome, monotonous, dreary, lackluster.
ANTONYMS exciting.
▶ verb **1** *the traffic forced him to* ***slow down*** **reduce speed,** go slower, decelerate, brake.
ANTONYMS accelerate.
2 *you need to* ***slow down*** **take it easy,** relax, ease up/off, take a break, slack off, let up; informal chill (out), hang loose.
3 *this would* ***slow up*** *our progress* **hold back/up,**

delay, retard, set back; restrict, check, curb, inhibit, impede, obstruct, hinder, hamper; archaic stay.

slowly ▶ **adverb 1** *Tom walked off slowly* **at a slow pace,** without hurrying, unhurriedly, steadily, at a leisurely pace, at a snail's pace; Music adagio, lento, largo.
ANTONYMS quickly.
2 *her health is improving slowly* **gradually,** bit by bit, little by little, slowly but surely, step by step.
ANTONYMS by leaps and bounds.

sluggish ▶ **adjective 1** *Alex felt tired and sluggish* **lethargic,** listless, lacking in energy, lifeless, inert, inactive, slow, torpid, languid, apathetic, weary, tired, fatigued, sleepy, drowsy, enervated; lazy, idle, indolent, slothful, sluggardly, logy; Medicine asthenic; informal dozy, dopey.
ANTONYMS vigorous.
2 *the economy is sluggish* **inactive,** quiet, slow, slack, flat, depressed, stagnant.
ANTONYMS brisk.

slumber ▶ **verb** literary *the child slumbered fitfully* See **SLEEP** (verb).
▶ **noun** literary *an uneasy slumber* See **SLEEP** (noun).

slump ▶ **verb 1** *he slumped into a chair* **sit heavily,** flop, flump, collapse, sink, fall; informal plunk oneself.
2 *housing prices slumped* **fall steeply,** plummet, tumble, drop, go down; informal crash, nosedive.
3 *reading standards have slumped* **decline,** deteriorate, degenerate, worsen, slip; informal go downhill.
▶ **noun 1** *a slump in profits* **steep fall,** drop, tumble, downturn, downswing, slide; informal decline, decrease, nosedive.
ANTONYMS rise.
2 *an economic slump* **recession,** economic decline, depression, slowdown, stagnation.
ANTONYMS boom.

slur ▶ **verb** *she was slurring her words* **mumble,** speak unclearly, garble.
▶ **noun** *a gross slur* **insult,** slight, slander, slanderous statement, aspersion, smear, allegation.

slut ▶ **noun** *she dressed like a slut and didn't act much better* **promiscuous woman,** prostitute, whore; informal tart, floozy, tramp, hooker, hustler; dated scarlet woman, loose woman, hussy, trollop; archaic harlot, strumpet, wanton.

sly ▶ **adjective 1** *she's rather sly* **cunning,** crafty, clever, wily, artful, guileful, tricky, scheming, devious, deceitful, duplicitous, dishonest, underhanded, sneaky; archaic subtle.
2 *a sly grin* **roguish,** mischievous, impish, playful, wicked, arch, knowing.
3 *she took a sly sip of water* **surreptitious,** furtive, stealthy, covert.
– PHRASES **on the sly** *he's dating Peggy on the sly* **in secret,** secretly, furtively, surreptitiously, covertly, clandestinely, on the quiet, behind someone's back; informal on the QT.

smack[1] ▶ **noun 1** *she gave him a smack* **slap,** clout, cuff, blow, spank, rap, swat, crack, thump, punch, karate chop; informal whack, thwack, clip, wallop, swipe, bop, belt, bash, sock.
2 *the package landed with a smack* **bang,** crash, crack, thud, thump.
3 informal *a smack on the lips* **kiss,** peck, smooch; informal smacker.
▶ **verb 1** *he tried to smack her* **slap,** hit, strike, spank, cuff, clout, thump, punch, swat; box someone's ears; informal whack, clip, wallop, swipe, bop, belt, bash, sock, slug.
2 *the waiter smacked a plate down* **bang,** slam, crash, thump; sling, fling; informal plunk.
▶ **adverb** informal *smack in the middle* **exactly,** precisely, straight, right, directly, squarely, dead, plumb, point-blank; informal slap, bang, smack dab.

smack[2] ▶ **noun 1** *the beer has a smack of hops* **taste,** flavor, savor.
2 *a smack of bitterness in his words* **trace,** tinge, touch, suggestion, hint, overtone, suspicion, whisper.
– PHRASES **smack of 1** *the tea smacked of tannin* **taste of,** have the flavor of. **2** *the plan smacked of self-promotion* **suggest,** hint at, have overtones of, give the impression of, have the stamp of, seem like; smell of, reek of.

smack[3] ▶ **noun** informal *they were shooting smack in the alley* **heroin.**

small ▶ **adjective 1** *a small apartment* **little,** compact, bijou, tiny, miniature, mini; minute, microscopic, minuscule; toy, baby; poky, cramped, boxy; informal teeny, teensy, itsy-bitsy, itty-bitty, pocket-sized, half-pint, little-bitty; Scottish wee.
ANTONYMS big, large.
2 *a very small man* **short,** little, petite, diminutive, elfin, tiny; puny, undersized, stunted, dwarfish, midget, pygmy, Lilliputian; Scottish wee; informal teeny, pint-sized.
ANTONYMS large, tall, heavily built.
3 *a few small changes* **slight,** minor, unimportant, trifling, trivial, insignificant, inconsequential, negligible, nugatory, infinitesimal; informal minuscule, piffling, piddling.
ANTONYMS major, substantial.
4 *small helpings* **inadequate,** meager, insufficient, ungenerous; informal measly, stingy, mingy, pathetic.
ANTONYMS ample, generous.
5 *they made him feel small* **foolish,** stupid, insignificant, unimportant; embarrassed, humiliated, uncomfortable, mortified, ashamed; crushed.
ANTONYMS proud.
6 *a small business* **small-scale,** modest, unpretentious, humble.
ANTONYMS big, large-scale, substantial.

CHOOSE THE RIGHT WORD

small, diminutive, little, miniature, minute, petite, tiny

Why do we call a house **small** and a woman **petite**? *Small* and **little** are used interchangeably to describe people or things of reduced dimensions, but *small* is preferred when describing something concrete that is of less than the usual size, quantity, value, or importance (*a small matter to discuss; a* *small room; a small price to pay*). *Little* more often refers to concepts (*through little fault of his own; an issue of little importance*) or to a more drastic reduction in scale (*a little shopping cart just like the one her mother used*). **Diminutive** and *petite* intensify the meaning of *small*, particularly with reference to women's figures that are very trim and compact (*with her diminutive figure, she had to shop in stores that specialized in petite sizes*). **Tiny** is used to describe what is extremely small, often to the point where it can be seen only by looking closely (*a tiny flaw in the material; a tiny insect*), while **minute** not only describes what is seen with difficulty but may also refer to a very small amount of something (*minute traces of gunpowder on his glove*). **Miniature** applies specifically to a copy, a model, or a representation of something on a very small scale (*a child's mobile consisting of miniature farm animals*).

small-minded ▶ adjective *they were too small-minded to listen to our views on interracial marriage* **narrow-minded,** petty, mean-spirited, uncharitable; close-minded, shortsighted, myopic, blinkered, inward-looking, unimaginative, parochial, provincial, insular, small-town; intolerant, illiberal, conservative, hidebound, dyed-in-the-wool, set in one's ways, inflexible; prejudiced, bigoted.
ANTONYMS tolerant.

small-time ▶ adjective *a small-time thief from New Haven* **minor,** small-scale; petty, unimportant, insignificant, inconsequential, minor-league; informal penny-ante, piddling, two-bit, bush-league, picayune.
ANTONYMS major.

smart ▶ adjective **1** informal *he's the smart one* **clever,** bright, intelligent, sharp-witted, quick-witted, shrewd, astute, able; perceptive, percipient; informal brainy, savvy, quick on the uptake.
ANTONYMS stupid.
2 *you look very smart* **well-dressed,** stylish, chic, fashionable, modish, elegant, neat, spruce, trim, dapper; informal snazzy, natty, snappy, sharp, cool, spiffy, fly, kicky.
ANTONYMS scruffy.
3 *a smart restaurant* **fashionable,** stylish, high-class, exclusive, chic, fancy, upscale, upmarket, high-toned; informal trendy, posh, ritzy, plush, classy, swanky, glitzy, swank.
ANTONYMS downmarket.
4 *a smart pace* **brisk,** quick, fast, rapid, swift, lively, spanking, energetic, vigorous; informal snappy, cracking.
ANTONYMS slow.
5 *a smart blow on the snout* **sharp,** severe, forceful, violent.
ANTONYMS gentle.
▶ verb **1** *her eyes were smarting* **sting,** burn, tingle, prickle; hurt, ache.
2 *she smarted at the accusations* **feel annoyed,** feel upset, take offense, feel aggrieved, feel indignant, be put out, feel hurt.

smash ▶ verb **1** *he smashed a window* **break,** shatter, splinter, crack, shiver; informal bust.
2 *she's smashed the car* **crash,** wreck, write off; informal total.
3 *they smashed into a wall* **crash into,** collide with, hit, strike, ram, smack into, slam into, plow into, run into, bump into, impact.
4 *Don smashed him over the head* **hit,** strike, thump, punch, smack; informal whack, bash, bop, clout, wallop, crown, slug.
5 *he smashed their hopes of glory* **destroy,** wreck, ruin, shatter, dash, crush, devastate, demolish, overturn, scotch; informal put the kibosh on, scuttle.
▶ noun **1** *the smash of glass* **breaking,** shattering, crash.
2 *it was a terrible smash* **crash,** collision, accident, wreck; informal pileup, smash-up.
3 informal *a box-office smash* **success,** sensation, sellout, triumph; informal (smash) hit, blockbuster, winner, knockout, wow, barn burner, biggie.

smattering ▶ noun *it's mostly modern, with a smattering of art deco* **bit,** modicum, touch, soupçon; nodding acquaintance; informal smidgen, smidge, tad.

smear ▶ verb **1** *the table was smeared with grease* **streak,** smudge, mark, soil, dirty; informal splotch; literary besmear.
2 *smear the meat with olive oil* **cover,** coat, grease; literary bedaub.
3 *she smeared sunblock on her skin* **spread,** rub, daub, slap, slather, smother, plaster, slick; apply; literary besmear.
4 *they are trying to smear our reputation* **sully,** tarnish, blacken, drag through the mud, taint, damage, defame, discredit, malign, slander, libel, slur; informal do a hatchet job on; formal calumniate, impugn; literary besmirch.
▶ noun **1** *smears of blood* **streak,** smudge, daub, dab, spot, patch, blotch, mark; informal splotch.
2 *they printed smears about his closest aides* **false accusation,** lie, untruth, slur, slander, libel, defamation, calumny.

smell ▶ noun *the smell of the kitchen* **odor,** aroma, fragrance, scent, perfume, redolence; bouquet, nose; stench, fetor, stink, reek, whiff; informal funk; literary miasma.
▶ verb **1** *he smelled her perfume* get a sniff of, scent, detect.
2 *the dogs smelled each other* **sniff,** nose.
3 *the cellar smells* **stink,** reek, have a bad smell, whiff.
4 *it smells like a hoax to me* **smack of,** have the hallmark(s) of, seem like, have the air of, suggest.

CHOOSE THE RIGHT WORD

smell, aroma, bouquet, fragrance, odor, perfume, scent, stench, stink

Everyone appreciates the **fragrance** of fresh-cut flowers, but the **stench** from the paper mill across town is usually unwelcome. Both have a distinctive **smell**, which is the most general of these words for what is perceived through the nose, but there is a big difference between a pleasant smell and a foul one. An **odor** may be either pleasant or unpleasant, but it suggests a smell that is clearly recognizable and can usually be traced to a single source (*the pungent odor of onions*). An **aroma** is a pleasing and distinctive odor that is usually penetrating or pervasive (*the aroma of fresh-ground coffee*), while **bouquet** refers to a delicate aroma, such as that of a fine wine (*after swirling the wine around in her glass, she sniffed the bouquet*). A **scent** is usually delicate and pleasing, with an emphasis on the source rather than on an olfactory impression (*the scent of balsam associated with Christmas*). *Fragrance* and **perfume** are both associated with flowers, but *fragrance* is more delicate; a *perfume* may be so rich and strong that it is repulsive or overpowering (*the air was so dense with the perfume of lilacs that I had to go indoors*). *Stench* and **stink** are reserved for smells that are foul, strong, and pervasive, although *stink* implies a sharper sensation, while *stench* refers to a more sickening one (*the stink of sweaty gym clothes; the stench of a rotting animal*).

smelly ▶ adjective *get that smelly wet dog off the sofa* **foul-smelling,** stinking, reeking, fetid, malodorous, pungent, rank, noxious, mephitic; off, gamy, high; musty, fusty; informal stinky, humming, funky; Brit. informal minging, pongy; literary miasmic, noisome.

smile ▶ verb *he smiled at her* **beam,** grin (from ear to ear), dimple, twinkle; smirk, simper; leer.
ANTONYMS frown.
▶ noun *the smile on Sara's face* **beam,** grin, twinkle; smirk, simper; leer.

CHOOSE THE RIGHT WORD

smile, grin, smirk, simper

The facial expression created by turning the corners of the mouth upward is commonly known as a **smile**. It can convey a wide range of emotion, from pleasure, approval, or amusement to insincerity and disinterest (*his complaint was met with a blank smile*). A **grin** is a wide smile that suggests spontaneous cheerfulness, warmth, pleasure, or amusement (*her teasing provoked an affectionate grin*). But *grin* may also describe a ferocious baring of the teeth or an angry grimace (*the grin of a skeleton*). A **simper**, on the other hand, is an expression of smugness and self-righteousness (*her simper of superiority*) as well as a silly or affected smile (*she curtsied with a girlish simper*). **Smirk** also implies an affected or self-conscious smile, but one that expresses derision or hostility (*to trick someone and then smirk as he makes a fool of himself*).

smirk ▶ verb *I hate the way they just sit there smirking* **smile smugly,** simper, snicker, snigger; leer.

smitten ▶ adjective 1 *he was smitten with cholera* **struck down,** laid low, suffering, affected, afflicted, plagued, stricken.
2 *Jane's smitten with you* **infatuated with,** besotted with, in love with, obsessed with, head over heels; enamored of, attracted to, taken with; captivated by, enchanted by, under someone's spell, moonstruck by; informal bowled over by, swept off one's feet by, crazy about, mad about, keen on, hot on/for, gone on, sweet on, gaga for.

smog ▶ noun *the smog in LA is intolerable* **fog,** haze; fumes, smoke, pollution.

smoke ▶ verb 1 *the fire was smoking* **smolder,** emit smoke; archaic reek.
2 *he smoked his cigarette* **puff on,** draw on, pull on; inhale; light; informal drag on, toke.
3 *they smoke their salmon* **cure,** preserve, dry.
▶ noun *the smoke from the bonfire* **fumes,** exhaust, gas, vapor; smog.

smoky ▶ adjective 1 *the smoky atmosphere* **smoke-filled,** sooty, smoggy, hazy, foggy, murky, thick.
2 *her smoky eyes* **gray,** sooty, dark, black.

smolder ▶ verb 1 *the bonfire still smoldered* **smoke,** glow, burn.
2 *she was smoldering with resentment* **seethe,** boil, fume, burn, simmer, be boiling over, be beside oneself; informal be livid.

smooth ▶ adjective 1 *the smooth flat rocks* **even,** level, flat, plane; unwrinkled, featureless; glassy, glossy, silky, polished.
ANTONYMS uneven, rough.
2 *his face was smooth* **clean-shaven,** hairless.
ANTONYMS rough, hairy.
3 *a smooth sauce* **creamy,** velvety, blended.
ANTONYMS lumpy.
4 *a smooth sea* **calm,** still, tranquil, undisturbed, unruffled, even, flat, waveless, like a millpond.
ANTONYMS rough, choppy.
5 *the smooth running of the equipment* **steady,** regular, uninterrupted, unbroken, fluid, fluent; straightforward, easy, effortless, trouble-free, seamless.
ANTONYMS irregular, jerky.
6 *a smooth wine* **mellow,** mild, agreeable, pleasant.
ANTONYMS harsh, bitter.
7 *the smooth tone of the clarinet* **dulcet,** soft, soothing, mellow, sweet, silvery, honeyed, mellifluous, melodious, lilting, lyrical, harmonious.
ANTONYMS raucous.
8 *a smooth, confident man* **suave,** urbane, sophisticated, polished, debonair; courteous, gracious, glib, slick, ingratiating, unctuous; informal smarmy.
ANTONYMS gauche.
▶ verb 1 *she smoothed the soil* **flatten,** level (out/off), even out/off; press, roll, steamroll, iron, plane.
2 *a plan to smooth the way for the agreement* **ease,** facilitate, clear the way for, pave the way for, expedite, assist, aid, help, oil the wheels of, lubricate.

smother ▶ verb 1 *she tried to smother her baby* **suffocate,** asphyxiate, stifle, choke.
2 *we smothered the flames* **extinguish,** put out, snuff out, dampen, douse, stamp out, choke.
3 *we smothered ourselves with sunscreen* **smear,** daub, spread, cover; literary besmear, bedaub.

4 *their granny always smothers them with affection* **overwhelm,** inundate, envelop, cocoon.
5 *she smothered a sigh* **stifle,** muffle, strangle, repress, suppress, hold back, fight back, bite back, swallow, contain, bottle up, conceal, hide; bite one's lip; informal keep a/the lid on.

smudge ▶ noun *a smudge of ink* **streak,** smear, mark, stain, blotch, stripe, blob, dab; informal splotch.
▶ verb 1 *her face was smudged with dust* **streak,** mark, dirty, soil, blotch, blacken, smear, blot, daub, stain; informal splotch; literary bedaub, besmirch.
2 *she smudged her makeup* **smear,** streak, mess up.

smug ▶ adjective *he was feeling smug after his win* **self-satisfied,** self-congratulatory, complacent, superior, pleased with oneself, self-approving.

smuggler ▶ noun *it was a small uncharted island frequented by smugglers* **trafficker,** runner, courier; informal mule, moonshiner, rum-runner.

snack ▶ noun *she made herself a snack* **light meal,** collation, treat, refreshments, lunch, nibbles, tidbit(s); informal bite (to eat).
▶ verb *don't snack on sugary foods* **eat between meals,** nibble, munch; informal graze, nosh.

snag ▶ noun 1 *the snag is that this might affect inflation* **complication,** difficulty, catch, hitch, hiccup, obstacle, stumbling block, pitfall, problem, impediment, hindrance, inconvenience, setback, hurdle, disadvantage, downside, drawback.
2 *smooth rails with no snags* **sharp projection,** jag; thorn, spur.
3 *a snag in her stocking* **tear,** rip, hole, gash, slash; run.
▶ verb 1 *she snagged her stockings* **tear,** rip.
2 *the zipper snagged on the fabric* **catch,** get caught, hook.

snap ▶ verb 1 *the ruler snapped* **break,** fracture, splinter, come apart, split, crack; informal bust.
2 *she snapped after years of violence* **flare up,** lose one's self-control, freak out, go to pieces, get worked up; informal crack up, lose one's cool, blow one's top, fly off the handle.
3 *a dog was snapping at his heels* **bite**; gnash its teeth.
4 *"Be quiet!" Anna snapped* **say roughly,** say brusquely, say abruptly, say angrily, bark, snarl, growl; retort, rejoin, retaliate; informal jump down someone's throat.
▶ noun 1 *she closed her purse with a snap* **click,** crack, pop.
2 *a cold snap* **period,** spell, time, interval, stretch, patch.
3 informal *vacation snaps* **photograph,** picture, photo, shot, snapshot, print, slide, frame, still; informal mug shot.
4 *it's a snap to put together* **an easy task**; informal a piece of cake, a cinch, a breeze, child's play, kid's stuff, duck soup.
– PHRASES **snap out of it** informal *you can't tell a clinically depressed person to just snap out of it* **recover,** get a grip, pull oneself together, get over it, get better, cheer up, perk up; informal buck up. **snap up** *customers are snapping up these DVDs as fast as we can put them out* **buy eagerly,** accept eagerly, jump at, take advantage of, grab, seize (on), grasp with both hands, pounce on.

snappy ▶ adjective informal 1 *a snappy catchphrase* **concise,** succinct, memorable, catchy, neat, clever, crisp, pithy, witty, incisive, brief, short.
ANTONYMS long-winded.
2 *a snappy dresser* **smart,** fashionable, stylish, chic, modish, elegant, neat, spruce, trim, dapper; informal snazzy, natty, sharp, nifty, cool, hip, styling, spiffy, fly.
ANTONYMS slovenly.
– PHRASES **make it snappy** *make it snappy, Trina, the Watsons will be here in five minutes* **hurry (up),** be quick (about it), get a move on, look lively, speed up; informal get cracking, step on it, move it, buck up, shake a leg; dated make haste.

snare ▶ noun 1 *the hare was caught in a snare* **trap,** gin, net, noose.
2 *avoid the snares of the new law* **pitfall,** trap, catch, danger, hazard, peril; web, mesh.
▶ verb 1 *game birds were snared* **trap,** catch, net, bag, ensnare, entrap.
2 *he managed to snare an heiress* **ensnare,** catch, get hold of, bag, hook, land.

snarl[1] ▶ verb 1 *the wolves are snarling* **growl,** gnash one's teeth.
2 *"Shut up!" he snarled* **say roughly,** say brusquely, say nastily, bark, snap, growl; informal jump down someone's throat.

snarl[2] ▶ verb 1 *the rope got snarled up in a bush* **tangle,** entangle, entwine, enmesh, ravel, knot, foul.
2 *this case has snarled up the court process* **complicate,** confuse, muddle, jumble; informal mess up.

snatch ▶ verb 1 *she snatched the sandwich* **grab,** seize, take hold of, get one's hands on, take, pluck; grasp at, clutch at.
2 informal *someone snatched my bag* See STEAL (sense 1 of the verb).
3 informal *she snatched the newborn from the hospital* See ABDUCT.
4 *he snatched victory* **seize,** pluck, wrest, achieve, secure, obtain; scrape.
▶ noun 1 *brief snatches of sleep* **period,** spell, time, fit, bout, interval, stretch.
2 *a snatch of conversation* **fragment,** snippet, bit, scrap, part, extract, excerpt, portion.

sneak ▶ verb 1 *I sneaked out* **creep,** slink, steal, slip, slide, sidle, edge, move furtively, tiptoe, pussyfoot, pad, prowl.
2 *she sneaked a camera in* **smuggle,** bring/take surreptitiously, bring/take secretly, bring/take illicitly, spirit, slip.
3 *he sneaked a doughnut* **steal,** take furtively, take surreptitiously; informal snatch.
▶ adjective 1 *a sneak attack* **furtive,** secret, stealthy, sly, surreptitious, clandestine, covert.
2 *a sneak preview* **exclusive,** private, quick.

sneaking ▶ adjective 1 *she had a sneaking admiration for him* **secret,** private, hidden, concealed, unvoiced, undisclosed, undeclared, unavowed.
2 *a sneaking feeling* **niggling,** nagging, lurking, insidious, lingering, gnawing, persistent.

sneer ▶ noun 1 *she had a sneer on her face* **smirk,**

curl of the lip, disparaging smile, contemptuous smile, cruel smile.
2 *the sneers of others* **jibe,** barb, jeer, taunt, insult, slight, affront, slur; informal dig.
▶ **verb 1** *he looked at me and sneered* **smirk,** curl one's lip, smile disparagingly, smile contemptuously, smile cruelly.
2 *it is easy to* ***sneer at*** *them* **scoff at,** scorn, disdain, mock, jeer at, hold in contempt, ridicule, deride, insult, slight, slur.

snicker ▶ **verb** *they all snickered at her* **giggle,** titter, snigger, chortle, simper, laugh.
▶ **noun** *he could not suppress a snicker* **giggle,** titter, snigger, chortle, simper.

sniff ▶ **verb 1** *she sniffed and blew her nose* **inhale,** breathe in; snuffle.
2 *Sandra sniffed the socks and grimaced* **smell,** scent, get a whiff of.
▶ **noun 1** *she gave a loud sniff* **snuffle,** inhalation.
2 *a sniff of fresh air* **smell,** scent, whiff; lungful.
3 informal *the first sniff of trouble* **indication,** hint, whiff, inkling, suggestion, whisper, trace, sign, suspicion.
– PHRASES **sniff at** *how dare you sniff at me just because I'm poor?* **scorn,** disdain, hold in contempt, look down one's nose at, treat as inferior, look down on, sneer at, scoff at; informal turn one's nose up at. **sniff out** informal *McMahon and Romero were sent uptown to sniff out the source of these letters* **detect,** find, discover, bring to light, track down, dig up, hunt out, ferret out, root out, uncover, unearth.

snip ▶ **verb 1** *an usher snipped our tickets* **cut,** clip, slit, nick, notch.
2 ***snip off*** *the faded flowers* **cut off,** trim (off), clip, prune, chop off, lop (off), dock, crop, sever, detach, remove, take off.
▶ **noun 1** *make snips along the edge* **cut,** slit, nick, notch, incision.
2 *snips of wallpaper* **scrap,** snippet, cutting, shred, remnant, fragment, sliver, bit, piece.

snippet ▶ **noun** *any snippet of information you can share would be appreciated* **piece,** bit, scrap, fragment, particle, shred; excerpt, extract.

snivel ▶ **verb 1** *he slumped in a chair, sniveling* **sniffle,** snuffle, whimper, whine, weep, cry; informal blubber, boo-hoo.
2 *don't snivel about what you get* **complain,** mutter, grumble, grouse, groan, carp, bleat, whine; informal gripe, moan, grouch, beef, bellyache, whinge, sound off, kvetch.

snobbery ▶ **noun** *they were raised in an environment of complacent snobbery* **affectation,** pretension, pretentiousness, arrogance, haughtiness, airs and graces, elitism; disdain, condescension, superciliousness; informal snootiness, uppitiness.

snobbish ▶ **adjective** *the snobbish distinction between art and craft* **elitist,** snobby, superior, supercilious; arrogant, haughty, disdainful, condescending; pretentious, affected; informal snooty, uppity, high and mighty, la-di-da, stuck-up, hoity-toity, snotty.

snoop informal ▶ **verb 1** *don't* ***snoop into*** *our affairs* **pry into,** inquire into/about, be inquisitive about/of, be curious about, poke about/around, be a busybody about, poke one's nose into; interfere in/with, meddle in/with, intrude on; informal be nosy about.
2 *they snooped around the building* **investigate,** explore, search, nose, have a good look; prowl around.
▶ **noun** *he went for a snoop around* **search,** nose, look, prowl, ferret, poke, investigation.

snooze informal ▶ **noun** *a good place for a snooze* **nap,** doze, sleep, rest, siesta, catnap; informal forty winks; literary slumber.
▶ **verb** *she gently snoozed* **nap,** doze, sleep, rest, take a siesta, catnap, drop off; informal snatch forty winks, get some shut-eye, put one's head down, catch some Zs; literary slumber.

snub ▶ **verb** *they snubbed their hosts* **rebuff,** spurn, repulse, cold-shoulder, brush off, give the cold shoulder to, keep at arm's length; ignore; insult, slight, affront, humiliate; informal freeze out, stiff, give someone the brush-off.
▶ **noun** *a very public snub* **rebuff,** repulse, slap in the face; humiliation, insult, slight, affront; informal brush-off, kiss-off, put-down.

snug ▶ **adjective 1** *our tents were snug* **cozy,** comfortable, warm, welcoming, restful, reassuring, intimate, sheltered, secure; informal comfy.
ANTONYMS bleak, unwelcoming.
2 *a snug dress* **tight,** skintight, close-fitting, form-fitting, figure-hugging, slinky.
ANTONYMS loose.

snuggle ▶ **verb** *Kent and Maris snuggled by the fire* **nestle,** curl up, huddle (up), cuddle up, nuzzle, settle.

soak ▶ **verb 1** *soak the beans in water* **immerse,** steep, submerge, submerse, dip, dunk, bathe, douse, marinate, souse.
2 *we got soaked outside* **drench,** wet through, saturate, waterlog, deluge, inundate, submerge, drown, swamp.
3 *the sweat* ***soaked through*** *his clothes* **permeate,** penetrate, percolate, seep into, spread through, infuse, impregnate.
4 *use towels to* ***soak up*** *the water* **absorb,** suck up, blot (up), mop (up), sponge up, sop up.

soaking ▶ **adjective** *good Lord, look at these soaking children* **drenched,** wet (through), soaked (through), sodden, soggy, waterlogged, saturated, sopping wet, dripping wet, wringing wet.
ANTONYMS parched.

soar ▶ **verb 1** *the bird soared into the air* **fly,** wing, ascend, climb, rise; take off, take flight.
ANTONYMS plummet.
2 *the gulls soared on the winds* **glide,** plane, float, drift, wheel, hover.
3 *the cost of living soared* **increase,** escalate, shoot up, rise, spiral; informal go through the roof, skyrocket.

sob ▶ **verb** *must she sob during every romantic scene?* **weep,** cry, shed tears, snivel, whimper; howl, bawl; informal blubber, boo-hoo.

sober ▶ **adjective 1** *the driver was clearly sober* **not drunk,** clearheaded; teetotal, abstinent, abstemious, dry; informal on the wagon.
ANTONYMS drunk.
2 *a sober view of life* **serious,** solemn, sensible, thoughtful, grave, somber, staid, levelheaded, businesslike, down-to-earth, commonsensical,

pragmatic, conservative; unemotional, dispassionate, objective, matter-of-fact, no-nonsense, rational, logical, straightforward.
ANTONYMS frivolous.
3 *a sober suit* **somber,** subdued; severe; conventional, traditional, quiet, drab, plain.
ANTONYMS flamboyant.
▶ **verb 1** *I ought to sober up* **quit drinking,** dry out, become sober.
2 *his expression sobered her* **make serious,** subdue, calm down, quiet, steady; bring down to earth, make someone stop and think, give someone pause for thought.

sobriety ▶ **noun 1** *she noted his sobriety* **soberness,** clearheadedness; abstinence, teetotalism, nonindulgence, abstemiousness, temperance.
2 *the mayor is a model of sobriety* **seriousness,** solemnity, gravity, gravitas, dignity, levelheadedness, common sense, pragmatism, practicality, self-control, self-restraint, conservatism.

so-called ▶ **adjective** *your so-called dream date is hitting on our waitress* **inappropriately named,** supposed, alleged, presumed, ostensible, reputed; nominal, titular, self-styled, professed, would-be, self-appointed, soi-disant.

sociable ▶ **adjective** *it was a sociable group, but he would rather have been with his own friends* **friendly,** affable, companionable, gregarious, convivial, amicable, cordial, warm, genial; communicative, responsive, forthcoming, open, outgoing, extrovert, hail-fellow-well-met, approachable; informal chummy, clubby.
ANTONYMS unfriendly.

social ▶ **adjective 1** *a major social problem* **communal,** community, collective, group, general, popular, civil, public, societal.
ANTONYMS individual.
2 *a social club* **recreational,** leisure, entertainment, amusement.
3 *a uniquely social animal* **gregarious,** interactional; organized.
▶ **noun** *the club has a social once a month* **party,** gathering, function, get-together, soirée; celebration, reunion, jamboree; informal bash, shindig, do.

socialize ▶ **verb** *these are not the type of people we want you socializing with* **interact,** converse, be sociable, mix, mingle, get together, meet, fraternize, consort; entertain, go out; informal hobnob.

society ▶ **noun 1** *a danger to society* **the community,** the (general) public, the people, the population; civilization, humankind, mankind, humanity.
2 *an industrial society* **culture,** community, civilization, nation, population.
3 *Sir Paul will help you enter society* **high society,** polite society, the upper classes, the elite, the smart set, the beautiful people, the beau monde, the haut monde; informal the upper crust, the top drawer.
4 *a local history society* **association,** club, group, circle, fellowship, guild, lodge, fraternity, brotherhood, sisterhood, sorority, league, union, alliance.
5 *the society of others* **company,** companionship, fellowship, friendship, comradeship, camaraderie.

sodden ▶ **adjective 1** *his clothes were sodden* **soaking,** soaked (through), wet (through), saturated, drenched, sopping wet, wringing wet.
ANTONYMS dry.
2 *sodden fields* **waterlogged,** soggy, saturated, boggy, swampy, miry, marshy; heavy, soft.
ANTONYMS arid.

soft ▶ **adjective 1** *soft fruit* **mushy,** squashy, pulpy, pappy, slushy, squishy, doughy; informal gooey.
ANTONYMS hard.
2 *soft ground* **swampy,** marshy, boggy, miry, oozy; heavy, squelchy.
ANTONYMS firm.
3 *a soft cushion* **squashy,** spongy, compressible, supple, springy, pliable, pliant, resilient, malleable.
ANTONYMS hard.
4 *soft fabric* **velvety,** smooth, fleecy, downy, furry, silky, silken, satiny.
ANTONYMS rough, harsh.
5 *a soft wind* **gentle,** light, mild, moderate.
ANTONYMS strong.
6 *soft light* **dim,** low, faint, subdued, muted, mellow.
ANTONYMS harsh.
7 *soft colors* **pale,** pastel, muted, understated, restrained, subdued, subtle.
ANTONYMS lurid.
8 *soft voices* **quiet,** low, faint, muted, subdued, muffled, hushed, whispered, stifled, murmured, gentle, dulcet; indistinct, inaudible.
ANTONYMS strident, clear.
9 *soft outlines* **blurred,** vague, hazy, misty, foggy, nebulous, fuzzy, blurry, indistinct, unclear.
ANTONYMS sharp.
10 *he seduced her with soft words* **kind,** gentle, sympathetic, soothing, tender, sensitive, affectionate, loving, amorous, warm, sweet, sentimental, pretty; informal mushy, slushy, schmaltzy, sappy.
ANTONYMS harsh.
11 *she's too soft with her students* **lenient,** easygoing, tolerant, forgiving, forbearing, indulgent, clement, permissive, liberal, lax.
ANTONYMS strict.
12 informal *he's soft in the head* **foolish,** stupid, simple, brainless, mindless; mad, scatterbrained, featherbrained; slow, weak, feeble; informal dopey, dippy, scatty, loopy, flaky.
ANTONYMS sensible.

soften ▶ **verb 1** *she tried to soften the blow of new service cuts* **alleviate,** ease, relieve, soothe, take the edge off, assuage, cushion, moderate, mitigate, palliate, diminish, blunt, deaden.
2 *the winds softened* **die down,** abate, subside, moderate, let up, calm, diminish, slacken, weaken.
– PHRASES **soften up** *she knows how to soften up Dad just before reaching into his wallet* **charm,** win over, persuade, influence, weaken, disarm, sweeten, butter up, soft-soap.

soggy ▶ **adjective** *the cushions are completely soggy from last night's rain* **mushy,** squashy, pulpy, slushy, squishy; swampy, marshy, boggy, miry; soaking, soaked through, wet, saturated, drenched.

soil[1] ▶ noun **1** *acid soil* **earth,** loam, dirt, clay, gumbo; ground.
2 *Canadian soil* **territory,** land, domain, dominion, region, country.

soil[2] ▶ verb **1** *he soiled his tie* **dirty,** stain, splash, spot, spatter, splatter, smear, smudge, sully, spoil, foul; literary begrime.
2 *our reputation is being soiled* **dishonor,** damage, sully, stain, blacken, tarnish, taint, blemish, defile, blot, smear, drag through the mud; literary besmirch.

sojourn formal ▶ noun *a sojourn in France* **stay,** visit, stop, stopover; vacation.
▶ verb *they sojourned in the monastery* **stay,** live, put up, stop (over), lodge, room, board; vacation.

solace ▶ noun *they found solace in each other* **comfort,** consolation, cheer, support, relief.
▶ verb *she was solaced with tea and sympathy* **comfort,** console, cheer, support, soothe, calm.

soldier ▶ noun *her daddy was a soldier in the Continental Army* **fighter,** trooper, serviceman, servicewoman; warrior; GI; peacekeeper; archaic man-at-arms.
– PHRASES **soldier on** informal See **PERSEVERE**.

solecism ▶ noun **1** *a poem marred by solecisms* **(grammatical) mistake,** error, blunder; informal howler, blooper.
2 *it would have been a solecism to answer* **faux pas,** gaffe, impropriety, social indiscretion, infelicity, slip, error, blunder, lapse; informal slip-up, boo-boo, goof, blooper, flub.

solemn ▶ adjective **1** *a solemn occasion* **dignified,** ceremonious, ceremonial, stately, formal, courtly, majestic; imposing, awe-inspiring, splendid, magnificent, grand.
ANTONYMS frivolous.
2 *he looked very solemn* **serious,** grave, sober, somber, unsmiling, stern, grim, dour, humorless; pensive, meditative, thoughtful.
ANTONYMS lighthearted.
3 *a solemn promise* **sincere,** earnest, honest, genuine, firm, heartfelt, wholehearted, sworn.
ANTONYMS insincere.

solicit ▶ verb **1** *Phil tried to solicit his help* **ask for,** request, seek, apply for, put in for, call for, press for, beg, plead for. See note at **BEG**.
2 *they are solicited for their opinions* **ask,** petition, importune, implore, plead with, entreat, appeal to, lobby, beg, supplicate, call on, press; literary beseech.

solicitous ▶ adjective *she was always solicitous about the welfare of her students* **concerned,** caring, considerate, attentive, mindful, thoughtful, interested; anxious, worried.

solid ▶ adjective **1** *the ice cream was solid* **hard,** rock-hard, rigid, firm, solidified, set, frozen, concrete.
ANTONYMS liquid, gaseous.
2 *solid gold* **pure,** 24-carat, unalloyed, unadulterated, genuine.
ANTONYMS alloyed, plated, hollow.
3 *a solid line* **continuous,** uninterrupted, unbroken, nonstop, undivided.
ANTONYMS broken.
4 *solid houses* **well-built,** sound, substantial, strong, sturdy, durable.
ANTONYMS flimsy.
5 *a solid argument* **well-founded,** valid, sound, reasonable, logical, authoritative, convincing, cogent, plausible, credible, reliable.
ANTONYMS untenable, incoherent.
6 *a solid friendship* **dependable,** reliable, firm, unshakable, trustworthy, stable, steadfast, staunch, constant, rock-steady.
ANTONYMS unreliable.
7 *solid citizens* **sensible,** dependable, trustworthy, decent, law-abiding, upright, upstanding, worthy.
8 *the company is very solid* **financially sound,** secure, creditworthy, profit-making, solvent, in credit, in the black.
9 *solid support from their colleagues* **unanimous,** united, consistent, undivided, wholehearted.
ANTONYMS divided.

solidarity ▶ noun *our solidarity is what gives us the credibility and power to make changes* **unanimity,** unity, like-mindedness, agreement, accord, harmony, consensus, concurrence, cooperation, cohesion, fraternity, mutual support; formal concord.

solidify ▶ verb *the mixture will solidify in about nine hours at room temperature* **harden,** set, freeze, thicken, stiffen, congeal, cake, dry, bake; ossify, calcify, fossilize, petrify.
ANTONYMS liquefy.

solitary ▶ adjective **1** *a solitary life* **lonely,** companionless, unaccompanied, by oneself, on one's own, alone, friendless; antisocial, unsociable, withdrawn, reclusive, cloistered, hermitic, incommunicado, lonesome.
ANTONYMS sociable.
2 *solitary farmsteads* **isolated,** remote, lonely, out of the way, in the back of beyond, outlying, off the beaten track/path, godforsaken, obscure, inaccessible, cutoff; secluded, private, sequestered, desolate, in the backwoods; informal in the sticks, in the middle of nowhere, in the boondocks, in the back woods; literary lone.
ANTONYMS accessible.
3 *a solitary piece of evidence* **single,** lone, sole, unique; only, one, individual; odd.

solitude ▶ noun **1** *she savored her solitude* **loneliness,** solitariness, isolation, seclusion, sequestration, withdrawal, privacy, peace.
2 (**solitudes**) *solitudes in the north of the state* **wilderness,** rural area, wilds, backwoods; desert, emptiness, wasteland; the bush, backcountry; informal the sticks, the boondocks.

CHOOSE THE RIGHT WORD

solitude, alienation, desolation, disaffection, estrangement, lonesomeness, solitude

Loneliness, which refers to a lack of companionship and is often associated with unhappiness, should not be confused with **solitude,** which is the state of being alone or cut off from all human contact (*the solitude of the lighthouse keeper*). You can be in the midst of a crowd of people and still experience *loneliness*, but not *solitude*, since you are not physically alone. Similarly, if you enjoy being alone, you can have solitude without loneliness. **Lonesomeness** is more intense than *loneliness*, suggesting the downheartedness you may experience when a loved one is absent (*she experienced lonesomeness following the death of her dog*). **Desolation** is more intense still, referring to a state of being utterly alone or forsaken (*the widow's desolation*). *Desolation* can also indicate a state of ruin or barrenness (*the desolation of the volcanic islands*). **Alienation**, **disaffection**, and **estrangement** have less to do with being or feeling alone and more to do with emotions that change over time. *Alienation* is a word that suggests a feeling of unrelatedness, especially a feeling of distance from your social or intellectual environment (*alienation from society*). *Disaffection* suggests that you now feel indifference or even distaste toward someone of you were once fond of (*a wife's growing disaffection for her husband*), while *estrangement* is a voluntary disaffection that can result in complete separation and strong feelings of dislike or hatred (*a daughter's estrangement from her parents*).

solution ▶ **noun 1** *an easy solution to the problem* **answer,** result, resolution, way out, fix, panacea; key, formula, explanation, interpretation.
2 *a solution of ammonia in water* **mixture,** mix, blend, compound, suspension, tincture, infusion, emulsion.

solve ▶ **verb** *has anyone ever solved this riddle?* **resolve,** answer, work out, find a solution to, find the key to, puzzle out, fathom, decipher, decode, clear up, straighten out, get to the bottom of, unravel, piece together, explain; informal figure out, crack.

solvent ▶ **adjective** *after years in debt, he finally knew what it meant to be solvent* **financially sound,** debt-free, in the black, in credit, creditworthy, solid, secure, profit-making; Finance unleveraged.

somber ▶ **adjective 1** *somber clothes* **dark,** drab, dull, dingy; restrained, subdued, sober, funereal.
ANTONYMS bright.
2 *a somber expression* **solemn,** earnest, serious, grave, sober, unsmiling, stern, grim, dour, humorless; gloomy, depressed, sad, melancholy, dismal, doleful, mournful, lugubrious.
ANTONYMS cheerful.

somebody ▶ **noun** *she wanted to be a somebody* **important person,** VIP, public figure, notable, dignitary, worthy; someone, (big/household) name, celebrity, star, superstar; grandee, luminary, leading light; informal celeb, bigwig, big shot, big cheese, hotshot, megastar.
ANTONYMS nonentity, no-name.

someday ▶ **adverb** *someday I'll live in the countryside* **sometime,** one (fine) day, one of these days, at a future date, sooner or later, by and by, in due course, in the fullness of time, in the long run.
ANTONYMS never.

somehow ▶ **adverb** *I knew that somehow I would find a way to buy that car* **by some means,** by any means, in some way, one way or another, no matter how, by fair means or foul, by hook or by crook, come what may.

sometime ▶ **adverb 1** *I'll visit sometime* **someday,** one day, one of these (fine) days, at a future date, sooner or later, by and by, in due course, in the fullness of time, in the long run.
ANTONYMS never.
2 *it happened sometime on Sunday* **at some time,** at some point; during, in the course of.
▶ **adjective** *the sometime editor of the paper* **former,** past, previous, prior, foregoing, late, erstwhile, one-time, ex-; formal quondam.

sometimes ▶ **adverb** *sometimes we have supper down on the beach* **occasionally,** from time to time, now and then, every so often, once in a while, on occasion, at times, off and on, at intervals, periodically, sporadically, spasmodically, intermittently.

somnolent ▶ **adjective 1** *he felt somnolent after lunch* **sleepy,** drowsy, tired, languid, dozy, groggy, lethargic, sluggish, enervated, torpid; informal snoozy, dopey, yawny; literary slumberous.
2 *a somnolent village* **quiet,** restful, tranquil, calm, peaceful, relaxing, soothing, undisturbed, untroubled.

song ▶ **noun 1** *a beautiful song* **air,** strain, ditty, melody, tune, number, track, anthem, hymn, chanty, chantey, ballad, aria.
2 *the song of the birds* **call(s),** chirping, cheeping, peeping, chirruping, warble(s), warbling, trilling, twitter; birdsong.
– PHRASES **song and dance** informal *why does he have to make such a song and dance out of everything?* See **FUSS** (sense 1 of the noun).

sonorous ▶ **adjective 1** *a sonorous voice* **resonant,** rich, full, round, booming, deep, clear, mellow, orotund, fruity, strong, resounding, reverberant.
2 *sonorous words of condemnation* **impressive,** imposing, grandiloquent, magniloquent, high-flown, lofty, orotund, bombastic, grandiose, pompous, pretentious, overblown, turgid; oratorical, rhetorical; informal highfalutin.

soon ▶ **adverb 1** *we'll be there soon* **shortly,** presently, in the near future, before long, in a little while, in a minute, in a moment, in an instant, in a bit, in the twinkling of an eye, in no time, before you know it, any minute (now), any day (now), by and by; informal pronto, in a jiffy; dated directly, anon.
2 *how soon can you get here?* **early,** quickly, promptly, speedily, punctually.

soothe ▶ **verb 1** *Rachel tried to soothe him* **calm (down),** pacify, comfort, hush, quiet, subdue, settle (down), lull, tranquilize; appease, conciliate, mollify.
ANTONYMS agitate.
2 *an anesthetic to soothe the pain* **alleviate,** ease, relieve, take the edge off, assuage, allay, lessen, palliate, diminish, decrease, dull, blunt, deaden.
ANTONYMS aggravate.

soothsayer ▶ noun *the most respected of the king's soothsayers* **seer,** oracle, augur, prophet/prophetess, sage, prognosticator, diviner, fortune teller, crystal-gazer, clairvoyant, psychic; literary sibyl; rare haruspex.

sophisticated ▶ adjective 1 *sophisticated techniques* **advanced,** modern, state of the art, the latest, new, up-to-the-minute; innovative, trailblazing, revolutionary, futuristic, avant-garde; complex, complicated, intricate, highly evolved.
ANTONYMS crude.
2 *a sophisticated woman* **worldly,** worldly-wise, experienced, enlightened, cosmopolitan, knowledgeable; urbane, cultured, cultivated, civilized, polished, refined; elegant, stylish; informal cool. See note at **URBANE.**
ANTONYMS naive.

sophistication ▶ noun *the shabbiest of work clothes could not disguise his sophistication* **worldliness,** experience; urbanity, culture, civilization, polish, refinement; elegance, style, poise, finesse, savoir faire; informal cool.

sophistry ▶ noun 1 *to claim this is pure sophistry* **specious reasoning,** fallacy, sophism, casuistry.
2 *a speech full of sophistries* **fallacious argument,** sophism, fallacy; Logic paralogism.

soporific ▶ adjective 1 *soporific drugs* **sleep-inducing,** sedative, somnolent, calmative, tranquilizing, narcotic, opiate; drowsy, sleepy, somniferous; Medicine hypnotic.
ANTONYMS invigorating.
2 *a soporific TV drama* **boring,** tedious, tired, dreary, turgid, dry, mind-numbing.
▶ noun *she was given a soporific* **sleeping pill,** sedative, calmative, tranquilizer, narcotic, opiate; Medicine hypnotic.
ANTONYMS stimulant.

sorcerer, sorceress ▶ noun *he was convinced that a sorceress had cast an evil spell upon his household* **wizard,** witch, magician, warlock, enchanter, enchantress, magus; witch doctor; archaic mage.

sorcery ▶ noun *the practice of sorcery was strictly forbidden* (**black**) **magic,** the black arts, witchcraft, wizardry, enchantment, spells, incantation, witching, witchery, thaumaturgy.

sordid ▶ adjective 1 *a sordid love affair* **sleazy,** dirty, seedy, seamy, unsavory, tawdry, cheap, debased, degenerate, dishonorable, disreputable, discreditable, contemptible, ignominious, shameful, abhorrent.
ANTONYMS respectable.
2 *a sordid little street* **squalid,** slummy, insalubrious, dirty, filthy, mucky, grimy, shabby, messy, soiled, scummy, unclean; informal cruddy, grungy, crummy, scuzzy.
ANTONYMS immaculate.

sore ▶ adjective 1 *a sore leg* **painful,** hurting, hurt, aching, throbbing, smarting, stinging, agonizing, excruciating; inflamed, sensitive, tender, raw, bruised, wounded, injured.
2 *we are in sore need of you* **dire,** urgent, pressing, desperate, parlous, critical, crucial, acute, grave, serious, drastic, extreme, life-and-death, great, terrible; formal exigent.
3 informal *they were sore at us* **upset,** angry, annoyed, cross, furious, vexed, displeased, disgruntled, dissatisfied, exasperated, irritated, galled, irked, put out, aggrieved, offended, affronted, piqued, nettled; informal aggravated, miffed, peeved, riled, teed off, ticked off.
▶ noun *a sore on his leg* **inflammation,** swelling, lesion; wound, scrape, abrasion, cut, laceration, graze, contusion, bruise; ulcer, boil, abscess, carbuncle.

sorrow ▶ noun 1 *he felt sorrow at her death* **sadness,** unhappiness, misery, despondency, regret, depression, despair, desolation, dejection, wretchedness, gloom, dolefulness, melancholy, woe, heartache, grief; literary dolor.
ANTONYMS joy.
2 *the sorrows of life* **trouble,** difficulty, problem, adversity, misery, woe, affliction, trial, tribulation, misfortune, pain, setback, reverse, blow, failure, tragedy.
ANTONYMS joy.
▶ verb *they sorrowed over her grave* **mourn,** lament, grieve, be sad, be miserable, be despondent, despair, suffer, ache, agonize, anguish, pine, weep, wail. See note at **MOURN.**
ANTONYMS rejoice.

sorrowful ▶ adjective 1 *sorrowful eyes* **sad,** unhappy, dejected, regretful, downcast, miserable, downhearted, despondent, despairing, disconsolate, desolate, glum, gloomy, doleful, dismal, melancholy, mournful, woeful, woebegone, forlorn, crestfallen, heartbroken; informal blue, down in/at the mouth, down in the dumps.
2 *sorrowful news* **tragic,** sad, unhappy, awful, miserable, sorry, pitiful; traumatic, upsetting, depressing, distressing, dispiriting, heartbreaking, harrowing; formal grievous.

sorry ▶ adjective 1 *I was sorry to hear about his accident* **sad,** unhappy, sorrowful, distressed, upset, downcast, downhearted, disheartened, despondent; heartbroken, inconsolable, grief-stricken.
ANTONYMS glad.
2 *he felt sorry for her* **full of pity,** sympathetic, compassionate, moved, consoling, empathetic, concerned.
ANTONYMS unsympathetic.
3 *I'm sorry if I was brusque* **regretful,** remorseful, contrite, repentant, rueful, penitent, apologetic, abject, guilty, ashamed, sheepish, shamefaced.
ANTONYMS unrepentant.
4 *he looks a sorry sight* **pitiful,** pitiable, heart-rending, distressing; unfortunate, unhappy, wretched, unlucky, shameful, regrettable, awful.
▶ exclamation *"Hey, that's my foot!" "Sorry!"* **apologies,** excuse me, pardon me, forgive me, my mistake; informal my bad.

sort ▶ noun 1 *what sort of book is it?* **type,** kind, nature, manner, variety, class, category, style; caliber, quality, form, group, set, bracket, genre, species, family, order, generation, vintage, make, model, brand, stamp, stripe, ilk, cast, grain, mold.
2 informal *he's a good sort* **person,** individual, soul, creature, human being; character, customer; informal fellow, type.

▶ **verb** *they sorted things of similar size* **classify,** class, categorize, catalog, grade, group; organize, arrange, order, marshal, assemble, systematize, systemize, pigeonhole, sort out.

– PHRASES **out of sorts 1** *I'm feeling out of sorts* **unwell,** ill, poorly, sick, queasy, nauseous, peaked, run-down, below par; informal under the weather, funny, lousy, rotten, awful, crappy, off. **2** *he's out of sorts because she turned him down* **grumpy,** irritable, crabby; unhappy, sad, miserable, down, depressed, gloomy, glum, forlorn, low, in a blue funk; informal blue, down in the dumps. **sort of** informal **1** *you look sort of familiar* **slightly,** faintly, remotely, vaguely; somewhat, moderately, quite, rather, fairly, reasonably, relatively; informal pretty, kind of, kinda. **2** *he sort of pirouetted* **as it were,** kind of, somehow. **sort out** *they must sort out their problems* **resolve,** settle, solve, fix, work out, straighten out, deal with, put right, set right, rectify, iron out; answer, explain, fathom, unravel, clear up; informal sew up, hammer out, thrash out, patch up, figure out.

sortie ▶ **noun 1** *a sortie against their besiegers* **foray,** sally, charge, offensive, attack, assault, onset, onslaught, thrust, drive.
2 *a bomber sortie* **raid,** flight, mission, operation, op.

so-so ▶ **adjective** informal *the appetizers were exceptional, but the chowder was so-so* **mediocre,** indifferent, average, middle-of-the-road, middling, moderate, ordinary, adequate, fair; uninspired, undistinguished, unexceptional, unremarkable, run-of-the-mill, lackluster, 'comme ci, comme ça'; informal no great shakes, not up to much, okay.

soul ▶ **noun 1** *seeing the soul through the eyes* **spirit,** psyche, (inner) self, inner being, life force, vital force; individuality, makeup, subconscious, anima; Philosophy pneuma; Hinduism atman.
2 *he is the soul of discretion* **embodiment,** personification, incarnation, epitome, quintessence, essence; model, exemplification, exemplar, image, manifestation.
3 *not a soul in sight* **person,** human being, individual, man, woman, mortal, creature.
4 *their music lacked soul* **inspiration,** feeling, emotion, passion, animation, intensity, fervor, ardor, enthusiasm, warmth, energy, vitality, spirit.

sound[1] ▶ **noun 1** *the sound of the car* **noise,** note; din, racket, row, hubbub; resonance, reverberation.
ANTONYMS silence.
2 *she did not make a sound* **utterance,** cry, word, noise, peep.
3 *the sound of the flute* **music,** tone, notes.
4 *I don't like the sound of that* **idea,** thought, concept, prospect, description.
▶ **verb 1** *the buzzer sounded* **make a noise,** resonate, resound, reverberate, go off, blare; ring, chime, peal.
2 *drivers must sound their horns* **blow,** blast, toot, blare; operate, set off; ring.
3 *do you sound the "h"?* **pronounce,** verbalize, voice, enunciate, articulate, vocalize, say.
4 *she sounded a warning* **utter,** voice, deliver, express, speak, announce, pronounce.
5 *it **sounds like** a crazy idea* **appear,** look (like), seem, strike someone as being, give every indication of being, come across as.

sound[2] ▶ **adjective 1** *your heart is sound* **healthy,** in good condition, in good shape, fit, hale and hearty, in fine fettle; undamaged, unimpaired.
ANTONYMS unhealthy.
2 *a sound building* **well-built,** solid, substantial, strong, sturdy, durable, stable, intact, unimpaired.
ANTONYMS unsafe, flimsy.
3 *sound advice* **well-founded,** valid, reasonable, logical, weighty, authoritative, reliable, well-grounded.
4 *a sound judge of character* **reliable,** dependable, trustworthy, fair; good, sensible, wise, judicious, sagacious, shrewd, perceptive.
ANTONYMS unreliable.
5 *financially sound* **solvent,** debt-free, in the black, in credit, creditworthy, secure, solid.
ANTONYMS insolvent, light.
6 *a sound sleep* **deep,** undisturbed, uninterrupted, untroubled, peaceful.
ANTONYMS light.

sound[3] ▶ **verb** *sound the depth of the river* **measure,** gauge, determine, test, investigate, survey, plumb, fathom, probe.
– PHRASES **sound out** *if you'll just sound them out, you might learn something useful* **investigate,** test, check, examine, probe, research, look into; canvass, survey, poll, question, interview, sample; informal pump.

sound[4] ▶ **noun** *an oil spill in the sound* **channel,** (sea) passage, strait(s), narrows, waterway; inlet, arm (of the sea), fjord, creek, bay; estuary.

sour ▶ **adjective 1** *sour wine* **acid,** acidic, acidy, acidulated, tart, bitter, sharp, vinegary, pungent; technical acerbic.
ANTONYMS sweet.
2 *sour milk* **bad,** off, turned, curdled, rancid, rank, foul, fetid; (of beer) skunky.
ANTONYMS fresh.
3 *a sour old man* **embittered,** resentful, rancorous, jaundiced, bitter; nasty, spiteful, irritable, peevish, fractious, cross, crabby, crotchety, cantankerous, disagreeable, petulant, querulous, grumpy, bad-tempered, ill-humored, sullen, surly, sulky, churlish; informal grouchy, cranky.
ANTONYMS amiable.
▶ **verb 1** *the war had soured him* **embitter,** disillusion, disenchant, poison, alienate; dissatisfy, frustrate.
2 *the dispute soured relations* **spoil,** mar, damage, harm, impair, wreck, upset, poison, blight, tarnish.
ANTONYMS improve.

source ▶ **noun 1** *the source of the river* **spring,** origin, headspring, headwater(s); literary wellspring.
2 *the source of the rumor* **origin,** birthplace, spring, fountainhead, fount, starting point, ground zero; history, provenance, derivation, root, beginning, genesis, start, rise; author, originator, initiator, inventor. See note at **ORIGIN**.

3 *a historian uses primary and secondary sources* **reference,** authority, material, document, informant.

souvenir ▶ noun *keep the key ring as a souvenir* **memento,** keepsake, reminder, remembrance, token, memorial; bomboniere; trophy, relic.

sovereign ▶ noun *the daughter of their beloved sovereign* **ruler,** monarch, crowned head, head of state, potentate, suzerain, overlord, dynast, leader; king, queen, emperor, empress, prince, princess, czar, royal duke, regent, mogul, emir, sheikh, sultan, maharaja, raja.
▶ adjective **1** *sovereign control* **supreme,** absolute, unlimited, unrestricted, boundless, ultimate, total, unconditional, full; principal, chief, dominant, predominant, ruling; royal, regal, monarchical.
2 *a sovereign state* **independent,** autonomous, self-governing, self-determining; nonaligned, free.

sovereignty ▶ noun **1** *their sovereignty over the islands* **jurisdiction,** rule, supremacy, dominion, power, ascendancy, suzerainty, hegemony, domination, authority, control, influence. See note at JURISDICTION.
2 *the colony demanded full sovereignty* **autonomy,** independence, self-government, self-rule, home rule, self-determination, freedom.

sow ▶ verb **1** *sow the seeds in rows* **plant,** scatter, spread, disperse, strew, disseminate, distribute, broadcast; drill, seed.
2 *the new policy has sown confusion* **cause,** bring about, occasion, create, lead to, produce, spread, engender, generate, prompt, initiate, precipitate, trigger, provoke; culminate in, entail, necessitate; foster, foment; literary beget.

space ▶ noun **1** *there was not enough space* **room,** capacity, area, volume, expanse, extent, scope, latitude, margin, leeway, play, clearance.
2 *green spaces in the city* **area,** expanse, stretch, sweep, tract.
3 *the space between the timbers* **gap,** interval, opening, aperture, cavity, cranny, fissure, crack, interstice, lacuna.
4 *write your name in the appropriate space* **blank,** gap, box; place.
5 *a space of seven years* **period,** span, time, duration, stretch, course, interval.
6 *the first woman in space* **outer space,** deep space; the universe, the galaxy, the solar system; infinity.
▶ verb *the chairs were spaced widely* **position,** arrange, range, array, dispose, lay out, locate, situate, set, stand.

spacious ▶ adjective *spacious accommodations* **roomy,** capacious, palatial, airy, sizable, generous, large, big, vast, immense; extensive, expansive, sweeping, rolling, rambling, open; formal commodious.
ANTONYMS cramped.

span ▶ noun **1** *a six-foot wing span* **extent,** length, width, reach, stretch, spread, distance, range.
2 *the span of one working day* **period,** space, time, duration, course, interval.
▶ verb **1** *an arch spanned the stream* **bridge,** cross, traverse, pass over.
2 *his career spanned twenty years* **last,** cover, extend, spread over, comprise.

spank ▶ verb *he would never dream of spanking his children* **smack,** slap, hit, cuff; informal wallop, belt, whack, tan someone's hide.

spar ▶ verb *they sparred over every little thing* **quarrel,** argue, fight, disagree, differ, be at odds, be at variance, fall out, dispute, squabble, wrangle, bandy words, cross swords, lock horns, be at loggerheads; informal scrap, spat.

spare ▶ adjective **1** *a spare set of keys* **extra,** supplementary, additional, second, other, alternative, alternate; emergency, reserve, backup, relief, fallback, substitute; fresh.
2 *they sold off the spare land* **surplus,** superfluous, excessive, extra; redundant, unnecessary, inessential, unessential, unneeded, uncalled for, dispensable, disposable, expendable, unwanted; informal going begging.
3 *your spare time* **free,** leisure, own.
4 *a man of spare build* See THIN (sense 3 of the adjective). See also note at THIN.
▶ verb **1** *sorry, I can't spare a quarter* **afford,** do without, manage without, dispense with, part with, give, provide.
2 *their captors eventually spared them* **pardon,** let off, forgive, reprieve, release, free; leave uninjured, leave unhurt; be merciful to, show mercy to, have mercy on, be lenient to, have pity on.

sparing ▶ adjective *a fiercely sparing man, he died rich and friendless* **thrifty,** economical, frugal, canny, careful, prudent, cautious; mean, miserly, niggardly, parsimonious, close-fisted, penny-pinching, ungenerous, close, grasping; informal stingy, cheap, tightfisted, tight, mingy, money-grubbing. See note at ECONOMICAL.
ANTONYMS lavish.

spark ▶ noun **1** *a spark of light* **flash,** glint, twinkle, flicker, flare, pinprick.
2 *not a spark of truth in the story* **particle,** iota, jot, whit, glimmer, atom, bit, trace, vestige, ounce, shred, crumb, grain, mite, hint, touch, suggestion, whisper, scintilla; informal smidgen, tad.
▶ verb *the trial sparked a furious debate* **cause,** give rise to, lead to, occasion, bring about, start, initiate, precipitate, prompt, trigger (off), provoke, stimulate, stir up.

sparkle ▶ verb **1** *her earrings sparkled* **glitter,** glint, glisten, twinkle, flash, blink, wink, shimmer, shine, gleam; literary coruscate, glister.
2 *she sparkled as the hostess* **be lively,** be vivacious, be animated, be ebullient, be exuberant, be bubbly, be effervescent, be witty, be full of life.
▶ noun *the sparkle of the pool* **glitter,** glint, twinkle, flicker, shimmer, flash, shine, gleam; literary coruscation.

sparse ▶ adjective *areas of sparse population* **scant,** scanty, scattered, scarce, infrequent, few and far between; meager, paltry, skimpy, limited, in short supply.
ANTONYMS abundant.

spartan ▶ adjective *the monk's spartan cell* **austere,** harsh, hard, frugal, stringent, rigorous, strict, stern, severe; ascetic, abstemious; bleak, joyless, grim, bare, stark, plain.

ANTONYMS luxurious.

spasm ▶ noun **1** *a muscle spasm* **contraction,** convulsion, cramp; twitch, jerk, tic, shudder, shiver, tremor.
2 *a spasm of coughing* **fit,** paroxysm, attack, burst, bout, seizure, outburst, outbreak, access.

spasmodic ▶ adjective *the car chugged up the road with spasmodic lurches* **intermittent,** fitful, irregular, sporadic, erratic, occasional, infrequent, scattered, patchy, isolated, periodic, periodical, on and off; informal herky-jerky.

spate ▶ noun *a spate of interest in military memorabilia* **series,** succession, run, cluster, string, rash, epidemic, outbreak, wave, flurry, rush, flood, deluge, torrent.

spatter ▶ verb *the curtains were spattered with champagne* **splash,** bespatter, splatter, spray, sprinkle, shower, speck, speckle, fleck, mottle, blotch, mark, cover; informal splotch.

spawn ▶ verb *that one brief statement has spawned a blitz of criticism* **give rise to,** bring about, occasion, generate, engender, originate; lead to, result in, effect, induce, initiate, start, set off, precipitate, trigger; breed, bear; literary beget.

speak ▶ verb **1** *she refused to speak about it* **talk,** say anything/something; utter, state, declare, tell, voice, express, pronounce, articulate, enunciate, vocalize, verbalize.
2 *we spoke the other day* **converse,** have a conversation, talk, communicate, chat, pass the time of day, have a word, gossip; informal have a confab, chew the fat; natter, shoot the breeze; formal confabulate.
3 *the minister spoke for two hours* **give a speech,** talk, lecture, hold forth, discourse, expound, expatiate, orate, sermonize, pontificate, declaim; informal spout, spiel, speechify, jaw, sound off.
4 *he was **spoken of** as a promising student* **mention,** talk about, discuss, refer to, remark on, allude to, describe.
5 *her expression spoke disbelief* **indicate,** show, display, register, reveal, betray, exhibit, manifest, express, convey, impart, bespeak, communicate, evidence; suggest, denote, reflect; formal evince.
6 *you must **speak to** him about his rudeness* **reprimand,** rebuke, admonish, chastise, chide, upbraid, reprove, reproach, scold, remonstrate with, take to task; informal tell off, dress down, rap over the knuckles, come down on, give someone what for; formal castigate.
– PHRASES **speak for 1** *she speaks for the Arts Council* **represent,** act for, appear for, express the views of, be spokesperson for. **2** *I spoke for the motion* **advocate,** champion, uphold, defend, support, promote, recommend, back, endorse, sponsor, espouse. **speak out** *if you've got a grievance, then speak out* **speak publicly,** speak openly, speak frankly, speak one's mind, sound off, stand up and be counted. **speak up** *speak up so we can hear you* **speak loudly,** speak clearly, raise one's voice; shout, yell, bellow; informal holler.

speaker ▶ noun *Reverend Graham is one of the guest speakers* **speechmaker,** lecturer, talker, speechifier, orator, declaimer, rhetorician; spokesperson, spokesman/woman, mouthpiece; reader, lector, commentator, broadcaster, narrator; informal spieler; historical demagogue, rhetor.

spearhead ▶ noun **1** *a Bronze Age spearhead* **spear tip,** spear point.
2 *the spearhead of the struggle against fascism* **leader(s),** driving force; forefront, front runner(s), front line, vanguard, van, cutting edge.
▶ verb *she spearheaded the campaign* **lead,** head, front; lead the way, be in the van, be in the vanguard.

special ▶ adjective **1** *a very special person* **exceptional,** unusual, singular, uncommon, notable, noteworthy, remarkable, outstanding, unique.
ANTONYMS ordinary.
2 *our town's special character* **distinctive,** distinct, individual, particular, characteristic, specific, peculiar, idiosyncratic.
ANTONYMS general.
3 *a special occasion* **momentous,** significant, memorable, signal, important, historic, festive, gala, red-letter.
4 *a special tool for cutting tiles* **specific,** particular, purpose-built, tailor-made, custom-built/made.

specialist ▶ noun *he's an electronics specialist* **expert,** authority, pundit, professional; connoisseur; master, maestro, adept, virtuoso; informal pro, buff, ace, whiz, hotshot, maven.
ANTONYMS amateur.

specialty ▶ noun **1** *his specialty was watercolors* **forte,** strong point, strength, métier, strong suit, talent, skill, bent, gift; Brit. speciality; informal bag, thing, cup of tea.
2 *a specialty of the region* **delicacy**; Brit. speciality, fine food/product, traditional food/product.

species ▶ noun *there are several species of spadefoot toad* **type,** kind, sort; genus, family, order, breed, strain, variety, class, classification, category, set, bracket; style, manner, form, genre; generation, vintage.

specific ▶ adjective **1** *a specific purpose* **particular,** specified, fixed, set, determined, distinct, definite; single, individual, peculiar, discrete, express, precise.
ANTONYMS general.
2 *I gave specific instructions* **detailed,** explicit, express, clear-cut, unequivocal, precise, exact, meticulous, strict, definite.
ANTONYMS vague.

specification ▶ noun **1** *the clear specification of objectives* **statement,** identification, definition, description, setting out, framing, designation, detailing, enumeration; stipulation, prescription.
2 (**specifications**) *a shelter built to their specifications* **instructions,** guidelines, parameters, stipulations, requirements, conditions, provisions, restrictions, order; description, details; informal specs.

specify ▶ verb *specify your color preferences* **state,** name, identify, define, describe, set out, frame, itemize, detail, list, spell out, enumerate, particularize, cite, instance; stipulate, prescribe.

specimen ▶ noun *a specimen of his handwriting* **sample,** example, instance, illustration, demonstration, exemplification; bit, snippet; model, prototype, pattern, dummy, pilot, trial, taster, tester.

specious ▶ adjective *specious reasoning* **misleading,** deceptive, false, fallacious, unsound, spurious, casuistic, sophistic.

speck ▶ noun **1** *a mere speck in the distance* **dot,** pinprick, spot, fleck, speckle.
2 *a speck of dust* **particle,** grain, atom, molecule; bit, trace.

speckled ▶ adjective *speckled eggs* **flecked,** speckly, specked, freckled, freckly, spotted, spotty, dotted, mottled, dappled.

spectacle ▶ noun **1** *a spectacle fit for a monarch* **display,** show, pageant, parade, performance, exhibition, extravaganza, spectacular.
2 *they were rather an odd spectacle* **sight,** vision, scene, prospect, vista, picture.
3 *don't make a spectacle of yourself* **exhibition,** laughingstock, fool, curiosity.

spectacular ▶ adjective **1** *a spectacular victory* **impressive,** magnificent, splendid, dazzling, sensational, dramatic, remarkable, outstanding, memorable, unforgettable.
ANTONYMS unimpressive.
2 *a spectacular view* **striking,** picturesque, eye-catching, breathtaking, arresting, glorious; informal out of this world.
ANTONYMS unimpressive, dull.

spectator ▶ noun *the stands are brimming with eager spectators* **watcher,** viewer, observer, onlooker, looker-on, bystander, witness; commentator, reporter, monitor; literary beholder.
ANTONYMS participant.

specter ▶ noun **1** *the specters in the crypt* **ghost,** phantom, apparition, spirit, wraith, shadow, presence; informal spook; literary phantasm, shade.
2 *the looming specter of war* **threat,** menace, shadow, cloud; prospect; danger, peril, fear, dread.

speculate ▶ verb **1** *they speculated about my private life* **conjecture,** theorize, hypothesize, guess, surmise; think, wonder, muse.
2 *investors* ***speculate on*** *the stock market* **gamble on,** take a risk on, venture in, wager on; invest in, play.

speculative ▶ adjective **1** *any discussion is largely speculative* **conjectural,** suppositional, theoretical, hypothetical, putative, academic, notional, abstract; tentative, unproven, unfounded, groundless, unsubstantiated.
2 *a speculative investment* **risky,** hazardous, unsafe, uncertain, unpredictable; informal chancy, dicey, iffy.

speech ▶ noun **1** *he doesn't have the power of speech* **speaking,** talking, verbal expression, verbal communication.
2 *her speech was slurred* **diction,** elocution, articulation, enunciation, pronunciation; utterance, words.
3 *an after-dinner speech* **talk,** address, lecture, discourse, oration, disquisition, peroration, deliverance, presentation; sermon, homily; monologue, soliloquy; informal spiel.
4 *Spanish popular speech* **language,** tongue, parlance, idiom, dialect, vernacular, patois; informal lingo, patter, -speak, -ese.

speechless ▶ adjective *her talk of divorce left him speechless* **lost for words,** at a loss (for words), dumbstruck, dumbfounded, bereft of speech, tongue-tied, inarticulate, mute, dumb, voiceless, silent; informal mum.
ANTONYMS verbose.

speed ▶ noun **1** *the speed of their progress* **rate,** pace, tempo, momentum.
2 *the speed with which they responded* **rapidity,** swiftness, speediness, quickness, dispatch, promptness, immediacy, briskness, sharpness; haste, hurry, precipitateness; acceleration, velocity; informal lick, clip; literary celerity.
▶ verb **1** *I sped home* **hurry,** rush, dash, run, race, sprint, bolt, dart, gallop, career, charge, shoot, hurtle, careen, hare, fly, zoom, scurry, scuttle, scamper, hasten; informal tear, belt, pelt, scoot, zip, zap, whip, hotfoot it, bomb, hightail it.
2 *he was caught speeding* **drive too fast,** exceed the speed limit.
3 *a holiday will speed his recovery* **hasten,** expedite, speed up, accelerate, advance, further, promote, boost, stimulate, aid, assist, facilitate.
ANTONYMS slow, hinder.

speedy ▶ adjective **1** *a speedy reply* **rapid,** swift, quick, fast; prompt, immediate, expeditious, express, brisk, sharp; whirlwind, lightning, meteoric; hasty, hurried, precipitate, breakneck, rushed; informal PDQ (pretty damn quick), snappy, quickie.
ANTONYMS slow.
2 *a speedy little car* **fast,** high-speed; informal nippy, zippy, peppy; literary fleet.
ANTONYMS slow.

spell[1] ▶ verb *the drought spelled disaster for them* **signal,** signify, mean, amount to, add up to, constitute; portend, augur, herald, bode, promise; involve; literary betoken, foretoken, forebode.
– PHRASES **spell out** *allow us to spell out the plan in detail* **explain,** make clear, make plain, elucidate, clarify; specify, itemize, detail, enumerate, list, expound, particularize, catalog.

spell[2] ▶ noun **1** *the witch recited a spell* **incantation,** charm, conjuration, formula; (**spells**) magic, sorcery, witchcraft, hex, curse.
2 *she surrendered to his spell* **influence,** (animal) magnetism, charisma, allure, lure, charm, attraction, enticement; magic, romance, mystique.
– PHRASES **cast a spell on** *it's as if this town cast a spell on me* **bewitch,** enchant, entrance; curse, jinx, witch, hex.

spell[3] ▶ noun **1** *a spell of dry weather* **period,** time, interval, season, stretch, run, course, streak, patch.
2 *a spell of dizziness* **bout,** fit, attack.

spellbinding ▶ adjective *a spellbinding tale set in the Far East* **fascinating,** enthralling, entrancing, bewitching, captivating, riveting, engrossing, gripping, absorbing, compelling, compulsive, mesmerizing, hypnotic; informal unputdownable.
ANTONYMS boring.

spellbound ▶ adjective *the audience was spellbound* **enthralled,** fascinated, rapt, riveted, transfixed, gripped, captivated, bewitched, enchanted, mesmerized, hypnotized; informal hooked.

spend ▶ verb **1** *she spent $185 on shoes* **pay out,** dish out, expend, disburse; squander, waste, fritter away; lavish; informal fork out, lay out, shell out, cough up, drop, blow, splurge, pony up.
2 *the morning was spent gardening* **pass,** occupy, fill, take up, while away.
3 *I've spent hours on this essay* **put in,** devote; waste.
4 *the storm had spent its force* **use up,** consume, exhaust, deplete, drain.

spendthrift ▶ noun *he is such a spendthrift* **profligate,** prodigal, squanderer, waster; informal big spender.
ANTONYMS miser.
▶ adjective *his spendthrift father* **profligate,** improvident, thriftless, wasteful, extravagant, prodigal.
ANTONYMS frugal.

spent ▶ adjective **1** *a spent force* **used up,** consumed, exhausted, finished, depleted, drained; informal burnt out.
2 *that's enough—I'm spent* **exhausted,** tired (out), weary, worn out, dog-tired, on one's last legs, drained, fatigued, ready to drop; informal done in, all in, dead on one's feet, dead beat, bushed, wiped out, frazzled, whacked, pooped, tuckered out.

spew ▶ verb *factories spewed out yellow smoke* **emit,** discharge, eject, expel, belch out, pour out, spout, gush, spurt, disgorge.

sphere ▶ noun **1** *a glass sphere* **globe,** ball, orb, spheroid, globule, round; bubble.
2 *our sphere of influence* **area,** field, compass, orbit; range, scope, extent.
3 *the sphere of foreign affairs* **domain,** realm, province, field, area, territory, arena, department.

spherical ▶ adjective *a spherical Japanese lantern* **round,** globular, globose, globoid, globe-shaped, spheroidal, spheric. See note at ROUND.

spice ▶ noun **1** *the spices in curry powder* **seasoning,** flavoring, condiment.
2 *the risk added spice to their affair* **excitement,** interest, color, piquancy, zest; an edge; informal a kick; literary salt.
– PHRASES **spice up** *they spiced up the party with some wild dancing* **enliven,** make more exciting, vitalize, perk up, put some life into, ginger up, galvanize, electrify, boost; informal pep up, jazz up, buck up.

spicy ▶ adjective **1** *a spicy casserole* **hot,** peppery, piquant, picante; spiced, seasoned; tasty, zesty, strong, pungent.
ANTONYMS bland.
2 *spicy stories* **entertaining,** colorful, lively, spirited, exciting, piquant, zesty; risqué, racy, scandalous, ribald, titillating, bawdy, naughty, salacious, dirty, smutty; informal raunchy, juicy, saucy.
ANTONYMS boring.

spike ▶ noun **1** *a metal spike* **prong,** barb, point; skewer, stake, spit; tine, pin; spur; Mountaineering piton.
2 *the spikes of a cactus* **thorn,** spine, prickle, bristle; Zoology spicule.
▶ verb **1** *she spiked an oyster* **impale,** spear, skewer; pierce, penetrate, perforate, stab, stick, transfix; literary transpierce.
2 informal *his drink was spiked with drugs* **adulterate,** contaminate, drug, lace; informal dope, doctor, cut.

spill ▶ verb **1** *Kevin spilled his drink* **knock over,** tip over, upset, overturn.
2 *the bath water spilled onto the floor* **overflow,** flow, pour, run, slop, slosh, splash; leak, escape; archaic overbrim.
3 *students spilled out of the building* **stream,** pour, surge, swarm, flood, throng, crowd.
4 *the horse spilled its rider* **unseat,** throw, dislodge, unhorse.
5 informal *he's spilling out his troubles to her* **reveal,** disclose, divulge, blurt out, babble, betray, tell; informal blab.
▶ noun **1** *an oil spill* **spillage,** leak, leakage, overflow, flood.
2 *she took a spill in the opening race* **fall,** tumble; informal header, cropper, nosedive.
– PHRASES **spill the beans** informal *somebody spilled the beans about the surprise party* **reveal all,** tell all, give the game away, talk; informal let the cat out of the bag, blab, come clean.

spin ▶ verb **1** *the bike wheels are spinning* **revolve,** rotate, turn, go round, whirl, gyrate, circle.
2 *she spun around to face him* **whirl,** wheel, twirl, turn, swing, twist, swivel, pirouette, pivot.
3 *her head was spinning* **reel,** whirl, go around, swim.
4 *she spun an amusing yarn* **tell,** recount, relate, narrate; weave, concoct, invent, fabricate, make up.
▶ noun **1** *a spin of the wheel* **rotation,** revolution, turn, whirl, twirl, gyration.
2 *a positive spin on the campaign* **slant,** angle, twist, bias.
3 *a quick spin to the grocery store* **trip,** jaunt, outing, excursion, journey; drive, ride, run, turn, airing, joyride.
– PHRASES **spin out** *the longer you can spin out the negotiations the better* **prolong,** protract, draw out, drag out, string out, extend, carry on, continue; fill out, pad out.

spine ▶ noun **1** *he injured his spine* **backbone,** spinal column, vertebral column; back; technical rachis.
2 *the spine of his philosophy* **core,** center, cornerstone, foundation, basis.
3 *the spines of a porcupine* **needle,** quill, bristle, barb, spike, prickle; thorn; technical spicule.

spine-chilling ▶ adjective *a spine-chilling ghost story* **terrifying,** blood-curdling, petrifying, hair-raising, frightening, scaring, chilling, horrifying, fearsome; eerie, sinister, bone-chilling, ghostly; eldritch; informal scary, creepy, spooky.
ANTONYMS comforting, reassuring.

spineless ▶ adjective *Flora could have smacked him for being so spineless* **weak,** weak-willed, weak-kneed, feeble, soft, ineffectual, irresolute, indecisive; **cowardly,** timid, timorous, fearful,

faint-hearted, pusillanimous, craven, unmanly, namby-pamby, lily-livered, chicken-hearted; informal wimpish, wimpy, sissy, wussy, chicken, yellow, yellow-bellied, gutless.
ANTONYMS bold, brave, strong-willed.

spiral ▶ adjective *a spiral column of smoke* **coiled,** helical, corkscrew, curling, winding, twisting, whorled; technical voluted, helicoid, helicoidal.
▶ noun *a spiral of smoke* **coil,** helix, corkscrew, curl, twist, gyre, whorl, scroll; technical volute, volution.
▶ verb 1 *smoke spiraled up* **coil,** wind, swirl, twist, wreathe, snake, gyrate; literary gyre.
2 *prices spiraled* **soar,** shoot up, rocket, increase rapidly, rise rapidly, escalate, climb; informal skyrocket, go through the roof.
ANTONYMS fall.
3 *the economy is* ***spiraling downward*** **deteriorate,** decline, degenerate, worsen, get worse; informal go downhill, take a nosedive, go to pot, go to the dogs, hit the skids, go down the tubes.
ANTONYMS improve.

spire ▶ noun *the spire of a nearby church* **steeple,** flèche.

spirit ▶ noun 1 *harmony between body and spirit* **soul,** psyche, (inner) self, inner being, inner man/woman, mind, ego, id; Philosophy pneuma.
ANTONYMS body, flesh.
2 *a spirit haunts the island* **ghost,** presence; informal spook.
3 *that's the spirit* **attitude,** frame of mind, way of thinking, point of view, outlook, thoughts, ideas.
4 *she was in good spirits when I left* **mood,** frame of mind, state of mind, emotional state, humor, temper.
5 *team spirit* **morale,** esprit de corps.
6 *the spirit of the age* **ethos,** prevailing tendency, motivating force, essence, quintessence; atmosphere, mood, feeling, climate; attitudes, beliefs, principles, standards, ethics.
7 *his spirit never failed him* **courage,** bravery, pluck, valor, strength of character, fortitude, backbone, mettle, stoutheartedness, determination, resolution, resolve, fight, grit; informal guts, spunk, sand, moxie.
8 *they played with great spirit* **enthusiasm,** eagerness, keenness, liveliness, vivacity, vivaciousness, animation, energy, verve, vigor, dynamism, zest, dash, élan, panache, sparkle, exuberance, gusto, brio, pep, fervor, zeal, fire, passion; informal get-up-and-go.
9 *the spirit of the law* **real/true meaning,** true intention, essence, substance.
10 *he drinks spirits* **strong liquor/drink**; informal hard stuff, firewater, hooch.
– PHRASES **spirit away** *they made up a story about having been spirited away by gypsies* **whisk away/off,** make off with, make disappear, run away with, abscond with, carry off, steal away, abduct, kidnap, snatch, seize.

spirited ▶ adjective *spirited young dancers* **lively,** vivacious, vibrant, full of life, vital, animated, high-spirited, sparkling, sprightly, energetic, active, vigorous, dynamic, dashing, enthusiastic, passionate; determined, resolute, purposeful; informal feisty, spunky, take-charge, gutsy, peppy.
ANTONYMS timid, apathetic, lifeless.

spiritless ▶ adjective *a spiritless performance* **apathetic,** passive, unenthusiastic, lifeless, listless, weak, feeble, spineless, languid, bloodless, insipid, characterless, submissive, meek, irresolute, indecisive; lackluster, flat, colorless, passionless, uninspired, wooden, dry, anemic, vapid, dull, boring, wishy-washy.
ANTONYMS spirited, lively.

spiritual ▶ adjective 1 *your spiritual self* **nonmaterial,** incorporeal, intangible; inner, mental, psychological; transcendent, ethereal, otherworldly, mystic, mystical, metaphysical; rare extramundane.
ANTONYMS physical.
2 *spiritual writings* **religious,** sacred, divine, holy, nonsecular, church, ecclesiastical, faith-based, devotional.
ANTONYMS secular.

spit[1] ▶ verb 1 *Cranston coughed and spat* **expectorate**; informal hawk, gob.
2 *"Go to hell," she spat* **snap,** say angrily, hiss.
3 *the fat began to spit* **sizzle,** hiss; crackle, sputter.
▶ noun *he made the mashed-up paper into a paste with spit* **spittle,** saliva, sputum, slobber, dribble, drool.

spit[2] ▶ noun *chicken cooked on a spit* **skewer,** brochette, rotisserie.

spite ▶ noun *he said it out of spite* **malice,** malevolence, ill will, vindictiveness, vengefulness, revenge, malignity, evil intentions, animus, enmity; informal bitchiness, cattiness; literary maleficence.
ANTONYMS benevolence.
▶ verb *he did it to spite me* **upset,** hurt, make miserable, grieve, distress, wound, pain, torment, injure.
ANTONYMS please.
– PHRASES **in spite of** *in spite of their mutual dislike, he had helped her* **despite,** notwithstanding, regardless of, for all; undeterred by, in defiance of, in the face of; even though, although.

spiteful ▶ adjective *they made spiteful remarks about Paula* **malicious,** malevolent, evil-intentioned, vindictive, vengeful, malign, mean, nasty, hurtful, mischievous, wounding, cruel, unkind; informal bitchy, catty; literary malefic, maleficent. See note at **VINDICTIVE.**
ANTONYMS benevolent.

splash ▶ verb 1 *splash your face with cool water* **sprinkle,** spray, shower, splatter, slosh, slop, squirt; daub; wet.
2 *his boots were splashed with mud* **spatter,** bespatter, splatter, speck, speckle, blotch, smear, stain, mark; informal splotch.
3 *waves splashed against the pier* **swash,** wash, break, lap; dash, beat, lash, batter, crash, buffet; literary plash.
4 *children splashed in the water* **paddle,** wade, slosh; wallow; informal splosh; rare plash.
5 *the story was splashed across the front pages* **blazon,** display, spread, plaster, trumpet, publicize; informal splatter.
▶ noun 1 *a splash of grease on his shirt* **spot,** blob,

dab, daub, smudge, smear, speck, fleck; mark, stain; informal splotch.
2 *a splash of soda water* **drop,** dash, bit, spot, soupçon, dribble, driblet.
3 *a splash of color* **patch,** burst, streak.
– PHRASES **make a splash** informal *he always believed he would make a splash in Washington* **cause a sensation,** cause a stir, attract attention, draw attention to oneself/itself, get noticed, make an impression, make an impact.

spleen ▶ **noun** *that doesn't give you the right to vent your spleen on me* **bad temper,** bad mood, ill temper, ill humor, anger, wrath, vexation, annoyance, irritation, displeasure, dissatisfaction, resentment, rancor; spite, ill feeling, malice, maliciousness, bitterness, animosity, antipathy, hostility, malevolence, venom, gall, malignance, malignity, acrimony, bile, hatred, hate; literary ire, choler.
ANTONYMS good humor.

splendid ▶ **adjective 1** *splendid costumes* **magnificent,** sumptuous, grand, impressive, imposing, superb, spectacular, resplendent, opulent, luxurious, deluxe, rich, fine, costly, expensive, lavish, ornate, gorgeous, glorious, dazzling, elegant, regal, handsome, beautiful; stately, majestic, princely, noble, proud, palatial; informal plush, posh, swanky, spiffy, ritzy, splendiferous, swank; literary brave.
ANTONYMS modest.
2 informal *we had a splendid holiday* **excellent,** wonderful, marvelous, superb, glorious, sublime, lovely, delightful, first-class, first-rate, blue-chip; informal super, great, amazing, fantastic, terrific, tremendous, phenomenal, sensational, heavenly, gorgeous, dreamy, grand, fabulous, fab, awesome, magic, ace, cool, mean, wicked, far out, A1, out of this world, killer; smashing, dandy, neat, divine, swell; archaic goodly.
ANTONYMS awful.

splendor ▶ **noun** *a wedding long remembered for its splendor* **magnificence,** sumptuousness, grandeur, impressiveness, resplendence, opulence, luxury, richness, fineness, lavishness, ornateness, glory, beauty, elegance; majesty, stateliness; informal ritziness, splendiferousness.
ANTONYMS ordinariness, simplicity, modesty.

splice ▶ **verb 1** *the ropes are spliced together* **interweave,** braid, plait, entwine, intertwine, interlace, knit, mesh; Nautical marry.
2 *we had to splice the two sections* **join,** attach, stick together, unite; blend, mix together.

splinter ▶ **noun** *a splinter of wood* **sliver,** shiver, chip, shard; fragment, piece, bit, shred; (**splinters**) matchwood, flinders.
▶ **verb** *the windshield splintered* **shatter,** break into tiny pieces, smash, smash into smithereens, fracture, split, crack, disintegrate, crumble.

split ▶ **verb 1** *the ax split the wood* **break,** chop, cut, hew, lop, cleave; snap, crack.
2 *the ice cracked and split* **break apart,** fracture, rupture, fissure, snap, come apart, splinter.
3 *her dress was split* **tear,** rip, slash, slit; literary rend.
4 *the issue could split the party* **divide,** disunite, separate, sever; bisect, partition; literary tear asunder.
ANTONYMS unite, unify.
5 *they split the money between them* **share (out),** divide (up), apportion, allocate, allot, distribute, dole out, parcel out, measure out; carve up, slice up; informal divvy up.
6 *the path split* **fork,** divide, bifurcate, diverge, branch.
ANTONYMS converge, merge.
7 *they* **split up** *last year* **break up,** separate, part, part company, become estranged; divorce, get divorced.
ANTONYMS get together, marry.
8 informal *let's split* See LEAVE[1] (sense 1).
▶ **noun 1** *a split in the rock face* **crack,** fissure, cleft, crevice, break, fracture, breach.
2 *a split in the curtain* **rip,** tear, cut, rent, slash, slit.
3 *a split in the governing party* **division,** rift, breach, schism, rupture, partition, separation, severance, scission, breakup.
4 *the acrimonious split with his wife* **breakup,** split-up, separation, parting, estrangement, rift; divorce; informal splitsville.
– PHRASES **split hairs** *while you're splitting hairs over who's the better parent, no one is watching the kids* **quibble,** cavil, carp, niggle, chop logic; informal nitpick; archaic pettifog.

spoil ▶ **verb 1** *too much sun spoils the complexion* **mar,** damage, impair, blemish, disfigure, blight, flaw, deface, scar, injure, harm; ruin, destroy, wreck; be a blot on the landscape.
ANTONYMS improve, enhance.
2 *rain spoiled my plans* **ruin,** wreck, destroy, upset, undo, mess up, make a mess of, dash, sabotage, scotch, torpedo; informal foul up, louse up, muck up, screw up, put the kibosh on, scuttle, do for, throw a (monkey) wrench in the works of, deep-six; archaic bring to naught.
ANTONYMS further, help.
3 *his sisters spoil him* **overindulge,** pamper, indulge, mollycoddle, cosset, coddle, baby, wait on hand and foot, kill with kindness; nanny.
ANTONYMS neglect, be strict with.
4 *stockpiled food may spoil* **go bad,** go off, go rancid, turn, go sour, go moldy, go rotten, rot, perish.
ANTONYMS keep.
– PHRASES **spoiling for** *it's obvious he's spoiling for a fight* **eager for,** itching for, looking for, keen to have, after, bent on, longing for.

spoils ▶ **plural noun 1** *the spoils of war* **booty,** loot, stolen goods, plunder, ill-gotten gains, haul, pickings; informal swag, boodle.
2 *the spoils of office* **benefits,** advantages, perks, prize; formal perquisites.

spoilsport ▶ **noun** *what spoilsport turned down the music?* **killjoy,** misery, damper; informal wet blanket, party pooper.

spoken ▶ **adjective** *spoken communication* **verbal,** oral, vocal, viva voce, uttered, said, stated; unwritten; by word of mouth.
ANTONYMS nonverbal, written.
– PHRASES **spoken for 1** *the money is spoken for* **reserved,** set aside, claimed, owned, booked.
2 *Claudine is spoken for* **attached,** going out with someone, in a relationship; informal going steady, taken.

spokesman, spokeswoman ▶ noun *he's the spokesman for our athletics program* **spokesperson,** representative, agent, mouthpiece, voice, official; informal spin doctor, PR person.

sponge ▶ verb **1** *I'll sponge your face* **wash,** clean, wipe, swab; mop, rinse, sluice, swill.
2 informal *he lived by **sponging off** others* **scrounge off/from,** be a parasite on, beg from; live off; informal freeload on, cadge from, bum off, mooch off.

sponger ▶ noun informal *Ida's good fortune brought out all the spongers in the family* **parasite,** hanger-on, leech, scrounger, beggar; informal freeloader, cadger, bum, bloodsucker, mooch, moocher, bottom feeder, schnorrer.

spongy ▶ adjective *a spongy layer of foam* **soft,** squashy, cushioned, cushiony, compressible, yielding; springy, resilient, elastic; porous, absorbent, permeable; technical spongiform.
ANTONYMS hard, solid.

sponsor ▶ noun *the money came from sponsors* **backer,** patron, promoter, benefactor, benefactress, supporter, partner, contributor, subscriber, friend, guarantor, underwriter; informal angel.
▶ verb *a bank sponsored the event* **finance,** put up the money for, fund, subsidize, back, promote, support, contribute to, be a patron of, guarantee, underwrite; informal foot the bill for, pick up the tab for, bankroll.

spontaneous ▶ adjective **1** *a spontaneous display of affection* **unplanned,** unpremeditated, unrehearsed, impulsive, impetuous, unstudied, impromptu, spur-of-the-moment, extempore, extemporaneous; unforced, voluntary, unconstrained, unprompted, unbidden, unsolicited; informal off-the-cuff.
ANTONYMS planned, calculated.
2 *a spontaneous reaction to danger* **reflex,** automatic, mechanical, natural, knee-jerk, involuntary, unthinking, unconscious, instinctive, instinctual, visceral; informal gut.
ANTONYMS conscious, voluntary.
3 *a spontaneous kind of person* **natural,** uninhibited, relaxed, unselfconscious, unaffected, open, genuine, easy, free and easy; impulsive, impetuous.
ANTONYMS inhibited.

CHOOSE THE RIGHT WORD

spontaneous, impromptu, improvised, impulsive, offhand, spontaneous, unpremeditated

If you're the kind of person who acts first and thinks about it later, your friends are likely to describe you as **spontaneous**, which means that you behave in a very natural way, without prompting or premeditation (*a spontaneous embrace; a spontaneous burst of applause*). Or they may call you **impulsive**, which has somewhat less positive connotations, suggesting someone who is governed by his or her own moods and whims without regard for others. Although *impulsive* behavior may be admirable (*his impulsive generosity prompted him to empty his pockets*), it is just as likely to be ugly or disruptive (*impulsive buying; an impulsive temper*). **Offhand** also has negative overtones, implying behavior that is spontaneous to the point of being cavalier or brusque (*her offhand remarks offended them*). **Unpremeditated** is a more formal term, often used in a legal context to describe an impulsive crime committed without forethought (*unpremeditated murder*). In the world of public speaking, an **extemporaneous** speech is one that is delivered without referring to a written text, although the speaker may have been aware that he or she would be called upon to speak, while an **impromptu** speech is one that the speaker was not expecting to give. **Improvised** is often used in the context of a musical or theatrical performance, suggesting a basic structure within which the performers are free to play in a spontaneous manner (*by its very nature, jazz is improvised*). But it has broader applications as well; in fact, anything that is devised on the spur of the moment may be described as *improvised*.

sporadic ▶ adjective *partly cloudy with sporadic showers* **occasional,** infrequent, irregular, periodic, scattered, patchy, isolated, odd; intermittent, spasmodic, fitful, desultory, erratic, unpredictable.
ANTONYMS frequent, steady, continuous.

sport ▶ noun **1** *we did a lot of sports* **(competitive) game(s),** physical recreation, physical activity, physical exercise, athletics; pastime.
2 dated *they were rogues out for a bit of sport* **fun,** pleasure, enjoyment, entertainment, amusement, diversion.
▶ verb *he sported a beard* **wear,** have on, dress in; **display,** exhibit, show off, flourish, parade, flaunt.

sporting ▶ adjective *they encourage sporting behavior among the boys* **sportsmanlike,** generous, gentlemanly, considerate; fair, just, honorable, decent.
ANTONYMS dirty, unfair.

spot ▶ noun **1** *a grease spot on the wall* **mark,** patch, dot, fleck, smudge, smear, stain, blotch, blot, splash; informal splotch.
2 *a secluded spot* **place,** location, site, position, point, situation, scene, setting, locale, locality, area, neighborhood, region; venue; technical locus.
3 *social policy has a regular spot on the agenda* **position,** place, slot, space.
4 informal *in a tight spot* **predicament,** mess, difficulty, trouble, plight, corner, quandary, dilemma; informal fix, jam, hole, sticky situation, can of worms, pickle, scrape, hot water, Catch-22.
▶ verb **1** *she spotted him in his car* **notice,** see, observe, note, discern, detect, perceive, make out, recognize, identify, locate; catch sight of, glimpse; literary behold, espy.
2 *her clothes were spotted with grease* **stain,** mark, fleck, speckle, smudge, streak, splash,

spatter; informal splotch.

– PHRASES **on the spot** *violators will be arrested on the spot* **immediately,** at once, right away, without delay, without hesitation, that instant, directly, there and then, then and there, forthwith, instantly, summarily, straightaway, in short order; archaic straightway.

spotless ▶ **adjective 1** *the kitchen was spotless* **perfectly clean,** ultra-clean, pristine, immaculate, shining, shiny, gleaming, spick-and-span.
ANTONYMS dirty.
2 *a spotless reputation* **unblemished,** unsullied, untarnished, untainted, unstained, pure, whiter than white, innocent, impeccable, blameless, irreproachable, above reproach; informal squeaky clean, Teflon.
ANTONYMS tarnished, impure.

spotlight ▶ **noun** *she was constantly in the spotlight* **public eye,** glare of publicity, limelight, center stage; focus of public/media attention.
▶ **verb** *this article spotlights the problem* **focus attention on,** highlight, point up, draw/call attention to, give prominence to, throw into relief, turn the spotlight on, bring to the fore.

spotted ▶ **adjective 1** *spotted leaves* **mottled,** dappled, speckled, flecked, freckled, freckly, dotted, stippled, brindle(d); informal splotchy.
ANTONYMS plain.
2 *a black-and-white spotted dress* **polka-dot,** dotted.
ANTONYMS plain.

spouse ▶ **noun** *are spouses invited to the office party?* **(life) partner,** mate, consort; informal better half, other half. See also **HUSBAND, WIFE.**

spout ▶ **verb 1** *lava was spouting from the crater* **spurt,** gush, spew, erupt, shoot, squirt, spray; disgorge, discharge, emit, belch forth.
2 *there he is, **spouting off** about religion, as usual* **hold forth,** sound off, go on, talk at length, expatiate; informal mouth off, speechify, spiel.
▶ **noun** *a can with a spout* **nozzle,** lip.

sprawl ▶ **verb 1** *he sprawled on a sofa* **stretch out,** lounge, loll, lie, recline, drape oneself, slump, flop, slouch.
2 *the town sprawled ahead of them* **spread,** stretch, extend, be strung out, be scattered, straggle, spill.

spray[1] ▶ **noun 1** *a spray of water* **shower,** sprinkling, sprinkle, jet, mist, drizzle; spume, spindrift; foam, froth.
2 *a perfume spray* **atomizer,** vaporizer, aerosol, sprinkler; nebulizer.
▶ **verb 1** *water was sprayed around* **sprinkle,** shower, spatter; scatter, disperse, diffuse; mist; douche; literary besprinkle.
2 *water sprayed into the air* **spout,** jet, gush, spurt, shoot, squirt.

spray[2] ▶ **noun 1** *a spray of holly* **sprig,** twig.
2 *a spray of flowers* **bouquet,** bunch, posy, nosegay; corsage.

spread ▶ **verb 1** *he spread the map out* **lay out,** open out, unfurl, unroll, roll out; straighten out, fan out; stretch out, extend; literary outspread.
ANTONYMS fold up.
2 *the landscape **spread out** below* **extend,** stretch (out), open out, be displayed, be exhibited, be on show; sprawl (out).
3 *papers were spread all over his desk* **scatter,** strew, disperse, distribute.
4 *he's been spreading rumors* **disseminate,** circulate, pass on, put about, communicate, diffuse, make public, make known, purvey, broadcast, publicize, propagate, promulgate; repeat; literary bruit about/abroad.
ANTONYMS suppress.
5 *she spread cold cream on her face* **smear,** daub, plaster, slather, lather, apply, put; smooth, rub.
6 *he spread the toast with butter* **cover,** coat, layer, daub; smother.
▶ **noun 1** *the spread of learning* **expansion,** proliferation, extension, growth; dissemination, diffusion, transmission, propagation.
2 *a spread of six feet* **span,** width, extent, stretch, reach.
3 *the immense spread of the heavens* **expanse,** area, sweep, stretch.
4 *a wide spread of subjects* **range,** span, spectrum, sweep; variety.
5 informal *the caterers laid on a huge spread* **large/elaborate meal,** feast, banquet; informal blowout, nosh.

spree ▶ **noun** *a spending spree* **binge,** bout, orgy, splurge, session.

sprig ▶ **noun** *a sprig of mistletoe* **small stem,** spray, twig.

sprightly ▶ **adjective** *sprightly Irish folk dancers* **spry,** lively, agile, nimble, energetic, active, full of energy, vigorous, spirited, animated, vivacious, frisky; informal full of vim and vigor.
ANTONYMS doddery, lethargic.

spring ▶ **verb 1** *the cat sprang off her lap* **leap,** jump, bound, vault, hop.
2 *the branch sprang back* **fly,** whip, flick, whisk, kick, bounce.
3 *all art springs from feelings* **originate,** derive, arise, stem, emanate, proceed, issue, evolve, come.
4 *fifty men sprang from nowhere* **appear suddenly,** appear unexpectedly, materialize, pop up, shoot up, sprout, develop quickly; proliferate, mushroom.
5 *he sprang the truth on me* **announce suddenly/unexpectedly,** reveal suddenly/unexpectedly, surprise someone with.
▶ **noun 1** *with a sudden spring he leapt on to the table* **leap,** jump, bound, vault, hop; pounce.
2 *the mattress has lost its spring* **springiness,** bounciness, bounce, resilience, elasticity, flexibility, stretch, stretchiness, give.
3 *there was a spring in his step* **buoyancy,** bounce, energy, liveliness, jauntiness, sprightliness, confidence.
4 *a mineral spring* **source,** geyser; literary wellspring, fount.
5 *the spring from which all her emotions poured* **origin,** source, fountainhead, root, roots, basis; informal ground zero.

springy ▶ **adjective** *the earth was springy beneath her feet* **elastic,** stretchy, stretchable, tensile; flexible, pliant, pliable, whippy; bouncy, resilient, spongy.

ANTONYMS rigid, squashy.

sprinkle ▶ verb 1 *he sprinkled water over the towel* **splash,** trickle, spray, shower; spatter.
2 *sprinkle sesame seeds over the top* **scatter,** strew; drizzle, pepper.
3 *sprinkle the cake with powdered sugar* **dredge,** dust.
4 *the sky was sprinkled with stars* **dot,** stipple, stud, fleck, speckle, spot, pepper; scatter, cover.

sprinkling ▶ noun 1 *a sprinkling of nutmeg* **scattering,** sprinkle, scatter, dusting; pinch, dash.
2 *mainly women, but a sprinkling of men* **few,** one or two, couple, handful, small number, trickle, scattering.

sprint ▶ verb *the lead racers sprinted past our corner at about two o'clock* **run,** race, dart, rush, dash, hasten, hurry, scurry, scamper, hare, bolt, fly, gallop, career, charge, shoot, hurtle, speed, zoom, go like lightning, go hell-bent for leather, go like the wind; jog, trot; informal tear, pelt, scoot, hotfoot it, belt, zip, whip, bomb, hightail it, barrel.
ANTONYMS walk.

sprite ▶ noun *by light of moon the woodland sprites do dance and play* **fairy,** elf, pixie, imp, brownie, puck, peri, leprechaun; nymph, sylph, naiad.

sprout ▶ verb 1 *the weeds begin to sprout* **germinate,** put/send out shoots, bud, burgeon.
2 *he had sprouted a beard* **grow,** develop, put/send out.
3 *parsley sprouted from the pot* **spring up,** shoot up, come up, grow, burgeon, develop, appear.

spruce ▶ adjective *the captain looked very spruce* **neat,** well-groomed, well-turned-out, well-dressed, smart, trim, dapper, elegant, chic; informal natty, snazzy, spiffy.
ANTONYMS untidy.
▶ verb 1 *the cottage had been* ***spruced up*** **smarten (up),** tidy, neaten, put in order, clean, upgrade, renovate; informal do up, gussy up.
2 *Sarah wanted to* ***spruce herself up*** **groom,** tidy, smarten (up), preen, primp; informal titivate, doll up.

spry ▶ adjective *isn't Aunt Helen spry for her age?* **sprightly,** lively, agile, nimble, energetic, active, full of energy, full of vim and vigor, vigorous, spirited, animated, vivacious, frisky, peppy.
ANTONYMS doddery, lethargic.

spume ▶ noun *the boat left a wake of white spume* **foam,** froth, surf, spindrift, bubbles.

spunk ▶ noun informal *it took a lot of spunk to blow the whistle on your own boss* **courage,** bravery, valor, nerve, confidence, daring, audacity, pluck, spirit, grit, mettle, spine, backbone; informal guts, gumption, moxie; dated, or humorous derring-do.

spur ▶ noun 1 *competition can be a spur* **stimulus,** incentive, encouragement, inducement, impetus, prod, motivation, inspiration, catalyst, springboard; informal kick up the backside, shot in the arm.
ANTONYMS disincentive, discouragement.
2 *a spur of bone* **projection,** spike, point; technical process.
▶ verb *the thought spurred him into action* **stimulate,** encourage, prompt, propel, prod, induce, impel, motivate, move, galvanize, inspire, incentivize, urge, drive, egg on, stir; incite, goad, provoke, prick, sting, light a fire under.
ANTONYMS discourage.
– PHRASES **on the spur of the moment** *the decision had been made on the spur of the moment* **impulsively,** on impulse, impetuously, without thinking, without premeditation, unpremeditatedly, impromptu, extempore, spontaneously; informal off the cuff.

spurious ▶ adjective *an attempt to be excused due to some spurious medical condition* **bogus,** fake, false, counterfeit, forged, fraudulent, sham, artificial, imitation, simulated, feigned, deceptive, misleading, specious; informal phony, pretend.
ANTONYMS genuine.

> CHOOSE THE RIGHT WORD
>
> **spurious, apocryphal, artificial, counterfeit, ersatz, synthetic**
>
> These adjectives pertain to what is false or not what it appears to be, although not all have negative connotations. **Artificial** implies manmade, especially in imitation of something natural (*artificial flowers; artificial turf*). A **synthetic** substance or material is one produced by a chemical process and used as a substitute for the natural substance it resembles (*boots made from synthetic rubber*). Something that is **counterfeit** is an imitation of something else—usually something rarer, finer, or more valuable—and is intended to deceive or defraud (*counterfeit bills*). **Spurious** also means false rather than true or genuine, but it carries no strong implication of being an imitation (*spurious letters falsely attributed to Winston Churchill*). **Ersatz** refers to an artificial substitute that is usually inferior (*ersatz tea made from tree bark and herbs*). The meaning of **apocryphal**, however, is much more restricted. It applies to accounts of the past that are widely circulated but whose truth or accuracy are doubtful (*an apocryphal story about George Washington as a boy*).

spurn ▶ verb *he's been spurned by every woman he ever loved* **reject,** rebuff, scorn, turn down, treat with contempt, disdain, look down one's nose at, despise; snub, slight, jilt, dismiss, brush off, turn one's back on; give someone the cold shoulder, cold-shoulder; informal turn one's nose up at, give someone the brush-off, kick in the teeth, give someone the bum's rush.
ANTONYMS welcome, accept.

spurt ▶ verb *water spurted from the tap* **squirt,** shoot, jet, erupt, gush, pour, stream, pump, surge, spew, course, well, spring, burst; disgorge, discharge, emit, belch forth, expel, eject.
▶ noun 1 *a spurt of water* **squirt,** jet, spout, gush, stream, rush, surge, flood, cascade, torrent.
2 *a spurt of courage* **burst,** fit, bout, rush, spate,

surge, attack, outburst, blaze.
3 *the sprinter put on a spurt* **burst of speed,** turn of speed, sprint, rush, burst of energy.

spy ▶ noun *a foreign spy* **secret agent,** intelligence agent, double agent, undercover agent, counterspy, mole, sleeper, plant, scout; informal snooper; archaic intelligencer.
▶ verb **1** *she spied for the West* **be a spy,** gather intelligence, work for the secret service; informal snoop.
2 *investigators* ***spied on*** *them* **observe furtively,** keep under surveillance/observation, watch, keep a watch on, keep an eye on.
3 *she spied a coffee shop* **notice,** observe, see, spot, sight, catch sight of, glimpse, make out, discern, detect; informal clap/lay/set eyes on; literary espy, behold, descry.

squabble ▶ noun *there was a squabble over which way they should go* **quarrel,** disagreement, argument, contretemps, falling-out, dispute, clash, blowup, altercation, shouting match, row, exchange, war of words; informal tiff, set-to, run-in, spat, scrap, rhubarb. See note at QUARREL.
▶ verb *the boys were squabbling over a ball* **quarrel,** argue, bicker, fall out, disagree, have words, dispute, spar, cross swords, lock horns, be at loggerheads; informal scrap.

squad ▶ noun **1** *an assassination squad* **team,** crew, gang, band, cell, body, mob, outfit, force.
2 *a firing squad* **detachment,** detail, unit, platoon, battery, troop, patrol, squadron, cadre, commando.

squalid ▶ adjective **1** *a squalid prison* **dirty,** filthy, grubby, grimy, mucky, slummy, foul, vile, poor, sorry, wretched, miserable, mean, seedy, shabby, sordid, insalubrious; **neglected,** uncared-for, broken-down, run-down, down-at-heel, down-at-the-heel(s), depressed, dilapidated, ramshackle, tumbledown, gone to rack and ruin, crumbling, decaying; informal scruffy, crummy, ratty, flea-bitten.
ANTONYMS clean, pleasant.
2 *a squalid deal with the opposition* **improper,** sordid, unseemly, unsavory, sleazy, seedy, seamy, shoddy, cheap, base, low, corrupt, dishonest, dishonorable, disreputable, despicable, discreditable, disgraceful, contemptible, shameful, underhanded.
ANTONYMS proper, decent.

squalor ▶ noun *they lived in squalor* **dirt,** filth, grubbiness, grime, muck, foulness, vileness, poverty, wretchedness, meanness, seediness, shabbiness, sordidness, sleaziness, **neglect,** decay, dilapidation; informal scruffiness, crumminess, grunge, rattiness.
ANTONYMS cleanliness, pleasantness, smartness.

squander ▶ verb *they squander their profits on expensive cars* **waste,** misspend, misuse, throw away, fritter away, spend recklessly, spend unwisely, spend like water; informal blow, go through, splurge, drop, pour down the drain.
ANTONYMS manage, make good use of, save.

square ▶ noun **1** *a shop in the square* market square, marketplace, plaza, piazza.
2 informal *you're such a square!* **(old) fogey,** conservative, traditionalist, conformist, bourgeois, fossil; informal stick-in-the-mud, fuddy-duddy, prig, stuffed shirt.
ANTONYMS trendy.
▶ adjective **1** *a square table* **quadrilateral,** rectangular, oblong, right-angled, at right angles, perpendicular; straight, level, parallel, horizontal, upright, vertical, true, plane.
ANTONYMS crooked, uneven.
2 *the sides were square at halftime* **level,** even, drawn, equal, tied; neck and neck, nip and tuck, side by side, evenly matched; informal even-steven(s).
ANTONYMS uneven.
3 *I'm going to be square with you* **fair,** honest, just, equitable, straight, true, upright, aboveboard, ethical, decent, proper; informal on the level.
ANTONYMS underhanded.
4 informal *don't be square!* **old-fashioned,** behind the times, out of date, conservative, traditionalist, conventional, conformist, bourgeois, straitlaced, fogeyish, stuffy; informal stick-in-the-mud, fuddy-duddy.
ANTONYMS trendy.
▶ verb **1** *the theory does not square with the data* **agree,** tally, be in agreement, be consistent, match up, correspond, fit, coincide, accord, conform, be compatible.
2 *his goal squared the match 1–1* **level,** even, make equal.
3 *would you* ***square up*** *the bill?* **pay,** settle, discharge, clear, meet.
4 *Bob squared things with his boss* **resolve,** sort out, settle, clear up, work out, iron out, smooth over, straighten out, deal with, put right, set right, put to rights, rectify, remedy; informal patch up.

squash ▶ verb **1** *the fruit got squashed* **crush,** squeeze, flatten, compress, press, smash, distort, pound, trample, stamp on; pulp, mash, cream, liquidize, beat, pulverize; informal squish, squoosh, smoosh.
2 *she squashed her clothes inside the bag* **force,** ram, thrust, push, cram, jam, stuff, pack, compress, squeeze, wedge, press.
3 *the proposal was immediately squashed* **reject,** block, cancel, scotch, frustrate, thwart, suppress, put a stop to, nip in the bud, put the lid on; informal put the kibosh on, stymie, scuttle, deep-six.
▶ noun *a side order of steamed squash* acorn squash, butternut squash, crookneck squash, Hubbard squash, scallop squash, spaghetti squash, summer squash, winter squash, zucchini, pumpkin, (vegetable) marrow.

squat ▶ verb **1** *I was squatting on the floor* **crouch (down),** hunker (down), sit on one's haunches, sit on one's heels.
2 *they are squatting on private land* **occupy illegally,** set up residence, dwell, settle, live.
▶ adjective *he was muscular and squat* **stocky,** thickset, dumpy, stubby, stumpy, short, small; informal humorous vertically challenged.
▶ noun informal *they gave me squat* See NOTHING.

squawk ▶ verb & noun *a pheasant squawked | the gull gave a squawk* **screech,** squeal, shriek, scream, croak, crow, caw, cluck, cackle, hoot, cry, call.

squeak ▶ noun & verb **1** *the vole's squeak | the rat*

squeaked **peep,** cheep, pipe, squeal, tweet, yelp, whimper.
2 *the squeak of the hinge | the hinges of the gate squeaked* **screech,** creak, scrape, grate, rasp, jar, groan.

squeal ▶ **noun** *the harsh squeal of a fox* **screech,** scream, shriek, squawk.
▶ **verb 1** *a dog squealed* **screech,** scream, shriek, squawk.
2 *the bookies only squealed because we beat them* **complain,** protest, object, grouse, grumble, whine, wail, carp, squawk; informal kick up a fuss, gripe, grouch, bellyache, moan, bitch, beef, whinge.
3 informal *he* ***squealed on*** *the rest of the gang to the police* **inform on,** tell tales on; report, give away, be disloyal to, sell out, stab in the back; informal rat on, rat out, snitch on, put the finger on, finger, sell down the river.

squeamish ▶ **adjective 1** *I'm too squeamish to gut fish | are you squeamish about a little blood?* **easily nauseated,** nervous; (**squeamish about**) **put off by,** not able to stand the sight of.
2 *less squeamish nations will sell them arms* **scrupulous,** principled, fastidious, particular, punctilious, honorable, upright, upstanding, high-minded, righteous, right-minded, moral, ethical.

squeeze ▶ **verb 1** *I squeezed the bottle* **compress,** press, crush, squash, pinch, nip, grasp, grip, clutch, flatten.
2 *squeeze the juice from both oranges* **extract,** press, force, express.
3 *Sally squeezed her feet into the sandals* **force,** thrust, cram, ram, jam, stuff, pack, wedge, press, squash.
4 *we all squeezed into Steve's van* **crowd,** crush, cram, pack, jam, squash, wedge oneself, shove, push, force one's way.
5 *he would squeeze more money out of Bill* **extort,** force, extract, wrest, wring, milk; informal bleed.
▶ **noun 1** *he gave her hand a squeeze* **press,** pinch, nip; grasp, grip, clutch, hug, clasp; compression.
2 *it was a tight squeeze in the tiny hall* **crush,** jam, squash, press, huddle; congestion.
3 *a squeeze of lemon juice* **few drops,** dash, splash, dribble, trickle, spot, hint, touch.

squire ▶ **noun 1** *the squire of the village* **landowner,** landholder, landlord, lord of the manor, country gentleman.
2 historical *his squire carried a banner* **attendant,** courtier, equerry, aide, steward, page boy.

squirm ▶ **verb 1** *I tried to squirm away* **wriggle,** wiggle, writhe, twist, slide, slither, turn, shift, fidget, jiggle, twitch, thresh, flounder, flail, toss and turn.
2 *he squirmed as everyone laughed* **wince,** shudder, feel embarrassed, feel ashamed.

squirt ▶ **verb 1** *a jet of ink squirted out of the tube* **spurt,** shoot, spray, fountain, jet, erupt; gush, rush, pump, surge, stream, spew, well, spring, burst, issue, emanate; emit, belch forth, expel, eject.
2 *she squirted me with cologne* **splash,** wet, spray, shower, spatter, splatter, sprinkle; literary besprinkle.
▶ **noun 1** *a squirt of water* **spurt,** jet, spray, fountain, gush, stream, surge.
2 informal *he was just a little squirt* **impudent person,** insignificant person, gnat, insect; informal pipsqueak, whippersnapper, picayune.

stab ▶ **verb 1** *a soldier stabbed the civilian* **knife,** run through, skewer, spear, bayonet, gore, spike, stick, impale, transfix, pierce, prick, puncture; literary transpierce.
2 *she stabbed at the earth with a fork* **lunge,** thrust, jab, poke, prod, dig.
▶ **noun 1** *a stab in the leg* **knife wound,** puncture, incision, prick, cut, perforation.
2 *they made stabs into the air* **lunge,** thrust, jab, poke, prod, dig, punch.
3 *a stab of pain* **twinge,** pang, throb, spasm, cramp, dart, prick, flash, thrill.
4 informal *he took a stab at writing* **attempt,** try, effort, endeavor; guess; informal go, shot, crack, bash, whack; formal essay.
– PHRASES **stab in the back** *just two months after I got her hired, she stabbed me in the back* **betray,** be disloyal to, be unfaithful to, desert, break one's promise to, double-cross, break faith with, sell out, play false, inform on/against; informal tell on, sell down the river, squeal on, rat out, finger.

stability ▶ **noun 1** *the stability of playground equipment* **firmness,** solidity, steadiness, strength, security, safety.
2 *his mental stability* **balance of mind,** mental health, sanity, normality, soundness, rationality, reason, sense.
3 *the stability of their relationship* **steadiness,** firmness, solidity, strength, durability, lasting nature, enduring nature, permanence, changelessness, invariability, immutability, indestructibility, reliability, dependability.

stable ▶ **adjective 1** *a stable tent* **firm,** solid, steady, secure, fixed, fast, safe, moored, anchored, stuck down, immovable.
ANTONYMS rickety, wobbly.
2 *a stable person* **well-balanced,** of sound mind, compos mentis, sane, normal, right in the head, rational, steady, reasonable, sensible, sober, down-to-earth, matter-of-fact, having both one's feet on the ground; informal all there.
ANTONYMS unbalanced.
3 *a stable relationship* **secure,** solid, strong, steady, firm, sure, steadfast, unwavering, unvarying, unfaltering, unfluctuating; established, abiding, durable, enduring, lasting, permanent, reliable, dependable.
ANTONYMS rocky, changeable.

stack ▶ **noun 1** *a stack of boxes* **heap,** pile, mound, mountain, pyramid, tower.
2 *a stack of hay* **haystack,** rick, hayrick, mow, shock, haycock; dated cock.
3 informal *a stack of money* See LOT (pronoun).
4 **chimney,** smokestack, funnel, exhaust pipe.
▶ **verb 1** *Leo was stacking plates* **heap** (**up**), pile (up), make a heap/pile/stack of; assemble, put together, collect, hoard, store, stockpile.
2 *they stacked the shelves* **load,** fill (up), lade, pack, charge, stuff, cram; stock.
ANTONYMS empty.

stadium ▶ **noun** *the stadium houses a soccer field and two athletic fields* **arena,** field, ground; bowl, amphitheater, coliseum, ring, dome, manège; track, course, racetrack, racecourse, raceway, speedway, velodrome, sportsplex; Brit. pitch.

staff ▶ noun **1** *there is a reluctance to take on new staff* **employees,** workers, workforce, personnel, human resources, manpower, labor.
2 *he carried a wooden staff* **stick,** stave, pole, crook.
3 *a staff of office* **rod,** tipstaff, cane, mace, wand, scepter, crozier, verge; Greek Mythology caduceus.
▶ verb *the center is staffed by teachers* **man,** people, crew, work, operate, occupy.

stage ▶ noun **1** *this stage of the development* **phase,** period, juncture, step, point, time, moment, instant, level.
2 *the last stage of the race* **part,** section, portion, stretch, leg, lap, circuit.
3 *a theater stage* **platform,** dais, stand, grandstand, staging, apron, rostrum, podium; bandstand, bandshell; catwalk.
4 *she has written for the stage* **theater,** drama, dramatics, dramatic arts, thespianism; informal boards.
5 *the political stage* **scene,** setting; context, frame, sphere, field, realm, arena, backdrop; affairs.
▶ verb **1** *they staged two plays* **put on,** put before the public, present, produce, mount, direct; perform, act, give.
2 *workers staged a protest* **organize,** arrange, coordinate, lay on, put together, get together, set up; orchestrate, choreograph, mastermind, engineer; take part in, participate in, join in.

stagger ▶ verb **1** *he staggered to the door* **lurch,** walk unsteadily, reel, sway, teeter, totter, stumble, wobble.
2 *I was absolutely staggered* **amaze,** astound, astonish, surprise, startle, stun, confound, dumbfound, stupefy, daze, take aback, leave open-mouthed, leave aghast; informal flabbergast, bowl over.
3 *meetings are staggered throughout the day* **spread (out),** space (out), time at intervals.

stagnant ▶ adjective **1** *stagnant water* **still,** motionless, static, stationary, standing, dead, slack; **foul,** stale, putrid, smelly.
ANTONYMS flowing, fresh.
2 *a stagnant economy* **inactive,** sluggish, slow-moving, lethargic, static, flat, depressed, declining, moribund, dying, dead, dormant.
ANTONYMS active, vibrant.

stagnate ▶ verb **1** *obstructions allow water to stagnate* **stop flowing,** become stagnant, become trapped; stand; become foul, become stale; fester, putrefy.
ANTONYMS flow.
2 *exports stagnated* **languish,** decline, deteriorate, fall, become stagnant, do nothing, stand still, tread water, be sluggish.
ANTONYMS boom.

staid ▶ adjective *I'm not some staid librarian, you know* **sedate,** respectable, quiet, serious, serious-minded, steady, conventional, traditional, unadventurous, unenterprising, set in one's ways, sober, proper, decorous, formal, stuffy, stiff, priggish; informal starchy, buttoned-down, stick-in-the-mud.
ANTONYMS frivolous, daring, informal.

stain ▶ verb **1** *her clothing was stained with blood* **discolor,** blemish, soil, mark, muddy, spot, spatter, splatter, smear, splash, smudge, blotch, blacken; literary imbrue.
2 *the report stained his reputation* **damage,** injure, harm, sully, blacken, tarnish, taint, smear, bring discredit to, dishonor, drag through the mud; literary besmirch.
3 *the wood was stained* **color,** tint, dye, tinge, pigment.
▶ noun **1** *a mud stain* **mark,** spot, spatter, splatter, blotch, smudge, smear.
2 *a stain on his character* **blemish,** injury, taint, blot, smear, discredit, dishonor; damage.
3 *dark wood stain* **tint,** color, dye, tinge, pigment, colorant.

stake[1] ▶ noun *a stake in the ground* **post,** pole, stick, spike, upright, support, prop, strut, pale, paling, picket, pile, piling, cane.
▶ verb **1** *the plants have to be staked* **prop up,** tie up, tether, support, hold up, brace, truss.
2 *he staked his claim* **assert,** declare, proclaim, state, make, lay, put in.
– PHRASES **stake out 1** *builders staked out the plot* **mark off/out,** demarcate, measure out, delimit, fence off, section off, close off, shut off, cordon off. **2** informal *the police staked out his apartment* **observe,** watch, keep an eye on, keep under observation, keep watch on, monitor, keep under surveillance, surveil; informal keep tabs on, keep a tab on, case.

stake[2] ▶ noun **1** *playing dice for high stakes* **bet,** wager, ante.
2 *they are racing for record stakes* **prize money,** purse, pot, winnings.
3 *low down in the popularity stakes* **competition,** contest, battle, challenge, rivalry, race, running, struggle, scramble.
4 *a 40 percent stake in the business* **share,** interest, ownership, involvement.
▶ verb *he staked all his week's pay* **bet,** wager, lay, put on, gamble, chance, venture, risk, hazard.

stale ▶ adjective **1** *stale food* **old,** past its best, off, dry, hard, musty, rancid, overstored.
ANTONYMS fresh.
2 *stale air* **stuffy,** close, musty, fusty, stagnant.
ANTONYMS fresh.
3 *stale beer* **flat,** turned, spoiled, off, insipid, tasteless.
4 *stale jokes* **hackneyed,** tired, worn out, overworked, threadbare, warmed-up, banal, trite, clichéd, platitudinous, unoriginal, unimaginative, uninspired, flat; out of date, outdated, outmoded, passé, archaic, obsolete; warmed-over; informal old hat, corny, unfunny, played out.
ANTONYMS original.

stalemate ▶ noun *the talks had reached a stalemate* **deadlock,** impasse, standoff; draw, tie, dead heat.

stalk[1] ▶ noun *the stalk of a plant* **stem,** shoot, trunk, stock, cane, bine, bent; Brit. haulm, straw, reed.

stalk[2] ▶ verb **1** *a cat was stalking a rabbit* **creep up on,** trail, follow, shadow, track down, go after, be after, course, hunt; informal tail, still-hunt.

2 *she stalked out* **strut,** stride, march, flounce, storm, stomp, sweep.

stall ▶ noun 1 *a market stall* **stand,** table, counter, booth, kiosk.
2 *stalls for larger animals* **pen,** coop, sty, corral, enclosure, compartment.
▶ verb 1 *the government has stalled the project* **obstruct,** impede, interfere with, hinder, hamper, block, interrupt, hold up, hold back, thwart, balk, sabotage, delay, stonewall, check, stop, halt, derail, put a brake on; informal stymie.
2 *the project has stalled* **stop,** fizzle, flatline, die, reach an impasse, hit a roadblock.
3 *quit stalling* **use delaying tactics,** play for time, temporize, gain time, procrastinate, hedge, beat around the bush, drag one's feet, delay, filibuster, stonewall, give someone the runaround.
4 *stall him for a bit* **delay,** divert, distract; **hold off,** stave off, fend off, keep off, ward off, keep at bay.

stalwart ▶ adjective *a stalwart supporter of the cause* **staunch,** loyal, faithful, committed, devoted, dedicated, dependable, reliable, steady, constant, trusty, solid, hard-working, steadfast, redoubtable, unwavering.
ANTONYMS disloyal, unfaithful, unreliable.

stamina ▶ noun *I felt my stamina weakening* **endurance,** staying power, tirelessness, fortitude, strength, energy, toughness, determination, tenacity, perseverance, grit.

stammer ▶ verb *he began to stammer* **stutter,** stumble over one's words, hesitate, falter, pause, halt, splutter.
▶ noun *he had a stammer* **stutter,** speech impediment, speech defect.

stamp ▶ verb 1 *he **stamped on** my toe* **trample (on),** step on, tread on, tramp on, stomp on; **crush,** squash, flatten.
2 *John stamped off, muttering* **stomp,** stump, clomp, clump.
3 *the name is stamped on the cover* **imprint,** print, impress, punch, inscribe, emboss, brand, frank.
4 *his face was stamped on Martha's memory* **fix,** inscribe, etch, carve, imprint, impress.
5 *his style stamps him as a player to watch* **identify,** characterize, brand, distinguish, classify, mark out, set apart, single out.
▶ noun 1 *the stamp of authority* **mark,** hallmark, indication, sign, seal, sure sign, telltale sign, quality, smack, smell, savor, air.
2 *he was of a very different stamp* **type,** kind, sort, variety, class, category, classification, style, description, condition, caliber, status, quality, nature, ilk, kidney, cast, grain, mold, stripe.
– PHRASES **stamp out** *Miller's promise to stamp out crime on these streets is, at best, a naive fantasy* **put an end/stop to,** end, stop, crush, put down, crack down on, curb, nip in the bud, scotch, squash, quash, quell, subdue, suppress, extinguish, stifle, abolish, get rid of, eliminate, eradicate, beat, overcome, defeat, destroy, wipe out; informal put the kibosh on, clean house.

stampede ▶ noun *the noise caused a stampede* **charge,** panic, rush, flight, rout.
▶ verb *the sheep stampeded* **bolt,** charge, flee, take flight; race, rush, career, sweep, run.

stance ▶ noun 1 *a natural golfer's stance* **posture,** body position, pose, attitude.
2 *a liberal stance* **attitude,** stand, point of view, viewpoint, opinion, way of thinking, outlook, standpoint, position, angle, perspective, approach, line, policy.

stand ▶ verb 1 *Lionel stood in the doorway* **be on one's feet,** be upright, be erect, be vertical.
ANTONYMS sit, lie.
2 *the men **stood up*** **rise,** get/rise to one's feet, get up, straighten up, pick oneself up, find one's feet, be upstanding; formal arise.
ANTONYMS sit down, lie down.
3 *today a house stands on the site* **be,** exist, be situated, be located, be positioned, be sited, have been built.
4 *he stood the book on the shelf* **put,** set, set up, erect, up-end, place, position, locate, prop, lean, stick, install, arrange; informal park.
5 *my decision stands* **remain in force,** remain valid/effective/operative, remain in operation, hold, hold good, apply, be the case, exist.
6 *her heart could not stand the strain* **withstand,** endure, bear, put up with, take, cope with, handle, sustain, resist, stand up to.
7 informal *I can't stand arrogance* **endure,** tolerate, bear, put up with, take, abide, support, countenance; informal swallow, stomach; formal brook.
▶ noun 1 *the party's stand on immigration* **attitude,** stance, point of view, viewpoint, opinion, way of thinking, outlook, standpoint, position, approach, thinking, policy, line.
2 *a stand against tyranny* **opposition,** resistance, objection, hostility, animosity.
3 *a large mirror on a stand* **base,** support, mounting, platform, rest, plinth, bottom; tripod, rack, trivet.
4 *a beer stand* **stall,** counter, booth, kiosk, tent.
5 *a taxi stand* stop, station, park, bay.
6 *the train drew to a stand* **stop,** halt, standstill, dead stop.
7 *a stand of trees* **copse,** thicket, grove, bush, woodlot.
– PHRASES **stand by 1** *stand by for further instructions* **wait,** be prepared, be in (a state of) readiness, be ready for action, be on full alert, wait in the wings. **2** *she stood by her husband* **remain/be loyal to,** stick with/by, remain/be true to, stand up for, support, back up, defend, stick up for. **3** *the government must stand by its pledges* **abide by,** keep (to), adhere to, hold to, stick to, observe, comply with. **stand down** *tell the troops to stand down* **relax,** stand easy, come off full alert. **stand for 1** *BC stands for British Columbia* **mean,** be an abbreviation of, represent, signify, denote, indicate, symbolize. **2** informal *I won't stand for any nonsense* **put up with,** endure, tolerate, accept, take, abide, support, countenance; informal swallow, stomach; formal brook. **3** *we stand for animal welfare* **advocate,** champion, uphold, defend, stand up for, support, back, endorse, be in favor of, promote, recommend, urge. **stand in** *during Coach Clement's absence, Mr. Maynard will stand in* **deputize,** act, act as deputy, substitute, fill in, sit in, do duty, take over, act as locum, be a proxy, cover, hold the fort, step into the breach; replace, relieve, take

over from; informal sub, fill someone's shoes, step into someone's shoes, pinch-hit. **stand out 1** *his veins stood out* **project,** stick out, bulge (out), be proud, jut (out). **2** *she stood out in the crowd* **be noticeable,** be visible, be obvious, be conspicuous, stick out, be striking, be distinctive, be prominent, attract attention, catch the eye, leap out, show up; informal stick/stand out like a sore thumb. **stand up 1** *after 200 years, his theory still stands up* **remain/be valid,** be sound, be plausible, hold water, hold up, stand questioning, survive investigation, bear examination, be verifiable. **2** *that creep Roger stood up his blind date* **fail to keep a date with,** fail to meet, fail to keep an appointment with, jilt. **stand up for** *dozens of Mr. Merlin's students stood up for him at the hearing* **support,** defend, back, back up, stick up for, champion, promote, uphold, take someone's part, take the side of, side with. **stand up to 1** *she stood up to her parents* **defy,** confront, challenge, resist, take on, put up a fight against, argue with, take a stand against. **2** *the old house has stood up to the war* **withstand,** survive, come through (unscathed), outlast, outlive, weather, ride out, ward off.

standard ▶ noun **1** *the standard of her work* **quality,** level, grade, caliber, merit, excellence. **2** *a safety standard* **guideline,** norm, yardstick, benchmark, measure, criterion, guide, touchstone, model, pattern, example, exemplar. **3** *a standard to live by* **principle,** ideal; (**standards**) code of behavior, code of honor, morals, scruples, ethics. **4** *the regiment's standard* **flag,** banner, pennant, ensign, color(s), banderole, guidon; Nautical burgee.
▶ adjective **1** *the standard way of doing it* **normal,** usual, typical, stock, common, ordinary, customary, conventional, wonted, established, settled, set, fixed, traditional, prevailing.
ANTONYMS unusual, special.
2 *the standard work on the subject* **definitive,** established, classic, recognized, accepted, authoritative, most reliable, exhaustive.

standardize ▶ verb *teachers have been asked to standardize their final exams* **systematize,** make consistent, make uniform, make comparable, regulate, normalize, bring into line, equalize, homogenize, regiment.

stand-in ▶ noun *a stand-in for the minister* **substitute,** replacement, deputy, surrogate, proxy, understudy, locum, supply, fill-in, cover, relief, stopgap; informal temp, pinch-hitter; (body) double, stuntman.
▶ adjective *a stand-in goaltender* **substitute,** replacement, deputy, fill-in, stopgap, supply, surrogate, relief, acting, temporary, provisional, caretaker; informal pinch-hitting.

standing ▶ noun **1** *his standing in the community* **status,** rank, ranking, position; reputation, estimation, stature; dated station. **2** *a person of some standing* **seniority,** rank, eminence, prominence, prestige, repute, stature, esteem, importance, account, consequence, influence, distinction; informal clout. **3** *a squabble of long standing* **duration,** existence, continuance, endurance, life, history.
▶ adjective **1** *standing stones* **upright,** erect, vertical, plumb, upended, on end, perpendicular; on one's feet.
ANTONYMS flat, lying down, seated.
2 *standing water* **stagnant,** still, motionless, static, stationary, dead, slack.
ANTONYMS flowing.
3 *a standing invitation* **permanent,** perpetual, everlasting, continuing, abiding, indefinite, open-ended; regular, repeated.
ANTONYMS temporary, occasional.

standoff ▶ noun *a nuclear standoff* **deadlock,** stalemate, impasse; draw, tie, dead heat; suspension of hostilities, lull.

standoffish ▶ adjective informal *a standoffish prig* **aloof,** distant, remote, detached, withdrawn, reserved, uncommunicative, unforthcoming, unapproachable, unresponsive, unfriendly, unsociable, introspective, introverted.
ANTONYMS friendly, approachable, sociable.

standpoint ▶ noun *she writes on religion from the standpoint of a believer* **point of view,** viewpoint, vantage point, attitude, stance, view, opinion, position, way of thinking, outlook, perspective.

standstill ▶ noun *negotiations have come to a standstill* **halt,** stop, dead stop, stand, gridlock.

staple ▶ adjective *rice is their staple crop* **main,** principal, chief, major, primary, leading, foremost, first, most important, predominant, dominant, (most) prominent, basic, standard, prime, premier; informal number-one.

star ▶ noun **1** *the sky was full of stars* **celestial body,** heavenly body, sun; asteroid, planet. **2** *the stars of the film* **principal,** leading lady/man, lead, female/male lead, hero, heroine.
ANTONYMS extra, bit player.
3 *a star of the world of chess* **celebrity,** superstar, big name, famous name, household name, someone, somebody, lion, leading light, VIP, personality, personage, luminary; informal celeb, big shot, megastar.
ANTONYMS nobody.
▶ adjective **1** *a star pupil* **brilliant,** talented, gifted, able, exceptional, outstanding, bright, clever, masterly, consummate, precocious, prodigious. **2** *the star attraction* **top,** leading, best, greatest, foremost, major, preeminent, champion.
ANTONYMS poor, minor.

stare ▶ verb *staring out the window* **gaze,** gape, goggle, glare, ogle, peer; informal gawk, rubberneck.

stark ▶ adjective **1** *a stark silhouette* **sharp,** sharply defined, well-focused, crisp, distinct, obvious, evident, clear, clear-cut, graphic, striking.
ANTONYMS fuzzy, indistinct.
2 *a stark landscape* **desolate,** bare, barren, arid, vacant, empty, forsaken, godforsaken, bleak, somber, depressing, cheerless, joyless; literary drear.
ANTONYMS pleasant.
3 *a stark room* **austere,** severe, bleak, plain, simple, bare, unadorned, unembellished, undecorated.
ANTONYMS ornate.

4 *stark terror* **sheer,** utter, complete, absolute, total, pure, downright, out-and-out, outright; rank, thorough, consummate, unqualified, unmitigated, unalloyed.
5 *the stark facts* **blunt,** bald, bare, simple, basic, plain, unvarnished, harsh, grim.
ANTONYMS disguised.
▶ adverb *stark naked* **completely,** totally, utterly, absolutely, downright, dead, entirely, wholly, fully, quite, altogether, thoroughly, truly, one hundred percent.

start ▶ verb 1 *the meeting starts at 7:45* **begin,** commence, get underway, go ahead, get going; informal kick off.
ANTONYMS finish.
2 *this was how her illness had started* **arise,** come into being, begin, commence, be born, come into existence, appear, arrive, come forth, establish oneself, emerge, erupt, burst out, originate, develop.
ANTONYMS clear up, end.
3 *she started her own charity* **establish,** set up, found, create, bring into being, institute, initiate, inaugurate, introduce, open, launch, float, kick-start, jump-start, get something off the ground, pioneer, organize, mastermind; informal kick something off.
ANTONYMS end.
4 *we had better start now if we want to finish the job* **commence,** make a start, begin, take the first step, make the first move, get going, go ahead, set things moving, start/get/set the ball rolling, buckle to/down, turn to; informal get moving, get cracking, get down to, get to it, get down to business, get the show on the road, take the plunge, kick off, get off one's backside, fire away.
ANTONYMS stop, give up, procrastinate.
5 *he started across the field* **set off,** set out, start out, set forth, begin one's journey, get on the road, depart, leave, get underway, make a start, sally forth, embark, sail; informal hit the road.
ANTONYMS arrive, stay.
6 *you can start the machine* **activate,** set in motion, switch on, start up, turn on, fire up; energize, actuate, set off, start off, set something going/moving.
ANTONYMS stop, shut down, close down.
7 *the machine started* **begin working,** start up, get going, spring into life.
ANTONYMS stop.
8 *"Oh my!" she said, starting* **flinch,** jerk, jump, twitch, recoil, shy, shrink, blench, wince.
▶ noun 1 *the start of the event* **beginning,** commencement, inception.
ANTONYMS end.
2 *the start of her illness* **onset,** commencement, emergence, (first) appearance, arrival, eruption, dawn, birth; informal square one.
3 *a quarter of an hour's start* **lead,** head start, advantage.
ANTONYMS handicap.
4 *a start in life* **advantageous beginning,** flying start, helping hand, lift, assistance, support, encouragement, boost, kick-start; informal break, leg up.
ANTONYMS handicap.
5 *she awoke with a start* **jerk,** twitch, flinch, wince, spasm, convulsion, jump.

startle ▶ verb *naturally their screaming startled me* **surprise,** frighten, scare, alarm, give someone a shock/fright/jolt, make someone jump; **perturb,** unsettle, agitate, disturb, disconcert, disquiet; informal give someone a turn, make someone jump out of their skin, freak someone out.
ANTONYMS put at ease.

startling ▶ adjective *startling news awaited him at Naples* **surprising,** astonishing, amazing, unexpected, unforeseen, staggering, shocking, stunning; extraordinary, remarkable, dramatic; disturbing, unsettling, perturbing, disconcerting, disquieting; frightening, alarming, scary.
ANTONYMS predictable, ordinary.

starvation ▶ noun *half of the people here face starvation* **extreme hunger,** lack of food, famine, undernourishment, malnourishment, fasting; deprivation of food; death from lack of food.

starving ▶ adjective *the world's starving children* **dying of hunger,** deprived of food, undernourished, malnourished, starved, half-starved; very hungry, ravenous, famished, empty, hollow; fasting.
ANTONYMS full.

state[1] ▶ noun 1 *the state of the economy* **condition,** shape, situation, circumstances, position; predicament, plight.
2 informal *don't get into a state* **fluster,** frenzy, fever, fret, panic, state of agitation/anxiety; informal flap, tizzy, dither, stew, sweat.
3 informal *your room is in a state* **mess,** chaos, disorder, disarray, confusion, muddle, heap, shambles; clutter, untidiness, disorganization, imbroglio.
4 *an autonomous state* **country,** nation, land, sovereign state, nation state, kingdom, realm, power, republic, confederation, federation.
5 *the country is divided into thirty-two states* **province,** federal state, region, territory, canton, department, county, district, shire.
6 *the power of the state* **government,** parliament, administration, regime, authorities.
▶ adjective *a state visit to China* **ceremonial,** official, formal, governmental, national, public.
ANTONYMS unofficial, private, informal.

state[2] ▶ verb *I stated my views* **express,** voice, utter, put into words, declare, affirm, assert, announce, make known, put across/over, communicate, air, reveal, disclose, divulge, proclaim, present, expound; set out, set down; informal come out with.

stated ▶ adjective *the stated aim of the program* **specified,** fixed, settled, set, agreed, declared, designated, laid down.
ANTONYMS undefined, irregular, tacit.

stately ▶ adjective *a stately mansion on the hill* **dignified,** majestic, ceremonious, courtly, imposing, impressive, solemn, awe-inspiring, regal, elegant, grand, glorious, splendid, magnificent, resplendent; slow-moving, measured, deliberate.

statement ▶ noun *how do you respond to the president's statement about homeland security?* **declaration,** expression of views/facts, affirmation, assertion, announcement, utterance, communication, proclamation, presentation, expounding; account, testimony, evidence, report, bulletin, communiqué.

static ▶ adjective **1** *static prices* **unchanged,** fixed, stable, steady, unchanging, changeless, unvarying, invariable, constant, consistent.
ANTONYMS variable.
2 *a static display* **stationary,** motionless, immobile, unmoving, still, stock-still, at a standstill, at rest, not moving a muscle, like a statue, rooted to the spot, frozen, inactive, inert, lifeless, inanimate.
ANTONYMS mobile, active, dynamic.

station ▶ noun **1** *a train station* **stopping place,** stop, halt, stage; terminus, terminal, depot.
2 *a research station* **establishment,** base, camp; post, depot; mission; site, facility, installation, yard.
3 *a police station* **office,** depot, base, headquarters, precinct, station house, detachment; informal cop shop.
4 *a radio station* **channel,** broadcasting organization; wavelength.
5 *the watchman resumed his station* **post,** position, place.
6 dated *Karen was getting ideas above her station* **rank,** place, status, position in society, social class, stratum, level, grade; caste; archaic condition, degree.
▶ verb *the regiment was stationed at Camp Pendleton* **put on duty,** post, position, place; establish, install; deploy, base, garrison.

stationary ▶ adjective **1** *a stationary car* **static,** parked, stopped, motionless, immobile, unmoving, still, stock-still, at a standstill, at rest; not moving a muscle, like a statue, rooted to the spot, frozen, inactive, inert, lifeless, inanimate.
ANTONYMS moving.
2 *a stationary population* **unchanging,** unvarying, invariable, constant, consistent, unchanged, changeless, fixed, stable, steady.
ANTONYMS shifting.

statue ▶ noun *a statue of Alexander Hamilton* **sculpture,** figure, effigy, statuette, figurine, idol; carving, bronze, graven image, model; bust, head.

statuesque ▶ adjective *statuesque beauty queens* **tall and dignified,** imposing, striking, stately, majestic, noble, magnificent, splendid, impressive, regal.

stature ▶ noun **1** *she was small in stature* **height,** tallness; size, build.
2 *an architect of international stature* **reputation,** repute, standing, status, position, prestige, distinction, eminence, preeminence, prominence, importance, influence, note, fame, celebrity, renown, acclaim.

status ▶ noun **1** *the status of women* **standing,** rank, ranking, position, social position, level, place, estimation; dated station.
2 *wealth and status* **prestige,** kudos, cachet, standing, stature, regard, fame, note, renown, honor, esteem, image, importance, prominence, consequence, distinction, influence, authority, eminence.
3 *the current status of the project* **state,** position, condition, shape, stage.

staunch ▶ adjective *a staunch supporter* **stalwart,** loyal, faithful, committed, devoted, dedicated, dependable, reliable, steady, constant, trusty, hard-working, steadfast, redoubtable, unwavering, tireless. See note at RESOLUTE.
ANTONYMS disloyal, unfaithful, unreliable.

stave ▶ verb
– PHRASES **stave off** *here, eat some crackers to stave off your hunger* **avert,** prevent, avoid, counter, preclude, forestall, nip in the bud; ward off, fend off, head off, keep off, keep at bay.

stay[1] ▶ verb **1** *he stayed where he was* **remain** (**behind**), stay behind, stay put; wait, linger, stick, be left, hold on, hang on, lodge; informal hang around; archaic bide, tarry.
ANTONYMS leave.
2 *they won't stay hidden* **continue** (**to be**), remain, keep, persist in being, carry on being, go on being.
3 *our aunt is staying with us* **visit,** spend time, put up, stop (off/over); lodge, room, board, have rooms, be housed, be accommodated, be quartered, be billeted, vacation; formal sojourn; archaic bide.
4 *legal proceedings were stayed* **postpone,** put off, delay, defer, put back, hold over/off; adjourn, suspend, prorogue, put over, table, lay on the table, take a rain check on; Law continue; informal put on ice, put on the back burner.
ANTONYMS advance.
5 literary *we must stay the enemy's advance* **delay,** slow down/up, hold back/up, set back, keep back, put back, put a brake on, retard; hinder, hamper, obstruct, inhibit, impede, curb, check, restrain, restrict, arrest; informal throw a (monkey) wrench in the works of.
ANTONYMS promote.
▶ noun **1** *a stay at a hotel* **visit,** stop, stop-off, stopover, overnight, break, vacation; formal sojourn.
2 *a stay of judgment* **postponement,** putting off, delay, deferment, deferral, putting back; adjournment, suspension, prorogation, tabling.

stay[2] ▶ noun *the stays holding up the mast* **strut, wire,** brace, tether, guy, prop, rod, support, truss; Nautical shroud.
▶ verb *her masts were well stayed* **brace,** tether, strut, wire, guy, prop, support, truss.

steadfast ▶ adjective **1** *a steadfast friend* **loyal,** faithful, committed, devoted, dedicated, dependable, reliable, steady, true, constant, staunch, solid, trusty.
ANTONYMS disloyal.
2 *a steadfast policy* **firm,** determined, resolute, relentless, implacable, single-minded; unchanging, unwavering, unhesitating, unfaltering, unswerving, unyielding, unflinching, uncompromising.
ANTONYMS irresolute.

steady ▶ adjective **1** *the ladder must be steady* **stable,** firm, fixed, secure, fast, safe, immovable, unshakable, dependable; anchored, moored, jammed, rooted, braced.
ANTONYMS unstable, loose.
2 *keep the camera steady* **motionless,** still, unshaking, static, stationary, unmoving.
ANTONYMS shaky.

3 *a steady gaze* **fixed,** intent, unwavering, unfaltering.
ANTONYMS darting.
4 *a steady young student* **sensible,** levelheaded, rational, settled, mature, down-to-earth, full of common sense, reliable, dependable, sound, sober, serious-minded, responsible, serious.
ANTONYMS flighty, immature, impulsive.
5 *a steady income* **constant,** unchanging, regular, consistent, invariable; continuous, continual, unceasing, ceaseless, perpetual, unremitting, unwavering, unfaltering, unending, endless, around/round-the-clock, all-year-round.
ANTONYMS fluctuating, sporadic.
6 *a steady boyfriend* **regular,** usual, established, settled, firm, devoted, faithful.
ANTONYMS occasional.
▶ **verb 1** *he steadied the rifle* **stabilize,** hold steady; brace, support; balance, poise; secure, fix, make fast.
2 *she needed to steady her nerves* **calm,** soothe, quiet, compose, settle; subdue, quell, control, get a grip on.

steal ▶ **verb 1** *the burglars stole a fax machine* **purloin,** thieve, take, take for oneself, help oneself to, loot, pilfer, run off with, abscond with, carry off, shoplift; embezzle, misappropriate; informal walk off with, rob, swipe, snatch, nab, rip off, lift, "liberate", "borrow", filch, pinch, heist; Brit. informal nick; formal peculate.
2 *his work was stolen by his tutor* **plagiarize,** copy, pass off as one's own, pirate, poach, borrow; informal rip off, lift, pinch, crib; Brit. informal nick.
3 *he stole a kiss* **snatch,** sneak, get stealthily/surreptitiously.
4 *he stole out of the room* **creep,** sneak, slink, slip, slide, glide, tiptoe, sidle, edge.
▶ **noun** informal *at $30 it's a steal* See **BARGAIN** (sense 1 of the noun).

stealing ▶ **noun** *he was convicted of stealing* **theft,** thieving, thievery, robbery, larceny, burglary, shoplifting, pilfering, pilferage, looting, misappropriation; embezzlement; formal peculation.

stealth ▶ **noun** *the stealth of a cat burglar* **furtiveness,** secretiveness, secrecy, surreptitiousness, sneakiness, slyness.
ANTONYMS openness.

stealthy ▶ **adjective** *she was a natural for such stealthy activities* **furtive,** secretive, secret, surreptitious, sneaking, sly, clandestine, covert, conspiratorial. See note at **SECRET**.
ANTONYMS open.

steam ▶ **noun 1** *steam from the kettle* **water vapor,** condensation, mist, haze, fog, moisture.
2 *he ran out of steam* **energy,** vigor, vitality, stamina, enthusiasm; **momentum,** impetus, force, strength, thrust, impulse, push, drive; speed, pace.
– PHRASES **steamed up** informal **1** *he got steamed up about forgetting his papers* **agitated**.
2 *they get steamed up about the media* See **ANGRY** (sense 1). **let/blow off steam** informal *you'll go nuts if you don't let off steam once in a while* **give vent to one's feelings,** speak one's mind, speak out, sound off, lose one's inhibitions, let oneself go; use up surplus energy.

steamy ▶ **adjective 1** *the steamy jungle* **humid,** muggy, sticky, dripping, moist, damp, clammy, sultry, sweaty, steaming.
2 informal *a steamy love scene* See **EROTIC**.
3 informal *they had a steamy affair* **passionate,** torrid, amorous, ardent, lustful; informal sizzling, hot, red-hot.

steel ▶ **verb**
– PHRASES **steel oneself** *the coach gives us tips on how to steel ourselves before a game* **brace oneself,** nerve oneself, summon (up) one's courage, screw up one's courage, gear oneself up, prepare oneself, get in the right frame of mind; fortify oneself, harden oneself; informal psych oneself up; literary gird (up) one's loins.

steely ▶ **adjective 1** *steely light* **blue-gray,** gray, steel-colored, steel-gray, iron-gray.
2 *steely muscles* **hard,** firm, toned, rigid, stiff, tense, tensed, taut.
ANTONYMS flabby.
3 *steely eyes* **cruel,** unfeeling, merciless, ruthless, pitiless, heartless, hard-hearted, hard, stony, cold-blooded, cold-hearted, harsh, callous, severe, unrelenting, unpitying, unforgiving, uncaring, unsympathetic; literary adamantine.
ANTONYMS kind.
4 *steely determination* **resolute,** firm, steadfast, dogged, single-minded; bitter, burning, ferocious, fanatical; ruthless, iron, grim, gritty; unquenchable, unflinching, unswerving, unfaltering, untiring, unwavering.
ANTONYMS halfhearted.

steep[1] ▶ **adjective 1** *steep cliffs* **precipitous,** sheer, abrupt, sharp, perpendicular, vertical, bluff, vertiginous.
ANTONYMS gentle.
2 *a steep increase* **sharp,** sudden, precipitate, precipitous, rapid.
ANTONYMS gradual.
3 informal *steep prices* **expensive,** costly, high, stiff; unreasonable, excessive, exorbitant, extortionate, outrageous, prohibitive, dear.
ANTONYMS reasonable.

steep[2] ▶ **verb 1** *the ham is then steeped in brine* **marinade,** marinate, soak, souse, macerate; pickle.
2 *winding sheets were steeped in mercury sulfate* **soak,** saturate, immerse, wet through, drench; technical ret.
3 *a city steeped in history* **imbue with,** fill with, permeate with, pervade by, suffuse with, infuse with, soak in.

steeple ▶ **noun** *a solitary gull perched atop the church steeple* **spire,** tower; bell tower, belfry, campanile; minaret.

steer ▶ **verb 1** *he steered the boat* **guide,** direct, maneuver, drive, pilot, navigate; Nautical con, helm.
2 *Luke steered her down the path* **guide,** conduct, direct, lead, take, usher, shepherd, marshal, herd.
– PHRASES **steer clear of** *mind my words and steer clear of that man* **keep away from,** keep one's distance from, keep at arm's length, give a wide berth to, avoid, avoid dealing with, have nothing to do with, shun, eschew.

stem[1] ▶ noun *a plant stem* **stalk,** shoot, trunk, stock, cane, bine.
– PHRASES **stem from** *this type of behavior often stems from a childhood of abuse and neglect* **have its origins in,** arise from, originate from, spring from, derive from, come from, emanate from, flow from, proceed from; **be caused by,** be brought on/about by, be produced by.

stem[2] ▶ verb *he stemmed the flow of blood* **staunch,** stop, halt, check, hold back, restrict, control, contain, curb; block, dam; slow, lessen, reduce, diminish, stanch; archaic stay.

stench ▶ noun *the stench from the basement was vile* **stink,** reek, whiff, fetor, funk; literary miasma. See note at SMELL.

stentorian ▶ adjective *his stentorian voice resonated throughout the theater* **loud,** thundering, thunderous, ear-splitting, deafening; powerful, strong, carrying; booming, resonant; strident.
ANTONYMS quiet, soft.

step ▶ noun **1** *Frank took a step forward* **pace,** stride.
2 *she heard a step on the stairs* **footstep,** footfall, tread.
3 *she left the room with a springy step* **gait,** walk, tread.
4 *it is only a step to the river* **short distance,** stone's throw, spitting distance; informal 'a hop, skip, and jump'.
5 *the top step* **stair,** tread; **(steps) stairs,** staircase, stairway.
6 *each step of the ladder* **rung,** tread.
7 *resigning is a very serious step* **course of action,** measure, move, act, action, initiative, maneuver, operation, tactic.
8 *a significant step toward a cease-fire* **advance,** development, move, movement; breakthrough.
9 *the first step on the managerial ladder* **stage,** level, grade, rank, degree; notch, rung.
▶ verb **1** *she stepped gingerly through the snow* **walk,** move, tread, pace, stride.
2 *the bull **stepped on** the farmer's foot* **tread on,** stamp on, trample (on); squash, crush, flatten.
– PHRASES **in step** *he is in step with mainstream thinking* **in accord,** in accordance, in harmony, in agreement, in tune, in line, in keeping, in conformity, compatible. **mind/watch one's step** *just watch your step when Mrs. Kline gets here* **be careful,** take care, step/tread carefully, exercise care/caution, mind how one goes, look out, watch out, be wary, be on one's guard, be on the qui vive. **out of step** *the paper was often out of step with public opinion* **at odds,** at variance, in disagreement, out of tune, out of line, not in keeping, out of harmony. **step by step** *I followed the directions step by step* **one step at a time,** bit by bit, gradually, in stages, by degrees, slowly, steadily. **step down** *it's time for Rowland to step down* **resign,** quit, stand down, give up one's post/job, bow out, abdicate; pack it in, call it quits. **step in 1** *nobody stepped in to save the bank* **intervene,** intercede, involve oneself, become/get involved, take a hand.
2 *I stepped in for a sick colleague* **stand in,** sit in, fill in, cover, substitute, take over; replace, take someone's place; informal sub. **step on it** informal *if we don't step on it we'll miss the boat* **hurry up,** get a move on, speed up, go faster, be quick; informal get cracking, get moving, step on the gas; dated make haste. **step up 1** *the army stepped up its offensive* **increase,** intensify, strengthen, augment, escalate; informal up, crank up.
2 *I stepped up my pace* **speed up,** increase, accelerate, quicken, hasten.

stereotype ▶ noun *the stereotype of the rancher* **standard/conventional image,** received idea, cliché, hackneyed idea, formula.
▶ verb *women in detective novels are often stereotyped as femmes fatales* **typecast,** pigeonhole, conventionalize, categorize, label, tag.

stereotyped ▶ adjective *the stereotyped image of a stewardess* **stock,** conventional, stereotypical, standard, formulaic, predictable; hackneyed, clichéd, cliché-ridden, banal, trite, unoriginal; typecast; informal corny, old hat.
ANTONYMS unconventional, original.

sterile ▶ adjective **1** *mules are sterile* **infertile,** unable to reproduce/conceive, unable to have children/young; archaic barren.
ANTONYMS fertile, fecund.
2 *sterile desert* **unproductive,** infertile, unfruitful, uncultivatable, barren.
ANTONYMS fertile, productive, rich.
3 *a sterile debate* **pointless,** unproductive, unfruitful, unrewarding, useless, unprofitable, profitless, futile, vain, idle; archaic bootless.
ANTONYMS fruitful.
4 *sterile academicism* **unimaginative,** uninspired, uninspiring, unoriginal, stale, lifeless, musty, phlegmatic.
ANTONYMS creative, original.
5 *sterile conditions* **aseptic,** sterilized, germ-free, antiseptic, disinfected; uncontaminated, unpolluted, pure, clean; sanitary, hygienic. See note at SANITARY.
ANTONYMS septic.

sterilize ▶ verb **1** *the scalpel was first sterilized* **disinfect,** fumigate, decontaminate, sanitize; pasteurize; clean, cleanse, purify; technical autoclave.
ANTONYMS contaminate.
2 *over 6.5 million people were sterilized* **make unable to have children,** make infertile, hysterectomize, vasectomize, have one's tubes tied, have a tubal ligation, have a salpingectomy.
3 *sterilizing domestic animals* **neuter,** castrate, spay, geld, cut, fix, desex, alter, doctor.

sterling ▶ adjective *this is a sterling example of the power of a positive attitude* **excellent,** first-rate, first-class, exceptional, outstanding, splendid, superlative, praiseworthy, laudable, commendable, admirable, valuable, worthy, deserving.
ANTONYMS poor, unexceptional.

stern[1] ▶ adjective **1** *a stern expression* **serious,** unsmiling, frowning, severe, forbidding, grim, unfriendly, austere, dour, stony, flinty, steely, unrelenting, unforgiving, unbending, unsympathetic, disapproving.
ANTONYMS genial, friendly.
2 *stern measures* **strict,** severe, stringent, harsh, drastic, hard, tough, extreme, rigid, ruthless, rigorous, exacting, demanding,

uncompromising, unsparing, inflexible, authoritarian, draconian. See note at **SEVERE**.
ANTONYMS lenient, lax.

stern[2] ▶ **noun** *the stern of the ship* **rear (end),** back, after end, poop, transom, tail.
ANTONYMS bow.

stew ▶ **noun 1** *we ate a hearty stew* ragout, casserole, fricassee.
2 informal *she's in a stew about that parking ticket* **mood,** flap, panic, fluster, fret, fuss, sweat, lather, tizzy, dither, twitter, state; literary pother.
▶ **verb 1** *stew the meat for an hour* **braise,** simmer, boil.
2 informal *there's no point stewing about it* See **WORRY** (sense 1 of the verb).
3 informal *the girls sat stewing in the heat* **swelter,** be very hot, perspire, sweat; informal roast, bake, cook, be boiling.

stick[1] ▶ **noun 1** *a fire made of sticks* **piece of wood,** twig, small branch.
2 *he walks with a stick* **walking stick,** cane, staff, alpenstock, crook, crutch.
3 *the plants need supporting on sticks* **cane,** pole, post, stake, upright.
4 *he beat me with a stick* **club,** cudgel, bludgeon, shillelagh; truncheon, baton; cane, birch, switch, rod.
– PHRASES **the sticks** informal *she didn't want him to know that she'd grown up in the sticks* **the country,** the countryside, rural areas; the backwoods, the back of beyond, the wilds, the hinterland, a backwater, the backcountry, the backland, the middle of nowhere, the boondocks, the boonies, hicksville.

stick[2] ▶ **verb 1** *he stuck his fork into the sausage* **thrust,** push, insert, jab, poke, dig, plunge.
2 *the bristles* **stuck into** *her skin* **pierce,** penetrate, puncture, prick, stab.
3 *the cup stuck to its saucer* **adhere,** cling, be fixed, be glued.
4 *stick the stamp there* **affix,** attach, fasten, fix; paste, glue, gum, tape, Scotch-tape, pin, tack.
5 *the wheels stuck in the mud* **become trapped,** become jammed, jam, catch, become wedged, become lodged, become fixed, become embedded.
6 *that sticks in his mind* **remain,** stay, linger, dwell, persist, continue, last, endure, burn.
7 *the charges won't stick* **be upheld,** hold, be believed; informal hold water.
8 informal *just stick that sandwich on my desk* **put (down),** place, set (down), lay (down), deposit, position; leave, stow; informal dump, park, pop, plunk.
– PHRASES **stick at** *anything you stick at will eventually get done* **persevere with,** persist with, keep at, work at, continue with, carry on with, not give up with, hammer away at, stay with; go the distance, stay the course; informal soldier on with, hang in there. **stick by** *Rodney stuck by me when everyone else bailed out* **be loyal to,** be faithful to, be true to, stand by, keep faith with, keep one's promise to. **stick it out** *I think I can stick it out for another two weeks* **put up with it,** grin and bear it, keep at it, keep going, stay with it, see it through; persevere, persist, carry on, struggle on; informal hang in there, soldier on, tough it out, nail one's colors to the mast. **stick out 1** *his front teeth stuck out* **protrude,** jut (out), project, stand out, extend, poke out; bulge, overhang.
2 *they stuck out in their strange clothes* **be noticeable,** be visible, be obvious, be conspicuous, stand out, be obtrusive, be prominent, attract attention, catch the eye, leap out, show up; informal stick/stand out like a sore thumb. **stick to** *he stuck to his promise* **abide by,** keep, adhere to, hold to, comply with, fulfill, make good, stand by. **stick up for** *after what she did, not even her family would stick up for her* **support,** take someone's side, side with, be on the side of, stand by, stand up for, take someone's part, defend, come to the defense of, champion, speak up for, fight for.

sticky ▶ **adjective 1** *sticky tape* **(self-)adhesive,** gummed, self-stick; technical adherent.
2 *sticky clay* **glutinous,** viscous, viscid, gluey, tacky, gummy, treacly, syrupy; mucilaginous; informal gooey, icky, gloppy.
ANTONYMS dry.
3 *sticky weather* **humid,** muggy, close, sultry, steamy, sweaty, oppressive, heavy.
ANTONYMS fresh, cool.
4 *a sticky situation* **awkward,** difficult, tricky, ticklish, problematic, delicate, touch-and-go, touchy, embarrassing, sensitive, uncomfortable; informal hairy.
ANTONYMS easy.

stiff ▶ **adjective 1** *stiff cardboard* **rigid,** hard, firm, inelastic, inflexible.
ANTONYMS flexible, plastic, limp.
2 *a stiff paste* **semisolid,** viscous, viscid, thick, stiffened, firm.
ANTONYMS runny.
3 *I'm stiff all over* **aching,** achy, painful; arthritic, rheumatic; informal creaky, rusty.
ANTONYMS supple, limber.
4 *a rather stiff manner* **formal,** reserved, unfriendly, chilly, cold, frigid, icy, austere, wooden, forced, strained, stilted; informal starchy, uptight, standoffish.
ANTONYMS relaxed, informal.
5 *a stiff fine* **harsh,** severe, heavy, crippling, punishing, stringent, drastic, draconian.
ANTONYMS lenient, mild.
6 *stiff resistance* **vigorous,** determined, full of determination, strong, spirited, resolute, tenacious, steely, four-square, unflagging, unyielding, dogged, stubborn, obdurate, rock-ribbed.
ANTONYMS halfhearted.
7 *a stiff climb* **difficult,** hard, arduous, tough, strenuous, laborious, uphill, exacting, tiring, demanding, formidable, challenging, punishing, grueling; informal killing, hellish.
ANTONYMS easy.
8 *a stiff breeze* **strong,** fresh, brisk.
ANTONYMS gentle.
9 *a stiff drink* **strong,** potent, alcoholic.
ANTONYMS weak.

stiffen ▶ **verb 1** *stir until the mixture stiffens* **become stiff,** thicken; set, become solid, solidify, harden, jell, congeal, coagulate, clot.
ANTONYMS soften, liquefy.
2 *she stiffened her muscles | without exercise, joints will stiffen* **make/become stiff,** tense

(up), tighten, tauten.
ANTONYMS relax.
3 *intimidation stiffened their resolve* **strengthen,** harden, toughen, fortify, reinforce, give a boost to.
ANTONYMS weaken.

stifle ▶ verb 1 *she stifled him with a pillow* **suffocate,** choke, asphyxiate, smother, gag.
2 *Eleanor stifled a giggle* **suppress,** smother, restrain, fight back, choke back, gulp back, check, swallow, curb, silence.
ANTONYMS let out.
3 *cartels stifle competition* **constrain,** hinder, hamper, impede, hold back, curb, check, restrain, prevent, inhibit, suppress.
ANTONYMS encourage.

stigma ▶ noun *the stigma of bankruptcy* **shame,** disgrace, dishonor, ignominy, opprobrium, humiliation, (bad) reputation.
ANTONYMS honor, credit.

still ▶ adjective 1 *the parrot lay still* **motionless,** unmoving, not moving a muscle, stock-still, immobile, inanimate, like a statue, as if turned to stone, rooted to the spot, transfixed, static, stationary.
ANTONYMS moving, active.
2 *a still night* **quiet,** silent, hushed, soundless, noiseless, undisturbed; **calm,** peaceful, serene, windless; literary stilly.
ANTONYMS noisy.
3 *the lake was still* **calm,** flat, even, smooth, placid, tranquil, pacific, waveless, glassy, like a millpond, unruffled, stagnant.
ANTONYMS rough, turbulent.
▶ noun *the still of the night* **quietness,** quiet, quietude, silence, stillness, hush, soundlessness; calm, tranquility, peace, serenity.
ANTONYMS noise, disturbance, hubbub.
▶ adverb 1 *she's still running in circles* **up to this time,** up to the present time, until now, even now, yet.
2 *He's crazy. Still, he's good for dinner conversation* **nevertheless,** nonetheless, regardless, all the same, just the same, anyway, anyhow, even so, yet, but, however, notwithstanding, despite that, in spite of that, for all that, be that as it may, in any event, at any rate; informal still and all, anyhoo.
▶ verb 1 *she stilled the crowd* **quiet,** silence, hush; calm, settle, pacify, soothe, lull, allay, subdue.
ANTONYMS stir up.
2 *the wind stilled* **abate,** die down, lessen, subside, ease up/off, let up, moderate, slacken, weaken.
ANTONYMS get stronger.

stilted ▶ adjective *a few minutes of stilted conversation* **strained,** forced, contrived, constrained, labored, stiff, self-conscious, awkward, unnatural, wooden.
ANTONYMS natural, effortless, spontaneous.

stimulant ▶ noun 1 *caffeine is a stimulant* **tonic,** restorative; antidepressant; informal pep pill, upper, pick-me-up, bracer, happy pill; Medicine analeptic.
ANTONYMS sedative, downer.
2 *a stimulant to discussion* **stimulus,** incentive, encouragement, impetus, inducement, boost, spur, prompt; informal shot in the arm.
ANTONYMS deterrent.

stimulate ▶ verb *we're looking for ways to stimulate tourism* **encourage,** act as a stimulus/incentive/impetus/spur to, prompt, prod, move, motivate, trigger, spark, spur on, galvanize, activate, kindle, fire, fire with enthusiasm, fuel, whet, nourish; inspire, incentivize, inspirit, rouse, excite, animate, electrify, jump-start, light a fire under. See notes at ENCOURAGE, QUICKEN.
ANTONYMS discourage.

stimulating ▶ adjective 1 *a stimulating effect on the circulation* **restorative,** tonic, invigorating, bracing, energizing, reviving, refreshing, revitalizing, revivifying; Medicine analeptic.
ANTONYMS sedative.
2 *a stimulating lecture* **thought-provoking,** interesting, fascinating, inspiring, inspirational, lively, sparkling, exciting, stirring, rousing, intriguing, giving one food for thought, refreshing; provocative, challenging; informal buzzy.
ANTONYMS uninspiring, uninteresting, boring.

stimulus ▶ noun *this sports facility has been a stimulus to the economic restoration of our city* **spur,** stimulant, encouragement, impetus, boost, prompt, prod, incentive, inducement, inspiration; motivation, impulse; informal shot in the arm.
ANTONYMS deterrent, discouragement.

sting ▶ noun 1 *a bee sting* **prick,** wound, injury, puncture.
2 *this cream will take the sting away* **smart,** pricking; pain, soreness, hurt, irritation.
3 *the sting of his betrayal* **heartache,** heartbreak, agony, torture, torment, hurt, pain, anguish.
4 *there was a sting in her words* **sharpness,** severity, bite, edge, pointedness, asperity; sarcasm, acrimony, malice, spite, venom.
5 informal *the victim of a sting* **swindle,** fraud, deception; trickery, sharp practice; informal rip-off, con, fiddle, bunco.
▶ verb 1 *she was stung by a scorpion* **prick,** wound, bite; poison.
2 *the smoke made her eyes sting* **smart,** burn, hurt, be irritated, be sore.
3 *the criticism stung her* **upset,** wound, cut to the quick, sear, grieve, hurt, pain, torment, mortify.
4 *he was stung into action* **provoke,** goad, incite, spur, prick, prod, rouse, drive, galvanize.
ANTONYMS deter.
5 informal *they stung a bank for thousands* **swindle,** defraud, cheat, fleece, gull; informal rip off, screw, shaft, bilk, do, rook, diddle, take for a ride, chisel, gouge.

stingy ▶ adjective informal *you can think I'm stingy all you want, I'm not giving you a penny* **mean,** miserly, niggardly, close-fisted, parsimonious, penny-pinching, cheeseparing, Scroogelike; informal tightfisted, cheap, tight, mingy, money-grubbing.
ANTONYMS generous, liberal.

stink ▶ verb 1 *his clothes stank of sweat* **reek,** smell (foul/bad/disgusting), stink/smell to high heaven.

2 informal *the idea stinks* **be very unpleasant,** be abhorrent, be despicable, be contemptible, be disgusting, be vile, be foul; informal suck.
3 informal *the whole affair stinks of a setup* **smack,** reek, give the impression, have all the hallmarks; strongly suggest.
▶ **noun 1** *the stink of a dirty diaper* **stench,** reek, fetor, foul/bad smell; informal funk; literary miasma. See note at **SMELL**.
2 informal *a big stink about the new proposals* **fuss,** commotion, rumpus, ruckus, trouble, outcry, uproar, brouhaha, furor; informal song and dance, to-do, hoo-ha.

stint ▶ **verb** *we saved by stinting on food* **skimp on,** scrimp on, be economical with, economize on, be sparing with, hold back on, be frugal with; be mean with, be parsimonious with; limit, restrict; informal be stingy with, be mingy with, be tight with.
▶ **noun** *a two-week stint in the office* **spell,** stretch, turn, session, term, shift, tour of duty.

stipulate ▶ **verb** *the document stipulates certain conditions* **specify,** set down, set out, lay down; demand, require, insist on, make a condition of, prescribe, impose; Law provide.

stipulation ▶ **noun** *the foundation could use the Lynde name, with the stipulation that a Lynde would always sit on the board of directors* **condition,** precondition, proviso, provision, prerequisite, specification; demand, requirement; rider, caveat, qualification.

stir ▶ **verb 1** *stir the mixture well* **mix,** blend, agitate; beat, whip, whisk, fold in.
2 *Travis stirred in his sleep* **move slightly,** change one's position, shift.
3 *a breeze stirred the leaves* **disturb,** rustle, shake, move, flutter, agitate.
4 *she finally stirred at ten o'clock* **get up,** get out of bed, rouse oneself, rise; **wake (up),** awaken; informal rise and shine, surface, show signs of life; formal arise; literary waken.
ANTONYMS go to bed, retire.
5 *I never stirred from here* **move,** budge, make a move, shift, go away; leave.
ANTONYMS stay, stay put.
6 *symbolism can stir the imagination* **arouse,** rouse, fire, kindle, inspire, stimulate, excite, awaken, quicken; literary waken.
ANTONYMS stultify.
7 *the war stirred him to action* **spur,** drive, rouse, prompt, propel, prod, motivate, encourage; urge, impel; provoke, goad, prick, sting, incite, light a fire under.
▶ **noun** *the news caused a stir* **commotion,** disturbance, fuss, excitement, turmoil, sensation; informal to-do, hoo-ha, hullabaloo, flap, splash.
– PHRASES **stir up** *his remarks stirred up a furor* **whip up,** work up, foment, fan the flames of, trigger, spark off, precipitate, excite, provoke, incite, ignite.

stirring ▶ **adjective** *a stirring portrait of his life as a missionary* **exciting,** thrilling, rousing, stimulating, moving, inspiring, inspirational, passionate, impassioned, emotional, heady.
ANTONYMS boring, pedestrian.

stitch ▶ **noun** *he was panting and had a stitch* **sharp pain,** stabbing pain, shooting pain, stab of pain, pang, twinge, spasm.
▶ **verb** *the seams are stitched by hand* **sew,** baste, tack; seam, hem; darn.

stock ▶ **noun 1** *the store carries little stock* **merchandise,** goods, wares, items/articles for sale, inventory.
2 *a stock of fuel* **store,** supply, stockpile, reserve, hoard, cache, bank, accumulation, quantity, collection.
3 *farm stock* **animals,** livestock, beasts; flocks, herds.
4 (**stocks**) *blue-chip stocks* **shares,** securities, equities, bonds.
5 *her stock is low with most voters* **popularity,** favor, regard, estimation, standing, status, reputation, name, prestige.
6 *his mother was of French stock* **descent,** ancestry, origin(s), parentage, pedigree, lineage, line (of descent), heritage, birth, extraction, family, blood, bloodline.
7 *chicken stock* **bouillon,** broth, consommé.
8 *the stock of a weapon* **handle,** butt, haft, grip, shaft, shank.
▶ **adjective 1** *a stock size* **standard,** regular, normal, established, set; common, readily/widely available; staple.
ANTONYMS nonstandard.
2 *the stock response* **usual,** routine, predictable, set, standard, staple, customary, familiar, conventional, traditional, stereotyped, clichéd, hackneyed, unoriginal, formulaic.
ANTONYMS original, unusual.
▶ **verb 1** *we stock organic food* **sell,** carry, keep (in stock), offer, have (for sale), retail, supply.
2 *the fridge was well stocked with milk* **supply,** provide, furnish, provision, equip, fill, load.
– PHRASES **in stock** *what brands of dog food do you have in stock?* **for/on sale,** (immediately) available, on the shelf. **stock up on/with** *people are stocking up on batteries and water* **amass supplies of,** stockpile, hoard, cache, lay in, buy up/in, put away/by, put/set aside, collect, accumulate, save; informal squirrel away, salt away, stash away. **take stock of** *let's take stock of our current situation* **review,** assess, appraise, evaluate; informal size up.

stockings ▶ **plural noun** *you'll need a pair of black stockings* **nylons,** pantyhose, tights; hosiery, hose, leotards; knee-highs.

stockpile ▶ **noun** *a stockpile of weapons* **stock,** store, supply, accumulation, collection, reserve, hoard, cache; informal stash.
▶ **verb** *food had been stockpiled* **store up,** amass, accumulate, store (up), stock up on, hoard, cache, collect, lay in, put away, put/set aside, put by, put away for a rainy day, stow away, save; informal salt away, stash away.

stock-still ▶ **adjective** *two stock-still deer were not more than twenty feet away from us* **motionless,** completely still, unmoving, not moving a muscle, immobile, like a statue/stone, rooted to the spot, transfixed, paralyzed, petrified, static, stationary.
ANTONYMS moving, active.

stocky ▶ **adjective** *he was short but stocky, and his physical strength was amazing* **thickset,** sturdy, heavily built, chunky, burly, strapping, brawny, solid, heavy, heavyset, hefty, beefy, blocky.

ANTONYMS slender, skinny.

stodgy ▶ adjective **1** *stodgy writing* **boring,** dull, uninteresting, dreary, turgid, tedious, dry, unimaginative, uninspired, unexciting, unoriginal, monotonous, humdrum, prosaic, staid, heavy going; informal deadly, square.
ANTONYMS interesting, lively.
2 *a stodgy pudding* **solid,** substantial, filling, hearty, heavy, starchy, indigestible.
ANTONYMS light.

stoicism ▶ noun *she accepted her sufferings with remarkable stoicism* **patience,** forbearance, resignation, fortitude, endurance, acceptance, tolerance, phlegm.
ANTONYMS intolerance.

stolid ▶ adjective *her stolid facade is somewhat unnerving* **impassive,** phlegmatic, unemotional, cool, calm, placid, unexcitable; dependable; unimaginative, dull.
ANTONYMS emotional, lively, imaginative.

stomach ▶ noun **1** *a stomach pain* **abdomen,** belly, gut, middle; informal tummy, insides.
2 *his fat stomach* **paunch,** potbelly, beer belly, girth; informal beer gut, pot, tummy, spare tire, breadbasket, middle-aged spread.
3 *he had no stomach for it* **appetite,** taste, hunger, thirst; inclination, desire, relish, fancy.
▶ verb **1** *I can't stomach butter* **digest,** keep down, manage to eat/consume, tolerate, take.
2 *they couldn't stomach the sight* **tolerate,** put up with, take, stand, endure, bear; informal hack, abide.

stone ▶ noun **1** *someone threw a stone at me* **rock,** pebble, boulder.
2 *a commemorative stone* **tablet,** monument, monolith, obelisk; gravestone, headstone, tombstone.
3 *paving stones* **slab,** flagstone, flag, cobble.
4 *what beautiful stones in her tiara* **gem,** gemstone, jewel, semiprecious stone, brilliant; informal rock, sparkler.
5 *a peach stone* **kernel,** seed, pip, pit.

stony ▶ adjective **1** *a stony path* **rocky,** pebbly, gravelly, shingly; rough, hard.
ANTONYMS smooth.
2 *a stony stare* **unfriendly,** hostile, cold, chilly, frosty, icy; hard, flinty, steely, stern, severe; fixed, expressionless, blank, poker-faced, deadpan; unfeeling, uncaring, unsympathetic, indifferent, cold-hearted, callous, heartless, hard-hearted, stony-hearted, merciless, pitiless.
ANTONYMS friendly, sympathetic.

stooge ▶ noun **1** *a government stooge* **underling,** minion, lackey, subordinate; henchman; **puppet,** pawn, cat's paw; informal sidekick.
2 *a comedian's stooge* **butt,** foil, straight man.

stoop ▶ verb **1** *she stooped to pick up the pen* **bend (over/down),** lean over/down, crouch (down).
2 *he stooped his head* **lower,** bend, incline, bow, duck.
3 *he stoops when he walks* **hunch one's shoulders,** walk with a stoop, be round-shouldered.
4 *Davis would stoop to committing a crime* **lower oneself,** sink, descend, resort; go as far as, sink as low as.
▶ noun **1** *a man with a stoop* **hunch,** round shoulders; curvature of the spine; Medicine kyphosis.
2 *we sat on the front stoop and watched the passers-by* **porch,** steps, platform, veranda, terrace.

stop ▶ verb **1** *we can't stop the decline* **put an end/stop/halt to,** bring to an end/stop/halt/close/standstill, end, halt; finish, terminate, discontinue, cut short, interrupt, nip in the bud; deactivate, shut down.
ANTONYMS start, begin, continue.
2 *he stopped smoking* **cease,** discontinue, desist from, break off; give up, abandon, abstain from, cut out; informal quit, leave off, knock off, pack in, lay off, give over.
3 *the car stopped* **pull up,** draw up, come to a stop/halt, come to rest, pull in, pull over; park.
4 *the music stopped* **conclude,** come to an end/stop/standstill, cease, end, finish, draw to a close, be over, terminate; pause, break off; peter out, fade away.
5 *divers stopped the flow of oil* **stem,** staunch, hold back, check, curb, block, dam; archaic stay.
6 *the police stopped her leaving* **prevent,** hinder, obstruct, impede, block, bar, preclude; dissuade from.
ANTONYMS encourage.
7 *the council stopped the housing project* **thwart,** balk, foil, frustrate, stand in the way of; scotch, derail; informal put paid to, put the kibosh on, put a stop to, do for, stymie, scuttle, deep-six.
ANTONYMS expedite.
8 *just stop the bottle with your thumb* **block (up),** plug, close (up), fill (up); seal, caulk, bung up; technical occlude.
▶ noun **1** *all business came to a stop* **halt,** end, finish, close, standstill; cessation, conclusion, stoppage, discontinuation.
ANTONYMS start, beginning, continuation.
2 *a brief stop in the town* **break,** stopover, stop-off, stay, visit; formal sojourn.
3 *the next stop is Central Park* **stopping place,** halt, station.
– PHRASES **put a stop to** *how can we put a stop to this senseless violence?* See **STOP** (sense 1 of the verb), **STOP** (sense 7 of the verb). **stop off/over** *we decided to stop over in Denver* **break one's journey,** take a break, pause, linger; stay, remain, put up, lodge, rest; formal sojourn.

stopgap ▶ noun *that old plane was merely a stopgap* **temporary solution/fix,** expedient, makeshift; substitute, stand-in, pinch-hitter.
▶ adjective *a stopgap measure* **temporary,** provisional, interim, pro tem, short-term, working, makeshift, emergency; caretaker, acting, stand-in, fill-in.
ANTONYMS permanent.

stopover ▶ noun *our stopover in Dallas lasted two weeks* **break,** stop, stop-off, layover, overnight, visit, stay; formal sojourn.

stoppage ▶ noun **1** *the stoppage of production* **discontinuation,** stopping, halting, cessation, termination, end, finish; interruption, suspension, breaking off.
ANTONYMS start, continuation.
2 *a stoppage of the blood supply* **obstruction,** blocking, blockage, block; Medicine occlusion, stasis.

3 *a stoppage over pay* **strike,** walkout; industrial action.

stopper ▶ noun *the stopper is not keeping the water from running out* **plug,** cork, bung, spigot, spile, seal.

store ▶ noun **1** *a store of money* **stock,** supply, stockpile, hoard, cache, reserve, bank, pool; informal war chest, pork barrel.
2 *a grain store* **storeroom,** storehouse, repository, depository, stockroom, depot, warehouse, magazine; informal lockup.
3 *ship's stores* **supplies,** provisions, stocks, necessities; food, rations, provender; materials, equipment, hardware; Military matériel, accoutrements; Nautical chandlery.
4 *a hardware store* **shop,** (retail) outlet, boutique, department store, chain store, emporium; supermarket, superstore, megastore.
▶ verb *rabbits don't store food* **keep,** keep in reserve, stockpile, lay in, put/set aside, put away/by, put away for a rainy day, save, collect, accumulate, hoard, cache; informal squirrel away, salt away, stash away.
ANTONYMS use, discard.
– PHRASES **set (great) store by** *Gwen set great store by good manners* **value,** attach great importance to, put a high value on, put a premium on; **think highly of,** hold in (high) regard, have a high opinion of; informal rate.

storm ▶ noun **1** *battered by a storm* **windstorm,** tempest, whirlwind, gale, strong wind, high wind, squall; cyclone, tornado, twister, dust devil, dust storm; rainstorm, thunderstorm, thundershower; monsoon, typhoon, hurricane, tropical storm; hailstorm, snowstorm, blizzard.
2 *a storm of bullets* **volley,** salvo, fusillade, barrage, cannonade; shower, spray, hail, rain.
3 *there was a storm over his remarks* **uproar,** outcry, fuss, furor, brouhaha, rumpus, trouble, hue and cry, controversy; informal to-do, hoo-ha, hullabaloo, ballyhoo, stink, row.
4 *a storm of protest* **outburst,** outbreak, explosion, eruption, outpouring, surge, blaze, flare-up, wave.
▶ verb **1** *she stormed out* **stride angrily,** stomp, march, stalk, flounce, stamp.
2 *his mother stormed at him* **rant,** rave, shout, bellow, roar, thunder, rage.
3 *police stormed the building* **attack,** charge, rush, assail, descend on, swoop on. See note at ATTACK.

stormy ▶ adjective **1** *stormy weather* **blustery,** squally, windy, gusty, blowy; rainy, thundery, snowy; wild, tempestuous, turbulent, violent, rough, foul.
ANTONYMS calm, fine.
2 *a stormy debate* **angry,** heated, fiery, fierce, furious, passionate, lively.
ANTONYMS peaceful.

story ▶ noun **1** *a story about his summer in Hawaii* **tale,** narrative, account, anecdote; informal yarn, spiel.
2 *the novel has a good story* **plot,** story line, scenario, libretto.
3 *the story appeared in the papers* **news item,** news report, article, feature, piece.
4 *there have been a lot of stories going around* **rumor,** piece of gossip, whisper; speculation.
5 *Harper changed his story* **testimony,** statement, report, account, version.
6 *Ellie never told stories* See FALSEHOOD (sense 1).

stout ▶ adjective **1** *a short stout man* **fat,** plump, portly, rotund, dumpy, chunky, corpulent; stocky, burly, bulky, hefty, heavyset, solidly built, thickset; informal tubby, pudgy, zaftig, corn-fed.
ANTONYMS thin, slender.
2 *stout leather shoes* **strong,** sturdy, solid, substantial, robust, tough, durable, hardwearing.
ANTONYMS fragile, flimsy.
3 *stout resistance* **determined,** vigorous, forceful, spirited; staunch, steadfast, stalwart, firm, resolute, unyielding, dogged; brave, bold, courageous, valiant, valorous, gallant, fearless, doughty, intrepid; informal gutsy, spunky.
ANTONYMS halfhearted, feeble.

stouthearted ▶ adjective *we stand in awe of these stouthearted heroes* **brave,** determined, courageous, bold, plucky, spirited, valiant, valorous, gallant, fearless, doughty, intrepid, stalwart; informal gutsy, spunky.

stove ▶ noun *there's a pot of coffee on the stove* **oven,** range, wood stove, wood-burning stove, potbellied stove, Franklin stove; trademark Coleman stove.

stow ▶ verb *Barney stowed her bags in the trunk* **pack,** load, store, place, put (away), deposit, stash.
ANTONYMS unload.
– PHRASES **stow away** *you'd better stow away until the air clears* **hide,** conceal oneself, travel secretly.

straddle ▶ verb **1** *she straddled the motorbike* **sit/stand astride,** bestride, mount, get on.
2 *a mountain range straddling the border* **lie on both sides of,** extend across, span.
3 *he straddled the issue of taxes* **be equivocal about,** be undecided about, equivocate about, vacillate about, waver about, waffle on; informal sit on the fence regarding.

strafe ▶ verb *enemy aircraft strafed our carriers* **bomb,** shell, bombard, fire on, machine-gun, rake with gunfire, enfilade; archaic fusillade.

straggle ▶ verb *we were straggling toward the end, but we weren't the last ones to cross the finish line* **trail,** lag, dawdle, walk slowly, dally, lollygag; fall behind, bring up the rear.

straight ▶ adjective **1** *a long, straight road* **unswerving,** undeviating, linear, as straight as an arrow, uncurving, unbending.
ANTONYMS winding, zigzag.
2 *that picture isn't straight* **level,** even, in line, aligned, square; vertical, upright, perpendicular; horizontal.
ANTONYMS askew, crooked.
3 *we must get the place straight* **in order,** (neat and) tidy, neat, shipshape, orderly, spick-and-span, organized, arranged, sorted out, straightened out.
ANTONYMS untidy, messy.
4 *a straight answer* **honest,** direct, frank, candid, truthful, sincere, forthright, straightforward, plain-spoken, blunt, straight from the shoulder, unequivocal, unambiguous;

informal upfront.
ANTONYMS indirect, evasive.
5 *straight thinking* **logical,** rational, clear, lucid, sound, coherent.
ANTONYMS irrational, illogical.
6 *three straight wins* **successive,** in succession, consecutive, in a row, running.
7 *straight brandy* **undiluted,** neat, pure, straight up.
ANTONYMS diluted.
8 informal *she's very straight* **respectable,** conventional, conservative, traditional, old-fashioned, straitlaced; informal stuffy, square, fuddy-duddy.
▶ **adverb 1** *he looked me straight in the eyes* **right,** directly, squarely, full; informal smack, bang, spang, smack dab.
2 *she drove straight home* **directly,** right, by a direct route.
3 *I'll call you straight back* **right away,** straightaway, immediately, directly, at once; archaic straightway.
4 *I told her straight* **frankly,** directly, candidly, honestly, forthrightly, plainly, point-blank, bluntly, flatly, straight from the shoulder, without beating about the bush, without mincing words, unequivocally, unambiguously, in plain English, to someone's face, straight up.
5 *he can't think straight* **logically,** rationally, clearly, lucidly, coherently, cogently.
– PHRASES **go straight** *maybe a few nights in jail will inspire him to go straight* **reform,** mend one's ways, turn over a new leaf, get back on the straight and narrow. **straight away** *I'll be there straightaway* **at once,** right away, (right) now, this/that (very) minute, this/that instant, immediately, instantly, directly, forthwith, without further/more ado, promptly, quickly, without delay, then and there, here and now, as soon as possible, ASAP, as quickly as possible, in short order; informal straight off, PDQ, pretty damn quick, pronto, lickety-split; archaic straightway. **straight from the shoulder** *I have to tell you the truth straight from the shoulder* See **STRAIGHT** (sense 4 of the adverb).

straighten ▶ **verb 1** *Rory straightened his tie* **make straight,** adjust, arrange, rearrange, (make) tidy, spruce up.
2 *we must straighten things out with Violet* **put/set right,** sort out, clear up, settle, resolve, put in order, regularize, rectify, remedy; informal patch up.
3 *he straightened up* **stand up** (**straight**), stand upright.

straightforward ▶ **adjective 1** *the process was remarkably straightforward* **uncomplicated,** simple, easy, effortless, painless, undemanding, plain sailing, child's play; informal as easy as pie, a piece of cake, a cinch, a snip, a breeze, a cakewalk, duck soup, a snap.
ANTONYMS complicated.
2 *a straightforward man* **honest,** frank, candid, open, truthful, sincere, on the level; forthright, plain-speaking, direct, unambiguous; informal upfront, on the up and up.
ANTONYMS evasive.

strain[1] ▶ **verb 1** *take care that you don't strain yourself* **overtax,** overwork, overextend, overreach, drive too far; exhaust, wear out; overdo it; informal knock oneself out.
2 *you have strained a muscle* **injure,** damage, pull, wrench, twist, sprain.
3 *we strained to haul the guns up the slope* **struggle,** labor, toil, make every effort, try very hard, break one's back, push/drive oneself to the limit; informal pull out all the stops, go all out, bust a gut.
4 *the flood of refugees is straining the relief services* **make excessive demands on,** overtax, be too much for, test, tax, put a strain on.
5 *the bear strained at the chain* **pull,** tug, heave, haul, jerk; informal yank.
6 archaic *she strained the infant to her bosom* **clasp,** press, clutch, hold tight; embrace, hug, enfold, envelop.
7 *strain the mixture* **sieve,** sift, filter, screen, riddle; rare filtrate.
▶ **noun 1** *the rope snapped under the strain* **tension,** tightness, tautness.
2 *muscle strain* **injury,** sprain, wrench, twist.
3 *the strain of her job* **pressure,** demands, burdens; stress; informal hassle.
4 *Nancy was showing signs of strain* **stress,** (nervous) tension; exhaustion, fatigue, pressure of work, overwork.
5 *the strains of Brahms's lullaby* **sound,** music; melody, tune.

strain[2] ▶ **noun 1** *a different strain of flu* **variety,** kind, type, sort; breed, genus.
2 *McCallum was of Puritan strain* **descent,** ancestry, origin(s), parentage, lineage, extraction, family, roots.
3 *there was a strain of insanity in the family* **tendency,** susceptibility, propensity, proneness; trait, disposition.
4 *a strain of solemnity* **element,** strand, vein, note, trace, touch, suggestion, hint.

strained ▶ **adjective 1** *relations between them were strained* **awkward,** tense, uneasy, uncomfortable, edgy, difficult, troubled.
ANTONYMS friendly.
2 *Jean's strained face* **drawn,** careworn, worn, pinched, tired, exhausted, drained, haggard.
3 *a strained smile* **forced,** constrained, unnatural; artificial, insincere, false, affected, put-on.
ANTONYMS natural.

strainer ▶ **noun** *pour the noodles into a strainer* **sieve,** colander, filter, sifter, riddle, screen; archaic griddle.

strait ▶ **noun 1** *a strait about six miles wide* **channel,** sound, inlet, stretch of water.
2 *the company is in desperate straits* **a bad/difficult situation,** difficulty, trouble, crisis, a mess, a predicament, a plight; informal hot/deep water, a jam, a hole, a bind, a fix, a scrape.

straitened ▶ **adjective** *our straitened circumstances improved once Desmond got his first teaching job* **impoverished,** poverty-stricken, poor, destitute, penniless, as poor as a church mouse, in penury, impecunious, unable to make ends meet, in reduced circumstances; informal (flat) broke, strapped (for cash); formal penurious.

straitlaced ▶ **adjective** *our straitlaced relatives were horrified by Stacey's punk hairdo* **prim**

(**and proper**), prudish, puritanical, prissy, conservative, old-fashioned, stuffy, staid, narrow-minded; informal starchy, square, fuddy-duddy.
ANTONYMS broad-minded.

strand[1] ▶ **noun 1** *strands of wool* **thread,** filament, fiber; length, ply.
2 *the various strands of the ecological movement* **element,** component, factor, ingredient, aspect, feature, strain.

strand[2] ▶ **noun** literary *a walk along the strand* **seashore,** shore, beach, sands, foreshore, shoreline, seaside, waterfront, front, waterside.

stranded ▶ **adjective 1** *a stranded ship* **beached,** grounded, run aground, high and dry; shipwrecked, wrecked, marooned.
2 *she was stranded in a strange city* **helpless,** without resources, in difficulties; in the lurch, abandoned, deserted.

strange ▶ **adjective 1** *strange things have been happening* **unusual,** odd, curious, peculiar, funny, bizarre, weird, uncanny, queer, unexpected, unfamiliar, atypical, anomalous, out of the ordinary, extraordinary, puzzling, mystifying, mysterious, perplexing, baffling, unaccountable, inexplicable, singular, freakish; suspicious, questionable; eerie, unnatural; informal fishy, bizarro, creepy, spooky.
ANTONYMS ordinary, usual.
2 *strange clothes* **weird,** eccentric, odd, peculiar, funny, bizarre, unusual; unconventional, outlandish, freakish, quirky, zany; informal wacky, way out, freaky, kooky, offbeat, off the wall, screwy, wacko.
ANTONYMS normal, conventional.
3 *visiting a strange house* **unfamiliar,** unknown, new.
ANTONYMS familiar.
4 *Jean was feeling strange* **ill,** unwell, poorly, peaked; informal under the weather, funny, peculiar, lousy, off; dated queer.
ANTONYMS well.
5 *she felt strange with him* **ill at ease,** uneasy, uncomfortable, awkward, self-conscious.
ANTONYMS relaxed.

stranger ▶ **noun** *they were taught to fear strangers* **newcomer,** new arrival, visitor, outsider, newbie.
– PHRASES **a stranger to** *I'm afraid I'm a stranger to these automated methods* **unaccustomed to,** unfamiliar with, unused to, new to, fresh to, inexperienced in; archaic strange to.

strangle ▶ **verb 1** *the victim was strangled with a scarf* **throttle,** choke, garrote; informal strangulate.
2 *she strangled a sob* **suppress,** smother, stifle, repress, restrain, fight back, choke back.
3 *bureaucracy is strangling commercial activity* **hamper,** hinder, impede, restrict, inhibit, curb, check, constrain, squash, crush, suppress, repress.

strap ▶ **noun** *thick leather straps* **thong,** tie, band, belt.
▶ **verb 1** *a bag was strapped to the bicycle* **fasten,** secure, tie, bind, make fast, lash, truss.
2 *his knee was strapped up* **bandage,** bind.
3 *his father strapped him* See LASH (sense 1 of the verb).

stratagem ▶ **noun** *Warren devised a series of stratagems to win their confidence* **plan,** scheme, tactic, maneuver, ploy, device, trick, ruse, plot, machination, dodge; subterfuge, artifice, wile; archaic shift.

> USAGE
> **stratagem**
> The mistaken spelling *strategem* (on the analogy of *strategy*) appears about 20% as often as the correct spelling *stratagem*. Though the words *stratagem* and *strategy* are etymologically related, they came into English by different routes, and their spellings diverged merely as a matter of long-standing convention. What happened is that the Latin *strategema* became *stratagema* in Romance languages such as French. (The *Century Dictionary* calls the Romance spelling "erroneous.") *Stratagem* came into English in the fifteenth century, through French. But it wasn't until the early nineteenth century that English and American writers borrowed *strategy* (originally a Greek term) from Latin. Hence our incongruous spellings today. — **BG**

strategic ▶ **adjective** *his lawyers were known for their strategic defense methods* **planned,** calculated, tactical, politic, judicious, prudent, shrewd.

strategy ▶ **noun 1** *the government's economic strategy* **master plan,** grand design, game plan, plan (of action), action plan, policy, program; tactics.
2 *military strategy* **the art of war,** (military) tactics.

stratum ▶ **noun 1** *a stratum of flint* **layer,** vein, seam, lode, bed.
2 *this stratum of society* **level,** class, echelon, rank, grade, group, set; caste; dated station, estate.

stray ▶ **verb 1** *the gazelle had strayed from the herd* **wander off,** go astray, get separated, get lost.
2 *we strayed from our original topic* **digress,** deviate, wander, get sidetracked, go off at a tangent, veer off; get off the subject.
3 *the young men were likely to stray* **be unfaithful,** have affairs, cheat, philander; informal play around, play the field.
4 *forgive me, Father, for I have strayed* **sin,** transgress, err, go astray; archaic trespass.
▶ **adjective 1** *a stray dog* **homeless,** lost, strayed, gone astray, abandoned.
2 *a stray bullet* **random,** chance, freak, unexpected, isolated, lone, single.
▶ **noun** *she adopted three strays* **homeless animal,** stray dog/cat, waif.

streak ▶ **noun 1** *a streak of orange light* **band,** line, strip, stripe, vein, slash, ray.
2 *green streaks on her legs* **mark,** smear, smudge, stain, blotch; informal splotch.
3 *a streak of self-destructiveness* **element,** vein, touch, strain; trait, characteristic.
4 *a winning streak* **period,** spell, stretch, run, patch.

▶ **verb 1** *the sky was streaked with red* **stripe,** band, fleck.
2 *overalls streaked with paint* **mark,** daub, smear; informal splotch.

stream ▶ **noun 1** *a mountain stream* **creek,** river, rivulet, rill, runnel, streamlet, freshet; tributary; bourn; brook.
2 *a stream of boiling water* **jet,** flow, rush, gush, surge, torrent, flood, cascade, outpouring, outflow; technical efflux.
3 *a steady stream of visitors* **succession,** flow, series, string.
▶ **verb 1** *tears were streaming down her face* **flow,** pour, course, run, gush, surge, flood, cascade, spill.
2 *children streamed out of the classrooms* **pour,** surge, charge, flood, swarm, pile, crowd.
3 *a flag streamed from the mast* **flutter,** float, flap, fly, blow, waft, wave.

streamer ▶ **noun** *streamers fluttered from every post and pole along the parade route* **pennant,** pennon, flag, banderole, banner.

streamlined ▶ **adjective 1** *streamlined cars* **aerodynamic,** smooth, sleek.
2 *a streamlined organization* **efficient,** smooth-running, well run, slick; time-saving, labor-saving.

street ▶ **noun** *Amsterdam's narrow cobbled streets* **road,** thoroughfare, avenue, drive, crescent, boulevard; side street/road, lane, highway.
– PHRASES **the man/woman in the street** *they claim to be interested in what the man in the street has to say, but that hardly seems the case* **an ordinary person,** Mr./Ms. Average; informal Joe Public, John Q. Public, Joe Blow, Joe Schmo, schmo, John Doe, Joe Sixpack. **on the streets** *many of these teens have parents who don't care that their kids are on the streets* **homeless,** down and out, of no fixed abode.

strength ▶ **noun 1** *enormous physical strength* **power,** brawn, muscle, muscularity, burliness, sturdiness, robustness, toughness, hardiness; vigor, force, might; informal beef; literary thew.
ANTONYMS weakness, frailty.
2 *Oliver began to regain his strength* **health,** fitness, vigor, stamina.
ANTONYMS infirmity.
3 *her great inner strength* **fortitude,** resilience, spirit, backbone, strength of character; courage, bravery, pluck, pluckiness, courageousness, grit, mettle; informal guts, spunk.
ANTONYMS vulnerability.
4 *the strength of the retaining wall* **robustness,** sturdiness, firmness, toughness, soundness, solidity, durability.
ANTONYMS weakness.
5 *China's military strength* **power,** influence, dominance, ascendancy, supremacy; informal clout; literary puissance.
ANTONYMS weakness, impotence.
6 *the strength of feeling against the president* **intensity,** vehemence, force, forcefulness, depth, ardor, fervor.
ANTONYMS half-heartedness.
7 *the strength of their argument* **cogency,** forcefulness, force, weight, power, potency, persuasiveness, soundness, validity.
ANTONYMS weakness, ineffectiveness.
8 *what are your strengths?* **strong point,** advantage, asset, forte, aptitude, talent, skill; specialty.
ANTONYMS failing, flaw, limitation.
9 *the strength of the army* **size,** extent, magnitude.
ANTONYMS weakness.
– PHRASES **on the strength of** *she got into Princeton on the strength of her essays* **because of,** by virtue of, on the basis of.

strengthen ▶ **verb 1** *calcium strengthens growing bones* **fortify,** make strong/stronger, build up, give strength to.
ANTONYMS weaken.
2 *engineers strengthened the walls* **reinforce,** make stronger, buttress, shore up, underpin.
3 *how does this process strengthen the glass?* **toughen,** temper, anneal.
4 *the wind had strengthened* **become strong/stronger,** gain strength, intensify, pick up.
ANTONYMS die down.
5 *his insistence strengthened her determination* **fortify,** bolster, make stronger, boost, reinforce, harden, stiffen, toughen, fuel.
ANTONYMS weaken.
6 *they strengthened their efforts* **redouble,** step up, increase, escalate; informal up, crank up, beef up.
ANTONYMS relax, decrease.
7 *the argument is strengthened by this evidence* **reinforce,** lend more weight to; support, substantiate, back up, confirm, bear out, corroborate.
ANTONYMS undermine.

strenuous ▶ **adjective 1** *a strenuous climb* **arduous,** difficult, hard, tough, taxing, demanding, exacting, exhausting, tiring, grueling, back-breaking; informal killing; archaic toilsome.
ANTONYMS easy.
2 *strenuous efforts* **vigorous,** energetic, zealous, forceful, strong, spirited, intense, determined, resolute, tenacious, tireless, indefatigable, dogged; formal pertinacious.
ANTONYMS halfhearted.

stress ▶ **noun 1** *he's under a lot of stress* **strain,** pressure, (nervous) tension, worry, anxiety, trouble, difficulty; informal hassle.
2 *laying greater stress on education* **emphasis,** importance, weight.
3 *the stress falls on the first syllable* **emphasis,** accent, accentuation; beat; Prosody ictus.
4 *the stress is uniform across the bar* **pressure,** tension, strain.
▶ **verb 1** *they stressed the need for reform* **emphasize,** draw attention to, underline, underscore, point up, place emphasis on, lay stress on, highlight, accentuate, press home.
ANTONYMS play down.
2 *the last syllable is stressed* **place the emphasis on,** emphasize, place the accent on.
3 *all the staff were stressed* **overstretch,** overtax, push to the limit, pressure, make tense, worry, harass; informal hassle.

stretch ▶ **verb 1** *this material stretches* **be elastic,** be stretchy, be tensile.
2 *he stretched the elastic* **pull (out),** draw out, extend, lengthen, elongate, expand.

3 *stretch your weekend into a vacation* **prolong,** lengthen, make longer, extend, spin out.
ANTONYMS shorten.
4 *my budget won't* ***stretch to*** *a new car* **be sufficient for,** be enough for, cover; afford, have the money for.
5 *the court case stretched their finances* **put a strain on,** overtax, overextend, drain, sap.
6 *stretching the truth* **bend,** strain, distort, exaggerate, embellish.
7 *she* ***stretched out*** *her hand to him* **reach out,** hold out, extend, outstretch, proffer; literary outreach.
ANTONYMS withdraw.
8 *he stretched his arms* **extend,** straighten (out).
9 *she* ***stretched out*** *on the sofa* **lie down,** recline, lean back, be recumbent, sprawl, lounge, loll.
10 *the desert stretches for miles* **extend,** spread, continue.
▶ **noun 1** *magnificent stretches of forest* **expanse,** area, tract, belt, sweep, extent.
2 *a four-hour stretch* **period,** time, spell, run, stint, session, shift.
3 informal *a ten-year stretch* **(prison) sentence,** (prison) term, stint, rap.
▶ **adjective** *stretch fabrics* **stretchy,** stretchable, elastic.

strict ▶ **adjective 1** *a strict interpretation of the law* **precise,** exact, literal, faithful, accurate, rigorous, careful, meticulous, pedantic.
ANTONYMS loose, imprecise.
2 *strict controls on spending* **stringent,** rigorous, severe, harsh, hard, rigid, tough, ironclad. See note at **SEVERE.**
ANTONYMS liberal.
3 *strict parents* **stern,** severe, harsh, uncompromising, authoritarian, governessy, firm, austere.
ANTONYMS lenient.
4 *this will be treated in strict confidence* **absolute,** utter, complete, total.
5 *a strict Roman Catholic* **orthodox,** devout, conscientious.
ANTONYMS moderate, liberal.

stricture ▶ **noun 1** *the constant strictures of the nuns* **criticism,** censure, condemnation, reproof, reproach, admonishment, animadversion.
ANTONYMS praise.
2 *the strictures on Victorian women* **constraint,** restriction, limitation, restraint, curb, impediment, barrier, obstacle.
ANTONYMS freedom.
3 *an intestinal stricture* **narrowing,** constriction.

stride ▶ **verb** *she came striding down the path* **march,** pace, step.
▶ **noun** *long swinging strides* **(long/large) step,** pace.
– PHRASES **take something in one's stride** *he seem to be taking the news in his stride* **deal with easily,** cope with easily, not bat an eyelid.

strident ▶ **adjective** *a strident voice interrupted the consultation* **harsh,** raucous, rough, grating, rasping, jarring, loud, shrill, screeching, piercing, ear-piercing. See note at **VOCIFEROUS.**
ANTONYMS soft.

strife ▶ **noun** *these countries have been immersed in political strife for more than a hundred years* **conflict,** friction, discord, disagreement, dissension, dispute, argument, quarreling, wrangling, bickering, controversy; ill/bad feeling, falling-out, bad blood, hostility, animosity.
ANTONYMS peace.

strike ▶ **verb 1** *the teacher struck Mary* **hit,** slap, smack, beat, thrash, spank, thump, punch, cuff; cane, lash, whip, club; informal clout, schmuck, wallop, belt, whack, thwack, bash, clobber, bop, cold-cock; literary smite.
2 *he struck the gong* **bang,** beat, hit; informal bash, wallop.
3 *the car struck a tree* **crash into,** collide with, hit, run into, bump into, smash into, impact.
4 *Jennifer struck the ball* **hit,** drive, propel; informal clout, wallop, swipe.
5 *he struck a match* **ignite,** light.
6 *she was asleep when the killer struck* **attack,** set upon someone, fall on someone, assault someone.
7 *the disease is striking 3,000 people a year* **affect,** afflict, attack, hit.
8 *striking a balance* **achieve,** reach, arrive at, find, attain, establish.
9 *we have struck a bargain* **agree (on),** come to an agreement on, settle on; informal clinch.
10 *he struck a heroic pose* **assume,** adopt, take on/up, affect, cop.
11 *they have struck oil* **discover,** find, come upon, hit.
12 *a thought struck her* **occur to,** come to (mind), dawn on one, hit, spring to mind, enter one's head.
13 *you strike me as intelligent* **seem to,** appear to, come across to, give the impression to.
14 *drivers are striking* **take industrial action,** go on strike, down tools, walk out, hit the bricks.
15 *the commodore struck his flag* **lower,** take down, bring down.
16 *we should strike south* **go,** make one's way, head, forge.
▶ **noun 1** *a 48-hour strike* **industrial action,** walkout, job action, stoppage.
2 *a military strike* **(air) attack,** assault, bombing, raid.
3 *a gold strike* **find,** discovery.
– PHRASES **strike out** *strike out the old phone number* **delete,** cross out, erase, rub out. **strike up 1** *the band struck up another tune* **begin to play,** start playing. **2** *we struck up a friendship* **begin,** start, commence, embark on, establish.

striking ▶ **adjective 1** *Lizzie bears a striking resemblance to her sister* **noticeable,** obvious, conspicuous, impactful, evident, marked, notable, unmistakable, strong; remarkable, extraordinary, incredible, amazing, astounding, astonishing, staggering. See note at **NOTICEABLE.**
ANTONYMS unremarkable.
2 *Kenya's striking landscape* **impressive,** imposing, grand, splendid, magnificent, spectacular, breathtaking, superb, marvelous, wonderful, stunning, staggering, sensational,

dramatic.
ANTONYMS unimpressive.
3 *what a striking young couple* **stunning,** attractive, good-looking, beautiful, glamorous, gorgeous, prepossessing, ravishing, handsome, pretty; informal knockout, drop-dead gorgeous; archaic fair, comely.
ANTONYMS unremarkable, unattractive.

string ▶ **noun 1** *a knotted piece of string* **twine,** cord, yarn, thread, strand.
2 *a string of convenience stores* **chain,** group, firm, company.
3 *a string of convictions* **series,** succession, chain, sequence, run, streak.
4 *a string of wagons* **line,** train, procession, queue, file, column, convoy, cavalcade.
5 *a string of pearls* **strand,** rope, necklace.
6 *a guaranteed loan with no strings* **condition,** qualification, provision, proviso, caveat, stipulation, rider, prerequisite, limitation, limit, constraint, restriction; informal catch.
▶ **verb 1** *lights were strung across the promenade* **hang,** suspend, sling, stretch, run; thread, loop, festoon.
2 *beads strung on a silver chain* **thread,** loop, link.
– PHRASES **string along 1** *must your sister always string along?* **go along,** come too, accompany someone, join someone. **2** *I think Daisy is just stringing poor Dave along* **mislead,** deceive, take advantage of, dupe, hoax, fool, make a fool of, play with, toy with, dally with, trifle with; informal lead up the garden path, take for a ride. **string out 1** *stringing out a story* **spin out,** drag out, lengthen. **2** *airfields strung out along the Gulf* **spread out,** space out, distribute, scatter. **string up** informal *Dawes and his boys went after Lucius, threatening to string him up* **hang,** lynch, gibbet.

stringent ▶ **adjective** *stringent regulations* **strict,** firm, rigid, rigorous, severe, harsh, tough, tight, exacting, demanding, inflexible, hard and fast.

stringy ▶ **adjective 1** *stringy hair* **straggly,** lank, thin.
2 *a stringy brunette* **lanky,** gangling, gangly, rangy, wiry, bony, skinny, scrawny, thin, spare, gaunt.
3 *stringy meat* **fibrous,** gristly, sinewy, chewy, tough, leathery.

strip[1] ▶ **verb 1** *he stripped and got into bed* **undress,** strip off, take one's clothes off, unclothe, disrobe, strip naked.
ANTONYMS dress.
2 ***stripping off*** *paint* **peel (off),** remove, take off, scrape (off), rub off, clean off.
3 *they* ***stripped her of*** *her doctorate* **take away from someone,** dispossess someone of, deprive someone of, confiscate, divest someone of, relieve someone of.
4 *they* ***stripped down*** *my engine* **dismantle,** disassemble, take to bits/pieces, take apart.
ANTONYMS assemble.
5 *the house had been stripped* **empty,** clear, clean out, plunder, rob, burgle, burglarize, loot, pillage, ransack, despoil, sack.

strip[2] ▶ **noun** *a strip of paper* **(narrow) piece,** bit, band, belt, ribbon, slip, shred.

stripe ▶ **noun** *it's a red jacket with a white stripe down each sleeve* **line,** band, strip, belt, bar, streak, vein, flash, blaze; technical stria, striation.

striped ▶ **adjective** *a tropical plant with large striped leaves* barred, lined, banded, stripy; streaky, variegated; technical striated.

stripling ▶ **noun** *it's natural for these striplings to get into a bit of trouble now and then* **youth,** adolescent, youngster, boy, schoolboy, lad, teenager, juvenile, minor, young man; informal kid, young 'un, whippersnapper, shaver.

strive ▶ **verb 1** *I shall strive to be virtuous* **try (hard),** attempt, endeavor, aim, venture, make an effort, exert oneself, do one's best, do all one can, do one's utmost, labor, work; informal go all out, give it one's best shot, pull out all the stops; formal essay.
2 *scholars must strive against bias* **struggle,** fight, battle, combat; campaign, crusade.

stroke ▶ **noun 1** *five strokes of the ax* **blow,** hit, thump, punch, slap, smack, cuff, knock; informal wallop, clout, whack, thwack, bash, swipe; archaic smite.
2 *she hit the green in three strokes* **shot,** hit, strike.
3 *light upward strokes* **movement,** action, motion.
4 *a stroke of genius* **feat,** accomplishment, achievement, master stroke.
5 *broad brush strokes* **mark,** line.
6 *the budget was full of bold strokes* **detail,** touch, point.
7 *he suffered a stroke* **thrombosis,** seizure; Medicine ictus.
▶ **verb** *she stroked the cat* **caress,** fondle, pat, pet, touch, rub, massage, soothe.

stroll ▶ **verb** *they strolled along the river* **saunter,** amble, wander, meander, ramble, promenade, walk, go for a walk, stretch one's legs, get some air; informal mosey; formal perambulate.
▶ **noun** *a stroll in the park* **saunter,** amble, wander, walk, turn, promenade; informal mosey; dated constitutional; formal perambulation.

strong ▶ **adjective 1** *Ben is a strong lad* **powerful,** muscular, brawny, powerfully built, strapping, sturdy, burly, meaty, robust, athletic, tough, rugged, lusty, strong as an ox/horse; informal beefy, hunky, husky; dated stalwart.
ANTONYMS weak, puny.
2 *a strong character* **forceful,** determined, spirited, self-assertive, tough, tenacious, indomitable, formidable, redoubtable, strong-minded; informal gutsy, feisty.
ANTONYMS weak.
3 *a strong fortress* **secure,** well-built, indestructible, well fortified, well protected, impregnable, solid.
4 *strong cotton bags* **durable,** hardwearing, heavy-duty, industrial-strength, tough, sturdy, well-made, long-lasting.
ANTONYMS weak, flimsy.
5 *the current is very strong* **forceful,** powerful, vigorous, fierce, intense.
ANTONYMS gentle.
6 *a strong interest in literature* **keen,** eager, passionate, fervent.
7 *strong feelings* **intense,** forceful, passionate,

ardent, fervent, fervid, deep-seated; literary perfervid.
8 *a strong supporter* **keen,** eager, enthusiastic, dedicated, staunch, loyal, steadfast.
9 *strong arguments* **compelling,** cogent, forceful, powerful, potent, weighty, convincing, sound, valid, well-founded, persuasive, influential.
ANTONYMS weak, unconvincing.
10 *a need for strong action* **firm,** forceful, drastic, extreme.
11 *she bore a very strong resemblance to Vera* **marked,** striking, noticeable, pronounced, distinct, definite, unmistakable, notable.
ANTONYMS slight.
12 *a strong voice* **loud,** powerful, forceful, resonant, sonorous, rich, deep, booming.
ANTONYMS weak, quiet.
13 *strong language* **bad,** foul, obscene, profane.
14 *a strong blue color* **intense,** deep, rich, bright, brilliant, vivid.
ANTONYMS pale.
15 *strong lights* **bright,** brilliant, dazzling, glaring.
16 *strong black coffee* **concentrated,** undiluted, potent.
ANTONYMS weak, mild.
17 *strong cheese* **highly flavored,** flavorful, piquant, tangy, spicy.
ANTONYMS mild.
18 *strong drink* **alcoholic,** intoxicating, hard, stiff; formal spirituous.
ANTONYMS soft, nonalcoholic.

strongbox ▶ **noun** *there was nothing in the strongbox but some worthless old stocks* **safe,** safety deposit box, cash/money box.

stronghold ▶ **noun 1** *the enemy stronghold* **fortress,** fort, castle, citadel, garrison.
2 *a liberal stronghold* **bastion,** center, hotbed, safe seat.

strong-minded ▶ **adjective** *a strong-minded social reformer* **determined,** firm, resolute, purposeful, strong-willed, uncompromising, unbending, forceful, persistent, tenacious, dogged; informal gutsy, spunky.

strong-willed ▶ **adjective** *you strong-willed recruits had better prepare yourselves to get broken* **determined,** resolute, stubborn, obstinate, willful, headstrong, strong-minded, self-willed, unbending, unyielding, intransigent, intractable, obdurate, recalcitrant; formal refractory.

structure ▶ **noun 1** *a vast Gothic structure* **building,** edifice, construction, erection, pile.
2 *the structure of local government* **construction,** form, formation, shape, composition, anatomy, makeup, constitution; organization, system, arrangement, design, framework, configuration, pattern.
▶ **verb** *the program is structured around periods of home study* **arrange,** organize, design, shape, construct, build, put together.

struggle ▶ **verb 1** *they struggled to do better* **strive,** try hard, endeavor, make every effort, do one's best/utmost, bend over backwards, put oneself out; informal go all out, give it one's best shot; formal essay.
2 *James struggled with the intruders* **fight,** grapple, wrestle, scuffle, brawl, spar; informal scrap.
3 *the teams struggled to be first* **compete,** contend, vie, fight, battle, jockey.
4 *she struggled over the dunes* **scramble,** flounder, stumble, fight/battle one's way, labor.
▶ **noun 1** *the struggle for justice* **endeavor,** striving, effort, exertion, labor; campaign, battle, crusade, drive, push.
2 *they were arrested without a struggle* **fight,** scuffle, brawl, tussle, wrestling bout, skirmish, fracas, melee; breach of the peace; informal scrap.
3 *many perished in the struggle* **conflict,** fight, battle, confrontation, clash, skirmish; hostilities, fighting, war, warfare, campaign.
4 *a struggle within the leadership* **contest,** competition, fight, clash; rivalry, friction, feuding, conflict, tug-of-war, turf war.
5 *life has been a struggle for me* **effort,** trial, trouble, stress, strain, battle; informal grind, hassle.

strut ▶ **verb** *he strutted around his vast office* **swagger,** swank, parade, stride, sweep, sashay.

stub ▶ **noun 1** *a cigarette stub* **butt,** (tail) end.
2 *a ticket stub* **counterfoil,** ticket slip, tab.
3 *a stub of pencil* **stump,** remnant, (tail) end.

stubborn ▶ **adjective 1** *you're too stubborn to admit it* **obstinate,** headstrong, willful, strong-willed, pigheaded, obdurate, difficult, contrary, perverse, recalcitrant, inflexible, iron-willed, uncompromising, unbending; informal stiff-necked, bloody-minded, balky; formal pertinacious, refractory, contumacious.
ANTONYMS compliant.
2 *stubborn stains* **indelible,** permanent, persistent, tenacious, resistant.

CHOOSE THE RIGHT WORD

stubborn, dogged, intractable, obdurate, obstinate, pertinacious, perverse

If you're the kind of person who takes a stand and then refuses to back down, your friends might say you have a **stubborn** disposition, a word that implies an innate resistance to any attempt to change one's purpose, course, or opinion. People who are *stubborn* by nature exhibit this kind of behavior in most situations, but they might be **obstinate** in a particular instance (*a stubborn child, he was obstinate in his refusal to eat vegetables*). *Obstinate* implies sticking persistently to an opinion, purpose, or course of action, especially in the face of persuasion or attack. While *obstinate* is usually a negative term, **dogged** can be either positive or negative, implying both tenacious, often sullen, persistence (*dogged pursuit of a college degree, even though he knew he would end up in the family business*) and great determination (*dogged loyalty to a cause*). **Obdurate** usually connotes a stubborn resistance marked by harshness and lack of feeling (*obdurate in ignoring their pleas*), while **intractable** means stubborn in a headstrong sense and difficult for others to control or manage (*intractable pain*). No matter how stubborn you are, you probably don't want to be called **pertinacious**, which implies persistence to the point of being annoying or unreasonable (*a pertinacious panhandler*).

stubby ▶ adjective *a small stubby man with glasses* **dumpy,** stocky, chunky, chubby, squat; short, stumpy, dwarfish; informal vertically challenged.
ANTONYMS slender, tall.

stuck ▶ adjective **1** *a message was stuck to his screen* **fixed,** fastened, attached, glued, pinned.
2 *the gate was stuck* **immovable,** stuck fast, jammed.
3 *if you get stuck, leave a blank* **baffled,** beaten, at a loss, at one's wits' end; informal stumped, bogged down, flummoxed, fazed, bamboozled.
– PHRASES **stuck on** informal *no one knew that Kit was stuck on his brother's wife* **infatuated with,** besotted with, smitten with, (head over heels) in love with, obsessed with; informal crazy about, mad about, wild about, carrying a torch for.
stuck with *she's always getting stuck with the neighbors' kids* **lumbered with,** left with, made responsible for.

stuck-up ▶ adjective informal See CONCEITED.

student ▶ noun **1** *a college student* **scholar,** undergraduate, graduate, grad student, postdoctoral fellow; freshman, sophomore, junior, senior.
2 *high school student* **pupil,** schoolchild, schoolboy, schoolgirl, scholar.
3 *a nursing student* **trainee,** apprentice, probationer, recruit, intern, novice; informal rookie.

studied ▶ adjective *the words were said with studied politeness* **deliberate,** careful, considered, conscious, calculated, intentional; affected, forced, strained, artificial.

studio ▶ noun *the artist's studio* **workshop,** workroom, atelier, workspace.

studious ▶ adjective **1** *a studious nature* **scholarly,** academic, bookish, intellectual, erudite, learned, donnish.
2 *studious attention* **diligent,** careful, attentive, assiduous, painstaking, thorough, meticulous.
3 *his studious absence from public view* **deliberate,** willful, conscious, intentional.

study ▶ noun **1** *two years of study* **learning,** education, schooling, academic work, scholarship, tuition, research; informal cramming.
2 *a study of global warming* **investigation,** inquiry, research, examination, analysis, review, survey.
3 *Father was in his study* **office,** workroom, studio.
4 *a critical study* **essay,** article, work, review, paper, dissertation, disquisition.
▶ verb **1** *Anne studied hard* **work,** review; informal cram, hit the books.
2 *he studied electronics* **learn,** read, be taught.
3 *Thomas was studying child development* **investigate,** inquire into, research, look into, examine, analyze, explore, review, appraise, conduct a survey of.
4 *she studied her friend thoughtfully* **scrutinize,** examine, inspect, consider, regard, look at, eye, observe, watch, survey; informal check out, eyeball.
– PHRASES **in a brown study** *you'll often catch a student in a brown study on a warm spring day like today* **lost in thought,** in a reverie, musing, ruminating, cogitating, dreaming, daydreaming; informal miles away.

stuff ▶ noun **1** *suede is tough stuff* **material,** fabric, cloth, textile; matter, substance.
2 *first-aid stuff* **items,** articles, objects, goods, equipment; informal things, bits and pieces, odds and ends.
3 *all my stuff is in the suitcase* **belongings,** (personal) possessions, effects, goods (and chattels), paraphernalia; informal gear, things.
4 *he knows his stuff* **facts,** information, data, subject.
▶ verb **1** *stuffing pillows* **fill,** pack, pad, upholster.
2 *Robyn stuffed her clothes into a bag* **shove,** thrust, push, ram, cram, squeeze, force, jam, pack, pile, stick.
3 informal *they **stuffed themselves with** chocolate* **fill oneself with,** gorge oneself with/on, overindulge oneself with; gobble, devour, wolf; informal pig out on, make a pig of oneself with/on.
4 *my nose was **stuffed up*** **block (up),** congest, obstruct.

stuffing ▶ noun **1** *the stuffing is coming out of the armchair* **padding,** wadding, filling, upholstery, packing, filler.
2 *sage and onion stuffing* dressing, filling, forcemeat, salpicon.
– PHRASES **knock the stuffing out of** informal *news of Pam's engagement knocked the stuffing out of Bob* **devastate,** shatter, crush, shock.

stuffy ▶ adjective **1** *a stuffy atmosphere* **airless,** close, musty, stale.
ANTONYMS airy.
2 *a stuffy young man* **staid,** sedate, sober, prim, priggish, straitlaced, conformist, conservative, old-fashioned, governessy; informal square, straight, starchy, fuddy-duddy.
ANTONYMS laid-back, modern.
3 *a stuffy nose* **blocked,** stuffed up, congested.
ANTONYMS clear.

stultify ▶ verb **1** *social welfare was stultified by international trade regulations* **hamper,** impede, thwart, frustrate, foil, suppress, smother.
2 *he stultifies her with too much gentleness* **bore,** make bored, dull, numb, benumb, stupefy.

stumble ▶ verb **1** *she stumbled and fell heavily* **trip (over/up),** lose one's balance, lose/miss one's footing, slip.
2 *he stumbled back home* **stagger,** totter, teeter, dodder, blunder, hobble, move clumsily.
3 *she stumbled through her speech* **stammer,** stutter, hesitate, falter, speak haltingly; informal fluff/flub one's lines.
– PHRASES **stumble across/on** *I stumbled across these old photographs in the attic* **come across/upon,** chance on, happen on, bump into, light on; discover, find, unearth, uncover; informal dig up.

stump ▶ verb *we could never stump Mr. Marlowe with our riddles* **baffle,** perplex, puzzle, confuse, confound, defeat, put at a loss; informal flummox, throw, floor, discombobulate.

stun ▶ verb **1** *a glancing blow stunned Gary* **daze,** stupefy, knock unconscious, knock out, lay out.
2 *she was stunned by the news* **astound,** amaze, astonish, dumbfound, stupefy, stagger, shock, take aback; informal flabbergast, bowl over.

stunning ▶ adjective **1** *a stunning win* **remarkable,** extraordinary, staggering, incredible, outstanding, amazing, astonishing, marvelous, phenomenal, splendid; informal fabulous, fantastic, tremendous, jaw-dropping.
ANTONYMS ordinary.
2 *she was looking stunning* See BEAUTIFUL.

stunt[1] ▶ verb *a disease that stunts growth* **inhibit,** impede, hamper, hinder, restrict, retard, slow, curb, check.
ANTONYMS encourage.

stunt[2] ▶ noun *acrobatic stunts* **feat,** exploit, trick.

stunted ▶ adjective *a stunted geranium* **small,** undersize(d), diminutive.

stupefaction ▶ noun **1** *alcoholic stupefaction* **oblivion,** obliviousness, unconsciousness, insensibility, stupor, daze.
2 *Don shook his head in stupefaction* **bewilderment,** confusion, perplexity, wonder, amazement, astonishment.

stupefy ▶ verb **1** *the blow had stupefied her* **stun,** daze, knock unconscious, knock out, lay out.
2 *they were stupefied from the wine* **drug,** sedate, tranquilize, intoxicate, inebriate; informal dope.
3 *the cost stupefied us* **shock,** stun, astound, dumbfound, overwhelm, stagger, amaze, astonish, take aback, take someone's breath away; informal flabbergast, bowl over, floor.

stupendous ▶ adjective **1** *stupendous achievements* **amazing,** astounding, astonishing, extraordinary, remarkable, phenomenal, staggering, breathtaking; informal fantastic, mind-boggling, awesome; literary wondrous.
ANTONYMS ordinary.
2 *a building of stupendous size* **colossal,** immense, vast, gigantic, massive, mammoth, huge, enormous.
ANTONYMS minute.

stupid ▶ adjective **1** *they're rather stupid* **unintelligent,** ignorant, dense, foolish, dull-witted, slow, simpleminded, vacuous, vapid, idiotic, imbecilic, imbecile, obtuse, doltish; informal thick, dim, dimwitted, dumb, dopey, dozy, moronic, cretinous, pea-brained, halfwitted, soft in the head, brain-dead, boneheaded, thickheaded, wooden-headed, muttonheaded, daft.
ANTONYMS intelligent.
2 *that was a really stupid thing to do* **foolish,** silly, unintelligent, idiotic, scatterbrained, nonsensical, senseless, unthinking, ill-advised, ill-considered, unwise, injudicious; inane, absurd, ludicrous, ridiculous, laughable, risible, fatuous, asinine, mad, insane, lunatic; informal crazy, dopey, cracked, half-baked, dimwitted, cockeyed, harebrained, lamebrained, nutty, batty, cuckoo, loony, loopy.
ANTONYMS sensible.
3 *he drank himself stupid* **into a stupor,** into a daze, into oblivion; stupefied, dazed, unconscious.
ANTONYMS alert.

CHOOSE THE RIGHT WORD

stupid, asinine, dense, dull, dumb, obtuse, slow, unintelligent

If you want to impugn someone's intelligence, the options are almost limitless. You can call the person **stupid**, a term that implies a sluggish, slow-witted lack of intelligence. **Asinine** is a harsher word, implying asslike or foolish behavior rather than slow-wittedness (*a woman her age looked asinine in a miniskirt*). Calling someone **dumb** is risky, because it is not only an informal word (*you dumb bunny!*), but because it also means mute and is associated with the offensive expression "deaf and dumb," used to describe people who cannot hear or speak. **Dense** implies an inability to understand even simple facts or instructions (*too dense to get the joke*), while **dull** suggests a sluggishness of mind unrelieved by any hint of quickness, brightness, or liveliness (*a dull stare*). **Slow** also implies a lack of quickness in comprehension or reaction and is often used as a euphemistic substitute for *stupid* (*he was a little slow intellectually*). **Obtuse** is a more formal word for slow-wittedness, but with a strong undercurrent of scorn (*it almost seemed as though he were being deliberately obtuse*). You can't go wrong with a word like **unintelligent**, which is probably the most objective term for low mental ability and the least likely to provoke an angry response (*unintelligent answers to the teacher's questions*).

stupidity ▶ noun **1** *he cursed their stupidity* **lack of intelligence,** foolishness, denseness, brainlessness, ignorance, dull-wittedness, slow-wittedness, doltishness, slowness; informal thickness, dimness, dopiness.
2 *the stupidity of the question* **foolishness,** folly, silliness, idiocy, brainlessness, senselessness, injudiciousness, ineptitude, inaneness, inanity, absurdity, ludicrousness, ridiculousness, fatuousness, madness, insanity, lunacy; informal craziness.

stupor ▶ noun *they left him slumped in a drunken stupor* **daze,** state of unconsciousness, torpor, insensibility, oblivion.

sturdy ▶ adjective **1** *a sturdy lad* **strapping,** well-built, muscular, athletic, strong, hefty, brawny, powerful, solid, burly, rugged, robust, tough, hardy, lusty; informal husky, beefy, meaty; dated stalwart; literary thewy.
ANTONYMS puny, frail.
2 *sturdy boots* **robust,** strong, strongly made, well built, solid, stout, tough, resilient, durable, long-lasting, hardwearing.
ANTONYMS weak, flimsy.
3 *sturdy resistance* **vigorous,** strong, stalwart, firm, determined, resolute, staunch, steadfast.
ANTONYMS weak.

stutter ▶ verb *he stuttered over a word* **stammer,**

stumble, falter.
▶ **noun** *a bad stutter* **stammer,** speech impediment, speech defect.

style ▶ **noun 1** *differing styles of management* **manner,** way, technique, method, methodology, approach, system, mode, form, modus operandi; informal MO.
2 *a nondirective style of counseling* **type,** kind, variety, sort, genre, school, brand, pattern, model.
3 *wearing clothes with style* **flair,** stylishness, elegance, grace, gracefulness, poise, polish, suaveness, sophistication, urbanity, chic, dash, panache, élan; informal class, pizzazz.
4 *Laura traveled in style* **comfort,** luxury, elegance, opulence, lavishness.
5 *modern styles* **fashion,** trend, vogue, mode.
▶ **verb 1** *sportswear styled by Karl* **design,** fashion, tailor.
2 *men who were styled "knight"* **call,** name, title, entitle, dub, designate, term, label, tag, nickname; formal denominate.

stylish ▶ **adjective** *a stylish raincoat* **fashionable,** modish, voguish, modern, up to date; smart, sophisticated, elegant, chic, dapper, dashing; informal trendy, natty, classy, nifty, ritzy, snazzy, fly, kicky, tony, spiffy.
ANTONYMS unfashionable.

suave ▶ **adjective** *your clothes should show what a suave man you are* **charming,** sophisticated, debonair, urbane, polished, refined, poised, self-possessed, dignified, civilized, gentlemanly, gallant; smooth, polite, well-mannered, civil, courteous, affable, tactful, diplomatic. See note at **URBANE**.
ANTONYMS unsophisticated.

subconscious ▶ **adjective** *subconscious desires* **unconscious,** latent, suppressed, repressed, subliminal, dormant, underlying, innermost; informal bottled up.
▶ **noun** *the creative powers of the subconscious* **(unconscious) mind,** imagination, inner(most) self, psyche.

subdue ▶ **verb 1** *he subdued all his enemies* **conquer,** defeat, vanquish, overcome, overwhelm, crush, quash, beat, trounce, subjugate, suppress, bring someone to their knees; informal lick, thrash, hammer.
2 *she could not subdue her longing* **curb,** restrain, hold back, constrain, contain, repress, suppress, stifle, smother, keep in check, rein in, control, master, quell; informal keep a/the lid on.

subdued ▶ **adjective 1** *Lewis's subdued air* **somber,** low-spirited, downcast, sad, dejected, depressed, gloomy, despondent, dispirited, disheartened, forlorn, woebegone; withdrawn, preoccupied; informal down in/at the mouth, down in the dumps, in the doldrums, in a blue funk.
ANTONYMS cheerful, lively.
2 *subdued voices* **hushed,** muted, quiet, low, soft, faint, muffled, indistinct.
ANTONYMS loud.
3 *subdued light* **dim,** muted, softened, soft, lowered, subtle.
ANTONYMS bright.

subject ▶ **noun 1** *the subject of this chapter* **theme,** subject matter, topic, issue, question, concern, point; substance, essence, gist.
2 *popular university subjects* **branch of study,** discipline, field.
3 *six subjects did the trials* **participant,** volunteer; informal guinea pig.
4 *Her Majesty's subjects* **citizen,** national; taxpayer, voter.
5 *a loyal subject* **liege,** liegeman, vassal, henchman, follower.
▶ **verb** *they were* ***subjected to*** *violence* **put through,** treat with, expose to.
– PHRASES **subject to 1** *it is subject to budgetary approval* **conditional on,** contingent on, dependent on. **2** *horses are subject to coughs* **susceptible to,** liable to, prone to, vulnerable to, predisposed to, at risk of. **3** *we are all subject to the law* **bound by,** constrained by, accountable to.

subjective ▶ **adjective** *a subjective analysis* **personal,** individual, emotional, instinctive, intuitive.
ANTONYMS objective.

subjugate ▶ **verb** *the Normans had subjugated most of Ireland's Gaelic population* **conquer,** vanquish, defeat, crush, quash, bring someone to their knees, enslave, subdue, suppress.
ANTONYMS liberate.

sublime ▶ **adjective 1** *sublime music* **exalted,** elevated, noble, lofty, awe-inspiring, majestic, magnificent, glorious, superb, wonderful, marvelous, splendid; informal fantastic, fabulous, terrific, heavenly, divine, out of this world.
2 *the sublime confidence of youth* **supreme,** total, complete, utter, consummate.

submerge ▶ **verb 1** *the U-boat submerged* **go under water,** dive, sink.
ANTONYMS surface.
2 *submerge the bowl in water* **immerse,** plunge, sink.
3 *the farmland was submerged* **flood,** inundate, deluge, swamp.
4 *she was submerged in work* **overwhelm,** inundate, deluge, swamp, bury, engulf, snow under.

submission ▶ **noun 1** *submission to authority* **yielding,** capitulation, acceptance, consent, compliance.
ANTONYMS defiance.
2 *Tim raised his hands in submission* **surrender,** capitulation, resignation, defeat.
3 *he wanted her total submission* **compliance,** submissiveness, acquiescence, passivity, obedience, docility, deference, subservience, servility, subjection.
ANTONYMS defiance, resistance.
4 *a report for submission to the Board* **presentation,** presenting, proffering, tendering, proposal, proposing.
5 *his original submission* **proposal,** suggestion, proposition, recommendation.
6 *the judge rejected her submission* **argument,** assertion, contention, statement, claim, allegation.

submissive ▶ **adjective** *she's far from being a submissive woman* **compliant,** yielding, acquiescent, unassertive, passive, obedient, biddable, dutiful, docile, pliant; informal under someone's thumb.

submit ▸ verb 1 *she submitted under duress* **give in/way,** yield, back down, cave in, capitulate; surrender, knuckle under.
ANTONYMS resist, defy.
2 *he refused to **submit to** their authority* **be governed by,** abide by, be regulated by, comply with, accept, adhere to, be subject to, agree to, consent to, conform to.
ANTONYMS resist, defy.
3 *we submitted an unopposed bid* **put forward,** present, offer, proffer, tender, propose, suggest, float; put in, send in, register.
ANTONYMS withdraw.
4 *they submitted that the judgment was inappropriate* **contend,** assert, argue, state, claim, posit, postulate.

subnormal ▸ adjective *subnormal trade activity* **below average,** below normal, low, poor, subpar.

subordinate ▸ adjective 1 *subordinate staff* **lower-ranking,** junior, lower, supporting.
ANTONYMS senior.
2 *a subordinate rule* **secondary,** lesser, minor, subsidiary, subservient, ancillary, auxiliary, peripheral, marginal; supplementary, accessory.
ANTONYMS central.
▸ noun *the manager and his subordinates* **junior,** assistant, second (in command), number two, right-hand man/woman, deputy, aide, underling, minion; informal sidekick, second banana.
ANTONYMS superior.

sub rosa ▸ adverb formal *the committee operates sub rosa* **in secret,** secretly, in private, privately, behind closed doors, in camera.
ANTONYMS openly.

subscribe ▸ verb 1 *we **subscribe to** several news magazines* **pay a subscription for,** have a subscription to, take, buy regularly.
2 *I subscribe to the ballet* **have season tickets,** have a subscription.
3 *I can't **subscribe to** that theory* **agree with,** accept, believe in, endorse, back, support, champion, buy into; formal accede to.
4 formal *he subscribed the document* **sign,** countersign, initial, autograph, witness.

subsequent ▸ adjective *the subsequent months* **following,** ensuing, succeeding, later, future, coming, to come, next.
ANTONYMS previous.
– PHRASES **subsequent to** *tell us what happened in the hours subsequent to the shooting* **following,** after, at the close/end of.

subservient ▸ adjective 1 *subservient women* **submissive,** deferential, compliant, obedient, dutiful, biddable, docile, passive, unassertive, subdued, downtrodden; informal under someone's thumb. See note at **OBSEQUIOUS**.
ANTONYMS independent.
2 *individual rights are subservient to the interests of the state* **subordinate,** secondary, subsidiary, peripheral, ancillary, auxiliary, less important.
ANTONYMS superior.

subside ▸ verb 1 *wait until the storm subsides* **abate,** let up, quiet down, calm, slacken (off), ease (up), relent, die down, recede, lessen, soften, diminish, decline, dwindle, weaken, fade, wane, ebb.
ANTONYMS intensify.
2 *the floodwaters have subsided* **recede,** ebb, fall, go down, get lower, abate.
ANTONYMS rise.
3 *the volcano is gradually subsiding* **sink,** settle, cave in, collapse, crumple, give way.

subsidiary ▸ adjective *a subsidiary company* **subordinate,** secondary, ancillary, auxiliary, subservient, supplementary, peripheral.
ANTONYMS principal.
▸ noun *two major subsidiaries* **subordinate company,** branch, branch plant, division, subdivision, derivative, subset, offshoot.

subsidize ▸ verb *they have agreed to subsidize the after-school program* **give money to,** pay a subsidy to, contribute to, invest in, sponsor, support, fund, finance, underwrite; informal shell out for, fork out for, cough up for; bankroll.

subsidy ▸ noun *the theater receives a subsidy of 1.7 million dollars a year* **grant,** allowance, endowment, contribution, donation, bursary, handout; backing, support, sponsorship, finance, funding; formal benefaction.

subsist ▸ verb 1 *he subsists on his pension* **survive,** live, stay alive, exist, eke out an existence; support oneself, manage, get along/by, make (both) ends meet.
2 *the tenant's rights of occupation subsist* **continue,** last, persist, endure, prevail, carry on, remain.

subsistence ▸ noun 1 *they depend on fish for subsistence* **survival,** existence, living, life, sustenance, nourishment.
2 *the money needed for his subsistence* **maintenance,** keep, upkeep, livelihood, room and board, board, nourishment, food.

substance ▸ noun 1 *an organic substance* **material,** matter, stuff.
2 *ghostly figures with no substance* **solidity,** body, corporeality; density, mass, weight, shape, structure.
3 *none of the objections has any substance* **meaningfulness,** significance, importance, import, validity, foundation; formal moment.
4 *the substance of the tale is very thin* **content,** subject matter, theme, message, essence.
5 *the Huskies are a team of substance* **character,** backbone, mettle.
6 *independent men of substance* **wealth,** fortune, riches, affluence, prosperity, money, means.

substantial ▸ adjective 1 *substantial beings* **real,** true, actual; physical, solid, material, concrete, corporeal.
2 *substantial progress had been made* **considerable,** real, significant, important, tectonic, notable, major, valuable, useful.
3 *substantial damages* **sizable,** considerable, significant, large, ample, appreciable, goodly.
4 *substantial oak beams* **sturdy,** solid, stout, thick, strong, well built, durable, long-lasting, hardwearing.
5 *rugby players with substantial builds* **hefty,** stout, sturdy, large, solid, bulky, burly, well built, portly.
6 *substantial landowners* **successful,** profitable,

prosperous, wealthy, affluent, moneyed, well-to-do, rich; informal loaded, stinking rich.
7 *substantial agreement* **fundamental,** essential, basic.

substantially ▶ adverb 1 *the cost has fallen substantially* **considerably,** significantly, to a great/large extent, greatly, markedly, appreciably.
ANTONYMS slightly.
2 *the draft was substantially accepted* **largely,** for the most part, by and large, on the whole, in the main, mainly, in essence, basically, fundamentally, to all intents and purposes.

substantiate ▶ verb *can you substantiate your allegations?* **prove,** show to be true, give substance to, support, uphold, bear out, justify, vindicate, validate, corroborate, verify, authenticate, confirm, endorse, give credence to.
ANTONYMS disprove.

substitute ▶ noun *substitutes for permanent employees* **replacement,** deputy, relief, proxy, reserve, surrogate, cover, stand-in, locum (tenens), understudy; informal sub, pinch-hitter.
▶ adjective *a substitute teacher* **acting,** supply, replacement, deputy, relief, reserve, surrogate, stand-in, temporary, caretaker, interim, provisional.
ANTONYMS permanent.
▶ verb 1 *cottage cheese can be substituted for yogurt* **exchange,** replace, use instead of, use as an alternative to, use in place of, swap.
2 *the senate was empowered to substitute for the president* **deputize,** act as deputy, act as a substitute, stand in, cover; replace, relieve, take over from; informal sub, fill someone's boots/shoes.

subterfuge ▶ noun 1 *the use of subterfuge by journalists* **trickery,** intrigue, deviousness, deceit, deception, dishonesty, cheating, duplicity, guile, cunning, craftiness, chicanery, pretense, fraud, fraudulence.
2 *a disreputable subterfuge* **trick,** hoax, ruse, wile, ploy, stratagem, artifice, dodge, bluff, pretense, deception, fraud, blind, smokescreen; informal con, scam.

subtle ▶ adjective 1 *subtle colors* **understated,** muted, subdued; delicate, faint, pale, soft, indistinct.
2 *subtle distinctions* **fine,** fine-drawn, nice, hair-splitting.
3 *a subtle mind* **astute,** keen, quick, fine, acute, sharp, shrewd, perceptive, discerning, discriminating, penetrating, sagacious, wise, clever, intelligent.
4 *a subtle plan* **ingenious,** clever, cunning, crafty, wily, artful, devious.

subtlety ▶ noun 1 *the subtlety of the flavor* **delicacy,** delicateness, subtleness; understatedness, mutedness, softness.
2 *classification is fraught with subtlety* **fineness,** subtleness, niceness, nicety, nuance.
3 *the subtlety of the human mind* **astuteness,** keenness, acuteness, sharpness, canniness, shrewdness, perceptiveness, discernment, discrimination, percipience, perspicacity, wisdom, cleverness, intelligence.
4 *the subtlety of their tactics* **ingenuity,** cleverness, skillfulness, adroitness, cunning, guile, craftiness, wiliness, artfulness, deviousness.

subtract ▶ verb *we'll subtract the cost of shipping* **take away/off,** deduct, debit, dock; informal knock off, minus.
ANTONYMS add.

suburb ▶ noun *a fast-growing suburb just west of Albany | you'll need a car if you move to the suburbs* **residential area,** dormitory area, bedroom community, commutershed, commuter belt, exurb; (**suburbs**) suburbia, the burbs.

suburban ▶ adjective 1 *a suburban area* **residential,** commuter, dormitory.
2 *her drab suburban existence* **dull,** boring, uninteresting, conventional, ordinary, commonplace, unremarkable, unexceptional; provincial, unsophisticated, parochial, bourgeois, middle-class, white-picket-fence.

subversive ▶ adjective *subversive activities* **disruptive,** troublemaking, inflammatory, insurrectionary; seditious, revolutionary, rebellious, rebel, renegade, dissident.
▶ noun *a dangerous subversive* **troublemaker,** dissident, agitator, revolutionary, renegade, rebel.

subvert ▶ verb 1 *a plot to subvert the state* **destabilize,** unsettle, overthrow, overturn; bring down, topple, depose, oust; disrupt, wreak havoc on, sabotage, ruin, undermine, weaken, damage.
2 *attempts to subvert Soviet youth* **corrupt,** pervert, deprave, contaminate, poison, embitter.

subway ▶ noun *taking the subway to Yankee Stadium* underground (rail system), metro, train; Brit. informal tube.

succeed ▶ verb 1 *Darwin succeeded where others had failed* **triumph,** achieve success, be successful, do well, flourish, thrive; informal make it, make the grade, make a name for oneself.
ANTONYMS fail.
2 *the plan succeeded* **be successful,** turn out well, work (out), be effective; informal come off, pay off.
ANTONYMS fail, flop.
3 *upon Taylor's death, his vice president succeeded him* **replace,** take the place of, take over from, follow, supersede; informal step into someone's shoes.
ANTONYMS precede.
4 *he* ***succeeded to*** *the throne* **inherit,** assume, acquire, attain; formal accede to.
ANTONYMS renounce, abdicate.
5 *embarrassment was succeeded by fear* **follow,** come after, follow after.
ANTONYMS precede.

succeeding ▶ adjective *strands of DNA are reproduced through succeeding generations* **subsequent,** successive, following, ensuing, later, future, coming.

success ▶ noun 1 *the success of the scheme* **favorable outcome,** successfulness, successful result, triumph.
ANTONYMS failure.
2 *the trappings of success* **prosperity,** affluence,

wealth, riches, opulence.
ANTONYMS poverty.
3 *a box-office success* **triumph,** best seller, blockbuster, sellout; informal (smash) hit, megahit, winner.
ANTONYMS failure, flop.
4 *an overnight success* **star,** superstar, celebrity, big name, household name; informal celeb, megastar.
ANTONYMS nobody.

successful ▶ adjective **1** *what can we do to make this campaign successful?* **victorious,** triumphant; fortunate, lucky; effective; informal socko, in like Flynn.
2 *a successful designer* **prosperous,** affluent, wealthy, rich; doing well, famous, eminent, top.
3 *successful companies* **flourishing,** thriving, booming, buoyant, doing well, profitable, moneymaking, lucrative.

USAGE

in like Flynn

This phrase, meaning "assured of success," first became widespread during World War II as an allusion to the actor Errol Flynn's legendary prowess in seducing women. (In 1942, Flynn was prosecuted for the statutory rape of two teenage girls—and was acquitted.) Today the phrase has generally lost any sexual connotation—e.g.: • "By these standards, Gore should be in like Flynn." (*Commercial Appeal*[Memphis]; Feb. 13, 2000.) • "Based on the results of our Triangle Census, you'll be in like Flynn." (*News & Observer*[Raleigh]; Mar. 27, 2000.) • "Follow the formula, and you're in like Flynn." (*BusinessWeek,* Aug. 7, 2000.) The phrase has been the subject of wordplay and consequent confusion. In 1966 appeared *Our Man Flint,* a film starring James Coburn and spoofing the James Bond series; the following year, its sequel, *In Like Flint,* was released. The popularity of these films—especially the latter with its pun on *in like Flynn*—sparked lingering confusion about what the proper phrase should be. Thus, during coverage of the 2000 Republican Convention, Mark Shields, a PBS commentator, said that George W. Bush might be "in like Flynn, or in like Flint—whatever we say" (PBS Convention Coverage, Aug. 3, 2000). This confusion had already surfaced in print—e.g.: "Yep, with my peacoat, I was in like Flint [read *Flynn*], I thought, able to hubbub with the highbrows or hang with the homeboys." (*News & Observer* [Raleigh]; Jan. 11, 1998) (in this example, *hubbub* should probably be *hobnob*). "If you want to be 'in like Flint [read *Flynn*],' there has to be a measure of exclusivity." Larry Lipson, (*Daily News* [L.A.]; Aug. 27, 1999.) "Finder praises Gawande as a quick learner. If he failed to incorporate advice initially, says Finder, 'the second time he was in like Flint [read *Flynn*].'" (*Boston Globe,* Nov. 10, 1999.) Although this usage occasionally appears in tongue-in-cheek references to Flint, Michigan, and to flint as stone, it shouldn't appear in sentences such as those just quoted. Errol Flynn is reported to have resented the phrase, but it will always be linked etymologically to him.
— BG

succession ▶ noun **1** *a succession of exciting events* **sequence,** series, progression, chain, cycle, round, string, train, line, run, flow, stream.
2 *his succession to the throne* **accession,** elevation, assumption.
– PHRASES **in succession** *the next four houses went up in succession, in a matter of just a few months* **one after the other,** in a row, consecutively, successively, in sequence.

successor ▶ noun *Mary was the rightful successor to the English throne* **heir (apparent),** inheritor, next-in-line.
ANTONYMS predecessor.

succinct ▶ adjective *what is your succinct appraisal of our situation?* **concise,** short (and sweet), brief, compact, condensed, crisp, laconic, terse, to the point, pithy, epigrammatic, synoptic, gnomic; formal compendious. See note at TERSE.
ANTONYMS verbose.

succor ▶ noun *providing succor in times of need* **aid,** help, a helping hand, assistance; comfort, ease, relief, support, TLC.
▶ verb *the prisoners were succored* **help,** aid, bring aid to, give/render assistance to, assist, lend a (helping) hand to; minister to, care for, comfort, bring relief to, support, take care of, look after, attend to.

succulent ▶ adjective *succulent black grapes* **juicy,** moist, luscious, soft, tender; choice, mouthwatering, appetizing, tasty, delicious; informal scrumptious.
ANTONYMS dry.

succumb ▶ verb **1** *she succumbed to temptation* **yield,** give in/way, submit, surrender, capitulate, cave in.
ANTONYMS resist.
2 *he **succumbed to** the disease* **die from/of;** catch, develop, contract, fall ill with; informal come down with.
ANTONYMS withstand.

suck ▶ verb **1** *they sucked orange juice through straws* **sip,** sup, siphon, slurp, draw, drink.
2 *Fran **sucked in** a deep breath* **draw,** breathe, gasp; inhale, inspire.
3 *they got **sucked into** petty crime* **implicate in,** involve in, draw into; informal mix up in.
4 informal *the weather sucks* **be very bad,** be awful, be terrible, be dreadful, be horrible; informal stink.
– PHRASES **suck up to** informal *they suck up to him, hanging on to his every word* **grovel to,** creep to, toady to, be obsequious to, be sycophantic to, kowtow to, bow and scrape to, truckle to; fawn on; informal lick someone's boots, be all over, brown-nose.

suckle ▶ verb *the lioness sucked her cubs* **breast-feed,** feed, nurse.

sudden ▶ adjective *a sudden change in plans*

unexpected, unforeseen, unanticipated, unlooked-for; immediate, instantaneous, instant, precipitous, precipitate, abrupt, rapid, swift, quick.

suddenly ▶ adverb *suddenly the scene shifts to the year 1954* **immediately,** instantaneously, instantly, straightaway, all of a sudden, all at once, promptly, abruptly, swiftly; unexpectedly, without warning, without notice, out of the blue; informal straight off, in a flash, like a shot.
ANTONYMS gradually.

suds ▶ plural noun *a detergent low in suds* **lather,** foam, froth, bubbles, soap.

sue ▶ verb **1** *he sued the contractor for negligence* **take legal action against,** take to court, bring an action/suit against, proceed against, prefer/bring charges against.
2 *suing for peace* **appeal for,** petition for, ask for, solicit (for), request, seek.

suffer ▶ verb **1** *I hate to see him suffer* **hurt,** ache, be in pain, feel pain; be in distress, be upset, be miserable.
2 *she suffers from asthma* **be afflicted by/with,** be affected by, be troubled with, have.
3 *the nation suffered a humiliating defeat* **undergo,** experience, be subjected to, receive, endure, face.
4 *the school's reputation has suffered* **be impaired,** be damaged, deteriorate, decline.
5 archaic *he was obliged to suffer her intimate proximity* **tolerate,** put up with, bear, stand, abide, endure; formal brook.
6 archaic *my conscience would not suffer me to accept* **allow,** permit, let, give leave to, sanction.

suffering ▶ noun *the suffering of these refugees defied description* **hardship,** distress, misery, wretchedness, adversity, tribulation; pain, agony, anguish, trauma, torment, torture, hurt, affliction, sadness, unhappiness, sorrow, grief, woe, angst, heartache, heartbreak, stress; literary dolor.

suffice ▶ verb *a simple yes or no will suffice* **be enough,** be sufficient, be adequate, do, serve, meet requirements, satisfy demands, answer/meet one's needs, answer/serve the purpose; informal fit/fill the bill.

sufficient ▶ adjective *there was sufficient evidence to justify a charge* **enough,** plenty of, ample; adequate, satisfactory.
ANTONYMS inadequate.

suffocate ▶ verb *it appears that the victim has been suffocated with a bed pillow* **smother,** asphyxiate, stifle; choke, strangle.

suffrage ▶ noun *suffrage for women is not yet a universal condition* **franchise,** right to vote, the vote, enfranchisement, ballot.

suffuse ▶ verb *the room was suffused with soft, pink light* **permeate,** spread over, spread throughout, cover, bathe, pervade, wash, saturate, imbue.

sugary ▶ adjective **1** *sugary snacks* **sweet,** sugared, sugar-coated, candied.
ANTONYMS sour.
2 *sugary romance* **sentimental,** mawkish, cloying, sickly (sweet), saccharine, syrupy; informal sappy, schmaltzy, slushy, mushy, sloppy, cutesy, corny.

suggest ▶ verb **1** *Ruth suggested a vacation* **propose,** put forward, recommend, advocate; advise, urge, encourage, counsel.
2 *evidence suggests that teenagers are responsive to price increases* **indicate,** lead to the belief, argue, demonstrate, show; formal evince.
3 *sources suggest that the prime minister will change his cabinet* **hint,** insinuate, imply, intimate, indicate; informal put ideas into one's head.
4 *the seduction scenes suggest his guilt and her loneliness* **convey,** express, communicate, impart, imply, intimate, smack of, evoke, conjure up; formal evince.

suggestion ▶ noun **1** *some suggestions for tackling this problem* **proposal,** proposition, motion, submission, recommendation; advice, counsel, hint, tip, clue, idea, trial balloon.
2 *the suggestion of a smirk* **hint,** trace, touch, suspicion, dash, soupçon, tinge; ghost, semblance, shadow, glimmer, impression, whisper.
3 *there is no suggestion that he was party to a conspiracy* **insinuation,** hint, implication, intimation, innuendo, imputation.

suggestive ▶ adjective **1** *suggestive remarks* **indecent,** indelicate, improper, unseemly, sexual, sexy, smutty, dirty, ribald, bawdy, racy, risqué, lewd, vulgar, coarse, salacious.
2 *an odor suggestive of a brewery* **redolent,** evocative, reminiscent; characteristic, indicative, typical.

suit ▶ noun **1** *a pinstriped suit* **outfit,** set of clothes, ensemble.
2 informal *suits in faraway boardrooms* **businessman, businesswoman,** executive, bureaucrat, administrator, manager.
3 *a medical malpractice suit* **legal action,** lawsuit, (court) case, action, (legal/judicial) proceedings, litigation.
4 *they spurned his suit* **entreaty,** request, plea, appeal, petition, supplication, application.
5 dated *his suit came to nothing* **courtship,** wooing, attentions.
▶ verb **1** *blue really suits you* **become,** work for, look good on, look attractive on, flatter.
2 *savings plans to suit all customers* **be convenient for,** be acceptable to, be suitable for, meet the requirements of; informal fit the bill for.
3 *recipes ideally suited to students* **make appropriate to/for,** tailor, fashion, adjust, adapt, modify, fit, gear, design.

suitable ▶ adjective **1** *suitable employment opportunities* **acceptable,** satisfactory, fitting; informal right up someone's alley.
ANTONYMS inappropriate.
2 *a drama suitable for all ages* **appropriate,** fitting, fit, acceptable, right.
ANTONYMS inappropriate.
3 *music suitable for a lively dinner party* **appropriate to/for,** suited to, befitting, in keeping with; informal cut out for.
ANTONYMS unfit.
4 *they treated him with suitable respect* **proper,** seemly, decent, appropriate, fitting, befitting, correct, due.

5 *suitable candidates* **well qualified,** well-suited, appropriate, fitting.
ANTONYMS unfit.

suitcase ▶ noun *the old brown suitcase had survived two ocean voyages and more train and bus trips than she could ever calculate* **travel bag,** traveling bag, case, valise, overnight case, portmanteau, vanity case, garment bag, backpack, duffel bag; (**suitcases**) luggage, baggage.

suite ▶ noun *we were quite comfortable in our suite at the Biltmore* **apartment,** rooms, set of rooms; Brit. flat.

suitor ▶ noun *Rosie routinely rejected the suitors who sought her affections, until Laurence came along* **admirer,** wooer, boyfriend, sweetheart, lover, beau; literary swain.

sulk ▶ verb *Dad was sulking* **mope,** brood, be sullen, have a long face, be in a bad mood, be in a huff, be grumpy, be moody; informal be down in the dumps.
▶ noun *she sank into a deep sulk* (**bad**) **mood,** fit of ill humor, fit of pique, pet, huff, (bad) temper; the sulks, the blues.

sulky ▶ adjective *sulky faces* **sullen,** surly, moping, pouting, moody, sour, piqued, petulant, brooding, broody, disgruntled, ill-humored, in a bad mood, out of humor, fed up, put out; bad-tempered, grumpy, huffy, glum, gloomy, morose; informal grouchy, crabby, cranky.
ANTONYMS cheerful.

sullen ▶ adjective *a bunch of sullen, spoiled brats* **surly,** sulky, pouting, sour, morose, resentful, glum, moody, gloomy, grumpy, bad-tempered, ill-tempered; unresponsive, uncommunicative, farouche, uncivil, unfriendly. See note at **GLUM**.
ANTONYMS cheerful.

sultry ▶ adjective **1** *a sultry day* **humid,** close, airless, stifling, oppressive, muggy, sticky, sweltering, tropical, heavy; hot; informal boiling, roasting.
ANTONYMS refreshing.
2 *a sultry film star* **passionate,** attractive, sensual, sexy, voluptuous, erotic, seductive.

sum ▶ noun **1** *a large sum of money* **amount,** quantity, volume.
2 *just a small sum* **amount of money,** price, charge, fee, cost.
3 *the sum of two numbers* (**sum**) **total,** grand total, tally, aggregate, summation.
ANTONYMS difference.
4 *the sum of his wisdom* **entirety,** totality, total, whole, aggregate, summation, beginning and end.
5 *we did sums at school* (**arithmetical**) **problem,** calculation; (**sums**) arithmetic, mathematics, math, computation.
– PHRASES **sum up 1** *one reviewer summed it up as "compelling"* **evaluate,** assess, appraise, rate, gauge, judge, deem, adjudge, estimate, form an opinion of. **2** *he summed up his reasons* **summarize,** make/give a summary of, précis, outline, give an outline of, recapitulate, review; informal recap.

summarily ▶ adverb *accused of treason, he was summarily executed* **immediately,** instantly, right away, straightaway, at once, on the spot, promptly; speedily, swiftly, rapidly, without delay; arbitrarily, without formality, peremptorily, without due process.

summarize ▶ verb *he summarized these ideas in a single phrase* **sum up,** abridge, condense, encapsulate, outline, give an outline of, put in a nutshell, recapitulate, give/make a summary of, give a synopsis of, précis, synopsize, give the gist of; informal recap.

summary ▶ noun *a summary of the findings* **synopsis,** précis, résumé, abstract, digest, encapsulation, abbreviated version; outline, sketch, rundown, review, summing-up, overview, recapitulation, epitome; informal recap.
▶ adjective **1** *a summary financial statement* **abridged,** abbreviated, shortened, condensed, concise, capsule, succinct, short, brief, pithy; formal compendious.
2 *summary execution* **immediate,** instant, instantaneous, on-the-spot; speedy, swift, rapid, without delay, sudden; arbitrary, without formality, peremptory.

summit ▶ noun **1** *the summit of Mount Washington* (**mountain**) **top,** peak, crest, crown, apex, tip, cap, hilltop.
ANTONYMS base, bottom.
2 *the summits of world literature* **acme,** peak, height, pinnacle, zenith, climax, high point/spot, highlight, crowning glory, capstone, best, finest, nonpareil.
ANTONYMS nadir.
3 *the next superpower summit* **meeting,** negotiation, conference, talk(s), discussion.

summon ▶ verb **1** *the embassy summoned her* **send for,** call for, request the presence of; ask, invite.
2 *they were summoned as witnesses* **serve with a summons,** summons, subpoena, cite, serve with a citation.
3 *the chair summoned a meeting* **convene,** assemble, order, call, announce; formal convoke.
4 *he summoned the courage to move closer* **muster,** gather, collect, rally, screw up.
5 *summoning up their memories of home* **call to mind,** call up/forth, conjure up, evoke, recall, revive, arouse, kindle, awaken, spark (off).
6 *they summoned spirits of the dead* **conjure up,** call up, invoke.

summons ▶ noun **1** *the court issued a summons* **writ,** subpoena, warrant, court order; Law citation.
2 *a summons to go to the boss's office* **order,** directive, command, instruction, demand, decree, injunction, edict, call, request.
▶ verb *he was summonsed to appear in court* **serve with a summons,** summon, subpoena, cite, serve with a citation.

sumptuous ▶ adjective *sumptuous brocade drapes* **lavish,** luxurious, opulent, magnificent, resplendent, gorgeous, splendid, grand, lavishly appointed, palatial, rich; informal plush, ritzy.
ANTONYMS plain.

sunder ▶ verb literary *his father and he were sundered by religious differences* **divide,** split, cleave, separate, rend, sever, rive.

sundry ▶ adjective *wings, radiators, and sundry other items were sent out to various workshops* **various,** varied, miscellaneous, assorted, mixed, diverse, diversified; several, numerous, many, manifold, multifarious, multitudinous; literary divers.

sunken ▶ adjective **1** *sunken eyes* **hollowed,** hollow, depressed, deep-set, concave, indented.
2 *a sunken garden* **below ground level,** at a lower level, lowered.

sunless ▶ adjective **1** *a cold sunless day* **dark,** overcast, cloudy, gray, gloomy, dismal, murky, dull.
2 *the sunless side of the house* **shady,** shadowy, dark, gloomy.

sunlight ▶ noun *avoid sunlight when taking this medication* **daylight,** (the) sun, sunshine, the sun's rays, (natural) light.

sunny ▶ adjective **1** *a sunny day* **bright,** sunshiny, sunlit, clear, fine, cloudless, without a cloud in the sky, sun-drenched.
ANTONYMS cloudy.
2 *a sunny disposition* **cheerful,** cheery, happy, lighthearted, bright, merry, joyful, bubbly, blithe, jolly, jovial, animated, buoyant, ebullient, upbeat, vivacious.
ANTONYMS miserable.
3 *look on the sunny side* **optimistic,** rosy, bright, hopeful, auspicious, favorable.
ANTONYMS sad, pessimistic.

sunrise ▶ noun *the infantry advanced at sunrise* **dawn,** crack of dawn, daybreak, break of day, sun-up, first light, (early) morning, cock crow; literary aurora.

sunset ▶ noun *the blossoms close at sunset* **sundown,** nightfall, close of day, twilight, dusk, evening; literary eventide, gloaming.

sunshine ▶ noun **1** *relaxing in the sunshine* **sunlight,** sun, sun's rays, daylight, (natural) light.
2 *his smile was all sunshine* **happiness,** cheerfulness, cheer, gladness, laughter, gaiety, merriment, joy, joyfulness, blitheness, joviality, jollity.

superb ▶ adjective **1** *he scored a superb goal* **excellent,** superlative, first-rate, first-class, outstanding, remarkable, marvelous, magnificent, wonderful, splendid, admirable, noteworthy, impressive, fine, exquisite, exceptional, glorious; informal great, fantastic, fabulous, terrific, super, awesome, ace, cool, A1, brilliant, killer.
ANTONYMS poor, inferior.
2 *a superb diamond necklace* **magnificent,** majestic, splendid, grand, impressive, imposing, awe-inspiring, breathtaking; gorgeous.
ANTONYMS poor, inferior.

supercilious ▶ adjective *a supercilious young clerk* **arrogant,** haughty, conceited, disdainful, overbearing, pompous, condescending, superior, patronizing, imperious, proud, snobbish, snobby, smug, scornful, sneering; informal hoity-toity, high and mighty, uppity, snooty, stuck-up, snotty, snot-nosed, jumped up, too big for one's britches.

superficial ▶ adjective **1** *superficial burns* **surface,** exterior, external, outer, outside, slight.
ANTONYMS deep, thorough.
2 *a superficial friendship* **shallow,** surface, skin-deep, artificial; empty, hollow, meaningless.
ANTONYMS deep, significant.
3 *a superficial investigation* **cursory,** perfunctory, casual, sketchy, desultory, token, slapdash, offhand, rushed, hasty, hurried.
ANTONYMS comprehensive, thorough.
4 *a superficial resemblance* **apparent,** seeming, outward, ostensible, cosmetic, slight.
ANTONYMS genuine, authentic.
5 *a superficial analysis* **trivial,** lightweight, two-dimensional.
ANTONYMS profound.
6 *a superficial person* **facile,** shallow, flippant, empty-headed, trivial, frivolous, silly, inane.
ANTONYMS deep, thoughtful.

CHOOSE THE RIGHT WORD

superficial, cursory, hasty, slapdash, shallow

No one wants to be accused of being **superficial** or **shallow**, two adjectives that literally indicate a lack of depth (*a superficial wound; a shallow grave*). *Superficial* suggests too much concern with the surface or obvious aspects of something, and it is considered a derogatory term because it connotes a personality that is not genuine or sincere. *Shallow* is even more derogatory because it implies not only a refusal to explore something deeply but an inability to feel, sympathize, or understand. It is unlikely that a *shallow* person, in other words, will ever have more than superficial relationships with his or her peers. **Cursory**, which may or may not be a derogatory term, suggests a lack of thoroughness or attention to detail (*a cursory glance at the newspaper*), while **hasty** emphasizes a refusal or inability to spend the necessary time on something (*a hasty review of the facts*). If you are **slapdash** in your approach, it means that you are both careless and hasty (*a slapdash job of cleaning up*).

superfluous ▶ adjective **1** *superfluous material* **surplus (to requirements),** nonessential, redundant, unneeded, excess, extra, (to) spare, remaining, unused, left over, in excess, waste.
ANTONYMS necessary, essential.
2 *words seemed superfluous* **unnecessary,** unneeded, redundant, uncalled for, unwarranted.
ANTONYMS necessary.

superhuman ▶ adjective **1** *a superhuman effort* **extraordinary,** phenomenal, prodigious, stupendous, exceptional, remarkable, immense, heroic.
ANTONYMS average, unremarkable.
2 *superhuman power* **divine,** holy, heavenly.
3 *superhuman beings* **supernatural,** preternatural, paranormal, otherworldly, unearthly; rare extramundane.
ANTONYMS mundane.

superintend ▶ verb *he was expected to superintend a grand banquet* **supervise,** oversee, be in charge of, be in control of, preside over, direct, administer, manage, run, be responsible for.

superintendent ▶ noun **1** *the superintendent of the museum* **manager,** director, administrator, supervisor, overseer, controller, chief, head, governor; informal boss.
2 *the building's superintendent* **caretaker,** janitor, warden, porter.

superior ▶ adjective **1** *a superior officer* **higher-ranking,** higher-level, senior, higher, higher-up.
ANTONYMS junior, inferior.
2 *the superior candidate* **better,** more expert, more skillful; worthier, fitter, preferred.
ANTONYMS worse, inferior.
3 *superior workmanship* **high-quality**; finer, better, higher-grade, of higher quality, greater; accomplished, expert.
ANTONYMS low-quality, inferior.
4 *superior chocolate* **good-quality,** high-quality, first-class, first-rate, top-quality; choice, select, exclusive, prime, prize, fine, excellent, best, choicest, finest.
ANTONYMS low-quality, inferior.
5 *a superior hotel* **high-class,** upper-class, select, exclusive, upscale, upmarket, five-star; informal classy, posh.
ANTONYMS downmarket, inferior.
6 *Hamish regarded her with superior amusement* **condescending,** supercilious, patronizing, haughty, disdainful, pompous, snobbish; informal high and mighty, hoity-toity, snooty, stuck-up.
ANTONYMS humble, modest.
▶ noun *my immediate superior* **manager,** chief, supervisor, senior, controller, foreman; informal boss.
ANTONYMS subordinate.

superiority ▶ noun *the military superiority of the North* **supremacy,** advantage, lead, dominance, primacy, ascendancy, eminence.

superlative ▶ adjective *a superlative photographer* **excellent,** magnificent, wonderful, marvelous, supreme, consummate, outstanding, remarkable, fine, choice, first-rate, first-class, premier, prime, unsurpassed, unequaled, unparalleled, unrivaled, preeminent; informal crack, ace, wicked, brilliant.
ANTONYMS mediocre.

supernatural ▶ adjective **1** *supernatural powers* **paranormal,** psychic, magic, magical, occult, mystic, mystical, superhuman, supernormal; rare extramundane.
2 *a supernatural being* **ghostly,** phantom, spectral, otherworldly, unearthly, unnatural.

supersede ▶ verb *I was superseded by much younger men* **replace,** take the place of, take over from, succeed; supplant, displace, oust, overthrow, remove, unseat; informal fill someone's shoes/boots. See note at REPLACE.

supervise ▶ verb **1** *he had to supervise the loading* **oversee,** superintend, be in charge of, preside over, direct, manage, run, look after, be responsible for, govern, organize, handle, micromanage.
2 *you may need to supervise the patient* **watch,** oversee, keep an eye on, observe, monitor, mind; invigilate.

supervision ▶ noun **1** *the supervision of the banking system* **administration,** management, control, charge; superintendence, regulation, government, governance.
2 *keep your children under supervision* **observation,** guidance, custody, charge, safekeeping, care, guardianship; control.

supervisor ▶ noun *the supervisor of sector B* **manager,** director, overseer, controller, superintendent, governor, chief, head; steward, foreman; informal boss.

supine ▶ adjective **1** *she lay supine on the sand* **flat on one's back,** face upward, facing upward, flat, horizontal, recumbent, stretched out.
ANTONYMS prone, upright.
2 *the supine media* **weak,** spineless, yielding, effete; docile, acquiescent, pliant, submissive, passive, inert, spiritless.
ANTONYMS strong.

supper ▶ noun *I had a bowl of chili for my supper* **dinner,** evening meal, main meal; snack, mealtime; formal repast; literary refection.

supplant ▶ verb **1** *paved highways supplanted the network of dirt roads* **replace,** supersede, displace, take over from, substitute for, override.
2 *the man he supplanted as prime minister* **oust,** usurp, overthrow, remove, topple, unseat, depose, dethrone; succeed, come after; informal fill someone's shoes/boots.

supple ▶ adjective **1** *her supple body* **lithe,** limber, lissome, willowy, flexible, loose-limbed, agile, acrobatic, nimble, double-jointed. See note at FLEXIBLE.
ANTONYMS stiff.
2 *supple leather* **pliant,** pliable, flexible, soft, bendable, workable, malleable, stretchy, elastic, springy, yielding, rubbery.
ANTONYMS inflexible, rigid.

supplement ▶ noun **1** *a mouse is a keyboard supplement* **addition,** accessory, supplementation, supplementary, extra, add-on, adjunct, appendage; Computing peripheral.
2 *a single room supplement* **surcharge,** addition, increase.
3 *a supplement to the essay* **appendix,** addendum, adhesion, end matter, tailpiece, codicil, postscript, addition, coda.
4 *a special supplement with today's paper* **pullout,** insert, extra section.
▶ verb *they supplemented their incomes by waiting tables on weekends* **augment,** increase, add to, boost, swell, amplify, enlarge, top up.

supplementary ▶ adjective **1** *supplementary income* **additional,** supplemental, extra, more, further; add-on, subsidiary, auxiliary, ancillary.
2 *a supplementary index* **appended,** attached, added, extra, accompanying.

suppliant ▶ noun *they were not mere suppliants* **petitioner,** supplicant, pleader, beggar, applicant.
▶ adjective *those around her were suppliant* **pleading,** begging, imploring, entreating, supplicating; on bended knee.

supplicate ▶ verb *he supplicated the governor for leniency* **entreat,** beg, plead with, implore, petition, appeal to, call on, urge, enjoin, importune, sue, ask, request; literary beseech.

supply ▶ verb **1** *they supplied money to rebels* **give,** contribute, provide, furnish, donate, bestow, grant, endow, impart; dispense, disburse, allocate, assign; informal fork out, shell out.
2 *the lake supplies the city with water* **provide,** furnish, endow, serve, confer; equip, arm.
3 *windmills supply their power needs* **satisfy,** meet, fulfill, cater for.
▶ noun **1** *a limited supply of food* **stock,** store, reserve, reservoir, stockpile, hoard, cache; storehouse, repository; fund, mine, bank.
2 *the supply of liquor* **provision,** dissemination, distribution, serving.
3 (**supplies**) *go to the grocery store for supplies* **provisions,** stores, stocks, rations, food, foodstuffs, eatables, produce, necessities; informal eats; formal comestibles.

support ▶ verb **1** *a roof supported by pillars* **hold up,** bear, carry, prop up, keep up, brace, shore up, underpin, buttress, reinforce, undergird.
2 *he struggled to support his family* **provide for,** maintain, sustain, keep, take care of, look after.
3 *she supported him to the end* **comfort,** encourage, sustain, buoy up, hearten, fortify, console, solace, reassure; informal buck up.
ANTONYMS neglect, abandon.
4 *evidence to support the argument* **substantiate,** back up, bear out, corroborate, confirm, attest to, verify, prove, validate, authenticate, endorse, ratify, undergird.
ANTONYMS contradict, undermine.
5 *the money supports charitable projects* **help,** aid, assist; contribute to, back, subsidize, fund, finance; informal bankroll.
6 *an independent candidate supported by locals* **back,** champion, help, assist, aid, abet, favor, encourage; vote for, stand behind, defend; sponsor, second, promote, endorse, sanction; informal throw one's weight behind.
ANTONYMS oppose.
7 *they support human rights* **advocate,** promote, champion, back, espouse, be in favor of, recommend, defend, subscribe to.
▶ noun **1** *bridge supports* **pillar,** post, prop, upright, crutch, plinth, brace, buttress; base, substructure, foundation, underpinning.
2 *she pays support for her ex-husband* **maintenance,** keep, sustenance, subsistence; alimony.
3 *I was lucky to have their support* **encouragement,** friendship, strength, consolation, solace, succor, relief.
4 *he was a great support* **comfort,** help, assistance, tower of strength, prop, mainstay.
5 *support for community services* **contributions,** backing, donations, money, subsidy, funding, funds, finance, capital.
6 *they voiced their support for him* **backing,** help, assistance, aid, endorsement, approval; votes, patronage.
7 *a surge in support for decentralization* **advocacy,** backing, promotion, championship, espousal, defense, recommendation.

supporter ▶ noun **1** *supporters of gun control* **advocate,** backer, adherent, promoter, champion, defender, upholder, crusader, proponent, campaigner, apologist; informal cheerleader.
2 *Republican supporters* **backer,** helper, adherent, follower, ally, voter, disciple; member.
3 *the charity relies on its supporters* **contributor,** donor, benefactor, sponsor, backer, patron, well-wisher.
4 *the team's supporters* **fan,** follower, enthusiast, devotee, admirer; informal buff, addict, groupie.

supportive ▶ adjective **1** *a supportive teacher* **encouraging,** caring, sympathetic, reassuring, understanding, concerned, helpful, kind, kindly; informal boosterish.
2 *we are supportive of the proposal* **in favor of,** favorable to, pro, on the side of, sympathetic to, well-disposed to, receptive to.

suppose ▶ verb **1** *I suppose he's used to this* **assume,** presume, expect, dare say, take it (as read); believe, think, fancy, suspect, sense, trust; guess, surmise, reckon, conjecture, deduce, infer, gather; formal opine.
2 *suppose you had a spacecraft* **assume,** imagine, (let's) say; hypothesize, theorize, speculate.
3 *the theory supposes rational players* **require,** presuppose, imply, assume; call for, need.

supposed ▶ adjective **1** *the supposed phenomena* **apparent,** ostensible, seeming, alleged, putative, reputed, rumored, claimed, purported; professed, declared, assumed, presumed.
2 *I'm supposed to meet him at 8:30* **meant,** intended, expected; required, obliged.

supposition ▶ noun *her supposition is based on previous results* **belief,** surmise, idea, notion, suspicion, conjecture, speculation, inference, theory, hypothesis, postulation, guess, feeling, hunch, assumption, presumption.

suppress ▶ verb **1** *they could suppress the rebellion* **subdue,** repress, crush, quell, quash, squash, stamp out; defeat, conquer, overpower, put down, crack down on; end, stop, terminate, halt.
ANTONYMS incite, encourage.
2 *she suppressed her irritation* **conceal,** restrain, stifle, smother, bottle up, hold back, control, check, curb, contain, bridle, inhibit, keep a rein on, put a lid on.
ANTONYMS express.
3 *the report was suppressed* **censor,** keep secret, conceal, hide, hush up, gag, withhold, cover up, stifle; ban, proscribe, outlaw; sweep under the carpet.
ANTONYMS disclose, publicize.

suppurate ▶ verb *the lesions are suppurating* **fester,** form pus, discharge, run, weep, become septic.

supremacy ▶ noun *the supremacy of oppressive leadership anywhere in the world is bad for everyone in the world* **ascendancy,** predominance, primacy, dominion, hegemony, authority, mastery, control, power, rule, sovereignty, influence; dominance, superiority, advantage, the upper hand, the whip hand, the edge; distinction, greatness.

supreme ▶ adjective **1** *the supreme commander* **highest ranking,** chief, head, top, foremost, principal, superior, premier, first, prime; greatest, dominant, predominant, preeminent.

ANTONYMS subordinate, inferior.
2 *a supreme achievement* **extraordinary,** remarkable, incredible, phenomenal, rare, exceptional, outstanding, great, incomparable, unparalleled, peerless.
ANTONYMS minimum.
3 *the supreme sacrifice* **ultimate,** final, last; utmost, extreme, greatest, highest.
ANTONYMS insignificant.

sure ▶ adjective **1** *I am sure that they didn't know* **certain,** positive, convinced, confident, definite, assured, satisfied, persuaded; unhesitating, unwavering, unshakable.
ANTONYMS uncertain, doubtful.
2 *someone was sure to be blamed* **bound,** likely, destined, fated.
ANTONYMS unlikely.
3 *a sure winner with the children* **guaranteed,** unfailing, infallible, unerring, assured, certain, inevitable; informal sure-fire.
ANTONYMS uncertain, unlikely.
4 *he entered in the sure knowledge that he would win* **unquestionable,** indisputable, irrefutable, incontrovertible, undeniable, indubitable, undoubted, absolute, categorical, true, certain; obvious, evident, plain, clear, conclusive, definite.
5 *a sure sign that he's worried* **reliable,** dependable, trustworthy, unfailing, infallible, certain, unambiguous, true, foolproof, established, effective; informal sure-fire; formal efficacious.
6 *the sure hand of the soloist* **firm,** steady, stable, secure, confident, steadfast, unfaltering, unwavering.
▶ exclamation *"Can I come too?" "Sure."* **yes,** all right, of course, indeed, certainly, absolutely, agreed; informal OK, yeah, yep, uh-huh, you bet, I'll say, sure thing.
– PHRASES **be sure to** *be sure to feed the cat* **remember to,** don't forget to, see that you, mind that you, take care to, be certain to. **for sure** informal *I'll be there for sure* **definitely,** surely, certainly, without doubt, without question, undoubtedly, indubitably, absolutely, undeniably, unmistakably. **make sure** *make sure that all the doors are locked* **check,** confirm, make certain, ensure, assure; verify, corroborate, substantiate.

surely ▶ adverb **1** *surely you remembered?* **it must be the case that,** assuredly, without question.
2 *I will surely die* **certainly,** for sure, definitely, undoubtedly, without doubt, doubtless, indubitably, unquestionably, without fail, inevitably.
3 *slowly but surely manipulating the public* **firmly,** steadily, confidently, assuredly, unhesitatingly, unfalteringly, unswervingly, determinedly, doggedly, tenaciously.

surety ▶ noun **1** *she's a surety for his obligations* **guarantor,** sponsor.
2 *a $10,000 surety* **pledge,** collateral, guaranty, guarantee, bond, assurance, insurance, deposit; security, indemnity, indemnification; earnest.

surface ▶ noun **1** *the surface of the door* **outside,** exterior; top, side; finish, veneer.
ANTONYMS inside, interior.
2 *the surface of police culture* **outward appearance,** facade.
3 *a floured surface* counter, table.
▶ adjective *surface appearances* **superficial,** external, exterior, outward, ostensible, apparent, cosmetic, skin deep.
ANTONYMS underlying.
▶ verb **1** *a submarine surfaced* **come to the surface,** come up, rise.
ANTONYMS dive.
2 *the idea first surfaced in the sixties* **emerge,** arise, appear, come to light, crop up, materialize, spring up.
3 informal *she eventually surfaces for breakfast* **get up,** get out of bed, rise, wake, awaken, appear.
– PHRASES **on the surface** *it sounded plausible enough on the surface* **at first glance,** to the casual eye, outwardly, to all appearances, apparently, ostensibly, superficially, externally.

surfeit ▶ noun *a surfeit of apples* **excess,** surplus, abundance, oversupply, superabundance, superfluity, glut, avalanche, deluge; overdose; informal bellyful.
ANTONYMS lack.
▶ verb *we'll all be surfeited with food* **satiate,** sate, gorge, overfeed, overfill, glut, cram, stuff, overindulge, fill; saturate.

surge ▶ noun **1** *a surge of water* **gush,** rush, outpouring, stream, flow.
2 *a surge in public support* **increase,** rise, growth, upswing, upsurge, groundswell, escalation, leap.
3 *a sudden surge of anger* **rush,** uprush, storm, torrent, blaze, outburst, eruption.
4 *the surge of sea* **swell,** heaving, rolling, roll, swirling; tide.
▶ verb **1** *the water surged into people's homes* **gush,** rush, stream, flow, burst, pour, cascade, spill, overflow, sweep, roll.
2 *the stock surged 47.63 points* **increase,** rise, grow, escalate, leap.
3 *the sea surged* **swell,** heave, rise, roll.

surly ▶ adjective *we've had complaints from customers about your surly disposition* **sullen,** sulky, moody, sour, unfriendly, unpleasant, scowling, unsmiling; bad-tempered, grumpy, crotchety, prickly, cantankerous, irascible, testy, short-tempered; abrupt, brusque, curt, gruff, churlish, ill-humored, crabby, cranky, uncivil; informal grouchy. See note at **BRUSQUE**.
ANTONYMS pleasant.

surmise ▶ verb *I can only surmise that they're plotting against me* **guess,** conjecture, suspect, deduce, infer, conclude, theorize, speculate, divine; assume, presume, suppose, understand, gather, feel, sense, think, believe, imagine, fancy, reckon; formal opine.

surmount ▶ verb **1** *his reputation surmounts language barriers* **overcome,** conquer, prevail over, triumph over, beat, vanquish; clear, cross, pass over; resist, endure.
2 *they surmounted the ridge* **climb over,** top, ascend, scale, mount.
ANTONYMS descend.
3 *the dome is surmounted by a statue* **cap,** top, crown, finish.

surname ▶ noun *his real surname is MacNeil* **family name,** last name; patronymic.

surpass ▶ verb *these students surpassed their classmates* **excel,** exceed, transcend; outdo, outshine, outstrip, outclass, overshadow, eclipse; improve on, top, trump, cap, beat, better, outperform; informal leapfrog.

surplus ▶ noun *a surplus of grain* **excess,** surfeit, superabundance, superfluity, oversupply, glut, profusion, plethora; remainder, residue, remains, leftovers.
ANTONYMS dearth.
▶ adjective *surplus adhesive* **excess,** leftover, unused, remaining, extra, additional, spare; superfluous, redundant, unwanted, unneeded, dispensable, expendable.
ANTONYMS insufficient.

surprise ▶ noun **1** *Kate looked at me in surprise* **astonishment,** amazement, wonder, incredulity, bewilderment, stupefaction, disbelief.
2 *the test came as a big surprise* **shock,** bolt from the blue, bombshell, revelation, rude awakening, eye-opener, wake-up call; informal shocker.
▶ verb **1** *I was so surprised that I dropped it* **astonish,** amaze, startle, astound, stun, stagger, shock; leave open-mouthed, take someone's breath away, dumbfound, stupefy, daze, take aback, shake up; informal bowl over, floor, flabbergast.
2 *she surprised a burglar* **take by surprise,** catch unawares, catch off guard, catch red-handed, catch in the act.

surprised ▶ adjective *Lenore's unexpected return surprised everyone* **astonished,** amazed, astounded, startled, stunned, staggered, nonplussed, shocked, taken aback, stupefied, dumbfounded, dumbstruck, speechless, thunderstruck, confounded, shaken up; informal bowled over, flabbergasted, floored, flummoxed.

surprising ▶ adjective *the results of the study were surprising* **unexpected,** unforeseen, unpredictable; astonishing, amazing, startling, astounding, staggering, incredible, extraordinary, breathtaking, remarkable; informal mind-blowing.

surrender ▶ verb **1** *the army surrendered* **capitulate,** give in, give (oneself) up, give way, yield, concede (defeat), submit, climb down, back down, cave in, relent, crumble; lay down one's arms, raise the white flag, throw in the towel.
ANTONYMS resist.
2 *they surrendered power to the workers* **give up,** relinquish, renounce, forgo, forswear; cede, abdicate, waive, forfeit, sacrifice; hand over, turn over, yield, resign, transfer, grant. See note at RELINQUISH.
ANTONYMS seize.
3 *don't surrender all hope of changing things* **abandon,** give up, cast aside.
▶ noun *the ordeal ended with their peaceful surrender* **capitulation,** submission, yielding, succumbing, acquiescence; fall, defeat, resignation.

surreptitious ▶ adjective *a surreptitious glance* **secret,** secretive, stealthy, clandestine, sneaky, sly, furtive; concealed, hidden, undercover, covert, veiled, cloak-and-dagger. See note at SECRET.
ANTONYMS blatant.

surround ▶ verb *we were surrounded by cops* **encircle,** enclose, encompass, ring; fence in, hem in, confine, bound, circumscribe, cut off; besiege, trap. See note at CIRCUMSCRIBE.

surrounding ▶ adjective *tenants in the surrounding buildings were evacuated as a precaution* **neighboring,** nearby, near, neighborhood, local; adjoining, adjacent, bordering, abutting; encircling, encompassing.

surroundings ▶ plural noun *the surroundings were unfamiliar* **environment,** setting, milieu, background, backdrop; conditions, circumstances, situation, context; vicinity, locality, habitat.

surveillance ▶ noun *we learned later that we had been under surveillance* **observation,** scrutiny, watch, view, inspection, supervision; spying, espionage, infiltration, reconnaissance; informal bugging, wiretapping, recon.

survey ▶ verb **1** *he surveyed his work* **look at,** look over, observe, view, contemplate, regard, gaze at, stare at, eye; scrutinize, examine, inspect, scan, study, consider, review, take stock of; informal size up; literary behold.
2 *they surveyed 4,000 drug users* **interview,** question, canvass, poll, cross-examine, investigate, research, study, probe, sample.
▶ noun **1** *a survey of the current literature* **study,** review, consideration, overview; scrutiny, examination, inspection, appraisal.
2 *a survey of sexual behavior* **poll,** review, investigation, inquiry, study, probe, questionnaire, census, research.

survive ▶ verb **1** *he survived by escaping through a hole* **remain alive,** live, sustain oneself, pull through, get through, hold on/out, make it, keep body and soul together.
2 *the theater must survive* **continue,** remain, persist, endure, live on, persevere, abide, go on, carry on, be extant, exist.
3 *he **was survived by** his sons* **outlive,** outlast; live longer than.

susceptible ▶ adjective **1** *susceptible children* **impressionable,** credulous, gullible, innocent, ingenuous, naive, easily led; defenseless, vulnerable; persuadable, tractable; sensitive, responsive, thin-skinned.
ANTONYMS skeptical, streetwise.
2 *people **susceptible to** blackmail* **open to,** receptive to, vulnerable to; an easy target for.
3 *he is **susceptible to** ulcers* **liable to,** prone to, subject to, inclined to, predisposed to, disposed to, given to, at risk of.
ANTONYMS immune, resistant.

suspect ▶ verb **1** *I suspected she'd made a mistake* **have a suspicion,** have a feeling, feel, (be inclined to) think, fancy, reckon, guess, surmise, conjecture, conclude, have a hunch; suppose, presume, deduce, infer, sense, imagine; fear.
2 *he had no reason to suspect my honesty* **doubt,** distrust, mistrust, have misgivings about, be skeptical about, have qualms about, be suspicious of, be wary of, harbor reservations about.

▶ noun *a murder suspect* **suspected person,** accused, defendant.
▶ adjective *a suspect package* **suspicious,** dubious, doubtful, untrustworthy; odd, queer; informal fishy, funny, shady.

suspend ▶ verb **1** *the court case was suspended* **adjourn,** interrupt, break off, postpone, delay, defer, shelve, put off, put on hold, intermit, prorogue, hold over, hold in abeyance; cut short, discontinue, dissolve, disband, terminate, table; informal put on ice, put on the back burner, mothball, take a rain check on. See note at POSTPONE.
2 *he was suspended from his duties* **exclude,** debar, remove, eliminate, expel, eject.
3 *lights were suspended from the ceiling* **hang,** sling, string; swing, dangle.

suspense ▶ noun *I can't bear the suspense* **tension,** uncertainty, doubt, anticipation, expectation, expectancy, excitement, anxiety, apprehension, strain.
– PHRASES **in suspense** *he left us waiting in suspense for hours* **eagerly,** agog, with bated breath, on tenterhooks; on edge, anxious, edgy, jumpy, keyed up, uneasy, antsy, uptight, jittery.

suspension ▶ noun **1** *the suspension of army operations* **adjournment,** interruption, postponement, delay, deferral, deferment, stay, prorogation; armistice; cessation, end, halt, stoppage, dissolution, disbandment, termination.
2 *his suspension from school* **exclusion,** debarment, removal, elimination, expulsion, ejection.

suspicion ▶ noun **1** *she had a suspicion that he didn't like her* **intuition,** feeling, impression, inkling, hunch, fancy, notion, supposition, belief, idea, theory; presentiment, premonition; informal gut feeling, sixth sense.
2 *I confronted him with my suspicions* **misgiving,** doubt, qualm, reservation, hesitation, question; skepticism, uncertainty, distrust, mistrust.
3 *wine with a suspicion of soda* **trace,** touch, suggestion, hint, soupçon, tinge, shade, whiff, bit, drop, dash, taste, jot, mite.

suspicious ▶ adjective **1** *she gave him a suspicious look* **doubtful,** unsure, dubious, wary, chary, skeptical, distrustful, mistrustful, disbelieving, cynical.
ANTONYMS trusting.
2 *a highly suspicious character* **disreputable,** unsavory, dubious, suspect, dishonest-looking, funny-looking, slippery; informal shifty, shady.
ANTONYMS upright, reputable.
3 *she disappeared in suspicious circumstances* **questionable,** odd, strange, dubious, irregular, queer, funny, doubtful, mysterious, murky; informal fishy.
ANTONYMS innocent.

sustain ▶ verb **1** *the balcony might not sustain the weight* **bear,** support, carry, stand, keep up, prop up, shore up, underpin.
2 *her memories sustained her* **comfort,** help, assist, encourage, succor, support, give strength to, buoy up, carry, cheer up, hearten; informal buck up.
3 *they were unable to sustain a coalition* **continue,** carry on, keep up, keep alive, maintain, preserve, conserve, perpetuate, retain.
4 *she had bread and cheese to sustain her* **nourish,** feed, nurture; maintain, preserve, keep alive, keep going, provide for.
5 *she sustained slight injuries* **undergo,** experience, suffer, endure.
6 *the allegation was not sustained* **uphold,** validate, ratify, vindicate, confirm, endorse; verify, corroborate, substantiate, bear out, prove, authenticate, back up, evidence, justify.

sustained ▶ adjective *her sustained battle against alcoholism* **continuous,** ongoing, steady, continual, constant, prolonged, persistent, nonstop, perpetual, unabating, relentless, rolling, unrelieved, unbroken, never-ending, incessant, unceasing, ceaseless, around/round-the-clock.
ANTONYMS sporadic.

sustenance ▶ noun **1** *the creature needs sustenance* **nourishment,** food, nutriment, nutrition, provisions, provender, rations; informal grub, chow; formal comestibles; literary viands; dated victuals.
2 *the sustenance of his family* **support,** maintenance, keep, living, livelihood, subsistence, income.

swagger ▶ verb **1** *we swaggered into the arena* **strut,** parade, stride; walk confidently; informal sashay.
2 *try to swagger less and instead show some humility* **boast,** brag, bluster, crow, gloat; strut, posture, blow one's own horn, lord it; informal show off, swank.
▶ noun **1** *a slight swagger in his stride* **strut**; confidence, arrogance, ostentation.
2 *he was full of swagger* **bluster,** braggadocio, bumptiousness, vainglory; informal swank.

swallow ▶ verb **1** *she couldn't swallow anything* **eat,** gulp down, consume, devour, put away; ingest, assimilate; drink, guzzle, quaff, imbibe, sup, slug; informal polish off, swig, chug, swill, down, scoff.
2 *I can't swallow any more of your insults* **tolerate,** endure, stand, put up with, bear, abide, countenance, stomach, take, accept; informal hack; formal brook.
3 *he swallowed my story* **believe,** credit, accept, trust; informal fall for, buy, go for, 'swallow hook, line, and sinker'.
4 *she swallowed her pride* **restrain,** repress, suppress, hold back, fight back; overcome, check, control, curb, rein in; silence, muffle, stifle, smother, hide, bottle up; informal keep a/the lid on.
– PHRASES **swallow up 1** *the darkness swallowed them up* **engulf,** swamp, devour, overwhelm, overcome. **2** *the colleges were swallowed up by universities* **take over,** engulf, absorb, assimilate, incorporate.

swamp ▶ noun *her horse got stuck in a swamp* **marsh,** bog, muskeg, quagmire, mire, morass, fen; quicksand, bayou; archaic quag.
▶ verb **1** *the rain was swamping the dry roads* **flood,** inundate, deluge, immerse; soak, drench, saturate.

2 *he was swamped by media attention* **overwhelm,** inundate, flood, deluge, engulf, snow under, overload, overpower, weigh down, besiege, beset.

swampy ▶ **adjective** *the swampy acreage behind the orchard* **marshy,** boggy, fenny, miry; soft, soggy, muddy, spongy, heavy, squelchy, waterlogged, sodden, wet; archaic quaggy.

swap ▶ **verb 1** *I swapped my stereo for some hockey equipment* **exchange,** trade, barter, interchange, bargain; switch, change, replace.
2 *we swapped jokes* **bandy,** exchange, trade, reciprocate.
▶ **noun** *a job swap* **exchange,** interchange, trade, switch, trade-off, substitution; informal switcheroo.

swarm ▶ **noun 1** *a swarm of bees* **hive,** flock, collection.
2 *a swarm of gendarmes* **crowd,** multitude, horde, host, mob, gang, throng, mass, army, troop, herd, pack; literary myriad.
▶ **verb** *reporters were swarming all over the place* **flock,** crowd, throng, surge, stream.
– PHRASES **be swarming with** *the woods were swarming with biting flies* **be crowded with,** be thronged with, be overrun with, be full of, abound in, be teeming with, be aswarm with, bristle with, be alive with, be crawling with, be infested with, overflow with, be prolific in, be abundant in; informal be thick with.

swarthy ▶ **adjective** *his swarthy complexion* **dark-skinned,** olive-skinned, dusky, tanned, saturnine, black; archaic swart.
ANTONYMS pale.

swashbuckling ▶ **adjective** *a swashbuckling hero of silent films* **daring,** heroic, daredevil, dashing, adventurous, bold, valiant, valorous, fearless, lionhearted, dauntless, devil-may-care; gallant, chivalrous, romantic.
ANTONYMS timid.

swathe ▶ **verb** *his hands were swathed in bandages* **wrap,** envelop, bind, swaddle, bandage, cover, shroud, drape, wind, enfold, sheathe.

sway ▶ **verb 1** *the curtains swayed in the breeze* **swing,** shake, oscillate, undulate, move to and fro, move back and forth.
2 *she swayed on her feet* **stagger,** wobble, rock, lurch, reel, roll, list, stumble, pitch.
3 *we are swayed by the media* **influence,** affect, bias, persuade, win over; manipulate, bend, mold.
4 *you must not be swayed by emotion* **rule,** govern, dominate, control, guide.
▶ **noun 1** *the sway of her hips* **swing,** roll, shake, oscillation, undulation.
2 *his opinions have a lot of sway* **clout,** influence, power, weight, authority, control. See note at JURISDICTION.
– PHRASES **hold sway** *they had held sway in France for a quarter of a century* **hold power,** wield power, exercise power, have jurisdiction, have authority, have dominion, rule, be in control, predominate; have the upper hand, have the edge, have the whip hand, have mastery; informal run the show, be in the driver's seat, be in the saddle.

swear ▶ **verb 1** *they swore to marry each other* **promise,** vow, pledge, give one's word, take an oath, undertake, guarantee; Law depose; formal aver.
2 *she swore she would never go back* **insist,** avow, pronounce, declare, proclaim, assert, profess, maintain, contend, emphasize, stress; formal aver.
3 *Kate spilled wine and swore* **curse,** blaspheme, utter profanities, utter oaths, use bad language, take the Lord's name in vain; informal cuss; archaic execrate.
– PHRASES **swear by** informal *we swear by these all-weather tires* **express confidence in,** have faith in, trust, believe in; set store by, value; informal rate. **swear off** informal *I swore off hard liquor years ago* **renounce,** forswear, forgo, abstain from, go without, shun, avoid, eschew, steer clear of; give up, dispense with, stop, discontinue, drop; informal kick, quit.

swearing ▶ **noun** *they had to bleep out all the swearing* **bad language,** strong language, cursing, blaspheming, blasphemy; profanities, obscenities, curses, oaths, expletives, swear words; informal cussing, four-letter words; formal imprecation.

sweat ▶ **noun 1** *he was drenched with sweat* **perspiration,** moisture, dampness, wetness; Medicine diaphoresis.
2 informal *he got into such a sweat about that girl* **fluster,** panic, frenzy, fever, pother; informal state, flap, tizzy, dither, stew, lather.
3 informal *the sweat of the working classes* **labor,** hard work, toil(s), effort(s), exertion(s), industry, drudgery, slog; informal grind, elbow grease.
▶ **verb 1** *she was sweating heavily* **perspire,** swelter, glow; be damp, be wet; secrete.
2 *I've sweated over this for six months* **work (hard),** work like a Trojan, labor, toil, slog, slave, work one's fingers to the bone; informal plug away; archaic drudge.
3 *he sweated over his mistakes* **worry,** agonize, fuss, panic, fret, lose sleep; informal be on pins and needles, be in a state, be in a flap, be in a stew, torture oneself, torment oneself.

sweaty ▶ **adjective** *his sweaty palms* **perspiring,** sweating, clammy, sticky, glowing; moist, damp.

sweep ▶ **verb 1** *she swept the floor* **brush,** clean, scrub, wipe, mop, dust, scour; informal do.
2 *I swept the crumbs off* **remove,** brush, clean, clear, whisk.
3 *he was swept out to sea* **carry,** pull, drag, tow.
4 *riots swept the country* **engulf,** overwhelm, flood.
5 *he swept down the stairs* **glide,** sail, breeze, drift, flit, flounce; stride, stroll, swagger.
6 *a limousine swept past* **glide,** sail, rush, race, streak, speed, fly, zoom, whiz, hurtle; informal tear, whip.
7 *police swept the conference room* **search,** probe, check, explore, go through, scour, comb.
▶ **noun 1** *a great sweep of his hand* **gesture,** stroke, wave, movement.
2 *a security sweep* **search,** hunt, exploration, probe.
3 *a long sweep of golden sand* **expanse,** tract, stretch, extent, plain.
4 *the broad sweep of our interests* **range,** span,

scope, compass, reach, spread, ambit, gamut, spectrum, extent. See note at RANGE.
– PHRASES **sweep aside** *you can't sweep aside these allegations forever* **disregard,** ignore, take no notice of, dismiss, shrug off, forget about, brush aside. **sweep under the carpet** *their grievances could no longer be swept under the carpet* **hide,** conceal, suppress, hush up, keep quiet about, censor, gag, withhold, cover up, stifle.

sweeping ▶ adjective **1** *sweeping changes* **extensive,** wide-ranging, global, broad, comprehensive, all-inclusive, all-embracing, far-reaching, across the board; thorough, radical; informal wall-to-wall.
ANTONYMS limited, narrow.
2 *a sweeping victory* **overwhelming,** decisive, thorough, complete, total, absolute, out-and-out, unqualified, landslide.
ANTONYMS narrow.
3 *sweeping statements* **wholesale,** blanket, generalized, all-inclusive, unqualified, indiscriminate, universal, oversimplified, imprecise.
ANTONYMS narrow, focused.
4 *sweeping banks of flowers* **broad,** extensive, expansive, vast, spacious, boundless, panoramic.
ANTONYMS small.

sweet ▶ adjective **1** *sweet cinnamon buns* **sugary,** sweetened, saccharine; sugared, honeyed, candied, glacé; sickly, cloying.
ANTONYMS sour, savory.
2 *the sweet scent of roses* **fragrant,** aromatic, perfumed; literary ambrosial.
3 *her sweet voice* **dulcet,** melodious, lyrical, mellifluous, musical, tuneful, soft, harmonious, silvery, honeyed, mellow, rich, golden.
ANTONYMS harsh, discordant.
4 *life was still sweet* **pleasant,** pleasing, pleasurable, agreeable, delightful, nice, satisfying, gratifying, good, acceptable, fine; informal lovely, great.
ANTONYMS harsh, disagreeable.
5 *the sweet April air* **pure,** wholesome, fresh, clean, clear.
ANTONYMS harsh, rotten.
6 *she has a sweet nature* **likable,** appealing, engaging, amiable, pleasant, agreeable, genial, friendly, nice, kind, thoughtful, considerate; charming, enchanting, captivating, delightful, lovely.
ANTONYMS nasty.
7 *she looks quite sweet* **cute,** lovable, adorable, endearing, charming, attractive, dear.
8 *my sweet Lydia* **dear,** dearest, darling, beloved, loved, cherished, precious, treasured.
▶ noun **1** (**sweets**) *trying to cut back on sweets* **desserts,** treats, cakes, cookies, pastries.
2 *happy birthday, my sweet!* **dear,** darling, dearest, love, sweetheart, beloved, honey, hon, pet, treasure, angel.
– PHRASES **sweet on** informal *it's obvious that Sam is sweet on Joanie* **fond of,** taken with, attracted to, in love with, enamored of, captivated by, infatuated with, keen on, devoted to, smitten with, moonstruck by; informal mad about, bowled over by.

sweeten ▶ verb **1** *sweeten the milk with honey* **make sweet,** add sugar to, sugar, sugar-coat.
2 *he chewed gum to sweeten his breath* **freshen,** refresh, purify, deodorize, perfume.
3 *try to sweeten the bad news* **soften,** ease, alleviate, mitigate, temper, cushion; embellish, embroider.
4 informal *a bigger dividend to sweeten shareholders* **mollify,** placate, soothe, soften up, pacify, appease, win over.

sweetheart ▶ noun **1** *you look lovely, sweetheart* **darling,** dear, dearest, love, beloved, sweet; informal honey, hon, sweetie, sugar, baby, babe.
2 *my high-school sweetheart* **lover,** love, girlfriend, boyfriend, beloved, significant other, lady love, loved one, suitor, admirer; informal steady, flame, main squeeze; valentine; literary swain; dated beau; archaic paramour.

swell ▶ verb **1** *her lip swelled up* **expand,** bulge, distend, inflate, dilate, bloat, puff up, balloon, fatten, fill out, tumefy.
ANTONYMS shrink, contract.
2 *the population swelled* **grow,** enlarge, increase, expand, rise, escalate, multiply, proliferate, snowball, mushroom.
ANTONYMS wane, decrease.
3 *she swelled with pride* **be filled,** be bursting, brim, overflow.
4 *the program swelled enrollments* **increase,** enlarge, augment, boost, top up, step up, multiply.
ANTONYMS decrease.
5 *the music swelled to fill the house* **grow loud,** grow louder, amplify, crescendo, intensify, heighten.
ANTONYMS quiet.
▶ noun **1** *a brief swell in the volume* **increase,** rise, escalation, surge, boost.
ANTONYMS decrease, dip.
2 *a heavy swell on the sea* **surge,** wave, undulation, roll.
▶ adjective informal dated *a swell idea* **excellent,** marvelous, wonderful, splendid, magnificent, superb; informal super, great, fantastic.
ANTONYMS bad.

swelling ▶ noun *use ice to reduce the swelling* **bump,** lump, bulge, protuberance, enlargement, distension, prominence, protrusion, node, nodule, tumescence; boil, blister, bunion, carbuncle.

sweltering ▶ adjective *a sweltering afternoon* **hot,** stifling, humid, sultry, sticky, muggy, close, stuffy; tropical, torrid, searing, blistering; informal boiling (hot), baking, roasting, sizzling.
ANTONYMS freezing.

swerve ▶ verb *a car swerved into her path* **veer,** deviate, skew, diverge, sheer, weave, zigzag, change direction; Sailing tack.
▶ noun *the bowler regulated his swerve* **curve,** curl, deviation, twist.

swift ▶ adjective **1** *a swift decision* **prompt,** rapid, sudden, immediate, instant, instantaneous; abrupt, hasty, hurried, precipitate, headlong.
ANTONYMS unhurried.
2 *swift runners* **fast,** rapid, quick, speedy, high-speed, fast-paced, brisk, lively; express, breakneck; fleet-footed; informal nippy, supersonic.
ANTONYMS slow, sluggish.

swill ▶ verb informal *she was swilling beers* **drink,** quaff, swallow, down, gulp, drain, imbibe, sup, slurp, consume, slug; informal swig, knock back, toss off, put away, chug, chugalug.
▶ noun 1 informal *she took a swill of coffee* **gulp,** swallow, drink, draft, mouthful, slug; informal swig.
2 *swill for the pigs* **pigswill,** mash, slops, scraps, refuse, scourings, leftovers; archaic hogwash.

swim ▶ verb 1 *they swam in the pool* **bathe,** take a dip, splash around; float, tread water, paddle.
2 *his food was **swimming in** gravy* **be saturated in,** be drenched in, be soaked in, be steeped in, be immersed in, be covered in, be drowning in, be full of.

swimmingly ▶ adverb *everything was going swimmingly* **well,** smoothly, easily, effortlessly, like clockwork, without a hitch, as planned, to plan; informal like a dream, like magic.

swindle ▶ verb *I was swindled out of money | he's been swindling clients for years* **defraud,** cheat, trick, dupe, deceive, fool, hoax, hoodwink, bamboozle; informal fleece, con, bilk, sting, hose, diddle, rip off, take for a ride, pull a fast one on, put one over on, take to the cleaners, gull, stiff, euchre, hornswoggle; literary cozen.
▶ noun *an insurance swindle* **fraud,** trick, deception, deceit, cheat, sham, artifice, ruse, dodge, racket, wile; sharp practice; informal con, fiddle, diddle, rip-off, flimflam, bunco.

swindler ▶ noun *the guy collecting for the hospital fund was a swindler* **fraudster,** fraud, confidence man, confidence trickster, trickster, cheat, rogue, mountebank, charlatan, impostor, hoaxer; informal con man, con artist, scam artist, shyster, gonif, shark, sharp, hustler, phony, crook, snake oil salesman.

swing ▶ verb 1 *the sign swung in the wind* **sway,** oscillate, move back and forth, move to and fro, wave, wag, rock, flutter, flap.
2 *Helen swung the bottle* **brandish,** wave, flourish, wield, shake, wag, twirl.
3 *this road swings off to the north* **curve,** bend, veer, turn, bear, wind, twist, deviate, slew, skew, drift, head.
4 *the balance swung from one party to the other* **change,** fluctuate, shift, alter, oscillate, waver, alternate, seesaw, yo-yo, vary.
5 informal *if we keep trying, we can swing this deal* **accomplish,** achieve, obtain, acquire, get, secure, net, win, attain, bag, hook; informal wangle, land.
▶ noun 1 *a swing of the pendulum* **oscillation,** sway, wave.
2 *a swing to the New Democrats in this constituency* **change,** move; turnaround, turnabout, reversal, about face, volte face, change of heart, U-turn, sea change.
3 *a swing toward plain food* **trend,** tendency, drift, movement.
4 *a mood swing* **fluctuation,** change, shift, variation, oscillation.

swirl ▶ verb *the snow swirled around them* **whirl,** eddy, billow, spiral, circulate, revolve, spin, twist; flow, stream, surge, seethe.

switch ▶ noun 1 *the switch on top of the telephone* **button,** lever, control, dial, rocker.
2 *a switch from direct to indirect taxation* **change,** move, shift, transition, transformation; reversal, turnaround, U-turn, changeover, transfer, conversion; substitution, exchange.
3 *a switch of willow* **branch,** twig, stick, rod.
▶ verb 1 *he switched sides* **change,** shift; reverse; informal chop and change.
2 *he managed to switch envelopes* **exchange,** swap, interchange, trade, substitute, replace, rotate.
– PHRASES **switch on** *switch on the air conditioning* **turn on,** put on, flick on, activate, start, power up, set going, set in motion, operate, initiate, actuate, initialize, energize; toggle, flip, throw. **switch off** *who switched off the fan?* **turn off,** shut off, flick off, power down, stop, cut, halt, deactivate; toggle, flip.

swollen ▶ adjective *the rivers are swollen | swollen glands* **distended,** expanded, enlarged, bulging, inflated, dilated, bloated, puffed up, puffy, tumescent, tumid; inflamed, varicose.

swoop ▶ verb 1 *pigeons swooped down after the grain* **dive,** descend, sweep, pounce, plunge, pitch, nosedive; rush, dart, speed, zoom.
2 *police **swooped on** the building* **raid,** pounce on, attack, assault, assail, charge, bust.

sword ▶ noun *a ceremonial sword* **blade,** foil, broadsword, épée, cutlass, rapier, saber, scimitar; literary brand.
– PHRASES **cross swords** *Larry is crossing swords with his brother-in-law again* **quarrel,** disagree, dispute, wrangle, bicker, be at odds, be at loggerheads, lock horns; fight, contend; informal scrap.

sybaritic ▶ adjective *she regretted having left her homespun past for this sybaritic life with Lanzo* **luxurious,** extravagant, lavish, self-indulgent, pleasure-seeking, sensual, voluptuous, hedonistic, epicurean, lotus-eating, libertine, debauched, decadent. See note at SENSUOUS.
– ANTONYMS ascetic.

sycophant ▶ noun *I thought you wanted a competent assistant, not a nodding sycophant* yes-man, bootlicker, brown-noser, toady, lickspittle, flatterer, flunky, lackey, spaniel, doormat, stooge, cringer, suck, suck-up.

sycophantic ▶ adjective *his clique of sycophantic friends* **obsequious,** servile, subservient, deferential, groveling, toadying, fawning, flattering, ingratiating, cringing, unctuous, slavish; informal smarmy, bootlicking, brown-nosing.

symbol ▶ noun 1 *the lotus is the symbol of purity* **emblem,** token, sign, representation, figure, image; metaphor, allegory; icon.
2 *the chemical symbol for helium* **sign,** character, mark, letter, ideogram.
3 *the Red Cross symbol* **logo,** emblem, badge, stamp, trademark, crest, insignia, coat of arms, seal, device, monogram, hallmark, flag, motif, icon. See note at EMBLEM.

symbolic ▶ adjective 1 *the Colosseum is symbolic of the Roman Empire* **emblematic,** representative, typical, characteristic, symptomatic.
2 *symbolic language* **figurative,** representative, illustrative, emblematic, metaphorical, allegorical, parabolic, allusive, suggestive; meaningful, significant.

ANTONYMS literal.

symbolize ▶ verb *the wheel symbolizes the power of peaceful change* **represent,** stand for, be a sign of, exemplify; denote, signify, mean, indicate, convey, express, imply, suggest, allude to; embody, epitomize, encapsulate, personify, typify; literary betoken.

symmetrical ▶ adjective *the two doves on the flag are symmetrical* **regular,** uniform, consistent; evenly shaped, aligned, equal; mirror image; balanced, proportional, even.

symmetry ▶ noun *the garden is laid out with perfect symmetry* **regularity,** evenness, uniformity, consistency, conformity, correspondence, equality; balance, proportions; formal concord.

sympathetic ▶ adjective **1** *a sympathetic listener* **compassionate,** caring, concerned, solicitous, empathetic, understanding, sensitive; commiserative, pitying, consoling, comforting, supportive, encouraging; considerate, kind, tenderhearted; informal boosterish.
ANTONYMS unfeeling.
2 *the most sympathetic character in the book* **likable,** pleasant, agreeable, congenial, friendly, genial, simpatico.
ANTONYMS unfriendly.
3 *I was **sympathetic to** his cause* **in favor of,** in sympathy with, pro, on the side of, supportive of, encouraging of; well-disposed to, favorably disposed to, receptive to.
ANTONYMS indifferent, opposed.

sympathize ▶ verb **1** *I do **sympathize with** the poor creature* **pity,** feel sorry for, show compassion for, commiserate with, offer condolences to, feel for, show concern for, show interest for; console, comfort, solace, soothe, support, encourage; empathize with, identify with, understand, relate to.
2 *they **sympathize with** the critique* **agree with,** support, be in favor of, go along with, favor, approve of, back, side with.

sympathizer ▶ noun *his Confederate brothers accused him of being a Yankee sympathizer* **supporter,** backer, well-wisher, advocate, ally, partisan; collaborator, fraternizer, conspirator, quisling.

sympathy ▶ noun **1** *he shows sympathy for the poor* **compassion,** caring, concern, solicitude, empathy; commiseration, pity, condolence, comfort, solace, support, encouragement; consideration, kindness.
ANTONYMS indifference.
2 *sympathy with a fellow journalist* **rapport,** fellow feeling, affinity, empathy, harmony, accord, compatibility; fellowship, camaraderie.
ANTONYMS hostility.
3 *their sympathy with the Communists* **agreement,** favor, approval, approbation, support, encouragement, partiality; association, alignment, affiliation.
ANTONYMS disapproval.

symptom ▶ noun **1** *the symptoms of the disease* **manifestation,** indication, indicator, sign, mark, feature, trait; Medicine prodrome.
2 *a symptom of the country's present turmoil* **expression,** sign, indication, mark, token, manifestation; portent, warning, clue, hint; testimony, evidence, proof; result, consequence, product. See note at **SIGN**.

symptomatic ▶ adjective *they worried that her lethargy was symptomatic of depression* **indicative,** characteristic, suggestive, typical, representative, symbolic.

synthesis ▶ noun *the synthesis of their diverse styles makes for a wonderful new sound in country music* **combination,** union, amalgam, blend, mixture, compound, fusion, composite, alloy; unification, amalgamation, marrying.

synthetic ▶ adjective *synthetic leather* **artificial,** fake, imitation, faux, mock, simulated, ersatz, substitute; pseudo, so-called; man-made, manufactured, fabricated; informal phony, pretend. See note at **SPURIOUS**.
ANTONYMS natural.

syrupy ▶ adjective **1** *syrupy medicine* **oversweet,** sweet, sugary, treacly, honeyed, saccharine; thick, sticky, gluey, viscid, glutinous; informal gooey.
2 *syrupy romantic drivel* **sentimental,** mawkish, cloying, sickly, saccharine, trite; informal soppy, schmaltzy, mushy, slushy, sloppy, lovey-dovey, cheesy, corny.

system ▶ noun **1** *a system of canals* **structure,** organization, arrangement, complex, network; informal setup.
2 *a system for regulating sales* **method,** methodology, technique, process, procedure, approach, practice; means, way, mode, framework, modus operandi; scheme, plan, policy, program, regimen, formula, routine.
3 *there was no system in his work* **order,** method, orderliness, systematization, planning, logic, routine.
4 *youngsters have no faith in **the system*** **the establishment,** the administration, the authorities, the powers that be; bureaucracy, officialdom; the status quo.

systematic ▶ adjective *the systematic firing of one department head after another* **structured,** methodical, organized, orderly, planned, systematized, regular, routine, standardized, standard; logical, coherent, consistent; efficient, businesslike, practical; informal left-brained.
ANTONYMS disorganized.

Tt

tab ▸ noun 1 *his name is on the tab of his jacket* tag, label, flap.
2 informal *the company will pick up the tab* **bill,** invoice, account, charge, check, expense, cost.

table ▸ noun 1 *put the plates on the table* bench, buffet, stand, counter, work surface; desk; bar.
2 *he provides an excellent table* **meal,** food, fare, menu, nourishment; eatables, provisions; informal spread, grub, chow, eats, nosh; literary viands; dated victuals.
3 *the report has numerous tables* **chart,** diagram, figure, graph, plan; list, tabulation, index.
▸ verb *the council tabled the issue until April* **postpone,** delay, defer, sideline, put on the back burner.

tableau ▸ noun 1 *mythic tableaux* **picture,** painting, representation, illustration, image.
2 *the first act consists of a series of tableaux* **pageant,** tableau vivant, parade, diorama, scene.
3 *a domestic tableau around the fireplace* **scene,** arrangement, grouping, group; picture, spectacle, image, vignette.

tablet ▸ noun 1 *a carved tablet* **slab,** stone, panel, plaque, plate, sign.
2 *a headache tablet* **pill,** capsule, lozenge, caplet, pastille, drop, pilule; informal tab.
3 *a writing tablet* **pad,** notepad, memo pad, notebook, scratchpad.

taboo ▸ noun *the taboo against healing on the Sabbath* **prohibition,** proscription, veto, interdiction, interdict, ban, restriction.
▸ adjective *taboo subjects* **forbidden,** prohibited, banned, proscribed, interdicted, outlawed, illegal, illicit, unlawful, restricted, off limits; unmentionable, unspeakable, unutterable, unsayable, ineffable; rude, impolite.
ANTONYMS acceptable.

tabulate ▸ verb *we tabulate the phone-in pledges every twenty minutes* **chart,** arrange, order, organize, systematize, systemize, catalog, list, index, classify, class, codify; compile, group, log, grade, rate.

tacit ▸ adjective *tacit promises* **implicit,** understood, implied, hinted, suggested; unspoken, unstated, unsaid, unexpressed, unvoiced; taken for granted, taken as read, inferred.
ANTONYMS explicit.

taciturn ▸ adjective *our taciturn daughter has suddenly become a little chatty* **untalkative,** uncommunicative, reticent, unforthcoming, quiet, secretive, tight-lipped, buttoned-up, close-mouthed; silent, mute, dumb, inarticulate; reserved, withdrawn.
ANTONYMS talkative.

tack ▸ noun 1 *tacks held the carpet down* **pin,** thumbtack, pushpin, nail, staple, rivet, stud.
2 *the boat bowled past on the opposite tack* **heading,** bearing, course, track, path, line.
3 *Mitchell wisely changed his tack* **approach,** way, method; policy, procedure, technique, tactic, plan, strategy, stratagem; path, line, angle, direction, course.
▸ verb 1 *a photo tacked to the wall* **pin,** nail, staple, fix, fasten, attach, secure, affix.
2 *the dress was roughly tacked together* **stitch,** baste, sew, bind.
3 *the yachts tacked back and forth* **zigzag,** change direction, change course, swerve, veer; Nautical go about, come about, beat.
4 *poems* ***tacked on*** *at the end of the book* **add (on),** append, join, stick (on).

tackle ▸ noun 1 *fishing tackle* **gear,** equipment, apparatus, kit, hardware; implements, instruments, accoutrements, paraphernalia, trappings, appurtenances; informal things, stuff, bits and pieces; archaic equipage.
2 *lifting tackle* **pulleys,** gear, hoist, crane, winch, davit, windlass, sheave.
3 *a tackle by the linebacker* **block,** interception, challenge, attack.
▸ verb 1 *we must tackle environmental problems* **come to grips with,** address, get to work on, set one's hand to, approach, take on, attend to, see to, try to sort out; deal with, take care of, handle, manage; informal have a crack at, have a go at.
2 *he tackled a masked intruder* **confront,** face up to, take on, contend with, challenge, attack; seize, grab, grapple with, intercept, block, stop; bring down, floor, fell; informal have a go at.

tacky[1] ▸ adjective *the paint was still tacky* **sticky,** wet, gluey, gummy, adhesive, viscous, viscid, treacly; informal gooey.

tacky[2] ▸ adjective *a tacky game show* **tawdry, tasteless,** kitsch, kitschy, vulgar, crude, garish, gaudy, showy, trashy, cheesy, cheap, common, second-rate.
ANTONYMS tasteful.

tact ▸ noun *Dr. Porter has a lot to learn about timing and tact* **diplomacy,** tactfulness, sensitivity, understanding, thoughtfulness, consideration, delicacy, discretion, prudence, judiciousness, subtlety, savoir faire; informal savvy.

tactful ▸ adjective *tactful criticism* **diplomatic,** discreet, considerate, sensitive, understanding, thoughtful, delicate, judicious, politic, perceptive, subtle; courteous, polite, decorous, respectful; informal savvy.

tactic ▶ **noun 1** *a tax-saving tactic* **strategy,** scheme, stratagem, plan, maneuver; method, expedient, gambit, move, approach, tack; device, trick, ploy, dodge, ruse, machination, contrivance; informal wangle; archaic shift.
2 *our fleet's superior tactics* **strategy,** policy, campaign, battle plans, game plans, maneuvers, logistics; generalship, organization, planning, direction, orchestration.

tactical ▶ **adjective** *they met secretly to discuss their next tactical move* **calculated,** planned, strategic; prudent, politic, diplomatic, judicious, shrewd, cunning, artful.

tactless ▶ **adjective** *it was a cruel, tactless thing to say* **insensitive,** inconsiderate, thoughtless, indelicate, undiplomatic, impolitic, indiscreet, unsubtle, clumsy, heavy-handed, graceless, awkward, inept, gauche; blunt, frank, outspoken, abrupt, gruff, rough, crude, coarse; imprudent, injudicious, unwise; rude, impolite, uncouth, discourteous, crass, tasteless, disrespectful, boorish.

tag ▶ **noun 1** *a price tag* **label,** ticket, badge, mark, marker, tab, sticker, stub, counterfoil, flag.
2 *he gained a "bad boy" tag* **designation,** label, description, characterization, identity; nickname, name, epithet, title, sobriquet; informal handle, moniker; formal denomination, appellation.
3 *tags from Shakespeare* **quotation,** quote, tag line, phrase, platitude, cliché, excerpt; saying, proverb, maxim, adage, aphorism, motto, epigram; slogan, catchphrase.
▶ **verb 1** *bottles tagged with colored stickers* **label,** mark, ticket, identify, flag, indicate.
2 *she is tagged as a "thinking" actor* **label,** class, categorize, characterize, designate, describe, identify, classify; mark, stamp, brand, pigeonhole, stereotype, typecast, compartmentalize, typify; name, call, title, entitle, dub, term, style.
3 *a poem* ***tagged on*** *as an afterthought* **add,** tack on, join; attach, append, stick on.
4 *he was* ***tagging along*** *behind her* **follow,** trail; come after, go after, shadow, dog; accompany, attend, escort; informal tail.

tail ▶ **noun 1** *the dog's tail* brush, scut, dock; tail feathers; hindquarters.
ANTONYMS head, front.
2 *the tail of the plane* **rear,** end, back, extremity; bottom.
ANTONYMS head, front.
3 *the tail of the hunting season* **close,** end, conclusion, tail end.
ANTONYMS beginning, start.
4 informal *put a tail on that suspect* **detective,** investigator, shadow; informal sleuth, private eye, gumshoe.
▶ **verb** informal *the paparazzi tailed them* **follow,** shadow, stalk, trail, track, hunt, hound, dog, pursue, chase.
– PHRASES **on someone's tail** *a police car stayed on his tail* **close behind,** following closely, (hard) on someone's heels. **tail off/away** *her voice tailed off* **fade,** wane, ebb, dwindle, decrease, lessen, diminish, decline, subside, abate, drop off, peter out, taper off; let up, ease off, die away, die down, come to an end. **turn tail** *I was so shocked, I just turned tail* **run away,** flee, bolt, make off, take to one's heels, cut and run, beat a (hasty) retreat; informal scram, skedaddle, vamoose.

tailor ▶ **noun** *the finest tailor in Memphis* **outfitter,** dressmaker, couturier, fashion designer, designer; clothier, costumer, seamstress.
▶ **verb** *services can be tailored to customer requirements* **customize,** adapt, adjust, modify, change, convert, alter, attune, mold, gear, fit, cut, shape, tune.

taint ▶ **noun** *the taint of corruption* **trace,** touch, suggestion, hint, tinge; stain, blot, blemish, stigma, black mark, discredit, dishonor, disgrace, shame.
▶ **verb 1** *the wilderness is tainted by pollution* **contaminate,** pollute, adulterate, infect, blight, spoil, soil, ruin, destroy; literary befoul. See note at **POLLUTE**.
ANTONYMS clean.
2 *those fraudsters taint the reputation of legitimate claimants* **tarnish,** sully, blacken, stain, blot, blemish, stigmatize, mar, corrupt, defile, soil, muddy, damage, harm, hurt; drag through the mud; literary besmirch.
ANTONYMS improve.

take ▶ **verb 1** *she took his hand* **lay hold of,** get hold of; grasp, grip, clasp, clutch, grab.
ANTONYMS give.
2 *he took an envelope from his pocket* **remove,** pull, draw, withdraw, extract, fish.
ANTONYMS give.
3 *a passage taken from my book* **extract,** quote, cite, excerpt, derive, abstract, copy, cull.
4 *she took a little wine* **drink,** imbibe; consume, swallow, eat, ingest.
5 *many prisoners were taken* **capture,** seize, catch, arrest, apprehend, take into custody; carry off, abduct.
ANTONYMS liberate, free.
6 *someone's taken my car* **steal,** remove, appropriate, make off with, pilfer, purloin; informal filch, swipe, snaffle, pinch.
ANTONYMS give back, restore.
7 *take four from the total* **subtract,** deduct, remove; discount; informal knock off, minus.
ANTONYMS add.
8 *all the seats had been taken* **occupy,** use, utilize, fill, hold; reserve, engage; informal bag.
9 *I have taken a room nearby* **rent,** lease, hire, charter; reserve, book, engage.
10 *I took the job* **accept,** undertake, take on.
ANTONYMS refuse, turn down.
11 *I'd take this over the other option* **pick,** choose, select; prefer, favor, opt for, vote for.
ANTONYMS refuse, turn down.
12 *take, for instance, Altoona* **consider,** contemplate, ponder, think about, mull over, examine, study, meditate over, ruminate about.
13 *she took his temperature* **ascertain,** determine, establish, measure, find out, discover; calculate, compute, evaluate, rate, assess, appraise, gauge.
14 *he took notes* **write,** note (down), jot (down), scribble, scrawl, record, register,

document, minute.

15 *I took the package to Wilmington* **bring,** carry, bear, transport, convey, move, transfer, ferry; informal cart, tote.

16 *the police took her home* **escort,** accompany, help, assist, show, lead, guide, see, usher, shepherd, convey.

17 *he took the train* **travel on/by,** journey on, go via; use.

18 *the town takes its name from the lake* **derive,** get, obtain, come by, acquire, pick up.

19 *she took the prize for best speaker* **receive,** obtain, gain, get, acquire, collect, accept, be awarded; secure, come by, win, earn, pick up, carry off; informal land, bag, net, scoop.

20 *I took the chance to postpone it* **act on,** take advantage of, capitalize on, use, exploit, make the most of, leap at, jump at, pounce on, seize, grasp, grab, accept.

ANTONYMS ignore, miss.

21 *he took great pleasure in painting* **derive,** draw, acquire, obtain, get, gain, extract, procure; experience, undergo, feel.

22 *Liz took the news badly* **receive,** respond to, react to, meet, greet; deal with, cope with.

23 *do you take me for a fool?* **regard as,** consider to be, view as, see as, believe to be, reckon to be, imagine to be, deem to be.

24 *I take it that you are hungry* **assume,** presume, suppose, imagine, expect, reckon, gather, dare say, trust, surmise, deduce, guess, conjecture, fancy, suspect.

25 *I take your point* **understand,** grasp, get, comprehend, apprehend, see, follow; accept, appreciate, acknowledge, sympathize with, agree with.

26 *Shirley was very taken with him* **captivate,** enchant, charm, delight, attract, beguile, enthrall, entrance, infatuate, dazzle; amuse, divert, entertain; informal tickle someone's fancy.

27 *I can't take much more* **endure,** bear, tolerate, stand, put up with, abide, stomach, accept, allow, countenance, support, shoulder; formal brook; archaic suffer.

28 *applicants must take a test* **carry out,** do, complete, write, conduct, perform, execute, discharge, accomplish, fulfill.

29 *I took drama, French, and art history* **study,** learn, have lessons in; take up, pursue; informal do.

30 *the journey took six hours* **last,** continue for, go on for, carry on for; require, call for, need, necessitate, entail, involve.

31 *it would take an expert to know that* **require,** need, necessitate, demand, call for, entail, involve.

32 *I take size six shoes* **wear,** use; require, need.

33 *the dye did not take* **be effective,** take effect, hold, root, be productive, be effectual, be useful; work, operate, succeed, function; formal be efficacious.

▶ **noun 1** *the whalers' commercial take* **catch,** haul, bag, yield, net.

2 *the state's tax take* **revenue,** income, gain, profit; takings, proceeds, returns, receipts, winnings, pickings, earnings, spoils; purse.

3 *a clapperboard for the start of each take* **scene,** sequence, film clip, clip.

4 *a fresh take on gender issues* **view of,** reading of, version of, interpretation of, understanding of, account of, analysis of, approach to.

– PHRASES **take after** *Sandy takes after his adventurous Uncle Lenny* **resemble,** look like; remind one of, make one think of, recall, conjure up, suggest, evoke; informal favor, be a chip off the old block. **take apart 1** *we took the machine apart* **dismantle,** pull to pieces, pull apart, disassemble, break up; tear down, demolish, destroy, wreck. **2** informal *the scene was taken apart by the director* See CRITICIZE. **take someone back 1** *the dream took me back to Vienna* **evoke,** remind one of, conjure up, summon up; echo, suggest. **2** *I will never take her back* **be reconciled (to),** forgive, pardon, excuse, exonerate, absolve; let bygones be bygones, bury the hatchet. **take something back 1** *I take back every word* **retract,** withdraw, renounce, disclaim, unsay, disavow, recant, repudiate; formal abjure. **2** *I must take the keys back* **return,** bring back, give back, restore. **take something down** *I took down everything she said* **write down,** note down, jot down, set down, record, commit to paper, register, draft, document, minute, pen. **take someone in 1** *she took in paying guests* **accommodate,** board, house, feed, put up, admit, receive; harbor. **2** *you were taken in by a hoax* **deceive,** delude, hoodwink, mislead, trick, dupe, fool, cheat, defraud, swindle, outwit, gull, hoax, bamboozle; informal con, put one over on. **take something in 1** *she could hardly take in the news* **comprehend,** understand, grasp, follow, absorb; informal get. **2** *this route takes in some great scenery* **include,** encompass, embrace, contain, comprise, cover, incorporate, comprehend, hold. **take someone in hand** *part of your job is to take young Master Jonathon in hand* **control,** be in charge of, dominate, master; reform, improve, correct, change, rehabilitate. **take something in hand** *are you willing to take this project in hand?* **deal with,** apply oneself to, come to grips with, set one's hand to, grapple with, take on, attend to, see to, sort out, take care of, handle, manage. **take it out of someone** *the final lap has taken it out of Johnson* **exhaust,** drain, enervate, tire, fatigue, wear out, weary, debilitate; informal poop. **take off 1** *the horse took off at great speed* **run away/off,** flee, abscond, take flight, decamp, leave, go, depart, make off, bolt, take to one's heels, escape; informal split, clear off, skedaddle, vamoose. **2** *the plane took off* **become airborne,** take to the air, take wing; lift off, blast off. **3** *the idea really took off* **succeed,** do well, become popular, catch on, prosper, flourish, thrive, boom. **take someone on 1** *there was no challenger to take him on* **compete against,** oppose, challenge, confront, face, fight, vie with, contend with, stand up to. **2** *we took on extra staff* **engage,** hire, employ, enroll, enlist, sign up; informal take on board. **take something on 1** *he took on more responsibility* **undertake,** accept, assume, shoulder, acquire, carry, bear. **2** *the study took on political meaning* **acquire,** assume, come to have. **take one's time** *if the place were on fire, Mark would still take his time* **go slowly,** dally, dawdle, delay, linger, drag one's feet, waste time, kill time; informal dilly-dally, lollygag; archaic tarry. **take someone out** **1** *he asked if he could take her out* **go out with,** escort, partner, accompany, go with; romance; informal date, see, go steady with; dated court, woo. **2** informal *the sniper took them all out* **kill,** murder, assassinate, dispatch, execute, finish off, eliminate, exterminate, terminate; informal do in, do away with, bump off, rub out, mow down; literary slay. **take something over** *the workers were stunned to learn that a rival corporation had taken over their company* **assume control of,** take charge of, take command of. **take to** **1** *he took to carrying his money in his sock* **make a habit of,** resort to, turn to, have recourse to (start/begin); start, begin, commence. **2** *Ruth took to the cat instantly* **like,** get on with, be friendly toward; informal take a shine to. **3** *the dog has really taken to racing* **become good at,** develop an ability for; like, enjoy. **take something up** **1** *she took up abstract painting* **engage in,** practice; begin, start, commence. **2** *the meetings took up all her time* **consume,** fill, absorb, use, occupy; waste, squander. **3** *her cousin took up the story* **resume,** recommence, restart, carry on, continue, pick up, return to. **4** *he took up their offer of a job* **accept,** say yes to, agree to, adopt; formal accede to. **5** *take the skirt up an inch* **shorten,** turn up; raise, lift. **take up with** *Burt has taken up with the kids in the ski club* **become friends with,** (begin to) go around with, fall in with, string along with, get involved with, start seeing; informal (begin to) hang out with.

takeoff ▶ noun **1** *the plane performed a safe takeoff* **departure,** liftoff, launch, blastoff; ascent, flight.
ANTONYMS touchdown.
2 informal *a takeoff of a talent show* **parody,** pastiche, mockery, caricature, travesty, satire, lampoon, mimicry, imitation, impersonation, impression; informal sendup, spoof.

takings ▶ plural noun *his takings from the race were substantial* **proceeds,** returns, receipts, earnings, winnings, pickings, spoils; profit, gain, income, revenue; gate, purse.

tale ▶ noun **1** *a tale of witches* **story,** narrative, anecdote, report, account, history; legend, fable, myth, parable, allegory, saga; informal yarn. **2** *she told tales to her mother* **lie,** fib, falsehood, story, untruth, fabrication, fiction; informal tall story, fairy tale, fairy story, cock-and-bull story.

talent ▶ noun *a natural talent for dancing* **flair,** aptitude, facility, gift, knack, technique, touch, bent, ability, expertise, capacity, faculty; strength, forte, genius, brilliance; dexterity, skill, artistry.

talented ▶ adjective *a talented sculptor* **gifted,** skillful, skilled, accomplished, brilliant, expert, consummate, masterly, adroit, dexterous, able, competent, apt, capable, deft, adept, proficient; informal crack, ace.
ANTONYMS inept.

talk ▶ verb **1** *I was talking to a friend* **speak,** chat, chatter, gossip, prattle, babble, rattle on, blather; informal yak, gab, jaw, chew the fat, natter, rap.
2 *you're talking garbage* **utter,** speak, say, voice, express, articulate, pronounce, verbalize, vocalize.
3 *they were able to talk in peace* **converse,** communicate, speak, confer, consult; negotiate, parley; informal have a confab, chew the fat, rap; formal confabulate.
4 *he* ***talked of*** *suicide* **mention,** refer to, speak about, discuss.
5 *he learned to talk Cree* **speak (in),** talk in, communicate in, converse in, express oneself in; use.
6 *nothing would make her talk* **confess,** speak out, speak up, reveal all, tell tales, give the game away, open one's mouth; informal come clean, blab, squeal, let the cat out of the bag, spill the beans, sing, rat.
7 *the others will talk* **gossip,** pass comment, make remarks; criticize.
▶ noun **1** *he was bored with all this talk* **chatter,** gossip, prattle, jabbering, babbling, gabbling; informal yakking, gabbing, nattering.
2 *she needed a talk with Jim* **conversation,** chat, discussion, tête-à-tête, heart-to-heart, dialogue, parley, powwow, consultation, conference, meeting; informal confab, jaw, chitchat, gossip; formal colloquy, confabulation.
3 **(talks)** *peace talks* **negotiations,** discussions; conference, summit, meeting, consultation, dialogue, symposium, seminar, conclave, parley; mediation, arbitration; informal powwow.
4 *she gave a talk on her travels* **lecture,** speech, address, discourse, oration, presentation, report, sermon; informal spiel.
5 *there was talk of a takeover* **gossip,** rumor, hearsay, tittle-tattle; news, report.
6 informal *he's all talk* **boasting,** bragging, idle talk, bombast, braggadocio; informal hot air, mouth.
7 *baby talk* **speech,** language, slang, idiom, idiolect; words; informal lingo, -ese.
– PHRASES **talk back to** *nobody talks back to Mr. Lynde* **answer back (to),** be impertinent to, be cheeky to, be rude to; contradict, argue with, disagree with. **talk big** informal See BOAST (sense 1 of the verb). **talk down to** *he routinely talks down to women* **condescend to,** patronize, look down one's nose at, put down. **talk someone into something** *don't even try to talk me into giving you another loan* **persuade into,** argue into, cajole into, coax into, bring around to, inveigle into, wheedle into, sweet-talk into, prevail on someone to; informal hustle into, fast-talk into.

talkative ▶ adjective *the talkative person in the seat next to mine* **chatty,** loquacious, garrulous, voluble, conversational, communicative; gossipy, babbling, blathering; long-winded, wordy, verbose, prolix; informal gabby, mouthy, motormouthed, talky.
ANTONYMS taciturn.

CHOOSE THE RIGHT WORD

talkative, garrulous, glib, loquacious, voluble

Someone who likes to talk frequently or at length might be described as **talkative** (*he* *was the most talkative person I'd ever met*). This word implies a readiness to engage in talk, while **loquacious** implies an inclination to talk incessantly or to keep up a constant flow of chatter (*a loquacious woman who never seemed to tire of hearing her own voice*). **Glib** and **voluble** pertain to the ease with which someone is able to converse or speak, although *voluble* may be used in either an approving or a critical sense (*a voluble speaker who was in great demand; a voluble neighbor who could not keep a secret*). *Glib* is almost always negative, referring to a superficial or slick way of speaking (*the glib manner of a used-car salesperson*). **Garrulous** also has negative overtones, implying a tedious or rambling talkativeness, usually about trivial things (*a garrulous old man who bored everyone with his stories about "the old days"*).

talker ▶ noun *Sue's husband is a real talker* **conversationalist,** speaker, communicator; chatterbox, motormouth, gossip, flibbertigibbet.

talking-to ▶ noun informal *if you ask me, that kid needs a good talking-to* See REPRIMAND (noun).

tall ▶ adjective 1 *a tall man* **big,** large, huge, towering, colossal, gigantic, giant, monstrous; leggy; informal long.
ANTONYMS short, small.
2 *tall buildings* **high,** big, lofty, towering, elevated, sky-high; multistory.
ANTONYMS low.
3 *she's five feet tall* **in height,** high, from head to toe; from top to bottom.
ANTONYMS wide.
4 *a tall tale* **unlikely,** improbable, exaggerated, far-fetched, implausible, dubious, unbelievable, incredible, absurd, untrue; informal cock-and-bull.
ANTONYMS credible, believable.
5 *a tall order* **demanding,** exacting, difficult; unreasonable, impossible.
ANTONYMS easy.

tally ▶ noun 1 *he keeps a tally of the score* **running total,** count, record, reckoning, register, account, roll; census, poll.
2 *her tally of 22 victories* **total,** score, count, sum.
▶ verb 1 *these statistics tally with government figures* **correspond with,** agree with, accord with, concur with, coincide with, match, fit, be consistent with, conform to, equate with, harmonize with, be in tune with, dovetail, correlate with/to, parallel; informal square with, jibe with.
ANTONYMS disagree, differ.
2 *votes were tallied with abacuses* **count,** calculate, add up, total, compute; figure out, work out, reckon, measure, quantify, tot up; formal enumerate.

tame ▶ adjective 1 *a tame elephant* **domesticated,** domestic, docile, tamed, broken, trained; gentle, mild; pet, housebroken; chiefly Brit. house-trained.
ANTONYMS wild, fierce.
2 informal *he has a tame lawyer* **amenable,** biddable, cooperative, willing, obedient, tractable, acquiescent, docile, submissive, compliant, meek.
ANTONYMS uncooperative.
3 *it was a pretty tame affair* **unexciting,** uninteresting, uninspiring, dull, bland, flat, insipid, spiritless, pedestrian, colorless, run-of-the-mill, mediocre, ordinary, humdrum, boring; harmless, safe, inoffensive.
ANTONYMS exciting.
▶ verb 1 *wild rabbits can be tamed* **domesticate,** break, train, master, subdue.
2 *she learned to tame her emotions* **subdue,** curb, control, calm, master, moderate, overcome, discipline, suppress, repress, mellow, temper, soften, bridle, get a grip on; informal lick.

tamper ▶ verb 1 *she saw them* ***tampering with*** *her car* **interfere with,** monkey around with, meddle with, tinker with, fiddle with, fool around with, play around with; doctor, alter, change, adjust, damage, deface, vandalize; informal mess around with.
2 *the defendant* ***tampered with*** *the jury* **influence,** get at, rig, manipulate, bribe, corrupt, bias; informal fix.

tan ▶ adjective *a tan waistcoat* **yellowish-brown,** light brown, pale brown, beige, tawny.
▶ verb 1 *use a sunscreen to help you tan* **become suntanned,** get a suntan, brown, go/get/become brown, bronze.
2 informal *I'll tan his hide* See THRASH (sense 1).

tang ▶ noun *there's a lovely tang to the glaze* **flavor,** taste, savor; sharpness, zest, bite, edge, smack, piquancy, spice; smell, odor, aroma, fragrance, perfume, redolence; informal kick, pep.

tangible ▶ adjective *I'd prefer a reward more tangible than praise—say, cash* **touchable,** palpable, material, physical, real, substantial, corporeal, solid, concrete; visible, noticeable; actual, definite, clear, clear-cut, distinct, manifest, evident, unmistakable, perceptible, discernible.
ANTONYMS abstract.

CHOOSE THE RIGHT WORD

tangible, appreciable, corporeal, palpable, perceptible, sensible

Anything that can be grasped, either with the hand or with the mind, is **tangible** (*tangible assets; tangible objects*). **Palpable,** like *tangible*, means capable of being touched or felt (*a palpable mist*), but it is often applied to whatever evokes a tactile response from the body (*a palpable chill in the room*). **Perceptible** is used to describe something that just crosses the border between invisibility and visibility or some other sense barrier (*a perceptible change in her tone of voice; a perceptible odor of garlic*). **Sensible** (in this sense) means that which can clearly be perceived through the senses or which makes a strong impression on the mind through the medium of sensations. In contrast to *perceptible*, something that is *sensible* is more obvious or immediately recognized (*a sensible shift in the tenor of the conversation*). **Corporeal** means bodily or material, in contrast to things that are immaterial or spiritual (*corporeal goods*). Something that is **appreciable** is large enough to be measured, valued, estimated, or considered significant. An *appreciable* change in temperature, for example, can be determined by looking at a thermometer; a *palpable* change in temperature may be slight, but still great enough to be felt; and a *perceptible* change in temperature might be so slight that it almost—but not quite—escapes notice.

tangle ▶ verb **1** *the wool got tangled* **entangle,** snarl, catch, entwine, twist, ravel, knot, enmesh, coil, mat, jumble, muddle.
2 *he tangled with his old rival* **come into conflict,** dispute, argue, quarrel, fight, wrangle, squabble, contend, cross swords, lock horns.
▶ noun **1** *a tangle of branches* **snarl,** mass, knot, mesh, mishmash.
2 *the defense got into an awful tangle* **muddle,** jumble, mix-up, confusion, shambles.

tangled ▶ adjective **1** *tangled hair* **knotted,** knotty, raveled, entangled, snarled (up), twisted, matted, tangly, messy; tousled, unkempt; informal mussed up.
2 *a tangled bureaucratic mess* **confused,** jumbled, mixed up, messy, chaotic, complicated, involved, complex, intricate, knotty, tortuous.
ANTONYMS simple, straightforward.

tank ▶ noun **1** *a hot water tank* **container,** receptacle, vat, cistern, repository, reservoir, basin.
2 *a tank full of fish* **aquarium,** bowl.
3 *the army's use of tanks* **armored vehicle,** armored car, combat vehicle; panzer.

tantalize ▶ verb *Steve was tantalized by Liliana's exotic eyes* **tease,** torment, torture, bait; tempt, entice, lure, allure, beguile; excite, fascinate, titillate, intrigue.

tantamount ▶ adjective *this is **tantamount to** mutiny* **equivalent to,** equal to, as good as, more or less, much the same as, comparable to, on a par with, commensurate with. See note at SAME.

tantrum ▶ noun *how can you tolerate his tantrums?* **fit of temper,** fit of rage, fit, outburst, pet, paroxysm, frenzy, bad mood, mood, huff, scene; informal hissy fit.

tap¹ ▶ noun **1** *she turned the tap on* **faucet,** valve, stopcock, cock, spout, spigot, spile.
2 *a phone tap in the embassy* **listening device,** wiretap, wire, bug, bugging device, (hidden) microphone, (hidden) mic, receiver.
▶ verb **1** *several barrels were tapped* **drain,** bleed, milk; broach, open.
2 *butlers were tapping ale* **pour (out),** draw off, siphon off, pump out, decant.
3 *their telephones are tapped* **bug,** wiretap, monitor, overhear, eavesdrop on, spy on.
4 *the resources were to be tapped for our benefit* **draw on,** exploit, milk, mine, use, utilize, turn to account.
– PHRASES **on tap 1** *beers on tap* **on draft,** from barrels, cask-conditioned. **2** informal *trained staff are on tap* **on hand,** at hand, available, ready, handy, accessible, standing by.

tap² ▶ verb **1** *she tapped on the door* **knock,** rap, strike, beat, drum.
2 *Dad tapped me on the knee* **pat,** hit, strike, slap, jab, poke, dig.
▶ noun **1** *a sharp tap at the door* **knock,** rap, drumming.
2 *a tap on the shoulder* **pat,** blow, slap, jab, poke, dig.

tape ▶ noun **1** *a package tied with tape* **binding,** ribbon, string, braid.
2 *secure the bandage with tape* **adhesive tape,** sticky tape, masking tape, duct tape; trademark Scotch Tape.
3 *they recorded the interview on tape* **audiocassette/videocassette,** (a) reel, (a) spool; video, VHS.
▶ verb **1** *a card was taped to the box* **bind,** stick, fix, fasten, secure, attach; tie, strap.
2 *they **taped off** the area* **cordon (off),** seal (off), close (off), shut (off), mark (off), fence (off); isolate, segregate.
3 *police taped his confession* **record,** tape-record, capture on tape; video.
4 *tape your ankle* **bind,** wrap, bandage.

taper ▶ verb **1** *the leaves taper at the tip* **narrow,** thin (out), come to a point, attenuate.
ANTONYMS thicken, swell.
2 *the meetings soon **tapered off*** **decrease,** lessen, dwindle, diminish, reduce, decline, die down, peter out, wane, ebb, slacken (off), fall off, let up, thin out.
ANTONYMS increase.

target ▶ noun **1** *targets at a range of 200 meters* **mark,** bull's-eye, goal.
2 *eagles can spot their target from half a mile* **prey,** quarry, game, kill.
3 *their profit target* **objective,** goal, aim, end; plan, intention, intent, design, aspiration, ambition, ideal, desire, wish.
4 *she was the target for a wave of abuse* **victim,** butt, recipient, focus, object, subject.
▶ verb **1** *he was targeted by a gunman* **pick out,** single out, earmark, fix on; attack, aim at, fire at.
2 *the product is **targeted at** a specific market* **aim at,** direct at, level at, intend for, focus on.
– PHRASES **on target 1** *the shot was on target* **accurate,** precise, unerring, sure, on the mark. **2** *the project was on target* **on schedule,** on track, on course, on time.

tariff ▶ noun *the lower tariffs across the border* **tax,** duty, toll, excise, levy, charge, rate, fee, countervail; price list.

tarnish ▶ verb **1** *gold does not tarnish easily* **discolor,** rust, oxidize, corrode, stain, dull, blacken.
ANTONYMS polish, brighten.
2 *it tarnished his reputation* **sully,** blacken, stain, blemish, blot, taint, soil, ruin, disgrace, mar, damage, harm, hurt, undermine, dishonor, stigmatize; literary besmirch.
ANTONYMS enhance.
▶ noun **1** *the tarnish on the candlesticks* **discoloration,** oxidation, rust; film.
2 *the tarnish on his reputation* **smear,** stain, blemish, blot, taint, stigma.

tart ▶ noun *a lemon tart* **pastry,** flan, tartlet, quiche, pie.

task ▶ noun *a daunting task* **job,** duty, chore, charge, assignment, detail, mission, engagement, occupation, undertaking, exercise, business, responsibility, burden, endeavor, enterprise, venture.
– PHRASES **take someone to task** *Bryce took me to task for having "borrowed" his car* **rebuke,** reprimand, reprove, reproach, remonstrate with, upbraid, scold, berate, castigate, lecture, censure, criticize, admonish, chide, chasten, arraign; informal tell off, bawl out, give someone a dressing-down.

taste ▶ noun **1** *a distinctive sharp taste* **flavor,** savor, relish, tang, smack.
2 *he was dying for a taste of brandy* **mouthful,** drop, bit, sip, nip, swallow, touch, soupçon, dash, modicum.
3 *it's too sweet for my taste* **palate,** taste buds, appetite, stomach.
4 *a taste for adventure* **liking,** love, fondness, fancy, desire, preference, penchant, predilection, inclination, partiality; hankering, appetite, hunger, thirst, relish.
ANTONYMS dislike.
5 *my first* ***taste of*** *prison* **experience of/with,** impression of; exposure to, contact with, involvement with.
6 *the house was furnished with taste* **judgment,** discrimination, discernment, tastefulness, refinement, finesse, elegance, grace, style.
ANTONYMS tastelessness, tackiness.
7 *the photo was rejected on grounds of taste* **decorum,** propriety, etiquette, politeness, delicacy, nicety, sensitivity, discretion, tastefulness.
ANTONYMS dislike.
▶ verb **1** *Adam tasted the wine* **sample,** test, try, savor; sip, sup.
2 *he could taste blood on his lip* **perceive,** discern, make out, distinguish.
3 *a beer that* ***tasted of*** *pumpkin* **have a/the flavor of,** savor of, smack of, be reminiscent of; suggest.
4 *it'll be good to taste real coffee again* **consume,** drink, partake of; eat, devour.
5 *he tasted defeat* **experience,** encounter, come face to face with, come up against, undergo; know.

tasteful ▶ adjective *the decor is simple and tasteful* **aesthetically pleasing,** in good taste, refined, cultured, elegant, stylish, smart, chic, attractive, exquisite.
ANTONYMS tasteless, tacky.

tasteless ▶ adjective **1** *the vegetables are tasteless* **flavorless,** bland, insipid, unappetizing, savorless, watery, weak.
ANTONYMS tasty, appetizing.
2 *tasteless leather paneling* **vulgar,** crude, tawdry, garish, gaudy, loud, trashy, showy, ostentatious, cheap, chintzy, kitschy, kitsch, inelegant; informal tacky.
ANTONYMS refined, tasteful.
3 *a tasteless remark* **crude,** vulgar, indelicate, uncouth, unseemly, crass, tactless, gauche, undiplomatic, indiscreet, inappropriate, offensive.
ANTONYMS tasteful, seemly.

tasty ▶ adjective *a tasty meal* **delicious,** palatable, luscious, mouthwatering, delectable, ambrosial, toothsome, dainty, flavorful; appetizing, tempting; informal yummy, scrumptious, finger-licking, lip-smacking, melt-in-your/the-mouth.
ANTONYMS bland, insipid.

tattle ▶ verb **1** *we were tattling about him* **gossip,** chatter, chat, prattle, babble, jabber, gabble, rattle on; informal chinwag, jaw, yak, gab, natter, tittle-tattle, chitchat.
2 *I would tattle on her if I had evidence* **inform;** report, talk, tell all, spill the beans; informal squeal, sing, let the cat out of the bag.
▶ noun *tabloid tattle* **gossip,** rumor, tittle-tattle, hearsay, scandal.

taunt ▶ noun *the taunts of his classmates* **jeer,** jibe, sneer, insult, barb, catcall; informal dig, put-down; (**taunts**) teasing, provocation, goading, derision, mockery.
▶ verb *she taunted him about his job* **jeer at,** sneer at, scoff at, poke fun at, make fun of, get at, insult, tease, chaff, torment, goad, ridicule, deride, mock, heckle, ride; informal rib, needle.

taut ▶ adjective **1** *the rope was taut* **tight,** stretched, rigid.
ANTONYMS slack, loose.
2 *her muscles remained taut* **flexed,** tense, hard, solid, firm, rigid, stiff.
ANTONYMS relaxed.
3 *a taut expression* **fraught,** strained, stressed, tense; informal uptight.

tautology ▶ noun *avoid such tautology as "let's all work together, everyone, as a team" by saying simply "let's work together"* **pleonasm,** repetition, reiteration, redundancy, superfluity, duplication.

tawdry ▶ adjective *the tawdry rings she wore on her fingers* **gaudy,** flashy, showy, garish, loud; tasteless, vulgar, trashy, junky, shoddy, shabby, gimcrack, chintzy, kitsch, kitsch; informal tacky, cheesy, schlocky.
ANTONYMS tasteful.

tax ▶ noun **1** *they have to pay tax on the interest* **duty,** tariff, excise, customs, dues; levy, toll, impost, tithe, charge, fee.
ANTONYMS rebate.
2 *a heavy tax on one's attention* **burden,** load, weight, demand, strain, pressure, stress, drain, imposition.
▶ verb **1** *they tax foreign companies more harshly* **charge (duty on),** tithe; formal mulct.
2 *his whining taxed her patience* **strain,** stretch, overburden, overload, encumber, push too far; overwhelm, try, wear out, exhaust, sap, drain, weary, weaken.

taxing ▶ adjective *restaurant work can be taxing* **demanding,** exacting, challenging, burdensome, arduous, onerous, difficult, hard, tough, laborious, back-breaking, strenuous, rigorous, punishing; tiring, exhausting, enervating, wearing, stressful; informal murderous.
ANTONYMS easy.

teach ▶ verb **1** *Alison teaches small children* **educate,** instruct, school, tutor, coach, train; enlighten, illuminate, verse, edify, indoctrinate;

drill, discipline.
2 *I taught yoga* **give lessons in,** lecture in, be a teacher of; demonstrate, instill, inculcate.
3 *she taught me how to love* **train,** show, guide, instruct, explain to, demonstrate to.

teacher ▶ noun *the new physics teacher used to be a nun* **educator,** tutor, instructor, master, mistress, governess, educationist, preceptor; coach, trainer; lecturer, professor, don; guide, mentor, guru, counselor; substitute teacher, sub; informal teach; formal pedagogue; historical schoolman, schoolmarm.

team ▶ noun **1** *the sales team* **group,** squad, company, party, crew, troupe, band, side, lineup, phalanx; informal bunch, gang, posse.
2 *a team of horses* **pair,** span, yoke, duo, set, tandem.
▶ verb **1** *the horses are teamed in pairs* **harness,** yoke, hitch, couple.
2 *you could* ***team up*** *with another artist for an exhibition* **join (forces),** collaborate, get together, work together; unite, combine, cooperate, link, ally, associate.

tear[1] ▶ verb **1** *I tore up the letter* **rip up,** rip in two, pull to pieces, shred.
2 *his flesh was torn* **lacerate,** cut (open), gash, slash, scratch, hack, pierce, stab; injure, wound.
3 *the traumas* ***tore*** *her family* ***apart*** **divide,** split, sever, break up, disunite, rupture; literary rend, sunder, cleave.
ANTONYMS unite.
4 *Gina tore the book from his hands* **snatch,** grab, seize, rip, wrench, wrest, pull, pluck; informal yank.
5 informal *Jack tore down the street* **sprint,** race, run, dart, rush, dash, hasten, hurry, bolt, fly, career, charge, shoot, hurtle, careen, speed, whiz, zoom, go like lightning, go like the wind; informal pelt, scoot, hotfoot it, belt, zip, whip, bomb, hightail it.
ANTONYMS stroll, amble.
▶ noun *a tear in her dress* **rip,** hole, split, slash, slit; snag.
– PHRASES **tear down** *they tore down the old barn* **demolish,** knock down, raze, raze to the ground, flatten, level, bulldoze; dismantle, disassemble.

tear[2] ▶ noun *tears in her eyes* **teardrop**; drop, droplet.
– PHRASES **in tears** *he was nearly in tears* **crying,** weeping, sobbing, wailing, howling, bawling, whimpering; tearful, upset; informal weepy, teary, blubbering.

tearful ▶ adjective **1** *Bess was tearful* **in tears,** with tears in one's eyes, choked up, crying, weeping, sobbing, sniveling; close to tears, emotional, upset, distressed, sad, unhappy; informal weepy, teary, misty-eyed; formal lachrymose.
ANTONYMS laughing, smiling.
2 *a tearful farewell* **emotional,** upsetting, distressing, sad, heartbreaking, sorrowful; poignant, moving, touching, tear-jerking; literary dolorous.
ANTONYMS cheerful.

tease ▶ verb *Larry's dentist is the dork he used to tease in sixth grade* **make fun of,** poke fun at, laugh at, guy, make a monkey (out) of; taunt, bait, goad, pick on; deride, mock, ridicule; informal rib, josh, pull/yank someone's chain, razz.

technical ▶ adjective **1** *an important technical achievement* practical, scientific, technological, high-tech.
2 *this might seem very technical* **specialist,** specialized, scientific; complex, complicated, esoteric.
3 *a technical fault* **mechanical.**

technique ▶ noun **1** *different techniques for solving the problem* **method,** approach, procedure, system, modus operandi, MO, way; means, strategy, tack, tactic, line; routine, practice.
2 *I was impressed with his technique* **skill,** ability, proficiency, expertise, mastery, talent, genius, artistry, craftsmanship; aptitude, adroitness, deftness, dexterity, facility, competence; performance, delivery; informal know-how.

tedious ▶ adjective *work on the assembly line was tedious* **boring,** dull, monotonous, repetitive, unrelieved, unvaried, uneventful; characterless, colorless, lifeless, insipid, uninteresting, unexciting, uninspiring, flat, bland, dry, stale, tired, lackluster, stodgy, dreary, mundane, monochrome; mind-numbing, soul-destroying, wearisome, tiring, tiresome, irksome, trying, frustrating; informal deadly, not up to much, humdrum, ho-hum, blah, dullsville, 'same old, same old'.
ANTONYMS exciting.

tedium ▶ noun **1** *she loathed the tedium of housework* **monotony,** boredom, ennui, uniformity, routine, dreariness, dryness, banality, vapidity, insipidity.
ANTONYMS variety.
2 *I dozed off during the tedium of the third act* **tedious passage,** tedious moments, tedious period of time, flatness, longueur.

teem ▶ verb *the pond once* ***teemed with*** *fish* **be full of,** be filled with, be alive with, be brimming with, abound in, be swarming with, be aswarm with; be packed with, be crawling with, be overrun by, bristle with, seethe with, be thick with; be jam-packed with, be chock-full of.

teenage ▶ adjective *a teenage hairstyle* **adolescent,** teenaged, youthful, young, juvenile; informal teen.

teenager ▶ noun *he's been counseling teenagers for twenty years* **adolescent,** youth, young person, minor, juvenile; informal teen, teenybopper.

teeter ▶ verb **1** *Daisy teetered toward them* **totter,** wobble, toddle, sway, stagger, stumble, reel, lurch, pitch.
2 *the situation teetered between tragedy and farce* **seesaw,** veer, fluctuate, oscillate, swing, alternate, waver.

telegram ▶ noun historical *the message arrived by telegram* telex; informal wire; dated radiogram; historical cable, cablegram.

telepathy ▶ noun *he claims he knew about Dylan's past through telepathy* **mind-reading,** thought transference; extrasensory perception,

ESP; clairvoyance, sixth sense; psychometry.

telephone ▸ noun *she picked up the telephone* **phone,** cell phone, cellular phone, cell; handset, receiver; informal blower, horn.
▸ verb *he telephoned me last night* **phone,** call, ring; get, reach; dated dial; informal call up, give someone a buzz, get on the blower to, get someone on the horn.

telescope ▸ noun *a pocket telescope* **spyglass,** glass; informal scope.
▸ verb **1** *the front of the car was telescoped* **concertina,** compact, compress, crush, squash.
2 *his recent employment experience can be telescoped into a short paragraph* **condense,** shorten, reduce, abbreviate, abridge, summarize, précis, abstract, shrink, consolidate; truncate, curtail.

television ▸ noun *what's on television this evening?* **TV**; informal the small screen, the idiot box, the tube, the boob tube, the box.

tell ▸ verb **1** *why didn't you tell me before?* **inform,** notify, apprise, let know, make aware, acquaint with, advise, put in the picture, brief, fill in; alert, warn; informal clue in/up.
2 *she told the story slowly* **relate,** recount, narrate, unfold, report, recite, describe, sketch, weave, spin; utter, voice, state, declare, communicate, impart, divulge.
3 *she told him to leave* **instruct,** order, command, direct, charge, enjoin, call on, require; literary bid.
4 *I tell you, I did nothing wrong* **assure,** promise, give one's word, swear, guarantee.
5 *the figures tell a different story* **reveal,** show, indicate, be evidence of, disclose, convey, signify.
6 *promise you won't tell?* **give the game away,** talk, tell tales, tattle; informal spill the beans, let the cat out of the bag, blab.
7 *she was bound to* **tell on** *him* **inform on,** tell tales on, give away, denounce, sell out; informal blow the whistle on, rat on, squeal on, finger.
8 *it was hard to tell what he said* **ascertain,** determine, work out, make out, deduce, discern, perceive, see, identify, recognize, understand, comprehend; informal figure out; Brit. informal suss out.
9 *he couldn't tell one from the other* **distinguish,** differentiate, discriminate.
10 *the strain began to* **tell on** *him* **take its toll,** leave its mark; affect.
– PHRASES **tell off** informal *oh, brother, did he ever tell you off* See **REPRIMAND** (verb).

telling ▸ adjective *a telling critique of the military mind* **revealing,** significant, weighty, important, meaningful, influential, striking, potent, powerful, compelling.
ANTONYMS insignificant.

telltale ▸ adjective *the telltale blush on her face* **revealing,** revelatory, suggestive, meaningful, significant, meaning; informal giveaway.

temerity ▸ noun *I doubt they'll have the temerity to print these accusations* **audacity,** nerve, effrontery, impudence, impertinence, cheek, gall, presumption; daring; informal face, front, neck, chutzpah.

CHOOSE THE RIGHT WORD

temerity, audacity, effrontery, foolhardiness, gall, impetuosity, rashness

The line that divides boldness from foolishness or stupidity is often a fine one. Someone who rushes hastily into a situation without thinking about the consequences might be accused of **rashness**, while **temerity** implies exposing oneself needlessly to danger while failing to estimate one's chances of success (*she had the temerity to criticize her teacher in front of the class*). **Audacity** describes a different kind of boldness, one that disregards moral standards or social conventions (*he had the audacity to ask her if she would mind paying for the trip*). Someone who behaves with **foolhardiness** is reckless or downright foolish (*climbing the mountain after dark was foolhardiness and everyone knew it*), while **impetuosity** describes an eager impulsiveness or behavior that is sudden, rash, and sometimes violent (*his impetuosity had landed him in trouble before*). **Gall** and **effrontery** are always derogatory terms. *Effrontery* is a more formal word for the flagrant disregard of the rules of propriety and courtesy (*she had the effrontery to call the president by his first name*), while *gall* is more colloquial and suggests outright insolence (*he was the only one who had the gall to tell the boss off*).

temper ▸ noun **1** *he walked out in a temper* **fit of rage,** rage, fury, fit of pique, tantrum, bad mood, mood, sulk, huff; informal grump, snit, hissy fit.
2 *a display of temper* **anger,** fury, rage, annoyance, vexation, irritation, irritability, ill humor, spleen, pique, petulance, testiness, tetchiness, touchiness, crabbiness; literary ire, choler.
3 *she struggled to keep her temper* **composure,** equanimity, self-control, self-possession, sangfroid, calm, good humor; informal cool.
▸ verb **1** *the steel is tempered by heat* **harden,** strengthen, toughen, fortify, anneal.
2 *their idealism is tempered with realism* **moderate,** modify, modulate, mitigate, alleviate, reduce, weaken, lighten, soften. See note at **ALLEVIATE**.
– PHRASES **lose one's temper** *calm down, there's no need to lose your temper* **get angry,** fly into a rage, erupt, lose control, go berserk, breathe fire, flare up, boil over; informal go mad, go crazy, go bananas, have a fit, see red, fly off the handle, blow one's top, hit the roof, go off the deep end, go ape, flip, freak out.

temperament ▸ noun *Haley's dog has the nicest temperament* **disposition,** nature, character, personality, makeup, constitution, mind, spirit; stamp, mettle, mold; mood, frame of mind, attitude, outlook, humor.

temperamental ▸ adjective **1** *a temperamental chef* **volatile,** excitable, emotional, mercurial,

capricious, erratic, unpredictable, changeable, inconsistent; hotheaded, fiery, quick-tempered, irritable, irascible, impatient; touchy, moody, sensitive, oversensitive, high-strung, neurotic, melodramatic.
ANTONYMS placid.
2 *a temperamental dislike of conflict* **inherent,** innate, natural, inborn, constitutional, deep-rooted, ingrained, congenital.

temperance ▶ noun *a strict advocate of temperance* **teetotalism,** abstinence, abstention, sobriety, self-restraint; prohibition. See note at ABSTINENCE.
ANTONYMS alcoholism.

temperate ▶ adjective **1** *temperate climates* **mild,** clement, benign, gentle, balmy.
ANTONYMS extreme.
2 *he was temperate in his consumption of food* **self-restrained,** restrained, moderate, self-controlled, disciplined; abstemious, self-denying, austere, ascetic; teetotal, abstinent.
ANTONYMS immoderate.

tempest ▶ noun *the skies opened and a tempest erupted* **storm,** gale, hurricane; tornado, whirlwind, cyclone, typhoon.

tempestuous ▶ adjective **1** *the fair weather passed and the day became tempestuous* **stormy,** blustery, squally, wild, turbulent, windy, gusty, blowy, rainy; foul, nasty, inclement.
ANTONYMS calm, fine.
2 *the tempestuous political environment* **turbulent,** stormy, tumultuous, wild, lively, heated, explosive, feverish, frenetic, frenzied.
ANTONYMS peaceful.
3 *a tempestuous woman* **emotional,** passionate, impassioned, fiery, intense; temperamental, volatile, excitable, mercurial, capricious, unpredictable, quick-tempered.
ANTONYMS calm, placid.

temple ▶ noun *at the altar of the temple* **house of God,** house of worship, shrine, sanctuary; church, cathedral, mosque, synagogue, shul; archaic fane.

tempo ▶ noun **1** *the tempo of the music* **speed,** cadence, rhythm, beat, time, pulse; measure, meter.
2 *the tempo of life in Western society* **pace,** rate, speed, velocity.

temporal ▶ adjective *the temporal aspects of church government* **secular,** nonspiritual, worldly, profane, material, mundane, earthly, terrestrial; nonreligious, areligious, lay.
ANTONYMS spiritual.

temporarily ▶ adverb **1** *the girl was temporarily placed with a foster family* **for the time being,** for the moment, for now, for the present, in the interim, for the nonce, in/for the meantime, in the meanwhile; provisionally, pro tem; informal for the minute.
ANTONYMS permanently.
2 *he was temporarily blinded by the light* **briefly,** for a short time, momentarily, fleetingly.
ANTONYMS permanently.

temporary ▶ adjective **1** *temporary accommodations | the temporary captain* **nonpermanent,** short-term, interim; provisional, pro tem, makeshift, stopgap; acting, fill-in, stand-in, caretaker.
ANTONYMS permanent.
2 *a temporary loss of self-control* **brief,** short-lived, momentary, fleeting, passing.
ANTONYMS lasting.

CHOOSE THE RIGHT WORD

temporary, ephemeral, evanescent, fleeting, transient, transitory

Things that don't last long are called **temporary**, which emphasizes a measurable but limited duration (*a temporary appointment as chief of staff*). Something that is **fleeting** passes almost instantaneously and cannot be caught or held (*a fleeting thought; a fleeting glimpse*). **Transient** also applies to something that lasts or stays only a short time (*transient house guests*), while **transitory** refers to something that is destined to pass away or come to an end (*the transitory pleasure of eating*). **Evanescent** and **ephemeral** describe what is even more short-lived. *Ephemeral* literally means lasting for only a single day, but is often used to describe anything that is slight and perishable (*his fame was ephemeral*). *Evanescent* is a more lyrical word for whatever vanishes almost as soon as it appears. In other words, a job might be *temporary*, an emotion *fleeting*, a visitor *transient*, a woman's beauty *transitory*, and glory *ephemeral*, but the flash of a bird's wing across the sky would have to be called *evanescent*.

tempt ▶ verb **1** *the manager tried to tempt him to stay* **entice,** persuade, convince, inveigle, induce, cajole, coax, woo; informal sweet-talk.
ANTONYMS discourage, deter.
2 *more customers are being tempted by credit* **allure,** attract, appeal to, whet the appetite of; lure, seduce, beguile, tantalize, draw.
ANTONYMS repel, put off.

CHOOSE THE RIGHT WORD

tempt, allure, beguile, entice, inveigle, lure, seduce

When we are under the influence of a powerful attraction, particularly to something that is wrong or unwise, we are **tempted**. **Entice** implies that a crafty or skillful person has attracted us by offering a reward or pleasure (*she was enticed into joining the group by a personal plea from its handsome leader*), while **inveigle** suggests that we are enticed through the use of deception or cajolery (*inveigled into supporting the plan*). If someone **lures** us, it suggests that we have been tempted or influenced for fraudulent or destructive purposes or attracted to something harmful or evil (*lured by gang members*). **Allure** may also suggest that we have been deliberately tempted against our will, but the connotations here are often sexual (*allured by her dark green eyes*). **Seduce** carries heavy sexual connotations (*seduced by an older woman*), although it can simply mean prompted to action against our will (*seduced by a clever sales pitch*). While **beguile** at one time referred exclusively to the use of deception to lead someone astray, nowadays it can also refer to the use of subtle devices to lead someone on (*a local festival designed to beguile the tourists*).

temptation ▶ noun 1 *Mary resisted the temptation to answer back* **desire,** urge, itch, impulse, inclination.
2 *the temptations of Las Vegas* **lure,** allurement, enticement, seduction, attraction, draw, pull; siren song.
3 *the temptation of travel to exotic locations* **allure,** appeal, attraction, fascination.

tempting ▶ adjective 1 *a tempting opportunity* **enticing,** alluring, attractive, appealing, inviting, captivating, seductive, beguiling, fascinating, tantalizing; irresistible.
ANTONYMS off-putting, uninviting.
2 *a plate of tempting cakes* **appetizing,** mouthwatering, delicious, toothsome; informal scrumptious, yummy, lip-smacking.
ANTONYMS unappetizing.

tenable ▶ adjective *O'Leary's confession has certainly made Cohn's alibi more tenable* **defensible,** justifiable, supportable, sustainable, arguable, able to hold water, reasonable, sensible, rational, sound, viable, plausible, credible, believable, conceivable.
ANTONYMS indefensible.

tenacious ▶ adjective 1 *his tenacious grip* **firm,** tight, fast, clinging; strong, forceful, powerful, unshakable, immovable, iron.
ANTONYMS weak, loose.
2 *a tenacious opponent* **persevering,** persistent, determined, dogged, strong-willed, tireless, indefatigable, resolute, patient, unflagging, staunch, steadfast, untiring, unwavering, unswerving, unshakable, unyielding, insistent; stubborn, intransigent, obstinate, obdurate, stiff-necked; rock-ribbed; pertinacious.
ANTONYMS irresolute.

tenacity ▶ noun *she practices her gymnastics routine with the tenacity of a bulldog* **persistence,** determination, perseverance, doggedness, strength of purpose, tirelessness, indefatigability, resolution, resoluteness, resolve, firmness, patience, purposefulness, staunchness, steadfastness, staying power, endurance, stamina, stubbornness, intransigence, obstinacy, obduracy, pertinacity. See note at COURAGE.

tenant ▶ noun *the tenants' rent is due on the first of each month* **occupant,** resident, inhabitant; renter, leaseholder, lessee, lodger, roomer; squatter.
ANTONYMS owner, freeholder.

tend[1] ▶ verb 1 *I tend to get very involved in my work* **be inclined,** be apt, be disposed, be prone, be liable, have a tendency, have a propensity.
2 *some of the younger voters tended toward the tabloid press* **incline,** lean, gravitate, move; prefer, favor, trend.

tend[2] ▶ verb *she tended her garden* **look after,** take care of, care for, minister to, attend to, see to, wait on; watch over, keep an eye on, mind, protect, watch, guard, supervise; nurse, nurture, cherish.
ANTONYMS neglect.

tendency ▶ noun 1 *his tendency to take the law into his own hands* **propensity,** proclivity, proneness, aptness, likelihood, inclination, disposition, predisposition, bent, leaning, penchant, predilection, susceptibility, liability; readiness; habit.
2 *this tendency toward cohabitation* **trend,** movement, drift, swing, gravitation, direction, course; orientation, bias.

tender[1] ▶ adjective 1 *a gentle, tender man* **caring,** kind, kindly, kindhearted, softhearted, tenderhearted, compassionate, sympathetic, warm, warmhearted, solicitous, fatherly, motherly, maternal, gentle, mild, benevolent, generous, giving, humane.
ANTONYMS hard-hearted, callous.
2 *a tender kiss* **affectionate,** fond, loving, emotional, warm, gentle, soft; amorous, adoring; informal lovey-dovey.
3 *simmer until the meat is tender* **easily chewed,** chewable, soft; succulent, juicy; tenderized, fork-tender.
ANTONYMS tough.
4 *tender plants* **delicate,** easily damaged, fragile, vulnerable.
ANTONYMS hardy.
5 *her ankle was swollen and tender* **sore,** painful, sensitive, inflamed, raw, red, chafed, bruised, irritated; hurting, aching, throbbing, smarting.
6 *the tender age of fifteen* **young,** youthful, early; impressionable, inexperienced, immature, unseasoned, juvenile, callow, green, raw, unripe, wet behind the ears.
ANTONYMS advanced.
7 *the issue of conscription was a particularly tender one* **difficult,** delicate, touchy, tricky, awkward, problematic, troublesome, thorny, ticklish; controversial, emotive; informal sticky.
ANTONYMS straightforward.

tender[2] ▶ verb 1 *she tendered her resignation* **offer,** proffer, present, put forward, propose, suggest, advance, submit, extend, give, render; hand in.
2 *firms of interior decorators tendered for the work* **put in a bid,** bid, quote, give an estimate.
▶ noun *six contractors were invited to submit tenders* **bid,** offer, quotation, quote, estimate, price; proposal, submission, pitch.

tenderness ▶ noun 1 *I felt an enormous tenderness for her* **affection,** fondness, love, devotion, loving kindness, emotion, sentiment.
2 *with unexpected tenderness, he told her what had happened* **kindness,** kindliness, kindheartedness, tenderheartedness, compassion, care, concern, sympathy, humanity, warmth, fatherliness, motherliness, gentleness, benevolence, generosity.
3 *abdominal tenderness* **soreness,** pain,

inflammation, irritation, bruising; ache, aching, smarting, throbbing.

tenet ▶ noun *the fundamental tenet of Marxism* **principle,** belief, doctrine, precept, creed, credo, article of faith, axiom, dogma, canon; theory, thesis, premise, conviction, idea, view, opinion, position; (**tenets**) ideology, code of belief, teaching(s).

tenor ▶ noun **1** *the general tenor of his speech* **sense,** meaning, theme, drift, thread, import, purport, intent, intention, burden, thrust, significance, message; gist, tone, essence, substance, spirit, feel.
2 *the even tenor of life in the village* **course,** direction, movement, drift, current, trend.

tense ▶ adjective **1** *the tense muscles of his neck* **taut,** tight, rigid, stretched, strained, stiff.
ANTONYMS slack, loose.
2 *Loretta was feeling tense and irritable* **anxious,** nervous, on edge, edgy, antsy, strained, stressed, under pressure, agitated, ill at ease, fretful, uneasy, restless, strung out, worked up, wound up, keyed up, overwrought, jumpy, on tenterhooks, with one's stomach in knots, worried, apprehensive, panicky; informal uptight, het up, stressed out, jittery, twitchy, squirrelly, in a state, a bundle of nerves.
ANTONYMS relaxed, calm.
3 *a tense moment* **nerve-racking,** stressful, anxious, worrying, fraught, charged, strained, nail-biting, suspenseful, uneasy, difficult, uncomfortable; exciting, cliffhanging, knife-edge; informal hairy, white-knuckle.
ANTONYMS relaxing.
▶ verb *Hebden tensed his muscles* **tighten,** tauten, tense up, flex, contract, brace, stiffen; screw up, knot, strain, stretch, squinch up.
ANTONYMS relax.

tension ▶ noun **1** *the tension of the rope* **tightness,** tautness, rigidity; pull, traction.
2 *the tension was unbearable* **strain,** stress, anxiety, pressure; worry, apprehensiveness, apprehension, agitation, nerves, nervousness, jumpiness, edginess, restlessness; suspense, uncertainty, anticipation, excitement; informal heebie-jeebies, butterflies (in one's stomach), collywobbles.
3 *months of tension between the military and the government* **strained relations,** strain; ill feeling, friction, antagonism, antipathy, hostility, enmity.

tentative ▶ adjective **1** *tentative arrangements | a tentative conclusion* **provisional,** unconfirmed, penciled in, iffy, preliminary, to be confirmed, subject to confirmation; speculative, conjectural, sketchy, untried, unproven, exploratory, experimental, trial, test, pilot.
ANTONYMS definite.
2 *he took a few tentative steps* **hesitant,** uncertain, cautious, timid, hesitating, faltering, shaky, unsteady, halting; wavering, unsure.
ANTONYMS confident.

tenterhooks ▶ plural noun
– PHRASES **on tenterhooks** *she's been on tenterhooks ever since the job interview* **in suspense,** waiting with bated breath; anxious, nervous, apprehensive, worried, worried sick, on edge, edgy, antsy, tense, strained, stressed, agitated, restless, worked up, keyed up, jumpy, with one's stomach in knots, with one's heart in one's mouth; informal with butterflies in one's stomach, jittery, twitchy, in a state, uptight, het up; squirrelly.

tenuous ▶ adjective **1** *a tenuous connection* **slight,** insubstantial, meager, flimsy, weak, doubtful, dubious, questionable, suspect; vague, nebulous, hazy.
ANTONYMS convincing, strong.
2 *a tenuous thread* **fine,** thin, slender, delicate, wispy, gossamer, fragile.
ANTONYMS thick, strong.

tepid ▶ adjective **1** *tepid water* **lukewarm,** warmish, slightly warm; at room temperature.
ANTONYMS hot, cold.
2 *a tepid response* **unenthusiastic,** apathetic, muted, halfhearted, so-so, 'comme ci, comme ça', indifferent, subdued, cool, lukewarm, uninterested, unenthused.
ANTONYMS passionate, enthusiastic.

term ▶ noun **1** *scientific and technical terms* **word,** expression, phrase, turn of phrase, idiom, locution; name, title, designation, label, moniker; formal appellation, denomination, descriptor.
2 (**terms**) *a protest in the strongest terms* **language,** mode of expression, manner of speaking, phraseology, terminology; words, expressions.
3 (**terms**) *the terms of the contract* **conditions,** stipulations, specifications, provisions, provisos, qualifications, particulars, small print, details, points.
4 (**terms**) *a policy offering more favorable terms* **rates,** prices, charges, costs, fees; tariff.
5 *the director is elected for a two-year term* **period,** period of time, time, length of time, spell, stint, duration; stretch, run; period of office, incumbency.
6 archaic *the whole term of your natural life* **duration,** length, span.
7 *the summer term* **session,** semester, trimester, quarter; intersession.
▶ verb *he has been termed the father of modern theology* **call,** name, entitle, title, style, designate, describe as, dub, label, brand, tag, bill, nickname; formal denominate.
– PHRASES **come to terms 1** *the two sides came to terms* **reach an agreement/understanding,** make a deal, reach a compromise, meet each other halfway. **2** *she eventually came to terms with her situation* **accept,** come to accept, reconcile oneself to, learn to live with, become resigned to, make the best of; face up to.

terminal ▶ adjective **1** *a terminal illness* **incurable,** untreatable, inoperable; fatal, mortal, deadly; Medicine immedicable.
2 *terminal patients* **incurable,** dying; near death, on one's deathbed, on one's last legs, with one foot in the grave.
3 *a terminal bonus may be payable when a policy matures* **final,** last, concluding, closing, end.
▶ noun **1** *a railroad terminal* **station,** last stop, end of the line; depot; chiefly Brit. terminus.
2 *a computer terminal* **workstation,** VDT, visual display terminal.

terminate ▸ verb **1** *the project was terminated* **bring to an end,** end, abort, curtail, bring to a close/conclusion, close, conclude, finish, stop, put an end to, wind up, wrap up, discontinue, cease, kill, cut short, ax; informal pull the plug on, can.
ANTONYMS begin, start, continue.
2 *ten employees were terminated* **fire,** ax; downsize; informal can, cut.
ANTONYMS hire.
3 *this bus terminates at Granville Street* **end its journey,** finish up, stop.

termination ▸ noun *the termination of the after-school music program* **ending,** end, closing, close, conclusion, finish, stopping, winding up, discontinuance, discontinuation; cancellation, dissolution; informal windup.
ANTONYMS start, beginning.

terminology ▸ noun *medical terminology* **phraseology,** terms, expressions, words, language, lexicon, parlance, vocabulary, wording, nomenclature; usage, idiom; jargon, cant, argot; informal lingo, -speak, -ese.

terrible ▸ adjective **1** *a terrible crime | terrible injuries* **dreadful,** awful, appalling, horrific, horrifying, horrible, horrendous, atrocious, abominable, deplorable, egregious, abhorrent, frightful, shocking, hideous, ghastly, grim, dire, unspeakable, gruesome, monstrous, sickening, heinous, vile; serious, grave, acute; formal grievous.
ANTONYMS minor, negligible.
2 *a terrible smell* **repulsive,** disgusting, awful, dreadful, ghastly, horrid, horrible, vile, foul, abominable, frightful, loathsome, revolting, nasty, odious, nauseating, repellent, horrendous, hideous, appalling, offensive, objectionable, obnoxious, gruesome, putrid, noisome, yucky, godawful, gross.
ANTONYMS nice, delightful, pleasant.
3 *he was in terrible pain* **severe,** extreme, intense, acute, excruciating, agonizing, unbearable, intolerable, unendurable.
ANTONYMS slight.
4 *that's a terrible thing to say* **unkind,** nasty, unpleasant, foul, obnoxious, vile, contemptible, despicable, wretched, shabby; spiteful, mean, malicious, poisonous, mean-spirited, cruel, hateful, hurtful; unfair, uncharitable, uncalled for, below the belt, unwarranted.
ANTONYMS kind, nice.
5 *the movie was terrible* **very bad,** dreadful, awful, deplorable, atrocious, hopeless, worthless, useless, poor, pathetic, pitiful, lamentable, appalling, abysmal; informal lame, lousy, brutal, painful, crappy.
ANTONYMS brilliant, excellent.
6 *I feel terrible. I've been in bed all day* **ill,** sick, queasy, poorly, unwell, nauseous, nauseated, peaked, green around the gills; dizzy, groggy; informal under the weather, lousy, crummy, awful, dreadful, crappy; rare peakish.
ANTONYMS well.
7 *she still feels terrible about what she did to John* **guilty,** conscience-stricken, remorseful, guilt-ridden, ashamed, chastened, contrite, sorry, sick, bad, awful.
ANTONYMS untroubled, unashamed.

terribly ▸ adverb **1** *she's not terribly upset* **very,** extremely, particularly, hugely, intensely, really, terrifically, tremendously, immensely, dreadfully, incredibly, remarkably, extraordinarily, seriously; informal real, mighty, awful, majorly.
2 *he played terribly* **very badly,** atrociously, deplorably, awfully, dreadfully, appallingly, execrably, abysmally, pitifully.
3 *I shall miss you terribly* **very much,** greatly, a great deal, a lot; informal tons, loads, big time.

terrific ▸ adjective **1** *a terrific all-star cast* **marvelous,** wonderful, sensational, outstanding, great, superb, excellent, first-rate, first-class, dazzling, out of this world, breathtaking; fantastic, fabulous, super, blue-ribbon, magic; informal cool, wicked, awesome, bang-up, dandy, mean.
2 *a terrific bang* **tremendous,** huge, massive, enormous, gigantic, colossal, mighty, great, prodigious, formidable, monstrous, sizable, considerable; intense, extreme, extraordinary; informal whopping, humongous; deafening.

terrify ▸ verb *that crazy driver terrified us* **petrify,** horrify, frighten, scare, scare stiff, scare/frighten to death, scare/frighten the living daylights out of, scare/frighten the life out of, scare/frighten someone out of their wits, scare witless, strike terror into, put the fear of God into; terrorize, paralyze, transfix; informal scare the pants off, scare the bejesus out of.

territory ▸ noun **1** *the island is a U.S. territory* **area,** area of land, region, enclave; country, state, land, colony, dominion, protectorate, fief, dependency, possession, jurisdiction, holding; section, turf.
2 *mountainous territory* **terrain,** land, ground, countryside.
3 *linguistic puzzles are Stina's territory* **domain,** area of concern/interest/knowledge, province, department, field, preserve, bailiwick, sphere, arena, realm, world.

terror ▸ noun **1** *she screamed in terror* **extreme fear,** dread, horror, fear and trembling, fright, alarm, panic.
2 informal *that child is a little terror* **rascal,** rogue, rapscallion, devil, imp, monkey, mischief-maker, troublemaker, scalawag, scamp; informal holy terror, horror, hellion, varmint; archaic scapegrace.

terrorize ▸ verb *terrorized by racist thugs* **persecute,** victimize, torment, harass, tyrannize, intimidate, menace, threaten, bully, browbeat; scare, frighten, terrify, petrify.

terse ▸ adjective *we were offended by her terse answers* **brief,** short, to the point, concise, succinct, crisp, pithy, incisive, trenchant, short and sweet, laconic, elliptical; **brusque,** abrupt, curt, clipped, blunt, pointed, ungracious, gruff.
ANTONYMS long-winded, polite.

CHOOSE THE RIGHT WORD

terse, concise, laconic, pithy, succinct

If you don't like to mince words, you'll make every effort to be **concise** in both your writing and speaking, which means to remove all superfluous details (*a concise summary of everything that happened*). **Succinct** is very close in meaning to *concise*, although it emphasizes compression and compactness in addition to brevity (*succinct instructions for what to do in an emergency*). If you're **laconic**, you are brief to the point of being curt, brusque, or even uncommunicative (*his laconic reply left many questions unanswered*). **Terse** can also mean clipped or abrupt (*a terse command*), but it usually connotes something that is both concise and polished (*a terse style of writing that was much admired*). A **pithy** statement is not only succinct but full of substance and meaning (*a pithy argument that no one could counter*).

test ▶ noun **1** *a series of scientific tests* **trial,** experiment, test case, case study, pilot study, trial run, tryout, dry run; check, examination, assessment, evaluation, appraisal, investigation, inspection, analysis, scrutiny, study, probe, exploration; screening; technical assay.
2 *candidates may be required to take a test* **exam,** examination, quiz.
▶ verb **1** *a small-scale prototype was tested* **try out,** put to the test, put through its paces, experiment with, pilot; check, examine, assess, evaluate, appraise, investigate, analyze, scrutinize, study, probe, explore, trial; sample; screen; technical assay.
2 *such behavior would test any marriage* **put a strain on,** strain, tax, try; make demands on, stretch, challenge.

testament ▶ noun *an achievement that is a testament to his professionalism and dedication* **testimony,** witness, evidence, proof, attestation; demonstration, indication, symbol, exemplification; monument, tribute.

testify ▶ verb **1** *you may be required to testify in court* **give evidence,** bear witness, be a witness, give one's testimony, attest; Law make a deposition.
2 *he testified that he had been threatened by a fellow officer* **attest,** swear, state on oath, state, declare, assert, affirm; allege, submit, claim; Law depose.
3 *the exhibits* **testify to** *the talents of the local sculptors* **be evidence/proof of,** attest to, confirm, prove, corroborate, substantiate, bear out; show, demonstrate, bear witness to, speak to, indicate, reveal, bespeak.

testimonial ▶ noun *a glowing testimonial* **recommendation,** reference, character reference, letter of recommendation, commendation, endorsement, blurb.

testimony ▶ noun **1** *Smith was in court to hear her testimony* **evidence,** sworn statement, attestation, affidavit; statement, declaration, assertion, affirmation; allegation, submission, claim; Law deposition.
2 *the work is a* **testimony to** *his professional commitment* **testament to,** proof of, evidence of, attestation to, witness to; confirmation of, verification of, corroboration of; demonstration of, illustration of, indication of.

testy ▶ adjective *what's made you so testy today?* **irritable,** tetchy, cranky, ornery, cantankerous, irascible, bad-tempered, grumpy, grouchy, crotchety, petulant, crabby, crusty, curmudgeonly, ill-tempered, ill-humored, peevish, cross, fractious, pettish, prickly, short-fused, waspish, snappish, snippy.
ANTONYMS good-humored.

tether ▶ verb *the horse had been tethered to a post* **tie,** tie up, hitch, rope, chain; fasten, bind, fetter, secure.
ANTONYMS unleash.
▶ noun *a dog on a tether* **rope,** chain, cord, leash, lead; restraint, fetter; halter.

text ▶ noun **1** *a text that explores pain and grief* **book,** work, written work, printed work, document.
2 *the pictures are clear and relate well to the text* **words,** wording, writing; content, body, main body; narrative, story.
3 *academic texts* **textbook,** book, material.
4 *a text from the First Book of Samuel* **passage,** extract, excerpt, quotation, verse, line; reading.

texture ▶ noun *the texture of the burlap is coarse and nubby* **feel,** touch; appearance, finish, surface, grain; quality, consistency; weave, nap.

thank ▶ verb *the boss thanked us for our special effort* **express (one's) gratitude to,** express one's thanks to, offer/extend thanks to, say thank you to, show one's appreciation to, credit, recognize, bless.

thankful ▶ adjective *she was thankful that the evening was over* **grateful,** appreciative, filled with gratitude, relieved.

thankless ▶ adjective **1** *a thankless task* **unenviable,** difficult, unpleasant, unrewarding; unappreciated, unrecognized, unacknowledged.
ANTONYMS rewarding.
2 *her thankless children* **ungrateful,** unappreciative, unthankful, ingrate.
ANTONYMS grateful.

thanks ▶ plural noun *they expressed their thanks and wished her well* **gratitude,** appreciation; acknowledgment, recognition, credit.
▶ exclamation *thanks for being so helpful* **thank you,** many thanks, thanks very much, thanks a lot, thank you kindly, much obliged, much appreciated, bless you; informal thanks a million.
– PHRASES **thanks to** *thanks to the untiring support of my wife, I've gotten back on my feet* **as a result of,** owing to, due to, because of, through, as a consequence of, on account of, by virtue of, by dint of, by reason of.

thaw ▶ verb *allow the ice cream to thaw for about ten minutes before folding in the other ingredients* **melt,** unfreeze, soften, liquefy, dissolve; defrost, warm.
ANTONYMS freeze.
▶ noun **1** *spring thaw* **runoff,** debacle, ice-out.
2 *a thaw in relations* **improvement,** relaxation, coming-to-terms, rapprochement.

theater ▶ noun **1** *the local theater* **playhouse,** auditorium, amphitheater; cinema, movie theater, movie house; dated nickelodeon.
2 *what made you want to go into* **the theater**? **acting,** performing, the stage; drama, the dramatic arts, dramaturgy, the thespian art;

show business, Broadway; informal the boards, show biz.
3 *the lecture theater* **hall,** room, auditorium.
4 *the Pacific theater of the war* **scene,** arena, field/sphere/place of action, setting, site.

theatrical ▶ **adjective 1** *a theatrical career* **stage,** dramatic, thespian, dramaturgical; show-business; informal show-biz; formal histrionic.
2 *Henry looked over his shoulder with theatrical caution* **exaggerated,** ostentatious, stagy, showy, melodramatic, overacted, overdone, histrionic, over-the-top, artificial, affected, mannered; informal hammy, ham, camp.

theft ▶ **noun** *the theft was reported on Thursday morning* **robbery,** stealing, thieving, larceny, thievery, shoplifting, burglary, misappropriation, appropriation, embezzlement; raid, holdup; informal heist, stickup; five-finger discount, rip-off; formal peculation.

theme ▶ **noun 1** *the theme of her speech* **subject,** topic, subject matter, matter, thesis, argument, text, burden, concern, thrust, message; thread, motif, keynote.
2 *the first violin takes up the theme* **melody,** tune, air; motif, leitmotif.
3 *the band played a medley of popular TV show themes* **song,** theme song, jingle.

then ▶ **adverb 1** *I was living in Cairo then* **at that time,** in those days; at that point (in time), at that moment, on that occasion.
2 *she won the first and then the second game* **next,** after that, afterward/afterward, subsequently, later.
3 *and then there's another problem* **in addition,** also, besides, as well, additionally, on top of that, over and above that, moreover, furthermore, what's more, to boot; too.
4 *well, if that's what he wants, then he should leave* **in that case,** that being so, it follows that.

theological ▶ **adjective** *theological writings* **religious,** scriptural, ecclesiastical, doctrinal; divine, holy.

theoretical ▶ **adjective** *it's just a theoretical situation* **hypothetical,** abstract, conjectural, academic, suppositional, speculative, notional, postulatory, what-if, assumed, presumed, untested, unproven, unsubstantiated.
ANTONYMS actual, real.

theorize ▶ **verb** *Darwin theorized that the atolls marked the sites of vanished volcanoes* **speculate,** conjecture, hypothesize, philosophize, postulate, propose, posit, suppose.

theory ▶ **noun 1** *I reckon that confirms my theory* **hypothesis,** thesis, conjecture, supposition, speculation, postulation, postulate, proposition, premise, surmise, assumption, presupposition; opinion, view, belief, contention.
2 *modern economic theory* **principles,** ideas, concepts; philosophy, ideology, system of ideas, science.
– PHRASES **in theory** *in theory, your idea sounds great, but can it be practically applied?* **in principle,** on paper, in the abstract, all things being equal, in an ideal world; hypothetically, theoretically, supposedly.

therapeutic ▶ **adjective** *the therapeutic effects of acupuncture* **healing,** curative, remedial, medicinal, restorative, salubrious, health-giving, tonic, reparative, corrective, beneficial, good, salutary.
ANTONYMS harmful.

therapy ▶ **noun 1** *a wide range of complementary therapies* **treatment,** remedy, cure.
2 *he's currently in therapy* **psychotherapy,** psychoanalysis, analysis, counseling.

thereabouts ▶ **adverb 1** *the land thereabouts* **near there,** around there, in that area.
2 *they sold it for five million* ***or thereabouts*** **approximately,** roughly, or so, give or take, plus or minus, in round numbers, in the ballpark of.

thereafter ▶ **adverb** *thereafter their fortunes suffered a deep decline* **after that,** following that, afterward/afterward, subsequently, then, next.

therefore ▶ **adverb** *Rodriguez was injured and therefore unable to play* **consequently,** so, as a result, hence, thus, accordingly, for that reason, ergo, that being the case, on that account; formal whence; archaic wherefore.

thesis ▶ **noun 1** *the central thesis of his lecture* **theory,** contention, argument, line of argument, proposal, proposition, idea, claim, premise, assumption, hypothesis, postulation, supposition.
2 *a doctoral thesis* **dissertation,** essay, paper, treatise, disquisition, composition, monograph, study.

thick ▶ **adjective 1** *the walls are five feet thick* **in extent/diameter,** across, wide, broad, deep.
2 *his short, thick legs* **stocky,** sturdy, stubby, chunky, blocky, hefty, thickset, burly, beefy, meaty, big, solid; fat, stout, plump.
ANTONYMS thin, slender.
3 *a thick winter sweater* **chunky,** bulky, heavy; cable-knit, woolly.
ANTONYMS thin, lightweight.
4 *the arena was thick with skaters* **crowded,** swarming, filled, packed, teeming, seething, buzzing, crawling, crammed, solid, overflowing, choked, jammed, congested; informal jam-packed, chockablock, stuffed.
5 *the thick summer vegetation* **plentiful,** abundant, profuse, luxuriant, bushy, rich, riotous, exuberant; rank, rampant; dense, impenetrable, impassable; informal jungly.
ANTONYMS meager, sparse.
6 *a thick paste* **viscous,** gooey, syrupy, firm, stiff, heavy; clotted, coagulated, viscid, semisolid, gelatinous; concentrated.
ANTONYMS runny, thin.
7 *thick fog* **dense,** heavy, opaque, impenetrable, soupy, murky.
ANTONYMS light.
8 informal *he's a bit thick* See **STUPID** (sense 1).
9 *Guy's voice was thick with desire* **husky,** hoarse, throaty, guttural, gravelly, rough.
ANTONYMS clear, shrill.
10 *a thick Scottish accent* **obvious,** pronounced, marked, broad, strong, rich, decided, distinct.
ANTONYMS faint, vague.
▶ **noun** *in the thick of the crisis* **midst,** center, hub, middle, core, heart.

thicken ▶ **verb** *stir the sauce as it thickens*

become **thick/thicker,** stiffen, condense; solidify, firm up, set, jell, congeal, clot, coagulate, cake, inspissate.

thicket ▶ noun *rabbits taking refuge in the thicket* **copse,** coppice, grove, brake, covert, clump; wood, woodlot, bush.

thickness ▶ noun **1** *the wall is several feet in thickness* **width,** breadth, depth, diameter.
2 *several thicknesses of limestone* **layer,** stratum, stratification, seam, vein; sheet, lamina.

thickset ▶ adjective *a thickset Caucasian male in his thirties* **stocky,** sturdy, big-boned, heavily built, well-built, chunky, burly, strapping, brawny, solid, blocky, heavy, hefty, beefy, meaty.
ANTONYMS slight.

thick-skinned ▶ adjective *these guards have gotten pretty thick-skinned over the years* **insensitive,** unfeeling, tough, hardened, callous, case-hardened; informal hard-boiled.
ANTONYMS sensitive.

thief ▶ noun *the thief is at large* **robber,** burglar, housebreaker, cat burglar, rustler, shoplifter, pickpocket, purse snatcher, sneak thief, mugger; embezzler, swindler, plunderer; criminal, villain; kleptomaniac; bandit, pirate, highwayman; informal crook; literary brigand.

thieve ▶ verb *before we were out of diapers, we were learning how to thieve anything that wasn't nailed down* **steal,** take, purloin, help oneself to, snatch, pilfer; embezzle, misappropriate; have one's fingers/hand in the till, rob; swipe, make off with, finagle, lift, "liberate", "borrow", filch, snaffle, pinch, heist; formal peculate.

thin ▶ adjective **1** *a thin white line* **narrow,** fine, attenuated.
ANTONYMS thick, broad.
2 *a thin cotton nightdress* **lightweight,** light, fine, delicate, floaty, flimsy, diaphanous, gossamer, insubstantial; sheer, gauzy, filmy, transparent, see-through; paper-thin.
ANTONYMS thick, heavy.
3 *a tall, thin woman* **slim,** lean, slender, rangy, willowy, svelte, sylphlike, spare, slight; **skinny,** underweight, scrawny, waiflike, scraggy, bony, angular, rawboned, hollow-cheeked, gaunt, skin-and-bones, emaciated, skeletal, wasted, pinched, undernourished, underfed; lanky, spindly, gangly, gangling, weedy; informal anorexic, like a bag of bones.
ANTONYMS plump, overweight, fat.
4 *his thin gray hair* **sparse,** scanty, wispy, thinning.
ANTONYMS thick, abundant.
5 *a bowl of thin soup* **watery,** weak, dilute, diluted; runny.
ANTONYMS thick, hearty.
6 *her thin voice* **weak,** faint, feeble, small, soft; reedy.
ANTONYMS strong, loud.
7 *the plot is very thin* **insubstantial,** flimsy, slight, feeble, lame, poor, weak, tenuous, inadequate, insufficient, unconvincing, unbelievable, implausible.
ANTONYMS meaty, convincing.
▶ verb **1** *some paint must be* ***thinned down*** *before use* **dilute,** water down, weaken.
2 *the crowds were beginning to* ***thin out*** **disperse,** dissipate, scatter; become less dense, become less in number, decrease, diminish, dwindle.

> CHOOSE THE RIGHT WORD
>
> **thin, gaunt, lean, skinny, slender, spare, svelte**
>
> You can't be too rich or too **thin**, but you can be too **skinny**. *Thin* describes someone whose weight is naturally low in proportion to his or her height, although it may also imply that the person is underweight (*she looked pale and thin after her operation*). *Skinny* is a more blunt and derogatory term for someone who is too thin, and it often implies underdevelopment (*a skinny little boy; a tall, skinny fashion model*). Most people would rather be called **slender**, which combines thinness with gracefulness and good proportions (*the slender legs of a Queen Anne table*), or better yet, **svelte**, a complimentary term that implies a slim, elegant figure (*after six months of dieting, she looked so svelte I hardly recognized her*). **Lean** and **spare** are used to describe people who are naturally thin, although *spare* suggests a more muscular leanness (*a tall, spare man who looked like Abraham Lincoln*). **Gaunt**, on the other hand, means so thin that the angularity of the bones can be seen beneath the skin (*looking gaunt after her latest bout with cancer*).

thing ▶ noun **1** *the room was full of strange things* **object,** article, item, artifact, commodity; device, gadget, instrument, utensil, tool, implement; entity, body; informal whatsit, whatchamacallit; Brit. thingummy, thingy, thingamabob, thingamajig, doohickey, doodad, dingus.
2 (**things**) *I'll come back tomorrow to collect my things* **belongings,** possessions, stuff, property, worldly goods, effects, personal effects, trappings, paraphernalia, bits and pieces, luggage, baggage, bags; informal gear, junk; Law goods and chattels.
3 (**things**) *his gardening things* **equipment,** apparatus, gear, kit, tackle, stuff; implements, tools, utensils; accoutrements.
4 *I've got several things to do today* **activity,** act, action, deed, undertaking, exploit, feat; task, job, chore.
5 *I've got other things on my mind just now* **thought,** notion, idea; concern, matter, worry, preoccupation.
6 *I keep remembering things he said* **remark,** statement, comment, utterance, observation, declaration, pronouncement.
7 *quite a few odd things happened* **incident,** episode, event, happening, occurrence, phenomenon.
8 (**things**) *how are things with you?* **matters,** affairs, circumstances, conditions, relations; state of affairs, situation, life.
9 *one of the things I like about you is your optimism* **characteristic,** quality, attribute,

property, trait, feature, point, aspect, facet, quirk.
10 *there's another thing you should know* **fact,** piece of information, point, detail, particular, factor.
11 *the thing is, I'm not sure if it's what I want* **fact of the matter,** fact, point, issue, problem.
12 *you lucky thing!* **person,** soul, creature, wretch; informal devil, bastard.
13 *Twylla developed a **thing about** noise* **phobia of/about,** fear of, dislike of, aversion to, problem with; obsession with, fixation about; informal hang-up.
14 *she had a **thing about** men who wore glasses* **penchant for,** preference for, taste for, inclination for, partiality for, predilection for, soft spot for, weakness for, fondness for, fancy for, liking for, love for; fetish for, obsession with, fixation on/with.
15 *books aren't really my thing* **what one likes,** what interests one; informal one's cup of tea, one's bag, what turns one on.
16 *it's the latest thing* **fashion,** trend, style, rage, fad.

think ▶ **verb 1** *I think he's gone home* **believe,** be of the opinion, be of the view, be under the impression; expect, imagine, anticipate; surmise, suppose, conjecture, guess, fancy; conclude, determine, reason; informal reckon, figure; formal opine.
2 *his family was thought to be enormously rich* **deem,** judge, hold, reckon, consider, presume, estimate; regard (as), view (as).
3 *Jack thought for a moment* **ponder,** reflect, deliberate, consider, meditate, contemplate, muse, ruminate, be lost in thought, be in a brown study, brood; concentrate, brainstorm, rack one's brains; put on one's thinking cap, sleep on it; formal cogitate.
4 *she **thought of** all the visits she had made to her father* **recall,** remember, recollect, call to mind, think back to.
5 *she forced herself to **think of** how he must be feeling* **imagine,** picture, visualize, envisage, consider; dream about, fantasize about.
– PHRASES **think better of** *Donnie was going to crash his ex-girlfriend's wedding, but he thought better of it* **have second thoughts about,** think twice about, think again about, change one's mind about; reconsider, decide against; informal get cold feet about. **think over** *take a few days to think over the proposal* **consider,** contemplate, deliberate about, mull over, ponder, chew over, chew on, reflect on, muse on, ruminate on. **think up** *I'm sure by Friday we'll have thought up a great idea for the presentation* **devise,** dream up, conjure up, come up with, invent, create, concoct, make up; hit on.

thinker ▶ **noun** *one of the most influential economic thinkers of the century* **theorist,** philosopher, scholar, savant, sage, intellectual, intellect, ideologist, ideologue; mind, brain, brainiac, genius.

thinking ▶ **adjective** *he seemed a thinking man* **intelligent,** sensible, reasonable, rational; logical, analytical; thoughtful, reflective, meditative, contemplative, pensive, shrewd, philosophical, sagacious.
ANTONYMS stupid, irrational.
▶ **noun** *the thinking behind the campaign* **reasoning,** logic, idea(s), theory, line of thought, philosophy, beliefs; opinion(s), view(s), thoughts, position, judgment, assessment, evaluation.

thin-skinned ▶ **adjective** *you can't benefit from constructive criticism if you're going to be so thin-skinned* **sensitive,** oversensitive, hypersensitive, easily offended, easily hurt, touchy, defensive.
ANTONYMS insensitive, unfeeling.

third-rate ▶ **adjective** *a third-rate hotel* **substandard,** bad, inferior, poor, poor-quality, low-grade, inadequate, unsatisfactory, unacceptable, not up to snuff, not up to scratch; appalling, abysmal, atrocious, awful, terrible, dreadful, execrable, godawful, miserable, pitiful; jerry-built, shoddy, chintzy, tinpot, trashy; cheapjack; informal lousy, rotten, bum, crummy, crappy.
ANTONYMS excellent.

thirst ▶ **noun 1** *I need a drink—I'm dying of thirst* **thirstiness,** dryness; dehydration.
2 *his thirst for knowledge* **craving,** desire, longing, yearning, hunger, hankering, keenness, eagerness, lust, appetite; informal yen, itch.
▶ **verb** *she **thirsted for** power* **crave,** want, covet, desire, hunger for, burn for, lust after, hanker after, have one's heart set on; wish, long.

thirsty ▶ **adjective 1** *the boys were hot and thirsty* **longing for a drink,** dry, dehydrated; informal parched, gasping.
2 *the thirsty soil* **dry,** arid, dried up/out, bone-dry, parched, baked, desiccated.
3 *she was thirsty for power* **eager,** hungry, greedy, thirsting, craving, longing, yearning, lusting, burning, desirous, hankering; informal itching, dying.

thong ▶ **noun** *leather thongs fastened to the quiver* **strip,** band, cord, string, lash, tie, belt, strap, tape, rope, tether.

thorn ▶ **noun** *a thorn in her finger* **prickle,** spike, barb, spine.

thorny ▶ **adjective 1** *dense thorny undergrowth* **prickly,** spiky, barbed, spiny, sharp; technical spinose, spinous.
2 *the thorny subject of confidentiality* **problematic,** tricky, ticklish, touchy, delicate, controversial, awkward, difficult, knotty, tough, taxing, trying, troublesome; complicated, complex, involved, intricate; vexed, sticky.

thorough ▶ **adjective 1** *a thorough investigation* **rigorous,** in-depth, exhaustive, thoroughgoing, minute, detailed, close, meticulous, methodical, careful, complete, comprehensive, full, extensive, widespread, sweeping, all-embracing, all-inclusive.
ANTONYMS superficial, cursory, partial.
2 *he is slow but thorough* **meticulous,** scrupulous, assiduous, conscientious, painstaking, methodical, careful, diligent, industrious, hard-working.
ANTONYMS careless.
3 *the child is being a thorough nuisance* **utter,**

downright, thoroughgoing, absolute, complete, total, out-and-out, arrant, real, perfect, sheer, unqualified, unmitigated.

thoroughbred ▶ adjective *thoroughbred horses* **purebred,** pedigree, pure, pure-blooded, blooded.

thoroughfare ▶ noun *avoiding the busy thoroughfares* **route,** passageway, waterway, throughway; main road, highway, freeway, street, road, roadway, avenue, boulevard.

thoroughly ▶ adverb 1 *we will investigate all complaints thoroughly* **rigorously,** in depth, exhaustively, minutely, closely, in detail, meticulously, scrupulously, assiduously, conscientiously, painstakingly, methodically, carefully, comprehensively, fully, from A to Z, from soup to nuts.
2 *she is thoroughly spoiled* **utterly,** downright, absolutely, completely, totally, entirely, one-hundred-percent, really, perfectly, positively, in every respect, through and through; informal plain, to the hilt.

though ▶ conjunction *though she smiled bravely, she looked pale and tired* **although,** even though/if, in spite of the fact that, despite the fact that, notwithstanding (the fact) that, for all that.
▶ adverb *it seems impossible, but you can try, though* **nevertheless,** nonetheless, even so, however, be that as it may, for all that, despite that, having said that; informal still and all.

thought ▶ noun 1 *what are your thoughts on the matter?* **idea,** notion, opinion, view, impression, feeling, theory; judgment, assessment, conclusion. See note at IDEA.
2 *he gave up any thought of getting a degree* **hope,** aspiration, ambition, dream; intention, idea, plan, design, aim.
3 *it only took a moment's thought* **thinking,** contemplation, musing, pondering, consideration, reflection, introspection, deliberation, rumination, meditation, brooding, reverie, concentration; formal cogitation.

thoughtful ▶ adjective 1 *a thoughtful expression* **pensive,** reflective, contemplative, musing, meditative, introspective, philosophical, ruminative, absorbed, engrossed, rapt, preoccupied, lost in thought, deep in thought, in a brown study, brooding; formal cogitative.
ANTONYMS vacant.
2 *how very thoughtful of you!* **considerate,** caring, attentive, understanding, sympathetic, solicitous, concerned, helpful, obliging, neighborly, unselfish, kind, compassionate, charitable.
ANTONYMS inconsiderate.

thoughtless ▶ adjective 1 *I'm so sorry—how thoughtless of me* **inconsiderate,** uncaring, insensitive, uncharitable, unkind, flippant, tactless, undiplomatic, indiscreet, remiss.
ANTONYMS considerate.
2 *a few minutes of thoughtless pleasure* **unthinking,** heedless, careless, unmindful, unguarded, absentminded; injudicious, ill-advised, ill-considered, imprudent, unwise, foolish, frivolous, silly, stupid, reckless, rash, precipitate, negligent, neglectful.
ANTONYMS careful.

thrash ▶ verb 1 *she thrashed him across the head and shoulders* **hit,** beat, strike, batter, thump, hammer, pound, rain blows on; assault, attack; cudgel, club; informal wallop, belt, bash, whup, whack, thwack, clout, clobber, pummel, slug, tan, sock, beat the (living) daylights out of.
2 *he was thrashing around in pain* **flail,** writhe, thresh, jerk, toss, twist, twitch.
– PHRASES **thrash out 1** *thrash out a problem* **resolve,** settle, sort out, work out, straighten out, iron out, clear up; talk through, discuss, debate. **2** *thrash out an agreement* **work out,** negotiate, agree on, bring about, hammer out, hammer together, hash out, produce, effect.

thread ▶ noun 1 *a needle and thread* cotton, filament, fiber; yarn, string, twine.
2 literary *the Fraser was a thread of silver below them* **streak,** strand, stripe, line, strip, seam, vein.
3 *she lost the thread of the conversation* **gist,** train of thought, drift, direction; theme, motif, tenor; story line, plot.
▶ verb 1 *he threaded the rope through a pulley* **pass,** string, work, ease, push, poke.
2 *she threaded her way through the tables* **weave,** inch, wind, squeeze, make.

threadbare ▶ adjective *a threadbare carpet* **worn,** well-worn, old, thin, worn out, holey, moth-eaten, mangy, ragged, frayed, tattered, battered; decrepit, shabby, scruffy, unkempt; having seen better days, falling apart at the seams, falling to pieces, tatty, ratty, the worse for wear, raggedy, dog-eared; informal raggedy-ass.

threat ▶ noun 1 *Maggie ignored his threats* **threatening remark,** warning, ultimatum.
2 *a possible threat to aircraft* **danger,** peril, hazard, menace, risk.
3 *the company faces the threat of liquidation proceedings* **possibility,** prospect, chance, probability, likelihood, risk.

threaten ▶ verb 1 *how dare you threaten me?* **menace,** intimidate, browbeat, bully, blackmail, terrorize; make/issue threats to.
2 *these events could threaten the stability of Europe* **endanger,** be a danger to, be a threat to, jeopardize, imperil, put at risk, put in jeopardy.
3 *the gray skies threatened snow* **foreshadow,** bode, warn of, presage, augur, portend, herald, be a harbinger of, indicate, point to, be a sign of, signal, spell; literary foretoken.
4 *as rain threatened, the party moved indoors* **seem likely,** seem imminent, be on the horizon, be brewing, be gathering, be looming, be on the way, be impending; hang over someone.

threatening ▶ adjective 1 *a threatening letter* **menacing,** intimidating, bullying, frightening, hostile; formal minatory.
2 *banks of threatening clouds* **ominous,** sinister, menacing, alarming, portentous, dark, black, thunderous.

threesome ▶ noun *a talented threesome* **trio,** triumvirate, triad, trinity, troika; triplets.

threshold ▶ noun 1 *the threshold of the church* **doorstep,** doorway, entrance, entry, door, gate, gateway, portal, doorsill.
2 *the threshold of a new era* **start,** beginning, commencement, brink, verge, cusp, dawn,

inception, day one, opening, debut; informal kickoff.

3 *the human threshold of pain* **lower limit,** minimum.

thrift ▶ noun *she learned her sense of thrift from her mother* **frugality,** economy, economizing, thriftiness, providence, prudence, good management, good husbandry, saving, scrimping and saving, abstemiousness; parsimony, penny-pinching, austerity.
ANTONYMS extravagance.

thrifty ▶ adjective *these kids have no idea what it means to be thrifty* **frugal,** economical, sparing, careful with money, penny-wise, provident, prudent, abstemious; parsimonious, penny-pinching, cheap. See note at ECONOMICAL.
ANTONYMS extravagant.

thrill ▶ noun **1** *the thrill of jumping out of an airplane* **excitement,** feeling of excitement, stimulation, adrenaline rush, pleasure, tingle; fun, enjoyment, amusement, delight, joy; informal buzz, high, rush, kick, charge.

2 *a thrill of excitement ran through her* **wave,** shiver, rush, surge, flash, blaze, tremor, quiver, flutter, shudder, frisson.

▶ verb **1** *his words thrilled her* **excite,** stimulate, arouse, rouse, inspire, delight, exhilarate, intoxicate, stir, charge up, electrify, galvanize, move, fire (with enthusiasm), fire someone's imagination; informal give someone a buzz, give someone a kick, give someone a charge.
ANTONYMS bore.

2 *he thrilled at the sound of her voice* **be/feel excited,** tingle, quiver; informal get a buzz out of, get a kick out of, get a charge out of.

thrilling ▶ adjective *a thrilling race* **exciting,** stirring, action-packed, breathtaking, rip-roaring, spine-tingling, gripping, riveting, fascinating, dramatic, hair-raising, mind-blowing; rousing, stimulating, moving, inspiring, inspirational, electrifying, heady.
ANTONYMS boring.

thrive ▶ verb *the roses in the west garden are thriving | business generally thrives this time of year* **flourish,** prosper, burgeon, bloom, blossom, mushroom, do well, advance, succeed, boom.
ANTONYMS decline, wither.

thriving ▶ adjective *real estate continues to be a thriving industry* **flourishing,** prosperous, prospering, growing, developing, burgeoning, blooming, healthy, successful, booming, mushrooming, profitable, expanding; informal going strong, going from strength to strength.
ANTONYMS moribund.

throat ▶ noun *an inflamed throat* **gullet,** esophagus; windpipe, trachea, gorge; maw, neck, jowl.

throb ▶ verb *her arms and legs throbbed with tiredness* **pulsate,** beat, pulse, palpitate, pound, thud, thump, drum, thrum, pitter-patter, go pit-a-pat, quiver; rare quop.

▶ noun *the throb of the ship's engines* **pulsation,** beat, beating, pulse, palpitation, pounding, thudding, thumping, drumming, thrumming.

throes ▶ plural noun *the throes of childbirth* **agony,** pain, pangs, spasms, torment, suffering, torture; literary travail.

– PHRASES **in the throes of** *we're in the throes of hurricane preparations* **in the middle of,** in the process of, in the midst of, busy with, occupied with, taken up with/by, involved in, dealing with; struggling with, wrestling with, grappling with.

throne ▶ noun *the czar risked losing his throne* **sovereign power,** sovereignty, rule, dominion.

throng ▶ noun *a throng of people blocked her way* **crowd,** horde, mass, multitude, host, army, herd, flock, drove, swarm, mob, sea, troop, pack, crush; collection, company, gathering, assembly, congregation; informal gaggle, bunch, gang.

▶ verb **1** *people thronged to see the play* **flock,** stream, swarm, troop, pour in.

2 *visitors thronged around him* **crowd,** cluster, mill, swarm, surge, congregate, gather.

throttle ▶ verb **1** *he tried to throttle her* **choke,** strangle, strangulate, garrote, gag.

2 *attempts to throttle the criminal supply of drugs* **suppress,** inhibit, stifle, control, restrain, check, contain, choke off, put a/the lid on; stop, put an end to, end, stamp out.

through ▶ preposition **1** *we drove through the tunnel* **into and out of,** to the other side of, to the far side of, from one side to the other of.

2 *he got the job through an advertisement* **by means of,** by way of, by dint of, via, using, thanks to, by virtue of, as a result of, as a consequence of, on account of, owing to, because of.

3 *he worked through the night* **throughout,** all through, for the whole of, for the duration of, until/to the end of.

▶ adverb *as soon as we opened the gate they came streaming through* **from one side to the other,** from one end to another, in and out the other side.

▶ adjective *a through train* **direct,** nonstop.

– PHRASES **through and through** *he was a city kid through and through* **in every respect,** to the core; thoroughly, utterly, absolutely, completely, totally, wholly, fully, entirely, unconditionally, unreservedly, altogether, out-and-out.

throughout ▶ preposition **1** *it had repercussions throughout the Middle East* **all over,** across, in every part of, everywhere in, all through, right through, all around.

2 *she remained fit throughout her life* **all through,** all, for the duration of, for the whole of, until the end of.

throw ▶ verb **1** *she threw the ball back* **hurl,** toss, fling, pitch, cast, lob, launch, catapult, project, propel; bowl; informal chuck, heave, sling, peg, let fly with.

2 *he threw another punch* **deliver,** give, land.

3 *she threw a withering glance at him* **direct,** cast, send, dart, shoot.

4 *the horse threw its rider* **unseat,** dislodge.

5 *her question threw me* **disconcert,** unnerve, fluster, ruffle, agitate, discomfit, put off, throw off balance, discountenance, unsettle, confuse; informal rattle, faze, flummox, baffle, befuddle, discombobulate.

6 *he threw a farewell party for them* **give,** host, hold, have, provide, put on, lay out, arrange,

organize.
7 *books were thrown all over her desk* **strew,** cast, scatter, disperse.
8 *he threw his keys on the table* **toss,** deposit, throw down, put down, dump, drop, plunk, plonk, plump.
▶ **noun 1** *we were allowed two throws each* **lob,** pitch; go, turn; bowl, ball.
2 *the loveseat was decorated with a red throw* **blanket,** afghan, covering, fabric; shawl.
– PHRASES **throw something away 1** *she hated throwing old clothes away* **discard,** throw out, dispose of, get rid of, do away with, toss out, scrap, clear out, dump, jettison; informal chuck (away/out), deep-six, ditch. **2** *the Tigers threw away a 3–0 lead* **squander,** waste, fritter away, fail to exploit, lose, let slip; informal blow. **throw someone out** *the duke and his family were thrown out* **expel,** eject, evict, drive out, force out, oust, remove; get rid of, depose, topple, unseat, overthrow, bring down, overturn, dislodge, displace, supplant, show someone the door; banish, deport, exile; informal boot out, kick out, give someone the boot. **throw something out 1** *throw out this moldy food* See THROW SOMETHING AWAY (sense 1) above. **2** *his case was thrown out* **reject,** dismiss, turn down, refuse, disallow, veto; informal give the thumbs down to. **throw up** informal See VOMIT (sense 1 of the verb).

thrust ▶ **verb 1** *she thrust her hands into her pockets* **shove,** push, force, plunge, stick, drive, propel, ram, poke, jam.
2 *fame had been thrust on him* **force,** foist, impose, inflict.
3 *he thrust his way past her* **push,** shove, force, elbow, shoulder, barge, bulldoze.
▶ **noun 1** *a hard thrust* **shove,** push, lunge, poke.
2 *a thrust led by Canadian forces* **advance,** push, drive, attack, assault, onslaught, offensive, charge, sortie, foray, raid, sally, invasion, incursion.
3 *only one engine is producing thrust* **force,** propulsive force, propulsion, power, impetus, momentum.
4 *the thrust of the speech* **gist,** substance, drift, burden, meaning, sense, theme, message, import, tenor.

thud ▶ **noun & verb** *it landed with a thud | bullets thudded into the ground* **thump,** thunk, clunk, clonk, crash, smack, bang; stomp, stamp, clump, clomp; informal wham, whump.

thug ▶ **noun** *one of Capone's thugs* **ruffian,** hooligan, vandal, hoodlum, gangster, villain, criminal; informal tough, bruiser, goon, heavy, enforcer, hired gun, hood.

thumb ▶ **noun** *the thumb on his left hand* technical **pollex,** opposable digit.
▶ **verb 1** *he thumbed through his notebook* **leaf,** flick, flip, riffle, skim, browse, look.
2 *his dictionaries were thumbed and ink-stained* **soil,** mark, make dog-eared.
3 *he was thumbing his way across Mexico* **hitchhike;** informal hitch, hitch/thumb a lift.
– PHRASES **all thumbs** *don't let Anthony carry the punch bowl—he's all thumbs* **clumsy,** klutzy, awkward, maladroit, inept, unskillful, heavy-handed, inexpert, butterfingered, ham-fisted. **thumbs down** informal *the budget increase has been given a thumbs down* **rejection,** refusal, veto, no, negation, rebuff; informal red light. **thumbs up** informal *we got the board's thumbs up for the land grant* **approval,** seal of approval, endorsement; permission, authorization, consent, yes, leave, authority, sanction, ratification, license, dispensation, nod, assent, blessing, rubber stamp, clearance; informal go-ahead, OK, A-OK, green light, say-so.

thumbnail ▶ **adjective** *a thumbnail sketch of the political climate* **concise,** short, brief, succinct, to the point, compact, crisp, short and sweet, quick, rapid; miniature, mini, small.

thump ▶ **verb 1** *the two men kicked and thumped him* **hit,** strike, beat, batter, pound, knock, rap, smack, thwack, pummel, punch, thrash, cuff, box someone's ears; informal bash, bop, clout, clobber, sock, swipe, slug, lash, whack, wallop, beat the (living) daylights out of, belt, tan, lay into, let someone have it, whup; literary smite.
2 *her heart thumped with fright* **throb,** pound, thud, hammer, pulsate, pulse, pump, palpitate, race, beat heavily.
▶ **noun** *she put the box down with a thump* **thud,** thunk, clunk, clonk, crash, smack, bang.

thunder ▶ **noun 1** *thunder and lightning* **thunderclap,** peal of thunder, roll of thunder, rumble of thunder, crack of thunder, crash of thunder; literary thunderbolt.
2 *the ceaseless thunder of the traffic* **rumble,** rumbling, boom, booming, roar, roaring, pounding, thud, thudding, crash, crashing, reverberation.
▶ **verb 1** *below me the surf thrashed and thundered* **rumble,** boom, roar, pound, thud, thump, bang; resound, reverberate, beat.
2 *she **thundered against** the evils of the age* **rail against,** fulminate against, inveigh against, rage against/about, rant about; condemn, denounce.
3 *"Answer me!" he thundered* **roar,** bellow, bark, yell, shout, bawl; informal holler.

thundering ▶ **adjective** See THUNDEROUS.

thunderous ▶ **adjective** *a thunderous noise* **very loud,** tumultuous, booming, roaring, resounding, reverberating, reverberant, ringing, deafening, ear-splitting, noisy, overloud, stentorian, thundering.

thunderstruck ▶ **adjective** *Charles was so thunderstruck that his voice was barely audible* **astonished,** amazed, astounded, staggered, surprised, startled, stunned, shocked, aghast, taken aback, dumbfounded, floored, blown away, dumbstruck, stupefied, dazed, speechless; informal flabbergasted.

thus ▶ **adverb 1** *the studio handled production, thus cutting its costs* **consequently,** as a consequence, in consequence, thereby, so, that being so, therefore, ergo, accordingly, hence, as a result, for that reason, ipso facto, because of that, on that account.
2 *all decent aristocrats act thus* **like that,** in that way, so, like so.
– PHRASES **thus far** *thus far, we've avoided any unanticipated expenditures* **so far,** until now, up until now, up to now, up to this point, hitherto.

> USAGE
> **thus**
> There is never a need to expand the adverb *thus* to "thusly."

thwack ▶ noun *the plastic ruler made a loud thwack on the desk* **slap,** whack, smack, wallop.
▶ verb See THUMP (sense 1 of the verb).

thwart ▶ verb *their plans to attack the embassy were thwarted* **foil,** frustrate, stand in the way of, forestall, derail, dash; stop, check, block, stonewall, prevent, defeat, impede, hinder, obstruct; informal put a crimp in, put the kibosh on, scotch, scuttle, do for, stymie.
ANTONYMS facilitate.

> CHOOSE THE RIGHT WORD
> **thwart, baffle, balk, foil, frustrate, inhibit**
> These verbs refer to the various ways in which we can outwit or overcome opposing forces. **Thwart** suggests using cleverness rather than force to bring about the defeat of an enemy or to block progress toward an objective (*thwart a rebellion; have one's goals thwarted by lack of education*). **Balk** also emphasizes setting up barriers (*a sudden reversal that balked their hopes for a speedy resolution*), but it is used more often as an intransitive verb meaning to stop at an obstacle and refuse to proceed (*he balked at appearing in front of the angry crowd*). To **baffle** is to cause defeat by bewildering or confusing (*the police were baffled by the lack of evidence*), while **foil** means to throw off course so as to discourage further effort (*her plan to arrive early was foiled by heavy traffic*). **Frustrate** implies rendering all attempts or efforts useless (*frustrated by the increasingly bad weather, they decided to work indoors*), while **inhibit** suggests forcing something into inaction (*to inhibit wage increases by raising corporate taxes*). Both *frustrate* and *inhibit* are used in a psychological context to suggest barriers that impede normal development or prevent the realization of natural desires (*he was both frustrated by her refusal to acknowledge his presence and inhibited by his own shyness*).

tic ▶ noun *a tic under his left eye* **twitch,** spasm, jerk, tremor; quirk.

tick ▶ noun **1** *the tick of his watch* **ticking,** tick-tock, click, clicking, tap, tapping.
2 *put a tick against the item of your choice* **check mark,** check, stroke, mark.
▶ verb **1** *the clock ticks* **click,** tock, tick-tock, tap.
2 *time is **ticking away*** **pass,** elapse, go, continue, advance, wear on, roll on, fly, run out, vanish.
– PHRASES **tick off 1** *that really ticked me off* **annoy,** irritate, rile, rattle, anger, antagonize, make someone mad, get on someone's nerves, get to, get someone's back up. **2** *tick off a list* **check off**; count off, cross off.

ticket ▶ noun *present your ticket at the gate* **pass,** authorization, permit, token, coupon, voucher; transfer.

tickle ▶ noun *a tickle in her throat* **tingle,** itch, irritation.
▶ verb **1** *he tried to tickle her under the chin* **stroke,** pet, tease, chuck.
2 *she found something that tickled her imagination* **stimulate,** interest, appeal to, arouse, titillate, excite.
– PHRASES **tickled pink** *the kids were tickled pink when we mentioned Disney World* **delighted,** thrilled, tickled to death, jumping for joy, high as a kite, pleased as punch, over the moon.

ticklish ▶ adjective *the issue has been made more ticklish since the factors of race and gender have entered the picture* **difficult,** problematic, tricky, touchy, delicate, sensitive, tender, awkward, prickly, thorny, tough; vexed, sticky.

tidbit ▶ noun **1** *a tidbit of information* **morsel,** piece, scrap, item, bit, nugget.
2 *tasty tidbits* **delicacy,** dainty, snack, nibble, appetizer, hors d'oeuvre, goody, dipper, finger food, nibbly.

tide ▶ noun **1** *ships come up the river with the tide* **tidewater,** ebb and flow, tidal flow.
2 *the tide of history* **course,** movement, direction, trend, current, drift, run, turn, tendency, tenor.
– PHRASES **tide someone over** *these canned goods should tide us over until the storm is over and the power is restored* **sustain,** keep someone going, keep someone afloat, keep someone's head above water, see someone through; keep the wolf from the door; help out, assist, aid.

tidings ▶ plural noun literary *what tidings do you bring us from across the wide ocean?* **news,** information, intelligence, word, reports, dispatches, notification, communication, latest; informal info, scuttlebutt, lowdown, scoop.

tidy ▶ adjective **1** *a tidy room* **neat,** neat and tidy, orderly, well-ordered, in (good) order, well-kept, shipshape, in apple-pie order, immaculate, spick-and-span, uncluttered, straight, trim, spruce.
ANTONYMS messy.
2 *he's a very tidy person* **neat,** trim, spruce, dapper, well-groomed, organized, well-organized, methodical, meticulous; fastidious; informal natty.
ANTONYMS scruffy, messy.
3 informal *a tidy sum* **large,** sizable, considerable, substantial, generous, significant, appreciable, handsome, respectable, ample, decent, goodly.
ANTONYMS small, paltry.
▶ verb **1** *I'd better **tidy up** the living room* **put in order,** clear up, sort out, straighten (up), clean up, spruce up, declutter.
2 *she **tidied herself up** in the bathroom* **groom oneself,** spruce oneself up, freshen oneself up, smarten oneself up; informal titivate oneself.

tie ▶ verb **1** *they tied Max to a chair* **bind,** tie up, tether, hitch, strap, truss, fetter, rope, chain, make fast, moor, lash, attach, fasten, fix, secure, join, connect, link, couple.
2 *he bent to tie his shoelaces* **do up,** lace, knot.
3 *a bonus deal **tied to** a productivity agreement* **link to,** connect to, couple to/with, relate to,

join to, marry to; make conditional on, bind up with.
4 *they tied for second place* **draw,** be equal, be even, be neck and neck.
▶ **noun 1** *he tightened the ties of his robe* **lace,** string, cord, fastening, fastener.
2 *a collar and tie* **necktie,** bow tie, string tie, bolo tie.
3 *family ties* **bond,** connection, link, relationship, attachment, affiliation, allegiance, friendship; kinship, interdependence.
4 *there was a tie for first place* **draw,** dead heat, deadlock.
– PHRASES **tie someone down** *she was afraid of getting tied down* **restrict,** restrain, limit, constrain, trammel, confine, cramp, hamper, handicap, hamstring, encumber, shackle, inhibit. **tie in** *how do these revisions tie in with the ultimate plan?* **be consistent,** tally, agree, be in agreement, accord, concur, fit in, harmonize, be in tune, dovetail, correspond, match; square, jibe. **tie someone/something up 1** *robbers tied her up and ransacked her home* **bind,** bind hand and foot, truss (up), fetter, chain up. **2** *he is tied up in meetings all morning* **occupy,** engage, keep busy. **3** *her capital is tied up in real estate* **lock,** bind up, trap; entangle.

tier ▶ **noun 1** *tiers of empty seats* **row,** line; layer, level; balcony.
2 *the most senior tier of management* **grade,** gradation, echelon, rank, stratum, level, rung on the ladder.

tight ▶ **adjective 1** *a tight grip* **firm,** fast, secure, fixed, clenched.
ANTONYMS relaxed.
2 *the rope was tight* **taut,** rigid, stiff, tense, stretched, strained.
ANTONYMS slack.
3 *tight jeans* **tight-fitting,** close-fitting, form-fitting, narrow, figure-hugging, skintight; informal sprayed-on.
ANTONYMS loose, baggy.
4 *a tight mass of fibers* **compact,** compacted, compressed, dense, solid.
ANTONYMS loose.
5 *a tight space* **small,** tiny, narrow, limited, restricted, confined, cramped, constricted, uncomfortable; rare incommodious.
ANTONYMS roomy, generous.
6 *tight control over the family's finances* **strict,** rigorous, stringent, tough, rigid, firm, uncompromising.
ANTONYMS lax.
7 *a tight schedule* **busy,** rigorous, packed, nonstop.
ANTONYMS open.
8 *he's in a tight spot* **difficult,** tricky, delicate, awkward, problematic, worrying, precarious; informal sticky.
ANTONYMS problem-free.
9 *a tight piece of writing* **succinct,** concise, pithy, incisive, crisp, condensed, well structured, clean, to the point.
ANTONYMS wordy, flowery.
10 *a tight race* **close,** even, evenly matched, well-matched; hard-fought, neck and neck.
ANTONYMS open.
11 *money is tight these days* **limited,** restricted, in short supply, scarce, depleted, diminished, low, inadequate, insufficient.
ANTONYMS plentiful, abundant.
12 *she is tight with the big movie stars* **close,** friendly, intimate, connected, close-knit, tight-knit, on good terms, buddy-buddy.

tighten ▶ **verb 1** *she tightened the rope* **pull taut,** tauten, pull tight, stretch, tense.
ANTONYMS loosen, slacken.
2 *he tightened his lips* **narrow,** constrict, contract, compress, screw up, pucker, purse, squinch up.
ANTONYMS relax.
3 *security in the area has been tightened* **increase,** make stricter, toughen up, heighten, scale up.
ANTONYMS relax.

till[1] ▶ **noun** *she counted the money in the till* **cash register,** cash drawer(s), cashbox, strongbox; checkout.

till[2] ▶ **verb** *he went back to tilling the land* **cultivate,** work, farm, plow, dig, hoe, turn over, prepare.

till[3] ▶ **preposition & conjunction 1** *he'll be in London till July* **until,** to, up to, through (to), up until, as late as.
2 *we didn't know about this till yesterday* **before,** prior to, previous to, up to, up until, earlier than.

USAGE

till, until

Till is, like *until,* a bona fide preposition and conjunction. Though less formal than *until, till* is neither colloquial nor substandard. As Anthony Burgess put it, "In nonpoetic English we use 'till' and 'until' indifferently." (*A Mouthful of Air*; 1992.) It's especially common in British English—e.g.:

- "After the First World War, Hatay, named by Ataturk after the Hittites, fell into the hands of the French, who did not return it till 1939." (*Independent* [UK]; Apr. 1, 1995.)
- "He works from dawn till dusk, six days a week." (*Daily Telegraph* [UK]; Mar. 31, 1997.)

And it still occurs in American English—e.g.: "In medium skillet, sauté the garlic till golden. Add onion, wait till brown." (*Palm Beach Post*; Mar. 23, 1995.)

But the myth of the word's low standing persists. Some writers and editors mistakenly think that *till* deserves a bracketed *sic*—e.g.: "'Trading in cotton futures was not practiced till [sic] after the close of the Civil War, spot cotton being quoted like other stocks in cents, halves, quarters, etc.'" (*School Science and Mathematics*; Apr. 1, 1997 [in which the *sic* appeared in the original source being quoted].)

If a form deserves a *sic,* it's the incorrect *'til.* Worse yet is *'till,* which is abominable—e.g.: "A month or two remain 'till [read *till*] you grab your dancing shoes, plus a crew of pals or that special date." (*Denver Post*; Mar. 21, 1997.) — **BG**

tilt ▶ verb *you'll have to tilt the sofa to fit it through the door* **slope,** tip, lean, list, bank, slant, incline, pitch, cant, angle.
– PHRASES **(at) full tilt** *our toboggans went down the icy slope at full tilt* **(at) full speed,** at top speed, full bore, as fast as one's legs can carry one, at a gallop, helter-skelter, headlong, pell-mell, at breakneck speed, with great force, with full force; informal like crazy, like mad, hell-bent for leather, a mile a minute, like the wind, like a bat out of hell, like (greased) lightning, lickety-split, full blast, all out, with a vengeance; literary apace.

timber ▶ noun *some eighty acres of marketable timber | expertly milled timbers* **wood,** lumber, logs; trees, sawlogs; hardwood, softwood; beam, spar, plank, batten, lath, board, joist, rafter.

time ▶ noun **1** *what time is it?* **hour;** dated o'clock.
2 *late at night was the best time to leave* **moment,** point, point in time, occasion, hour, minute, second, instant, juncture, stage.
3 *he worked there for a time* **while,** spell, stretch, stint, span, season, interval, period, period of time, length of time, duration, phase, stage, term, patch.
4 *the time of the dinosaurs* **era,** age, epoch, period, years, days; generation, date.
5 *I've known a lot of cats in my time* **lifetime,** life, life span, days, time on earth, existence.
6 *he had been a professional actor in his time* **heyday,** day, best days, best years, glory days, prime, peak, Golden Age.
7 **(the times)** *the times are a-changing* **conditions,** circumstances; life, the state of affairs, the way of the world.
8 *tunes in waltz time* **rhythm,** tempo, beat; meter, measure, pattern.
▶ verb **1** *the events were timed perfectly* **schedule,** set, set up, arrange, organize, coordinate, fix, line up, slot in, prearrange, timetable, plan; slate.
2 *we timed ourselves to prepare for the race* **measure,** clock, record one's time.
– PHRASES **ahead of time** *get to the airport ahead of time* **early,** in good time, with time to spare, in advance. **ahead of one's/its time** *Leonardo was ahead of his time in almost all endeavors | a laser procedure that is ahead of its time* **revolutionary,** avant-garde, futuristic, innovatory, innovative, trailblazing, pioneering, groundbreaking, advanced, cutting edge. **all the time** *their bleeping dog barks all the time* **constantly,** the entire time, around/round the clock, day and night, night and day, 'morning, noon, and night', 'day in, day out', at all times, always, nonstop, without a break, ceaselessly, endlessly, unfailingly, incessantly, perpetually, permanently, interminably, continuously, continually, eternally, unremittingly, remorselessly, relentlessly, unrelentingly; informal 24-7; archaic without surcease. **at one time** *she was a nurse at one time* **formerly,** previously, once, in the past, at one point, once upon a time, time was when, one fine day, in days/times gone by, in times past, in the (good) old days, long ago, back in the day; literary in days/times of yore; archaic erstwhile, whilom. **at the same time 1** *they arrived at the same time* **simultaneously,** at the same instant, at the same moment, together, all together, as a group, at once, at one and the same time; in unison, in concert, in chorus, in synchrony, as one, in tandem. **2** *Curt seems like a nice guy—at the same time I'm not sure I would trust him* **nonetheless,** even so, however, but, still, yet, though, on the other hand; in spite of that, despite that, be that as it may, for all that, that said; notwithstanding, regardless, anyway, anyhow, still and all. **at times** *she is at times cruel and ruthless* **occasionally,** sometimes, from time to time, now and then, every so often, once in a while, on occasion, off and on, at intervals, periodically, sporadically. **behind the times** *the older I get, the less I think my parents are behind the times* **old-fashioned,** out of date, outmoded, outdated, dated, old, passé; informal square, not with it, old-school, horse-and-buggy, fusty. **for the time being** *we're living in the cottage for the time being* **for now,** for the moment, for the present, in the interim, for the nonce, in/for the meantime, in the meanwhile, for a short time, briefly; temporarily, provisionally, pro tem. **from time to time** See AT TIMES above. **in no time** *I'll be dressed in no time* **(very) soon,** in a second, in an instant, in a minute, in a moment, in a trice, in a flash, shortly, any second, any minute (now), momentarily; informal in a jiffy, in a sec, in two shakes of a lamb's tail, in a snap; formal directly. **in good time** *don't worry, Father will get here in good time* **punctually,** promptly, on time, early, with time to spare, ahead of time, ahead of schedule. **in time 1** *I came back in time for the party* **early enough,** in good time, punctually, on time, not too late, with time to spare, on schedule. **2** *in time, she'll forgot about it* **eventually,** in the end, in due course, by and by, finally, after a while; one day, some day, sometime, sooner or later. **many a time** *many a time they had gone to bed hungry* **frequently,** regularly, often, very often, all the time, habitually, customarily, routinely; again and again, time and again, over and over again, repeatedly, recurrently, continually, oftentimes; literary oft, ofttimes. **on time** *please make sure you show up to class, and be on time* **punctually,** in good time, to/on schedule, when expected, on the dot. **time after time** *the camera produces excellent results time after time* **repeatedly,** frequently, often, again and again, over and over (again), time and (time) again, many times, many a time; persistently, recurrently, constantly, continually, oftentimes; literary oft, ofttimes.

timeless ▶ adjective *the timeless appeal of a well-crafted rocking chair* **lasting,** enduring, classic, ageless, permanent, perennial, abiding, unfailing, unchanging, unvarying, never-changing, changeless, unfading, unending, undying, immortal, eternal, everlasting, immutable.
ANTONYMS ephemeral.

timely ▶ adjective *his refresher course on giving CPR proved to be very timely* **opportune,** well-timed, at the right time, convenient, appropriate, expedient, seasonable, felicitous.

CHOOSE THE RIGHT WORD

timely, opportune, propitious, seasonable

Some people seem to have a knack for doing or saying the right thing at the right time. A **timely** act or remark is one that comes at a moment when it is of genuine value or service (*a timely interruption*), while an **opportune** one comes in the nick of time, as if by design, and exactly meets the needs of the occasion (*a storm came up at an opportune moment, squelching enthusiasm for the fight*). **Seasonable** applies to whatever is suited to the season of the year or fits in with the needs of the moment or the character of the occasion (*seasonable weather; a seasonable menu for a cold winter day*). **Propitious** means presenting favorable conditions. In other words, while a warm day in December might not be *seasonable*, it might very well be *propitious* for the sailor setting off on a round-the-world cruise.

timetable ▶ noun *a bus timetable | I have a very full timetable* **schedule,** program, agenda, calendar; list, itinerary, timeline.

timid ▶ adjective *I was too timid to ask for what I wanted* **apprehensive,** fearful, easily frightened, afraid, faint-hearted, timorous, nervous, scared, frightened, cowardly, pusillanimous, spineless; shy, diffident, self-effacing; informal wimpish, wimpy, yellow, chicken, mousy, gutless, sissy, lily-livered, candy-assed, weak-kneed.
ANTONYMS bold.

timorous ▶ adjective See TIMID.

tincture ▶ noun **1** *tincture of iodine* **solution,** suspension, infusion, elixir.
2 *a tincture of bitterness* See TINGE (sense 2 of the noun).

tinge ▶ verb **1** *a mass of white blossom tinged with pink* **tint,** color, stain, shade, wash.
2 *his optimism is tinged with realism* **influence,** affect, touch, flavor, color, modify; taint.
▶ noun **1** *the light had a blue tinge to it* **tint,** color, shade, tone, hue.
2 *a tinge of cynicism* **trace,** note, touch, suggestion, hint, bit, scintilla, savor, flavor, element, modicum, streak, vein, suspicion, soupçon, tincture.

tingle ▶ verb *her flesh still tingled from the shock* **prickle,** sting; tremble, quiver, shiver.
▶ noun *she felt a tingle of anticipation* **thrill,** buzz, quiver, shiver, tingling, sting, stinging; tremor.

tinker ▶ verb *a mechanic was* ***tinkering with*** *the engine* **fiddle with,** adjust, fix, try to mend, play about with, fool with, futz with; tamper with, interfere with, mess about with, meddle with.

tinkle ▶ verb **1** *the bell tinkled* **ring,** jingle, jangle, chime, peal, ding, ping.
2 *cool water tinkled in the stone fountain* **splash,** purl, babble, burble; literary plash.
▶ noun *the tinkle of sleigh bells* **ring,** chime, ding, ping, jingle, jangle, tintinnabulation.

tinsel ▶ noun *the tinsel of Hollywood* **ostentation,** showiness, show, glitter, flamboyance, gaudiness; attractiveness, glamour; informal flashiness, ritz, glitz, garishness, razzle-dazzle, razzmatazz, eye candy.

tint ▶ noun **1** *the sky was taking on an apricot tint* **shade,** color, tone, hue, pigmentation, tinge, cast, tincture, flush, blush, wash.
2 *a hair tint* **dye,** coloring, rinse, highlights, lowlights.

tiny ▶ adjective *what are these tiny red insects on my houseplants?* **minute,** minuscule, microscopic, nanoscale, infinitesimal, very small, little, mini, diminutive, miniature, scaled down, baby, toy, dwarf, pygmy, peewee, Lilliputian; informal teeny, teeny-weeny, teensy, teensy-weensy, itty-bitty, itsy-bitsy, eensy, eensy-weensy, little-bitty; bite-sized, pint-sized; chiefly Scottish wee. See note at SMALL.
ANTONYMS huge.

tip[1] ▶ noun *the swords we use in the play have blunt tips | the tip of the iceberg* **point,** end, extremity, head, sharp end, spike, prong, tine, nib; top, summit, apex, cusp, crown, crest, pinnacle, vertex.

tip[2] ▶ verb **1** *the boat tipped over* **overturn,** turn over, topple (over), fall (over); keel over, capsize, flip, turn turtle; Nautical pitchpole.
2 *a whale could tip over a small boat* **upset,** overturn, topple over, turn over, knock over, push over, upend, capsize, roll, flip.
3 *the car tipped to one side* **lean,** tilt, list, slope, bank, slant, incline, pitch, cant, heel, careen.

tip[3] ▶ noun **1** *a generous tip* **gratuity,** baksheesh; present, gift, reward.
2 *useful tips* **piece of advice,** suggestion, word of advice, pointer, recommendation; clue, hint, steer, tip-off; word to the wise.

tip-off ▶ noun *police have received an anonymous tip-off* **piece of information,** warning, lead, forewarning; hint, clue; advice, information, notification.

tipsy ▶ adjective *you're too tipsy to be driving home* **merry,** half-drunk, lightheaded, woozy, mellow, slightly drunk, lubricated. See note at DRUNK.
ANTONYMS sober.

tirade ▶ noun *both attorneys were stunned when the judge launched into a tirade* **diatribe,** harangue, rant, onslaught, attack, polemic, denunciation, broadside, fulmination, condemnation, censure, invective, criticism, tongue-lashing; blast; lecture; literary philippic.

tire ▶ verb **1** *he began to tire as the ascent grew steeper* **weaken,** grow weak, flag, wilt, droop; deteriorate.
2 *the journey had tired her* **fatigue,** tire out, exhaust, wear out, drain, weary, frazzle, overtire, enervate; informal knock out, do in, wear to a frazzle.
3 *we are* ***tired of*** *your difficult behavior* **weary of,** get fed up with, get sick of, get bored with, get impatient with; informal have had it up to here with, have had enough of.

tired ▶ adjective **1** *you're just tired from traveling* **exhausted,** worn out, weary, fatigued, dog-tired, dead beat, bone-tired, ready to drop, drained, zonked, wasted, enervated, jaded;

informal done in, bushed, whipped, bagged, knocked out, wiped out, pooped, tuckered out.
ANTONYMS energetic, wide awake, fresh.
2 *are you* ***tired of*** *having him here?* **fed up with,** weary of, bored with/by, sick (to death) of; informal up to here with.
3 *tired jokes* **hackneyed,** overused, overworked, worn out, stale, clichéd, hoary, stock, stereotyped, predictable, unimaginative, unoriginal, uninspired, dull, boring, routine; informal old hat, corny.
ANTONYMS lively, fresh.

> CHOOSE THE RIGHT WORD
>
> **tired, exhausted, fatigued, tuckered, weary**
>
> **Tired** is what you are after you've cleaned the house, spent two hours reading a dull report, or trained for a marathon; it means that you are drained of your strength and energy, without giving any indication of degree. **Weary**, on the other hand, is how you feel after you've had to interrupt your dinner five or six times to answer the phone. It implies not only a depletion of energy but also the vexation that accompanies having to put up with something that is, or has become, disagreeable. **Exhausted** means that you are totally drained of strength and energy, a condition that may even be irreversible (*exhausted by battling a terminal disease*). **Fatigued** is a more precise word than either *tired* or *weary*; it implies a loss of energy through strain, illness, or overwork to the point where rest or sleep is essential (*fatigued after working a 24-hour shift*). **Tuckered** is an informal word that comes close in meaning to *fatigued* or *exhausted*, but often carries the suggestion of loss of breath (*tuckered out after running up six flights of stairs*).

tireless ▶ adjective *their tireless efforts to reclaim the Hudson have given us a remarkably cleaner river* **indefatigable,** energetic, vigorous, industrious, hard-working, determined, enthusiastic, keen, zealous, spirited, dynamic, dogged, tenacious, persevering, untiring, unwearying, unremitting, unflagging, indomitable.
ANTONYMS lazy.

tiresome ▶ adjective *the word is that she just couldn't stand one more day of his tiresome obsession with computer games* **boring,** dull, tedious, insipid, wearisome, wearing, uninteresting, uneventful, humdrum, monotonous, mind-numbing; annoying, irritating, trying, irksome, vexing, troublesome, bothersome, nettlesome; informal aggravating, pesky.
ANTONYMS interesting, pleasant.

tiring ▶ adjective *it was very tiring work* **exhausting,** wearying, taxing, fatiguing, wearing, enervating, draining; hard, heavy, arduous, strenuous, onerous, uphill, demanding, grueling; informal murderous.

tissue ▶ noun **1** *living tissue* **matter,** material, substance; flesh.
2 *a box of tissues* **facial tissue**; trademark Kleenex.

titillate ▶ verb *the dancers titillated the audience* **arouse,** excite, tantalize, stimulate, stir, thrill, interest, attract, fascinate; informal turn on.
ANTONYMS bore.

titillating ▶ adjective *a titillating rendition of "Baby, It's Cold Outside"* **arousing,** exciting, stimulating, sexy, thrilling, provocative, tantalizing, interesting, fascinating; suggestive, salacious, erotic.
ANTONYMS boring.

title ▶ noun **1** *the title of the work* **name,** heading, legend, label, caption, inscription.
2 *the company publishes 400 titles a year* **publication,** work, book, newspaper, paper, magazine, periodical.
3 *the title of governor general* **designation,** name, form of address, honorific; epithet, rank, office, position, job title; informal moniker, handle, tag; formal appellation, denomination; sobriquet.
4 *an Olympic title* **championship,** crown, first place; laurels, palm.
5 *the landlord is obliged to prove his* ***title to the land*** **ownership of,** proprietorship of, possession of, holding of, freehold of, entitlement to, right to, claim to.
▶ verb *a paper titled "Immigration Today"* **call,** entitle, name, dub, designate, style, term; formal denominate.

titter ▶ verb & noun *she caused a few titters | the people at out table started to titter* **giggle,** snicker, twitter, tee-hee, chuckle, laugh, chortle.

titular ▶ adjective **1** *the titular head of a university* **nominal,** in title only, in name only, ceremonial, honorary, so-called; token, puppet.
2 *the book's titular hero* **eponymous,** identifying.

toady ▶ noun *a conniving little toady* **sycophant,** brown-noser, lickspittle, flatterer, flunky, lackey, trained seal, doormat, stooge, cringer; informal bootlicker, suck-up, yes-man; vulgar slang kiss-ass, ass-kisser.
▶ verb *she imagined him* ***toadying to*** *his rich clients* **grovel to,** ingratiate oneself with, be obsequious to, kowtow to, pander to, crawl to, truckle to, bow and scrape to, curry favor with, make up to, fawn on/over, slaver over, flatter, adulate, suck up to, lick the boots of, butter up.

toast ▶ noun **1** *he raised his glass in a toast* **tribute,** salute, salutation; archaic pledge.
2 *he was the toast of Toledo* **darling,** favorite, pet, heroine, hero; talk; fair-haired boy/girl.
▶ verb **1** *she toasted her hands in front of the fire* **warm,** warm up, heat, heat up.
2 *we toasted the couple with champagne* **drink (to) the health of,** drink to, salute, honor, pay tribute to.

today ▶ adverb **1** *the work must be finished today* **this day,** this very day, this morning, this afternoon, this evening.
2 *the complex tasks demanded of computers today* **nowadays,** these days, at the present time, in these times, in this day and age, now, currently, at the moment, at present, at

this moment in time; in the present climate, presently.

toddle ▶ verb 1 *the child toddled toward him* **totter,** teeter, wobble, falter, waddle, stumble.
2 informal *I toddled down to the quay* **amble,** wander, meander, stroll, saunter; informal mosey, toodle, tootle, putter.

to-do ▶ noun informal *the to-do in the street finally prompted a call to the police* **commotion,** fuss, ado, excitement, agitation, stir, palaver, confusion, disturbance, brouhaha, fracas, uproar, furor, tempest in a teapot, much ado about nothing; informal hoo-ha, ballyhoo, hullabaloo; Brit. informal kerfuffle.

together ▶ adverb 1 *friends who work together* **with each other,** in conjunction, jointly, in cooperation, in collaboration, in partnership, in combination, in league, in tandem, side by side, hand in hand, shoulder to shoulder, cheek by jowl; in collusion, hand in glove; informal in cahoots.
ANTONYMS separately.
2 *they both spoke together* **simultaneously,** at the same time, at one and the same time, at once, all together, as a group, in unison, in concert, in chorus, as one, with one accord.
ANTONYMS separately.
▶ adjective informal *a very together young woman* See LEVELHEADED.

toil ▶ verb 1 *she toiled all night* **work hard,** labor, exert oneself, slave (away), grind away, strive, work one's fingers to the bone, put one's nose to the grindstone; informal slog away, plug away, beaver away, work one's butt off, sweat blood; literary travail; archaic drudge, moil. See note at LABOR.
ANTONYMS rest, relax.
2 *she began to toil up the cliff path* **struggle,** trudge, tramp, tromp, traipse, slog, plod, trek, drag oneself; informal schlep.
▶ noun *a life of toil* **hard work,** labor, exertion, slaving, drudgery, effort, industry, 'blood, sweat, and tears'; slogging, elbow grease; literary travail; archaic moil.

toilet ▶ noun *he left to use the toilet* See BATHROOM.

token ▶ noun 1 *a token of our appreciation* **symbol,** sign, emblem, badge, representation, indication, mark, manifestation, expression, pledge, demonstration, recognition; evidence, proof. See note at SIGN.
2 *he kept the menu as a token of their wedding anniversary* **memento,** souvenir, keepsake, reminder, remembrance, memorial. See note at EMBLEM.
▶ adjective *token resistance* **symbolic,** emblematic; perfunctory, slight, nominal, minimal, minor, mild, superficial, inconsequential.

tolerable ▶ adjective 1 *a tolerable noise level* **bearable,** endurable, supportable, acceptable.
ANTONYMS intolerable.
2 *he had a tolerable voice* **fairly good,** passable, adequate, all right, acceptable, satisfactory, not (too) bad, average, fair; mediocre, middling, ordinary, indifferent, unremarkable, unexceptional; informal OK, so-so, 'comme ci, comme ça', nothing to write home about, no great shakes.
ANTONYMS unacceptable, exceptional.

tolerance ▶ noun 1 *an attitude of tolerance toward other people* **acceptance,** toleration; open-mindedness, broad-mindedness, forbearance, liberality, liberalism; patience, charity, indulgence, understanding.
2 *she has a low* **tolerance to** *alcohol* **endurance of, resistance to,** resilience to, resistance to, immunity to.

tolerant ▶ adjective *a tolerant attitude toward other religions* **open-minded,** forbearing, broad-minded, liberal, unprejudiced, unbiased; patient, long-suffering, understanding, forgiving, charitable, lenient, indulgent, permissive, easygoing, lax; informal laid-back.
ANTONYMS intolerant.

tolerate ▶ verb 1 *a regime unwilling to tolerate dissent* **allow,** permit, condone, accept, swallow, countenance; formal brook; archaic suffer.
2 *he couldn't tolerate her mood swings any longer* **endure,** put up with, bear, take, stand, support, stomach, deal with; abide.

toleration ▶ noun *her father demonstrated little toleration where her boyfriends were concerned* **acceptance,** tolerance, endurance; forbearance, sufferance, liberality, open-mindedness, broad-mindedness, liberalism; patience, charity, indulgence, understanding.

toll[1] ▶ noun 1 *a highway toll* **charge,** fee, payment, levy, tariff, tax.
2 *the toll of dead and injured* **number,** count, tally, total, sum total, grand total, sum; record, list.
3 *the toll on the environment has been high* **adverse effect(s),** detriment, harm, damage, injury, impact, hurt; cost, price, loss, disadvantage, suffering, penalty.

toll[2] ▶ verb *I heard the bell toll* **ring (out),** chime, strike, peal; sound, ding, dong, clang, bong, resound, reverberate; literary knell.

tomb ▶ noun *the tomb of old Mr. Momphreys* **burial chamber,** sepulcher, mausoleum, vault, crypt, catacomb; last/final resting place, grave, barrow, burial mound; historical charnel house.

tombstone ▶ noun *the writing on the tombstone* **gravestone,** headstone, stone; memorial, monument.

tome ▶ noun *he expects us to read this tome by Monday* **volume,** book, work, opus, publication, title.

tomfoolery ▶ noun *Mrs. Marks had no patience for tomfoolery* **silliness,** fooling around, clowning, shenanigans, capers, antics, pranks, tricks, buffoonery, skylarking, nonsense, horseplay, monkey business, mischief, foolishness, foolery, fandango.

tone ▶ noun 1 *the tone of the tuba* **timbre,** sound, sound quality, voice, voice quality, color, tonality.
2 *the somewhat impatient tone of his letter* **mood,** air, spirit, feel, sound, flavor, note, attitude, character, nature, manner, temper; tenor, vein, drift, gist.
3 *a dial tone* **note,** signal, beep, bleep.
4 *tones of burgundy and firebrick red* **shade,** color, hue, tint, tinge.
– PHRASES **tone down** *the pastels in the upholstery will help to tone down the color*

scheme **soften,** lighten, mute, subdue, mellow; **moderate,** modify, modulate, mitigate, temper, dampen.

tongue ▶ **noun 1** *a foreign tongue* **language,** dialect, patois, vernacular, mother tongue, native tongue, heritage language, lingua franca; informal lingo.
2 *her sharp tongue* **way/manner of speaking,** speech, choice of words, parlance.

tongue-tied ▶ **adjective** *he was tongue-tied with strangers* **lost for words,** speechless, unable to get a word out, struck dumb, dumbstruck; mute, dumb, silent; informal mum.
ANTONYMS loquacious.

tonic ▶ **noun 1** *ginseng can be used as a natural tonic* **stimulant,** restorative, refresher, medicine; informal pick-me-up; Medicine analeptic.
2 *we found the change of scene a tonic* **stimulant,** boost, fillip; informal shot in the arm, pick-me-up.

too ▶ **adverb 1** *invasion would be too risky* **excessively,** overly, over, unduly, immoderately, inordinately, unreasonably, extremely, exorbitantly, very; informal too-too.
2 *he was unhappy, too, you know* **also,** as well, in addition, additionally, into the bargain, besides, furthermore, moreover, on top of that, to boot, likewise.

tool ▶ **noun 1** *garden tools* **implement,** utensil, instrument, device, apparatus, gadget, appliance, machine, contrivance, contraption; informal gizmo.
2 *the beautiful Estella is Miss Havisham's tool* **puppet,** pawn, creature, cat's paw; minion, lackey, instrument, organ; informal stooge.
▶ **verb** *tool leather into a saddle* **work,** fashion, shape, cut; ornament, embellish, decorate, chase.

CHOOSE THE RIGHT WORD

tool, apparatus, appliance, implement, instrument, utensil

A wrench is a **tool**, meaning that it is a device held in and manipulated by the hand and used by a mechanic, plumber, carpenter, or other laborer to work, shape, move, or transform material (*he couldn't fix the drawer without the right tools*). An **implement** is a broader term referring to any tool or mechanical device used for a particular purpose (*agricultural implements*). A washing machine is an **appliance**, which refers to a mechanical or power-driven device, especially for household use (*the newly-married couple went shopping for appliances*). A **utensil** is a hand-held implement for domestic use (*eating utensils*), while an **instrument** is used for scientific or artistic purposes (*musical instrument; surgical instrument*). **Apparatus** refers to a collection of distinct instruments, tools, or other devices that are used in connection or combination with one another for a certain purpose (*the gym was open, but the exercise apparatus had not been set up*).

top ▶ **noun 1** *the top of the cliff* **summit,** peak, pinnacle, crest, crown, brow, head, tip, apex, vertex.
ANTONYMS bottom, base.
2 *the top of the table* **upper part,** upper surface, upper layer.
3 *the carrots' green tops* **leaves,** shoots, stem, stalk.
ANTONYMS root, tuber.
4 *the top of the coffee jar* **lid,** cap, cover, stopper, cork.
5 *a short-sleeved top* **shirt,** jersey, sweatshirt, sweater, pullover, vest; T-shirt, tank top; blouse.
6 *by 1981 he was at the top of his profession* **high point,** height, peak, pinnacle, zenith, acme, culmination, climax, prime.
ANTONYMS low point.
▶ **adjective 1** *the top floor* **highest,** topmost, uppermost.
ANTONYMS bottom, lowest.
2 *the world's top scientists* **foremost,** leading, principal, preeminent, greatest, best, finest, elite; informal top-notch, number one, blue-ribbon, blue-chip.
3 *the organization's top management* **upper,** chief, principal, main, leading, highest, highest-ranking, ruling, commanding, most powerful, most important.
4 *a top Paris hotel* **prime,** excellent, superb, superior, choice, select, top-quality, top-grade, first-rate, first-class, grade A, best, finest, premier, superlative, second to none, nonpareil; informal A1, top-notch, blue-ribbon, blue-chip, number one.
ANTONYMS mediocre, inferior.
5 *they are traveling at top speed* **maximum,** maximal, greatest, utmost.
ANTONYMS lowest, minimum.
▶ **verb 1** *sales are expected to top $1.3 billion* **exceed,** surpass, go beyond, better, best, beat, outstrip, outdo, outshine, eclipse, go one better than, cap.
2 *their debut CD is currently topping the charts* **lead,** head, be at the top of.
3 *chocolate mousse topped with whipped cream* **cover,** cap, coat, smother; finish, garnish.
– PHRASES **over the top** *the lavish dessert buffet after that meal was simply over the top* **excessive,** immoderate, inordinate, extreme, exaggerated, extravagant, overblown, too much, unreasonable, hyperbolic, disproportionate, undue, unwarranted, uncalled for, unnecessary, going too far. **top up** *remember to top up your gas tank before heading back to Houston* **fill,** refill, refresh, freshen, replenish, recharge, resupply; supplement, add to, augment.

topic ▶ **noun** *today's topic is skin care* **subject,** subject matter, theme, issue, matter, point, talking point, question, concern, argument, thesis, text, keynote.

topical ▶ **adjective** *let's stick to topical issues* **current,** up-to-date, up-to-the-minute, contemporary, recent, relevant; newsworthy, in the news.
ANTONYMS out-of-date.

topmost ▶ **adjective** See UPPERMOST (sense 1).

top-notch ▶ **adjective** informal *Rebecca is one of our top-notch salespeople* **first-class,** first-rate, top-quality, five-star; superior, prime, premier, premium, grade A, blue-chip, blue-ribbon, superlative, best, finest, select, exclusive, excellent, superb, outstanding, unbeatable, splendid, of the highest order, top-of-the-line, top-flight, top-grade; informal bang-up, A1.

topple ▸ verb **1** *she toppled over* **fall,** fall over, tumble, overturn, tip over, keel over, collapse; lose one's balance.
2 *protesters toppled a huge statue* **knock over,** upset, push over, tip over, fell, upend.
3 *a plot to topple the government* **overthrow,** oust, unseat, overturn, bring down, defeat, get rid of, dislodge, eject.

topsy-turvy ▸ adjective **1** *a topsy-turvy flag* **upside down,** wrong side up, inverted, reversed, upset; informal bassackward, ass-backward.
ANTONYMS right side up.
2 *everything in the apartment was topsy-turvy* **in disarray,** in a mess, in a muddle, in disorder, disordered, jumbled, in chaos, chaotic, disorganized, awry, upside down, at sixes and sevens; informal every which way, higgledy-piggledy.
ANTONYMS neat, ordered.

torment ▸ noun **1** *months of mental and emotional torment* **agony,** suffering, torture, pain, anguish, misery, distress, affliction, trauma, wretchedness; hell, purgatory.
2 *it was a torment to see him like that* **ordeal,** affliction, scourge, curse, plague, bane, thorn in someone's side/flesh, cross to bear; sorrow, tribulation, trouble.
▸ verb **1** *she was tormented by shame* **torture,** afflict, rack, harrow, plague, haunt, bedevil, distress, agonize.
2 *she began to torment the two younger boys* **tease,** taunt, bait, harass, provoke, goad, plague, bother, trouble, persecute; informal needle.

torn ▸ adjective **1** *a torn shirt* **ripped,** rent, cut, slit; ragged, tattered, in tatters, in ribbons.
2 *she was torn between the two options* **wavering,** vacillating, irresolute, dithering, uncertain, unsure, undecided, split, of two minds.

tornado ▸ noun See STORM (sense 1 of the noun).

torpid ▸ adjective *torpid tourists traveled tired through the tropics* **lethargic,** sluggish, inert, inactive, slow, lifeless; languid, listless, lazy, idle, indolent, slothful, supine, passive, apathetic, phlegmatic, somnolent, sleepy, weary, tired.
ANTONYMS energetic.

torpor ▸ noun *the feeling of torpor lingered for weeks* **lethargy,** sluggishness, inertia, inactivity, lifelessness, listlessness, languor, lassitude, laziness, idleness, indolence, sloth, acedia, passivity, somnolence, weariness, sleepiness.

torrent ▸ noun **1** *a torrent of water* **flood,** deluge, inundation, spate, cascade, cataract, rush, stream, current, flow, overflow, tide.
2 *a torrent of abuse* **outburst,** outpouring, stream, flood, volley, barrage, tide, spate.
ANTONYMS trickle.

torrid ▸ adjective **1** *a torrid summer* **hot,** dry, scorching, searing, blazing, blistering, sweltering, burning, sultry; informal boiling (hot), baking (hot), sizzling.
ANTONYMS cold, wet.
2 *a torrid affair* **passionate,** ardent, lustful, amorous; informal steamy, sultry, sizzling, hot.
ANTONYMS passionless.

tortuous ▸ adjective **1** *a tortuous route* **twisting,** twisty, twisting and turning, winding, windy, zigzag, sinuous, snaky, serpentine, meandering, circuitous.
ANTONYMS straight.
2 *a tortuous argument* **convoluted,** complicated, complex, labyrinthine, tangled, tangly, involved, confusing, difficult to follow, involuted, lengthy, overlong, circuitous.
ANTONYMS straightforward.

torture ▸ noun **1** *acts of torture* **infliction of pain,** abuse, ill-treatment, maltreatment, persecution; sadism.
2 *the torture of losing a loved one* **torment,** agony, suffering, pain, anguish, misery, distress, heartbreak, affliction, scourge, trauma, wretchedness; hell, purgatory.
▸ verb **1** *the security forces routinely tortured suspects* **inflict pain on,** ill-treat, abuse, mistreat, maltreat, persecute.
2 *he was tortured by grief* **torment,** rack, afflict, harrow, plague, agonize, scourge, crucify.

toss ▸ verb **1** *he tossed the ball over the fence* **throw,** hurl, fling, sling, cast, pitch, lob, project; informal heave, chuck.
2 *he tossed a coin and it landed heads* **flip,** flick.
3 *the ship tossed about on the waves* **pitch,** lurch, rock, roll, plunge, reel, list, keel, sway, wallow, flounder.
4 *she tossed about in her sleep* **thrash,** squirm, wriggle, writhe, fidget, turn.
5 *toss the salad ingredients together* **shake,** stir, turn, mix, combine.

total ▸ adjective **1** *the total cost* **entire,** complete, whole, full, comprehensive, combined, aggregate, gross, overall, final.
ANTONYMS partial.
2 *a total success* **complete,** utter, absolute, thorough, out-and-out, outright, all-out, sheer, perfect, consummate, arrant, positive, rank, unmitigated, unqualified, unreserved, categorical.
ANTONYMS partial.
▸ noun *a total of $160,000* **sum,** sum total, grand total, aggregate, result; whole, entirety, totality.
▸ verb **1** *the prize money totaled $33,050* **add up to,** amount to, come to, run to, make, work out to.
2 *she totaled up her score* **add (up),** count, reckon, tot up, tally, compute, work out.

totalitarian ▸ adjective *Saddam's totalitarian regime* **autocratic,** undemocratic, one-party, dictatorial, tyrannical, despotic, fascist, oppressive, repressive, illiberal; authoritarian, autarchic, absolute, absolutist; dystopian.
ANTONYMS democratic.

totality ▸ noun *the concept is difficult to grasp in its totality* **entirety,** wholeness, fullness, completeness; whole, total, aggregate, sum, sum total; all, everything.

totally ▸ adverb *the decor is totally pink*

completely, entirely, wholly, thoroughly, fully, utterly, absolutely, perfectly, unreservedly, unconditionally, quite, altogether, downright; in every way, in every respect, one hundred percent, every inch, to the hilt; informal flat out, to the max.
ANTONYMS partly.

totter ▶ verb **1** *arm in arm, they tottered across the lawn* **teeter,** dodder, walk unsteadily, stagger, wobble, stumble, shuffle, shamble, toddle; reel, sway, roll, lurch.
2 *the foundations began to heave and totter* **shake,** sway, tremble, quiver, teeter, shudder, rock, quake; chiefly Brit. judder.

touch ▶ verb **1** *his shoes were touching the end of the bed* **be in contact with,** come into contact with, meet, join, connect with, converge with, be contiguous with, be against.
2 *he touched her cheek* **press lightly,** tap, pat; feel, stroke, fondle, caress, pet; brush, graze, put a hand to.
3 *nobody can touch her when she's on her game* **compare with,** rival, compete with, come/get close to, be on a par with, equal, match, be a match for, be in the same class/league as, measure up to; better, beat; informal hold a candle to.
4 *you're not supposed to touch the computer* **handle,** hold, pick up, move; meddle with, play about with, fiddle with, interfere with, tamper with, disturb, lay a finger on; use, employ, make use of.
5 *people whose lives have been touched by the recession* **affect,** impact, have an effect on, have an impact on, make a difference to, change.
6 *years later she wrote to tell them how much their kindnesses had touched her* **affect,** move, tug at someone's heartstrings; leave an impression on, have an effect on.
▶ noun **1** *he felt her touch on his shoulder* **tap,** pat; stroke, caress; brush, graze; hand.
2 *his political touch* **skill,** skillfulness, expertise, dexterity, deftness, adroitness, adeptness, ability, talent, flair, facility, proficiency, mastery, knack, technique, approach, style.
3 *a touch of sadness* **trace,** bit, grain, hint, suggestion, suspicion, scintilla, tinge, overtone, undertone, note; dash, taste, drop, dab, dribble, pinch, speck, soupçon.
4 *the oil lamps are a nice touch* **detail,** feature, point; addition, accessory.
5 *have you been in touch with him?* **contact,** communication, correspondence; connection, association, interaction.
– PHRASES **touch down** *the plane is expected to touch down in San Juan* **land,** alight, come down, put down, arrive. **touch off** *the action touched off a string of protests* **cause,** spark, trigger, start, set in motion, ignite, stir up, provoke, give rise to, lead to, generate, set off. **touch on/upon** *his speech is sure to touch on the subject of school vouchers* **refer to,** mention, comment on, speak on, remark on, bring up, raise, broach, allude to; cover, deal with. **touch something up 1** *these paints are handy for touching up small areas* **repaint,** retouch, patch, fix; renovate, refurbish, revamp. **2** *the editor touched up my prose* **improve,** enhance, make better, refine, give the finishing touches to; informal tweak.

touch-and-go ▶ adjective *his recovery is touch-and-go* **uncertain,** precarious, risky, chancy, hazardous, dangerous, critical, suspenseful, cliffhanging, hanging by a thread; informal dicey.
ANTONYMS certain.

touching ▶ adjective *a touching tribute to their mother* **moving,** affecting, heartwarming, emotional, emotive, tender, sentimental; poignant, sad, tearjerker, tearjerking. See note at **MOVING**.

touchstone ▶ noun *the declaration was considered a touchstone for Soviet dissidents* **criterion,** standard, yardstick, benchmark, barometer, bellwether, litmus test; measure, point of reference, norm, gauge, test, guide, exemplar, model, pattern.

touchy ▶ adjective **1** *Arnie can be so touchy* **sensitive,** oversensitive, hypersensitive, easily offended, thin-skinned, high-strung, tense; irritable, dyspeptic, tetchy, testy, crotchety, peevish, waspish, querulous, bad-tempered, petulant, pettish, cranky, fractious, choleric.
ANTONYMS affable, good-humored.
2 *a touchy subject* **delicate,** sensitive, tricky, ticklish, thorny, prickly, embarrassing, awkward, difficult; contentious, controversial.

tough ▶ adjective **1** *tough leather gloves* **durable,** strong, resilient, sturdy, rugged, solid, stout, long-lasting, heavy-duty, industrial-strength, well-built, made to last.
ANTONYMS soft, flimsy, fragile.
2 *the steak was tough* **chewy,** leathery, gristly, stringy, fibrous.
ANTONYMS tender.
3 *she'll survive—she's tough* **robust,** resilient, strong, hardy, rugged, flinty, fit; stalwart, tough as nails.
ANTONYMS weak.
4 *another tough report from the auditor* **strict,** stern, severe, stringent, rigorous, hard, firm, hard-hitting, uncompromising; unsentimental, unsympathetic.
ANTONYMS soft, light, lenient.
5 *that exercise sure was tough* **arduous,** onerous, strenuous, grueling, exacting, difficult, demanding, hard, taxing, tiring, exhausting, punishing, laborious, stressful, back-breaking, Herculean; archaic toilsome.
ANTONYMS easy.
6 *these are tough questions* **difficult,** hard, baffling, knotty, thorny, tricky.
ANTONYMS easy.
▶ noun *a gang of toughs* **ruffian,** thug, goon, hoodlum, hooligan; informal roughneck, hood, heavy, bruiser, yahoo.

toughen ▶ verb **1** *the process toughens the wood fibers* **strengthen,** fortify, reinforce, harden, temper, anneal.
2 *measures to* ***toughen up*** *prison discipline* **make stricter,** make more severe, stiffen, tighten up; informal beef up.

tour ▶ noun **1** *we enjoyed a two-week* ***tour of*** *Italy* **trip to/through,** excursion to/through, journey to/through, expedition to/through, jaunt to/through, outing to/through; trek to/through, safari to/through; archaic peregrination

to/through.
2 *a tour of the factory* **visit,** inspection, guided tour.
▶ **verb 1** *this hotel is well placed for touring the Cariboo* **travel around,** explore, discover, vacation in, visit.
2 *the governor toured the factory* **visit,** go around/through, walk around/through, inspect; informal check out.
– PHRASES **tour of duty** *a six-month tour of duty abroad* **stint,** stretch, spell, turn, assignment, period of service.

tourist ▶ **noun** *the islands teem with tourists* **vacationer,** traveler, sightseer, visitor, backpacker, globetrotter, day tripper, out-of-towner.
ANTONYMS local.

tournament ▶ **noun 1** *a golf tournament* **competition,** contest, championship, meeting, tourney, meet, event, match, round robin.
2 historical *a knight preparing for a tournament* **joust,** tilt; the lists.

tousled ▶ **adjective** *tousled hair* **untidy,** disheveled, wind-blown, messy, disordered, disarranged, messed up, rumpled, uncombed, ungroomed, tangled, wild, unkempt; informal mussed up.
ANTONYMS neat, tidy.

tout ▶ **verb 1** *street merchants were touting their wares* **peddle,** sell, hawk, offer for sale, promote.
2 *cab drivers were* ***touting for*** *business* **solicit,** seek, drum up; ask for, petition for, appeal for.
3 *she's being touted as the next party leader* **recommend,** speak of, extol, advocate, talk of; predict.

tow ▶ **verb** *the car was towed back to the garage* **pull,** haul, drag, draw, tug, lug.
– PHRASES **in tow** *he arrived with his new girlfriend in tow* **in attendance,** by one's side, alongside, in one's charge; accompanying, following, tagging along.

toward, towards ▶ **preposition 1** *they were driving toward her apartment* **in the direction of,** to; on the way to, on the road to, en route to.
2 *toward evening, dark clouds gathered* **just before,** shortly before, near, around, approaching, close to, coming to, getting on for.
3 *her attitude toward politics* **with regard to,** as regards, regarding, in regard to, respecting, in relation to, concerning, about, apropos, vis-à-vis.
4 *some money toward the cost of a new house* **as a contribution to,** for, to help with.

tower ▶ **noun** *a church tower* **steeple,** spire; minaret; turret; bell tower, belfry, campanile; skyscraper, high-rise, edifice; transmission tower.
▶ **verb 1** *snow-capped peaks towered over the valley* **soar,** rise, rear, loom; overshadow, overhang, hang over, dominate.
2 *she* ***towered over*** *most other theologians of her generation* **eclipse,** overshadow, outshine, outclass, surpass, dominate, be head and shoulders above, put someone/something in the shade.

towering ▶ **adjective 1** *a towering skyscraper* **high,** tall, lofty, soaring, sky-high, multistory; giant, gigantic, enormous, huge, massive; informal ginormous.
2 *a towering intellect* **outstanding,** preeminent, leading, foremost, finest, top, surpassing, supreme, great, incomparable, unrivaled, unsurpassed, peerless.

town ▶ **noun** *they live in a town just outside Milwaukee* **municipality,** township, conurbation, urban area; city, capital, metropolis, megalopolis, megacity, burg; small town, whistle-stop.

toxic ▶ **adjective** *toxic houseplants* **poisonous,** virulent, noxious, deadly, dangerous, harmful, injurious, pernicious.
ANTONYMS harmless.

toy ▶ **noun** *Santa left a bundle of toys* **plaything,** game; gadget, device; trinket, knickknack, gizmo.
▶ **adjective 1** *a toy gun* **model,** imitation, replica, fake; miniature.
2 *a toy poodle* **miniature,** small, tiny, diminutive, dwarf, midget, pygmy.
– PHRASES **toy with 1** *I was toying with the idea of writing a book* **think about,** consider, flirt with, entertain the possibility of; kick around. **2** *Adam toyed with his glasses* **fiddle with,** play with, fidget with, twiddle; finger. **3** *she toyed with her food* **nibble,** pick at, peck at, eat listlessly, eat like a bird. **4** *you are toying with my emotions* **trifle with,** play with, play havoc with, amuse oneself with, mess with, be flippant with.

trace ▶ **verb 1** *police hope to trace the owner of the vehicle* **track down,** find, discover, detect, unearth, turn up, hunt down, ferret out.
2 *she traced a pattern in the sand with her toe* **draw,** outline, mark, sketch.
3 *the analysis traces the origins of cowboy poetry* **outline,** map out, follow, sketch out, delineate, depict, show, indicate.
▶ **noun 1** *no trace had been found of the runaways* **vestige,** sign, mark, indication, evidence, clue; trail, tracks, marks, prints, footprints, spoor; remains, remnant, relic.
2 *a trace of bitterness crept into her voice* **bit,** touch, hint, suggestion, suspicion, shadow, whiff; drop, dash, tinge, speck, shred, iota; smidgen, tad.

CHOOSE THE RIGHT WORD

trace, remnant, track, trail, vestige

You can follow the **track** of a deer in the snow, the **trace** of a sleigh, or the **trail** of someone who has just cut down a Christmas tree and is dragging it back to the car. A *track* is a line or a series of marks left by the passage of something or someone; it often refers specifically to a line of footprints or a path worn into the ground by the feet (*to follow the track of a grizzly bear*). *Trace* may refer to a line or a rut made by someone or something that has been present or passed by; it may also refer to a mark serving as evidence that something has happened or been there (*traces of mud throughout the house; the telephoto shots have a trace* *of a camera shake*). *Trail* may refer to the track created by the passage of animals or people, or to the mark or marks left by something being dragged along a surface (*they followed the trail of the injured dog*). **Vestige** and **remnant** come closer in meaning to *trace*, as they refer to what remains after something has passed away. A *vestige* is always slight when compared to what it recalls (*the last vestiges of a great civilization*), while a *remnant* is a fragment or scrap of something (*all that remained of the historic tapestry after the fire was a few scorched remnants*).

track ▶ noun **1** *a gravel track* **path,** pathway, footpath, lane, trail, route, way, course.
2 *the final lap of the track* **course,** racetrack, raceway; velodrome.
3 (**tracks**) *he found the tracks of a wolverine* **traces,** marks, prints, footprints, trail, spoor.
4 *we followed the track of the hurricane* **course,** path, line, route, way, trajectory, wake.
5 *railroad tracks* **rail,** line.
6 *the album's title track* **song,** recording, number, piece.
▶ verb *he tracked a bear for 40 miles* **follow,** trail, trace, pursue, shadow, stalk, keep an eye on, keep in sight; informal tail.
– PHRASES **keep track of** *the electronic log keeps track of your blood-glucose readings* **monitor,** follow, keep up with, keep an eye on; keep in touch with, keep up to date with; informal keep tabs on. **track down** *Captain Pearce vowed that they would track down the killer* **discover,** find, detect, hunt down/out, unearth, uncover, turn up, dig up, ferret out, bring to light. **on track** *the fund-raising is on track* **on course,** on an even keel, on schedule.

tract[1] ▶ noun *large tracts of land* **area,** region, expanse, sweep, stretch, extent, belt, swathe, zone.

tract[2] ▶ noun *a political tract* **treatise,** essay, article, paper, work, monograph, disquisition, dissertation, thesis, homily, tractate; pamphlet, booklet, chapbook, leaflet.

tractable ▶ adjective *our preschool teachers disagree with the statement that children are becoming less tractable every year* **malleable,** manageable, amenable, pliable, governable, yielding, complaisant, compliant, game, persuadable, accommodating, docile, biddable, obliging, obedient, submissive, meek.
ANTONYMS recalcitrant.

trade ▶ noun **1** *the illicit trade in stolen cattle* **commerce,** buying and selling, dealing, traffic, trafficking, business, marketing, merchandising; dealings, transactions, deal-making.
2 *we shook hands as we made the trade* **exchange,** transaction, swap, trade-off; archaic truck.
3 *the glazier's trade* **craft,** occupation, job, career, profession, business, line of work, line, métier, vocation, calling, walk of life, field; work, employment, livelihood.
▶ verb **1** *he made his fortune* ***trading in*** *beaver pelts* **deal (in),** buy and sell, traffic (in), market, merchandise, peddle, vend; informal hawk, run.
2 *the business is trading at a loss* **operate,** run, do business.
3 *I traded the old machine for a newer model* **swap,** exchange, switch; barter, trade in.
– PHRASES **trade on** *he trades on his friendship with powerful people* **exploit,** take advantage of, capitalize on, profit from, use, make use of; milk; informal cash in on.

trademark ▶ noun **1** *the company's trademark* **logo,** brand, emblem, sign, mark, stamp, symbol, badge, crest, monogram, colophon; brand name, trade name, proprietary name.
2 *it had all the trademarks of a Mafia hit* **characteristic,** hallmark, calling card, sign, trait, quality, attribute, feature, peculiarity, idiosyncrasy, quirk.

trader ▶ noun *a commodities trader* **dealer,** merchant, buyer, seller, buyer and seller, marketeer, merchandiser, broker, agent; distributor, vendor, purveyor, monger, supplier, trafficker; retailer, wholesaler; storekeeper, shopkeeper; wheeler-dealer.

tradition ▶ noun **1** *during a maiden speech, by tradition, everyone keeps absolutely silent* **historical convention,** unwritten law, mores; oral history, lore, folklore.
2 *an age-old tradition* **custom,** practice, convention, ritual, observance, way, usage, habit, institution; formal praxis.

traditional ▶ adjective **1** *traditional Christmas fare* **long-established,** customary, time-honored, established, classic, accustomed, standard, regular, normal, conventional, usual, orthodox, habitual, set, fixed, routine, ritual; old, age-old, ancestral.
2 *traditional beliefs* **handed-down,** folk, unwritten, oral.

traduce ▶ verb *you dare to traduce my family?* **defame,** slander, speak ill of, misrepresent, malign, vilify, denigrate, disparage, slur, impugn, smear, besmirch, run down, blacken the name of, cast aspersions on; informal badmouth, dis.

traffic ▶ noun **1** *the bridge is not open to traffic* **vehicles**; cars, trucks.
2 *they might be stuck in traffic* **a traffic jam,** congestion, a gridlock, a holdup, a bottleneck, a tie-up; informal a snarl-up, a logjam.
3 *the illegal traffic in stolen art* **trade,** trading, trafficking, dealing, commerce, business, buying and selling; smuggling, bootlegging, black market; dealings, transactions.
▶ verb *he confessed to* ***trafficking in*** *narcotics* **trade (in),** deal (in), do business in, buy and sell; smuggle, bootleg; informal run, push.

tragedy ▶ noun *the flood was the worst tragedy in the city's history* **disaster,** calamity, catastrophe, cataclysm, misfortune, mishap, blow, trial, tribulation, affliction, adversity.

tragic ▶ adjective **1** *a tragic accident* **disastrous,** calamitous, catastrophic, cataclysmic, devastating, terrible, dreadful, awful, appalling, dismal, horrendous; fatal, deadly, mortal, lethal.
ANTONYMS fortunate, lucky.
2 *a tragic tale* **sad,** unhappy, pathetic, moving, distressing, depressing, painful, harrowing,

heart-rending, piteous, wretched, sorry; melancholy, doleful, mournful, miserable, gut-wrenching.
ANTONYMS joyful, happy.
3 *a tragic waste of talent* **regrettable,** shameful, terrible, horrible, awful, deplorable, lamentable, piteous, dreadful, grievous.

trail ▶ **noun 1** *he left a trail of clues | a trail of devastation* **series,** string, chain, succession, sequence; aftermath, wake. See note at TRACE.
2 *wolves on the trail of their prey* **track,** spoor, path, scent; traces, marks, signs, prints, footprints.
3 *the airplane's vapor trail* **wake,** contrail, tail, stream.
4 *a trail of ants* **line,** column, train, file, procession, string, chain, convoy; lineup.
5 *provincial parks with nature trails* **path,** pathway, way, footpath, walk, track, course, route.
▶ **verb 1** *her robe trailed along the ground* **drag,** sweep, swish, be drawn; dangle, hang (down), droop.
2 *the roses grew wild, their stems trailing over the banks* **hang,** droop, fall, spill, cascade.
3 *Filteau suspected that they were trailing him* **follow,** pursue, track, shadow, stalk, hunt (down); informal tail.
4 *the defending champions were trailing 3–1 in the second period* **lose,** be down, be behind, lag behind.
5 *her voice trailed off* **fade,** tail off/away, grow faint, die away, dwindle, taper off, subside, peter out, fizzle out.

train ▶ **verb 1** *an engineer trained in remote-sensing techniques* **instruct,** teach, coach, tutor, school, educate, prime, drill, ground; inculcate, indoctrinate, initiate, break in.
2 *she's training to be a hairdresser* **study,** learn, prepare, take instruction.
3 *with the Olympics in mind, athletes are training hard* **exercise,** do exercises, work out, get into shape, practice, prepare.
4 *she trained the gun on his chest* **aim,** point, direct, level, focus; zero in.
▶ **noun 1** *the train for Youngstown* locomotive, subway, monorail; informal iron horse; baby talk choo choo.
2 *a minister and his train of attendants* **retinue,** entourage, cortège, following, staff, household.
3 *a train of elephants* **procession,** line, file, column, convoy, cavalcade, caravan, string, succession, trail.
4 *a bizarre train of events* **chain,** string, series, sequence, succession, set, course, cycle, concatenation.

trainer ▶ **noun** *my personal trainer at the gym* **coach,** instructor, teacher, tutor; handler.

training ▶ **noun 1** *in-house training for staff* **instruction,** teaching, coaching, tuition, tutoring, guidance, schooling, education, orientation; indoctrination, inculcation, initiation.
2 *four months' hard training before the tournament* **exercise,** exercises, working out, conditioning; practice, preparation.

trait ▶ **noun** *elaborating on the truth is just one of her personality traits* **characteristic,** attribute, feature, quality, property; habit, custom, mannerism, idiosyncrasy, peculiarity, quirk, oddity, foible.

traitor ▶ **noun** *convicted traitors will be executed* **betrayer,** backstabber, double-crosser, renegade, fifth columnist; turncoat, defector, deserter; collaborator, informer, mole, snitch, double agent; Judas, Benedict Arnold, quisling; informal snake in the grass, two-timer, rat, scab, fink.

traitorous ▶ **adjective** *his dealings with a traitorous party* **treacherous,** disloyal, treasonous, renegade, backstabbing; double-crossing, double-dealing, faithless, unfaithful, two-faced, duplicitous, deceitful, false; informal two-timing; literary perfidious.
ANTONYMS loyal.

trajectory ▶ **noun** *the missile's trajectory* **course,** path, route, track, line, orbit.

trammel literary ▶ **noun** *the trammels of domesticity* **restraint,** constraint, curb, check, impediment, obstacle, barrier, handicap, bar, hindrance, encumbrance, disadvantage, drawback, shackles, fetters, bonds.
▶ **verb** *those less trammeled by convention than himself* **restrict,** restrain, constrain, hamper, confine, hinder, handicap, obstruct, impede, hold back, tie down, hamstring, shackle, fetter.

tramp ▶ **verb** *we tramped across France* **trudge,** tromp, plod, galumph, stamp, trample, lumber, clump, clomp, stump, stomp; trek, slog, schlep, drag oneself, walk, hike, march, traipse.
▶ **noun 1** *a wandering old tramp* **vagrant,** vagabond, street person, hobo, homeless person, down-and-out; traveler, drifter, derelict, beggar, mendicant, bag lady, bum.
2 *the regular tramp of the sentry's boots* **footstep,** tromp, step, footfall, tread, stamp, stomp.

trample ▶ **verb 1** *someone had trampled on the tulips* **tread,** tramp, stamp, stomp, walk over; squash, crush, flatten.
2 *we do nothing but* **trample over** *their feelings* **treat with contempt,** disregard, show no consideration for, abuse; encroach on, infringe (on).

trance ▶ **noun** *he pretended to be in a trance* **daze,** stupor, hypnotic state, half-conscious state, dream, reverie, fugue state.

tranquil ▶ **adjective 1** *the lake's tranquil waters* **peaceful,** calm, calming, still, serene, placid, restful, quiet, relaxing, undisturbed, limpid, pacific.
ANTONYMS disturbed.
2 *Martha smiled, perfectly tranquil* **calm,** serene, relaxed, unruffled, unperturbed, unflustered, untroubled, composed, 'calm, cool, and collected'; equable, even-tempered, placid, unflappable. See note at CALM.
ANTONYMS excitable.

tranquilize ▶ **verb** *the horse was tranquilized* **sedate,** put under sedation, narcotize, anesthetize, etherize, drug.

tranquilizer ▶ **noun** *don't have any wine if you're taking tranquilizers* **sedative,** barbiturate, calmative, sleeping pill, depressant, narcotic, opiate; informal downer.

ANTONYMS stimulant.

transact ▶ verb *no business will be transacted on the day after Christmas* **conduct,** carry out, negotiate, do, perform, execute, take care of, discharge; settle, conclude, finish, accomplish.

transaction ▶ noun **1** *property transactions* **deal,** business deal, undertaking, arrangement, bargain, negotiation, agreement, settlement; proceedings.
2 *the bank statement records your transactions* **debit,** credit, deposit, withdrawal.
3 *the transaction of government business* **conduct,** carrying out, negotiation, performance, execution.

transcend ▶ verb **1** *an issue that transcended party politics* **go beyond,** rise above, cut across.
2 *his exploits far transcended those of his predecessors* **surpass,** exceed, beat, cap, tower above, outdo, outclass, outstrip, leave behind, outshine, eclipse, overshadow, throw into the shade, upstage, top.

transcendent ▶ adjective **1** *the search for a transcendent level of knowledge* **mystical,** mystic, transcendental, spiritual, divine; metaphysical.
2 *a transcendent genius* **incomparable,** matchless, peerless, unrivaled, inimitable, beyond compare/comparison, unparalleled, unequaled, without equal, second to none, unsurpassed, unsurpassable, nonpareil; exceptional, consummate, unique, perfect, rare, surpassing, magnificent.

transcendental ▶ adjective See **TRANSCENDENT** (sense 1).

transcribe ▶ verb **1** *each interview was taped and transcribed* **write out,** write down, copy down, put in writing, put on paper, render.
2 *a person who can take and transcribe shorthand* **transliterate,** interpret, translate.

transcript ▶ noun **1** *a radio transcript* **written version,** printed version, script, text, transliteration, record, reproduction.
2 *university transcript* **student record,** grades, report card.

transfer ▶ verb **1** *the hostages were transferred to a safe house* **move,** convey, take, bring, shift, remove, carry, transport; transplant, relocate, resettle.
2 *the property was transferred to his wife* **hand over,** pass on, make over, turn over, sign over, consign, devolve, assign, delegate.
▶ noun **1** *he died shortly after his transfer to hospital* **move,** conveyance, transferral, transference, shift, relocation, removal, switch, transplantation.
2 *keep your bus transfer in your pocket* **ticket,** pass; receipt, proof of purchase.

transfix ▶ verb **1** *she was transfixed by the images on the screen* **mesmerize,** hypnotize, spellbind, bewitch, captivate, entrance, enthrall, fascinate, absorb, enrapture, grip, hook, rivet, paralyze.
2 *a field mouse is transfixed by the owl's curved talons* **impale,** stab, spear, pierce, spike, skewer, gore, stick, run through.

transform ▶ verb *the old inn has been transformed into an outpatient medical facility* **change,** alter, convert, metamorphose, transfigure, transmute, mutate; revolutionize, overhaul; remodel, reshape, redo, reconstruct, rebuild, reorganize, rearrange, rework, renew, revamp, remake, retool; informal transmogrify, morph.

transformation ▶ noun *the transformation of the sales department has been dramatic* **change,** alteration, mutation, conversion, metamorphosis, transfiguration, transmutation, sea change; revolution, overhaul; remodeling, reshaping, redoing, reconstruction, rebuilding, reorganization, rearrangement, reworking, renewal, revamp, remaking, remake; informal transmogrification, morphing.

transgress ▶ verb **1** *if they transgress, the punishment is harsh* **misbehave,** behave badly, break the law, err, fall from grace, stray from the straight and narrow, sin, do wrong, go astray; archaic trespass.
2 *she had transgressed an unwritten social law* **infringe,** breach, contravene, disobey, defy, violate, break, flout.

transgression ▶ noun **1** *a punishment for past transgressions* **offense,** crime, sin, wrong, wrongdoing, misdemeanor, impropriety, infraction, misdeed, lawbreaking; error, lapse, peccadillo, fault; archaic trespass.
2 *Adam's transgression of God's law* **infringement,** breach, contravention, violation, defiance, disobedience, nonobservance. See note at **SIN**.

transgressor ▶ noun *grant these transgressors forgiveness* **offender,** miscreant, lawbreaker, criminal, villain, felon, malefactor, guilty party, culprit; sinner, evildoer; archaic trespasser, miscreant.

transient ▶ adjective *our interest in the environment must not be transient* **transitory,** temporary, short-lived, short-term, ephemeral, impermanent, brief, short, momentary, fleeting, passing, here today and gone tomorrow; literary evanescent, fugitive. See note at **TEMPORARY**.
ANTONYMS permanent.
▶ noun *the plight of poor transients* **hobo,** vagrant, vagabond, street person, homeless person, down-and-out; traveler, drifter, derelict.

transit ▶ noun **1** *public transit* **transportation,** transport, mass transit, bus system, subway system.
2 *the transit of goods between states* **transportation,** transport, movement, flow, conveyance, shipping, shipment, trucking, carriage, transfer.
– PHRASES **in transit** *the building supplies are in transit* **en route,** on the journey, on the way, on the road.

transition ▶ noun *the transition from school to work* **change,** passage, move, transformation, conversion, metamorphosis, alteration, handover, changeover; segue, shift, switch, jump, leap, progression; progress, development, evolution, flux.

transitional ▶ adjective **1** *a transitional period* **changeover,** interim; changing, fluid, in flux, unsettled, intermediate, liminal.
2 *the transitional government* **interim,**

temporary, provisional, pro tem, acting, caretaker.

transitory ▶ adjective *transitory fashions* **transient,** temporary, brief, short, short-lived, short-term, impermanent, ephemeral, momentary, fleeting, passing, here today and gone tomorrow; literary evanescent, fugitive. See note at TEMPORARY.
ANTONYMS permanent.

translate ▶ verb **1** *the German original had been translated into English* **render,** put, express, convert, change; transcribe, transliterate.
2 *be prepared to translate plenty of jargon* **render,** paraphrase, reword, rephrase, convert, decipher, decode, gloss, explain.
3 *interesting ideas cannot always be translated into effective movies* **adapt,** change, convert, transform, alter, turn, transmute; informal transmogrify, morph.

translation ▶ noun *the translation of the Bible into English* **rendition,** rendering, conversion; transcription, transliteration.

transmission ▶ noun **1** *the transmission of ideas* **spread,** transferral, communication, conveyance; dissemination, circulation, transference.
2 *a live transmission* **broadcast,** program, show, airing, podcast.
3 *her car had a faulty transmission* **power train,** drivetrain.

transmit ▶ verb **1** *the use of computers to transmit information* **transfer,** pass on, hand on, communicate, convey, impart, channel, carry, relay, forward, dispatch; disseminate, spread, circulate.
2 *the program will be transmitted on Sunday* **broadcast,** relay, send out, air, televise, podcast.

transparency ▶ noun **1** *the transparency of the glass* **translucency,** limpidity, clearness, clarity.
2 *color transparencies* **slide,** acetate.
3 *the new government aims for better transparency* **openness,** accountability, straightforwardness, candor.

transparent ▶ adjective **1** *transparent blue water* **clear,** crystal clear, see-through, translucent, pellucid, limpid, glassy, vitreous.
ANTONYMS opaque, cloudy.
2 *fine transparent fabrics* **see-through,** sheer, filmy, gauzy, diaphanous, translucent.
ANTONYMS thick.
3 *a transparent attempt to win favor* **obvious,** evident, self-evident, undisguised, unconcealed, conspicuous, patent, clear, crystal clear, plain, (as) plain as the nose on your face, apparent, unmistakable, easily discerned, manifest, palpable, indisputable, unambiguous, unequivocal.
ANTONYMS ambiguous, obscure.

transpire ▶ verb **1** *it transpired that her family had moved away* **become known,** emerge, come to light, be revealed, turn out, come out, be discovered, prove to be the case, unfold.
2 *I'm going to find out exactly what transpired* **happen,** occur, take place, arise, come about, materialize, turn up, chance, befall, ensue; literary come to pass. See note at HAPPEN.

> USAGE
> **transpire**
> The common use of *transpire* to mean 'occur, happen' (*I'm going to find out exactly what transpired*) is a loose extension of an earlier meaning, 'come to be known' (*it transpired that Mark had been baptized a Catholic*). This loose sense of 'happen,' which is now more common in American usage than the sense of 'come to be known,' was first recorded in American English toward the end of the eighteenth century and has been listed in American dictionaries from the nineteenth century. Careful writers should note, however, that in cases where *occur* or *happen* would do just as well, the use of *transpire* may strike readers as an affectation or as jargon.

transplant ▶ verb **1** *our headquarters will be transplanted to Pennsylvania* **transfer,** move, remove, shift, relocate, take.
2 *the seedlings should be transplanted in larger pots* **replant,** repot, relocate.
3 *kidneys must be transplanted within 48 hours of removal* **transfer,** implant.

transport ▶ verb *barges transport the lumber from the mill* **convey,** carry, take, transfer, move, shift, send, deliver, bear, ship, ferry, haul; informal cart.
▶ noun **1** *alternative forms of transport* **transit,** conveyance, means/method of transport; travel, getting around; vehicle, car, truck, train.
2 See note at RAPTURE.

transpose ▶ verb **1** *the blue and black plates were transposed* **interchange,** exchange, switch, swap (around), reverse, invert, flip.
2 *the themes are transposed from the sphere of love to that of work* **transfer,** shift, relocate, transplant, move, displace.

transverse ▶ adjective *a transverse bar* **crosswise,** crossways, cross, horizontal, diagonal, oblique, slanted.

trap ▶ noun **1** *an animal caught in a trap* **snare,** net, mesh, deadfall, leghold (trap), pitfall.
2 *the question was set as a trap* **trick,** ploy, ruse, deception, subterfuge; booby trap, ambush, setup.
3 informal *shut your trap!* See MOUTH (sense 1 of the noun).
▶ verb **1** *police trapped the two men and arrested them* **snare,** entrap, ensnare, lay a trap for; capture, catch, bag, corner, ambush.
2 *a rat trapped in a barn* **confine,** cut off, corner, shut in, pen in, hem in; imprison, hold captive.
3 *I hoped to trap him into an admission* **trick,** dupe, deceive, lure, inveigle, beguile, fool, hoodwink; catch, trip up.

trappings ▶ plural noun *surrounded by the trappings of royalty* **accessories,** accoutrements, appurtenances, trimmings, frills, accompaniments, extras, ornamentation, adornment, decoration; regalia, panoply, paraphernalia, apparatus, finery, equipment, gear, effects, things, bits and pieces.

trash ▶ noun 1 *the subway entrance was blocked with trash* **garbage,** refuse, waste, litter, junk, debris, detritus, rubbish.
2 *if they read at all, they read trash* **junk,** dross, dreck, drivel, nonsense, trivia, pulp, pulp fiction, pap, garbage, rubbish; informal crap, schlock.
3 informal *that family is trash* **scum,** vermin, the dregs of society, the lowest of the low; informal the scum of the earth, dirt, riffraff.
▶ verb 1 *the apartment had been totally trashed* **wreck,** ruin, destroy, wreak havoc on, devastate; vandalize, tear up, bust up, smash; informal total.
2 *his play was trashed by the critics* **criticize, lambaste,** censure, attack, insult, abuse, malign, give a bad press to, condemn, flay, savage, pan, knock, take to pieces, take/pull apart, crucify, hammer, slam, bash, trash talk, roast, maul, rubbish, pummel; informal bad-mouth, bitch about.

trauma ▶ noun 1 *the trauma of divorce* **shock,** upheaval, distress, stress, strain, pain, anguish, suffering, upset, agony, misery, sorrow, grief, heartache, heartbreak, torture; ordeal, trial, tribulation, trouble, worry, anxiety; nightmare, hell, hellishness.
2 *the trauma to the liver* **injury,** damage, wound; cut, laceration, lesion, abrasion, contusion.

traumatic ▶ adjective *the enduring pain of this traumatic event* **disturbing,** shocking, distressing, upsetting, heartbreaking, painful, scarring, jolting, agonizing, hurtful, stressful, damaging, injurious, harmful, awful, terrible, devastating, harrowing.

travel ▶ verb 1 *Tim spent much of his time traveling abroad* **journey,** tour, take a trip, voyage, explore, go sightseeing, globe-trot, backpack, gallivant; archaic peregrinate.
2 *we traveled the length and breadth of the island* **journey through,** cross, traverse, cover; roam, wander, rove, range, trek.
3 *light travels faster than sound* **move,** be transmitted.
▶ noun (**travels**) *she amassed great wealth during her travels* **journeys,** expeditions, trips, tours, excursions, voyages, treks, safaris, explorations, wanderings, odysseys, pilgrimages, jaunts, junkets; traveling, touring, sightseeing, backpacking, globe-trotting, gallivanting; archaic peregrinations.

traveler ▶ noun *thousands of travelers were left stranded* **tourist,** vacationer, sightseer, visitor, globe-trotter, backpacker; pilgrim, wanderer, drifter, nomad, migrant; passenger, commuter, fare.

traveling ▶ adjective *in those days, many a tired traveling man would stop at Aunt Dilly's for some hot soup and a warm bath* **nomadic,** itinerant, peripatetic, wandering, roaming, roving, wayfaring, migrant, vagrant, of no fixed address.

traverse ▶ verb 1 *he traversed the deserts of Iran* **travel over/across,** cross, journey over/across, pass over; cover; ply; wander, roam, range.
2 *a ditch traversed by a wooden bridge* **cross,** bridge, span; extend across, lie across, stretch across.

travesty ▶ noun *a travesty of justice* **perversion of,** distortion of, corruption of, misrepresentation of, poor imitation of, poor substitute for, mockery of, parody of, caricature of; farce of, charade of, pantomime of, sham of, spoof of; informal apology for, (poor) excuse for. See note at CARICATURE.

treacherous ▶ adjective 1 *her treacherous brother betrayed her* **traitorous,** disloyal, faithless, unfaithful, duplicitous, deceitful, deceptive, false, backstabbing, double-crossing, double-dealing, two-faced, weaselly, untrustworthy, unreliable; apostate, renegade, two-timing; literary perfidious.
ANTONYMS loyal, faithful.
2 *treacherous driving conditions* **dangerous,** hazardous, perilous, unsafe, precarious, risky, deceptive, unreliable; informal dicey, hairy.
ANTONYMS safe, reliable.

treachery ▶ noun *Myrna never forgave Warren his treachery* **betrayal,** disloyalty, faithlessness, unfaithfulness, infidelity, breach of trust, duplicity, dirty tricks, deceit, deception, chicanery, stab in the back, backstabbing, double-dealing, untrustworthiness; treason, two-timing; literary perfidy.

tread ▶ verb 1 *he trod purposefully down the hall* **walk,** step, stride, pace, go; march, tramp, plod, thump, stomp, trudge.
2 *the snow had been* **trodden down** *by the horses* **crush,** flatten, press down, squash; trample on, tramp on, stamp on, stomp on.
▶ noun *we heard her heavy tread on the stairs* **step,** footstep, footfall, tramp, thump; clip-clop.

treason ▶ noun *the treason of Benedict Arnold will be recounted for centuries* **treachery,** disloyalty, betrayal, faithlessness; sedition, subversion, mutiny, rebellion; high treason, lèse-majesté; apostasy; literary perfidy.
ANTONYMS allegiance, loyalty.

treasonable ▶ adjective *treasonable offenses against the king* **traitorous,** treasonous, treacherous, disloyal; seditious, subversive, mutinous, rebellious; literary perfidious.
ANTONYMS loyal.

treasure ▶ noun 1 *a casket of treasure* **riches,** valuables, jewels, gems, gold, silver, precious metals, money, cash; wealth, fortune; treasure trove.
2 *art treasures* **valuable object,** valuable, work of art, masterpiece, precious item.
3 informal *she's a real treasure* **paragon,** gem, angel, find, star, one of a kind, one in a million.
▶ verb *I treasure the photographs I took of Jack* **cherish,** hold dear, prize, value greatly; adore, dote on, love, be devoted to, worship, venerate.

treat ▶ verb 1 *Charlotte treated him very badly* **behave toward,** act toward; deal with, handle; literary use.
2 *police are treating the fires as arson* **regard,** consider, view, look upon, think of.
3 *the book treats its subject with insight and responsibility* **tackle,** deal with, handle, discuss, present, explore, investigate, approach; consider, study, analyze.
4 *she was treated at St. Paul's Hospital* **give medical care (to),** nurse, care for, tend (to), help, give treatment (to), attend (to),

administer (to); medicate.
5 *the plants may prove useful in treating cancer* **cure,** heal, remedy; fight, combat.
6 *she* ***treated him to*** *an expensive meal* **buy (for) someone,** take someone out for, give (to) someone; pay for (for someone); foot the bill for, pick up the tab for.
7 *delegates were* ***treated to*** *an Indonesian dance show* **regale with,** entertain with/by, fête with, amuse with, divert with.
▶ **noun 1** *a birthday treat* **celebration,** entertainment, amusement; surprise; party, excursion, outing, special event.
2 *I bought you some chocolate as a treat* **present,** gift; delicacy, luxury, indulgence, extravagance, guilty pleasure; informal goodie.
3 *it was a real treat to see them* **pleasure,** delight, boon, thrill, joy.

treatise ▶ **noun** *a treatise on the principles of democracy* **disquisition,** essay, paper, work, exposition, discourse, dissertation, thesis, monograph, opus, oeuvre, study, critique; tract, pamphlet, account.

treatment ▶ **noun 1** *the company's treatment of its workers* **behavior toward,** conduct toward; handling of, dealings with, management of.
2 *she's responding well to treatment* **medical care,** therapy, nursing, ministrations; medication, drugs, medicaments; cure, remedy.
3 *her treatment of the topic* **discussion,** handling, investigation, exploration, consideration, study, analysis, critique; approach, methodology.

treaty ▶ **noun** *several terms of the treaty were casually violated* **agreement,** settlement, pact, deal, entente, concordat, accord, protocol, convention, contract, covenant, bargain, pledge; concord, compact.

trek ▶ **noun** *a three-day trek across the desert* **journey,** trip, expedition, safari, odyssey, voyage; hike, march, slog, tramp, walk; long haul.
▶ **verb** *we trekked through the jungle* **hike,** tramp, march, slog, footslog, trudge, traipse, walk; travel, journey; informal **hoof it.**

trellis ▶ **noun** *rambling roses scrambled up the trellis* **lattice,** framework, espalier, arbor; network, mesh; grille, grid, grating; latticework; technical reticulation.

tremble ▶ **verb 1** *Joe's hands were trembling* **shake,** shake like a leaf, quiver, twitch, jerk; quaver, waver.
2 *the entire building trembled* **shake,** shudder, quake, wobble, rock, vibrate, move, sway, totter, teeter; chiefly Brit. judder. See note at SHAKE.
3 *she trembled at the thought of what he had in store for her* **be afraid,** be frightened, be apprehensive, worry, shake in one's boots; quail, quake, shrink, blench.
▶ **noun** *the slight tremble in her hands* **tremor,** shake, shakiness, trembling, quiver, quaking, twitch, vibration, unsteadiness.
ANTONYMS steadiness.

tremendous ▶ **adjective 1** *tremendous sums of money* **huge,** enormous, immense, colossal, massive, prodigious, stupendous, monumental, mammoth, vast, gigantic, giant, mighty, epic, titanic, towering, king-size(d), jumbo, gargantuan, Herculean; substantial, considerable, Brobdingnagian; informal whopping, astronomical, humongous, ginormous.
ANTONYMS tiny, small, slight.
2 *a tremendous explosion* **very loud,** deafening, ear-splitting, booming, thundering, thunderous, resounding.
ANTONYMS soft.
3 informal *I've seen him play and he's tremendous* **excellent,** splendid, wonderful, marvelous, magnificent, superb, sublime, lovely, delightful, too good to be true; informal super, great, amazing, fantastic, terrific, sensational, heavenly, divine, fabulous, awesome, to die for, magic, wicked, mind-blowing, splendiferous, far out, out of this world, brilliant, boss, swell.
ANTONYMS bad, poor.

tremor ▶ **noun 1** *the sudden tremor of her hands* **trembling,** shaking, shakiness, tremble, shake, quivering, quiver, twitching, twitch, tic; quavering, quaver, quake, palpitation.
2 *a tremor of fear ran through her* **shiver,** frisson, spasm, thrill, tingle, stab, dart, wave, surge, rush, ripple.
3 *the epicenter of the tremor* **earthquake,** earth tremor, shock; informal quake.

tremulous ▶ **adjective 1** *a tremulous voice* **shaky,** trembling, shaking, unsteady, quavering, wavering, quivering, quivery, quaking, weak, warbly, trembly.
ANTONYMS steady.
2 *a tremulous smile* **timid,** diffident, shy, hesitant, uncertain, nervous, jittery, timorous, frightened, scared, anxious, apprehensive; informal trepidatious.
ANTONYMS confident.

trench ▶ **noun** *plant seeds in shallow trenches to conserve moisture* **ditch,** channel, trough, excavation, furrow, rut, conduit, cut, drain, duct, waterway, watercourse; entrenchment, moat; Archaeology fosse.

trenchant ▶ **adjective** *trenchant criticism of her leadership* **incisive,** penetrating, sharp, keen, insightful, acute, focused, shrewd, razor-sharp, piercing; vigorous, forceful, strong, potent, telling, emphatic, forthright; mordant, cutting, biting, acerbic, pungent.
ANTONYMS vague.

trend ▶ **noun 1** *an upward trend in unemployment* **tendency,** movement, drift, swing, shift, course, current, direction, progression, inclination, leaning; bias, bent.
2 *the latest trend in dance music* **fashion,** vogue, style, mode, craze, mania, rage; informal fad, thing, flavor of the month.
▶ **verb** *interest rates are trending up* **move,** go, head, drift, gravitate, swing, shift, turn, incline, tend, lean, veer.

trepidation ▶ **noun** *he sat in the waiting room, full of trepidation* **fear,** apprehension, dread, fearfulness, fright, agitation, anxiety, worry, nervousness, tension, misgivings, unease, uneasiness, foreboding, disquiet, dismay, consternation, alarm, panic; informal butterflies (in one's stomach), jitteriness, the jitters, the creeps, the shivers, a cold sweat, the heebie-jeebies, the willies, the shakes, jim-jams, collywobbles, cold feet.
ANTONYMS equanimity, composure.

trespass ▶ verb **1** *there is no excuse for trespassing on railroad property* **intrude on,** encroach on, enter without permission, invade.
2 *I must not **trespass on** your good nature* **take advantage of,** impose on, play on, exploit, abuse; encroach on, infringe on.
3 archaic *he would be the last among us to trespass* **sin,** transgress, offend, do wrong, err, go astray, fall from grace, stray from the straight and narrow.
▶ noun **1** *his alleged trespass on private land* **unlawful entry,** intrusion, encroachment, invasion.
2 archaic *he asked forgiveness for his trespasses* **sin,** wrong, wrongdoing, transgression, crime, offense, misdeed, misdemeanor, error, lapse, fall from grace.

trespasser ▶ noun *trespassers will be prosecuted* **intruder**, interloper, unwelcome visitor, encroacher.

tresses ▶ plural noun *her strawberry blonde tresses* **hair,** head of hair, mane, mop of hair, shock of hair, shag of hair; locks, curls, ringlets.

trial ▶ noun **1** *the trial is expected to last several weeks* **court case,** case, assize, lawsuit, suit, hearing, inquiry, tribunal, litigation, legal proceedings, judicial proceedings, proceedings, legal action; court-martial; appeal, retrial.
2 *the product is undergoing clinical trials* **test,** tryout, experiment, pilot study; examination, check, assessment, evaluation, appraisal; trial/test period, trial/test run, beta test, dry run.
3 *she could be a bit of a trial at times* **nuisance,** pest, irritant, problem, ordeal, inconvenience, plague, thorn in one's side, one's cross to bear; bore; informal pain, pain in the neck, pain in the butt, headache, drag, bother, nightmare, albatross; nudnik, burr under someone's saddle.
4 *a long account of her trials and tribulations* **trouble**, anxiety, worry, burden, affliction, ordeal, tribulation, adversity, hardship, trying time, tragedy, trauma, setback, difficulty, problem, misfortune, bad luck, mishap, misadventure; informal hassle; literary travails.
▶ adjective *a three-month trial period* **test,** experimental, pilot, exploratory, probationary, provisional.

tribe ▶ noun *nomadic tribes of the Sahara* **ethnic group,** people, band, nation; family, dynasty, house, clan, sept.

tribulation ▶ noun **1** *the tribulations of her personal life* **trouble,** difficulty, problem, worry, anxiety, burden, cross to bear, ordeal, trial, adversity, hardship, tragedy, sorrow, trauma, affliction; setback, blow; informal hassle; literary travail.
2 *his time of tribulation was just beginning* **suffering,** distress, trouble, misery, wretchedness, unhappiness, sadness, heartache, woe, grief, sorrow, pain, anguish, agony; literary travail.

tributary ▶ noun *the countless tributaries of the mighty Mississippi* **headwater,** creek, branch, fork, feeder, side stream, side channel, snye.

tribute ▶ noun **1** *tributes flooded in from friends and colleagues* **accolade,** praise, commendation, salute, testimonial, homage, eulogy, paean, panegyric; congratulations, compliments, plaudits, appreciation; gift, present, offering; bouquet; formal encomium.
ANTONYMS criticism, condemnation.
2 *it is a tribute to his courage that he ever played again* **testimony,** indication, manifestation, testament, evidence, proof, attestation.
– PHRASES **pay tribute to** *the players on both teams paid tribute to the retiring Ripken* **praise,** sing the praises of, speak highly of, commend, acclaim, tip one's hat to, applaud, salute, honor, show appreciation of, recognize, acknowledge, pay homage to, extol; formal laud.

trick ▶ noun **1** *he's capable of any mean trick | their clever little trick cost us $500* **stratagem,** ploy, ruse, scheme, device, maneuver, contrivance, machination, artifice, wile, dodge; deceit, deception, trickery, subterfuge, chicanery, swindle, hoax, fraud, confidence trick; informal con, setup, rip-off, game, scam, sting, flimflam, bunco; archaic shift, fetch, rig.
2 *I think she's playing a trick on us* **practical joke,** joke, prank, jape, spoof, gag, put-on.
3 *conjuring tricks* **feat,** stunt; (**tricks**) **sleight of hand,** legerdemain, prestidigitation; magic.
4 (**tricks**) *the tricks of the trade* **knack,** art, skills, techniques; secrets, shortcuts.
▶ verb *many people have been tricked by con artists with fake IDs* **deceive,** delude, hoodwink, mislead, take in, dupe, fool, double-cross, cheat, defraud, swindle, gull, hoax, bamboozle, entrap; informal con, bilk, diddle, rook, put one over on, pull a fast one on, pull the wool over someone's eyes, take for a ride, shaft, flimflam, sucker, snooker; literary cozen, illude; archaic chicane.
– PHRASES **do the trick** informal *here, these two aspirins should do the trick* **be effective,** work, solve the problem, fill/fit the bill. **trick of the light** *it was probably just a trick of the light* **illusion,** optical illusion, figment of the imagination; mirage.

trickery ▶ noun *she suspects me of trickery* **deception**, deceit, dishonesty, cheating, duplicity, double-dealing, legerdemain, sleight of hand, guile, craftiness, deviousness, subterfuge, skulduggery, chicanery, fraud, fraudulence, swindling; formal pettifoggery; informal monkey business, funny business.
ANTONYMS honesty.

trickle ▶ verb *blood was trickling from two cuts in his lip* **drip,** dribble, ooze, leak, seep, percolate, spill.
ANTONYMS pour, gush.
▶ noun *trickles of water* **dribble,** drip, thin stream, rivulet.

trickster ▶ noun *she spent her whole life loving and protecting a brother who was never better than the lowest of tricksters* **swindler,** cheat, fraud, fraudster; charlatan, mountebank, quack, impostor, sham, hoaxer; rogue, villain, shyster, scoundrel; informal con man, con artist, sharp, shark, flimflammer, grifter, scam artist, bunco artist, chiseler.

tricky ▶ adjective **1** *a tricky situation* **difficult,** awkward, problematic, delicate, ticklish, sensitive, embarrassing, touchy; risky, uncertain, precarious, touch-and-go; thorny, knotty, complex, complicated; informal sticky, hairy, dicey.

ANTONYMS straightforward, uncomplicated.
2 *a tricky and unscrupulous politician* **cunning,** crafty, wily, guileful, artful, devious, sly, scheming, slippery, slick, calculating, designing, sharp, shrewd, astute, canny; duplicitous, dishonest, deceitful.
ANTONYMS honest.

trifle ▶ **noun 1** *we needn't bother the principal over such trifles* **unimportant thing,** trivial thing, triviality, thing of no importance, thing of no consequence, bagatelle, inessential, nothing; technicality, nonissue; (**trifles**) trivia, minutiae, flummery, small potatoes.
2 *we wrapped up a few trifles as party favors* **bauble,** trinket, knickknack, gimcrack, gewgaw, toy; informal whatnot.
3 *he bought it for **a trifle*** **next to nothing,** a very small amount; a pittance; informal peanuts, chump change.
– PHRASES **a trifle** *Candace is a trifle miffed at Brad* **a little,** a bit, somewhat, a touch, a mite, a whit; informal a tad. **trifle with** *you should never have trifled with her emotions* **play with,** amuse oneself with, toy with, dally with, be flippant with, flirt with, play fast and loose with, mess about with; dated sport with.

trifling ▶ **adjective** *a trifling matter* **trivial,** unimportant, insignificant, inconsequential, petty, minor, of little/no account, of little/no consequence, footling, pettifogging, incidental; silly, idle, insipid, superficial, small, tiny, inconsiderable, nominal, negligible, nugatory; informal piddling; formal exiguous.
ANTONYMS important.

trigger ▶ **verb 1** *the incident triggered an acrimonious debate* **precipitate,** prompt, elicit, trigger off, set off, spark (off), touch off, provoke, stir up; cause, give rise to, launch, lead to, set in motion, occasion, bring about, generate, engender, begin, start, initiate; literary enkindle.
2 *thieves triggered the alarm* **activate,** set off, set going, trip.

trim ▶ **verb 1** *his hair had been washed and trimmed* **cut,** crop, bob, shorten, clip, snip, shear, barber; neaten, shape, tidy up.
2 ***trim off** the lower leaves using a sharp knife* **cut off,** remove, take off, chop off, lop off; prune.
3 *production costs need to be trimmed* **reduce,** decrease, cut down, cut back on, scale down, prune, slim down, pare down, dock.
4 *the story was severely trimmed for the movie version* **shorten,** abridge, condense, abbreviate, telescope, truncate.
5 *a pair of black leather gloves trimmed with fake fur* **decorate,** adorn, ornament, embellish; edge, pipe, border, hem, fringe.
▶ **noun 1** *white curtains with a tasteful blue trim* **decoration,** trimming, ornamentation, adornment, embellishment; border, edging, piping, rickrack, hem, fringe, frill, frippery.
2 *an unruly mop in need of a trim* **haircut,** cut, barbering, clip, snip; pruning, tidying up.
▶ **adjective 1** *a trim little villa* **neat,** tidy, neat and tidy, orderly, in (good) order, uncluttered, well-kept, well-maintained, shipshape, spruce, in apple-pie order, immaculate, spick-and-span.
ANTONYMS untidy, messy.
2 *she does Pilates to stay trim* **slim,** in shape, slender, lean, sleek, willowy, lissome, svelte; streamlined.
ANTONYMS fat.

trimming ▶ **noun 1** *a black dress with lace trimming* See **TRIM** (sense 1 of the noun).
2 (**trimmings**) *roast turkey with all the trimmings* **accompaniments,** extras, frills, fixings, accessories, accoutrements, trappings, paraphernalia; garnishing, garnish.

trinket ▶ **noun** *he brought back some lovely little trinkets from the South Seas* **knickknack,** bauble, ornament, bibelot, curio, trifle, gimcrack, gewgaw, toy, novelty; informal whatnot, doohickey, tchotchke; dated kickshaw.

trio ▶ **noun** *a talented trio from East Orange will sing the closing hymn* **threesome,** triumvirate, triad, trinity, troika; triplets.

trip ▶ **verb 1** *he tripped on the loose stones* **stumble,** lose one's footing, catch one's foot, slip, lose one's balance, fall, fall down, tumble, topple, take a spill, wipe out.
2 *students often **trip up** by forgetting to add a bibliography* **make a mistake,** miscalculate, make a blunder, blunder, go wrong, make an error, err; informal slip up, screw up, make a boo-boo, goof up, mess up, fluff.
3 *the question was intended to trip him up* **catch out,** trick, outwit, outsmart; throw off balance, disconcert, unsettle, discountenance, discomfit, throw, wrong-foot.
4 *they tripped merrily along the path* **skip,** run, dance, prance, bound, spring, scamper.
5 *Hoffman tripped the alarm* **set off,** activate, trigger; turn on.
▶ **noun 1** *a trip to Oahu* **excursion,** outing, jaunt; **vacation,** visit, tour, journey, expedition, voyage; drive, run, day out, day trip, road trip, cruise, junket, spin; rare peregrination. See note at **JOURNEY**.
2 *a trip down icy front steps can be a devastating accident* **stumble,** slip, misstep, false step; fall, tumble, spill.

triple ▶ **adjective 1** *a triple alliance* **three-way,** tripartite; threefold, trifold.
2 *they paid her triple the standard fee* **three times,** treble.

trite ▶ **adjective** *critics were put off by the trite dialogue* **banal,** hackneyed, clichéd, platitudinous, vapid, commonplace, stock, conventional, stereotyped, overused, overdone, overworked, stale, worn out, timeworn, tired, hoary, hack, unimaginative, unoriginal, uninteresting, dull; informal old hat, corny, cornball, cheesy, boilerplate.
ANTONYMS original, imaginative.

triumph ▶ **noun 1** *Gretzky's many triumphs* **victory,** win, conquest, success; achievement, feat, accomplishment.
ANTONYMS defeat.
2 *his eyes shone with triumph* **jubilation,** exultation, elation, delight, joy, happiness, glee, pride, satisfaction.
ANTONYMS disappointment.
3 *a triumph of their ingenuity* **tour de force,** masterpiece, coup, wonder, sensation, master stroke, feat.

ANTONYMS failure.

▶ **verb 1** *she triumphed in the tournament* **win,** succeed, come first, clinch first place, be victorious, carry the day, prevail, take the honors, come out on top.
ANTONYMS lose, fail.
2 *they had no chance of* ***triumphing over*** *the Democrats in the third district* **defeat,** beat, conquer, trounce, vanquish, overcome, overpower, overwhelm, get the better of; bring someone to their knees, prevail against, subdue, subjugate; informal lick, best.

triumphant ▶ **adjective 1** *the triumphant Swedish team* **victorious,** successful, winning, conquering, all-conquering; undefeated, unbeaten.
ANTONYMS unsuccessful, defeated.
2 *a triumphant expression* **jubilant,** exultant, elated, rejoicing, joyful, joyous, delighted, gleeful, proud, gloating.
ANTONYMS disappointed, despondent.

trivia ▶ **plural noun** *his head is overflowing with obscure trivia* **minutiae,** minor details, petty detail, niceties, technicalities, trivialities, trifles, trumpery, nonessentials, ephemera; informal small potatoes, peanuts.

trivial ▶ **adjective 1** *trivial problems* **unimportant,** banal, trite, commonplace, insignificant, inconsequential, minor, of no account, of no consequence, of no importance; incidental, inessential, nonessential, petty, trifling, trumpery, pettifogging, footling, small, slight, little, inconsiderable, negligible, paltry, nugatory; informal piddling, picayune, nickel-and-dime, penny-ante; trademark Mickey Mouse.
ANTONYMS important, significant, life-and-death.
2 *I used to be quite a trivial person* **frivolous,** superficial, shallow, unthinking, airheaded, featherbrained, lightweight, foolish, silly, trite.
ANTONYMS profound, serious.

triviality ▶ **noun 1** *the triviality of the subject matter* **unimportance,** insignificance, inconsequence, inconsequentiality, pettiness, banality.
2 *he need not concern himself with such trivialities* **minor detail,** thing of no importance/consequence, trifle, nonessential, nothing; technicality; (**trivialities**) trivia, minutiae.

troop ▶ **noun** (**troops**) *Ethiopian troops were stationed there* **soldiers,** armed forces, servicemen, servicewomen, infantry; peacekeepers; guards, escorts; the services, the army, the military.

▶ **verb** *we trooped out of the hall* **walk,** march, file, proceed; flock, crowd, throng, stream, swarm, surge, spill.

trophy ▶ **noun 1** *a swimming trophy* **cup,** medal; prize, award.
2 *a cabinet full of trophies from his travels* **souvenir,** memento, keepsake; spoils, booty.

tropical ▶ **adjective** *tropical weather* **very hot,** sweltering, boiling, scorching, humid, sultry, steamy, sticky, oppressive, stifling, suffocating, heavy, equatorial.
ANTONYMS cold, arctic.

trouble ▶ **noun 1** *you've caused enough trouble already* **problems,** difficulty, bother, inconvenience, worry, concern, anxiety, distress, stress, strife, agitation, harassment, hassle, unpleasantness.
2 *she poured out all her troubles* **problem,** misfortune, difficulty, trial, tribulation, trauma, burden, pain, woe, grief, heartache, misery, affliction, vexation, suffering.
3 *he's gone to a lot of trouble to help you* **effort,** inconvenience, fuss, bother, exertion, work, labor; pains, care, attention, thought.
4 *Rodney has been no trouble at all* **nuisance,** bother, inconvenience, irritation, irritant, problem, trial, pest, thorn in someone's flesh/side, headache, pain, pain in the neck/backside, drag; informal pain in the butt, burr under someone's saddle, nudnik.
5 *you're too gullible, that's your trouble* **shortcoming,** flaw, weakness, weak point, failing, fault, imperfection, defect, blemish; problem, difficulty.
6 *he had a history of heart trouble* **disease,** illness, sickness, ailments, complaints, problems; disorder, disability.
7 *the crash was due to engine trouble* **malfunction,** dysfunction, failure, breakdown.
8 *a game marred by serious crowd trouble* **disturbance,** disorder, unrest, unruliness, fighting, fracas, breach of the peace.

▶ **verb 1** *this matter had been troubling her for some time* **worry,** bother, concern, disturb, upset, agitate, distress, perturb, annoy, irritate, vex, irk, nag, niggle, prey on someone's mind, weigh down, burden; informal bug.
2 *he* ***was troubled by*** *bouts of ill health* **be afflicted by,** be burdened with; suffer from, be cursed with, be plagued by.
3 *there is nothing you need trouble about* **worry,** upset oneself, fret, be anxious, be concerned, concern oneself.
4 *don't trouble to see me out* **bother,** take the trouble, go to the trouble, exert oneself, go out of one's way.
5 *I'm sorry to trouble you* **inconvenience,** bother, impose on, disturb, put out, pester, hassle; formal discommode.

– PHRASES **in trouble** *he comes to visit only when he's in trouble* **in difficulty,** in difficulties, in a mess, in a bad way, in a predicament, in dire straits; informal in a fix, in a pickle, in a tight corner/spot, in a hole, in hot water, up a tree, up a/the creek, up against it.

troublemaker ▶ **noun** *I have little use for my former friends, who were, for the most part, troublemakers* **rabble-rouser,** rogue, scourge, agitator, agent provocateur, ringleader; incendiary, firebrand, demagogue; scandalmonger, gossipmonger, meddler, nuisance, mischief-maker, hell raiser; informal badass.

troublesome ▶ **adjective 1** *a troublesome problem* **annoying,** irritating, exasperating, maddening, infuriating, irksome, pesky, vexatious, vexing, bothersome, nettlesome, tiresome, worrying, worrisome, disturbing, upsetting, niggling, nagging; difficult, awkward, problematic, taxing; informal aggravating.
ANTONYMS simple, straightforward.

2 *a troublesome child* **difficult,** awkward, trying, demanding, uncooperative, rebellious, unmanageable, unruly, obstreperous, disruptive, badly behaved, disobedient, naughty, recalcitrant, high-maintenance; formal refractory.
ANTONYMS obedient, cooperative.

trough ▶ **noun 1** *a large feeding trough* **manger,** feeder, bunk, rack, crib, feed box; waterer.
2 *a thirty-foot trough* **channel,** conduit, trench, ditch, gully, drain, culvert, cut, flume, gutter; rain gutter.

trounce ▶ **verb** *Turner scored a season-high 19 points when the UConn women trounced St. Joseph's 87–34* **defeat convincingly,** rout, crush, overwhelm; informal hammer, clobber, thrash, whip, drub, shellac, cream, skunk, pulverize, massacre, crucify, demolish, destroy, blow away, annihilate, make mincemeat of, wipe the floor with, walk all over, murder.

troupe ▶ **noun** *our theater troupe is on tour* **group,** company, band, ensemble, set; cast.

truancy ▶ **noun** *the Board of Ed wants to know why truancy in the high school is at an all-time high* **absenteeism,** nonattendance, playing truant, truanting; informal playing hooky, skipping; booking out.

truant ▶ **noun** *the truants were sent to Mr. Maurer's office* **absentee,** runaway.
– PHRASES **play truant** *more than half of the freshman class staged a protest by playing truant on Monday* stay away from school; informal skip school, skip, play hooky; book out.

truce ▶ **noun** *news of the truce spread quickly among the locals* **cease-fire,** armistice, suspension of hostilities, peace, entente; respite, lull; informal letup.

truculent ▶ **adjective** *a number of staffers have complained that Wilson is too truculent to work with* **defiant,** aggressive, antagonistic, combative, belligerent, pugnacious, confrontational, ready for a fight, obstreperous, argumentative, quarrelsome, uncooperative; bad-tempered, ornery, short-tempered, cross, snappish, cranky; feisty, spoiling for a fight.
ANTONYMS cooperative, amiable.

trudge ▶ **verb** *they trudged through two miles of wet snow* **plod,** tramp, tromp, drag oneself, walk heavily, walk slowly, plow, slog, toil, trek; informal traipse, galumph.

true ▶ **adjective 1** *you'll see that what I say is true* **correct,** accurate, right, verifiable, in accordance with the facts, what actually/really happened, well-documented, the case, so; literal, factual, unelaborated, unvarnished.
ANTONYMS untrue, false, fallacious.
2 *people are still willing to pay for true craftsmanship* **genuine,** authentic, real, actual, bona fide, proper; honest-to-goodness, kosher, legit, the real McCoy.
ANTONYMS bogus, phony.
3 *the true owner of the goods* **rightful,** legitimate, legal, lawful, authorized, bona fide, de jure.
ANTONYMS de facto.
4 *the necessity for true repentance* **sincere,** genuine, real, unfeigned, heartfelt, hearty, from the heart.
ANTONYMS insincere, feigned.
5 *a true friend* **loyal,** faithful, constant, devoted, staunch, steadfast, true-blue, unswerving, unwavering; trustworthy, trusty, reliable, dependable.
ANTONYMS disloyal, faithless.
6 *a true reflection of life in the 50s* **accurate,** true to life, faithful, telling it like it is, fact-based, realistic, close, lifelike.
ANTONYMS inaccurate.

truly ▶ **adverb 1** *tell me truly what you want* **truthfully,** honestly, frankly, sincerely, candidly, openly, to someone's face, laying one's cards on the table; informal pulling no punches.
2 *I'm truly grateful to them* **sincerely,** genuinely, really, indeed, from the bottom of one's heart, heartily, profoundly; very, surely, extremely, immensely, thoroughly, positively, completely, tremendously, totally, incredibly, awfully; formal most; informal sure.
3 *this is truly a miracle* **without (a) doubt,** unquestionably, undoubtedly, certainly, surely, definitely, beyond doubt, beyond question, indubitably, undeniably, beyond the shadow of a doubt; in truth, really, in reality, actually, in fact; archaic forsooth, verily.
4 *exams do not truly reflect children's abilities* **accurately,** correctly, exactly, precisely, faithfully; informal to a T.

trump ▶ **verb** *by wearing the simplest of dresses, she had trumped them all* **outshine,** outclass, upstage, put in the shade, eclipse, surpass, outdo, outperform; beat, better, top, cap; informal be a cut above, be head and shoulders above, leave standing.

trumpet ▶ **verb 1** *the elephant trumpeted* call out, bellow, roar, yell, cry out, toot, bugle, holler.
2 *companies trumpeted their success* **proclaim,** announce, declare, herald, celebrate, shout from the rooftops.

truncate ▶ **verb** *the program may need to be truncated* **shorten,** cut, cut short, curtail, bring to an untimely end; abbreviate, condense, reduce, prune.
ANTONYMS lengthen, extend.

truncheon ▶ **noun** See BLUDGEON (noun).

trunk ▶ **noun 1** *the trunk of a tree* **main stem,** bole.
2 *the trunk of her car* **luggage compartment,** back.
3 *his powerful trunk* **torso,** body, upper body.
4 *an elephant's trunk* **proboscis,** nose, snout.
5 *a steamer trunk* **chest,** box, crate, coffer; case.

truss ▶ **noun** *three steel trusses* **support,** buttress, joist, brace, beam, prop, strut, stay, stanchion, pier.
▶ **verb** *she taught us how to truss the hens before roasting* **tie up,** bind, chain up; pinion, fetter, tether, secure; swaddle, wrap.

trust ▶ **noun 1** *good relationships are built on trust* **confidence,** belief, faith, certainty, assurance, conviction, credence; reliance.
ANTONYMS distrust, mistrust, doubt.
2 *a position of trust* **responsibility,** duty, obligation.

3 *the money is to be held in trust for his son* **safekeeping,** protection, charge, care, custody; trusteeship.

▶ **verb 1** *I should never have trusted her* **put one's trust in,** have faith in, have (every) confidence in, believe in, pin one's hopes/faith on, confide in.

ANTONYMS distrust, mistrust, doubt.

2 *he can be trusted to carry out an impartial investigation* **rely on,** depend on, bank on, count on, be sure of.

3 *I trust we shall meet again* **hope,** expect, take it, assume, presume, suppose.

4 *they don't like to trust their money to anyone outside the family* **entrust,** consign, commit, give, hand over, turn over, assign.

trustworthy ▶ **adjective** *a trustworthy citizen* **reliable,** dependable, honest, honorable, upright, principled, true, truthful, as good as one's word, ethical, virtuous, incorruptible, unimpeachable, above suspicion; responsible, sensible, levelheaded; loyal, faithful, staunch, steadfast, trusty; safe, sound, reputable, discreet; informal on the level, straight-up.

ANTONYMS unreliable.

trusty ▶ **adjective** *a cowboy and his trusty horse* **reliable,** dependable, trustworthy, unfailing, fail-safe, trusted, tried and true; loyal, faithful, true, staunch, steadfast, constant, unswerving, unwavering.

ANTONYMS unreliable.

truth ▶ **noun 1** *he doubted the truth of her statement* **veracity,** truthfulness, verity, sincerity, candor, honesty; accuracy, correctness, validity, factuality, authenticity.

ANTONYMS dishonesty, falseness.

2 *it's the truth, I swear* **what actually happened,** the case, so; the gospel (truth), the honest truth.

ANTONYMS lies.

3 *truth is stranger than fiction* **fact(s),** reality, real life, actuality.

ANTONYMS fiction.

4 *scientific truths* **fact,** verity, certainty, certitude; law, principle.

ANTONYMS lie, falsehood.

– PHRASES **in truth** *in truth, their marriage was rocky from the start* **in fact,** in actual fact, as it happens, in point of fact, in reality, really, actually, to tell the truth, if truth be told.

truthful ▶ **adjective 1** *truthful behavior* **honest,** sincere, trustworthy, genuine; candid, frank, straight-shooting, open, forthright, straight, upfront, on the level, on the up and up.

ANTONYMS deceitful, deceptive.

2 *a truthful account* **true,** accurate, correct, factual, faithful, reliable; unvarnished, unembellished, unidealized; formal veracious, veridical.

ANTONYMS inaccurate, untrue.

try ▶ **verb 1** *try to help him* **attempt,** endeavor, venture, make an effort, exert oneself, strive, do one's best, do one's utmost, move heaven and earth; undertake, aim, take it upon oneself; informal have a go, give it one's best shot, bend over backwards, bust a gut, do one's damnedest, pull out all the stops, go all out, knock oneself out; formal essay.

2 *try it and see what you think* **test,** put to the test, sample, taste, inspect, investigate, examine, appraise, evaluate, assess; informal check out, give something a whirl, test drive.

3 *Mary tried everyone's patience* **tax,** strain, test, stretch, sap, drain, exhaust, wear out.

4 *the case is to be tried by a jury* **adjudicate,** consider, hear, adjudge, examine.

▶ **noun** *I'll have one last try* **attempt,** effort, endeavor; informal go, shot, crack, stab; formal essay.

– PHRASES **try something out** *they volunteered to try out the new system* **test,** trial, experiment with, pilot; put through its paces; assess, evaluate.

trying ▶ **adjective 1** *a trying day* **stressful,** taxing, demanding, difficult, tough, hard, pressured, frustrating, fraught; arduous, grueling, tiring, exhausting; informal hellish. See note at HARD.

ANTONYMS easy, painless.

2 *Steve was very trying* **annoying,** irritating, exasperating, maddening, infuriating; tiresome, irksome, troublesome, bothersome, vexing; informal aggravating.

ANTONYMS accommodating.

tuck ▶ **verb 1** *he tucked his shirt into his pants* **push,** insert, slip, fold; thrust, stuff, stick, cram.

2 *the dress was tucked all over* **pleat,** gather, fold, ruffle.

3 *he tucked the knife behind his seat* **hide,** conceal, secrete; store, stow, stash.

▶ **noun** *a dress with tucks* **pleat,** gather, fold, ruffle.

– PHRASES **tuck in** *Toby tucked the children in after reading them a story* **put to bed,** settle down, cover up; make comfortable.

tug ▶ **verb 1** *Ben tugged at her sleeve* **pull (at),** pluck, tweak, twitch, jerk, wrench; catch hold of, yank (at).

2 *she tugged him toward the door* **drag,** pull, lug, draw, haul, heave, tow.

▶ **noun** *one good tug would loosen it* **pull,** jerk, wrench, heave, yank.

tuition ▶ **noun 1** *students go broke paying the increased tuition* **fees,** charges, bill.

2 *her skill improved with tuition* **instruction,** teaching, coaching, tutoring, tutelage, lessons, education, schooling; training, drill, preparation, guidance.

tumble ▶ **verb 1** *he tumbled over* **fall (over),** fall down, topple over, lose one's balance, keel over, take a spill, go headlong, go head over heels, trip, stumble; informal come a cropper.

2 *they all tumbled from the room* **hurry,** rush, scramble, scurry, bound, pile, bundle.

3 *a creek tumbled over the rocks* **cascade,** fall, flow, pour, spill, stream.

4 *oil prices tumbled* **plummet,** plunge, fall, dive, nosedive, drop, slump, slide, decrease, decline, crash.

ANTONYMS rise.

▶ **noun 1** *I took a tumble in the bushes* **fall,** trip, spill; informal nosedive.

2 *a tumble in share prices* **drop,** fall, plunge, dive, nosedive, slump, decline, collapse; informal crash.

ANTONYMS rise.

tumbledown ▶ **adjective** *a tumbledown shack in the woods* **dilapidated,** ramshackle, decrepit, neglected, beat-up, run-down, falling to pieces, decaying, derelict, crumbling; rickety, shaky.

tumor ▸ noun *a biopsy of the tumor* **cancerous growth,** malignant growth, cancer, malignancy; lump, growth, swelling, fibroid; Medicine carcinoma, sarcoma.

tumult ▸ noun **1** *she added her voice to the tumult* **clamor,** din, noise, racket, uproar, hue and cry, commotion, ruckus, maelstrom, rumpus, hubbub, pandemonium, babel, bedlam, brouhaha, furor, fracas, melee, frenzy; informal hullabaloo.
ANTONYMS silence.
2 *years of political tumult* **turmoil,** confusion, disorder, disarray, unrest, chaos, turbulence, mayhem, maelstrom, havoc, upheaval, ferment, agitation, trouble.
ANTONYMS tranquility.

tumultuous ▸ adjective **1** *tumultuous applause* **loud,** deafening, thunderous, uproarious, noisy, clamorous, vociferous, vehement.
ANTONYMS soft.
2 *their tumultuous relationship* **tempestuous,** stormy, turbulent, passionate, intense, explosive, violent, volatile, full of ups and downs, roller-coaster.
ANTONYMS peaceful, uneventful.
3 *a tumultuous crowd* **disorderly,** unruly, rowdy, turbulent, boisterous, excited, agitated, restless, wild, riotous, frenzied.
ANTONYMS orderly.

tune ▸ noun *she hummed a cheerful tune* **melody,** air, strain, theme; song, jingle, ditty.
▸ verb **1** *they tuned their guitars* **adjust,** fine-tune, tune up.
2 *a body clock tuned to the lunar cycle* **attune,** adapt, adjust, fine-tune; regulate, modulate.
– PHRASES **change one's tune** *our "Bachelor Bob" seems to have changed his tune about settling down and raising a family* **change one's mind,** do a U-turn, have a change of heart; do an about-face; informal do a one-eighty, pull a U-ey. **in tune** *are any of the candidates really in tune with the voters?* **in accord,** in keeping, in accordance, in agreement, in harmony, in step, in line, in sympathy, compatible. **tune up** *most of these old cash registers just need to be tuned up a bit* **tweak,** adjust, fine-tune, calibrate, maintain, improve, ameliorate, enhance.

tuneful ▸ adjective *an evening of tuneful songs* **melodious,** melodic, musical, mellifluous, dulcet, euphonious, harmonious, lyrical, lilting, sweet.
ANTONYMS discordant.

tunnel ▸ noun *a tunnel under the hills* **underground passage,** underpass, subway; shaft; burrow, hole; historical mine.
▸ verb *he tunneled under the fence* **dig,** burrow, mine, bore, drill.

turbulent ▸ adjective **1** *the country's turbulent past* **tempestuous,** stormy, unstable, unsettled, tumultuous, chaotic; violent, anarchic, lawless.
ANTONYMS peaceful.
2 *turbulent seas* **rough,** stormy, tempestuous, storm-tossed, heavy, violent, wild, roiling, raging, seething, choppy, agitated, boisterous.
ANTONYMS calm.

turf ▸ noun **1** *they walked over a patch of turf* **grass,** lawn, sod.
2 *she was keen to protect her turf* **territory,** domain, province, preserve, sphere of influence; stomping ground, stamping ground; bailiwick.

turgid ▸ adjective **1** *his turgid prose* **bombastic,** pompous, overblown, inflated, tumid, high-flown, puffed up, affected, pretentious, grandiose, florid, ornate, grandiloquent, orotund; informal highfalutin, purple.
ANTONYMS simple.
2 *the tissues become turgid* **swollen,** distended, tumescent, engorged, bloated, tumid.

turmoil ▸ noun *political turmoil* **confusion,** upheaval, turbulence, tumult, disorder, disturbance, agitation, ferment, unrest, disquiet, trouble, disruption, chaos, mayhem; uncertainty.
ANTONYMS peace.
– PHRASES **in turmoil** *Michel's sudden death left the family in turmoil* **confused,** chaotic, in chaos, topsy-turvy, at sixes and sevens; reeling, disorientated; informal all over the place.

turn ▸ verb **1** *the wheels were still turning* **go around,** revolve, rotate, spin, roll, circle, wheel, whirl, twirl, gyrate, swivel, pivot.
2 *I turned and headed back* **change direction,** change course, make a U-turn, about-face, turn around/about; informal pull a U-ey, do a one-eighty.
3 *the car turned the corner* **go around,** round, negotiate, take.
4 *the path turned to right and left* **bend,** curve, wind, veer, twist, meander, snake, zigzag.
5 *he* ***turned*** *his gun* ***on*** *Lenny* **aim at,** point at, level at, direct at, train on.
6 *he turned his ankle* **sprain,** twist, wrench; hurt.
7 *their honeymoon* ***turned into*** *a nightmare* **become,** develop into, turn out to be; be transformed into, metamorphose into, descend into, grow into.
8 *Emma turned red* **become,** go, grow, get.
9 *he turned the house into apartments* **convert,** change, transform, make; adapt, modify, rebuild, reconstruct.
10 *I've just turned forty* **reach,** get to, become, hit.
11 *she* ***turned to*** *politics* **take up,** become involved in, go into, enter, undertake.
12 *we can now* ***turn to*** *another topic* **move on to,** go on to, proceed to, consider, attend to, address; take up, switch to.
▸ noun **1** *a turn of the wheel* **rotation,** revolution, spin, whirl, gyration, swivel.
2 *a turn to the left* **change of direction,** veer, divergence.
3 *we're approaching the turn* **bend,** corner, turning, turnoff, junction, crossroads.
4 *you'll get your turn in a minute* **opportunity,** chance, say; stint, time; try; informal go, shot, stab, crack.
5 *she did me some good turns* **service,** deed, act; favor, kindness.
– PHRASES **at every turn** *her name seemed to come up at every turn* **repeatedly,** recurrently, all the time, always, constantly, again and again. **in turn** *let's consider these three points in*

turn **one after the other,** one by one, one at a time, in succession, successively, sequentially. **take a turn for the better** *his luck took a turn for the better* **improve,** pick up, look up, perk up, rally, turn the corner; recover, revive. **take a turn for the worse** *even the doctors were surprised when Richie took a turn for the worse* **deteriorate,** worsen, decline; informal go downhill. **turn against** *after his father died, Bruce turned against his stepmother* **become hostile to,** take a dislike to, betray, double-cross. **turn away** *I know you're hurt, but please don't turn us away* **send away,** reject, rebuff, repel, cold-shoulder; informal send packing. **turn back** *just before boarding the ferry, Clint changed his mind and turned back* **retrace one's steps,** go back, return; retreat. **turn down 1** *his novel was turned down* **reject,** refuse, decline, spurn, rebuff. **2** *Pete turned the volume down* **reduce,** lower, decrease, lessen; muffle, mute. **turn in 1** *he turned in his brother to the police* **betray,** inform on, denounce, sell out, stab someone in the back; blow the whistle on, rat on, squeal on, finger. **2** *we turned in the entrance forms just in time* **hand in/over/back,** give in, submit, surrender, give up; deliver, return. **3** *I usually turn in before 10 o'clock* **go to bed,** retire, go to sleep, call it a day; informal hit the hay, hit the sack. **turn of events** *she was unprepared for this turn of events* **development,** incident, occurrence, happening, circumstance, surprise. **turn of phrase** *a clever turn of phrase* **expression,** idiom, phrase, term, word, aphorism. **turn off 1** *his so-called jokes really turn me off* **put off,** leave cold, repel, disgust, revolt, offend; disenchant, alienate; bore, gross out. **2** *please turn off the garage lights* **switch off,** shut off, turn out; extinguish; deactivate; informal kill, cut, power down. **turn on 1** *the decision turned on the law* **depend on,** rest on, hinge on, be contingent on, be decided by. **2** *okay, I admit it—his green eyes turn me on* See AROUSE (sense 3). **3** *I'll turn on the generator* **switch on,** start up, activate, trip, power up. **4** *it began as a simple disagreement, but then he turned on us like a mad dog* **attack,** set on, fall on, let fly at, lash out at, hit out at; informal lay into, tear into, let someone have it, bite someone's head off, jump down someone's throat; light into. **turn on to** *Christie has turned me on to the health benefits of yoga* **introduce someone to,** get someone into, pique someone's interest in. **turn out 1** *a huge crowd turned out* **come,** be present, attend, appear, turn up, arrive; assemble, gather, show up. **2** *it turned out that she had been abroad* **transpire,** emerge, come to light, become apparent, become clear. **3** *things didn't turn out as I'd intended* **happen,** occur, come about; develop, proceed; work out, come out, end up, pan out, result; formal eventuate. **4** *it's about time she turned out that bum of a boyfriend* **throw out,** eject, evict, expel, oust, drum out, banish; informal kick out, send packing, boot out, show someone the door. **5** *turn out the light* See TURN OFF (sense 2) above. **6** *they turn out a million engines a year* **produce,** make, manufacture, fabricate, generate, put out, churn out. **turn over 1** *the crate fell off the back of the truck and turned over* **overturn,** upturn, capsize, keel over, flip, turn turtle, be upended, tip. **2** *I turned over a few pages* **flip over,** flick through, leaf through. **3** *she turned the proposal over in her mind* **think about,** think over, consider, ponder, contemplate, reflect on, chew over, mull over, muse on, ruminate on. **4** *he turned over the business to his brother* **transfer,** hand over, pass on, consign, commit. **turn someone's stomach** *the sight of blood turns my stomach* **nauseate someone,** sicken someone, make someone sick. **turn to** *I always had my grandparents to turn to* **seek help from,** have recourse to, approach, apply to, appeal to; take to, resort to. **turn up 1** *the missing documents turned up* **be found,** be discovered, be located, reappear. **2** *the police turned up* **arrive,** appear, present oneself, show up, show, show one's face. **3** *something better will turn up* **present itself,** offer itself, occur, happen, crop up, appear. **4** *she turned up the treble* **increase,** raise, amplify, intensify. **5** *they turned up lots of information* **discover,** uncover, unearth, find, dig up, ferret out, root out, expose.

turning point ▶ noun *the turning point in their relationship* **crossroads,** critical moment, decisive moment, moment of truth, watershed, crisis, landmark.

turnout ▶ noun *the producers were overjoyed with the turnout* **attendance,** audience, crowd, gathering, showing, throng, assembly, assemblage, congregation, number; participation.

turnover ▶ noun **1** *an annual turnover of $2.25 million* **(gross) revenue,** income, yield; sales, gross.
2 *a high turnover of staff* **rate of replacement,** change, movement.

tussle ▶ noun *his glasses were smashed in the tussle* **scuffle,** fight, struggle, skirmish, brawl, scrum, rough-and-tumble, free-for-all, fracas, fray, rumpus, melee; informal spat, scrap, roughhouse, tug-of-war.
▶ verb *demonstrators tussled with police* **scuffle,** fight, struggle, brawl, grapple, wrestle, clash; informal scrap, roughhouse.

tutor ▶ noun *a history tutor* **teacher,** instructor, educator, lecturer, trainer, mentor; formal pedagogue.
▶ verb *he was tutored at home* **teach,** instruct, educate, school, coach, train, drill.

TV ▶ noun See TELEVISION.

twaddle ▶ noun informal See NONSENSE (sense 1 of the noun). See also note at NONSENSE.

tweak ▶ verb **1** *she tweaked his nose* **pull,** jerk, tug, twist, twitch, pinch, squeeze.
2 *the product can be tweaked to suit your needs* **adjust,** modify, alter, change, adapt; refine.
▶ noun **1** *he gave her hair a tweak* **pull,** jerk, tug, twist, pinch, twitch, squeeze.
2 *a few minor tweaks were required* **adjustment,** modification, alteration, change; refinement.

twig ▶ noun *leafy twigs* **stick,** sprig, shoot, stem, branchlet.

twilight ▶ noun 1 *we arrived at twilight* **dusk,** sunset, sundown, nightfall, evening, close of day, day's end; literary eventide, gloaming.
ANTONYMS dawn, daybreak.
2 *it was scarcely visible in the twilight* **half-light,** semidarkness, gloom.
3 *the twilight of his career* **decline,** waning, ebb; autumn, final years, tail end.
ANTONYMS dawn, peak, height.
▶ adjective *a twilight world* **shadowy,** dark, shady, dim, gloomy, obscure, crepuscular, twilit.

twin ▶ noun *a bedroom that was the twin of her own* **duplicate,** double, carbon copy, exact likeness, mirror image, replica, look-alike, doppelgänger, clone; counterpart, match, pair; informal dead ringer, spitting image.
▶ adjective 1 *twin peaks* **matching,** identical, matched, paired.
2 *the twin aims of conservation and recreation* **twofold,** double, dual; related, linked, connected; corresponding, parallel, complementary, equivalent.
▶ verb *the company twinned its brewing with distilling* **combine,** join, link, couple, pair.

twine ▶ noun *a ball of twine* **string,** cord, thread, yarn.
▶ verb 1 *she twined her arms around him* **wind,** entwine, wrap, wreathe.
2 *ivy twined around the tree* **entwine (itself),** coil, loop, twist, spiral, curl; weave, interlace, intertwine, braid.

twinge ▶ noun 1 *twinges in her stomach* **pain,** spasm, ache, throb; cramp, stitch.
2 *a twinge of guilt* **pang,** prick, qualm, scruple, misgiving.

twinkle ▶ noun & verb *a twinkle in her eye | the lights of the city twinkled below me* **glitter,** sparkle, shine, glimmer, shimmer, glint, gleam, flicker, flash, wink; literary glister.

twinkling ▶ adjective *twinkling white lights graced the gazebo* **sparkling,** glistening, glittering, glimmering, glinting, gleaming, flickering, winking, shining, scintillating, lambent; literary coruscating.

twirl ▶ verb 1 *he twirled the gun around* **spin,** whirl, turn, pivot, swivel, twist, revolve, rotate.
2 *she twirled her hair around her finger* **wind,** twist, coil, curl, wrap.
▶ noun *she did a quick twirl* **pirouette,** spin, whirl, turn, twist, rotation, revolution, gyration, twizzle.

twist ▶ verb 1 *the impact twisted the chassis* **crumple,** crush, buckle, mangle, warp, deform, distort.
2 *her face twisted with rage* **contort,** screw up.
3 *Ma anxiously twisted a handkerchief* **wring,** squeeze.
4 *he twisted around in his seat* **turn (around),** swivel (around), spin (around), pivot, rotate, revolve.
5 *she twisted out of his grasp* **wriggle,** squirm, worm one's way, wiggle.
6 *I twisted my ankle* **sprain,** wrench, turn.
7 *you are twisting my words* **distort,** misrepresent, change, alter, pervert, falsify, warp, skew, misinterpret, misconstrue, misstate, misquote; garble.
8 *he twisted the radio knob* **twiddle,** adjust, turn, rotate, swivel.
9 *she twisted her hair around her finger* **wind,** twirl, coil, curl, wrap.
10 *the wires were twisted together* **intertwine,** twine, interlace, weave, plait, braid, coil, wind.
11 *the road twisted and turned* **wind,** bend, curve, turn, meander, weave, zigzag, swerve, snake.
▶ noun 1 *a twist of the wrist* **turn,** twirl, spin, rotation; flick.
2 *the twists of the road* **bend,** curve, turn, zigzag, kink.
3 *the twists of the plot* **convolution,** complication, complexity, intricacy; surprise, revelation.
4 *a modern twist on an old theme* **interpretation,** slant, outlook, angle, approach, treatment; variation, change, difference.
– PHRASES **twist someone's arm** *I didn't want to go with them, but Hazel twisted my arm* **pressurize someone,** coerce someone, force someone; persuade someone; informal lean on someone, browbeat someone, strong-arm someone, bulldoze someone, railroad someone, put the screws to/on someone.

twit ▶ noun informal See **FOOL** (sense 1 of the noun).

twitch ▶ verb *he twitched and then lay still* **jerk,** convulse, have a spasm, quiver, tremble, shiver, shudder.
▶ noun 1 *a twitch of her lips* **spasm,** convulsion, quiver, tremor, shiver, shudder, small movement; tic.
2 *he gave a twitch at his mustache* **pull,** tug, tweak, yank, jerk.
3 *he felt a twitch in his left side* **pang,** twinge, dart, stab, prick.

twitter ▶ verb 1 *sparrows twittered under the eaves* **chirp,** chirrup, cheep, tweet, peep, chatter, trill, warble, sing.
2 *stop twittering about Francis* **blather,** jabber, blabber, chatter, chitter, gabble, go on, blab, rattle, yap, prattle, babble, blither, ramble; informal yak, quack, yabber, talk someone's ear off.
▶ noun 1 *a bird's twitter* **chirp,** chirrup, cheep, tweet, peep, trill, warble, song.
2 *her nonstop twitter* **prattle,** chatter, babble, talk, gabble, blabber; informal yakking.

two-faced ▶ adjective *her two-faced ex* **deceitful,** insincere, double-dealing, hypocritical, backstabbing, false, fickle, untrustworthy, duplicitous, deceiving, dissembling, dishonest; disloyal, treacherous, faithless, traitorous, cheating, lying, weaselly; literary perfidious.
ANTONYMS sincere.

tycoon ▶ noun *a newspaper tycoon* **magnate,** mogul, industrialist, businessman, financier, entrepreneur, captain of industry, millionaire, multimillionaire, merchant prince; informal big shot, bigwig, honcho, supremo, big wheel, kahuna; derogatory fat cat, robber baron.

type ▶ noun 1 *a pastor of the old-fashioned type* **kind,** sort, variety, class, category, set, genre, species, order, breed, race; style, nature, manner, rank; generation, vintage; stamp, ilk, cast, grain, mold, stripe, brand, flavor. See note at **EMBLEM.**

2 *sporty types* **person,** individual, character, sort.
3 *italic type* **print,** font, typeface, face, characters, lettering, letters.

typhoon ▶ noun See STORM (sense 1 of the noun).

typical ▶ adjective 1 *a typical example of art deco* **representative,** classic, quintessential, archetypal, model, prototypical, stereotypical, paradigmatic.
ANTONYMS atypical, unusual, abnormal.
2 *a fairly typical day* **normal,** average, ordinary, standard, regular, routine, run-of-the-mill, conventional, unremarkable, unsurprising, unexceptional; informal blah. See note at NORMAL.
ANTONYMS atypical, unusual, exceptional.
3 *it's typical of him to forget* **characteristic,** in keeping, usual, normal, par for the course, predictable, true to form; customary, habitual.
ANTONYMS uncharacteristic.

typify ▶ verb *the girls' basketball team typifies the school spirit of our student body* **epitomize,** exemplify, characterize, be representative of; personify, embody, be emblematic of.

tyrannical ▶ adjective *a tyrannical government* **dictatorial,** despotic, autocratic, oppressive, repressive, totalitarian, undemocratic, illiberal; authoritarian, high-handed, imperious, harsh, strict, iron-handed, iron-fisted, severe, cruel, brutal, ruthless.
ANTONYMS liberal.

tyrannize ▶ verb *she tyrannized her daughter-in-law* **dominate,** dictate to, browbeat, intimidate, bully, lord it over; persecute, victimize, torment, terrorize; oppress, repress, crush, subjugate; informal push around.

tyranny ▶ noun *they will not soon forget the brutal tyranny of Amin* **despotism,** absolute power, autocracy, dictatorship, totalitarianism, Fascism; oppression, repression, subjugation, enslavement; authoritarianism, bullying, severity, cruelty, brutality, ruthlessness.

tyrant ▶ noun *dare we envision a world free from tyrants?* **dictator,** despot, autocrat, authoritarian, oppressor; slave driver, martinet, bully, megalomaniac.

Uu

ubiquitous ▶ adjective *the ubiquitous golden arches of burgerdom* **omnipresent,** ever-present, everywhere, all over the place, pervasive, universal, worldwide, global; rife, prevalent, far-reaching, inescapable.
ANTONYMS rare.

ugly ▶ adjective **1** *an ugly face* **unattractive,** unappealing, unpleasant, hideous, unlovely, unprepossessing, unsightly, horrible, frightful, awful, ghastly, vile, revolting, repellent, repulsive, repugnant; grotesque, disgusting, monstrous, reptilian, misshapen, deformed, disfigured, plug-ugly, butt-ugly; homely, plain, not much to look at.
ANTONYMS beautiful.
2 *things got pretty ugly* **unpleasant,** nasty, disagreeable, alarming, tense, charged, serious, grave; dangerous, perilous, threatening, menacing, hostile, ominous, sinister.
ANTONYMS pleasant.
3 *an ugly rumor* **horrible,** despicable, reprehensible, nasty, appalling, objectionable, offensive, obnoxious, vile, dishonorable, rotten, vicious, spiteful.

ulcer ▶ noun *something to soothe the ulcers in his mouth* **sore,** ulceration, abscess, boil, carbuncle, blister, gumboil, cyst; Medicine aphtha, chancre, furuncle.

ulterior ▶ adjective *his ulterior objectives were disguised by feigned concern* **underlying,** undisclosed, undivulged, concealed, hidden, covert, secret, personal, private, selfish.
ANTONYMS overt.

ultimate ▶ adjective **1** *the ultimate collapse of their empire* **eventual,** final, concluding, terminal, end; resulting, ensuing, consequent, subsequent.
2 *ultimate truths about civilization* **fundamental,** basic, primary, elementary, elemental, absolute, central, key, crucial, essential, pivotal.
3 *the ultimate gift for cat lovers* **best,** ideal, perfect, greatest, supreme, paramount, superlative, highest, utmost, optimum, quintessential.
▶ noun *the ultimate in Bohemian chic* **utmost,** optimum, last word, height, epitome, peak, pinnacle, acme, zenith, nonpareil, dernier cri, ne plus ultra; (**the ultimate**) informal da bomb; dated informal the bee's knees, the cat's pajamas/whiskers/meow.

ultimately ▶ adverb **1** *the money will ultimately belong to us* **eventually,** in the end, in the long run, at length, finally, sooner or later, in time, in the fullness of time, when all is said and done, one day, some day, sometime, over the long haul; informal when push comes to shove.
2 *two ultimately contradictory reasons* **fundamentally,** basically, primarily, essentially, at heart, deep down.

umbrage ▶ noun
– PHRASES **take umbrage** *I would take umbrage at that if I thought you were serious* **take offense,** take exception, be aggrieved, be affronted, be annoyed, be angry, be indignant, be put out, be insulted, be hurt, be piqued, be resentful, be disgruntled, go into a huff, be miffed, have one's nose put out of joint, chafe.

umbrella ▶ noun **1** *they huddled under the umbrella* parasol, sunshade.
2 *the groups worked under the umbrella of the Arts Coalition* **aegis,** auspices, patronage, protection, guardianship, support, backing, agency, guidance, care, charge, responsibility, cover.

umpire ▶ noun *the umpire reversed his decision* **referec,** linesman, adjudicator, arbitrator, judge, moderator, official; ref, ump.
▶ verb *he umpired a boat race* **referee,** adjudicate, arbitrate, judge, moderate, oversee, officiate; informal ref, ump.

umpteen ▶ adjective See **COUNTLESS**.

unable ▶ adjective *I'm unable to fix the leak* **powerless,** impotent, at a loss, inadequate, incompetent, unfit, unqualified, incapable.

unabridged ▶ adjective *the unabridged version is in two volumes* **complete,** entire, whole, full-length, intact, uncut, unshortened, unexpurgated.

unacceptable ▶ adjective *the repair job on the gutters was unacceptable* **intolerable,** insufferable, unsatisfactory, inadmissible, inappropriate, unsuitable, undesirable, unreasonable, insupportable; offensive, obnoxious, disagreeable, disgraceful, deplorable, beyond the pale, bad; a bit much, too much, not on.
ANTONYMS satisfactory.

unaccompanied ▶ adjective *when Howard arrived at the dance he was unaccompanied* **alone,** on one's own, by oneself, solo, lone, solitary, single-handed; unescorted, unattended, unchaperoned; informal by one's lonesome.

unaccountable ▶ adjective **1** *for some unaccountable reason, the dogs have been pacing the floor all evening* **inexplicable,** insoluble, incomprehensible, unfathomable, impenetrable, puzzling, perplexing, baffling,

bewildering, mystifying, mysterious, inscrutable, peculiar, strange, queer, odd, obscure; informal weird, freaky.
2 *a private company unaccountable to voters* **not answerable,** not liable, not responsible; free, exempt, immune; unsupervised.

unaccustomed ▶ adjective **1** *she was unaccustomed to being bossed around* **unused to,** new to, fresh to; unfamiliar with, inexperienced in, unconversant with, unacquainted with.
ANTONYMS habitual.
2 *he showed unaccustomed emotion* **unusual,** unfamiliar, uncommon, unwonted, exceptional, unprecedented, extraordinary, rare, surprising, abnormal, atypical.
ANTONYMS habitual.

unaffected ▶ adjective **1** *they are unaffected by the change in command* **unchanged by,** unaltered by, uninfluenced by; untouched by, unmoved by, unresponsive to; proof against, impervious to, immune to.
ANTONYMS influenced.
2 *his manner was unaffected* **unassuming,** unpretentious, down-to-earth, natural, easy, uninhibited, open, artless, guileless, ingenuous, unsophisticated, genuine, real, sincere, honest, earnest, wholehearted, heartfelt, true, bona fide, frank; informal upfront.
ANTONYMS pretentious, false.

unanimous ▶ adjective **1** *doctors were unanimous about the effects* **united,** in agreement, in accord, of one mind, of the same mind, in harmony, concordant, undivided, as one.
ANTONYMS divided.
2 *a unanimous vote* **uniform,** consistent, united, concerted, congruent.

unanswerable ▶ adjective **1** *an unanswerable case* **irrefutable,** indisputable, undeniable, incontestable, incontrovertible, irrefragable; conclusive, absolute, positive.
ANTONYMS weak, flawed.
2 *unanswerable questions* **insoluble,** unsolvable, inexplicable, unexplainable.
ANTONYMS obvious.

unapproachable ▶ adjective **1** *unapproachable islands* **inaccessible,** unreachable, remote, out of the way, isolated, far-flung, off the beaten track/path; informal in the middle of nowhere, in the sticks, in the boondocks.
ANTONYMS accessible.
2 *her boss appeared unapproachable* **aloof,** distant, remote, detached, reserved, withdrawn, uncommunicative, guarded, unresponsive, unforthcoming, unfriendly, unsympathetic, unsociable; cool, cold, frosty, stiff, haughty, superior, formal, intimidating; informal standoffish, stuck-up.
ANTONYMS friendly.

unarmed ▶ adjective *they fired into a crowd of unarmed civilians* **defenseless,** weaponless; unprotected, undefended, unguarded, unshielded, vulnerable, exposed, assailable, open to attack.

unassailable ▶ adjective **1** *an unassailable fortress* **impregnable,** invulnerable, impenetrable, inviolable, invincible, unconquerable; secure, safe, strong, indestructible.
ANTONYMS defenseless.
2 *his logic was unassailable* **indisputable,** undeniable, unquestionable, incontestable, incontrovertible, irrefutable, indubitable, watertight, sound, rock-solid, good, sure, manifest, patent, obvious.

unassuming ▶ adjective *she's not quite the unassuming ingénue she seems to be* **modest,** self-effacing, humble, meek, bashful, reserved, diffident; unobtrusive, unostentatious, low-key, unpretentious, unaffected, natural, artless, ingenuous.

unattached ▶ adjective **1** *they were both unattached* **single,** unmarried, unwed, uncommitted, available, at large, footloose and fancy free, on one's own; unloved.
ANTONYMS married.
2 *we are unattached to any organization* **unaffiliated,** unallied; autonomous, independent, nonaligned, self-governing, neutral, separate, unconnected, detached.
ANTONYMS affiliated.

unattended ▶ adjective **1** *his cries went unattended* **ignored,** disregarded, neglected, passed over, unheeded.
2 *an unattended vehicle* **unguarded,** unwatched, alone, solitary; abandoned.
3 *she had to walk there unattended* **unaccompanied,** unescorted, partnerless, unchaperoned, alone, on one's own, by oneself, solo; informal by one's lonesome.

unauthorized ▶ adjective *you can't hold an unauthorized meeting in a town building* **unofficial,** unsanctioned, unaccredited, unlicensed, unwarranted, unapproved, bootleg, pirated; wildcat; disallowed, prohibited, out of bounds, banned, barred, forbidden, outlawed, illegal, illegitimate, illicit, proscribed.
ANTONYMS official.

unavoidable ▶ adjective *it was an unavoidable mishap* **inescapable,** inevitable, inexorable, assured, certain, predestined, predetermined, fated, ineluctable; necessary, compulsory, required, obligatory, mandatory.

unaware ▶ adjective *the vice president claimed to be unaware of the arms deal* **ignorant,** unknowing, unconscious, heedless, unmindful, oblivious, incognizant, unsuspecting, uninformed, unenlightened, unwitting, innocent; inattentive, unobservant, unperceptive, blind; informal in the dark; literary nescient.
ANTONYMS conscious.

unawares ▶ adverb **1** *brigands caught them unawares* **by surprise,** unexpectedly, without warning, suddenly, abruptly, unprepared, off-guard; informal with one's pants down, napping.
ANTONYMS prepared.
2 *the chipmunk, unawares, approached the waiting cat* **unknowingly,** unwittingly, unconsciously; unintentionally, inadvertently, accidentally, by mistake.
ANTONYMS knowingly.

unbalanced ▶ adjective **1** *he is unbalanced and dangerous* **unstable,** mentally ill, deranged, demented, disturbed, unhinged, insane, mad,

out of one's mind; informal crazy, loopy, loony, nuts, nutso, nutty, cracked, bushed, screwy, batty, dotty, cuckoo, bonkers, squirrelly; dated touched.
ANTONYMS sane.
2 *a most unbalanced article* **biased,** prejudiced, one-sided, partisan, inequitable, unjust, unfair, parti pris.
ANTONYMS unbiased.

unbearable ▶ **adjective** *the cold made the waiting even more unbearable* **intolerable,** insufferable, insupportable, unendurable, unacceptable, unmanageable, overpowering; informal too much.
ANTONYMS tolerable.

unbeatable ▶ **adjective** *the Cubs were unbeatable in April* **invincible,** unstoppable, unassailable, indomitable, unconquerable, unsurpassable, matchless, peerless, nonpareil; supreme.

unbecoming ▶ **adjective 1** *an unbecoming sundress* **unflattering,** unattractive, unsightly, plain, ugly, homely, hideous; unsuitable, ill-fitting.
ANTONYMS flattering.
2 *as a representative of this state, your conduct was unbecoming* **inappropriate,** unfitting, unbefitting, unsuitable, unsuited, inapt, indecorous, out of keeping, untoward, incorrect, unacceptable; unworthy, improper, unseemly, undignified.
ANTONYMS appropriate.

unbelievable ▶ **adjective** *an unbelievable story | the grandeur of this casino is unbelievable* **incredible,** beyond belief, inconceivable, unthinkable, unimaginable; unconvincing, far-fetched, dubious, implausible, improbable, unrealistic; informal hard to swallow.
ANTONYMS credible.

unbeliever ▶ **noun** *many of the faithful were once unbelievers* **infidel,** heretic, heathen, nonbeliever, atheist, agnostic, pagan, nihilist, apostate, freethinker, dissenter, nonconformist; disbeliever, skeptic, cynic, doubter, doubting Thomas, questioner, scoffer.
ANTONYMS believer.

unbending ▶ **adjective** *she resented the demands of her unbending father* **inflexible,** rigid, strict, austere, stern, tough, firm, uncompromising, unyielding, hard line, resolute, determined, unrelenting, relentless, inexorable, intransigent, immovable; unfeeling, unemotional, stiff, forbidding, unfriendly.

unbiased ▶ **adjective** *we need an unbiased opinion* **impartial,** unprejudiced, neutral, nonpartisan, disinterested, detached, dispassionate, objective, value-free, open-minded, equitable, evenhanded, fair.
ANTONYMS prejudiced.

unborn ▶ **adjective** *smoking can be harmful to your unborn child* **embryonic,** fetal, in utero; expected.

unbounded ▶ **adjective** *unbounded enthusiasm* **unlimited,** boundless, limitless, illimitable; unrestrained, unrestricted, unconstrained, uncontrolled, unchecked, unbridled, rampant; untold, immeasurable, endless, unending, interminable, everlasting, infinite, inexhaustible.
ANTONYMS limited.

unbreakable ▶ **adjective** *unbreakable dishes* **indestructible,** shatterproof, durable, long-lasting; reinforced, sturdy, tough, stout, resistant, infrangible, heavy-duty, industrial-strength.
ANTONYMS fragile.

unbridled ▶ **adjective** *the unbridled spirit in these young players is very contagious* **unrestrained,** unconstrained, uncontrolled, uninhibited, unrestricted, unchecked, unmufflered, uncurbed, rampant, runaway, irrepressible, unstoppable, intemperate, immoderate.
ANTONYMS restrained.

unbroken ▶ **adjective 1** *the last unbroken window* **undamaged,** unimpaired, unharmed, unscathed, untouched, sound, intact, whole, perfect.
2 *an unbroken horse* **untamed,** undomesticated, untrained, wild, feral.
3 *an unbroken chain of victories* **uninterrupted,** continuous, endless, constant, unremitting, perpetual; unobstructed.
4 *his record is still unbroken* **unbeaten,** undefeated, unsurpassed, unrivaled, unmatched, supreme, intact.

unburden ▶ **verb** *she had a sudden wish to* ***unburden herself*** **open one's heart,** confess, confide, tell all; informal come clean, fess up, spill one's guts, let it all out.

uncanny ▶ **adjective 1** *the silence was uncanny* **eerie,** unnatural, unearthly, preternatural, supernatural, otherworldly, ghostly, mysterious, strange, unsettling, abnormal, weird, bizarre, surreal, eldritch; informal creepy, spooky, freakish, freaky.
2 *an uncanny resemblance* **striking,** remarkable, extraordinary, exceptional, incredible, noteworthy, notable, arresting.

unceremonious ▶ **adjective 1** *an unceremonious dismissal* **abrupt,** sudden, hasty, hurried, summary, perfunctory, undignified; rude, impolite, discourteous, offhand.
2 *an unceremonious man* **informal,** casual, relaxed, easygoing, familiar, natural, laid-back.
ANTONYMS formal.

uncertain ▶ **adjective 1** *the outcome is uncertain* **unknown,** debatable, open to question, in doubt, undetermined, unsure, in the balance, up in the air; unpredictable, unforeseeable, incalculable; risky, chancy, dicey; informal iffy.
ANTONYMS predictable, settled.
2 *its origin is uncertain* **vague,** unclear, fuzzy, ambiguous, unknown, unascertainable, obscure, arcane.
3 *uncertain weather* **changeable,** variable, irregular, unpredictable, unreliable, unsettled, erratic, fluctuating.
4 *Ed was uncertain about what to do* **unsure,** doubtful, dubious, undecided, irresolute, hesitant, blowing hot and cold, vacillating, vague, unclear, ambivalent, of two minds.
ANTONYMS sure.
5 *an uncertain smile* **hesitant,** tentative, faltering, unsure, unconfident.
ANTONYMS confident.

uncertainty ▶ **noun 1** *the uncertainty of the*

stock market **unpredictability,** unreliability, riskiness, chanciness, precariousness, changeability, variability, inconstancy, fickleness, caprice.
ANTONYMS predictability.
2 *uncertainty about the future is always bad for morale* **doubt,** lack of certainty, indecision, irresolution, hesitancy, unsureness, doubtfulness, wavering, vacillation, equivocation, vagueness, haziness, ambivalence, lack of conviction, disquiet, wariness, chariness, leeriness, skepticism; queries, questions; formal dubiety.
3 *she pushed the anxious uncertainties out of her mind* **doubt,** qualm, misgiving, apprehension, quandary, reservation, scruple, second thought, query, question, question mark, suspicion.
4 *there was uncertainty in his voice* **hesitancy,** hesitation, tentativeness, unsureness, lack of confidence, diffidence, doubtfulness, doubt.
ANTONYMS confidence.

CHOOSE THE RIGHT WORD

uncertainty, doubt, dubiety, skepticism

If you're not sure about something, you're probably experiencing a degree of **uncertainty**, which is a general term covering everything from a mere lack of absolute certainty (*uncertainty about the time of the dinner party*) to an almost complete lack of knowledge that makes it impossible to do more than guess at the result or outcome (*uncertainty about the country's future*). **Doubt** implies both uncertainty and an inability to make a decision because the evidence is insufficient (*considerable doubt as to her innocence*). **Dubiety** comes closer in meaning to *uncertainty* than to *doubt*, because it stresses a lack of sureness rather than an inability to reach a decision; but unlike *uncertainty*, it connotes wavering or fluctuating between one conclusion and another (*no one could fail to notice the dubiety in his voice*). If you exhibit **skepticism**, you are not so much uncertain as unwilling to believe. It usually refers to an habitual state of mind or to a customary reaction (*she always listened to his excuses with skepticism*).

unchangeable ▸ adjective *the political climate in this town is unchangeable* **unalterable,** immutable, invariable, changeless, fixed, hard and fast, cast-iron, ironclad, set/cast/carved in stone, dyed-in-the-wool, established, permanent, enduring, abiding, lasting, indestructible, ineradicable, irreversible.
ANTONYMS variable.

uncharitable ▸ adjective *in the end, the uncharitable old miser has a change of heart and becomes the benevolent hero* **mean,** mean-spirited, unkind, selfish, self-centered, inconsiderate, thoughtless, insensitive, unfriendly, unsympathetic, hard-hearted, uncaring, unfeeling, ungenerous, ungracious, unfair.

uncharted ▸ adjective *they approached the uncharted territory with some trepidation* **unexplored,** undiscovered, unmapped, untraveled, unfamiliar, untrodden, unplumbed, unknown.

uncivil ▸ adjective *she apologized to her family for Rusty's uncivil words* **impolite,** rude, discourteous, disrespectful, unmannerly, bad-mannered, impertinent, impudent, ungracious; brusque, sharp, curt, offhand, gruff, churlish, snippy. See note at RUDE.
ANTONYMS polite.

uncivilized ▸ adjective *we had been taught that working-class people were inferior and uncivilized* **uncouth,** coarse, rough, boorish, vulgar, philistine, uneducated, uncultured, uncultivated, benighted, unsophisticated, unpolished; ill-bred, ill-mannered, thuggish, loutish, redneck; barbarian, primitive, savage, brutish; archaic rude.

unclean ▸ adjective **1** *unclean premises* **dirty,** filthy, grubby, grimy, mucky, foul, impure, tainted, grungy, sullied, soiled, unwashed; polluted, contaminated, infected, unsanitary, unhygienic, unhealthy, disease-ridden.
ANTONYMS pure, clean.
2 *an unclean meat* **impure**; forbidden, taboo.
ANTONYMS kosher.

uncomfortable ▸ adjective **1** *an uncomfortable chair* **painful,** disagreeable, intolerable, unbearable, confining, cramped.
2 *I felt uncomfortable in her presence* **uneasy,** awkward, nervous, tense, ill-at-ease, strained, edgy, restless, embarrassed, troubled, worried, anxious, fraught, rattled, twitchy, discombobulated, antsy.
ANTONYMS relaxed.

uncommitted ▸ adjective **1** *uncommitted voters* **floating,** undecided, nonpartisan, unaffiliated, neutral, nonaligned, impartial, independent, undeclared, uncertain; informal sitting on the fence.
ANTONYMS aligned.
2 *the uncommitted male* **unmarried,** unattached, unwed, partnerless; footloose and fancy free, available, single, lone.
ANTONYMS attached.

uncommon ▸ adjective **1** *an uncommon occurrence* **unusual,** abnormal, rare, atypical, unconventional, unfamiliar, strange, odd, curious, extraordinary, outlandish, novel, singular, peculiar, bizarre; alien, weird, oddball, offbeat; scarce, few and far between, exceptional, isolated, infrequent, irregular, seldom seen.
2 *an uncommon capacity for hard work* **remarkable,** extraordinary, exceptional, singular, particular, marked, outstanding, noteworthy, significant, especial, special, signal, superior, unique, unparalleled, prodigious, unearthly; informal mind-boggling.

uncommonly ▸ adverb *the cherry blossoms are uncommonly magnificent this year* **unusually,** remarkably, extraordinarily, exceptionally, singularly, particularly, especially, decidedly, notably, eminently, extremely, very.

uncommunicative ▸ adjective *their*

uncommunicative dinner guests made the evening seem terribly long **taciturn,** quiet, unforthcoming, reserved, reticent, laconic, tongue-tied, mute, silent, tight-lipped, close-mouthed; guarded, secretive, close, private; distant, remote, aloof, curt, withdrawn, unsociable, farouche; informal mum, standoffish.
ANTONYMS talkative.

uncompromising ▶ **adjective** *two uncompromising parties will never reach a common ground* **inflexible,** unbending, unyielding, unshakable, resolute, rigid, hard-line, immovable, intractable, inexorable, firm, determined, obstinate, stubborn, adamant, obdurate, intransigent, headstrong, stiff-necked, pigheaded, single-minded, bloody-minded.
ANTONYMS flexible.

unconcerned ▶ **adjective 1** *she is unconcerned about their responses* **indifferent,** unmoved, apathetic, uninterested, incurious, dispassionate, heedless, impassive, unmindful.
ANTONYMS interested.
2 *he tried to look unconcerned* **untroubled,** unworried, unruffled, insouciant, nonchalant, blasé, carefree, casual, blithe, relaxed, at ease, 'calm, cool, and collected'; informal laid-back, poker-faced.
ANTONYMS anxious.

unconditional ▶ **adjective** *they gave their mom's new husband an unconditional welcome* **wholehearted,** unqualified, unreserved, unlimited, unrestricted, unmitigated, unquestioning; complete, total, entire, full, absolute, out-and-out, unequivocal.

unconnected ▶ **adjective 1** *the ground wire was unconnected* **detached,** disconnected, loose.
ANTONYMS attached.
2 *unconnected tasks* **unrelated,** dissociated, separate, independent, distinct, different, disparate, discrete.
ANTONYMS related.
3 *unconnected chains of thought* **disjointed,** incoherent, disconnected, rambling, wandering, diffuse, disorderly, haphazard, disorganized, garbled, mixed, muddled, aimless.
ANTONYMS coherent.

unconscionable ▶ **adjective 1** *the unconscionable use of test animals* **unethical,** amoral, immoral, unprincipled, indefensible, unforgivable, wrong; unscrupulous, unfair, underhanded, dishonorable.
ANTONYMS ethical.
2 *we waited an unconscionable length of time* **excessive,** unreasonable, unwarranted, uncalled for, unfair, inordinate, immoderate, undue, inexcusable, unforgivable, unnecessary, needless; informal over the top.
ANTONYMS acceptable.

unconscious ▶ **adjective 1** *she made sure he was unconscious* **insensible,** senseless, insentient, insensate, comatose, inert, knocked out, stunned; motionless, immobile, prostrate; informal out cold, out like a light, out of it, down for the count, passed out, dead to the world.
2 *she was* ***unconscious of*** *the pain* **heedless of,** unmindful of, disregarding of, oblivious to, insensible to, impervious to, unaffected by, unconcerned by, indifferent to; unaware of, unknowing of, ignorant of, incognizant of.
ANTONYMS aware.
3 *an unconscious desire* **subconscious,** latent, suppressed, subliminal, sleeping, dormant, inherent, instinctive, involuntary, uncontrolled, spontaneous; unintentional, unthinking, unwitting, inadvertent; informal gut.
ANTONYMS voluntary.
▶ **noun** *fantasies raging in the unconscious* **subconscious,** psyche, ego, id, inner self.

uncontrollable ▶ **adjective 1** *the crowds were uncontrollable* **unmanageable,** out of control, ungovernable, wild, unruly, disorderly, recalcitrant, turbulent, disobedient, delinquent, defiant, undisciplined; formal refractory.
ANTONYMS compliant.
2 *an uncontrollable rage* **unstoppable,** irrepressible, ungovernable, unquenchable; wild, violent, frenzied, furious, mad, hysterical, passionate, out of control.

unconventional ▶ **adjective** *her unconventional sense of humor didn't sit well with some of the audience* **unusual,** irregular, unorthodox, unfamiliar, uncommon, unwonted, out of the ordinary, atypical, singular, alternative, different; new, novel, innovative, groundbreaking, pioneering, original, unprecedented; eccentric, idiosyncratic, quirky, odd, strange, bizarre, weird, outlandish, curious; abnormal, anomalous, aberrant, extraordinary; nonconformist, Bohemian, avant-garde; informal far out, offbeat, off the wall, wacky, madcap, oddball, zany, hippie, kooky, wacko.
ANTONYMS orthodox.

uncoordinated ▶ **adjective** *you'd be surprised how many uncoordinated hopefuls show up for these dance auditions* **clumsy,** awkward, blundering, bumbling, lumbering, flat-footed, heavy-handed, graceless, gawky, ungainly, ungraceful; inept, unhandy, unskillful, inexpert, maladroit, bungling; informal klutzy, butterfingered, ham-fisted, ham-handed, all thumbs.
ANTONYMS dexterous.

uncouth ▶ **adjective** *I was hoping you'd be less uncouth in public* **uncivilized,** uncultured, uncultivated, unrefined, unpolished, unsophisticated, bush-league, common, plebeian, low, rough, rough-hewn, coarse, loutish, boorish, oafish, troglodyte; churlish, uncivil, rude, impolite, discourteous, disrespectful, unmannerly, bad-mannered, ill-bred, indecorous, crass, indelicate; vulgar, crude, raunchy. See note at **RUDE**.
ANTONYMS refined.

uncover ▶ **verb 1** *she uncovered the new artwork* **expose,** reveal, lay bare; unwrap, unveil; strip, denude.
2 *they uncovered a money-laundering plot* **detect,** discover, come across, stumble on, chance on, find, turn up, unearth, dig up; expose, unveil, unmask, disclose, reveal, lay bare, make known, make public, bring to light, blow the lid off, blow the whistle on, pull the plug on.

unctuous ▶ **adjective** *she sees through his*

unctuous manners **sycophantic,** ingratiating, obsequious, fawning, servile, groveling, subservient, cringing, humble, hypocritical, insincere, gushing, effusive; glib, smooth, slick, slippery, oily, greasy; smarmy, slimy.

undaunted ▶ **adjective** *through all our crises, Cal has been the undaunted one* **unafraid,** undismayed, unflinching, unshrinking, unabashed, fearless, dauntless, intrepid, bold, valiant, brave, courageous, plucky, gritty, indomitable, confident, audacious, daring; informal gutsy, spunky.
ANTONYMS fearful.

undecided ▶ **adjective** *Gavin is hoping to win over the majority of undecided voters* **unresolved,** uncertain, unsure, unclear, unsettled, indefinite, undetermined, unknown, in the balance, up in the air, debatable, arguable, moot, open to question, doubtful, dubious, borderline, ambiguous, vague; indecisive, irresolute, hesitant, tentative, wavering, vacillating, uncommitted, ambivalent, of two minds, torn, fence-sitting, on the fence; informal iffy, wishy-washy.
ANTONYMS certain.

undefined ▶ **adjective 1** *some matters are still undefined* **unspecified,** unexplained, unspecific, indeterminate, unsettled; unclear, woolly, imprecise, inexact, indefinite, vague, fuzzy.
ANTONYMS definite, specific.
2 *undefined shapes* **indistinct,** indefinite, formless, indistinguishable, vague, amorphous, hazy, misty, shadowy, nebulous, blurred, blurry.
ANTONYMS clear, distinct.

undeniable ▶ **adjective** *her willingness to work is undeniable* **indisputable,** indubitable, unquestionable, beyond doubt, beyond question, undebatable, incontrovertible, incontestable, irrefutable, unassailable; certain, sure, definite, positive, conclusive, plain, obvious, unmistakable, self-evident, patent, emphatic, categorical, unequivocal.
ANTONYMS questionable.

under ▶ **preposition 1** *they hid under a bush* **beneath,** below, underneath.
ANTONYMS above, over.
2 *the rent is under $450* **less than,** lower than, below.
ANTONYMS more than, over.
3 *branch managers are under the retail director* **subordinate to,** junior to, inferior to, subservient to, answerable to, responsible to, subject to, controlled by.
ANTONYMS above, over.
4 *the town was under water* **flooded by,** immersed in, submerged by, sunk in, engulfed by, inundated by.
ANTONYMS above.
5 *forty homes are under construction* **undergoing,** in the process of.
6 *our finances are under pressure* **subject to,** liable to, at the mercy of.
▶ **adverb** *coughing and spluttering she went under* **down,** lower, below, underneath, beneath; underwater.

undercover ▶ **adjective** *she does undercover work for the insurance company* **covert,** secret, clandestine, incognito, underground, surreptitious, furtive, cloak-and-dagger, stealthy, hidden, concealed, backstairs, closet; informal hush-hush, sneaky, on the QT.
ANTONYMS overt.

undercurrent ▶ **noun 1** *dangerous undercurrents in the cove* **undertow,** underflow; riptide.
2 *the undercurrent of despair in his words* **undertone,** overtone, suggestion, connotation, intimation, hint, nuance, trace, suspicion, whisper, tinge; feeling, atmosphere, aura, echo; informal vibe.

undercut ▶ **verb 1** *the firm undercut their rivals* **charge less than,** undersell, underprice, underbid.
2 *his authority was being undercut* **undermine,** weaken, impair, sap, threaten, subvert, sabotage, ruin, destabilize, wreck.

underdog ▶ **noun** *yesterday's underdog is today's champion* **long shot,** dark horse, weaker one, little guy, David; downtrodden, victim, loser, fall guy.

underestimate ▶ **verb** *underestimating the opposition was our biggest mistake* **underrate,** undervalue, lowball, do an injustice to, be wrong about, sell short, play down, understate; minimize, de-emphasize, underemphasize, diminish, gloss over, trivialize; miscalculate, misjudge, misconstrue, misread.
ANTONYMS exaggerate.

undergo ▶ **verb** *she underwent a lengthy cross-examination* **go through,** experience, undertake, face, submit to, be subjected to, come in for, receive, sustain, endure, brave, bear, tolerate, stand, withstand, weather.

underground ▶ **adjective 1** *an underground parking garage* **subterranean,** buried, sunken, subsurface, basement.
2 *underground trade* **clandestine,** secret, surreptitious, covert, undercover, closet, cloak-and-dagger, back-alley, backstairs, black-market, hidden, sneaky, furtive; resistance, subversive; informal hush-hush.
3 *the underground art scene* **alternative,** radical, revolutionary, unconventional, unorthodox, avant-garde, counterculture, experimental, innovative.
▶ **adverb 1** *the insects live underground* **below ground,** in the earth, subterraneously.
2 *the rebels went underground* **into hiding,** into seclusion, undercover, to earth, to ground.

undergrowth ▶ **noun** *the undergrowth is a habitat for various small mammals and certain birds* **shrubbery,** vegetation, underbrush, greenery, ground cover, underwood, brushwood, brush, scrub, bush, covert, thicket, copse; bushes, plants, brambles, herbage; technical herbaceous layer.

underline ▶ **verb 1** *she underlined a phrase* **underscore,** mark, pick out, emphasize, highlight.
2 *the program underlines the benefits of exercise* **emphasize,** stress, highlight, accentuate, accent, focus on, spotlight, point up, play up.

underling ▶ **noun** *he dishes out orders to his underlings* **subordinate,** inferior, junior, minion, lackey, subaltern, flunky, menial, vassal, subject, hireling, servant, henchman,

factotum; informal gofer.
ANTONYMS boss.

underlying ▶ adjective 1 *the underlying aims of the research* **fundamental,** basic, primary, prime, central, principal, root, chief, cardinal, key, elementary, intrinsic, essential.
2 *an underlying feeling of irritation* **latent,** repressed, suppressed, unrevealed, undisclosed, unexpressed, concealed, hidden, masked.

undermine ▶ verb 1 *their integrity is being undermined* **subvert,** undercut, sabotage, threaten, weaken, compromise, diminish, reduce, impair, mar, spoil, ruin, damage, hurt, injure, cripple, sap, shake; informal drag through the mud.
ANTONYMS strengthen, enhance.
2 *rivers undermined their banks* **erode,** wear away, eat away at.

underprivileged ▶ adjective *he spends his summers backpacking with underprivileged children from his hometown* **needy,** deprived, disadvantaged, poor, destitute, in need, in straitened circumstances, impoverished, poverty-stricken, on the poverty line, indigent, lower-class; formal penurious.
ANTONYMS wealthy.

underrate ▶ verb *for years the girls' athletic program was underrated* **undervalue,** underestimate, do an injustice to, sell short, play down, understate, minimize, diminish, downgrade, trivialize.
ANTONYMS exaggerate.

undersized ▶ adjective *the lack of nutrients will result in undersized tomatoes* **underdeveloped,** stunted, small, short, little, tiny, petite, slight, compact, miniature, mini, diminutive, dwarfish, pygmy, pint-sized, pocket-sized, baby, teeny-weeny, itsy-bitsy, itty-bitty, vertically challenged.
ANTONYMS overgrown.

understand ▶ verb 1 *he couldn't understand anything we said* **comprehend,** grasp, take in, see, apprehend, follow, make sense of, fathom; unravel, decipher, interpret; informal figure out, work out, make head(s) or tail(s) of, get one's head around, get the drift of, catch on to, get; Brit. informal twig.
2 *she understood how hard he'd worked* **appreciate,** recognize, realize, acknowledge, know, be aware of, be conscious of; informal be wise to; formal be cognizant of.
3 *I understand that you wish to go* **believe,** gather, take it, hear (tell), notice, see, learn; conclude, infer, assume, surmise, fancy.
▶ exclamation *I want out, understand?* get it, get the picture, see, right, know what I mean, get my drift, capisce, comprende.

understanding ▶ noun 1 *test your understanding of the language* **comprehension,** apprehension, grasp, mastery, appreciation, assimilation, absorption; knowledge, awareness, insight, skill, expertise, proficiency; informal know-how; formal cognizance.
ANTONYMS ignorance.
2 *it was my understanding that this was free* **belief,** perception, view, conviction, feeling, opinion, intuition, impression, assumption, supposition, inference, interpretation.
3 *she treated me with understanding* **compassion,** sympathy, pity, feeling, concern, consideration, kindness, sensitivity, decency, humanity, charity, goodwill, mercy, tolerance.
ANTONYMS indifference.
4 *we had a tacit understanding* **agreement,** arrangement, deal, bargain, settlement, pledge, pact, compact, contract, covenant, bond, meeting of minds.
▶ adjective *an understanding friend* **compassionate,** sympathetic, sensitive, considerate, tender, kind, thoughtful, tolerant, patient, forbearing, lenient, merciful, forgiving, humane; approachable, supportive, perceptive.

understate ▶ verb *let's not understate the importance of the coaching staff* **play down,** downplay, underrate, underplay, de-emphasize, trivialize, minimize, diminish, downgrade, brush aside, gloss over, put it mildly; informal soft-pedal, sell short.
ANTONYMS exaggerate.

understudy ▶ noun *Mark's understudy got better reviews than Mark himself did* **stand-in,** substitute, replacement, reserve, fill-in, locum, proxy, backup, relief, standby, stopgap; informal sub, pinch-hitter.

undertake ▶ verb *are you ready to undertake this challenge?* **tackle,** take on, assume, shoulder, handle, manage, deal with, be responsible for; engage in, take part in, go about, set about, get down to, come to grips with, embark on; attempt, try, endeavor; informal have a go at; formal essay.

undertaker ▶ noun *in those days, an epidemic of the flu would have the undertaker working around the clock* **funeral director,** mortician.

undertone ▶ noun 1 *he said something in an undertone* **low voice,** murmur, whisper, mutter.
2 *the story's dark undertones* **undercurrent,** overtone, suggestion, nuance, vein, atmosphere, aura, tenor, flavor, tinge; vibrations.

undervalue ▶ verb *I didn't mean to undervalue your contributions* **underrate,** underestimate, play down, understate, underemphasize, diminish, minimize, downgrade, reduce, brush aside, gloss over, trivialize, underprice; informal sell short.

underwater ▶ adjective *an underwater laboratory* **submerged,** immersed, sunken, subaqueous, subsurface; undersea, subsea, submarine.

underwear ▶ noun *he always managed to leave half of his underwear at camp* undergarment(s), underthings, underclothes, lingerie; foundation garment(s); informal undies, drawers, skivvies.

underworld ▶ noun 1 *Osiris, god of the underworld* **the netherworld,** the nether regions, hell, the abyss; eternal damnation; Sheol, Hades, Gehenna, Tophet; informal the other place; literary the pit.
ANTONYMS heaven.
2 *the city's violent underworld* **criminal world,** gangland; criminals, gangsters; informal mobsters.

underwrite ▶ verb *a local businesswoman has agreed to underwrite our charter* **sponsor,** support, back, insure, guarantee, indemnify, subsidize, pay for, finance, fund; informal foot the bill for, bankroll.

undesirable ▶ adjective **1** *undesirable side effects* **unpleasant,** disagreeable, objectionable, nasty, unwelcome, unwanted, unfortunate, inconvenient, infelicitous.
ANTONYMS pleasant.
2 *some very undesirable people* **unpleasant,** disagreeable, obnoxious, nasty, vile, unsavory, awful, repulsive, repellent, objectionable, abhorrent, loathsome, hateful, detestable, deplorable, appalling, insufferable, intolerable, despicable, contemptible, odious, terrible, dreadful, frightful, ghastly, horrible, horrid.
ANTONYMS pleasant, agreeable.
▶ noun *the bar was full of undesirables* **outcast,** lowlife, misfit, deviant, unsavory character, pariah, leper, untouchable, freak.

undisciplined ▶ adjective *you've never seen such a bunch of undisciplined kids and pets under one roof* **unruly,** disorderly, disobedient, badly behaved, recalcitrant, restive, wayward, delinquent, rebellious, refractory, insubordinate, disruptive, errant, out of control, uncontrollable, wild, naughty; disorganized, unsystematic, unmethodical, lax, slapdash, slipshod, sloppy.

undisguised ▶ adjective *he regarded her with undisguised affection* **obvious,** evident, patent, manifest, transparent, overt, unconcealed, unhidden, unmistakable, undeniable, plain, clear, clear-cut, explicit, naked, visible; blatant, flagrant, glaring, bold.

undisputed ▶ adjective *his military preeminence was undisputed* **uncontested,** indubitable, undoubted, incontestable, unchallenged, incontrovertible, unequivocal, undeniable, irrefutable, unmistakable, sure, certain, definite, accepted, acknowledged, recognized.
ANTONYMS doubtful.

undistinguished ▶ adjective *an undistinguished career as a claims adjuster* **unexceptional,** indifferent, run-of-the-mill, middle-of-the-road, ordinary, average, commonplace, mediocre, humdrum, lackluster, forgettable, uninspired, uneventful, unremarkable, inconsequential, featureless, nondescript, middling, moderate; informal garden-variety, by-the-numbers, nothing special, no great shakes, nothing to write home about, OK, so-so, 'comme ci, comme ça', bush-league, blah, plain-vanilla.
ANTONYMS extraordinary.

undo ▶ verb **1** *he undid another button* **unfasten,** unbutton, unhook, untie, unlace; unlock, unbolt; loosen, disentangle, extricate, release, detach, free, open; disconnect, disengage, separate.
ANTONYMS fasten.
2 *they will undo a decision by the superior court* **revoke,** overrule, overturn, repeal, rescind, reverse, retract, countermand, cancel, annul, nullify, invalidate, void, negate; Law vacate; formal abrogate.
ANTONYMS ratify.
3 *she undid much of the good work done* **ruin,** undermine, subvert, overturn, scotch, sabotage, spoil, impair, mar, destroy, wreck, eradicate, obliterate; cancel out, neutralize, thwart, foil, frustrate, hamper, hinder, obstruct; informal blow, put the kibosh on, foul up, scuttle.
ANTONYMS enhance.

undoing ▶ noun **1** *she plotted the emperor's undoing* **downfall,** defeat, conquest, deposition, overthrow, ruin, ruination, elimination, end, collapse, failure, fall, fall from grace, debasement; Waterloo.
2 *their complacency was their undoing* **fatal flaw,** Achilles heel, weakness, weak point, failing, nemesis, affliction, curse.

undone ▶ adjective **1** *some work was left undone* **unfinished,** incomplete, half-done, unaccomplished, unfulfilled, unconcluded; omitted, neglected, disregarded, ignored; remaining, outstanding, deferred, pending, on ice; informal on the back burner.
ANTONYMS finished.
2 formal *she had lost and was utterly undone* **done for,** finished, ruined, destroyed, doomed, lost, defeated, beaten; informal washed up, toast.
ANTONYMS successful.

undoubted ▶ adjective *their undoubted friendship* **undisputed,** unchallenged, unquestioned, indubitable, incontrovertible, irrefutable, incontestable, sure, certain, unmistakable; definite, accepted, acknowledged, recognized.

undoubtedly ▶ adverb *they are undoubtedly guilty* **doubtless,** indubitably, doubtlessly, no doubt, without (a) doubt, unquestionably, without question, indisputably, undeniably, incontrovertibly, clearly, obviously, patently, certainly, definitely, surely, of course, indeed. See note at CLEARLY.

undress ▶ verb *he undressed and got into bed* **strip (off),** disrobe, take off one's clothes, peel down.
– PHRASES **in a state of undress** *she waltzed in while I was in a state of undress* **naked,** (in the) nude, bare, stripped, unclothed, undressed, unclad; informal in one's birthday suit, in the raw, in the buff, au naturel, buck-naked, butt-naked, mother-naked.

undue ▶ adjective *we didn't intend to add undue stress to your situation* **excessive,** immoderate, intemperate, inordinate, disproportionate; uncalled for, unneeded, unnecessary, needless, unwarranted, unjustified, unreasonable; inappropriate, unmerited, unsuitable, improper.
ANTONYMS appropriate.

unduly ▶ adverb See EXCESSIVELY.

undying ▶ adjective *his undying devotion to Aunt Myrna* **abiding,** lasting, enduring, permanent, constant, infinite; unceasing, perpetual, ceaseless, incessant, unending, never-ending, unfading, amaranthine; immortal, eternal, deathless.

unearth ▶ verb **1** *workers unearthed an artillery shell* **dig up,** excavate, exhume, disinter, root out, unbury.
2 *I unearthed an interesting fact* **discover,** uncover, find, come across, stumble upon, hit on, bring to light, expose, turn up, hunt out.

unearthly ▶ adjective *an unearthly chill in the air* **otherworldly,** supernatural, preternatural, alien; ghostly, spectral, phantom, mysterious,

spine-chilling, hair-raising; uncanny, eerie, strange, weird, unnatural, bizarre, surreal; eldritch; informal spooky, creepy, scary.
ANTONYMS normal.

uneasy ▶ adjective **1** *the doctor made him feel uneasy* **worried,** anxious, troubled, disturbed, agitated, rattled, nervous, tense, overwrought, edgy, jumpy, apprehensive, restless, discomfited, perturbed, fearful, uncomfortable, unsettled; informal jittery, antsy, trepidatious.
ANTONYMS calm, at ease.
2 *he had an uneasy feeling* **worrying,** disturbing, troubling, alarming, disquieting, unsettling, disconcerting, upsetting, nagging, niggling.
3 *the victory ensured an uneasy peace* **tense,** awkward, strained, fraught; precarious, unstable, insecure.
ANTONYMS stable.

unemotional ▶ adjective *an effective clinician must remain unemotional when the patient is most out of control* **reserved,** undemonstrative, sober, restrained, passionless, perfunctory, emotionless, unsentimental, unexcitable, impassive, apathetic, phlegmatic, stoical, equable; cool, cold, frigid, unfeeling, callous.

unemployed ▶ adjective *most of my former colleagues are still unemployed* **jobless,** out-of-work, between jobs, unwaged, unoccupied, laid off, idle; on welfare; Brit. redundant.

unending ▶ adjective *the unending noise from that construction site is making us crazy* **endless,** never-ending, interminable, perpetual, eternal, amaranthine, ceaseless, incessant, unceasing, nonstop, uninterrupted, continuous, continual, constant, persistent, recurring, unbroken, unabating, unremitting, relentless. See note at ETERNAL.

unenviable ▶ adjective **disagreeable,** nasty, unpleasant, undesirable, unfortunate, unlucky, horrible, thankless; unwanted.

unequal ▶ adjective **1** *they are unequal in length* **different,** dissimilar, unalike, unlike, disparate, unmatched, uneven, irregular, varying, variable, asymmetrical.
ANTONYMS identical.
2 *the unequal distribution of wealth* **unfair,** unjust, disproportionate, inequitable, biased, askew.
ANTONYMS fair.
3 *an unequal contest* **one-sided,** uneven, unfair, ill-matched, unbalanced, lopsided, skewed.
ANTONYMS evenly balanced, fair.
4 *she felt unequal to the task* **inadequate for,** incapable of, unqualified for, unsuited to, incompetent at, not up to; informal not cut out for.
ANTONYMS competent.

unequaled ▶ adjective **unbeaten,** matchless, unmatched, unrivaled, unsurpassed, unparalleled, peerless, incomparable, inimitable, unique, second to none, in a class of its/one's own.

unequivocal ▶ adjective *the report's advice was unequivocal* **unambiguous,** unmistakable, indisputable, incontrovertible, indubitable, undeniable; clear, clear-cut, plain, plain-spoken, explicit, specific, categorical, straightforward, blunt, candid, emphatic, manifest.
ANTONYMS ambiguous.

unethical ▶ adjective **immoral,** amoral, unprincipled, unscrupulous, dishonorable, dishonest, wrong, deceitful, unconscionable, unfair, fraudulent, underhanded, wicked, evil, sneaky, corrupt; unprofessional, improper.

uneven ▶ adjective **1** *uneven ground* **bumpy,** rough, lumpy, stony, rocky, rugged, potholed, rutted, pitted, jagged.
ANTONYMS flat, smooth.
2 *uneven teeth* **irregular,** unequal, unbalanced, misaligned, lopsided, askew, crooked, asymmetrical, unsymmetrical.
ANTONYMS regular.
3 *uneven quality* **inconsistent,** variable, varying, fluctuating, irregular, erratic, patchy; choppy, unsteady.
ANTONYMS consistent.
4 *an uneven contest* **one-sided,** unequal, unfair, unjust, inequitable, ill-matched, unbalanced, David and Goliath.
ANTONYMS fair.

uneventful ▶ adjective *our flight was, thankfully, quite uneventful* **unexciting,** uninteresting, monotonous, boring, dull, tedious, humdrum, routine, unvaried, ordinary, run-of-the-mill, pedestrian, mundane, predictable; informal blah.
ANTONYMS exciting.

unexceptional ▶ adjective *an adequate but unexceptional hotel* **ordinary,** average, typical, everyday, mediocre, run-of-the-mill, middle-of-the-road, indifferent; informal OK, blah, so-so, 'comme ci, comme ça', nothing special, no great shakes, fair-to-middling.

unexpected ▶ adjective *an unexpected change in plans* **unforeseen,** unanticipated, unpredicted, unlooked-for, sudden, abrupt, surprising, unannounced.

unfair ▶ adjective **1** *the trial was unfair* **unjust,** inequitable, prejudiced, biased, discriminatory; one-sided, unequal, uneven, unbalanced, partisan, partial, skewed.
ANTONYMS just.
2 *his comments were unfair* **undeserved,** unmerited, uncalled for, unreasonable, unjustified.
ANTONYMS justified.
3 *unfair play* **unsportsmanlike,** unsporting, dirty, below the belt, underhanded, dishonorable.
ANTONYMS sporting.
4 *you're being very unfair* **inconsiderate,** thoughtless, insensitive, selfish, spiteful, mean, unkind, unreasonable; hypercritical, overcritical.

unfaithful ▶ adjective **1** *her husband had been unfaithful* **adulterous,** faithless, fickle, untrue, inconstant; unchaste, cheating, philandering, two-timing.
2 *an unfaithful friend* **disloyal,** treacherous, traitorous, untrustworthy, unreliable, undependable, fair-weather, false, two-faced, double-crossing, deceitful; literary perfidious.
ANTONYMS loyal.

unfamiliar ▶ adjective **1** *an unfamiliar part of the city* **unknown,** new, strange, foreign, alien;

unexplored, uncharted.
2 *the unfamiliar sounds* **unusual,** uncommon, unconventional, novel, different, exotic, unorthodox, odd, peculiar, curious, uncharacteristic, anomalous, abnormal, out of the ordinary.
3 *investors* ***unfamiliar with*** *the stock market* **unacquainted with,** unused to, unaccustomed to, unconversant with, unversed in, inexperienced in, uninformed of, unschooled in, unenlightened of, ignorant of, not cognizant of, new to, a stranger to.

unfashionable ▶ adjective *a pair of unfashionable shoes will ruin the whole look* **out,** out of date, outdated, old-fashioned, outmoded, out of style, dated, unstylish, passé, démodé, unhip, uncool, nerdy, dowdy, frumpy, lame, unsexy, old hat, square.

unfasten ▶ verb *Ron unfastened his belt* **undo,** open, disconnect, remove, untie, unbutton, unzip, unlash, loose, loosen, free, unlock, unbolt.

unfavorable ▶ adjective **1** *unfavorable comments* **adverse,** critical, hostile, inimical, unfriendly, unsympathetic, negative, scathing; discouraging, disapproving, uncomplimentary, unflattering.
ANTONYMS positive.
2 *the unfavorable economic climate* **gloomy,** adverse, inauspicious, unpropitious, disadvantageous; unsuitable, inappropriate, inopportune.
ANTONYMS advantageous.

unfeeling ▶ adjective *humiliating Don in front of his children was an unfeeling thing to do* **uncaring,** unsympathetic, unemotional, uncharitable; heartless, hard-hearted, hard, harsh, austere, cold, cold-hearted, cold-blooded, insensitive, callous.
ANTONYMS compassionate.

unfit ▶ adjective **1** *that party is* ***unfit*** *to govern* | ***unfit*** *for service* **unqualified,** unsuitable, unsuited, inappropriate, unequipped, inadequate, not designed; incapable of, unable to, not up to, not equal to, unworthy of; informal not cut out for, not up to scratch.
ANTONYMS suitable.
2 *unfit and overweight children* **unhealthy,** out of shape, in poor condition/shape.
ANTONYMS (physically) fit.

unflattering ▶ adjective **1** *an unflattering review* **unfavorable,** uncomplimentary, harsh, unsympathetic, critical, negative, hostile, scathing.
ANTONYMS complimentary.
2 *an unflattering dress* **unattractive,** unbecoming, unsightly, ugly, homely, plain, ill-fitting.
ANTONYMS becoming.

unfold ▶ verb **1** *May unfolded the map* **open out,** spread out, flatten, straighten out, unroll, unfurl.
2 *I watched the events unfold* **develop,** evolve, happen, take place, occur, transpire, progress, play out.

unforeseen ▶ adjective *the problems with the bus were, of course, unforeseen* **unpredicted,** unexpected, unanticipated, unplanned, not bargained for, surprising.
ANTONYMS expected.

unforgettable ▶ adjective *the trip to Indonesia was unforgettable* **memorable,** not/never to be forgotten, haunting, catchy; striking, impressive, outstanding, extraordinary, exceptional.
ANTONYMS unexceptional.

unforgivable ▶ adjective *he had committed the unforgivable sin—he had informed on his friends* **inexcusable,** unpardonable, unjustifiable, indefensible.
ANTONYMS venial.

unfortunate ▶ adjective **1** *unfortunate people* **unlucky,** hapless, jinxed, out of luck, luckless, wretched, miserable, forlorn, poor, pitiful; informal down on one's luck.
ANTONYMS lucky.
2 *an unfortunate start to our vacation* **adverse,** disadvantageous, unfavorable, unlucky, unwelcome, unpromising, inauspicious, unpropitious, bad; formal grievous.
ANTONYMS auspicious.
3 *an unfortunate remark* **regrettable,** inappropriate, unsuitable, infelicitous, unbecoming, inopportune, tactless, injudicious.
ANTONYMS tactful, appropriate.

unfounded ▶ adjective *unfounded speculation* **groundless,** baseless, unsubstantiated, unproven, unsupported, uncorroborated, unconfirmed, unverified, unattested, unjustified, without basis, without foundation; specious, speculative, conjectural, idle; false, untrue.
ANTONYMS proven.

unfriendly ▶ adjective **1** *an unfriendly look* **hostile,** disagreeable, antagonistic, aggressive; ill-natured, unpleasant, surly, sour, uncongenial; inhospitable, unneighborly, unwelcoming, unkind, unsympathetic; unsociable, antisocial; aloof, stiff, cold, cool, frosty, distant, unapproachable; informal standoffish, starchy.
ANTONYMS amiable.
2 *an unfriendly wind* **unfavorable,** unhelpful, disadvantageous, unpropitious, inauspicious, hostile.
ANTONYMS favorable.
3 *environmentally unfriendly* **harmful,** damaging, destructive, disrespectful.

ungainly ▶ adjective *they were as ungainly as fifth-grade boys taking dance lessons in a foot of snow* **awkward,** clumsy, klutzy, ungraceful, graceless, inelegant, gawky, maladroit, gauche, uncoordinated; archaic lubberly.
ANTONYMS graceful.

ungodly ▶ adjective **1** *ungodly behavior* **unholy,** godless, irreligious, impious, blasphemous, sacrilegious, profane; immoral, corrupt, depraved, sinful, wicked, evil, iniquitous.
2 *he called at an ungodly hour* **unreasonable,** unsocial, antisocial, unearthly, godforsaken.

ungrateful ▶ adjective *she's been so generous to those ungrateful children* **unappreciative,** unthankful, thankless, ungracious, churlish.
ANTONYMS thankful.

unguarded ▸ adjective **1** *an unguarded frontier* **undefended,** unprotected, unfortified; vulnerable, insecure, open to attack.
2 *an unguarded remark* **careless,** indiscreet, incautious, thoughtless, rash, reckless, foolhardy, foolish, imprudent, injudicious, ill-considered, ill-judged, insensitive; unwary, inattentive, off guard, distracted, absentminded; candid, open; literary temerarious.

unhappy ▸ adjective **1** *the unhappy boy cried all night* **sad,** miserable, sorrowful, dejected, despondent, disconsolate, morose, broken-hearted, heartbroken, hurting, down, downcast, dispirited, downhearted, depressed, melancholy, mournful, gloomy, glum, lugubrious, despairing, doleful, forlorn, woebegone, woeful, long-faced, joyless, cheerless; informal down in the dumps, down in/at the mouth, blue.
ANTONYMS cheerful.
2 *in the unhappy event of litigation* **unfortunate,** unlucky, luckless; ill-starred, ill-fated, doomed; regrettable, lamentable; informal jinxed; literary star-crossed.
3 *I was unhappy with the service I received* **dissatisfied,** displeased, discontented, disappointed, disgruntled, angry; informal PO'd.

unhealthy ▸ adjective **1** *an unhealthy lifestyle* **harmful,** detrimental, destructive, injurious, damaging, deleterious; malign, noxious, poisonous, insalubrious, baleful.
2 *an unhealthy pallor* **sickly,** ill, unwell, in poor health, ailing, sick, indisposed, weak, wan, sallow, frail, delicate, infirm, washed out, run-down.
3 *an unhealthy obsession with toenails* **unwholesome,** morbid, macabre, twisted, abnormal, warped, depraved, unnatural; informal sick, wrong.

unheard of ▸ adjective *these medical procedures were unheard of just ten years ago* **unprecedented,** exceptional, extraordinary, out of the ordinary, unthought of, undreamed of, unbelievable, inconceivable, unimaginable, unthinkable; **unknown,** unfamiliar, new.
ANTONYMS common, well-known.

unheeded ▸ adjective *he was soon reminded of his parents' unheeded warnings* **disregarded,** ignored, neglected, overlooked, unnoted, unrecognized.

unhinged ▸ adjective *he was completely unhinged just because we were a few minutes late* **deranged,** demented, unbalanced, unglued, crazed, mad, insane, disturbed, out of one's mind, out of one's tree; informal crazy, mental, nutso, bonkers, batty, loopy, loco, postal, bananas, touched.
ANTONYMS sane.

unholy ▸ adjective **1** *a grin of unholy amusement* **ungodly,** godless, irreligious, impious, blasphemous, sacrilegious, profane, irreverent; wicked, evil, immoral, corrupt, depraved, sinful.
2 *an unholy alliance* **unnatural,** unusual, improbable, made in Hell.

unhurried ▸ adjective *we live at an unhurried pace around here* **leisurely,** easy, easygoing, relaxed, slow, deliberate, measured, calm.
ANTONYMS hasty.

unidentified ▸ adjective *an unidentified caller said he knew the whereabouts of Lyle* **unknown,** unnamed, anonymous, incognito, nameless, unfamiliar, strange, mysterious.
ANTONYMS known.

unification ▸ noun *the costs of German unification* **union,** merger, fusion, fusing, amalgamation, coalition, combination, confederation, federation, synthesis, joining.

uniform ▸ adjective **1** *a uniform temperature* **constant,** consistent, steady, invariable, unvarying, unfluctuating, unchanging, stable, static, regular, fixed, even, equal.
ANTONYMS variable.
2 *pieces of uniform size* **identical,** matching, similar, equal; same, like, homogeneous, consistent.
ANTONYMS varied.
▸ noun *a soldier in uniform* **costume,** livery, regalia, suit, ensemble, outfit; colors; informal getup, monkey suit, rig, gear; archaic habit.

uniformity ▸ noun **1** *uniformity in tax law* **constancy,** consistency, conformity, invariability, stability, regularity, evenness, homogeneity, equality, harmony.
ANTONYMS variation.
2 *a dull uniformity* **monotony,** tedium, tediousness, dullness, dreariness, flatness, sameness.
ANTONYMS variety.

unify ▸ verb *he unified the confederacy into a powerful entity* **unite,** bring together, join (together), marry, merge, fuse, amalgamate, integrate, coalesce, combine, blend, mix, meld, bind, consolidate.
ANTONYMS separate.

unimaginable ▸ adjective *the phone bills have been unimaginable* **unthinkable,** inconceivable, indescribable, incredible, unbelievable, unheard of, unthought of, untold, mind-boggling, undreamed of, beyond one's wildest dreams.

unimaginative ▸ adjective *the biggest letdown is the dessert menu, which is quite unimaginative* **uninspired,** uninventive, unoriginal, uncreative, commonplace, pedestrian, mundane, institutional, ordinary, routine, matter-of-fact, humdrum, workaday, run-of-the-mill, by-the-numbers, hackneyed, trite, hoary.

unimportant ▸ adjective *the details are unimportant at this stage* **insignificant,** inconsequential, insubstantial, immaterial, trivial, minor, venial, trifling, of little/no importance, of little/no consequence, of no account, no-account, irrelevant, peripheral, extraneous, petty, paltry, derisory, weightless, small; informal piddling.

uninhabited ▸ adjective *most of the village has been uninhabited since the epidemic in the seventies* **unpopulated,** unpeopled, unsettled, vacant, empty, unoccupied; unlived-in, untenanted.

uninhibited ▸ adjective **1** *uninhibited dancing* **unrestrained,** unrepressed, abandoned, wild, reckless; unrestricted, unmuffled, uncontrolled, unchecked, intemperate, wanton,

loose; informal gung-ho.
ANTONYMS controlled.
2 *I'm pretty uninhibited* **unreserved,** unrepressed, liberated, unselfconscious, free and easy, free-spirited, relaxed, informal, open, outgoing, extrovert, outspoken, candid, frank, forthright; informal upfront, jiggy.
ANTONYMS repressed.

unintelligible ▶ adjective **1** *unintelligible sounds* **incomprehensible,** indiscernible, mumbled, indistinct, unclear, slurred, inarticulate, incoherent, garbled.
2 *unintelligible logic* **impenetrable,** baffling, perplexing, inscrutable, opaque, cryptic, abstruse, unfathomable, incoherent, incomprehensible, as clear as mud, impossible to follow.
3 *unintelligible graffiti* **illegible,** indecipherable, unreadable, hieroglyphic.

unintentional ▶ adjective *I assure you, the insult was unintentional* **unintended,** accidental, inadvertent, involuntary, unwitting, unthinking, unpremeditated, unconscious; random, fortuitous, serendipitous, fluky.
ANTONYMS deliberate.

uninterested ▶ adjective *I couldn't live with someone* ***uninterested in*** *world affairs* **indifferent to,** unconcerned with, incurious about, uninvolved with/in, apathetic to, lukewarm about, unenthusiastic about, bored with. See notes at **DISINTERESTED.**

uninteresting ▶ adjective *an uninteresting book about genealogy* **unexciting,** boring, dull, tiresome, wearisome, soporific, tedious, jejune, lifeless, lackluster, humdrum, colorless, soulless, bland, insipid, banal, dry, dreary, drab, pedestrian, lacking; informal blah, samey.
ANTONYMS exciting.

uninterrupted ▶ adjective *an uninterrupted 55 minutes of your favorite music* **unbroken,** continuous, continual, constant, nonstop, ceaseless; undisturbed, untroubled.
ANTONYMS intermittent.

uninviting ▶ adjective *the bed looked cold and uninviting* **unappealing,** unattractive, unappetizing, off-putting; bleak, cheerless, dreary, dismal, depressing, grim, inhospitable, forbidding.
ANTONYMS tempting.

union ▶ noun **1** *the union of art and nature* **unification,** uniting, joining, merging, merger, fusion, fusing, amalgamation, coalition, combination, synthesis, blend, blending, mingling; **marriage,** wedding, alliance, civil union; coupling.
ANTONYMS separation, parting.
2 *the workers joined a union* **association,** labor union, trade union, league, guild, confederation, federation, brotherhood, organization.

unique ▶ adjective **1** *each site is unique* **distinctive,** distinct, individual, special, idiosyncratic; single, sole, lone, unrepeated, unrepeatable, solitary, exclusive, rare, uncommon, unusual, sui generis; informal one-off, one-of-a-kind, once-in-a-lifetime, one-shot.
2 *a unique insight* **remarkable,** special, singular, noteworthy, notable, extraordinary; unequaled, unparalleled, unmatched, unsurpassed, unrivaled, peerless, nonpareil, incomparable; formal unexampled.
3 *species unique to the island* **peculiar,** specific, limited.

> USAGE
> **unique**
> Strictly speaking, *unique* means "being one of a kind," not "unusual." Hence the phrases *very unique, quite unique, how unique,* and the like are slovenly. *The Oxford English Dictionary* notes that this tendency to hyperbole—to use *unique* when all that is meant is "uncommon, unusual, remarkable"—began in the nineteenth century. However old it is, the tendency is worth resisting.
>
> Unless the thing is the only one of its kind, rarity does not make it unique. For instance, if a thing is one in a million, logically there would be two things in two million. Rare indeed but not unique. Who can demand responsible use of the language from an ad writer who is reckless enough to say, in a national advertisement, that a certain luxury sedan is "so unique, it's capable of thought"? And what are we to make of the following examples?
>
> - "This year the consensus among the development executives seems to be that there are some fantastically funny, very exciting, very, very unique talents here." (*Time*; Aug. 16, 1993.)
> - "Residents of college basketball's most unique unincorporated village were in place yesterday afternoon, the day before their Blue Devils will face North Carolina." (*New York Times*; Feb. 2, 1995.)
>
> Arguably, our modern culture lacks and does not want absolutes, in intellectual life or in language. But stick with the uncomparable *unique*, and you may stand out as almost unique. — **BG**

unison ▶ noun
– PHRASES **in unison** *they lifted their arms in unison* **simultaneously,** at (one and) the same time, (all) at once, (all) together.

unit ▶ noun **1** *the family is the fundamental unit of society* **component,** element, building block, constituent; subdivision.
2 *a unit of currency* **quantity,** measure, denomination.
3 *a guerrilla unit* **detachment,** contingent, division, company, squadron, corps, regiment, brigade, platoon, battalion; cell, faction.

unite ▶ verb **1** *uniting the municipalities* **unify,** join, link, connect, combine, amalgamate, fuse, weld, bond, wed, marry, bring together, knit together, splice. See note at **JOIN.**
ANTONYMS divide.
2 *environmentalists and union activists united to demand changes* **join together,** join forces, combine, band together, ally, cooperate,

collaborate, work together, pull together, team up, hitch up, hook up, twin.
ANTONYMS split.

united ▶ adjective **1** *a united Germany* **unified,** integrated, amalgamated, joined, merged; federal, confederate.
2 *a united response* **common,** shared, joint, combined, communal, cooperative, collective, collaborative, concerted; Brit. informal joined-up.
3 *they were united in their views* **unanimous,** in agreement, agreed, in unison, of the same opinion, like-minded, as one, in accord, in harmony, in unity.

unity ▶ noun **1** *European unity* **union,** unification, integration, amalgamation; coalition, federation, confederation.
ANTONYMS division.
2 *unity between alliance members* **harmony,** accord, cooperation, collaboration, agreement, consensus, solidarity; formal concord, concordance.
ANTONYMS strife, discord.
3 *the organic unity of the universe* **oneness,** singleness, wholeness, uniformity, homogeneity.

universal ▶ adjective *the universal features of language* **general,** ubiquitous, comprehensive, common, omnipresent, all-inclusive, all-embracing, across-the-board; global, worldwide, international, widespread; formal catholic.

CHOOSE THE RIGHT WORD

universal, catholic, common, ecumenical, general, generic

Something that is **universal** applies to every case or individual in a class or category (*a universal practice among aboriginal tribesmen; a universal truth*). **General**, on the other hand, is less precise; it implies applicability to all or most of a group or class, whether the members of that group are clearly defined or only casually associated (*a drug that has come into general use among women but has not yet won the universal acceptance of doctors*). **Generic** is often used in place of *general* when referring to every member of a genus or clearly-defined scientific category (*a generic characteristic of insects*); with reference to language, it means referring to both men and women (*a generic pronoun*). **Common** implies participation or sharing by all members of a class (*a common interest in French culture*) or frequently occurring (*a common complaint*). **Catholic** implies a wide-ranging or inclusive attitude (*known for his catholic tastes in music*), while **ecumenical** means pertaining to the whole Christian church or promoting unity among religious groups or divisions (*an ecumenical marriage ceremony*).

universally ▶ adverb *it was universally accepted that no man married merely for love* **generally,** widely, commonly, across the board, all over.

universe ▶ noun **1** *the physical universe* **cosmos,** macrocosm, totality; infinity, all existence, Creation; space, outer space, firmament.
2 *the universe of computer hardware* **world,** sphere, domain, preserve, milieu, province.

unjust ▶ adjective **1** *the assessment was unjust* **unfair,** prejudiced, prejudicial, biased, inequitable, discriminatory, partisan, partial, one-sided, jaundiced.
ANTONYMS fair.
2 *an unjust attack* **wrongful,** unfair, undeserved, unmerited, unwarranted, uncalled for, unreasonable, unjustifiable, undue, gratuitous.
ANTONYMS fair, reasonable.

unjustifiable ▶ adjective **1** *an unjustifiable extravagance* **indefensible,** inexcusable, unforgivable, unpardonable, uncalled for, gratuitous, without justification, unwarrantable; excessive, immoderate.
ANTONYMS reasonable.
2 *an unjustifiable slur on his character* **groundless,** unfounded, baseless, unsubstantiated, unconfirmed, uncorroborated, indefensible, irrational.

unkempt ▶ adjective *unkempt hair* **untidy,** messy, scruffy, straggly, disordered, disheveled, disarranged, rumpled, wind-blown, ungroomed, bedraggled, in a mess, mussed, messed up; tousled, uncombed.
ANTONYMS tidy.

unkind ▶ adjective *everyone was being rude and unkind to him* **uncharitable,** unpleasant, disagreeable, nasty, mean, mean-spirited, cruel, vindictive, vicious, spiteful, malicious, callous, unsympathetic, unfeeling, uncaring, unsparing, hurtful, ill-natured, hard-hearted, cold-hearted; unfriendly, uncivil, inconsiderate, insensitive, hostile; informal bitchy, catty.

unknown ▶ adjective **1** *the future is unknown* **uncertain,** undisclosed, unrevealed, secret; undetermined, undecided, unresolved, unsettled, unsure, unascertained.
ANTONYMS decided.
2 *unknown country* **unexplored,** uncharted, unmapped, untraveled, undiscovered, unfamiliar, unheard of, new, novel, strange.
ANTONYMS familiar.
3 *persons unknown* **unidentified,** anonymous, unnamed, nameless; faceless, hidden.
ANTONYMS identified, named.
4 *unknown artists* **obscure,** unrecognized, unheard of, unsung, overlooked, unheralded, minor, insignificant, unimportant.
ANTONYMS familiar.
▶ noun *the overseas ballots are a big unknown* **mystery,** unknown quantity, uncertainty, ambiguity, variable, anyone's guess; informal crapshoot.

unlawful ▶ adjective *unlawful imports of drugs* **illegal,** illicit, illegitimate, against the law; criminal, felonious; prohibited, banned, outlawed, proscribed, forbidden.
ANTONYMS legal.

unlike ▶ preposition **1** *the familiar artichoke is totally unlike a Jerusalem artichoke* **different from,** dissimilar to.
ANTONYMS similar to.
2 *unlike Bob, Regis enjoyed swing dancing* **in contrast to,** as opposed to.

ANTONYMS similarly to.
▶ **adjective** *a meeting of unlike minds* **dissimilar,** unalike, disparate, contrasting, antithetical, different, diverse, incongruous, heterogeneous, mismatched, divergent, at variance, varying, at odds; informal poles apart, like night and day, like apples and oranges.

unlikely ▶ **adjective 1** *it is unlikely they will ever recover* **improbable,** doubtful, dubious.
ANTONYMS probable.
2 *an unlikely story* **implausible,** improbable, questionable, unconvincing, far-fetched, unrealistic, incredible, unbelievable, inconceivable, unimaginable; absurd, preposterous; informal tall.
ANTONYMS believable.

unlimited ▶ **adjective 1** *unlimited supplies of water* **inexhaustible,** limitless, illimitable, boundless, immeasurable, incalculable, untold, infinite, endless, bottomless, never-ending.
ANTONYMS finite.
2 *unlimited travel* **unrestricted,** unconstrained, unrestrained, unchecked, unbridled, uncurbed.
ANTONYMS restricted.
3 *unlimited power* **total,** unqualified, unconditional, unrestricted, absolute, supreme.
ANTONYMS conditional, restricted.

unload ▶ **verb 1** *we unloaded the van* **unpack,** empty.
2 *they unloaded the cases from the truck* **remove,** offload, discharge.
3 *the government unloaded its 20 percent stake* **sell,** discard, jettison, offload, get rid of, dispose of; palm something off (on someone), foist something (on someone), fob something off (on someone); informal dump, ditch, get shut of.
4 *she unloaded her troubles* **divulge,** talk about, open up about, pour out, vent, give vent to, get something off one's chest.

unlock ▶ **verb** *I unlocked the door and led the way in* **unbolt,** unlatch, unbar, unfasten, open.

unloved ▶ **adjective** *Melanie felt lonely and unloved* **unwanted,** uncared-for, friendless, unvalued; rejected, unwelcome, shunned, spurned, neglected, abandoned.

unlucky ▶ **adjective 1** *he was unlucky not to score* **unfortunate,** luckless, out of luck, jinxed, hapless, ill-fated, ill-starred, unhappy; informal down on one's luck; literary star-crossed.
ANTONYMS fortunate.
2 *an unlucky number* **unfavorable,** inauspicious, unpropitious, ominous, cursed, ill-fated, ill-omened, disadvantageous, unfortunate.
ANTONYMS favorable.

unmanageable ▶ **adjective 1** *the huge project was unmanageable* **troublesome,** awkward, inconvenient; cumbersome, bulky, unwieldy.
2 *his behavior was becoming unmanageable* **uncontrollable,** ungovernable, unruly, disorderly, out of hand, difficult, disruptive, undisciplined, wayward, refractory, restive; archaic contumacious.

unmanly ▶ **adjective** *he was on the verge of tears, but did not wish to appear unmanly* **effeminate,** effete, unmasculine, womanish, epicene; weak, limp-wristed, soft, timid, timorous; informal sissy, swishy, wimpish, wimpy, nancy, pansy, camp.
ANTONYMS virile.

unmarried ▶ **adjective** *all of my siblings are happily unmarried* **single,** unwed, unwedded; spinster, bachelor; unattached, available, eligible, free.

unmistakable ▶ **adjective** *the taste of ginger is unmistakable* **distinctive,** distinct, telltale, indisputable, indubitable, undoubted, unambiguous, unequivocal; plain, clear, clear-cut, definite, obvious, unmissable, evident, self-evident, manifest, patent, pronounced, as plain as the nose on your face, as clear as day.

unmitigated ▶ **adjective** *the raid was an unmitigated disaster* **absolute,** unqualified, categorical, complete, total, downright, outright, utter, out-and-out, undiluted, unequivocal, untempered, veritable, perfect, consummate, pure, sheer. See note at **SEVERE.**

unmoved ▶ **adjective 1** *he was totally unmoved by her outburst* **unaffected,** untouched, unimpressed, aloof, cool, cold, dry-eyed; unconcerned, uncaring, unsympathetic, unreceptive, indifferent, impassive, unemotional, stoical, phlegmatic, equable, nonchalant; impervious (to), oblivious (to), heedless (of), deaf to.
2 *he remained unmoved on the crucial issues* **steadfast,** firm, unwavering, unswerving, resolved, resolute, decided, unswayed, uninfluenced, inflexible, unbending, intransigent, implacable, adamant.

unnatural ▶ **adjective 1** *the life of a circus bear is completely unnatural* **abnormal,** unusual, uncommon, extraordinary, strange, odd, peculiar, unorthodox, exceptional, irregular, atypical, untypical; freakish, freaky, uncanny.
ANTONYMS normal.
2 *a flash of unnatural color* **artificial,** man-made, synthetic, manufactured, inorganic, genetically engineered.
ANTONYMS genuine.
3 *unnatural vice* **perverted,** warped, aberrant, twisted, deviant, depraved, degenerate; informal kinky, sick.
4 *her voice sounded unnatural* **affected,** artificial, mannered, stilted, forced, labored, strained, false, fake, theatrical, insincere, ersatz; informal put on, phony.

unnecessary ▶ **adjective** *extra blankets are unnecessary* **unneeded,** nonessential, inessential, not required, uncalled for, useless, unwarranted, unwanted, undesired, dispensable, unimportant, optional, extraneous, gratuitous, expendable, noncore, disposable, redundant, pointless, purposeless.
ANTONYMS essential.

unnerve ▶ **verb** *the bleakness of his gaze unnerved her* **demoralize,** discourage, dishearten, dispirit, daunt, alarm, frighten, dismay, disconcert, discompose, perturb, upset, discomfit, take aback, unsettle, disquiet, fluster, agitate, shake, ruffle, throw off balance; informal rattle, faze, shake up, discombobulate.
ANTONYMS hearten.

unobtrusive ▶ **adjective** *she was unobtrusive and shy* **inconspicuous,** unnoticeable, low-

key, discreet, circumspect, understated, unostentatious.
ANTONYMS extrovert, conspicuous.

unoccupied ▸ adjective 1 *an unoccupied house* **vacant,** empty, uninhabited, unlived-in, untenanted, abandoned; free, available.
ANTONYMS inhabited.
2 *an unoccupied territory* **uninhabited,** unpopulated, unpeopled, unsettled.
ANTONYMS inhabited, populated.
3 *many young people were unoccupied* **at leisure,** idle, free, with time on one's hands, at a loose end; unemployed, without work.
ANTONYMS busy.

unofficial ▸ adjective 1 *unofficial figures* **unconfirmed,** unauthenticated, uncorroborated, unsubstantiated, provisional, off the record.
ANTONYMS confirmed.
2 *an unofficial committee* **informal,** casual; unauthorized, unsanctioned, unaccredited.
ANTONYMS formal.

unorthodox ▸ adjective *Hobson's unorthodox views denied him an academic career* **unconventional,** unusual, radical, nonconformist, avant-garde, eccentric, maverick, strange, idiosyncratic; heterodox, heretical, dissenting; informal off-the-wall, way out, offbeat, kooky.
ANTONYMS conventional.

unpalatable ▸ adjective 1 *unpalatable food* **unappetizing,** unappealing, unsavory, inedible, uneatable; disgusting, rancid, revolting, nauseating, tasteless, flavorless, gross.
ANTONYMS tasty.
2 *the unpalatable truth* **disagreeable,** unpleasant, regrettable, unwelcome, lamentable, hard to swallow, hard to take.

unparalleled ▸ adjective *an unparalleled opportunity to change society* **exceptional,** unique, singular, rare, unequaled, unprecedented, without parallel, without equal, nonpareil, matchless, peerless, unrivaled, unsurpassed, unexcelled, incomparable, second to none; formal unexampled.

unperturbed ▸ adjective *Daniel was unperturbed by the outburst* **untroubled,** undisturbed, unworried, unconcerned, unmoved, unflustered, unruffled, undismayed, impassive; calm, composed, cool, collected, unemotional, self-possessed, self-assured, levelheaded, unfazed, nonplussed, laid-back.

unpleasant ▸ adjective 1 *a very unpleasant situation* **disagreeable,** irksome, troublesome, annoying, irritating, vexatious, displeasing, distressing, nasty, horrible, terrible, awful, dreadful, hateful, miserable, invidious, objectionable, offensive, obnoxious, repugnant, repulsive, repellent, revolting, disgusting, distasteful, nauseating, unsavory.
ANTONYMS agreeable.
2 *an unpleasant man* **unlikable,** unlovable, disagreeable; unfriendly, rude, impolite, obnoxious, nasty, spiteful, mean, mean-spirited; insufferable, unbearable, annoying, irritating.
ANTONYMS likable.

unpopular ▸ adjective *he was unpopular at school* **disliked,** friendless, unliked, unloved, loathed, despised; unwelcome, avoided, ignored, rejected, outcast, shunned, spurned, cold-shouldered, ostracized; unfashionable, unhip, out.

unprecedented ▸ adjective *warfare on an unprecedented scale* **unheard of,** unknown, new, novel, groundbreaking, revolutionary, pioneering, epoch-making; unparalleled, unequaled, unmatched, unrivaled, without parallel, without equal, out of the ordinary, unusual, exceptional, singular, unique; formal unexampled.

unpredictable ▸ adjective 1 *unpredictable results* **unforeseeable,** uncertain, unsure, doubtful, dubious, iffy, dicey, in the balance, up in the air.
2 *unpredictable behavior* **erratic,** moody, volatile, unstable, capricious, temperamental, mercurial, changeable, variable; 'on-again, off-again'.

unpremeditated ▸ adjective *she later regretted her unpremeditated response* **unplanned,** spontaneous, unprepared, impromptu, spur-of-the-moment, unrehearsed, ad lib, improvised, extemporaneous; informal off-the-cuff, off the top of one's head. See note at SPONTANEOUS.
ANTONYMS planned.

unpretentious ▸ adjective 1 *he was thoroughly unpretentious* **unaffected,** modest, unassuming, without airs, natural, straightforward, open, honest, sincere, frank, ingenuous.
2 *an unpretentious hotel* **simple,** plain, modest, humble, unostentatious, unsophisticated, folksy, no-frills.

unprincipled ▸ adjective *he is an unprincipled opportunist* **immoral,** unethical, amoral, unscrupulous, Machiavellian, dishonorable, dishonest, deceitful, devious, corrupt, crooked, wicked, evil, villainous, shameless, base, low; libertine, licentious.
ANTONYMS ethical.

unproductive ▸ adjective 1 *unproductive soil* **infertile,** sterile, barren, arid, unfruitful, poor.
ANTONYMS fertile.
2 *unproductive meetings* **fruitless,** futile, vain, idle, useless, worthless, valueless, pointless, ineffective, ineffectual, unprofitable, unrewarding.
ANTONYMS fruitful.

unprofessional ▸ adjective 1 *unprofessional conduct* **improper,** unethical, unprincipled, unscrupulous, dishonorable, disreputable, unseemly, unbecoming, indecorous.
2 *you don't want to hire unprofessional roofers* **amateurish,** amateur, unskilled, unskillful, inexpert, unqualified, inexperienced, incompetent, second-rate, inefficient.

unpromising ▸ adjective *they were not deterred by this unpromising start* **inauspicious,** unfavorable, unpropitious, discouraging, disheartening, gloomy, bleak, black, portentous, ominous, ill-omened.
ANTONYMS auspicious.

unqualified ▸ adjective 1 *an unqualified accountant* **untrained,** inexperienced;

unlicensed, quack.
2 *those unqualified to look after children* **unsuitable,** unsuited, unfit, ineligible, incompetent, unable, incapable, unprepared, ill-equipped, ill-prepared.
3 *unqualified support* **unconditional,** unreserved, unlimited, without reservations, categorical, unequivocal, unambiguous, wholehearted; complete, absolute, downright, undivided, total, utter.

unquestionable ▶ adjective *the sincerity of his beliefs is unquestionable* **indubitable,** undoubted, beyond question, beyond doubt, indisputable, undeniable, irrefutable, incontestable, incontrovertible, unequivocal; certain, sure, definite, self-evident, evident, manifest, obvious, apparent, patent.

unravel ▶ verb **1** *he unraveled the strands* **untangle,** disentangle, separate out, unwind, untwist, unsnarl, unthread.
ANTONYMS entangle.
2 *detectives are trying to unravel the mystery* **solve,** resolve, clear up, puzzle out, unscramble, get to the bottom of, explain, clarify, make head(s) or tail(s) of; figure out, dope out.
ANTONYMS complicate.
3 *society is starting to unravel* **fall apart,** fail, collapse, go wrong, deteriorate, go downhill, fray.
ANTONYMS succeed.

unreal ▶ adjective **1** *an unreal world of monsters and fairies* **imaginary,** fictitious, pretend, make-believe, made-up, dreamed-up, mock, false, illusory, chimerical, mythical, fanciful; hypothetical, theoretical; informal phony.
2 informal *that roller coaster was totally unreal* **incredible,** fantastic, unbelievable, out of this world.

unrealistic ▶ adjective **1** *unrealistic expectations* **impractical,** impracticable, unfeasible, nonviable; unreasonable, irrational, illogical, senseless, silly, foolish, fanciful, idealistic, quixotic, romantic, starry-eyed, blue-sky, pie in the sky; chiefly Brit. informal airy-fairy.
ANTONYMS pragmatic.
2 *unrealistic images* **unlifelike,** nonrealistic, unnatural, nonrepresentational, abstract; unbelievable, implausible.
ANTONYMS lifelike.

unreasonable ▶ adjective **1** *an unreasonable officer* **uncooperative,** unhelpful, disobliging, unaccommodating, awkward, contrary, difficult; obstinate, obdurate, willful, headstrong, pigheaded, cussed, intractable, intransigent, inflexible; irrational, illogical, prejudiced, intolerant.
2 *unreasonable demands* **unacceptable,** preposterous, outrageous, ridiculous; excessive, impossible, immoderate, disproportionate, undue, inordinate, intolerable, unjustified, unwarranted, uncalled for. See note at ABSURD.

unrefined ▶ adjective **1** *unrefined clay* **unprocessed,** untreated, crude, raw, natural, unprepared, unfinished.
ANTONYMS processed.
2 *unrefined people* **uncultured,** uncultivated, uncivilized, uneducated, unsophisticated; boorish, lumpen, oafish, loutish, coarse, vulgar, rude, rough, uncouth.
ANTONYMS cultured.

unrelenting ▶ adjective **1** *the unrelenting heat* **continual,** constant, continuous, relentless, unremitting, unabating, unflagging, uninterrupted, unrelieved, incessant, unceasing, ceaseless, endless, unending, persistent, nonstop.
ANTONYMS intermittent.
2 *an unrelenting opponent* **implacable,** inflexible, uncompromising, unyielding, unbending, relentless, determined, dogged, tenacious, steadfast, tireless, indefatigable, unflagging, unshakable, unswerving, unwavering.

unreliable ▶ adjective **1** *unreliable volunteers* **undependable,** untrustworthy, irresponsible, fickle, fair-weather, capricious, erratic, unpredictable, inconstant, faithless, temperamental; informal hinky.
2 *an unreliable indicator* **questionable,** open to doubt, doubtful, dubious, suspect, unsound, tenuous, uncertain, fallible; risky, chancy, inaccurate; informal iffy, dicey.

unrepentant ▶ adjective *how can you expect to be forgiven if you're unrepentant?* **remorseless,** unrepenting, impenitent, unashamed, shameless, unapologetic, unabashed.

unreserved ▶ adjective **1** *unreserved support* **unconditional,** unqualified, without reservations, unlimited, categorical, unequivocal, unambiguous; absolute, complete, thorough, wholehearted, full, total, utter, undivided.
ANTONYMS qualified.
2 *unreserved seats* **not booked,** unallocated, unoccupied, free, empty, vacant, available.
ANTONYMS booked.

unresolved ▶ adjective *as long as this issue is unresolved we cannot move ahead* **undecided,** unsettled, undetermined, uncertain, open, pending, open to debate/question, moot, doubtful, on the table, in play, in doubt, up in the air.
ANTONYMS decided.

unrest ▶ noun *social unrest* **disruption,** disturbance, trouble, turmoil, turbulence, disorder, chaos, anarchy; discord, disquiet, dissension, dissent, strife, protest, rebellion, uprising, rioting.
ANTONYMS peace.

unrestricted ▶ adjective *this area is reserved for unrestricted play* **unlimited,** open, free, freewheeling, clear, unhindered, unimpeded, unhampered, unchecked, unqualified, unrestrained, unconstrained, unblocked, unbounded, unconfined, rampant.
ANTONYMS limited.

unrivaled ▶ adjective *an unrivaled collection of rare coins* **unequaled,** without equal, unparalleled, without parallel, unmatched, unsurpassed, unexcelled, incomparable, beyond compare, inimitable, second to none, nonpareil.

unruly ▶ adjective *I can't take care of your unruly brats* **disorderly,** rowdy, wild, unmanageable, uncontrollable, disobedient, disruptive,

undisciplined, restive, wayward, willful, headstrong, irrepressible, obstreperous, difficult, intractable, out of hand, recalcitrant; boisterous, lively, rambunctious, refractory; archaic contumacious.
ANTONYMS disciplined.

unsaid ▶ adjective *our unsaid feelings for one another* **unspoken,** unuttered, unstated, unexpressed, unvoiced, suppressed; tacit, implicit, not spelled out, implied; understood, inferred.

unsavory ▶ adjective 1 *unsavory portions of food* **unpalatable,** unappetizing, distasteful, disagreeable, unappealing, repugnant, off-putting, unattractive; inedible, uneatable, disgusting, revolting, nauseating, sickening, foul, raunchy, nasty, vile; tasteless, bland, flavorless; informal yucky.
ANTONYMS tasty, appetizing.
2 *an unsavory character* **disreputable,** unpleasant, undesirable, disagreeable, nasty, mean, rough; immoral, degenerate, dishonorable, dishonest, unprincipled, unscrupulous, low, villainous; informal shady, crooked.
ANTONYMS reputable.

unscrupulous ▶ adjective *we didn't want to believe that someone in our group could be that unscrupulous* **unprincipled,** unethical, immoral, conscienceless, shameless, reprobate, exploitative, corrupt, dishonest, dishonorable, deceitful, devious, underhanded, unsavory, disreputable, evil, wicked, villainous, Machiavellian; informal crooked, shady, hinky; dated dastardly.

unseat ▶ verb 1 *the horse unseated his rider* **dislodge,** throw, dismount, upset, unhorse.
2 *an attempt to unseat the party leader* **depose,** oust, remove from office, topple, overthrow, bring down, overturn, eject, dislodge, supplant; usurp.

unseemly ▶ adjective *their unseemly behavior at Donna's baby shower* **improper,** unbecoming, unfitting, unbefitting, unworthy, undignified, indiscreet, indelicate, indecorous, ungentlemanly, unladylike.
ANTONYMS decorous.

unselfish ▶ adjective *his unselfish motives* **altruistic,** selfless, self-denying, self-sacrificing; generous, giving, magnanimous, philanthropic, public-spirited, charitable, benevolent, caring, kind, considerate, thoughtful, noble.

unsettle ▶ verb *all this talk of death was unsettling him* **unnerve,** upset, disturb, disquiet, perturb, discomfit, disconcert, alarm, dismay, trouble, bother, agitate, fluster, ruffle, shake (up), throw, unbalance, destabilize; informal rattle, faze, pull the rug (out) from under.

unsettled ▶ adjective 1 *an unsettled life* **aimless,** directionless, purposeless, without purpose; rootless, nomadic.
2 *an unsettled child* **restless,** restive, fidgety, anxious, worried, troubled, fretful; agitated, ruffled, uneasy, disconcerted, discomposed, unnerved, ill at ease, edgy, on edge, tense, nervous, apprehensive, disturbed, perturbed, unstrung; informal rattled, fazed.
3 *unsettled weather* **changeable,** changing, variable, varying, inconstant, inconsistent, ever-changing, erratic, unstable, undependable, unreliable, uncertain, unpredictable, protean.
4 *the question is still unsettled* **undecided,** to be decided, unresolved, undetermined, moot, uncertain, open to debate, doubtful, in doubt, up in the air, in a state of uncertainty.
5 *the debt remains unsettled* **unpaid,** payable, outstanding, owing, owed, to be paid, due, undischarged, delinquent, past due.
6 *unsettled areas* **uninhabited,** unpopulated, unpeopled, unoccupied, desolate, lonely.

unshakable ▶ adjective *she finally came to trust Hal's unshakable love* **steadfast,** resolute, staunch, firm, decided, determined, unswerving, unwavering; unyielding, inflexible, dogged, obstinate, obdurate, tenacious, persistent, indefatigable, tireless, unflagging, unremitting, unrelenting, relentless.

unsightly ▶ adjective *unsightly stains on the wall* **ugly,** unattractive, unprepossessing, unlovely, disagreeable, displeasing, hideous, horrible, repulsive, revolting, offensive, grotesque, monstrous, gross, ghastly.
ANTONYMS attractive.

unskilled ▶ adjective *the unskilled workforce* **untrained,** unqualified; manual, blue-collar, laboring, menial; inexpert, inexperienced, unpracticed, amateurish, unprofessional.

unsociable ▶ adjective *we found him to be stiff and unsociable* **unfriendly,** uncongenial, unneighborly, unapproachable, introverted, reticent, reserved, withdrawn, aloof, distant, remote, detached, unsocial, antisocial, asocial, taciturn, silent, quiet; informal standoffish.
ANTONYMS friendly.

unsolicited ▶ adjective *their unsolicited opinions* **uninvited,** unsought, unasked-for, unrequested.

unsophisticated ▶ adjective 1 *she seemed a bit unsophisticated* **unworldly,** naive, unrefined, simple, innocent, ignorant, green, immature, callow, inexperienced, childlike, artless, guileless, ingenuous, natural, unaffected, unassuming, unpretentious; informal cheesy. See note at GULLIBLE.
2 *unsophisticated software* **simple,** crude, low-tech, basic, rudimentary, primitive, rough and ready, homespun, bush-league; straightforward, uncomplicated, uninvolved.

unsound ▶ adjective 1 *structurally unsound* **weak,** rickety, flimsy, wobbly, unstable, crumbling, damaged, rotten, ramshackle, shoddy, insubstantial, unsafe, dangerous.
ANTONYMS strong.
2 *this plan appears unsound* **untenable,** flawed, defective, faulty, ill-founded, flimsy, unreliable, questionable, dubious, tenuous, suspect, fallacious, fallible; informal iffy.
3 *of unsound mind* **disordered,** deranged, disturbed, demented, unstable, unbalanced, unhinged, addled, insane.
ANTONYMS sane.

unspeakable ▶ adjective 1 *unspeakable delights* **indescribable,** beyond description,

inexpressible, unutterable, indefinable, unimaginable, inconceivable.
2 *an unspeakable crime* **horrific,** awful, appalling, dreadful, horrifying, horrendous, abominable, frightful, fearful, shocking, ghastly, gruesome, monstrous, heinous, egregious, deplorable, despicable, execrable, vile.

unspoiled ▶ adjective *the unspoiled landscape* **immaculate,** perfect, pristine, virgin, unimpaired, unblemished, unharmed, unflawed, undamaged, untouched, unmarked, untainted, as good as new/before.

unspoken ▶ adjective *they had an unspoken understanding* **unstated,** unexpressed, unuttered, unsaid, unvoiced, unarticulated, undeclared, not spelt out; tacit, implicit, implied, understood, unwritten.
ANTONYMS explicit.

unstable ▶ adjective **1** *that old ladder looks unstable* **unsteady,** rocky, wobbly, tippy; rickety, shaky, unsafe, insecure, precarious.
ANTONYMS steady.
2 *unstable coffee prices* **changeable,** volatile, variable, fluctuating, irregular, unpredictable, capricious, erratic, 'on-again, off-again'.
ANTONYMS fixed, firm.
3 *he was mentally unstable* **unbalanced,** of unsound mind, mentally ill, deranged, demented, disturbed, unhinged, volatile; informal kooky.
ANTONYMS balanced, of sound mind.

unstudied ▶ adjective *his unstudied grace* **natural,** easy, spontaneous, unaffected, unforced, uncontrived, unstilted, unpretentious, ingenuous, without airs, artless.

unsubstantiated ▶ adjective *unsubstantiated rumors* **unconfirmed,** unsupported, uncorroborated, unverified, unattested, unproven; unfounded, groundless, baseless, without foundation, unjustified.

unsuccessful ▶ adjective **1** *an unsuccessful attempt* **failed,** ineffective, fruitless, profitless, unproductive, abortive; vain, futile, useless, pointless, worthless, luckless.
2 *an unsuccessful business* **unprofitable,** loss-making.
3 *an unsuccessful candidate* **failed,** losing, beaten; unlucky, out of luck; informal losingest.

unsuitable ▶ adjective **1** *the product is unsuitable for your needs* **inappropriate,** unsuited, wrong, ill-suited, inapt, inapplicable, unacceptable, unfitting, unbefitting, incompatible, out of place, out of keeping, misplaced; formal inapposite.
ANTONYMS appropriate.
2 *an unsuitable moment for belching* **inopportune,** infelicitous, inappropriate, wrong, unfortunate; formal malapropos.
ANTONYMS opportune.

unsung ▶ adjective *no victory is without its unsung heroes* **unacknowledged,** uncelebrated, unacclaimed, unapplauded, unhailed, unheralded; neglected, unrecognized, overlooked, forgotten.
ANTONYMS celebrated.

unsure ▶ adjective **1** *she felt very unsure* **unconfident,** unassertive, insecure, hesitant, diffident, anxious, apprehensive.
ANTONYMS confident.
2 *Sally was unsure what to do* **undecided,** irresolute, dithering, equivocating, vacillating, of two minds, wishy-washy, in a quandary.
ANTONYMS decided.
3 *some teachers are unsure about the proposed strike* **dubious,** doubtful, skeptical, uncertain, unconvinced.
ANTONYMS convinced.
4 *the date is unsure* **not fixed,** undecided, uncertain.
ANTONYMS fixed.

unsuspecting ▶ adjective *it's a trap deliberately set for unsuspecting first-time buyers* **unsuspicious,** unwary, unaware, unconscious, ignorant, unwitting; trusting, gullible, credulous, ingenuous, naive, wide-eyed.
ANTONYMS wary.

unsympathetic ▶ adjective **1** *unsympathetic staff* **uncaring,** unconcerned, unfriendly, unfeeling, apathetic, insensitive, indifferent, unkind, pitiless, thoughtless, heartless, hard-hearted, stony, callous.
ANTONYMS caring.
2 *the government was **unsympathetic to** these views* **opposed to,** against, (dead) set against, antagonistic to, ill-disposed to; informal anti.
3 *an unsympathetic character* **unlikable,** dislikable, disagreeable, unpleasant, unappealing, off-putting, objectionable, unsavory; unfriendly.
ANTONYMS likable.

untangle ▶ verb **1** *I untangled the fishing tackle* **disentangle,** unravel, unsnarl, straighten out, untwist, untwine, unknot.
2 *untangling a mystery* **solve,** find the/an answer to, resolve, puzzle out, work out, fathom, clear up, clarify, get to the bottom of; informal figure out.

untenable ▶ adjective *these untenable explanations are not helping your case* **indefensible,** insupportable, unsustainable, unjustified, unjustifiable, flimsy, weak, shaky.

unthinkable ▶ adjective *winning the lottery is just too unthinkable* **unimaginable,** inconceivable, unbelievable, incredible, beyond belief, implausible, preposterous.

unthinking ▶ adjective **1** *an unthinking lout* **thoughtless,** inconsiderate, insensitive; tactless, undiplomatic, indiscreet.
ANTONYMS thoughtful.
2 *an unthinking remark* **absentminded,** heedless, thoughtless, careless, injudicious, imprudent, unwise, foolish, reckless, rash, precipitate; involuntary, inadvertent, unintentional, spontaneous, impulsive, unpremeditated.
ANTONYMS intentional.

untidy ▶ adjective **1** *untidy hair* **scruffy,** tousled, disheveled, unkempt, messy, disordered, disarranged, messed up, rumpled, bedraggled, uncombed, ungroomed, straggly, ruffled, tangled, matted, wind-blown, raddled; informal mussed up, raggedy.
ANTONYMS neat.
2 *the room was untidy* **disordered,** messy, in

a mess, disorderly, disorganized, in disorder, cluttered, in a muddle, muddled, in chaos, chaotic, haywire, topsy-turvy, in disarray, at sixes and sevens; informal higgledy-piggledy.
ANTONYMS neat, orderly.

untie ▶ verb *untie the team of horses* **undo,** unknot, unbind, unfasten, unlace, untether, unhitch, unmoor; (turn) loose, (set) free, release, let go, unshackle.

untimely ▶ adjective 1 *an untimely interruption* **ill-timed,** badly timed, mistimed; inopportune, inappropriate, unseasonable; inconvenient, unwelcome, infelicitous; formal malapropos.
ANTONYMS opportune.
2 *his untimely death* **premature,** (too) early, too soon, before time, unexpected.
ANTONYMS expected.

untiring ▶ adjective *these kids have been untiring in their efforts to get to the championship* **vigorous,** energetic, determined, resolute, enthusiastic, keen, zealous, spirited, dogged, tenacious, persistent, persevering, staunch; tireless, unflagging, unfailing, unfaltering, unwavering, indefatigable, unrelenting, unswerving; formal pertinacious.

untold ▶ adjective 1 *untold quantities* **boundless,** immeasurable, incalculable, limitless, unlimited, infinite, measureless; countless, innumerable, endless, numberless, uncountable; numerous, many, multiple; literary multitudinous, myriad.
ANTONYMS limited.
2 *the untold story* **unreported,** overlooked, ignored; hidden, secret, unrecounted, unrevealed, undisclosed, undivulged, unpublished.

untoward ▶ adjective 1 *an untoward occurrence* **inconvenient,** unlucky, unexpected, unforeseen, surprising, unusual; unwelcome, unfavorable, adverse, unfortunate, infelicitous; formal malapropos.
2 *untoward behavior* **improper,** unseemly; perverse.

untroubled ▶ adjective *they all thought I was untroubled, but I was really falling to pieces* **unworried,** unperturbed, unconcerned, unruffled, undismayed, unbothered, unalarmed, unflustered; insouciant, nonchalant, composed, blasé, carefree, calm, serene, tranquil, relaxed, halcyon, comfortable, at ease, happy-go-lucky, blissful, laid-back, mellow; informal supercool.

untrue ▶ adjective 1 *these suggestions are totally untrue* **false,** untruthful, fabricated, made up, invented, concocted, trumped up; erroneous, wrong, incorrect, inaccurate; fallacious, fictitious, unsound, unfounded, baseless, misguided.
ANTONYMS correct.
2 *he was untrue to his friends* **unfaithful,** disloyal, faithless, false, treacherous, traitorous, deceitful, deceiving, duplicitous, double-dealing, insincere, unreliable, undependable, inconstant; informal two-timing; literary perfidious.
ANTONYMS faithful.

untrustworthy ▶ adjective *the group's untrustworthy treasurer* **dishonest,** deceitful, double-dealing, treacherous, traitorous, two-faced, duplicitous, mendacious, dishonorable, unprincipled, unscrupulous, corrupt, slippery; unreliable, undependable, fly-by-night, capricious, fickle; informal hinky.
ANTONYMS reliable.

untruth ▶ noun 1 *a patent untruth* **lie,** falsehood, fib, fabrication, invention, falsification, half-truth, exaggeration; story, myth, piece of fiction; informal tall story, fairy tale, cock-and-bull story, whopper.
2 *the total untruth of the story* **falsity,** falsehood, falseness, untruthfulness, fictitiousness; fabrication, dishonesty, deceit, deceitfulness, inaccuracy, unreliability.

untruthful ▶ adjective 1 *the answers may be untruthful* **false,** untrue, fabricated, made up, invented, trumped up; erroneous, wrong, incorrect, inaccurate, fallacious, fictitious.
2 *an untruthful person* **lying,** mendacious, dishonest, deceitful, duplicitous, false, double-dealing, two-faced, untrustworthy, dishonorable; informal crooked; literary perfidious.
ANTONYMS honest.

unusual ▶ adjective *an unusual color for a marigold* **uncommon,** abnormal, atypical, unexpected, surprising, unfamiliar, different; strange, odd, curious, out of the ordinary, extraordinary, unorthodox, unconventional, outlandish, singular, special, unique, peculiar, bizarre; rare, scarce, few and far between, thin on the ground, exceptional, isolated, occasional, infrequent; informal weird, offbeat, out there, freaky.
ANTONYMS common.

unutterable ▶ adjective See UNSPEAKABLE.

unveil ▶ verb *this afternoon they are unveiling the details of yesterday's invasion* **reveal,** present, display, show, exhibit, put on display; release, launch, bring out; disclose, divulge, make known, make public, publish, broadcast, communicate.

unwarranted ▶ adjective 1 *the criticism is unwarranted* **unjustified,** uncalled for, unnecessary, unreasonable, unjust, groundless, excessive, gratuitous, immoderate, disproportionate, undue, unconscionable, unjustifiable, indefensible, inexcusable, unforgivable, unpardonable.
ANTONYMS justified.
2 *an unwarranted invasion of privacy* **unauthorized,** unsanctioned, unapproved, uncertified, unlicensed; illegal, unlawful, illicit, illegitimate.
ANTONYMS legal.

unwelcome ▶ adjective 1 *I was made to feel unwelcome* **unwanted,** uninvited, unaccepted, excluded, rejected.
2 *even a small increase is unwelcome* **undesirable,** undesired, unpopular, unfortunate, disappointing, upsetting, distressing, disagreeable, displeasing; regrettable, deplorable, objectionable, lamentable.

unwell ▶ adjective *I felt unwell as soon as we hit the open sea* **ill,** sick, indisposed, ailing, not (very) well, not too good, lousy, bad, rough, not oneself, under/below par, groggy, peaked, queasy, woozy, nauseous, nauseated; off, poorly, wretched, dead; under the weather; funny, weird; informal crappy, pukey.

unwieldy ▸ adjective *an unwieldy trunk full of old clothes* **cumbersome,** unmanageable, unmaneuverable; awkward, clumsy, massive, heavy, hefty, ponderous, bulky, weighty.
ANTONYMS manageable.

unwilling ▸ adjective **1** *unwilling conscripts* **reluctant,** unenthusiastic, hesitant, resistant, grudging, involuntary, forced.
ANTONYMS keen.
2 *he was unwilling to take on that responsibility* **disinclined,** reluctant, averse, loath; (**be unwilling to do something**) not have the heart to, balk at, refuse to, demur at, shy away from, flinch from, shrink from, have qualms about, have misgivings about, have reservations about.
ANTONYMS keen.

unwind ▸ verb **1** *Ella unwound the scarf from her neck* **unroll,** uncoil, unravel, untwine, untwist, disentangle, open (out), straighten (out).
2 *he liked to unwind after work* **relax,** loosen up, ease up/off, slow down, de-stress, unbend, rest, put one's feet up, sit back, take it easy, take a load off; informal wind down, mellow (out), let it all hang out, veg, hang loose, chill (out).

unwise ▸ adjective *it would have been unwise to argue* **injudicious,** ill-advised, ill-judged, imprudent, inexpedient, foolish, silly, inadvisable, impolitic, misguided, foolhardy, irresponsible, impetuous, rash, hasty, overhasty, reckless.
ANTONYMS sensible.

unwitting ▸ adjective **1** *an unwitting accomplice* **unknowing,** unconscious, unsuspecting, oblivious, unaware, innocent, in the dark.
ANTONYMS knowing.
2 *an unwitting mistake* **unintentional,** unintended, inadvertent, involuntary, unconscious, accidental.
ANTONYMS conscious.

unworldly ▸ adjective **1** *a gauche, unworldly girl* **naive,** simple, inexperienced, innocent, green, raw, callow, immature, ignorant, gullible, ingenuous, artless, guileless, childlike, trusting, credulous; nonmaterialistic.
2 *unworldly beauty* **unearthly,** otherworldly, ethereal, ghostly, preternatural, supernatural, paranormal, mystical.

unworthy ▸ adjective **1** *he was unworthy of trust* **undeserving,** ineligible, unqualified, unfit.
ANTONYMS deserving.
2 *unworthy behavior* **unbecoming,** unsuitable, inappropriate, unbefitting, unfitting, unseemly, improper; discreditable, shameful, dishonorable, despicable, ignoble, contemptible, reprehensible.
ANTONYMS becoming.

upbraid ▸ verb *we were upbraided for leaving the back door unlocked* **reprimand,** rebuke, admonish, chastise, chide, reprove, reproach, scold, berate, take to task, lambaste, give someone a piece of one's mind, give someone a tongue-lashing, rake/haul over the coals, lecture; informal tell off, give someone a talking-to, tear a strip off (of), dress down, give someone an earful, rap over the knuckles, bawl out, lay into, chew out, ream out; formal castigate; rare reprehend. See note at **SCOLD**.

upbringing ▸ noun *tell us a little about your upbringing* **childhood,** early life, formative years, teaching, education, instruction, tutelage, care, rearing, raising, breeding.

upgrade ▸ verb **1** *there are plans to upgrade the rail system* **improve,** modernize, update, bring up to date, make better, ameliorate, reform; rehabilitate, recondition, refurbish, spruce up, renovate, rejuvenate, overhaul; bring up to code.
ANTONYMS downgrade.
2 *he was upgraded to a seat in the cabinet* **promote,** give promotion to, elevate, move up, raise.
ANTONYMS demote.

upheaval ▸ noun *the upheaval caused by wartime evacuation* **disruption,** disturbance, trouble, turbulence, disorder, confusion, turmoil, pandemonium, chaos, mayhem, cataclysm, shakeup, debacle; revolution, change, craziness.

uphill ▸ adjective **1** *an uphill path* **upward,** rising, ascending, climbing.
ANTONYMS downhill.
2 *an uphill struggle* **arduous,** difficult, hard, tough, taxing, demanding, exacting, stiff, formidable, exhausting, tiring, wearisome, laborious, grueling, back-breaking, punishing, burdensome, onerous, Herculean; informal no picnic, killing; archaic toilsome.
ANTONYMS easy.

uphold ▸ verb **1** *the court upheld his claim for damages* **confirm,** endorse, sustain, approve, agree to, support; champion, defend.
ANTONYMS overturn, oppose.
2 *they've a tradition to uphold* **maintain,** sustain, continue, preserve, protect, champion, defend, keep, hold to, keep alive, keep going, back (up), stand by.
ANTONYMS abandon.

upkeep ▸ noun *the upkeep of the kennel can be quite expensive* **maintenance,** repair(s), service, servicing, preservation, conservation; running; care, support, keep, subsistence.

uplift ▸ verb *she needs something to uplift her spirits* **boost,** raise, buoy up, lift, cheer up, perk up, enliven, brighten up, lighten, stimulate, inspire, revive, restore; informal buck up.

upper ▸ adjective **1** *the upper floor* **higher,** superior; top; informal nosebleed.
ANTONYMS lower.
2 *the upper echelons of the party* **senior,** superior, higher-level, higher-ranking, top, loftier.
ANTONYMS junior, inferior.
– PHRASES **the upper hand** *it remains to be seen which party will have the upper hand in this election* **an advantage,** the edge, the whip hand, a lead, a head start, ascendancy, superiority, supremacy, sway, control, power, mastery, dominance, command, leverage.

upper-class ▸ adjective *our upper-class relations look down on us* **aristocratic,** noble, of noble birth, patrician, titled, blue-blooded, high-born, well-born, elite, born with a silver spoon in one's mouth; rich, wealthy; upscale, upmarket, upper-crust, high-class, tony, top-drawer, classy, posh, uptown; landowning, landed; archaic gentle, of gentle birth.

uppermost ▶ adjective **1** *the uppermost branches* **highest,** top, topmost.
2 *their own problems remained uppermost in their minds* **predominant,** of greatest importance, to the fore, foremost, first, primary, dominant, principal, chief, main, paramount, supreme, preponderant, major.

upright ▶ adjective **1** *an upright position* **vertical,** perpendicular, plumb, straight (up), straight up and down, standing, bolt upright, erect, on end; on one's feet.
ANTONYMS horizontal.
2 *an upright member of the community* **honest,** honorable, upstanding, respectable, high-minded, law-abiding, right-minded, worthy, moral, ethical, righteous, decent, scrupulous, conscientious, good, virtuous, principled, of principle, noble, incorruptible.
ANTONYMS dishonorable.

uprising ▶ noun *the uprising was put down by government forces* **rebellion,** revolt, insurrection, mutiny, revolution, insurgence, intifada, rioting, riot; civil disobedience, unrest, anarchy, coup, coup d'état, putsch.

CHOOSE THE RIGHT WORD

uprising, insurgency, insurrection, mutiny, putsch, rebellion, revolution

There are a number of ways to defy the established order or overthrow a government. You can stage an **uprising**, which is a broad term referring to a small and usually unsuccessful act of popular resistance (*uprisings among angry workers all over the country*). An uprising is often the first sign of a general or widespread **rebellion**, which is an act of armed resistance against a government or authority; this term is usually applied after the fact to describe an act of resistance that has failed (*a rebellion against the landowners*). If it is successful, however, a rebellion may become a **revolution**, which often implies a war or an outbreak of violence (*the American Revolution*). Although a *revolution* usually involves the overthrow of a government or political system by the people, it can also be used to describe any drastic change in ideas, economic institutions, or moral values (*the sexual revolution*). An **insurrection** is an organized effort to seize power, especially political power, while an **insurgency** is usually aided by foreign powers. If you're on a ship, you can stage a **mutiny**, which is an insurrection against military or naval authority. But if you're relying on speed and surprise to catch the authorities off guard, you'll want to stage a **putsch**, which is a small, popular uprising or planned attempt to seize power.

uproar ▶ noun **1** *the uproar in the kitchen continued for some time* **turmoil,** disorder, confusion, chaos, commotion, disturbance, rumpus, ruckus, tumult, turbulence, mayhem, pandemonium, bedlam, noise, din, clamor, hubbub, racket; shouting, yelling, babel; informal hullabaloo, hoo-ha, brouhaha.
ANTONYMS calm.
2 *there was an uproar when she was dismissed* **outcry,** furor, protest; fuss, reaction, backlash, commotion, hue and cry; informal hullabaloo, stink, rhubarb, firestorm.
ANTONYMS acquiescence.

uproarious ▶ adjective **1** *an uproarious party* **riotous,** rowdy, noisy, loud, wild, unrestrained, unruly, rip-roaring, rollicking, boisterous, rambunctious, knockabout.
ANTONYMS quiet.
2 *an uproarious joke* **hilarious,** hysterical, rib-tickling, gut-busting, priceless, side-splitting, knee-slapping, thigh-slapping.
ANTONYMS solemn.

upset ▶ verb **1** *the accusation upset her* **distress,** trouble, perturb, dismay, disturb, discompose, unsettle, disconcert, disquiet, worry, bother, agitate, fluster, throw, ruffle, unnerve, shake; hurt, sadden, grieve.
2 *he upset a tureen of soup* **knock over,** overturn, upend, tip over, flip, topple (over); spill.
3 *the dam will upset the ecological balance* **disrupt,** interfere with, disturb, throw out, throw into confusion, throw off balance, mess with/up.
4 *the Indians upset the Angels 9-0* **defeat,** beat, topple; surprise, embarrass.
▶ noun **1** *a stomach upset* **complaint,** disorder, ailment, illness, sickness, malady; informal bug.
2 *the Oilers' victory was a remarkable upset* **surprise win,** shocker.
▶ adjective **1** *the loss made Jane upset* **distressed,** troubled, perturbed, dismayed, disturbed, unsettled, disconcerted, worried, bothered, anxious, agitated, flustered, ruffled, unnerved, shaken, unstrung; hurt, saddened, grieved; informal cut up, choked.
ANTONYMS unperturbed, calm.
2 *an upset stomach* **disturbed,** unsettled, queasy, bad, hurting, poorly.

upshot ▶ noun *the upshot of this conflict of interests was a compromise* **result,** end result, consequence, outcome, conclusion; effect, repercussion, reverberations, ramification, aftereffect, payoff.
ANTONYMS cause.

upside down ▶ adjective *an upside-down canoe* **upturned,** upended, inverted, wrong side up, overturned; capsized, flipped.
– PHRASES **turned upside down** *the apartment was turned upside down* **in disarray,** in disorder, jumbled up, in a mess, in a muddle, untidy, disorganized, chaotic, all over the place, in chaos, in confusion, topsy-turvy, at sixes and sevens; informal higgledy-piggledy.

upstanding ▶ adjective *an upstanding citizen* **honest,** honorable, upright, respectable, high-minded, law-abiding, right-minded, worthy, trustworthy, moral, ethical, righteous, decent,

good, virtuous, principled, of principle, noble, incorruptible, straightforward.
ANTONYMS dishonorable.

upstart ▶ noun *these upstarts, they don't know their place* **parvenu,** arriviste, nouveau riche, status seeker, social climber, a jumped-up ——, johnny-come-lately.

up-to-date ▶ adjective **1** *up-to-date equipment* **modern,** contemporary, the latest, state-of-the-art, cutting-edge, leading-edge, new, present-day, up-to-the-minute; advanced; mod.
ANTONYMS out of date, old-fashioned.
2 *the newsletter will keep you up-to-date* **informed,** up to speed, in the picture, in touch, au fait, au courant, conversant, familiar, knowledgeable, acquainted, aware, clued in.

upturn ▶ noun *we've enjoyed an upturn in sales this quarter* **improvement,** upswing, turn for the better; recovery, revival, rally, resurgence, increase, rise, hike, jump, leap, upsurge, boost, escalation.
ANTONYMS fall, slump.

upward ▶ adjective *an upward trend* **rising,** on the rise, ascending, climbing, mounting; uphill.
ANTONYMS downward.
▶ adverb (also **upwards**) *the smoke drifts upward | he inched his way upwards* **up,** upward, higher, uphill, upslope; to the top, skyward, heavenward.
ANTONYMS downward.
– PHRASES **upward(s) of** *he makes upwards of $500 per session* **more than,** above, over, in excess of, exceeding, beyond, greater than.

urban ▶ adjective *crimes rates are significantly higher in urban areas* **town,** city, municipal, civic, metropolitan, built-up, inner-city, downtown, suburban; urbanized, citified, townie.
ANTONYMS rural.

urbane ▶ adjective *the urbane English professor* **suave,** sophisticated, debonair, worldly, cultivated, cultured, civilized, cosmopolitan; smooth, polished, refined, self-possessed; courteous, polite, well-mannered, mannerly, civil, charming, gentlemanly, gallant.
ANTONYMS uncouth, unsophisticated.

CHOOSE THE RIGHT WORD

urbane, cosmopolitan, genteel, sophisticated, suave

In his long career as a film star, Cary Grant was known for playing **urbane, sophisticated** roles. *Urbane* in this context suggests the social poise and polished manner of someone who is well-traveled and well-bred, while *sophisticated* means worldly-wise as opposed to naive (*a sophisticated young girl who had spent her childhood in Paris and London*). **Cosmopolitan** describes someone who is at home anywhere in the world and is free from provincial attitudes (*a cosmopolitan man who could charm women of all ages and nationalities*), while **suave** suggests the gracious social behavior of *urbane* combined with a certain glibness or superficial politeness (*she was taken in by his expensive clothes and suave manner*). At one time **genteel** meant well-bred or refined, but nowadays it has connotations of self-consciousness or pretentiousness (*too genteel to drink wine from a juice glass*).

urchin ▶ noun *Mrs. Duffy made frequent complaints about the urchins who played stickball on her street* **ragamuffin,** waif, stray; imp, rascal, street urchin; derogatory guttersnipe; scapegrace; dated gamin.

urge ▶ verb **1** *she urged him to try again* **encourage,** exhort, enjoin, press, entreat, implore, call on, appeal to, beg, plead with, coax; egg on, prod, prompt, spur, goad, incite, push, pressure, pressurize; formal adjure; literary beseech.
2 *she urged her horse down the lane* **spur (on),** force, drive, impel, propel.
3 *I urge caution in interpreting these results* **advise,** counsel, advocate, recommend, suggest, advance.
▶ noun *his urge to travel* **desire,** wish, need, compulsion, longing, yearning, hankering, craving, appetite, hunger, thirst; fancy, impulse, impetus; informal yen, itch.

urgent ▶ adjective **1** *the urgent need for more funding* **acute,** pressing, dire, desperate, critical, serious, grave, intense, crying, burning, compelling, extreme, exigent, high-priority, top-priority; life-and-death. See note at CRUCIAL.
2 *an urgent whisper* **insistent,** persistent, importunate, earnest, pleading, begging.

urinate ▶ verb *it was a bit of a culture shock to see men urinating out on the street* relieve oneself, pass water, make water; informal pee, take a leak, piddle, tinkle, (take a) whiz, piss; formal micturate.

usable ▶ adjective *the postage meter on the third floor will not be usable until further notice* **ready/fit for use,** able to be used, at someone's disposal, disposable; working, in working order, functioning, functional, serviceable, operational, up and running, accessible.

usage ▶ noun **1** *energy usage* **use,** consumption, utilization.
2 *the usage of equipment* **use,** utilization, operation, manipulation, running, handling.
3 *the intricacies of English usage* **phraseology,** parlance, idiom, way of speaking/writing, mode of expression, style; idiolect.
4 *the usages of polite society* **custom,** practice, habit, tradition, convention, rule, observance; way, procedure, form, wont; formal praxis; (**usages**) mores.

use ▶ verb **1** *she used her key to open the front door* **utilize,** make use of, avail oneself of, employ, work, operate, wield, ply, apply, maneuver, manipulate, put to use, put/press into service.
2 *the court will use its discretion in making an order* **exercise,** employ, bring into play, practice, apply, exert, bring to bear.
3 *he just felt used* **take advantage of,** exploit, manipulate, take liberties with, impose on, abuse; capitalize on, profit from, trade on, milk; informal walk all over.
4 *we have used all the available funds* **consume,**

get/go through, exhaust, deplete, expend, spend; waste, fritter away, squander, dissipate, run out of.

▶ noun 1 *the use of such weapons* **utilization,** usage, application, employment, operation, manipulation.

2 *what is the use of that?* **advantage,** benefit, service, utility, usefulness, help, good, gain, avail, profit, value, worth, point, object, purpose, sense, reason.

3 *composers have not found much use for the device* **need,** necessity, call, demand, requirement.

used ▶ adjective *a used car* **secondhand,** preowned, nearly new, old; worn, hand-me-down, castoff, recycled, warmed-over; informal preloved.

ANTONYMS new.

– PHRASES **used to** *I'm not used to such fine dining* **accustomed to,** no stranger to, familiar with, at home with, in the habit of, an old hand at, experienced in, versed in, conversant with, acquainted with.

useful ▶ adjective 1 *a useful multipurpose tool* **functional,** practical, handy, convenient, utilitarian, serviceable, of use, of service.

ANTONYMS useless.

2 *a useful experience* **beneficial,** advantageous, helpful, worthwhile, profitable, rewarding, productive, constructive, valuable, fruitful.

ANTONYMS disadvantageous.

useless ▶ adjective 1 *useless attempts* **futile,** to no avail, (in) vain, pointless, to no purpose, unavailing, hopeless, ineffectual, ineffective, to no effect, fruitless, unprofitable, profitless, unproductive; archaic bootless.

ANTONYMS useful, beneficial.

2 *useless machines* **unusable,** broken, kaput, defunct, dud, faulty.

3 informal *he was a useless worker* **incompetent,** inept, ineffective, incapable, unemployable, inadequate, hopeless, no-account, bad; informal pathetic.

ANTONYMS competent.

usher ▶ verb *she ushered him to a window seat* **escort,** accompany, take, show, see, lead, conduct, guide, steer, shepherd, marshal.

▶ noun *ushers showed them to their seats* **guide,** attendant, escort, sidesman.

– PHRASES **usher in** *Henry Ford's assembly line ushered in an era of unprecedented productivity* **herald,** mark the start of, signal, ring in, show in, set the scene for, pave the way for; start, begin, introduce, open the door to, get going, set in motion, get underway, kick off, launch.

usual ▶ adjective *meatloaf is their usual Wednesday special* **habitual,** customary, accustomed, wonted, normal, routine, regular, standard, typical, established, set, settled, stock, conventional, traditional, expected, predictable, familiar; average, general, ordinary, everyday. See note at **NORMAL**.

ANTONYMS exceptional.

usually ▶ adverb *he usually arrived home about one o'clock* **normally,** generally, habitually, customarily, routinely, typically, ordinarily, commonly, conventionally, traditionally; as a rule, in general, more often than not, in the main, mainly, mostly, for the most part, nine times out of ten.

usurp ▶ verb 1 *Richard usurped the throne* **seize,** take over, take possession of, take, commandeer, wrest, assume, expropriate.

2 *the Hanoverian dynasty had usurped the Stuarts* **oust,** overthrow, remove, topple, unseat, depose, dethrone; supplant, replace.

utilitarian ▶ adjective *she traded in her sporty little coupe for a utilitarian station wagon* **practical,** functional, pragmatic, serviceable, useful, sensible, efficient, utility, workaday, no-frills; plain, unadorned, undecorative.

ANTONYMS decorative.

utility ▶ noun 1 *we have increased the machine's utility* **usefulness,** use, benefit, value, advantage, advantageousness, help, helpfulness, effectiveness, avail; formal efficacy.

2 *an important public utility* **service,** service provider, organization, corporation, institution.

utilize ▶ verb *the foam pellets are utilized to make lightweight insulation* **use,** make use of, put to use, employ, avail oneself of, bring/press into service, bring into play, deploy, draw on, exploit, harness.

utmost ▶ adjective *a matter of the utmost importance* **greatest,** highest, maximum, most, uttermost; extreme, supreme, paramount.

▶ noun *a plot that stretches credulity to the utmost* **maximum,** uttermost, limit; informal max.

utter[1] ▶ adjective *that's utter garbage* **complete,** total, absolute, thorough, perfect, downright, out-and-out, outright, thoroughgoing, all-out, sheer, arrant, wholesale, rank, pure, real, veritable, consummate, categorical, unmitigated, unqualified, unadulterated, unalloyed.

utter[2] ▶ verb 1 *he uttered an exasperated snort* **emit,** let out, give, produce.

2 *he hardly uttered a word* **say,** speak, voice, express, articulate, pronounce, enunciate, verbalize, vocalize.

utterance ▶ noun *your snide utterances are not appreciated* **remark,** comment, word, statement, observation, declaration, pronouncement; exclamation, assertion.

utterly ▶ adverb *this is utterly ridiculous* **completely,** totally, absolutely, entirely, wholly, fully, thoroughly, quite, altogether, one hundred percent, downright, outright, in all respects, unconditionally, perfectly, really, to the hilt, to the core; dead.

Vv

vacancy ▸ noun **1** *there are vacancies for computer technicians* **opening,** position, post, job, opportunity, place.
2 *a hotel vacancy* **room available,** space for rent.

vacant ▸ adjective **1** *a vacant house* **empty,** unoccupied, available, not in use, free, unfilled; uninhabited, untenanted.
ANTONYMS full, occupied.
2 *a vacant look* **blank,** expressionless, unresponsive, emotionless, impassive, uninterested, vacuous, empty, absent, glazed, glassy; unintelligent, dull-witted, dense, brainless, empty-headed; informal zombified, lobotomized.
ANTONYMS expressive.

vacate ▸ verb **1** *he was forced to vacate the premises* **leave,** move out of, evacuate, quit, depart from; abandon, desert.
ANTONYMS occupy, inhabit.
2 *he will be vacating his post next year* **resign from,** leave, stand down from, give up, bow out of, relinquish, retire from, quit.
ANTONYMS take up.

vacation ▸ noun *their summer vacations in Hawaii* **break,** time off, recess, leave, leave of absence, furlough, sabbatical; **trip,** tour; chiefly Brit. holiday; formal sojourn.
▸ verb *I was vacationing in Europe with my family* **travel,** tour, stay, visit, stop over; formal sojourn.

vacillate ▸ verb *I vacillated between teaching and journalism* **dither,** waver, be indecisive, be undecided, be ambivalent, hesitate, be of two minds, blow hot and cold, keep changing one's mind, be conflicted; fluctuate, oscillate, hem and haw; informal dilly-dally, shilly-shally.

vacuous ▸ adjective *that vacuous laugh of his drives me nuts* **silly,** inane, unintelligent, insipid, foolish, stupid, fatuous, idiotic, brainless, witless, vapid, vacant, empty-headed; informal dumb, moronic, brain-dead, fluffy, fluffball.
ANTONYMS intelligent.

vacuum ▸ noun **1** *people longing to fill the spiritual vacuum in their lives* **emptiness,** void, nothingness, vacancy, absence, black hole.
2 *the political vacuum left by the emperor's death* **gap,** space, lacuna, void.
3 informal *I need to replace the bag in the vacuum* **vacuum cleaner,** vac; trademark Dustbuster, Hoover.

vagabond ▸ noun & adjective See VAGRANT (noun).

vagary ▸ noun *the vagaries of the weather* **change,** fluctuation, variation, quirk, peculiarity, oddity, eccentricity, unpredictability, caprice, foible, whim, whimsy, fancy.

vagrant ▸ noun *a temporary home for vagrants* **street person,** homeless person, tramp, hobo, drifter, down-and-out, derelict, beggar; itinerant, wanderer, nomad, traveler, vagabond, transient; informal bag lady, bum; literary wayfarer.
▸ adjective *vagrant beggars* **homeless,** drifting, transient, roving, roaming, itinerant, wandering, nomadic, traveling, vagabond, rootless, of no fixed address/abode; archaic errant.

vague ▸ adjective **1** *a vague shape* **indistinct,** indefinite, indeterminate, unclear, ill-defined; hazy, fuzzy, misty, blurred, blurry, out of focus, faint, shadowy, dim, obscure, nebulous, amorphous, diaphanous.
ANTONYMS clear, precise.
2 *a vague description* **imprecise,** rough, approximate, inexact, nonspecific, generalized, ambiguous, equivocal, hazy, woolly.
ANTONYMS clear, precise.
3 *they had only vague plans* **hazy,** uncertain, undecided, unsure, unclear, unsettled, indefinite, indeterminate, unconfirmed, up in the air, speculative, sketchy.
ANTONYMS firm.
4 *she was so vague in everyday life* **absentminded,** forgetful, dreamy, abstracted, with one's head in the clouds, scatty, scattered, not with it.
ANTONYMS organized, together.

vaguely ▸ adverb **1** *she looks vaguely familiar* **slightly,** a little, a bit, somewhat, rather, in a way; faintly, obscurely; informal sort of, kind of, kinda.
ANTONYMS very.
2 *he fired his rifle vaguely in our direction* **roughly,** more or less, approximately.
ANTONYMS exactly.
3 *he smiled vaguely* **absentmindedly,** abstractedly, vacantly.

vain ▸ adjective **1** *he was vain about his looks* **conceited,** narcissistic, self-loving, in love with oneself, self-admiring, self-regarding, self-obsessed, egocentric, egotistic, egotistical; proud, arrogant, boastful, cocky, cocksure, immodest, swaggering; informal big-headed; literary vainglorious.
ANTONYMS modest.
2 *a vain attempt* **futile,** useless, pointless, to no purpose, hopeless, in vain; ineffective, ineffectual, inefficacious, impotent, unavailing, to no avail, fruitless, profitless, unrewarding, unproductive, unsuccessful, failed, abortive,

for nothing; thwarted, frustrated, foiled; archaic bootless.
ANTONYMS successful.
– PHRASES **in vain 1** *they tried in vain to save him* **unsuccessfully,** without success, to no avail, to no purpose, fruitlessly. **2** *his efforts were in vain* See VAIN (sense 2). **3** *she took the Lord's name in vain* **irreverently,** casually, disrespectfully, flippantly.

valedictory ▶ **noun** *at their fifty-year reunion, Estelle Carver read the valedictory that she had delivered in 1954* **speech,** address, lecture, declamation.
▶ **adjective** *a valedictory message* **farewell,** goodbye, leaving, parting; last, final.

valiant ▶ **adjective** *a valiant warrior | her valiant efforts* **brave,** courageous, valorous, intrepid, heroic, gallant, lionhearted, bold, fearless, daring, audacious; unflinching, unshrinking, unafraid, dauntless, undaunted, doughty, tough, indomitable, mettlesome, stouthearted, spirited, plucky; informal game, gutsy, spunky.
ANTONYMS cowardly.

valid ▶ **adjective 1** *a valid criticism* **well-founded,** sound, reasonable, rational, logical, justifiable, defensible, viable, bona fide; cogent, effective, powerful, potent, convincing, credible, forceful, strong, solid, weighty. See note at BELIEVABLE.
2 *a valid contract* **legally binding,** lawful, legal, legitimate, official, signed and sealed, contractual; in force, current, in effect, effective; informal legit.
3 *valid information* **legitimate,** authentic, authoritative, reliable, bona fide.

validate ▶ **verb 1** *clinical trials now exist to validate this claim* **prove,** substantiate, corroborate, verify, support, back up, bear out, lend force to, confirm, justify, vindicate, authenticate.
ANTONYMS disprove.
2 *250 certificates need to be validated* **ratify,** endorse, approve, agree to, accept, authorize, legalize, legitimize, warrant, license, certify, recognize.
ANTONYMS reject, revoke.

valley ▶ **noun** *the homes in the valley are subject to mudslides* **dale,** vale; hollow, basin, gully, gorge, ravine, coulee, trough, canyon, rift; glen; literary dell.

valor ▶ **noun** *medals awarded for acts of valor* **bravery,** courage, pluck, nerve, daring, fearlessness, audacity, boldness, dauntlessness, stout-heartedness, heroism, backbone, spirit; informal guts, true grit, spunk; moxie.
ANTONYMS cowardice.

valuable ▶ **adjective 1** *a valuable watch* **precious,** costly, pricey, expensive, dear, high-priced, high-cost, high-end, upscale, big-ticket; worth its weight in gold, priceless.
ANTONYMS cheap, worthless.
2 *a valuable contribution* **useful,** helpful, beneficial, invaluable, crucial, productive, constructive, effective, advantageous, worthwhile, worthy, important.
ANTONYMS useless.

value ▶ **noun 1** *houses exceeding $250,000 in value* **price,** cost, worth; market price, monetary value, face value.
2 *the value of adequate preparation cannot be understated* **worth,** usefulness, advantage, benefit, gain, profit, good, help, merit, helpfulness, avail; importance, significance.
3 *society's values are passed on to us as children* **principles,** ethics, moral code, morals, standards, code of behavior.
▶ **verb 1** *his estate was valued at $345,000* **evaluate,** assess, estimate, appraise, price, put/set a price on.
2 *she valued his opinion* **think highly of,** have a high opinion of, hold in high regard, rate highly, esteem, set (great) store by, put stock in, appreciate, respect; prize, cherish, treasure.

valued ▶ **adjective** *this is my most valued piece of crystal* **cherished,** treasured, dear, prized; esteemed, respected, highly regarded, appreciated, important.

vamp ▶ **noun** informal *a tawny-haired vamp* **seductress,** temptress, siren, femme fatale, sex kitten, trollop, home wrecker, man-eater; flirt, coquette, tease.

vanguard ▶ **noun** *she was in the vanguard of the labor movement | they were destined to become the vanguard of space exploration* **forefront,** advance guard, spearhead, front, front line, fore, van, lead, cutting edge; avant-garde, leaders, founders, founding fathers, pioneers, trailblazers, trendsetters, innovators, groundbreakers.
ANTONYMS rear, followers.

vanish ▶ **verb 1** *he vanished without a trace* **disappear,** be lost to sight/view, become invisible, vanish into thin air, recede from view, dematerialize.
ANTONYMS appear, materialize.
2 *all hope of freedom vanished* **fade,** fade away, evaporate, vaporize, melt away, come to an end, end, cease to exist, pass away, die out, be no more.
ANTONYMS endure, materialize.

vanity ▶ **noun 1** *she had none of the vanity often associated with beautiful women* **conceit,** narcissism, self-love, self-admiration, self-absorption, self-regard, egotism; pride, arrogance, boastfulness, cockiness, swagger, rodomontade; informal big-headedness; literary vainglory. See notes at EGOTISM, PRIDE.
ANTONYMS modesty.
2 *the vanity of all desires of the will* **futility,** uselessness, pointlessness, worthlessness, fruitlessness.

vanquish ▶ **verb** *I promise you, we shall vanquish our enemy and reclaim what is rightfully ours* **conquer,** defeat, beat, trounce, rout, triumph over, be victorious over, get the better of, worst, upset; overcome, overwhelm, overpower, overthrow, subdue, subjugate, quell, quash, crush, bring someone to their knees, tear someone apart; informal lick, hammer, clobber, thrash, smash, demolish, wipe the floor with, make mincemeat of, massacre, slaughter, annihilate, cream, skunk, shellac.

vapid ▶ **adjective** *a tuneful but vapid musical comedy* **insipid,** uninspired, colorless, uninteresting, feeble, flat, dull, boring, tedious, tired, unexciting, uninspiring, unimaginative,

lifeless, tame, vacuous, bland, trite, jejune.
ANTONYMS lively, colorful.

variable ▶ adjective *the weather on the shoreline is known for being variable* **changeable,** changing, varying, shifting, fluctuating, irregular, inconstant, inconsistent, fluid, unsteady, unstable, unsettled, fitful, mutable, protean, wavering, vacillating, capricious, fickle, volatile, unpredictable, mercurial, unreliable; informal up and down.
ANTONYMS constant.
▶ noun *there are other variables to consider* **factor,** element, ingredient, quantity, unknown quantity, condition.

variance ▶ noun *the variance between the two groups is slight* **difference,** variation, discrepancy, dissimilarity, disagreement, conflict, divergence, deviation, contrast, contradiction, imbalance, incongruity.
– PHRASES **at variance 1** *his recollections were* ***at variance with*** *documentary evidence* **inconsistent,** at odds, not in keeping, out of keeping, out of line, out of step, in conflict, in disagreement. **2** *science and religion need not be at variance* **conflicting,** in conflict, in disagreement, in opposition; different, differing, divergent, discrepant, dissimilar, contrary, incompatible, contradictory, irreconcilable, incongruous; at cross purposes, at loggerheads, in dispute.

variant ▶ noun *there are a number of variants of the same idea* **variation,** form, alternative, adaptation, alteration, modification, permutation, version, analog.
▶ adjective *a variant spelling* **alternative,** other, different, substitute, divergent, derived, modified.

variation ▶ noun **1** *regional variations in farming practice* **difference,** dissimilarity; disparity, contrast, discrepancy, imbalance; technical differential.
2 *opening times are subject to variation* **change,** alteration, modification; diversification.
3 *there was very little variation from an understood pattern* **deviation,** variance, divergence, departure, fluctuation.
4 *hurling is an Irish variation of field hockey* **variant,** form, alternative form; development, adaptation, alteration, mutation, transformation, diversification, modification.

varied ▶ adjective *her varied interests keep her extremely busy* **diverse,** assorted, miscellaneous, mixed, sundry, heterogeneous, wide-ranging, manifold, multifarious; disparate, motley.

variegated ▶ adjective *variegated leaves* **multicolored,** multicolor, many-colored, many-hued, polychromatic, varicolored, colorful, prismatic, rainbow, kaleidoscopic; mottled, striated, marbled, streaked, speckled, flecked, dappled; informal splotchy.
ANTONYMS plain, monochrome.

variety ▶ noun **1** *the lack of variety in the curriculum* **diversity,** variation, diversification, heterogeneity, multifariousness, change, choice, difference.
ANTONYMS uniformity.
2 *a wide variety of flowers and shrubs* **assortment,** miscellany, range, array, collection, selection, mixture, medley, multiplicity; mixed bag, motley collection, potpourri, hodgepodge.
3 *fifty varieties of pasta* **sort,** kind, type, class, category, style, form; make, model, brand; strain, breed, genus.

various ▶ adjective *there are various styles to choose from* **diverse,** different, differing, varied, varying, a variety of, assorted, mixed, myriad, sundry, miscellaneous, heterogeneous, disparate, motley; several, a number of, an assortment of; literary divers.

varnish ▶ noun & verb *two coats of varnish | she varnished the woodwork* **lacquer,** shellac, finish, japan, enamel, glaze; polish, wax.

vary ▶ verb **1** *estimates of the development cost vary* **differ,** be different, be dissimilar, conflict.
2 *rates of interest can vary over time* **fluctuate,** rise and fall, go up and down, change, alter, shift, swing, deviate, differ.
3 *the diaphragm is used for varying the aperture of the lens* **modify,** change, alter, transform, adjust, regulate, control, set; diversify, reshape; informal tweak.

vast ▶ adjective *a vast holding of farmland* **huge,** extensive, expansive, broad, wide, sweeping, boundless, immeasurable, limitless, infinite; enormous, immense, great, massive, colossal, tremendous, mighty, prodigious, gigantic, gargantuan, mammoth, monumental; giant, towering, mountainous, titanic, Brobdingnagian; informal jumbo, mega, monster, whopping, humongous, astronomical, ginormous.
ANTONYMS tiny.

vault[1] ▶ noun **1** *the highest Gothic vault in Europe* **arched roof,** dome, arch.
2 *the vault under the church* **cellar,** basement, underground chamber; crypt, catacomb, burial chamber.
3 *valuables stored in the vault* **safe,** safety deposit box, repository, coffer, strongroom.

vault[2] ▶ verb *he* ***vaulted over*** *the gate* **jump over,** leap over, spring over, bound over; hurdle, clear.

vaunt ▶ verb *their much vaunted record of accuracy* **boast about,** brag about, make much of, crow about, parade, flaunt; acclaim, trumpet, praise, extol, celebrate; informal show off about, hype; formal laud.

veer ▶ verb *we then saw the car veer suddenly to the right* **turn,** swerve, curve, swing, sheer, career, weave, wheel; change direction, change course, go off course, deviate.

vegetate ▶ verb *ever since school ended, he just vegetates* **do nothing,** relax, rest, idle, languish, laze, lounge, loll; stagnate; informal veg, bum around, hang out, zone out, lollygag.

vegetation ▶ noun *lush tropical vegetation* **plants,** flora; greenery, foliage, herbage, verdure.

vehemence ▶ noun *the recruiters were told to speak with unwavering vehemence* **passion,** force, forcefulness, ardor, fervor, violence, urgency, strength, vigor, intensity, keenness, feeling, enthusiasm, zeal.

vehement ▶ adjective *her vehement arguments persuaded them to save the housing project*

passionate, forceful, ardent, impassioned, heated, spirited, urgent, fervent, violent, fierce, fiery, strong, forcible, powerful, emphatic, vigorous, intense, earnest, keen, enthusiastic, zealous.
ANTONYMS mild, apathetic.

vehicle ▶ noun **1** *a stolen vehicle* **means of transport,** conveyance, motor vehicle.
2 *a vehicle for the communication of original ideas* **channel,** medium, conduit, means, means of expression, agency, agent, instrument, mechanism, organ, apparatus.

veil ▶ noun **1** *a thin veil of high cloud made the sun hazy* **covering,** cover, screen, curtain, mantle, cloak, mask, blanket, shroud, canopy, cloud, pall.
2 *the women wore black veils* **mask,** scarf, kerchief, head covering, headdress; dupatta, purdah, mantilla, chador, hijab, yashmak.
▶ verb *the peak was veiled in mist* **envelop,** surround, swathe, enfold, cover, conceal, hide, screen, shield, cloak, blanket, shroud; obscure; literary enshroud, mantle.

veiled ▶ adjective *veiled threats* **disguised,** camouflaged, masked, covert, hidden, concealed, suppressed, underlying, implicit, implied, indirect.
ANTONYMS overt.

vein ▶ noun **1** *a vein in his neck pulsed* **blood vessel.**
2 *the mineral veins in the rock* **layer,** lode, seam, stratum, stratification, deposit, pipe.
3 *white marble with gray veins* **streak,** marking, mark, line, stripe, strip, band, thread, strand; technical stria, striation.
4 *he closes the article in a humorous vein* **mood,** frame of mind, temper, disposition, attitude, tenor, tone, key, spirit, character, fashion, feel, flavor, quality, atmosphere, humor; manner, mode, way, style.

velocity ▶ noun *light travels at a constant velocity* **speed,** pace, rate, tempo, momentum, impetus; swiftness, rapidity; literary fleetness, celerity.

venal ▶ adjective *they ran the town according to their own venal system of "law and order"* **corrupt,** corruptible, bribable, open to bribery; dishonest, dishonorable, untrustworthy, unscrupulous, unprincipled; mercenary, greedy; informal crooked.
ANTONYMS honorable, honest.

vendetta ▶ noun *the vendetta between our families is older than our grandparents* **feud,** blood feud, quarrel, argument, falling-out, dispute, fight, war; bad blood, enmity, rivalry, conflict, strife.

vendor ▶ noun *most of the vendors on Main Street are participating in Saturday's sidewalk sales* **retailer,** seller, dealer, trader, purveyor, storekeeper, shopkeeper, merchant; salesperson, supplier, peddler, hawker; scalper, huckster, trafficker.

veneer ▶ noun **1** *American cherry wood with a maple veneer* **surface,** lamination, layer, overlay, facing, covering, finish, exterior, cladding, laminate.
2 *a veneer of sophistication* **facade,** front, false front, show, outward display, appearance, impression, semblance, guise, disguise, mask, masquerade, pretense, camouflage, cover, window dressing.

venerable ▶ adjective *the venerable Martin Steed joined our faculty in 1962* **respected,** venerated, revered, honored, esteemed, hallowed, august, distinguished, eminent, great, grand.

vengeance ▶ noun *your appetite for vengeance has destroyed your life* **revenge,** retribution, retaliation, payback, requital, reprisal, satisfaction, an eye for an eye (and a tooth for a tooth).
– PHRASES **with a vengeance** *she returned to the stage with a vengeance* **vigorously,** strenuously, energetically, with a will, with all the stops out, for all one is worth, all out, flat out, at full tilt; informal hammer and tongs, like crazy, like mad, like gangbusters.

venial ▶ adjective *the venial indiscretions of my youth* **forgivable,** pardonable, excusable, allowable, permissible; slight, minor, unimportant, insignificant, trivial, trifling.
ANTONYMS unforgivable, mortal.

venom ▶ noun **1** *snake venom* **poison,** toxin; archaic bane.
2 *his voice was full of venom* **rancor,** malevolence, vitriol, spite, vindictiveness, malice, maliciousness, ill will, acrimony, animosity, animus, bitterness, antagonism, hostility, bile, hate, hatred; informal bitchiness, cattiness.

venomous ▶ adjective **1** *a venomous snake | the spider's venomous bite* **poisonous,** toxic; dangerous, deadly, lethal, fatal, mortal.
ANTONYMS harmless.
2 *venomous remarks* **vicious,** spiteful, rancorous, malevolent, vitriolic, vindictive, malicious, poisonous, virulent, bitter, acidic, acrimonious, caustic, antagonistic, hostile, cruel; informal bitchy, catty; literary malefic, maleficent. See note at **VINDICTIVE.**
ANTONYMS kind, benevolent.

vent ▶ noun *an air vent* **duct,** flue, shaft, well, passage, airway; outlet, inlet, opening, aperture, hole, gap, orifice.
▶ verb *the crowd vented their fury on the police* **release,** air, give vent to, give free rein to, let out, pour out, express, give expression to, voice, give voice to, verbalize, ventilate, discuss, talk over, communicate.

ventilate ▶ verb *ventilate all work areas* **air,** aerate, air out, oxygenate, air-condition, fan; freshen, cool.

venture ▶ noun *a business venture* **enterprise,** undertaking, project, initiative, scheme, operation, endeavor, speculation, plunge, gamble, gambit, experiment.
▶ verb **1** *we ventured across the country* **set out,** go, travel, journey.
2 *may I venture an opinion?* **put forward,** advance, proffer, offer, volunteer, air, suggest, submit, propose, moot.
3 *I ventured to ask her to come and dine with me* **dare,** be/make so bold as, presume; take the liberty of, stick one's neck out, go out on a limb.

veracious ▶ adjective formal See **TRUTHFUL** (sense 2).

verbal ▶ adjective *a verbal agreement* **oral,** spoken, stated, said, verbalized, expressed; unwritten, word-of-mouth.

verbatim ▶ adverb *I memorized his monologue verbatim* **word for word,** letter for letter, line for line, to the letter, literally, exactly, precisely, accurately, closely, faithfully.

verbose ▶ adjective *try not to be so verbose when you're being interviewed* **wordy,** loquacious, garrulous, talkative, voluble; long-winded, flatulent, lengthy, prolix, tautological, pleonastic, periphrastic, circumlocutory, circuitous, wandering, discursive, digressive, rambling; informal mouthy, gabby, chatty, motormouthed.
ANTONYMS succinct, laconic.

verdict ▶ noun *the judge's verdict is final* **judgment,** adjudication, decision, finding, ruling, decree, resolution, pronouncement, conclusion, opinion; Law determination.

verge ▶ noun **1** *the verge of the lake* **edge,** border, margin, side, brink, rim, lip; fringe, boundary, perimeter, outskirts; literary skirt. See note at **BORDER**.
2 *Spain was on the verge of an economic crisis* **brink,** threshold, edge, point.
▶ verb *a degree of caution that* ***verged on*** *the obsessive* **approach,** border on, come close/near to, be tantamount to; tend toward, approximate to, resemble.

verification ▶ noun *they may require further verification* **confirmation,** substantiation, proof, corroboration, support, attestation, validation, authentication, endorsement.

verify ▶ verb **1** *the evidence verifies my claim* **substantiate,** confirm, prove, corroborate, back up, bear out, justify, support, uphold, attest to, testify to, validate, authenticate, endorse, certify.
ANTONYMS refute.
2 *we need to verify those figures* **test,** double-check, check out, establish the truth of.

vernacular ▶ noun **1** *he wrote in* ***the vernacular*** *to reach a wider audience* **everyday language,** colloquial language, conversational language, common parlance, demotic, lay terms.
2 informal *the preppy vernacular of Orange County* **language,** dialect, regional language, regionalisms, patois, parlance; idiom, slang, jargon; informal lingo, -speak, -ese. See note at **DIALECT**.

versatile ▶ adjective *she's our most versatile player* **adaptable,** flexible, all-around, multifaceted, multitalented, resourceful; adjustable, multipurpose, all-purpose, handy; rare polytropic.

verse ▶ noun **1** *Elizabethan verse* **poetry,** versification, poetic form; poems, balladry, lyrics, lines, doggerel; literary poesy.
ANTONYMS prose.
2 *a verse he'd composed for our anniversary* **poem,** lyric, ballad, sonnet, ode, limerick, rhyme, ditty, lay.
3 *a poem with sixty verses* **stanza,** canto, couplet; strophe.

version ▶ noun **1** *his version of events* **account,** report, statement, description, record, story, rendering, interpretation, explanation, understanding, reading, impression, side, take.
2 *the Japanese version will be published next year* **edition,** translation, impression.
3 *they replaced coal-burning furnaces with gas versions* **form,** sort, kind, type, variety, variant, model.

vertical ▶ adjective *workers enter through a vertical shaft* **upright,** erect, perpendicular, plumb, straight up and down, on end, standing, upstanding, bolt upright.
ANTONYMS horizontal.

vertigo ▶ noun *the steep narrow stairs give me vertigo* **dizziness,** giddiness, lightheadedness, loss of balance.

verve ▶ noun *the kids performed with joyful verve* **enthusiasm,** vigor, energy, pep, dynamism, élan, vitality, vivacity, buoyancy, liveliness, animation, zest, sparkle, charisma, spirit, ebullience, exuberance, life, brio, gusto, eagerness, keenness, passion, zeal, relish, feeling, ardor, fire; informal zing, zip, vim, pizzazz, oomph, get-up-and-go.

very ▶ adverb *that's very kind of you* **extremely,** exceedingly, exceptionally, extraordinarily, tremendously, immensely, hugely, intensely, acutely, abundantly, singularly, uncommonly, decidedly, particularly, supremely, highly, remarkably, really, truly, mightily, ever so; informal terrifically, awfully, fearfully, terribly, devilishly, majorly, seriously, mega, ultra, damn, damned; dead, real, way, mighty, awful, darned; archaic exceeding.
ANTONYMS slightly.
▶ adjective **1** *those were his very words* **exact,** actual, precise.
2 *the very thought of food made her feel ill* **mere,** simple, pure; sheer.

vessel ▶ noun **1** *a fishing vessel* **boat,** ship, craft, watercraft; literary bark/barque.
2 *pour the mixture into a heatproof vessel* **container,** receptacle; basin, bowl, pan, pot; urn, tank, cask, barrel, drum, vat.

vest ▶ verb *executive power is* ***vested in*** *the president* **confer on,** entrust to, invest in, bestow on, grant to, give to, put in the hands of; endow in, lodge in, lay on, place on.

vestibule ▶ noun *brochures are available in the vestibule* **entrance hall,** hall, hallway, entrance, porch, portico, foyer, lobby, anteroom, narthex, antechamber, waiting room.

vestige ▶ noun **1** *the last vestiges of colonialism* **remnant,** fragment, relic, echo, indication, sign, trace, residue, mark, legacy, reminder; remains. See note at **TRACE**.
2 *she showed no vestige of emotion* **bit,** touch, hint, suggestion, suspicion, shadow, scrap, tinge, speck, shred, jot, iota, whit, scintilla, glimmer; informal smidgen, tad, titch, tinch.

vestigial ▶ adjective **1** *vestigial limbs* **rudimentary,** undeveloped; nonfunctional; Biology primitive.
2 *he felt a vestigial flicker of anger from last night* **remaining,** surviving, residual, leftover, lingering.

veteran ▶ noun *a veteran of 16 political campaigns* **old hand,** past master, doyen, vet;

informal old-timer, old stager, old warhorse.
ANTONYMS novice.
▶ **adjective** *a veteran diplomat* **long-serving,** seasoned, old, hardened; adept, expert, well trained, practiced, experienced, senior; informal battle-scarred.

veto ▶ **noun** *the president's right of veto* **rejection,** dismissal; prohibition, proscription, embargo, ban, interdict, check; informal thumbs down, red light.
ANTONYMS approval.
▶ **verb** *five nations vetoed the proposal* **reject,** turn down, throw out, dismiss; prohibit, forbid, interdict, proscribe, disallow, embargo, ban, rule out, say no to; informal kill, put the kibosh on, give the thumbs down to, give the red light to.
ANTONYMS approve.

vex ▶ **verb** *Alice was vexed by his remarks* **annoy,** irritate, anger, infuriate, exasperate, irk, gall, pique, put out, antagonize, nettle, get on someone's nerves, ruffle someone's feathers, rattle someone's cage, make someone's hackles rise, rub the wrong way; informal aggravate, peeve, miff, rile, needle, get (to), bug, get someone's goat, get someone's back up, get someone's dander up, tee off, tick off, burn up, rankle.

vexation ▶ **noun** *she stamped her foot in vexation* **annoyance,** irritation, exasperation, indignation, anger, crossness, displeasure, pique, bile, disgruntlement, bad mood; informal aggravation.

vexed ▶ **adjective 1** *a vexed expression* **annoyed,** irritated, cross, angry, infuriated, exasperated, irked, piqued, nettled, displeased, put out, disgruntled; informal aggravated, peeved, miffed, riled, hacked off, hot under the collar, teed off, ticked off, sore, bent out of shape; PO'd; archaic wroth.
2 *the vexed issue of immigration* **disputed,** in dispute, contested, in contention, contentious, debated, at issue, controversial, moot; problematic, difficult, knotty, thorny, ticklish, tense.

viable ▶ **adjective** *it doesn't sound like a viable solution* **feasible,** workable, practicable, practical, usable, possible, realistic, achievable, attainable, realizable; informal doable.
ANTONYMS impracticable.

vibrant ▶ **adjective 1** *a vibrant and passionate woman* **spirited,** lively, full of life, energetic, vigorous, vital, full of vim and vigor, animated, sparkling, effervescent, vivacious, dynamic, stimulating, exciting, passionate, fiery; informal peppy, feisty.
ANTONYMS listless, dull.
2 *vibrant colors* **vivid,** bright, striking, brilliant, strong, rich, colorful, bold.
ANTONYMS washed out, pale.
3 *his vibrant voice* **resonant,** sonorous, reverberant, resounding, ringing, echoing; strong, rich, full, round.
ANTONYMS soft, feeble.

vibrate ▶ **verb 1** *the floor beneath them vibrated* **quiver,** shake, tremble, shiver, shudder, throb, pulsate, rattle; rock, wobble, oscillate, waver, swing, sway, move to and fro; chiefly Brit. judder.
2 *a low rumbling sound began to vibrate through the car* **reverberate,** resonate, resound, ring, echo.

vibration ▶ **noun** *loose bolts are causing the vibration* **tremor,** shaking, quivering, quaking, shuddering, throb, throbbing, pulsation; chiefly Brit. judder, juddering.

vicarious ▶ **adjective** *I had the vicarious thrill of knowing my wife was to be named the next university president* **indirect,** secondhand, secondary, derivative, derived, surrogate, substitute; empathetic, empathic.

vice ▶ **noun 1** *youngsters driven to vice* **immorality,** wrongdoing, wickedness, badness, evil, iniquity, villainy, corruption, misconduct, misdeeds; sin, sinfulness, ungodliness; depravity, degeneracy, dissolution, dissipation, debauchery, decadence, lechery, perversion; crime, transgression; formal turpitude; archaic trespass. See note at **SIN**.
ANTONYMS virtue.
2 *smoking is my only vice* **shortcoming,** failing, flaw, fault, bad habit, defect, weakness, deficiency, limitation, imperfection, blemish, foible, frailty.
ANTONYMS virtue.

vice versa ▶ **adverb** *dancers can teach actors a lot and vice versa* **conversely,** inversely, contrariwise; reciprocally, the other way around/round.

vicinity ▶ **noun** *many female artists and writers live in the vicinity* **neighborhood,** surrounding area, locality, locale, area, local area, district, region, quarter, zone; environs, surroundings, precincts; informal neck of the woods.
– PHRASES **in the vicinity of** *his fortune is in the vicinity of four billion dollars* **around,** about, nearly, circa, approaching, roughly, approximating, approximately, something like, more or less; in the region of, in the neighborhood of, near to, close to.

vicious ▶ **adjective 1** *a vicious killer* **brutal,** ferocious, savage, violent, dangerous, ruthless, remorseless, merciless, heartless, callous, cruel, harsh, cold-blooded, inhuman, fierce, barbarous, barbaric, brutish, bloodthirsty, fiendish, sadistic, monstrous, murderous, homicidal; informal smash-mouth.
ANTONYMS gentle.
2 *a vicious hate campaign* **malicious,** malevolent, malignant, malign, spiteful, hateful, vindictive, venomous, poisonous, rancorous, mean, cruel, bitter, cutting, acrimonious, hostile, nasty; defamatory, slanderous; informal catty.
ANTONYMS benevolent, kindly.

vicissitude ▶ **noun** *the vicissitude of our love* **change,** alteration, shift, reversal, twist, turn, downturn, variation; inconstancy, instability, uncertainty, chanciness, unpredictability, fickleness, variability, changeability, fluctuation, vacillation; ups and downs.

victim ▶ **noun 1** *a victim of crime* **sufferer,** injured party, casualty; fatality, loss; loser.
2 *the victim of a con game* **target,** object, subject, focus, recipient, butt.
3 *a born victim* **loser,** prey, stooge, dupe,

sucker, quarry, fool, fall guy, chump; informal patsy, sap.
4 *he offered himself as a victim* **sacrifice,** offering, burnt offering, scapegoat.
– PHRASES **fall victim to** *they fell victim to the flu* **fall ill with,** be stricken with, catch, develop, contract, pick up; succumb to.

victimize ▶ **verb** *a government that victimizes the most needy and defenseless* **persecute,** pick on, push around, bully, abuse, discriminate against, ill-treat, mistreat, maltreat, terrorize, hector; exploit, prey on, take advantage of, dupe, cheat, double-cross, get at, have it in for, give someone a hard time, hassle, lean on, gang up on.

victor ▶ **verb** *to the victors go all the sponsorship opportunities* **winner,** champion, conqueror, conquering hero, vanquisher, hero; prize winner, gold medalist; informal champ, top dog.
ANTONYMS loser.

victorious ▶ **adjective** *the victorious Romanians brought home the gold* **triumphant,** conquering, vanquishing, winning, champion, successful, top, first.

victuals ▶ **plural noun** dated See FOOD (sense 1).

vie ▶ **verb** *the brothers had always vied for favoritism* **compete,** contend, contest, struggle, fight, battle, cross swords, lock horns, buck, jockey; war, feud.

view ▶ **noun 1** *the view from her apartment* **outlook,** prospect, panorama, vista, scene, aspect, perspective, spectacle, sight; scenery, landscape.
2 *we agree with this view* **opinion,** point of view, viewpoint, belief, judgment, thinking, notion, idea, conviction, persuasion, attitude, feeling, sentiment, concept, hypothesis, theory; stance, standpoint, philosophy, doctrine, dogma, approach, take. See note at OPINION.
3 *the church came into view* **sight,** perspective, vision, visibility.
▶ **verb 1** *they viewed the landscape* **look at,** eye, observe, gaze at, stare at, ogle, contemplate, watch, scan, regard, take in, survey, inspect, scrutinize; informal check out, get a load of, eyeball; literary espy, behold.
2 *the law was viewed as a last resort* **consider,** regard, look upon, see, perceive, judge, deem, reckon.
– PHRASES **in view of** *in view of this new evidence, we would like to reconsider our decision* **considering,** bearing in mind, taking into account, on account of, in (the) light of, owing to, because of, as a result of, given. **on view** *the Garbo memorabilia will be on view until Thursday* **on display,** on exhibition, on show.

viewer ▶ **noun** *one of our lucky viewers will win a trip to Mexico* **watcher,** spectator, onlooker, looker-on, observer, member of the audience; (**viewers**) audience, crowd; literary beholder.

viewpoint ▶ **noun** *I understand your viewpoint* See VIEW (sense 2 of the noun).

vigilant ▶ **adjective** *we've become more vigilant since the neighbors were robbed* **watchful,** observant, attentive, alert, eagle-eyed, hawk-eyed, on the lookout, on one's toes, on the qui vive; wide awake, wakeful, unwinking, on one's guard, cautious, wary, circumspect, heedful, mindful; informal beady-eyed.
ANTONYMS inattentive.

> CHOOSE THE RIGHT WORD
>
> **vigilant, careful, cautious, circumspect, wary, watchful, alert**
>
> All of these adjectives connote being on the lookout for danger or opportunity. **Watchful** is the most general term, meaning closely observant (*a watchful young man who noticed everything*). If you're **vigilant**, you are watchful for a purpose (*to be vigilant in the presence of one's enemies*), and **wary** suggests being on the lookout for treachery or trickery (*wary of his neighbor's motives in offering to move the fence*). If you're **alert**, you are quick to apprehend a danger, an opportunity, or an emergency (*she was much more alert after a good night's sleep*), and if you're **careful**, you may be able to avoid danger or error altogether. **Cautious** and **circumspect** also emphasize the avoidance of danger or unpleasant situations. To be *circumspect* is to be watchful in all directions and with regard to all possible consequences (*these journalists have to be circumspect, not criticizing anyone too harshly*); to be *cautious* is to guard against contingencies (*a cautious approach to treating illness*).

vigor ▶ **noun** *they ran with great vigor* **robustness,** health, hardiness, strength, sturdiness, toughness; bloom, radiance, energy, life, vitality, virility, verve, spirit; zeal, passion, determination, dynamism, zest, pep, drive, force; informal oomph, get-up-and-go, zing, piss and vinegar.
ANTONYMS lethargy.

vigorous ▶ **adjective 1** *the child was vigorous* **robust,** healthy, hale and hearty, strong, sturdy, fit; hardy, tough, athletic; bouncing, thriving, flourishing, blooming; energetic, lively, active, perky, spirited, vibrant, vital, zestful; informal peppy, bouncy, in the pink.
ANTONYMS weak, frail.
2 *a vigorous defense of policy* **strenuous,** powerful, forceful, spirited, mettlesome, determined, aggressive, two-fisted, driving, eager, zealous, ardent, fervent, vehement, passionate; tough, robust, thorough, blunt, hard-hitting; informal punchy.
ANTONYMS weak, feeble.

vigorously ▶ **adverb** *she pedaled vigorously* **strenuously,** strongly, powerfully, forcefully, energetically, heartily, vehemently, for dear life, for all one is worth, all out, fiercely, hard; informal like mad, like crazy, like gangbusters.

vile ▶ **adjective** *a vile smell | his vile crimes* **foul,** nasty, unpleasant, bad, disagreeable, horrid, horrible, dreadful, abominable, atrocious, offensive, obnoxious, odious, unsavory, repulsive, disgusting, distasteful, loathsome, hateful, nauseating, sickening; disgraceful, appalling, shocking, sorry, shabby, shameful, dishonorable, execrable, heinous, abhorrent, deplorable, monstrous, wicked, evil, iniquitous,

nefarious, depraved, debased; contemptible, despicable, reprehensible; informal gross, godawful, lowdown, lousy; archaic scurvy. See note at **DEPRAVED**.
ANTONYMS pleasant.

vilify ▶ verb *the press has eagerly vilified Smith and her attorneys* **disparage,** denigrate, defame, run down, revile, abuse, speak ill of, criticize, condemn, denounce; malign, slander, libel, slur; informal tear apart/into, lay into, slam, badmouth, dis, crucify; formal derogate, calumniate. See note at **MALIGN**.
ANTONYMS commend.

villain ▶ noun *my favorite Disney villain was Cruella* **criminal,** lawbreaker, offender, felon, convict, malefactor, wrongdoer; gangster, gunman, thief, robber; rogue, reprobate, ruffian, hoodlum; miscreant, scoundrel; Law malfeasant; informal crook, con, bad guy, baddy, lowlife; dated cad, knave; archaic blackguard.

villainous ▶ adjective *a taut thriller in which the hero makes a subtle shift from virtuous to villainous* **wicked,** evil, iniquitous, sinful, nefarious, vile, foul, monstrous, outrageous, atrocious, abominable, reprehensible, hateful, odious, contemptible, horrible, heinous, egregious, diabolical, flagitious, fiendish, vicious, murderous; criminal, illicit, unlawful, illegal, lawless; immoral, corrupt, degenerate, sordid, depraved, dishonest, dishonorable, unscrupulous, unprincipled; informal crooked, bent, lowdown, dirty, shady; dated dastardly.
ANTONYMS virtuous.

vindicate ▶ verb **1** *he was vindicated by the jury* **acquit,** clear, absolve, exonerate; discharge, liberate, free; informal let off, let off the hook; formal exculpate. See note at **ABSOLVE**.
2 *I had fully vindicated my contention* **justify,** warrant, substantiate, ratify, authenticate, verify, confirm, corroborate, prove, defend, support, back up, bear out, evidence, endorse.

vindictive ▶ adjective *in her memoirs she revealed that Drake had been a vindictive ex-lover* **vengeful,** revengeful, unforgiving, resentful, acrimonious, bitter; spiteful, mean, rancorous, venomous, malicious, malevolent, nasty, mean-spirited, cruel, unkind; informal catty.
ANTONYMS forgiving.

CHOOSE THE RIGHT WORD

vindictive, rancorous, spiteful, vengeful, venomous

Someone who is motivated by a desire to get even might be described as **vindictive**, a word that suggests harboring grudges for imagined wrongs (*a vindictive person who had alienated friends and neighbors alike*). **Spiteful** is a stronger term, implying a bitter or vicious vindictiveness (*a spiteful child who broke the toy she had been forced to share*). **Vengeful** implies a strong urge to actually seek vengeance (*vengeful after losing her husband in hit-and-run accident*). Someone who is **rancorous** suffers from a deep-seated and lasting bitterness, although it does not imply a desire to hurt or to be vindictive (*his rancorous nature made him difficult to befriend*). **Venomous** takes its meaning from "venom" referring to someone or something of a spiteful, malignant nature and suggesting a poisonous sting (*a critic's venomous attack on the author's first novel*).

vintage ▶ noun **1** *1986 was a classic vintage for the Cabernet Sauvignon* **year.**
2 *furniture of Louis XV vintage* **period,** era, epoch, time, origin; genre, style, kind, sort, type.
▶ adjective **1** *vintage French wine* **high-quality,** quality, choice, select, prime, superior, best.
2 *vintage automobiles* **classic,** ageless, timeless; old, antique, heritage, historic.
3 *his reaction was vintage Tom* **characteristic,** typical, pure, prime, trademark.

violate ▶ verb **1** *this violates fundamental human rights* **contravene,** breach, infringe, break, transgress, overstep, disobey, defy, flout; disregard, ignore, trample on.
ANTONYMS comply with.
2 *they felt their privacy had been violated* **invade,** trespass upon, encroach upon, intrude upon; disrespect.
ANTONYMS respect.
3 *the tomb was violated* **desecrate,** profane, defile, degrade, debase; damage, vandalize, deface, destroy.
4 *he drugged and then violated her* **rape,** sexually assault, assault, force oneself on, abuse, attack, molest, interfere with; archaic defile, deflower, dishonor, ruin; literary ravish.

violence ▶ noun **1** *violence against women* **brutality,** brute force, ferocity, savagery, cruelty, sadism, barbarity, brutishness.
2 *the protest ended in violence* **fighting,** fights, bloodshed, brawling, disorder, rioting, hostility, turbulence, mayhem.
3 *the violence of the blow* **forcefulness,** force, power, strength, might, savagery, ferocity, brutality.
4 *the violence of his passion* **intensity,** severity, strength, force, vehemence, power, potency, fervency, ferocity, fury, fire.

violent ▶ adjective **1** *he gets violent when drunk* **brutal,** vicious, savage, rough, aggressive, abusive, physically abusive, threatening, fierce, physical, wild, ferocious; barbarous, barbaric, thuggish, pugnacious, cutthroat, smash-mouth, homicidal, murderous, cruel.
ANTONYMS gentle.
2 *a violent blow* **powerful,** forceful, hard, sharp, smart, strong, vigorous, mighty, hefty; savage, ferocious, brutal, vicious.
ANTONYMS weak.
3 *violent jealousy* **intense,** extreme, strong, powerful, vehement, intemperate, unbridled, uncontrollable, ungovernable, inordinate, consuming, passionate.
ANTONYMS mild.
4 *a violent movie* **gory,** gruesome, grisly, full of violence.

virgin ▶ noun *she remained a virgin* chaste woman/man, celibate; literary maiden, maid, vestal, ingenue.
▶ adjective **1** *virgin forest* **untouched,** unspoiled, untainted, immaculate, pristine, flawless;

spotless, unsullied, unpolluted, undefiled, perfect; unchanged, intact; unexplored, uncharted, unmapped.
2 *virgin girls* **chaste,** virginal, celibate, abstinent; maiden, maidenly; pure, uncorrupted, undefiled, unsullied, innocent; literary vestal.

virginal ▶ adjective See VIRGIN (sense 2 of the adjective).

virile ▶ adjective *the strong, virile hero* **manly,** masculine, male; strong, tough, vigorous, robust, muscular, muscly, brawny, rugged, sturdy, lusty, husky; red-blooded, fertile; informal macho, butch, beefy, hunky, testosteronic. See note at MALE.
ANTONYMS effeminate.

virtual ▶ adjective **1** *a virtual guarantee* **effective,** in effect, near, near enough, essential, practical, to all intents and purposes.
2 *a virtual shopping environment* **simulated,** artificial, imitation, make-believe; computer-generated, online, virtual reality.

virtually ▶ adverb *the building is virtually empty* **effectively,** in effect, all but, more or less, practically, almost, nearly, close to, verging on, just about, as good as, essentially, to all intents and purposes, roughly, approximately; informal pretty much, pretty well; literary well-nigh, nigh on.

virtue ▶ noun **1** *the simple virtue of farm life* **goodness,** virtuousness, righteousness, morality, integrity, dignity, rectitude, honor, decency, respectability, nobility, worthiness, purity; principles, ethics. See note at GOODNESS.
ANTONYMS vice, iniquity.
2 *promptness was not one of his virtues* **strong point,** good point, good quality, asset, forte, attribute, strength, talent, feature.
ANTONYMS failing.
3 *I can see no virtue in this* **merit,** advantage, benefit, usefulness, strength, efficacy, plus, point.
ANTONYMS disadvantage.
– PHRASES **by virtue of** *they hold the posts by virtue of family connections* **because of,** on account of, by dint of, by means of, by way of, via, through, as a result of, as a consequence of, on the strength of, owing to, thanks to, due to, by reason of.

virtuosity ▶ noun *the architect's virtuosity* **skill,** skillfulness, mastery, expertise, prowess, proficiency, ability, aptitude; excellence, brilliance, talent, genius, artistry, flair, panache, finesse, wizardry; informal know-how, chops.

virtuoso ▶ noun *the pianist is clearly a virtuoso* **genius,** expert, master, past master, maestro, artist, prodigy, marvel, adept, professional, doyen, veteran; star, champion; informal hotshot, wizard, magician, pro, ace.
ANTONYMS beginner.
▶ adjective *a virtuoso violinist* **skillful,** expert, accomplished, masterly, master, consummate, proficient, talented, gifted, adept, good, capable; impressive, outstanding, exceptional, magnificent, supreme, first-rate, stellar, brilliant, excellent; informal superb, mean, ace.
ANTONYMS incompetent.

virtuous ▶ adjective *they were entirely virtuous in their endeavors* **righteous,** good, pure, whiter than white, saintly, angelic, moral, ethical, upright, upstanding, high-minded, principled, exemplary; law-abiding, irreproachable, blameless, guiltless, unimpeachable, immaculate, honest, honorable, reputable, laudable, decent, respectable, noble, worthy, meritorious; informal squeaky clean. See note at MORAL.

virulent ▶ adjective **1** *virulent herbicides* **poisonous,** toxic, venomous, noxious, deadly, lethal, fatal, dangerous, harmful, injurious, pernicious, damaging, destructive; literary deathly.
ANTONYMS harmless, nontoxic.
2 *a virulent epidemic* **infectious,** infective, contagious, communicable, transmittable, transmissible, spreading, pestilential; informal catching.
ANTONYMS noncontagious.
3 *a virulent attack on morals* **vitriolic,** malicious, malevolent, hostile, spiteful, venomous, vicious, vindictive, bitter, sharp, rancorous, acrimonious, scathing, caustic, withering, nasty, savage, harsh.
ANTONYMS benevolent, amicable.

visible ▶ adjective *there are no visible scratches* **perceptible,** perceivable, seeable, observable, noticeable, detectable, discernible; in sight, in/on view, on display; evident, apparent, manifest, transparent, plain, clear, conspicuous, front-and-center, obvious, patent, unmistakable, unconcealed, undisguised, prominent, salient, striking, glaring.

vision ▶ noun **1** *her vision was blurred by tears* **eyesight,** sight, observation, (visual) perception; eyes; view, perspective.
2 *the psychic was troubled by visions of the dead* **apparition,** hallucination, illusion, mirage, specter, phantom, ghost, wraith, manifestation; literary phantasm, shade.
3 *visions of a better future* **dream,** daydream, reverie; plan, hope; fantasy, pipe dream, delusion.
4 *his speech lacked vision* **imagination,** creativity, inventiveness, innovation, inspiration, intuition, perception, insight, foresight, prescience.
5 *Melissa was a vision in lilac* **beautiful sight,** feast for the eyes, pleasure to behold, delight, dream, beauty, picture, joy, marvel; informal sight for sore eyes, stunner, knockout, looker, eye-catcher, peach.

visionary ▶ adjective **1** *a visionary person* **inspired,** imaginative, creative, inventive, ingenious, enterprising, innovative; insightful, perceptive, intuitive, prescient, discerning, shrewd, wise, clever, resourceful; idealistic, romantic, quixotic, dreamy; informal starry-eyed.
2 archaic *a visionary image* See IMAGINARY.
▶ noun *a visionary pictured him in hell* **seer,** mystic, oracle, prophet/prophetess, soothsayer, augur, diviner, clairvoyant, crystal-gazer, medium; literary sibyl.

visit ▶ verb **1** *I visited my dear uncle* **call on,** pay a visit to, go to see, look in on; stay with; stop by, drop by; informal go see; pop in on, drop in on, look up.

2 *she never visits* **stop by,** drop by, pay a visit, call; informal pop in, drop in.
3 *Alex was visiting the Yukon* **stay in,** stop over in, spend time in, vacation in; tour, explore, see.
▶ **noun 1** *she paid a visit to her mom* **call,** social call, visitation.
2 *a visit to the museum* **trip to,** tour of, look around; stopover at, stay at; vacation at; formal sojourn at.

visitation ▶ **noun 1** *the bishop's visitations* **visit,** official, tour of inspection, survey, examination.
2 *a visitation from God* **apparition,** vision, appearance, manifestation, materialization.
3 *Jehovah punished them by visitations* **affliction,** scourge, bane, curse, plague, blight, disaster, tragedy, catastrophe; punishment, retribution, vengeance.

visitor ▶ **noun 1** *I am expecting a visitor* **guest,** caller, house guest; company; archaic visitant.
2 *the monument attracts thousands of visitors each month* **tourist,** traveler, vacationer, day tripper, sightseer; pilgrim, habitué; foreigner, outsider, stranger, alien.

visual ▶ **adjective 1** *visual defects* **optical,** optic, ocular, eye; vision, sight.
2 *a visual indication that the alarm works* **visible,** perceptible, perceivable, discernible.
▶ **noun** *the speaker used excellent visuals* **graphic,** visual aid, image, illustration, diagram, display; show and tell.

visualize ▶ **verb** *Grampa's colorful tales made it easy to visualize his childhood adventures* **envisage,** envision, conjure up, picture, call to mind, see, imagine, evoke, dream up, fantasize about, conceptualize, contemplate, conceive of.

vital ▶ **adjective 1** *it is vital that action be taken soon* **essential,** of the essence, critical, crucial, key, indispensable, integral, all-important, imperative, mandatory, requisite, urgent, pressing, burning, compelling, high-priority, life-and-death.
ANTONYMS unimportant, peripheral.
2 *the vital organs* **major,** main, chief; essential, necessary.
ANTONYMS minor, dispensable.
3 *he is young and vital* **lively,** energetic, active, sprightly, spry, spirited, vivacious, exuberant, bouncy, enthusiastic, vibrant, zestful, sparkling, dynamic, virile, vigorous, lusty, hale and hearty; informal peppy, spunky, full of beans, bright-eyed and bushy-tailed. See note at ALIVE.
ANTONYMS listless.

vitality ▶ **noun** *the bright weather has revived my vitality* **liveliness,** life, energy, spirit, vivacity, exuberance, buoyancy, bounce, élan, verve, vim, pep, brio, zest, sparkle, dynamism, passion, fire, vigor, drive, punch; get-up-and-go.

vitriolic ▶ **adjective** *a vitriolic attack on the government* **acrimonious,** rancorous, bitter, caustic, mordant, acerbic, trenchant, virulent, spiteful, savage, venomous, poisonous, malicious, splenetic; nasty, mean, cruel, unkind, harsh, hostile, vindictive, vicious, scathing, barbed, wounding, sharp, cutting, withering, sarcastic; informal bitchy, catty.

vituperation ▶ **noun** *in public he hid well the vituperation he dispensed at home* **invective,** condemnation, opprobrium, scolding, criticism, disapprobation, fault-finding; blame, abuse, insults, vilification, denunciation, obloquy, denigration, disparagement, slander, libel, defamation, slurs, aspersions; vitriol, venom; informal flak; formal castigation. See note at SCOLD.
ANTONYMS praise.

vivacious ▶ **adjective** *their vivacious daughter had become moody and morose* **lively,** spirited, bubbly, ebullient, buoyant, sparkling, lighthearted, jaunty, merry, happy, jolly, full of fun, cheery, cheerful, perky, sunny, breezy, enthusiastic, irrepressible, vibrant, vital, zestful, energetic, effervescent, dynamic; informal peppy, bouncy, upbeat, chirpy.
ANTONYMS dull.

vivid ▶ **adjective 1** *a vivid blue sea* **bright,** colorful, brilliant, radiant, vibrant, glaring, strong, bold, deep, intense, rich, warm.
ANTONYMS dull.
2 *a vivid account of urban poverty* **graphic,** evocative, realistic, lifelike, faithful, authentic, clear, detailed, lucid, eloquent, striking, arresting, impressive, colorful, rich, dramatic, lively, stimulating, interesting, fascinating, scintillating; memorable, powerful, stirring, moving, telling, haunting. See note at GRAPHIC.
ANTONYMS vague.

vocabulary ▶ **noun 1** *technical vocabulary* **language,** lexicon, lexis, words; diction, terminology, phraseology, nomenclature, terms, expressions, parlance, idiom, jargon, vernacular, argot, cant; informal vocab, lingo, -speak, -ese.
2 *she is improving her vocabulary* **word power,** lexicon, command of language; informal vocab.

vocal ▶ **adjective 1** *vocal sounds* **vocalized,** voiced, uttered, articulated, oral; spoken, viva voce, said.
2 *a vocal critic of the government* **vociferous,** outspoken, forthright, plain-spoken, expressive, blunt, frank, candid, open; vehement, strident, vigorous, emphatic, insistent, forceful, zealous, clamorous, loudmouthed.
▶ **plural noun** (**vocals**) *we'll record the vocals later* **voices,** singing; harmonies.

vocation ▶ **noun** *forestry is my vocation* **calling,** life's work, mission, purpose, function; profession, occupation, career, job, employment, trade, craft, business, line, line of work, métier.

vociferous ▶ **adjective** See VOCAL (sense 2 of the adjective).

CHOOSE THE RIGHT WORD

vociferous, boisterous, clamorous, obstreperous, strident

An angry crowd might be **vociferous**, which implies loud and unrestrained shouting or crying out (*a vociferous argument*). A happy crowd might be **boisterous**, which implies noisy exuberance or high-spirited rowdiness (*a boisterous celebration of spring*). A crowd that wants something is likely to be **clamorous**, which suggests an urgent or insistent vociferousness in demanding or protesting something. If people's demands are not met, they might become **obstreperous**, which means noisy in an unruly and aggressive way, usually in defiance of authority (*an obstreperous child*). **Strident** suggests a harsh, grating loudness that is particularly distressing to the ear (*her strident voice could be heard throughout the building*).

vogue ▶ **noun** *retro accessories are enjoying a new vogue* **fashion,** trend, fad, craze, rage, enthusiasm, passion, obsession, mania; fashionableness, popularity, currency, favor; informal trendiness.

– PHRASES **in vogue** *denim's been in vogue my whole lifetime* **fashionable,** voguish, stylish, modish, up-to-date, up-to-the-minute, du jour, modern, current; prevalent, popular, in favor, in demand, sought-after, all the rage; chic, chi-chi, smart, tony, kicky, le dernier cri; trendy, hip, cool, big, happening, now, in, with it.

voice ▶ **noun 1** *she lost her voice* **power of speech.**
2 *he gave voice to his anger* **expression,** utterance, verbalization, vocalization.
3 *we speak with one voice* **opinion,** view, feeling, wish, desire, will; (**voice of the people**) vox populi; informal vox pop.
4 *citizens must have a voice in this* **say,** influence, vote, input, role, representation, seat at the table.
5 *a powerful voice for conservation* **spokesperson,** speaker, champion, representative, mouthpiece, intermediary; forum, vehicle, instrument, channel, organ, agent.
▶ **verb** *they voiced their opposition* **express,** vocalize, communicate, articulate, declare, state, assert, reveal, proclaim, announce, publish, publicize, make public, make known, table, air, vent; utter, say, speak; informal come out with.

void ▶ **noun** *the void of space* **vacuum,** emptiness, nothingness, nullity, blankness, vacuity; empty space, blank space, space, gap, cavity, chasm, abyss, gulf, pit, black hole.
▶ **verb** *the contract was voided* **invalidate,** annul, nullify; negate, quash, cancel, countermand, repeal, revoke, rescind, retract, withdraw, reverse, undo, abolish; Law vacate; formal abrogate.
ANTONYMS validate.
▶ **adjective 1** *vast void spaces* **empty,** vacant, blank, bare, clear, free, unfilled, unoccupied, uninhabited.
ANTONYMS full.
2 *a country void of man or beast* **devoid of,** empty of, vacant of, bereft of, free from; lacking, wanting, without, with nary a.
ANTONYMS occupied.
3 *the election was void* **invalid,** null, ineffective, nonviable, useless, worthless, nugatory.
ANTONYMS valid.

CHOOSE THE RIGHT WORD

void, abrogate, annul, invalidate, negate, nullify

To **void** a check, to **invalidate** a claim, to **abrogate** a law, and to **annul** a marriage all refer to the same basic activity, which is putting an end to something or depriving it of validity, force, or authority. But these verbs are not always interchangeable. *Annul* is the most general term, meaning to end something that exists or to declare that it never really existed (*the charter was annulled before it could be challenged*). *Abrogate* implies the exercise of legal authority (*Congress abrogated the treaty between the two warring factions*), while **nullify** means to deprive something of its value or effectiveness (*nullify the enemy's attempt to establish communications*). *Void* and *invalidate* are often used interchangeably as they both mean to make null or worthless (*void a legal document by tearing it up; invalidate a check by putting the wrong date on it*). **Negate** means to prove an assertion false (*her version of the story negated everything her brother had said*) or to nullify or make something ineffective (*the study's findings were negated by its author's arrest for fraud*).

volatile ▶ **adjective 1** *a volatile personality* **unpredictable,** changeable, variable, inconstant, inconsistent, erratic, irregular, unstable, turbulent, blowing hot and cold, varying, shifting, fluctuating, fluid, mutable; mercurial, capricious, whimsical, fickle, flighty, impulsive, temperamental, high-strung, excitable, emotional, fiery, moody, tempestuous.
ANTONYMS stable, constant.
2 *the atmosphere is too volatile for an election* **tense,** strained, fraught, uneasy, uncomfortable, charged, explosive, inflammatory, turbulent; informal nail-biting, ready to blow.
ANTONYMS stable, calm.
3 *a volatile organic compound* **evaporative,** vaporous; explosive, inflammable; unstable, labile.
ANTONYMS stable.

volition ▶ **noun**
– PHRASES **of one's own volition** *I joined the army of my own volition* **of one's own free will,** of one's own accord, by choice, by preference; voluntarily, willingly, readily, freely, intentionally, consciously, deliberately, on purpose, purposely; gladly, with pleasure.

volley ▶ **noun** *a volley of rifle shots* **barrage,** cannonade, battery, bombardment, salvo, discharge, fusillade; storm, hail, shower, deluge, torrent; historical broadside.

voluble ▶ **adjective** *she was as voluble as her husband was silent* **talkative,** loquacious, garrulous, verbose, wordy, chatty, gossipy, effusive, gushing, forthcoming, conversational, communicative, expansive; articulate, fluent; informal mouthy, motormouthed, gabby, gassy, windy, talky. See note at TALKATIVE.
ANTONYMS taciturn.

volume ▶ **noun 1** *a volume from the library* **book,** publication, tome, hardback, paperback, title; manual, almanac, compendium.
2 *a glass syringe of known volume* **capacity,** cubic measure, size, magnitude, mass,

bulk, extent; dimensions, proportions, measurements.
3 *a huge volume of water* **quantity,** amount, proportion, measure, mass, bulk.
4 *she turned the volume down* **loudness,** sound, amplification; informal decibels.

voluminous ▶ **adjective** *the clown's voluminous trousers* **capacious,** roomy, spacious, ample, full, big, large, bulky, extensive, sizable, generous; billowing, baggy, loose-fitting; formal commodious.

voluntarily ▶ **adverb** *they agreed to leave the country voluntarily* **freely,** of one's own free will, of one's own accord, of one's own volition, by choice, by preference; willingly, readily, intentionally, deliberately, on purpose, purposely, spontaneously; gladly, with pleasure.

voluntary ▶ **adjective 1** *attendance is voluntary* **optional,** discretionary, elective, noncompulsory, volitional; Law permissive.
ANTONYMS compulsory, obligatory.
2 *voluntary work* **unpaid,** unsalaried, unwaged, for free, without charge, for nothing; honorary, volunteer; Law pro bono (publico).
ANTONYMS paid.

volunteer ▶ **verb 1** *I volunteered my services* **offer,** tender, proffer, put forward, put up, venture.
2 *he volunteered as a driver* **offer one's services,** present oneself, make oneself available, sign up.
▶ **noun** *each volunteer was tested three times* **subject,** participant, case, patient; informal guinea pig.

voluptuous ▶ **adjective 1** *a voluptuous model* **curvaceous,** shapely, ample, buxom, full-figured; seductive, alluring, comely, sultry, sensuous, sexy, womanly; Junoesque, Rubenesque; informal bodacious, curvy, busty, stacked, built, slinky. See note at **SENSUOUS**.
ANTONYMS scrawny.
2 *she was voluptuous by nature* **hedonistic,** sybaritic, epicurean, pleasure-loving, self-indulgent; decadent, intemperate, immoderate, dissolute, sensual, licentious.
ANTONYMS ascetic.

vomit ▶ **verb 1** *he needed to vomit* **be sick,** spew, heave, retch, gag, get sick; informal throw up, puke, purge, hurl, barf, upchuck, ralph.
2 *I vomited my breakfast* **regurgitate,** bring up, spew up, cough up, lose; informal throw up, puke, spit up.
▶ **noun** *a coat stained with vomit* **vomitus;** informal puke, spew, barf.

voracious ▶ **adjective** *her voracious appetite* **insatiable,** unquenchable, unappeasable, prodigious, uncontrollable, compulsive, gluttonous, greedy, rapacious; enthusiastic, eager, keen, avid, desirous, hungry, ravenous; informal piggish; rare esurient.

vortex ▶ **noun** *a whirling vortex of smoke* **whirlwind,** cyclone, whirlpool, gyre, maelstrom, eddy, swirl, spiral; black hole.

vote ▶ **noun 1** *a rigged vote* **ballot,** poll, election, referendum, plebiscite; show of hands.
2 *women finally got the vote* **suffrage,** voting rights, franchise, enfranchisement; voice, say.
▶ **verb 1** *only half of them voted* **go to the polls,** cast one's vote, cast one's ballot.
2 *he was* **voted in** *as secretary* **elect,** return, select, choose, pick, adopt, appoint, designate, opt for, decide on.
3 *I vote we have one more game* **suggest,** propose, recommend, advocate, move, submit.

vouch ▶ **verb**
– PHRASES **vouch for** *I can vouch for his honesty* **attest to,** confirm, affirm, verify, swear to, testify to, bear out, back up, support, stick up for, go to bat for, corroborate, substantiate, prove, uphold, sponsor, give credence to, endorse, certify, warrant, validate.

voucher ▶ **noun** *present your voucher to the attendant at the front door* **coupon,** token, ticket, license, permit, pass; chit, slip, stub; informal ducat, comp.

vow ▶ **noun** *a vow of silence* **oath,** pledge, promise, bond, covenant, commitment, avowal, profession, affirmation, attestation, assurance, guarantee; word, word of honor; formal troth.
▶ **verb** *I vowed to do better* **swear,** pledge, promise, avow, undertake, engage, make a commitment, give one's word, guarantee; archaic plight.

voyage ▶ **noun** *the voyage lasted 120 days* **journey,** trip, expedition, excursion, tour; hike, trek, travels; pilgrimage, quest, crusade, odyssey; cruise, passage, flight, drive, road trip. See note at **JOURNEY**.
▶ **verb** *he voyaged through Peru* **travel,** journey, tour, globe-trot; sail, steam, cruise, fly, drive; informal gallivant; archaic peregrinate.

vulgar ▶ **adjective 1** *a vulgar joke* **rude,** indecent, indelicate, offensive, distasteful, coarse, crude, ribald, risqué, naughty, suggestive, racy, earthy, off-color, bawdy, obscene, profane, lewd, salacious, smutty, dirty, filthy, pornographic, X-rated; informal sleazy, raunchy, blue, locker-room; saucy, salty; euphemistic adult.
ANTONYMS decent, inoffensive.
2 *the decor was lavish but vulgar* **tasteless,** crass, tawdry, ostentatious, flamboyant, overdone, showy, gaudy, garish, brassy, kitsch, kitschy, tinselly, loud; informal flash, flashy, tacky.
ANTONYMS tasteful, restrained.
3 *it is vulgar to belch in public* **impolite,** ill-mannered, unmannerly, rude, indecorous, unseemly, ill-bred, boorish, uncouth, crude, rough; unsophisticated, unrefined, common, low-minded; unladylike, ungentlemanly.
ANTONYMS genteel, decorous.

Ww

wad ▸ **noun 1** *a wad of cotton* **lump,** clump, mass, pad, swab, hunk, wedge, ball, cake, nugget; bit, piece, plug.
2 *a wad of $20 bills* **bundle,** roll, pile, stack, sheaf, bankroll.
3 *a wad of tobacco* **quid,** twist, plug, chew, chaw.
▸ **verb** *he wadded up his napkin* **crumple,** stuff, press, gather, pack, wrap.

wadding ▸ **noun** *the wadding in the quilt is all lumpy* **stuffing,** filling, filler, packing, padding, cushioning, quilting; (cotton) batting, (cotton) batten.

waddle ▸ **verb** *after seven weeks in a hospital bed, it's normal to waddle a bit* **toddle,** dodder, totter, wobble, shuffle; duckwalk.

wade ▸ **verb 1** *they waded in the icy water* **paddle,** wallow, dabble; informal splosh.
2 *I had to wade through some hefty documents* **plow,** plod, trawl, labor, toil; study, browse; informal splash, slog.

waft ▸ **verb 1** *smoke wafted through the air* **drift,** float, glide, whirl, travel.
2 *a breeze wafted the smell toward us* **convey,** carry, transport, bear; blow, puff.

wag[1] ▸ **verb 1** *the dog's tail wagged frantically* **swing,** swish, switch, sway, shake, quiver, twitch, whip, bob; informal waggle.
2 *he wagged his stick at them* **shake,** wave, wiggle, waggle, flourish, brandish.

wag[2] ▸ **noun** *he's a bit of a wag* See **JOKER**.

wage ▸ **noun 1** (usu. **wages**) *the farm workers' wages | a fair wage* **pay,** payment, remuneration, salary, stipend, fee, honorarium; income, revenue; profit, gain, reward; earnings, paycheck; Brit. pay packet; formal emolument.
2 (**wages**) *the wages of sin is death* **reward,** recompense, retribution; returns, deserts.
▸ **verb** *they waged war on the guerrillas* **engage in,** carry on, conduct, execute, pursue, prosecute, proceed with.

wager ▸ **noun** *a wager of $100* **bet,** gamble, speculation; stake, pledge, ante.
▸ **verb** *I'll wager ten bucks on the home team* **bet,** gamble, lay odds, put money on; stake, pledge, risk, venture, hazard, chance.

waggle ▸ **verb** informal See **WAG**[1].

waif ▸ **noun** *a homeless waif* **ragamuffin,** urchin; foundling, orphan, stray; derogatory guttersnipe; dated gamin.

wail ▸ **noun** *a wail of anguish* **howl,** bawl, yowl, cry, moan, groan; shriek, scream, holler, yelp.
▸ **verb** *the children began to wail* **howl,** weep, cry, sob, moan, groan, keen, lament, yowl, snivel, whimper, whine, bawl, shriek, scream, yelp, caterwaul; informal blubber.

wait ▸ **verb 1** *Jill waited while Jack fetched the water* **stay (put),** remain, rest, stop, halt, pause; linger, loiter, dally; informal stick around, hang out, hang around, kill time, waste time, kick one's heels, twiddle one's thumbs; archaic tarry.
2 *Joey waited until she nodded* **hold on,** hold back, bide one's time, hang fire, mark time, stand by, sit tight, hold one's horses.
3 *they were waiting for the kettle to boil* **await;** anticipate, look forward, long, pine, yearn, expect, be ready.
4 *the movie will have to wait* **be postponed,** be delayed, be put off, be deferred; informal be put on the back burner, be put on ice.
▸ **noun** *a long wait* **delay,** holdup, interval, interlude, intermission, pause, break, stay, cessation, suspension, stoppage, halt, interruption, lull, respite, recess, moratorium, hiatus, gap, rest.
– PHRASES **wait on** *he waits on her as if he were a paid servant* **serve,** attend to, tend (to), cater for/to; minister to, take care of, look after, see to. **wait up 1** *she waited up for him every night* **stay awake,** stay up, keep vigil. **2** *hey, wait up!* **stop,** slow down, hold on, wait for me.

waive ▸ **verb 1** *he waived his right to a hearing* **relinquish,** renounce, give up, abandon, surrender, cede, sign away, yield, reject, dispense with, abdicate, sacrifice, refuse, turn down, spurn. See note at **RELINQUISH**.
2 *the manager waived the rules* **disregard,** ignore, overlook, set aside, forgo, drop.

wake ▸ **verb 1** *at 4:30 am Mark woke up* **awake,** waken, awaken, rouse oneself, stir, come to, come round, bestir oneself; get up, get out of bed; formal arise.
ANTONYMS sleep.
2 *she woke her husband* **rouse,** arouse, waken.
3 *a shock woke him up a bit* **activate,** stimulate, galvanize, enliven, animate, stir up, spur on, buoy, invigorate, revitalize; informal perk up, pep up.
4 *they* **woke up to** *what we were saying* **realize,** become aware of, become conscious of, become mindful of, clue in to.
5 *the name woke an old memory* **evoke,** conjure up, rouse, stir, revive, awaken, rekindle, rejuvenate, stimulate.
ANTONYMS suppress.
▸ **noun** *a mourner at a wake* **vigil,** watch; funeral.

wakeful ▸ **adjective 1** *he had been wakeful all night* **awake,** restless, restive, tossing and turning.

ANTONYMS asleep.
2 *I was suddenly wakeful* **alert,** watchful, vigilant, on the lookout, on one's guard, attentive, heedful, wary.
ANTONYMS inattentive.

waken ▶ **verb** See **WAKE** (sense 1 of the verb), **WAKE** (sense 2 of the verb).

walk ▶ **verb 1** *they walked along the road* **stroll,** saunter, amble, trudge, plod, dawdle, hike, tramp, tromp, slog, stomp, trek, march, stride, sashay, glide, troop, patrol, wander, ramble, tread, prowl, promenade, roam, traipse; stretch one's legs; informal mosey, hoof it; formal perambulate.
2 *he walked her home* **accompany,** escort, guide, show, see, usher, take, chaperone, steer, shepherd.
▶ **noun 1** *their country walks* **stroll,** saunter, amble, promenade; ramble, hike, tramp, march; turn; dated constitutional.
2 *the map shows several nature walks* See **TRAIL** (sense 5 of the noun).
3 *he shoveled the front walk* **path,** pathway, walkway, sidewalk.
4 *her elegant walk* **gait,** step, stride, tread.
– PHRASES **walk all over** informal **1** *be firm or he'll walk all over you* **take advantage of,** impose on, exploit, use, abuse, misuse, manipulate, take liberties with; informal take for a ride, run rings around. **2** *we walked all over the home team* See **TROUNCE**. **walk off/away with 1** informal *she walked off with my wallet* See **STEAL** (sense 1 of the verb). **2** *he walked off with four awards* **win easily,** win hands down, attain, earn, gain, garner, receive, acquire, secure, collect, pick up, net; informal bag. **walk of life** *we come from different walks of life* **class,** status, rank, caste, sphere, arena; profession, career, vocation, job, occupation, employment, business, trade, craft; province, field. **walk out 1** *he walked out in a temper* **leave,** depart, get up and go, storm off/out, flounce out, absent oneself; informal take off. **2** *teachers walked out in protest* **(go on) strike,** stop work; protest, mutiny, revolt. **walk out on** *did you hear that Sierra walked out on Curt?* **desert,** abandon, leave, betray, throw over, jilt, run out on; informal dump, ditch.

walker ▶ **noun** *a vigorous walker* **hiker,** rambler, traveler, roamer, rover, pedestrian; literary wayfarer.

walkout ▶ **noun** *workers staged a walkout at 10:45 this morning* **strike,** stoppage, industrial action, job action, revolt, rebellion.

walkover ▶ **noun** *after yesterday's walkover, today's tight game was especially exciting* **easy victory,** rout, landslide; informal piece of cake, pushover, cinch, breeze, picnic, laugher, whitewash; informal duck soup.

wall ▶ **noun 1** *brick walls* **barrier,** partition, enclosure, screen, panel, divider; bulkhead.
2 *an ancient city wall* **fortification,** rampart, barricade, bulwark, stockade.
3 *break down the walls that stop world trade* **obstacle,** barrier, fence; impediment, hindrance, block, roadblock, check.
▶ **verb 1** *tenements **walled in** the courtyard* **enclose,** bound, encircle, confine, hem, close in, shut in, fence in.
2 *the doorway had been **walled up*** **block,** seal, close, brick up.
– PHRASES **go to the wall for** informal *I never asked you to go the wall for me* **risk everything for,** do anything for, put one's life on the line for. **off the wall** informal *his outfits are really off the wall* See **UNCONVENTIONAL**.

wallet ▶ **noun** *I've got maybe two or three dollars in my wallet* **purse,** change purse; billfold, pocketbook, fanny pack.

wallow ▶ **verb 1** *pigs wallow in the mud* **loll about/around,** roll about/around, lie about/around, splash about/around; slosh, wade, paddle; informal splosh.
2 *a ship wallowing in stormy seas* **roll,** lurch, toss, plunge, pitch, reel, rock, flounder, keel, list; labor.
3 *she seems to wallow in self-pity* **luxuriate,** bask, take pleasure, take satisfaction, indulge (oneself), delight, revel, glory; enjoy, like, love, relish, savor; informal get a kick out of, get off on.

wan ▶ **adjective 1** *she looked so wan and frail* **pale,** pallid, ashen, white, gray; anemic, colorless, bloodless, waxen, chalky, pasty, peaked, sickly, washed out, drained, drawn, ghostly. See note at **PALE**[2].
ANTONYMS flushed.
2 *the wan light of the moon* **dim,** faint, weak, feeble, pale, watery, washy.
ANTONYMS bright.

wand ▶ **noun** *the magician's wand* **baton,** stick, staff, bar, dowel, rod; twig, cane, birch, switch; historical caduceus.

wander ▶ **verb 1** *I wandered around the mansion* **stroll,** amble, saunter, walk, dawdle, potter, ramble, meander; roam, rove, range, drift, prowl; informal traipse, mosey, tootle, mooch.
2 *we are wandering from the point* **stray,** depart, diverge, veer, swerve, deviate, digress, drift, get sidetracked.

wanderer ▶ **noun** *a wanderer in the wilderness* **traveler,** rambler, hiker, migrant, globetrotter, roamer, rover; itinerant, rolling stone, nomad; tramp, transient, drifter, vagabond, vagrant; informal hobo, bum; literary wayfarer.

wane ▶ **verb** *time-lapse photography shows the moon waning* **decline,** diminish, decrease, dwindle, shrink, tail off, ebb, fade (away), lessen, peter out, fall off, recede, slump, flag, weaken, give way, wither, crumble, evaporate, disintegrate, die out; literary evanesce.
ANTONYMS wax, grow.

want ▶ **verb 1** *do you want more coffee?* **desire,** wish for, hope for, aspire to, fancy, care for, like; long for, yearn for, crave, hanker after, hunger for, thirst for, cry out for, covet; need; informal have a yen for, have a jones for, be dying for.
2 informal *you **want to** be more careful* **should,** ought to, need to, must.
3 *this mollycoddled generation **wants for** nothing* **lack,** be without, have need of, be devoid of, be bereft of, be missing. See note at **LACK**.
▶ **noun 1** *his want of vigilance* **lack,** absence, nonexistence, unavailability; dearth, deficiency, inadequacy, insufficiency, paucity, shortage, scarcity, deficit.

2 *a time of want* **need,** neediness, austerity, privation, deprivation, poverty, impoverishment, penury, destitution; famine, drought.
3 *all her wants would be taken care of* **wish,** desire, demand, longing, yearning, fancy, craving, hankering; need, requirement; informal yen.

wanting ▸ adjective **1** *the defenses were found wanting* **deficient,** inadequate, lacking, insufficient, imperfect, unacceptable, unsatisfactory, flawed, faulty, defective, unsound, substandard, inferior, second-rate, poor, shoddy.
ANTONYMS sufficient.
2 *millions were left wanting for food* **without,** lacking, deprived of, devoid of, bereft of, in need of, out of; deficient in, short on; informal minus.

wanton ▸ adjective **1** *wanton destruction* **deliberate,** willful, malicious, spiteful, wicked, cruel; gratuitous, unprovoked, motiveless, arbitrary, groundless, unjustifiable, needless, unnecessary, uncalled for, senseless, pointless, purposeless, meaningless, empty, random; capricious.
ANTONYMS justifiable.
2 *a wanton seductress* **promiscuous,** immoral, immodest, indecent, shameless, unchaste, fast, loose, impure, abandoned, lustful, lecherous, lascivious, libidinous, licentious, dissolute, debauched, degenerate, corrupt, whorish, disreputable.
ANTONYMS chaste.

war ▸ noun **1** *the Napoleonic wars* **conflict,** warfare, combat, fighting, (military) action, bloodshed, struggle; battle, skirmish, fight, clash, engagement, encounter; offensive, attack, campaign; hostilities; jihad, crusade.
ANTONYMS peace.
2 *the war against drugs* **campaign,** crusade, battle, fight, struggle, movement, drive.
▸ verb *rival empires* ***warred against*** *each other* **fight (against),** battle (against), combat (against), wage war against, take up arms against; feud with, quarrel with, struggle with/against, contend with, wrangle with, cross swords with; attack, engage (against), take on, skirmish with.

ward ▸ noun **1** *the surgical ward* **room,** department, unit, area, wing.
2 *the majority of voters in our ward are over the age of 50* **district,** constituency, division, quarter, zone, parish.
3 *the boy is my ward* **dependent,** charge, protégé.
– PHRASES **ward off 1** *we use this lotion to ward off gnats* **fend off,** repel, repulse, beat back, chase away; informal send packing. **2** *she warded off the blow* **parry,** avert, deflect, block; evade, avoid, dodge. **3** *garlic is worn to ward off evil spirits* **rebuff,** avert, keep at bay, fend off, stave off, turn away, repel, resist, prevent, obstruct, foil, frustrate, thwart, check, stop.

warden ▸ noun **1** *a park warden* **ranger;** custodian, keeper, guardian, protector; superintendent, caretaker, supervisor.
2 *his behavior was reported to the warden* **governor,** executive, president, official; jailer, keeper; informal screw.

wardrobe ▸ noun **1** *she bought new shirts to expand his wardrobe* **collection of clothes;** garments, attire, outfits; trousseau.
2 chiefly Brit. *she opened the wardrobe* **(clothes) closet,** armoire, locker, cupboard, cabinet.

warehouse ▸ noun *twelve DVD players were stolen from the warehouse* **depot,** distribution center, storehouse, store, storeroom, depository, storage, entrepôt, stockroom; granary; Military magazine.

wares ▸ plural noun *on Saturdays, the weaver would come into town with his wares* **merchandise,** goods, products, produce, stock, commodities; lines, range; informal stuff.

warfare ▸ noun *neither side seems ready to end this warfare* **fighting,** war, combat, conflict, (military) action, hostilities; bloodshed, battles, skirmishes.

warlike ▸ adjective *warlike leaders* **aggressive,** belligerent, warring, bellicose, pugnacious, combative, bloodthirsty, jingoistic, hostile, threatening, quarrelsome; militaristic, militant, warmongering.

warlock ▸ noun *Samantha's father, the warlock Maurice* **sorcerer,** wizard, magus, (black) magician, enchanter; archaic mage.

warm ▸ adjective **1** *a warm kitchen* **hot,** cozy, snug; informal toasty.
ANTONYMS cold, cool.
2 *a warm day in spring* **balmy,** summery, sultry, hot, mild, temperate; sunny, fine.
ANTONYMS cold, chilly.
3 *warm water* **heated,** tepid, lukewarm.
ANTONYMS cold, chilled.
4 *a warm sweater* **thick,** thermal, winter, woolly, fleecy, chunky.
ANTONYMS light, summery.
5 *a warm welcome* **friendly,** cordial, amiable, genial, kind, pleasant, fond; welcoming, hospitable, benevolent, benign, charitable; sincere, genuine, wholehearted, heartfelt, enthusiastic, eager, hearty.
ANTONYMS unfriendly, hostile.
▸ verb *warm the soup in that pan* **heat (up),** reheat, cook; thaw (out), melt, warm up, microwave; informal zap, nuke.
ANTONYMS chill.
– PHRASES **warm to 1** *everyone warmed to him* **like,** take to, get on (well) with, hit it off with, be on good terms with. **2** *he couldn't warm to the notion* **be enthusiastic about,** be supportive of, be excited about, get into. **warm up 1** *I run in place a bit just to warm up* **limber up,** loosen up, stretch, work out, exercise; prepare, rehearse. **2** *the emcee warmed up the crowd* **enliven,** liven, stimulate, animate, rouse, stir, excite; informal get going.

warmth ▸ noun **1** *the warmth of the fire* **heat,** warmness, hotness, fieriness; coziness.
2 *the warmth of their welcome* **friendliness,** amiability, geniality, cordiality, kindness, tenderness, fondness; benevolence, charity; enthusiasm, eagerness, ardor, fervor, energy, effusiveness.

warn ▸ verb **1** *David warned her about the cat* **notify,** alert, apprise, inform, tell, make someone aware, forewarn, remind, give notice;

informal tip off.
2 *police are warning galleries to be alert* **advise,** exhort, urge, counsel, caution.

warning ▶ noun **1** *the earthquake came without warning* **(advance) notice,** forewarning, alert; hint, signal, sign, alarm bells; informal tip-off, heads-up, red flag.
2 *a health warning* **caution,** advisory, notification, information; exhortation, injunction; advice.
3 *a warning of things to come* **omen,** premonition, foreboding, prophecy, prediction, forecast, token, portent, signal, sign; literary foretoken.
4 *his sentence is a warning to other drunk drivers* **example,** deterrent, lesson, caution, exemplar, message, moral.
5 *a written warning* **admonition,** remonstrance, reprimand, censure, caution; informal dressing-down, talking-to.

warrant ▶ noun **1** *a warrant for his arrest* **authorization,** order, license, permit, document; writ, summons, subpoena; mandate, decree, fiat, edict.
2 *a travel warrant* **voucher,** slip, ticket, coupon, pass.
▶ verb **1** *the charges warranted a severe sentence* **justify,** vindicate, call for, sanction, validate; permit, authorize; deserve, excuse, account for, legitimize; support, license, approve of; merit, qualify for, rate, be worthy of, be deserving of.
2 *we warrant that the texts do not infringe copyright* **guarantee,** affirm, swear, promise, vow, pledge, undertake, state, assert, declare, profess, attest; vouch, testify, bear witness; formal aver.

warring ▶ adjective *warring tribes* **opposing,** conflicting, at war, fighting, battling, quarreling; competing, hostile, rival.

warrior ▶ noun *fearsome warriors* **fighter,** soldier, serviceman, combatant, mercenary.

wary ▶ adjective **1** *he was trained to be wary* **cautious,** careful, circumspect, on one's guard, chary, alert, on the lookout, on one's toes, on the qui vive; attentive, heedful, watchful, vigilant, observant; informal wide awake. See note at **VIGILANT.**
ANTONYMS inattentive.
2 *we are wary of strangers* **suspicious,** chary, leery, careful, distrustful, mistrustful, skeptical, doubtful, dubious.
ANTONYMS trustful.

wash ▶ verb **1** *he is washing in the guest bathroom* **clean oneself**; bathe, take a bath, shower, soak, freshen up; formal perform one's ablutions.
2 *he washed her socks* **clean,** cleanse, rinse, launder, scour; shampoo, lather, sponge, scrub, wipe; sluice, douse, swab, disinfect; literary lave.
ANTONYMS soil.
3 *waves washed against the hull* **splash,** lap, splosh, dash, crash, break, beat, surge, ripple, roll.
4 *the wreckage was washed downriver* **sweep,** carry, convey, transport.
5 *it **washed up** on my front lawn* **land,** come to rest, be deposited, be beached.
6 *guilt **washed over** her* **surge through,** rush through, course through, flood over, flow over; affect, overcome.
7 informal *this story just won't wash* **be accepted,** be acceptable, be plausible, be convincing, hold up, hold water, stand up, bear scrutiny; do.
▶ noun **1** *she needs a wash* **clean,** shower, dip, bath, soak; formal ablutions.
2 *that shirt should go in the wash* **laundry,** washing.
3 *antiseptic skin wash* **lotion,** salve, preparation, rinse, liquid; liniment.
4 *the wash of the boat* **backwash,** wake, trail, path.
5 *the wash of the waves on the beach* **surge,** flow, swell, sweep, rise and fall, roll, splash.
6 *a light watercolor wash* **paint,** stain, film, coat, coating; tint, glaze.
– PHRASES **wash one's hands of** *I'm going to wash my hands of the whole business* **disown,** renounce, reject, forswear, disavow, give up on, turn one's back on, cast aside, abandon; formal abjure. **wash up** *you kids can wash up after dinner* **wash the dishes,** do the dishes, clean up.

washed out ▶ adjective **1** *a washed-out denim jacket* **faded,** bleached, decolorized, stonewashed; pale, light, drab, muted.
ANTONYMS bold.
2 *he looked washed out after his exams* **exhausted,** tired, worn out, weary, fatigued, spent, drained, enervated, run-down; informal done in, dog-tired, bushed, beat, zonked, pooped, tuckered out.
ANTONYMS energetic.

waspish ▶ adjective *he's a waspish old geezer* **irritable,** touchy, testy, cross, snappish, cantankerous, splenetic, short-tempered, bad-tempered, moody, ornery, crotchety, crabby; informal grouchy.

waste ▶ verb **1** *he doesn't like to waste money* **squander,** misspend, misuse, fritter away, throw away, lavish, dissipate, throw around; informal blow, splurge.
ANTONYMS conserve.
2 *these children are **wasting away** in the streets* **grow weak,** grow thin, shrink, decline, wilt, fade, flag, deteriorate, degenerate, languish.
ANTONYMS flourish, thrive.
3 *the disease wasted his legs* **emaciate,** atrophy, wither, debilitate, shrivel, shrink, weaken, enfeeble. See note at **RAVAGE.**
4 informal *I saw them waste the guy* See **MURDER** (sense 1 of the verb).
▶ adjective **1** *waste material* **unwanted,** excess, superfluous, left over, scrap, useless, worthless; unusable, unprofitable.
2 *waste ground* **uncultivated,** barren, desert, arid, bare; desolate, void, uninhabited, unpopulated; wild.
▶ noun **1** *a waste of money* **misuse,** misapplication, misemployment, abuse; extravagance, wastefulness, lavishness.
2 *household waste* **garbage,** rubbish, trash, refuse, litter, debris, flotsam and jetsam, dross, junk, detritus, scrap; dregs, scraps; sewage, effluent.
3 (usu. **wastes**) *the frozen wastes of the Arctic* **desert,** wasteland, wilderness, wilds, emptiness.
– PHRASES **lay waste** See **LAY**[1].

wasted ▶ adjective **1** *a wasted effort* **squandered,** misspent, misdirected, misused, dissipated; pointless, useless, needless, unnecessary; vain,

fruitless.
2 *a wasted opportunity* **missed,** lost, forfeited, neglected, squandered, bungled; informal down the drain.
3 *I'm wasted in this job* **underemployed in/for,** underused in, too good for, above.
4 *his wasted legs* **emaciated,** atrophied, withered, shriveled, weak, frail, shrunken, skeletal, rickety, scrawny, wizened.
5 informal *everybody at the party was wasted* See DRUNK.

wasteful ▶ adjective *a wasteful use of fuel* **prodigal,** profligate, uneconomical, inefficient, extravagant, lavish, excessive, imprudent, improvident, intemperate; thriftless, spendthrift; needless, useless.
ANTONYMS frugal.

watch ▶ verb **1** *she watched him as he spoke* **observe,** view, look at, eye, gaze at, stare at, gape at, peer at; contemplate, survey, keep an eye on; inspect, scrutinize, scan, examine, study, ogle, gawk at, regard, mark; informal check out, get a load of, eyeball; literary behold.
ANTONYMS ignore.
2 *he was being watched by the police* **spy on,** keep in sight, track, monitor, survey, follow, keep under surveillance; informal keep tabs on, stake out.
3 *will you watch the kids?* **look after,** mind, keep an eye on, take care of, supervise, tend, attend to; guard, safeguard, protect, babysit.
ANTONYMS neglect.
4 *we stayed to watch the boat* **guard,** protect, shield, defend, safeguard; cover, patrol, police.
5 *watch what you say* **be careful,** mind, be aware of, pay attention to, consider, pay heed to.
▶ noun **1** *Bill looked at his watch* **timepiece,** chronometer; wristwatch, pocket watch, stopwatch.
2 *we kept watch on the yacht* **guard,** vigil, lookout, an eye; observation, surveillance, vigilance.
– PHRASES **watch out/it/yourself** *watch it, Bob, or you'll go over the edge | hey, you kids, watch yourselves!* **be careful,** be watchful, be on your guard, beware, be wary, be cautious, look out, pay attention, take heed, take care, keep an eye open/out, keep one's eyes peeled, be vigilant.

watchdog ▶ noun **1** *they use watchdogs to ward off trespassers* **guard dog.**
2 *a consumer watchdog* **ombudsman,** monitor, scrutineer, inspector, supervisor; custodian, guardian, protector.

watcher ▶ noun *the crime scene brought out your typical collection of watchers* **onlooker,** spectator, observer, viewer, fly on the wall; witness, bystander, looker-on; spy; informal rubberneck; literary beholder.

watchful ▶ adjective *the watchful eye of their mother* **observant,** alert, vigilant, attentive, awake, aware, heedful, sharp-eyed, eagle-eyed, hawk-eyed; on the lookout, on the qui vive, wary, cautious, careful, canny, chary. See note at VIGILANT.

watchman ▶ noun *the morning watchman comes on duty at half past five* **security guard,** custodian, warden; sentry, guard, patrolman, lookout, sentinel, scout, watch.

watchword ▶ noun *Quality First is the watchword of our company* **guiding principle,** motto, slogan, maxim, mantra, catchphrase, byword, shibboleth; informal buzzword.

water ▶ noun **1** *a glass of water* H_2O; dated Adam's ale.
2 *a house down by the water* **sea,** ocean; lake, river; drink.
▶ verb **1** *water the plants* **sprinkle,** moisten, dampen, wet, spray, splash; soak, douse, souse, drench, saturate; hose (down).
2 *my mouth watered* **moisten,** become wet, salivate; informal drool.
– PHRASES **hold water** *your story just doesn't hold water* **be tenable,** ring true, bear scrutiny, make sense, stand up, hold up, be convincing, be plausible, be sound. **water down 1** *staff had watered down the drinks* **dilute,** thin (out), weaken; adulterate, doctor, mix; informal cut.
2 *the proposals were watered down* **moderate,** temper, mitigate, tone down, soften, tame; understate, play down, soft-pedal.

waterfall ▶ noun *a family of otters was frolicking in the waterfall* **cascade,** cataract, falls, chute.

watertight ▶ adjective **1** *a watertight container* **impermeable,** impervious, (hermetically) sealed; waterproof, water-repellent, water-resistant.
ANTONYMS leaky.
2 *a watertight alibi* **indisputable,** unquestionable, incontrovertible, irrefutable, unassailable, impregnable; foolproof, sound, flawless, airtight, bulletproof, conclusive.
ANTONYMS flawed.

watery ▶ adjective **1** *a watery discharge* **liquid,** fluid, aqueous; technical hydrous.
ANTONYMS solid, thick.
2 *a watery meadow* **wet,** damp, moist, sodden, soggy, squelchy, slushy, soft; saturated, waterlogged; boggy, marshy, swampy, miry, muddy.
ANTONYMS dry.
3 *watery soup* **thin,** runny, weak, sloppy, dilute, diluted; tasteless, flavorless, insipid, bland.
ANTONYMS thick, hearty.
4 *the light was watery and gray* **pale,** wan, faint, weak, feeble; informal wishy-washy, washy.
ANTONYMS bright.
5 *watery eyes* **tearful,** teary, weepy, moist, rheumy; formal lachrymose.
ANTONYMS dry.

wave ▶ verb **1** *he waved his flag in triumph* **brandish,** shake, swish, move to and fro, move up and down, wag, sweep, swing, flourish, wield; flick, flutter.
2 *the grass waved in the breeze* **ripple,** flutter, undulate, stir, flap, sway, billow, shake, quiver, move.
3 *the waiter waved them closer* **gesture,** gesticulate, signal, beckon, motion.
▶ noun **1** *she gave him a friendly wave* **gesture,** gesticulation; signal, sign, motion; salute.
2 *he surfs the Malibu waves* **breaker,** roller, comber, boomer, ripple, white horse, bore, big kahuna; (**waves**) swell, surf, froth; backwash.
3 *a wave of emigration* **flow,** rush, surge, flood, stream, tide, deluge, spate.
4 *a wave of self-pity* **surge,** rush, stab, dart,

upsurge, groundswell; thrill, frisson; feeling.
5 *his hair grew in thick waves* **curl,** kink, corkscrew, twist, ringlet, coil.
6 *electromagnetic waves* ripple, vibration, oscillation.
PHRASES **make waves** informal *just be quiet and don't make waves* **cause trouble,** be disruptive, be troublesome; make an impression, get noticed. **wave aside** *he waved aside her protest* **dismiss,** reject, brush aside, shrug off, disregard, ignore, discount, play down; informal pooh-pooh. **wave down** *she had no luck waving down a cab* **flag down,** hail, stop, summon, call, accost.

waver ▶ **verb 1** *the candlelight wavered in the draft* **flicker,** quiver, twinkle, glimmer, wink, blink.
2 *his voice wavered* **falter,** wobble, tremble, quaver, shake.
3 *he wavered between the choices* **be undecided,** be irresolute, hesitate, dither, equivocate, vacillate, waffle, fluctuate; think twice, change one's mind, blow hot and cold; informal shilly-shally, sit on the fence.

wavy ▶ **adjective** *wavy hair | a screen filled with wavy lines* **curly,** curvy, curved, undulating, squiggly, rippled, crinkly, kinked, zigzag.

wax ▶ **verb** *the moon is waxing* **get bigger,** increase, enlarge.
ANTONYMS wane.
– PHRASES **wax lyrical** *sorry, I didn't mean to wax lyrical about the good old days* **be enthusiastic,** enthuse, eulogize, rave, gush, get carried away.

way ▶ **noun 1** *a way of reducing the damage* **method,** process, procedure, technique, system; plan, strategy, scheme; means, mechanism, approach.
2 *she kissed him in her brisk way* **manner,** style, fashion, mode; modus operandi, MO.
3 *I've changed my ways* **practice,** wont, habit, custom, policy, procedure, convention, routine, modus vivendi; trait, attribute, peculiarity, idiosyncrasy; conduct, behavior, manner, style, nature, personality, temperament, disposition, character.
4 *which way leads home?* **route,** course, direction; road, street, track, path.
5 *I'll go out the back way* **door,** gate, exit, entrance, entry; route.
6 *a short way downstream* **distance,** length, stretch, journey; space, interval, span.
7 *April is a long way away* **time,** stretch, term, span, duration.
8 *a car coming the other way* **direction,** bearing, course, orientation, line, tack.
9 *in some ways, he may be better off* **respect,** regard, aspect, facet, sense, angle; detail, point, particular.
10 *the country is in a bad way* **state,** condition, situation, circumstances, position; predicament, plight; informal shape.
– PHRASES **by the way** *by the way, Roy is back in town* **incidentally,** by the by, in passing, en passant, as an aside. **give way 1** *the government gave way and passed the bill* **yield,** back down, surrender, capitulate, concede defeat, give in, submit, succumb; acquiesce, agree, assent; informal throw in the towel/sponge, cave in.
2 *the door gave way* **collapse,** give, cave in, fall in, come apart, crumple, buckle. **3** *grief gave way to guilt* **be replaced by,** be succeeded by, be followed by, be supplanted by. **on the way** *help is on the way* **coming,** imminent, forthcoming, approaching, impending, close, near, on us; proceeding, en route, in transit.

wayfarer ▶ **noun** literary See **WANDERER**.

waylay ▶ **verb 1** *we were waylaid and robbed* **ambush,** hold up, attack, assail, rob; informal mug, stick up.
2 *several people waylaid her for an interview* **accost,** detain, intercept, take aside, pounce on, importune; informal buttonhole.

wayward ▶ **adjective** *a wayward child* **willful,** headstrong, stubborn, obstinate, obdurate, perverse, contrary, disobedient, insubordinate, undisciplined; rebellious, defiant, uncooperative, recalcitrant, unruly, wild, unmanageable, erratic; difficult, impossible; formal refractory.
ANTONYMS docile.

weak ▶ **adjective 1** *they are too weak to move* **frail,** feeble, delicate, fragile; infirm, sick, sickly, debilitated, incapacitated, ailing, indisposed, decrepit; tired, fatigued, exhausted, anemic; informal weedy.
ANTONYMS strong.
2 *weak eyesight* **inadequate,** poor, feeble; defective, faulty, deficient, imperfect, substandard.
ANTONYMS strong, powerful, convincing, resolute, bright, loud.
3 *a weak excuse* **unconvincing,** untenable, tenuous, implausible, unsatisfactory, poor, inadequate, feeble, flimsy, lame, hollow; informal pathetic.
ANTONYMS strong, powerful.
4 *I was too weak to be a rebel* **spineless,** craven, cowardly, pusillanimous, timid; irresolute, indecisive, ineffectual, inept, effete, meek, tame, ineffective, impotent, soft, faint-hearted; informal yellow, weak-kneed, gutless, chicken.
ANTONYMS strong, resolute.
5 *a weak light* **dim,** pale, wan, faint, feeble, muted.
ANTONYMS strong, bright.
6 *a weak voice* **indistinct,** muffled, muted, hushed, low, faint, thready, thin.
ANTONYMS strong, loud.
7 *weak coffee* **watery,** diluted, dilute, watered down, thin, tasteless, flavorless, bland, insipid, wishy-washy.
ANTONYMS strong, powerful.
8 *a weak smile* **unenthusiastic,** feeble, halfhearted, lame.

CHOOSE THE RIGHT WORD

weak, debilitated, decrepit, feeble, frail, infirm

Someone who is **weak** lacks physical, mental, or moral strength (*a weak heart; a weak excuse; too weak to resist temptation*). But there's nothing to suggest what the cause of this lack of strength might be. Someone who is **frail**, on the other hand, is weak because he or she has a slight build or delicate constitution (*a small, frail man*). Calling someone **feeble** implies that his or her weakness is pitiable (*too feeble to get out of bed*); when applied to things, *feeble* means faint or inadequate (*a feeble light*). **Infirm** suggests a loss of soundness, as from aging or illness (*poverty and illness had made him infirm*). **Debilitated** and **decrepit** also suggest that strength once present has been lost. But while someone who is young may be *debilitated* by disease, *decrepit* specifically refers to a loss of strength due to advanced age or long use (*a decrepit old woman who seldom left her house; a decrepit building that would soon be torn down*).

weaken ▶ verb 1 *the virus weakened him terribly* **enfeeble,** debilitate, incapacitate, sap, enervate, tire, exhaust, wear out; wither, cripple, disable, emasculate.
2 *she tried to weaken the blow for him* **reduce,** decrease, diminish, soften, lessen, moderate, temper, dilute, blunt, mitigate.
3 *our morale weakened* **decrease,** dwindle, diminish, wane, ebb, subside, peter out, fizzle out, tail off, decline, falter.
4 *the move weakened her authority* **impair,** undermine, erode, eat away at, compromise; invalidate, negate, discredit.

weakling ▶ noun *a ninety-pound weakling* **pushover,** namby-pamby, coward, milksop; informal wimp, weed, sissy, twinkie, drip, softie, doormat, chicken, yellow-belly, scaredy-cat, wuss.

weakness ▶ noun 1 *with old age came weakness* **frailty,** feebleness, enfeeblement, fragility, delicacy; infirmity, sickness, sickliness, debility, incapacity, impotence, indisposition, decrepitude, vulnerability.
2 *he has worked on his weaknesses* **fault,** flaw, defect, deficiency, weak point, failing, shortcoming, weak link, imperfection, Achilles heel, foible.
3 *a weakness for champagne* **fondness,** liking, partiality, preference, love, penchant, soft spot, predilection, inclination, taste, eye; enthusiasm, appetite; susceptibility.
4 *the president was accused of weakness* **timidity,** cowardliness, pusillanimity; indecision, irresolution, ineffectuality, ineptitude, impotence, meekness, powerlessness, ineffectiveness.
5 *the weakness of this argument* **untenability,** implausibility, poverty, inadequacy, transparency; flimsiness, hollowness.
6 *the weakness of the sound* **indistinctness,** mutedness, faintness, feebleness, lowness; dimness, paleness.

wealth ▶ noun 1 *a gentleman of wealth* **affluence,** prosperity, riches, means, substance, fortune; money, cash, lucre, capital, treasure, finance; assets, possessions, resources, funds; property, stock, reserves, securities, holdings; informal wherewithal, dough, moola.
ANTONYMS poverty.
2 *a wealth of information* **abundance,** profusion, mine, store, treasury, bounty, bonanza, cornucopia, myriad; informal lot, load, heap, mass, mountain, stack, ton; formal plenitude.
ANTONYMS dearth.

wealthy ▶ adjective *our wealthy neighbors have an indoor swimming pool* **rich,** affluent, moneyed, well off, well-to-do, prosperous, comfortable, propertied; of substance; informal well-heeled, rolling in it, in the money, made of money, filthy rich, stinking rich, loaded, flush.
ANTONYMS poor.

CHOOSE THE RIGHT WORD

wealthy, affluent, flush, opulent, prosperous, rich, well-to-do

If you have an abundance of money, you are **rich**. Another term for *rich* is **wealthy**, which may further imply that you are an established and prominent member of the community whose lifestyle is in keeping with your income (*a wealthy family whose influence on public opinion could not be ignored*). **Affluent** comes from the Latin word meaning to flow, and it connotes a generous income (*an affluent neighborhood*), while **opulent** suggests lavish spending or an ostentatious display of wealth (*an opulent mansion with every imaginable luxury*). One may come from an *affluent* family, in other words, and not have a particularly *opulent* lifestyle. If you're **prosperous**, you are thriving or flourishing (*a prosperous merchant; a prosperous business*). While *prosperous* suggests an economic situation that is on the rise, **flush** means having plenty of money on hand at a particular time (*she was feeling flush after receiving her first paycheck*). **Well-to-do** implies a generous income, enough to support comfortable living but not necessarily enough to be considered rich (*they were known as a well-to-do family with a strong commitment to educating their children*).

wear ▶ verb 1 *he wore a suit* **dress in,** be clothed in, have on, sport, model; put on, don.
2 *Barbara wore a smile* **bear,** have (on one's face), show, display, exhibit; give, put on, assume.
3 *the bricks have been **worn down*** **erode,** abrade, rub away, grind away, wash away, crumble (away), wear down; corrode, eat away (at), dissolve.
4 *the tires are wearing well* **last,** endure, hold up, bear up, prove durable.
▶ noun 1 *you won't get much wear out of that* **use,** wearing, service, utility, value; informal mileage.
2 *evening wear* **clothes,** clothing, garments, dress, attire, garb, wardrobe; informal getup, gear, togs, duds; formal apparel; literary array.
3 *the varnish will withstand wear* **damage,** friction, erosion, attrition, abrasion; weathering.
– PHRASES **wear down** *he wore down her resistance* **gradually overcome,** slowly reduce, erode, wear away, exhaust, undermine. **wear off** *the novelty soon wore off* **fade,** diminish,

lessen, dwindle, decrease, wane, ebb, peter out, fizzle out, pall, disappear, run out. **wear on** *the afternoon wore on* **pass,** elapse, proceed, advance, progress, go by, roll by, march on, slip by/away, fly by/past. **wear out 1** *the fabric will eventually wear out* **deteriorate,** become worn, wear thin, fray, become threadbare, wear through. **2** *the grandkids wore me out* **fatigue,** tire out, weary, exhaust, drain, sap, overtax, enervate, debilitate, jade, prostrate; informal poop, frazzle, do in.

wearing ▶ **adjective** See WEARISOME.

wearisome ▶ **adjective** *the wearisome job of shingling the roof* **tiring,** exhausting, wearying, fatiguing, enervating, draining, sapping, stressful, wearing, crushing; demanding, exacting, taxing, trying, challenging, burdensome, arduous, grueling, punishing, grinding, onerous, difficult, hard, tough, heavy, laborious, back-breaking, crippling, strenuous, rigorous, uphill; tiresome, irksome, weary, boring, dull, tedious, monotonous, humdrum, prosaic, unexciting, uninteresting.

weary ▶ **adjective 1** *he was weary after cycling* **tired,** worn out, exhausted, fatigued, sapped, burnt-out, dog-tired, spent, drained, prostrate, enervated; informal all in, done in, beat, ready to drop, bushed, worn to a frazzle, pooped, tuckered out. See note at TIRED.
ANTONYMS fresh, energetic.
2 *she was* ***weary of*** *the arguments* **tired of,** fed up with, bored by, sick of, burnt-out on; informal have had it up to here with.
ANTONYMS enthusiastic.
3 *a weary journey* **tiring,** exhausting, wearying, fatiguing, enervating, draining, sapping, wearing, trying, demanding, taxing, arduous, grueling, difficult, hard, tough.
ANTONYMS refreshing.

weather ▶ **noun** *what's the weather like?* **forecast,** outlook; meteorological conditions, climate, atmospheric pressure, temperature; elements.
▶ **verb** *we weathered the recession* **survive,** come through, ride out, pull through; withstand, endure, rise above, surmount, overcome, resist, brave; informal stick out.
– PHRASES **under the weather** informal *we were sorry to hear that Dottie's been under the weather* See ILL (sense 1 of the adjective).

weave ▶ **verb 1** *flowers were woven into their hair* **entwine,** lace, twist, knit, intertwine, braid, plait, loop.
2 *he weaves colorful plots* **invent,** make up, fabricate, construct, create, contrive, spin; tell, recount, relate.
3 *he had to weave his way through the crowds* **thread,** wind, wend; dodge, zigzag.

web ▶ **noun 1** *a spider's web* **mesh,** net, lattice, latticework, lacework, webbing; gauze, gossamer.
2 *a web of friendships* **network,** nexus, complex, set, chain; tissue.
3 *visit us on the Web* **Internet,** World Wide Web, Net, information superhighway, Infobahn, cyberspace.
▶ **adjective** *a web environment* **online,** Internet, virtual, digital, cyber, web-based, e-.

wed ▶ **verb 1** *they are old enough to wed* **marry,** get married, become husband and wife; informal tie the knot, walk down the aisle, get hitched, take the plunge.
ANTONYMS divorce, separate.
2 *he will wed his girlfriend* **marry,** take as one's wife/husband, lead to the altar; informal make an honest woman of; archaic espouse.
ANTONYMS divorce, jilt.
3 *she wedded the two forms of spirituality* **unite,** unify, join, combine, amalgamate, fuse, integrate, bond, merge, meld, splice.

wedded ▶ **adjective 1** *wedded bliss* **married,** matrimonial, marital, conjugal, nuptial; Law spousal; literary connubial.
2 *she is* ***wedded to*** *her work* **dedicated to,** devoted to, attached to, fixated on, single-minded about.

wedge ▶ **noun 1** *the door was secured by a wedge* **doorstop,** chock, block, stop.
2 *a wedge of cheese* **hunk,** segment, triangle, slice, section; chunk, lump, slab, block, piece.
▶ **verb** *she wedged her case between two bags* **squeeze,** cram, jam, ram, force, push, shove; informal stuff.

weed ▶ **verb**
– PHRASES **weed out** *first we weed out the unqualified candidates* **isolate,** separate out, sort out, sift out, winnow out, filter out, set apart, segregate; eliminate, get rid of, remove, cut, chop; informal lose.

weekly ▶ **adjective** *weekly installments* **once a week**; lasting a week; formal hebdomadal.
▶ **adverb** *the directors meet weekly* **once a week,** every week, each week, on a weekly basis; by the week, per week, a week.

weep ▶ **verb** *even the toughest soldiers wept* **cry,** shed tears, sob, snivel, whimper, whine, wail, bawl; informal boo-hoo, blubber.

weepy ▶ **adjective** *there were a lot a weepy people in the audience* **tearful,** close to tears, upset, distressed, sad, unhappy; in tears, crying, weeping, sniveling; informal teary, misty-eyed, choked-up; formal lachrymose.

weigh ▶ **verb 1** *she weighs the fruit* **measure the weight of,** put on the scales; heft.
2 *he weighed 170 lb.* **have a weight of,** tip the scales at, weigh in at.
3 *the situation* ***weighed*** *heavily* ***on*** *him* **oppress,** lie heavy on, burden, hang over, gnaw at, prey on (one's mind); trouble, worry, bother, disturb, get down, depress, haunt, nag, torment, plague.
4 *he has to weigh his options* **consider,** contemplate, think about, mull over, chew over, reflect on, ruminate about, muse on; assess, appraise, analyze, investigate, inquire into, look into, examine, review, explore, take stock of.
5 *they need to weigh benefit against risk* **balance,** evaluate, compare, juxtapose, contrast, measure.
– PHRASES **weigh down** *my fishing gear weighed me down* **burden,** saddle, overload, overburden, encumber, hamper, handicap.

weight ▶ **noun 1** *the weight of the book* **heaviness,** mass, load, burden, pressure, force; poundage, tonnage.
2 *his recommendation will carry great*

weight **influence**, force, leverage, sway, pull, importance, significance, consequence, value, substance, power, authority; informal clout.
3 *a weight off her mind* **burden**, load, millstone, albatross, encumbrance; trouble, worry, pressure, strain.
4 *the weight of the evidence is against him* **preponderance**, majority, bulk, body, lion's share, predominance; most, almost all.

weighty ▶ **adjective 1** *a weighty tome* **heavy**, thick, bulky, hefty, cumbersome, ponderous. See note at **HEAVY**.
ANTONYMS light.
2 *a weighty subject* **important**, significant, momentous, consequential, far-reaching, impactful, key, major, big, vital, critical, crucial; serious, grave, solemn.
ANTONYMS unimportant, trivial.
3 *a weighty responsibility* **burdensome**, onerous, heavy, oppressive, taxing, troublesome, solemn.
4 *weighty arguments* **compelling**, cogent, strong, forceful, powerful, beefy, potent, effective, sound, valid, telling; impressive, persuasive, convincing, influential, authoritative.
ANTONYMS weak.

weird ▶ **adjective 1** *weird apparitions* **uncanny**, eerie, unnatural, supernatural, unearthly, otherworldly, ghostly, mysterious, strange, abnormal, unusual; eldritch; informal creepy, spooky, freaky.
ANTONYMS normal.
2 *a weird sense of humor* **bizarre**, quirky, outlandish, eccentric, unconventional, unorthodox, idiosyncratic, surreal, crazy, peculiar, odd, strange, queer, freakish, zany, madcap, outré; informal bizarro, wacky, freaky, way-out, offbeat, off the wall, wacko.
ANTONYMS conventional.
– PHRASES **weird out** *I'm a little weirded out by his spiky blue hair* **disturb**, freak out, unnerve, unsettle, alarm, alienate.

welcome ▶ **noun** *I appreciate the welcome I got from your parents* **greeting**, salutation; reception, hospitality; red carpet (treatment).
▶ **verb 1** *welcome your guests in their own language* **greet**, salute, receive, meet, usher in.
2 *we welcomed their decision* **be pleased by**, be glad about, approve of, appreciate, embrace; informal give the thumbs up to.
▶ **adjective** *welcome news* **pleasing**, agreeable, encouraging, gratifying, heartening, promising, favorable, pleasant, refreshing; gladly received, wanted, appreciated, popular, desirable.

welfare ▶ **noun 1** *the welfare of children* **well-being**, health, comfort, security, safety, protection, prosperity, success, fortune; interest, good.
2 *we cannot claim welfare* social security, social assistance, benefit, public assistance; pension, credit, support; sick pay, unemployment benefit; informal the dole.

well[1] ▶ **adverb 1** *he behaves well* **satisfactorily**, nicely, correctly, properly, fittingly, suitably, appropriately; decently, fairly, kindly, generously, honestly.
ANTONYMS badly.
2 *they get along well* **harmoniously**, agreeably, pleasantly, nicely, happily, amicably, amiably, peaceably; informal famously.
ANTONYMS badly.
3 *he plays the piano well* **skillfully**, ably, competently, proficiently, adeptly, deftly, expertly, admirably, excellently.
ANTONYMS poorly.
4 *I know her well* **intimately**, thoroughly, deeply, profoundly, personally.
ANTONYMS barely.
5 *they studied the recipe well* **carefully**, closely, attentively, rigorously, in depth, exhaustively, in detail, meticulously, scrupulously, conscientiously, methodically, completely, comprehensively, fully, extensively, thoroughly, effectively.
ANTONYMS negligently.
6 *they speak well of him* **admiringly**, highly, approvingly, favorably, appreciatively, warmly, enthusiastically, positively, glowingly.
ANTONYMS disparagingly.
7 *she makes enough money to live well* **comfortably**, in (the lap of) luxury, prosperously.
8 *you may well be right* **quite possibly**, conceivably, probably; undoubtedly, certainly, unquestionably.
9 *he is well over forty* **considerably**, very much, a great deal, substantially, easily, comfortably, significantly.
ANTONYMS barely.
10 *she could well afford it* **easily**, comfortably, readily, effortlessly.
ANTONYMS barely.
▶ **adjective 1** *she was completely well again* **healthy**, fine, fit, robust, strong, vigorous, blooming, thriving, hale and hearty, in good shape, in good condition, in fine fettle; informal in the pink.
ANTONYMS ill.
2 *all is not well* **satisfactory**, all right, fine, in order, as it should be, acceptable; informal OK, hunky-dory, jake.
ANTONYMS unsatisfactory.
3 *it would be well to tell us in advance* **advisable**, sensible, prudent, politic, commonsensical, wise, judicious, expedient, recommended, advantageous, beneficial, profitable, desirable; a good idea.
ANTONYMS inadvisable.
– PHRASES **as well** *I'll have the shrimp cocktail as well* **too**, also, in addition, additionally, into the bargain, besides, furthermore, moreover, likewise, to boot. **as well as** *we sell books as well as newspapers* **together with**, along with, besides, plus, and, with, on top of, not to mention, to say nothing of, let alone. **well done** *well done, Robbie, your voice has never been better* **congratulations**, bravo, right on, congrats, my compliments, good work, three cheers, felicitations.

well[2] ▶ **noun 1** *she drew water from the well* borehole, bore, spring, waterhole.
2 *he's a bottomless well of forgiveness* **source**, supply, fount, reservoir, wellspring, mine, fund, treasury.
▶ **verb** *tears welled from her eyes* **flow**, spill, stream, run, rush, gush, roll, cascade, flood, spout; seep, trickle; burst, issue, upwell.

well-advised ▶ adjective *I'm not sure this is a well-advised investment* **wise,** prudent, sensible.

well-being ▶ noun See WELFARE (sense 1).

well-bred ▶ adjective *a well-bred youngster such as yourself should not be cavorting with people of their station* **well brought up,** polite, civil, mannerly, courteous, respectful; ladylike, gentlemanly, genteel, cultivated, urbane, proper, refined, patrician, polished, well-behaved.

well-built ▶ adjective *we need a couple of well-built guys to move these bookcases* **sturdy,** strapping, brawny, burly, hefty, muscular, muscly, strong, rugged, lusty, Herculean; informal hunky, beefy, husky, hulking.
ANTONYMS puny.

well-known ▶ adjective **1** *well-known principles* **familiar,** widely known, popular, common, everyday, established.
ANTONYMS abstruse.
2 *a well-known family of architects* **famous,** famed, prominent, notable, renowned, distinguished, eminent, illustrious, celebrated, acclaimed, recognized, important; notorious.
ANTONYMS obscure.

well-nigh ▶ adverb *enforcing the recycling ordinance is well-nigh impossible* **almost,** nearly, just about, more or less, practically, virtually, all but, as good as, nearing, close to, approaching; roughly, approximately; informal pretty much, nigh on.

well off ▶ adjective **1** *her family's very well off* See WELL-TO-DO.
2 *the prisoners were relatively well off* **fortunate,** lucky, comfortable; informal sitting pretty.
3 *the island is not **well off for** harbors* **well supplied with,** well stocked with, well furnished with, well equipped with; well situated for.

well-read ▶ adjective *a well-read history professor* **knowledgeable,** well-informed, well versed, erudite, scholarly, literate, educated, cultured, bookish, studious; dated lettered.
ANTONYMS ignorant.

well-spoken ▶ adjective *what a bright, well-spoken young man* **articulate,** eloquent, coherent, nicely spoken; refined, polite.

well-to-do ▶ adjective *her well-to-do Uncle Leroy* **wealthy,** rich, affluent, moneyed, well off, prosperous, comfortable, propertied; informal rolling in it, in the money, loaded, well-heeled, flush, made of money, on easy street. See note at WEALTHY.

wet ▶ adjective **1** *wet clothes* **damp,** moist, soaked, drenched, saturated, sopping, dripping, soggy; waterlogged.
ANTONYMS dry.
2 *it was cold and wet* **rainy,** raining, pouring, teeming, inclement, showery, drizzly, drizzling; damp; humid, muggy.
ANTONYMS dry.
3 *the paint is still wet* **sticky,** tacky; fresh.
ANTONYMS dry.
4 *a wet mortar mix* **aqueous,** watery, sloppy.
ANTONYMS dry.
▶ verb *wet the clothes before ironing them* **dampen,** damp, moisten; sprinkle, spray, splash, spritz; soak, saturate, flood, douse, souse, drench.
ANTONYMS dry.
▶ noun **1** *the wet of his tears* **wetness,** damp, moisture, moistness, sogginess; wateriness.
2 *the race was held in the wet* **rain,** drizzle, precipitation; spray, dew, damp.

wharf ▶ noun *there are no available boat slips at this wharf* **quay,** pier, dock, berth, landing, jetty; harbor, dockyard, marina.

wheedle ▶ verb *she wheedled us into hiring her brother* **coax,** cajole, inveigle, induce, entice, charm, tempt, beguile, blandish, flatter, persuade, influence, win someone over, bring someone around, convince, prevail on, get around; informal sweet-talk, soft-soap.

wheel ▶ noun *a wagon wheel* disk, hoop, ring, circle.
▶ verb **1** *she wheeled the trolley away* **push,** trundle, roll.
2 *the flock of doves wheeled around* **turn,** go around, circle, orbit.
– PHRASES **at/behind the wheel** *were you at the wheel when the accident occurred?* **driving,** steering, in the driver's seat.

wheeze ▶ verb *the air was full of ash, and they coughed and wheezed* **breathe noisily,** gasp, whistle, hiss, rasp, croak, pant, cough.

whereabouts ▶ plural noun *his whereabouts remain secret* **location,** position, site, place, situation, spot, point, vicinity; home, address, locale, neighborhood; bearings, orientation.

wherewithal ▶ noun *he has the wherewithal to start up his own business* **money,** cash, capital, finance(s), funds; resources, means, ability, capability; informal dough, loot, necessary, boodle, bucks.

whet ▶ verb **1** *he whetted his knife on a stone* **sharpen,** hone, strop, grind, file.
ANTONYMS blunt.
2 *something to whet your appetite* **stimulate,** excite, arouse, rouse, kindle, trigger, spark, quicken, stir, inspire, animate, waken, fuel, fire, activate, tempt, galvanize.
ANTONYMS dull, spoil.

whiff ▶ noun **1** *I caught a whiff of perfume* **faint smell,** trace, sniff, scent, odor, aroma.
2 *the faintest whiff of irony* **trace,** hint, suggestion, impression, suspicion, soupçon, smidgen, nuance, intimation, tinge, vein, shred, whisper, air, element, overtone.
3 *whiffs of smoke from the boiler* **puff,** gust, flurry, breath, draft, waft.

while ▶ noun *we chatted for a while* **time,** spell, stretch, stint, span, interval, period; duration, phase, patch.
▶ verb *tennis helped to while away the time* **pass,** spend, occupy, use up, fritter, kill.

whim ▶ noun **1** *she bought it on a whim* **impulse,** urge, notion, fancy, foible, caprice, conceit, vagary, inclination, megrim.
2 *human whim* **capriciousness,** whimsy, caprice, volatility, fickleness, idiosyncrasy.

whimper ▶ noun & verb *we heard her whimpers from downstairs | why is he whimpering?*

whine, cry, sob, moan, snivel, wail, groan; mewl, bleat.

whimsical ▶ adjective **1** *a whimsical sense of humor* **fanciful,** playful, mischievous, waggish, quaint, quizzical, curious, droll; eccentric, quirky, idiosyncratic, unconventional, outlandish, queer, fey; informal offbeat, freaky.
2 *the whimsical arbitrariness of autocracy* **volatile,** capricious, fickle, changeable, unpredictable, variable, erratic, mercurial, mutable, inconstant, inconsistent, unstable, protean.

whine ▶ noun & verb **1** *a whine from the kennel | she heard an animal whine* **whimper,** cry, mewl, howl, yowl.
2 *the motor's whine | the motor whined* **hum,** drone.
3 *his latest whine was about the long hours | stop whining!* **complaint** [noun], **complain** [verb], grouse, grumble, murmur; informal gripe, moan, grouch, whinge, bellyache, beef.

whip ▶ noun *he would use a whip on his dogs* **lash,** scourge, strap, belt, rod, bullwhip; historical cat-o'-nine-tails.
▶ verb **1** *he whipped the boy* **flog,** scourge, flagellate, lash, strap, belt, thrash, beat, tan someone's hide.
2 *whip the cream* **whisk,** beat.
3 *she whipped her listeners into a frenzy* **rouse,** stir up, excite, galvanize, electrify, stimulate, inspire, fire up, get someone going, inflame, agitate, goad, provoke.
4 informal *he whipped around the corner* See DASH (sense 1 of the verb).
5 informal *then she whipped out a revolver* **pull,** whisk, pluck, jerk.

whirl ▶ verb **1** *leaves whirled in eddies* **rotate,** circle, wheel, turn, revolve, orbit, spin, twirl.
2 *they whirled past* **hurry,** race, dash, rush, run, sprint, bolt, dart, gallop, career, charge, shoot, hurtle, fly, speed, scurry; informal tear, belt, pelt, scoot, bomb, hightail it.
3 *his mind was whirling* **spin,** reel, swim.
▶ noun **1** *a whirl of dust* **swirl,** flurry, eddy.
2 *the mad social whirl* **hurly-burly,** activity, bustle, rush, flurry, fuss, turmoil, merry-go-round.
3 *Laura's mind was in a whirl* **spin,** daze, stupor, muddle, jumble; confusion; informal dither.

whirlpool ▶ noun **1** *a river full of whirlpools* **eddy,** vortex, maelstrom.
2 *the health club has a whirlpool* **hot tub**; trademark Jacuzzi.

whirlwind ▶ noun **1** *the building was hit by a whirlwind* **tornado,** hurricane, typhoon, cyclone, vortex, twister, dust devil.
2 *a whirlwind of activity* **maelstrom,** welter, bedlam, mayhem, babel, swirl, tumult, hurly-burly, commotion, confusion; informal madhouse, three-ring circus.
▶ adjective *a whirlwind romance* **rapid,** lightning, headlong, impulsive, breakneck, meteoric, sudden, swift, fast, quick, speedy, dizzying; informal quickie.

whisk ▶ verb **1** *the cable car will whisk you to the top* **speed,** hurry, rush, sweep, hurtle, shoot.
2 *she whisked the cloth away* **pull,** snatch, pluck, tug, jerk; informal whip, yank.
3 *he whisked out of sight* **dash,** rush, race, bolt, dart, gallop, career, charge, shoot, hurtle, fly, speed, zoom, scurry, scuttle, scamper; informal tear, belt, pelt, scoot, zip, whip.
4 *she whisked the hair from her face* **flick,** brush, sweep, wave.
5 *whisk the egg yolks* **whip,** beat, mix.

whisper ▶ verb **1** *Alison whispered in his ear* **murmur,** mutter, mumble, speak softly, breathe; hiss; formal susurrate.
ANTONYMS shout.
2 literary *the wind whispered in the grass* **rustle,** murmur, sigh, moan, whoosh, whir, swish, blow, breathe.
ANTONYMS roar.
▶ noun **1** *she spoke in a whisper* **murmur,** mutter, mumble, low voice, undertone; rare sibilation, susurration.
2 literary *the wind died to a whisper* **rustle,** murmur, sigh, whoosh, swish.
3 *I heard the whisper that he's left town* **rumor,** story, report, speculation, insinuation, suggestion, hint; informal buzz.
4 *not a whisper of interest* See WHIT.

whit ▶ noun *they gave him not a whit of consideration* **scrap,** bit, speck, iota, jot, atom, crumb, shred, grain, mite, touch, trace, shadow, suggestion, whisper, suspicion, scintilla, modicum; informal smidgen, smidge.

white ▶ adjective **1** *a clean white bandage* **colorless,** unpigmented, bleached, natural; snowy, milky, chalky, ivory.
2 *her face was white with fear* **pale,** pallid, wan, ashen, bloodless, waxen, chalky, pasty, washed out, drained, drawn, ghostly, deathly.
3 *white hair* **snowy,** gray, silver, silvery, hoary, grizzled.
4 *the early white settlers* **Caucasian,** European.

white-collar ▶ adjective *white-collar workers* **clerical,** administrative, professional, executive, salaried, office.

whiten ▶ verb *the sun has whitened the pink towels* **make white,** make pale, bleach, blanch, lighten, fade.

whitewash ▶ noun **1** *the report was a whitewash* **cover-up,** camouflage, deception, facade, veneer, pretext.
ANTONYMS exposé.
2 informal *a four-game whitewash* **walkover,** rout, landslide; informal pushover, cinch, breeze.
▶ verb *don't whitewash what happened* **cover up,** sweep under the carpet, hush up, suppress, draw a veil over, conceal, veil, obscure, keep secret; gloss over, downplay, soft-pedal.
ANTONYMS expose.

whittle ▶ verb **1** *he sat whittling a piece of wood* **pare,** shave, trim, carve, shape, model.
2 *his powers were **whittled away*** **erode,** wear away, eat away, reduce, diminish, undermine, weaken, subvert, compromise, impair, impede, hinder, cripple, disable, enfeeble, sap.
3 *the ten teams have been **whittled down** to six* **reduce,** cut down, cut back, prune, trim, slim down, pare down, shrink, decrease, diminish.

whole ▶ adjective **1** *the whole report* **entire,** complete, full, unabridged, uncut.
ANTONYMS incomplete.

2 *they unearthed a whole humanoid skull* **intact,** in one piece, unbroken; undamaged, unmarked, perfect.
▶ **noun 1** *a single whole* **entity,** unit, body, discrete item, ensemble.
2 *the whole of the year* **all,** every part, the lot, the sum, the sum total, the entirety.
– PHRASES **on the whole** *on the whole, they lived peaceably* **overall,** all in all, all things considered, for the most part, in the main, in general, generally, generally speaking, as a rule, as a general rule, by and large; normally, usually, more often than not, almost always, most of the time, typically, ordinarily.

wholehearted ▶ **adjective** *you have my wholehearted support* **committed,** positive, emphatic, devoted, dedicated, enthusiastic, unshakable, unswerving; unqualified, unstinting, unreserved, without reservations, unconditional, unequivocal, unmitigated; complete, full, total, absolute.
ANTONYMS halfhearted.

wholesale ▶ **adverb** *the images were removed wholesale* **extensively,** on a large scale, comprehensively; indiscriminately, without exception, across the board.
ANTONYMS selectively.
▶ **adjective** *wholesale destruction* **extensive,** widespread, large-scale, wide-ranging, comprehensive, total, mass; indiscriminate.
ANTONYMS partial.

wholesome ▶ **adjective 1** *wholesome food* **healthy,** health-giving, healthful, good (for one), nutritious, nourishing; natural, uncontaminated, organic.
2 *wholesome fun* **good,** ethical, moral, clean, virtuous, pure, innocent, chaste; uplifting, edifying, proper, correct, decent, harmless; informal squeaky clean.

wholly ▶ **adverb 1** *the measures were wholly inadequate* **completely,** totally, absolutely, entirely, fully, thoroughly, utterly, quite, perfectly, downright, in every respect, in all respects; informal one hundred percent, 'lock, stock, and barrel'.
2 *they rely wholly on you* **exclusively,** only, solely, purely, alone.

whoop ▶ **noun & verb** *whoops of delight | he whooped for joy* **shout,** cry, call, yell, roar, scream, shriek, screech, cheer, hoot; informal holler.

whore ▶ **noun** *the whores on the street* See PROSTITUTE.
▶ **verb 1** *she spent her life whoring* **work as a prostitute,** sell one's body, sell oneself, be on the streets.
2 *the men whored and drank* **use prostitutes;** archaic wench.

wicked ▶ **adjective 1** *wicked deeds* **evil,** sinful, immoral, wrong, morally wrong, wrongful, bad, iniquitous, corrupt, base, mean, vile; villainous, nefarious, erring, foul, monstrous, shocking, outrageous, atrocious, abominable, depraved, reprehensible, hateful, detestable, despicable, odious, contemptible, horrible, heinous, egregious, execrable, fiendish, vicious, murderous, black-hearted, barbarous; criminal, illicit, unlawful, illegal, lawless, felonious, dishonest, unscrupulous; Law malfeasant; informal crooked; dated dastardly.
ANTONYMS virtuous.
2 *the wind was wicked* **nasty,** harsh, formidable, unpleasant, foul, bad, disagreeable, irksome, troublesome, displeasing, uncomfortable, annoying, irritating, hateful, detestable.
ANTONYMS agreeable.
3 *a wicked sense of humor* **mischievous,** playful, naughty, impish, roguish, arch, puckish, cheeky.
4 informal *Sophie makes wicked cakes* See EXCELLENT.

wide ▶ **adjective 1** *a wide river* **broad,** extensive, spacious, vast, spread out.
ANTONYMS narrow.
2 *their eyes were wide with shock* **fully open,** dilated, gaping, staring, wide open.
ANTONYMS closed.
3 *a wide range of opinion* **comprehensive,** broad, extensive, diverse, full, ample, large, large-scale, wide-ranging, exhaustive, general, all-inclusive.
ANTONYMS limited, restricted.
4 *her shot was wide* **off target,** off the mark, inaccurate.
ANTONYMS on target.
▶ **adverb 1** *he opened his eyes wide* **fully,** to the fullest/furthest extent, as far/much as possible, all the way, completely.
2 *he shot wide* **off target,** inaccurately.
– PHRASES **wide open 1** *their mouths were wide open* **agape,** yawning, open wide, fully open.
2 *the championship is wide open* **undecided,** unpredictable, uncertain, unsure, in the balance, up in the air; informal anyone's/anybody's guess. **3** *they were* ***wide open to*** *attacks* **vulnerable to,** exposed to, unprotected from, undefended from, at risk of, in danger of.

wide-eyed ▶ **adjective 1** *the onlookers were wide-eyed as the spaceship descended* **surprised,** flabbergasted, amazed, astonished, astounded, stunned, staggered, goggle-eyed, pop-eyed, open-mouthed, dumbstruck; enthralled, fascinated, gripped.
2 *a wide-eyed youth in a wicked world* **innocent,** naive, impressionable, ingenuous, childlike, credulous, trusting, unquestioning, unsophisticated, gullible.

widen ▶ **verb 1** *a proposal to widen the highway* **broaden,** make/become wider, open up/out, expand, extend, enlarge.
2 *the organization must widen its support* **increase,** augment, boost, swell, enlarge.

widespread ▶ **adjective** *widespread starvation* **general,** extensive, universal, common, global, worldwide, international, omnipresent, ubiquitous, across the board, blanket, sweeping, wholesale; predominant, prevalent, rife, broad, rampant, pervasive.
ANTONYMS limited.

width ▶ **noun 1** *the width of the river* **breadth,** broadness, wideness, thickness, span, diameter, girth.
ANTONYMS length.
2 *the width of experience required* **range,** breadth, compass, scope, span, spectrum, scale, extent, extensiveness, comprehensiveness.
ANTONYMS narrowness.

wield ▶ verb **1** *he was wielding a sword* **brandish,** flourish, wave, swing; use, employ, handle.
2 *he has wielded power since 1972* **exercise,** exert, hold, maintain, command, control.

wife ▶ noun *after seventeen years, he was still madly in love with his wife* **spouse,** partner, life partner, mate, consort, woman, helpmate, helpmeet, bride; informal old lady, wifey, better half, other half, missus, ball and chain, significant other.

wild ▶ adjective **1** *wild animals* **untamed,** undomesticated, feral; fierce, ferocious, savage, untamable.
ANTONYMS tame.
2 *wild flowers* **uncultivated,** native, indigenous.
ANTONYMS cultivated.
3 *wild tribes* **primitive,** uncivilized, uncultured; savage, barbarous, barbaric.
ANTONYMS civilized.
4 *wild country* **uninhabited,** unpopulated, uncultivated; rugged, rough, inhospitable, desolate, barren.
5 *wild weather* **stormy,** squally, tempestuous, turbulent.
ANTONYMS calm.
6 *her wild black hair* **disheveled,** tousled, tangled, windswept, untidy, unkempt, mussed up.
ANTONYMS tidy.
7 *wild behavior* **uncontrolled,** unrestrained, out of control, undisciplined, unruly, rowdy, disorderly, riotous, corybantic.
ANTONYMS self-disciplined, disciplined.
8 *wild with excitement* **very excited,** delirious, in a frenzy; tumultuous, passionate, vehement, unrestrained.
ANTONYMS calm.
9 informal *I was wild with jealousy* **distraught,** frantic, beside oneself, in a frenzy, hysterical, deranged, berserk; informal mad, crazy.
10 informal *Hank went wild when he found out* See FURIOUS (sense 1).
11 informal *his family wasn't **wild about** me* **enamored of,** (very) enthusiastic about, (very) keen on, infatuated with, smitten with; informal crazy about, blown away by, mad about, nuts about.
ANTONYMS indifferent, unenthusiastic.
12 *Bill's wild schemes* **madcap,** ridiculous, ludicrous, foolish, rash, stupid, foolhardy, idiotic, absurd, silly, ill-considered, senseless, nonsensical; impractical, impracticable, unworkable; informal crazy, crackpot, cockeyed, harebrained, cockamamie, loopy.
ANTONYMS sensible, practical.
13 *a wild guess* **random,** arbitrary, haphazard, hit-or-miss, uninformed.
ANTONYMS considered.
– PHRASES **run wild 1** *the children are running wild* **run amok,** run riot, get out of control, be undisciplined. **2** *the garden had run wild* **grow unchecked,** grow profusely, run riot, ramble.

wilderness ▶ noun **1** *the Siberian wilderness* **wilds,** wastes, bush, bush country, bushland, inhospitable region; desert, backcountry, outback, great outdoors; informal boondocks, boonies.
2 *the urban wilderness* **wasteland,** no man's land; informal wilds.
▶ adjective *wilderness activities* **outdoor recreation,** ecotourism, adventure, backcountry.

will[1] ▶ verb *accidents will happen* **tend to,** have a tendency to, are bound to, do, are going to, must.

will[2] ▶ noun **1** *the will to succeed* **determination,** willpower, strength of character, resolution, resolve, resoluteness, single-mindedness, purposefulness, drive, commitment, dedication, doggedness, tenacity, tenaciousness, staying power.
2 *they stayed against their will* **desire,** wish, preference, inclination, intention, intent, volition.
3 *God's will* **wish,** desire, decision, choice; decree, command.
4 *the dead man's will* **testament,** last will and testament, bequest.
▶ verb **1** *do what you will* **want,** wish, please, see/think fit, think best, like, choose, prefer.
2 *God willed it* **decree,** order, ordain, command.
3 *she willed the money to her husband* **bequeath,** leave, hand down, pass on, settle on; Law devise.
– PHRASES **at will** *he thought he could walk in and out of my life at will* **as one pleases,** as one thinks fit, to suit oneself, at whim.

willful ▶ adjective **1** *willful destruction* **deliberate,** intentional, done on purpose, premeditated, planned, conscious.
ANTONYMS accidental, unintentional.
2 *a willful child* **headstrong,** strong-willed, obstinate, stubborn, pigheaded, recalcitrant, uncooperative, obstreperous, ungovernable, unmanageable; balky; formal refractory, contumacious.
ANTONYMS biddable, amenable.

willing ▶ adjective **1** *I'm willing to give it a try* **ready,** prepared, disposed, inclined, of a mind, minded; happy, glad, pleased, agreeable, amenable; informal game.
ANTONYMS reluctant, disinclined.
2 *willing help* **readily given,** willingly given, ungrudging, volunteered.
ANTONYMS grudging.

willingly ▶ adverb *I willingly agreed to make a donation* **voluntarily,** of one's own free will, of one's own accord; readily, without reluctance, ungrudgingly, cheerfully, happily, gladly, with pleasure.

willingness ▶ noun *we appreciate your willingness to help* **readiness,** inclination, will, wish, desire, alacrity.

willpower ▶ noun See WILL[2] (sense 1 of the noun).

wilt ▶ verb **1** *the roses had begun to wilt* **droop,** sag, become limp, flop; wither, shrivel (up).
ANTONYMS flourish, thrive.
2 *we wilted in the heat* **languish,** flag, droop, become listless, tire, wane.
ANTONYMS perk up.

wily ▶ adjective *a wily old rascal* **shrewd,** clever, sharp, sharp-witted, astute, canny, smart; crafty, cunning, artful, sly, scheming, calculating,

devious; informal clueful, tricky, foxy; archaic subtle.
ANTONYMS naive.

win ▶ **verb 1** *he won the race* **take,** be the victor in, be the winner of, come first in, take first prize in, triumph in, be successful in.
ANTONYMS lose.
2 *Claire knew he would win* **be the winner,** come in first, be victorious, carry the day, win the day, come out on top, succeed, triumph, prevail.
ANTONYMS lose.
3 *he won a cash prize* **secure,** gain, garner, collect, pick up, walk away/off with, carry off; informal land, net, bag, scoop.
4 *she won his heart* **captivate,** steal, snare, capture.
▶ **noun** *a 1–0 win* **victory,** triumph, conquest.
ANTONYMS defeat.
– PHRASES **win over** *do you really believe that flowers and jewelry are enough to win her over?* **persuade,** convince, sway, prevail on; seduce.

wince ▶ **verb** *he winced at the pain* **grimace,** make a face, flinch, blanch, start.
▶ **noun** *a wince of pain* **grimace,** flinch, start.

CHOOSE THE RIGHT WORD
wince, cower, cringe, flinch, recoil
The same individual might **wince** when receiving a flu shot, **flinch** from a difficult task, and **cower** in fear at the approach of a tornado. All of these verbs mean to draw back in alarm, disgust, faintheartedness, or servility, but there are subtle differences among them. To *wince* is to make a slight recoiling movement, often an involuntary contraction of the facial features, in response to pain or discomfort (*to wince when a singer misses a high note*), while *flinch* may imply a similar drawing-back motion or, more abstractly, a reluctance or avoidance (*to tackle the job without flinching*). *Cower* and **cringe** both refer to stooped postures, although *cower* is usually associated with fearful trembling (*he cowered in the doorway*) while *cringe* is usually linked to servile, cowardly, or fawning behavior (*she cringed before her father's authority*). More than any of the other verbs here, **recoil** suggests a physical movement away from something (*recoil at the sight of a poisonous snake*), although that movement may also be psychological (*recoil at the very thought of a family reunion*).

wind[1] ▶ **noun 1** *the trees were swaying in the wind* **breeze,** current of air; gale, hurricane; literary zephyr.
2 *Jez got his wind back* **breath.**
3 *the discomfort of holding back one's wind* **flatulence,** gas; informal fart(s), farting; formal flatus.
– PHRASES **get wind of** informal *White House officials got wind of the plan* **hear about/of,** learn about/of, find out about, pick up on, be told about/of, be informed of; informal hear (about) through the grapevine. **in the wind** *we fear that civil war is in the wind* **on the way,** coming, about to happen, in the offing, in the air, on the horizon, approaching, looming, brewing, afoot; informal in the cards.

wind[2] ▶ **verb 1** *this road winds dangerously* **twist and turn,** twist, bend, curve, loop, zigzag, weave, snake.
2 *she wound a towel around her waist* **wrap,** furl, entwine, lace, loop.
3 *he wound the yarn into a ball* **coil,** roll, twist, twine.
– PHRASES **wind down 1** informal *they needed to wind down* **relax,** unwind, calm down, cool down/off, ease up/off, take it easy, rest, put one's feet up; informal take a load off, hang loose, chill, chill out, kick back. **2** *the summer was winding down* **draw to a close,** come to an end, tail off, taper off, slack off, slacken off, slow down, die, die down. **wind up 1** *let's wind up this meeting and go to lunch* **conclude,** bring to an end/close, end, terminate; informal wrap up. **2** informal *I never thought that Jerry would wind up in real estate* **end up,** finish up, find oneself.

winded ▶ **adjective** *he is winded just from walking up the stairs* **out of breath,** breathless, gasping for breath, panting, hyperventilating; informal huffing and puffing.

windfall ▶ **noun** *the inheritance from Uncle Larry was an unexpected windfall* **bonanza,** jackpot, pennies from heaven, stroke/piece of luck, godsend, manna from heaven.

winding ▶ **noun** *the windings of the stream* **twist,** turn, turning, bend, loop, curve, zigzag, meander.
▶ **adjective** *the winding country roads* **twisting and turning,** meandering, windy, twisty, bending, curving, zigzag, zigzagging, serpentine, sinuous, snaking, tortuous; rare flexuous.
ANTONYMS straight.

window ▶ **noun** *there are two small windows on the south side* opening, aperture.

windy ▶ **adjective 1** *a windy day* **breezy,** blowy, blustery, gusty; wild, stormy, squally, tempestuous, boisterous.
ANTONYMS still.
2 *a windy hillside* **windswept,** exposed, open to the elements, bare, bleak.
ANTONYMS sheltered.

wing ▶ **noun 1** *a bird's wings* literary pinion.
2 *the east wing of the house* **part,** section, side; annex, extension, bump-out, ell.
3 *the radical wing of the party* **faction,** camp, arm, branch, group, section, set, coterie, cabal; side, end.
▶ **verb 1** *a seagull winged its way over the sea* **fly,** glide, soar.
2 *the bomb winged past* **hurtle,** speed, shoot, whiz, zoom, streak, fly.
3 *the hunter only winged the hawk* **wound,** graze, hit.
– PHRASES **wing it** informal *if you don't know all the words, just wing it* **improvise,** play it by ear, extemporize, ad lib, fly by the seat of one's pants, fake it.

wink ▶ **verb 1** *he winked an eye at her* **blink,** flutter, bat.
2 *the diamond winked in the moonlight* **sparkle,**

twinkle, flash, glitter, gleam, shine, scintillate.
– PHRASES **wink at** *too many people on the payroll were willing to wink at the corruption in high places* **turn a blind eye to,** close one's eyes to, ignore, overlook, disregard; connive at, condone, tolerate.

winner ▸ noun *the winners receive trophies at the closing ceremony* **victor,** champion, conqueror, vanquisher, hero; medalist; informal champ, top dog, world-beater.
ANTONYMS loser.

winning ▸ adjective **1** *the winning team* **victorious,** successful, triumphant, vanquishing, conquering; first, first-place, top, leading.
2 *a winning smile* **engaging,** charming, appealing, endearing, sweet, cute, winsome, attractive, pretty, prepossessing, fetching, lovely, lovable, adorable, delightful, disarming, captivating, bewitching.

winnings ▸ plural noun *he put all his winnings into a college fund* **prize money,** gains, prize, booty, spoils, loot; proceeds, profits, earnings, takings, purse.

winnow ▸ verb *the chaff is winnowed from the grain* **separate (out),** divide, segregate, sort out, sift out, filter out; isolate, narrow down; remove, get rid of.

wintry ▸ adjective **1** *wintry weather* **bleak,** cold, chilly, chill, frosty, freezing, icy, snowy, blizzardy, arctic, glacial, bitter, raw, hypothermic; informal nippy.
ANTONYMS summery, hot.
2 *a wintry smile* **unfriendly,** unwelcoming, cool, cold, frosty, frigid, dismal, cheerless.
ANTONYMS friendly, warm.

wipe ▸ verb **1** *Beth wiped the table* **rub,** mop, sponge, swab; clean, dry, polish, towel.
2 *he **wiped** the marks **off** the window* **rub off,** clean off, remove from, get rid of from, take off from, erase from, efface from.
3 *she wiped the memory from her mind* **obliterate,** expunge, erase, blot out.
▸ noun *he gave the table a wipe* **rub,** mop, sponge, swab; clean, polish.
– PHRASES **wipe out 1** *the influenza of 1918 wiped out entire families* **destroy,** annihilate, eradicate, eliminate; slaughter, massacre, kill, exterminate; demolish, raze to the ground; informal take out, zap, waste; literary slay.
2 *I wiped out the file accidentally* **erase,** delete, trash, zap, kill, nuke.

wiry ▸ adjective **1** *a wiry man* **sinewy,** athletic, strong; lean, spare, thin, stringy, skinny.
ANTONYMS flabby, frail.
2 *wiry hair* **coarse,** rough, stiff; curly, wavy.
ANTONYMS straight, smooth.

wisdom ▸ noun **1** *we questioned the wisdom of the decision* **sagacity,** intelligence, sense, common sense, shrewdness, astuteness, smartness, judiciousness, judgment, prudence, circumspection; logic, rationale, rationality, soundness, advisability.
ANTONYMS folly, stupidity.
2 *the wisdom of the East* **knowledge,** learning, erudition, sophistication, scholarship, philosophy; lore. See note at **KNOWLEDGE.**

wise ▸ adjective **1** *a wise old man* **sage,** sagacious, intelligent, clever, learned, knowledgeable, enlightened; astute, smart, shrewd, sharp-witted, canny, knowing; sensible, prudent, discerning, discriminating, sophisticated, judicious, perceptive, insightful, perspicacious; rational, logical, sound, sane; formal sapient.
ANTONYMS foolish.
2 *wise course of action* See **SENSIBLE.**
– PHRASES **wise to** informal *countless generations of local fishermen have been wise to these riptides* **aware of,** familiar with, acquainted with; formal cognizant of.

wisecrack ▸ noun informal *her parents were not amused by Lenny's wisecracks* **joke,** witticism, quip, jest, sally; pun, bon mot; informal crack, gag, funny, one-liner, zinger.

wish ▸ verb **1** *I **wished for** power* **desire,** want, hope for, covet, dream of, long for, yearn for, crave, hunger for, lust after; aspire to, be desirous of, set one's heart on, seek, fancy, hanker after; informal have a yen for, itch for.
2 *they can do as they wish* **want,** desire, feel inclined, feel like, care; choose, please, think fit.
3 *I wish you to send them a message* **want,** desire, require.
4 *I wished him farewell* **bid.**
▸ noun **1** *his wish to own a Mercedes* **desire,** longing, yearning, inclination, urge, whim, craving, hunger; hope, aspiration, aim, ambition, dream; informal hankering, yen, itch.
2 *her parents' wishes* **request,** requirement, bidding, instruction, direction, demand, entreaty, order, command; want, desire; will; literary behest.

wishy-washy ▸ adjective **1** *he's so wishy-washy* **feeble,** ineffectual, weak, vapid, effete, gutless, spineless, limp, namby-pamby, spiritless, indecisive, characterless; pathetic.
ANTONYMS strong, decisive.
2 *wishy-washy soup* **watery,** weak, thin; tasteless, flavorless, insipid.
ANTONYMS tasty.
3 *a wishy-washy color* **pale,** insipid, pallid, muted, pastel.
ANTONYMS vibrant.

wistful ▸ adjective *the old photos gave me a wistful feeling* **nostalgic,** yearning, longing; plaintive, regretful, rueful, melancholy, mournful, elegiac; pensive, reflective, contemplative.

wit ▸ noun **1** (**wits**) *he needed all his wits to escape* **intelligence,** shrewdness, astuteness, cleverness, canniness, sense, common sense, wisdom, sagacity, judgment, acumen, insight; brains, mind; informal gumption, savvy, horse sense, smarts, street smarts.
2 *my sparkling wit* **wittiness,** humor, funniness, drollery, esprit; repartee, badinage, banter, wordplay; jokes, witticisms, quips, puns.
3 *she's such a wit* **comedian,** humorist, comic, joker, jokester; informal wag, card, funnyman.

CHOOSE THE RIGHT WORD

wit, humor, irony, repartee, sarcasm, satire

If you're good at perceiving analogies between dissimilar things and expressing them in quick, sharp, spontaneous observations or remarks, you have **wit**. **Humor**, on the other hand, is the ability to perceive what is comical, ridiculous, or ludicrous in a situation or character, and to express it in a way that makes others see or feel the same thing. It suggests more sympathy, tolerance, and kindliness than *wit* (*she maintained a sense of humor in the midst of trying circumstances*). **Irony** is the implicit humor in the contradiction between what is meant and what is expressed, or in the discrepancy between appearance and reality. An example would be to shout, in the midst of a hurricane, "What a perfect day for a wedding!" Although **sarcasm** may take the form of irony, it is less subtle and is often used harshly or bitterly to wound or ridicule someone. Unlike irony, however, *sarcasm* depends on tone of voice for its effect (*"a fine friend you turned out to be!" he said, with obvious sarcasm*). **Satire** usually implies the use of sarcasm or irony for the purpose of ridicule or criticism, often directed at institutions or political figures (*she wrote political satire for the comedy team*). If you are good at making quick, witty replies, you will be known for your **repartee**, which is the art of responding pointedly and skillfully with wit or humor in a conversational exchange (*no one could compete with her witty repartee*).

witch ▶ **noun 1** *the witch cast a spell* **sorceress,** enchantress, necromancer; Wiccan; archaic pythoness.
2 informal *she's a nasty old witch* **hag,** crone, harpy, harridan, she-devil; informal battle-ax.

witchcraft ▶ **noun** *they've practiced witchcraft on this island for centuries* **sorcery,** black magic, white magic, magic, witching, witchery, wizardry; spells, incantations; Wicca; rare thaumaturgy.

withdraw ▶ **verb 1** *she withdrew her hand from his* **remove,** extract, pull out, take out; take back, take away.
ANTONYMS insert.
2 *the ban on advertising was withdrawn* **abolish,** cancel, lift, set aside, end, stop, remove, reverse, revoke, rescind, repeal, annul, void.
ANTONYMS introduce.
3 *she withdrew the allegation* **retract,** take back, go back on, recant, disavow, disclaim, repudiate, renounce, abjure; back down, climb down, backtrack, backpedal, do a U-turn, eat one's words.
ANTONYMS put forward.
4 *the troops **withdrew from** the city* **leave,** pull out of, evacuate, quit, (beat a) retreat from.
ANTONYMS enter.
5 *his partner **withdrew from** the project* **pull out of,** back out of, bow out of; get cold feet.
6 *they withdrew to their rooms* **retire,** retreat, adjourn, decamp; leave, depart, absent oneself; formal repair; dated remove; literary betake oneself.

withdrawal ▶ **noun 1** *the withdrawal of subsidies* **removal,** abolition, cancellation, discontinuation, termination, elimination.
2 *the withdrawal of the troops* **departure,** pullout, exit, exodus, evacuation, retreat.
3 *she's suffering the effects of withdrawal* **detoxification**; informal detox, (going) cold turkey.

withdrawn ▶ **adjective** *Kate has become so withdrawn since Lucius left for the Gulf* **introverted,** unsociable, inhibited, uncommunicative, unforthcoming, quiet, taciturn, reticent, reserved, retiring, private, reclusive; shy, timid; aloof, indrawn; informal standoffish.
ANTONYMS outgoing.

wither ▶ **verb 1** *the flowers withered in the sun* **shrivel (up),** dry up; wilt, droop, go limp, fade, perish; shrink, waste away, atrophy.
ANTONYMS thrive, flourish.
2 *her confidence withered* **diminish,** dwindle, shrink, lessen, fade, ebb, wane; evaporate, disappear.
ANTONYMS grow.

withhold ▶ **verb 1** *he withheld the information* **hold back,** keep back, refuse to give; retain, hold on to; hide, conceal, keep secret; informal sit on.
2 *she could not withhold her tears* **suppress,** repress, hold back, fight back, choke back, control, check, restrain, contain.

within ▶ **preposition 1** *within the prison walls* **inside,** in, enclosed by, surrounded by; within the bounds of, within the confines of.
ANTONYMS outside.
2 *within a few hours* **in less than,** in under, in no more than, after only.

without ▶ **preposition 1** *thousands were without food* **lacking,** short of, deprived of, in need of, wanting, needing, requiring.
2 *I don't want to go without you* **unaccompanied by,** unescorted by; in the absence of; informal sans, minus.

withstand ▶ **verb** *it was a miracle that they were able to withstand the brutal winter* **resist,** weather, survive, endure, cope with, stand, tolerate, bear, stomach, defy, brave, hold out against, tough out, bear up against; stand up to, face, confront.

witness ▶ **noun 1** *witnesses claimed that he started the fight* **observer,** onlooker, eyewitness, spectator, viewer, watcher; bystander, passerby.
2 *she cross-examined the witness* **deponent,** testifier.
▶ **verb 1** *who witnessed the incident?* **see,** observe, watch, view, notice, spot; be present at, attend; literary behold; informal get a look at.
2 *Canada witnessed a cultural explosion* **undergo,** experience, go through, see; enjoy; suffer.
3 *the will is correctly witnessed* **countersign,** sign, endorse, validate; notarize.
– PHRASES **bear witness to** *his diary bears witness to his lifelong struggle with depression* **attest to,** testify to, confirm, evidence, prove, verify, corroborate, substantiate; show, demonstrate, indicate, reveal, bespeak.

witticism ▶ **noun** *the publisher asked her to put some of her witticisms in a weekly feature* **joke,** quip, jest, pun, play on words, bon mot; informal one-liner, gag, funny, crack, wisecrack, zinger.

witty ▶ adjective *it was a pleasure to sit and listen to their witty conversations* **humorous,** amusing, droll, funny, comic, comical; jocular, facetious, waggish, tongue-in-cheek; sparkling, scintillating, entertaining; clever, quick-witted.

wizard ▶ noun 1 *the wizard cast a spell over them* **sorcerer,** warlock, magus, (black) magician, necromancer, enchanter; archaic mage.
2 *a financial wizard* **genius,** expert, master, virtuoso, maestro, marvel, Wunderkind, guru; informal hotshot, demon, whiz kid, buff, pro, ace; maven.

wizened ▶ adjective *their wizened faces said much about the hard lives they had endured* **wrinkled,** lined, creased, shriveled (up), withered, weather-beaten, shrunken, gnarled, aged.

wobble ▶ verb 1 *the table wobbled* **rock,** teeter, jiggle, sway, seesaw, shake.
2 *he wobbled across to the door* **teeter,** totter, stagger; lurch.
3 *her voice wobbled* **tremble,** shake, quiver, quaver, waver.
▶ noun 1 *she stood up with a wobble* **totter,** teeter, sway.
2 *the operatic wobble in her voice* **tremor,** quiver, quaver, trembling, vibrato.

woe ▶ noun 1 *a tale of woe* **misery,** sorrow, distress, wretchedness, sadness, unhappiness, heartache, heartbreak, despondency, despair, depression, regret, gloom, melancholy; adversity, misfortune, disaster, suffering, hardship; literary dolor.
ANTONYMS joy, happiness.
2 *financial woes* **trouble,** difficulty, problem, trial, tribulation, misfortune, setback, reverse.

woebegone ▶ adjective *we were not prepared to find Thom in such a woebegone condition* **sad,** unhappy, miserable, dejected, disconsolate, forlorn, crestfallen, downcast, glum, gloomy, doleful, downhearted, heavy-hearted, despondent, melancholy, sorrowful, mournful, woeful, plaintive, depressed, wretched, desolate; informal down in/at the mouth, down in the dumps, blue.
ANTONYMS cheerful.

woeful ▶ adjective 1 *her face was woeful* See **WOEBEGONE.**
2 *a woeful ballad* **tragic,** sad, miserable, cheerless, gloomy, sorry, pitiful, pathetic, traumatic, depressing, heartbreaking, heart-rending, tear-jerking, gut-wrenching.
ANTONYMS cheerful, uplifting.
3 *the team's woeful performance* **lamentable,** awful, terrible, atrocious, disgraceful, deplorable, shameful, hopeless, dreadful; substandard, poor, inadequate, inferior, unsatisfactory; informal rotten, appalling, crummy, pathetic, pitiful, lousy, abysmal, dire, crappy, lame, brutal.
ANTONYMS excellent.

wolf ▶ noun informal *he's a bit of a wolf* See **WOMANIZER.**
▶ verb *he **wolfed down** his breakfast* **devour,** gobble (up), guzzle, gulp down, bolt (down); informal put away, demolish, shovel in/down, scoff (down), scarf (up).

woman ▶ noun 1 *a woman got out of the car* **lady,** girl, female; matron; Scottish lass, lassie; informal chick, girlie, sister, dame, broad, gal; grrrl; literary maid, maiden, damsel; archaic wench, gentlewoman; (**women**) womenfolk.
2 *he found himself a new woman* **girlfriend,** sweetheart, partner, significant other, inamorata, lover, mistress; fiancée; wife, spouse; informal missus, better half, main squeeze, squeeze, babe, baby; dated lady friend, lady love.

womanish ▶ adjective *Andrew's first stage role was that of a womanish baker from Brooklyn* **effeminate,** girlish, girly, unmanly, unmasculine, epicene.
ANTONYMS manly.

womanizer ▶ noun informal *her friends tried to warn her about his reputation as a womanizer* **philanderer,** Don Juan, Casanova, Romeo, Lothario, playboy, ladies' man, flirt, seducer, rake, roué, lecher, libertine, debauchee; informal skirt-chaser, wolf, ladykiller, lech.

womankind ▶ noun *we are mindful of the plight of womankind throughout the world* **women**; woman, the female sex, womenkind, womanhood, womenfolk; informal the gentler sex.

womanly ▶ adjective 1 *womanly virtues* **feminine,** female; archaic feminal.
ANTONYMS masculine.
2 *her womanly figure* **voluptuous,** curvaceous, shapely, ample, buxom, full-figured; Junoesque, Rubenesque; informal curvy, busty.
ANTONYMS boyish.

wonder ▶ noun 1 *she was speechless with wonder* **awe,** admiration, wonderment, fascination; surprise, astonishment, stupefaction, amazement.
2 *the wonders of nature* **marvel,** miracle, phenomenon, sensation, spectacle, beauty; curiosity; informal humdinger.
▶ verb 1 *I wondered what was on her mind* **ponder,** think about, meditate on, reflect on, muse on, puzzle over, speculate about, conjecture; be curious about.
2 *people wondered at such bravery* **marvel,** be amazed, be astonished, stand in awe, be dumbfounded, gape, goggle; informal be flabbergasted.

wonderful ▶ adjective *a wonderful vacation in Europe* **marvelous,** magnificent, superb, glorious, sublime, lovely, delightful; informal super, great, fantastic, terrific, tremendous, sensational, incredible, fabulous, fab, out of this world, awesome, magic, wicked, far out, killer, brilliant, peachy, dandy, neat, swell.
ANTONYMS awful.

wont ▶ adjective *he was wont to arise at 5:30* **accustomed,** used, given, inclined.
▶ noun *Paul drove fast, as was his wont* **custom,** habit, way, practice, convention, rule.

woo ▶ verb dated 1 *Richard wooed Joan all through their college years* **romantically pursue,** pursue, chase (after); dated court, pay court to, romance, seek the hand of, set one's cap for/at, make love to.
2 *the party wooed voters with promises* **seek,** pursue, curry favor with, try to win, try to

attract, try to cultivate.
3 *an attempt to woo him out of retirement* **entice,** tempt, coax, persuade, wheedle; informal sweet-talk.

wood ▶ noun **1** *there should be enough wood left over to make a small shelf* **lumber,** timber, planks, planking; logs, sawlogs.
2 (usu. **woods**) *a walk through the woods* **forest,** woodland, trees; copse, coppice, grove, bush, woodlot.

wooded ▶ adjective *the wooded area behind the library* **forested,** treed, tree-covered, woody; literary sylvan.

wooden ▶ adjective **1** *a wooden door* **wood,** timber, woody; ligneous.
2 *his wooden posture* **stilted,** stiff, unnatural, awkward, leaden; dry, flat, stodgy, lifeless, passionless, spiritless, soulless.
3 *her face was wooden* **expressionless,** impassive, poker-faced, emotionless, blank, vacant, unresponsive.

woolgathering ▶ noun *lost in her daily woolgathering* **daydreaming,** reverie, dreaming, musing, abstraction, preoccupation; absentmindedness, forgetfulness.

woolly ▶ adjective **1** *a woolly hat* **woolen,** wool, fleecy.
2 *a sheep's woolly coat* **fleecy,** shaggy, hairy, fluffy, flocculent.
3 *woolly generalizations* **vague,** ill-defined, hazy, unclear, fuzzy, blurry, foggy, nebulous, imprecise, inexact, indefinite; confused, muddled.

word ▶ noun **1** *the Italian word for "ham"* **term,** name, expression, designation, locution, vocable; formal appellation.
2 *his words were meant kindly* **remark,** comment, observation, statement, utterance, pronouncement.
3 (**words**) *I've got three weeks to learn the words* **script,** lyrics, libretto.
4 *I give you my word* **promise,** word of honor, assurance, guarantee, undertaking; pledge, vow, oath, bond; formal troth.
5 *I want a word with you* **talk,** conversation, chat, tête-à-tête, heart-to-heart, one-to-one, man-to-man; discussion, consultation; informal confab, powwow; formal confabulation.
6 *there's no word from the hospital* **news,** information, communication, intelligence; message, report, communiqué, dispatch, bulletin; informal info, dope; literary tidings.
7 *word has it he's turned over a new leaf* **rumor,** hearsay, talk, gossip; informal the grapevine, the word on the street.
8 *I'm waiting for the word from HQ* **instruction,** order, command; signal, prompt, cue, tip-off; informal go-ahead, thumbs up, green light.
9 *Heather's word was law* **command,** order, decree, edict; bidding, will.
10 *our word now must be success* **motto,** watchword, slogan, catchword, buzzword.
▶ verb *the question was carefully worded* **phrase,** express, put, couch, frame, formulate, style; say, utter.
– PHRASES **have words** *we had words, and Jason walked out* **quarrel,** argue, disagree, squabble, bicker, fight, wrangle, dispute, fall out, clash, row. **in a word** *in a word, it was a miserable day for sailing* **briefly,** to be brief, in short, in a nutshell, to come to the point, to cut a long story short, not to put too fine a point on it; to sum up, to summarize, in summary. **word for word 1** *they took down the speeches word for word* **verbatim,** letter for letter, to the letter; exactly, faithfully. **2** *a word-for-word translation* **verbatim,** literal, exact, direct, accurate, faithful; unadulterated, unabridged.

wordy ▶ adjective *a wordy sermon* **long-winded,** verbose, prolix, lengthy, protracted, long-drawn-out, overlong, rambling, circumlocutory, periphrastic, pleonastic; loquacious, garrulous, voluble; informal windy.
ANTONYMS succinct.

work ▶ noun **1** *a day's work in the fields* **labor,** toil, slog, drudgery, exertion, effort, industry, service; informal grind, sweat, elbow grease; literary travail. See note at LABOR.
ANTONYMS leisure, rest.
2 *I'm looking for work* **employment,** a job, a position, a situation, a post; an occupation, a profession, a career, a vocation, a calling; wage labor; tasks, jobs, duties, assignments, projects; chores.
ANTONYMS unemployment, retirement.
3 *works of literature* **composition,** piece, creation; opus, oeuvre.
4 (**works**) *the complete works of Shakespeare* **writings,** oeuvre, canon, output.
5 *this is the work of a radical faction* **handiwork,** doing, act, deed.
6 (**works**) *a lifetime spent doing good works* **deeds,** acts, actions.
7 informal (**the works**) *for only $60 you can get the works* **everything,** the full treatment; informal the lot, the whole shebang, the full nine yards, the whole kit and caboodle, the whole ball of wax.
▶ verb **1** *staff worked late into the night* **toil,** labor, exert oneself, slave (away); keep at it, put one's nose to the grindstone; informal slog (away), plug away, put one's back into it, knock oneself out, sweat blood; literary travail.
ANTONYMS rest, play.
2 *he worked in education for years* **be employed,** have a job, earn one's living, do business.
3 *farmers worked the land* **cultivate,** farm, till, plow.
4 *his car was working perfectly* **function,** go, run, operate; informal behave.
5 *how do I work this machine?* **operate,** use, handle, control, manipulate, run.
6 *their ploy worked* **succeed,** work out, turn out well, go as planned, get results, be effective; informal come off, pay off, do/turn the trick.
ANTONYMS fail.
7 *makeup can work miracles* **bring about,** accomplish, achieve, produce, perform, create, engender, contrive, effect.
8 informal *can you **work it** so I can get in for free?* **arrange it/things,** manipulate it/things, contrive it; pull strings, fix it, swing it, wangle it.
9 *he worked the crowd into a frenzy* **stir (up),** excite, drive, move, rouse, fire, galvanize; whip up, agitate.
10 *work the mixture into a paste* **knead,**

squeeze, form; mix, stir, blend.
11 *he worked the blade into the padlock* **maneuver,** manipulate, guide, edge.
12 *her mouth worked furiously* **twitch,** quiver, convulse.
13 *he worked his way through the crowd* **maneuver,** make, thread, wind, weave, wend.
– PHRASES **work on** *leave Hank to me—I'll work on him* **persuade,** manipulate, influence; coax, cajole, wheedle, soften up, sweet-talk; informal twist someone's arm, lean on. **work out 1** *the bill works out to $50* **amount to,** add up to, come to, total. **2** *my idea worked out* See WORK (sense 6 of the verb). **3** *things didn't work out the way she planned* **end up,** turn out, go, come out, develop; happen, occur; informal pan out. **4** *he works out at the local gym* **exercise,** train. **5** *work out what you can afford* **calculate,** compute, determine, reckon (up). **6** *I'm trying to work out what she meant* **understand,** comprehend, sort out, make sense of, get to the bottom of, make head(s) or tail(s) of, unravel, decipher, decode, puzzle out; informal figure out. **7** *they worked out a plan* **devise,** formulate, draw up, put together, develop, construct, arrange, organize, contrive, concoct; hammer out, negotiate. **work up** *he couldn't work up any enthusiasm* **stimulate,** rouse, raise, arouse, awaken, excite.

workable ▶ adjective *a workable household budget* **practicable,** feasible, viable, possible, achievable; realistic, reasonable, sensible, practical; informal doable.
ANTONYMS impracticable.

workaday ▶ adjective *workaday prose | our workaday lives* **ordinary,** average, run-of-the-mill, middle-of-the-road, conventional, unremarkable, unexceptional, humdrum, undistinguished, commonplace, mundane, pedestrian; routine, everyday, day-to-day, garden-variety, standard; informal nothing to write home about, dime a dozen.
ANTONYMS exceptional.

worker ▶ noun **1** *a strike by 500 workers* **employee,** member of staff; workman, laborer, hand, operative, operator; proletarian; artisan, craftsman, craftswoman; wage earner, breadwinner.
2 informal *I have a reputation for being a worker* **hard worker,** toiler, workhorse; informal busy bee, eager beaver, workaholic, wheelhorse.

working ▶ adjective **1** *working mothers* **employed,** in (gainful) employment, in work, waged.
ANTONYMS unemployed, out of work.
2 *a working windmill* **functioning,** operating, running, active, operational, functional, serviceable; informal up and running.
ANTONYMS broken, faulty.
3 *a working knowledge of contract law* **sufficient,** adequate, viable; useful, effective.
▶ noun **1** *the working of a carburetor* **functioning,** operation, running, action, performance.
2 (**workings**) *the workings of a watch* **mechanism,** machinery, parts, movement, action, works; informal insides.

workmanship ▶ noun *the workmanship evidenced in these chairs is superb* **craftsmanship,** artistry, craft, art, artisanship, handiwork; skill, expertise, technique.

workout ▶ noun *cool down gradually after your workout* **exercise session,** training session, drill; warm-up; exercises, aerobics, isometrics, callisthenics.

workshop ▶ noun **1** *the craftsmen had a chilly workshop* **workroom,** studio, atelier; factory, plant.
2 *a workshop on combating stress* **study group,** discussion group, seminar, class; support group.

world ▶ noun **1** *he traveled the world* **earth,** globe, planet, sphere.
2 *life on other worlds* **planet,** moon, star, heavenly body, orb.
3 *the academic world* **sphere,** society, circle, arena, milieu, province, domain, orbit, preserve, realm, field, discipline, area, sector.
4 *she would show **the world** that she was strong* **everyone,** everybody, people, mankind, humankind, humanity, the (general) public, the population, the populace, all and sundry, 'every Tom, Dick, and Harry'.
5 *a world of difference* **huge amount,** good deal, great deal, abundance, wealth, profusion, mountain; informal heap, lot, load, ton.
6 *she renounced **the world*** **society,** material things, secular interests, temporal concerns, earthly concerns.
– PHRASES **on top of the world** informal *at age twenty, I was on top of the world* See OVERJOYED. **out of this world** informal *the scampi at Vinnie's is out of this world* See WONDERFUL.

worldly ▶ adjective **1** *his youth was wasted on worldly pursuits* **earthly,** terrestrial, temporal, mundane; mortal, human, material, materialistic, physical, carnal, fleshly, bodily, corporeal, sensual.
ANTONYMS spiritual.
2 *a worldly woman* **sophisticated,** experienced, worldly-wise, knowledgeable, knowing, enlightened, shrewd, mature, seasoned, cosmopolitan, streetwise, street-smart, urbane, cultivated, cultured.
ANTONYMS unsophisticated, naive.

worldwide ▶ adjective *a worldwide effort to combat AIDS* **global,** international, intercontinental, universal; ubiquitous, extensive, widespread, far-reaching, wide-ranging, all-embracing.
ANTONYMS local.

worn ▶ adjective **1** *his hat was worn* **shabby,** worn out, threadbare, tattered, in tatters, holey, falling to pieces, ragged, frayed, well-used, moth-eaten, scruffy, having seen better days; informal tatty, ratty, the worse for wear, raggedy, dog-eared.
ANTONYMS smart, new.
2 *her face looked worn* **worn-out.**

worried ▶ adjective *Father Douglas came to sit with the worried parents* **anxious,** perturbed, troubled, bothered, concerned, upset, distressed, distraught, disquieted, uneasy, fretful, agitated, nervous, edgy, on edge, tense, overwrought, worked up, keyed up, jumpy, stressed, strung out; apprehensive, fearful, afraid, frightened, scared; informal uptight, a bundle of nerves, on tenterhooks, jittery,

twitchy, in a stew, in a sweat, het up, rattled, antsy, squirrelly, trepidatious.
ANTONYMS carefree, unconcerned.

worry ▶ verb **1** *she worries about his health* **fret,** be concerned, be anxious, agonize, brood, panic, lose sleep, get worked up, get stressed, get in a state, stew, torment oneself.
2 *is something worrying you?* **trouble,** bother, make anxious, disturb, distress, upset, concern, disquiet, fret, agitate, unsettle, perturb, scare, fluster, stress, tax, torment, plague, bedevil; prey on one's mind, weigh down, gnaw at, rattle; informal bug, get to, dig at, nag.
▶ noun **1** *I'm beside myself with worry* **anxiety,** perturbation, distress, concern, uneasiness, unease, disquiet, fretfulness, restlessness, nervousness, nerves, agitation, edginess, tension, stress; apprehension, fear, dread, trepidation, misgiving, angst; informal butterflies (in the stomach), the willies, the heebie-jeebies.
2 *the rats are a worry* **problem,** cause for concern, issue; nuisance, pest, plague, trial, trouble, vexation, bane, bugbear; informal pain, pain in the neck, headache, hassle, stress.

worsen ▶ verb **1** *insomnia can worsen a patient's distress* **aggravate,** exacerbate, compound, add to, intensify, increase, magnify, heighten, inflame, augment; informal add fuel to the fire of.
ANTONYMS improve.
2 *the recession worsened* **deteriorate,** degenerate, decline, regress; informal go downhill, go to pot, go to the dogs, hit the skids, nosedive.
ANTONYMS improve, recover.

worship ▶ noun **1** *the worship of idols* **reverence,** veneration, adoration, glorification, glory, exaltation; devotion, praise, thanksgiving, homage, honor; archaic magnification.
2 *morning worship* **service,** religious rite, prayer, praise, devotion, religious observance.
3 *he contemplated her with worship* **admiration,** adulation, idolization, lionization, hero-worship.
▶ verb *they worship pagan gods* **revere,** reverence, venerate, pay homage to, honor, adore, praise, pray to, glorify, exalt, extol; hold dear, cherish, treasure, esteem, adulate, idolize, deify, hero-worship, lionize; follow, look up to; informal put on a pedestal; formal laud; archaic magnify. See note at **REVERE**.

worst ▶ verb *they were worsted by the Czechs in the first round* **defeat,** beat, prevail over, triumph over, trounce, rout, vanquish, conquer, master, overcome, overwhelm, overpower, crush; outdo, outclass, outstrip, surpass; informal thrash, smash, lick, best, clobber, drub, slaughter, murder, wipe out, crucify, demolish, wipe the floor with, take to the cleaners, walk all over, make mincemeat of, shellac, cream, whup.

worth ▶ noun **1** *evidence of the rug's worth* **value,** price, cost; valuation, quotation, estimate.
2 *the intrinsic worth of education* **benefit,** advantage, use, value, virtue, utility, service, profit, help, aid; desirability, appeal; significance, sense; informal mileage, percentage; archaic behoof.
3 *a sense of personal worth* **worthiness,** merit, value, excellence, caliber, quality, stature, eminence, consequence, importance, significance, distinction.

worthless ▶ adjective **1** *the item was worthless* **valueless**; poor quality, inferior, second-rate, third-rate, low-grade, cheap, shoddy, tawdry, cheesy; informal crummy, nickel-and-dime.
ANTONYMS valuable, precious.
2 *his conclusions are worthless* **useless,** (of) no use, ineffective, ineffectual, fruitless, unproductive, unavailing, pointless, nugatory, valueless, inadequate, deficient, meaningless, senseless, insubstantial, empty, hollow, trifling, petty, inconsequential, lame, paltry, pathetic, no-account.
ANTONYMS useful.
3 *his worthless son* **good-for-nothing,** ne'er-do-well, useless, despicable, contemptible, low, ignominious, corrupt, villainous, degenerate, shiftless, feckless; informal no-good, lousy, no-account.

worthwhile ▶ adjective *a worthwhile expenditure of time* **valuable,** useful, of use, of service, beneficial, rewarding, advantageous, positive, helpful, profitable, gainful, fruitful, productive, lucrative, constructive, effective, effectual, meaningful, worthy.

worthy ▶ adjective *a worthy citizen* **virtuous,** righteous, good, moral, ethical, upright, upstanding, high-minded, principled, exemplary; law-abiding, irreproachable, blameless, guiltless, unimpeachable, honest, honorable, reputable, decent, respectable, noble, meritorious; pure, saintly, angelic; informal squeaky clean.
ANTONYMS disreputable.
▶ noun *local worthies* **dignitary,** personage, VIP, notable, notability, pillar of society, luminary, leading light, big name, grandee; informal heavyweight, bigwig, top dog, big shot, big cheese, big wheel, big kahuna.
ANTONYMS nobody.
– PHRASES **be worthy of** *your opinions are worthy of our consideration* **deserve,** merit, warrant, rate, justify, earn, be entitled to, qualify for.

wound ▶ noun **1** *a chest wound* **injury,** lesion, cut, gash, laceration, tear, slash; graze, scratch, abrasion; bruise, contusion; Medicine trauma.
2 *the wounds inflicted by the media* **insult,** blow, slight, offense, affront; hurt, damage, injury, pain, distress, grief, anguish, torment.
▶ verb **1** *he was critically wounded* **injure,** hurt, harm; maim, mutilate, disable, incapacitate, cripple; lacerate, cut, graze, gash, stab, slash.
2 *her words had wounded him* **hurt,** scar, damage, injure; insult, slight, offend, affront, distress, disturb, upset, trouble; grieve, sadden, pain, cut, sting, shock, traumatize, torment.

wraith ▶ noun *from a gray and billowy fog the wraith did appear* **ghost,** specter, spirit, phantom, apparition, manifestation; informal spook; literary shade, phantasm.

wrangle ▶ noun *a wrangle over money* **argument,** dispute, disagreement, quarrel, falling-out, fight, squabble, turf war, altercation, war of words, shouting match, tiff, tug-of-war; informal set-to, run-in, row. See note at **QUARREL**.
▶ verb *we wrangled over the details* **argue,** quarrel,

bicker, squabble, fall out, have words, disagree, be at odds, fight, battle, feud, clash; informal scrap.

wrap ▶ verb **1** *she wrapped herself in a towel* **swathe,** bundle, swaddle, muffle, cloak, enfold, envelop, encase, cover, fold, wind.
2 *I wrapped the vase carefully* **package,** pack, pack up, bundle, bundle up; gift-wrap.
▶ noun *he put a wrap around her* **shawl,** stole, cloak, cape, mantle, scarf, poncho, serape, pelisse.
– PHRASES **wrap up** *wrap up well—it's cold* **dress warmly,** bundle up. **wrap something up** informal *our objective is to wrap up the Pendleton case by the end of the month* **conclude,** finish, end, wind up, terminate, stop, cease, finalize, complete, tie up; informal sew up.

wrapper ▶ noun *a candy wrapper* **wrapping,** wrap, packaging, paper, cover, covering; jacket, sheath.

wrath ▶ noun *I refuse to subject myself any longer to her wrath* **anger,** rage, fury, outrage, spleen, vexation, (high) dudgeon, crossness, displeasure, annoyance, irritation; literary ire, choler.
ANTONYMS happiness.

wreath ▶ noun *a wreath of dried flowers* **garland,** circlet, chaplet, crown, festoon, lei; ring, loop, circle.

wreathe ▶ verb **1** *a pulpit wreathed in holly* **festoon,** garland, drape, cover, bedeck, deck, decorate, ornament, adorn.
2 *blue smoke wreathed upward* **spiral,** coil, loop, wind, curl, twist, snake, curve.

wreck ▶ noun **1** *salvage teams landed on the wreck* **shipwreck,** sunken ship, derelict; shell, hull; wreckage.
2 *the wreck of a stolen car* **wreckage,** debris, remainder, ruins, remains.
▶ verb **1** *he had wrecked her car* **demolish,** crash, smash up, damage, destroy; vandalize, deface, desecrate; informal trash, total.
2 *his ship was wrecked* **shipwreck,** sink, capsize, run aground.
3 *the crisis wrecked his plans* **ruin,** spoil, disrupt, undo, put a stop to, frustrate, blight, crush, quash, dash, destroy, scotch, shatter, devastate, sabotage; informal mess up, screw up, foul up, put paid to, scupper, scuttle, stymie, put the kibosh on, nix.

wreckage ▶ noun See WRECK (sense 1 of the noun), WRECK (sense 2 of the noun).

wrench ▶ noun **1** *she felt a wrench on her shoulders* **tug,** pull, jerk, jolt, heave; informal yank.
2 *hold the piston with a wrench* monkey wrench.
3 *leaving was an immense wrench* **traumatic event,** painful parting; pang, trauma.
▶ verb **1** *he wrenched the gun from her hand* **tug,** pull, jerk, wrest, heave, twist, pluck, grab, seize, snatch, force, pry, jimmy; informal yank.
2 *she wrenched her ankle* **sprain,** twist, turn, strain, pull; injure, hurt.

wrest ▶ verb *he wrested the broom from Angela's grasp* **wrench,** snatch, seize, grab, pry, pluck, tug, pull, jerk, dislodge, remove; informal yank.

wrestle ▶ verb *words were exchanged, and then they began wrestling* | *she wrestled with her conscience* **grapple,** fight, struggle, contend, vie, battle, wrangle; scuffle, tussle, brawl; informal scrap, wrassle, rassle.

wretch ▶ noun **1** *the wretches killed themselves* **poor creature,** poor soul, poor thing, poor unfortunate; informal poor devil.
2 *I wouldn't trust the old wretch* **scoundrel,** villain, ruffian, rogue, rascal, reprobate, criminal, miscreant, good-for-nothing; informal heel, creep, louse, rat, swine, dog, lowlife, scumbag, scumbucket, scuzzball, sleazeball, sleazebag; informal archaic blackguard, picaroon.

wretched ▶ adjective **1** *I felt so wretched without you* **miserable,** unhappy, sad, heartbroken, grief-stricken, sorrowful, sorry for oneself, distressed, desolate, devastated, despairing, disconsolate, downcast, dejected, crestfallen, cheerless, depressed, melancholy, morose, gloomy, mournful, doleful, dismal, forlorn, woebegone; informal blue; literary dolorous.
ANTONYMS cheerful.
2 *I feel wretched* **ill,** unwell, poorly, sick, below par; informal under the weather, out of sorts.
ANTONYMS well.
3 *their living conditions are wretched* **harsh,** hard, grim, stark, difficult; poor, impoverished; pitiful, pathetic, miserable, cheerless, sordid, shabby, seedy, unhealthy, insalubrious, dilapidated; informal scummy.
ANTONYMS comfortable, luxurious.
4 *the wretched dweller in the shantytown* **unfortunate,** unlucky, luckless, ill-starred, blighted, hapless, poor, pitiable, downtrodden, oppressed; literary star-crossed.
ANTONYMS cheerful, well, comfortable, fortunate, excellent.
5 *he's a wretched coward* **despicable,** contemptible, reprehensible, base, vile, loathsome, hateful, detestable, odious, ignoble, shameful, shabby, worthless; informal dirty, rotten, lowdown, lousy.
ANTONYMS fortunate.
6 *wretched weather* **terrible,** awful, dire, atrocious, dreadful, bad, poor, lamentable, deplorable; informal godawful.
ANTONYMS excellent.
7 *I don't want the wretched money* informal **damn,** damned, blessed, cursed, flaming, confounded, rotten, blasted, bloody.

wriggle ▶ verb **1** *she tried to hug him but he wriggled* **squirm,** writhe, wiggle, jiggle, jerk, thresh, flounder, flail, twitch, twist and turn; snake, worm, slither.
2 *he* ***wriggled out of*** *his responsibilities* **avoid,** shirk, dodge, evade, elude, sidestep; escape from; informal duck.

wring ▶ verb **1** ***wring out*** *the clothes* **twist,** squeeze, screw, scrunch, knead, press, mangle.
2 *concessions were wrung from the government* **extract,** elicit, force, exact, wrest, wrench, squeeze, milk; informal bleed.
3 *his expression wrung her heart* **rend,** tear at, harrow, pierce, stab, wound, rack; distress, pain, hurt.

wrinkle ▶ noun **1** *fine wrinkles around her mouth* **crease,** fold, pucker, line, crinkle, furrow, ridge, groove; informal crow's feet, laugh line.
2 *the project has some wrinkles to iron out* **difficulty,** snag, hitch, drawback, imperfection, problem.

▶ verb *his coattails **wrinkled up*** **crease,** pucker, gather, crinkle, crimp, crumple, rumple, scrunch up.

writ ▶ noun *they were served with a writ* **summons,** subpoena, warrant, arraignment, indictment, citation, court order.

write ▶ verb **1** *he wrote her name in the book* **put in writing,** write down, jot down, put down, note, take down, record, register, log, list; inscribe, sign, scribble, scrawl, pencil.
2 *Jacqueline wrote a poem* **compose,** draft, think up, formulate, compile, pen, dash off, produce.
3 *he had her address and promised to write* **correspond,** write a letter, communicate, get/stay in touch, keep in contact, email; informal drop someone a line.
– PHRASES **write off 1** *they have had to write off loans* **forget about,** disregard, give up on, cancel, annul. **2** *she wrote off the cost of the computer* **deduct,** claim. **3** *who would write off a player of his stature?* **disregard,** dismiss, ignore.

writer ▶ noun *my favorite American writer* **author,** wordsmith, man/woman of letters, penman; novelist, essayist, biographer; journalist, columnist, correspondent; scriptwriter, playwright, dramatist, dramaturge, tragedian; poet; informal scribbler, scribe, hack.

writhe ▶ verb *she writhed about in pain* **squirm,** wriggle, thrash, flail, toss, toss and turn, twist, twist and turn, struggle.

writing ▶ noun **1** *I can't read his writing* **handwriting,** script, print, hand; penmanship, calligraphy, chirography; informal scribble, scrawl, chicken scratch.
2 (**writings**) *the writings of Woodrow Wilson* **works,** compositions, books, publications, oeuvre; papers, articles, essays.

wrong ▶ adjective **1** *the wrong answer* **incorrect,** mistaken, in error, erroneous, inaccurate, inexact, imprecise, fallacious, wide of the mark, off target, unsound, faulty; informal out.
ANTONYMS right, correct.
2 *he knew he had said the wrong thing* **inappropriate,** unsuitable, inapt, inapposite, undesirable; ill-advised, ill-considered, ill-judged, impolitic, injudicious, infelicitous, unfitting, out of keeping, improper; informal out of order.
ANTONYMS appropriate.
3 *I've done nothing wrong* **illegal,** unlawful, illicit, criminal, dishonest, dishonorable, corrupt; unethical, immoral, bad, wicked, sinful, iniquitous, nefarious, blameworthy, reprehensible; informal crooked.
ANTONYMS ethical, legal.
4 *there's something wrong with the engine* **amiss,** awry, out of order, not right, faulty, flawed, defective.
▶ adverb *she guessed wrong* **incorrectly,** wrongly, inaccurately, erroneously, mistakenly, in error.
▶ noun **1** *the difference between right and wrong* **immorality,** sin, sinfulness, wickedness, evil; unlawfulness, crime, corruption, villainy, dishonesty, injustice, wrongdoing, misconduct, transgression.
ANTONYMS right, virtue.
2 *an attempt to make up for past wrongs* **misdeed,** offense, injury, crime, transgression, violation, peccadillo, sin; injustice, outrage, atrocity; Law tort; archaic trespass.
▶ verb **1** *she was determined to forget the man who had wronged her* **ill-use,** mistreat, do an injustice to, do wrong to, ill-treat, abuse, harm, hurt, injure.
2 *perhaps I am wronging him* **malign,** misrepresent, do a disservice to, impugn, defame, slander, libel.
– PHRASES **get wrong** *don't get me wrong, I usually like Italian food* **misunderstand,** misinterpret, misconstrue, mistake, misread, take amiss; get the wrong idea/impression; informal be barking up the wrong tree. **go wrong 1** *I've gone wrong somewhere* **make a mistake,** make an error, make a blunder, blunder, miscalculate, trip up; informal slip up, goof, screw up, make a boo-boo, fluff, flub. **2** *their plans went wrong* **go awry,** go amiss, go off course, fail, be unsuccessful, fall through, come to nothing; backfire, misfire, rebound; informal come to grief, come a cropper, go up in smoke, go adrift. **3** *the radio's gone wrong* **break down,** malfunction, fail, stop working, crash, give out; informal be on the blink, conk out, go kaput, go on the fritz. **in the wrong** *just admit that you're in the wrong* **to blame,** blameworthy, at fault, reprehensible, responsible, culpable, answerable, guilty; archaic peccant.

wrongdoer ▶ noun *the wrongdoers in our neighborhood were essentially harmless until the Hanovers moved in* **offender,** lawbreaker, criminal, felon, delinquent, villain, culprit, evildoer, sinner, transgressor, malefactor, miscreant, rogue, scoundrel; informal crook; Law malfeasant; archaic trespasser.

wrongful ▶ adjective *a wrongful arrest* **unjustified,** unwarranted, unjust, unfair, undue, undeserved, unreasonable, groundless, indefensible, inappropriate, improper, unlawful, illegal, illegitimate.
ANTONYMS rightful, fair.

wry ▶ adjective **1** *his wry humor* **ironic,** sardonic, satirical, mocking, sarcastic; dry, droll, witty, humorous.
2 *a wry expression* **unimpressed,** displeased, annoyed, irritated, irked, vexed, piqued, disgruntled, dissatisfied; informal peeved.

Xx

X-ray ▶ **noun** *the X-ray shows a clean break* **radiograph,** radiogram, X-ray image/picture/photograph, roentgenogram.

Yy

yank ▶ verb informal *give the rope a quick yank* **jerk,** pull, tug, wrench; snatch, seize.

yap ▶ verb **1** *the dogs yapped at his heels* **bark,** woof, yelp, yip.
2 informal *what are they yapping about now?* See BABBLE (sense 1 of the verb).

yardstick ▶ noun *many of the financial yardsticks known to our grandparents are simply not appropriate for today's investors* **standard,** measure, gauge, scale, guide, guideline, indicator, test, touchstone, barometer, criterion, benchmark, point of reference, model, pattern, template.

yarn ▶ noun **1** *you need to use a fine yarn* **thread,** cotton, wool, fiber, filament; ply.
2 informal *a far-fetched yarn* **story,** tale, anecdote, saga, narrative; informal tall tale, tall story, fish story, cock-and-bull story, shaggy-dog story, spiel.

yawning ▶ adjective *a yawning hole where the door once was* **gaping,** wide open, wide, cavernous, deep; huge, great, big.

year ▶ noun *he held the office for one year* **twelve-month period,** twelve-month session, annum; calendar year, fiscal year, FY; archaic twelvemonth.
– PHRASES **year in, year out** *we hear the same excuses, year in, year out* **repeatedly,** again and again, time and (time) again, time after time, over and over (again); 'week in, week out', 'day in, day out', inexorably, recurrently; continuously, continually, constantly, nonstop, habitually, regularly, without a break, unfailingly, always.

yearly ▶ adjective *a yearly payment* **annual,** once a year, every year, each year, per annum.
▶ adverb *the guide is published yearly* **annually,** once a year, per annum, by the year, every year, each year.

yearn ▶ verb *he* ***yearned for*** *a second chance* **long for,** pine for, crave, desire, want, wish for, hanker for, covet, lust after/for, pant for, hunger for, burn for, thirst for, ache for, eat one's heart out for, have one's heart set on; informal have a yen for, itch for.

yearning ▶ noun *a yearning for the mountains* **longing,** craving, desire, want, wish, hankering, urge, hunger, thirst, appetite, lust, ache; informal yen, itch.

yell ▶ verb *he yelled in agony* **cry out,** call out, shout, howl, yowl, wail, scream, shriek, screech, yelp, squeal; roar, bawl; informal holler.
▶ noun *a yell of rage* **cry,** shout, howl, yowl, scream, shriek, screech, yelp, squeal; roar; informal holler.

yen ▶ noun informal *I've got a yen for chocolate cake* **hankering,** yearning, longing, craving, urge, desire, want, wish, hunger, thirst, lust, appetite, ache; fancy, inclination; informal itch.

yes ▶ exclamation *yes, I'll come to your party* **all right,** very well, of course, by all means, sure, certainly, absolutely, indeed, right, affirmative, in the affirmative, agreed, roger; Nautical aye aye; informal yeah, yep, yup, ya, uh-huh, okay, OK, okey-dokey, okey-doke; archaic yea, aye.
ANTONYMS no.

yet ▶ adverb **1** *he hasn't made up his mind yet* **so far,** thus far, as yet, up till/to now, until now.
2 *don't celebrate just yet* **now,** right now, at this time; already, so soon.
3 *he was doing nothing, yet he appeared purposeful* **nevertheless,** nonetheless, even so, but, however, still, notwithstanding, despite that, in spite of that, for all that, all the same, just the same, at the same time, be that as it may; archaic natheless.
4 *he supplied yet more unsolicited advice* **even,** still, further, in addition, additionally, besides, into the bargain, to boot, on top (of that).

yield ▶ verb **1** *too many projects yield poor returns* **produce,** bear, give, supply, provide, afford, return, bring in, earn, realize, generate, deliver, offer, pay out; informal rake in.
2 *the nobility yielded power to the capitalists* **relinquish,** surrender, cede, remit, part with, hand over; make over, bequeath, leave. See note at RELINQUISH.
ANTONYMS withhold, retain.
3 *the duke was forced to yield* **surrender,** capitulate, submit, relent, admit defeat, back down, climb down, give in, give up the struggle, lay down one's arms, raise/show the white flag; informal throw in the towel, cave in.
4 *he* ***yielded to*** *her demands* **give in to,** give way to, submit to, bow down to, comply with, agree to, consent to, go along with; grant, permit, allow; informal cave in to; formal accede to.
ANTONYMS resist, defy.
5 *the floorboards yielded underfoot* **bend,** give, give way.
▶ noun *risky investments usually have higher yields* **profit,** gain, return, dividend, earnings.

yoke ▶ noun **1** *the horses were loosened from the yoke* **harness,** collar, coupling.
2 *countries struggling under the yoke of imperialism* **tyranny,** oppression, domination, hegemony, enslavement, servitude, subjugation, subjection, bondage, thrall; bonds, chains, fetters, shackles.

3 *the yoke of marriage* **bond,** tie, connection, link.

▶ **verb 1** *a pair of oxen were yoked together* **harness,** hitch, couple, tether, fasten, attach, join.

2 *their aim of yoking biology and mechanics* **unite,** join, marry, link, connect; tie, bind, bond.

yokel ▶ **noun** *unless you want trouble, don't mess with the local yokels* **bumpkin,** peasant, provincial, rustic, country cousin, countryman, countrywoman; informal hayseed, hillbilly, hick, rube, clodhopper, yahoo.

young ▶ **adjective 1** *young people* **youthful,** juvenile; junior, adolescent, teenage; in the springtime of life, in one's salad days.
ANTONYMS old, elderly, mature.

2 *she's very young for her age* **immature,** childish, inexperienced, unsophisticated, naive, unworldly; informal wet behind the ears.
ANTONYMS old, elderly, mature.

3 *the young microbrewery industry* **fledgling,** developing, budding, in its infancy, emerging.
ANTONYMS old, elderly, mature.

▶ **noun 1** *a robin feeding its young* **offspring,** progeny, family, babies.

2 (**the young**) *the young don't care nowadays* **young people,** children, boys and girls, youngsters, youth, the younger generation, juveniles, minors; informal young 'uns, kids.

youngster ▶ **noun** *a new magazine for youngsters* **child,** teenager, adolescent, youth, juvenile, minor, junior; boy, girl; lass, lad; whippersnapper, stripling; informal kid, young 'un, teen.

youth ▶ **noun 1** *he had been a keen sportsman in his youth* **early years,** young days, salad days, teens, teenage years, adolescence, boyhood, girlhood, childhood; minority; formal juvenescence.
ANTONYMS adulthood, old age.

2 *she had kept her youth and beauty* **youthfulness,** freshness, bloom, vigor, energy.
ANTONYMS maturity.

3 *local youths* **young person/man/woman,** boy, girl, juvenile, teenager, adolescent, junior, minor; informal teen, kid.

4 *the youth of the nation* **young people,** young, younger generation, next generation.
ANTONYMS elderly.

youthful ▶ **adjective** *a youthful new leader* **young-looking,** spry, sprightly, vigorous, active; young, boyish, girlish; fresh-faced, in the springtime of life, in one's salad days.
ANTONYMS old, elderly.

CHOOSE THE RIGHT WORD

youthful, adolescent, callow, immature, juvenile, puerile

Everyone wants to look **youthful**, an adjective that means possessing, or appearing to possess, the qualities associated with youth (*a youthful enthusiasm for the job*). But no one wants to be called **immature**, which means childish or emotionally underdeveloped and usually pertains to behavior and attitudes rather than to physical appearance (*still immature despite the fact that he was almost thirty*). **Juvenile** suggests immaturity of mind or body and is applied especially to things that are designed for boys and girls in their early teens (*juvenile books*), while **adolescent** applies to the period between puberty and maturity and suggests the physical awkwardness and emotional instability associated with the teenage years (*an adolescent response to criticism*). Young men in particular are often described as **callow**, which means immature in terms of experience (*a callow youth who had never lived away from his family*). Of all these words, **puerile** is probably the most insulting, because it is so often used to describe adults who display the immature behavior of a child (*a puerile piece of writing; a puerile revolt against his aging parents*).

Zz

zany ▶ **adjective** *the zany humor of the Marx Brothers* **eccentric,** peculiar, odd, unconventional, strange, bizarre, weird; mad, crazy, comic, madcap, funny, quirky, idiosyncratic; informal wacky, screwy, nutty, oddball, off the wall; daft; kooky, wacko, bizarro.
ANTONYMS conventional, sensible.

zap ▶ **verb** informal **1** *they were zapped by antiradar missiles* See DESTROY (sense 5).
2 *race cars zapped past* See SPEED (sense 1 of the verb).
3 *she zapped a chicken burger for lunch* **nuke,** microwave.

zeal ▶ **noun** *Ross's zeal for football* **passion,** ardor, love, fervor, fire, avidity, devotion, enthusiasm, eagerness, keenness, appetite, relish, gusto, vigor, energy, intensity; fanaticism.
ANTONYMS apathy, indifference.

zealot ▶ **noun** *York was too much of a zealot for the party to endorse seriously* **fanatic,** enthusiast, extremist, radical, young Turk, diehard, true believer, activist, militant; bigot, dogmatist, sectarian, partisan; informal fiend, maniac, ultra, nut; eager beaver.

> CHOOSE THE RIGHT WORD
>
> **zealot, bigot, enthusiast, extremist, fanatic**
>
> An **enthusiast** displays an intense and eager interest in something (*a skydiving enthusiast*). A **fanatic** is not only intense and eager but possibly irrational in his or her enthusiasm; *fanatic* suggests extreme devotion and a willingness to go to any length to maintain or carry out one's beliefs (*a fly-fishing fanatic who hired a helicopter to reach his favorite stream*). A **zealot** exhibits not only extreme devotion but vehement activity in support of a cause or goal (*a feminist zealot who spent most of her time campaigning for women's rights*). An **extremist** is a supporter of extreme doctrines or practices, particularly in a political context (*a paramilitary extremist who anticipated the overthrow of the government*). But it is the **bigot** who causes the most trouble, exhibiting obstinate and often blind devotion to his or her beliefs and opinions. In contrast to *fanatic* and *zealot*, the term *bigot* implies intolerance and contempt for those who do not agree (*a bigot who could not accept his daughter's decision to marry outside her religion*).

zealous ▶ **adjective** *a zealous worker* **fervent,** ardent, fervid, fanatical, passionate, impassioned, devout, devoted, committed, dedicated, hard-core, enthusiastic, eager, keen, overkeen, avid, card-carrying, vigorous, energetic, intense, fierce; literary perfervid. See note at EAGER.
ANTONYMS apathetic, indifferent.

zenith ▶ **noun** *at the zenith of his power | the view from the mountain's zenith* **highest point,** high point, crowning point, height, top, acme, peak, pinnacle, apex, apogee, crown, crest, summit, climax, culmination, prime, meridian.
ANTONYMS nadir.

zero ▶ **noun** *I rated my chances at zero* **nothing,** nothing at all, nil, none, naught/nought; informal zilch, nix, zip, nada, diddly-squat.
– PHRASES **zero in on** *each study group will zero in on a different aspect of the ecosystem* **focus on,** focus attention on, center on, concentrate on, home in on, fix on, pinpoint, highlight, spotlight; informal zoom in on.

zero hour ▶ **noun** *as zero hour approached, thirty ships swung into position* **the appointed time,** the critical moment, the moment of truth, the point/moment of decision, the Rubicon, the crux; informal the crunch.

zest ▶ **noun** **1** *she had a great zest for life* **enthusiasm,** gusto, relish, appetite, eagerness, keenness, avidity, zeal, fervor, ardor, passion; verve, vigor, liveliness, sparkle, fire, animation, vitality, dynamism, energy, brio, pep, spirit, exuberance, high spirits, joie de vivre; informal zing, zip, oomph, vim, pizzazz, get-up-and-go.
ANTONYMS apathy, indifference.
2 *the lemon pepper and cilantro will add zest to the sauce | he wanted to put some zest to his life* **piquancy,** tang, flavor, savor, taste, spice, spiciness, relish, bite; excitement, interest, an edge; informal kick, punch, zing, oomph.
ANTONYMS blandness.
3 *the grated zest of an orange* **rind,** peel, skin.

zing ▶ **noun** informal See ZEST (sense 1).

zip informal ▶ **noun** *he's full of zip* See ENERGY.
▶ **verb** *I zipped along the highway* See SPEED (sense 1 of the verb).

zone ▶ **noun** *the search continued in the zone south of the river* **area,** sector, section, belt, stretch, region, territory, district, quarter, precinct, locality, neighborhood, province.

zoom ▶ **verb** informal *a lone car zoomed across the desert road* **whiz,** zip, whip, buzz, hurtle, speed, rush, streak, shoot, race, bolt, dash, run, flash, blast, charge, fly, careen, career, go like the wind; informal belt, scoot, tear, go like a bat out of hell, bomb, hightail, clip.

– PHRASES **zoom in on** *zoom in on the rabbit in the background* **enlarge,** magnify, close in on, focus in on.